Oxford Dictionary of National Biography

IN ASSOCIATION WITH

The British Academy

From the earliest times to the year 2000

Edited by

H. C. G. Matthew

and

Brian Harrison

Volume 56

Usk–Wallich

OXFORD

UNIVERSITY PRESS

OXFORD

UNIVERSITY PRESS

Great Clarendon Street, Oxford OX2 6DP

Oxford University Press is a department of the University of Oxford.
It furthers the University's objective of excellence in research, scholarship,
and education by publishing worldwide in

Oxford New York

Auckland Bangkok Buenos Aires Cape Town
Chennai Dar es Salaam Delhi Hong Kong Istanbul Karachi
Kolkata Kuala Lumpur Madrid Melbourne Mexico City Mumbai Nairobi
São Paulo Shanghai Taipei Tokyo Toronto

Oxford is a registered trade mark of Oxford University Press
in the UK and in certain other countries

Published in the United States
by Oxford University Press Inc., New York

First published 2004

British Library Cataloguing in Publication Data
Data available

Library of Congress Cataloging in Publication Data
Data available: for details see volume 1, p. iv

ISBN 0-19-861406-3 (this volume)
ISBN 0-19-861411-X (set of sixty volumes)

Text captured by Alliance Phototypesetters, Pondicherry
Illustrations reproduced and archived by
Alliance Graphics Ltd, UK
Typeset in OUP Swift by Interactive Sciences Limited, Gloucester
Printed in Great Britain on acid-free paper by
Butler and Tanner Ltd,
Frome, Somerset

LIST OF ABBREVIATIONS

1 General abbreviations

AB	bachelor of arts
ABC	Australian Broadcasting Corporation
ABC TV	ABC Television
act.	active
A$	Australian dollar
AD	*anno domini*
AFC	Air Force Cross
AIDS	acquired immune deficiency syndrome
AK	Alaska
AL	Alabama
A level	advanced level [examination]
ALS	associate of the Linnean Society
AM	master of arts
AMICE	associate member of the Institution of Civil Engineers
ANZAC	Australian and New Zealand Army Corps
appx *pl.* appxs	appendix(es)
AR	Arkansas
ARA	associate of the Royal Academy
ARCA	associate of the Royal College of Art
ARCM	associate of the Royal College of Music
ARCO	associate of the Royal College of Organists
ARIBA	associate of the Royal Institute of British Architects
ARP	air-raid precautions
ARRC	associate of the Royal Red Cross
ARSA	associate of the Royal Scottish Academy
art.	article / item
ASC	Army Service Corps
Asch	Austrian Schilling
ASDIC	Antisubmarine Detection Investigation Committee
ATS	Auxiliary Territorial Service
ATV	Associated Television
Aug	August
AZ	Arizona
b.	born
BA	bachelor of arts
BA (Admin.)	bachelor of arts (administration)
BAFTA	British Academy of Film and Television Arts
BAO	bachelor of arts in obstetrics
bap.	baptized
BBC	British Broadcasting Corporation / Company
BC	before Christ
BCE	before the common (*or* Christian) era
BCE	bachelor of civil engineering
BCG	bacillus of Calmette and Guérin [inoculation against tuberculosis]
BCh	bachelor of surgery
BChir	bachelor of surgery
BCL	bachelor of civil law

BCnL	bachelor of canon law
BCom	bachelor of commerce
BD	bachelor of divinity
BEd	bachelor of education
BEng	bachelor of engineering
bk *pl.* bks	book(s)
BL	bachelor of law / letters / literature
BLitt	bachelor of letters
BM	bachelor of medicine
BMus	bachelor of music
BP	before present
BP	British Petroleum
Bros.	Brothers
BS	(1) bachelor of science; (2) bachelor of surgery; (3) British standard
BSc	bachelor of science
BSc (Econ.)	bachelor of science (economics)
BSc (Eng.)	bachelor of science (engineering)
bt	baronet
BTh	bachelor of theology
bur.	buried
C.	command [identifier for published parliamentary papers]
c.	*circa*
c.	*capitulum pl. capitula*: chapter(s)
CA	California
Cantab.	Cantabrigiensis
cap.	*capitulum pl. capitula*: chapter(s)
CB	companion of the Bath
CBE	commander of the Order of the British Empire
CBS	Columbia Broadcasting System
cc	cubic centimetres
C$	Canadian dollar
CD	compact disc
Cd	command [identifier for published parliamentary papers]
CE	Common (*or* Christian) Era
cent.	century
cf.	compare
CH	Companion of Honour
chap.	chapter
ChB	bachelor of surgery
CI	Imperial Order of the Crown of India
CIA	Central Intelligence Agency
CID	Criminal Investigation Department
CIE	companion of the Order of the Indian Empire
Cie	Compagnie
CLit	companion of literature
CM	master of surgery
cm	centimetre(s)

Cmd	command [identifier for published parliamentary papers]	edn	edition
CMG	companion of the Order of St Michael and St George	EEC	European Economic Community
		EFTA	European Free Trade Association
Cmnd	command [identifier for published parliamentary papers]	EICS	East India Company Service
		EMI	Electrical and Musical Industries (Ltd)
CO	Colorado	Eng.	English
Co.	company	enl.	enlarged
co.	county	ENSA	Entertainments National Service Association
col. *pl.* cols.	column(s)	ep. *pl.* epp.	*epistola(e)*
Corp.	corporation	ESP	extra-sensory perception
CSE	certificate of secondary education	esp.	especially
CSI	companion of the Order of the Star of India	esq.	esquire
CT	Connecticut	est.	estimate / estimated
CVO	commander of the Royal Victorian Order	EU	European Union
cwt	hundredweight	ex	sold by (*lit.* out of)
$	(American) dollar	excl.	excludes / excluding
d.	(1) penny (pence); (2) died	exh.	exhibited
DBE	dame commander of the Order of the British Empire	exh. cat.	exhibition catalogue
		f. *pl.* ff.	following [pages]
DCH	diploma in child health	FA	Football Association
DCh	doctor of surgery	FACP	fellow of the American College of Physicians
DCL	doctor of civil law	facs.	facsimile
DCnL	doctor of canon law	FANY	First Aid Nursing Yeomanry
DCVO	dame commander of the Royal Victorian Order	FBA	fellow of the British Academy
DD	doctor of divinity	FBI	Federation of British Industries
DE	Delaware	FCS	fellow of the Chemical Society
Dec	December	Feb	February
dem.	demolished	FEng	fellow of the Fellowship of Engineering
DEng	doctor of engineering	FFCM	fellow of the Faculty of Community Medicine
des.	destroyed	FGS	fellow of the Geological Society
DFC	Distinguished Flying Cross	fig.	figure
DipEd	diploma in education	FIMechE	fellow of the Institution of Mechanical Engineers
DipPsych	diploma in psychiatry		
diss.	dissertation	FL	Florida
DL	deputy lieutenant	*fl.*	*floruit*
DLitt	doctor of letters	FLS	fellow of the Linnean Society
DLittCelt	doctor of Celtic letters	FM	frequency modulation
DM	(1) Deutschmark; (2) doctor of medicine; (3) doctor of musical arts	fol. *pl.* fols.	folio(s)
		Fr	French francs
DMus	doctor of music	Fr.	French
DNA	dioxyribonucleic acid	FRAeS	fellow of the Royal Aeronautical Society
doc.	document	FRAI	fellow of the Royal Anthropological Institute
DOL	doctor of oriental learning	FRAM	fellow of the Royal Academy of Music
DPH	diploma in public health	FRAS	(1) fellow of the Royal Asiatic Society; (2) fellow of the Royal Astronomical Society
DPhil	doctor of philosophy		
DPM	diploma in psychological medicine	FRCM	fellow of the Royal College of Music
DSC	Distinguished Service Cross	FRCO	fellow of the Royal College of Organists
DSc	doctor of science	FRCOG	fellow of the Royal College of Obstetricians and Gynaecologists
DSc (Econ.)	doctor of science (economics)		
DSc (Eng.)	doctor of science (engineering)	FRCP(C)	fellow of the Royal College of Physicians of Canada
DSM	Distinguished Service Medal		
DSO	companion of the Distinguished Service Order	FRCP (Edin.)	fellow of the Royal College of Physicians of Edinburgh
DSocSc	doctor of social science		
DTech	doctor of technology	FRCP (Lond.)	fellow of the Royal College of Physicians of London
DTh	doctor of theology		
DTM	diploma in tropical medicine	FRCPath	fellow of the Royal College of Pathologists
DTMH	diploma in tropical medicine and hygiene	FRCPsych	fellow of the Royal College of Psychiatrists
DU	doctor of the university	FRCS	fellow of the Royal College of Surgeons
DUniv	doctor of the university	FRGS	fellow of the Royal Geographical Society
dwt	pennyweight	FRIBA	fellow of the Royal Institute of British Architects
EC	European Community	FRICS	fellow of the Royal Institute of Chartered Surveyors
ed. *pl.* eds.	edited / edited by / editor(s)		
Edin.	Edinburgh	FRS	fellow of the Royal Society
		FRSA	fellow of the Royal Society of Arts

FRSCM	fellow of the Royal School of Church Music	ISO	companion of the Imperial Service Order
FRSE	fellow of the Royal Society of Edinburgh	It.	Italian
FRSL	fellow of the Royal Society of Literature	ITA	Independent Television Authority
FSA	fellow of the Society of Antiquaries	ITV	Independent Television
ft	foot *pl.* feet	Jan	January
FTCL	fellow of Trinity College of Music, London	JP	justice of the peace
ft-lb per min.	foot-pounds per minute [unit of horsepower]	jun.	junior
FZS	fellow of the Zoological Society	KB	knight of the Order of the Bath
GA	Georgia	KBE	knight commander of the Order of the British Empire
GBE	knight or dame grand cross of the Order of the British Empire	KC	king's counsel
GCB	knight grand cross of the Order of the Bath	kcal	kilocalorie
GCE	general certificate of education	KCB	knight commander of the Order of the Bath
GCH	knight grand cross of the Royal Guelphic Order	KCH	knight commander of the Royal Guelphic Order
GCHQ	government communications headquarters	KCIE	knight commander of the Order of the Indian Empire
GCIE	knight grand commander of the Order of the Indian Empire	KCMG	knight commander of the Order of St Michael and St George
GCMG	knight or dame grand cross of the Order of St Michael and St George	KCSI	knight commander of the Order of the Star of India
GCSE	general certificate of secondary education	KCVO	knight commander of the Royal Victorian Order
GCSI	knight grand commander of the Order of the Star of India	keV	kilo-electron-volt
GCStJ	bailiff or dame grand cross of the order of St John of Jerusalem	KG	knight of the Order of the Garter
		KGB	[Soviet committee of state security]
GCVO	knight or dame grand cross of the Royal Victorian Order	KH	knight of the Royal Guelphic Order
		KLM	Koninklijke Luchtvaart Maatschappij (Royal Dutch Air Lines)
GEC	General Electric Company		
Ger.	German	km	kilometre(s)
GI	government (*or* general) issue	KP	knight of the Order of St Patrick
GMT	Greenwich mean time	KS	Kansas
GP	general practitioner	KT	knight of the Order of the Thistle
GPU	[Soviet special police unit]	kt	knight
GSO	general staff officer	KY	Kentucky
Heb.	Hebrew	£	pound(s) sterling
HEICS	Honourable East India Company Service	£E	Egyptian pound
HI	Hawaii	L	lira *pl.* lire
HIV	human immunodeficiency virus	l. *pl.* ll.	line(s)
HK$	Hong Kong dollar	LA	Lousiana
HM	his / her majesty('s)	LAA	light anti-aircraft
HMAS	his / her majesty's Australian ship	LAH	licentiate of the Apothecaries' Hall, Dublin
HMNZS	his / her majesty's New Zealand ship	Lat.	Latin
HMS	his / her majesty's ship	lb	pound(s), unit of weight
HMSO	His / Her Majesty's Stationery Office	LDS	licence in dental surgery
HMV	His Master's Voice	*lit.*	literally
Hon.	Honourable	LittB	bachelor of letters
hp	horsepower	LittD	doctor of letters
hr	hour(s)	LKQCPI	licentiate of the King and Queen's College of Physicians, Ireland
HRH	his / her royal highness		
HTV	Harlech Television	LLA	lady literate in arts
IA	Iowa	LLB	bachelor of laws
ibid.	*ibidem*: in the same place	LLD	doctor of laws
ICI	Imperial Chemical Industries (Ltd)	LLM	master of laws
ID	Idaho	LM	licentiate in midwifery
IL	Illinois	LP	long-playing record
illus.	illustration	LRAM	licentiate of the Royal Academy of Music
illustr.	illustrated	LRCP	licentiate of the Royal College of Physicians
IN	Indiana	LRCPS (Glasgow)	licentiate of the Royal College of Physicians and Surgeons of Glasgow
in.	inch(es)		
Inc.	Incorporated	LRCS	licentiate of the Royal College of Surgeons
incl.	includes / including	LSA	licentiate of the Society of Apothecaries
IOU	I owe you	LSD	lysergic acid diethylamide
IQ	intelligence quotient	LVO	lieutenant of the Royal Victorian Order
Ir£	Irish pound	M. *pl.* MM.	Monsieur *pl.* Messieurs
IRA	Irish Republican Army	m	metre(s)

m. *pl.* mm.	membrane(s)	ND	North Dakota
MA	(1) Massachusetts; (2) master of arts	n.d.	no date
MAI	master of engineering	NE	Nebraska
MB	bachelor of medicine	*nem. con.*	*nemine contradicente*: unanimously
MBA	master of business administration	new ser.	new series
MBE	member of the Order of the British Empire	NH	New Hampshire
MC	Military Cross	NHS	National Health Service
MCC	Marylebone Cricket Club	NJ	New Jersey
MCh	master of surgery	NKVD	[Soviet people's commissariat for internal affairs]
MChir	master of surgery		
MCom	master of commerce	NM	New Mexico
MD	(1) doctor of medicine; (2) Maryland	nm	nanometre(s)
MDMA	methylenedioxymethamphetamine	no. *pl.* nos.	number(s)
ME	Maine	Nov	November
MEd	master of education	n.p.	no place [of publication]
MEng	master of engineering	NS	new style
MEP	member of the European parliament	NV	Nevada
MG	Morris Garages	NY	New York
MGM	Metro-Goldwyn-Mayer	NZBS	New Zealand Broadcasting Service
Mgr	Monsignor	OBE	officer of the Order of the British Empire
MI	(1) Michigan; (2) military intelligence	obit.	obituary
MI1c	[secret intelligence department]	Oct	October
MI5	[military intelligence department]	OCTU	officer cadets training unit
MI6	[secret intelligence department]	OECD	Organization for Economic Co-operation and Development
MI9	[secret escape service]		
MICE	member of the Institution of Civil Engineers	OEEC	Organization for European Economic Co-operation
MIEE	member of the Institution of Electrical Engineers		
		OFM	order of Friars Minor [Franciscans]
min.	minute(s)	OFMCap	Ordine Frati Minori Cappucini: member of the Capuchin order
Mk	mark		
ML	(1) licentiate of medicine; (2) master of laws	OH	Ohio
MLitt	master of letters	OK	Oklahoma
Mlle	Mademoiselle	O level	ordinary level [examination]
mm	millimetre(s)	OM	Order of Merit
Mme	Madame	OP	order of Preachers [Dominicans]
MN	Minnesota	op. *pl.* opp.	opus *pl.* opera
MO	Missouri	OPEC	Organization of Petroleum Exporting Countries
MOH	medical officer of health	OR	Oregon
MP	member of parliament	orig.	original
m.p.h.	miles per hour	os	old style
MPhil	master of philosophy	OSB	Order of St Benedict
MRCP	member of the Royal College of Physicians	OTC	Officers' Training Corps
MRCS	member of the Royal College of Surgeons	OWS	Old Watercolour Society
MRCVS	member of the Royal College of Veterinary Surgeons	Oxon.	Oxoniensis
		p. *pl.* pp.	page(s)
MRIA	member of the Royal Irish Academy	PA	Pennsylvania
MS	(1) master of science; (2) Mississippi	p.a.	per annum
MS *pl.* MSS	manuscript(s)	para.	paragraph
MSc	master of science	PAYE	pay as you earn
MSc (Econ.)	master of science (economics)	pbk *pl.* pbks	paperback(s)
MT	Montana	*per.*	[during the] period
MusB	bachelor of music	PhD	doctor of philosophy
MusBac	bachelor of music	pl.	(1) plate(s); (2) plural
MusD	doctor of music	priv. coll.	private collection
MV	motor vessel	pt *pl.* pts	part(s)
MVO	member of the Royal Victorian Order	pubd	published
n. *pl.* nn.	note(s)	PVC	polyvinyl chloride
NAAFI	Navy, Army, and Air Force Institutes	q. *pl.* qq.	(1) question(s); (2) quire(s)
NASA	National Aeronautics and Space Administration	QC	queen's counsel
NATO	North Atlantic Treaty Organization	R	rand
NBC	National Broadcasting Corporation	R.	Rex / Regina
NC	North Carolina	r	recto
NCO	non-commissioned officer	r.	reigned / ruled
		RA	Royal Academy / Royal Academician

RAC	Royal Automobile Club		Skr	Swedish krona
RAF	Royal Air Force		Span.	Spanish
RAFVR	Royal Air Force Volunteer Reserve		SPCK	Society for Promoting Christian Knowledge
RAM	[member of the] Royal Academy of Music		SS	(1) Santissimi; (2) Schutzstaffel; (3) steam ship
RAMC	Royal Army Medical Corps		STB	bachelor of theology
RCA	Royal College of Art		STD	doctor of theology
RCNC	Royal Corps of Naval Constructors		STM	master of theology
RCOG	Royal College of Obstetricians and Gynaecologists		STP	doctor of theology
RDI	royal designer for industry		*supp.*	supposedly
RE	Royal Engineers		suppl. *pl.* suppls.	supplement(s)
repr. *pl.* reprs.	reprint(s) / reprinted		s.v.	*sub verbo* / *sub voce*: under the word / heading
repro.	reproduced		SY	steam yacht
rev.	revised / revised by / reviser / revision		TA	Territorial Army
Revd	Reverend		TASS	[Soviet news agency]
RHA	Royal Hibernian Academy		TB	tuberculosis (*lit.* tubercle bacillus)
RI	(1) Rhode Island; (2) Royal Institute of Painters in Water-Colours		TD	(1) *teachtaí dála* (member of the Dáil); (2) territorial decoration
RIBA	Royal Institute of British Architects		TN	Tennessee
RIN	Royal Indian Navy		TNT	trinitrotoluene
RM	Reichsmark		trans.	translated / translated by / translation / translator
RMS	Royal Mail steamer		TT	tourist trophy
RN	Royal Navy		TUC	Trades Union Congress
RNA	ribonucleic acid		TX	Texas
RNAS	Royal Naval Air Service		U-boat	*Unterseeboot*: submarine
RNR	Royal Naval Reserve		Ufa	Universum-Film AG
RNVR	Royal Naval Volunteer Reserve		UMIST	University of Manchester Institute of Science and Technology
RO	Record Office		UN	United Nations
r.p.m.	revolutions per minute		UNESCO	United Nations Educational, Scientific, and Cultural Organization
RRS	royal research ship			
Rs	rupees		UNICEF	United Nations International Children's Emergency Fund
RSA	(1) Royal Scottish Academician; (2) Royal Society of Arts		unpubd	unpublished
RSPCA	Royal Society for the Prevention of Cruelty to Animals		USS	United States ship
Rt Hon.	Right Honourable		UT	Utah
Rt Revd	Right Reverend		*v*	verso
RUC	Royal Ulster Constabulary		v.	versus
Russ.	Russian		VA	Virginia
RWS	Royal Watercolour Society		VAD	Voluntary Aid Detachment
S4C	Sianel Pedwar Cymru		VC	Victoria Cross
s.	shilling(s)		VE-day	victory in Europe day
s.a.	*sub anno*: under the year		Ven.	Venerable
SABC	South African Broadcasting Corporation		VJ-day	victory over Japan day
SAS	Special Air Service		vol. *pl.* vols.	volume(s)
SC	South Carolina		VT	Vermont
ScD	doctor of science		WA	Washington [state]
S$	Singapore dollar		WAAC	Women's Auxiliary Army Corps
SD	South Dakota		WAAF	Women's Auxiliary Air Force
sec.	second(s)		WEA	Workers' Educational Association
sel.	selected		WHO	World Health Organization
sen.	senior		WI	Wisconsin
Sept	September		WRAF	Women's Royal Air Force
ser.	series		WRNS	Women's Royal Naval Service
SHAPE	supreme headquarters allied powers, Europe		WV	West Virginia
SIDRO	Société Internationale d'Énergie Hydro-Électrique		WVS	Women's Voluntary Service
sig. *pl.* sigs.	signature(s)		WY	Wyoming
sing.	singular		¥	yen
SIS	Secret Intelligence Service		YMCA	Young Men's Christian Association
SJ	Society of Jesus		YWCA	Young Women's Christian Association

2 Institution abbreviations

All Souls Oxf.	All Souls College, Oxford
AM Oxf.	Ashmolean Museum, Oxford
Balliol Oxf.	Balliol College, Oxford
BBC WAC	BBC Written Archives Centre, Reading
Beds. & Luton ARS	Bedfordshire and Luton Archives and Record Service, Bedford
Berks. RO	Berkshire Record Office, Reading
BFI	British Film Institute, London
BFI NFTVA	British Film Institute, London, National Film and Television Archive
BGS	British Geological Survey, Keyworth, Nottingham
Birm. CA	Birmingham Central Library, Birmingham City Archives
Birm. CL	Birmingham Central Library
BL	British Library, London
BL NSA	British Library, London, National Sound Archive
BL OIOC	British Library, London, Oriental and India Office Collections
BLPES	London School of Economics and Political Science, British Library of Political and Economic Science
BM	British Museum, London
Bodl. Oxf.	Bodleian Library, Oxford
Bodl. RH	Bodleian Library of Commonwealth and African Studies at Rhodes House, Oxford
Borth. Inst.	Borthwick Institute of Historical Research, University of York
Boston PL	Boston Public Library, Massachusetts
Bristol RO	Bristol Record Office
Bucks. RLSS	Buckinghamshire Records and Local Studies Service, Aylesbury
CAC Cam.	Churchill College, Cambridge, Churchill Archives Centre
Cambs. AS	Cambridgeshire Archive Service
CCC Cam.	Corpus Christi College, Cambridge
CCC Oxf.	Corpus Christi College, Oxford
Ches. & Chester ALSS	Cheshire and Chester Archives and Local Studies Service
Christ Church Oxf.	Christ Church, Oxford
Christies	Christies, London
City Westm. AC	City of Westminster Archives Centre, London
CKS	Centre for Kentish Studies, Maidstone
CLRO	Corporation of London Records Office
Coll. Arms	College of Arms, London
Col. U.	Columbia University, New York
Cornwall RO	Cornwall Record Office, Truro
Courtauld Inst.	Courtauld Institute of Art, London
CUL	Cambridge University Library
Cumbria AS	Cumbria Archive Service
Derbys. RO	Derbyshire Record Office, Matlock
Devon RO	Devon Record Office, Exeter
Dorset RO	Dorset Record Office, Dorchester
Duke U.	Duke University, Durham, North Carolina
Duke U., Perkins L.	Duke University, Durham, North Carolina, William R. Perkins Library
Durham Cath. CL	Durham Cathedral, chapter library
Durham RO	Durham Record Office
DWL	Dr Williams's Library, London
Essex RO	Essex Record Office
E. Sussex RO	East Sussex Record Office, Lewes
Eton	Eton College, Berkshire
FM Cam.	Fitzwilliam Museum, Cambridge
Folger	Folger Shakespeare Library, Washington, DC
Garr. Club	Garrick Club, London
Girton Cam.	Girton College, Cambridge
GL	Guildhall Library, London
Glos. RO	Gloucestershire Record Office, Gloucester
Gon. & Caius Cam.	Gonville and Caius College, Cambridge
Gov. Art Coll.	Government Art Collection
GS Lond.	Geological Society of London
Hants. RO	Hampshire Record Office, Winchester
Harris Man. Oxf.	Harris Manchester College, Oxford
Harvard TC	Harvard Theatre Collection, Harvard University, Cambridge, Massachusetts, Nathan Marsh Pusey Library
Harvard U.	Harvard University, Cambridge, Massachusetts
Harvard U., Houghton L.	Harvard University, Cambridge, Massachusetts, Houghton Library
Herefs. RO	Herefordshire Record Office, Hereford
Herts. ALS	Hertfordshire Archives and Local Studies, Hertford
Hist. Soc. Penn.	Historical Society of Pennsylvania, Philadelphia
HLRO	House of Lords Record Office, London
Hult. Arch.	Hulton Archive, London and New York
Hunt. L.	Huntington Library, San Marino, California
ICL	Imperial College, London
Inst. CE	Institution of Civil Engineers, London
Inst. EE	Institution of Electrical Engineers, London
IWM	Imperial War Museum, London
IWM FVA	Imperial War Museum, London, Film and Video Archive
IWM SA	Imperial War Museum, London, Sound Archive
JRL	John Rylands University Library of Manchester
King's AC Cam.	King's College Archives Centre, Cambridge
King's Cam.	King's College, Cambridge
King's Lond.	King's College, London
King's Lond., Liddell Hart C.	King's College, London, Liddell Hart Centre for Military Archives
Lancs. RO	Lancashire Record Office, Preston
L. Cong.	Library of Congress, Washington, DC
Leics. RO	Leicestershire, Leicester, and Rutland Record Office, Leicester
Lincs. Arch.	Lincolnshire Archives, Lincoln
Linn. Soc.	Linnean Society of London
LMA	London Metropolitan Archives
LPL	Lambeth Palace, London
Lpool RO	Liverpool Record Office and Local Studies Service
LUL	London University Library
Magd. Cam.	Magdalene College, Cambridge
Magd. Oxf.	Magdalen College, Oxford
Man. City Gall.	Manchester City Galleries
Man. CL	Manchester Central Library
Mass. Hist. Soc.	Massachusetts Historical Society, Boston
Merton Oxf.	Merton College, Oxford
MHS Oxf.	Museum of the History of Science, Oxford
Mitchell L., Glas.	Mitchell Library, Glasgow
Mitchell L., NSW	State Library of New South Wales, Sydney, Mitchell Library
Morgan L.	Pierpont Morgan Library, New York
NA Canada	National Archives of Canada, Ottawa
NA Ire.	National Archives of Ireland, Dublin
NAM	National Army Museum, London
NA Scot.	National Archives of Scotland, Edinburgh
News Int. RO	News International Record Office, London
NG Ire.	National Gallery of Ireland, Dublin

NG Scot.	National Gallery of Scotland, Edinburgh
NHM	Natural History Museum, London
NL Aus.	National Library of Australia, Canberra
NL Ire.	National Library of Ireland, Dublin
NL NZ	National Library of New Zealand, Wellington
NL NZ, Turnbull L.	National Library of New Zealand, Wellington, Alexander Turnbull Library
NL Scot.	National Library of Scotland, Edinburgh
NL Wales	National Library of Wales, Aberystwyth
NMG Wales	National Museum and Gallery of Wales, Cardiff
NMM	National Maritime Museum, London
Norfolk RO	Norfolk Record Office, Norwich
Northants. RO	Northamptonshire Record Office, Northampton
Northumbd RO	Northumberland Record Office
Notts. Arch.	Nottinghamshire Archives, Nottingham
NPG	National Portrait Gallery, London
NRA	National Archives, London, Historical Manuscripts Commission, National Register of Archives
Nuffield Oxf.	Nuffield College, Oxford
N. Yorks. CRO	North Yorkshire County Record Office, Northallerton
NYPL	New York Public Library
Oxf. UA	Oxford University Archives
Oxf. U. Mus. NH	Oxford University Museum of Natural History
Oxon. RO	Oxfordshire Record Office, Oxford
Pembroke Cam.	Pembroke College, Cambridge
PRO	National Archives, London, Public Record Office
PRO NIre.	Public Record Office for Northern Ireland, Belfast
Pusey Oxf.	Pusey House, Oxford
RA	Royal Academy of Arts, London
Ransom HRC	Harry Ransom Humanities Research Center, University of Texas, Austin
RAS	Royal Astronomical Society, London
RBG Kew	Royal Botanic Gardens, Kew, London
RCP Lond.	Royal College of Physicians of London
RCS Eng.	Royal College of Surgeons of England, London
RGS	Royal Geographical Society, London
RIBA	Royal Institute of British Architects, London
RIBA BAL	Royal Institute of British Architects, London, British Architectural Library
Royal Arch.	Royal Archives, Windsor Castle, Berkshire [by gracious permission of her majesty the queen]
Royal Irish Acad.	Royal Irish Academy, Dublin
Royal Scot. Acad.	Royal Scottish Academy, Edinburgh
RS	Royal Society, London
RSA	Royal Society of Arts, London
RS Friends, Lond.	Religious Society of Friends, London
St Ant. Oxf.	St Antony's College, Oxford
St John Cam.	St John's College, Cambridge
S. Antiquaries, Lond.	Society of Antiquaries of London
Sci. Mus.	Science Museum, London
Scot. NPG	Scottish National Portrait Gallery, Edinburgh
Scott Polar RI	University of Cambridge, Scott Polar Research Institute
Sheff. Arch.	Sheffield Archives
Shrops. RRC	Shropshire Records and Research Centre, Shrewsbury
SOAS	School of Oriental and African Studies, London
Som. ARS	Somerset Archive and Record Service, Taunton
Staffs. RO	Staffordshire Record Office, Stafford
Suffolk RO	Suffolk Record Office
Surrey HC	Surrey History Centre, Woking
TCD	Trinity College, Dublin
Trinity Cam.	Trinity College, Cambridge
U. Aberdeen	University of Aberdeen
U. Birm.	University of Birmingham
U. Birm. L.	University of Birmingham Library
U. Cal.	University of California
U. Cam.	University of Cambridge
UCL	University College, London
U. Durham	University of Durham
U. Durham L.	University of Durham Library
U. Edin.	University of Edinburgh
U. Edin., New Coll.	University of Edinburgh, New College
U. Edin., New Coll. L.	University of Edinburgh, New College Library
U. Edin. L.	University of Edinburgh Library
U. Glas.	University of Glasgow
U. Glas. L.	University of Glasgow Library
U. Hull	University of Hull
U. Hull, Brynmor Jones L.	University of Hull, Brynmor Jones Library
U. Leeds	University of Leeds
U. Leeds, Brotherton L.	University of Leeds, Brotherton Library
U. Lond.	University of London
U. Lpool	University of Liverpool
U. Lpool L.	University of Liverpool Library
U. Mich.	University of Michigan, Ann Arbor
U. Mich., Clements L.	University of Michigan, Ann Arbor, William L. Clements Library
U. Newcastle	University of Newcastle upon Tyne
U. Newcastle, Robinson L.	University of Newcastle upon Tyne, Robinson Library
U. Nott.	University of Nottingham
U. Nott. L.	University of Nottingham Library
U. Oxf.	University of Oxford
U. Reading	University of Reading
U. Reading L.	University of Reading Library
U. St Andr.	University of St Andrews
U. St Andr. L.	University of St Andrews Library
U. Southampton	University of Southampton
U. Southampton L.	University of Southampton Library
U. Sussex	University of Sussex, Brighton
U. Texas	University of Texas, Austin
U. Wales	University of Wales
U. Warwick Mod. RC	University of Warwick, Coventry, Modern Records Centre
V&A	Victoria and Albert Museum, London
V&A NAL	Victoria and Albert Museum, London, National Art Library
Warks. CRO	Warwickshire County Record Office, Warwick
Wellcome L.	Wellcome Library for the History and Understanding of Medicine, London
Westm. DA	Westminster Diocesan Archives, London
Wilts. & Swindon RO	Wiltshire and Swindon Record Office, Trowbridge
Worcs. RO	Worcestershire Record Office, Worcester
W. Sussex RO	West Sussex Record Office, Chichester
W. Yorks. AS	West Yorkshire Archive Service
Yale U.	Yale University, New Haven, Connecticut
Yale U., Beinecke L.	Yale University, New Haven, Connecticut, Beinecke Rare Book and Manuscript Library
Yale U. CBA	Yale University, New Haven, Connecticut, Yale Center for British Art

3 Bibliographic abbreviations

Adams, *Drama* — W. D. Adams, *A dictionary of the drama*, 1: *A–G* (1904); 2: *H–Z* (1956) [vol. 2 microfilm only]

AFM — J O'Donovan, ed. and trans., *Annala rioghachta Eireann | Annals of the kingdom of Ireland by the four masters*, 7 vols. (1848–51); 2nd edn (1856); 3rd edn (1990)

Allibone, *Dict.* — S. A. Allibone, *A critical dictionary of English literature and British and American authors*, 3 vols. (1859–71); suppl. by J. F. Kirk, 2 vols. (1891)

ANB — J. A. Garraty and M. C. Carnes, eds., *American national biography*, 24 vols. (1999)

Anderson, *Scot. nat.* — W. Anderson, *The Scottish nation, or, The surnames, families, literature, honours, and biographical history of the people of Scotland*, 3 vols. (1859–63)

Ann. mon. — H. R. Luard, ed., *Annales monastici*, 5 vols., Rolls Series, 36 (1864–9)

Ann. Ulster — S. Mac Airt and G. Mac Niocaill, eds., *Annals of Ulster (to AD 1131)* (1983)

APC — *Acts of the privy council of England*, new ser., 46 vols. (1890–1964)

APS — *The acts of the parliaments of Scotland*, 12 vols. in 13 (1814–75)

Arber, *Regs. Stationers* — F. Arber, ed., *A transcript of the registers of the Company of Stationers of London, 1554–1640 AD*, 5 vols. (1875–94)

ArchR — *Architectural Review*

ASC — D. Whitelock, D. C. Douglas, and S. I. Tucker, ed. and trans., *The Anglo-Saxon Chronicle: a revised translation* (1961)

AS chart. — P. H. Sawyer, *Anglo-Saxon charters: an annotated list and bibliography*, Royal Historical Society Guides and Handbooks (1968)

AusDB — D. Pike and others, eds., *Australian dictionary of biography*, 16 vols. (1966–2002)

Baker, *Serjeants* — J. H. Baker, *The order of serjeants at law*, SeldS, suppl. ser., 5 (1984)

Bale, *Cat.* — J. Bale, *Scriptorum illustrium Maioris Brytannie, quam nunc Angliam et Scotiam vocant: catalogus*, 2 vols. in 1 (Basel, 1557–9); facs. edn (1971)

Bale, *Index* — J. Bale, *Index Britanniae scriptorum*, ed. R. L. Poole and M. Bateson (1902); facs. edn (1990)

BBCS — *Bulletin of the Board of Celtic Studies*

BDMBR — J. O. Baylen and N. J. Gossman, eds., *Biographical dictionary of modern British radicals*, 3 vols. in 4 (1979–88)

Bede, *Hist. eccl.* — *Bede's Ecclesiastical history of the English people*, ed. and trans. B. Colgrave and R. A. B. Mynors, OMT (1969); repr. (1991)

Bénézit, *Dict.* — E. Bénézit, *Dictionnaire critique et documentaire des peintres, sculpteurs, dessinateurs et graveurs*, 3 vols. (Paris, 1911–23); new edn, 8 vols. (1948–66), repr. (1966); 3rd edn, rev. and enl., 10 vols. (1976); 4th edn, 14 vols. (1999)

BIHR — *Bulletin of the Institute of Historical Research*

Birch, *Seals* — W. de Birch, *Catalogue of seals in the department of manuscripts in the British Museum*, 6 vols. (1887–1900)

Bishop Burnet's History — *Bishop Burnet's History of his own time*, ed. M. J. Routh, 2nd edn, 6 vols. (1833)

Blackwood — *Blackwood's [Edinburgh] Magazine*, 328 vols. (1817–1980)

Blain, Clements & Grundy, *Feminist comp.* — V. Blain, P. Clements, and I. Grundy, eds., *The feminist companion to literature in English* (1990)

BL cat. — *The British Library general catalogue of printed books* [in 360 vols. with suppls., also CD-ROM and online]

BMJ — *British Medical Journal*

Boase & Courtney, *Bibl. Corn.* — G. C. Boase and W. P. Courtney, *Bibliotheca Cornubiensis: a catalogue of the writings … of Cornishmen*, 3 vols. (1874–82)

Boase, *Mod. Eng. biog.* — F. Boase, *Modern English biography: containing many thousand concise memoirs of persons who have died since the year 1850*, 6 vols. (privately printed, Truro, 1892–1921); repr. (1965)

Boswell, *Life* — *Boswell's Life of Johnson: together with Journal of a tour to the Hebrides and Johnson's Diary of a journey into north Wales*, ed. G. B. Hill, enl. edn, rev. L. F. Powell, 6 vols. (1934–50); 2nd edn (1964); repr. (1971)

Brown & Stratton, *Brit. mus.* — J. D. Brown and S. S. Stratton, *British musical biography* (1897)

Bryan, *Painters* — M. Bryan, *A biographical and critical dictionary of painters and engravers*, 2 vols. (1816); new edn, ed. G. Stanley (1849); new edn, ed. R. E. Graves and W. Armstrong, 2 vols. (1886–9); [4th edn], ed. G. C. Williamson, 5 vols. (1903–5) [various reprs.]

Burke, *Gen. GB* — J. Burke, *A genealogical and heraldic history of the commoners of Great Britain and Ireland*, 4 vols. (1833–8); new edn as *A genealogical and heraldic dictionary of the landed gentry of Great Britain and Ireland*, 3 vols. [1843–9] [many later edns]

Burke, *Gen. Ire.* — J. B. Burke, *A genealogical and heraldic history of the landed gentry of Ireland* (1899); 2nd edn (1904); 3rd edn (1912); 4th edn (1958); 5th edn as *Burke's Irish family records* (1976)

Burke, *Peerage* — J. Burke, *A general* [later edns *A genealogical*] *and heraldic dictionary of the peerage and baronetage of the United Kingdom* [later edns *the British empire*] (1829–)

Burney, *Hist. mus.* — C. Burney, *A general history of music, from the earliest ages to the present period*, 4 vols. (1776–89)

Burtchaell & Sadleir, *Alum. Dubl.* — G. D. Burtchaell and T. U. Sadleir, *Alumni Dublinenses: a register of the students, graduates, and provosts of Trinity College* (1924); [2nd edn], with suppl., in 2 pts (1935)

Calamy rev. — A. G. Matthews, *Calamy revised* (1934); repr. (1988)

CCI — *Calendar of confirmations and inventories granted and given up in the several commissariots of Scotland* (1876–)

CCIR — *Calendar of the close rolls preserved in the Public Record Office*, 47 vols. (1892–1963)

CDS — J. Bain, ed., *Calendar of documents relating to Scotland*, 4 vols., PRO (1881–8); suppl. vol. 5, ed. G. G. Simpson and J. D. Galbraith [1986]

CEPR letters — W. H. Bliss, C. Johnson, and J. Twemlow, eds., *Calendar of entries in the papal registers relating to Great Britain and Ireland: papal letters* (1893–)

CGPLA — *Calendars of the grants of probate and letters of administration* [in 4 ser.: *England & Wales, Northern Ireland, Ireland*, and *Éire*]

Chambers, *Scots.* — R. Chambers, ed., *A biographical dictionary of eminent Scotsmen*, 4 vols. (1832–5)

Chancery records — chancery records pubd by the PRO

Chancery records (RC) — chancery records pubd by the Record Commissions

CIPM	Calendar of inquisitions post mortem, [20 vols.], PRO (1904–); also Henry VII, 3 vols. (1898–1955)
Clarendon, Hist. rebellion	E. Hyde, earl of Clarendon, The history of the rebellion and civil wars in England, 6 vols. (1888); repr. (1958) and (1992)
Cobbett, Parl. hist.	W. Cobbett and J. Wright, eds., Cobbett's Parliamentary history of England, 36 vols. (1806–1820)
Colvin, Archs.	H. Colvin, A biographical dictionary of British architects, 1600–1840, 3rd edn (1995)
Cooper, Ath. Cantab.	C. H. Cooper and T. Cooper, Athenae Cantabrigienses, 3 vols. (1858–1913); repr. (1967)
CPR	Calendar of the patent rolls preserved in the Public Record Office (1891–)
Crockford	Crockford's Clerical Directory
CS	Camden Society
CSP	Calendar of state papers [in 11 ser.: domestic, Scotland, Scottish series, Ireland, colonial, Commonwealth, foreign, Spain [at Simancas], Rome, Milan, and Venice]
CYS	Canterbury and York Society
DAB	Dictionary of American biography, 21 vols. (1928–36), repr. in 11 vols. (1964); 10 suppls. (1944–96)
DBB	D. J. Jeremy, ed., Dictionary of business biography, 5 vols. (1984–6)
DCB	G. W. Brown and others, Dictionary of Canadian biography, [14 vols.] (1966–)
Debrett's Peerage	Debrett's Peerage (1803–) [sometimes Debrett's Illustrated peerage]
Desmond, Botanists	R. Desmond, Dictionary of British and Irish botanists and horticulturists (1977); rev. edn (1994)
Dir. Brit. archs.	A. Felstead, J. Franklin, and L. Pinfield, eds., Directory of British architects, 1834–1900 (1993); 2nd edn, ed. A. Brodie and others, 2 vols. (2001)
DLB	J. M. Bellamy and J. Saville, eds., Dictionary of labour biography, [10 vols.] (1972–)
DLitB	Dictionary of Literary Biography
DNB	Dictionary of national biography, 63 vols. (1885–1900), suppl., 3 vols. (1901); repr. in 22 vols. (1908–9); 10 further suppls. (1912–96); Missing persons (1993)
DNZB	W. H. Oliver and C. Orange, eds., The dictionary of New Zealand biography, 5 vols. (1990–2000)
DSAB	W. J. de Kock and others, eds., Dictionary of South African biography, 5 vols. (1968–87)
DSB	C. C. Gillispie and F. L. Holmes, eds., Dictionary of scientific biography, 16 vols. (1970–80); repr. in 8 vols. (1981); 2 vol. suppl. (1990)
DSBB	A. Slaven and S. Checkland, eds., Dictionary of Scottish business biography, 1860–1960, 2 vols. (1986–90)
DSCHT	N. M. de S. Cameron and others, eds., Dictionary of Scottish church history and theology (1993)
Dugdale, Monasticon	W. Dugdale, Monasticon Anglicanum, 3 vols. (1655–72); 2nd edn, 3 vols. (1661–82); new edn, ed. J. Caley, J. Ellis, and B. Bandinel, 6 vols. in 8 pts (1817–30); repr. (1846) and (1970)
DWB	J. E. Lloyd and others, eds., Dictionary of Welsh biography down to 1940 (1959) [Eng. trans. of Y bywgraffiadur Cymreig hyd 1940, 2nd edn (1954)]
EdinR	Edinburgh Review, or, Critical Journal
EETS	Early English Text Society
Emden, Cam.	A. B. Emden, A biographical register of the University of Cambridge to 1500 (1963)
Emden, Oxf.	A. B. Emden, A biographical register of the University of Oxford to AD 1500, 3 vols. (1957–9); also A biographical register of the University of Oxford, AD 1501 to 1540 (1974)
EngHR	English Historical Review
Engraved Brit. ports.	F. M. O'Donoghue and H. M. Hake, Catalogue of engraved British portraits preserved in the department of prints and drawings in the British Museum, 6 vols. (1908–25)
ER	The English Reports, 178 vols. (1900–32)
ESTC	English short title catalogue, 1475–1800 [CD-ROM and online]
Evelyn, Diary	The diary of John Evelyn, ed. E. S. De Beer, 6 vols. (1955); repr. (2000)
Farington, Diary	The diary of Joseph Farington, ed. K. Garlick and others, 17 vols. (1978–98)
Fasti Angl. (Hardy)	J. Le Neve, Fasti ecclesiae Anglicanae, ed. T. D. Hardy, 3 vols. (1854)
Fasti Angl., 1066–1300	[J. Le Neve], Fasti ecclesiae Anglicanae, 1066–1300, ed. D. E. Greenway and J. S. Barrow, [8 vols.] (1968–)
Fasti Angl., 1300–1541	[J. Le Neve], Fasti ecclesiae Anglicanae, 1300–1541, 12 vols. (1962–7)
Fasti Angl., 1541–1857	[J. Le Neve], Fasti ecclesiae Anglicanae, 1541–1857, ed. J. M. Horn, D. M. Smith, and D. S. Bailey, [9 vols.] (1969–)
Fasti Scot.	H. Scott, Fasti ecclesiae Scoticanae, 3 vols. in 6 (1871); new edn, [11 vols.] (1915–)
FO List	Foreign Office List
Fortescue, Brit. army	J. W. Fortescue, A history of the British army, 13 vols. (1899–1930)
Foss, Judges	E. Foss, The judges of England, 9 vols. (1848–64); repr. (1966)
Foster, Alum. Oxon.	J. Foster, ed., Alumni Oxonienses: the members of the University of Oxford, 1715–1886, 4 vols. (1887–8); later edn (1891); also Alumni Oxonienses … 1500–1714, 4 vols. (1891–2); 8 vol. repr. (1968) and (2000)
Fuller, Worthies	T. Fuller, The history of the worthies of England, 4 pts (1662); new edn, 2 vols., ed. J. Nichols (1811); new edn, 3 vols., ed. P. A. Nuttall (1840); repr. (1965)
GEC, Baronetage	G. E. Cokayne, Complete baronetage, 6 vols. (1900–09); repr. (1983) [microprint]
GEC, Peerage	G. E. C. [G. E. Cokayne], The complete peerage of England, Scotland, Ireland, Great Britain, and the United Kingdom, 8 vols. (1887–98); new edn, ed. V. Gibbs and others, 14 vols. in 15 (1910–98); microprint repr. (1982) and (1987)
Genest, Eng. stage	J. Genest, Some account of the English stage from the Restoration in 1660 to 1830, 10 vols. (1832); repr. [New York, 1965]
Gillow, Lit. biog. hist.	J. Gillow, A literary and biographical history or bibliographical dictionary of the English Catholics, from the breach with Rome, in 1534, to the present time, 5 vols. [1885–1902]; repr. (1961); repr. with preface by C. Gillow (1999)
Gir. Camb. opera	Giraldi Cambrensis opera, ed. J. S. Brewer, J. F. Dimock, and G. F. Warner, 8 vols., Rolls Series, 21 (1861–91)
GJ	Geographical Journal

Gladstone, *Diaries*	*The Gladstone diaries: with cabinet minutes and prime-ministerial correspondence*, ed. M. R. D. Foot and H. C. G. Matthew, 14 vols. (1968–94)
GM	*Gentleman's Magazine*
Graves, *Artists*	A. Graves, ed., *A dictionary of artists who have exhibited works in the principal London exhibitions of oil paintings from 1760 to 1880* (1884); new edn (1895); 3rd edn (1901); facs. edn (1969); repr. [1970], (1973), and (1984)
Graves, *Brit. Inst.*	A. Graves, *The British Institution, 1806–1867: a complete dictionary of contributors and their work from the foundation of the institution* (1875); facs. edn (1908); repr. (1969)
Graves, *RA exhibitors*	A. Graves, *The Royal Academy of Arts: a complete dictionary of contributors and their work from its foundation in 1769 to 1904*, 8 vols. (1905–6); repr. in 4 vols. (1970) and (1972)
Graves, *Soc. Artists*	A. Graves, *The Society of Artists of Great Britain, 1760–1791, the Free Society of Artists, 1761–1783: a complete dictionary* (1907); facs. edn (1969)
Greaves & Zaller, *BDBR*	R. L. Greaves and R. Zaller, eds., *Biographical dictionary of British radicals in the seventeenth century*, 3 vols. (1982–4)
Grove, *Dict. mus.*	G. Grove, ed., *A dictionary of music and musicians*, 5 vols. (1878–90); 2nd edn, ed. J. A. Fuller Maitland (1904–10); 3rd edn, ed. H. C. Colles (1927); 4th edn with suppl. (1940); 5th edn, ed. E. Blom, 9 vols. (1954); suppl. (1961) [see also *New Grove*]
Hall, *Dramatic ports.*	L. A. Hall, *Catalogue of dramatic portraits in the theatre collection of the Harvard College library*, 4 vols. (1930–34)
Hansard	*Hansard's parliamentary debates*, ser. 1–5 (1803–)
Highfill, Burnim & Langhans, *BDA*	P. H. Highfill, K. A. Burnim, and E. A. Langhans, *A biographical dictionary of actors, actresses, musicians, dancers, managers, and other stage personnel in London, 1660–1800*, 16 vols. (1973–93)
Hist. U. Oxf.	T. H. Aston, ed., *The history of the University of Oxford*, 8 vols. (1984–2000) [1: *The early Oxford schools*, ed. J. I. Catto (1984); 2: *Late medieval Oxford*, ed. J. I. Catto and R. Evans (1992); 3: *The collegiate university*, ed. J. McConica (1986); 4: *Seventeenth-century Oxford*, ed. N. Tyacke (1997); 5: *The eighteenth century*, ed. L. S. Sutherland and L. G. Mitchell (1986); 6–7: *Nineteenth-century Oxford*, ed. M. G. Brock and M. C. Curthoys (1997–2000); 8: *The twentieth century*, ed. B. Harrison (2000)]
HJ	*Historical Journal*
HMC	Historical Manuscripts Commission
Holdsworth, *Eng. law*	W. S. Holdsworth, *A history of English law*, ed. A. L. Goodhart and H. L. Hanbury, 17 vols. (1903–72)
HoP, *Commons*	*The history of parliament: the House of Commons* [1386–1421, ed. J. S. Roskell, L. Clark, and C. Rawcliffe, 4 vols. (1992); 1509–1558, ed. S. T. Bindoff, 3 vols. (1982); 1558–1603, ed. P. W. Hasler, 3 vols. (1981); 1660–1690, ed. B. D. Henning, 3 vols. (1983); 1690–1715, ed. D. W. Hayton, E. Cruickshanks, and S. Handley, 5 vols. (2002); 1715–1754, ed. R. Sedgwick, 2 vols. (1970); 1754–1790, ed. L. Namier and J. Brooke, 3 vols. (1964), repr. (1985); 1790–1820, ed. R. G. Thorne, 5 vols. (1986); in draft (used with permission): 1422–1504, 1604–1629, 1640–1660, and 1820–1832]
IGI	*International Genealogical Index*, Church of Jesus Christ of the Latterday Saints
ILN	*Illustrated London News*
IMC	Irish Manuscripts Commission
Irving, *Scots.*	J. Irving, ed., *The book of Scotsmen eminent for achievements in arms and arts, church and state, law, legislation and literature, commerce, science, travel and philanthropy* (1881)
JCS	*Journal of the Chemical Society*
JHC	*Journals of the House of Commons*
JHL	*Journals of the House of Lords*
John of Worcester, *Chron.*	*The chronicle of John of Worcester*, ed. R. R. Darlington and P. McGurk, trans. J. Bray and P. McGurk, 3 vols., OMT (1995–) [vol. 1 forthcoming]
Keeler, *Long Parliament*	M. F. Keeler, *The Long Parliament, 1640–1641: a biographical study of its members* (1954)
Kelly, *Handbk*	*The upper ten thousand: an alphabetical list of all members of noble families*, 3 vols. (1875–7); continued as *Kelly's handbook of the upper ten thousand for 1878* [1879], 2 vols. (1878–9); continued as *Kelly's handbook to the titled, landed and official classes*, 94 vols. (1880–1973)
LondG	*London Gazette*
LP Henry VIII	J. S. Brewer, J. Gairdner, and R. H. Brodie, eds., *Letters and papers, foreign and domestic, of the reign of Henry VIII*, 23 vols. in 38 (1862–1932); repr. (1965)
Mallalieu, *Watercolour artists*	H. L. Mallalieu, *The dictionary of British watercolour artists up to 1820*, 3 vols. (1976–90); vol. 1, 2nd edn (1986)
Memoirs FRS	*Biographical Memoirs of Fellows of the Royal Society*
MGH	Monumenta Germaniae Historica
MT	*Musical Times*
Munk, *Roll*	W. Munk, *The roll of the Royal College of Physicians of London*, 2 vols. (1861); 2nd edn, 3 vols. (1878)
N&Q	*Notes and Queries*
New Grove	S. Sadie, ed., *The new Grove dictionary of music and musicians*, 20 vols. (1980); 2nd edn, 29 vols. (2001) [also online edn; see also Grove, *Dict. mus.*]
Nichols, *Illustrations*	J. Nichols and J. B. Nichols, *Illustrations of the literary history of the eighteenth century*, 8 vols. (1817–58)
Nichols, *Lit. anecdotes*	J. Nichols, *Literary anecdotes of the eighteenth century*, 9 vols. (1812–16); facs. edn (1966)
Obits. FRS	*Obituary Notices of Fellows of the Royal Society*
O'Byrne, *Naval biog. dict.*	W. R. O'Byrne, *A naval biographical dictionary* (1849); repr. (1990); [2nd edn], 2 vols. (1861)
OHS	Oxford Historical Society
Old Westminsters	*The record of Old Westminsters*, 1–2, ed. G. F. R. Barker and A. H. Stenning (1928); suppl. 1, ed. J. B. Whitmore and G. R. Y. Radcliffe [1938]; 3, ed. J. B. Whitmore, G. R. Y. Radcliffe, and D. C. Simpson (1963); suppl. 2, ed. F. E. Pagan (1978); 4, ed. F. E. Pagan and H. E. Pagan (1992)
OMT	Oxford Medieval Texts
Ordericus Vitalis, *Eccl. hist.*	*The ecclesiastical history of Orderic Vitalis*, ed. and trans. M. Chibnall, 6 vols., OMT (1969–80); repr. (1990)
Paris, *Chron.*	*Matthaei Parisiensis, monachi sancti Albani, chronica majora*, ed. H. R. Luard, Rolls Series, 7 vols. (1872–83)
Parl. papers	*Parliamentary papers* (1801–)
PBA	*Proceedings of the British Academy*

Pepys, *Diary*	*The diary of Samuel Pepys*, ed. R. Latham and W. Matthews, 11 vols. (1970–83); repr. (1995) and (2000)
Pevsner	N. Pevsner and others, *Buildings of England* series
PICE	*Proceedings of the Institution of Civil Engineers*
Pipe rolls	*The great roll of the pipe for . . .*, PRSoc. (1884–)
PRO	Public Record Office
PRS	*Proceedings of the Royal Society of London*
PRSoc.	Pipe Roll Society
PTRS	*Philosophical Transactions of the Royal Society*
QR	*Quarterly Review*
RC	Record Commissions
Redgrave, *Artists*	S. Redgrave, *A dictionary of artists of the English school* (1874); rev. edn (1878); repr. (1970)
Reg. Oxf.	C. W. Boase and A. Clark, eds., *Register of the University of Oxford*, 5 vols., OHS, 1, 10–12, 14 (1885–9)
Reg. PCS	J. H. Burton and others, eds., *The register of the privy council of Scotland*, 1st ser., 14 vols. (1877–98); 2nd ser., 8 vols. (1899–1908); 3rd ser., [16 vols.] (1908–70)
Reg. RAN	H. W. C. Davis and others, eds., *Regesta regum Anglo-Normannorum, 1066–1154*, 4 vols. (1913–69)
RIBA Journal	*Journal of the Royal Institute of British Architects* [later *RIBA Journal*]
RotP	J. Strachey, ed., *Rotuli parliamentorum ut et petitiones, et placita in parliamento*, 6 vols. (1767–77)
RotS	D. Macpherson, J. Caley, and W. Illingworth, eds., *Rotuli Scotiae in Turri Londinensi et in domo capitulari Westmonasteriensi asservati*, 2 vols., RC, 14 (1814–19)
RS	Record(s) Society
Rymer, *Foedera*	T. Rymer and R. Sanderson, eds., *Foedera, conventiones, literae et cuiuscunque generis acta publica inter reges Angliae et alios quosvis imperatores, reges, pontifices, principes, vel communitates*, 20 vols. (1704–35); 2nd edn, 20 vols. (1726–35); 3rd edn, 10 vols. (1739–45); facs. edn (1967); new edn, ed. A. Clarke, J. Caley, and F. Holbrooke, 4 vols., RC, 50 (1816–30)
Sainty, *Judges*	J. Sainty, ed., *The judges of England, 1272–1990*, SeldS, suppl. ser., 10 (1993)
Sainty, *King's counsel*	J. Sainty, ed., *A list of English law officers and king's counsel*, SeldS, suppl. ser., 7 (1987)
SCH	Studies in Church History
Scots peerage	J. B. Paul, ed. *The Scots peerage, founded on Wood's edition of Sir Robert Douglas's Peerage of Scotland, containing an historical and genealogical account of the nobility of that kingdom*, 9 vols. (1904–14)
SeldS	Selden Society
SHR	*Scottish Historical Review*
State trials	T. B. Howell and T. J. Howell, eds., *Cobbett's Complete collection of state trials*, 34 vols. (1809–28)
STC, 1475–1640	A. W. Pollard, G. R. Redgrave, and others, eds., *A short-title catalogue of . . . English books . . . 1475–1640* (1926); 2nd edn, ed. W. A. Jackson, F. S. Ferguson, and K. F. Pantzer, 3 vols. (1976–91) [see also Wing, *STC*]
STS	Scottish Text Society
SurtS	Surtees Society
Symeon of Durham, *Opera*	*Symeonis monachi opera omnia*, ed. T. Arnold, 2 vols., Rolls Series, 75 (1882–5); repr. (1965)
Tanner, *Bibl. Brit.-Hib.*	T. Tanner, *Bibliotheca Britannico-Hibernica*, ed. D. Wilkins (1748); repr. (1963)
Thieme & Becker, *Allgemeines Lexikon*	U. Thieme, F. Becker, and H. Vollmer, eds., *Allgemeines Lexikon der bildenden Künstler von der Antike bis zur Gegenwart*, 37 vols. (Leipzig, 1907–50); repr. (1961–5), (1983), and (1992)
Thurloe, *State papers*	*A collection of the state papers of John Thurloe*, ed. T. Birch, 7 vols. (1742)
TLS	*Times Literary Supplement*
Tout, *Admin. hist.*	T. F. Tout, *Chapters in the administrative history of mediaeval England: the wardrobe, the chamber, and the small seals*, 6 vols. (1920–33); repr. (1967)
TRHS	*Transactions of the Royal Historical Society*
VCH	H. A. Doubleday and others, eds., *The Victoria history of the counties of England*, [88 vols.] (1900–)
Venn, *Alum. Cant.*	J. Venn and J. A. Venn, *Alumni Cantabrigienses: a biographical list of all known students, graduates, and holders of office at the University of Cambridge, from the earliest times to 1900*, 10 vols. (1922–54); repr. in 2 vols. (1974–8)
Vertue, *Note books*	[G. Vertue], *Note books*, ed. K. Esdaile, earl of Ilchester, and H. M. Hake, 6 vols., Walpole Society, 18, 20, 22, 24, 26, 30 (1930–55)
VF	*Vanity Fair*
Walford, *County families*	E. Walford, *The county families of the United Kingdom, or, Royal manual of the titled and untitled aristocracy of Great Britain and Ireland* (1860)
Walker rev.	A. G. Matthews, *Walker revised: being a revision of John Walker's Sufferings of the clergy during the grand rebellion, 1642–60* (1948); repr. (1988)
Walpole, *Corr.*	*The Yale edition of Horace Walpole's correspondence*, ed. W. S. Lewis, 48 vols. (1937–83)
Ward, *Men of the reign*	T. H. Ward, ed., *Men of the reign: a biographical dictionary of eminent persons of British and colonial birth who have died during the reign of Queen Victoria* (1885); repr. (Graz, 1968)
Waterhouse, *18c painters*	E. Waterhouse, *The dictionary of 18th century painters in oils and crayons* (1981); repr. as *British 18th century painters in oils and crayons* (1991), vol. 2 of *Dictionary of British art*
Watt, *Bibl. Brit.*	R. Watt, *Bibliotheca Britannica, or, A general index to British and foreign literature*, 4 vols. (1824) [many reprs.]
Wellesley index	W. E. Houghton, ed., *The Wellesley index to Victorian periodicals, 1824–1900*, 5 vols. (1966–89); new edn (1999) [CD-ROM]
Wing, *STC*	D. Wing, ed., *Short-title catalogue of . . . English books . . . 1641–1700*, 3 vols. (1945–51); 2nd edn (1972–88); rev. and enl. edn, ed. J. J. Morrison, C. W. Nelson, and M. Seccombe, 4 vols. (1994–8) [see also *STC, 1475–1640*]
Wisden	*John Wisden's Cricketer's Almanack*
Wood, *Ath. Oxon.*	A. Wood, *Athenae Oxonienses . . . to which are added the Fasti*, 2 vols. (1691–2); 2nd edn (1721); new edn, 4 vols., ed. P. Bliss (1813–20); repr. (1967) and (1969)
Wood, *Vic. painters*	C. Wood, *Dictionary of Victorian painters* (1971); 2nd edn (1978); 3rd edn as *Victorian painters*, 2 vols. (1995), vol. 4 of *Dictionary of British art*
WW	*Who's who* (1849–)
WWBMP	M. Stenton and S. Lees, eds., *Who's who of British members of parliament*, 4 vols. (1976–81)
WWW	*Who was who* (1929–)

Usk, Adam (*c.*1350–1430), chronicler, was born in the Monmouthshire town of Usk about the middle of the fourteenth century. His first patron was Edmund Mortimer, earl of March and lord of Usk, who sent him to Oxford, where in 1387 he was *extraordinarius* in canon law. He says in his chronicle that he was the leader of the Welsh faction in the student riots at Oxford in 1388–9, and that he held a chair of civil law there, before working for seven years (presumably 1395–1402) as an advocate in the court of the archbishop of Canterbury, Thomas Arundel. It was probably as a member of the archbishop's entourage that he attended the parliament of September 1397, in which Arundel was exiled from the realm. When Arundel and Henry Bolingbroke returned to England in July 1399, Usk joined them at Bristol and accompanied their march to Chester, of which he provides a circumstantial account. In September 1399 he was appointed to the committee that determined the grounds for Richard II's deposition and Henry's accession, and on 21 September visited Richard in the Tower of London, where, notwithstanding his hostility to Richard's style of kingship, he was much moved by the king's plight.

The earl of March had died in 1398; despite the fact that the earl's eight-year-old son's claim to the throne was overlooked in 1399, Usk soon accommodated himself to the new regime, and during the next two years his career was at its height. He received several benefices, and was regularly employed as advocate and counsellor both by Henry IV and by various magnates and prelates. Archbishop Arundel now became his foremost patron. On 19 February 1402, however, Usk left England for Rome. It is often asserted that he was compelled to leave after being convicted of horse-stealing at Westminster, but his real aim in going to Rome was to seek clerical preferment. In Rome, he was taken under the protection of Cardinal Balthasar Cossa (later Pope John XXIII), and became a papal chaplain and auditor of causes of the Apostolic Palace. His attempts to secure for himself the sees of St David's and Hereford, both of which fell vacant in 1404, aroused the anger of Henry IV, and rumours (not unfounded) now reached England that he was sympathetic to Owain Glyn Dŵr's Welsh revolt. During the Roman uprising of August 1405 he fled with Pope Innocent VII to Viterbo, returning with him to Rome in March 1406.

In June 1406 Usk left Rome and made his way back to Bruges, where he met Richard Brugge, Lancaster king of arms, who warned him not to return to England on account of the king's wrath. According to his own account, he spent the next two years wandering through France, making a living from his legal qualifications. In fact, it seems that in the winter of 1406–7 he went to Avignon, where the antipope Benedict XII provided him to the bishopric of Llandaff, presumably with Glyn Dŵr's agreement. When news of this reached England in 1407, Usk was declared a rebel and deprived of all his benefices. He also had some contact with the rebel earl of Northumberland at this time, though he declined to accompany Northumberland on his fatal invasion of England in February 1408. Meeting Richard Brugge again in Paris, Usk promised to make his way back to Wales, where he would pretend to be one of Glyn Dŵr's men, then slip away to join Edward, Lord Charlton, at Welshpool in the hope of gaining a pardon from the king. This he managed to do, though not without some alarms, and only after being obliged to spend some two years as a 'poor chaplain' at Welshpool before, on 20 March 1411, the king agreed to pardon him, at the request of Charlton and David Holbache, esquire.

Usk now returned to England, where Arundel restored him to his former post in the archiepiscopal administration and gave him the church of Merstham, Surrey, as his living. He never recovered his old influence, however, and after Arundel's death in February 1414, with his hopes of further promotion finally dashed, he seems to have spent more time in his native Wales, though in 1417 he sat on a committee of the convocation of Canterbury to secure promotion for graduates. His later years were uneventful by comparison with his earlier adventures, and by January 1429 he was said to be aged and suffering from 'long-standing incurable infirmities' (Holmes, 1.66). His will, dated 20 January 1430, was proved on 26 March. He asked to be buried before the statue of Our Lady in Usk church, where a memorial brass to him may still be seen.

Among the bequests in Usk's will was his copy of Higden's *Polychronicon*, which he left to his kinsman, Edward ab Adam. This is now BL, Add. MS 10104, and it includes, on folios 155–76, the first part (1377–1404) of the unique copy of his continuation of the *Polychronicon* from 1377 to 1421. The second part (1404–21) became detached from the British Library manuscript at some point between the seventeenth and nineteenth centuries, but was discovered *c.*1900 among the duke of Rutland's papers at Belvoir Castle, where it remains. The entire chronicle was edited by E. M. Thompson as *Chronicon Adae de Usk, 1377–1421* and published by the Royal Society of Literature in 1904. Usk began writing his chronicle in the spring of 1401, adding to it intermittently over the next twenty years. Its tone and content are heavily influenced by the author's personal experiences, and it contains a greater autobiographical element than almost any other late medieval English chronicle that has survived. It is at its fullest for the years 1397–1402, with valuable accounts of the parliament of 1397, the revolution of 1399, and the first two years of Henry IV's rule. The years 1402–14 are sparse on English affairs, but contain a good deal of information on the Glyn Dŵr revolt and the politics of the papal court at Rome (especially the turbulent years 1405–6). From 1414 onwards the chronicle once again concentrates on England (including a detailed description of the London pageants that marked Henry V's return from Agincourt), but from 1417 onwards the entries become ever briefer.

The passages on Richard II are characterized by hostility to the king's rule; those on Henry IV by an ambivalence occasioned partly by Usk's Welsh sympathies, and partly by his affection for the Mortimer family, whom some saw as having been denied the throne by Henry in 1399; while those on Henry V are lavish in their praise for the king, though tempered latterly by Usk's misgivings about the king's incessant demands for money. Dislike of taxation, and of secular encroachment upon the liberties of the church, are themes that run through the chronicle, as are a (characteristically Welsh) predilection for prophecy and topography. Although Usk does not always tell us the entire truth about himself, his chronicle nevertheless provides a fascinating picture of a man for whom the conflict of loyalties produced by the convulsive politics of the late fourteenth and early fifteenth centuries had become too acute.   C. GIVEN-WILSON

Sources *The chronicle of Adam Usk, 1377–1421*, ed. and trans. C. Given-Wilson, OMT (1997) · *Chronicon Adae de Usk*, ed. and trans. E. M. Thompson, 2nd edn (1904) · J. Norris-Jones, 'Adam Usk's epitaph', *Y Cymmrodor*, 31 (1921), 112–34 · C. Given-Wilson, 'The dating and structure of the chronicle of Adam Usk', *Welsh History Review / Cylchgrawn Hanes Cymru*, 17 (1994–5), 520–33 · J. E. Lloyd, *Owen Glendower* (1931) · *Chancery records* · *CEPR letters*, vols. 5–6 · PRO · BL, MSS · T. S. Holmes, ed., *The register of John Stafford, bishop of Bath and Wells, 1425–1443*, 1, Somerset RS, 31 (1915), 66
Archives Belvoir Castle, Leicestershire, MSS · BL, Add. MS 10104
Wealth at death see will, *Chronicon Adae de Usk*, introduction

Usk, Thomas (*c*.1354–1388), scrivener, author, and administrator, is remembered for his tragic role in the struggles for power around the throne of the young Richard II and as the author of the prose treatise *The Testament of Love*. In that work he refers to London as the 'place of his kindly engendrure' and the city in which he was 'forth growen' (ed. Skeat, I.vi.101; Shoaf, 97), and this is borne out by London documents which identify his father as a David Usk, a *hurer* ('cap maker'), and his mother as Alice, who jointly owned property 'beside Newgate' in 1364; by 1375 Alice was the wife of John Curson. There is further confirmation in the statement of the chronicler Henry Knighton that after his execution his head was set up over Newgate 'to disgrace his kinsfolk, who lived in that part of the city' (*Knighton's Chronicle*, 500). His exact date of birth is unknown; in the *Testament of Love* he talks of the events of 1381–3 as happening 'in my youth' (Skeat, I.vi.53; Shoaf, 94f.). However, he is mentioned in legal records of 1375–6 in the functions of mainpernor and attorney, which implies adult citizenship and the completion of a scrivener's apprenticeship by that time. By 1381 Usk was working as a *scriveyn*, or copyist, in the city of London, at a time when tension between the victualling and non-victualling guilds had reached its height, fuelled by anxiety about food supplies and rising prices. The power of the victuallers, in particular Sir Nicholas Brembre and Sir William Walworth, whose support had been crucial to the king during the peasants' revolt, was being challenged by John Northampton, a prominent member of the Drapers' Company, who looked for support both from the lower masters and ordinary citizenry of London and from John of Gaunt, duke of Lancaster.

Usk enters the documented history of the period, in August 1384, with his own *Appeal* (legal accusation) against John Northampton, John More, Richard Norbury, and William Essex. In this document he details his own part, first as one of Northampton's confidential clerks and later as an active collaborator, in Northampton's attempt during his two years as mayor (from October 1381 to October 1383) to undermine the power of the victualling guilds within the common council of the city and secure his own re-election. Although in reality there was much support in the city for Northampton's efforts to rein in the victuallers and bring down the price of food, Usk's accusation implied that Northampton and the three others were motivated solely by a desire for their own advancement. It was to this end, according to Usk, that they arranged to pack the meetings of the common council with their own supporters, pass legislation designed to reduce the power of aldermen and increase that of the guilds, challenge the retail monopoly of the victualling trades, and whip up feeling among the poor against the senior officers of the city.

Usk's position in the non-victuallers' faction progressed from that of a scrivener, employed 'to write thair billes' to that of 'ful helpere & promotour' (Chambers and Daunt, 23, 29–30). He confesses, for instance, to acting on Northampton's behalf to procure a parliamentary edict against usurers in the city that would permanently disqualify senior officers who were Northampton's adversaries, and attempting to influence the Commons in favour of the Northampton party's candidates. Usk also confesses to participating in dubious canvassing methods (such as the placing of armed men at the doors of the Guildhall to keep out rival supporters) in an attempt to secure the re-election of Northampton as mayor in October 1383. When Northampton's aims were thwarted by the election of Brembre, Usk was one of a delegation sent by Northampton to Gaunt to persuade him to intervene and overturn the election. As Gaunt refused to be drawn in, Northampton assembled his supporters from about thirty crafts and set out from Cheapside to carry a new election by weight of numbers, but he was dissuaded by the aldermen. Then, with Usk's active co-operation, he embarked on a course of popular agitation against Brembre, which culminated on 7 February 1384 in Northampton's arrest.

Usk himself was arrested in July or August 1384 and placed in the custody of the mayor. By 18 August, the day of the council at Reading at which Northampton was first arraigned, Usk had gone over to Brembre's party and written his *Appeal*, which was personally enacted before the king. Immediately afterwards he was returned to London under the jurisdiction of the mayor. He apparently took no personal part in the second trial of Northampton, and that of More and Norbury, in the Tower of London on 12 September, but the prosecution case was again based on his statement, in a Latin adaptation. Usk was formally pardoned 'for all treasons, felonies and other offences wherof he is indicted in the city of London' by a signet letter of 24 September 1384 (*CPR, 1381–5*, 467), but the intentions of the Brembre party remained equivocal. An exchequer document from July 1385 authorizes payment of expenses to Brembre for a period of custody lasting six months, and suggests the possibility of a trial of Usk himself on a charge of making false accusations against Northampton and his partners. Moreover, the autobiographical stratum of *The Testament of Love*, which transparently relates the events of 1381 to 1384, pictures Usk in prison and abandoned by those with whom he had allied himself. Though in this allegorical work his imprisonment can be read as metaphor, he is clearly at the time of writing (which must have been after 1384) at a low point in his fortunes and in doubt about his prospects.

In fact, Usk was not to enjoy any mark of royal favour until the following summer (1385), when, as a serjeant-at-arms of the king, he received a paid commission to raise ships and men for the relief of Damme. He enjoyed his position as a lowly member of the king's affinity for little more than two years. In August and September 1387 Thomas Usk, the king's serjeant-at-arms, is named as a mainpernor in deeds of commitment of several manors in Sussex and Kent to Nicholas Exton, a mayor of London belonging to the Brembre faction, and in the same year he was appointed under-sheriff of Middlesex at the king's request, conveyed to the mayor and sheriffs of London in a letter of the privy seal dated 2 September. By December, however, he was under arrest and at the mercy of the lords appellant.

In the following year Usk shared the fate of the circle of the king's advisers by whose influence he had briefly achieved preferment, when the lords appellant persuaded the Merciless Parliament to pass sentence of death on Michael de la Pole, Simon Burley, Robert de Vere, and others, for treasonably misleading the king. In the parliamentary proceedings Usk is named as an accomplice of Brembre in a conspiracy against the life of the duke of Gloucester, and one of the charges against Alexander Neville, archbishop of York, is that of advising the king to bestow lands and offices on Usk. On 4 March Usk himself was impeached of treason in full parliament and condemned to be drawn and hanged. It is reported by the Westminster chronicler that he went to his death with great piety and contrition, reciting funeral offices, but maintaining to the end his loyalty to the king and the truth of his accusations against Northampton. His execution at Tyburn was brutal: 'Thomas Usk was hanged and immediately taken down and, after about thirty strokes of the axe, beheaded' (*Westminster Chronicle*, 315).

The Testament of Love, Usk's only known composition apart from the *Appeal*, is a prose treatise in English in three books. It was first printed, from a manuscript since lost, by William Thynne in his 1532 edition of the works of Chaucer, to whom the work was sometimes attributed until the true author was identified in the late nineteenth century by Henry Bradley. In 1897 Thynne's print became the basis of a conjecturally restored text edited by W. W. Skeat in volume 7 (*Chaucerian and other Pieces*) of his *Complete Works of Geoffrey Chaucer*.

Written in the form of a Boethian dialogue between a prisoner and a Lady Love who appears to him in a vision, it shows textual knowledge of recent works of Chaucer, including *The Hous of Fame*, *Boece*, and *Troilus and Criseyde*. Chaucer himself is referred to by the Lady Love as the author of 'the boke of Troilus' and 'myne owne trewe servaunt, the noble philosophical poete in English' (ed. Skeat, III.iv.248–9, 258–9; Shoaf, 266). Usk has evidently been influenced by his reading of Chaucer in his discussions of such topics as fortune and the freedom of the will, and in his portrayal of the character Love as representative of both earthly and divine love. But his book is far from being a slavish imitation of the *Boece*. It draws on a number of other sources than Chaucer, including the *Polychronicon* of Ranulf Higden and writings of St Anselm on predestination, grace, and free will. Its genre is that of many-layered allegory, allowing a number of parallel interpretations on various figural and actual levels; its aim, apparently, is to vindicate his political choices and actions through a presentation of his philosophy of life. The narrator himself expounds the multiple significances of his character Margaret, who is named repeatedly as his mistress and potential benefactress in his conversations with Love: she is (like the margarite or pearl) 'grace, lerning, or wisdom of god, or els holy church' (Skeat, III.ix.102–3; Shoaf, 305). The identification of Margaret with holy church convinced Skeat that Usk's object was to clear himself of the taint of Lollardy. The suggestion of heresy can, however, also be read as political allegory, in which case he is pleading for acceptance as a penitent by the royal party. On yet another level of interpretation Margaret is clearly a 'deedly [mortal]' woman (Skeat, II.xii.121; Shoaf, 217), who is addressed as his courtly mistress in an acrostic composed of the first letter of the prologue and each of the book's thirty-three chapters: 'Margarete of virtw have merci on thin Vsk'. Usk was himself witness at Reading to the effective intervention of Queen Anne to mitigate the punishment of Northampton and it is possible that his *Testament* has a similar aim in relation to himself in the period after his pardon in September 1384, while he was still in danger of being disposed of by the court circle as of no further use.

For all its obscurity, the *Testament of Love* is important as an early example of the use of the vernacular in an original prose composition and as exhibiting the response to Chaucer's works of a contemporary reader and disciple. Its baffling versatility is a fitting tribute to a writer and politician who has been described as a 'supple code-switcher' in all his doings.   RONALD WALDRON

Sources corporation of London documents, GL, hustings rolls 91/186, 187; 103/38, 39, 279; 108/47 • A. H. Thomas and P. E. Jones, eds., *Calendar of plea and memoranda rolls preserved among the archives of the corporation of the City of London at the Guildhall*, 2 (1929) • R. R. Sharpe, ed., *Calendar of letter-books preserved in the archives of the corporation of the City of London*, [12 vols.] (1899–1912), vols. G–H • R. R. Sharpe, ed., *Calendar of wills proved and enrolled in the court of husting, London, AD 1258 – AD 1688*, 2 vols. (1889–90) • H. T. Riley, ed., *Memorials of London and London life in the XIIIth, XIVth, and XVth centuries* (1868) • exchequer issue rolls, PRO, E403/508/m.17; E403/510/m.6 • miscellanea of the exchequer, PRO, E163/5/28 • *Chancery records* • R. W. Chambers and M. Daunt, eds., *A book of London English, 1384–1425* (1931), 18–31 [Usk's *Appeal*] • T. Usk, 'The testament of love', *Chaucerian and other pieces*, ed. W. Skeat (1897), [vol. 7] of *The complete works of Geoffrey Chaucer* (1894–7), xviii–xxxi, 1–144 • T. Usk, *The testament of love*, ed. R. A. Shoaf (1998) • A. Middleton, 'Thomas Usk's "perdurable letters": the *Testament of love* from script to print', *Studies in Bibliography*, 51 (1998), 63–116 • E. Powell and G. M. Trevelyan, eds., *The peasants' rising and the Lollards* (1899) • *RotP*, vol. 3 • L. C. Hector and B. F. Harvey, eds. and trans., *The Westminster chronicle, 1381–1394*, OMT (1982) • *Knighton's chronicle, 1337–1396*, ed.

and trans. G. H. Martin, OMT (1995) [Lat. orig., *Chronica de eventibus Angliae a tempore regis Edgari usque mortem regis Ricardi Secundi*, with parallel Eng. text] · P. Nightingale, *A medieval mercantile community: the Grocers' Company and the politics and trade of London, 1000–1485* (1995) · R. Bird, *The turbulent London of Richard II* (1949) · R. Bressie, 'The date of Thomas Usk's *Testament of love*', *Modern Philology*, 26 (1928–9), 17–29 · P. Strohm, 'The textual vicissitudes of Usk's *Appeal*', in P. Strohm, *Hochon's arrow* (1992), 145–60
Archives PRO, miscellanea of the exchequer, E 163/5/28 no. 9

Ussher, Ambrose (*c*.1582–1629), Church of Ireland clergyman and scholar, was born in Dublin, one of the ten children of Arland Ussher (*d.* 1598), a clerk of chancery, and his wife, Margaret, the daughter of James Stanyhurst and Anna Fitzsimons. He was the younger and only surviving brother of James *Ussher, the future archbishop of Armagh. Ussher may have studied at Cambridge. He was definitely a student at Trinity College, Dublin, graduating BA by 1601, proceeding MA by 1605, and, according to James Ware, being also awarded a BD. He served both as librarian and as a lecturer and was elected fellow on 7 March 1611.

Little is known about Ussher's public career. He wrote on his brother's behalf to the mathematician Henry Briggs in 1606, and was described the following year by the orientalist William Eyre as a 'most learned young man'. By 1615 he had secured two rectories in co. Louth, Darver and Mansfieldstown, but he had given these up by 1622. There are two reasons for his relative anonymity. First, incapacity: from late 1608 to mid-1609 his Trinity salary was paid to his brother James because of his 'sickness' (Mahaffy, *Particular Book*, fol. 36b). In fact he was so mentally ill during this period that he was put under restraint. Second, he devoted a considerable amount of his time to study and writing. There survive well over thirty of his manuscript sermons, commentaries, and lengthy books (TCD, Manuscripts Room), suggesting an extremely wide range—from Arabic, where he compiled a dictionary and grammar, to controversial and systematic theology, attacking Bellarmine in particular, to astronomy, and even to politics, where he composed a 'Discourse of the question of Scotland's union with England' (TCD, MS 287).

Ussher's most interesting achievement is his translation of the Bible: three manuscript volumes survive containing nearly all the Old Testament, and less than half of the New Testament—all of Romans, Revelation, and some of the minor epistles, and part of John and Corinthians. Begun well before but completed just after the Authorized Version of 1609, it was, to say the least, unfortunately timed. Ussher sought to rescue the project with a dedication to James, over-optimistically asserting that the king, unlike his Catholic adversaries, wanted as many different biblical translations as possible. Ussher contrasted the derivative nature of the Authorized Version which had, he claimed, sucked up the juice from all the old and worn translations, with the freshness of his own approach. But although he trumpeted over one thousand 'changes of matter', his translation, in fact, differed only marginally from those of Tyndale and his successors. Nevertheless, it was more than just an academic exercise. It reads well.

Like Tyndale, he is sensitive to the challenge of conveying the relationship between Hebrew word order and sense in his English translation. He also confirms the judgement that the Authorized Version scholars deliberately used anachronistic phrases, by himself choosing more colloquial and fresh translations: 'you' rather than 'ye'; 'to' rather than 'unto'; 'lust' rather than 'concupiscence'. He clearly intended his manuscript works for a wider audience—two were dedicated to Irish lord deputies, but none, bar the first twenty-eight pages of a catechism, was ever printed.

Ussher died suddenly and unmarried in 1629 and was buried in Dublin on 4 March. His best epitaph is perhaps that of his brother's biographer, Richard Parr, who described him as 'a very learned young man, who died too early'.   ALAN FORD

Sources *The whole works of … James Ussher*, ed. C. R. Elrington and J. H. Todd, 17 vols. (1847–64), vol. 1, p. 315; vol. 15, pp. 22, 426 · J. P. Mahaffy, ed., *The particular book of Trinity College, Dublin* (1904) · *The whole works of Sir James Ware concerning Ireland*, ed. and trans. W. Harris, rev. edn, 2/2 (1764), 128–9 · J. P. Mahaffy, *An epoch in Irish history: Trinity College, Dublin, its foundation and early fortunes, 1591–1660* (1903), 121–3 · J. B. Leslie, *Armagh clergy and parishes* (1911), 208, 368 · *Fourth report*, HMC, 3 (1874), 598–9 · college muniments, TCD, P/1/52 · W. B. Wright, *The Ussher memoirs* (1889)
Archives TCD, Old Library, translation of Bible, MS 68 · TCD, Old Library, Arabic and Hebrew grammatical collection, MSS 221 and 222 · TCD, Old Library, theological disputation, MSS 285–286 · TCD, Old Library, sermons and other MSS, incl. discourse on union of Scotland and England, MS 287 · TCD, Old Library, misc. works, MSS 788–789 · TCD, Old Library, Hebrew and Latin notes, MS 290 · TCD, Old Library, treatises against Roman Catholic church, MS 291 · TCD, Old Library, translation of Psalm, MS 1210 · TCD, Old Library, Arabic notes, MS 1514

Ussher, Henry (*c*.1550–1613), Church of Ireland archbishop of Armagh, one of eight children (five sons and three daughters) of Thomas Ussher (1499–1566) and Margaret (*d.* 1597), daughter of Henry Geydon, alderman of Dublin, was born in Dublin about 1550. James *Ussher, a successor as archbishop of Armagh, was the son of his brother Arland and Margaret Stanihurst, sister to Richard Stanihurst. There were three branches of the old established Ussher family active in civic life in Dublin in the second half of the sixteenth century, Henry belonging to that of St Nicholas's parish. An uncle, Alderman John Ussher of Bridgefoot Street, was the publisher in 1571 of the first Irish language book ever printed in Ireland, a protestant catechism.

Henry Ussher entered Magdalene College, Cambridge, matriculating on 2 May 1567, and graduated BA in the first quarter of 1570. His studies continued at Paris and at Oxford, where he entered University College, was incorporated BA on 1 July 1572 and graduated MA on 11 July 1572. His first preferment was the treasurership of Christ Church, Dublin (1573). On 12 March 1580 he was made archdeacon of Dublin by Archbishop Adam Loftus, with whom the Usshers were connected by marriage. He married, about 1573, Margaret, daughter of Thomas Eliot of Balrisk, co. Meath; they had eight sons and two daughters. His second wife was Mary Smith (who survived him); they had three daughters.

Ussher was a leading agent in two campaigns for an Irish university. Negatively, he was an emissary from Archbishop Loftus to the English privy council in London on two occasions in the winter and spring of 1584–5. On the first visit he bore a petition which was designed to undermine the scheme for the foundation of a university college based on the revenues of St Patrick's Cathedral, Dublin, a project being advanced by the lord deputy, Sir John Perrot. Loftus was successful in frustrating the project which was abandoned in June 1585.

Positively, Ussher was involved in the scheme of the early 1590s to set up an academy on the site of the former monastery of All Hallows, near Dublin. The municipal corporation, the original grantee of the property, offered the site for the erection of a college. Ussher was again sent to London, this time to further the scheme of which Loftus thoroughly approved, with letters dated 4 November 1591. On 13 January 1592 he received a warrant (dated 21 December) granting the royal assent for the establishment. On 3 March 1592 the foundation charter passed the great seal. Ussher was named in it as one of the three fellows; he never, however, acted as such, nor was he one of the original benefactors.

On the death of John *Garvey, his brother-in-law, on 2 March 1595, Ussher succeeded him as archbishop of Armagh and primate of Ireland; he was appointed on 22 July 1595 and was consecrated the following day. Described as 'very perfect in the Irish language' (*CSP Ire.*, 1592–6, 311), he was deemed suitable for appointment because he was 'of good years, wise, well learned and of sincere life' (Morrin, 402). Owing to the poverty of the see, he was allowed to continue to hold the archdeaconry of Dublin *in commendam*. Blaming the predecessor of Garvey, Archbishop Thomas Long, for alienating church lands, he sought protection from Sir Robert Cecil against the complaints of disaffected landholders whose 'unreasonable leases' had caused 'utter havock in the primacy' (*CSP Ire.*, 1592–6, 508).

Ussher's archiepiscopal career was overshadowed by the disruption caused in central Ulster by the Nine Years' War until 1603 and the subsequent mopping up of the rebellion. By the time peace was established in the region he was nearing the end of his life. The poor state of his archdiocese and his own lassitude are attested to in the account of Lord Deputy Chichester's visit to Armagh in 1605. Angered at the dilapidation of the cathedral church and the alienation of livings for vicars choral by the dean, the lord deputy rounded on Ussher, who was in his entourage, ordering him to appoint a minister to Armagh, to preach in Irish every summer and to appropriate the tithes and profits of the college of vicars for the maintenance of scholars from Ulster at Trinity College.

Ussher died at Termonfeckin on Easter Sunday, 2 April 1613, and was buried in St Peter's Church, Drogheda. His widow married William Fitzwilliams of Dundrum in 1614. His youngest son, Robert *Ussher, who was educated at Trinity, became provost of the university and later was promoted to the episcopal see of Kildare.

Henry Ussher's main contribution to the intellectual and cultural life of his time lies in his being of the first generation of Reformation churchmen to emerge from the local milieu. Steeped as he was in the traditions and aspirations of the English ecclesio-political establishment in Ireland, he was fully committed to the credal position of the Anglican church. He was also fully supportive of the drive for a native seminary for the training of ministers in the reformed religion in Ireland, but not at the expense (as he and others saw it) of the depleted revenues of the church in Dublin. Instead he backed enthusiastically the plan for a college on a former monastic site, and his support was manifested in his sending of his own offspring for their education there. COLM LENNON

Sources *CSP Ire.*, 1574–85, 468, 537, 544; 1588–92, 437; 1592–6, 317, 508, 525; 1603–6, 317; 1611–14, 81 · J. Morrin, ed., *Calendar of the patent and close rolls of chancery in Ireland, of the reigns of Henry VIII, Edward VI, Mary, and Elizabeth*, 2 (1862), 321, 402 · W. B. Wright, *The Ussher memoirs* (1889), 30–42 · J. Murray, 'The Tudor diocese of Dublin: episcopal government, ecclesiastical politics and the enforcement of the reformation, c.1534–1590', PhD diss., TCD, 1997, 365–6 · C. Lennon, '"The bowels of the city's bounty": the municipality of Dublin and the foundation of Trinity College in 1592', *Long Room*, 37 (1992), 10–16 · *DNB* · C. Lennon, *The lords of Dublin in the age of the Reformation* (1989), 88, 135–7, 274 · H. J. Lawlor, *The fasti of St Patrick's, Dublin* (1930), 79
Likenesses oils, 17th cent., episcopal palace, Armagh; repro. in Wright, *Ussher memoirs*, facing p. 44
Wealth at death at least £300 owed to his estate; income from lease of tithes of seven rectories; at least three houses, in Drogheda, Dublin, and Termonfeckin: Wright, *Ussher memoirs*, 47–8

Ussher, Henry (1741–1790), astronomer, was the fourth son of the seven children of Revd Samuel Ussher (1694–1771), rector of Dunganstown, co. Wicklow, and his wife, Frances, the daughter of Revd Philip Walsh of Blessington and his wife, Catherine. He was descended from a notable Irish family whose former members included James Ussher, archbishop of Armagh from 1624 to 1656. From 1756 to 1790 he was associated with Trinity College, Dublin, where he became a scholar in 1759. He graduated BA in 1761, MA in 1764, and BD and DD in 1779, gained a fellowship in 1764, and was lecturer in mathematics from 1769 to 1770. He was then appointed university preacher and professor of divinity, and became a senior fellow in 1781. He resigned his previous professorship on his appointment to the new post of Andrews' professor of astronomy from 14 December 1784, and took up residence at Dunsink observatory, co. Dublin, in August 1785. He had established himself as the fellow best qualified in astronomical calculation and in meteorological work prior to this appointment. On behalf of the college he consulted with Nevil Maskelyne, the astronomer royal of England at Greenwich, as to the design of major observing equipment to be installed at the new observatory, which was built according to his requirements on land that had belonged to the family of the wife of the Revd Daniel Beaufort. The Beauforts were at one time neighbours to the Usshers in Mecklenbergh Street, Dublin, where Ussher had set up a small observatory with a telescope and transit instrument in 1774.

Equipment for Dunsink was ordered from Jesse Ramsden of London (1735–1800), together with two pendulum clocks by John Arnold & Son. A 4¼ inch achromatic telescope mounted as a transit instrument was delivered in 1785. Of the other instruments ordered, two equatorial telescopes were never delivered, and serious delays affected the huge 'vertical circle' which, following the design of the 5 foot Palermo circle by Ramsden, was at first intended to be 10 feet in diameter. Eventually, eighteen years after Ussher's death, and eight years after Ramsden's, an 8 foot circle was delivered to Ussher's successor, the Revd John Brinkley.

The construction of Dunsink observatory, deriving, as was the professorship, from the legacy of Provost Andrews, owed a great deal to the co-operation of Ussher and Maskelyne, and is described in some detail by Ussher in the first paper published in the *Transactions of the Royal Irish Academy* (1, 1787, 3–21). Ussher, with his special interest in meteorology, is credited with the design of the first permanent observing room (his meridian room) in which meteorological factors were taken into account—circulation of air being a prime consideration. The rotating dome on the top of the 1785 building was an early design, following that of Kew observatory, and stone pillars supporting the instruments, including the intended equatorial telescope under the rotating dome, rested on bedrock, independently of the adjacent walls. This was the earliest example of such construction, which became commonplace thereafter.

The establishment of Dunsink was Ussher's principal life work. His other notable contribution was undoubtedly the instruction given to Francis, the younger son of the Revd Daniel Beaufort, Ussher's observing assistant for five months from November 1788, which prepared him for his successful and influential career as hydrographer of the Royal Navy.

Ussher was a founder member of the Royal Irish Academy, and his contributions to the *Transactions* include investigations of instrumental and meteorological factors; these and unpublished material remaining at Dunsink indicate his care and concern for details. A note in the *Transactions* on the rotation period of Saturn derived from observations of the planet's apparent ellipticity and Ussher's very remarkable observation of the aurora borealis in daylight in 1788 testify to his awareness of physical considerations in interpreting observations. Ussher was elected to fellowship of the Royal Society of London in 1785, the year the Irish Academy was founded.

Ussher's marriage to Margaret Burne, a member of a prominent Dublin family, produced eight children. The eldest son, Sir Thomas *Ussher RN (1779–1848), captained the ship that took Napoleon to Elba in 1814. Ussher died suddenly at his home in Harcourt Street, Dublin, on 8 May 1790, his last entry in the Dunsink weather diary being on 5 May, and was buried in the chapel of Trinity College. His death was thought to have been hastened by excessive night work in cold, damp conditions. The board of Trinity College promised a pension for his widow and grants towards publication of his sermons (50 guineas) and his astronomical papers (20 guineas); it also ordered a bust to be provided at the observatory in his memory and

announced a prize essay on 'The death of Ussher'. Only the essay prize —and possibly the widow's pension—were awarded.   P. A. WAYMAN

Sources W. B. S. Taylor, *History of the University of Dublin* (1845) · P. A. Wayman, *Dunsink observatory, 1785–1985: a bicentennial history* (1987) · J. P. Mahaffy and others, *The book of Trinity College, Dublin, 1591–1891* (1892) · *DNB* · A. Friendly, *Beaufort of the Admiralty* (1977) · H. Ussher, 'Account of the observatory belonging to Trinity College, Dublin', *Transactions of the Royal Irish Academy*, 1: Science (1786–7), 3–21 · I. Duff, 'Henry Ussher and the early history of Dunsink observatory: a bicentennial note', *Journal of the British Astronomical Association*, 94 (1983–4), 18–21 · W. B. Wright, *The Ussher memoirs* (1889) · P. A. Wayman, 'Henry Ussher at Dunsink, 1783–1790', *Irish Astronomical Journal*, 10 (1971–2), 121–8
Archives Dunsink observatory, Dublin
Likenesses drawing, repro. in Wright, *Ussher memoirs*

Ussher, James (1581–1656), Church of Ireland archbishop of Armagh and scholar, was born in Nicholas Street, Dublin, on 4 January 1581, the fifth of ten children of Arland Ussher (*d.* 1598), one of the clerks of chancery, and his wife, Margaret (*d.* 1626), daughter of James Stanyhurst, gentleman, of Corduff, co. Dublin, and Anna Fitzsimons; Ambrose *Ussher (*c.*1582–1629) was his only surviving brother. Both his parents came from prominent Anglo-Irish families, and James was brought up in a prosperous Dublin household. Though some branches of the family had opted for Catholicism by the end of the sixteenth century, James's side (with the notable exception of his mother) were protestant, and his uncle Henry Ussher was Church of Ireland archbishop of Armagh from 1595 to 1613.

Early education and Trinity College, Dublin, 1594–1618
According to Nicholas Bernard, his first biographer, who provides many unique (and, of course, unverifiable) details of his early life, Ussher was taught to read, rather incongruously, by two aunts blind from infancy. As an eight-year-old he was sent to the nearby Dublin Free School kept by two firmly protestant Scottish graduates, James Hamilton and James Fullerton. When the new Irish university, Trinity College, Dublin, was opened in 1594, Ussher entered as one of the first scholars, and was joined by Hamilton and Fullerton as two of its first fellows. This was a crucial choice: although it was founded to educate the youth of Ireland, Trinity's commitment to the Reformation ultimately ensured that it had a much narrower remit—to train the protestant élite for church and state in a largely Catholic country. More than that, Trinity's protestantism was of an uncompromising type: its first real provost was the English presbyterian leader Walter Travers, who entertained in Trinity his fellow presbyterian Humphrey Fenn, and it was, not surprisingly, dogged in its early decades by accusations that it harboured puritans. The young Ussher therefore encountered at Trinity a firmly Calvinist outlook which shaped his theology and may also have influenced his later tolerance towards nonconformity.

Ussher had gained his BA by 1598, and in the same year his father (who had wanted him to become a lawyer) died, leaving him free to pursue a career in the ministry. In 1599 he impressed the earl of Essex at a public disputation in

James Ussher (1581–1656), by Sir Peter Lely, c.1654

Trinity, and he proceeded MA on 6 February 1601. Generally, both through his own efforts, and through those of his teachers, he received a thorough academic grounding, learning Greek and Hebrew (and subsequently several other ancient languages), being taught divinity by Travers and being introduced to Ramist logic, and commencing his lifelong fascination with biblical chronology. He also, again according to Bernard, launched himself at the age of twenty on the immense and eighteen-year-long task of reading through the entire corpus of the Latin and Greek church fathers. In 1600 he made the transition from student to fellow, and was awarded the degrees of BD in 1607 and DD in 1612. He was ordained in December 1601, having obtained a dispensation allowing him to be made priest before the canonical age.

As a fellow, Ussher was active both outside and within the university as a preacher and teacher. He was one of a trio of Trinity fellows who provided three weekly public lectures in Christ Church, Dublin. In 1602 he also preached to Catholic congregations during a brief campaign to force recusants to attend protestant services. The suspension of this campaign on the orders of the lord deputy, Charles Blount, Lord Mountjoy, led him to attack official toleration of Catholicism in a sermon on Ezekiel 4: 6, in which he predicted a judgement after forty years. He was presented by Archbishop Adam Loftus of Dublin to the chancellorship of St Patrick's Cathedral in 1605 (illegally, as it turned out; the mistake was rectified by a royal appointment to the post on 12 July 1611), and served the prebend of Finglas, where he preached every Sunday. Inside the college he acted as catechist, and from 1607 as professor of theological controversies. He was chosen

vice-chancellor on 2 March 1615, and became vice-provost on 13 May 1616. Together with Luke Challoner, the vice-provost of Trinity until his death in 1613, Ussher made expeditions to London in 1602, 1606, and 1609 to buy books for the college, and make contact with English literati, including Henry Briggs, John Davenant, Sir Henry Savile, and William Camden. The last-mentioned asked him to contribute material about Ireland for the 1607 edition of *Britannia*.

The main focus of Ussher's early academic career was anti-Catholic theology and history. While still a student, he had challenged his Catholic relative the Jesuit Henry Fitzsimon, then imprisoned in Dublin Castle, to a public disputation on the identification of the pope with Antichrist. Fitzsimon declined to take on the callow youth, but the thrust of Ussher's scholarly interest was confirmed by his lectures as professor, which consisted of a detailed refutation of the theological works of Robert Bellarmine, the great Jesuit controversialist. In 1613 he married Phoebe, daughter of Luke Challoner and Rose Ball, and published his first work, *Gravissimae quaestionis, de Christianarum ecclesiarum … continua successione et statu, historica explicatio*. This demonstrated what became the hallmarks of Ussher's published work: thorough and impartial scholarship which demonstrated a rare gift for discovering and printing crucial primary sources; often, however, allied to a rather more partial and polemical subtext. The main substance of the work was a meticulous and path-breaking account of many medieval heretical groups, based upon extensive and often original manuscript research. But it also had an underlying polemical purpose: this was to trace the rise of Antichrist in the Roman Catholic church, especially from the eleventh century, and to demonstrate how the purity of the Christian gospel was preserved in the later middle ages by groups such as the Cathars and Waldensians. Hence Ussher sought to emphasize the proto-protestant elements of the heretics, and discard as Catholic distortions evidence which contradicted this. According to the table of contents, the work was to extend up to the Reformation, but the latter part was never completed; Ussher abandoned the narrative in the early twelfth century, thus leaving it unclear just how radical he was prepared to be in tracing a non-episcopal descent for the protestant churches through an at times bizarre collection of heretics.

Ussher was also involved in drawing up the Church of Ireland's first full confession of faith—the articles passed by convocation in 1615. Bernard claimed that Ussher as a member of the lower house was appointed as 'a principal person' to draw them up (N. Bernard, *Judgement of the Archbishop of Armagh*, 1657, 67). Ussher's grandson later argued that this simply meant that he acted as a kind of clerk or editor, collating the results of the discussions of the two houses of convocation. Modern scholars have tended to interpret his role differently, seeing him as the primary drafter of the Irish articles, a view supported by the overlap between one of his catechisms and some of the articles. Given the complete absence of sources about the working of the convocation, it is impossible to decide with any precision how far he wrote or merely edited the articles. Three things are clear, however: first, the Irish articles were a considerable advance upon the Thirty-Nine Articles, on which they were based—they were fuller, more hostile to Roman Catholicism, much more explicitly Calvinist, incorporating the Lambeth articles—indeed, they acted as a fascinating link between the Elizabethan settlement and the Westminster confession; second, and as a result, they allowed the Irish church to accommodate a far wider range of opinions on the puritan wing than was possible in the Church of England—they were, for instance, more flexible on the issue of episcopacy, and, crucially, they did not require subscription; and third, Ussher was closely associated, and, as is apparent from his later career, fully supported the theological stance of the Irish articles.

Bishop and politician, 1619–1624 The five years after 1619 dramatically altered Ussher's status and reputation, transforming him from an Irish university professor to a public figure known in England as well as Ireland for his erudition and judiciousness. The key to his new prominence seems to have been his meeting (precise date unknown) with James I. He arrived in England in 1619 (for what turned out to be a two-year stay) with a recommendation from the Irish privy council stressing that, despite rumours to the contrary, he was not puritan, but rather 'an excellent and painful preacher, a modest man, abounding in goodness, and his life and doctrine so agreeable, as those who agree not with him are yet constrained to love and admire him' (Parr, 15–16). His only child, Elizabeth, was born in London and baptized on 19 September that year at St Dunstan-in-the-East. Always partial to a scholar–cleric, James on 16 January 1621 nominated him to succeed George Montgomery as bishop of Meath, an appointment welcomed at the highest level in Ireland— the Irish lord deputy, Oliver St John, Lord Grandison, wrote to him: 'there is none here but are exceeding glad that you are called thereunto, even some Papists themselves have testified their gladness of it' (*Works*, 1.52). Ussher's rapid rise was confirmed when he was invited to preach before the two houses of the English parliament on 18 February 1621 during a joint communion service. The invitation placed him in an interesting position. The king wanted him to use the occasion to urge parliament to grant supply as quickly as possible. But the invitation seems to have come from the firmly protestant circle around the earl of Pembroke, concerned about James's reluctance to support the protestant cause in Europe, and impressed with the strongly anti-Catholic tone of Ussher's sermons since his arrival in London. Typically, Ussher sought to please both parties, reminding the assembled company that 'God loves a giver', before going on to urge firm measures against idolatrous, anti-Christian papists.

Ussher remained in England until the summer, and as a result was not consecrated bishop of Meath until 2 December 1621. Even at this stage the competing demands on his time—episcopal, political, and scholarly—were evident. He had, obviously, many responsibilities in his diocese. As

early as July he had been engaged in a dispute with Archbishop Christopher Hampton of Armagh over whether or not he could exercise episcopal jurisdiction before consecration. His first major administrative task was to compile what was, in effect if not in name, a detailed visitation, reporting on the condition of his large diocese to the commissioners sent over from England in 1622. His reply, one of the most detailed, demonstrates that the ministry in Meath, while one of the best equipped in Ireland with preaching ministers, nevertheless was not without its problems, suffering from lay appropriation of benefices, financial difficulties, and decaying church fabric, not to mention the irrefragable determination of the local Irish population to resist all the blandishments and bullying of the protestant church, state, and clergy. Ussher had also to deal with the legally complex and politically sensitive issue of tithing.

Yet Ussher could spend little time in his diocese because of his political and academic commitments. He was now a national figure, a member of the Irish privy council, chosen to preach at the swearing-in on 8 September of the new lord deputy, Henry Cary, Viscount Falkland. Nor was he content with clerical platitudes: at the inauguration he used the pulpit to deliver a clear anti-Catholic and politically loaded message, basing his sermon on Romans 13: 'Let every soul be subject unto the higher powers', taking as his particular text 'for he beareth not the sword in vain: for he is the minister of God, a revenger to execute wrath upon him that doeth evil'. Ussher's call for the new lord deputy firmly to enforce the laws against recusancy caused considerable and understandable concern among the Irish Catholics, who were hoping that James's pursuit of a Spanish marriage for his son might lead him to be more tolerant in his treatment of his Catholic subjects. The subsequent furore, in which Catholics claimed that Ussher had stated that 'the sword had rusted too long in the sheath' (*Works*, 15.181), led to a reprimand for Ussher from Hampton, who called on him to withdraw his offensive remarks and suggested that in future he spend more time in his diocese. But his views were not all that dissimilar to those of the Dublin administration, and in November 1622 the authorities chose him to address a gathering in Dublin of recusant officials who had refused the oath of supremacy: his speech was subsequently published and earned him a commendatory letter from the king.

In addition to his new role as ecclesiastical politician Ussher was determined to maintain his former commitment to academic research and writing. Though he had resigned his professorship on being appointed bishop in 1621, he still used his regular and often lengthy trips to England both to exploit English libraries and also to maintain his extensive contacts with leading scholars such as John Selden, Henry Spelman, and Robert Cotton. One significant result of his researches was a small treatise entitled (in its 1631 edition) *A Discourse of the Religion Anciently Professed by the Irish and British*, first printed in 1622 as an appendix to a work published by Ussher's friend the Irish judge Christopher Sibthorpe. This set out to examine the early history of the Irish church, and, through a typically Ussherian combination of meticulous scholarship and the anachronistic imposition of later religious concepts and divisions, showed to his satisfaction that the Celtic church in Ireland had been, essentially, protestant. Ussher thus provided the Church of Ireland with its classic origin myth, legitimizing both its descent from the early Irish church and its possession of that church's cathedrals, churches, and livings. This claim formed the basis for countless histories of the Church of Ireland, right down to the twentieth century.

In late summer 1623 Ussher returned to England, where he researched for his major work on 'the antiquities of the British church before and since the Christian faith was received by the English nation' (Parr, 24). This time he remained away until March 1626, delayed in England by a serious fever which laid him low for a considerable period. His priorities were indicated clearly by the letter he secured from James which excused him from his episcopal duties so that he could pursue his project. Certainly the king saw him as a major scholarly and ecclesiastical figure. On 20 June 1624 he preached before James at Wanstead on the universality of the church of Christ, and towards the end of 1624 came his second major scholarly publication, a lengthy work of controversial anti-Catholic theology dedicated to King James, *An Answer to a Challenge Made by a Jesuit in Ireland*. The challenge was to prove that the doctrines held by the Roman Catholic church were not in all respects those of the early Christian church. Ussher unleashed his many years of patristic and historical scholarship to prove that the medieval and modern papacy had strayed from early purity in the familiar controversial areas of real presence, confession, purgatory, prayer for the dead, prayer to saints, images, free will, and merits. In November 1625 he was invited by Lord and Lady Mordaunt (later earl and countess of Peterborough) to visit their home at Drayton in Northamptonshire to engage in a debate with a Catholic priest. The rigour of his arguments routed the priest, and confirmed the wavering Mordaunts in the protestant faith.

Archbishop and politician, 1625–1635 On 3 January 1625 Archbishop Hampton died. With James favourably disposed, and his patron, the puritan Mary, Lady Vere, lobbying secretary of state Edward Conway, Lord Conway, Ussher was nominated to the primacy on 29 January 1625. When he returned to Ireland in 1626 for his consecration, he found that political tensions were rising. As England moved to war with Spain, King Charles sought to secure his Irish flank against Spanish attack by negotiating with the Irish Catholics, hitherto excluded from political and legal office in Ireland, for a financial contribution to the upkeep of the army. In return Charles offered them a series of concessions (including, initially, religious toleration), which became known as the Graces.

The prospect of sharing power with what he viewed as anti-Christian papists greatly alarmed Ussher, and he called a secret meeting of the Irish bishops at his house in Drogheda in November 1626, which drew up a classic statement of early modern intolerance:

> The religion of the papists is superstitious and idolatrous; their faith and doctrine, erroneous and heretical; their church in respect of both, apostatical. To give them therefore a toleration, or to consent that they might freely exercise their religion, and profess their faith and doctrine, is a grievous sin.   (Parr, 28)

Conscious that talks between the Irish Catholics and Charles might break down, Ussher initially refrained from publicizing the statement. But by April 1627, with negotiations seemingly moving to a successful conclusion, his doubts were made public in a series of sermons preached in Dublin by Ussher, Archbishop Archibald Hamilton of Cashel, and Bishop George Downham of Derry, with the last-mentioned leading the way on 23 April in Christ Church Cathedral, where he read out the bishops' statement and asked: 'Are not many among us for gain and outward respects, willing and ready to consent to a toleration of false religion?' (Bodl. Oxf., MS Carte 1, fol. 86r). That the Irish authorities at least were sympathetic to Ussher's position is suggested by the invitation to the primate to address the assembly called to discuss the Graces on 30 April, so that he could urge all those present to make a contribution to the defence of the country, an occasion which he also used to defend the bishops' outspokenness. In the end the Graces were never officially confirmed by parliament.

After the departure of Lord Falkland in 1629, the two Irish lords justices, Adam Loftus, Viscount Loftus, and Richard Boyle, earl of Cork, filled a long interregnum before the arrival of Thomas Wentworth as lord deputy in 1633. They were finally able to give vent to the innate anti-Catholicism of Irish protestants, and set about closing down Catholic religious houses and imposing conformity. Amid hopes that the new lord deputy would continue this crusade, Ussher made contact with a rising star in the English ecclesiastical scene, William Laud, archbishop of Canterbury from 1633, seeking to exploit his growing influence over patronage and policy to the benefit of the Irish church. It was to Laud that he explained his own preferred solution to the government's financial problems: since the Irish Catholics were the main source of the state's insecurity, it was only just that they should be made to pay for the support of an army through the imposition of fines for their recusancy. When Wentworth finally arrived in Ireland in 1633, however, it gradually became apparent that both secular and ecclesiastical policy was to be markedly different.

Soon after his arrival Wentworth won over Ussher to the idea of postponing enforcement of the penal laws against Catholics by telling him that only when the Church of Ireland was properly resourced and provided with suitable clergy could the enforcement of conformity begin. And, indeed, one of the signal achievements of Wentworth in Ireland was the generous re-endowment of the established church as possessions and benefices detained by laymen were confiscated and returned to their rightful clerical owners, a development greatly welcomed by Ussher. On 26 June 1634 the long-pending dispute between the sees of Armagh and Dublin for the primacy of all Ireland was decided by Wentworth in favour of Armagh, and on 14 July Ussher preached the sermon at the opening of the Irish parliament. But the other ecclesiastical policies of Laud and his allies in England and Ireland were less welcome to him. His firm Calvinism could not stomach the rise of Arminianizing clerics, nor could he accept the underlying thrust of Wentworth's and Laud's drive to harmonize the Irish and English churches, part of Charles's and Laud's wider interest in establishing greater conformity among the protestant churches in these islands.

The turning point came in 1634, when Wentworth called parliament and, with it, convocation. With the help of their chief agent in Ireland, John Bramhall, bishop of Derry, Laud and Wentworth set about replacing the Irish articles of 1615 with the thirty-nine English articles, and imposing the English canons of 1604 on the Church of Ireland. The instinctively independent and Calvinist Irish church was horrified at what was seen as a threat to its distinctive character, and Ussher was to the forefront in seeking to oppose the designs of Wentworth and Bramhall. After a series of battles in the lower house, Wentworth accepted a compromise over the articles: the thirty-nine were adopted, but the Irish articles were not thereby annulled, and Ussher, for one, subsequently insisted that clergy assent to both sets. The canons were equally contentious: Wentworth found out, rather belatedly, that convocation had gone through the English canons one by one marking those which they were unwilling to adopt. They were, for instance, deeply hostile to any references to subscription, as likely to restrict the considerable latitude afforded to puritans by the Church of Ireland. Ussher's attitude on this issue can be judged by his response to Wentworth's request to draft an Irish version of the fourth English canon, which provided for subscription to the Thirty-Nine Articles. Ussher's draft read:

> we do approve the book of Articles of Religion agreed upon by the … Convocation holden at London in … 1562 … So that if hereafter any minister shall presume to teach anything contrary to the doctrine delivered therein; upon refusal of the correction of his error, he shall be deprived of all … ecclesiastical benefices … (Sheffield City Libraries, Wentworth Woodhouse muniments, vol. 20/172)

The limp 'approval' required by this draft was, from the point of view of Wentworth, wholly useless. Wentworth had as a result to draft his own version, which he bullied convocation into accepting:

> we do receive and approve the book of Articles of Religion agreed upon by the … Convocation holden at London in … 1562 … if any hereafter shall affirm, that any of these articles are in any part superstitious or erroneous, or such as he may not with good conscience subscribe unto, let him be excommunicated … (Constitutions and Canons Ecclesiastical, Dublin, 1783, canon 1)

The depth of feeling on Ussher's side was a surprise to Wentworth, who reported to Laud that Ussher had refused to accept the English canons verbatim 'lest Ireland might become subject to the Church of England, as the Province of York is to that of Canterbury. Needs forsooth, we must be a church of ourselves' (Radcliffe, 1.381).

As a result, a new set of Irish canons had to be drafted, on the basis of their English counterpart.

A further indication of the change in theological emphasis in the Church of Ireland came with the appointment in August 1634 of William Chappell as provost of Trinity College. As Ussher was well aware, Chappell, formerly John Milton's tutor at Christ's College, Cambridge, was an Arminian, in the strict theological sense of the term, and his appointment marked a major effort on the part of Laud and Wentworth to reform the Calvinist college by replacing both its statutes and its fellows. The subsequent clash between Chappell and the old guard led Ussher to side with the latter. With the firm support of Wentworth and Laud, Chappell triumphed, however, and Ussher was by the mid-1630s deeply disillusioned about what he saw as the rise of Arminianism in Ireland.

By the end of 1635 it was apparent that there had been a significant shift in power within the Church of Ireland; Ussher, though still formally primate of all Ireland, had lost de facto responsibility for the everyday running of the Irish church to Bramhall; while power to formulate policy was now in the hands of Laud. Ussher was sensitive to this shift: though he remained on friendly terms with Wentworth, dedicating his 1638 work Immanuel to the lord lieutenant, and, indeed, Wentworth retained a guarded respect for the scholar–archbishop, nevertheless, Ussher increasingly withdrew from public life. His correspondence with Laud petered out (Laud in August 1637 complained that he had not heard from Ussher for two years), his trips to England ceased, and he beat a symbolic retreat from Dublin, choosing to live instead in Drogheda, where he had not only his episcopal residence but also his library, and was able to concentrate upon his archdiocese and his research.

As archbishop Ussher was undoubtedly a thorough administrator, but more reactive than active, generally opting for conciliation rather than confrontation. Some historians have claimed that he had a serious disagreement with William Bedell (bishop of Kilmore, 1629–42) over the latter's determination to use the Irish language to evangelize the native population, but this is to misinterpret the evidence. Bedell's efforts to root out abuses among his clergy and corruption in his ecclesiastical courts received a sympathetic hearing from Ussher, but he could do little to help his fellow prelate. Ussher's behaviour when faced with complaints in the early 1630s about the nonconformity of some Church of Ireland clergy in the dioceses of Down and Connor was typical of his approach: he sought to have proceedings against them stayed in the hope that they could continue in their livings. Not surprisingly the nonconformist clergy thought that Ussher was sufficiently sympathetic to tolerate their continued presence in the Church of Ireland.

The studious archbishop, 1631–1639 Ussher had already in 1631 published a history of the controversies surrounding the ninth-century monk Gotteschalc of Orbais. Though apparently obscure, these possessed an acute contemporary relevance, for Gottschalc's primary concern had been to defend a strict doctrine of double predestination.

Ussher's account of the medieval arguments was, naturally, scholarly and original, but it could also be read as a coded attack upon Arminian doctrines from an Augustinian perspective. Indeed, the book opened with an account of the rise of the Pelagian heresy, often used by Calvinist scholars in the 1630s—as, for example, by Ussher's friend Samuel Ward—as one of the few means left which they could use to attack Arminianism in print. In the following year, 1632, he turned his attention to Irish history again, producing *Veterum epistolarum Hibernicarum sylloge*, a pathbreaking scholarly edition of letters and texts relating to the medieval Irish church which brought together for the first time a remarkable range of essential primary sources. Again, his work was not without contemporary significance, for among the documents were those that showed the early Irish church differing with Rome over Easter, and the papacy establishing its control over the church in Ireland, marking the end, as Ussher saw it, of its early freedom from Roman domination.

In 1639 came the culmination of Ussher's researches into the early history of Britain and Ireland, with the publication of his *Britannicarum ecclesiarum antiquitates*, a monumental work that set out to trace the development of Christianity in these islands from its misty origins to the end of the seventh century. Though it is true that Ussher still believed the mythical story of King Lucius, and even accepted the missionary activities of Joseph of Arimathea in Britain, the *Antiquitates* nevertheless represented 'the most scholarly, extensive and coherent account of the origin and spread of Christianity in Britain that had yet appeared' (Parry, 139). During the 1630s, as his historical interests matured, it became evident that the fiercely anti-Catholic and apocalyptic tone of his earlier writings was much less prominent. But one contemporary concern remained evident in *Antiquitates*—Ussher's anti-Arminianism: the work contained yet another treatment of the efforts to stamp out Pelagianism in Britain.

Between king and parliament, 1640–1649 The dramatic change in political circumstances in 1640, when Charles's growing difficulties in England, Scotland, and Ireland finally forced him to recall parliament, ended Ussher's isolation. In March 1640 Ussher preached the sermon at the opening of the Irish parliament, and in the following month he set out once more for England—never, as it turned out, to return to Ireland. In England, though he settled down again to his usual pattern of scholarly research and preaching, just as in the early 1620s he also became involved in national ecclesiastical politics. But this time he was a much more significant figure. With his firm but moderate Calvinism and his international reputation for scholarship, his opinion was sought and his support courted by both king and parliament. He moved easily in both circles. Over the period 1641–2 he was linked to three leading parliamentary figures, the earl of Warwick, John Pym, and the earl of Bedford. He stayed in London at Warwick's house, reportedly meeting with Pym, and preached regularly from 14 February 1641 to 6 November 1642 at Covent Garden, whose vestry was controlled by Bedford. And he was prepared to criticize the excesses of the

Laudian regime, joining with other newly rehabilitated clergy such as Bishop John Williams and William Twisse in a House of Lords committee established on 1 March 1641, which drew up a list of innovations in doctrine, discipline, and liturgy (though again it should be noted that the ever cautious Ussher dissociated himself from an unauthorized published account of their conclusions). Most significant of all, during this period he toyed with the idea of a compromise between episcopacy and presbyterianism. Though not published until after his death, his *Reduction of Episcopacy* probably circulated in London during this period (though its precise history in manuscript is far from clear), offering an alternative to the puritan demand for the elimination of bishops root and branch.

Not surprisingly, therefore, after Ussher was deprived of his home and his income by the Irish rising of October 1641, parliament was prepared to grant him a pension of £400. However, in a neat illustration of his value to both sides, the king also sought to provide for him, granting him in February 1642 the temporalities of the vacant see of Carlisle. And indeed for all his Calvinism, he was, it must always be remembered, a bishop and a firm royalist. It was Ussher who advised Charles in May 1641 that he need not sign the earl of Strafford's bill of attainder (at least, that is the most credible of various conflicting accounts of Charles's consultation with his bishops over this delicate matter of conscience), it was to Ussher that Charles entrusted his last message to Strafford before his execution on 12 May, and it was Ussher who attended Strafford on the scaffold, and gave a laudatory account of Strafford's bravery when facing death. Equally, though prepared to modify episcopacy, Ussher was still a stout defender of the institution. Throughout the period 1641–4 he used all his historical skills to demonstrate that episcopacy had been instituted in the early days of the church, producing a series of five works: *The judgement of Doctor Rainolds touching the original of episcopacy. More largely enlarged out of antiquity by James Ussher* (1641); *A Geographical and Historical Disquisition, Touching Asia* and *The Original of Bishops and Metropolitans* (both published as part of *Certain Brief Treatises*, 1641); and two treatises on the Ignatian epistles, both published in 1644. The first of these stimulated John Milton to a reply which was exactly the opposite to Ussher's flat prose style and cautious conclusions. The last two represent one of Ussher's great scholarly achievements: through alert textual detective work he sorted the true from the false letters of the early church father Ignatius, and showed conclusively that those of his letters which contained some of the earliest information about the superior role of bishops in the church were genuine. Though, as Milton aggressively indicated, such historical acuteness was not always acceptable to the hotter sort of protestants, modern scholarship has made only minor adjustments to Ussher's conclusions.

As king and parliament moved closer to war, in late 1642 Ussher moved to Oxford. The purpose was to pursue his studies, and this is perfectly believable, but it also placed him in one of the key royalist centres of power, close to the king. Cautious as ever, he did, it is true, seek and gain parliamentary permission to move with his family to Oxford. But as divisions hardened, it was no longer possible to straddle both camps, and in Oxford he firmly committed himself to the king. On several occasions in 1643–4 he preached before Charles. He also offered him advice on Irish affairs, though here the king's desperate desire for accommodation with the confederate Irish—in particular his willingness to grant a formal toleration of Catholicism—ran directly counter to the primate's instinctive anti-popery. In July 1643 parliament made one last attempt to gain Ussher's support, inviting him to attend the Westminster assembly. His peremptory refusal to take up his position or even to recognize the assembly ended parliamentary hopes that his Calvinism and anti-Catholicism might outweigh his royalism.

Now identified with the royal cause, Ussher inevitably suffered as its position worsened. In March 1645 he left Oxford in the entourage of Prince Charles, to make for Bristol, and thence moved to Cardiff, where his son-in-law Sir Timothy Tyrrell was the royalist governor. There he remained for nearly a year, continuing his studies, and preaching before Charles when the king arrived in Cardiff following the battle of Naseby. As the royalist position deteriorated, Ussher considered emigrating to France, but instead opted to remain in Wales, removing himself and his family to stay with Lady Stradling in her castle at St Donats in Glamorgan. After a dangerous encounter with what he termed 'the rude Welsh', which led to the loss of many of his papers, he arrived safely at St Donats, where he immediately began ransacking the considerable library. In June 1646 he had to leave Wales and made for London, where he came under the protection of his friend the countess of Peterborough, who put him up at her various houses for the remainder of his life. The return of such a noted royal supporter did not go unnoticed, especially since he took up a preaching position at Lincoln's Inn early in 1647, and later in the same year he was summoned to appear before parliamentary commissioners. Though they insisted that he take the negative oath, his friends in parliament ensured that this was never pressed, and he returned unmolested to his preaching.

Ussher's prominence on the national stage was not, however, completely over. In 1648 Charles, imprisoned on the Isle of Wight, sought the advice of leading clerics, and Ussher was allowed to travel to see him on 7 November. Hopes on the parliamentary side that Ussher might persuade the king to moderate his religious principles proved unavailing, as the primate seized the opportunity of a sermon before the king on his birthday on 19 November to reassert the divine source of royal authority and insist that 'If any professor of religion do rebel against the king, that is a scandal to religion' (*Works*, 13.261). When, on 30 January 1649, the king was executed, Ussher watched and wept from the roof of the countess of Peterborough's house in London.

Ussher the scholar, 1647–1655 Apart from his preaching, Ussher's focus now was his research and writing. Just as he had begun his academic career with chronology and the church fathers, so too he returned to the same subjects during his last years, abandoning his interest in polemical theology and Irish history. In 1647 he published *De Romanae ecclesiae symbolo vetere … diatriba*, which provided a learned and distinctive answer to that classic patristic problem: the origin of the creeds. In the following year a treatise on the calendar appeared: *De Macedonum et Asianorum anno solari dissertatio: cum Graecorum astronomorum parapegmate, ad Macedonici et Juliani anni rationes accommodato*. This was a technical preamble to his last great published works, *Annales veteris testamenti* (1650) and its continuation, *Annalium pars posterior* (1654). Of all Ussher's works this was the one that gained most international recognition; this was hardly surprising, since it provided a convincing answer to the great theological and cosmological question of the day—the date of the foundation of the world. What Ussher did was to exploit his vast knowledge of ancient languages, calendars, and history and match it to his biblical scholarship to construct a comprehensive chronology which linked together biblical and ancient history. Then, once the Bible was firmly anchored in history, he could count backwards from known biblical dates, through the internal chronology of the Bible, back to Adam. To modern writers, for whom the premiss is ridiculous, Ussher's work seems both fanciful and pedantic in the extreme. But once one grants the premiss, the edifice which he erected on it can be recognized for what it is: a highly impressive piece of scholarship. He was of course building upon the work of earlier writers such as Joseph Justus Scaliger, and his precise dating of the foundation of the world to 23 October 4004 BC was, inevitably, challenged by subsequent scholars who disputed details of his interpretation, but the idea that the world was created roughly 4000 years before Christ became fixed in popular consciousness in the English-speaking world largely thanks to Ussher's labours. The popularity of his work was attested both by its rapid translation into English and by the many subsequent editions until well into the eighteenth century. His final work, published in 1655, dealt with the controversy between Buxtorf and Arnold Boate on the one hand, and Capellanus on the other, over the accuracy of the Hebrew and Septuagint texts of the Old Testament.

Though for the most part Ussher lived in semi-retirement in the 1650s, focusing upon his studies, he was still viewed by both sides as a man of influence. In November 1654, when the protectorate parliament sought the advice of ten divines about how to draw up a fundamental statement of the Christian faith which might unite the feuding religious groups in England, he was one of those invited. According to the royalist Robert Waring, he dismissed the offer out of hand, 'as if he should … set up a new religion with them who had destroyed the old religion and episcopacy' (McNeill, 389). According to the somewhat less reliable Richard Baxter, he turned down the offer for himself but co-operated with the efforts of his replacement, Baxter. Ussher's continued loyalty to his episcopal friends was confirmed when restrictions on Anglican clergy and laity were tightened following Penruddock's rising in 1655. It was Ussher who was chosen to petition Cromwell to seek redress. He saw the protector twice, but failed to persuade him to change his policy.

Death and afterlife　In February 1656 Ussher left London for the countess of Peterborough's house in Reigate, where he continued his studies. On 20 March he complained of a violent pain in his side at supper. He took to his bed in great pain, and having prayed with the countess's chaplain, took leave of the countess, thanking her for her long hospitality. He died of an internal haemorrhage about one o'clock in the afternoon of 21 March, his last words being 'O Lord forgive me, especially my sins of omission' (*Works*, 1.277). His friends intended to bury him privately at Reigate, but Cromwell intervened, offering to pay for a state funeral. Ussher's former chaplain Nicholas Bernard organized the service, and Ussher was buried before a large congregation in St Erasmus's Chapel in Westminster Abbey on 17 April 1656, with Bernard himself preaching the sermon, subsequently published as *The Life and Death of … Dr James Usher* (1656).

Indeed, Bernard continued to work for Ussher almost as hard after his death as he had before it, carefully guarding and shrewdly shaping and reshaping the primate's reputation in response to the rapidly changing political situation in the latter days of the Commonwealth. In a series of books published between 1656 and 1659 Bernard released previously unpublished works which showed Ussher as a moderate but tolerant episcopalian, providing through his *Reduction of Episcopacy* and his flexible attitude towards extempore prayers a basis on which to construct a more comprehensive protestant church. After the Restoration, however, Bernard changed tack, emphasizing instead Ussher's orthodox adherence to the forms and formularies of the Church of England. The publication in 1661 by Bishop Robert Sanderson of Ussher's posthumous *The Power Communicated by God to the Prince, and the Obedience Required of the Subject*, a round assertion of the illegality of resistance to a divinely appointed monarch, helped to fix an alternative vision of Ussher as a firm royalist and stout defender of the status quo. But his sympathy for and friendship with puritans ensured that he was revered in the nonconformist tradition too—he was the only prelate included in Samuel Clarke's classic *Lives* of the puritan saints, where he received the remarkable encomium: 'he was then so far from a prelatical spirit, that on the contrary he was an advocate for, and patron of godly and conscientious nonconformists' (Clarke, 286).

Ussher's posthumous reputation underwent a further shift in the 1680s as it was adapted to meet the threat of Catholic rule. One of his other chaplains, Richard Parr, published in 1686 a second life of Ussher, together with a large collection of his letters. Parr also emphasized Ussher's Anglican moderation, eliminating many of the puritan associations and friendships which had featured in Bernard's *Life*. But, making an obvious contemporary point, he retained, and emphasized, Ussher's fierce anti-Catholicism. The relevance of this to James II's rule was not lost, and Parr only managed to get the book past the censors by removing several unacceptable passages. At the same time Ussher's afterlife had a more popular

dimension. Towards the end of his life he had uttered several gloomy prognostications of the future travails of protestantism at the hands of the Catholic enemy; these, together with a sermon early in the 1600s, which seemingly forecast the 1641 rising, gave him the status of prophet. *Strange and remarkable prophecies and predictions of the holy, learned and excellent James Ussher* was published first in 1678, and reprinted in England and abroad in the 1680s; it went through numerous subsequent editions at times of religious crisis, being last published as a broadside against the popish threat posed to the Church of England by the Oxford Movement in 1846.

Even in the nineteenth and twentieth centuries Ussher managed to divide historians. His high-church biographer, and editor of the somewhat unsatisfactory edition of his complete works, Charles Elrington, clashed in 1849 with the noted presbyterian historian James Seaton Reid about where Ussher was to be placed on the protestant ecclesiological spectrum. The biography of Ussher by R. B. Knox (1967), though written by a Presbyterian, strives to show that Ussher, somewhat anachronistically, was an orthodox 'Anglican'. In fact, he was typical of the moderate Calvinism of the Jacobean church, opposed to Laudianism and all that entailed, seeing himself as a part of the wider continental reformed traditions. Theologically he was a Calvinist who along with Bishop John Davenant popularized (among academics at least) the idea of hypothetical universalism as a way round the bleaker implications of double predestination. Although, after he was safely dead, a high-church polemicist, Thomas Pierce, claimed that Ussher had towards the end of his life privately renounced the excesses of Calvinism and become a good Arminian, this is about as believable a claim as those made by Catholic opponents that he had considered converting to Catholicism after the disasters of the civil war.

The difficulty in pinning down the real Ussher, and his consequent exploitation by both high- and low-church protestant traditions as 'one of their own', was partly a product of his scholarly method and partly a result of his character. As has been seen, he was a cautious scholar, happiest surrounded by manuscripts in a library. Though he did indeed write polemical works, his style was neither aggressive nor outspoken, but rather consisted in the slow building up of citations, sources, and references. Where he did try to make a contemporary point in print, it was rarely overt and never outspoken. This style was matched by his personality. The surviving portraits of Ussher are remarkably consistent in the portrayal of an archetypal clerical scholar—pure, calm, judicious, and somewhat subfusc. Contemporary accounts of the primate emphasize his disinterested, mild manner, his dedication to learning, and his lack of interest in worldly power. However, though noble, these virtues do not necessarily sit easily with the responsibilities of a seventeenth-century bishop. And, indeed, one distinguished historian, Gilbert Burnet, identified his major fault as his inability to lead: 'he was not made for the governing part of his function. He had too gentle a soul to manage that rough work of reforming abuses' (Burnet, 86). The history of the relations in the 1630s between Ussher and Bedell, though somewhat misrepresented by some historians, nevertheless suggests a clear contrast between the vigorous and determined Bedell, tackling the abuses in the ecclesiastical courts and the ministry in his diocese and seeking to preach in Irish, and Ussher, sympathetic but less active and far less optimistic about the possibility of actually changing the status quo, and interested in the Irish language as a research tool, but not able himself to preach in it. Richard Parr sought to defend Ussher from Burnet's charge, arguing that the trust which several lords deputies exhibited in him proved his 'abilities in matters of govt, when ever he would give his mind to them' (Parr, 35). But the parting caveat is crucial. Though indeed a highly efficient administrator, Ussher did not always give his mind to his episcopal duties: a simple analysis of the time he spent in Meath when bishop of Meath confirms this. And in the 1630s he made a clear choice—or, arguably, he had the choice made for him by Wentworth and Bramhall—to leave to one side the role of the primate as leader of the church and to concentrate instead upon his scholarly research.

Whatever the disputes over Ussher's administrative abilities as a bishop, there is no argument over his standing as a scholar and churchman. His long-term legacy includes the first detailed academic treatment of the early Irish church, the creation of an identity myth for Irish protestantism, the identification of the genuine Ignatian epistles, and even, in extreme fundamentalist circles, the defence of creationism. In terms of his contemporaries he was also noted for his pastoral and spiritual skills. Deeply prayerful, he was repeatedly approached for spiritual advice, comfort, and assistance during his career. His expertise as a controversialist made him the natural choice to rescue Roman Catholics for the protestant faith—this was, after all, the foundation of his friendship with the countess of Peterborough. His spiritual sensitivity similarly recommended him as counsellor for those who were dying. Thus in 1655, when Elizabeth, the wife of Sir Hugh Cholmley, was asked whom she wished to attend her on her deathbed, she chose Ussher.

But it is on his scholarship that Ussher's reputation ultimately rests. Here the range of his achievements was extraordinary—spanning the Bible, theology, patristics, Irish history, ancient history, ancient languages, chronology, and the calendar. When Selden called his friend 'learned to miracle' (Bernard, 9), he was, of course, exaggerating: but only slightly. He was not a flamboyant scholar, but the depth and breadth of his knowledge rightly earned him the admiration and respect not just of his contemporaries in the republic of letters across Europe, but also of politicians and ecclesiastical leaders of all persuasions. ALAN FORD

Sources *The whole works of … James Ussher*, ed. C. R. Elrington and J. H. Todd, 17 vols. (1847–64) [vol. 1 incl. lengthy life by Elrington] · N. Bernard, *The life and death of … Dr James Usher* (1656) · S. Clarke, *A general martyrology* (1677) · [G. Burnet], *The life of William Bedell* (1685) · R. Parr, ed., *The life of the most reverend father in God, James Usher … with a collection of three hundred letters* (1686) · G. Radcliffe, *The earl of Strafforde's letters and dispatches, with an essay towards his life*, ed. W. Knowler, 2 vols. (1739) · C. McNeill, ed., *The Tanner letters*, IMC (1943) · A. Ford, 'Correspondence between archbishops Ussher and Laud', *Archivium Hibernicum*, 46 (1991–2), 5–21 · W. O'Sullivan, ed., 'Correspondence of David Rothe and James Ussher, 1619–23', *Cellectanea Hibernica*, 36–7 (1994–5), 7–49 · W. M. Abbott, 'James Ussher and "Ussherian" episcopacy, 1640–1656: the primate and his *Reduction* manuscript', *Albion*, 22 (1990), 237–59 · J. Barr, 'Why the world was created in 4004 B.C.: Archbishop Ussher and biblical chronology', *Bulletin of the John Rylands Library*, 67 (1984–5), 575–608 · *The memoirs and memorials of Sir Hugh Cholmley of Whitby, 1600–1657*, ed. J. Binns, Yorkshire Archaeological Society, 153 (2000) · A. Capern, '"Slipperye times and dangerous dayes": James Ussher and the Calvinist reformation of Britain, 1560–1660', PhD diss., University of New South Wales, 1991 · D. C. Douglas, *English scholars* (1939) · A. Ford, 'James Ussher and the creation of an Irish protestant identity', *British consciousness and identity*, ed. B. I. Bradshaw and P. Roberts (1998), 185–212 · A. Ford, 'James Ussher and the godly price in early seventeenth-century Ireland', *Political ideology in Ireland, 1541–1641*, ed. H. Morgan (1999), 203–28 · C. Giblin, 'Aegidius Chaissy, O. F. M., and James Ussher, protestant archbishop of Armagh', *Irish Ecclesiastical Record*, 5th ser., 85 (1956), 393–405 · A. Gwynn, 'Archbishop Ussher and Fr Brendan O'Connor', *Father Luke Wadding: commemorative volume*, ed. Franciscan Fathers dún Mhuire, Killiney (1957), 263–83 · R. B. Knox, *James Ussher archbishop of Armagh* (1967) · U. Lotz-Heumann, 'The protestant interpretation of history in Ireland: the case of James Ussher's *Discourse*', *Protestant history and identity in sixteenth century Europe: the later Reformation*, ed. B. Gordon (1996), vol. 2, pp. 107–21 · J. Leerssen, 'Archbishop Ussher and Gaelic culture', *Studia Hibernica*, 22–3 (1982–3), 50–58 · J. McCafferty, 'St Patrick for the Church of England: James Ussher's *Discourse*', *Bullán*, 3 (1998), 87–102 · J. McCafferty, '"God bless your free Church of Ireland": Wentworth, Laud, Bramhall and the Irish convocation of 1634', *The political world of Thomas Wentworth, earl of Strafford, 1621–1641*, ed. J. F. Merritt (1996), 187–208 · W. S. O'Sullivan, 'Review of R. B. Knox, "James Ussher archbishop of Armagh"', *Irish Historical Studies*, 16 (1968–9), 215–19 · G. Parry, *Trophies of time: English antiquarians of the seventeenth century* (1995) · H. Trevor-Roper, 'James Ussher, archbishop of Armagh', *Catholics, Anglicans and puritans* (1989), 120–65 · W. B. Wright, *The Ussher memoirs* (1889)

Archives BL, verbatim account of speech at Dublin Castle · Bodl. Oxf., collectanea · Bodl. Oxf., papers · Hunt. L., corresp. · TCD, corresp. | BL, Sloane MSS, corresp. with J. Dury

Likenesses oils, 1641, Jesus College, Oxford; repro. in R. Lane Poole, *Catalogue of portraits in the possession of the University, Colleges, City, and County of Oxford*, 3 vols. (1912–26), vol. 1, p. 51 · W. Fletcher, oils, 1644, Bodl. Oxf. · P. Lely, portrait, *c.*1654, priv. coll. [*see illus.*] · oils, *c.*1654 (after P. Lely), Chatsworth, Derbyshire; version, NPG · E. Findon, engraving (after portrait in TCD), repro. in *Whole works*, ed. Elrington and Todd, 1, frontispiece · W. Marshall, line engraving, BM, NPG; repro. in J. Ussher, *A body of divinity* (1647) · G. Stodard, engraving; copy, priv. coll. · portrait, Church of Ireland; repro. in www.arm.ac.uk/history/ussher.html, 1 Nov 2002

Ussher, Robert (*c.*1592–1642), Church of Ireland bishop of Kildare, was born in Ireland, the eighth son of Henry *Ussher (*c.*1550–1613), archdeacon of Dublin and from 1595 archbishop of Armagh, and his first wife, Margaret Smart, *née* Eliot. He was educated at Trinity College, Dublin, graduating BA in 1612, proceeding MA in 1614, serving as a fellow from 1611 to 1617 and as vice-provost from 1615 to 1617, and gaining his BD in 1621. Briefly appointed as rector of Ardtrea, co. Londonderry, in 1617, he became in the same year prebendary at St Audoen's (St Patrick's,

Dublin), which he held until 1636. Among the other livings he acquired were the rectory of Moylagh, in the diocese of Meath, in 1623 and the prebend of Dromaragh (Dromore), which he held from 1629 to 1634. He married Jane Kynaston of Pontesbury, Shropshire, and had six children.

In April 1627 Ussher was chosen provost of Trinity College, Dublin, in an abortive election by disgruntled junior fellows. The senior fellows refused to accept him, and William Bedell was subsequently appointed. When Bedell resigned in 1629, and Archbishop Laud failed to persuade his favoured candidate to accept the post, Ussher, with the strong backing of his cousin Archbishop James Ussher of Armagh, emerged as a compromise candidate. He was nominated by the king on 29 June 1629, elected by the fellows on 4 August, and formally admitted on 14 January 1630. Under Ussher the college grew significantly, acquiring three confiscated Catholic mass houses, but his provostship was marred by faction: two fellows dissented from his election, and he found it difficult to keep order. By 1634 Laud and Lord Deputy Wentworth wanted rid of this 'weak man' (Wentworth Woodhouse muniments, Sheffield City Library, 6.45). Although Wentworth was in fact willing to offer him a bishopric, Ussher gave up the provostship in August for the archdeaconry of Meath. In his place Wentworth imposed the much more formidable William Chappell. Even Ussher's cousin accepted that he was unable to govern the college effectively. The problem was partly its constitution—the statutes gave the provost very little independent power—but also Robert Ussher's own ineffectiveness: 'albeit he be a very honest man … yet is of too soft and gentle a disposition to rule so heady a company' (Whole Works, 15.574). He was not without pastoral talents, however, Ware characterizing him as an assiduous preacher, 'remarkable for his pulpit abilities' (Whole Works, 1.392). On 19 October 1635 he was nominated to the see of Kildare, and was consecrated on 25 February 1636. Here he unsuccessfully sought to regain see lands alienated by his predecessors. After the 1641 rising he fled to his in-laws at Pontesbury, where he died on 7 September 1642.   ALAN FORD

Sources H. J. Lawlor, *The fasti of St Patrick's, Dublin* (1930), 148 · J. B. Leslie, *Armagh clergy and parishes* (1911), 108 · *The whole works of Sir James Ware concerning Ireland*, ed. and trans. W. Harris, 1 (1739), 392–3 · W. B. Wright, *The Ussher memoirs* (1889), 55–7 · *Calendar of the Irish patent rolls of James I* (before 1830); facs. edn as *Irish patent rolls of James I* (1966), 565 · *The works of the most reverend father in God, William Laud*, 6, ed. J. Bliss (1857), 261, 267 · *The whole works of … James Ussher*, ed. C. R. Elrington and J. H. Todd, 17 vols. (1847–64), vol. 1, pp. 100f.; vol. 15, pp. 445f., 449f., 456 · E. S. Shuckburgh, ed., *Two biographies of William Bedell, bishop of Kilmore, with a selection of his letters and an unpublished treatise* (1902), 300 · Ware's annals, TCD, MS 6404, fol. 62r · muniments, college register, TCD, V/5/1, 25–47 · *DNB* · E. B. Fryde and others, eds., *Handbook of British chronology*, 3rd edn, Royal Historical Society Guides and Handbooks, 2 (1986)
Archives TCD, corresp. and papers

Ussher, Sir Thomas (1779–1848), naval officer, was the eldest son of the astronomer Dr Henry *Ussher (1741–1790) and his wife, Mary Burne. In January 1791, under the patronage of Colonel William Burton Conyngham MP, the uncle of the late Marquess Conyngham, he entered the navy on the *Squirrel* on the home station and on the west coast of Africa. He was present in the *Invincible* in the action of 1 June 1794, and in 1795–6 was successively in the *Prince George*, *Glory*, and *Thunderer*, the flagships of Sir Hugh Cloberry Christian, by whom he was appointed acting lieutenant of the *Minotaur*. In May 1796 he served on shore with a party of seamen at the capture of St Lucia. He was afterwards acting lieutenant of the brig *Pelican* (rank confirmed 17 July 1797), was repeatedly engaged with French and Spanish privateers, and on 5 April 1798, in attempting to cut out one in the Augustine River near Cumberland harbour (Guantanamo) in Cuba, he was severely wounded in the right thigh. While in the *Pelican* he is said to have been in upwards of twenty boat engagements. In May 1799 he was appointed to the *Trent*, and in her returned to England in September 1800.

Ussher's many wounds obliged him to remain on shore for some months, but in June 1801 he was appointed to command the cutter *Nox*, stationed at Weymouth in attendance on the king. In September 1803 he commanded the cutter *Joseph*, and in April 1804 the brig *Colpoys* (14 guns) attached to the fleet off Brest under Admiral Cornwallis. His vigilance and energy in quest of intelligence repeatedly obtained the admiral's approval. Later on, the *Colpoys* was employed in the Bay of Biscay and on the north coast of Spain. On 18 October 1806 Ussher was promoted commander and appointed to the sloop *Redwing* (18 guns), in which he was chiefly employed in protecting the trade against the Spanish gunboats and privateers near Gibraltar. He was repeatedly engaged with the gunboats or armed vessels, often against a great numerical superiority, and especially on 7 May 1808, near Cape Trafalgar, when he met seven armed vessels convoying twelve coasters. Of the nineteen only three escaped, eight of the others being sunk and eight taken; the loss to the enemy, of men killed, drowned, or taken prisoner, was returned as 240. On Lord Collingwood's report of this and other gallant services, Ussher was promoted to post rank by commission dated 24 May 1808. After his return home he was entertained at Dublin at a public dinner and presented with the freedom of the city.

In 1809 Ussher commanded the *Leyden* (64 guns) in the operations in the Scheldt. While in command of the frigate *Hyacinth* (26 guns) in the Mediterranean (1811–12), on 29 April 1812 he led a boat attack against several privateers moored in the port of Malaga; in the face of murderous musketry fire from the shore, which killed or wounded 68 out of 149, he brought out two of the largest privateers and did what damage he could to the others. Although the enterprise was not fully successful, the commander-in-chief and the Admiralty signified their approval of Ussher's conduct, and in October he was moved to the *Euryalus* (36 guns), from which, in February 1813, he was transferred to the *Undaunted* (38 guns). In both he was employed in the blockade of Toulon and along the south coast of France. In April 1814, when he was in the *Undaunted* close to Marseilles, a deputation of the mayor and chief men of the city came on board to acquaint him of Napoleon's abdication and of the formation of a provisional government. Almost immediately afterwards he received instructions to prepare to convey the ex-emperor to Elba, and at Fréjus on 28 April received him on board. On the 30th he anchored at Porto Ferrajo, and on 3 May Napoleon landed. The *Undaunted* remained at Elba until the ex-emperor's baggage had been landed from the transports and then sailed for Genoa. At the end of June, Ussher was moved into the *Duncan* (74 guns), in which he shortly afterwards returned to England. On 4 June 1815 he was made a CB, and on 2 December 1815 he was awarded a pension of £200 a year for wounds; on 24 July 1830 he was appointed equerry to Queen Adelaide, and in 1831 he was made a KCH and was knighted. From 1831 to 1838 he was successively superintendent of the dockyards at Bermuda and Halifax. He was promoted rear-admiral on 9 November 1846, and in July 1847 was appointed commander-in-chief at Queenstown.

Ussher had married Elizabeth, the daughter of Thomas Foster of Grove House, Buckinghamshire. They had two daughters and three sons, of whom the eldest, Thomas Neville, chargé d'affaires at Haiti, died on 13 April 1885; the second, Sydney Henry, a naval captain, died in 1863; and the third, Edward Pellew Hammett, a lieutenant-colonel in the Royal Marines, died in 1878. Ussher wrote *A Narrative of Events Connected with the First Abdication of Napoleon* (1841), which was reprinted with a portrait and memoir in *Napoleon's Last Voyages* (1895). He died at the Admiralty House, Queenstown, co. Cork, Ireland, on 6 January 1848. J. K. LAUGHTON, *rev.* ANDREW LAMBERT

Sources E. D. H. E. Napier, *The life and correspondence of Admiral Sir Charles Napier*, 2 vols. (1862) · Burke, *Gen. GB* (1894) · O'Byrne, *Naval biog. dict.* · *GM*, 2nd ser., 29 (1848), 435 · J. Marshall, *Royal naval biography*, suppl. 1 (1827) · P. Mackesy, *The war in the Mediterranean, 1803–1810* (1957)
Likenesses portrait, c.1830–1833, NMM · portrait, repro. in T. Ussher, *A narrative of events connected with the first abdication of Napoleon* (1841)

Utenhove, Jan (1516–1566), Reformed theologian and author, was born in Ghent, into a distinguished family of Dutch scholars and intellectuals.

Family background and education A number of Utenhove's relatives enjoyed close relations with Erasmus, and the complexity of links within this family has caused much confusion regarding Jan Utenhove's precise relationship with other well-known authors in the clan. In fact there were two branches of the Utenhove family—the Van Markegen, which included the well-known poet Karel Utenhove (*d.* 1600), sometimes erroneously described as Jan Utenhove's son or nephew, and the Van der Gracht. Jan Utenhove was part of the latter branch, the second son of Tijkaert (*d.* 19 Aug 1549), a captain in the army of Charles V. But the wider family network certainly provided Jan Utenhove with a web of connections which went to the heart of the humanist élite of the Southern Netherlands. Nicklaas Utenhove (Van Markegen) was a personal friend of Erasmus, and his son Karel was at one time the great humanist's amanuensis at Basel. Through these important connections Utenhove also came into contact with others who would be close collaborators in later career, including John à Lasco and Marten Micron.

Utenhove studied in Louvain, and like many with his humanist interests he became a highly accomplished linguist, knowing Latin, Greek, German, and French as well as Dutch. It was also probably in Louvain that he met Joris Cassander, the eirenic theologian who sought to mediate between Catholic and protestant faiths. Although Cassander would ultimately remain within the Catholic church, his influence may have partly been responsible for Utenhove's conversion to Reformed protestantism, though there were others with similar interests in the Ghent reformist circles in which he moved.

Move to England In 1544 the emperor moved to clamp down on the reformist intellectuals, who had previously enjoyed a great deal of freedom to pursue their scholarly interests without necessarily opting for outright dissent. A number were arrested and executed; Jan Utenhove was among those compromised in the investigations who felt it necessary to withdraw from his homeland. He journeyed first to Cologne and thence to Aachen and Strasbourg, where his potential as an influential recruit to the Reformation was recognized. After a brief period of activity in the French and Dutch exile congregations at Strasbourg he joined the important cadre of Strasbourg reformers (which also included Bucer, Fagius, Peter Martyr, and Valérand Poullain) who accepted Archbishop Thomas Cranmer's invitation to move to England and assist the process of reformation.

In England Utenhove first settled in Canterbury, as Cranmer's guest. Here he and François Pérussel seem together to have been responsible for the foundation of a small French-speaking congregation. In November 1548 Utenhove wrote to Fagius from Canterbury referring to 'nostra Gallica Ecclesia'. A few months later he received enthusiastic congratulations from Peter Martyr on the foundation of the congregation. The Canterbury congregation seems to have been small, and of short duration; in any case, early in 1549 Utenhove left England once again, and journeyed to Zürich. Here he made a good impression on Heinrich Bullinger, not least by expounding a eucharistic theology compatible with that of the Swiss church. On his return to England, Utenhove would hereafter be closely associated with the group of 'Zürichers' who kept Bullinger closely informed of developments at the English court and who exerted their influence to conform the English reformation settlement to that of the Helvetic model.

Back in London, Utenhove (like Marten Micron) lodged in the house of John Hooper, the leading English representative of the Zürich affinity. While Hooper ultimately moved to Gloucester to take up his new appointment as bishop both his guests remained in London to play their part in the establishment of the new London stranger churches. Micron would be named as one of the earliest ministers; Utenhove would play a scarcely less important role as one of the first four elders. In the three short years of the church's initial existence, Utenhove played a critical role, along with Micron and the church's superintendent, John à Lasco, in framing the worship traditions. He was responsible for Dutch translations of several of the church's core documents, notably à Lasco's statement of doctrine, the *Compendium doctrinae*, translated by Utenhove as *Een Cort begrijp der Leeringhen van die waerachtighe ende eender Ghemeynten Gods ende Christi* (1551). Utenhove was also responsible for a Dutch version of à Lasco's Emden catechism, *De Catechismus, oft kinder leere, diemen to London, inde Duysche ghemeynte is ghebruyckende* (1551). But his most substantial original achievement was the Dutch versification of the Psalms, set in train during the London years, and gradually brought to completion through the remainder of Utenhove's life. In adopting the congregational singing of the psalms as a core part of their worship, the London stranger churches were heavily influenced by the example of the Strasbourg French church, of which Calvin was briefly minister between 1538 and 1541. Calvin exported the practice back to Geneva, where a complete version of the French metrical translation of the psalms was completed by 1561. The London Dutch enthusiastically adopted the practice, though without slavishly following the French example in their choice of musical models. In London, Utenhove prepared first a core collection of ten translations, generally using models drawn from German sources, and the early Dutch collection known as the *Souterliedekens*. The influence of the French Marot/Beza psalms would become more profound as the project progressed.

Emden and Poland On the death of Edward VI in 1553 it was swiftly clear that the London foreign church would not survive the change of regime. Utenhove joined the leaders of the church in seeking a new refuge, and when à Lasco and his colleagues set off in two Danish ships from Gravesend on 17 September Utenhove was of the party. The later tribulation of the church, denied the refuge they had confidently expected in Denmark, and subsequently in several north German cities, is mostly known from Utenhove's full and indignant narrative, published as the *Simplex et fidelis narratio de instituta ac demum dissipata Belgarum, aliorumque perigrinorum in Anglia, ecclesia* (1560). The larger of the two vessels was blown off course and only arrived at the Danish court in November, by when the Lutheran court preachers had poisoned the king's mind against the refugees: while à Lasco and Utenhove set off overland to return to Emden, others of the refugees survived a brutal journey across the North Sea to north Germany, where a succession of Lutheran cities denied them permission to settle. The community was finally reunited in Emden, where they were assured of a welcome in à Lasco's former church. Rather than being organized here as a separate congregation, as in London, the exiles were quickly absorbed into the local church structure.

In Emden, Utenhove excused himself from formal office, preferring to resume the ambitious literary ventures interrupted by the London church's dissolution. Among the exiles were a number of the printers who had worked for the church in London; they brought with them some capital and, crucially, the necessary expertise and special fonts of type necessary for the printing of music. In Emden, therefore, Utenhove was able to publish several greatly expanded versions of his London psalm collections: by 1559 these numbered sixty-four in all. It is known from a rare surviving letter that these psalms were in use in the small secret congregations which during these years gathered in the Netherlands. In 1555 the minister of the Antwerp Reformed congregation reported to an Emden bookseller: 'I also occasionally sell one of my Lord Utenhove's psalters, and I would also certainly sell more if they were not so expensive' (Duke, Lewis, and Pettegree, 135).

Utenhove also embarked on another venture in Emden which was to prove far less successful, a new Dutch translation of the New Testament. This enterprise was a response to a perceived need in scholarly circles for a version more faithful to the original languages, and Utenhove was in principle well qualified to undertake such a task. Many of his fellow Emden exiles, including Micron and the Bible scholar Gualter Delenus were enlisted to assist. But, fatally, Utenhove was also determined to produce a translation which would be comprehensible in all parts of the Netherlands, avoiding local dialect forms. It employed a 'cleansed' language which included the invention of new forms for several simple words, and not surprisingly left its intended audience largely baffled. A large edition of 2500 copies was produced, but most remained unsold; the publisher was forced to recoup some of his losses by selling off the paper intended for a projected folio edition. The press was brought to the brink of collapse, not helped by the success of a rival (and far more derivative) Bible translation produced by a competing Emden firm. The project also left an enduring legacy of acrimony among the participants.

By this time Utenhove had in any case left Emden, having decided to accompany à Lasco when the former London superintendent heeded the call to return to assist the upbuilding of the Reformation in his native Poland. These were difficult and frustrating years for à Lasco; Utenhove occupied his time with further scholarly projects, including the *Rationes quaedam* (1560), a collection of proofs against the Lutheran doctrine of the Lord's supper. His engagement in this controversial writing reflected the bitter turn to inter-confessional controversy since the eruption of the second sacramentarian controversy earlier in the decade. He and à Lasco had been instrumental in stimulating John Calvin to take up the cudgels against the Hamburg minister Joachim Westphal at the beginnings of the dispute; now Utenhove persisted in the publication of his *Simplex narratio* against the advice of the Genevan reformer, who believed that it would be better to let the matter drop.

Return to London The accession of Elizabeth in November 1558 opened the final chapter in Utenhove's life. It was immediately clear that the hoped-for restoration of the London churches would require that the strangers could once again call on a spokesman of stature. In December

1559 Utenhove arrived back in London, carrying with him the original foundation charter. The restoration of the churches was completed early in 1560, though without the extraordinary liberties that had proved so controversial in the earlier reign: now the post of superintendent was filled by the bishop of London, Edmund Grindal. In this new climate the church relied heavily on the diplomatic skills and connections of Jan Utenhove, in the absence of à Lasco and Micron indisputably the church's leading personality. He once again took on the office of elder and performed signal service, offering strong support to his colleague Pieter Delenus and his fellow elders in the dispute with Adriaan van Haemstede. When plague broke out in 1563 Utenhove undertook to render members' wills into Latin so that they could be proved in the English courts. He also acted as an invaluable link between the exile community and sympathizers—often former exiles—at court. In 1563–4 these connections were put to good use, when a trade dispute with the government of the Netherlands closed the Antwerp mart and dictated an urgent need to establish an alternative continental outlet for English cloth. The ruling counts of East Friesland proposed Emden, their small but friendly northern German port which had proved such a hospitable refuge for Dutch and English protestants during the reign of Mary. Utenhove, with firsthand experience of Emden and an established relationship with the leading personalities in both London and East Friesland, was a natural choice to act as broker. Delegates from both England and East Friesland lent on Utenhove for advice, and he for his part attempted to expedite proceedings in vigorous correspondence with Grindal and Cecil. His efforts had their reward when in February 1564 a treaty was signed moving the English mart to Emden.

The Dutch church repaid Utenhove's faithful service by continuing to promote the use of his psalm translations. One of the first decisions of the newly restored church (10 January 1561) was to order a new printing of the psalms, now one hundred in number. The task was committed to the London printer John Day, with whom the church had connections dating back to the reign of Edward VI. The first edition sold so quickly that a second was necessary within two months. The *Hondert Psalmen* showed the growing influence of the French Marot/Beza versions, particularly in the use of melodies taken from the French Genevan psalters.

Achievement During the remaining years of Utenhove's life much of his energies were devoted to completing his translation of the Psalms. His will suggests that this task was completed in the summer of 1563, though he himself did not have the chance to see them through to publication before his own death on 6 January 1566. His will left profits from the publication to be shared between the Dutch church and his widow, Anna (*née* van Horne); after her death the church was to have the whole profit. Spurred by this potential income the church moved swiftly after Utenhove's death to have the psalms published. In December 1566 the whole psalter was finally issued, published by John Day, and with a preface furnished by the minister of the Dutch church, Godfried van Winghen. Its influence, however, was short-lived. The year 1566 also saw the publication of a competing versification, that of Pieter Dathenus, a former collaborator with Utenhove who had nevertheless been highly critical of Utenhove's use of language both in his translation of the New Testament and in his work on the psalms. Dathenus's simpler, less literary language, combined with a more complete fidelity to the melodies of the French Marot/Beza psalms, ensured that his version soon established its supremacy in the Netherlands, though the London church remained faithful to their own translation for some years to come. Utenhove left his widow in reasonable circumstances; in 1568 she presided over a large household of fourteen souls in the liberties of Christ Church, Aldgate. The children named in this return were boarders: Utenhove seems to have entered into marriage comparatively late in life (there is no mention of a wife in the records of the Dutch church until 1559), and apparently there were no children. Neither he nor his wife mention family in their respective wills; on the death of Anna in 1571 the bulk of their property was left to the Dutch church.

Although his Psalms would not ultimately establish themselves as the basis for worship in the Dutch Reformed church, Utenhove's influence as a writer, theologian, and church organizer in several different locations should not be underestimated. He remains an astonishing exemplar of the multifaceted talent of the group of international scholars and theologians who contributed so much to the development of Reformed protestantism in this critical period of the development of the Reformation.   ANDREW PETTEGREE

Sources F. Pijper, *Jan Utenhove: zijn leven en zijne werken* (1883) · D. Nauta and others, eds., *Biografisch lexicon voor de geschiedenis van het Nederlandse protestantisme*, 3 vols. (Kampen, 1978–88) · A. Pettegree, *Foreign protestant communities in sixteenth-century London* (1986) · A. Pettegree, *Emden and the Dutch revolt: exile and the development of reformed protestantism* (1992) · A. Pettegree, 'The London exile community and the second sacramentarian controversy', in A. Pettegree, *Marian protestantism: six studies* (1996), 55–85 · R. A. Leaver, *'Goostly Psalmes and Spirituall Songes': English and Dutch metrical psalms from Coverdale to Utenhove, 1535–1566* (1991) · A. A. van Schelven, ed., *Kerkeraads-protocollen der Nederduitsche vluchtelingenkerk to Londen, 1560–1563*, Historisch Genootschap te Utrecht, 3rd ser., 43 (1921) · J. ten Doornkaat Koolman, 'Jan Utenhoves Besuch bei Heinrich Bullinger im Jahre 1549', *Zwingliana*, 14 (1974–8), 263–73 · S. J. Lenselink, *De Nederlanse Psalmberijmingen van de Souterliedekens tot Datheen* (1969) · *STC, 1475–1640*, nos. 2738.7, 2739, 15260 · G. D. Ramsay, *The City of London in international politics at the accession of Elizabeth Tudor* (1975) · A. Duke, G. Lewis, and A. Pettegree, *Calvinism in Europe: a collection of documents* (1992) · will, PRO, PROB 11/54, sig. 6

Uther Pendragon (*supp. fl.* **late 5th cent.?**). *See under* Arthur (*supp. fl.* in or before 6th cent.).

Uthred [Uchtryd, Uchtredus] (*d.* **1148**), bishop of Llandaff, was probably that same Uchtredus, archdeacon of Llandaff, who attested the settlement between Bishop Urban and Robert, earl of Gloucester, at Woodstock in 1126. The same archdeacon accompanied Urban to Rome in 1131 and

1134. His name is northern English, though it does not necessarily follow that Uthred had any English blood in him. Uthred succeeded Urban as bishop of Llandaff in 1140 after a vacancy of about six years. His nomination must have been through King Stephen, as Archbishop Theobald would not otherwise have consecrated him; but his see was in the area controlled by Earl Robert in the interests of the Empress Matilda, and he is found associated with the earl in his curia, and is addressed by his writs.

Bishop Uthred does not come well out of the sources. Gerald of Wales makes the chapter of St David's talk of him, in a letter to the pope, as being ill-educated and a disgrace to his office (but St David's sources are unlikely to be kind to a bishop of Llandaff in the twelfth century). He was at one point in his career suspended from his office by Archbishop Theobald. Relations with Gilbert Foliot, abbot of Gloucester, were frequently quarrelsome, largely because of the abbot's robust defence of his house's extensive interests in the diocese of Llandaff. Foliot did, however, make protestations of friendship to Uthred, and solicited his assistance at times. Uthred seems, from these collisions, to have been assertive of the rights of his church and office. Llanthony sources also indicate that he was an innovative administrator, constituting a Welsh cleric as dean to exert authority over central Gwent and farm episcopal dues. He courted the lay powers of his diocese, working with the earl of Gloucester, and marrying a daughter, Angharad, to Iorwerth, brother of King Morgan ab Owain of Glamorgan. It is clear that he was very much a Welsh *claswr*, a member of one of the hereditary priestly families that dominated the church in south Wales, even after the Norman conquests there. His son, Robert, attempted to assert a hereditary claim on the diocese after Uthred's death and greatly troubled Bishop Nicholas, a regular cleric. The sour portrait of this Robert by John of Salisbury as a family man, acquisitive and aggressive in the assertion of traditional rights, might well apply to his father. Uthred died in 1148 and is honoured with a brief encomium in the Welsh chronicles.   DAVID CROUCH

Sources T. Jones, ed. and trans., *Brut y tywysogyon, or, The chronicle of the princes: Red Book of Hergest* (1955) · J. G. Evans and J. Rhys, eds., *The text of the Book of Llan Dâv reproduced from the Gwysaney manuscript* (1893) · D. Crouch, ed., *Llandaff episcopal acta, 1140–1287*, South Wales and Monmouth RS, 5 (1988) · *Florentii Wigorniensis monachi chronicon ex chronicis*, ed. B. Thorpe, 2 vols., EHS, 10 (1848–9) · *Gir. Camb. opera* · *Letters and charters of Gilbert Foliot*, ed. A. Morey and others (1967) · *The letters of John of Salisbury*, ed. and trans. H. E. Butler and W. J. Millor, rev. C. N. L. Brooke, 2 vols., OMT (1979–86) [Lat. orig. with parallel Eng. text]

Uthwatt, Augustus Andrewes, Baron Uthwatt (1879–1949), lawyer, was born on 25 April 1879 at Ballarat, Victoria, Australia, the third of six sons of Thomas Andrewes Uthwatt (1846–1927), who later inherited the lordship of the manor of Maids Moreton, Buckinghamshire, and his wife, Annie (d. 1928), daughter of William O'Donnell Hazlitt, of Dunmow, co. Donegal. He was educated at Ballarat College in Victoria, and at Melbourne University, gaining his BA with first-class honours in 1899, and proceeding to the LLB. In 1901 he left Australia to study at Balliol College,

Oxford, where he gained the degree of BCL with second-class honours in 1903, and was elected Vinerian scholar in 1904. He was made an honorary fellow of the college in 1947.

Uthwatt was called to the bar in 1904 by Gray's Inn, where he subsequently became a bencher (1927). He was a pupil in the chambers of the equity lawyer Robert John Parker. During the First World War he was rejected for military service on health grounds, and rather than continue to profit at the bar in the enforced absence of many of his competitors, he worked for the newly formed Ministry of Food, to which he was appointed legal adviser in 1916. His work there developed the novel technique of using orders of council, which were applied to the administration of defence of the realm regulations and the implementation of food controls, as he drafted hundreds of orders in the absence of precedents. He declined the offer of a knighthood in recognition of his war service.

At the end of the war Uthwatt returned to his career at the bar, building a large practice in equity and conveyancing, and taking on many commercial and revenue cases. His style of advocacy was remembered as being concise and unflamboyant. On 6 August 1927 he married Mary Baxter (d. 1951), the daughter of the Revd Charles Edwin Meeres, vicar of Eastry, Kent; she had previously been married to John Lewis James Bonhote. They had no children, though Uthwatt did have an adopted daughter.

Uthwatt became a member of the Council for Legal Education in 1929. In 1934 he was appointed junior counsel on the Chancery side to the Treasury and the Board of Trade, and to the attorney-general in charity matters. He was treasurer of Gray's Inn (1939–40) and vice-treasurer (1941). In 1941 he was appointed a judge of the Chancery Division of the High Court, and accepted a knighthood. He was promoted to the lords and judicial committee of the privy council in 1946, as a lord of appeal in ordinary, with a life peerage, as Baron Uthwatt. His career as a judge was relatively short, but he delivered a number of judgments which offered illuminating statements on difficult issues of law. His judgment in the Chancery Division in *Re Anstead* (1943) dealt with the tangled issues relating to the administration of estates, and the judgment of the judicial committee of the privy council which he delivered in *Perera (M. G.) v. Peiris* (1949) addressed the question of privilege in libel actions.

During the Second World War, Uthwatt chaired committees on the responsibility for repair of premises damaged by hostilities, on liability for war damage, and on the principles of assessment of war damage to property, which formed the background to the Landlord and Tenant (War Damages) Acts to distribute fairly between landlord and tenant the loss arising from war damage. He became best known for his chairmanship of another wartime committee, the expert committee on compensation and betterment, appointed in January 1941 to advise on ways to guard against speculation in land which might hamper plans for the post-war reconstruction. The Uthwatt report, published in September 1942, presented the principle that ownership of land did not imply an unqualified right of use. It advocated a central planning authority to authorize future development, and recommended that the state should take over the rights of development for all land outside built-up areas, and impose a levy on increases in annual site value. Although these recommendations were not fully implemented, the report formed an important background to the planning system introduced in the 1947 Town and Country Planning Act.

After the war Uthwatt chaired a committee on leasehold property, and resumed his work as a judge. At the time of his death he was hearing an appeal on the validity of a law nationalizing the Australian banks. He died suddenly, at his home, White Friars, Sandwich, Kent, on 24 April 1949. His body was cremated, and the funeral was held on 28 April at the parish church at Lathbury, in Buckinghamshire, in a service conducted by his brother, the Venerable W. A. Uthwatt.   J. W. BRUNYATE, *rev.* C. V. J. GRIFFITHS

Sources *The Times* (25 April 1949) · *The Times* (27 April 1949) · *The Times* (29 April 1949) · *The Times* (5 May 1949) · *The Times* (12 Sept 1949) · *WWW, 1941–50* · *Expert committee on compensation and betterment*, Cmd. 6386, Sept 1942 · private information (1959) · personal knowledge (1959) · Burke, *Gen. GB* (1937) ['Andrewes of Maids Moreton Manor']
Likenesses W. Stoneman, photograph, 1942, NPG
Wealth at death £47,799 13s. 5d.: probate, 5 Sept 1949, CGPLA Eng. & Wales

Utley, Thomas Edwin [Peter] **(1921–1988)**, journalist and political analyst, was born on 1 February 1921 in Hawarden, Flintshire, the second of five children (two sons, two daughters, and one deceased in infancy) of Thomas Cooper, chemist, of West Derby, Liverpool, and his wife, Emily Utley. In 1931 he was adopted by his maternal aunt, Anne Utley, by whose surname he was thenceforward known. He was born blind in one eye owing to infantile glaucoma and lost the sight of the other eye at the age of nine, but, with the help of a series of amanuenses, courageous determination, and a prodigious memory, offset this handicap almost completely in adult life. Educated privately, Utley took first-class honours in both parts one (1941) and two (1942) of the history tripos at Corpus Christi College, Cambridge.

Utley joined the Royal Institute of International Affairs (Chatham House) in 1942, as secretary to the Anglo-French relations post-war reconstruction group, and worked there until 1944, when he became a temporary foreign leader writer at *The Times* for one year. From 1945 to 1947 he was foreign leader writer at the *Sunday Times*. He spent a year at *The Observer* in 1947–8, and then rejoined *The Times* as a leader writer. He stayed there for six years, becoming associate editor of *The Spectator* in 1954–5. He married in 1951 Brigid Viola Mary, younger daughter of Dermot Michael Macgregor *Morrah, journalist, historian, and Arundel herald-extraordinary. There were two sons and two daughters of the marriage. In 1955 Utley began life as a freelance journalist and broadcaster, until in 1964 he joined the *Daily Telegraph* as a leader writer. He was that newspaper's chief assistant editor in 1986–7. From 1987 until his death a year later he was obituaries editor and a columnist at *The Times*.

Utley's frequently signed articles on political subjects gained for him a widespread reputation as a political philosopher, and during his later years he was regarded as its most articulate and reflective exponent by that wing of the Conservative Party which designated itself distinctively as high tory. The party in general during the last twenty years of his life was influenced more than it might have cared to admit by the views expressed in Utley's leading and other articles in the *Daily Telegraph*.

Never inclined to inhabit an ivory tower, Utley served as chairman of the Paddington Conservative Association in 1977–9 (president, 1979–80) and as consultant director (1980–88) of the research department of Conservative central office; but his only venture into practical politics, when he contested Antrim North at the general election of February 1974 against the sitting Democratic Unionist member, Ian Paisley, proved abortive. Northern Ireland was one of the many subjects to which he brought his ability to provide policy with a well-developed structure of logically sustainable argument; but this quality was most practically effective during the premiership (1979–90) of Margaret Thatcher, who held him in high regard. In some degree he paved the way intellectually for the changes in the direction of Conservative policy which she initiated and implemented. He also had an unswerving religious belief, and regretted changes to the Church of England which would damage its careful compromises.

A collection of Utley's signed publications appeared after his death under the title *A Tory Seer* (ed. Charles Moore and Simon Heffer, 1989). His own books included *Modern Political Thought* (1952), *Not Guilty: the Conservative Reply* (1957), *Occasion for Ombudsman* (1961), *Your Money and your Life* (1964), *Enoch Powell: the Man and his Thinking* (1968), and *Lessons of Ulster* (1975). His influence was magnified by the spellbinding effect which his fluent and incisive discourse produced, especially upon young hearers. It was not without significance that the group of younger officials who sat at his feet at the Conservative Research Department became known as the 'Utley play school'.

Utley (known to his many friends as Peter) was of striking, if frail, appearance; and those introduced to him sensed no disposition on his part to conceal the severity of the disability under which he laboured. He wore a black patch over his right eye. An inveterate smoker, unable to see where he flicked his ash, he caused Margaret Thatcher to bob up and down from her chair to move the ashtray in order to preserve the carpets.

Utley was overtaken by a cancer-induced stroke while working at his home, and died the following evening at the Cromwell Hospital, London, on 21 June 1988. A memorial service was held at St Martin-in-the-Fields, London, on 24 October 1988.   J. ENOCH POWELL, *rev.*

Sources *The Independent* (23 June 1988) · *The Times* (23 June 1988) · personal knowledge (1996) · private information (1996)
Likenesses photograph, repro. in *The Times*

Utley, Winifred [Freda] **(1899–1978)**, author and writer on politics, was born on 23 January 1899 in legal chambers at 1 King's Bench Walk in the Temple, London, the second and last child of Willie Herbert Utley (1866–1918) and his wife, Emily Williamson (1865–1945). Her father was studying to become a barrister but was a journalist by profession, being assistant editor and music critic of a leading Liberal paper, *The Star*. Her paternal grandfather was one of a long line of blacksmiths in the village of Utley, near Keighley in Yorkshire. She was educated privately at La Combe, Rolle, Lake Geneva, Switzerland (1909–11), Peterborough Lodge, Hampstead, London, and at Prior's Field, Godalming, Surrey (1911–15), passing the Cambridge higher local examination in 1915, but the sudden impoverishment of her family prevented her from going on to the University of Cambridge. In 1920 she enrolled on a journalism diploma course at King's College, London, and then in 1921—with a bursary from the central committee on women's training and employment of the Ministry of Labour—she registered for the BA honours course in history. Graduating with a first in 1923, she enrolled on an MA course and gained a distinction in 1925 for her thesis, 'The social and economic status of the collegia from Constantine to Theodosius II'. From 1926 to 1927 she held the Ratan Tata research studentship at the London School of Economics.

Plain featured, short-sighted, and hard of hearing, Freda Utley, as she was always known, remained a being born to believe. Her parents were radicals in their outlook and they educated their daughter in a rationalist and humanist mode. As an atheist she saw religion only as the shield of tyranny, intolerance, and cruelty. She became imbued with a passion for justice which proved as strong as any religious fervour. Aspiring to liberate mankind from immemorial oppression, she sought to usher in, through political activity, a new era of human freedom. First, she joined the Independent Labour Party and then in 1923 became secretary of the King's College Socialist Society. She was elected chairman of the London University Labour Party. In 1927, as vice-president of the University Labour Federation, she visited Russia, the 'Land of Promise' and then, as instructed, became a member of the Communist Party (1928–30). She stood for election in February 1928 as a Communist Party candidate to the London county council. She also translated from the German Vladimir Astrov's *Illustrated History of the Russian Revolution* (New York, 1928).

In 1928 Freda Utley travelled through Siberia to China and Japan. In Tokyo she pursued research in economic history for nine months. That period she always remembered as the happiest year of her life. She studied the bases of competition by Japan and India with the cotton industry of Lancashire. Her pioneering articles on comparative labour costs in the *Manchester Guardian Commercial* (25 April and 2 May 1929) established her reputation as an expert on the cotton industry. *Lancashire and the Far East* (1931) embodied the fruits of her research. It was both 'a study in modern imperialism' and an indictment of British policy in India: Beveridge refused to permit the publication of the work under the imprint of the London School of Economics. The book was, however, twice translated into Russian, in 1931 and again in 1934, and was also published in Japanese in 1936.

Freda Utley had made two fateful decisions. In 1928 she married a Russian citizen, Arkady Berdichevsky. In 1930 she emigrated to the USSR, where she lived in Moscow until 1936; their son, Jon Basil Utley, was born in Moscow in 1934. She served in succession as a member of the Anglo-American section of the Comintern and as a textile specialist at Promexport and at the commissariat of light industry. In 1932 she became a senior scientific worker at the Institute of World Economy and Politics of the Academy of Sciences, devoting herself to a study of the economy of Japan. Her husband had survived the purges of 1930–32 but was arrested on 11 April 1936 and sentenced to five years in prison. The arrest was due, she believed, to Margaret Cole, who had passed on to the authorities her own very sour verdict upon the Soviet regime (Utley, *Odyssey*, 86). She never saw Arkady again and left the Soviet Union 'with my political beliefs and my personal happiness alike shattered' (Utley, *Lost Illusion*, 1). Years passed by before she again became free in mind and in spirit.

In 1936 Freda Utley published the book which she had written in Russia from a Marxist perspective, *Japan's Feet of Clay*. The work sought to 'tear the veil from the face of Japanese tyranny' (Utley, *Lost Illusion*, 159) and proved to be comparable as an exposé to Katherine Mayo's *Mother India* (1927). It was banned in Japan but its message was diffused by the ideas of the Marxist Toichi Nawa (1906–1978), who stressed the link between Japan's need for raw materials and its expansionist policy. Freda called for Anglo-American economic sanctions against Japan and foretold, in their absence, the destruction of the British empire. Another book, *Japan's Gamble in China* (1937) reiterated the same warning. As 'Clayfoot Utley', Freda next served for six months as a war correspondent in Hankow (Hankou). Her experiences in the front line were embodied in the most impressive book *China at War* (1939), which represented a more balanced survey than *Japan's Feet of Clay* but renewed the plea for Anglo-American sanctions.

From 1939 until her death in 1978 Freda Utley lived in the USA. There she published a memorable commentary on her experience of Stalin's rule. She had last campaigned on behalf of the Communist Party in 1929 among the cotton operatives of Lancashire. She had not renewed her membership of the party after 1930. In Russia she speedily became disillusioned with the Soviet regime but kept a half-hitch upon her tongue throughout her years in 'the Hell of communist tyranny' (Utley, *Odyssey*, 305). *The Dream we Lost: Soviet Russia Then and Now* (1940) revised and abbreviated as *Lost Illusion* (1948), was one of the most bitter contributions ever penned to the literature of disillusion, and was written more in hatred than in sorrow. Freda had found the study of history unsatisfying as an academic pursuit. She had yearned to partake in the actual making of history, a hope which was, however, frustrated. She became a simple witness, and offered her testimony as 'the only Western writer who had known Russia both from inside and from below, sharing some of the hardships and all the fears of the forcibly silenced Russian people' (Utley, *Odyssey*, 255). The book contained a searing indictment of life endured in a virtual hell of human suffering under 'a savage and barbarous Asiatic despotism' (Utley, *Lost Illusion*, 94). Its publication marked the beginning of Freda's new career as a dedicated anti-communist. She had recognized that communism was in effect a substitute religion, but she still continued to believe in the rights of man. The book gave deep offence to the 'totalitarian liberal cohorts' of the Western intelligentsia (Utley, *Odyssey*, 270, 275). She had become 'a premature anti-Communist' and paid a heavy price for her conversion.

Freda Utley reached a mass audience through the medium of the *Reader's Digest* (November 1941). She found it difficult, however, for some years to secure contracts from publishers. Nor could she ever obtain an academic post. She was also denied American citizenship for five years (1940–44). In 1940 she had advocated the conclusion of a negotiated peace between Britain and Hitler. In 1942 she opposed American intervention in Europe and the allied demand for unconditional surrender, lest it should deliver the whole continent into the hands of Stalin. Thereafter she served as a correspondent for the *Reader's Digest* in China (1944–5) and in Germany (1948). *The High Cost of Vengeance* (1949) denounced allied post-war policy in Germany as stupid, wicked, vindictive, and disastrous, maintaining her reputation as a controversialist. *The China Story* (1951) sought to account for 'the loss of China' and investigated the influence of Owen Lattimore on American policy: it became for three months a best-seller. In 1950 Freda became an American citizen. She gave much help to Senator McCarthy but concluded that his campaign had been 'brief and abortive' (Utley, *Odyssey*, 279). After the Suez crisis of 1956 she undertook a tour of Asia and asked *Will the Middle East Go West?* (1957). The United States, she argued, had alienated Western-oriented Arabs by its pro-Israeli policy and might push the whole region into the communist camp.

In 1968 Freda Utley completed the first volume of her autobiography, which covered the years down to 1945 and devoted an indiscreet chapter to her friendship since 1924 with Bertrand Russell. She never, however, published the second volume, analysing the intricacies of Washington politics (1945–75). Possessed by a zest for thorough research, Freda spread her energies widely, perhaps too widely. Six of her eight books were translated into seven languages but their author never secured the recognition she sought. Disputatious by disposition, she always remained, in Rosa Luxemburg's phrase, 'the one who thinks differently' and an opponent in succession of the established regimes in England, Japan, Russia, and the USA. Russell Kirk aptly described her as 'thorny and indomitable … full of reproaches and resentments, possessed of acerbic wit, passionately didactic and remarkably readable' (Kirk, 32). Freda's material prospects were so blighted by her political views that her great talents ran to waste. She lost her faith in the inevitability of progress and in the perfectibility of man through the improvement of his material conditions. To the end she remained a modern Antigone, consumed by a savage indignation against injustice.

Freda Utley died on 22 January 1978, after suffering a stroke, in Georgetown University Hospital, Washington. Her book on post-war Germany, translated as *Kostspielige Rache* in 1950, was twice reprinted, in 1962 and again in 1993. Her contributions to the history of Asia and of the USSR remain of lasting value. *The China Story* (1951) was translated into Japanese in 1993. *Japan's Feet of Clay* (1936) was translated into Japanese in 1998 and was reprinted in the original English in 2000. *Lancashire and the Far East* (1931) had become an instant classic monograph of international economic history and was reprinted in 1996. An interim epitaph upon her may well be: 'just missed being great' (Utley, *Odyssey*, 36).   D. A. FARNIE

Sources F. Utley, *Lost illusion* (1948) · F. Utley, *Odyssey of a liberal: memoirs* (1970) · *Contemporary Authors: Permanent Series*, 81–4 (1979), 578–9 [incl. list of press sources;] · *Who was Who in America*, 7 (1981), 583 · *New York Times* (23 Jan 1978) · K. Sugihara, 'Economic motivations behind Japanese aggression in the late 1930s: perspectives of Freda Utley and Nawa Toichi', *Journal of Contemporary History*, 32 (1997), 259–80 · J. Hunter, preface, in F. Utley, *Japan's feet of clay* (2000), v–viii · D. A. Farnie and others, *Region and strategy in Britain and Japan: business in Lancashire and Kansai, 1890–1990* (2000) · D. A. Farnie, 'Freda Utley, 1898–1978: crusader for truth, freedom and justice', *Britain and Japan. Biographical portraits*, ed. H. Cortazzi (2002), vol. 4, pp. 361–71 · R. Kirk, 'Odyssey of a liberal', *New York Times Book Review* (19 April 1970), 32–3 · King's Lond., archives · FredaUtley.com, Oct 2002 · b. cert.

Archives Stanford University, California, Hoover Institution, papers

Likenesses Chase Ltd, photograph, 1950, priv. coll. · photograph, 1950, repro. in Kirk, 'Odyssey of a liberal', 33 · photographs, repro. in F. Utley, *China at war* (1939)

Utterson, Edward Vernon (*bap.* 1777, *d.* 1856), antiquary and literary editor, was baptized on 14 July 1777, the eldest son of John Utterson of Fareham, Hampshire, and his wife, Elizabeth. He was educated at Eton College and entered Trinity Hall, Cambridge, as a pensioner on 17 February 1794, matriculating in Michaelmas term 1797 and gaining an LLB in 1801. He was admitted to Lincoln's Inn on 31 October 1794 and became a barrister on 1 February 1802. On 2 May 1803 he married Sarah Elizabeth (*d.* 1851), daughter of T. Brown; she was the author of *Tales of the Dead* (1813). They had several children. Utterson was one of six clerks in chancery in 1815, a post from which he retired with full salary in 1842 when the office was abolished. He was elected a fellow of the Society of Antiquaries in 1807 and was an original member of the Roxburghe Club in 1812; he was also an Athenaeum member. His places of residence were at Newport, Isle of Wight, and at Beldornie Tower, Pelham Field, Ryde, at the latter of which he founded the Beldornie Press.

Utterson reprinted or edited a large variety of early works of English literature, notably a number by Samuel Rowlands. One of Rowlands's works, *The Night-Raven*, for example, was reprinted by him in 1841 in a limited edition of sixteen copies. A statement on a page after the title-page reads: 'This is one of Samuel Rowlands's productions, which, in spite of occasional indelicacy of language, and coarseness of allusion, possesses some claims on our attention from its illustration of contemporary manners, and reference to ancient literature'. There is no preliminary matter by Utterson, but *Select Pieces of Early Popular Poetry* (2 vols., 1817) has a 'Preface' of fourteen pages by him where, in addition to various scholarly and bibliographical matters, he writes 'The rigid moralist of the present day may perhaps feel inclined to censure the phraseology of some of these latter poems as occasionally swerving from the language of decency', but the standards for such matters were very different in earlier times (pp. xvii–xviii). This explanation will serve for others of Utterson's editions and reprints where the presence of questionable language occurs. 'Among the rarer and costlier books of Utterson's collection' were the first three folio Shakespeares and a lot of other now rare items, listed in Quaritch's *Contributions towards a Dictionary of English Book-Collectors* (1892–1921; reprint 1969).

In the 5 January 1856 issue of *Notes and Queries* John Payne Collier, writing from Maidenhead, began his note on 'Reprints of early English poetry' as follows:

> The late Mr. Edward Vernon Utterson, the editor of two well-known volumes of *'Early Popular Poetry'* (8vo., 1817), had, as is well known, a private press …, by which he reprinted a variety of highly curious poetical tracts, of dates between 1590 and 1620.

He went on to state that he had been given a copy of every one of these tracts and regretted that he had discovered a number of 'inaccuracies'. After attempting to explain how the inaccuracies might have occurred, he gave some fourteen examples of them. One week later in *Notes and Queries* he wrote, of his earlier note, 'I there spoke of Mr. E. V. Utterson as dead; I am most happy to be informed [by Utterson] that he is living and well'. He explained that, being of some distance from London and having mistakenly believed that he had been apprised of Utterson's death, he wrote the early note. He pointed out that he had written there that in his intercourse with Utterson he had 'always found him kind, liberal, and disinterested'. He concluded the later note by writing 'I think I know Mr. Utterson well enough to feel sure that he will accept the amends contained in this note'. One cannot, however, be sure that there are no further inaccuracies in Utterson's other reprints.

There were two sales of Utterson's books, besides one of engravings and one of pictures and other objects. The first book sale was during his lifetime, and ran for eight days from 19 to 27 April 1852, bringing in £4805. Utterson died on 14 July 1856 at Upper Brunswick Place, Hove, Brighton, and was buried at Fareham. The second auction ran for seven days from 20 to 27 March 1857 and brought in £4050.   ARTHUR SHERBO

Sources Venn, *Alum. Cant.* · B. Quaritch, ed., *Contributions towards a dictionary of English book-collectors*, 14 pts (1892–1921); repr. (1969) · *GM*, 2nd ser., 45 (1856)
Archives BL, letters to Philip Bliss, Add. MSS 34567–34581 · U. Edin., letters to David Laing
Likenesses J. Posselwhite, stipple (after J. Jackson), BM

Uttley [*née* Taylor], **Alice Jane** [*known as* Alison Uttley] (**1884–1976**), writer, was born on 17 December 1884 at Castle Top Farm, Matlock, Derbyshire, the elder child of

Alice Jane Uttley (1884–1976), by Jane Bown, 1965

Henry Taylor, farmer, and his wife, Hannah, *née* Dickens. A son, William Henry, was born to them a year later. Alice Taylor was first educated at home and at the Lea School in the village of Holloway, where, unusually for the time, she was encouraged to take an interest in geology and the scientific examination of natural phenomena. At the age of thirteen she gained a scholarship to the Lady Manners School, Bakewell, and here her enthusiasm for science was directed into more formal channels. She won several school prizes (for sport as well as for academic subjects) and in 1903 she gained a county major scholarship to Manchester University to read physics, taking her BSc degree in 1906 as only the second woman honours graduate of the university. She greatly enjoyed these years as a student, during which she lived in the residential Ashburne Hall, and the university in its turn was to recognize her achievements by making her an honorary LittD in 1970.

Having decided to become a teacher, Alice Taylor moved on to the training college at Cambridge (later Hughes Hall), and in 1908 she took up the post of physics teacher at the Fulham Secondary School for Girls in London. On 10 August 1911, at the Ethical Church, Paddington, London, she married James Arthur Uttley (1882/3–1930), a civil engineer working in Cheshire, and she moved with him to Knutsford where their only child, John Corin Taylor (1915–1978), was born. During the First World War her husband served with the Royal Engineers and suffered illness which permanently impaired his health, and in 1930 he died, leaving his wife with the need to earn a living for herself and her son, who was a scholar at Sedbergh School. At this time of crisis she received great support through her friendship with the former professor of philosophy at Manchester, Samuel Alexander, and he encouraged her to develop her latent talent for writing.

This had first manifested itself before her husband's death in articles written for magazines and in a little children's book published under the name Alison Uttley in 1929: *The Squirrel, the Hare and the Little Grey Rabbit*. Based on a story which she had invented to amuse her son, it exploited the popular device of recreating a rural society largely peopled by animals. Charmingly illustrated with muted watercolours by Margaret Tempest, it was to have over thirty successors (the last five accompanied by rather more heavy-handed pictures by Katherine Wigglesworth), and the series formed a reliable foundation upon which, in the second half of her long life, she was able to extend her reputation as a professional writer.

The nature of this reputation can clearly be gauged from Alison Uttley's first publication for an adult readership: *The Country Child* (1931). As she was later to say of her Little Grey Rabbit books, 'the country ways … were the country ways known to the author' and in this lightly fictionalized autobiography she set out to explore the rich experiences of her Derbyshire childhood. In simple but evocative prose she celebrated the life of a Victorian farming community, steeped in its own traditions, and although she was to go on to write more than a hundred books, almost all of them drew upon this powerful perception of a rural life still only marginally affected by the industrial revolution.

Alison Uttley's many books include several series of stories such as the Sam Pig books or the Tim Rabbit books, where a family of animals stands substitute for, and thus generalizes the experience of, a human family, and to these must be added numerous tales of magic for children and children's plays, most notably the full-length play on the life of Hans Christian Andersen, *The Washerwoman's Child* (1946). There were also successors to *The Country Child* in *Ambush of Young Days* (1937) and *The Farm on the Hill* (1941), and the novels *High Meadows* (1938) and *When All is Done* (1945), and there were numerous essay collections on country themes, beginning with *Country Hoard* (1943) and often made distinctive by the black and white illustrations of C. F. Tunnicliffe.

Alison Uttley's most original, and perhaps her most deeply-felt, work is the fantasy story *A Traveller in Time* (1939), in which there came together in near-perfect conjunction her childhood experiences at Castle Top Farm and her fascination with a plot that had been put under way by Anthony Babington in 1569 to rescue Mary, queen of Scots, from imprisonment in nearby Wingfield Manor. Careful research underlies the fabric of the romance, but the book draws too on her own lifelong interest in dreams, aspects of which she discussed in her annotated essay *The Stuff of Dreams* (1953).

Although she moved house several times after her husband's death, Alison Uttley soon came to make her home near Beaconsfield (at a house which she called Thackers after the farmhouse in *A Traveller in Time*) and it was here that she spent the rest of her life. She had a fairly strict working regime, recognizing the need for writers constantly to exercise their skills, and she proved to be a shrewd woman of business. Her time was not so full, though, as to exclude her enthusiasm for gardening, music, and cricket. She also had a keen interest in art and assembled a small but well-chosen collection of Flemish paintings.

Notwithstanding her intense feeling for the place of her childhood, and her affection for Manchester (not least Old Trafford), Alison Uttley developed strong ties with her adoptive county, which she was able to express in her lovingly detailed study *Buckinghamshire* (1950). Only after illness and a fall was she persuaded to leave Thackers and she died in hospital at Wycombe General Hospital, High Wycombe, on 7 May 1976. In her will she left many of her books and papers, together with an unsigned head portrait, to Manchester University.

BRIAN ALDERSON, rev.

Sources *The Times* (8 May 1976) · E. Saintsbury, *The world of Alison Uttley* (1980) · private information (1986) · b. cert. · m. cert. · d. cert.
Archives JRL, corresp., diaries, literary MSS, and papers
Likenesses J. Bown, photograph, 1965, priv. coll. [*see illus.*]
Wealth at death £113,643: probate, 12 Oct 1976, *CGPLA Eng. & Wales*

Uvarov, Sir Boris Petrovich (1889–1970), entomologist, was born at Uralsk in south-eastern Russia on 5 November 1889, the youngest of three sons of Pyotr P. Uvarov, a state bank employee, and his wife, Aleksandra. Early interested in collecting insects, after schooling at Uralsk from 1895 to 1902 he attended the School of Mining at Yekaterinoslav (1904–6) before studying biology in the University of St Petersburg, graduating with a first-class degree in 1910. In the same year he married Anna Fyodorovna Prodanyuk (d. 1968), daughter of F. and E. Fyodorov. The couple later had a son.

After graduation Uvarov held appointments in several provincial departments of agriculture and in 1915 at the age of twenty-seven he was made director of the Tiflis Bureau of Plant Protection. This involved the organization of plant protection stations in Transcaucasia and a thorough entomological exploration of the region. In 1919 he became lecturer in the State University in Tiflis and keeper of entomology and zoology in the State Museum of Georgia. In the face of rampant Georgian nationalism his position was difficult. But among the contingent of British troops in Georgia was Patrick A. Buxton, who provided a connecting link with London; and in 1920 Uvarov was given an appointment at the Imperial Bureau (later the Commonwealth Institute) of Entomology.

Uvarov had made extensive studies of locusts and grasshoppers in south-east Russia, establishing his reputation as a taxonomist. He had discovered that swarming and non-swarming locusts, which are so different in appearance that they had always been regarded as different species, were in fact phases of the same insect. This phase theory provided the basis for much of his outstanding contribution to the control of locust plagues.

Uvarov's official work at the bureau was the identification of insects sent in from all parts of the Commonwealth. However, he also found time to add to his already large output of papers on the taxonomy of grasshoppers; he wrote his classic book *Locusts and Grasshoppers* (1928) which was published in English and in Russian and was the handbook of 'acridologists' (to use Uvarov's own word) for some thirty years. He also prepared a very useful review of the discipline's literature in *Insect Nutrition and Metabolism* (1928) commissioned by the Empire Marketing

Sir Boris Petrovich Uvarov (1889–1970), by Pamela Chandler

Board, and an outstanding review, *Insects and Climate* (1931), again with the Empire Marketing Board.

In the late 1920s there were serious locust plagues in south-west Asia and in Africa. The Committee of Civil Research asked the Commonwealth Institute to undertake investigations into swarming locusts and Uvarov was given the task of organizing and supervising this project. His small unit, occupying very restricted quarters in the British Museum (Natural History) soon became the international centre for locust research. A series of scientific international anti-locust conferences was organized which served to formulate programmes and to co-ordinate international studies of the locust problem. They led to the establishment of permanent regional organizations aiming at a continuous study of each locust species in its natural haunts with a view to the prevention of locust plagues. This twin policy, of international co-operation and prevention of outbreaks by continuing field studies, was the keynote of Uvarov's teaching and was based in his theory of locust phases.

By 1938 the results were clear enough for an international plan to destroy locusts in their outbreak areas, preventing the build-up of populations to the crowded state, in which the phase change from the solitary to the gregarious form takes place and swarms spread widely over the surrounding countries. The outbreak of war in 1939 prevented the full operation of this plan, but the methods advocated were successfully used against the red locust and the migratory locust in Africa—species of which the outbreak areas had been discovered and

defined. In 1945 Uvarov's unit became the Anti-Locust Research Centre under the Colonial Office and during the next fourteen years the centre developed into the foremost laboratory in the world for research in and control of locusts.

Uvarov's advice was sought from many countries, even after his retirement. In 1959 he retired as director of the centre and devoted himself largely to the writing of a new book, *Grasshoppers and Locusts*. The first volume appeared in 1966 and the second was finally produced for publication in 1977 after his death by close colleagues.

Uvarov's output of scientific publications was prodigious—in the fields of botany, geography, biogeography, and ecology, as well as locust control. But his major contribution was to taxonomy: in the course of half a century he described 284 genera and over 900 species and subspecies of Orthoptera. His impact on acridoid systematics was considerable. The theory of locust phases was both a cause and an effect of this broad attitude of mind: he always stressed that the really significant phase differences were changes in physiology and behaviour which in turn increased or maintained the high density of populations. At one time the theory of phase transformation was discredited because it did not seem to apply to the greatest of all the plague locusts, the desert locust. But it was then realized that the desert locust underwent the same phase changes: these took place as the invading swarms, carried by convergent rain bearing winds, reproduced and multiplied in crowded conditions. Since there were no persisting outbreak areas for this locust different strategies had to be used for control. When a desert locust plague broke out in the early years of the Second World War, Uvarov was able to provide a sound biogeographical basis for the large-scale control campaigns. He did not consider that locust and grasshopper problems could ever be solved by chemical methods alone. He believed that a radical solution must be sought in the ecological regulation of populations (*Entomologicheskoye Obozreniye*, vol. 48, 1969).

Uvarov received many honours: CMG (1943), KCMG (1961), FRS (1950), commandeur de l'Ordre Royal de Lion (1948), and honorary DSc in the University of Madrid (1935). He served as president of the Royal Entomological Society of London (1959–61).

Uvarov was a person of small stature but immense toughness and vitality. He had a dry sense of humour, an ability to inspire young entomologists coming into locust research, and a capacity to foster the development of relevant fields of science of which he himself had little intimate knowledge or experience. Although he never seemed satisfied his purpose was honest, his objectives were desirable, and his methods and ideas were sound. He was naturalized in 1943. Uvarov died at his home, 36 Kingsley Avenue, Ealing, London, on 18 March 1970.

V. B. WIGGLESWORTH, *rev.* V. M. QUIRKE

Sources P. T. Haskell, *In memoriam*, Anti-Locust Research Centre, Centre for Overseas Pest Research (1970) [brochure] · V. B. Wigglesworth, *Memoirs FRS*, 17 (1971), 713–40 · personal knowledge (1981) · N. Waloff and G. B. Popov, 'Uvarov, 1889–1970, the father of acridology', *Annual Review of Entomology*, 35 (1990), 1–24 · *CGPLA Eng. & Wales* (1970)

Archives PRO, papers, AV 20 | Bodl. Oxf., corresp. with T. R. E. Southwood

Likenesses P. Chandler, photograph, RS [*see illus.*] · photograph, Royal Entomological Society, London

Wealth at death £20,308: probate, 1970, *CGPLA Eng. & Wales*

Uvedale, Sir Edmund (d. 1606), soldier, was the second son of Sir Francis Uvedale (d. 1589), landowner, of Horton in Dorset, and Katherine, daughter of John La Zouche, eighth Baron Zouche, of Harringworth, Northamptonshire. His uncle Henry Uvedale of Moor Crichel, Dorset, also had a son called Sir Edmund Uvedale, with whom he has been confused. Alternative spellings of the family name are Uvedall, Udall, and Woodall. Uvedale's family was notable for its protestant connections. His grandfather Sir William *Uvedale was 'a friend to the reforming party' (*DNB*) while his kinsman Richard *Uvedale was one of the key members of the Dudley conspiracy against Mary in 1555–6 and was executed. The firebrand puritan John Udall was also related, though more distantly. Thus it is not surprising that much of Uvedale's career was spent in the Netherlands, fighting against the Spanish.

Uvedale has been identified with a Udall who was master of the revels at Lincoln's Inn in 1565, but this may have been his distant cousin William Uvedale of Wickham, Hampshire. The first definite evidence of Uvedale is a letter from him, written while serving in the Anglo-Welsh regiment commanded by Thomas Morgan around Antwerp in 1584–5, to Sir Francis Walsingham, principal secretary, lamenting that, as he saw it, 'the better part' of the locals 'are rather desirous of our destruction than willing to relieve [our] necessity' (*CSP for.*, 19.254). He writes authoritatively but does not appear in any list of Morgan's captains at this time, so may have been a junior officer. He went home at some stage that spring, but returned in summer 1585. He was captain of one of the first companies of the expeditionary force led by Sir John Norris to land, arriving in the Netherlands on 31 July. Some time between 12 and 21 August he was captured by the Spanish, but was ransomed for a sum that 'exceeds 340 angels' (ibid., 19.683) in time to join the muster held at Utrecht on 14 September. He commanded a company of 150 foot in Elizabeth I's pay for the next dozen years.

Uvedale was probably a servant of Sir Philip Sidney. He distinguished himself at the battle at Zutphen in September 1586 where Sidney was mortally wounded. In summer the next year he served in the garrison that heroically (albeit unsuccessfully) defended Sluys and was among those singled out for praise by the commander, Sir Roger Williams. He was also lauded in an elegy on Sidney's death written by the prominent poet George Whetstone, then serving as commissary of musters in the English army. However, at Bergen op Zoom in September 1587—after the garrison of Sluys arrived back at English lines, but before the elegy on Sidney had been published—Uvedale killed Whetstone in a duel fought over the commissary's accusations that the captain had committed muster fraud. Uvedale was cleared of murder at a court martial, but

more than six months later the matter was still being pursued: his old colonel Morgan was one who thought he should be retried and punished.

Perhaps because of Uvedale's Sidney connection, he was able to shrug off these problems. Indeed, in 1588 he was one of a number of captains knighted by Peregrine Bertie, Baron Willoughby de Eresby, lieutenant-general in the Netherlands. Then on 12 October 1591 Uvedale succeeded Sir William Borlase as marshal of Flushing, a post he held at least until 1597. Uvedale's superior as governor was Sir Robert Sidney, himself a client of Robert Devereux, earl of Essex. Further, his brother, Thomas Uvedale, was a servant of Essex. He offered his services to the earl after returning to England but was declined. Like Sidney, he also prudently established himself as a client of the Cecils. In early 1593 Uvedale admitted to a friend that 'I have not written to [Lord Burghley] long tyme', who had let him know 'that he doth exepecket I should wright heme of soch newes as are in this kontrie' (*De L'Isle and Dudley MSS*, 2.132). He tried to maintain good relations with Sir Robert Cecil, principal secretary. Consequently, in December 1595 he was confident of success in a suit for payment of 'his old Accounts', making 'no Doubt but to obtain yt in 12 dayes, because all the Lords doe promes to further yt, and none will cross yt' (Collins, 1.377). Accusations of financial irregularity continued to dog him, but Uvedale was clearly a player of the game of patronage, as well as a brave soldier.

Uvedale married Mary (d. 1637), daughter of Sir William and Lady Dorothy Dormer of Wing, Buckinghamshire, and widow of Lord Anthony Browne. The Dormers were staunchly Catholic. This marriage probably took place after 1592. The couple had no known children. By late spring 1597 Uvedale was probably past his prime and left Flushing, but kept an active interest in military affairs back in England. He initially returned home to Dorset, which he had visited at least three times during the 1590s to attend to lands he inherited from his father. He became an important figure in local affairs, being appointed keeper of Kingston Lacy, Dorset, part of the duchy of Lancaster, in 1598, and a member of the quorum of the commission of the peace and deputy lieutenant of Dorset from about 1601. In 1598 he moved to London, where he was appointed surveyor-general of the forces within England—his cousin by marriage Robert Williams was his deputy for Dorset. The following year Uvedale inspected the fortifications around the Solent and was appointed sergeant-major-general of the army gathered to defend against the threat of another Spanish armada. By 1601 he was a commissioner for the musters in Dorset, and that year he was elected MP for the county. He was helped by the fact that his elder brother Thomas Uvedale was sheriff at the time of the election, but he was also supported by the lord lieutenant, Thomas Howard, Viscount Bindon, who signed himself to him as 'your very loving friend and kinsman' (HoP, *Commons, 1558–1603*, 3.545). Uvedale was now wealthy enough to give £50 to the library of Sir Thomas Bodley (former English ambassador to the Dutch republic) at Oxford in 1603.

Uvedale died on 6 April 1606, leaving his house and land at Poole to his wife. A request in his will that no ceremony be used at his funeral (which was honoured, though a memorial was erected at Wimborne Minster) and bequests to the poor of five parishes are perhaps a last indication of godly fervour.
D. J. B. TRIM

Sources C. Izard, *George Whetstone: mid-Elizabethan gentleman of letters* (1942) · *Report on the manuscripts of Lord De L'Isle and Dudley*, 6 vols., HMC, 77 (1925–66), vols. 2–3 · *HoP, Commons, 1558–1603*, vol. 3 · W. P. Baildon, ed., *The records of the Honorable Society of Lincoln's Inn: the black books*, 1 (1897) · R. Williams, *A briefe discourse of warre* (1590); repr. in *The works of Sir Roger Williams*, ed. J. X. Evans (1972), 1–51 · *APC, 1600–01* · *Letters of Sir Thomas Bodley to Thomas James*, ed. G. W. Wheeler (1926); repr. (1985) · *CSP for.*, 1584–6 · PRO, Audit Office, AO 1/292/1096 · PRO, Exchequer, E 351/240–41 · BL, Harley MS 168 · BL, Egerton MS 1694 · *Calendar of the manuscripts of the most hon. the marquis of Salisbury*, 24 vols., HMC, 9 (1883–1976), vols. 6–9 · H. Sydney and others, *Letters and memorials of state*, ed. A. Collins, 2 vols. (1746) · Nationaal Archief, The Hague, Archief van Johan van Oldenbarnevelt, 2943 · Bodl. Oxf., MSS Rawl. B. 83, 139 · W. A. Shaw, *The knights of England*, 2 (1906), 87
Archives PRO, state papers

Uvedale [Woodhall], **John** (*d.* 1549), administrator, was the son of Juliana Skoore, of Banwell, Somerset (*d.* 1542). The family name was Woodall, or Woodhall, but Uvedale adopted the coat of arms and esquire status of the gentry family of Uvedale of Wickham, Hampshire. No close familial connection has been discovered, although Uvedale's early life is obscure. His mother died in 1542, leaving all her goods to George, the illegitimate son of Uvedale's deceased brother, Thomas Woodall. The only other certain relative was his namesake, John Uvedale (*d.* 1559), esquire, of Waltham on the Wolde, Leicestershire.

It is unlikely that Uvedale was the John Uvedale who served as a purveyor of wagons for the royal household from 1487 until 1509. The purveyor attended Henry VII's funeral in that capacity, whereas Uvedale was already, from 1503, a clerk in the signet office. When Uvedale in 1548 emphasized his long service to the crown, he mentioned only the signet appointment of 1503. By the award of Thomas Howard, second duke of Norfolk, Uvedale was on 25 November 1517 sworn in as clerk of the pells in the receipt of the exchequer in survivorship with the incumbent, Robert Blackwell of Bedfordshire. He was sworn in again, alone, on 2 November 1520 following Blackwell's death. The post was in the gift of Lord Treasurer Norfolk. Uvedale had connections to the Howard family from at least 1513, when he received royal funds intended for Lord Thomas Howard; he subsequently witnessed the duke's will in May 1520. Although he retained his exchequer office until death, Uvedale served in person only from 1517 to 1525. In the latter year he was appointed secretary to the duke of Richmond's newly established council, a body intended to serve as a council for the north with headquarters at Sheriff Hutton, Yorkshire. Thereafter Uvedale's exchequer duties were delegated to successive deputies, including his long-time clerk and eventual son-in-law Gilbert Claydon of Binkley, Cambridgeshire. In June 1523 Uvedale added the exchequer position of farmer of the aulnage of cloth in Hampshire and Wiltshire to his developing list of sinecures; he had already, at an uncertain date, secured the keepership of Brasted Park, Kent. By 1525 at the latest he had married, taking as his spouse a sister of Thomas Brightman, a tavern-keeper in Westminster and usher and cryer of king's bench.

The appointment to Richmond's council began an association with the north of England that would continue through the remainder of Uvedale's career and eventually establish him among the Yorkshire gentry. He held office first as secretary to the duke of Richmond until 1536 and then as secretary to the council of the north up to his death in 1549. Uvedale, however, initially held more than provincial aspirations. In 1528 he almost lost his secretaryship when he sought advancement in London from Thomas Wolsey. At court during most of the early 1530s, in 1533 he obtained the office of clerk of the signet in north and south Wales, and entered the Reformation Parliament in a by-election of 1533 or 1534, possibly sitting for the borough of Berwick. Uvedale's opportunity appeared to come in 1533 when Thomas Cromwell secured for him the promising position of secretary to Anne Boleyn. However, the queen's execution in 1536 and the rejuvenation of the council of the north under Thomas Howard, third duke of Norfolk, following the Pilgrimage of Grace led to Uvedale's return to Yorkshire. Initially disappointed by this development, in December 1537 he unsuccessfully petitioned Cromwell for a new position at court. None the less, in 1538 Uvedale was added to the commissions of the peace for the North, East, and West Ridings, and was increasingly drawn into the contentious public affairs of the period. In 1537 he surveyed Bridlington and Jervaulx abbeys and assisted Norfolk in examining seditious persons; in 1539 he served as a commissioner to take the surrender of five Yorkshire priories. Upon reconstitution of the council of the north in 1545, Uvedale was reaffirmed as secretary, appointed to the council, and sworn a master in chancery for the taking of recognizances.

The Anglo-Scottish wars of the 1540s brought Uvedale to national prominence. From August 1542 until his death Uvedale was actively engaged in the fiscal administration of England's war effort. Initially Uvedale served as paymaster to the forces under the control of successive lord wardens of the east and middle marches. He was then placed in control of finances for the 1546 invasion of Scotland under Edward Seymour, earl of Hertford, disbursing the bulk of the direct campaign expenses, over £113,000. He played a similarly prominent role in the period 1547–9 as under-treasurer for the Scottish war. From his base at Newcastle upon Tyne, and with a staff of twelve, Uvedale was painstaking in his attention to detail. Although he held the trust and confidence of Seymour as lord protector, Uvedale's final years were marred by increasing infirmity of body and a growing anxiety for the plight of diseased and mistreated servicemen who suffered from the inability of the government to pay their wages promptly. In June 1548 he quarrelled with the lord warden, William Grey, Lord Grey of Wilton, over the existence of a secret fund which the privy council had ordered Uvedale to keep under his own control. Thereafter, the treasurer's efforts to be allowed to render his accounts and retire from service increased. Eventually he was permitted to return to London in August 1549 to clear his account for the years up to 1547. Death followed within months, and his final account was submitted and cleared by his son and heir in June 1550.

Uvedale prospered in royal service. In the five years 1542–7 alone, as a paymaster he earned for himself and his clerks £1130. In addition to his varied official responsibilities and sinecures, Uvedale specialized in the exploitation of mines and minerals. In 1529 he leased all rights to iron and coal in the forest of Teesdale within the lordship of Barnard Castle, Durham, paying the crown one-twentieth of the proceeds. He and Cromwell were among the lessees of lead mines in Dartmoor Forest in 1534. On 30 November 1537 Uvedale leased all lead and coal mines and rights in Nidderdale, Yorkshire, from Byland monastery for forty years, at a yearly rent of three-twentieths of the proceeds; the rights of Uvedale's heir would be contested later by Sir John York, the purchaser of the estate. Uvedale established his family seat at Marrick Priory in the North Riding. In September 1539 he had taken the surrender of the house on behalf of the crown, but had already, in January 1538, sought Cromwell's assistance in securing a favourable lease upon the dissolution. His persistence was rewarded with a twenty-one-year lease of the house, demesne, and parsonage on 6 June 1541. On 8 June 1545 Uvedale purchased the estate in fee, paying £364 0s. 6d. for property valued by the crown in 1550 at £16 11s. 2d per annum.

Uvedale adopted protestantism during the 1530s, stating in his last will and testament of 24 October 1546 that his soul would be preserved by the grace of Christ alone, not by any works or deeds. In 1538 he advocated the total suppression of the monasteries as God's undoubted will, and in 1540 he encouraged Cromwell to move the king to order that several bibles be placed in every cathedral and collegiate church of the realm, for people of all ages to read and study. In his old age Uvedale represented himself as a godly, ethical agent of the crown who had pursued his career free from crime or misbehaviour. He died on 20 October 1549.

There were two children of Uvedale's marriage: a daughter, Ursula, married to Gilbert Claydon by 1546, and a son and heir, Avery. The age of the latter was given as twenty-four in the inquisition post mortem of April 1550. He was educated at the Middle Temple, and by 1551 was a serjeant-at-law and gentleman usher to Edward VI. By his father's will Avery inherited all the landed estate.

J. D. ALSOP

Sources HoP, Commons, 1509–58 · J. D. Alsop, 'The exchequer of receipt in the reign of Edward VI', PhD diss., U. Cam., 1978, 350–52 · PRO, E 351/211 · will, PRO, PROB 11/33, fols. 43v–44 · PRO, SP 15/1/60, 82, 134, 136, 138; SP 15/2/20, 67, 70, 171–2; SP 15/4/70 · BL, Add. MS 32657, fols. 24, 26–7, 33–4 · LP Henry VIII · PRO, C 142/90/92 · PRO, REQ 2/2/4 · PRO, STAC 3/5/75 · PRO, E 36/266, fols. 70v, 73v · PRO, E 36/253, fol. 17 · PRO, E 36/132 · PRO, E 165/9 · PRO, E 314/20/9 · PRO, E 314/20/28 · PRO, E 101/674/2 · PRO, E 351/212 · PRO, E 405/190–498 · PRO, SP1/18, fols. 266–73 · PRO, SP1/229, fol. 7 · PRO, SP1/297, fols. 200–09 · PRO, SP1/243, fols. 41–2 · PRO, PROB 11/21, fol. 176 · PRO, PROB 11/42B, fol. 393 · BL, Stowe MS 146, fol. 59 · Calendar of the manuscripts of the marquis of Bath preserved at Longleat, Wiltshire, 5 vols., HMC, 58 (1904–80), vol. 4, pp. 30–31, 44–5, 64, 73 · APC · CPR, 1547–8, 92; 1549–51, 294; 1553, 344
Archives BL, corresp., Add. MSS 32646–32657, passim | PRO, state papers, Henry VIII (Cromwell's papers), corresp., SP 1 · PRO, state papers, Scotland, corresp., SP 15/1, 2, 4
Wealth at death prosperous: will, PRO, PROB 11/33, fols. 43v–44

Uvedale, Richard (b. before **1508**, d. **1556**), conspirator, was born by 1508, being of age when he succeeded to his property in 1528, the fourth of five sons of Sir William Uvedale (c.1484–1528), landowner, and his wife, Dorothy (d. 1530), daughter and coheir of Thomas Troyes of Kilmeston, Hampshire, who later married Lord Edmund Howard and so became the stepmother of the future queen, Katherine Howard. His grandfather was Sir William Uvedale of Wickham, Hampshire. He had three sisters; his eldest brother was Sir Arthur Uvedale (b. 1502x4, d. 1537/8) and his other brothers were William, John, and Francis. He shared lands in Surrey worth £80 p.a. with William and was liable to distraint of knighthood in 1547. Nothing is known of his education.

Richard Uvedale seems to have fought in France in 1544 and Sir Richard Long, a gentleman of the privy chamber, procured for him the captaincy of the new fortress at Hasilworth, Portsmouth, by May 1546. He continued as captain until at least 1552, but soon thereafter took command of Yarmouth Castle on the Isle of Wight. He seems to have lived on an inherited estate at Chelsham, Surrey, and at Chilling, apparently 2 miles from Calshot Point, Hampshire, which were convenient for the hunting in which he was often mentioned as participating. A life of apparently unburdensome duty and social consequence as a country gentleman was brought to an untimely end when Uvedale became entangled in plans hatched by Sir Henry Dudley to oppose Mary I's Spanish marriage. This conspiracy had a degree of support from France which Dudley exaggerated for recruiting purposes.

Uvedale was not mentioned in connection with early conspiratorial meetings in London, and it was consistently denied that he knew of the scheme to rob the exchequer that caused the plot to start to unravel. His role was vital, however, because he commanded a substantial coastal garrison and, if the conspiracy was to have any hope of success, it was essential that large numbers of French troops could be landed swiftly and the local gentry rally to the cause. In February 1556 Uvedale assisted John Throckmorton in conveying Dudley to France. He claimed the plot was revealed to him as Dudley embarked, having been led to believe until that point that he was merely assisting him in avoiding his creditors. He stressed that Dudley and Throckmorton had conversations, sometimes in French, which he did not hear or, if he did, could not understand, and wrote ciphered letters which he did not see. But he clearly was well acquainted with Throckmorton at least, who apparently owed him money.

Uvedale was very exposed when the government became suspicious of the activities of certain people in the vicinity of the Solent. Interrogation of those concerned with Dudley's departure showed clearly that he connived at voyages to France without licence. Rather pointlessly, Uvedale denied knowing these witnesses but admitted on 23 March the fact of arranging Dudley's departure, while disclaiming knowledge of his enterprises. Probably among those arrested on 18 March and taken to the Tower of London, he was lodged near the Bell Tower. Throckmorton feared that 'Udall beynge very sickly as also for the feare of the tortoure wyll co[n]fesse' anything (PRO, SP 11/8/53)—with reason. From this point, Uvedale was first to extend the privy council's knowledge, gratuitously incriminating himself.

Uvedale was interrogated on 23 March, confessed on 24–25 March and was questioned again three times between 15 and 24 April. A detailed, if garbled, account of his activities was put together by the privy council and formed, as was intended from the outset, the case against him. On 24 March he confessed that he had largely concurred in Dudley's sudden proposition before departure that, when the latter returned with about ten ships to expel the Spaniards from the realm, Uvedale should help by 'pegging' the coastal artillery and that he should 'see what he coulde doo aboute Portesmouthe' (PRO, SP 11/7/32). He professed to have been lukewarm and of limited usefulness, but this may reflect an attempt to deflect blame as each conspirator accused his fellows and downplayed his own role. During the interrogation on 25 March, he altered his initial account by adding that, far from Dudley springing it on him, he now remembered that Throckmorton had mentioned the plan earlier in the week. John Bedell, another prisoner, said that on a later occasion he had heard Uvedale again promise to sabotage the artillery. The interrogators noted that Bedell showed Uvedale to be an '[a]better' of the plot, and this doomed his feeble self-exculpations. His indictment stressed that he had reaffirmed his commitment to Throckmorton at Chelsham as late as 14 March, four days before the arrests.

The other conspirators seemed to regard Uvedale as useful because of his role as garrison commander, hoping he could raise up to 1000 professional soldiers. This was stressed in negotiations with the French. His complicity was unpardonable, despite government caution, because of the importance of his office. John White, the sheriff of Hampshire, believed Uvedale could raise 2000 men from the Isle of Wight, Sussex, and Portsmouth, and noted darkly that 'Rytche Woddall & other had appointed to take in th'armor of the countres of Southampto[n]' (PRO, SP 11/8/62).

Along with Throckmorton, Uvedale was tried on 21 April 1556 at Southwark. It was fruitless now to plead not guilty, and he was executed at Tyburn on the 28th; after quartering, his head was set up on London Bridge. White secured Uvedale's Hampshire lands; his paternal inheritance in Surrey probably survived as it was in trust, since the holdings there of his nephew William Uvedale (d. 1569) were undiminished by his attainder. Uvedale died unmarried.

JULIAN LOCK

Sources G. Leveson-Gower, 'Notices of the family of Uvedale of Titsey, Surrey, and Wickham, Hampshire', *Surrey Archaeological Collections*, 3 (1865), 63–192 · D. M. Loades, *Two Tudor conspiracies* (1965), 153n, 171, 187, 189, 193n, 194, 200, 210, 215–16, 218–20, 222, 226–7, 230–31, 237, 258–60, 263, 267 · *LP Henry VIII*, vols. 20/1, 21/2 · *CSP dom.*, *1553–8* · state papers, domestic, Mary, PRO, SP 11 · *Report of the Deputy Keeper of the Public Records*, 4 (1843), appx 2, 252–3 · queen's bench, crown side indictments: 'Baga de secretis', PRO, KB 8/33 · will, PRO, PROB 11/23, sig. 4 [Sir William Uvedale, 1528] · *The diary of Henry Machyn, citizen and merchant-taylor of London, from AD 1550 to AD 1563*, ed. J. G. Nichols, CS, 42 (1848)

Uvedale, Robert (1642–1722), schoolteacher and botanist, was born on 25 May 1642 in the parish of St Margaret, Westminster, the third son of eleven children of Robert Uvedale (d. 1683), innkeeper, and his wife, Margaret, formerly Smith. Robert was the eldest of the seven children to survive infancy. The family was a very minor offshoot of a younger branch of the Dorset Uvedales, an armigerous branch of an important family originating in Cumberland.

While Uvedale was at Westminster School the scholars were taken to see the state funeral of Cromwell on 11 November 1658. As the bier passed, he darted out and seized the small satin escutcheon, and later had it framed and backed by a Latin inscription describing its acquisition. The seizure of this trophy gained his descendants some fame in later years. When Uvedale was admitted to Trinity College, Cambridge, on 10 May 1659, John Ray was fellow and tutor at Trinity and perhaps instilled a love of botany in his young scholar. Uvedale graduated in 1663 and was elected fellow the following year, when he was appointed master at the free school in Enfield, Middlesex. However, he became involved in a difficult lawsuit in chancery over the agreements to board children and the quality of the teaching, matters not being helped by his opening his own school, the Palace, nearby. The case dragged on until 1676, and though he effectively won, Uvedale resigned from the free school that year and concentrated on his own school. He resigned his fellowship to marry, on 20 June 1678, Mary (1656–1740), second daughter of Edward *Stephens of Cherrington; they raised a family of five sons and six daughters. His own school prospered and by 1721 he had sent twenty-six boys, many sons of local aristocracy and gentry, and including his own three sons, to Trinity College.

Although he was never elected a fellow of the Royal Society, Uvedale was informed of its activities. James Petiver lent him its *Philosophical Transactions* and gave him books, and Sir Hans Sloane was a correspondent. In 1682 Uvedale was made LLD. He had signed for deacon's orders in 1666, was ordained priest in 1692, and collated to the wealthy rectory of Orpington, Kent, although he probably seldom went there. He was rector of Barking, Suffolk in 1700 and held various Suffolk livings.

In 1691 John Gibson, describing gardens near London, wrote of Uvedale's garden, which lay along the south side of Church Street, Enfield:

> Dr Uvedale … is become master of the greatest and choicest collection of exotic greens that is perhaps anywhere in this land. His greens take up six or seven houses … His orange trees and largest myrtles fill up his biggest house … those more nice and curious plants that need closer keeping are in warmer rooms and some of them stoved when he thinks fit.

His flowers are choice, his stock numerous, and his culture of them very methodical. (Gibson, 188)

Uvedale's correspondents in Europe and the Far East were responsible for sending him seeds and plants of these exotics, but he endeavoured to collect widely from within Britain, complaining bitterly about the inadequacies of the carriers and postal services when his precious packages went astray.

Uvedale also assembled a herbarium, now part of the Sloane herbarium in the Natural History Museum. He was perhaps the first fully to appreciate the value of recording where and when, and by whom, species were found. Many famous botanists came to visit him. From 1712 he became increasingly infirm, and was obliged to undergo several operations to drain fluid from what he described as a tumour. The third operation was successful, and although suffering from gout, he survived; he died at Enfield on 17 August 1722.

Thomas Uvedale (*fl.* 1712), described in the *Dictionary of National Biography* as brother of Robert, is now shown to have been a collateral relative. He lived at Hampton Wick and was also a correspondent of Sloane, to whom he sent some plants, now in the Sloane herbarium. He published in 1712 a two-volume *Memoirs of Philip de Comines* (2nd edn 1720), translated from a French original and reissued in *Military Classics* (1817). Robert's own brother **Thomas Uvedale** (*bap.* 1651, *d.* 1703), who was baptized on 12 January 1651, was an innkeeper like their father. He died in 1703.

G. S. BOULGER, rev. ANITA McCONNELL

Sources J. G. L. Burnby and A. E. Robinson, *And they blew exceeding fine: Robert Uvedale, 1642–1722* (1976) · *Extracts from the literary and scientific correspondence of Richard Richardson*, ed. D. Turner (1835), 15–17, 24–5 · J. Gibson, 'An account of several gardens near London', *Archaeologia*, 12 (1796), 181–92, esp. 188 · W. R., 'Cedars of Lebanon in England', *Gardeners' Chronicle*, 3rd ser., 8 (1890), 505–6 · E. A. Fry, 'The majesty escutcheon', *Notes and Queries for Somerset and Dorset*, 19 (1927–9), 14–17 · IGI
Archives BL, letters to Sir Hans Sloane and J. Petiver
Likenesses portrait, repro. in Burnby and Robinson, *And they blew exceeding fine*, 7

Uvedale, Thomas (*bap.* 1651, *d.* **1703**). *See under* Uvedale, Robert (1642–1722).

Uvedale, Thomas (*fl.* 1712). *See under* Uvedale, Robert (1642–1722).

Uvedale, Sir William (1454/5–1525), administrator, was the son and heir of Sir Thomas Uvedale (*c.*1410–1474), of Wickham, Hampshire, an influential member of that county's gentry, and of his first wife, Margaret Kingston. Margaret died some time between 1457 and 1463, when Sir Thomas married again; his second wife was Elizabeth, widow of William Sidney. About 1477 William Uvedale married Anne, the daughter of Elizabeth's first marriage. William's first public employment appears to have been as a commissioner against piracy in 1477. He became a JP for Hampshire in 1478, and a subsidy commissioner in 1483. Already attached to the royal household, he was to have been knighted at Edward V's coronation.

Though given custody of Portchester Castle, Hampshire, by Richard III to replace Sir Edward Woodville, in the autumn of 1483 Uvedale joined the conspiracy of the duke of Buckingham (whose family his father had served) against the new king. He was attainted, though pardoned corporal penalties in January 1485. Rapidly restored by Henry VII, he was created a knight of the Bath on 29 November 1489, and became a knight of the royal body in 1504. He was Hampshire's sheriff three times (1479–80, 1486–7, 1492–3), and twice member for parliament (1491, 1495), but stayed off the county's peace commission between 1486 and 1494. Even from 1497 to 1507, he was only recorded at two out of nineteen documented sessions, one being the trial in 1505 of his fellow courtier William Sandys (*d.* 1540) for illegal maintenance.

Early in 1493 Uvedale became a member of oyer and terminer and peace commissions for Gloucestershire, Worcestershire, Herefordshire, and Shropshire. He was also a JP in Cornwall from 1494, but had been dropped by 1502; and he held commissions in Devon against rebels in 1497. Useful to Henry VII in counties strange to him, Uvedale came to serve above all in the Welsh marches.

In 1501 Uvedale was formally appointed as councillor to Arthur, prince of Wales (*d.* 1502), but he was already serving under William Smith (*d.* 1514), bishop of Coventry and Lichfield, in the council of the marches. In 1497 he authorized a financial levy as the council's comptroller, while in 1514 he followed Smith in signing articles against disorders in Shropshire. In 1505 Chester was added to the usual four marcher shires in which he was commissioned to deliver gaols. In 1508 he was appointed to a judicial eyre through the lordships of Usk, Caerleon, and Trelleck. In 1511 he arbitrated between Shrewsbury Abbey and the town while in 1517 he joined an enclosure inquisition in Herefordshire, Worcestershire, and Gloucestershire. Uvedale also acquired a more personal interest in the region. He acted as steward of Abberley, Shrawley, Elmley Lovett, and Salwarpe, all in Worcestershire, from 1504 until his death, and as keeper of the king's forests of Brengewood and Wigmore in Herefordshire from 1512. He was also keeper from 1506 of the nearby Huntington Forest of the third duke of Buckingham.

In 1509 Uvedale was said to be dividing his residence between Wickham, Ludlow, and London, but he does seem later to have had more time for Hampshire affairs—despite some carelessness with his knighthood, it is perhaps more likely to have been he rather than his younger namesake who was a commissioner of array at Portchester in 1522 and for the subsidy of 1523 but a reluctant Hampshire contributor to the forced loan of 1522/3. Uvedale died on 2 January 1525, followed some three years later by his heir, another Sir William (*c.*1484–1528). The latter seems to have inherited a landed income over £200.

A contemporary **Sir William Uvedale** (*d.* 1542) of More Crichell, Dorset, was son of Henry Uvedale (*c.*1460–1515x18) and Edith Pool of Gloucestershire. His father, an esquire of Henry VII's household (in 1508 gentleman usher) had been member of parliament for Wilton (1491), customer of Poole, keeper of Corfe Castle, and sheriff of

Somerset and Dorset for 1503–4. Probably the two Sir Williams were first cousins twice removed, their common ancestor being Sir Thomas's father, Sir John Uvedale.

Between 1511 and 1515 Uvedale secured the reversion of his father's posts of launder—keeper of the lawns, or open ground—of Clarendon Forest, Wiltshire, and bailiff of Purbeck, Dorset. He also seems to have followed him as gentleman usher to the king. From 1515 he acted as customs comptroller at Poole. Having found it prudent to obtain a pardon in 1527 for malversations, he was reappointed the following year. He became collector of the London wool customs from 1522 until 1535, when he relinquished the post to William Thynne (d. 1546). From 1522 to 1534 he also acted as the duchy of Lancaster's feodary for Dorset, Somerset, Wiltshire, and Hampshire.

Uvedale became a JP for Dorset in 1522, and a subsidy commissioner there in 1523 and 1534. Nominated for the shrievalty but never chosen, he was, however, knighted on 30 May 1533 at Anne Boleyn's coronation. Sir William was prompt to enter the monastic land-market in 1536, and subsequently acquired lands in Wiltshire and Dorset formerly held by the houses of Wilton and Cerne—the latter estate, at Kimmeridge, adjoined his existing Purbeck property, and cost him over £200.

Uvedale had married Jane Dawson of Norfolk; an apparent reference to this in a letter of William Blount, fourth Lord Mountjoy (d. 1534)—who described Uvedale as 'my servant' (BL, Stowe MSS, MS 147, fol. 16)—suggests 1513. His will, made on 10 September 1542 and proved on 31 October, mentions four sons and one daughter; all the sons appear to have been minors. He bequeathed his soul to God and the 'company of heaven', omitting the usual mention of the Virgin Mary—a courtier-like compromise. He was buried in St Katherine's Church in London.

JULIAN LOCK

Sources LP Henry VIII · Chancery records · G. Leveson-Gower, 'Notices of the family of Uvedale of Titsey, Surrey, and Wickham, Hampshire', Surrey Archaeological Collections, 3 (1865), 63–192 · E. A. Fry, 'The Uvedale family of Dorset', Notes and Queries for Somerset and Dorset, 19 (1927–9), 54–62 · D. A. Luckett, 'Crown patronage and local administration in Berkshire, Dorset, Hampshire, Oxfordshire, Somerset and Wiltshire, 1485–1509', DPhil diss., U. Oxf., 1992 · Chester warrants, PRO, CHES 1/2 · W. Jerdan, ed., Rutland papers: original documents illustrative of the courts and times of Henry VII and Henry VIII, CS, 21 (1842) · C. G. Bayne and W. H. Dunham, eds., Select cases in the council of Henry VII, SeldS, 75 (1958) · J. C. Wedgwood and A. D. Holt, History of parliament, 1: Biographies of the members of the Commons house, 1439–1509 (1936), 899–901 · Worcestershire County Record Office, Berington MSS, BA 81 1, (705:24) · PRO, Prerogative court of Canterbury Wills, PROB 11/29/10 · customs accounts, PRO, E122 · BL, Stowe MSS, MS 147, fol. 16
Wealth at death approximately £200 landed income; £17 annuities; £80 cash; 240 sheep assigned: will, PRO, PROB 11/29/10

Uvedale, Sir William (d. 1542). See under Uvedale, Sir William (1454/5–1525).

Uwins, Cyril Frank (1896–1972), aviator, was born at 2 Carmichael Road, South Norwood, Croydon, on 2 August 1896, the elder son (there were no daughters) of Frank Uwins, a wood broker, and his wife, Annie Henton. He was educated at the Whitgift School, Croydon, where he developed a schoolboy interest in kites—an appropriate introduction to an aeronautical career. When the First World War broke out in 1914 he joined a London regiment and in 1916 managed to achieve a transfer to the Royal Flying Corps. The following year, on a ferry flight from Hounslow aerodrome to St Omer in France, the engine failed in the Morane-Parasol monoplane he was flying and in the ensuing crash Uwins broke his neck. He suffered from a stiff neck for the rest of his life.

Once he was out of hospital Uwins was judged medically unfit for active service, and on 25 October 1918 he was posted to the Bristol Aeroplane Company's works at Filton to succeed Captain Joseph Hammond of the Royal Flying Corps, Bristol's test pilot from 19 January 1917, who had been killed flying an American-built Bristol fighter.

Uwins's first test flight—on 26 October 1918, the day after he joined Bristol—was in a Bristol Scout F (B 3991). Six months later, on 1 May 1919, he was demobilized from the Royal Air Force and formally joined the Bristol Aeroplane Company. On that same day, still in uniform, he made the first post-war commercial air flight in Britain when he flew the Bristol Company's general manager, Herbert Thomas, from Filton to Hounslow aerodrome in a Bristol Tourer Coupé (M 1460)—a civil variant of the wartime Bristol fighter.

During the next thirty years Uwins made the first flights of every new Bristol aeroplane, ranging from the heavy twin-engine Bristol Braemar triplane of February 1918, through the little Bristol Brownie ultra-light monoplane of August 1926 (in which he gained third place in the Lympne light aeroplane trials), to the Bristol Bulldog single-seat biplane fighter of May 1927, and the Bristol Blenheim twin-engine bomber of June 1936 to the Bristol type 170 freighter of December 1945.

The fifty-eight prototype aircraft which Uwins flew, and the very large number of production machines, spanned the transformation of aeronautical design from the simple wooden fabric-covered biplane of the First World War to the all-metal stressed-skin monoplane with retractable undercarriage and variable-pitch propellers. Uwins coped with them all in a steady, careful, self-possessed, and taciturn manner and, through skill—and a measure of good luck—survived. Indeed, though he had many close calls, he had no serious accident. Eventually he headed a team of eight assistant test pilots, none of whom ever made the first flight of a new aeroplane while Uwins was in charge.

In the course of his work, on 16 September 1932—almost exactly halfway through his test-flying career—Uwins regained for Britain the world's aeroplane height record by climbing to 43,976 feet (nearly 8½ miles), flying an open cockpit Vickers Vespa biplane with a specially tuned Bristol Pegasus engine. The climb took a hundred minutes, the descent twenty minutes. On the way down Uwins ran out of fuel and made a successful forced landing in a field near Chippenham. For this feat he was awarded the Britannia trophy.

Uwin's phlegmatic and somewhat austere nature went to the extent that, when intercom arrangements were developed between pilot and flight observer in two-seat aircraft, he insisted he could speak to the flight observer but the flight observer could never answer back. In any discussion he habitually ended the briefest of conversations with, 'We won't say anything more about that'. Tall, quiet, with aquiline features and—from middle age—plentiful white hair, Uwins was absorbed in his work; he never smoked, drank sparingly, and allowed himself one major holiday each year, in the south of France.

Uwins retired as deputy chairman of the Bristol Aeroplane Company in 1964 following its merger with Vickers and the English Electric Company to form the British Aircraft Corporation. He was awarded the silver medal for aeronautics of the Royal Aeronautical Society, of which he became a fellow, and he was made an honorary MSc of Bristol University in 1964. He was president of the Society of British Aircraft Constructors from 1956 to 1958 and a member of the Air Registration Board from 1959 to 1964. He won the AFC in 1937 and was appointed OBE in 1943.

Uwins was twice married: first in 1919 to Joyce Marguerite, the daughter of Charles Ernest Boucher, a director of a local company. They had two daughters. Joyce Uwins was killed in a motor-car accident in 1950. He married, secondly, in 1955, Naomi Short, the widow of Captain E. D. Short of the King's regiment and the daughter of Henry Augustus Scott-Barrett. Uwins died on 11 September 1972 at the Lansdown Nursing Home, Bath.

PETER G. MASEFIELD, *rev.*

Sources C. H. Barnes, *Bristol aircraft since 1910* (1964) · personal knowledge (1986) · *The Times* (12 Sept 1972) · *WWW* · *CGPLA Eng. & Wales* (1973)
Wealth at death £79,952: probate, 9 Sept 1973, *CGPLA Eng. & Wales*

Uwins, David (1780–1837), physician, was born in London, the second son of Thomas Uwins (*d.* 1816), a clerk in the Bank of England, and his wife, Sarah (*d.* 1824), and the brother of the artist Thomas *Uwins RA. Uwins's father 'had no desire for his boys than they should be honest tradesmen' (Uwins, 1.6). The boys attended a school run by a Mr Crole in Islington, London.

Uwins was a little man with a large head and a long pale face. He trained in London hospitals, and went on to graduate MD (Edinburgh) on 12 September 1803. After his return to London he worked for a short time as assistant physician at the Finsbury Dispensary, and then set up in practice in Aylesbury, Buckinghamshire. On 22 December 1807 he obtained the licentiate of the Royal College of Physicians. He married shortly before he was elected physician to the City Dispensary in London in 1815. He was afterwards elected physician to the new Finsbury and Central Dispensary.

Uwins's attention was first drawn to homoeopathy in 1826 by his brother Thomas, who was living in Naples and whose friend Frederic Quin had done much there to popularize the system. At this time Uwins had just published his *Compendium of Theoretical and Practical Medicine* (1825), one of several conventional textbooks written by him. Already approaching middle age he did not find homoeopathy immediately attractive and he was never a complete convert to its practice. When Quin went to London in 1827 their first meeting was not a success. Uwins continued his conventional career, being appointed in 1828 as physician to the lunatic asylum at Peckham. His observations there formed the basis of his *Treatise on those disorders of the brain and nervous system which are usually considered, and called mental* (1833). This was a successful book which greatly enhanced his professional reputation.

However, no doubt encouraged by his brother, who claimed that he owed everything to Quin, Uwins and Quin became friends. Uwins started to use homoeopathic remedies and was present in 1837 at the first (unsuccessful) attempt to form a British homoeopathic society.

In 1836 an eminent homoeopathic physician, Dr Belluomini, was unjustly accused of quackery by the medical journals and popular press, and of gross misconduct in connection with the death of a patient. So malicious was the abuse that even the editor of *The Lancet* was driven to protest. Uwins, who had a strong sense of what was acceptable conduct in medicine, was very upset by these events. He therefore sought, from fairness, to put forward his own protest. Although he had the reputation of being the worst of speakers, he read a paper at the Medical Society of London and published a pamphlet entitled *Homeopathy and Allopathy, or, Large, Small, and Atomic Doses* (1836?). In this he described some of the astonishing cures that had been effected by homoeopathy and he praised Quin's professional honesty.

By this declaration Uwins became publicly associated with a system of medicine that most doctors regarded as anathema. It brought upon him the censure of former friends and colleagues from which his professional eminence could not shield him. He had always been of a highly nervous temperament and the stress of these events together with worry about financial matters proved too much for him. His health broke down and he died of 'nervous fever' at his house, 19 Bedford Row, Holborn, London, on 22 September 1837, and was buried at Kensal Green cemetery.

BERNARD LEARY

Sources *DNB* · Munk, *Roll* · S. Uwins, *A memoir of Thomas Uwins*, 2 vols. (1858) · E. Hamilton, *A memoir of F. H. F. Quin* (privately printed, [London], 1879) · *The Lancet* (12 Nov 1836), 267 · *Handbook of Kensal Green cemetery* (1853) · d. cert.

Uwins, Thomas (1782–1857), painter, illustrator, and art administrator, was born on 24 February 1782 at Hermes Hill, Pentonville, London, the youngest of four children of Thomas Uwins (*d.* 1816), clerk of the Bank of England, and his wife, Sarah (*d.* 1824). He had some limited instruction from his sister's drawing master and six years with his brothers as a day scholar at Mr Crole's school, Queen's Head Lane, Islington, after which Uwins's parents took Alderman Boydell's advice and apprenticed him in 1797 to the engraver Benjamin Smith, in whose workshop he learned a trade he hated under the assistant, William Holl. Uwins's drawing talent enabled him to enter the Royal Academy Schools in December 1798 and in 1801 he quit his apprenticeship.

From 1799 Uwins exhibited miniature portraits in the Royal Academy exhibitions, followed from 1807 by small designs and book illustrations. Employers included J. Walker of Paternoster Row, Charles Warren, and from 1808 Rudolph Ackermann, for whom he contributed fashion figures to the *Repository of Art* and occasional articles signed Arbiter Elegantarium. He also drew in watercolour representative figures for major Ackermann publications, notably *Westminster Abbey* (1812), *Oxford University* (1814), *Cambridge University* (1815), and *Public Schools* (1816).

In 1809 Thomas Heaphy proposed Uwins for the Society of Painters in Water Colours, and in the following summers he sketched rural subjects, excelling with hop picking at Farnham in 1811 and, in 1818, the vintage in Burgundy following a visit to Paris. Elected a full member of the society in 1810, Uwins served as secretary in 1813–14 and 1816–18 but his progress was interrupted when he resigned in 1818 to concentrate on book illustrations, mainly of English authors, at which he was now adept. This was in order to repay the Society of Arts the whole of a debt of £800 incurred as joint guarantor with Charles Warren, who had a family to support. The grind of this miniature work over two years damaged his eyesight and in 1821 Uwins moved to Edinburgh on the recommendation of the sculptor Samuel Joseph, in the hope of obtaining higher prices for portraits in oil and chalk; he also executed three large transparencies of George IV's visit in 1822 and drawings for Walter Scott's novels.

A devoted son, Uwins returned to London before his mother's death in August 1824, and shortly afterwards left for Italy in search of a better climate for his health. His letters to his brothers, Zechariah and David, published by his wife in a *Memoir* (1858), chart his progress through Geneva and Florence, where he was seriously ill, to Rome in November. Welcomed there by English artists, of whom Charles Eastlake became a particular friend, and dazzled by the city's splendours he decided to stay the winter to study and copy the old masters.

Uwins's visit to Naples the following spring was prolonged by commissions and hospitality from the influential Sir Richard Acton. His health restored, he enjoyed considerable success with portraits of British and Austrian visitors while still finding time for drawings for ladies' albums and annuals that he sent to his brothers for distribution to London publishers. In July 1826 a patron, Mr Crosier Raine, conveyed him to Venice; this and the journey back to Naples alone through the great cities gave Uwins a wide knowledge of Italian art that was to stand him in good stead.

By now Uwins felt that he was accepted as the representative of the English school in Naples. Modest to a fault and conscious of his inadequate training as an oil painter, he took advice from the visiting David Wilkie and from Joseph Severn in Rome, while Eastlake urged him to paint larger than mere cabinet size. After submitting to cruel criticism from his old watercolour society friend William Havell, who proved an exhausting companion late in 1828 when they shared a house at the foot of Vesuvius, Uwins considered himself a better painter. His confidence was boosted further by Sir Thomas Lawrence's letters expressing his esteem for Uwins who, unable to comply with his

earlier request for copying in the Sistine Chapel, had given Lawrence alternative drawings and was rewarded with a commission for a painting. The leading London dealers, the Woodburns, were also interested in the Italian peasant paintings, a 'new class of subjects' (Uwins, 2.191) that Uwins developed to become his future support.

From 1829 Uwins sent these Italian subjects to the British Institution and, from 1830, to the Royal Academy. *The (Neapolitan) Saint Manufactory* (Leicester Art Gallery) that revealed his contempt for the trappings of Roman Catholicism proved a great success in the academy's exhibition of 1832: this followed his return to England after time in Rome where he received his nephew James, who painted similar scenes, and who exhibited in London from 1839 to 1850. In 1833 Thomas Uwins was elected associate of the Royal Academy, then full member in 1838; in 1844 he was appointed librarian. Uwins's favourite subject was *Neapolitans Dancing the Tarantella*, first shown in 1830; a later version, probably exhibited at the Royal Academy in 1842 as *The Lesson* (V&A), was one of four works bought by John Sheepshanks. Another important collector of British art, Robert Vernon, bought *The Chapeau de Brigand* (Tate collection), shown in 1839 and rightly deemed 'delicious'.

Uwins had left Italy with mixed feelings but his fears of ill health and penury in a damp climate proved groundless. Earlier in life he described himself as 'a little meagre swarthy figure' (Herrmann, 241); he grew quite distinguished with age and fitted easily into continental life, learning French and then some Italian, and his access to the best Neapolitan society and appreciation of the old masters prepared him for an acquaintance with Prince Albert, whom he met as one of the artists chosen to work on the fresco of Comus in the Queen's Pavilion, Buckingham Palace Gardens (des.) in 1843. To his amazement he was appointed in 1845 surveyor of pictures to Queen Victoria and completed the first *catalogue raisonné* of the Royal Collection six years later.

Elected in 1821, Uwins now found time to become an active member of the Sketching Society that included many friends, notably the Chalon brothers, and enjoyed royal approval. His miniature portraits such as that of the *Bishop of Chichester* (BM) of 1816 and rural subjects in watercolour gave way in Italy to local scenes in pen and wash (examples in the British Museum), the medium chosen by the group who were depicted in 1836 by their member, John Partridge (drawing; BM), who also painted Uwins's portrait (NPG).

In 1847 Uwins was chosen to succeed Eastlake as keeper of the National Gallery, then sharing the Trafalgar Square building with the Royal Academy. On duty four days a week he found himself responsible to the trustees for a shambolic institution attracting some 3000 people daily, too many bringing their own refreshment. Uwins had to answer questions from the parliamentary select committees of 1850 and 1853 including questions on the cleaning of pictures: these revealed him an advocate of little more than a silk handkerchief or warm water, whereas John Seguier, the restorer, had his own instructions to use stronger methods. The need to strengthen the administration was obvious and on Uwins's retirement a director was appointed, among other changes.

Meanwhile in 1851 Uwins visited Venice with Woodburn on National Gallery business and advised against the purchase of the Manfridi collection: he also travelled in England in pursuit of commissions for his own paintings, which were exhibited at the Royal Academy up to his death as well as in Manchester and Liverpool. On his first holiday in 1850 he had unexpectedly married on 18 September an old friend, Sarah Kirby (d. 1861?), and found great happiness; but the strain of his three appointments told and he succumbed to illness in January 1855 and left his Kensington house for retirement in Staines. He died there on 26 August 1857 sustained to the last by his Christian faith, and was buried in the new burial-ground adjoining the church. On 3 June 1858 his studio sale at Christies made nearly £745.   FELICITY OWEN

Sources S. Uwins, *A memoir of Thomas Uwins*, 2 vols. (1858); repr. in 1 vol. (1978) · *DNB* · Graves, *RA exhibitors* · J. L. Roget, *A history of the 'Old Water-Colour' Society*, 2 vols. (1891) · J. Phillips, *Thomas Uwins RA* (1989) [exhibition catalogue, Gallery Downstairs, London] · L. Herrmann, *The Connoisseur*, 159 (1965), 236–41 · R. Parkinson, ed., *Catalogue of British oil paintings, 1820–1860* (1990) [catalogue of V&A] · 'Select committee on the National Gallery', *Parl. papers* (1850), vol. 15, no. 612; (1852–3), vol. 35, no. 867
Archives RA, letters to T. Lawrence and C. Eastlake
Likenesses J. Partridge, pencil drawing, 1825, NPG · J. Partridge, group portrait, pencil, ink, and wash drawing, 1836 (*A Meeting of the Sketching Society*), BM · J. Partridge, oils, 1836, NPG · C. H. Lear, black chalk drawing, 1845, NPG · G. H. White, pencil drawing, c.1845, NPG · J. Smyth, line engraving, 1847 (after T. H. Illidge), BM, NPG; repro. in *Art Union* (1847)
Wealth at death £744 19s. od.—value of art sold 3 June 1858; Uwins's own paintings, drawings, and engravings; contents of his studio plus a few watercolours and drawings by friends, mostly Sketching Society members: Christie's sale catalogue

Uxbridge. For this title name *see* Paget, Henry, first earl of Uxbridge (c.1663–1743); Paget, Henry, second earl of Uxbridge (*bap.* 1719, *d.* 1769) [*see under* Paget, Henry, first earl of Uxbridge (c.1663–1743)].

Vaart, Jan vander (1647–1727), painter, was born in Haarlem of unknown parents and trained under Thomas Wyck. He arrived in England c.1674 and worked as a painter of landscapes with small figures, small portraits, and still-lifes. Vertue comments on the *trompe-l'œil* success of many of his paintings, especially his 'very surprizing pictures of dead partridges that have deceiv'd the sight being so naturally painted' as well as 'fiddles he has painted so deceiveingly to the eye' (Vertue, *Note books*, 3.21), the last referring to the violin he painted for the second duke of Devonshire on the back of the door of the state music room at Chatsworth (still *in situ*). According to Marshall Smith (who initially confuses 'Vaude-Vert', as he calls him, with Vanderbank), vander Vaart 'Paints a *Face* and *Posture* very well, *Landskip, Foul, etc* extraordinary fine and is to be Rank'd amongst the great Masters of the *Age*' (M. S., 25–6).

Between 1685 and 1687 vander Vaart was employed by Willem Wissing as a drapery and landscape painter; an example of their association is the full-length *Frances Stewart, Duchess of Richmond and Lennox* (NPG). He later collaborated with the German-born artist Johann Kerseboom, producing such joint works as *Thomas Osborne, Duke of Leeds* of 1704. From 1687 he also practised as an independent portrait painter working in the style of Wissing. Among his sitters were the Shirley family, the family of the first Earl Ferrers, signed and dated 1688; Mary II (priv. coll.); and Mary Sayer, countess of Pembroke (priv. coll.).

A number of vander Vaart's portraits were engraved in mezzotint by Bernard Lens for the print publisher Edward Cooper. This particular print technique was closely associated with vander Vaart, who was among its earliest practitioners in England. Chaloner Smith records nine mezzotints by him: *Charles II*, *Thomas Killegrew*, and *James, Duke of Monmouth* after Willem Wissing; *Colonel Robert Feilding*, *Lady Essex Finch*, and *Elizabeth, Duchess of Somerset* after Lely; *Ann, Duchess of Monmouth* after Kneller; *Oliver Plunkett* by Garret Morphey; and *Edward Wetenhall* by vander Vaart himself. Most of these were produced either for Edward Cooper or his fellow print publisher Richard Tompson. Vander Vaart also taught the highly successful young printmaker John Smith how to make mezzotints.

In 1713 poor eyesight forced him to give up his portrait practice although vander Vaart seems to have been able to continue working and established a successful restoration business from his house in Covent Garden's piazza. Respected by fellow artists, he appears never to have married and left as his main heir his nephew and executor the painter John Arnold, with whom he lived and worked for over thirty years. Vander Vaart made his will on 17 January 1727, which was proved on 29 March 1727. He died in London between these dates and was buried at St Paul's, Covent Garden, under the right-hand aisle approaching the altar.   DIANA DETHLOFF

Sources Vertue, *Note books*, 3.11, 21, 32 · M. S. [M. Smith], *The art of painting: according to the theory and practise of the best Italian, French and Germane masters* (1693), 25–6 · J. C. Smith, *British mezzotinto portraits*, 4 vols. in 5 (1878–84) · A. Griffiths and R. A. Gerard, *The print in Stuart Britain, 1603–1689* (1998), 217, 232, 239 [exhibition catalogue, BM, 8 May – 20 Sept 1998] · M. K. Talley, *Portrait painting in England: studies in the technical literature before 1700* (1981), 378 · will, PRO, 11/614, sig. 77
Wealth at death left money and property to brother's family: will, PRO, PROB 11/614, fols. 253r–254r

Vacarius (c.1120–c.1200), civil lawyer, who introduced the revived Roman civil law into England, was almost certainly of Lombard origin. He studied civil law at Bologna, where he attained the title *magister*. About 1143 Archbishop Theobald brought him to Canterbury to join the team, led by John of Salisbury, which assisted Theobald in his struggle with the papal legate, Henry de Blois. According to John, Vacarius and his use of Roman law incurred the censure of King Stephen, Henry's brother. In the late 1150s Vacarius transferred to the service of Roger de Pont l'Évêque, archbishop of York, who had previously been archdeacon of Canterbury, and remained based in the northern province for the rest of his long life. In 1164 he acted as agent in Paris for the archbishop, who in 1166 gave him the prebend of Norwell in the collegiate church of Southwell. He took orders, probably after his arrival in England. In 1171 he accompanied the archbishop to France when the latter was summoned to clear himself of charges arising out of his involvement in the Becket dispute. After Roger de Pont l'Évêque's death in 1181 Vacarius seems to have concerned himself primarily with the affairs of the Southwell canons and with his duties as rector of Norwell, where he had no vicar.

There is considerable documentary evidence for Vacarius's activities as a man of affairs. He appears as a witness, usually to grants or confirmations, but on a number of occasions to judgments or settlements of disputes, in two charters of Theobald in the 1150s, and then to eight of Roger, three of Roger's successor, Geoffrey, and five of the Southwell canons. His reputation as a jurist ensured that he was chosen as a papal judge-delegate in several cases. In the early 1190s Vacarius obtained papal permission to grant half his church at Norwell to his nephew Reginald, and in 1198, when he must have been nearly eighty, Innocent III nominated him to preach the crusade in the province of York, doubtless as a tribute to his local distinction. Vacarius died about 1200.

Vacarius's main claim to fame is as the compiler of the *Liber pauperum*, an anthology of extracts, sometimes abbreviated, from Justinian's *Code* and *Digest*, distributed in nine books in imitation of the *Code* (as it was understood in the twelfth century). The books are divided, according to subject matter, into titles taken from the *Code*, and the number of extracts within each title ranges from one to fifty. In the prologue Vacarius explains that, as the work was intended for poor students, it had to be cheap and capable of being read in a short time. The selection of extracts was based, he said, on their scientific interest and practical use; the work was intended not for professional civil lawyers but for others, presumably canonists and secular lawyers. Civil law in England was viewed as a general jurisprudential supplement to canon law, which had more practical importance. That the *Liber pauperum* was the main medium of civil-law teaching in England around 1200 is attested by the large number of manuscripts, mostly in fragmentary form, that survive from that period. The main texts on each topic are supplemented by texts from other titles of the *Digest* and *Code* and by explanatory glosses. Most of these glosses are anonymous. They are based on the teaching of the Bolognese school and reflect the opinions of its principal professors, but some refer expressly to Vacarius's views, which are occasionally cited even in continental glosses. He was particularly interested in general principles of law, in legal procedure, and in the authority of custom and was clearly a teacher of note. One may properly speak of a Vacarian school in England.

Precisely where and when Vacarius taught is not, however, so clear. The once widespread idea that he taught civil law in Oxford in the 1150s has been disproved by Sir Richard Southern, and the composition of the *Liber*, formerly thought to be of that period, is now considered to be more probably dated in the 1170s or 1180s. The place of

his instruction was possibly Oxford or possibly Northampton, seat of a short-lived twelfth-century *studium*, where Vacarius himself says that he spent some time *causa studendi* (which may mean for studying or teaching, or both). Another possibility is Lincoln, which had an important cathedral school that certainly taught canon law, and was only about 16 miles from Vacarius's rectory at Norwell. It is certain that in the 1190s the *Liber pauperum* was used as the main text of a flourishing school of civil law in Oxford, whose students, notorious for their arrogance, were known as *pauperistae*, but the master himself was then probably too old to have participated personally.

Apart from the *Liber pauperum*, Vacarius wrote three treatises on theological and canon-law themes. The earliest work, the *Tractatus de assumpto homine*, was probably written in the 1160s. It concerns the controversy over the manner of union between the divine and human natures of Christ and aims to convince a friend, 'B', who had adopted the views of Gilbert de la Porrée and Peter Lombard, of the error of his ways. Vacarius shows no familiarity with current theological debates, and bases his argument on Augustine, Boethius, and civil-law doctrines of possession.

The second work, the *Summa de matrimonio*, was written shortly afterwards and is concerned with the moment when a marriage comes into being: is it physical consummation (Gratian) or the exchange of present promises (Peter Lombard)? Although this was a canon-law problem, Vacarius is critical of canon law as being unscientific and, in an apparent reference to Gratian's *Decretum*, refers scornfully to those who toil in vain to bring the discord of contradictions into concord. In his view what makes a marriage is the delivery of the wife to her husband, that is, *traditio*, the word in civil law for the delivery of goods following sale or gift.

The *Liber super multiplices et varios errores* is a reply to a theological tract written by an old friend from his student days, Hugo Speroni of Piacenza, and sent by the hand of Vacarius's nephew Leonard, who visited his uncle in England. It dates from the 1170s or early 1180s. Once again, where arguments based on canon law would be expected, Vacarius ignores them in favour of civil-law similes.

PETER STEIN

Sources R. W. Southern, 'Master Vacarius and the beginning of an English academic tradition', *Medieval learning and literature: essays presented to Richard William Hunt*, ed. J. J. G. Alexander and M. T. Gibson (1976), 257–86 • F. de Zulueta and P. Stein, *The teaching of Roman law around 1200*, SeldS, suppl. ser., 8 (1990) • P. Stein, 'The Vacarian school', *Journal of Legal History*, 13 (1992), 23–31 • *The Liber pauperum of Vacarius*, ed. F. de Zulueta, SeldS, 44 (1927) • F. W. Maitland, 'Magistri Vacarii summa de matrimonio', *Law Quarterly Review*, 13 (1897), 133–43, 270–87 • N. M. Haring, 'The *Tractatus de assumpto homine* by Magister Vacarius', *Mediaeval Studies*, 21 (1959), 147–75 • P. Ilarino da Milano, 'L'eresia di U. Speroni nella configurazione di maestro Vacario', *Studi e Testi*, 115 (1945)

Vachell, Ada Marian [*known as* Sister Ada] (**1866–1923**), worker for disabled people, was born on 27 December 1866, at 14 Charles Street, Cardiff, daughter of William Vachell (1827–1910), iron merchant and three times mayor of Cardiff, and his wife, Marian or Mary Anne, daughter of William Fedden of Clifton. Scarlet fever claimed the lives of two of Ada's brothers and left her frail and partially deaf, and shortly afterwards, about 1875, she, her parents, and a surviving younger son, Arthur, moved to her mother's home city of Bristol. After a patchy education Ada began charitable work in Bristol, but it was not until 1895 that she began the work with disabled people which was to dominate her life. Physical disability then condemned sufferers to a life of economic dependence and social isolation, and chronic pain compounded by boredom often led to drunkenness. In 1895 Miss Vachell visited Grace Thyrza Kimmins's Guild of the Brave Poor Things, which was inspired by Mrs (Juliana Horatia) Ewing's *Story of a Short Life* (1885). Her 'cripples' were emboldened with flags and banners to fight the misery and dependence which their conditions brought and to be 'Laetus sorte mea' ('happy in my lot').

Vachell took the idea to Bristol and founded the Guild of the Poor Things there on 13 February 1896. Sister Ada, as she became known, began social meetings for disabled people to combat boredom and isolation, and went on to place many of them (boys more easily than girls) in apprenticeships, the guild paying the premium, and to take on summer country holidays as many as she could (82 in 1899, and 147 by 1904). With medals and mottoes, flags and banners, 'cripples' were encouraged to 'face about manfully and bear cheerfully what inevitable hardness life holds. But though we feel this, it can never lessen our deep pity, our lovingest sympathy. Life is not easy to any Poor Thing. They are all men and women—even little children of sorrows. They are all acquainted with grief' (Unwin, 123). She had a band of voluntary helpers, but she always remained at the heart of the guild, doing everything from raising money to visiting disabled people in the workhouse.

With help from guild members who had found work, and from factory girls of the Hand-in-Hand social club which Miss Vachell had earlier helped to run, the guild grew steadily, reaching 200 members in 1906. From its first premises in Stratton Street, it moved to Broad Plain by March 1896. In May 1906 it opened a purpose-built holiday home at Churchill, Somerset, and on 27 June 1913 opened purpose-built premises at the Guild Heritage, Braggs Lane, Bristol. In 1899 Miss Vachell helped to found the Bristol Invalid Children's School, which was modelled on Mrs Humphry Ward's work at the Passmore Edwards Settlement in Tavistock Place, London.

Sister Ada seems to have been a quite remarkable person—undogmatic, non-judgemental, hard-working, cheerful, compassionate, and able to see and solve problems. A devout Christian, she worshipped with Anglicans, Unitarians, and Quakers alike, and demanded of her guild members allegiance to no particular creed. A convinced abstainer, she organized a temperance group within the guild, but membership was optional, and she wrote of a woman who had drunk herself to death, 'There's a great content that we haven't to sort out the good and evil in people, haven't to judge, *can't* judge,—but that with God

all is seen and allowed for and understood' (Unwin, 41). The name Poor Things had been her choice, but she was happy to change it to the Guild of the Handicapped after young male members found the expression 'poor things' hindered their chance of finding work. From comfortable circumstances and physically weak, she undertook exhausting manual work, such as giving daily baths to twenty guild members on holiday in a farmhouse with no bathroom. She talked of soldierly discipline and decked her meeting-rooms with flags and banners, but ensured that guild holidays were marked by freedom and lack of rules, and remarked of her members that 'Heroes are with us yet, and some live upon parish pay' (Unwin, 49).

Miss Vachell, who as well as pursuing her voluntary work kept an interest in the theatre and advocated women's suffrage, died suddenly of pneumonia on 29 December 1923 at her home, Foley Cottage, Hampton Road, Clifton, Bristol. After a funeral service attended by weeping crowds at Bristol Cathedral on 2 January 1924, her body was cremated at Golders Green crematorium the next day. A tablet raised in the cathedral to her memory bears the guild emblem of crutch and sword. Nearly one hundred years later the state had taken over much of the guild's work, and its administration costs per member were becoming too large. It was decided to cease activity from January 1987 and use the guild's by then considerable assets to give grants to individual disabled people so that Miss Vachell's work would continue.

ELIZABETH BAIGENT

Sources F. M. Unwin, *Ada Vachell of Bristol* (1928) · CGPLA Eng. & Wales (1910) [William Vachell] · b. cert. · d. cert. · *Bristol Times and Mirror* (11 April 1913) · private information (2004) · CGPLA Eng. & Wales (1924) · Bristol RO, Records of the Bristol Guild of the Handicapped, 39842 · I. Vachell and A. C. Vachell, *A short account or history of the family of Vachell* (1900)
Archives Bristol RO, Bristol Guild of the Handicapped MSS
Wealth at death £13,974 7s. 9d.: probate, 7 Feb 1924, CGPLA Eng. & Wales

Vachell, Horace Annesley (1861–1955), novelist, was born at Sydenham, Kent, on 30 October 1861, the eldest of the three sons of Richard Tanfield Vachell (d. 1868) of Coptfold Hall, Essex, and his wife, Georgina (d. 1910), daughter of Arthur Lyttelton Annesley of Arley Castle, Staffordshire. He was a distant kinsman of the schoolmaster and clergyman Edward Lyttelton and the lawyer and politician Alfred Lyttelton. Part of his boyhood was spent at Hursley, near Winchester, whose cathedral made a profound mark upon his spirit. Vachell was educated at Harrow School and at the Royal Military College, Sandhurst, where in 1881 he won the half-mile race against Woolwich. Afterwards he served for a time as lieutenant in the rifle brigade; but he spent most of the 1880s in California. There, in 1889, he married Lydie Phillips (d. 1895), daughter of C. H. Phillips of San Luis Obispo, managing director of a land company, with whom Vachell went into partnership. Vachell and his wife had one son who became a captain in the Royal Flying Corps and died as a result of an aeroplane accident in 1915, and one daughter, Lydie, whose birth in 1895 was followed by the death of her mother.

Horace Annesley Vachell (1861–1955), by James Russell & Sons

and circumstances of English upper-middle-class life over a long period. He was a fellow of the Royal Society of Literature.

Vachell had at all times a distinguished appearance, particularly in his later years, when his noble head and silvery hair gave him both dignity and panache. He affected a high stiff collar, stock, and morning coat, and his voice, musical and precise, with its clipped Edwardian diction, enhanced the charm of his talk. He was a generous and vivid raconteur: his stage reminiscences were exceptionally lively, covering a period of vigorous development and change in the English theatre. He kept to the end of his life an alert mind and a delight in good food and good wine. His home, Widcombe Manor, near Bath, an old house of great beauty, he enriched with books and pictures and fine furniture. The terraced garden was his particular pride, and in it was set a superb fountain brought from Italy. In his last years he moved, much to his grief, into a smaller house at Sherborne. He died on 10 January 1955 at Widcombe Manor.

L. A. G. STRONG, *rev.* ANNETTE PEACH

Sources H. A. Vachell, *Distant fields* (1937) · personal knowledge (1971) · H. A. Vachell, *Methuselah's diary* (1949) · H. A. Vachell, *More from Methuselah* (1951) · reviews, *TLS* (1902–54) · H. A. Vachell, *Quinneys'*, 22nd impression (1969) · H. A. Vachell, *Vicar's walk* (1933) [repr 1972] · D. Newsome, *Godliness and good learning* (1961) · *CGPLA Eng. & Wales* (1955)

Archives A. P. Watt & Co., London · Hunt. L., letters · NRA, corresp. and literary papers · U. Cal., Berkeley · University of North Carolina, Chapel Hill | BL, corresp. with Society of Authors, Add. MSS 56838, 63339, 63455 · Richmond Local Studies Library, London, corresp. with Douglas Sladen

Likenesses photograph, 1937, repro. in Vachell, *Distant fields*, facing p. 46 · photograph, 1949, repro. in Vachell, *Methuselah's diary*, frontispiece · photograph, 1951, repro. in Vachell, *More from Methuselah*, frontispiece · H. Furniss, ink caricature, NPG · J. Russell & Sons, photograph, NPG [*see illus.*]

Wealth at death £25,583 4s. 11d.: probate, 1955, *CGPLA Eng. & Wales*

Before 1900 Vachell had returned to England and settled down to his long career as a writer. Independent means were an undoubted help, but, as he himself admitted, success came easily. By the time he ceased work he had written more than fifty novels and volumes of short stories; fourteen plays, several of them adapted from his novels; numerous collections of essays; and several autobiographical books, the last of them, *More from Methuselah* (1951), published when he was in his ninetieth year. Conspicuous among the novels are *John Charity* (1900), *Brothers* (1904), and his first great popular success, *The Hill* (1905), a school story with Harrow as its scene. Later works are *Her Son* (1907), *The Fourth Dimension* (1920), and *The Fifth Commandment* (1932). *Vicar's Walk* (1933; repr. 1972) is noted for its descriptions of Wells Cathedral.

Vachell's most famous play, *Quinneys'* (1915; 22nd impression, 1969), gave Henry Ainley a Yorkshire role which was probably his greatest success in a character part. *Quinneys'* was followed in 1916 by the oddly titled *Fishpingle*. Of the essays, *Little Tyrannies* (1940) gives a characteristic sample, and the last autobiography but one, *Methuselah's Diary* (1949), showed Vachell's rambling, intimate kindly commentary still in full flower. In any of his chosen media he was not an important writer; he may be placed somewhere between John Galsworthy and popular writers such as W. J. Locke and E. Temple Thurston. He wrote honestly and carefully, and his work illuminates, with shrewdness and good humour, the beliefs, customs,

Vacher, Charles (1818–1883), watercolour painter, was the third son of Thomas Vacher, a leading stationer and bookseller. He was born at his father's premises, 29 Parliament Street, Westminster, on 22 June 1818. (The building was demolished in 1898 to make way for road widening and the new government offices.) His brothers Thomas Brittain Vacher (1805–1880) and George Vacher continued their father's business, publishing *Vacher's Parliamentary Companion* from 1832; the business survives as Vacher Dod Publications. They also set up a charity, known as the Vacher Endowments, and donated the pulpits in St Margaret's, Westminster, the parliamentary church where they served as wardens, and where Charles Vacher was probably baptized. T. B. Vacher was a keen amateur artist, and there are examples of his sketches in the Victoria and Albert Museum.

Charles Vacher was a pupil at the Royal Academy Schools, and in 1839 he went to Italy, to study further in Rome, and remained there until 1843. In 1838 and 1839 his first exhibits at the Royal Academy had been views of a well and of a street at Bacharach on the Rhine, so he had presumably already visited Germany. Later he made many more continental and Near Eastern tours. Vacher specialized in Italian subjects but there were also a few views of Algeria and an increasing number of Egypt. In 1846 he was one of the many British and American artists with studios in Rome who were visited by the marine painter Edward William Cooke.

On his return to England, Vacher was elected an associate of the New Society of Painters in Water Colours, to which he had been introduced by his friend the lithographer and painter Louis Haghe; he became a full member in 1850. In that year he also exhibited a French subject at the Royal Hibernian Academy, and three years later he appeared, for the only time, at the Royal Scottish Academy with two north African pictures and one of Venice. He also exhibited at the Royal Manchester Institution from 1842. Otherwise he concentrated on the London market, showing 324 works at the New Society of Painters in Water Colours alone, from his election to 1881.

Charles Vacher's brother Thomas married in 1850, and on his return from Rome Charles moved from the family home to 31 Upper Charlotte Street, London. On 16 July 1857 he married Jane, daughter of James Mathewson Allan, and the couple settled at 4 The Boltons, West Brompton. Here Vacher died, of progressive cerebrospinal paralysis, on 21 July 1883; he was buried in Kensal Green cemetery. There were no children of the marriage, and his widow and nephews were the executors of his will, in which he left £45,847 3s. 7d., a very considerable sum for a painter. He was a rapid and detailed worker, and left more than 2000 sketches at his death; his finished watercolours are well composed and robustly coloured. His remaining works were sold at Christies on 21 February 1884. There are examples in the British Museum and in the Victoria and Albert Museum, London; the Grundy Art Gallery, Blackpool; the Glasgow Art Gallery; and Portsmouth City Museum.　　　　　　　　　　HUON MALLALIEU

Sources DNB · Mallalieu, *Watercolour artists* · L. Binyon, *Catalogue of drawings by British artists and artists of foreign origin working in Great Britain*, 4 vols. (1898–1907) · private information (2004) [Vacher Dod Publications] · Wood, *Vic. painters* · m. cert. · d. cert. · *CGPLA Eng. & Wales* (1883)

Likenesses T. Harwood, oils, c.1840, priv. coll.; formerly in possession of family, 1899 · W. D. Kennedy, oils, 1850, priv. coll.; formerly in possession of family, 1899 · C. Vacher, self-portrait, watercolour, priv. coll.; formerly in possession of family, 1899

Wealth at death £45,847 3s. 7d.: probate, 29 Aug 1883, *CGPLA Eng. & Wales*

Vadis, Aegidius de. See Duwes, Giles (d. 1535).

Vagliano, Panayis Athanase (1814–1902), merchant and shipowner, was born in the village of Keramies on the Greek island of Cephalonia, the fifth of the eight children of Anastase Vagliano (1775–1842) and his wife, Fronia. By the end of the nineteenth century he had become one of the leading Greek businessmen in the City of London.

After a brief spell as a seaman Vagliano entered commerce first as a trader at the Cephalonian port of Argostolion before joining his brothers Marino and Andreas in Russia some time around 1840 to set up Vaglianos Bros., a successful grain-exporting and shipping concern operating out of Taganrog. They also became involved in the export of grain from the Danube basin, and Panayis is believed to have run their operations in the port of Galatz in the 1850s. Vaglianos Bros. reputedly made very high profits during the Crimean War, shipping grain from the Sea of Azov to Constantinople.

The brothers developed an extensive branch network within Russia providing credits to Russian grain producers, whose produce they exported to western Europe. After the Crimean War, when British insurance underwriters were for a time reluctant to insure Greek ships, the company helped their compatriots by shipping their cargoes uninsured and exclusively on Greek ships. Vaglianos Bros. continued to combine merchanting with shipping, and between 1870 and 1905 they accounted for more than 10 per cent of the Greek-owned fleet.

In 1858 Panayis Vagliano moved to London, where he set up a grain-dealing and banking house, which he ran for forty-four years. Here he represented the interests of other Greek grain concerns as well as those of Vaglianos Bros. His contacts with the well-established Greek merchant community in the City of London expedited his membership of the Baltic exchange. In the 1860s Vagliano opened the first shipping office in London to deal exclusively with Greek-owned shipping. For forty years this functioned as the main link between Greek shipping interests and the London maritime market. Before 1910 Greek law prohibited the use of ships as collateral for loans, but Vagliano offered a way around this proscription. He granted loans to Greek shipowners at rates of interest of 7 to 8 per cent for the purchase of ships. In so doing he played a key role in the switch of Greek shipping from sail to steam, as well as making good profits for his enterprise. As Vagliano himself put it, it had been his desire to see 'all Greek seafarers turn into shipowners and the seas covered with a thick forest of Greek masts' (Lemos, 106). It earned for him the accolade of 'father of modern Greek shipping'.

Vagliano generally had the reputation of being a hardworking and shrewd businessman. Even so, in 1890 he sued the Bank of England for accepting cheques forged by a dishonest director of his company. But Vagliano himself was unable to distinguish between the allegedly forged and genuine signatures and he lost the case. His accounts with the Bank of England were closed as a result.

Although austere in his personal life, Vagliano was a generous benefactor and took his place among Greece's most important philanthropists. In 1888 he gave a large donation towards the building of the Greek National Library in Athens. He also donated £1600, one-twentieth of the total cost, towards the building of the St Sophia Greek Orthodox Church in London, and in 1881 he acted as presiding churchwarden during its consecration. He was married to Catherine (Kata) Vegdatopoulo, but the date of the marriage is unknown.

Immensely wealthy (his estate at death being nearly £3 million), Vagliano left £500,000 in his will to be used for educational and charitable purposes in his native Cephalonia. He arranged for the remains of his brother Marino, who had died in Taganrog in 1896, to be transferred to England to be buried in London's Norwood cemetery. Following his own death, on 25 January 1902 at 16 Dawson Place, Kensington, London, Panayis Vagliano was buried beside him. He left no heirs, his only child, Christophore, having died in infancy, and his business interests passed to his brothers' descendants.   STUART THOMPSTONE

Sources M. D. Sturdza, *Dictionnaire historique et généalogique des grandes familles de Grèce, d'Albanie et de Constantinople* (1983), 442–3 · A. G. Lemos, *Modern Greek seamen* (1971), 77–8 · G. Harlaftis, *A history of Greek-owned shipping: the making of an international tramp fleet, 1830 to the present day* (1996) · T. Catsiyannis, 'The Greek community in London', 1990 · S. R. Thompstone, 'The organisation and financing of Russian foreign trade before 1914', PhD diss., U. Lond., 1991 · d. cert. · *CGPLA Eng. & Wales* (1902)
Archives Bank of England, London, Freshfield MSS, F12 · Bank of England, London, secretary's files, G15/173
Likenesses photograph, repro. in Harlaftis, *History of Greek-owned shipping* · portrait (after statue), repro. in Catsiyannis, 'The Greek community in London' · statue, Athens?
Wealth at death £2,888,095 7s. 8d.: probate, 25 Feb 1902, *CGPLA Eng. & Wales*

Vaizey [*née* Bell; *other married name* Mansergh], **Jessie** (1856–1917), writer, was born on 3 October 1856 at 47 Myrtle Street South, Mount Pleasant, in Liverpool, the second of the seven children of David Bell (*b. c.*1814), shipping agent and insurance broker, and his wife, Elizabeth Morrish, *née* Barton (*b. c.*1821); both parents were Scottish. Jessie depicted their happy family life in her semi-autobiographical novel *Salt of Life* (1915). She and her elder sister were educated at home by a governess and then by a tutor, who encouraged her youthful writing. She had from childhood told stories to her siblings and in her middle teens won a newspaper short-story competition. She apparently continued to write for pleasure but published nothing until after her first husband's death.

On 19 July 1883, at the parish church of Llangollen, Denbighshire, Wales, Jessie married Henry Mansergh (1852–1894), a cotton broker, and continued living in the more affluent suburbs of Liverpool. A daughter was born in 1886, but the marriage was troubled, possibly by Henry Mansergh's addiction to alcohol or drugs. After his death of kidney disease on 28 May 1894, probably to supplement her income, 'Mrs Henry Mansergh' appears in print as the author of short stories and magazine serials, some of which were later published in volume form. Her first book, *A Girl in Springtime* (1897), had been serialized in the *Girls' Own Paper* as early as August 1894.

Another short-story competition (won with an entry sent in surreptitiously by her young daughter) brought the prize of a cruise to the eastern Mediterranean and Egypt, where Jessie met George de Horne Vaizey (1857–1927), an insurance broker of Essex stock but with a proud strain of Dutch ancestry. They married in Liverpool on 19 March 1898, the circumstances of their meeting giving rise to a family joke that 'granny won grandfather in a competition'.

As Mrs George de Horne Vaizey, Jessie continued to write prolifically. She and her husband settled first at Broxbourne, Hertfordshire, where their son George (who also became a novelist) was born in 1900. Two years later Jessie contracted typhoid, and was left with a crippling form of arthritis which confined her to a wheelchair and caused her more or less constant pain. Yet she managed to remain cheerful, witty, and well-dressed, and even to go on with her hobby of embroidering needlework pictures.

Jessie Vaizey wrote principally for and about women, but it was the handful of her books for girls which brought her lasting popularity. Her first success in this field was *About Peggy Savile* (1900), but her resounding triumph was *Pixie O'Shaughnessy* (1902). This heroine was not the first wild Irish girl in school-story fiction, but her naïvety, charm, and thoughtfulness made her particularly bewitching, and the book was to be reprinted as late as 1940. *Pixie*'s Irish background was derived from a brief holiday visit, just as Egypt had supplied the setting for *A Rose-Coloured Thread* (1898), Liverpool for several books, Hertfordshire for *A Houseful of Girls* (1901), and London flats for others.

In 1910 the Vaizeys moved to The Pryors, a large block of flats overlooking Hampstead Heath, where the outlook gave Jessie much pleasure. Jessie Vaizey died on 23 January 1917, following an operation for an appendix abscess, having been sustained in all the troubles of her life by her strong Presbyterian faith. She had been much distressed by the outbreak of the First World War, although she did not allow it to shadow her writing. Jessie Vaizey preferred to give her stories happy endings, but they were not always conventional ones and she was well aware of the sadder side of life. Her most interesting books lay bare two of the dilemmas then facing middle-class young women: the lack of meaningful occupation for the well-to-do (for instance in *Grizel Married*, 1915) and the scarcity of gainful employment for the poverty-stricken (as in *The Daughters of a Genius*, 1903, and particularly *The Independence of Claire*, 1915). This perception, and her careful delineations of middle-class society, memorably distinguish her work from the mass of merely romantic contemporary fiction.

HILARY CLARE

Sources A. G. H., 'Mrs. George de Horne Vaizey: some memories by an intimate friend', *Girls' Own Paper Annual*, 38 (1917), 379–80 · Mrs G. de H. Vaizey, *Salt of life* (1915) · G. Vaizey, *A lineage and a city: an Essex family cycle* (1970) [autobiographical novel by son] · private information (2004) · b. cert. · m. certs. · d. cert. · d. cert. [Henry Mansergh]
Likenesses photograph, repro. in A. G. H., 'Mrs. George de Horne Vaizey' · photograph, priv. coll.
Wealth at death £558 12s.: probate, 19 March 1917, *CGPLA Eng. & Wales*

Vaizey, John Ernest, Baron Vaizey (1929–1984), economist, was born on 1 October 1929 at 60 Woolwich Road, East Greenwich, the younger child and only son of Ernest Vaizey, wharfinger, and his wife, Lucy Butler Hart. He was educated at Colfe's Grammar School, Lewisham, until in December 1943 he was suddenly struck down by osteomyelitis. Lying on his stomach, encased in plaster, he suffered acute pain for the next two years. He encapsulated the experience in a minor masterpiece of autobiography,

Scenes from Institutional Life (1959, repr. 1986). It is a deeply moving account of insensitive nursing in an inadequately supplied wartime hospital, varied by touches of humour, for he could never be solemn or sad for long. Those painful years gave him, he says, 'a sense of urgency and effort'. It was as if he guessed that he would have a short life and must pack all he could into it.

He completed his school education at Queen Mary's Hospital school, Carshalton, Surrey, and won an open exhibition at Cambridge. '"Any more for Jesus?" the porters at the station cried evangelically', so he says, when he arrived. But he was bound for Queens' College, which he had pricked with a pin on a list in the local library at Lewisham. In 1949 he obtained a second class (division I) in part one of the economics tripos, and in 1951 he gained a first class in part two. After a year in Geneva as a research officer at the United Nations Economic Commission in Europe, he was elected in 1953 to a fellowship at St Catharine's College, Cambridge, together with a five-year university lectureship. In 1956 he moved to Oxford as a university lecturer in economics and economic history. He hated the place, and left in 1960 for a research post at the London University Institute of Education. He was there for two years, and in 1961 made a most happy marriage to Marina Stansky, a graduate of Harvard and Cambridge, and a distinguished art critic. She was the daughter of Lyman Stansky, a lawyer, of New York. They were to have two sons and a daughter.

Vaizey was offered, and surprisingly accepted, a fellowship at Worcester College, Oxford, in 1962, and became a convert to the Oxford he had once disliked so much. During his two periods in Oxford he produced his major contribution in his chosen field, the virtually unexplored subject of educational finance. *The Costs of Education* (1958) showed that official statistics had been mere surmise. The accepted belief that the slump of 1931 had caused disastrous cuts in educational expenditure was demonstrated as a myth: on the contrary, real per capita expenditure rose in the 1930s. He followed this up with numerous books and papers and conference addresses where he expressed a vigorous but unpopular minority view for over twenty years. Although the economics of education was to be his main theme—the subject of some eighteen works written either by himself or in conjunction with others—it was not his only interest. He wrote a history of Guinness's brewery (with Patrick Lynch, 1960) and one of the British steel industry (1974); *Capitalism* (1971); *Social Democracy* (1971); and *The Squandered Peace* (1983), a survey of world history from 1945 to 1975. He also produced two light-hearted novels, *Barometer Man* (1966) and *The Sleepless Lunch* (1968).

Vaizey was of Anglo-Irish descent and had the bubbling wit, the sense of humour, and the power of oratory that often go with that inheritance. He was fascinated by Ireland, also by Portugal where he did much work for the Gulbenkian Foundation. His other favourite country was Australia, but this affection led to an unhappy episode. In 1966 he had become professor of economics at Brunel University and in 1974 head of its school of social sciences, which was largely his creation. But in 1975 he suddenly accepted the vice-chancellorship of Monash University, Melbourne. He came, he saw, he withdrew, to the consternation of his friends, though they knew that he was volatile and impulsive.

In 1976 he was made a life peer in the resignation honours list of Harold Wilson. Yet, although he had been in one sense of the word a 'socialist' from early youth, he was becoming increasingly disillusioned with the Labour Party, and in 1978 he resigned. He was one of a group of former Labour intellectuals whose faith had been shaken by the manoeuvres of the Callaghan administration, among them his friend Hugh Thomas. He proclaimed his reasons on television in the run-up to the 1979 general election and henceforth took the Conservative whip. He knew and admired Margaret Thatcher, and he was among those whom she consulted. Towards the end of his life he took much interest in the economics of the health service. His *National Health* (1984) is remarkably prophetic. In 1982 he was appointed principal of the King George VI and Queen Elizabeth Foundation of St Catharine at Cumberland Lodge in the Great Park of Windsor. Within two years he had rescued its finances and revitalized its staff.

In talk irreverent, amusing, even outrageous ('Trots the lot' was his description of the Labour front bench in the House of Lords), Vaizey was a fundamentally serious person who packed an immense amount into a short life—over forty books; consultancies and visiting professorships galore; directorships (mostly unpaid); membership of innumerable councils and committees. He was very religious, describing himself as 'a deeply flawed Puritan', though in fact he was a devout high Anglican. He was a loyal, almost passionate, friend, but he could also be a formidable enemy, especially of those whom he regarded as pompous or priggish.

Vaizey received honorary doctorates from the universities of Brunel (1970) and Adelaide (1974), and was appointed to the order of El Sabio in Spain in 1969. His health was always precarious. He had serious heart surgery in 1980, from which he narrowly recovered, and again in 1984, from which he did not. He died in St Thomas's Hospital, London, on 19 July 1984. ROBERT BLAKE, *rev.*

Sources *The Times* (20 July 1984) · *The Times* (23 July 1984) · J. Vaizey, *Scenes from institutional life* (1959); [2nd edn] (1986) · personal knowledge (1990) · private information (1990) · *CGPLA Eng. & Wales* (1984)
Archives U. Leeds, Brotherton L., corresp. with Lord Bottomley | SOUND BL NSA, performance recordings
Wealth at death £108,181: probate, 8 Oct 1984, *CGPLA Eng. & Wales*

Vale, Samuel (1797–1848), actor, was born on 3 October 1797 in London, where his father was the proprietor of a toy shop. After finishing school he was placed in his father's shop, but was soon attracted to the theatre on seeing Edmund Kean perform at Drury Lane. In opposition to his father's wishes he began to study drama, and in 1813 he ran away from home and joined a small company under Harrison at Leatherhead.

Under the name Dornton (after the hero of Holcroft's

Samuel Vale
(1797–1848), by
John Rogers, pubd
1827 (after Thomas
Charles Wageman)
[as the Idle
Apprentice]

The Road to Ruin), he made his stage début at the age of seventeen, playing Realize in *The Will*; the attempt was a failure, and again he ran away to try his luck by turns in Worthing, Arundel, and Portsmouth. After reaching Gosport he was first taken on by Nicholson to play—not very successfully—a long part in *The Fishermen of Baghdad*, and was then offered an engagement in 1815 by Thornton at Arundel. Now he dropped the name Dornton, and as Mr Brown played the first successful role of his career, Montalban in John Tobin's *The Honeymoon*, to the Juliana of Elizabeth Edwin. After this he steadily rose in popularity until his own father came to see him act (Count Virolet in Colman's *The Mountaineers* and Charles in *The Village Lawyer*) and was forced to acknowledge his son's talents in his chosen career. A reconciliation followed, and Vale took an engagement under Henry at Minehead, Somerset, playing, *inter alia*, Young Norval, Selim in *Blue Beard*, and Young Malcolm. He then moved to Fisher's Exeter circuit, now using the name Vincent, and remained with the company for eighteen months. At Torquay he became very popular playing in *John Bull, or, An Englishman's Fireside*, and *The Review, or, Jack of All Trades*. In January 1819 he used his own name for the first time when he opened in Norwich as Careless in *The School for Scandal*. He remained on the Norwich circuit for two years, and then joined Crisp's Cheltenham circuit, touring Cheltenham, Worcester, and Ludlow.

In October 1820 Vale made his London début, as Buckingham in *Rochester*, at the Olympic under Barlow and Reeve; Vale's father had apparently exerted his influence to get the engagement for his son. At the end of the season, however, he retired to the provinces once more, and played Hawthorn to the Rosetta of Maria Tree at Cheltenham. Perhaps his most successful role in this period was Nicholas Twill in *Too Late for Dinner*, also at Cheltenham. He was back at the Olympic as Logic in *Tom and Jerry* in October 1821, then migrated to Sadler's Wells under Egerton. He also performed at the Surrey, and is said to

have sung 'The Good Old Days of Adam and Eve' at least 500 times.

Vale achieved prominence on the London stage between 1831 and 1848, when he first took the part of Simon Spatterdash in Samuel Beazley's musical farce *The Boarding House, or, Five Hours at Brighton*, a role with which his name became closely identified. It prompted 'Sam Valerisms', idiosyncratic and illogical verbal comparisons—'"Why here we are all mustarded", as the roast beef said to the Welsh rabbit' and '"When a man is ashamed to show the front of his face let him turn around and show the back of it", as the turnstile said to the weather-cock'—for which Vale is remembered today, immortalized by Charles Dickens as Sam Weller in *The Pickwick Papers* (1836).

Vale went on to play many parts at the Royal Coburg Theatre and at the Surrey, his most popular role at the latter house being Dummie Dunnaker in Ben Webster's version of *Paul Clifford, or, The Highwayman of 1770* (1832). In 1835 he joined D. W. Osbaldiston's company at Covent Garden, where he remained until 1837, playing in popular burlettas. Vale continued to act for the rest of his life, but the latter part of his career was undistinguished by any significant achievement. He died on 3 March 1848.

NILANJANA BANERJI

Sources *Oxberry's Dramatic Biography*, new ser., 1/3 (1827), 37–50 · Hall, *Dramatic ports.* · *DNB* · *GM*, 2nd ser., 29 (1848) · *Birmingham Daily Gazette* (9 May 1882) · A. Nicoll, *A history of English drama, 1660–1900*, 6 vols. (1952–9) · *N&Q*, 6th ser., 5 (1882)
Likenesses J. Rogers, stipple engraving, pubd 1827 (after T. C. Wageman), NPG [*see illus.*] · five portraits, Harvard TC · portrait, repro. in *Oxberry's Dramatic Biography* · portrait, repro. in Cumberland, *Minor theatre* (1837)

Valence, Aymer de. *See* Lusignan, Aymer de (*c.*1228–1260).

Valence, Aymer de, eleventh earl of Pembroke (*d.* 1324), magnate, was the son of William de *Valence (*d.* 1296), the half-brother of *Henry III, and therefore closely related to both the kings of England who ruled during his lifetime; through his mother, William de Valence's wife, Joan de Munchensi (*d.* 1307), he was descended from the Marshal earls of Pembroke.

Birth and family The date and place of birth of Aymer de Valence are both unknown. The evidence of proofs of age suggests a date somewhere between 1270 and 1275, but his father's return to England in January 1273, after crusading with the Lord Edward, implies a date towards the end of this period. Since William de Valence spent a considerable part of 1273 and 1274 on royal business in the vicinity of Limoges, and in close proximity to his own French lands, there is at least a possibility that his wife accompanied him and that Aymer was born in France. Although Aymer took his family name either from Valence, a few kilometres south-east of Lusignan and on the outskirts of Couhé south of Poitiers, or from another Valence north of Angoulême and north-east of Montignac, there is no positive evidence to support either of them as his actual birthplace.

Aymer was his parents' third and only surviving son. His eldest brother, John, died in 1277 and was buried in Westminster Abbey, close to his sister Margaret (*d.* 1276). Until

William de Valence the younger was killed in Wales in June 1282 Aymer had been destined for an ecclesiastical career, like his uncle and namesake in the reign of Henry III: a petition to the pope in May 1282 requesting that Aymer be provided with a plurality of benefices described him as 'a youth of good ability, recommended by his study of letters and his manners and merits' (PRO, SC1/13/204; *CClR, 1279–1288*, 188).

French inheritance As the ultimate heir of both his parents, Aymer de Valence held lands in England, Wales, and Ireland, and would have occupied a leading place in English magnate society whatever the politics of the time. However he was also one of the last holders of an English earldom to be closely linked with France both by descent and by the tenure of land. He was the grandson of Hugues (X) de Lusignan, count of La Marche (d. 1249) and of *Isabella of Angoulême (c.1188–1246) and widow of King John of England, who belonged to two of the great families of Poitou in central France. On the death of his father in May 1296 Valence inherited Rancon (held from the bishop of Limoges); Bellac and Champagnac (held from the abbess of La Règle at Limoges), all to the north of Limoges and within the county of La Marche; and Montignac (held from the bishop of Angoulême) on the River Charente, a few kilometres to the north of Angoulême, of which county it formed part. When Guiard de Lusignan, the last count of La Marche and Angoulême, died in 1308, Valence's claims to succeed to these strategically placed territories were sufficiently strong for Philippe IV of France to buy them out in 1309 in return for 1000 livres tournois and Valence's liege homage. He visited France at least six times between 1296 and 1307, and on eleven occasions (mainly on official business) between 1307 and his death there in 1324. The magnificent Valence casket decorated with the arms of the families to whom Aymer was related, which was made for either William or Aymer and is now in the Victoria and Albert Museum, shows very vividly the extent of his continental connections.

Marriages and illegitimate son Valence's ties with France were strengthened by his two marriages. The first was to Beatrice, daughter of Raoul de Clermont, lord of Nesle in Picardy and constable of France, and took place before 18 October 1295. A single surviving letter from Beatrice, calling herself 'la soune lyge compayne e amye' to Valence in 1296 (PRO, SC1/18/183), suggests an affectionate relationship between the two, but otherwise little is known about her. Beatrice died in September 1320, and was buried in the church of the Benedictine priory at Stratford-le-Bow in Middlesex. On 5 July 1321 in Paris, Aymer married Mary de *St Pol (c.1304–1377), daughter of Gui de Châtillon, count of St Pol and butler of France. She brought to the marriage lands at Tours-en-Vimeu, Thièvre, Oreville, and Fréacans, in the area of the Pas-de-Calais, which she retained until 1372.

There is no record of any children by either of Valence's marriages, but he had an illegitimate son, Henry de Valence, with an unknown partner. This relationship may be one source of the tradition, for which there is no evidence, that Valence married an unnamed daughter of the count of Bar. The fact that he was briefly held prisoner in Bar in 1317 may also have something to do with the story. Henry de Valence was a knight who served in his father's retinue between 1315 and 1319; in 1317–18 he was a hostage for Aymer in Bar; he died in 1322, leaving a widow named Margery.

Service to Edward I Aymer de Valence's first recorded action was to accompany his father on a diplomatic mission to Cambrai early in 1296; at Westminster on 14 July 1297 he took the oath of fealty to Prince Edward as Edward I's successor; in the same year he was knighted and in 1297–8 accompanied Edward I to Flanders. He was involved in diplomatic negotiations with France in 1297, in 1299 (the treaty for Edward I's remarriage), 1301, 1302, and 1303, and in 1304 was to have joined Prince Edward on his proposed visit to France to do homage for Aquitaine. He fought in Scotland, at Falkirk, in 1298, and again in 1299, 1300 (the siege of Caerlaverock), 1301, and 1302. In 1303 he commanded the English forces south of the Forth, and in April 1306 was appointed captain of the north after the killing of his brother-in-law John Comyn by Robert Bruce, whom he defeated at Methven in June. Although in May 1307 he was himself defeated by Bruce at Loudoun Hill, in August he was appointed by the new king, Edward II, as keeper of Scotland.

The dispute over Gaveston On 26 October 1307, following his mother's death, Aymer de Valence succeeded to the title and to the lands of the earldom of Pembroke in England, Wales, and Ireland (the lordship of Wexford). In November 1307 he went to France to complete arrangements for Edward II's marriage to Isabella, daughter of Philippe IV of France, and in mid-January 1308 he conducted Edward from Dover to Boulogne, where the king was married on 25 January. Although the new earl of Pembroke had witnessed the charter creating Gaveston earl of Cornwall on 6 August 1307, it is likely that by 1308 he was becoming concerned about the arrogance of Gaveston's behaviour. However Pembroke's involvement in the 'Boulogne declaration' of 31 January 1308 was primarily caused by the need to end the financial and administrative abuses of royal government which had continued from the reign of Edward I. There is no indication of any personal hostility between Pembroke and the king. Pembroke helped to persuade Edward II to accept magnate demands for Gaveston's exile in May 1308, but in March 1309 went to Avignon on Edward's behalf in a successful attempt to persuade the pope to sanction Gaveston's return to England. Pembroke's political attitude soon changed, however, partly because of the king's failure to implement the reforms agreed at Stamford in August 1309, but also because of the behaviour of Gaveston, who bestowed one of his notorious nicknames on Pembroke, whom he allegedly described as Joseph the Jew 'because he was pale and tall' (*Historia Anglicana*, 1, 115).

In March 1310 Pembroke was elected as one of the *lords ordainer who were reluctantly authorized by the king to draw up a programme of reform. Despite several appeals from Edward II, Pembroke maintained his distance from the court, and in September 1310 refused to join Edward and Gaveston in a new campaign in Scotland, although he did send a token force to observe the letter of his military obligations. Pembroke played an active part in the drafting of the ordinances, whose publication he witnessed on 27 September 1311. In March 1312 Pembroke was appointed by an assembly of prelates and magnates to pursue and capture Gaveston, who had returned to England from his latest exile in late 1311 or early 1312. On 17 May Pembroke and the earl of Surrey besieged Gaveston in Scarborough Castle; and on 19 May Gaveston surrendered to Pembroke, who guaranteed his safety until 1 August. After a meeting with the king at York, Gaveston was placed in Pembroke's personal custody and taken south. On 9 June Pembroke and Gaveston reached Deddington in Oxfordshire, where Pembroke left him and a few retainers at the rector's house while he visited his wife at his manor of Bampton about 20 miles away. On the morning of 10 June the earl of Warwick seized Gaveston, took him to Warwick and, with the approval of the earl of Lancaster and other magnates, executed him nearby on 19 June.

This act removed any ambiguity in Pembroke's relations with the king. Pembroke probably continued to support the principles of reform as contained in the ordinances, but his support of his fellow ordainers was ended by this blow to his honour. Until the actions of the Despensers after 1318 again placed a strain upon his loyalty, Pembroke remained clearly on the king's side.

Service to Edward II, 1312–1316 In August 1312 Pembroke visited Paris to enlist Philippe IV's aid in negotiating with the ordainers; on 20–21 September, at great risk to his personal safety, he attempted to ensure the loyalty of the city of London to the king; and he took an active part in the negotiations which led to a peace treaty between Edward II and his opponents on 20 December 1312. In February and March 1313 he went to Paris to arrange for a personal meeting between Edward II and Philippe IV to resolve Anglo-French disputes in Aquitaine, and accompanied Edward and Isabella to Paris in June and July. He again accompanied Edward to France for a meeting with Philippe IV at Montreuil in December 1313.

In April 1314 Pembroke was appointed as the king's lieutenant in Scotland, in advance of the campaign to relieve Stirling which culminated in the disastrous English defeat at Bannockburn on 24 June. Pembroke was close to the king, and intervened to lead him away from the battle to safety at Dunbar and thence to Berwick.

On 2 January 1315 Pembroke attended Gaveston's reburial at Langley; in May and June he visited Paris on behalf of Edward II to obtain confirmation from the new French king, Louis X, of previous Anglo-French agreements; between July and October 1315 he organized the defence of the northern borders from Scottish attack. In February 1316 he deputized for the king at the opening of the Lincoln parliament, at which the earl of Lancaster was nominated as the king's chief councillor, and was a member of the committee appointed to consider reform of the realm and the royal household. In July he helped to end the resistance of Bristol to royal authority.

Capture and ransom In December 1316 Pembroke was appointed to lead an embassy to the newly elected pope, John XXII, to obtain support against the Scots, achieve financial concessions, and possibly to free Edward from his oath to uphold the ordinances. In early May 1317, as Pembroke was returning from Avignon, he was taken prisoner at Étampes and taken to an unknown destination in the county of Bar on the borders between France and the empire where he was forced to agree to a ransom of £10,400. His captor, Jean de Lamouilly, who came from Bar, had served in various Scottish garrisons between 1299 and 1312. Lamouilly's wages were apparently in arrears but it is also likely that Count Édouard of Bar used Pembroke's capture to punish Edward II for the treatment in England of his sister Joan, the estranged wife of the earl of Surrey. Pembroke was freed from captivity before the end of June 1317. The burden of paying his ransom and of redeeming the hostages he left behind in Bar left him with severe financial problems for the rest of his life.

Political manoeuvrings, 1317–1320 The Avignon embassy has also traditionally, but incorrectly, been seen as the occasion on which Pembroke began the formation of a so-called 'middle party', designed to win control over the royal government at the expense of Thomas, earl of Lancaster. Even had he wished to do so, Pembroke's financial problems would have deprived him of the necessary freedom of action. In fact his main motivation in the critical period of English politics between 1316 and 1318 was to do whatever he could to avoid the outbreak of civil war between the king's supporters and those of the earl of Lancaster. On 1 November 1317 Pembroke contracted to serve the king for life in peace and war, while on 24 November he and Bartholomew Badlesmere made a contract with one of the current royal favourites, Roger Damory, with the intention of ensuring the latter's future good behaviour.

The possible dangers had been shown all too clearly on 1 October 1317, when Pembroke had barely succeeded in persuading the king not to attack Lancaster in his castle of Pontefract. Pembroke also played an important role, along with other magnates, the leading English clergy, and two papal envoys, in the tortuous negotiations which concluded in the treaty agreed between Edward II and Lancaster at Leake on 9 August 1318. Pembroke was a prominent member of the standing royal council of prelates and magnates which was established at the York parliament in October 1318. In March 1319 he sat at the chapter house of St Paul's Cathedral to hear the complaints of the citizens of London. In August 1319 Pembroke made his will (which is not extant) before taking part in September in the unsuccessful siege of Berwick; and in December he helped to negotiate a two-year truce with the Scots.

The civil war and its aftermath, 1320–1324 In February 1320 Pembroke was appointed to be keeper of the realm during the king's proposed visit to France to do homage for Aquitaine, and was reappointed during June and July when the king made his delayed visit. However, real power was increasingly being exercised by the younger Hugh Despenser and his father. The death of Pembroke's wife in September, and his lack of a legitimate male heir, gave him a good excuse to go to France to arrange for a second marriage. Pembroke left England in late November 1320 and returned in late March 1321, shortly before the attack on the Despensers by Hereford and Mortimer. Pembroke again left England in late May to marry Mary de St Pol in Paris and returned to England in late July. He then played a crucial role in persuading Edward II to agree to the exile of the Despensers, after warning the king that even his loyalty might be in question if the king refused.

However, Pembroke was not trusted by the opponents of the Despensers, and this fact, as well as his own natural inclination, brought him back openly to the king's side in the civil war that followed. Pembroke was present at the siege of Leeds Castle in October, and in December consented to the return of the Despensers from exile. He was active in the campaign against the contrariants, and was one of the earls who judged the earl of Lancaster guilty of treason on 21 March 1322. Pembroke's reputation was however compromised by the events of 1321–2. The king's enemies considered that he had betrayed them, while in May 1322 the king, under the influence of the Despensers, forced Pembroke to make a pledge of loyalty 'for certain reasons he was given to understand' (*CCIR, 1318–1323*, 563–4).

Pembroke took part in the unsuccessful Scottish campaign in the late summer of 1322, and on 14 October was in the English army defeated by the Scots on Blackhowmoor, near Old Byland in Yorkshire. He negotiated the thirteen-year truce that was agreed with the Scots in May 1323. In June 1324 he was sent to France to settle the St Sardos dispute. He never reached Paris, dying suddenly on 23 June, probably near St Riquier in Picardy. Pembroke's body was returned to London on 31 July, and he was buried in Westminster Abbey near the high altar on 1 August. Although his death was almost certainly natural, writers hostile to him claimed that he was poisoned, and that his lack of a male heir was a divine punishment for his part in Lancaster's death, while his widow and coheirs suffered harassment in revenge for Pembroke's support of the Despensers' opponents in 1321. Long before his death Pembroke had been overtaken by events beyond his control.

Mary de St Pol outlived Pembroke by over fifty years, devoting herself to a life of piety; she died in England in March 1377 at the Franciscan priory of Denny near Cambridge, which she herself had founded in 1339, and where she was buried. In memory of her husband she commissioned the fine stone tomb in Westminster Abbey, and a chantry—now part of the chapel of St John the Baptist; she installed a memorial window in the new church of the Greyfriars in London; and in 1347 founded Pembroke College in Cambridge. In 1363 one of the scholars of the college, Jakob Nielsen from Denmark (James Nicholas of Dacia), wrote an ingenious if rather tortuous poem in Aymer's honour.

Assessment: a conflict of loyalties While he possessed considerable talents as an administrator, diplomat, and military commander, in politics Pembroke was not a natural leader but was by birth and experience an upholder of tradition, whose usual inclination was to serve his royal cousins and the crown they represented to the best of his ability. Although he played a prominent and constructive part in the many crises of the reign of Edward II, his loyalty and integrity were severely tested by the influence exercised over Edward and his government by Piers Gaveston and by Hugh Despenser the younger. Had he lived beyond 1324 he would certainly have been forced to make a choice between serving Edward, transferring his allegiance to Isabella and Mortimer, or even in the last resort withdrawing to his French lands. Since England and France were then on the verge of open war, his death may also have saved him from another difficult choice between allegiances.

Pembroke's leading retainers included his nephew John Hastings, lord of Abergavenny and father of Laurence Hastings, Pembroke's eventual successor as earl in 1339. Another nephew, John Comyn, was the son of John Comyn of Badenoch who was killed by Robert Bruce in 1306, and was himself killed fighting Robert at Bannockburn in 1314. In 1297 Thomas Berkeley, senior, and his son Maurice made an indenture for military service with Pembroke. They, and other members of the Berkeley family, and other associates of the Berkeleys, remained as regular retainers of Pembroke until they quarrelled with him in 1317 and moved to the service of Roger Mortimer of Wigmore. One of the many ironies of Pembroke's career is that Thomas Berkeley, junior, Thomas Gurney, and John Maltravers, the custodians of the deposed Edward II at Berkeley Castle in 1327, were all former members of Pembroke's retinue. Another prominent Pembroke retainer was John Darcy, who made an indenture for life service in 1309 and served him until 1323, when he was appointed justiciar of Ireland. Darcy was later to serve as steward of the royal household from 1337 and was present at the battle of Crécy in 1346. Pembroke evidently inspired loyalty and affection among some at least of his retainers, since in 1323 Darcy regretted having to leave his good master and lord—'son bon maistre e seigneur' (PRO, SC8/239/11949).

J. R. S. PHILLIPS

Sources J. R. S. Phillips, *Aymer de Valence, earl of Pembroke, 1307–1324: baronial politics in the reign of Edward II* (1972) · J. R. S. Phillips, 'The "middle party" and the negotiating of the treaty of Leake, 1318: a reinterpretation', *BIHR*, 46 (1973), 11–27 · T. F. Tout, *The place of the reign of Edward II in English history: based upon the Ford lectures delivered in the University of Oxford in 1913* (1914); 2nd edn, rev. H. Johnstone (1936) · J. C. Davies, *The baronial opposition to Edward II* (1918); repr. (1967) · J. R. Maddicott, *Thomas of Lancaster, 1307–1322: a study in the reign of Edward II* (1970) · M. Vale, *The Angevin legacy and the Hundred Years War, 1250–1340* (1990) · C. Bémont, *Simon de Montfort, earl of Leicester, 1208–1265*, trans. E. F. Jacob, new edn (1930) · J. P. Trabut-Cussac, *L'Administration anglaise en Gascogne sous Henry III et Édouard I de 1254 à 1307* (Geneva, 1972) · F. R. Lewis, 'William de Valence', *Aberystwyth Studies*, 13 (1934), 11–35 · F. R. Lewis, 'William de Valence', *Aberystwyth Studies*, 14 (1936), 69–92 · H. Jenkinson, 'Mary de Sancto Paulo, foundress of Pembroke College, Cambridge',

Archaeologia, 66 (1915), 401–46 · L. E. Tanner, 'The countess of Pembroke and Westminster Abbey', *Gazette* [Pembroke College Cambridge Society], 33 (1959), 9–13 · J. Alexander and P. Binski, eds., *Age of chivalry: art in Plantagenet England, 1200–1400* (1987) [exhibition catalogue, RA] · P. Binski, *Westminster Abbey and the Plantagenets: kingship and the representation of power, 1200–1400* (1995) · PRO, Special Collections [esp. SC1 (ancient correspondence); SC8 (ancient petitions)] · *Chancery records* · *Thomae Walsingham, quondam monachi S. Albani, historia Anglicana*, ed. H. T. Riley, 2 vols., pt 1 of *Chronica monasterii S. Albani*, Rolls Series, 28 (1863–4), vol. 1

Likenesses tomb with stone effigy, 1326?–1329, Westminster Abbey; repro. in Binski, *Westminster Abbey and the Plantagenets*, 114 · seal, PRO, E 329/87

Wealth at death £3000 p.a.—value of English, Welsh, and Irish lands: Phillips, *Aymer de Valence*, 233, 243–5

William de Valence, earl of Pembroke (*d.* 1296), tomb effigy

Valence [Lusignan], William de, earl of Pembroke

Valence [Lusignan], **William de**, earl of Pembroke (*d.* 1296), magnate, was the fourth or fifth son of *Isabella of Angoulême, widow of King John, and her second husband, whom she married in 1220, Hugues (X) de Lusignan, count of La Marche. He was born probably at Valence, a hamlet of Couhé (Vienne), some 20 miles south of Poitiers: the date is unknown, but F. R. Lewis has argued for the period 1227–31, when Isabella was, astonishingly, aged over forty. His childhood, otherwise obscure, witnessed the near ruination of the powerful Lusignans in 1241–2 in a rebellion against the Capetians supported by Henry III. After its failure his parents went into retirement, and partitioned their lands between their sons in 1242, assigning Valence the castellanies of Montignac, Bellac, Rancon, and Champagnac; but he had still not reached his majority in June 1246.

Early career and acquisitions in England In the summer of 1247 the Lusignans accepted Henry III's invitation to visit England. Valence and his brother Aymer de *Lusignan (*d.* 1260) and sister Alice and a few adherents settled at court, whereas two elder brothers, Guy and Geoffroi, and others, returned home with pensions. Henry hoped thereby to cultivate clients among the Poitevin nobility, to advance his interests against the Capetians, and to protect Gascony. There is some truth, however, in the chroniclers' assertion that Valence really owed his advancement to Henry's affection and plans to create a strengthened royal family in England. Henry arranged his marriage on 13 August 1247 to Joan (*d.* 1307), daughter of Warin de *Munchensi (*d.* 1255), who, thanks to her brother's recent death, was a coheir to £703 p.a. of the Marshal estate; thus Valence became in the right of his wife lord of Wexford, and lord of Pembroke and Goodrich castles. Probably as part of the marriage contract, Henry granted him in 1247 Hertford Castle at pleasure (for life from 1249) and a double money fee: 500 marks p.a. for life, with an additional £500 p.a., the latter eventually to be replaced by lands held in fee. There were a handful of other lucrative perquisites which enabled him to purchase the west-country Pont de l'Arche estate in 1252 and the Northumbrian Bertram lands in the 1260s. Consequently, on 22 August 1248, during his first return to Poitou, Valence ceded Montignac to his brother Geoffroi.

Although Valence was almost constantly at court for the next ten years in England, Matthew Paris's account of his influence, much coloured by later events, is not entirely supported by the records. At first he was often unruly, probably because the king was too slow to replace his money fee with lands. Henry ceremoniously knighted him at Westminster on 13 October 1247. Until 1249 he was active in tournaments, for which the king temporarily confiscated his estates in October 1249. These tournaments won him the earliest English knights for his retinue, together with powerful friends, such as his brother-in-law John de Warenne, earl of Surrey (*d.* 1304), and Richard de Clare, earl of Gloucester (*d.* 1262). Valence took the cross with Henry III on 6 March 1250 at the Great Hall at Westminster, but in November 1251 the king closed all ports to prevent his going on crusade independently to rescue Louis IX. Although this may have been one of his attempts to extract more grants from Henry, Valence did make some preparations for crusade, leasing assets and securing papal promises of 2200 marks (part of which was paid by the mid-1250s). By early 1252 Henry had replaced Valence's money-fee of 500 marks p.a. with large wardships, such as that of Fitzjohn of Warkworth, Northumberland (held until 1268), and had begun to find him additional manors.

The Lusignans and their rivals, 1252–1258 In 1252 the importance of the Lusignans was greatly increased for a while by the outbreak of rebellion in Gascony, which they were instrumental in crushing. In January Valence joined the royal council, arbitrating in Henry's dispute with

Simon de Montfort (d. 1265) over the lieutenancy of Gascony. The Lusignans now began to quarrel arrogantly with magnates, confident that the king would not punish them. In October 1252 Valence raided the lands of the bishop of Ely at Hatfield, and at the end of the year he joined his brother Aymer, bishop-elect of Winchester, in the notorious raid on the palaces of Boniface of Savoy, the archbishop of Canterbury. From this point onwards, if Matthew Paris and others are to be believed, the court was divided by struggles between the Lusignans and the queen's family, the Savoyards. Valence retained the friendship of the earl of Gloucester whose heir, Gilbert de Clare (d. 1295), married his niece Alice, in January 1253, and shortly after that they went on an unsuccessful tournamenting expedition to France. By October 1253 Valence joined Henry III in Gascony where the Lusignans raised a large force of over 100 Poitevin knights for the campaign. Valence helped to settle the border areas of Bergerac and Gensac and to arbitrate in the dispute between Simon de Montfort and Gaston de Béarn over Bigorre. Characteristically, he tried further to pressurize Henry for lands, but obtained only the promise of a large wardship. During the winter of 1254 he accompanied Henry back to England via Paris and in 1255 was rewarded with the wardship for a year of his rich kinsman, William de *Munchensi (d. 1287).

From 1255 to 1257 Valence remained high in the king's affections, but the records do not show him active in formulating policy; he was excluded by older rivals, especially Savoyards. In September 1255 he went north with the king and took a small part in negotiations concerning the minority of Alexander III, king of Scots. In the following month, at Windsor, he merely witnessed the king's acceptance of the 'Sicilian business'; this is often mistaken as evidence that he proposed it. Even in January 1256 Henry ordered Valence to be consulted over Gascony only 'if expedient'. Only over the acceptance of the crown of Germany, by Richard, earl of Cornwall, at Christmas 1256 is it possible that Valence much influenced events.

The war with Llywelyn ap Gruffudd of Wales which broke out in 1256, however, suddenly made Valence indispensable in his own right as a marcher lord. Many of his estates were threatened. From the spring of 1257 his men of Pembroke under Roger of Leyburn were fighting against the Welsh at Carmarthen but he remained at court, witnessing on 10 April an ordinance on household economies and, no doubt, taking the councillors' oath of about that date reported in the Burton annals. In August he joined the king's ineffectual campaign at Deganwy where, according to John of Wallingford, he quarrelled with Humphrey (IV) de Bohun, earl of Hereford. When in April 1258 the truce with Llywelyn ended and the Welsh of Cemais raided Pembroke itself, Valence demanded revenge in parliament and accused Simon de Montfort and the earl of Gloucester of treachery. This helped precipitate the 'sworn conspiracy' of these two earls and five other magnates—all courtiers—on 12 April, which brought about the baronial reform movement and the Lusignans' eventual downfall.

Valence's rivals at court were afraid of the Lusignans' growing hold over the king and his heir. After Richard of Cornwall's departure for Germany in April 1257 Henry III increasingly turned to them for advice and financial assistance. Valence lent Henry 1100 marks in November 1257 and shortly afterwards, according to Matthew Paris, mortgaged Stamford and Grantham from the Lord Edward. An alliance then arose between Valence and Edward, whose lands were also threatened by the Welsh. Such developments, if unchecked, promised to give the Lusignans an indefinite monopoly on power. Their many enemies were enraged. Old quarrels again came to the surface. Litigants high and low had been denied justice against them, especially thanks to the king's order of about November 1256 (noted by Matthew Paris) forbidding any writ to be filed in chancery against them or other favourites. Their feud with the queen's family has been noted. Valence himself had sparred over rights in Pembrokeshire and Ireland with the earl of Hereford and his son. In 1257 his officials clashed with Simon de Montfort, provoking another confrontation in parliament in May. These disputes were complicated by their being rivals for land-grants from the king, where Henry favoured Valence. Valence also gained at the expense of other claimants on royal patronage, such as stewards of the household. His friendship with Edward even drove him apart from the earl of Gloucester, Edward's rival on the march. Thus, by 1258, although rising royal favourites, Valence and his brothers were politically isolated at court. Peter of Savoy and Montfort now advocated peace negotiations with Louis IX, undercutting the Lusignans' position. Thanks to the harshness of their estate officials, particularly Valence's notorious steward, William de Bussay, the Lusignans were accorded little sympathy in provincial society either. Indeed, they may even have been thought responsible for advising Henry's harsh rule of the localities, in order to raise money for the recent Welsh war. The Lusignans had become a major part of the general grievances accumulating against Henry III's personal rule.

Opposition to reform, and exile The reform movement begun in April 1258, designed to win the king the support of the 'community of the realm', was deftly exploited by Valence's enemies. Although he and his brothers swore to support it, and were even nominated by the king onto the committee of twenty-four to draw up reforms, they soon fell foul of the new regime. Valence continued to frustrate Montfort's patronage claims and when, at the great Oxford parliament of June 1258, it was mooted to resume all alienations made from the crown, he refused his consent, only, according to Paris, to meet Montfort's riposte 'either you give up your castles or you lose your head' (Paris, *Chron.*, 5.697–8). The Lusignans and their supporters, the Lord Edward and John de Warenne, fled at the end of the month to Bishop Aymer's castle at Winchester; however, they were easily forced to capitulate on 5 July and, after Valence refused the option to remain in custody until reforms were complete, they chose exile, sailing on 14 July. Valence accepted a pension of 3000 marks and the council placed his lands under some of his men, the revenues deposited at the New Temple, a remarkable arrangement that permitted his return; but the council later confiscated 1500 marks from his account.

Valence and his brothers reached Boulogne, where they eluded an ambush from Henry de Montfort bent on avenging his father. Despite the opposition of Louis IX's wife, the sister of the queen of England, the Lusignans were allowed passage to Poitou; Louis may have believed their expulsion indicated that the peace treaty under negotiation between himself and Henry III would now go ahead. Valence's wife, displeased by the council's financial arrangements for her, was allowed to join him in exile in December. Meanwhile, efforts were made to prevent his smuggling money out of the country and, indeed, his steward, William de Bussay, was apprehended in November 1258 when he attempted to return. In the following months Bussay and a handful of Valence's bailiffs were tried and imprisoned for their oppressions.

Valence at first attempted to consolidate his interests in Poitou, but soon became involved in plots for his return. On 2 March 1259 he purchased property in Limoges, and then reacquired Montignac from his brother, for he styled himself 'Lord of Pembroke and Montignac', in a remission of rights granted to Charroux Abbey on 7 and 14 October (Monsabert, 246–8). By December he was at Paris where he met secretly with Simon de Montfort who had quarrelled with the baronial regime. Here, allegedly at the king's instigation, they settled their private differences and prepared for Valence's return with the support of Montfort's new ally, the Lord Edward. Their plans were foiled by the failure of Edward's rising in the spring of 1260, but this alliance held firm. From August to October 1260 Valence was ordered by Edward to defend Lourdes and Tarbes in Bigorre for Montfort against Esquivat de Chabanais; and in the truce with Chabanais at Tarbes on 2 October he represented Montfort. On 27 November he met Edward at Paris, probably again to discuss returning, but Aymer de Lusignan's death on 4 December at Paris forced another postponement.

Return to the king's side, 1261–1265 Valence returned thanks to Henry III's overthrow of the provisions of Oxford in 1261. The king could, even in February, appoint Valence's retainer Geoffrey de Gascelin constable of Hertford. However, Valence's loyalties were at first unclear, because on 27 March the king attempted to prevent him landing with the Lord Edward, then still in opposition. When he did return with Edward at about Easter (24 April) it was possibly 'by assent of the barons [who opposed Henry's recovery of power]' (*Liber de antiquis legibus*, 49), and because he swore at Dover his oath to the provisions of Oxford and to answer those who had complaint against him (*Flores historiarum*, 2.466). Valence may have flirted with opposition to secure himself the best terms from his Savoyard rivals at court. But the king, none the less, easily detached him from Edward and Montfort, receiving him at Rochester on 30 April to peace with restoration of all lands.

For the remainder of 1261 Valence concentrated on repairing his estates. In 1262 he was more frequently at court, but, thanks to the Savoyards, his influence was much reduced. He was unable to secure his henchmen pardons or, until 10 July, to get the king to compensate him for his exile; he was still awaiting full payment in March 1263. In July 1262 he accompanied Henry III to France and with Henry of Almain, the king's nephew, attempted unsuccessfully to reconcile the king to the new earl of Gloucester, Gilbert de Clare. Valence left the king in August, perhaps in anger, for although Henry III ordered him to return to him in France on 14 October, he was still in London on 11 November. Henry III only detached him from Clare by a grant of part of the latter's lands on 10 December, increased in July 1263 to £500, with promise of a further £500 in September. Thus, Valence did not support Clare and Almain's uprising with Simon de Montfort in 1263 and, indeed, Clare long resented this betrayal.

For the remainder of the barons' wars Valence remained loyal to the king. In February 1263 he represented Henry at Paris to secure concessions made by Louis IX; he probably proceeded to Poitou to receive on Henry's behalf the homage of the vicomte de Turenne and others. In October he accompanied Henry for the Boulogne conference before the French king, at about the same time receiving the Cressy wardship. During the fighting against Montfortians in 1264 he was frequently in the Lord Edward's force, for example at the battle of Northampton on 5 April, in revenge for which the Londoners attacked his property and stole his money deposited at the Temple. At the battle of Lewes on 14 May he fought on the right wing in Edward's squadron with John de Warenne, but made his escape with Warenne and Geoffroi de Lusignan to Pevensey Castle and the continent. His lands were forfeit, Pembroke going to the rebel earl of Gloucester and Goodrich to Humphrey (V) de Bohun (known as the younger). Valence returned a year later, landing in Pembroke in May 1265 with John de Warenne, a number of Lusignans, and a substantial force; this fanned a general marcher revolt against Simon de Montfort. Edward escaped from captivity and with Valence surprised Simon de Montfort the younger at Kenilworth and defeated Montfort himself at Evesham on 4 August 1265. Valence joined the siege of the remaining Montfortians at Kenilworth and in May 1266, with John de Warenne, punished rebels at Bury St Edmunds. He was well rewarded with the lands of Montfortians, for example Humphrey de Bohun junior, Roger Bertram, and William de Munchensi. He played no part in drawing up the dictum of Kenilworth and, indeed, seems to have opposed it, his harshness driving Munchensi into further rebellion. Valence clashed repeatedly with the renegade earl of Gloucester when they seized rebels' lands. In 1269 Valence, John de Warenne, and Henry of Almain conspired against the rebel Robert de Ferrers, earl of Derby, and secured his lands for Edmund, earl of Lancaster. In 1267–8 Henry III finally replaced Valence's money-fee of £500 p.a. with lands, mainly in East Anglia.

Crusade and service under Edward I From 1264 Valence revived his friendship with the Lord Edward. On 24 June 1268 at the parliament at Northampton he took the cross with Edward, John de Warenne, and Henry of Almain, promising under one of the earliest known military contracts to recruit nineteen knights for 2000 marks. In July 1268 he again visited Pembroke and was in Ireland, probably for the first time, in the spring of 1270, taking custody of Maurice Fitzgerald's heir whose wardship he and his daughter, Agnes, purchased from his fellow crusader, Thomas de Clare. On 20 August following he sailed for the Holy Land with Edward. His movements there are not known, but he acquired a cross with a foot of gold and emeralds (which his daughter-in-law was later to bequeath to Westminster Abbey). Following the attempt on Edward's life at Acre he was one of the executors of the prince's will, made on 18 June 1272, but he left the crusade early, in August, perhaps through fear for his estates at the hands of his old enemy, the earl of Gloucester. He returned independently to London on 11 January 1273, ahead of Edward, now king. On 7 June he was hunting illegally with his retinue in Hampshire.

Valence held many commands in Gascony and Wales under Edward I. On 3 September 1273 he received for Edward the fealty of the citizens of Limoges. He remained in Gascony with the king, but was reported illegally hunting in Hampshire on 29 November. He returned to Limoges in July 1274 to honour Edward's promise to defend the citizens, appointing a seneschal and besieging the vicomtesse de Limoges's castle at Aixe. On 19 August he attended Edward's coronation at Westminster. On 4 September he was again hunting illegally with his retinue in Hampshire. In February 1275 he represented Edward at the Paris *parlement* at Candlemas, receiving Gaston de Béarn's challenge to do single combat with Edward. Valence returned by May and Edward duly granted him the constableship of Cilgerran Castle and the wardship of the heirs of Roger de Somery, on condition that he paid some of the king's debts.

Valence played an active part in the campaign of 1277 against Llywelyn ap Gruffudd. With Prince Edmund he led a second army which marched up the coast from Pembroke and reached Aberystwyth by 25 July, where they laid the foundations of the new castle. They drove Llywelyn north into Snowdonia. Valence returned to Pembroke on 3 October, but by 27 December he was at Marwell, Hampshire.

After a quiet year spent mainly at court Valence was in June 1279 sent to receive the Agenais, ceded to Edward I under the treaty of Amiens. He entered Agen on 8 August and two days later installed Jean de Grailly as seneschal. After an embassy to the king of Castile in November, in January 1280 he returned to Agen where he laid the foundations of Tournon and the *bastide* of Valence d'Agen. He returned to London by 6 June and remained in England for the next two years.

Valence fought in the final struggle against Llywelyn; in July 1282 the king appointed him to replace the earl of Gloucester as commander in west Wales, and rewarded him with the wardship for a year of his son-in-law, John Hastings, lord of Abergavenny. Valence's son, William the younger, had been killed by the Welsh on 16 June in an ambush near Llandeilo. After mustering another force at Carmarthen on 6 December against Llywelyn's last sortie, he crushed a further rebellion in Cardiganshire in January. He left Aberystwyth in April with over 1000 men and captured Prince Dafydd's last stronghold, Castell y Bere, in a ten-day siege. From September to Christmas 1284 he accompanied Edward I on his triumphal tour of Wales. It is notable, however, that Edward did not reward his loyalty with increased lands or liberties on the march; indeed, in 1285, despite Valence's personal remonstration at Aberystwyth, Edward ordered royal justices into Pembrokeshire to hear appeals by the earl of Hereford and the burgesses of Haverfordwest against Valence, a significant royal intrusion into marcher liberties.

From September 1286 to June 1289 Valence accompanied Edward to Gascony; he fell ill with fever at Saintes in November 1286. In September 1289 he helped negotiate at Salisbury the proposed marriage between Prince Edward and Margaret, the Maid of Norway. From January to March 1291 he was appointed to adjudicate in the feud on the Welsh march between the earls of Gloucester and Hereford; however, he and other marchers, fearing further royal assaults on their liberties, intervened to prevent Edward I carrying out the sentence. In the following August he assisted the king in the preliminary hearings of the Scottish succession at Berwick. On 10 December, at Westminster Abbey, he witnessed Edward's grant of the heart of Henry III to the nuns of Fontevraud for reburial. On 5 February 1292, at Westminster, the king appointed him one of the five to regulate tournaments under the laws of arms. In the summer he returned with the king to Norham, declaring that the Scottish succession should be decided according to English law, which favoured John de Balliol. In October, at Berwick, he was one of those marchers who granted Edward a fifteenth, provided that it would not constitute a precedent. In October 1294 the king sent him, with Roger (IV) Bigod, earl of Norfolk, to hold south Wales against the revolt of Madog ap Llywelyn.

Death and assessment In January 1296 Valence, accompanied by his son Aymer de *Valence (d. 1324), headed an embassy to Cambrai in a fruitless attempt to negotiate between Edward I and Philippe IV of France. Despite old age, he may have been involved in a skirmish, for he returned to England wounded and was met at Dover by a litter sent by his wife. He died at his manor of Brabourne in Kent on 16 May. John Leland's account that he was slain by the French at Bayonne on 13 June must, therefore, be incorrect. Valence was buried near Henry III at Westminster Abbey in the chapel of St Edmund and St Thomas the Martyr where his monument, an expensive piece of foreign workmanship, remains—a canopied stone altar-tomb bearing his effigy in wood covered with copper gilt, in full armour with heraldry and inscription, decorated in Limoges enamel. Valence was survived by his wife, Joan, who retained the title of countess of Pembroke, Pembroke and Goodrich castles, and Wexford until her death in September 1307. They had three sons: John, who died in childhood in January 1277, buried in the chapel of Edward the Confessor, Westminster Abbey, where his grave-slab survives; William the younger, who was killed by the Welsh on 16 June 1282, and who may be buried at Dorchester Abbey, Oxfordshire; and Aymer, born 1270x75, who succeeded in 1296 as lord of Montignac and in 1307 as earl of Pembroke. There were also four daughters: Isabel (d. 1305), who married in 1275 John Hastings (d. 1313); Margaret, who died in childhood on 24 March 1276 and was buried with John de Valence at Westminster Abbey; Agnes (d. 1310), who married first, in 1266, Maurice Fitzgerald (d. 1268), second Hugh de Balliol (d. 1271), and third Jean d'Avesnes (d. 1283); and Joan, who married John Comyn, lord of Badenoch (d. 1306).

Valence was never created an earl by Henry III or Edward I. On his seal, and in most of his charters, he merely styled himself 'lord of Pembroke'. His wife, in fact, only inherited part of the Marshal earldom of Pembroke. However, control of the Pembrokeshire county court may have led to his assumption of the title of earl in documents by the late 1280s, and in the 1290s Edward I occasionally accepted it, even summoning him to parliament as earl in 1295, a unique example of informal elevation, perhaps an inexpensive reward for Valence's loyalty. His relationship with the king was always one of dependence as much as kinship. His scattered estates, a half held by marriage, were worth some £1500 p.a., relatively modest for an 'earl'; his income needed royal grants, such as wardships, to increase it by an average of £1000 p.a., which prevented him from pursuing an independent political line or developing a large retinue. Thus, his benefactions were modest: mainly to Pembroke Priory and the foundation of a hospital at Tenby. His disputes with the Clares and Bohuns arose from their being fellow Marshal coheirs whose claims much reduced the extent of Pembroke. Valence pursued another vendetta against the Munchensis, culminating in his unsuccessful attempt in 1289 to have William de Munchensi's surviving daughter, Dionysia, bastardized; he was almost certainly supported by his wife, who hated the descendants of her father Warin de Munchensi's second marriage, who deprived her of the family inheritance. But Valence's poor reputation has been much exaggerated: in 1270, for example, he refused to be dishonest and break open a private letter (Shirley, 2.345). He inspired the lasting affection of his wife and his brother-in-law, John de Warenne, one of his executors. Vilified as an 'alien' in the reign of Henry III, his interests were, in fact, overwhelmingly English, justifying the Dunstable annalist's epitaph of *satis fidelis regno Anglie* ('sufficiently faithful to the kingdom of England'; *Ann. Mon.*, 3.400).

H. W. RIDGEWAY

Sources Chancery records · PRO · R. F. Treharne and I. J. Sanders, eds., *Documents of the baronial movement of reform and rebellion, 1258–1267* (1973) · Rymer, *Foedera* · *Calendar of inquisitions miscellaneous (chancery)*, PRO, 1 (1916) · A. Teulet and others, eds., *Layettes du trésor des chartes*, 5 vols. (Paris, 1863–1909), vol. 2, pp. 498–9, 623–4 · G. Thomas, *Cartulaire des comtes de La Marche et d'Angoulême* (1934) · D. P. de Monsabert, 'Chartes et documents pour servir à l'histoire de l'Abbaie de Charroux', *Archives Historiques du Poitou*, 39 (1910) · *A descriptive catalogue of ancient deeds in the Public Record Office*, 6 vols. (1890–1915) · *RotP*, vol. 1 · W. W. Shirley, ed., *Royal and other historical letters illustrative of the reign of Henry III*, 2 vols., Rolls Series, 27 (1862–6) · F. Michel, C. Bémont, and Y. Renouard, eds., *Rôles Gascons*, 4 vols. (1885–1962), vols. 1–3 · H. S. Sweetman and G. F. Handcock, eds., *Calendar of documents relating to Ireland*, 5 vols., PRO (1875–86), vols. 1–2 · *Littere Wallie*, ed. J. G. Edwards (1940) · I. H. Jeayes, *Descriptive catalogue of the charters and muniments in the possession of the Rt. Hon. Lord Fitzhardinge at Berkeley Castle* (1892) · Dugdale, *Monasticon*, new edn · N. H. Nicolas, ed., *Testamenta vetusta: being illustrations from wills*, 1 (1826), 100 · Paris, *Chron.* · *Ann. mon.* · *The historical works of Gervase of Canterbury*, ed. W. Stubbs, 2 vols., Rolls Series, 73 (1879–80) · H. R. Luard, ed., *Flores historiarum*, 3 vols., Rolls Series, 95 (1890) · T. Stapleton, ed., *De antiquis legibus liber: cronica majorum et vicecomitum Londoniarum*, CS, 34 (1846) · [W. Rishanger], *The chronicle of William de Rishanger, of the barons' wars*, ed. J. O. Halliwell, CS, 15 (1840) · *Willelmi Rishanger … chronica et annales*, ed. H. T. Riley, pt 2 of *Chronica monasterii S. Albani*, Rolls Series, 28 (1865) · R. Vaughan, 'The chronicle of John of Wallingford', *EngHR*, 73 (1958), 66–77 · F. R. Lewis, 'William de Valence, pt 1', *Aberystwyth Studies*, 13 (1934), 13–35 · F. R. Lewis, 'William de Valence, pt 2', *Aberystwyth Studies*, 14 (1936), 72–91 · H. Ridgeway, 'William de Valence and his *familiares*', *Historical Research*, 65 (1992), 239–57 · H. W. Ridgeway, 'Foreign favourites and Henry III's problems of patronage, 1247–58', *EngHR*, 104 (1989), 590–610 · H. W. Ridgeway, 'The Lord Edward and the Provisions of Oxford (1258): a study in faction', *Thirteenth century England: proceedings of the Newcastle upon Tyne conference* [Newcastle upon Tyne 1985], ed. P. R. Coss and S. D. Lloyd, 1 (1986), 89–99 · D. A. Carpenter, 'What happened in 1258?', *War and government in the middle ages: essays in honour of J. O. Prestwich*, ed. J. B. Gillingham and J. C. Holt (1984) · J. R. Maddicott, *Simon de Montfort* (1994) · P. J. Lankester, 'A military effigy in Dorchester Abbey, Oxon.', *Oxoniensia*, 52 (1987), 145–72, esp. 155–9 · J. E. Lloyd, *A history of Wales from the earliest times to the Edwardian conquest*, 2nd edn, 2 vols. (1912) · J. E. Morris, *The Welsh wars of Edward I* (1901) · M. Prestwich, *Edward I* (1988) · J. R. S. Phillips, *Aymer de Valence, earl of Pembroke, 1307–1324: baronial politics in the reign of Edward II* (1972) · S. D. Lloyd, *English society and the crusade, 1216–1307* (1988) · J. P. Trabut-Cussac, *L'Administration anglaise en Gascogne sous Henry III et Édouard I de 1254 à 1307* (Geneva, 1972)
Likenesses tomb effigy, Westminster Abbey, London [*see illus.*]

Valentia. For this title name *see* Annesley, Francis, second Viscount Valentia (*bap.* 1586, *d.* 1660).

Valentine family (*per. c.*1685–1845), musicians, were central to musical life in Leicester for over a century, and many enjoyed wider careers. As many members of the family had the same forename, it can be difficult to distinguish biographical evidence conclusively. Thomas Follintine, 'a stranger' (Hartopp, 1884), perhaps from Melton Mowbray, Leicestershire, where Thomas, son of Thomas Follentine, was baptized on 28 April 1667, probably moved to Leicester about 1670 and was granted freeman status as a town wait on 2 April 1684. His eldest sons, Thomas (*bap.* 1667?, *d.* 1721) and Henry (*bap.* 1670?), were appointed waits in 1685. Henry was organist at St Martin's, Leicester, in 1701, and in 1703 was the first to become a freeman as a musician. He built the organ at Ashbourne, Derbyshire, in 1710, and later became a maltster. The younger Thomas's six surviving sons were all musicians, including David (*bap.* 1698), organist at Ludlow about 1730, and Mark (*bap.* 1701), appointed organist at St Martin's, Leicester, in 1745 at a salary of £10 10s. per annum but sacked, following complaints, in 1748.

The most adventurous of the younger Thomas's brothers seems to have been **Robert Valentine** [Follintine] (*bap.* 1674), composer, baptized at St Martin's, Leicester, on 16 January 1674, the son of Thomas Follintine and his wife, Sarah (*d.* 1684?). Further information about his life is mostly circumstantial. His education is unrecorded, and he did not become a town wait. By 1708 he was established in Rome, where his *Sonate di flauto* op. 2 was published with a dedication to Sir Thomas Samwell, later MP for Coventry, who was in Italy on his grand tour. Between April 1708 and March 1710 he was employed as an oboist at the Ruspoli palace in Rome, and he may have moved to Naples in 1710, as his *Twelve Sonatas* op. 3 (1710) is dedicated to John Fleetwood, the British consul there, and one of his concertos appears in a Naples manuscript of 1725. His *Twelve Solos* op. 12 (1730) was dedicated to the duke dell' Oratino, a Neapolitan nobleman. He is supposed to have returned to England in 1731, when his complete works were published by John Walsh, but there are no mentions of concert appearances in the London newspapers, and details of his death are unknown. He composed many tuneful sonatas and concertos, mostly for the recorder or flute, which remained popular among amateur musicians. Manuscripts of his compositions can be found at the Naples conservatory, at Uppsala University and Rostock University, and in the Biblioteca Comunale, Assisi, the Herzog-August-Bibliothek, Wolfenbüttel, and the British Library.

John Valentine (*bap.* 1730, *d.* 1791), composer, was the grandson of the younger Thomas Valentine (*bap.* 1667?, *d.* 1721) and thus Robert Valentine's great-nephew. He was baptized at St Margaret's, Leicester, on 7 June 1730, the son of John Valentine (*bap.* 1699, *d.* in or before 1754) and his wife, Sarah (1693?–1763?). No record of his education exists, but he was probably apprenticed to his father, or an uncle, and he was made a freeman of Leicester on 16 April 1754. He married Tabitha Simpson (*b.* 1728) on 1 May 1755 at Aylestone, Leicestershire, and by 1759 he owned a music shop in New Bond Street, Leicester, which he later transferred to the Market Place by 1768, and then to Belgrave Gate by 1774. According to Kroeger he performed at concerts throughout the midlands from Matlock Bath to Market Harborough, primarily as a violinist, but he taught everything from the harpsichord to the french horn: in 1769 he advertised his fees—10s. 6d. entrance, and 15s. a quarter—in the *Leicester and Nottingham Journal*, together with a comprehensive selection of instruments and music for sale. He composed mostly music for amateurs, including three sets of marches and *Eight easy symphonies … designed for & dedicated to, all junior performers and musical societies*, op. 6. On 27 February 1762 his only theatrical piece, *The Epithalamium in the Tragedy of Isabella, or, The Fatal Marriage*, was performed in Leicester by Durravan's Company of Comedians, and on 5 May 1763, a day of thanksgiving following the treaty of Paris, his *Ode to Peace* 'was performed in a grand chorus of voices and instruments' (Thompson, 113). His other compositions include *Thirty*

Psalm Tunes and a sycophantic *Ode on the Birthday of the Marquis of Granby*. Some of his manuscript compositions are in the British Library. He died in Leicester on 10 September 1791 and was buried at St Margaret's, Leicester, on 12 September 1791.

Three of his children became musicians, the most prominent being **Ann Valentine** (*bap.* 1762, *d.* 1845), who was baptized at St Martin's, Leicester, on 15 March 1762. She probably received her musical training from her father, and in 1777 she performed a harpsichord concerto at 'Mr Valentine's Annual Concert at Rugby' (Kroeger, 450). William Gardiner, whose writings are entertaining but not always totally reliable, noted that she usually played music by Handel, either an organ concerto or a harpsichord lesson, as the 'wretched little piano fortes of the day' (Gardiner, 67) were not suitable for concerts. About 1785 she was appointed organist at St Margaret's, Leicester, and from 1791 she lived in Belgrave Gate, where she perhaps continued to run her father's music shop. She composed *Ten sonatas for the piano forte or harpsichord with an accompaniment for the violin or german-flute* op. 1, *A Collect for the Sixth Sunday after Trinity*, a song, 'Ye Gentlest Gales', and seven piano pieces. According to the records of St Margaret's, when she died on 13 October 1845 she was living at Coleshill, presumably in Warwickshire; she was buried at St Margaret's on 20 October 1845.

Sarah Valentine (1771–1843), Ann's younger sister, lived with her at Belgrave Gate and was also a professional musician. Her only known composition is *The British March and Quickstep … for the Pianoforte*: a copy, bound with a collection of Ann's music, is in the Lilly Library, Indiana University. In 1800 Sarah replaced Miss Greatorex as organist at St Martin's, Leicester, receiving 150 votes against the one vote received by Frederick Hill, the other candidate. Another versatile member of the family was a brother of Sarah and Ann, Thomas Valentine (1757–1800), the eldest son of John, who performed in a concert as a singer and violinist in 1771. In 1774 he advertised in the *Leicester and Nottingham Journal* as a harpsichord teacher and tuner, and by 1784 an announcement in the same newspaper of a 'musical meeting' at Ashby-de-la-Zouch, where he was to play first violin, described him as a member of the Covent Garden theatre. According to his obituary, also in the *Leicester and Nottingham Journal*, when he died at Wrexham, Denbighshire, he was organist to Sir Watkins Williams Wynn at Ruabon, and his military compositions were particularly admired.

In March 1773 a concert advertised for Thomas's benefit broke a mutual contract between John and his first cousin Henry Valentine (*b.* 1725), who owned a music shop in East Gate, Leicester, and played the oboe. According to a notice Henry placed in the *Leicester and Nottingham Journal*, he and John had agreed to share all profits of benefit concerts equally, and so he appealed to the 'impartial public' to support him in a future concert of his own. This took place in June 1773, but the conflict was apparently short-lived, as by September Henry and John again organized a joint benefit concert.

A Mrs Valentine, whose first name is not recorded, frequently took part in Leicester concerts. In 1765 she sang a cantata by John Stanley and a song with guitar accompaniment at a Valentine benefit concert, by 1767 she had her own series of benefit concerts, and in 1774 she performed on the musical glasses. It seems that she was Mary Geary, the wife of Henry: Kroeger surmises that she was probably not John's wife, Tabitha, as she sang at Henry's concert in June 1773 when the cousins were in dispute.

According to Gardiner, the fortnightly subscription concerts in Leicester were a financial success because the performers were mostly amateurs and 'Misses Ann and Fanny, and Messrs John and Henry Valentine, and Robert jun.' (Gardiner, 67) were paid only 2s. 6d. a night. Works played included 'the concertos of Corelli, Handel, Geminiani, Stanley, and Avison; the symphonies of Martini, Stamitz, Abell, Maldere, Vanhall, and Ditters' (ibid.) and a sinfonia by Haydn, whose music had apparently not been heard in Leicester before. Robert Valentine (b. 1762) and Fanny Valentine (b. 1770) were children of Henry and Mary: Fanny, who for a short time was also an actress, sang 'grave songs from Handel's oratorios, and now and then a Vauxhall ballad' (ibid., 67–8), and Robert, who became a freeman in 1784, may have been 'Mr Valentine, the professor', who in 1794 took part with William Gardiner and Abbé Dobler in a performance of Beethoven's violin trio in E♭ 'well before any of Beethoven's works had been heard elsewhere in England' (ibid., 113).

After Ann's death in 1845 no further Valentines seem to have been important to the musical life of Leicester, but the British Library catalogue contains many works by others who may have been members of the same family, including John, who wrote *The Elements of Practical Harmony, or What is Generally Called Thorough Base* (1834), and Thomas, who composed over 150 piano pieces, mostly arrangements of popular airs with variations.

SALLY DRAGE

Sources M. Medforth, 'The Valentines of Leicester: a reappraisal of an 18th-century musical family', *MT*, 122 (1981), 812–18 · K. Kroeger, 'John Valentine: eighteenth-century music-master in the English midlands', *Notes*, 44 (1987–8), 444–55 · C. Johnson, preface, in A. Valentine, *Ten sonatas for the piano forte or harpsichord with an accompaniment for the violin or german-flute* (1994) · P. Young, preface, in R. Valentine, *Concerto in D major for flute or oboe, strings and continuo* (1967) · M. Medforth, 'Valentine, Robert', *New Grove*, 2nd edn · M. Medforth, 'Valentine, John', *New Grove*, 2nd edn · H. Hartopp, ed., *Register of freemen of Leicester, 1196–1770* (1927) · T. North, ed., *The accounts of the churchwardens of St Martin's, Leicester, 1489–1844* (1884) · W. Gardiner, *Music and friends*, 1 (1838) · J. Thompson, *The history of Leicester in the eighteenth century* (1871) · will, Leics. RO, PR/T/SMP/749 [John Valentine] · parish register, Leicester, St Margaret, 12 Sept 1791, Leics. RO [burial: John Valentine] · parish register, Leicester, St Margaret, 20 Oct 1845, Leics. RO [burial: Ann Valentine] · IGI

Wealth at death under £300; John Valentine: will, Leics. RO, PR/T/SMP/749

Valentine, Ann (bap. **1762**, d. **1845**). *See under* Valentine family (per. c.1685–1845).

Valentine, Benjamin (d. in or before **1653**), politician, is of obscure background, although his origins may have been in Cheshire. Certainly he was of no significant fortune. He

married at an unknown date Elizabeth, daughter of Matthew Springham, and had a son, Matthew, who was of St Clement Danes, Middlesex, at the time of his death in 1654.

Valentine became involved in the west country political network overseen by the Herberts, earls of Pembroke, and was a friend of Sir John Eliot. In 1624, with William Coryton, he enjoined Arthur Brett, a relative of the earl of Middlesex banned from court, to return under Pembroke's protection. Valentine was returned to parliament for St Germans in 1628 and in the same year attacked the King's favourite, the duke of Buckingham, portraying him as a public enemy in the Commons' remonstrance debate. In 1629 he was one of the Eliot group and called for the punishment of the customs officers. In the demonstration of 2 March against the adjournment of the parliament he joined Denzil Holles in holding down Speaker Finch. Professing his loyalty to the king, Valentine supported the reading of Eliot's resolutions against religious and fiscal innovation. He was thus squarely in potentially revolutionary territory. Arrested with eight other MPs, he refused to answer to council concerning the events in the Commons.

Valentine stayed the course as a recalcitrant prisoner in the major state case of 1629–30 which did much to bring about Charles I's personal rule. Subject to Star Chamber charges which eventually lapsed, Valentine and five others sued for writs of habeas corpus on 6 May 1629, seeking bail. In king's bench he relied on the telling argument, invoking the petition of right, made by Sir Edward Littleton for John Selden. Charles subverted the law in preventing the prisoners from being brought to court to be bailed, and Valentine remained in the Tower. The petition of the county of Cornwall in September for the prisoners' release reflected his links with the west. At the new legal term in October 1629 the king offered the prisoners bail with a good behaviour bond, seeking their submission to his authority and rationalization of their arbitrary treatment. Most refused and were remanded to prison. The three ringleaders in the Commons—Eliot, Holles, and Valentine—were transferred from the Tower to the Marshalsea on 29 October. Continuing their protest they forced the crown to try them for seditious conduct and speeches in parliament. Henry Calthorpe and Robert Mason represented Valentine. The defendants entered a plea against jurisdiction, maintaining that only parliament could judge them, but were ruled against and found guilty in king's bench. Valentine was imprisoned at the king's pleasure and fined £500—less than the others, being of less ability to pay. The Long Parliament condemned the entire proceedings, awarding compensation, and in 1667 both houses upheld its resolutions. Although enjoying relaxed conditions of confinement until 1632, Valentine continued recalcitrant and imprisoned until 1640, when Charles released him in an apparently conciliatory gesture prior to the meeting of the Short Parliament.

Although he was once more returned for St Germans to

the Long Parliament, Valentine was not politically active but took the protestation of 5 May 1641 and the covenant in 1643. Apparently taking no part in the civil wars, in February 1649 he subscribed to the Commons' vote of 5 December in favour of the Newport negotiations. He thus does not appear to have been ultimately a committed revolutionary. He died some time in or before 1653 and his place in history rests upon his actions, however factious or ideological, in dissenting from the Caroline regime of the late 1620s.   L. J. REEVE

Sources DNB · L. J. Reeve, *Charles I and the road to personal rule* (1989) · L. J. Reeve, 'The legal status of the petition of right', *HJ*, 29 (1986), 257–77 · L. J. Reeve, 'The arguments in king's bench in 1629 concerning the imprisonment of John Selden and other members of the House of Commons', *Journal of British Studies*, 25 (1986), 264–87 · W. Notestein and F. H. Relf, eds., *Commons debates for 1629* (1921) · *State trials* · S. R. Gardiner, *History of England from the accession of James I to the outbreak of the civil war*, 10 vols. (1883–4) · C. Russell, *Parliaments and English politics, 1621–1629* (1979) · C. Russell, *The fall of the British monarchies, 1637–1642* (1991) · K. M. Sharpe, ed., *Faction and parliament: essays on early Stuart history* (1978) · D. Underdown, *Pride's Purge: politics in the puritan revolution* (1971) · R. Lockyer, *Buckingham: the life and political career of George Villiers, first duke of Buckingham, 1592–1628* (1981) · B. Worden, *The Rump Parliament, 1648–1653* (1974) · E. S. Cope, *Politics without parliaments, 1629–1640* (1987) · H. Hulme, *The life of Sir John Eliot* (1957) · D. Brunton and D. H. Pennington, *Members of the Long Parliament* (1954) · J. Forster, *Sir John Eliot: a biography*, 2 vols. (1864)
Archives PRO, State Papers, Domestic, Car. 1 SP16
Wealth at death almost certainly died poor, dependent upon parliamentary handouts: Underdown, *Pride's Purge*, 242 · paid compensation by the Long Parliament: DNB

Valentine, Charles Wilfrid (1879–1964), psychologist and educationist, was born on 16 August 1879 at Halton Road, Runcorn, Cheshire, one of the eight children of Henry Valentine (*b*. 1841), a Wesleyan Methodist minister, and his wife, Sophia Woodcock. He attended Nottingham high school and then Preston grammar school, leaving at seventeen to teach in a small boarding-school. Nevertheless, after seven years of teaching at various secondary schools, interspersed with largely self-financed degree studies, Valentine's university education was eventually both thorough and extensive. He obtained a BA from London University (taken externally at University College, Aberystwyth, where he was an exhibitioner), an MA from Cambridge gained with a double first in philosophy and psychology in 1909 (as a foundation scholar in moral sciences at Downing College), and a DPhil from St Andrews in 1913. He also spent part of 1908 as a student at the Würzburg laboratory of Oswald Külpe in Germany, where he steeped himself in the new experimental investigation of what were then termed the higher mental functions, including imagery and thinking. What seemed particularly to impress Valentine and also Cyril Burt, a fellow student at Würzburg who became a lifelong friend, was the work on human learning, memory, and experimental pedagogy, especially that by Ernst Meumann.

On returning from Germany, Valentine obtained his first academic post at twenty-nine and spent the next five years until 1914 as lecturer in psychology to St Andrews

provincial committee, working also as assistant in education at the University of St Andrews for four of them. During his tenure at St Andrews he married, on 4 January 1911, (Margaret) Ethel Rothwell Jackson (1887/8–1956), daughter of Arthur Jackson, retired mechanical engineer; there were three sons and a daughter from this union. After a further five years as professor of education at Queen's University, Belfast, he became professor of education at the University of Birmingham in 1919, a post he held until his retirement in 1946.

In Birmingham, Valentine's considerable talents as teacher, writer, and researcher flourished as he established what was in effect the first major centre for educational psychology in the UK. His broad and eclectic education, together with his wide teaching experience, helped him to command the shifting borderland between psychology and education, where formidable psychological, statistical, and also social skills were vital. Over this long period his research into such topics as child development, transfer of training, imagery, mental testing, home and classroom discipline, the reliability of examinations, and the questionable place of Latin in the curriculum gave rise to more than fifty papers and sixteen books (most of which went into several editions). The most influential of these were *Psychology and its Bearing on Education* (1950), *Intelligence Tests for Children* (1948), and *The Difficult Child and the Problems of Discipline* (1940). Like Sully, Binet, and Piaget before him he made his systematic observation of his own children's development the basis of one of his major works: *The Psychology of Early Childhood* (1942).

Valentine probably also found his other academic love, the psychology of aesthetics, as early as 1908 in Würzburg; Burt claims that they were both surprised by Külpe's strong interest in the subject. In any event Valentine's earliest published book, *An Introduction to the Experimental Psychology of Beauty* (1913), was on what he termed his 'hobby'. This apparently minor interest continued to fascinate him. His last published work on the subject, *The Experimental Psychology of Beauty*, appeared in 1962, only two years before his death. An interest in aspects of Freudian thinking, in particular in the psychology of dreams and the light that they cast on the unconscious, occupied him for many years, culminating in the publication of *Dreams and the Unconscious* (1921). A revised edition appeared in 1928 under the title *The New Psychology of the Unconscious*. He also enthusiastically embraced the problems of military education in the Second World War, even to the extent of enduring the rigours of army basic training though nearing retirement age. The outcome of this work appeared in the two short but typically practical and down-to-earth books, *Principles of Army Instruction* (1942) and *The Human Factor in the Army* (1943).

Among Valentine's other major contributions to British academic life was his role as founder and editor for nearly ten years of *The Forum of Education*, and then of its successor, the *British Journal of Educational Psychology*, which he edited and managed for a further unprecedented twenty-five years from its creation in 1931. During his tenure the *Journal* was committed to championing the contribution that a distinctively British psychology had made to education. He was also associated with various societies that supported psychology; he was president of Section J (psychology) of the British Association of Science in 1930 and president of the British Psychological Society for 1947–8. Earlier he had also served with considerable success on local bodies, for example as chairman of the Birmingham higher education subcommittee from 1919 to 1925, a considerable coup for someone barely settled into his major academic position. Still writing to within a few months of the end, Valentine died at his home, the White House, 92 Silver Street, Wythall, Worcestershire, on 26 May 1964.   A. D. LOVIE and P. LOVIE

Sources *British Journal of Psychology*, 55 (1964), 385–90 · *British Journal of Educational Psychology*, 34 (1964), 219–22 · *The Times* (29 May 1964) · L. B. Birch, 'List of publications by C. W. Valentine', *British Journal of Educational Psychology*, 26 (1956), 3–7 · C. Burt, 'The contributions of Professor C. W. Valentine to psychology', *British Journal of Educational Psychology*, 26 (1956), 8–14 · *WWW, 1961–70* · L. Zusne, *Names in the history of psychology* (Washington, 1975), 350–51 · b. cert. · m. cert. · d. cert. · *CGPLA Eng. & Wales* (1964)
Likenesses photograph, British Psychological Society, Leicester, Grace Rawlings Visual Archive; repro. in *British Journal of Psychology*, 55 (1964), facing p. 385 · photograph, British Psychological Society, Leicester, Grace Rawlings Visual Archive; repro. in *British Journal of Educational Psychology*, 34 (1964), facing p. 219
Wealth at death £18,021: probate, 4 Aug 1964, *CGPLA Eng. & Wales*

Valentine, Dickie [*real name* Richard Bryce] (**1929–1971**), singer and impressionist, was born at St Pancras, London, on 4 November 1929, the son of a lorry driver. At the age of three he appeared in the film *Jack's the Boy*, starring Jack Hulbert and Cicely Courtneidge. At fourteen he became a page-boy at Manchester's Palace Theatre, a role he repeated for a while at the London Palladium before being sacked for cheekiness. So he must have found it satisfying when he found himself topping the bill at the Palladium in his mid-twenties.

Bryce was able to take a course of singing lessons through the generosity of the Canadian stage star Bill O'Connor, who met Bryce while he was working as a backstage call-boy at Her Majesty's Theatre, Haymarket. He honed his craft performing as a featured singer with the big bands that were so popular during and after the war, and it was when he joined Ted Heath's band on St Valentine's day in 1949 that he conceived the idea for his stage surname. His rise to fame took place in the early 1950s when he became a romantic idol; so huge was his fan club that, for its annual meeting of 1957, the Royal Albert Hall was booked and filled to capacity. On 27 October 1954 he married Elizabeth Flynn (*b.* 1932/3), daughter of John Flynn, an engineer of Regent Street, London. At this point he was at the height of his success; that same year he released his first number one hit record, 'Finger of Suspicion' (jointly written by Paul Mann and Al Lewis). His subsequent acclaim led to his being invited to appear on television in the USA, on such shows as those of Eddie Fisher and Ed Sullivan. He had a number of other chart hits with Decca records, including another number one in 1955 with 'Christmas Alphabet', written by Buddy Kaye (with

Jules Loman's collaboration). From then on he was eclipsed by the craze for rock and roll. A brief flirtation with this genre in 1956, *Dickie Valentine's Rock 'n' Roll Party Medley*, proved unsuccessful—it was, indeed, something he himself described as the biggest 'clanger' he had ever dropped. In 1959 he signed to Pye, where his recording manager was Tony Hatch, and in that year enjoyed his last top twenty hit with 'One More Sunrise'.

Valentine had always possessed another string to his bow, however, and that was his talent for impressions: these included a melodramatic Al Jolson, an operatic Mario Lanza, and a lachrymose Johnny Ray. Being himself a singer with no gimmicks or obvious mannerisms, he was keenly alert to the idiosyncrasies of others. He was given his own show on Independent Television in 1966. His first marriage, from which there were two children, ended in divorce in 1967, and on 1 June 1968 he married Wendy Ann Wayne, *née* Cook (*b.* 1943/4), an actress.

During this period Valentine began to fade from the media spotlight, although he remained in demand as a cabaret artist, and received invitations and bookings from clubs throughout the world. Early in 1971 he made a tour of Australia. However, on 6 May that year he was killed while returning from performing at a club in Wales, after the car in which he was travelling struck a bridge support at Glangrwyney, Brecknockshire. His pianist, Syd Boatman, and drummer, Dave Pearson, were also fatally injured in the same accident.

Valentine was of stocky build and possessed a winning smile. His singing style was notable for having a wider dynamic range than that associated with the typical dance band crooner. His controlled legato and well-shaped musical phrases in romantic ballads were enhanced by a velvety vocal timbre. He was admired for his warm and sincere personality and, in the narrow confines and hot-house atmosphere of the recording studio, was appreciated for his co-operative, modest, and professional manner.   DEREK B. SCOTT

Sources *The Times* (7 May 1971) · C. Larkin, ed., *The encyclopedia of popular music*, 3rd edn (1998), 5597–8 · www.45-rpm.org.uk/biogs. htm [UK artists biography index] · T. Hatch and B. Gladwell, *Crescendo International*, 9/3 (June 1971) · *Variety*, 262/230 (12 May 1971) · *Melody Maker*, 46/4 (15 May 1971) · m. certs. · d. cert.
Likenesses photograph, repro. in Hatch and Gladwell, *Crescendo International*, 3
Wealth at death £55,365: probate, 17 Aug 1971, *CGPLA Eng. & Wales*

Valentine, Greta Mary (1907–1998). *See under* Crowley, Aleister (1875–1947).

Valentine, James (**1815–1879**), engraver and photographer, was born on 12 June 1815 in Dundee, the second of the five children of John Valentine (1792–1868), linen weaver, and his wife, Mary Watson (*bap.* 1790, *d.* 1866), daughter of Andrew Watson, a Dundee shipmaster and his wife, Elizabeth Elder. After schooling in Dundee, he was sent to Edinburgh to study art. He returned to Dundee in 1832 to set up an engraving and copperplate printing business with his father, who had taken up a new trade

James Valentine (1815–1879), by Valentine Studio

cutting wooden blocks for linen printing. On 28 August 1837 he married Christina Marshall (1812/13–1842), daughter of John Marshall, shoemaker. In June 1838, days before the birth of his first child, he announced that he was no longer a partner in Valentine & Son and was setting up on his own account as an engraver and copperplate and lithographic printer in the Overgate in Dundee. After giving birth to their third child in November 1841, his wife died on 3 May 1842 of lung disease. The only son of this marriage, John (1841–1867), became a pioneer photographer in Hawaii. On 5 December 1843 James Valentine married his second wife, Rachel Dobson (1817–1879), in Glasgow.

Valentine prospered; he rarely described himself in the same way twice in the Dundee directory, but the mainstay of his business was the engraving, printing, and supplying of business stationery. In 1840 he became a member of the guildry and in 1845 a burgess, both evidence of his progress in the Dundee business establishment. About 1849 he met the colourful American social campaigner Elihu Burritt; he was involved in publicity for Burritt's visit to Dundee, producing engraved illustrated envelopes supporting his varied causes, which included universal brotherhood, arbitration for war, freedom of commerce, and (more mundanely) penny postage overseas. By 1851 Valentine had fourteen employees; in that year he decided to add portrait photography to his firm's activities, having become interested in this new invention as an aid to engraving. To equip himself, he studied 'in M. Billoch's photographic academy in Paris' and corresponded 'with some of the best French and English photographers' (Dundee Public Library, Lamb MS 215 (2)).

This enterprise proved to be so profitable that in 1855 Valentine erected one of the largest photographic glasshouses in Britain. By the end of the decade portrait photography came first in his advertisements and he was retailing photographs of local worthies. In the early 1860s—after instruction in the studio of Francis Frith in Reigate, Surrey—he added landscape photography to his repertory, aided by the ingenious conversion of a barouche into a mobile dark-room and by the entry into the business of his eldest son by his second marriage, William Dobson Valentine. In 1864 he solicited the Queen Victoria's attention with topographical photographs, including one of Queenswell in Glen Mark, and was rewarded with commissions for views of Scottish scenery. In 1868 he obtained the royal warrant as 'photographer to the queen', the second in Scotland to do so after George Washington Wilson of Aberdeen. This side of his business rapidly developed: the sale of view scraps for prices ranging from 1s. to 3s. 6d. and elegant albums from half a guinea to 12 guineas gave rise to a large printing works at 152 and 154 Perth Road, Dundee. The 12,000 wet-plate collodion negatives which Valentine prepared were not markedly different in quality from those of his competitors in the landscape photograph trade aiming at upper- and middle-class tourists, but he excelled in the organization of his business and the presentation of his products.

James Valentine was a staunch member of the Congregational church, initially attending the Castle Street Chapel and from 1867, after a disagreement when he headed a list of eighty-three dissident members, becoming a member of the Panmure Street Chapel. (His son James (1846–1918) became a Congregational minister at Peterborough.) He died at his home, 19 Thomson Street, Dundee, on 19 June 1879 and was buried in Balgay cemetery in Dundee. His second wife survived him by seven weeks. He had laid the foundations of a firm which, under his sons and grandsons, became the longest-surviving and possibly the largest of British photographic publishers. He was immediately succeeded by his sons William Dobson Valentine (1844–1907) and George Dobson Valentine (1852–1890). The main collection of James Valentine's photographs is in the Valentine archive in St Andrews University Library, but examples are also found in most general photograph collections in Britain and in many overseas.   R. N. SMART

Sources *Dundee Advertiser* (20 June 1879) · R. Smart, '"Famous throughout the world": Valentine & Sons Ltd., Dundee', *Review of Scottish Culture*, 4 (1988), 75–87 · R. Smart, 'James Valentine, 1859–79', *Mood of the moment: master works of photography from the University of St Andrews*, ed. M. Kemp (1995), 14–15 · directories, Dundee, 1809–79 · *Dundee Advertiser* (8 June 1838) · *Dundee Advertiser* (13 July 1855) · Dundee Public Library, Lamb MSS, 215 (2) · James Valentine advertising brochure, 1859, Dundee Public Library · *British Journal Photographic Almanac and Photographers Daily Companion* (1867), 100–01 · *British Journal of Photography* (12 Aug 1864), 295 · census returns for Dundee, 1841, 1851, 1861, 1871 · records of Castle Street Chapel, Dundee City Archives · records of Panmure Street Chapel, Dundee City Archives · index to Howff burial-ground, Dundee City Archives · burgess-roll, Dundee City Archives · m. reg. Scot. [J. Valentine and C. Marshall] · d. cert. · parish register (birth), 12 June 1815, Dundee · parish registers (births and baptisms), Dundee, 1790

[John Valentine and M. Watson] · parish registers (births and baptisms), Dundee, 1792 [John Valentine and M. Watson] · *The Call* (10 Nov 1868) [John Valentine] · parish register (birth), 1 Feb 1817, Glasgow Gorbals [R. Dobson] · tombstone(s?), Balgay cemetery, Dundee [James Valentine and Rachel Valentine]

Archives U. St Andr., collection

Likenesses T. Rodger, photograph, *c*.1855, U. St Andr., GDV Album 6.81 · Valentine Studio, cabinet photograph, *c*.1865, U. St Andr., GDV Album 1.8 · Valentine Studio, cabinet photograph, *c*.1865, U. St Andr., GDV Album 2.10 · Valentine Studio, photograph, *c*.1870, U. St Andr. · Valentine Studio, tinted print on bevelled glass, U. St Andr., Valentine archive [*see illus.*]

Wealth at death £4240 1*s*. 2*d*.: confirmation, 31 Oct 1879, *CCI*

Valentine, John (*bap*. 1730, *d*. 1791). *See under* Valentine family (*per. c*.1685–1845).

Valentine, Robert (*bap*. 1674). *See under* Valentine family (*per. c*.1685–1845).

Valera, Cipriano de (*c*.1532–*c*.1606), theologian and translator, was probably born in Valera la Vieja in the Badajoz province of Spain; he graduated in logic and philosophy from the University of Seville and then entered the monastery of the Observant Hieronymites at San Isidoro del Campo near Seville. In the 1550s monks at San Isidoro, including Cassiodoro de Reina, as well as Valera, were taking up a protestant position. Faced with an investigation by the Inquisition in 1557, Valera and fellow protestants fled to Geneva, where they joined the Italian church in the city but were later given a place of worship of their own. Following Elizabeth's accession, Valera left Geneva for England, where he probably joined the Spanish congregation which met under the ministry of Reina in the London church of St Mary Axe. He was incorporated as BA at Cambridge on 9 February 1560. A royal mandate of 12 January 1561 made him a fellow of Magdalene.

In Spain Valera was burnt in effigy by the Inquisition in April 1562 and he came to be listed in the Index as 'the Spanish heretic'. On 12 June 1563 at Cambridge he took the degree of MA, incorporated at Oxford on 21 February 1566. He served as college treasurer at Magdalene from 1564 to 1566, but between 1561 and 1568 he registered many more absences from college than any other fellow, and in 1568 he settled in London, where in January 1569 he was recorded as a member of the French protestant church. He married a woman named Anne, with whom he had a son, baptized Isaac, and two other children, one of them perhaps a daughter named Judith. He was listed as a schoolmaster in May 1571, and again in 1573, when he was named in the will of a Spanish refugee. He was poor, and he and his family received doles of money during the 1570s and early 1580s. By 1583 Valera, his wife, and son Isaac were recorded as members of the London Italian church and he was listed as a preacher in that year.

In 1588, the Armada year, Valera published his first work, the anti-Catholic *Dos tratados: el primo es del papa, ... el segundo es de la missa* ('Two treatises, the first on the pope, the second on the mass'). It is possible that the earl of Leicester was the patron for this work. The fact that London was omitted as the place of publication and the name of the English printer Hispanicized suggests that the book

was intended for import into Spain. In 1594 he published another *tratado* (*Tratado para confirmar los pobres cativos de Berveria en la catolica fe*) which, ostensibly intended to offer consolation to captives of the Barbary pirates, may have alluded to the persecution of religious dissidents in Spain. Some copies of this treatise also carry an attack, aimed at a Spanish-speaking readership, on bogus miracles that Valera alleged against the prioress of a convent in Lisbon. In 1596 came Valera's tribute to Calvin—a translation into Spanish of Calvin's *Catechism*—and in the same year his *El Testamento Nuevo de nuestro Señor Jesu Christo* (1596). This 'New Testament of our Lord Jesus Christ', with its publishing details once more concealed so as to reach a readership within Spain, was the first instalment of a revision of the Bible in Spanish published by Reina at Basel in 1569.

During the late 1590s Valera extended his work as a mediator of Calvinist protestantism in Spanish with his version of Calvin's *Institutes*, *Institucion de la religion Christiana*, published in London in 1597 and amended for Spanish readers. In 1599 he composed the preface for *Catholico reformado*, a Spanish translation of a work by William Perkins, and in 1600, anonymously, *Aviso a los de la iglesia Romana sobre la indiccion del jubileo*, an attack on the papal holy year then being celebrated in Rome. Finally he completed his revision of Reina, published in Holland as *La Biblia, que es los sacros libros del Vieio y Nueuo Testamento, segunda edicion, revisita y conferida con los textos Hebreos y Griegos y con diversas translaciones, por Cypriano de Valera* ('The Bible, that is, the holy books of the Old and New Testament, revised and compared with the Hebrew and Greek texts and with various translations', 1602). The publication costs may have been met by Prince Christian I of Anhalt-Bernberg; the work was dedicated to Count Maurice of Nassau, the stadholder of Holland. Valera travelled to Amsterdam in November 1602 to supervise the printing and went on to Middleburg, but most probably returned to London where he died, probably about 1606. His work on the Bible in Spanish can be considered his most lasting achievement.
                                                          MICHAEL MULLETT

Sources A. Ramírez, 'Un testimonio inedito de Cipriano de Valera', *Bibliothèque d'Humanisme et Renaissance*, 30 (1968), 145–6 · Venn, *Alum. Cant.*, 1/4.293 · A. G. Kinder, *Spanish protestants and reformers in the sixteenth century: a bibliography* (1983), 14, D12; 16, D39 · Wood, *Ath. Oxon.: Fasti* (1820), 169 · Foster, *Alum. Oxon., 1500–1714*, 3.1553 · A. G. Kinder, 'Further unpublished material and some notes on Cipriano de Valera', *Bibliothèque d'Humanisme et Renaissance*, 30 (1969), 169–71 · P. Collinson, *Archbishop Grindal, 1519–1583: the struggle for a reformed church* (1979), 144 · S. L. Greenslade, ed., *The Cambridge history of the Bible: the West from the Reformation to the present day* (1963), 128, 354 · A. G. Kinder, 'Cipriano de Valera, Spanish reformer (1532?–1602?)', *Bulletin of Hispanic Studies*, 46 (1969), 109–19

Valera, Eamon De (1882–1975), taoiseach and president of Éire, was born on 14 October 1882 at the Nursery and Child's Hospital, Lexington Avenue, New York. There is dispute about the details of his birth. He was the son of a Spanish father, Juan Vivion De Valera (1864/5?–1885?), variously described as an artist and a sculptor, and an Irish mother, Catherine Coll (*b*. 1856). Rumours that he was really the son of a local farmer in Ireland named Atkinson

Eamon De Valera (1882–1975), by Sir John Lavery, 1921

for whom his mother worked as a maidservant are unfounded—she left for America on 2 October 1879, three years before the birth of her son—but careful research has failed to discover any record of the marriage of De Valera and Catherine Coll. There is a discrepancy also in the baptismal record; he was christened Edward, but the name registered was George, and his authorized biography states that this was not altered to Eamon until he was under sentence of death in 1916, when his mother produced a copy of the certificate to prove his American citizenship. His place of birth, the Nursery and Child's Hospital, was, according to one biographer, a place for destitute and abandoned children: 'hardly the sort of place to leave a child if she had a home … in which to place it' (Coogan, 9). This question of De Valera's legitimacy recurred throughout his career, and was used by his enemies to discredit him. Juan Vivion De Valera (some records give his surname as De Valero, and his first names are occasionally transposed) disappeared from his son's life in 1885; the best calculation is that he died in the early part of that year at Denver, Colorado, where he had gone to seek medical advice (he was suffering from tuberculosis). In April 1885 Catherine's brother Ned Coll took the child to Ireland; she subsequently married Charles Wheelwright, a groom and a carriage driver, and settled at Rochester, New York.

Early career De Valera's childhood, spent at Bruree, co. Limerick, was marked by a lack of affection and the requirement to work hard around the farm—an experience very different from the rural idyll that he later recalled. He began his education in the grey schoolhouse in Bruree, where he was known as Eddie Coll, following the Irish custom of naming a child with no living or discernible father after the mother's maiden name. Subsequently he attended the Christian Brothers' Secondary School at Charleville, a significant establishment for the education of young boys into the nationalist version of the Irish past. In 1898 he was accepted into Blackrock College in Dublin, with a £20-a-year scholarship for three years. He was happy as a boarder there, thanking God for his deliverance from Bruree. Two years later he went to University College, Blackrock, an extension of the secondary school, and in 1903 entered Rockwell College as a mathematics lecturer, gaining a pass degree in mathematics in 1904 from the Royal University. He then took various teaching posts while living in Blackrock College. In 1908 he set out to learn Irish as a means of obtaining a post in the National University of Ireland. One of his teachers was Sinéad Flanagan (1878–1975), four years his senior, whom he married on 8 January 1910. The first of their seven children (five sons and two daughters) was born in 1911.

So far there was little to suggest that De Valera would follow a revolutionary career. But like many of his contemporaries he was drawn into politics by the dramatic events surrounding the battle over the third Home Rule Bill which the Liberal prime minister, H. H. Asquith, introduced into the House of Commons in April 1912. Irish unionists, spearheaded by Ulster unionists, vowed to resist home rule by all means necessary, and the Ulster unionists formed the Ulster Volunteer Force in 1913 to use force if need be. Nationalists replied on 25 November by forming the Irish Volunteers in which De Valera enlisted, thereby embarking on the rough and dangerous sea of Irish politics. He took part in the gun-running episode at Howth, co. Dublin, when both constitutional and volunteer leaders emulated the Ulster Volunteer Force's earlier adventure at Larne in April, and landed boatloads of arms from Germany. When, in September 1914, the leader of the Home Rule Party, John Redmond, followed up his support of the British war effort by urging the volunteers to fight 'wherever the firing line extends' (Coogan, 56), De Valera went with the minority who split from the movement in protest.

From the Easter rising to civil war, 1916–1923 De Valera took no part in planning the Easter rising of 1916, though he had risen through the ranks of the Irish Volunteers, being appointed to the 3rd division which was given the task of covering the Beggar's Bush military barracks. He was a member of the Irish Republican Brotherhood, but left after the rising, a decision which significantly affected his later career. His participation in the rising (in which he expected to be killed) caused him some personal anguish, and he wrote to his wife that he knew she would not think 'it was selfishness nor callous indifference or senseless optimism that made me so calm when I was about to offer up you and the children as sacrifice' (Coogan, 63). This was a turning point in their married life, for from now on De Valera became a public figure, a man frequently on the run, and a figure remote from his family. His wife, for her part, remained firmly in the background.

At the end of Easter week De Valera (who proved himself an effective commander) gave himself up to the British army, leaving his men to make their own surrender. Controversy dogged him over this decision, which he took to save his men from summary execution; he was also angry at the failure of the Dublin people to support the rebels. A military court sentenced him to death on 8 May, but this was commuted to penal servitude for life. De Valera was the only commandant to be spared execution, but this was not, as sometimes asserted, because of his American citizenship; the army merely felt that it had shot enough prisoners to set an example. In prison he showed the qualities of leadership that characterized his later career, combining the ability to be a good listener with a sense of authority. In June 1917 he was released under a general amnesty and in July he won the East Clare constituency for Sinn Féin. He appeared in his volunteer uniform but assured the voters that he had learned his nationalism 'listening to the sermons that were given by the patriotic priests' (Boyce, 315–16) and that Ireland did not need another Easter week. On 25 October he became president of Sinn Féin, as the candidate who could unite the supporters of the Irish Republican Brotherhood with Arthur Griffith's monarchical views of an Ireland with its king, lords, and commons. His skill at reconciling the apparently irreconcilable was demonstrated in the slogan he devised for the movement, which 'aims at securing the International recognition of Ireland as an independent Irish republic. Having achieved this status the Irish People may by referendum freely choose their own form of government' (Coogan, 96). Four days after the Sinn Féin convention he was elected president of the Irish Volunteers, now dominated by the Irish Republican Brotherhood, but he refused to rejoin, claiming that to do so would be to contradict his Catholic principles. Sinn Féin now rose to the ascendant, helped by the British effort to impose conscription on Ireland in April 1918, but De Valera was arrested in May and imprisoned in Lincoln gaol, from which he escaped in February 1919. Soon Ireland was engulfed in a war between the IRA and the crown forces, spearheaded by the Royal Irish Constabulary and the 'black and tan' recruits to the force. De Valera played no part in this conflict: he was in hiding until he left to gather support for the cause in the United States of America in June 1919, where he remained until December 1920, by which time the Better Government of Ireland Act which partitioned Ireland had completed its legislative process. His fortunes in America were mixed; he had no support from President Wilson, whose call for national self-determination could hardly be applied to the possessions of his wartime ally. But De Valera was a most successful fund-raiser, securing nearly $6 million through two issues of 'republican bonds', a larger sum of money than was raised in Ireland. He worked tirelessly to promote the Irish republican cause, though he provoked some consternation when he suggested that Ireland might have the same relationship with Britain as Cuba with the United States. He fell foul of rivalries in the Irish-American community, and his Cuban analogy alienated John Devoy's Clan na Gael. But overall his American visit was a success, especially in combating Lloyd George's attempts to equate Britain's fight for the union with that of the US federal government in its war on the confederacy. When he returned to Ireland he urged a more regular form of warfare, with battle offered by 'about 500 men on each side' (T. Ryle Dwyer, 47), in preference to ambushes, assassinations, and minor engagements. He claimed that Sinn Féin were not 'political doctrinaires' (ibid., 48) and assured Britain that a free Ireland would not threaten her security.

It is all the more surprising, therefore, that following a truce between the crown forces and the IRA in July 1921, De Valera should emerge over the next six months as the leading opponent of the compromise—dominion status for Ireland with certain safeguards for British defence—that Michael Collins and Arthur Griffith had negotiated with the British government by December. Moreover, while refusing to go to London in October (following preliminary sparring with Lloyd George in August) he tried to keep the negotiations in his hands. This made the task of the Irish plenipotentiaries more difficult, and left him open to the accusation that he knew a compromise must be accepted, but did not wish to be accused of 'betraying' the republic. De Valera claimed that he remained in Ireland to rally the nation should talks break down; but his failure to acknowledge the central point—that it was the acceptance of the invitation to treat that must lead to a compromise—and his denunciation of the signatories of the Anglo-Irish treaty of 6 December provoked the bitterness that soured a whole political generation—and succeeding ones. The problem was this: that De Valera had hit upon his own solution to the problem of reconciling imperialism and nationalism, his concept of 'external association', whereby Ireland would not be in the empire, but would be associated with it for certain purposes, such as foreign policy. This, he hoped, would find a common denominator that would maintain republican unity, which would in turn oblige the British government to reopen negotiations: a very doubtful prospect, despite the crumbling of Lloyd George's coalition. And there is no doubt that De Valera saw those who signed the treaty as having sold out and betrayed their country: 'When the Articles of Agreement were brought over here', he said, 'I felt as though the plague were being introduced into the country' (Garvin, 151). De Valera cannot be held responsible for the civil war that followed; the IRA would have split anyway. But he threw his whole political weight and prestige behind the enemies of the settlement, and his moralistic style was calculated to put the signatories in the dock, with De Valera acting as the conscience of the (republican) nation. The debate in the Dáil in December 1921 ended with the worst possible result: a victory for the pro-treatyites by sixty-four votes to fifty-seven, too narrow to be conclusive. Efforts to prevent divisions leading to civil war failed, and by June 1922 De Valera was on the path that seemed to lead into the political wilderness.

From civil war to government, 1922–1932 De Valera was rejected as president of the Dáil following the pro-treaty vote on 22 January 1922, but in September he assumed the role of president of the Irish republic on the invitation of the anti-treaty or 'irregular' forces. He played no significant part in the brutal fighting that characterized the war. As it petered out in summer 1923 he was again in prison, this time arrested by the free state when he appeared at an election rally in co. Clare in July 1923. He was released a year later, but his political instincts reasserted themselves. He knew that if he clung to the notion that the Irish state did not legally exist, then he and his followers would be marginalized by the fact that the state was 'the natural repository of popular power' (Bew, Hazelkorn, and Patterson, 28), and it was up to republicans to get hold of that repository. On 16 May 1926 he launched a new political party, Fianna Fáil ('Soldiers of destiny'), to lead the 'soldiers of the rearguard' (Coogan, 366). This led to an irrevocable breach with Sinn Féin, and the gap widened when De Valera insisted upon entering the Irish parliament (Dáil), subscribing—with mental reservations—to the oath of allegiance required of deputies, claiming that he had merely signed his name 'in the same way as I would sign an autograph in a newspaper' (T. Ryle Dwyer, 14). His decision was justified by events. In the general election of 1927 Fianna Fáil won forty-four seats; this total rose to seventy-two seats in 1932, when the party took office with Labour support. In 1933, with seventy-seven seats, Fianna Fáil formed a single-party government.

Political ascendancy De Valera was now entering his period of ascendancy in Irish politics. His party's success was founded on its appeal to the rural voter, especially the small farmer, but he also won support from labourers, especially through a scheme to build cottages for rural workers and married labourers. He created a formidable constituency organization, founded a newspaper, the *Irish Press*, and raised funds in America. But he confronted two major issues, both rising from his political past: his relationship with militant republicans, and with the Roman Catholic church. De Valera always praised the anti-treaty IRA as the salt of the political earth, and in May 1928 his colleague, Sean Lemass, described Fianna Fáil as a 'slightly constitutional party' (T. Ryle Dwyer, 344). Party members walked with the IRA to the hallowed grave of the republican hero, Theobald Wolfe Tone. But once in office De Valera emphasized that republicanism had come home, and that any other source of military force, besides that of the state, was no longer justified. He still hesitated to declare such a source illegal, but his government showed itself a stern enemy both of the threat from the right, in the shape of Eoin O'Duffy's quasi-fascist Blueshirt movement (really a pro-treaty offshoot raised to defend the threatened free state), and from dissidents in the IRA who now began to eye De Valera as a possible betrayer of the cause. However, his republicanism now took a more pragmatic form, as manifested in his drive to weaken the Anglo-Irish connection in the 1930s, and by his waging of an 'economic war' with Britain, sparked off by his refusal to repay moneys due from British funding of the land purchase acts of the late nineteenth and early twentieth centuries. His shifting of the state towards greater freedom helped him deal with his second great problem: what to do about the Roman Catholic church. De Valera admired Wolfe Tone; but he took his politics from Daniel O'Connell, who from the 1820s onwards had forged close bonds between nationalism and religion in Ireland. In 1933 his government taxed imported papers as a means of guarding against secular foreign influences; in 1935 it criminalized the sale of contraceptive devices; in preparing his constitution of 1937 he was careful to consult with Jesuits and other clerical advisers on what he eventually defined as the 'special position' of the Roman Catholic church as the faith professed by the vast majority of Irish citizens. The non-Catholic churches were satisfied with this wording, which reflected De Valera's tolerance, shown also in his ignoring of criticism from Cardinal Joseph MacRory and two Jesuits that the use of the term Church of Ireland was nothing less than the authoritative approval of lying propaganda. He dabbled with the idea of vocationalism; the constitution contained provision for the direct election of members of the Irish senate by any functional or vocational group, in substitution for an equal number of members elected in the manner otherwise prescribed. But this came to nothing and Catholic intellectuals throughout Europe abandoned the idea after the Second World War. In all this he contrived to show the hierarchy that he was a consultant of their views, not a conduit for them. And his courting of the church showed that De Valera combined hard-headed appreciation of where political power lay in Ireland, with a genuine vision of an Irish nation whose genius 'always stressed spiritual and intellectual rather than material values' (K. Mullarkey, 'Ireland, the pope and vocationalism: the impact of the encyclical Quadragesimo Anno', in Augusteijn, 105). His constitution of 1937 emphasized the centrality of the family in Irish life, which for him required the woman to stay at home and provide the stable centre for the stormy world of men (as his own wife had always done). Catholic culture also influenced the articles on private property, education, personal rights, and directive social principles.

These measures hardly endeared De Valera to Irish and especially to Ulster protestants. And it was this lacuna in his political thinking that later generations, bearing in mind the Ulster crisis that broke in 1968, have criticized. But this arose from his firm conviction that the nation state was indeed the best, the only, framework through which men (and he meant men) could lead the fullest, freest, most spiritual lives, the lives that God intended them to lead. This led him in 1934 to suggest that the solution to Ireland's minority problem was that Ulster unionists could be resettled in their British homeland, while Irish citizens living in Great Britain could replace them in Ireland: an expedient that neither group, arguably, would have found acceptable. He simply could not comprehend the unionist objection to his vision, and this was why his constitution of 1937 claimed that Ireland was a state encompassing the whole island, though temporarily deprived of the North. The real criticism of him lies in his attempt to whip up the partition issue for narrow political advantage; this, however, well illustrates the combination of visionary ideas and fighting instinct that characterized his political style.

De Valera's greatest test came between 1938 and 1945. He used Ireland's position in the League of Nations to warn of the dangers of international tension which could lead to war; and as the peace of Europe grew more fragile he was determined to keep Ireland out of the conflict. He won his most important concession in Anglo-Irish talks in 1938 when Neville Chamberlain, eager to appease Ireland and thus secure the United Kingdom's western flank, conceded sovereignty over the 'treaty ports', bases used by the Royal Navy under the terms of the 1921 agreement. When war broke out De Valera defended Irish neutrality, while inclining towards the British in matters such as the repatriation of air-force pilots who baled out over Irish soil. Yet, as in the past, his cautious political judgement seemed to desert him, when on hearing of the death of Hitler he offered his condolences through the German ambassador. This he later described as merely good diplomatic manners, but the gesture ignored the misery endured by Europe (including the German people) throughout the Nazi regime. However, he not only retrieved the situation; he responded to Winston Churchill's strictures on his 'frolicking with the Germans and later with the Japanese' in a broadcast on 17 June, in which he asked Churchill if he could not find it in his heart to acknowledge 'that there is a small nation that stood alone, not only for a year or two, but for several hundred years against aggression' (Coogan, 611). De Valera was now indeed the uncrowned king of Ireland, being celebrated as such in a street ballad of the day (O Faolain, 10)—and the inheritor of the mantle of that other 'chief', Charles Stewart Parnell.

Elder statesman, 1945–1975 From now on De Valera's mantle began to slip. He showed that he was still capable of winning elections—he lost power in 1948, but regained office in 1951 and in 1957 won an overall majority, the first since the election of 1944. But he suffered from discontent within his party as the new men, led by Sean Lemass, began to press for the modernization of economic policy. Emigration from Ireland had increased. There were allegations of corruption. His eyesight, which had not been good since the 1930s, worsened. He showed something of his old skills when, following the collapse of the Fine Gael-led coalition government in 1951 over the role of the Catholic church in state welfare policy, he introduced welfare measures while keeping the hierarchy on his side. In 1957 he interned IRA men engaged in a 'war' against Northern Ireland, again without conceding his republican credentials. Fianna Fáil showed that it could attract a wider constituency, appealing to businessmen and men of property, a kind of 'middle Ireland'. But De Valera suffered a humiliation in 1959 when he stood down as leader of the party and taoiseach and ran his campaign for the presidency of Ireland with a recommendation to the electorate to abandon proportional representation for the British 'first past

the post' system, which would have guaranteed Fianna Fáil almost permanent power. He was elected president, but his proposed electoral reform was rejected.

On 25 June 1959 De Valera was inaugurated as president. He held the office for nearly fourteen years, carrying out his ceremonial duties with his usual mixture of charm and dignity. In 1966 he visibly disturbed the new Fianna Fáil men at the Easter rising commemoration when he spoke of his dream of a Gaelic Irish nation. He was by now quite blind, but stood again for another term as president, which he held when the Northern Ireland crisis broke in 1968–9. Characteristically, his intervention was primarily motivated by his desire to save Fianna Fáil party unity rather than alleviate what was, admittedly, a predicament which no one could control. On 25 June 1973 he retired from public life. In January 1975 his wife died on the eve of their 65th wedding anniversary. In March he received the freedom of the city of Dublin, adding this to his many honours, including the order of Christ, bestowed on him by Pope John XXIII. He died in a Dublin nursing home, after a brief illness, on 29 August 1975. He was buried in Glasnevin cemetery on 2 September.

De Valera was a tall man, 6 feet 1 inch in height, and his athletic build (he had been a keen rugby player in his youth) and long back earned him the nickname the Long Fellow. Photographs and portraits reflect both his physical and political transformation from fiery young revolutionary to elder statesman. He was devout, and liked the company of Jesuits; but he made it clear that when he disagreed with his church, then his church was mistaken. This was his attitude to anyone with whom he disagreed. He was a dry, uninspiring orator, but his natural air of authority commanded attention and respect. He frequently resorted to casuistry, but his younger habit of making reckless statements gave way to a growing pragmatism and to political exigencies. He could be generous and he believed (and often with justification) that he meant well. He lacked any real understanding of Ulster unionists, despite an often sentimental attitude to them as sadly misguided members of the Irish nation.

Reputation De Valera's career has undergone considerable historiographical revision since the rather fulsome official biography written by the earl of Longford and Thomas P. O'Neill in 1970. A film *Michael Collins* (1996), directed by Neil Jordan, cast him in a particularly unfavourable light. But he was always a controversial political figure, and this was reflected in his anxiety to set the record straight; that is, to ensure that it portrayed him in more favourable terms. His chief contribution to Irish politics was to make Fianna Fáil the natural party of government, and to give it a sound democratic base which endured the storms of late twentieth-century Irish political life. But his ultimate purpose, to use this party to mould the Ireland that he dreamed of—Gaelic-speaking, rural, filled with comely maidens and athletic young men who would not succumb to the materialism of the modern world— remained, and remains, unfulfilled.

D. GEORGE BOYCE

Sources F. Pakenham, earl of Longford and T. P. O'Neill, *De Valera* (1974) · T. P. Coogan, *De Valera: long fellow, long shadow* (1993) · T. Ryle Dwyer, *De Valera: the man and the myths* (Dublin, 1991) · M. Laffan, *The resurrection of Ireland: the Sinn Féin Party, 1916–1923* (1999) · J. Bowman, *De Valera and the Ulster question, 1917–1973* (1982) · R. Fisk, *In time of war* (1983) · D. G. Boyce, *Nationalism in Ireland* (1995) · T. Garvin, *The evolution of Irish nationalist politics* (Dublin, 1981) · S. Faughnan, 'The Jesuits and the drafting of the Irish constitution of 1937', *Irish Historical Studies*, 26 (1988–9), 79–102 · D. Keogh, *Twentieth century Ireland* (Dublin, 1994) · P. Bew, E. Hazelkorn, and H. Patterson, *The dynamics of Irish politics* (1989) · M. C. Bromage, *De Valera and the march of a nation* (1967) · B. Farrell, *De Valera's constitution and ours* (Dublin, 1988) · J. Augusteijn, ed., *Ireland in the 1930s: new perspectives* (Dublin, 1999) · J. Steffan, *The long fellow: the story of the great Irish patriot* (1996) · S. O Faolain, *The life story of Eamon de Valera* (1933) · *DNB*

Archives Blackrock College, archives · Franciscan Library, Killiney, co. Dublin · NL Ire. · PRO, papers, CO 904 | HLRO, corresp. with David Lloyd George · NA Ire., departments of executive council, taoiseach, and foreign affairs · NL Ire., MSS of Frank Gallagher, Mary MacSwiney, Sean T. G. O'Kelly · NL Ire., letters to John L. Burke · PRO, Cabinet, Foreign Office and Dominions Office papers · University College, Dublin, MSS of Ernest Blyth, Desmond Fitzgerald, Sean McEntee, Patrick McGilligan | FILM RTE, Dublin, *The age of De Valera*, 1982 · RTE, Dublin, *The treaty*, 1991

Likenesses C. C. Bradshaw, oils, 1916, NG Ire. · photographs, 1917–18, Hult. Arch. · J. Lavery, oils, 1921, Hugh Lane Gallery, Dublin [*see illus.*] · S. O'Sullivan, drawing, 1931, NG Ire. · H. Coster, photographs, 1939, NPG · L. Whelan, oils, 1955, Commissioners of Public Works, Dublin · J. Connor, bronze bust, 1968, NG Ire. · B. Partridge, pen and ink, and watercolour caricature, NPG; repro. in *Punch Almanack* (1922) · B. Partridge, pen-and-ink caricature, NPG; repro. in *Punch* (4 Feb 1942) · photographs, repro. in Coogan, *De Valera*, following p. 16 · portrait, repro. in Pakenham and O'Neill, *De Valera*

Wealth at death £3185: probate, 11 Aug 1976, *CGPLA Éire*

Valerius Pansa, Gaius (*fl.* 120). *See under* Roman officials (*act.* AD 43–410).

Valette, (Pierre) Adolphe (1876–1942), painter, was born on 13 October 1876 at 28 rue de Roanne, St Étienne, France, the third son of Ferdinand Jean Baptiste Valette (*b.* 1846, *d.* before 1919), armourer and army captain, and Magdelaine Brondel (*b. c.*1847), seamstress, both from the Loire region, who married on 12 March 1872. Valette generally omitted Pierre from his signature: possibly he was called Adolphe at home to distinguish him from his paternal grandfather. In France, Valette's art is barely known but in England, particularly in Manchester where he resided for many years and produced his most important paintings, he is renowned for two reasons: first, for a remarkable series of impressionist views of the city, and second, for his influence on the painter L. S. Lowry.

From the age of fifteen Valette undertook commercial work to support his artistic studies. At L'École Régionale des Arts Industriels, St Étienne, where he studied from 1891 to 1895, he won prizes for drawing and was regarded as a brilliant pupil. He received further artistic awards in Lyons from 1896 to 1899 and, while studying at the École des Arts Decoratifs, Bordeaux, from 1901 to 1904, he gained a travelling scholarship. The outbreak of the Russo-Japanese war prevented Valette visiting Japan (Japanese art being fashionable at the time) so he came to England. He apparently enrolled at Birkbeck College, London,

although no records survive to confirm this. By November 1905 he was studying at the Manchester Municipal School of Art; the following year he became a teacher, principally of life drawing, at which he excelled. He retired from the school through illness in 1920. In 1928 he returned to France where he travelled and painted until his death.

Valette, who generally wore sombre suits and a hat, gave the impression of being tall and slender. His hair and eyes were dark and most self-portraits show him bearded. By nature he was modest and sensitive and he was a very popular teacher, revered for his knowledge and skill. His best-known pupil, L. S. Lowry, once expressed to John Rothenstein the importance of his influence:

> I cannot overestimate the effect on me at that time of the coming into this drab city of Adolphe Valette, full of the French Impressionists, aware of everything that was going on in Paris. He had a freshness and breadth of experience that exhilarated his students. (Rothenstein, 81)

Among his many pupils were James Fitton RA (1889–1982), David Ghilchick (1872–1974), later an illustrator for *Punch*, and Sam Rabin (1903–1991), a painter-sculptor turned wrestler. On 13 October 1909 Valette married a well-born Brazilian art student, Gabriela Louisa de Bolivar (1881/1886–1917). She was his favourite model until her early death from tuberculosis. Their only child, Peter (1910–1929), died from tuberculous meningitis while still an apprentice mercantile marine. On 1 October 1919 Valette married (Helena) Andrée Pallez (*c.*1878–1973), a lecturer in French at Manchester University. She helped to support him financially and after his death preserved much of his work.

Despite his heavy teaching commitments Valette's artistic output was considerable. Besides a vast number of academic studies, this comprises paintings, drawings, including pastel and watercolour, engravings, etchings, and lithographs. Valette experimented stylistically. His early figurative work shows symbolist influences while landscapes executed after his arrival in England are largely impressionist in style up to 1913. After this he adopted a loosely post-impressionist manner. Several early family portraits reflect the casual approach and intimate mood of the Nabis school, but later portraits show the influence of Augustus John and Sir William Orpen. The summit of Valette's career is a series of large impressionistic Manchester scenes painted from spontaneous, subtly toned Whistlerian studies made on the spot. Monumental in scale and carefully structured, they show an Edwardian city in a process of rapid change: trams and horse-drawn vehicles jostle side-by-side and in the twilight even rows of lights on tall commercial buildings glisten through a damp and foggy gloom and on the still canals. Valette's regular strokes of pigment applied to an unprimed canvas or over a tonal ground suggest forms disappearing into mist, fog, or drizzling rain, a favourite effect of Monet and other impressionists. Valette's decision to remain in Manchester perhaps originated in the city's affinities with the large commercial cities of Bordeaux and Lyons where he had previously studied and worked. These paintings were shown in a major exhibition of his work held in a Manchester furniture showroom in 1918. A further exhibition was held there in 1920. After his return to France, Valette contributed mainly to the salons in St Étienne and Lyons. He died in a French hospital on 18 April 1942. Manchester City Galleries holds the largest collection of his work, including eight Manchester scenes, a self-portrait, and a number of studies. A few examples of Valette's work can also be found in other museums and galleries in Salford, Preston, and Stockport, and in St Étienne and Roubaix in France.   SANDRA MARTIN

Sources S. Martin, *Adolphe Valette: a French influence in Manchester* (1994) [exhibition catalogue, Man. City Gall., 16 July – 4 Sept 1994] · [S. A. Martin], *Adolphe Valette* (1976) [exhibition catalogue, Man. City Gall., 6 Oct – 14 Nov 1976] · press cuttings and copies of cuttings, Man. City Gall. · private information (2004) · J. Rothenstein, *Modern English painters*, 2: *Lewis to Moore* (1956) · Archives Municipales, St Étienne, France · d. cert. [Gabriela Louisa de Bolivar] · m. cert. · *Manchester Guardian* (19 Aug 1942?)
Archives Man. City Gall. · Musée d'Art Moderne, St Etienne · Tib Lane Gallery, Manchester | Manchester Metropolitan University, records of Municipal School of Art | FILM Granada TV, Manchester, short film
Likenesses photographs, 1910, repro. in Martin, *Adolphe Valette* · A. Valette, self-portrait, crayon on paper, 1912, priv. coll. · A. Valette, self-portrait, oils, c.1912, priv. coll. · A. Valette, self-portrait, oil on linen, c.1914–1917, Man. City Gall. · A. Valette, self-portrait, oils, c.1920, Sefton Samuels collection · photographs, 1936–9, repro. in Martin, *Adolphe Valette* · A. Valette, three self-portraits, oils, priv. colls.

Valiente [*née* Dominy], **Doreen Edith** (1922–1999), witch, was born on 4 January 1922 at 1 High Street, Colliers Wood, Mitcham, Surrey, the daughter of Harry Dominy (*d.* in or before 1944), architect, and his wife, Edith Annie Richardson (*d.* 1964). Her father came from Cerne Abbas in Dorset, and she grew up in that county, retaining a strong Dorset accent throughout her life. Little is known of her upbringing, although she apparently attended a convent school until she was fifteen: in later years she regarded the lack of higher education as an intellectual asset, promoting independent thought. It was also important to her that she identified at an early age with witches, riding round the streets on a broomstick. When she was nine she had the first of many visions of a spirit world. By her late adolescence she was a practising clairvoyant, although her regular occupation was as a secretary. She was working as such in Cardiff when, on 31 January 1941, she married a merchant seaman, Joanis Vlachopoulos. Months later he went missing at sea, presumed dead. On 29 May 1944 she married Casimiro Valiente (1917/18–1972), a restaurant cook and refugee from the Spanish Civil War. After the end of the war the couple settled in Bournemouth.

Throughout this period, Doreen Valiente retained an interest in magic, reading voraciously and attending meetings of theosophists and spiritualists. In September 1952 she read an interview with the occultist Cecil Williamson in the magazine *Illustrated*, in which he claimed that witchcraft was still practised by covens in Britain. She wrote to him, and he passed her letter to Gerald Gardner, the publicist of the Wicca religion, the modern religion of pagan witchcraft. She was initiated at a house in Christchurch, Dorset, at midsummer 1953. She then joined Gardner's coven, which met in north London, and he rapidly utilized her talent for writing poetry and for ritual. During the next few years she produced some of the major works of Wicca, including the enduring version of the most important, *The Charge of the Goddess*. She also became high priestess of the coven, but quarrelled with Gardner in 1957 over what she thought was his excessive quest for publicity. She departed from the coven, taking a faction with her, which she ran as a separate group until the early 1960s. Her involvement with Wicca had produced a final strain upon her marriage, which was dissolved in the late 1950s, and she moved to Brighton near the end of that decade.

In 1962 Valiente published her first book, *Where Witchcraft Lives*, an account of past and present witchcraft in Sussex, in which she posed as a disinterested observer. The death of her Christian mother in 1964 enabled her to acknowledge her beliefs publicly, and she began to address local societies and write magazine articles openly as a witch. In 1964 she was made president of the first national body of modern witches, the Witchcraft Research Association, and joined the coven of Robert Cochrane, Britain's most prominent male witch after the death of Gardner. The collapse of both in 1966 led to a period of withdrawal, from which Valiente emerged in 1971 to encourage the foundation of a national pagan front, and then as the author of three important books, which established her as a public figure. In the first, *An ABC of Witchcraft Past and Present* (1973), she provided her own history of witchcraft; the second, *Natural Magic* (1975), was a handbook of practical magic; and the third, *Witchcraft for Tomorrow* (1978), was a book of ritual for witches who wished to set up their own covens.

In 1978 Valiente found domestic happiness with Ronald Cooke, who lived with her until his death in 1997. In 1989 she published *The Rebirth of Witchcraft*, a semi-autobiographical history of modern witchcraft, and the following year was co-author, with Evan John Jones, of *Witchcraft: a Tradition Renewed*, a handbook of pagan witchcraft based on Cochrane's tradition. She died from cancer in the Sackville Nursing Home, Sackville Road, Hove, on 1 September 1999 and was cremated at Brighton crematorium nine days later, with a Wiccan service; those arranging it had received 8000 messages from her admirers. She left her collection of books and magical artefacts to the Centre for Pagan Studies at Maresfield, Sussex, of which she had been patron. A strong-minded, independent, and modest person, of striking integrity and creative power, Doreen Valiente deserves the title of mother of modern pagan witchcraft.   RONALD HUTTON

Sources D. Valiente, *The rebirth of witchcraft* (Phoenix, 1989) · Gerald Gardner papers, priv. coll., Toronto · Doreen Valiente papers, priv. coll., Sussex · Doreen Valiente papers, priv. coll., Surrey · personal knowledge (2004) · private information (2004) · *The Times* (27 Sept 1999) · *Daily Telegraph* (10 Sept 1999) · *The Independent* (20 Sept 1999) · b. cert. · m. cert. [Casimiro Valiente] · d. cert. · www.doreenvaliente.com
Archives priv. colls.

Likenesses photograph (in old age), repro. in *The Times* · photograph (in old age), repro. in *Daily Telegraph* · photograph (in old age), repro. in *The Independent*

Wealth at death under £200,000—gross; under £70,000—net: probate, 1 Nov 1999, *CGPLA Eng. & Wales*

Vallance, (Gerald) Aylmer (1892–1955), journalist, was born at Partick in Lanarkshire on 4 July 1892, the son of a shawl manufacturer, George Henry Vallance, and his wife, Agnes Felton. Although baptized George Alexander Gerald, he later changed his names to Gerald Aylmer. His educational achievements were exceptional. He won an open scholarship to Edinburgh's leading public school, Fettes College, where his academic prowess earned him a succession of prizes. As head boy Vallance crowned his school career by winning an open classical scholarship to Balliol College, where he gained a first in classical moderations (1913). The outbreak of the First World War prevented him from completing his studies. He was commissioned in the Somerset light infantry—by some accounts because he was too drunk to realize he had enlisted—and was posted to India. He was transferred to the intelligence corps in 1915, and allegedly played the 'great game' in the Himalayas. The former classicist had discovered a natural aptitude for soldiering. He graduated from Staff College at Quetta in 1917, and ended the war as brigade-major of the 2nd Indian division. Mature beyond his years, and with little incentive to re-enter the ivory tower, Vallance looked to a post where he could draw upon his fascination with economics as well as his obvious administrative skills. Thus, from 1919 to 1928 he held the post of general secretary of the National Maritime Board, while at the same time beginning to write on financial matters.

Vallance's reputation as a freelance writer grew, as did the range of topics he was prepared to tackle. An attractive and affable character, always identifiable in a crowd by his height and large pointed beard (a later nickname was 'the Admiral'), the bespectacled Vallance became a familiar sight in Fleet Street. He was thus already known as a journalist when, in 1929, Sir Walter Layton invited him to leave commerce and join *The Economist*, where he became assistant editor. In 1930 Layton became chairman of the board of the *News Chronicle*, a mid-market newspaper born out of the old and by now obsolete Liberal dailies. He made increasing use of Vallance in creating a popular and genuinely independent alternative to the more Conservative *Daily Mail* and the *Daily Express*. The remoulding and remarketing of the *News Chronicle* was taking too long, so in 1933 Vallance became editor, making an immediate impact. Decisive, well-organized, and experienced in handling even the prickliest of editorial or printing personnel, Vallance quickly learned how to put a paper to bed *and* dine well at the Savoy Grill. He then focused upon recruiting fresh talent. Vernon Bartlett, already well known on the wireless, found a new home with the *News Chronicle* after being sacked by the BBC, while Gerald Barry applied proven talent as an editor to the features desk. Younger writers later enjoyed distinguished careers elsewhere in Fleet Street or inside the BBC, the Design Council, and other similarly august bodies. Vallance placed

great store on his paper's coverage of the City and of industry, establishing a reputation for incisive reporting and coverage that lasted long after his enforced resignation early in 1936.

As an editor—ironically the only post he ever held in the newspaper industry—Vallance operated with quiet efficiency, while at the same time ensuring that the *News Chronicle* acquired a much sharper political edge, witness its deep antipathy towards the British Union of Fascists. Old Liberal loyalties were in effect abandoned, and the post-1931 rebirth of the Labour Party welcomed. This increasingly antagonized those directors who remained loyal to the Liberal cause; no less shocking were the stories of their editor's sexual exploits. Vallance's undisguised glee at the Liberals' losses in the 1935 general election, when added to his notoriety as a heavy drinker and an office philanderer, left Layton with no alternative but to accede to the board's insistence on dismissal.

Vallance's editorship of the *News Chronicle* proved to be the high point of his career. In 1937 he joined the *New Statesman* as assistant editor to Kingsley Martin, and stayed there until his death nearly twenty years later. Not that Vallance's relationship with Martin was always harmonious. By the early fifties an outstanding debt had generated much ill will, with Martin increasingly critical of his colleague's chaotic personal finances and complicated private life. Nevertheless, in his memoirs Martin was generous in his praise of an unusual personality whose intellect and intelligence were matched by a wide range of practical skills: a typical weekend in the thirties would see Vallance drive north to a castle leased in the borders, fly fish for trout and then cook his catch, find time to work on his next book, entertain his travelling companion, and be back in London in time to chair an editorial conference first thing on Monday morning. When not writing on the great issues of the day, Vallance drew upon a myriad of hobbies and interests in order to entertain his readers. Ironically, despite his own financial misfortunes, Vallance was always a shrewd commentator on money matters, and this extended to his two most significant inter-war books: *The Centre of the World* (1935—about the City of London) and *Hire-Purchase* (1939).

Vallance was an important counterweight to Kingsley Martin, always remaining calm under pressure, endeavouring to ensure editorial consistency, encouraging a collegial atmosphere within the Great Turnstile offices, and invariably offering sound advice. Only rarely did Vallance's personal politics, increasingly sympathetic to the Communist Party, get the better of him, and then even Martin would tremble at his assistant's highly convincing prediction of capitalism's imminent demise.

Vallance relished playing Cassandra whenever his editor was in earshot, and a return to uniform in 1939 offered endless opportunities. As a lieutenant-colonel in the War Office, Vallance resumed intelligence work, liaising with the press in a news management role. In addition he wrote several pamphlets for the Army Bureau of Current Affairs. Vallance still wrote regularly for the *New Statesman*—anonymously, but no doubt with War Office approval. However, there is evidence to suggest that ano-nymity offered the opportunity to complement pro-allied propaganda with items which Vallance's superiors would most certainly not have sanctioned. Thus, the *New States-man* during and after the Second World War consistently supported the communists in Yugoslavia, and indeed Vallance named his son after Tito. Similarly, the assistant editor must shoulder much of the responsibility for a widely shared view that after 1945 his paper was too willing for too long to give Stalin the benefit of the doubt.

As an editor Vallance was the consummate professional, never allowing his private life to undermine the quality of his work. He applied the same high level of efficiency and enthusiasm to whatever job he was asked to undertake, and he rarely made enemies. Good humoured, genuinely funny, and ever ready to entertain with an anecdote from an exciting and eventful life, he was always capable of bringing out the best in his colleagues, many of whom owed their careers to his early tutelage.

Vallance was married three times. His first wife was Phyllis Taylor Birnstingl, the daughter of J. K. Reid of Edgbaston and a widow with two daughters. The marriage lasted from 1928 until it was dissolved in 1940. Vallance then married Helen, divorced wife of J. R. H. Chisholm and the daughter of Philip Gosse, a medical practitioner. This second marriage produced one son and one daughter, but again ended in divorce. Finally, in 1950 Vallance married Ute Christina Fischinger, the daughter of Max Ferdinand Fischinger, a German army officer. In his last five years Vallance was beset by creditors and bedevilled by illness, but he enjoyed a rare period of domestic stability. After a lifetime of sexual adventures he died in London, on 24 November 1955, a happily married man.

ADRIAN SMITH

Sources G. Cox, 'The editor who made love — and great news', *British Journalism Review*, 7/3 (1996), 16–24 • C. H. Rolph, *Kingsley: the life, letters and diaries of Kingsley Martin* (1973) • E. Hyams, *The 'New Statesman': the history of the first fifty years, 1913–1963* (1963) • K. Martin, ed., *Editor: a second volume of autobiography, 1931–1945* (1968) • *DNB* • I. Elliott, ed., *The Balliol College register, 1900–1950*, 3rd edn (privately printed, Oxford, 1953) • *CGPLA Eng. & Wales* (1956)
Archives BL, corresp. with Society of Authors, Add. MS 56838
Wealth at death £6443 7s. 2d.: administration, 6 March 1956, *CGPLA Eng. & Wales*

Vallance, William Fleming (1827–1904), landscape and marine painter, was born at Paisley on 13 February 1827, the youngest son in the family of six sons and one daughter of David Vallance, tobacco manufacturer, and his wife, Margaret Warden. William, whose father died in William's childhood, was sent at a very early age to work in a weaver's shop; but on the family's subsequent removal to Leith he was apprenticed in 1841 as a carver and gilder to Messrs Aitken Dott in Edinburgh. During his apprenticeship he began to draw, and made a little money by drawing chalk portraits; but he was twenty-three before he received any proper instruction. He then worked for a short time in the Trustees' Academy under E. Dallas, and later, from 1855, he studied under Robert Scott Lauder. Vallance first exhibited at the Royal Scottish Academy in 1849, but it was not until 1857 that he took up art as a profession.

On 2 January 1856 Vallance married in Edinburgh Elizabeth Mackie Bell (b. c.1834), daughter of James Bell; they had two sons and six daughters. His earlier work had been chiefly portraiture and genre. After 1870 he painted, principally in co. Wicklow, Connemara, and co. Galway, a series of pictures of Irish life and character, humorous in figure and incident, and fresh in landscape setting. In the 1870s he also travelled to the south of France and Italy where the intensity of Mediterranean light made an impact on his work, for example, *Venice* (1877; Perth Museum and Art Gallery). But a year or two spent in Leith in childhood had left its impress on his mind, and it was as a painter of the sea and shipping that he was eventually best-known. His first pictures of this kind hovered between the Dutch convention and the freer and higher-pitched art of his own contemporaries and countrymen. Gradually the influence of the latter prevailed, and in such pictures as his Royal Scottish Academy diploma work *Reading the War News* (1871; Royal Scottish Academy, Edinburgh), *The Busy Clyde* (1880), and *Knocking on the Harbour Walls* (1884) he attained a certain charm of silvery lighting, painting with considerable, if somewhat flimsy, dexterity. Probably, however, his feeling for nature found its most vital expression in the watercolours, often in body colour, which he painted out of doors. He made extensive studies of the sea and sky, and in the 1860s accompanied William McTaggart to Cadzow Forest, Lanarkshire.

Vallance was elected associate of the Royal Scottish Academy in 1875, and became an academician in 1881. Towards the end of his life he suffered from ill health which restricted his productivity. He was admitted to the asylum in the parish of Lasswade, Edinburgh, where he died on 30 August 1904. He was buried in Newington cemetery in Edinburgh on 3 September 1904 and was survived by his wife and family.

J. L. CAW, rev. JOANNA SODEN

Sources private information (1912) • *Glasgow Evening News* (1888) • *The Scotsman* (1 Sept 1904) • *Annual Report of the Council of the Royal Scottish Academy of Painting, Sculpture, and Architecture*, 77 (1904), 11–12 • C. B. de Laperriere, ed., *The Royal Scottish Academy exhibitors, 1826–1990*, 4 vols. (1991), vol. 4, pp. 353–6 • J. L. Caw, *Scottish painting past and present, 1620–1908* (1908), 263 • P. J. M. McEwan, *Dictionary of Scottish art and architecture* (1994), 584 • Bryan, *Painters* (1909–10), 5.230 • J. Halsby and P. Harris, *The dictionary of Scottish painters, 1600 to the present*, 2nd edn (1998), 225 • Royal Scot. Acad. • m. cert. • d. cert.
Archives Royal Scot. Acad., letter collection
Likenesses J. B. Abercromby, wash drawing, 1898, Scot. NPG • J. Moffat, photograph, Royal Society of Arts, Edinburgh • Messrs Nesbit & Lothian, photograph, Royal Society of Arts, Edinburgh • J. Pettie, chalk drawing (as young man); in possession of his widow, 1912

Vallancey, Charles (c.1726–1812), antiquary and military surveyor, was born in Flanders of French Huguenot parents (the name was originally De Vallance) who had moved to Windsor after his father was appointed to the royal service. Educated at Eton College and the recently established Royal Military Academy at Woolwich, he was commissioned as an ensign in the 10th regiment of foot in

1747. About 1750 his regiment was sent to Ireland, where he remained for the rest of his life. He acquired a sound technical knowledge of his profession, translating two French works as *Essay on Fortification*, published in 1757, and *The Field Engineer* (1758), and he took part in the action to repel the landing of Thurot at Carrickfergus in February 1760. But official recognition and promotion came slowly. On 26 January 1762, as Captain Vallancey, he transferred to the engineers as the second military engineer (engineer-in-ordinary) in the Irish service. The position of first engineer at that time was a purchased sinecure, a source of professional frustration to Vallancey, and it was not until 1793 that he became director of engineers with the rank of major-general. He was promoted lieutenant-general in 1798 and general in 1803, and was then generously allowed to retire on full pay.

In 1769 Vallancey reported on the ruinous state of Irish coastal defences and embarked on a major programme of map-making and a detailed military survey which was, however, still unfinished when he retired. In this work he was particularly encouraged by Lord Townshend, the lord lieutenant, his contemporary at Eton and a former soldier who respected his abilities and tried to obtain a pension to help support his wife and ten children. Eventually a pension was paid to his four marriageable daughters and gratuities were awarded in 1776, 1781, and 1786, together with additional pay to support his survey work. He designed the fortifications in Cork harbour in the 1780s, and was put in command of them in 1790, claiming after the French landing at Bantry Bay that his shore defences had kept the invader away from Cork. In 1798 he drew up a scheme for the defence of Dublin in the event of rebellion.

But Vallancey was actually much more interested in the ancient past. His survey work had brought him into fascinated contact with passage graves, stone forts, and other Irish antiquities. Since he knew little Irish, at least to begin with, he worked closely with patriotic Irish-speaking scholars such as Theophilus O'Flanagan and Charles O'Conor who copied and translated manuscripts for him, sharing and sometimes disciplining his rather uncritical enthusiasm for the ancient glories of Irish civilization. This collaboration coincided with the general revival of interest in the Celtic past, stimulated by Mac-Pherson's *Ossian* (1760). In 1772 the Royal Dublin Society established an antiquities committee, of which Vallancey was joint secretary. This was followed in 1785 by the inauguration of the Royal Irish Academy, of which he was a founder member. His most enduring contribution to Irish scholarship was to help the academy acquire the Book of Lecan in 1787 and to purchase for it the Leabhar Breac ('Speckled book') in 1789, two of the great fifteenth-century manuscript compilations of ancient materials.

Vallancey's own far-flung antiquarian researches led to a long series of eccentric and disorganized publications, including *An essay on the antiquity of the Irish language: being a collation of Irish with the Punic language* (1772), *A Vindication of the Ancient History of Ireland* (1786), and the compendious *Collectanea de rebus Hibernicis* (1770–1804), in which he argued obsessively on the basis of often dubious philological, historical, mythological, and archaeological evidence for an ultimately Eastern, possibly Phoenician or Persian, origin for ancient Irish civilization, brought to Ireland by Indo-Scythian migration. Although he became a fellow of the Royal Society in 1784, and the politician Henry Flood wanted him to be the first holder of an endowed chair of Irish at Trinity College, Dublin, many of his contemporaries were sceptical of his scholarly judgement and Phoenician fantasies. The great orientalist Sir William Jones, who gave him assistance with Indian matters, privately thought his work 'very stupid' (Jones, 2.768). But, despite his frequent absurdities, his local observations and collections of manuscript material and his capacity to energize others to get things done laid the foundations for major advances in the study of Irish prehistory and mythology in the century after his death. He was often wrong-headed, but not always wrong. Modern scholarship has given him some credit for anticipating more scientific theories of Indo-European culture and for realizing the value of myth as a form of historical evidence. He was probably wrong in claiming evidence of Mithraism at the ancient burial site at Newgrange but right in assuming connections with sun worship. His last published work, *An Account of the Ancient Stone Amphitheatre Lately Discovered in the County of Kerry* (1812), wrongly identifies Staigue Fort as an amphitheatre, adducing irrelevant Indian parallels, but rightly assigns it to a very early period. Vallancey who, according to J. H. Andrews, married four times, died in Dublin on 8 August 1812.

NORMAN VANCE

Sources J. H. Andrews, 'Charles Vallancey and the map of Ireland', *GJ*, 132 (1966), 48–61 · C. O'Halloran, 'An English orientalist in Ireland: Charles Vallancey (1726–1812)', *Forging in the smithy*, ed. J. Leerssen and others (1995), 161–73 · *DNB* · *Belfast Magazine*, 11 (1813), 297–300 · J. Millar, *List of all the officers in the horse dragoons and foot, on the Irish establishment for 1755* (1755) · *List of general and field officers, 1754–1868* (1754–1868) · *The letters of Sir William Jones*, ed. G. Cannon, 2 vols. (1970) · *The manuscripts and correspondence of James, first earl of Charlemont*, 2 vols., HMC, 28 (1891–4) · J. Redington and R. A. Roberts, eds., *Calendar of home office papers of the reign of George III*, 3: 1770–1772, PRO (1881) · *The correspondence of Thomas Percy and John Pinkerton*, ed. H. H. Wood (1985), vol. 8 of *The Percy letters*, ed. C. Brooks, D. N. Smith, and A. F. Falconer (1944–88) · T. Ó Raifeartaigh, *The Royal Irish Academy: a bicentennial history, 1785–1985* (1985) · *GM*, 1st ser., 82/2 (1812), 289–91

Archives Harvard U., Houghton L., Irish MSS · Royal Irish Acad., scientific notebooks | BL, Add. MSS · BL, unpublished 'Essay on military surveys' (1779) presented to King, Map Room MSS · Hunt. L., letters to Charles O'Conor · NRA, corresp. with Sir Joseph Banks · PRO NIre., corresp. with John Foster, D 207/96 · TCD, letters to Joseph Cooper Walker

Likenesses G. Chinnery, oils, c.1800, Royal Irish Acad. · attrib. H. D. Hamilton, pastel on paper, NG Ire. · portrait, Royal Irish Acad.; repro. in Raifeartaigh, ed., *The Royal Irish Academy* · stipple (after G. Chinnery), NG Ire.; repro. in C. Vallancey, *Collectanea de rebus Hibernicis*, 6 vols. (1804)

Vallans, William (*fl. c.*1577–1590), poet, was born in Hertfordshire, the son of John Valans, to whom the author addressed the tailpiece (from internal evidence composed *c.*1577) to his influential river-poem *A tale of two swannes: wherein is comprehended the original and increase of the river Lee, commonly called Ware-river* (1590). Vallans's preface explains that he is publishing the poem in order to 'make better known to the world, my countrie or place of byrth'; and to 'encourage those worthy Poets, who have written *Epithalamion Thamesis*, to publish the same'. The reference is thought to be to Edmund Spenser's projected work of that name, 'long since … promised', which he described in a letter to Gabriel Harvey published in 1580; and to William Camden's 'De connubio Tamae et Isis'—a Latin work scattered through successive editions of his *Britannia* (1586–1607).

Vallans's likening of his work to a swansong, 'being fully resolved to leave my country', has never been satisfactorily explained. It is illustrated by a quotation from Thomas Watson's *Amyntas* (1585) alongside Abraham Fraunce's translation from *The Lamentations of Amyntas* (1587). The poem, a chorographical blank-verse description of Hertfordshire, is the earliest extant river-marriage poem in English, predating Spenser's *Epithalamion* (1596), the related sequence in *The Faerie Queene* (IV.xi.9–53), and Michael Drayton's *Polyolbion* (1612–22). Its formal device (the journey to London of 'two Cignets of esteeme') is developed from that of *Cygnea cantio* (1545) by John Leland, a copy of whose *Naeniae* (1545) Vallans owned. His antiquarian scholarship is revealed in an explanatory 'Commentarie' that includes specific praise (as 'a diligent searcher and preserver of antiquities') for John Stow—the 'good aged … cytezyn' to whom the manuscript poem by 'Wm Vallans Salter' (dated 1582; BL, Harley MS 36780, fol. 129) is apparently addressed ('what payns to seeke old wrytten bookes').

No relevant records of the Salters' Company survive, but Vallans's literary career seems to have been established by 1578, when he supplied commendatory verses to John Wharton's invective against usury, *Whartons Dream*. Thomas Hearne reprinted *A Tale of Two Swannes* in his edition of Leland's *Itinerary* (vol. 5, 1711), from what seems its sole surviving copy (annotated by Thomas Rawlinson), and there suggested Vallans's authorship of *The Honourable Prentice* (1615), a slim collection of historical narratives in prose by 'W. V.' (including an account of the medieval mercenary Sir John Hawkwood), 'composed some few yeeres since, for my owne recreation', and dedicated to his 'respected friend' Robert Valens. W. V.'s identity remains conjectural, as does the relevance of the marriage of a William Valence to Martha Potts, at St Dunstan-in-the-West, London, on 4 October 1576, probably the same man as was buried there 'out of Lincolnes Inne' on 24 December 1601.   NICK DE SOMOGYI

Sources J. B. Oruch, 'Spenser, Camden, and the poetic marriages of rivers', *Studies in Philology*, 64 (1967), 606–24 · C. G. Osgood, 'Spenser's English rivers', *Transactions of the Connecticut Academy of the Arts and Sciences*, 23 (1920), 65–108 · *The itinerary of John Leland the antiquary*, ed. T. Hearne, 5 (1711) · T. P. Roche, *The kindly flame: a study of the third and fourth books of Spenser's 'Faerie Queene'* (1964), esp. 167–84 · E. Brydges, *Restituta, or, Titles, extracts, and characters of old books in English literature*, 4 vols. (1814–16), vol. 4, pp. 444–5 · T. Warton, *The history of English poetry*, new edn, 3 vols. (1840) · L. Bradner, *Musae Anglicanae: a history of Anglo-Latin poetry, 1500–1925* (1940) · J. Hunter, 'Chorus Vatum Anglicanorum: collections concerning the poets and verse-writers of the English nation', 1843, BL, Add. MS 24488, 186–7
Archives BL, Harley MS 367, fol. 129

Valognes, Hamo de [Hamo fitz Geoffrey] (*d.* 1202/3), justiciar of Ireland, was the son of Geoffrey de Valognes, lord of one of the two manors of Titsey in Surrey. In 1086 Titsey had been held by Hamo the sheriff, and was subsequently inherited by his niece Mabel, who married Robert, earl of Gloucester (*d.* 1147). Hamo de Valognes began his career as a prominent seigneurial official in the household of Robert's son, William, earl of Gloucester. He appears frequently in charters in his capacity as the earl's constable, an office he occupied at least as early as 1158. That he was an important member of the earl's household is apparent from the order of witnesses in numerous charters, where he ranked second to the seneschal, Richard of Kardif, Countess Hawisia, or Robert, brother of the earl. Valognes was therefore a tested and experienced official when he entered the service of John, lord of Ireland, when the latter became earl of Gloucester in 1189.

It was thus likely that John would make use of Valognes's experience in his expanding Irish lordship. He was a witness in an important grant of land in Uriel to Peter Pipard in 1193, and must have been well versed in Irish affairs when John appointed him as his justiciar of Ireland, following the restoration of that lordship by King Richard in 1195. John entrusted Valognes with the task of enforcing his claim to the custody of episcopal temporalities during vacancies, even when they lay within the territories of the great liberties. Some such policy must have underlain the seizure of the see of Leighlin in the liberty of Leinster by Valognes, probably in 1197, in order to prevent the bishop-elect's consecration, perhaps on the grounds that the bishop had not sworn fealty in respect of the temporalities of the see. Since neither Henry II nor John appears to have exercised the royal right in regard to temporalities existing within the liberties before Valognes intervened, the dispute was bound to create a conflict between church and state. In September 1198 Innocent III admonished John in the severest terms for the actions of his justiciar in preventing the consecration of the bishop-elect, and in compelling John Cumin, archbishop of Dublin, to seek refuge in exile in Normandy. Innocent seems to link the Leighlin episode with the exile, which suggests that the archbishop had—understandably in the circumstances—failed to recognize John's claims in regard to the see. Thus began a bitter dispute in which Valognes was excommunicated and the see of Dublin placed under interdict by the archbishop. But neither Innocent's pointed reference to the fate of King Uzziah, who was stricken with leprosy for disregarding the privileges of the priesthood (2 Chronicles, 26: 18–20), nor the reports of a miraculously bleeding crucifix rescued by the archbishop from his cathedral, made the slightest impression on John or King Richard. Eventually John partially relented in deference to repeated pleas from the pope to allow the old archbishop to return after seven years in exile, but he never yielded on the issues in dispute.

Perhaps as a measure to cool the situation Valognes was

succeeded as justiciar by Meiler fitz Henry before John's accession to the throne in 1199, but not before he had surveyed the lands and liberties of the archbishopric of Armagh. This suggests that John sought to extend his royal prerogatives in relation to the primatial see as in the case of Leighlin. Valognes's justiciarship clearly marks a decisive advance in the definition of church–state relations in Ireland by regarding all bishops as tenants-in-chief in respect of their temporalities. His retirement from office enabled him to be reconciled to the archbishop by means of a suitable gift of land 'for the injuries and wrongs done to the church of Dublin by him and his when he was justiciar of Ireland' (McNeill, 27). He continued to enjoy royal favour, receiving from the king the grant of the lordship of Askeaton in Limerick in September 1199, followed by a commission as sheriff of Cambridge and Huntingdon three months later. The Irish lordship was a significant addition to the lands he already held of the earl of Gloucester in Surrey and Kent. However, he had to surrender his offices by royal command on 30 March 1202 when illness rendered him too feeble to conduct his duties. He died before 27 May 1203, when Hugh de Neville was granted custody of his lands and his sons. His son and heir, Hamo, eventually acquired seisin of Askeaton in 1215, which suggests that he was only nine years old when his father died.   C. A. EMPEY

Sources *Chronica magistri Rogeri de Hovedene*, ed. W. Stubbs, 4, Rolls Series, 51 (1871), vol. 4 · M. P. Sheehy, ed., *Pontificia Hibernica: medieval papal chancery documents concerning Ireland, 640–1261*, 2 vols. (1962–5) · T. D. Hardy, ed., *Rotuli chartarum in Turri Londinensi asservati*, RC, 36 (1837) · H. S. Sweetman and G. F. Handcock, eds., *Calendar of documents relating to Ireland*, 5 vols., PRO (1875–86), vol. 1 · R. B. Patterson, ed., *Earldom of Gloucester charters* (1973) · T. D. Hardy, ed., *Rotuli de oblatis et finibus*, RC (1835) · T. D. Hardy, ed., *Rotuli litterarum patentium*, RC (1835) · C. McNeill, ed., *Calendar of Archbishop Alen's register, c.1172–1534* (1950) · E. Curtis, ed., *Calendar of Ormond deeds*, IMC, 1: *1172–1350* (1932) · H. G. Richardson and G. O. Sayles, *The administration of Ireland, 1172–1377* (1963) · M. Murphy, 'Balancing the concerns of church and state: the archbishops of Dublin, 1181–1228', *Colony and frontier in medieval Ireland: essays presented to J. F. Lydon*, ed. T. B. Barry and others (1995), 41–56 · C. A. Empey, 'The settlement of the kingdom of Limerick', *England and Ireland in the later middle ages: essays in honour of Jocelyn Otway-Ruthven*, ed. J. Lydon (1981) · *VCH Surrey*, vol. 4

Valognes, Philip de (d. 1215), administrator, was the third of five sons of Roger de Valognes (d. c.1141), lord of the English honour of Valognes, centred upon Bennington, Hertfordshire, and his wife, Agnes, who can safely be identified as a daughter of John fitz Richard, lord of Saxlingham, Norfolk. Philip's elder brothers, Peter (d. 1158) and Robert (d. 1184), succeeded in turn to the family's English estates, originally acquired soon after 1066 by their Norman grandfather. Agnes was a sister of Eustace fitz John, a notable ally of David I of Scotland, and Peter married a niece of Ada de Warenne, David's daughter-in-law. Philip was therefore well placed to embark on a Scottish career with his younger brother Roger, who eventually became lord of East Kilbride, Lanarkshire. Almost immediately after arriving in Scotland, Philip de Valognes became chief chamberlain of King William the Lion and served as such from 1165 to c.1171 and again from c.1193 to the king's

death (4 December 1214). Early in 1215 Alexander II reappointed him, and he died in office.

The chamberlain of Scotland was the crown's principal financial officer, and there is a tantalizing reference in a later inventory of Scottish records, made in 1296, to a roll of accounts, apparently dating from 1201–15, which began with the heading 'the twentieth account of Philip ...' The surname is unrecoverable; but it seems likely that Philip de Valognes's tenure of the chamberlainship gave a new impetus to administrative centralization in Scotland, through the introduction of a court of audit to watch over and maximize royal revenues. His services, however, were by no means limited to the fiscal sphere. A leading confidant of King William, he was almost constantly at his side, and remained a key member of the royal household even while the chamberlainship was held by Walter of Berkeley (c.1171–c.1193). In December 1174 Valognes was one of the magnates of Scotland required to find hostages under the treaty of Falaise. About this time he was defeated by William (I) Marshal at a tournament in Maine, though not before impressing as the best Scottish knight on the field. He probably campaigned with William the Lion in Moray and Ross in 1179, and in 1209 he was employed in Scottish negotiations with King John of England. Accusations that Walter of St Albans had bribed him to procure Walter's appointment in 1207 as bishop of Glasgow were investigated by the papacy in 1219. The rewards of royal service brought Valognes grants of Benvie and Panmure in Angus and Ringwood in Roxburghshire. He gained Torpenhow, Cumberland, from the lord of Galloway, and he claimed to be the heir of his own younger brother Geoffrey (d. c.1190) for lands in Northumberland and other English counties. His claims were disputed by his niece Gunnora and her husband, Robert fitz Walter, to whom the honour of Valognes had descended from Gunnora's father, Philip's brother Robert de Valognes; but Philip was partly successful when in 1208 King John accepted his proffer of 300 marks, ten palfreys, and two hounds. After his death on 5 November 1215, Philip de Valognes was buried in the chapter house of Melrose Abbey, and the chamberlainship of Scotland passed as a hereditary office to his only son, William, whose mother remains unidentified.

Philip de Valognes also had a daughter, Sibyl (d. 1222), who married Robert (V) de Stuteville (d. 1213), and their son Eustace (d. 1241) became lord of the Stuteville baronies of Cottingham, Yorkshire, and Liddel Strength, Cumberland. William de Valognes, who died in 1219 and was buried beside his father at Melrose, was succeeded by the three daughters of his marriage to Lora, or Loretta, daughter of Saer de Quincy, earl of Winchester. Lora, the eldest, carried the chamberlainship to her husband, Henry de Balliol, of Cavers, Roxburghshire; Christiana married Peter de Maule, ancestor of the earls of Panmure; and Isabel married David Comyn of West Linton, Peeblesshire. In 1233 William's daughters had livery of the honour of Valognes as coheirs of Christiana, daughter of Gunnora and Robert fitz Walter.   KEITH STRINGER

Sources G. W. S. Barrow, ed., *Regesta regum Scottorum*, 2 (1971) · A. O. Anderson, ed. and trans., *Early sources of Scottish history, AD 500*

to 1286, 2 (1922); repr. with corrections (1990) · W. Bower, *Scotichronicon*, ed. D. E. R. Watt and others, new edn, 9 vols. (1987–98), vols. 4, 5 · W. P. Hedley, *Northumberland families*, 2 vols., Society of Antiquaries of Newcastle upon Tyne, Record Series (1968–70) · G. W. S. Barrow, *The Anglo-Norman era in Scottish history* (1980) · A. A. M. Duncan, *Scotland: the making of the kingdom* (1975), vol. 1 of *The Edinburgh history of Scotland*, ed. G. Donaldson (1965–75) · W. T. Lancaster, *The early history of Ripley and the Ingilby family* (1918) · T. D. Hardy, ed., *Rotuli de oblatis et finibus*, RC (1835) · W. Farrer and others, eds., *Early Yorkshire charters*, 12 vols. (1914–65), vol. 9
Likenesses seal, NA Scot.

Valpy, Abraham John (1787–1854), classical scholar and printer, was the second son of Richard *Valpy (1754–1836), a schoolmaster, and his second wife, Mary, daughter of Henry Benwell of Caversham, Oxfordshire. After being trained under his father at Reading grammar school, he matriculated from Pembroke College, Oxford, on 25 April 1805. He was elected on 30 March 1808 Bennet (Ossulston) scholar of his college, graduated BA in 1809, MA in 1811, and was a fellow of the college for a short time from 7 June 1811. In 1809 he printed for private circulation a slim and elegant volume containing the Latin hexameter poems which he had unsuccessfully submitted for a university prize in 1806, 1807, and 1808.

Valpy published at Reading in December 1804, while still a schoolboy, and with a dedication to his fellow pupils, a volume of excerpts from Cicero's letters, which reached a fifth edition in 1829. He and his father shared the hope that he might rival the fame of Aldus and Stephanus as a printer and editor of classical works, and with this object in view he was bound nominal apprentice to a freeman of London, Humphrey Gregory Pridden. In 1807 he was admitted a liveryman of the Stationers' Company.

Valpy married at Burrington, Somerset, on 25 February 1813, Harriet, third daughter of Sydenham Teast Wylde, vicar of that parish; there were to be no children. He opened business in Took's Court, Chancery Lane, moving in 1822 to Red Lion Passage, Fleet Street, where William Bowyer, the English printer whom Valpy hoped to equal in reputation for learning, had ended his business career in 1777. For many years he published, either under his own editing or under the supervision of some classical scholar, numerous works, especially in ancient literature. The chief work edited by himself was a version of Brotier's *Tacitus*, which came out in 1812 in five volumes, and was later reissued more than once. His principal assistants in editing were Edward Henry Barker of Thetford, George Burges, George Dyer, and the Revd Thomas Smart Hughes. Most of the volumes that he published bore on the title-page the Greek digamma, which he adopted as a trade mark and monogram; he is said to have placed it on his carriage.

Valpy started the *Classical Journal* in 1810, continuing it until December 1829, and from March 1813 to December 1828 brought out *The Pamphleteer*, 'a collection of the best pamphlets of the day', in fifty-eight quarterly parts; contributors included George Canning, William Wilberforce, William Huskisson, Stamford Raffles, and Jeremy Bentham. His first great speculation was the reissue of the *Thesaurus Graecæ Linguae* of Stephanus. Edited by Barker, it

Abraham John Valpy (1787–1854), by H. S. Turner, pubd 1831 (after Eden Upton Eddis, 1831)

came out between 1816 and 1828 in twelve volumes. This vast enterprise suffered from a crushing article published in 1820 by Charles James Blomfield (later bishop of London) in the 1820 *Quarterly Review*.

Between 1819 and 1830 Valpy reissued in 141 volumes new versions of the Delphin classics under the editorial care of George Dyer, and from January 1822 to December 1825 he was patron, printer, and publisher of a periodical called *The Museum*. In 1830–34 he brought out the Family Classical Library: English Translations of Greek and Latin Classics, in fifty-two volumes, and in 1831 he started an Epitome of English Literature, in the philosophical portion of which appeared abridgements of Paley's *Moral Philosophy* and *Evidences of Christianity*, and Locke's *Essay on the Human Understanding*. An edition of the plays and poems of Shakespeare was published by him in fifteen volumes (1832–4), and in 1834 he began a serial work on the *National Gallery of Painting and Sculpture*, although only four half-crown parts saw the light.

About 1837 Valpy sold his printing materials, parted with his large stock of books and copyrights, and retired into private life. From that time he applied his energies to the University Life Assurance Company and other undertakings in which he was interested either as a director or shareholder. He died on 19 November 1854 at his home in St John's Wood Road, London, where his widow died ten years later, on 19 June 1864.

W. P. COURTNEY, *rev.* RICHARD JENKYNS

Sources *GM*, 1st ser., 83/1 (1813), 282 · *GM*, 2nd ser., 43 (1855), 204–5 · *GM*, 3rd ser., 16 (1864), 126 · Foster, *Alum. Oxon.* · A. J. Valpy, *Catalogue of classical works in Greek, Latin, and English* (1831) · Nichols, *Lit. anecdotes*, 9.759 · *N&Q*, 3rd ser., 6 (1864), 51, 96, 135–6 · review, *QR*, 22 (1819–20), 302–48 · private information (1899) [George Wood, bursar of Pembroke College] · A. P. Burke, *Family records* (1897)
Archives U. Reading L., business papers | BL, letters to Philip Bliss, Add. MSS 34568–34579 *passim* · BL, letters to Lord Grenville, Add. MS 58995
Likenesses H. S. Turner, engraving, pubd 1831 (after E. U. Eddis, 1831), NPG [*see illus.*] · oils; formerly in possession of G. C. B. Valpy, 1899

Valpy, Edward (1764–1832), classical scholar, was born at Reading, the fourth son of Richard Valpy of St John's, Jersey, and his wife, Catherine, daughter of John Chevalier. He went to school at Bury St Edmunds and was admitted to Trinity College, Cambridge, in 1781, although as a 'ten-year man' he deferred matriculation until he graduated BD in 1810. He became rector of Stanford Dingley, Berkshire. On 20 December 1800 he married Anne, daughter of Thomas Western of Great Abington, Cambridgeshire, and widow of Chaloner Byng Baldock, vicar of Milton Abbey, Dorset. They had a son, the Revd Edward John Western Valpy (d. 1830), whom Valpy presented to the living of Stanford Dingley in 1825.

Valpy acted for many years as a master at Reading School under his brother, Richard *Valpy. In 1810 he was elected high master of Norwich School, which greatly improved and expanded under his direction; he is said to have raised the number of pupils from 8 to 300 in his first two years. He published a popular textbook on Latin style, *Elegantiae Latinae* (1803), and an edition of the Greek Testament, with notes, in three volumes (1815). In 1819 Valpy became rector of All Saints', Thwaite, and vicar of St Mary's, South Walsham, both in Norfolk. He held these livings until his death at Yarmouth on 15 April 1832.

W. W. WROTH, *rev.* RICHARD SMAIL

Sources GM, 1st ser., 70 (1800), 1288 · GM, 1st ser., 100/1 (1830), 280 · GM, 1st ser., 102/1 (1832), 373 · Venn, *Alum. Cant.* · *General history of Norfolk*, 2 (1829), 977, 1051, 1351 · J. Foster, ed., *Index ecclesiasticus, or, Alphabetical lists of all ecclesiastical dignitaries in England and Wales since the Reformation* (1890)

Valpy, Francis Edward Jackson (1797–1882). *See under* Valpy, Richard (1754–1836).

Valpy, Richard (1754–1836), schoolmaster, was born at his father's landed estate in St John's, Jersey, on 7 December 1754, the eldest of the six children of Richard Valpy and Catherine, daughter of John Chevalier. His younger brother was Edward *Valpy. After some local schooling, in 1764 he was sent to the college of Valognes, Normandy, where he became fluent in French but acquired an accent that some found execrable. In 1769 he transferred to Southampton grammar school and subsequently to Guildford grammar school, where as a pupil he published by subscription a volume of nondescript verses, entitled *Practical Blossoms*.

At Southampton, Valpy had longed for a naval career, only to be dissuaded by his mother's entreaties. Shortly afterwards his enthusiasm shifted to acting and he resolved to call on Richard Garrick for advice, but his courage failed him on that actor's doorstep. Instead, in 1773 he entered Pembroke College, Oxford, as a Morley scholar. Having graduated BA, and following his ordination, in 1777 he became second master at Bury St Edmunds School. In June of the following year he married Martha, daughter of John Cornelius of Caundé, Guernsey; they had a daughter. In 1781 he was appointed headmaster of Reading School, and on 30 May 1782 he married, second, Mary, daughter of Henry Benwell of Caversham and sister of his pupil William *Benwell. Mary, who was totally deaf, gave

Richard Valpy (1754–1836), by Charles Turner, pubd 1811 (after John Opie, exh. RA 1801)

birth to six sons and four daughters. The second son was Abraham *Valpy.

Reading School was at that time struggling, with only twenty-three pupils. By 1791 Valpy had raised their numbers to 120, of whom many were the sons of Berkshire magnates and gentry. His boarding fees of £50–£60 a year were steep but he energetically tackled the poor state of the school buildings. He persuaded Reading corporation to lease him the headmaster's house, at that time rented on an annual basis, for the period of three lives; he added a hall, a library, and an extra wing. Teaching took place in the basement of the town hall, constantly disrupted by the noise of borough business overhead; the civic fathers having refused to pay for new premises, in 1790 Valpy built a separate schoolroom with his own funds. Hitherto boarders had been billeted in the town but he leased from the corporation the abbey's former hospitium, remembered as both insanitary and draughty.

Notwithstanding these physical discomforts pupils held Valpy in high esteem and affection. Accepting him as a mighty flogger they relished his playing the part, as an actor manqué, of a character unafraid to mock himself. He made all the boys take plenty of exercise, from cricket to swimming, but his reputation rested mainly on the high quality of his scholarship. In 1788 he was elected fellow of the Society of Antiquaries, and a few years later he proceeded BD and DD. Of the pupils he encouraged a number are noticed in the *Oxford Dictionary of National Biography*: Bulkeley Bandinel, Sir William Bolland, Peter Paul Dobree, John Jackson (1811–1885), Sir John Keane, John Lemprière, Henry Alworth and John Merewether, and Sir Thomas Noon Talfourd. His alumni were regularly supportive; in 1800 they subscribed for a portrait of him by John Opie, and after his death they erected a statue of him, by Samuel Nixon, in St Laurence's Church, Reading.

Valpy was a tall and imposing figure who had a passionate interest—fuelled by an exceptionally retentive mind—in politics, military and naval affairs, agriculture, and education, especially of the poor. Early in his life he had gambled heavily. He fostered among pupils a love of English literature, then rare in schools, and adapted English as well as Greek and Latin plays for the boys to perform. During the triennial visitation of the school from Oxford he organized plays in the town hall to benefit local charities. He declined two bishoprics and also the headmastership of Rugby, disliking that school's curriculum and fees and citing Mrs Valpy's reluctance to move.

Valpy's textbooks made him widely known; a Greek grammar and Latin grammar (1809) were followed by *Latin delectus* (1814) and *Greek delectus* (1816), which offered passages for translation into English, and by works on mythology and history. Some townspeople, resentful of their free school being turned into an academy for the well off, complained that the classics were crowding out more useful mathematical and commercial subjects. Such hostility to the school clearly encouraged Reading corporation to deny it much-needed funds, and it never developed, as comparable foundations were doing, into a great nineteenth-century independent school. Valpy stayed on for too long, not retiring until he was in his mid-seventies in 1830, leaving behind only sixty-five pupils. He moved to the rectory at Stradishall, Suffolk, a living he had held since 1787. By then his sight was failing and he became accident-prone. He died on 28 March 1836, at his eldest son's house in Earl's Terrace, Kensington, London, after breaking his leg in a fall, and was buried in Kensal Green. His wife had predeceased him.

Valpy's sixth and youngest son, **Francis Edward Jackson Valpy** (1797–1882), Church of England clergyman and schoolmaster, was born at the headmaster's house, Reading School, on 22 February 1797. He was educated at Reading School and, from 1815, at Trinity College, Cambridge, where he was a Bell scholar and where he graduated BA in 1819. Six years later, in 1825, he married Eliza, daughter of John Pullen of Canonbury; they had eight sons. In 1826 he was ordained and in 1830 he was made headmaster of Reading School. He inherited a court judgment, ignored by his father, requiring grammar schools to teach classics free to local pupils. Reading people, still aggrieved over the school, disinclined the corporation to repair the increasingly crumbling leasehold premises. Though Valpy resembled his father in scholarship and preaching eloquence he was not an inspiring teacher and lacked the decisiveness required to overcome the school's problems with the town. By 1837 it had only twenty boarders and seventeen day-boys, nine with free places.

In 1839 Valpy resigned and, until 1842, he taught at Burton upon Trent School. From 1845 to 1873 he was rector of Garveston, Norfolk, where in 1866 he married his second wife, Mary, daughter of John Champion of Guernsey. He published several Greek textbooks, etymological dictionaries of Greek and Latin, editions of Sophocles' *Ajax* and *Electra*, and *The Course of Nature … in Vindication of Scripture*. He died on 28 November 1882 in London, whither he had retired, at 10 Regent's Park Terrace, Gloucester Gate, and was buried at Garveston. He left £11,500.

T. A. B. CORLEY

Sources *DNB* · *GM*, 2nd ser., 6 (1836), 553–5 · M. Naxton, *The history of Reading School* (1986) · C. Coates, *The history and antiquities of Reading* (1802) · J. J. Cooper, *Some worthies of Reading* (1923) · W. M. Childs, *The town of Reading during the early part of the nineteenth century* (1910); repr. (1967), 69–73 · Foster, *Alum. Oxon.* · *VCH Berkshire*, 2.258 · O. Oldfellow [B. Brockett], *Our school, or, Scraps and scrapes in schoolboy life* (1857) · *The Times* (5 April 1836) · Venn, *Alum. Cant.* · Boase, *Mod. Eng. biog.*, 3.1072 · J. Doran, *The history and antiquities of the town and borough of Reading* (1835) · *Clergy List* (1858) · *Clergy List* (1868) · *Reading Mercury* (13 July 1839) · *Reading Mercury* (2 Dec 1882) · *Reading Mercury* (Jan 1922) · *The Times* (30 Nov 1882) · *Berkshire Chronicle* (2 Dec 1882)

Likenesses J. Opie, oils, 1801, Reading Corporation, Berkshire · C. Turner, mezzotint, pubd 1811 (after J. Opie, exh. RA 1801), BM [*see illus.*] · S. Nixon, statue, 1838, St Lawrence's Church, Reading · J. H. Nixon, lithograph (after S. Nixon), BM

Wealth at death £11,516 2s. 11d.—Francis Edward Jackson Valpy: resworn probate, April 1883, *CGPLA Eng. & Wales*

Van. For names including this prefix (also van de, van den, van der) *see under* the substantive element of the name; for example, for Sir Anthony Van Dyck *see* Dyck, Sir Anthony Van; for Sir Laurens van der Post *see* Post, Sir Laurens Jan van der.

Vanbrugh, Charles (1720–1745). *See under* Vanbrugh, Sir John (1664–1726).

Vanbrugh, Dame Irene [*real name* Irene Barnes] (1872–1949), actress, was born at Exeter on 2 December 1872, the fourth and youngest daughter of the Revd Reginald Henry Barnes (d. 1889), prebendary of Exeter Cathedral and vicar of Heavitree, and his wife, Frances Mary Emily, daughter of William Nation, barrister. The Nations were an old Exeter family, members of which had given great support to the theatre and had helped in the discovery of Edmund Kean. Irene was the fifth child in a family of six, Violet *Vanbrugh being the eldest and Sir Kenneth Ralph *Barnes the youngest. The stage name Vanbrugh was first adopted by Violet at the suggestion of Ellen Terry, who remained throughout her life an invaluable friend. Violet's successful entry upon a stage career under J. L. Toole in 1886 set Irene an example rare in those days among strictly brought-up daughters of professional men. Irene was educated at Exeter high school and by prolonged trips to the continent with her father, and at a school near Earls Court, recommended by Ellen Terry, when the family removed to London. Like Violet, Irene had a spell of training under Sarah Thorne at the Theatre Royal, Margate,

Dame Irene Vanbrugh (1872–1949), by Flora Lion, 1913

where she made her first stage appearance in August 1888, as Phoebe in *As You Like It*. On Boxing day of the same year she made her London début, on the recommendation of Lewis Carroll, as the White Queen and the Jack of hearts in a revival of *Alice in Wonderland* at the Globe Theatre in Newcastle Street, Strand. She then again followed Violet's lead by joining Toole's company. She played a big round of parts in already popular plays such as Dion Boucicault's *Dot* and H. J. Byron's *Uncle Dick's Darling*. With Toole she toured Australia in 1890. On her return, still with Toole, she made her first original creations as Thea Tesman in the first play by James Barrie, his burlesque *Ibsen's Ghost* (1891), and as Bell Golightly in his *Walker, London* (1892). She then joined Herbert Tree at the Haymarket Theatre as Lettice in *The Tempter* (1893) by H. A. Jones. In the following year she moved to the St James's Theatre and played a number of secondary parts under the management of George Alexander, afterwards joining the company of her brother-in-law, Arthur Bourchier, at the Royalty Theatre and on an American visit. On her return to London at the Court Theatre in 1898 she created Rose in *Trelawny of the 'Wells'* by Arthur Pinero, and, during the same season, Stella in Robert Marshall's *His Excellency the Governor*.

Then came Irene Vanbrugh's first great triumph, her Sophy Fullgarney in the production by John Hare at the Globe Theatre of Pinero's *The Gay Lord Quex* (1899). As with many of her creations, Irene Vanbrugh's intelligence, sympathy, and alertness avoided extravagance in a subtle expression of class-contrast. This gave the character an intensity of appeal that was at the time something quite

new. In 1901 she married Dion *Boucicault the younger (1859–1929), who became her manager in 1915 and who acted with her until his death. There were to be no children. Her Letty in Pinero's play of that name at the Duke of York's Theatre (1903) was a less memorable success than some of those that had gone before. It was at the St James's Theatre as Nina Jesson in Pinero's *His House in Order* (1906)—a delicately temperamental study of the second wife of a pompous member of parliament—that Irene Vanbrugh touched the heights once more. She also scored notably as Marise in *The Thief*, adapted from Henry Bernstein, at the St James's Theatre (1907). Her Zoe Blundell, too, in Pinero's *Mid-Channel* at the same theatre (1909) was specially worthy of remembrance. She gave another poignant performance in the title part of W. Somerset Maugham's play *Grace* at the Duke of York's Theatre (1910). She created many other attractive characters of a quite different order, such as Lady Mary Lasenby in Barrie's *The Admirable Crichton* at the Duke of York's Theatre (1902); Kate, in his one-act play *The Twelve-Pound Look* at the Hippodrome (1911); and Rosalind in his one-act play of that name, also produced at the Duke of York's Theatre (1912). In this she was commanded to appear before the king at Queen Alexandra's birthday party at Sandringham. Norah Marsh in Maugham's *The Land of Promise* at the Duke of York's Theatre (1914) was an achievement of high merit, but its deserved success suffered from the outbreak of war. She was more fortunate with her Olivia in A. A. Milne's *Mr Pim Passes By* at the New Theatre (1920). Even so, she never excelled her early Pinero creations.

One of Irene Vanbrugh's latest and most appreciated successes was in Norman Ginsbury's *Viceroy Sarah*, in which she succeeded Edith Evans as the duchess of Marlborough for the run at the Whitehall Theatre (1935). She appeared three times in plays by G. B. Shaw, the last being as Catherine of Braganza in *In Good King Charles's Golden Days* when it was produced at the Malvern festival in 1939 and was afterwards presented in London at the New Theatre in 1940, only to be stopped by the war. During the battle of Britain she carried out a characteristic piece of war work by giving, with Violet Vanbrugh and Donald Wolfit, extracts from *The Merry Wives of Windsor* at the Strand Theatre during lunchtime.

Irene Vanbrugh, who was appointed DBE in 1941, celebrated her golden jubilee at a testimonial matinée in His Majesty's Theatre on 20 June 1938. At this she appeared in an act from *The Gay Lord Quex* and in one from A. A. Milne's *Belinda*, in which she had been seen at the New Theatre in 1918, and also in the title part of Barrie's *Rosalind*. The performance was attended by Queen Elizabeth and it realized over £2000, which was divided between the Elizabeth Garrett Anderson Hospital and the Theatrical Ladies' Guild. Irene Vanbrugh was constant in her promotion of every theatrical good cause; she was a particularly keen supporter of the Royal Academy of Dramatic Art, both because her brother, Sir Kenneth Barnes, was its first principal and because she was deeply conscious of its value to the art and welfare of the theatre. Notable among her charity performances was her appearance as Lady Gay Spanker in an 'all-star' revival at the St James's Theatre of her father-in-law's famous comedy, *London Assurance* (1913), given in aid of King George's Pension Fund for Actors and Actresses. In 1919 to avert selling the Academy of Dramatic Art theatre, then partly completed, she had the old film *Masks and Faces* remade with a star cast, as well as Shaw, Pinero, Barrie, and Sir Squire Bancroft sitting round at a council meeting.

Although Irene Vanbrugh allowed nothing to deter her main interest from the living theatre, which she loved and in the future of which she believed with her whole heart, she found time from 1933 to appear in a number of films, including *Head of the Family, Catherine the Great* (1934), *The Way of Youth, Escape me Never* (1935), *Wings of the Morning* (1937), and *Knight without Armour* (1937). Towards the close of her life she wrote an autobiography entitled *To Tell my Story* (1948). It contains some well-informed character sketches of the dramatists, actors, actresses, and others with whom she worked, as well as letters from Pinero, Barrie, Shaw, and others, and vivid glimpses of life in America, Australia, and other parts of the world visited during her tours. In her writings and otherwise she gave the impression of having enjoyed a career of manifold opportunity and fulfilment. Dame Irene Vanbrugh died in the National Hospital, Queen Square, London, after a short illness, on 30 November 1949.   S. R. LITTLEWOOD, *rev.*

Sources I. Vanbrugh, *To tell my story* (1948) · J. Parker, ed., *Who's who in the theatre*, 6th edn (1930) · personal knowledge (1959) · private information (1959) · *CGPLA Eng. & Wales* (1950)
Archives University of Rochester, New York, Rush Rhees Library, corresp. and papers | Richmond Local Studies Library, London, letters to Douglas Sladen |FILM BFI NFTVA, actuality footage · BFI NFTVA, documentary footage
Likenesses O. Birley, oils, *c.*1907, National Gallery of Victoria, Melbourne, Australia · F. Lion, lithograph, 1913, NPG [*see illus.*] · C. Buchel, oils, 1923, Royal Academy of Dramatic Art, London · U. Bradley, oils, Royal Academy of Dramatic Art, London · Mrs. A. Broom, photograph, NPG · C. Buchel, oils; in possession of Kenneth Barnes, in 1959 · C. Buchel & Hassell, lithograph, NPG · H. Coster, photographs, NPG · J. Lavery, oils; in possession of Michael Barnes, in 1959 · J. Oppenheimer, oils; in possession of the artist, in 1959 · W. Rothenstein, portrait (as Rose Trelawney); in possession of G. Spiegleberg, in 1959 · S. J. Solomon, portrait, oils; in possession of Colin Anderson, in 1959
Wealth at death £16,973 14s. 2d.: probate, 3 Feb 1950, *CGPLA Eng. & Wales*

Vanbrugh, Sir John (1664–1726), playwright and architect, was born probably on 24 January 1664, the day of his baptism at home, in the parish of St Nicholas Acons, London. His parents were Giles Vanbrugh (1631–1689), a London merchant of Flemish extraction, and Elizabeth (*c.*1637–1711), widow of Thomas Barker and daughter of Sir Dudley Carleton of Clerkenwell and Imber Court, Surrey. Variant spellings of the surname include Vanbrook, which John Vanbrugh occasionally signed and was probably phonetic. The form 'Vanburgh' was never used in the family, whose crest contained a bridge (*brug* in Flemish).

Early life John Vanbrugh was his parents' fourth child (of nineteen) and eldest surviving son. His grandfather Gillis

Sir John Vanbrugh (1664–1726), by Sir Godfrey Kneller, *c.*1704–10

reached London in 1616 from Haarlem, where many Antwerp protestants had fled during the late sixteenth-century religious persecution; the Vanbrughs dealt in cloth. The Carletons, connected by marriage with several English noble families, were to be significant for John Vanbrugh's career. In the period of the plague and the great fire it is uncertain when Giles's family left London, but by October 1667 they had settled in Chester, an Irish Sea and Atlantic port in decline through silting of the River Dee. Giles's interests diversified to include property, lead, and grain, as well as Caribbean sugar. The familiar half-truth is that he was a 'sugar-baker' (refiner), but as a gentleman his connection with the established Chester refiner Anthony Henthorne was probably financial.

There are no records of Vanbrugh's education, either at the King's School in Chester or elsewhere, but he may, like his uncle Peter (and possibly his father), have had a tutor. Like his parents, he jealously guarded his personal privacy; his surviving correspondence shows him generally silent about failures (in trade, the army, the Far East, and France) and reticent about any enterprise until it was firmly supported (most notably his conversion to architecture). As an adult he knew literary and colloquial French, wrote a good hand, and practised Shelton's shorthand—all useful accomplishments for a commercial career. His father had travelled in Europe for three years; the value of the son's experiences abroad was neither direct nor immediate. There is no truth whatever in the tradition that he studied architecture for three years in France.

The search for a vocation In 1681 Vanbrugh was working in the London wine business of his paternal cousin William

Matthews, but the business failed. The following year he was 'entertained' (taken into service) for five years as a factor in the East India Company, and on 4 May 1683, underwritten by his father and his uncle William, he sailed in the *Scipio* with a cargo for Surat. He was commended by his employers but found the life neither congenial nor profitable, and after little more than a year he took ship for London, where he arrived in August 1685. He was the only English architect of his time with firsthand knowledge of the Far East, and twelve months in total at sea would have left him time, as it did for the architect Sir William Chambers in the 1740s, for book learning.

Not satisfied with the efforts of his father's family to find him suitable employment, Vanbrugh turned to his mother's in the person of Theophilus Hastings, seventh earl of Huntingdon, warden of royal forests south of the Trent, and colonel of an infantry regiment. Vanbrugh's letter of 28 December 1685 implies the hope of civil employment; instead on 30 January 1686 he was commissioned ensign in Huntingdon's regiment. After joining at Hull, he marched to London for James II's review at Blackheath. He learned that both his colonel and his captain were Roman Catholics, and the atmosphere of the camp under the Catholic king was increasingly popish—sufficient reason for Vanbrugh, staunchly protestant like his father, to extricate himself. Before the regiment moved north in August he had purchased his freedom. A year later he was in the household of another kinsman, James Bertie, first earl of Abingdon, with three of the latter's nephews, including Robert Bertie, Lord Willoughby (afterwards first duke of Ancaster). In September 1687 Vanbrugh and the nephews received the freedom of Oxford, revoked by the king five months later with Abingdon's stewardship of the city.

In September 1688 Vanbrugh was in France with Willoughby, and incautiously praised William of Orange, newly at war with France and preparing to invade England. He was arrested, perhaps less for his indiscretion than for his noble connection and the supposition that he might be a valuable hostage; he was imprisoned in the citadel at Calais. In October 1690, his father having died, his mother tried unsuccessfully to secure an exchange with a young Jacobite officer. She managed to alleviate his conditions somewhat by transferring money to him from a sinecure obtained for him by Willoughby, then chancellor of the duchy of Lancaster. Nevertheless his health deteriorated, and after much negotiation he was transferred in April 1691 to better quarters at Vincennes. He divined that the original cause, and even date, of his arrest had been forgotten, and in July he approached the court of James II at St Germain, begging help as (he falsely claimed) a loyal adherent of the exiled king. His story was not challenged, but the French began to intercept his letters. Eventually he managed to smuggle out a letter to his mother, revealing the complex game of spy exchange in which he had become a pawn. Early in 1692 he was promoted to the Bastille, and in November he was released in a complicated exchange. After some weeks at liberty in Paris on parole he reached England, without papers, at the end of March 1693. He kept his sinecure, an auditorship in the duchy of Lancaster, paying a deputy until his resignation in 1702.

Vanbrugh was an early member of the whig political and literary Kit-Cat Club, 'generally mentioned', according to Horace Walpole, 'as a set of wits, in reality the patriots that saved Britain' (*Anecdotes of Painting in England*, life of Kneller). Its serious aim was to secure the protestant succession against the heirs of James II, but for Vanbrugh its importance included the provision in later years of several architectural clients. However, the direction of his life appears still uncertain. He was restless; he had spent half his twenties unjustly imprisoned: he told Daniel Finch, second earl of Nottingham, who as secretary of state was entitled to the truth, that he was never a spy. Revenge against the French must have been one motive for obtaining a captaincy in the marine regiment of Thomas Osborne, marquess of Carmarthen, another kinsman. After the disastrous naval engagement of 7–8 June 1694 at Camaret Bay, off Brest, Carmarthen published his *Journal of the Brest-Expedition* (1694) to justify his own actions; incidentally he praised the bravery of Vanbrugh, who 'in a great many things was extremely Serviceable both by his advice and otherwise' (p. 38). Vanbrugh is not known to have seen further action; on 20 August 1698, after the end of the French war, he retired on half pay. By then he had seen the successful production of four of his works on the London stage, including the two original masterpieces that were to earn him lasting fame.

The dramatist It is reasonable to suppose that, living in the West End of London, Vanbrugh often visited the Restoration theatre. On 21 November 1696 his comedy *The Relapse* opened at the Drury Lane theatre. In the ensuing eighteen months it was followed by a second comedy, *The Provok'd Wife* (Lincoln's Inn Fields, April 1697), and two adaptations of French plays: *Aesop*, from Edme Boursault's *Les fables d'Ésope*, and *The Country House*, from a one-act play by Florent Carton de Dancourt. The two original plays were successful and popular, and were reprinted and revived often during the following half-century; no doubt it was their success that led Vanbrugh to make, and the managers to stage, the adaptations. Between 1700 and 1707 he contributed six more stage works, but he had also become deeply involved in architecture and other concerns.

According to its prologue, *The Relapse* was 'Got, Conceiv'd, and Born in Six Weeks space'; the affectation of rapid composition was less unusual than the astonishing success of a first play. However, both success and surprise were characteristic of Vanbrugh. In fact *The Relapse* was written early in 1696, soon after the production of Colley Cibber's *Love's Last Shift*, to which it is a sequel; its staging was deferred until the winter for management reasons. *The Provok'd Wife* opened only five months later, but its origins are no simpler. In 1698 Vanbrugh himself wrote that it was 'writ many years ago, and when I was very young' (*Plays*, 1.207). This may have been special pleading in response to Jeremy Collier (see below) and the play shows familiarity not only with comedies of the 1670s but also with topical issues of the 1690s. Probably its conception came from his first experience of the London stage in 1681, but its eventual birth in a revised form revealed a work of equal maturity.

The Relapse is also the first instance of Vanbrugh's disposition to improve on an existing model. As a novice, he wanted to tell a more credible story than Cibber's—also a successful first play by a young but established actor—whose optimistic ending with the libertine's pious reform he found too good to last. He kept four of Cibber's main characters as well as three of the original cast, including Cibber himself as Sir Novelty Fashion, elevated by Vanbrugh to Lord Foppington. Vanbrugh's main plot makes the hero relapse, but he also continued the secondary plot involving Sir Novelty and his penniless younger brother, and exposing the serious social and personal problems of primogeniture, the system by which the eldest son inherits the whole estate, his siblings nothing. However, the sermon is sugared for most of the audience as the younger brother outwits the elder and secures the rustic heiress as his bride.

Vanbrugh's claim in the prologue to hasty writing and little structure ('in too much haste … writ to be o'ercharged with either Plot or Wit') is disingenuous, for the writing reveals both a remarkable naturalness and considerable artifice. Many passages printed as prose are in fact metrical, which suggests an intuitive facility; more remarkable is the impression of entirely artless prose, capturing the language of his day, the sounds and rhythms of speech, and the mannerisms of diverse characters. Moreover, the major and minor plots are easily and skilfully interwoven, with a symmetry that is certainly deliberate and indeed architectural. Cibber was generous in his tribute, praising not only the 'Spirit, Ease and Readiness' of his pen but also the 'clear and lively Simplicity in his Wit, that neither wants the Ornament of learning, nor has the least Smell of the Lamp in it' (Cibber, 122).

The Provok'd Wife, no less shrewd or entertaining, is even more closely constructed and addresses—with a light touch—even weightier matters. The wife is wedded to the aptly named Sir John Brute, who married her 'because I had a mind to lie with her, and she would not let me' (II. II.i), while she married for money. Divorce was not a realistic option: it was rare and costly, involving a private bill in the House of Lords, and even if successful, it compromised the parties' social standing. The unhappy couple's problems thus remain unsolved at the final curtain, and their mutual detestation is poignantly contrasted with the discovery by young Heartfree and Bellinda of true love, the 'one inestimable Lot, in which the only Heaven on Earth is written' (v. iv). Sir John's wickedness is not limited to carnality and drunkenness; although in the play's swift pace some of the audience may miss it, Act IV opens as he comes fresh from killing a man in a street brawl.

In April 1698, a year after the première of *The Provok'd Wife*, Jeremy Collier published his *Short View of the Immorality and Profaneness of the English Stage*, probably the best-known of many pamphlets in a long and often heated debate between the Calvinist view of plays as fiction, and therefore falsehood, and the classical Aristotelian idea of the stage as a world parallel to everyday life with the capacity, as through a mirror, to instruct as well as to entertain.

Collier's renown is largely due to Vanbrugh's response, *A Short Vindication of the Relapse and the Provok'd Wife*, published on 8 June 1698. Collier accused Vanbrugh of immoral characters, profane language, and dramatic and literary incompetence. In fact Vanbrugh's characters neither speak nor behave exceptionally, although his success made him an obvious (though not unique) target. His reply, energetic and elegant, used wit, hyperbole, and ridicule to expose Collier as often wide of the mark and defective in logic. In the nearest he came to stating a theory of comedy, Vanbrugh pressed the Aristotelian view that the theatre educates: 'The Business of Comedy is to shew People what they shou'd do, by representing them upon the Stage, doing what they shou'd not do' (*Plays*, 1.206). Vanbrugh had become a shrewd observer of people; he also belittled Collier's attempts at literary criticism, although he ignored the specific charge that some of his characters behaved neither reasonably nor probably. This charge is still made, although before the time of Ibsen and Pinero producers were not worried by inconsistency. One modern editor of Vanbrugh rightly emphasizes that 'on the stage these problems disappear. When events are so funny and move so fast there is no time to think how they arose' (J. L. Smith, Introduction to *The Provok'd Wife*, 1974, xx). Collier replied in print, and by the end of 1700 over thirty pamphlets had been published, for or against. Some actors in *The Provok'd Wife* were prosecuted for uttering profanities on stage. But the Restoration comedy of amorality was in decline and Vanbrugh's creative faculties were turning to architecture.

The art of adaptation Vanbrugh was an expert translator and adapter. *Aesop* (Drury Lane, December 1696) was not a drama but a musical entertainment, with singing, dancing, and comic acts wrapped around a simple love story. The prologue's claim to 'no Bawdy' notwithstanding, some of the humour is earthy, apparently escaping Collier's notice. In May 1697 Vanbrugh added a short second part (unrelated to Boursault's *Ésope à la cour*, which it antedates). *The Country House* (Drury Lane, January 1698) made two acts out of Dancourt's one, but remained an afterpiece. The *Maison de campagne* is not a country house in the modern English sense, and the plot concerns the owner's inability to deter visitors, even strangers, who expect free lodging. Finally the owner returns to Paris; the condition of his daughter's marriage is that the groom also takes the house. Vanbrugh was free with the original, not only adapting French regional and linguistic references for an English audience but also using vivid and varied language to animate stereotypical characters.

In his adaptation of *The Pilgrim* (Drury Lane, April 1700) Vanbrugh followed closely John Fletcher's play of c.1621, while modernizing and to some extent expurgating the language. *The False Friend* (Drury Lane, February 1702), from Le Sage's *Le traître puni*, and *The Mistake* (27 December 1705), from Molière's *Le dépit amoureux*, are set in Spain. Le

Sage's play, like *The Pilgrim*, adapted a serious story of love, honour, and betrayal, by Francisco de Rojas Zorilla; in the second play Vanbrugh moved the scene from Molière's Paris. In this latter story of mistaken identity of person and gender, finally happily resolved, Vanbrugh replaced Molière's verse by lively prose, some of it metrical. *The Mistake* was acted in the new Queen's Theatre in the Haymarket, as was *The Confederacy* (30 October 1705), based on Dancourt's *Les bourgeoises à la mode*. Here Vanbrugh added humour and substance to Dancourt's rather straight characters, most of whom in this story of lustful husbands, extravagant and scheming wives, and dishonest young men, are in a no better state at the finish. Two other compositions are lost: one act of *Squire Trelooby* (the others by Congreve and William Walsh; Lincoln's Inn Fields, 30 March 1704) from Molière and an afterpiece from Molière, *The Cuckold in Conceit* (Queen's Theatre, 22 March 1707).

The architect of Castle Howard 'Van's Genius without Thought or Lecture', wrote Jonathan Swift in 1706, 'Is hugely turnd to architecture' (*The History of Vanbrug's House*, 1706). Three years earlier Swift had already lampooned Vanbrugh's pretensions to both architecture and heraldry (*Vanbrug's House*, 1703), but by 1706 Vanbrugh was very much in the public eye and the later poem also mentions Blenheim. 'Vanbrug's house' was the small one (known since Swift's satire as Goose-Pie House) which he obtained permission to build in 1701, for himself in the ruins of Whitehall Palace. The implications of 'hugely', the first allusion to the scale of his architecture, are less significant than those of 'without thought or lecture'. There is no documentary evidence of either premeditation or preparation for this new change of career; however, although Swift's view may have been the common one—and has never been questioned—it was illusory. It seems extraordinary that his first commission should be a palatial house as ostentatious as any in the preceding century; yet it is explicable. Castle Howard, Yorkshire, was designed for Charles Howard, third earl of Carlisle, five years Vanbrugh's junior, a Kit-Cat colleague and a Carleton kinsman. Carlisle leased the gutted castle of Henderskelfe and its estate from his grandmother on 31 October 1698. By that time William Talman, whom he had asked to design a new house, must have inspected the site, but by the following spring when Carlisle again visited Yorkshire, Vanbrugh was competing with Talman and seeking to replace him.

According to Vanbrugh's letter of Christmas day 1699 (*Letters*, 4–5) designs had been made, revised, and approved, and site works and quarrying started; in the previous summer he had 'seen most of the great Houses of the North', including Chatsworth, where the duke of Devonshire had recently dismissed Talman. The letter's tone suggests what some of the architectural detailing confirms, that Vanbrugh wanted to surpass his prototypes; Castle Howard was to be better architecture than Chatsworth and grander, with the earl's and countess's matching state suites along the south front as in a royal house. Vanbrugh's mansion is a baroque palace in all but name, profusely decorated, with the central building encased in a giant pilaster order and surmounted by a large dome. It faces north and south in sympathy with the lie of the landscape, whereas Talman's design faced east and west. Second, before the end of 1699 Vanbrugh had decided to raise the entrance hall into an over-large cupola, a feature unprecedented in English domestic architecture, giving the interior its unique majesty and the exterior its dramatic silhouette.

Vanbrugh's entry into architecture depended on his own—and Carlisle's—confidence and the collaboration of the established architect Nicholas Hawksmoor; the seeds had been sown in the rising post-fire London of 1681, perhaps among the Anglo-Indian monuments of Surat, and surely during his time on parole in Paris, already an impressive city with many modern classical buildings. What he still lacked to realize his vision was supplied by Hawksmoor, introduced officially to Carlisle in the spring of 1700 but already indispensable; the surviving preliminary drawings (mostly in the V&A) include small ones in Vanbrugh's untrained hand and Hawksmoor's corresponding professional larger ones. The relationship between Vanbrugh and Hawksmoor was initially between the Renaissance gentleman architect, engaging in a liberal art, and the practised professional, but it soon became the close partnership that produced Castle Howard and Blenheim. Their letters make clear that Hawksmoor regarded Vanbrugh as the begetter of these commissions, himself as (in his own words) 'the loving Nurse that almost thinks the child his own' (BL, Add. MS 61353, fol. 239).

Vanbrugh both relied on and learned from Hawksmoor's experience, technical knowledge, draughtsmanship, and repertory of design detail. Moreover, it was Hawksmoor's grasp of the classical orders and his feeling for the eloquence of masonry that generated both the style of these two great houses and that of Vanbrugh's plainer independent works. How they met is unknown, but it was probably no later than Vanbrugh's entry to the theatre world. They had associates in common. Vanbrugh's marine commander, Lord Carmarthen, was the brother-in-law of William Fermor, first Baron Leominster, for whom Hawksmoor was building Easton Neston. Vanbrugh's court connections brought him close to the office of works; moreover his cousin William Vanbrugh was secretary to the commission for building Greenwich Hospital, where Hawksmoor was Sir Christopher Wren's assistant. From May 1700 Carlisle would pay him £40 a year plus £50 for the annual summer journey that he, like Vanbrugh, would make to Yorkshire.

By the summer of 1712 Castle Howard was ready for occupation. Vanbrugh subsequently reported that Carlisle was pleased with his house's practical virtues: it was warm, dry, draught-free, and therefore economical to run. Vanbrugh's attribution of these virtues to his own good design principles show that considerable 'thought and lecture' had preceded the commission. However, leaving the west side uncompleted, Carlisle turned his attention to the garden and garden buildings, and the western side was built to Sir Thomas Robinson's design for the fourth earl, and still unfinished at the latter's death in 1758.

Solvency and status Vanbrugh seems to have been paid little or nothing for Castle Howard; his rewards were Carlisle's patronage and lifelong hospitality. In 1702 his marine's half pay was badly in arrears, and neither architecture nor the theatre could offer a steady and solid income. This may explain his commission on 10 March 1702 as captain in the new foot regiment of George Hastings, eighth earl of Huntingdon—his original colonel's son. Two months later, on 4 May, Queen Anne's declaration of war on France cast military service in a different light, and Vanbrugh promptly found a substitute and resigned. Meanwhile he had received a better offer: on 20 May his appointment was confirmed as comptroller of her majesty's works in place of Talman. Other architectural clients were disenchanted with Talman; so, in a different capacity, was his superior in the works, Sir Christopher Wren. Carlisle, briefly lord treasurer in 1702, was undoubtedly the power behind Vanbrugh's appointment, even though he left office shortly before. The salary was modest, but the post brought official houses which could be rented to tenants. Whitehall regarded the post as a useless sinecure, but Vanbrugh meant to outperform Talman in public as in private architecture. Moreover, since Wren was seventy it was reasonable to have another senior officer in the works. Vanbrugh could be critical of Wren's pragmatic and sometimes easy-going attitude to bureaucracy. In 1704, describing to the lord treasurer contractual irregularities at the Orangery being built at Kensington Palace, he complained that Wren had considered the matter not worth pursuing. Vanbrugh's concern, and the fact that he made unspecified changes to the design of the building (of which Wren was nominally the architect) are insufficient grounds for denying its authorship to Hawksmoor, the resident designer at Kensington, of whose style it is entirely characteristic. Relations with Wren improved. Vanbrugh later hoped to succeed him as surveyor-general, but when offered the post (around 1715) declined 'out of Tenderness' for Wren (*Letters*, 123).

Vanbrugh justified the Treasury's confidence and, except for a gap in 1713–14, retained the post of comptroller until his death. His introduction and advancement in the College of Arms, however, were—and remain—controversial. On 21 June 1703 the obsolete office of Carlisle herald was revived to enable him to proceed the following March to Clarenceux herald, second only to Garter herald. When in 1725 he sold his office to Knox Ward, he told a friend he had 'got leave to dispose in earnest, of a Place I got in jest' (*Letters*, 170). This antonymy occurs often in Vanbrugh's writing, and its significance should not be overstated. His colleagues' initial opposition ought to have been directed as much to Lord Carlisle, who as deputy earl marshal arranged both appointments and against whose wishes they were powerless; however, as in other areas, Vanbrugh duly made more friends than enemies. The pageantry of state occasions appealed to his theatrical sense, his duties were not onerous, and he appears to have performed them well. In his later years they are detailed

in his *Journal of All Receipts Payments and other Transactions* (printed in Downes, *Vanbrugh*), and in the opinion of a modern herald and historian, although the appointment was 'incongruous', he was 'possibly the most distinguished man who has ever worn a herald's tabard' (A. R. Wagner, *Heralds of England*, 1967, 326). In May–June 1706 Lord Halifax and Vanbrugh (representing the octogenarian Garter king of arms) led a delegation to Hanover to confer the Order of the Garter on Prince George, the future George II; Vanbrugh probably had leisure to see the formal gardens developing at Herrenhausen, the elector of Hanover's summer palace.

At the age of forty Vanbrugh's ambition, energy, and capability must have seemed boundless, as he assumed the role of impresario. By June 1703 he had purchased, for £2000, a site on the west side of the Haymarket, hoping by the end of the year to finish a new theatre. As both developer and architect he envisaged a building 'very different from any Other House in being' (*Letters*, 4) and half as big again as the first substantial purpose-built Restoration playhouse, Drury Lane, built thirty years earlier. It was widely known that the venture, to be called the Queen's Theatre, had the support, moral and—less reliably—financial, of the Kit-Cat Club, whose pledged subscriptions were intended to pay for it; the default of subscribers was but the first of many troubles. Vanbrugh and William Congreve were licensed as joint managers on 14 December 1704, but legal and financial difficulties had delayed the foundation until 18 April 1704 and, although Queen Anne attended a preliminary concert in November 1704, the official opening was not until 9 April 1705. The first production was an opera, Giacomo Greber's *The Loves of Ergasto*. The acoustics of the auditorium, which was very high, did not favour speech, and the house soon proved more suited to music. The problem was compounded by sheer size, which made the house, at the west end of town, difficult to fill. Nevertheless, from August the Queen's Theatre was dedicated to plays and Drury Lane to operas, an arrangement not reversed until the end of 1707. In 1708 the theatre closed early, before reopening on 14 December with changes to both the stage and auditorium and an enlarged orchestra pit.

As theatre manager Vanbrugh was unlucky, but not unusually so. At the end of 1705 Congreve left him in sole charge. Opera was expensive, and Vanbrugh's repeated attempts to economize always ended with the thought that if the queen would give a patronal subsidy all would be well. On 14 August 1706 he leased the theatre to Owen *Swiny for seven years, but early in 1708 he bought out Swiny, paying him as manager; however, before the closure for alteration on 20 May Swiny was again in control. In 1712 Swiny left England, bankrupt. Vanbrugh did not venture again into management; he kept his financial interest until 1720, when, after his marriage, he sold the building to his brother Charles and the properties and wardrobe to Drury Lane. The modified theatre survived until its comprehensive remodelling in 1782.

Blenheim Vanbrugh's most famous building—the centre of comment both favourable and adverse—is Blenheim.

The name is Anglicized from Blindheim, the village on the Bavarian Danube near which the forces of the grand alliance under John Churchill, first duke of Marlborough, and Eugène of Savoy defeated France and Bavaria on 3 August 1704. Although the War of the Spanish Succession was far from over, this battle was decisive for the alliance. At home, both Marlborough and his duchess were in high favour with Queen Anne, who considered a hero's reward appropriate. Parliament ratified the grant of the royal manor of Woodstock, Oxfordshire, in March 1705, but Marlborough knew of it unofficially several months earlier.

Blenheim, like Castle Howard, is a palace, although it did not acquire that title until the nineteenth century. It exceeded Castle Howard in most respects; it is larger, and its encasing giant order is interlaced with a second smaller order. It is emblazoned with sculpted emblems of victory; its dramatic and jagged skyline shocked Georgian sensibility but came to be admired in the Romantic era.

Much of Blenheim's commissioning is known only from legal depositions made years later, when unpaid construction bills led to litigation. The duke, in his mid-fifties, was looking forward to retirement at the end of hostilities; according to Vanbrugh's evidence in 1720, Marlborough, on winter leave, approached him around Christmas 1704, intending to build a house—at his own expense—in Woodstock Park, and the following February architect and client met on site. Between these two meetings Marlborough saw the model for Castle Howard. According to Vanbrugh (*Letters*, 179), Marlborough did not want Wren as his architect; probably the great commander had already discovered the character of Vanbrugh's work, but the model would have removed any doubts.

Marlborough requested a design similar to Carlisle's, with such additions as a gallery. Assuming stability in prices, the sum he intended, £40,000, exceeded the cost of Carlisle's house; Blenheim was to outshine Castle Howard, while emulating not only its grandeur but also its symmetrical and—for a palace—convenient plan. Almost everything at Blenheim is larger, the cost (ultimately about £300,000) six or seven or eight times greater than Castle Howard. Most of this was paid by the Treasury, the rest by the Marlboroughs. After their fall from grace, and indeed after the queen's death, no document was found confirming the extension of royal bounty from the estate to a house; however, it was never disproved, and the organization of the work leaves little doubt of the substance, generally accepted at the time, of the gift. A Treasury warrant of 9 June 1705 appointed Vanbrugh, as the duke's agent, surveyor of the Blenheim works. Hawksmoor was appointed assistant surveyor, and the office was a microcosm of the royal works.

Blenheim's standards were to be of the highest, although Vanbrugh properly sought competitive prices for the work, 'that the Appearance of every thing may exceed the Cost' (*Letters*, 23). As an ardent admirer of the duke, he regarded the project, as he wrote in 1710, 'much more as an intended Monument of the Queens Glory than

a private Habitation for the Duke' (ibid., 45–6). (After Marlborough's death his widow refashioned Blenheim's image into a personal monument to her husband.) From the outset carved martial trophies were to embellish the roofline. Vanbrugh and Hawksmoor worked empirically and by experiment, even making changes during the course of building. It must have seemed the ideal commission, supported by the public purse as long as the queen's favour lasted, and initially without limit. Site work began soon after Marlborough's February visit, and on 18 June an impressive foundation-stone was laid. Four days later Vanbrugh proposed to his client the first significant alteration, enlarging the hall and adding a colossal portico and the attic storey that floods this north-facing room with light. Other changes followed. Early in 1707 the whole building was heightened, including the giant order; consequently the Doric was replaced by the slenderer Corinthian. Six large turrets added excitement to the roofline, their complex forms undoubtedly developed by Hawksmoor. The house was also, like Castle Howard, extended to either side by additional courtyards providing ampler services and stables. Marlborough accepted all these enhancements; his duchess, who mistrusted all architects, was never happy. Her extreme displeasure was reserved for the Grand Bridge, a viaduct to carry the northern avenue, aligned on the entrance, across the valley of the small River Glyme. This avenue was seldom used, the practical approach being from the east through Woodstock town, but the huge arched bridge with its sparse and massive decorative features gave Blenheim a unique scenic grandeur even before 1764, when Lancelot 'Capability' Brown dammed the stream into the lake, a body of water more appropriate than the original small watercourse at the bottom of the valley.

Building did not proceed smoothly. Contractors accepted the Treasury as a reliable, albeit a slow, payer; however, payments were in arrears by June 1706, with serious effects on the local economy. By the summer of 1710 the whole project was in doubt as costs rose and the Marlboroughs lost favour; Edward Strong, the principal mason, laid off most of his workforce in September, and the following month the duchess closed the building season prematurely. The beginning of 1711 saw her dismissal from court and the end of that year the duke's from command. When Treasury payments ceased altogether on 1 June 1712 they had reached £233,000, with almost £45,000 outstanding, but the house was quite uninhabitable. The Marlboroughs spent 1713 and half of 1714 in exile, before returning to England on 2 August, the day after Anne's death. In May 1716 Marlborough suffered a stroke, and when building work resumed the contracts were made directly with the couple, not with the crown. But on 8 November 1716 Vanbrugh, provoked beyond patience by the duchess's unreasonable criticism, resigned. For the next six years she relied on the advice of James Moore, a cabinet-maker; by 1719 she was able to move with her ailing husband into the still incomplete house. In 1721 they sued Vanbrugh, Hawksmoor, and 419 other defendants for conspiracy—with little effect, although Lord Macclesfield granted a perpetual injunction to prevent Vanbrugh from suing the crown for the remaining arrears of his salary, of which he had received one third, £800, in March 1716. Marlborough died in June 1722; by then Moore had outrun his competence. Hawksmoor, whose connection with Blenheim had never officially ended, and who had offered his help in April, took charge until 1725, and designed among other things the Long Library and the Woodstock gate.

Blenheim was finished, after a fashion, without the colonnade and triumphal gate intended to close the north forecourt, or much of the west (stable) range. The Grand Bridge had become usable in 1721 with the completion of earthworks for the approach road. In August 1725, through the intervention of Sir Robert Walpole, Vanbrugh secured the remainder of his Blenheim arrears. A month previously he had been refused entry to Woodstock Park and could only glimpse his masterpiece over the rectory garden wall.

Kimbolton Castle and Vanbrugh's personal style Blenheim and Castle Howard are collaborative works with Hawksmoor. Their exteriors are remarkable for their surface enrichment and carved detailing; Hawksmoor had used this 'decorated' style, derived from the works of Wren and seventeenth-century French architects, at Easton Neston. In the early summer of 1707 Vanbrugh was called to Kimbolton, Huntingdon, by the countess of Manchester (while Charles Montague, fourth earl, a Kit-Cat associate, was in Venice) because the south front had collapsed. Kimbolton was a four-square fortified house, refurbished from the 1520s onwards; most recently the interior courtyard had been remodelled in the 1690s in a domestic classical style. The local mason's proposals were asymmetrical and inadequate; Vanbrugh took Hawksmoor to Kimbolton, and after consultation a new design for the south range was approved by the countess and forwarded to the earl on 18 July. Hawksmoor acted only as draughtsman. 'As to the Outside', wrote Vanbrugh, 'I thought 'twas absolutely best to give it Something of the Castle Air, tho' at the Same time to make it regular' (*Letters*, 14). Old stone could be recycled into smooth ashlar, with regular sash-windows and a battlemented skyline, effectively hiding the concave bow of the façade. For his design Vanbrugh cited the precedent of Hugh May's work at Windsor Castle in the 1670s; in a further letter he hoped that Kimbolton would exhibit 'a Manly Beauty' and—more significantly—demonstrate his belief that 'certainly the Figure and Proportions make the most pleasing Fabrick, And not the delicacy of the Ornaments' (*Letters*, 15)—the nearest we have to a statement of his aesthetic creed. His patron was evidently pleased, for within three years most of the exterior had been rebuilt to match the south range, with a new suite of state rooms. Although in 1719 Manchester celebrated his elevation to a dukedom by commissioning from the Florentine Alessandro Galilei a somewhat incongruous giant portico on the east, Kimbolton is in essence a plain classically based house with battlements.

As early as 1701 Vanbrugh's little house at Whitehall (dem. 1898) already exemplified a plainer architectural mode, also developed by Hawksmoor in the 1690s and later exploited in his London churches. It is also, broadly speaking, the style of Vanbrugh's later independent designs, although the two architects' works are usually distinguishable: Vanbrugh's lack the complex formal abstraction of, for example, the Kensington Orangery. At Kimbolton the 'castle air' probably meant no more than the appearance of a castle, but it acquired wider associations in some of his later works. His experience of fortified buildings embraced not only the ancient walls of Chester and York but also the bastions and gatehouses of Vincennes and Paris. Moreover the vigorous skyline of Blenheim owes no more to Hawksmoor's detailing than to Vanbrugh's knowledge of the prodigy houses of the reigns of Elizabeth I and James I: the dramatic and castle-like relationships of mass at Hardwick Hall and Wollaton Hall were inspired, like the writing of Shakespeare and Spenser, by Elizabethan romantic neo-medievalism. Later, in 1722, Vanbrugh directed alterations to the medieval west range—containing the great hall—of Lumley Castle, Durham, 'making regular' and classicizing the fenestration by blocking the old openings and inserting large sash-windows with oval lights above them.

On 13 May 1709 Vanbrugh leased Chargate farm in Esher, Surrey, with permission to rebuild the farmhouse appropriately. The work was probably complete before his mother's death there in August 1711. Elizabeth Vanbrugh was exceptionally discreet about her finances, but she probably paid for the house as a family home for the architect's unmarried sisters and younger brothers. Any hope of this vanished three years later when he sold the estate. Chargate's plan and appearance are known from office drawings; its H-plan suggests the reuse of a Tudor house's foundations. It had indeed 'something of the castle air' on a small scale—all the rooms were small—with battlements and segmental-headed sash-windows like Kimbolton. It was built of brick, and its turrets and prominent chimneys look both back to earlier domestic architecture and forward to Vanbrugh's later work.

At Chargate the windows were without architraves, appearing merely punched out of sheer wall surfaces. In his next major commission, Kings Weston, Gloucestershire (1710–14), some of the windows are treated likewise; others are surrounded merely by broad shallow bands. Kings Weston was built for Edward Southwell in fine limestone ashlar quarried from the park. The interior took many years to finish, and additions were made in the 1760s by Robert Mylne; however, Vanbrugh was certainly responsible for the plan, the impressive newel staircase in the centre, and the elevations, each treated differently. The entrance front has an applied portico of giant but unfluted Corinthian pilasters with a pediment; the other fronts are astylar. The crowning rooftop arcade forms an open attic, containing all the chimney flues and making a highly picturesque effect from a distance.

Kings Weston is the plainest of Vanbrugh's houses. He and Hawksmoor were not alone in the first years of the eighteenth century in envisaging a plain architecture based on the classical canons implicit in the writings of

Vitruvius and Palladio. Vanbrugh probably read Vitruvius in French, and by 1703 he owned Roland Fréart's accurate French edition of Palladio; the only architectural book mentioned in his letters, he valued it for 'the Plans of most of the Houses he built' (*Letters*, 9). He could have claimed to be the first English Palladian of the century; he was, however, attracted not by the potential of a pattern book but by Palladio's skill as a domestic planner and his practical common sense. There was nothing orthodox in Vanbrugh's attitude to the Renaissance, but Palladio's frugal exterior elevations suited his preference for 'figure' over ornament, and the 'castle air' could be accommodated to it.

Vanbrugh at fifty: politics and official life On 21 September 1711 Vanbrugh was appointed to the Fifty New Churches commission (he also sat on its initial working committee and submitted several designs for churches). His *Proposals* or general recommendations (printed in Downes, *Vanbrugh*, 257–8) appear superficially very different from Wren's paper of 1711 with their emphasis on the churches' 'Solemn and Awfull Appearance'; however, they contain much very practical advice. His support, like Wren's, was undoubtedly valuable to Hawksmoor as one of the two permanent surveyors. The new commission of 2 December 1715 included no architects; however, by then Vanbrugh's fortune had turned twice.

Vanbrugh paid dearly for his loyalty to Marlborough. On 25 January 1713, writing to the mayor of Woodstock about the duke's proposal to pave the market place, he mentioned the 'continual plague and bitter persecution he has most barbarously been followed with for two years past' (*Letters*, 54). His letter, intercepted, was made public; Vanbrugh denied any political intent, but on 15 April his patent as comptroller was revoked. Both Thomas Archer and William Talman applied to replace him but the post was left vacant. A man with more enemies than Vanbrugh would have been in greater danger; he was also fortunate in not depending on his official houses for shelter, and as his salary was usually years in arrears his finances were not immediately affected. He visited Chester in the summer and spent the last quarter of 1713 at Castle Howard.

The queen's death in August 1714 and changes in government and administration permitted reinstatement. On 18 September, George I landed at Greenwich and knighted Vanbrugh there; the citation was for his Hanover excursion, but the prime mover was Marlborough. In November, Vanbrugh advised Halifax on the reform of the office of works and on 24 January 1715 he was reappointed comptroller. On 15 June he received the new post (created for him, according to Hawksmoor, and probably instigated by Carlisle) of surveyor of gardens and waters. In this capacity he designed the castellated water tower built the following year on Kensington Palace Green (des.). Concurrently he designed rooms and chimney-pieces for the prince of Wales's apartments at Hampton Court. Halifax's reforms included the establishment in May 1715 of a new board of works, which made Wren's authority nominal. Until Wren's dismissal in April 1718 Vanbrugh attended

almost nine in every ten meetings, one motive undoubtedly being concern for his ageing colleague. He was instrumental in the downfall of the incompetent William Benson, who succeeded Wren; when Benson was dismissed after little over a year, Vanbrugh was disappointed not to replace him. On 1 August 1716 he had succeeded Wren as surveyor to Greenwich Hospital, a post he held for life, but without major new works there.

Personal and family; the Greenwich estate On 1 January 1715 Vanbrugh opened a *Journal of All Receipts Payments and other Transactions* which, apart from a few missing pages, chronicles most events until his death. The tone of a memorandum on the first page suggests a turning point of which the new journal was symbolic. Impending reinstatement at Whitehall was accompanied by improvements in his finances. On 14 October 1714 he had sold Chargate with its contents. In May 1715 he mortgaged the Haymarket Theatre to his younger brother Charles for £2500; moreover, while Charles was home from sea he paid Vanbrugh a sum for board and lodging almost equalling the mortgage interest he received. The journal shows that Vanbrugh made little use of banks and ran a complex loan and investment system among his siblings. On 9 March 1717, as a replacement for Chargate, he leased a house in Palace Yard near Greenwich Hospital, with option to purchase, from Sir William Saunderson.

By then another change was impending. Lady Mary Wortley Montagu had flippantly reported him as considering 'the Honourable state of matrimony' (*Letters*, ed. R. Halsband, 1965, 1.201) as early as October 1713 and identified the family, if not the individual, as the Yarburghs of Heslington, near York. As with other major decisions, this one was far more premeditated than he admitted. A year after leasing the Greenwich house, in a letter (30 April 1718, probably to a daughter of Lord Carlisle) he confided a lover's dilemma: he was in 'a Sort of retirement here at Greenwich' because the 'Heslington Lady … keeps me from your gay meetings at York, by [being] there, and from those at London, by being absent' (BL, Add. MS 32686, fols. 104–5). Next Christmas he described the weather at Castle Howard to Lord Newcastle as 'so bloody Cold, I have almost a mind to Marry to keep myself warm' (*Letters*, 107).

Secrecy continued: only ten days after the event did Vanbrugh inform Lord Newcastle of his marriage on 14 January 1719 to Henrietta Maria (1693–1776), daughter of Colonel James Yarburgh, Vanbrugh's contemporary and a former aide-de-camp to Marlborough. She was charming and practical, and the marriage was apparently both fruitful and happy. In June 1722 Vanbrugh told the publisher and secretary of the Kit-Cat Club, Jacob Tonson, his young wife was 'Special good'; by then he was 'two Boys strong in the Nursery but am forbid getting any more this Season' (*Letters*, 146). The elder son, Charles [*see below*], was born on 20 October 1720; the younger, John, was born on 14 February 1722 but lived just over a year. He was buried on 28 March 1723 at Walton-on-Thames, where he had been sent to a family property to be nursed.

Vanbrugh had headed the family since his mother's

death in 1711, and in 1718 he began to develop a private hamlet at the top of Greenwich Hill towards Blackheath, an area becoming fashionable. On 3 March he leased about 12 acres from Sir Michael Biddulph. By June he was buying bricks; Richard Billinghurst, a master bricklayer with contracts at the Royal Hospital, took charge of constructing a house, of London stock brick, at the north-west corner of the triangular estate; it was habitable before the lease on Saunderson's house expired in March 1720. A battlemented building with a circular stair tower in the centre and square corner turrets, it justified the name—and the air—of Vanbrugh Castle. It was modest in size and symmetrical, with small convenient rooms like those of Chargate and unrivalled views over the Thames valley and estuary. Accidentally the castle became the prototype for the bigger asymmetrical mock castles of the late eighteenth century, for by 1724 Vanbrugh had enlarged it to one side by about half; the extension, also symmetrical, contained a big room on each floor, but made the whole irregular. By then he had also built small houses for his brothers Charles and Philip and two 'white towers', four-storey miniature castles of white bricks, as well as a habitable gatehouse at the southern corner. All except Vanbrugh Castle were demolished early in the twentieth century.

Major works after 1715 'One may find a great deal of Pleasure', Vanbrugh wrote to Tonson in 1719, 'in building a Palace for another; when one shou'd find very little, in living in't ones Self' (*Letters*, 122). In his last decade Vanbrugh undertook four more great house commissions. The nucleus of Claremont, for Thomas Pelham-Holles, earl of Clare and first duke of Newcastle, was his own Chargate, which Holles had bought from him. By replacing battlements by attic parapets and adding a central pediment and a coat of plaster the house was easily classicized. Vanbrugh cut away the sloping ground in front to make a podium, with long arcaded wings extending on either side at the lower level, to a total length of 90 metres. The transformation was completed in 1720 with a huge two-storey 'great room' behind one wing. Claremont's effect depended on its size, its many round-headed openings, turrets, and tall chimneys, some of the last joined in pairs by arches. The whole was demolished about 1763 except for some impressive garden walls and the Belvedere (1715) on the hill behind, a turreted rehearsal for the Kensington water tower and Vanbrugh Castle, with extensive views from the roof.

Eastbury, Dorset, was begun for George Doddington of the Admiralty in 1718 after two or three years' designing. Only a wing was built before Doddington's death in 1720; the main house was started in 1722 to a reduced plan for his nephew George Bubb Doddington, and completed by Roger Morris in 1738. With its corner towers, its deep forecourt flanked by service wings, and the dramatic attic Vanbrugh intended over the centre, Eastbury approached Blenheim's grandeur but neither its real size nor its visual complexity; however, Morris omitted the attic and added a Palladian pediment to Vanbrugh's four-square hexastyle portico. Eastbury's size embarrassed later owners, one of

whom in 1775 demolished it with gunpowder except for part of the stable wing, now a self-contained house, and one massive courtyard gateway.

The fate of Seaton Delaval, Northumberland (1720–28), was not very much better; the service wings survive, but the main house, although roofed and conserved, has been a dramatic shell since a fire in 1822. Seaton was built for Admiral George Delaval to replace an older house; the main pile was Vanbrugh's tribute to Elizabethan Wollaton, not only in its dramatic massing of towers and turrets, but also in its interior planning; like Wollaton, it had a two-storey hall with a big attic room over it.

Of the last great house, Grimsthorpe Castle, Lincolnshire, only one range of four was built. The late Tudor courtyard house belonged to Robert Bertie, first duke of Ancaster, Vanbrugh's kinsman and companion in France in 1688. Vanbrugh's complete design was engraved and published in Colen Campbell's *Vitruvius Britannicus* (1725). Its unexecuted south front paraphrases Campbell's design for Houghton, Norfolk, of which Vanbrugh could have had advance knowledge; the constituents and disposition are very similar but the proportions are quite different. Eventually only the north (entrance) range was built, begun in 1722 and finished for the second duke shortly after Vanbrugh's death. Grimsthorpe's detailing is sparing and fastidious, but not conventional, with internal doorcases derived from an engraving of one of Michelangelo's least orthodox exemplars.

Vanbrugh's final tribute to Palladio is the most equivocal: the Belvedere or Temple of the Four Winds at Castle Howard (1725–8), which, as correspondence shows, was executed faithfully by Hawksmoor (the interior was fitted in 1738–9 after the latter's death). Of the several English buildings consciously based on Palladio's Rotonda near Vicenza—a domed square building with porticoes on all sides—this is the smallest but is alone, like its prototype, a day building designed for a different prospect for every time of day. The figure and proportions are remote from Palladio's but set on a contour 500 metres from the house, it seems closer, even in dull weather, to the spirit of Mediterranean antiquity than any other English building of its time.

The last years of a professional Another unsuccessful contender for the surveyorship in 1719 was the painter Sir James Thornhill. Such people, Vanbrugh wrote, 'just learn enough of [architecture] to help fill up their Pictures' (*Letters*, 117); the strength of his contempt for 'a Painter made Surveyor of the Works' confirms how completely he saw himself, with an active comptrollership and several spectacular great houses to his credit, as a professional architect. Approaching sixty, he still enjoyed reasonable health for his years and his time, although he reduced his commitments: on 5 July 1725 he sold the office of Clarenceux herald. His travels around England indicate a sound constitution, and three of his sisters lived to eighty or beyond. Marriage brought a coach-and-four, but on his own he liked a calash, the equestrian equivalent of a small sports car; his driving was 'none of the slowest' (*Letters*, 106). However, life in French prisons may have taken its toll. On

30 August 1725 he made a will, quickly and privately after an unprecedented asthmatic attack. On 3 February 1726 the complaint was 'still sticking close to me' (*N&Q*, 36, 1989, 468), but he was active, and attended four board of works meetings in March. The last was on 23 March; three days later, on 26 March 1726, he died at his Whitehall house, of quinsy. He was buried on 31 March in the family vault under the north aisle of St Stephen Walbrook; his will, unwitnessed, was authenticated by a servant and a cousin. Henrietta Maria, who outlived him by fifty years, died at Whitehall about 22 April 1776 and was buried in the family vault on 3 May.

Among Vanbrugh's papers were three acts and one scene of a play, *A Journey to London*; Cibber adapted and completed this as *The Provok'd Husband*, which opened at Drury Lane on 10 January 1728. Cibber printed Vanbrugh's manuscript (now lost) with his own; its date is uncertain but some of the allusions are appropriate to the early 1720s. Moreover, Vanbrugh's play can be seen as a reaction to the new genre of sentimental comedy of which the prime example is Richard Steele's *The Conscious Lovers* (1722)—moral, decorous, and tasteful—in a profession of faith in the old genre, which delivers a moral lesson by showing the characters 'doing what they shou'd not do'. Vanbrugh's themes were familiar—battles of the sexes and generations, and between rural naïvety and metropolitan intrigue—but Cibber converted a brilliant and relentless farce into a competent and successful comedy.

Vanbrugh's achievement Vanbrugh did nothing by halves. He had the gift of presenting complexity to others as simple, but not simplistic; even to his architectural clients he used clear, non-technical language. His two original comedies are brilliant, not only because they are both entertaining and serious, but because they present contrived situations and ridiculous characters as credible, crafted and often metrical speech as natural. His apparently casual style, praised by contemporaries such as Cibber and Pope, is the same as that of all but his earliest letters.

Vanbrugh the architect does not cite the Vitruvian tripos of commodity, firmness, and delight, but it is implicit in both his writing and practice. Convenience was cause for pride; his structures are massive and conventional, and the new churches should, he told the commission, stand for a thousand years; 'the most *pleasing* Fabrick' (*Letters*, 15) was the end to be gained. He sought the spirit rather than the letter of Vitruvius and Palladio. Although initially his buildings may seem accidentally composed, they are as carefully considered as his fluent stage works, but only for Castle Howard is there evidence from drawings (and there in partnership) of how his designs developed. His eye for shape, mass, and texture paralleled his ear for language and speech. He understood that mere size is not the same as scale, which for him was proportionate to the human figure. Of his houses Blenheim is inevitably the archetype; Seaton Delaval, for all its damaged and weathered state, best captures the romantic element in baroque art with its combination of elegant but sparing detail, varied textures, rugged massing, and dramatic outlines. He also appreciated that buildings do not exist in isolation. Although 'a Vanbrugh garden' has some meaning, he was not a garden designer but worked with the leading practitioners—George London and Stephen Switzer at Castle Howard, Henry Wise at Blenheim, Charles Bridgeman at Stowe. He designed garden buildings, from elegant temples at Stowe and Eastbury to mock-fortified walls around Castle Howard. With Hawksmoor he deferentially allowed Carlisle to take the credit for the Castle Howard landscape, but in truth the ideas came from all three.

Vanbrugh had few followers in either drama or architecture not only because his creations were inimitable, but because he was working at the end of a period. Collier's attack represents a change in theatrical taste just as the *Letter Concerning Design* of Anthony Ashley Cooper, third earl of Shaftesbury, which attacked Blenheim, marks a reversion from baroque architecture. Nevertheless the original comedies are not forgotten even today. In architecture Vanbrugh was less influential than he undoubtedly hoped. He seems to have believed that as surveyor he could have provided, better than orthodox Palladians, the British style called for in Shaftesbury's essay, which circulated in London during 1712 although it was not published until 1732. As second officer in a period of little crown building, Vanbrugh's power was limited.

Vanbrugh's name is associated with two surviving albums of drawings. The 'Kings Weston Book' (Glos. RO, 33746) is a compilation of the early 1720s by an anonymous Somerset mason and surveyor; it contains not only drawings of Kings Weston but also a series of designs for little houses similar in concept and style to Vanbrugh's Greenwich estate. None is in Vanbrugh's hand, but they appear to be copied from his originals. The Elton Hall book (V&A, E.2124–1992) contains original drawings by Vanbrugh and by Sir Edward Lovett Pearce, his cousin through his mother's sister. About the time of Vanbrugh's death Pearce began architectural practice in Dublin; in some drawings it is hardly possible to distinguish hands, and although there is no evidence beyond the album and the kinship Pearce was probably Vanbrugh's assistant and informal pupil.

About fifty years after his death Vanbrugh the author of racy comedies and overwhelming buildings began to be revalued. Sheridan, who understood him, adapted *The Relapse* for a different public as *A Trip to Scarborough* (1777). In architecture praise came from artists rather than critics. In 1773 Robert and James Adam, while mindful of 'barbarisms and absurdities', praised Vanbrugh's movement: 'the rise and fall, the advance and recess, with other diversity of form, in the different parts of a building' (*Works in Architecture*, 1.2).

More surprising is the perceptive appraisal in the 'Thirteenth discourse' of Sir Joshua Reynolds, of Vanbrugh as 'an Architect who composed like a Painter' (*Discourses*, 1959, 244). Vanbrugh foreshadowed the late eighteenth-century Picturesque in his unsuccessful attempt to save old Woodstock Manor in 1709. He invoked both romantic association and the enhancement of the otherwise dull view north from Blenheim. Henry II, 'One of the Bravest and most Warlike of the English Kings', had installed there his mistress Rosamund Clifford; the now ruined buildings could become 'One of the Most Agreable Objects that the best of Landskip Painters can invent' (*Letters*, 29–30). His own drawing (now lost) supported his argument. Nevertheless, Reynolds meant more than Picturesque effects, for in figure composition the elements are simple and universal, yet infinitely variable. He would have ridiculed, had he known of it, Vanbrugh's propensity for naïvely adding smoke to the chimneys in his elevations, but he understood Vanbrugh's baroque composition in few large units rather than many small ones, the colossal couplet of pillars rather than the repetition of many. Vanbrugh did not design stage scenery—his plays involved people in conventional settings—and the relationship and distinction between his two creative areas is deeper: they grow separately from the same mind, and one might add to Reynolds's sentence that he composed his plays with the eye, and ear, of a dramatist.

The Gothic revival did nothing for Vanbrugh's reputation: his own medievalizing buildings contain not a single pointed arch. Nevertheless, at the height of the Gothic revival he was included among the classical architects portrayed on the base of the Albert Memorial (1872) beside Inigo Jones, Wren, and Palladio. Something of his spirit informed the great Victorian civic monuments, although he was seen as an amateur, a maverick, and no more serious than his own stage characters. His significance emerged only in the 1920s, at the same time that England rediscovered the European baroque, in particular with the publication in 1928 of H. A. Tipping and C. Hussey's profusely illustrated *The Works of Sir John Vanbrugh and his School* and G. Webb's edition of his correspondence. Subsequent research revealed the serious man of the two best portraits—by Kneller and Thomas Murray (both NPG)—who combined the industrious Vanbrugh merchant ethic and the Carleton social ease, hardened and tempered by experience. The realization that in Hawksmoor he had at least an equal embarrassed anyone with space for only one hero at a time, but eventually the truth was accepted that both were very exceptional men.

Charles Vanbrugh (1720–1745), soldier, first and only surviving son of Sir John Vanbrugh, was born on 20 October 1720 at Greenwich or Whitehall and was thus in his sixth year when his father died; Lord Carlisle was his godfather. At eight he went to the school of a Mr Le Plas. On 6 September 1731 he played Scipio in a performance in Vanbrugh Castle of James Thomson's *Sophonisba, or, Hannibal's Overthrow*. The cast were children of the nobility and gentry, and the play had previously been acted by juveniles in London. He was at Westminster School from 1732 to 1736, when his mother paid for him to learn Italian, before completing his education in Lausanne. On 29 April 1738 he was enrolled there in the Compagnie des Nobles Fusillers. In March 1740 he was in London and showed his father's houses and designs to Jacob Friedrich, Baron Bielfeld. As ensign in the Coldstream Guards he was in Flanders by the autumn of 1743. He was wounded in the battle of Fontenoy, Hainault, on 11 May 1745 and died soon after midnight; he was buried at Ath on 13 May. He was unmarried. His comrade Joseph Yorke (later Lord Dover) wrote to Jack Jones, an old family servant, a moving account of his death. Charles showed great promise. His vocabulary and propensity to 'Rhyming and … dry joking' at twenty months (Vanbrugh, *Letters*, 149) were more than paternal fantasy, for surviving letters have his father's wit and betray varied reading. Bielfeld found him 'a young man of real merit' (Whistler, *Sir John Vanbrugh*, 294–5).

KERRY DOWNES

Sources *The complete works of Sir John Vanbrugh*, ed. B. Dobrée, 1–3: *The plays* (1927) • *The complete works of Sir John Vanbrugh*, ed. G. Webb, 4: *The letters* (1928) • K. Downes, *Vanbrugh* (1977) • K. Downes, *Sir John Vanbrugh: a biography* (1987) • L. Whistler, *The imagination of Vanbrugh and his fellow artists* (1954) • H. M. Colvin and M. Craig, eds., *Architectural drawings in the library of Elton Hall by Sir John Vanbrugh and Sir Edward Lovett Pearce* (1964) • P. Beal and others, *Index of English literary manuscripts*, ed. P. J. Croft and others, [4 vols. in 11 pts] (1980–), vol. 2 • J. Milhous and R. D. Hume, *Vice-chamberlain Coke's theatrical papers, 1706–1715* (1982) • H. A. Tipping and C. Hussey, *English homes* (1928), 4/2: *The works of Sir John Vanbrugh and his school* • C. Ridgway and R. Williams, eds., *Sir John Vanbrugh and landscape architecture in baroque England* (2000) • L. Whistler, *Sir John Vanbrugh, architect and dramatist* (1938) • C. Cibber, *An apology for the life of Colley Cibber*, new edn, ed. B. R. S. Fone (1968) • P. Holland, *The ornament of action: text and performance in Restoration comedy* (1979) • W. H. Godfrey, A. Wagner, and H. Stanford London, *The College of Arms, Queen Victoria Street* (1963) • D. Green, *Blenheim Palace* (1951) • H. M. Colvin and others, eds., *The history of the king's works*, 5 (1976) • J. W. Krutch, *Comedy and conscience after the Restoration* (1924) • C. Leech, T. W. Craik, L. Potter, and others, eds., *The Revels history of drama in English*, 8 vols. (1975–83), vol. 5 • A. Nicoll, *Restoration drama, 1660–1700*, 4th edn (1952), vol. 1 of *A history of English drama, 1660–1900*; *The early eighteenth century*, 3rd edn (1952), vol. 2 of *A history of English drama, 1660–1900* • L. Hotson, *The Commonwealth and Restoration stage* (1928) • J. Milhous, 'New light on Vanbrugh's Haymarket Theatre project', *Theatre Survey*, 17/2 (1976), 143–61 • P. Muschke and J. Fleischer, 'A re-evaluation of Vanbrugh', *Publications of the Modern Language Association*, 49 (1934), 848–89 • L. B. Faller, 'Between jest and earnest: the comedy of Sir John Vanbrugh', *Modern Philology*, 72 (1974–5), 17–29 • C. Saumarez Smith, *The building of Castle Howard* (1990) • parish register, City of London, St Nicolas Acons, 24 Jan 1664 [baptism] • parish register, City of London, St Stephen Wallbrook, 31 March 1726 [burial]

Archives BL, papers, incl. those relating to building Blenheim Palace, Add. MSS 19592–19601, 61172, 61353–61354, 61356; Lansdowne MS 817 • Borth. Inst., corresp. and receipts • Folger, papers • Harvard U., Houghton L., papers • Hunt. L., papers • Princeton University, New Jersey, papers • PRO • PRO, LC • V&A, drawings for Castle Howard, Kimbolton Castle, and Kings Weston • Yale U., Beinecke L., papers | BL, letters to vice-chamberlain Coke, Add. MS 78607 • BL, corresp. with Henry Joyres and William Boulter, Add. MS 19605 • BL, corresp. with duke of Marlborough and duchess of Marlborough, Add. MSS 61353, 61655 • BL, corresp. with duke of Newcastle, Add. MSS 32687, 33064 • BL, corresp. with Treasury, Add. MSS 19602, 19605, 61353, 61356, 70046 • Castle Howard, North Yorkshire, letters to third earl of Carlisle

Likenesses G. Kneller, oils, *c.*1704–1710, NPG [*see illus.*] • J. Simon, mezzotint, after 1715 (after G. Kneller) • attrib. T. Murray, oils, *c.*1718–1719, NPG • attrib. J. Richardson, oils, *c.*1725, RIBA; version, Coll. Arms • J. Faber, mezzotint, 1733 (after G. Kneller)

Vanbrugh, Violet [*real name* Violet Augusta Mary Barnes] **(1867–1942)**, actress, was born at Exeter on 11 June 1867, the eldest child of the Revd Reginald Henry Barnes (*d.*

1889), prebendary of Exeter Cathedral and vicar of Heavitree, and his wife, Frances Mary Emily Nation, and sister of Irene *Vanbrugh and Sir Kenneth Ralph *Barnes. After schooling in Exeter, France, and Germany, Violet determined to go on the stage at a time when this was by no means usual with girls of her education and social standing, and when there were no dramatic schools outside of the theatre itself. Remembering the advice of General Gordon, a friend of the family, to allow his children to follow their bent, her father permitted her to make the attempt. With £50 to spend and a nurse as companion she journeyed to London and after three months she succeeded in interesting Ellen Terry, on whose recommendation J. L. Toole gave Violet her first engagement: at Toole's Theatre in February 1886 she walked on in fantastic male costume as one of the crowd in F. C. Burnand's burlesque *Faust and Loose*. From there she went to the Criterion Theatre and had her first speaking part in London as Ellen in *The Little Pilgrim*. She then joined Sarah Thorne's repertory company at the Theatre Royal, Margate, Kent, where she had an invaluable training, learning a new part every week. In the autumn of the same year she rejoined Toole, playing Lady Anne in *The Butler* by the Herman Merivales, both on tour and afterwards in London. Among other parts in which she appeared with Toole were as May Fielding in Dion Boucicault's *Dot* and as Kitty Maitland in the Merivales' *The Don*. She then returned to Margate and gained valuable experience in a variety of parts. After returning to London in 1888 she joined W. H. Kendal and Madge Kendal, whom she accompanied on their first two American tours, having the great benefit of Madge Kendal's advice and example. Violet Vanbrugh played baronne de Préfont in A. W. Pinero's *The Ironmaster*, Lady Ingram in J. Palgrave Simpson's *A Scrap of Paper*, and other leading parts that fell to her quite unexpectedly when she was called upon to replace Olga Brandon, who at the last moment was unable to go. After two years in America Violet Vanbrugh returned to London, intending to rest. Shortly after her return an extraordinary and unexpected piece of good luck came when Henry Irving, with whom she had then a slight acquaintance, stopped a hansom cab in which she was driving and offered her there and then the part of Ann Boleyn in his production of *King Henry VIII* at the Lyceum Theatre. In this she duly appeared (5 January 1892), at the same time understudying Ellen Terry as Cordelia in *King Lear* and as Rosamund in Lord Tennyson's *Becket*.

In the following year Violet Vanbrugh was engaged by Augustin Daly to join his company at Daly's Theatre, headed by Ada Rehan, whom she understudied. Among the parts she played at Daly's in 1893–4 were Lady Sneerwell in Sheridan's *The School for Scandal*, Alithea in Garrick's *The Country Girl*, and Olivia in Shakespeare's *Twelfth Night*. In 1894 she married Arthur *Bourchier (1863–1927), who had been a member of Daly's company. She joined him, taking the title part in his *The Chili Widow* when he went into management at the Royalty Theatre, and she afterwards appeared as Stella in Herman Merivale's *The Queen's Proctor*—a version of *Divorçons*. With

Bourchier she went to America, and on her return in 1898 she created the part of Lady Beauvedere in J. O. Hobbes's *The Ambassador* with George Alexander at the St James's Theatre. She took the leading part in a succession of plays, most of them by contemporary authors, and many of them produced by Bourchier during his lease of the Garrick Theatre. In 1906 at Stratford upon Avon she played Lady Macbeth to her husband's Macbeth, the play being revived the same year at the Garrick Theatre. At Stratford also in 1910 she played Beatrice in *Much Ado about Nothing*. Both she and Arthur Bourchier were then engaged by Sir Herbert Tree at His Majesty's Theatre, where, in September of that year, she made a great success as Queen Katherine in *King Henry VIII*. In the following year she appeared in Tree's revival of *The Merry Wives of Windsor* as Mistress Ford to Ellen Terry's Mistress Page. At His Majesty's again in 1915 she played Queen Katherine in an 'all-star' revival of *King Henry VIII*, given in aid of King George's Pension Fund for Actors and Actresses.

From then onward Violet played many other parts, but Mistress Ford and Queen Katherine remained the characters for which she was chiefly remembered. She reappeared as Mistress Ford at the Hippodrome, Manchester, in 1934, with her sister Irene as Mistress Page, and again in a notable performance at the Ring Theatre, Blackfriars, in March 1937. In the June following both sisters took the same parts in a revival at the open-air theatre in Regent's Park. In the same year her golden jubilee as an actress was celebrated with a luncheon in her honour. She appeared in one or two films towards the close of her life, including a version of Shaw's *Pygmalion* in 1938, but she allowed nothing to interfere with her devotion to live theatre. She endowed every part that she took with an appealing dignity and charm. She was a pioneer, alike of her family and her generation, in taking up the stage as a calling for serious-minded middle-class girls, and she never forfeited her pride in high ideals on or off the stage. She wrote a delightful book of reminiscences which took the family motto for its title, *Dare to be Wise* (1925). Violet Vanbrugh divorced her husband in 1917. Her daughter, Prudence, also became an actress. Violet Vanbrugh died in London on 11 November 1942. S. R. LITTLEWOOD, rev.

Sources V. Vanbrugh, *Dare to be wise* (1925) · *The Times* (12 Nov 1942) · J. Parker, ed., *Who's who in the theatre*, 6th edn (1930) · personal knowledge (1959) · private information (1959)

Likenesses E. Kapp, drawing, 1919, Barber Institute of Fine Arts, Birmingham · Bassano, postcard, NPG · C. Buchel, chalk and wash drawing (as Lady Macbeth), Royal Shakespeare Theatre, Stratford upon Avon · C. Buchel, lithograph, NPG · C. Buchel, oils (as Queen Katherine in Shakespeare's *Henry VIII*), Royal Academy of Dramatic Art, London · Histed, photogravure, NPG

Wealth at death £3956 0s. 2d.: probate, 9 Jan 1943, *CGPLA Eng. & Wales*

Vance, Alfred Glenville [*real name* Alfred Peck Stevens] (1839?–1888), actor and singer, was probably born in London in 1839. He was placed in the office of a solicitor in Lincoln's Inn Fields. After early efforts as a provincial actor he accepted an engagement of 50s. a week at the Preston theatre, under Edmund Falconer, to play secondary parts, including harlequin. He then went on the Northampton circuit, and was eventually taken on by Copeland at Liverpool, where he opened a dancing academy. He also kept a dancing and fencing school in Carlisle. He reappeared on stage at the Theatre Royal, Manchester, and played a clown at the old Theatre Royal in Leeds. Up to this time he was professionally known as Alfred Glenville. When he left Leeds to tour with an entertainment he adopted the name of Alfred Glenville Vance. His most popular performance was in a monologue entertainment entitled *Touches of the Times*, in which he presented as many as twenty different characters. On the suggestion of J. J. Poole, at one time manager of the South London Music-Hall, Vance adopted the 'variety' stage and appeared at the Metropolitan, Philharmonic, and South London music-halls. He was a poor singer but a clever dancer, and his sketches of character took a firm hold on the public. All London rang with the words and tune of his 'The Chickaleery Cove' and other cockney songs. In 1864 he was at the London Pavilion music hall, and he was at various periods associated with the Strand (whose site later became occupied by the Gaiety Theatre) and the Canterbury music-halls. For many years he travelled round the country with what was called Vance's Concert Company. He also played the clown at the St James's Theatre under Chatterton's management, and appeared at many other houses. Among the songs which became popular and secured him royal recognition were 'Jolly Dogs' and 'Walking in the Zoo'. Later in his career he was known as 'the Great Vance'. On Wednesday 26 December 1888, at the Sun Music-Hall, Knightsbridge, when he had given two songs and had sung in the wig and robes of a judge three verses of a third called 'Are you Guilty?', Vance, who suffered from heart disease, collapsed in the wing, and was found to be dead. He was buried on 2 January 1889 at Nunhead cemetery.

JOSEPH KNIGHT, rev. NILANJANA BANERJI

Sources *The Era* (29 Dec 1888) • *The Times* (29 Dec 1888) • C. D. Stuart and A. J. Park, *The variety stage* (1895) • *The life and reminiscences of E. L. Blanchard, with notes from the diary of Wm. Blanchard*, ed. C. W. Scott and C. Howard, 2 vols. (1891) • *Era Almanack and Annual* (1890) • P. Hartnoll, ed., *The Oxford companion to the theatre* (1951); 2nd edn (1957); 3rd edn (1967) • P. Hartnoll, ed., *The concise Oxford companion to the theatre* (1972)
Wealth at death £39 7s. 5d.: probate, 10 Jan 1889, CGPLA Eng. & Wales

Vancouver, Charles (*bap.* 1756, *d.* 1815?), agricultural improver and writer, was baptized on 11 November 1756 at King's Lynn, the son of John Jasper Vancouver (*d.* 1773), deputy collector of customs at King's Lynn, and his wife, Bridget Berners. Both parents were Dutch, and he was an older brother of George *Vancouver the explorer. At an early age he was apprenticed to a great farmer in Norfolk. About 1776 Arthur Young secured for him a post in Ireland as bailiff to Lord Shelburne, at Rahan, King's county, where drainage of bog land was among his duties. By 1785 at the latest he was in Kentucky supervising the drainage, improvement, and settlement of an estate of 53,000 acres,

a scheme which is said to have run into difficulties. At this time he projected a multi-volume work entitled 'A general compendium … of chemical, experimental and natural philosophy', but the plan came to nothing.

Vancouver was back in England by 1793 when Sir John Sinclair (president of the board of agriculture), presumably at the instigation of Young (its secretary), asked him to write the volumes on the farming of Cambridgeshire and Essex in the board's series of *General Views* of agriculture in the English and Welsh counties. Vancouver's volumes were published in 1794 and 1795. About 1798–1805 he travelled again, perhaps supervising more work in Kentucky and making excursions through Pennsylvania, Virginia, and the western United States. It was probably also during these years that he became involved in fen drainage in the Netherlands. Certainly he was in the Netherlands in the late 1790s, and married Louise van Coeverden, a kinswoman, in 1798 or 1799. By 1806 at the latest he was back in England, working again for the board of agriculture, completing *General Views* of Devon (1808) and Hampshire (1810). He is said to have died in Virginia in 1815.

It is clear from his writings that Vancouver regarded himself as a practical expert, working under contract, on agricultural improvement, especially through land drainage and reclamation. His agricultural writings were a secondary activity and probably not more than six years of his life were devoted to them. They are, nevertheless, of very great value to rural and local historians for their detailed and acute observations on farming practice and rural life. Despite some obstruction from the farmers of Cambridgeshire (who feared that his survey was connected with taxation), and unlike some authors of the *General Views*, he visited, and collected statistics for, almost all of the county's parishes; his figures are still used by rural historians today. Likewise, his book on Devon's agriculture was based upon personal observation in almost all of the parishes of that huge county, although he did misplace some of them when he came to write up his report. His writing is always authoritative and comprehensive. It is especially enthusiastic when he contemplates plans for land reclamation: his design for improved drainage of part of the fens of eastern England, his ideas about the colonization of the New Forest in Hampshire, and his ambitious plans, based partly on his Irish experience, for reclamation of the peat bogs of Dartmoor.   H. S. A. FOX

Sources C. Vancouver, *General view of the agriculture of Hampshire, including the Isle of Wight* (1810) • C. Vancouver, *General view of the agriculture of the county of Devon* (1808) • C. Vancouver, 'Observations on the proposed Eau Brink cut for the further draining of the fens', in R. Parkinson, *General view of the agriculture of the county of Huntingdon* (1813), appx [written in 1794] • C. Vancouver, 'Observations on the proper persons and necessary capital for settling in the Kantuke district, Ohio, North America', *Annals of Agriculture*, 6 (1786), 405–11 • G. Vancouver, *A voyage of discovery to the north Pacific Ocean and round the world, 1791–1795*, ed. W. Kaye Lamb, 4 vols., Hakluyt Society (1984), vol. 1, pp. 2–269 • *Arthur Young's tour in Ireland (1776–1779)*, ed. A. W. Hutton, 2 vols. (1892) • R. H. Dillon, 'Charles Vancouver's plan', *Pacific Northwest Quarterly*, 41 (1950) • A. Mansvelt, 'Vancouver: a lost branch of the van Coeverden family',

British Columbia Historical News, 6 (1973), 20–23 · parish register (baptism), 11 Nov 1756, King's Lynn
Archives NL Wales, Cotes MSS
Likenesses J. Gillray, cartoon, 1796 (*The caneing in Conduit Street*), NPG

Vancouver, George (1757–1798), naval officer and hydrographer, was born in Fincham Street, King's Lynn, Norfolk, on 22 June 1757, the sixth and youngest child of John Jasper Vancouver (*d.* 1773), deputy collector of customs at King's Lynn, and his wife, Bridget Berners (1715–1768). His older brother was Charles *Vancouver, the agricultural improver. Having probably attended Lynn grammar school, on 22 January 1772 the fourteen-year-old Vancouver joined the *Resolution* at Deptford yard, where she was being fitted out for Captain Cook's second voyage to the Pacific (1772–5) to search for the legendary southern continent. Although rated as an able seaman Vancouver was in fact a young gentleman of the quarterdeck. During the voyage he received training from the expedition's astronomer, William Wales, in astronomical observations, surveying, and drawing, which he acknowledged in 1793 during his own voyage by naming the western entrance point of Portland inlet Wales Point. The voyage, under Cook's eagle eye, gave young Vancouver invaluable experience. He also took part in Cook's third voyage to the Pacific (1776–80) in search of a Pacific outlet to the north-west passage, sailing this time as a midshipman in Cook's consort the *Discovery*. Two charts drawn by Vancouver have survived from Cook's second voyage and one from his third. This last, in the library of the University of Wisconsin, Milwaukee, is a small-scale chart drawn on two sheets covering much of the area of the north-west coast of America he was later to survey himself.

On 19 October 1780, twelve days after the *Discovery* paid off, Vancouver passed the examination for lieutenant and on 9 December 1780 he joined the sloop *Martin* in that rank, employed first on escort and patrol duties in the English Channel and the North Sea and later in the West Indies. On 17 May 1782 he joined the *Fame*, remaining in her until she returned to Plymouth where she was paid off on 3 July 1783, when Vancouver was placed on half pay. In November 1784 he was appointed to the *Europa*, flagship of Admiral Alexander Innes, newly appointed commander-in-chief in the West Indies, and in her returned to Jamaica. In January 1786 Innes died and was succeeded by Commodore Sir Alan Gardner, who became a good friend and patron of Vancouver. In the autumn of 1787 Gardner instructed Vancouver to survey Port Royal and Kingston harbours assisted by Joseph Whidbey, newly appointed master of the *Europa*. The resulting chart, which was dedicated to Gardner, was published in London on 1 December. The *Europa* returned to England in September 1789 at the end of a five-year commission, by which time Vancouver had risen to become her first lieutenant.

Following the expulsion by Spanish frigates of two British whalers from Puerto Deseado on the coast of Patagonia, plans were drawn up in 1789 to send a vessel to the south Atlantic under an experienced commander skilled in surveying. A vessel of 330 tons, under construction in a private yard, was purchased and named *Discovery*. Henry Roberts, who had been on Cook's second and third voyages, was appointed in command with Vancouver as his first lieutenant. By the end of January 1790 the *Discovery* was ready to sail, but almost simultaneously news reached London of the seizure by Spain of British trading vessels at Nootka Sound on the north-west coast of America. In April John Meares, whose vessels had been seized, arrived in London and submitted a greatly exaggerated memorial to the British government. On 30 April a formidable fleet, which became known as the Spanish armament, was mobilized and the imminent departure of the *Discovery* was cancelled. Vancouver was appointed to the *Courageaux*, commanded by Gardner, with Whidbey as her master. On 28 October 1790 the Nootka Sound convention was signed in Madrid, which gave Great Britain almost everything she sought including, with great reluctance on the part of Spain, the restoration of the buildings and tracts of land seized by the Spaniards that Meares claimed he owned in Nootka Sound.

On 15 December 1790 the *Discovery* was recommissioned with Vancouver promoted commander in command, with the 133 ton brig *Chatham* (Lieutenant William R. Broughton) as consort. Vancouver's instructions, dated 8 March 1791, were diplomatic as well as exploratory. First he was to proceed to the Sandwich Islands (Hawaii) where he was to spend the winter surveying them. He was then to proceed to the north-west coast of America, which he was to explore from 30° to 60° N looking for 'any water-communication which may tend, in any considerable degree, to facilitate an intercourse for the purposes of commerce, between the north-west coast, and the country upon the opposite side of the continent' (Vancouver, 1.284), paying particular attention to the Strait of Juan de Fuca, just south of present-day Vancouver Island and then thought to be the entrance to a great inland sea. As convenient he was to visit Nootka Sound to receive back from the Spaniards the properties they had seized in 1789.

Vancouver sailed from Falmouth on 1 April 1791, proceeding to the north-west coast via the Cape of Good Hope. This enabled him to examine the south-west coast of Australia, where he became the European discoverer of King George Sound. He next visited Dusky Sound in New Zealand, where he spent three weeks wooding and watering his ship and making minor additions to Cook's survey. On his chart Cook had marked 'Nobody knows what' where he had been unable to complete the survey of a minor inlet. Vancouver completed the survey of this inlet and substituted on his chart 'Somebody knows what'. *En route* for Tahiti the two ships became separated and Broughton became the European discoverer of Chatham Island, east of New Zealand. After refitting his two ships in Tahiti, Vancouver next spent thirteen days in the Hawaiian Islands, visiting several of the islands hoping to find the store ship *Daedalus*, which he had expected to meet there.

On 16 April 1792 the north-west coast of America was sighted about 115 miles north of San Francisco Bay. Vancouver now began the first of three survey seasons on the north-west coast. Because of the length of coastline he was expected to examine Vancouver used a procedure known as a running survey, which Cook had perfected during his three Pacific voyages. To provide a rigid framework for his survey Vancouver relied on a series of observation spots, generally situated several hundred miles apart, where he landed his portable observatory. A great deal of the detailed survey work was carried out in a series of boat expeditions, with the two ships moving from one convenient anchorage to another. The first of these observation spots was established in Discovery Bay on the south side of Juan de Fuca Strait. From here boat parties were sent away to examine the adjacent waters, during which the extensive body of water now known as Puget Sound was discovered and surveyed. From the next anchorage Vancouver himself led a boat expedition to examine Howe Sound and Jervis inlet. On 22 June 1792, as he was returning to the *Discovery*, he encountered two small Spanish vessels, the *Sutil* and *Mexicana*, which were also engaged in surveying operations under the command of Dionisio Alcalá-Galiano. For a short time the two expeditions carried out a joint survey, but having learned that Spanish negotiator Juan Francisco de la Bodega y Quadra was waiting for him in Nootka Sound and that the *Daedalus* had arrived there, Vancouver could not afford to wait and so arrived in Nootka Sound before the Spanish vessels and thus became the first European to establish the insularity of Vancouver Island and that Juan de Fuca Strait was not the entrance to a great inland sea.

On his arrival in Nootka Sound, Vancouver learned that the captain of the *Daedalus* and William Gooch, who was to join the expedition as its astronomer, had been murdered in Oahu, one of the Hawaiian Islands. This unfortunate news meant that Vancouver and Whidbey not only had to make almost all the necessary astronomical observations between them but they had to compute them as well, a very tedious procedure.

Vancouver was warmly greeted by Bodega y Quadra, but their negotiations, extending over three weeks, soon ran into difficulties. Vancouver expected to receive back the whole of Nootka Sound, whereas Bodega y Quadra was prepared to deliver only a small area where Meares had built a hut in 1788. Having reached an impasse the two negotiators agreed to refer the matter back to their respective governments and await further instructions.

From Nootka Sound, Vancouver sailed for San Francisco and Monterey, but on the way south he detached the *Chatham* to examine a river which the American Robert Gray had entered in the *Columbia* in May 1792. Broughton succeeded, with difficulty, in crossing the bar and then led a boat expedition 100 miles upstream to a position about 18 miles above the site of present-day Portland. On reaching Monterey, Vancouver was greeted once more by Bodega y Quadra, but with no fresh instructions for either party Broughton was sent back to London, via Mexico City and Spain, to obtain them, Zachary Mudge, the *Discovery*'s first lieutenant, having already been sent back from Nootka Sound on a similar mission.

Vancouver spent the following winter in the Hawaiian Islands; in May 1793 he was back on the north-west coast to continue his survey and by September he had charted the coast to 56° N. At the end of the 1793 season Vancouver again called at Monterey and afterwards at San Diego before tracing the coast to 30° N and sailing for the Hawaiian Islands to spend the winter there.

During his third and last visit to the Hawaiian Islands, Vancouver completed their survey, but also involved himself in the islands' affairs, encouraging their unification under Kamehameha, the principal chief of the island of Hawaii. At the same time he persuaded Kamehameha to cede the islands to Great Britain, but the act of cession was not ratified in London.

Vancouver began his 1794 season in Cook inlet, the northern limit of his survey, working his way south to join up with his previous season's work, his final anchorage being in a bay on the south-eastern side of Baranof Island which Vancouver appropriately named Port Conclusion. By happy coincidence he was promoted to post captain on 28 August 1794, six days after completing his survey.

Considering the difficulties facing him, Vancouver's survey is remarkably accurate and for the greater part of the nineteenth century his atlas was the only reliable authority for navigating the remoter parts of British Columbia and Alaska. His latitudes are very close to modern values, but his longitudes are less so, particularly in his final season when bad weather prevented him from obtaining any lunar distances. Of all the men who served under Cook, Vancouver was the only one whose work as a hydrographic surveyor placed him in the same class as his mentor. The care Vancouver took with the health of his crew during this voyage also mirrored Cook's achievements, with only one man dying of disease, another of poisoning, and four by drowning.

On the voyage home calls were made at Monterey, Valparaiso, and St Helena, from where the *Discovery* sailed in convoy, anchoring off the mouth of the River Shannon on 13 September 1795. From here Vancouver travelled directly to London to report to the Admiralty, rejoining his ship when she arrived in the Thames on 20 October after a voyage lasting for over four and a half years.

On his return Vancouver's achievements did not receive the recognition that they deserved, mainly because of reports that he had acted harshly towards some of his subordinates. During the voyage his relationship with Archibald Menzies, the expedition's naturalist and botanist, had been difficult and Vancouver's threat to court-martial Menzies was only averted by the intervention of Sir Joseph Banks. Thomas Pitt, heir of Lord Camelford, and one of the *Discovery*'s midshipmen, proved unbalanced and disruptive. In consequence Vancouver sent him home in the *Daedalus* from Hawaii in 1794. On the expedition's return Pitt, by now Lord Camelford, challenged Vancouver to a duel and meeting him by chance in Conduit Street attempted to assault him, giving rise to a notorious cartoon by James Gillray entitled 'The Caneing in Conduit Street'. In consequence Camelford was bound over to keep the peace.

In November 1795 Vancouver settled on half pay in

Petersham, near Richmond Park, Surrey, to revise his journal, of which the manuscript is now lost, for publication. During the final season on the north-west coast he had been ill and had been unable to take part in any of the boat expeditions. Back in England his health continued to deteriorate and on 12 May 1798 he died unmarried, aged forty, with his narrative still uncompleted. His brother John completed his *Voyage* which was published in 1798 in an attractive edition, consisting of three quarto volumes and a folio atlas. A second edition of six octavo volumes followed in 1801. Vancouver was buried in St Peter's Church, Petersham, on 18 May 1798, where his grave is marked by a plain headstone.

Almost all the names given by Vancouver on the north-west coast of America have survived, most notably Vancouver Island, originally named Quadra and Vancouver's Island by Vancouver at his friend Bodega y Quadra's request that he should name some port or island after them both. When in 1884 the Canadian Pacific Railway was nearing completion, Vancouver was the name chosen for the city-to-be on Burrard inlet that was to be its western terminus.   ANDREW C. F. DAVID

Sources G. Vancouver, *A voyage of discovery to the north Pacific Ocean and round the world, 1791–1795*, ed. W. Kaye Lamb, 4 vols., Hakluyt Society (1984) · B. Anderson, *Surveyor of the sea: the life and voyages of Captain George Vancouver* (1960) · G. Godwin, *Vancouver: a life, 1757–1798* (1930) · A. Gifford, *Captain Vancouver: a portrait of his life* (1986) · A. David, 'Vancouver's survey methods and surveys', *From maps to metaphors: the Pacific world of George Vancouver* (1993), 51–69 · J. M. Naish, *The interwoven lives of George Vancouver, Archibald Menzies, Joseph Whidbey and Peter Puget* (1996) · PRO, PROB 11/1312 · parish register, St Margaret, King's Lynn, 16 March 1761 [baptism]
Archives BL, logbooks of the *Discovery*, Add. MSS 17542–17551 · Hydrographic Office, Taunton, surveys · McGill University, Montreal, McLennan Library, papers and corresp. · NMM, lieutenant's logs · PRO, corresp.
Likenesses J. Gillray, caricature, coloured etching, pubd 1796 (*The caneing in Conduit Street*), NPG · oils, NPG
Wealth at death £5000: will, proved 22 Aug 1798, PRO, PROB 11/1312

Vandam, Albert Dresden (1843–1903), journalist and writer, born in London in March 1843, was the son of Mark Vandam, of Jewish descent, district commissioner for the Netherlands state lottery. Before he was thirteen he was sent to Paris, where he was privately educated and remained fifteen years. According to his own story, he was looked after in boyhood by two maternal great-uncles, who had been surgeons in Napoleon's army, had set up after Waterloo in private practice at Paris, enjoyed the *entrée* to Napoleon III's court, and entertained at their house the leaders of Parisian artistic society. Vandam claimed that his youth was passed among French people of importance, and that he also made the acquaintance of the theatrical and Bohemian worlds of the French capital.

Vandam began his career as a journalist during the Austro-Prussian War of 1866, writing for English papers, and he was correspondent for American papers during the Franco-Prussian War. After settling in London in 1871 he did translation from French and Dutch, and other literary work, occasionally going abroad on special assignments

for newspapers. From 1882 to 1887 he was again in Paris as correspondent for *The Globe*, subsequently making his home anew in London.

Vandam's *An Englishman in Paris*, published anonymously in 1892 (2 vols.), excited considerable curiosity. It collected apparently intimate gossip of the courts of Louis Philippe and Napoleon III. Vandam wrote again on French life and history, often depreciatingly, in *My Paris Note-Book* (1894), *French Men and French Manners* (1895), *Undercurrents of the Second Empire* (1897), and *Men and Manners of the Second Empire* (1904), but he did not repeat the success of his first effort. He also published some novels.

Vandam translated into English the autobiography of the sixteenth-century Pomeranian notary Bartholomew Sastrow, which he published as *Social Germany in Luther's Time* (1902, introduction by H. A. L. Fisher). He married Maria, daughter of Lewin Moseley, a London dentist. Vandam died at his home, 47A Manchester Street, Marylebone, London, on 26 October 1903.

LEWIS MELVILLE, *rev.* ROGER T. STEARN

Sources *The Times* (27 Oct 1903) · *WW* · A. D. Vandam, *My Paris note-book* (1894) · A. D. Vandam, *French men and French manners* (1895) · private information (1912) · *CGPLA Eng. & Wales* (1903)
Wealth at death £45: administration, 22 Dec 1903, *CGPLA Eng. & Wales*

Vandeleur, Sir John Ormsby (1763–1849), army officer, was the grandson of John Vandeleur of Kilrush, and son of Captain Richard Vandeleur (*d.* 1772), 9th dragoons, of Rutland, Queen's county, and his wife, Elinor, daughter of John Firman of Firmount. He received a commission as ensign in the 5th foot in December 1781, and was promoted lieutenant in the 67th in 1783. He served with the 67th in the West Indies, and, exchanging in 1788 into the 9th, was promoted captain on 9 March 1792. In October 1792 he exchanged into the 8th light dragoons, and was promoted major on 1 March 1794.

In April 1794 Vandeleur went with his regiment to Flanders to serve under the duke of York, took part in the principal actions of the campaign, and the retreat to Bremen. On the embarkation of the army for England in April 1795 Vandeleur remained with a small corps under General Dundas until December. In August 1796 he went to the Cape of Good Hope, and served in the operations under generals Craig and Dundas. On 1 January 1798 he was promoted lieutenant-colonel in the 8th light dragoons. In October 1802 he went with his regiment to India, and served as lieutenant-colonel with local rank of colonel in command of a brigade of cavalry under Lord Lake in the Maratha campaigns of 1803–5. At the battle of Laswari on 1 November 1803 Vandeleur turned the enemy's left flank and took 2000 prisoners, receiving the thanks of Lord Lake. He was similarly distinguished in November 1804 for the cavalry action at Fatehgarh, where the Maratha chief Holkar was surprised and defeated. Equally brilliant were his charge and recapture of artillery at Afzalghar on 2 March 1805.

In 1806 Vandeleur returned to England. On 16 April 1807 he exchanged into the 19th light dragoons, and on 25 April 1808 was promoted brevet colonel. On 4 June 1811 he was

Sir John Ormsby Vandeleur (1763–1849), by William Salter, 1835–8

promoted major-general, and appointed to command an infantry brigade of the light division in the Peninsula. Vandeleur led the division, after Craufurd received his mortal wound, to the assault of the breach of Ciudad Rodrigo on 19 January 1812, when he was severely wounded. He nevertheless took part in the battle of Salamanca on 22 June. In June 1813 he intercepted a French division and cut off one of its brigades, taking 300 prisoners and forcing the remainder to disperse in the mountains. On 21 June 1813 he was at the battle of Vitoria, and in July was appointed to command a brigade of light dragoons under Sir Thomas Graham (afterwards Lord Lynedoch), and later under Lord Niddry, and he was engaged in all the operations of that column, including the battle of the Nive. At the close of the Peninsular War he was selected to lead a division of British cavalry and artillery from Bordeaux to Calais.

In October 1814 Vandeleur was appointed to the staff of the British army in the Netherlands. He was given the colonelcy of the 19th light dragoons on 12 January 1815. He commanded the 4th cavalry brigade, consisting of the 11th, 12th, and 16th light dragoons, at the battle of Waterloo, and from the time that Lord Uxbridge was wounded and had to leave the field he commanded, as next senior, the whole of the British cavalry at Waterloo, and during the advance on Paris until Louis XVIII entered the capital. For his services in the Peninsula and the Netherlands he was made a KCB (military division) on 3 January 1815, and received the gold cross with clasps for Ciudad Rodrigo, Salamanca, Vitoria, and the Nive, and the Waterloo

medal. He was also made a knight of the second class of the Russian order of St Vladimir, and a commander of the Bavarian order of Maximilian Joseph.

The 19th light dragoons were disbanded in 1820, and in 1823 Vandeleur was made colonel of the 14th light dragoons, from which on 18 June 1830 he was transferred to that of the 16th lancers. He was promoted lieutenant-general on 19 July 1821, and general on 28 June 1838. He was made a CB in 1833.

Vandeleur married, in 1829, a daughter of the Revd John Glasse, and they had a son and a daughter, Ellen, wife of Colonel (afterwards General) Richard Greaves, for some twenty years assistant military secretary to the commander of the forces in Ireland, and afterwards colonel of the 40th foot. Vandeleur died on 1 November 1849 at his house in Merrion Square, Dublin.

R. H. VETCH, *rev.* ROGER T. STEARN

Sources PRO, War Office records · dispatches, *LondG* · W. Siborne, *History of the war in France and Belgium in 1815*, 2 vols. (1844) · W. F. P. Napier, *History of the war in the Peninsula and in the south of France*, new edn, 6 vols. (1886) · W. Thorn, *Memoir of the war in India, 1803–6* (1818) · *GM*, 2nd ser., 34 (1850), 672 · *Colburn's United Service Magazine*, 3 (1849), 639 · J. Philippart, ed., *The royal military calendar*, 3rd edn, 5 vols. (1820) · private information (1899) · Burke, *Gen. GB* · A. J. Guy, ed., *The road to Waterloo: the British army and the struggle against revolutionary and Napoleonic France, 1793–1815* (1990) · R. Muir, *Britain and the defeat of Napoleon, 1807–1815* (1996)

Archives TCD, papers, incl. Waterloo campaign | PRO NIre., letters to Henry Stewart

Likenesses W. Salter, oils, 1835–8, NPG [*see illus.*] · Z. Belliard, engraving (after portrait) · W. Salter, group portrait, oils (*The Waterloo Banquet at Apsley House*), Wellington Museum, London; oil study, *c.*1834–40, NPG

Vandenhoff, Charlotte Elizabeth (1818–1860). *See under* Vandenhoff, John M. (1790–1861).

Vandenhoff, George (1820–1885). *See under* Vandenhoff, John M. (1790–1861).

Vandenhoff, John M. (1790–1861), actor, was born on 31 March 1790 in Salisbury, where his family, of Dutch extraction and said to have come to Britain in the train of William of Orange, appear to have been dyers. He was educated at the Jesuits' college in Stonyhurst, Lancashire, with a view to his becoming a priest. For a year he taught classics in a school. His first appearance on the stage was at Salisbury, on 11 May 1808, as Osmond in M. G. Lewis's *The Castle Spectre*. After playing at Exeter, Weymouth, and elsewhere with Edmund Kean, and at Swansea with John Cooper, he made his first appearance at Bath in October 1813 as Jaffier in Otway's *Venice Preserv'd*. In 1814 he became a member of the company at the English Opera House (Lyceum) under Arnold, where he was the original Count d'Herleim in *Frederick the Great*. The same year he made his first appearance in Liverpool, where he became a great favourite. After playing in Manchester, Dublin, and elsewhere, in December 1820, as Vandenhoff from Liverpool, he made his début at Covent Garden, as King Lear. During the season he was seen as Sir Giles Overreach, Coriolanus, Pizarro, and Rolla. He also played Rob Roy, Gambia in *The Slave*, and Mirandola in place of W. C. Macready, who was ill. He was the first Leicester in *Kenilworth*.

In 1822 Vandenhoff retired, in some disgust, at the treatment he received from his manager, who seemed inclined to allot the best parts to Charles Young, Macready, or Charles Kemble. Vandenhoff's subsequent decision to perform in Liverpool, however, led to what became known as the 'Salter riots', the object of which was to drive Vandenhoff away and secure his position for Salter, a local actor. The situation was resolved by the managers Banks and Lewis, who engaged both tragedians and alternated them in the leading characters in such plays as *Othello*, *Julius Caesar*, and *Venice Preserv'd*, until Vandenhoff came to be acknowledged as the better actor and Salter gradually receded. In 1822 Vandenhoff also appeared in Edinburgh as Coriolanus; he returned there in 1826 as Macbeth, and again in February 1830, when he played Cassius and Othello. He was a favourite in the city, where his Coriolanus inspired great enthusiasm. He appears to have played there between the months of January and March for many consecutive years. In 1834 he was seen at the Haymarket in *Hamlet*. In 1835–6 he played at both Drury Lane and Covent Garden—alternate nights being given to opera. On the transference of Talfourd's *Ion* from Covent Garden to the Haymarket in 1836, Vandenhoff played Adrastus, in which, however, he was not very successful. In September 1837 he went to America and made his début at the National Theatre in New York; he went on to play Caius Marcus in *Coriolanus* at the Chesnut Street Theatre, Philadelphia.

On his return to England, when Macready opened Covent Garden in September 1838, Vandenhoff became a member of the company, and played Richelieu, Falconbridge, Cassius, Hotspur, and many other parts. After 1839, when Macready's management of Covent Garden ceased, Vandenhoff appeared chiefly in the provinces, although he was seen occasionally at Drury Lane.

In January 1857 Vandenhoff, with his daughter, paid a starring visit to Edinburgh; his last performance there was on 26 February, as Wolsey in *Henry VIII*, with Henry Irving playing Surrey. On 29 October 1858, at Liverpool, Vandenhoff took his farewell of the stage as Brutus and Wolsey. He died on 4 October 1861 at his home, 34 North Bank, Regent's Park, London.

Vandenhoff left several children, most of whom also took to the stage. A son, **George Vandenhoff** (1820–1885), actor and lawyer, born on 18 February 1820, made his début at Covent Garden on 14 October 1839, as Leon in Beaumont and Fletcher's *Rule a Wife and Have a Wife*. Among other parts later played by him at that theatre was Mercutio in Madame Vestris's production of *Romeo and Juliet*. In August 1842 he took his farewell of the English stage, as Hamlet, and migrated to America, where he made his début, as Hamlet once again, at the Park Theatre, New York, followed by appearances at the Walnut Street Theatre, Philadelphia. For the next ten years he lived mainly in New York, where he staged a translation of Sophocles' *Antigone* with music by Mendelssohn (1845), played Claude Melnotte at Wallack's Theatre (1852), gave poetry readings, and taught elocution. On 20 August 1855, in Boston, he married an actress, Miss Mackean, who had appeared in New York and Philadelphia, but on her marriage decided to retire from the stage. Soon Vandenhoff returned to England. He ceased to act after he was called to the bar in November 1858. He continued to give poetry readings, however, and published a volume of theatrical anecdotes, *Dramatic Reminiscences* (1860). His final appearance on stage was with Geneviève Ward in 1878, when he played Wolsey in *Henry VIII* and Gloster in *Jane Shore*.

The only one of John Vandenhoff's children to attain celebrity status on the English stage was his daughter **Charlotte Elizabeth Vandenhoff** (1818–1860), who was born in Liverpool and made her first appearance at Drury Lane as Juliet on 11 April 1836. She went from there to Covent Garden and the Haymarket, and succeeded in establishing herself as a capable actress in parts in which delicacy and feeling rather than strength or passion were required. She won acceptance as Imogen, Cordelia, and Pauline in *The Lady of Lyons*, and in 1837, at the Haymarket, was the first Lydia in Sheridan Knowles's *The Love Chase*. In October 1839 she made her American début at the National Theatre, New York, as Julia in *The Hunchback*, a role she repeated in November at the Chesnut Street Theatre, Philadelphia. Her chief triumph was as Antigone in a translation from Sophocles at Covent Garden on 2 January 1845, in which her father played Creon. In January 1855, at the St James's, she was Alcestis in a translation by Spicer from Euripides. She was fair in hair and complexion, symmetrical, with gentle mobile features, and was taxed, perhaps unjustly, with imitating Helen Faucit. Charlotte Vandenhoff retained her maiden name to the last, though she married, on 7 July 1856 by licence at St Mary's Church, Hull, Thomas Swinbourne, an actor well known in the provinces and not unknown in London. This marriage she sought within a month to repudiate. She revisited America in 1858. She was taken ill in Birmingham, and died in Handsworth on 31 July 1860. She was the author of *Woman's Heart*, produced in 1852 at the Haymarket, a comedy in which she herself played the heroine.

JOSEPH KNIGHT, rev. NILANJANA BANERJI

Sources *The Era* (13 Oct 1861) • Ward, *Men of the reign* • *The life and reminiscences of E. L. Blanchard, with notes from the diary of Wm. Blanchard*, ed. C. W. Scott and C. Howard, 2 vols. (1891) • *Actors by Daylight*, 1 (1838) • P. Hartnoll, ed., *The Oxford companion to the theatre* (1951); 2nd edn (1957); 3rd edn (1967) • P. Hartnoll, ed., *The concise Oxford companion to the theatre* (1972) • T. A. Brown, *History of the American stage* (1870) • J. C. Dibdin, *The annals of the Edinburgh stage* (1888) • *The Era* (5 Aug 1860) • Hall, *Dramatic ports.* • G. Vandenhoff, *Dramatic reminiscences, or, actors and actresses of England and America*, ed. H. S. Carleton (1860) • J. W. Marston, *Our recent actors*, 2 vols. (1888) • *CGPLA Eng. & Wales* (1860)

Likenesses portrait, repro. in *Cornucopia* (Jan 1821) • prints, BM, NPG • six prints, Harvard TC

Wealth at death under £3000: probate, 2 Nov 1861, *CGPLA Eng. & Wales* • under £2000—Charlotte Elizabeth Vandenhoff: administration, 21 Sept 1860, *CGPLA Eng. & Wales*

Vandeput, George (d. 1800), naval officer, was an illegitimate son of Sir George Vandeput, baronet (d. 1784); details of his mother are unknown. On 24 September 1759, while serving as a midshipman of the *Neptune*, flagship of Sir

Charles Saunders in the St Lawrence, Vandeput was promoted lieutenant of the *Shrewsbury*, commanded by Captain Hugh Palliser. He continued with Palliser in the *Shrewsbury* until the peace in 1763. On 17 April of the following year he was promoted to the command of the sloop *Goree*, and on 20 June 1765 he was posted to the *Surprize* (20 guns). In August 1766 he was moved to the *Boreas*, and in June 1767 to the frigate *Carysfort* (28 guns) for the Mediterranean, where he was for the next three years. He was then for another three years in the *Solebay*, on the home station, and, in December 1773, after several temporary commands, he commissioned the *Asia* for the North American station.

Here Vandeput remained for three years, for the most part at, or in the neighbourhood of, Boston and New York. It appears to have been off New York in 1776—the details are only vaguely given and the incident is not mentioned in Vandeput's letters, or in the ship's log—that a tender of the *Asia* captured a small vessel laden with gunpowder. Whether by accident or caution, Vandeput ordered her to lie off for the night at some little distance; and this led to one of the prisoners, in his terror, confessing that in one of the barrels was a musket-lock, which would be fired by clockwork at a given time. It had been hoped that the barrels of powder would be at once put into the *Asia*'s magazine and the coasting vessel allowed to go free. In 1777 the *Asia* returned to England, and having been refitted was sent to the East Indies. She came home with convoy in the beginning of 1781, and in the following year Vandeput, in the *Atlas* (98 guns), took part in the relief of Gibraltar and the desultory action off Cape Spartel on 20 October. He is said by Burke to have assumed the title of baronet after his father's death on 17 June 1784. If so, it was not acknowledged by the Admiralty, nor in his official position.

After the peace Vandeput commanded the yacht *Princess Augusta* until, on 1 February 1793, he was promoted rear-admiral. On 4 July 1794 he was made vice-admiral, and through 1795 had command of a small squadron in the North Sea. In 1796, with his flag in the *St Albans*, he was employed on convoy service to Lisbon and the Mediterranean; and in 1797, still in the *St Albans*, he commanded the squadron on the coast of North America. Towards the end of the year he shifted his flag to the *Resolution*, and in 1798 to the *Asia*. He was promoted to the rank of admiral on 14 February 1799. He died suddenly, on board the *Asia*, at sea on 14 March 1800. His body was sent, by the *Cleopatra*, to Providence, and there buried. He left an illegitimate son, George, who is also said to have called himself a baronet.

J. K. LAUGHTON, *rev.* NICHOLAS TRACY

Sources Murray to Nepean; letters from North American squadron, 18 March 1800, PRO, ADM 1/494, fol. 8; ADM 1/494–5 · log of HMS Asia, PRO, ADM 51/67

Vanderbank, John (1694–1739), painter and draughtsman, was born probably in London on 9 September 1694, and was baptized on 19 September at St Giles-in-the-Fields, the elder son of John Vanderbank (*d.* 1717), well-to-

do proprietor of the Soho Tapestry Manufactory and chief arras maker to the crown, of Great Queen Street, London, and his wife, Sarah (*d.* 1727). He was one of the first students at Kneller's academy in Great Queen Street, 1711, later taken over by Sir James Thornhill; as it declined, Vanderbank and Louis Chéron opened a new academy in October 1720, in or just off St Martin's Lane (perhaps in Peter Court), notably holding life classes with male and female models, attended by (among others) Hogarth, Joseph Highmore, John Ellys, and James Seymour. This academy closed soon after May 1724, when Vanderbank fled to France for some five months to avoid imprisonment for debt. Vertue notes that he 'livd very extravagantly. keeping. a chariot horses a mistres drinking & country house a purpose for her' (Vertue, *Note books*, 3.98). At some point during 1724 (perhaps in France), Vanderbank married his 'mistres', an actress called Anne (surname unknown), deemed by Vertue to be 'a Vain empty wooman' (ibid.).

Vanderbank worked chiefly as a portraitist (also painting some allegorical subjects) and illustrator. From 1720 he began to establish a portrait practice, developing a free, painterly style, described by Vertue as 'greatness of pencilling, spirit and composition' (Vertue, *Note books*) and partly derived from admiration for works by Rubens and Van Dyck, some of which he studiously copied. During 1724–9 Vanderbank was repeatedly in debt and confined within the liberties of the Fleet prison. In 1727 his mother died, having prudently left her assets to her younger son, Moses (*b.* *c.*1695, *d.* after 1745), also a painter, out of reach of John's creditors. Moses' sale of the family's tapestry interests in 1729 (to John Ellys) enabled him to discharge John's debts. From 1729 John Vanderbank occupied a house in Holles Street, Cavendish Square, rent-free (thanks to a generous patron and landlord who, however, appropriated the contents of his studio after his death) and living 'galantly or freely according to the custom of the Age' (Vertue, *Note books*, 3.97).

Portraiture, Vanderbank's most promising source of income, might (in Vertue's opinion, *Note books*, 5.98) have made him, after Kneller's death, the leading portraitist of his day, had he exerted himself more. His most characterful portraits include two of Sir Isaac Newton, portrayed in the last years of his life, in his own hair (1725; versions RSA and Trinity College, Cambridge) and wigged (1726; RSA); the painter George Lambert (untraced; engraved by Faber, 1727); the sculptor John Michael Rysbrack (*c.*1728; NPG); the poet James Thomson (Scottish National Portrait Gallery, Edinburgh); and the eccentric Newmarket trainer Tregonwell Frampton (*c.*1725; Christies, 27 May 1988). By contrast, many of Vanderbank's more formal portraits of 'persons of Quality', male or female, betray a lack of rapport with his sitters and a tendency to rely on stock poses, sometimes directly derived from Van Dyck. Vertue noted that he (perhaps regularly) used the services of the drapery painter Joseph van Aken. Waterhouse considered that Vanderbank's masterpiece was the large full-length of Queen Caroline (1736; Goodwood House, Chichester,

Sussex). At least thirty of his portraits were engraved, by John Faber junior, George White, and others. Vanderbank painted three allegorical subjects incorporating an equestrian portrait of George I for the decoration of the staircase at 11 Bedford Row, London, and contributed *The Apotheosis, or, Death of the King* (1727; Christies, 15 November 1996) to the series of ten paintings by various artists (including Chéron and Pieter Angelis) engraved in 1728, advertised by John Bowles as *Ten Prints of the Reign of King Charles the First.*

As draughtsman and illustrator, Vanderbank demonstrates a verve and originality lacking in his portraiture. A series of pen, ink, and wash drawings of horses and riders being trained in the exercises of *haute école*, perhaps drawn in the early 1720s when the artist 'was himself a Disciple in our Riding-Schools', was engraved and published by Joseph Sympson in 1729 as *Twenty Five Actions of the Manage Horse*; these drawings (now dispersed in various collections including the Tate collection, the British Museum, London, the Huntington Art Gallery, San Marino, California, and the Yale Center for British Art, New Haven, Connecticut) were widely copied and pirated. In 1723 Vanderbank was commissioned by the publishers J. and R. Tonson to illustrate *Don Quixote*, in the original Spanish; this eventually appeared as a lavish four-volume quarto edition in 1738, with sixty-eight engraved plates after Vanderbank. This project, for which Vanderbank's initial designs were preferred over Hogarth's, appears to have preoccupied Vanderbank, perhaps almost empathetically, for the remainder of his life, resulting in three sets of drawings: first sketched (collection British Museum), then finished for the engraver's use (collection Pierpont Morgan Library, New York), then drawn afresh, elaborated, and fully finished (collection British Museum), as well as a series of some thirty-five small freely painted oil panels (various museum and private collections; see Hammelmann, 3–15). Vanderbank also illustrated or designed frontispieces for various volumes of plays. Two self-portraits in pen and ink are known (NPG, dated 1738; and V&A). Vanderbank died at his home in Holles Street on 23 December 1739, aged forty-five, survived by his wife. Vertue noted that 'he left no children behind him by this wooman' (Vertue, *Note books*, 3.98).   JUDY EGERTON

Sources Vertue, *Note books*, 2.94, 126–8; 3.2, 3–5, 11, 12, 15, 20, 38, 44, 54, 57–8, 82, 85, 89, 97–8, 105, 124; 5.1, 14; 4.6, 38 · H. Hammelmann, *Book illustrators in eighteenth-century England*, ed. T. S. R. Boase (1975), 79–86 · [E. Croft-Murray], typescript of biographical notice, *c.*1968, BM, department of prints and drawings · E. Croft-Murray, *Decorative painting in England, 1537–1837*, 1 (1962), 260a–b · E. Croft-Murray, *Decorative painting in England, 1537–1837*, 2 (1970), 221a, 289b, 321a–b · E. Waterhouse, *Painting in Britain, 1530–1790* (1953), 125 · H. A. Hammelmann, 'John Vanderbank's *Don Quixote*', *Master Drawings*, 7 (1969), 3–15 · J. Ingamells, 'John Vanderbank and Don Quixote', *Preview, City of York Art Gallery Quarterly*, 21 (1968), 763–7 · J. Kerslake, *National Portrait Gallery: early Georgian portraits*, 1 (1977), 238–9, 283 · K. Eustace, *Michael Rysbrack: sculptor, 1694–1770* (1982), 64, cat. no. 2 [exhibition catalogue, City of Bristol Museum and Art Gallery, Bristol, 6 March – 1 May 1982] · parish register, London, St Giles-in-the-Fields, 19 Sept 1694 [baptism]
Likenesses J. Vanderbank, self-portrait, pen-and-ink drawing, 1738, NPG · J. Vanderbank, self-portrait, pen-and-ink drawing, V&A

Vanderbank [Vandrebanc], **Peter** (1649–1697), engraver, is traditionally and plausibly said to have been born in Paris and to have trained under François de Poilly. He always signed his plates with his name written in the French way, and it is only in a few advertisements and in later sources that it is given as Vanderbank. The prime information about his life is recorded by George Vertue, who was given it by one of his sons in 1743. He was brought to London in 1674 by the painter Henri Gascar, and his first plate in England was a large head of Charles II after a Gascar painting made in 1675. The following year he made a second head of Charles, this time after a portrait by Gascar's great rival, Peter Lely. These plates were by far the finest that had been made in England up to that date, and secured both Vanderbank's position and his independence. So when Gascar fled back to France at the outbreak of the Popish Plot fever in 1678, Vanderbank stayed, although he was probably also a Catholic.

Vanderbank initially published his own plates, but later worked mostly for other publishers and booksellers. In his earlier period he concentrated almost entirely on portraits, which, unusually for an engraver of the period, he made from paintings rather than his own life drawings. In later years he turned his hand to other types of print, including three very large etchings after Verrio's now destroyed ceilings at Windsor Castle; they are almost the only visual record we have of these paintings.

According to Vertue, Vanderbank married a Miss Forester, who brought him a dowry of £500. When, for reasons that are still obscure, his fortunes declined, he retired to her brother's estate at Bradfield in Hertfordshire, where he died. He was buried in the parish church of Cottered-cum-Bradfield on 4 October 1697. His widow sold his plates to the printseller Christopher Browne, and his three sons 'went to sea, or shifted about being not otherwise provided for' (Vertue, 5.19). He was no relation of the painter and illustrator John Vanderbank the younger (1694–1739), whose father was a tapestry weaver in Soho. His prints are be found in many public collections, including the British Museum.

ANTONY GRIFFITHS

Sources DNB · Vertue, *Note books* · BL, Add. MS 23078, fols. 46–7 · A. Griffiths and R. A. Gerard, *The print in Stuart Britain, 1603–1689* (1998), 217–24, 248, 296, 302–3 [exhibition catalogue, BM, 8 May – 20 Sept 1998]
Likenesses P. Vandrebanc, self-portrait, pen-and-ink drawing, 1738, NPG · G. Kneller, chalk drawing, BM; repro. in L. Stainton and C. White, *Drawing in England from Hilliard to Hogarth* (1987), following p. 185 · G. White, mezzotint (after G. Kneller), BM, NPG
Wealth at death 'His forthunes declined'; sons were not provided for

Vandergucht, Benjamin (1753–1794). *See under* Vandergucht, Gerard (1696/7–1776).

Vandergucht, Gerard (1696/7–1776), engraver and art dealer, was the son of the engraver Michael Vandergucht, born in Antwerp. **Michael Vandergucht** (1660–1725) was a pupil of Philip Bouttats and was admitted to the Antwerp Guild of St Luke in 1673. He was in England by July 1688, when a set of Roman emperors that he had engraved for Christopher Browne was advertised in the *Term Catalogues*. He was employed chiefly to engrave portraits, book illustrations, and architectural prints. As Vertue noted, he always worked in pure engraving and never practised etching, so that his output was rather stiff and old-fashioned by the time of his death. He was living in Queen Street, Bloomsbury, by 1713 and trained his sons Gerard and John, as well as George Vertue and James Smith. He occasionally painted portraits and conversation pieces. According to Vertue he 'was much afflicted with the Gout many years before he died' (Vertue, *Note books*, 3.62), at his house in Bloomsbury on 16 October 1725. He was buried in the churchyard of St Giles-in-the-Fields.

Taught to engrave by his father, Gerard Vandergucht received instruction in drawing by Louis Chéron and from 1713 at the academy in Great Queen Street. Having learned to draw expressively, he mastered etching, abandoning 'his Fathers stiff manner of Engraveing' (Vertue, *Note books*, 6.188). Vertue credits him with being the first English-born engraver to imitate successfully the then novel and fashionable French manner of blending etching with engraving in order to combine the advantages of free drawing with engraved detail and tonal gradation. This skill recommended him to James Thornhill, who employed him to engrave four designs for the cupola of St Paul's Cathedral (1719). Another four were commissioned from Frenchmen, including Bernard Baron and Claude Du Bosc, 'then the only Men in that way, of Etching & graving mixt together in London' (ibid.). In 1722 Vandergucht accompanied Dr Stukeley on an antiquarian tour, and he became, along with Vertue, the favourite artist of the antiquarians, engraving several important Roman finds. He worked for printsellers and booksellers until his father's death in 1725, when he took over Michael Vandergucht's house, the Golden Head in Queen Street, near the new church on the south side of Bloomsbury Square. On 24 August that year he married Mary Liney of St Marylebone.

Vandergucht's first important publications on his own account were sets of copies of French prints of Charles Coypel's *Don Quixote* tapestries and of the *Labours of Hercules*, after Chéron. For the next twenty-five years he was a leading engraver and publisher of history prints, antiquities, and decorative subjects. His output was very varied and included plates to William Cheseldon's *The Anatomy of the Human Body* and Batty Langley's *Pomona, or, The Fruit-Garden Illustrated* (1729), as well as reproductions of old master paintings and decorative sets, such as *Eight Curious Prints of Fowl and Fish* (1735). Robert White and Francis Patton were apprenticed to him in the 1730s, when he was also one of the leading artists who petitioned with William Hogarth for the Copyright Act of 1735. One of his last publications was a view of Philadelphia (1755), for which he organized the English part of the subscription.

By 1734 Vandergucht was also advertising himself as a dealer in historical portraits and antique marble busts, and about 1760 he retired from engraving to concentrate on this aspect of his business. He moved in 1758 to Vandyke's Head in Great Brook Street, near Grosvenor Square, where he sold old and modern Italian, Dutch, French, and Flemish prints, drawings, and paintings as well as antique and modern statues, busts, and bronzes. In addition he supplied artists' equipment and offered to frame prints and to clean and repair pictures. He was a member of the Society for the Encouragement of Arts, Manufactures, and Commerce and a respected authority on the arts. Vandergucht died at his house in Great Brook Street in his eightieth year on 18 March 1776. A sale of the 'very capital collection of pictures, by the most eminent Italian, French, Flemish and Dutch masters; remarkable fine bronzes, marble busts, statues &c. of the late Mr. Gerard Vandergucht deceased, distinguished for his superior knowledge in the vertu' was held by Christie and Ansell on 6 March 1777.

John Vandergucht (b. c.1699, d. in or after 1730), engraver, was born in London, the second son of Michael Vandergucht. He was taught by his father 'to age 17 or 18 and then sent to Germany, Bohemia &c', after which he returned to London and worked for himself in opposition to his brother Gerard: as Vertue wryly observed, 'there never was any grat harmony between the brothers'. John Vandergucht engraved small plates of history and portraits 'pretty neatly'. But 'he was much afflicted with the gout a distemper his father had, in a great degree and the son at 15 or 20 Had it first, (low diet or some quacking experiments) being taken ill of a violent feaver carried him off in a small time aged only about 31' (Vertue, *Note books*, 3.62). In April 1730 he was still living in Great Wild Street, Drury Lane, but he presumably died soon afterwards.

Benjamin Vandergucht (1753–1794), painter and picture dealer, was said to be a twin, 'the last and thirty-second child of Gerard and his only wife, Mary, who outlived him', to die in 1794 (*Anecdotes of Painting*, 221). He studied at the St Martin's Lane Academy and the Royal Academy Schools and exhibited with the Free Society and the Royal Academy. He specialized in theatrical scenes and was patronized by David Garrick, but gave up painting about 1787 to concentrate on dealing and picture restoration. In 1789 he published some prints of French revolutionary scenes. He was drowned crossing the River Thames at Chiswick on 16 September 1794, leaving a wife and eleven children.

TIMOTHY CLAYTON

Sources Vertue, *Note books* · T. Clayton, *The English print, 1688–1802* (1997) · R. Hyde, *A prospect of Britain: the town panoramas of Samuel and Nathaniel Buck* (1994) · C. T. von Murr, *Journal zur Kunstgeschichte*, 4 (1777), 15 · I. Bignamini, 'George Vertue, art historian, and art institutions in London, 1689–1768', *Walpole Society*, 54 (1988), 1–148 · E. Arber, ed., *The term catalogues, 1668–1709*, 3 vols. (privately printed, London, 1903–6) · Farington, *Diary* · Waterhouse, *18c painters* · *Country Journal, or, The Craftsman* (4 April 1730) · *A catalogue of the very capital collection of pictures … remarkable fine bronzes, marble busts, statues &c. of the late Mr Gerard Vandergucht* (1777) [sale catalogue, Christie and Ansell, London, 6 March 1777] · H. Walpole, *Anecdotes of painting in England … collected by the late George Vertue, and now digested and published*, 3rd edn, 5 (1782), 221

Likenesses W. Stukeley, Indian ink drawing, 1721, BM • J. Caldwall, etching (after B. Vandergucht), NPG

Vandergucht, John (*b. c.*1699, *d.* in or after **1730**). *See under* Vandergucht, Gerard (1696/7–1776).

Vandergucht, Michael (**1660–1725**). *See under* Vandergucht, Gerard (1696/7–1776).

Vanderlint, Jacob (*d.* **1740**), economic theorist, was an immigrant from the Low Countries who became a timber merchant at Blackfriars, London. In 1734 he published *Money answers all things, or, An essay to make money sufficiently plentiful amongst all ranks of people and increase our foreign and domestick trade*. In this work Vanderlint, motivated by what he saw as England's economic decline since 1688, and concerned at the poverty and high level of unemployment, proposed an increase in the money supply in order to achieve a better balance of trade and hence promote economic recovery: 'plenty of money never fails to make trade flourish'. He believed in free trade ('there should never be any restraints of any kind on trade'; p. 33), and that peace was the foundation of the happiness of a nation and would promote freedom of trade, which would lead to full employment. He wanted to create a more equal society by increasing the amount of land under cultivation and distributing it among the people, as he believed that the happiest and most powerful society was one 'that abounds most with middling people' (p. 100).

Vanderlint anticipated Hume's ideas on money and international trade, and he was highly praised by Marx, who regarded him as one of the leading defenders of the working classes. He died in February 1740.

ANNE PIMLOTT BAKER

Sources T. W. Hutchinson, *Before Adam Smith: the emergence of political economy, 1662–1776* (1988), 129–33 • D. Vickers, *Studies in the theory of money, 1690–1776* (1959), 170–84 • Allibone, *Dict.* • *DNB*

Van der Myn, Herman. *See* Mijn, Heroman van der (*c.*1684–1741).

Van Dyck, Sir Anthony. *See* Dyck, Sir Anthony Van (1599–1641).

Vandyke, Peter (**1729–1799**), painter, was born in the Netherlands. He was possibly related to Philip Van Dyk (1680–1753), a well-known portrait painter in Amsterdam. That he went to England at the invitation of Sir Joshua Reynolds to assist in painting draperies is partially recorded in an inscription on the verso of his well-known portrait of Samuel Taylor Coleridge (1795; National Portrait Gallery, London), where it is stated that 'This portrait was painted by Mr Vandyck, a descendant of the great Van Dyck, invited over from Holland by Sir Joshua Reynolds—1796' (Walker, 1.118). He exhibited a few pictures at the Incorporated Society of Artists in 1762 and 1764, and six portraits at the Free Society of Artists in 1767. It seems that Vandyke experienced difficulty in establishing himself as a portrait painter in London: in 1771 the Free Society of Artists voted to give 10 guineas to 'Mr. Vandyke' then in distress (Whitley, 1.190). His whole-length portrait of a

tennis player is reproduced in Waterhouse, page 386. Vandyke settled at Bristol where he continued to paint portraits. For the publisher and bookseller Joseph Cottle he painted the portrait of Coleridge mentioned above and those of Robert Southey (1795; National Portrait Gallery, London), Charles Lamb, and Cottle himself. The portrait of Coleridge was engraved by Richard Woodman and reproduced in Cottle's *Early Recollections* (1837), where Vandyke was also described as 'a descendant of the great Vandyke' (Cottle, 1.xxxvi).

> He was invited over from Holland by the late Sir Joshua Reynolds, to assist him in his portraits, particularly in the drapery department; in which capacity he remained with him many years. Mr. Vandyke afterwards settled at Bristol, and obtained just celebrity for his likenesses. (Cottle, 1.xxxi)

While Cottle thought that Vandyke's 'portrait of Coleridge did him great credit … exhibiting Mr. C. in one of his animated conversations, the expression of which the painter has in a good degree preserved' (ibid.), Coleridge described his facial appearance at that time as 'a mere carcase of a face, fat, flabby, & expressive chiefly of inexpression' (*Collected Letters of Samuel Taylor Coleridge*, ed. E. L. Griggs, 1, 1956, 259). Vandyke's portraits of Coleridge and Southey were included in the 'Romantic icons' exhibition held at the Wordsworth Museum, Dove Cottage, and at the National Portrait Gallery, London, in 1995–6. Peter Vandyke died in 1799.

ANNETTE PEACH

Sources J. Cottle, *Early recollections; chiefly relating to the late Samuel Taylor Coleridge, during his long residence in Bristol*, 2 vols. (1837) • R. Walker, *National Portrait Gallery: Regency portraits*, 1 (1985), 118 • Redgrave, *Artists* • M. D. Paley, *Portraits of Coleridge* (1999) • Waterhouse, *18c painters* • R. Woof and S. Hebron, *Romantic icons* (1999) [exhibition catalogue, NPG at Dove Cottage, Grasmere, 1995–6] • W. T. Whitley, *Artists and their friends in England, 1700–1799*, 1 (1928), 190

Vane, Anne (*d.* **1736**), royal mistress, was the eldest daughter of Gilbert Vane, second Baron Barnard (*bap.* 1678, *d.* 1753), owner of the Raby estate in co. Durham, and his wife, Mary (1682–1728), daughter of Morgan Randyll (*b.* 1649, *d.* after 1738), of Chilworth, Surrey, a London alderman and MP for Guildford on several occasions between 1679 and 1722. She became a maid of honour to Caroline, princess of Wales, on 18 August 1725; the princess and her husband, later George II, probably made the appointment to maintain their connections with the opposition to the Walpole administration, as both the Vane and Randyll families were tories. Anne continued in service when Caroline became queen, in 1727.

Anne Vane's mother had been described in the will of Christopher Vane, first Baron Barnard (*d.* 1723), as 'scandalous' (GEC, *Peerage*, 1.425), and Lady Barnard's reputation may well have encouraged similar expectations of her daughter. Gossip started to accrue around Anne Vane in autumn 1730, when her journey to Bath for health reasons—she was spitting blood, perhaps a sign of tuberculosis—occasioned the rumour that she was pregnant. Vane denied the accusation but she was compromised in the eyes of her fellow courtiers. It was rumoured that she

Anne Vane (d. 1736), by John Faber junior (after John Vanderbank, 1729)

had wished to marry William *Stanhope, first Baron, and later first earl of, Harrington (1683?–1756), but 'he forsook her, having gained his ends without it' (*Egmont Diary*, 1.236). During 1731 she became sexually involved with John *Hervey, Baron Hervey of Ickworth (1696–1743), and then with *Frederick Lewis, prince of Wales (1707–1751). Hervey and Frederick had enjoyed an intense friendship, and when it became clear that Vane was pregnant with a child that she publicly declared to be the prince's, Hervey wrote to her, claiming that she had turned Frederick against him. Others also were horrified by the liaison; John Perceval, first earl of Egmont, wrote that 'the woman will put the Prince on several things that may hurt both him and others' (ibid.), describing Vane as 'this fat and ill-shaped dwarf' with 'neither sense nor wit' (ibid., 1.235).

Vane was dismissed as maid of honour to Queen Caroline in January 1732 and was installed by the prince in a house in Soho Square, where she held court as his mistress. She later moved to a house on St James's Street, where she gave birth to a boy, Cornwall Fitz-Frederick Vane, on 5 June 1732. Publicly she was now the mother of the prince's son but Hervey and Harrington disputed the child's paternity. Ridicule from the press followed: Hogarth's double portrait of Henry VIII and Anne Boleyn was amended to show caricatures of Frederick and Vane. A poem, *Vanella in the Straw*, published in 1732, and *The Fair Concubine, or, The Secret History of the Beautiful Vanella* also appeared, both of which alluded to Vane's previous relationship with Hervey and suggested that he had fathered an earlier child. Vane had a further child with the prince, a

daughter, in April 1733 but the girl only lived for a few hours.

According to Hervey, by April 1734 he and Vane were again having sexual relations. She continued to live from the £1600 a year that Frederick paid her and kept a house in Wimbledon and in Grosvenor Street, where she had moved late in 1732. Vane became a channel through which Hervey learned details of the prince's political manoeuvres; if Frederick also used her as a political agent Hervey did not profess to be aware of it.

In 1735 changes in the prince's life led to Vane's eclipse. His betrothal to Augusta of Saxe-Gotha was settled, and he also became close to Lady Archibald Hamilton, who was more discreet about the nature of her friendship with him than Vane. In September 1735 Vane was told by the prince that 'decency required that he should quit correspondence with herself' (*Egmont Diary*, 2.198) and that 'she should go immediately into Holland or France, or any other place she would choose out of England' (Hervey, 2.476). Advised by Hervey (who wrote her letters for her), she succeeded in negotiating a more favourable settlement, which allowed her to remain in London at her Grosvenor Street house and keep her annual £1600 allowance.

Vane thus remained a source of potential embarrassment to the prince on the eve of his wedding, but she was by now suffering from 'cholics, loss of appetite, and general decay' (*Egmont Diary*, 2.483) and in November 1735 she moved to Bath. Her son died in London on 20 February 1736. Vane herself died in Bath on 27 March, and was buried at Bath Abbey. The next month a tragedy, *Vanella*, was published, depicting her as the cast-off mistress of Prince Adonis, dying from his neglect.

Anne Vane's memory was not powerful enough to stop Frederick from reinventing himself as an uxorious family man and defender of patriotic interests against a scheming court. In 1749 Samuel Johnson's *The Vanity of Human Wishes* coupled her with Catherine Sedley, mistress of James II, as examples of the ill fortune of women who became the lovers of royalty:

> Yet Vane could tell what ills from beauty spring;
> And Sedley curs'd the form that pleased a king.
> (Halsband, 397)

Vane lacked the political sense or experience to make any lasting impression as a royal mistress. She had little interest in politics except as court intrigue, and to Frederick she was probably only someone with whom he could prove his virility and thus his dynastic significance. She was unlikely ever to have been a player—as opposed to only a pawn—in the highly factional court of George II.

MATTHEW KILBURN

Sources R. Halsband, 'A prince, a lord, and a maid of honour [2 pts]', *History Today*, 23 (1973), 305–12, 391–7 • John, Lord Hervey, *Some materials towards memoirs of the reign of King George II*, ed. R. Sedgwick, 3 vols. (1931) • *Manuscripts of the earl of Egmont: diary of Viscount Percival, afterwards first earl of Egmont*, 3 vols., HMC, 63 (1920–23), vol. 1, pp. 218, 225, 235, 264–5, 280, 390; vol. 2, pp. 14, 198 • *Letters to and from Henrietta countess of Suffolk*, ed. J. W. Croker, 2 vols. (1824), vol. 1, pp. 407–10 • *Report on the manuscripts of the late*

Reginald Rawdon Hastings, 4 vols., HMC, 78 (1928–47), vol. 3, pp. 10–12, 16–17 • Walpole, *Corr.*, 41.448–52 • *GM*, 1st ser., 6 (1736), 111, 168 • GEC, *Peerage* • Burke, *Peerage* (1999) • J. C. Sainty, 'Office-holders in modern Britain: household of Princess Caroline, 1714–27', www. ihrinfo.ac.uk/office/caroline.html, 26 March 2003
Archives BL, letter to Lady Suffolk, Add. MS 22629, fol. 28
Likenesses J. Faber, engraving, 1729, BM; repro. in Halsband, 'A prince, a lord', 311 • J. Amigoni, oils, 1735, priv. coll.; repro. in Halsband, 'A prince, a lord', 393 • J. Faber junior, mezzotint (after J. Vanderbank, 1729), BM, NPG [*see illus.*] • line engraving, BM; repro. in *The fair concubine, or, The secret history of the beautiful Vanella*

Vane, Charles (*d.* 1720), pirate, is of unknown origins and parentage. Aside from the published and manuscript accounts of the trial which sent him to the gallows the main source for his life and career is the pseudonymous Captain Charles Johnson's *A General History of the Robberies and Murders of the Most Notorious Pyrates* (1724).

Vane is first heard of in the Gulf of Florida plundering Spaniards who were salvaging silver out of wrecks from their plate fleet of 1715. Although (according to the later testimony of Captain Vincent Pearce of HMS *Phoenix*) Vane surrendered himself to obtain the king's pardon toward the end of March 1718, this reformation did not last. Before the month was out Vane and several compatriots, who had squandered their ill-gotten gains, set out, allegedly in a canoe, to begin anew their criminal careers. By the end of July, over the course of various acts of piracy, they had worked themselves up to a band of seventy-five men and several ships. On New Providence, principal island of the Bahamas and a notorious haunt of pirate bands, Captain Vane

> had the impudence to come ashore with his sword in hand, threaten to burn the principal houses of the town, and to make examples of many of the people; and though he committed no murders, his behaviour was extremely insolent to all who were not as great villains as himself. He reigned here as Governor 20 days, stopped all vessels which came in, and would suffer none to go out. Being informed of a Governor being sent from England, he swore, while he was in the harbour, he would suffer no other Governor there himself. (Johnson, 111–12)

Alexander Gilmore, a master aboard the *John and Elizabeth*, which was seized by Vane off the island of Abaco on 29 March reports

> [t]hat in their Passage, the Prisoner at the Bar [Robert Hudson] covered his Piece at the Deponent, and said, Damn your Blood, I'll kill you, for sending me on the Mainyard in the Storm; That Charles Vane interposed, and prevented him at that time, and protected him afterwards, during his stay on Board. (*Tryals of Captains John Rackham and other Pirates*, 36)

Other piracies for which Vane was eventually charged included attacks on the *Betty* (17 April), the *Fortune* (22 April), and the *Richard and John* (23 May), all off Crooked Island. Vane's intention to refit for a voyage from New Providence to Brazil was abandoned with the arrival of Woodes Rogers, the real governor, on 24 July. The pirate apparently again attempted to secure a pardon on his own terms, but not being accorded a speedy answer, he burnt a

prize, slipped out of the harbour, and sailed off under piratical colours. With two subsequently captured sloops he and his men arrived at a small island 'where they shared their booty and spent some time in a riotous manner of living, as is the custom of Pirates' (Johnson, 105). Running low on provisions, they cruised near the Windward Islands in May, and subsequently haunted 'the track the Old England ships take in their voyage to the American Colonies' (ibid.). Three months later, off South Carolina, there was dissension in the group, with some pirates under Vane's deputy, Yeats, seeking the king's pardon. Vane cruised in the area hoping to seize his traitorous ex-colleagues, without success, but took a few prizes and was able through them to set Colonel Rhet, a local pirate hunter, on the wrong track. Sailing north Vane seized a prize off Long Island, but subsequently caught a tartar, a ship stronger than its pursuer, in the form of a French man-of-war. John Rakham, Vane's quartermaster, urged '[t]hat though she had more guns and a greater weight of metal, they might board her and then the best boys would carry the day' (Johnson, 108). While Vane as captain prevailed in his counsel of flight he was deposed the next day and was turned out in a small sloop with his mate, Robert Deal, and fifteen followers. They sailed for the Caribbean, making captures off north-west Jamaica and arriving in the Bay of Honduras on 16 December. Careening on Bonacca, they set out on a cruise in February 1719 only to run into a 'violent tornado', which wrecked Vane's vessel and drowned most of his crew. He survived several weeks on an island through the kindness of fishermen, before a Jamaican vessel captained by one Halford, an old friend and ex-buccaneer, appeared. Vane requested transport but was told by Halford, 'Charles, I shan't trust you aboard my ship unless I carry you a prisoner; for I shall have you caballing with my men, knock me on the head, and run away with my ship a-pirating'. The Jamaican captain kindly added, however, that he would return in about a month 'and if I find you upon the island when I come back I'll carry you to Jamaica and hang you'. When Vane hesitated at Halford's suggestion to steal a fisherman's dory for his escape, Halford concluded '[s]tay there and be d—nd if you are so squeamish' (Johnson, 109–10). Although Vane did manage to ship before the mast in another vessel he failed to avoid his fate. An unlucky chance meeting of that ship with Captain Halford resulted in Vane's exposure, and Halford, true to his promise, took the pirate to Jamaica in irons. On 22 March 1720 Charles Vane was brought to trial before a court of Admiralty in St Jago de la Vega. Found guilty of piracy he was executed at Gallows Point, Port Royal, on 29 March with his body subsequently hung in chains on Gun Quay.

SAMUEL PYEATT MENEFEE

Sources *The tryals of Captains John Rackham and other pirates* (1721) [copy at PRO, CO 137/14] • C. Johnson, *A general history of the robberies and murders of the most notorious pirates*, 4th edn (1726–8); repr., ed. A. L. Hayward (1926) • *CSP col.*, vols. 30–32 • P. W. Coldham, *English adventurers and emigrants, 1661–1733: abstracts of examinations in the high court of admiralty with reference to colonial America* (1985) • Marine Research Society, *The pirates own book: authentic narratives of the most* *celebrated sea robbers* (1837); (1993) • P. Bosse, *The pirates' who's who: giving particulars of the lives and deaths of the pirates and buccaneers* (1924) • high court of admiralty, instance and prize courts, examinations and answers, 1717–1722, PRO, HCA 13/86

Vane [*formerly* Stewart], **Charles William**, **third marquess of Londonderry** (1778–1854), army officer and diplomatist, was the only son of Robert *Stewart, first marquess of Londonderry (1739–1821), and his second wife, Frances (*d.* 18 January 1833, aged eighty-two), eldest daughter of Charles Pratt, first Earl Camden. He was born in Mary Street, Dublin, on 18 May 1778, and was thus nine years younger than his half-brother, Robert *Stewart, second marquess, better known as Lord Castlereagh. Charles was raised as an Anglican, in contrast to the family's Presbyterian tradition, and was educated at Eton College (1790–94), where at the age of thirteen he narrowly escaped drowning in a vain attempt to save the life of his schoolfellow Lord Waldegrave.

Early military service At the age of sixteen, on 11 October 1794, he was commissioned an ensign in a newly raised regiment of foot (Macnamara's), in which he became lieutenant on 30 October and captain on 12 November. He obtained a majority in the 106th foot on 31 July 1795, but both this and his former regiment were disbanded in that year. He was employed on the staff of Lord Moira's corps in the campaign of 1794–5 in the Netherlands. He then accompanied Colonel Craufurd to the headquarters of the Austrian army, and served with it in the campaigns of 1795–6 on the Rhine and upper Danube. At Donauworth he was struck by a bullet, the ball entering the right side of his face, passing under his nose, and lodging in his left cheek, subsequently leaving his sight impaired.

Having briefly served as aide-de-camp to his uncle, Lord Camden, the lord lieutenant of Ireland, on 4 August 1796 Stewart obtained a majority in the 5th dragoons (Royal Irish); he became lieutenant-colonel of the regiment on 1 January 1797. The 5th dragoons served in Ireland during the uprising of 1798, but were disbanded as potentially disloyal on 8 April 1799. Lord Cornwallis, however, expressed the hope that since Stewart's individual exertions had been 'as meritorious as possible' his worth should not be 'suffered to pass unnoticed', and with the concurrence of the duke of York he was within four days made lieutenant-colonel of the 18th light dragoons (Charles, marquess of Londonderry, *Memoirs*, 1st ser., 2.105–6, 112). Stewart served in the short campaign of 1799 in the Netherlands. He was attached to Abercromby's division on 19 September, and to Pulteney's on 2 October, and was again slightly wounded on outpost duty at Schagenburg on 10 October. On 25 September 1803 he was made aide-de-camp to the king and colonel in the army. Shortly afterwards he was appointed under-secretary in Ireland. He had been elected member for Thomastown in the Irish parliament in March 1800, and for County Londonderry (where his family owned estates) in May; after the union he was member for County Londonderry in the imperial parliament from 1801 until 1814, serving as under-

Charles William Vane [Stewart], **third marquess of Londonderry** (1778–1854), by Sir Thomas Lawrence, 1812

secretary to his half-brother at the war department in 1807.

The Peninsular War In August 1808 Stewart left his office for a time to command the hussar brigade in the corps sent out to Portugal under Sir John Moore. The brigade, composed of the 18th and the King's German hussars, to which the 10th hussars were later added, covered Hope's advance on Madrid and Salamanca in November, and afterwards the retreat of the whole army on Corunna. Stewart was critical of Moore, who in turn thought Stewart a 'very silly fellow' (Fortescue, *Brit. army*, 6.319), though publicly he praised Stewart and Paget for the spirit they had inspired in the cavalry. Stewart returned to England and to his office in January 1809, but in April 1809, on the recommendation of Castlereagh, he went back to Portugal as adjutant-general under Sir Arthur Wellesley (later Viscount Wellington), with the rank of brigadier-general. He was promoted major-general on 25 July, and served as adjutant-general throughout the campaigns of 1810 and 1811. Stewart was full of praise for Wellington, but the latter shared Moore's reservations, especially as regards the pretensions Stewart brought to his position as adjutant-general. *The Times* commented that 'it was never pretended that the Marquis of Londonderry possessed the qualities of a great military commander', but added that 'there never was a braver soldier in the British army' (*The Times*, 7 March 1854, 9). At Rueda his dashing attack unfortunately gave away the British positions; at Oporto his charge with a squadron of the 14th dragoons resulted in severe casualties. No one doubted his gallantry; Wellington mentioned him in his dispatches following Busaco and Fuentes de Oñoro; he singled him out for repeated praise for his actions at Oporto, while the French commander, Foy, described his action as 'un charge incroyable'. The thanks of the House of Commons were voted to him after Talavera, and Wellington told Liverpool that Stewart behaved with 'his usual gallantry' at Cuidad Rodrigo (Oman, 341; *Despatches, Correspondence*, 2nd ser., 4.321–4, 5.309). Wellington, however, refused to trust him with a substantial cavalry command, telling the duke of York that, with his defective sight and hearing, his gallantry would be apt to lead him into difficulties 'from which even the superiority of our men and horses would not be able to extricate our cavalry'. Years later, Wellington told Croker that Stewart used to harass the cavalry to death by constant patrols and reconnaissances. This, he added, 'I was obliged to forbid, but he refused to obey me' (*Supplementary Despatches*, 7.165–6; *Croker*, 1.346). Moore, with some justification, and Wellington with less, believed Stewart intrigued in London behind their backs. His direct line to the war department was unsettling to his commanders, for, as Wellington told Croker in 1826, 'Castlereagh had a real respect for Charles's understanding, and a high opinion of his good sense and discretion. This seems incomprehensible to us who knew the two men' (*Croker*, 1.346).

Diplomacy With the rejection of his repeated requests for a new cavalry command, on the return of his half-brother to office as foreign secretary, Stewart embarked on a diplomatic career. As he later confessed to Lord Clarendon, though he had 'no trade but the sword', a 'smatter' of diplomacy had come his way (Londonderry to Clarendon, 19 Nov 1851). Having been made KB on 1 February 1813, and having received the Portuguese order of the Tower and Sword on 27 March (he was to receive the gold medal with one clasp in the following year for his services in the Peninsula), Stewart was appointed on 9 April 1813 British minister to the court of Berlin; he was 'specially charged with the military superintendent, so far as Great Britain is concerned, of the Prussian and Swedish armies'. He reached the headquarters of the allies at Dresden on 26 April, and signed the formal treaty of alliance between Great Britain, Russia, and Prussia. To his chagrin he missed the battle at Lutzen; but he was actively engaged at Bautzen, and he took part in Blucher's cavalry stroke at Haynau on 26 May. He helped to storm one of the redoubts at Dresden, and was severely wounded at Kulm. At Leipzig (16 October) Blucher gave him the command of his reserve cavalry, and he captured a battery at the head of the Brandenburg hussars. He was said, as ambassador, to be 'always at the post of danger', and 'to have no other object in view than to go in quest of death wherever it is most likely to be found' (*Supplementary Despatches*, 8.353).

But it was in bringing pressure upon Bernadotte that Stewart was of most service to the cause of the allies. Recognizing Bernadotte's reluctance to attack his countrymen, Stewart, using 'outrageous' plain speaking, brought him to undertake a limited advance at Leipzig (Brett-James, 204–5), and he prevented the completion of a convention under which Davout would have been allowed to

return to France with 30,000 troops. During the campaign of 1814 Stewart, who had been made colonel of the 25th light dragoons on 20 November 1813, was present at the actions of La Rothière, Fère-Champenoise, and Montmartre, and at the entry into Paris on 31 March. He was promoted lieutenant-general on 4 June.

Bernadotte 'a préféré ses intérêts à ses passions' (ibid., 212), in creating Stewart knight grand cross of the sword of Sweden (25 October 1813), but his elevation to the peerage as Baron Stewart of Stewart's Court and Bally-lawn, co. Donegal, rumours of which were abroad in 1813, but which was finally gazetted on 1 July 1814, marked genuine regard for his services, as well as Castlereagh's favour. He also received the order of the Black Eagle (30 September 1813), and of the Red Eagle (12 March 1814) of Prussia, and the Russian order of St George (fourth class) (30 September 1813). He received an honorary DCL from Oxford (16 June 1814) and an honorary LLD from Cambridge (July 1814), and was sworn of the privy council on 22 July 1814. On the enlargement of the Bath he received the GCB (January 1815), and in March 1816 the GCH.

Ambassador at Vienna On 27 August 1814 Stewart was appointed ambassador at Vienna. He assisted Castlereagh, and afterwards Wellington, in the negotiations of the congress there, being especially concerned with the affairs of Switzerland. His chief function, and one in which his skill was acknowledged, was as a verbatim note-taker, but Castlereagh also used him as a trusted messenger to England. At Vienna his love of finery in dress earned him the name 'the golden peacock' and made him ridiculous; his drinking attracted unfavourable comment; and his womanizing shocked the diarist Charles Greville, as well as attracting the attention of the Austrian secret police. As well as patronizing the brothels of Vienna, as a handsome widower, Stewart's name had been linked with Lady Priscilla Burghersh and the Princess Bagration, before he resumed an affair, begun while recuperating from his wound at Kulm, with the duchess of Sagan. Nevertheless Castlereagh confirmed him as British representative at the congresses of Troppau in 1820, and Laybach in 1821, and he was at Verona with Wellington in 1822. More sceptical of Metternich that the gullible Aberdeen, Stewart played the difficult role assigned to him, of participating without committing his government, with some skill.

Marquess of Londonderry By his brother's death on 12 August 1822 Stewart became marquess of Londonderry, and when he found that Canning was to take the Foreign Office he tendered his resignation; but at Canning's request he remained until the end of the year to assist Wellington at Verona. Nevertheless he sought to persuade fellow ambassadors, such as Cathcart, to help in resisting the new foreign secretary. His devotion to his brother, which was to persist throughout his life, was largely responsible for his hatred of Canning, and also made him suspicious of Wellington, leading to hostility between the two men at Verona, and setting a pattern of alternating distrust of, and regard for, the duke that was also to remain a feature of Stewart's career. In 1823, on his return from Verona, he demanded of Liverpool a diplomatic pension, causing the prime minister (who had already experienced great difficulties with Stewart's demands for the reversion of his brother's command of the County Londonderry militia, and the granting of the British peerage promised to his late brother) to write on the offending letter 'This is too bad', a phrase that was to be thrown at Stewart, now Londonderry, by his enemies for the rest of his life. The prime minister and others saw him as greedy and grasping; for his part Stewart pointed out that he had resigned the lordship of the bedchamber he had held since 1814, as well as resigning the governorship of Fort Charles in Jamaica (to which he had been appointed in 1809) to facilitate the government's arrangements with Bloomfield.

Marriages and politics On 8 August 1804 Stewart had married Lady Catherine Bligh (*b*. 1774), daughter of the third earl of Darnley. She died on 11 February 1812, while he was on his way home from Spain, leaving one son. On 3 April 1819 he married, against the protests of her family, Frances Anne Emily Vane-Tempest (*d*. 1865) [*see* Vane, Frances Anne], only daughter of Sir Harry Vane-Tempest, and of Anne, *suo jure* countess of Antrim, and heir to very large estates in co. Durham and the north of Ireland. On his marriage he took the surname Vane, and on 28 March 1823 he was created Earl Vane and Viscount Seaham in the peerage of the United Kingdom, with remainder to the eldest son by his second marriage.

Having failed in an attempt, prompted by his own and his sister-in-law's antipathy to Canning, to establish an independent political connection with Camden and other associates of his late brother, the new Lord Londonderry devoted himself to establishing a political power base in Ireland and co. Durham. In co. Down he renewed his family's alliance with the Hills; in Durham he achieved, until 1831, a similar understanding with the Lambtons. This latter, though surviving the accession to office of Lord Grey, with whom Londonderry, once again estranged from Wellington, expressed sympathy, failed to survive the Reform Bill, of which Londonderry became one of the most bitter opponents, being at one point almost dragged from his horse by a pro-reform mob, and having to be forcibly restrained in his place in the Lords from interrupting William IV's dissolution in 1831.

As a reward for his considerable expenditure in the Conservative cause, amounting in his own estimation to £30,000, in 1835, during Peel's short administration, he was offered and accepted the embassy at St Petersburg; the appointment was, however, bitterly attacked in the House of Commons on 13 March, on the grounds of Londonderry's unsuitability as an ambassador, and his pro-Russian stance on the Polish revolt. Wellington, as foreign secretary, had told Greville:

> that he was not particularly partial to the man, nor ever had been; but that he was very fit for that post, was an excellent ambassador, procured more information and obtained more insight into the affairs of a foreign court than anybody, and that he was the best relater of what passed at a conference,

and wrote the best account of a conversation, of any man he knew. (*Greville Memoirs*, 15 March 1835)

But in the face of the Commons' attack Londonderry, to save the government embarrassment, withdrew. Partly in compensation Peel offered Londonderry his old job at Vienna in 1841 (in spite of Queen Victoria's request that Londonderry should not be offered employment), but Londonderry's sense of self-importance and pretensions to other office (he wanted the Paris embassy, or the lord lieutenant of Ireland) made him decline. He nevertheless remained a supporter of Peel until 1850, though the latter failed to appreciate the complex local factors which induced Londonderry to support John Bright at the Durham City by-election of July 1843, in preference to a Conservative. Similar local considerations also induced him to oppose his own son at County Down in 1852.

In co. Durham he threw himself enthusiastically into his second wife's coal concerns, investing heavily in property, and recruiting the foremost mining viewer of his day, John Buddle, as his agent. Seaham harbour was commissioned and built by him, exporting its first coal in 1831. That year also saw Londonderry settle a coal strike, following a face-to-face meeting with the union leader, Thomas Hepburn, to the disgust of his fellow owners. High expectations were held out that he would perform a similar function in the 1844 coal strike, and miners' delegates appealed to him to arbitrate the dispute. When, however, Londonderry refused to do so, the miners turned against him; his habit of issuing paternalistic ukases played into the hands of his critics, and popular mythology from then on unjustly cast him as the arch villain of the north-east coal trade, citing his opposition to the Coal Mines Act of 1842 as evidence for their view. Though Londonderry was in theory a wealthy man, the fluctuations of the coal trade, his electioneering expenditure, and his personal extravagance meant that he was always in financial difficulties—so much so that in 1834 it was feared he would follow his half-brother's example of suicide.

Londonderry fought two duels, the first against Cornet Battier, of the 10th hussars, of which he had become colonel on 3 February 1820, for which he was soundly reprimanded by the Horse Guards; and the second against Henry Grattan the younger in 1839 for an alleged slight over the so-called 'bedchamber' crisis. In each case Londonderry received his adversary's fire, and then discharged his own pistol in the air.

Last years On 10 January 1837 Londonderry became general, and on 21 June 1843 he was transferred from the 10th hussars to the 2nd Life Guards. He had been appointed governor of co. Londonderry in 1823, and one of the joint-governors of co. Down in 1824; and he was made lord lieutenant of Durham on 27 April 1842. His lingering military ambitions were rebuffed by Derby, to whom he had transferred his political allegiance, when the latter declined to appoint him MGO in 1852. Derby, however, sought to compensate him on 19 January 1853 by awarding him the Garter made vacant by Wellington's death.

Londonderry was one of the pallbearers at Wellington's funeral, but he did not long survive his old chief. He died at his home, Holdernesse House, Park Lane, London, on 6 March 1854, from influenza, and was buried on 16 March at Long Newton, near Wynyard Park, co. Durham, where his widow (who died on 20 January 1865, after continuing, to the admiration of Londonderry's friend, Disraeli, to manage the colliery enterprises following his death) built a 'memorial-room' for the insignia of his orders and other relics of him. An equestrian statue of him by Gaetano Monti was unveiled in the market place at Durham by Disraeli on 2 December 1861.

Londonderry's only son from his first marriage, Frederick William Robert Stewart (1805–1872), succeeded as fourth marquess of Londonderry. Londonderry had three sons and four daughters from his second marriage. The eldest of these sons, George Henry Robert Charles William Vane-Tempest (1821–1884), succeeded him as Earl Vane, and (by the death of his half-brother) became fifth marquess of Londonderry on 25 November 1872.

E. M. LLOYD, rev. A. J. HEESOM

Sources E. Londonderry, *Frances Anne: the life and times of Frances Anne, marchioness of Londonderry, and her husband Charles, third marquess of Londonderry* (1958) · A. Alison, *The lives of Lord Castlereagh and Sir Charles Stewart*, 3 vols. (1861) · R. W. Sturgess, *Aristocrat in business; the third marquess of Londonderry as coalowner and portbuilder* (1975) · *Despatches, correspondence, and memoranda of Field Marshal Arthur, duke of Wellington*, ed. A. R. Wellesley, second duke of Wellington, 8 vols. (1867–80) · *Supplementary despatches (correspondence) and memoranda of Field Marshal Arthur, duke of Wellington*, ed. A. R. Wellesley, second duke of Wellington, 15 vols. (1858–72) · marquess of Londonderry [C. S. H. Vane-Tempest-Stewart], *Narrative of the Peninsular War, from 1808 to 1813*, 2nd edn (1828) · marquess of Londonderry [C. S. H. Vane-Tempest-Stewart], *Narrative of the war in Germany and France, in 1813 and 1814* (1830) · *Memoirs and correspondence of Viscount Castlereagh, second marquess of Londonderry*, ed. C. Vane, marquess of Londonderry, 12 vols. (1848–53), vols. 1–4 · *The Greville memoirs, 1814–1860*, ed. L. Strachey and R. Fulford, 8 vols. (1938) · A. J. Heesom, 'Entrepreneurial paternalism: the third Lord Londonderry (1778–1854) and the coal trade', *Durham University Journal*, 66 (1973–4), 238–56 · A. J. Heesom, 'Legitimate versus illegitimate influence: aristocratic electioneering in mid-Victorian Britain', *Parliamentary History*, 7 (1988), 282–305 · R. W. Sturgess, 'The Londonderry Trust, 1819–54', *Archaeologia Aeliana*, 5th ser., 10 (1982), 179–92 · C. E. Hiskey, 'John Buddle (1773–1843): agent and entrepreneur in the north-east coal trade', MLitt diss., U. Durham, 1978 · A. J. Heesom, 'The northern coal miners and the opposition to the Coal Mines Act of 1842', *International Review of Social History*, 25 (1980), 236–71 · Fortescue, *Brit. army*, vol. 6 · *The Croker papers: the correspondence and diaries of … John Wilson Croker*, ed. L. J. Jennings, 3 vols. (1884) · C. W. C. Oman, *A history of the Peninsular War*, 7 vols. (1902–30) · A. Brett-James, ed., *General Wilson's Journal, 1812–1814* (1964) · *The Times* (7 March 1854) · GEC, *Peerage*
Archives CKS, family MSS · Durham RO, corresp. and papers · PRO NIre., corresp. and papers, D 3030; D3084/C/A | BL, corresp. with Lord Aberdeen, Add. MSS 43238–43254 · BL, corresp. with Sir William A'Court, Add. MSS 41531–41532 · BL, corresp. with Sir Robert Gordon, Add. MS 43212 · BL, corresp. with Prince Lieven and Princess Lieven, Add. MSS 47292, 47298, 47374–47377 · BL, corresp. with earl of Liverpool, Add. MSS 38256–38299, 38378, 38571–38576, *passim* · BL, corresp. with Sir Hudson Lowe, Add. MSS 20111–20114, 20191–20192 · BL, corresp. with third Viscount Melbourne, Add. MSS 60411–60415 · BL, letters to John Moore, Add. MS 57543 · BL, corresp. with Sir Robert Peel, Add. MSS 40225–40609, *passim* · BL, corresp. with Sir George Rose, Add. MS 42791 · BL, corresp. with Lord Westmorland, M/512/3 · Bodl. Oxf., corresp. with Benjamin Disraeli · Durham RO, letters to Cuthbert Sharp · Hunt. L., letters to Grenville family · Lambton estate office, Lambton Park, Chester-le-Street, co. Durham, corresp. with earl of Durham · Liverpool Central Library, letters to fourteenth earl of Derby · Lpool RO, letters to fourteenth earl of Derby · McGill University, Montreal, McLennan Library, corresp. with Lord Hardinge · Niedersächsisches Hauptstaatsarchiv Hannover, letters to duke of Cumberland · RA, corresp. with Thomas Lawrence · U. Southampton, letters to duke of Wellington · W. Sussex RO, letters to duke of Richmond · Woburn Abbey, letters to Lord George William Russell

Likenesses T. Lawrence, oils, 1812, NPG [*see illus.*] · T. Lawrence, oils, 1818 · attrib. I. Cruickshank, pencil and wash sketch, *c*.1835, NPG · J. Bouet, pencil drawing, 1851, U. Durham · R. Monti, bronze statue, 1861, Market Place, Durham · J. Doyle, satirical sketches, BM, NPG; repro. in H. T. Ryall, *Portraits of eminent conservatives and statesmen* (1836) · J. Hopwood, stipple (after T. Lawrence), BM · J. Jenkins, stipple (after J. Bostock), BM, NPG; repro. in *Military Panorama* (1813) · engraving, Durham RO, D/Lo/F 657 (3) · marble effigy, Wynyard Hall, co. Durham

Wealth at death £335,000; debts of £50,000: GEC, *Peerage*; Sturgess, 'The Londonderry Trust'; will

Vane [*née* Hawes; *other married name* Hamilton], **Frances Anne**, Viscountess Vane (*bap.* 1715, *d.* 1788), memoirist, was probably born at her father's house in Winchester Street, London, and was baptized on 14 January 1715 at St Peter-le-Poer, Old Broad Street, London, the daughter of Francis Hawes (*d.* 1764) and his wife, Susanna. Her father had amassed a substantial fortune from his career as clerk to the treasurer of the navy and as a stockbroker, with assets of £165,587 in 1721, including Purley Hall, near Reading, Berkshire, and an admired art collection. He was appointed a director of the South Sea Company in February 1715, and had a share in devising the plan grossly to inflate the price of the company's stock, the so-called South Sea Bubble. He was included in the Sufferer's Act of 1721, and of the £40,000 he declared to the government's assessors, all except £31 0s. 2¼d. was confiscated to be redistributed among company shareholders.

Frances grew up with her family in financial difficulties, which allowed her little or no dowry. Her beauty and vivacity—she was supposedly the finest minuet dancer in England—evidently made up for her comparative poverty, however, and in May 1733 she married Lord William Hamilton, second son of James *Hamilton, fourth duke of Hamilton and first duke of Brandon. On 11 July 1734 Lord William died at his house in Pall Mall, and ten months later, on 19 May 1735 at St Marylebone, Frances married William Holles Vane, second Viscount Vane (1714–1789). Lord Vane was infatuated with his beautiful young wife, but Frances made no secret of the fact that she despised her second husband, and almost immediately embarked on a series of highly public liaisons. For approximately the next thirty years her sexual adventures and extravagant spending caused Viscount Vane both social embarrassment and financial difficulty.

Though Viscount Vane remained devoted to Frances, her contempt for him manifested itself not only in her repeated elopements and attempts legally to separate, but in the publication in 1751 of 'Memoirs of a Lady of Quality', which remains the main source for her life. This, a chronicle of her exploits during those periods when she managed to escape him, appeared as Chapter 88 of Tobias

Frances Anne Vane, Viscountess Vane (*bap.* 1715, *d.* 1788), by unknown artist

Smollett's novel *The Adventures of Peregrine Pickle*. Published anonymously, the account none the less left readers in no doubt as to the identity of the 'lady of quality', though there was some question as to its authorship. It now seems that the narrative was in fact written by Frances Vane, but revised for publication by Dr John Shebbeare. It is written in the style of the amatory fiction popularized in England in the late seventeenth and early eighteenth centuries by writers such as Aphra Behn, Delarivier Manley, and Eliza Haywood.

Describing her father's initial attempts to end her relationship with the equally impoverished Lord William Hamilton, Lady Vane writes:

> I sent a letter to my lover, who, when he received it, had almost fainted away, believing that I should be locked up in the country, and snatched for ever from his arms. Tortured with these apprehensions, he changed cloaths [*sic*] immediately, and taking horse, resolved to follow me whithersoever we should go. (Vane, 437)

In recounting Hamilton's untimely death she depicts herself as a romantic heroine and model of sensibility, emotionally devastated by the loss of her husband. Horace Walpole viewed her in a somewhat different light, and in a gossipy letter to Horace Mann dated 23 November 1741, he confided:

> Lady Townshend told me that when [Lady Vane's] first husband Lord William Hamilton died, she said that she had

no comfort but in the Blessed Sacrament—though at the same time she lay with an hundred other men. I said, that was not extraordinary; it was what she meant by the Sacrament—the *receiving the body and blood*. (Walpole, *Corr.*, 17.210)

The 'Memoirs' describe how Lady Vane's family pressured her into her second marriage to Lord Vane, who is portrayed as foolish, ugly, and sexually impotent—a man whose sexual attempts 'were like the pawings of an imp, sent from hell to teize [*sic*] and torment some guilty wretch' (Vane, 451). Descriptions such as these are used to defend her behaviour by depicting her as an innocent beauty, ripe for the wiles of the man she claimed was her first extramarital lover, Sewallis Shirley (1709-1765), a son of Robert Shirley, first Earl Ferrers, with whom she eloped while visiting Paris with her husband in summer 1736 and then lived with in Brussels. Lord Vane attempted to win her back with desperate measures: in August 1736 he was reported as riding post several times through Boulogne, and allegedly 'had forty or fifty people riding over France in quest of her' (GEC, *Peerage*, 12/2.215). In January 1737 he offered £100 reward in the newspapers to anyone who could locate her; John Perceval, first earl of Egmont, thought him 'a very silly young man, half mad, half fool' (ibid.). These efforts naturally failed to conciliate Lady Vane, and when Shirley abandoned her in 1738, she became the mistress of Augustus Berkeley, fourth earl of Berkeley (1716–1755), and they remained lovers until late 1741. Other admirers, such as Sir Thomas Aston, fourth baronet (*d.* 1744), a Cheshire landowner and whig politician opposed to Walpole, and Hugh Fortescue, Earl Clinton (*d.* 1751), are mentioned in the 'Memoirs', and though Lady Vane denied that these men were ever anything more to her than friends, her husband—and society at large—remained unconvinced.

What contemporaries found so shocking was that Lady Vane, far from trying to preserve a reputation for sexual purity, should instead effectively advertise her adultery. While other memoirists such as Laetitia Pilkington, Teresia Constantia Phillips, and George Anne Bellamy used their apologetic texts to claim that they had been calumniated, and to express remorse for their frailties, Lady Vane unrepentantly publicized the details of her tumultuous affairs. After the candour with which she accounts for her first sexual digression, her tone for the remainder of her narrative vacillates uneasily between a refreshing denial of contemporary social and moral mores, and the need at least partially to vindicate her behaviour and character by blaming her family, her husband, and a hypocritical world. In the height of happiness with her first lover, Mr Shirley, for example, Vane describes herself as scornful of society's opinion:

> the world had now given me up, and I renounced the world with the most perfect resignation. I weighed in my own breast what I should lose in point of character, with what I suffered in my peace at home, and found, that my reputation was not to be preserved, except at the expense of my quiet … I therefore determined to give up a few ceremonial visits, and empty professions, for the more substantial enjoyments of life. (Vane, 463)

It is this attitude which fascinated and horrified contemporary readers. Horace Walpole expressed titillated shock in a letter to Horace Mann in 1751, stating:

> My Lady Vane has literally published the memoirs of her own life, only suppressing part of her lovers, no part of the success of the others with her: a degree of profligacy not to be accounted for; she does not want money, none of her stallions will raise her credit; and the number, all she had to brag of, concealed! (Walpole, *Corr.*, 20.230)

Writing to Sarah Chapone on 11 January 1751, the novelist and printer Samuel Richardson declared that *Peregrine Pickle* was 'a bad Book, which contains the bad Story of a wicked Woman' (*Selected Letters*, 173). He referred to Lady Vane and other scandalous memoirists as 'a Set of Wretches, wishing to perpetuate their Infamy' (ibid., *n.*). It is perhaps appropriate that the most measured response to Lady Vane's narrative should come from another woman, and one who had also been a runaway bride. Lady Mary Wortley Montagu's reaction to the 'Memoirs' did not reflect the malicious tittle-tattle of Horace Walpole or the moral outrage of Richardson, but instead demonstrated objective pity and social wisdom. As Montagu observed in a letter to her daughter Lady Bute on 16 February 1752, '[Frances Vane's] History, rightly considered, would be more instructive to young Women than any Sermon I know. They may see there the mortifications and variety of misery are the unavoidable consequences of Galantrys [*sic*]' (*Complete Letters*, 3.2).

Lady Vane remained socially active following the publication of her 'Memoirs'. Horace Walpole heard of her at Bath in October 1766: 'since it is too late for her now to go anywhere else' (Walpole, *Corr.*, 30.131). This may be a reference to her shattered reputation, or to the ill health that affected her later years. Bath was one of the resorts where she would allegedly take houses 'with no other view than to get them furnished, and then sell the furniture for half what it cost, to get a little cash in her pocket' (*GM*, 1st ser., 59/1, 1789, 403). After about twenty years in which she was bedridden, during which she is said to have considered converting to Catholicism, she died on 31 March 1788 at her house in Hill Street, Mayfair, Westminster, where she lived apart from her husband. She had no children from her marriages. She was buried in the Vane family vault in Shipborne, Kent. Lord Vane's expensive attempts to recapture his wife, and his requirement to support her erratic lifestyle and separate household, had forced him to live as a debtor within the rules of the king's bench for a period, to let his country seat in Kent, and sell his estate in Staffordshire and also his reversion of the Holles family estates. He died at his home in Downing Street, London, on 5 April 1789. EMMA PLASKITT

Sources F. Vane, 'Memoirs of a lady of quality', in T. Smollett, *The adventures of Peregrine Pickle*, ed. J. L. Clifford, rev. P.-G. Boucé (1983), 432–540 · *DNB* · Walpole, *Corr.*, 14.48; 17.209–10, 459; 20.230, 439; 37.1 · *The complete letters of Lady Mary Wortley Montagu*, ed. R. Halsband, 3 (1967), 3.2–3 · *Selected letters of Samuel Richardson*, ed. J. Carroll (1964), 173 · F. A. Nussbaum, *The autobiographical subject: gender and ideology in eighteenth-century England* (1989), 181–2 · C. Brant, 'Speaking of women: scandal and the law in the mid-eighteenth century', *Women, texts, and histories, 1575–1760*, ed. C. Brant and D. Purkiss (1992), 242–70 · W. Austin Flanders, 'The significance of

Smollett's *Memoirs of a lady of quality*', *Genre*, 8 (1975), 146–54 · G. S. Rousseau, 'Controversy or collusion? The "Lady Vane" tracts', *N&Q*, 217 (1972), 375–8 · R. Putney, 'Smollett and Lady Vane's memoirs', *Philological Quarterly*, 25 (1946), 120–26 · E. Plaskitt, '"The Beauteous Frame": the treatment of female sexual reputation in selected prose by Eliza Haywood, Samuel Richardson, and Frances Burney', DPhil diss., U. Oxf., 1999, 47–9 · J. Duncomb, *The Feminiad: a poem* (1754), 15 · 'The heroines, or, Modern memoirs', *London Magazine*, 20 (1751), 136 · *GM*, 1st ser., 3 (1733), 268 · *GM*, 1st ser., 5 (1735), 275 · *GM*, 1st ser., 58 (1788), 368, 461 · *GM*, 1st ser., 59 (1789), 403 · GEC, *Peerage* · E. Cruickshanks, 'Aston, Sir Thomas', HoP, *Commons, 1715–54* · IGI

Archives BL, letters to Lord Hardwicke, Add. MS 35597, fols. 364, 368

Likenesses line engraving, 1787, BM · painting, priv. coll. [*see illus.*]

Vane, Frances Anne, marchioness of Londonderry (1800–1865), society hostess and businesswoman, was born on 17 January 1800 in St James's Square, London, the only child of Sir Henry (Harry) Vane-Tempest, baronet (1771–1813), and his wife, Anne Catherine MacDonnell, in her own right countess of Antrim (d. 1834). Disappointed in their hopes of a son, her parents neglected Lady Frances Anne: she recalled in 1848 that 'Never was any child so harshly treated as I was by my Father, Mother, and Governess. I met with nothing but cuffs and abuse' (*Frances Anne*, 14). At the same time the child had impressed upon her by servants and other relations, particularly her aunt Frances Taylor, a sense of her position as the heir to the family fortunes of some £60,000 a year. The mixture of flattery and abuse, fawning and neglect, inevitably damaged her character, and she became by her own account 'sly, artful, and deceiving' (ibid.); haughty arrogance, which was to be her defining characteristic, also became ingrained. The death of her father brought her into possession of vast estates in co. Durham but also into conflict with her mother. Hence Frances Anne was made a ward in chancery, and at thirteen was given her own establishment and had her first love affair (with the brother of a suitor of her mother). By the time she was sixteen she had been the object of proposals from Lord O'Neil (twice her age) and the duke of Leinster, who had travelled over from Ireland specifically to inspect the heiress. In 1818 she met Charles William Stewart, Baron Stewart (1778–1854) [*see* Vane, Charles William], heir presumptive to his half-brother Robert *Stewart, then Viscount Castlereagh and from 1821 second marquess of Londonderry. Stewart, a forty-year-old widower with a young son, was ambassador in Vienna, and had a reputation as a ladies' man. Lady Antrim encouraged the relationship, but Mrs Taylor (the other guardian) opposed it. Only after the case was heard in the court of chancery did the marriage go ahead, on 3 April 1819.

It was an ideal match. Frances Anne's pride met its equal in her ultra-conservative husband, and he revelled in the vast wealth and territorial power which the match brought him. (In 1829 he changed his own surname to Vane to reflect the importance of the connection.) In Vienna, Lady Stewart flaunted her wealth—especially her ever-increasing collection of jewellery—and her new position, to the amusement of some and the disgust of others. Mrs Bradford, the wife of the embassy chaplain, described

Frances Anne Vane, marchioness of Londonderry (1800–1865), by Simon Jacques Rochard

the couple: 'She, decked out like the Queen of Golconda seated on a Sofa, receives you with *freezing* pomp and the atmosphere which surrounds her is *awful* and *chilling*. He is her most humble slave' (*More Letters from Martha Wilmot*, 35). The pride of the Stewarts offended people more important than Mrs Bradford: the Austrian imperial family refused for some time to have social contact with the embassy after they offended against court protocol. But another emperor, Alexander I of Russia, was greatly taken with Lady Stewart on their first meeting in November 1820, and when they met again in 1822, after the successive deaths of Stewart's father and brother, the relationship between the new Lady Londonderry and the tsar, pursued at the congress of Verona, became the talk of Europe. The congress, however, saw the end of Londonderry's ambassadorial career, and they returned to England in 1823.

Londonderry's political career faltered henceforward: his extreme toryism even alienated him from the duke of Wellington. But the couple maintained a glittering presence in London, where they entertained the Conservative aristocracy and political aspirants at Holdernesse House on Park Lane, and devoted themselves to the maintenance of their interest at Mount Stewart in co. Down, and at Wynyard Park and Seaham Hall in co. Durham, all of which properties they either purchased or substantially remodelled at great expense: Wynyard Park was remodelled by Philip Wyatt at a cost of some £147,000, only to burn down partially in 1841 and be rebuilt by Bonomi with the expenditure of a further £40,000. After the death of her mother, Lady Londonderry inherited further property

in co. Antrim, where she built herself a retreat, Garron Tower. The couple's income was huge, and was enhanced by the dramatic expansion of their industrial interests. Their family, too, was large: after an early miscarriage in 1819, Frances Anne had had a son in Vienna on 26 April 1821. He was followed by a daughter in 1822, another miscarriage, and two more sons and three daughters, one of whom died as an infant. Her youngest child was born in February 1836; five months later the Londonderrys travelled to Russia via Berlin, where they spent several months before returning via Warsaw in April 1837. Lady Londonderry's vivid account of what was then a most unusual holiday destination for British aristocrats was eventually published in 1973. In her own lifetime she published her account of two further journeys as *Narrative of a Visit to the Courts of Vienna, Constantinople, Athens, Naples, etc* (1844).

While her husband was alive, Lady Londonderry was, if not typical of her class, then at least an exaggerated caricature of it: autocratic, extravagant, and proud, she was Jane Austen's Lady Catherine de Bourgh made flesh. It was in her widowhood that she finally came into her own, in all senses of that phrase, and she rapidly took control of the empire she had brought to the Londonderry family after her husband's death on 6 March 1854. Far from handing control of the huge coalmining and coal-shipping concern that was the basis of her fortune over to her sons or agents, and retiring into obscurity, Lady Londonderry soon established herself at Seaham Hall as the active and effective head of the business. Benjamin Disraeli, who had been something of a protégé of hers, visited her at Seaham in 1861, and described her life:

> on the shores of the German Ocean [North Sea], surrounded by her collieries and her blast furnaces and her railroads and the unceasing telegraphs, with a port hewn out of the solid rock, screw steamers and four thousand pitmen under her control … she has a regular office … and here she transacts, with innumerable agents, immense business—and I remember her five-and-twenty years ago a mere fine lady; nay, the finest in London! But one must find excitement if one has brains. (*Letters … Londonderry*, 268)

In addition to the business enterprises, Lady Londonderry was active in the electoral politics of the county and city of Durham; her contributions to the election funds of Conservative candidates and the scale of her local commercial and industrial operations gave her an authoritative voice in the process. She was likewise active in providing Anglican churches and schools, especially in Seaham, a town which had come into existence solely to serve the Londonderrys' industrial interests. She spent the summers at Garron Tower in co. Antrim, where she continued to entertain in the grand style, and where she took an active and admonitory interest in the agricultural practices of her tenants. Unlike most women of the period, she regularly addressed large gatherings of her tenants and employees, delivering speeches at tenants' dinners and at the huge fêtes held for the Durham colliers.

Frances Anne Londonderry did not inspire affection, but she earned the respect which she required. Some of her family proved troublesome: her eldest daughter, Frances (*d.* 1899), married the seventh duke of Marlborough, and the second, Alexandrina (1823–1879), who was named after the tsar of Russia, became countess of Portarlington, but the youngest daughter, Lady Adelaide (*d.* 1882), disgraced the family by eloping with her brother's tutor. The eldest son, George (1821–1884), was inoffensive enough, and succeeded his half-brother as fifth marquess of Londonderry in 1872. But Lord Ernest (1836–1885) fell in with a press-gang, and had to be bought a commission in the army, from which he was subsequently cashiered. And Lord Adolphus (1825–1864), who was his mother's favourite child and the member for North Durham, married Lady Susan Pelham-Clinton against her family's wishes, became insane, and had to be medically restrained. His death in 1864 was a great blow to Lady Londonderry.

Having suffered for some years from liver disease and an 'enfeebled heart', Lady Londonderry died on 20 January 1865 at Seaham Hall, and was buried in the family vault in the parish church at Long Newton, co. Durham, bedecked in her turquoise rings. Her personal estate was probated at under £400,000 in England (Londonderry had left her a life interest in the estates and houses which she had brought to the marriage), and under £25,000 in Ireland. Her will included a careful catalogue of her jewels, which were to be distributed among her family strictly according to her instructions. Appointing her son to the Order of St Patrick in 1874, Disraeli recalled her as 'a *grande dame* who was kind to me when a youth, though she was a tyrant in her way' (*Letters … Bradford*, 1.74–5).   K. D. REYNOLDS

Sources Edith, marchioness of Londonderry, *Frances Anne* (1958) · K. D. Reynolds, *Aristocratic women and political society in Victorian Britain* (1998) · *Letters from Benjamin Disraeli to Frances Anne, marchioness of Londonderry, 1837–1861*, ed. Edith, marchioness of Londonderry (1938) · *The Russian journal of Lady Londonderry*, ed. W. A. L. Seaman and J. R. Sewell (1973) · *Letters of Disraeli to Lady Bradford and Lady Chesterfield*, ed. marquis of Zetland, 2 vols. (1929) · *The Creevey papers*, ed. J. Gore, rev. edn (1963) · *More letters from Martha Wilmot*, ed. Edith, marchioness of Londonderry and H. M. Hyde (1935) · Burke, *Peerage* (1901) · d. cert. · will · *CGPLA Eng. & Wales* (1865) · *CGPLA Ire.* (1865)
Archives Durham RO, corresp. and papers · PRO NIre., corresp. and papers, travel journal
Likenesses T. Lawrence, oils, 1818, repro. in Londonderry, *Frances Anne*; priv. coll. · J. Ender, drawing, 1820, repro. in Londonderry, *Frances Anne*; priv. coll. · T. Lawrence, double portrait, oils (with her son), repro. in Londonderry, *Frances Anne*; priv. coll. · S. J. Rochard, miniature, priv. coll. [*see illus.*] · portrait (in middle age), repro. in Londonderry, *Frances Anne*; priv. coll. · portraits, repro. in Londonderry, *Frances Anne*
Wealth at death under £400,000: probate, 7 June 1865, *CGPLA Eng. & Wales* · under £25,000: probate, 22 June 1865, *CGPLA Ire.*

Vane, Sir Francis Patrick Fletcher, fifth baronet (1861–1934), army officer and boy scout leader, was born on 16 October 1861 in Dublin, the only son of Frederick Henry Fletcher Vane (1807–1894), a younger son of the second baronet and formerly lieutenant in the 12th lancers, and his wife, Rosa Linda (*d.* 1895), fourth daughter of John Moore of Prospect House, Galway. The family claimed descent from Sir Henry Vane, knighted at the battle of Poitiers in 1356, and the baronetcy was created in 1786.

Vane grew up in Sidmouth, Devon, and was educated at the Misses Hills' preparatory school, Cheltenham, where he was 'lonely, miserable, and terribly homesick' (Vane, *Agin the Governments*, 12); briefly at Charterhouse School (1873–4), where he was bullied and unhappy; by private tutors in the country; at Tours in 1876; and at the Oxford Military College, Cowley (January 1876 to December 1877), a private military school preparing for Woolwich and Sandhurst entrance and militia examinations. He was 'enormously proud' (ibid., 26) of his uniform, and one of 'a pretty wild lot' (ibid.). He entered the regular army through the militia 'back door'; in October 1878 he was commissioned lieutenant in the 3rd battalion, Worcestershire regiment. He wanted to enter the family regiment, the Coldstream Guards, but there were no vacancies, so in August 1882 he transferred to the 2nd battalion, Scots Guards. He was so ragged by other officers that he resigned in May 1883 and transferred to the submarine miners, Royal Engineers, at Chatham and Gosport; they operated the electrically fired anti-ship harbour-defence minefields. He resigned his commission and in 1886 was a resident at Toynbee Hall, Whitechapel, which he saw as a revival of chivalry and where he raised a working boys' cadet corps. An enthusiastic cyclist, from April 1888 to May 1889 he was a captain in the 26th Middlesex cyclist volunteers; contrary to his later claim, he was not its commanding officer.

Vane married, on 15 December 1888, Anna Oliphant da Costa Ricci (*d.* 1922), third daughter of Baron da Costa Ricci, of the Portuguese legation. In 1889 Vane was made a knight commander of the Portuguese military order of Christ. He was involved in the Anglo-Siberian Trading Syndicate and in 1891 became a member of Lloyds. Proud of his lineage and family baronetcy, and enthusiastic for genealogy and heraldry, he established with others the Honourable Society of the Baronetage (1898), to purify the baronetage of false claimants. He resided in France, returning after the Fashoda crisis (1898).

Vane had volunteered for every war since the Second Anglo-Afghan War, and in 1899 offered his services for the Second South African War, 'being of a soldier race, and trained as such, no other action was possible for me' (Vane, *Pax Britannica*, x). In January 1900 he was appointed captain in a militia unit, the 3rd battalion, King's Own (Royal Lancaster regiment). On the voyage out he was inoculated against typhoid, which may later have saved his life, as he was in Bloemfontein during the typhoid epidemic. He served in South Africa from 1900 to 1902, with intervals of home sick leave. He was a cavalry transport officer, commandant at Karree and Glen (1901), and judge of a military court in Western District, Cape Colony, commanded a small column in Cape Colony, was a JP in Orange River Colony and raised a force of loyal burghers at Karee, visited concentration camps, and became known for his 'alleged pro-Boerism' (ibid., 188). Like other British officers he was relatively sympathetic to the Boers and hostile to the mining capitalists and Jews: 'the people we disliked the most were the Johannesburg Jews' (ibid., 12). He apparently shared Boer attitudes to non-Europeans, accepting Boer shooting of them. Opposing the arming of 'semi-savage auxiliaries' (ibid., 163), he approved the exclusion of non-Europeans from the pavements: 'there must be a distinction between the privileges of the white and the black' (ibid., 77). He became convinced of the need to conciliate the Boers. He returned to England in 1902, and his belief in reconciliation and his criticism of aspects of British conduct of the war—he especially disliked farm burning, which he considered 'useless and inexcusable' (Vane, *Agin the Governments*, 138)—brought him into contact with British Liberal pro-Boers. From 1902 to 1903 he was back in South Africa, investigating the post-war situation and reporting for the *Daily News* and other Liberal publications, and was criticized by the South African loyalist press. In 1905 he published *Pax Britannica in South Africa*, his 'thoughts and experiences' of South Africa during and after the war. Sympathetic to the Boers, urging reconciliation, and unsympathetic to the blacks, it criticized British destruction and looting but, while regretting the mortality in the concentration camps, claimed that there was 'no intentional cruelty' (Vane, *Pax Britannica*, 135), and praised Emily Hobhouse's 'painful exposure' of them (ibid.).

Vane's father had been 'verging in politics on Republicanism' (Vane, *Agin the Governments*, 1), and Vane was a Liberal, though also 'an imperialist bordering on Jingoism' (Vane, *Pax Britannica*, 227). In the general election of 1906 he was Liberal candidate at the 'Metropolis of Beer', the Burton upon Trent division of Staffordshire, where he lost to the Liberal Unionist, a brewer. Vane was subsequently prospective Liberal parliamentary candidate for the Cockermouth division of Cumberland. He supported compulsory military training, as advocated by Lord Roberts, though not conscription. In June 1908, following the death of his cousin Sir Henry Ralph Fletcher Vane, fourth baronet, he inherited the baronetcy and property. However, this did not enrich him because litigation in the 1860s between his father and Sir Henry, disputing who was the rightful heir, had cost about £50,000 and left the estate heavily encumbered: Vane alleged that this consequence had been 'really caused by the lawyers on both sides' (Vane, *Agin the Governments*, 185) and called the case 'the curse of my life' (ibid., 6). After Sir Henry's death the estate was placed in a trust, the income from which was to pay off the mortgage. Nevertheless Vane continued to enjoy a comfortable private income. He described himself in 1909 as a radical and a 'social reformer of a very advanced type' (*On Certain Fundamentals*, 1909, 22). He advocated reform of the House of Lords and condemned the sale of honours for party funds. Active in Liberal and pacifist circles and a proponent of socialism, he attended the seventeenth International Peace Congress in London in 1908. He supported the suffragettes, too, participating in their meetings and processions.

In 1908 Vane, who since his time at Toynbee Hall had been interested in the organization of boy cadets, supported Baden-Powell's new Boy Scout movement. Baden-Powell, a Carthusian contemporary, in 1909 appointed Vane commissioner for London, partly to disarm socialist and pacifist criticism of the movement. Scouting had grown rapidly, attracting men of conflicting ideals and aspirations, and two issues were especially divisive: the use of democratic or authoritarian control, and militarism. Enthusiastic, Vane worked hard at organizing scouting in London. He emphasized its peaceful, civilian potential, denying that it was military, and gained support for it from the Cadburys and other Quakers. He distrusted the 'militarist clique around Baden Powell' (Vane, *Agin the Governments*, 211) and wanted a more democratic structure. He warned Baden-Powell of the 'suspicion and dislike' of headquarters by 'a very large proportion of active men' in the organization (Jeal, 404). The conflict between Vane and headquarters was partly personality clash and partly power struggle. Baden-Powell was determined to retain control of the movement but was indecisive and reluctant to act against Vane. Under pressure at headquarters from J. Archibald Kyle, the manager, and Major-General Sir Edmond Roche Elles, the chief commissioner—who both threatened resignation—Baden-Powell dismissed Vane in November 1909. Vane may have been, and Baden-Powell have believed he was, homosexual: rumours circulated about Vane and boys.

Vane was amazed at his dismissal, and protested. In December 1909 he accepted an invitation to be president of the British Boy Scouts (BBS), which had grown out of the Battersea Boy Scouts' secession from Baden-Powell's organization in May 1909 and was backed by Cassell's popular boys' weekly *Chums*. Vane's organization was joined by many London and Birmingham scout troops, and some well-known Liberals—including Charles Masterman, Barrow Cadbury, and W. T. Stead—joined his committee. In 1910 reportedly about a third of United Kingdom boy scouts were members of the BBS, which spread to the dominions. In February 1910 Vane formed the National Peace Scouts, a loose federation of the BBS with the Boys' Life Brigade (a pacifist rival of the Boys' Brigade), and waged a tactical media offensive—which included his pamphlet *The Boy Knight* (1910)—against Baden-Powell's movement, alleging its militarism and contrasting his own peace scouts. In summer 1910 he was a founder of the Italian boy scouts (Esploratori). In November 1911 he founded the Order of World Scouts and became its first grand scoutmaster (1911–12); by 1912 his and Baden-Powell's organizations were competing worldwide. Vane spent much of his own money on his scout movement, overcommitted himself, and in August 1912 was declared bankrupt. The BBS survived, but rapidly declined in numbers and importance; according to Tim Jeal 'Baden-Powell was very lucky to have escaped in this way' (Jeal, 408). Thereafter Vane and the BBS were almost ignored in scouting historiography until publication of Jeal's *Baden-Powell* in 1989.

In 1913, as the suffragette movement escalated, Sylvia Pankhurst's East London Federation intermittently fought the police in the East End. She appealed for an ex-army man to help them with 'drilling'. Vane responded, and in November assumed the title of 'leader' of her 'People's Army' and 'People's Training Corps'. He did little, then withdrew to Italy. Sylvia Pankhurst wrote that he was a 'broken reed' (Pankhurst, 507). In July 1914 Vane published his anti-war pamphlet *The Other Illusions*, contrasting the glamorous image of war with its horrific, sordid, and immoral reality, and advocating socialism. But in 1914 Vane supported the war and encouraged recruitment. He was appointed a major in the 9th service battalion of the Royal Munster Fusiliers in Dublin. In 1916 he published *The Principles of Military Art*, considering training, tactics, and morale, and urging conciliation of Germany. He helped to suppress the Easter rising of 1916. Shocked at the shooting by Captain J. C. Bowen-Colthurst of Francis Sheehy-Skeffington, a pacifist, and others, he went to London and reported it to Kitchener and John Redmond. He pressed for an inquiry and official action against Bowen-Colthurst, and was relegated to unemployment.

In the general election of 1918 Vane actively supported Liberal and Labour candidates. After the war he lived for several years in Italy, where he loathed the fascists and their persecution of boy scouts. His first wife having died in 1922, he married in 1927 Kathleen, daughter of George Henry Crosbie of Kipp, Dumfriesshire. His publications included articles in the *Contemporary Review* and other periodicals, and his memoirs, *Agin the Governments* (1929). He was well-meaning, generous, 'a genuine "knight errant"' (Jeal, 407) determined to right wrongs, if eccentric and egotistical. He died on 10 June 1934 in St Thomas's Hospital, Lambeth, London, and was cremated on 15 June at Golders Green crematorium, London. His wife survived him. There were no children of either of his marriages, and the baronetcy became extinct.   ROGER T. STEARN

Sources F. P. F Vane, *Agin the governments: memories and adventures of Sir Francis Fletcher Vane, bt* (1929) · F. P. F. Vane, *Pax Britannica in South Africa* (1905) · *WWW*, 1929–40 · Burke, *Peerage* (1924) · *Debrett's Peerage* (1924) · F. K. W. Girdlestone, E. T. Hardman, and A. H. Tod, eds., *Charterhouse register, 1872–1900* (1904) · J. Tecklenborough [H. Naidley], *Seven years' cadet-life: containing the records of the Oxford Military College* (1885) · *Monthly Army List* (1882–3) · *Official Army List* (Jan 1901) · *The Friend* (17 April 1911) · *The Times* (11 June 1934) · *The Times* (18 June 1934) · T. Jeal, *Baden-Powell* (1995) · J. Springhall, *Youth, empire and society: British youth movements, 1883–1940* (1977) · M. Rosenthal, *The character factory: Baden-Powell and the origins of the Boy Scout movement* (1986) · R. H. MacDonald, *Sons of the empire: the frontier and the Boy Scout movement, 1890–1918* (1993) · K. Surridge, '"All you soldiers are what we call pro-Boer": the military critique of the South African War, 1899–1902', *History*, new ser., 82 (1997), 582–600 · R. T. Stearn, 'Oxford Military College, 1876–1896', *Soldiers of the Queen*, 83 (Dec 1995), 6–15 · A. Warren, 'Sir Robert Baden-Powell, the Scout movement and citizen training in Great Britain, 1900–1920', *EngHR*, 101 (1986), 376–98 · J. Springhall, A. Summers, and A. Warren, 'Debate', *EngHR*, 102 (1987), 934–50 · British Boy Scouts website, Sept 2002 · *CGPLA Eng. & Wales* (1934) · F. P. F. Vane, *The boy knight: essays and addresses on the evolution of the Boy Scout movement* (1910) · E. S. Pankhurst, *The suffragette movement: an intimate account of persons and ideals* (1931) · A. Rosen, *Rise up, women! The militant campaign of the Women's Social and Political Union, 1903–1914* (1974) · P. Laity, *The British peace movement, 1870–1914* (2001) · M. J. Foster, 'The Peace Scouts: the British Boy Scouts, their successes and failure', PhD diss., International Institute of Integrative Medicine, Corpus Christi, Texas, 2003 · M. J. Dedman, 'Economic and social factors affecting the development of youth organizations for civilian boys in Britain between 1880 and 1914', PhD diss., London School of Economics and Political Science, 1985

Archives Scout Association Archives, Gilwell, corresp. with R. S. S. Baden-Powell

Likenesses Lafayette Ltd, photograph, *c*.1915, repro. in Vane, *Agin the governments*, frontispiece

Wealth at death £193 18*s*. 6*d*.: administration, 2 Oct 1934, *CGPLA Eng. & Wales*

Vane, Sir Henry (1589–1655), administrator and diplomat, was born on 18 February 1589, the eldest son of Henry Vane (or Fane; 1560–1596) of Hadlow, Kent, and his second wife, Margaret (*d*. 1630), daughter of Roger Twysden. He matriculated at Brasenose College, Oxford, on 15 June 1604 and entered Gray's Inn as a student in 1606. On 3 March 1611 he received a knighthood from James I and the following year, on 27 March, he married Frances (1592–1663), coheir of Thomas Darcy of Tolleshunt D'Arcy, Essex, with whom he eventually had seven sons and five daughters.

Rise to favour Shortly thereafter Vane decided 'to put myself into court and bought a carver's place by means of the friendship of Sir Thomas Overbury, which cost me £5000' (*DNB*). In 1613 he purchased a third part of the subpoena office in chancery from Sir Edward George for a further £3000 from his wife's marriage portion, and in 1617 the office of cofferer in the household of Charles, prince of Wales, from Sir David Foulis. During this period he also began his long record of parliamentary service, representing Lostwithiel in 1614 and Carlisle in 1621. He would eventually sit in every session during his lifetime except 1629, when he was out of the country, and the Barebone's Parliament of 1652. He continued to sit for Carlisle in the parliaments of 1624, 1625, and 1626, and was MP for Thetford, Norfolk, in 1628 and for Wilton, Wiltshire, in both the Short and Long parliaments.

Vane's investment in court posts paid off handsomely as he ingratiated himself with James I, who granted him a reversion for forty years to the whole subpoena office, and Prince Charles, who included him in the select group of servants summoned to attend him in Madrid in 1623. Vane's career seems to have suffered a temporary setback owing to a quarrel with Buckingham that, according to a later report by a Venetian ambassador, obliged him to retire to the Netherlands. The Venetian's comment that Vane was a supporter of the Spanish match which had ended so disastrously may explain this dispute (*CSP Venice, 1629–32*, 141). In any case it proved only a momentary obstacle, since in April 1625, shortly after Charles's accession, Archbishop Tobie Matthew reported that Vane had been received back into Buckingham's favour, adding, 'he has long been rooted in the king's heart and has a world of great friends at court' (*CSP dom., 1625–6*, 10). Along with Marmaduke Darrell, Vane now became joint cofferer of the king's household. He was also given a mission to the Netherlands, on which he set out in August 1626, although none of the dispatches appear to survive among the state papers for Holland.

The embassy to The Hague In March 1629 Vane was again given a diplomatic assignment, as a private emissary to

Sir Henry Vane (1589–1655), by Michiel Janszoon van
Miereveldt, 1630

the prince of Orange and Charles's brother-in-law and sister, Frederick V and Elizabeth, the exiled elector and electress palatine and titular king and queen of Bohemia. His
main task was to explain Charles's decision to treat for
peace with France and Spain. After about a month, during
which the treaty with France was concluded, he was summoned back to London for consultations. Charles promised to send Vane back to The Hague the moment it
became clear where his negotiations with Madrid were
leading but delayed doing so until autumn, thereby
exacerbating Dutch suspicions. In September the king's
permanent resident at The Hague, Dudley Carleton the
younger, learned of secret discussions for a truce between
Spain and the Netherlands, which had been encouraged
by Dutch fears that Charles was about to conclude a separate peace without consulting his allies. Carleton therefore
urgently requested his colleague's return. Vane finally
arrived in late October, this time as an extraordinary
ambassador empowered to deal with the states of Holland
as well as the prince of Orange. His instructions reflected
Charles's impatience and condescension toward the
Netherlands. If the Dutch accused the British government
of treating with Madrid without consulting them Vane
was to turn the tables by accusing them of violating their
treaty obligations to the British crown by commencing
truce negotiations without informing London. If, however, 'the Prince of Orange and States bear that respect to
us as becomes them' Vane was to solicit their advice and
offer to mediate with Madrid on their behalf. He was also
to seek justice for the massacre of English merchants at
Amboyna, in modern Indonesia, by the Dutch East India
Company in 1623, and to reassure Frederick and Elizabeth

that he would continue to seek their restitution to lands
from which they had been driven by Spanish and imperial
armies.

Although the Dutch responded politely to his embassy,
Vane soon concluded that they no longer trusted Charles
and were inclined to make the best peace they could in
their own interests, although this would mean abandoning Frederick V. In addition their response concerning
Amboyna was so unsatisfactory that he refused to receive
it. Despite this lack of success he continued to support the
Anglo-Dutch alliance and war with Spain. His experience
in the Netherlands also drove home to him the adverse
affects that Charles's lack of money was having on his
European reputation and the need to demonstrate that
Britain was still capable of effective military efforts. On
hearing reports of the dissolution of the 1629 parliament
he wrote to the earl of Carlisle urging the Council to:

> resolve and execute with courage, for it is high time to
> vindicate the King's honour and that of the nation, which
> will never be effected until you put ships to sea and act
> something abroad, which will also make you esteemed at
> home.   (PRO, SP 84/139/92)

He warned his superiors that their failure to pay the pension of Elizabeth of Bohemia had seriously damaged Britain's reputation and he lobbied for the payment of English royal debts to Dutch merchants with a persistence
that provoked a sharp rebuke from his patron Sir Richard
Weston, the lord treasurer. He also asked for and received
funds with which to bribe Dutch politicians. Although the
bitter factional divisions characteristic of Dutch politics
disgusted Vane—reminding him, he said, of the recent
parliament—he felt confident that with proper management a pro-British party could be brought to power (PRO,
SP 84/140 fol. 160). In a policy memorandum for the king
written in July 1630, when he was again summoned home
for consultations, he warned that Madrid would use all
available means to alienate Britain from its protestant
allies, advised continuing the Dutch alliance, and
exhorted Charles to 'put your affairs at home in such
order as that the world may take notice that by the next
spring you will be capable of making war, or treating with
your sword in your hand' (PRO, SP 84/141, fols. 192–4).

Vane's superiors in London had decided otherwise, however, and Vane was sent back to The Hague with the
unenviable task of defending Charles's view that making
peace with Spain did not mean abandoning his allies but
merely amounted to an effort to achieve their common
objectives by alternative means. This did not prove easy.
Immediately after his arrival Vane received a surprise visit
from the king of Bohemia, brandishing the letter his wife
had just received from her brother, who remonstrated bitterly against Charles's conduct, complained that he 'saw
himself left by all the world … and so burst out into a passionate weeping' (PRO, SP 84/141, fol. 307). Although Vane
managed to cajole Elizabeth into saying she trusted her
brother's wisdom, Frederick had not finished his protests.
He next threatened that if his wife's English pension were
not paid he would send her back to London, break up his
household, and retire into obscurity with two servants.

Although the prince of Orange avoided such melodrama, he said he was unable to understand why Charles thought peace negotiations could prove of any benefit. Vane meanwhile grew increasingly impatient with the Dutch. Fortunately, neither side wanted an open breach, so the embassy ended with outward demonstrations of accord that masked the mutual suspicions and recriminations that now characterized Anglo-Dutch relations.

Embassy to Sweden and domestic administration, 1631–1638 Vane's conduct of his embassy pleased his superiors, earning him a seat on the privy council and a new diplomatic assignment in 1631, to attempt to negotiate an agreement with Gustavus Adolphus, king of Sweden, for the reconquest and restoration of Frederick's hereditary principality of the Palatinate, which had been overrun by Spanish and imperial armies. Vane initially received a warm welcome but his relationship with the Swedish king soon cooled as it became clear that Gustavus would agree to British requests only in return for much more substantial assistance than the few thousand volunteers and £10,000 a month Charles was prepared to offer. Vane soon also realized that the Swedish king was prepared to sacrifice the Palatinate in return for the support of France and the neutrality of Bavaria and other Catholic German principalities in his war with the emperor. Even if he did liberate it by arms, he was not inclined to turn it over to Frederick except on humiliating terms. Gustavus Adolphus, in turn, believed or pretended to believe that Vane had deliberately sabotaged his good relations with Charles I in order to serve his pro-Spanish patrons in London. The embassy therefore ended in open failure. This did not displease friends of Charles and Vane on the council, however, who were sceptical of the Swedish alliance from the start.

The Dutch and German embassies appear to have helped Vane consolidate his influence at court. He corresponded during his absences abroad with a large network of influential friends, including Hispanophiles like Richard Weston, Francis Cottington, and the earl of Arundel, but also figures far more sympathetic to protestant causes, such as the earls of Holland, Bedford, and Pembroke. In July 1630 Thomas Roe jealously told Elizabeth of Bohemia that she should rely on Vane for information about the English court, since he 'is of the cabinet and one of those that can read whispers' (*CSP dom.*, 1629–31, 306). Although he did not yet hold an office of the front rank, Vane played an active administrative role in a variety of areas. As comptroller of the household, an office he held from 1629, and a member of the board of the green cloth, he was responsible for overseeing the provisioning of the court. His diligence earned him a promotion to the post of treasurer of the household in 1639. Vane also helped to set up an independent household for Prince Charles and Princess Mary in 1633. Between 1632 and 1638 he was an active participant on the admiralty commission that oversaw the creation of the ship-money fleet. Simultaneously he helped regulate the manufacture and sale of gunpowder as a saltpetre commissioner. He also served on the high

commission from 1633 to 1641, and on various *ad hoc* committees of the council charged with investigations into such matters as the administration of the poor laws, the use of able bodied felons in 'discoveries and other foreign employments' (*CSP dom.*, 1631–3, 547), the regulation of the great wardrobe, the enforcement of proclamations against unlicensed building in London, the conduct of the admiralty between the death of Buckingham in 1629 and the appointment of the earl of Northumberland as lord admiral in 1638, and the expenditure of secret service money. In 1638 he oversaw the preparations for the arrival in England of Marie de' Medici, the king's mother-in-law and queen mother of France.

Secretary of state Vane's career reached its apogee between 1639 and 1641, during the escalating confrontation provoked by Charles I's attempt to impose ecclesiastical reforms on Scotland. At the outset of this period he and the earl of Arundel emerged as close confidants of the king during the early planning of the first military campaign against the covenanters. He was named, along with the marquess of Hamilton, the earl of Pembroke, and Secretary Sir John Coke, to the select committee appointed in January 1639 to oversee preparations for the king's own journey north. He travelled to the frontier that spring and returned briefly to London in May, when he engaged in a heated exchange with the earl of Bristol over the wisdom of allowing Charles to preside over the military campaign in person but was back in the north in time to witness the king's unexpected entrance into a conference between the English and Scottish commanders on 12 June. In early July he and the earl of Lindsey were reported to be the only two privy councillors in attendance on Charles in the north. He attended the truce negotiations that took place that month, sending guardedly optimistic reports back to London on the chances for a peaceful resolution to the conflict, and was appointed to the council of war in December. Over the winter he remained active in preparations for a new campaign.

On 3 February 1640 Vane was appointed secretary of state after the aged Coke was forced into retirement. As an exceptional favour he was allowed to retain his position as treasurer of the household. He owed his elevation to the queen and the marquess of Hamilton, who prevailed over the opposition of Thomas Wentworth. Vane was given responsibility for relations with France, the Dutch republic, Germany, and the Baltic region, while his colleague Sir Francis Windebank oversaw diplomacy with Italy, Spain, and the Spanish Netherlands. Domestic correspondence was to be divided equally. During the Short Parliament, Vane acted as the crown's leading spokesman in the Commons and on 4 May proposed a compromise by which Charles would agree to surrender ship money in exchange for twelve subsidies. The Commons' failure to accept this offer quickly caused Charles to lose patience and end the session the following day. Clarendon later blamed Vane's mismanagement for this outcome, almost certainly unfairly.

Vane again accompanied Charles to the north in the

summer of 1640, sending frequent reports back to Winde-bank and the council in London. These reveal his growing disillusionment with the king's policy as he became more convinced that shortages of money and supplies were hampering military preparations, and of the depth and breadth of English sympathy for the Scottish cause. He had always believed that England needed to unite intern-ally so as to protect its honour and the interests of its allies through effective action abroad. In the past he had often blamed parliamentary intransigence and puritan excesses for the kingdom's divisions but he now began to worry that Charles's determination to fight an unpopular war with an undisciplined army and a nearly empty treas-ury was having disastrous effects on the kingdom's mor-ale. By August he was lamenting the danger of mutiny in the English forces, the lack of money to supply them, the disorder of the king's affairs, and the prospect that if the Scots 'advance southward it is then to be apprehended they have certainly a party amongst us' (*CSP dom.*, 1640, 549, 630, 641–2; Russell, 148–9).

The fall of Strafford Vane's misgivings about the war with Scotland worsened his relations with Wentworth. The two men had enjoyed an amicable relationship as late as the summer of 1639, when Wentworth used Vane as an intermediary to pass on advice about the Scottish crisis to the king, but they became bitter rivals soon afterwards. Wentworth gratuitously affronted Vane when he was ele-vated to the peerage on 12 January 1640 by taking, along-side the earldom of Strafford, the title to the barony of Raby, the secretary's main seat in co. Durham. Shortly thereafter Sir Richard Cave reported that the court 'is div-ided into a double faction; the Lieutenant of Ireland goes on still in a close high way; Sir H. Vane marches after him in a more open posture … fiery feud there is between them'. During the early months of the Long Parliament, Vane belonged to a moderate group on the council that wanted to reconcile Charles to his people by persuading him to abandon his provocative Scottish policies. He sup-plied information to the parliamentary committee in Edinburgh and eventually became the key witness in the impeachment proceedings against Strafford, as the only member of the council prepared to testify that the lord lieutenant had advised using the Irish army to subdue England. The absence of a corroborating witness weak-ened the force of this revelation, especially after the earl of Bristol revealed that Vane had recalled his colleague's incriminating words only after three interrogations. But on 10 April Sir Henry *Vane the younger produced a copy of his father's notes of the fateful council meeting, which he claimed to have found while searching his father's study for other papers. The elder Vane displayed consider-able irritation with his son for revealing this document but Clarendon and other contemporaries suspected secret collusion between them, whether justifiably or not it is now impossible to determine. Whatever the case, the revelation of Vane's notes helped seal the fate of his bitter rival.

On the day that the Lords voted Strafford's attainder Vane wrote to Sir Thomas Roe:

> God send us now a happy end of our troubles and good peace … I hope my next will tell you that he [Charles] is resolved to reconcile himself with his people, and to rely on their counsels, there being now no other [way] left. (*CSP dom.*, 1640–41, 571)

Since Windebank had by now fled to the continent, Vane had become the only secretary of state. He once more accompanied the king to Scotland in the summer of 1641 and in August naïvely reported that Charles was recovering the love of his subjects, 'so that I assure myself by next spring he will be useful to his friends abroad, to the comfort of all the reformed churches' (*CSP dom.*, 1641–3, 101). But news of the outbreak of the Irish rising and renewed friction between the king and the Long Parlia-ment soon shattered his optimism. 'Three kingdoms in this condition, no money and little affection, should be well thought of, and the Catholic Romish princes abroad all drawing to a peace … we cannot be happy if we change not our counsels' (ibid., 149). Unfortunately his support for compromise, together with his role in Strafford's destruction, had by this time alienated both his former patron Henrietta Maria and the king. In early December he was dismissed from all his offices at court.

Death and assessment For some time Vane remained an active member of parliament but his influence gradually waned. Pym moved on 13 December 1641 to have him added to parliament's committee for Irish affairs. The next year he was appointed parliament's lord lieutenant of Durham, although this was a largely meaningless office since the county had fallen under royalist control. In 1644 he was included on the committee for both kingdoms but the Commons rejected a motion to name him to the coun-cil of state in 1650. Although he represented Kent in the first protectorate parliament his political career was by then effectively over. His death about May 1655 gave rise to royalist reports that he had committed suicide from remorse over his role in Strafford's attainder. Although no solid evidence supports this claim, Vane's will does con-tain an unusually bleak opening formula, describing his life as 'nothing but vanity and vexation', suggesting that he died an unhappy man (will).

Vane's posthumous reputation has continued to suffer from disapproval of his role in Strafford's demise and a particularly venomous portrait by the earl of Clarendon, who described him as an 'illiterate' time-server of medi-ocre abilities, who joined the court to enrich himself, rose to a position for which he was utterly unqualified, and betrayed the king because of personal malice against a more able rival (Clarendon, *Hist. rebellion*, 2.548). The abun-dant documentary evidence for Vane's career—much of it still largely unexplored by historians—reveals a less damning picture. He was a competent and diligent admin-istrator and a reasonably shrewd diplomat. Like most suc-cessful courtiers he did enrich himself while serving the crown, increasing his estate from an annual rental value of about £460 at the start of his adult life to roughly £3000 by 1640. The profits of office allowed him to purchase the manor of Fairlawn in Kent for £4000 and the seignories of Raby, Barnard Castle, and Long Newton in Durham for

£18,000. The earl of Bedford also drew him in as an early investor in the drainage of the Lincolnshire fens. But if he looked after his own financial interests, Vane was also capable of real generosity. His efforts to help Dutch merchants secure payments of debts owed them by the English crown has already been mentioned. When the painter Gerrit van Honthorst asked his assistance in obtaining prompt payment for portraits he had completed for Charles I, Vane paid for them with his own purse and was reimbursed later by the crown. During the development of Covent Garden, Vane bought a house lot and planted it with fruit trees as a public amenity.

Vane was not an unprincipled time-server but a moderate pragmatist. He instinctively favoured protestant alliances, largely because he shared the contemporary phobia of 'popish kings', but he had few illusions that religious solidarity alone could ever provide an adequate foundation for foreign policy. He disliked the fractiousness of Dutch politics and he saw more clearly than many contemporaries that Gustavus Adolphus was more interested in extending his own power in Germany than in restoring the rights of defeated protestant rulers like Frederick V. Above all he recognized that even sympathetic European powers would serve Stuart interests only if they believed they might obtain tangible benefits by doing so, which meant that for Charles to achieve anything in Europe he needed to find the resources necessary to wage war. For this reason Vane disliked parliaments that threatened to weaken the crown's fiscal position and undermine the king's reputation abroad, but favoured ship money. His initial response, when confronted with Scottish defiance of Charles's ecclesiastical policies, was to support a decisive display of force followed by acts of royal clemency, once the king's authority had been re-established. But when he realized that a military campaign might fail and that the English political nation was becoming bitterly divided by the king's Scottish policies he changed his mind and became an advocate of conciliation. His repeatedly expressed hope amid the deepening political crisis of 1641 that Charles would somehow regain the love of his people and then go on to assist other protestant states against popish kings might have been naïve, but it was far from cynical. Unfortunately his preference for conciliation and dislike of partisan quarrels that disrupted the practical ability to get things done ultimately satisfied neither the king and queen, nor the more determined leaders of the Long Parliament.

R. MALCOLM SMUTS

Sources CSP dom., 1610–49 · state papers foreign, Holland, Jan 1629–July 1630, PRO, SP84/139–142 · DNB · CSP Venice, 1628–32 · negotiations of Sir Henry Vane with Gustavus Adolphus, BL, Egerton MS 2541, fols. 181–94 · S. R. Gardiner, History of England from the accession of James I to the outbreak of the civil war, 1603–1642, 10 vols. (1883–4), vols. 4–6 · Clarendon, Hist. rebellion · K. Sharpe, The personal rule of Charles I (1992) · C. Hibbard, Charles I and the Popish Plot (1983) · Vane and other correspondence, BL, Egerton MS 2533 · signet office docquet books, 1627–38, PRO, SO3/9–11 · state papers foreign, Sweden, 1628–32, PRO, SP95/3 · will, PRO, PROB 11/245, fols. 421–2 · L. J. Reeve, Charles I and the road to personal rule (1989) · Sheffield Public Library, Wentworth Woodhouse muniments, StrP10b

[microfilm] · J. E. Mousley, 'Fane, Henry II', HoP, Commons, 1558–1603 · C. Russell, The fall of the British monarchies, 1637–1642 (1991)
Archives Durham RO, deeds and papers, D/LO | BL, official summary of his embassy to Gustavus Adolphus, Egerton MS 2541, fols. 181–94 · BL, letters to Sir Edward Nicholas, Egerton MS 2533 · Durham RO, letters to Lord Dorchester, D/LO/F1020 [copies] · PRO, oration to Gustavus Adolphus, 1632, SP95/2, fol. 231 · PRO, missions to the Netherlands, SP84/139–142 · PRO, letters and documents relating to Vane, SP 16, passim
Likenesses M. J. van Miereveldt, portrait, 1630; Sotheby's, 13 July 1988, lot 20 [see illus.] · Van Dyck, oils; in possession of Sir Henry Vane, in 1866 · oils (after M. J. van Miereveldt), NPG; version, Raby Castle, Durham
Wealth at death substantial; portions of £2000 each to two daughters; also numerous smaller bequests: will, PRO, PROB 11/245, fols. 421–2

Vane, Sir Henry, the younger

Vane, Sir Henry, the younger (1613–1662), politician and author, was born near Debden, Essex, and was baptized at Debden on 26 May 1613, the first of the eleven children of Sir Henry *Vane the elder (1589–1655), a Kentish landowner and rising courtier, and his wife, Frances (1592–1663), daughter of Thomas Darcy of Tolleshunt D'Arcy, Essex.

Early years, 1613–1635 Vane's parents were of the greater English gentry, and this patrician heritage determined his education and early ambitions. At Westminster School the boy not only profited from the usual humanist instruction in the classics but eagerly conformed to the dominant culture of 'Good-fellowship' because it seemed 'the only means of accomplishing a Gentleman'. In his mid-teens, however, Vane underwent an intense spiritual crisis, causing him to lament his past lifestyle as 'disloyalty to God, prophaneness … a way of sin', and to rejoice in hope of salvation by his newfound 'knowledge of the only true God and Jesus Christ' (Tryal, 87). From this divine revelation he dated his inner resolve to follow the dictates of conscience, yet these, at first, required little outward change. Though his devoted disciple and biographer, George Sikes, suggests that Vane immediately separated from his 'former Jolly Company' (Sikes, 8), contemporary friends were getting witty letters, without any mention of godliness, three years after his conversion. During this period Vane had completed his education in the conventional manner with a few months at Magdalen Hall, Oxford, where he neither matriculated nor, according to a near contemporary, lived with 'great exactness', then a foreign tour including Paris and the protestant intellectual centres of Geneva, Leiden, and possibly Saumur (Clarendon, Hist. rebellion, 3.34).

In 1631 Sir Henry Vane secured his son's appointment as aide to Sir Robert Anstruther, ambassador at the court of Emperor Ferdinand II. Six months in Vienna gave the younger Vane a valuable training in diplomacy; his reports, accurately forecasting the failure of the negotiations to restore the elector palatine's lands, display a keen understanding of European power politics. Upon his return family friends observed a 'great improvement' in the eighteen-year-old—'his French [is] good, his discourse discreet, his fashion comely and fair' (CSP dom., 1631–3, 294). Charles I granted him a 'gracious and attentive' audience, commended his recent conduct, and raised hopes of

Sir Henry Vane the younger (1613–1662), by Sir Peter Lely, c.1650

a place in the privy chamber (*CSP dom.*, *1631–3*, 266). But his father's critics, resenting his premature advancement, greeted him less cordially, and his initial disappointment probably owed much to their hostility. Had Vane himself objected to the position he would surely have informed his parents of his scruples, just as he had previously announced his aversion to a military career. That no alternative preferment subsequently came his way was almost certainly due to his growing dissatisfaction with the ceremonies of the Church of England, to which Archbishop Laud was enforcing uniformity more rigorously than ever, especially at that microcosm of hierarchical order, the Caroline court. The exact stages of Vane's progress from apparent conformity to adamant dissent remain obscure. Not so the denouement. In 1635, after two years resisting parental and episcopal pressure to receive the sacrament kneeling, Vane resolved upon emigration to New England. Rumour ascribed this startling development to the 'Persuasions' of Sir Nathaniel Rich and John Pym, prominent colonial investors opposed to Laudianism. The elder Vane, who had consented only when the king restricted his heir's absence to three years, suspected 'conventicles and plots'. Though he consulted godly friends, including Pym and the Connecticut patentees, from whom he accepted a commission, the decision to suffer the 'losses of all other things' for the sake of 'sweet peace' with God was Vane's alone. Grieved by his father's reproachful distrust he vehemently affirmed his determination to do nothing unsanctioned by both 'honour and a good conscience' (*CSP dom.*, *1635*, 261). Godliness and gentility were thus, for Vane, entirely compatible.

New England, 1635–1637 Vane reached Massachusetts on 6 October 1635. Despite Vane's long hair and fashionable dress, which affronted some of the stricter emigrants, the colony's leaders warmly welcomed the 'young gentleman of excellent parts' who had renounced the court for the 'obedience of the gospel'. Instead of proceeding to Connecticut, Vane settled in Boston, where he revelled in freedom 'to enjoy the ordinances of Christ in their purity', and fellowship with the spiritual élite, who heard his conversion narrative and admitted him into church membership on 1 November (Winthrop, 1.162). Directing his diplomatic skills to the goal of godly reconciliation rapidly brought Vane official recognition. Later that autumn the town meeting forbade residents to sue each other until he and two elders had first attempted to resolve the dispute. Vane's deep concern for Christian unity also inspired him to volunteer his services at a higher level. Learning of recent conflicts between former governors John Winthrop and Thomas Dudley he convened a meeting of magistrates and ministers at which he appealed for frankness and 'a more firm and friendly uniting of minds'. The result was a superficial affirmation of harmony, and a set of articles enjoining 'more strictness in civil government and military discipline' (Winthrop, 1.170). Little as his elders may have relished his intervention Vane's prestige continued to grow. On 3 March 1636 he became a freeman of the Massachusetts corporation, and a commissioner for military affairs. The 25th of May saw his elevation to the highest office. Though the election of an inexperienced youth less than eight months after his arrival has, with hindsight, attracted much criticism, it made perfect sense to contemporaries. At twenty-three Vane had already shown himself a 'wise and godly gentleman', committed to New England's welfare (Winthrop, 1.201). As a privy councillor's son he might ease the strained relations between the Congregationalist colony and Whitehall; in handling local business he would have expert advisers—deputy governor John Winthrop and the council.

Vane's term as governor began well. Saluted by the English ships in harbour—an unprecedented honour—he turned the captains' respect for his high connections to the colony's advantage. His first achievement was an agreement regulating entry procedures and reducing the risk of disorderly conduct by crewmen ashore; his second a tactful compromise between the colonists who failed to fly the king's colours for fear of idolatry—displaying the popish cross of St George—and the sailors who consequently suspected them of disloyalty. Notwithstanding these small successes Vane warned his father that the situation was 'very tumultuous', because of the uncertainty surrounding the charter and the threat from Native Americans aided by the French (*CSP col.*, 1.239). Though his diplomacy failed to prevent the onset of hostilities with the Pequot tribe, it did secure peace with the Narragansetts and the purchase of Rhode Island as a refuge for separatist settlers. Foremost among these was Roger Williams, who had helped Vane in the negotiations and became his close friend.

That Vane's governorship ended disastrously was due not to mismanagement of external dangers but, ironically, to unforeseen results of the very godliness that had made him an attractive candidate. Vane perceived 'God's ends' for Massachusetts as 'not trade ... but the profession of ... truth', and this priority proved his undoing when religious controversy erupted that autumn (Willcock, 34). Instead of remaining aloof for unity's sake the governor plunged into the fray, using his position to champion the so-called Antinomian party, comprising Anne Hutchinson, John Wheelwright, and a majority of the Boston church. Ranged against them were Winthrop and most ministers and members of the outlying churches. When his arguments failed to convince this formidable opposition Vane despaired. In December he offered his resignation, alleging urgent private business in England. Questioned, he tearfully denied valuing his property above the public interest, and disclosed his real reason: desire to escape 'the inevitable danger ... of God's judgments ... for these differences ... and the scandalous imputations brought upon himself, as if he should be the cause of all' (Winthrop, 1.202–3). Though he retracted these passionate words the self-centred attempt to desert his post did nothing for Vane's prestige. Only the protests of the Boston church against their leader's premature departure persuaded him to stay and continue the unequal struggle. In May's election Winthrop triumphed. Vane, reduced to a humble delegate for Boston, ostentatiously shunned his late deputy's society and denounced his policies in writing. Thus Winthrop's defence of a new decree excluding settlers with 'dangerous opinions' evoked a vigorous refutation from Vane, who reasoned that the magistrates' assumption of this power contravened the laws of both Christ and the king. To no avail. Vane quit Massachusetts on 3 August 1637, before he could suffer the banishment that soon befell his faction.

Vane's turbulent transatlantic sojourn had significant consequences. Besides an enduring solicitude for the colonists, which moved him to assist both Rhode Island and Massachusetts so effectively that even Winthrop pronounced him a 'true friend to New England' (Winthrop, 2.256), the young man learned spiritual and political lessons which strongly influenced his subsequent career. For the first—and last—time in his life he had formally professed himself the 'obedient child' of a congenial church, where he absorbed such controversial doctrines as 'assurance by immediate revelation' from the Holy Spirit and the universal antithesis between the few recipients of this grace and their undiscerning opponents, the many Christians still under the first covenant of works (Winthrop, 1.203, 206). Henceforth Vane trusted neither episcopacy nor the 'most refined' ecclesiastical forms and their clerical administrators to protect the godly. Instead, he turned to politics. The *Brief Answer* to Winthrop adduced biblical arguments that 'a Christian commonwealth' must not make laws giving 'that without limitation to man, which is proper to God', and this contrast between divine and human judgment would distinguish all his later writings against persecution (Hutchinson, 95). Openly avowing sublime truths while he was governor proved counterproductive, however. It was surely the humiliating experience of leading a despised and isolated faction to defeat that taught Vane the danger of frankness, and the practical necessity of proceeding via alliances with the less enlightened, while concealing his own emotions and 'utmost aims' (Sikes, 8–9). The resultant imperturbability impressed both admirers, who saw in it the renunciation of 'all unbecoming passions', and adversaries, who condemned it as 'rare dissimulation' (Rowe, *Sir Henry Vane ... a Study*, 278; Clarendon, *Hist. rebellion*, 7.266).

Rise to eminence, 1637–1643 From the maelstrom of Massachusetts politics Vane retreated to the comparative calm of the family estates in England. Such was his discretion that contemporary commentators could not tell whether he retained the 'misgrounded Opinions' responsible for his emigration; Edward Hyde recalled that he seemed 'much reformed in those extravagances' (Knowles, 2.116; Clarendon, *Hist. rebellion*, 3.34). Sir Henry Vane began to promote his son's rehabilitation at court, an object for which the puritan magnate Algernon Percy, earl of Northumberland and lord high admiral, also exerted himself. After initial setbacks their applications succeeded in January 1639, when the king made Vane joint treasurer of the navy with Sir William Russell. This office, worth £800 p.a., was no sinecure: that year's work included preparing ship-money accounts and complex cost estimates for the Scottish war. Vane discharged these duties diligently, pleasing Northumberland, who in December directed the port of Hull to elect him as one of their burgesses in the forthcoming parliament. That corporation jibbed at the peremptory recommendation of an 'unknown' gentleman, but yielded when his father's influence relieved it of a lawsuit long pending in the exchequer (Rowe, 'Sir Henry Vane ... as MP', 22). Preoccupied with admiralty business and marriage negotiations Vane played little part in the Short Parliament of April–May 1640. On 23 June the king knighted him. Eight days later Henry married sixteen-year-old Frances (1623/4–1679), daughter of Sir Christopher Wray of Ashby, Lincolnshire. The couple enjoyed an annual income of £1400 largely derived from the navy and the properties in Kent and Durham which his father now settled on him.

The first year of the Long Parliament, where he again represented Hull, transformed Sir Henry Vane the younger from a prosperous official who appeared 'well satisfied and composed to the government' into one of the 'chief Opposers of the Court Party' (Clarendon, *Hist. rebellion*, 3.34; Rowe, *Sir Henry Vane ... a Study*, 277). In fact, Vane's apparent contentment had never amounted to more than superficial acquiescence. Months before parliament met he had secretly searched his father's papers for material incriminating the authoritarian earl of Strafford, enemy to both his family and the godly network in which Vane increasingly, albeit unobtrusively, participated. Vane's new relatives, the Wrays, were principled opponents of ship money and Laudianism; his old friend Pym, to whom he confided the 'proof' of Strafford's treason, brought him into close contact with John Hampden, Oliver St John, and other orchestrators of the campaign against popery and arbitrary government. From January 1641 Vane began to serve on major committees and speak to naval questions. Strafford's trial, in April, brought his first blaze of notoriety. To justify betraying his father's trust Vane pleaded the higher patriotic duty enjoined by 'conscience', and so persuaded many MPs of his 'integrity and merit'. Others were sceptical, however, and the incident engendered his reputation as a 'most false person' (Clarendon, *Hist. rebellion*, 3.135, 137; Wood, *Ath. Oxon.*, 3.579). To these aspersions the summer added religious radicalism, as Vane, with Oliver Cromwell and Sir Arthur Hesilrige, drafted and ardently defended the 'root and branch' bill against episcopacy. A published speech vividly conveys not just the 'rottenness' of an antichristian system assailing both 'Civil freedome' and 'the very life and power of Godlinesse', but the wonder—and urgency—of this providential opportunity to eradicate 'the mystery of iniquity' and achieve a 'perfect reformation' making 'all things ... new' (Vane, *Speech ... Against Episcopall-Government*, 5, 8, 7, 5, 2, 3). Yet Vane's apocalyptic vision was firmly anchored in reality: he proposed gradual change, from bishops to diocesan commissions drawn equally from clergy and laity. That autumn he pressed for the bishops' exclusion from the House of Lords, and co-authored the ecclesiastical sections of the grand remonstrance. By December, when the king dismissed both Vanes from their offices, the younger was so 'much esteemed in the Commons' that it sought his reinstatement (*CSP dom.*, 1641–3, 211).

As England drifted into civil war Vane's star continued to rise. Following the abortive attempt on the five members in January 1642 he devised the apt declaration affirming the Commons' commitment to legal process, and was prominent during the adjournment to the Guildhall. Clarendon, who best knew Vane personally from 1640 to 1642, remembered his 'great natural parts ... quick conception ... very ready, sharp and weighty expression'; Edmund Ludlow cherished similar memories of his 'quick apprehension ... strong memory ... piercing judgment ... great foresight ... free and gracefull utterance' (Clarendon, *Hist. rebellion*, 3.34; Ludlow, *Voyce*, 314). These talents, suitably directed, proved exceedingly useful to Pym. Vane's fervent devotion to parliament's cause—which he conceived eschatologically, as 'the CAUSE of GOD ... for the Promoting of the Kingdom of his dear Son'—made him a powerful advocate of practical measures to protect 'Liberties and Religion' from 'oppression and violence' (*Tryal*, 90; *Three Speeches*, 5, 7). In July he headed a committee sent to vindicate the militia ordinance at the Kent assizes; November found him explaining parliament's position and successfully soliciting co-operation from its principal ally, the City—the first of many such missions. Though remaining at Westminster while Hampden, Cromwell, Hesilrige, and other colleagues took the field occasioned erroneous speculation that he was 'timorous', Vane excelled in administrative roles, serving on Pym's executive committee of safety, and, from August 1642, as sole treasurer of the navy, appointed by ordinance.

By 1643 Vane was an influential member of the emerging 'war party' in parliament. Sharply critical of the defensive strategy and peace initiatives favoured by some lawyers and such peers as Lord-General Essex, he counselled prosecuting the conflict aggressively by obtaining Scottish military aid. Pym concurred. That summer Vane led the parliamentary commission that negotiated the solemn league and covenant—perhaps his finest, undoubtedly his most controversial, diplomatic coup. Clarendon, whose royal master lost most thereby, depicted the Scots as deserving victims of Vane's remarkable 'ability ... to cozen and deceive'; Archibald Johnston bitterly complained that Vane had subtly substituted a flexible 'politick engyn' for the precise, permanent union that the covenanters, in 'simplicity of heart', had envisaged (Clarendon, *Hist. rebellion*, 7.267; *Diary of Sir Archibald Johnston*, 3.171). Contemporary evidence, however, does not support allegations of deliberate deceit. Tact he certainly used, concealing his separatist sympathies, and capitalizing on the covenanters' readiness to esteem him a 'very gracious youth', a fellow foe of episcopacy, now become 'one of the gravest and ablest' Englishmen (*Letters and Journals of Robert Baillie*, 1.306, 2.89). But Vane made no secret of parliament's preference for a purely 'civil League', and even after acceding to a 'religious Covenant', endeavoured to 'keepe a door open in England to Independencie'—that is, avoid an infeasible commitment to divine-right presbyterianism (ibid., 2.90). This he accomplished by qualifying the church reform clause with the unexceptionable phrase 'according to the Word of God'. That the Scots did not foresee that this authority might sanction alternative forms, and so 'cast all loose', was not his fault (*Diary of Sir Archibald Johnston*, 3.171). Vane himself took the covenant seriously, as befitted one of the few oaths he ever swore. For him, though, its obligations were not, primarily, to Scotland or the Stuart monarchy, but to the 'Cause of God', whose 'Supream Rule' the British nations explicitly accepted by adopting it. Looking back, he affirmed his loyalty to these 'righteous and holy ends', rather than the 'form and words' (*Tryal*, 61). Blind adherence to the 'old government' (*Diary of Thomas Burton*, 3.177–8) enshrined in the latter, amid changed circumstances, was no better than idolatry; the real covenant breakers were the literalists who abandoned the 'true sense' for 'other ends' (*Tryal*, 61).

Uses of power, 1643–1648 The covenant signalled Sir Henry Vane's arrival at the heart of British public life, where he remained through almost a decade of war, revolution, and unsettlement. Excepting a few short, but significant, episodes of withdrawal, these were years of intensive labour in multifarious capacities. Admiralty records, committee and council minutes, together with the Commons' *Journal* confirm contemporary testimony to his 'unwearied Industry', and, at critical moments, 'constant attendance' leaving 'scarce any leisure to eat ..., converse with his nearest Relations, or ... mind his Family affairs' (*Reliquiae Baxterianae*, 75; Nickolls, 78; Sikes, 105). Yet neither diligence nor even brilliance could give Vane complete control of the collective entity that was the Long Parliament. His power always depended on the responses of others. Though his oratory could be extremely persuasive—Algernon Sidney recalled that 'he often used to bring over the Parliament to his Single Opinion, when their own sentiments … till his were heard, had a different tendency'—it was not invariably decisive (Rowe, *Sir Henry Vane … a Study*, 278–9). Vane suffered significant defeats; overall, his influence fluctuated considerably. To evaluate this phase of his career it is necessary to examine both his constant interests and the particular course he steered through the turbulent political waters.

By 1644 Vane, the chief surviving architect of the Scottish alliance since Pym's death the previous December, had become a major leader in his own right. It was to him that the king, hoping to exploit parliament's divisions, addressed peace feelers promising liberty of conscience in January. Ably assisted by St John, who now led the middle group, Vane thwarted an attempt by Essex to arraign him for his part in these negotiations, and obtained the Commons' thanks for his role in exposing the latest City plot. The ensuing months saw Vane's mastery of parliamentary procedure facilitate a further setback for the peace party—the establishment of a new executive, the committee of both kingdoms. This body, consisting of peers, MPs, and Scottish representatives, enjoyed greater powers to manage the war than its predecessor. Vane frequently acted as its spokesman in the Commons; in June he personally conveyed its instructions to Manchester, Fairfax, and the Scots besieging York. Rumours that this mission camouflaged unsuccessful canvassing among these commanders for the king's deposition lack foundation. Extant correspondence gives no hint of friction. Vane's letters emphasize practical problems, urging the distant committee to accept expert analysis of the military situation; gratified by such deference to their opinion, the generals praised Vane's 'fidelity and ability' (*CSP dom.*, 1644, 288).

Cordial relations with Manchester and the Scots were short-lived. Committed as ever to winning the war Vane altered tactics that autumn when it became clear that Scottish intervention had not delivered the decisive victory anticipated. Once the covenanters' 'most intime friend', Vane now offended them by challenging clerical authority, questioning the reported size of their army—which parliament paid—and, with Cromwell, openly advocating 'liberty for sects' (*Letters and Journals of Robert Baillie*, 2.231, 235–6). The Scots responded by moving towards the peace party, which showed increasing sympathy for presbyterianism, albeit the Erastian variety; their former allies, the war party and middle group, they labelled 'independents' after their congregationalist opponents in the Westminster assembly. From reliance on Scottish arms this faction turned to restructuring the English forces, removing inept or superfluous officers, and rekindling parliamentarian morale. Central to their programme was the self-denying ordinance, which Vane seconded on 9 December. By debarring MPs from all civil or military offices self-denial not only displaced Manchester, Essex, and other proponents of peace, but countered damaging suspicions that personal gain motivated the war's supporters, while appealing strongly to the godly. A last-minute exemption for those officials reappointed by

parliament after the king discharged them enabled Vane to remain naval treasurer. Sidney credited him with counselling the creation of the New Model Army from several formerly divided regional commands. Vane certainly endorsed this reorganization warmly; on 21 January 1645 he joined Cromwell as teller for the motion constituting Sir Thomas Fairfax the new lord-general. As a parliamentary commissioner at Uxbridge in February he observed the Scots' failure to convert the king to presbyterianism; when the talks collapsed the Commons again sent him to secure the City's help in financing the coming campaign. This crowned the winter's reforms with the long-awaited military success: the New Model's annihilation of the royalist field army at Naseby, for which Vane moved the thanksgiving. Not just this victory, but parliament's ultimate triumph in the civil war owed much to his efforts. Well might certain colonels soon to enter the house remember him as 'the cheife steeresman of publique affaires during the late warres', who contributed 'not less … to the Obtaining of Victories than the Valour of the Generals' (Ludlow, *Voyce*, 310; Rowe, *Sir Henry Vane … a Study*, 279).

Victory, ironically, diminished Vane's influence. From 1645–6 he and St John gradually lost control of the central executive committees, then the house itself, to a resurgent peace party, political presbyterians led by Holles and Stapleton. What separated the independent minority in parliament from Holles was less religion *per se*—Hesilrige embraced presbyterianism, while Vane and Cromwell opposed any rigid discipline stifling tender consciences—than distrust of the king, and dislike of disbandment of the army. After repeatedly losing divisions Vane withdrew: in December 1646 he obtained permission to sell his office, and during the presbyterian ascendancy of the next six months seldom attended the Commons or committees. Thus, though he remained intimate with Cromwell, another absentee, he played no direct part in the developing conflict between parliament and the New Model until June 1647, when he was commissioned to negotiate. Despite sympathy for the army's demands he initially deprecated its march on London, but changed his mind on perceiving that the greater danger to parliament was the presbyterian mob, which had 'threatned to … cutt [him] in pieces' (Firth, 1.136). On 30 July the speakers, several peers, and fifty-eight MPs, including Vane, requested Fairfax's protection. Once military occupation of the capital had restored power to the independents Vane resumed regular attendance. He continued to mediate between parliament and army, seeking resolution of the soldiers' grievances, sponsoring the officers' suggested settlement, *The Heads of Proposals*, in the house, and assisting to defeat an extremist motion against further approaches to the king. This moderation, together with his closeness to Cromwell, inspired distrustful London radicals to publish fresh attacks on his integrity. In September the Leveller leader, John Lilburne, who had earlier denounced Vane and St John as 'unworthy covetous earthworms', accused Cromwell and Vane of designing 'to keep the poor people everlastingly … in bondage' (Lilburne, 5;

Rowe, *Sir Henry Vane … a Study*, 97). Self-advancement at the people's expense was definitely not Vane's conscious goal—he afterwards denied pursuing 'private gainful ends', while a contemporary witness, the chairman of the navy committee, no independent, confirms that he discharged his duties as treasurer with 'much clearnesse and freedome from any corruption' (*Tryal*, 46–7; Rowe, *Sir Henry Vane … a Study*, 134). Yet Lilburne's suspicions accurately reflect the ideological gulf dividing the populist, undeferential Levellers from such socially conservative 'silken Independents' as Vane.

Vane's conservatism became still more apparent in 1648. Despite the king's engagement with the Scots, which exasperated the officers and many MPs, Vane disapproved of the vote of no addresses to the king, passed in his absence. In April, he joined presbyterians and moderate independents in revamping the 1646 declaration against altering the fundamental government by king, Lords, and Commons. Though the army's departure from London to fight the second civil war facilitated a presbyterian revival in parliament Vane remained an active administrator, concentrating on problems arising from the naval mutiny. The emergency over, parliament appointed him one of fifteen commissioners—nine presbyterians and six independents—to treat with the king at Newport. Far from discouraging concessions, or delaying matters for the army's benefit, as his detractors later alleged, Vane sincerely, though unavailingly, strove to bring the king to an agreement resembling *The Heads of Proposals*. Vane's comparative disregard for 'outward dispensations'—recent victories evidencing divine displeasure with the king—troubled Cromwell, who no longer saw a need for even 'moderate episcopacy' (*Letters and Speeches*, 1.358; Firth, 2.51); he affectionately warned his 'dear brother' against 'medling with the accursed thing', and advised an 'honourable retreat' (*Letters and Speeches*, 1.358; Firth, 2.50, 51). The mounting dissatisfaction of the army and its radical allies dismayed Vane as much as his fellow commissioners, yet he, unlike them, did not panic, but rather tried to dissuade the Commons from pronouncing the king's answers sufficient to continue the treaty. His inability to carry the crucial vote of 5 December on this question prompted Colonel Pride's famous purge of the presbyterian majority. To this assault on parliamentary privilege Vane's immediate reaction, shared by many former 'royal Independents', was voluntary retirement, avoiding involvement in the king's trial or its prerequisite, the truncated Commons' unilateral assumption of both legislative and executive power. He could therefore truthfully assert that he was 'never a first mover but always a follower', who bore no responsibility for the revolution (*Tryal*, 44).

Uses of power, 1649–1653 Confronted with the accomplished fact, however, Vane rapidly progressed from passive consternation to energetic support of the nascent Commonwealth. Six weeks after the purge he accepted Cromwell's arguments for resuming his seat; on 14 February 1649 he was elected to the new executive, the council

of state. Although his scruples contributed to the substitution of a simple engagement of loyalty for the contentious abjuration of kingship that the regicides expected of councillors, Vane's early hesitation issued in convinced republicanism rather than conformist loyalism. Thus his initial scepticism concerning claims that revolution had 'restored' freedom became faith in the people's pre-existent 'natural right' to self-government (*Brief Lives*, 194; Vane, *Healing Question*, 2). To justify jettisoning the former constitution Vane not only echoed Cromwell's invocation of providence and the 'necessity' created by the king's obduracy and the Lords' dissent but championed the Commons' prerogative to safeguard the 'Liberty … of the whole' as they saw fit (*Diary of Thomas Burton*, 3.173; *Tryal*, 108). The 'little remnant of the Parliament' he regarded as no mere expedient, still less the army's puppet, but an authentic 'representative of the nation' (*Diary of Thomas Burton*, 3.176). Satisfaction with its legitimacy did not blind Vane to parliament's deficiencies. By the summer of 1651 the members' 'continuall contestation and brabling' despite divine deliverances had exhausted his former confidence in their 'good aymes'; he correctly anticipated still 'greater tryalls and difficultys' in seeking a righteous settlement (Nickolls, 78, 19, 79). To achieve that end Vane, unlike Hesilrige, would not consider the Long Parliament indispensable. Yet he consistently opposed reviving monarchy or otherwise repudiating 1649—the moment when 'as a seale set to … their Authority' parliament 'caused justice to be done upon the late King' so vindicating the cause and laying the foundations of freedom and prosperity (*Proceeds of the Protector*, 7; *Diary of Thomas Burton*, 3.173).

That the insecure and isolated English Commonwealth of 1649 survived to unify Britain and win international renown owed much to Vane's work. Besides organizing vital supplies and reinforcements for Cromwell's victorious campaigns in Ireland and Scotland, Vane managed the fleet that destroyed the royalists' squadron, reduced their last territories, defeated the Dutch, and intimidated England's other neighbours. His competence impressed contemporaries. Roger Williams in 1652 thought 'the navy … mostly depending on [Vane's] care'; Hesilrige attested parliament's reliance on his 'providence', while Sidney considered Vane 'an absolute Master' of such matters, and attributed the invention of the frigate to his genius—an overstatement reflecting his instigation of a major shipbuilding programme including over thirty new frigates (*Letters of Roger Williams*, 253–4; *Diary of Thomas Burton*, 3.442; Rowe, *Sir Henry Vane … a Study*, 279). Vane also advocated incentives for sailors and improvements in naval administration and finance. Among the latter was his request, in June 1650, to resign the treasurership, recommending that his successor receive a salary instead of a percentage; though Vane received compensatory lands, substantial savings resulted. The Commonwealth further profited from Vane's diplomatic skills. John Milton, who overheard many discussions, applauded his ability to 'unfold the drift of hollow states'. Vane himself asserted that his policy aimed at exploiting foreign rivalries 'for the interest of England' (Nickolls, 41). From at least the early 1640s he had favoured closer ties with the protestant Dutch republic: in 1651 he strongly supported St John and Strickland's mission to propose union, and tried to prevent war despite their failure. Vane had more success in promoting a union conferring English liberties upon, rather than simply annexing, conquered Scotland, where he spent the winter of 1651–2 as a parliamentary commissioner. On 16 March 1652 he reported the Scots' nominal assent; thereafter, he actively participated in the committee preparing the incorporation bill. Vane also pursued long-standing interests in the colonies, especially New England. As a member of parliament's committee for plantations Vane had helped to procure Rhode Island's charter in 1644; the spring of 1653 saw him assist Williams to secure its confirmation.

More precious than colonial welfare to both Vane and Williams was the defence of religious liberty from any coercive national church. In this enterprise they had collaborated since 1644, when Vane delighted Williams with a 'heavenly speech' against suppressing 'any … if sober, though never so different' (Williams, *Bloudy Tenent*, preface), and horrified the Scots by not only supporting parliament's 'accommodation order' for reconciliation or protection of 'tender consciences' but deploring its non-extension from ecclesiological to doctrinal differences (*Baillie*, 2.235, 236). Though powerless to prevent the draconian blasphemy legislation of 1648 and 1650 Vane interceded for individuals, including anti-Trinitarian writers John Biddle and John Fry; twice he exhorted Massachusetts to toleration. By 1652 congregationalism had replaced presbyterianism as the main threat in old as well as New England. In February the Independent divines presented parliament with *The Humble Proposals*, which alarmed separatists by advising severe restrictions on their freedom to preach, worship, and publish. The Baptists petitioned; Williams protested in a series of tracts; Milton implored Cromwell to 'save free conscience'. Vane's response was the anonymous publication, in June, of *Zeal Examined, or, A Discourse for Liberty of Conscience*, his first major work, mostly written in 1651. This text, contending that even idolaters should not be punished for their religion, expounds Vane's concept of complete freedom from magisterial constraint in spiritual matters. Its well-organized, intensely biblical argument denounces the tendency of the 'Principle of Antichrist'—persecution—to resurface in 'every new Form', so deceiving believers (Vane, *Zeal*, preface). Vane dismisses Old Testament teaching on the magistrate's religious responsibilities as applicable only to national Israel, and movingly appeals instead to New Testament principles of patient love towards less enlightened consciences, whether Christian or not. The 'Interest of Protestants', who deny any infallible human arbiter, is, he insists, to encourage unlimited study and debate, not attempt enforcement of a hypocritical conformity (Vane, *Zeal*, 4). *Zeal Examined* may well have inspired Milton's poetic tribute to Vane's perfect comprehension of 'spiritual power and civil'; it certainly helped to redirect the controversy (Polizzotto, 578–

9). Parliament's committee eventually recommended the *Humble Proposals* without their most contested elements.

The contrast between Milton's sonnets to Vane and Cromwell—unqualified admiration versus apprehensive entreaty—mirrors the growing distance between these statesmen by 1652. Both were antiformalists who abhorred oppression of godly consciences, yet whereas Cromwell equally detested impious abuses of liberty Vane thought that even the Ranters' 'grosse mistakes' might be perversions of 'true and high discoveries' (Vane, *Zeal*, 33, 34). Cromwell favoured a moderate established church with able ordained preachers, whom he heard respectfully; Vane confessed himself a 'backe friend' to the clergy, whose authority he utterly rejected (Nickolls, 84). Nor were their differences confined to religious policy. In January 1650 Vane had reported, from parliament's first committee considering its successor, a plan to reapportion constituencies but recruit new members only for those vacant. This compromise between the need to make parliament more representative and the danger that an unreconciled electorate would return candidates hostile to the republic seemed self-interested to Cromwell and the army, who urged a dissolution. Vane's identification with the recruiter scheme probably explains his exclusion from both the September 1652 committee to prepare the bill for an entirely new representative body, and the winter's informal conferences with the increasingly impatient officers. Vane did, however, attend the final meeting, on 19 April 1653, and was the 'very chiefest' of the MPs who consented to attempt the bill's deferral pending further discussion of Cromwell's proposal that parliament entrust power to a smaller body until elections became safe (Woolrych, 64). When Cromwell forcibly emptied the house next day he especially blamed Vane, alleging 'that he might have prevented this extraordinary course, but he was a Juggler' without 'common honesty' (Blencowe, 141). These bitter reproaches reveal less about Vane's actual responsibility for the disaster than Cromwell's disappointment, perhaps exacerbated by overconfidence in his friend's ability to sway parliament. That Hesilrige, Vane's victorious adversary in several encounters, and now the bill's main sponsor, instigated the fatal move to rush it through that morning over protests from the army's allies is much more likely than deliberate double-crossing by Vane, who may have genuinely supported Cromwell's interim solution—he would suggest a similar expedient in October 1659. The involuntary dissolution strained their long friendship to breaking point: repelled by its illegal violence Vane retired from government.

Retirement, 1653–1656 Retreat was Sir Henry Vane's habitual reaction to disagreeable political developments. What distinguished this instance was its length—three years—and its ending in active opposition rather than renewed power. The durability of his dissatisfaction surprised enemies and friends alike. In June 1653 a royalist newswriter reported that Vane had declined the chance of nomination to the new assembly, but expected his surrender upon a 'little entreaty'; Williams observed that he was still 'daily missed and courted' the following summer

(Thurloe, *State papers*, 1.265; *Letters of Roger Williams*, 260). Cromwell would doubtless have welcomed Vane's assistance as warmly as he did that of other able former MPs. That Vane remained aloof, neither endorsing nor denouncing the army's successive expedients, was not because of personal animosity against Cromwell, towards whom he professed himself 'still the same as ever ... in true friendship' as late as 1655 (Thurloe, *State papers*, 4.329). Rather, his conduct was directed by the 'passive principles'— 'seeking God and waiting only upon him'—which Cromwell had criticized in 1648 (*Proceeds of the Protector*, 6; Cust, 217). Thus Vane greeted England's reversion to a semi-monarchical regime—the protectorate—by concluding that God was 'weaning his every day more and more from all worldly concerns, as well in Government as other things, and making them look for Protection only in and by himself' (Cust, 219). Godly detachment did not, however, imply indifference. Vane's letters to his friend and neighbour Richard Cust, nominee for Lincolnshire, in the winter of 1653–4 display a keen, if pessimistic, assessment of the situation. Whereas many radicals expected the nominated assembly to enact major reforms, even herald the millennium, Vane feared complacency and anticipated imminent proof 'whether our faces be set Sionward, filled with the expectation of Christ's heavenly appearance, or whether we be going back to the City spiritually called Sodom'. The Fifth Monarchists' sanguine predictions that Christ's kingdom would 'settle them in ... worldly glory, light and power' he deemed erroneous, citing scriptural prophecies that its advent would be 'very terrible and dark', bringing judgments on the 'Hypocrites in Zion' (Cust, 218). Vane's doubts concerning the political 'Hopes yet visible' by mid-December were such that he dared not do any the least service, but set instead an example of entire prostration before providence (Cust, 219).

Resignation enabled Vane to enjoy the domestic life for which he had sometimes hankered amid the pressures of public business. His marriage had proved extremely successful. Frances not only bore him fifteen children, but provided practical, emotional, and spiritual support. Roger Williams celebrated Lady Vane's piety in a pamphlet dedication; Ludlow thought her 'very godly and virtuous ... very desirable in all respects' (Ludlow, *Voyce*, 315). To please her Vane had, in 1650, purchased Lincolnshire property centred on Belleau, which was their principal residence until his father's death in 1655, after which they spent more time at Raby Castle, co. Durham. Of their progeny, three sons and seven daughters survived infancy. Although Vane entrusted the general 'care of his domestic affairs intirely' to his wife's competent management, he assumed personal responsibility for the family's edification (Rowe, *Sir Henry Vane ... a Study*, 279). Each evening his household and any others 'Providentially there' heard him pray and expound scripture. Where Vane differed from most godly householders was in preferring 'this Family-way of Religion' to virtually every form of public worship. No sabbatarian he nevertheless allotted more

time to Sunday's religious exercises; his habit of preaching at home on this day appalled strict presbyterians (Sikes, 50, 156–7, 49). Vane's extant sermons, preserved by his daughter Margaret, are perfectly intelligible, first interpreting, then applying the chosen texts. Among the listeners who derived 'great Comfort' was John Rogers, himself a minister. Besides appreciating that Vane spoke 'clearly, soundly and discriminatively', Rogers esteemed his 'godly *Family* ... a *Church*, a *Court* and an *University* of the highest, best and most *Liberal Sciences*' (Rogers, 21, 22, 21). The most important student was Henry, the eldest son, who received a secluded education quite unlike his father's. Instead of sending him to school or college Vane engaged a reliable tutor—his talented disciple Henry Stubbe—and subsequently vetoed a continental tour for fear that the 'corrupt opinions ... of forraign Popish Countries' might infect his heir; when Henry eventually joined a diplomatic mission the destination was protestant Scandinavia (*Vindication*, 7).

Retirement was, supremely, a time of reflection, in which Vane discerned both the 'opportunity' and 'duty' (Vane, *Meditations*, preface) to promulgate his 'Witness ... to this Age' (ibid., title-page). The result, completed by April 1655, was *The Retired Mans Meditations*, his longest and most complex work, uniquely published under his name in his lifetime. Conceived as a 'leisurely survey', diffuse, repetitive, and saturated in biblical metaphor, this book is far less accessible than those which present a specific argument. Its allegorical approach to scripture baffled many, especially those trained in scholastic methodology. Richard Baxter judged Vane's doctrines 'so clowdily formed that few could understand them', Gilbert Burnet complained that he omitted the 'necessary key', while Martin Finch produced his detailed *Animadversions* upon Vane's deviations from conventional exegesis and Calvinist orthodoxy (*Reliquiae Baxterianae*, 75; *Burnet's History*, 1.279). Such attempts to discredit his teaching are offset by the enthusiasm of others: Henry Stubbe hailed the *Meditations* as 'the most glorious Truths ... witnessed unto these 1500 years' (Stubbe, 8), while George Sikes insisted that they gave 'the fairest aim to England, truly to understand its case', and ascribed clerical critics' incomprehension to unregeneracy (Sikes, 130). Vane himself acknowledged that the 'more Theoretical' early chapters might seem 'knotty and abstruse', and pleaded the 'insufficiency of expression' to convey sublime subjects—the nature of God and revelation; the condition of man; the conflict of good and evil (Vane, *Meditations*, preface). To dismiss these difficult sections as speculative rambling is to overlook their importance for both his own world-view and his reconciliatory enterprise. Vane hoped that his insights might resolve the controversies raging between Trinitarians and Socinians, Arminians and Calvinists, and so prove universally beneficial. Readers of all degrees of illumination he exhorted to renounce self-interest, and use the *Meditations*, together with the Bible, as a mirror wherein to examine themselves and determine the right course to follow. The preface encouraged perseverance by promising that later chapters were so much 'more practical' that even the 'lowest capacities' would find them 'very easie and familiar'.

The latter part of the *Meditations* does, indeed, address major practical questions, albeit obliquely. Vane's tripartite understanding of humanity may seem abstract, but actually explains the main tragedy of 1653—godly fragmentation—as well as that 1650s phenomenon, the rise of the Quakers. It also generates the radical conclusion that the saints should not demand power on an exclusive basis, but co-operate with upright natural men and those still under the first covenant in so far as these advance Christ's cause. No faction can single-handedly initiate the millennial kingdom. All saints must first attain perfection by enduring persecution from earthly governments dominated either by openly ungodly men or the apostate visible church. Thus Vane countered the Fifth Monarchists' call to precipitate action; he did not, however, embrace the opposite extreme of passively shunning government itself as intrinsically antichristian. A fascinating chapter contends that magistracy has a vital place in God's design, that it is rightly instituted by man's 'rational and voluntary' subjection to gain justice in external matters, and that it will share in the ultimate redemption of creation (Vane, *Meditations*, 385). No form, not even the Mosaic law, has any right to permanency. Rather, it is essential to move 'forward, and ... be still enquiring and learning out more of Christs mind'; upright rulers must always be prepared to yield to such 'higher discoveries' (ibid., 389, 391). Vane urged the use of 'all lawful and righteous means' to study and seek to implement Christ's impartial rule (ibid., 393). In England's case recent providences plainly indicated what to pursue—the 'cause and interest' of the 'good people ... in reference to both Civil' and 'Christian liberties'. God could not intend to abandon this work, but would grant instruction if 'applications [were] made in a way of righteousness' (ibid., 394). Godly and 'good men' might then by 'free debate and common consent' (ibid., 394, 395) attempt to create a government repudiating self-interest and matching God's 'original pattern' as closely as possible (ibid., 395). Failure to achieve a 'happy union' on this basis would, Vane warned, constitute hypocritical negligence, incurring judgment at Christ's coming. Though he did not name the protectorate its inconsistency with the ideal was clearly implied.

Opposition, 1656–1659 Embedded deep in the *Meditations*, Vane's political reflections made little impact. In 1656, however, they resurfaced with amplification in his best-selling pamphlet, *A Healing Question*. Vane left retirement that spring in hope of influencing a government in crisis, its confidence sapped by the setbacks of 1655. Change was imminent: the question was the direction—forward to a reformed republic, or back towards monarchy. In March Cromwell disclosed his perplexity in a fast-day declaration which deplored divisions and announced that he awaited 'a conviction' enabling him to 'find out his provocation', and recover God's 'blessed presence' (O. Cromwell, 'A declaration of his highness inviting the people of England and Wales to a day of solemn fasting and humiliation on March 28, 1656', 1656, unpaginated). Interpreting

this as the righteous application for guidance which he had desired Vane composed a constructive reply—the *Healing Question*, prescribing the divine cure for the nation's ills: representative government created by explicit agreement of a reunited 'good Party'. Of central importance was the contention that the latter constituted an easily recognizable 'Society by themselves', distinguished by constant commitment to the cause, expressed through prayer, active service, or financial aid, and common faith that it was approaching fulfilment in 1649 (Vane, *Healing Question*, 9, 2). This excluded all those disaffected by the revolution. Recent divisions stemmed from the reluctance of a powerful section—the army leadership—to admit the 'whole body of the good People' to exercise the 'right of natural soveraignty' that the providential conquest of their enemies had confirmed (ibid., 11, 13). Self-determination was essential to a 'durable and solid settlement'. It was also feasible, since 'well qualified' delegates were available (ibid., 16, 19). Vane proposed a constitutional convention, chosen by the entire party, followed by individual members' ratification of its resolutions as the unalterable law. Although this procedure might legitimize any form Vane advised that a supreme legislature, sitting at regular intervals, was the safest option, if restrained by certain 'fundamental ... conditions'—an Act of Oblivion, a separate, but subordinate, executive, and, of course, non-interference in religious matters. Restricting political participation to all the 'refined party' not only precluded a parliament representing ungodly monarchists, but promised the widest possible basis to the projected republic (ibid., 20, 18, 7). Thus Vane offered a more positive and realistic solution than most republican critics, whose recommendations ranged from hazardous free elections to restoring the reputedly corrupt and oligarchical remnant of the Long Parliament.

The *Healing Question* contrasted with other criticisms of the protectorate in manner as well as matter. Where these frequently indulged in vitriolic vilification of Cromwell and the army, Vane's approach was restrained, reasonable, and above all eirenical, exhorting every group within the honest party to humbly confess their 'mutual offence' in a 'spirit of self-denial and love' (Vane, *Healing Question*, 21, 22). Innovations since 1653 he ascribed to 'temptation' rather than 'malicious design', and downplayed their hurtful effects (ibid., 23). Vane insisted that the soldiers and their 'honest and wise general' should 'not be despaired of', but were, indeed, indispensable to the 'outward safety of the whole body' (ibid., 12, 1, 12). His reunionist rhetoric not only emphasized the perils and principles shared by all factions, but skilfully addressed the particular concerns of each. Fifth Monarchists, for example, were encouraged to espouse unity as the 'onely remedy' capable, under God, of 'bringing in Christ ... as the chiefe Ruler' (ibid., 21). Legalistic sticklers for the Long Parliament's exclusive authority were reminded that 'former Lawes' scarcely justified its past actions: true legitimacy derived from the 'Law of Successe' and the 'inward warrant of Justice and Righteousness' (ibid., 9). Cromwellians, however, were assured that they would gain much, and lose nothing rightfully theirs, by 'submitting themselves' under 'their own Supreme Judicature' (ibid., 11). Preparing for this end was even their duty, as 'faithful Guardians to the Commonwealth … in its nonage' (ibid., 13). Thus Vane's short-term expectations were moderate; unlike many opponents of the protectorate he did not demand an instant surrender of power or revolution. But this very moderation would make the government appear far more odious in rejecting his proposals than if he had condemned it straight away. The 'good party' could test the protector's professed loyalty to the cause by his response to the *Healing Question*'s plea for the restoration of their rights.

Cromwell's initial response to *A Healing Question* seemed positive. After circulating among his council between April and May the manuscript was licensed for publication in the 'ordinary way'—unlike the clandestine printing of overtly treasonable texts (*Proceeds of the Protector*, 4). Secretary John Thurloe, a hostile witness, admitted that it was at first 'applauded' (Thurloe, *State papers*, 5.122). But the triumph of conservative counsels in June, when Cromwell decided to call another parliament, rendered the *Healing Question* highly subversive, since it implicitly denied the protectorate's legitimacy, and presented a compelling alternative. Not all the 'good party' resisted its appeal. Vane himself remained active and confident, giving the government reason to fear him as a leader of a nationwide network engaged in a well co-ordinated campaign to promote dissident candidates who might transform the new parliament into just such a convention as he had suggested. Despite his defeat in the Lincolnshire elections Vane's charisma made him too dangerous to be left unchecked. In August the council denounced the *Healing Question* as a 'seditious book … tending to the disturbance of the present Government', and ordered Vane to give substantial security for his good conduct; refusal brought him imprisonment at Carisbrooke Castle on the Isle of Wight (*CSP dom.*, 1656–7, 101). Meanwhile, an officially sponsored refutation, insinuating that the pamphlet aimed to revive the purged parliament, had appeared. The alteration in his treatment convinced Vane of Cromwell's apostasy. Orders to isolate him notwithstanding, his bitter disillusionment reached the world in *The Proceeds of the Protector (So-called) and his Council Against Sir Henry Vane*. This taxed Cromwell with pride, backsliding, and betraying the cause by refusing subjection to his 'earthly Head', the 'good people' assembled in parliament, and coveting 'the Throne in spirituals as well as Temporals' (*Proceeds of the Protector*, 8). Beneath the godly veneer Vane detected a revival of the Stuarts' absolutist policies, and passionately implored his old friend to repent and be reconciled to the saints before ruin befell them all.

Although Oliver was unmoved Vane's eloquence converted others, including the articulate Fifth Monarchist, John Rogers, his fellow prisoner, who in 1659 acclaimed the *Healing Question* as a 'great *Means of Blessing* towards the *Recovering* … of this *poor* ISLAND' (Rogers, 41). A new edition produced in the same year (despite the '1660' date printed on it), advertising its 'main substance' as 'very seasonable, and of much use', testified to persistent demand (Vane, *Healing Question*, 1660 edn, postscript). *A Healing Question* was, indeed, of enduring relevance—not least as a source of the powerful slogan, the 'Good Old Cause', that did so much to undermine Richard Cromwell's tenuous hold on the army. The writing and reception of the book marked Vane's transition from an uneasy, meditative neutrality to concrete political objectives and advocacy. Carisbrooke confirmed his belief that suffering for conscientious 'witness' was inevitable, even salutary, yet did not inspire him to court martyrdom. Released in December 1656 he remained the government's quiet, but implacable, opponent, resisting pressure from legal and military threats to his Raby estates, and continuing to promote 'good party' solidarity. One means to this end was dialogue with those other persecuted witnesses, the Quakers. Undeterred by an acrimonious meeting with George Fox, Vane established cordial contacts with various prominent Friends, including his Durham neighbours Anthony Pearson, Edward Burrough, and Richard Hubberthorn, who counted him among those politicians most 'open to hear Counsel' and advance 'good things' (Caton MS, fol. 400, 403). Even in the political wilderness Vane's ideas, influence, and associations alarmed the protector's adherents: 1658 saw Richard Baxter's first attempt to destroy his reputation by branding him an intolerable 'masked Papist', head of a mysterious and subversive sect (Baxter, *Key*, preface).

Return to power, 1659 In January 1659 Sir Henry Vane re-entered public life as member for Whitchurch, Hampshire, in the last protectorate parliament. This rotten borough he secured with help from local republican dignitary Robert Wallop, after government influence blocked his candidacy at Hull and Bristol. Vane's election evidenced the cohesion of the opposition network; when parliament met, his appeals for 'love and unity' amid diversity paid further short-term dividends. Hesilrige, for instance, became so close a confederate that one disgusted MP accused him of trying 'to make himself and Vane the great Hogen-Mogens to rule the Commonwealth' (*Diary of Thomas Burton*, 4.221). Where these two led, others followed—old parliamentary colleagues, such as Thomas Scot, Edmund Ludlow, and Henry Neville, joining disaffected former officers from republican colonels Matthew Alured and John Okey to former Cromwellians John Lambert and William Packer. Though an oft-defeated minority indoors the commonwealthsmen had significant support outside from the London radicals and a rising tide of nostalgic propaganda aimed at a discontented army. Far from conspiring to embroil the latter with parliament Vane advocated conciliating the soldiers by redressing their grievances, so encouraging proper subordination to the people's deputies. Army independence did not attract him: his attempt, with Hesilrige, to enter the guarded house on April 23 indicated disapprobation of a dissolution dictated by the military. Nor had Vane set out to wreck this parliament by time-wasting; rather, he sought—without success—to persuade it to reverse the conservative trends of 1656–9. His speeches, much less long-winded than Hesilrige's, not only stressed the devolution of authority from the defunct ancient constitution to the present representative, but offered constructive criticisms of the protectorate. Existing foundations could, he thought, sustain a 'new superstructure' built upon that 'safe and rational' principle, the accountability to parliament of all office-holders (*Diary of Thomas Burton*, 3.177, 176). Vane advised MPs to 'adopt' Richard Cromwell and constrain him to serve the 'public interest' by rejecting such monarchical recrudescences as the legislative veto, unsupervised command of the armed forces, and a lifelong settled revenue (*Diary of Thomas Burton*, 3.180, 320). Thus Vane's immediate goals were limited to safeguarding liberty by extensive constitutional reform.

Vane ultimately aspired, however, to a government with foundations 'firm and deep as in the Word of God' capable of making the people 'holy as well as … free'. Debates in Richard's parliament had revealed an important new challenge to this virtuous vision: James Harrington's concept of an economically determined commonwealth based on immutable 'orders' deduced from 'humane Prudence' (Vane, *Needful Corrective*, 9, 2, 5, 1). Vane's response was *A Needful Corrective or Ballance in Popular Government*, a published letter to Harrington which wooed his followers by praising his learning and 'the essentials' of his model (ibid., 2). Writing as an anonymous '*Advocate for the Godly Man*', Vane questioned Harrington's confidence in the automatic ability of correct orders to compel 'the depraved, corrupted and self-interested will of man in the great Body … the People' to 'espouse their true publick interest' (ibid., 2, 6, 7). Only an 'extraordinary effusion of [the] Spirit upon all flesh' could make the nation 'truly free' to establish a government by its own willpower (ibid., 7); wisdom would therefore confine 'the right … of a free Citizen', at least temporarily, to a qualified élite corresponding to the good party (ibid., 8). This body should elect a 'Ruling Senate' and 'Representatives' to sit as a single assembly—similar nomenclature masking another major deviation from Harrington's bicameral system (ibid., 9, 7). Vane pressed his constitution's superior claim to be 'the most exact platforme of the purest kind of popular Government', derived from '*Israels* Commonwealth' (ibid., 10). The emphasis upon 'Divine Institution' was, of course, calculated to appeal to the godly, as was the assertion of the value of 'true godliness' despite the counterfeit variety's prevalence (ibid., 2). But Vane also went further than Fifth Monarchists in bridging the gap between the mundane and the millennial, recommending 'ordinary means' (ibid., 10) as a potential pathway to the 'perfect day' when the 'judgment of such a restored People … in their Assemblies … may not so much be the judgment of Man, as of the Lord himself, their King' (ibid., 11). Thus the *Needful Corrective* presented the godly republic as an attractive and eminently feasible alternative, synthesizing scripture and the best contemporary thought so as to court the widest possible support.

The protectorate's effective collapse afforded Vane a golden opportunity to promote his righteous constitution in central politics, delegating its detailed defence in print to Henry Stubbe and John Rogers. A preliminary problem was the need for an authority competent and plausible enough to fill the governmental vacuum and inaugurate a permanent republic. The solution—restoring the parliament expelled in April 1653—owed much to Vane, who hosted the private negotiations which induced the army to trust the republican leaders, upon verbal pledges to move the house in favour of the officers' desires; these included a 'select senate' resembling that proposed in the *Corrective*. When MPs discussed settlement that summer Vane invoked scripture to defend such a senate, representing a worthy minority, against majoritarian arguments from the irreligious Henry Neville, a Harringtonian. At September's constitutional committee, however, Vane advanced resolutions omitting disputed specifics like the senate in order to establish vital principles: rejection of any single person for representative government restrained by 'fundamentals', including toleration for Trinitarians acknowledging biblical inspiration. Only October's crisis prevented this compromise from receiving parliamentary approval. Since the commonwealth he envisaged, unlike Harrington's, required voluntary co-operation from all those eligible to participate Vane pursued consensus in practice as well as theory. Thus he resisted calls to debar or severely penalize penitent Cromwellians, supported a generous Indemnity Act, and sought to smooth the sometimes troubled relations between parliament and army by urging conciliatory courses upon the former and explaining controversial policies to the latter. The one actual civilian among the seven commissioners purging the officer corps, Vane developed close links with the grandees, especially Lambert, and so incurred a share in Hesilrige's growing suspicions of that brilliant commander. October saw Hesilrige's infectious distrust and determination to demonstrate parliament's 'absolute power' foil the more flexible Vane's best efforts, first to dissuade MPs from the antimilitary precautions that provoked their second expulsion, then to achieve a rapprochement continuing legal government by the council of state until parliament's readmission on conditions acceptable to the army. Prior to that point Vane had contended with relative success to facilitate progress towards settlement and contain the internal differences that threatened the Commonwealth.

But this was not the sum of Vane's contribution to the restored republic of May–October 1659. Parliament reinstated him as councillor and admiralty commissioner, and appointed him to numerous important committees. In July the council allocated him the convenient Whitehall suite that he had occupied until 1653. Once again he worked, with an energy equalled by very few, on business ranging from finance to national security, while somehow finding time to relieve imprisoned Quakers, and renew services to his Hull constituents. Foreign policy remained a speciality: Vane presented nearly all reports concerning it, and attended most diplomatic conferences. The French ambassador, Bordeaux, thought him the 'principal minister', and commended his tactful civility; from the Netherlands, de Witt distinguished Vane as the one to impress. While Vane's diplomacy aimed at honourable peace with all England's neighbours, it revived the early republic's particular inclination for alliance, and ultimately coalescence, with the United Provinces. Nearer home Vane resumed his interest in perfecting union with Scotland, towards which parliament made significant advances. Amid the emergency of the summer royalist rising Vane became colonel of a volunteer regiment raised by London's separatist congregations. Their choice of him illustrates his popularity in radical circles; his acceptance resulted from prudential reluctance to offend rather than any change in his lifelong disinclination to military service. Though this appointment fuelled conservative fears that he headed an armed and fanatical faction there is little doubt that Vane's role was, as he afterwards stated, 'honorary and titular' (*Tryal*, 49).

From October to December 1659 Vane played a conspicuous, yet equivocal, political part. Despite the failure of his attempts at reconciliation he did not despair of the Commonwealth's prospects, but interpreted the disruptions as heralding 'the glorious appearance of the Kingdom of God' (*Diary of Sir Archibald Johnston*, 3.149). Although he disapproved of parliament's forcible interruption he did not condemn the officers, who counted him an ally, and called him to their temporary executive, the committee of safety. To their dismay Vane and his closest civilian associate, Richard Salway, quitted that body's main sessions in protest at its usurpation of legislative powers, and declined all diplomatic or administrative duties, except those relating to the admiralty, for which they held valid parliamentary commissions. Vane's scruples did not, however, extend to the committee's subcommittee on the government, where he produced an 'Agreement of the people', including a fundamental of toleration, which encountered fierce opposition from the presbyterian zealot Archibald Johnston. Lambert's departure to lead the expedition against Monck lost Vane his ablest military backer. His hopes of determining the constitution suffered a further setback in mid-November, when the treaty between the armies accorded equal weight to the antisectarian Monck, and transferred responsibility for settlement to a general council of officers rather than a representative of the 'good people'. As England drifted towards anarchy Vane contemplated withdrawal, since he found himself increasingly marginalized and mistrusted by senior officers anxious to placate the 'sober godly' opponents of radical reformation. He stayed on, however, until December, when he and Salway consented to mediate between the committee and Lawson's channel fleet, which had just declared for parliament. Their confidence that 'they had kept themselves free and so might agree both partyes' was misplaced: Lawson's advisers suspected them of having 'too far espoused' the army's interest (*Diary of Sir Archibald Johnston*, 3.171; *Memoirs of Edmund*

Ludlow, 2.180). Failure of this conference sealed the committee's fate; on 24 December 1659 the London regiments recalled parliament.

Exclusion to execution, 1660–1662 Parliament's second return ended Sir Henry Vane's career. On 9 January 1660 he was summoned to face charges of 'Crimes, Miscarriages and Misdemeanours' committed during the interruption (*An Exact Accompt*, no. 55, 589). Unimpressed by the nice distinctions that he employed to disprove illegal activity, MPs voted to cancel his membership and banish him to Raby. In the same week his regiment was disbanded. Yet Vane lingered in London, pleading ill health, until mid-February, when parliament, prompted by his suspicious enemy General Monck, enforced his removal to Belleau. Despite expulsion Vane featured largely in the torrent of execration engulfing the Rump Parliament. Similar calumnies the previous year had evoked vigorous vindications of Vane's integrity, but now few of his demoralized admirers dared defend him. Though sensible of his danger, as one of the most hated republican leaders Vane neither fled nor submitted at the Restoration. Vengeance soon overtook him. In June the Convention Commons unanimously resolved to except him from the Indemnity Act as to all but life; on 1 July he was arrested at his Hampstead house. In exchange for Vane's entire exclusion the Lords joined the Commons in petitioning that he and Lambert might be spared death, as non-regicides, if prosecuted. To this Charles II assented on 30 August.

Imprisonment—in the Tower until October 1661, thereafter in the Scilly Isles—gave Vane ample opportunity for reflection. When permitted paper and ink he wrote profusely, producing three substantial theological treatises, and various shorter meditations, all published posthumously. These works reveal that adversity only strengthened Vane's confidence in the cause, and his divine calling to encourage, guide, and awaken the saints by his testimony and example. Ever a realist, Vane did not minimize the severity or injustice of the present sufferings. Rather, he offered biblical consolation and explanation to those despondent and bewildered by the 'black shade which God hath drawn over his work' (*Tryal*, 77). Eclipse had justly befallen the cause, not for inherent evil, but because it was 'not so prudently and righteously managed as it might and ought to have been' (ibid., 120). Sincere repentance might yet result in renewed deliverance and service. Meanwhile, those who had preserved a 'good Conscience' need not fear the 'unrestrained Power and revengeful mind' of their enemies (ibid., 119). Temporary experience of defeat fulfilled prophecies which also guaranteed ultimate triumph. Against the Fifth Monarchists' violent counsels Vane contended that the saints should simply 'depend upon God, for the avenging of his people even when all humane ability to perform it is vanished' (Vane, *Two Treatises*, 2). Vane's last writings advocate passive expectancy more strongly than ever before: virtuous action had become both less feasible and—with 'the near Approaching *Day* of the *Lord*'—less necessary (ibid., title-page).

That the faithful patience Vane enjoined was not stoical

apathy is plain from his final public appearances. In 1662 the government responded to the Cavalier Parliament's repeated requests for his punishment by bringing him back to the Tower and preparing charges that his services to the Commonwealth constituted treason against Charles II. At his trial in king's bench on 6 June Vane vehemently denied doing anything 'morally evil': his constant motives had been 'Honour, Justice, Reason and Conscience', the 'principles of that Righteous Cause' which he would never repudiate (*Tryal*, 26, 47, 43). He had not acted independently, but by the 'then regnant' authority of parliament, which no lesser court could challenge (ibid., 46). Like Lilburne before him Vane protested that his treatment contravened the 'lawfull Liberties of English-men', and raised numerous legal objections, which were cursorily dismissed (ibid., 76). The guilty verdict was inevitable. On 11 June Vane was condemned to die despite the king's promise—only the 'penitent', his judges declared, deserved mercy (ibid., 54). Lambert, who professed remorse, was reprieved. Vane invited martyrdom by defiant self-defence. The sentence, commuted to beheading, was executed at Tower Hill on 14 June. Vane faced death calmly, even joyfully, in hope that it might strengthen 'the Faith of many', bring 'others … to the knowledge of the Truth', and so hasten the promised 'Resurrection' of the 'glorious Cause' (ibid., 80). His courage and dignity on the scaffold, amid official harassment that curtailed his speech, greatly impressed hostile observers. Vane was buried privately on 15 June in the family vault at Shipborne, Kent.

Assessment Contemporaries of all persuasions acknowledged Sir Henry Vane's importance. Charles II believed him 'too dangerous … to let live' (Bryant, 128); Algernon Sidney thought his death 'intollerable grievous' to England, whose 'greatest ornament' he was (Rowe, *Sir Henry Vane … a Study*, 282). Anthony Wood pronounced Vane 'the Proteus of the times … an inventor … of whimseys in religion' and 'crotchets in the state'; George Sikes portrayed him as a 'faithful watchman and able Patriot', with 'remarkable insight [into] the Politie of the true Commonwealth' (Wood, *Ath. Oxon.*, 3. 582; Sikes, 105, 107). To Archibald Johnston he became the 'Achitophel' whose 'politik, deceitful, double false waye' threatened God's ordinances; Edmund Ludlow deemed him not merely a 'choyce martyr of Christ' but 'a polititian truely pious and a Christian truly politique' (*Diary of Sir Archibald Johnston*, 3.164, 165; Ludlow, *Voyce*, 313, 314). Machiavellian or martyr? Historiography has since oscillated between these interpretations of his character. But the strength of contemporary reactions to Vane reflects the impact of his ideas as much as his personal qualities. Most politicians are not thinkers; most theorists are not actors. Vane was both. After over a decade of intense activity he began, in the 1650s, to publish his vision of the righteous republic. Though enemies dismissed his works as incomprehensible or impracticable, they in fact reveal a coherent world-view derived primarily from scripture, yet adapted to the needs of the moment. Unlike Harrington, Vane was not mesmerized by idealized institutions. Unswerving in his dedication to

the cause of God and the principles befitting its adherents he remained a political pragmatist, flexible as to specific forms. In contrast to the narrow sectarian rule that some desired, Vane's godly republicanism was genuinely eirenical, perceiving that goodness was not confined to the saints, and pursuing the reconciliation of all those formerly united under the banner of civil and Christian liberty. This understudied ideological legacy survived the débâcle of 1659 to influence the subsequent development of republicanism on both sides of the Atlantic.

RUTH E. MAYERS

Sources The tryal of Sir Henry Vane, knight, at the kings bench, Westminster, June the 2nd & 6th 1662 (1662) • [H. Vane], Zeal examined (1652) • H. Vane, The retired mans meditations (1655) • [H. Vane], A healing question (1656) • The proceeds of the protector (so-called) and his council against Sir Henry Vane, knight (1656) • [H. Vane], A needful corrective or ballance in popular government (1659) • H. Vane, Two treatises (1662) • H. Vane, Sr. Henry Vane his speech in the House of Commons, at a committee for the bill against episcopall-government (1641) • Three speeches spoken in Guild-hall concerning his majesties refusall of a treaty of peace, and what is to be done thereupon (1642) • G. Sikes, The life and death of Sir Henry Vane, kt. (1662) • A vindication of that prudent and honourable knight, Sir Henry Vane (1659) • H. Stubbe, Malice rebuked (1659) • J. Rogers, Diapoliteia (1659) • E. Ludlow, A voyce from the watch tower, ed. A. B. Worden, CS, 4th ser., 21 (1978) • The memoirs of Edmund Ludlow, ed. C. H. Firth, 2 vols. (1894) • V. A. Rowe, Sir Henry Vane the younger: a study in political and administrative history (1970) [incl. A. Sidney, 'The character of Sir Henry Vane jnr', appx F] • Wood, Ath. Oxon., new edn, vol. 3 • Reliquiae Baxterianae, or, Mr Richard Baxter's narrative of the most memorable passages of his life and times, ed. M. Sylvester, 1 vol. in 3 pts (1696) • R. Baxter, A key for Catholicks (1659) • Clarendon, Hist. rebellion • CSP dom., 1631-3; 1635; 1638-9; 1641-4; 1656-7; 1660-61 • CSP col., vol. 1 • Thurloe, State papers • Original letters and papers of state addressed to Oliver Cromwell … found among the political collections of Mr John Milton, ed. J. Nickolls (1743) • C. Dalton, History of the Wrays of Glentworth, 2 (1881) • Diary of Thomas Burton, ed. J. T. Rutt, 4 vols. (1828) • Diary of Sir Archibald Johnston of Wariston, 3, ed. J. D. Ogilvie, Scottish History Society, 3rd ser., 34 (1940) • Letters of Roger Williams (1874) • R. Williams, The bloudy tenent, of persecution (1644) • John Winthrop's journal: 'History of New England', 1630-1649, ed. J. K. Hosmer, 2 vols. (1908) • H. Vane, A brief answer to a certain declaration, Hutchinson papers, ed. W. Whitmore and W. Appleton, 1 (1864) • The letters and journals of Robert Baillie, ed. D. Laing, 3 vols. (1841-2), vols. 1-2 • W. Knowles, ed., The earle of Strafford's letters and dispatches, 2 vols. (1739) • Bishop Burnet's History of his own time: with the suppressed passages of the first volume, ed. M. J. Routh, 6 vols. (1823), vol. 1 • The Clarke papers, ed. C. H. Firth, 4 vols., CS, new ser., 49, 54, 61-2 (1891-1901) • E. Cust, Records of the Cust family of Pinchbeck, Stamford and Belton in Lincolnshire, 1479-1700 (1898) • The letters and speeches of Oliver Cromwell, ed. T. Carlyle, 1 (1849) • RS Friends, Lond., MS vol. S81, Caton MS 3 • J. Willcock, Life of Sir Henry Vane the younger, statesman and mystic (1913) • A. Bryant, ed., The letters, speeches and declarations of King Charles II (1935) • V. A. Rowe, 'Sir Henry Vane the younger as MP for Hull', N&Q, 204 (1959), 19-24 • A. Woolrych, Commonwealth to protectorate, pbk edn (2000) • M. Guizot, Histoire du protectorat de Richard Cromwell et du rétablissement des Stuart, 2 vols. (1856) • An exact accompt of the daily proceedings in parliament, no. 53 (30 Dec 1659-6 Jan 1660); no. 55 (14-21 Jan 1660) • The remonstrance and protestation of the well-affected people of the cities of London, Westminster, and the other cities (1659) • J. Lilburne, Jonah's cry out of the whale's belly [1647] [Thomason tract E 400(5)] • T. Hutchinson, A collection of original papers relative to the history of the colony of Massachusetts (1769) • C. Polizzotto, 'The campaign against The humble proposals of 1652', Journal of Ecclesiastical History, 38 (1987), 569-81 • DNB • Aubrey's Brief lives, ed. O. L. Dick (1949); pbk edn (1992) • R. W. Blencowe, ed., Sydney papers: consisting

of a journal of the earl of Leicester, and original letters of Algernon Sydney (1825)
Archives V&A NAL, sermon and letter · Worcester College, Oxford, corresp.
Likenesses P. Lely, oils, c.1650, Raby Castle, co. Durham [see illus.] · W. Dobson, oils, NPG · W. Faithorne, line engraving, BM, NPG; repro. in Sikes, Life

Vane [Fane], **Thomas** (b. **1599/1600**), Church of England clergyman and Roman Catholic convert, was born in Kent, matriculated from Jesus College, Oxford, on 26 April 1616 aged sixteen, and transferred in 1618 to Christ's College, Cambridge, where he graduated BA in 1620 and MA in 1623. He was ordained deacon and priest at Peterborough in April 1621 and was appointed chaplain-extraordinary to Charles I and rector of the rich west Kent living of Crayford, possibly by means of family patronage, in 1626. Edward Hasted, in his history of Kent, omits him from his list of rectors of Crayford, perhaps influenced by the rector's subsequent abandonment of the Church of England, leaving a gap from the year of Vane's appointment to the point at which his successor was eventually appointed, in 1648.

It seems likely that at least as early as the 1630s Vane was exhibiting Arminian sacramental preferences which presaged his conversion to Catholicism and which seem to have divided his parish: in July 1633 the last significant step taken by the archbishop of Canterbury, George Abbot, was in the form of an arbitration to impose on Crayford church a distinctly high-church manner of reverently receiving 'the body and blood of Our Lord and Saviour Jesus Christ' (VCH Kent, 2.91). The rector took his Cambridge DD in 1640 but was soon to leave the Church of England and, becoming a Catholic, gave up his benefice and, apparently with his wife, travelled to France and Italy. He was awarded a medical degree in a continental university and changed his career to the practice of medicine.

Educated in theology to an advanced degree Vane also took up authorship on behalf of the Catholic faith. His A Lost Sheep Returned Home, published in Paris in 1643, around the time of his departure for the continent, was dedicated to Charles I's Catholic queen, Henrietta Maria, and explained the motives for his change of faith. It drew a defence of the historical authenticity of the Church of England from the historian Edward Chisenhall and went through five editions between 1643 and 1666. His historical work, An Answer to a Libell (Paris, 1646), was a defence of the Catholic Church's Fourth Lateran Council, which in 1215 established the doctrine of transubstantiation in the Eucharist. Dedicated to Sir Kenelm Digby, it had earlier been issued attached to Miles Pinckney's Occasional Discourses (1646). A third book, Wisdom and innocence, or, Prudence and simplicity in the examples of the shepherd and the dove, propounded by Our Lord, was published in 1652 with a dedication to the earl of Westmorland.

Vane was a remarkable but shadowy character, difficult to trace. He may or may not have been the Thomas Fane who died in Kent in 1692 at the age of ninety.

MICHAEL MULLETT

Sources Gillow, Lit. biog. hist., 5.563–4 · Venn, Alum. Cant. · Foster, Alum. Oxon. · E. Hasted, The history and topographical survey of the county of Kent, 2nd edn, 5 (1798), 152 · VCH Kent, 2.91 · P. Clark, English provincial society from the Reformation to the revolution: religion, politics and society in Kent, 1500–1640 (1977), 362 · DNB · T. H. Clancy, English Catholic books, 1641–1700: a bibliography, rev. edn (1996)

Vane, William Harry, first duke of Cleveland (1766–1842), aristocrat, was the son of Henry Vane, second earl of Darlington (1726–1792), and Margaret (d. 1800), daughter of Robert Lowther and sister of James Lowther, first earl of Lonsdale. He was born on 27 July 1766 in St James's Square, London, and was educated by a private tutor, William Lipscomb, and at Christ Church, Oxford, where he matriculated in 1783. He married, first, on 17 September 1787, Lady Katherine Margaret (1766–1807), second daughter and coheir of Harry *Powlett or Paulet, sixth duke of Bolton; they had three sons and five daughters. He married, second, on 27 July 1813, Elizabeth (1777–1861), daughter of Robert Russell, market gardener, of Newton, Yorkshire. His second wife had been his mistress for some years, and previously that of Thomas Coutts, the banker. She inherited substantially under her husband's will.

As Viscount Barnard he was MP for Totnes in 1788–90, and for Winchelsea (which his father had recently purchased) in 1790–92. His political allegiances fluctuated; he started as a whig, but generally supported Pitt, until succeeding as earl of Darlington on 8 September 1792. Thereafter he became increasingly alienated from Pitt, who was unwilling to elevate Darlington in the peerage. He supported the ministries of Canning and Wellington as an independent. Although he seldom spoke in the House of Lords, he was an advocate of political reform, and presented there a petition from South Shields on the subject on 3 March 1829. He proved himself throughout an influential supporter of the bill, and willing enough to abandon his six borough seats. Indeed, he was said to have purchased the seats to ensure his marquessate, and given them up to gain a dukedom: he was created marquess of Cleveland in 1827 and duke of Cleveland in 1833. However, his support for reform was such that he disinherited his elder sons (who had become tories) in favour of his youngest son, Lord Harry Vane, who remained a whig.

The duke was more notable as a sportsman than as a politician. Living at Raby Castle, co. Durham, for a considerable portion of every year, he proved himself an enthusiastic upholder of every form of sport. He began to hunt his father's hounds in 1787, and spared no expense on his kennel. His hounds were renowned for their speed, and were divided into two packs, one of large breed and one of small; with these he hunted on alternate days. After each day's hunting it was his habit to enter an account of the day's sport in a diary, portions of which were privately published at the close of every season. He paid considerable sums of money to his tenants for the preservation of foxes, and on their behalf he successfully opposed the first Stockton and Darlington Railway in 1820, because in its course it encroached on a favourite cover. In 1835 he divided his celebrated pack between his son-in-law, Mark Milbanke, and himself, and the old district of the hunt was at the same time apportioned. Almost equally enthusiastic in his patronage of the turf, he maintained a magnificent stud, and was rewarded by winning the St Leger with his horse Chorister in 1831.

The duke of Cleveland died in Cleveland House, St James's Square, on 29 January 1842, and was buried in Staindrop church, co. Durham, where a monument was erected to his memory. He was succeeded in the title by each of his three sons in turn, none of whom had any legitimate heirs. Lord Brougham, whom Cleveland had introduced to the House of Commons as member for Winchelsea and who was a lifelong friend, was one of the executors of a will that left almost £1 million in addition to huge estates, around £1,250,000 in consols, and plate and jewels to the value of a further £1 million.

WILLIAM CARR, *rev.* K. D. REYNOLDS

Sources GEC, *Peerage* · *GM*, 2nd ser., 17 (1842), 543–5 · Burke, *Peerage* · P. Mandler, *Aristocratic government in the age of reform: whigs and liberals, 1830–1852* (1990) · *The Times* (31 Jan 1842) · *Morning Post* (31 Jan 1842)
Archives BL, family papers, Add. MS 43507 | U. Durham L., corresp. with Lord Grey
Likenesses A. W. Devis, oils, *c.*1810, Harris Museum and Art Gallery, Preston · J. Downman, pencil and watercolour drawing, 1813, Smith College Museum of Art, Northampton, Massachusetts · W. T. Fry, stipple, pubd 1821, BM, NPG · J. Doyle, lithograph, pubd 1833, NPG · F. Chantrey, pencil drawing, NPG · Devis, portrait; in possession of Milbanke family, Birmingham, 1899 · Fry, engraving (after Devis) · R. Westmacott, recumbent figure on monument, Staindrop, co. Durham · miniatures, Raby Castle, co. Durham · portraits, Raby Castle, co. Durham
Wealth at death under £1,000,000 personalty; £1,250,000 consols; approx. £1,000,000 jewels and plate; also estates valued at approx. £50,000 p.a. in Yorkshire and elsewhere in England: GEC, *Peerage*; *GM*, 545; will

Vanessa. *See* Homrigh, Esther Van (1688–1723).

Van Haecken, Joseph. *See* Aken, Joseph van (c.1699–1749).

VanKoughnet [Vankoughnet], **Philip Michael Matthew Scott** (1822–1869), politician and judge in Canada, was born on 21 January 1822 at Cornwall, Stormont county, Ontario, the eldest son of Lieutenant-Colonel Philip VanKoughnet and his wife, Harriet Sophia, the daughter of Matthew Scott of Carrick-on-Suir, co. Tipperary. The family, which was originally named von Gochnat, emigrated from Colmar in Alsace in 1750, and settled in what later became the town of Springfield, Massachusetts. Michael VanKoughnet (1751–1832), grandfather of Philip, was a loyalist and took refuge in 1783 in Cornwall, old province of Quebec, where he died in October 1832, leaving three sons and a daughter from his marriage with Eve, the daughter of John Bolton Empey. The eldest son, Philip VanKoughnet (1790–1873), born on 2 April 1790, served at the battle of Crysler's Farm on 11 November 1813 and commanded the fifth battalion of the Canadian incorporated militia at the battle of the Windmill, Prescott, on 13 November 1837. He was also for thirty years a member of the legislature of Upper Canada, and, on its union with Lower Canada in 1841, the legislative council. At his death he was chairman of the board of arbitrators for the dominion. He died at Cornwall on 17 May 1873, leaving eight sons and five daughters.

The younger Philip VanKoughnet was educated at the Eastern District grammar school before serving under his father in the militia in 1837. The experience led him to give up thoughts of entering the church and he turned instead to law. He began his studies in Cornwall in 1838, then moved to Toronto, and was admitted to the bar in 1843. He specialized in equity law and rapidly established his reputation and a successful practice, enabling him to marry in November 1845 Elizabeth, the daughter of Colonel Barker Turner. He was appointed queen's counsel in 1850, served on the council of the University of Trinity College, and lectured there on equity jurisprudence.

In 1856 VanKoughnet was persuaded by his longstanding friend John A. Macdonald to become president of the executive council and minister of agriculture. In the latter post he was active and efficient, paying particular attention to combating crop damage by pests. Also in 1856 he was elected to the legislative council as member for the Rideau district. In 1858 he became commissioner of crown lands and in 1860 chief superintendent of Indian affairs, in which post he had some success in settling longrunning land claims. He initiated the system of selling townships *en bloc*, which led to a rapid opening up of new areas for colonization. He also encouraged and organized western exploring expeditions and promoted improvements in transport infrastructure, particularly railways.

In 1862 VanKoughnet was appointed chancellor of the court of chancery of Upper Canada. He held this office with distinction until his death, having declined Macdonald's offer in 1868 of the office of chief justice. He died at Toronto on 7 November 1869 after a short illness and was survived by his wife and their two sons. Although he was helped by his close friendship with Macdonald, his achievements were due in large measure to his industry, keen mind, and legal acumen.

G. LE G. NORGATE, *rev.* ELIZABETH BAIGENT

Sources *The Times* (10 Nov 1869) · *DCB*, vol. 9 · G. M. Rose, *Cyclopaedia of Canadian biography* (1888) · R. S. Lambert, *Renewing nature's wealth* (1967)

Vanlore, Sir Peter [*formerly* Pieter van Loor] (c.1547–1627), merchant and moneylender, was born in Utrecht in the Netherlands, the third son of Maurice van Loor and his wife, Stephania. He arrived in England about 1568. By 1571 he was lodging with one William Pickarde in the parish of St Dunstan-in-the-West, London; by March 1578, when he was called before the privy council to account for his activities, he was operating as a jewel merchant in the city. Before 19 July 1585, when he was living in the parish of St Benet Sherehog, he had married Jacoba or Jacomina, daughter of Henry Teighbott.

The foundations of Vanlore's extensive fortune seem to have been laid in the 1590s through the supply of jewellery to the royal court. On 17 December 1594 the queen authorized payment of £1700 to him for a single pearl chain. Profits increased dramatically with the accession of James I: in the first eighteen months of his reign the king spent £30,000 on Vanlore's gems and continued to patronize him thereafter, although in 1619 Vanlore bought £18,000 worth of the queen's jewels back to fund a royal progress. While not quite in the league of Philip Burlamachi, like William Courteen he also became one of the most prominent alien merchants lending money to the crown, advancing at least £35,000 by 1625. With Sir Baptist Hickes and Sir William Cockayne he lent an equal share of £30,000 to the government in 1621 to subsidize the proposed Palatinate expedition. In return the king knighted him at Whitehall on 5 November, but he had to wait until after Charles I's accession, and lend further, in order to secure any repayment.

Other securities came in the form of licences. In January 1604 Vanlore was granted a licence to export 15,000 broadcloths for ten years free of duty. The following year he led a syndicate which bought similar concessions from the courtiers Sir Philip Herbert and Sir James Hay and sold them on to the Merchant Adventurers at a profit. Like his fellow syndicate member Arthur Ingram and their mutual friend Lionel Cranfield, subsequently earl of Middlesex and lord treasurer, Vanlore also speculated in crown lands, acquiring temporary interests in manors in Sedgemoor, Gloucestershire, Oxfordshire, Devon, and elsewhere. While he evidently continued to make regular use of his city contacts from his residence in Fenchurch Street, in 1604 he bought the manor of Tilehurst, near Reading, Berkshire, and over the years he consolidated his property in the locality through purchase and foreclosing mortgages. In 1625 the privy council intervened to assert, against the counter-claims of Sir Richard Lydall, his possession of the manor of Sonning, also in Berkshire, which had come to him as a creditor of the earl of Kellie. By the end of his life:

> Sir Peter owned one of the largest estates in Berkshire and, although he had not occupied any important administrative office in the shire, he possessed a great potential influence over county affairs and a social parity with any of his fellow landowners. (Durston, 209)

Yet as a major crown creditor and a conspicuously successful immigrant, Vanlore had been, and had felt himself to be, vulnerable. His naturalization, finalized on 5 May 1610, was no protection against the Star Chamber case brought in 1619 against him and other Dutch merchant strangers alleging illegal export of bullion. The charges were almost certainly fabricated as a pretext for the crown to duck its financial obligations, and Vanlore secured some mitigation in sentence by pleading successfully that he was pursuing business for the earl of Dunbar, Lord Fenton, the earl of Somerset, and others, but the lawsuit bred insecurity. On 1 January 1620 John Chamberlain reported to Sir Dudley Carleton that Vanlore had 'said that when he had ended this busines he wold bid England farewell'. To the observation that his £8000 fine (reduced to £7000):

> was no great loss to him, beeing otherwise so well feathered having goode store of land in England … he aunswered he had children here to leave yt to, but for himself he wold go to save his skin, for they that upon such witnes could take away

his goods might when they pleased take his life. (*Letters of John Chamberlain*, 279–80)

In the event, Vanlore remained in England until his death on 6 September 1627. His will of 29 June that year reveals strong ties both to his native community and to the establishment of his adopted country. Sir Paul Bayning was an overseer and Lord Keeper Sir Thomas Coventry among special friends singled out; the Dutch church, his local parish, and Christ's Hospital all received legacies. This bifurcation was repeated in his children's marriages: those of Peter (*bap.* 1586) to Susanna Becke of Antwerp and of Elizabeth to Hans van den Bernden; those of Jacquemine (*bap.* 1587, *d.* 1606) to Johannes De *Laet, newly arrived immigrant, and of Anne to Sir Charles *Caesar, master of chancery and third generation immigrant; and those of Mary to Sir Edward Powell, eventually master of requests, and Catherine to Sir Thomas *Glemham. Vanlore left each of his grandchildren £1000, but it is unclear to what extent his estate was ever fully reimbursed for his loans: in July 1628 his widow, Jacoba, and her son-in-law Powell were still seeking £13,000 due from the crown. Peter the younger obtained a baronetcy on 6 September that year, but the estates so spectacularly built up were dispersed when he died in 1645 leaving three daughters.

VIVIENNE LARMINIE

Sources *CSP dom.*, 1594–1628 · *The letters of John Chamberlain*, ed. N. E. McClure, 2 (1939), 245–51, 275–8, 405 · R. E. G. Kirk and E. F. Kirk, eds., *Returns of aliens dwelling in the city and suburbs of London, from the reign of Henry VIII to that of James I*, Huguenot Society of London, 10/1 (1900) · will, PRO, PROB 11/152, sig. 88 · PRO, PROB 11/153, sig. 28 [sentence] · W. J. C. Moens, ed., *The marriage, baptism, and burial registers, 1571 to 1874, of the Dutch church, Austin Friars* (1884) · *VCH Berkshire*, 4.101 · W. H. Rylands, ed., *The four visitations of Berkshire*, 1, Harleian Society, 56 (1907), 137 · W. A. Shaw, ed., *Letters of denization and acts of naturalization for aliens in England and Ireland, 1603–1700*, Huguenot Society of London, 18 (1911), 14, 56, 77, 105 · C. G. Durston, 'Berkshire and its county gentry, 1625–1649', PhD diss., U. Reading, 1977 · M. Prestwich, *Cranfield: politics and profits under the early Stuarts* (1966) · R. Ashton, *The crown and the money market, 1603–1640* (1960) · R. Ashton, *The city and the court, 1603–1643* (1979), 19 · GEC, *Baronetage*

Vannes, Peter (*c.*1488–1563), diplomat and dean of Salisbury, was born in Lucca, Italy, the son of Stefano Vanni of Lucca. Vannes was the kinsman of Andrea Ammonius, a close friend of Erasmus, Latin secretary to Henry VIII, and one of the many Italian humanists who enjoyed favour at the English court. Vannes referred to himself as Ammonius's kinsman (*consobrinus*), but their exact relationship has not been established, with some sources suggesting that Ammonius was Vannes's maternal uncle, and others that the two men were cousins. In 1513 Ammonius brought Vannes to England and employed him as his assistant. Silvestro Gigli, bishop of Worcester and a fellow Lucchese, introduced Vannes to Cardinal Wolsey, who retained him as his Latin secretary in 1514. Ammonius's death three years later, in August 1517, prompted Vannes to write immediately to Wolsey seeking some living previously held by his late kinsman. At the same time, a distraught Erasmus entrusted Vannes with the task of destroying or forwarding any of his extant correspondence with Ammonius. Exasperated at the slow response to his request, Erasmus berated Vannes in subsequent letters, calling him a 'monster' and complaining that he had none of the spirit of his relative Ammonius.

In 1523 Vannes was incorporated a bachelor of theology at Cambridge, possibly because he had already taken that degree on the continent. Although he was unsuccessful in his efforts to become bishop of Lucca in 1526, he had sufficient patronage and influence to acquire several ecclesiastical livings in England: by 1530 he held prebends in the cathedrals of Hereford (Cublington) and Salisbury (South Grantham and Bedwyn), Bedwyn having been previously held by the illegitimate son of Wolsey, Thomas Winter.

Vannes began his diplomatic career in earnest in 1527 when, with Cuthbert Tunstall, Sir Thomas More, and other luminaries, he accompanied Wolsey to France to establish a league between England, the Holy Roman empire, France, and Venice. In late November 1528 he and Sir Francis Bryan were sent to Rome as special ambassadors to the pope, each receiving a daily wage of 26s. 8d. Masquerading as an embassy to warn the papacy against agreeing to an imperial peace proposal, the mission was actually intended to induce Pope Clement VII to pronounce Henry VIII's marriage to Katherine of Aragon void *ab initio*. The ambassadors had other objectives, too, including that of disproving the authenticity of a brief which undermined Henry's arguments for the divorce by removing disabilities found in the original dispensation for the marriage. Vannes was encouraged to use whatever means necessary to secure support, including hiring advocates, bribing cardinals, and even threatening the pope with the withdrawal of English allegiance to Rome. If all else failed, Vannes was instructed to seek Clement VII's approval for Henry to have two wives, 'making the children of the second marriage legitimate as well as those of the first, whereof some great reasons and precedents, especially in the Old Testament, appear' (*LP Henry VIII*, 4/2, no. 4977). On their journey Vannes and Bryan stopped in France to meet the French king, François I, in mid-December, and finally arrived in Rome on 28 January 1529. Clement's ill health delayed the English embassy until late March, when the ambassadors met him informally; they only had a formal audience on 1 April. After the failure of the mission Bryan went to France to serve as ambassador, while Vannes returned to England, travelling via Paris to promote the divorce with the French king and clergy.

Vannes survived the fall of his patron Wolsey, an event that did not impede his advancement. Indeed, some time after 1528 he became Latin secretary to Henry VIII. Appointed collector of papal taxes in England on 17 July 1533, he travelled later that year to Rome, Avignon, and Marseilles in his new capacity. He also continued to accumulate benefices, acquiring prebends in the dioceses of Bath and Wells (Compton Dundon) in May 1534 and York (Bole) in February 1535. He was appointed archdeacon of Worcester in May 1534, and was formally installed as dean of Salisbury on 3 February 1540, a post he appears to have held *de facto* since 1536, and one that he retained until 28 March 1563. In 1541 he became rector of

Tredington, Worcestershire, and acquired the further prebends of Caddington Major in St Paul's in April 1542 and Shipton in Salisbury in 1543. In 1545 he received a special pension of £26 13s. 4d. from King Henry VIII College, Oxford, as compensation for the canonry he had held in that college until its dissolution.

Upon his accession Edward VI retained Vannes as his Latin secretary with an annual salary of 40 marks. He was reappointed for life on 13 December 1549. Shortly thereafter, in May 1550, Vannes was appointed English ambassador to Venice with a salary of 40s. a day. He visited his native Lucca in November 1551. The protestant Edwardian regime instructed Vannes to keep close watch over Englishmen travelling in Italy, especially those with Catholic tendencies who sought out Cardinal Pole and his circle. Vannes continued to serve as ambassador during the first half of Mary's reign, when he prudently adopted a pro-imperial position. He may also have acted as the queen's spokesman in justifying her determination to execute Thomas Cranmer in spite of his recantation. During his tenure abroad Vannes became involved in some highly questionable activities. In 1554 he hired assassins who attempted to kill Sir Peter Carew. Circumstantial evidence suggests Vannes's involvement in the mysterious death in 1556 of Edward Courtenay, earl of Devon; it is possible that Vannes had him poisoned to foil a plot to marry the earl to Mary's sister, Elizabeth, and then take the English throne. In any event, Vannes requested his recall immediately after Courtenay's demise on 18 September, and returned to English soil some time after October 1556. Queen Elizabeth disregarded any unsavoury rumours and allowed Vannes to retain his livings after 1558.

Vannes died between 28 March and 1 May 1563, leaving two wills, both dated 1 July 1562. His affairs took some time to settle, with one will granted probate on 21 May 1563 and the other being confirmed and proved a full year later, on 10 July 1564. He provided very well for his family: his sister Margaret received a comfortable living for the remainder of her life, and his brother's illegitimate daughter, also named Margaret, was given a dowry of 300 crowns (*scutos*). Vannes's principal heir, a 'Benedict Hudson, alias Vannes', was most probably his illegitimate son; not only did Vannes bequeath Benedict's mother, Alice, a cow and a valuable bed, but, much more telling, he also left Benedict all family lands in his native Lucca. It may be a pointer to his court connections that he left to Sir William Petre, royal secretary from 1544 to 1557, a 'new black satin robe adorned with black velvet newly acquired from Venice' (PRO, PROB 11/46, fol. 173v).

Vannes's standing at the English court attracted Italian humanists seeking patronage. Ortensio Lando, eager to honour a fellow Lucchese, dedicated his 1550 work *Miscellaneae questiones* to him. It was through Vannes that Pietro Aretino in 1542 sent a copy of his second volume of letters to Henry VIII, to whom it was dedicated. Other literary figures appreciated Vannes's friendship, among them John Leland, who commemorated their relationship in an ode. L. E. HUNT

Sources LP Henry VIII · P. G. Bietenholz and T. B. Deutscher, eds., *Contemporaries of Erasmus* (1985–7) · Cooper, *Ath. Cantab.*, 1.220–21 · G. M. Bell, *A handlist of British diplomatic representatives, 1509–1688*, Royal Historical Society Guides and Handbooks, 16 (1990) · K. R. Bartlett, *The English in Italy, 1525–1559* (1991) · C. Pizzi, *Un amico di Erasmo: l'umanista Andrea Ammonio* (1956) · *The correspondence of Erasmus*, ed. and trans. R. A. B. Mynors and others, 22 vols. (1974–94) [annotated by W. K. Ferguson] · W. Page, ed., *The certificates of the commissioners appointed to survey the chantries, guilds, hospitals, etc., in the county of York. Part II*, SurtS, 92 (1895), 526 · W. Wilkie, *The cardinal protectors of England* (1974) · W. U. Bullock, 'The "lost" Miscellaneae questions of Ortensio Lando', *Italian Studies*, 2 (1938–9), 49–64 · J. Strype, *Ecclesiastical memorials*, 3 vols. (1822) · G. de C. Parmiter, *The king's great matter: a study in Anglo-papal relations, 1527–1534* (1967) · J. Leland, *Encomia* (1774), vol. 5 of *De rebus Britannicis collectanea* · J. Strype, *The life of Sir John Cheke* (1821) · Wood, *Ath. Oxon.*, 1st edn · Emden, *Oxf.*, 4.590–91 · BL, Harley MSS 5008–5009 · *Fasti Angl., 1541–1857*, [St Paul's, London] · *Fasti Angl., 1541–1857*, [York] · *Fasti Angl., 1541–1857*, [Bath and Wells] · *Fasti Angl., 1541–1857*, [Salisbury] · *Fasti Angl., 1541–1857*, [Ely] · Venn, *Alum. Cant.*, 1/4.294 · D. MacCulloch, *Thomas Cranmer: a life* (1996) · will, PRO, PROB 11/46, fols. 161v–162r; 173r–v
Archives BL, Harley 5008 & 5009 | PRO, Kew, State Papers – domestic, foreign, Spanish, Venetian · letters and papers of Henry VIII
Wealth at death see wills, PRO, PROB 11/46, fols. 161v–162r; 173r–v

Vans, Sir Patrick. *See* Vaus, Sir Patrick, Lord Barnbarroch (*d.* 1597).

Vansittart, Edward Westby (1818–1904), naval officer, born at Bisham Abbey near Maidenhead, Berkshire, on 20 July 1818, was the third son of the five children of Vice-Admiral Henry *Vansittart (1777–1843) of Eastwood, Woodstock, Canada, and his wife, Mary Charity (*d.* 1834), the daughter of the Revd John Pennefather. He entered the navy as a first-class volunteer in June 1831, and attended the Royal Naval College, Portsmouth. As a midshipman of the *Jaseur* he served on the east coast of Spain during the First Carlist War (1834–6). Having passed his examination on 2 August 1837, he served as mate in the *Wellesley*, the flagship on the East India station, and was present at the capture of Karachi in February 1839 and at other operations in the Persian Gulf. In December 1841 he was appointed to the *Cornwallis* (72 guns), the flagship of Sir William Parker on the East Indies and China station, and in her took part in the operations in the Yangtze (Yangzi) River, including the capture of the Woosung (Wusong) batteries on 16 June 1842. He was mentioned in dispatches and was promoted lieutenant on 16 September 1842. In February 1843 he was appointed to the sloop *Serpent* (16 guns), and remained in her in the East Indies for three years.

After a short period on the *Gladiator* in the channel, Vansittart in December 1846 joined the *Hibernia* (104 guns), the flagship of Sir William Parker in the Mediterranean. During the Portuguese rebellion of 1846–7 he acted as aide-de-camp to Parker, and was present at the surrender of the Portuguese rebel fleet off Oporto. On 1 January 1849 he was appointed first lieutenant of the royal yacht *Victoria and Albert*, and on 23 October of that year was promoted commander.

In August 1852 Vansittart commissioned the new iron-clad sloop *Bittern* for the China station, where he was involved in the suppression of piracy and was mentioned in dispatches. During the Crimean War the *Bittern* was attached to the squadron blockading De Castries Bay in the Gulf of Tartary. In September and October 1855 Vansittart destroyed a large number of pirate junks and the pirate stronghold of Sheipoo and rescued a party of British ladies from the pirates. He was thanked by the Chinese authorities, and received a testimonial and presentation from the British and foreign merchants. On 9 January 1856 he was promoted captain. In November 1859 he was appointed to the frigate *Ariadne*, which in 1860 went out to Canada and back escorting the battleship *Hero*, in which the prince of Wales visited the North American colonies. The *Ariadne* then returned to the North American station for a full commission. In September 1864 Vansittart commissioned the new ironclad *Achilles* for the channel squadron, and remained in command of her for four years. He was made a CB in March 1867 and was awarded a good service pension in November 1869. In September 1871 he commissioned another new ironclad, the *Sultan*, for the channel squadron, in which he was senior captain, and continued in her until he retired, on 20 July 1873. He was promoted rear-admiral, retired, on 19 January 1874, and vice-admiral on 1 February 1879. He died at his home, Brierden, Selden Road, Worthing, on 19 October 1904.

Vansittart, a tall and strongly built man, was an outstanding ship-handler and noted for his opposition to higher authority. His selection for the prize commands of the *Ariadne*, the *Achilles*, and the *Sultan* reflected his standing in the service.

L. G. C. LAUGHTON, *rev.* ANDREW LAMBERT

Sources G. S. Graham, *The China station: war and diplomacy, 1830–1860* (1978) · R. A. Courtemanche, *No need of glory: the British navy in American waters, 1860–1864* (1977) · G. Ballard, *The black battlefleet* (1980) · *The Times* (20 Oct 1904) · O'Byrne, *Naval biog. dict.* · WWW · Kelly, *Handbk* (1891)
Wealth at death £19,076 5s. 6d.: probate, 29 Nov 1904, CGPLA Eng. & Wales

Vansittart, George Henry (1768–1824), army officer, born on 16 July 1768, was the eldest son of George Vansittart (1745–1825), of Bengal and Bisham Abbey, Berkshire, MP for Berkshire (1784–1812), and his wife, Sarah, daughter of the Revd Sir James Stonhouse, baronet, of Radley, Berkshire. Henry *Vansittart (1777–1843) was his younger brother. Henry Vansittart (1732–1770?) and Robert Vansittart (1728–1789) were his uncles. He was educated under Dr Warton at Winchester College, at a military academy at Strasbourg (when aged fifteen), and at Christ Church, Oxford, where he matriculated on 7 November 1785.

After obtaining a commission as ensign in the 19th foot on 18 October 1786, he was allowed a year's leave to study military science at Brunswick and attend the Prussian manoeuvres. He became lieutenant on 25 December 1787, exchanged to the 38th foot on 12 March 1788, and obtained a company in the 18th on 23 June 1790. He joined it at Gibraltar, went with it to Toulon in 1793 to support the anti-Jacobin Toulonnais, took part in the defence, and was one of the last men to leave. He became major in the New South Wales Corps on 20 November 1793, and lieutenant-colonel of the 95th rifles on 21 February 1794. He took part with it in the expedition to the Cape under Sir Alured Clarke in 1795. He was made colonel in the army on 26 January 1797; but the 95th was broken up in the course of that year, and for the next three years he was on half pay and in the Berkshire militia, which his uncle, Colonel Arthur Vansittart, had previously commanded.

On 10 April 1801 Vansittart became lieutenant-colonel of the 68th foot, went with it to the West Indies, and was present at the capture of St Lucia in June 1803. On 25 September he was promoted major-general, and served on the staff in England from 1804 to 1806, and in Ireland from 1806 to 1810, when he became lieutenant-general (25 July). While in command of the Oxford district he received the degree of DCL on 26 June 1805. He was made colonel of the 12th reserve battalion on 9 July 1803, and was transferred to the 1st garrison battalion on 25 February 1805. The colours of this battalion were afterwards presented to him, and later hung in the great hall in Bisham Abbey. He became general on 19 July 1821.

On 29 October 1818 Vansittart married Anna Maria, daughter and coheir of Thomas Copson of Sheppey Hall, Leicestershire. She survived him, with one son, George Henry (1823–1885); a second son, Augustus Arthur (1824–1882), was born posthumously. Vansittart died on 4 February 1824. E. M. LLOYD, rev. ROGER T. STEARN

Sources GM, 1st ser., 94/1 (1824) · J. Philippart, ed., The royal military calendar, 3rd edn, 5 vols. (1820) · Burke, Gen. GB · private information (1898) · A. J. Guy, ed., The road to Waterloo: the British army and the struggle against revolutionary and Napoleonic France, 1793–1815 (1990) · T. C. W. Blanning, The French revolutionary wars, 1787–1802 (1996) · M. Crook, Toulon in war and revolution (1991) · Foster, Alum. Oxon.

Vansittart [née Lowe], **Henrietta** (1833–1883), engineer, was probably born in Bermondsey, London, the eldest in the family of four daughters and two sons of James *Lowe (1796–1866), a smoke-jack maker and inventor, and his wife, Mary (d. 1872), the eldest daughter of George Barnes of Ewell, squire. Her education is unknown, although both parents had connections with the Seymours of Syon House. By 1852 James Lowe was reduced to poverty and Bermondsey had become a slum. On 25 July 1855 in the British embassy, Paris, Henrietta married Frederick Vansittart (d. 1902), a lieutenant of the 14th dragoons, the son of William Vansittart of the Shottesbrooke family of White Waltham. They had no children. He sold his commission in 1856 and bought 18 Clarges Street, London. Henrietta did not lose interest in her impecunious father and within two years she was with him aboard HMS Bullfinch for the trials of his new screw propeller. By 1859 she and Edward Bulwer-*Lytton (later first earl of Lytton) (1831–1891) were having a secret affair. In 1860 Benjamin Disraeli thought she had such a hold on Lytton that it was affecting his attendance at the house. The friendship lasted until 1871.

Following her father's death in October 1866 Vansittart carried on his pioneering work on the development of the screw propeller for steamships. In 1868 she obtained patent no. 2877 for the Lowe-Vansittart propeller. The Times of 24 September 1869 reported the Admiralty trials of the propeller when fitted to HMS Druid, and the part played by Vansittart even though she was a married woman. In 1871 the Lowe-Vansittart propeller was awarded a first-class diploma at the Kensington exhibition, and similar awards followed worldwide. Meanwhile it had been fitted to many warships and liners, including the Scandinavian and Lusitania.

Vansittart's obituary in the Journal of the London Association of Foreman Engineers and Draughtsmen recalled that 'she was a remarkable personage with a great knowledge of engineering matters and considerable versatility of talent', and:

> how cheery and thoughtful for the happiness of others she was … she was the only lady, it is believed, who ever wrote and read a scientific paper, illustrated by diagrams and drawings made by herself, before the members of a Scientific Institution.

This referred to a paper presented in 1876.

In September 1882 Vansittart visited the Tynemouth exhibition. She did not pay the £600 for renewal of her patent, and the day after it was due was ordered by magistrates to be detained in the county lunatic asylum at Coxlodge, Gosforth, near Newcastle upon Tyne, having been found wandering by the police. She died there on 8 February 1883 of acute mania and anthrax.

B. M. E. O'MAHONEY, rev.

Sources Journal of the London Association of Foreman Engineers and Draughtsmen (March 1883) · B. M. E. O'Mahoney, 'Britain's first woman engineer', Woman Engineer, 13/4 (April 1983) · H. Vansittart, letters to Edward Bulwer-Lytton, Herts. ALS, D/EK c25/136 · d. cert. · m. cert. · CGPLA Eng. & Wales (1883)

Wealth at death £821 2s. 8d.: probate, 3 Aug 1883, CGPLA Eng. & Wales

Vansittart, Henry (1732–1770?), East India Company servant and governor of Bengal, born on 3 June 1732 at his father's house in Ormond Street, London, was the third son of Arthur van Sittart (1692–1760) of Shottesbrooke, Berkshire, and his wife, Martha, who was the eldest daughter and coheir of Sir John Stonhouse of Radley, who had been comptroller of Queen Anne's household. Robert *Vansittart was his elder brother, and George, his younger brother, who also served in Bengal, was the father of General George Henry *Vansittart and Vice-Admiral Henry *Vansittart. It was this generation that began spelling the name as a single word. Merchants and traders, the family traced its origin to Siddard, a town in the province of Limburg in the Netherlands, but Henry's ancestors had moved to Julich and eventually to Danzig, and from there his grandfather Peter van Sittart went to London about 1670. Having made a fortune in trading with Russia, India, and the south seas, he became a governor of the Russia Company and a director of the East India Company. His son Arthur, Henry's father, was also involved in both of the trading companies, from which he made a large fortune. By then the family were living in Reading, where

Henry Vansittart (1732–1770?), by Sir Joshua Reynolds, c.1753–4

Henry probably attended the grammar school before going to Winchester College.

Early career In 1745 Vansittart was given an appointment by the East India Company as a writer at their establishment at Fort St David, Madras. Some accounts have suggested, without giving any details, that he was sent to India at thirteen by his father to get him out of England since he was a dissolute and unruly youth (*DNB*), but a writer was, in effect, an apprentice who copied letters and other documents under the direction of more senior officials, and not until 1751 was sixteen made the minimum age for such appointments in the company's service. They were sought after as an opportunity to make money, especially by families like the van Sittarts, with a long connection to the East India Company. When Vansittart arrived at Fort St David to begin his career as a writer, it was a subsidiary establishment of Fort St George, about 50 miles to the north, the company's headquarters in south India. It was close to Pondicherry, and when the rival French trading company the Compagnie des Indes Orientales attacked Fort St David in 1746–7, he took part in its successful defence. He also began the study of Persian, which was the formal language of communication with Mughal officials, and while English writers praised his skill, a Frenchman said no Indian could understand him (Woodruff, 1.116), which would not preclude a good reading knowledge. Robert Clive was another recently arrived young company servant at Fort St David, and he and Vansittart began a close friendship, although later they became opponents when the company was involved in party struggles in England. In 1749 Fort St George was captured by the French,

and Fort St David became the seat of the company's government in the Madras region until 1752, when it was returned to Fort St George. The move to Fort St David probably helped Vansittart's advancement, for in 1750 he was promoted to the grade of factor, or agent responsible for the sale and purchase of the company's goods in his area. At this time the company's servants were essentially private traders licensed by the company, not full-time civilian employees as was later the case. While serving its commercial needs, their positions gave servants the opportunity for political involvement, which, combined with the right to trade on their own account, and through deals of various kinds with Indian rulers and merchants, made it possible for even a young man like Vansittart to amass a considerable fortune very quickly. Although no exact details are known, he had made enough in five or six years to return to England from Madras in 1751.

Vansittart now enjoyed the pleasures of an eighteenth-century rake, if contemporary accounts are true, for he became a member, along with his two brothers Arthur and Robert, of Sir Francis Dashwood's Hell-Fire Club whose members were said to engage in parodies of the mass, sexual orgies, and political conspiracies. Vansittart had his portrait painted by William Hogarth in 1753 dressed as a monk, and was said to have brought a baboon from India, which he had dressed as a chaplain for the club. In addition to these pastimes Vansittart apparently gambled heavily and lost much of his money before returning to Fort St George in 1753.

While England and France were at peace, the French and English trading companies in India were engaged in local wars, and at the end of 1753 Dupleix, the great French commander in India, agreed to discuss peace. Vansittart was one of the two East India Company commissaries who met the French at Sadras during 21–6 January 1754, and, while the negotiations failed, the senior officials were impressed by Vansittart's skill. He became a junior merchant and then in 1756 a senior merchant, giving him more authority and more opportunities for private trade. He also became secretary, as well as Persian translator, to the secret committee, which consisted of the governor and four other members of his council and dealt with Indian rulers. In the following year he became a member of the council itself and 'searcher of the seagate', a position of profit and responsibility.

An important concern of the council and secret committee at the time was the company's relationship to the most powerful ruler in the region, the nawab of Arcot. While the commander of the company's armies in 1754 proposed deposing him and taking over his territories, the council hesitated, on the grounds that the company lacked experience to manage such a large territory. A similar situation was to face Vansittart a few years later in Bengal, with even more momentous consequences. Another major concern of the council was prompted by the outbreak of war between France and Britain in 1756, when Madras was attacked in February 1759 by the comte de Lally, the commandant of all the French possessions in

India. Vansittart became acting governor while the French were besieging Fort St George.

Contemporary accounts give little information about Vansittart's private life, but whatever his youthful indiscretions, after his return to Madras he appears to have become a respectable family man. On 1 June 1754 he married Emilia Morse (d. 1819), daughter of Nicolas Morse, the governor of Madras. They had two daughters, Emilia and Sophie, and five sons, Henry, Arthur, Robert, George, and Nicholas *Vansittart.

Governor of Bengal Robert Clive, now governor of Bengal, planned to return to England. He urged Laurence Sulivan, one of the most powerful figures in the company in London, to bring Vansittart from Madras to Bengal as governor as the best hope for maintaining the company's position there. Vansittart was appointed governor of Bengal by the company on 8 November 1759, but he did not arrive in Calcutta until July 1760, after the French threat to Madras had lessened. The language of the appointment letter—as president of the council and governor of Fort William and the company's settlements in Bengal, Bihar, and Orissa—sounds impressive, but the power and prestige with which the title resonates comes from a later time. Decisions were made by majority vote, and the majority of Vansittart's council were from the beginning opposed to him, partly as an outsider from Madras who, in their view, had usurped a place that by right of seniority belonged to them. However, the councils protests went unheeded as the directors supported Vansittart. The acting governor, John Zephaniah Holwell, felt especially aggrieved, but Vansittart in general accepted the plans he had made for dealing with the most pressing problem, relations with *Mir Jafar Ali Khan [see under Bengal, nawabs of], the nawab of Bengal, and he afterwards defended Vansittart when he was attacked by his enemies in London.

Vansittart arrived in Bengal to find not only a hostile council, but, as he put it, 'the treasury was so low, and our resources so much drained, that we were obliged to put an entire stop to our investment [the goods that were purchased to be exported to Europe] and it was with the utmost difficulty the current expenses of the settlement could be provided for' (Vansittart, 1.14). His explanation for this situation, a few years after Clive had seemed to deliver the wealth of Bengal to the company, centred on the treaty that had been made with Mir Jafar to overthrow the nawab of Bengal and give the throne to him. By the treaty the company was to raise an army, which would be under its complete control but paid for by the nawab and at his service when required. The nawab had failed to provide the promised money, and Vansittart was faced with a mutinous army that had not been paid for months. The nawab was losing control of his own administration and, so far from being able to pay the arrears, asked Vansittart for loans. To add to his difficulties, no money had been sent from London, as the directors had assumed that the money from the nawab would pay for the investment and, in addition, Madras and Bombay had been told that they would have to depend on Bengal for their needs. From his

recent experience he knew how much Madras needed supplies because of the war with the French for the control of the Carnatic, which, he pointed out, was 'an interesting object for the English nation' but a very expensive one for the company. Since there was no hope of getting money directly from the nawab, he soon concluded that the only solution was to get him to cede outright large territories to the company, from which it could collect the taxes. When Vansittart went to see him in October 1760, it became clear that the nawab was willing to see himself and his state ruined rather than put 'more power and more resources of money in our hands' (ibid., 1.15). Vansittart was convinced that the only course of action left open, if he was to save the company's foothold in Bengal, was the overthrow of Mir Jafar in favour of his son-in-law *Mir Kasim [see under Bengal, nawabs of], who, quite apart from the company, was already intriguing against him. Vansittart tried to save the nawab's reputation by suggesting that he could retain his title, with Mir Kasim as his deputy. However, he refused this offer, and turned over all power to Mir Kasim and went to live in Calcutta. Mir Kasim had already signed a treaty on 27 September 1760 giving the company what Vansittart wanted: full control of the three rich districts of Burdwan, Midnapore, and Chittagong. Often spoken of as a creature of Vansittart and the British, it is probable that Mir Kasim would have overthrown the nawab without their intrusion and without the costs that accrued from Vansittart's arrangement.

Vansittart always referred in his writings to these events as 'the revolution', and believed that people were in general pleased with it, as evidenced by the fact that there had been no resistance, and 'not a drop of blood spilt' (Vansittart, 1.53). When the directors heard what had happened, they were also pleased; they told the council in Calcutta that they realized the revolution was principally due to Vansittart and 'returned him thanks for his great services' (ibid., 2.177). Warren Hastings was an active participant in bringing about the changes, and he remained Vansittart's most loyal supporter in the council and among the senior officials in charge of the company's factories. Almost immediately challenges to Vansittart's authority came from these officials, especially those at Patna.

Patna, one of the most important inland posts, became the focus of Vansittart's troubles when the company's military officers there, Lieutenant-Colonel Eyre Coote and Major John Carnac, supported Ramnarian, the deputy governor of the region appointed by the previous nawab, in his refusal to submit his accounts to Mir Kasim. Their stand contravened the orders of Vansittart, who was anxious to remain on good terms with the nawab. Coote and Carnac continued to defy him and insulted the nawab, so Vansittart recalled them, leaving Ramnarian at the mercy of Mir Kasim, who had him put to death. This led to the charge then and later that Vansittart had sacrificed a friend of the British in order to placate and strengthen the nawab, instead of weakening him, which would have been in the company's interest.

The most serious dispute involving Vansittart, the

nawab, the company's servants, and London developed over the private inland trade of the company's servants. The company itself had been free from paying duties on goods they were exporting through the use of permits, or *dastaks*, granted to them by the Mughal authorities. After the battle of Plassey the private merchants began to use them for internal as well as external trade. Furthermore, the British traders employed Indian agents, *gomastahs*, who oppressed the Indian merchants by forcing them to sell goods at low prices. Mir Kasim realized that this misuse of the permits was depriving him of duties as well as ruining the local traders, and that the company's agents, both British and Indian, were setting up what amounted to their own system of law and order. He appealed to Vansittart to put a stop to what in 1758 the directors in London had called the 'scandalous prostitution' of the permits, and Vansittart saw the justice of the nawab's complaints. Along with Hastings he went to negotiate with the nawab at his capital, and they reached what seemed to him a fair settlement: the company's servants could participate in the inland trade on the payment of a 9 per cent duty, which was much less than Indian traders paid. However, when Vansittart reported this settlement early in 1763, the council, with its hostile majority, rejected it out of hand as one more concession by the governor to the nawab. Two members of the council accused Vansittart of having made a private arrangement with the nawab to protect his own private trade, but they could produce no evidence. When the nawab learned that Vansittart's agreement with him had been rejected by the council, he took the dramatic step of removing all duties on trade, for Indians as well as for the British. The council were enraged and Vansittart's plea that Britons could compete in a system of free trade with Indians and other foreigners was disregarded. The majority argued that by remitting the duties the nawab had declared war on the company, and the army should be prepared to march to force the nawab to restore the duties or to face the consequences of being deposed.

The nawab prepared for war, which began after the company's agent at Patna, William Ellis, one of Vansittart's bitterest enemies, attacked the nawab's forces in June 1763. When Ellis and the other Europeans with him were captured and put to death, the council insisted that war was inevitable. Vansittart was against war, as he felt that Mir Kasim had been driven to desperation by the actions of Ellis, and he also opposed the council's plans to replace Mir Kasim with the old nawab, Mir Jafar, who would obviously be a puppet of the council majority. Vansittart and Hastings were attacked in the council as profiting from their relationship with Mir Kasim, a murderer of Britons, but being powerless before the majority, and unwilling to show publicly the extent of the divisions, Vansittart signed the declaration of war on 7 July 1763. The conflict dragged on for over a year until Mir Kasim's defeat, along with his allies the nawab of Oudh and the Mughal emperor Shah Alam, at Buxar on 23 October 1764, perhaps the most important of all British military victories in India as it gave the company effective territorial control of vast areas of Bengal and Bihar.

This, however, was no triumph for Vansittart, who had long since wearied of India. Frustrated by the opposition in the council, and suffering from what may have been malaria, he had planned to resign in December 1763, but the majority of the council surprisingly urged him to stay until a successor could be appointed. He agreed to do so, not leaving until December 1764.

Return to England Back in England Vansittart became involved in the complex and shifting politics of the proprietors and directors of the East India Company, where Robert Clive, once his chief supporter but now estranged because of Vansittart's deposing of Mir Jafar, vied with Laurence Sulivan for influence in the company and parliament. Vansittart sided with Sulivan in these contests. Clive's supporters, especially Luke Scrafton, assailed his record and his personal character in speeches, newspaper articles, and books, which were answered with equal venom by Vansittart's friends. The most interesting production of the literary war, however, came from Vansittart himself. Before he had left Bengal, he had sent copies of relevant documents to his friends in London, published as *Original Papers Relative to the Disturbances in Bengal*, which he used as the basis for his remarkable book *A Narrative of the Transaction in Bengal from 1760 to 1764*, which, while defending his own policies and vindicating his character, provided details of the often very cogent counter-arguments of his opponents as well as numerous letters from the nawabs of Bengal.

Vansittart was elected to parliament for the borough of Reading on 16 March 1768, using his connections to further his own and his friends' interests in the company and in parliament. His main concerns at this time seem to have been financial. How much money he had actually made in India is not known, but his brother George later remarked that one needed £50,000 to retire, and he probably had made at least that much. His enemies accused him, in fact, of 'trying to encircle the general trade of Bengal under his own direction', but it was assumed that governors of Bengal would be very wealthy men, for, without apology, 'they were in India to get rich' (Marshall, *East Indian Fortunes*, 217, 115, 3). He was able to buy an estate and a house in Berkshire, but he had difficulty in transferring his Indian money back to Britain. Remitting money from India, because of the company's rules, was often harder than making it, and Vansittart thought of returning to India to retrieve what he could of his fortune. His situation was made worse by heavy losses that he had sustained as a result of his involvement in the company's politics in London.

In 1769 elections took place for the directors of the governing body of the East India Company. Since voting rights depended on stock ownership, Vansittart, in alliance with Laurence Sulivan, organized a complex system of borrowing money to buy stock. However, an unexpected financial crisis ruined many speculators in the company's stocks, with Vansittart among those hardest hit. Hope for his salvation came with news of the disastrous state of the company's affairs in India. The crisis prompted the decision to send out three commissioners with power to override the councils which had given such trouble to Vansittart and other governors. It was assumed that there would be opportunity of great financial gain for the commissioners, and Vansittart's friends, hoping that he would be saved from further ruin, got him appointed. He was balanced by an opponent, Luke Scrafton, and by Francis Forde, regarded as somewhat neutral in the company's internal politics, who had served with Vansittart in Madras. The commissioners sailed in September 1769, and were in Cape Town on 27 December, but the ship apparently foundered some time later, for it was never heard of again. How desperately Vansittart needed money was shown when his executors found he had virtually no resources in England, except the properties in Berkshire and Greenwich.

It was an anticlimactic end for someone who, ten years before, Clive and other well-wishers had thought best suited to be governor of Bengal and to secure it for Britain. Historians of British India, looking back on the building of an empire, have not, however, dealt kindly with his reputation, measuring him against the great conquerors—Clive, Hastings, and Wellesley. Thus H. H. Dodwell, one of the most influential, summarized his career by saying that he proved 'lamentably deficient in the art of government', for 'he could neither judge men, nor manage them, nor read the future' (Dodwell, 215–16). That Vansittart did not look at mid-eighteenth-century India and see it as a field for fulfilling Britain's imperial destiny is perfectly true. None the less what emerges from the record is a perceptive, humane intelligence, aware that the complex political organizations of the Mughals and their successor states were undergoing enormous changes, but that it was best to wait and try to understand what was happening and why. Perhaps this is what he was implying when he once wrote to Hastings that 'I love peace and quietness and have learnt to make allowances for the different tempers and passions of men' (Vansittart, 2.175).

AINSLIE T. EMBREE

Sources DNB · biographical series, 1702–1948, BL OIOC · personal records, BL OIOC, O/6 · biographical index, BL OIOC · BL OIOC, Home misc., 92, 196/6, 95/3, 100/12, 191/15, 204 · dispatches to Bengal, 1760–64, BL OIOC · H. Vansittart, *A narrative of the transactions in Bengal from 1760–1764*, ed. A. C. Banerjee (1976) · P. J. Marshall, *East Indian fortunes: the British in Bengal in the eighteenth century* (1976) · L. S. Sutherland, *The East India Company in eighteenth century politics* (1952) · H. H. Dodwell, *Dupleix and Clive: the beginning of empire* (1920) · D. McCormick, *The Hell-Fire Club* (1958) · G. H. Khan, *Seir Mutaqherin* (1789) · K. K. Datta and others, eds., *Fort William–India House correspondence*, 3 (1968) · H. D. Love, *Vestiges of old Madras, 1640–1800*, 4 vols. (1913) · L. Scrafton, *Observations on Mr. Vansittart's 'Narrative'* (1767) · P. J. Marshall, *Bengal—the British bridgehead: eastern India, 1740–1828* (1987), 2/2 of The new Cambridge history of India, ed. G. Johnson and others · J. Z. Howell, *A defence of Mr. Vansittart's conduct* (1774) · P. Woodruff [P. Mason], *The men who ruled India*, pbk edn (1963)

Archives BL, register of papers relating to English and Dutch East Indies, Add. MS 34123 | BL, narrative of transactions in Bengal, letters to Warren Hastings, Add. MSS 29211, 29132 · BL OIOC,

corresp. with John Carnac, MS Eur. F 128 · Bodl. Oxf., corresp. with Laurence Sulivan · Surrey HC, letters to John Frederick

Likenesses J. Reynolds, oils, c.1753–1754, FM Cam. [*see illus.*] · Dance, painting, 1768; in possession of Lord Haldon in 1899 · S. W. Reynolds, mezzotint, pubd 1822 (after J. Reynolds), BM, NPG · Hogarth, painting; at Shottesbrooke, Berkshire, in 1899

Wealth at death estate near Reading; house in Greenwich: Marshall, *East India fortunes*

Vansittart, Henry (1777–1843), naval officer, the fifth son of George Vansittart (1745–1825) of Bisham Abbey, Berkshire, and his wife, Sarah, the daughter of the Revd Sir James Stonhouse, bt, was born in George Street, Hanover Square, London, on 17 April 1777. George Henry *Vansittart was his elder brother, Henry Vansittart, governor of Bengal, was his uncle, and Nicholas Vansittart, first Baron Bexley, was his first cousin. Having been entered on the books of the guardship *Scipio* in the Medway in October 1788, he was afterwards nominally in the guardship *Boyne* in the Thames, and probably actually served in the *Pegasus* on the Newfoundland station in 1791. In 1792 he was in the *Hannibal*, stationed at Plymouth, and in 1793 went out to the Mediterranean in the *Princess Royal*, the flagship of Rear-Admiral Goodall. During the siege of Toulon by the republican army he was severely wounded. After the evacuation he was moved into the frigate *L'Aigle*, with Captain Samuel Hood, served at the siege of Calvi, and was in October 1794 moved into the *Victory*, in which he returned to England. On 21 February 1795 he was promoted lieutenant of the *Stately* (64 guns), in which he was present at the capture of the Cape of Good Hope and of the Dutch squadron in Saldanha Bay. He was then moved into the *Monarch*, the flagship of Rear-Admiral George Elphinstone (later Viscount Keith), and returned in her to England.

Vansittart was next appointed to the *Queen Charlotte*, Keith's flagship in the channel, and on 30 May 1798 was promoted commander of the sloop *Hermes*. From her he was moved to the *Bonetta*, which he took out to Jamaica, and on 13 February 1801 he was posted to the *Abergavenny* (54 guns), stationed at Port Royal. In July he returned to England in the *Thunderer* (74 guns). After a few months on half pay he was appointed, in April 1802, to the frigate *Magicienne*, from which, in January 1803, he was moved to the *Fortunée* (36 guns). He remained commander of this ship for upwards of nine years, in the North Sea, off Boulogne, in the channel, in the West Indies, and in the Mediterranean, mostly cruising and convoying. He married, in 1809, Mary Charity (d. 1834), the daughter of the Revd John Pennefather, with whom he had five children, among them Edward Westby *Vansittart. From August 1812 to March 1814 he was on the *Clarence* (74 guns). With the exception of a few months in 1801–2 he had served continuously from 1791. He became rear-admiral on 22 July 1830 and vice-admiral on 23 November 1841. He died on 21 March 1843 at his seat, Eastwood, Woodstock, Canada.

J. K. LAUGHTON, rev. ANDREW LAMBERT

Sources D. Syrett and R. L. DiNardo, *The commissioned sea officers of the Royal Navy, 1660–1815*, rev. edn, Occasional Publications of the Navy RS, 1 (1994) · *GM*, 2nd ser., 20 (1843), 110 · O'Byrne, *Naval biog. dict.* · Burke, *Gen. GB* (1898)

Likenesses M. Gauci, lithograph (after C. R. Bone), BM

Vansittart, Nicholas, first Baron Bexley (1766–1851), politician, was born on 29 April 1766 in Old Burlington Street, London, the fifth and youngest son of Henry *Vansittart (1732–1770?), governor of Bengal, and his wife, Emilia (d. 1819), daughter of Nicholas Morse, governor of Madras. In 1770, after the loss of his father at sea, Nicholas was placed under the guardianship of his uncles Sir Robert Palk and Colonel Arthur Vansittart of Shottesbrooke. He was educated at Mr Gilpin's school at Cheam in Surrey, and at Christ Church, Oxford, where he matriculated on 29 March 1784 and graduated BA in 1787 and MA in 1791. He received the honorary degree of DCL on 16 June 1814. He became a student of Lincoln's Inn on 21 April 1788, was called to the bar on 26 May 1791, and became a bencher of Lincoln's Inn on 12 November 1812.

Conservative politician In the 1790s Vansittart took three steps which were greatly to help him in his pursuit of a political career. First, as a newly qualified barrister he attended the Crown and Rolls debating society in Chancery Lane, although throughout his life his voice remained feeble and indistinct. Second, between 1793 and 1796 he wrote four pamphlets supportive of the younger Pitt's fiscal and foreign policies, which gave him something of a financial reputation. Third, he made a number of useful political contacts by serving, from 1797, in the fashionable City of London and Westminster light horse volunteers 'which positively bristled with MPs and future ministers of the Crown' (Gash, 26). He was returned as MP for Hastings on 25 May 1796, and subsequently represented Old Sarum (1808–12), East Grinstead (1812), and the Treasury borough of Harwich from 1812 until his elevation to the peerage in 1823. Such closed boroughs in the unreformed parliament suited Vansittart as he did not have to rely upon his mediocre skills as a public speaker to get himself elected and once elected he did not need to pay much, if any, attention to constituency affairs.

Politically Vansittart attached himself to Henry Addington, his cousin and another of Mr Gilpin's alumni. He was rewarded in February 1801 with the task of leading a mission on behalf of the Addington administration to Copenhagen to persuade the Danes to leave Tsar Paul's Northern League and abandon the policy of armed neutrality. When it became clear that the Danes were not amenable to persuasion, however, Vansittart reported to Addington that nothing remained but to strike a speedy and severe blow, and this was duly administered by Nelson at the battle of Copenhagen on 2 April 1801.

In March Vansittart had been appointed joint secretary of the Treasury by Addington and he held this office until the ministry's resignation on 26 April 1804. He returned to office in January 1805 as secretary for Ireland and a privy councillor, despite Pitt's reservations regarding Catholic reaction to the appointment and doubts regarding Vansittart's debating ability. These obstacles were overcome thanks to the good offices of the duke of Cumberland, Addington's insistence that office be found for his closest supporters as a condition of his entering the ministry (as Lord Sidmouth and lord president of the council), and Bragge-Bathurst's declining the post. Sidmouth left

Nicholas Vansittart, first Baron Bexley (1766–1851), by T. A. Dean, pubd 1838 (after Sir Thomas Lawrence, c.1824)

the administration in July but Vansittart did not follow his patron's example until September. His undistinguished tenure of office had, however, been marred by his finding himself at odds with his lord lieutenant, Lord Hardwicke.

Vansittart returned to the secretaryship to the Treasury when the Sidmouth connection entered Grenville's 'ministry of all the talents' in January 1806, only to resign with Sidmouth in March 1807 shortly before the administration was turned out. He played no part in Portland's ministry although his growing reputation as a financier and parliamentarian was confirmed by his carrying unopposed thirty-eight resolutions during debate on the resumption of cash payments (20 June 1809).

Vansittart married the Hon. Catherine Isabella (1778–1810), second daughter of William *Eden, first Baron Auckland, on 22 July 1806. Such was his wife's ill health, however, that he temporarily withdrew from public life in the spring of 1809 in order to accompany her on rest cures at Malvern and Torquay. The deterioration in his wife's health explains his declining Perceval's offer of the exchequer on 13 October, though he may well also have been influenced in his decision by the fact that Sidmouth was offered no place and he did not wish to desert his friend, or did not feel that it was politic to be seen to be deserting his patron. He was at least able to be at his wife's side when she died at Torquay on 10 August 1810 aged only thirty-two.

On 24 April 1811, in response to the report of the bullion committee and Francis Horner's call for the resumption of cash payments within two years, Vansittart resumed his active political career by tabling his own anti-bullionist resolutions. He played a leading role in the debates which culminated in defeat of Horner's proposal on 9 May and thus allowed the Perceval administration to pursue its vigorous prosecution of the war effort.

Chancellor of the exchequer Sidmouth entered Perceval's government as lord president of council in April 1812 but failed to secure the exchequer for Vansittart who, on reflection, preferred to stay out of office rather than take the proffered post of a junior lordship of the Treasury. In the event, however, Vansittart returned to office on 20 May as the replacement of the assassinated prime minister in his role as chancellor of the exchequer.

Few chancellors can have been faced with a more daunting set of circumstances on entering office. Massive population growth (up from 10.5 million in 1801 to 12 million in 1811) both fuelled Malthusian fears of famine and helped account for the quadrupling of poor rates between 1775 and 1817. Moreover, the war waged with France since 1793 (with only the fourteen-month respite brought about by the peace of Amiens in 1802) was equally unprecedented and deleterious in its impact, with the national debt increasing from £238 million in 1793 to £902 million in 1816. As if war with France was not bad enough, the attempt to break the continental system by restricting the scope for neutrals to trade with Napoleonic Europe not only induced recession at home but pushed the United States into declaring war on Great Britain in the very month of Vansittart's first budget. Last but not least, the new chancellor was aware that even if these wars could be brought to a victorious conclusion their close would pose questions of comparable magnitude and complexity in the shape of managing the transition from a wartime to a peacetime economy and accommodating the demand for the immediate relief of wartime taxation. Such a political and economic context would have tested the most adroit chancellor and certainly proved more than a match for Vansittart, notwithstanding his links with Rothschilds and Barings, and the financial advice he received from the Revd Henry Beeke.

Vansittart's first budget, of June 1812, was in reality Perceval's last (with the qualification that Vansittart preferred to add to existing taxes on male servants, carriages, horses, and dogs, than tax private brewing establishments) and he only set his own mark on the national finances with his 'new plan of finance' of March 1813, which in practice involved raising loans for the sinking fund and increasing the customs by 25 per cent.

Vansittart acted as Castlereagh's deputy in the Commons while the foreign secretary and leader of the house attended the negotiations for the first treaty of Paris from April to May 1814. He was, however, both politically and financially ill-equipped to appease the clamour both inside and outside parliament for immediate peacetime economy and relief from taxation. Napoleon's escape from Elba obliged him to defer premature speculation regarding alternatives to the income tax and impose unprecedentedly high taxation in his budget of 14 June 1815.

The victory at Waterloo (four days later) increased the pressures on the exchequer to relax its demands on the public but Vansittart's room for manoeuvre was severely constrained by the size of the national debt (the interest payments on which amounted to roughly 80 per cent of government expenditure) while the transition to peacetime accentuated, where it did not create, economic difficulties which included recession, rising unemployment, and increasing local taxation.

Matters were made worse by the government's loss of about a quarter of its revenue in 1816, following its failure to retain the income tax and decision not to renew the malt tax, as this delayed both the resumption of cash payments and pursuit of the policy of freeing trade. Indeed, it was not until 1819 that a phased return to the gold standard was approved, and in the meantime Vansittart had been forced to have recourse to both the money market and increased indirect taxation.

If Vansittart was not the author of the government's financial difficulties he can certainly be accused of playing its hand badly in attempting to retain the income tax in 1816. First, by announcing on 9 February that discontinuation of the tax was dependent on ratification of the treaty of Ghent by the American senate (thereby formally ending the Anglo-American War of 1812–14), the government appeared to vindicate the popular view that it was only a wartime levy. Second, the substantial concessions proposed by the exchequer, which included lowering the standard rate from 2s. to 1s. in the pound so as to relinquish £7,500,000 of revenue per annum, were announced too late to have any chance of countering the arguments of those favouring repeal. Third, the government failed to make the most of those arguments in favour of the tax which MPs might have found most persuasive, such as the claim that it offered the prospect of deriving a steady and growing revenue from trade at a time when it appeared to be better able to make a contribution to the national coffers than the landed interest. The net result was that the income tax was lost by thirty-seven votes and the restoration of sound national finances was delayed by at least three years.

1819 was marked not only by the reimposition of the malt tax but also by the first of a series of raids on the sinking fund which hastened the depreciation in Vansittart's own stock and which led to Lady Bathurst describing him as 'a millstone about their necks' who was not got rid of by his colleagues because 'they had scruples about telling him he was inefficient' (*Greville Memoirs*, 72). Arbuthnot wrote to Castlereagh that Vansittart was 'abused, ridiculed & deserted by everybody', it being

> declared of him by all parties & all description of men, that altho' in private life a good man, there is no belief to be attached to a word he says, as he one day declares in the House that no funding will be required, & the next day it is generally known that there must be a great funding.

In the City 'he has fallen lower than could be imagined' with the 'Bank most loud against him' (*Correspondence of Charles Arbuthnot*, 16–17). The low esteem in which Vansittart was generally now held in the house was demonstrated on 14 June 1821 when a motion for the repeal of the tax on horses employed in agriculture was carried against him. Confidence in his abilities slumped still further when his 1822 scheme to relieve some of the immediate burden of service pensions fell foul of the market place.

However, it would be misleading to attribute Vansittart's retention of office so long purely to the wish of his cabinet colleagues not to hurt his feelings. Other, less altruistic, calculations were involved. Thus when it was suggested in March 1821 that the ministry should be strengthened in the Commons (among other changes) by Peel taking the exchequer and Vansittart moving to the Board of Control, Castlereagh effectively scotched the idea by objecting that such a change might undermine his own position as leader of the House of Commons. His argument that 'Mr. Peel had never done any thing to entitle him to so high a place as the one proposed' (*Journal of Mrs Arbuthnot*, 1.82) ironically echoed George Rose's 1809 comment on the suggestion that Vansittart should receive the exchequer, that it was 'much more than he is worth, either from talents or experience' (Gray, 361).

The latter judgement seemed to be borne out by events as Vansittart appeared incapable of imposing his will as chancellor. He argued in vain for the retention of the income tax in 1816 and his stewardship was marked by no innovations of note: the 1819 decision to embark on a phased return to the gold standard, for example, being due to the deliberations of the select committee on the currency chaired by Peel rather than to the chancellor himself.

Certainly Vansittart's chancellorship was insufficiently distinguished to ensure his continued retention of that office when the question of strengthening the administration by readmitting Canning was resumed following Londonderry's suicide in 1822. George Canning had entertained a low opinion of Vansittart from the very outset of Liverpool's premiership, writing to Arbuthnot on 18 July 1812 that the disputed lead in the Commons between Castlereagh and himself might be put 'in abeyance ... if continuing nominally with the Chancp. of the Ex. in a third hand—even in Van's' (*Correspondence of Charles Arbuthnot*, 8). By 1822 Canning's lieutenant, Huskisson (who had always hated Vansittart's lack of 'system' and hand-to-mouth financial expedients), was referring privately to the chancellor as 'the real **blot** and **sin** of the Government' and his confidant, Croker, could only pay the backhanded compliment of asserting that Vansittart 'though not a very creditable Chancellor of the Exchequer, was a very useful one' given his facility, over the previous year, of giving up his principles and eating his words (*Croker Papers*, 1.229). However, an apparently inexhaustible capacity to consume humble pie, albeit with seemingly genuine humility, is no qualification for high office and Vansittart was persuaded in December 1822 to make way at the exchequer for Robinson in return for a peerage, a pension of £3000 per annum, and Bragge-Bathurst's place in the cabinet as chancellor of the duchy of Lancaster.

Evangelical peer George IV was prepared to confer the peerage on Vansittart not only out of a sense of the value of his past services but also out of the high estimation in which he held his private character. Vansittart was not only a lifelong engager in evangelical good works but exuded 'perpetual good nature', and by this stage his 'white hairs and unworldly gentleness' and the 'primitive simplicity of his manner' had resulted in his acquiring 'the sort of veneration with which men are accustomed to regard a saintly priest' (*The Times*, 12 Feb 1851, 5). He was created Baron Bexley of Bexley in Kent on 1 March 1823 and proceeded to play a mostly ornamental role in the Lords. Canning was engaged in an unsuccessful intrigue to exclude him from office shortly before the close of Liverpool's premiership but found it convenient to court him when he succeeded Liverpool as premier in 1827 (Aspinall, 198).

Although having initially indicated a willingness to continue in office, Bexley was among the 'protestant' tories led by the duke of Wellington who resigned when the king invited Canning to succeed Lord Liverpool as prime minister. However, he was ultimately persuaded to withdraw his resignation and retain his position thanks to the king's personal entreaty, the example of the duke of Clarence in taking office (as lord high admiral), and Canning's reassurances that he would balance 'protestants' and 'Catholics' in his administration, although at the time Bexley represented the sole survivor of the 'protestant' party from Liverpool's cabinet. These political somersaults were thus bound to give the impression in ultra circles that Bexley was more concerned to cling to office than to cleave to principle. Thus Lord Howard de Walden characterized him as 'a little hypocritical evangelical sneaking fox' (Aspinall, 129): an impression which was no doubt strengthened by the king's outburst that he would make Bexley his prime minister when Goderich presented him with difficulties in forming an administration in September 1827 (*Journal of Mrs Arbuthnot*, 2.141).

Not surprisingly Bexley lost office when the king turned to Wellington to form an administration in January 1828 and he thereafter devoted himself primarily to charitable and religious works including support for King's College, London, the Greenwich Hospital (of which he was a director), the port of Harwich (of which he was a high steward), the British and Foreign Bible Mission (of which he was the sometime president), and the Church Missionary and Prayer Book and Homily societies.

Bexley died on 8 February 1851 at his country residence, Foot's Cray, Kent. His peerage became extinct. His political career was long and distinguished in terms of his tenure of office. It would, however, be difficult to deny that he was promoted above his abilities and that more than most chancellors he was buffeted by the economy he sought to control, and deserves as little credit for the favourable legacy he bestowed on his successor (a surplus revenue of £7,000,000 per annum) as he deserves blame for the unfavourable legacy which he himself inherited. He owed his initial success in politics largely to his Sidmouthite connections. His chancellorship proved him to be no better at arithmetic than he was at rhetoric. He lasted as long as he did as chancellor because Liverpool's affection for him outlived his confidence in his abilities and because Castlereagh regarded him, unlike Canning, as no threat to his leadership of the Commons. Ironically, Vansittart, as Bexley, enjoyed an extended lease of his post-exchequer political life at the hands of his long-standing critic Canning, precisely because he had by this time achieved iconic status as a tame 'protestant' veteran of Liverpool's administration.

Historians generally take the view of most of Vansittart's contemporaries in seeing him as a man of unexceptional abilities who unsurprisingly experienced considerable difficulties in holding an office of first-rate importance in a period of national crisis. Such a view reinforces the indisputable fact that Vansittart's greatest political talent, and one not to be sneered at, was that for survival.   JOHN PLOWRIGHT

Sources DNB · The Times (12 Feb 1851) · 'Vansittart, Nicholas', HoP, Commons · N. Gash, Lord Liverpool (1984) · The Greville memoirs, 1814–1860, ed. L. Strachey and R. Fulford, 8 vols. (1938) · The correspondence of Charles Arbuthnot, ed. A. Aspinall, CS, 3rd ser., 65 (1941) · The journal of Mrs Arbuthnot, 1820–1832, ed. F. Bamford and the duke of Wellington [G. Wellesley], 2 vols. (1950) · The Croker papers: the correspondence and diaries of ... John Wilson Croker, ed. L. J. Jennings, 1 (1884) · A. Aspinall, ed., The formation of Canning's ministry, February to August 1827, CS, 3rd ser., 59 (1937) · D. Gray, Spencer Perceval: the evangelical prime minister, 1762–1812 (1963) · B. Hilton, Corn, cash, commerce: the economic policies of the tory governments, 1815–1830 (1977)
Archives BL, corresp. and papers, Add. MSS 31229–31237 · LPL, corresp. | Bexley Local Studies and Archive Centre, Bexley Heath, letters to John Charles Herries · BL, letters to the Comte d'Antraigues, Add. MS 57537 · BL, letters to Lord Auckland, Add. MSS 34456–34461 passim · BL, corresp. with Lord Grenville, Add. MS 58960 · BL, corresp. with Lord Hardwicke, Add. MSS 35560–35767 · BL, corresp. with John Charles Herries, Add. MS 57403 · BL, corresp. with first and second earls of Liverpool, Add. MSS 38260–38574 passim · BL, corresp. with Sir Robert Peel, Add. MSS 40221–40862 · Devon RO, corresp. with Lord Sidmouth · PRO NIre., corresp. with Lord Castlereagh, D3030
Likenesses W. Owen, oils, 1815; at Christ Church Oxf. in 1899 · T. Lawrence, oils, c.1824; at Kirkleatham Hall, Yorkshire, in 1899 · C. Turner, mezzotint, pubd 1836 (after J. Rand), BM, NPG · T. A. Dean, stipple, pubd 1838 (after T. Lawrence, c.1824), BM, NPG [see illus.] · G. M. Zornlin, pencil drawing, 1848, NPG · T. A. Dean, stipple (after T. Lawrence, c.1824), BM, NPG; repro. in Jerdan, National portrait gallery of illustrious and eminent personages (1831) · J. Doyle, group caricature, pen over pencil (A small tea party of superannuated politicians), BM · W. Owen, oils; at Guildhall, Harwich, Essex, in 1899 · Scriven, engraving (after P. Stephanoff) · P. Stephanoff, watercolour study (for Coronation of George IV), V&A

Vansittart, Robert (1728–1789), jurist, was born on 28 December 1728 at Great Ormond Street, London, the second son of Arthur van Sittart (1691–1760), merchant, of Shottesbrooke, Berkshire, and his wife, Martha, eldest daughter of Sir John Stonhouse, baronet, of Radley, Berkshire, comptroller of the household to Queen Anne. Henry *Vansittart (1732–1770?) governor of Bengal, was his younger brother.

Vansittart was educated at Reading School and at Winchester College. He matriculated from Trinity College, Oxford, on 3 April 1745, was elected a fellow of All Souls

College in 1748, and graduated BCL in 1751 and DCL in 1757. In 1753 he was called to the bar by the society of the Inner Temple. On 17 May 1760 he was nominated high steward of Monmouth, in 1763 recorder of Maidenhead, in 1764 recorder of Newbury, and in 1770 recorder of Windsor. In 1767 he was appointed by the crown regius professor of civil law in the University of Oxford, a post he held until his death. For some years before his appointment he performed the duties of public orator for his predecessor, Robert Jenner.

Vansittart was a close friend of the painters George Knapton and William Hogarth, as well as of the poets Paul Whitehead and William Cowper. In Italy he met Goethe, who named a character in one of his comedies after him. Through the classical scholar Joseph Warton, Vansittart became a friend of Dr Johnson, who regarded him with much affection, and who was invited to visit India with him by his brother Henry. In 1759, in a festive moment, Dr Johnson, while on a visit to Oxford, proposed that they should scale the walls of All Souls together; but Vansittart declined. On another occasion, while Vansittart was edifying Boswell with a lengthy story about a flea, Johnson burst in with 'It is a pity, sir, that you have not seen a lion; for a flea has taken you such a time that a lion must have served you for a twelve-month' (Boswell, Life, 2.194).

Vansittart, who was elected a fellow of the Society of Antiquaries on 4 June 1767, undertook antiquarian pursuits in his spare time. In the year of his election he edited *Certain Ancient Tracts Concerning the Management of Landed Property*, which consisted of reprints of Gentian Hervet's translation *Xenophon's Treatise of the Householde* (1534), and Sir Anthony Fitzherbert's *Boke of Husbandry* (1534) and *Surveyinge* (1539).

Vansittart was a man of licentious and debauched habits and, like his brother Henry, was a member of the 'Franciscans of Medmenham', otherwise known as the 'Hell-Fire Club'. To this society he presented with great pomp a baboon sent from India by Henry, to which Sir Francis Dashwood was accustomed to administer the eucharist at their meetings. As a young man, he was painted by Hogarth wearing a kerchief in the colours of the 'Franciscans', wound in turban fashion over the head, embroidered with the motto 'Love and Friendship'. On 23 August 1773 Mrs Thrale described Vansittart to Johnson as 'very ill and very wild, I fancy he wants a governess' (Redford, 2.113).

Vansittart died at Oxford, unmarried, on 31 January 1789, and was buried in a vault in the chapel of All Souls College. He was tall and very thin, and the members of the Oxford bar gave the name of Counsellor Van to a sharp-pointed rock on the River Wye from a fancied resemblance (Bloomfield, 23).

E. I. CARLYLE, rev. ROBERT BROWN

Sources private information (1899) · Boswell, Life · The letters of Samuel Johnson, ed. B. Redford, 5 vols. (1992–4) · J. L. Clifford, Dictionary Johnson (1979) · Johnsonian miscellanies, ed. G. B. Hill, 2 vols. (1897) · Autobiography, letters and literary remains of Mrs Piozzi, ed. A. Hayward, 2 vols. (1861) · Foster, Alum. Oxon. · GM, 1st ser., 59

(1789), 182 • E. Towers, *Dashwood: the man and the myth* (1986) • R. Bloomfield, *The banks of Wye: a poem in four books* (1823) • HoP, *Commons, 1754–90* • E. Craster, *Monumental inscriptions in the chapel of All Souls College, Oxford* (1969) • *Hist. U. Oxf.* 5: *18th-cent. Oxf.*

Likenesses W. Hogarth, portrait (as a young man); formerly in Shottesbrooke collection • J. Reynolds, portrait (in later life); formerly in Shottesbrooke collection

Vansittart, Robert Gilbert, Baron Vansittart (1881–1957), diplomatist, was born at Wilton House, Farnham, on 25 June 1881, the eldest of three sons among the six children of Captain Robert Arnold Vansittart (1851–1938), army officer, and his wife, Alice (1854–1919), third daughter of Gilbert James Blane, landowner, of Foliejon Park, near Windsor. The Vansittart family's origins can be traced to the small town of Sittard on the Dutch–German border, opposite Cologne, and later to the Hanse city of Danzig. It was from here that Peter Van Sittard, the founder of the English branch of the family, arrived in London in 1674. A merchant adventurer in the classic mould, he amassed a great fortune by trading with the East India Company. Many of his progeny led distinguished public careers in law, the armed forces, and politics. Five years after Vansittart's birth, his father unexpectedly inherited an estate of some 2000 acres at Foots Cray, Kent. Vansittart—or Van, as he was familiarly known to both his closest friends and his bitterest enemies—remembered his childhood, whiled away in well-to-do if not overly affluent circumstances, as 'jolly and humdrum' (*Mist Procession*, 16).

At the age of seven Vansittart was dispatched to St Neot's, a preparatory school near Winchfield. In 1893 he arrived at Eton College, where he spent a full seven years. He did not shine on the playing fields. His finest sporting deeds were reserved for tennis and boxing; in team games he was less successful, barely scraping into the cricket team as twelfth man. His special talent lay in foreign languages. In 1899 he excelled himself by carrying off both the French and German prince consort prizes, a rare, if not unique, accomplishment. A member of the Eton Society (Pop), Vansittart finished his time at Eton as captain of the Oppidans. He displayed a noticeable liking for amateur theatricals and speechifying. Caught up by the nationalist fervour at the outbreak of the Second South African War, he inspired the Fourth of June celebrations with his stirring renditions of patriotic perorations such as 'White Man's Burden' or 'To the race'. The young orator, according to the *Eton College Chronicle*, 'held the audience spellbound by the vibrating earnestness of his voice'.

Bent on a diplomatic career, Vansittart travelled the continent for over two years improving his proficiency in French and German. In Germany he encountered an intense anti-British hysteria, engendered by the ramifications of the Second South African War. On one occasion he was challenged to a duel, a predicament from which he escaped by revealing an admirable diplomatic technique. His early experiences in Germany perhaps laid the foundation for his subsequent attitude towards the Germans, and that led him, eventually, with growing experience, to

Robert Gilbert Vansittart, Baron Vansittart (1881–1957), by Howard Coster, 1938

promulgate the doctrine of 'original German sin' in international relations; conversely, the warmth of his reception in Paris won him over as an inveterate Francophile. These were to be the twin leitmotifs of his future European policy.

In March 1903 Vansittart sat for the diplomatic examination and passed out top of the list. In October 1903 he was appointed to the Paris embassy, where he was promoted third secretary in March 1905, passed on examination in public law in December 1905, and was appointed MVO in April 1906. In April 1907 he was transferred to Tehran. He was promoted second secretary in December 1908, and transferred to Cairo in January 1909. In August 1911 ill health brought him back to the Foreign Office, where he was to spend the remainder of his career. Incisive of thought, diligent, and energetic, possessed of a forceful character and the necessary social graces, Vansittart was soon earmarked as a high-flyer. But not only his routine work brought Vansittart to the attention of his peers and masters. Since his days at Eton, Vansittart had harboured literary ambitions. Occasionally, he contemplated abandoning diplomacy for the profession of a full-time writer. While in Paris he wrote a play in French, *Les parias*, that ran for six weeks at the Théâtre Molière, a singular feat for a young unpaid attaché, and one that augmented his reputation for brilliance. It marked the beginning of a parallel calling as a dramatist, poet, and novelist. Vansittart's most celebrated piece, *The Singing Caravan* (1933), which read as a kind of *Canterbury Tales* set in Persia, ran into several editions and was much admired by his distant kinsman T. E. Lawrence.

By 1914 Vansittart had attained the rank of assistant clerk. On the outbreak of war he was appointed head of the Swedish section of the newly created contraband department. He came to form a deep attachment towards his immediate chief, Eyre Crowe, a legendary Foreign Office figure: both shared a common view regarding the German menace. In 1916 he was assigned to direct the prisoners of war department under Lord Newton, a post he regarded with little enthusiasm. However, dealing with the treatment of prisoners on a day-to-day basis provided him with conclusive proof of German barbarism. He harboured no doubt that the Germans were committing atrocities on a massive scale. The war also brought personal tragedy. Arnold, his younger brother, was killed in action at Ypres. As Vansittart confessed, his private loss polarized his anti-German convictions. 'The personal element should not affect policy', he admitted, 'but one cannot prevent experience from confirming conclusions already reached. Why ask for strength to reverse them?' (*Mist Procession*, 22).

From 'Backwater Bob' under Lord Newton, Vansittart suddenly became 'brilliant' again (*Mist Procession*, 198–9) when he was included, with the rank of first secretary, in the British delegation to the Paris peace conference. At the conference Vansittart dealt mainly with the Turkish settlement, a topic that also absorbed the foreign secretary, Lord Curzon. Impressed with Vansittart's competence and diplomatic skills, Curzon appointed him as his private secretary in December 1920. Now holding the rank of assistant secretary, Vansittart worked under Curzon until January 1924. Meanwhile, he had been made a CMG in June 1920, and had, on 7 September 1921, married Gladys (1892–1928), the only daughter of General William Christian Heppenheimer, financier and army officer, of New Jersey, USA. They had one daughter, Cynthia, born in 1922.

Following the change of government in January 1924, Vansittart returned to regular Foreign Office work as head of the American department. Furthering Anglo-American relations was not an easy task, though he succeeded in resolving the thorny question of wartime blockade claims. At the same time, his dealings with the United States reinforced his ambivalence towards Americans, a state of mind typical of so many of his class and generation. Later, he would be heard referring to them as 'this untrustworthy race' (minutes of 5 Feb 1934, FO 371/17593). In February 1928 he was promoted to assistant under-secretary and joined the staff at 10 Downing Street, where he acted as private secretary to prime ministers Stanley Baldwin and Ramsay MacDonald. Once again, he performed well. Two years later, though not to everyone's satisfaction, Vansittart was appointed permanent under-secretary at the Foreign Office, in January 1930. Aged only forty-eight, he had attained the top post of his profession. He had been advanced to KCB in June 1929 and, as befitted

his new status, he was appointed GCMG in January 1931. On 29 July 1931 he married for the second time, following the tragic death of his first wife in July 1928. His bride, Sarita Enriqueta, was the widow of Vansittart's late colleague, Sir Colville Adrian de Rune Barclay, and the daughter of Herbert Ward, artist and explorer, of 105, avenue Malakoff, Paris. Vansittart himself had little private income: his father's intemperate forays on the stock exchange had squandered most of the family's assets. But Sarita was a considerable heiress (her income at the time was estimated at £40,000 per annum) and her money enabled them to live in princely splendour. They acquired Denham Place, a magnificent William and Mary manor house in Buckinghamshire, standing in almost 100 acres of gardens, and modelled on Hampton Court, where they employed a staff of twelve servants and five gardeners. When in London, they lived in almost equal splendour at 44 Park Street, Grosvenor Square. Vansittart's immediate family also expanded, to include not only his daughter but also Sarita's three sons from her previous marriage. Sarita introduced into his life a stability and balance that had been lacking since 1928. Their marriage lasted until Vansittart's death in 1957. To observers, the overwhelming impression of their union was one of 'conjugal bliss' (private information).

In May 1930 Vansittart detected the discredited figure of 'Old Adam', the symbol of pre-1914 diplomatic practice, at large again in Europe (Vansittart, 'An aspect of international relations in 1930', FO 371/14350, C3358/3358/62). By 1933, with Hitler's accession to power, he identified with absolute certainty Old Adam's current address, and expanded on the ramifications of allowing him to rampage at will throughout Europe. Unless checked, he wrote:

> The present regime in Germany will, on past and present form, loose off another European war just so soon as it feels strong enough … we are considering very crude people, who have very few ideas in their noddles but brute force and militarism. (Minutes of 6 May 1933, Vnst 2/3, Vansittart MSS)

Vansittart never deviated from this view. But how would he combat the German menace? First, by redefining the aims of British strategy, by isolating Germany as Britain's most immediate danger, and then by boosting the British defence programme to meet this changed order of priorities. Well out of the public eye as a member of high-powered government committees, Vansittart laboured ceaselessly to realize these aims.

At the same time, Vansittart did not rule out a diplomatic option, either by an overall European arrangement with Germany, or, should that prove impossible, by constructing a diplomatic front to rein in Germany. One such attempt collapsed in the wake of the public outcry over the Hoare–Laval pact, a plan to shore up an Anglo-French-Italian combination by resolving the Italo-Ethiopian war to Italy's distinct advantage. Although the cabinet had backed the plan, much of the blame for the débâcle was levelled at Vansittart, who had tenaciously promoted it. Vansittart lost influence, never to regain it. Eden, the new foreign secretary, had already determined to get rid of him, and this was confirmed when Neville Chamberlain became prime minister in May 1937. Vansittart's techniques also worked against him. His memoranda, drafted in a convoluted, epigrammatic style, faintly condescending in tone, warning of terrible dangers if his advice went unheeded, all too often irritated his political masters. In January 1938 Vansittart was 'kicked upstairs', assuming the high-sounding, but politically meaningless, title of chief diplomatic adviser to the government; he was at the same time advanced to GCB.

For the next three years Vansittart functioned in a state of limbo. His advice was rarely sought, and if given, it fell on deaf ears. When the war he had long prophesied broke out, he, at least, held no doubt as to its cause. 'The Nazi regime' had been set on war from the outset. But no less, 'the Prussian military caste and system are always there on The Day … we are fighting the German Army and the German people on whom the Army is based. We are fighting the *real*, and not the "accidental" Germany' (memorandum, 28 Nov 1939, FO 371/22986, C19495/15/18). In a series of broadcasts, later published as *Black Record* (1941), Vansittart expanded upon these themes. In some quarters, his anti-Germanism was viewed as excessive, even paranoid. Hostile questions were raised in parliament. Numerous critics suggested that a civil servant should not be allowed to air such controversial issues in public. In July 1941 Vansittart decided to resign from the service. In recognition of his long public service, he was raised to the peerage as Baron Vansittart of Denham; he had been appointed a privy councillor the previous year.

However, Vansittart did not retire from public life. He spoke frequently in the House of Lords, continuing his campaign against Germany. After the war, he gained a reputation as a cold war warrior, as he regularly castigated the Soviet Union's record. What emerged was his utter loathing for all forms of totalitarianism: 'Commu-Nazis', as he termed them. Concurrently, he wrote a series of polemical works explaining and justifying his own record, the most influential of which were *Lessons of my Life* (1943) and *Bones of Contention* (n.d.). Vansittart's autobiography, *The Mist Procession*, a perceptive account of his times, included some discerning and amusing pen portraits of the main characters, even if marred, occasionally, by an over-elaborate style. It was published posthumously in 1958. Vansittart's final sentence—'Mine is a story of failure, but it throws light on my time which failed too'—was a disarmingly generous, even-handed verdict on his life's work. No doubt the times had frustrated him. But in one crucial respect he had prevailed. Few men of his generation perceived with greater clarity the predominant menace of the times through which they lived.

In the autumn of 1956 Vansittart spoke out strongly against Nasser's seizure of the Suez Canal, denouncing the Egyptian president as a squalid imitation of the European dictators he had challenged in the 1930s. Opposed to any policy of scuttle, he was deeply depressed by Eden's inept handling of the crisis. These were to be his last public statements on matters of foreign policy. For some time Vansittart had been suffering from a heart condition. His ailment gradually worsened. Confined to his bed, he contracted a severe chill from which he never recovered. On 14 February 1957 Vansittart died, peacefully and without pain, at Denham Place, aged seventy-five years. He was cremated, according to his wishes. No national memorial was raised in his honour, but in the shadow of Denham church there lies a stone, now somewhat faded, to his memory.

NORMAN ROSE

Sources CAC Cam., Vansittart MSS · PRO, FO 371, 800 · cabinet papers and minutes · *Hansard 5L* · *Hansard 5C* · Lord Vansittart [R. G. Vansittart], *The mist procession: the autobiography of Lord Vansittart* (1958) · N. Rose, *Vansittart: study of a diplomat* (1978) · private information (2004) · *DNB* · *The Times* (15 Feb 1957) · I. G. Colvin, *Vansittart in office: an historic survey of the origins of the Second World War based on the papers of Sir Robert Vansittart* (1965) · *CGPLA Eng. & Wales* (1957) · Burke, *Peerage* · *WWW* · d. cert. · b. cert.

Archives CAC Cam., corresp. and papers · CAC Cam., corresp. and papers relating to Malta | BL, corresp. with Society of Authors, Add. MS 63339 · Bodl. Oxf., corresp. with Gilbert Murray · Bodl. Oxf., corresp. with Sir Horace Rumbold · Bodl. Oxf., corresp. with Lord Simon · Bodl. Oxf., letters to E. J. Thompson, MS Eng. Hist. c. 5321 · CAC Cam., Christie MSS · CAC Cam., Hankey MSS · CAC Cam., corresp. with Sir Eric Phipps · CAC Cam., corresp. with Sir E. L. Spears · CUL, letters to Stanley Baldwin and others · CUL, letters to Sir Samuel Hoare · CUL, Templewood MSS · HLRO, letters to Herbert Samuel, A 155/9 · JRL, letters to *Manchester Guardian* · PRO NIre., corresp. with Lord Londonderry, D 3099/4/20 · Queen's University, Belfast, letters to Otto Kyllmann, MS 18/19 · U. Warwick Mod. RC, letters to A. P. Young, MSS 242/X/VA | FILM BFI NFTVA, documentary footage · BFI NFTVA, news footage | SOUND BL NSA, sound recording · IWM SA, recorded talk

Likenesses W. Stoneman, photographs, 1930–52, NPG · H. Coster, photograph, 1938, NPG [*see illus.*] · C. Ware, photograph, 22 April 1938, Hult. Arch. · photographs, 11 Nov 1938, Hult. Arch. · A. R. Thomson, oils, exh. 1942, NPG · C. Beaton, photograph, NPG · H. Coster, photographs, NPG · photograph, repro. in J. Connell, *The Office* (1958), facing p. 160 · photographs, repro. in Rose, *Vansittart*

Wealth at death £59,262 4*s.*: probate, 27 June 1957, *CGPLA Eng. & Wales*

Vardill [*married name* Niven], **Anna Jane** (1781–1852), poet, was born on 19 November 1781 in London, the only child of the Revd Dr John Vardill (1749–1811) and his wife (*d.* 1826). Her father, who was born in New York state, moved to England in 1774. He was a loyalist spy, a professor, and a clergyman who served as rector of Skirbeck and Fishtoft in Lincolnshire, from 1791 until his death in 1811. He wrote at least one play, *The Unknown*, which was performed at the Surrey Theatre in 1819.

Vardill grew up in Galloway, London, and Lincolnshire. Her father provided the strongest influence on her education. In the preface to her first published work, *Poems and translations, from the minor Greek poets and others, written chiefly between the ages of ten and sixteen, by a lady* (1809), she states that '[a] most indulgent father … found amusement in familiarizing his only child with the Poets of Antiquity' (Vardill, iv). This first published volume went to three editions. It contains precocious translations of Anacreon, Sappho, Theocritus, Horace, and others, in addition to original works such as 'The rights of woman, a burlesque essay', in which Vardill cites a wide range of supposed authorities on the subject and satirizes both sexes before concluding that woman's role should be that of prime minister to man's king.

Vardill published *The Pleasures of Human Life: a Poem*, in 1812. Like much of her work, this poem is an effective imitation of a particular style—Augustan, in this case—and a tribute to her father, who had died the previous year. From 1813 to 1822, as 'V', she produced a number of works in the style of various Romantic poets, including Walter Scott, Robert Southey, and Lord Byron, for the *European Magazine*. Her most famous contribution to the magazine was a continuation of Samuel Taylor Coleridge's 'Christabel', published in April 1815, over a year before Coleridge's original appeared in print. She had heard the poem read aloud in December 1814 by Henry Crabb Robinson, a family friend who later became her mother's executor. 'Christobell' demonstrates Vardill's remarkable ability to imitate contemporary poetic forms, allowing the previously inaccessible Romantic idiom to filter into popular literary culture.

After her marriage to James Niven (*d.* 1830) in 1822, Vardill moved from London to his estate at Kirkcudbright in Scotland. Their only child, Agnes, was born in 1825. After her husband's death Vardill returned to England, where she divided her time between London and Skipton until her death in Skipton on 4 June 1852.

MEGAN A. STEPHAN

Sources Blain, Clements & Grundy, *Feminist comp.*, 1110 · F. S. Schwarzbach, 'Anna Jane Vardill', *An encyclopedia of British women writers*, ed. P. Schlueter and J. Schlueter (1998), 641–2 · *Diary, reminiscences, and correspondence of Henry Crabb Robinson*, ed. T. Sadler, 3 vols. (1869), vol. 1, p. 465, vol. 2, pp. 158–9, 363, 376 · [A. J. Vardill], *Poems and translations, from the minor Greek poets and others, written chiefly between the ages of ten and sixteen, by a lady* (1809) · R. Inglis, *N&Q*, 2nd ser., 2 (1856), 437 · D. H. Reiman, 'Christobell, or, The case of the sequel preemptive', *Wordsworth Circle*, 6 (1975), 283–9 · R. Haven, 'Anna Vardill Niven's Christobell: an addendum', *Wordsworth Circle*, 7 (1976), 117–18 · 'Vardill, John', *Concise dictionary of American biography*, 3rd edn (1980), 1082 · Watt, *Bibl. Brit.*, 2.923 · Allibone, *Dict.* · 'Anna Jane Vardill, later Niven', *The Cambridge bibliography of English literature*, ed. J. Shattock, 3rd edn, 4: *1800–1900* (1999), 486

Vardon, Henry William [Harry] (1870–1937), golfer, was born at Marais, Grouville, Jersey, on 9 May 1870, one of eight children of Philippe George Vardon, a gardener, and his wife, Elizabeth Augustine Bouchard. Harry, as he was always known, did little at school, but was drawn to golf when the course for the Royal Jersey Golf Club was laid out near his home in 1878. With friends he took up the game in a rough, ready, yet committed way and worked occasionally as a caddy. He left school aged just twelve, working first on a farm, then in the service of a local doctor, before being employed in 1887 as a gardener by Major Spofforth, captain of the Royal Jersey Golf Club. Spofforth encouraged the young man's golf, and Vardon quickly became the leading local artisan player.

In 1890 Vardon was appointed professional to a new course established at Studley Royal, Yorkshire, prompted by his younger brother, Tom, himself an accomplished golfer who had already moved to the mainland. He quickly tired of the limited opportunities there and

Henry William [Harry] **Vardon** (1870–1937), by Clement Flower, 1913 [*The Triumvirate*: Vardon (right) with John H. Taylor (left) and James Braid (centre)]

moved across the Pennines to Bury in Lancashire, where he was the professional until in 1896 he moved again to Ganton. He first entered the open championship in 1893 and gave warning of his ability by finishing sixth the following year. It was in 1896 that Vardon broke through to the highest level. He began by comfortably beating J. H. Taylor, open champion in 1894 and 1895, in an exhibition match before going on to win the open himself at Muirfield, beating Taylor in a play-off. He was to win the open five more times (at Prestwick in 1898, 1903, and 1914, and at Sandwich in 1899 and 1911), a feat still unmatched in 2000, and came second on four other occasions. In 1900 he won the US open championship, coming second on the two other occasions he entered—most famously in a play-off to the young local amateur Francis Ouimet at Brookline in 1913 but also notably when aged fifty. Other significant successes came at the inaugural German open in 1911 and the *News of the World* match play championship the following year at Sunningdale.

The so-called 'triumvirate' of Vardon, Taylor, and James Braid dominated golf in Britain in the twenty years before the First World War, though the absolute peak of Vardon's golf was played between 1898 and 1903. After his second open victory his 'long-sustained spell of first-class form [was] little short of phenomenal' (*Golf*, 17/427, 16 Sept 1898, 22), and in 1899 he was judged virtually unbeatable, going 'up and down the country winning tournaments and breaking records, trampling down all opponents in his juggernaut stride' (*The Times*, 22 March 1937, 14). He was styled by some the Napoleon of Golf, more commonly the Greyhound. Such supremacy bore witness to a natural athleticism allied to an iron will. He practised assiduously until he had mastered every shot and on the course was 'Gifted with a rare control of himself which nothing could ruffle' (Taylor, 89), his powerful concentration allowing him 'to sink into the game' (Kirkaldy, 137). He championed two major innovations of technique: first, the use of the overlapping grip which had been developed some years before, such that it is now universally called the 'Vardon grip', and second, a much more upright swing than that favoured by the hitherto dominant Scots players, probably allowing him to hit down the line longer than most. His ball striking was rhythmic, authoritative, and pure; from both tee and fairway the straightness of his hitting was legendary. Bernard Darwin, the great observer of the game, could not 'imagine anybody hitting the ball better than Harry Vardon' (Darwin, 159).

Vardon's supremacy could not last for ever, but its end was hastened by two factors. While winning at Prestwick in 1903 his health broke down seriously from tuberculosis. He spent many months recovering at Mundesley Sanatorium in Norfolk, and though he returned to competitive golf in 1904 ill health often dogged him thereafter. Second, his putting became highly erratic. If this had never been the strongest part of his game, after the turn of the century it became his undoing. In today's language he probably suffered from the 'yips', causing him to stab or jerk at short putts, though he himself believed it was caused by an old footballing injury to his right hand. After 1920 his game fell away markedly and he concentrated on teaching at the South Hertfordshire club at Totteridge, which he had joined as professional in 1902 and served happily until his death.

In his prime Vardon was a great sporting figure, akin in stature to the cricketer W. G. Grace. He was, indeed, both a beneficiary of and a stimulus to the first great era of the growth of golf in England and the United States. An expanding middle class, with increasing amounts of time and money to spare, was embracing the game as never before, and a large railway network enabled thousands of spectators to witness championships and exhibition matches. That he was counted as an Englishman (although born and brought up in Jersey) challenging the Scots at their own game only added to the sense of occasion—most piquantly in his famous challenge match against Willie Park jun. in 1899. Vardon was well aware of golf's widening appeal. He criss-crossed Britain and parts of Ireland and France, and made three long trips to North America, taking the game to old and new audiences by playing against other champions, local professionals, and leading amateurs. The effort in this was immense (and may have contributed to his ill health), yet he lost very rarely indeed. As a counterpart to this evangelicalism he also designed fourteen golf courses, several of them associated with flourishing polite resorts, as at Llandrindod Wells, or prosperous suburbs, as at Sandy Lodge. He reached a wider audience still by publishing successfully

on the game. *The Complete Golfer* went through thirteen editions from 1905 before a revised edition was issued in 1914. *How to Play Golf* was published in 1912 and was followed by a chapter on driving in *Success at Golf* (1913), *Progressive Golf* (1922), and *My Golfing Life* (1933). If these books are clear and effective, there is a hint of regret in each, perhaps for what might have been, but also at the introduction after 1900 of the modern rubber or Haskell ball, which he strongly believed had made the game less skilful.

Golf was Vardon's life. Like many champions he had a prodigious determination. Yet to his peers there was little that was selfish or distant about him. Taylor noticed that he was 'Kindly and considerate and without harshness, he looked upon the world with tolerance and understanding' (Taylor, 117). Whether his wife agreed is uncertain. He married Jessie Bryant (1869/70–1946), an ironer of St Helier, Jersey, the daughter of John Bryant, ginger beer maker, on 15 November 1891 when she was already pregnant. Vardon was in England when his son, Clarence Henry, was born in June 1892, but saw the child die on 5 August. He was unable to persuade his wife to join him in England until 1896, but soon after their reunion she suffered a miscarriage. The marriage was to remain childless and appears to have been a detached one, his wife showing little interest in his achievements or in any social life. In the 1920s, after he had given up hope of further golfing triumphs, Vardon found some comfort with Gladys Matilda (Tilly) Howell (1892–1963), a dancer, with whom he had a son, Peter, born on 23 January 1926 (Howell).

Vardon died at his home, 14 Totteridge Lane, Totteridge, near London, on 20 March 1937 and was buried in St Andrew's parish church, Totteridge, four days later. *The Times* quickly published an obituary that was unstinting in its praise. 'He did what only a very great player can do; he raised the general conception of what was possible in his game and forced his nearest rivals to attain a higher standard by attempting that which they would otherwise have deemed impossible'. At his funeral, homage was paid by Taylor, Braid, Ted Ray, and Sandy Herd, between them winners of twelve open championships and two US open championships.   JULIAN HOPPIT

Sources A. Howell, *Harry Vardon: the revealing story of a champion golfer* (1991) · H. Vardon, *My golfing life* (1933) · L. Viney, ed., *The royal and ancient book of golf records* (1991) · E. H. Ballard, *The story of South Herts golf club* (1987) · J. H. Taylor, *Golf: my life's work* (1943) · A. Kirkaldy, *Fifty years of golf: my memories* (1921) · B. Darwin, *The world that Fred made: an autobiography* (1955) · b. cert. · m. cert. · *The Times* (22 March 1937) · *DNB* · *CGPLA Eng. & Wales* (1937) · b. cert. [Peter Howell]

Archives FILM BFI NFTVA, news footage · BFI NFTVA, sports footage · BFI NFTVA, actuality footage

Likenesses C. Flower, group portrait, 1913, Royal and Ancient Golf Club, St Andrews [*see illus.*]

Wealth at death £11,153 2s. 1d.: resworn probate, 14 July 1937, *CGPLA Eng. & Wales*

Vardon, Thomas (1799–1867), librarian, was the son of Thomas Vardon of Gracechurch Street, London, and his wife, Elizabeth Bryant Tarbutt. His early life is obscure and nothing is known of his education. He married Laura Ann Stapylton Johnson, daughter of the Revd A. Johnson of

South Stoke, Somerset, about 1829. In February 1828 Vardon was appointed a clerk in the House of Commons and in June of that year he was appointed to the post of librarian of the house, which he held concurrently with his clerkship until September 1831.

The house had had a librarian only since 1818, but Vardon began immediately to expand the job into a kind of parliamentary factotum, and into spheres which the more senior officers of the house had left untouched. In this he was aided by the inauguration of a commodious new library, designed by Sir John Soane, in the year of his appointment, and by a vigorous and equally enthusiastic assistant, Thomas Erskine May. After the fire of 1834, expansion continued in a well-planned and convenient temporary library, and, after 1852, in the magnificent suite of four—soon expanded to six—fine rooms designed by Charles Barry and A. W. N. Pugin, the centrepiece of public-room provision in the new Palace of Westminster.

Vardon made himself and his department indispensable to the house. 'There is no subject', he told a select committee in 1835, '… on which I am not called upon to afford instant information' ('Standing committee on the library', evidence, 11–12). These are words which might be expected of a modern computer-equipped reference librarian, but in the 1830s they were singular indeed. They signalled the beginning of the House of Commons library as an institution in which the main resources were the intellect, knowledge, and ability of the staff, rather than the shelves of books—perhaps the first example in the world of a library of talents rather than of bibliographical sources. Meanwhile, the development of the collection had not been neglected; in fact, Vardon had built up the stock of the library almost from nothing after the fire of 1834. By 1860 it was far wider than the original idea of a library of historical, parliamentary, and constitutional information, and was particularly rich in political, economic, and topographical works. Under Vardon, and often by him, classified sets of parliamentary papers were assembled, and indexing of journals and reports went forward. As he took care to have the new library suite designed as a place of relaxation as well as one of study, it rapidly became the principal social as well as intellectual centre of the house.

Vardon died at his extensive house (as large as the clerk's) in the Palace of Westminster on 12 April 1867, from heart disease; he was survived by his wife, a son, and two daughters, and left in his will, in a series of trusts, some £80,000. Before Vardon's appointment the House of Commons library could have faded from existence at any time, unnoticed; with his tenure, it became a central pillar of parliamentary life.   C. C. POND

Sources W. R. McKay and J. C. Sainty, eds., *Clerks in the House of Commons, 1363–1989* (1989), 95 · D. Menhennet, *The House of Commons library: a history* (1991), 26–7 · 'Standing committee on the library of the House of Commons', *Parl. papers* (1835), 18.11–12, no. 104 · d. cert.

Archives House of Commons | UCL, letters to Society for the Diffusion of Useful Knowledge

Likenesses R. Dighton, portrait, *c.*1850; copies, Librarian's office, House of Commons; Vardon Room, House of Commons

Wealth at death under £80,000: probate, 23 May 1867, *CGPLA Eng. & Wales*

Vardy, John (1717/18–1765), architect, was born in Durham, where he was baptized on 20 February 1718. He was the second son of Ralph and Mary Vardy; his father was a labourer turned gardener, and John was one of at least seven children. He is next recorded in May 1736, when he was appointed clerk of the works at the Queen's House, Greenwich, at the age of only eighteen. There is no indication of how he made the transition as, unlike most of his colleagues in the office of works, his name does not appear in the records of any appropriate trade guilds. His subsequent official appointments were as clerk of the works at Hampton Court (1745–6), at Whitehall, Westminster, and St James's (1746–54), and at Kensington (1754–61). In 1756 he was made clerk at Chelsea Hospital, and from 1749 to 1763 he was surveyor to the Royal Mint.

During the first ten years of his career Vardy seems to have established himself as an unofficial personal assistant to William Kent, preparing drawings for projects such as the Treasury building overlooking Horse Guards Parade (begun in 1733) and the Houses of Parliament. In 1741 he drew and engraved Kent's gothick pulpit design for York Minster, and three years later he made his sole venture into publishing with a volume of fifty plates entitled *Some Designs of Mr. Inigo Jones and Mr. William Kent*, thirty-three of which were devoted to buildings, furniture, vases, and other artefacts by the latter architect. Vardy performed a particular service both to contemporaries and to posterity by including the gothick court of king's bench and Gloucester Cathedral choir screen, as well as engraving separately the gothicized Esher Place. Apart from Batty Langley's *Gothic Architecture Improved* (published initially in 1741–2), these were the earliest appearances in print of the new gothick style.

In his official capacity Vardy was responsible (jointly with William Robinson) for supervising the posthumous execution of Kent's scheme for the Horse Guards in Whitehall (1750–59), and for designing the 'new stone building' at Westminster as accommodation for the king's bench records and exchequer bill offices: designed in 1753, it was partly realized in 1755–8, finally completed in 1821, and demolished in 1883. His 1748 design for a new royal palace in Whitehall (exhibited 1761) is not known to have survived.

Like his office of works colleagues Isaac Ware and Henry Flitcroft, Vardy was essentially an architectural civil servant whose reputation rests mainly on private commissions, though most of these have been demolished or altered. His style, in both classical and gothick idioms, was formed by his close contact with Kent. This is seen in his earliest datable independent project, an unexecuted design (1746) for a four-towered mansion for the Hon. Richard Arundell, and in his design (1754; also unexecuted) for a British museum, the one indebted to Holkham, the other to Kent's parliament schemes. His classical designs are generally in a restrained Palladian manner, as with Milton (later Dorchester) House, Park Lane (*c.*1751; dem. 1849) for Baron Milton, first earl of Dorchester;

Woodcote Park, Epsom, Surrey, a stylistically attributable design of the 1750s for Frederick Calvert, the sixth Baron Baltimore (burnt 1934 and rebuilt); and the remodelling of Hackwood Park in Hampshire for the fifth duke of Bolton (c.1761–3; altered out of recognition in 1805–13). However, fashionable rococo leanings can be detected in some of his garden building designs, in the plasterwork he designed for the interior of Milton House, and in his furniture designs for Hackwood and elsewhere. For Milton Abbey in Dorset he offered his client, Lord Milton, both Palladian and gothick options; work seems to have been started on the gothick scheme in 1753, but it was left unfinished and subsequently replaced by a house designed by Sir William Chambers. At Spencer House overlooking Green Park, London (1755–60, for the first Earl Spencer), the exterior and ground-floor rooms were completed to Vardy's Palladian scheme, but for the first-floor rooms he was superseded by the neo-classicist James 'Athenian' Stuart, despite his own attempts to introduce neo-classical motifs to his designs.

Vardy died in London on 17 May 1765 at the age of forty-seven. His will, which shows him to have been comfortably off, with property in Derby Street, Westminster, and Egham, Surrey, mentions his wife (whose name is not given), brother Thomas (a carver who executed his furniture designs), daughters Margaret and Elisabeth, and sons Edward and John; to the last (also an architect) he left 'all my books, drawings, instruments and matters relating to architecture'.   ROGER WHITE

Sources R. White, 'John Vardy', *The architectural outsiders*, ed. R. Brown (1985), 63–81 · Colvin, *Archs.* · H. M. Wood, ed., *The registers of St Mary-le-Bow, in the city of Durham* (privately printed, 1912) · H. M. Wood, ed., *The registers of St. Mary in the South Bailey, in the city of Durham* (privately printed, 1908) · R. White, 'Isaac Ware and Chesterfield House', *The rococo in England*, ed. C. Hind (1986), 175–92 · H. M. Colvin and others, eds., *The history of the king's works*, 5 (1976), 425–30, pl. 64A–B · will, PRO, PROB 11/909, sig. 239
Archives Hackwood Park, Hampshire · RIBA · Sir John Soane's Museum, London · V&A
Wealth at death owned property: will, PRO, PROB 11/909, sig. 239

Varey, John Earl (1922–1999), scholar of Spanish literature, was born on 26 August 1922 at 15 Fielding Crescent, Blackburn, Lancashire, the son of Harold Varey, elementary schoolmaster, and his wife, Dorothy Halstead, *née* Yates. He grew up in his birthplace, attending Blackburn grammar school, and developed a lifelong devotion to Blackburn Rovers, an enduring Lancashire accent, and a strong—but straight-faced—sense of humour. Awarded an open exhibition to Emmanuel College, he went up to Cambridge in 1941. The war interrupted his undergraduate career, and from 1942 to 1945 he was a navigator with bomber and transport commands; he flew in numerous sorties over Germany and survived a period when the life expectancy of bomber aircrew was short. He ended the war as a flight lieutenant.

Cambridge after the war fell under the intellectual spell of F. R. Leavis and William Empson. Their close readings of literary texts were certainly an influence, but Varey also had a passion for classical theatre in performance, a passion which dated back to puppets in childhood. After a first in part two of the tripos, he married, on 5 June 1948, Cicely Rainford (Micky) Virgo, bank clerk, of Eccles, Lancashire, and daughter of William Henry Virgo, sales manager. They had three sons, one of whom died young, and one daughter. In the same year Varey began his doctoral research on the history of puppets in Spain. The topic might seem far from classical theatre, but, as Varey argued, puppeteers were licensed by the theatre authorities, much of their material was related to classical subject matter, and the relevant documents were preserved in the same archives. The thesis was finished on schedule in 1951, but the passionate interest continued: in the design, construction, and operation of playhouses, in actors, in staging, and in the dramatists themselves: Tirso de Molina, Lope de Vega, but particularly Pedro Calderón de la Barca.

In 1952 Westfield College, then in Hampstead, decided to make its first full-time appointment in Spanish, and chose Varey as assistant lecturer. Gradually, as he became lecturer, reader (1957), and professor (1963), he turned his department into one of the best in Britain. At the same time he became involved in the complexities of administration in a large federal university: he was dean of Westfield's faculty of arts (1966–8), vice-principal (1968–70), and principal (1984–9); in the university he was elected to the senate and academic council, which he chaired from 1980 to 1983; and he also chaired numerous other committees, the most important of which was the management committee of the Warburg Institute. His most difficult—and most successful—task was to oversee the merger of Westfield with Queen Mary College, which was completed in the year of his retirement. His patience and level-headedness helped to preserve the ethos of both institutions, although he could be induced, during this period, to make acid comments about government policies in higher education.

One of Varey's greatest legacies to scholarship was his foundation, in 1963, of Tamesis Books, which by the time of his death had published, in all areas of Hispanic studies, over 200 monographs, editions, or facsimiles; its most important series, *Fuentes para la historia del teatro en España*, ran to thirty-five volumes. Understandably, this was the series in which Varey was most involved (with Norman Shergold and, later, Charles Davis), but as Tamesis's general editor until his death he read the proofs of all the volumes. Other projects in which he played a major role were the research project on the history of the theatre and the two Grant and Cutler series, Critical Guides to Spanish Texts and Research Bibliographies and Checklists, of which he was the joint general editor. He also found time to produce twenty books and over 100 articles of his own, to lecture at over 100 venues in three continents, and to acquire (with the help of Micky and their children Nicholas, Alison, and Michael, in the family home in Platts Lane, Hampstead), an international reputation for hospitality.

Such dedication to Spanish literature, to Westfield, and

to the University of London, did not go unrecognized. Varey was president of the Association of Hispanists of Great Britain and Ireland (1979–81), an 'illustrious son of Madrid' (1980), an honorary life member of the University of London Union (1980), a corresponding member of the Real Academia Española (1981), a fellow of the British Academy (1985), and an honorary member of the Instituto de Estudios Madrileños (1988; the first foreigner to receive the honour). He was awarded an honorary doctorate by Cambridge University in 1981. On his retirement in 1989 he received two congratulatory volumes of essays: one from colleagues and pupils in Westfield, the other international. His active retirement was hampered by illness; he died at University College Hospital, London, on 28 March 1999. He was survived by his wife and three children.

To Hispanists, Varey was one of the great scholars of classical Spanish drama, with an unrivalled knowledge of theatres and performance. To non-Hispanists he was a prodigiously energetic and skilful administrator. Those who knew little of the golden age of Spanish drama, and even less of Calderón, came to see that these topics were worthy of interest and respect. Few scholars have done more for their subject. DON W. CRUICKSHANK

Sources *The Independent* (1 April 1999) · *Daily Telegraph* (13 April 1999) · *The Guardian* (4 May 1999) · *The Times* (10 May 1999) · *WWW* · personal knowledge (2004) · private information (2004) · b. cert. · m. cert. · d. cert.

Likenesses photograph, repro. in *The Independent* · photograph, repro. in *Daily Telegraph*

Wealth at death under £200,000—gross; under £100,000—net: probate, 23 Aug 1999, *CGPLA Eng. & Wales*

Varley, (Samuel) Alfred (1832–1921). *See under* Varley, Cromwell Fleetwood (1828–1883).

Varley, Cornelius (1781–1873), landscape painter and inventor of optical apparatus, was born on 21 November 1781 at the Blue Post tavern in Mare Street, Hackney, the third of five children of Richard Varley (d. 1791) and his second wife, Hannah Fleetwood, a descendant of General Charles Fleetwood and Oliver Cromwell's daughter Bridget. When Varley was ten years old his father died leaving the family inadequately provided for, and the large house in Hackney was vacated for a dark court opposite St Luke's Hospital in Old Street. Varley's elder brother, John *Varley (1778–1842), became a famous watercolour artist, a profession also taken up by his younger brother William Fleetwood *Varley (1785–1856) [*see under* Varley, John (1778–1842)], and his younger sister, Elizabeth, who married the artist William Mulready in 1803. Two years after his father's death, Cornelius's uncle Samuel Varley, a watchmaker, jeweller, and natural philosopher, took charge of him. Varley later wrote in his autobiography that it was his uncle who opened his eyes to the wonders of science. Cornelius began to make lenses and microscopes and assisted his uncle in his chemical experiments and public lectures when the latter founded the Chemical and Philosophical Society at Hatton House in 1794, one of the forerunners of the Royal Institution. In 1800, however, Samuel Varley gave up his own business

and the Hatton House lectures to work for Charles, third Earl Stanhope, and Cornelius Varley determined to become an artist like his elder brother. Instead of undergoing another apprenticeship, he taught himself by sketching from nature in the company of his brother John with whom he lived at Charles Street, Covent Garden. John introduced Cornelius to the influential patron of watercolour artists, Thomas Monro. Through Monro, Varley met George, fifth earl of Essex, who recommended him to his first students.

Within a year of the start of his new career Varley was invited to teach the Bacon Schutz family at Gillingham Hall, Norfolk, and the Rous family at Henham Hall in Suffolk. After spending the winter of 1801–2 in Suffolk he returned to London to teach drawing and perspective. In June 1802 Varley travelled to north Wales with his brother John and Thomas Webster (1772–1844), a young architect who was later to become a prominent member of the Geological Society of London. He returned to Wales in 1803 with the artists Joshua Cristall and William Havell and again on his own in 1805. His sketches from these trips and another to St Albans in 1804 constitute some of his most significant output. Rather than showing a concern for one single impression or the construction of a successfully controlled pictorial space, they concentrate on the detailed observation of different landscape features as they appear at a particular moment rendered in colour on the spot. During and after his lifetime these works were not valued. In a review of the sale of Varley's work at Christies, the *Telegraph* of 16 July 1875 saw little interest in the sketches, stating that 'we have got far beyond such work as his'. In the second half of the twentieth century, however, his work became appreciated for its freshness and its role in pioneering a 'naturalistic' mode of landscape depiction. The rediscovery of his drawings in the family's collection in the early 1970s finally opened up a new assessment. Varley's early watercolour drawings, such as *Ross Market Place, Herefordshire* (V&A), one of his earliest exhibits, shown in 1805 at the Society of Painters in Water Colours (SPWC) (of which Varley was a founding member), are remarkable for their attention to detail and to changing atmospheric effects.

Yet most of the works Varley exhibited publicly in the first two decades of the century bear poetic titles that indicate their more conventionally idealistic character. He exhibited work at the Royal Academy from 1803, and at the SPWC after its foundation in 1804. Varley did not sell many works in exhibitions, however. In 1809 he published a series of etchings and lithographs entitled *Shipping, barges, fishing boats, and other vessels, commonly met with on the British coasts, rivers and canals* which does not seem to have been a great success, and only the first part was published. Although in 1819 the SPWC awarded him one of its first three prizes for the encouragement of the production of important work, Varley's main occupation from 1814 was once again as an optical manufacturer.

In 1809 Varley invented the graphic telescope, a drawing instrument which combined the portability of the camera obscura with the two-way mirror arrangement of William

Hyde Wollaston's camera lucida. Its much improved lens system allowed it to be used for objects or views of greatly varying size and distance. Varley patented the graphic telescope in 1811, but found that manufacturers were not able to work to his exacting specifications; this was perhaps a reason why he set up his own workshop. He had, however, never entirely abandoned his scientific interests after leaving his uncle's house. From 1804 until 1844 his name appears on many engraved illustrations in the *Transactions of the Society of Arts*, and he became a full member of the society in 1814. In 1807 and 1809 he contributed to the emerging science of meteorology by publishing two articles on atmospheric phenomena in the *Philosophical Magazine*, based on observations collected during his sketching trips to Wales in 1803 and 1805. He also became involved in the City Philosophical Society where he met the scientist Michael Faraday. After Faraday's election as director of the laboratories at the Royal Institution, Varley was invited to lecture there on the graphic telescope in 1826, and again during the 1830s, returning annually between 1838 and 1861.

In 1821 Varley married Elizabeth Livermore Straker, a cousin of Faraday's own future wife. They had three daughters and seven sons, two of whom, Cromwell Fleetwood *Varley and Frederick Henry *Varley, became eminent as electrical engineers. Through the artist John Linnell's *Journals* (vol. 1, FM Cam.) we know that Varley attended the services of the Revd John Martin at the Baptist church at Keppel Street, Bloomsbury, about 1811. He was a member of the Sandemanian sect from 1833 to 1847.

In 1839 Varley co-founded the Royal Microscopic Society and contributed a series of communications to its *Transactions*. In contrast to his work as an artist, he achieved recognition during his lifetime for developing optical instruments, receiving two silver medals from the Society of Arts in 1831 and in 1833, as well as an Isis gold medal for improvements in the construction of microscopes in 1841. Varley's distinction as a manufacturer was acknowledged when he and his sons mounted a display at the Great Exhibition in 1851. He was awarded a prize medal for his graphic telescope and its supporting table which by then had come to be widely used by artists such as John Sell Cotman and the land surveyor Thomas Hornor (1785–1844) when, in 1820, the latter drew his great panorama of London from St Paul's Cathedral for the Colosseum in Regent's Park. In 1845 Varley published a *Treatise on Optical Drawing Instruments*. He never, however, entirely gave up his work as an artist and continued to exhibit at the Royal Academy until 1859, at Suffolk Street, and four times at the British Institution between 1815 and 1840. Not many pictures produced after 1814 are known to have survived, but the few that are, together with the titles given in the exhibition catalogues, show that the split between composed works bearing poetic titles and detailed topographical studies continued into his later life. A photograph taken of Varley in the studio of the family towards the end of his life shows a small man of stocky build with a white beard, deep-set eyes, and bushy eyebrows. Throughout his

life he regularly attended scientific meetings and soirées. He was known for his range of knowledge, wide interests, and rapid speech. He died at 19 South Grove West, Stoke Newington, London, on 2 October 1873, at the age of nearly ninety-two years. Examples of his work are to be found in the Victoria and Albert Museum and British Museum, London, Tate Collection, Fitzwilliam Museum, Cambridge, Ashmolean Museum, Oxford, and the Yale Center for British Art, New Haven, Connecticut.

CHARLOTTE KLONK

Sources *Cornelius Varley's narrative written by himself* [n.d.] · C. Klonk, 'Sketching from nature: John and Cornelius Varley and their circle', *Science and the perception of nature: British landscape art in the late eighteenth and early nineteenth centuries* (1996), 101–47 · *Brief notice of the life and labours of the late Cornelius Varley* (1874) · M. Pidgley, 'Cornelius Varley, Cotman, and the graphic telescope', *Burlington Magazine*, 114 (1972), 781–6 · P. Colnaghi and D. Colnaghi, *Exhibition of drawings and watercolours by Cornelius Varley* (1973) [exhibition catalogue, Colnaghi's Gallery, London, 21 Feb – 16 March 1973] · B. S. Long, 'Cornelius Varley', *Old Water-Colour Society's Club*, 14 (1936–7), 1–10 · J. L. Roget, *A history of the 'Old Water-Colour' Society*, 1 (1891) · A. T. Story, *The life of John Linnell*, 2 vols. (1892) · A. Story, *James Holmes and John Varley* (1894) · J. J. Jenkins, 'Papers: file Cornelius Varley', [n.d.], Bankside Gallery, London, Royal Watercolour Society · C. M. Kauffmann, *John Varley, 1778–1842* (1984) · Graves, *Artists*, 3rd edn · CGPLA Eng. & Wales (1873) · d. cert.

Archives V&A NAL, papers relating to his career and to his scientific interests, and fragments of an autobiography

Likenesses Messrs Varley Brothers, photograph, priv. coll.; repro. in *ILN* (25 Oct 1873), 389 · wood-engraving (after photograph), BM; repro. in *ILN* (1873)

Wealth at death under £200: probate, 7 Nov 1873, *CGPLA Eng. & Wales*

Varley, Cromwell Fleetwood (1828–1883), telegraph engineer, was born at Kentish Town, London, on 6 April 1828, the second of the ten children of the artist and inventor Cornelius *Varley (1781–1873) and his wife, Elizabeth Livermore Straker. He claimed descent from Oliver Cromwell and General Charles Fleetwood, for whom he was named. His family was associated with the London Sandemanian congregation, as was the experimental philosopher Michael Faraday (1791–1867). In later years, however, Varley came to regard the Sandemanians as a 'very narrow-minded sect'.

After completing his schooling at St Saviour's Grammar School, Southwark, Varley joined the newly formed Electric Telegraph Company in 1846; he rose to become chief engineer for the London area by 1852 and for the entire company by 1861. Soon after joining the company he devised an electrical method for locating faults in the insulation of underground lines, thus facilitating their repair. This method, known as the 'Varley loop test', was in use for many years. Similar techniques later proved of great value on submarine cables, aided by the employment of standardized resistance coils, which Varley helped introduce into telegraphic practice. He was among the first to trace the retardation and distortion of signals on underground lines to the effects of electrostatic induction, and in 1854 patented a double-current key that lessened the problem by using pulses of alternating polarity to discharge the line. Varley developed a variety of improved testing instruments and relays, and in 1870 patented the 'cymaphen', a type of harmonic telegraph that could transmit musical tones and, in a later variant, articulate speech. He also devised a simple way to use small electrical charges to generate much larger ones, and 'Varley's multiplier' became the basis of widely used electrostatic machines.

Varley's most important work came in submarine telegraphy. After the failure of the short-lived first Atlantic cable in 1858, he was appointed to a joint investigative committee established by the British government and the Atlantic Telegraph Company. Its 1861 report helped restore enough confidence in the technology for a second attempt to span the Atlantic to be launched in 1865, with Varley now serving as chief electrician. Although the 1865 cable snapped during laying, a renewed attempt the following year succeeded; moreover, the broken cable was then grappled and brought to the surface, spliced, and also completed from Ireland to Newfoundland. Varley devised many improvements in cable testing and signalling techniques in the 1860s, including the use of condensers and 'curbed' transmission to sharpen signals, and artificial cables to mimic the effects of distributed resistance and capacitance. A strong-jawed man with muttonchop whiskers and a receding hairline, Varley soon became a leading figure among telegraph engineers. He had a shrewd business sense, and the patent partnership he formed in 1865 with the physicist William Thomson (later Lord Kelvin; 1824-1907) and the electrical engineer Fleeming Jenkin (1833-1885) eventually brought all three men large royalties from cable companies.

Varley was elected a member of the Institution of Civil Engineers in 1865 and a fellow of the Royal Society in 1871. In the latter year he was also a founder member of the Society of Telegraph Engineers (later the Institution of Electrical Engineers). He wrote widely on telegraphic and electrical subjects, and in 1871 published a paper in the *Proceedings of the Royal Society* on electrical discharges in rarefied gases, in which he suggested that cathode rays were streams of tiny electrified particles, later identified as electrons. A convinced spiritualist, he helped introduce the physicist William Crookes (1832-1919) to the subject in 1867, and in 1874 used a cable galvanometer to investigate the 'materializations' of the medium Florence Cook (1856-1904).

Varley had two sons and two daughters with his first wife, Ellen Rouse, whom he married on 4 October 1855. On returning from a trip abroad on cable business, Varley found that she had gone off to live with Ion Perdicaris, a wealthy Greek-American, whom she had met at Malvern in 1871. After the divorce was granted in 1873, she and the children settled with Perdicaris at Tangier. In 1904 Varley's elder son, also named Cromwell, was kidnapped along with Perdicaris by Moroccan bandits, precipitating an international incident before both men were released unharmed. On 11 January 1877 Varley married Heleanor Jessie Smith of Forres, Scotland. After several years of failing health, he died at Cromwell House, Bexleyheath,

Kent, on 2 September 1883, and was buried on 6 September at Christ Church, Bexley.

(Samuel) Alfred Varley (1832-1921) followed his brother Cromwell into the Electric Telegraph Company, entering its Manchester workshops in 1852. He supervised the first field telegraphs used in the Crimean War and published influential papers on cable signalling in 1858-9. In 1861 he took over running a London telegraph factory owned by his father. He and Cromwell had a bitter falling out, and in later years the two brothers denounced each other for a variety of real and imagined slights and betrayals. His marriage in 1860 to Emily Andrews brought them seven children, of whom at least three survived him, although it seems that Emily left him after the children were grown.

Alfred Varley's lack of business acumen kept him from reaping the full rewards of his work. In 1866 he was one of several nearly simultaneous inventors of the self-exciting dynamo, which freed the generation of electric currents from reliance on permanent magnets. This was eventually recognized as a fundamental advance, as was Varley's later invention of compound winding, but his patents on both lapsed before they became commercially valuable. Soured by business failures and the lack of recognition given to his pioneering contributions, he became known in the late 1880s as a vocal critic of electrical engineers' increasing reliance on mathematical theory. He was awarded a civil-list pension in 1894, and later retired to Winchester, where he died at his house, Abbottsacre Lodge, Abbott's Road, on 4 August 1921. He was buried in the city's new cemetery on 9 August.   BRUCE J. HUNT

Sources A. G. Lee, 'The Varley brothers: Cromwell Fleetwood Varley and Samuel Alfred Varley', *Journal of the Institution of Electrical Engineers*, 71 (1932), 958–64 • *The Times* (5 Sept 1883) • *PICE*, 77 (1883–4), 373–81 • R. J. Noakes, 'Telegraphy is an occult art: Cromwell Fleetwood Varley and the diffusion of electricity to the other world', *British Journal for the History of Science*, 32 (1999), 421–59 • J. V. Jeffery, 'The Varley family: engineers and artists', *Notes and Records of the Royal Society*, 51 (1997), 263–79 • private information (2004) [John Varley Jeffery, great-nephew] • *The Electrician*, 11 (1883), 397–8 • *Electrical Review*, 13 (1883), 203–4 • *Engineering* (7 Sept 1883), 222 • *The Times* (8 Aug 1921) [Samuel Alfred Varley] • *Electrical Review*, 89 (1921), 221 [Samuel Alfred Varley] • *Nature*, 107 (1921), 789–90 [Samuel Alfred Varley] • private information (2004) [John F. Varley, great-grandson] • C. Bright, *Submarine telegraphs: their history, construction, and working* (1898) • C. Smith and M. N. Wise, *Energy and empire: a biographical study of Lord Kelvin* (1989) • G. N. Cantor, *Michael Faraday: Sandemanian and scientist* (1991) • *Report on spiritualism by the committee of the London Dialectical Society* (1871), 157–72 [evidence of C. F. Varley, 25 May 1869] • T. H. Hall, *The spiritualists: the story of Florence Cook and William Crookes* (1962) • C. J. Stephenson, 'Further comments on Cromwell Varley's electrical test on Florence Cook', *Proceedings of the Society for Psychical Research*, 54 (1963–6), 363–417 • *Report of the British Association for the Advancement of Science* (1854–1921) • 'Varley v. Varley and Perdicaris', *The Times* (1 Feb 1873), 11 • B. W. Tuchman, 'Perdicaris alive or Raisuli dead', *American Heritage*, 10 (1959), 18–21, 98–101 • *CGPLA Eng. & Wales* (1883) • *CGPLA Eng. & Wales* (1921) [Samuel Alfred Varley] • m. cert., 1855 • *DNB*

Archives BL, Alfred Russel Wallace Collection • CUL, letters to Lord Kelvin • ICL, Rayleigh collection [Samuel Alfred Varley] • U. Glas. L., corresp. with Lord Kelvin

Likenesses F. Jenkin, drawing, 1869, repro. in R. L. Stevenson, 'Memoir', in S. Colvin and J. A. Ewing, *Papers literary, scientific, &c by*

the late Fleeming Jenkin, 2 vols. (1887), vol. 1, facing p. cx · pencil drawing, *c.*1876–1879, Inst. EE · engraving, repro. in *The Atlantic telegraph: its history from the commencement of the undertaking in 1854, to the return of the 'Great Eastern' in 1865* (1865), facing p. 56 · photograph, priv. coll. · photograph (Samuel Alfred Varley), repro. in *Electrical Review* (9 Sept 1892) · vignette, repro. in *The City* (5 May 1883)

Wealth at death £42,157 14*s.* 6*d.*: probate, 25 Oct 1883, *CGPLA Eng. & Wales* · probably very little: Samuel Alfred Varley

Varley, Frederick Henry (1842–1916), electrical engineer, was born at 1 Charles Street, Somers Town, London, on 18 December 1842, the youngest of the seven sons of Cornelius *Varley (1781–1873), scientific instrument maker and watercolour artist, and his wife, Elizabeth Livermore Straker. He was educated privately in Islington and his subsequent engineering career was probably influenced by his father's interest in science. Another strong influence was that of his brother Cromwell Fleetwood *Varley (1828–1883). In 1859 Frederick joined the family firm, which made telegraph components and testing apparatus, many of which were for his brother. In 1865 he was involved in tests on the Atlantic telegraph cable, and in 1868 he acted as assistant engineer on the Lowestoft–Norderney section of the Reuter cable. He and his brother Octavius went into business as consulting engineers and manufacturers of cable testing equipments and instruments. Octavius died in 1871 but Varley used the title O. and F. H. Varley until the 1880s. During his career Varley took out several patents for telegraph apparatus including double current galvanometers and keys, ink-writing Morse instruments, and a system of block signalling for railways.

Varley's subsequent areas of interest mirrored the growth of the electrical industry. In the late 1870s he produced flexible carbons for arc lamps, which he patented in 1882, and a lamp in which light was produced by passing electricity through a constantly falling stream of powdered carbon. He later developed an incandescent lamp filament by soaking fibres in compounds of boron, but the Varley diaphanous filament was not a success, partly due to the domination of the lamp industry by Swan and Edison's patents. Varley also produced and patented batteries and electric motors, and in 1881 helped Cromwell Fleetwood Varley with improvements to the cymaphen, his device for transmitting musical tones. Before the outbreak of the First World War Varley was working on A. T. Johnson's tuned reed wireless system. As well as electrical equipment he developed porous stone wicks for oil and petroleum lamps, and in 1890 he patented photographic apparatus.

Like his brother Cromwell Fleetwood Varley, Frederick Varley was interested in spiritualism and the scientific recording of phenomena produced by mediums. In 1879 Charles Blackburn, a spiritualist investigator, commissioned him to build apparatus for recording the weight of mediums during seances. This was used on 7 October 1879 to monitor a medium called Mr Haxby. Another interest was shooting, and he designed apparatus for indicating target scores automatically. He also published a pocket book of marksmen's target diagrams in 1867.

Throughout his life Varley lived in the Stoke Newington

area of London, which was also the site of his father's works. He died at 82 Newington Green Road, on 12 March 1916.   TIM PROCTER

Sources *Journal of the Institution of Electrical Engineers*, 54 (1916), 688 · biographical sketch, *Electrician Blue Book* [electrical trades directory] (1914), lxxxviii · J. V. Jeffery, 'The Varley family: engineers and artists', *Notes and Records of the Royal Society*, 51 (1997), 263–79 · F. H. Varley, 'Improvements in the production of the electric light', *Journal of the Society of Telegraph Engineers*, 9 (1880), 331 · W. H. Harrison, 'New discoveries in spiritualism', *The Spiritualist and Journal of Psychological Science*, 15 (1879), 186–90 · b. cert. · d. cert. · A. G. Debus and others, eds., *World who's who in science* (1968) [Cornelius Varley]

Varley, Henry (1835–1912), evangelist, was born on 25 October 1835 in Tattershall, Lincolnshire, the youngest of four sons and seven children of John Varley, brewer and maltster, of Tattershall, and his wife, Mary. He was educated at Lincoln until his mother's death in 1845 and then attended a boarding-school in Kibworth, Leicestershire (1845–6). At the age of eleven he went to London to work, eventually becoming a butcher employed by Thomas Pickworth, a staunch Calvinist. In 1851 Varley, whose mother had been a devout Anglican evangelical, experienced an evangelical conversion through the preaching of Baptist W. Noel, a well-known Baptist minister. He was baptized as a believer and joined Noel's church. In 1854 he emigrated to Australia where his early hopes as a gold-digger were disappointed, but where he prospered as a butcher near Melbourne, buying his own business in Geelong in 1855. On returning to England in 1857 he married, on 20 October, Sarah Pickworth, the third daughter of his former employer, and established himself as a successful butcher in Notting Hill, London.

Varley's business success was soon eclipsed by his evangelistic preaching; his rapport with the working poor led him to establish a church for his converts. In 1860 Varley and Thomas Pickworth each gave £1100 to build a tabernacle in Notting Hill, which accommodated 1000 people. Varley was its unpaid minister until 1882 and experimented with various means of evangelizing and meeting the social needs of the poor. Particularly original among these was the annual Butcher's Festival. His ideas had a significant influence on the American evangelist D. L. Moody in 1867 and later in 1872. Varley often preached for C. H. Spurgeon and, like Spurgeon, declined ordination; unlike Spurgeon he refused to be identified as a Baptist. Many of his associates thought him close to the Open Brethren. In 1869 he sold his business and began preaching throughout Britain. In 1874 he toured Canada and the United States. This was the first of a series of overseas crusades: Australia and New Zealand (1876–8), America (1884), the Cape Colony (1886), and Australia (1886–8). In 1888 he settled in Melbourne for health reasons but continued to travel widely, preaching repeatedly in Britain as well as in Singapore (1891), India (1892–3), America (1893–4, 1895, 1897–9, 1901–2), Canada (1897, 1898), Norway (1903), and Germany (1903).

Varley was one of a number of itinerant lay evangelists who emerged after the 1858–9 religious revival. Gradually his sermons moved away from emotional appeals to more reasoned ones; in this he had much in common with such British 'gentleman evangelists' of his day as Brownlow North. His preaching reflected emphases then popular with British evangelicals: the controversial Holiness teaching promoted by the Keswick Convention, anti-Catholicism, temperance, opposition to Anglo-Catholic ritualism, and vehement campaigns against international prostitution rings. Varley embraced premillennialism, which reinforced his pessimistic view of the direction of Victorian society. He was fearless in his attacks on public figures whose actions he considered unconscionable. Varley was also known for his purity lectures, aimed at making men serious, sober, and sexually abstemious. He wrote many religious tracts and books, of which *The Evangel of the Risen Christ* and *Christ's Coming Kingdom* (3rd edn, 1893) had a notable success. Varley died at the Belvedere Mansion Hotel, 61 King's Road, Brighton, on 30 March 1912, and was buried in Brighton extra-mural cemetery on 4 April. He was survived by six sons and two daughters.

D. M. Lewis, *rev.* Timothy C. F. Stunt

Sources H. Varley, *Henry Varley's life story* (1913) • J. Pollock, *Moody without Sankey* (1966), 68–9, 94 • C. M. Davies, *Unorthodox London, or, Phases of religious life in the metropolis* (1873), 58–62
Likenesses photograph, *c*.1905, repro. in Varley, *Henry Varley's life story*, frontispiece
Wealth at death £2,375 12s. 11d.: administration, 1912, CGPLA Eng. & Wales

Varley, John (1778–1842), watercolour painter and art teacher, was born on 17 August 1778 in a converted inn, the Blue Post, Mare Street, Hackney, Middlesex. He was the eldest of five children of Richard Varley (*d.* 1791) of Epworth, Lincolnshire, and his second wife, Hannah Fleetwood. By family tradition his mother was descended from Oliver Cromwell's daughter Bridget. Richard Varley's profession is unknown, but his brother Samuel Varley was a manufacturer of scientific instruments. In spite of parental disapproval, Richard Varley's three sons, John Varley, Cornelius *Varley (1781–1873), and William Fleetwood Varley [*see below*], became artists, as did his daughter Elizabeth, who married the painter William Mulready.

Early career, 1791–1805 At the age of thirteen John Varley was apprenticed to a silversmith, but his father's death in 1791 left the family in poverty, and forced a move to lodgings opposite St Luke's Hospital in Old Street, Hoxton. Varley was next placed with a law stationer but his heart was in sketching and his mother was persuaded to support him. After a brief time with a portrait painter in Holborn, at fifteen or sixteen he became a pupil and assistant to Joseph Charles Barrow, who held an evening drawing school at 12 Furnival's Inn Court, Holborn; François Louis Francia was his fellow assistant. In 1796, while out sketching, Varley made the acquaintance of John Preston Neale. The two men formed a lasting friendship and frequently 'sallied forth in search of the picturesque' (Roget, 1.169) in the villages around north-east London. Barrow took him on a sketching tour to Peterborough and in 1798 Varley exhibited a drawing of Peterborough Cathedral at the

John Varley (1778–1842), self-portrait, *c*.1800

Royal Academy, before becoming a regular exhibitor there until 1804.

Varley's first tour to Wales in 1798 or 1799 laid the foundation of his art, providing him with inspiration and subject matter for the rest of his life. At this time Varley became acquainted with Dr Thomas Monro, taking part in the drawing sessions at the 'Monro academy' in the Adelphi Terrace from 1800 and visiting Monro at his country home, Fetcham Cottage, near Leatherhead. On Monro's advice Varley left Hoxton and moved to the West End, to live first with his brother Cornelius in Charles Street, Covent Garden, and then from 1801 at 2 Harris Place, Pantheon, Oxford Street. It was at this time that he is first recorded taking pupils. In 1802 he visited north Wales again and also became a member of the Sketching Society, chaired by John Sell Cotman, to draw subjects of literary inspiration. His marriage to Esther Gisborne (*d.* 1824) in the following year produced five sons and three daughters but was not, according to the painter John Linnell and other friends, a happy one. Linnell provides a picture of Varley's heavy build and imposing physique, describing him as 'bull like in strength and figure'. Varley was a keen pugilist, though his skill was said to be marred by his ungainliness. He was also 'a man of the most generous impulses … but deficient in sagacity and most easily imposed upon by the crafty' (Linnell, autobiography, 10).

Varley's early work may be divided into three groups: topographical views of English and Welsh towns, Welsh landscapes, and more informal studies from nature. The topographical views, mostly of Hereford (many in Hereford Art Gallery), Leominster, Chester, and Conwy (examples in the V&A), tend to conform to a pattern of rows of houses on a central receding street, reminiscent of the work of Thomas Hearne, with the addition of the picturesque irregularity of half-timbered houses, peeling paintwork, and crumbling masonry. The second group, of Welsh mountain views, form the bulk of his output throughout his career, though it is the earlier examples that most convincingly portray the awe-inspiring character of mountain scenery. Both in technique and composition they owe a prime debt to Thomas Girtin, and ultimately to Richard Wilson, whose *Snowdon from Llyn Nantle* (Walker Art Gallery, Liverpool) was the progenitor of such Welsh views. These early watercolours are more naturalistic than later examples, with the views represented showing a regard for topographical accuracy. Nevertheless, Varley followed William Gilpin's advice in adapting nature to the requirements of composition. Distant mountains, for example, are brought nearer the picture plane to form a focal point. Indeed, as early as 1804, in his views of Bala Lake and Moel Hebog (V&A), the tonality follows in detail the rules Varley published later in his own *A Treatise on the Principles of Landscape Design* of 1816–17: shadow in the foreground, succeeded by a mass of light contrasting with a middle tone in the further distance. In selecting his viewpoints Varley, like his contemporaries, followed the numerous pictorial models which had been called into being by the rapid increase of tourism and travel books in the eighteenth century.

The third category of Varley's early watercolours were informal studies of the English landscape, several of them inscribed with the rubric 'Studies from nature'. They were usually panoramic views clearly based on direct observation but with the addition of the Claudean framing device of trees if the composition demanded, for example *Polesden* (1800; Laing Art Gallery, Newcastle upon Tyne). At this time Varley developed his landscape compositions to produce works dominated by unbroken, unmodulated layers of wash with sharply defined edges, for example *Harlech Castle and Tygwyn Ferry* (1804; Yale U. CBA), which are closely comparable to Cotman's work of the same period.

Years of success, 1805–1812: teacher and astrologer Varley played a significant role in the establishment of the Society of Painters in Water Colours in November 1804, which marked a significant rise in the status of that art form. He took a leading part in the society's early years and enjoyed a considerable personal success at its exhibitions. To the first, in 1805, he contributed forty-two watercolours out of a total of 275, of which thirty were sold for a total of £139 13s. He continued to be the society's most prolific exhibitor, with an average of forty-four works in the exhibitions between 1805 and 1812. His ability to produce numerous fresh drawings for an opening earned them the sobriquet of 'Varley's hot rolls'. His principal buyers were members of the aristocracy and landed gentry: Sir Henry Englefield, Lord Essex, Thomas Hope, Lord Ossulston, William Ord, Sir John Swinburne, Walter Fawkes, and Edward Lascelles, later earl of Harewood.

Varley was equally well known as a teacher of both professional artists and well-born amateurs. By about 1805–6 many of the rising generation of artists were his pupils.

Mulready, Linnell, W. H. Hunt, William Turner of Oxford, and Copley Fielding, all in their teens, lived at his house for a sum of about £100 a year. David Cox and Peter DeWint, both in their early twenties, also took some lessons at this period. Varley was a firm believer in principles of composition which he published in very dogmatic terms. Paradoxically, however, he was praised by contemporaries for encouraging his pupils to draw from nature and offering only the most general supervision. According to Linnell, 'Copying drawings formed no part of the pupils' employment; they were constantly drawing from nature or trying to compose' (Linnell, autobiography, 7), and it is from the evidence of his pupils more than from his own work that Varley has been accorded recognition as a father figure of *plein-air* painting in early nineteenth-century Britain. Yet it was as a teacher of well-born ladies at a guinea an hour that Varley enhanced his earnings and cemented his relationship with his patrons, and it was here that he applied his principles of composition which his pupils imbibed by copying his drawings.

One of Varley's pupils, Elizabeth Turner, daughter of the Yarmouth banker Dawson Turner, who took lessons from him in 1822, described another aspect of his character: 'With all his nobility of mind he unites a more childish simplicity and credulity, and he entirely believes in astrology, palmistry, raising of ghosts and seeing of visions' (Kauffmann, 39). Astrology, in which Varley fervently believed, had long ceased to command respect in such sophisticated circles. Nevertheless, there were many who admired his prognostications, of which there are countless stories, not least that he foretold the fire that burnt down his house in 1825. It was his belief in visions that cemented his friendship with William Blake, whom he encouraged to envision and draw portraits of historical and imaginary figures during their evening sessions at Varley's house in Great Titchfield Street between 1819 and 1825. Many of Blake's figures were drawn into two of Varley's sketchbooks. Varley also shared Blake's interest in J. C. Lavater's theories of physiognomy, which sought to demonstrate that a man's innate qualities determine his outward appearance. In his own *Treatise on Zodiacal Physiognomy*, of which the first and only part was published in 1828, Varley located the mainspring of human physiognomy in the basic astrological belief that the influence of the heavens at the moment of birth accounts for the differing physical characteristics, abilities, and temperaments of mankind. However, apart from the profile heads which illustrate the *Treatise* (preparatory drawings in the Tate collection), there is no discernible influence of his astrological interest on his work as a painter.

In 1808 Varley made a tour of Northumberland, sketching the coastal castles, and henceforth Northumberland, like Wales, provided a reservoir of motifs and locations upon which he drew for the rest of his career. His work continued to be dominated by a simple flat wash style until about 1812, when he introduced more strictly classical motifs derived from seventeenth-century epic and pastoral landscape, for example, *Suburbs of an Ancient City* (1808; Tate collection).

Teaching manuals, lean years and revival, 1813–1842 In 1812 declining sales, owing partly to monotony of output, forced the Society of Painters in Water Colours to admit oil painters, and from 1813–1820 its name was changed to the Society of Painters in Oil and Water Colours. In the years 1816–21 the average number of works Varley exhibited dwindled to a mere eight; this decline in exhibited work mirrors a general reduction in his output. However, his name was kept before the public's eye with the publication of his *Treatise on the Principles of Landscape Design* in 1816–17. This was in the tradition of illustrated teaching manuals which had proliferated since the 1790s. The works of Claude and Gaspard Poussin served as his main models, and were combined with picturesque theories of variety and intricacy. The basic theme of the *Treatise*, that 'emphasis must always be on the principal subject', also appears in several other such manuals, but Varley's publication is distinguished by its extreme formalism. His other publications in this field include *Treatise on the Art of Drawing in Perspective* (1815–20), and three shorter manuals: *A Practical Treatise on the Art of Drawing* (c.1815–20), *Precepts of Landscape Drawing* (c.1818), and *Studies of Trees* (1818–19), as well as the more interesting *John Varley's List of Colours* (1816), which gives nineteen colour samples, with brief advice on their use.

At this time Varley produced formulaic paintings by applying Claudean compositional arrangements to Welsh scenery, as for example in *Landscape with Harlech Castle* of c.1815–25 (V&A) and also, in strong contrast, several of his more direct, informal views of the Thames at Millbank and Lambeth (*Millbank Penitentiary*, 1816; Museum of London). Thames views had formed part of his repertory since 1806, but these sketches of Millbank, several inscribed 'study from nature', are less finished and lighter in tonality than his more formal compositions of the villages of Chiswick and Chelsea. In the 1820s he tried to fall in with the prevailing taste for works of moral or literary content, exhibiting illustrations to the Bible, or to Milton, Byron, and Scott at the Society of Painters, but such subjects remain relatively rare in his *œuvre*.

These were lean years for Varley, with eight children to support, few watercolours to exhibit, and little financial sense. From 1819 Linnell was inundated with requests for loans and in 1820 Varley was declared bankrupt and gaoled. Indeed, although there was a temporary revival in the number of works he exhibited at the Society of Painters in Water Colours in 1823–6, and also a display of his work at his house in Great Titchfield Street, Varley appears to have remained insolvent throughout the 1820s and early 1830s. His wife, Esther, died in 1824 and he married Delvalle (b. c.1800), daughter of his friend the engraver Wilson Lowry, in the following year; this union proved to be happier and produced two more children. With the increasing importance of middle-class patronage during the 1830s dealers began to compete with the annual exhibitions for sales of works; in commercial dealings Varley depended first on Samuel Woodburn and then on William Vokins, who became a personal friend.

The last years of his life saw a revival of Varley's fortunes based on a complete change of style. From the later 1830s he moved away from topographical subjects to concentrate on imaginary landscape compositions. Many of these were small, postcard-size sketches characterized by bold, rapid brushstrokes in dark brown wash. A more fundamental change of palette, inspired by the glowing, mystical landscapes of Samuel Palmer, followed in 1839–40. The sketchy brown wash technique was amplified by the introduction of dark red and purple colours and the use of coarse wove paper. In the final phase, 1841–2, he extended the use of hot tonalities with contrasting pink, purple, and orange areas and experimented with an increasing use of gum. These late works have an expressive intensity not seen in Varley's art since his early years, and in 1841 he once again exhibited thirty watercolours and sold twenty-four. Sadly, this revival of fortunes came too late to save him from the financial difficulties that had dogged him, and he died on 17 November 1842 at the house of William Vokins, 5 John Street, Oxford Street, London. His second wife survived him.

Varley's reputation was summarized in his obituaries and in the early histories (Redgrave and Redgrave, 201; Kauffmann, 65). He was accorded the recognition due to one of the leading watercolourists of his day, but there was also an awareness of the monotony of his vast output. In his best work he rivals Girtin and Cotman, but he exhibited over 700 watercolours at the watercolour societies, a relatively small proportion of his total output (there are also a few oils), and his reputation never survived the ensuing glut of his work.

Varley's family William Fleetwood Varley (1785–1856) appears to have been taught by his brother John, with whom he was still living at 2 Harris Place, Oxford Street, London, in 1804. His watercolours, of which fifteen are in the Victoria and Albert Museum, London, reflect different aspects of John's style. He lived in London and exhibited at the Royal Academy between 1804 and 1818, but his principal reputation was as a drawing master in Cornwall, Bath, and Oxford. A brief publication, *A Few Observations on Art* (1816), was followed by his fuller treatise *Observations on Colouring and Sketching from Nature* (1820), a teaching manual of more practical use than many of its peers. While living in Oxford he was nearly burnt to death in a fire caused by undergraduates, an event from which he never fully recovered, and after which he apparently gave up working. This must have been after 1825, the date of his latest watercolour in the Victoria and Albert Museum, London. He died in Ramsgate in 1856.

Of John Varley's ten children, two became professional painters: Albert Fleetwood (1804–1876) and Charles Smith (1811–1887). **John Varley** (1850–1933), son of Albert Fleetwood and his wife, Caroline Roper, was born on 26 January 1850, at New Road, Fulham, London. He achieved a considerable reputation for his views, in watercolour and oil, of Egypt, particularly street scenes of Cairo, and views of the Nile, and also of India and Japan, France and Italy, which he exhibited at the Royal Academy between 1876 and 1895, and which were the subject of one-person shows in London in 1904 and 1913. Like his grandfather, he was interested in astrology and the occult. He and his wife, Isabella, *née* Pollexfen, aunt of the poet W. B. Yeats, whom he married in 1876, were drawn to theosophy and were members of the inner circle gathered round Madame Blavatsky in 1883–4. He died of cancer at the Imperial Nursing Home, Montpellier Parade, Cheltenham, on 20 May 1933, leaving at least one daughter. C. M. KAUFFMANN

Sources C. M. Kauffmann, *John Varley, 1778–1842* (1984) · A. Lyles, 'John Varley's early work', *Old Water-Colour Society's Club*, 59 (1984), 1–22 · A. Lyles, 'John Varley's Thames', *Old Water-Colour Society's Club*, 63 (1994), 1–37 · A. Lyles, 'John Varley: a catalogue of his watercolours and drawings in the British Museum', MA diss., Courtauld Inst., 1980 · A. Bury, *John Varley of the Old Society* (1946) · R. Redgrave and S. Redgrave, *A century of British painters* (1866) · J. L. Roget, *A history of the 'Old Water-Colour' Society*, 2 vols. (1891) · A. T. Story, *The life of John Linnell* (1892) · A. T. Story, *James Holmes and John Varley* (1894) · J. Bayard, *Works of splendor and imagination: the exhibition watercolour, 1770–1870* (1981) [exhibition catalogue, Yale U. CBA] · M. Hardie, *Watercolour painting in Britain*, 2 (1967) · P. Curry, *A confusion of prophets: Victorian and Edwardian astrology* (1992) · D. Linnell, *Blake, Palmer, Linnell & co.: the life of John Linnell* (1994) · J. Dobai, *Die Kunstliteratur des Klassizismus und der Romantik in England*, 3: *1790–1840* (1977), 1172 ff. · J. Linnell, MS autobiography, V&A NAL · b. cert. [John Varley junior] · d. cert. [John Varley junior]
Archives Bankside Gallery, London, Old Watercolour Society, J. J. Jenkins papers · FM Cam., John Linnell archive, incl. his journal, autobiography, and corresp. · V&A NAL, Old Watercolour Society price books, 1805, 1807, 1808–1812
Likenesses J. Varley, self-portrait, drawing, *c*.1800; Sothebys, 13 Nov 1980, lot 43 [*see illus.*] · W. Lowry, pencil, 1804, priv. coll. · J. Linnell, watercolour drawing, *c*.1810, V&A · W. Mulready, black chalk, *c*.1814, BM · W. Mulready, miniature, oils, 1814, NPG · W. Blake, pencil drawing, *c*.1820–1825, NPG · J. Linnell, double portrait, pencil drawing, 1821 (with William Blake), FM Cam. · J. Linnell, oils, AM Oxf. · portraits, repro. in R. Walker, *Regency portraits* (1985)
Wealth at death declared bankrupt in 1820 and in debt for much of the period 1820 until death · £2151 16*s*. 9*d*.—John Varley junior: administration with will, resworn, 1933

Varley, John (1850–1933). *See under* Varley, John (1778–1842).

Varley, Julia (1871–1952), trade unionist, was born on 16 March 1871 in Horton, Bradford, the first child of Richard Varley, an engine tenter (a skilled worsted mill worker), and his wife, Martha Ann Alderson. Her maternal great-grandfather, Joseph Alderson, who died in 1886, was a veteran of Peterloo and the Chartist campaigns. Julia Varley attended St Andrew's School, Listerhills, Bradford, and the Quaker Sunday school, but because of family circumstances left school at the age of twelve, and became a part-time mill worker, soon progressing to full-time weaver.

Julia Varley joined the Weavers and Textile Workers' Union and by the age of fifteen had become Bradford branch secretary. On her mother's death she had to give up full-time mill work to care for her younger sisters and brothers, but this did not stop her union work, remarkable at a time when few women were members of unions, let alone active in them. Her involvement increased with the Manningham Mills strike of 1890–91; she became the first woman member of the Bradford Trades Council as secretary of her union branch, and served on its executive committee from 1899 to 1906.

This marked a considerable broadening of Julia Varley's activities away from 'pure' union activity. In 1903 she was appointed by Bradford corporation to inquire into employment conditions and assist in the organization of school meals. She served on the Bradford board of (poor law) guardians from 1904 to 1907. This brought her into contact with tramping women, whose conditions she determined to investigate at first hand. She therefore disguised herself and tramped from Leeds to Liverpool, ostensibly in search of an errant husband, sleeping in casual wards on the way. She followed this up with a similar tour of London doss-houses. She also became a suffragette and was twice imprisoned in 1907. By comparison with her doss-house and casual ward experiences, she found food and accommodation in Holloway quite good.

At this time Julia Varley had also become involved with Mary Macarthur and the National Federation of Women Workers (NFWW), and in 1907 they succeeded in establishing a branch of the NFWW among the female small-chain makers of Cradley Heath. The agitation begun by the NFWW was taken up and given high-profile national publicity by the women's suffrage press and the Anti-Sweating League, with the result that small-chain making was included within the provisions of the 1909 Trade Boards Act. In 1909 Edward Cadbury invited her to Birmingham to organize women workers; she immediately established an NFWW branch at Bournville, which affiliated to the Birmingham Trades Council, with Julia Varley as branch delegate. In January 1910 she was elected to the executive (again the first woman in both positions), and was immediately involved in successful campaigns concerned with pay and conditions of bakers and chain makers. However, the attempt to establish a branch of the newly formed Workers' Union (WU) in the potteries at Bilston not only failed, but involved her in physical violence.

By 1912, Julia Varley's involvement with the WU had come to convince her that men and women should organize in a single union, and she transferred her allegiance to it from the NFWW. Its heartland was in the Black Country, and in the hard but ultimately successful 1913 metalworkers' strikes Julia Varley played a major part in rallying the strikers' women to the cause. A strike among Cornish clay miners was less successful. However, a major change to the WU's fortunes occurred with the First World War, when the influx of new, especially female, labour into munitions led to a sharp increase in membership, particularly among women; from 5000 in 1914, the WU's women membership had risen to over 80,000 by 1918. Until August 1915 Julia Varley was the WU's only woman organizer, and she continued to organize actively right through the war, despite having to undergo a major throat operation early in 1917.

Nevertheless, the war brought to an end Julia Varley's connection with the Birmingham Trades Council, which had initially given qualified support to war work, but soon changed its position, especially after the introduction of conscription in 1916. This apparent lack of patriotism caused Julia Varley and a number of other council members to form a breakaway body, the Birmingham Trade

Union Industrial Council, which ceased activity in 1918, when most of its members reaffiliated to the Birmingham Trades Council. However, Julia Varley apparently remained unreconciled.

In general at this time Julia Varley seems to have become more favourable to certain official institutions. In 1917–18 she was selected to serve on two bodies set up by the Ministry of Labour: first, the Labour Advisory Board, responsible for investigating and reporting on the working of labour exchanges; the second was as part of a commission of five representative women sent to investigate rumours of immoral behaviour by WAACs in France (the committee found the rumours groundless). More controversially, she accepted an invitation to serve on the executive of the National Alliance of Employers and Employed, a body regarded with deep suspicion by most of the trade union movement; the executive committee of her own WU gave her permission to join provided it was made clear that she was acting in a purely personal capacity.

After the war Julia Varley continued as chief woman organizer for the WU, and, after their 1929 merger, for the Transport and General Workers' Union, until 1936. She was elected to the newly established general council of the TUC as one of two representatives of women workers from 1921 to 1924, and from 1926 to 1935; in this capacity she attended various International Labour Organization conferences in Geneva, Rome, and Vienna. She served on various government committees, notably on the working of the labour exchanges, and the condition of women and young persons under the two-shift system. She became involved in the work of the Society for the Overseas Settlement of British Women, and in 1925 travelled with a group of emigrants to Canada. As a member of the executive committee of the Industrial Welfare Society, she got to know the duke of York (later George VI). Another unexpected friend was Nancy Astor, who apparently warmed to a fellow rebel. In 1931 she was appointed OBE for her public work, and in March 1936 she finally retired from the trade union movement and active participation in public life, though still taking an active interest from her home at 42 Hay Green Lane, Bournville.

Julia Varley worked to assure women's position within the trade union movement as a whole, rather than (like Mary Macarthur) in separate unions. She achieved high position in one of the country's largest unions, and with it a prominent place in public life, which she enjoyed. She was sturdily built, wore pince-nez, and habitually had a determined expression. Her general approach was forthright, though she was capable of kindness and affection. Throughout the 1930s her eyesight gradually failed to the point of total blindness, though she still kept contact with the TUC and the local church. She died of a stroke on 24 November 1952 at 32 Hampden Street, Bradford, the home of her sisters, Mrs Martha Jarrett and Mrs Jessie Wooller; and after a service in All Saints' Church, Bradford, she was buried in Undercliffe cemetery.   DAVID DOUGHAN

Sources S. Lewenhak, *Women and trade unions: an outline history of women in the British trade union movement* (1977) · J. Bellamy, M.

'Espinasse, and E. Taylor, 'Varley, Julia', *DLB*, vol. 5 · M. G. Bondfield, *A life's work* [1948] · H. Swaffer, 'Julia Varley's swan song', *Daily Herald* (27 May 1935) · *Labour Woman* (Jan 1953) · b. cert. · d. cert.
Archives U. Hull, Brynmor Jones L., corresp. and papers
Likenesses photograph, repro. in Swaffer, 'Julia Varley's swan song'
Wealth at death £1419 14s. 3d.: probate, 5 March 1953, *CGPLA Eng. & Wales*

Varley, William Fleetwood (1785–1856). *See under* Varley, John (1778–1842).

Varlo, Charles (b. c.1725, d. in or after 1795), agriculturist, was born in Yorkshire about 1725. He visited Ireland at the age of twenty-one, and spent some time with Edward Synge (1659–1741), bishop of Elphin. While in Ireland, he was employed by the linen board to advise flax-farmers on how to improve the quality of their flax, as he came from a part of Yorkshire well known for flax farming. By 1748 he had a farm in co. Leitrim, and was experimenting in the growing of turnips. At the age of twenty-seven he married, and bought more land. He brought over English labourers and farm implements. It used to be thought that Varlo was the inventor of the Rotherham plough, which was in wide use by the end of the eighteenth century, but in fact this had been patented in 1730.

In 1760 the prohibition on the export of Irish cattle to England was removed, and Varlo sold his land in Ireland and prepared to bring his cattle over to England. This was a very unpopular move: Varlo's cattle were slaughtered by the mob in the streets of Dublin in May 1760, and he himself had a very narrow escape. With the help of the duke of Bedford, lord lieutenant of Ireland, he managed to get some compensation from the government, and he appears to have begun cattle farming in England, probably in Yorkshire. In 1764 he perfected a harrowing and sowing machine. He also invented a winnowing machine which he perfected in 1772, and a machine designed to remove friction.

In 1784, while he was living in Sloane Square, in London, Varlo became involved in a somewhat ludicrous episode. He had bought papers and charters supposedly granted by Charles I to Sir Edward Plowden, entitling him to colonize New Albion (later New Jersey) in America. This attempt at colonization had failed and in Charles II's reign the charter was superseded by a new grant to the duke of York. Armed with his papers (which were probably forgeries), Varlo went out to the American colonies in 1784 hoping to be recognized as governor of the province of New Jersey and to take over one-third of the territory. The case was tried before the colonial courts, but Varlo's claim was dismissed. Varlo nevertheless printed his documents in America in a thirty-page pamphlet. Before returning to England he travelled for a year through New England, Maryland, and Virginia (where he met George Washington). Once back in Britain he unsuccessfully petitioned the king and the prince of Wales in the hope of getting some of the money granted to American loyalists.

Varlo wrote widely on agricultural topics, with observations made on his travels in England and in America. His works include *The Yorkshire Farmer* (1766), *A New System of*

Husbandry (1770, 5th edn 1785), and *The Floating Ideas of Nature, Suited to the Philosopher, Farmer, and Mechanic* (1796).

It is not known when Varlo died, but he appears to have been living in Southampton Row, New Road, Paddington, Middlesex, on 24 February 1795, when Sir John Sinclair sent him a formal letter of thanks for certain suggestions made by Varlo to the board of agriculture about the offering of premiums for the cultivation of maize.

ERNEST CLARKE, *rev.* ANNE PIMLOTT BAKER

Sources C. Varlo, preface, *The floating ideas of nature*, 2 (1796) [Varlo's letters to the prince of Wales] • C. Varlo, *The modern farmers guide: a new system of husbandry … to which is prefixed a short abstract of the author's life and travels*, 2 vols. (1768) • J. W. Raimo, *Biographical directory of American colonial and revolutionary governors, 1607–1789* (1980)

Vasey, Sir Ernest Albert (1901–1984), politician in Kenya and businessman, was born on 27 August 1901 in Maryport, Cumberland, the son of Ernest Albert Vasey, an actor. His mother, whose name is unknown, was described as a repertory actress. Vasey's early life was peripatetic. His formal education ended when he left the Bromley national school aged twelve. He followed various trades on his way to achieving a more secure position, working as a Manchester club pageboy, a newspaper vendor, a blacksmith, a cobbler, and a household furnishing salesman, and in the mines. Between 1929 and 1937 Vasey was active in west midlands Conservative politics, earning a reputation as a powerful speaker, and serving on Shrewsbury town council and on the executive committee of the National Conservative Association, as well as being involved with the West Midlands Unionist Association and the Junior Imperial League. On 19 July 1923 he married Norah May (*b.* 1900/01), daughter of William Percy Mitchell, a master household furnisher. The couple had a son.

A holiday in Kenya in 1935 marked the start of Vasey's long association with the colony, and he settled there in 1937. Resolved never to enter politics again, he followed a business career, eventually serving on the boards of various companies, including the Bata Shoe Company Ltd. In 1938, however, at the suggestion of Gwladys, Lady Delamere, he stood successfully for election to the Nairobi municipal council, remaining a member until 1950. As mayor in 1941–2, he worked for an increase in African representation, securing during his second term in office (1944–6) the addition of two nominated African representatives to the council. In 1944 he married Hannah Strauss (*d.* 1981); they had one son. In 1945 Vasey was elected legislative councillor for Nairobi North. In this capacity he pressed for greater direction in government policy towards industry, and helped bring about the creation of a ministry of commerce in 1948.

In 1950 Vasey crossed the floor to join the colonial government, becoming only the second European from outside the colonial service to be appointed by the government to the executive council and receiving under the new 'member system' the portfolio for health, local government, and education. He later claimed that he had joined the government in order to articulate his 'moderate' views more freely and to establish himself as an effective leader of all races (Vasey to P. Rogers, 20 Dec 1952, Vasey MSS, box 1, file 3). Some, however, thought that the switch of allegiance reflected his failure to attract sufficient support among elected European members in the legislative council to secure his own election (Blundell, 76). In 1952 Vasey was appointed minister of finance in a bid by the administration to end the political stand-off with European settlers over fiscal policy by promoting an unofficial. He remained in the post until 1959. Vasey was one of the key political figures in Kenya throughout the Mau Mau emergency. He reformed the treasury along more professional lines, and secured the addition of development to his portfolio in 1954 under the Lyttelton constitution. Protecting funds intended for development and attracting additional British financial assistance while ensuring that emergency expenditure did not result in British control over Kenyan finances, Vasey successfully steered the Kenyan economy through the emergency. He helped Kenya to establish strong connections with aid agencies at a relatively early stage, upheld confidence among investors, and urged government encouragement of new industries and the creation of the Nairobi stock exchange, established in 1954, as well as a loans scheme to assist African traders.

Admired by officials as a skilful administrator, Vasey played up his position as an unofficial, threatening resignation on several occasions when it strengthened his hand in negotiations with the Colonial Office and the Kenyan administration. Characterized by British officials in 1949 as 'a red hot settler' (Tignor, 309), Vasey, a member of the Capricorn Africa Society, was progressive politically, financing W. W. W. Awori's newspaper *Radio Posta* in the late 1940s, and consistently advocating greater African political advance, calling for instance for the introduction of a common roll. He was the most effective of settler politicians in securing multiracial support, working closely with Asian community leaders, although sometimes privately dismissive of Asian suitability for political office (ibid.). Vasey formed the Unofficial Members' Organization in 1948 to provide a forum in which members representing all races could meet, and, in 1955, instituted a series of secret meetings with European, Asian, and African community leaders to discuss constitutional advance. In 1959 he was rumoured to be considering forming a multiracial party. Regarded as a man of great integrity, Vasey's robust and opinionated style and his political views left him, however, without significant support among European unofficials, and during his last years at the Treasury criticism of him culminated in demands for an inquiry into Kenya's fiscal policies.

Despite having been a significant influence behind the introduction in 1957 of multiracial representation through an electoral college, Vasey failed to gain election in 1958 to the legislative council as a special elected member owing to an African boycott. He resigned from the council of ministers and in 1959 was invited by Julius Nyerere to Tanganyika, where he was minister of finance and economics from 1959 to 1960 and minister for finance from 1960 to 1962. From 1962 to 1966 he was an economic adviser to the World Bank, and between 1963 and 1966 resident representative in Pakistan for the International Bank for Reconstruction and Development. Returning to Kenya in 1966, Vasey sought a quieter life, working as a financial consultant with, among others, the International Finance Corporation. He chaired several important official inquiries, including an inquiry into local government in Zanzibar (1954). He also published various papers on Kenyan economic and political development.

Vasey's early theatrical associations inspired a lifelong love. He acted from an early age, tried dramatic writing (a one-scene play published in 1933 debated the social costs of industry), and became a partner in a Nairobi playhouse/cinema and managing director in the British East African cinema syndicate, the New Theatre Ltd. He was made CMG in 1945, awarded the insignia of the second class of the Brilliant Star of Zanzibar in 1955, and made a freeman of Nairobi in 1957, KBE in 1959, and in 1966 Hilal-i-Quaid-i-Azam of Pakistan. He died in Nairobi on 10 January 1984, predeceased by his second wife.   SARAH STOCKWELL

Sources *The Times* (12 Jan 1984), 12 • Bodl. RH, Vasey MSS • R. L. Tignor, *Capitalism and nationalism at the end of empire: state and business in decolonizing Egypt, Nigeria, and Kenya, 1945–1963* (1998), pt 3 • D. Throup, *Economic and social origins of Mau Mau, 1945–53* (1987), 283 • B. Berman, *Control and crisis in colonial Kenya: dialectic of domination* (1990), 284, 404–5 • M. McWilliam, 'Economic policy and the Kenya settlers, 1945–1948', *Essays in imperial government presented to Margery Perham*, ed. K. Robinson and F. Madden (1963), 171–92 • M. Blundell, *So rough a wind: the Kenya memoirs of Sir Michael Blundell* (1964), 76 • P. Murphy, *Party politics and decolonization: the conservative party and British colonial policy in tropical Africa, 1951–1964* (1995), 178–9 • B. A. Ogot, *Historical dictionary of Kenya* (1981), 209–10 • WWW, 1981–90

Archives Bodl. RH, financial papers relating to Kenya and Tanganyika • Kenya National Archives, Nairobi

Vashon, James (1742–1827), naval officer, son of James Volant Vashon (*bap.* 1707), Church of England clergyman at Eye in Herefordshire and lecturer of Ludlow, was born at Ludlow on 9 August 1742. He entered the navy in August 1755 on the *Revenge*, with Captain Frederick Cornewall, a local figure of property and influence. In the *Revenge* Vashon was present at the battle of Minorca on 20 May 1756, and when Cornewall returned to England as a witness in the trial of Admiral John Byng he transferred into the *Lancaster*, with Captain George Edgcumbe, and took part in the capture of Louisbourg in July 1758. The *Lancaster* then served in the West Indies, as part of the force under Commodore John Moore in the capture of Guadeloupe.

Vashon was then moved to the *Cambridge*, Moore's flagship, and continued in her, under Captain Goostrey and Rear-Admiral Charles Holmes at Jamaica. While there he frequently served in the *Boreas*, a cruising frigate, and experienced some sharp boat service in cutting out enemy privateers. Holmes died in November 1761, and on 1 July 1762 Goostrey was killed in the attack on the Morro Castle at Havana. In summer 1761 Goostrey is said to have asked Holmes to make Vashon a lieutenant. Holmes demurred,

saying he looked such a boy, but he would make him one in time. The death of both patrons nullified this plan, and though he passed his lieutenant's examination on 7 September 1763, and continued serving without interruption on the Newfoundland station and the West Indies, he was not promoted until 1 June 1774, when Sir George Rodney made him a lieutenant of the *Maidstone*. After she received a refit in England he sailed in her in 1777 to the coast of North America, under the command of Captain Alan Gardner, and spent the early months of 1778 in active cruising.

In March, Vashon commanded the boats which set fire to a ship they had driven on shore, where she was defended by several field-pieces. In July he carried intelligence of the French fleet to Lord Howe at New York and, having rejoined the *Maidstone*, assisted in capturing the privateer *Lion*. Vashon, with twenty-four men, was put on the *Lion*, but the worsening weather prevented further communication, and the situation of the prize crew with some two hundred prisoners grew precarious. The ship was also in a sinking condition, but Vashon succeeded in keeping the *Lion*'s crew at the pumps, and so brought the prize safely to Antigua. For this service he was promoted to the rank of commander on 5 August 1779, and ordered home; and on 29 August 1779 he married Jane Bethell at Ludlow.

Vashon was appointed to the *Alert*, in which he returned to the West Indies. He was sent home with dispatches from Jamaica early in 1781, was for some time attached to the fleet in the North Sea under Sir Hyde Parker, and in December went again to the West Indies with Rodney, where the *Alert* was stationed off Martinique as a lookout ship. He was with the fleet off Dominica at the battle of the Saints (12 April 1782), when he took possession of the *Glorieuse*, and was active in saving survivors from the explosion of the *César*. He was promoted captain of the *Prince William* by a commission dated the same day. Rodney soon afterwards appointed him flag captain of the *Formidable*, a mark of esteem, and, on Rodney's recall Vashon was moved into the frigate *Sibyl*, which he commanded until the peace.

From 1786 to 1789 Vashon was captain of the *Europa*, with Commodore Gardner's broad pennant, and in the Spanish armament of 1790 he commanded the *Ardent* (64 guns) and in 1793 was appointed to the *St Albans* (64 guns), employed on convoy service to the Mediterranean and to Jamaica. He afterwards commanded the *Pompée* (80 guns) in the Channel Fleet off Brest, and during the mutiny at Spithead. Following its conclusion a new and dangerous outbreak occurred in the *Pompée* and though this was promptly quelled and the ringleaders tried by court martial and sentenced to death, Vashon applied to be relieved from the command. He commanded in turn the *Neptune* (98 guns), the *Dreadnought* (98 guns) in 1801–2, and the *Princess Royal* (90 guns) from 1803 until his promotion to the rank of rear-admiral on 23 April 1804.

The command of so many large second rates indicates recognition of solid though not brilliant, professional skills, yet further significant duties eluded Vashon, and

for four years he commanded the ships at Leith and on the coast of Scotland. He was made a vice-admiral on 28 April 1808, and admiral on 4 June 1814. He died at Ludlow on 20 October 1827, and was survived by a son, then in holy orders.
J. K. LAUGHTON, rev. P. L. C. WEBB

Sources Admiralty 'in letters', PRO, ADM 1 · J. Ralfe, *The naval biography of Great Britain*, 4 vols. (1828) · J. Marshall, *Royal naval biography*, 4 vols. (1823–35) [with 4 suppls.] · D. Syrett and R. L. DiNardo, *The commissioned sea officers of the Royal Navy, 1660–1815*, rev. edn, Occasional Publications of the Navy RS, 1 (1994) · *GM*, 1st ser., 97/2 (1827), 465 · IGI

Archives NMM, letters to Lord Keith · PRO, Admiralty 'in letters', ADM 1

Likenesses J. Young, mezzotint, pubd 1809 (after G. Watson), BM, NMM

Vassa, Gustavus. *See* Equiano, Olaudah (*c*.1745–1797).

Vassall, Elizabeth. *See* Fox, Elizabeth Vassall, Lady Holland (1771?–1845).

Vassall, John (*d*. 1625), shipowner and colonial adventurer, was of French descent; his family, probably Huguenots, originated from near Caen in Normandy. Little is known of his parents or early career, though he apparently acquired a reputation as a competent authority on maritime matters, and was consulted by the high court of admiralty in suits concerning wreck in 1577 and mariners' wages in 1597. His seafaring career probably included voyages into the Mediterranean, to Leghorn and Genoa, during the early 1580s. In 1588 he set out two vessels to serve in the Armada campaign, serving as captain of one of them, the *Samuel* (140 tons). In 1594 he was rewarded for building four ships in association with Thomas Barnes and Bartholomew Matthewson. He was a prominent member of the Trinity House of Deptford, serving as an elder brother during the early seventeenth century, when he was involved in a wide range of maritime business. In 1609 he joined the Virginia Company of London, with an adventure of £25.

Vassall married three times. His first wife was Anne Howes, whom he married at the church of St Dunstan and All Saints, Stepney, on 25 September 1569. Following her death he married Anna Russell (*d*. 1593), on 4 September 1580; their children included four sons and one daughter, among whom were Samuel *Vassall (*bap*. 1586, *d*. 1667), MP and Virginia merchant, and William [*see below*]. On 27 March 1594, after the death of his second wife, Vassall married Judith (*d*. 1629), widow of Thomas Scott of Colchester and London, and third daughter of Stephen Borough of Stepney, with whom he had four daughters and two sons. A prominent and respected member of the maritime community in London, Vassall acquired various landed interests in the City and in Essex, including the lease on the parsonage and rectory of Eastwood, where he lived for a while, becoming a friend and neighbour of Samuel Purchas. In his will of 29 April 1625 he made generous provision for his wife and his surviving children. He died at Stepney, and was buried in the parish church on 13 September 1625.

William Vassall (1592–1655), born on 27 August 1592 at Stepney, was the fourth son of John and Anna Vassall. Little evidence survives for his education or early career. On 9 June 1613 he married Anna, daughter of George King of Cold Norton, Essex, with whom he had five daughters and a son, John (*c*.1625–1688). He was a leading figure in establishing the Massachusetts Bay Company during 1629, when he was selected as a member of council and assistant. In 1630 he and his family emigrated to the colony, leaving their home in Prittlewell, Essex, though they returned to England the following year, going back to Massachusetts in 1635. After a brief stay at Roxbury, however, Vassall moved to Scituate in Plymouth plantation, where he acquired land along the North River and soon became a prominent figure in the local community. In partnership with his brother Samuel he was very active commercially throughout the 1630s and 1640s. In 1642 he was chosen as one of the deputies for Scituate, and served on the council of war during a time of disturbed relations with the indigenous people.

By the early 1640s Vassall was embroiled in controversy with the colonial authorities concerning membership of the church. In 1646 he was involved in a petition to relax restrictions on admission to the church, though it was dismissed by Edward Johnson as the work of 'persons of a Linsiwolsie disposition, some for Prelacy, some for Presbytery, and some for Plebsbytery' (J. Franklin Jameson, ed., *Johnson's Wonder-Working Providence, 1628–1651*, New York, 1910, 240). Vassall returned to London, where he tried to pursue his case with parliament. John Child's *New England's Jonas Cast up in London* (1647) was heavily influenced by him, but it had little impact. In 1648 he migrated to Barbados, acquiring an estate in St Michael's parish. Able and hard-working, he was soon prominent within the colonial community. In 1652 he was a commissioner of the highways. During 1655 he was appointed a commissioner for implementing the Navigation Acts; he was also chosen to serve in the recently established prize office. He died in Barbados later in the year, with property in the colony and a huge estate in New England. He was buried in Barbados in 1655.

Spencer Thomas Vassall (1764–1807), army officer, a direct descendant of William Vassall, was born on 7 April 1764 in Massachusetts, the second son of John Vassall (1738–1797), merchant and planter, and his wife, Elizabeth Oliver (*d*. 1807). His parents returned to England as a result of the political and military conflict in North America, settling at Bristol and subsequently at Bath. Apparently Vassall was educated at a foreign academy before joining the 59th regiment of foot as an ensign, at the age of twelve. Thereafter he acquired extensive experience, serving in varying capacities and campaigns with the regiment. As a young lieutenant he earned renown during the siege of Gibraltar in 1782. He took part in two campaigns in Flanders during the French Revolutionary Wars, when he was allegedly nearly executed on suspicion of being a spy. He also served as a senior officer in Antigua. He purchased the lieutenant-colonelcy of the 38th regiment, which he took command of in 1801. Under his leadership it became known as 'the Crack Regiment in Ireland' (*Memoir of … Lieutenant-Colonel Vassall*, 18). In 1806 he participated in the capture of the Cape of Good Hope, where he served briefly as commandant. During his years in the service he became respected for his professional abilities; apparently, he was highly regarded by Sir John Moore, with whom he was compared.

Vassall married Catherine Brandreth Backhouse, daughter of J. Evans, clergyman, on 30 June 1795. They had two sons and two daughters. His last campaign was with the ill-fated expedition to seize Buenos Aires in 1807. He was injured during the capture of Montevideo, on 3 February, and died from his wounds on 7 February 1807. Although his body was interred in the grand church of Montevideo, his remains were brought back to England and placed in a family vault in St Paul's, Bristol, to which a monument, designed by Flaxman, was added. He died leaving property in Britain and Jamaica to be held in trust for his widow and children. JOHN C. APPLEBY

(William) John Christopher Vassall (1924–1996), by F. Shepherd, 1975

Sources W. Vassall, *Vassall pedigree, 1500 to 1890* (1890) · genealogical notes on the Vassall family from 1588 to 1831, BL, Add. MS 51806, fols. 133–40 · *CSP dom.*, 1547–80; 1581–94; 1628–9 · G. G. Harris, ed., *Trinity House of Deptford: transactions, 1609–35*, London RS, 19 (1983) · J. S. Corbett, ed., *Papers relating to the navy during the Spanish war, 1585–1587*, Navy RS, 11 (1898) · A list of ships set out against the Spanish in 1588, BL, Harley MS 168, fol. 177 · *The Winthrop papers*, ed. W. C. Ford and others, 2 (1931) · *The journal of John Winthrop, 1630–1649*, ed. R. S. Dunn, J. Savage, and L. Yeandle (1996) · N. B. Shurtleff and D. Pulsifer, eds., *Records of the colony of New Plymouth in New England*, 12 vols. (1855–61), vols. 1, 2, 11, 12 · N. B. Shurtleff, ed., *Records of the governor and company of the Massachusetts Bay in New England*, 5 vols. in 6 (1853–4), vol. 1 · *Memoir of the life of Lieutenant-Colonel Vassall* (1819) · J. D. Grainger, ed., *The Royal Navy in the River Plate, 1806–1807*, Navy RS, 135 (1996) · *GM*, 1st ser., 77 (1807), 161, 362, 386 · E. A. Jones, *The loyalists of Massachusetts: their memorials, petitions and claims* (1930) · will, PRO, PROB 11/146, sig. 99 · will, PRO, PROB 11/265, sig. 246 [William Vassall] · will, PRO, PROB 11/1465, sig. 629 [Spencer Thomas Vassall]

Archives BL, Add. MS 34181 · BL, Add. MS 51806 · Trinity House, London, records

Wealth at death property in Barbados, and a large estate in New England; William Vassall · property in Britain and Jamaica; Spencer Thomas Vassall

Vassall [later Phillips], (**William**) **John Christopher** (1924–1996), Admiralty official and spy, was born on 20 September 1924 at St Bartholomew's Hospital, London, where his father, William Vassall, was a long-serving chaplain and his mother, Mabel Andrea Sellicks, was a nurse. Educated at a boarding-school at Seaford in Sussex, he went to Monmouth School at the age of thirteen. His obituary in *The Times* noted that he was 'a mediocre scholar with no enthusiasm for games, [though] he had the reputation as the best-dressed boy in the school, but also acquired the nickname "Serf", for his servility towards his elders and eagerness to please' (*The Times*). At the age of seventeen he volunteered for the Royal Air Force, but was rejected. He also failed to get into Keble College, Oxford. After jobs in a City branch of the Midland Bank and as a temporary clerk in the Admiralty he was conscripted into the Royal Air Force in 1943 and trained as an RAF photographer, serving with 137 wing in western Europe. After the war he joined the civil service and in 1948 gained a posting with the Admiralty. In 1952, at the height of the cold war, he was sent to Moscow on the staff of the naval attaché: although a very lowly employee, he grandly described himself on his business cards as 'junior attaché', and was rebuked for turning up at social occasions thought to be too elevated for his grade.

Unsurprisingly Vassall was unhappy with the protocol and snobberies of embassy life and sought friends outside. A homosexual at a time when such practices were unlawful in Britain and the Soviet Union, he was vulnerable to entrapment by the KGB. He made the acquaintance of a Pole named Mikhailsky, who introduced him to the secret world of homosexual Moscow. It was at a party in 1954 that he was photographed in a variety of compromising positions. There followed a classic entrapment, with the KGB using threats of exposure, which quickly gave way to flattery and financial inducements. From 1954 until his arrest in 1962 Vassall supplied his Soviet controllers with an unceasing flow of documents, first from the Moscow embassy, then from the Admiralty in London. His treachery inflicted untold damage as, at various times in his career, he had access to critical information. At the time Vassall claimed that he did not regard his actions as espionage. He never, for example, thought of confiding in the British ambassador or the naval attaché, whom he considered cold, aloof, and forbidding: curiously the ambassador later said he would have arranged for Vassall to be returned home, 'as had been done in one or two other cases' (*The Times*).

Back at the Admiralty, Vassall's lifestyle began to outstrip his civil service income. He took a flat in Dolphin Square, Pimlico, and started to wear Savile Row suits and take foreign holidays. Eventually the lifestyle brought him to the attention of the authorities and a secret raid at his flat uncovered a range of incriminating evidence. That another spy had been uncovered at the heart of the British state led to a scandal that destabilized the Macmillan government a year before the Profumo affair led to the downfall of the prime minister. A range of security issues were raised, and after the trial of the hapless Vassall—most of which was heard *in camera*, and which ended with an eighteen-year sentence—the Radcliffe inquiry was established to investigate. The inquiry did not achieve any concrete results, except the gaoling of two journalists, for refusing to reveal their sources, and a former junior minister at the Admiralty. A former political correspondent of the *Sunday Telegraph* called the tribunal 'a massive cover-up' (*Daily Telegraph*, 6 Dec 1996).

Vassall had converted to Roman Catholicism in 1953, and was regularly visited by Lord Longford. He was released ten years into his sentence, and spent some time in a monastery, writing a volume of self-serving memoirs (*Vassall*, 1975) in which he described himself as a 'pygmy of a spy'. He changed his name to Phillips, found a job as a clerk with the British Records Association, and lived for the rest of his life in quiet obscurity in London's St John's Wood. He died of a heart attack on 18 November 1996 in St Mary's Hospital, Praed Street, Westminster, and was cremated; it was not until nearly three weeks later that his death came to the attention of the press.

PETER MARTLAND

Sources P. Wright, *Spycatcher* (1987) · C. Andrew and O. Gordievsky, *KGB: the inside story of its foreign operations, from Lenin to Gorbachev* (1990) · *The Times* (6 Dec 1996) · *The Independent* (9 Dec 1996) · *Daily Telegraph* (6 Dec 1996) · b. cert. · d. cert. · W. J. C. Vassall, *Vassall: the autobiography of a spy* (1975)
Likenesses F. Shepherd, photograph, 1975, News International Syndication, London [*see illus.*] · photograph, repro. in *The Times* · photograph, repro. in *Daily Telegraph* · photograph, repro. in *The Independent*
Wealth at death under £180,000: probate, 6 Jan 1997, *CGPLA Eng. & Wales*

Vassall, Samuel (*bap.* 1586, *d.* 1667), merchant and politician, was born in London and baptized at Stepney on 5 June 1586, the second of the five children of John *Vassall (*d.* 1625), mariner and shipowner, and his second wife, Anna Russell (*d.* 1593) of Ratcliffe. His father was a man of French background, whose family moved to England because of the religious conflict in France. Little is known of Vassall's education or early career, though he may have been an apprentice with Abraham Cartwright, a wealthy London draper, for whom he served as a factor in Italy during the 1620s. Vassall married Cartwright's daughter, Frances, with whom he had eight children, two of whom died young.

During the early seventeenth century Vassall acquired extensive interests in trade, shipping, and colonial enterprise. By 1619 he was a member of the Drapers' Company, in which he served as a warden from 1636 to 1637 and as an assistant from 1636 to 1659. He was also a member of the Levant Company, serving as an assistant in 1625, 1628, and 1640. In 1628 he inherited a share of £4100 in the second joint-stock of the East India Company, from his father-in-law. Much of his overseas trade was in cloth, which was exported to markets in the Mediterranean and the American colonies in exchange for goods such as currants, silk, tobacco, hemp, and flax. During the 1620s he was briefly involved in privateering, setting out the *Thomas* of London with letters of marque against France in

1627. About the same time he purchased a group of Moorish prisoners who were to be shipped as slaves to Leghorn. He regularly used his own vessels in the new transatlantic trades with Virginia and the West Indies, in occasional partnership with young city traders such as Maurice Thompson. With his brother William *Vassall [see under Vassall, John], he was a founder member of the Massachusetts Bay Company in 1629, when he was elected as an assistant. In 1630, in association with his brother-in-law, Peter Andrews, he was involved in a project to establish a colony in Carolina; although the enterprise failed, as late as 1663 Vassall was defending his rights in the region.

Vassall was an ambitious entrepreneur, who was prepared to take risks to further his business interests. He claimed to be the sole English trader with Ragusa, where he built up a flourishing trade in high-quality cloth during the 1620s and 1630s. According to the Venetian ambassador, by the mid-1630s he was experimenting with a new fringed cloth, which other members of the Levant Company were unable to make. From Ragusa, Vassall sent most of his cloth to markets in Hungary, though he was forced out of this trade after 1636 by the city authorities of Ragusa. In December 1637 the Venetian ambassador was trying to persuade him to relocate his business to Venice, but the negotiations that followed were difficult and unsuccessful. Despite the pressure of other commitments, during the 1640s he was one of a small group of London merchants engaged in the development of the slave trade with Barbados, although his commercial ventures in west Africa led to accusations of interloping from the Guinea Company. By 1648 he was attempting to establish a trade with Brazil, under licence from the king of Portugal.

At key times during the 1620s and 1630s Vassall's business activities became entangled with politics. In 1627 he was imprisoned for opposing the forced loan in the City. The following year he refused to pay impositions on currants, for which he was subsequently jailed for contempt of court. Furthermore, in 1630 he opposed the continued levy of tonnage and poundage without parliamentary approval. After refusing to pay ship money in 1635 he was imprisoned and some of his plate was seized, though it was later returned. In September 1639, during the political crisis that grew out of the Scottish war, his house was searched and a number of papers, including covenanting tracts and a remonstrance against ship money, were seized. He was arrested again in July 1640, allegedly for organizing a petition among the inhabitants of London, to be presented to the king. Later in the year he complained to parliament that he had been committed sixteen times, for which he claimed £20,000 in damages for loss of trade and injury to his credit.

Despite little experience in City politics or administration, Vassall was elected as one of the MPs for London to the Short and Long parliaments. Throughout the 1640s he was involved in a wide range of business, supporting and promoting the cause of the parliamentary leadership against Charles I, while looking after his own interests. In

October 1641 he made a speech in the Commons on behalf of the Turkey merchants, and was instrumental in the passing of a prohibition against the import of currants from Venetian territories. He was also a supporter of John Pym's proposal for a company for America and Africa. He was involved in discussions for a loan from the City to parliament in November 1641, and in sending relief to Ireland later in the year. He was appointed to serve on committees for Virginia in December 1640, and for the relief of captives in Algiers in November 1641. These official duties increased following the outbreak of the civil war. In September 1642 he became one of the commissioners for the navy. At varying times thereafter several of his ships were hired for state service, though thinly veiled charges of corruption by Andrewes Burrell were dismissed as self-interested and ill-informed. In November 1643 he was appointed to the commission for plantations. In addition he was nominated to serve on committees for levying the assessment within London in 1642; for Barbados in 1643; for regulating the price of tobacco in 1644; for the excise and the assessment for the Scottish army in 1645; for bishops' lands and scandalous offences in 1646; and for the relief of Ireland, as well as scandalous offences, in 1648. In 1644 he was a prominent witness in the trial of Archbishop William Laud. Apparently he held Laud responsible for his imprisonment for refusing to pay tonnage and poundage, and claimed that the archbishop had warned him 'that he did eat the bread out of the King's children's mouths; and that if he were in another country he would be hanged for it' (Works of … Laud, 4.102).

Like the other members for London, Vassall played a leading role in organizing the parliamentarian war effort in the City, not only in managing financial assessments but also in administering decrees, such as the new model ordinance of February 1645. In July 1646 he was nominated as one of the commissioners for the conservation of the peace between England and Scotland. As a supporter of the presbyterian middle group, however, he was purged from parliament in 1648. He seems to have been in difficult financial circumstances during the 1650s. In April 1654 he petitioned the lord protector for assistance, claiming not to have received any of the compensation, amounting to £10,445 12s. 2d., that parliament had voted for him. Following further petitions to Cromwell and the council of state he was in October 1655 awarded £2591 17s. 6d. with interest. He continued to petition the protectorate for assistance, after receiving only £1000 of this total. Both his petitions of 1654 and 1657 were printed, but in response to the latter he was told to apply to parliament for help, as there was no revenue left in Cromwell's hands to satisfy the debt. In June 1658 he was again in custody, possibly as a result of his financial situation. In February 1660 he was constituted one of the commissioners for customs in London, though the appointment was probably short-lived. Little evidence survives for Vassall's activities after 1660. He may have owned property at Bedale in Yorkshire, in addition to his landed interests in Massachusetts. He died in obscure circumstances overseas, possibly in

Massachusetts, in 1667; letters of administration were granted to his son Henry on 24 October 1667, and confirmed the following month.　　　JOHN C. APPLEBY

Sources C. H. Firth and R. S. Rait, eds., *Acts and ordinances of the interregnum, 1642–1660*, 3 vols. (1911) · CSP dom., 1625–49; 1652–9 · CSP col., vol. 1 · CSP Venice, 1632–43 · APC, 1627–31 · *The journal of Sir Simonds D'Ewes from the first recess of the Long Parliament to the withdrawal of King Charles from London*, ed. W. H. Coates (1942) · L. F. Stock, ed., *Proceedings and debates of the British parliaments respecting North America*, 1: 1542–1688 (1924) · V. Pearl, *London and the outbreak of the puritan revolution: city government and national politics, 1625–1643* (1961) · R. Brenner, *Merchants and revolution: commercial change, political conflict, and London's overseas traders, 1550–1653* (1993) · K. R. Andrews, *Ships, money, and politics: seafaring and naval enterprise in the reign of Charles I* (1991) · *Two discourses of the navy, 1638 and 1659, by John Holland; also … 1660, by Sir Robert Slyngesbie*, ed. J. R. Tanner, Navy RS, 7 (1896) · W. Vassall, *Vassall pedigree 1500 to 1890* (1858) · *The works of the most reverend father in God, William Laud*, ed. J. Bliss and W. Scott, 7 vols. (1847–60) · A. Brown, ed., *The genesis of the United States*, 2 vols. (1890) · genealogical notes on the Vassall family, BL, Add. MS 51806, fols. 133–40 · D. Underdown, *Pride's Purge: politics in the puritan revolution* (1971) · *The visitation of London, anno Domini 1633, 1634, and 1635, made by Sir Henry St George*, ed. J. J. Howard and J. L. Chester, 2 vols., Harleian Society, 15, 17 (1880–83) · libels, high court of admiralty, 1646–52, PRO, HCA 24/108–110 · K. Lindley, *Popular politics and religion in civil war London* (1997) · letters of administration, Oct–Nov 1667, PRO, PROB 6/42, fols. 136v, 142r–v
Archives BL, genealogical notes on Vassall family, Add. MS 51806, fols. 133–140 | PRO, high court of admiralty, libels
Wealth at death administration, Oct/Nov 1667, PRO, PROB 6/42, fols. 136v, 142r–v

Vassall, Spencer Thomas (1764–1807). *See under* Vassall, John (d. 1625).

Vassall, William (1592–1655). *See under* Vassall, John (d. 1625).

Vaughan family (*per. c.*1400–*c.*1504), gentry of Tretower and Hergest, was prominent in the eastern march of Wales and the Herefordshire borderland. According to later pedigrees Walter Sais (the Englishman), a soldier, settled near Tretower, moved to Bredwardine, Herefordshire, after marrying Sir Walter Bredwardine's daughter. An elder son, Roger Hen (the elder), married a daughter of Sir Walter Devereux of Weobley, and the links between the two families remained strong. Their son was known as Roger Fychan (the younger). **Roger Fychan** [Vaughan] (d. 1415) married Gwladus (d. 1454), daughter of Sir *Dafydd Gam from near Brecon; he and his father-in-law died at Agincourt in 1415. The Mortimer and Stafford lordships and the rising houses of Devereux and Herbert were the circles in which the prolific Vaughan family prospered, to become one of the most prominent Anglo-Welsh families in the southern borderland. The three sons of Roger Fychan—Watkyn, Thomas, and Roger [*see below*]—were established at the main Vaughan residences of Bredwardine, Hergest, and Tretower, having been brought up with their half-brothers, William [*see* Herbert, William, first earl of Pembroke] and Richard Herbert, after the widowed Gwladus married Sir William ap Thomas of Raglan. The Vaughans proved staunch Yorkists during the Wars of the Roses, and Roger Vaughan was the duke of York's receiver of Builth as early as 1442–3.

Watkyn [Walter] **Vaughan** (*d.* 1456) inherited Bredwardine. He married Elizabeth, daughter of Sir Henry Wogan of Pembrokeshire, whose wife was Sir William ap Thomas's daughter. At Easter 1456 he was murdered at Bredwardine and his kinsmen William Herbert and Walter Devereux forcibly arranged the trial and execution of the culprits at Hereford. His numerous offspring included his heir, **Sir Thomas Vaughan** [Thomas ap Watkyn Vaughan] (*fl. c.*1456), who married Eleanor, daughter of the Herefordshire esquire Robert Whitney; he was knighted, presumably by Edward IV, whom his brother William served as custodian of Aberystwyth Castle (under Walter Devereux, now Lord Ferrers). Tradition suggests that William accompanied Devereux to subdue northern England for Edward IV in 1462, and that he slew the earl of Warwick at Barnet in 1471. He was certainly bailiff of Brecon in 1475 and Richard III sought to retain his loyalty in 1484 with an annuity of 10 marks. The Vaughans of Bredwardine patronized Welsh poets who, in turn, wrote elegies for them and praised their Yorkist endeavours.

Watkyn's next brother, **Thomas ap Roger Vaughan** (*c.*1400–1469), married Elen Gethin, daughter of Cadwgan ap Dafydd. Thomas had a long-standing interest from the mid-1440s in the Stafford lordship of Huntington, which was near his house at Hergest, and in the Stafford lordships of Brecon and Hay; in September 1461 Edward IV appointed him receiver of Brecon, Hay, and Huntington during the minority of the duke of Buckingham. This reinforced an allegiance to the Yorkist regime that he shared with his brothers, and Watkyn, Thomas, and Roger fought with their Herbert kinsmen at Edgcote in 1469, when Thomas lost his life. He was buried at Kington church, near Hergest, where his tomb may still be seen; his widow was still living near Presteigne in 1474. Their three sons, Watkyn [*see below*], Richard, and Roger, and a daughter Alice (or Elizabeth), wife of Robert Whitney, were as generous as the Bredwardine Vaughans in patronizing Welsh poets, and collections of prose and poetry are known as the Red Book of Hergest (Bodl. Oxf., Jesus College MS 111) and the White Book of Hergest (since destroyed); though not compiled under Vaughan patronage, these books were apparently acquired by the Vaughans in the later fifteenth century. The eldest son, **Watkyn Vaughan** [Watkyn ap Thomas ap Roger] (*d.* 1504), married Sybil Baskerville, a granddaughter of Sir Walter Devereux, and controlled the lordship of Huntington between 1475 and 1499, and, more intermittently, neighbouring lordships too. He died on 6 January 1504.

Sir Roger Vaughan (*d.* 1471), the third son of Roger Fychan of Bredwardine, was the most prominent of all. He was the first Vaughan to reside at Tretower, which appears to have been a gift from William Herbert, and which he turned into an imposing fortified manor house. He was closely associated with his Herbert and Devereux kinsmen, whom he joined on the Yorkist side at Mortimer's Cross in February 1461; Roger is said to have led Owen Tudor to execution at Hereford after the battle. Vaughans, Herberts, and Devereux were responsible for securing Wales for Edward IV: Roger was steward and receiver of Cantref Selyf, Alexanderston, and Pencelli; he helped to quell a Carmarthenshire rising in 1465, and he was knighted. On 16 February 1470 he was appointed constable of Cardigan Castle, but after the Lancastrian defeat at Tewkesbury in May 1471 he was captured by Jasper Tudor and beheaded at Chepstow, an act that poisoned the Vaughans' relations with the Tudors. Welsh poets urged revenge for the defeat of the Herberts and their allies at Edgcote, and for Jasper Tudor's treachery at Chepstow. The four daughters of Roger and his first wife, Denise, daughter of Thomas ap Philip Vaughan of Talgarth, married prominent gentry in southern Wales. Of his numerous sons, the eldest, **Thomas Vaughan** (*d. c.*1493), not to be confused with Thomas *Vaughan (*d.* 1483), was an esquire of the body to Edward IV, and when the duke of Buckingham rebelled against Richard III in October 1483, he and his relatives denied the duke Welsh aid and sacked his castle at Brecon. King Richard rewarded him with the stewardship of Brecon, Hay, and Huntington for life on 4 March 1484. Henry Tudor's accession posed a threat to the Vaughans, and in 1486 Thomas again raided Brecon Castle; a general pardon from Henry VII on 2 April 1487 gave him some security, but his three sons were not prominent thereafter.　　　　　　　　R. A. GRIFFITHS

Sources H. T. Evans, *Wales and the Wars of the Roses* (1915) • P. C. Bartrum, ed., *Welsh genealogies, AD 300–1400*, 8 vols. (1974), vol. 2, p. 243 • P. C. Bartrum, ed., *Welsh genealogies, AD 1400–1500*, 18 vols. (1983), vol. 3, pp. 451–67 • R. A. Griffiths and R. S. Thomas, *The principality of Wales in the later middle ages: the structure and personnel of government*, 1: *South Wales, 1277–1536* (1972) • T. B. Pugh, ed., *The marcher lordships of south Wales, 1415–1536: select documents* (1963) • T. Jones, *History of Brecknockshire*, new edn, 4 vols. (1909) • *Chancery records* • *The poetical works of Lewis Glyn Cothi*, ed. [J. Jones and W. Davies], 2 vols. (1837) • A. Herbert, 'Herefordshire, 1413–61: some aspects of society and public order', *Patronage, the crown and the provinces in later medieval England*, ed. R. A. Griffiths (1981), 103–22 • R. A. Griffiths and R. S. Thomas, *The making of the Tudor dynasty* (1985) • *CIPM, Henry VII*, 3, no. 492 [Watkyn Vaughan] • *Three books of Polydore Vergil's 'English history'*, ed. H. Ellis, CS, 29 (1844), 155

Vaughan, Arthur (1868–1915), geologist, was born on 7 March 1868 at 34A Pembroke Square, London, the son of William Vaughan, a civil service clerk and later actuary to the Board of Trade, and his wife, Julia Ward. From University College School, he entered University College, London, in 1885, gaining a first-class degree in mathematics. He then entered Trinity College, Cambridge, with a mathematical scholarship and in 1891 was awarded first-class honours in the part two mathematical physics tripos. In the same year, on 28 July, he married Frances Catherine (*d.* 1962), daughter of Walter Hawkes, butcher. On leaving Cambridge he accepted a post as senior science master at the army coaching establishment in Clifton, Bristol. There he remained until 1910 when he was offered a lectureship in geology at Oxford University.

While at University College, Vaughan had come under the influence of Professor Bonney, then also president of the Geological Society of London. Thus Vaughan's earliest scientific papers were on the physics of the earth. However, soon after his move to Bristol, Vaughan came under the twin influences of Edward Wilson (curator of the Bristol Museum) and Sidney Reynolds (professor of geology at the University College in Bristol)—influences which led him into the fields of stratigraphy and palaeontology.

In all, Vaughan published twenty-six geological papers, mainly on palaeontology and stratigraphy of the Lower Carboniferous Limestone in the Bristol district. It was his mastery of this field which was to win him the Oxford lectureship and world renown. Vaughan demonstrated persuasively, on the basis of examining strata exposed in the Avon Gorge in Bristol, that there was a sequence of coral and brachiopod species in the limestones and that this could be used for detailed correlation with strata in other areas. In the Avon Gorge limestones, Vaughan established twelve biozones, each characterized by a distinctive species and fossil assemblage, through 800 metres of sediment from the base of the Carboniferous to the beginning of the Millstone Grits (a span later recognized as 30 million years). At the time, this was an immense leap in precision correlation. Vaughan soon extended his correlation to south Wales and to Ireland, and later to Belgium, demonstrating the wide validity of his principles. Some of Vaughan's contemporaries had doubts, and thought that the species ranges represented not time zones but environmental habitats, which might disappear, only to reappear again at a later time, in perhaps another place; so the correlation could be ecological and not evolutionary. Notwithstanding these doubts, the Vaughan scheme was adopted throughout Britain and used for over sixty years until a lithologically based stratigraphy was introduced in the late 1960s. Vaughan's pioneering researches were based on painstaking and prolonged fieldwork, often done in his spare time, with little if any financial support, and often while suffering from poor health. They earned him many distinctions and his contributions have played a major role in the evolution of understanding of Lower Carboniferous stratigraphy.

Vaughan courageously fought increasing limitations to physical activity during the last decade of his life. His outstanding mental powers for clear-sighted logical analysis remained with him to the end. To his many friends he was always genial and loyal. He died at his home, 315 Woodstock Road, Oxford, on 3 December 1915, survived by his wife and two children.　ROBERT J. G. SAVAGE

Sources S. H. R[eynolds], 'Arthur Vaughan', *Geological Magazine*, new ser., 6th decade, 3 (1916), 92–6 · A. Vaughan, 'The Carboniferous Limestone series (Avonian) of the Avon gorge', *Proceedings of the Bristol Naturalists Society*, 4/1, 74–168 · corresp., A. Vaughan with F. A. Bather and A. S. Woodward, 1904–12, NHM · corresp., A. Vaughan with J. W. Tutcher and H. V. Wickes, 1898–1915, Bristol City Museum and Art Gallery · J. H. Milton, *Arthur Vaughan memorial fund* (privately printed, 1916?) · A. S. Woodward, *Quarterly Journal of the Geological Society*, 72 (1916), lvii–lviii · E. A. Vincent, *Geology and mineralogy at Oxford, 1860–1986* (1994) · m. cert.

Archives Oxf. U. Mus. NH, notebooks | Bristol City Museum and Art Gallery, corresp. with J. W. Tutcher and W. H. V. Wickes · NHM, corresp. with F. A. Bather and A. S. Woodward

Likenesses photograph, repro. in R[eynolds], 'Arthur Vaughan', pl. V, p. 93

Wealth at death £3393 13s. 10d.: probate, 18 Feb 1916, *CGPLA Eng. & Wales*

Vaughan, Benjamin (1751–1835), diplomatist and political reformer, was born on 19 April 1751 in Jamaica, the eldest of the eleven children of Samuel Vaughan, a London merchant and West India planter of Welsh extraction, and Sarah, daughter of Benjamin Hallowell, a Boston merchant and founder of Hallowell, Maine. Vaughan's father operated his prosperous business from premises at Dunster's Court, London, and met his wife through an unsuccessful business partnership with her father. Soon after marrying Benjamin's parents moved to Jamaica, but returned to London after his birth to reside at Wanstead. Vaughan was sent to Henry Newcome's school at Hackney and on 27 August 1765 he was admitted to Lincoln's Inn. The following year, along with his brother William *Vaughan (1752–1850), he was sent to the Warrington Academy and resided with the eminent dissenter Joseph Priestley. After three years' study at Warrington, Vaughan went to Trinity College, Cambridge, despite the fact that Unitarians could not graduate, remaining there until 1771, when he apparently began once more to study law, in the Inner Temple. By 1779 Vaughan had determined to marry Sarah Manning (d. 1835), daughter of William Manning, a London merchant, but her father insisted that he acquire a profession to rely on if necessary, since both families' fortunes depended on West Indian trade. Thus, in 1780, Vaughan enrolled at the University of Edinburgh to study medicine, though he never practised the field, preferring instead to join Manning's business. He returned to London to marry Sarah on 30 June 1781 at the church of St Dunstan-in-the-East; the marriage produced three sons and four daughters.

Through his father Vaughan was first introduced to politics. Samuel Vaughan was an active reformer as a member of the Society of the Supporters of the Bill of Rights in the 1760s and a friend of John Wilkes and John Horne Tooke. He was also a member of the Club of Honest Whigs, the meetings of which Benjamin sometimes attended, whereby he associated with the likes of Priestley, Richard Price, and James Burgh. In 1767 Vaughan also became acquainted with Benjamin Franklin, with whom he was to develop a close friendship and admiration, resulting in the publication of the comprehensive *Political, Miscellaneous and Philosophical Pieces … Written by Benjamin Franklin* (1780). At other times, Vaughan was variously occupied with his father's business, spending twelve months in the early 1770s managing a plantation in Jamaica and then directing the London company from 1775 to 1777. Around this time, probably through his association with Horne Tooke and as a frequenter of parliamentary debates, Vaughan became known to Lord Shelburne, by whom he was often employed as an adviser and private secretary, and as such was an active and important mediator in Paris during the Anglo-American peace negotiations of 1782–3.

In 1783 Vaughan returned to London to restart work for Manning and lived with his family at Jefferies Square. Engaging himself in his hobbies of music and bird breeding, Vaughan also entertained on a regular basis reform-minded men like Price, Priestley, Thomas Paine, and Samuel Romilly. About 1783 he also thought of establishing a newspaper, and served on a six-man board advising the government on behalf of the Committee of West Indian Merchants and Planters. He was, in addition, a part of the Association for Promoting the Discovery of the Interior Parts of Africa, and wrote a long, unpublished manuscript entitled 'The political state of the Austrian Netherlands'. For twelve months from January 1788 Vaughan's attention turned to editing his short-lived periodical, *The Repository*, and writing *New and Old Principles of Trade Compared* (1788).

Following the outbreak of revolution in France, Vaughan made a number of visits to Paris and was one of the privileged, though not impressed, few who sat near the royal box at the Fête de la Fédération on 14 July 1790. That same year, writing as A Christian Politician, Vaughan composed *A Collection of Testimonies in Favour of Religious Liberty* (1790), which he followed, in the year between July 1792 and June 1793, with a series of letters criticizing William Pitt's government in the *Morning Chronicle*, under the pseudonym A Calm Observer, and published collectively as *Letters on the Subject of the Concert of Princes and the Dismemberment of Poland and France* (1793) and *Two Papers by the Calm Observer* (1795). Vaughan also published his *Comments on the Proposed War with France* (1793), wrote an introduction to David Ramsay's *History of the American Revolution* (1793), and edited with Richard Price two volumes of *Works of the Late Doctor Franklin* (1793). His enthusiasm for writing in these years, however, was not matched by his somewhat reticent term of office following his election to parliament in February 1792 as a member for Calne. Despite the numerous opportunities to voice his opinions, Vaughan apparently spoke only once, in February 1794, on account of William Wilberforce's bills for the abolition of the slave trade.

In 1794, with the arrest of William Stone, brother of John Hurford Stone, an outspoken pro-French businessman living in Paris, the authorities found a letter from Vaughan, and he was subsequently summoned in May to appear before the privy council. Vaughan, however, fled to France without his family, taking refuge at Passy before being detained in a former Carmelite convent. By 27 June 1794 he had been released and travelled to Switzerland, where he spent time in Geneva, Bern, and Basel, and was befriended by the wealthy Fellensberg family and local liberals including Johann-Ludwig Iselin, J. L. Le Grand, and François Fesch. In 1795 he seemed determined to move to America, thus urging his wife and family to travel to Boston, where they arrived in September. Vaughan, however, stayed in Basel in the hope of promoting peace, and he made several trips to Paris on a false passport bearing the name John Martin and identifying him as an American citizen. In February and March 1796 he completed *De l'état politique et economic de la France sous sa Constitution de l'An III* (1796), which was published in Strasbourg, and for the next twelve months he lived outside Paris in the country house of Fulwar Skipwith, an American consul, and established a textile factory in partnership with the Stone brothers.

Eventually, in July 1797, Vaughan joined his family in America, where they settled on inherited lands at Hallowell. Here, he retired from active politics, although he maintained an active mind through his writing efforts, which included *Travels of a philosopher, or, Observations on the manners and arts of various nations in Africa and Asia* (1797), *An abridgement of the second edition of a work by Dr. Currie … on the use of water in diseases of the human frame* (1799), *The Rural Socrates* (1800), *Remarks on a Dangerous Mistake Made as to the Eastern Boundary of Louisiana* (1814), and frequent contributions to local agricultural and medical journals. He devoted much of his time at Hallowell to promoting scientific and literary societies and as such was one of the founders of the Maine Historical Society and the Maine Medical Society, and he often opened his large personal library for use by scholars. Largely on account of this kind of patronage, Vaughan was bestowed an honorary doctor of laws degree from Harvard in 1807 and Bowdoin in 1812. He also dedicated much of his time in the final years to maintaining his extensive investments and properties in Maine, which included a lumber company he owned with his brother Charles Vaughan (1759–1839). Troubled by gout in his later years, Vaughan's duties became increasingly difficult, and he died on 7 December 1835.

MICHAEL T. DAVIS

Sources C. C. Murray, 'Benjamin Vaughan (1751–1835): the life of an Anglo-American intellectual', PhD diss., Columbia University, 1989 · J. G. Alger, *Englishmen in the French Revolution* (1889) · R. H. Gardiner, 'Memoir of Benjamin Vaughan', *Maine Historical Society Collections*, 1st ser., 6 (1859), 84–92 · J. H. Sheppard, 'Reminiscences and genealogy of the Vaughan family', *New England Historical and Genealogical Register*, 19 (1865), 543–56 · *DNB*

Archives American Philosophical Society, Philadelphia, personal and family corresp. and papers · American Philosophical Society, Philadelphia, John Vaughan MSS · Bowdoin College Library, Brunswick, Maine · Hist. Soc. Penn. · U. Mich., Clements L. | Bodl. Oxf., letters to Lord Lansdowne · Franklin Institute, Philadelphia, Pennsylvania, Samuel Vaughan MSS · NRA, priv. coll., letters to Lord Lansdowne · U. Mich., Clements L., Shelburne MSS

Likenesses F. Cotes, oils, 1765, Museum of Fine Arts, Boston

Wealth at death extensive property and investments

Vaughan, Bernard John (1847–1922), Jesuit, was born at Courtfield, the family home near Ross-on-Wye, on 20 September 1847, the sixth son in the family of thirteen children born to Colonel John Francis Vaughan (1808–1880) and his first wife, Elizabeth Louisa (1810–1853), third daughter of John Rolls of Hendre, Monmouth, the grandfather of the first Baron Llangattock. The Vaughans were an old Catholic recusant family. Four of John and Eliza Vaughan's five daughters became nuns (the fifth was prevented from doing so by poor health); of their eight sons, six became priests and three bishops—Herbert Alfred *Vaughan, cardinal-archbishop of Westminster; Roger William *Vaughan, archbishop of Sydney; and John Stephen Vaughan, auxiliary bishop of Salford.

After being taught at home Vaughan began his formal education in 1859 at Stonyhurst College, which had been given to the Jesuits by his great-grandfather, Thomas Weld of Lulworth, the father of Cardinal Thomas Weld. At school Vaughan did not distinguish himself either academically or at sport. He decided to become a priest and a

Jesuit, and entered the noviciate of the Society of Jesus at Manresa House, Roehampton, in December 1866. He spent the years preceding his ordination in 1880 in the study of philosophy and theology, mainly at St Beuno's College, north Wales, and in teaching at Stonyhurst and Beaumont colleges.

Having completed his course of studies Vaughan received in 1883 his appointment to the Jesuit church of the Holy Name in Manchester, a city which he came to love. There he soon began to show the gifts as a preacher and public speaker that were to make him famous. His distinguished bearing and impassioned style of oratory, his ability to choose topics of interest to his hearers and to deal with them in a striking manner, and his skill as a raconteur and in repartee made him much in demand for sermons and public meetings. His use of rhetorical devices and sensational methods led some contemporaries to call his oratory artificial, but there was no doubting his sincerity. His skill in debate and quick sense of humour greatly helped him to convey his message to his listeners. He was not afraid of controversy, and in 1895 gave a course of ten lectures in the Free Trade Hall in Manchester on the claims of the Catholic church in reply to views expressed by the bishop of Manchester.

Vaughan's reputation as a preacher was not long confined to Manchester. He preached the Lenten course in 1897 in the church of San Silvestro in Rome and in 1898 on the Riviera, where his hearers at Cannes included the prince of Wales, who asked for the manuscript of his sermon on St Mary Magdalen. As there was no manuscript, Vaughan wrote out the sermon, 'The woman that was a sinner', from his notes and presented it to the prince, with whom a close friendship developed. The sermon was published in 1898. Vaughan's reputation as a preacher and speaker and, possibly, his friendship with the prince of Wales led to his being moved in 1901 from Manchester to the Jesuit church in Farm Street, Mayfair, where his sermons over the next twenty years were well attended. Many of his sermons and addresses were published, including The Sins of Society (1905), Society, Sin and the Saviour (1907), and Socialism: is it Liberty or Tyranny? (1909). He also spoke at public meetings about the social evils of the day—low wages, housing conditions, the need for more hospital care and orphanages, and injustice in its many forms. In June 1902, soon after his arrival in London, he brought an action for libel against a newspaper, The Rock, which had been fulminating against Jesuits in general and individually, and was awarded damages. This brought him more public notice.

In addition to his preaching and public speaking Vaughan gave much of his time to work among the poor, both in Manchester and in the East End of London; some have thought that this work was the dominating interest in his life. Soon after his arrival in London he took a room in the East End and began to spend one day a week preaching and reciting public prayers in the streets. In 1911 he organized a grand mission that lasted three weeks, with processions, bands, and sermons in the churches and outside. He persuaded Madame Adelina Patti to go to London in 1904 and 1908 for concerts in the Albert Hall to raise money for good works in the East End.

In the years before the First World War, Vaughan made preaching tours in Rome, Ireland, Canada, the United States, Japan, and China. During the war he was frequently invited to preach and give lectures in aid of war charities and patriotic causes. In 1922 he went on a tour of South Africa. Critics claim that Vaughan deliberately courted publicity. This may be true, but it was not for his own sake. His object was to make his message—spiritual, theological, or on the subject of social reform—known and accepted as widely as possible. A priest with whom he worked in the East End considered him one of the humblest priests he had ever met.

Vaughan was ill on his return from South Africa in 1922 (throughout much of his life he had suffered from exhaustion) and he died on 31 October 1922 at Manresa House, Roehampton, his general condition weakened by insomnia and nervous strain. He was buried at Kensal Green Roman Catholic cemetery, London, on 3 November.

GEOFFREY HOLT

Sources C. C. Martindale, Bernard Vaughan (1923) · J. G. Snead-Cox, Life of Cardinal Vaughan, 2 vols. (1910) · B. J. Vaughan, 'Letters and notices', 1923, Archives of the British Province of the Society of Jesus, London [vol. 38], 120–63 · G. Holt, 'Vaughan, Bernard', Dictionnaire de spiritualité ascétique et mystique: doctrine et histoire, ed. M. Viller and others (1937–95) · E. F. Sutcliffe, Bibliography of the English province of the Society of Jesus, 1773–1953 (1957)
Archives Archives of the British Province of the Society of Jesus, London | FILM BFI NFTVA, news footage · BFI NFTVA, propaganda footage (Hepworth Manufacturing Company)
Likenesses photographs, c.1880–1922, Archives of the British Province of the Society of Jesus, London · G. C. Beresford, two photographs, 1905, NPG · H. Herkomer, portrait, 1908, Stonyhurst College, Lancashire · A. Garratt, watercolour, 1910, NPG · Russell & Sons, photograph, NPG · Sarony & Co., photogravure, NPG · Spy [L. Ward], caricature, mechanical reproduction, NPG; repro. in VF (30 Jan 1907) · portrait, Archives of the British Province of the Society of Jesus, London
Wealth at death £710: probate, 22 Feb 1923, CGPLA Eng. & Wales

Vaughan, Charles John (1816–1897), headmaster and dean of Llandaff, was born on 6 August 1816 at Leicester, the second son of the Revd Edward Thomas Vaughan (1772–1829), vicar of St Martin's, Leicester, and his wife, Agnes Pares, also of Leicester. The family consisted of five sons and five daughters. Vaughan was educated at Rugby School (1829–34) where he was a member of the inner circle of Thomas Arnold's pupils. He matriculated at Trinity College, Cambridge, in 1834 and, after winning a series of university prizes, he was bracketed equal with the fourth Lord Lyttelton as senior classic and chancellor's medallist in 1838. He was elected to a fellowship at Trinity in 1839 (MA 1841; DD 1845), which he vacated in 1842. He was vicar of St Martin's, Leicester, from 1841 to 1844, when he was elected headmaster of Harrow School after having been an unsuccessful candidate for Rugby when Arnold died in 1842. Vaughan took over a school which was in very poor shape. In fifteen years he transformed its fortunes and won it a position among the leading public

Charles John Vaughan (1816–1897), by George Richmond, 1866–7

schools. When he arrived, there were about seventy boys; when he left, about four hundred and sixty. While at Harrow, in 1850, he married Catherine Maria Stanley (1821–1899), sister of a former Rugby schoolfellow, A. P. Stanley.

Vaughan was a good scholar, albeit on rather narrow lines, and a strong disciplinarian. He favoured a monitorial system on the Rugby pattern, and defended this in a pamphlet (1853) when there had been publicity over a case in which a boy had been severely beaten by a monitor. During his time the school chapel was rebuilt, and his sermons and religious teaching exerted a strong influence. He appointed able men to the staff, was highly regarded by his colleagues, and remained in friendly contact with many of them long after he had left Harrow. Unlike most Victorian headmasters, Vaughan, with his wife, took a strong interest in local affairs. He was the first chairman of the Harrow local board, and he did something to meet the complaints of the parishioners about their exclusion from the benefits of the school by founding the English Class in 1853, against the wishes of his governors, where local boys could learn Latin and English subjects at modest cost. This later grew into the lower school of John Lyon.

Many of Vaughan's old boys spoke of him very warmly, but as one of them wrote, 'There was an element of inscrutability about him … He found it convenient to see through others without being seen through himself' (L. A. Tollemache, *Old and Odd Memories*, 1908, 119). Vaughan

resigned his headmastership in 1859. Since the publication of Phyllis Grosskurth's biography of John Addington Symonds (1964) and of her edition of Symonds's memoirs (1984), it has been generally accepted that Vaughan resigned as the result of pressure from Symonds's father, Dr Symonds, who had been told by his son (a former Harrovian) that the headmaster had sent 'a series of passionate letters' to another boy who was a fellow monitor. When Dr Symonds learned about the letters, he insisted, it is said, that if exposure were to be avoided, Vaughan should resign and should not accept any higher preferment in the church. *The Times* obituary states that Vaughan had been offered two bishoprics. In 1860 the prime minister, Palmerston, who was also chairman of the Harrow governors, offered him the see of Rochester. Vaughan accepted it, and then withdrew a few days later. According to J. A. Symonds (though he dates these events to 1863), this withdrawal had been enforced by Dr Symonds. The story presents many difficulties: on the one hand Vaughan certainly withdrew his acceptance of the see and, when he died, he directed that no biography should be written; on the other hand the dates are discrepant and there is no evidence other than J. A. Symonds's statements. He himself was not the recipient of the letters and at the time of the alleged events he was in a highly excited mental state as he strove to come to terms with his own homosexuality. His credibility as a witness must be considered in relation to all these pressures. It seems impossible to go beyond a 'not proven' verdict; but in 1862 Vaughan was offered and refused another (unspecified) high office.

In 1860 Vaughan was appointed vicar of Doncaster, where he threw himself with great energy and success into the work of a large town parish. He was on excellent terms with the corporation, he behaved with courage during a cholera epidemic, and, in a setting very different from that of Harrow, he accomplished a good deal for education, playing a major part in resuscitating the town's moribund grammar school, which was re-opened in 1862. Only a few years later the Taunton commission described it as one of the leading grammar schools in Yorkshire. When he left Doncaster in 1869 the local press was full of tributes which were clearly much more than conventional. He had, it was said, 'laboured and helped with a generosity unexampled for the spiritual and temporal benefit of his parishioners' (*Doncaster, Nottingham, and Lincoln Gazette*, 10 Sept 1869).

It was at Doncaster that Vaughan began what was to be the most important work of his later life—the preparing of young men for ordination. He had announced his intention to receive young graduates in a Cambridge University sermon in 1861, and by the time he left Doncaster, 120 of the so-called 'doves' had been trained by him, 100 of whom came to the town from all over the country for special services. Vaughan was master of the Temple from 1869 to 1894, combining this from 1879 with the deanery of Llandaff, which he held until he died. In London he developed the considerable reputation as a preacher which he had gained at Harrow and at Doncaster. His published work consisted largely of sermons and of commentaries on some of the epistles, and he was a member of the committee which produced the Revised New Testament. The training of the 'doves' continued almost until the end of his life; in all some 450 men passed through his hands. Two of them, Randall Davidson, archbishop of Canterbury from 1903 to 1928, and the Cambridge medievalist G. G. Coulton, have left accounts of their training. Vaughan concentrated on the detailed study of the Greek Testament and on regular sermon preparation, while all the men did regular parish work under a local clergyman. Both Coulton and Davidson commented on the absence of party spirit and the encouragement to men to form their own opinions.

At Llandaff, Vaughan became a major figure in Welsh life. He was much respected by nonconformists and co-operated with men of all opinions. In 1880 he re-founded the cathedral school, which his bishop called 'the Dean's favourite child'. He played an important part in the foundation of the university college in 1883, and was one of the two representatives sent to plead the case before the arbitrators that the new south Wales college should be located in Cardiff. He was a steady friend and supporter of the first principal, John Viriamu Jones, and he was president of the college in 1894–6. At this time his health broke down. He suffered from bronchitis and paralysis and he steadily weakened until he died on 15 October 1897, at the deanery, Llandaff. In its obituary, the *Cardiff Times* wrote that 'in his death the whole Principality has lost a friend'. When he was buried in the cathedral precincts on 20 October, his funeral was attended by a very large concourse of mourners which included a formal delegation of the local nonconformist ministers and nearly half of all the students he had prepared for ordination.   JOHN ROACH

Sources F. D. How, *Six great schoolmasters: Hawtrey, Moberly, Kennedy, Vaughan, Temple, Bradley* (1904) • C. Vaughan, 'Dean Vaughan', *Welsh political and educational leaders in the Victorian era*, ed. J. V. Morgan (1908), 407–28 • E. W. Howson, G. T. Warner, and others, eds., *Harrow School* (1898), 108–14 • R. R. Williams, 'A neglected Victorian divine: Vaughan of Llandaff', *Church Quarterly Review*, 154 (1953), 72–85 • *The memoirs of John Addington Symonds*, ed. P. Grosskurth (1984) • P. Grosskurth, *John Addington Symonds: a biography* (1964) • Letters to Lord Palmerston, 1854–62, Broadlands Papers • *The Times* (16 Oct 1897) • *The Times* (18 Oct 1897) • *Guardian* (20 Oct 1897) • *Guardian* (27 Oct 1897) • *Cardiff Times and South Wales Weekly News* (23 Oct 1897) • *Cardiff Times and South Wales Weekly News* (30 Oct 1897) • *Doncaster, Nottingham, and Lincoln Gazette* (2 July 1869) • *Doncaster, Nottingham, and Lincoln Gazette* (16 July 1869) • *Doncaster, Nottingham, and Lincoln Gazette* (27 Aug–10 Sept 1869) • *CGPLA Eng. & Wales* (1897) • Venn, *Alum. Cant.* • *DNB* • R. E. Prothero and G. G. Bradley, *The life and correspondence of Arthur Penrhyn Stanley*, 1 (1894), 7

Archives All Souls Oxf., corresp. with Sir Charles Richard Vaughan • BL, Dalrymple MSS • BL, letters to W. E. Gladstone, Add. MSS 44377–44510, *passim* • BL, corresp. with Macmillans, Add. MS 55113 • Durham Cath. CL, letters to J. B. Lightfoot • Leics. RO, letters relating to education of R. F. Martin • NL Scot., letters to Sir Charles Dalrymple

Likenesses G. Richmond, chalk drawing, 1853, Inner Temple, London • G. Richmond, oils, 1866–7, Harrow School, Middlesex [*see illus.*] • Jamson, photograph, *c*.1870, Hall Cross comprehensive school (formerly Doncaster grammar school), Doncaster • W. W.

Ouless, oils, 1895, Trinity Cam. • E. O. Ford, marble medallion, 1898, Harrow School, Middlesex • W. G. John, marble effigy, *c*.1900, Llandaff Cathedral, Oudoceus chapel • Elliott & Fry, carte-de-visite, NPG • Lock & Whitfield, woodburytype photograph, NPG; repro. in T. Cooper, *Men of mark: a gallery of contemporary portraits* (1882) • London Stereoscopic Co., cabinet photograph, NPG • S. A. Walker, cabinet photograph, NPG • carte-de-visite, NPG • chromolithograph caricature, NPG; repro. in *VF* (24 Aug 1872) • photographs, NPG

Wealth at death £22,208 12s. 5d.: probate, 16 Nov 1897, *CGPLA Eng. & Wales*

Vaughan, Sir Charles Richard (1774–1849), diplomatist, son of James Vaughan, physician, of Leicester, and Hester, daughter of John Smalley (who had married a daughter of Sir Richard Halford), was born at Leicester on 20 December 1774. His brothers were Sir Henry *Halford (Vaughan), who dropped this last name; Sir John *Vaughan (1769–1839), baron of the exchequer; and Peter Vaughan, warden of Merton College, Oxford. Charles Vaughan was educated at Rugby School, where he entered on 22 January 1788, and at Merton College, Oxford, matriculating on 26 October 1791. He graduated BA in 1796 and MA in 1798, in which year he was also elected a fellow of All Souls. He intended to follow the medical profession, attending lectures in both Edinburgh and London, and took the degree of MB in 1800. He was, however, elected Radcliffe travelling fellow on 4 December 1800, and spent the next three years in Germany, France, and Spain. In 1804 he visited Constantinople, Asia Minor, and Syria. The following year he made his way from Aleppo to Persia, fell ill near the Caspian, and was indebted perhaps for his life to the kindness of some Russian officers. With them he sailed for the Volga in November, was shut out by the ice, and had to spend the winter on the desert island of Kulali, but eventually arrived at Astrakhan in April 1806, reaching England by way of St Petersburg on 11 August 1806.

In 1808, in a private capacity, Vaughan accompanied Charles Stuart (afterwards Lord Stuart de Rothesay) to Spain, and was present at the assembly of the northern juntas at Lugo; thence he went to Madrid, and travelled to Saragossa with Colonel Charles William Doyle. On his return to Madrid he was sent with dispatches relating to the battle of Tudela to Sir John Moore at Salamanca, and returned to England in December 1808. In 1809 he published his *Narrative of the Siege of Saragossa*, which reached a fifth edition within the year.

In 1809 Vaughan was also appointed private secretary to Henry Bathurst, third Earl Bathurst, secretary for foreign affairs. On 5 January 1810 he became secretary of legation (later of embassy) in Spain, whither he returned with the minister, Henry Wellesley. He was sent to Britain in 1811 to give information as to the state of politics in Spain. He acted as minister-plenipotentiary during the absence of his chief from August 1815 until December 1816, and his correspondence during these years throws much light on Spanish politics. On 5 April 1820 he went to Paris as secretary of embassy under his old friend Sir Charles Stuart, and on 8 February 1823 became minister-plenipotentiary to the confederated states of Switzerland. He was appointed envoy-extraordinary and minister-plenipotentiary to the United States in 1825, and on 23 March he was made privy councillor. Between 11 July and 13 August 1826 he travelled nearly 1800 miles in the United States; three years later he accomplished another long tour. From 1831 to 1833 he was on leave of absence in England, and during this time had a personal conference with the king on American affairs. In 1833 he was created knight grand cross of the Royal Guelphic Order of Hanover. Ill health caused his retirement from Washington in October 1835. Though, in Sir Charles Webster's view, a man of 'no great ability' (Webster, 1.69), he dealt with important matters such as the Canadian boundary, the Latin American republics, the slave trade, and the tariff. On one occasion he was fiercely reprimanded by Canning for exceeding instructions (Temperley, 288). Palmerston thought him 'a steady sensible man, though not very showy' (Bourne, 466).

In 1835 Vaughan made a protracted tour of the continent. On 4 March 1837 he was sent on a special embassy to Constantinople, and proceeded by way of Malta, where he heard that the mission was no longer required; he therefore went to Venice, and thence travelled home through Italy and Switzerland. In such travel he spent most of the years that were left to him. He left minute itineraries of his later journeys. He died unmarried in Hertford Street, Mayfair, Westminster, on 15 June 1849.

C. A. HARRIS, *rev.* H. C. G. MATTHEW

Sources private information (1899) · *GM*, 2nd ser., 32 (1849), 204 · H. Temperley, *The foreign policy of Canning, 1822–1827* (1925) · C. K. Webster, *The foreign policy of Palmerston, 1830–1841*, 2 vols. (1951) · K. Bourne, *Palmerston: the early years, 1784–1841* (1982)

Archives All Souls Oxf., corresp. and papers | BL, corresp. with Lord Holland, Add. MS 51616 · Leics. RO, corresp. with Sir Henry Halford · NA Scot., letters to Sir Charles Murray · U. Southampton L., corresp. with Lord Palmerston

Likenesses T. Lawrence, oils, after 1820, All Souls Oxf. · S. Cousins, mezzotint, 1832 (after T. Lawrence), BM, NPG

Vaughan, Cuthbert (*c.*1519–1563), soldier, is of unknown parentage. He began his military career in 1546, serving as a captain at Boulogne. One year later he was a captain at the siege of Leith. He continued this military service during Edward's reign, for which he was rewarded in late 1551 with the office of bailiff of the lordships of Marche and Oye in Calais. During Mary's reign he was involved in Wyatt's rebellion: on 13 February 1554 he was indicted at Westminster for offences committed in Middlesex, and for marching to London in order to seize the Tower. For this he was condemned to death. He then provided evidence against another of the rebels, Sir Nicholas Throckmorton, and was subsequently released on a bond of 300 crowns. He did not suffer much: although he lost some of his lands, he successfully petitioned Mary for their restoration after his release. This clemency may have been due to the intervention of Philip, who sought to reconcile many of the rebels to the state; by the end of the reign he was on Philip's pension list.

In 1557 Vaughan was summoned to court to raise 300 men and lead them, as captain, to Berwick; the men were mustered at Tower Hill. Several of these men deserted in Scotland but were subsequently found and hanged. For his service in Scotland he received lands and further restorations. Vaughan married Elizabeth, daughter of Thomas Roydon and Margaret Whettenhall. She survived him by more than thirty years: she died on 19 August 1595 and was buried on 15 November at East Peckham church in Kent. Vaughan was her second husband, the first being William Twysden and the third Thomas Goulding. The recusant Jane *Wiseman was said to be their daughter. Early in 1558 Vaughan became involved in a land dispute with the son of his wife's first husband, Thomas Twysden. Early in Elizabeth's reign he was again sent to command at Berwick. Lord Eure, the commander there, sent him home complaining that he was insubordinate; Vaughan had refused to deliver his muster book when demanded by Eure's clerk. On his way back to court he carried a report on the state of Scotland and the protestant rebels there, a commission organized by the earl of Westmorland so that Vaughan might retain some credit. The privy council reinstated him on 21 January 1559. He then took part in the English intervention in the Scottish Reformation crisis of 1559–60. In July 1559 he was sent to survey the fortifications at Aymouth, while in April 1560 he was involved in the siege of Leith. In late April he was praised for his valiant conduct in assaulting the town of Pelham, for which he received the appellation 'the general of Pelham', reported by Randolph (*CSP Scot.*, 1547–63, 429–30, n. 826). He was later listed as one of the captains who had served best under Lord Grey. Cecil acknowledged his good services and saw that he was rewarded with a grant of marches in Kent and Sussex.

In 1562 Vaughan was appointed as muster master and comptroller of the English garrison then occupying Newhaven. On 28 September he and Sir Adrian Poynings left Portsmouth to take the first troops across to Newhaven. He argued over various matters with Poynings. Later rumours emerged in London that he was misappropriating money, and he was subsequently investigated, but was not charged. His work comprised musters, upkeep of fortifications, and general administration. On arrival at Newhaven he was quick to emphasize the strategic value of defending the town of Rouen. At one point he was asked to reform the church service used at the garrison: considered too radical, it was to be brought into line with the established service in England. He died on 23 July 1563, succumbing to the plague which was decimating the English garrison at Newhaven. Vaughan's religion seems to have been of the more 'advanced' sort. It is clear that he steadfastly opposed the reintroduction of Catholicism in Mary's reign, and his subsequent exile may have been important in the development of his religious beliefs. His wife, Elizabeth, was a noted puritan patron. Moreover, in December 1562 he expressed the hope that the parliament of the next year would make a more full reform of religion than that already in use. Despite his many years of loyal and valiant service, Vaughan was not the easiest man to work with. His opinions were strong, and he was not one to back down; he quarrelled extensively with Poynings, for example, as to what the best way for the English to enter the town of Newhaven might be. His career was dogged by accusations of insubordination and fiscal misappropriation. Nothing was ever proved, however, and he was held in some esteem by Cecil. Perhaps his firm convictions aroused ill feeling in others: he seems to have been a committed protestant and a solid military man.

C. P. CROLY

Sources LP Henry VIII, vol. 19 · APC, 1552–70 · CPR, 1554–7; 1558–66 · CSP for., Elizabeth, vols. 1–6 · CSP dom., 1547–80 · CSP Scot., 1547–63 · D. M. Loades, Two Tudor conspiracies (1965) · A. L. Rowse, Ralegh and the Throckmortons (1962) · BL, Harley MS 169 · PRO, SP 12/vol. 15; SP 15/vol. 8; SP 70/vols. 42–7 · Bodl. Oxf., MS Tanner 90 · P. Forbes, A full view of the public transactions in the reign of Queen Elizabeth, 2 vols. (1740–41)

Archives BL, Harley MS 169 · Bodl. Oxf., MS Tanner 90

David James Vaughan (1825– 1905), by unknown photographer

Vaughan, David James (1825–1905), Church of England clergyman and social reformer, born at St Martin's vicarage, Leicester, on 2 August 1825, was the sixth and youngest son of Edward Thomas Vaughan (1772–1829), fellow of Trinity College, Cambridge, and vicar of St Martin's, Leicester, and his second wife, Agnes, daughter of John Pares of The Newarke, Leicester. Charles John *Vaughan, master of the Temple, and General Sir John Luther Vaughan GCB were elder brothers. James Vaughan, a physician of Leicester and one of the founders of the Leicester Infirmary, was his grandfather, and his uncles included Sir Henry *Halford, physician; Sir John *Vaughan, father of Henry Halford Vaughan; and Sir Charles Richard *Vaughan.

Vaughan was educated first at the Leicester collegiate school, under W. H. Thompson, afterwards master of Trinity College, Cambridge, and in August 1840 he went to Rugby School, first under Thomas Arnold and then under A. C. Tait. In 1844 he won a scholarship at Trinity College, Cambridge, and next year the Bell university scholarship, along with his friend John Llewelyn Davies. In 1847 he was Browne medallist for Latin ode and epigrams; and in 1847 and 1848 he obtained the members' prize for a Latin essay. In 1848 he was bracketed fifth classic with Llewelyn Davies, and he was twenty-fourth senior optime. He graduated BA in 1848, proceeded MA in 1851, and was a fellow of Trinity College from 1850 to 1858. On 11 January 1859 he married Margaret, daughter of John Greg of Escowbeck, Lancashire.

Vaughan, Llewelyn Davies, and Brooke Foss Westcott, all fellows of Trinity, formed at Cambridge a lifelong friendship. The three were among the earliest members of the Cambridge Philological Society. In 1852 Vaughan and Llewelyn Davies brought out together a translation of Plato's Republic, with introduction, analysis, and notes. Llewelyn Davies undertook the first five books, and Vaughan the last five, each author submitting his work to the other for correction or amendment. The analysis was the work of Vaughan, while Llewelyn Davies was responsible for the introduction. In various reprints, this was for many years a standard edition, regarded by many as more accurate, if less stylish, than Jowett's translation. The translators sold their copyright for £60.

After initial hesitation, Vaughan was ordained deacon in 1853, and began his pastoral work in Leicester, living on his fellowship, and serving as honorary curate, first to his eldest brother at St Martin's, and then at St John's Church. In 1854 he was ordained priest, and in 1855 he succeeded Llewelyn Davies as incumbent of St Mark's, Whitechapel. In 1860 he was appointed vicar of St Martin's, Leicester, and master of Wyggeston's Hospital. The living was then in the gift of the crown, and had been held by his father and two of his brothers continuously since 1802, save for an interval of twelve years. In the case of each of the three sons the appointment was made at the request of the parishioners. Vaughan refused all subsequent offers of preferment, including a residentiary canonry at Peterborough and the lucrative living of Battersea, which Earl Spencer offered him in 1872. He accepted an honorary canonry of Peterborough in 1872, and he was rural dean of Leicester from 1875 to 1884 and from 1888 to 1891. In June 1894 he was made honorary DD of Durham University.

In early life Vaughan was influenced by the liberal theology of John Macleod Campbell, to whom he dedicated his Christian Evidences (1864), and while in London he, like Llewelyn Davies, came under the influence of F. D. Maurice. Maurice's example as social and educational reformer largely moulded Vaughan's career. Vaughan's teaching on the atonement and inspiration was at the outset called in question, but he soon concentrated his interests in social questions, to which he brought a broad public spirit and sympathy. His educational initiatives were no less successful, and perhaps more enduring, than those of Maurice and his colleagues in London. In 1862 he started in Leicester, on the lines of the Working Men's College founded by Maurice in London in 1854, a working men's reading-room and institute in one of the parish schools. He arranged classes and lectures, taught by volunteers, and the numbers attending them grew steadily. In 1868 there were 400 adults under instruction, and the name of the institute was changed to 'college', as being in Vaughan's words 'not only a school of sound learning, but also a home for Christian intercourse and brotherly love'. At one time the Leicester Working Men's College was educating 2300 students. In addition to Sunday morning and evening classes, night classes, and advanced classes, there were established a provident society, sick benefit society, and book club. Some of the students became leading manufacturers in Leicester, and several filled the office of mayor. Vaughan was president of the college for forty-three years. The college was rebuilt in the 1960s and remains the chief site for adult education in Leicester; it became part of the future University of Leicester in 1929.

On Sunday afternoons, in St Martin's Church, Vaughan gave addresses on social and industrial as well as religious themes to working men, including members of the great friendly societies in Leicester, and students of the college. The first, 'The Christian aspect and use of politics', was delivered on 13 February 1870. Some of his Sunday afternoon addresses were published in 1894 as *Questions of the Day*. Vaughan was chairman of the first Leicester school board in 1871, and exercised a moderating influence over stormy deliberations. During an epidemic of smallpox in 1871 he constantly visited the patients in the improvised hospital, and from that time to near the end of his life he regularly ministered to the staff and patients of the borough isolation hospital.

In 1893 failing health compelled him to resign his parish, and he retired to Wyggeston's Hospital on the outskirts of the town. He continued to act as chairman of the Institution of District Nurses, president of the Leicester Working Men's College, and honorary chaplain to the isolation hospital. He died at the master's house at Wyggeston's Hospital on 30 July 1905, and was buried at the Welford Road cemetery, Leicester. His wife died on 21 February 1911 and was buried beside her husband.

To commemorate Vaughan's work at St Martin's, as well as that of his father and two brothers, a new south porch was erected at St Martin's Church in 1896–7 at the cost of £3000. After his death a new Vaughan Working Men's College was built in Great Central Street and Holy Bones, Leicester, as a memorial to him, at the cost of £8000. The building was formally opened by Sir Oliver Lodge on 12 October 1908. It is now Vaughan College in St Nicholas Street, Leicester.

W. G. D. FLETCHER, *rev.* H. C. G. MATTHEW

Sources *The Times* (31 July 1905) · *The Guardian* (9 Aug 1905) · *Leicester Advertiser* (5 Aug 1905) · *Leicester Chronicle and Mercury* (12 May 1877) · *Leicester Chronicle and Mercury* (17 Oct 1908) · *The Wyvern* (7 July 1893) · A. J. Allaway, *Leicestershire Archaeological and Historical Society Transactions*, 33 (1957), 45–58 · A. Westcott, *Life of Brooke Foss Westcott*, 2 vols. (1903) · private information (1912)
Likenesses C. H. Jeens, stipple, BM · photograph, repro. in Allaway, 'David James Vaughan', 44 · photograph, University of Leicester, Vaughan College [*see illus.*]
Wealth at death £4007 7s. 8d.: probate, 9 Sept 1905, *CGPLA Eng. & Wales*

Vaughan [Fychan], **Edward** (early 1450s–1522/3), bishop of St David's, was almost certainly a Welshman, born somewhere in south Wales in the early 1450s. His parentage is unknown. He was educated at Cambridge University, where he was admitted as bachelor of canon law in either 1474 or 1475, and he incepted as doctor of canon law in 1482. He may have stayed on at Cambridge or returned home for a time, for it was not until 1487 that he received his first known preferment, as rector of St Matthew's Church, Friday Street, London, and portioner in the church of St Probus, Cornwall. These were granted presumably in anticipation of his ordination as subdeacon on 1 March, deacon on 22 March, and priest on 5 April 1488. He was made archdeacon of Lewes, Chichester diocese, in the same year. His clerical preferment, mainly in the dioceses of London and Chichester, has been fully recorded by A. B. Emden and in Le Neve's *Fasti ecclesiae Anglicanae*. He had already held prebends in St Paul's Cathedral when he was rewarded with the lucrative and prestigious office of treasurer there, together with its prebend of Broomesbury, in 1503. In London he gained a reputation for generosity and public spirit, building a house there for his successors and distributing 500 marks to the poor in time of dearth. In 1504 he became precentor of Abergwili and prebendary of Llanbister.

Vaughan was appointed bishop of St David's by papal provision on 13 July 1509 and consecrated by Archbishop Warham on 22 July the same year. He brought down to St David's, to act as choirmaster, a talented English organist and composer, John Norman, some of whose music has survived. By experience a careful manager, he commissioned a new copy of the Black Book of St David's (a fourteenth-century survey of the episcopal estates) in 1516, and in 1517 he renewed the appropriation of the church of Llansanffraid, Cardiganshire, to the vicars-choral to help them repair and maintain their houses within the close.

At St David's, however, Vaughan's reputation rests chiefly and securely on his building work. John Leland, who had visited St David's within two decades of the bishop's death, records that he built the chapel of Holy Trinity, the chapel of St Justinian, and the great barn at Lamphey, and that he repaired the castle of Llawhaden and built a new chapel there. Later authorities have attributed to him other building work at his palace at Lamphey, including the chapel, where a perpendicular-style east window has survived. At the cathedral he was responsible for the roof of the lady chapel and its ante-chapel, the south porch, and the third stage of the tower, although neither of the two latter, as W. Basil Jones caustically remarked, 'would confer immortality on his taste in architecture' (Jones and Freeman, 309). This was to be expected, for the diocese was in a depressed state and the money was just not available for lavish, large-scale reparations—witness the long list of tax exemptions that the bishop recorded in his register for 1513 and 1517 to religious houses and churches that had been 'diminished, impoverished and destroyed by wars, fires, inundations of rivers and other misfortunes and chances' (Isaacson, 2.790–803, 818–27). Holy Trinity chapel, however, with its fine ashlar finish and fan vaulting, remains one of the glories of the cathedral. It was constructed in an empty, enclosed, roofless space east of the presbytery, an area described by George Owen as 'the most vile and filthy place in the whole church' (Robson, 58). Built at the bishop's own expense, it was designed to be his resting-place and chantry chapel. It has been acclaimed as 'one of the finest pieces of Perpendicular work in the Principality' (Williams, 433). The same high-quality work can be seen in the traceried east window of the chapel at Lamphey Palace where the bishop seems to have spent his retirement. Here he rationalized the building of the palace in an attempt, as C. A. Ralegh Radford argued, 'to concentrate the life of the palace in one block and under one roof, abandoning the extensive establishment laid out in the more spacious days of the thirteenth and fourteenth centuries' (Radford, 12).

Vaughan died in late 1522 or early 1523 (certainly before 27 January 1523 when his will, dated 20 May 1521, was proved), and was buried in Holy Trinity chapel where, in Browne Willis's day, a brass memorial was still attached to his marble grave marker, lauding him as a supporter and ornament of his country who had managed and augmented the talents that God had given him skilfully, wisely, and well. He left numerous bequests to religious houses within his diocese and the large sum of £40 for a priest to sing masses for six years to secure the repose of his soul.   F. G. COWLEY

Sources P. A. Robson, *The cathedral church of St. David's: a short history and description of the fabric and episcopal buildings* (1901), 58 • *Fasti Angl., 1300–1541*, [Chichester], 14 • *Fasti Angl., 1300–1541*, [St Paul's, London], 16, 21, 39, 58 • *Fasti Angl., 1300–1541*, [Welsh dioceses], 55–6 • Emden, *Cam.*, 607–8 • *Joannis Lelandi antiquarii de rebus Britannicis collectanea*, ed. T. Hearne, [3rd edn], 6 vols. (1774), vol. 2, p. 324 • B. Willis, *A survey of the cathedral church of St David's* (1717), 15, 19–21, 68, 77–8, 117–18 • W. B. Jones and E. A. Freeman, *The history and antiquities of St David's* (1856) • Cooper, *Ath. Cantab.*, 1.26 • R. F. Isaacson, ed. and trans., *The episcopal registers of the diocese of St David's, 1397–1518*, 2 vols. in 3, Honourable Society of Cymmrodorion, Cymmrodorion Record Series (1917–20) • G. Williams, *The Welsh church from conquest to Reformation*, rev. edn (1976), 432–3, 518, 564, 566 • E. Yardley, *Menevia sacra*, ed. F. Green (1927), 85–6 • C. A. R. Radford, 'The palace of the bishops of St David's at Lamphey, Pembrokeshire', *Archaeologia Cambrensis*, 93 (1935), 1–14 • will, PRO, PROB 11/21, sig. 2
Archives NL Wales, episcopal register

Vaughan, Frankie [real name Frank Fruim Ableson] (1928–1999), popular singer, was born on 3 February 1928 at Liverpool Maternity Hospital, the son of Isaac Ableson, an upholsterer, and his wife, Leah, née Cossack, a seamstress. He was the grandson of Russian Jewish immigrants and was later inspired to take the stage name Frankie Vaughan from his maternal grandmother, who referred to him as her 'number vawn' grandson. At fourteen he won a scholarship to study at the Lancaster College of Art, and he held a place at Leeds University before being called up to the army towards the end of the Second World War. During his enlistment he sang in a number of camp concerts. He was demobbed in 1949 and enrolled at Leeds College of Art as a student teacher. On 6 June 1951 he married Stella Shock (b. 1929/30), daughter of Bernard Shock, a market trader. While taking a commercial art course, his singing at a college revue at Leeds Empire Theatre so impressed the manager that it was suggested that he should seek the agent Billy Marsh, who handled newcomers to show business. Vaughan initially preferred the notionally safer world of commercial art, but when the commissions ran dry, he sought out Marsh, who was impressed by his voice

and booked him for the circuit of northern variety theatres. Vaughan had arrived, and after his first year of touring was earning £150 per week.

While appearing in her show *New Stars and Old Favourites*, Vaughan met the female music-hall star and male impersonator Hetty King. Their encounter profoundly affected his career, as King coached him to develop for his own act the top hat and tails routine that she used. Subsequently, Vaughan was famed for the nonchalant style in which he would arrive on the stage dressed in a tuxedo, smile at the audience, swing his cane, and push his top hat or boater over his eyes at a jaunty angle.

King also advised him to find a signature tune, and Vaughan found it in the Victorian number 'Give me the Moonlight', which he made his own. He became known as 'Mr Moonlight', and would deliver his trademark song in a relaxed manner, often accompanied with an athletic high kick which delighted his audiences. However, it was not only Vaughan's performing style which marked him out as a major star in the 1950s. His voice was noted for its Liverpudlian twang, its cued chuckle (to tie in with his high kick), and the hint it gave of his Jewish origins. Like his idol the Jewish-American singer and entertainer Al Jolson, Vaughan had sung in the choir of his local synagogue.

Throughout the 1950s Vaughan enjoyed tremendous recording success. His first record was 'That Old Piano Roll Blues' and this was followed by a string of hits which kept him in the top thirty singles charts. These included 'Kisses Sweeter than Wine', 'Can't get Along without You', and almost inevitably 'Give me the Moonlight'. His most successful hit was 'The Green door', a memorable chestnut later revived by Shakin' Stevens and the punk band The Cramps. Alongside his chart success, Vaughan began a film career which culminated with a trip to Hollywood to appear in a supporting role with Marilyn Monroe and Yves Montand in the film *Let's Make Love* (1960). However, he took an instant dislike to Hollywood and the film was not a success, its production having been plagued by difficulties, not helped by Monroe's off-screen affair with Montand. Monroe was rumoured to have attempted to seduce Vaughan too but he resisted, and cited familial reasons for his early return to London. He did, however, perform for several seasons in Las Vegas during the 1950s and 1960s.

Despite the significant changes which took place in popular music during the 1960s and 1970s, Vaughan retained his star status. He continued his recording career and headlined at the London Palladium and at numerous summer shows at the Talk of the Town, which attracted family audiences. He also received greater exposure on television and appeared in Britain on *Sunday Night at the Palladium* and in America on *The Ed Sullivan Show*. In 1985 Vaughan successfully took over the lead in the West End musical *42nd Street*. This role proved to be his swansong, as he was forced to leave the cast after a year when he contracted peritonitis, having ignored the onset of the illness amid the show's hectic performance schedule. Although he had always been an advocate of physical exercise, he was dogged by ill health for the rest of his life. He was forced to have surgery after rupturing an artery in 1992 and underwent heart surgery in his final years.

Vaughan was renowned for his charity work, and he received several honours (including appointment as OBE in 1965 and CBE in 1997) for his support of the British Boys' Clubs Association: he had once been a member of one such club, and had donated the royalties of 'Green door' to the cause. In 1964 he was appointed to a committee dealing with juvenile delinquency, and successfully negotiated a deal with young Glaswegian gang members to turn in their weapons and accept an amnesty agreement.

Frankie Vaughan died on 17 September 1999 at the Churchill Hospital, Oxford. He was buried at Bushey Jewish cemetery, Hertfordshire. He was survived by his wife, Stella, and two sons and a daughter. He had remained a popular and versatile entertainer throughout his career, and received plaudits from his peers, who described him as a 'loveable and regular guy' who had achieved the affection of the British public.   MARK WHEELER

Sources *The Guardian* (18 Sept 1999), 22 · *The Independent* (18 Sept 1999), 7 · *The Scotsman* (20 Sept 1999) · 'Fuller up: the dead musician directory', elvispelvis.com · P. Probert and A. Probert, 'Great singers', www.greatsingers-groups.com/Frankie Vaughan.html · news report of final illness, www.grimsby-online.co.uk/articles/showbusiness/article124.html · www.findagrave.com · b. cert. · m. cert. · d. cert.
Archives Liverpool John Moores University, MSS, music MSS | FILM BFI NFTVA, documentary footage
Likenesses photographs, Hult. Arch.

Vaughan, Sir Gruffudd, fychan (*d.* 1447), soldier, was the son of Gruffudd ab Ieuan ap Madog of Powys and his wife, Mallt (Maud), daughter of Griffri ap Rhys Bongam of Broniarth. The father was implicated in Glyn Dŵr's rebellion and his estates (valued at 20 marks) were forfeited in 1404. Of Broniarth and Trelydan in Powys, the son was one of that breed of independent Welsh gentry (*uchelwyr*) who prospered after Glyn Dŵr's rebellion in the service of marcher lords, in Vaughan's case the lords of Powys and the Stafford lords of Caus. Lack of evidence obscures much of his career, and the native Welsh poetry addressed to him concentrates primarily on his military prowess. Gruffudd Vaughan was apparently not involved in the rebellion; a later pedigree identifies him as a burgess in Welshpool in 1406, though the identification is uncertain. He may have accompanied Henry V to France, but the tradition that he was made a knight-banneret at Agincourt (1415) is unsubstantiated. In November 1417 Vaughan and his brother, Ieuan ap Gruffudd, described as gentlemen, with two others made themselves notorious by capturing, on their ancestral estate at Broniarth, Sir John Oldcastle, the Lollard upon whose head a price of 1000 marks had been set. Various privileges were granted them for this act—including a pardon of murders and felonies and the right to hold their lands free of certain rents and services—by a charter dated 6 July 1419 from Edward Charlton, lord of Powys, to whom they had delivered Oldcastle at Welshpool. At Shrewsbury on 4 March 1421, in the presence of Henry V, the duke of Gloucester, and the earl of Stafford, the four captors acknowledged that they had received their portion of the reward from Charlton.

According to the poet Hywel Cilan, Vaughan was honoured in London and then knighted, with others, in a town beyond Rouen, presumably an allusion to service in France. If, as Hywel states (and the poet Lewys Glyn Cothi repeats), he was 'aureated' by Henry VI and his counsellors, this may have occurred when the king visited Rouen and Paris in 1430–32; the earl of Stafford was in the royal entourage. As a knight Vaughan was in receipt of an annuity of 5 marks from Stafford by 1441–2. In the following year he appears in the retinue of Sir Christopher Talbot, the youngest son of the earl of Shrewsbury and a notable jouster: on 10 August 1443 his lance pierced Talbot's heart at Caus and, as a result, Vaughan and his son Rheinallt (or Reynold) were outlawed and a price of 500 marks was placed on the father's head. His capture was effected by Henry Grey, count of Tancarville and one of the heirs of the Charltons of Powys, who summoned Sir Gruffudd to Powis Castle and gave what Sir Gruffudd considered a 'safe conduct'. Immediately on his arrival within the courtyard he was summarily beheaded, on 9 July 1447. This event was the occasion of poetical laments by Lewys Glyn Cothi and Dafydd Llwyd of Mathafarn. On 20 July 1447 a treasury warrant was issued for the payment of the 500 marks to Grey. The deed has been attributed to jealousy on Grey's part because Sir Gruffudd claimed descent from the ancient princes of Powys, and may have laid claim to some of Grey's lands. His sons Rheinallt and Dafydd accepted a pardon on 21 December 1448.

Sir Gruffudd married first Margaret, daughter and coheir of Gruffudd ap Jenkin of Broniarth, and second Margaret, daughter of Madog of Hope. He had three sons and three daughters. The eldest son was David Llwyd (*d.* 1489) of Leighton, ancestor of the Lloyds of Marrington, Marton, and Stockton; the second, Cadwalader, was ancestor of the Lloyds of Maes-mawr; and the third, Rheinallt, was ancestor of the Wynnes of Garth and of the Lloyds of Broniarth and Gaerfawr.
                      A. F. POLLARD, *rev.* R. A. GRIFFITHS

Sources E. D. Jones, 'Some fifteenth-century Welsh poetry relating to Montgomeryshire', *Montgomeryshire Collections*, 52 (1951–2), 3–21 · *Chancery records* · *Gwaith Hywel Cilan*, ed. L. Jones (1963), 47–9, 68–9 · *Gwaith Lewys Glyn Cothi*, ed. D. Johnston (1995), 447–8, 619–20 · *Gwaith Dafydd Llwyd o Fathafarn*, ed. W. L. Richards (1964), 120–22, 205 · C. Rawcliffe, *The Staffords, earls of Stafford and dukes of Buckingham, 1394–1521*, Cambridge Studies in Medieval Life and Thought, 3rd ser., 11 (1978) · P. C. Bartrum, ed., *Welsh genealogies, AD 300–1400*, 8 vols. (1974), vol. 3, pp. 480–81, 591 · J. P. Collier, ed., *Trevelyan papers*, 1 (1857), 26–7 · R. M. Jones, 'Y Ddraig Lwyd', *Ysgrifau Beirniadol*, 18 (1992), 164–88

Vaughan, Dame Helen Charlotte Isabella Gwynne- [*née* Helen Charlotte Isabella Fraser] (1879–1967), mycologist and women's activist, was born on 21 January 1879, at Chapel Street, Westminster, London, the elder daughter of Captain Arthur H. Fraser (1852–1884), Scots Guards, and his wife, Lucy Jane (1855/6–1939), novelist, daughter of Major Robert Fergusson, Royal Ayrshire and militia rifles. Both the Frasers and the Fergussons were old Scottish families, the Frasers having estates in Aberdeenshire and

Dame Helen Charlotte Isabella Gwynne-Vaughan (1879–1967), by Lafayette, 1929

the Fergussons belonging to the ancient gentry of Ayrshire. Arthur Fraser died in 1884; in 1887 his widow married Francis Hay-Newton, the son of her father's second wife. Her stepfather being a member of the consular service, Helen Fraser spent several years of her childhood abroad, her education being provided by governesses. She spent one year (1895–6) at Cheltenham Ladies' College, where she enjoyed the intellectual challenge, if not the discipline, and in 1896 came out at the Gordon Highlanders' ball in Aberdeen. For the next three years, without much enthusiasm, she followed the round of social activities of an upper-class girl of the time. However, two summers spent with her mother and sister in London girls' clubs introduced her to working-class women, an experience which made her very aware of her own leadership abilities.

In 1899, having overcome the opposition of her family, Helen Fraser began study for the Oxford entrance examinations at the ladies' department of King's College, London. She stayed on as one of the first women students at King's College (Carter medal, botany, 1902; BSc in botany with second-class honours, 1904). She was then demonstrator for a year to mycologist V. H. Blackman at University College, having previously assisted him in research on rust fungi. In 1905 she became demonstrator to botanist Margaret Benson at Royal Holloway College and the following year was appointed assistant lecturer. Work in girls' clubs, support of the more moderate wing of the

women's suffrage movement, and, with Dr Louisa Garrett Anderson, the founding of a University of London suffrage society were further concerns. Despite these many duties and interests she continued with her research, cytological studies on the stages of development of reproductive systems of fungi (begun with Blackman). A new field at the time, it was the area in which she was to work throughout her scientific career. After receiving her DSc in 1907 she obtained a lectureship at University College, Nottingham.

Tall, well built, and fair, with large grey eyes and a deep, pleasant voice, she was a strikingly attractive young woman. Unlike most of her female colleagues she dressed fashionably. She had a marked aristocratic aloofness, however, and maintained her distance, particularly from men of her own age. She looked rather towards older, established scientists, and thanks to her social connections made friends among them. Confident and energetic, she published several papers and entered into university politics. In 1909, helped by a recommendation from David Thomas Gwynne-Vaughan (1871–1915), former head of the botany department at Birkbeck College, London, she succeeded to his post. She was one of the youngest applicants and the only woman. In 1911 she married Gwynne-Vaughan, then at Queen's University, Belfast. She kept her Birkbeck post, but throughout the four years until his death from tuberculosis in 1915 they succeeded in spending at least half of each year together.

Early in 1917 Helen Gwynne-Vaughan was appointed chief controller of the Women's Army Auxiliary Corps then being formed to alleviate military manpower shortages. Her appointment was due largely to family connections and her association with Louisa Garrett Anderson, already involved in army medical work; it gave her immense satisfaction, fitting in with her leadership aspirations and the Fraser family tradition of military service. As head of women's units in France she led a corps which eventually reached 10,000, the recruits serving in capacities ranging from cooks to machine maintenance technicians.

An able and energetic organizer, although something of a strict disciplinarian, Helen Gwynne-Vaughan overcame much prejudice and obstruction from senior army officers; further, her corps successfully weathered a series of unfounded accusations in the home press of immoral conduct. Official recognition of her achievements came in January 1918 when she became the first woman to be appointed a military CBE; three months later, in recognition of its work during the battle of Ypres, the corps was renamed Queen Mary's Army Auxiliary Corps, with the queen as titular commander-in-chief.

In September 1918, with considerable reluctance, Helen Gwynne-Vaughan accepted the appointment of head of the Women's Royal Air Force. Profiting from her earlier experience she was able during her fifteen-month tenure to streamline this large unit's then chaotic administration and form an efficient machine. She was created DBE shortly before her resignation in December 1919.

Dame Helen's remarkably successful use of the opportunities the war had offered transformed her from a minor academic to a public figure. In 1920, aged forty-one and at the height of her powers, she applied for the regius professorship of botany at Aberdeen University. Unsuccessful, she remained at Birkbeck and in 1921 was appointed professor. Birkbeck was then upgraded to a school and admitted to the senate of London University. Her administrative talents and ability to secure the services of distinguished men from other institutions as part-time lecturers led to high standards of instruction, and the research school she founded attracted outstanding students, British and foreign. A stimulating teacher herself, she also returned with vigour to her cytological studies of the genetics of reproduction in fungi, and published about ten important papers over the next fifteen years. Although she was attacked strongly for her persistent support of the theory of two nuclear fusions and two reductions in the life cycle of the Ascomycetes group (ideas disproved by 1950), her contributions to basic studies in fungal genetics were notable. She also published two books, *Fungi: Ascomycetes, Ustilaginales, Uredinales* (1922) and (with B. Barnes) *The Structure and Development of the Fungi* (1927). Generally regarded as a good, detailed, taxonomic outline, the latter became a standard university text. She received the Linnean Society's Trail medal in 1920 and served on its council in 1921–4. Further professional recognition came in 1928 when she was president of both the Mycological Society and section K of the British Association. She was also active in university governance and served one four-year term on the university senate.

In the 1920s Dame Helen made several attempts to enter political life. After standing unsuccessfully for North Camberwell in London county council elections in 1922, she fought three subsequent general elections as Conservative candidate for the same constituency. Very much one of the old governing class, out of sympathy with the major social planning policies of the time, she was not successful. However, her public status was such that she was frequently consulted by prominent administrators, and served on government committees and on a royal commission on food prices. In 1929 she was appointed GBE for public and scientific services.

Dame Helen kept close ties with the women's services, including temporary organizations for the training of women officers. From one of these, by the late 1930s, an Auxiliary Territorial Service (ATS) instruction school was developed; from her position of commandant of this school she sought and secured, by July 1939, the post of first director of the ATS. The late start, inadequate preparation, and shortage of suitably trained officers meant that embodiment and mobilization of the expanded ATS went badly. Dame Helen, then over sixty and out of step with the times, too apt to encourage appointment of officers for their social class rather than ability, and sometimes difficult to deal with, was replaced. She returned to Birkbeck College in July 1941 and remained there until her retirement (as professor emeritus) in 1944.

Still a striking, handsome woman with lively interests,

Dame Helen remained active, working full time as honorary secretary of the London branch of the Soldiers', Sailors', and Air Force Association until 1962. She also served on committees of the old comrades associations of the army and air force where she had tremendous prestige. Her autobiographical *Service with the Army* had appeared in 1942.

The original architect of the present women's army corps, Dame Helen was one of the most distinguished women of her era. Her achievements in two such different fields as academic mycology and service administration were exceptional. Although considered by many abrupt and inflexible, she could be generous and warm-hearted, and she inspired great admiration among many of her staff. In middle age she became a vegetarian and lived very frugally; latterly she was severely affected by arthritis. She spent her last three years at the RAF Convalescent Home, Sussexdown, Storrington, Sussex, where she died on 26 August 1967. Following cremation her ashes were sent to Scotland for deposit in the Fraser family vault.

MARY R. S. CREESE

Sources M. Izzard, *A heroine in her time* (1969) · *Transactions of the British Mycological Society*, 51 (1968), 177–8 · DNB · *The Times* (22 Jan 1962) · *The Times* (30 Aug 1967) · *The Times* (3 Nov 1967) · G. C. Ainsworth, *Introduction to the history of mycology* (1976) · H. C. I. Gwynne-Vaughan, *Service with the army* [1942] · S. Bidwell, *The Women's Royal Army Corps* (1977) · *CGPLA Eng. & Wales* (1968) · W. E. Dick, 'Professor Dame Helen Gwynne-Vaughan, GBE, DSc', *Discovery* (July 1944), 199–200, 219 **Archives** NAM, military corresp. and papers · Women's Royal Army Corps Museum, Guildford | U. Glas., letters to F. O. Bower **Likenesses** P. de Laszlo, oils, 1909, Birkbeck College, London; repro. in Izzard, *A heroine in her time* · W. Orpen, oils, 1918, IWM · Lafayette, photograph, c.1928, repro. in *Transactions of the British Mycological Society*, facing p. 177 · Lafayette, photograph, 1929, NPG [*see illus.*] · J. Allan, bronze sculpture, 1953 · photograph, repro. in *The Times* (22 Jan 1962) · photograph, repro. in *The Times* (30 Aug 1967) · photograph, repro. in *ILN* (9 Sept 1967) · photographs, repro. in Izzard, *A heroine in her time* **Wealth at death** £16,777: probate, 21 March 1968, *CGPLA Eng. & Wales*

Vaughan, Sir Henry (1587?–1660/61), royalist army officer, was the sixth son of Walter Vaughan (d. 1598) of Golden Grove, Carmarthenshire, and Mary Rice (d. before 1588), daughter of Sir Walter Rice of Newton; he was the brother of the poet and promoter of Newfoundland, William *Vaughan, and John *Vaughan, first earl of Carbery. He settled at Derwydd, Llandybïe, Carmarthenshire, about 1602 or 1603, having married a widow, Sage Rice (*fl.* 1590–1640), the only child of the heir of that house, Elizabeth, first wife of John Gwyn William. Vaughan was sheriff for Carmarthenshire in 1619–1620, and represented Carmarthen Boroughs in successive parliaments from 1621 to 1629, except for the 1625 parliament, when he was unseated after a double return. He was elected as representative for the county on 26 March 1640 and again on 5 November 1640. During the Long Parliament he was nominated as a commissioner to root out scandalous ministers in a bill that was proceeding through the Commons. However, on 7 April 1642 a long-time opponent of his family, Hugh Grundy, presented a petition to parliament alleging misconduct against him in his care of the church, and sought to have him removed as a commissioner. Vaughan held six parish churches which he had obtained from Sir Henry Percy, son of the earl of Northumberland, at a rent of £750 a year. Grundy claimed that he grossly underpaid the curates and employed 'six unworthy and scandalous persons that are no preachers' in these churches. He further alleged that Vaughan entertained papists in his house and employed recusants in his own service (HLRO, Main MSS, 1644).

At the outbreak of civil war Vaughan closely followed the position of his nephew Richard Vaughan, second earl of Carbery, who had been given command of the royalist forces in south-west Wales. Indeed one commentator, writing shortly after the Restoration, described Vaughan as 'principled and actuated' by Carbery (E. D. Jones, ed., 'The gentry of south west Wales in the civil war', *National Library of Wales Journal*, 11, 1959–60, 143). In 1642 he was nominated as a commissioner of array in Carmarthenshire, and made lieutenant-colonel of the foot in Carbery's regiment. On 14 January 1643 he was knighted by Charles I at Oxford and on 26 October the king appointed him sergeant-major-general of the royalist forces in the counties of Carmarthen, Cardigan, and Pembroke. Vaughan moved into these counties and was described as 'the instrument of much mischief', apparently treating his opponents with some brutality (Phillips, 2.142). He was disabled from sitting in the Commons on 5 February 1644. Vaughan based his headquarters at Haverfordwest but abandoned that town in March 1644, reputedly after a panic induced by a stampede of frightened cattle, which was mistaken for the parliamentarian troops of Rowland Laugharne. He fled to Carmarthen, but that town was also taken by parliament a few weeks later.

Vaughan returned to Oxford and sat in the king's parliament there. He was taken prisoner at the battle of Naseby on 14 June 1645, and on 18 June was brought before the House of Commons and committed to the Tower, where he remained until his removal to the Fleet on 1 October 1647. Vaughan wrote to his wife from prison on 29 July 1648 that he was 'like to be in a starving condicion' (Jones, 'Cadets', 139). On 27 April 1644 a fine of £160 had been set for him by the parliamentarian authorities and on 20 August 1645 he was assessed at £500, by the committee for compounding, his estate being valued at £600 a year. He was in severe financial difficulties, however, and about this time assessed his debts at £3603, including £20 for his 'lodging and diet' in the Tower. He informed the authorities that 'all the demeans where I live was my wife's, and the best part of my estate was my wife's inheritance' (Carmarthenshire RO, Cawdor (Vaughan) MS 22/658).

Supporting the view that Vaughan's conduct in the war was particularly vicious is the fact of his exclusion from any pardon under the Newcastle propositions of 1646. He was similarly exempted from the general pardon of 13 October 1648, being described as a 'capital offender'. A parliamentarian writer described him as '"Act-all", now prisoner in the Tower for all [the family?]', brother to 'the honest Richard (Tell-all)' (*The Earle of Carberyes Pedegree*,

1646). His strong affection for the king's cause was also indicated by a royalist song of 1647:

Sir Harry Vaughan looks as grave
As any beard can make him.
Those [who] come poore prisoners to see
Doe for our Patriarke take him.
Old Harry is a right true blue,
As valiant as Pendraggon,
And would be loyall to his king
Had King Charles ne'er a rag on.
(Jones, 'Cadets', 140)

Though it was reported that Vaughan was in prison in London until 1659, he was listed as a potential royal activist in Carmarthenshire during 1658. He made his will on 27 November 1660 but died at Derwydd, Llandybïe, before 5 January 1661, when an inventory of his goods was drawn up; his will was proved at Carmarthen on 22 January. His eldest son, John, predeceased him so the estate devolved on his second son, also **Sir Henry Vaughan** (*c.*1613–1676). He was a lieutenant-colonel in his father's regiment, and was first noticed in arms when Tenby was captured by Cromwell in 1648 during the second civil war. In his father's letter from prison of July 1648, Henry was described as being a 'prisoner in Denby Castle'. A contemporary pamphlet called him 'Sergeant-Major' but his memorial inscription gives his rank as 'Colonel' (Phillips, 2.378; Harrison, 12, 84). After the Restoration he was knighted at Whitehall, on 9 January 1662. He was appointed as captain of the foot for the borough of Carmarthen in 1662 by the earl of Carbery, and served as mayor for the town in 1670. He was returned as MP for the county of Carmarthen at a by-election in January 1668, but a question arose over his eligibility to sit as he had been outlawed for debt. After consideration it was decided that his election should stand, and he retained the seat until his death (caused by a fall from his horse) on 26 December 1676. It has been suggested that he was 'interested in Parliament solely as a refuge from his creditors: he made no recorded speeches and sat on no committees, but he loyally supported the court party' (Naylor and Jagger, 3.628). He was buried at Llandybïe church, where an elaborate monument was erected to his memory by his widow, Elizabeth (*d.* 1694), eldest daughter and coheir of William Herbert of Coldbrook, Monmouthshire. Many writers have erroneously assumed the existence of only one Sir Henry Vaughan, while some have still further confounded them with their namesake, who hailed from Cilcennin, Cardiganshire.

LLOYD BOWEN

Sources DNB • F. Jones, 'Cadets of Golden Grove, pt 2: Vaughan of Derwydd', *Transactions of the Honourable Society of Cymmrodorion* (1974–5), 132–61 • Carmarthenshire RO, Cawdor (Vaughan) MSS • NL Wales, Derwydd MSS • J. R. Phillips, *Memoirs of the civil war in Wales and the marches, 1642–1649*, 2 vols. (1874) • P. R. Newman, *Royalist officers in England and Wales, 1642–1660: a biographical dictionary* (1981), 385–6 • JHC, 1–9 (1547–1687) • M. A. E. Green, ed., *Calendar of the proceedings of the committee for compounding … 1643–1660*, 5 vols., PRO (1889–92) • M. A. E. Green, ed., *Calendar of the proceedings of the committee for advance of money, 1642–1656*, 3 vols., PRO (1888) • L. Naylor and G. Jagger, 'Vaughan, Sir Henry', HoP, *Commons, 1660–90*, 3.627–8 • W. A. Shaw, *The knights of England*, 2 vols. (1906) • main papers of the House of Lords, HLRO • [R. J. Harrison], *Some notices of the Stepney family* (privately printed, London, 1870) • F. Jones, 'The

Vaughans of Golden Grove', *Transactions of the Honourable Society of Cymmrodorion* (1963), 96–145 • will, NL Wales, SD/probate/1682/84 [Henry Vaughan the younger]
Archives Carmarthenshire RO, Cawdor (Vaughan) MSS • NL Wales, Derwydd MSS
Likenesses portrait, *c*.1644, Derwydd House, Carmarthenshire • funeral effigy (Henry Vaughan the younger), Llandybïe church, Carmarthenshire
Wealth at death estate value £600 p.a., 1645: Green, ed., *Calendar of the committee for the advance of money*, 588 • apparently indebted: NL Wales, SD/probate/1660/89

Vaughan, Sir Henry (*c*.1613–1676). *See under* Vaughan, Sir Henry (1587?–1660/61).

Vaughan, Henry (1621–1695), writer and translator of devotional works, was born at Newton by Usk in the parish of Llansanffraid (St Bridget's), Brecknockshire, the eldest known child of Thomas Vaughan (*c*.1586–1658), of Tretower, and Denise Jenkin (*b. c*.1593), only daughter and heir of David and Gwenllian Morgan, of Llansanffraid. Vaughan was the elder of twins; his brother Thomas *Vaughan (1621–1666) was also an author, under the pseudonym Eugenius Philalethes. Vaughan could claim kinship with two powerful Welsh families, one Catholic and one protestant. His paternal grandmother, Frances, was the natural daughter of Thomas Somerset, who spent some twenty-four years in the Tower of London for his adherence to Catholicism. As she survived into Vaughan's boyhood, there may have been some direct Catholic influence upon his early nurturing. Vaughan shared a common ancestry with the Herbert family through the daughter of the famous warrior of Agincourt Dafydd ap Llywelyn, the 'Davy Gam, esquire' of Shakespeare's *Henry V*. He is not known to have claimed kinship with George Herbert, but must surely have been aware of the connection.

Education Thomas later remarked that '*English* is a *Language* the *Author* was *not born to*' (*Works of Thomas Vaughan*, 94). Their father, however, had a command of English, and they were probably bilingual. Both boys were sent to school under Matthew Herbert, rector of Llangattock, and both wrote tributes to him. Since their interest was so clearly shared, the two brothers' intimate acquaintance with hermeticism may have dated from those years. Herbert doubtless reinforced the devotion to church and monarchy that the boys would have learned at home. Like several others among Vaughan's clerical acquaintances, he was to prove uncompromising during the interregnum, suffering sequestration and imprisonment and narrowly avoiding banishment.

The buttery books of Jesus College, Oxford, show that Thomas was admitted to the college in May 1638 (Hutchinson, 30), and it has long been assumed that Henry went up at the same time, though Wood states that 'he made his first entry into Jesus College in Michaelmas term 1638, aged 17 years' (Wood, *Ath. Oxon.*, 926). There is no clear record, as there is in Thomas's case, to establish Henry's residence or matriculation, but the assumption of his association with Oxford, supported by his inclusion in *Athenae Oxonienses*, is reasonable enough. He informed Aubrey, who wrote to him on Wood's behalf, 'I stayed not

att Oxford to take any degree' (*Works of Henry Vaughan*, 687). Recent research in the Jesus College archives suggests that 'Henry did not enter Jesus College before 1641, unless he did so in 1639 without matriculating or paying an admission fee, and left before the record in the surviving Buttery Books resumes in December of that year' (Allen, 'The Vaughans at Jesus College, Oxford, 1638–48'). The suggestion that Henry went to Oxford some time after Thomas may be strengthened by a comparison of the poems each wrote for the 1651 edition of the *Comedies, Tragi-Comedies, with Other Poems* of William Cartwright, who had died in 1643. Thomas had clearly attended Cartwright's lectures, which were the great draw of the time ('When He did read, how did we flock to hear!'; *Works of Thomas Vaughan*, 582), while Henry apparently had not, since he begins his verses 'I did but see thee' (*Complete Poems*, 88). On the other hand Hutchinson thought that a reference, in 'On Sir Thomas Bodley's library; the author being then in Oxford', to the library being T-shaped ('all our fame / Meets here to speak one letter of thy name') suggests a date before 1640, when the addition of the Selden end produced the shape of an H (Hutchinson, 31).

It was quite usual for elder sons of the gentry not to graduate, and to proceed to the inns of court. In the letter to Aubrey already cited, dated 15 June 1673, Vaughan wrote that he 'was sent to London, beinge then designed by my father for the study of the Law, which the sudden eruption of our late civil warres wholie frustrated' (*Works of Henry Vaughan*, 687). If he indeed left London upon the outbreak of civil war, that would have been soon after Charles raised his standard at Nottingham on 22 August 1642. The mist which surrounds Vaughan's Oxford career is not dispelled by Aubrey, who writes '*Eugenius Philalethes* was of Jesus College. Whither Henry was I have forgotten; but he was a Clarke sometime to Judge Sir Marmaduke Lloyd' (*Brief Lives*, 303). Such employment seems probable enough: Vaughan said that he had been sent to London to study law, and he and Lloyd had their ardent royalism in common. Vaughan could have held this position from 1642 to 1645; Lloyd was taken prisoner at the siege of Hereford in December 1645, fined, and dismissed from his position as judge.

Apart from the periods of study, at Llangattock, Oxford, and one of the inns of court, Vaughan's life was spent in his native village. His first wife was Catherine Wise, daughter of Richard and Lucy Wise of Gilsdon Hall, Coleshill, Warwickshire. They were probably married before the publication of *Poems* in 1646, and had four children, Thomas, Lucy, Frances, and Catherine. The date of Catherine Wise's death is unknown, but the elegy 'Fair and Young Light' in the 1655 *Silex scintillans* probably celebrates her memory.

Military service The Latin poem addressed to posterity prefaced to *Olor Iscanus* (1651) was once thought to indicate that Vaughan had not fought in the civil war; a more likely interpretation is that he had not fought on the wrong side, had not taken part in the 'great overthrow' which had swept away the church, the monarch, and the peace of the kingdom. His 'An elegy on the death of Mr. R. W. Slain in the late unfortunate differences at Rowton Heath, near Chester, 1645' clearly suggests that he participated in that battle. Further, among the 'Captaines' taken prisoner on 24 September 1645 after the royalist defeat at Rowton Heath we find Thomas Vaughan. Henry Vaughan seems to have been among the survivors of Rowton Heath who withdrew to Beeston Castle, about 9 miles south-east of Chester, which surrendered in November 1645 (*Works of Thomas Vaughan*, 6). In the splendid humorous poem 'Upon a cloak lent him by Mr. J. Ridsley' Vaughan refers to 'that day, when we / Left craggy *Beeston*, and the fatal *Dee*' (*Complete Poems*, 84). Moreover, his name appears in a list, dated 1663, of officers claiming their share in relief promised by the crown, just where we would expect it, along with 'Cap. Tho. Vaughan' in the company of Colonel Sir Herbert Price, of Brecon Priory (Hutchinson, 64–5). Vaughan's younger brother William (*b. c.*1628) died on 14 July 1648, possibly as a result of wounds or sickness incurred during the second civil war, and Vaughan mourned William's death in a series of fine elegies.

Vaughan as poet, translator, and writer of devotional prose Henry Vaughan's first volume, *Poems, with the Tenth Satire of Juvenal Englished*, appeared in 1646. The civil war had been in progress for four years, and Vaughan had by then seen military service. Two major causes of distress were still in the future: the death of his beloved younger brother William in 1648, and the execution of Charles I in 1649. The title-page indicated the author's status as gentleman, and its preface is addressed to 'Gentlemen' whose 'more refined spirits out-wing these dull Times, and soar above the drudgery of dirty intelligence'. Vaughan claims detachment, yet he reminds his readers that they are living in 'the dregs of an age'. He is aware that his love poems might seem anachronistic; the echoes of Habington's *Castara*, a celebration of wedded chastity, would have appealed to Charles I and Henrietta Maria. In reference to his translation he describes Juvenal as one whose pen 'had as much true passion, for the infirmities of that state, as we should have pity, to the distractions of our own' (*Complete Poems*, 31). He hints darkly, and with good reason, at topical application.

In the *Poems* of 1646 we find, lightly handled, themes and interests that will take on deeper resonance in the later *Silex* (the theme of the restoration of all things, for example, in 'To my Ingenuous Friend, R. W.' and in 'Upon the Priory Grove'). On the other hand, some of the more successful poems differ markedly from Vaughan's mature verse, suggesting that religious lyricism was not his sole talent. Lines 35–56 of 'A Rhapsody' indicate that Vaughan had used his eyes and imagination to some purpose during his time in London; lines 27–36 of 'To Amoret Weeping' show that Vaughan had read or heard the Jacobean dramatists with attention: he captures their manner, their concreteness of moral perception, very well. 'A Rhapsody' also suggests that in spite of his claim to detachment, Vaughan had been considerably stirred by the political events of the time.

Olor Iscanus, published in 1651 but with a preface dated 17 December 1647, is the book one might expect from a young royalist of that time and place. Vaughan writes a joking poem on his poverty (the royalist ruined in his fortunes); he writes verse letters to his friends (as royalists scattered by their adversities did); he writes elegies for acquaintances slain in battle; he participates (at one remove in the case of Fletcher and directly in the case of Cartwright) in two of the great royalist publishing ventures of the time. One royalist theme, treated in the secular verse with uncommon *gravitas*, is that of retirement. Vaughan treats this theme mostly through translation, of the poems of Ovid written during his banishment, of those of Boethius written during his imprisonment. Vaughan's treatment of the Horatian theme of the royalist contentedly retired to his estates is unconventional. In translating the Polish Jesuit neo-Latin poet Casimir Sarbiewski, he answers Horace's 'Beatus ille' ode with the reflection that the

> worldly he …
> Ploughing his own *fields*, seldom can
> Be justly styled, *the blessed man*,

for 'That title only fits a *Saint*', who

> can gladly part
> With *house* and *lands*, and leave
> … [the] loud strife
> Of this world for a better life.
> (*Complete Poems*, 127)

In *Silex scintillans* the theme of retirement deepens into the theme of hiddenness. There we see it in such poems as 'The Book', where the world of all that has lived within nature is hidden in the artefact which is the book, waiting for that day when God will 'make all new again' (*Complete Poems*, 310); we see it in the alchemical imagery of the poem 'Holy Scriptures', when Vaughan addresses the Bible and says,

> In thee the hidden stone, the *manna* lies,
> Thou art the great *elixir*, rare and choice;
> (ibid., 198)

we see it in 'The Timber', where Vaughan relates death to new life, to the growing up of fresh groves and the shooting of green branches, 'While the low *violet* thrives at their root' (ibid., 262); we see it in 'The Seed Growing Secretly', with its typical reference to that 'Dear, secret *greenness*!' which is nursed below the level of tempests and winds, and whose growth is apparent only to God (ibid., 277); we see it even more movingly expressed in the elegiac poem 'I Walked the Other Day', in which the poet represents himself as digging in winter in a place where he had once

> seen the soil to yield
> A gallant flower,

and there

> saw the warm recluse alone to lie
> Where fresh and green
> He lived of us unseen.
> (ibid., 240–41)

We see it, finally, in the hidden God of 'The Night', in whom there is a 'deep but dazzling darkness', and in whose night the poet wishes to 'live invisible and dim' (ibid., 290).

In virtually all these examples the theme of hiddenness

is linked with the theme of potentiality, as expressed through notions like new growth, alchemical transmutation, resurrection of the dead. If our 'life is hid with Christ in God' (Colossians 3: 3), then the possibility of new life, of transfiguration, is there. Vaughan brings together the notion of potentiality as expressed through alchemical philosophy and the same notion as expressed through the parables of the kingdom, in which mustard seeds grow into great trees, or scattered seed brings forth a hundredfold, in which, that is, hidden and apparently insignificant things gather to a greatness. Vaughan's response in such poems as these is religious and spiritual rather than directly political. Nevertheless, it is a spiritual response to a political situation. Whether drawing on Dante or on more ancient sources, Vaughan was aware of the polysemous possibilities of poetry; so much in his world is hidden, quietly biding its time, waiting for a new life, that the alert and sympathetic contemporary reader may have seen in such images hidden and buried royalism and Anglicanism waiting for their potentialities to be actualized, for their new day to dawn.

Most of Vaughan's work in prose consists of translations, the titles of which make clear their application to historical circumstance, for example *Of the Benefit wee may Get by our Enemies*, *The Praise and Happinesse of the Countrie-Life*, *The World Contemned*, *Of Temperance and Patience*. A significant original work is *The Mount of Olives, or, Solitary Devotions* (1652). Vaughan may well have thought of it as an alternative to the Book of Common Prayer, use of which was proscribed. It is interesting that, in spite of the Anglican rite being banned, Vaughan provides prayers, a meditation, and admonitions in relation to receiving 'the holy Communion', as well as 'A Prayer in Time of Persecution and Heresie' (*Works of Henry Vaughan*, 160–66). It seems probable that clandestine services were held, yet in the Brecon gaol records for the relevant period only one prosecution for use of the Book of Common Prayer has been found.

Vaughan as medical practitioner In his letter to Aubrey of 15 June 1673 Vaughan wrote that his brother's employment was in 'physic and Chymistrie', and added, 'My profession also is physic, whch I have practised now for many years with good success (I thank god!) & a repute big enough for a person of greater parts than my selfe.' Both Hutchinson and the two women, Gwenllian Morgan and Louise Guiney, on whose researches he based his biography, gave careful attention to the questions of when Vaughan is likely to have begun work as a medical practitioner and where he received his medical degree. They found no evidence that Vaughan had graduated in medicine from any British or European university. Legal documents dated 1677, 1690, 1691, 1693, and 1695 refer to Vaughan as doctor of medicine or of 'physick', but he himself does not use the title, referring to himself only as 'Physitian' (Hutchinson, 190). He is described as 'M.D.' on his gravestone. Hutchinson conceded that the College of Physicians would probably have been unable to enforce regulations against unlicensed practitioners in a county so remote as Brecknockshire; but he thought it unlikely that 'a man of

honour like Henry Vaughan would have adopted the custom of none too scrupulous astrologers, or have suffered popular use to give him a degree to which he was not entitled' (ibid., 193). Such an assumption may well be anachronistic; it certainly dates from an era when the literary persona of the author of *Silex scintillans* was assumed to be virtually identical with the man himself. In Vaughan's translation of Heinrich Nolle, *Hermetical Physick* (1655), we find 'And after all the coyl of Academical licentiated Doctors, he onely is the true Physician, created so by the light of Nature, to whom Nature her selfe hath taught and manifested her proper and genuine operations by Experience' (*Works of Henry Vaughan*, 581). The first nine words of this sentence are Vaughan's interpolation, and suggest that if he was acting as a physician by 1655, he was unlicensed.

The twinship and obviously shared intellectual interests of Thomas and Henry make some comparison of their careers relevant. Thomas was evicted from his living in 1650, and needed a source of income. In a letter of May 1650 Samuel Hartlib noted that he 'for some years hath tried Chymical or Physical Conclusions', and we also learn from Hartlib that in that year there was a project to form a 'chymical club' of which Vaughan was to be a member. It seems likely that this society was actually formed (*Works of Thomas Vaughan*, 11–13). Thomas was married on 28 September 1651, and his wife, Rebecca, died on 17 April 1658. He writes in his manuscript notebook 'Aqua vitae: non vitis' (BL, Sloane MS 1741) that he had employed himself all her lifetime 'in the Acquisition of some naturall secrets' (*Works of Thomas Vaughan*, 588). There is also an apparent reference to Henry Vaughan's first wife staying with them in London and making, with Rebecca, 'a great glass of eye-water' (ibid., 17). Thomas Vaughan's alchemical and 'philosophical' publications run from 1650 to 1655. He seems to have been working at 'physick' for some considerable time before 1655, the date before which, Hutchinson argued, Henry could not have given himself to continuous medical training. If Hartlib is to be trusted, Thomas's work in 'physick' began before 1650. If Henry Vaughan's position as a legal clerk ended in or before 1645, it is likely enough that he would have needed at least some supplementary income. His father was a younger son, there is reference in the verse to poverty, and, given its strongly royalist leanings, the family is unlikely to have prospered financially during the civil war. Vaughan's clerical neighbour Rowland Watkyns, who was dispossessed in 1648, probably practised as a physician while he was deprived of his living, and he and Vaughan may have been rivals. If a dispossessed cleric could have been an unlicensed practitioner, why not the elder son of a poor royalist gentry family who had completed no other professional training? After all, Vaughan's interest in hermetic authors, whose writing had practical as well as theoretical implications, can be documented from the poems as early as 1650.

Since Hutchinson's biography, further evidence that Vaughan was taking a strong interest in medicine before 1655 has come to light. Fourteen medical books he once owned are now in the Library Company of Philadelphia. Probably Vaughan's widow at his death sent them to Bristol, the nearest market, where they were purchased by Dr William Logan, then practising medicine in Bristol. Logan's library was sent to America after his death, and incorporated into the library of his brother James Logan, William Penn's agent. One of the books, Jean Pecquet's *Experimenta nova anatomica* (Paris, 1651), was first owned by Thomas Vaughan, the flyleaf bearing his signature and the motto *Deo duce: comite natura*, with the date 1652, which presumably represents the date on which Thomas acquired this work. On page 107 there is a marginal note in Henry's hand concerning the cause and cure of fever and dropsy, signed 'H:V:S'. The form of signature suggests that Henry owned, or had access to, and felt free to write in, this book while he was still thinking of himself as Silurist (a native of the district anciently inhabited by the Silures), since books of a later date are signed simply 'Vaughan'. Nicholas Fonteyn's treatise on paediatric medicine *Commentarius in Sebastianum Austrium: de puerorum morbis* carries the autograph signature and motto '*Henr: Vaughan Siluris. 1654. Salus mea ex Agno*'. The earliest work which bears both the signature 'Vaughan' and the date of acquisition was published in 1669, and acquired by Vaughan in 1676. The collection shows that he began to buy medical books at least as early as 1654 and continued to do so until 1682. No book signed merely 'Vaughan' has any religious motto in his hand.

Aubrey thought of Vaughan as taking a strong and informed interest in natural history; on 27 November 1675 he wrote to Anthony Wood that he was sending to his cousin Vaughan for the 'Naturall History' of Brecknockshire and of 'other circumjacent counties: no man fitter' (Hutchinson, 212). This request was in connection with a natural history of England and Wales projected by Dr Robert Plott, keeper of the Ashmolean Museum at Oxford. Vaughan replied to Aubrey on 9 December 1675, assuring him that he would take care to assist Plott 'with a short account of natures Dispensatorie heer', and requesting Aubrey to acquaint him 'with the method of his writinge' (*Works of Henry Vaughan*, 692). As it was not until 1681 that Aubrey forwarded queries from Plott to Vaughan, it is scarcely surprising that nothing came of Vaughan's collaboration. However, Vaughan's marginalia to Simon Paulli's *Quadripartitum botanicum*, acquired for 12s. in 1682, suggest that his interest in natural history persisted. Vaughan did not complete this project, but roughly 400 plants are given their common English names; medicinal properties attributed to some are mentioned; and the note on *Agnus castis* suggests that Vaughan retained in his seventh decade that respect for Catholicism, evident in his translations, which he may well have learned as a child from his grandmother. He gives the English name as 'Park-leafs, or Chaste tree', adding the note 'A kind of withie, of which the most holy monks & nuns make them girdles' (p. 188).

Later life After the death of his first wife Vaughan married her sister Elizabeth Wise (*b.* 1630). There were four children of the second marriage: Grisell, Lucy, Rachel, and

Henry. It has been found surprising that a devout Anglican should have married his deceased wife's sister. The table of kindred and affinity would have made the validity of such a marriage challengeable; however, under the Commonwealth that document shared the fate of the Book of Common Prayer, and the Act for Marriages of 1653 did not touch upon the prohibited degrees. The totally unworldly, devoted Anglican of *Silex scintillans* was a literary construct, only partially representative of Vaughan's non-literary self. It was natural enough that his dead wife's sister would help to care for his children. 'Isaac's Marriage', in the 1650 *Silex scintillans*, indicates that Vaughan had given thought to that biblical marriage which the Book of Common Prayer held up as an example, and which involved marriage with a kinswoman 'in-law'.

Vaughan's own statements indicate three significant periods of illness. In the preface to the 1655 *Silex scintillans*, he intimated that he was 'nigh unto death' when he wrote the last poems in it (*Complete Poems*, 143). The title-page of *Flores solitudinis* (1654) states that the pieces in it were 'Collected in his Sicknesse and Retirement', suggesting a protracted illness (*Works of Henry Vaughan*, 211). In 1662 he wrote to the commissioners of account, who had been appointed to inquire into alleged misuse of tithes, 'I had not fayled to wayt upon you my selfe, if weaknes, & other violent effects of a late feaver, had not resisted my real intentions' (Hutchinson, 199). Aubrey records that he wrote to Vaughan 'on that very day that the Pr[ince] of Orange came to London'—18 December 1688 (ibid., 209). On 25 March 1689 Vaughan wrote to Wood, 'I received a letter in the beginning of my sicknes from my Cousin John Awbrey about those inquiries you make now. … but it was my misfortune to continue so very weak and such a forlorn Clinic, that I could not to this day return him an answer' (*Works of Henry Vaughan*, 694). Such glimpses of Vaughan as we have in his later years derive from two principal sources. First, a correspondence with Aubrey and Wood began with a letter of 15 June 1673 to Aubrey, giving an account of his and Thomas's publications, and ended with another, also to Aubrey, of 9 October 1694, on the subject of Welsh bards (ibid., 689–97). He refers to himself and Thomas as 'low & forgotten things' and expresses pleasure that their names are to be 'revived, & shine in the Historie of the Universitie' (ibid., 689, 692). This correspondence is interesting, but not rich in biographical fact.

The other source is less happy, consisting of lawsuits indicating serious tensions within Vaughan's family, especially between the children of his first and second marriages. By an indenture dated 1689 Vaughan and his wife gave the Newton estate to his eldest son, with Thomas agreeing in return to pay £100 each to the children of the second marriage, to allow his father £30 a year for life, and his stepmother £20 a year after his father's death. However, this affair was not concluded until 1694. Thomas did not make the agreed payments to the children of the second marriage, and alleged that his father and stepmother had 'in a most clandestine manner … taken away the said articles and indenture … and cut the signatures there-from' (Hutchinson, 230). The matter was finally settled out of court and an agreement was reached which acknowledged Thomas's right to the estate. In 1693 Vaughan's daughter Catherine, whose hand had been burnt when she was an infant and who was lame, peti-tioned the justices of the great sessions to 'order her father to give her necessary maintenance' (ibid., 232). The judge of assize awarded her £6 a year, but this appears not to have been paid, and Catherine received no support from the local magistrates. In a second petition to the next meeting of the great sessions she complained that she had received only 2s. 6d. This occasioned a bitter letter from Vaughan to the judge who had made the award: 'your Lordship will give me leave to tell you that among hea-thens noe parents were ever compelled to maintain or relieve disobedient & rebellious children, that both des-pise and vilifie their parents' (*Works of Henry Vaughan*, 699). The case seems to have been concluded by the local mag-istrates ordering a quarterly payment of 15s. At some time after the house at Newton was conveyed to his son Thomas in 1689, Vaughan and Elizabeth moved to a cot-tage in Sgethrog; its lintel-stone may be seen at the foot of Vaughan's gravestone. On it are inscribed the initials HᵛE over the date 1689; however, it is unclear when they actu-ally vacated Newton.

There is no portrait of Vaughan, and no description of his appearance. Aubrey wrote that he was 'ingeniose, but prowd and humorous', that is, capricious or moody (*Brief Lives*, 303). This seems an apt description of Thomas Vaughan. The brothers may have been identical twins. Thomas Powell wrote of them, 'Not only your *faces*, but your *wits* are *twins*' (*Complete Poems*, 67), and the second half of this seems apt enough. Stevie Davies considers the fact of Vaughan's twinship central to understanding of his personality and, by extension, his work.

Death and reputation The cause of Vaughan's death is unknown; he died in Brecknockshire in 1695, on 23 April, like Shakespeare before him, and Wordsworth after him. His wife survived him. He died intestate, and his posses-sions were valued at £49 4s.: not much, but almost ten times what his father's had been at his death in 1658. Vaughan's gravestone, of unusual size and thickness, may still be seen in St Bridget's churchyard, Llansanffraid. Vaughan was buried not inside the church, as was fairly usual for gentlemen at that time, but in the churchyard, a statement of humility perhaps. At the top is written in Latin: 'Henry Vaughan, Silurist, Doctor of Medicine. He died on April 23 in the year of our salvation 1695 and in the 73rd year of his age.' (Vaughan's age at death, as recorded on his gravestone, is at odds with the now generally accepted year of his birth.) Immediately below is the family's coat of arms: a statement of claim to gentlemanly status. Below that is written in Latin: 'What he wished on his tomb: unprofitable servant, greatest of sinners, here I lie; glory to God; may He have mercy.' The combination of worldliness and humility is not merely conventional: memorials to the gentry of that time were apt to celebrate

the virtues of class, such as free-handed hospitality, rather than Christianity's more rigorous virtues.

The gravestone, a kind of retrospective, sums Vaughan up as gentleman, Silurist, medical man, and Christian. Arguably he came at last to present himself under two principal aspects, of gentleman and of Christian, which are, as George Herbert clearly saw when he wrote 'Church Monuments', in some tension with one another.

Vaughan anticipates the Romantics in expressing a lov-ing appreciation of the natural world. His sense of the sac-redness of nature may be related to his reading in the her-metic books. These speak of a god transcendent, hidden, utterly beyond all sense and thought; but also of a god nearer than was the Lord in the garden of Eden, a god moreover whose presence is uninterrupted. Of all para-doxes, this is the most favoured by the hermetic writers. To the author of the fifth *libellus*, as to Henry Vaughan, the Lord manifested himself 'ungrudgingly through all the universe'; he 'beheld God's image with his eyes, and laid hold on it with his hands' (*Hermetica*, ed. W. Scott, 4 vols., 1924–36, 1.159). Since he creates by emanation, there is no sharp distinction between God and his universe. No place is especially sacred, because every place is sacred; to use Vaughan's words, God is 'in all things, though invisibly' (*Complete Poems*, 242), and 'each bush / And oak doth know I AM' (ibid., 193). Such a viewpoint had its appeal for a mid-century Anglican who had lost his accustomed liturgy and his former places of worship. Vaughan's devotion to the God who manifested himself ungrudgingly through the universe surely marks a new phase of religious sensibility in seventeenth-century England.

As Vaughan's nineteenth-century editors and his twentieth-century biographer were clergymen, it is not surprising that they found him most interesting as a reli-gious poet. *Silex scintillans* is indeed as great a sequence of religious lyrics as we have. However, discussion of Vaughan, for some considerable time after the appear-ance of Hutchinson's *Life* in 1947, tacitly accepted his view that 'We can admire his loyalty to his ideals in Church and State, and yet regret that the calm and remote air of his divine poems and devotional pieces should so often be ruf-fled by these political and ecclesiastical outbursts' (Hutch-inson, 109). Since then, however, criticism has been increasingly focused on Vaughan's religio-political inten-tions (religion and politics were scarcely separable), which can be descried even in poems in which polemical intent is not obvious. The founding, in the year of the ter-centenary of his death, of a society devoted to the study and celebration of his work and that of his brother has resulted in an increase of critical attention. This is a wel-come development; the ratio of work, during the second half of the twentieth century, on Marvell and Herbert to that on Vaughan is unjustified. While much interesting criticism has sharpened our sense of Vaughan as a poet of political purpose, it does not follow that his understand-ing of political processes was superior. What then about his work makes it worthy of continued attention?

As one of the defeated, Vaughan wore his rue with a dif-ference, in two senses. His finest lyrics challenge the best in their age; his achievements in rhythm have no peer until Hopkins; and if others had a better understanding of political process, none of his contemporaries understood better than he the relatedness of all living things and their relationship to what we call the inanimate world. He understood the New Testament's most important passage on the theology of nature, Romans 8: 19–22, as modern theologians do. What the science of his time could not prove, the intuition of the poet could express. Jurgen Moltmann understood well when he prefaced his *God in Creation* with Vaughan's poem 'The Book', which asserts the unity of creation and the value of all creatures. Victorian criticism of the metaphysicals may often seem dated, but it was astute of H. C. Beeching, introducing E. K. Chambers's edition of Vaughan's poems in 1896, to sense the force of an observation first made of Wordsworth and say that Vaughan too 'makes us feel that Nature is not a mere collection of phenomena, but infuses into her least approach some sense of her mysterious whole'. At the beginning of the twenty-first century some students of 'environmental literature' consider it anachronistic to think of 'ecological consciousness' as anything but a post-Darwinian phenomenon. Closer study of Vaughan, as of Milton, his greatest contemporary on the other side of the political divide, might convince them otherwise.

ALAN RUDRUM

Sources F. E. Hutchinson, *Henry Vaughan: a life and interpretation* (1947) · *The works of Henry Vaughan*, ed. L. C. Martin, 2nd edn (1957) · *Henry Vaughan: the complete poems*, ed. A. Rudrum, rev. reprint (1983) · *The works of Thomas Vaughan*, ed. A. Rudrum (1984) · *Aubrey's Brief lives*, ed. O. L. Dick (1960) · Wood, *Ath. Oxon.*, 2nd edn · B. Allen, 'Henry Vaughan at Oxford', *Jesus College Record* (1997–8), 23–7 · B. Allen, 'The Vaughans at Jesus College, Oxford, 1638–48' [fuller version of 'Henry Vaughan at Oxford', forthcoming in *Scintilla*] · S. Davies, *Henry Vaughan* (1995) · E. Wolf, 'Some books of early English provenance in the Library Company of Philadelphia', *Book Collector*, 9/3 (1960), 275–84 · N. Fonteyn, *Commentarius in Sebastianum Austrium: de puerorum morbis* (Amsterdam, 1642) · J. Pecquet, *Experimenta nova anatomica* (Paris, 1651) · S. Paulli, *Quadripartitum botanicum* (Strasbourg, 1667–8) · A. Rudrum, 'Henry Vaughan, the liberation of the creatures, and seventeenth century English Calvinism', *Seventeenth Century*, 4/1 (1989), 33–54 · A. Rudrum, ed., *Essential articles for the study of Henry Vaughan* (1987) · R. Watkyns, *Flamma sine fumo, or, Poems without fictions. Hereunto are annexed the causes, symptoms, or signes of several diseases with their cures, and also the diversity of urines, with their causes in poetical measure* (1662) · *The poems of Henry Vaughan*, ed. E. K. Chambers (1896) [with an introduction by H. C. Beeching] · J. Moltmann, *God in creation: a new theology of creation and the spirit of God*, trans. M. Kohl (1991) · P. W. Thomas, 'The language of light: Henry Vaughan and the puritans', *Scintilla*, 3 (1999), 9–29

Archives Bodl. Oxf., MS autog. c. 9, fol. 81 · LPL · NL Wales | Bodl. Oxf., MS Aubrey 13, fols. 337, 338, 340 · Bodl. Oxf., MS Wood F 39, fols. 216, 227 · Bodl. Oxf., MS Wood F 45, fol. 68

Wealth at death £49 4s.: wills, 1695 21 Llansantffrayd, Llandaff RO, Brecknockshire

Vaughan, Henry (1809–1899), art collector, son of George Vaughan and his wife, Elizabeth Andrews, was born into a Quaker family on 17 April 1809 in Southwark, London, where his father carried on a successful business as a hat manufacturer. He was privately educated at Walthamstow, and on the death of his father in 1828 succeeded to a large fortune. He spent much time travelling and became

a cultivated, enthusiastic, and eclectic collector of works of art, especially of prints and drawings by J. W. M. Turner, with whom he was personally acquainted. He was a member of the Athenaeum, was elected FSA in 1879, and was one of the founders and most active members of the Burlington Fine Arts Club. Though undoubtedly one of the outstanding English collectors of his time, and a generous lender to exhibitions and museums, he appears to have been something of a recluse, whose reputation is largely based on his important gifts and bequests to British museums. He died, unmarried, on 26 November 1899, at 28 Cumberland Terrace, Regent's Park, London, where he had lived since 1834.

In 1886 Vaughan had presented (anonymously) John Constable's celebrated *Hay Wain* to the National Gallery, having purchased it at Christies twenty years earlier. In 1887 he gave five important Michelangelo drawings, all bought at the Woodburn sale in 1860, to the British Museum. By his will Vaughan distributed his wealth among various medical charities and hospitals, and the bulk of his art collections among museums. Thus the British Museum department of prints and drawings received a further 555 items, including fifty-seven old master drawings, over 300 drawings by John Flaxman, Thomas Lawrence, and Thomas Stothard, and, above all, nearly a hundred proofs of Turner's *Liber Studiorum* and twenty-three drawings connected with it. Some of the drawings were transferred from Vaughan's bequest to the National Gallery, which also received various sculptures and Italian and British paintings (the latter now in the Tate collection). To the Victoria and Albert Museum he assigned his collections of stained glass and carved panels, six Turner watercolours, and the full-scale studies for Constable's *Hay Wain* and *Leaping Horse*, which had been on loan to that museum since 1862. To University College, London, he bequeathed the remainder of his *Liber* prints, his collection of Constable mezzotints, his Rembrandt etchings and other prints, and a number of English drawings. The rest of Vaughan's outstanding and scholarly collection of Turner watercolours—he was described by Ruskin as 'a great Turner man' (Dawson, 39)—was divided between Edinburgh and Dublin. The National Gallery of Scotland received a representative selection of thirty-nine drawings, and a similar group of thirty-one drawings went to the National Gallery of Ireland.

LUKE HERRMANN

Sources *The Times* (27 Nov 1899) · *The Times* (3 Jan 1900) · *The Times* (8 May 1901) · *The Athenaeum* (2 Dec 1899), 767 · will and 3 codicils, probate granted, London, 1899 · d. cert. · *DNB* · *CGPLA Eng. & Wales* (1899) · B. Dawson, *Turner in the National Gallery of Ireland* (1988)

Wealth at death £230,002 2s. 11d.: probate, 27 Dec 1899, *CGPLA Eng. & Wales*

Vaughan, Henry Halford (1811–1885), historian, was born at 1 Montague Place, London, on 27 August 1811, the second son of Sir John *Vaughan (1769–1839), subsequently justice of common pleas, and his first wife, the Hon. Augusta St John (d. 1813), daughter of Henry Beauchamp, twelfth Baron St John of Bletso. In 1822 Vaughan went to Rugby School where Thomas Arnold, according to his son

Henry Halford Vaughan (1811–1885), by Julia Margaret Cameron

Matthew, considered him the ablest boy in the school. (His prize essay there was published in 1829.) He matriculated at Christ Church, Oxford, in 1829, and was awarded a Fell exhibition, often, but not in his case, the preliminary to a studentship. His contemporaries included W. E. Gladstone and H. G. Liddell. Vaughan took a first class in *literae humaniores* in 1833, and in 1835 was elected to a fellowship at Oriel, one of the most coveted distinctions in Oxford, having, it was reputed, read nothing beforehand except Bacon's *Advancement of Learning*. He was awarded the chancellor's prize in 1836 for an English essay (highly praised by Mark Pattison) on 'The effects of a national taste for general and diffusive reading'. Vaughan was called to the bar at Lincoln's Inn in 1838 but never practised as a barrister, and in 1839 became clerk of assize for the South Wales circuit, which gave him a permanent income of £500 a year plus fees. In 1839 he stood for election to the recently revived praelectorship of logic (subsequently the Wykeham professorship), but was defeated because of his unwillingness to reside in Oxford and the bitter opposition of the Newmanites who accused him of heresy for questioning scriptural authority as the sole basis of morality. In 1842 he was deprived of his fellowship for refusing to take holy orders; in the same year he acted as a special poor law commissioner, inquiring into the employment of women and children in agriculture. Undeterred by failure, he sought election to the White professorship of

moral philosophy in 1841 and 1846, and for a second time to the praelectorship of logic in 1848.

In 1848, Vaughan was appointed professor of modern history at Oxford. As the nominee of a prime minister committed to university reform, the first layman to hold the chair, and the victim of Tractarian hostility and obsolete statutes, he was enthusiastically welcomed by the radical reformers who included Liddell, A. P. Stanley, Mark Pattison, and Benjamin Jowett. In his two inaugural lectures delivered shortly before the creation of the school of jurisprudence and history, Vaughan enunciated a scientific and evolutionary view of history then novel in Oxford. History was defined as 'a disclosure of the critical changes in the condition of society', and although it did not repeat itself was subject to laws discovered by observation and by 'instincts of expectation', a concept later echoed in a famous phrase of Pasteur. Although Lord John Russell was dissuaded from appointing him to the royal commission on Oxford University in 1850, Vaughan had immense influence on the commission's recommendations for reviving the professoriate through his friendship with Liddell, who was a commissioner and was said to idolize Vaughan. In evidence often anticipating Mark Pattison, Vaughan proposed a body of professors who would 'investigate, reflect, and write', even if they were not very active as lecturers, pursuing learning for its own sake wherever it led. The university was to be governed by an intellectual oligarchy of mainly lay professors with a permanent majority in reformed institutions and in five faculties, including a separate faculty of theology. Lay fellowships were to be increased and college endowments redistributed. Vaughan's idea of a university not only strengthened the university at the expense of the colleges but advocated a secular university imposed by the state and divorced from the Church of England. He was bitterly attacked by Pusey, who accused him of Germanizing the university, and defended himself in *Oxford Reform and Oxford Professors* (1854). An acrimonious correspondence with Pusey was published in a *Postscript* in the same year. As opinion polarized, Vaughan became the champion of a radically reformed professoriate.

Gladstone, who piloted the Oxford Bill through parliament in 1854, judged that the professorial question would be best left to the university, but Vaughan believed the collegiate and Anglican character of Oxford made legislation essential to implement the commission's proposals. Petitions to a sympathetic Lord John Russell having failed, Vaughan, without the support of the radical reformers except for Liddell and apparently ready to see the bill fail, took the drastic step of lobbying the anti-clerical dissenting opposition in parliament by preparing briefs and drafting amendments. His allies deserted when concessions were offered on religious tests, but obstruction caused such serious delays that Gladstone was forced to make sweeping revisions to the bill, none of which favoured the professoriate, and complained of the opposition offered by 'the *London* portion of the Oxford Reformers' (Vaughan resided in Hampstead). As a reformer Vaughan was an original and powerful advocate, but his intransigence won few converts, and he undoubtedly contributed to the animus towards professors in general which lingered in Oxford for many years.

From 1849 to 1856, except in 1855, Vaughan went annually to Oxford to lecture on English and continental history to the reign of King John, but only the inaugural lectures were published. His audiences were spellbound by his eloquence and presence. Liddell wrote that:

> His features were large, well-defined, and mobile, especially his eyes [which] were fixed on you with an intensity of expression that seemed to pierce to your very soul. He had an immense 'fell' of rough hair [which] gave a sort of wild Olympian character to his head. (H. L. Thompson, *Henry George Liddell*, 1899, 124–5)

Of his lecture on the death of William I, George Butler recorded, 'the lecture was a powerful, poetical, and sometimes sublime oration … Vaughan is almost too brilliant, both in conversation and in lecturing. He dazzles one' (J. E. Butler, *Recollections of George Butler*, n.d., 88). So well attended were his lectures in 1852 that he transferred to the Sheldonian. Yet Vaughan's contribution to the establishment of historical studies at Oxford was negligible, and neither Goldwin Smith, Freeman, nor Stubbs mentioned him in their inaugural lectures. A principal cause of his lack of influence was a refusal to live in Oxford. He disliked Oxford society and preferred the intellectual Bohemian salon at Little Holland House, to which he was introduced by his wife's aunt Mrs Thoby Prinsep, and where he was affectionately known as Boodh (Buddha). For study he preferred the London Library, of which he was a foundation subscriber, to the Bodleian. Above all, his elevated conception of the professoriate was irreconcilable with the prevalent view in Oxford that, at least until more fellowships in new studies were provided by the reform of college statutes, the professor ought to be a superior tutor. To Vaughan this meant that learning was sacrificed to education and was replaced by the drudgery of 'hand-to-mouth' lecturing with almost continuous residence. The irony of a radical reformer perpetuating the longstanding abuse of non-resident professors was not lost on Vaughan's detractors. Owing to his non-residence, he was never an examiner, he was not consulted when special subjects were introduced in 1855, and he was ineligible for election to the hebdomadal council, the governing body of the university. When Oriel endowed the chair on condition that the incumbent resided, Vaughan resigned in March 1858, despite the pleas of Jowett and others who even petitioned Palmerston on his behalf.

In 1861, Vaughan served on the public schools commission where Lord Lyttelton praised his 'laborious industry, fertility of thought and subtlety of expression', while regretting that 'his practical wisdom is not commensurate' (BL, Add. MS 44239, fol. 235). Vaughan contributed an account of Rugby and a remarkable minority report on mental development and liberal education in which he advocated the teaching of natural science. As with university reform, many of his ideas later gained acceptance.

Vaughan retired to Upton Castle, Pembrokeshire, in 1867, intending to complete the philosophical treatise on the origin of moral ideas which had occupied him since the 1840s. He was initially influenced by Hume and later by the study of history and anthropology, but the complexity of the subject and its long gestation eventually overwhelmed him. Substantial fragments of the manuscript survive but inexplicable losses have destroyed its coherence. Vaughan believed that many of his ideas were appropriated by J. M. Wilson and T. Fowler in *Progressive Morality*, which was printed in 1875 but not published until after Vaughan's death. He published a three-volume work on Shakespeare's tragedies (1878–86).

On 21 August 1856, Vaughan married Adeline Maria Jackson (1837–1881), the eighteen-year-old daughter of John Jackson MD and Maria Pattle. It was, said Goldwin Smith, 'the most startling event of the kind since the marriage of Luther' (Oxford, Christ Church Archives, MS Estates 117, fol. 22v). The surviving children were William Wyamar *Vaughan (headmaster of Rugby), Augusta, Margaret, Millicent, and Emma. Vaughan died at Upton Castle on 19 April 1885. The *Oxford Review* recalled the impress which he 'stamped on the best men of his day' by his 'rare and commanding intellect', but Goldwin Smith described his life as 'one of genius, mournfully, almost tragically, thrown away' (G. Smith, *Reminiscences*, 1911, 274).

E. G. W. BILL

Sources E. G. W. Bill, *University reform in nineteenth-century Oxford: a study of Henry Halford Vaughan, 1811–1885* (1973) · Bodl. Oxf., MSS Vaughan · *Report of the Oxford University Commission* (1852) · BL, Gladstone MSS · *Report of the public schools commission* (1864) · *Oxford Magazine* (6 May 1885), 196–7 · *Oxford Review*, 1/12 (13 May 1885), 285–6 · CGPLA Eng. & Wales (1885)

Archives Bodl. Oxf., corresp. and papers | All Souls Oxf., letters to Sir C. R. Vaughan · BL, Gladstone MSS · LPL, letters to Lord Selborne

Likenesses J. M. Cameron, photograph, Bodl. Oxf. · J. M. Cameron, photograph, NPG [*see illus.*] · G. F. Watts, crayon drawing, priv. coll.

Wealth at death £17,505 8s. 4d.: administration, 17 June 1885, CGPLA Eng. & Wales

Vaughan, Herbert Alfred Henry Joseph Thomas (1832–1903),

cardinal-archbishop of Westminster, was born on 15 April 1832 in Gloucester, where his paternal grandfather William Michael Vaughan (1781–1861), lord of the manors of Welsh Bicknor and Ruardean, was residing with his family on account of the health of his first wife Teresa Marie, sister of Cardinal Thomas Weld of Lulworth. The ancestral seat of the Vaughans was Courtfield, situated on a secluded bend of the river near Ross-on-Wye in Herefordshire, a place which had helped to sustain the family's adherence to recusancy since the sixteenth century.

Early life and education, 1832–1849 Herbert Vaughan was the eldest of thirteen children of Colonel John Francis Vaughan (1808–1880) and his first wife, Elizabeth Louisa Rolls (1810–1853), a convert to Rome and the third daughter of John and Martha Rolls of Hendre, a large estate some 13 miles from Courtfield. Two of Vaughan's brothers were raised to the episcopate—Roger William *Vaughan (1834–1883), a monk of Downside, who became coadjutor of Sydney in 1873 and succeeded to the archbishopric in

Herbert Alfred Henry Joseph Thomas Vaughan (1832–1903), by London Stereoscopic Co.

1877, and John (1853–1925), who became auxiliary bishop in 1909 to Louis Charles Casartelli, fourth bishop of Salford. Three other brothers were priests—Kenelm (1840–1909), ordained by his uncle, the bishop of Plymouth, in 1865 when *in articulo mortis* from the consumption endemic in the family, but who was to recover to engage in apostolic work; Joseph (1841–1896), a Benedictine who established Fort Augustus Abbey in Scotland in 1876; and Bernard John *Vaughan (1847–1922), a much sought-after Jesuit preacher. Of Vaughan's five sisters, four became nuns—Gwladys (1838–1880) joined the Visitation order in Boulogne; Helen (1839–1861) entered the Sisters of Charity in London and died shortly afterwards; Clare (1843–1862) became a Poor Clare in Amiens and died after nine months there; and Mary (1845–1884) became prioress of the Augustinian convent in Newton Abbot. To have so many members of the immediate family in the priesthood or the religious life forged a singular cohesiveness among the brothers and sisters.

In 1841 Vaughan went to school at Stonyhurst, a mansion made over to the Jesuits in 1794 by his great-grandfather; his Jesuit uncle, Richard Vaughan (1826–1899), was involved in a redesign of the college buildings that reached fruition in the 1850s. Despite the family ties Vaughan was unhappy, missing the bucolic pursuits of Courtfield. Realizing he was not thriving, his father removed him after four years and, following a short sojourn during 1845–6 in the small school at Downside, sent him to the Jesuits at Brugelette in Belgium. There, for three years, he was engaged in a period of systematic study, finding the continental system of education congenial.

Priesthood and early career, 1849–1872 At sixteen Vaughan conceived a desire for the priesthood, intending to serve the Welsh mission. He entered the Collegio Romano taking lodgings near the piazza della Minerva, accommodation he was to share briefly with the Cambridge convert of 1851 Aubrey de Vere. This was an exciting period to be in Rome for young Englishmen seeking ordination to the priesthood. A Roman Catholic hierarchy had been restored to England on 29 September 1850 by Pius IX and political furore had arisen at home upon the issue of Cardinal Wiseman's first pastoral letter. Converts were also much in evidence in Rome since the submissions of John Henry Newman in 1845 and Henry Edward Manning in 1851. Vaughan was himself a striking addition to Roman society; de Vere records how he stood amazed at Vaughan's physical beauty when they first met, describing him as handsome, refined, and innocent as a child. It was in the autumn of 1852, when he moved to the Accademia dei Nobili Ecclesiastici, that Vaughan encountered the strong personality of Manning, whose mass he began to serve daily at 6 a.m. A warm and enduring friendship was established between them, enhanced by their shared enthusiasm for Rome and their growing devotion to the person of Pius IX.

Wiseman requested Manning's return to England in 1853 to establish a community of diocesan priests similar to that founded by Charles Borromeo in Milan in 1578. Such a body was intended to become a force in elevating the status of the English secular clergy, and be capable of responding quickly to diocesan needs. Manning was initially cautious, but Vaughan quickly saw the potential. Unfortunately, however, Vaughan's mother had died in childbirth in January 1853 and his sense of loss militated against him making any long-term plans. Visits to Courtfield enhanced his depression and he was eventually sent to stay with an uncle who had a residence in Florence. Concern about health led to Vaughan's ordination before the canonical age. He was twenty-two and, after ordination in Lucca on 28 October 1854, celebrated his first mass in the church of the Annunziata in Florence.

Aware of Vaughan's desire to work in the ministry of priestly formation, Wiseman offered him the vice-presidency of St Edmund's College near Ware. Extraordinary as the appointment seems, Wiseman did not possess experienced priests with the vision to realize that the clergy could no longer be trained simply as self-effacing dispensers of the sacraments—ignorant of European thought and unfamiliar with Rome. The president of St Edmund's was William Weathers, a convert and theologian of some ability, who was sufficiently robust to support William G. Ward as a lay professor to the divines and yet sufficiently insecure to resent the arrival of Vaughan at St Edmund's and, later, members of Manning's new community, the Oblates of St Charles. It is a measure of

Manning's charity that he subsequently recommended Weathers to assist with the preparatory work of the First Vatican Council and then had him appointed as auxiliary bishop of Westminster.

Opposition to Vaughan at St Edmund's centred upon the influence of George Errington, appointed Wiseman's coadjutor in the year of Vaughan's arrival. Unyieldingly reactionary, resentful of innovation, and hostile to convert clergy, Errington lacked Wiseman's internationalism and urbanity. Frederick Faber thought Errington spent his energies as a bishop in placing obstacles before those seen to be doing good. Inflaming fears and jealousies and stubborn to a degree, Wiseman's coadjutor was to lead the diocesan chapter in open revolt before Pius IX removed him from office in 1862.

Vaughan was a founding member of the Oblates of St Charles in 1857, the original group including, with Manning, three other priests, one of whom was Wiseman's nephew, and two clerical students at Rome, one being Charles J. Laprimaudaye, formerly vicar of Lavington. Vaughan was to remain loyal to his oblation after Manning, in the interests of peace, withdrew the Oblates from their teaching commitments at St Edmund's. Vaughan, indeed, continued to attend chapter meetings of the Oblate community even after his elevation to the episcopacy.

Manning encouraged Vaughan in the establishment of 'a house of studies' that would train students for foreign missionary work. Such an apostolate was considered to be within the scope of the Oblates' rule. Manning, furthermore, thought it would bring a special blessing as the first institution of its kind in England. On 25 September 1857 the chapter of the Oblates approved the new work as the special apostolate of Herbert Vaughan.

Armed with the support of all but one of the English bishops gathered at Oscott College in 1863, Vaughan embarked upon a fund-raising campaign in the Americas that would occupy him for the final two years of Wiseman's life. Visiting South America, he was horrified at what he saw of the quality and disposition of some of the clergy; in Peru, in particular, he was convinced that the church would benefit from the suppression of some friaries and monasteries. In Rio he witnessed the evils of slavery at first hand, and this convinced him of the importance of the work on which he had set his mind.

On his appointment to the see of Westminster in 1865 Manning recalled his fellow Oblate, suggesting the time was ripe to initiate the new work on English soil. For his part Manning organized the largest Catholic meeting since the Reformation in St James's Hall, Piccadilly, to launch the enterprise. Within eighteen months Vaughan had sufficient funds to establish St Joseph's College at Mill Hill. The money he collected on his travels (some £10,000 in cash, with promises of more to come) could henceforward be devoted to maintenance of the students and establishment of bursaries. Manning also put Vaughan in contact with Lady Elizabeth Herbert of Lea, widow of Sir Sidney Herbert, who, for the remainder of her life, was to

devote time and resources to the enterprise and find spiritual consolation in the foundation of the work. The need to have a literary organ that would enable Vaughan to carry forward the missionary apostolate and reach a wide audience impelled him to buy *The Tablet* in 1865, a development that was to be enhanced in 1878 by his acquisition of the *Dublin Review*, a gift of W. G. Ward.

Twelve months before Vaughan was raised to the episcopate, the main college buildings at Mill Hill were free of debt; there were thirty-six students in training and the first missionary assignment, working with emancipated black slaves in the southern states of America, had been undertaken. Vaughan was to remain superior-general of the missionaries throughout his life.

Bishop of Salford, 1872–1892 It was with a certain incredulity that the clergy of the Salford diocese learned in 1872 that Herbert Vaughan was to be their new bishop. His predecessor, William Turner (1799–1872), had been a sturdy Lancastrian with a wealth of pastoral experience. He had built many churches and opened schools, and he had devoted himself to providing for the spiritual welfare of immigrant Irish Catholics in the years following the great famine of 1845. Vaughan, on the other hand, had been engaged in specialist ministries, was of gentry stock, and knew little of the industrial belt of Lancashire and the needs of its people.

Consecrated by Manning in Salford Cathedral on 28 October 1872, somewhat ironically together with William Weathers who at the same time was made titular bishop of Amycla, Vaughan entered upon his new duties with characteristic dedication. The diocese was missionary terrain and he viewed its Catholic population of some 196,000 souls as ready for spiritual evangelization. His twenty-year ministry was concentrated upon the priesthood, children, and the poor. Dutch, Belgian, German, and Irish priests were brought into the diocese to enhance the number of native clergy, and he established for some years a pastoral centre in the bishop's house that helped to cement new relationships. Recently ordained priests spent a year of acclimatization in the centre before being deployed to a mission. Schools and orphanages were opened and Vaughan established both the Catholic Protection and Rescue Society and a new congregation of nuns, the Franciscan Missionary Sisters of St Joseph, to assist with the apostolate for destitute and orphaned children. More than forty new missions were opened and he organized the publication and dissemination of Catholic Truth Society tracts and pamphlets.

Vaughan's time in Lancashire, however, was blighted by a bitter dispute with the Jesuits, which had national implications. In 1873 the Jesuit provincial in England intimated that the Society of Jesus was planning to open a school in Manchester for the secondary education of children of the commercial and business classes. Vaughan refused to countenance the proposal because it would threaten a new diocesan venture to which he was committed and which was aimed at meeting the same need. The provincial protested, but Vaughan remained resolute. The provincial then declared that because of ecclesiastical exemptions granted to the society in 1540 and renewed in 1814, the Jesuits did not need episcopal approval in order to go ahead with the plan. The position was serious, and in 1875, while Vaughan was on Mill Hill business in the United States, the society went ahead with its declared intention and opened the school. Vaughan appealed to Rome, determined to resign his see if not supported. To avoid further deterioration in relationships, and with the advice of Rome, Vaughan held discussions with the Jesuit general, who eventually instructed the English provincial to close the school. The dispute had been acrimonious, but Vaughan went ahead with the establishment of his own school, St Bede's College, and in 1888 set up St Bede's-on-the-Rhine, in Metternich's old palace at Bonn, to provide courses in German for his Lancashire boys. The English bishops decided to have the whole matter of their rights *vis-à-vis* the Jesuits and other religious orders and congregations clarified at Rome. Vaughan, along with the bishop of Clifton, William Clifford, acted as agent of the hierarchy for the purpose and the issue of the bull *Romanos pontifices* in 1881, which was a considerable vindication of Vaughan's earlier stance. Religious orders subsequently had to secure permission from the local ordinary and the Holy See before establishing a residence, church, or school.

In 1883 Vaughan founded in his diocese the Voluntary Schools Association to assist Manning in his national campaign to reopen the 1870 elementary education settlement. Manning was seeking a royal commission into denominational grievances about the funding of church schools. Vaughan fully supported Manning in his attempt to use the general election of 1885 to force the church schools issue to the top of the political agenda. The campaign had an influence on the establishment of the Cross commission by Lord Salisbury in 1886 to inquire into the working of the 1870 Education Act, and Manning was appointed a member.

Archbishop of Westminster, 1892–1902 Vaughan was in his sixtieth year when Manning died from bronchitis on 14 January 1892. He knew that he was the first choice on the diocesan *terna* for Westminster and the choice of his fellow bishops. Manning had hoped Vaughan would succeed him. Vaughan, however, did not relish the possibility of a move to London or the leadership role that would be thrust upon him. He wrote to the pope to try to prevent what seemed inevitable, but Rome had reacted to the death of Manning with uncharacteristic rapidity. Only ten weeks elapsed, all due processes having been observed, before Leo XIII appointed Vaughan to the archbishopric. Enthronement took place on 8 May 1892 in the pro-cathedral at Kensington at a subdued ceremony with only one other bishop present. The diocese was still in mourning. Vaughan declared he owed to Manning 'obligations, intellectual, moral and personal—obligations of a friendship, of a more deep and enduring kind than I can find words to portray' (McCormack, 229).

Although he attempted to model himself upon his predecessor, Vaughan found difficulty in cultivating Manning's ease of manner with all classes of people. He disliked

having to deal with senior government ministers and civil servants, and admitted to J. G. Snead-Cox, his friend and subsequent biographer, that he found visiting the poor in their homes a trial. Nevertheless, Vaughan had a deep spiritual life, a love of the diocesan clergy, and considerable experience of dealing with social problems.

Vaughan received the pallium, symbol of unity with Rome, at a ceremony attended by all the Roman Catholic bishops in Brompton Oratory on 16 August 1892, the first time the pallium had been conferred on English soil since Reginald Pole received it in Bow church on 25 March 1556. Both Wiseman and Manning had received it in Rome. Less than a year after the impressive ceremony, Vaughan was awarded a cardinal's red hat on 16 January 1893, his titular church in Rome being Santi Andrea e Gregorio on the Coelian Hill.

Turning his attention immediately to seminary training, the new archbishop considered diocesan seminaries to be wasteful of human and material resources, and advocated the need for a strong central seminary that would serve several dioceses. Manning had wished to have seminary training in line with the prescriptions of the Council of Trent, and to that end he had disaggregated the divines from the lay boys at St Edmund's and established a seminary for the former in Hammersmith. Under Vaughan this was closed, and Oscott College was used to cater for the needs of six dioceses (including Westminster) and the vicariate of Wales. The arrangement operated during Vaughan's lifetime, but his successor withdrew the Westminster students and returned them to St Edmund's.

Vaughan continued the policy of agitation for reform of the school board system and lived to see it abolished by the Education Act of 1902, which enabled the day-to-day operational costs of Catholic elementary schools to be met from public moneys. Vaughan did not live to see the liberal onslaughts of 1906–8, which attempted—albeit unsuccessfully—to unpack the settlement.

Faced with demands from leading members of the aristocracy that Catholics should be permitted to attend Oxford and Cambridge and that the episcopal policy operational since 1865 be reviewed, Vaughan tried to rally the bishops in a new attempt to set up a Catholic university or university college. Meeting with little response, he realized that demands for attendance at Oxbridge were being fed by the expansion of provincial university colleges in the second half of the nineteenth century—institutions at which attendance for Catholics had not been prohibited by Rome. Vaughan was outraged by dispensations some bishops had given freely to favoured sons of the aristocracy wishing to go to Oxford. By September 1894 he thought it better that Rome should be petitioned by the bishops themselves for the removal of the ban, rather than be dragged along by the force of the lay agitation. The voting of the hierarchy on the issue in September 1894 was close. Seven bishops supported Vaughan's idea, six opposed, and there was one absentee. In 1896 the ban was lifted by Rome on the condition that spiritual safeguards be put in place. It was re-emphasized, however, that there should be a Catholic university in England.

In relations with the Church of England, Vaughan lacked Manning's insight and experience. This was particularly noticeable when Viscount Halifax and the Abbé Fernand Portal (a teacher in the local seminary in Cahors in France) selected the matter of the validity of Anglican orders as a first step in developing a case for eventual reunion of the two churches. If the problem of orders could be resolved, other doctrinal issues, it was thought, might be tackled. Vaughan wanted such ecumenical discussions to take place, if at all, in a context in which the English hierarchy was not ignored. As things stood, there was a danger that the bishops would be kept in the dark and Rome, too, misled. In 1895, therefore, he urged the establishment by Rome of a committee made up of a number of international scholars to examine the validity of Anglican orders. The outcome of its deliberations was the issuing of 'Apostolicae curae' in 1896, which indicated that Anglican orders were invalid because of a lack of proper continuity and defect in intention.

Manning had purchased the site for his successor to begin building a cathedral for Westminster. Vaughan saw the construction of such an edifice as symbolic of the coming of age of the restored hierarchy. In 1894 he appointed John Francis Bentley as architect, and selected the Byzantine style because it was cost-effective and the outer shell could be rapidly completed, leaving the internal furnishing to be undertaken later. (Construction of the cathedral began in 1895 and building had progressed sufficiently by 1903 for Vaughan's requiem to be held there.) After much wrangling with English and French Benedictines and in face of the determination of the Westminster chapter, Vaughan established a house of secular clergy or chaplains with the responsibility for liturgy and for recitation of the Divine Office in the cathedral. It was a decision that was to endure.

Death and reputation The stresses of ten years of work in London took their toll on Vaughan's health. Never robust, he began to suffer increasingly from dropsy, and in the summer of 1902 had to go to Bad Nauheim for treatment. On his return, he convalesced with Lord and Lady Edmund Talbot at Derwent House before returning to London in December. After three months of continuing decline he realized he was not going to recover, and went to stay at Mill Hill where he remained until his death on 19 June 1903. He made a formal public profession of faith the day before his death in the presence of the vicar-general, three canons of the chapter, and a small community of priests, students, and relatives. He was seventy-one years of age and, following a public requiem in his new cathedral and a second one at Mill Hill, he was buried on 26 June in the garden of St Joseph's College in fulfilment of his expressed wish.

Vaughan's upbringing, education, social relationships, and rapid rise to positions of authority and leadership within the ecclesiastical establishment have led to his pastoral style being considered remote, cold, and mechanical. His aristocratic features and bearing, however,

formed but a façade beneath which there was a man of deep, if somewhat austere, spirituality, utterly dedicated to the social and missionary enterprise of the church, and an opponent of religious liberalism and indifferentism. Manning (who advised Vaughan to laugh more), Lady Herbert of Lea, the men and boys of his missionary institute, and the students at St Edmund's College were convinced of his innate compassion for people. He can be seen as one of the last of the great Victorian prelates, but also as one who encapsulated within himself the main virtues of the dying recusant tradition within Catholicism.

V. A. MCCLELLAND

Sources J. G. Snead-Cox, *The life of Cardinal Vaughan*, 2 vols. (1910) · A. McCormack, *Cardinal Vaughan* (1966) · R. O'Neil, *Cardinal Herbert Vaughan* (1995) · M. Vaughan, *Courtfield and the Vaughans* (1989) · *Letters of Herbert Cardinal Vaughan to Lady Herbert of Lea, 1867–1903*, ed. S. Leslie (1942) · V. A. McClelland, *Cardinal Manning: his public life and influence, 1865–1892* (1962) · V. A. McClelland, *English Roman Catholics and higher education, 1830–1903* (1973) · E. R. Norman, *The English Catholic church in the nineteenth century* (1984) · S. M. P. Reilly, *Aubrey de Vere: Victorian observer* (1956) · J. Berkeley, *Lulworth and the Welds* (1971) · C. A. Bolton, *Salford diocese and its Catholic past: a survey* (1950) · M. Walsh, *'The Tablet', 1840–1990: a commemorative history* (1990) · R. Kollar, *Westminster Cathedral: from dream to reality* (1987)
Archives St Joseph's College, Mill Hill, London, archives · Wardley Hall, Worsley, Manchester, Salford Roman Catholic diocesan archives · Westm. DA, corresp. and papers | Borth. Inst., corresp. with second Viscount Halifax · LPL, corresp. with Archbishop Benson · LPL, letters to Athelstan Riley · LPL, corresp. with Temple · U. St Andr., letters to Wilfrid Ward · Westm. DA, letters to E. H. Thompson · Wilts. & Swindon RO, corresp. with Sidney Herbert and Elizabeth Herbert
Likenesses London Stereoscopic Co., photograph, NPG [*see illus.*] · Spy [L. Ward], chromolithograph caricature, repro. in *VF*, 39 (7 Jan 1893), 6 · recumbent figure, Westminster Cathedral, London
Wealth at death £743 5*s*. 8*d*.: probate, 11 Aug 1903, *CGPLA Eng. & Wales*

Vaughan [*married name* Morgan]**, Hilda Campbell** (1892–1985), novelist, was born in a house known as The Castle in Builth Wells, Brecknockshire, on 12 June 1892, the youngest daughter of Hugh Vaughan Vaughan (1852–1936) and his wife, Eva, *née* Campbell, of Dunoon, Argyll. Her father's surname had been assumed by royal licence in lieu of Thomas in 1885; the family traced its descent from the Vaughans of whom the poet Henry Vaughan, the Silurist, was the most illustrious member. Hilda Vaughan's father, a successful country solicitor, held various public appointments and offices in Radnorshire, becoming clerk of the peace and under sheriff and clerk of the county council and its education committee. It is with Radnorshire, where most of her novels are set, that Hilda Vaughan is generally associated.

Educated privately, though sketchily, by a succession of governesses, she remained at home until the outbreak of the First World War in 1914, during which she first came into contact with the harsher realities of life while serving in a Red Cross hospital and then, for three years, as organizing secretary of the Women's Land Army in Brecknockshire and Radnorshire. At the war's end she left home for London and, while taking a writing course at Bedford College, met the novelist Charles Langbridge *Morgan (1894–

1958), who had just been appointed junior drama critic on the staff of *The Times*. They married on 6 June 1923, and took a flat in More's Garden, Chelsea, where they were to remain for nine years until their removal to a house in Campden Hill Square. Their shared ambition to become writers drew them together, as her husband's letters reveal, but her subsequent career was somewhat overshadowed by his reputation—especially after publication of *The Fountain* in 1932—as one of the foremost English novelists of his day. There were two children of the marriage: Roger Morgan, the former librarian of the House of Lords and previously of the House of Commons, and Shirley Morgan, who married the marquess of Anglesey.

Hilda Vaughan's first novel, *The Battle to the Weak* (1925), set near Builth Wells, is a didactic work which exploits her knowledge of the topography, speech, and atmosphere of Radnorshire, but also reflects her own struggle to achieve recognition in her own right. Her third novel, *The Invader* (1928), is a comedy and perhaps the most authentically Welsh of all her works, and in *Her Father's House* (1930) she again makes use of her native place. Her most successful novel, *The Soldier and the Gentlewoman* (1932), set in Carmarthenshire and published by Victor Gollancz, was a new departure into ironic tragedy; it was dramatized by Laurier Lister and Dorothy Massingham, and produced at the Vaudeville Theatre, London, in 1933. Her subsequent novels, *The Curtain Rises* (1935), *Harvest Home* (1936), *Pardon and Peace* (1945), *Iron and Gold* (1948), and *The Candle and the Light* (1954), are romantic in theme but realistic and unsentimental in their acute observation of human character, particularly in adversity; compassion is at their heart. The fourth of these was first published in the United States, to which Charles Morgan had sent his wife and children during the Second World War, under the title *The Fair Woman* (1942). She also wrote two plays in collaboration with Laurier Lister: *She Too was Young* (1938), performed at Wyndhams Theatre, London, concurrently with her husband's *The Flashing Stream*, and *Forsaking All Other*, which was never staged. Her most exquisite writing is found in the novella *A Thing of Nought* (1934; revised edition 1948), a tale of star-crossed love told with great economy and again set in the hills of Radnorshire.

In 1957 the Morgans visited the West Indies for the benefit of Charles's health, but the relief was only temporary and he died the following year, after which, her own health affected, Hilda Vaughan published no more novels. A statement about her religious faith, which bordered on the quasi-mystical, is to be found in her introduction to an edition of Thomas Traherne's *Centuries of Meditations*, published in 1960. Apart from the autobiographical essays 'A country childhood' and 'Far away: not long ago', which first appeared in *Lovat Dickson's Magazine* in 1934 and 1935, this was the only occasion on which she wrote about herself. She was elected a fellow of the Royal Society of Literature in 1963.

Hilda Vaughan died on 4 November 1985 at Hazlewell Nursing Home, 29/31 Hazlewell Road, Putney, and was buried at Diserth, Radnorshire.   MEIC STEPHENS

Sources C. W. Newman, *Hilda Vaughan* (1981) · G. F. Adam, *Three contemporary Anglo-Welsh novelists: Jack Jones, Rhys Davies and Hilda Vaughan* (1948) · H. Vaughan, 'A country childhood', *Lovat Dickson's Magazine*, 3/4 (Oct 1934), 417–33 · H. Vaughan, 'Far away: not long ago', *Lovat Dickson's Magazine*, 4/1 (Jan 1935), 71–84 · personal knowledge (2004) · private information (2004) [daughter] · *Selected letters of Charles Morgan*, ed. E. Lewis (1967) · d. cert. · b. cert. · m. cert. · H. Vaughan, *Iron and gold*, ed. J. Aaron (2002)

Archives NL Wales, letters to R. E. Roberts and Harriet Roberts

Likenesses C. Fremantle, portrait, priv. coll.; repro. in Newman, *Hilda Vaughan*

Vaughan [*married name* Gourlay], **Dame Janet Maria** (1899–1993), haematologist and radiobiologist, was born on 18 October 1899 at 4 Albert Road, Clifton, Bristol, the eldest of the four children of William Wyamar *Vaughan (1865–1938), schoolmaster, and his first wife, Margaret, *née* Symonds (1869–1925), third daughter of John Addington *Symonds (1840–1893), writer and historian. She had two younger brothers, and a younger sister who died in childhood. At the time of her birth her father was an assistant master at Clifton College; he was later headmaster of Giggleswick School (1904–10), master of Wellington College (1910–21), and headmaster of Rugby School (1921–31).

Janet Vaughan was educated at home until she was fifteen, and then at North Foreland Lodge, a school for young ladies. At school she developed an interest in history, politics, current affairs, and questions of poverty and social justice, but not in the foreign languages that she was supposed to learn, causing the headmistress to tell Janet's father that she was 'clearly too stupid to be worth educating' (Vaughan, 'Jottings'). She determined, nevertheless, to become a doctor, in the hope that this would give her a background that would enable her to influence society, and she applied for entry to Somerville College, Oxford. After twice failing she passed the compulsory Oxford entrance examination in Latin, Greek, and arithmetic, and entered Somerville in Michaelmas term 1919 to read medicine, with the full support of her parents. Tutored by J. B. S. Haldane, she was introduced into the Huxley and Haldane families in Oxford and, despite having no previous knowledge of science other than 'a little lady-like botany' (ibid.), she obtained first-class honours in physiology in 1922.

Vaughan completed her clinical studies at University College Hospital (UCH) in 1925 but when, in the same year, her mother died she abandoned her intention to become a physician and trained at UCH as a clinical pathologist, so as to have time to run her father's home at the weekends. Learning of Professor George Minot's work in the USA on the effect of liver in pernicious anaemia, she surreptitiously arranged for liver to be given to a patient, who then made a remarkable recovery, which the treating physician attributed to his prescription of arsenic. Encouraged by Sir Charles Harington, she prepared extracts from minced liver at home and, after trying them herself (because dogs vomited them up), she obtained permission to test them on further patients. The results were uniformly good and provided her with the material for her DM, obtained in 1931.

In 1929 Vaughan's father remarried and she felt able to

Dame Janet Maria Vaughan (1899–1993), by Elliott & Fry, 1945

travel abroad; a Rockefeller fellowship enabled her to work with Minot for a year in Boston. On her return Beit Memorial and Leverhulme fellowships enabled her to conduct research at the London Hospital medical school on the relationship of disorders of haematopoiesis to changes in bone. On 13 September 1930 she married David Gourlay (1889/90–1963), then a civil servant in the Post Office and, later, founder of the Wayfarer's Travel Agency; he was the son of David Gourlay, building contractor, and had been a co-resident in the multiply occupied house in which Vaughan had lived when working at UCH. They had two daughters, Mary (b. 1933) and Priscilla (b. 1935). In 1934 Vaughan was appointed assistant in clinical pathology at the new British Postgraduate Medical School, which put her in charge of the routine haematological and blood transfusion services at the Hammersmith Hospital. In the same year she published her book *The Anaemias*, which rapidly became the standard text on the subject.

Vaughan's socialist sympathies had been strengthened by the appalling conditions of life that she saw in the London slums during her clinical training and by her subsequent experience of the frequency of nutritional anaemia, and they led her to take an active part in the Committee for Spanish Medical Aid in support of the government forces in the Spanish Civil War. She learned in consequence that stored blood had been successfully used in treating casualties. Blood transfusion was still a primitive process in the UK, requiring fresh blood to be obtained for each patient, and she made preparations for storing blood on a small scale at Hammersmith Hospital.

Convinced of the imminence of war after the Munich agreement, she drew up plans, with a few like-minded colleagues, for a national transfusion service. These were accepted by the government; the Medical Research Council (MRC) was made responsible for running the service and Vaughan was put in charge of the north-west London depot for the duration of the war. As the end of the war approached the MRC sent her to Brussels to help to resuscitate liberated but famished British prisoners, and then to Belsen to assess the value of concentrated protein preparations for former prisoners on the verge of dying from starvation—an experience that she described as 'trying to do science in hell' (Vaughan, 'Jottings').

Vaughan meanwhile had been elected principal of Somerville, which had emerged from the war with increased undergraduate numbers, a reduced teaching strength, run-down buildings, and precarious finances. She brought to the task energy and persistence, and a sense of optimism that was of crucial importance in overcoming the difficulties of the period. She left the college, twenty-two years later, greatly enlarged in numbers and buildings, with sound finances and a commitment to science as well as to the humanities. She was remembered by students as someone who valued them as individuals and was deeply concerned about their personal welfare. Her comment in 1992 on Somerville's decision to admit men is characteristic: 'I think the time had come for it. I am not sorry at all. I think it's very exciting actually' (*The Times*, 4 Feb 1992, 4).

Despite her college commitments Vaughan found time for active scientific research and external social responsibility. The explosion of nuclear weapons had focused attention on the effects of irradiation from ingested radionuclides, and she headed a small multi-disciplinary group, funded by the MRC, to investigate the biological effects of bone-seeking radioisotopes. The work revealed important differences between the effects of the different radioactive elements, and Vaughan was soon recognized as a world authority on the effects of plutonium. After retirement in 1967 she published *The Physiology of Bone* (1970), which went to three editions, and *The Effects of Radiation on the Skeleton* (1973).

Vaughan served on many local and national committees—as founding trustee of the Nuffield Foundation (1943–67); as a member of the royal commission on equal pay (1944–6), of the Phillips Committee on the Economic and Financial Problems of the Provision for Old Age (1953–4), and of two task groups of the International Committee for Radiological Protection (1967 and 1969); and as chairman of the Oxford Regional Hospital Board (1950–51). She was appointed OBE in 1944 and DBE in 1957, elected FRCP in 1939, and FRS in 1979, and awarded honorary degrees by seven universities. She died on 9 January 1993 at the Churchill Hospital, Oxford, of bronchopneumonia. She was survived by her two daughters. RICHARD DOLL

Sources M. Owen, *Memoirs FRS*, 41 (1995), 483–98 • *The Times* (11 Jan 1993) • Munk, *Roll* • P. Adams, *Somerville for women: an Oxford college, 1879–1993* (1996) • *Janet Maria Vaughan: a memorial tribute* (1993) [Somerville College] • J. M. Vaughan, 'Jottings', Somerville College,

Oxford [autobiography; differently paginated versions] · L. Caldicott, 'Janet Vaughan', *Women of our century* (1984) · V. Brittain, *Testament of youth* (1933) · *WWW*, 1991–5 · personal knowledge (2004) · private information (2004) · b. cert. · m. cert. · d. cert. · *CGPLA Eng. & Wales* (1993)
Archives Somerville College, Oxford, 'Jottings' (autobiographical notes) · Wellcome L., personal papers | Harvard U., Francis A. Countway Library of Medicine, Minot corresp.
Likenesses three photographs, 1919–79, repro. in Owen, *Memoirs FRS*, 482 · Elliott & Fry, photograph, 1945, NPG [*see illus.*] · D. Gordine, bust, Somerville College, Oxford · C. R. Lange, portrait, Somerville College, Oxford
Wealth at death under £125,000: probate, 23 Feb 1993, *CGPLA Eng. & Wales*

Vaughan, John, first earl of Carbery (1574/5–1634), courtier and politician, was the eldest son of Walter Vaughan (d. 1598) of Golden Grove, Llanfihangel Aberbythych, Carmarthenshire, and Mary (d. before 1588), daughter of Sir Walter Rice of Newton, Carmarthenshire. Sir William *Vaughan (c.1575–1641) and Sir Henry *Vaughan (1587?–1660/61) were his brothers. He matriculated, aged seventeen, from Jesus College, Oxford, on 4 February 1592, and entered the Inner Temple in 1596. His early career was influenced by his ties with Robert Devereux, second earl of Essex, whom his father also followed. The earl described Vaughan as his 'servant' in 1598; on 13 February that year Vaughan married Margaret, daughter of Sir Gelly Meyrick, Essex's steward and man of business in Wales (PRO, C115/100/7409). This marriage ended by 1614 after producing two sons, the elder of whom was Richard *Vaughan, second earl, and he then married Jane Meredith (*née* Palmer). Vaughan followed Essex on his expedition to Ireland in 1599, when the earl knighted him. These ties caused suspicion to fall on Vaughan after the Essex revolt of 1601, and he felt the need to demonstrate his innocence to Sir Robert Cecil after reports circulated of his complicity in the plot. Vaughan was also removed from the commission of the peace in Carmarthenshire for a time while his political loyalties were in question. It was possibly with a view to defending his reputation that he represented Carmarthenshire in the parliament of 1601.

Vaughan's campaign to clear his name was successful, and was probably aided by the accession of a new monarch in 1603. For a period he busied himself with local office and consolidated his position in Carmarthenshire, until he initiated a campaign to secure a post in the prospective household of Prince Charles. In 1614 he approached the king's favourite, the earl of Somerset, asking him to intercede with James I on his behalf, and also wrote to Sir Henry Neville requesting to be 'sworn in the place I have desired' (PRO, SP 14/78/64). His efforts were rewarded with the profitable position of comptroller when Prince Charles's household was created in 1616. Vaughan now acquired a house in Fulham, where he sheltered Sir Francis Bacon after his impeachment in the 1621 parliament. Vaughan also sat in this assembly, again representing Carmarthenshire. It was during the parliamentary recess that King James elevated him to an Irish barony, as baron of Mullingar, and this caused Vaughan some difficulties when parliament reconvened in November, as

some members questioned whether his title disqualified him from sitting in the Commons. This probably helps explain why he never again sought election to parliament.

Vaughan's position in the prince's household meant he was one of the servants who followed Charles into Spain in 1623 when he left to expedite his marriage to the infanta. The trip caused him some difficulties, however, with reports entering England that he had become a Catholic, while he later recalled that the expedition had cost him between £3000 and £4000.

Charles's accession in 1625, rather than furthering Vaughan's career at court, actually occasioned its cessation. He was removed as comptroller, and although he was reported to be in line for some monetary reimbursement, no further court appointment was forthcoming. In 1628 he approached Sir John Coke requesting compensation for his losses on the Spanish trip, and estimated that his time in service had cost him £20,000. Nevertheless, this did not stop him addressing the duke of Buckingham with a request that he 'work my re-establishing into my precedent place', but his entreaties were to no avail (PRO, SP 16/86/16). His elevation to an Irish earldom in 1628, when he was created earl of Carbery, may have been some form of compensation, but, like many others, he may simply have paid for the honour. He lived out the rest of his life at Golden Grove where he made a nuncupative will on 29 April 1634, bequeathing his estates to his only surviving son and heir, Richard, the future royalist lieutenant-general. Vaughan died at Golden Grove on 6 May 1634 and was buried in the family vault in the parish church of Llandeilo Fawr, Carmarthenshire.   LLOYD BOWEN

Sources F. Jones, 'The Vaughans of Golden Grove', *Transactions of the Honourable Society of Cymmrodorion* (1963), 96–145 · *Calendar of the manuscripts of the most hon. the marquis of Salisbury*, 24 vols., HMC, 9 (1883–1976), esp. vol. 11 · *CSP dom.*, 1603–28 · T. I. Jeffreys Jones, ed., *Exchequer proceedings concerning Wales, in tempore James I* (1955) · GEC, *Peerage* · L. Dunn, *Visitations of Wales and part of the marches; between … 1586 and 1613*, ed. S. R. Heyrick (1846), vol. 1, pp. 213–14 · HoP, *Commons, 1558–1603* · I. ab Owen Edwards, *A catalogue of star chamber proceedings relating to Wales* (1929) · *JHC*, 1 (1547–1628) · *The works of Francis Bacon*, ed. J. Spedding, R. L. Ellis, and D. D. Heath, 14 vols. (1857–74), vol. 14 · *The letters of John Chamberlain*, ed. N. E. McClure, 2 (1939) · *The manuscripts of the Earl Cowper*, 3 vols., HMC, 23 (1888–9), vol. 1, p. 369 · Foster, *Alum. Oxon.* · PRO, C 115/100/7409 · PRO, SP 14/78/64 · PRO, SP 16/86/16
Archives Carmarthenshire RO, Cawdor MSS
Wealth at death £428 p.a. as comptroller; presumably considerable wealth from extensive Carmarthenshire estates

Vaughan, Sir John (1603–1674), judge, was born on 14 September 1603 at Trawscoed, Cardiganshire, the eldest of the eight children of Edward Vaughan (d. 1635), esquire, and Lettice, daughter of John Stedman, Strata Florida, Cardiganshire. In 1625 he married Jane Stedman (d. 1680) of Cilcennin, Cardiganshire. Vaughan was educated at the King's School, Worcester (1613–18), and at Christ Church, Oxford (1618–21), though he did not graduate. He was admitted to the Inner Temple in November 1621, was called to the bar in 1630, and became a bencher in 1660. It was in the Star Chamber that he first made his name. In 1628 he entered the Commons as member for Cardigan borough and would represent it again in the Short and Long parliaments. Like Edward Hyde, he opposed the extraordinary measures adopted during the period of Charles I's personal rule. He helped to prepare charges against Laud and to fashion the Triennial Act, but although he participated in the early proceedings against Strafford he drew the line at attainder, as being unconstitutional. Hyde, the future earl of Clarendon, with whom he was then friendly, later said that Vaughan was 'without inclination to any change of government' (*Life of … Clarendon*, 1.31). In short he was a constitutional royalist, and so remained.

Vaughan returned home before the outbreak of the civil war. Marriage settlements and the purchase of eight Cardiganshire granges, formerly belonging to the dissolved monastery of Strata Florida, led to a perceptible increase in the annual rental of the Trawscoed estate, estimated to be about £1200 before his death. In an economically poor county he was thus regarded as one of the leading gentry. At first he loyally supported the royalists. The fall of Tenby in March 1643 disturbed him and he was soon placing some order upon the undisciplined Cardiganshire trained bands. Reprisals followed. In January 1645 his house was totally plundered and in September he was disabled from sitting in parliament. The assertion that he helped parliamentary forces to capture Aberystwyth Castle cannot be corroborated and only his own testimony records that he compounded for his estate. When the Cromwellian government encouraged moderate men to return to public life Vaughan refused even to exercise his profession. Vaughan seldom emerged during these turbulent years into the clear light of day, leading Clarendon to the reasonable conclusion that he lived 'as near an innocent life as the iniquity of that time would permit' (*Life of … Clarendon*, 1.31).

Vaughan represented Cardiganshire in the Cavalier Parliament from 1661 to 1668. His silver-tongued eloquence was widely admired. In praising Sir Thomas Littleton, Pepys declared that he was 'the usual second to the great Vaughan' (Pepys, *Diary*, 7.210). He opposed the repeal of the Triennial Act, expressly desired by the king. In the 1668 dispute concerning Thomas Skinner he may justly be regarded as the architect of the victory of the Commons over the Lords, who henceforth abandoned all attempts to exercise original jurisdiction in civil cases when the parties were commoners. As a debater he is best remembered for his sustained attack on Clarendon who, he was now convinced, was a menace to constitutional government.

Vaughan was knighted on 20 May 1668 and sworn chief justice of the court of common pleas on 23 May. His presidency preceded the period when party faction influenced judicial appointments. He defended the court of common pleas against the jurisdiction of the courts of king's bench, chancery, and Admiralty. His authoritative opinion helped to preserve the Welsh court of great sessions from the encroachment of the Westminster courts until its extinction in 1831. In *Thomas v. Sorrell* (1674) he showed that an act of parliament could not be suspended except by legislative power. His fame chiefly rests upon *Bushell's*

case (1670). Edward Bushell was a member of the jury fined for persistently acquitting the Quakers William Penn and William Mead for holding an unlawful assembly. Bushell, imprisoned for refusal to pay, sued out a writ of habeas corpus which was returned to the court of common pleas. Vaughan demonstrated beyond doubt that jurors, not the judge, are to decide questions of fact. Ever since *Bushell's case* juries who have honestly felt that they could not follow the direction of a judge have retired to consider their verdict under the full protection of Vaughan's historic judgment, and his name is appropriately included on a plaque in the Old Bailey which commemorates the endurance of Bushell and his fellow jurors. Lord Campbell considered him to be a 'really consummate common law judge' (J. Campbell, *Lives of the Chief Justices*, 3, 1857, 2).

Occasionally said to be aloof and opinionated, Vaughan was nevertheless much esteemed by a constellation of able men. John Selden dedicated to him his *Vindiciae … Marie Clausi* (1653) and Vaughan was one of the executors of his splendid library at length placed in the 'Selden end' of the Bodleian Library. John Evelyn thought him 'a very wise and learned person' (Evelyn, *Diary*, 514). Matthew Hale loved to converse with Vaughan, his Acton neighbour, while Aubrey records that Thomas Hobbes delighted to visit Vaughan, his 'great acquaintance', thrice weekly (*Brief Lives*, 1.369). Vaughan died on 10 December 1674 at Serjeants' Inn and was buried twelve days later in the Temple Church where the latitudinarian Edward Stillingfleet paid him high tribute. His only son, Edward, briefly a lord commissioner for the Admiralty, published his father's *Reports* in 1677 and a corrected version in 1706.

J. GWYNN WILLIAMS

Sources J. G. Williams, 'Sir John Vaughan of Trawscoed, 1603–1674', *National Library of Wales Journal*, 8 (1953–4), 33–48, 121–46, 225–41 • [E. Vaughan], preface, in *The reports and arguments of that learned judge, Sir John Vaughan … published by his son, Edward Vaughan*, 2nd edn (1706) • F. Green, ed., *Calendar of deeds and documents*, 2: *The Crosswood deeds* (1927) • J. M. Howells, 'The Crosswood estate', *Ceredigion*, 3 (1956–9), 70–88 • L. Naylor and G. Jagger, 'Vaughan, John', *HoP, Commons, 1660–90*, 3.628–30 • *DWB* • *The life of Edward, earl of Clarendon … written by himself*, 2 vols. (1857), vol. 1 • K. A. Esdaile, *Temple church monuments* (1933) • *Brief lives, chiefly of contemporaries, set down by John Aubrey, between the years 1669 and 1696*, ed. A. Clark, 2 vols. (1898)

Archives NL Wales, Crosswood collection of deeds and documents

Likenesses J. M. Wright, oils, 1671, Inner Temple, London • R. White, line engraving, BM, NPG; repro. in *Reports* • M. Wright, portrait; originally Guildhall, London • portrait, priv. coll. • portrait, Gwysaney, near Mold, Flintshire • portrait, repro. in P. Yorke, *The royal tribes of Wales* (1799), 111

Wealth at death approx. £1200 annual rental from Trawscoed estate: will, Green, ed., *Crosswood*, 418

Vaughan, John, third earl of Carbery (*bap.* 1639, *d.* 1713), politician and colonial governor, was baptized on 18 July 1639 at St Dunstan-in-the-West, London, the second son of Richard *Vaughan, second earl of Carbery (1600?–1686), and his second wife, Frances (1620/1621–1650), daughter and coheir of Sir James Altham of Oxhey in Watford, Hertfordshire. He was educated at home at Golden Grove, Llanfihangel Aberbythych, Carmarthenshire, by Dr Jeremy

Taylor, who was chaplain to the family under the second earl's protection during the protectorate. Despite being royalists, the Carberys benefited from the personal favour of Cromwell, who admired Frances Vaughan's piety. Vaughan matriculated from Christ Church, Oxford, in 1656 and proceeded to the Inner Temple in 1658. He was knighted at Charles II's coronation in 1661 and became MP for the borough of Carmarthen in the same year. In parliament Vaughan was a fierce promoter of the king's personal interests, especially those involving providing money for Charles. He opposed Lord Chancellor Clarendon's austerity measures, and played a role in Clarendon's impeachment in 1667. Vaughan's activities caused Pepys to declare him 'one of the lewdest fellows of the age, worse than Sir Charles Sedley', and Clarendon described him as having 'as ill a face as fame' (Pepys, 8.532 and n). Vaughan enjoyed life in Restoration London to the fullest. He was fond of the theatre and especially of the plays of John Dryden for whom he wrote a poetic prologue to *The Conquest of Granada*. He became his father's heir in 1667 upon his elder brother's death and claimed the courtesy title Lord Vaughan. He married Mary Brown, of Green Castle, Carmarthen, a couple of years before her death in 1674; they had no children.

Vaughan was appointed governor of Jamaica in 1674. He intended to run Jamaica's government with the English parliament as a model. His instructions for running the island from the king and the lords of trade and plantations included stopping piracy, encouraging planting of sugar, and negotiating prices of slaves with the Royal African Company. He was in constant conflict with his lieutenant-governor, the ex-buccaneer Sir Henry Morgan, and with the Jamaican assembly, which opposed his tough measures against pirates. In piracy cases the accused were often supported by Morgan as they were prosecuted by Vaughan. Vaughan made piracy an executable offence in 1677 when the Jamaican assembly was given the right to issue death sentences without appeal. None of the laws passed by the Jamaican assembly under Vaughan were given the royal assent, but his leadership marks the start of the constitutional history of the island. He corresponded with Henry Oldenburg, secretary to the Royal Society, while on Jamaica, and thereby kept up with all the latest scientific developments in London. An element of scandal followed Vaughan throughout his life from his time in Jamaica; he was accused by his enemies of selling his Welsh servants, including his clergyman, into slavery on the island. Vaughan was an unpopular governor, and the assembly failed to vote him an income for his last year on the island. He suffered from ill health in the tropical climate and was no doubt happy to return to London in 1678.

Vaughan regained his place in parliament as MP for the county of Carmarthen (1679–81, 1685–6). Despite his dubious reputation his life and career flourished after his return from Jamaica. His friend Dryden dedicated his coarsest comedy, *The Kind Keeper, or, Mr Limberham*, to Vaughan in 1680. The play was forced to close after only three days, even in the relaxed moral world of Restoration London, though Dryden had been initially confident that his learned and witty patron would protect the play, which had first been performed when Vaughan was away in Jamaica. Vaughan married Lady Anne Savile (1663–1690), daughter of George Savile, first marquess of Halifax, in 1682. With her he had his only surviving legitimate child and heir, Anne, before his wife died in childbirth in 1690. On the death of his father in December 1686 Vaughan became third earl of Carbery and also inherited the baronies of Mullengar and Emlyn. His wide learning and love of mathematics were acknowledged when he became president of the Royal Society in 1686; he held the position for three years. He supported the accession of William and Mary in 1688 and remained a member of the whig establishment until his death. He built a house at Tite Street, Chelsea, subsequently called Gough House after a later owner, which was his chief London residence. The earl was a member of the Kit-Cat Club, and his portrait was painted by Kneller as one of the famous collection commemorating the club. It is now on display at Beningbrough Hall. Carbery died suddenly on 16 January 1713 while returning to Chelsea after visiting his banker in London. He was buried in Westminster Abbey on 28 January in St John the Baptist's chapel. His titles died with him, and his daughter inherited the wealth he carefully accumulated throughout his life. She married, almost immediately after her father's death, Charles Powlett. The marriage was unhappy, and she died without children in 1751. Carbery's house at Chelsea was demolished in 1966.

K. GRUDZIEN BASTON

Sources Pepys, *Diary*, 8.532; 9.71 · W. J. Gardner, *A history of Jamaica*, new edn (1909) · F. Cundall, *The governors of Jamaica in the seventeenth century* (1936) · K. Lane, *Blood and silver: a history of piracy in the Caribbean and Central America* (1999) · J. Caulfield, *Memoirs of the celebrated persons comprising the Kit-Cat Club* (1821) · *The works of John Dryden*, 14: *Plays: The kind keeper, The Spanish fryar, The Duke of Guise, and The vindication*, ed. V. A. Dearing and A. Roper (1993), 3–6 · T. Faulkner, *An historical and topographical description of Chelsea and its environs*, [new edn], 2 (1829) · A. Beaver, *Memorials of old Chelsea* (1892) · GEC, *Peerage* · J. L. Chester, ed., *The marriage, baptismal, and burial registers of the collegiate church or abbey of St Peter, Westminster*, Harleian Society, 10 (1876) · Foster, *Alum. Oxon.* · G. R. De Beer, 'Chelsea and the Royal Society', *Chelsea Society Annual Report* (1947) · J. E. Lloyd, *A history of Carmarthenshire*, 2 (1939) · DNB · PRO, PROB 11/531, fols. 231r–232r · L. Naylor and G. Jagger, 'Vaughan, Hon. John', HoP, *Commons, 1660–90*

Archives Francis Jones Archives, West Wales Genealogy, Brandy Books · Longleat House, Wiltshire, marquis of Bath collection, papers concerning Jamaica

Likenesses oils, *c*.1674–1678, Golden Grove, Carmarthenshire; repro. in R. A. G. Howard and K. S. Campbell, *Catalogue of the pictures at Golden Grove* (1904) · G. Kneller, oils, *c*.1700–1710, NPG; [displayed at Beningbrough Hall, Yorkshire] · J. Faber junior, mezzotint, 1733 (after G. Kneller, *c*.1700–1710), BM, NPG; reversed · Cooper, engraving (after G. Kneller, *c*.1700–1710), BL; repro. in Caulfield, *Memoirs of the celebrated persons*, facing p. 124 · G. Kneller, oils (after his earlier work), repro. in R. A. G. Howard and K. S. Campbell, *Catalogue of the pictures at Golden Grove* (1904) · J. Simon, engraving (after G. Kneller, *c*.1700–1710), BM; repro. in Cundall, *Governors of Jamaica*, facing p. 18 · J. Simon, mezzotint (after G. Kneller), BM, NPG

Wealth at death £4000—per annum, plus 'a great personal estate': letter from Ralph Palmer to Viscount Fermaugh, 27 Jan 1713, A. Beaver, *Memorials of old Chelsea* (1892)

Vaughan, Sir John (*c.*1731–1795), army officer, was the second son of Wilmot Vaughan, third Viscount Lisburne (*d.* 1766), of Crosswood (Trawscoed), Cardiganshire, and his wife, Elizabeth (*d.* 1764), daughter of Thomas Watson of Berwick upon Tweed and Grindon Ridge, Northumberland. Without prospects, as the younger son of an impecunious holder of an Irish peerage, Vaughan embarked early on a military career, becoming a second lieutenant in the marines in 1746. The political connections of his whig family, his own military aptitude, and the opportunities of wartime ensured his steady promotion. He became a cornet of dragoons in 1748, lieutenant in 1751, and captain in 1754, and served in Germany early in the Seven Years' War. In 1759 he raised the 94th foot, becoming its lieutenant-colonel in 1760. This regiment, the Royal Welsh volunteers, served in North America and the West Indies, where Vaughan distinguished himself at the capture of Martinique in 1762. When the regiment disbanded later that year Vaughan transferred to the command of the 16th foot, serving in North America until 1767 and then in Ireland; he was promoted colonel in 1772. In 1775 he became colonel of the 46th foot and took them to America. In 1774 he had entered parliament as MP for the venal freeman borough of Berwick upon Tweed, where the Vaughan brothers had inherited the interest of their childless uncle, another Thomas Watson; he represented that constituency until his death. Military duties in the American War restricted his attendance in parliament, where, like his brother Wilmot, the fourth viscount and first earl of Lisburne, who sat on the Admiralty board from 1770 to 1782, he was a supporter of Lord North's ministry. He also sat in the Irish parliament for St Johnstown from 1776 to 1783.

Vaughan rose to military prominence during the American War of Independence, making a name for himself as a bold battlefield commander. In 1776 he led attacks at the battles of Brooklyn Heights and Manhattan Island prior to the capture of New York city. Later that year he was wounded at the battle of White Plains. Promoted major-general in August 1777, Vaughan had a horse shot from under him when storming Fort Montgomery two months later. He was commended for his bravery by General Sir Henry Clinton, who suggested that the fort should be renamed Fort Vaughan. Vaughan then commanded the small army of 2000 men dispatched by Clinton in a vain attempt to reach General Burgoyne before his surrender at Saratoga. His burning of the town of Aesopus (later Kingston, New York)—which he alleged was 'a Nursery for almost every Villain in the Country' (Hurst, 29)—outraged the Americans, who called him General Aesopus. His force burned and destroyed farms until within 46 miles of Albany, then returned to New York city. George III in 1778 ordered that Vaughan be informed of royal approbation of his spirited behaviour. In 1779 Vaughan commanded part of Clinton's second expedition up the Hudson River, and left New York in December. He returned to Britain, and was given a dormant commission to succeed Lord Cornwallis as commander in the southern American colonies in case Cornwallis declined to return there. When Cornwallis did go back, Vaughan was sent to command in the Leeward Islands, arriving in Barbados in February 1780. He promptly reversed the previous defensive strategy of scattered garrisons by collecting a force of 5000 men to attack French islands, but his plans were foiled by Admiral Rodney's inability to win control of West Indian waters. Vaughan had to remain inactive until, on news of the war with the United Provinces, he initiated the capture in February 1781 by Rodney and himself of the Dutch island of St Eustatius, an international entrepôt and the main supply base for the American war. Both Vaughan and Rodney busied themselves for some months in arranging the disposal of the vast plunder; Vaughan's share was 9.2 per cent, £150,000. Much of what was sent back to England was intercepted by the French fleet. Sixty-four civil claims were lodged against the two commanders by British merchants who contended that the confiscation of their goods on St Eustatius was illegal, cases which dragged on until 1793. In Vaughan's only known speech in parliament, on 4 December 1781, he defended himself against Edmund Burke's charge that he had made a personal fortune from St Eustatius. He claimed that 'neither directly nor indirectly … had he made a single shilling from the business' (HoP, *Commons, 1754–90*, 3.576).

After the war Vaughan, who was promoted to lieutenant-general on 20 November 1782, retired from active military service. Among his rewards was the governorship of Berwick Castle, bestowed in 1780 after he had held that of Fort William for a year. Both this post and the colonelcy of the 46th foot he retained until his death. Such sources of income do not explain the considerable wealth he acquired. As early as 1773 he paid £10,000 for an estate in Cardiganshire, and he now made other purchases and gave large loans to his brother. This circumstance puts into perspective his 1781 parliamentary denial that he had profited from the St Eustatius booty. In parliament Vaughan supported the Shelburne ministry of 1782–3, apparently in the hope of being appointed governor of Canada or Gibraltar. Disappointed, he joined his brother Lord Lisburne in support of the 1783 Fox–North coalition, and later opposed the ministry of the younger Pitt. However, in 1788 he admitted personal respect for the prime minister, and made it known that some mark of royal approval of his military services would secure his political allegiance. Pitt demurred, in view of his previous hostility, and Vaughan remained in opposition until won over by being made KB in 1792. In the French Revolutionary Wars he was recalled to army duties. In 1794 he was appointed to succeed Sir John Grey as army commander-in-chief in the Windward Islands. It was a thankless task, as he was beset by slave risings and Carib uprisings instigated by French revolutionaries, and was denied the soldiers needed to reinforce his fever-ridden troops. His proposal to raise black regiments was vetoed by the secretary for war, Henry Dundas, at the behest of the British plantation-owners, a decision against which Vaughan protested vigorously as the subordination of the national interest to private advantage, and which he partly defied. He died, unmarried, reportedly of a bowel complaint, though poison was also suspected, in Martinique on 30 June 1795, with the military conflict still unresolved; he was buried at Mamhead, Devon.

PETER D. G. THOMAS

Sources G. Morgan, *A Welsh house and its family: the Vaughans of Trawsgoed* (1997) · Fortescue, *Brit. army*, vols. 3–4 · P. Mackesy, *The war for America, 1775–1783* (1964) · HoP, *Commons, 1754–90* · HoP, *Commons, 1790–1820* · DNB · M. Duffy, *Soldiers, sugar, and sea power: the British expeditions to the West Indies and the war against revolutionary France* (1987) · R. Blanco, ed., *The American revolution, 1775–1783: an encyclopedia*, 2 vols. (1993) · R. Hurst, *The golden rock: an episode in the American War of Independence, 1775–1783* (1996) · GM, 1st ser., 65 (1795), 703–4
Archives BL, corresp. and papers, Egerton MSS 2134–2137 · NL Wales, corresp. and papers · U. Mich., Clements L., corresp. and papers | PRO, War Office papers · PRO, letters to Lord Rodney, box 26 · U. Mich., Clements L., corresp. with Thomas Gage
Likenesses probably B. West, portrait, repro. in Morgan, *A Welsh house and its family* · portrait, Trawscoed (Crosswood), Cardiganshire
Wealth at death presumably a lot more than £10,000; received £150,000 following the capture of St Eustatius in 1781

Vaughan, Sir John (1769–1839), judge, was born in Leicester on 11 February 1769, the third son of James Vaughan MD of Leicester and his wife, Hester, daughter of John Smalley, alderman, also of Leicester. Charles Richard *Vaughan and Sir Henry *Halford were his brothers. Educated at Rugby School, he matriculated at Queen's College, Oxford, on 17 October 1785. Leaving Oxford without a degree, he was admitted to Lincoln's Inn on 11 February 1786, and was called to the bar on 30 June 1791. Vaughan joined the midland circuit, where his style of advocacy brought him popularity with juries. Elected recorder of Leicester on 14 February 1798, he was created serjeant-at-law on 12 February 1799. A strong supporter of Pitt, he threw himself into the movement for raising funds for the war with France by public subscription.

On 20 December 1803 Vaughan married his first wife, Augusta (d. 1813), second daughter of Henry Beauchamp, thirteenth Baron St John of Bletso. They had six children: Henry Halford *Vaughan, another son, and four daughters.

Vaughan was appointed solicitor-general to Queen Charlotte on 1 May 1814, being promoted to attorney-general in the Trinity vacation 1816, and in the Easter term 1816 was appointed king's serjeant. As such in March 1820 he conducted the crown's case against Sir Francis Burdett for seditious libel following Burdett's comments upon the 'Peterloo massacre' of 1819. In August 1821 Vaughan led for the crown in the prosecution for seditious conspiracy of George Edmonds and others who had resolved to elect a 'legislatorial attorney' to represent Birmingham in parliament.

On 4 August 1823 Vaughan married his second wife, Louisa (1785–1860), eldest daughter of Sir Charles William Rouse-Boughton, bt, and widow of St Andrew, fourteenth Baron St John of Bletso; they had a son and a daughter.

On 23 February 1827 Vaughan was raised to the exchequer bench following the resignation of Sir Robert Graham and was knighted on 24 November 1828. His reputation for legal learning was not high, and it was said that he owed his judicial appointment to the influence of his brother Sir Henry Halford, though he was credited with a sound understanding both of court practice and of human character. He was one of the judges to whom was referred in 1829 the Irish case of *Harding* v. *Pollock*, on the question of whether the right of appointing clerks of the peace for a county was vested in the crown or in the *custos rotulorum* of the county, his opinion being given against the crown.

On 29 April 1834 Vaughan was transferred to the court of common pleas, and in June of the same year was sworn of the privy council and admitted to the Oxford degree of DCL. Consulted in the Camoys peerage case in 1839 about the rules regulating the determination of abeyances of baronies, he concurred in the judgment of Chief Justice Tindal.

Vaughan died of heart disease on 25 September 1839 at his home, Eastbury Lodge, near Watford, Hertfordshire, and was buried in the burial-ground of the parish of Wistow, Leicestershire. His brother Sir Henry Halford placed a mural tablet to his memory in Wistow church.

J. M. RIGG, rev. N. G. JONES

Sources E. Foss, *Biographia juridica: a biographical dictionary of the judges of England … 1066–1870* (1870) · GM, 2nd ser., 12 (1839), 648–9 · 'The recent judicial changes: memoir of Mr Justice Vaughan', *Legal Observer*, 19 (1839–40), 33–4 · E. G. W. Bill, *University reform in nineteenth-century Oxford: a study of Henry Halford Vaughan, 1811–1885* (1973), 5–7 · W. Munk, *The life of Sir Henry Halford* (1895), 8–9 · R. Walton, *Random recollections of the midland circuit* (1869), 12–14 · d. cert.
Archives All Souls Oxf., letters to Sir Charles Richard Vaughan
Likenesses school of T. Lawrence, oils (in robes of baron of exchequer), Lamport Hall, Northamptonshire · Pickersgill, portrait; at Leicester town hall in 1899 · portrait; formerly at Wistow Hall, Leicestershire, 1899

Vaughan, John [Jacky] (1799–1868), ironmaster, was born in Worcester on 21 December 1799, a son of John Vaughan, subsequently at Sir Josiah Guest's Dowlais ironworks. He had at least two brothers. He joined his father as an ironworker in south Wales, progressing at Dowlais to become a foreman.

About 1825 Vaughan took a post in Carlisle as manager of a small ironworks, and in 1832 he was appointed mill manager for Losh, Wilson, and Bell's Walker ironworks near Newcastle upon Tyne. In 1839 Vaughan and Henry W. F. Bolckow agreed to enter into partnership to exploit the iron trade, Bolckow to provide the initial £10,000 capital, and profits to be shared equally. The partners opened their works at Middlesbrough in 1841, making iron castings and wrought products. Vaughan in 1845–6 erected four iron blast furnaces at Witton Park in co. Durham.

In 1850 Vaughan decided to mine the seam of ironstone cropping out on the Cleveland Hills east of Middlesbrough, soon erecting nine blast furnaces for its treatment and establishing the commercial viability of Cleveland iron. In 1855 the partners' output of manufactured iron exceeded 120,000 tons; they employed 4000 people and consumed 600,000 tons of coal. In succeeding years they continued to expand while others, attracted by their success, also produced iron in the district.

Jacky Vaughan was one of the great 'working' ironmasters. From nothing he amassed a fortune estimated at close to £1 million by a combination of sustained hard work and practical technical ability. After 1855 his grip on the business slackened; in 1864, when the partnership was converted into a joint-stock company with industrial assets valued at about £1 million, Vaughan became deputy chairman of Bolckow, Vaughan & Co. Ltd.

For many years Vaughan was a Wesleyan Methodist, but then he turned towards the Church of England. He joined the first board of Tees conservancy commissioners in 1852, and a year later was among Middlesbrough's first councillors, becoming the town's third mayor in 1855. He was appointed JP and a deputy lieutenant for the North Riding of Yorkshire.

Vaughan was twice married, first, in the 1820s, to Eleanor Downing (or Downie) of Cumberland, with whom he had four sons but who died about 1834; and, second, to a widow, originally Anne Poole of Newcastle upon Tyne, sister of Henry Bolckow's first wife. The youngest son by his first marriage, Thomas, survived to inherit the major part of the estate, including Gunnergate Hall in Yorkshire. By his second marriage John Vaughan had no children of his own, but his wife's three children by previous marriages took his name. He died at his house, 1 Hyde Park Gate, London, on 16 September 1868.   J. K. ALMOND, rev.

Sources J. S. Jeans, *Pioneers of the Cleveland iron trade* (1875) • W. H. Burnett, *Old Cleveland … local writers and local worthies* (1886) • C. A. Hempstead, ed., *Cleveland iron and steel: background and 19th century history* (1979) • R. Gott, *Henry Bolckow, founder of Teesside* (1968) • newspaper clippings, Middlesbrough Central Reference Library • d. cert.

Wealth at death under £180,000: probate, 16 Sept 1869, *CGPLA Eng. & Wales*

Vaughan, Kate [*real name* Catherine Candelon or Candelin] (1852?–1903), actress and dancer, born in London, was the elder daughter of a musician who played in the orchestra of the Grecian Theatre, City Road. After receiving some preliminary training in the dancing academy conducted by Mrs Benjamin Oliver Conquest of that theatre, she took finishing lessons from John D'Auban, and, with her sister Susie, made her début as a dancer, as one of the Sisters Vaughan, in 1870 at the Metropolitan music-hall. Early in 1872 she took a small part at the Royal Court Theatre in *In re Becca*, a travesty of Andrew Halliday's recent Drury Lane drama *Rebecca*. In 1873 the Sisters Vaughan danced the 'grand ballet' of the Furies in W. F. Vandervell's version of Offenbach's *Orpheus in the Underworld*, and Kate, as the Spirit of Darkness, startled the audience by her novelty costume of black skirt and black tights relieved by gilt trimmings. She frequently wore black gloves, and inaugurated the skirt-dance, a sedate forerunner of the can-can, in which the manipulation of voluminous gossamer draperies played a part just as important as the actual steps: one observer described her as 'a terpsichorean poem'. On 1 December 1873 W. E. Gladstone attended a performance of *Antony and Cleopatra* at Drury Lane, and commented, 'Miss K. Vaughan in the ballet, dressed in black and gold, danced marvellously' (*Diaries*). At the same house, at Christmas 1875, she played the leading character of Zemira in Edward Blanchard's pantomime *Beauty and the Beast*, displaying abilities as a burlesque actress of an arch and refined type.

A notable seven years' association with the Gaiety began on 26 August 1876, when Vaughan appeared as Maritana in H. J. Byron's extravaganza *Little Don Caesar*. Thenceforth she formed, with Nellie Farren, Edward Terry, and E. W. Royce, one of a quartet that delighted London in a long succession of merry burlesques by Byron, F. C. Burnand, and Robert Reece, in which her waltzing with Royce was particularly enjoyed by audiences. Her last performance at the Gaiety was as Lili in Burnand's burlesque drama *Blue Beard* (12 March 1883).

On 3 June 1884 Vaughan became the second wife of Colonel the Hon. Frederick Arthur Wellesley (1844–1931), the

Kate Vaughan (1852?–1903), by W. & D. Downey, 1880 [as Morgiana in the burlesque *The Forty Thieves*]

third son of Henry Richard Charles *Wellesley, the first Earl Cowley. Her absence from the stage was, however, short-lived: in the summer of 1885 she danced at Her Majesty's in the spectacular ballet *Excelsior*, and, although appearing for only two minutes nightly, proved a great attraction. Thereafter from reasons of health she abandoned dancing for old comedy, in which she showed unsuspected talent. She had already appeared as First Niece in *The Critic* at the Gaiety for John Parry's farewell benefit (7 February 1877). In 1886 she organized the Vaughan–Conway comedy company in conjunction with H. B. Conway, and made a successful tour of the provinces. After dissolving the partnership she began a season of management at the Opera Comique on 5 February 1887. She appeared there as Lydia Languish in *The Rivals*, as Miss Hardcastle to the Young Marlow of Forbes Robertson, and as Peg Woffington in Charles Reade's *Masks and Faces* to the Triplet of James Fernandez. The chief success of the season was the revival of *The School for Scandal*, in which she made an admirable Lady Teazle. In a later provincial tour she delighted audiences by her performance as Peggy in David Garrick's *The Country Girl* and as the title character in Hermann Vezin's *The Little Viscount*. At Terry's Theatre on 30 April 1894 she returned to burlesque as Kitty Seabrook in Arthur Branscombe's extravaganza *King Kodak*, but her old magic had departed. In 1896, after a testimonial performance at the Gaiety, she went to Australia for her health. She was divorced by her husband the following year. In the summer of 1898 she had a short season at Terry's Theatre in her old-comedy characterizations. In 1902 failing health necessitated a visit to South Africa, but a theatrical tour which she opened at Cape Town proved unsuccessful. She died at Johannesburg on 21 February 1903.

In point of grace, magnetism, and spirituality, Kate Vaughan was the greatest English dancer of her century. She owed little to early training and much to innate refinement and an exquisite sense of rhythm. A woman of varied accomplishments, she was a capable actress in old comedy.   W. J. Lawrence, *rev.* J. Gilliland

Sources *The life and reminiscences of E. L. Blanchard, with notes from the diary of Wm. Blanchard*, ed. C. W. Scott and C. Howard, 2 vols. (1891) • *Daily Telegraph* (24 Feb 1903) • C. Scott, *The drama of yesterday and today*, 2 vols. (1899) • J. Hollingshead, *Gaiety chronicles* (1898) • E. Reid and H. Compton, eds., *The dramatic peerage* [1891] • G. Vuillier, *A history of dancing from the earliest ages to our own times*, ed. and trans. J. Grego (1898) • C. E. Pascoe, ed., *The dramatic list*, 2nd edn (1880) • Hall, *Dramatic ports.* • Burke, *Peerage* • R. Pearsall, *The worm in the bud* (1969) • Gladstone, *Diaries*
Likenesses W. & D. Downey, photograph, 1880, Theatre Museum, London [*see illus.*] • Jack, watercolour, in or before 1897 (as Morgiana in *The Forty Thieves*) • W. & D. Downey, woodburytype photograph, repro. in W. Downey and D. Downey, *The cabinet portrait gallery*, 1 (1890) • Kingsbury & Notcutt, photograph, NPG • four prints, Harvard TC • photographs, NPG • portrait, repro. in *Theatre Magazine* (May 1881) • portrait?, repro. in Scott, *Drama* • portrait?, repro. in Hollingshead, *Gaiety chronicles*

Vaughan, (John) Keith (1912–1977), painter and book illustrator, was born at Selsey, Sussex, on 23 August 1912, the elder son (there were no daughters) of Eric George Story Vaughan, a civil engineer, and his wife, Gladys Regina Marion Mackintosh. The parents separated in 1922. On the paternal side his grandfather and great-grandfather were successful London cabinet-makers and came of a long line of craftsmen. From 1921 to 1930 he was an unhappy boarder at Christ's Hospital, Horsham, Sussex, but the art master of the time, H. A. Rigby, stimulated his interest in the visual arts, especially in landscape drawing. On leaving school, however, a vocation was not clear to him, and in 1931 he took employment with Lintas, a Unilever advertising agency, an occupation which, fortunately, left him energy to develop skills in painting and photography and to study the work of the masters, Cézanne, Matisse, and Picasso in particular. On a visit to Paris in 1937 he was greatly impressed by Gauguin. During this period he also frequented the ballet, an experience which was seminal to his later work.

Vaughan was a slow developer, and he was lucky that when he left Lintas in 1939 he was able to spend a year painting in the country. On the outbreak of war he was a conscientious objector. He joined the Pioneer Corps in 1941 and for most of his time in the service worked as a clerk and German interpreter at the prisoner-of-war camp at Malton, Yorkshire, where he found time to draw and to work in gouache and also to write. The journal which he began in 1939 and continued throughout his life was published in extracts selected and illustrated by himself in 1966. His introvert and reticent nature inhibited professional progress in this field, but he was a natural writer and during the war he graduated into the company of John Lehmann and his friends, and contributed to Penguin *New Writing* in 1944–6; in 1949 he made lithograph illustrations for Norman Cameron's translation of Rimbaud's *Une saison en enfer* which Lehmann published.

Vaughan's first exhibition of drawings was held in 1942 at the Reid and Lefèvre Gallery, London, where in 1946 he also exhibited paintings. He had never received a formal art training but at the same time as he was slowly making his name as an artist he established himself as a teacher, at Camberwell School of Arts and Crafts (1946–8), at the Central School of Arts and Crafts (1948–57) and from 1954 as a visiting teacher at the Slade School of Fine Art. He was visiting resident artist at Iowa State University in 1959.

The subject matter of Vaughan's painting is confined almost entirely to landscape and the male nude. The patterned grey-green and ochreous spaces of the Sussex downs had impressed their images on him in his schooldays, and experiments in photographing groups of bathers at Pagham on the Sussex coast in 1939 developed his interest and experience in figure-group composition. The many variations on this latter theme (which he liked to call an 'assembly'), which occupied him over decades, owed much to Cézanne, whereas his landscapes are often in the spirit, if not the vocabulary, of Graham Sutherland. Study of Cézanne's late bathing groups stiffened his intellectual approach to painting at the right moment. It would have been all too easy for him to have developed an idiom of more facile appeal. As it was he pushed himself almost to the clumsy in such experimental works as *Leaping Figure* (1951; Tate collection). His rich palette of ochre, corn-yellow, olive-green, deep blues, and white was intensely personal, growing more Mediterranean in its verve when he began to respond with some passion to the painting of Nicolas de Stael. There were many influences on him, John Minton (with whom he once shared a house) and John Craxton notably among his contemporaries; but his work always had a character apart. His reduction of the human figure to near impersonality and his spreading of colour into wide and formal patterning are symptomatic of this somewhat withdrawn attitude. He was essentially a private artist and received few public commissions, the best known being the *Theseus* mural for the dome of discovery at the Festival of Britain in 1951, and in 1955 a tile-mural for a bus shelter in Corby new town whose abstract design so baffled the local authority that it was bricked up.

Having signified assent Vaughan was elected an associate of the Royal Academy in 1960 but resigned within a month. In 1964 he was elected an honorary fellow of the Royal College of Art, and in 1965 was appointed CBE. He held a number of exhibitions in this country, was given one-man shows in New York, Los Angeles, Buenos Aires, and São Paulo, and was accorded a retrospective exhibition at the Whitechapel Art Gallery in 1962. He never married. Threatened by cancer, he committed suicide at his Hampstead home, 9 Belsize Park, on 4 November 1977.   KENNETH GARLICK, rev.

Sources *The Times* (8 Nov 1977) · J. B. and P. C., *The Times* (14 Nov 1977) · K. Vaughan, *Journal and drawings, 1936–1965* (1966) · *Keith Vaughan: images of man* (1981) [exhibition catalogue, Geffrye Museum, London] · MSS, catalogues, Tate collection · private information (1986) · M. Yorke, *The spirit of place* (1988) · *CGPLA Eng. & Wales* (1978)
Archives Tate collection
Likenesses J. H. Lewinski, photographs, *c.*1950, NPG · F. H. Maw, photographs, *c.*1950, NPG · K. Vaughan, self-portrait, pen and black ink, crayon, and gouache drawing, 1950, NPG · D. Berwin, photograph, 1951, Hult. Arch. · K. Vaughan, self-portrait, repro. in *Art News and Review* (8 April 1950)
Wealth at death £146,343: probate, 6 April 1978, *CGPLA Eng. & Wales*

Vaughan, Rachel. *See* Russell, Rachel (*bap.* 1637, *d.* 1723).

Vaughan, Rice (*d. c.*1672), lawyer, was the second son of Henry Vaughan of Gelli-goch, Machynlleth, and Mary, daughter of Maurice Wynn of Glyn, near Harlech. He attended Shrewsbury School (1615), entered Gray's Inn (1638), and was called to the bar on 20 June 1648. Vaughan sided with parliament in the civil wars and became a member of the committee for Cardiganshire, Pembrokeshire, and Carmarthenshire. He failed to be elected MP for Merioneth in 1654 and petitioned the council of state formally on 24 August 1654 because of the alleged irregularities and corrupt practices of the sheriff, Maurice Lewis, who, in collusion with Edward Vaughan of Llwydiarth, ensured that John Vaughan of Cefnbodig, near Llanycil, Merioneth, was elected. In the previous year, however, Rice Vaughan had been appointed prothonotary for Denbighshire and Montgomeryshire in the court of great sessions, having petitioned for the post on 3 January 1646. He served in the commission for sequestration from 1649,

examined with others the miscarriages of the trustees and surveyors for the sale of forfeited estates, and was actively engaged with the business of the council of state in 1656. In 1659 he served as judge of great sessions for the Anglesey circuit (Williams, 100). Vaughan's subsequent career is unclear, but he appears to have been imprisoned in the Tower for two years from May 1665.

Vaughan wrote three works at least, namely *A Plea for the Common Laws of England* (1651), a pamphlet addressed to the House of Commons replying to Hugh Peter's book *A Good Work for a Good Magistrate*; *Practica Walliae, or, The Proceedings in the Great Sessions of Wales* (1672), which was published posthumously; and *A Discourse of Coin and Coinage* (1675), again published posthumously and edited by Henry Vaughan, 'the Silurist'. Vaughan was part of a group of lawyers that was 'opposed to all law reform or did not want changes to go further than those made during the Interregnum' (Veall, 99). In *A Plea for the Common Laws of England* he claimed that common laws were 'one of the most excellent and humane laws that any nation had'. They had not been imposed by any king

> but consisted of laudable and righteous customs, based on reason and convenience, in common use over hundreds of years. As for the defects that did remain, Parliament was gradually throwing off the chaff; the task could not be done all at once.   (ibid., 24)

J. GWYNFOR JONES

Sources J. Foster, *The register of admissions to Gray's Inn, 1521–1889, together with the register of marriages in Gray's Inn chapel, 1695–1754* (privately printed, London, 1889) · *CSP dom.*, 1654, 299–300 · W. R. Williams, *The history of the great sessions in Wales, 1542–1830* (privately printed, Brecon, 1899), 100–03 · *DWB*, 1005 · D. Veall, *The popular movement for law reform, 1640–1660* (1970)
Wealth at death not known, but about £1500

Vaughan, Richard (*c.*1553–1607), bishop of London, was born at Dyffryn, Llŷn, Caernarvonshire, second son of Thomas ap Robert Vaughan (Vychan) and his wife (*née* Griffin). If, as has been assumed, Vaughan pursued his studies under the auspices of his kinsman John *Aylmer, future bishop of London, it was without initial financial assistance. It was only as a sizar that on 16 November 1569 he matriculated from St John's College, Cambridge, where his tutor was John Becon. It was presumably as a result of his own efforts that he was admitted a scholar on Lady Margaret's foundation on 6 November 1573. Indeed Vaughan's kinship with Aylmer, whose wife was born Judith King (alias Bures), may date only from 25 June 1581 when Vaughan married Joan Bewers at Great Dunmow, Essex.

Having graduated BA in 1574 and proceeded MA in 1577, Vaughan gave his age as 'about' twenty-four when ordained deacon and priest by Aylmer on 21 and 22 December 1577, as a master of arts of Chipping Ongar, Essex. As curate there he received a diocesan preaching licence on 4 January 1578.

Vaughan thus began his career as protégé of an influential godly family: the patron of the living was the future attorney-general of the court of wards, James Morice, and the incumbent rector Thomas Morice. On 22 April 1578, on

Richard Vaughan (*c*.1553–1607), by unknown artist

Thomas's resignation, Vaughan succeeded to the rectory, resigning when instituted on 24 November 1580 to nearby Little Canfield. On 24 February 1582, only months after his marriage there, Aylmer collated Vaughan vicar of Great Dunmow, which he held in plurality with Little Canfield until January 1591. He then seems to have resigned both livings. On 19 August 1591 he was instituted rector of Moreton, Essex, once again at the presentation of James Morice and a kinsman, John Morice.

Meanwhile Vaughan's route to higher preferment had been smoothed by Aylmer. Collated prebendary of Holborn in St Paul's on 18 November 1583, he was promoted archdeacon of Middlesex on 26 October 1588. Having already proceeded BTh he was granted the degree of DTh in 1589. While no act books survive for his tenure Vaughan appears to have been an active, sympathetic *oculus episcopi*, contriving to win the confidence of the moderate puritan clergy whom Aylmer was always disposed to harry. In this he resembled John Still, archdeacon of Sudbury, evidently a close friend. Vaughan was granted letters patent for the prebend of Combe IX in Wells, *sede vacante*, and instituted by Archbishop John Whitgift on 5 February 1593, six days before Still's consecration as bishop of Bath and Wells. Still had presumably requested his appointment.

Sir John Puckering, lord keeper from May 1592, made Vaughan examining chaplain of clerics applying for the crown's ecclesiastical patronage in his gift. Sir John Harington noted with approval that he was 'precise' in that office, turning away unsatisfactory candidates, and described Vaughan in his prime as mild, 'very prompt and ready in speache, and withall facetious' (Harington, 2.49). It was perhaps a reference to his Welsh origins, which,

indeed, Vaughan never forgot, maintaining a series of Welsh curates in his Essex livings. When William Morgan dedicated his Welsh translation of the Bible to Elizabeth in 1588, he named Vaughan, 'provost of St John's Hospital at Lutterworth', as one of the six scholars who had given him particular assistance (Hughes, 85).

Thus by October 1594, perhaps prompted by Robert Devereux, second earl of Essex, Lord Burghley and Robert Cecil were proposing Vaughan for a Welsh bishopric. Whitgift approved his candidacy and urged his selection for Bangor. Probably not yet forty-three, Vaughan was elected on 22 November 1595 and consecrated on 25 January 1596, conscientiously resigning all his preferments in London diocese. Since Bangor was poorly endowed, its bishops traditionally enjoyed other privileges: thus Vaughan was granted the archdeaconry of Anglesey *in commendam*, his revenues from his predecessor's resignation (the crown therefore claiming no *sede vacante* profit), and five years to discharge his first fruits. Thereafter his rise was rapid. At Christmas 1596 Essex promised to promote his candidacy for Salisbury and his name was one of three being canvassed in April 1597. He may have refused it for financial reasons, as did others during 1596–7, and in the event he followed Hugh Bellot at Chester, as he had already done at Bangor.

Vaughan's election was confirmed on 4 June 1597 and again he received favourable financial terms: five years to pay his first fruits, the cancellation of sums 'behind' for Bangor, and restitution of the temporalities from Bellot's death, fully twelve months earlier. He also held the valuable rectory of Bangor Is-coed, Flintshire, throughout his tenure. In August 1597 he expressed to Robert Cecil his unqualified satisfaction with these arrangements.

During his years at Chester, Vaughan became preoccupied with the suppression of Catholicism, firing off to Cecil a vivid series of letters on the subject. In 1604 he alleged that he had 'reclaimed' over 600 recusants in three years, yet his visitation that year revealed more than 3500 known recusants in Lancashire. Although in 1601 he threatened to deprive eight nonconforming ministers for failing to wear the surplice, he did not in the event remove any of them and he stoutly defended his choice of Richard Midgeley as queen's preacher in Lancashire. At the Hampton Court conference in 1604, when Laurence Chaderton obtained a measure of tolerance from James I for the nonconforming Lancashire ministers, Vaughan was instructed not to proceed against them too peremptorily. He probably had no intention of doing so: although during his visitation later that year he dutifully attempted to enforce the new canons, which enshrined the three articles which Whitgift had first promulgated in 1583, he acted with restraint and again no minister was deprived.

Vaughan was translated to London in 1604 and enthroned in St Paul's on 26 December; his selection as successor to the disciplinarian Richard Bancroft is not easy to account for. King James perhaps gambled that an energetic anti-Catholic was more likely in so radical a diocese to win over nonconformist consciences than a man of more conservative stamp. Yet Vaughan arrived at Fulham to discover that James had now become obsessed with the question of clerical conformity and was pressing for the removal of all who refused to accept the new canons. He seems to have played his hand with consummate skill, to the extent that James commended his 'industry'. John Chamberlain reported in February 1605 that, while proceeding 'slowly', he had finally silenced 'all that continue disobedient', adding that he was much commended for 'gravitie, wisdome, learning, mildnes and temperance, even among that faction' and was held 'every way the most sufficient man of that coate' (McClure, 1.203).

Indeed during 1605 Vaughan sanctioned the deprivation of only two city incumbents, while a mere handful, of whom Stephen Egerton and Anthony Wotton were the most prominent, were suspended. Between April and June, Vaughan also appears, pending his primary visitation, to have tacitly issued an amnesty to those Essex and Hertfordshire clergy who remained under threat as a result of Bancroft's last visitation in 1604. Following his visitation in October only about thirty men were subsequently examined for nonconformist practices and none was deprived as a result. Many radical incumbents, including Thomas Stoughton, vicar of Coggeshall, Essex, escaped further summons altogether. Stoughton's deprivation in 1606 was probably the culmination of earlier high commission proceedings against him and was perhaps sanctioned by Vaughan only with reluctance.

Harington proposed that Vaughan's efficiency was impaired by illness. He grew corpulent 'of a sudden' and shortly after reaching London 'fell into that drowsie disease of which he after dyed, growing thereby unfit for that place', which required 'a *Vigilantius*, and not a *Dormitantius*' (Harington, 2.50). This is misleading evidence. There can be little doubt that Vaughan's leniency towards nonconformity was dictated by his own abiding sympathies. Richard Rogers recorded that after the discovery of the Gunpowder Plot he restored 'the Most Suspended Ministers' (Knappen, 32). Thus did he apparently attempt to reverse the trend of 1604 by laying stress on the church's anti-Catholic, rather than its conformist, stance. On 30 May 1606 Rogers celebrated eighteen months' freedom in the pulpit with the telling comment 'The Bishop my good friend'. Finally he noted the 'sorry news' of the death of 'our Bp. Vaughan, who ... permitted the godly ministers to live peaceably and enjoy their liberty' (ibid.). No other prelate of his generation was accorded such an epitaph by a leading nonconformist.

Vaughan died of apoplexy on 30 March 1607 and was buried in Bishop Kemp's chapel in St Paul's with a memorial inscription, destroyed in the great fire of 1666. He was succeeded by Thomas Ravis, a prelate of more authoritarian cast.

Vaughan and his wife, Joan, are credited with three sons and six daughters, of whom Elizabeth, wife of Thomas Mallory, dean of Chester, became mother of the royalist clergyman Thomas Mallory, whilst Dorothy married John Jegon, later bishop of Norwich. Katherine was baptized at Stanford Rivers, Essex, on 29 January 1596, four days after Vaughan's consecration. This circumstance has led to the assumption, which cannot be substantiated, that he was rector there. The brief document which he wrote as bishop of Chester on 19 April 1601, accepted as his will, was no more than a list of assets to be equally divided between his (here unnamed) wife and children. It was not witnessed and named no executor, but on the basis of it letters of administration were granted to his widow on 15 April 1607.

Vaughan published nothing except some early Latin verses and two sermons printed in 1599, but his visitation articles for London, based on three sets by Bancroft, proved the most influential of the Jacobean church. *Vaughanus redivivus*, a virtually impenetrable hagiography in Latin by his kinsman John *Williams, archbishop of York, survives in manuscript (BL, Harley MS 6495, art.6).

BRETT USHER

Sources Venn, *Alum. Cant.*, 1/4.295 • W. Hughes, *Diocesan histories: Bangor* (1911) • GL, MS 9535/1, fols. 158r, 159r [ordination] • J. Harington, *Nugae antiquae*, ed. T. Park and H. Harington, 2 vols. (1804) • *Calendar of the manuscripts of the most hon. the marquis of Salisbury*, 4–19, HMC, 9 (1892–1965) • *CSP dom., 1598–1601* • *The letters of John Chamberlain*, ed. N. E. McClure, 2 vols. (1939) • K. Fincham, *Prelate as pastor: the episcopate of James I* (1990) • K. Fincham, ed., *Visitation articles and injunctions of the early Stuart church*, 1 (1994) • LMA, DL/C/617, 618, 304, 305 [diocesan act bks of office] • *Two Elizabethan puritan diaries, by Richard Rogers and Samuel Ward*, ed. M. M. Knappen, SCH, 2 [1933] • will, PRO, PROB 11/109, sig. 32 • Essex RO, DP/11/1 [Great Dunmow parish records] • C. Haigh, *Reformation and resistance in Tudor Lancashire* (1975)

Archives Bangor, diocesan records of Bangor • Chester, diocesan records of Chester • London, diocesan records of London | Hatfield House, Hertfordshire, letters to Robert Cecil, bishop of Chester • PRO, state papers domestic, letters to government

Likenesses C. Janssen?, portrait, Fulham Palace • Passe, line engraving, BM, NPG; repro. in H. Holland, *Herōologia* (1620) • engravings • oils, Bodl. Oxf. [*see illus.*]

Wealth at death probably moderate; estate divided equally between wife and children: will, PRO, PROB 11/109, sig. 32

Vaughan, Richard, second earl of Carbery (1600?–1686), royalist army officer, was the principal magnate of southwest Wales during the mid-seventeenth century, and its leading local royalist during the great civil war. He was the elder of two sons of John *Vaughan (1574/5–1634) of Golden Grove, Carmarthenshire (later first earl of Carbery), and his first wife, Margaret Meyrick, daughter of the soldier and courtier Sir Gelly Meyrick, and was probably born in 1600; the dearth of local records for this period makes it possible only to surmise the date of birth from later references to his age. It is known that he travelled to Spain in his youth, perhaps accompanying his father in the train of the prince of Wales in 1623. The first contemporary notices of him come with his elections to represent Carmarthenshire in the parliaments between 1624 and 1629. He was knighted at the coronation of Charles I in February 1626, and succeeded to the earldom on his father's death in 1634. On 15 February 1638 he was admitted a member of Gray's Inn. Carbery first married Bridget Lloyd, daughter of Thomas Lloyd of Llanllŷr, Cardiganshire. Neither the inception nor the end of the marriage can be dated, but she was dead by 8 August 1637, when he wed again. His new wife reflected his widening

Richard Vaughan, second earl of Carbery (1600?–1686), by unknown artist

horizons, being Frances Altham (1620/21–1650), daughter of Sir James Altham of Oxhey in Watford, Hertfordshire. She was the mother of Carbery's two sons, Francis (d. 1667), first husband of Lady Rachel Wriothesley, the future Lady Rachel Russell (1637–1723), and John *Vaughan (bap. 1639, d. 1713), who was to succeed his father as earl of Carbery.

The parliamentarian propagandist John Vicars called Carbery a man of 'pride and menacing insolencies' (John Vicars, Magnalia Dei Anglicana, or, England's Parliamentary-Chronicle, 4 parts, 1646, 2.177), but if this comment is not a mere reflection of partisan hostility then it can at least be said that his fiery character was not related to ambition; the very paucity of reference to him before the outbreak of civil war argues for an unusual lack of interest in national affairs. He played no part in the politics of the Short or Long parliaments, and at the opening of the war itself he was such a dark horse that parliament appointed him to execute its militia ordinance in Carmarthenshire and Cardiganshire, while the king clearly trusted him likewise to act as his own most distinguished supporter in the region. It was Charles who was correct, but we have no trace of his actions until a regiment raised by him and led by his uncle Henry *Vaughan reached the royal army in January 1643. On 4 April, as part of the establishment of regional royalist commands, Carbery himself was commissioned lieutenant-general of the three south-western Welsh counties and instructed to secure them for the king's cause, with a system of county committees intended to provide him with the money and recruits for a local army. Carmarthenshire and Cardiganshire were firmly royalist, but in Pembrokeshire the towns of Tenby

and Pembroke contained a party sympathetic to parliament, and thus the new-made general certainly had work to do. He seems, however, to have preferred to observe an informal local truce; as the parliamentarians of those seaports did not trouble him, so he left them in peace, and both waited for the war to be resolved elsewhere.

This amicable situation was ended by Charles's truce with the Irish insurgents in September 1643, and his decision to withdraw the royal army in Ireland to reinforce the English royalists. The ports of Pembrokeshire were thus placed in a vital strategic position, perfectly positioned for use as parliamentarian bases to disrupt the flow of soldiers to the king, and their reduction by his supporters became an urgent matter. Carbery set about it on 18 August, as the armistice with the Irish seemed to be certain, by persuading most of the Pembrokeshire gentry to declare their intention of helping him to secure Tenby and Pembroke, and provide him with £2000 towards any necessary military action. It seems likely that the earl was hoping that no such action would in fact be necessary, and that this show of strength would cow the ports into compliance; and this is what initially occurred. On 30 August the corporation of Tenby had declared for the king, and by 24 October that of Pembroke had done the same. Carbery appeared to have secured a total and bloodless victory, and was lavishly rewarded. On 24 October he was given an English peerage as Baron Vaughan of Emlyn and on 17 November he was commissioned governor of Milford Haven, a position which gave him direct military control of Pembroke and any outlying forts along the inlet leading to it. It may have been this commission which precipitated a rising among the parliamentarian zealots in Pembroke, led by John Poyer, who seized the port and made actual warfare inevitable at last.

Carbery himself had absolutely no experience of war, and no aptitude for it; nor did he have the services of a gifted veteran. In these circumstances he did his best, issuing a declaration on 11 January 1644 which called up the militia of his three counties to besiege Pembroke, and settled county rates to pay them. These forces were drawn into the towns and castles around Pembroke, and a new fort built across the Haven, and left to blockade the town into surrender, without risking a direct attack upon it. In the absence of siege guns or experienced soldiers this was probably all that he could have done, but the strategy underestimated the enterprise both of parliament and of its adherents in Pembroke. The former relieved the port with a naval squadron, and the latter included the sort of talented veteran whom Carbery lacked, in the person of Rowland Laugharne. On 22 February, reinforced by the sailors from the squadron, Laugharne commenced a series of assaults upon the royalist garrisons around Pembroke, and took them one after the other, including Tenby. Carbery's fatal mistake had been to keep no mobile force in reserve, and so he was unable to halt this process. By the end of March 1644 he had lost the whole of Pembrokeshire, and was recalled to the royal court at Oxford to account for the disaster. His departure—and perhaps his leadership—left the local royalists completely demoralized, and in April, Laugharne took possession of Carmarthenshire and Cardiganshire as well, without resistance. Carbery had lost the entire region of his command.

At Oxford, Carbery was personally exonerated from blame, but it was obvious that he would have to surrender his commission to a proven soldier, so on 8 May 1644 he commenced his journey back to Wales as adviser to his replacement as commander in the south-west, Charles Gerard. After this he vanishes from view for the remainder of the war, apparently retiring to his seat at Golden Grove to sit it out. When Laugharne made a second, and final, conquest of Carmarthenshire in November 1645, parliament resolved that Carbery should be fined £4500 for his former actions. He was, however, defended by Laugharne himself, who wrote to the speaker of the Commons on 18 November, explaining that the earl promised to be an eager and reliable collaborator and that his local standing would make him very useful to parliament in settling the region. Laugharne therefore requested that the fine be remitted. He was opposed by the Pembrokeshire county committee, which had more bitter memories of Carbery as a former opponent. The balance was tipped when the earl himself went to London to plead his case and to mobilize old and new friends in his behalf; Sir John Meyrick and the earl of Essex seem to have been especially influential in achieving the decision of the Commons to cancel the fine upon 16 February 1646. The formalities of this discharge were not completed until 9 April 1647, but after that he was safe.

Carbery repaid his new masters well, by his utter refusal to support the uprising against them in south Wales in April and May 1648, when his old enemies Poyer and Laugharne made common cause with most of the region's royalists and declared for the king. Whatever compelled his decision—caution after his previous narrow escape or a disinclination to ally with former local foes—it proved prudent, as the uprising was crushed while he continued inactive and undisturbed at Golden Grove. A local tale that he narrowly evaded capture by Cromwell, who was instead entertained and charmed by his wife, is a fiction. Throughout the interregnum he led a retired and comfortable life, achieving some vicarious literary fame as the patron of Jeremy Taylor. While a guest in his house, this Anglican divine published several of his most notable works, from *The Great Exemplar* (1649) to the collection of sermons published in 1655 under the title *Golden Grove*. Countess Frances died on 9 October 1650, leaving Carbery to make a last and most prestigious match in July 1652, with Lady Alice Egerton, eleventh and youngest daughter of John *Egerton, first earl of Bridgewater (1579–1649). She was to outlive him by two and a half years, dying in July 1689.

At the Restoration, Carbery was appointed president of the newly re-established council of Wales and the marches, an honour which reflected both his former services as a royalist leader and his status as the foremost resident Welsh peer. He carried out his duties with apparent diligence until 1672, when he was dismissed because of a public scandal concerning his alleged ill treatment, extending to physical mutilation, of servants and tenants on his estate at Dryslwyn, Carmarthenshire. The main legacy of his tenure of the presidency was a literary one, resulting from his patronage of Samuel Butler whom he made his secretary, and steward of Ludlow Castle, the seat of the council; it seems to have been there that Butler wrote the first part of *Hudibras*. After his disgrace Carbery slips from public view; he died on 3 December 1686, probably at Golden Grove, and is presumed to have been buried in Llandeilo Fawr parish church.

Carbery deserves some honour as a patron of letters and a conscientious administrator, but it is very clear that his contemporaries felt more respect for his social position than his personality. He never showed any interest in politics, and his role as a general was forced upon him and became one of the most inglorious of the civil war. His conduct in that war can be praised for prudence and realism rather than for any other virtues, and it is clear that his own taste was for a quiet life as a provincial nobleman; his part in national history may almost be described as accidental.   RONALD HUTTON

Sources F. Jones, 'The Vaughans of Golden Grove', *Transactions of the Honourable Society of Cymmrodorion* (1963), 96–145 · PRO, SP 16/497/148 · *His majesties declaration to all his … subjects in … Cornwall, &c* [with] *The agreement of the Maior, Aldermen and Inhabitants of the towne of Tenby* (1643) · *Mercurius Aulicus* (24 Oct 1643) · *Mercurius Aulicus* (11 Jan 1644) · PRO, SP 19/126, fols. 105–8 · *A true relation of the success of Captain Swanley … (1644) · A true relation of the proceedings of Colonel Laugharne* (1644) · Bodl. Oxf., MS Firth C7, fol. 14 · Bodl. Oxf., MS Firth C8, fols. 346–2 · Bodl. Oxf., MS Dugdale 19, fols. 11–13 · *The earl of Carberyes pedigree* (1646) · W. O. Pughe, ed., *The Cambrian register*, 1 (1796), 164 · *Second report*, HMC, 1/2 (1871); repr. (1874), appx, p. 88 · V. B. Heltzel, ed., 'Richard, earl of Carbery's advice to his son', *Huntington Library Bulletin*, 11 (1937), 59–105
Likenesses portrait, repro. in J. E. Lloyd, *A history of Carmarthenshire*, 2 vols. (1939), vol. 2, facing p. 26 · portrait, Carmarthenshire County Museum [*see illus.*]

Vaughan, Robert (1795–1868), Congregational minister, of Welsh descent, was born in Bristol on 14 October 1795. His parents belonged to the established church. He had no early advantages of education, but showed a taste for historical reading, one of his first purchases being a copy of Sir Walter Ralegh's *History of the World*. He came under the influence of William Thorp (1771–1833), Independent minister at Castle Green, Bristol, who trained him for the ministry and from whom he took his early, over-demonstrative style of preaching.

While still a student Vaughan was invited to serve Angel Street Congregational Church, Worcester, and was ordained on 4 July 1819; among his ordainers were William Jay and John Angell James. He married in 1822 Susanna Ryall of Melcombe Regis, Dorset. They had several children: Robert Alfred *Vaughan was the eldest son; the eldest daughter married Dr Carl Buch, principal of Government College at Bareilly, upper India, who was murdered in 1857 at the outbreak of the Indian mutiny. In March 1825 Vaughan accepted a call to Hornton Street, Kensington, in succession to John Leifchild.

Through the publication of his *Life and Opinions of John de*

Robert Vaughan (1795–1868), by Samuel Bellin, pubd 1850 (after Philip Westcott)

Wycliffe (1828) and *Memorials of the Stuart Dynasty* (1831) Vaughan gained some reputation as a historical writer. In 1833 he was appointed to the chair of history in University College, London, and he published his introductory lecture, *On the Study of General History*, in 1834. In the same year he delivered the Congregational lecture, a series of disquisitions published as *Causes of the Corruption of Christianity* (1834). His connection with University College brought him into contact with whig leaders, and increased his influence as a preacher; people of social position, including Harriet, duchess of Sutherland, were drawn to his services. In 1836 he received a DD from Glasgow University. He continued his historical research, and published the *Protectorate of Oliver Cromwell* (2 vols., 1838) and *The History of England under the House of Stuart* (1840).

In 1843 Vaughan succeeded Gilbert Wardlaw as president and professor of theology at the Lancashire Independent college, which moved on 26 April to new buildings at Whalley Range, Manchester. He published his inaugural discourse, *Protestant Nonconformity*, in 1843. He was dissatisfied with the tone of the *Eclectic Review*, which, under the editorship of Thomas Price, was favouring the militant policy of Edward Miall. Vaughan was opposed to radical political dissent. Only during his last year did he embrace the principles of the Liberation Society. He was also opposed to the voluntary principle in education. To present his own views he launched the *British Quarterly Review*, bringing out the first number in January 1845. During the twenty years of his editorship he kept it at a high intellectual level and, while retaining its nonconformist character and its theological conservatism, admitted on other topics a wide range of writers of different schools. Some of his own articles were collected in *Essays on History, Philosophy, and Theology* (2 vols., 1849). The *British Quarterly Review* was his most influential contribution to the hold that Congregationalism was to achieve in the great centres of population by 1870. Such an outcome coincided with the view that he had expressed in his book *The Age of Great Cities* (1843) that Congregationalism was the authentic religion of urban industrial society. In 1846 Vaughan occupied the chair of the Congregational Union. Returning to the subject of his first publication, he edited for the Wycliffe Society *Tracts and Treatises of John de Wycliffe … with … Memoir* (1845), and published *John de Wycliffe, DD: a Monograph* (1853).

Vaughan was not entirely fitted to be a successful president of the Lancashire Independent college. He had no competence in dogmatic theology and his manner towards students was reserved and undemonstrative. He resigned his post on 20 July 1857, in great perturbation of mind, in the wake of the bitter controversy over the endorsement of the principles of higher criticism by his colleague Dr Samuel Davidson. Although Vaughan voted against Davidson in the college committee, he did not initiate the action. He was succeeded by Henry Rogers (1806–1877).

After ministering for a short time to a small congregation at Uxbridge, Vaughan retired to St John's Wood, and occupied himself with literary work, publishing *Revolutions in English History* (3 vols., 1859–63) and taking his part in the nonconformist publications occasioned by the bicentenary of the Act of Uniformity of 1662. It was a speech by Vaughan at the Congregational Union in autumn 1861 that was the main inspiration for the bicentenary commemoration of 1862. In 1867 Vaughan accepted a call to a newly formed congregation at Torquay. Scarcely had he moved there when he was seized with congestion of the brain followed by typhus. He died at Torquay on 15 June 1868, and was buried there.

Vaughan was a man of striking presence and great platform power, but otherwise he was not popular, and his ministerial career was not as successful as those of contemporaries such as William Jay, John Angell James, and Thomas Binney. However, beside the works specified above and single sermons and speeches, other books of his are significant, particularly because they provide provocative comments on contemporary religious life: *Thoughts on the … State of Religious Parties in England* (1838); *Congregationalism … in Relation to … Modern Society* (1842); *The Modern Pulpit* (1842); and *English Nonconformity* (1862).

ALEXANDER GORDON, *rev.* R. TUDUR JONES

Sources *Robert Vaughan: a memorial* (1869) · 'In memoriam;– Rev. Dr. Vaughan', *British Quarterly Review*, 49/97 (Jan 1869), 160–88 · 'The Rev. Robert Vaughan', *Evangelical Magazine and Missionary Chronicle*, [3rd ser.], 10 (1868), 447–55 · *Congregational Year Book* (1869), 288–91 · E. J. Evans and W. F. Hurndall, eds., *Pulpit memorials* (1878), 261–81 · J. Thompson, *Lancashire Independent College, 1843–93* (1893) · R. Tudur Jones, *Congregationalism in England, 1662–1962* (1962) · A. Peel, *The Congregational two hundred, 1530–1948* (1948)

Archives UCL, letters to Society for the Diffusion of Useful Knowledge
Likenesses R. Woodman, stipple, pubd 1825, NPG · W. Holl, stipple, pubd 1830 (after J. R. Wildman), BM, NPG; repro. in *Evangelical Magazine* · S. Bellin, mezzotint, pubd 1850 (after P. Westcott), BM, NPG [*see illus.*] · engraving (after portrait), repro. in *Robert Vaughan*
Wealth at death under £7000: resworn probate, May 1879, *CGPLA Eng. & Wales* (1868)

Vaughan, Robert Alfred (1823–1857), Congregational minister and writer, was born at Worcester on 18 March 1823, the eldest child of Robert *Vaughan (1795–1868), also a Congregational minister, and his wife, Susanna, *née* Ryall. He was two months premature and never robust. Educated first by his father, he entered University College School, London, in 1836 at the age of thirteen. He passed on to University College, from which he graduated BA with classical honours in 1842. Vaughan's prevailing tastes were literary, and he believed that the life of a scholar clergyman would be congenial to his reserved temperament. In 1843 he became a student in the Lancashire Independent college, Manchester, under his father's presidency. Next year he published his first piece, *The Witch of Endor*, an unremarkable three-act dramatic poem. On his father's encouragement, he read Origen for a long, scholarly article published in the *British Quarterly* (October 1845). It won the commendations of Sir James Stephen and Sir Thomas Noon Talfourd. In 1846 he contributed a dramatic piece, 'Edwin and Elgiva', to the *London University Magazine*.

Having finished his course in Manchester, Vaughan spent a session (1846–7) at the University of Halle, where he came under the influence of Julius Müller and Tholuck. A religious and psychological crisis made him doubt his vocation for a time. He decided that the work of his life was to be the production of a series of ecclesiastical dramas to illustrate the history of the church. Between June and October 1847 he travelled in Italy with his father.

In April 1848 Vaughan became assistant to the octogenarian William Jay at Argyle Chapel, Bath. It was an unfortunate appointment. The congregation were accustomed to Jay's forceful preaching and not all of them took kindly to the very different style of an introverted, scholarly young man who while he was at the chapel was writing articles for the *British Quarterly* on Schleiermacher and Savonarola and planning his work on the mystics. A few months after his installation, on 7 June 1848 he married Jane (*b.* 1827/8), the only child of James Finlay, a bookseller, of Newcastle upon Tyne. With his new financial responsibilities in mind, he stated that the condition of his remaining at the chapel was to be co-pastor with Jay. This was not acceptable either to Jay or to the deacons, and Vaughan therefore resigned, preaching his last sermon on 24 March 1850.

Accepting a call from Ebenezer Chapel, Steelhouse Lane, Birmingham, Vaughan was ordained there on 8 September 1850. The fact that the ordination prayer was offered by John Angell James shows that he had not lost the confidence of the Congregationalist establishment.

However, he was unsuited, both in health and temperament, to minister to a large congregation. While his health declined, he overworked himself in his study. He was learning Spanish and Dutch (being already proficient in French, German, and Italian) to gain access to the writings of mystics, and was contributing constantly to the *British Quarterly*. In the autumn of 1854 he visited Glasgow, but declined a call to succeed Ralph Wardlaw. He returned home ill. In the spring of 1855 he showed symptoms of tuberculosis; he resigned his charge, preaching his last sermon on 24 June. In August he put to press his *Hours with the Mystics*, which was published in March 1856.

This followed Vaughan's own design and interspersed a series of dialogues with studies in narrative form. The literally minded reviewer in the *Christian Observer* declared, 'This sort of literary olio is not at all to our taste' (*Christian Observer*, 1856, 573). The book is extremely broad in scope, ranging from the early oriental mystics, the Neoplatonists, and the Sufis to Teresa of Avila, George Fox, and the Swedenborgians. The overall approach is sympathetic, but infused with Vaughan's English protestant prejudices.

The brief remainder of Vaughan's life was that of an invalid at Bournemouth, St John's Wood, and Westbourne Park, London. Yet he continued to contribute articles to *Fraser's Magazine* as well as to the *British Quarterly*. He died at 19 Alexander Street, Westbourne Park, on 26 October 1857; his wife survived him. An enlarged edition of *Hours with the Mystics* appeared in 1860, edited by his father, while a third edition (1880) was edited by his son Wycliffe Vaughan. ALEXANDER GORDON, *rev.* ANNE STOTT

Sources R. A. Vaughan, *Essays and remains*, 1 (1858), ix–cxiv · R. A. Vaughan, *Hours with the mystics*, ed. [W. Vaughan], 3rd edn, 2 vols. (1880), v–xxiv · *Eclectic Review*, 6th ser., 4 (1858), 252–67 · E. White, ed., *Positive religion versus negative morality* (1857) · *Autobiography of the Rev. William Jay*, ed. G. Redford and J. A. James, 3rd edn (1855), 220 · IGI
Likenesses M. and N. Hannart, stipple, repro. in Vaughan, *Essays and remains*

Vaughan, Robert Powell (1591/2–1667), antiquary, was the only son of Hywel Fychan ap Gruffydd ap Hywel (*d.* 1639) of Gwengraig, near Dolgellau, and his wife, Margaret, second daughter of Edward Owen of Hengwrt, Merioneth, and granddaughter of Lewis *Owen (*d.* 1555), baron of the exchequer of north Wales. On 4 December 1612 he matriculated from Oriel College, Oxford, at the age of twenty, but he left without taking a degree. He married Catherine (1594–1663), daughter of Griffith Nanney, with whom he had four sons and four daughters: Howell Vaughan of Vanner, later sheriff of Merioneth, Ynyr, Hugh, Griffith, Margaret, Jane, Elin, and Ann. His father had acquired Hengwrt from Catherine's brother-in-law by a mortgage but Hywel never lived there himself. Robert was still living at Gwengraig in 1624 and possibly moved to Hengwrt on his marriage, although the date of this is not known. He was on the commission of the peace for Merioneth.

Vaughan's only real publication was *British Antiquities Revisited* (1662) which was largely concerned with the debate over which of the sons of Rhodri Mawr (d. 878) was the eldest; a debate to which the most notable other contribution was that of George Owen's 'An aunswer to north-Wales men that would maintayne Anarawd to be the eldest of his brethren and the superior prince of Wales'. It also included a correction of the pedigree of the earl of Carbery that had appeared in Percy Enderbie's *Cambria triumphans* (1661), making the distinction between Gwaethfoed of Powys and Gwaethfoed of Ceredigion, as well as a short tract on the five royal tribes of Wales. For Vaughan a history ought 'to testifie the truth by consent of the tymes, and immediate succession of princes, otherwise will appear like a broken chaine, wantinge some necessarie linkes to unite the whole' and he thus produced *British Antiquities* 'cheefeley out of a desire to cleere the way for a perfect historie of Wales, yf any shall undertake it'.

Vaughan's other historical labours were also matters of translation and supplementation rather than original writing. He translated *Brut y Twysogion* for James Ussher. In 1663 he also commenced printing an expanded version of David Powel's *Historie of Cambria* before discovering that his material had been used without permission in Enderby's *Cambria triumphans*. Only 128 pages had been printed at that stage and all but a few copies were sold for waste paper. He is also thought to have had a large hand in the writing of Thomas Ellis's *Memoirs of Owen Glendowr*. Other works by Vaughan include *Trioedd ynys Prydain*, a scripture concordance, and a collection of Welsh proverbs with translations. He had John Meredith enquire the cost of publishing the latter two in London in 1655.

Vaughan died on Ascension day (16 May) 1667. In his will he asked to be buried at Dolgellau. He left what has been regarded as the 'premier collection' of Welsh manuscripts, both in quantitative and qualitative terms. It included the oldest manuscripts of the laws of Wales, of Arthurian and other romances, and of the holy grail, together with an early translation of part of Matthew's gospel, historical and medieval theological works, and a very substantial amount of poetry. Disputes over the manuscripts went to law and in 1697 Edward Lhuyd described the library as 'much rifld' (R. T. Gunther, *Early Science in Oxford*, 14, 1945, 348), but the collection remained largely intact, and incorporated into the Peniarth collection donated by Sir John Williams it formed a cornerstone of the National Library of Wales's collection when it was established at Aberystwyth. Vaughan's collection of books fared less well, being finally dispersed in the early nineteenth century, but various catalogues of both manuscripts and books are extant (Tibbott, Davies, and Jones). 'Robert Vaughan and his library' was set by the council of the national eisteddfod as a topic for a major essay in the late 1940s.   MIHAIL DAFYDD EVANS

Sources E. D. Jones, 'Robert Vaughan of Hengwrt', *Journal of the Merioneth Historical and Record Society*, 1 (1949–51), 21–30 • R. Morgan, 'Robert Vaughan of Hengwrt', *Journal of the Merioneth Historical and Record Society*, 8 (1977–80), 397–408 • T. E. Parry, 'Llythyrau Robert Vaughan gyda rhagymadrodd a nodiadau', MA diss., U. Wales, 1961 • Foster, *Alum. Oxon.* • *DWB* • G. Tibbott, W. L. Davies, and E. D. Jones, 'Introduction to handlist of Peniarth manuscripts', *Handlist of manuscripts in the National Library of Wales*, 1 [1940], iii–xxiii **Archives** Cardiff Central Library, corresp., notebooks, and papers • NL Wales, papers: Hengwrt MSS, MSS 472, 5262, 9092–9095, 11058 • Shrops. RRC, Merionethshire Inquisitions, MS 188

Vaughan, Sir Roger (d. 1471). *See under* Vaughan family (*per.* c.1400–c.1504).

Vaughan, Roger William [*name in religion* Bede] (1834–1883), Roman Catholic archbishop of Sydney, born at Courtfield, near Ross-on-Wye, Herefordshire, on 9 January 1834, was the second of the thirteen children of Colonel John Francis Vaughan (1808–1880) of Courtfield, and his first wife, Elizabeth Louisa (1810–1853), daughter of John Rolls of Hendre, Monmouthshire. Four of the five daughters of the marriage became nuns, and of the six sons who became priests, two besides Roger were appointed bishops: Herbert *Vaughan, cardinal-archbishop of Westminster, and John, auxiliary bishop of Salford; another brother, Bernard John *Vaughan, became a Jesuit priest.

At the age of six Vaughan was sent to a private boarding-school in Monmouth, but was withdrawn in 1842 because of poor health. He was to suffer from a weak heart throughout his life. In 1850 he entered St Gregory's College at Downside, near Bath, and on completing his studies joined the Benedictine community there, entering the noviciate on 12 September 1853 and taking his solemn vows on 5 October 1854. The following year he was sent at his father's expense to study in Rome, where he resided at the Benedictine abbey of St Paul's-outside-the-Walls. There he was ordained priest in April 1859. On returning to England he spent two years in charge of the mission at Downside before being appointed in November 1861 professor of metaphysics and moral philosophy at the priory of St Michael at Belmont, Hereford, recently established as the common noviciate and house of studies of the English Benedictine congregation. It also served as the cathedral priory of the diocese of Newport and Menevia. Vaughan was elected prior in 1862, at the early age of twenty-eight, and was twice re-elected. Under his leadership Belmont became a centre of monastic and liturgical renewal. His interest in Thomism bore fruit in the two-volume *Life and Labours of St Thomas of Aquin*, which he published in 1871.

As early as 1866 the ageing archbishop of Sydney, John Bede Polding (1794–1877), himself a Downside monk, had tried to obtain Vaughan as his coadjutor, with right of succession, but it was not until February 1873 that Vaughan accepted the appointment. His pedigree commended him to the British government, but not to the largely Irish Australian episcopate, who had hoped for the appointment of one of their number. Consecrated at Liverpool on 9 March 1873 by Cardinal Manning, Vaughan arrived in Sydney to a tumultuous welcome on 16 December. He took up residence at St John's College, and soon established a style more assertive and decisive than that of Polding, by now universally venerated, but a spent force. His imposing stature and dignified manner were of advantage to him in his dealings with the New South Wales government. On the death of Polding in March 1877 he entered into full possession of the metropolitan see of Sydney. He proved combative and even confrontational, taking the bold step of setting up a separate Catholic elementary school system, independent of state aid. He introduced new teaching orders to run the schools, which more than doubled in number between 1873 and 1883. In carrying through this policy he had to face the opposition not only of the state premier, Sir Henry Parkes, but also of some of his own suffragans, who resented his avowed determination to break what he termed 'the Irish masonry'. His other major achievement was the successful raising of funds for the construction of St Mary's Cathedral. He presided over its dedication on 8 September 1882.

The strain of conflict and personal isolation took its toll of Vaughan's health. In April 1883 he left Sydney for a European tour which was to have culminated in an *ad limina* visit to Rome. He landed at Liverpool on 16 August and proceeded the following day to his uncle's house at Ince Blundell Hall, Lancashire. There, on the night of 17–18 August, he died suddenly of a heart attack. He was buried temporarily at Ince Blundell. His death marked the end of the special relationship of the English Benedictines with the Australian church—an association which had begun with William Ullathorne. His Irish successor, Patrick (later Cardinal) Moran, declined to pay the costs of having his predecessor's remains brought to Sydney. They were removed to Belmont in 1887 and remained there until 1946, when on the initiative of Cardinal Gilroy, archbishop of Sydney, they were finally interred in St Mary's Cathedral, Sydney.   G. MARTIN MURPHY

Sources *AusDB* • F. O'Donoghue, *The bishop of Botany Bay: the life of John Bede Polding, Australia's first Catholic archbishop* (1982) • B. Whelan, *History of Belmont Abbey* (1959), 55–64 • M. Vaughan, *Courtfield and the Vaughans* (1989), 85–91 • J. T. Donovan, *The most revd Roger Bede Vaughan: life and labours* (1883) • H. N. Birt, *Benedictine pioneers in Australia*, 2 vols. (1911) • J. C. Hedley, memoir, *Downside Review*, 3 (1884), 1–27
Archives Sydney Roman Catholic Archdiocesan Archives, corresp. and papers | Downside Abbey, near Bath, corresp. with Ephrem Guy • NL Wales, Courtfield MSS
Likenesses engraving, repro. in Hedley, *Downside Review* • oils, Belmont Abbey, Hereford
Wealth at death £61,828—in Australia: *AusDB* • £1309 9s. 7d.: administration with will, 6 May 1884, *CGPLA Eng. & Wales*

Vaughan, Rowland (c.1590–1667), translator and poet, was as he himself says 'ennyd iau' ('a little younger'; NL Wales, Wrexham 3, 125) than Hugh Nannau, who was born in 1588. He was born at Caer-gai, Llanuwchllyn, the eldest son of John Vaughan of Caer-gai, a manor situated not far from Bala in Merioneth, and his wife, Ellen (or Elin) of the family of Nannau, another manor, situated near Dolgellau in the same county. There is no record of what school he attended, but he did spend at least some time in Oxford, probably at the university there. He refers to this in a letter to a Dr Siôn Elis prefixed to his own translation *Yr arfer o weddi yr Arglwydd* ('The practice of the Lord's prayer', 1658): 'pan fûm yn brith sugno peth ar fronnau eich mammaeth dda chwi, Rhydychen' ('when, after a fashion, I suckled at the breasts of your foster mother, Oxford'). There is no record of his having taken a degree.

Vaughan married Jane, the daughter and heir of Edward Price of Tref Prysg (or Coed Prysg) in Llanuwchllyn, Merioneth. In an elegy composed on his death Hugh Cadwaladr does not mention Vaughan's wife so, presumably, she predeceased her husband. He names six children: John, Edward, William, Elin, Elsbeth, and Marged. In his *Pedigrees of Anglesey and Carnarvonshire Families* (1914) J. E. Griffiths records that Vaughan and his wife had eight children, four boys and four girls. He does not mention William, and the other two names he records are Gabriel and Mary. So it may be that there were nine children all told. The eldest, John, entered Hart Hall, Oxford, in 1635. He later married Catherine, daughter of William Wynne of Y Glyn, Llanaber, Merioneth.

Rowland Vaughan's father, John, was high sheriff of Merioneth in 1613 and 1620; Rowland held the same office in 1642, and his son and heir, John, was high sheriff in 1670. During the turbulent period of the civil war Rowland Vaughan was a staunch royalist in politics and a staunch Anglican in his religion. A contemporary poet, William Phylip, refers to Vaughan being away 'in the war' (W. L. Davies, 'Phylipiaid Ardudwy', *Y Cymmrodor* 42.233). Another poet, Hugh Cadwaladr, refers to his 'bearing arms in war' (NL Wales, 11990, 571). It is said that he was a 'Captain' at the battle of Naseby in 1645 (D. Williams, *A History of Modern Wales*, 1950, 109). His home, Caer-gai, was burnt by parliamentary forces in the same year. His inheritance was given to his nephew. After 1645 it is likely that Vaughan spent some time in hiding, in Cilgellan, on the slopes of Aran Benllyn in Merioneth, and in 1650 he was imprisoned at Caerleon. About that time he began to translate *Eikon Basilike*, purportedly written by Charles I. The translation was left incomplete, and never published. After the wars it was only as a result of years of litigation that he succeeded in regaining his patrimony. He built a new house at Caer-gai, and died there on 18 September 1667.

Rowland Vaughan was a poet, the type 'living on his own food' as it was said—in order to differentiate him and others from poets who attempted to make a living by composing praise poetry to the gentry. His strict-metre poems are what could be expected of a seventeenth-century Welsh squire liking, as he himself said of a friend, 'yn hoffi march a gwalch a milgi' ('liking a horse and a hawk and a hound'; Ellis, 144). His free-metre poetry is of a religious and didactic nature, or is used for political propaganda.

But it is as a translator that Rowland Vaughan is best-known, especially as the translator of *Yr ymarfer o dduwioldeb* (1630), his version of Lewis Bayly's *The Practice of Piety*. Other works published by him, such as *Yr arfer o weddi yr Arglwydd* (1658), a translation of *The Practice of the Lord's Prayer* by John Despagne, provide practical guidance on devotional matters, or hold forth against nonconformists—*Ymddiffyniad rhag pla o schism* (1658), a translation of *A Defence Against the Plague of Schism* by William Brough, is an example. Papists were also told that they had strayed from the true path of the Christian faith. To his way of thinking both they and the nonconformists should be, as he was, devoted members of the Church of England. All his translations fit into the tradition of devotional translations that dominated Welsh prose in the seventeenth century.

In his address to the reader of *Yr ymarfer o dduwioldeb* Vaughan makes the interesting comment that he gained the 'weak mastery' that he had of Welsh letters from his love of the strict-metre poems called *cywyddau* ('deall, mai wrth fwrw fy serch ar gywyddau cymraeg y cefais i y gyfrwyddyd wan sydd gennif').   GWYN THOMAS

Sources G. Thomas, 'Changes in the tradition of Welsh poetry in north Wales in the seventeenth century', DPhil diss., U. Oxf., 1966 · G. Thomas, 'Rowland Vaughan', *Y traddodiad rhyddiaith*, ed. G. Bowen (1970) · *DWB* · M. Ellis, 'Cyflwyniad Rowland Vaughan "Caergai" i'w gyfieithiad o *Eikon Basilike*', *National Library of Wales Journal*, 1 (1939–40), 141–4 · *Carolau a dyri'au duwiol* (1688) · NL Wales, Wrexham 3, 125 · NL Wales, 11990, 571

Vaughan, Simon. *See* Fychan, Simwnt (*d.* 1606).

Vaughan, Stephen (*b.* in or before **1502**, *d.* **1549**), merchant and administrator, was born into the London branch of the Vaughan family, which was of Welsh descent and had joined the ranks of the London mercantile community in the fifteenth century. His father is thought to have been an undistinguished London mercer, who was still alive in 1535 and probably educated his son at St Paul's School. Stephen Vaughan spoke in later life as though he knew John Colet.

Vaughan followed in his father's footsteps, embarking on a commercial career. He was an active member of the Merchant Adventurers. Each year his business caused him to pursue a hectic peripatetic course between the Low Country marts, about which he recorded:

> after the exigencies of the same, so that I am never at rest. I am now at Barrugh [Bergen op Zoom], now at Bruce [Bruges], now at Gamut [Ghent], now here now there, so that not without exceeding trouble can I satisfy to all those to whom I minister … as to please all if it were possible. (BL, Cotton MS Galba B.x, fol. 9r)

Unfortunately, such sources relating to his commercial activities only describe his later years as a merchant. He was held in high regard by the mercantile community and received a pension from the Merchant Adventurers from 1529. On the death of Sir John Hackett in October 1534 he acted as chief factor for the English merchants operating at Antwerp, residing at the English House. Finally, on the death of John Hutton on 5 September 1538, Vaughan was chosen to succeed him both as governor of the company and as Henry VIII's ambassador in the Low Countries. The years 1538 to 1539 marked a high point, not only in his career as a mercer and merchant adventurer but also in his developing role as a diplomat in the service of Sir Thomas Cromwell, principal secretary, and the crown.

Servant to Cromwell and to the crown, c.1520–1539 As early as March 1524 Vaughan was in Cromwell's service and rose with his master. During the 1520s the two men developed a strong, enduring, and mutually supportive relationship. Vaughan enjoyed the hospitality of his master and the wide acquaintanceship that it afforded. It was through Cromwell's influence, for instance, that he was employed by Cardinal Thomas Wolsey, archbishop of York, to 'write the evidence' for his college at Oxford (Richardson, 18). In return Vaughan assisted Cromwell in business negotiations and, as a personal spy during his frequent trips to the Low Countries, he kept him informed of rumours and significant political trends there. Nor was this a fair-weather friendship.

With Cromwell's initial disgrace, following the fall of Wolsey in 1529, he found in Vaughan a true and loyal friend. His letters to his master at this fateful time are worth quoting in full. Writing on 30 October he declared:

> I commend me unto you and am greatly in doubt how you are entreated in this sudden overthrow of my lord your master [Wolsey]. I never longed for to hear from you as now, and like as a true heart is never overthrown with no tempest, like so cannot the same in your trouble, but be now much more thrifty to know your state, and more greedy to show you, if it were possible, by works how much it counteth to serve you. Wherefore, if there be any service in the world which I may do for you, let me have knowledge and be assured of me as of yourself … Though I hear many things of you which please me no, yet do I doubt but your truth and wisdom shall deliver you from danger. You are more hated for your master's sake than for anything which I think you have wrongfully done any man.   (PRO, SP 1/55, fol. 246r)

Vaughan wrote on 3 February 1530 from Bergen op Zoom, immediately following Cromwell's restoration to favour, telling him how relieved he was to learn that his master had weathered the storm successfully. 'You now sail in a sure haven', he observed, but hastened to warn him against further complications, 'a merry semblance of weather often trusteth men into dangerous seas, not thinking to be suddenly oppressed with tempest, when unawares they be prevented and brought in great jeopardy' (PRO, SP 1/56, fol. 252r). Such steadfast and unstinting support was given, moreover, at a time when he was beset with his own problems. No longer able to depend on Cromwell's protection he fell prey to internecine struggles of a religious nature, which in 1529 wrought havoc within the ranks of the Merchant Adventurers. He was cited to appear before Cuthbert Tunstall, bishop of London, on charges of heresy at the instigation of Hutton, the then governor of the company, charges from which he only finally freed himself in 1531.

With Cromwell's return to Henry's favour in 1530, the heat went out of this affair and Vaughan was once again able to pursue his career based as it was on his intimate association with his master and friend. Throughout the years 1530 to 1539 life was hectic for Vaughan as he combined the roles of diplomat and merchant. November 1530 again saw him in the Low Countries. Cromwell dispatched him to find William Tyndale, in order to urge him to return to England, a task that not only absorbed much of Vaughan's time during the years 1530 and 1531 but also ultimately proved completely fruitless. Neither his lack of success nor the king's resultant displeasure seems to have set back his career as a diplomat. Another four major missions followed between 1532 and 1539, during which time he never gave up his mercantile activities. In December 1532 he was sent to France to report on the political situation, returning to Calais by the end of July 1533. Almost immediately thereafter, on 28 July, he left that city to join

Christopher Mont at Antwerp, from where the two men set out to undertake negotiations with the German princes, a mission that finished only in December. Then after a year's respite, during which he became chief factor for the English merchants operating at Antwerp, he was again employed in 1535, in the role of confidential messenger, on a secret mission to Denmark. Returning to England in January 1536 he was sent by the king to observe an interview between Eustache Chapuys and Katherine of Aragon, which took place just before 'the Dowager's' death. His role on this occasion, as the imperial ambassador made clear to Charles V, was to 'spy on my movements and report what I might say or do during my visit' (*CSP Spain, 1536–8*, no. 3). Vaughan married Margery (*d.* 1544), whose brother John Gwyneth was his executor. They had a son, Stephen (*b.* 1536/7), and two daughters, Anne *Locke (*c.*1530–1590x1607) and Jane. Finally, in the autumn of 1538 he accompanied Thomas Wriothesley, clerk of the signet, on an embassy to the Low Countries to establish closer amity and to confer with the regent, Mary of Hungary, regarding Henry's proposed marriage with Christina, dowager duchess of Milan. When these negotiations broke down Wriothesley returned home in March 1539. Vaughan remained in Brussels as resident ambassador and governor of the Merchant Adventurers. It was in this capacity that he entertained Anne of Cleves on her passage to England in December 1539, accompanying her to London, where they arrived at Christmas. He returned to Brussels in January 1540.

The 1530s saw Vaughan rise rapidly in the service of the crown, yet the rewards for his devoted service were limited in comparison with leading courtiers. In July 1531 he was appointed writer of the king's books, which carried an annual salary of £20. In 1533, as a reward for his work in Germany, he was granted an annuity of £20 and in 1534 he was appointed as clerk of dispensations and faculties in chancery, a post that he held *in absentia*. Nor did he fare as well as he might have expected from Cromwell, who obtained for him the priory of St Mary Spital, in Shoreditch, London, and secured for his wife her appointment as silk-woman to Anne Boleyn. At least until 1544 he still relied on his earnings as a merchant.

Royal agent, 1539–1546 From 1539 to 1544 Vaughan's work for the crown in the Low Countries was mainly of a commercial character. Following his return to Brussels in January 1540 he became embroiled in the economic turmoil of the summer and autumn before returning to Flanders in 1541 to assist Sir Edward Carne in securing the repeal of imperial legislation impeding English commerce. With the long-awaited outbreak of war between Valois and Habsburg in July 1542, Vaughan's service to the crown centred on the recruitment of mercenaries and raising loans on the Antwerp bourse. In March 1544 he was appointed commissary in the Low Countries and Germany and was dispatched with Thomas Chamberlain to recruit mercenaries to operate with the English army. This task was vitally important because Henry needed more professional soldiers. For three months Vaughan and Chamberlain pursued a hazardous course. Vaughan's

life was on more than one occasion threatened, before he was able to bring this motley array of recruits (or at least some of them) to join the king's army at Calais.

Only with this work completed was Vaughan permitted to arrange his oft-requested passage to London to be at the bedside of his ailing wife—and even then he arrived too late. She had died on 16 September, ten days before his arrival. Nor did an uncaring privy council leave him long to grieve. In October he was back in Antwerp and only after the strongest representations was he allowed in early November to make a hurried trip home to put his affairs in order—on the condition that he returned to the continent by 21 October. Most pressing was the task of providing for the care of his children. Vaughan's thoughts thus turned to marrying again but, confined as he was to the Low Countries, this was no easy task. Pleas to find him a wife addressed to the king's secretary, Sir William Paget, and then to Baron Wriothesley, lord chancellor, produced no result. Indeed it was to be another year before in February 1546 he found himself another partner—Margery Brinklow (*d.* 1557), the impoverished widow of the London mercer Henry Brinklow, who died in 1545/6. Even then, so little could he be spared from his official duties that his new bride had to pass over to Calais, where the couple were married in the private chapel of Sir George Brooke, ninth Lord Cobham, deputy of Calais, on or shortly after 27 April. They had no children.

From the time of his appointment as the crown's chief financial agent in the Low Countries in May 1544 until his resignation from the post on 8 September 1546, whatever his personal problems, Vaughan was rarely absent from Antwerp. Ever since the fateful instruction in May 1544 when, amid a myriad of fund-raising schemes, the king ordered Vaughan to raise a loan on the Antwerp bourse, his stay in that city was virtually uninterrupted. Under his guidance, during the years from 1544 to 1546 Henry's mounting debts were managed with exemplary care. Secure in the support of the privy council, initially Vaughan's primary concern was with gaining some knowledge of the labyrinthine tactics of the denizens of the bourse—the southern German merchant bankers, brokers like Jaspar Ducci, and underwriters. Exploiting Vaughan's ignorance of market operations during his first year as royal factor, these men managed to milk the English crown by creating a major difference between the nominal and real interest rates on loans raised for it. Vaughan, however, was an apt pupil. Before leaving his post he was able to cut through the tangle of financial ploys. He simplified the process for negotiations and established direct links with the Antwerp agents of the southern German merchant bankers, which allowed him to reduce transactions costs and the real interest rate paid by the English crown. By the accession of Edward VI in 1547, Vaughan had managed to establish a place for the crown on the Antwerp market, which was commensurate with its true credit standing.

Yet once again, in spite of giving up his mercantile activity and devoting himself wholeheartedly to the exigencies of royal service, he was not as well rewarded as he might have expected to be. In November 1542 he was the recipient of seven small pieces of property in London. He acquired a better position as under-treasurer at the Tower of London mint on 25 March 1544, which brought with it an annual salary of £133 13s. 4d. It was to this post and the clerkship of faculties in chancery that he returned after his resignation in September 1546. He lived in London with his new wife until his death there on 25 December 1549. He was buried at St Mary-le-Bow, London. It would be difficult to disagree with W. C. Richardson's view that Vaughan rose from obscurity and despite years of devoted royal service, during which he firmly established English crown finance at Antwerp, died inconspicuously, and was soon forgotten.　　　　　　　　　　　　IAN BLANCHARD

Sources W. C. Richardson, *Stephen Vaughan, financial agent of Henry VIII: a study of financial relations with the Low Countries* [1953] · I. Blanchard, 'English royal borrowing at Antwerp, 1544–1574', *Finances publiques et finances privées au bas moyen âge: actes du colloque tenu à Gand le 5–6 mai 1995*, ed. M. Boone and W. Prevenier (1996), 57–74 · I. Blanchard, *International lead production and trade in the 'age of the Saigerprozess', 1460–1560* (Stuttgart, 1994), 170–72 · *LP Henry VIII*, vols. 5–14, 17, 19 · HoP, *Commons, 1509–58* · M. L. Robertson, 'Thomas Cromwell's servants: the ministerial household in early Tudor government and society', PhD diss., U. Cal., Los Angeles, 1975 · G. J. Millar, *Tudor mercenaries and auxiliaries, 1485–1547* (Charlottesville, VA, 1980)
Archives BL, corresp. with Cobham, Harley MS 283 · BL, corresp. with Henry VIII, Thomas Cromwell, etc., Cotton MSS
Wealth at death property with annual rent of £26 6s. 8d. and house at St Mary Spital: HoP, *Commons, 1509–58*

Vaughan, Sir Thomas (d. 1483), courtier, was the son of Robert Vaughan of Monmouth and his wife, Margaret; claims that he was related to the Vaughans of Brecknockshire are not substantiated [see Vaughan family (*per. c.*1400–*c.*1504)]. He entered royal service, perhaps with Beaufort patronage—on 30 March 1443 John Beaufort, earl of Somerset (d. 1444), urged his grant of denizenship. In 1446, as king's esquire, he was appointed steward and receiver of the Beauchamp estates in Herefordshire and the marches, but by 1450 he had moved to London as an esquire for the body, and (18 July) master of the king's ordnance for life. He was well rewarded, became a king's serjeant, and acquired a house named Garlick in Stepney which was a meeting-place of the influential. By 1456 he was a councillor of the king's half-brother, Jasper Tudor (d. 1495). Vaughan was employed as an envoy to Burgundy (1457–8), and he sat as MP for Marlborough (1455–6) and JP for Middlesex (1457–8). In 1459 the approaching conflict between Queen Margaret and Richard, duke of York, made him reassess his loyalties, and it was later alleged that he entered into a conspiracy with York's friends (4 July). He was among the Yorkists dispersed at Ludford Bridge (12 October), and was attainted in the Coventry parliament in December; but he returned with the Yorkist lords from Calais in 1460. Once they had captured Henry VI at Northampton (10 July), Vaughan resumed mastership of the ordnance and became keeper of the great wardrobe. He soon—between 28 July and 18 October—married Eleanor, daughter of Sir Thomas Arundel of Betchworth, Surrey, and widow of the Lancastrian Sir

Thomas Brown; for £1000 Vaughan secured Brown's forfeited estates in south-east England. Queen Margaret's victory at St Albans (17 February 1461) caused him to flee with York's treasure, but he was captured at sea by French pirates.

Louis XI resisted Margaret's request that he hand Vaughan over to her, and in October 1461 Edward IV contributed £200 to his ransom. He returned to Yorkist service in 1462 as esquire for the body and (June 1465) keeper of the great wardrobe, treasurer of the chamber, and master of the king's jewels. Thereafter he was a favoured and protected royal servant, who was again employed on embassies to Burgundy, France, and the Hanse, and was appointed JP in Kent, Surrey, and Sussex (1464–6), and sheriff of Surrey–Sussex (1466–7). In January 1469 he became keeper of the hanaper.

Vaughan may have shared Edward IV's exile in 1470–71; after the king's return he assumed further responsibilities, especially in royal estate management. In July 1471 he was appointed chamberlain and councillor of the prince of Wales, and was prominent in supervising his estates and his upbringing. In the 1470s he was a central figure in exploiting the estates that fell to the crown, including those of Mowbray (1477) and Clarence (1478), and in developing the prince's council in Wales and the marches; as a king's councillor he was knighted in 1475 and was MP for Cornwall in 1478. Vaughan had close relations with prominent nobles, including the Woodvilles and Richard of Gloucester—the latter resided at Garlick in 1473–4; at Westminster he built a mansion (*c.*1474) which seems to have served as a residence for the prince. When Edward IV died (9 April 1483) Vaughan was with the prince at Ludlow. He was in the party which left on 24 April to accompany Edward V to his coronation. They were intercepted by Gloucester and the duke of Buckingham, and Vaughan, along with Richard Grey and Sir Richard Haute, was arrested in the king's lodgings at Stony Stratford on 30 April, accused of plotting against Gloucester. By now an 'aged knight' (*Crowland Chronicle Continuations*), he was confined at Pontefract. Some weeks later, he was condemned and on 25 June executed, a victim of Edward IV's trust and Richard of Gloucester's ambition.　　　R. A. GRIFFITHS

Sources *Chancery records* · PRO · Rymer, *Foedera*, 2nd edn · *RotP* · N. H. Nicolas, ed., *Proceedings and ordinances of the privy council of England*, 7 vols., RC, 26 (1834–7) · E. D. Jones, 'The parentage of Sir Thomas Vaughan', *National Library of Wales Journal*, 8 (1953–4), 349 · N. Pronay and J. Cox, eds., *The Crowland chronicle continuations, 1459–1486* (1986) · C. L. Kingsford, ed., *Chronicles of London* (1905) · C. L. Kingsford, *English historical literature in the fifteenth century* (1913) · A. F. Sutton and P. W. Hammond, eds., *The coronation of Richard III: the extant documents* (1983) · C. L. Scofield, *The life and reign of Edward the Fourth*, 2 vols. (1923) · C. Ross, *Edward IV* (1974)
Likenesses brass, V&A

Vaughan, Sir Thomas (*fl. c.*1456). *See under* Vaughan family (*per. c.*1400–*c.*1504).

Vaughan, Thomas (d. *c.*1493). *See under* Vaughan family (*per. c.*1400–*c.*1504).

Vaughan, Thomas (1621–1666), hermetic philosopher and alchemist, was the son of Thomas Vaughan (*c.*1586–1658)

of Llansanffraid (St Bridget's), Brecknockshire, and his wife, Denise Jenkin (*b. c.*1593), daughter and heir of David Morgan of Llansanffraid. Thomas and his elder twin brother, the poet Henry *Vaughan, were born at Newton by Usk and were the oldest surviving children of the marriage for whom there is clear evidence. Although no portrait is known of either Henry or Thomas, they may have been identical twins, since their similar appearance in adulthood was remarked upon by their friend Thomas Powell in a poem prefacing Henry's *Olor Iscanus* (1651). Allusions in the brothers' writings indicate that the family was bilingual in Welsh and English.

Education and early career Between 1632 and 1638 Henry and Thomas were tutored by the rector of nearby Llangattock, Matthew Herbert, to whom both brothers later wrote verses that indicated their affection and respect. They were then sent to Oxford; Thomas Vaughan was admitted to Jesus College on 4 May 1638, matriculated on 14 December 1638, was promoted from commoner to scholar in May 1641, and took his BA degree on 18 February 1642. Early in his Oxford years he demonstrated his royalist sympathies in a Latin poem contributed to a volume celebrating the birth of Henry, duke of Gloucester, *Horti Carolini rosa altera* (1640). He also became an admirer of William Cartwright, to whose posthumously published *Comedies, Tragi-Comedies, with other Poems* (1651) he was to contribute a complimentary poem. The latter part of his time at Jesus was disrupted by the civil war; Henry Vaughan, in his 1673 letter to John Aubrey retailing biographical information about himself and his twin, says only that Thomas remained at Oxford for ten or twelve years, 'and (I thinke) he could be noe lesse than M^r of Arts' (H. Vaughan to Aubrey, 1673, Bodl. Oxf., MS Wood F.39, fol. 216), but he was clearly unsure of the details.

Henry is more definite about Thomas's ordination: 'ordayned minister by bishop Mainwaringe & presented to the Rectorie of St Brigets by his kinsman Sr George Vaughan' (H. Vaughan to Aubrey, 1673, Bodl. Oxf., MS Wood F.39 fol. 216). No date is given, but the previous rector of Llansanffraid died in 1643 or 1644, and by 1645 Thomas would have reached the age of twenty-four, the legal minimum for ordination as a priest. However, he did not long enjoy the benefice. Although he is described as rector of Llansanffraid in Michaelmas term 1649, in a lawsuit that he brought for trespass on a plot of ground known as Little Island, sequestrations were being carried out against Anglican clergy and royalist sympathizers in Wales from as early as 1645, and in 1650 Thomas Vaughan was formally evicted under the Act for Better Propagation and Preaching the Gospel in Wales, Ejecting Ministers and Schoolmasters, and Redresse of Grievances. The propagators' charges against him were that he was 'a comōn drunkard, a common swearer, no preacher, a whoremast^r, & in armes personally against ye Parliament' (Bodl. Oxf., MS Walker e.7, fol. 213b).

Evidence from their own writings and from other records corroborates this last charge: the Vaughan twins did indeed take up arms in the royalist cause. Both were probably present at the defeat suffered by the king's forces at Rowton Heath near Chester on 24 September 1645, and a Captain Thomas Vaughan is mentioned in a list of royalist officers taken prisoner, along with a Captain Henshaw. This may be a cousin of Vaughan's associate Thomas Henshaw, to whom Vaughan dedicated *Magia Adamica* in 1650, describing him as his 'best of Friends'. In July 1648 the Vaughans' younger brother William died as a result of what Thomas described in *The Man-Mouse* as a 'glorious imployment' (*The Man-Mouse*, 1650, 85), which perhaps alludes to a fatal injury suffered in the royalist cause; he himself seems to have been at Oxford at the time, as the preface to *Anthroposophia theomagica* is dated 'Oxonii 48' and the book itself concludes with an apology to the effect that it was 'compos'd in *Haste*, and in my *Dayes of Mourning*, on the *sad Occurence of a Brother's Death*'.

By May 1650, on the evidence of Hartlib's 'Ephemerides', Vaughan ('the author of Anthroposophia', as Hartlib calls him) and Thomas Henshaw were living at Kensington and collaborating on alchemical enterprises. Henshaw's circle of alchemical acquaintance was wide, and his family connections included William Backhouse of Swallowfield; if he were not already acquainted with them, Vaughan could have been introduced by Henshaw to men like Robert Child (who included Vaughan in his plans for a 'chymical club') and Elias Ashmole.

Publication and controversy Vaughan's first tracts on hermetic philosophy, *Anthroposophia theomagica* and *Anima magica abscondita*, were issued together in 1650. They attracted considerable interest in his own circle, as well as the hostile attentions of the Cambridge Platonist Henry More. They were followed in the same year by *Magia Adamica*, issued with *The Man-Mouse*, and in 1651 by *Lumen de lumine*, issued with *The Second Wash*, the latter items in both volumes being Vaughan's refutations of More. All these titles appeared under Vaughan's pseudonym of 'Eugenius Philalethes' and were brought out by the same publisher, Humphrey Blunden, known for his interest in occult writers, including Boehme. He is likely to be the same H. Blunden who appended a verse postscript to *Anima magica abscondita* and who was reputed a 'happy Operatour in Chymistrie' (H. More, 'The second lash', in *Enthusiasmus triumphatus*, 1656 edn, 208).

The dedication of *Anthroposophia theomagica* to the Rosicrucian brotherhood may be only one nail in the coffin of Vaughan's credibility in the eyes of posterity, but responses among his contemporaries were more mixed. His vehement anti-Aristotelianism and his espousal of such authorities as the fabulous antique sage Hermes Trismegistus, the occult philosopher Cornelius Agrippa, the cabbalist Johann Reuchlin, and the alchemist Michael Sendivogius positioned him in an intellectual milieu that attracted, even if fleetingly, some of the most original minds of his time. Henry More attacked him in frivolous or scatological terms in two publications: *Observations upon 'Anthroposophia theomagica', and 'Anima magica abscondita'* (1650) and *The Second Lash of Alazonomastix* (1651). Vaughan responded in kind in his point-by-point counterblasts, *The Man-Mouse* and *The Second Wash*. Neither party comes well out of this exchange, but underlying the Oxford versus Cambridge logomachy and *odium academicum* there is a serious confrontation between two opposing world-views: Vaughan's magical, hermetic, and cabbalistic, More's anti-enthusiastic and (somewhat incoherently) Cartesian.

Vaughan was clearly given to cantankerous criticism, and not only in his controversy with More. His comments on Ashmole's *Theatrum chemicum Britannicum* (1652), themselves acidly annotated in cipher by Ashmole (Bodl. Oxf., MS Rawl. D 864 fol. 222), include remarks on the level of 'ha ha hie. Sympleton' and 'Away Animal thou liest'. Of the ending of 'The Magistery' (*Theatrum chemicum Britannicum*, 342–3) by Ashmole's alchemical mentor William Backhouse:

> Oh happy man that understands
> This Medicen to atchieve!

Vaughan sneered 'The author was never so happy', to which Ashmole retorted 'If the observator was as happy he would be more modest in his censures'. None the less, Ashmole's annotated copy of Pierre Borel's *Bibliotheca chimica* (Bodl. Oxf., MS Ashmole 1374) shows that he possessed all Vaughan's philosophical publications.

Vaughan's next work, *Aula lucis*, came out in 1652 under the initials 'S. N.' (the last letters of his names) but despite the change of pseudonym and publisher it is vouched for as his by Henry Vaughan. It has been suggested that the dedicatee, 'Seleucus Abantiades', who, Vaughan says, knew him from his childhood, was Matthew Herbert. Also in 1652 Vaughan published an English version by an unidentified translator of the key Rosicrucian text, the *Fama et confessio*. To this *Fame and Confession of the Fraternitie of R: C:* Vaughan added an extensive preface. For his final philosophical discourse, *Euphrates, or, The Waters of the East* (1655), he reverted to the pseudonym of Eugenius Philalethes; its publisher was Humphrey Moseley, who was also Henry Vaughan's publisher. Finally, in 1657, Vaughan wrote an introduction to *The Chymists Key*, Henry's translation of Heinrich Nolle's *De generatione rerum naturalium liber*. The 'Discourse' of his own to which he alludes in the concluding words of this piece was apparently never published, and no further work of his appeared in print in his lifetime. Nor did any work achieve a second edition, although *Magia Adamica* and *Euphrates* were reissued in 1656 and 1671 respectively.

Marriage, later career, and death Vaughan married on 28 September 1651; his wife's name was Rebecca, but that and the details that Vaughan himself preserved about their life together are all that is definitely known about her. She died on 17 April 1658, probably in London at lodgings owned by a Mistress Highgate, with whom Vaughan left some of her belongings. On 26 April Rebecca's burial was recorded at Meppershall in Bedfordshire, which led Hutchinson to suggest that she came from there. The name Rebecca occurs in the family of the ejected rector of Meppershall, Timothy Archer, but there is no evidence for the existence of a Rebecca Archer who might have been Thomas Vaughan's wife.

On the evidence of Vaughan's notebook 'Aqua vitae: non vitis' (BL, MS Sloane 1741), the marriage was a happy one. He appears to have begun 'Aqua vitae' shortly after Rebecca's death; the title-page motto suggests that he saw it partly as therapy for his grief, and many pages are adorned with their joint initials, T. R. V., and pious exclamations. It seems that the Vaughans had supported themselves by the 'naturall secrets' ('Aqua vitae', fol. 105*v*) that enabled them to practise chemical medicine, and 'Aqua vitae' was intended in the first instance as a record of the alchemical work Vaughan carried out with his wife's encouragement. Rebecca, too, was active in the preparation of medicaments, as among her belongings listed by Vaughan after her death was 'a great glass full of eye-water, made att the Pinner of Wakefield, by my deare wife, and my sister vaughan [Henry's first wife Catherine], who are both now with god'. (Hutchinson identifies the Pinner (or Pinder) of Wakefield as an inn in the parish of St Pancras, half a mile north of Gray's Inn; prior to living there, the Vaughans had lodged at a Mr Coalman's in Holborn.)

Vaughan continued to make additions to 'Aqua vitae' for several years, the latest dated entry being an alchemical extraction on 8 August 1662, but the dreams and premonitions and affectionate remembrances of his wife were mainly written down in the year following her death, to April 1659. The entry for 9 April 1659 suggests that there may have been some truth in the propagators' accusation of disorderly behaviour against Vaughan, since he describes a dream encounter with 'a certaine person, with whom I had in former times revelled away many yeares in drinking' (fol. 103).

Towards the end of the 1650s Vaughan became involved in an unfortunate episode with a chemical practitioner of apparently parliamentarian sympathies called Edward Bolnest. A typical alchemical imbroglio, it began with Bolnest's advancing money to Vaughan on the understanding that Vaughan would disclose to him the secrets of his art, only to be disappointed. Vaughan's counterclaim, in a deposition dated 18 May 1661 (Chanc. Pro. Hamilton 354.45) that shows him to have been living at the time in the parish of St Giles-in-the-Fields, hinged on Bolnest's threats and violence in his attempts to recover the moneys and goods he believed that Vaughan had accepted under false pretences. There is apparently no record of how or if the dispute was resolved.

The political and religious settlement after the Restoration would have been to Vaughan's liking, but, for whatever reason, he did not reclaim the Llansanffraid living. Possibly he had hopes of advancement from his new patron, Sir Robert Moray; Moray was not only a good chemist but also a favourite with Charles II, whom he assisted in chemical operations in the royal laboratory in Whitehall. At the end of 1665 Moray withdrew from London to Albury, between Oxford and Thame, because of the plague; there he kept himself occupied with chemical experiments. Vaughan seems to have joined him, as it was in the house of Samuel Kem, minister at Albury, that Vaughan suddenly died on 27 February 1666. Wood, in noting the circumstances, cited an unidentified Harris of

Jesus College as his source: 'Eugenius Philalethes died as twere suddenly when he was operating strong mercurie, some of which by chance getting up into his nose killed him' (Wood, 3, col. 722). The expenses of Vaughan's burial at Albury on 1 March were paid by Moray, to whom, according to Henry Vaughan, Vaughan left all his books and manuscripts.

The canon of Vaughan's works is based on information given by Henry Vaughan to Aubrey in 1673, supplemented by Ashmole's *Bibliotheca chimica* list. *A Brief Naturall History* by 'Eugenius Philalethes' (1669), though placed among Thomas Vaughan's oeuvre by William Cooper in his *Catalogue of Chymicall Books* (1675), was rejected from the canon by Anthony Wood on stylistic grounds. One posthumous publication should, however, be added. Those of Thomas's Latin poems that were available to Henry were published by the latter as a separate section at the back of *Thalia rediviva* (1678); they conclude with a note to the effect that many other pieces were lacking, among them 'Alcippus et Jacintha', described as 'Poema heroicum absolutissimum' (*Thalia rediviva*, 93), having been left behind in Oxford. Besides conventional love poems to 'Stella' and some complimentary verse, Thomas's contributions to *Thalia rediviva* include epitaphs on Charles I and Archbishop Laud, a virulent satire on an unidentified political opponent under the name of Vertumnus, and a series on the executed royalist Colonel John Morris, hero of the siege of Pontefract in 1648. Apart from these Latin poems and the *Horti Carolini rosa altera* and Cartwright poems already discussed, he also contributed complimentary verses in English to his brother's *Olor Iscanus* and in Latin to Thomas Powell's *Elementa opticae* (1651).

Vaughan in retrospect Vaughan's reputation has undergone both neglect and misrepresentation at the hands of posterity, and his standing among his contemporaries was ambiguous. In character he was capable both of the coarseness and arrogance seen in his dealings with More and Ashmole and of the reflective tenderness of the memoranda in 'Aqua vitae'. Of himself he observed in his postscript to *The Fame and Confession* that his nature was 'more *Melancholy* then *Sociable*' (*The Fame and Confession*, 57). As a prose stylist too he ranged from the lyricism of his description of Thalia and the *prima materia* in *Lumen de lumine* to the crude invective of his polemics with More. In the latter he 'Clevelandized', affecting a prose version of the swaggering satire of John Cleveland, the royalist poet of whom there are many echoes in his writings. Vaughan may well have known Cleveland personally after Cleveland had abandoned Cambridge for Oxford in the mid-1640s; Cleveland had many imitators, but in Vaughan's case the taunting of More, the Cambridge man, in the language of this prestigious refugee from the other university would have had a particular piquancy.

Opinions about Vaughan differed sharply at the time of his first publications. Child and Hartlib both alluded to his books in terms that suggest they caused a stir among the natural philosophers, and in late 1650 George Starkey was planning a refutation (which seems never to have been written, or not to have survived). As regards his fame as an alchemical operator, Hartlib in his 'Ephemerides' seems to be inclined to give Vaughan the benefit of the doubt over whether he possessed the *Menstruum Universale* or *prima materia*; the passage is obscure, but seems to indicate that the experience that Robert Boyle had had of this substance—whatever it might have been—corroborated Vaughan's. Vaughan gives a recipe for the *Menstruum Universale* in 'Aqua vitae' (fol. 12v.) About this time, Backhouse told Ashmole that Vaughan was experimenting on the spirit of saltpetre 'and of late he added May-dew to it' (Bodl. Oxf., MS Rawl. D 864 fol. 207).

Although some took Vaughan and his work seriously, there were contemporary detractors other than Henry More. For instance, John Gaule's *Mus-mantia* (1652)—the title is an obvious pun on Vaughan's *Man-Mouse*—contains much detailed quotation derived from a hostile reading of *Magia Adamica*. Later Vaughan received the back-handed compliment of being among the victims of the many and various plagiarisms of John Heydon, particularly in *The Harmony of the World* (1662). Samuel Butler pokes fun at Vaughan in part 1 of *Hudibras* (1663) as one of the gurus of the mystical squire Ralpho and also in his prose portrait 'An Hermetic Philosopher'. In a more serious vein, Samuel Parker, bishop of Oxford, debunks 'our late English *Rosie Crusians*' and singles out 'the controversial Rencountres of Eugenius Philalethes', along with the writings of Heydon, as examples of language unbecoming philosophical discourse (*A Free and Impartial Censure, of the Platonick Philosophie*, 2nd edn, 1667, 75). Swift complained in 1704 that *Anthroposophia theomagica* was 'a Piece of the most unintelligible Fustian, that, perhaps, was ever publish'd in any Language' (*A Tale of a Tub*, 1704). Notwithstanding this, Vaughan's writings were known in continental Europe, and in the late seventeenth and first half of the eighteenth centuries several of his works were circulated in German translation.

Nineteenth-century enthusiasm for the occult brought a new lease of life to Vaughan's reputation as a Rosicrucian and as the purported possessor of the elixir of life, and he was endowed in occultist circles with the character of a magus. It is largely in this context and for this readership that A. E. Waite prepared his collected edition of Vaughan's works for the Theosophical Society (1919). Only in the last third of the twentieth century did the reassessment of Rosicrucianism against the background of seventeenth-century philosophy and politics enable a fresh look to be taken at those who associated themselves with the movement; the intellectual bases of alchemy too, stripped of the pretensions and secrecy of its more dubious practitioners, likewise came under serious reappraisal, and both trends served to situate Vaughan more securely in the intellectual milieu of his day. Vaughan certainly preferred to think of himself as a philosopher: 'for *Alchymie* in the common acceptation, and as it is a *torture of metalls*, I did never believe; much less did I study it' (*Euphrates*, sig. A3–3ᵛ). JENNIFER SPEAKE

Sources *The works of Thomas Vaughan*, ed. A. Rudrum (1984) • F. E. Hutchinson, *Henry Vaughan* (1947) • T. Vaughan, 'Aqua vitae', 1658–62, BL, MS Sloane 1741 • *Thomas and Rebecca Vaughan's 'Aqua vitae, non*

vitis', ed. D. R. Dickson (2001) · A. M. Guinsburg, 'Henry More, Thomas Vaughan and the late Renaissance magical tradition', *Ambix*, 27 (1980), 36–58 · F. B. Burnham, 'The More–Vaughan controversy: the revolt against philosophical enthusiasm', *Journal of the History of Ideas*, 35 (1974), 33–49 · J. Ferguson, ed., *Bibliotheca chemica*, 2 vols. (1906) · *Elias Ashmole (1617–1692): his autobiographical and historical notes*, ed. C. H. Josten, 5 vols. (1966 [i.e. 1967]), vol. 2, p. 575 · Wood, *Ath. Oxon.* · H. Vaughan, letter to Aubrey, 1673, Bodl. Oxf., MS Wood F.39, fol. 216 · Bodl. Oxf., MS Walker, e.7, fol. 213b · Bodl. Oxf., MS Rawl. D. 864

Vaughan, Thomas (*fl.* **1772–1820**), playwright, was the son of a lawyer, and was educated in the same profession. He obtained the post of clerk to the commission of peace of the city of Westminster, and about 1782 became captain of a company of the Westminster Volunteers..He had a great love of the stage, and devoted much of his leisure time to dramatic literature. In 1772 he wrote a series of essays in the *Morning Post* on the Richmond Theatre. In 1776 he produced a farce entitled *Love's Metamorphoses*, which was acted for Mrs Wrighten's benefit at Drury Lane on 15 April. It was afterwards rejected by John Philip Kemble, manager of Drury Lane, in 1789, and by George Colman the younger, manager of the Haymarket, in 1791. Vaughan published it in 1791, under the title *Love's Vagaries*, with a dedication to the rejectors. In 1776 he published another farce, entitled *The Hotel, or, The Double Valet*, which appeared at Drury Lane on 21 November. His next dramatic venture was *Deception*, a political comedy, which was acted at Drury Lane on 28 September 1784. None of Vaughan's plays possessed much merit, and they met with no success. He was the author of a novel entitled *Fashionable Follies* (1782), which had some vogue; one reviewer called it 'The best of his writings' (*European Magazine*, 58). He republished it in 1810 with considerable additions, and with a dedication to Colman, with whom he had formerly quarrelled, and who bestowed on him the nickname of Dapper. Though much earlier, *The Retort* (1761), a reply to Churchill's *Rosciad*, which contained an allusion to Vaughan as 'Dapper', is also assigned to him (Churchill, 31n.; *New Cambridge Bibliography of English Literature*, 2.859). He was a friend of Sheridan, and is said to have been the original of Dangle in *The Critic*.

E. I. CARLYLE, *rev.* GRANT P. CERNY

Sources *The new Cambridge bibliography of English literature*, [2nd edn], 2, ed. G. Watson (1971), 859 · *European Magazine and London Review*, 1 (1782), 30–31, 58 · D. E. Baker, *Biographia dramatica, or, A companion to the playhouse*, rev. I. Reed, new edn, rev. S. Jones, 1/2 (1812), 725–6 · C. Churchill, *The Rosciad and The Apology*, ed. R. W. Lowe (1891), 31n. · Genest, *Eng. stage*, 5.494, 546; 6.332 · *N&Q*, 9th ser., 4 (1899), 4

Vaughan, Thomas (**1782–1843**), singer, was born in Norwich, where he was a chorister at the cathedral under John Christmas Beckwith. His father died while Vaughan, still very young, was preparing to enter the musical profession, which he was able to do under the patronage of Canon Charles Smith. In June 1799 he was elected lay clerk of St George's Chapel, Windsor, where he attracted the notice of George III. On 28 May 1803 he was admitted a gentleman of the Chapel Royal, and about the same time became vicar-choral of St Paul's Cathedral and lay vicar of Westminster Abbey. In 1806 he married Miss Tennant, a soprano singer well known from 1797 in oratorio performances. After some nine or ten years of married life they separated, and Mrs Vaughan was heard, as Mrs Tennant, at Drury Lane Theatre.

In 1811 Vaughan joined Charles Knyvett in establishing vocal subscription concerts in opposition to the Vocal Concerts; but on the death of Samuel Harrison in 1812 the two enterprises were merged, and from 1813 Vaughan became principal tenor soloist at all the prominent concerts and festivals. He sang at the Three Choirs festivals from 1805 to 1836, and took part in the performance of Beethoven's ninth symphony in 1825. For twenty-five years he was the leading singer of oratorio in England. He died on 9 January 1843 at a friend's house near Birmingham, and was buried on the 17th in the west cloister of Westminster Abbey.

L. M. MIDDLETON, *rev.* ANNE PIMLOTT BAKER

Sources Brown & Stratton, *Brit. mus.* · Grove, *Dict. mus.* · *GM*, 2nd ser., 19 (1843), 212–13 · *The Athenaeum* (14 Jan 1843), 39 · *Musical World* (12 Jan 1843), 20

Vaughan, Watkyn (*d.* 1456). *See under* Vaughan family (*per. c.*1400–*c.*1504).

Vaughan, Watkyn (*d.* 1504). *See under* Vaughan family (*per. c.*1400–*c.*1504).

Vaughan, Sir William [*pseud.* Orpheus junior] (*c.***1575–1641**), writer and promoter of colonization in Newfoundland, was the second son of Walter Vaughan (*d.* 1598), twice member of parliament, of Golden Grove, Llanfihangel Aberbythych, Carmarthenshire, and his first wife, Mary (*d.* before 1588), daughter of Sir Walter Rice of Newton, Dinefwr, Carmarthenshire. William matriculated, along with his elder brother John *Vaughan (created earl of Carbery in 1628), from Jesus College, Oxford, on 4 February 1592, and graduated BA on 1 March 1595 and MA on 16 November 1597. Sir Henry *Vaughan, royalist army officer, was a younger brother. William supplicated for the degree of BCL on 3 December 1600. As a young man he travelled extensively in France and Italy, and also visited Vienna, where he received a doctorate in law, being incorporated DCL at Oxford on 23 June 1605.

Vaughan showed early his aptitude for writing accomplished poetry, especially of a religious nature, in Latin. While at Oxford he published *Erōtopaignion pium* (1597) and *Erotopainion pium*, part 2 (1598), containing verse paraphrases of the Bible. The contents of the two publications again appeared in the more widely known *Poematum libellus* (1598). This volume also contains an encomiastic ode addressed to Robert Devereux, earl of Essex (with whose family the Vaughans were closely connected); 'De sphaerarum ordine', a didactic cycle of verses on the sun, moon, and planets; and a section entitled 'Palaemonis amores philosophici', seventeen poems in which themes from classical poets like Catullus and Ovid are combined with sonnet-like effusions of a Petrarchan nature. Also included in *Poematum libellus* is a memorial poem on the death of Vaughan's father ('Speculum humanae condicionis'), which was also printed separately.

In 1600 Vaughan's most famous work appeared, *The Golden-Grove, Moralized in Three Bookes* (a second edition, 'now lately reviewed and enlarged by the Author', was published in 1608). The title recalls both the name of the Vaughan family home (the work is dedicated to William's brother John) and 'the golden grove of the ancient Hesperides'. Among liminary Latin verses to greet the work are poems by notable Oxford contemporaries of the two brothers, among them John Williams and Griffith Powell (both Carmarthenshire men who became principal of Jesus College), and the Latin dramatist Matthew Gwinne. The prose text of *The Golden-Grove* is written in English, and presents a learned and elaborate treatise 'very necessary for all such as would know how to governe themselves, their houses or their countrey'. The arrangement is in three books, dealing in Aristotelian fashion with the religious and moral ('virtue'), economic ('family'), and political ('civility' or 'commonwealth') aspects of human life. Vaughan is particularly sensitive to social relationships; he displays advanced views on farming and estate management, and his concern for the plight of yeomen (as in his native Carmarthenshire) foreshadows his later commitment to colonial enterprises: 'There is no life more pleasant than a Yeomans life … But now a dayes yeomanrie is decayed, hospitalitie gone to wracke, and husbandrie almost quite fallen' (1608 edition, sig. v4ii–iii). Throughout *The Golden-Grove* quotations from classical authors abound, notably Persius, on whose satires Vaughan says in his preface that he had prepared an unpublished commentary. Other references to literary matters also give an indication of some of Vaughan's attitudes. In book 1 he delivers a diatribe against 'stage playes', but in book 3 the 'excellency' of true poetry is extolled. From the time of Moses and Homer poets 'were the first that observed the sacred operations of nature' (sig. Z1v), and poetry the chief cause of the heathen's 'civility'. 'Neither is our owne age altogether to be dispraysed' (sig. Z7r), and he singles out the earl of Surrey, Sir Philip Sidney, and James VI of Scotland for special mention.

Details of Vaughan's life in the years immediately after returning from his European tour are patchy. In the early 1600s he married Elizabeth, daughter and heir of David ap Robert of Llangyndeyrn. Her home, Tor-y-coed (which Vaughan sometimes quaintly spelt 'Terra-Coed'), thereafter became his main residence. A son of the marriage, Francis, appears to have died young. Further tragedy came upon the family in January 1608, when the house was struck by lightning and Elizabeth Vaughan killed. Vaughan himself escaped, one of several preservations that he came to interpret as signs of divine calling to special service. His wife's death affected him deeply, and for a time he appears to have suffered from something close to religious mania. He was also the victim of insinuations about the circumstances of his wife's death. To refute these he wrote a strangely mystical work entitled *The spirit of detraction conjured and convicted in seven circles: a work both divine and morall, fit to be perused by the libertines of the age, who endeavour by their detracting and derogatory speeches to* embezell the glory of God and the credit of their neighbours (1611).

Another of Vaughan's early interests was medicine. In 1600, the same year as the first edition of *The Golden-Grove*, he published *Naturall and Artificiall Directions for Health*, a work that he was to revise and enlarge through several editions and under slightly different titles (*Approved Directions for Health*; *Directions for Health*) for the rest of his life. This work, like *The Golden-Grove*, was in part occasioned by his concern for the condition of ordinary people, and his directions, 'derived from the best Phisitians, as well as moderne as antient', come under six headings: 'air, fire and water'; 'food and nourishment'; 'evacuations, as purgations, Tobacco taking, etc.'; 'infirmities, humours, and death'; 'perturbations of the mind, and spiritual sicknesses'; 'quarterly, monthly, and daily diet with Medicines to prolong life'.

William Vaughan married as his second wife Anne (d. 1672), daughter of John Christmas of Colchester, and with her had one son, Edward, and five daughters, Margaret, Jane, Dorothy, Mary, and Anne. As became a member of his family, he was involved in the public affairs of Carmarthenshire and was sheriff of the county for 1616. His major concern, however, from 1616 onwards was with promoting colonization in the New World, in part as a hoped-for means of alleviating social and economic problems of the kind that he had described in *The Golden-Grove*. Various possibilities were considered, but in the end his choice fell on Newfoundland. In 1610 'a company of adventurers' had been granted, by James I, territory in Newfoundland for the purposes of colonial development. In 1616 Vaughan purchased from the company land south of a line extending from Placentia Bay to Caplin Bay on the Avalon peninsula, on the eastern part of the island. In token of its Welsh origin, the colony was named Cambriol. The first group of settlers was sent out in 1617, at Vaughan's expense, to the Aquafort area, and a governor, Captain Richard Whitbourne, was appointed in 1618. Whitbourne reorganized the colony, and made Renews its centre. The venture proved, however, extremely precarious, and by 1619 the colony had collapsed, although some of the settlers probably remained. According to the autobiographical material in *The Newlanders Cure*, Vaughan assigned part of his land to Henry Cary, Viscount Falkland, and another portion to Sir George Calvert. Nevertheless, his interest in Newfoundland remained unabated: 'my Zeale to Newfoundland is not frozen', he wrote in 1630 (*The Newlanders Cure*, sig. A5v). Although there is no hard evidence to support the claim, often made, that Vaughan himself visited the territory on the Avalon peninsula, his attempts to promote it continued throughout the 1620s. In 1625 he published a Latin poem, 'Cambrensium Caroleia', in honour of the marriage of Charles I, and included with it John Mason's map of Newfoundland. This shows names of many Welsh towns and counties, and also Vaughan's Cove and Golden Grove.

Mason's map was also included in the most extraordinary of all Vaughan's works, written under the pseudonym Orpheus junior: *The golden fleece divided into three parts, under which are discovered the errours of religion, the vices and decayes of the kingdome, and lastly the wayes to get wealth, and to restore trading so much complayned of: transported from Cambrioll Colchos, out of the southermost part of the iland, commonly called the Newfoundland, by Orpheus junior, for the generall and perpetuall good of Great Britaine* (1626). The work fancifully draws a parallel between the mission conducted by Jason and his fellow Argonauts to win the golden fleece and the opportunities offered to colonists, especially Orpheus junior's 'countreymen of Wales', in Newfoundland. The book abounds with classical allusions, many of them symbolically interpreted. The god Apollo is shown passing judgment in religious, political, economic, and moral matters. Leading historical figures are brought before him to plead the cause of their actions, and are approved or otherwise by the god. The 'Cambrioll Colchos' of Newfoundland is finally shown to be the answer to all ills. Although *The Golden Fleece* is a rambling work, and bigoted in its hostility to Roman Catholicism, it remains a remarkable piece of colonial propaganda, and is one of the earliest books concerned with America.

In 1626 Vaughan's anti-Catholic passion found further expression in the publication of *The New-Found Politicke*, a translation by Vaughan, John Florio, and another, unnamed, author of selections from Traiano Boccalini's *Ragguagli di Parnaso*. Dedicated to Charles I, the work is an earnest, although indirect, warning against concluding any alliance with Spain. In 1630 a further medical work, *The Newlanders Cure*, came from Vaughan's pen. The book is primarily aimed at emigrants undertaking the voyage to the New World, and in particular discusses remedies for scurvy and other likely complaints. The knowledgeable discussion of colonists' ailments has sometimes been taken to signify that Vaughan did at last cross the Atlantic in the late 1620s, but the autobiographical material contained in the dedication strongly suggests that visiting Newfoundland was for him still only a dream rather than a realized fact.

In 1628 Vaughan was knighted, in Ireland. As far as is known, he lived for the rest of his life in Carmarthenshire, and 'consoled himself for the failure of his dreams with his meditations and writings upon religion' (Cell, *Newfoundland*, 26). At the end of his life he produced two bulky books of verse, *The church militant, historically continued from the yeare of our Saviours incarnation 33 untill this present 1640* (1640) and *The soules exercise in the daily contemplation of our Saviours birth, life, passion, and resurrection* (1641). 'Poor, Cambriol's Lord', to use Robert Hayman's appellation for Vaughan, died in August 1641, probably at Tor-y-coed, and was buried at Llangyndeyrn 'without vain pomp', as was enjoined in his will (dated 14 August and proved at Carmarthen on 27 August 1641).   CERI DAVIES

Sources DNB · G. T. Cell, 'Vaughan, Sir William', *DCB*, vol. 1 · D. L. Thomas, 'Iscennen and Golden Grove', *Transactions of the Honourable Society of Cymmrodorion* (1940), 115–29 · G. T. Cell, ed., *Newfoundland discovered: English attempts at colonisation, 1610–1630*, Hakluyt Society, new ser., 160 (1982) · E. W. Jones, 'Y wladfa gyntaf: Cambriola a Syr William Vaughan', *National Library of Wales Journal*, 30 (1998), 231–68 · W. K. D. Davies, 'The Welsh in Canada: a geographical overview', *The Welsh in Canada*, ed. M. E. Chamberlain (1986), 16–19 · L. Bradner, *Musae Anglicanae: a history of Anglo-Latin poetry, 1500–1925* (1940), 51–2 · 'Will of Sir William Vaughan', *Transactions of the Carmarthenshire Antiquarian Society*, 10 (1914–15), 70 · J. W. Binns, *Intellectual culture in Elizabethan and Jacobean England: the Latin writings of the age* (1990) · A. G. Prys-Jones, *The story of Carmarthenshire*, 2 (1972), 129–68 · J. J. Jones, 'The golden fleece', *National Library of Wales Journal*, 3 (1943–4), 58–60 · F. A. Yates, *John Florio: the life of an Italian in Shakespeare's England* (1934), 85–6, 260–64, 301–9 · Reg. Oxf. · W. A. Shaw, *The knights of England*, 2 (1906), 194
Archives Berks. RO, letters to Sir Nicholas Carew

Vaughan, Sir William (*d.* 1649), royalist army officer, was the son and heir of a Shropshire or Herefordshire family, and entered Shrewsbury School on 30 January 1596. He learned his military skills in Europe, and in 1620 may have served as a captain in Lord Cromwell's regiment of foot, raised for Mansfeld's expedition to the Netherlands. By 27 July 1639 he had decided to serve the king in the bishops' wars, and late in 1641 he led a troop in the earl of Carnarvon's regiment of horse, sent to Ireland to help suppress the October rebellion. After commanding Sir Richard Grenvile's cavalry at Rathconnell (7 February 1643) he carried news of the victory to Dublin, and was knighted by the marquess of Ormond.

Vaughan was made a colonel, and, in charge of over 300 horse, part of a large body of reinforcements sent by Ormond to relieve Chester, he joined Lord Byron's forces there early in February 1644, and played an important role in Shropshire and north Wales for the remainder of the war. He helped Colonel Robert Ellice capture Apley Castle, Shropshire (24 March 1644), and rout Thomas Mytton at Longford the following day. His regiment then joined Prince Rupert's army, and Vaughan was probably at the storming of Bolton on 28 May and the siege of Liverpool (7–12 June). He served with Byron on the royalist right wing at Marston Moor on 2 July, and was with him in the disastrous rout at Montgomery on 18 September. Byron complained of how little Vaughan contributed to the action; but, earlier in the month, Vaughan and Sir Michael Erneley had broken Sir Thomas Myddleton's army there, before settling down to besiege the castle. On 28 September he garrisoned Shrawardine Castle in Shropshire, of which he had been appointed governor, but two weeks later, on 13 October, he was taken prisoner by Mytton while on his knees receiving communion in Shrawardine church. Allowed back into the castle, on the pretext of persuading it to surrender, he failed to re-emerge, and within a fortnight defeated Sir John Price at Welshpool.

During the winter Vaughan was made general of Shropshire. He had put his troops into garrisons all over the county—at Dawley House, Lilleshall Abbey, Caws Castle, Leigh Hall, and High Ercall—with his parson brother commanding Shrawardine itself. Unscrupulously living off the country and confiscating the property of local parliamentarians, the best-documented example being his robbery from the drapers of Dolgellau of £140 and sundry cloths (27 November 1644), Vaughan acquired the sobriquet 'the Devil of Shrawardine' (*Mercurius Aulicus*, 1 Feb 1644). But his actions were effective: he cut off Myddleton from his Shropshire colleagues, and ensured that his men were well paid, clothed, and housed; and his regiment emerged from winter quarters 400 strong, a number rivalling Rupert's own regiment, usually the strongest in the royalist army. During the early 1640s Vaughan was a member of the close circle of Thomas Chaloner, headmaster of Shrewsbury School, who met regularly at The Sextry inn in the town.

After being defeated and captured by Cromwell at Bampton, Oxfordshire (27 April 1645), Vaughan was soon exchanged, and he beat off some Shropshire horse near Wenlock on 9 May before joining the king eight days later on his march from Oxford to Chester. He was present at the storming of Leicester (30 May); and at Naseby (14 June), in the second line of the royalist right wing, he participated in the great charge which pierced Ireton's opposing troops. After the defeat he fell back on Shropshire, where local clubmen in the south-west of the county were withholding supplies from the royalist garrisons, and the parliamentarian forces had captured Caws and Shrawardine (24–5 June) and were besieging High Ercall.

Vaughan defeated his opponents at Broncroft Castle (4 July) and the following day relieved High Ercall, capturing nearly 400 prisoners, whom he used to help ransom royalist foot taken at Naseby. He joined the king at Ludlow on 7 August, and was with him at Doncaster (19 August) and Huntingdon (23 August). Towards the end of the month Vaughan burnt Bishop's Castle, and he was present at the defeat at Rowton Heath (24 September). After accompanying the king to Newark, in October he was appointed general of the horse in Wales and the marches, and promised to continue provisioning Chester from north Wales. He defeated Sydenham Poyntz at Drayton in mid-October, and managed to get a supply of brimstone into Chester before being crushed by Michael Jones and Mytton, with a much larger force, at Denbigh on 1 November, while he waited for the Caernarvonshire levies to arrive. Vaughan's routed cavalry retreated to Knighton, Radnorshire, where they broke up on 13 November. He found temporary quarters at Leominster, but was then forced back on Worcester. Early in December he was ordered to renew the attempt to relieve Chester, but each time he managed to weld together his troops in Herefordshire and Shropshire for the task, strong sallies by Jones or Mytton scattered them, and he was denied admittance to Ludlow.

On 9 December Vaughan was reported to be quartered between Bridgnorth and Bewdley with 1000 men; after burning the village of Wrockwardine, Vaughan again relieved High Ercall, and in January 1646 joined Lord Astley at Bridgnorth in the frustrated hope of amalgamating with Lord St Paul's Welsh troops in a further assault on Chester. Instead he retreated with Astley to Worcester, and finally abandoned the attempt on 29 January. February saw Vaughan engaged in further raids in the marches, especially at Clun, Presteigne, and Leintwardine, and at the end of the month he plundered Richard Jones of Trewern, Radnorshire, of over £400 and the very rings from his wife's fingers. Early in March he rejoined Astley, and he was with him when the royalist forces were comprehensively defeated by Sir William Brereton at Stow on the Wold, Gloucestershire, on 21 March.

Vaughan, though wounded, escaped capture and made his way to The Hague, where in November 1648 Rupert gave him command of a ship, in which he seems to have crossed over to Ireland. He became major-general of horse under Ormond. When, at Rathmines on 2 August 1649, Michael Jones surprised the royalists, Vaughan led the counter-charge, only to be killed fighting bravely at the head of his men. On 8 October 1651, leave to compound for his estates was granted to Charles Vaughan, his administrator. Vaughan's main overall achievement was, in every adversity, to keep his regiment of horse up to strength; in this regard no royalist commander achieved more, and the spectres of his cavalrymen are rumoured still to canter across the Shropshire countryside.

BASIL MORGAN

Sources P. Young, *Naseby, 1645* (1985) · *DNB* · R. Hutton, *The royalist war effort, 1642–1646*, pbk edn (1984) · J. E. Auden, 'The war services of some Shropshire officers in the king's army', *Transactions of the Shropshire Archaeological and Natural History Society*, 4th ser., 2 (1912), 215–93 · R. N. Dore, *The civil wars in Cheshire* (1966) · R. H. Morris, *The siege of Chester, 1643–1646* (1924) · P. R. Newman, *Royalist officers in England and Wales, 1642–1660: a biographical dictionary* (1981) · G. W. Fisher, *Annals of Shrewsbury School*, rev. J. S. Hill (1899) · E. Calvert, ed., *Shrewsbury School regestum scholarium, 1562–1635: admittances and readmittances* [1892]

Vaughan, William (*bap.* **1640**, *d.* **1719**), merchant and colonial official, was baptized on 3 January 1640, probably in Wales, the first of three children of George Vaughan (*bap.* 1615, *d.* 1699) and Mary Boxall (*d.* 1645). His paternal grandfather was Sir Roger Vaughan, a member of the minor Glamorgan gentry. He was living at an early age in London, the protégé of Sir Josiah Child, a prominent and wealthy London merchant, who made a fortune supplying the navy and later virtually ruled the East India Company. Vaughan was sent to New England as a representative of the merchant house to investigate the prospects of the lumber trade which had been boosted by the demand generated by the Anglo-Dutch wars. He had arrived in Portsmouth, New Hampshire, by 1666. He married Margaret (*d.* 1690), the daughter of Richard Cutt, in 1668 and became a partner in the Cutt fishery trade, which he inherited after Cutt's death in 1676.

By the 1680s Vaughan was a leading merchant and politician in Portsmouth and remained so until his death. In the charter granted by Charles II constituting New Hampshire as a separate province from Massachusetts, he was named as one of the councillors of the new royal colony. The royal governor was attempting to make the Piscataqua region a model for the effective implementation of trade regulations. Vaughan and other traders used their political and commercial influence to undermine the royal governor and acted as if the region was a free port. When an official tried to search a vessel owned by him, the infuriated Vaughan beat him so badly with a cane that it took him several months to recover. In 1683 he was deprived of his seat on the council. Vaughan spent nine months in prison in 1684 for gathering dispositions, signed by nearly half of the adult male population, complaining that the proprietary government threatened total ruin to New Hampshire. In July 1684 the privy council ordered a full investigation and the governor was removed from office; the evidence provided by Vaughan from prison to the agent in London had helped the case, but the continuing support of Sir Josiah Child was perhaps more crucial. Vaughan was part of a group that tended to think and act in terms of New England looking to Boston as their capital, supporting the position of Congregationalism, liberty, hard money, and property against those who saw New Hampshire as an independent beachhead of royal authority in New England. As well as a commission in the militia, Vaughan held a succession of offices in the province: he was a justice of the common pleas from 1680 to 1686, and, reappointed to the council in 1692, he continued to be a member until 1698. For a brief period in the 1690s Vaughan and a few others assumed total executive control in New Hampshire. From 1706 to 1715 he was the president of the council and at the same time chief justice of the superior court. He died at Portsmouth on 12 November 1719. The Vaughans continued to be one of the leading families of New Hampshire as exemplified by his son George, who became lieutenant-governor in 1715.   HYWEL MEILYR DAVIES

Sources C. E. Clark, *The eastern frontier: the settlement of northern New England, 1610–1763* (1970) · J. R. Daniel, *Colonial New Hampshire: a history* (1981) · D. E. Van Deventer, *The emergence of provincial New Hampshire, 1623–1741* (1976) · G. E. Hodgdon, *Reminiscences and genealogical record of the Vaughan family of New Hampshire* (1918)
Archives New Hampshire Historical Society, Concord, family papers

Vaughan, William (*b.* *c.*1716, *d.* in or after **1780**), army officer in the Jacobite and Spanish service, was the third son of John Vaughan (1675–1752) of Courtfield, near Ross, Herefordshire, and his second wife, Elizabeth, daughter of Philip Jones of Llan-arth Fawr, Monmouthshire. Both families were recusant. After the landing of Prince Charles Edward, the Young Pretender, in Scotland in 1745, William Vaughan left Monmouthshire for the north, in the company of David Morgan (executed for high treason, 30 July 1746), who 'seldom kept company with any Gentleman of his Neighbourhood' (*Complete History of the Trials of the Rebels*, quoted in Blaikie, *Origins*, 172), and Francis Townley, of Townley Hall. They joined the prince's army at Preston on 27 November, with 'some few common people, but no numbers as was expected' (Blaikie, *Itinerary*, 28). Vaughan was at first attached to the prince's life-guards, but subsequently served as lieutenant-colonel in the Manchester regiment. He was present at Culloden, but succeeded in effecting his escape into France. His name was included on a list of rebels guilty of treason (22 May 1747), and he was later excepted from the general act of pardon.

Early in 1747 Vaughan accompanied Prince Charles on his journey from Paris to Madrid, and on Charles's recommendation was admitted into the Spanish service, with the rank of lieutenant-colonel, in the regiment called Hibernia. In this he served over twenty-nine years, attaining in December 1773 the rank of major-general. On 26 October 1777 he was appointed *mariscal de campo*, or 'major-

general', of the royal armies, but towards the end of 1778 he joined the Spanish expedition to Buenos Aires. He is last mentioned in the Spanish records under the date of 29 March 1780 as being nominated to serve with the troops under the general command of Don Vittoria de Navia. He probably died soon after.

Vaughan's elder brother, Richard (*b.* 1708), the second son, also took part in the Jacobite rising, joined the duke of Perth's division, and was also present at Culloden. He was indicted, by Justice Henry Fielding of Bow Street, for forging English banknotes. He also subsequently entered the Spanish service, and died in that country, having married a Spanish lady, Doña Francesca, with whom he had a daughter, Elizabeth (who married the count of Kilmallock, colonel in the Spanish service), and a son, William (1740–1796), who succeeded to the Courtfield estate, and continued the line, Cardinal Vaughan and Roger William Vaughan, Roman Catholic archbishop of Sydney, being his great-grandsons.   M. R. GLOZIER

Sources *DNB* · Archivo General de Simancas, war office archives · W. B. Blaikie, ed., *Itinerary of Prince Charles Edward Stuart*, Scottish History Society, 23 (1897) · W. B. Blaikie, ed., *Origins of the 'Forty-Five and the papers relating to that rising*, Scottish History Society, 2nd ser., vol. 2 (1916) · Burke, *Gen. GB* · *Cambrian Journal*, [new ser., 4] (1861), 310–11 · *Lettres de noblesse, 1669–1790; Lettres d'anoblissement de confirmation ou de maintenu de noblesse, enregistrées à la chambre des comptes de Paris, de 1635 à 1787*, 146/bis; *Lettres de naturalité et lettres de légitimation, 1635–1787*, 151/bis, Centre Accueil de la Recherche des Archives Nationales, Paris, O^{1}54 · R. Challoner, *A short history of the first beginning and progress of the protestant religion*, 12 vols. (1735) · G. T. Clark, *Limbus patrum Morganiae et Glamorganiae* (1886) · A. C. Ewald, *The life and times of Prince Charles Stuart*, 2 vols. (1875); new edn (1883); 3rd edn (1904), vol. 2, p. 147 · M. H. Massue de Ruvigny, ed., *The Jacobite peerage* (1904); repr. (1974), 239, 242
Archives Spanish war office, Salamanca

Vaughan, William (1752–1850), promoter of the London docks, was born in London on 22 September 1752, the second son of Samuel Vaughan, a London merchant, and his wife, Sarah, daughter of Benjamin Hallowell of Boston, Massachusetts. He received a good education, first at Newcome's school at Hackney, Middlesex, then at the academy at Warrington in Lancashire, where he and his elder brother Benjamin *Vaughan resided with the eminent Dr Joseph Priestley. His studies were much directed to geography, history, travels, and voyages of discovery. After leaving school he entered his father's business, and soon became prominent in mercantile and commercial affairs. In 1783 he was elected a director of the Royal Exchange Assurance Corporation, and continued in it, as director, sub-governor, and governor, until 1829.

In 1791 Vaughan endeavoured to form a society for the promotion of English canals, and, with this end in view, made a collection, in three folio volumes, of plans and descriptions relating to the subject. Failing in his objective, he turned his attention to docks, on which he became one of the first authorities. From 1793 to 1797 he published a series of pamphlets and tracts advocating the construction of docks for the port of London, and on 22 April 1796 he gave evidence before a parliamentary committee in favour of the bill for establishing wet docks. In 1839 he published many of these papers, prefaced by a memoir of his own life. The great development of London as a port must be regarded as partly due to his unceasing exertions.

During the naval mutiny at the Nore in 1797 Vaughan formed one of the committee of London merchants convened to meet at the Royal Exchange to take prompt measures to restore tranquillity. He proved extremely active, and independently drew up a short address to the seamen which was put in circulation by the naval authorities.

Vaughan was for many years a fellow of the Royal Society, the Linnean Society, and the Royal Astronomical Society, and a member of numerous societies dedicated to the physical and moral welfare of various groups in England and North America. He was a member of the New England corporation, and filled the office of governor until 1829. As a member of the Society for Bettering the Condition and Improving the Comforts of the Poor, he was involved in 1815 in establishing the first savings bank in London, at Leicester Place, Westminster. He was a governor of Christ's Hospital and an honorary member of the Society of Civil Engineers. Beset by failing sight in old age, and apparently unmarried, Vaughan died in London on 5 May 1850, at his residence, 70 Fenchurch Street.

E. I. CARLYLE, *rev.* ANITA McCONNELL

Sources I. S. Greeves, *London docks, 1800–1980: a civil engineering history* (1980) · W. Vaughan, 'Narrative', in W. Vaughan, *Tracts on docks and commerce* (1839), 4–22 · *GM*, 2nd ser., 33 (1850), 681
Archives Birm. CL, letters to Boulton family
Likenesses F. Chantrey, marble bust, 1811, NPG · D. Alexander, drawing, repro. in Vaughan, *Tracts on docks and commerce*

Vaughan, William Wyamar (1865–1938), schoolmaster, was born at Hampstead on 25 February 1865, the younger son of Henry Halford *Vaughan (1811–1885), regius professor of modern history at Oxford, and his wife, Adeline Maria (1837–1881), daughter of John Jackson MD, of the East India Company's service, the leading English physician in Calcutta. He was grandson of the judge Sir John *Vaughan (1769–1839), great-nephew of the physician Sir Henry Halford, and first cousin through his mother of H. A. L. Fisher and Sir W. W. Fisher. He was educated at Rugby School, New College, Oxford (1884–8), where he gained seconds in classical moderations and *literae humaniores*, and the University of Paris.

After fourteen years (1890–1904) spent as assistant master at Clifton College, where he was for long head of the modern side, Vaughan was appointed headmaster of Giggleswick School. Six years later (1910) he became master of Wellington College and in 1921 returned to his old school, Rugby, as the first lay headmaster since its very early days. Unlike his recent predecessors at Rugby, Vaughan had not been a don, and his interests were not confined to the sixth form or even to the classics. During his period at Rugby a number of major building projects were undertaken at the school. He retired in July 1931, and went to live at Princes Risborough, Buckinghamshire. He was appointed MVO in 1920 and received the honorary degree of DLitt from Oxford University in 1931.

Vaughan was twice married: first, in 1898, to Margaret (1869–1925), daughter of John Addington *Symonds (1840–1893), with whom he had four children, including Janet *Vaughan, who became principal of Somerville College, Oxford; his second marriage in 1929, was to Elizabeth, daughter of John Geldard, of Settle.

Vaughan was president of the Modern Language Association in 1915, of the Incorporated Association of Headmasters in 1916, of the Science Masters Association in 1919, and of the educational section of the British Association in 1925, and after his retirement his services were ever in great request on educational bodies. In 1932 he presided over the International Congress of Secondary Teachers and in 1935 he became chairman of the Central Council for School Broadcasting. He also served on the consultative committee of the Board of Education (1920–26), on the government committee for considering the place of science in education, and on the Teachers' Registration Council (1928–32), and he visited the Gold Coast as a member of the advisory committee on education in the colonies. It was as a delegate to the Indian Science Congress that he went to Agra in December 1937. While visiting the Taj Mahal he fell and broke his thigh. His leg was amputated, but he died of pneumonia at the Thomason Hospital, Agra, on 4 February 1938.

Broad-shouldered, broad-minded, and large-hearted, Vaughan would have been a prominent figure in any walk of life: but that which he chose was particularly well suited to bring out his qualities. In him a rapid and sometimes explosive reaction to folly, neglect, or wrongdoing was tempered by a strong sense of justice, deep sympathies, and a keen sense of humour. He was fond of boys and understood them and he had a remarkable power of remembering their names and characteristics. In a time of much searching of heart in the educational world he showed that new ideas and methods could be assimilated without sacrificing what was valuable in the old; that freedom was not incompatible with discipline nor science with the humanities; and that school education was only the beginning of what should be a lifelong activity.

H. C. BRADBY, *rev.* M. C. CURTHOYS

Sources *The Times* (5 Feb 1938) · personal knowledge (1949) · J. B. H. Simpson, *Rugby since Arnold* (1967) · *CGPLA Eng. & Wales* (1938)
Archives Rugby School, Warwickshire, corresp. and papers | Bodl. Oxf., corresp. with his father, H. H. Vaughan
Likenesses W. Rothenstein, drawing, 1932, repro. in Simpson, *Rugby since Arnold*, facing p. 196 · G. Harcourt, oils, Wellington College, Berkshire · G. Philpot, oils, Rugby School, Warwickshire · W. Rothenstein, drawing, Wellington College, Berkshire
Wealth at death £38,478 5s. 9d.: probate, 10 March 1938, *CGPLA Eng. & Wales*

Vaus, John (*c*.1484–*c*.1539), grammarian, came of a well-established family in the city and diocese of Aberdeen, where a number of its members served as aldermen, councillors, and priests throughout the fifteenth century. It is not known, however, whether John Vaus was born in Aberdeen; records in the Vatican archives merely state that he was the son of a priest and an unmarried woman, that Pope Alexander VI had dispensed him from his illegitimacy on 23 June 1503 in order to allow him to proceed to the priesthood and be beneficed, and that on 14 June 1504 Julius II had confirmed him as vicar of Alness in the diocese of Ross while he was still a student at the University of Aberdeen. From these facts and the later statements of Hector Boece, it is possible to argue that he was born about 1484, attended the cathedral grammar school in Old Aberdeen under his kinsman Alexander Vaus, and was a student in the arts faculty at the university under Hector Boece between 1500 and 1504 before the foundation of King's College in 1505. It would also appear that when Boece was appointed principal of that college in 1505, he sent Vaus for further studies in Paris, where the latter graduated MA in 1505.

The date at which Vaus returned to take up his appointment as the grammarian employed to teach Latin at Aberdeen University (one of the earliest recorded) is not known, but during his first stay in Paris he is known to have made the acquaintance of such publishers as Josse Bade of the Ascensius Press and to have purchased a number of works on Latin grammar. He is known to have visited Paris again in 1523 to oversee the publication of his commentary on the first part of the *Doctrinale* of Alexander de Villa Dei, along with the printing of his translation into Scots of the *Ars minor* of Aelius Donatus, and with that of his own *Rudimenta puerorum in artem grammaticam*, a textbook which was still being reprinted, with changes and additions, at the Ascensius Press in 1553. Indeed, a study of the twenty-eight incunables in Aberdeen University Library which Vaus once possessed shows him to have been familiar with a wide range of textbooks on Latin grammar and on the principles governing the language and its literature; taken together with the warm tributes paid to his teaching ability by Hector Boece and his own students, they reveal him to have been both an industrious and elegant master of his subject, and to have given a flying start to the university's early development in humanist studies. In 1520, during his period of office as grammarian, Vaus is also noted as being chaplain of the Holy Name of Jesus altar at St Nicholas parish church in Aberdeen, and he is likewise recorded as having gifted an image of the crucified Christ to hang above the organ loft on the rood screen in King's College chapel. The date of his death is unknown, but his successor, Theophilus Stewart, is named as the university grammarian in a document dated 12 April 1539, while another university record confirms Vaus as being deceased in 1542.

LESLIE J. MACFARLANE

Sources *Hectoris Boetii murthlacensium et aberdonensium episcoporum vitae*, ed. and trans. J. Moir, New Spalding Club, 12 (1894) · *CEPR letters*, 17/1.1298; 18.345 · U. Aberdeen L., special libraries and archives, John Vaus Collection of Incunables · *Book of Sasines II*, Aberdeen City Archives, fol. 149r · J. Durkan and A. Ross, *Early Scottish libraries* (1961), 155–7, 187 · L. Delisle, 'L'imprimeur parisien Josse Bade et le professeur écossais Jean Vaus', *Bibliothèque de l'École des Chartes*, 57 (1896), 1–12 · C. Innes, ed., *Fasti Aberdonenses ... 1494–1854*, Spalding Club, 26 (1854), preface, xxii–xxiii · P. J. Anderson, ed., *Officers and graduates of University and King's College, Aberdeen, MVD–MDCCCLX*, New Spalding Club, 11 (1893), 45 · F. C. Eeles, *King's College Chapel Aberdeen* (1956), 21, 44 · L. J. Macfarlane, *William Elphinstone and the kingdom of Scotland, 1431–1514: the struggle for order*, quincentenary edn (1995), 324, 335, 365–9, 390 · R. R. Bolgar, *The classical heritage and its beneficiaries* (1963) · W. S. Mitchell, ed., *Catalogue of the incunabula in Aberdeen University Library* (1968)
Archives U. Aberdeen L., special libraries and archives, incunables [which John Vaus is known to have possessed, and many of which bear his signature of ownership]

Vaus [Vans], **Sir Patrick**, **Lord Barnbarroch** (*d.* 1597), diplomat and judge, was the second son of Sir John Vaus of Barnbarroch, Wigtownshire, and his wife, Janet, only child of Sir Samuel MacCulloch of Myreton, keeper of the palace of Linlithgow. Vaus was intended for the church and became rector of Wigtown, but succeeded to the family estates on the death of his elder brother, Alexander, in 1568; he later (May 1580) granted a nineteen-year 'tack' of the parsonage and vicarage of Wigtown.

Vaus was threatened with escheat in October 1570 for absenting himself from the royal host, but on 1 January 1576 he was appointed an ordinary lord of session, with the title Lord Barnbarroch. By 1580 he had married Katherine Kennedy (*d.* in or after 1593), and they had four sons: his heir, John, later one of the gentlemen of the chamber to James VI, and Patrick, Robert, and Alexander. Vaus also had a natural son, Richard, who was granted precept of legitimation on 1 May 1577. Probably knighted in the 1580s, Vaus was admitted on 21 April 1587 to membership of the privy council, and in the following month he and Peter Young went on embassy to Denmark to arrange for the marriage of James VI with Anne of Denmark; Vaus later accompanied James VI to Norway and witnessed the marriage, on 23 November 1589. In October 1589 the king granted him a new charter of his lands in *blench ferm* in recognition of his services in Denmark, incorporated in the free barony of Bar. In August 1591 these lands were incorporated into the free barony of Barnbarroch. However, Vaus evidently had trouble collecting taxes assigned to him in Kyle Stewart on account of 'expenssis maid at his ambassadrie', as he complained to the privy council in February 1589 (*Reg. PCS*, 353).

In the parliaments of 1592 and 1593 Vaus was elected a lord of the articles, while in June 1592 he was granted an annual pension of £200 Scots. In January 1597, when the king returned to Edinburgh after the previous month's anti-Catholic riot, Vaus was among those called upon to attend James in arms at the 'mercat croce' for 'reduceing of certane disordourit personis ... to his Majesteis obediens' (*Reg. PCS*, 355). Vaus died, presumably in Edinburgh, later that year, on 22 July 1597.

DAVIE HORSBURGH

Sources M. Livingstone, D. Hay Fleming, and others, eds., *Registrum secreti sigilli regum Scotorum / The register of the privy seal of Scotland*, 6–7 (1963–6) · *Reg. PCS*, 1st ser., vols. 4–5 · J. M. Thomson and others, eds., *Registrum magni sigilli regum Scotorum / The register of the great seal of Scotland*, 11 vols. (1882–1914), vols. 5–6 · *DNB* · G. Donaldson, *Scotland: James V to James VII* (1965), vol. 3 of *The Edinburgh history of Scotland* (1965–75)
Wealth at death substantial estate

Vautor, Thomas (*fl.* 1592–1619), composer, first appears as a household musician in the family of Mary Beaumont of Glenfield, Leicestershire. On her first marriage in 1592 he passed into the service of her husband, Sir George Villiers, at Brooksby. Following Sir George's death in 1606, his widow moved with her sons to Goadby, also in Leicestershire, where on 19 June she married Sir William Rayner, who himself died four months later. She subsequently married Sir Thomas Compton. In 1616 Vautor was admitted BMus at Oxford. By this time Lady Compton's son, George Villiers, was rising in the king's favour; upon his creation as marquess of Buckingham in 1618 Vautor dedicated to him his only collection of madrigals, entitled *The first set: being songs of divers ayres and natures, of five and six parts: apt for viols and voices* (1619).

This volume contains Vautor's only known music, but it suffices to reveal him as one of the most interesting minor composers of this rich period in English music. Its twenty-two items are markedly varied and, as Vautor's preface makes clear, were composed over an extended period, some pieces dating from its dedicatee's 'tender yeares'. These probably include the three lively *ballets* that open the collection, and which are in a typical 1590s style. Vautor was not a contributor to *The Triumphs of Oriana* (1601), the collection of madrigals published in honour of the ageing Queen Elizabeth, but 'Shepherds and nymphs', included in his own collection and ending 'Farewell, fair Oriana', is a posthumous tribute to that sovereign. Two pieces are explicit elegies, the first a pair of madrigals, 'Melpomene, bewail' with 'Whilst fatal sisters', for Prince Henry (*d.* 1612), the second 'Weep, weep, mine eyes', for Sir Thomas Beaumont of Stoughton, Leicestershire (*d.* 1614); curiously, both are viol-accompanied duets in an antiquated 'grave' style more characteristic of early Elizabethan music, though the former concludes with a six-voice, madrigalian-style chorus that is thoroughly up-to-date. In the sharpest contrast to these sober pieces is 'Mother, I will have a husband', a torrent of babble from a girl intent on matrimony at all costs.

The remaining pieces further reveal Vautor's range and quality—some of them may be counted among the finest of English madrigals. To name but two: 'Sweet Suffolk owl', whose initial chattering declamation and lively word painting are deftly balanced by its conclusion's haunting melancholy, and the pair of madrigals, 'Lock up, fair lids' with 'And yet, O dream' (a setting of a sonnet by Sir Philip Sidney), impressive for its often spacious paragraphs laced with quietly expressive dissonance, and its masterly use of chromaticism and word painting. Nothing is known of Vautor after the publication of his madrigal volume.   DAVID BROWN

Sources T. Vautor, *The first set: being songs of divers ayres and natures* (1619), preface · *New Grove*, 2nd edn · E. H. Fellowes, *The English madrigal composers*, 2nd edn (1950) · GEC, *Peerage* · *DNB*

Vautort, de, family (*per.* 1086–1274), barons, were descended from **Reginald** [i] **de Vautort** (*fl.* 1086–1123). His family, prominent in the service of Robert, count of Mortain (*d.* 1091), is traditionally said to have originated from Vautorte (Mayenne), some 20 miles south of Mortain, though Torteval (Calvados) now seems more likely. By 1086 Count Robert had granted the Vautorts substantial estates in the west country, then in the tenure of Reginald [i]. They comprised some fifty-five manors in south Devon

and south-east Cornwall (with a further two in Somerset), of which Trematon, with a castle and market in evidence by 1086, became the natural centre. Reginald is later found in the retinue of Count Robert's son, William, and he lived on until at least 1123, witnessing a royal charter in that year in the company of other west-country barons. By 1129 he, with a brother Ralph, had founded the Benedictine priory of Modbury, Devon, dependent on the abbey of St Pierre-sur-Dives (Calvados). If evidence of 1212 is correct, it was probably about this time that Henry I granted to the family the manors of Maker, King's Tamerton, and Sutton Vautort, Devon.

Reginald's son and heir, **Roger** [i] **de Vautort** (*d. c.*1163), in evidence from 1129, confirmed the foundation at Modbury, adding to its benefactions the church of St Stephen near Trematon (now in Saltash). At the beginning of Stephen's reign he may have given his allegiance to the new king but when Reginald, one of Henry I's illegitimate sons and a leading supporter of the Empress Matilda, was made earl of Cornwall in 1140, Roger became subject to his lordship. He was Reginald's principal subtenant, holding his estates for the service of fifty-nine knights, and is found witnessing the earl's charter in favour of the borough of Truro and two others, in favour of Launceston Priory, in the earl's company. His heir was **Ralph** [i] **de Vautort** (*d.* 1171/2), the son of Roger and his wife, Emma. Ralph issued two charters in favour of Modbury Priory; the wardship of his son and heir, **Roger** [ii] **de Vautort** (1164x6–1206), was granted in 1171 or 1172, when Ralph [i] also paid scutage. Until Roger came of age (in 1186 or 1187), his estates were in the hands of an uncle, Johel de Vautort, from whom descended a cadet branch of the family holding lands of the earls of Devon.

Roger [ii] de Vautort is found in the retinue of William de Vernon, earl of Devon, in the early 1190s and then in Richard I's army in Normandy. He found favour with King John, receiving from the king the royal manor of Callington, Cornwall, on his marriage to one Alesia. Shortly before his death, in November 1206, he substantially increased the family's estates by obtaining from the king a promise of the Nonant family's share of the honour of Totnes, Devon, known thereafter as the honour of Harberton, which was to escheat to the crown on the fall of William de Briouze.

Roger [ii]'s heir was his son **Reginald** [ii] **de Vautort** (*d.* 1245) who came of age about 1211. He appears to have remained loyal to the king in the mounting political crisis of John's reign and, on Henry III's accession, was witness to the first reissue of Magna Carta. It was doubtless in recognition of his loyalty that, shortly afterwards, he was confirmed in the honour of Harberton. He was sheriff of Cornwall in 1221 and 1224 and later served the king in a number of minor ways, but including, in 1242, a successful mission against the rebel William de Marisco, who had seized Lundy island. He assumed the Nonant family's role as principal patron of Buckfast Priory and took a great interest in the fortunes of Modbury Priory, on one occasion, in 1240, removing a dishonest and disreputable prior from his post. He also issued charters in favour of the priories of St Michael's Mount, Cornwall, and St Nicholas, Exeter, and confirmed to his burgesses of Saltash (first in evidence in 1201) the privileges conferred on them by 'his ancestors'. He married Joan, one of the three daughters of Thomas *Basset of Headington, Oxfordshire. This brought him a claim to land in Colyton, Devon, which was disputed over a long period by Walter de Dunstanville.

Under Reginald [ii] the family reached its apogee, his joint tenure of the honours of Trematon and Harberton making Reginald one of the leading landholders in that part of the west country. Thereafter the family went into decline. Reginald [ii] had no surviving children and his estates therefore passed to his brother **Ralph** [ii] **de Vautort** (*d.* 1257), who seems to have initiated a process of alienating the family estates. His heir, **Reginald** [iii] **de Vautort** (*d.* 1269), the son of Ralph and his wife, Joan, succeeded as a minor. Reginald [iii] may, in fact, never have come of age, for though he married one Hawise during his minority, he is otherwise scarcely recorded. When he died childless in 1269, he was succeeded by his uncle **Roger** [iii] **de Vautort** (*d.* 1274), a man allegedly of weak intellect who immediately alienated large parts of the family estates. The honour of Trematon passed in that year to Richard, earl of Cornwall, and at the same time other extensive grants were made to the bishop of Exeter and Alexander of Okeston, who had married Joan, the widow of his brother, Ralph [ii]. Roger [iii] died, childless, late in 1274, and his remaining estates escheated to the crown, encumbered with debts, mostly incurred before 1269, totalling nearly £500. These lands remained in the king's hands for thirty years, being eventually partitioned between Peter Corbet and Henry Pomeroy, descended from Roger [ii] de Vautort's two sisters.

Though one of the leading landholders in south-east Cornwall and adjoining parts of Devon, the Vautort family, with no other estates outside the west country, remained generally remote from national politics. Although they achieved considerable local status after the acquisition of the honour of Harberton, they were also intermittently overshadowed by the earls of Cornwall, and when the male line faltered the family was unable to resist Earl Richard's expansionist ambitions.

ROBERT BEARMAN

Sources *Pipe rolls* · *Chancery records* · Modbury Priory deeds and cartulary, Eton · 'Buckfast Abbey cartulary', *Reg. John de Grandisson, bishop of Exeter*, ed. F. C. Hingeston Randolph, 3 (1899) · *Curia regis rolls preserved in the Public Record Office* (1922–) · P. L. Hull, ed., *The cartulary of Launceston Priory (Lambeth Palace MS. 719): a calendar*, Devon and Cornwall RS, new ser., 30 (1987) · A. Farley, ed., *Domesday Book*, 2 vols. (1783) · H. C. M. Lyte and others, eds., *Liber feodorum: the book of fees*, 3 vols. (1920–31) · O. J. Reichel and others, eds., *Devon feet of fines*, 2 vols., Devon and Cornwall RS (1912–39) · M. Beresford, *New towns of the middle ages* (1967) · J. H. Rowe, ed., *Cornwall feet of fines*, 2 vols., Devon and Cornwall RS, old ser., 8 (1914–50) · I. J. Sanders, *English baronies: a study of their origin and descent, 1086–1327* (1960) · R. Bearman, ed., *Charters of the Redvers family and the earldom of Devon, 1090–1217*, Devon and Cornwall RS, new ser., 37 (1994) · P. L. Hull, ed., *The cartulary of St. Michael's Mount*, Devon and Cornwall RS, new ser., 5 (1962) · [W. Illingworth], ed., *Rotuli hundredorum*

temp. Hen. III et Edw. I, RC, 1 (1812), 56 · K. S. B. Keats-Rohan, *Domesday people I* (1999)

Vautort, Ralph de (*d.* 1171/2). *See under* Vautort, de, family (*per.* 1086–1274).

Vautort, Ralph de (*d.* 1257). *See under* Vautort, de, family (*per.* 1086–1274).

Vautort, Reginald de (*fl.* 1086–1123). *See under* Vautort, de, family (*per.* 1086–1274).

Vautort, Reginald de (*d.* 1245). *See under* Vautort, de, family (*per.* 1086–1274).

Vautort, Reginald de (*d.* 1269). *See under* Vautort, de, family (*per.* 1086–1274).

Vautort, Roger de (*d. c.*1163). *See under* Vautort, de, family (*per.* 1086–1274).

Vautort, Roger de (1164x6–1206). *See under* Vautort, de, family (*per.* 1086–1274).

Vautort, Roger de (*d.* 1274). *See under* Vautort, de, family (*per.* 1086–1274).

Vautrollier, Thomas (*d.* 1587), bookseller and printer, was born in Troyes, France. He was among the large number of French immigrants who came to England at the beginning of the reign of Elizabeth. After settling in London, he soon found employment in the book trade, first as a bookbinder and then as a bookseller in partnership with another French immigrant, Jean Desserans. He was granted letters of denization on 9 March 1562, and was admitted as a 'brother' (a form of associate membership) of the Stationers' Company on 2 October 1564 (Arber, *Regs. Stationers*, 1.279). As only a brother rather than a full freeman, Vautrollier was technically not allowed to operate a printing press without direct permission from the crown. Nevertheless, he was printing from 1570 when he dissolved the partnership with Desserans and began to print on his own account, beginning a thoroughly successful career that won him a reputation as one of London's most accomplished printers. Between 1570 and 1587 he published some 150 books, including a number of extremely rich and lavish volumes: the tax assessments on his property in the Blackfriars reveal that this work also brought him considerable prosperity.

The first book entered by Vautrollier in the Stationers' Company registers was a writing book of the French schoolmaster Jean de Beauchesne which was published in 1570 (the first such writing book to be published in England). This first project set the tone for his future career in several important respects. From this point Vautrollier would establish an important niche market, bringing to the English public translations of books from the French; these ranged from Beauchesne, through the poetry of Guillaume du Bartas, to political tracts such as the life of the martyred Huguenot leader Gaspard de Coligny. Vautrollier also brought to the Beauchesne project the typographical sophistication and style that would characterize all of his work and exploit his connections with the sophisticated European book world. In London, Vautrollier functioned from an early stage as an agent for the Antwerp printer Christopher Plantin, though his own printing types were obtained from two French giants of the art, Robert Granjon and Claude Garamond. Vautrollier also patronized the influential Huguenot designer Pierre Haultin, whose nephew Jerome was working in England at this time.

Vautrollier was deeply committed to the protestant church. In London, like so many of his co-religionists, he joined the French stranger church (to which he would leave £3 at his death), and a number of his most important projects reveal his close ties to the protestant hierarchy. In 1574 he published an English translation of Calvin's *Institutes*, the first of a number of Calvin editions that included four editions of this work in Latin. At a time when demand for Latin books was still overwhelmingly met by imports Vautrollier was one of the few printers with the confidence and resources to take on such a substantial project, in this case in partnership with the English author and theologian Edmund Bunny. Vautrollier also published an edition of Bunny's hugely popular abridgement of the *Institutes*. More singular still was Vautrollier's initiative in publishing a series of the work of Martin Luther, in most cases the first editions of Luther's biblical commentaries for many years. To Vautrollier falls much of the credit for keeping Luther in the public eye during an era when Calvinist theology ruled the roost. Vautrollier's work and protestant sympathies won approval in high places and valuable official patronage.

In April 1573 Vautrollier was granted a ten-year patent for two Latin texts, and the following year, on 19 June 1574, he received a further ten-year privilege to print a number of Latin works, including Beza's Latin New Testament and works by Cicero, Ovid, and Pierre Ramus; he was allowed to employ 'six woorkemen Ffrenchmen or Du[t]chemen' to help him (Arber, *Regs. Stationers*, 2.746). As this suggests, Vautrollier continued to specialize in educational books, through which he established (particularly with the privilege for the modish Ramus) close connections with Cambridge University. He also continued to print primers and schoolbooks for elementary education, particularly the work of the French schoolmaster Claude Holyband.

The growth of Vautrollier's business caused predictable tensions with competitors in the London publishing trade. In 1578 he was fined 10s. for printing the *Special and Chosen Sermons of Dr Martin Luther* without licence, the first of a number of bruising encounters with the regulatory authorities. One such clash led to his temporarily withdrawing from London and settling in Scotland during the 1580s after he had incurred the displeasure of the privy council for printing the work of the visionary Italian philosopher Giordano Bruno. The departure north was not, however, unprepared. Vautrollier's connections with Scotland were of sufficiently long standing to make him fully aware of the commercial opportunities north of the border. In 1577 he had printed two books for the Scottish bookseller Henry Charteris and by 1580 he was systematically engaged in the book trade in Edinburgh. In that year

the town council of Edinburgh demanded from him payment for books he had imported from London. In 1582 a complaint was made against him for retailing and binding books while not free of the burgh. But in Scotland, too, Vautrollier had friends in high places. He supplied schoolbooks to James VI through his tutor Peter Young, and in 1580 the general assembly of the Church of Scotland had recommended that he be given licence and privilege to print in Scotland, arguing the 'great necessity of a printer within this country'. Vautrollier set out for Scotland in the spring of 1583, only for the ships in which he had entrusted his precious cargo of books and printing materials to be waylaid and plundered by pirates. Vautrollier persevered and with official encouragement eight books were published under his name in Edinburgh in 1584. But even with royal patronage, there seems to have been insufficient business to justify his remaining there, and the following year he returned to London.

In a 1582 report on printing privileges, Christopher Barker, the queen's printer, felt Vautrollier was not fully exploiting his patents, and that 'he doth yet, neither great good, nor great harme withall' (Arber, *Regs. Stationers*, 1.144). This did not prevent a 1582–3 privy council commission into the printing trade recommending that Vautrollier's patent be opened up in order to benefit poorer printers. In 1583 and 1586 his London printing house was recorded as operating two printing presses. His wife, Jacqueline (*d.* after 1588), seems to have been an active member of the business; on 17 July 1581 she was granted permission by the Stationers' Company to finish printing an edition of Cicero 'in her husbandes absence' (Greg and Boswell, 11).

In 1583 Vautrollier was noted as being infirm, but he did not die until some point between 10 July 1587 when he drew up his will and 22 July 1587 when the will was proved. He bequeathed to his son Manassess the press he had used in Edinburgh; three other children, Thomas (who later became a bookseller in London), Simon, and James, were also mentioned in the will. Jacqueline continued the business on her own for a short time, although on 4 March 1588 the Stationers' Company ordered that she 'shall not at anye tyme or tymes hereafter prynte anye manner of Booke or Bookes whatsoeu[r], as well by Reason that her husband at the tyme of his decease was noe prynter'; shortly afterwards she married Richard Field, a former apprentice of her husband, in whose name the printing business was carried on (Greg and Boswell, 26).

ANDREW PETTEGREE

Sources W. R. LeFanu, 'Thomas Vautrollier, printer and bookseller', *Proceedings of the Huguenot Society*, 20 (1958–64), 12–25 · C. Clair, 'Thomas Vautrollier', *Gutenberg Jahrbuch* (1960), 223–8 · C. Clair, 'Refugee printers and publishers in Britain during the Tudor period', *Proceedings of the Huguenot Society*, 21 (1970–76), 115–23 · R. Dickson and J. P. Edmond, *Annals of Scotish printing* (1890), 377–93 · A. Mann, *The Scottish book trade, 1500–1720* (2000) · H. R. Plomer, *Abstracts from the wills of English printers* (1903), 27–9 · D. McKitterick, *A history of Cambridge University Press*, 1 (1992) · R. Peter and J.-F. Gilmont, *Bibliotheca Calviniana*, 3 (Geneva, 2000), nos. 76/4, 79/3, 83/5, 84/5, 85/1, 78/5, 79/3, 74/2 · R. E. G. Kirk and E. F. Kirk, eds., *Returns of aliens dwelling in the city and suburbs of London*, *from the reign of Henry VIII to that of James I*, 4 vols., Huguenot Society of London, 10 (1900–08), vol. 1, p. 392; vol. 2, pp. 179, 182, 252, 355; vol. 3, p. 411 • Arber, *Regs. Stationers* • P. Blayney, 'William Cecil and the stationers', *The Stationers' Company and the book trade, 1550–1990*, ed. R. Myers and M. Harris, St Paul's Bibliographies (1997), 11–34 • W. W. Greg and E. Boswell, eds., *Records of the court of the Stationers' Company, 1576 to 1602, from register B* (1930) • W. W. Greg, ed., *A companion to Arber* (1967) • *CPR, 1572–5*, 93

Vaux, Anne (*bap.* 1562, *d.* in or after 1637), recusant, was the third daughter of William *Vaux, third Baron Vaux of Harrowden (1535–1595), and his first wife, Elizabeth, daughter of John *Beaumont, master of the rolls from 1550 to 1552. Anne was baptized at Irthlingborough, Northamptonshire, on 9 July 1562; her mother was buried in the same parish on 12 August that year.

The family was strongly attached to Catholicism. For several years Anne Vaux worked hard and took considerable risks on behalf of the Jesuit provincial, Father Henry Garnett, to whom she was clearly devoted. Anne and her widowed sister, Eleanor *Brooksby, used their wealth to rent houses where missionary priests might meet in safety. One such property was White Webbs in Enfield Chase. In 1604 Anne Vaux, under the assumed name Mrs Perkins, and Garnett were dwelling in a house at Wandsworth, and both there and at White Webbs they were visited by, among others, her 'cousin german removed' Francis Tresham, the final man to be admitted to the Gunpowder Plot in 1605 (PRO, SP 14/216/212). Tresham's aunt, Mary, was Anne's stepmother. During the summer of 1605 Anne accompanied Garnett and other prominent English recusants on the much publicized 'pilgrimage' to St Winifred's Well (Holywell), Flintshire. Although kept in ignorance of the conspirators' plans Anne certainly had her suspicions: White Webbs was visited by several Gunpowder Plot conspirators that summer and autumn, and on the way to Holywell she had noted the 'fine horses' in the stables of Catholic houses, later recalling how she had 'feared these wild heads had something in hand, and prayed him [Garnett] for God's sake to talke with Mr Catesbye and to hinder any thinge that possibly he might' (PRO, SP 14/216/200).

A theory that Anne Vaux wrote the warning letter to Lord Monteagle which ultimately frustrated the Gunpowder Plot rests solely on perceived similarities between her handwriting and the 'disguised hand' used by the author; it lacks credibility (Nicholls, 214). She was at Coughton Court in late October and early November. When the plot was discovered she was arrested, but swiftly discharged on Lewis Pickering's bond. She concealed the fugitive Garnett in his vain efforts to avoid capture at Hindlip, Worcester, the home of Thomas Abington (or Habington). Garnett was arrested there on 25 January and conveyed to the Tower of London.

The ever-loyal Anne Vaux followed Garnett to the capital and managed to establish a channel of communications through his gaoler, writing to Garnett in an invisible ink at the foot of innocuous messages about spectacles and unpaid bills. Unfortunately, the gaoler passed every letter to the authorities. Anne was arrested in March and

joined Garnett in the Tower. Records survive for her examinations on 11 and 24 March, in which she insisted on her innocence from any complicity in treason while admitting to the by now well-documented visits of conspirators to her various residences. She was released in August 1606, and was in part responsible for publicizing 'Garnett's straw', an ear of corn, allegedly from the straw spread around the scaffold at Garnett's execution, which upon magnification appeared to carry a likeness of the dead man.

For many years the two Vaux sisters lived quietly at Shoby on the Brooksbys' Leicestershire estates, harbouring the Jesuit Father William Wright. In 1625 they were convicted of recusancy at Leicester Castle, but neither paid the fine demanded. After Eleanor Brooksby's death that same year, Anne, still with Father Wright in tow, moved to Stanley Grange in Derbyshire. There she kept what amounted to a school for the sons of Catholic gentlefolk: an attempt was made by the ecclesiastical authorities to suppress the establishment in 1635, but this may not have been entirely successful. The last extant reference to Anne Vaux comes in a parish register entry for the death of one of her servants in February 1637. Stanley Grange, however, long remained a centre for Jesuit activities in England.　　　　　　　　　　MARK NICHOLLS

Sources PRO, SP 14/216 • G. Anstruther, *Vaux of Harrowden: a recusant family* (1953) • GEC, *Peerage* • M. Nicholls, *Investigating Gunpowder Plot* (1991)

Vaux, Edward (1588–1661). *See under* Vaux, Thomas, second Baron Vaux (1509–1556).

Vaux, Henry (*c.*1559–1587). *See under* Vaux, William, third Baron Vaux (1535–1595).

Vaux, Laurence (1519–1585), Roman Catholic priest, was born in Bolton-le-Moors, Lancashire. He appears from the similarity in their coats of arms to have been distantly related to the Vaux family of Harrowden. He seems to have moved from Manchester grammar school to Queen's College, Oxford, and then to Corpus Christi College, where he attracted the attention of James Brooks, who was a fellow of the college and was bishop of Gloucester in Mary's reign, when Vaux served him as a chaplain. Cuthbert Scott, the bishop of Chester, ordained him priest in the collegiate church at Manchester on 24 September 1542. With the Edwardian dissolution of the college Vaux received a pension of £8 13*s.* 4*d.* In 1548 he was listed as a curate of Manchester church with a yearly salary of £12 19*s.* 6*d.* In 1556 he was admitted BTh at Oxford. In 1558 he became warden of the refounded collegiate church at Manchester. Towards the end of Mary's reign the college was used as a prison for protestants, but Vaux was never accused of cruelty.

After Elizabeth's first parliament passed the Acts of Uniformity and Supremacy, Vaux fled Manchester and took with him some of the college plate and vestments. Dodd reports that he went to Ireland where he fell in among brigands who robbed him of all his substance. Vaux himself did not mention the loss of the college plate, however, and he left some of it in his will. Vaux gave no indication why he had gone to Ireland, but his stay there was short, because he was hiding in Lancashire in 1561. His religious work came to the attention of the council who ordered him to remain in Worcestershire. Shortly after this Vaux left England and settled in Louvain, where he found his former bishop, Cuthbert Scott, who died on 3 October 1564. Vaux seems to have kept a school there.

During Vaux's stay in Louvain, Pope Pius V appointed Thomas Harding and Nicholas Sander apostolic delegates for England with faculties to be communicated to priests in England. The pope also forbade English Catholics to attend services in the Church of England. In 1566 Vaux visited Rome and was present at a papal consistory where the pope explained the faculties he had granted to Harding and Sander; Vaux was to communicate that explanation to them. After Vaux told Sander and Harding of the pope's directives they suggested that Vaux and William Allen return to England to announce the papal ban on attending the Church of England. They could not go themselves because they were involved in a pamphlet war with protestant divines which would make them marked men in England. Sander wrote a pastoral letter announcing the papal ban which Vaux and Allen were to circulate among their friends. Sander's letter does not survive, but Vaux also wrote a letter which preserved Sander's principal points. Vaux's work in Lancashire spreading the news of the papal prohibition again attracted the attention of the government, and a warrant was issued for his arrest.

Vaux was back in Louvain in 1567, having left England at the same time as Allen. While teaching at his school Vaux wrote a catechism for his students which he had printed as *A Catechisme, or Christian Doctrine, Necessary for Children and Ignorant People* (Louvain, 1567). It was his only publication, although another edition appeared at Antwerp in 1574, and two further editions in 1583. While similar in some ways to Bonner's 1555 *A Profitable and Necessary Doctrine*, the catechism differed in others. Vaux, like Bonner, avoided some controversial topics such as saints, purgatory, transubstantiation, and indulgences. Where Bonner's catechism treated holy water simply as a reminder of baptism, Vaux endowed it with apotropaic powers. The most significant difference between Bonner and Vaux is that Vaux defined salvation as resulting from faith and works as distinct from the Marian position, which cited faith alone joined with charity. Vaux's catechism also reproduced the medieval canon law for marriage. On 10 August 1572, the feast of St Laurence, he became a novice in the canons regular of St Augustine. Upon his entrance he received a letter from Thomas Goldwell, Marian bishop of St Asaph and a religious exile in Rome. Before taking his religious vows on 3 May 1573 he executed legal documents to preserve the Manchester plate and property 'until such time as the college should be restored to the Catholic faith' (*DNB*). Vaux was later elected sub-prior and may have returned to England to seek vocations for the foundation of an English community.

In 1580 William Allen persuaded the superior-general of the Society of Jesus to begin an English mission. Gregory XIII realized that the only Catholic bishop left in England

was Bishop Watson, who had been in confinement for years. He decided to send Bishop Goldwell back to England and with him his friend Laurence Vaux; Goldwell's presence in England would restore regular ecclesiastical government, and may have been based on the hope of limited toleration that was expected to result from the negotiations for the French match. By the time that the party of missionaries left Rome the negotiations had failed. Because of the publicity attending the departure of Campion and Persons for England, Goldwell did not leave the continent; Vaux, however, did. Upon his arrival he and another priest were turned over to the English by a French spy who had sailed the channel with them. After his initial examination Vaux was imprisoned at the Gatehouse at Westminster where the conditions were not bad. His letters describe the neat room he had and the quality of the food, all of which cost him £16 per year. In April 1584 Vaux was moved to the less comfortable Clink, apparently because copies of his catechism began circulating in the Manchester area. In 1585 he appeared before John Aylmer, bishop of London, and other royal commissioners. Aylmer asked Vaux if he were any relation to the Vaux who had written the popish catechism; Vaux admitted that the catechism was his. The bishop thought that Vaux should be executed, but Lord Burghley seems to have intervened for him. He died in the Clink some time in 1585. The cause of death is unknown. The Jesuit John Gibbons lists him as a martyr in his *Concertatio*, but that term is not normally used to describe those who died for their faith while in prison. The chronicle of the convent of St Martin in Louvain claimed that he was 'famished to death' (Gibson, 187). JOHN J. LAROCCA

Sources T. G. Law, introduction, in L. Vaux, *A catechisme, or Christian doctrine*, Chetham Society, new ser., 4 (1885) · *DNB* · V. Scully, 'Lawrence Vaux', *The Catholic encyclopedia*, ed. C. G. Herbermann and others, 15 (1912) · C. Dodd [H. Tootell], *The church history of England, from the year 1500, to the year 1688*, 3 vols. (1737–42) · Wood, *Ath. Oxon.*, new edn, 1.384 · J. E. Bailey, ed., *Inventories of goods in the churches and chapels of Lancashire, 1552*, Chetham Society, 107 (1879) · T. E. Gibson, *Lydiate Hall and its associations* (1876) · J. Molanus, *L'histoire de la ville de Louvain* (1861) · T. M. Veech, *Dr Nicholas Sanders and the English Reformation, 1530–1581* (1935) · Gillow, *Lit. biog. hist.*, vol. 5 · P. Guilday, *The English Catholic refugees on the continent, 1558–1795* (1914) · *CSP dom., addenda, 1547–65*

Archives Chetham's Library, Manchester, papers

Vaux, Nicholas, first Baron Vaux (c.1460–1523), courtier and soldier, was of an old Northamptonshire family. The Vaux estate of Harrowden had been acquired through the marriage of Margaret Vaux, Nicholas's great-aunt, to William Harrowden early in the fifteenth century. Nicholas's father, **Sir William Vaux** (1437–1471), married before 22 December 1456 Katharine Peniston (*d.* in or after 1509) of Provence, probably a lady-in-waiting to Margaret of Anjou. William Vaux, who was knighted about 1460, was attainted in November 1461 by Edward IV's first parliament, and he was next noted by Fortescue among the exiles in St Mighel with Queen Margaret in a letter of 13 December 1464. Vaux returned to England, probably with the queen in 1471, as he died on the field of Tewkesbury on 4 May and was buried in Tewkesbury Abbey. Katharine

Vaux was among the ladies taken after the battle with Queen Margaret, and was said to have returned to France with the queen in January 1476. In February 1478 Edward IV granted Katharine life interest in the manors of Stanton and Markham, which she had held with Vaux, because she 'hath none erthly thing for her and her children to lyve upon' (PRO, C81/863/4673). Those children were Nicholas and his sister Jane, or Joan, who married Sir Richard Guildford, perhaps by November 1487, as a Dame Joana Guildford is listed among the ladies attending Elizabeth of York's coronation.

Early life and local service Nicholas Vaux's childhood is obscure; he may have lived in the household of Margaret, countess of Richmond, given the comment in a pedigree that he 'floruit summa gratia apud Margaretam comitissam Richmundiae' (*DNB*). Certainly Vaux rapidly found favour under Henry VII. In Henry's first parliament Vaux petitioned for, and was granted, reversal of his father's attainder and the return of his lands; and on 2 November 1485, as an esquire of the body, he gained the stewardships of Olney and Newport Pagnell in Buckinghamshire. Throughout his life he performed his share of local service in his home county of Northamptonshire, through regular inclusion in commissions of the peace and for matters ranging from gaol delivery to sewers, and he was sheriff of Northamptonshire for the years commencing 5 November 1495, 5 November 1501, and 10 November 1516. Further fruits of royal favour included a grant on 1 June 1502 of the constableship of Rockingham Castle and stewardship of the lordships of Rockingham, Brigstock, and King's Cliffe with various associated offices.

Some time early in Henry's VII's reign Vaux married Elizabeth, daughter of Lord Fitzhugh and widow of Sir William Parr. They had three daughters: Katharine, who married Sir George Throckmorton; Ann, who married Thomas, Lord Strange; and Alice, who married Sir Richard Sapcote. After Elizabeth's death (before July 1507), Vaux made an advantageous second marriage before February 1508 with Anne (*b. c.*1489, *d.* in or before 1523), daughter of Sir Thomas Green, who inherited lands in York, Kent, Nottinghamshire, Northamptonshire, Buckinghamshire, Leicestershire, and Lincolnshire on her father's death in December 1506. Vaux paid heavily for the marriage. His children with Anne were: Margaret, who married Sir Francis Poulteney; Bridget, who married Maurice Welsh; Maud, who married Sir John Fermor; and two sons, Thomas *Vaux, who married Vaux's ward Elizabeth Cheyne, and William.

Diplomatic and military service Anstruther described Vaux as a jouster, courtier, and soldier, and his courtly and military talents were particularly exercised in French affairs. He was knighted on 16 June 1487 at Stoke, and made banneret in June 1497 after Blackheath, but though nominated several times for the Order of the Garter he was never chosen. On 23 December 1488 Vaux was among those commissioned in Northamptonshire to muster archers for the king's expedition to Brittany. He was with the knights who met the French delegates in 1492 during the settlement of the treaty of Étaples. In 1500 he accompanied Henry VII to Calais for his meeting with the archduke. An indenture dated 1 June 1502 appointed Vaux lieutenant of Guînes, and Henry VIII renewed Vaux's indenture at Guînes as 'keeper, governor, surveyor and lieutenant' for twenty years from 6 October 1509. Vaux's tenure in France was graced by triumphs and trials. He was called to serve in the vanguard of the king's army with 300 men under Lord Lisle in the campaign that captured Thérouanne and Tournai in April 1513; he fought at the battle of the spurs, but was forced to flee for his life from the ambush of a supply train travelling from Calais to the army at Thérouanne about 27–9 June. When policy turned to alliance, Vaux and his wife were summoned on 4 September 1514 to join the escort of Henry VIII's sister Mary to Abbeville for her marriage to Louis XII, and Vaux attended the marriage ceremony on 9 October.

From 1518 to 1520 Vaux was at the centre of Anglo-French affairs. On 9 November 1518 he was commissioned along with the earl of Worcester, the bishop of Ely, and Thomas Docwra to receive François I's oath accepting the treaty of London, which established peace and a marriage agreement between Henry VIII's daughter Mary and the dauphin François, and surrendered Tournai to the French on payment of 50,000 francs. Vaux was received by François with the other ambassadors on 12 December and was present at Notre Dame in Paris two days later when François gave his oath. On 30 January 1519 he was in Tournai with Worcester, Docwra, and Sir Edward Belknap, and on 10 February the town was surrendered. Vaux's next task was to prepare for the Field of Cloth of Gold; he served on the commission to appoint the time and place of the meeting. In January 1520 François I asked for Vaux to assist the earl of Worcester in choosing a place for the meeting, in lieu of the sieur de Chastillon. On 17 March Vaux, Belknap, and Sir William Sandys 'landyed at Caleys' charged with 'the makynge of a palace before the castle gate of Gwines' and making other necessary arrangements for lodgings, feasting, jousting, and fortifications (J. G. Nichols, ed., *A Chronicle of Calais in the Reigns of Henry VII and Henry VIII to the Year 1540*, CS, 35, 1845, 18). Vaux appears to have had a major role in supervising the building and had no easy time of it, judging by his letters to Wolsey of March, April, and May 1520, complaining of dilatory provisioners and lack of money. He was summoned as a knight of Northamptonshire to be present with Henry at the meeting. On 7 June 1520, the day the festivities commenced, he and the other English ambassadors had audience with François I.

Vaux's life was not without controversy. Treason was hinted against him in a letter of September 1504 or 1505 in which Sir Hugh Conway, then treasurer of Calais, claimed that Vaux and Antony Browne, lieutenant of Calais, had indicated that if the Tudor dynasty were challenged they 'should make ther peaxce hoo ever the worlde tourne' (Gairdner, 1.231–40). An anonymous letter to Wolsey of 1520 touching on the duke of Buckingham's treason also included articles of indenture between Vaux and Henry VII for Guînes, and advised Wolsey to review them and determine if Vaux had fulfilled the terms. Vaux was present at Buckingham's indictment for treason, on 8 May 1521 in the London Guildhall, and with Sir William Sandys led the duke through London to the Tower after his conviction. He was mentioned as briefly harbouring a chaplain of Buckingham's after his death, but does not seem to have suffered from this incident.

Court life Vaux's jousting appearances seemed more for service or show than sport. He and his brother-in-law Sir Richard Guildford were prominent at the jousts held for the marriage of Prince Arthur and Katherine of Aragon; according to one chronicler they 'were ever for the most party in the feld every day of the justes … and by them the Kynges Grace did sende his myende and messages into the feld' (Kipling, 65/543-9). Vaux played a similar role at the Field of Cloth of Gold, keeping order on the field rather than jousting, not surprisingly considering his age. On and off the field, his rich apparel prompted comment. At the wedding jousts he and Guildford wore 'great and massy cheynes of golde abought ther nekkes' (ibid., 65/547). The day of the marriage, Vaux wore 'a goune of purpyll velvet the which was pygth or sett wyth pesis of gold soo thyk & massy, that yt was Reportid to be worth In gold beside the sylk & furre M li'. Two days later he wore a 'coler of Essis' which weighed 'viiiC li. of noblys' (Thomas and Thornley, 311-12). Vaux made another notable appearance at the jousts to celebrate the birth of a prince to Henry VIII and Queen Katherine in February 1511. On the second day of the tourney, he wore 'a gown of Goldsmyth werk to the knees and theryn a Furre of Rygth broun & Fyne Sablys of grete valu' (ibid., 371).

The family was well represented at other court functions: a Lady Vaux, probably Katharine, was at Prince Arthur's baptism in September 1486. In 1487 Vaux was one of twelve knights of the body who alternated in bearing a canopy over Queen Elizabeth's litter as she was borne through London to Westminster before her coronation, while Katharine Vaux was with the queen when she sat in state the day after her coronation. Vaux was at the feast to celebrate Prince Henry's creation as duke of York at All Hallows in 1494, and was one of the knights with Prince Henry when he met Katherine of Aragon at St George's Field to escort her into the city of London in November 1501. He was in procession and presumably at the feast to celebrate the receipt of Wolsey's red hat in November 1515 and was among those who bore the canopy over the Princess Mary at her baptism, on 20 February 1516.

Vaux may have resided mainly at Harrowden after 1486; on 27 July 1511, Henry VIII visited 'Sir Nicholas Vaux's place', presumably Harrowden. Yet recognizances of February and July 1517, and October 1518, also describe him as of Norton, Northamptonshire (probably Green's Norton, part of his wife's inheritance), and Norton as well as Harrowden figures in his will. From 1502 his duties took him between Northamptonshire and France, and Anstruther suggests he spent winters in England and the rest of the year at Guînes. Vaux's interest in improving his lands led him into enclosure, and a 1517 survey discovered offences against the acts forbidding enclosures on his lands in

Buckinghamshire, Northamptonshire, and Bedfordshire, for which he was later pardoned. He also had to seek pardon in 1518 for failing to appear to submit accounts for his term as sheriff.

It was said that Vaux 'lieth very sore' in Guînes on 22 September 1522, but death held off until after his creation, before 28 April 1523, as first Baron Vaux of Harrowden. A letter of 14 May said Vaux was very ill, and he probably died that same day at the hospital of the knights of St John of Jerusalem in Clerkenwell. His will requested burial at Harrowden, Blackfriars in London, or Guînes, depending on his residence at death, and it is believed he was buried at Blackfriars.   L. L. FORD

Sources G. Anstruther, *Vaux of Harrowden: a recusant family* (1953), 3-37 · *LP Henry VIII*, vols. 1-3 · *CPR, 1485-1509* · GEC, *Peerage*, new edn, 12.216-19 · J. Gairdner, ed., *Letters and papers illustrative of the reigns of Richard III and Henry VII*, 1, Rolls Series, 24 (1861), 231-40; appx A, pts 6 and 7, 388-404, 404-17 · J. Wake, ed., *Northamptonshire past and present, Journal of the Northamptonshire Record Society*, vol. 2 in six parts (1962), 191, 202, 315, 321 · J. Bruce, ed., *Letters and papers of the Verney family down to the end of the year 1639*, CS, 56 (1853), 3, 12, 18-20, 32-3 · G. Kipling, ed., *The receyt of the Ladie Kateryne*, EETS, 296 (1990), 65, 157 · *The chronicles of the White Rose of York: historical fragments relating to the reign of King Edward the Fourth* (1845), 127-8 · BL, Cotton MS Julius B.xii, fols. 23v, 30r, 37r-v, 42v · PRO, Duchy of Lancaster, 5/4, fols. 77r, 93v · PRO, C65/106, m. 10-13 · *CIPM, Henry VII*, 1, no. 295; 3, nos. 43, 87, 247, 1004, 1162 · H. Ellis, ed., *The pylgrymage of Sir Richard Guylforde to the Holy Land, AD 1506*, CS, 51 (1851), xi-xiii, 5, 80 · A. H. Thomas and I. D. Thornley, eds., *The great chronicle of London* (1938) · *The works of Sir John Fortescue*, ed. T. Fortescue, 1 (1869), 21-31 · *VCH Northamptonshire*, vol. 4 · W. A. Shaw, *The knights of England*, 2 (1906), 29 · J. Anstis, ed., *The register of the most noble order of the Garter*, 2 (1724), 237-60, *passim* · Dugdale, *Monasticon*, new edn, 2.53-9

Vaux, Thomas, second Baron Vaux (1509-1556), poet, was born on 25 April 1509, one of the two sons of Nicholas *Vaux, first Baron Vaux of Harrowden (c.1460-1523), courtier and soldier, and his second wife, Anne (b. c.1489, d. in or before 1523), daughter of Sir Thomas Green of Boughton and Green's Norton, Northamptonshire, and his wife, Jane. Just after his fourteenth birthday in 1523, Vaux married Elizabeth (1504x9-1556), daughter of Sir Thomas Cheyne of Fen Ditton, Cambridgeshire, and of Thenford and Irthlingborough, Northamptonshire, and his second wife, Anne, daughter of Sir William Parr. They had two sons and two daughters. One of their sons was William *Vaux, third Baron Vaux of Harrowden (1535-1595). Vaux is said to have been educated at Cambridge University, but there is no surviving evidence for this.

In July 1527 Vaux was a member of Cardinal Wolsey's retinue on his embassy to France, where he negotiated with François I at Amiens. He first sat in parliament in 1529, and attended King Henry VIII and Anne Boleyn on their visit to François I at Calais in September 1532, taking twelve retainers with him. On 18 April of that year a man of his name wrote to the duke of Norfolk from Ampthill, revealing his unhappiness with his role in relation to the king's treatment of Katherine of Aragon (BL, Cotton MS Otho C.x, fol. 177), but this was probably not Lord Vaux. On 30 May 1533 Vaux was created a knight of the Bath for the coronation of Anne Boleyn on the next day. In March 1535

Thomas Vaux, second Baron Vaux (1509–1556), by Hans Holbein the younger, early 1530s

he signed a document acknowledging the payment to him of £280 by Roger Chomley for the manor of Newington Luces, Kent; the other witnesses were Sir Thomas Wyatt and Sir Thomas Poynings.

Vaux's only public office seems to have been that of governor of Jersey which he held from January to August 1536: he sold the office on to Edward Seymour, Viscount Beauchamp, for £150. It seems likely that at about this time he withdrew from the court and retired to his Northamptonshire estates, probably because his religious views were opposed to the growing influence of protestantism. Except for one day in November 1547, he did not attend parliament between 1534 and 1554. With other noblemen he attended the third of a series of disputations on questions appointed by the royal visitors at Cambridge University on 24–5 June 1549, and was part of Queen Mary's train at her coronation.

Vaux is usually associated with the courtly poets Sir Thomas Wyatt and Henry Howard, earl of Surrey. Vaux's poems are all original compositions rather than translations or imitations. They are mainly concerned with the trials of love and strike moralizing, sentencious, and occasionally religious notes. On a few occasions Vaux produces an unexpected metrical effect and a fresh or intimate tone, but his meaning is sometimes obscure. In *The Arte of English Poesie* (1589), George Puttenham included Vaux among the 'new company of courtly makers' who sprang up during the reign of King Henry VIII. Beginning the long confusion between father and son by calling him Nicholas Vaux, Puttenham described him as 'a man of much facillitie in vulgar makings', adding that 'his commendation lyeth chiefly in the facillitie of his meetre, and the aptnesse of his descriptions such as he taketh upon him to make, namely in sundry of his Songs, wherein he sheweth the counterfait action very lively & pleasantly' (Puttenham, 60, 62). Elsewhere, again getting his first name wrong, Puttenham describes Vaux as 'a noble gentleman,

and much delighted in vulgar making, & a man otherwise of no great learning but having herein a marvelous facillitie' (ibid., 239).

The canon of Vaux's surviving poetry is small. Describing the figure of '*Pragamatographia.* or the Counterfait action', Puttenham quoted twenty-two lines of a poem which he attributed to Vaux. The complete poem of fifty-six lines, with a few textual changes, was printed, without attribution, under the title 'Thassault of Cupide upon the Fort where the Lovers Hart Lay Wounded and how he was Taken' in Richard Tottel's *Songes and Sonnetes* (1557), a year after Vaux's death. The poem (no. 211 in *Tottel's Miscellany*) remained popular during the rest of the century: it was adapted and printed by John Awdely (*c.*1560), registered for publication as a ballad in 1565–6, adapted again in *A Gorgeous Gallery of Gallant Inventions* (1578), where it is described as 'To the tune, when Cupid scaled first the Fort', and copied in a manuscript miscellany (BL, Harley MS 6910) in the mid-1590s.

The following poem in Tottel's miscellany (no. 212 in Rollins's edition), headed 'The Aged Lover Renounceth Love' and beginning 'I Lothe that I did love', is again unattributed, but ascribed to Vaux in two contemporary manuscript miscellanies (Bodl. Oxf., MS Ashmole 48 and BL, Harley MS 1703); in the second of these it is said to have been written during the reign of Queen Mary. It was registered as a ballad for publication in 1563–4, and perhaps again in 1579; in his *Posies* of 1575, George Gascoigne referred to the poem's first line as written by Vaux, and 'thought by some to be made upon his death bed' (*Posies*, sig. ¶ ¶ iiir). The poem's first line also supplies the name of a tune for a poem in *A Gorgeous Gallery*: two more or less contemporary settings of the tune are known. It is a corrupt version of three stanzas (1, 3, and 8) of this poem which the gravedigger sings in *Hamlet* (v.i).

Two other poems in Tottel's miscellany have been attributed to Vaux in two manuscripts once owned by the Harington family. BL, Add. MS 28635, and the collection of poems, now at Arundel Castle, which is known as the Arundel Harington manuscript both have copies of the sonnet entitled 'The Frailtie and Hurtfulnes of Beautie' which begins 'Brittle beautie, that nature made so fraile' and of the alliterative epigram 'Against an Unstedfast Woman' (respectively, nos. 9 and 217 in Rollins's edition of Tottel and nos. 298 and 299 in the edition of the *Arundel Harington Manuscript* by R. Hughey). Puttenham printed his own imitation of the first of these 'made to daunt the insolence of a beautifull woman' (Puttenham, 123). Two further poems in the Arundel Harington manuscript can be associated with Vaux. One, a short poem beginning 'Syns by examples daylye we are taught' (no. 173 in Hughey's edition), is unique to the manuscript and attributed to him in it. The second, beginning 'When I looke back and in my self behold' (no. 22 in Hughey's edition), is one of fifteen poems printed above Vaux's name in the collection *The Paradise of Dainty Devices* (1576), where it has the title 'Of the Instabilitie of Youth' (no. 17). In addition to being copied in the Harington family collection, BL, Add. MS 28635, it is also found in two late sixteenth-century manuscript miscellanies (BL, Add. MSS 26737 and 30076): in the second of these it appears to be used as a song, and music for it survives, perhaps by Robert Parsons, in the Bodleian Library (MS mus. sch. e. 423). A shorter version of the poem, which seems to be independent of these sources, was printed in the Harington family collection *Nugae antiquae* in 1769 with the heading 'SONNET *wrote in the Tower*, 1554', with the implication that the poem was by John Harington the elder. The other poems attributed to Vaux in *The Paradise* are nos. 8 ('In his Extreame Sycknesse'), 16, 37 (another version is in *A Gorgeous Gallery of Gallant Inventions* of 1578), 48, 71 ('How can the tree but wast', for which musical settings survive), 80–81, 87–92, and 113 in Rollins's edition: nos. 48 and 88 are probably by William Hunnis.

In March 1556 Vaux was recorded as living at Arnold, Nottinghamshire; the date of his death is not known, but he was buried in October of that year. His wife died on 20 November, and it is likely that both were victims of the plague. He was succeeded by his son William.

There are two different drawings of Vaux by Hans Holbein the younger in the Royal Collection and one of his wife: they probably date from before 1536 and were executed in preparation for a pair of portraits of the couple. No painted versions are known of the portrait of Lord Vaux, but early painted versions of the picture of Lady Vaux are at Hampton Court and Prague, and probably derive from a lost original by Holbein.

Edward Vaux, fourth Baron Vaux of Harrowden (1588–1661), was born on 13 September 1588, the son of George Vaux (1564–1594) and his wife, Elizabeth (*fl.* 1585–1625), daughter of John Roper, first Baron Teynham, and his wife, Elizabeth. Edward was the grandson of William Vaux, the third baron, and the great-grandson of Thomas Vaux, the second baron, inheriting a strong devotion to Roman Catholicism.

Vaux was a ward of Queen Elizabeth I, but his mother bought back the wardship in or before Hilary term 1598, and he was brought up by his mother and her sisters-in-law, Anne Vaux and Eleanor, the wife of Edward Brooksby. He was educated with other boys by private tutors at Harrowden. From 1598 his mother sheltered the Jesuit priest John Gerard there, and mother and son were both suspected of being implicated in the Gunpowder Plot. Vaux travelled to Italy with Sir Oliver Manners in 1609–11, and was committed to the Fleet on his return for refusing to take the oath of allegiance. Sentenced to perpetual imprisonment and the loss of all his lands, he was pardoned and transferred to the custody of the dean of Westminster, George Montaigne, or Mountain, in October 1612, had his forfeited lands restored, and was released on the payment of sureties of £1500 in 1614–15. He attended parliament, served as a colonel of an English regiment in the Spanish service in Flanders in 1622–4, and, after a search of his house at Boughton for arms, was again committed to the Fleet for a short period in November 1625. During the civil war, in which he seems not to have taken an active part, his recusancy resulted in the confiscation of his estates.

In 1632, within five weeks of her husband's death, Vaux married Elizabeth (1586–1658), widow of William Knollys, first earl of Banbury, the daughter of Thomas Howard, first earl of Suffolk, and his second wife, Catherine. Vaux had probably lived with her while her husband was alive, and the couple had two sons, Edward (1627–*c*.1645) and Nicholas (*b.* 1631), who bore the surname Vaux. He died on 8 September 1661, and was buried at Dorking, having settled the whole of his estates on his son Nicholas, so excluding his own lawful heirs. Edward Vaux was succeeded in the title by his only surviving brother, Henry Vaux (*c*.1591–1663), fifth Baron Vaux of Harrowden, who died unmarried and without children. The title then fell into abeyance until it was revived on 12 March 1838 by George Charles Mostyn of Kiddington (1804–1883) who claimed it through his mother and the families of Vaux, Simeon, and Butler. The House of Lords decided in favour of Mostyn's claim to the title in preference to that of Edward Bourchier Hartopp; a third coheir, Robert Henry Herbert, twelfth earl of Pembroke, did not pursue his claim. Mostyn and Hartopp both traced their descent to daughters (Mary and Catharine, respectively) of George Vaux, the son of William Vaux, the third baron. H. R. WOUDHUYSEN

Sources GEC, *Peerage* · G. Anstruther, *Vaux of Harrowden: a recusant family* (1953) · G. Puttenham, *The arte of English poetry*, ed. G. D. Willcock and A. Walker (1936) · *Tottel's miscellany*, ed. H. E. Rollins, rev. edn, 2 vols. (1966) · R. Hughey, ed., *The Arundel Harington manuscript of Tudor poetry*, 2 vols. (1960) · *The paradise of dainty devices* (1576–1606), ed. H. E. Rollins (1927)
Likenesses H. Holbein the younger, coloured chalks, ink, and metalpoint drawing, 1530–34, Royal Collection [*see illus.*] · H. Holbein the younger, chalk, pen and ink drawing, Royal Collection

Vaux, Sir William (1437–1471). *See under* Vaux, Nicholas, first Baron Vaux (*c*.1460–1523).

Vaux, William, **third Baron Vaux** (1535–1595), recusant and priest harbourer, was probably born at Harrowden, Northamptonshire, in August 1535, the son of Thomas *Vaux, second Baron Vaux (1509–1556), and Elizabeth (1504x9–1556), daughter and heir of Sir Thomas Cheyne of Irthlingborough. William succeeded to the title upon the death of his father in October 1556, and at some time before 1 June 1557 he married Elizabeth, daughter of Sir John Beaumont of Grace Dieu, Leicestershire. They had four children: Henry [*see below*], Eleanor *Brooksby (*c*.1560–1625), Elizabeth (*b.* 1561), and Anne *Vaux (*bap.* 1562, *d.* in or after 1637). Upon the death of his first wife (12 August 1562) William married Mary, daughter of John Tresham of Rushton and sister of Sir Thomas Tresham. They had five children: George (1564–1594), Edward (*d.* 1585), Ambrose (*d.* 1626), Muriel, and Catherine.

On 20 January 1558 Vaux took his seat in the House of Lords and appeared there several times during the final year of Mary Tudor's reign. After her death he was one of the noblemen appointed to escort the new queen, Elizabeth, from Hatfield to London. He stayed away from parliament in 1559 and gave his proxy to the earl of Bedford, a protestant. Despite being known as a Catholic in 1567 and being listed as a supporter of the queen of the Scots he was a commissioner for musters in 1569–70, on a committee dealing with vagabonds and the eating of meat at forbidden times in 1572, and on a commission for gaol delivery in 1578–9. Persons believed that Vaux was arrested after the invasion of Ireland, but he was still at liberty at that time because he signed the certificate of musters on 22 September 1580 and sat in parliament on 19 January 1581. The queen and council viewed Vaux as a loyal subject despite his recusancy and support for Mary Stuart until his association with the Jesuit Edmund Campion.

In 1567 or 1568 Vaux looked for a competent tutor for his precocious son Henry. He decided upon Campion, who accepted the invitation and spent several months at Harrowden. Campion's letter to Henry, written on the eve of his departure from Oxford to Ireland in July 1570, testified to his deep friendship with the Vaux family and to the cultivated atmosphere in which Henry was raised. Vaux's troubles began after Campion's capture at the end of July 1581. On 6 August the privy council instructed Sir Walter Mildmay to summon Vaux and commit him to the custody of someone sound in religion because it was believed that Campion had stayed at his house. On 18 August he was questioned in the presence of members of the privy council. He and Sir Thomas Tresham were asked to swear that Campion had stayed at their houses. Both refused and were committed to the Fleet as close prisoners. Along with Tresham and others Vaux appeared before Star Chamber on 15 November. Asked again if Campion had stayed at his house, Vaux replied: 'And as to the receiving of Mr. Campion I (albeit I confess he was school master to some of my boys) yet deny that he was at my house. I say that he was not there to my knowledge, whereof reprove me [that is prove me wrong], and let me be punished with that punishment I deserve' (Anstruther, 122). They remained close prisoners after the trial. None the less at least once, c.7 January 1582, he and the other Catholic prisoners attended a clandestine mass in the Fleet. For this offence he and Tresham were fined 100 marks each. During his imprisonment his daughter Elizabeth entered the Poor Clares in Rouen in March 1582, and his sons Edward and Ambrose visited the English College in Rome in April. George visited the college in Rheims later the same year. Interestingly Vaux was never tried for sending his children abroad. About 19 April 1583 he and Tresham were released. During his imprisonment he had conveyed land to his sons so that it could not be seized to pay his recusancy fines.

Vaux was forced to remain in the London area, and rented a house in Hackney which was frequented by priests, as the council knew. Because of his fines and his conveyances of land, he could not pay his levy for light horse and lances. Lord Vaux's house received attention in the winter of 1585–6 as the site of an exorcism performed by the Jesuit William Weston upon a servant of Anthony Babington, later infamous for his role in the Babington plot. On 7 December 1587 Vaux was committed to the care of the archbishop of Canterbury. He was released in February 1589 when he appeared in the House of Lords. In 1590 Vaux was allowed to go to Northamptonshire for the first time in nine years. By this date his physical and mental health had deteriorated. In 1591 a government spy commented of Vaux and Thomas Tresham that they were good subjects and opposed the plans of the Spanish. The spy found their loyalty most remarkable. Vaux died on 30 August 1595 at Irthlingborough. The title passed to his grandson Edward *Vaux [see under Vaux, Thomas, second Baron Vaux (1509–1556)], first-born son of George Vaux and Elizabeth Roper.

Henry Vaux (c.1559–1587) was most likely born at Harrowden, the oldest son of William, third Baron Vaux, and Elizabeth Beaumont. He was an especially talented child, and by the age of thirteen was writing poetry in English and Latin. In 1571 Lord Vaux entrusted the care of the children of his marriage with Elizabeth Beaumont to her mother (also named Elizabeth) for ten years. He paid £20 annually for Henry and £10 annually for each of his sisters. Presumably the children received most of their education at Grace Dieu. In 1580 Henry Vaux was a member of an association of Catholic laymen, organized by George Gilbert to meet and support recently arrived priests and to conduct them to Catholic households. By 1583 he refused to marry because of his desire to become a priest. Consequently he and Lord Vaux drafted an agreement whereby the title and inheritance was settled on his half-brother George after an annuity had been set aside for Henry. Henry postponed his departure for the continent to study for orders until he constructed a safe network for clergy in England.

Throughout the 1580s Henry provided accommodation for and assistance to priests. He attended the meeting of leading recusants, priests, and Jesuits in Hoxton in the spring of 1585 that resulted in the establishment of a fund for the support of the clergy. Henry promised 100 marks to the fund. Periodically he was named in interrogations and confessions. On 5 November 1586 Henry was captured when the Vaux house in Hackney was raided. After examination by the privy council he was sent to the Marshalsea prison. Because of the deterioration of his health he was released for three months on 22 May 1587. He went to stay with his sister Eleanor Brooksby at Great Ashby, where he died of consumption on 19 November 1587. In a letter to Claudio Acquaviva, Jesuit father general, on 16 April 1596, Henry Garnet claimed that Henry Vaux pronounced the simple vows of the Society of Jesus immediately before his death. Few seem to have been aware of the vows. Indeed the Jesuit John Gerard wrote that the only thing that caused Henry Vaux regret on his deathbed was that he could not then be admitted into the society.

JOHN J. LARocca

Sources DNB · G. Anstruther, *Vaux of Harrowden: a recusant family* (1953) · J. Strype, *Annals of the Reformation and establishment of religion … during Queen Elizabeth's happy reign*, 2nd edn, 3 (1728) · T. M. McCoog, *English and Welsh Jesuits, 1555–1650*, 2, Catholic RS, 75 (1995) · A. Morey, *The Catholic subjects of Elizabeth I* (1978) · W. R. Trimble, *The Catholic laity in Elizabethan England, 1558–1603* (1964) · P. Caraman, *Henry Garnet, 1555–1606, and the Gunpowder Plot* (1964) · J. Gerard, *The autobiography of a hunted priest*, trans. P. Caraman (1988) · *The condition of Catholics under James I: Father Gerard's narrative of the*

Gunpowder Plot, ed. J. Morris (1871) • *Miscellanea*, II, Catholic RS, 2 (1906) • *CSP dom.*, 1547–80; 1591–4 • *CSP Rome*, 1558–71

Vaux, William Sandys Wright (1818–1885), antiquary, only son of William Vaux (1783/4–1844), Church of England clergyman, sometime prebendary of Winchester and probably vicar of Romsey, Hampshire, was born on 28 February 1818. He was educated at Westminster School from 1831 to 1836, and matriculated at Balliol College, Oxford, on 18 March 1836; he graduated BA in 1840 and proceeded MA in 1842. On 13 April 1841 he entered the department of antiquities of the British Museum as a first-class assistant. When the department was split on the retirement of the keeper, Edward Hawkins, he became on 21 January 1861 the first keeper of coins and medals. He married, on 11 July 1861, Louisa, eldest daughter of Francis Rivington of Harley Street, London.

Vaux's administration of the department was criticized following the abrupt departure of Frederic Madden junior in 1868. In July 1870 he appears to have had a breakdown and disappeared without warning, only to be located at Portsea. He was subsequently obliged to appear before a trustees' committee investigating losses from the collection, but was cleared of blame and allowed in October 1870 to resign with a pension. From 1871 to 1876 Vaux was engaged in cataloguing the coins in the Bodleian Library.

From 1846 Vaux was a member of the council of the Numismatic Society. In 1852 he became one of the secretaries, and for some time assisted John Yonge Akerman in editing the first series of the *Numismatic Chronicle*, in which he himself wrote twenty-five papers. He was president of the society from 1855 to 1874. For many years the society met in Vaux's rooms in Gate Street, Lincoln's Inn Fields. On 4 June 1868 he became a fellow of the Royal Society. From November 1875 to his death he was the secretary of the Royal Asiatic Society of Great Britain and Ireland, and for many years he was secretary to the Royal Society of Literature and was a fellow of the Society of Antiquaries. He was also connected with the early development of the Oxford Movement in London, and his rooms were a frequent place of meeting for the subcommittees connected with the London Church Union and the foreign chaplaincies. He died at his home, 102 Cheyne Walk, Chelsea, London, on 21 June 1885.

Vaux's knowledge was large and varied, more especially in all that related to oriental antiquities. His *Nineveh and Persepolis* (1850; 4th edn, 1855) is still of interest and did much to popularize the discoveries of Layard and others. He was responsible for *Inscriptions in the Phoenician Character … Discovered on the Site of Carthage, etc* (1863; lithographed facsimile), a transliteration into Hebrew characters with Latin translation. In 1864–5 he worked with A. W. Franks revising Hawkins's *Catalogue of British Medals*, which eventually appeared in 1885. He also wrote: *Handbook to the antiquities in the British Museum: a description of the remains of Greek, Assyrian, Egyptian, and Etruscan art* (1851), *Ancient History from the Monuments: Persia from the Earliest Period to the Arab Conquest* (1875; rev. edn by Prof. A. H. Sayce, 1893), and *Ancient History from the Monuments: Greek*

Cities and Islands of Asia Minor (1877). In 1854 he edited for the Hakluyt Society *The World Encompassed by Sir F. Drake*.

Vaux's contribution as a numismatist is not now regarded as of great significance. Little cataloguing took place during his keepership and he wrote relatively few articles. He is described as 'kind-hearted and unselfish' with 'a large circle of friends and acquaintances' (*Proceedings*, 145).

G. C. BOASE, *rev.* M. L. CAYGILL

Sources corresp., BM • *Numismatic Chronicle*, 3rd ser. 6 (1886), 18–19 • private information (2004) [A. Burnett] • *Proceedings of the Society of Antiquaries of London*, 2nd ser., 11 (1885–7), 145 • *The Times* (24 June 1885) • Foster, *Alum. Oxon.* • *GM*, 2nd ser., 23 (1845), 326
Archives BM
Wealth at death £858 14*s.* 6*d.*: resworn probate, Jan 1887, *CGPLA Eng. & Wales* (1886)

Vavasour [*married names* Finch, Richardson], **Anne** (*fl.* 1580–1621), lady of the royal household, was the daughter of Henry Vavasour of Copmanthorpe, Yorkshire, and Margaret Knyvet. Sworn as a gentlewoman of the bedchamber to Queen Elizabeth in 1580, she was serving within the year as one of the six maids of honour. This title proved all too ephemeral, for shortly after her arrival at court she became the mistress of Edward de *Vere, seventeenth earl of Oxford (1550–1604), and on 23 March 1581 gave birth to his son in the maidens' chamber. The queen sent both parents to the Tower. Their son, Edward Vere, went on to a military career in the Netherlands and a knighthood (1607), probably under the tutelage of his paternal relatives Sir Francis and Sir Horace Vere.

By 1590 Anne had married one John Finch, but was probably already the mistress of the queen's champion at tilt, Sir Henry *Lee (1533–1611), with whom she also had a son, Thomas Vavasour, alias Freeman. Anne and Sir Henry lived openly together at Ditchley in Oxfordshire and his other country houses; indeed, they entertained Queen Anne at a lodge near Woodstock in September 1608. At Lee's death in 1611 Anne inherited a jointure worth £700. By 1618 she had married a John Richardson, unmindful, apparently, that her first husband, Finch, was yet living. Lee's heir sued her for bigamy in the court of high commission, where she was fined £2000 in 1621. A tomb with a quatrain verse epitaph was prepared for Anne in St Peter's Chapel at Quarrendon, where Sir Henry was buried:

> Under this stone entombed lies a fair & worthy Dame
> Daughter to Henry Vavasour, Anne Vavasour her name.
> She living with Sir Henry Lee, for love long time did dwell
> Death could not part them but here they rest within one cell.
> (Lysons, and Lysons, 624)

No further details of her career or death have come to light.

Anne is associated with several Elizabethan lyrics, none of which she is likely to have written. The text of 'Though I seem strange, sweet friend, be thou not so' in Folger MS V.a.89, pages 8–9, is subscribed 'Vavaser', but 'La. B. to N.' in the British Library's Harley MS 6910, folio 145*r–v*. A partial text in Harley MS 7392 (2), folio 40, was at first assigned to 'H W'; the initials were later crossed out in favour of 'Ball.', quite possibly an abbreviation for 'ballad' in this anthology. The Folger manuscript also ascribes its copy of

Anne Vavasour (*fl.* 1580–1621), attrib. John de Critz the elder, *c.*1605

a poem on the Oxford–Vavasour liaison (beginning 'Sitting alone upon my thought') to Anne; she and Oxford are named in connection with other manuscript versions of the poem, apparently to identify them as the principals in the work rather than its authors.

Anne is often confused with another Anne Vavasour who also served as a maid of honour *c.*1601–3. In 1603 she married Sir Richard Warburton of London (*d.* 1610), the third son of Peter Warburton of Hefferston Grange, Weaversham, Cheshire, with Alice, daughter of John Cooper. Their son Cecil was Warburton's heir. This Anne was related to Anne Clifford and in the service of Lucy, countess of Bedford, before coming to court. She attended Elizabeth's funeral and received a pension of £66 13*s.* 4*d.* early in James's reign.   STEVEN W. MAY

Sources E. K. Chambers, *Sir Henry Lee* (1936) · New year's gift list, 1581, Eton, MS 192 · S. W. May, ed., *The poems of Edward de Vere, seventeenth earl of Oxford, and of Robert Devereux, second earl of Essex* (1980) · Folger, Folger MS V.a.89, 8–9 · BL, Harley MS 6910, fol. 145r–v · Bodl. Oxf., MS Rawl. poet. 85, fol. 17 · HoP, *Commons, 1558–1603* · D. Lysons and S. Lysons, *Magna Britannia*, 1 (1806)

Likenesses attrib. J. de Critz the elder, portrait, *c.*1605, Worshipful Company of Armourers and Brasiers, London [*see illus.*] · attrib. M. Gheeraerts, portrait, repro. in Chambers, *Sir Henry Lee*, 151

Vavasour, Sir John (*d.* 1506), judge, was the eldest son of John Vavasour of Spaldington in Yorkshire, and his wife Isabel, daughter and coheir of Thomas de la Hay, lord of Spaldington. He studied law at the Inner Temple. His first employment in court recorded in the year-books took place in Trinity term 1467, and in Trinity term 1478 he was invested with the order of the coif. He acted as legal adviser to various corporations and individuals, including Richard, duke of Gloucester. On 15 June 1483, in the last fortnight of the reign of Edward V, he was nominated a king's serjeant, an appointment renewed by Richard III and Henry VII. On 23 September 1485 he was appointed second justice at Lancaster, and was promoted to chief justice there in 1495. In the first year of Henry VII's reign the king and the earl of Northumberland put forward candidates for the post of recorder of York, but the corporation defended its autonomy and elected Vavasour (who had acted for the city for some years) in spring 1486. He continued in office until his appointment as puisne justice of the common pleas on 17 October 1489. He was knighted in 1501.

Vavasour married, possibly as his second wife, Elizabeth (*d.* 1509), daughter of Robert Tailboys, son of Sir William *Tailboys. She was the widow of an unidentified Greystoke, probably Sir Robert (*d.* 1483). In 1494 she and Vavasour were estranged, with Vavasour denying her any share of his land unless she repaid £700 she had taken away; but matters were apparently settled by 1502 when Vavasour granted her a life interest in Badsworth, Yorkshire. In the sixteenth century Vavasour was remembered as 'a very homely man and rude of condycyons and lovyd never to spend mych money' (*Testamenta Eboracensia*, 4.90). From a memorial dated 1505–6 it appears that he was concerned in Sir Richard Empson's lawsuit against Sir Robert Plumpton, and that he allowed himself to be influenced by Empson. Vavasour was discharged as judge on 16 October 1506. He died without issue on 26 November 1506 and was buried in St Helen's, Bishopgate, London. His heir was Peter, son of his brother William.

E. I. CARLYLE, *rev.* ROSEMARY HORROX

Sources E. W. Ives, *The common lawyers of pre-Reformation England* (1983) · *The reports of Sir John Spelman*, ed. J. H. Baker, 2 vols., SeldS, 93–4 (1977–8) · Foss, *Judges* · L. C. Attreed, ed., *The York House books, 1461–1490*, 2 vols. (1991) · E. W. Ives, 'The reputation of the common lawyers in English society, 1450–1550', *University of Birmingham Historical Journal*, 7 (1960), 130–61 · [J. Raine], ed., *Testamenta Eboracensia*, 4, SurtS, 53 (1869) · T. Stapleton, ed., *Plumpton correspondence*, CS, 4 (1839) · will, PRO, PROB 11/15, sig. 16 · *CIPM, Henry VII*, 3, nos. 275, 276, 849

Vavasour, Thomas (*d.* 1585), physician and recusant, was a younger son of Sir Peter Vavasour (*d.* in or after 1556) of Spaldington, Yorkshire, and Elizabeth Windsor; the family was a cadet branch of the Vavasours of Hazelwood Castle. Thomas Vavasour was educated at St John's College, Cambridge, in the 1530s (BA, 1536; MA, 1538). Elected a fellow of Clare College in 1539, he transferred to Henry VIII's new foundation of Trinity College in 1547, serving first as steward and then as junior bursar. His religious commitment first became apparent in the course of Nicholas Ridley's visitation of the university in June 1549, during which Vavasour was a thorn in the bishop of Rochester's flesh. He was listed second among eight senior fellows of Trinity who were described as a nest of papists, posted a Latin pasquinade against the visitors, and extemporized a marvellous counter to one of Ridley's arguments during the famous public disputation about the eucharist. Ridley advanced a pointed sorites: 'what Christ took, that he blessed; what he blessed, that he brake; what he brake, that he gave; ergo, what he received [that is, bread], he gave, etc.' Vavasour immediately cut in:

> God took a rib out of Adam's side; what he took, he built; what he built, he brought; what he brought, he gave to Adam to be his wife; but he took a rib: ergo, he gave a rib to Adam to wife. (*Acts and Monuments*, 6.331)

Many years later, Edmund Grindal, then archbishop of York, was to remind William Cecil of the character of this man—they had been contemporaries at St John's in the 1530s. Vavasour was now making trouble for him in York, and Grindal recalled him as 'sophistical, disdainful, and eluding arguments with irrision' (Nicholson, 350).

Soon after the disputation Vavasour left England for Italy. While his later career suggests that his motives may have been as much religious as professional, his avowed purpose—to study medicine—was legitimate enough for him to remain in receipt of his stipend from Trinity. Having graduated MD at Venice in December 1553 he returned to England with Mary Tudor upon the throne and the mass once more upon the altar. He continues to appear in the Trinity College accounts until 1555 (the accounts for 1556–9 are unfortunately lost), but presumably resigned his fellowship by November 1556, when he was licensed for medical practice by the recently founded Royal College of Physicians. By 1561 he was married to Dorothy Kent, and in the 1560s took up residence with his wife in the parish of Holy Trinity Goodramgate, York. Their house stood on Common School Lane, beside Archbishop Holgate's School.

The 'alteration of religion' under Queen Elizabeth was coolly received in York, and Thomas Vavasour was from the start a ringleader of Catholic survival and resistance. The arrival of more determined ecclesiastical leadership in the later 1560s, beginning with Matthew Hutton's appointment as dean in 1567, led to a clamp-down on Catholic activities. Vavasour was summoned before the York high commission in 1568, but, as later reported to William Cecil, his influential friends ensured that officials turned a blind eye, and the oft-repeated summons proved impossible to serve. In due course he was excommunicated for contumacy, and no doubt savoured the irony of the penalty. With the outbreak of the rising of the northern earls (1569), however, he found it expedient to go into hiding. Eventually, in 1574, he was pinned down at his York residence in what seems to have been England's earliest priest's hole. He was in effect starved out, and after his arrest he was in due course brought before the high commission. In Grindal's words, the commissioners:

> knowing his disposition to talk, thought it not good to commit the said Dr Vavasour to the castle of York, where some other like affected remain prisoners; but rather to a solitary prison in the Queen's majesty's castle at Hull, where he shall only talk to the walls.   (Nicholson, 351)

Apart from a period of house arrest in 1575–7 and a brief release on parole in 1579, he spent the rest of his life there. Ministering to the sick of the gaol during an outbreak of disease, he himself fell ill and died on 12 May 1585. He was buried in Drypool churchyard, Hull.

Under Vavasour's wife, Dorothy, the household remained a centre of York Catholicism until the 1580s. Edmund Campion said mass there during his sensational tour of England in 1580. Two of their sons, Thomas and James, went abroad to study for the priesthood in the Catholic seminaries. Thomas died tragically in 1587, murdered by his guide in Puglia while on a fund-raising trip for the English College at Rome. Dorothy herself was arrested in 1581, in the aftermath of Campion's tour, and spent the rest of her life in the gaols of the Ousegate Bridge in York, together with other female recusants. There she contracted gaol fever, and died on 26 October 1587, with her companions Mary Hutton and Alice Oldcorne dying the day before and the day after. Those who die in gaol are not usually accorded the title of martyr, but there can be little doubt that the Vavasours gave up everything for their faith, undergoing not a short agony, but years of hardship and suffering and the disintegration of their immediate family. Yet not in vain: descendants and relatives of the Vavasours remained prominent in Yorkshire recusancy well into the seventeenth century.   RICHARD REX

Sources R. Rex, 'Thomas Vavasour', *Recusant History*, 20 (1990–91), 436–54 · J. Lamb, ed., *A collection of letters, statutes and other documents … illustrative of the history of the University of Cambridge during the Reformation* (1838), 120 · *The acts and monuments of John Foxe*, ed. S. R. Cattley, 8 vols. (1837–41), vol. 6, pp. 328–32 · senior bursars' accounts, Trinity Cam. · 'Fr Grene's MS, Book F', *Records of the English province of the Society of Jesus*, ed. H. Foley, 3 (1878), 214–57 · J. Morris, ed., *The troubles of our Catholic forefathers related by themselves*, 3 (1877) · J. C. H. Aveling, *Catholic recusancy in the city of York, 1558–1791*, Catholic RS, monograph ser., 2 (1970) · T. F. Knox and others, eds., *The first and second diaries of the English College, Douay* (1878) · W. Nicholson, ed., *The remains of Edmund Grindal*, Parker Society, 9 (1843), 350–51 · M. Hodgetts, 'A topographical index of hiding places', *Recusant History*, 16 (1982–3), 146–216

Vavasour, Sir William, baronet (*d.* 1659), royalist army officer, was the younger surviving son of Sir Thomas Vavasour (*d.* 1620) of Copmanthorpe, Yorkshire, and Skellingthorpe, Lincolnshire, knight marshal to James I, and his wife, Mary Dodges. Like his elder brother, Sir Charles (*d.* 1644), William saw military service in Europe before returning to England in 1639, and he married a Dutch woman whose name is not known. He later married Olivia (1620–1714), daughter of Brian Stapleton (or Stapylton) of Mytton, Yorkshire. His family was related to the strongly Catholic Vavasours of Hazelwood, Yorkshire, who supplied several notable royalist officers, but is not known to have been Catholic itself.

During the second bishops' war of 1640 Vavasour was a

colonel of foot. On 9 November 1641 the Commons named him to the council of war for Ireland, but later the same month his involvement in the army plot emerged and he accompanied Charles I during the attempted arrest of the five members on 4 January 1642. Consequently the Commons vetoed his appointment in the Irish expedition. At the outbreak of the civil war he became lieutenant-colonel of the king's life guard of foot under Lord Willoughby. He was captured at the battle of Edgehill and imprisoned at Warwick Castle, but escaped or was released before 10 April 1643 and rejoined the court in Oxford. On 14 June 1643 he was appointed commander-in-chief in the five counties of Herefordshire, Monmouthshire, Glamorgan, Brecknockshire, and Radnorshire, nominally under Richard Herbert, second Baron Herbert of Cherbury. The aim was to reconstitute Herbert's shattered command in those counties, and Vavasour worked with local commissioners to raise men and money. On 17 July he was made a baronet and governor of Hereford, and later that month he briefly besieged Brilliana, Lady Harley, at Brampton Bryan. His 1500 foot and horse were then subsumed into the main royal army.

Vavasour led the Welsh forces at the siege of Gloucester in August and commanded one of four foot brigades at the first battle of Newbury on 21 September where his men suffered heavily. He returned to his command in October and was named colonel-general of the five counties on 10 November. He spent eight months based mainly at Tewkesbury, where his council of war was based, fighting to reduce Colonel Edward Massey's Gloucester garrison. For some months Massey was in desperate straits. However, Vavasour's success was short-lived. Between December 1643 and February 1644 Massey's deputy, Captain Backhouse, inveigled him into a fake plot to betray Gloucester. This wasted considerable time and his secretive behaviour alienated Vavasour's council of war; Massey's chaplain, John Corbet, says that Vavasour 'was complained of, reviled and cursed and at once lost every opportunity of action and advancement in the king's service' (Corbet, 87). He fell foul of Herbert, who resented being sidelined, while Sir John Winter, governor of the Forest of Dean, and Colonel Nicholas Mynne, his former lieutenant-colonel, increasingly ignored his orders from February onwards; the successive governors of Berkeley Castle were never his to command.

As it became clear that Prince Rupert would replace Herbert and exercise a real command, Vavasour pinned his hopes on becoming commander-in-chief in Gloucestershire. He cleared the forest in February and stormed Painswick on 29 March, which he did partly 'to repaire his credit' (Corbet, 88). On 12 April he was appointed commander-in-chief in Gloucestershire but much of his force had already been reassigned elsewhere and he could not prevent a vital convoy slipping into Gloucester, enabling Massey to take the offensive. The publication of the Backhouse plot in May added to his humiliation. When Herbert resigned his command in June he secured Vavasour's dismissal in favour of Mynne. After Mynne's death in action on 2 August Vavasour was reappointed governor of

Hereford but he did not take the post up, for reasons unknown. Despite being promoted field marshal-general in the same month he never held command again.

Vavasour shared Rupert's disgrace after the fall of Bristol in March 1645 and resumed his military career abroad in 1646. Little is known of his later years. Presumably Vavasour had no estates, because the parliamentarian committees never troubled him. In August 1656 he was briefly back in England, where the council of state authorized him to raise volunteers and press prisoners to serve Charles X of Sweden. Vavasour was killed in action at the siege of Copenhagen, possibly on 18 February 1659; his widow was granted letters of administration on 11 March. It was said that the Swedish king asked for his body to be recovered and that it came back stripped, with the ears cut off. He was survived by a daughter, born in Drury Lane in 1654.   ANDREW WARMINGTON

Sources P. R. Newman, *The old service: royalist regimental colonels and the civil war, 1642–1646* (1993) · J. Corbet, 'An historicall relation of the military government of Gloucester', *Bibliotheca Gloucestrensis*, ed. [J. Washbourne], 1 (privately printed, Gloucester, 1823), 1–152 · R. Hutton, *The royalist war effort, 1642–1646*, 2nd edn (1999) · *CSP dom., 1640–41; 1644–5; 1656* · P. R. Newman, *Royalist officers in England and Wales, 1642–1660: a biographical dictionary* (1981) · G. A. Harrison, 'Royalist organisation in Gloucestershire and Bristol, 1642–1646', MA diss., University of Manchester, 1961 · *A true relation of a wicked plot* (1644) [Thomason tract E 45(12)] · corresp. of Prince Rupert, BL, Add. MSS 18980–18981 · *The journal of Sir Simonds D'Ewes from the first recess of the Long Parliament to the withdrawal of King Charles from London*, ed. W. H. Coates (1942); repr. (1970) · W. H. Coates, A. Steele Young, and V. F. Snow, eds., *The private journals of the Long Parliament*, 1: *3 January to 5 March 1642* (1982) · 'A journal of Sir William Vavasour's military motions', Bodl. Oxf., MS Clarendon 27, fols. 73–6 · *Dugdale's visitation of Yorkshire, with additions*, ed. J. W. Clay, 1 (1899), 177 · GEC, *Baronetage*, 2.212, 2.78
Archives BL, letters to Prince Rupert, Add. MSS 18980–18981

Veal [Veel], **Edward** (1632/3–1708), clergyman, ejected minister, and nonconformist tutor, is of uncertain origins. He is perhaps the son of the Lancashire gentleman Edward Veal of Laughton who was an elder of the seventh Lancashire classis in 1646. It has, however, also been suggested that he was probably born in Gloucestershire. He matriculated at Christ Church, Oxford, on 27 February 1651, graduating BA in 1652 and proceeding MA on 21 February 1654. From 1655 he was minister of Dunboyne, co. Meath, on a stipend of £40 per annum under the civil establishment of Henry Cromwell; he was ordained at Winwick, Lancashire, by the fourth Lancashire presbyterian classis on a call from his Irish parish on 14 August 1657. Nevertheless, in March 1655 it was by a petition of the Independent churches of Ireland that Veal was proposed as one of a raft of eight men suitable to remedy the lack of godly fellows at Trinity College, Dublin, and was duly one of the five elected fellows; he had been promoted to a senior fellowship by 24 November 1656. He was created BD there on 3 July 1661. Shortly afterwards he was deprived of both parish and fellowship for his nonconformity to the re-established Church of Ireland and, having received a certificate (dated 31 December 1661) testifying to his usefulness from Stephen Charnock and six other nonconformist divines, he left Ireland in January 1662. The certificate described him as:

> a learned, orthodox, and ordained minister, of a sober, pious and peaceable conversation, who during his abode in the college, was eminently useful for the instruction of youth, and whose ministry hath been often exercised … with great satisfaction to the Godly.   (Calamy, *Continuation*, 1.83)

He became chaplain to the former parliamentarian general Sir William Waller, after whose death in 1668 he became pastor to a small congregation in the East End of London. In 1669 it was reported that at Stepney 'one Mr Veale, an Independent hath lately set up a meeting in this parish, And first sollicited for Subscriptions, before he would come' (*Calamy rev.*, 501). This must be the same meeting over which he presided (if not in precisely the same location) near or in Globe Alley, Wapping; that was broken up by the authorities in 1670 but Veal took out a licence as its presbyterian minister under the declaration of indulgence two years later. In 1689 he was certified as a preacher in the parish of Whitechapel (consistent with the congregation at Wapping, to which he himself alluded in 1703). He also ran an academy at Wapping for ministerial students, for which he suffered prosecution. Among his pupils were Samuel Wesley (*bap.* 1662, *d.* 1735), the father of John and Charles Wesley; despite his later career in the Church of England, at the time that he attended Veal's academy in the late 1670s Wesley was intended for the Independent ministry. Veal gave up the academy about 1680. The apparent ambiguities over his denominational label reflect, no doubt, both the insensitivities and carelessness in reporting of the authorities and even more the fluidities of association within Restoration dissent. It is probably most significant that Veal was co-editor of works by Stephen Charnock, like himself an Independent in Ireland in the 1650s who found himself comfortable within Restoration presbyterianism; he also contributed along with other presbyterian divines to the continuation of Matthew Poole's *Annotations upon the Holy Bible* (1683).

Having lost his voice 'and ability to speak out of the pulpit' and having 'thought fit to supply the want of it', Veal published *Practical Discourses* on sin, wickedness, and Christ as healer and saviour (Veel, sig. A2). Another volume of *Practical Discourses* followed in 1705. Besides these he wrote many sermons on a variety of topics such as 'what spiritual knowledge they ought to seek for that desire to be saved'. Many of these were published in the various editions of the *Morning Exercises*, the majority being republished in James Nichols's *The Morning Exercises at Cripplegate* (1844).

By late November 1705, when he made his will, Veal had retired south of the river to suburban Peckham. His wife (whose name is unknown) had died before him and the only kin mentioned in his will were a sister, Martha, to whom he left £5 for mourning and 'my Pools Annotations on the Scripture in two Volumes in Folio'; his widowed sister-in-law; and his unmarried daughter, Katherine, who received the bulk of the estate (PRO, PROB 11/502, sig. 157).

Veal died on 6 June 1708, aged seventy-five. He had originally wished to be buried in Battersea, but was in fact buried in the parish church of Wapping on 13 June. His funeral sermon was preached by Thomas Simmons, his successor as pastor to the Wapping congregation. Preaching on a text from 2 Timothy, Simmons declared that 'every part of the apostle's character may be accommodated to the case of our deceased friend and father' who had been 'very laborious in his attempts to pull down the strongholds of sin and Satan, in the souls of other men' (Simmons, 41–2).

ALEXANDER GORDON, *rev.* CAROLINE L. LEACHMAN

Sources E. Calamy, *A continuation of the account of the ministers … who were ejected and silenced after the Restoration in 1660*, 2 vols. (1727), vol. 1, pp. 81–4 · E. Calamy, ed., *An abridgement of Mr. Baxter's history of his life and times, with an account of the ministers, &c., who were ejected after the Restauration of King Charles II*, 2nd edn, 2 vols. (1713), vol. 2, p. 57 · *Calamy rev.*, 501 · E. Veel, *Practical discourses* (1703) · T. Simmons, *The conqueror crowned: a funeral sermon on occasion of the death of the late Reverend and learned divine Mr Edward Veel* (1708) · Wood, *Ath. Oxon.: Fasti* (1820), 164–5, 177 · will, PRO, PROB 11/502, sig. 157
Wealth at death see will, PRO, PROB 11/502, sig. 157; *Calamy rev.*, 501

Veale, Sir Douglas (1891–1973), university administrator, was born in Bristol on 2 April 1891, the third and youngest son (there were no daughters) of Edward Woodhouse Veale, solicitor, and his wife, Maud Mary Rootham. He was educated at Bristol grammar school which he left in 1910 with a classical scholarship to Corpus Christi College, Oxford, where he was placed in the first class in classical honour moderations in 1912 and in the second class in *literae humaniores* in 1914.

Veale was called up as a territorial to serve in the 4th battalion of the Gloucestershire regiment. He took the civil service examinations, was appointed a second-class clerk under the Local Government Board, married in 1914 Evelyn Annie (*d.* 1970), daughter of James Alexander Henderson, surveyor, of Westbury-on-Trym, Bristol, and rejoined his battalion to see service as a captain in France and Belgium in 1915. He was invalided home to become adjutant to the reserve battalion but in 1917 was released to take up his clerkship.

Veale was soon marked out for promotion as the board itself burgeoned into the Ministry of Health. By 1920 he was private secretary to the permanent secretary and from 1921 to 1928 private secretary to successive ministers of health from Christopher Addison onwards. It was Veale who supplied Sir Alfred Mond—and thereby the cabinet—with the formula 'the British Commonwealth of Nations' during the negotiations over the Irish treaty of 1921. In 1926 he became a principal. As Neville Chamberlain's private secretary he played a major role, with his friend and colleague Sir Maurice Gwyer, in implementing the complicated Local Government Act of 1929; he was appointed CBE that year.

It was evident in Whitehall that Veale was striding to the top, but Oxford's pull proved stronger. The Asquith commission had recommended in 1922 that the central administration of the university should be strengthened and the post of registrar should become an appointment of far greater significance. In 1930 Veale was appointed registrar from a strong field.

Oxford colleges were at that time reluctant to accept central guidance, and Veale was the object of early suspicion, as a young man in a hurry (and he remained both young and in a hurry all his life). But his tirelessness, accessibility, knowledge, and supple draftsmanship soon made him indispensable. As a fellow (1930) of his old college, the smallest in Oxford, he was sensitive to college susceptibilities and his own particular experience of Whitehall made him sensitive also to town–gown relations. He was patient, impartial (but not so impartial as to lose impetus), energetic, and imperturbable. He worked his small staff hard but took personal responsibility for any error, never forgetting how Maurice Hankey had once saved his own face by letting Veale be blamed for one of Hankey's rare omissions. He always went to a meeting knowing what he expected to be the result and wrote the minutes of hebdomadal council in advance, leaving narrow spaces for the dissenting view. He was never a 'mere administrator' but he liked clear decisions and yielded no sympathy to the self-indulgent who rejoiced in making university politics the art of the impossible. He had the rapid knack of harnessing the soaring imagination of others to the longer haul without developing tunnel vision.

It was significant that Veale's favourite vice-chancellor, among the many he served so strenuously, should be A. D. Lindsay, the master of Balliol, and the least effective in Veale's view Sir Richard Livingstone, the president of Veale's own college.

Veale's integrity was combined with ingenuity in unobtrusively exercising influence. As time went on his contemporaries in Whitehall became very important men and Whitehall itself became increasingly important to Oxford as the Treasury and the University Grants Committee came to play a more significant part in its future. Veale did not scruple to use them and all his own widespread friendships to the hilt. His hospitality was at once generous and purposeful.

Veale was a principal architect of the modern Oxford University, preparing it well for the dramatic changes which followed his retirement. Inevitably the Clarendon Building, in those days the abode of the university offices, was known as the Hotel de Veale. The various Nuffield benefactions were in part the result of his skill in steering vision into practicality. He was keenly interested in the Commonwealth, and was a forceful ally to the Colonial Office and its Oxford connections, to Sir Ralph Furse, Sir Charles Jeffries, and Dame Margery Perham. The medical world of city and university owes him a particular debt; likewise the Oxford Society, the Historic Buildings Appeal, the Oxford Preservation Trust, Dorset House, the Casson Trust, St Antony's College, and St Edmund Hall, of which he became an honorary fellow in 1958 (the same year as that in which he was made an honorary fellow of his own college). Outside Oxford his favourite charity was the Abbey School at Malvern of which he was chairman and where his two daughters were educated. Retiring as

registrar (1958) he remained as energetic as ever. He was also remarkably fit—a great walker and a keen tennis player who at the age of eighty-one complained that doubles in the university parks did not give him enough exercise. He worked hard to get his genial way and usually did; but he never repined at defeat: he was a strong swimmer. Knowing his own worth, he was cheerful but serious-minded, a stout Anglican, staunch to the Arnoldian values of a generation too few of whom survived Flanders. Silent at the major bodies which he serviced, for he always briefed his chairman so well that words by him were unnecessary, he would in compensation read aloud to his wife of an evening the book of *his* choice. Lady Veale (he was knighted in 1954) was a person of quiet strength and whimsical humour. It was a most happy marriage. They were survived by three children: John, musician and film critic; (Evelyn) Margaret, widow of R. B. McCallum, master of Pembroke College, Oxford; and Janet.

Veale died in Oxford on 27 September 1973 at the Acland Hospital, the extension of which owed much to his efforts long before. Veale was an honorary DCL of Oxford (1958) and honorary LLD of Melbourne (1948). He is commemorated in Oxford by a carving of his head in the archway leading from the Bodleian quadrangle to the Clarendon Building and by sheltered housing in Headington named after him.   E. T. WILLIAMS, *rev.* H. G. JUDGE

Sources *The Times* (29 Sept 1973) · *Oxford Times* (5 Oct 1973) · K. Wheare, *Oxford*, 26/1 (1974) · R. Heussler, *Yesterday's rulers: the making of the British colonial service* (1963) · R. D. Furse, *Aucuparius: recollections of a recruiting officer* (1962) · *The Lyttelton Hart-Davis letters: correspondence of George Lyttelton and Rupert Hart-Davis*, ed. R. Hart-Davis, 4 (1982) · D. Dilks, *Neville Chamberlain*, 1 (1984) · *Hist. U. Oxf.* 8: *20th cent.* · personal knowledge (1986) · private information (1986)
Archives BL, corresp. with Albert Mansbridge, Add. MS 65257A · Bodl. Oxf., corresp. with Nevill Coghill, MSS Eng. lett. c. 798–809 · Bodl. Oxf., corresp. with Lord Monckton · Bodl. RH, corresp. with Margery Perham · Nuffield Oxf., corresp. with Lord Cherwell
Likenesses M. Batten, stone bust, 1953, Bodl. Oxf. · W. Stoneman, photograph, 1955, NPG
Wealth at death £139,757: probate, 1974, *CGPLA Eng. & Wales*

Veale, George (*b.* 1757, *d.* in or before 1833), viola player, was baptized on 2 October 1757 at St Andrew's Church, Holborn, London, the son of Timothy Veale and his wife, Elizabeth. He was first heard of in 1784, when he took part in the Handel memorial concerts. He played in the Covent Garden Theatre band and took part in the oratorio performances at the Drury Lane Theatre. He was admitted to the Royal Society of Musicians in 1788, and during the 1790s played in the annual concerts in St Paul's Cathedral sponsored by the Royal Society of Musicians. From 1812 to 1817 he played in the band at Drury Lane.

It used to be thought (incorrectly) that Veale was the pseudonymous author of a satire on Dr Burney's *Musical Tour* entitled *Musical Travels through England* (1774), which appeared under the name of Joel Collier. The second edition contains a fictitious account of the last illness and death of Collier. It was later suggested that it was written partly by John Laurence Bicknell and partly by Peter Beckford.

Veale had died by 6 January 1833, when the Royal Society of Musicians gave his sister £12 to cover his funeral expenses.   ANNE PIMLOTT BAKER

Sources Highfill, Burnim & Langhans, *BDA* · *IGI* · Allibone, *Dict.*
Wealth at death sister was given £12 by the Royal Society of Musicians for funeral expenses, suggesting poverty

Veale, Richard (1687?–1756), master mariner and privateer, was probably the son of Richard Veale, a fuller, who was born on 20 January 1687 and baptized in St George's, Exeter, on 30 January. Another son, Joseph, became receiver of taxes for Devon. Veale married twice. His first wife, Margaret Brown, died in July 1734; they had two children, but both had died in infancy. On 6 May 1735 he married Jane (*bap.* 1716, *d.* 1754), daughter of James King, a City merchant.

After extensive experience as a master Veale was commissioned in 1744, when the war against Spain was formally extended to France, as commander of the *Hunter*, a private man-of-war. He subsequently commanded the privateers *Inspector* and *Dreadnought*.

Veale's successes as a privateer included the capture of an English privateer from a French man-of-war which had taken her; and after a running sea fight, the capture of a valuable French privateer. But they were offset when several owners of the *Hunter* brought proceedings against him in the court of chancery in June 1746, and by the earlier wreck of the *Inspector* in Tangier Bay in January 1746, with the loss of ninety-six men and the imprisonment of most of the rest of the crew. Veale was rescued by HMS *Phoenix*. The last survivors were not freed until 1750, and an account of their suffering was published by a member of the crew in the following year.

By 1749 Veale had resumed his career as a merchant mariner—in command of the *Queen of Portugal*, on which he carried Henry Fielding to Lisbon in 1754. Fielding has left a vivid picture of Veale. He presents him as a mercurial figure: a brave and good-natured man who was a father to his sailors, but who 'wore a sword of no ordinary length by his side, with which he swaggered in his cabin, among the wretches his passengers, whom he had stowed in cupboards on each side' and had 'a voice capable of deafening all others' (Fielding, 29). Veale died two years after his second wife, in June 1756. His will was proved in the prerogative court of Canterbury on 19 October 1756.

E. W. L. KEYMER

Sources H. Fielding, *The journal of a voyage to Lisbon*, ed. T. Keymer (1996) · parish register, Hand Alley Chapel, 1716, PRO, RG4/4138 · parish register, St George, Exeter, 30 Jan 1687 [baptism] · will, PRO, PROB 11/825/284 · marriage allegation, faculty office, 2 May 1735, LPL · rate book, 1921–3, Southwark Local Studies Library · *Lloyd's Lists* (1741–55) · W. A. Shaw, ed., *Calendar of treasury books and papers*, 4, PRO (1901), 356 · act book, PRO, HCA 3/72/334 · letters of marque, PRO, HCA 25/32, HCA 25/34, and HCA 25/35 · sentences, PRO, HCA 34/32 and HCA 34/33 · appeals, PRO, HCA 43/9 · *The correspondence of Henry and Sarah Fielding*, ed. M. C. Battestin and C. T. Probyn (1993), 104 · chancery proceedings, PRO, C9/343/89 · petition, PRO, SP 35/2/9
Archives LPL, marriage allegations · PRO, chancery proceedings, C9, C11, C24, and C33 · PRO, HCA classes 3, 25, 26, 32, 34, and 43

Wealth at death part owner of the Saudades: act book, PRO, HCA 3/72/334 · bequests of over £300: PRO, PROB 11/825/284 · possibly owned a house: Fielding, *Journal*, 24

Vedder, David (*bap.* 1789, *d.* 1854), poet, son of a small landowner, was baptized on 29 December 1789 in the parish of Deerness, near Kirkwall, Orkney, the son of John Vedder and Jean Shewrie. His father died when he was young, and he was educated by his mother. She died when he was about twelve, and he went to sea as a cabin boy. Ten years later he became captain of a Greenland whaler, which he commanded for several years. In 1815 he was appointed first officer of an armed cruiser, and in 1820 became a tide surveyor, officiating successively at Montrose, Kirkcaldy, Dundee, and Leith.

Vedder wrote and translated verse from an early age, publishing his first poem in his early twenties. In 1828 he published *The Covenanters' Communion and other Poems*. In 1830, after a quarrel with Henry Glassington Bell, editor of the *Edinburgh Literary Journal*, Vedder set up the rival *Edinburgh Literary Gazette*, which was supported by De Quincey among others. In 1832 he published *Orcadian Sketches*, a prose and verse miscellany, as well as a popular *Memoir of Sir Walter Scott*. In 1839 he edited *Poetical Remains of Robert Fraser*, a Kirkcaldy poet, together with a memoir. He contributed text for Walter Geikie's *Etchings* in 1841, and the following year he published *Poems, Legendary, Lyrical, and Descriptive*, illustrated by Geikie. Among these his lyric 'The Temple of Nature' was a favourite with Thomas Chalmers, who often recited it to his students. The same year Vedder collaborated with Frederick Schenck in *The Pictorial Gift-Book of Lays and Lithographs*. In 1852 he published his *Story of Reynard the Fox*, with lithographs by Schenck and MacFarlane, considered on its appearance 'by far the best edition of this famous story yet presented in English' (*Literary Gazette*, 1852, 789). He was a contributor to many anthologies and magazines, including the supplementary volume of George Thomson's *Scottish Melodies*, Blackie's *Book of Scottish Song* (1844), *Whistle-Binkie* (1853), Constable's *Edinburgh Magazine*, the *Christian Herald*, *Tait's Magazine*, and *Chambers's Journal*. A posthumous volume of Vedder's *Poems, Lyrics, and Sketches* was published in 1878, with a memoir by George Gilfillan, who remembers him as 'tall, considerably above 6 feet, rotund, red faced, and with a world of sagacity in his rugged features, and of warmth in his big heart' (Gilfillan, xiv).

Retiring on a pension in 1852, Vedder died of kidney disease at 173 Causewayside, Newington, Edinburgh, on 11 February 1854, and was buried in the Grange cemetery, Edinburgh. He was survived by his widow, a son in the Royal Navy, and two daughters, one of whom was married to Frederick Schenck, a well-known Edinburgh lithographer.

T. W. BAYNE, *rev.* SARAH COUPER

Sources G. Gilfillan, 'Memoir', in D. Vedder, *Poems, lyrics, and sketches* (1878) · C. Rogers, *The modern Scottish minstrel, or, The songs of Scotland of the past half-century*, 3 (1856), 143–5 · *United Presbyterian Magazine*, 8 (1854), 209–15 · J. G. Wilson, ed., *The poets and poetry of Scotland*, 2 (1877), 117–18 · Chambers, *Scots.* (1870) · R. Inglis, *The dramatic writers of Scotland* (1868) · *IGI* · *Literary Gazette* (23 Oct 1852), 789 · bur. reg. Scot.
Archives BL, letters to George Thomson, Add. MS 35265

Veel, Edward. *See* Veel, Edward (1632/3–1708).

Veel, Robert (1647/8–*c*.1674), poet, probably born at Alveston, Gloucestershire, was the younger son of William Veel (*d.* 1656), of Symondshall, Gloucestershire, and Elizabeth (*d.* in or before 1656), daughter of Robert Culliford. Veel's family had been impoverished by the post-civil war sequestrations of the estates of his father and his grandfather, the royalist plotter Colonel Thomas *Veel. His father's will, while leaving Robert £500 when he came of age, also made provisions for binding him as an apprentice. Veel entered St Edmund Hall as a commoner at the age of fifteen on 25 April 1663 and spent ten terms at Oxford, but he did not take a degree. He later went to London, presumably after coming into his inheritance in 1668 or 1669. There, according to Wood, he 'lived after the manner of poets in a debauch'd way, and wrote partly for the use of his idle and vain Companions, but more to gain Money to carry on the Trade of Folly' (Wood, *Ath. Oxon.*, 1.517). In 1672 Veel published *New Court-Songs and Poems* under the name R. V. gent., dedicating it to 'Mr. T. D.'. It has been suggested that this was the playwright and poet Thomas D'Urfey; however, this is unlikely as D'Urfey was only born in 1653. Collections like these were quite in vogue at the time among young aspiring blades about town, but few of the 129 *New Court-Songs and Poems* are of any literary merit. The majority are love poems in rhyming couplets addressed to various of the poet's muses, most commonly 'Clariza', interspersed with loyal odes, drinking songs, and some savagely misogynist celebrations of bachelorhood and the roistering life. 'A Rant Against Marriage' puts it plainest:

And when with Sorrow their [bachelors'] hearts are sunk
They may go to the Tavern, and be drunk
And never be dogg'd by a Bitcherly Punk
To ask them why, or wherefore.

The best is 'Snow', a more mature poem which defuses worldly vanity by comparing individuals to snowflakes which might fall on a palace or a dunghill but which are all doomed to be melted by the sun. It is not possible, however, to say which pieces are Veel's own; some, indeed, have attributed the whole collection to Robert Vine. Wood records that Veel also published 'Poor Robin's Intelligence', which appeared in a half-sheet weekly in 1672 or 1673, and that this attack on 'the Misses of the Town' provoked a retort from one 'K. C.' entitled 'Poor Robin's Elegy, or, The Imposter Silenc'd'. Veel died about 1674, leaving no children. His grave is unknown.

ANDREW WARMINGTON

Sources Wood, *Ath. Oxon.*, 2nd edn, vol. 1 · R. V. [R. Veel], *New court-songs and poems* (1672) · S. Rudder, *A new history of Gloucestershire* (1779) · R. Atkyns, *The ancient and present state of Glostershire*, 2 pts in 1 (1712) · will, Glos. RO, D225 F14 [William Veel] · W. T. Lowndes, *The bibliographer's manual of English literature*, ed. H. G. Bohn, 6 (1894) · DNB

Veel, Thomas (*c*.1591–1663/4), royalist army officer and conspirator, was born at Alveston, Gloucestershire, the third or fourth son of Nicholas Veel and his wife, the daughter of Robert Bridges of Combe, Gloucestershire. He was also the scion of an ancient family of minor gentry, who leased another Gloucestershire estate at Symondshall in Wotton under Edge from the Berkeleys of Berkeley Castle, with whom they had strong historic ties. Veel married first Dorothy Wynneate, with whom he had a son, William (*d.* 1656), father of the poet Robert *Veel, and three daughters. He also had two more sons, Nicholas and Thomas, with a second wife whose name is unknown.

According to one source, Veel saw military service overseas, though he may only have been a trained bands colonel (Newman). He was one of the earliest and most active royalists in the county from the outset of the civil war, defying the efforts of John Smyth to hold the Berkeley interest neutral. He was named to the royalist commission of the peace in March 1643, then appointed governor of Berkeley Castle in November 1643 after the resignation of Captain Maxwell. According to John Corbet the troops under his command were formidable only in plunder, hemmed in as they were by parliamentarian garrisons at nearby Slimbridge and Frampton. Veel was dismissed as governor in August 1644, apparently because the earl of Bristol wished to place Colonel Richard Power there, but he remained in arms at least until June 1645. He later compounded for his estates, paying £704 13*s*. 4*d*., after enduring plundering, sequestration, and other charges which, on top of heavy debts, quite ruined the estate. A descendant's claims that Veel was related to the presbyterian royalist (and former parliamentarian governor of Gloucester) Sir Edward Massey, that he raised a horse regiment which fought alongside Massey at Worcester on 3 September 1651, and that he escaped to the continent afterwards are unproven and implausible. However, Massey certainly trusted the Veel family implicitly, writing later that they were 'all zealously his Ma[jes]ties servants' (*Nicholas Papers*, 4.158–9).

After Penruddock's abortive rising of February 1656 and the rise of the 'action party' among royalist plotters, Veel became a pivotal figure in local plans for an uprising against the interregnum regimes. These plans varied over the years but generally revolved around his raising up to 3000 men to take Gloucester and Bristol in preparation for a landing. Charles II sent him blank recruiting commissions in November 1656 and again in May 1659. Massey spent several months in hiding at the Veel family house in Symondshall in mid-1659 while organizing a revolt. On 31 July, shortly before this was due to start, troops from the Gloucester garrison arrested Veel, his two surviving sons, and his grandson (another Thomas), then Massey himself. The estates were briefly re-sequestered. Both Thomas the grandson and Nicholas were imprisoned, and Nicholas was imprisoned again in Hurst Castle in September. The former, who had fled when the estates were ordered to be sequestered, returned to assault the commissioners' agent in November and taunt him that Monck was coming from Scotland to restore the king.

After the Restoration, mindful of Veel's huge sacrifices, Charles and Clarendon discussed several ways of rewarding him. These included the profits from the sale of a baronetcy, the rights to certain bonds from merchants bound over for defrauding the customs, the rights to smuggled

French goods, a share of receipts from the West Indies from the commissioners of prizes, and the lease of the ballast office. However, as Clarendon admitted, Veel repeatedly lost out to less deserving petitioners. In 1661 his son Nicholas and grandson Thomas were granted the office of making and registering assurances in London, which they held in trust for Veel to pay him profits which were worth over £400 per year. They later became county collectors of the royal and additional aids and the hearth tax and embarked on chequered careers in the royal service, facing constant resistance from JPs and the populace until they lost their positions, poorer by thousands of pounds, in 1668. By then Colonel Thomas Veel was dead, having died at some point between 7 October 1663, when he made the final codicil to his will, and 26 May 1664, when the will was proved; he was buried in Alveston church.

ANDREW WARMINGTON

Sources W. Veel, 'Copy of a letter from King Charles the Second to Colonel Thomas Veel', *Archaeologica*, 14 (1801), 75–83 • Glos. RO, D 225, F 12–14 • S. Rudder, *A new history of Gloucestershire* (1779) • R. Atkyns, *The ancient and present state of Glostershire* (1712) • M. A. E. Green, ed., *Calendar of the proceedings of the committee for compounding … 1643–1660*, 5 vols., PRO (1889–92) • D. Underdown, *Royalist conspiracy in England, 1649–1660* (1960) • *CSP dom.*, 1660–70 • W. A. Shaw, ed., *Calendar of treasury books*, 1–3, PRO (1904–8) • *The Clarke papers*, ed. C. H. Firth, 4 vols., CS, new ser., 49, 54, 61–2 (1891–1901) • BL, Add. MSS 33588–33589 • J. Corbet, *Historicall relation of the military government of Gloucester*, ed. J. Washbourne, *Bibliotheca Gloucestrensis* (1823) • will, PRO, PROB 11/320, sigs. 74 and 91 • *The Nicholas papers*, ed. G. F. Warner, 4, CS, 3rd ser., 31 (1920) • PRO, SP 23/243/162 • P. R. Newman, *Royalist officers in England and Wales, 1642–1660: a biographical dictionary* (1981)

Archives Glos. RO, corresp. and family papers, D225

Wealth at death settled most of lands on son before death, but left bequests over £1000; office of assurances apparently valued over £400: will, PRO, PROB 11/320, sigs. 74 and 91

Veil, Charles Marie de (1630–1685×91), religious convert and biblical commentator, was born in the Jewish quarter of Metz, then an imperial city, but from 1648 part of France, the grandson of Jaquetiel David (*d.* 1679) and son of David Weil (*d.* 1645), a rabbi who presided over the synagogue in that town, and his wife, Magdelaine. His original given name is unknown. In 1652 there arrived in Metz a new Catholic archdeacon, Jacques-Bénigne Bossuet, who shared in the current apocalyptic excitement of both Christians and Jewish cabbalists and the conviction of the former of an imminent large-scale conversion of the Jews. His first convert was the son of an influential Jewish doctor, and the rabbi's young son soon followed. Such a triumph came quickly to the ears of the authorities, and Veil was taken up by the governor of Metz, Marshall Charles Schomberg, and his wife, Marie, and on 8 September 1654 was baptized into the Catholic church, taking their names. The following year his brother Daniel was also baptized, and was sponsored by Louis XIV himself, taking the name Louis-Compiègne.

Soon after his conversion Veil entered an Augustinian seminary, and he was later ordained at Angers as a priest of the Augustinian order; probably he was for many years a member and lecturer of the chapter at Toussaints. By 1672 he had been appointed a professor. However, Veil was increasingly influenced by the Jansenists, especially Bishop Henri Arnauld and his brother Antoine Arnauld. He defended Jansenist theses on 16 April 1674 for his doctoral degree, and joined the Geneviève (often called Gallican) reformed offshoot of the Augustinian order. In October 1674, as doctor of theology in the Royal Academy of Angers and priest and canon of the Gallican congregation, he published at Angers a commentary on the gospels of Matthew and Mark. In 1676, after a brief stay in Paris as a member of the community of Cathérine, Val des Ecoliers (now united with the Gallican order), he became prior of St Ambrose at Melun. During this period he attended a study circle at the quarters of Bossuet, now tutor to the dauphin at St Germain. Jansenism, meanwhile, had been denounced as Calvinism in Catholic clothing; the seminary at Angers was shut down and Antoine Arnauld was forced to flee to the Netherlands. Veil had become acquainted with several prominent Huguenots of the church at Charenton near Paris. In August 1677, having himself departed for the Netherlands, he was converted to protestantism. By that November he was in England, and with the support of Jean Maximilien de l'Angle, one of the ministers of the French church in the Savoy, successfully lobbied the secretary of state, Joseph Williamson, for asylum.

The famous scholar was welcomed in Anglican circles and set about revising his commentary on Matthew and Mark in respect of passages which he had once taken to support Catholic rites. On 2 March 1678 Bossuet wrote urging de Veil, as he was known in England, to return to France, promising that he had no reason to fear, but the appeal came to nothing. De Veil was received into the Church of England on 1 April 1678 and was soon allowed into the ministry. The bishop of London, Henry Compton, allowed him to use the library at Fulham Palace and did not insist on his re-ordination; de Veil was required only to take the oath of supremacy, and to promise conformity according to the Book of Common Prayer and the Thirty-Nine Articles. It is possible that he was received into a noble household, possibly to the family of Viscount Ranelagh, whose wife was sister to Robert Boyle. Certainly de Veil wrote from Fulham on 14 May 1678 to Boyle, siding with him against the proposition of the Hebraist Richard Simon that, given the obscurity of the scriptures, tradition must play a decisive role in determining the meaning of the Bible. Simon retorted by asking de Veil what, in that case, was the basis for the baptism of infants, for he knew of no scriptural warrant for it. Veil had no ready answer, and avoided the question in the published version of his revised commentary on Mark, dedicated to Bishop Compton. The publication of two other works, *A Song of Songs* and *Twelve Minor Prophets*, both revised in a strongly protestant direction, led to the cancellation on 9 January 1680 of his doctoral degree by the University of Angers.

De Veil's next project was a commentary on the Acts of the Apostles, and it seems that during the preparation of this work, unable to answer Simon's question, he underwent his last conversion. Perhaps he encountered the work of Henry Jessey, who had written about the readmission of the Jews to England, or that of Francis Bampfield, John Tombes, or Hanserd Knollys, all respected scholars who had rejected infant baptism. It appears that about this time he met and married a servant at Fulham Palace, who was a Baptist and arranged a meeting with Knollys. He became a Baptist by Easter 1684, and quickly lost all his influential friends and means of support. He became friendly with Nehemiah Cox of the church of Petty France. The churches of his new denomination rarely paid their ministers, but an exception was made in the case of de Veil, and they, 'on consideration of his abilities, on his dismission from his place, raised him a salary, which he enjoyed till his death' (Crosby, 4.259). When his commentary on Acts appeared in 1684 it 'calmly presented their case as a part of a fine piece of scholarship' (Whitley, 31). In the last years of his life de Veil was a pastor to a congregation in Gracechurch Street in the City of London. Though this was near the area where Huguenots were settling in refuge from the persecution in France, it was considered too risky to employ him in proselytizing among them, and his activities during this period are obscure. The date and circumstances of his death are unknown, but it is clear that it took place between September 1685 and 1691.   STEPHEN WRIGHT

Sources W. T. Whitley, 'Charles Marie de Veil', *Baptist Quarterly*, 5 (1930–31), 74–85, 118–29, 177–89 · T. Crosby, *The history of the English Baptists, from the Reformation to the beginning of the reign of King George I*, 4 vols. (1738–40)

Veil, Sir Thomas de (1684–1746), magistrate, is a figure whose early life is obscure. According to his contemporary biographer (*Memoirs of the Life and Times of Sir Thomas Deveil*, 5–6) he was born in St Paul's Churchyard, London, in 1684 and was the son of the Revd Dr Hans de Veil, a Church of England clergyman. This de Veil later became, thanks to the patronage of Bishop John Tillotson, librarian at Lambeth Palace.

Only the place and date of birth may, however, be correct. For although the registers of St Augustine, Watling Street, London, record the birth of a Thomas de Veil in the parish on 21 November 1684, this man was the son of Lewis de Compiègne de Veil and his wife, Anne. De Veil is said to have been apprenticed to a mercer near Cheapside and then, when his master's business failed, to have become a soldier. Certainly, upon the outbreak of the War of the Spanish Succession, he enlisted as a volunteer and served with distinction. He fought at Cadiz and Vigo in 1702 and at Almanza in 1707, and by 1713, when the war ended and he was retired on half pay, had attained the rank of captain of dragoons.

Little is known about de Veil's family life. He married his first wife, Anne Hancock, on 27 January 1704 at St Martin-in-the-Fields, Westminster. After her death he married three times, but none of his wives survived him. His third wife was called Kingsman; the names of the others are not known. He is said to have fathered twenty-five children. De Veil was appointed to the commissions of the peace for Middlesex and Westminster in 1729, and opened his first office in Leicester Fields (Leicester Square). From there he

moved to Thrift Street, Soho, and thence, in 1739 or 1740, to Bow Street. Ambitious, courageous, and active, he did much to prosecute crime and maintain public order in the metropolis. In 1735 he was instrumental in breaking the formidable gang of robbers led by William Wreathock, a Hatton Garden attorney; in 1736–7 he bravely attempted to enforce Sir Robert Walpole's ill-conceived Gin Act; and in 1741 his efforts secured the conviction of James Hall, who murdered his master, John Penny, principal of Clement's Inn. Hall was executed. Such was his zeal that the government turned to de Veil whenever it needed a magistrate's services. In this capacity he acted as a 'court justice' and although this was not an official appointment he was rewarded by Treasury grants, by an appointment as inspector-general of exports and imports (with a salary of £500 per annum) in 1738, and by a knighthood in 1744.

De Veil's stern enforcement of the penal code may not have endeared him to the poor, however, and his exertions in the interests of the powerful frequently incurred popular resentment. Thus, in 1744, at the behest of 'great people', de Veil attempted to prevent a meeting of footmen protesting at the employment of foreign servants. The footmen marched upon his house in Bow Street; he arrested three of their number, but the others stormed the house and released the men. By 1746 de Veil had become the leading metropolitan magistrate, was a colonel in the Westminster militia, and sat on the commissions of the peace for Essex, Surrey, and Hertfordshire. On 6 October 1746, after examining a prisoner at Bow Street, he suffered an apoplectic stroke. He died the next morning and was buried at Denham, Buckinghamshire, on the 11th. His treatise, *Observations on the Practice of a Justice of the Peace* (1747), was published posthumously.

De Veil is sometimes cited as a classic example of the venal trading justice, but this is an extreme view. No clear evidence of corruption has ever been adduced against him and, although he lived magnificently, he possessed income other than that derived from fees as a magistrate. His eminence established Bow Street as an important centre of magisterial activity. Two years after his death his house there was occupied by Henry Fielding and thus became the birthplace of the Bow Street runners.

PHILIP SUGDEN

Sources *Memoirs of the life and times of Sir Thomas Deveil, knight* (1748) · 'Sir Thomas De Veil's life', *GM*, 1st ser., 17 (1747), 562–4 · parish register, London, St Augustine, Watling Street, 4 Dec 1684, GL, MS 8872/2 [baptism] · details of military service, BL, Add. MS 33054, fols. 100–01 · *Select trials at the sessions house in the Old Bailey*, 4 vols. (1742) · W. A. Shaw, ed., *Calendar of treasury books and papers*, 5 vols., PRO (1897–1903) · P. Pringle, *The thief-takers* (1958) · S. Webb and B. Webb, *English local government*, 1: *The parish and the county* (1906) · A. Babington, *A house in Bow Street* (1969) · IGI

Archives BL, MSS, Add. MSS 32702, fol. 165; 33054, fols. 100, 240, 242; 33057, fol. 487; 47013A, fols. 115–119b | BL, Stowe MS 256, fol. 106b

Likenesses T. Ryley, mezzotint, 1747 (after De la Cour), BL

Veitch family (*per.* 1768–1929), horticulturists, ran important nurseries in Devon and London and commissioned several notable plant hunting expeditions. The first family member to come to notice was **John Veitch** (1752–

1839), who was born in Jedburgh, Roxburghshire, and, having trained at a nursery in Edinburgh, was employed in a London nursery about 1768. He then went to be steward to Sir Thomas Ackland's estate at Killerton, near Exeter, Devon, where his son James [i] Veitch was born on 25 January 1792. About 1800 John Veitch founded a tree nursery at Budlake, near Killerton. He was also responsible for tree plantings at Luscombe Castle and Poltimore House in Devon. In 1832 he moved to Mount Radford, Exeter, where his son James had recently bought land for a new nursery. John died at Mount Radford in 1839.

James [i] **Veitch** (1792–1863) was trained in his father's nursery at Budlake from 1800 to 1810. He developed the new nursery at Mount Radford from about 1830 and, in partnership with his son James [ii] Veitch, acquired the Exotic Nursery of Joseph Knight and Thomas A. Perry, on the King's Road, Chelsea, in 1853. In the 1840s he employed as plant collectors William Lobb in South America and his brother Thomas Lobb in Asia. James died at Exeter on 14 May 1863, leaving two sons, James [ii] and Robert Toswill.

James [ii] **Veitch** (1815–1869) was born at Exeter on 24 May 1815. He moved to Chelsea in 1853 as business partner to his father; the following year he relinquished his interest in the Exeter nursery, which was thenceforth run separately. The Veitch memorial medal was instituted in his honour. He died at his home, Stanley House, King's Road, Chelsea, on 10 September 1869, leaving three sons.

Shortly after James [ii] Veitch became involved with the Chelsea nursery, about 1856 or 1857, his younger brother, **Robert Toswill Veitch** (1823–1885), returned from the Cape of Good Hope, where he had been farming, to take charge of the Exeter nursery. In 1864 he established nurseries at New North Road and High Street, Exeter, trading as Robert Veitch & Son. He died in Torquay, Devon, on 18 January 1885.

Robert Toswill's son **Peter Christian Massyn Veitch** (1850–1929) was born at the Cape of Good Hope. He collected plants for the Veitch firm in Australasia between 1875 and 1878 before going to Britain to succeed his father in charge of the Exeter branch of the business. He received the Victoria medal of honour of the Royal Horticultural Society in 1916. He died in Exeter, Devon, on 9 March 1929. His daughter, Anna Mildred (1889–1949), became managing director of Robert Veitch & Son Ltd.

Meanwhile in the running of the Chelsea nursery James [ii] Veitch was succeeded after 1865 by his three sons, **John Gould** [i] **Veitch** (1839–1870), Harry James [see below], and **Arthur Veitch** (1844–1880). Arthur was born in Exeter on 24 February 1844 and became a partner in the family firm, but died young on 25 September 1880 at 16 Edith Grove, Fulham Road, London. He left a widow, Emily Eliza. Arthur's eldest brother, John Gould [i], was born at Exeter on 17 April 1839. He visited the Far East in 1860 and Australasia in 1864, bringing back many trees which were new to Britain. He was elected fellow of the Linnean Society in 1866. He married Jane Hodge and they had two sons, James Herbert (1868–1907) and **John Gould** [ii] **Veitch** (1869–1914). He died in 1870.

John Gould [ii] was born on 19 July 1869 at Kingston Hill, Surrey. After attending Westminster School he was admitted to Trinity College, Cambridge, and graduated BA in 1890 and MA in 1894. He won soccer blues at Cambridge in 1888–91 and went on to play for England in the Corinthians' (gentlemen amateurs') game against Wales in 1894. He was described as 'an ivory-faced hero with a black moustache' (Grayson, 119) and 'a brilliant dribbler in the best Westminster tradition, with a deadly shot that brought him 60 goals in 68 games for the Corinthians' (ibid.). On 16 December 1894 he married Dorothy Maud, widow of Carl Richard G. Le Doux. He lived at 22 Homefield Road, Wimbledon, Surrey, and died at Wimbledon on 3 October 1914.

John Gould [ii] was a partner in the family firm, but far more important to the business was his elder brother, **James Herbert Veitch** (1868–1907), who was born at Chelsea on 1 May 1868. He was educated at Crawford College, Maidenhead, and in technical subjects in Germany and France before starting work at the Chelsea nursery in 1885. He continued to work there and at Coombe Wood, Surrey, at Langley, Buckinghamshire, and at Feltham, Middlesex. He was elected fellow of the Linnean Society in 1889 and the Horticultural Society. From 1891 to 1893 he toured the world collecting plants for the nursery and published accounts of his travels in the *Gardener's Chronicle* (1892–4) and as *A Traveller's Notes* (1896). In 1898 James Veitch & Sons was formed into a limited company of which James Herbert became managing director. James Herbert prepared *Hortus Veitchii*, privately published in 1906, an invaluable history of the family firm. Shortly after this poor health obliged him to retire from business and his uncle Harry James came out of retirement to take over from him. He died of paralysis at Exeter on 13 November 1907. He was survived by his widow, Lucy Elizabeth Wood, whom he had married in 1898. They had no children.

Sir Harry James Veitch (1840–1924) was born at Exeter on 29 June 1840. He was educated at Exeter grammar school and continued his training at Altona, near Hamburg, and at Paris with the firm of Vilmorin-Andrieux. He joined the Chelsea branch of the firm in 1858 or 1859 and worked at Chelsea, Coombe Wood, and Langley. He took a particular interest in plant hunting and was instrumental in commissioning the notable expeditions of Richard Pearce, a gardener at the Exeter Veitch nursery, to China, Peru, and Bolivia in 1859 and afterwards; of Frederick William Burbidge to Borneo in 1877; and of Ernest Henry Wilson to China and Tibet in 1899–1902 and 1903–5. (Appropriately Wilson received the Veitch memorial medal in 1906.) During Harry James's time at the nursery it established its reputation for orchid hybridization and the successful introduction to British gardens of many exotics. He retired from the firm in 1900, but came out of retirement to manage the firm between 1906 and 1914. (In the years immediately preceding 1914 the firm declined rapidly, and in 1914 much stock had to be sold off.) He was elected fellow of the Linnean Society in 1886. He received the Victoria medal of honour of the Royal Horticultural

Society in 1906, and later served as the society's treasurer and vice-president. He was knighted in 1912. He published a manual of Coniferae in 1881 and of orchidaceous plants (1887–94), both of which contain much information about the plants brought to Britain by the firm's collectors. He died at East Burnham Park, Slough, on 6 July 1924. In 1867 he had married Louisa Mary (d. 1921), daughter of Frederick W. Johnston of Stoke Newington. Like James Herbert and his wife they had no children, and, as there was no successor in the family to take over the business, the nursery at Coombe Wood was sold.   ELIZABETH BAIGENT

Sources Desmond, *Botanists*, rev. edn · *WWW* · Venn, *Alum. Cant.* · Burke, *Peerage* · 'Veitch, James Herbert', *DNB* · 'Veitch, Sir Harry James', *DNB* · E. Grayson, *Corinthians and cricketers* (1957) · J. H. Veitch, *Hortus Veitchii* (privately printed, 1906) · *CGPLA Eng. & Wales* (1869) · *CGPLA Eng. & Wales* (1880) · *CGPLA Eng. & Wales* (1907) · *CGPLA Eng. & Wales* (1914) · *CGPLA Eng. & Wales* (1925) · *CGPLA Eng. & Wales* (1929)
Wealth at death £2687 9s. 3d.—James Herbert Veitch: probate, 1907, *CGPLA Eng. & Wales* · under £70,000—James Veitch: probate, 1869, *CGPLA Eng. & Wales* · £1496 8s. 7d.—John Gould Veitch: probate, 1914, *CGPLA Eng. & Wales* · £79,385 9s.—Sir Harry James Veitch: probate, 1925, *CGPLA Eng. & Wales* · £15,803 9s. 10d.—Peter Christian Massyn Veitch: probate, 25 May 1929, *CGPLA Eng. & Wales* · under £30,000—Arthur Veitch: probate, 1880, *CGPLA Eng. & Wales*

Veitch, Arthur (1844–1880). *See under* Veitch family (*per.* 1768–1929).

Veitch, Colin Campbell McKechnie (1881–1938), footballer and journalist, was born on 22 May 1881 at his parents' home, 130 Byker Bank, in a poor area of Newcastle upon Tyne. His father, James Veitch, worked as a poor-law relieving officer. His mother was Sarah Ann (formerly Kidd) and there were three elder brothers, James, Gerald, and Norman. It was a socialist family, which believed in education and improvement. Colin went to the Heaton science and art school and in October 1898 signed indentures as a pupil teacher at the North View School, Heaton. He was later active in the local socialist Sunday school. But it was not only his studies at which he stood out but also football, the sporting craze of the 1890s.

As a youngster Veitch had played football in Heaton Park, close to his home, and at school, and his talent must have been obvious from the start. By 1894 he was captain of Newcastle boys and making a reputation with a succession of junior clubs—Larkspur, Dalton, and Malcolm Rovers, a Heaton team with whom he won an early medal. He played for Rutherford College and after playing in several friendlies for Newcastle United he signed as a professional in 1899; he made his first team début in October. It was not until the second half of the 1902–3 season that he was one of several new players given the chance to stave off relegation and became the linchpin of a side which almost dominated English football until 1911: Newcastle were champions of the league in 1905, 1907, and 1909, FA cup winners in 1910, and, remarkably, losing finalists four times, in 1905, 1906, 1908, and 1911.

During this period Veitch was often one of the Newcastle half-backs. Regularly captain, he often helped the directors pick the team, and used his intelligence to stiffen the short-passing game with some tactical leavening. He was probably one of the early exponents of the pre-match discussion and the half-time team talk so beloved of the modern football manager but so mysterious in form and impact. He played six times for England between 1906 and 1909 and his versatility was reflected in his appearance in every position in the Newcastle side except in goal. This perhaps explained his otherwise obscure nickname—'Double Width'.

With his socialist background it was not surprising that when the players' union, formed in the winter of 1907–8, tried to abolish the social and financial restrictions on professional footballers, Veitch was an active participant. The union's programme embraced the abolition of the maximum wage, freedom of contract, a percentage of any transfer fee to players, and the right to seek legal redress in conflicts with the clubs. The campaign failed, partly owing to the difficulty of organizing a group of workers uncertain about the benefits of collective bargaining, but mainly because of the intransigence and hostility of the employers at the Football Association and Football League. Veitch was not a militant. He believed in compromise through negotiation and he was very disappointed at the small gains made, the main one being that a match bonus for wins and draws could be paid for the first time. He was chairman of the union from 1911 to 1918.

By then Veitch had been serving for over two years in France, where he was commissioned as a lieutenant in the Royal Garrison Artillery. After demobilization he returned to football as reserve team coach at Newcastle, where he established one of the first nursery teams, Newcastle Swifts, with the aim of spotting and developing local footballing talent. The ensuing depression led to economies, the Swifts were disbanded, and he was sacked in 1926. He became manager of second division Bradford City in August 1926 but left after eighteen months, following the club's relegation to the third division. He had written articles for both the local and national press while still a player, and in July 1929 he joined the *Newcastle Evening Chronicle* group of newspapers as a sports reporter.

Football and journalism were more than enough to bring social celebrity on Tyneside but Veitch had another life which also kept him in the public eye. He was a star of the Newcastle Operatic Society, an amateur society which he joined in 1901. Two of his brothers were already members. The repertoire consisted largely of Gilbert and Sullivan and by 1911 Veitch had risen from the ranks of the chorus to deputy musical director and conductor. He also met his first wife there, Minnie Cole. They were married in 1907, a marriage brought to an end by her death in December 1924.

The Veitch family were also active in the *Clarion* movement, which had been formed to make socialists: they sang in the Newcastle *Clarion* choir and enjoyed the sociability and physical *joie de vivre* of the Newcastle *Clarion* cycling club. In June 1911 Veitch and Minnie, together with his brother Norman and his wife and four others, had set up the Newcastle *Clarion* Dramatic Society with the aim of both putting on plays and making money which would benefit the movement. All plays were to be applicable to socialism or other advanced subjects, but by 1924 the aim had become the furtherance of art by the production of plays, the development of players, and the founding of the People's Playhouse. In 1929 it became the People's Theatre Company, severing its connections with socialism. Colin Veitch acted, directed, and wrote music. In 1931 he married for the second time. Greta Mary Burke was a professional actress who had taken part in several People's Theatre productions. The couple had a house built in the Gosforth district of Newcastle. The house had a first-floor balcony and it was said that the couple would perform the famous scene from *Romeo and Juliet* in full view of the rest of the street.

Veitch was twice in the 1920s asked to stand as the prospective Labour candidate for the Newcastle East parliamentary constituency, though on each occasion he refused. He was taken ill in June 1938. He went to Switzerland to recuperate but pneumonia caused complications and he died at Bern on 26 August 1938. On the following day, the first of the 1938–9 football season, the crowd before United's home match with Plymouth stood silently for two minutes in memory of a footballer and a man who was out of the ordinary. Greta Veitch died in March 1968 and left the bulk of her £19,000 estate for a Burke-Veitch scholarship intended to enable a woman or girl born in Northumberland or Durham to study at the Royal College of Dramatic Art. TONY MASON

Sources D. A. Highton, 'Colin Veitch, footballer', MA diss., University of Northumbria, 1995 · J. Harding, *For the good of the game* (1991) · T. Mason, *Association football and English society, 1863–1915* (1980) · *Sunday Sun* (May–Aug 1931) · B. Hunt, *Northern goalfields* (1989) · *Newcastle Journal* (29 Aug 1938) · b. cert. · *CGPLA Eng. & Wales* (1938) · *Newcastle Evening Chronicle* (27 Aug 1968)
Wealth at death £3371 0s. 3d.: probate, 11 Nov 1938, *CGPLA Eng. & Wales*

Veitch, Sir Harry James (1840–1924). *See under* Veitch family (*per.* 1768–1929).

Veitch, James, Lord Elliock (1712–1793), judge, was born on 25 September 1712, the eldest son of William Veitch (d. 1747) of Boigend and Elliock in Dumfriesshire, and his wife, Christian Thomson, daughter of a provost of Peebles. Educated at Edinburgh University and at Leiden University (which he entered in 1733), and perhaps also at Halle, Veitch began his legal career as an apprentice to his father, an eminent writer to the signet. He was called to the bar on 15 February 1738. Shortly afterwards he went abroad to continue his studies in Holland and Germany, where his 'abilities and conversation' attracted the attention of Crown Prince Frederick of Prussia (from 1740 Frederick II, 'the Great'), who persuaded him to cut short his grand tour and remain at his court for some years.

Veitch was a sociable character with an attractive personality, sharp mind, and wide range of interests. On his return to Scotland he became a popular member of Edinburgh legal and literati circles. He also kept up a correspondence with Frederick. On 13 July 1747 he was appointed sheriff-depute of the county of Peebles, one of the first wave of legally qualified and salaried sheriffs-depute appointed following the Heritable Jurisdictions Act of 1747.

Politically Veitch had connections with Charles Douglas, third duke of Queensberry, who in 1755 brought him in as member for Dumfriesshire, a constituency dominated by the Queensberry family. At Westminster, Veitch appears to have taken a fairly independent line. Despite the approaches of Newcastle, he voted against Newcastle and Fox over the Minorca enquiry in 1757. A member of the committee to prepare the Scottish Militia Bill of 1760, he objected to Pitt's proposal to 'draw the Highland line' and seems to have abstained in the vote on the bill on 15 April.

Later that year Newcastle, anxious to secure a parliamentary seat for Thomas Miller, the new lord advocate, advised Miller to propose to Queensberry that if Veitch were promoted to the bench on the first vacancy, Queensberry might bring in Miller in his place. Queensberry agreed to the proposal. On 22 October 1760 Andrew Macdowall, Lord Bankton, died. A month later, on 22 November, Miller, 'from long and intimate acquaintance', recommended Veitch to Hardwicke for the vacancy:

> He is a man of great worth and as much in the favour and esteem of his country as any man I know, and though he has not had much practice at the bar yet he is a man of learning and solid knowledge of the law and I observe that the prospect of his promotion gives very general satisfaction both to the judges and to the bar. (BL, Add. MS 35449, fol. 284)

Veitch duly resigned in February 1761 and took his seat on the bench on 6 March with the title of Lord Elliock. He was a well-respected judge, with a scholarly bent. He was appointed a commissioner for the forfeited estates in 1767, a deputy governor of the Royal Bank of Scotland in 1776, and a commissioner for fisheries and manufactures the following year. He died at his home in St Andrew's Square, Edinburgh, on 1 July 1793. He was unmarried and his estates were inherited by his nephew.

RICHARD SCOTT

Sources E. Haden-Guest, 'Veitch, James', HoP, *Commons, 1754–90* · G. Brunton and D. Haig, *An historical account of the senators of the college of justice, from its institution in MDXXXII* (1832) · DNB · GM, 1st ser., 63 (1793), 675 · BL, Add. MS 35449
Likenesses H. Raeburn, portrait, priv. coll. · H. Raeburn, portrait, priv. coll. · G. Watson, portrait, priv. coll. · B. West, portrait, priv. coll.

Veitch, James (1792–1863). *See under* Veitch family (*per.* 1768–1929).

Veitch, James (1815–1869). *See under* Veitch family (*per.* 1768–1929).

Veitch, James Herbert (1868–1907). *See under* Veitch family (*per.* 1768–1929).

Veitch, John (1752–1839). *See under* Veitch family (*per.* 1768–1929).

Veitch, John (1829–1894), philosopher, born in Biggiesknowe, Peebles, on 24 October 1829, was the eldest and only surviving child of Sergeant James Veitch, a Peninsular War veteran, and his wife, Nancy Ritchie. Both parents, particularly the mother, held those high ideals of the value of education characteristic of some of the Scottish peasantry. Until sixteen years of age Veitch was educated successively at Mr Smith's 'adventure' school and at the high school of Peebles. In 1845 he proceeded to Edinburgh University, where he at once gained a bursary or entrance scholarship.

Two years before, at the time of the Disruption, Veitch, with his parents, had joined the Free Church of Scotland, and, after one session's attendance at Edinburgh University, he entered the New College there, just instituted for the benefit of Free Church students. Here he first met Professor A. Campbell Fraser, who became his lifelong friend. The year 1848 found him back at the university, hearing the brilliant lectures of John Wilson and of Sir William Hamilton, by whom Veitch was profoundly influenced. Originally destined for the ministry of the Free Church, he turned his attention in 1850 to theology but was repelled by the dogmatic tendencies of the day. Until 1856 he supported himself by private tuition.

In 1856 Veitch was appointed assistant to Sir William Hamilton in the chair of logic and metaphysics in the University of Edinburgh. Hamilton's death took place in the same year, and was followed by the transference of Campbell Fraser from the professorship of philosophy in New College. Veitch continued in his position as assistant to Fraser until, in May 1860, he was elected to the chair of logic, rhetoric, and metaphysics in the University of St Andrews. During the same period he aided his chief in the editorial work of the *North British Review*. Veitch's duties at St Andrews required him to teach English literature as well as philosophy, and he began studies in the literature and antiquities of the Scottish border. At this period his friends included many remarkable men, among others James David Forbes, James Frederick Ferrier, John Tulloch, William Young Sellar, and John Campbell Shairp. On 17 June 1862 he married Eliza Hill Wilson, only daughter of George Wilson of Dalmarnock and Auchineden. They had no children.

In the summer of 1864 Veitch was elected to the professorship of logic and rhetoric in the University of Glasgow, which he occupied until his death. Six months of the year were thenceforth spent in Glasgow, and the remainder in Peebles, where he built a residence, The Loanings, and enjoyed unique opportunities of studying the scenery, history, literature, and lore of his native borderland. He took an active part in the leading border associations, in the politics of Peeblesshire, and in various benevolent institutions. In 1872 he received the honorary degree of LLD from Edinburgh University. He died at The Loanings on 3 September 1894 and was buried in the Old Town in Peebles. His wife survived him.

As a thinker Veitch was at odds with the chief movements of his day, and by adopting an extreme, and often contemptuous, attitude of criticism, he precluded himself from having a formative influence on the thousands of students who came under his care. Those of them who knew him intimately were affected by his personal character, not by his lectures. One former pupil, J. H. Muirhead, commented that 'Veitch's real interest was not in philosophy at all except, as with so many in these theology-ridden days, as it seemed to provide a rod with which to chastise Hume and assert the rights of uncritical belief' (Drummond and Bulloch, 228). Contemporaries judged him to be limited to the work of criticism, incapable of much original thought. His critique of idealism in *Knowing and Being* (1889), some of whose themes were continued in *Dualism and Monism* (1895), demonstrated the exhaustion of the Scottish school of philosophy, pitting a naive realism against the new problems posed by T. H. Green's reading of Kant and Hegel. His philosophical publications also include translations of Descartes, and memoirs of Dugald Stewart (1857) and William Hamilton (1869), both of which are strictly biographical, attempting only limited accounts of their subjects' thought. His *Hamilton* (1882) was an exhaustive statement of Hamilton's contribution to philosophy.

Inborn inclination, extraordinary opportunity, and rare power of observation combined in the production of Veitch's work on *The History and Poetry of the Scottish Border* (2 vols., 1893). The same qualities reveal themselves in the fine volumes on *The Feeling for Nature in Scottish Poetry* (2 vols., 1887), as well as in his three small books of verse, *The Tweed, and Other Poems* (1875), *Hillside Rhymes* (1872), and *Merlin and Other Poems* (1889). The poems are less successful than the prose works. Occasionally they reach a high level, but always within a limited range.

R. M. WENLEY, *rev.* C. A. CREFFIELD

Sources M. R. L. Bryce, *John Veitch: memoir* (1896) · R. M. Wenley, 'Introductory essay', in J. Veitch, *Dualism and monism* (1895) · R. Metz, *A hundred years of British philosophy*, ed. J. H. Muirhead, trans. J. W. Harvey (1938) [Ger. orig., *Die philophischen Strömungen der Gegenwart in Grossbritannien* (1935)] · *Wellesley index* · A. L. Drummond and J. Bulloch, *The church in late Victorian Scotland* (1978) · *CCI* (1895)
Archives NL Scot., corresp. | NL Scot., corresp. with Blackwoods · NL Scot., letters to Alexander Campbell Fraser
Likenesses monument, U. Glas. · monument, Summit of Cademuir Hill · monument, Peebles · monument, Glasgow · photographs, repro. in Bryce, *John Veitch*
Wealth at death £3086 17s. 2d.: confirmation, 29 Nov 1894, *CCI* · £594 15s. 9d.: additional estate, 19 March 1895, *CCI*

Veitch, John Gould (1839–1870). *See under* Veitch family (*per.* 1768–1929).

Veitch, John Gould (1869–1914). *See under* Veitch family (*per.* 1768–1929).

Veitch [*née* Fairlie], **Marion** (1639–1722), diarist, was born in Edinburgh and baptized in the abbey kirk of Holyroodhouse in the Canongate in Edinburgh on 20 December 1639, the daughter of James Fairlie (*b.* 1606), an Edinburgh shoemaker, and his wife, Euphan Kincaid. When she was six she went to live with relatives in the parish of Lanark, where she grew up and was probably educated privately. She married the Presbyterian minister William *Veitch (1640–1722), in the High Kirk of Lanark on 23 November 1664, after which the couple moved to the nearby village of Dunsyre. The marriage produced five daughters and five sons, among them the future governor of Nova Scotia Samuel *Vetch.

William Veitch was constantly harassed by the authorities, often away from his family for long periods, living under a false name and sometimes even in exile abroad. As a result Marion's life was one of frequent moves, and she was out of Scotland for many years. While in England she lived at Hanham Hall, Northumberland (1672–7), Stanton Hall in the same county (1677–85), and Newcastle (1685–8), sometimes with and sometimes without her husband. With the restoration of presbyterianism in Scotland by the revolution of 1688, the Veitches' lives became easier, and William was called as minister to Peebles and later Dumfries, where the couple lived until their deaths.

Marion Veitch kept a journal, which covered her life from her marriage to her later years in Dumfries, and which was printed for the Free Church of Scotland in Edinburgh in 1846. It describes the affairs of herself and her family, and provides an interesting insight into the thought of a dedicated covenanting presbyterian at a time when the kirk was suffering its greatest persecution. Marion died at Dumfries on 9 May 1722, one day after her husband, and was buried with him in the same grave in St Michael's Church in Dumfries.   ALEXANDER DU TOIT

Sources K. W. H. Howard, *Marion Veitch: the memoirs, life and times of a Scots covenanting family (1639–1732)* (1992) · M. Veitch, 'An account of the Lord's gracious dealing with me, and of his remarkable hearing and answering my supplications', *Memoir of Mrs William Veitch, Mr Thomas Hog of Kiltearn, Mr Henry Erskine, and Mr John Carstairs* (1846), 1–60 · *Fasti Scot.*, new edn, 2.265
Archives NL Scot., Advocates' Library, MS 'An account of the Lord's gracious dealing with me, and of his remarkable hearing and answering my supplications'

Veitch, Peter Christian Massyn (1850–1929). *See under* Veitch family (*per.* 1768–1929).

Veitch, Robert Toswill (1823–1885). *See under* Veitch family (*per.* 1768–1929).

Veitch, William [*alias* William Johnston, George Johnston] (1640–1722), Church of Scotland minister, was born at Roberton, Lanarkshire, on 27 April 1640, the fifth son of John Veitch (1589–1673), minister of that parish, and his wife, Elizabeth Johnston, daughter of a Glasgow merchant. He studied at the University of Glasgow, graduated MA in 1659, and was awarded the title of laureate. The following year he became tutor to the family of Sir Andrew Ker of Greenhead, and was later governor to Greenhead's son at the University of Edinburgh. His memoirs suggest that the eminent presbyterian John Livingstone persuaded him to become a minister. He joined the family of Sir Hugh Campbell of Calder as chaplain in 1663, though he was forced by the local bishop to leave about September 1664. On 23 November the same year he married Marion Fairlie (1639–1722) [*see* Veitch, Marion] of the family of Braid, with whom he had five sons and five daughters.

In 1667 Veitch joined the presbyterian Pentland rising and was sent by the rebels to Edinburgh to seek the advice of Sir James Stewart of Goodtrees. He was captured but later freed, after which he fled as an outlaw to England,

where he adopted his mother's name, being known as William or George Johnston. For some time he was chaplain to the wife of the mayor of Newcastle, and, after preaching both in London and in other places in the north of England, he was in 1671 ordained minister of a meeting-house at Fallowlees in Northumberland, where his wife and sons William and Samuel *Vetch joined him. He afterwards preached at Hanham Hall in the parish of Rothbury, also in Northumberland; four years later he removed to Stanton Hall in the parish of Longhorsley.

On 16 January 1679 Veitch was arrested and, having been suspended on 22 February before the committee of public affairs in Edinburgh, was imprisoned on the Bass Rock. However, on 17 July he was set at liberty (possibly at the intercession of Sir James Dalrymple of Stair and the first earl of Shaftesbury, among others) and returned to Northumberland. When in 1681 Archibald Campbell, earl of Argyll, escaped from prison, Veitch not only sheltered him in his house, but also used his own experience as a fugitive to conduct the earl safely to London. Two years later Veitch had to make his own escape to the United Provinces, but during the Monmouth rising of 1685 he was sent to Northumberland to foment an outbreak there. The failure of Argyll's parallel uprising in Scotland put an end to the project, and after remaining for some time in hiding under various names, Veitch became minister of a meeting-house at Beverley, Yorkshire, where he remained for six or seven months.

After the declarations of indulgence of James VII and II, Veitch returned to Scotland and was called to the parish of Whittonhall, Morebattle, in the presbytery of Kelso, where he was admitted in April 1688. He was translated successively in 1690 to Peebles and in 1694 to Dumfries, and was a member of the general assembly of the Church of Scotland from 1690 to 1692. He published four sermons in the 1690s and two tracts against Catholicism in 1718 and 1720. He demitted his charge on 19 May 1715, and died, probably at Dumfries, on 8 May 1722; his wife died a day later. He was buried at Dumfries parish church. Several of his children had predeceased him, including William, who had died during the ill-fated Darien expedition in 1699. Samuel (1668–1732) became the first governor of Nova Scotia.   GINNY GARDNER

Sources *DNB* · *Fasti Scot.*, 2.81, 265, 3.323 · *Memoirs of Mr William Veitch, and George Brysson*, ed. T. McCrie (1825) · C. S. Terry, *The Pentland rising and Rullion Green* (1905)
Likenesses portrait, priv. coll.

Veitch, William (1794–1885), classical scholar, son of a miller and farmer, was born at Spittal-on-Rule in the parish of Bedrule, Roxburghshire. He received his elementary education at Jedburgh, and studied for the church at Edinburgh University, where Edward Irving and Thomas Carlyle were among his contemporaries. He became a licentiate of the Church of Scotland, and preached occasionally before the secession of 1843, afterwards devoting himself to research and tuition. He failed to gain the Edinburgh Greek chair in 1851, when John Stuart Blackie was preferred. He continued to read with advanced classical pupils, and to advise and assist scholarly writers. In 1866

William Veitch (1794–1885), by James Irvine

he received the honorary degree of LLD from Edinburgh University. Fond of sport, and a skilled raconteur, he died a bachelor at 7 North West Circus Place, Edinburgh on 8 July 1885, and was buried in the Dean cemetery of the city.

Veitch is chiefly remembered for his *Greek Verbs, Irregular and Defective*, an important work which was revised and expanded several times after its publication in 1848. In it Veitch listed the forms of irregular verbs found in literary texts, but the work's value was limited by the lack of evidence from inscriptions, and his researches were completed before the discovery of most papyri. He also edited various Greek and Latin texts and wrote numerous reviews. His lexicographical expertise was often called upon for the preparation and revision of classical dictionaries and other works of reference, including a new edition of Liddell and Scott's Greek lexicon.

T. W. BAYNE, *rev.* RICHARD SMAIL

Sources *The Scotsman* (10 July 1885) · *The Scottish Church*, 1 (1885), 412–19 · Irving, *Scots.* · D. W. Thompson, *Daydreams of a schoolmaster* (1864) · J. E. Sandys, *A history of classical scholarship*, 3 (1908), 427 · *CCI* (1885)
Likenesses J. Irvine, portrait, Scot. NPG [*see illus.*]
Wealth at death £11,488 14*s.* 4*d.*: confirmation, 19 Aug 1885, *CCI*

Velde, Willem van de, the elder (1611–1693). *See under* Velde, Willem van de, the younger (1633–1707).

Velde, Willem [William] **van de, the younger** (1633–1707), marine painter, was born at Leiden, Netherlands, and was baptized there on 18 December 1633 in the Hooglandsche Kerk. He was the son of the marine artist **Willem van de Velde the elder** (1611–1693) and his wife,

Judith, *née* Van Leeuwen, whom he had married on 19 August 1631. Van de Velde the elder was born in Leiden, the son of Willemsz van de Velde, master of a transport vessel. He spent his entire life drawing ships and small craft and was much in demand for his meticulously detailed grisailles (*penschilderingen* or 'pen paintings' drawn in ink on a prepared white canvas or oak panel). He was constantly at sea with the Dutch fleet, sometimes as an independent observer, sometimes in an official capacity, and he was present at several of the major sea battles of the Anglo-Dutch Wars.

Van de Velde the younger was initially the pupil of his father but about 1648 he moved to Weesp to study under Simon de Vlieger. In 1652 he was living in Amsterdam, where on 23 March that year he married Petronella le Maine. The marriage was dissolved a year later. He took up work in his father's studio and his earliest paintings were signed by his father as head of the family studio. In 1666 he married Magdalena Walraven in Amsterdam. He had precocious gifts as an artist and many of his most celebrated calm scenes with shipping were painted while he was still in his twenties. A fine example is *Calm: a Wijdschip and a Kaag in an Inlet Close to a Sea Wall* (National Gallery, London). He was only thirty-two when he painted *Calm: Dutch Ships Coming to Anchor* (Wallace Collection, London), which is regarded by many as his masterpiece. The picture was commissioned by Admiral Cornelis Tromp and shows the *Liefde*, his flagship at the battle of Lowestoft. During the winter of 1672–3 van de Velde and his father moved to London where they took up residence in Greenwich and were provided with a studio in the Queen's House by Charles II. In February 1674 a royal warrant was issued which ordered:

> the Salary of One hundred pounds per annum unto William Vandevelde the elder for taking and making Draughts of Sea Fights, and the like Salary of One Hundred pounds per annum unto William Vandevelde the younger for putting the said Draughts into Colours for Our particular use.
> (king's bills, February 1673/4, PRO, SO 7/40)

The subject matter of the younger van de Velde's paintings changed after his move to England. Instead of groups of anonymous fishing vessels in calms he tended to paint portraits of particular ships such as royal yachts and men-of-war, as well as paintings of sea battles and storms. One reason for the change was the nature of the commissions that he received from his English patrons, and the other reason may have been the influence of Ludolf Bakhuizen who had become popular in the 1670s and specialized in dramatic storm scenes. One of the most impressive examples of van de Velde the younger's storm scenes is *The English Ship Resolution in a Gale*, while the most spectacular of his sea battles is his vast canvas *The Gouden Leeuw at the Battle of the Texel*. Both these paintings are in the National Maritime Museum, London.

Unlike his father, van de Velde the younger did not make a regular practice of sailing with the English or the Dutch fleets and most of his battle pictures were painted from sketches made by his father. After the latter's death in December 1693, however, it became necessary for him to be present at important maritime events, and an order from the English Admiralty dated 18 May 1694 indicates his official role. Soon afterwards he joined the fleet commanded by Admiral Russell and spent a year in the Mediterranean. Freed from his father's obsession with accuracy his later pictures were painted in a more fluid style and some of his smaller pictures have the immediacy of oil sketches. Van de Velde died in Westminster, or possibly Greenwich, in 1707 and was buried on 17 April alongside his father in the church of St James, Piccadilly, London.

Van de Velde's work inspired several generations of English marine artists. Samuel Scott, Dominic Serres, and Nicholas Pocock were among the many eighteenth-century artists known to have copied his pictures, while Turner, Constable, and Clarkson Stanfield were among his admirers in the nineteenth century. The major collections of his work in Britain are in the National Gallery, London; the Royal Collection; the Wallace Collection; and the National Maritime Museum. In Holland the Rijksmuseum, Amsterdam, and the Mauritshuis in The Hague have many of his paintings; and the Amsterdam Historisch Museum has one of his masterpieces, *The Gouden Leeuw off Amsterdam*, a sweeping view of shipping on the River IJ painted for the city of Amsterdam in 1686.

DAVID CORDINGLY

Sources M. S. Robinson, *The paintings of the Willem van de Veldes*, 2 vols. (1990) [catalogue raisonée] • M. S. Robinson, *Van de Velde drawings in the National Maritime Museum*, 2 vols. (1958–74) • M. S. Robinson and R. E. J. Weber, *The Willem van de Velde drawings in the Boymans van Beuningen Museum*, 3 vols. (Rotterdam, 1979) • R. E. J. Weber, 'The artistic relationship between the ship draughtsman Willem van de Velde the elder and his son the marine painter in the year 1664', *Master Drawings*, 17/2 (1979), 152–61 • *The art of the Van de Veldes: paintings and drawings by the great Dutch marine artists and their English followers* (1982) [exhibition catalogue, National Maritime Museum, London, 23 June – 5 Dec 1982] • G. Kauffman, ed., *Zeichner der Admiralität: Marinezeichnungen und Gemälde von Willem van de Velde dem Älteren und dem Jüngeren* (Herford, Germany, 1981) [exhibition catalogue, Altonaer Museum, Hamburg, 3 June – 6 Sept 1981] • church register, Hooglandsche Kerk, Leiden, 18 Dec 1633 [baptism] • parish register, London, Piccadilly, St James's, 17 April 1707 [burial]
Likenesses C. van der Helst, oils, *c.*1672, Rijksmuseum, Amsterdam • J. Smith, mezzotint, 1707 (after painting by G. Kneller, 1680), BM, NPG

Veley, Margaret (1843–1887), novelist and poet, was born on 12 May 1843 at Braintree, Essex, the second daughter of Augustus Charles Veley, a solicitor of Swiss extraction, and his wife, Sophia, daughter of Thomas Ludbey, rector of Cranham. Her father's practice was mainly occupied with the ecclesiastical business of the district. Veley was educated at home, with the exception of one term spent at Queen's College, Tufnell Park, London. She was proficient in French and well read in French literature. In contrast to the conservatism of her family, she developed quite liberal political and religious views, leaving a post as a Sunday school teacher when a new clergyman, to whose views she was opposed, was hired.

Veley began writing both prose and verse early, though she published nothing until 1870. Her first poem, 'Michaelmas Daisies', appeared in *The Spectator* in April of that

year, and in September she published a short story, 'Milly's First Love', in *Blackwood's Edinburgh Magazine*. In 1872 she began her first and best-known novel, *For Percival*, a story of 'womanly self-sacrifice' (Blain, Clements & Grundy, *Feminist comp.*, 1111) which appeared as a serial in the *Cornhill Magazine* (September–December 1878), then under the editorship of Leslie Stephen. It was immediately published in book form and was well received. Written in a clear and pointed style, it shows a strong sense of humour and keen perception of character.

The deaths of two of Veley's married sisters in 1877 and 1885 and of her father in 1879 strongly affected her later writings. In 1880 she moved to London. The stories 'Mrs. Austin' and 'Damocles' appeared serially in the *Cornhill Magazine* in 1880 and 1882 respectively. *Mitchelhurst Place* appeared serially in *Macmillan's Magazine* in 1884. A two-volume edition was printed that year, and an edition in one volume in 1885. *A Garden of Memories* ran through the *English Illustrated Magazine* from July to September 1886 and was published in two volumes in 1887.

Veley died, unmarried, at her home at 45 Matheson Road, West Kensington, London, on 7 December 1887 after a short illness. She was buried on 10 December in Braintree cemetery. A posthumous volume of her poems, *A Marriage of Shadows and other Poems*, published in 1888, contained a biographical preface by Leslie Stephen.

ELIZABETH LEE, rev. MEGAN A. STEPHAN

Sources Allibone, *Dict.* • L. Stephen, preface, in M. Veley, *A marriage of shadows and other poems* (1888) • Blain, Clements & Grundy, *Feminist comp.* • CGPLA Eng. & Wales (1888)
Archives NL Scot., letters to Blackwoods
Wealth at death £1148 2s. 6d.: probate, 3 Jan 1888, CGPLA Eng. & Wales

Velley, Thomas (bap. 1748, d. 1806), botanist, baptized on 1 June 1748 at Chipping Ongar, Essex, was the son of the Revd Thomas Velley of that town and his wife, Jane. He matriculated from St John's College, Oxford, on 19 March 1766, and graduated BCL in 1772 and DCL in 1787. On 6 October 1785 he married Jane Hammond: they had five children. He served in the Oxford militia, ranked as major in 1781 and lieutenant-colonel in 1799, retiring in 1802.

Velley lived for many years at Portland Place, Bath, taking no part in legal affairs, but devoting himself to botany, especially to the study of algae. He collected in Essex, the Isle of Wight, and along the south coast. He was the friend and correspondent of Sir James Edward Smith, Dawson Turner, John Stackhouse, Sir Thomas Gery Cullum, Sir William Watson, and Richard Relhan, and became a fellow of the Linnean Society in 1792. Velley's botanical works were *Coloured figures of marine plants found on the southern coast of England, illustrated with descriptions* (1795), with five coloured plates, and three papers.

Returning from London to Bath on 6 June 1806, Velley jumped from a runaway stagecoach at Reading, fell, and hit his head violently on the ground. He died, without regaining consciousness, on 8 June, and was buried in the church of St Mary the Virgin, Reading, five days later. His extensive and annotated herbarium, illustrated by numerous dissections and microscopic drawings of grasses and other flowering plants, and especially of algae, was offered by his widow to the Linnean Society in 1809. When it declined, the collection was purchased by William Roscoe for the Liverpool Botanic Garden. Sir James Edward Smith in 1798 gave the name *Velleia* to an Australasian genus of flowering plants in Velley's honour.   G. S. BOULGER, rev. ANITA MCCONNELL

Sources H. Blackler, 'The herbarium of Thomas Velley, 1748–1806', *North Western Naturalist*, 13/1 (1938), 72–8 · *GM*, 1st ser., 76 (1806), 588 · *Bath Chronicle* (12 June 1806) · will, PRO, PROB 11/1448 sig 680
Archives Merseyside Maritime Museum, Liverpool, herbarium | Linn. Soc., letters to Sir James Smith

Venables, Edmund (1819–1895), Church of England clergyman and antiquary, born at 17 Queenhithe, London, on 5 July 1819, was the third son of William Venables (*d.* 1840), a papermaker and stationer and alderman of London, who was lord mayor in 1826 and MP for London in 1831–2. His mother, Ann Ruth Fromow, was of Huguenot descent. Venables was educated at Merchant Taylors' School, London, from July 1830, and became the captain of the school. In 1838 he matriculated from Pembroke College, Cambridge, where he was Stuart's exhibitioner and scholar in 1839. In 1842 he graduated BA, being third wrangler and fifth in the second class in the classical tripos. In 1845 he proceeded MA, and he was admitted *ad eundem* at Oxford on 17 December 1856. While an undergraduate he developed an interest in antiquarian studies and shared in the foundation of the Cambridge Camden Society. In 1845 he became a member of the Royal Archaeological Institute and contributed many papers to its journal.

Venables was ordained by the bishop of Chichester in 1844 as curate to Archdeacon Julius Hare (1795–1855), rector of Herstmonceaux in Sussex; he remained there until 1853. In 1846 he was ordained priest by the bishop of Norwich. On 8 September 1847 he married at St Michael's Church, Highgate, Caroline Mary Tebbs, the daughter of Henry Tebbs of Southwood Hall, Highgate, a proctor of Doctors' Commons. They had one son and six daughters. From 1853 to 1855 Venables was curate at Bonchurch in the Isle of Wight; for some years after, he continued to live there, tutoring pupils. With the assistance of some local naturalists he compiled a guide to the island, which was published in 1860. Drawing mainly from the contents of this volume, he also published a shorter work entitled *A Guide to the Undercliff of the Isle of Wight* (1867).

Venables was appointed by Bishop John Jackson as his examining chaplain at Lincoln, and continued in that position when his diocesan was translated to London. In 1865 he was appointed prebendary of Carlton with Thurlby in Lincoln Cathedral, and in 1867 precentor and canon-residentiary. From that time Venables identified himself completely with Lincoln, haunting the minster and its library, and revelling in the antiquarian charm of the city, which inspired many occasional papers. An essay by Venables on Lincoln Cathedral was included in 1893 in a volume of *Our English Minsters*, and printed separately in 1898. He contributed an essay on 'The architecture of the cathedrals of England considered historically' to J. S. Howson's

Essays on Cathedrals (1872); and he undertook, though he did not live to finish, a volume on the *Episcopal Palaces of England*. This was published in 1895, with accounts of seven of the palaces being by Venables. He also edited the fourth edition of Murray's *Handbook for Wiltshire, Dorsetshire, and Somersetshire* in 1882 and published an *Historical Sketch of Bere Regis, Dorset* in the same year.

Venables also edited theological and devotional works. In 1864 he translated Karl Wieseler's *Chronological Synopsis of the Four Gospels*, which was included in 1877 in Bohn's Theological Library, and he edited in 1869 a translation by his brother G. H. Venables of Bleek's *Introduction to the Old Testament*, reproduced in 1875 in Bohn's Ecclesiastical Library. For the Clarendon Press series he edited in 1879 Bunyan's *Pilgrim's Progress* and *Grace Abounding*; his life of John Bunyan appeared in 1888 in the Great Writers series, and in 1883 he edited Lancelot Andrewes's *Private Devotions*. He also contributed to William Smith's *Dictionary of the Bible* (1860–65), Smith's *Dictionary of Christian Antiquities* (1875–80), Smith's *Dictionary of Christian Biography* (1877–87), the *Encyclopaedia Britannica*, Kitto's *A Cyclopaedia of Biblical Literature*, and to the *Dictionary of National Biography*. He was also a frequent writer for the *Saturday Review*, *The Athenaeum*, *The Guardian*, and *Good Words*.

Venables died of influenza at the precentory, Lincoln, on 5 March 1895. His wife, who was suffering from the same illness, died the following day. They were buried on 9 March in the same grave in the cloisters of Lincoln Cathedral. Two of their daughters survived them.

    W. P. COURTNEY, rev. NILANJANA BANERJI

Sources *Lincoln Gazette and Lincolnshire Times* (9 March 1895), 5 · Venn, *Alum. Cant.* · *Manchester Guardian* (6 March 1895), 5 · C. J. Robinson, ed., *A register of the scholars admitted into Merchant Taylors' School, from AD 1562 to 1874*, 2 (1883) · *The Athenaeum* (9 March 1895), 319 · A. J. C. Hare, *Memorials of a quiet life*, 13th edn, 3 (1876), 247–9
Archives BL, letters to W. E. Gladstone, Add. MSS 44403–44514 · CUL, letters to Sir George Stokes · Durham Cath. CL, letters to J. B. Lightfoot
Wealth at death £20,787 15s. 8d.: probate, 17 April 1895, CGPLA Eng. & Wales

Venables, Edward Frederick (1815–1858), indigo planter and volunteer soldier, was born on 5 May 1815, the third son of Lazarus Jones Venables (1772–1856), barrister, of Liverpool and Woodhill, Shropshire, and his wife, Alice, daughter of Thomas Jolley of Liverpool. He early went to India as an indigo planter. He married in 1851 Eliza Power, daughter of R. H. Kinchant of Park Hall, Oswestry, Shropshire; they had no children. Venables, two elder brothers having died, inherited from his father in 1856 the family estates near Oswestry.

At the time of the outbreak of the Indian mutiny Venables was settled near Azamgarh in the North-Western Provinces. After the rising of the 17th native infantry on 3 June 1857 he left Azamgarh for Ghazipur. Some planters and clerks had been left behind, and Venables and another planter, M. P. Dunn—'two men cast in the heroic type' (Malleson, *The Indian Mutiny of 1857*, 184)—determined to rescue them. No help was provided by the commissioner of the division, and when they set out on 16 June they had only a few Indian mounted constables, given them by A. Ross, the magistrate at Ghazipur. To these, however, Venables was able to add some of the tenants on his own estates at Dohrighat and a few refugees from surrounding villages. Having obtained the assistance of Ali Bakh, a collector, from within the town, Venables compelled the 13th irregular cavalry to abandon Azamgarh and reoccupied it. On 10 July he took the offensive against the mutineers with seventy-five mounted constables, an old gun, and a loyal Sepoy regiment. He stormed the police station and released his friends. When, however, on 16 July he attacked the Rajputs of the Palwar clan at Koilsa, he was deserted by his Sepoys and had to re-enter Azamgarh. Two days later reinforcements reached him, but most of them he sent to Ghazipur. On 20 July he marched out again with the rest, and, though compelled to retire before superior forces, the retreat, in which Venables himself led the cavalry, was so masterly that the rebels very soon retired from before Azamgarh. But on 29 July, under orders from Commissioner Tucker, it was once more evacuated, Venables retiring a second time to Ghazipur. But Azamgarh having been in August occupied by the Nepalese allies, Venables again took part in an advance on it. On 19 September, when the rebels were surprised at Mandori, he, though only a volunteer, commanded the cavalry, was first up to the first gun taken, and killed three men with his own hand. The mutineers then offered 500 rupees for his head.

Venables next rode as a volunteer with General Sir Thomas Harte Franks in his march from eastern Oudh to Lucknow, and rendered outstanding service. In the early spring of 1858 he had retired to Allahabad in broken health and spirits, and was looking forward to a return to England, when Lord Canning persuaded him to again volunteer his services at Azamgarh. His judgement and local knowledge were of great value to Lord Mark Kerr and Sir E. Lugard. With the former Venables re-entered Azamgarh on 6 April. While engaged in the pursuit of Koor Singh after his defeat by Lugard on 15 April he was mortally wounded, and he died four days later, on 19 April.

When, the following June, the Calcutta chamber of commerce met to consider a memorial to Venables, Lord Canning, the governor-general, wrote commending his intrepidity, energy, and calm temper, and his 'thoroughly just appreciation of the people and circumstances with which he had to deal'. He was considered one of the heroes of the mutiny. His younger brother became heir to his estates.   G. LE G. NORGATE, *rev.* ROGER T. STEARN

Sources Burke, *Gen. GB* · J. W. Kaye and G. B. Malleson, *Kaye's and Malleson's History of the Indian mutiny of 1857–8*, 4–5 (1889) · H. G. Keene, *Fifty-seven* (1883) · *Annual Register* (1858) · Ward, *Men of the reign* · G. B. Malleson, *The Indian mutiny of 1857*, 4th edn (1892) · C. Hibbert, *The great mutiny, India, 1857* (1978) · Boase, *Mod. Eng. biog.*

Venables, George Stovin (1810–1888), barrister and journalist, born on 18 June 1810 at Kirkethorpe, Yorkshire, was the second son of Richard Venables of Llysdinam Hall, Brecknockshire, archdeacon of Carmarthen and for twenty-five years chairman of the Radnorshire quarter sessions. George's mother was Sophia, daughter of George Lister of Girsby, Lincolnshire. He was educated at Charterhouse School at the same time as William Makepeace Thackeray, whose nose he is alleged to have broken in a fight. He proceeded to Jesus College, Cambridge, and in 1831 won the chancellor's medal for English verse, the subject being the 'North-West Passage'. He graduated BA in 1832 and MA in 1835, was elected a fellow of Jesus College (1835–68), and acted as tutor from 1835 to 1838.

Venables was called to the bar by the Inner Temple in June 1836, and joined the Oxford circuit, but eventually devoted himself to parliamentary practice, being made a queen's counsel in 1863. Simultaneously he pursued an anonymous career in journalism, setting the highest standards for journalism as a vehicle for political thought and for publishing faithful reports of public life. On 1 November 1855 he wrote the leading article in the first issue of the *Saturday Review* and continued to make regular weekly contributions to the paper for more than thirty years. From 1857 onwards he also compiled, for at least twenty-five consecutive years, the summary of events published in *The Times* on the last day of every year. He also contributed to the *Literary Review*, the *Victoria Regia*, and *Macmillan's Magazine*. The only work published in his own name was his memoir of his closest friend, Henry Lushington, which was printed as a preface to Lushington's *Italian War* (1859). He had also printed privately in 1848, in conjunction with Henry Lushington, a volume of poems entitled *Joint Compositions*. Venables retired from legal practice with a considerable fortune in 1882 and became the high sheriff of Radnor in 1884. He died on 6 October 1888 at his home, 67 Curzon Street, Mayfair, London.

The impression made by Venables upon many of the most distinguished of his contemporaries was that he was almost unequalled in the extraordinary force and charm of his character. As an advocate he displayed the most remarkable memory and powers of expression. He was considered a close friend by many leading figures of the day, such as Thackeray, Lord Tennyson, and Sir James Fitzjames Stephen. A year before his death a number of his friends, including Sir James Stephen, erected a window as a memorial of Venables and his two brothers, the Revd Richard Venables of Llysdinam Hall and Joseph Henry Venables (1813–1866), barrister, in the church at Llysdinam, which he had built and endowed. It was inscribed 'Conditori hujus ecclesiæ amicissimi quidam'. Thackeray is alleged to have founded the character of George Warrington in *Pendennis* partly upon Venables. Tennyson accepted from Venables a line in 'The Princess' ('If that hypothesis of theirs be sound'); the poem is dedicated to Henry Lushington. On hearing of his friend's death, Sir James Stephen wrote an article of warm appreciation on Venables in the *Saturday Review*.

HERBERT STEPHEN, *rev.* NILANJANA BANERJI

Sources Venn, *Alum. Cant.* · *Saturday Review*, 66 (1888), 419–20 · L. Stephen, *The life of Sir James Fitzjames Stephen* (1895) · Burke, *Gen. GB* · J. Foster, *Men-at-the-bar: a biographical hand-list of the members of*

the various inns of court, 2nd edn (1885) · Allibone, Dict. · H. Tennyson, Alfred Lord Tennyson: a memoir by his son, 2 vols. (1897)

Archives NL Wales, journal, diaries, corresp., and papers | BL, letters to T. H. S. Escott, Add. MS 58795

Likenesses attrib. A. C. Sterling, salt print photograph, 1846–9, NPG · J. Collier, portrait; at Llysdinam Hall, Newbridge-on-Wye, in 1899 · chalk drawing, Jesus College, Cambridge

Wealth at death £154,350 4s. 8d.: resworn probate, June 1889, CGPLA Eng. & Wales (1888)

Sir Percy
Frederick Ronald
Venables (1904–
1979), by Walter
Bird, 1963

Venables, Sir Percy Frederick Ronald [Peter] (1904–1979), educationist and university administrator, was born on 5 August 1904 at Birkenhead, the second of the seven children of Percy Venables, a Post Office clerk, and his wife, Ethel Kate Paull. Peter, as he was known, was educated at Birkenhead secondary school and the Birkenhead Institute and subsequently, from 1922, at Liverpool University, where he was to spend eight years. In 1925 he obtained a first-class honours BSc degree in chemistry. He also represented the university at rugby in which, as his chunky figure dictated, he was a front row forward.

Venables's first intention was to enter schoolteaching and with this in mind he spent a further year taking the education diploma in 1926. He was diverted, however, into chemical research and spent two years as a research student working on the photosynthesis of nitrogen compounds. His thesis on this subject earned him a PhD degree in 1928 and a research fellowship, which he held until 1930.

In 1930 Venables was appointed to a lectureship in chemistry at the Leicester College of Technology. Here he threw himself into the challenges of teaching during the dark days of the depression and he left himself little time for further research. He published several papers on chemical analysis and also, as co-author, a slim volume entitled A Chemistry Course for Painters and Decorators (1933), a title which was perhaps the first indication of his lasting commitment to the technical education of the underprivileged. In 1936 he moved from Leicester to become head of the chemistry department at the South-East Essex Technical College, and in 1941 he was appointed principal of the Municipal College in Southend-on-Sea. Thus by the age of thirty-seven he had already established himself as an academic administrator. It was a wise move, for his great gifts as an administrator were called on continuously thereafter and he cannot have regretted that he abandoned a career in chemical research.

It was while Venables was a lecturer in Leicester that he married in 1932 Ethel Craig, daughter of Alfred Howell, a wharfinger of Middlesbrough. This was a match of intellectual equals; she, too, was a graduate in chemistry but, as Venables himself put it, they were both 'lapsed chemists'—he into administration, she into educational psychology, in which she graduated PhD in 1956. In later years she became an authority on marriage guidance. They were a devoted couple, sharing for forty-seven years not only intellectual but social and cultural interests, and establishing close links with the worlds of music, theatre, and art. They had two sons and two daughters; their younger daughter, Clare, who made a career in the theatre, succeeded Joan Littlewood as director of the Stratford Theatre.

In 1947 Venables was appointed principal of the Royal Technical College, Salford. For nine years he was intimately involved in the process of creation of the eight colleges of advanced technology (CATs), of which his institution was one. This was the first attempt to upgrade technical education in Britain, which still tended to classify engineers as artisans rather than professionals. In 1955 Venables published his first major work, Technical Education, and, in the same year, moved from Salford to the Birmingham CAT, where he was to remain until his retirement in 1969. He was again involved in the process of upgrading for his new institution became Aston University and he himself became a vice-chancellor in 1966. Throughout all this period of stress and change Venables clung to his visions of expanded opportunities for vocational training for all who could benefit, and of vocational training that was in no sense narrow but was instead an education for a full and rewarding life. In articles and speeches he pressed for close links between education and industry and was a tireless advocate of the sandwich course as a means to this end. His second major work, Higher Education Developments: the Technological Universities, 1956–76, was published in 1978.

Despite the pressures of his appointments Venables found time to undertake a very large range of services of many kinds. He was president of the Association of Principals of Technical Institutions (1953–4) and president of the Manchester Literary and Philosophical Society (1954–6). His government appointments included membership of the Central Advisory Council for Education (England) (1956–60), of the Advisory Council on Scientific Policy (1962–4), of the Northern Ireland committee on university and higher technical education (1963–4), and of the committee on manpower resources (1965–8). With a fine impartiality he was concurrently chairman (1965–9) both of the Independent Television Authority's adult education advisory committee and of the BBC further education advisory council. In 1969–73 he was vice-president of the British Association for Commercial and Industrial Education (BACIE) and in 1971–7 president of the National Institute of Adult Education. In addition to all this he was a member of the West Midlands Economic Planning Council (1965–8) and of the Midlands Electricity Board (1967–73).

In 1967, having been elected vice-chairman of the Committee of Vice-Chancellors and Principals of the United Kingdom, Venables was asked by Jennie Lee, the minister of state at the Department of Education and Science, to become chairman of the planning committee of the Open University. To the astonishment of his vice-cancellarian colleagues he accepted. The planning committee was dissolved in 1969 when the Open University received its royal charter, which named Venables first pro-chancellor and chairman of council, a position he held for five years.

Venables was punctilious as chairman, never encroaching on the job of the vice-chancellor. He saw his role as that of ensuring that the policies of the university were in harmony with the spirit of the charter, with the views of the lay members of the governing body, and with the motivation and commitment of the staff. This he accomplished with a lightness of touch and a firmness of purpose. He was a wonderful chairman, always totally prepared, willing to listen patiently to all who wished to speak, however foolishly, summarizing with unerring insight any consensus that he perceived, and able to give a lead when there was no consensus by offering his own well-thought-out suggestion.

It was a measure of the trust in his total integrity which Venables inspired that he was recalled from retirement to be chairman of the university's committee on continuing education. By 1975 the first objective of the university, namely the provision of courses leading to a first degree, had been largely accomplished. But another objective, 'to provide for the educational well-being of the community generally', was still to be tackled. This phrase, almost certainly drafted by Venables himself, covers all the egalitarian and humanitarian ideas that had inspired him throughout his life. It could be implemented through the provision of continuing education. The report of the committee was published in 1977.

This was the last formal contribution that Venables made to the Open University, of which he had been, as it were, the consultant architect, while others erected the buildings. Venables was knighted in 1963 and received honorary degrees from Aston (1969), Sussex (1971), and the Open University (1973). He was made an honorary fellow of the University of Manchester Institute of Science and Technology (1970), and of Chelsea College (1973). He became a fellow of the Royal Institute of Chemistry in 1938.

Despite his many commitments, about which he was conscientious in the extreme, Venables was a warm and friendly man with an impish sense of humour, making his wisecracks with a completely dead-pan face. He had endless patience, sympathy, and goodwill towards those who worked with him. He died, after a short illness, at his home, 15 Forest Road, Moseley, Birmingham, on 17 June 1979.   WALTER PERRY, *rev.*

Sources *The Times* (23 Nov 1979) • C. A. Russell, 'Sir Peter Venables, 1904–1979', *Chemistry in Britain*, 16 (1980), 555 • personal knowledge (1986) • private information (1986) • *CGPLA Eng. & Wales* (1979)
Archives ICL, corresp. with Lord Jackson
Likenesses W. Bird, photograph, 1963, NPG [*see illus.*] • D. Poole, portrait, 1974, Open University, Milton Keynes, Walton Hall
Wealth at death £39,294: probate, 5 Dec 1979, *CGPLA Eng. & Wales*

Venables, Robert (1612/13–1687), parliamentarian army officer, was the son of Robert Venables, gentleman, of Antrobus, Cheshire, and Ellen, daughter of Richard Simcox of Rudheath, Cheshire. His father could trace his ancestry back to the Norman conquest, but he was the head of the cadet branch of the Venables, while his mother's father and brother were on the cusp of the gentry and yeomanry, regularly serving as grand jurymen at assizes and quarter sessions.

When the civil war broke out in 1642 Venables volunteered for service and was commissioned a captain in the parliamentarian army being assembled in Cheshire by Sir William Brereton. He was reported to have been captured at an untidy skirmish at Westhoughton, Lancashire, but was soon released and served in his own county and in Lancashire throughout the first civil war, as captain and then lieutenant-colonel of the regiment of Robert Duckenfield and then of Brereton himself. In 1644 he distinguished himself in the defence of Nantwich and he was seriously wounded at the siege of Chester; but by the spring of 1645 he was governor of Tarvin, the town that acted as headquarters for the siege operations at Chester, just 5 miles away. The letter books of Sir William Brereton reveal him as a key member of the council of war that planned that siege, and one of Brereton's main allies in the feuds within the Cheshire committees and between Brereton and his fellow generals in neighbouring counties. He was one of the signatories of the articles under which Chester finally surrendered on 1 February 1646, and he was one of those whom Brereton recommended to parliament for appointment as governor of this strategically vital town. Instead he was put in charge of a force that was sent to reduce the remaining royalist garrisons in north Wales.

Venables remained in arms in 1647 and 1648 but was also active as a civil commissioner, and spent much time trying in vain to secure payment of arrears of £2113. In summer 1647 mutineers in Nantwich imprisoned members of the county committee and held them to ransom for their arrears, and he borrowed another £232 to end the crisis. A year later he was still awaiting compensation. Late in 1648 he was called up to army headquarters in London, and on 15 December, still a lieutenant-colonel, he was put in charge of a committee of lower-ranking officers charged with finding 'the best ways and grounds for the speedy bringing of the king to justice' (*Clarke*, 2.132).

In April 1649 Venables was commissioned a full colonel and ordered to raise a fresh regiment for Ireland. The names of his junior officers and NCOs suggest that he raised it in Cheshire. He crossed to Dublin in July, ahead of the main contingent of Cromwell's army of conquest, and joined Major-General Michael Jones (himself commander at the siege of Chester for several months in 1645) in time to take part in the crushing defeat of the king's lord lieutenant, the marquess of Ormond, at Rathmines on 5 August. He and his regiment then joined Cromwell and he was given the great responsibility of leading them to storm the breach at Drogheda after the first wave had been driven back with heavy casualties. It was also Venables's pikemen who prevented the drawbridge across the river that ran through the town from being raised and who made possible the massacre of the garrison on the north side of the town.

After the capture of Drogheda, Cromwell divided his army and sent Venables with three full regiments north to join up with the brutalized Sir Charles Coote for a ruthless reimposition of protestant control of Ulster. He moved steadily north, summoning and taking the surrender of Dundalk, Newry, Carlingford, and Belfast before relieving Coote in Derry. He then defeated Colonel Mark Trevor in a stiff engagement at Dromore. Cromwell was full of praise for his northern commander in a series of letters to Westminster.

In 1650 Venables and Coote continued the process of securing Ulster. They joined forces in June to crush the army of Ulster, commanded (following the death of Owen Roe O'Neill) by Bishop Heber McMahon of Clogher, at the battle of Scariffhollis (21 June; near Letterkenny in co. Donegal), putting 3000 men to the sword and summarily executing many prisoners. By the summer only Charlemont in the whole of Ulster lay in Catholic hands, and after a failed assault in which 800 English were killed, Coote and Venables accepted its surrender on terms (14 August). But securing all the towns and crushing the armies did not bring peace. Venables now became all too literally bogged down in a guerrilla war against 'tories' in north Connaught and south-west Ulster that was to last for another two years, though he was also involved in the campaigns that led to the defeat of the final formal army of Catholics—that of the earl of Clanricarde in Connaught.

By 1653 Ireland was pacified. Venables had fought a hard war, and had condoned, if he had not himself ordered, atrocities against those who had surrendered to mercy (that is, on conditions which left their lives at the mercy and discretion of the victors). He had shown courage, resolution, and grit. He had also shown forbearance. Being in a subsidiary theatre, his men had been poorly paid, poorly supplied, and—at least, once Cromwell had returned to Britain—poorly recognized. He was later to write an account of his service in Ulster, 'for all which,' he sourly added, 'I never received further reward than a letter of thanks' (Narrative, 3).

Venables spent his last months in Ireland in bitter dispute with resettled presbyterian ministers who were trying to reimpose a strict confessional church on the model of their Scottish homeland. At one point he threatened to transplant them to Munster. Little is known of his own religion, other than that he was ascetically protestant and almost certainly a Congregationalist. He was also very active in drawing up the regulations for putting the severe Act of Settlement into effect in 1653. He lobbied hard on his own behalf and that of his men for satisfaction of arrears, and in December 1651 he received land to the value of £1223 in part settlement of his own. But many of those who fought with him remained unsatisfied and in May 1654 he returned from Ireland to lobby on their behalf.

Venables's arrival coincided with the secret decision of the council of state to mount a surprise attack on the Spanish West Indies, and in August he was privily asked by Cromwell to command the military expedition (he agreed, though he was not formally commissioned until December). For twelve years he had been toughened by war and had become a fearless and resilient soldier. Cromwell admired what he had achieved in the bleak winter of relentless rain when they were both in Ireland. It was a big promotion to put him in charge of what was intended to be the first stage of a fundamental assault on the Spanish islands and mainland colonies in and around the Caribbean. In a few short weeks he was to bring ruin and ignominy on himself. He had just married (in June 1654) for a second time in mysterious circumstances. (His first wife was Elizabeth, daughter of Thomas Rudyard of Rudyard, Staffordshire, gentleman, but the date of their marriage and her death are not known.) His second wife, Elizabeth (c.1614–1689), widow of Thomas Lee of Darnhall, Cheshire, and daughter of Samuel Aldersey of Chester, later said that it was a marriage based on duty and in fulfilment of a promise rashly entered into ('my engagement to him was before his going to Ireland; what it was is best known to himself And if he be willing as myself to bury it in silence, it shall never be repeated'; Townshend, 24). It was a loveless match with someone who disliked his politics, disdained his religion, and disapproved of his manners. She escorted him to the Indies, but asserted that 'the success was very ill, for the work of God was not like to be done by the Devil's instruments. A wicked army it was, and sent out without arms or provisions' (ibid., 28). Venables himself claimed that his intentions were honourable: he had attempted 'to promote the gospel and serve the country' (Narrative, 7). Perhaps his first error had been to take his new wife with him.

The council in its wisdom decided to share authority over the campaign between a general (Venables) and an admiral (William Penn) who had to make decisions with the advice and consent of three civilians with extensive knowledge of the Caribbean (this was the first real mistake). This group, with other veteran merchants from the area, planned the expedition. They put together an army of 1000 veterans and 8000 'volunteer' soldiers (this was the second mistake). They ordered the wrong food and forgot to take anything for storing water—this on a tropical campaign (the third mistake). They had thirty-eight sound vessels to convey them and to take on any Spanish naval vessels they encountered (this was not a mistake). The commanders were given a free choice of target and considered Hispaniola (Dominica), St John's Island (Puerto Rico), or the area to the south of the Orinoco. Once they reached the Bahamas and took on extra supplies and 2000 extra troops, they decided on Hispaniola. It was intrinsically a good choice for it was fertile and well placed to launch further expeditions.

They sailed in the last fortnight of December in two squadrons, and arrived four weeks later in Barbados. They refreshed themselves, planned their expedition for two months and then sailed for Hispaniola, arriving on 13 April. By this time Venables and Penn were barely on speaking terms, and full of so much mutual mistrust that Venables seems genuinely to have suspected that Penn would offload him and his men and depart, leaving them marooned. There were bitter disputes about the division of supplies and inadequate contingency plans for Penn to come to Venables's assistance if he got into trouble.

The weather was foul: torrential tropical rain that ruined the gunpowder, caused the biscuits to rot, and made the rivers unfordable. Over-confident planning and under-confident soldiers proved a fatal combination. Having telegraphed their intentions to the Spaniards, they lost the element of surprise. After landing with 8000 men 40 miles from San Domingo they marched disconsolately through inhospitable wooded terrain and were twice ambushed by the Spanish (18 and 25 April). Venables lost about a third of his men and, bitterly complaining of their cowardice, got Penn to take him and the remainder off, though not without some delay. Very much as a means of saving face and seeking a compensatory triumph, Venables ordered Penn to take him to Jamaica, a less developed and economically (as it seemed) less promising island. Here he quickly gained a pyrrhic victory. He landed on 10 May and took the surrender of the capital on 17 May, but not before much of the garrison and many of the inhabitants had taken to the hills. Venables was faced with the prospect of a guerrilla campaign as stubborn as that fought by the tories in Ireland. He began the thankless task of rooting them out, but fell ill with a tropical fever.

Penn, fearing the consequences of this failure, abandoned Venables, and sailed for home with half the fleet on 25 June, determined to get his side of the story in first. On discovering this, Venables set off in hot pursuit in a vessel called the *Marston Moor*, but he failed to overtake Penn. He arrived in Portsmouth on 9 September 1655 'almost a skeleton, and so weak he could neither stand nor ride' (*Portland MSS*, 2.97). This did not spare him (or Penn) a spell in the Tower of London as a wrathful council and a distraught Cromwell (brooding on why God had deserted him in this great cause in which he had invested much hope) pondered whom to hold responsible. On 30 October Venables was released from prison but relieved of all his military commands. He retreated to Cheshire, far from the complaints of Cromwell if not those of Mrs Venables. He was effectively in disgrace for the rest of the protectorate.

Although some royalist sources later claimed that in his bitterness at his treatment Venables turned towards supporting a Restoration, there is little evidence of it. Although he lived close to the epicentre of support for Sir George Booth's pro-Stuart rebellion in August 1659 he took no part. On the other hand, when George Monck marched south in January he named Venables governor of Chester. Sir Edward Hyde sounded out loyalist gentry in Cheshire about whether it was safe to leave him in post once the king returned. He had heard good things of his political loyalty, but was troubled by his reputation for Independency in religion. So Venables was replaced.

Venables lived out the rest of his life in provincial obscurity. He bought a house at Wincham in Cheshire, less draughty and with more modern amenities than the rambling house at Antrobus where he had lived hitherto. He held no office and though he was questioned in early 1664 about possible involvement in the Farnley Wood Plot which was led by ex-Cromwellian soldiers, he was exonerated. He may have sheltered a fugitive (William Veitch) after the Pentland rising in 1667, and he seems to have remained a nonconformist in religion, but he was no political activist. He published a quietist tract—*The Experienced Angler, or, Angling Improved*—in 1662, with an epistle by Isaak Walton. It ran through five editions in his lifetime.

Venables's was a life of frustration. He served loyally in the civil war in England, and tenaciously in Ireland from 1649 to 1654. But he never received the recognition he deserved and he had to spend the years of peace seeking compensation for what he was owed. He was over-promoted and under-supported in a high-profile fiasco in the Caribbean that cost him his reputation. He had to live out his life as a disgraced man with a sharp-tongued wife who disapproved of all he stood for. 'There hath some cross passages fallen out betwixt me and [General Venables]', she wrote, 'upon which I have resolved never to proceed farther, but continue as I was' (Townshend, 24). Even the marriages he arranged for his son and daughter turned out badly: 'to relate the cross and unhandsome passages that fell out in these marriages are not only too tedious to relate but would be a grief to those that do yet survive', Elizabeth wrote (ibid., 28). But one senses that he never heard the end of it and that death did not come too soon to him; he died at Wincham in his seventy-fifth year, and was buried in July 1687.   JOHN MORRILL

Sources I. Gentles, *The New Model Army in England, Ireland, and Scotland, 1645–1653* (1992) • R. N. Dore, *The civil wars in Cheshire* (1966) • J. S. Morrill, *Cheshire, 1630–1660* (1974) • *The letter books of Sir William Brereton*, ed. R. N. Dore, Lancashire and Cheshire Records Society, 123, 128 (1984–90) • E. Robinson, *A discourse of the warr in Lancashire … betweene King Charles and the parliament*, ed. W. Beamont, Chetham Society, 62 (1864) • L. P. Townshend, ed., *Some account of General Robert Venables … with the autobiographical memoranda or diary of his widow, Elizabeth Venables*, Chetham Society, 83 (1872) • *The writings and speeches of Oliver Cromwell*, ed. W. C. Abbott and C. D. Crane, 4 vols. (1937–47), vols. 2, 3 • J. S. Wheeler, *Cromwell in Ireland* (2000) • C. H. Firth and G. Davies, *The regimental history of Cromwell's army*, 2 (1940) • *The narrative of General Venables*, ed. C. H. Firth, CS, new ser., 60 (1900) • S. A. G. Taylor, *The western design* (1969) • S. R. Gardiner, *History of the Commonwealth and protectorate, 1649–1656*, new edn, 4 vols. (1903), vol. 4 • K. O. Kupperman, 'Errand to the Indies', *William* and Mary Quarterly, 45 (1988), 70–99 • P. Sutton, The Jamaica campaign: the Cromwellian West Indies campaign (1990) • R. W. Bridges, Annals of Jamaica (1837) • Seventh report, HMC, 6 (1879) [Francis Barrington letters] • F. C. Cundell and J. L. Pietersz, Jamaica under the Spaniards (1913) • The Clarke papers, ed. C. H. Firth, 4 vols., CS, new ser., 49, 54, 61–2 (1891–1901) • The manuscripts of his grace the duke of Portland, 10 vols., HMC, 29 (1891–1931), vol. 2 • will, Ches. & Chester ALSS, WS 1687

Vendramini, Francesco (1780–1856). *See under* Vendramini, Giovanni (1769–1839).

Vendramini, Giovanni (1769–1839), engraver and architect, was born at Roncade, near Bassano, then under Venetian rule. In Bassano he studied architecture with Antonio Gaidon, but preferred engraving, particularly stipple, which he practised in the studio of Antonio Suntach. Vendramini was invited to London by Luigi Schiavonetti (1765–1810), who was also from Bassano and for whom Vendramini worked for three years. They were among the many 'distinguished young men' who paid 'high premiums' to follow Francesco Bartolozzi (1725–1815) to Britain to learn the secret of stipple-engraving (Baily, 28). As one of Bartolozzi's ablest pupils, Vendramini succeeded to his master's workshop and house at North End in Fulham when Bartolozzi left for Lisbon in 1802. Among Vendramini's earliest and most renowned works are the five plates he engraved for the set of thirteen *Cries of London*, after Francis Wheatley (1747–1801), between 1793 and 1797. Published by Colnaghi & Co., this series was supervised by Schiavonetti. Vendramini subsequently took over Schiavonetti's engraving business at 12 Michaels Street, Brompton. Other early stipple works include *St John the Baptist*, after Raphael, and *The Power of Love*, after Pellegrini.

In February 1802, by a marriage licence dated 5 February, Vendramini married a British woman of Portuguese origin, Lucy de Faria, with whom he had two daughters. Between 1802 and 1805 he produced a number of large-scale engravings after the panoramic paintings by Sir Robert Kerr Porter, among them *The Storming of Seringapatam*, *The Passage of the Alps by the Russians under Suvarrow*, and *The Death of Sir Ralph Abercromby*, which were published by John P. Thompson. During this same period he engraved Porter's *Twenty-Six Illustrations to Anacreon*, published on 4 June 1805. On the back of this success, in 1805 Vendramini went to St Petersburg and later to Moscow, where he worked for Tsar Alexander I for two years. Among his profitable commissions produced there was the engraved portrait *Catherine, Empress of Russia* and his only known colour aquatint, *The Conflagration of Moscow, Sept 14 1812*. So successful was his work in Russia that Vendramini was unable to leave the country without the help of the ambassador for Naples and Duke Sarcopkiolo, who enabled him to cross the border as a diplomatic courier. After his return to Britain he concentrated on producing faithful large stipple plates of Italian old masters, notably *Leda*, after Leonardo da Vinci, *The Vision of St Catherine*, after Paul Veronese, *St Sebastian*, after Spagnoletto, *The Raising of Lazarus*, after Sebastiano del Piombo (now in the National

Gallery), and a *Deposition*, after Donatello. He also produced several prints after Cipriani (*Amorini*) and H. Singleton (Pomfret's *Love Triumphant over Reason*). Of contemporary interest was his set of sixteen portraits of European leaders who visited London between 1814 and 1815, which were published by him at 14 Brompton Row. Among the more notable portraits he is known to have engraved are *Miss Maria Theresa Decamp as Urania*, after P. Jean (1802), *William Wilberforce*, after H. Edridge (1809), *Sir Peter Francis Bourgeois*, after Sir W. Beechey (1811), and *Joseph Nollekens*, after F. Abbot (1816); these and others of his works are in the collections of the Victoria and Albert Museum and the British Museum. Vendramini died, a widower, of 'disease of the brain' at his house at 91 Quadrant, Regent Street, London, on 8 February 1839.

Francesco Vendramini (1780–1856), engraver and architect, and the brother of Giovanni, was born in Bassano and appears to have followed Giovanni to London. It is not known if he married, but his daughter, Julia Frances Vendramini, was baptized at St Paul's, Covent Garden, in 1803. He accompanied his brother to St Petersburg, where in 1808 he became a member of the Academy of Fine Arts. In 1824 he returned to Bassano, intending to settle there. After only fifteen days, however, he moved to Florence, where he lived for eleven years and engraved many plates. He was offered a post in Rome as engraver to the pontificate, but returned to Russia to live and worked as an architect until his death, on 2 February 1856. Francesco too worked in stipple, in the style of Bartolozzi, and in line-engraving. His works include a number of portraits of contemporary Russian personalities, in particular *Alexander I*, after St Aubin (1819). In Bassano he produced portraits of living illustrious Italians and reproduced prints after Reni, Maratti, Ribera, and Titian, whose *Death of Peter Martyr* is described as his finest and best-known print. At the time of his death he held the status of professor in St Petersburg. Among joint printing collaborations with his brother is the portrait of *Kurakin* (Prince Aleksandr Borisovich), after Barowikowski.   JULIA NURSE

Sources Bénézit, *Dict.* • Thieme & Becker, *Allgemeines Lexikon* • M. C. Le-Blanc, *Manuel de l'amateur d'estampes* (Paris, 1889), vol. 4, p. 103 • *Apollo*, 10 (1929), 254–5 • J. T. H. Baily, *F. Bartolozzi: a biographical essay* (1907), xxviii, xxix, xxxix • *Engraved Brit. ports.*, vol. 6, p. 704 • J. H. Slater, *Engravings and their value: a complete guide to the collection and prices of all classes of prints* (1929); repr. (1978), vol. 6, p. 645 • F. Harvey, 'Stipple engraving as practised in England, 1760–1810', *Print Collector's Quarterly*, 17/1 (1930), 49–71 [includes illustrations of Vendramini's plates for the *Cries of London* on p. 61 ('Hot spice gingerbread smoking hot')] • D. Alexander and R. Godfrey, *Painters and engraving: the reproductive print from Hogarth to Wilkie* (Yale, 1980), 45–6 • D. Alexander, 'Vendramini, Giovanni', *The dictionary of art*, ed. J. Turner (1996) • L. Sevrolini, *Dizionario illustrato degli incisori italiani, moderni e contemporanei* (1955) • *Art Union*, 1 (1839), 61 • admon, PRO, PROB 6/215, fol. 315r • d. cert.

Venetian painters in Britain (*act.* 1708–*c.*1750), decorative painters, were linked by kinship or close professional practice. Giovanni Antonio Pellegrini, Marco Ricci and Sebastiano Ricci, Antonio Bellucci, and Jacopo Amigoni worked mainly as decorative painters at various stages in England between 1708 and 1739. All were connected with

London theatre and musical life, and on the whole their patrons were prominent whigs. Their artistic achievement in England is hard to judge since relatively little of their work survives *in situ*, or indeed at all. Though they were not Venetians by birth, the work of Giuseppe Grisoni and Antonio Joli in England places them within this group.

Marco Ricci (1676–1730) was born on 5 June 1676 at Belluno, in the republic of Venice, the son of Gerolamo Ricci, a landscape painter, and Gerolama Trevissoi. He probably trained with his uncle, Sebastiano Ricci [*see below*], and is said to have fled to Dalmatia, where he was apprenticed to a landscape painter, after having killed a gondolier in a brawl. With Pellegrini he was invited to England in 1708 by the British ambassador at Venice, Charles Montagu, then earl and later first duke of Manchester. **Giovanni Antonio Pellegrini** (1675–1741) was born on 29 April 1675 in the parish of San Polo, Venice, the son of Antonio Pellegrini, a glove maker. Montagu's secretary, Christian Cole, a close friend of Rosalba Carriera, whose sister Angela (*d.* 1760) had married Pellegrini in early January 1704, may have suggested their names. By 1708 Pellegrini was a painter of high repute who had made use of Marco Ricci's services as a landscape specialist. Already well travelled, Pellegrini had worked with his master Paolo Pagani (1661–1716) in Moravia and Vienna in the early 1690s, and had visited Rome from 1699 to 1701. His free, spirited handling and vivid colouring were indebted to his study of the late baroque of Luca Giordano and Giovanni Battista Gaulli. Marco Ricci was an eccentric, unstable character, whose career is poorly documented, but he worked in Florence and probably visited Rome. He painted classical landscapes, picturesque Veneto scenes, capriccios, and tempestuous landscapes indebted to Salvador Rosa and Alessandro Magnasco.

When he invited Pellegrini and Marco Ricci to London, Manchester's concerns were for the renovation of Kimbolton Castle, Huntingdonshire, by Vanbrugh, and the success of the new opera house in Haymarket, London, to which he hoped to attract first-rate Italian singers. After their arrival in late October 1708, the pair worked on the decoration of the hall and staircase at Manchester House (des.) and on scenery for two opera productions of 1709 under the management of Owen McSwiney. In 1709–10 Charles Howard, third earl of Carlisle, employed them at Castle Howard in Yorkshire, recently completed by Vanbrugh, together with the north Italian stuccoists Giovanni Bagutti and Plura. The extensive decoration, largely destroyed by fire in 1940, included scenes from the *Iliad*, an unusual choice which may owe more to the tradition of theatre and opera than to conventional baroque iconography. Pellegrini and Ricci also worked for the young Richard Boyle, third earl of Burlington (or for his mother, Juliana), probably then painting the scenes from the *Metamorphoses*, now at Narford Hall, Norfolk, which were apparently presented to Sir Andrew Fountaine after Colen Campbell's reorganization of Burlington House. Fountaine also independently commissioned paintings from Pellegrini. About 1711–12 William Henry Bentinck, second

duke of Portland, employed Pellegrini at his house in St James's Square, London, for a fee of £800 according to Vertue, suggesting that the decorations (des. 1748 during rebuilding) were substantial. Pellegrini's last major commission before he left for Düsseldorf in early summer 1713 was at Kimbolton Castle, where he painted the chapel, the grand staircase, and another room. Here and in the Narford canvases his radiant colour, sensuous brushwork, and often Veronese-inspired designs reveal his strengths as a virtuoso late baroque artist. The relative freedom allowed by his whig patrons, who were unencumbered by rigid patterns of patronage, together with his new-found interest in the work of Van Dyck and Rubens, had a dynamic effect on his style. For the first time Pellegrini painted family portraits, for Manchester and Carlisle and perhaps for the dramatist and dealer Peter Le Motteux, and he produced many cabinet pictures of biblical and mythological heroines for what must have been a demanding market.

While Marco Ricci had worked independently on theatre decoration in 1710, there is no evidence in the Carriera correspondence to support Vertue's account that the two painters had quarrelled. Marco Ricci travelled to Venice in summer 1711, accompanying the singer Catherine Tofts, and he returned with his uncle in the winter. **Sebastiano Ricci** (*bap.* 1659, *d.* 1734) was baptized on 1 August 1659 at Belluno, in the republic of Venice, the son of Livio Ricci and his wife, Andreana. In Venice he was apprenticed to Federico Cervelli (*b. c.*1625, *d.* before 1700). Following a number of romantic entanglements, including a possible marriage to Anna Maria Venanza, on 12 September 1696 he married Maddalena Vandermer (*c.*1663–1742). Ricci's early career involved long sojourns in Bologna (where he learned the guitar), Parma, Rome, and Milan. Except for a trip to Vienna in 1701–2, he was mainly based in Venice from 1696 until 1706 when he joined Marco Ricci at the Florentine court. Sebastiano Ricci's travels enabled him to study the best of Italian art, from the proto-baroque of Correggio in Parma to the energetic and witty classicism of Annibale Carracci at the Palazzo Farnese in Rome. In Venice in 1708 he painted a lyrical homage to Veronese in a celebrated altarpiece for San Giorgio Maggiore. Perhaps he went to London, as Vertue recounts, to mortify Pellegrini; perhaps he was invited by Queen Anne, as Pascoli states; more likely he was grasping the opportunity to compete for the prestigious commission of the dome of St Paul's Cathedral, for a rumour to that effect had reached John Talman in Rome by November 1711. Pellegrini had already entered the public competition of 1709, and he and Sir James Thornhill were invited in February 1710 to paint 'little cupolas' or models: it is unlikely that *The Trinity and Saints* (V&A; repr. Knox, pl. 42) of 1710 relates to this, as it had already been decided that the subjects were to come from the Acts of the Apostles. The commission was not resolved until June 1715, and Ricci's involvement is undocumented. Instead he found a lavish patron in Lord Burlington, who in 1712–13 commissioned monumental canvases of mythological subjects for the staircase of Burlington House, London, and a variety of others on biblical or classical themes, some of which were installed in his villa at Chiswick in the late 1720s. Handel also enjoyed Burlington's patronage in this period, and would have known Pellegrini and the Riccis—some of their paintings were in his collection. Other whig figures who commissioned work from Sebastiano Ricci include Richard Arundell, a friend of Fountaine, and the duke of Portland, who paid £1000 for decorative work at Portland House completed by the summer of 1713 (largely destroyed through rebuilding, 1748). This included a ceiling with *The Choice of Hercules* as a centrepiece, recalling the earl of Shaftesbury's espousal of the subject in 1712 as an illumination of his moral philosophy (dem. 1938). In the autumn Sebastiano and Marco Ricci decorated the duke's chapel at Bulstrode House (des. by rebuilding, 1862). Sebastiano Ricci is not documented at Kneller's Academy, where Pellegrini was one of the directors (and was active in life-drawing classes); however, he presented an allegory on the peace of Utrecht to the Painter–Stainers' Company, perhaps at the time when Handel's Utrecht *Te Deum* was performed. While little is known of Marco's independent work, his landscapes were clearly popular and the many versions that exist of his *Opera Rehearsal*, including one at Castle Howard (1709–10; repr. Scarpa Sonino, *Ricci*, fig. 59), a playful group portrait, attest to the popularity of this early exercise in sardonic social observation.

Portland, Burlington, and probably other patrons who employed both painters, could compare Pellegrini's sketchy, festive style with Sebastiano Ricci's powerful, dynamic manner. A more versatile, inventive artist, Ricci adapted his style to suit the developing classicizing taste of English patrons, looking to the Roman and Bolognese artists whom they admired as well as to the qualities of Veronese. Charles Talbot, first duke of Shrewsbury, an admirer of the Roman baroque, was keen to have Ricci decorate the prince of Wales's bedchamber; however, Lord Halifax insisted that the commission go to Thornhill, for the sake of his career and for the encouragement of English artists. Possibly Shrewsbury obtained for Ricci instead the commission to paint the *Resurrection* mural at Chelsea Hospital in 1714–15. In late summer 1715 Sebastiano Ricci left England, since he is documented in Milan in September; Marco Ricci presumably left with him. In Venice the pair continued to collaborate and to work for British patrons, painting two of the allegorical tombs of whig worthies commissioned by Owen McSwiney in the early 1720s, and numerous works for Joseph (later Consul) Smith. Both were closely associated with Venetian theatre and opera. Sebastiano Ricci bought a handsome apartment in the calle del Salvadego with his English wealth where Marco resided until his death on 21 January 1730. He was unmarried. He was buried on 22 January in the Venetian church of San Moisè. In London Marco had painted atmospheric landscapes in gouache on kidskin, a technique taken up by Joseph Goupy, and he probably made caricatures there too; he explored these new genres with great originality in his remaining years in Venice,

while also experimenting with etching from 1723. Sebastiano enjoyed a high international reputation in his late career as a painter who had rediscovered the values of Veronese. He died in Venice on 15 May 1734. Pellegrini's later career was a peripatetic one. After two profitable years at the court of Düsseldorf, followed by a sojourn in the Netherlands, he was again invited to England in 1719 by the British ambassador at The Hague, William Cadogan, to decorate his country house (des. by fire before 1770). During these months, from May to late October, Pellegrini may also have worked on the staircase decoration at Cowdray House, Sussex, for Lord Montacute (des. 1793 by fire) and perhaps for Sir Andrew Fountaine at Narford. For the remaining twenty-two years of his life Pellegrini worked all over Europe, especially for the courts of Dresden, Würzburg, Vienna, and Mannheim, while also painting the enormous ceiling of the 'Salle Mississippi' at the Banque Royale in Paris for John Law in 1720 (des. 1722 during renovations). He died on 2 November 1741 in Venice and was buried there in the church of San Vidal on 3 November.

The commercial success of Pellegrini and the Riccis in England may have induced other painters to try their luck there. Niccolò Cassana (1659–1713), active in Venice from 1698 as the agent of Grand Duke Ferdinand and a friend of Sebastiano Ricci, went to London c.1710—invited, according to C. F. Ratti, to paint portraits for Queen Anne. Vertue records that he and Sebastiano engaged in picture dealing, supplying the nobility with often dubious old masters. Vincenzo Damini (b. c.1690x92, d. after 1749), a follower of Pellegrini, is said to have come from Düsseldorf to London, and Vertue notes that he arrived about 1713, but he may not have arrived until 1719–20. He left for Italy in 1730, accompanied by his pupil, the unconventional and talented Giles Hussey. Vertue associated Damini with Francesco Riario, a Bolognese history painter, one of whose few documented works is a portrait of John Devoto (*fl.* 1708–1752), a painter of Genoese parentage who worked as a stage designer from 1718 at Drury Lane, London, and elsewhere. The Flemish-born **Giuseppe Grisoni** (1699–1769) was born at Mons on 24 October 1699. Of his parents nothing is known. He studied in Florence and Rome and came to England with John Talman in 1715, working as a draughtsman. He developed as a portraitist and history painter, decorating a ceiling at Canons for James Brydges, first duke of Chandos. His depiction of Colley Cibber as Lord Foppington in Vanbrugh's *The Relapse* (Garrick Club, London; repr. Ashton no. 116) is a rare early theatrical portrait, while a painting showing one of the masquerades at the King's Theatre organized by John James Heidegger (V&A; exh. NPG, 1985, no. 105) may be by his hand. In 1724 Grisoni married an Englishwoman, Anne St John (d. 1739?), to whom he had given drawing lessons, and returned to Italy in 1728, taking with him William Hoare as his pupil. He worked successfully in Florence until 1740 and subsequently in Rome, where he died in 1769, as a sculptor and history painter. Little is known of the career of Francesco Sleter (c.1685–1775), who called himself a Venetian, although undocumented in contemporary Venetian sources. He is first recorded in England as working for the duke of Chandos at Canons in 1719; he probably decorated the state rooms at Grimsthorpe Castle for Peregrine Bertie, second duke of Ancaster, after Vanbrugh completed the building in 1724; here his style is close to Bellucci's. Sleter is later documented in 1731, painting murals based on Spenser's *Faerie Queene* for the Temple of Venus at Stowe, Buckinghamshire, while in 1732 he provided grisaille decoration for Benjamin Styles at Moor Park, Hertfordshire. In the mid- and late 1730s he was paid for ceiling decorations at Mereworth Castle (Kent) for John Fane, later seventh earl of Westmorland; he died at Mereworth in 1775.

The most celebrated artist to arrive in these years was **Antonio Bellucci** (1654–1726). He was born on 19 February 1654 in Venice and baptized there in the church of Santa Maria Formosa on 26 February, the son of Giovan Battista Bellucci and Caterina Volpato. He studied drawing in Dalmatia (Sebenico) with a nobleman, Domenico Difnico, and some time before 1680 married Maria, with whom he had three children baptized in June 1680, 1683, and 1684 in Venice. Bellucci had gained fame in his native Venice in the 1680s, developing a neo-Veronesian manner which was also indebted to Bolognese and Roman baroque art. Although he worked periodically on religious and secular commissions in Venice, he was essentially a successful court painter, celebrating the glory of the ruling Liechtenstein family at Vienna (1692–1703) and the Wittelsbach at Düsseldorf (1706–16) with allegorical cycles enshrining their virtues. In 1716 at the death of his patron, the elector Johann Wilhelm, Bellucci left Düsseldorf for London, no doubt encouraged by Pellegrini. His reputation went before him, and he decorated an unspecified house in Pall Mall on his arrival. Little is known of his patrons, and by comparison with the versatile Ricci, he may have seemed old-fashioned. His major patron was the first duke of Chandos, who brought together the leading history painters of the day at Canons, together with the stuccoists Giovanni Bagutti and Giuseppe Artari, who had also worked in Germany. Handel was still director of music at Canons in 1719, and Bellucci could well have known him from Düsseldorf. Among other decorations (des. *c.*1747–8), he painted the enormous library ceiling with a complex allegory recalling the rhetoric he had employed for the elector palatine. His canvases from the ceiling of the chapel, completed by August 1720, survive at Great Witley church, Worcestershire, while the four paintings commissioned by the duke for St Lawrence's Church, Little Stanmore, Whitchurch, Middlesex, survive *in situ*. At Chandos House in St James's Square, London, Bellucci decorated the duke's visiting room and picture room (des. by rebuilding, 1735). He may have felt at home in England to some extent, especially when Pellegrini returned, or when the antiquarian and connoisseur Anton Maria Zanetti, a close friend of the Riccis and Pellegrini, visited in summer 1721; moreover he would have known Giacomo Leoni from the Düsseldorf court. However, Bellucci suffered from gout, and left in July 1722, working in the Veneto until his death at the family home

in Pieve di Soligo on 29 August 1726. His son Giovanni Battista Bellucci (1684–1760) remained, making his career as a portraitist in England and Ireland; his portrait of the librettist Paolo Rolli (priv. coll.; exh. NPG, 1985, no. 90) evokes the family's associations with London musical life.

It has been convincingly argued that the first generation of whig nobility admired the mercantile, oligarchic republic of Venice and associated its civic virtues with the architectural style of Palladio, hence the position of Palladianism as the English national style by the 1720s. The employment of artists who worked in the manner of Veronese by prominent whigs has been seen as a deliberate reinforcement of this analogy with the cultural as well as political virtues of Venice. It can be objected that Pellegrini's major decorative projects were associated with Vanbrugh, and that he and the Riccis had more in common with the cosmopolitan world of Italian music and of late baroque decoration than with the essentially protestant and rational ethos of English Palladianism. However, as distinct from large-scale history painting in oil on plaster, Pellegrini and Sebastiano Ricci could also provide canvases to be inset in decorative surrounds in Palladian interiors. Sebastiano Ricci's work was undoubtedly favoured by Burlington; moreover, he designed the frontispiece to Leoni's *The Architecture of A. Palladio* (1715), to which he and Marco Ricci were subscribers. Sebastiano was the most successful of this group of Venetians in England: Vertue reported the death in 1734 of this 'excellent and famous painter', noting that his works in England would remain 'a Monument of Fame—to him and to the Honour of this Nation' (Vertue, *Note books*, 3.65). But in general by the 1720s the established taste for Italian opera and for Veronese-inspired history painting tended to raise nationalistic hackles, leading to a movement in favour of a more robust, naturalistic 'English' style in music, theatre, and art. The Venetian painter whom this affected most strongly was Jacopo Amigoni.

Born in Venice, the son of Pietro Amigoni and Caterina Fischi, **Jacopo Amigoni** (*c.*1680x85–1752), whose name also appears as Giacomo Amiconi in various sources, is recorded as 'abroad' in 1711, and, according to Vertue, who may have had the information at first hand, he was a pupil of Bellucci at Düsseldorf. Certainly Amigoni's career was made in Germany, particularly at the court of the elector Max II Emanuel von Wittelsbach; he worked at Nymphenburg, Schleissheim, and the abbey of Ottobeuren from 1716 to 1729, visiting Venice, Rome, and Naples in 1728–9. His pupil Joseph Wagner (1706–1780) was to join him in London in 1732. Receptive to both French and Venetian influences, Amigoni's art evolved from a lightened Bellucci-like manner to a delicate, cosmopolitan style, with cool, powdery colours and a finish evoking the softness of pastel. In late 1729 Amigoni travelled to London with his sister Carlotta (a painter and engraver) and an Italian opera singer, presumably one engaged by Handel on his trip to Germany in that year.

Amigoni decorated the staircase of Lord Tankerville's house in St James's Square, London, in early 1730 (des. by rebuilding *c.*1753), collaborating with the Lombard *quadraturist* Gaetano Brunetti (*d.* 1758). He worked elsewhere with Brunetti (who was also a scene-painter) including the staircase of the duke of Chandos's new residence at Cavendish Square in 1735 (des.). His paintings, generally on canvas rather than plaster, attracted fashionable attention: the queen visited Lord Tankerville's house to view his work in 1732, while the staircase decoration for the Spanish ambassador at Powis House (des.) provided the catalyst for controversy in 1734. Amigoni was attacked by James Ralph in the *Weekly Register* as a foreigner who painted in an overblown and superficial manner, compared with the more wholesome and realistic qualities of English art. Although this attack was held up for ridicule by Bavius in the *Grub Street Journal*, Ralph's views were shared if not encouraged by Hogarth, whose animosity towards Amigoni in particular was inflamed by the action of Benjamin Styles in publicly rejecting Thornhill's history paintings for the hall at Moor Park. Styles turned to Amigoni instead in 1732 for some light-hearted Ovidian scenes, with grisaille paintings by Sleter in the upper level, the whole set amid elegant stucco-work by Bagutti. Another possible bone of contention was Amigoni's decoration of the rebuilt Covent Garden Theatre for Hogarth's friend John Rich in 1732 (lost in renovations, 1782). Hogarth prevented Amigoni from obtaining the commission for the staircase at St Bartholomew's Hospital in 1734 by volunteering himself for the task. Amigoni was identified with Italian opera through his close friendship with the famous castrato Farinelli, in London from 1734, and his marriage on 17 May 1738 to Maria Antonia Marchesini (La Lucchesina), the opera singer who made her London début at the King's Theatre in 1737. He may have collaborated with George Lambert on the scenery for Handel's opera *Atalanta* in 1736. Meanwhile, Amigoni set up a print studio with Wagner (a business partnership that was to continue until his death) which produced prints after Amigoni's paintings, including portraits and a group, *Cries of London*, while prints after Canaletto were planned. Doubtless competition with Hogarth and Arthur Pond fuelled the studio's energies; moreover, as the taste for allegorical and mythological decorative paintings was receding, Amigoni's activities diversified. However, he continued to work as a history painter, painting a ceiling for Thomas Wentworth, first earl of Strafford, in 1735 and probably collaborating with Sleter at Mereworth Castle in 1736–9, although payments are recorded only to Sleter. Charles Howard negotiated with Amigoni in 1731 and in 1736–7 for four paintings, *The Labours of Hercules*, for Hawksmoor's Tempietto at Castle Howard (which were apparently never executed): knowing his patron's tastes, Amigoni cited Pellegrini's prices. Amigoni painted small-scale histories exquisitely on copper for *The Temple of the Four Monarchies of the World* (Royal Collection), the complex musical clock designed by Charles Clay, with sculptural ornament by Rysbrack and Roubiliac, and music by Handel, Geminiani, and Corelli, which was purchased by Augusta, princess of Wales, in 1743.

Although Amigoni was more successful in some ways as a portraitist of fashionable society than Hogarth, the limitations of his elegant, courtly style were recognized. Queen Caroline and the prince of Wales sat to him, and apart from painting other members of the royal family he portrayed sitters such as the young Charles Frederick, subsequently an important patron of Andrea Casali, while his allegorical portrait of Farinelli (National Museum, Bucharest; repr. Scarpa Sonino, *Amigoni*, 88) was admired in his studio in 1735. Amigoni and Wagner returned to Venice in mid-1739. There he painted altarpieces and decorative works for an international clientele, remaining in contact with Farinelli, who had left London for Madrid in 1737. At Farinelli's instigation Amigoni was invited to become first painter to Fernando VI: from 1747 until his death on 22 August 1752 in the Calle del Barquillo, Madrid, he worked on fresco decoration, court portraits, and stage designs. He was buried on 23 August in the church of San José, Madrid.

Amigoni may have encouraged Antonio Canal, called Canaletto, to visit England, and **Antonio Joli** (*c.*1700–1777) was able to benefit from the latter's popularity with the English. A talented painter of stage scenery and *vedute*, Joli was born in Modena, where he studied perspective under Raffaello Rinaldi before becoming a pupil of Giovanni Paolo Panini in Rome. He worked for the theatre in Modena, and in Venice from 1732 until 1742, where he married. After travelling to Germany he settled in London from 1744 to 1748 or 1749. Joli was taken up by Heidegger, working for him at the King's Theatre and decorating his house in Richmond with landscapes and capriccios. Farinelli must have known Joli's theatrical work, for he was invited to the Spanish court in 1749. Joli left Madrid for Italy in 1754, and was a founder member of the Venetian Academy in 1755, but by the late 1750s was in Naples, working on a large group of topographical views for John, Lord Brudenell. He worked in Naples from 1762 as a painter of scenery, of court life, and of sparkling *vedute*. Joli died on 29 April 1777 in Naples, survived by his wife.

CATHERINE WHISTLER

Sources L. G. Hennessey, *Jacopo Amigoni (c.1685–1752): an artistic biography with a catalogue of his Venetian paintings* (Ann Arbor, 1983) · A. Scarpa Sonino, *Jacopo Amigoni* (Soncino, 1994) · F. Magani, *Antonio Bellucci: catalogo ragionato* (Rimini, 1995) · F. M. N. Gabburri, *Vite di artisti* [unpublished at his death in 1742], in *Settecento Pisano*, ed. R. P. Ciardi (Pisa, 1990), appx. 1, ed. A. Tosi, *Giuseppe Grisoni*, p. 350 · *La pittura in Italia: il Settecento* (Milan, 1990), Giuseppe Grisoni, p. 745; Antonio Joli, p. 752 [with extensive bibliographies] · *In the shadow of Vesuvius: views of Naples from baroque to Romanticism, 1631–1830* (Naples, 1990), 124–5 [exhibition catalogue, Accademia Italiana, London] · G. Knox, *Antonio Pellegrini (1675–1741)* (1995) · A. Bettagno, ed., *Antonio Pellegrini: il maestro veneto del Rococò alle corti d'Europa* [n.d.] [exhibition catalogue, Venice, 1998] · D. Succi and A. Delneri, eds., *Marco Ricci e il paesaggio veneto del Settecento* (Venice, 1993) [exhibition catalogue, Belluno] · A. Scarpa Sonino, *Marco Ricci* (Milan, 1991) · J. Daniels, *Sebastiano Ricci* (1976) · J. Daniels, *L'opera completa di Sebastiano Ricci* (Milan, 1976) · J. Daniels, 'Sebastiano Ricci in England', *Atti del congresso internazionale di studi su Sebastiano Ricci e il suo tempo* (Milan, 1976), 68–82 · L. Moretti, 'Documenti e appunti su Sebastiano Ricci', *Saggi e Memorie di Storia dell'Arte*, 11 (1978), 97–125 · A. Rizzi, ed., *Sebastiano Ricci* (Udine, 1989) [exhibition catalogue] · *Rosalba Carriera: lettere, diari, frammenti*, ed. B. Sani, 2 vols. (Florence, 1985) [for Giovanni Antonio Pellegrini,

Marco and Sebastiano Ricci, and Antonio Bellucci] · C. Gibson-Wood, 'The political background to Thornhill's paintings in St Paul's Cathedral', *Journal of the Warburg and Courtauld Institutes*, 56 (1993), 229–37 · J. Urrea Fernández, *La pintura italiana del siglo XVIII en España* (Valladolid, 1977) [Jacopo Amigoni and Antonio Joli] · J. Simon, ed., *Handel: a celebration of his life and times, 1685–1759* (1985) [exhibition catalogue, NPG] · S. West, ed., *Italian culture in northern Europe in the eighteenth century* (1999) · F. Haskell, *Mecenati e pittori*, 3rd edn (Turin, 2000) · B. Redford, *Venice and the grand tour* (1996) · C. Saumarez Smith, *The building of Castle Howard* (1990); repr. (1997) · A. Laing, 'Foreign decorators and plasterers in England', *The rococo in England: a symposium*, ed. C. Hind (1986), 21–45 · J. Howard, 'Hogarth, Amigoni and "The rake's levee": new light on *A rake's progress*', *Apollo*, 146 (1997), 31–7 · F. Vivian, *Il Console Smith* (Vicenza, 1973) · I. Bignamini, 'George Vertue, art historian, and art institutions in London, 1689–1768', *Walpole Society*, 54 (1988), 1–148 · B. Ford, 'Sir Andrew Fountaine: one of the keenest virtuosi of his age', *Apollo*, 122 (1985), 352–63 · G. Wilson, 'One God! One Farinelli! Amigoni's portraits of a famous *castrato*', *Apollo*, 140 (1994), 45–51 · F. Russell, 'Canaletto and Joli at Chesterfield House', *Burlington Magazine*, 130 (1988), 627–30 · A. Meyric-Hughes and M. Royalton Kisch, 'Handel's art collection', *Apollo*, 146 (1997), 17–23 · F. J. Watson, 'A clock decorated by Amigoni in the English royal collection', *Studi in onore di Antonio Morassis (Arte Veneta)* (Venice, [1971]), 293–9 · B. Allen, 'Venetian painters in England in the earlier eighteenth century', *Canaletto and England*, ed. M. Liversidge and J. Farrington (1993), 30–37 [exhibition catalogue, Birmingham Gas Hall Exhibition Gallery, Birmingham, 14 Oct 1993 – 9 Jan 1994] · L. Maggioni, 'Anton Maria Zanetti tra Venezia, Parigi e Londra: incontri ed esperienze artistiche', *Per la storia del collezionismo italiano*, ed. C. de Benedictis (Florence, 1991), 91–109 · A. Compagnone, 'Vincenzo Damini', *Dizionario biografico degli Italiani*, 32 (Rome, 1986), 359–61 · T. C. Barnard and J. Clark, eds., *Lord Burlington: architecture, art and life* (1995) · Vertue, *Note books* · C. H. Collins Baker and M. Baker, *The life and circumstances of James Brydges, first duke of Chandos, patron of the liberal arts* (1949) [Antonio Bellucci, Giuseppe Grisoni] · L. Lanzi, *Storia pittorica della Italia* (Florence, 1824), 237–8 [Giuseppe Grisoni] · A. Longhi, *Compendio delle vite dei pittori veneziani* (Venice, 1762) · P. J. Mariette, *Abecedario* (Paris, 1857–8), vol. 4, pp. 93–4 [Giovanni Antonio Pellegrini] · W. Montagu, *Court and society from Elizabeth to Anne: edited from the papers at Kimbolton*, 2 vols. (1864) [Manchester in Venice] · P. A. Orlandi, *Abecedario pittorico* (Naples, 1763) [Antonio Bellucci] · L. Pascoli, *Vite de' pittori, scultori ed architetti moderni* (Rome, 1730–36), vol. 2, p. 385 [Ricci] · C. G. Ratti, *Delle vite de' pittori, scultori ed architetti genovesi* (Genoa, 1769), 15 [Niccolò Cassana] · T. Temanza, *Zibaldon*, ed. N. Ivanoff (Venice, 1963), 70 [Marco Ricci] · Thieme & Becker, *Allgemeines Lexikon* [Giuseppe Grisoni, birth date] · G. Tiraboschi, *Notizie de' pittori, scultori, incisori e architetti natii degli stati del Serenissimo Signor Duca di Modena* (Modena, 1786), 229–30 [Antonio Joli] · H. Walpole, *Anecdotes of painting in England: with some account of the principal artists*, ed. R. N. Wornum, new edn, 3 vols. (1849); repr. (1862) · F. Zava Bocazzi, 'Spigolature seicentesche', *Arte Veneta*, 32 (1978), 339 [Antonio Bellucci] · G. Ashton, *Pictures in the Garrick Club* (1997)

Likenesses A. Bellucci, self-portrait, oils, *c*.1684 (Antonio Bellucci), AM Oxf. · A. Bellucci, self-portrait, oils, 1700–26 (Antonio Bellucci), Uffizi, Florence · S. Ricci, self-portrait, oils, 1704 (Sebastiano Ricci), Uffizi, Florence · G. A. Pellegrini, self-portrait, oils, *c*.1722 (Giovanni Antonio Pellegrini), NPG · R. Carriera, pastel, 1724 (Sebastiano Ricci), Staatliche Kunsthalle, Karlsruhe · R. Carriera, pastel, 1724 (Marco Ricci), Staatliche Kunsthalle, Karlsruhe · G. Grisoni, self-portrait, oils, *c*.1750 (Giuseppe Grisoni), Uffizi, Florence · J. Amigoni, group portrait, oils, 1750–52 [Jacopo Amigoni with Carlo Broschi Farinelli, Pietro Metastasio, and Teresa Castellini), National Gallery of Victoria, Melbourne, Australia · G. A. Faldoni, etching (Sebastiano Ricci, after a lost self-portrait) · G. A. Faldoni, etching (Marco Ricci; after R. Carriera) · A. Longhi, etching (Jacopo Amigoni), repro. in Longhi, *Compendio*

Venn, Anne (*bap.* **1627**, *d.* **1654**), religious radical and diarist, was baptized in London on 1 January 1627 at All Hallows, Bread Street, the only daughter of John *Venn (*bap.* 1586, *d.* 1650), a silk merchant trading from his shop on Bread Street but originally from Lydiard St Lawrence in Somerset, and his second wife, Margaret (*b.* 1594), daughter of Geoffrey Langley of Colchester, Essex, and widow of two Londoners, John Elliot and John Scarborough.

The Venns were a godly and relatively prosperous London family. Although still an adolescent, at the end of the 1630s Anne Venn was allowed to accompany her parents regularly to secret puritan religious meetings. At the meetings, the Venns made the close acquaintance of the zealous divine Christopher Love who, as chaplain to her father's regiment during the civil war, lived with the family at Windsor Castle, where they had moved in October 1642, and for a time became Anne's spiritual confidant. John Venn, her father, had become a leading parliamentarian activist and later became a regicide. Unknown to her parents, from the age of nine Anne began to be tortured by the fear that she might be damned and subsequently kept a careful written record, very much in the genre of the puritan diarist or autobiographer, of her excruciating mental turmoil over an eighteen-year period until she at last gained some comforting assurance of salvation. The handwritten work, which she kept a close secret, was discovered in her closet along with several other godly devotional writings after her death and was published in 1658, organized into three books by her stepfather Thomas Weld, an Independent divine, under the title *A Wise Virgin's Lamp Burning*.

The work reveals a clearly well-educated and intelligent woman who sought spiritual reassurance by reading puritan works and attending godly sermons. Personally austere, she would not wear jewellery or vain clothes. She was intensely introspective, probably lonely and depressive, and may not have enjoyed robust health. Yet she could also be self-assertive, if not stubborn, at times when pursuing her spiritual goals. Although remaining on good terms with most of the godly whose acquaintance she made, she and her parents eventually became dissatisfied with Christopher Love and the newly imposed presbyterian settlement. About 1645 the family returned to London, living in Whitecross Street. Anne submitted herself to the required vetting for the sacrament of communion by elders in Love's parish of St Anne, Aldersgate, London, but the experience was blighted by a lack of inner conviction that she was fit to partake of it. The Venns moved out of London to Kensington about 1647, but found the local preaching unsatisfactory and later attended the ministry elsewhere. The sudden and unexpected death of John Venn during the night of 27–8 June 1650 was a great blow to Anne and her mother. By 1651 Anne had become totally disillusioned with presbyterianism and had fallen under the influence of the Independent divine and former chaplain to Sir Thomas Fairfax, Isaac Knight, the curate at Hammersmith in the chapelry of Fulham and later rector of Fulham. When Knight gathered an Independent church at Fulham in 1652, Anne and her mother joined the church and became active and enthusiastic members of it. At long last Anne was able to experience some spiritual peace.

Left a dowry of £1000 in her father's will, Anne never married. She died in Kensington in late December 1654 after a severe cold, but characteristically she maintained her diary until on the verge of death. In her will, made on 19 November 1653 and proved on 26 January 1655, she left bequests totalling £867. Among the beneficiaries were eight leading Independent divines, including Isaac Knight, and the poor of the gathered church at Fulham. She bequeathed her remaining goods, plate, jewels, household furnishing, and books to her mother, whom she appointed her executor.   KEITH LINDLEY

Sources A. Venn, *A wise virgin's lamp burning* (1658) · will, PRO, PROB 11/243/36 · will, PRO, PROB 11/213/123 (John Venn) · W. B. Bannerman, ed., *The registers of All Hallows, Bread Street, and of St John the Evangelist, Friday Street, London*, Harleian Society, register section, 43 (1913), 23 · HoP, *Commons, 1640–60* [draft] · *The visitation of London, anno Domini 1633, 1634, and 1635, made by Sir Henry St George*, 2, ed. J. J. Howard, Harleian Society, 17 (1883), 308 · A. Laurence, *Parliamentary army chaplains, 1642–1651*, Royal Historical Society Studies in History, 59 (1990), 141–2, 192 · J. Venn, *Annals of a clerical family* (1904), 223

Wealth at death £867 in bequests; goods; plate; jewels; household furnishings; books: will, PRO, PROB 11/243/36

Venn, Henry (1725–1797), Church of England clergyman, was born at Barnes, Surrey, on 2 March 1725, the third son of Richard *Venn (1691–1739), rector of St Antholin's, Watling Street, London, who was descended from an unbroken succession of clergymen from the time of the Reformation, and Maria Anna Isabella Margaretta Beatrix (*d.* 1762), daughter of John Ashton. After being educated at several private schools he entered St John's College, Cambridge, in June 1742, but in September he moved to Jesus College, having obtained a Rustat scholarship there. He graduated BA in 1745 and proceeded MA in 1749. In 1747 he was appointed by William Battie to one of the university scholarships that Battie had just founded. Venn was a noted university cricketer, but after playing in a match between Surrey and All England he gave away his bat, apparently because he was to be ordained and did not want to hear, 'Well played, Parson!' (Venn, *Life*, 70–71). He was ordained deacon in June 1747 and priest in June 1749, having been elected to a fellowship at Queens' College on 30 March of that year. He also began his ministerial career in 1749 and for a short time combined his college duties with officiating at Barton, Cambridgeshire, Wadenhoe, Northamptonshire, Little Hedingham, Essex, and other local places. He ceased to reside at Cambridge in 1750 and went as curate to Adam Langley, who held the livings of St Matthew, Friday Street, London, and West Horsley, Surrey. He served at St Matthew's during part of the summer and the rest of the year at West Horsley.

At West Horsley, Venn's family prayers were attended by about forty poor neighbours, some of whom he instructed in his home; and the number of communicants increased from twelve to sixty. The local clergy considered him an enthusiast and Methodist, but he continued to hold the

Henry Venn (1725–1797), by John Russell, 1787

strong high-church beliefs of his father, as contained in *The Whole Duty of Man*. At the same time his ministry there gave him time for reading, and he began to doubt the outlook of this book. He was now influenced by another book, William Law's *A Serious Call to a Devout and Holy Life*, and he sought to practise its moral and spiritual precepts.

In 1754 Venn became curate of Clapham and was elected lecturer at two London churches—St Alban, Wood Street, and St Swithin London Stone, Cannon Street. The number of sermons required from him led him to learn to preach without reading from a manuscript, and he preached extempore or from short notes for the rest of his life. He had to relinquish his fellowship at Cambridge in 1757, when he married Eling, daughter of Thomas Bishop, minister of the Tower Church, Ipswich. They had one son, John, and four daughters, of whom the eldest, Eling, married Charles Elliott and was the mother of Edward Bishop Elliott and Henry Venn Elliott.

Clapham was already becoming an evangelical centre, and there Venn came under the influence of John Thornton (1720–1790), the banker, who bought the advowson of Clapham, and other early Methodists such as George Whitefield and the countess of Huntingdon. He became closely attached also to John Wesley himself—too closely, thought Samuel Walker (1740–1761)—until about 1758, when he was 'brought to believe for himself' (Sidney, 435). A severe illness in 1756 kept him from work for eight months, but gave him more time for self-examination and consideration upon this matter. During that time he began to write his devotional book *The Complete Duty of Man*, which was finally published in 1763. As its title indicates, it was connected with *The Whole Duty of Man*. Venn wished to remedy what he considered were the defects of that book and set out the moral duties required by the evangelical approach. It was a popular book, and twenty editions had been sold by the early years of the next century.

Venn published also in 1760 a sermon on *The Duty of a Parish Priest and the Incomparable Pleasure of a Life Devoted to the Care of Souls*, which expressed his attachment to the authority and responsibility of the Anglican ministry. He was determined to remain within the Church of England, and among his objections to the Methodists, he wrote in 1763, was that they 'made the ground of their Assurance an inward fleeting instead of the faithfulness of Jehovah, the sensation of a fluctuating heart instead of the unchangeable promises of God' (G. G. Cragg, *Grimshaw of Haworth*, 1947, 71).

In 1759 William Legge, second earl of Dartmouth (1731–1801), who had been converted by Lady Huntingdon, induced Sir John Ramsden, the patron, to appoint Venn as vicar of Huddersfield. In accepting this post he suffered a financial loss. His annual stipend there was only £100, which he found inadequate, even though Lord Dartmouth and John Thornton made further contributions to it. While not yet a factory town, Huddersfield's long-established textile industry was now already expanding sufficiently to make it a large village. The parish covered a wide area inhabited by some 1400 families scattered about the countryside in outlying hamlets and farms. John Wesley went there in October 1757 and wrote, 'A wilder people I never saw in England' (*Journal of … John Wesley*, 4.210).

Venn found them 'utterly ignorant of the redemption that is in Jesus Christ' (Venn, *Life*, 25), but he gained them by preaching, praying, visiting, and welcoming enquirers in his vicarage. On Sundays at Huddersfield large crowds, many from a distance, soon filled the church to hear his sermons. He sought not only to teach them but also to train them as worshippers and communicants and to understand the prayer book. He twice delivered sermons explaining it, conducted courses of preparation before holy communion, introduced hymn-singing into the service, and catechized the younger members of the congregation. During weekdays he engaged also in open-air preaching and held services in private houses in the hamlets. In a letter written in 1762 to Lady Huntingdon he stated that during that year, apart from Sunday work, he 'generally preached eight or ten sermons in the week in distant parts of the parish' (Ryle). In addition to his parochial activities he accepted invitations from Lady Huntingdon, John Fletcher, and others to preach in various parts of England and south Wales.

Venn's last years at Huddersfield were hard for him. His financial difficulties increased. The upkeep of his family, travelling in his parish and elsewhere, and entertaining the many people who visited him were expensive. The death of his wife in 1767 saddened him and left him in the sole charge of five young children. His intense labours exhausted him and began to affect his health. He showed signs of consumption and was able to preach only once a fortnight, and even then the exertion incapacitated him for several days. In 1771 he was offered the living of Yelling, Huntingdonshire, which he accepted regretfully, saying, 'Nothing would have prevailed upon me to leave Huddersfield if my lungs had not received an irreparable injury' (Elliott-Binns, 323).

In July 1771 Venn married a widow, Catherine Smith (*d.* 1792), daughter of James Ascough, vicar of Highworth, Wiltshire. At the small village of Yelling he started with a congregation of twenty or thirty, but as his health recovered he achieved a like success there and generally went each year to preach for a few weeks in London. And, since Yelling was only 12 miles from Cambridge, he was visited by many of the younger members of the university, among whom were Charles Simeon, William Faris, Thomas Robinson, and Joseph Jowett. He exerted a strong personal influence upon them and also upon others with whom he engaged in an extensive correspondence. So his importance at Huddersfield, where he gained the first large place outside London for evangelicalism and became known as a preacher and writer, was succeeded by his effect at Yelling upon men who became prominent leaders of the movement in the country. After twenty years at Yelling, Venn's health collapsed. In the autumn of 1791 he engaged a permanent curate for the parish and after that seldom officiated in his church or elsewhere, but continued his conversation and writing. Early in 1797 he left Yelling and went to Clapham, where his son John was now rector. He died at Clapham on 24 June 1797 and was buried in the old churchyard.

Like most evangelicals, Venn was a moderate Calvinist. He wrote in 1775, 'Though the doctrines of Grace are clear to me, I am still no friend to High Calvinism' (Venn, *Life*, 32). After his ordination he adopted a strict manner of life and rarely went to mixed parties, but he was always genial and happy, with, a vicar of Brighton remarked, 'a cheerful, open countenance' (Elliott-Binns, 131). He was a lively and effective preacher. One of his Huddersfield congregation recalled, 'When he got warm with his subject, he looked as if he would jump out of his pulpit. He made many weep' (Ryle, 167). And he was an attractive, sympathetic conversationalist, always ready to assist and advise those who came to him, whether from farm or university.

His son **John Venn** (1759–1813), Church of England clergyman, was born at Clapham on 9 March 1759 during his father's curacy there. He entered Sidney Sussex College, Cambridge, in October 1777, graduated BA in 1781, and proceeded MA in 1784. He was ordained deacon on 22 September 1782 and priest on 26 March 1783, as a curate to his father. He was rector of Little Dunham, Norfolk, from 1783 to 1792, and was the first rector to reside in the parish for seventy-five years. He founded a clerical society, the members of which met twice a year at his rectory to discuss common concerns. He married at Trinity Church, Hull, on 22 October 1789 Catherine, daughter of William King, merchant of Hull; she died on 15 April 1803. They had two surviving sons—Henry *Venn (1796–1873) and John, for many years vicar of St Peter's, Hereford—and also five daughters, of whom Jane Catherine, the second, married James (afterwards Sir James) Stephen and was mother of Sir James Fitzjames Stephen and of Sir Leslie Stephen. He married secondly Frances, daughter of John Turton of Clapham, in August 1812.

Venn was rector of Clapham from 1792 until his death, and was appointed by the trustees set up under the will of John Thornton. It was during his incumbency that the influential 'Clapham Sect' developed, and its members followed him as their pastor and spiritual guide. In 1799 he set up the Society for Bettering the Condition and Improving the Comforts of the Poor, which consisted of thirty members, who over tea every month in their houses arranged for visitors to distribute aid in the parish and in 1800 undertook a universal vaccination there. He upheld a strict way of life. In 1796 the inns in the parish had to abolish their skittle-grounds and cease all gaming in their premises; and he wrote about his children, 'With respect to parties, they never go to any where cards and dancing are introduced, neither do they learn to dance' (Hennell, 158). His parishioners' campaign against the slave trade and other religious and philanthropic causes gained his support. A founder and the first chairman of the Church Missionary Society in 1799, he asserted that it was to be conducted 'on the Church principle, not the High Church principle' (Cornish, 47). He shared in the dislike felt by many towards evangelicals at this time. When Hannah More was taken to Clapham in the carriage of Beilby Porteus, bishop of London, with whom she was staying, the coachman was told to put her down at the Bull's Head tavern instead of the rectory.

Venn's earnestness and spiritual fervour found expression in his eloquent and persuasive preaching. In addition, he displayed a cultivated intellect, a composed judgement, and a practical outlook. These qualities enabled him to exert a powerful influence upon his wealthy, notable congregation. He died at Clapham on 1 July 1813. His second wife survived him.

LEONARD W. COWIE

Sources J. Venn, The life and a selection from the letters of the late Rev. Henry Venn, 2nd edn (1839) • J. Venn, Annals of a clerical family (1904) • M. M. Hennell, John Venn and the Clapham Sect (1958) • 'Memoir of the author', H. Venn, The complete duty of man, new edn (1936) • J. C. Ryle, 'Henry Venn and his ministry', Five Christian leaders of the eighteenth century (1960) • L. E. Elliott-Binns, The early evangelicals: a religious and social study (1953) • J. Stephen, 'The Clapham sect', Essays in ecclesiastical biography, 2 (1849) • F. W. Cornish, The English church in the nineteenth century, 2 vols. (1910), vol. 8 of A history of the English church, ed. W. R. W. Stephens and W. Hunt (1899–1910), pt 1 • E. Sidney, The life of Samuel Walker, rev. edn (1838) • The journal of the Rev. John Wesley, ed. N. Curnock and others, 8 vols. (1909–16) • J. Hordern, 'Huddersfield, past and present', Warehouseman and Draper [suppl.] (29 Sept 1900) [U. Birm. L., special collections department]
Archives U. Birm. L., special collections department, letters and papers | Westminster College, Cambridge, corresp. with Selina, countess of Huntingdon
Likenesses J. Russell, chalk drawing, 1787, NPG [see illus.] • G. Adcock, stipple, pubd 1834, NPG • T. A. Dean, engraving (after M. Chamberlain, 1770), U. Birm.; repro. in Venn, Life

Venn, Henry (1796–1873), missionary society administrator, was born at Clapham, Surrey, on 10 February 1796, the fifth of eight children of John *Venn (1759–1813), rector of Clapham and a founder of the Church Missionary Society (CMS) [see under Venn, Henry], and his first wife, Catherine (d. 1803), daughter of William King, a merchant. He had one surviving brother, John, and five sisters, one of whom, Jane Catherine, married Sir James Stephen. His grandfather was Henry *Venn (1725–1797). He was brought up in the milieu of evangelical philanthropy and strong family interaction which characterized the leading evangelical Anglicans of the 'Clapham Sect'. He was taught by his father and, for a year, by Professor Farish of Cambridge, prior to entering Queens' College, Cambridge, in 1814. He graduated in 1818 as nineteenth wrangler. In 1819 he was elected fellow, and he was ordained deacon and priest in the following year. After a curacy in St Dunstan-in-the-West, London (1821–4), he returned to Queens' College and taught as a tutor; he also served as university proctor. He then became incumbent of Drypool, Hull (1827–34), and of St John's Holloway, Islington, London (1834–46). While at Drypool, on 21 January 1829 he married Martha Sykes (d. 1840), daughter of Nicholas Sykes of Swanland, a wealthy Hull businessman. They had two sons (John *Venn and Henry) and one daughter (Henrietta).

In 1841 Venn became honorary clerical secretary (part-time) of the CMS. He remained in this position until 1872 and became full-time secretary in 1846. In this central position in the leading evangelical Anglican missionary society, Venn's past experience and personal gifts blended in a remarkable way: he had had a missionary interest since his childhood; he had a good, analytical mind; he mixed easily with men of affairs; and he was a shrewd judge of people. Moreover, he was an excellent committee man, always master of his brief but prepared to compromise; and he was an excellent organizer and an assiduous correspondent. Above all he was a pragmatic thinker who sought to establish how best the gospel could be preached, and—an increasing preoccupation—how a native church could be established.

The CMS in 1841 was at a low ebb. Financially it faced a severe crisis. Its voluntary and evangelical character meant that it had been regarded with some suspicion by the ecclesiastical establishment. Venn, as a member of its committee, had already been a principal figure in establishing and justifying an accommodation with the Church of England hierarchy, which formally recognized bishops' rights in relation to the licensing of missionaries and thus paved the way for episcopal recognition of the CMS. As secretary, while retaining a vigorous commitment to voluntary missionary societies, Venn succeeded in moving the CMS to a position of greater acceptability within the Church of England, so that by 1870 virtually all the episcopal bench were vice-presidents of the society. The CMS finances, recruitment, and morale also improved. Venn's greatest contribution, however, was in mission strategy.

Henry Venn (1796–1873), by George Richmond, *c*.1831

The CMS supported the extension of the episcopate in New Zealand in 1841, but Venn was extremely frustrated by Bishop Selwyn's reluctance to ordain Maori on the grounds that they were insufficiently educated. Bishop Samuel Wilberforce and others pressed strongly for an increase in the episcopate overseas. Venn resisted the appointment of English 'missionary bishops' as a general principle because he feared that, in a context where the laity was not strong, an autocratic, authoritarian episcopal style would rapidly develop, making it impossible to appoint a 'native' bishop. This debate prompted him to think deeply about the shape of the church in newly missionized countries and it is with this thinking that he is most associated.

Together with his American collaborator Rufus Anderson (1796–1880), Venn began to identify the 'three selfs' principle (Shenk, *Henry Venn*, 31): that churches should be self-governing, self-supporting, and self-propagating—the true objective for the emerging churches. The originality of the principle can be exaggerated. Great missionaries such as the Serampore trio (William Carey, Joshua Marshman, and William Ward) and Alexander Duff had given considerable thought to the issues involved. The philanthropic, abolitionist context was one, moreover, where radical policies which had a high confidence in indigenous capacity were readily accepted. Where Venn and Anderson were ahead of their contemporaries was in their capacity to enunciate their thinking with a power and logical clarity that nobody else could match.

So far as England was concerned, Venn's grasp of missionary issues was unrivalled. He kept in close touch with missionaries, ecclesiastical leaders, politicians, and statesmen. He assiduously sought to establish what missionary principles the Bible, church history, and contemporary experience provided. By 1851, however, he was speaking of the need for missionaries to work themselves out of a job—'the euthanasia of a mission' (Williams, 4–5), and the central importance of indigenous (rather than missionary) pastors who should be close to the culture of their congregations. In the 1860s he became convinced that the dependence system of converts relying on the missionary was the great enemy to be resisted. He advocated structures which would facilitate the emergence of pastoral, governmental, and financial independence, and he stressed the importance of native churches reflecting their own cultures, both institutionally and liturgically. He also expected that these churches would become ecumenical and break from the denominational divisions of the missionary churches.

Venn was the architect of the elevation of his great friend Samuel Crowther (*c*.1806–1891), a former slave, to the episcopate in west Africa in 1864. He was disappointed that the missionaries effectively put themselves outside Crowther's episcopal control and came to the conclusion that 'the European element in a native church' was 'the great snare and hindrance to its growth' (Williams, 34). Missionaries, he argued, constantly underestimated the capacity of their converts. Consequently the only way forward was a significant measure of separation of the indigenous church from the church of soldiers, settlers, and missionaries. In his conviction that the emerging native church might have a large degree of independence and its own episcopate alongside the existing structures of the Church of England in the same area, he was moving to a more radical and controversial position than many contemporary Anglicans were prepared to countenance.

Although he was not an accomplished speaker and though he did not write systematically and for a wide general public, Venn had an authority within the CMS and, in lesser measure, within the Church of England, which made him an immensely influential missionary statesman both in his own day and subsequently. His papers, though mainly for internal CMS use, were brought together in his *Memoir* (1880) and ensured that his influence was perpetuated. It is indicative of his catholicity that the one major book Venn wrote was a study of the sixteenth-century Jesuit missionary Francis Xavier. It was not a success: few Victorian evangelicals wanted to read about counter-Reformation heroes.

Venn nevertheless brought ecclesiological issues to the centre of the agenda. He took other cultures seriously and he was confident that indigenous figures could lead in commerce and politics, as well as in church life. He constantly opposed missionary paternalism. He was consequently (and remains) much admired and revered by those indigenous Christians who shared his vision of self-government. Indeed, distinguished twentieth-century Nigerian historians regarded him as the ideological originator of Nigerian nationalism. Many significant later missiologists (G. Warneck and R. Allen for example) owed much to him. He served, as a recognized and respected evangelical Anglican leader, on two royal commissions—one on clerical subscription, in 1864, and the other on ritualism, in 1867.

Venn has been much criticized—for driving too sharp a wedge between church and mission; for moving too quickly to independence in areas such as Sierra Leone; for making self-support too central a condition for self-government; for being too 'church-centric' in his analysis; for being insufficiently sympathetic to the problems of the missionaries; and for not travelling outside Europe. It is not possible, however, to gainsay his immense impact. In his private life, Venn had sufficient wealth to live in moderate comfort. During his time with the CMS he lived first in north London, at Highgate and then in Highbury (1848–60), and he finally moved to East Sheen, Mortlake, Surrey, where he died, following a stroke, on 13 January 1873. He was buried in Mortlake cemetery.

C. PETER WILLIAMS

Sources J. F. A. Ajayi, 'Henry Venn and the policy of development', *Journal of the Historical Society of Nigeria*, 1 (1959), 331–42 • J. F. A. Ajayi, 'Nineteenth century origins of Nigerian nationalism', *Journal of the Historical Society of Nigeria*, 2 (1961), 196–212 • *Church Missionary Intelligencer* (1840–73) • W. Knight, ed., *The missionary secretariat of Henry Venn, BD* (1880) • W. Knight, ed., *Memoir of Henry Venn, BD*, new edn (1882) • W. R. Shenk, 'Rufus Anderson and Henry Venn', *International Bulletin of Missionary Research*, 5 (1981), 168–72 • W. R. Shenk, *Henry Venn—missionary statesman* (1983) • W. R. Shenk, 'The contribution of Henry Venn to mission thought', *Anvil*, 2 (1985), 25–42 • E. Stock, *The history of the Church Missionary Society: its environment, its men and its work*, 1–3 (1899) • M. Warren, ed., *To apply the gospel* (1971) • C. P. Williams, *The ideal of the self-governing church: a study in Victorian missionary strategy* (1990) • T. E. Yates, *Venn and Victorian bishops abroad: the missionary policies of Henry Venn and their repercussions upon the Anglican episcopate of the colonial period, 1841–1872* (1978)
Archives LPL • U. Birm. L., special collections department, corresp., diaries, and papers | BL, corresp. with W. E. Gladstone, Add. MSS 44368–44385 • Selwyn College, Cambridge, letters to Bishop Selwyn
Likenesses G. Richmond, drawing, c.1831, Queens' College, Cambridge [see illus.] • S. Cousins, mezzotint (after G. Richmond), BM • G. Richmond, portrait, Partnership House, Waterloo Road, London • bust, St Paul's Cathedral, London
Wealth at death under £6000: probate, 1 March 1873, CGPLA Eng. & Wales

Venn, John (bap. 1586, d. 1650), parliamentarian activist and regicide, was baptized at Lydiard St Lawrence in Somerset on 8 April 1586, the second son of Simon Venn, of yeoman stock, and his wife, Maud Lawrence. He was bound apprentice to the Merchant Taylors' Company in 1602, gained his freedom in 1610, and entered the livery in 1621. He became an assistant of the company in 1638, and warden in 1641–3, but was to be excused service as master in 1648 because of his commitments as an MP. In 1619 at Chelsea, Middlesex, Venn married Mary (d. 1625), daughter of Henry Wood, a London merchant, with whom he had a son. His second marriage, by licence dated 13 February 1626, at West Ham, Essex, was to Margaret (b. 1594), daughter of Geoffrey Langley of Colchester, Essex, widow of John Elliot and of John Scarborough (salter and haberdasher of London respectively); they had a son and a daughter. Five other children from the two marriages died in infancy.

From at least 1621 Venn had a silk shop in Bread Street and was busy establishing himself as a substantial trader in wool and silk with the west of England and Ireland. Like several future leading parliamentarians he also developed an interest in America without, in his case, ever becoming actively involved in colonial trade. He was one of the original members of the Massachusetts Bay Company, joining its governing body in 1629 and attending its meetings in England, and he was still holding company stock in 1644. He corresponded with John Winthrop in Massachusetts and had apparently considered emigrating himself. Although far from being the impoverished merchant of later royalist propaganda, he was not a member of the City's mercantile elite, only managing third rank in his ward in the 1640 listing of citizens according to their wealth.

Venn made an early impact in the civic arena. Having become a member of the Honourable Artillery Company in 1614, he gained prominence in City politics for the first time in 1631 when he was an unsuccessful anti-establishment candidate in a disputed artillery company election for the position of captain-leader. Nevertheless in subsequent years further promotion in the company followed—from an assistant in 1632 to captain-sergeant-major in 1636 and deputy president under Alderman Thomas Soames in 1639. Around the same time Venn was securing officer rank in the London trained bands; he was a captain in 1616 and by 1642 had become a lieutenant-colonel in the Yellow regiment under Sir John Wollaston. His early military interests and experience stood him in good stead during the war years of the 1640s. In 1631 Venn was chosen as churchwarden of All Hallows, Bread Street, a London parish renowned for its puritanism, and throughout the 1630s he and his second wife regularly attended puritan religious meetings, where they made the close acquaintance of the zealous divine Christopher Love. From at least 1638 Venn was also a leading member of common council, serving during the next four years on seven committees including two terms on the highly influential City lands committee.

Exceptionally active in radical politics in the early 1640s, Venn apparently enjoyed close links with William Fiennes, Viscount Saye and Sele. He also developed a highly effective political partnership with Isaac Penington, a fellow City militant, which gave them considerable powers of co-ordination and direction over radical action in the capital, and he seems to have had close links with the Scottish commissioners sent to London. Venn was a key figure in the organization of the London petition to the king of September 1640, calling for a parliament and outlining grievances, and in spring 1641 he was at the forefront of the City campaign for the trial and execution of the earl of Strafford. His popularity at this time was such that when Matthew Cradock (one of the London MPs) died Venn replaced him at a by-election on 1 June and thereby joined Penington in the Commons. He was to prove a most active MP, being nominated to 300 committees during his time in parliament. The campaign for godly reformation of the Church also drew his enthusiastic support. In October 1641, for example, he gave his support in the Commons to parish zealots in St Giles Cripplegate who had denounced their curate and one of the churchwardens for blocking the implementation of reforms sanctioned by the Commons. He presented a petition of London ministers on 20 December opposing the use of prayers that ran counter to their consciences and calling for the setting up of a national synod to initiate reform. Venn was later to lead the zealots in his own parish of All Hallows, Bread Street, in their endeavour to gain the presbyterian Lazarus Seaman as their minister, and he was reported to have joined Penington in a Commons attack on the rector of St Matthew's Friday Street, designed to help restore the puritan dissident Henry Burton to the living.

In the turbulent closing weeks of 1641 Venn found himself in the political spotlight. This period opened with a reminder of the limits of his influence among his fellow citizens when he failed to dissuade common council from entertaining the king on his return from Scotland. Yet Venn soon attracted from two fellow MPs the not entirely unfounded accusation that he, and possibly Penington too, had been guilty of orchestrating mass demonstrations outside parliament, aimed at intimidating MPs, during the debate on the grand remonstrance. In addition he had something of a following among London apprentices. Again, like Penington, Venn acted as an intermediary and informant between the City and parliament—most notably during the change of control over the London militia. Venn was also active in the campaign of July 1642 to remove the royalist Sir Richard Gurney from the mayoralty, thus clearing the way for Penington's promotion to that office. Both men later shared with two other citizens the distinction of being identified as traitors by the king for their role in disaffecting London from him.

Venn became a leading supporter of parliament's war effort. He helped to raise subscriptions of money, plate, and horse and provide the capital with gunpowder. On the outbreak of hostilities he became a colonel of foot in parliament's army and fought at Worcester on 23 September 1642. Appointed governor of Windsor Castle on the following 28 October, he successfully withstood an early attack by Prince Rupert and remained a constant threat to the royalists. Christopher Love, who had been appointed chaplain to Venn's regiment, joined Venn and his family in Windsor where he continued to exercise a strong influence over them. Venn also ensured that St George's Chapel was subjected to a godly purge. Removed from the governorship in June 1645 under the self-denying ordinance, he returned to London to continue his support for the war effort and became a prominent member of the army committee.

Despite his admiration for the presbyterian Love, Venn became a leading London Independent and, after the attempted presbyterian counter-revolution of 1647, he was appointed to the Independent-dominated London militia committee of September 1647. After the second civil war he was appointed to the high court of justice for the king's trial and was present at all but two of its sittings; he signed the death warrant [see also Regicides]. He was a busy committeeman in the Rump Parliament with army and financial matters claiming much of his attention. Venn's sudden and unexpected death during the night of 27/28 June 1650 gave rise to groundless rumours of suicide. His widow, Margaret, was the main beneficiary of his will, proved on 1 July, in which he left property in London, Somerset, and three other counties, and a debt of £4000 still due to him for his expenses at Windsor and a further £140 owed by the trustees for bishops' lands. Not long after his death his widow married Thomas Weld, an Independent divine. After the Restoration Venn's estates were said to have been forfeited for regicide. A diary kept by his daughter Anne (or Hannah) *Venn was published posthumously in 1658 while his son Thomas wrote *Military and maritime [sic] discipline* in 1672 and later became mayor of Bridgwater.

John Venn (*bap.* 1647, *d.* 1687), Church of England clergyman, was the son of Venn's cousin Simon Venn of Lydiard St Lawrence, and his wife, Jane. Baptized at Combe Florey, Somerset, on 17 August 1647, he matriculated at Balliol College, Oxford, on 10 May 1662, graduated BA in 1666, and proceeded MA in 1669; he was created BD and DD in 1685. He married Catherine Lowe, sister of Sir Edward Lowe, one of the masters in chancery. A fellow of Balliol, Venn was master of the college from 1678 to 1687 and vice-chancellor of the university in 1686–7. He also enjoyed clerical livings in Lincolnshire and Oxfordshire and, unlike his namesake, was a fervent upholder of church orthodoxy. He died on 8 October 1687 and was buried in Lydiard St Lawrence where he left an estate in his will, which was proved on 4 May 1688.

KEITH LINDLEY

Sources J. Venn, *Annals of a clerical family* (1904), 223–5, 227, 229 · will, PRO, PROB 11/213/123 · will of John Venn, PRO, PROB 11/391/70 · HoP, *Commons, 1690–1715* [draft] · K. Lindley, *Popular politics and religion in civil war London* (1997), 112, 149, 151–3, 189, 190, 412 · A. Venn, *A wise virgin's lamp burning* (1658) · journals, CLRO, court of common council, vol. 38, fol. 107; vol. 39, fols. 65, 111, 162; vol. 40, fols. 3, 31 · Merchant Taylors' Company, apprentice binding books, GL, microfilm 313, vol. 3, p. 94 · Merchant Taylors' Company court minutes, GL, microfilm 330, vol. 9, fols. 59, 60, 65, 70, 75, 77, 126, 128 · C. H. Firth and R. S. Rait, eds., *Acts and ordinances of the interregnum, 1642–1660*, 1 (1911), 38, 1007–8, 1255, 1261; 2 (1911), 123 · *The visitation of London, anno Domini 1633, 1634, and 1635, made by Sir Henry St George*, 2, ed. J. J. Howard, Harleian Society, 17 (1883), 308 · W. B. Bannerman, ed., *The registers of All Hallows, Bread Street, and of St John the Evangelist, Friday Street, London*, Harleian Society, register section, 43 (1913), 20–27, 179, 181, 186, 188, 190 · IGI · DNB · Foster, *Alum. Oxon.* · *The obituary of Richard Smyth ... being a catalogue of all such persons as he knew in their life*, ed. H. Ellis, CS, 44 (1849), 29 · 'Boyd's Inhabitants of London', Society of Genealogists, London, 10337, 10338 · V. Pearl, *London and the outbreak of the puritan revolution: city government and national politics, 1625–1643* (1961); repr. with corrections (1964), 187–9

Wealth at death property in London, Somerset, Lincolnshire, Essex, and Northamptonshire; £4000 owed; £140: will, PRO, PROB 11/213/123

Venn, John (*bap.* **1647**, *d.* **1687**). See under Venn, John (*bap.* 1586, *d.* 1650).

Venn, John (1759–1813). *See under* Venn, Henry (1725–1797).

Venn, John (1834–1923), philosopher and antiquary, was born on 4 August 1834 at Drypool, Hull, the first of the two children of Henry *Venn (1796–1873), fellow of Queens' College, Cambridge, evangelical divine, and secretary of the Church Missionary Society, and his wife, Martha Sykes (*d.* 1840), daughter of Nicholas Sykes, of Swanland, near Hull. The family on the father's side originated from Devon and was of considerable evangelical and intellectual eminence. His great-grandfather Henry Venn (1725–1797) was vicar of Huddersfield, author of *The Complete Duty of Man* (1763), and prominent with George Whitefield in the evangelical revival in Britain. His grandfather John *Venn (1759–1813) [*see under* Venn, Henry (1725–1797)] was the vicar of Clapham and a founder of the Church Missionary Society, a leading member of the influential evangelical reformers known as the 'Clapham Sect', with the Stephen, the Macaulay, and the Dicey families, and, with his friend William Wilberforce, an opponent of the slave trade.

After being educated initially by private tutors Venn attended Sir Roger Cholmeley's School, Highgate, and then Islington proprietary school. In October 1853 he entered Gonville and Caius College, Cambridge, representing the eighth generation of his family to be admitted to and to graduate from Cambridge or Oxford. Elected mathematical scholar in 1854, he was sixth wrangler in the mathematical tripos of 1857 and was elected fellow of his college a few months later. He was ordained deacon at Ely in 1858, and priest in 1859, and held curacies successively at Cheshunt, Hertfordshire, and at Mortlake, Surrey.

After taking his degree Venn's attention was drawn to such writers as Augustus De Morgan, George Boole, John Austin, and, particularly, John Stuart Mill, whose *Logic* profoundly affected his critical outlook. Other influences included the companionship of his cousins E. J. S. Dicey, A. V. Dicey, James Stephen, and Leslie Stephen. Unhappy with parochial work he returned to Cambridge in 1862 and applied the dry, organized, accurate, tight, and methodical habits of the 'Claphamites' to philosophy and scholarship, a process that led him through his Hulsean lectures upon *Some Characteristics of Belief, Scientific and Religious* (1869), and to his eventual resignation from the clergy in 1883. He remained, however, according to his son J. A. Venn, a man of religious conviction, and in later life often remarked that changes in accepted opinion concerning the Thirty-Nine Articles meant that he could consistently have retained his orders. Shortly after his return to Cambridge he was appointed as Caius's first 'catechist', a new series of college posts with a university-wide role. For a few months he acted simultaneously as curate of St Edward's Church. On 21 June 1867 he married Susanna Carnegie Edmonstone, daughter of the Revd Charles Welland Edmonstone. They had one child, John Archibald *Venn. Venn's academic appointment brought him into the philosophical circle around John Grote, Knightbridge professor of moral philosophy, which provided the impetus and direction for his philosophical career. The Grote Club met as a philosophical discussion group from 1862 until Grote's death in 1866 at Trumpington vicarage, and afterwards as the Grote Society at Trinity College, under Grote's successor, Frederick Denison Maurice. Venn discussed each chapter of *The Logic of Chance* (1866) with fellow conversationalists who included John Grote, Henry Sidgwick, Joseph Mayor, John Rickards Mozley, W. Aldis Wright, John Batteridge Pearson, and, after 1866, Alfred Marshall. This network provided the milieu and origins of the modern style of Cambridge philosophy with its conversational, common-sense, and analytic approach. As the first lecturers in moral sciences, Venn, Sidgwick, Mayor, and Marshall were the missionaries of the new style of professional philosopher in Britain whose influences outlasted the century and whose philosophy was characterized by a persistent and confident pursuit of intelligence and truth.

In *The Logic of Chance* Venn pioneered the frequency theory of probability, in which assertions of probability are understood as purely empirically based judgements of the recurrence of types of events over time, independent of an observer's feelings. As with much of his work, Venn is here exploring the logic and limits of belief. As with his Hulsean lectures, his advice is to err in favour of scepticism. His originality does not lie in the theory of probability which he developed, nor in his rejection of alternative theories, especially the idea that probability deals with graduations of beliefs. It is displayed in his patient analysis of the wide variety of different and yet legitimate uses of the term probability, which makes theorizing so complex and difficult, his recognition that probability theory had application to a limited proportion of human conduct, and his application of this to the moral sciences. For the former he rejected a mathematical in favour of an empirical approach, and aligned himself with the work of John Stuart Mill, who remained an influence and friend. In the social sciences he recognized that the science of human actions and that of natural events differed profoundly, as the objects of the former were liable to change under the impact of motive, and that the observer is liable to 'intrude' himself upon the objects and the statistics. Venn's international reputation depends upon his 1880 contribution to the use of diagrams as methods for testing propositions and syllogisms, and representing sets, their union and intersections, *On the Diagrammatic and Mechanical Representation of Propositions and Reasonings* (1880). Venn diagrams provide a simple, but highly versatile and functional, visual representation of logical relations using circles in various overlapping and intersecting positions. They are still used to test the validity of a syllogism.

In *Symbolic Logic* (1881) Venn adjudicated the debate between the leading logicians of the day, including W. S. Jevons and C. S. Pierce, on the application of George Boole's algebraic techniques. While claiming no originality, his achievements in reworking algebra and geometry for logic were pathfinding and profound. While recognizing that symbols have various meanings, he considered that there was a more common currency and language of symbols than in everyday forms of speech, which allowed symbolic logic greater purchase on problem-solving. His classificatory systems for propositions and types of symbols remain useful. His tendency to argue for a connection between everyday and formal logic, known as 'conventionalism', allies him closely to the modern Cambridge tradition. *The Principles of Empirical or Inductive Logic* (1889), based upon Cambridge lectures, was Venn's final major work on logic. Although he was originally sympathetic to Mill's inductive method, under Venn's dry, methodical, and 'Humean' inspection, the project is found wanting in terms of language, analysis, and above all, application, which Venn argued had led to fruitless controversy. Venn challenges the foundationalist claim that logic has a definite starting point, and the frequently used metaphors of chains and buildings with foundations. 'All these metaphors are misleading, unless it is expressly explained that any such starting point is a merely conventional one, assumed for convenience' (*The Principles of Empirical or Inductive Logic*, 116–17).

As with Grote and Sidgwick, Venn's contribution chiefly lies not in his writings but in the impetus he gave to the intellectual life of Cambridge, for he donated a library of logic books, lectured weekly, tutored, and examined generations of Cambridge philosophers into the next century. He set a style, standards, and methods that were replicated, and he impressed logicians in Cambridge, especially J. N. Keynes, J. M. Keynes, W. E. Johnson, C. D. Broad, A. J. Balfour, and his friends J. R. Seeley and Leslie Stephen, as well as, outside Cambridge, C. L. Dodgson, W. S. Jevons, K. Pearson, and A. V. Dicey. He was elected ScD and FRS in 1883, FSA in 1892, and president of his college in 1903.

Precisely the same skills that made Venn a profound philosopher were applied to his antiquarian and genealogical work on university history, which became his dominant interest from the mid-1880s. Generations of researchers have benefited from the detail and accuracy of a myriad of biographical reference books, most famously, *Annals of a Clerical Family* (1904), *Early Collegiate Life* (1923), *A Biographical History of Gonville and Caius College* (1897), and the *Alumni Cantabrigienses, from Earliest Times to 1900* (1922), latterly compiled with the help of his son.

Throughout his life Venn, a man of lean build, was a keen botanist, walker, and mountain climber. He died on 4 April 1923 at his home, Vicarsbrook, Chaucer Road, Cambridge, and was buried three days later near colleagues at Trumpington churchyard. His wife survived him.   JOHN R. GIBBINS

Sources H. T. Francis, 'In memoriam: John Venn', *The Caian*, 31 (1922–3), 100–24 • *PRS*, 110A (1926), x–xi • M. M. Hennell, *John Venn and the Clapham Sect* (1958) • W. Stockton, introduction, 1972, Gon. & Caius Cam., John Venn MSS catalogue • J. A. Venn, *Autobiography of John Venn*, Queen's College Library, Cambridge • B. Hilton, *The age of atonement: the influence of evangelicalism on social and economic thought, 1795–1865* (1988) • J. Passmore, *A hundred years of philosophy*, 2nd edn (1966); repr. (1968) • J. M. Keynes, *A treatise on probability* (1921) • I. Copi and C. Cohen, *Introduction to logic* (1994) • W. C. Salmon, 'John Venn's logic of chance', *Proceedings of the 1978 Pisa Conference on the History and Philosophy of Science*, 2 (1981), 125–38 • M. E. Baron, 'A note on the historical development of logic diagrams: Leibniz, Euler, and Venn', *Mathematical Gazette*, 53 (1969), 113–25 • J. R. Gibbins, 'John Grote, Cambridge University and the development of Victorian ideas', PhD diss., U. Newcastle, 1988 • R. Froman, *A young math book: Venn diagram* (1972) • *DNB* • *CGPLA Eng. & Wales* (1923)

Archives Gon. & Caius Cam., corresp. and papers • MHS Oxf., notes relating to studies of anthropometry • Society of Genealogists, London, genealogical research notes • U. Birm. L., special collections department, corresp. and papers | Trinity Cam., Mayor MSS • U. Glas. L., special collections department, letters to A. V. Dicey • UCL, letters to Sir Francis Galton • Wellcome L., letters to Sir Francis Galton

Likenesses E. Clifford, crayon drawing, 1889, Queens' College, Cambridge • C. E. Brock, oils, 1899, Gon. & Caius Cam. • J. Palmer Clarke, photograph, repro. in Francis, 'In memoriam: John Venn', 100

Wealth at death £17,807 11s.: probate, 9 June 1923, *CGPLA Eng. & Wales*

Venn, John Archibald (1883–1958), historian and college head, was born at Cambridge on 10 November 1883, the only child of John *Venn (1834–1923) of Gonville and Caius College and his wife, Susanna Carnegie, *née* Edmonstone. He was educated at Eastbourne College, admitted at Trinity College, Cambridge, in 1902, took a third class in both parts of the historical tripos, and proceeded BA 1905, MA 1909, and LittD 1929. In 1906 he married Lucy Marion (1882/3–1958), only child of Professor William *Ridgeway. They adopted a daughter in 1932. For several years Venn and his father, than whom he could not have had a more experienced teacher in prosopography, compiled historical data on members of the university, and their *Book of Matriculations and Degrees … 1544 to 1659* appeared in 1913. He also helped to edit five volumes published between 1911 and 1916 of an admissions register of his own college to 1900, and completed the second volume of John Peile's expansive and unfinished *Biographical Register of Christ's College* (1913). He played tennis and enjoyed ornithology and motoring; though not a player of the game he invented a bowling machine which bowled out the Australian cricketer V. T. Trumper in three successive deliveries.

After army service in the First World War, Venn worked as a statistician in the food production department from 1917 and he remained an adviser to the Ministry of Agriculture while pursuing an academic career. From 1921 until 1949 he held the Gilbey lectureship in the history and economics of agriculture at Cambridge, and also served on many international, national, and local committees and the councils of academic bodies such as the British Association for the Advancement of Science. His last major position of that kind was as chairman of a government commission on the sugar industry in British Guiana in 1948–9. Such appointments are listed in *Who Was Who, 1951–1960*. He was made a fellow of the Society of Antiquaries, and in recognition of the wartime evacuation of the medical school from London to Queens' a 'perpetual student of Bart's', a title which delighted him. Venn's interest in farming was almost exclusively academic and confined to its history and organization, but he contributed useful counsel when agriculture was the object of several experiments between the wars, and was not reluctant to expose economic fallacies and practical obstacles. He wrote a standard book, *Foundations of Agricultural Economics* (1923), enlarged in 1933, and other papers in the subject.

Venn was elected fellow of Queens' College, with which his family had been associated since the eighteenth century, in 1927, served as junior bursar, and while still junior fellow was elected its president in March 1932, when he became the youngest head of a Cambridge college. He was generous to Queens' in his lifetime and by his will, and with his wife was a hospitable host despite his own teetotalism. He was ambitious for Queens' and ready to delegate responsibilities to its officers and to support them. He also served on the council of the senate and as vice-chancellor during the exacting disruption of war (1941–3). His high sense of the traditional dignity of his offices as president and vice-chancellor and of the respect due to them rather than to himself personally meant that those who did not know him sometimes mistook formality for aloofness. After the war the university appointed him its first honorary keeper of the archives, and he largely established the post on a permanent footing. He was awarded a Coronation Medal in 1953 and was made CMG in 1956 for public services. He died at the president's lodge on 15 March 1958 after being in poor health for a year, and was buried on 20 March. His wife survived him by only ten days.

At heart Venn was always a historian. He published meticulous statistics of Oxford and Cambridge matriculations since 1544 in 1908 and 1930. Yet the work which occupied him for most of his life and for which he has been best remembered, the *Alumni Cantabrigienses: a biographical list of all known students, graduates and holders of office at the University of Cambridge from the earliest times to 1900*, was planned with his father. Two volumes of the first part to 1751 appeared before John Venn's death, and his son saw the series through to completion in a further eight massive, closely printed volumes between 1924 and 1954. He had many amanuenses but carefully controlled the entire labour of abstracting millions of facts from a wide variety of manuscript and published sources, and scrutinized all the proofs. He had the subject at his fingertips and, perhaps not surprisingly for one whose favourite author was Sir Thomas Browne, it provided him with endless anecdotes. The *Alumni* project was befriended and heavily subsidized by the syndics of the university press whose secretary, Sir Sydney Roberts, wrote of Venn's 'immense courage and determination' in accomplishing his vast plan (letter of 24 Jan 1959, registry file 3580/59). He was not a medievalist and his biographies down to 1500 were superseded by A. B. Emden's *Biographical Register* of 1963, but the bulk of the work, comprising more than 125,000 entries, has not been paralleled, let alone surpassed. Without them the social and academic history of Cambridge and of the English establishment at large written since the 1940s would have been much poorer.

JOHN D. PICKLES

Sources *The Times* (17 March 1958) • *Cambridge Review* (19 April 1958), 450 • *WWW*, 1951–60 • *The Dial* [Queens' College, Cambridge], 86 (1932), 3–4 • *The Dial* [Queens' College, Cambridge], 102 (1948), 23 • *Manchester Guardian* (17 March 1958) • private information (2004) • CUL, Cambridge University Press MSS • Cambridge University Registry, file 3580/59 • Venn, *Alum. Cant.*

Archives CUL • Gon. & Caius Cam., corresp. mainly with family members • Queens' College, Cambridge | BL, typescript of 'Evidence before the Agricultural Tribunal of Investigation 1923', 42254, fols. 324–350 • U. Birm. L., special collections department, letters from students relating to work on the Venn MSS

Likenesses E. J. Rosenberg, chalk drawing, 1885, Queens' College, Cambridge • Miss Wale, oils, 1893 • Miss Wheelwright, miniature, 1899 • Palmer Clarke, five photographs, 1914–1929?, Cambridge City Library, Cambridgeshire collection • T. S. La Fontaine, oils, 1930–1939?, Queens' College, Cambridge; repro. in *The Dial* (Easter 1948), 23 • W. Stoneman, photograph, 1947, NPG • photograph (in old age), repro. in *ILN* (22 March 1958)

Wealth at death £73,614 0s. 6d.: probate, 28 May 1958, *CGPLA Eng. & Wales*

Venn, Richard (1691–1739), Church of England clergyman and religious controversialist, the eldest and only surviving son of Dennis Venn (*d.* 1695), vicar of Holbeton, Devon, and his second wife, Patience Gay (*d.* 1712), was born at Holbeton on 7 January 1691. The family had a strong clerical tradition and his grandfather, the vicar of Otterton, had been one of the most prominent west country sufferers for his loyalty to the crown during the civil war. As a result of an injury suffered in childhood Venn could walk only with pain and difficulty, but his intrepid spirit and intellectual abilities remained unimpaired. After attending school at Modbury he went on to Blundell's in Tiverton—a contemporary here was Bampfylde Moore Carew—and thence, in 1709, to Cambridge, where he took up a closed scholarship at Sidney Sussex, graduating BA in 1713 and proceeding MA in 1716.

Venn moved to London and was ordained deacon in 1716 and priest in 1717; he became curate at St Giles Cripplegate, where the rector, Dr Thomas Bennet, was a noted high-churchman. In 1725 he became rector of St Antholin's, Watling Street, retaining a sinecure appointment worth £130 p.a. at St Giles's. He was also a preacher at Paul's Cross. His attitude towards the Hanoverian succession was ambiguous. He was not a nonjuror, but his tract *King George's Title Asserted* (1715), written in an attempt to persuade Thomas Baker to take the oaths, was argued without conviction. In 1716 he married Maria Anna Isabella Margaretta Beatrix (*d.* 1762), a god-daughter of Queen Mary of Modena and daughter of John *Ashton (*d.* 1691), the Jacobite executed for his part in the Preston plot in 1691. With her came several Stuart relics, which remained in the Venn family for generations, including a snuffbox made from a fragment of the Boscobel oak, a piece of the garter sash worn by King Charles I at his execution, and a picture of King James III. They had eight children, of whom four died in infancy or childhood. One son, Edward (1717–80), attended St John's College, Cambridge, and practised medicine at Ipswich; another was the evangelical minister Henry *Venn (1725–1797). Venn was a stern father, of whom family tradition related that 'the system of Solomon he preferred to that of Rousseau'

(J. Venn, 53), but he was also fair and affectionate, blessing his children at the end of every day.

Venn was an influential figure. He formed close friendships with Bishop Edmund Gibson and with the high tory MP John Barnard, lord mayor of London in 1737, and he was a prominent member of a metropolitan circle of high-church clergy that included William Berriman and Henry Stebbing. A consistent opponent of the dissenters, whom he equated with the rebellious sectarians of the 1640s, he resisted proposals to repeal the Corporation and Test Acts and wept when the Mortmain Act was passed in 1736. He attacked Daniel Neal's *History of the Puritans* (1732–8); led the successful campaign to prevent the latitudinarian Thomas Rundle from becoming bishop of Gloucester in 1734; called Conyers Middleton an 'apostate priest'; and was the first London clergyman to refuse his pulpit to George Whitefield, the Methodist, in 1737.

Venn died in London from smallpox on 16 February 1739, and was buried at St Antholin's. During his later years his views found frequent expression in the high-church *Weekly Miscellany*, edited by William Webster. His last published work, an anti-Methodist letter, appeared in that journal less than a week before his death. This and other letters, together with an extensive selection of his miscellaneous writings, was published by his widow under the title *Tracts and Sermons* (1740).

RICHARD SHARP

Sources J. Venn, *Annals of a clerical family* (1904) · R. Venn, *Tracts and sermons on several occasions*, ed. [M. Venn] (1740) · Venn, *Alum. Cant.* · *GM*, 1st ser., 9 (1739), 106 · *Walker rev.*, 125–6 · N. Sykes, *Edmund Gibson, bishop of London, 1669–1748: a study in politics & religion in the eighteenth century* (1926) · *Manuscripts of the earl of Egmont: diary of Viscount Percival, afterwards first earl of Egmont*, 3 vols., HMC, 63 (1920–23)

Vennar [Vennard], **Richard** (*bap.* 1564, *d.* 1615), author, was baptized on 25 January 1564 at the church of St Edmund, Salisbury, the second son of John Vennard (*c.*1520–1589), merchant (probably a mercer), and his wife, whose surname may have been Harris. Others called him Vennar and his name is so spelt in his autobiography, *An Apology* (1614). According to Vennar, Bishop Jewell baptized him in the presence of the earls of Bedford and Pembroke. He was educated by Adam Hill in Salisbury, then went to Balliol College, Oxford, as a fellow-commoner for two years, after which his father sent him with an Italian guide, a serving man, and a page to the courts of Henri III in Paris and Maximilian II in Vienna and home again through Germany. He 'forth-with' admitted himself to Lincoln's Inn, where he maintained 'sixe men, with horses sutable' (Vennar, *Apology*, 5–6). But since Henri set up his court in September 1574 and Maximilian died in October 1576, Vennar would have made his journey when he was ten to twelve years old, having already spent two years at Oxford. Moreover, he went to Barnard's Inn first, then on 10 June 1581 to Lincoln's Inn, where six years later he acquired special admission. He was there for twenty-six years without being called to the bar or practising law.

Vennar's father complained about his son's wasting

money and gave him £300 on condition that he demand no more. But when first his older brother died in 1588 and then his father in 1589, Vennar sued his brother's widow, Mary, in the Star Chamber for his father's estate. She soon married a lawyer in Lincoln's Inn, Richard Low, and they defeated Vennar, who in 1599 compounded for £150, though he thought he should have had thousands. This lawsuit sent Vennar to prison at least twice, for allegedly stealing documents and for debt, and therefore, Vennar thought, destroyed his reputation and his life. He also went to prison for a fraud in 1590–91, of which he was found innocent.

In 1600 Vennar made the first of three attempts to rehabilitate himself. He went to Scotland and found favour with James VI, but on his return was accused of disloyalty and spent more time in prison. He next tried unsuccessfully to be called to the bar and then took up a literary career. In 1601 and 1602 he produced a pious, protestant work in prose and verse, *The Right Way to Heaven*; a poem called *England's Joy*, on Lord Mountjoy's great victory at Kinsale; a much revised edition of *The Right Way*; and a play (now lost) also called *England's Joy*, which he said was to raise money for a return to Scotland. Later he wrote a (lost) broadside against papists and *The True Testimony of a Faithful Subject* (1605), a thanksgiving for the discovery of the Gunpowder Plot that includes part of *The Right Way*.

Vennar was and is mainly known for his attempt to mount his play. In a broadside, *Plot of the Play Called 'England's Joy'* (1602), he announced its performance at the Swan Playhouse on 6 November 1602. It was to consist of nine spectacular scenes acted, as report had it, by gentlemen and gentlewomen. According to Vennar spectators paid 12*s.* each and the actors were 'men of good birth, Schollers by profession'—not, apparently, women. Vennar duly appeared on stage and delivered six lines of the prologue, but then bailiffs arrested him for debt and effectually 'spoke an Epilogue instead'. Although he pocketed 'much mony', the authorities did not indict him (Vennar, *Apology*, 24–7).

A rather different story was soon current and has remained so. John Chamberlain explained it to Dudley Carleton on 19 November: Vennar

> gave out bills of a famous play on satterday was sevenight on the Banckside, to be acted only by certain gentlemen and gentlewomen of account, the price at comming in was two shillings or eighteen pence at least and when he had gotten most part of the money into his hands, he wold have shewed them a fayre payre of heeles, but he was not so nimble to get up on horsebacke, but that he was faine to forsake that course, and betake himself to the water, where he was pursued and taken and brought before the L: Cheife Justice [Sir John Popham], who wold make nothing of that but a iest and merriment, and bounde him over in five pound to appeare at the sessions: in the meane time the common people … revenged themselves upon the hangings curtaines chaires stooles walles and whatsoever came in theyre way very outragiously and made a great spoyle (PRO, SP 12/285, fol. 149*v.*)

Thereafter Vennar himself was derisively called England's Joy. The play was finally mounted by William Fennor in the spring of 1615.

Vennar was imprisoned at least three more times: for wronging lawyers at the Inner Temple, of which he was found guiltless and recompensed; for fraud while trying to raise money in 1606 to finance a masque, of which he was also found guiltless but remained in prison because he could not raise sureties for good behaviour; and for debt in 1614. During this last imprisonment, which was in the Wood Street compter, he wrote his *Apology* and died. He was buried at St Michael, Wood Street, on 13 October 1615, aged fifty-one. According to Fennor in 1616, Vennar had objected to fees demanded in the compter and been thrown into the black hole, where 'lying without a bedde, hee caught such an extreame cold in his legges, that it was not long before he departed this life' (W. Fennor, *Compter's Commonwealth*, 1617, 62–4).

In 1588 Vennar had a wife, Elizabeth (who apparently had recusant connections), and for two weeks in 1590 a son, Richard. He was estranged from his wife and 'children' in 1596 (PRO, SP 12/256, fol. 134) and was single and childless in 1614. His actions and their results made his claims to social distinction ridiculous, but his verse, usually in the six-line stanza of *Venus and Adonis*, is respectable in the manner of Daniel and Drayton, if often overblown, and his prose in the *Apology* is lively.   HERBERT BERRY

Sources H. Berry, 'Richard Vennor, England's Joy', *English Literary Renaissance*, 31 (2001), 240–65 · R. Vennar, *An apology* (1614) · parish register, Salisbury, St Edmund's, 1564, 1590, Wilts. & Swindon RO, MS 1901/1 [baptism] · PRO, PROB 11/74, fol. 129 [will, John Vennard] · letter from John Chamberlain to Dudley Carleton, 1602, PRO, SP 12/285, fol. 149v · W. P. Baildon, ed., *The records of the Honorable Society of Lincoln's Inn: admissions*, 1 (1896), 93 · W. P. Baildon, ed., *The records of the Honorable Society of Lincoln's Inn: the black books*, 2 (1898), 103 · Vennard family lawsuit, 1588–90, PRO, STAC. 5/V. 7/17 [John Vennard's deposition] · Vennard family lawsuit, 1588–90, PRO, STAC. 5/V. 4/28 [the answer] · Vennard family lawsuit, 1588–90, PRO, STAC. 5/V. 1/30 · APC, 1590–91 · R. Vennar, letter to Sir Robert Cecil, 1596, PRO, SP 12/256, fols. 134, 135 · C. Yelverton, letters to Sir Robert Cecil and Sir Edward Coke, 1601, Hatfield House, Cecil MSS, vol. 180, no. 9 · J. Taylor, *A cast over water* (1615) · parish register, London, St Michael, Wood Street, 13 Oct 1615, GL, MS 6530 [burial] · W. Fennor, *The compters common-wealth* (1617)
Wealth at death penury

Venner, Thomas (1608/9–1661), Fifth Monarchist, was probably born in Littleham, Devon. By 1633 he had moved to London, where he worked as a cooper and became a member of the Coopers' Company, probably in that year. Aged twenty-eight, he testified with the separatists Praisegod Barebone and Stephen More before the high court of admiralty in January 1637 regarding a shipment of wine to Virginia. He subsequently emigrated to Salem, Massachusetts, where he was admitted to its church on 25 February 1638 and became a freeman of the town the following month. A juryman in 1638 and 1640, he served as constable beginning in August 1642. Dissatisfied with life in Salem, he organized some of the settlers to move to Providence Island in the West Indies, but this endeavour apparently collapsed. Venner sold the 40 acres allocated to him in Salem and moved to Boston by 1644. With him were his wife, Alice (d. 1692), and son, Thomas [see below], baptized at Salem in May 1641; he and Alice would have two more children in Boston, Hannah (b. February 1645) and Samuel

(b. February 1650). Venner became a member of the artillery company in 1645, and in October 1648 he organized the coopers of Boston and Charlestown into a trading company.

Some time following the return of Venner and his family to London in October 1651, he embraced Fifth Monarchist tenets. By 1655 he was employed as a master cooper in the Tower, but he was arrested in June and dismissed for allegedly discussing Cromwell's assassination and plotting to blow up the Tower. The government did not take him very seriously, for he was free by winter, when he participated in meetings with other Fifth Monarchists, including John Portman and Arthur Squibb, and republicans such as John Okey and Thomas Lawson. Henry Vane's *The Healing Question* was the starting point for their discussions about possible joint political action, but they failed to achieve substantive agreement. Okey, Lawson, Portman, and others were arrested in the summer, and officials were searching for Venner. If he was detained, it was only briefly, for in early August he was holding meetings of his Fifth Monarchist congregation at Swan Alley, Coleman Street, London; copies of *Englands Remembrancers*, urging the godly to elect proponents of the Good Old Cause to parliament, were distributed. Apparently the members of the church, some of whom had been lured from John Rogers's congregation, were primarily young men and apprentices. During the winter of 1656–7 Venner planned an insurrection, organizing five groups of twenty-five members each, with only one person in each cell knowing details about the other units. Venner and Portman discussed possible co-operation, but Rogers, Thomas Harrison, and John Carew were opposed, while Christopher Feake and Livewell Chapman were apparently not approached. Venner's people obtained maps, telescopes, horses, weapons, and armour, and his son-in-law, William Medley, drafted a manifesto, *A Standard Set Up*. It proclaimed the saints' intention to establish theocratic government featuring a sanhedrin and a governing council, each elected by members of gathered churches, and biblically based laws. Land tenures would be reformed and copyhold abolished. The Vennerites intended to confiscate their enemies' property, depositing some of it in a public treasury to support God's work and distributing the rest equally among themselves. Proposed legal reforms, including a hierarchy of courts, beginning with monthly ones in market towns, were aimed at ending law as an instrument of social oppression; judges, like all other officials, would be chosen by the saints alone. The rebels intended to rendezvous at Mile End Green and then march into East Anglia, where they expected many recruits to join them. Venner asked his female followers to distribute copies of the manifesto. The rebels' standard depicted a red lion and the motto 'Who shall rouse him up?' As they assembled on 9 April, government troops arrested approximately twenty of them and seized weapons and 500 copies of the manifesto. Taken before Cromwell, Venner and his supporters refused to doff their hats and impolitely referred to the lord protector as 'thou'. Although Venner was not tried, he was incarcerated in the Tower until at least February 1659.

By December 1660, when Venner visited Exeter, he was again conspiring, now against the restored monarchy. On Sunday 6 January 1661 he called his followers to arms, urging them not to sheath their swords until the monarchy had been destroyed. Their new manifesto, *A Door of Hope*, called for an international crusade, financed by expropriated property, to defeat France, Spain, the Catholic states in Germany, and the papacy, and for a godly society free of poverty, taxation, primogeniture, and capital punishment for theft. With ensigns emblazoned 'The Lord God and Gideon' and the battle cry 'King Jesus, and the [regicides'] heads upon the gates', some fifty zealots, including at least one armed woman, rebelled. After temporarily seizing St Paul's, the Vennerites sparred with trained bands before retreating to Kenwood, where troops forced a further withdrawal to Aldersgate. Another rebel band repulsed two files of guards near Bishopsgate. After evading capture at Kenwood on Monday night, the rebels fought in a skirmish early on Wednesday morning near Leadenhall Street. Failing to apprehend the lord mayor or liberate prisoners from the compter, they were routed by the life guards in Wood Street. Venner himself had killed at least three of the approximately twenty loyalists who died, but the Vennerites suffered comparable losses, and Venner himself sustained nineteen wounds. Arraigned at the Old Bailey on the 17th, he initially refused to plead, instead launching into a discourse on the Fifth Monarchy. After finally pleading not guilty, he admitted having participated in the insurrection, but not as leader, for that had been Jesus's role. As Venner prepared to be hanged, drawn, and quartered before his meeting-house on 19 January 1661, he remained defiant, claiming to have acted 'according to the best light I had, and according to the best understanding that the Scripture will afford' (*Last Speech*, 4). By 21 January thirteen of his compatriots had been executed, and for good measure the government demolished his meeting-house. If the revolt was pathetic and desperate, as some historians have suggested, it was also a manifestation of Venner's fierce conviction that Christ's people, their triumph assured, were literally to take the field against the forces of Antichrist. Resolute in his faith, Venner was a misguided millenarian zealot.

Venner's elder son, **Thomas Venner** (*b.* 1641), baptized on 16 May 1641 at Salem, was also to follow his father as a rebel, taking part in the Monmouth rising of 1685. He served as an officer in an English regiment in the Netherlands, but joined Monmouth after he was cashiered. Commissioned lieutenant-colonel by the duke, Venner served in Monmouth's personal regiment, where Nathaniel Wade was one of his majors. An adviser to Lord Grey during the rebellion, Venner sustained a stomach wound at Bridport on 14 June. After learning of Argyll's defeat, he advised Monmouth to flee. When Grey prevailed on Monmouth to continue fighting, Venner and Thomas Parsons returned to the Netherlands, ostensibly at Robert Ferguson's request, to purchase weapons and ammunition with which to launch an uprising in Ireland. But this may have

been a story concocted by Captain John Tillier to save his own life following his capture. During the autumn of 1685 Venner was in Cleves, threatening to avenge his father's death. According to the informer Edmund Everard, he belonged to a faction of militant exiles that included Major John Manley, and was expecting the inauguration of Christ's earthly kingdom by 1688.

RICHARD L. GREAVES

Sources Thurloe, *State papers*, 5.248, 272–3; 6.163–4, 184–6, 188 · *The last speech and prayer with other passages of Thomas Venner … immediately before his execution* (1660) · *JHC*, 7 (1651–9), 521 · *A relation of the arraignment and trial of those who made the late rebellious insurrections in London* (1661) · C. E. Banks, 'Thomas Venner: the Boston winecooper and Fifth-Monarchy Man', *New England Historical and Genealogical Register*, 47 (1893), 437–44 · B. S. Capp, *The Fifth Monarchy Men: a study in seventeenth-century English millenarianism* (1972) · R. L. Greaves, *Deliver us from evil: the radical underground in Britain, 1660–1663* (1986) · *Kingdomes Intelligencer* (7–14 Jan 1661) · *Kingdomes Intelligencer* (14–21 Jan 1661) · *Kingdomes Intelligencer* (21–8 Jan 1661) · *Mercurius Publicus*, 1 (3–10 Jan 1661) · *Mercurius Publicus*, 3 (17–24 Jan 1661) · C. Burrage, 'The fifth monarchy insurrections', *EngHR*, 25 (1910), 722–47 · E. Ludlow, *A voyce from the watch tower*, ed. A. B. Worden, CS, 4th ser., 21 (1978) · B. S. Capp, 'Venner, Thomas', Greaves & Zaller, *BDBR*, 268–70 · W. M. Wigfield, *The Monmouth rebels, 1685*, Somerset RS, 79 (1985)
Archives BL, Add. MS 4459, fols. 111–22 · Bodl. Oxf., MS Rawl. A54
Likenesses portrait, repro. in E. Pagitt, *Heresiography* (1662), 280

Venner, Thomas (*b.* 1641). *See under* Venner, Thomas (1608/9–1661).

Venner, Tobias (1577–1660), physician and medical writer, was born near North Petherton, Somerset. Details of his early life and family are obscure, but at the age of eighteen he became an undergraduate at St Alban's Hall, Oxford, where he graduated BA on 1 February 1599. Venner then returned to Somerset and in 1601 married Agnes Jeffrye (*d.* 1634) at Bridgwater, having established himself as a medical practitioner in the area; they had a daughter and three sons. The girl died while still young and was buried at North Petherton in 1618.

By the time he obtained his BM and DM degrees in 1613, Venner was already visiting Bath between spring and autumn when the annual influx of the sick provided a lucrative trade for visiting physicians. Bath's hot mineral springs enjoyed a reputation for the successful treatment of skin problems, paralytic disorders, and painful conditions. The spa was popular with people from all ranks of society but bathing was confined to just three months of the year, so avoiding the hottest and coldest seasons, which were considered dangerous, though Venner challenged the wisdom of this statement in his publication *The Bathes of Bathe* (1620). Several earlier writers had published books about bathing which featured Bath but Venner was the first to write exclusively about the city's spa. His book undoubtedly helped to promote his image as a balneological specialist and encouraged visitors to consult a trained medical practitioner rather than one of the many quacks and charlatans who pervaded the city.

The Bathes of Bathe accompanied the initial part of another work by Venner on the preservation of health, entitled *Via recta ad vitam longam*, the final part of which he completed two years later. The book followed a traditional format, and discussed how the six 'non-naturals' (environment, diet, sleep, exercise, excretion, and the passions of the mind) affected the balance of the four humours (blood, phlegm, yellow bile, and black bile). Venner advocated the consumption of bran to prevent constipation, and regular cleaning of the teeth to prevent tooth decay and bad breath. He cautioned against drinking water conveyed through lead piping. He also published *A Briefe … Treatise Concerning the Taking of the Fume of Tobacco* (1621). Although he personally disliked its 'detestable savour' and deplored its immoderate recreational use, he recommended tobacco-smoking as a means of improving digestion and countering the malign effects of cold, misty weather and contagious air.

By 1630 the improvements which had been carried out to the bathing facilities at Bath were attracting even more patients and doctors. Venner was by then well established in the city, where he leased property near what was known as the Hot Bath. He continued his links with Bridgwater and rented land at Rhode, a small hamlet to the west of the town. His books were selling well and his three sons had graduated in medicine from Oxford University. However, within the space of three years Venner's wife and eldest son both died. His second wife, Mary Parker, also predeceased him, in 1646.

At the age of seventy-five, Venner was appointed physician to the Scudamore charity. This was a fund set up by Viscount John Scudamore in memory of his wife to provide free medical advice to poor strangers arriving in Bath and also to patients admitted to Bellot's Hospital, which had been founded in 1609 expressly to provide accommodation near the Hot Bath.

A contemporary biographer wrote rather disparagingly that whereas some men had guts in their brains, Dr Venner's brains were in his guts. Venner's writings suggest that he was a man of moderate habits and piety, so it was not surprising that during the Commonwealth period he espoused the puritan cause. His longevity certainly served to prove the efficacy of his regimen: he died at Bath on 27 March 1660 in his eighty-third year. He was buried in Bath Abbey, where for many years a monument, which is mentioned in Pepys's diary, commemorated his beneficence. He survived all his children; no Venners were mentioned in his will and he left no property, only money and a few named items which were bequeathed to various members of the Parker family, to which he was related through his second wife.   ROGER ROLLS

Sources Wood, *Ath. Oxon.* · Foster, *Alum. Oxon.* · E. Dwelly, ed., *Bishop's transcripts at Wells*, 1 (1913) · E. Dwelly, *Dwelly's parish records*, 2, 10 (1922) · E. Dwelly, *Dwelly's National records*, 2: *XVII century directory of Somerset* (1932) · K. Symons, *The grammar school of King Edward VI, Bath* (1934) · J. Wood, *A description of Bath*, 2nd edn (1765); repr. (1969) · E. Holland and M. Inskip, *Citizens of Bath* (1988) · F. Brown, ed., *Abstracts of Somersetshire wills*, 6 vols. (privately printed, London, 1887–90), vol. 2, p. 96; vol. 3, p. 54 · A. J. Jewers, ed., *The registers of the abbey church of SS Peter and Paul, Bath*, 2, Harleian Society, Register Section, 28 (1901) · P. R. James, *The baths of Bath in the 16th and early 17th centuries* (1938) · Bellot's admission and account book, Guildhall, Bath, Bath city archives · T. Guidott, *Lives and characters of the physicians of Bath* (1676) · J. Wroughton, *A community at war: the civil war in Bath and north Somerset, 1642–1650*, rev. edn (1992) · *Proceedings of the Bath Natural History & Antiquarian Field Club*, 3 (1877), 11

Likenesses W. Faithorne, line engraving, BM, NPG; repro. in T. Venner, *Via recta ad vitam longam* (1660)

Venning, John (1776–1858), prison reformer and philanthropist, was born at Totnes, Devon, on 20 May 1776, the son of Walter Venning, a merchant, and Mary Ann, his wife. He attended Totnes grammar school and, at the age of fourteen, followed his elder brother William to work for Jackson & Co., a London banking house with interests in Russia. In 1793 he was sent to St Petersburg by the firm; six years later he was joined there by his younger brother Walter *Venning (1781–1821). John Venning married Julia, the daughter of James Meybohm, a wealthy member of the large German merchant community in St Petersburg, on 13 September 1805.

Venning rapidly established himself in the expatriate merchant community in St Petersburg, meeting Tsar Alexander I in 1808 and becoming a familiar figure in polite Russian society. In 1807 Walter Venning returned to England; he came back to Russia in 1817 a committed evangelical and prison reformer. Shortly after, John Venning himself was converted, and he abandoned his social life of theatres and balls. Like other evangelicals, he cultivated an intense personal devotion to Christ, holding that all were sinners saved only through Christ's redemption. Committed to active charitable intervention for the salvation of all God's children, he took Walter's cue in embracing the work of the Society for the Improvement of Prison Discipline, which had been established in England in 1815. This society modelled its work on that of John Howard (1726–1790), the prison reformer, and campaigned for regulated prisons which provided education and instruction in the Christian faith, and reformed rather than brutalized prisoners. John Venning committed himself to reforming Russian prisons and to forwarding the work of the British and Foreign Bible Society, which had set up a Russian Bible Society in 1813, aiming to make vernacular Bibles available to every family in the empire. This agenda brought him close to Alexander I, whose mystical and ultra-conservative Christian spirituality had also led the tsar to an involvement with English Quakers, Methodists, and Baptists, as well as German Lutheran pietists. The tsar aimed to create a transformed society, impermeable to revolution and based on the word of God, education, and philanthropy.

Alexander was a frequent visitor to the Venning brothers, who in 1819 set up a Prison Discipline Society in St Petersburg. After Walter's death in 1821, John continued their work, revealing to the tsar the appalling conditions in Russian prisons. Emphasizing their extreme filth, the abuse of women, the lack of any medical or spiritual care, and the prevalence of disease, corruption, vice, overcrowding, and misery, Venning presented the prisons as hell come to earth. He was particularly horrified by the condition of the so-called 'exiles' sent to Siberian mines in chain-gangs. Venning reported directly to Alexander through Prince Galitzin and pressed for Howardian reforms, including the introduction of such health measures as exercise and basic hygiene, and the suppression of vices such as gambling, alcoholism, and promiscuity. He also suggested the adoption of work programmes in shoemaking, tailoring, and other trades, and, above all, he called for religious conversion based on distribution of Bibles and Bible teaching. Venning believed that crime stemmed from universal sinfulness: Satan's power flourishing in foul neglected neighbourhoods, fuelled by extravagance, addiction, and atheistic sedition. At the heart of his message was the imperative of trust in God and redemption through Christ.

Venning was given unlimited access to the prisons of Russia and carefully cultivated the support of leading Russians: indeed, during this period it was *de rigueur* for aspiring Russians to be seen to be engaged in philanthropic ventures. In 1821 he visited England and went to Newgate Prison with Elizabeth Fry, also getting to know the rest of the Gurney, Fry, and Hoare Quaker banking interests with whom Walter had worked closely. During this trip he established a Prison Discipline Society in Prussia and visited prisons in France before returning to St Petersburg in 1822.

Administration was very poor in Russia, and Venning frequently found the orders of the tsar were ignored because they had not been transmitted down. Moreover, he was often abused and menaced by officials whose profits and pleasures were threatened by reform; charges of peculation were trumped up against him in 1828 and dismissed without trial. Gradually the reforms which he sought began to be introduced in the great cities. However, by the mid-1820s Alexander's belief in philanthropic Western methods of securing reform was being undermined by the Russian Orthodox church and other deeply reactionary forces in Russia, which saw them as harbingers of foreign influence and liberalism. Obscurantist policies had already set in when Alexander I died in late 1825 and although his successor, Nicholas I, agreed to be patron of the St Petersburg Prison Discipline Society, he drastically reduced the field of activity of the Russian Bible Society. In May 1830 Venning and his wife returned to England and on medical advice remained there. His work of prison reform and Bible distribution was continued in Russia by the German doctor Frederich Haas of Moscow.

Venning also worked to secure the release of debtors from Russian prisons, but his philanthropy was wider than Bible distribution and prison reform. In November 1824, for example, he played a major role in setting up two houses of refuge after the terrible St Petersburg flood, and he secured funding from the imperial family to replace these with a permanent house with a hospital and work programme. In 1828 Venning persuaded the dowager empress to grant £40,000 to set up an enlightened lunatic asylum 5 miles from St Petersburg. Here he worked as governor to establish a regime based on the moral management system pioneered at The Retreat in York, and centred on the dignified treatment of inmates, exercise, kindness, good food, prayer, and scriptural instruction. In addition he and Walter were part of a committee which established two Lancaster schools, triggered by the visit to Alexander I of the Quakers William Allen and Stephen Grellet in 1818. The schools were paid for by the imperial family and other benefactors; one operated for poor Russian boys, the other for poor expatriate children. The one for Russians suffered from the government reaction against Lancaster schools in the mid-1820s, although it had been founded specifically to teach scripture, in direct challenge to Russian schools which, to the alarm of the authorities, were teaching French liberal philosophy.

On their return to England the Vennings settled at Surrey House, Surrey Street, Norwich (near the Gurneys of Earlham), and John became a significant figure in the Norwich City Mission. Although actual denomination meant far less to Venning than a vital personal relationship with Christ, he and his wife were Congregationalists, attending a church in Prince's Street, Norwich, from 1831 to 1858. After suffering acute abdominal pains for some time, he died at his home on 11 April 1858, leaving his wife and a son and daughter. John Venning was remembered as a kindly, hospitable, and cheerful man, warm-hearted in his beliefs, who had acted out his gratitude for and delight in Christ's redemption of the world in a strange and at times savage environment of autocratic policy making, immense human suffering, and intense distrust from Europhobic elements of the Russian state.

BILL FORSYTHE

Sources *Reports of the Committee of the Society for the Improvement of Prison Discipline, and Reformation of Juvenile Offenders*, 8 vols. (1818–32) · T. S. Henderson, *Memorials of John Venning esq.* (1862) · B. Hollingsworth, 'John Venning and prison reform in Russia, 1819–1830', *Slavonic and East European Review*, 48 (1970), 537–56 · J. C. Zacek, 'The Lancastrian schools movement in Russia', *Slavonic and East European Review*, 45 (1967), 343–67 · J. C. Zacek, 'The Russian Bible Society and the Orthodox church', *Church History*, 35 (1966), 411–37 · A. McConnell, *Tsar Alexander I: paternalistic reformer* (1970) · E. M. Almeding, *The Emperor Alexander I* (1964) · B. H. Sumner, *Survey of Russian history* (1961) · private information (2004) · J. C. Zacek, 'The Imperial Philanthropic Society in the reign of Alexander', *Canadian-American Slavic Studies*, 9/4 (1975), 427–36
Likenesses H. Adlard, portrait, *c.*1850, repro. in Henderson, *Memorials*, frontispiece
Wealth at death under £25,000: probate, 10 May 1858

Venning, Ralph (*c.*1622–1674), clergyman and ejected minister, was born in Devon, the son of Francis Venning and his wife, Joan. As a youth he became the first convert of George Hughes (1603/4–1667), vicar of Tavistock, whom Venning later recalled as 'gentle to me as a nurse which cherisheth her children' (*Mysteries and Revelations*, preface). He was educated at Emmanuel College, Cambridge, where he entered as a sizar on 1 April 1643 and graduated BA in 1646. Continuing at Emmanuel, the following year he issued the first of many publications, *Orthodox Paradoxes* and *Mysteries and Revelations*, an explanation of scriptural names, allusions, and metaphors, dedicated to Captain Francis West, lieutenant of the Tower of London, from whom Venning had received 'many favours'. On 16 February 1648 he was appointed chaplain at the Tower, but returned to Cambridge to proceed MA in 1650. He subsequently held a lectureship at St Olave's, Southwark, where he earned fame as a preacher and continued to publish sermons and devotional works such as *The New Command Renewed* (1650) and *Canaans Flowings* (1653).

During the protectorate Venning was one of those employed to examine candidates for chaplaincies in the navy. From 1654 he preached sermons at St Paul's before successive mayors of London. He was made an assistant to the Surrey commission of triers and ejectors on 29 September 1657 and lecturer at St Mary Magdalen, Milk Street, on 26 November 1658. On 14 December 1659 Richard Baxter advised an anxious John Greenborough that Venning was one of those 'godly orthodox men' who, despite their congregational principles and possible lack of ordination, 'you may thanke God you have such to heare' (Keeble and Nuttall, 1.421). In January 1661 he signed the congregational and Baptist *Renunciation and Declaration* against Thomas Venner. By a licence of 8 January 1661, which gave his parish as St Botolph without Bishopsgate, he married Hannah, widow of John Cope of London.

Venning was ejected under the Act of Uniformity in 1662; he was reported to be preaching unofficially in Southwark in 1663 and at the Wild Man, Cannon Street, the following year. At Southwark, Calamy recorded, Venning was 'a most importunate and prevalent pleader for the poor' who succeeded in raising 'some hundreds of pounds for them' each year (Calamy, *Abridgement*, 2.22–3). Sermons preached there many years earlier appeared in his *Sin, the Plague of Plagues* (1669). Under the declaration of indulgence Venning took out a licence in St Clement Eastcheap on 30 April 1672. Earlier he had become the co-pastor with Robert Bragge (1627–1704) of the Independent congregation at Pewterers' Hall, Fenchurch Street, and this charge he held until his death.

It seems that Venning and his wife had remained childless but that he had continued to hope that she might conceive. In an astoundingly laconic will, dated 8 January 1674, 'being in good health', he disposed in one short paragraph of much money. There were legacies amounting to £240 for various relations, £50 'to Christ's hospital for the blew coat children', £30 for poor ministers, and £10 for 'my honoured Mother Johan' and for his stepdaughter Hannah Cope; most of the rest went to his wife, then aged about forty, with one proviso: 'if I leave a child I give it £1000'. Less than two months later, while preaching at Joyners' Hall on Sunday afternoon, 1 March 1674, he was taken ill. He died on 10 March, aged about fifty-two, and was buried in Bunhill Fields; the funeral sermon was preached by his colleague Robert Bragge. *The Dead yet Speaking* (1674), *Venning's Remains, or, Christ's School* (1675), and *Mr Vennings Alarm to Unconverted Sinners* (1675) were the first of many posthumous editions of his works; some were still being reprinted even in the late nineteenth century.   STEPHEN WRIGHT

Sources *Calamy rev.*, 501–2 · Venn, *Alum. Cant.* · E. Calamy, ed., *An abridgement of Mr. Baxter's history of his life and times, with an account of the ministers, &c., who were ejected after the Restauration of King Charles II*, 2nd edn, 2 vols. (1713) · will, PRO, PROB 11/345, sig. 102 · *Calendar of the correspondence of Richard Baxter*, ed. N. H. Keeble and G. F. Nuttall, 2 vols. (1991) · B. Capp, *Cromwell's navy: the fleet and the English revolution, 1648–1660* (1989); pbk repr. (1992) · Wing, *STC*

Likenesses W. Hollar, etching, 1674, BM, NPG, V&A; repro. in R. Venning, *Venning's remains* (1675)

Wealth at death over £1000: will, PRO, PROB 11/345, sig. 102

Venning, Walter (1781–1821), philanthropist, was born at Totnes, Devon, on 15 November 1781, the youngest of three sons born to his father, Walter, a local merchant, and his wife, Mary Ann. He followed his two brothers to Totnes grammar school and thence to Jackson & Co., a London banking house with interests in St Petersburg, Russia. In 1799 he joined his brother John *Venning (1776–1858) at the St Petersburg branch of the company and remained there until 1807, when he returned to London. In 1810 he experienced an evangelical conversion, the impact of which was deepened by his mother's death in 1811. On 6 September 1811 he joined the Independents. He never married.

In 1815 the Gurney, Hoare, and Fry evangelical Quaker banking interests coalesced to form the London-based Society for the Improvement of Prison Discipline; Walter Venning became intensely involved with this society, which was established to implement the prison reformer John Howard's recommendations following his revelations of appalling conditions prevailing in prisons throughout Europe. He had argued that prisons should be rigorously supervised by the public authorities and administered according to proper health practices, with the provision of work, exercise, pastoral care, and aftercare, and appropriate classification of all prisoners.

Walter Venning returned to St Petersburg in 1817, where he influenced the conversion of his brother John. It was a propitious time for his mission: Tsar Alexander I was deeply committed to a mystical vision of vernacular scripture and Western-style philanthropy underpinning an ultra-conservative Christian society. This emphasis on the living word of God led him to support the British and Foreign Bible Society in its crusade to make the vernacular Bible available to every family in Russia. Indeed, at this time it was *de rigueur* for any aspiring Russian politician or aristocrat to be seen to be engaged in such work.

In 1817 Walter Venning was introduced by Revd John Paterson of the Bible Society to the Russian court and this led to a meeting with Prince Galitzin, one of Alexander's most influential ministers. Walter Venning was allowed to visit the prisons of St Petersburg and to report directly to Alexander. In 1818 he was invited to report on the prisons of Moscow; his report was translated into Russian by Princess Meshchersky. In this widely read document he depicted the prisons as grossly neglected and abusive environments: corruptly administered, full of dirt, violence, and drunkenness, they housed prisoners dying of preventable disease without any programmes of spiritual or moral reform or training for release. In the spring of 1819 the tsar agreed to the establishment of a Prison Discipline Society in St Petersburg, comprising Russians and British and other expatriates. On 5 May 1819 he visited the Venning brothers and showed much interest in the design of a model prison, based on John Howard's plans but adapted to the Russian climate. At the same time Walter

Venning was working with Princess Meshchersky to introduce Ladies' Visiting Committees to women prisoners in St Petersburg, in imitation of Elizabeth Fry's work. Some success was achieved in transforming places of terror and abuse into sober and ordered establishments offering employment and religious instruction.

Venning was also concerned with the Russian Bible Society and the Lancaster schools movement, which was introducing the monitorial teaching system in Russia. In 1818 the Quakers William Allen and Stephen Grellet visited Alexander, whom they had met in England four years earlier, and they criticized Russian Lancaster schools for teaching French philosophical writings and other secular texts which they viewed as seditious. Venning played a major role in setting up two Lancaster schools for scriptural and moral education in St Petersburg, one for poor Russian boys and one for expatriates, to ensure a proper religious and moral basis to this kind of education.

Just before these schools opened Walter Venning died at his brother John's home in St Petersburg on 10 January 1821 of typhoid, probably contracted while visiting prisoners. He was buried at the city's English chapel and a bronze monument erected in his memory. He was remembered for his intense enthusiasm for evangelical Christianity and prison reform. He had committed his life to the belief that the rich and powerful would find the true Christ in stewardship of the dispossessed, the poor, and the lost; by their good works they would create a truly Christian society united in charity, obligation, gratitude, and obedience. His work was continued by his brother John.   BILL FORSYTHE

Sources R. Knill, *Memoir of the life and character of W. Venning* (1822) • T. S. Henderson, *Memorials of John Venning esq.* (1862) • *Reports of the Committee of the Society for the Improvement of Prison Discipline, and Reformation of Juvenile Offenders*, 8 vols. (1818–32) • B. Hollingsworth, 'John Venning and prison reform in Russia, 1819–1830', *Slavonic and East European Review*, 48 (1970), 537–56 • J. C. Zacek, 'The Lancastrian schools movement in Russia', *Slavonic and East European Review*, 45 (1967), 343–67 • J. C. Zacek, 'The Russian Bible Society and the Orthodox church', *Church History*, 35 (1966), 411–37 • J. C. Zacek, 'The Imperial Philanthropic Society in the reign of Alexander I', *Canadian–American Slavic Studies*, 9/4 (1975), 427–36 • A. McConnell, *Tsar Alexander I: paternalistic reformer* (1970) • E. M. Almedrige, *The Emperor Alexander I* (1964) • B. H. Sumner, *Survey of Russian history* (1961) • private information (1997)
Likenesses R. Cooper, portrait, *c*.1820, repro. in Knill, *Memoir*

Vennor, Henry George (1840–1884), geologist and meteorologist, was born on 30 December 1840 in Montreal, Lower Canada, the son of Henry Vennor, hardware merchant, and his wife, Marion Paterson. He was educated at Philips School and the high school in Montreal before enrolling at McGill University in the late 1850s. There Vennor studied civil engineering, geology, mineralogy, and zoology under professors including Sir John William Dawson and Thomas Sterry Hunt, while simultaneously taking chemistry at the Montreal Medical College. After graduating with honours in 1860, he spent five years in the employ of the mercantile firm of Frothingham and Workman.

From an early age it became evident that Vennor possessed the aptitude and interests to be a naturalist. While still a schoolboy, he had assembled a collection of local reptiles (mostly snakes), preserved in alcohol and displayed at a provincial exhibition; it eventually became the property of McGill University. Part of his leisure time was devoted also at this time to studying the weather and amassing large collections of the birds and fossils of Montreal Island. By 1865 he had several papers on the ornithology of Canada published in the *Canadian Naturalist* and the *British American Magazine*. This was followed, in 1876, by the appearance of his book *Our Birds of Prey, or, The Eagles, Hawks, and Owls of Canada*.

Five years after graduating from college, Vennor embarked on a career in geology, working under Sir William Edmond Logan, director of the geological survey of Canada, on a survey of Manitoulin Island in Lake Huron. During this time his zeal as an amateur naturalist drove him to gather, in his free time, a collection of the birds he encountered, a collection subsequently donated to Queen's College, Kingston. In 1866 Vennor became a permanent staff member of the survey and began to develop detailed topographical maps of south-eastern Ontario and Pontiac county, Quebec. It was there that he conducted the majority of his field work during his years with the survey. In 1867 he published a ground-breaking paper on the stratigraphy of the Precambrian Shield in the Hastings county area in the *Quarterly Journal of the Geological Society of London* (23/1, 256–7); he was elected a fellow of the society in 1870. While mapping the geographical distributions of the Laurentian Mountains, he began to record in detail the economically significant mineral and metal deposits in the region. In the process, he discovered Precambrian gold in a mine in Hastings county in 1866. Initially he down-played the importance of this find, but it nevertheless led to a brief gold rush in the region.

Throughout his career Vennor actively promoted the interests of local mining operators and he was instrumental in directing their attention to the phosphate deposits in Ottawa county as early as 1872, a mining industry which boomed during the 1880s and remained profitable long thereafter. He continued to work for the geological survey on projects that traced the Precambrian formations of the Laurentian Mountains; he reported his findings in seven reports for the geological survey of Canada. Partly because these reports were never published, he came into conflict with Alfred Richard Cecil Selwyn, who was the survey's director from 1869 to 1895. The two men quarrelled frequently over working conditions and the preferential advancement of a younger generation of geologists, such as George Mercer Dawson, over the more experienced members of the survey. Vennor continued, meanwhile, to focus his efforts on promoting the economic development of local minerals until, in 1881, he was 'dismissed for using his position to traffic in phosphate lands in the Ottawa valley' (Zaslow, 136). He subsequently opened a consulting office in Montreal.

Over the years, Vennor developed a personal interest in

meteorology. Interested in weather forecasting, he compiled and compared data on weather patterns and believed that he had detected a 'law of recurrences' which allowed for a degree of predictability. After successfully forecasting Montreal's excessively mild Christmas and new year's day in 1875, he decided to begin publishing *Vennor's Almanac* annually from 1877. This venture was so successful in terms of distribution and critical acclaim that by 1881 he not only issued a separate American edition, but he also published *Vennor's Weather Bulletin* monthly throughout 1882 and part of 1883. Vennor died in Montreal on 8 June 1884 and was buried two days later. Walter Smith, who continued to publish the almanac after Vennor's death, claimed in the 1885 edition that Vennor was survived by a wife and three children, but no mention of them is made in any contemporary obituaries. TRENT A. MITCHELL

Sources M. Zaslow, *Reading the rocks: the story of the geological survey of Canada* (1975) · DCB, vol. 11 · J. G. Wilson and J. Fiske, eds., *Appleton's cyclopaedia of American biography*, 6 (1889), 276–77 · *The Gazette* [Montreal] (9 June 1884) · *The Examiner* [Charlottetown] (14 June 1884) · *Dominion Annual Register* (1884)
Archives Blacker Wood Library, Montreal, MSS

Ventners, Lawrence (*c.*1880–1947), bookmaker, was a well-known figure in the Garscube Road area of Glasgow, but nothing is known about his birth or parents. In common with a significant number of other bookies locally, Ventners was a Roman Catholic. He was popularly known as Lawrie.

Since the passing of the Betting Houses Act in 1853 it had been unlawful to accept bets for cash in premises away from a racecourse. Bookmakers evaded the law by taking bets on the street, a practice which was outlawed by the Street Betting Act of 1906. To avoid capture by the police, bookies then moved their operations into more secluded spots, and Ventners, like other Glasgow bookmakers, worked in closes, the entrances to tenement buildings. These were well used and easily approached by 'punters' (betters) but they could be well guarded by 'watchers' (look-outs).

In a city rent by sectarianism and discrimination bookmakers, like public house owners, 'came disproportionately from among the first or second generation Irish Catholic immigrants' (McGlennan to Chinn, letter 1, 2). Condemned by establishment leaders in church and local government (but not by the Roman Catholic church) as immoral and unchristian, bookies were also depicted as parasites who leached off the working class and who encouraged unwise expenditure. Yet the life of Lawrie Ventners is in stark contrast to that bleak and unflattering portrayal. Ordinary Glaswegians, according to later oral testimony, looked on him as 'the "patron saint" of the neighbourhood' (Ditty to Chinn, letter 2, 2). He was recalled as being a man 'who was always helping someone with their financial troubles'; and when he died 'the streets were black with mourners' (Moir to Chinn, letter 2, 5; *Daily Record* cutting). This positive view of Ventners was emphasized by a reporter who witnessed his funeral: the crowd was so great that mourners were six to eight deep

on both sides of the street for its whole length. Every window was crammed with spectators and special police were on duty. The reporter learned that this was not just a gathering of Ventners' clients, it was 'the massed tribute of his friends, the humble folk of Garscube Road and the congested area around'. People spoke of how Ventners had sent food to families in difficulties, of how he had saved others from eviction, and of how 'every week without fail a cripple received an envelope with enough in it to keep a roof over his head' (*Sunday Sun*, 15 June 1947).

A latter-day Robin Hood and working-class 'folk hero', Lawrie Ventners died in June 1947 and was buried in Glasgow on 15 June 1947. CARL CHINN

Sources *Sunday Sun* (15 June 1947) · Vince McGlennan, letter 1; Wilson Ditty, letter 2 [incl. cutting from the *Daily Record*]; John Moir, letter 2, U. Birm. L., special collections department, Carl Chinn bookmaking letters · C. Chinn, *Better betting with a decent feller: bookmakers, betting and the British working class, 1750–1990* (1991)

Ventris, Michael George Francis (1922–1956), architect and classical scholar, was born at Wheathampstead, Hertfordshire, on 12 July 1922, the only child of Edward Francis Vereker Ventris, an officer in the Indian army, and his wife, Dora Janasz, who was partly of Polish descent. He was educated at Stowe School, and went in 1940 to the Architectural Association school in London. He served as a navigator in the Royal Air Force during the Second World War, and married in 1942 Lois Elizabeth, daughter of Hugh William Knox-Niven, lieutenant-colonel, with whom he had a son and a daughter. After the war he completed his training as an architect, taking his diploma with honours in 1948. He worked as a member of the Ministry of Education development group of schools branch, and together with his wife designed their own house in Hampstead. His work had already attracted notice, and a brilliant career as an architect had been predicted for him. In 1956 he was awarded the first research fellowship offered by the *Architects' Journal*.

Ventris's fame, however, was the product of his hobby. From childhood he had been keenly interested in languages and scripts—at preparatory school in Switzerland he ran a club called La Kaboule—and a lecture by Sir Arthur Evans turned his attention at the age of fourteen to the problem of the undeciphered Minoan scripts. These, called by Evans Linear A and Linear B, were written on clay tablets by the prehistoric inhabitants of Crete and mainland Greece. The Linear B script, which Ventris eventually deciphered, may be dated roughly between 1400 and 1200 BC.

Ventris began by proposing, when only eighteen, in an article published in the *American Journal of Archaeology* for 1940, that the language was related to Etruscan; and he clung to this mistaken idea until his work forced him to recognize the existence of Greek in the texts. Returning to the problem after the war, he corresponded with the chief scholars all over the world who were working in this field, and circulated month by month reports on his own work. The publication in 1951 of the tablets found at Pylos in south-west Greece in 1939 provided him with a great increase of material, and his systematic analysis of this was the foundation of his success. The graphic system consists of about ninety syllabic signs, supplemented by numerals and rough pictograms, representing persons, objects, and commodities. Painstaking work combined with imaginative skill enabled him to establish connections between the syllabic signs, so that many of them could be linked as sharing the same vowel. In this way he built up a table, or 'grid' as he called it, showing the relationship of the signs before any had been given a phonetic value.

All that was then necessary was to find the values of a few signs, which would automatically determine the linked signs. This vital step was taken by means of some words which Ventris identified as Cretan place names; and the substitution of these values in other words immediately suggested a Greek interpretation. The Greek solution was first tentatively suggested in a privately circulated note dated 1 June 1952, and repeated with more confidence and examples in a broadcast talk a month later. He at once sought the help of Greek scholars in developing his theory, which he published with the collaboration of a young Cambridge academic, John Chadwick, as 'Evidence for Greek dialect in the Mycenean archives' (*Journal of Hellenic Studies*, 73, 1953, 84–103). The theory was at first treated with some scepticism, but within a year of the first announcement a new tablet was published which strikingly confirmed the values already proposed. This proof was accepted by the great majority of Greek scholars.

Ventris's only printed book was *Documents in Mycenaean Greek* (1956), again with the collaboration of Chadwick, which was on the point of publication at the time of his death. His achievement ranks not only with the great decipherments of the nineteenth century, with Grotefend, Rawlinson, and Champollion; but also with the archaeological discoveries of Schliemann and Evans, in opening up a new vista in Greek history. The demonstration that Greek was already spoken in Greece in the Mycenaean age was a satisfying confirmation of generally held views; but theories of the relationship of Crete and the mainland have had to be drastically revised. Knowledge of the Mycenaean dialect has thrown new light on the history of the Greek language; and the study of Mycenaean institutions as revealed by the tablets has provided much new material for comparison with Homer.

Ventris was appointed OBE in 1955; the University of Uppsala conferred upon him an honorary doctorate, and University College, London, made him an honorary research associate. In spite of honours he remained modest and unassuming; cheerful, witty, and versatile, he was never too busy to answer a request for help or to listen to a suggestion. His charm and skill as a linguist made him popular at international meetings.

Ventris was killed in an accident on the Barnet bypass, Hatfield, Hertfordshire, while driving alone in his car in the early hours of the morning of 6 September 1956. A fund was opened to create a studentship in his memory to encourage his two chief interests: architecture and Mycenaean civilization; and he was posthumously awarded the Kenyon medal for classical studies by the British Academy.   JOHN CHADWICK, *rev.*

Sources *The Times* (8 Sept 1956) · *The Times* (10 Sept 1956) · *The Times* (17 Sept 1956) · J. Chadwick, *The decipherment of Linear B* (1958) · private information (1971) · personal knowledge (1971) · M. Ventris and J. Chadwick, *Documents in Mycenaean Greek* (1956) · *CGPLA Eng. & Wales* (1956)

Archives U. Oxf., Sackler Library, notes on Minoan language

Wealth at death £72,761 11s. 9d.: probate, 5 Dec 1956, *CGPLA Eng. & Wales*

Ventris, Sir Peyton (1645–1691), judge and politician, was born in November 1645, the first surviving son of Edward Ventris (*d.* 1649) of the manor of Granhams in Great Shelford, Cambridgeshire, and of Mary, daughter of Sir John Brewse of Little Wenham, Suffolk, where Ventris was born. His father, a barrister of the Middle Temple, took no part in the civil war though he did profit from it, as he purchased his manor in 1646 from a compounding royalist. He died in 1649, leaving the bulk of his property to his eldest son, Peyton.

Ventris entered Jesus College, Cambridge, on 4 July 1660 and proceeded, without taking a degree, to the Middle Temple on 3 February 1664. He was called to the bar on 2 June 1671 and kept a chamber in Fleet Street above the Great Gate of the Middle Temple. Ventris enjoyed little success as a pleader. Having begun noting cases while a student, he now turned to reporting for his livelihood. The result was two volumes of reports, principally of arguments in king's bench and common pleas, published posthumously in 1696 and in many editions thereafter owing to their reputation for clarity, comprehensiveness, and accuracy.

Ventris married Margaret, the daughter and coheir of Henry Whiting, a shipowner of Coggeshall, Essex, and of Ipswich. They had five sons and one daughter. Ventris established his family in St Nicholas's parish, Ipswich, where in 1681 he became the town clerk and one of three counsel to the corporation. In July 1684 he lost these offices when his name was omitted from the town's new charter, perhaps owing to accusations that he had countenanced conventicles and because he had defended dissenters in king's bench. Despite apparent royal disfavour, Ventris was made a justice of the peace for Suffolk in 1685. His fortunes improved further when he inherited extensive properties from his father-in-law in 1687.

Ventris came to prominence only after the revolution of 1688. He was chosen to one of Ipswich's seats in the Convention Parliament in January 1689, where he reportedly voted against declaring the throne vacant by virtue of James II's departure from England. In his only recorded parliamentary speech Ventris defended the hereditary royal revenue. Ventris, along with other more prominent lawyers, took the oath as a serjeant-at-law on 2 May 1689. Two days later the king made him a justice of common pleas; a knighthood followed on 31 October 1689.

Like other justices, Ventris was often asked to comment

on legal cases heard in the House of Lords and on proposed legislation that would affect the operation of the law. But Ventris's recorded statements, both in court and in parliament, were few and brief compared to those of the more prominent jurists with whom he served. After a long illness Ventris died on 6 April 1691 at his house in Ipswich and was buried in the chancel of St Nicholas's Church, survived by his wife, his mother, five sons, and a daughter. Why Ventris, who had done little to distinguish himself professionally, had been advanced to the bench remains unclear, though his *Reports* endure as among the most important written during the Restoration.

PAUL D. HALLIDAY

Sources N. Luttrell, *A brief historical relation of state affairs from September 1678 to April 1714*, 6 vols. (1857) · HoP, *Commons, 1660–90* · Foss, *Judges*, 7.367–9 · Venn, *Alum. Cant.* · 'Ipswich in 1689', *N&Q*, 208 (1963), 48 · J. J. Muskett, *Suffolk manorial families* (1908), 129–30 · will, PRO, PROB 11/404 [also in Muskett, 130–31], 206v–207 · C. T. Martin, ed., *Minutes of parliament of the Middle Temple*, 4 vols. (1904–5) · J. Wodderspoon, *Memorials of the ancient town of Ipswich* (1850) · J. Hutchinson, ed., *A catalogue of notable Middle Templars: with brief biographical notices* (1902), 248 · *CSP dom., 1683–4; 1690–91* · VCH Cambridgeshire and the Isle of Ely, 8.211
Likenesses R. White, line engraving, 1696 (after J. Riley), BM, NPG; repro. in *The reports of Sir Peyton Ventris* (1696) · J. Riley, oils, Middle Temple, London
Wealth at death lands in Cambridgeshire, Essex, and Suffolk: will, PRO, PROB 11/404, fols. 206v–207

Venturi [*née* Ashurst], **Emilie** (1819/20?–1893), campaigner for women's rights and supporter of Italian independence, was probably born in 1819 or 1820, the youngest daughter of William Henry *Ashurst (d. 1855), a solicitor, and his wife, Elizabeth Ann, *née* Brown (d. 1854), of Muswell Hill, Middlesex. Elizabeth Ann *Ashurst, Caroline *Stansfeld, and Matilda Ashurst *Biggs were her sisters. Her father was a supporter of radical causes and his political sympathy for the rights of women was a central influence upon all his daughters.

William Ashurst wanted his daughters to have a practical education and Emilie received informal training as a legal clerk in his offices. Here she met Sydney Hawkes, a friend of James *Stansfeld who married her sister Caroline in 1844. She herself married Hawkes in the same year. In July the Ashurst family established contact with the Italian republican exile Giuseppe Mazzini, who became a close and intimate friend of all the sisters, but perhaps of Emilie most of all. She had shown a talent for drawing, portraiture in particular, and in 1846 was apprenticed to the artist Frank Stone. However, both she and her family were now actively involved in the cause of an independent Italian republic. In August 1846 she and Sydney travelled to Paris with her sister Caroline to make contact with exiled Italian supporters of Mazzini and establish a secret postal network. This clandestine work continued throughout the 1840s and 1850s. In the winter of 1848 she travelled in disguise across the Alps to bring money raised in England to the short-lived republican government in Rome. In the late 1840s she had also become Mazzini's literary and financial secretary in London. While she was immersed in the secret world of Italian republicanism,

and perhaps as a result of this, her marriage to Hawkes had begun to deteriorate. During 1850–51 Emilie lived in Genoa with her sister Matilda and studied under Fraschieri, president of the Genoa Academy of Painting. By 1854 an unsuccessful venture in the brewing industry had left Hawkes bankrupt. He had also started another relationship and was seeking a divorce. For Emilie the strain of this and of caring for her parents before their deaths brought on severe bouts of depression. With the family home at Muswell Hill gone, in 1857 she considered living with the freethinker G. J. Holyoake and his family. This came to nothing, but Holyoake helped her to sell some of her portraits: in 1846 she had painted Mazzini for his mother and in the 1850s she completed portraits of Ledru-Rollin and Kossuth. To Mazzini she poured out her sorrows: in October 1858 he replied:

> Your note, dearest Emilie … is one of the saddest you have ever written to me. To speak of yourself quietly as a dead person, to declare that even Art has lost its hold upon you, to say that you can neither love nor feel love, is nearly crushing to me. (*Mazzini's Letters to an English Family*, 2.112)

But there remained Emilie's work in the cause of Italy. After the failure of the republican movement in 1848–9, support in England was put on a more permanent footing with the creation in 1851 of the Society of the Friends of Italy, and Emilie was one of the original seventy-five women members of its council. Some Italian exiles resented her influence with Mazzini, notably Felice Orsini, one of Mazzini's paid agents, whose slanderous remarks towards her in the summer of 1858 were intercepted by James Stansfeld and led to a quarrel. When Orsini suggested that he and Stansfeld should meet in Belgium to settle the matter by a duel, Mazzini sent Orsini abroad, where, thoroughly alienated, he organized an assassination attempt on Napoleon III.

In the autumn of 1859, while on a visit to Italy, Emilie met Carlo Venturi, a Tyrolese Venetian who had deserted from the Austrian army in 1848 at the age of eighteen and fled to South America. Later he had fought with Garibaldi and risen to the rank of major. Their relationship soon blossomed. However, Venturi's situation in Italy was not safe and he hoped to return to South America. To prevent this, Mazzini employed him in Tyrol and Trentino in observation and map-making—he was an intelligence officer by training. Emilie returned to London, having learned that her divorce from Hawkes had at last been finalized, and she and Venturi were married in England on 6 June 1861. There they remained while Venturi kept himself in readiness for a call from Garibaldi to return to fight in Italy. Their financial situation was precarious and in September 1865 Carlo travelled to Milan to meet his family to secure financial support, but was rebuffed. He died of heart disease on 26 March 1866 aged thirty-six, while they were staying with friends in Wimbledon.

During the 1860s Emilie, who after Carlo's death was known as Madame Venturi, was fully engaged as Mazzini's literary editor. In 1862 she published *The Duties of Man*, a translation of his treatise, with the intention of bringing his ideas to a more popular audience. She was also involved in preparing an English translation of his collected writings, published in six volumes between 1864 and 1870. She also published several articles on Mazzini, including 'Joseph Mazzini: what he has done for Italy', which appeared in the *Contemporary Review* of October 1870. After Mazzini's death in 1872, she wrote a memoir of him, with two of his essays appended. Over the years she had collected his letters to her family. These were published in 1920–22 by her friend Elinor Richards as *Mazzini's Letters to an English Family, 1844–72* (in three volumes).

After Carlo Venturi's death Emilie lived in Carlyle Square, Chelsea, where she kept a political salon which attracted many celebrities of the time. She was an early supporter of Irish home rule and regarded the Irish leader Parnell as a second Mazzini. Her friend Justin McCarthy included a description of her in his *Portraits of the Sixties*:

> A wealth of hair, black in youth and silvery white in later years, was drawn back from a forehead that noted great intellectual powers, and well-marked eyebrows lent additional character to eyes whose direct, honest, fearless gaze made a lasting impression upon almost all who came into contact.   (McCarthy, 333)

Throughout her life a chronic respiratory condition kept her in poor health, yet she remained politically active. From the late 1860s she turned her energy towards domestic political questions. Like her sisters she was a lifelong advocate of female suffrage. In May 1866 she helped to organize the petition which John Stuart Mill presented to parliament. She was a prominent supporter of the campaign to repeal the Contagious Diseases Acts; these had created special powers in the naval and garrison towns for the compulsory medical inspection and treatment of women in lock hospitals. In 1869 she joined the executive of the Ladies' National Association for Repeal, led by Josephine Butler, and from 1871 to 1886 she edited the campaign's organ, *The Shield*. She played an important role in the successful campaign to reject the 1872–3 compromise bill of the home secretary, Henry Austin Bruce, and supported the parliamentary leadership of the campaign by James Stansfeld which led to the final victory of 1886. Between 1871 and 1883 she was a member of the Vigilance Association for the Defence of Personal Rights (and for the amendment of the law in points wherein it is injurious to women).

From 1876 Emilie was a member of the executive committee of the campaign to reform the married women's property law. This led in 1882 to legislation establishing the principle that married women should enjoy the same rights over property as unmarried women, and that husbands and wives should have separate interests in their property. Her interest in this question led her to take a more advanced position on the suffrage question. The National Society for Women's Suffrage had for many years supported a measure of reform aimed at enfranchising women who held the current property qualification; this effectively limited the measure to widows and spinsters who were ratepayers. In 1889 Emilie joined the newly founded Women's Franchise League (WFL), led by Elizabeth Wolstenholme Elmy, also a prominent figure in the Married Women's Property Committee. The WFL took the view that since married women now enjoyed equal rights to property they should enjoy the right to vote on the same basis. But a claim on behalf of all women was seen to imply universal adult suffrage, a step the national society was not yet prepared to embrace, on grounds of political expediency.

Venturi also engaged in small-scale philanthropic efforts to help women: with her sister Matilda she established a rescue home for prostitutes in Leicester.

Emilie Venturi was the author of two novels. Drawing on her Italian experiences, in 1871 she wrote a story entitled 'A Dull Day' which was circulated privately, about an Englishwoman who witnesses the escape of an Italian patriot. The second, *The Owl's Nest in the City: a Story*, published in 1876 under the pseudonym Edward Lovel, was apparently written in two weeks after a wager with Jane Carlyle that she could write a novel about love without revealing the sex of the author.

Emilie Venturi died of jaundice at her residence, 318 King's Road, Chelsea, on 16 March 1893, and was buried in the family plot at Highgate cemetery.

JONATHAN SPAIN

Sources *Mazzini's letters to an English family*, ed. E. F. Richards, 3 vols. (1920–22) · *Scritti editi ed inediti di Giuseppe Mazzini*, 94 vols. (Imola, 1906–43) · *Annual Register* (1893) · J. McCabe, *Life and letters of George Jacob Holyoake*, 1 (1908), 140, 287; 2 (1908), 202 · D. Mack Smith, *Mazzini* (1994) · M. St J. Packe, *The bombs of Orsini* (1957) · E. A. Daniels, *Jessie White Mario: Risorgimento revolutionary* (1972) · H. W. Rudman, *Italian nationalism and English letters* (1940) · J. W. Mario, *The birth of modern Italy* (1909) · J. L. Hammond and B. Hammond, *James Stansfeld: a Victorian champion of sexual equality* (1932) · J. McCarthy, *Portraits of the sixties* (1903) · J. R. Walkowitz, *Prostitution and Victorian society: women, class and the state* (1980) · L. Holcombe, *Wives and property: reform of married women's property law in nineteenth-century England* (1983) · O. Banks, *The biographical dictionary of British feminists*, 1 (1985) · P. Levine, *Victorian feminism, 1850–1900* (1987) · d. cert.
Likenesses portrait, repro. in Richards, ed., *Mazzini's letters to an English family*, vol. 1, p. 142 · portrait, repro. in Richards, ed., *Mazzini's letters to an English family*, vol. 3, p. 10
Wealth at death £3842 6s. 6d.: administration, 18 May 1893, CGPLA Eng. & Wales

Venutius (*fl.* AD 51–*c.*71), king in Britain, was a man of high rank, of the tribe of the Brigantes, which during the Roman period in Britain occupied almost the whole of the area from the Humber to the line of Hadrian's Wall, with the exception of what is now south-east Yorkshire and with the possible addition of territory in south-west Scotland. He was married to *Cartimandua, queen of the Brigantes. The Roman historian Tacitus, in his account of this period, the *Annals*, singles out Venutius as the outstanding British general after the capture of Caratacus in AD 51 and a man who had long been loyal to Rome, and protected by her, as noted in an earlier passage. This earlier reference to Venutius is not extant, so it must have been in the lost part of Tacitus, for AD 43–7. It may be assumed that Cartimandua's alliance with Rome, supported by Venutius, dated from the invasion in AD 43 or not long after. Venutius then quarrelled with Cartimandua; his brother and relations were captured by her; and an invasion of

Cartimandua's kingdom was launched as a response by a war band led by Venutius, presumably from the north, since Rome held the south. Roman forces were involved in supporting their ally, the queen, and were in the end successful in repelling the invasion. These events took place under the governor Didius Gallus, whose term of office was AD 52–7.

Tacitus had already written the history of the years AD 69–96 in the *Histories*, and in that account the story of Venutius and Cartimandua and its end is told in highly compressed form. Here it was the glory of having handed over Caratacus to the Romans that led to Cartimandua increasing in wealth and extravagance. She rejected Venutius in favour of his armour bearer Vellocatus, whom she took as her new consort. Venutius summoned allies and the Brigantes themselves revolted. Cartimandua sought support from Rome; she was rescued; but the kingdom was left to Venutius, with war against the Brigantes inevitable when Rome's hands were freed from the civil war in AD 69 that had given Venutius his opportunity. The story as told in the *Histories* seems at first to imply a much shorter time scale than the story in the *Annals*, but the beginning of the trouble is clearly stated to be not long after the capture of Caratacus and the final triumph of Venutius linked to the opportunity offered by Roman civil war in AD 69. It would appear, therefore, that Venutius nursed his grievances in exile from the early AD 50s to 69.

Sir Mortimer Wheeler thought that he had located Venutius's stronghold in the great defended enclosure at Stanwick, in north Yorkshire. More recent work and thinking rejects this notion and that of a 'battle of Stanwick' and sees Stanwick as an *oppidum*, a proto-urban centre, receiving luxury items from the Roman world, and therefore much more probably to be linked to the pro-Roman queen Cartimandua.

In Tacitus's terse description in the *Agricola* of the conquest of the Brigantes by Petillius Cerialis, there is no reference to Venutius. There may be one other reference, by the poet Statius, eulogizing the achievements of an earlier governor of Britain, Vettius Bolanus (AD 69–71), for the benefit of Bolanus's son and referring to the trophies Bolanus dedicated in Britain, among them the breastplate which he took from a British king. As it was Bolanus who rescued Cartimandua, it may not be too fanciful to see here a reference to Venutius. If so, Venutius survived this encounter, perhaps to perish in fighting against Cerialis, governor from AD 71 to 73 or 74.　　BRIAN DOBSON

Sources C. Tacitus, *The annals of imperial Rome*, ed. and trans. M. Grant, rev. edn (1989), 12, 40 · C. Tacitus, *The histories*, ed. and trans. K. Wellesley (1964), 3–5 · *Tacitus on Britain and Germany: a new translation of 'The Agricola' and 'The Germania'*, ed. and trans. H. Mattingley (1948); rev. as *The Agricola; and the Germania*, rev. S. A. Handford [1971] · Statius, *Silvae*, trans. D. A. Slater (1908)

Verax. *See* Gould, Nathaniel (1857–1919).

Verax, Theodorus. *See* Walker, Clement (d. 1651).

Verbruggen, Jan (*bap.* 1712, *d.* 1781), gun-founder, was baptized on 4 March 1712 in Enkhuizen in the Netherlands, but little is known about his origins or early years. He was taught by the Dutch seascapist Jan van Call the younger. He married Eva van Schaak (*d. c.*1739) in 1734; they had three children. Appointed master founder of the Dutch admiralty's Enkhuizen cannon foundry in 1740, in 1754 Verbruggen also took over the recently modernized state ordnance foundry at The Hague. However, after a few years he was suspended because of accusations of hiding flaws in guns.

In 1763 Verbruggen offered his services to the British government, without success; yet by 1769 circumstances had changed in Britain. Andrew Schalch, master founder, scarcely cast any guns, while, more seriously, the Board of Ordnance's two contract founders, Richard Gilpin and William Bowen, were reaching the end of their careers. It appeared that within a year there would be no one in Britain capable of casting brass guns. On 12 January 1770, in consequence, Jan and his son, Pieter [*see below*], were appointed master founders of the royal brass foundry at Woolwich at a joint wage of 12*s.* a day, the same rate as that at which Schalch had been engaged in 1718. They arrived in May 1770 and embarked on a programme to modernize the royal brass foundry. Their most important innovation was the introduction of horizontal boring for guns cast solid; previously guns were cast round a core and reamed out vertically. Solid boring for brass guns had been developed by the Swiss founder Jean Maritz in 1712 and adopted at The Hague in the 1750s. Other changes included rebuilding the furnaces and casting pits and the use of precast moulds for cascables, which permitted larger numbers of higher-quality guns to be cast more quickly.

The first Verbruggen guns passed proof in April 1774. Their cannon, mortars, and howitzers had a much better proof record than those of past founders. For the first time since its early years the royal brass foundry was able to provide all the brass guns required by the British services, and produced over one hundred guns a year during the American War of Independence. The Verbruggens carried out other services for the board, making machine parts, boring up foreign guns, and analysing metal from brass and iron guns.

Jan Verbruggen died at Woolwich on 27 October 1781 and was buried in the Dutch church at Austin Friars in the City of London. His son, Pieter, continued as master founder. **Pieter Verbruggen** (1735–1786) was born on 12 March 1735 at Enkhuizen, in the Netherlands, and educated in law at the University of Leiden. He subsequently worked with his father at The Hague. Under Pieter Verbruggen the royal brass foundry reached its apogee, finishing a total of 237 guns in 1782. However, with the ending of the American war there was a severe reduction. In 1783 147 guns were cast, but between 1784 and Pieter's death the annual total never rose above 13. From October 1783 the skilled workforce assembled by the Verbruggens began to be dispersed. Moreover, Pieter was in dispute with the board over payments; in September 1785 he complained he had had no money since 1782. Pieter Verbruggen married Wynefrede Kooystra on 21 September 1785 at Austin Friars; they had no children. He died on 20 February the following year, at Woolwich. He also was buried at the Dutch church at Austin Friars. His sisters, Catherine and Maria, took two years to settle his affairs with the board and returned to the Netherlands. The Verbruggens had been training a successor, Frederick Groves from the drawing office at Plymouth. However, after Pieter Verbruggen's death the royal brass foundry was reorganized; the position of master founder was abolished and the foundry came under the control of Thomas Blomefield, inspector of artillery. Groves resigned in disappointment.

A remarkable series of water-colours depicting the royal brass foundry under the Verbruggens, which have often been attributed to Jan or Pieter, has survived in the possession of the family. However, the high standard of water-colour technique, use of perspective, and fine detail are unlike the conventional Dutch seascapes Jan normally painted. Moreover the drawings seem to depict father and son at work. A more likely attribution is to one of three water-colourists associated with the Board of Ordnance: Paul Sandby, professor of drawing at Woolwich; Thomas Sandby, from the drawing office in the Tower of London; or Michael Angelo Rooker, who carried out highly detailed engravings of experiments for the board in 1778.

RUTH RHYNAS BROWN

Sources M. H. Jackson and C. de Beer, *Eighteenth century gunfounding* (1973) · minute books, board of ordnance, 1763–88, PRO, WO 47/63–111 · bill books, quarter books, board of ordnance, 1770–87, PRO, WO 51/245–WO 52/11–26 · C. de Beer, *The art of gunfounding* (1991) · GM
Archives Semeijns de Vries van Doesburgh Foundation, Netherlands | Eliott Memorial, Gibraltar, guns · Fort Nelson, Hampshire, royal armouries, guns · Museo del Ejército, Madrid, Spain, guns · Museum of Artillery, Woolwich, guns · PRO, Board of Ordnance MSS · Tower of London, royal armouries, guns
Likenesses portraits, *c.*1777 (Jan Verbruggen and Peter Verbruggen; the Verbruggen drawings), Semeijns de Vries van Doesburgh Foundation, the Netherlands
Wealth at death board of ordnance paid daughters £2000 for guns and copper: bill books, PRO, WO 52/23 & 26

Verbruggen, John (1670?–1708). *See under* Verbruggen, Susanna (*bap.* 1666, *d.* 1703).

Verbruggen, Pieter (1735–1786). *See under* Verbruggen, Jan (*bap.* 1712, *d.* 1781).

Verbruggen [née Percival; *other married name* Mountfort], **Susanna** (*bap.* 1666, *d.* 1703), actress, was baptized on 29 July 1666 at St Giles Cripplegate, London, the daughter of Thomas Percival (*d.* 1693?), a minor actor–manager in the Duke's and United Company, and his wife, Anne Terry. Her first recorded appearance is as Winifred in Thomas D'Urfey's *Sir Barnaby Whig*, for the King's Company at Drury Lane Theatre in the summer of 1681. In a letter dated 1684 Dryden already refers to her as 'a Comedian', a title that remained appropriate for the United Company actress who played mostly comic roles in more than sixty new plays between 1681 and 1703. As early as 1686 she had progressed not only to playing Nell, the leading role in Thomas Jevon's *The Devil of a Wife*, but also to delivering the epilogue—an indication of her rising appeal and importance as an actress.

On 22 June 1686, at St James's, Duke's Place, Aldgate,

Susanna Percival married the actor and playwright William *Mountfort (*c.*1664–1692); they had at least four children, although only two—Susanna and Mary—reached adulthood. As Mrs Mountfort, Susanna continued to gain recognition for her comic acting as well as her ability to play breeches parts: 'a more adroit pretty Fellow than is usually seen upon the Stage' (Cibber, 166). The dedicatory epistle to *Sir Anthony Love* (1690), the play containing what was arguably her most notable breeches role, praises not only her acting skills, but suggests that Thomas Southerne wrote the role of Sir Anthony specifically for the actress: 'as I made every Line for her, she has mended every Word for me; and by a Gaiety and Air, particular to her Action, turn'd every thing into the Genius of the Character' (*Works of Thomas Southerne*, 1.14–20).

The opportunity afforded by Susanna's marriage to Mountfort was capitalized on in their appearances as a 'gay couple', a productive union which ended when Mountfort was murdered on 9 or 10 December 1692 by Captain Richard Hill, aided by Lord Mohun (who was found not guilty of murder in 1693). Following her husband's death Mrs Mountfort continued to act in comedies, creating, among others, the notable character of the old maid, Lady Susan Malepart, in *The Maid's Last Prayer* (1693), a 'Youthful Virgin of five and forty, with a selling Rump, bow Leggs, a shining Face, and colly'd Eyebrows … sure she's an Original' (*Works of Thomas Southerne*, 1.70–72).

On 31 January 1694 Mrs Mountfort married John Verbruggen [*see below*], a promising young actor, at St Clement Danes and some time afterwards moved to the parish of St Martin-in-the-Fields. As Mrs Verbruggen she became one of London's best comic actresses, earning, in the year she got married, 50s. a week. Her last recorded roles, in 1703, were Hillaria in Thomas Baker's *Tunbridge Wells* and Whimsey in Richard Estcourt's *The Fair Example*, the latter on 10 April. According to an account written by Thomas Davies, Mrs Verbruggen died in childbirth later that year. She was buried at St Martin-in-the-Fields on 2 September 1703 and the child, Lewis Vanbrugen, was buried the following October. Another child, John George Verbruggen, the son of John and Susanna, was baptized at St Clement Danes on 23 November 1708, although no birth record has been traced (Highfill, Burnim & Langhans, *BDA*).

Susanna Verbruggen, a contemporary of Mrs Bracegirdle, appears not only to have carved out her own niche during her career but, according to one recent critic, to have influenced the repertory of the time through a willingness and ability to play, in addition to the charming heroines, 'ugly, foolish and low-life characters' (Howe, 84). As Cibber remarks, 'she was so fond of Humour, in what low Part soever to be found, that she would make no scruple of defacing her fair Form to come heartily into it' (Cibber, 165–7). Although no portrait has been traced, Tony Aston offers a flattering image of her as 'the most pleasant creature that ever appeared … she was a fine, fair Woman, plump, full-featured; her Face of a fine, smooth Oval, full of beautiful, well-dispos'd Moles on it, and on her Neck and Breast' (Highfill, Burnim & Langhans, *BDA*). Her diverse roles, variously described as the coquette, the stale virgin, the hoyden, the minx, the bawd, and the comic grotesque, give some idea of the humorous stock characters conjured ably by the actress, suggesting that both her popularity and Cibber's praise were not undeserved:

> Mistress of more variety of Humour than I ever knew in any one Woman Actress. This variety, too, was attended with an equal Vivacity, which made her excellent in Characters extremely different. ... Nothing, tho' ever so barren, if within the Bounds of Nature, could be flat in her Hands. She gave many heightening Touches to Characters but coldly written, and often made an Author vain of his Work that in it self had but little Merit. (Cibber, 165–7)

John Verbruggen (1670?–1708), also said to have appeared under the name Alexander early in his career, is first recorded in United Company records in 1688. After his marriage in 1694 he appeared exclusively under his own name, playing such characters as Ambrosio in D'Urfey's *Don Quixote* (1694) and Loveless in Cibber's *Love's Last Shift* (1697). At Lincoln's Inn Fields (where he held a share) his repertory ranged from Wilmore in Aphra Behn's *The Rover* to Oroonoko in Southerne's *Oroonoko* and Edgar in *King Lear*. Described by Aston as tall, well-built, but 'a little In-kneed, which gave him a shambling Gate, which was a Carelessness, and became him', the actor, a rival to both George Powell and Thomas Betterton, was described as being a 'rough diamond', untrained but natural, and able to 'touch tenderly the finer feelings, as well as excite the wilder emotions of the heart' (Doran, 1.61). Verbruggen was buried on 12 March 1708 at St Martin-in-the-Fields.   DEIRDRE E. HEDDON

Sources Highfill, Burnim & Langhans, *BDA* · E. Howe, *The first English actresses: women and drama, 1660–1700* (1992) · C. Cibber, *An apology for the life of Mr. Colley Cibber*, new edn, ed. R. W. Lowe, 2 vols. (1889) · J. Doran, *'Their majesties' servants': annals of the English stage*, 2 vols. (1864) · Genest, *Eng. stage* · S. B. Wells, ed., *A comparison between the two stages: a late Restoration book of the theatre* (1942); repr. (1971) · *The works of Thomas Southerne*, ed. R. Jordan and H. Love, 1 (1988) · A. Nicoll, *A history of English drama, 1660–1900*, 6 vols. (1923–59) · P. Holland, *The ornament of action: text and performance in Restoration comedy* (1979) · C. Leech, T. W. Craik, L. Potter, and others, eds., *The Revels history of drama in English*, [another edn], 8 vols. (1996) · *DNB*

Verdon [Verdun], **Bertram de** (*d.* 1192), judge and administrator, was the son of Norman de Verdon and Luceline, daughter of Geoffrey of *Clinton, chamberlain to Henry I. He is mentioned as adhering to Henry II against his rebel sons in 1173. In 1175 and the three following years he was regularly present as a baron at the sittings of the *curia regis*, and from 1175 to 1179, and probably later, served as itinerant justice in eight counties. He was also sheriff of Warwickshire and Leicestershire from 1168 to 1183. In March 1177 he was sent with others of the king's counsellors by Henry to Fernando II, king of León, to negotiate and announce his intention of making a pilgrimage to Santiago de Compostela.

Verdon accompanied John to Ireland in 1185 and remained as his seneschal of Ireland after John's return to England in the same year. Gerald of Wales mentions staying with him in Dublin and his house remained a well-known landmark in Dublin throughout the middle ages. He was also appointed custodian of the castle of Drogheda

following Hugh de Lacy's death in 1186. While in Ireland John granted him lands equivalent to the baronies of Upper and Lower Dundalk in the modern co. Louth, although the earliest surviving record of this grant comes from the years 1189–91. He established a manor at the site now known as Castletown, west of the present town of Dundalk, with a parish church dedicated to St John the Baptist. He, or possibly his son Nicholas, founded a house for the Crutched Friars dedicated to St Leonard at Seatown in Dundalk itself. He left Ireland before the end of 1189.

Verdon continued in the service of Richard I, witnessing charters at Canterbury on 1 December 1189 and at Westminster in January 1190, and accompanied Richard to the Holy Land. He was surety for Richard's peace with Tancred of Sicily in November 1190 and witnessed a charter at Messina on 23 January 1191. He arrived in Palestine in June 1191, and on 21 August was left with Stephen de Longchamp in charge of Acre and the queens of England and Sicily, and the daughter of the emperor of Cyprus, while Richard proceeded towards Jerusalem. Verdon died the following year (1192) at Jaffa. Among other religious benefactions he founded in 1176 the Cistercian abbey of Croxden in Staffordshire, where his chief lands were.

Verdon's first wife was Maud, daughter of Robert de Ferrers, earl of Derby (*d.* 1159), with whom he had no children. He and his second wife, Rohese, had six sons of whom two, Thomas and Nicholas, succeeded in turn to his estates. His one daughter, Lesceline, married Hugh de *Lacy, later earl of Ulster (*d.* 1242). Nicholas's only daughter and heir, Rohese, married Theobald Butler, and was grandmother of Theobald de *Verdon.

     W. E. RHODES, *rev.* B. SMITH

Sources A. Gwynn and R. N. Hadcock, *Medieval religious houses: Ireland* (1970) · A. J. Otway-Ruthven, 'The partition of the de Verdon lands in Ireland in 1332', *Proceedings of the Royal Irish Academy*, 66C (1967–8), 401–45 · J. Burke, *A general and heraldic dictionary of the peerages of England, Ireland and Scotland, extinct, dormant, and in abeyance* (1831)

Verdon [Verdun], **Theobald de**, first Lord Verdon (1248?–1309), baron, was the youngest surviving son and heir of Sir John de Verdon, who had holdings in Buckinghamshire, Leicestershire, Wiltshire, Warwickshire, and Staffordshire, and of Margaret, daughter of Gilbert de Lacy (*d.* 1230), and granddaughter and coheir of Walter de *Lacy (*d.* 1241), lord of Meath in Ireland, Weobley, Herefordshire, and Ewyas Lacy, Shropshire. Theobald's two elder brothers, Nicholas and John, were killed in Ireland in 1271, when Theobald was said to have been twenty-three years old, so that when his father died in 1274, he inherited a substantial estate stretching from the marches of Wales to Ireland. As a result of his inheritance, over the next thirty years, Verdon divided his time between England and Ireland and gradually became embroiled in the politics of these turbulent regions.

John de Verdon had strong ties to the crown, fighting for the royalists during the barons' wars, serving on behalf of the Lord Edward in 1261–3, going on crusade with Edward in 1270–72, and serving again in Ireland on his return, when his son Theobald acted as his attorney in England.

After his father died, Theobald de Verdon continued this tradition of royal service. He was in Ireland after 1275 and was summoned to serve in Wales in 1277, 1282, and again in 1283. Verdon's men helped to transport victuals from Ireland to Wales to provision the royal army there in 1282. Verdon garnered some royal favours in these years. At his request, Nicholas de Netterville, his household knight in Ireland, was excused from royal administrative service in 1284. In that same year Verdon was granted special permission to receive his Irishmen into the king's peace, and also obtained the right to hold markets on a number of his Irish manors.

Verdon was summoned to parliament in 1275 and again in 1283, to discuss the capture of Dafydd ap Gruffudd. In 1290 he was among the magnates who granted an aid for the marriage of the king's daughter, and he was summoned regularly to parliament after 1295. In 1291 he and several other Irish lords graciously granted Edward a fifteenth of their moveables and of those of their men in Ireland.

Despite his loyal service Verdon later encountered problems with Edward I, beginning in Ireland. Henry III had seized Walter de Lacy's liberty of Meath, and some of those liberties had been restored to the coparceners of Lacy's estate, Geoffrey de Geneville and John de Verdon, Theobald's father. Geneville's liberties were more extensive than those assigned to John, and an inquest in 1266 stated that the Lord Edward would lose at least 400 marks a year if John's liberty was held as freely as Geneville's. When Verdon complained about his loss in 1279, another inquest was conducted upholding the earlier verdict, after which Edward seized all of Theobald's liberties in Meath.

At about that time Verdon was engaged in a long-running dispute with Llanthony Priory in the Welsh marches. The prior, who held a virgate of land of him, was summoned to Verdon's court to answer for a trespass. When the prior did not appear, Verdon's men seized cattle and other goods belonging to the prior, and refused to release them when the prior asked. The prior then brought a plea of trespass against Verdon accusing his men of a variety of misdeeds, including assault and homicide. Edward I intervened and ordered Verdon and his men not to vex the prior. But when the sheriff of Hereford and his men went to Verdon's court at Ewyas Lacy to investigate the matter, they were assaulted by Verdon's steward and a crowd of Welshmen, numbering 600 according to the aggrieved sheriff. The abbot of Combe similarly brought a plea of trespass in 1290 against Verdon, who in 1291 was swept up in the war between the earls of Gloucester and Hereford. In January 1291, along with other lords from the Anglo-Welsh marches, Verdon was summoned to testify about the conflict before royal justices. In March he duly appeared, and like the other lords refused to testify, claiming that the king's demand violated their liberties and the custom of the march. He similarly refused to allow his men to be impanelled as jurors.

Edward seized Verdon's lands to compel him to answer for his trespasses against Llanthony and his disobedience of royal orders. Having recovered his lands, in October 1291 he came before the king and council at Abergavenny, at the same time that the earls of Gloucester and Hereford were arraigned. Like them, Verdon was found guilty, and was ordered to appear before the king and council in parliament in January 1292 for judgment. Edward was at first harsh. Verdon was committed to gaol, and forever disinherited of his liberty of Ewyas Lacy. Yet Edward relented. On account of the good services that Verdon and his ancestors had performed for the king, and because Verdon had voluntarily confessed and submitted himself to judgment, Edward declared that his liberty would be restored to his heirs after his death, and that he would have to pay a fine of 500 marks. Ewyas Lacy was taken into royal custody on 19 February, but then restored to Verdon the following June.

Despite this punishment Verdon continued to come into conflict with his neighbours. In 1299 the prior of Llanthony once again complained about Verdon and his subjects in Ewyas, asserting that they were harassing the prior's men. Two years later Verdon's followers were similarly accused of committing trespasses against Sir John Hastings, so that the king had to warn him to amend his ways or be prepared to accept the remedy.

Although only in his forties, there are signs that Verdon may have been growing infirm during the 1290s. In 1295 he was summoned to parliament and ordered to help the justiciar of Ireland raise men to fight in Scotland. That same year he granted his eldest son, John, lands out of his patrimony without royal permission, and was fined accordingly. When in 1297 he was ordered to come to the king with horses and arms to fight in Gascony, he wrote back that he could not attend because of his infirmity, and because John, whom he had wanted to serve in his place, had died. Edward did not like the excuse and replied that he recalled that Verdon's second son, another Theobald, appeared fit, and so should be sent to serve in his father's place. Verdon stayed in Ireland in 1297 and 1298, and was discharged from service against the Scots in 1299. In March 1300 the Irish besieged him in Roch Castle. When the king summoned him for military service again in 1301, he stipulated that Verdon could send his son in his place if he was disabled by illness. He would then have been about fifty-three years old. Nevertheless, he attended the parliament at Lincoln in 1301, where he was one of the witnesses to the letter of the barons to the pope, and continued to be summoned for royal service in Scotland until his death in 1309.

Verdon married Margery, who brought land in Bisley, Gloucestershire, to the marriage. They had several sons: John, who died in Ireland in 1297; Theobald, who inherited his father's estate; and their younger brothers, Robert, Nicholas, and Michael. In April 1302 Verdon arranged a marriage between the younger Theobald and Matilda, daughter of Edmund (I) de Mortimer, in which both families promised lands in Ireland to the couple. They were married at Wigmore on 27 July. Theobald de Verdon the elder died at Alton, Staffordshire, the head of his patrimony, on 24 August 1309, when he was about sixty-one years old. He was buried with great honour among his ancestors in Croxden Abbey on 13 October.

The younger **Theobald de Verdon**, first Lord Verdon (1278–1316), baron, born on 8 September 1278, served in Scotland on a number of occasions, including the Falkirk campaign of 1298, and was summoned regularly to parliament from 1299, being thereby considered to have become Lord Verdon in his own right. He was probably on friendly terms with Thomas of Lancaster, who in 1312 attended the funeral of Verdon's first wife. On 30 April 1313 he was made justiciar of Ireland, an appointment probably made at least in part in response to the revolt against the Irish government of Verdon's own brothers in 1312–13. But he did not take up office until 18 June 1314, and was replaced on 27 February 1315. Following the death of his wife Matilda in 1312, Verdon married, on 4 February 1316, Elizabeth de *Clare (1294/5–1360), sister of Gilbert de *Clare, earl of Gloucester (d. 1314), and widow of John de Burgh, until his death in 1313 heir to the earldom of Ulster. It was alleged that Verdon had abducted Elizabeth from Bristol Castle, but he claimed before the council that she had come out to meet him, and that they had been betrothed in Ireland. Verdon died at Alton on 27 July 1316, and was buried in Croxden Abbey. He left no male heir, but had three daughters from his first marriage, and a posthumous daughter from his second. The Verdon estates were accordingly partitioned among these coheiresses and their husbands: Joan, who married first John Montagu and second Thomas Furnival; Elizabeth, who married Sir Bartholomew *Burghersh (d. 1355); Margery, who married first William Blount, second Sir Mark Hose, and third Sir John Crophill; and Isabella, who married Henry *Ferrers, Lord Ferrers of Groby (d. 1343) [see under Ferrers family (per. c.1240–1445)].   SCOTT L. WAUGH

Sources GEC, *Peerage*, new edn, 12/2.249–52 · F. Palgrave, ed., *The parliamentary writs and writs of military summons*, 2 vols. in 4 (1827–34) · *RotP*, vol. 1 · *Chancery records* · Rymer, *Foedera*, new edn, vol. 4 · Dugdale, *Monasticon*, new edn, 5.661 · I. J. Sanders, *English baronies: a study of their origin and descent, 1086–1327* (1960), 95 · M. Prestwich, *Edward I* (1988), 351 · A. J. Otway-Ruthven, *A history of medieval Ireland* (1968); 2nd edn (1980), 208, 217 · R. R. Davies, *Lordship and society in the march of Wales, 1282–1400* (1978), 253, 260, 262, 265, 267, 283 · J. E. Morris, *The Welsh wars of Edward I* (1901), 22, 62, 79, 117, 229, 230, 238, 277 · A. J. Otway-Ruthven, 'The partition of the de Verdon lands in Ireland in 1332', *Proceedings of the Royal Irish Academy*, 66C (1967–8), 401–45 · G. Wrottesley, ed., 'Extracts form the plea rolls, AD 1272 to 1294', *Collections for a history of Staffordshire*, William Salt Archaeological Society, 6/1 (1885) · J. R. Maddicott, *Thomas of Lancaster, 1307–1322: a study in the reign of Edward II* (1970) · J. C. Ward, *English noblewomen in the later middle ages* (1992)

Verdon, Theobald de, first Lord Verdon (1278–1316). *See under* Verdon, Theobald de, first Lord Verdon (1248?–1309).

Verdun, Bertram de. *See* Verdon, Bertram de (d. 1192).

Vere. For this title name *see* individual entries under Vere; *see also* Beauclerk, Vere, Baron Vere of Hanworth (1699–1781).

Vere, de, family (*per.* 1080–1703). For members of this family *see* individual entries under Vere and related entries; for information on the family *see* Vere, Aubrey (II) de (d. 1141).

Vere, Agnes de. *See* Essex, Agnes of, countess of Oxford (b. 1151, d. in or after 1206).

Vere [*née* Cecil], **Anne de, countess of Oxford** (1556–1588), courtier, was born on 5 December 1556, the daughter of William *Cecil, first Baron Burghley (1520/21–1598), and his second wife, Mildred (1526–1589) [*see* Cecil, Mildred], daughter of Sir Anthony *Cooke. Anne presumably gained the equivalent of a grammar school education in the cultivated Cecil household. Writing to Lord Burghley in 1577, the German educator Johannes Sturm (Sturmius) expressed his understanding that Anne 'speaks Latin also' (4 Dec 1577, *CSP for.*, 1577–8, no. 469).

In 1569 Anne was contracted to marry Philip Sidney, but by July 1571 she was engaged to Burghley's ward, Edward de *Vere, seventeenth earl of Oxford (1550–1604). Oxford's biographers have speculated that Burghley engineered the match (despite his protestations to the contrary), yet Anne may have been an attractive as well as accomplished young lady. Her brother, Robert Cecil, thought so, at least; writing from dingy lodgings at Ostend in 1587 he observed that 'If my lady of Oxford were here, her bewty wold quickly be marred' (PRO, SP 84/21, fol. 242). De Vere married Anne at Westminster Abbey on 19 December 1571, with Queen Elizabeth and many prominent courtiers in attendance. The match, however, proved disastrous; Oxford denied the paternity of his daughter Elizabeth, who was born on 2 July 1575 while he travelled on the continent, and he lived apart from his wife until some time in 1582.

During the separation Anne maintained cordial relations with the queen; this is evidenced in her exchange of new year's gifts with her sovereign every year from 1575 to 1588. The countess received five book dedications, all between 1575 and 1581. In his dedication to Anne, Geoffrey Fenton described his *Golden Epistles* (1575) as a 'morall discourse' mingled with 'texts of divinitie' (sig. *2). The last two dedications are translated expositions of Ephesians, the first of Niels Hemmingsen's exposition, by Abraham Fleming (1580), the second, an anonymous translation of Chrysostom (1581). In between are two books by de Vere retainers who had already dedicated works to the earl. George Baker terms Anne 'his singular good Lady' (sig. A2) in the dedication to his translation *Newe Jewell of Health* (1576), from the work by Conrad Gesner. Similarly, John Brooke's *Christian Discourse* (1578), is dedicated to 'his singuler good ladie and mistres, the countesse of Oxenforde'. Brooke praises her humility and courtesy as well as her 'good inclination to vertue and godlinesse' (sig. A2, A3v). Baker praises her 'wit, learning, and authoritie' (sig. A2v), Fenton her 'learning and judgement' (sig. *2), and Fleming her regard for learning and 'zealous love to religion' (sig. *3).

BL, Lansdowne MS 104 preserves copies in Lord Burghley's hand of two letters that the countess sent to her husband in December 1581; in both she professes her devotion to de Vere and her desire for reconciliation.

Burghley has corrected several readings in the second letter. After her reconciliation with Oxford, Anne gave birth to three more daughters: Bridget (*b.* 6 April 1584), Susan (*b.* 26 May 1587), and Frances, who died an infant on 12 September 1587. The couple's only son, styled Lord Bolebec (Bulbeck), died within four days of his birth in May 1583. Anne died at Greenwich on 5 June 1588 and was buried at Westminster Abbey on 25 June.

In *Pandora* (1584), John Southern credited Anne with four sonnets and two quatrains memorializing her dead son. All six poems, however, are couched in Southern's uniquely arhythmic meters, which are neither accentual nor syllabic. The content of all six draw heavily as well on his favourite poet, Desportes. They could perhaps be translations of Anne's elegies in Latin or another language, but are probably prosopopoeias outright.

STEVEN W. MAY

Sources GEC, *Peerage*, new edn · *Calendar of the manuscripts of the most hon. the marquis of Salisbury*, 5, HMC, 9 (1894) · C. Read, *Mr Secretary Cecil and Queen Elizabeth* (1955) · HoP, *Commons, 1558–1603* · F. B. Williams, *Index of dedications and commendatory verses in English books before 1641* (1962) · CSP for., 1577–8, no. 469 · New year's gift list, 1575, Folger, Folger MS Z.d.14 · New year's gift lists, 1576, BL, Add. MS 4827 · New year's gift lists, 1577, PRO, C Misc. 3/39 · New year's gift lists, 1578, Society of Antiquaries, MS 537 · New year's gift list, 1581, Eton, MS 192 · New year's gift lists, 1582, BL, Harleian MS 1644 · New year's gift lists, 1584, BL, Egerton MS 3052 · New year's gift list, 1585, Folger, MS Z.d.16 · New year's gift lists, 1588, BL, Add. MS 8159 · J. Nichols, *The progresses and public processions of Queen Elizabeth*, new edn, 2 (1823), 249–75 · gaps, 1580, BL, Harl. MS 4698 · gaps, 1583, BL, Sloane MS 814 · S. W. May, 'The countess of Oxford's sonnets: a caveat', *English Language Notes*, 29/3 (1992), 9–19 · R. Smith, 'The sonnets of the countess of Oxford and Elizabeth I: translations from Desportes', *N&Q*, 239 (1994), 446–50 · E. Moody, 'Six elegiac poems, possibly by Anne Cecil de Vere', *English Literary Renaissance*, 19 (1989), 152–70 · PRO, SP 84/21, fols. 242–3
Archives BL, Lansdowne MS 104

Vere, Aubrey (II) de (*d.* 1141), administrator, was the son and successor of Aubrey (I) de Vere and Beatrice, his wife. While the family was from Ver, south of Coutances in Normandy, there is no evidence that Aubrey senior or his descendants held lands either there or in Brittany, with which they retained ties. The elder Aubrey was most probably the younger son of a Norman lord who prospered in England after the conquest, becoming a royal chamberlain. Probably born in the early 1080s, Aubrey junior married Alice (*d.* 1163?), daughter of Earl Gilbert de *Clare, before 1107. He was to become one of the most prominent royal administrators of the later years of the reign of Henry I and the early years of Stephen. It is likely that Aubrey (II) began his administrative career as royal chamberlain, possibly inheriting that office from his father when the latter died *c.*1112. By 1121 he was sheriff of Essex, and, later in that decade, of London and Middlesex. The extent of the king's confidence in de Vere is evident in his appointment as joint sheriff, with Richard Basset, to the custody of eleven counties in 1129–30. This unprecedented situation was probably part of an effort to collect arrears and to adjust the shrieval farms. While the king had levied one fine of 550 marks and four war-horses against him for having allowed a prisoner to escape, and

another of at least 100 marks for permission to resign the shrievalty of Essex and Hertfordshire, these fines had gone largely uncollected—another sign of royal favour. In 1133 Henry I bestowed the hereditary office of master chamberlain of England on de Vere; the office was to remain in the de Vere family until 1703. Although his royal service was primarily confined to England, he was at least twice with Henry I in Normandy.

When Aubrey de Vere's son William asserted that his father was 'justiciar of all England', and privy to important royal secrets, he seems to have meant that his father had travelled extensively as a justice, rather than that he had been chief justiciar of the realm. William of Malmesbury describes him as *causidicus*—a pleader or advocate—and skilled in the law. De Vere may have served as an itinerant justice under Henry I; he certainly did so in Stephen's reign. He had accepted Stephen's rule by Easter 1136, and when the king was summoned before an ecclesiastical council after his arrest of Roger of Salisbury and other bishops in 1139, he sent de Vere as his advocate. Aubrey de Vere was killed in a London riot on 15 May 1141, perhaps while supporting his son-in-law Geoffrey de *Mandeville, first earl of Essex (*d.* 1144).

Aubrey de Vere had at least nine children with Alice, who survived him for twenty-two years; as a widow she retired to St Osyth's Priory. They had five sons: Aubrey (III) de *Vere, his successor; Robert, who held a small Northamptonshire fief in 1166; Geoffrey, who served as sheriff of Shropshire from 1165 to 1170; William, who held the prebend of Nesden in St Paul's, London, before becoming a canon of St Osyth's Priory, Essex, and then bishop of Hereford (1186–98), and who wrote a life of St Osgyth; and Gilbert, prior of the order of the hospital of St John of Jerusalem in England (1195–7). Two of their four daughters became countesses: Rohese (Rohese de *Beauchamp [*see under* Beauchamp, de, family]) married successively Geoffrey de Mandeville, first earl of Essex, and Payn de *Beauchamp of Bedford [*see under* Beauchamp, de, family]; and Juliana, divorced by Hugh (I) Bigod, earl of Norfolk, married Walchelin Maminot of West Greenwich. Alice married Robert of Essex, then Roger fitz Richard of Warkworth; their fourth daughter was wife to Roger of Raimes.

De Vere inherited the barony of Castle Hedingham, with twenty-nine manors located mostly in the eastern counties. Like many Normans of the second generation in England, he expanded his patrimony, but did so primarily by acquiring mesne tenancies. He founded a Benedictine cell of St Melanie, Rennes, at Hatfield Broadoak, Essex, *c.*1135, and patronized his father's foundation, also Benedictine, of Earls Colne Priory, Essex. He also began construction of a stone keep at Hedingham, Essex, modelled upon the royal keep at Rochester. It survives relatively intact. His family was to prove one of the longest lasting in the history of the English aristocracy. His eldest son was made earl of Oxford in the year of Aubrey (II)'s death, and although its descent was several times transmitted through collaterals, and twice interrupted by forfeitures, the title nevertheless passed to no fewer than nineteen successive descendants, until the twentieth earl, also Aubrey de Vere, died without a male heir in 1703.

RaGena C. DeAragon

Sources Reg. RAN, vols. 2–3 · Pipe rolls, 31 Henry I · Dugdale, Monasticon, new edn · The itinerary of John Leland in or about the years 1535–1543, ed. L. Toulmin Smith, 11 pts in 5 vols. (1906–10) · William of Malmesbury, The Historia novella, ed. and trans. K. R. Potter (1955) · Paris, Chron. · English historical documents, 1, ed. D. Whitelock (1955) · Lambert of Ardres, Historia comitium Ghisnensium, Ecbasis cuiusdam captivi per tropologiam, ed. K. Strecker, Hanover, MGH Scriptores Rerum Germanicarum, 24 (Hanover, 1935) · Sir Christopher Hatton's Book of seals, ed. L. C. Loyd and D. M. Stenton, Northamptonshire RS, 15 (1950) · H. Hall, ed., The Red Book of the Exchequer, 3 vols., Rolls Series, 99 (1896) · M. Gervers, ed., The cartulary of the knights of St John of Jerusalem in England, 1, British Academy, Records of Social and Economic History, new ser., 6 (1982) · J. H. Round, Geoffrey de Mandeville: a study of the anarchy (1892) · J. A. Green, The government of England under Henry I (1986) · A. Farley, ed., Domesday Book, 2 vols. (1783)
Archives BL, Add. MSS · CUL | BL, Cotton MSS; Stowe MSS · Bodl. Oxf., Rawl. MSS · Essex RO, Chelmsford, Hedingham MSS
Wealth at death see Farley, ed., Domesday book

Vere, Aubrey (III) de, count of Guînes and earl of Oxford (d. 1194), magnate, was the son of Aubrey (II) de *Vere (d. 1141), royal chamberlain, and Alice (d. 1163?), daughter of Gilbert de *Clare, and sister of Gilbert fitz Gilbert de Clare, earl of Pembroke. By the time of his father's death Aubrey (III) was already politically prominent. His career was remarkable for the accumulation of large numbers of estates throughout England. In 1139 he had acquired the comital title by marrying Beatrice, the heir to her grandfather, Manasses, count of Guînes in the Pas-de-Calais (who enjoyed a moiety of the lordship of Folkestone and estates in the honour of Boulogne in Suffolk). He defected to the Empress Matilda in the aftermath of the capture of Stephen at Lincoln in February 1141. In May 1141 Count Aubrey succeeded his father, who had died in a riot in London. It would seem that he was briefly reconciled to the king after Stephen's release in September 1141, for there is a reference to the king's confirmation of the lands he had from his father. In 1141 the empress had offered him for his adherence the earldom of Cambridge, or, if that was not satisfactory, a choice of four other titles: he chose Oxford. She added to these grants the castle of Colchester. At this time Earl Aubrey was closely associated with his brother-in-law, Geoffrey de Mandeville, earl of Essex, and was arrested with him in 1143, having to surrender the castle of Canfield to secure his release. He was a character of some importance in East Anglia during the latter years of Stephen's reign. There seems every reason to believe (in view of the number of appearances in his charters) that Earl Aubrey acted as an auxiliary of Geoffrey de Mandeville, until the latter's death in 1144. If so, he would have spent a period in opposition to the king. But it is equally likely that after Mandeville's death, Earl Aubrey would have returned to neutrality; something that his close family connection with the loyalist Clares would have made easy to accomplish. Between 1144 and 1146 he was divorced from his wife, thus losing his connection with

Guînes. When he remarried he was clearly in King Stephen's obedience once more, for the king and queen contributed the manor of Ickleton, Cambridgeshire, to the marriage portion of the new countess, Euphemia, who had died by late 1153, and who was said on later evidence to have been the daughter of William de Cantilupe. The countess on her deathbed made a grant for the late queen's soul and that of her son, which was confirmed by the king.

In 1153 Earl Aubrey was with Stephen's army at the siege of Wallingford, and he attested the treaty of Westminster, which established the succession, in November 1153. With the accession of Henry II in 1154 Earl Aubrey was able to make good his claim to his comital rights in Oxfordshire, where the new king conceded him the third penny of the profits of justice in a charter of January 1156, and also allowed him succession to the chamberlainship of the exchequer which the earl's father had held. The castle of Colchester, however, was not confirmed to him. The earl attested royal charters until 1160, but thereafter disappears from the Plantagenet court for a time. He was active however on the king's behalf during the wars of 1173–4, joining the royalist army which defeated the earl of Leicester's invasion in Suffolk. He attended the king in England several times before Henry II's death in 1189, and was at the first coronation of King Richard in September of that year.

Earl Aubrey's later career was notable for the notorious divorce proceedings he took to rid himself of his third wife, Agnes of *Essex (b. 1151, d. in or after 1206), daughter of Henry of Essex, the royal constable, whom he married early in 1163 (when she was twelve) inopportunely just before her father's disgrace and ruin. Earl Aubrey pursued his case to Rome, where it was ultimately settled in Agnes's favour in 1171 or 1172. The earl had in the meantime kept his wife under close guard in one of his castles, refusing her leave to go out even to hear mass and refusing to acknowledge her as countess of Oxford. There does seem to have been a reconciliation between the pair ultimately: Countess Agnes attested several of his later charters and consented to an alienation of a rent from her marriage portion to Colne Priory; also all the earl's four sons were born from his marriage with Agnes (including the youngest, named Henry after his disgraced grandfather). Earl Aubrey died, probably in his late seventies, possibly even his early eighties, on 26 December 1194, and was buried at Colne Priory in Essex, being survived by Countess Agnes. He left four sons: his heir, Earl Aubrey (IV) de Vere, Ralph (who died before his elder brother), Robert de *Vere, who later succeeded to the earldom, and the Henry already mentioned. The chronicle of Lambert of Ardres calls him (perhaps as a pun on his surname) Aubrey Aper ('the Boar'). This is doubtless the source of the de Vere family's livery badge, a boar's head, found on their seals as early as the later thirteenth century. Later tradition calls him Aubrey the Grim from a mistranscription of aper as Asper.

Earl Aubrey's significance in the politics of the anarchy and the early Angevin monarchy is by no means small: his volatility and attachment to the Mandeville earls made Essex unstable in the 1140s and threatened the king's control of London. The remarkable thing is that he was able to achieve so much on so narrow a landed base. The *carta* of his honour of Hedingham reveals in 1166 a barony of merely 29¼ and ⅛ fees held in chief, and his earldom of Oxford brought no assets other than the annual third penny. The answer to this puzzle would seem to be the enormous wealth accumulated by his father as a leading royal justice. Through this, and through political favours, he followed his father's own work in accumulating a great demesne estate in Essex and Suffolk from many sources, the mechanics of which may be partly glimpsed through notes of the lost archive once at Hedingham. This tells of substantial conveyances from at least a dozen individuals, including the duke of Brittany, the earl of Hertford, the bishop of Ely, and the abbot of Bury St Edmunds. Earl Aubrey continued to patronize in lavish style his father's foundation of Colne Priory, and, in addition, confirmed gifts to his father's other foundation of Hatfield Regis. He also made modest grants to the nuns of Hedingham, whose house he perhaps founded.   DAVID CROUCH

Sources J. L. Fisher, ed., *Cartularium prioratus de Colne*, Essex Archaeological Society, occasional publications, 1 (1946) · Register of Hedingham, Essex County RO, D/DPr (Earls Colne Estate) 145 · Dugdale, *Monasticon*, new edn · S. A. Moore, ed., *Cartularium monasterii Sancti Johannis baptiste de Colecestria*, 2 vols., Roxburghe Club, 131 (1897) · Queens' College, Cambridge, mun. box 63 · D. C. Douglas, ed., *Feudal documents from the abbey of Bury St Edmunds*, British Academy, Records of Social and Economic History, 8 (1932) · P. Morant, *The history and antiquities of the county of Essex*, 2 vols. (1768) · *Reg. RAN*, 4.242, 634–5 · Vere family cartulary, Bodl. Oxf., MS Rawl. B. 248 · *Sir Christopher Hatton's Book of seals*, ed. L. C. Loyd and D. M. Stenton, Northamptonshire RS, 15 (1950) · GEC, *Peerage*, new edn · W. Stubbs, ed., *Gesta regis Henrici secundi Benedicti abbatis: the chronicle of the reigns of Henry II and Richard I, AD 1169–1192*, 2 vols., Rolls Series, 49 (1867) · Lambert of Ardres, *Chronicon Ghisnense et Ardense (918–1203)* (1855)

Archives Bodl. Oxf., MS Rawl. B.248 · Essex RO, Chelmsford, D/DPr 145

Likenesses seal, white wax, *c.*1139–1146, BL, Add. MS ch. 28329 · seal, white wax, 1143–76, BL, Cotton, ch. xxix.77

Vere, Aubrey de, tenth earl of Oxford (1338×40–1400), magnate, was the third son of John de *Vere, the seventh earl (1312–1360), and his wife, Maud (*d.* 1366), one of the four daughters and coheirs of Giles, Lord Badlesmere (*d.* 1338). Aubrey de Vere had married Alice (*d.* 11 May 1400), daughter of the Essex landowner John, Lord Fitzwalter (*d.* 1361), by 1386. On 13 July 1360 Aubrey's mother had granted her son the stewardship of the royal forest of Havering, Essex, for life, and after her death he received her jointure in Sawston, Cambridgeshire, and Calverton, Buckinghamshire, which his father had entailed on him. De Vere sought a career in the service of Edward, the Black Prince, with whom he was in Aquitaine in July 1366. Presumably as a consequence of good service to the prince in the Castilian campaign of 1367, he was knighted, and then in October he was retained by Prince Edward for life with the handsome annuity of £66 13s. 4d., later increased to £100. He was acting as the prince's secretary in September 1371. That month his surviving elder brother, Thomas,

earl of Oxford, died, leaving a son, Robert de *Vere, aged nine, as his heir. On 22 July 1375 the Black Prince appointed de Vere constable of Wallingford Castle, Berkshire, and steward both of its honour and that of St Valéry. De Vere's annuities were confirmed after the prince's death by the latter's son Richard, first as prince of Wales and afterwards as king.

Highly regarded by Richard's mother, Princess Joan, de Vere was among those servants of her husband (with a number of whom he had close personal links) who were to be at the heart of government in the early years of Richard II's minority. His later prominence had been foreshadowed at the end of Edward III's reign, when in 1377 Princess Joan sent him, with two other mediators, to try to compose the quarrel between her brother-in-law John of Gaunt, duke of Lancaster, and the citizens of London (the mission had little success), and he was also appointed to a mission to negotiate with the French crown. De Vere was appointed to the continual council which was set up to govern the realm in the parliament of 1378, and which functioned from November 1378 to January 1380: he put in 113 days' attendance. By January 1381 he was chamberlain of the household (an office hereditary to the earls of Oxford), and in March was appointed on a commission to negotiate Richard's marriage to Anne of Bohemia. During the peasants' revolt, de Vere was one of those who were in the Tower of London with the king when the rebels seized the city, and he bore the king's sword when Richard went to negotiate with them at Mile End.

De Vere did not exploit his chamberlainship to augment his estates, apparently preferring to see his nephew Robert, heir to the poorly endowed earldom, ascend in royal favour. Indeed, he may have engineered Robert's admission to the royal household. De Vere seems rather to have chosen to concentrate on maintaining the family interest in its main regional sphere, Essex, by securing firm control of royal offices and demesne estates there. On 1 February 1378 he received a grant of the constableship of Hadleigh Castle, in return for the surrender of his earlier Wallingford grant. On 25 June 1379 he received the keepership for life of three royal Essex parks (Rayleigh, Thunderly, and Hadleigh), notwithstanding grants of them to other royal servants, and, on 8 January 1380 he was granted the keeping of Rochford hundred. On 30 November 1381 he was licensed to stay in Hadleigh Castle for life with his household. He was well placed to protect his interests even against the weight of the house of Lancaster. During the peasants' revolt, and again in May 1382, his tenants at Stony Stratford, Buckinghamshire, attacked the men of Henry, earl of Derby, at Passenham, but Henry's attempt to gain redress from the king failed. On 4 October 1383 de Vere headed an embassy to negotiate with the French crown, and in 1385 he participated in Richard II's Scottish expedition, with a modest retinue of forty.

In 1387–8 the defeat by the lords appellant of de Vere's nephew, Robert, by now duke of Ireland, Robert's flight abroad, and his subsequent conviction for treason in the Merciless Parliament of 1388, constituted a grave family set-back. De Vere was compelled to give up the chamberlainship, and in January 1388 was expelled from the royal household. However, he was respected by the lords appellant: he was allowed to keep all his royal grants, and was consulted by their leader, the duke of Gloucester, on how to respond to a diplomatic initiative from the duke of Burgundy. When Robert de Vere died in exile in 1392, Richard was able in the 1393 parliament to restore to Aubrey, as his nephew's heir, the forfeited title and estates of the earldom. However, Oxford vainly petitioned in the parliaments of 1394 and January 1397 for the restoration of the chamberlainship, which the king had granted in 1390 to his half-brother John Holland, earl of Huntingdon. The highly partisan Commons in the parliament of 1399 alleged that Oxford had abandoned his hereditary right because of Richard's menaces.

Richard may therefore have regarded Oxford as unimportant, insufficiently supportive in 1387–8, and too closely connected with his opponents. The earl was on good terms with his wife's nephew Walter, Lord Fitzwalter, a friend of the duke of Gloucester, while on 3 August 1394 he was among the nobles who went surety for the earl of Arundel, who had highly offended the king. In 1399, however, the Commons alleged that Oxford's health and ability had grievously declined in the past few years. Henry refused their petition to restore the chamberlainship to him, after its surrender by Huntingdon. Oxford's expectation of his own demise is reflected in the indenture that he made with his feoffees, dated 1 November 1399, laying down the disposition of his properties in the case of Alice's surviving him, and during the minority of his son and heir, Richard. His own experience as a younger son was reflected in the careful provision for the sustenance of his younger son John, for his education 'in the schools', and entail. In January 1400 Huntingdon (to whose daughter Oxford had married his son Richard) sought refuge at Hadleigh Castle, after the failure of the 'Epiphany plot' to topple Henry IV; Oxford and his wife were there. The search was so intense that Huntingdon soon had to leave, to be caught and killed shortly afterwards. Oxford himself died less than two months later, on 23 April, probably at Hadleigh, and is likely to have been interred in the family's burial place, Earls Colne Priory, Essex.   ANTHONY GOODMAN

Sources J. F. Baldwin, *The king's council in England during the middle ages* (1913) · GEC, *Peerage*, new edn, 10.233-4; appx f · Chancery records · V. H. Galbraith, ed., *The Anonimalle chronicle, 1333 to 1381* (1927) · G. A. Holmes, *The estates of the higher nobility in fourteenth-century England* (1957) · K. B. McFarlane, *Lancastrian kings and Lollard knights* (1972) · RotP, vol. 3 · *Johannis de Trokelowe et Henrici de Blaneforde … chronica et annales*, ed. H. T. Riley, pt 3 of *Chronica monasterii S. Albani*, Rolls Series, 28 (1866) · N. Saul, *Richard II* (1997) · CIPM, vol. 18

Vere, Aubrey de, twentieth earl of Oxford (1627–1703), nobleman, was born in London on 28 February 1627, the oldest son of Robert de Vere, the nineteenth earl (*b.* after 1575, *d.* 1632), and his wife, Beatrice (or Bauck; *d.* 1653/1657), daughter of Sjerck van Hemmema, of Nufen,

Aubrey de Vere, twentieth earl of Oxford (1627-1703), by Sir Godfrey Kneller, *c.*1690

Friesland. His father, a descendant of John de Vere, fifteenth earl of Oxford, was accepted as nineteenth earl after a long debate in the House of Lords in April 1626. He possessed an inadequate estate in England and after securing his title returned to the Low Countries, where he had already made a career as a soldier in the Dutch army. On 7 August 1632 he was killed in the trenches before Maastricht, leaving his title, and very little else, to his five-year-old son.

Although Oxford had been born in London he was raised with his mother's family in Friesland. In 1638 he was granted £10 per annum in part-payment for his earldom's creation money, but his continuing poverty resulted in the appointment, in July 1641, of a committee of the House of Lords to consider his estate. His role in the first civil war is unclear; after the Restoration he claimed to have led a 'regiment of scholars' from Oxford for the king, but there is no hard evidence to prove this. By 1644 he was in the Low Countries serving as sergeant-major in Colonel Knightley's regiment in the Dutch service. On 10 December 1646 he was promoted colonel, commanding in Knightley's stead, a position he held until the peace of Westphalia. Despite his continental duties, however, he did find time to visit the city of his birth. On 18 June 1647 he eased his financial difficulties by marrying, at St Martin-in-the-Fields, the ten-year-old Anne Bayning (1637–1659), daughter and coheir of Paul, second Viscount Bayning of Sudbury. Her considerable fortune must have helped sustain Oxford as he embarked upon his career as a royalist conspirator. He was still in London in April 1651 when he challenged Lieutenant-Colonel Robert Sidney to a duel, which was prevented by the intervention of his friends.

Oxford's estate was sequestered in 1651 and on 20 June 1654 he was gaoled in the Tower, suspected of conspiring against the protector. In September 1656 he was considered for the post of general of the royalist forces in England in connection with a planned uprising: 'the Earl of Oxford appears to be a very fitting person as being free from any former engagement' (Ogle and others, 3.167). He spent much of the rest of the interregnum in or near London, where, under his royalist code name, Mr Waller, he worked for the king and feuded with his fellow conspirators. While committed to the exiled king, he found it difficult to work harmoniously with many of his agents, particularly John, Lord Mordaunt. On 15 August 1659 he was again committed to the Tower, this time suspected of complicity in Sir George Booth's rising. His wife, who accompanied him, died there on 14 September, and he was released on 29 September.

Oxford remained in London in the confused months preceding the Restoration, and in early spring 1660 was prominent in the agitation among the so-called 'new lords'—those who had never sat in the house during the civil wars—for their places in the chamber. He ultimately took his seat on 27 April and on 3 May was one of six peers nominated by the house to attend Charles II with an invitation to return to England. At the Restoration he was rewarded for his services. He was made knight of the Garter in May 1660 (and formally invested in April 1661), and bore the curtana at the king's coronation in April 1661, as well as at every subsequent coronation until his death. The king appointed him lord lieutenant of Essex, an office he held from August 1660 until February 1688 and again from October 1688 until 1703. As lord lieutenant he played a significant role in marshalling the militia of the home counties against the threat of Dutch invasion in 1667. In addition to his lieutenancy the king gave him command of the King's regiment of horse, or, as it was commonly known while he was its colonel, the Oxford Blues. As colonel of the Blues he participated in the suppression of Venner's rising in January 1661, and in 1678 the king promoted him lieutenant-general of horse and foot.

Charles II's favours bolstered Oxford's anaemic fortune; the king granted him several offices which provided the earl enough revenue to support—at times precariously—his title. He was a commissioner of claims at the coronation, and warden of the New Forest in 1667–8. More significantly he was chief justice in eyre of the forest south of Trent from June 1660 to January 1673. The office was, according to Roger North, of small use and great expense to the crown, but Charles II granted the place 'purely to gratify the Earl of Oxford who was one that ever wanted Royal boons' (North, 1.58). Oxford surrendered the office to the duke of Monmouth in 1673, in return for a gift of £5000 and an annuity of £2000. He was also the high steward of Colchester.

Evidently Oxford did not use the profits of office to cultivate civility. He lived riotously on the Piazza at Covent Garden in the 1660s. On one occasion in 1663 a brawl erupted among his guests, and was quelled only after the arrival of troops dispatched by the duke of Albemarle. One January morning in 1665 Samuel Pepys visited Oxford's house on business, and wrote 'his lordship was in bed at past ten o'clock: and Lord help us, so rude a dirty family I never saw in my life' (Pepys, 6.3). Some contemporaries were scandalized by Oxford's sham marriage to the well-known actress Hester *Davenport (1642–1717), who bore him a son, Aubrey (1664–1708), who later claimed, falsely, to be earl of Oxford. On 1 January 1673 he contracted a genuine marriage with Diana Kirke (d. 1719), daughter of George Kirke, groom of the bedchamber.

Through most of the 1660s and 1670s Oxford was a reliable supporter of the court. The king named him to the privy council in January 1670 and he protested against the passage of the Test Act in 1677. In 1678 he was made a gentleman of the bedchamber. He was dropped from the council in April 1679 during Shaftesbury's brief lord presidency, but returned following the earl's dismissal. In July 1680 he served as ambassador-extraordinary to Louis XIV, who was then touring near Calais. In 1684 he was one of Danby's sureties when the former lord treasurer was released from the Tower.

Oxford's position under James II was an ambivalent one. He supported James's accession, but lost his place in the bedchamber. In February 1688 he refused to push for the repeal of the penal laws and Test Act in his lieutenancy, defying the king's direct command. His example was important; Sir John Reresby wrote 'My lord of Oxford, the first earl of the realm (but low in his fortune) … tould the King plainly he could not persuade that to others which he was avers to in his own concience' (Memoirs of Sir John Reresby, 487). The consequence of this stance was his dismissal from his lieutenancy, regiment, and high stewardship of Colchester. James's desperate attempts to fend off the prince of Orange's invasion in late 1688 resulted in Oxford's restoration to the lieutenancy in October (replacing the ineffectual Catholic Lord Petre), and to his regiment in December. On 17 November he would not sign a petition calling for a free parliament, but by 8 December he had joined the prince, representing him at a meeting with the king's supporters at Hungerford.

Oxford's adroit change of sides secured William III's favour, and he continued in his places after the revolution. He served as lieutenant-general in the army and was present at the battle of the Boyne in 1690. In the House of Lords he generally allied himself with the whigs; in 1693 he attacked the tory secretary, Nottingham, over the bungled attack upon Brest, and defended the impeached whig Lord Somers in 1701. He served as speaker of the house from August 1700 to September 1701. By 1693 it was rumoured that he would give up command of his regiment 'on account of his great age' (Luttrell, 3.6) but he nevertheless continued in command for another decade.

After William III's death Oxford was reappointed to the privy council and, for the last time, bore the sword at a coronation—Queen Anne's in April 1702. He died at his house in Downing Street on 12 March 1703, aged seventy-six, and was buried in Westminster Abbey ten days later. His only surviving legitimate child was a daughter—Diana, duchess of St Albans—and so with him ended the de Vere earldom of Oxford, a title which stretched back to the reign of King Stephen.   VICTOR STATER

Sources GEC, *Peerage* · *CSP dom.*, 1651; 1660–61; 1667; 1686–8 · Pepys, *Diary* · *Calendar of the Clarendon state papers preserved in the Bodleian Library*, ed. O. Ogle and others, 5 vols. (1869–1970) · N. Luttrell, *A brief historical relation of state affairs from September 1678 to April 1714*, 6 vols. (1857) · R. North, *The lives of … Francis North … Dudley North … and … John North*, ed. A. Jessopp, 3 vols. (1890) · *Memoirs of Sir John Reresby*, ed. A. Browning (1936) · D. Underdown, *Royalist conspiracy in England, 1649–1660* (1960) · H. Horwitz, *Parliament, policy and politics in the reign of William III* (1977) · A. Swatland, *The House of Lords in the reign of Charles II* (1996)
Archives PRO, accounts, SP 46/87/176–227
Likenesses G. Kneller, oils, c.1690, NPG [*see illus.*] · G. Kneller, oils, Antony, Cornwall · attrib. G. Soest, oils, Dulwich College Gallery, London

Vere, Sir Aubrey De [*formerly* Aubrey Vere Hunt], **second baronet** (1788–1846), poet, was born on 28 August 1788, at Curragh Chase, Adare, co. Limerick, the eldest son of Sir Vere Hunt, first baronet (d. 1818), and his wife, Eleanor (d. 1820), only daughter of William Cecil Pery, Lord Glentworth, bishop of Limerick. He had a private tutor at Ambleside, Westmorland, and then went to Harrow School where he was a contemporary of Byron and Peel. On 12 May 1807 he married Mary (d. 1856), the eldest daughter of Stephen Edward Rice of Mount Trenchard, co. Limerick, and the sister of his closest friend. They had three daughters, two of whom died in adolescence, and five sons, including the poet Aubrey Thomas de *Vere (1814–1902), and the classical scholar Sir Stephen De *Vere (1812–1904).

De Vere succeeded to the baronetcy in 1818, and was a popular landlord. A loyalist, strongly in favour of Catholic emancipation, however, he failed to be elected when he stood for parliament about 1820. He contributed to *Harmonica* (1818), and his first major work was *Julian the Apostate*, published in 1822 while he was living in London. Another drama, *The Duke of Mercia*, followed in 1823.

Nevertheless, De Vere was mainly known as a sonneteer. 'The true basis of power' and the 'Lamentation of Ireland' were noted. He took the name by which he is known, De Vere, by letters patent on 15 March 1832. About this time, he became close to Wordsworth, who called his sonnets, attached to *Song of Faith* (1842), 'the most perfect of our age' (*Mary Tudor*, 1884). The drama *Mary Tudor* (1846) was written during De Vere's final illness; he died at Curragh Chase on 5 July 1846.   [ANON.], *rev.* JESSICA HININGS

Sources A. De Vere, the younger, *Recollections of Aubrey De Vere* (1897) · A. De Vere, *Mary Tudor* (1884) · Burke, *Gen. Ire.* (1912) · D. J. O'Donoghue, *The poets of Ireland: a biographical dictionary with bibliographical particulars*, 1 vol. in 3 pts (1892–3) · *The Times* (10 July 1846) ·

GM, 2nd ser., 26 (1846) · Ward, *Men of the reign* · A. J. Webb, *A compendium of Irish biography* (1878) · S. J. Kunitz and H. Haycraft, eds., *British authors of the nineteenth century* (1936) · R. Hogan, ed., *Dictionary of Irish literature*, rev. edn, 1 (1996), 347–8
Archives BL, corresp. with Sir Robert Peel, Add. MSS 40246, 40345, 40504 · TCD, letters to Grace O'Brien with poems

Vere, Aubrey Thomas de (1814–1902), poet, born on the family estate of Curragh Chase, Adare, co. Limerick, on 10 January 1814, was the third son of Aubrey Vere Hunt, later styled Sir Aubrey De *Vere, second baronet (1788–1846), and his wife, Mary (d. 1856), who was the eldest daughter of Stephen Edward Rice (d. 1831) of Mount Trenchard, co. Limerick, and sister of Thomas Spring *Rice, first Lord Monteagle (1790–1866). Aubrey's two elder brothers successively inherited the baronetcy. His father supported Catholic emancipation, so that, when the bill granting it was passed, young Aubrey climbed a pillar outside the house and waved a torch in the darkness. He was educated privately and one of his tutors, Edward Johnstone, aroused the boy's interest in Wordsworth, an enthusiasm that lasted for life. He entered Trinity College, Dublin, in 1832 where he studied in a desultory manner, concentrating on metaphysics and theology rather than on the more mundane aspects of a course which seemed to destine him for holy orders in the Church of Ireland, a path in line with his father's wishes for his third son. In 1837 he won a prize for an essay on theology, and the following year he left the college without committing himself to the church. He visited Oxford in 1838 and met John Henry (later Cardinal) Newman, who was a leading Tractarian, arguing for the reform of Anglicanism along traditional lines. De Vere admired Newman's sincerity and holiness, describing him as being like a 'youthful ascetic of the middle ages' (de Vere, 256). In 1839 de Vere visited Cambridge, where he discovered an entirely different intellectual climate in the Apostles club, where everything was openly discussed with complete freedom, and where traditional practices and the idea of authority were relentlessly questioned. His cousin Stephen Spring Rice was a member of this club and in their correspondence de Vere steadily withdraws from the Apostles' view that liberty is the freedom to do and think as one likes to a more orthodox position, conducive to settled concepts of authority and revealed truth. In one of his letters, he writes: 'Religio [means] *to bind again* … and how can you bind except by Doctrines reduced to their orthodox form and Duties explained, applied, and enforced?' (Ward, 59). Through his cousin's association with the Apostles, de Vere met Richard Monckton Milnes, poet and biographer of Keats, and James Spedding, the great editor of Francis Bacon. Although Tennyson was another Apostle, de Vere did not meet him until 1842. The year before, 1841, he had met Wordsworth, by then poet laureate, while in London attending to the publication of two books of poems by his father: *Sonnets* and *Song of Faith*. He was invited to the Lake District, where he fitted easily into Wordsworth's extended household, including Sara Coleridge, daughter of the poet, and Isabella Fenwick.

In 1842 de Vere published *The Waldenses and Other Poems*,

Aubrey Thomas de Vere (1814–1902), by Julia Margaret Cameron, c.1864

containing lyrics and meditations on religion, which he dedicated to the mathematician and astronomer William Rowan Hamilton, whom he had known at Trinity College, and with whom he had discussed belief and the evidence of nature. In 1843 appeared *The Search after Proserpine and Other Poems*, a copy of which he sent to Walter Savage Landor, whom he had long admired. Landor did not read the book for five years but when he did heaped praise upon it, and hailed de Vere as breathing the 'pure fresh air' of Greece (Taylor, 255). However, when he travelled in the Mediterranean in 1843 he found the Greeks 'a false people … never ashamed of being detected in a lie', as he wrote later in his *Picturesque Sketches of Greece and Turkey* (1850, 1.11). In 1845 he spent a good deal of time in London, where he met Thomas Carlyle and his wife, Jane Welsh, whom he greatly impressed with his youthful good looks, religious air, and contempt for society wit. His father, Sir Aubrey, was ailing at this time, and went to London for treatment, where he was looked after by his son, who approved of the paintings by Rembrandt and Correggio bought for Curragh Chase. In late autumn and early winter 1845 he went on a walking tour of Scotland; when he reached Edinburgh news began to arrive of the consequences of the failure of the potato crop that year in Ireland, the first onset of what was to become known as the great famine. His father died in July 1846, as the blight began to strike a second time. With his brothers Vere, Stephen, William, and Horace he threw himself into the organization of famine relief schemes, helped in the distribution of the Indian corn (maize) that was sent in to the areas where

starvation was rife, tried to work on the consciences of his fellow landlords encouraging them to commit resources to match those allocated from government, and attempted to supervise and regulate the process of emigration. De Vere also set up a scheme whereby women were engaged in a number of industries, and then faced the problem of disposing of manufactured goods for which there was no market. This extensive range of voluntary activities informed his study of Anglo-Irish political economy *English Misrule and Irish Misdeeds* (1848). He recognized a depth of anti-Irish feeling in England, and called for systematic emigration from a rural society that was uneconomic, as well as the redevelopment of agriculture along efficient lines. His direct experience of the famine in Limerick and in Clare informed his threnody on the disaster 'The Year of Sorrow—Ireland 1849', which he included in *Inisfail* (1861), a lyrical chronicle of Ireland, which sees it as an isle of destiny, whose people are fated to suffer affliction so they may accomplish a spiritual mission in the world. De Vere employs different forms and voices, from rhapsodic declamation to terse quatrains, to depict Ireland's varied history and traditions, but the thinking is fatalistic. Of Ireland he says, in the 'Introduction': 'Her Fatalism meant simply a profound sense of Religion' (*Inisfail*, xx).

By 1851 de Vere had taken the step to which he had been tending since meeting Newman in 1838. In 1850 he spent time in the company of Henry Edward (later Cardinal) Manning, and together they studied Aquinas and Dante. Manning left the Anglican church in April 1851; in the autumn he and de Vere set off for Rome, on a pilgrimage, and de Vere was accepted into the Catholic church at Avignon on 15 November, much to the dismay of Carlyle, who warned him against submitting himself to the bondage of traditional orthodoxy.

In 1854 the Irish Catholic hierarchy, in an attempt to establish a system of higher education for their congregation, appointed Newman to be first rector of the Catholic University of Ireland. Newman made a number of professorial appointments and established de Vere in the chair of political and social science, recognizing his candidate's experience of affairs, and his analysis of administrative and economic difficulties in Ireland. However, de Vere had no students and gave no lectures. He was working on a poetic task Pope Pius IX had suggested during an audience in Rome after his conversion in 1851: that he devote his imaginative energies to poems on the Virgin Mary and the saints of the church. The first instalment of this project appeared in 1857 as *May Carols, or, Ancilla domini*, which celebrate Mary as the mediatrix between the material and spiritual worlds, the means whereby the incarnation took place in human flesh. He sees her animating all beauty, and, in particular, flowing through the annual resurrection of spring. *Legends of St Patrick* (1872) versified episodes from the saint's life and his conversion of the Irish to Christianity, while *Legends of the Saxon Saints* (1879) undertook a similar task for St Cuthbert, Caedmon, and others. His approach to Catholic doctrine, and the way in which it might be expressed in poetry, had something in common with that of Gerard Manley Hopkins, the English Jesuit whom Newman brought to teach in the Catholic University. They were in most other respects very different. Mutual friends once arranged for them to meet at Howth, but de Vere was gone when Hopkins arrived. When he learned from his hosts that de Vere had a poor opinion of Dryden, Hopkins thought that he had 'not missed much'.

Alexander the Great (1874) and *St Thomas of Canterbury* (1876) were two leaden ventures into that sepulchre of imaginative energy: the Victorian verse-drama. Like many Victorians de Vere saw the early phases of culture as periods in which essential features of a people or a civilization were realized, hence his interest in early heroes and saints, and his desire to reanimate legendary styles of thought and feeling. *The Foray of Queen Maeve* (1882) was another such attempt at reading the early traces of culture and identity in Ireland; he based it on a manuscript translation of the Irish saga *Táin Bó Cuailnge* by Brian O'Looney in the Royal Irish Academy. *Constitutional and Unconstitutional Political Action* (1882), a pamphlet written in reaction to the murder in Phoenix Park of Lord Frederick Cavendish, the newly appointed chief secretary of Ireland, by the Invincibles, a Fenian splinter group, shows his commitment to non-violent reform. *Essays Literary and Ethical* (1889) mixes literary criticism with meditations on issues such as church property and materialism. His *Recollections* (1897) recalls a long life, many friendships, and his path towards a fixed set of religious convictions.

De Vere did not marry, but he seems to have been one of those for whom celibacy poses no difficulty. He died at Curragh Chase on 21 January 1902 and was buried in the churchyard at Askeaton, co. Limerick.

ROBERT WELCH

Sources S. M. Paraclita Reilly, *Aubrey de Vere: Victorian observer* (1956) · W. Ward, *Aubrey de Vere: a memoir* (1904) · H. Taylor, *Autobiography*, 2 vols. (1885) · A. De Vere, *Recollections* (1897) · R. Welch, *Irish poetry from Moore to Yeats* (1980)
Archives Curragh Chase, co. Limerick, family papers · NL Ire., papers · NRA, corresp. and literary papers | BL, letters to W. E. Gladstone, Add. MSS 44367–44785, *passim* · BL, corresp. with Macmillans, Add. MS 55009 · CUL, letters to Lord Acton · NL Ire., letters to Lord Emly · NL Ire., letters to R. P. Graves · NL Ire., letters to William Monsell · Syracuse University, New York, corresp. with Sir John Simeon · TCD, corresp. with Dowden · TCD, corresp. with C. Eliot Norton and others · U. Durham L., letters to Lord Grey · U. Glas. L., letters, mainly to W. Macneile Dixon · U. Reading L., letters to George Bell & Sons · U. St Andr. L., letters to Wilfrid Ward
Likenesses S. Lawrence, oils, 1820–29, Curragh Chase, co. Limerick · J. M. Cameron, photograph, *c.*1864, NPG [*see illus.*] · portrait, repro. in Ward, *Aubrey de Vere*
Wealth at death £799 12s. 11d.: probate, 19 Feb 1902, CGPLA Ire.

Vere, Sir Charles Broke (1779–1843), army officer, born on 21 February 1779, was the second son of Philip Bowes Broke (1749–1801) of Nacton, Suffolk, and his wife, Elizabeth (d. 1822), daughter and eventual heir of the Revd Charles Beaumont of Witnesham, Suffolk. Rear-Admiral Sir Philip Bowes Vere *Broke was his brother. Charles was commissioned ensign in the 5th foot on 23 June 1796; lieutenant on 7 December, and captain on 21 February 1799. He served with the 5th in the expedition to the Netherlands in that year. He was at the Royal Military College

Sir Charles Broke Vere (1779–1843), by Thomas Goff Lupton, pubd 1839 (after George Patten, *c.*1836)

from 1799 to 1803. In 1805, while on his way to join Lord Cathcart's expedition to the Elbe, he was wrecked on the Dutch coast, and made prisoner. He was soon released, and served in the force sent to South America under Craufurd in 1807. In the disastrous attack on Buenos Aires he was employed as assistant quartermaster-general. On 4 February 1808 he obtained a majority in the 5th.

After a short time on the staff in Ireland, Vere went to the Peninsula in 1809, and was appointed assistant quartermaster-general to the 4th division. He was present with it at Busaco, Albuera, Ciudad Rodrigo, Badajoz, and Salamanca; at Badajoz he was severely wounded while leading the men of the division to the breach in the Trinidad bastion. He was made brevet lieutenant-colonel on 27 April 1812. He had been removed from his regiment and made a permanent assistant quartermaster-general on 7 February 1811. During the campaigns of 1813–14 he was employed on the headquarters staff. He not only attended to the routine business but also drafted operation orders. He was present at Vitoria, the Pyrenees, Nivelle, Nive, Orthez, and Toulouse. He received the gold cross with five clasps, and was made KCB in January 1815. In the 1815 campaign he was at first attached to Hill's corps, and Hill in his report of 20 June expressed his particular thanks to him; when Sir William Howe de Lancey was killed in the battle of Waterloo, Wellington chose Broke, though he was not the senior, to perform the duty of quartermaster-general. Broke fulfilled this role during the latter half of the battle, and on the march to Paris, and he was afterwards deputy quartermaster-general in the army of occupation. He received the Russian order of Vladimir (second class) and the Netherlands order of Wilhelm (second class). He was placed on half pay on 4 July 1823, and was promoted colonel on 27 May 1825, when, on Wellington's recommendation, he was appointed aide-de-camp to the king. He held this post until 10 January 1837, when he became major-general. In 1822 he had taken the additional name of Vere. A Conservative, in 1832 he contested East Suffolk without success, but he was returned second on the poll in 1835, and unopposed in 1837, while he again defeated the whig candidate in 1841. He published a pamphlet, *The Danger of Opening the Ports to Foreign Corn at a Fixed Duty Considered* (1834). He died at Bath on 1 April 1843, and was buried at Nacton.   E. M. LLOYD, *rev.* ROGER T. STEARN

Sources *Annual Register* (1843) · *GM*, 2nd ser., 19 (1843) · J. G. Brighton, ed., *Admiral Sir P. V. B. Broke* (1866) · *The dispatches of … the duke of Wellington … from 1799 to 1818*, ed. J. Gurwood, 13 vols. in 12 (1834–9) · S. G. P. Ward, *Wellington's headquarters: a study of the administrative problems in the Peninsula, 1809–14* (1957) · *WWBMP* · A. J. Guy, ed., *The road to Waterloo: the British army and the struggle against revolutionary and Napoleonic France, 1793–1815* (1990) · R. Muir, *Britain and the defeat of Napoleon, 1807–1815* (1996)
Archives NAM, orders in Waterloo campaign · Suffolk RO, Ipswich, corresp. and papers
Likenesses H. R. Cook, print, pubd *c*.1814 (after G. Engleheart), BM · oils, *c*.1814 (after S. Lane), NMM · T. Blood, print, 1815, BM, NPG · T. G. Lupton, mezzotint, pubd 1839 (after G. Patten, *c*.1836), BM, NPG [*see illus.*] · R. J. Lane, lithograph (after G. Patten), NPG · W. Salter, group portrait, oils (*The Waterloo banquet at Apsley House*), Wellington Museum, London; oil study, *c*.1834–1840, NPG

Vere, Edward de, seventeenth earl of Oxford (1550–1604), courtier and poet, was born on 12 April 1550, probably at Castle Hedingham, Essex, the only son of John de *Vere, sixteenth earl of Oxford (1516–1562), and his second wife, Margery, daughter of Sir John Golding and half-sister of Arthur Golding, the translator of Ovid. Until his father's death he was known as Lord Bulbeck.

Education and early years Bulbeck matriculated as an impubes (immature) fellow-commoner of Queens' College, Cambridge, in November 1558, remaining for one academic year. He seems thereafter to have been tutored in the household of Sir Thomas Smith by Thomas Fowle. Upon his father's death on 3 August 1562 he succeeded to the earldom of Oxford and other hereditary dignities, including the ceremonial office of lord great chamberlain. His half-sister Katherine, daughter of his father's first wife, Dorothy, second daughter of Ralph Neville, fourth earl of Westmorland, challenged his legitimacy, claiming irregularities in their father's marriage to Margery Golding; Oxford was successfully defended by Arthur Golding, then his receiver. As a royal ward he came under the guardianship of William Cecil, master of the court of wards. Cecil drew up orders for his exercises and for his studies, which were put in the hands of Lawrence Nowell, dean of Lichfield: he learned French, Latin, penmanship, and dancing. An early taste for literature is evidenced in his purchases of books by Chaucer, Plutarch (in French), Cicero, and Plato (probably in Latin).

Oxford accompanied the queen on progress to Cambridge in August 1564, and to Oxford in September 1566.

Edward de Vere, seventeenth earl of Oxford (1550–1604), by unknown artist, 17th cent. [original, 1575]

Like others in the queen's retinue he was granted an unearned MA on each occasion. In July 1567, while practising the art of fencing with a Westminster tailor in the garden of Cecil House, he killed an unarmed and possibly inebriated undercook, Thomas Brincknell of Westminster. A coroner's jury which was openly influenced by Cecil, and which included Ralph Holinshed, spared Oxford, with the grotesque finding that Brincknell had committed suicide by 'running upon a point of a fence-sword of the said earl' (Murdin, 2.764). Oxford thus learned that he could commit no outrage which Cecil would not forgive and do his best to forget. On 24 October 1569, in the first of some eighty surviving letters and memoranda in English, and in his own hand, he begged Cecil to procure him some military duty. Though he desired a posting to the continent, he was sent to Scotland under the command of Thomas Radcliffe, third earl of Sussex, in or about April 1570. Upon coming of age on 12 April 1571 he took his seat in the House of Lords; in May he engaged in the tilt, tourney, and barrier in the queen's presence at Westminster. In August he was appointed to attend the French envoy, Paul de Foix, who travelled to England to discuss the queen's projected marriage to the duc d'Anjou. About the same time he declared an interest in Cecil's eldest daughter, Anne [*see* Vere, Anne de, countess of Oxford], then fourteen, and received the queen's consent to a marriage. Cecil—now Lord Burghley—explained to the earl of Rutland, evidently a disappointed rival, that he 'found in the earl more understanding than any stranger to him would think' (*Rutland MSS*, 1.95). The wedding, celebrated on 19 December 1571, was attended by the queen.

The marriage was a disaster. By March 1572 Oxford remonstrated with Burghley over the prosecution of Thomas Howard, fourth duke of Norfolk, and was suspected of arranging an abortive plot to rescue Norfolk from the Tower. On 22 September he entreated Burghley to procure him naval employment, but had to settle for life at court, where he openly flirted with the queen. 'My Lord of Oxford', wrote Gilbert Talbot to his father, the earl of Shrewsbury, on 11 May 1573:

> is lately grown into great credit; for the queen's Majesty delighteth more in his personage, and his dancing and valiantness, than any other. I think Sussex doth back him all that he can; if it were not for his fickle head, he would pass any of them shortly.   (Lodge, 2.100–01)

Talbot knew his man. Early in July 1574 Oxford departed without licence for Flanders, the refuge of northern English Catholic nobility. Enraged, the queen dispatched gentlemen pensioners, led by Thomas Bedingfield, to fetch him back. Having dutifully returned by the end of the month, in August Oxford and Burghley waited on the queen at Bristol with an apology. Conciliatory, she agreed to allow Oxford to travel abroad with licence. He left early in February 1575 and visited Paris and Strasbourg before making his way to Venice by April. Over the next year he visited Padua, Siena, and Milan, among other cities, finally decamping from Venice on 6 March 1576. He carried with him to Paris and Calais luxurious articles of dress and toilet, a Venetian choirboy named Orazio Cogno, and memories of a Venetian courtesan named Virginia Padoana. Waylaid by pirates on crossing the channel, Oxford was bereft of many of his souvenirs, finally landing at Dover on 20 April and returning to London by river-wherry to avoid meeting Anne—who in the interim had borne a daughter, Elizabeth—at Gravesend. The distraught Burghley declared that Oxford had been 'enticed by certain lewd persons to be a stranger to his wife' (Murdin, 2.778), apparently unable to conceive that his son-in-law preferred the company of the choirboy, whom he kept in his London lodgings for eleven months, giving rise to suspicions of pederasty. Oxford made himself fashionable by sporting imported embroidered gloves, sweet-bags, perfumed leather jerkins, and costly washes or perfumes, and ingratiated himself with the queen by presenting her with perfumed gloves trimmed with tufts or roses of coloured silk.

Courtier Oxford's eccentricities and irregularities of temper grew with his years. From 1577 to December 1580 he and his intimate friends Henry Howard and Charles Arundel flirted with Catholicism and sedition, amusing themselves at Oxford's table, while Oxford derided the queen, particularly her singing voice. Oxford nevertheless accompanied Elizabeth to Saffron Walden and Audley End in July 1578. Gabriel Harvey paid the earl conventional compliments in one of three dedications prefaced to the third book of his memorial volume, *Gratulationes Valdenses*. About the same time Harvey composed a satire of Oxford as an Italianated Englishman under the title 'Speculum Tuscanismi', describing him as clad in 'a little apish hatte, cowched fast to the pate, like an oyster', and in French cambric ruffs; as 'delicate in speach, queynte in araye: conceited in all poyntes … a passing singular odde man' (Spenser, sig. E2). Nash's charge that the earl caused his libeller to be imprisoned in the Fleet prison is not independently verifiable, and was denied by Harvey. In August 1579 Oxford insulted Sir Philip Sidney in the tennis court at Greenwich, calling him a 'puppy'. Sources differ on who initiated the ensuing written challenge, but the queen interposed on the earl's behalf, forbidding a duel and ordering Sidney to defer to Oxford's superior rank. Unwilling to bear the humiliation, Sidney retired from court. Oxford is reported to have plotted Sidney's murder.

On 16 December 1580 Oxford denounced Howard and Arundel to the queen as Catholic sympathizers. Hoist with his own petard, Oxford spent a few days in the Tower himself, but soon regained his freedom and won the prize in a tilt on 22 January 1581. On 23 March, however, the Yorkshire beauty and queen's maid of honour Anne *Vavasour, who had been Oxford's mistress since 1579, gave birth to a son, whereupon he found himself back in the Tower. He recovered his freedom in June, and in December was reconciled with his wife.

Domestic tranquillity was shattered again in March 1582, when Oxford fought a duel with Anne Vavasour's uncle Sir Thomas Knyvet. Both men were wounded, the earl more dangerously. Their quarrel continued on and off for a year, with deaths and injuries among retainers on both sides. In May 1583, at Ralegh's instigation, the queen and Oxford achieved a *modus vivendi*. In August 1585 he sailed with John Norris to the Netherlands; a letter from Burghley informing Oxford that he was to have command of the horse failed to reach him before his sudden return to England on 21 October in a fit of 'humour'. Still in the queen's graces, but impoverished, he petitioned her for a £1000 annuity, which she granted in 1586. In October of that year he became commissioner for the trial of Mary, queen of Scots, taking part in the proceedings at Fotheringhay and in the Star Chamber at Westminster. In 1588, during the Armada battle, Oxford volunteered for service at Tilbury but refused Leicester's request that he serve as governor of Harwich, thinking the position beneath him. When Oxford took his complaint to the queen, Leicester wrote to Walsingham: 'I am glad I am rid of my Lord Oxford, seeing he refuseth this and I pray you let me not be pressed any more for him what suit so ever he make' (PRO, SP 12/214(1), fols. 2–3). To cover the earl's dereliction of duty Burghley, in a propaganda pamphlet issued the same year, refashioned Oxford, along with other non-combatant noblemen, into national heroes.

Since 1569 Oxford had received votes for the Order of the Garter approximately proportional to the esteem in which he was held by the queen. After 1588 he received no more votes while she lived. He nevertheless performed the duties of a peer in the trials of Philip Howard, earl of Arundel, in 1589, and Essex in 1601. After Anne died of a fever in 1588, Oxford married again about January 1592. His second wife was Elizabeth, daughter and heir of Thomas Trentham of Rocester Priory, Staffordshire; she secured the lineage by giving birth to a son, Henry de *Vere (1593–1625), the future eighteenth earl. Moving from London, first to Stoke Newington and thence to Hackney, Oxford devoted his declining years to the endless pursuit of supplementary income, petitioning for the monopoly on fruit, oils, and wool; for the gauging of beer; for the pre-emption of tin in Cornwall and Devon (1595–9); for the governorship of Jersey; and for the presidency of Wales. His numerous letters to Burghley and to Robert Cecil reflect his endless disappointments. Bitter to the end, he plotted against the royal succession by a Scot. His signature is notably absent from the proclamation of 24 March 1603 and its first printed impression, though it was added to the second impression. At James I's coronation on 25 July Oxford secured fees due to the office of lord great chamberlain; his annuity was subsequently extended. Perhaps succumbing to the consequences of the high-risk behaviour of his youth, and following a decade of complaints about his health, he died on 24 June 1604 and was buried on 6 July in the churchyard of St Augustine, Hackney, without a memorial tomb.

Oxford was notorious in his own time for his effeminate dress, for his irregular life, and for squandering virtually his entire patrimony on personal extravagance. Exemplary was his purchase in 1580 of Fisher's Folly, so named because it had bankrupted its original builder, the London alderman Jasper Fisher. Unable to sustain the expense of maintaining the house, Oxford was forced to sell in 1588. Eternally short of funds, he did not scruple to burden lesser men with his debts. About 1591 the poet Thomas Churchyard hired lodgings for the earl at the house of Mrs Julian Penn, giving his own bond in lieu of cash. When Oxford neglected to pay the rent, Churchyard, in fear of arrest, sought sanctuary.

Oxford's first wife, Anne, died at the queen's palace at Greenwich on 5 June 1588, and was buried in state at Westminster Abbey on 25 June. Numerous elegies are preserved in the British Library (Lansdowne MS 104, fols. 195–214; Cotton MS Julius F. 10, fols. 112–115v, 132). Though she was well educated and is even said by Sturmius to have spoken Latin, the four epitaphs written after her son died at birth in May 1583, and attributed to Anne by John Southern in his *Pandora* of 1584, were in fact translations (doubtless by Southern himself) from the French poetry of Desportes. Anne's other children were: Elizabeth, born 2 July 1575, who married William Stanley, earl of Derby, at Greenwich on 26 January 1594 and died at Richmond on 10 March 1627; Bridget, born 6 April 1584, who married Francis, Lord Norris (afterwards earl of Berkshire) in May or June 1599; Frances, who died and was buried at Edmonton on 12 September 1587; and Susan, born 26 May 1587, who married Philip Herbert, earl of Montgomery, and died in 1628 or 1629. Oxford's second wife, Elizabeth, was buried at Hackney on 3 January 1613. The illegitimate son of the earl and Anne Vavasour, Edward Vere, distinguished himself as a soldier and died on 18 August 1629.

Poetry and book dedications Oxford evinced a genuine interest in music, and wrote verse of much lyric beauty.

Puttenham, and Meres in Puttenham's footsteps, reckoned him among 'the best for comedy' in his day but, although Oxford was a patron of a company of players from 1580 to 1602, no specimen of his dramatic compositions survives. Sixteen lyrical poems have been authenticated as his work, along with four more doubtful pieces. Most of his poems first appeared in poetical anthologies signed E. O., or E. of O. Amateurish verses 'To the reader', marred by heavy alliteration, together with a pompous letter from the earl to the translator, were prefixed to Bedingfield's translation of Cardanus's *Comfort* (1576), 'published by commandment of the right honourable the Earl of Oxenford'. These verses and an accompanying letter were composed about 1 January 1572, when Oxford was twenty-one. Seven poems, generally more successful, appeared in the *Paradise of Dainty Devices* (1576), and three more in *England's Parnassus* (1600); two of the latter, 'Doth sorrow fret thy soul?' and 'What plague is greater than the grief of mind?', together with 'Faction that ever dwells', appeared in the appendix to the publisher Newman's surreptitious edition of Sidney's *Astrophel and Stella* (1591). Others are found in *The Phoenix Nest* (1593) and in *England's Helicon* of 1600 ('The Shepherd's Commendation of his Nymph'). The earl is noticed in John Bodenham's *Belvedere, or, The Garden of the Muses* (1600). His most attractive poem, a dialogue between the poet and Desire, was first printed imperfectly in Puttenham's *Art of Poesy* (1589), and then more correctly in Breton's *Bower of Delights* (1597). A few others have been recovered by modern editors from the Rawlinson manuscripts in the Bodleian Library. The surviving poems go some way towards validating the opinion of William Webbe that among the courtier-poets in the early years of Elizabeth, 'in the rare devises of poetry, [Oxford] may challenge to him selfe the tytle of the most excellent among the rest' (Webbe, sig. C3v).

Some twenty-eight printed books were dedicated to Oxford between 1564 and 1599. Among the more important were *Euphues and his England* (1580), the work of his then servant John Lyly, and *Hekatompathia, or, Passionate Centurie of Love* (1582), dedicated to Oxford by Thomas Watson with the report that the earl had perused the collection before publication; and Edmund Spenser addressed a sonnet to him (among many other worthies) in the closing pages of his *Faerie Queene* (1590). Books of smaller account include two translations by Arthur Golding (1564, 1571); four translations by his sometime servant Anthony Munday (1579, 1580, 1588, 1595); *The English Secretarie* by Angel Day (1586); and two songbooks by John Farmer (1591, 1599). Claims by literary and historical amateurs, beginning with J. Thomas Looney in 1920 and embraced by Oxford's otherwise worthy biographer B. M. Ward, that Oxford wrote the poems and plays attributed by contemporaries to William Shakespeare, are without merit.

ALAN H. NELSON

Sources J. T. Looney, *Shakespeare identified in Edmund De Vere, seventeenth earl of Oxford*, ed. R. Loyd Miller, 3rd edn, with *The poems of Edward De Vere* [and other essays], 3 vols. (Port Washington, NY, 1975) • S. W. May, ed., *The poems of Edward de Vere, seventeenth earl of*

Oxford, and of Robert Devereux, second earl of Essex (1980) · A. H. Nelson, *Monstrous adversary: the life of Edward de Vere, 17th earl of Oxford* (2003) · B. M. Ward, *The seventeenth earl of Oxford, 1550–1604, from contemporary documents* (1928) · F. B. Williams, *Index of dedications and commendatory verses in English books before 1641* (1962) · Hatfield House, Burghley papers · PRO, SP 12, SP 15, state papers, Elizabethan · *A collection of state papers ... left by William Cecill, Lord Burghley*, ed. S. Haynes and W. Murdin, 2 vols. (1740–59) · Hunt. L., Egerton papers · *The manuscripts of his grace the duke of Rutland*, 4 vols., HMC, 24 (1888–1905) · E. Lodge, *Illustrations of British history, biography, and manners*, 3 vols. (1791) · E. Spenser, *Three proper, and wittie, familiar letters* (1580) · W. Webbe, *A discourse of English poetrie* (1586)

Likenesses oils, 17th cent. (after unknown portrait, 1575), priv. coll.; on loan to NPG [*see illus.*]

Vere [de Vere], **Sir Francis** (1560/61–1609), army officer and diplomat, was the second son of Geoffrey Vere (*c.*1525–1572?) and his wife, Elizabeth (*d.* 1615), daughter of Richard Harkyns (or Hardekyn) of Colchester, Essex. He was born in 1560 or early in 1561, at either Crepping Hall or Crustwick: both properties in Essex, owned by his father, who was the fourth son of John de *Vere, fifteenth earl of Oxford [*see under* Vere, John de, sixteenth earl of Oxford]. Thus Francis was close kin of the holders of the premier earldom in England—something he never forgot and which he used to his advantage.

Formative years Little is known of Vere's early life. His connection to the de Vere earls of Oxford was of use to him early, for John de *Vere, the sixteenth earl, left a legacy of £20 to him while he was still an infant. As befitted descendants of one of the foremost generals in the Wars of the Roses, Francis, his elder brother, John, and both his younger brothers, Robert and Horace *Vere, all received training in the art of war from a young gentlemen of puritan persuasion with some military experience, William Browne, who seems to have been a retainer of the family—perhaps of the senior branch rather than of Geoffrey Vere, who was not wealthy. Thus from an early stage the brothers were intended for, or at least had an interest in, military careers and, in the event, all served as soldiers (Browne, who was later knighted, served alongside the Veres in the Netherlands.)

In his late teens Francis Vere travelled through Europe, as did many young English gentlemen in this era. The English ambassador in Paris reported that 'two young Veres', clients of the earl of Oxford, were in France in July and September 1577, hoping to fight in the country's sixth war of religion since 1562, but with the royal (Catholic) army (*CSP for.*, 12.14, 192). The two were probably John and Francis (the latter then about seventeen) who were of course connected to Oxford. Moreover the chief royal general was the duke of Guise and in later life Francis recalled that he was in Paris 'when I was very young' where 'I was for a time with the Duke of Guise ... [but] was called thence by her Majesty's command and made to know the error of that course' (*Salisbury MSS*, 17.494). Presumably the two young Veres were simply seeking actual military experience, but in later life none of the brothers would have contemplated serving a Catholic prince against protestants:

Sir Francis Vere (1560/61–1609), by unknown artist, *c.*1590

indeed Horace was strongly Calvinist. Not much later Francis travelled to eastern Europe. In a letter of 1589 Sir Francis Aleyn described Vere (whom he called 'my brother') to his friend Anthony Bacon as 'he that made the voyage with me into Polonia' (LPL, MS 657, fol. 247), a trip attributed by Vere's early twentieth-century biographer Markham to 'about 1580' (Markham, 26).

Vere's biographers all agree that he had little or no military experience and none in the Netherlands before joining the royal army sent by Elizabeth to aid the Dutch republic in 1585. In fact he served in the Netherlands in 1581 and 1582. The Dutch at this time had some 3000 English soldiers in their employ—mercenaries, but also motivated by confessional zeal to aid their fellow protestants against the Spanish. Vere was a gentleman volunteer in the company of horse led by the famous Welsh professional soldier Roger Williams, whose lieutenant was John Vere: Williams later boasted that Francis's first service was 'under his charge', and both brothers are listed in Williams's muster roll of August 1582 (PRO, SP 78/24, fol. 132*r*; *CSP for.*, *May–December 1582*, 260). Francis Vere helped to suppress a potential mutiny against the general of the English in Dutch employ, John Norris. Vere and other gentlemen rankers rallied to their general with 'dagger drawn' and cowed the soldiers, who had gone unpaid for some time (*CSP for.*, *May–December 1582*, 258; Stowe, 805).

Thus Vere had a good deal of military experience, including an education in what contemporaries called the 'most fit school and nursery to nourish soldiers' of the time (Motley, 1382)—the Dutch revolt against Spain. The English army in the Netherlands, moulded by Vere in the

1590s, would in turn come to be regarded itself as a finishing school for soldiers.

Apprenticeship: the Netherlands, 1585-1589 In December 1585 Francis Vere, still only twenty-five, joined the English army of Robert Dudley, earl of Leicester, in the Netherlands. Late in February 1586 he joined the company of lancers commanded by his cousin, Peregrine Bertie, Baron Willoughby d'Eresby (which was in the states general's pay, so Vere was still in a sense a mercenary). Willoughby's troopers, including Vere, distinguished themselves in several actions against the Spanish in summer and autumn 1586 and in November of that year Vere received his first independent command, as captain of a company of foot in the royal army—the first time he was in the pay of his own nation.

Vere's company was originally in the garrison of Bergen-op-Zoom, commanded by Willoughby, but in summer 1587 was moved to Sluys, which from 8 June to 4 August 1587 was besieged by the duke of Parma, Spain's commander-in-chief and a 'new Alexander' according to contemporaries. Sluys eventually fell, despite great efforts to relieve it by Leicester, but under Vere's old commander, Williams, the garrison fought heroically before it was obliged to accept terms. Vere, twice wounded, made his reputation among both friend and foe by his gallantry. As Williams later recalled, Vere ('marked for the red mandilion' that he habitually wore) 'stood alwaies in the head of the armed men at the assaults'; and, being 'requested to retire' because of his wounds, 'answered, he had rather be kild ten times at a breach, than once in a house' (*The Works of Sir Roger Williams*, ed. J. X. Evans, 1972, 48).

Leicester's failure to relieve Sluys, combined with various misjudgements in his administration, led to his resignation and replacement in December 1587 by Willoughby. Vere was back in Bergen, which by autumn 1588 was Parma's new target. The Spanish hoped to wipe out the stain of the Armada's defeat. Instead the city's (mostly English) garrison inflicted on the new Alexander his first defeat. Vere was wounded again and distinguished himself in command of the partly detached forts that commanded Bergen's access to the sea; he was one of three officers singled out in Willoughby's dispatches to Elizabeth for bravery, and was knighted.

Vere was now given leave and returned home with a letter of introduction from Willoughby to Lord Burghley, Elizabeth's chief minister. Vere was already acquainted with Sir Francis Walsingham and Robert Devereux, earl of Essex, prominent counsellor and courtier, respectively. In short order he won the esteem of Burghley who in turn introduced him to Elizabeth; her impression of the young paladin was evidently also favourable. In February 1589, after spending the winter at his family home, Francis returned to the Netherlands, accompanied by his brother Robert.

The trip to England made Vere personally known to the greatest figures in the realm, allowing Willoughby, on Vere's return, to appoint him sergeant-major-general—effectively second in command of all English forces in the Netherlands. (Confusingly Vere was paid from 3 December 1588, but it seems clear he was not appointed until after his return to the Netherlands.) This was a remarkable achievement for a man still not quite thirty who had yet to exercise an independent command in the field, and who for all his connections was a mere younger son of a country gentleman. There was no doubt that Vere was valiant and honourable, the two most important qualities for a sixteenth-century general; and during the siege of Bergen he showed he was, in addition, 'a prudent adviser … a cautious commander and a resourceful contriver of stratagems' (Markham, 132–3). Even so, the appointment was still something of a gamble.

Vere's rapid rise owed much to Willoughby's patronage, but there were also strategic and political dimensions to his appointment. Willoughby had already asked to be relieved of command in the Netherlands for personal reasons and his sergeant-major-general would most likely replace him. He and Leicester had directed the Anglo-Dutch armies, but from 1589 England prosecuted the war against Spain by sending armies to France and even the Iberian peninsula. The numbers of English troops in the Netherlands dropped and did not reach the heights of the late 1580s again until the dawn of the seventeenth century. Those troops' commander-in-chief would thus be subordinate to the Dutch, rather than setting the operational agenda, and so did not have to be a peer. Furthermore Leicester and Willoughby had each exercised considerable political power, but often neither wisely nor well—Leicester, in particular, had affronted the queen by his vice-regal pretensions. The English army in the United Provinces was a potential power-base. Elizabeth and her ministers wanted as its commander a man who could not abuse his position. As long as he had the necessary basic military credentials, then modest domestic wealth and status might make him an attractive candidate for high military office, rather than otherwise.

In spring 1589 Willoughby duly retired to England; from May, Vere was formally in command of all English troops in the Netherlands, except those in the garrisons of the cautionary towns of Flushing and Brill (Dutch, but in English hands for the duration of hostilities) which remained under their respective governors. However, Vere kept the rank of sergeant-major-general: he was not appointed to the office of lieutenant-general, held by Leicester and Willoughby. If this reflected the fact that he was a commoner, not a peer, it also reflected the wish of the crown to keep control of its general across the narrow seas. Vere never forgot this, but would still be able to use his primacy in military affairs to achieve a social eminence that transcended his relatively modest origins.

Elizabeth's general, the states' auxiliary, 1589-1593 From August 1589 Vere was in sole charge of the English army of assistance in the Dutch republic. His appointment was a surprise to the Dutch—understandably so. However, Vere soon showed that he could exercise tact and discretion in dealing with England's allies, while he endeared himself to them by his energy and daring. He led from the front, but showed great ability from the very start of his command.

In October 1589 Vere led 900 English foot to join a small Dutch army in Gelderland (in the eastern Netherlands) under the province's stadholder, Count Adolf von Nieuwenaar. When the count was killed shortly after Vere's arrival the states of Gelderland, remarkably, asked Vere to take command. He won a victory in the field over a small Spanish army (in which his horse was killed and he was again wounded) before returning to the main part of the republic and going into winter quarters around Utrecht. He had attracted the attention of Maurice of Nassau, stadholder of the Netherlands and Zealand and captain-general of the United Provinces. In March 1590 Vere led a 600-strong English contingent (including his recently arrived brother Horace as well as Robert Vere) in the army under Maurice that stormed Breda. That summer Vere operated with a detached force in initial moves against Nijmegen and then in October he accompanied Maurice on a raid on Dunkirk in which Vere was again wounded.

Also wounded with him was Count van Solms, who had participated in the defence of Bergen. Both men were in Maurice's trusted inner circle of commanders, along with another veteran of Bergen, Marcelis Bacx; Count van Hohenlohe (who had been captain-general in the 1580s); Floris van Brederode; Daniel de Hertaing, seigneur de Marquette; and Maurice's cousin, William Louis of Nassau, stadholder of Friesland. If not quite the *diadochi* of Alexander the Great, they were still a remarkably talented group of soldiers. Each year in the 1590s Maurice went on campaign, each year reducing another great Spanish stronghold; each year it was these men who were chosen to accompany the prince. That Vere was one of this élite says much about him and about the trust placed in him at this time by Maurice and the states general. As a Dutch chronicler wrote, Vere was 'a stout and gallant man, greatly favoured by the States above any other foreigner' ('*een cloeck dapper man, den Landen boven alle andere vreemde seer aenghenaem*'; Orlers, 79).

1591 saw sweeping success for Maurice and the Dutch army. In May Vere's men put into practice a clever ruse (probably planned by Maurice, though Vere later claimed the credit) by which the city of Zutphen was taken without a siege. The army then moved on to Deventer, which four years earlier had been betrayed to Parma by an English Catholic governor. Maurice now retook it very swiftly, largely owing to the courage of his English troops (though Vere, again, later took to himself and his troops more credit than they were probably due). Maurice then moved on against the important city of Nijmegen. Investing such a fortress was a complex operation; siege lines covered many miles. Vere was given a detached command and handled it well; so effectively was Nijmegen blockaded that in the end no assault was necessary. Sir Francis was one of five officers singled out by the Dutch for praise at the end of 1591's operations.

The summers of the next two years witnessed less frenetic campaigning, but diplomacy was inevitably a major part of Vere's duties as commander of an expeditionary force in a foreign country. There was much scope for disagreement between the United Provinces and England over the English troops' conditions of service. Equally Elizabeth used the Netherlands as a strategic reserve of experienced troops to serve elsewhere. Sir John Norris, for example, commanded an English army in Brittany from 1591 to 1594, while Essex led an expedition to Normandy in 1592: both drew on English troops from the Netherlands. In addition Elizabeth had her own preferences for strategy in the Netherlands, but her priorities were not always those of the states general. The burden of arranging for the transfers of men and of requesting naval support from the states, and of cajoling the Dutch into the action recommended by Elizabeth, fell mostly on Sir Thomas Bodley, the English ambassador, but the English commander-in-chief was necessarily a party to such negotiations. Vere handled himself well and learned from Bodley's successes (and mistakes).

Meanwhile Vere was wounded when leading the English troops in the storm of Steenwijk in 1592, and ably seconded Maurice at the siege of St Geertruidenberg in 1593. It fell before the end of the summer and Vere was able to go home, where in the parliamentary elections of 1593 he was returned as MP for Leominster. He owed his election to the earl of Essex, who as part of a plan to monopolize the patronage of English military officers, 'cultivated Sir Francis Vere' (Hammer, 218). This was welcomed by Vere, who increasingly looked to the earl for patronage.

Vere did nothing of note in this parliament and it was his only real attempt to enter the English domestic political arena. He did not lack political skills, as his increasing involvement in diplomatic negotiations with the Dutch revealed. However, he lacked a power-base in England and generally was content to concentrate on military affairs; then, too, he was a significant player in Dutch affairs. How far he was valued by his allies was made clear during this visit home in late summer 1593, when the states general offered him a pension, on top of his salary from the English government. Unusually, Elizabeth permitted Vere to accept it, and in replying to the states general declared she, like they, knew Vere 'for a gentleman very well accomplished in all the virtues and perfections, as much civil as military' ('nous le cognoissons pour gentilhome si bien accomply en toutes vertus et perfections, tant civiles, qu'appertenantes a la guerre'; Nationaal Archief, liassen Engeland 5882–II, no. 291).

It is unsurprising, therefore, that the states now turned to Vere in an attempt to get more English troops. Maurice was planning in 1594 to reduce the great Spanish fortress of Groningen, key to the eastern Netherlands, which would inevitably be a lengthy and complex campaign, requiring a large army. Maurice wanted Elizabeth to enhance the English field army in the Netherlands, but the already considerable financial burden of England's multi-front war with Spain made Elizabeth reluctant to raise more troops. In autumn 1593, therefore, the states general contracted with Vere to raise a new, separate, English regiment of ten companies, at the states general's expense and to be paid by them, but commanded by Vere, who was empowered to choose all the officers. The desire to increase his authority and no doubt the desire to strike strong blows against the enemy led Vere to accept this commission, which was parallel to his queen's commission. He was once again, in some senses, a mercenary.

Serving two masters, 1594–1599 By March 1594 the companies of Vere's mercenary regiment were arriving in the Netherlands; they were quickly deployed to the campaign against Groningen. The siege, in which Vere was wounded again, lasted well into the summer, but on 15 July Maurice and William Louis, who commanded in the east for the states general, made a triumphal entry into the city. That autumn Vere operated in the north-east of France, whose king, Henri IV, was also at war with Spain: Vere led a Dutch contingent to aid the French. In the following year, 1595, Maurice contented himself with more modest operations, but had the worse of manoeuvrings against the Spanish, in the course of which the rival armies' cavalry clashed. In this action Robert Vere was killed. Evidence differs as to the circumstances, but one account indicates that he was murdered after being taken prisoner. This is not unlikely, for only a few weeks later Vere took a small Spanish fort and had half the defenders killed in cold blood. It was in some ways uncharacteristic and perhaps best explained as an act of revenge, but it does reveal the ruthlessness of which Vere was quite capable.

Now, however, Vere was recalled to national service. Essex had been given permission to lead an assault on Spain itself—a grand strategy of which Vere approved and which he may have helped Essex to formulate. Bodley had retired and it was Vere who obtained the support of the states general for the expedition, which he then joined with a thousand veterans. Essex was lord general and Vere lord marshal and lieutenant-general of the army accompanying the fleet, of which the rear-admiral was Sir Walter Ralegh. Ralegh was more important at court and claimed precedence over Vere, but Sir Francis would have none of it: 'there passed some wourdes' between the two, so hot that some feared it would ruin the venture (LPL, MS 657, fol. 5v). Essex eventually patched up the quarrel and, in the eventual storm and sack of Cadiz, Vere won considerable distinction—plus nearly £4000 worth of booty.

By January 1597 Vere was back in the Netherlands: his later claim that he spent the winter at court must be due to a lapse of memory or to the inchoate state of his memoirs. On 24 January 1597 Vere was instrumental in the complete rout of the Spanish army in the battle of Turnhout, in which his horse was killed under him again. Both at the time and in his *Commentaries* Vere took most of the credit, resulting in a bitter dispute with Sir Robert Sidney, governor of Flushing, who also fought well. In fact the credit was probably due equally to Hohenlohe, Solms, Vere, and Bacx, who all showed great initiative and tactical skill and 'were greatly honoured' by the Dutch (Orlers, 117). It was the first battlefield victory over Spanish troops for nearly twenty years.

That summer Essex led an expedition to the Azores:

Vere accompanied him, again as lord marshal. This venture ended in disappointment, largely because of Essex's mistakes—these included his treatment of Vere. The earl appointed his friend Lord Mountjoy as lieutenant-general, an office Sir Francis had expected, since he had executed it so capably at Cadiz. Vere could do little but accept his patron's decision, but injured pride and frustration at the mishandling of the expedition led him to turn decisively against Essex. On his return he also metaphorically crossed swords again with Sidney and Ralegh over military issues. Vere's increasing unwillingness to defer to anyone reflected his confidence in his own abilities and experience.

It also no doubt reflected Vere's own increasing security. The longer he held his position in the Netherlands, the more indispensable he became. Both English and Dutch governments had become accustomed to working with Sir Francis. This was manifested when in 1598 England and the United Provinces renegotiated the arrangements by which the war against Spain was prosecuted. A new treaty, most satisfactory to Elizabeth, was signed in London on 16 August 1598—but it resulted from hard bargaining conducted by the new English ambassador in the Hague, George Gilpin, and by Sir Francis Vere, who was accredited as special envoy to the states general and had conducted negotiations throughout June. Vere's reward came in the autumn, when he was made governor of the cautionary town of Brill—filling the vacancy left by the death of Lord Burgh, despite the hopes of lords Cromwell and Grey de Wilton, who lobbied hard for the post, and the opposition of Essex. Vere's good opinion of himself was shared by the queen and her new chief minister, Sir Robert Cecil.

The major provision of the treaty in 1598 was that all English field companies be put into the pay and under the command of the states general from January 1599. The cautionary garrisons were excluded and Elizabeth reserved ultimate authority over the rest, but almost all the English troops in the Netherlands were once again under Dutch control. As soon as the treaty went into effect in January 1599 Vere's sergeant-major-general's commission from Elizabeth was matched by one from the states general, making him 'generael over alle de compaignien Engelschen' and giving him the full burden ('last') and power ('macht') 'over die Engelsche Capiteynen, Officieren & soldaten' in Dutch pay (Nationaal Archief, archief van de staten-generaal, no. 12270, fol. 169; Nationaal Archief, Oldenbarnevelt archief, no. 2977). Vere was the only foreign general in the states' army and commanded all English troops in the Netherlands, save in Flushing, with a power that was almost absolute. However, his main paymaster was henceforth the Dutch republic, which was increasingly seeking to integrate all its foreign troops into a centralized military structure. Sir Francis Vere—basking in his new status—may not have foreseen it, but trouble lay ahead.

Apogee, 1599–1603 For the moment, however, Vere was still irreplaceable. He was the only man able to fulfil two functions: first he could command the English troops in the field effectively while being trusted by both sides to do justice to their own military priorities; second he was able both to convince the states to redeploy those troops to suit Elizabeth's strategic priorities and to persuade her to give additional assistance when the Dutch needed it. Vere was even a popular figure at home. In October 1599 a stage version of the battle of Turnhout attracted good audiences: the actor playing Vere was identifiable by his (false) beard and distinctive clothing, as one eyewitness affirmed—clearly Vere was now a public personality.

It was in these years indeed that Vere won his greatest fame. In summer 1600 he commanded one of the three divisions of the army with which Maurice made a daring amphibious invasion of Flanders. Outmanoeuvred by the Spanish under Archduke Albert of Austria, the Dutch army was brought to battle near Nieuwpoort on 2 July 1600. The result was the most celebrated battle of the Eighty Years' War between Spain and the Netherlands and a great victory for Maurice. It has been analysed many times and it seems clear that, again, Vere claimed more credit than he was due in his *Commentaries*. Maurice, in particular, is made to appear indecisive, and readers could easily conclude that Vere was chiefly responsible for the victory. Indeed while his dispatches at the time were taken by some Englishmen to show 'that the Ennemy was overthrowen by the Valor of the English, and the good Direction of Sir Francis Vere', others commented on the self-congratulatory note of Vere's 'letters to the counsaile'. The well-informed John Chamberlain wrote sardonically that these gave a 'relation … so partiall, as yf no man had strooke stroke but the English, and among the English no man almost but Sir Francis Vere.' Yet even Chamberlain did not doubt that Vere had played a great part. Indeed Elizabeth received letters from the Dutch government 'in commendation of our nation, but especially of his great service that day', and 'attributing the Victory to his good Order and Direction'; she herself declared Vere to be the worthiest captain of her time (Sydney and others, 2.204; *Letters of John Chamberlain*, 1.102). In fact Vere commanded the advance guard which made a skilful fighting withdrawal, and then, together with Maurice, led the counter-attack that swept the Spanish from the field in disarray. He was wounded in three places and again had his horse shot underneath him. He did not win the battle himself, but what he did was most praiseworthy.

Vere's heroic defence of Ostend followed in 1601. The siege of Ostend (one of the greatest of the century) from July 1601 to September 1604 is referred to in *Hamlet* and in the *Atheists Tragedie* of the Jacobean dramatist Cyril Tourneur, who himself served there. But for Vere's determined initial resistance the city would have fallen much earlier. The Dutch had advance warning of Spanish plans and deliberately shipped Vere into the city with 1500 extra troops, mostly English. He took command on 9 July 1601, four days after the town was invested by the archduke. Vere ensured that the port remained accessible to friendly shipping and was himself transported out by sea that summer, after being shot in the head. He returned in September and continued to conduct a vigorous defence, but

against overwhelming odds. By the beginning of December Vere's garrison had lost 40 per cent of its strength and a storm at sea had disrupted a Dutch fleet with reinforcements and supplies. He opened negotiations for a surrender, deliberately aimed at buying time; the fleet sailed in, Vere cancelled his negotiations, and the archduke was left 'growling and furious' (Motley, 3.86).

This is one of the more controversial episodes in Vere's career; at the time and later he was criticized, first by those who thought that the negotiations were meant seriously and that the withdrawal of the capitulation offer was only fortuitous; and second by those who felt he had acted dishonourably. His 'anti-parley' was defended in a pamphlet, possibly authored by Tourneur (*Extremities Urging the Lord General Sir F. Veare to Offer the Late Anti-parle with the Archduke Albertus*, 1602). In fact, such negotiations, aimed simply at spinning out time, were common in seventeenth-century warfare; and there is no doubt that the whole thing was a ruse, since the garrison council of war agreed to Vere's suggestion before the anti-parley was initiated. The ploy saved the city and was lauded by the garrison's officers, English, Dutch, and French—no more need be said.

On 7 January 1602 Albert unleashed his greatest assault yet, one designed to storm the entire fortress, rather than merely particular outworks. Vere himself briefly fought hand-to-hand in the breach to repel the main Spanish assault and the garrison held firm. Then, as the enemy retreated, Vere ordered the western sluice of the city to be opened and the retreat was turned into a disaster. A lull inevitably followed as the archduke endeavoured to make good his losses, and in March Vere was withdrawn, as the new campaign season would shortly start and his services were wanted in the field. He made a short trip home where he convinced Elizabeth to raise more troops for service in the Netherlands, then returned as commander of a division of over 7000 Englishmen in Maurice's army. Vere was at the height of his fame and success.

In consequence of his unique place in Anglo-Dutch relations, his diplomatic skill, his prowess in combat, and his popularity Vere had unique authority, greater than that of any other mercenaries in Dutch pay. For example, Vere controlled 'the apointing of all Captens' in the English forces (Sydney and others, 2.206). He was also able in these years effectively to thumb his nose at the English hierarchy (save for the queen and Cecil). Lord Grey and the earl of Northumberland fought at Nieuwpoort and Ostend respectively; both objected to having to serve under their social inferior. However, despite frequent complaints at Elizabeth's court, Grey was consistently obliged to defer to Vere; and Northumberland only avoided that fate by a precipitate return to England. In April 1602, during Vere's visit home following his triumph at Ostend, Northumberland challenged him to a duel. He received the dismissive reply that Vere 'thought it not reasonable to satisfie him after the manner he did require and therefore he would not doe it' (CUL, Add. MS 9276, fol. 6r)! Northumberland was, in any case, required by the queen to withdraw his challenge. It is unsurprising that Vere also defied the wishes of Essex, consciously choosing to ignore the earl's attempts to advance his clients in the English army; Vere told him to his face that 'the command of the [English] nation [in the Netherlands] belonged to me' (Arber, 137), leaving Essex 'much offended with Sir Francis Vere' (*Letters of John Chamberlain*, 1.68).

Increasingly, however, Vere's exercise of power was perceived as arbitrary. In 1603, for example, he was warned about the rumour that he had deliberately blocked the promotion of 'all Cornish men' because of a quarrel with a west-country captain, William Lower (BL, Add. MS 32464, p. 62). It was not only the envious Ralegh, Sidney, Grey, and Northumberland who resented Sir Francis; even two of his lieutenant-colonels, Sir Henry Docwra and Sir Callisthenes Brooke, fell out with him. When Vere's behaviour aroused 'a general discontentment' (Markham, 307), he took increasingly high-handed methods to maintain order, bullying at least one malcontent captain and winking at a brutal assault on another by his latest lieutenant-colonel, Sir John Ogle. Vere's high-handedness to his own countrymen weakened his position for it made him more dependent on the goodwill of the Dutch, which was becoming less and less unconditional.

Fall In the early to mid-1590s Maurice of Nassau initiated his celebrated military reforms which eventually helped the Dutch to win their independence. As a result by 1598 the army was both very proficient and under standardized and centralized authority. The autonomy of the republic's English troops, which owed much to Vere's unique position, went against this trend. From 1599 the Dutch expected the English troops, now in their pay, to be as subordinate to central authority as the many other mercenary contingents in their employ.

In 1601 attempts by Maurice to remove some English troops from Vere's command led to 'Hart burning between Sir Francis and his Excellency' (Sydney and others, 2.228). Between July and October 1602 Vere was almost incommunicado during a prolonged convalescence following a head wound while on campaign with Maurice. During this time George Gilpin, the experienced English ambassador in the Netherlands, died and was not immediately replaced. Vere believed that Maurice used his and Gilpin's absence to increase his authority over the English contingent: an English captain noted that Vere was 'nothing well pleased with … [Maurice's] dealings by him' (*Salisbury MSS*, 12.307).

However, at this stage (1602) the Dutch were still keen to stay on good terms with Vere, taking pains, for example, to ensure his pay was more up to date than that of most of his compatriots: thus in April 1603 he was paid 2600 guilders of his personal salary and perquisites which were in arrears, even though his accounts had not yet been finalized (Nationaal Archief, archief van de staten-generaal, no. 12503, fol. 368r). Evidently his services were still valued and his employers would have hoped that he could be induced to adapt to their wishes. However, Vere was then in dispute with the states general through much of the winter of 1602–3 over the terms of his and his soldiers' employment; and his old teacher Browne, now

lieutenant-governor of Flushing, reported that he was on poor terms with Maurice of Nassau. Vere was showing no signs of being willing to make the adjustments that the Dutch required. However, in his favour was the fact that he was still the favoured generalissimo of the head of state of the republic's major ally.

On 24 March 1603 Elizabeth died. Her successor, James of Scotland, had peace with Spain as his prime foreign policy objective. Maurice and the states had a golden opportunity to subjugate fully their English employees and made moves to limit further Vere's authority. They focused attention on Vere's judicial powers which were wholly exceptional: by 1603 all troops in the Dutch army were subject to the jurisdiction of the high court of military justice. Vere and his supporters, believing that 'the title of general was merely a show if he had to exercise its power without being able to administer justice' (Nationaal Archief, Oldenbarnevelt archief, no. 2971, fol. 2r), were determined to resist what Vere regarded as an intolerable encroachment on his authority.

As part of his strategy Vere returned home to win the support of the new king. He had already obtained the continuation of his governorship of Brill by letters patent of 16 April 1603. Vere had promptly proclaimed the Scottish king as king of England and he got on well with James I. Encouraged, Vere decided to bring his dispute with the Dutch to a head. At the end of 1603 he threatened to resign unless his authority over the English troops was confirmed on his terms. He evidently believed that, with the king's support secured, he was still irreplaceable. So confident was he that he made his bid while still in England. Courtiers wrote on his behalf to perceived allies within the Netherlands, and early in 1604 the new English ambassador, Sir Ralph Winwood, presented a strongly worded remonstrance to the council of state in support of Vere's requests. The stakes were high: as one English veteran turned diplomat observed, Vere was in effect seeking no less than 'absolute command of the English troops in Holland' (*CSP dom.*, 1603–10, 68).

Unfortunately for Vere by the time his proposals came before the republic's council of state, it would have heard of how 'the Spanish Ambassador [had been] publicqly feasted by the king on St Stephen's day' ('Journal of Levinus Munck', 249). It was obvious that James intended to make peace; his government's influence in Dutch military affairs, albeit still considerable, was inevitably reduced. In addition, the resentment Vere had aroused among the English officers in the Netherlands meant that the Dutch did not have to worry about disorder within their élite corps if they came to a parting of the ways. Consequently Vere's demands were refused. Having declared that if they were not met then his office of colonel-general of the English infantry would be 'nudum et inutile nomen' ('an empty and useless title'; Nationaal Archief, Oldenbarnevelt archief, no. 2971 fol. 1v), Vere was left with no choice but to resign and by April 1604 he had done so. In retrospect this was probably Maurice's intention from the start of his attempts to reduce Vere's judicial powers in 1603.

Vere was still governor of Brill; he could have remained

there, but, badly wounded in body in 1600, 1601, and 1602, and now wounded in pride, he returned to England, where he was welcomed at court. On both sides of the North Sea there was a readiness to pretend that Vere's resignation was due to ill health, which saved blushes all round. However, Vere did not retire; rather (in the language of industrial relations), he had suffered constructive dismissal.

Further career and death In 1605 the Dutch republic was left reeling by a great Spanish offensive which, it was obvious, would be renewed the following year. In December Vere returned to Brill (which had been governed by a deputy); he did so not simply to resume his governorship, but in the belief (shared by other observers) that the dire straits of the Dutch might compel them to restore his commission.

Maurice and other Dutch officials dropped hints of sympathy for their former general, but it cost them nothing to express regret at 'the clause in the treaty [of London] inhibiting the Governors of the cautionary townes to have command in these warres' (BL, Stowe MS 168, fol. 345v). Clemont Edmondes, who had carried Vere's dispatches from Nieuwpoort, reflected the reality when he wrote in March 1606 of 'the jelowsie which the house of Nassau hath of Sir Francis Vere of whom Counte Maurice speaketh much good but geveth litle furtherance' (BL, Stowe MS, fol. 356v). Ogle and Sir Horace Vere supported Sir Francis's return, but bitter opposition from leading English officers, such as Sir Edward Cecil, who was 'malcontent' at the prospect of having to resume a 'servile ranck' (De L'Isle and Dudley MSS, 3.257), provided a good excuse for Maurice to reject Vere without causing unpleasantness among his friends at the English court or in the Dutch army.

In the end, in 1606, the states general awarded a pension of 3000 guilders (some £300) per annum to Francis Vere; thus bought off, he returned to England, never to lead men in battle again.

In June 1606 Vere was appointed governor of Portsmouth, with subsidiary grants of other offices in that vicinity. It is notable that though England's coastal fortresses were generally run down in the years of peace that followed the treaty of London, 'enormous sums' were still spent on the defences of Portsmouth, the garrison and fortifications of which were 'still in reasonably good condition' on Vere's death (R. Stewart, The English Ordnance Office, 1585–1625: a Case Study in Bureaucracy, 1996, 119). It is a tribute to the prestige and influence of Sir Francis that he was able to buck the trend of James's pacifist policy in this way.

In later life love found the semi-retired soldier. On 26 October 1607 Vere married Elizabeth, daughter of John Dent, a citizen of London, and his second wife, Alice Grant. Elizabeth was only sixteen; Sir Francis was perhaps three times her age. However, the couple seem to have been happy enough in the short time that remained to them (and it is notable that the same month Horace Vere married a lady sixteen years his junior).

On 28 August 1609, without warning, Vere died. He left no will (a contemporary reported that he left his £300 annuity to the earl of Oxford, but it had been specified in the grant that it should go to Oxford on his death) and a commission for the administration of his property was issued to his widow on 30 August 1609. Their only child had predeceased him. Vere was buried in Westminster Abbey the day after his death, and a magnificent memorial was constructed in the chapel of St John. Modelled on the tomb of Engelbert of Nassau at Breda, it was an appropriate memorial to an Englishman who was among the internationally best known of his time.

The cause of Vere's relatively early death is unknown. However, early in 1605 Ambassador Winwood had observed of Vere's life in semi-retirement that it made 'his lyfe … unprofitible to the world, and perhaps, as unpleasing to himself' (BL, Stowe MS 168, fol. 345). Thus, a fellow soldier's speculation that Vere died 'because he had nothing to do' may not be far off the truth (J. M. Shuttleworth, ed., The Life of Lord Herbert of Cherbury, 1976, 72). However, Vere had also suffered so many wounds that his body may simply have been prematurely worn out.

The Commentaries At some point after 1604 Vere recorded his memoirs of several campaigns; these were published in 1657 as his Commentaries. To this surviving text Vere's posthumous editor, William Dillingham, a Cambridge academic, added narratives of Nieuwpoort and the parley at Ostend by Sir John Ogle, written some years earlier; and extracts from some of the publications of Henry Hexham, Vere's page at Ostend and, by the 1630s, a noted writer on military subjects. The resultant work is not only a key source for Vere's life, but one of the major sources for the history of England and the Netherlands in this period.

The Commentaries show Vere in a positive light and have been disparaged by some historians as a partisan publication. Other scholars stress that they were not published until forty-eight years after his death and then at the instigation of an antiquary; they assert that Vere wrote a private work intended to aid the military education of future English officers. The great military historian C. H. Firth noted that 'the object of the Commentaries was not autobiographical': they were 'designed to be communicated to a few other soldiers' (Arber, xvii), and Vere's biographer argued similarly (Markham).

However, there was a flourishing manuscript culture in seventeenth-century England: tracts circulated widely even if unpublished. Ogle had read a copy—but so had Cyril Tourneur, more professional writer than soldier (Arber, 162). The copy of Vere's writings that Dillingham originally saw was in the possession of the distinguished parliamentarian general Philip Skippon, who at the start of his career had served under the Veres, and the other copies he found were in the possession of Sir Francis Vere's great-nephews, grandchildren of Sir Horace: but of these, while Thomas, Lord Fairfax, was also a soldier, the earls of Clare and Westmorland were not. In short, the Commentaries are Vere's version of events for his family, friends, and a circle of admiring veterans, but he would have known the extent to which manuscripts circulated and were copied. Given his grievance over his treatment by Maurice, Vere surely wrote with half an eye on a wider public than simply his own friends and extended family, even if he never intended publication. Moreover, the work may have been left incomplete only by his death; it may be that he intended an autobiography modelled on the *Commentaires* of the distinguished French soldier Blaise de Monluc, of which Vere would certainly have been aware, rather than military reflections based on the example of Caesar's *Commentaries*.

In any event there is clearly a self-congratulatory aspect to Vere's writings. Even Ogle, Vere's trusted lieutenant, felt that his own role at Nieuwpoort had been understated by his former commander (Arber, 162). As noted above, John Chamberlain thought that Vere's Nieuwpoort dispatches were self-serving. Vere's original editor commented that Horace Vere's services were 'so eminent and considerable that they might easily have furnished another Commentary; had not his own exceeding modesty proved a stepmother to his deserved praises'—which suggests that he felt Sir Francis lacked modesty (ibid., 87). Vere's style in his *Commentaries* attracted opprobrious comment by Samuel Johnson and the great antiquary Thomas Birch, on the grounds that he tried to take the credit for all the actions he described (Markham, 359*n*.). Into the nineteenth and early twentieth centuries, historians simply accepted Vere's descriptions of events and lauded him accordingly, but historians writing from a Dutch perspective found Vere's tone distasteful; modern historians of the Netherlands have also questioned the accuracy of how he depicted his relationship with Maurice and his contribution to Dutch strategy (for example, van Deursen, 8; Borman, *passim*).

In spite of these caveats Vere was an eyewitness of the events he describes for some of which he is a unique source, and he wrote clearly. No one at the time, English or Dutch, questioned his bravery or tactical ability and he was still trusted by Maurice until very late, as even Dutch historians accept (such as van Deursen, 9). Properly used, the *Commentaries* are an excellent historical source, but given the bias that has been identified in the author, they need to be read carefully, they must always be compared with other accounts of events where possible, and where sources differ Vere's verdict on events should not be accepted simply on his say so. In short, the *Commentaries* should be treated like any seventeenth-century memoir, and neither privileged nor suspected unduly.

Character Vere was notable for his calculated rashness. His bravery at Sluys, Nieuwpoort, and Ostend and his frequent wounds all pay tribute to a valour that was remarkable even in an era when courage in combat was common. As we have seen, he was very quick to quarrel when he felt his interests or honour threatened. In this he was no worse than most of his fellow officers and better than some. However, this combativeness may have had a similar cause to Vere's desire, of which we have seen repeated examples, to be given all or most of the credit for actions in which he participated, even when not truly or wholly warranted. His palpable preoccupation with recognition, when his achievements would undoubtedly have brought

him great praise in any case, surely hints at a more profound anxiety. Rather than 'inordinate self-esteem' (Motley, 4.69), it is possible that Vere had just the opposite problem. For most of his time in the Netherlands he was notorious for 'his melancholic disposition' and though a year after he was obliged to retire Browne noted—in surprise—that 'he love[d] company and mirth' (*De L'Isle and Dudley MSS*, 3.257), for much of his life something plainly gnawed deep down in Francis Vere's soul.

None the less Vere commanded great devotion. Clemont Edmondes dedicated his best-selling translation of Caesar's *Commentaries* in 1600 to Vere, and Tourneur published an elegy lamenting his death. Hexham and Ogle remembered their old chief with affection and respect in their writings. Even his rival Edward Cecil, in a tactical treatise written in the 1620s, reminisced that 'The whole Army both reverenced him and stood in awe of him' (Dalton, 1.57). Not only former soldiers praised Vere: both the Dutch historian Isaac Dorislaus, holder of the first chair of history at Cambridge, and Thomas May, translator of Lucan and historian of the Long Parliament, viewed his victory at Nieuwpoort as comparable to those of the ancient Romans: there was no higher compliment in Renaissance Europe, where the Nassaus read ancient Roman authors when seeking tactical inspiration. Nor was such praise surprising. Vere was not just a victorious commander: he was also a man of humanistic sympathies. At the sack of Faro in 1596 he saved the library of the distinguished Spanish scholar Osorius and later deposited it in the Oxford University library, which had been refounded by his old colleague Bodley. Vere keenly supported Bodley's attempt to create a resource centre for protestant learning at Oxford: he was one of the first donors in 1598, and followed his £100 present then with regular donations in the following ten years, as well as further gifts of books in 1602, 1607, and 1609, including 'China books' (provenance unknown) (*Letters of Sir Thomas Bodley*, 168).

Achievements and reputation Vere became famous in Elizabethan England's great war against Spain, and was the mentor for a generation of English soldiers, many of whom went on to command in the civil wars of the 1640s. Today he is probably the best-known English military (as opposed to naval) commander of the late sixteenth and early seventeenth centuries, largely thanks to his *Commentaries*, and to a florid nineteenth-century biography, *The Fighting Veres*, by the eccentric Victorian admiral-turned-writer Sir Clements Markham. The existence of the *Commentaries*, a first-person narrative written in robust style, guaranteed the attention of future generations to its author. Vere was greatly praised by early nineteenth-century writers of military history, who took him as a standard example of a sixteenth-century general; one declared that of the English soldiers of Elizabeth's era 'there was none whose exploits more justly entitle him to the admiration of posterity than Sir Francis de Vere' (G. R. Gleig, *Lives of the most Eminent British Military Commanders*, 3 vols., 1831–2, 1.124–5). A strong attack on him in the 1870s by the great American historian of the Dutch revolt John

Lothrop Motley only added to Vere's renown, since Motley's pro-Dutch bias ensured that his negative assessments were not simply accepted. In 1888 Motley was in turn vigorously criticized by Markham in *The Fighting Veres*, the book that established its subject's fame. Nominally a double biography of Francis and his younger brother Horace, whose military career later matched his brother's, it devoted less than a third to Horace. Only in the last quarter of the twentieth century has there been sustained analysis by academic historians of English involvement in the Netherlands in the late Tudor and early Stuart periods. It has not produced any work on Vere (albeit Wernham's narrative histories of the Anglo-Spanish war are informative) other than a PhD thesis (Borman); but this focuses on his career as commander-in-chief of the royal English army in the Dutch republic between 1589 and 1603, is not a biography, and has not been published. So Vere, though relatively well known, has never been the subject of a full biography; most narratives of his life do not take into account recent scholarship on the period; and interested readers with normal library resources will be able to discover little more about him.

What verdict, then, can be reached on his career? Dutch historians highlight his ability at light infantry warfare (for example, Schulten and Schulten, 75), and his fighting withdrawal at Nieuwpoort was masterfully done, but he was also a good cavalry general, as he showed at Turnhout. His fighting qualities made him, according to Ogle, admittedly a devoted supporter, 'the fittest instrument … that [the Dutch] can advise of if they mean to make an active war' (*Salisbury MSS*, 16.306). However, Vere also demonstrated mastery of siege warfare, which was what Maurice valued him for throughout the 1590s. In addition he reorganized the English army in the 1590s, showing a talent for administration. Thus Motley's claim that though 'an efficient colonel, [Vere] was not a general to be relied upon in great affairs either in council or in the field' (Motley, 4.69) does not do justice to his all-round abilities.

On the other hand it is going too far to claim him as one of England's 'great captains'. Motley's claim contained a kernel of truth and was presumably based on the verdict of William Louis of Nassau that Vere (whom he knew well) was 'een goed kolonel' but needed further schooling before he could play the part of a general (van Deursen, 8n.). In virtually all the great actions in which he won distinction Vere was a subordinate. Maurice often accepted his advice (or so Vere claimed, though modern historians are more sceptical), and was often semi-detached from the main army, but Sir Francis never exercised a truly independent command (in contrast to Sir Horace) and even if Maurice took his advice every time Vere claimed, it was still the prince who had to make the decisions and bear the responsibility. All in all, Vere's talents were those of an excellent corps commander and/or a staff officer, rather than of an army commander. This judgement is of course anachronistic and approximate, but it offers a guide to where Sir Francis Vere should stand in the pantheon of English military greats. If this assessment is not as high as he (or some historians) would have liked, he was still a very able soldier and diplomat.

Vere is best summed up by contemporaries. In the words of a seventeenth-century biographer,

> though he were an honourable slip of that ancient tree of nobility [the earls of Oxford] … yet he brought more glory to the name of Vere, than he took of blood from the family. … He was amongst the Queen's swordmen, inferior to none, but superior to many.   (Naunton, 295–6)

Cecil elsewhere declared: 'Hee was the verie Dyall of the whole Army by whome wee knew when we should fight or not' (Dalton). It is an epitaph Sir Francis Vere might have chosen.   D. J. B. TRIM

Sources C. H. Firth, introduction, *An English garner*, 7: *Stuart tracts, 1603–1693*, ed. E. Arber and C. H. Firth (1903); repr. (1964) [incl. 'The *Commentaries* of Sir Francis Vere (1657)', ed. W. Dillingham] • C. R. Markham, *The fighting Veres: lives of Sir Francis Vere … and of Sir Horace Vere … Baron Vere de Tilbury* (1888) • T. J. Borman, 'Sir Francis Vere in the Netherlands, 1589–1603: a re-evaluation of his career as sergeant major general of Elizabeth I's troops', PhD diss., U. Hull, 1997 • J. L. Motley, *History of the United Netherlands: from the death of William the Silent to the Twelve Years Truce, 1609*, 4 vols. (New York, 1879–80) • D. J. B. Trim, 'Fighting "Jacob's wars": the employment of English and Welsh mercenaries in the European wars of religion; France and the Netherlands, 1562–1610', PhD diss., U. Lond., 2002 • PRO, exchequer, pipe office, declared accounts, E 351/240–1 • state papers: France, PRO, SP 78/22, 24 • state papers: Holland, PRO, SP 84 • Nationaal Archief, The Hague, archief van de raad van state, 12–24, 1232–8, 1525 • Nationaal Archief, The Hague, archief van de staten-generaal, liassen Engeland 5581–3; liassen Lopende 4891, 4900–2; staten van oorlog 8040–5; loketkast 12576; financial records, 12503, 12356 • Nationaal Archief, The Hague, Archief van Johan van Oldenbarnevelt, 2943–5, 2950, 2971, 2977 • BL, Stowe MS 168 • LPL, MS 657 • J. Orlers, *Den Nassauschen Laurencrans* (Leyden, 1610) [a contemporary Eng. edn, *The triumphs of Nassau*, trans. William Shute (1613), is unreliable] • N. Japikse and H. P. Rijperman, eds., *Resolutiën der Staten-Generaal van 1576 tot 1609*, 14 vols. (The Hague, 1915–70), vols. 7–14 • *Report on the manuscripts of Lord De L'Isle and Dudley*, 6 vols., HMC, 77 (1925–66), vols. 2–3 • *Calendar of the manuscripts of the most hon. the marquis of Salisbury*, 24 vols., HMC, 9 (1883–1976), vols. 4–18 • *Report on the manuscripts of the marquis of Downshire*, 6 vols. in 7, HMC, 75 (1924–95), vols. 3–4 • *CSP for., 1572–4; 1582; 1585–8* • R. B. Wernham, ed., *List and analysis of state papers, foreign series, Elizabeth I*, 7 vols. (1964–2000) • H. Sydney and others, *Letters and memorials of state*, ed. A. Collins, 2 vols. (1746) [Sydney Papers] • *The letters of John Chamberlain*, ed. N. E. McClure, 2 vols. (1939) • C. Tourneur, *A funerall poeme upon the death of the most worthie and true souldier Sir Francis Vere Knight, captaine of Portsmouth, lord gouvernour of his majesties cautionarie towne of Briell in Holland* (1609) • J. Stowe, *Annales of England*, ed. E. Howes, 1631 edn • R. Naunton, *Fragmenta regalia, or, Observations on the late Queen Elizabeth, her times and favourites, Memoirs of Robert Cary and fragmenta regalia*, ed. W. Scott (1806) • *APC, 1595–1604* • R. B. Wernham, *After the Armada: Elizabethan England and the struggle for western Europe, 1588–1595* (1984) • R. B. Wernham, *The return of the armadas: the last years of the Elizabethan war against Spain, 1595–1603* (1994) • P. E. J. Hammer, *The polarisation of Elizabethan politics: the political career of Robert Devereux, 2nd earl of Essex, 1585–1597* (1999) • A. Th. van Deursen, 'De raad van state en de generaliteit (1590–1616)', *Bijdragen voor de geschiedenis der Nederlanden*, 19 (1964–5), 1–48 • J. I. Israel, *The Dutch republic: its rise, greatness and fall* (1995) • 'The journal of Levinus Munck', ed. H. V. Jones, *EngHR*, 68 (1953), 234–58 • M. van der Hoeven, ed., *Exercise of arms: warfare in the Netherlands (1568–1648)* (1997) • C. M. Schulten and J. W. M. Schulten, *Het leger in de zeventiende eeuw* (Bussum, Netherlands, 1969) • C. Wilson, *Queen Elizabeth and the revolt of the Netherlands* (1970) • E. Belleroche, 'The "siege of Ostend", or, "The New Troy", 1601–1604', *Proceedings of the Huguenot*

Society of London, 3 (1888–91), 428–539 · H. J. Webb, Elizabethan military science: the books and the practice (1965) · J. R. Hale, War and society in Renaissance Europe, 1450–1620 (1985); repr. (1998) · Niew Nederlandsch biografisch woordenboek, ed. P. C. Molhuysen, P. J. Blok, L. Knappert, and K. H. Kossman, 10 vols. (1911–37) · W. C. Metcalfe, ed., The visitations of Essex, 1, Harleian Society, 13 (1878) · Letters of Sir Thomas Bodley to Thomas James, ed. G. W. Wheeler (1926); repr. (1985) · J. L. Chester, ed., The marriage, baptismal, and burial registers of the collegiate church or abbey of St Peter, Westminster, Harleian Society, 10 (1876) · W. A. Shaw, The knights of England, 2 vols. (1906) · F. G. Emmison, ed., Elizabethan life: wills of Essex gentry and merchants (1978) · C. Dalton, The life and times of General Sir Edward Cecil, Viscount Wimbledon … 1605–31, 2 vols. (1885)

Archives BL, papers, Harley MSS, vol. 168, fols. 120 et seq.; vol. 287, fols. 243–55; vol. 6844, fols. 77 et seq. · CUL, commentaries | Hatfield House, Hertfordshire, Cecil papers and manuscripts · Nationaal Archief, The Hague, archief van de staten-generaal, liassen Engeland; liassen Lopende · PRO, state papers, foreign, Holland, SP 84

Likenesses oils, c.1590, priv. coll.; on loan to NPG [see illus.] · R. Gaywood, etching (after memorial), BM, NPG · engraving (after portrait, c.1590), repro. in Markham, Fighting Veres, frontispiece · memorial, Westminster Abbey; repro. in Wilson, Queen Elizabeth, pl. iii

Vere, Henry de, eighteenth earl of Oxford (1593–1625), nobleman and soldier, was the only surviving son of Edward de *Vere, seventeenth earl of Oxford (1550–1604), and his second wife, Elizabeth Trentham (d. 1612/13). He was born on 24 February 1593 at Stoke Newington, Middlesex, and inherited his title on 24 June 1604. He was admitted to the Middle Temple in November 1604, and awarded an MA degree at Oxford on 30 August 1605 during a royal visit there. It seems unlikely that the earl absorbed much learning at either place, however, preferring what his mother described in 1611 as 'evil courses'. His financial situation was from the beginning precarious; in 1604 King James granted him a £200 pension, and in 1609 his mother, as his guardian, sought a parliamentary bill that would have allowed him to sell part of his estate.

While he was at least occasionally at court—serving as esquire to Prince Charles on his creation as duke of York in 1605, and becoming knight of the Bath at Prince Henry's assumption of the principality of Wales in 1610—Oxford preferred what some described as 'debauchery' away from Whitehall. In 1611 the king granted him the keepership of Havering Park, although James worried that he would not preserve the game there. Conflict with his mother, who described him as 'younge and nott able to advise himself' (BL, Add. MS 29549, fol. 31), bedevilled his youth, but her death in December 1612 or early January 1613 increased his income and allowed him to embark upon an extended tour of Europe. He remained overseas for over five years, first in the Spanish Netherlands, then France (he was in Paris in 1614), and finally, Venice. In Venice, with the king's approval, Oxford offered to raise 6000 men for the republic's service—an offer the senate declined. While in Venice he was unwarily drawn into a dispute at home. Lady Hatton attempted to derail the planned match of her daughter, Frances Coke, to Sir John Villiers, brother of James's favourite Buckingham, by claiming a pre-contract with Oxford. The king insisted upon the Villiers marriage, and the ploy failed. 'He

[Oxford] sends word he will come over and see what he must do, but it is doubtful whether her fair face and the large fortune offered will induce him to risk losing the favour of the King' (CSP dom., 1611–18, 482).

Oxford returned to England in October 1618, served in Queen Anne's funeral in May 1619, and in the same month took up his office as hereditary lord great chamberlain. But the European war beckoned, and was more attractive to the earl than a court now dominated by Buckingham. In June 1620 he joined his kinsman Sir Horace Vere as a captain in Vere's regiment. His 250 men were raised, the Venetian ambassador claimed, at Oxford's own expense—although given his poverty this seems a dubious assertion. After only a few months' service he left the Palatinate just before word arrived of the catastrophic defeat of Frederick's army at White Mountain, outside Prague. He landed in England on 11 November.

As a peer with firsthand experience of the war (limited though it was), Oxford was named by James to the council of war which in January and February 1621 considered how to rescue the elector palatine's fortunes. In the first session of the parliament of 1621, armed with two proxies and a feeling that his services were undervalued, he aligned himself with the so-called 'noble patriots' opposed to a Spanish match. Oxford spoke rashly about the match, and in July was gaoled for a short time in the Tower. The king suggested that he absent himself from parliament's second session, and then made sure of his absence by appointing him to command a fleet patrolling the English Channel in December. Oxford served at sea until March 1622, but was removed from command following another imbroglio with Buckingham. This time he unwisely intervened in the marriage of another Villiers brother, Christopher, to Elizabeth Norreys. He 'hoped the time would come when justice would be free, and not pass only through Buckingham's hands' (CSP dom., 1619–23, 328). For this Oxford once again went to the Tower. This time James was incensed and directed the attorney-general to prepare a Star Chamber prosecution. Held a close prisoner for twenty months, repeated efforts to gain Oxford's release failed due to the king's intransigence. Finally, on 30 December 1623, he was freed, thanks to the good offices of Prince Charles and Buckingham, hoping to smooth the waters before the upcoming parliamentary session. The duke further ingratiated himself with Oxford by supporting his planned match with Lady Diana (1596–1654), daughter of Thomas Cecil, second earl of Exeter. Lady Diana's beauty was matched by her £30,000 fortune, and the two were married as soon as Oxford was released, on 1 January 1624. Now reconciled—at least outwardly—to the royal favourite, in May 1624 Oxford took command of a regiment in the elector palatine's service in the Low Countries. There, in late May, he received a slight wound in his left arm in action before Terheiden. The injury evidently became infected, for he died of a fever at The Hague between 2 and 9 June 1625 NS. He was buried in Westminster Abbey on 15 July 1625. He left no children, and was succeeded by his second cousin Robert de Vere, nineteenth earl of Oxford.

VICTOR STATER

Sources GEC, *Peerage* · *CSP dom.*, 1611–25 · T. Cogswell, *The blessed revolution* (1989), 84, 100–01, 298 · S. R. Gardiner, *History of England from the accession of James I to the outbreak of the civil war*, 10 vols. (1883–4); repr. (1965), vols. 3–5 · Finch-Hatton MSS, BL, Add. MS 29549 · V. Snow, *Essex the rebel* (1970), 94–118 · L. Stone, *The crisis of the aristocracy, 1558–1641* (1965), 110, 596, 760 · will, PRO, PROB 11/146, sig. 75
Archives BL, letters, Add. MS 29549
Likenesses J. Payne, line engraving, BM · R. Vaughan, line engraving, BM, NPG · double portrait, line engraving (with Henry, third earl of Southampton), BM, NPG · oils (after, type of *c.*1620–1625), NPG · oils, Wilton House, Wiltshire
Wealth at death father died possessed of rental under £900 in 1604: Stone, *Crisis*, 760

Vere, Horace [Horatio], **Baron Vere of Tilbury** (1565–1635), army officer, was the youngest of four sons of Geoffrey Vere (*d.* 1572?) of Crepping Hall, Wakes Colne, Essex, and his wife, Elizabeth (*d.* 1615), daughter of Richard Harkyns (or Hardekyn) of Colchester. Geoffrey was the third son of John de *Vere, fifteenth earl of Oxford [*see under* Vere, John de, sixteenth earl of Oxford], so Horace was close kin of the premier earl of England, a title to which for a time he would even be heir presumptive. Most contemporary English sources (and all modern historians) give his name as Horace, but some English and all Dutch memoirs and manuscripts of the period give Horatio. His elder brother Sir Francis *Vere was also a celebrated military commander.

Early career Little is known of Horace Vere's early life. He and his elder brothers Robert and Francis were trained as boys in the military arts by William Browne (later knighted) and by the early 1580s Francis was fighting for the protestant cause in the Netherlands. He continued in service there after England joined the Dutch in war against Spain in 1585, and in February 1589 he was joined by Robert. In the following year Robert visited their widowed mother and returned with the youngest brother, now aged twenty-five (leaving Elizabeth Vere in the care of the eldest brother, John). What Horace had done up to this point is unknown.

In 1591, despite his inexperience, Vere was appointed lieutenant of his brother Francis's own company of foot. By June 1594, after the English troops had suffered heavy casualties, including at least three captains, while besieging Groningen, Sir Francis wrote to Lord Burghley, Elizabeth's chief minister, that 'My youngest brother for his experiences and trial made of his sufficiency shows himself very capable of the charge' (Markham, 194). Horace was duly promoted captain. Evidently he distinguished himself in this capacity, for in 1596 he was made lieutenant-colonel of Sir John Wingfield's regiment of foot in the army sent to attack Cadiz under the command of the earl of Essex. When Wingfield was slain in battle Horace took command of the 750-strong regiment and was knighted by Essex for his good service.

On his return Vere passed from Elizabeth's employ into the Dutch army. To supplement the forces in the queen's pay the states general of the United Provinces had commissioned Sir Francis in 1594 to raise an extra regiment of English troops as mercenaries. Late in 1596 Sir 'Oratius'

Horace Vere, Baron Vere of Tilbury (1565–1635), by Michiel Janszoon van Miereveldt, 1629

became the senior captain of the regiment (PRO, SP 84/54, fol. 107r). He spent the rest of his career in the service of the Dutch republic. This did not exclude also serving his sovereign but his primary paymaster henceforth would always be the United Provinces.

In 1599 all the English troops in the Netherlands, save for the garrisons of the 'cautionary towns' of Flushing and Brill, were transferred into Dutch pay. Sir Horace Vere distinguished himself in the bitter fighting around Bommel, in which a Spanish offensive was blunted and then driven back. In the celebrated battle of Nieuwpoort (2 July 1600), in which the English troops played a major part, Horace distinguished himself. He gathered six companies of English troops, with which he saved the Dutch artillery (which played an important part in the victory) before launching a charge that helped break up the Spanish momentum, allowing Sir Francis Vere and Prince Maurice, captain-general of the United Provinces, to launch a general counter-attack and sweep the Spanish to defeat. Sir Francis's narrative of the battle in his military memoirs does not do justice to his brother's role ('The *Commentaries*', 158–65). Sir John Ogle, a loyal lieutenant to both, implies that Sir Francis gave an imperfect account of Nieuwpoort because he could not be aware of all that had gone on, being caught up in the action. Surely, however, by the time Sir Francis wrote his memoir, he must have had an idea of what his own brother, at least, had done. He preferred to emphasize his own part in this famous battle at the expense not only of Sir Edward Cecil (another English officer with whom he had quarrelled bitterly by the time of writing), but even of his brother. A better idea of

Horace's role can be gained from the Dutch chronicler Orlers (Orlers, 1610, edn, 157).

The famous victory at Nieuwpoort was followed by the equally famous siege of Ostend. Vere alarmed Elizabeth in September 1600 when he wrote to her, warning of the city's vulnerability, and she ensured that its garrison was reinforced, mostly by English soldiers, before the siege commenced in July 1601. Eventually it lasted more than three years and the city became known as 'the New Troy' in consequence. The defence was originally commanded by Sir Francis Vere, ably seconded by his brother. In the massive Spanish assault of 7 January 1602 Sir Horace had charge of '12 weak companies' holding the vitally important post known as Sand Hill; it was here that the brunt of the Spanish assault would fall and Sir Horace was 'hurt in the leg, with a splinter', a potentially serious wound which he and his leg survived intact ('The *Commentaries*', 176, 183). In March 1602 both Veres were rotated out of Ostend with many of their troops and given a chance to rest. Sir Horace was given his elder brother's dispatches to carry to the new king, James VI and I, in April 1603.

In his prime James promptly made peace with Spain. He maintained English control over the cautionary towns and still permitted the Dutch republic to recruit English, Welsh, and Scottish troops, but England was no longer an ally of the United Provinces. This undermined Sir Francis Vere's position and he was obliged to resign his post as *generaal der infanterie* in 1604. At first no one replaced him. Sir Edward Cecil, grandson of Lord Burghley and nephew of the secretary of state, Sir Robert Cecil (later earl of Salisbury), was impatient with Sir Francis's supremacy and had already intrigued against his general. Consequently, initially the four English colonels, Henry Sutton, Cecil, Ogle, and Sir Horace, each answered only to the captain-general (Maurice) and the council of state. It was only after more than a year, during which Ogle could observe that 'Sir Horace Vere presses hard', that, on 3 May 1605, Horace was appointed *Generael over alle d'Engelsche compaignien* (*Salisbury MSS*, 17.156). His authority, even then, was more limited than his brother's: he would only 'superintend' the other colonels in the field, rather than having any administrative jurisdiction; this limitation on his authority was largely due to Cecil's refusal to be commanded by Vere (*De L'Isle and Dudley MSS*, 3.153–4; *Salisbury MSS*, 17.156–7).

However, Sir Horace Vere showed himself to be at least his brother's equal. In autumn 1604 he was commended by the states general for his distinguished conduct in the successful siege of Sluys. A year later he saved Maurice and the Dutch army at the battle of Mulheim (9 October 1605). The Dutch cavalry were commanded by Maurice's younger brother and heir, Prince Frederick Henry of Nassau, who had served with Vere at Sluys. Unfortunately his force was routed, throwing the entire states' army into danger. A retreat was necessary but there was 'every prospect of the movement being converted into a complete rout' (Markham, 376), unless time could be gained for Maurice to rally his troops. Vere now conceived and executed a bold plan, crossing the Ruhr with picked English companies and holding the passage of the river until Maurice had rallied the army, which then withdrew in good order. The Spanish general, the celebrated Spínola, 'declared that Sir Horace Vere had saved the army of the States' (ibid., 377).

As he defied the Spanish at the river crossing Vere must have truly seemed a latterday Horatius to the hard-pressed Nassau brothers. In the following year his primacy in the field went beyond mere 'superintendence'. Each English colonel kept control of 'the disposing of the business of his owne regiment' (that is, of internal administration), but henceforth were obliged to 'receive their directions' (that is, in military operations) from Sir Horace (*De L'Isle and Dudley MSS*, 3.283–4).

Vere exercised his new powers in the field only during 1607, for 1608 was taken up largely by the negotiations which resulted in 1609 in the beginning of the Twelve Years' Truce between Spain and the Dutch republic. Following the campaign season of 1607 he returned to England in October for a double celebration: his brother, aged forty-seven, married a woman thirty years younger than himself; in November 1607 Sir Horace, at forty-two, wed Lady Mary Hoby (1581–1671) [see Vere, Mary], aged twenty-six. The two had met the previous year when Horace was visiting home. The daughter of Sir John Tracy of Tuddington, Mary was the widow of William Hoby and had two small children. It was thus a convenient match for Mary, but Horace seems genuinely to have been in love. She followed him to the Netherlands (though not until July 1608) and in later life both clearly had great affection for each other. John Chamberlain's description of Sir Horace and his lady taking him sightseeing in the Netherlands in October 1608 is but one example of their ease in each other's company.

The Twelve Years' Truce and relations with the Dutch In 1609 Sir Francis Vere died. He had still been governor of Brill, a very desirable post which was promptly sought by Thomas Howard, earl of Arundel, and by Sir Edward Cecil, whose father, the earl of Exeter, wrote to his brother and Edward's uncle, the earl of Salisbury. However, though this was not a Dutch office, Prince Maurice recommended Sir Horace Vere and did so strongly enough to ensure that he was duly appointed successor to his brother. Vere held the office until 1616, when the English government finally returned the cautionary towns of Brill and Flushing to Dutch control. He was granted an annual pension of £800 in lieu of the office's pay and perquisites, but in any case it did not affect his standing in the republic, which by this time was secure.

Vere was on close terms with both Maurice and Frederick Henry of Nassau. His cordial relations with the former are particularly notable as personal differences between the prince and Sir Francis had been a major factor in the latter's enforced resignation. However, the younger Vere blamed Sir Edward Cecil for his brother's fate, rather than Maurice. Both Cecil and Sir Horace were colonels at the time; both rose to become generals in the Dutch service and were ennobled at home. However, they were at odds for many years, each seeking appointments at the other's expense and each endeavouring to prefer their own clients to commands over the other's. Despite Cecil's exalted connections in England Vere had the better of the rivalry, at least in the United Provinces. From 1610 he established himself in the affinity of Henry, prince of Wales, but his success was primarily due to his connection to the Nassaus. From at least 1606 Vere received preferential rates of pay and his clients generally had the best of the competition with Cecil's: one of them, Sir Edward Harwood, was even made a gentleman of Maurice's privy chamber. Moreover not only was Vere appointed governor of Brill in 1610, but he was preferred to the governorship of Utrecht in July 1618. This appointment came at the expense of Sir John Ogle who, during the Arminian troubles, sided with the opponents of Maurice. His replacement by Vere was thus doubly a gesture of trust.

No doubt it owed much to Vere's actions at Mulheim, but it must also have been due to a personal relationship between the two men. When, in 1610, Maurice decided at the last minute to accompany the army which besieged Jülich, Vere reported how 'his Excellencie hath desyred me to wayte upon him which I wold not refewse' (Trim, 349). Clearly they got on well.

Nevertheless Sir Horace carried less authority than had Sir Francis. The withdrawal of England from war against Spain in 1604 followed five years later by an armistice between Spain and the United Provinces naturally made the English troops in Dutch service less significant and this made it easier for their employers to reduce them to the same obedience to the republic as all its other soldiers. Vere himself reflected on the 'lymitations [with which] I … exersyse that command I have under the States', observing that the best way for an English or Welsh soldier to advance his career was to be 'knowen to the princypall persons that govern here' (Trim, 351). Indeed, his own successful career demonstrated this point.

The fullness of fame In 1620 the Palatinate, whose elector Frederick V's wife was Princess Elizabeth, daughter of James VI and I, faced invasion by Spanish troops, after Frederick's intervention in Bohemia. In May 1620 James finally responded to the appeals of his own subjects to intervene on his protestant son-in-law's behalf by permitting Count Dohna, the palatine envoy, to raise troops in England (but at his own expense). Consequently Dohna also wanted to chose the expedition's general. Sir Edward Cecil wanted the post and obtained the backing of the king's favourite, the duke of Buckingham. However, though Vere had not sought the command, Dohna chose him, much to Cecil's anger. Buckingham withdrew his support for the expedition, but such was the feeling for the protestant cause among the English gentry and nobility, and such was Vere's reputation, that there was no shortage of volunteers, including many from distinguished families: two of his captains were Robert Devereux, third earl of Essex, and Horace's own kinsman Henry de Vere, eighteenth earl of Oxford (whose impoverished inheritance had been relieved only by a generous legacy from Sir Francis Vere). However, owing to Dohna's financial difficulties,

it was not until 22 July that Vere and a force of 2200 volunteers sailed for the Netherlands. The following month Spínola's, Spanish army invaded the Palatinate.

Vere's force was reinforced in the Netherlands by men from the English regiments in Dutch pay and was accompanied into the Palatinate by a Dutch cavalry force under Frederick Henry. Vere outmanoeuvred Spínola and was able to effect a union with the army of the German protestant Evangelical Union, Frederick V's allies. That winter, however, the elector was utterly defeated at the battle of the White Mountain and, together with his 'winter queen', fled to his Nassau cousins in The Hague. In April 1621 the princes of the Evangelical Union broke up their army, agreeing to leave the Palatinate and the English army defending it to their fates. Vere carefully disposed the forces under his command to hold Mannheim, Heidelberg, and Frankenthal, key fortresses in the Lower Palatinate. Frankenthal was besieged in 1621, but was gallantly defended until Vere relieved the siege.

However, that year the imperialist general Tilly completed the conquest of the Upper Palatinate, while Vere's troops were ill-paid and suffering from disease. Early in 1622 James sent £30,000 to help his son-in-law, but much of it was diverted to Ernst, Count Mansfeld. The latter had been Frederick's general in Bohemia and the elector joined his army for an offensive that began in April 1622. Frederick actually reached Mannheim, where Vere was in command, but Tilly twice defeated Mansfeld's army and by June Frederick had retreated to the Netherlands once more. By late summer an overwhelming imperialist and Spanish army had assembled and the writing was on the wall. Heidelberg was stormed on 16 September 1622. Two weeks later Vere was obliged to surrender Mannheim, but he was granted the honours of war and took his surviving troops back to the Netherlands. He then returned to England.

Vere received an enthusiastic welcome. He was celebrated in verse by the dramatist and translator of Homer, George Chapman ('Pro Vero autumni lachrymae', 1622); Ben Jonson declared his deeds 'fit to be Sung by a Horace', hymning his 'fame … wonne/In th'eye of Europe, where thy deedes were done' (*Epigrammes*, 91); later, Thomas May dedicated book seven of his translation of Lucan, which deals with the battle of Pharsalia, to Vere, whose military prowess made him seem comparable to Caesar. Meanwhile on 16 February 1623 he was appointed mustermaster-general of the ordnance for life.

All this was appropriate recognition. Given Vere's lack of support it was remarkable that he had held back the Catholic tide so long. To hold virtually all the Lower Palatinate against Spanish attacks in 1621 was an impressive feat and had Vere been given greater resources things might have turned out differently.

Back in the Netherlands Maurice was in constantly poor health and the republic was militarily on the back foot. Vere quickly returned to the Netherlands and to active service. Breda, seat of the Nassau family, was closely besieged and in 1624–5 Vere was involved in the operations to relieve the siege. Hampered by Maurice's death on 23 April 1625, these failed; the city capitulated to Spínola.

It was a dark moment for the Dutch republic and made the worse for Vere since his young cousin, the earl of Oxford, died of wounds sustained at Breda. However, Sir Horace had distinguished himself in the fighting, carrying out another fighting withdrawal: the most difficult operation in warfare. He received further honours at home. In 1624 he was made a member of the council of war; Cecil and Ogle were also appointed, but neither were any longer in Dutch service—it was a signal honour for one who was a general in foreign pay. On 24 July 1625 Sir Horace was created Baron Vere of Tilbury (the title came from his estate in north-east Essex rather than from the Thames-side fort): appropriately the supporters granted to his arms carried shields, one with the arms of the Netherlands, the other with the arms of Zealand. He and his wife bought an estate at Clapton, near Hackney, where, aged sixty, he may have hoped to retire with his five daughters.

Last years Frederick Henry, who on Maurice's death had succeeded him as stadholder and captain-general, wanted his old comrade in arms in service again and Vere would not refuse the call. Vere was on the republic's council of war which, in 1628, decided to begin a counter-offensive by campaigning against the great fortress city of 's-Hertogenbosch. In 1629 Vere commanded a large English contingent in the prince of Orange's army. It included, among a host of noble officers and gentlemen volunteers, Robert de Vere, nineteenth earl of Oxford; Vere's son-in-law, John Holles, Lord Haughton; Thomas Fairfax (whose grandfather, Thomas, first Lord Fairfax, had fought with Vere in the 1590s, whose great-uncle Sir Charles had been killed at Ostend, and two of whose uncles had been killed in the Palatinate); and lords Doncaster, Fielding, and Craven. It was a long siege—Vere was rumoured to have been killed in June; a kinsman, Sir Edward Vere, was killed in August. Yet in September the city fell: the greatest Spanish defeat since the Armada.

Vere was able to spend more of his time in England during the following two years, though he was in the Netherlands in the summers (the campaign season). In 1632 another major offensive was launched, this time against Maastricht. Vere was commander of the English brigade, and on this occasion Frederick Henry went so far as to give him the power to confer knighthood. In this siege Vere's nephew Sir Simon Harcourt was badly wounded, while two English colonels were mortally wounded, both close to Vere: Sir Edward Harwood and the earl of Oxford. However, even though an imperialist army was sent to bolster Spanish attempts to relieve the siege, the sacrifices of Vere's kin and loyal followers were not in vain. Maastricht surrendered in August, leaving Spanish power in disarray.

Vere now entered virtual retirement. His only military duties were connected with the business of the ordnance office and he enjoyed the company of his family. By this time his three elder daughters had all been married. In 1626 Elizabeth had married John *Holles, who later succeeded as second earl of Clare; and in 1627 Mary had married Sir Roger Townshend; on his death in 1638 she married Mildmay *Fane, second earl of Westmorland. (Both daughters had been born in the Netherlands and had been the beneficiaries of a parliamentary act of naturalization in 1624.) Moreover in 1634 Catherine married Oliver St John, the notable lawyer and future parliamentarian leader; after his death she married John Poulett, son and heir of John, Lord Poulett of Hinton St George. In 1635 Vere's fourth daughter, Anne [see Fairfax, Anne], was betrothed to Thomas Fairfax.

Family matters, therefore, were well in hand when on 2 May 1635 Vere went to dine at Whitehall with his friend Sir Henry Vane, ambassador to The Hague, then on a trip home. Sir Horace, in his seventieth year, had a stroke and died within two hours. He was buried with great pomp on 8 May 1635 in Westminster Abbey, by the side of his brother Sir Francis, where both still lie.

Sir Horace Vere's will, dated 10 November 1634, was proved on 6 May 1635. It makes no mention of his daughters, but he had made a number of conveyances of his property the previous year and he left his remaining lands to Mary, 'my most loving wife', evidently trusting her to make appropriate dispositions for their children (PRO, PROB 11/168, fol. 7v). In 1637 Thomas Fairfax married Anne Vere; later, the Veres' youngest daughter, Dorothy, married John Wolstenholme of Stanmore, Middlesex. Mary Vere, Lady Vere of Tilbury, lived to be ninety, serving for a time as parliamentarian governor of Charles I's children Elizabeth and Henry, duke of Gloucester.

Character and religious views The Veres have been classified among 'the well-known Puritan families' of pre-civil war England (Heal and Holmes, 366). Sir Horace himself was a patron and protector of puritan ministers: from 1611 to 1619 the puritan minister William Ames was in Vere's personal service, and in 1620 he was chaplain of Sir Horace's regiment in Dutch pay. (Later, Sir Edward Harwood, Vere's client, helped get Ames a university appointment.) Vere appointed as chaplain of his regiment for palatine service the puritan minister Dr John Burgess.

Mary, Lady Vere's religious views were regarded by some contemporaries as 'of a Dutch complexion' (DNB) and it was to this she owed parliament's favour after the civil wars. It was probably the case that Horace married her because her views agreed with his own, rather than that she picked presbyterianism up in the Netherlands. In 1608, in his absence, she made a donation to Sir Thomas Bodley's Calvinist intellectual project at Oxford University. His wife's strong views; his own family background; his friendship with the princes of Orange (known as defenders of the Reformed church in the Netherlands); his appointment as governor of Utrecht in place of Sir John Ogle, tainted with Arminian sympathies; and his own patronage of 'godly' ministers exiled from England—all make it clear that Sir Horace was certainly a puritan and probably a presbyterian.

That Vere could live happily in England under Charles I, despite his firm views in favour of military intervention on the continent, and his almost certain puritan sympathies, was probably partly due to an instinctive allegiance to his king, which a close personal tie to the princely house of Orange must have reinforced. However, in addition Horace Vere quite simply got on with people. For example, even after Sir Francis fell out with Sir Robert Sidney, Horace and Sidney remained friends. Contemporaries also remarked on the steady nature of Sir Horace's temperament, though this was heightened by the contrast with his more choleric brother. A near-contemporary writer recorded that 'it was true of him what is said of the Caspian Sea, that it doth never ebb nor flow, observing a constant tenor neither elated or depressed with success' (Fuller, *Worthies*, 1.514). Ben Jonson praised Vere for his

> Humanitie, and pietie, which are
> As noble in great chiefes, as they are rare.
> And best become the valiant man to weare,
> Who more should seeke mens reverence, then feare.
> (*Epigrammes*, 91)

Horace Vere's friendship with the notoriously prickly Maurice of Nassau, and his ability to stay on good terms with almost all the English officers in the Netherlands (notable as a group for their hot-headed quarrelsomeness), along with the praise he garnered from his opponents all point to his essential likeableness.

Historical significance Most early modern English military commanders before the duke of Marlborough (other than Oliver Cromwell) have been largely ignored, but this is truer of Horace Vere than most. He is rarely the subject of even short essays in specialist periodicals; he has less than a third of C. R. Markham's putative double biography of the Vere brothers; and in general works of military history or biography it is Francis who attracts attention, with Horace often not even mentioned. This reflects that Francis, the elder, came first, that he commanded in a period of greater success for his employers, and that he was a gifted self-publicist. However, the younger brother was certainly as able a soldier and arguably more influential in the long term.

English troops commanded by Sir Francis Vere played a crucial part in the operations of the 1590s by which the future of the Dutch republic was secured, but the success of the great Dutch counter-offensive of that decade was really due to Maurice of Nassau and a group of highly proficient and professional officers of whom Sir Francis Vere, while a leading light, was only one. From about 1610 the senior officers serving the Nassaus, while still efficient, were mostly of a lesser calibre. Sir Francis Vere's record is thus partly made to look good by those around him, while the opposite is true of Sir Horace. In addition, he, unlike his brother, commanded an army in his own right. Francis commended himself to posterity by his apparently frank memoirs, which in fact serve to enhance the author's reputation at every point. Horace was a quieter, more modest man: Thomas Fuller observed that while he had 'as much valour' he had 'more meekness' than his elder brother (Fuller, *Worthies*, 1.514). Francis helped win the day

at Nieuwpoort and ensured that everybody knew it; Horace saved the day at Mulheim, but did not boast of the fact.

Moreover, Sir Horace Vere recognized that in the long term the English troops in Dutch employ could not be maintained as a separate force and, by keeping on good terms with first Maurice and then Frederick Henry, he ensured that a steady flow of Englishmen crossed the narrow seas and fought with the Dutch. England's insular inhabitants thus had an opportunity for valuable military experience, despite the long peace between 1604 and 1639; but they also had an escape valve for the stress resulting from their sovereign's refusal to intervene in the Thirty Years' War. Revisionist historians have not recognized that any unity in the English body politic in the 1620s and 1630s existed partly because many of those who were discontent with the Stuarts' religious and foreign policies had an opportunity to vent their frustrations.

Indeed, as contemporaries recognized, Sir Horace Vere's army was a 'Nurcery of Souldierie' (Hexham, 'epistle dedicatory'). Sir Horace was the teacher and patron of a whole generation of soldiers. In the 1640s they comprised a high proportion of both the cavalier and roundhead officer corps. Generals who had served under Sir Horace included the earl of Essex, Sir Thomas Fairfax, Philip Skippon, Sir William Waller, Philip, Lord Wharton, Sir Jacob Astley, Sir Nicholas Byron, Sir Thomas Glemham, and Sir Ralph Hopton; but Vere's veterans could be found at all levels of the royalist and parliamentarian armies. Many former protégés of the even-tempered Sir Horace were moderate in their conduct of what Waller, writing to Hopton, famously termed a 'war without an enemy'. George Monck, who brought about the restoration of Charles II, was one of Vere's particular protégés. Monck's decision to renew legitimate monarchy, rather than become a military dictator, was doubtless the result of his own character; but this had been moulded by Vere's influence at an early stage.

By his tactical astuteness, leadership, courtesy, courage, and magnanimity, and his influence on his contemporaries, Vere was a figure of genuine significance in seventeenth-century English and European history. He deserves to be more than just a footnote in history—and to be remembered in his own right, not just as an addendum to his brother.   D. J. B. TRIM

Sources C. R. Markham, *The fighting Veres* (1888) · D. J. B. Trim, 'Sir Horace Vere in Holland and the Rhineland, 1610–1612', *Historical Research*, 72 (1999), 334–51 · 'The *Commentaries* of Sir Francis Vere' [1657], *An English garner*, 7: *Stuart tracts, 1603–1693*, ed. E. Arber and C. H. Firth (1903) · *DNB* · P. C. Molhuysen, P. J. Blok, L. Knappert, and K. H. Kossman, eds., *Niew Nederlandsch biografisch woordenboek*, 10 vols. (1911–37), vol. 5 · J. Orlers, *Den Nassauschen Laurencrans* (Leyden, 1610) [English edn: *The triumphs of Nassou, or, A description and representation of all the victories both by land and sea, granted … to … the Estates Generall of the United Netherlands Provinces*, trans. William Shute (1613); the English translation, itself a translation from the French, is unreliable] · *Report on the manuscripts of Lord De L'Isle and Dudley*, 6 vols., HMC, 77 (1925–66) · *Calendar of the manuscripts of the most hon. the marquis of Salisbury*, 24 vols., HMC, 9 (1883–1976) · State Papers Holland, PRO, SP 84 · accounts of pay issued to troops serving for the defence of the Palatinate, 1622–1624, PRO, E 101/612/73 · will, PRO, PROB 11/168, fols. 7v–8v [sig. 45] · BL, Lansdowne MS 81 ·

Longleat House, Wiltshire, Devereux MS 2 · Nationaal Archief, The Hague, Archief van de Staten-Generaal, 8043–51 · Nationaal Archief, The Hague, Archief van Johan van Oldenbarnevelt, 2009 · Bodl. Oxf., MS Rawl. D. 859 · *CSP dom.*, *1603–35* · N. Japikse and H. H. P. Rijperman, eds., *Resolutiën der Staten-Generaal van 1576 tot 1609*, 14 vols. (The Hague, 1915–70), vols. 8–14; see also new ser., *1610–1670*, vol. 1 · *Dudley Carleton to John Chamberlain, 1603–1624: Jacobean letters*, ed. M. Lee (1972) · G. H. Wheeler, ed., *Letters of Sir Thomas Bodley to Thomas James* (1626); repr. (1985) · *The letters of John Chamberlain*, ed. N. E. McClure, 2 vols. (1939) · J. Israel, *The Dutch republic: its rise, greatness and fall, 1477–1806* (1995) · G. B. Johnston, ed., *Poems of Ben Jonson*, Muses Library edn (1954) · D. Norbrook, 'Lucan, Thomas May, and the creation of a republican literary culture', *Culture and politics in early Stuart England*, ed. K. Sharpe and P. Lake (1994), 45–66 · H. Hexham, *The principles of the art militarie: practised in the warres of the United Netherlands* (1637) · N. Tyacke, *The fortunes of English puritanism, 1603–1640* (1990) · H. H. Rowen, *The princes of Orange: the stadholders in the Dutch republic* (1988); paperback edn (1990) · M. Slade, *1569–1628: letters to the English ambassador*, ed. W. Nijenhuis, Publications of the Sir Thomas Browne Institute, new ser., 6 (1986) · F. Heal and C. Holmes, *The gentry in England and Wales, 1500–1700* (1994) · B. Donagan, 'Halcyon days and the literature of war: England's military education before 1642', *Past and Present*, 147 (1995), 65–100 · W. A. Shaw, *Knights of England*, 3 vols. (1906) · Fuller, *Worthies* (1840), 1.514 · GEC, *Peerage* · F. G. Emmison, ed., *Elizabethan life: wills of Essex gentry and merchants* (1978), 79 · W. C. Metcalfe, ed., *The visitations of Essex, 1552, 1558, 1570 and 1634*, Harleian Society, 13 (1878), pt. 1

Archives BL, letters to Lord Doncaster, Egerton MSS 2593–2594 · Koninklijke Bibliotheek, The Hague, handschriften, 34C18, 72D32/4, 121A2–3 · Nationaal Archief, The Hague, Archief van de Staten-Generaal, Liassen Lopende · PRO, state papers, foreign, Holland

Likenesses portrait, 17th cent., Hinton St George, Somerset · J. A. van Ravesteyn, oils, 1611, Mauritshuis, The Hague · M. J. van Miereveldt, oils, 1629, Ashdown House, Oxfordshire [*see illus.*] · M. J. van Miereveldt, oils, second version, 1629, NPG · F. Delaram, line engraving, BM, V&A · C. Janssen, portrait; in possession of marquis of Townsend in 1899; copy, Wentworth · attrib. C. Janssen, portrait; in possession of Sir H. St John in 1899 · Vertue, engraving (after C. Janssen), repro. in A. Collins, *Historical collections of the noble families of Cavendishe, Holles, Vere, Harley and Ogle, with the lives of the most remarkable persons* (1752) · engraving, repro. in Markham, *Fighting Veres*, 364 · two busts; at Welbeck Castle in 1899

Vere, John de, seventh earl of Oxford (1312–1360), magnate and soldier, was the only son of Alfonso de Vere (*d.* 1328) and his wife, Jane Foliot. Alfonso was the younger brother of Robert de Vere, sixth earl of Oxford, who died childless in 1331, and John thus succeeded to the earldom, and to the hereditary chamberlainship of England, in that year. In 1336 he married Maud, the second of the four daughters and coheir of Giles, Lord Badlesmere, of Badlesmere in Kent, who died in 1338.

Most of John de Vere's adult life was spent in the service of Edward III on campaigns in France and Scotland. He formed a close connection with William *Bohun, earl of Northampton, who was almost exactly the same age. The two were brothers-in-law: Northampton married Elizabeth, the third of Giles Badlesmere's four daughters; they campaigned together in France and Scotland, and were associated on various commissions in England. They died within nine months of one another in 1360. Oxford's military career began with the Scottish campaigns of the 1330s. In 1334–5 he served on the Roxburgh campaign, bringing a retinue of twenty-eight men-at-arms and

twelve mounted archers. He then took part in the summer campaign of 1335, on this occasion as a member of the retinue of Earl Warenne. When a French invasion threatened in 1339 he was appointed keeper of the 'maritime lands' in Essex; in November he put to sea in the king's service, and in March 1340 he served in Flanders with the earl of Warwick. In February 1342 he took part in a tournament at Dunstable, and Murimuth identifies him as one of the 'young earls of the kingdom' (*Adae Murimuth continuatio chronicarum*, 123) alongside Derby, Warwick, Northampton, Pembroke, and Suffolk, whom he contrasts with nobles such as Gloucester, Arundel, and Warenne who were absent from the tournament on account of their age and infirmity.

In August 1342 Oxford set out on his first major campaign in France, serving in Brittany with the earl of Northampton, who had been appointed Edward III's lieutenant there. The expedition relieved Brest, and on 30 September put the forces of Charles de Blois to flight at Morlaix in a hard-fought battle. In the following year Oxford served with Northampton on the expedition sent to Scotland to relieve Lochmaben Castle, and in 1345 he again campaigned with Northampton in Brittany. A later tradition has it that on their return his ships were blown so far off course that he and his retinue were forced ashore on the coast of Connacht, where their goods were pillaged by the local people. However, he was at Quimperlé in Brittany in January 1346, and it is possible that he and Northampton overwintered there.

In the summer of 1346 John de Vere joined Edward III's expedition to Normandy. He and Northampton may have gone to Normandy straight from Brittany. According to Froissart, Oxford fought alongside Edward, the Black Prince, at the battle of Crécy on 26 August, and was one of the commanders who sent word to the king asking for reinforcements, as the division was hard-pressed by the French. Edward replied with his famous message 'Let the boy win his spurs' (*Chroniques*, 3.183). Oxford then took part in the siege of Calais, but in 1348 he was said to be 'detained by severe sickness' (*CCIR, 1346–1349*, 598), and he did not campaign again until 1355, when he accompanied the Black Prince to Gascony. He then joined in the prince's famous raid into Languedoc, while early in the following year he is reported as campaigning in the area around Rocamadour in Quercy.

In the autumn of 1356 the Black Prince's army moved north and encountered the French at Poitiers on 19 September. John de Vere and the earl of Warwick were in command of the vanguard. During the battle Oxford took a group of archers to attack the flank of the French cavalry and brought them down, preventing them from overrunning the main body of English archers. After the battle he returned to Bordeaux, but as the negotiations for peace with France became more difficult he was summoned to a council in London on 10 October 1359, and subsequently joined the king on the Rheims campaign of 1359–60. He died, probably during the raid into Burgundy, on 23 or 24 January 1360. His body was brought home to England and buried in the family burial place at Earls Colne Priory in Essex.

Oxford had enjoyed an active military career, though none of the contemporary chroniclers suggests that he had exceptional prowess or that he acquired great fame on the battlefield. Indeed, Edward III did not reward him as generously as some of his other companions-in-arms. He never became a member of the Order of the Garter, unlike the earl of Northampton, and although he was permitted to re-enfeoff his estates so as to give his wife a substantial life interest in them, he enjoyed little royal patronage. In a sense, the de Veres were on the fringes of the titled nobility. Although their earldom was ancient, their inheritance, and thus their resources, were modest by comparison with their peers. The retinues he brought to his campaigns were small compared with those of his fellow earls. He managed to augment his inheritance with his wife's share of the Badlesmere inheritance, but this too was modest. Service in the king's wars was not obviously a source of reward or profit for Oxford; indeed, his wages were often assigned on the subsidy or paid in the form of grants of wool, and there is no evidence for a major building programme either at his main residence, Castle Hedingham in Essex, or at Earls Colne Priory, of which he was patron, even though the priory was damaged when the tower and crossing collapsed in 1356. In his will Oxford left only 100 marks for works at the priory.

Oxford's widow died in 1366. They had four sons and two daughters. Their eldest son, John, married Elizabeth, daughter of Hugh Courtenay, earl of Devon, but he died c.1350. Another son, Robert, is known to have died in his father's lifetime, but otherwise nothing is known about him. Both John and Robert were buried at Earls Colne Priory. Thomas, the elder surviving son, was born about 1336–7, married Maud, daughter of Sir Ralph *Ufford, and succeeded to the earldom on his father's death. Aubrey de *Vere, the younger surviving son, was born about 1338–40 and became tenth earl in 1393 on the restoration of the earldom after the exile and forfeiture of Thomas's son, Robert de *Vere, ninth earl of Oxford and duke of Ireland, Richard II's favourite. The elder daughter, Margaret, married first Henry, Lord Beaumont (d. 1369), second Sir Nicholas Loveyn of Penshurst, Kent, (d. c.1375), and third John *Devereux, Baron Devereux (d. 1393). John de Vere left 1000 marks in his will for the marriage portion of a second daughter, Matilda, but otherwise nothing is known of her.

If the instructions in his will were implemented, Oxford was buried on the south side of the choir of the lady chapel of Earls Colne Priory. His widow asked to be buried in the priory 'near the body of my worshipful lord Earl deceased' (Benton, 263). The alabaster effigies on one of the tombs known to have been in the priory in 1653, and of which a drawing survives, have been identified as those of John de Vere and his wife, but they appear to have been destroyed in the early eighteenth century. None of the tombs subsequently removed to St Stephen's Chapel near Bures in Suffolk has been identified as that of John de Vere.   ANTHONY TUCK

Sources Register of Archbishop Simon Islip, LPL [Microfilm, CUL] · Vere family cartulary, Bodl. Oxf., MS Rawl. B. 248 · exchequer, king's remembrancer, accounts various — indentures of war, PRO, E.101/68 · *Chancery records* · CIPM, vol. 5; 10, no. 638 · *Adae Murimuth continuatio chronicarum. Robertus de Avesbury de gestis mirabilibus regis Edwardi tertii*, ed. E. M. Thompson, Rolls Series, 93 (1889) · *Chronicon Galfridi le Baker de Swynebroke*, ed. E. M. Thompson (1889) · *Thomae Walsingham, quondam monachi S. Albani, historia Anglicana*, ed. H. T. Riley, 2 vols., pt 1 of *Chronica monasterii S. Albani*, Rolls Series, 28 (1863–4), vol. 1 · M. C. B. Dawes, ed., *Register of Edward, the Black Prince*, 4 vols., PRO (1930–33) · *Chroniques de J. Froissart*, ed. S. Luce and others, 3 (Paris, 1872) · W. Dugdale, *The baronage of England*, 2 vols. (1675–6), vol. 1 · DNB · GEC, *Peerage* · G. M. Benton, 'Essex wills', *Transactions of the Essex Archaeological Society*, new ser., 21 (1932–4), 234–69, esp. 263
Archives Bodl. Oxf., MS Rawl. B. 248
Likenesses drawing of effigy, repro. in Gough, *Sepulchral monuments*, 1, pt 2, pl. 52
Wealth at death estates: CIPM, 10

Vere, John de, twelfth earl of Oxford (1408–1462), magnate, was the elder son of Richard de Vere, eleventh earl of Oxford (1385?–1417), and his second wife, Alice, daughter of Sir Richard Sergeaux and widow of Guy de St Aubyn. He was born on 23 April 1408 at Castle Hedingham, the family seat in Essex. He inherited his title as a minor on his father's death in February 1417; custody of the heir and his estates was granted to Thomas Beaufort, duke of Exeter, who had established himself as the leading magnate in East Anglia during the previous decade. In 1425, still a minor, the earl married Elizabeth (c.1410–1473/4), daughter and heir of Sir John Howard. On the death of her grandfather in 1438, the couple took possession of her inheritance in Norfolk, Suffolk, Essex, and Cambridgeshire. The marriage was contracted without the king's licence—although Oxford was later to claim that it had been arranged by the advice of his guardian the duke of Exeter—and the earl was fined £2000, a sum that he had difficulty paying. The earldom of Oxford was among the poorest of the comital titles; in 1437 de Vere claimed that his lands were worth only £500 per year, although he may have exaggerated his poverty somewhat.

When Exeter died in 1426, custody of the Oxford estates was granted to the duke of Bedford. De Vere was granted livery of his inheritance on 4 July 1429. He had already been knighted, at the same time as the four-year-old king, in May 1426. During the 1430s and most of the 1440s, Oxford's political activity at a local level was concentrated in Essex, where the bulk of his estates lay. He was a regular member of the peace commission there from 1429, as well as serving on commissions to raise loans and levy taxes in the shire. He was also consistently appointed as a JP in Suffolk from 1438, and in Cambridgeshire from 1443; both were counties in which he held a number of manors. In February 1435 he secured a licence to travel to the Holy Land, but there is no evidence that he made the journey; certainly there was no significant interruption in his appointment to local commissions.

Oxford also began to be involved in political, military, and diplomatic activities at a national level. In July 1436 he mustered his retinue at Sandwich for the expedition to relieve Calais from Burgundian siege. In June 1439, with

Cardinal Beaufort and other envoys, he took part in the inconclusive negotiations with the French at Oye. Two years later he and his retinue accompanied the duke of York, the king's new lieutenant in France, to Normandy. In June 1450 the earl was among the nobles appointed to act against Cade's rebels.

In the late 1440s Oxford became significantly involved for the first time in politics in Norfolk, where some of his wife's estates lay. He had been appointed a JP in the shire once in 1438, but it was only from 1448 that he became a regular member of the peace commission there. In 1450, after the fall from power of William de la Pole, duke of Suffolk, Oxford took a leading role—together with John (VI) Mowbray, duke of Norfolk, and Sir John Fastolf—in attempts to undermine the local power of Suffolk's servants, who had dominated the region during the 1440s. Initially these attempts seemed to make some headway. In August 1450, for example, Oxford and the duke of Norfolk were appointed to lead a general commission of oyer and terminer in Norfolk and Suffolk, before which several of Suffolk's leading supporters were indicted. However, by the spring of 1451 Suffolk's associates—whose power in the region was wide-ranging and long-standing—were successfully regrouping under the leadership of Thomas, Lord Scales, and the widowed duchess of Suffolk. Despite the best attempts of Oxford, who spent a substantial amount of time at his wife's manor of Winch in western Norfolk during this period, and of the duke of Norfolk, Suffolk's men were acquitted of most of the charges laid against them, and by 1452 leading members of Suffolk's affinity, such as Sir Thomas Tuddenham and John Heydon, were again being appointed to office in the region.

It took some time for Oxford's allegiances to become clear as politics became increasingly divided and increasingly confused during the 1450s. He was a member of the protectorate council and was among the nobles appointed to the keeping of the seas in the spring of 1454, but does not seem to have had close associations either with the court or with the protector York at this point. Political division became armed confrontation at St Albans in May 1455, but neither Oxford nor the duke of Norfolk took part in the battle because they arrived a day too late. The earl does not seem to have established a decisive association with either camp until 1459, when he committed himself to the queen against York; in December of that year, and in the following April, he was appointed to lead anti-Yorkist commissions of array in Essex. By May 1460 his eldest son, Aubrey—who had recently married Anne, daughter of Humphrey *Stafford, duke of Buckingham—was reported by one of the Paston correspondents to be 'great with the Queen'.

The Yorkist victory at Northampton in July 1460 seems to have been followed by a period of illness—whether real or tactical—for Oxford; in November of that year he was exempted, 'in consideration of his infirmities', from appearing in person before the king or in council or parliament. If the earl was trying to maintain a low profile in the face of the new regime, it was an attempt that did not long survive the accession of Edward IV. In February 1462, with

his son Aubrey and Sir Thomas Tuddenham, Oxford's former opponent in Norfolk and now a fellow Lancastrian loyalist, the earl was arrested on charges of high treason and committed to the Tower of London. He was tried before the constable of England, John Tiptoft, earl of Worcester, and condemned to death. On 26 February he was beheaded on Tower Hill, and was buried in the church of the Austin friars in London. It was a dramatic end to a career of which the most consistent feature had apparently been Oxford's unwillingness to take sides in the developing political conflict until the last possible moment. His son Aubrey had been executed six days earlier; the earl was therefore succeeded by his second son, John de *Vere.   HELEN CASTOR

Sources Chancery records · The Paston letters, AD 1422–1509, ed. J. Gairdner, new edn, 6 vols. (1904) · CIPM, vol. 20 · J. Gairdner, ed., The historical collections of a citizen of London in the fifteenth century, CS, new ser., 17 (1876) · J. Gairdner, ed., Three fifteenth-century chronicles, CS, new ser., 28 (1880) · R. A. Griffiths, The reign of King Henry VI: the exercise of royal authority, 1422–1461 (1981) · J. L. Watts, Henry VI and the politics of kingship (1996) · N. H. Nicolas, ed., Proceedings and ordinances of the privy council of England, 7 vols., RC, 26 (1834–7) · Rymer, Foedera, 3rd edn · J. Stevenson, ed., Letters and papers illustrative of the wars of the English in France during the reign of Henry VI, king of England, 2 vols. in 3 pts, Rolls Series, 22 (1861–4) · P. A. Johnson, Duke Richard of York, 1411–1460 (1988) · GEC, Peerage · CPR, 1436–41, 71–2
Archives Bodl. Oxf., letters to John Paston
Wealth at death £500 p.a. as claimed by subject: CPR

Vere, John de, thirteenth earl of Oxford (1442–1513), magnate, was the second but eldest surviving son of John de *Vere, twelfth earl of Oxford (1408–1462), and Elizabeth (c.1410–1473/4), daughter and heir of Sir John Howard. He was born on 8 September 1442.

Restoration and early Lancastrian attachment Although his father and elder brother were convicted of treason and executed in February 1462, the new earl was treated in conciliatory fashion by Edward IV. Edward granted out few of the family's estates, leaving most in the keeping of de Vere administrators, and on 18 January 1464 Earl John had licence of entry on all his father's lands, a patrimony concentrated in East Anglia and in particular in north Essex and west Suffolk; what grantees there were were compensated by the king. In the parliament of 1464 Oxford secured the reversal of the attainder of Robert de Vere, duke of Ireland and earl of Oxford (d. 1392), passed in 1388. (Later in life he sometimes used Robert de Vere's title of marquess of Dublin in addition to those of earl of Oxford, Viscount Bulbeck, and Lord Scales). At the coronation of Elizabeth Woodville on 26 May 1465 he was created knight of the Bath and served both as great chamberlain of England (substituting for the absent earl of Warwick) and as chamberlain to the queen.

Yet Oxford's loyalty to the Yorkist regime had been by no means secured. In November 1468 he was imprisoned in the Tower of London and confessed to plotting with the Lancastrians. He was probably released before 7 January and was pardoned on 15 April 1469, but by early July he had joined George, duke of Clarence, and Richard Neville, earl of Warwick (the Kingmaker) in their opposition to the king, mobilizing his retinue for the Edgcote campaign. In the autumn, as Edward regained his freedom of action, his household men showed hostility to Oxford, and in the following spring, as Warwick and Clarence rebelled again, Oxford left England for the court in exile of Margaret of Anjou. He joined the Lancastrian leaders in their meetings with Warwick and Clarence in July, and in the invasion of England in September. He landed with Clarence, Warwick, and Jasper Tudor in Devon but moved to Essex to raise troops before marching to London, where he rejoined his allies on 8 October. On 13 October he bore the sword of state before the restored Henry VI in the procession to St Paul's for a ceremonial crown-wearing, and two days later he presided at the trial of John Tiptoft, earl of Worcester. He was one of the leading lords of the readeption regime.

Flight, surrender, imprisonment, and escape When Edward sought to invade in March 1471, Oxford prevented his landing in Norfolk, raised troops in East Anglia, and advanced to Newark. Confronted by Edward's superior forces he withdrew to Leicester, where his company was attacked and routed on 3 April. He joined Warwick at Coventry, counselled him against seeking compromise with Edward in the wake of Clarence's defection, and commanded the right wing at the battle of Barnet on 14 April. His men defeated those of Lord Hastings but fell to pillaging; when he did gather them together and return to the fight, it is reported that his badge of a mullet, or star with streams of light, was mistaken for Edward's sun in splendour and his men were shot at by their own side, causing them to cry treason and scatter. With his two brothers George and Thomas, William, Viscount Beaumont, and forty men, Oxford fled to Scotland, where he received a safe conduct on 28 April, and then to France. In the next two years he plotted with Archbishop Neville, mounted attacks on Calais, attempted a landing at St Osyth in Essex, and conducted a successful campaign of piracy from French and Scottish ports before seizing St Michael's Mount in Cornwall on 30 September 1473. There, with a force variously estimated by the chroniclers at 80 or 397 men, he was besieged, loosely at first by Sir Henry Bodrugan, then more vigorously by John Fortescue with 300 men and 4 ships. Wounded in the face by an arrow, offered pardon for his life, threatened with desertion by all but a handful of his followers, he finally surrendered on 15 February 1474, still accompanied by Beaumont and by his brothers.

Although he was imprisoned at Hammes Castle in the Calais pale and attainted early in 1475, Oxford remained a threat to Edward. In 1477 an impostor claiming to be the earl caused trouble in Cambridgeshire and Huntingdonshire, and in 1478 Oxford himself managed to scale the walls of Hammes Castle and leap into the moat, though contemporaries were unsure whether this was an attempt at escape or at suicide. He was if anything more dangerous to Richard III, who ordered his transfer to England on 28 October 1484, too late to prevent his escape to join Henry Tudor in the company of his gaoler James Blount. Henry

was reportedly delighted to secure the services of a Lancastrian partisan of such devotion and military experience. Oxford showed his mettle at once, returning to Hammes to relieve the garrison besieged there by Lord Dynham and bringing the soldiers back to augment Tudor's forces. At Bosworth he commanded Henry's vanguard and held his ground in fierce fighting in which John Howard, duke of Norfolk, leading Richard's vanguard, was killed.

The countess's tribulations Oxford's triumphant return brought to an end a period of great trial for his wife, Margaret Neville. She was the sixth daughter of Richard Neville, earl of Salisbury, and Alice Montagu, daughter and heir of the last Montagu earl of Salisbury; as sister of Warwick the Kingmaker and Archbishop Neville she presumably encouraged her husband's alliance with them. Although the earl was not attainted in 1471, his estates were confiscated and granted to Richard, duke of Gloucester, leaving Margaret completely without income: she had no inherited land, no claim to a jointure while her husband lived, and no children with land of their own. Nor could she look to her brothers for help, when two, Richard and John, were dead and the third, Archbishop George Neville, in disgrace. When she emerged from sanctuary at St Martin's-le-Grand in London, where she had taken refuge after Barnet, her prospects were so bleak that they attracted the comment of Philippe de Commines, who reported that she became dependent on charity or on what she could earn by her needle. She received some money from her husband's distant relative and her near neighbour John, Lord Howard, but from the king she had nothing but two general pardons in 1475 and 1479 until he granted her an annuity of £100 during her husband's lifetime in 1482. Her sufferings did not, however, impair her vigour, to judge by her involvement in Henry VII's court or by a letter of May 1486 in which she urged Sir John Paston to cut off the escape of Viscount Lovell following his unsuccessful rebellion. Her husband's kindness to the widowed duchess of Norfolk and his co-operation over the restoration of the Howard estates by 1494 may perhaps reflect her gratitude for the Howards' kindness to her. She died between 20 November 1506 and 14 January 1507 and was buried at Colne Priory, Essex.

Zenith of power under Henry VII In 1485 Oxford was immediately recognized as one of the great men of Henry VII's regime. This was evident at his arrival in London after Bosworth, when suitors flocked to petition him, and at the coronation, where he held the court of claims, having been recognized as hereditary lord great chamberlain, bore the king's train, and set the crown on Henry's head at the coronation banquet. He was appointed to significant offices: lord admiral (21 September 1485), chief steward of the duchy of Lancaster south of Trent, and constable of the Tower of London (both 22 September 1485). He was also granted various offices on the crown estates in Essex, Norfolk, and Suffolk. He rapidly assumed military and political leadership in East Anglia, as the Paston letters and the records of several boroughs and of the University of

Cambridge show. Many of the leaders of gentry society in Essex, Suffolk, Norfolk, and Cambridgeshire were his annuitants or associates: for instance seven of the ten known knights of the shire for Suffolk between 1485 and 1504 were drawn from his circle.

Oxford's power rested on a landed base combining his father's lands, his mother's lands, half the Scales lands to which he had a claim through his mother, some Mowbray estates forfeited by the Howards, and other grants from the king. In 1488–9 these brought him a net annual landed income of more than £1400, and by 1498–9 this had risen to more than £1600. From 1488 he also had custody of the lands of his old companion Beaumont, who had lost his reason but lived on in Oxford's care until 1507. After 1500 Oxford and his councillors took vigorous initiatives to off-set declining revenues from some of these estates, a necessary step in view of the large expenses of his house-hold, which were running at between £1400 and £1500 a year in 1498/9 and 1507. The success of his financial man-agement is attested by the £2500 in ready money and goods to the value of nearly £4400 inventoried at his death.

Oxford sat in Henry's council throughout the reign, though he was not one of the most regular attenders. By 1486 he was also a knight of the Garter. He was present at most major court occasions from the baptism of Prince Arthur in 1486, where he stood godfather, to the betrothal of Princess Mary and Charles of Habsburg in 1508. He com-manded the vanguard at the battle of Stoke in 1487 and again on the invasion of France in 1492, led many troops to join Henry against the Yorkshire rebels in 1489, and began the assault on the Cornish rebels at Blackheath in 1497. He presided as lord high steward at the trial of Edward, earl of Warwick, on 21 November 1499. As lord admiral he does not seem to have been much concerned with the navy, but he did assert his rights over wrecks and king's fish. He regularly entertained Henry VII on his progresses, but Francis Bacon's story that on one of these occasions Henry imposed a vast fine upon him for gathering illegal retainers to welcome the king is probably apocryphal. Oxford lived mostly at Wivenhoe, Essex, which he had inherited from his mother, and at Castle Hedingham, Essex. At the latter he was building in brick by 1490, add-ing domes to the turrets of the twelfth-century keep and constructing a new great hall, several towers, a curtain wall, and a bridge across the moat. Of these only the bridge survives. Oxford's jousting helm also survives, in the Bargello Museum in Florence. He kept an outstanding chapel choir and commissioned Caxton's edition of *The Four Sons of Aymon* in 1489.

Second marriage and death Oxford married his second wife, Elizabeth, daughter and coheir of Sir Richard Scrope and Eleanor Washbourne, between 28 November 1508 and 10 April 1509, following the death of her first hus-band, the earl's colleague Beaumont. Oxford made his tes-tament in April 1509 as Henry VII lay dying, but survived four years into the new reign, keeping his offices and co-operating with the Howards who were rising to domin-ate East Anglian politics. He died at Castle Hedingham on

10 March 1513 and was buried on 24 April with his ances-tors at Colne Priory, alongside his first wife in the lady chapel. Their tomb had been constructed as long before as 1488–9 by Henry Lorymere of London, marbler. Oxford's alabaster effigy was still in place in 1653 but had been des-troyed by 1736. Elizabeth lived until 26 June 1537, remain-ing active at court, and was buried with Beaumont at Wivenhoe, where their brass remains. Oxford had no children by either marriage and was succeeded by John, the son of his brother Sir George de Vere.   S. J. GUNN

Sources GEC, *Peerage* · C. L. Scofield, 'The early life of John de Vere, thirteenth earl of Oxford', *EngHR*, 29 (1914), 228–45 · A. Craw-ford, 'Victims of attainder: the Howard and de Vere women in the late fifteenth century', *Reading Medieval Studies*, 15 (1989), 59–74 · C. Rawcliffe and S. Flower, 'English noblemen and their advisers: consultation and collaboration in the later middle ages', *Journal of British Studies*, 25 (1986), 157–77 · R. Virgoe, 'The recovery of the Howards in East Anglia, 1485–1529', *Wealth and power in Tudor Eng-land: essays presented to S. T. Bindoff*, ed. E. W. Ives, R. J. Knecht, and J. J. Scarisbrick (1978), 1–20, esp. 8–16 · PRO · receiver-general's accounts, 1488–9, 1498–9, Essex RO, Chelmsford, D/DPr 135a, 139 · Essex RO, Chelmsford, Colchester chamberlain's accounts, D/Y2/3 · Essex RO, Chelmsford, Maldon chamberlain's accounts, D/B3/3/227 · household accounts, 1507, Longleat House, Wiltshire, misc. vol. 11 · W. H. St J. Hope, ed., 'The last testament and inven-tory of John de Veer, thirteenth earl of Oxford', *Archaeologia*, 66 (1915), 275–348 · *The Paston letters, 1422–1509 AD*, ed. J. Gairdner, new edn, 3 vols. (1872–5); repr. in 4 vols. (1910) · F. H. Fairweather, 'Colne Priory, Essex, and the burials of the earls of Oxford', *Archae-ologia*, 87 (1938), 275–95, esp. 288–91 · *An Inventory of the historical monuments in Essex*, 4 vols. (1916–23), 1.51–7 · C. G. Bayne and W. H. Dunham, eds., *Select cases in the council of Henry VII*, SeldS, 75 (1958) · A. H. Thomas and I. D. Thornley, eds., *The great chronicle of London* (1938) · S. Anglo, 'The foundation of the Tudor dynasty: the coron-ation and marriage of Henry VII', *Guildhall Miscellany*, 2 (1960–68), 7–9 · D. MacCulloch, *Suffolk and the Tudors: politics and religion in an English county, 1500–1600* (1986) · R. Horrox, *Richard III, a study of ser-vice*, Cambridge Studies in Medieval Life and Thought, 4th ser., 11 (1989) · P. W. Hammond, *The battles of Barnet and Tewkesbury* (1990) · B. Thomas and L. G. Boccia, *Armi Storiche del Museo Nazionale di Fir-enze, Palazzo del Bargello, restaurate dall'Aiuto Austriaco per Firenze* (1971), 52 · M. Bateson, ed., *Grace book B*, 1 (1903) · *Household books of John, duke of Norfolk, and Thomas, earl of Surrey*, ed. J. P. Collier, Rox-burghe Club, 61 (1844), 504–20 · Suffolk RO, Ipswich, borough of Eye accounts, EE2 · borough of Norwich accounts, Norfolk RO, 7f
Archives Essex RO, Chelmsford, Colne Priory collection, D/DPr
Likenesses H. Lorymere?, alabaster effigy, 1488–1489?, Colne Pri-ory, Essex · D. King, drawing (after alabaster effigy), repro. in Fair-weather, 'Colne Priory, Essex', pl. 89
Wealth at death £8206 17s. 8¾d.: *Archaeologia*, 66

Vere, John de, fifteenth earl of Oxford (1482–1540). *See under* Vere, John de, sixteenth earl of Oxford (1516–1562).

Vere, John de, sixteenth earl of Oxford (1516–1562), mag-nate and rake, was the eldest of four sons (there were also four daughters) of **John de Vere**, fifteenth earl of Oxford (1482–1540), and his second wife, Elizabeth Trussell (*b.* 1496, *d.* in or before 1527), daughter of Edward Trussell of Kibblestone, Staffordshire. He was born at Hedingham Castle, Essex, and educated privately.

The fifteenth earl of Oxford was the son of John de Vere and Alice Kilrington (alias Colbroke) and grandson of a younger son of Richard de Vere (*d.* 1417), the eleventh earl; he succeeded his second cousin John de Vere, fourteenth earl (1499–1526), whose disorderly personal life Cardinal

Wolsey had attempted to regulate, but which left him without legitimate issue. The cadet John had no heirs from his childhood marriage to Christian Foderingey (b. c.1481, d. in or before 1498), but paid the crown 2000 marks for the Trussell heiress and married her between 1507 and 1509. By 1509 de Vere was Henry VIII's esquire of the body; he was knighted serving him in France in 1513. He attended Henry at meetings with François I and Charles V in 1520. Wolsey's support helped him procure in 1526 a life grant of the great chamberlainship, which had descended in the senior line of his family, and he was made a knight of the Garter the following year. He signed the lords' petition against Wolsey on 1 December 1529. Associated with the divorce faction and by 1531 a royal councillor, Oxford bore the crown at Anne Boleyn's coronation, but later served on commissions trying her and her alleged lovers in 1536 and also the panels for the Courtenay conspiracy trials in 1538. Reputedly protestant, he was granted monastic lands in Essex worth £160 p.a. A Venetian report in 1531 asserted that he was 'a man of valour and authority … and it is his custom always to cavalcade with two hundred horse' (CSP Venice, 1527–33, 295). The fifteenth earl died at Earls Colne, Essex, on 21 March 1540 and was buried at Castle Hedingham on 12 April.

The sixteenth earl, who held the courtesy title Lord Bulbeck during his father's lifetime, lost any chance of succession to the great chamberlainship when Thomas Cromwell acquired it. He had joined his father in attending the king when he met Anne of Cleves at Blackheath in January 1540. He took part in Henry's Boulogne campaign of 1544 as captain of the rearguard, unusually bringing a contingent with firearms rather than horses. Oxford was one of the twelve chief mourners at Henry VIII's funeral, as later at Edward VI's. However, Stephen Gardiner complained that his players were disrupting the mourning a week after Henry's death. He was knighted at Edward VI's coronation.

Meanwhile, the earl's private life had established a pattern of disorder (recalling the fourteenth earl's), to which testimonies were collected in 1585 when the legitimacy of his heir was impugned. On 2 July 1536 he married Dorothy Neville, daughter of Ralph Neville, fourth earl of Westmorland (1498–1549), and Katherine Stafford; a great wedding reception, shared with two Manners–Neville matches, followed, attended by Henry VIII. The marriage settlement was confirmed by statute: altogether the union was rather firmer than he later wished. Dorothy bore him a daughter, Katherine (1538–1600), but left him on 6 June 1546. Thomas Howard, third duke of Norfolk, who had married her maternal aunt, tried to persuade Dorothy to return, 'but she said she wold never goe home agayne amongst such a bad comanye as were about the Earle of Oxford at that tyme' (Hunt. L., MS EL 5870). It included the notorious highwayman Thomas Robinson and such gamblers as John Lucas, master of requests, who was said to have won from Oxford 'the wardship of Mistress Roydon at dice' (Metcalfe, 235–6); perhaps also the company of players whose maintenance had been a family tradition since at least 1492. Oxford's 'unkynde

dealinge' with Dorothy by 1546 ranged from maintaining as a mistress Anne, servant of his tenant at Tilbury Hall, to apparently marrying bigamously Joan Jockey (d. 1585) of Earls Colne.

Family as well as religious disputes may have underlain the altercation in the presence chamber at Westminster in 1552 when Henry Neville, Lord Bergavenny, struck Oxford, drawing blood. Dorothy's death on 6 January 1548 might have provided opportunity to reduce Oxford's entanglements. Presumably it was after this that, with others, Sir Thomas Darcy and Edmund, Lord Sheffield, husbands of Oxford's sisters Elizabeth and Anne, had violently attacked Joan Jockey and 'cutt her nose' (Hunt. L., MS EL 5870), possibly to brand her a whore.

The incorrigible Oxford was already involved with Dorothy Fosser, his daughter Katherine's waiting woman. Darcy on 27 June 1547 informed Edward Seymour, duke of Somerset and protector, that the banns had twice been asked between them. Darcy, who suggested that Dorothy be replaced by the daughter of the local magnate Thomas, Lord Wentworth, also acted as Somerset's agent in having Dorothy physically removed and Oxford effectively treated as mentally incompetent. On 1 February 1548 Somerset induced the earl to promise Katherine to his younger son, Henry, enforced by the substantial bond of £6000. Somerset, who now had the great chamberlainship, also insisted on 'the clere extinction of his [Oxford's] pretenced clayme to the saide office' (APC, 1547–50, 93).

Oxford apparently again had banns asked for marriage to Dorothy Fosser, but suddenly abandoned this, compensating her with an annuity of £10. On 1 August 1548 he was married irregularly, without banns, to Margery Golding, daughter of John Golding of Belchamp St Paul, Essex, and half-sister of the translator Arthur Golding. With her he had the coveted male heir—unfortunately of contestable legitimacy after Oxford's vagaries—Edward de *Vere, later seventeenth earl of Oxford (1550–1604), and a daughter, Mary (d. 1624?), who married Peregrine Bertie, Lord Willoughby de Eresby. But the marriage gave Somerset a pretext to enforce the conveyance of most of Oxford's estates to himself (as trustee for the marriage project) and to impose a bond of £500 as security against alienations by him. These measures required statutory cancellation in 1552 after Somerset's fall. Eventually Katherine de Vere married Edward, Baron Windsor, and Henry Seymour married Jane Percy.

Drawing up his will on 21 December 1552, Oxford not only affirmed the royal supremacy, but insisted that his salvation was 'not to be Justyfied by eny good deede that ever I did, for I knowledge that all the Deedes and workes that ever I wroght were they never so righteous, be but as filthynes in the sight of God' (BL, Stowe Charter MS 633). Oxford's protestantism probably encouraged him to sign the letters patent of 16 June 1553 nominating Jane Grey to succeed Edward VI. According to Robert Wingfield, he imprisoned Clement Tusser in Hedingham Castle for proclaiming Mary, but Tusser successfully canvassed the support of Oxford's 'menial servants'. 'The earl professed himself much moved by their words' and encouraged his 'hundred common servants remarkable for their stature and strength' to confine the pro-Grey 'gentlemen' of his household, including several of the Golding family (Mac-Culloch, 264). He planned to take his men to join Mary, but was directed to secure Ipswich instead. Ostensible compulsion was useful insurance for his change of sides, but Oxford's adherence to Mary did not necessarily inspire great trust, though it did get him the great chamberlainship back (from William Parr, marquess of Northampton). In 1555 Oxford was instructed to assist with the burning of heretics at Colchester and Manningtree, which apparently he did, but the next year his opposition to Spanish marriage plans led to vague suspicion of implication in Henry Dudley's plot.

Oxford obtained from Elizabeth I confirmation of his great chamberlainship, which he claimed as his hereditary right, and also the lord lieutenancy of Essex. He sat to try Lord Wentworth—a competitor for local influence—for losing Calais. He entertained the Swedish prince John (wooing the queen for his brother) in September 1559 and Elizabeth herself in August 1561, having demonstrated his political reliability by his zeal first in 1560 against slanderers of the queen and then in spring 1561 against Sir Thomas Wharton and Sir Edward Waldegrave, Marian councillors and now frequenters of illegal masses.

Oxford died at Hedingham Castle on 3 August 1562 and was apparently buried in the church there (although his will had specified Earls Colne) on 31 August. His widow, Margery, married Christopher (or Charles) Tyrell, died on 2 December 1568, and was buried with the earl. Public spirited though his will might appear, the sixteenth earl's rakish and violent private life, set in a rather old-fashioned, oversized, and disorderly household, limited his capacity for a wider role. Unlike his father, he was not considered privy council or Garter material. He did at least preserve his wealth and standing as a magnate, unlike his own son.   JONATHAN HUGHES

Sources A. H. Nelson, 'Biography of Edward de Vere the seventeenth earl of Oxford' [unpublished], chap. 1 · *CSP dom.*, rev. edn, 1547–53 · Hunt. L., MS EL 5870 · BL, Stowe Charter MS 633 · *APC*, 1547–50, 1552–6 · *CPR*, 1580–83 · *CSP Venice*, 1527–33 · J. Stow, *A survey of London*, rev. edn (1603); repr. with introduction by C. L. Kingsford as *A survey of London*, 2 vols. (1908); repr. with addns (1971) · W. C. Metcalfe, ed., *The visitations of Essex*, 1, Harleian Society, 13 (1878) · E. G. Emmison, *Elizabethan life: wills of Essex gentry and merchants* (1978) · GEC, *Peerage* · H. Miller, *Henry VIII and the English nobility* (1986) · D. MacCulloch, 'The *Vita Mariae Angliae Reginae* of Robert Wingfield of Brantham', *Camden miscellany, XXVIII*, CS, 4th ser., 29 (1984), 181–301
Likenesses marble monument (fifteenth earl, with wife and children including the future sixteenth earl), Castle Hedingham church, Essex; repro. in *North-west Essex*, Royal Commission for Historic Monuments (1916), facing p. 50
Wealth at death 3000 marks in cash: will and testament, PRO, PROB 10/51; PRO, PROB 11/46, fols. 174v–176, abstracted Emmison, *Elizabethan life*, 1–4

Vere [*née* Tracy; *other married name* Hoby], **Mary**, **Lady Vere** (1581–1671), gentlewoman and patron of ministers, was born on 18 May 1581, the youngest daughter of Sir John Tracy (*d.* 1591) of Toddington, Gloucestershire, and his wife, Ann Throckmorton. Her mother died three days

later. When she was nineteen Mary married William Hoby (*d.* 1602?) of Hailes, Gloucestershire; during a brief marriage they had two sons, Philip (*d.* 1617) and William (*d.* 1623). In November 1607 she married Sir Horace *Vere, from 1625 Baron Vere of Tilbury (1565–1635). Vere had already established his military reputation in the Dutch wars against Spain and later served as governor of the cautionary town of Brill between 1609 and 1616. In the early 1620s he commanded the English volunteer force in the palatinate. The couple became strongly associated with the international Calvinist cause. While he was on campaign Vere supplied his wife with continental news about the wars, which she circulated to other members of her family. Lady Vere's interest in news continued after his death in 1635, and in 1637 she informed Sir Ferdinando Fairfax of a Swedish victory against imperial forces, which she observed 'will hinder the Emperor's design to send forces against the Low Countries' (Johnson, 1.313). Vere's death left her 'indebted', although she was the main beneficiary as well as the executor of his will. Nevertheless, in 1635 Lady Vere still hoped to raise dowries of between £3000 and £4000 for two of her daughters.

Vere employed a number of puritan clergy as his personal chaplains and Lady Vere shared his religious tastes. In 1649 the presbyterian cleric, John Geree, described her as 'an ancient mother in our Israel' (Geree, A2v). In particular Lady Vere celebrated the protestant credentials of the Tracy family, which were firmly rooted in the early days of the Reformation. William Gurnall recorded that Lady Vere 'took much delight' in the story of her ancestor William *Tracy (*d.* 1530), who was mentioned in Foxe's book of martyrs and whose remains were burnt after Archbishop Warham declared his will to be heretical in 1532 (Gurnall, 126–7). This incident was also recalled by Henry Hexham in the dedication to Lady Vere of his translation of Polyander's *A Disputation Against the Adoration of the Reliques of Saints Departed* (1611).

After her marriage to Sir Horace, Lady Vere developed a reputation as a patron of godly ministers and she corresponded with William Ames, John Burgess, John Davenport, John Dod, John Preston, Peter Senthill, Obadiah Sedgewick, and James Ussher. Ames, one of the Veres' chaplains, thanked her for 'your kindness toward me and mine [and] your respect unto my poor ministry' and Dod, vicar of Fawsley, wrote 'I make mention of you daily in my prayers'. Dod also noted in 1642 that Lady Vere was 'naturally addicted unto melancholy'. In 1624 Lady Vere used her influence with her sister Dorothy's husband, secretary of state Sir Edward Conway, to promote James Ussher as bishop of Meath. Ussher subsequently thanked Lady Vere for the 'effectual means', which she had used and asked her to thank Conway for his 'extraordinary kindness', although the two men had never met (BL, Add. MS 4275, fols. 8r, 182v, 184r, 32r). Lady Vere also successfully lobbied Conway to have John Davenport appointed vicar of St Stephen, Coleman Street, London, despite accusations that Davenport's support came only from a puritan faction. Nicholas Byfield, Thomas Gataker, and Richard Sibbes all dedicated religious works to Lady Vere and Sir

Horace. In his *Directions for the Private Reading of the Scriptures* (1618) Byfield particularly thanked them for the 'many favours I have received, but especially for all the incouragements wherewith I have been refreshed in observing your love to my ministerie' (A2r).

Lady Vere spent some time accompanying her husband in the Netherlands and two of their five daughters, Elizabeth and Mary, were born at The Hague and were naturalized by act of parliament in 1624. Through the marriages of her daughters and of her niece, Brilliana Conway (Brilliana *Harley), Lady Vere was brought into close contact with the puritan opposition to the crown. Her eldest daughter, Elizabeth (d. 1683), married, in 1626, John *Holles, from 1637 second earl of Clare; Mary (c.1611–1669) married Sir Roger Townshend and then Mildmay *Fane, from 1638 second earl of Westmorland; Catharine (b. 1612/13) married, in 1634, Oliver St John of Lidiard Tregose, and then, in 1641, John Poulett, from 1649 Lord Paulet; Anne [see Fairfax, Anne (1617/18–1665)] married, in 1637, Thomas *Fairfax (from 1648 Lord Fairfax); and Dorothy married John Wolstenholme. Lady Vere also acted as matchmaker in the marriage between Brilliana Conway and the Herefordshire puritan gentleman, Sir Robert Harley. Lady Vere acquainted Secretary Conway with Sir Robert's affection for his daughter and outlined his 'parentage, the abilities of his mind, his ripe discretion, his well-grounded religion', and last but not least the value of the Harley estates (BL, Add. MS 61989, fol. 81r). In 1642 the Harleys sent their eldest daughter, Brilliana, to live with Lady Vere at her home in Hackney and Lady Harley reminded her daughter of the respect in which they held Lady Vere—'believe it, there is not a wiser and better woman' (BL, Add. MS 70003, fol. 260r). In 1643 Lady Vere was briefly entrusted by parliament with the care of two of the king's children and in 1645 parliament granted her £1000 as part of the arrears of the sum of £2500 owed to her husband from the state. In January 1649 John Geree addressed the dedication of his *Might Overcoming Right* to Lady Vere and her daughter Anne Fairfax in the hope that they could persuade Sir Thomas Fairfax to save the king.

William Gurnall's funeral sermon for Lady Vere shows her life as an aged and pious widow. Twice daily she and her household worshipped God and on Sundays, after public worship, the sermon was repeated to her family. The servants were then called before her to give an account of the morning service and after supper she would join them in singing psalms. Twice a day Lady Vere would spend some hours alone in her closet reading the scriptures and other works of practical divinity, and every night she prayed with her female servants before retiring. She was renowned for her charity to the poor and sick, and Gurnall described her as 'a Protestant Dorcas, full of good works, and alms-deeds'. 'Few ever exceeded her, in loving and honouring' the 'faithful ministers of Christ' and he described her zeal in finding 'able and faithful ministers for those livings she had in her dispose'. On her deathbed in her 'acutest pains and greatest agonies' she continued in 'admiring and blessing God for his mercies' (Gurnall, 130, 138, 141, 145). She died on 25 December 1671

and was buried on 10 January 1672. Her funeral sermon was published with a series of epitaphs by Charles Darby, rector of Kediton in Suffolk, Edward Thomas, Simon Ford, Anthony Withers, and Richard Howlett.

JACQUELINE EALES

Sources W. Gurnall, *The Christian's labour and reward* (1672) · BL, Add. MS 4275 [correspondence to Lady Vere from ministers] · BL, Add. MS 61989, fol. 81r [correspondence to Lady Vere from ministers] · BL, Add. MS 70003, fol. 260r [correspondence to Lady Vere from ministers] · J. Eales, *Puritans and roundheads: the Harleys of Brampton Bryan and the outbreak of the English civil war* (1990) · G. W. Johnson, ed., *The Fairfax correspondence: memoirs of the reign of Charles the First*, 1 (1848) · PRO, SP 16/13/15 · PRO, SP 14/154/28 · PRO, SP 14/138/32 · J. Geree, *Might overcoming right* (1649) · JHC, 2 (1640–42), 148 · JHC, 4 (1644–6), 173 · A. Luders and others, eds., *Statutes of the realm*, 11 vols. in 12, RC (1810–28), vol. 4, p. lxxiv · A. Collins, *Historical collections of the noble families of Cavendishe, Holles, Vere, Harley and Ogle* (1752), 341–2 [will of Sir Horace Vere] · GEC, *Peerage*
Likenesses F. H. Van Hove, engraving, repro. in S. Clark, *The lives of sundry eminent persons in this later age* (1683)

Vere, Philippa de, countess of Oxford, marchioness of Dublin, and duchess of Ireland (b. 1367×70?, d. 1411). *See under* Vere, Robert de, ninth earl of Oxford, marquess of Dublin, and duke of Ireland (1362–1392).

Vere, Robert de, third earl of Oxford (d. 1221), magnate, was the third surviving son of Aubrey (III) de *Vere, the first earl (d. 1194), and of his third wife, Agnes of *Essex (b. 1151, d. in or after 1206). Little is known of him before 1207. Before his father's death in 1194 he attested several charters to monastic houses founded by the de Vere family, but his name does not appear on any charters issued by his elder brother Aubrey (IV), the second earl, and rarely on those of others. Before Michaelmas 1207 Robert married Isabel de *Bolebec, the aunt and namesake of Aubrey (IV)'s wife, who had died childless in either 1206 or 1207. The pipe roll of 1207 states that the first instalment of Isabel's fine for not being compelled to marry was in fact paid by her new husband, Robert de Vere. Isabel the niece had been the heir to the Bolebec estate, based upon Whitchurch in Buckinghamshire. Her own heirs were her two aunts, and Robert's marriage was clearly a de Vere strategy to retain control over at least half the Bolebec lands. It may also have recognized Robert as heir apparent to the earldom of Oxford. Despite two marriages Earl Aubrey failed to father a legitimate heir, and he was also predeceased by his next brother, Ralph. Robert and Isabel had one child, Hugh, later fourth earl of Oxford.

Robert de Vere succeeded his brother in October 1214. King John charged him 1000 marks for his relief and a wardship, but may not have confirmed him in the earldom and hereditary master chamberlainship; de Vere attested a royal charter issued in London on 15 January 1215 without a title. Earl Aubrey had been numbered among King John's cronies, but Robert de Vere joined the rebellion against John, one of six known rebel leaders who were descendants of his grandparents Aubrey de Vere and Alice de Clare and part of a large group whose holdings were predominantly in the eastern counties. The relief was high for a baronage of moderate extent such as de Vere's, but his primary grievance may have been John's withholding of the earldom. He attended the assembly of barons at Stamford in April 1215, and was named by Roger of Wendover as one of the principal promoters of discontent. The king must have agreed; he ordered that de Vere's lands be seized in mid-May, along with the estates of several others on Wendover's list. While de Vere was among the rebels at Runnymede, his role in the negotiations for Magna Carta is impossible to reconstruct. By 23 June the king had recognized him as earl of Oxford, for on that date the sheriff of Oxfordshire was ordered to pay Earl Robert the comital percentage of judicial fines from that county. The earl was one of the twenty-five barons elected to oversee the implementation of Magna Carta, and the fact that he attested writs issued to implement their judgments could indicate that he was deeply involved in rebel counsels, but the wavering course of his allegiance in 1215 and the years immediately following could equally well show that he was principally moved by external pressures. He was excommunicated by Pope Innocent III, and in late March 1216 John captured Oxford's primary castle at Hedingham, Essex, after a three-day siege. The earl was granted safe conduct to seek the king's forgiveness, yet within months he had offered his homage to Prince Louis of France at Rochester. After John's death Earl Robert recovered his lands, and he formally made his peace with the new regime in October 1217.

By 1220 the earl of Oxford was serving as an itinerant justice, and he presided in the *curia regis* in 1221; political considerations may have lain behind his judicial employment, but he may also have become conversant with the common law in his capacity as a landowner and local magnate. He patronized the Essex houses of Hatfield Broadoak Priory and Tilty Abbey, Osney Abbey in Oxfordshire, and the hospitallers. When the earl died, shortly before 25 October 1221, he was buried in the Benedictine priory of Hatfield Broadoak, although Earls Colne Priory was the traditional burial place of the de Vere family. His effigy rests in the parish church at Hatfield, where it was moved after the dissolution. Its shield differs from those of all other de Veres in that the silver mullet in the first quarter was borne not on a field gules, but on one of France ancient. No account explains these anomalies. Countess Isabel obtained the guardianship of their son, who was a minor, and his estates, which she exercised for approximately ten years. She died on 3 February 1245 and was buried at the Dominican friary in Oxford. Earl Hugh died in December 1263.   RaGena C. DeAragon

Sources *Pipe rolls* · Paris, *Chron.*, vols. 2, 5 · GEC, *Peerage*, new edn, 10.208–13 · H. Hall, ed., *The Red Book of the Exchequer*, 3 vols., Rolls Series, 99 (1896) · D. A. Carpenter, *The minority of Henry III* (1990) · *Seventh report*, HMC, 6 (1879) · *The itinerary of John Leland the antiquary*, ed. T. Hearne, 9 vols. (1710–12) · T. D. Hardy, ed., *Rotuli litterarum patentium*, RC (1835) · W. Camden, *Remains concerning Britain*, ed. J. Philipot and W. D. Gent, 7th edn (1674); repr. (1870) · C. Roberts, ed., *Excerpta è rotulis finium in Turri Londinensi asservatis, Henrico Tertio rege, AD 1216–1272*, 1, RC, 32 (1835), 74
Archives BL, Cotton MSS · BL, Harley MSS · BL, Stowe MSS · Bodl. Oxf., Rawl. MSS
Likenesses effigy, parish church, Hatfield Broadoak, Essex
Wealth at death see Hall, ed., *Red Book*

Vere, Robert de, ninth earl of Oxford, marquess of Dublin, and duke of Ireland (1362–1392), courtier, was the son of Thomas de Vere, eighth earl of Oxford (d. 1371), and Maud, daughter of Sir Ralph *Ufford (d. 1346).

The young courtier Robert de Vere was born on 16 January 1362, and was only nine years old when he succeeded to the earldom on the death of his father. His wardship remained in the king's hands, and he was brought up in the royal household. In October 1371 his marriage was granted to Enguerrand (VII) de *Coucy, earl of Bedford (c.1340–1397), and his wife, *Isabella (1332–1379), *Edward III's eldest daughter. The intention was that he should marry their younger daughter Philippa de Coucy [**Philippa de Vere** (1367x70?–1411)], who had been born at the king's residence at Eltham, and the marriage duly took place on or before 5 October 1376.

The de Vere family could trace their tenure of the earldom of Oxford back to the time of Stephen, but they were probably the most impoverished of the English earls, with a small inheritance mainly in Essex, Suffolk, and south Cambridgeshire. Robert de Vere's marriage to the king's granddaughter substantially enhanced the family's status, though he and his wife could not count on receiving a share of her father's inheritance. When Coucy resigned his allegiance in 1377, his inheritance passed into the hands of Richard II; it was granted to his wife with reversion of part of it to de Vere and Philippa, and some of it was later assigned for their maintenance, but de Vere may well have been disappointed in his expectation of territorial aggrandizement from his marriage. This may be one reason why he subsequently repudiated her in favour of a member of the household of Richard's consort, Anne of Bohemia.

By virtue of his upbringing in the royal household Robert de Vere was probably already known to the future Richard II. On St George's day (23 April) 1377, Richard (now prince of Wales) was knighted along with de Vere, his cousin Henry, earl of Derby, his uncle Thomas of Woodstock, and several other young nobles. De Vere, however, was soon to outstrip them all in favour and close friendship with the new king, who was five years his junior. It was alleged at the time of de Vere's downfall in 1388 that Sir Simon Burley (d. 1388) had introduced him to the king and encouraged Richard to grant the earl sole title to the share of the Coucy lands which he and his wife held jointly if his wife predeceased him. However, the hostility to Burley exhibited by the king's opponents in 1388 may have inclined them to exaggerate his part in de Vere's rise at court; it is also possible that his uncle, Aubrey de *Vere (d. 1400), who was acting chamberlain in the early years of Richard's reign and who, together with Burley, had substantial influence in the royal household, played a part in the earl's advancement.

In the early years of Richard II's reign, while de Vere was still under age, his presence at court went unremarked: he was merely one of a group of young men around the king, none of whom yet seemed marked out for particular favour. From 1384 onwards, however, Robert de Vere emerged as the king's closest and most lavishly rewarded friend. He had his own chambers in the king's residences at Eltham and Langley, and he was the recipient of extensive patronage. His opponents believed that he used his influence over the king to enrich himself. He was granted, for example, the reversion of the Audley inheritance in south-west England and the shrievalty of Rutland for life. In 1385 the king gave him the castle and lordship of Queenborough in Kent: the wording of the grant concludes 'the curse of God and St Edward and the king on any who do or attempt aught against this grant' (*CPR, 1381–5*, 542), and in July 1387 Richard appointed him chief justice of Chester.

Irish connections In December 1385 the king conferred on Robert de Vere the title marquess of Dublin, granting him palatine powers in Ireland, and probably in the same year he became a knight of the Garter. The de Vere family had disposed of its meagre interests in Ireland some twenty years earlier, and Robert himself had no links with or knowledge of the lordship, nor, it seemed, any serious intention of going there himself. The title of marquess aroused particular hostility among the lords. It had hitherto been unknown in England (it may have originated in central Europe), and it placed de Vere above all the earls in precedence; yet his rise owed everything to royal favour, and nothing to his own achievements.

To cover the costs that he (or more probably his deputy) would incur in Ireland, de Vere was granted immediate use of the revenues from the Audley lands, and the ransom of Jean de Penthièvre, son of Charles de Blois, claimant to the duchy of Brittany. Although de Vere himself never went to Ireland, his council concerned itself with Irish business, and in March 1386 he appointed Sir John Stanley (d. 1414) his deputy there. Stanley eventually took an expedition to Ireland in August 1387. Richard, however, was determined to raise de Vere still higher in rank, and on 13 October 1386 his marquessate was revoked and he was created duke of Ireland, where his powers were enhanced so that the king retained only de Vere's liege homage for the lordship. The king's closest friend, who was the first holder of the title of duke from outside the inner circles of the royal family, was now equal in status to Richard II's uncles of Lancaster, York, and Gloucester, and Walsingham records how indignant the other nobles were at the further promotion of such a mediocrity.

The king's favourite The nature of de Vere's influence over the king has provoked much speculation. There was certainly an emotional charge to the relationship, as there evidently was between de Vere and his second wife, but the English chroniclers find difficulty in explaining the hold he had over the king. Walsingham attributes it to magic spells cast by a friar in the royal household, and also hints at a sexual relationship. Although there are some similarities to the friendship between Edward II and Piers Gaveston, there is no evidence for a homosexual relationship between the two men, but the possibility of a formal compact of brotherhood, as has been suggested between Gaveston and Edward, should not be entirely ruled out. Froissart says that the king was so blinded by de Vere that

'if he had said black was white the king would not have gainsaid him' (*Œuvres*, 12.239). Froissart also, however, suggests that de Vere had an attractive side to his personality, for at the time of his exile he describes him as having 'sensitivity, honour, fair speech and great generosity' (*Chroniques*, 14.33).

By 1387 de Vere had acquired the means to live in some opulence. After his downfall he was found to have had at Chester silver plate worth nearly £100 and other possessions worth over £300. Among these were a set of wall or bed hangings embroidered with butterflies, other embroidered hangings, four liveries for his minstrels, and six liveries each for his valets and grooms.

Yet it was not just the favour shown to de Vere that aroused hostility, but also his own behaviour, especially his attempts to undermine the relationship between John of Gaunt, duke of Lancaster, and the king. De Vere may have had a hand in the episode at the Salisbury parliament in 1384 when a Carmelite friar accused Gaunt of treason. He denied any complicity in the affair, but the friar tried to implicate him, and it is perhaps significant that the friar had been saying mass before the king in de Vere's chamber immediately before he made the accusation. There is more reason to suppose that de Vere was implicated in the plot against Gaunt's life hatched in February 1385: Walsingham and the Monk of Evesham accuse the young men around the king of complicity in the plot, while the Monk of Westminster singles out de Vere and two other earls for specific mention. De Vere served with a substantial retinue on the king's expedition to Scotland in the summer of 1385, and Froissart says that his influence lay behind Richard's decision at Edinburgh to return home, rejecting Gaunt's advice to move further into Scotland. The Monk of Westminster, however, does not suggest that de Vere had any part in the decision.

Divorce and second marriage By 1386 Robert de Vere's standing with his fellow nobles was already low; what finally destroyed it was his repudiation of his wife in the following year and his marriage to **Agnes Lancecrona** [Agnes de Vere] (*fl.* 1382–1388), a lady of the royal household. Little is known about her origins. Walsingham believes that she was a saddler's daughter, but it has been suggested on the basis of her name that she belonged to a German (or possibly Netherlandish) noble family called Landskron. She had come to England with Queen Anne in 1382, and is described by the Monk of Westminster as a 'woman of the queen's chamber' (*Westminster Chronicle*, 188–9). She may indeed have been of German rather than Czech origin, but such a distinction would probably not have appeared significant at the English court in the 1380s. From the point of view of the English nobles and their wives, her lowly status, and her membership of a group of Bohemians around the queen who were generally unpopular, were quite sufficient for de Vere's affair with her to cause grave offence. His first wife was Edward III's granddaughter, and her royal uncles, notably Gloucester, were strongly protective of her and, later, sought to shield her from the consequences of her husband's disgrace and exile.

Westminster suggests that de Vere 'grew to detest' his first wife, who can scarcely have been out of her teens when he decided to divorce her. He lobbied for a divorce at the papal curia, allegedly with perjured witnesses. Froissart maintains that he had no good reason to divorce her, but did so for frivolous reasons. Although the editors of the Dieulacres chronicle cast doubt on whether the divorce was granted, the Monk of Westminster records that it was annulled by papal bull in October 1389, and it is therefore probably safe to assume that it did indeed take place. It is not clear, however, whether Agnes was enthusiastic about de Vere's advances: two of his retainers were later accused of abducting her and taking her to Chester, where de Vere was residing in the summer of 1387. After de Vere's downfall various items belonging to Agnes and her servants were found at Chester. They included two new saddles 'pour damoiselles de Boeme', and one old saddle in Bohemian style (PRO, E 36/66). These are the last traces of her: she disappeared from public view as suddenly as she had arrived.

From Radcot Bridge to Louvain Robert de Vere's marriage to Agnes Lancecrona, and the dishonouring of Edward III's granddaughter that it implied, was undoubtedly a major reason for the intensification of hostility to him in the summer and autumn of 1387. Walsingham suggests that the king supported de Vere's pursuit of Agnes Lancecrona, but that the king's uncles, especially Gloucester, were highly indignant at the affront to their niece. He goes on to say that Gloucester now looked for an opportunity to avenge the insult. For his part, the king came to rely on de Vere even more in these months, and the latter's appointment as justice of Chester was intended to ensure that the royal earldom, with its considerable military potential, was in safe hands. In November 1387 both the king and his opponents began to muster their forces. The duke of Gloucester and the earls of Arundel and Warwick (three of the future *lords appellant) appeared in arms at Harringay in mid-November, and accused de Vere, along with four other associates of the king, of treason. De Vere meanwhile was raising an army in Cheshire, which set out to march south in mid-December. On 20 December 1387 de Vere's army was routed by the appellants at Radcot Bridge in Oxfordshire. De Vere himself escaped, but many of his followers were killed, and de Vere displayed little military skill. Indeed, one source reports that some of his troops deserted even before they encountered the appellant army, while Walsingham goes so far as to suggest that de Vere himself contemplated flight before the battle, and had to have his courage reinforced by his men. Ralph, Lord Basset, seems to have spoken for many when he remarked that 'I am not going to offer to have my head broken for the duke of Ireland' (*Knighton's Chronicle*, 407).

The appellants' victory at Radcot Bridge was decisive: by the end of December Richard had agreed that de Vere and other lords who had been close to the king should be tried for treason in the Merciless Parliament which opened in February 1388. De Vere, of course, was tried in his absence. He was accused, along with four other leading familiars of the king, of accroaching royal power, of benefiting

improperly from royal patronage, of encouraging the king to resist the council imposed on him in the parliament of October 1386, and of manipulating the law for their own advantage. De Vere in particular was accused of separating England from Ireland by encouraging the king to grant him the lordship of Ireland without the assent of the community in either land, and of raising an army in Cheshire to destroy the duke of Gloucester and the other appellants. He was found guilty, and sentenced *in absentia* to death and forfeiture of all his lands and titles.

After the rout at Radcot Bridge de Vere escaped first of all to Bruges, and then to Dordrecht in Holland. The count of Holland, Albrecht of Bavaria, refused to countenance his presence in Dordrecht, and he moved on to Utrecht. In the late summer of 1389 he went to Paris, where he met his fellow exiles Michael de la Pole and Alexander Neville, the deposed archbishop of York (*d.* 1392). De la Pole died while de Vere was in Paris, and Walsingham says that he left de Vere such goods as he had been able to save from forfeiture. His estranged wife's father, Enguerrand de Coucy, however, was influential at the French court and was determined to drive him out of France. De Vere asked Charles VI of France to intercede on his behalf with the duchess of Brabant, who according to Froissart gave him leave to reside in Louvain. His mother visited him in 1391, and in February of the following year Richard II suggested that he should be allowed to return to England. The council objected, however, and his death shortly afterwards removed a potentially difficult issue for Richard. De Vere died some time before 5 August 1392, probably at or near Louvain: Thomas Otterbourne records that he was killed by a wild boar while out hunting, but his story is not confirmed by any other contemporary source.

Family fortunes Walsingham says that de Vere died in poverty and distress, but he had had some success during his exile in obtaining payment of instalments of the ransom of Jean de Penthièvre. The dukes of Berri and Burgundy agreed that he should be paid 27,600 francs of the ransom in 1388, but it is uncertain how much he had actually received by the time of his death. He had no children, and in January 1393 his uncle, Aubrey de Vere, who was his heir, successfully petitioned for the entailed lands of the earldom of Oxford and the title of earl to be restored to him.

Robert de Vere was buried at Louvain, but in September 1395 Richard II ordered that his body should be exhumed and brought to England for reburial at Earls Colne Priory, Essex, the family's burial place. Walsingham describes how, in a bizarre demonstration of his continued affection for his favourite, Richard had the coffin opened so that he could look upon de Vere's face and touch his fingers. De Vere's mother (though not, apparently, his estranged wife) and various bishops, abbots, and priors were present at the ceremony. None of the nobles came, however, 'because they had not yet digested the hatred they had for him' (*Trokelowe*, 185). His tomb does not survive.

After his exile, his first wife went to live with de Vere's

mother, who according to Westminster had strongly disapproved of her son's affair with Agnes Lancecrona, and held Philippa 'more dear than if she had been her own daughter' (*Westminster Chronicle*, 190–91). She was always known as the duchess of Ireland, despite her husband's forfeiture of the title, and Richard II ensured that she received an adequate maintenance. De Vere's mother farmed her exiled son's lands, and Philippa was granted an annuity of 100 marks from the revenues of these lands, rising to 300 marks after de Vere's death. In 1398 she was granted dower from her husband's estates. Early in Henry IV's reign she and her elder sister Mary agreed to divide their father's inheritance between them, with Philippa receiving the English and Mary the French lands. She was at court from time to time in Henry's reign, and accompanied Richard II's widow, Queen Isabella, to Calais on her way back to France in 1401. She died, in England, on 24 September 1411: it is not known where she is buried.

ANTHONY TUCK

Sources L. C. Hector and B. F. Harvey, eds. and trans., *The Westminster chronicle, 1381–1394*, OMT (1982) · *Knighton's chronicle, 1337–1396*, ed. and trans. G. H. Martin, OMT (1995) [Lat. orig., *Chronica de eventibus Angliae a tempore regis Edgari usque mortem regis Ricardi Secundi*, with parallel Eng. text] · *Johannis de Trokelowe et Henrici de Blaneforde … chronica et annales*, ed. H. T. Riley, pt 3 of *Chronica monasterii S. Albani*, Rolls Series, 28 (1866) · *Thomae Walsingham, quondam monachi S. Albani, historia Anglicana*, ed. H. T. Riley, 2 vols., pt 1 of *Chronica monasterii S. Albani*, Rolls Series, 28 (1863–4) · *Œuvres de Froissart*, ed. K. de Lettenhove, 14 (Brussels, 1872) · M. V. Clarke and V. H. Galbraith, eds., 'The deposition of Richard II', *Bulletin of the John Rylands University Library*, 14 (1930), 125–81, esp. 164–81 [chronicle of Dieulacres Abbey] · exchequer treasury of receipt, miscellaneous books, PRO, E 36/66 · *Chancery records* · *Calendar of inquisitions miscellaneous (chancery)*, 7 vols., PRO (1916–68) · *CIPM* · *RotP*, vol. 3 · *Duo rerum Anglicarum scriptores veteres, Thomas Otterbourne et Joh. Whethamstede*, ed. T. Hearne, 1 (1732) · A. Tuck, *Richard II and the English nobility* (1973) · P. Chaplais, *Piers Gaveston: Edward II's adoptive brother* (1994) · M. Jones, 'The ransom of Jean de Bretagne, count of Penthièvre: an aspect of English foreign policy, 1386–8', *BIHR*, 45 (1972), 7–26 · G. S. Haslop, 'Two entries from the register of John de Shirburn, abbot of Selby, 1369–1408', *Yorkshire Archaeological Journal*, 41 (1963–6), 287–96 · M. V. Clarke, 'Forfeitures and treason in 1388', *Fourteenth century studies*, ed. L. S. Sutherland and M. McKisack (1937), 115–45 · C. D. Ross, 'Forfeiture for treason in the reign of Richard II', *EngHR*, 71 (1956), 560–75 · P. Morgan, *War and society in medieval Cheshire, 1277–1403*, Chetham Society, 3rd ser., 34 (1987) · C. Given-Wilson, *The royal household and the king's affinity: service, politics and finance in England, 1360–1413* (1986) · R. Halliday, 'Robert de Vere, ninth earl of Oxford', *Medieval History*, 3 (1993), 71–85 · W. D. Macray, ed., *Chronicon abbatiae de Evesham, ad annum 1418*, Rolls Series, 29 (1863) · GEC, *Peerage* · N. Saul, *Richard II* (1997)

Vere, Sir Stephen Edward De, fourth baronet (1812–1904), philanthropist and classical scholar, was the son of Sir Aubrey De *Vere, second baronet (1788–1846), and his wife, Mary Rice (*d.* 1856); his younger brother was Aubrey Thomas de *Vere. He was born at Curragh Chase, Adare, co. Limerick, on 26 July 1812. He was educated at Trinity College, Dublin, and throughout his life shared the literary tastes of his family. After reading at Lincoln's Inn, he was called to the Irish bar in 1836. His life was dedicated to the service of his fellow countrymen, and he worked hard for the relief of the distress during the Irish famine. He

believed emigration to be the only panacea, and encouraged the young men to go out to Canada. Hearing of the terrible sufferings of the emigrants on the voyage, in May 1847 he went himself as a steerage passenger to Canada. The emigrant ships were sailing vessels, and the voyage took six weeks or more. Arriving in Canada he wrote a letter (30 November 1847) describing the appalling conditions aboard ship. His revelations were made public by the Colonial Office and had a powerful impact. De Vere's letter was cited in both houses of parliament in 1848, and his recommendations for new regulations were the basis for amendments to the passenger acts ensuring that proper accommodation was provided for emigrants.

De Vere's admiration of the Irish Catholic people led him to embrace the Roman Catholic religion, and his reception into that church took place during his visit to Canada in 1848. In 1851 he wrote a pamphlet defending the creation of a Catholic hierarchy in England.

De Vere was member of parliament for Limerick County (1854–9). He was a Liberal, supporting tenant right and Gladstone's land legislation, but he was opposed to home rule. He succeeded his brother Vere as fourth baronet in 1880. De Vere published *Translations from Horace* in 1886, together with some original verse. He died unmarried on 10 November 1904 at Foynes, co. Limerick, an island in the River Shannon and was buried there, by the door of the Roman Catholic church, which was built mainly by his exertions. A fountain was erected in the village during his lifetime to commemorate his work in the district. His kindness to his tenants was remarkable; they were permitted to help themselves to wood from the park, and even, it was said, to the deer. The baronetcy became extinct at his death.

ELIZABETH LEE, *rev.* M. C. CURTHOYS

Sources *The Times* (11 Nov 1904) · W. Ward, *Aubrey de Vere: a memoir* (1904), 183–4 · A. de Vere, *Recollections* (1897), 252–5 · O. MacDonagh, *A pattern of government growth* (1961) · WWBMP · 'Select committee … on colonization from Ireland: first report', *Parl. papers* (1847–8), 17.44–9, no. 415 · WWW

Archives TCD, journals, letter-books, and papers | NL Ire., letters to Lord Emly · NL Ire., Monsell MSS · PRO NIre., Wyndham-Quin MSS · University of Limerick Library, letters to Lord Dunraven

Wealth at death £4132 18*s*. 9*d*.: probate, 16 Feb 1905, *CGPLA Ire.* · £451 2*s*. 4*d*.—effects in England: Irish probate sealed in London, 27 Feb 1905, *CGPLA Ire.*

Vere, Thomas (*d.* 1682), jury foreman, was the son of Ralph Vere of Wrotham, Kent. He was apprenticed in 1635/6 to John Wright, a member of the Stationers' Company. He obtained his freedom in 1644, and between 1646 and 1680 he operated as a bookseller in the Old Bailey area.

Vere served as the foreman of the jury which tried the Quakers William Penn and William Mead at the Old Bailey before the mayor and recorder of London in September 1670. Penn and Meade had been arrested for conspiracy to commit a riot in Gracechurch Street on 14 August 1670. After an initial deliberation lasting one and a half hours, the jury split 8:4 for a guilty verdict. After being sent back again the jury found the defendants guilty of 'speaking in Gracechurch Street'. After being sent out again, they found Penn guilty of speaking or 'preaching' to an 'assembly', but found Meade not guilty. The judge then ordered the jury detained overnight, without food or drink. When they returned the same verdict twice more, the court threatened the jury with being carted about the city. The jury sent word of a new verdict, but the court adjourned until the following day, whereupon the jury found a unanimous verdict of not guilty. This enraged the bench, who imposed a fine of 40 marks upon each juror and ordered them detained until the fine was paid. Vere evidently paid his fine and was released, as he was not one of the four jurors, led by Edward Bushell, who sued out a writ of habeas corpus in the court of common pleas, and won the ruling that the fine had no basis in law and that the jury had been held without lawful cause.

Vere was elected a common councilman for the Farringdon Without ward in 1672 and 1675–7. He served as warden of the Stationers' Company in 1677 and as master in 1681. His will, dated 13 February 1682, referred to himself as 'citizen and stationer', and to his belief in his personal salvation 'with the elect children of God' (will). He asked to be buried in his local church of St Sepulchre, near to his 'late wife'. His will was proved later in 1682.

STUART HANDLEY

Sources will, GL, MS 9171/38, fols. 26r–28r · J. R. Woodhead, *The rulers of London, 1660–1689* (1965), 167 · H. R. Plomer and others, *A dictionary of the booksellers and printers who were at work in England, Scotland, and Ireland from 1641 to 1667* (1907), 186 · R. Myers, *The Stationers' Company archive: an account of the records, 1554–1984* (1990), 203 · C. W. Horle, *The Quakers and the English legal system, 1660–1688* (1988), 116 · T. A. Green, *Verdict according to conscience* (1985), 200–64 · *State trials*, 6.951–1026 · *The peoples ancient and just liberties asserted* (1670) · *The poems and letters of Andrew Marvell*, ed. H. Margoliouth, rev. P. Legouis, 3rd edn, 2 vols. (1971), 117–8, 318

Vereker, Charles, **second Viscount Gort** (1768–1842), soldier and politician, was the second son of Thomas Vereker of Roxborough, co. Limerick, and his wife, Juliana, sister of John Prendergast Smyth, first Viscount Gort. He was descended from a family of Flemish extraction, long settled in co. Limerick. At the age of fourteen he entered the Royal Navy, and, serving as a midshipman, participated in the relief of Gibraltar in 1782. Vereker's gallantry on this occasion received the warm acknowledgement of his commander; but after a few years' service he retired from the navy and purchased a commission in the army. In 1790 Vereker was returned for the borough of Limerick to the Irish parliament in the interest of his uncle, whose heir he had become. He retained this position until the union in 1800, and in 1802 was elected unopposed for the same constituency to Westminster; he held this seat down to his succession to the peerage in 1817.

He was twice married: first, on 7 November 1789, to Jane, widow of William Stamer of Carnelly, and daughter of Ralph Westropp of Attyflyn, who died on 19 February 1798; and, second, on 5 March 1810, to Elizabeth (*d.* 1858), daughter of John Palliser of Derryluskan, co. Tipperary. He had children by both marriages, two sons and three daughters.

In 1793 Vereker was appointed to the command of the Limerick militia, with the rank of lieutenant-colonel, and in that capacity he was in charge of the garrison at Sligo at the time of the French invasion during 1798. After his victory at Castlebar the French general, Humbert, desiring to join with the Ulster United Irishmen, marched on Sligo at the head of his whole force of 1600 men, accompanied by numerous Irish irregulars, and on the morning of 5 September he arrived at Colooney, a village within 5 miles of that town. Vereker, who had only 300 men at his disposal, had received orders not to risk an engagement, but believing that the French force at Colooney represented only a detachment of the main army, he marched out to meet it. After holding the enemy at bay for nearly two hours, Vereker retreated to Sligo with considerable casualties. He was himself severely wounded in the engagement. Humbert, conjecturing from Vereker's audacity that he was supported by the main body of the British army, diverted his march from Sligo. The significance of this clash was later exaggerated, but it did demonstrate that the Irish militia would not always run when under fire. For his services Vereker was voted the thanks of an Irish parliament anxious to assert its limited dependence on English forces; he also received a sword of honour from the city of Limerick. After considerable lobbying he was in 1803 awarded the privilege of adopting the motto 'Coloony', with a grant of supporters bearing the flag of the Limerick militia.

Vereker was a vigorous opponent of the union, against which he voted: he declared in the Commons in 1799 that 'having defended his country with his blood, there was nothing in the gift of the crown that could tempt him to betray it by his vote'. Yet, while he occasionally opposed the government's Irish defence measures, at Westminster he proved susceptible to offers of patronage. In 1803 the chief secretary declared him 'a very troublesome man, who is full of vanity, but warm in his attachments' (HoP, *Commons*, 447). In 1807 he was appointed a commissioner of the Treasury for Ireland. He also held the honorary offices of constable of Limerick Castle and governor of Galway. He succeeded his uncle in the viscountcy of Gort on 23 May 1817, having failed in 1816 to extract an earldom by means of conduct the viceroy found 'shabby' (HoP, *Commons*, 448). He was elected an Irish representative peer in 1823. He acted in general with the tory party, yet despite being virulently anti-Catholic and the controlling patron of Limerick corporation, Gort voted for Catholic emancipation in 1829, and for the Irish Corporation Act. He died at Dublin on 11 November 1842, and was succeeded by his eldest son, John Prendergast Vereker, third viscount.

C. L. FALKINER, *rev.* PETER GRAY

Sources HoP, *Commons* · T. Pakenham, *The year of liberty: the story of the great Irish rebellion of 1798* (1969) · T. Bartlett, *The fall and rise of the Irish nation: the Catholic question, 1690–1830* (1992) · *Annual Register* (1842) · *Freeman's Journal* [Dublin] (14 Nov 1842) · GM, 2nd ser., 18 (1842)

Archives BL, corresp. with Sir Robert Peel, Add. MSS 40221–40508 · PRO NIre., Wyndham-Quin MSS · University of Limerick Library, letters to Lord Dunraven

Likenesses J. Comerford, engraving, 1841, NL Ire. · C. Grey, pencil drawing, NG Ire.; repro. in *Dublin University Magazine* (1842), xix ·

J. Heath, stipple (after J. Comerford), BM, NPG; repro. in J. Barrington, *Historic memoirs* (1809) • J. Kirkwood, etching (after C. Grey), NG Ire.; repro. in *Dublin University Magazine* (1842), 19

Vereker, John Standish Surtees Prendergast, sixth Viscount Gort in the peerage of Ireland and first Viscount Gort in the peerage of the United Kingdom (1886–1946),

army officer, was born at 24 Chesham Place, London, on 10 July 1886, the elder son of John Gage Prendergast Vereker, fifth Viscount Gort (1849–1902), and his wife, Eleanor (*d.* 1933), daughter and coheir of Robert Smith *Surtees, novelist, of Hamsterley Hall, co. Durham. He was educated at Harrow School (*c.*1900–04), being a schoolboy there when he succeeded to the family honours in 1902, and attended the Royal Military College, Sandhurst (1905–6). He was gazetted ensign in the Grenadier Guards in 1905. On 23 February 1911 Gort married his cousin, Corinna Katherine Medlicott Vereker (1891–1940); they had two sons and a daughter. The marriage ended in divorce in 1925.

First World War service On the outbreak of war with Germany in August 1914, the month of his promotion to captain, Gort went to France as aide-de-camp to the commander of the 1st corps, Sir Douglas Haig. In 1915 he was appointed GSO3 to the 1st corps, and later he became brigade-major of the 4th (guards) brigade. He was present at the battles of Festubert and Loos. In July 1916 he was appointed GSO2 to the operations branch at general headquarters (GHQ). In January 1917 a special subsection of the operations branch was formed, with Gort as assistant to its chief, to work out details of the campaign for that year, which it was then hoped would include a landing from the sea behind the German front near Middelkerke. This was a landmark in staff organization: the conception of a planning staff without other duties was a novelty.

Gort was a competent staff officer, but his greatest gift was for leadership. In April 1917 he was appointed to command the 4th battalion, Grenadier Guards, shortly before the arduous offensive in Flanders. On the first day of that offensive, 31 July, in the battle of Pilckem Ridge, he was wounded, but, despite great pain, he remained until the captured ground had been consolidated. For his exploits on that occasion he received a bar to the DSO to which he had been appointed earlier in the year. He returned to lead his battalion in a later phase of the offensive. In November he was wounded again in the battle of Cambrai. In March 1918, now commanding the 1st battalion of his regiment, he played a part in stemming the German offensive at Arras. He was awarded a second bar to the DSO. Already he had acquired a reputation for the rarest gallantry, complete disregard of personal danger, and the power to keep alive in troops under his command a spirit of endeavour, untamed by loss and strain.

The great day of Gort's early career was 27 September 1918. The occasion was an episode in the victorious British offensive, the passage of the Canal du Nord and storming of the Hindenburg line near the village of Flesquières, in which he found himself temporarily in command of the 3rd guards brigade. The situation with which he was confronted was all too familiar: the brigade was to pass through and capture the third objective, but found that

John Standish Surtees Prendergast Vereker, sixth Viscount Gort in the peerage of Ireland and first Viscount Gort in the peerage of the United Kingdom (1886–1946), by Reginald Grenville Eves, 1940

the second had not been fully attained. Gort first led his own battalion up under very heavy fire to its starting line. He was then wounded, but personally directed a tank against an obstacle holding up the advance. The brigade's left flank was completely exposed, but he covered it with one of his battalions, the 1st Welsh Guards. Severely wounded for the second time, he struggled up from the stretcher on which he had been lying and continued to direct the attack. Later on he collapsed, but, recovering partially, he insisted on waiting until the success signals were seen. It was an extraordinary feat of physical courage and of will, for which he fittingly was awarded the VC. In the course of the war he was also awarded the MC and was eight times mentioned in dispatches.

Gort attended the Staff College, Camberley, on its reopening in 1919. In 1921, now a brevet lieutenant-colonel, he returned as instructor. He then reverted to regimental duty. In 1926 he became chief instructor at the senior officers' school at Sheerness, and his promotion to the rank of colonel was antedated to January 1925. He went on to command the Grenadier Guards and regimental district in 1930, became director of military training in India in 1932, and in 1936 went to the Staff College for the third time, now as commandant.

Chief of the Imperial General Staff The secretary of state for war, Leslie Hore-Belisha, wished to rejuvenate the higher appointments at the War Office. His eye fell upon Gort, who early in 1937 was still only fifty years of age. He was appointed military secretary to the secretary of state and later in the year chief of the Imperial General Staff (CIGS). He was promoted full general, skipping the intermediate rank of lieutenant-general. He was also appointed CB, and promoted KCB in 1938.

In early life Gort had acquired the ridiculous and inappropriate nickname Fat Boy, but he was later known familiarly as Jack. In what would now be termed his life-style he was austere and self-denying; indeed he seemed to delight in privations and expected others to do the same. On his appointment to the Staff College in 1936 one colonel remarked: 'He will have all the beds made of concrete and hosed down with cold water nightly' (Colville, 68). His suggestion that officers might use their leisure hours at Camberley learning to fly rather than following the drag hunt was not widely appreciated. He also had a schoolboy sense of fun which he never entirely outgrew. In his days as an instructor at the Staff College in the early 1920s he had been a ringleader in various rags, such as squirting hoses under the bedroom doors of those who retired too early on mess nights, and he was not above treating the war minister to similar horseplay in 1939.

In promoting Gort to the highest appointment in the army, Hore-Belisha hoped he had chosen a man who would supply the drive for pushing through overdue reforms, and that his character would appeal to the troops and enhance the service's reputation with the public. Sir Ronald Adam as his deputy would supply the brains and adroitness necessary in the chiefs of staff committee and the committee of imperial defence. Sir John Kennedy's opinion, that 'in the war office this fine fighting soldier was like a fish out of water' (Kennedy, 5), may be too severe, but it soon became apparent that Gort was not ideally suited to the position of CIGS. One of Gort's salient characteristics throughout his life was an obsession with detail, sometimes to the exclusion or neglect of the broader picture. Nevertheless, he became CIGS at a time when the energetic and ambitious Hore-Belisha was bringing army reform to the forefront of British politics, and he played an important part in the great improvements that were accomplished before the outbreak of war. His most important achievement was to get the army's continental commitment recognized by the government (finally achieved in February 1939)—with the resultant rush to get its equipment, weapons, and transport modernized—and part of the Territorial Army earmarked for development as its eventual reserve. Though he remained ignorant of the French army's weaknesses, Gort was convinced that Germany was Britain's most likely enemy, that the field force must be ready for dispatch to France, and that the pre-1939 plan to send only two divisions was a completely inadequate contribution to an alliance.

Quite apart from the blighting of individual careers, it was a tragedy for the British army that Gort and Hore-Belisha proved unable to work amicably together; indeed for several months before the outbreak of war Hore-Belisha and his chief military adviser were barely on speaking terms and saw as little of each other as possible. To judge by the diaries of Sir H. R. Pownall and Sir W. E.

Ironside, all the fault was on Hore-Belisha's side, but Gort's biographer corrects this impression, pointing out that the CIGS offered his political chief no affection or understanding and little credit for his many admirable reforms. A less formal CIGS, capable of overlooking or even laughing at the war minister's irritating mannerisms and methods, might have gained the latter's confidence and achieved a working relationship.

Commander-in-chief of the field force, 1939–1940 The government's omission to appoint a commander-in-chief of the field force before the declaration of war on 3 September 1939 caused ill feeling and confusion among the three possible choices (Sir J. G. Dill, Ironside, and the least likely candidate, Gort). Whether or not Gort pressed for the appointment of commander-in-chief is uncertain, but he was evidently delighted to escape from Hore-Belisha and the War Office, where he was succeeded by Ironside. Gort, like H. A. Alexander, made no secret of the fact that he enjoyed the excitement of war. 'Here we go again, marching to war' was his first remark on reaching the Staff College to form his headquarters, and he added, 'I can't expect everybody to be as thrilled as I am'.

Gort's position in the allied command structure was a curious one. His headquarters had liaison with General M.-G. Gamelin's (general headquarters), but he was not under Gamelin's orders. The British field force was included in the First Army group under General Billotte but—initially at any rate—Gort was to receive his orders from General Alphonse Georges, French commander of the armies on the north-eastern front. Like his predecessor Sir John French in 1914, Gort was granted the right to appeal to his own government should he consider that French orders (or, as it turned out, lack of them) might endanger his troops. The two original corps commanders, Dill and Sir Alan Brooke, expressed criticisms of the field force's equipment, tactics, and training, feeling that Gort was too complacent and too obsessed with detail. In their turn Gort and Pownall, his chief of staff, suspected the corps commanders of 'bellyaching' and defeatism. Too much of Gort's time was taken up with ceremonial visits to the French and in entertaining a stream of distinguished visitors at general headquarters, but in any case he believed in delegating a large measure of responsibility for training to his subordinates. Montgomery made some sharp criticisms of Gort's leadership in his *Memoirs*, but allowed that he had an impossible task in running a great headquarters as well as exercising direct command over the fighting and administrative forces. The plan was for Gort to appoint two army commanders under him when four corps were assembled, but only three were in place by May 1940.

On a substantial operational issue, Gort was unhappy about Gamelin's proposal to abandon the frontier defences and advance into Belgium to the line of the River Dyle (Plan D) in the event of a German attack. Gort, Pownall, and Ironside were all present at Vincennes on 9 November when Gamelin explained his plans and the safeguards against being surprised in the open, and none of them objected. Gort suppressed his reservations in the interests of allied unity: he was under French direction and would advance when told to without reference to his government. In retrospect this acquiescence in an extremely risky plan was to be widely criticized as a dereliction of duty.

The final rift with Hore-Belisha resulted directly from the minister's visit to the field force in mid-November. It seems unlikely that Gort himself intrigued against the war minister, but he had a trusted 'hatchet man' in Pownall and must have been broadly aware of his clandestine efforts. But, in contrast to Pownall, who rejoiced, Gort was surprised at Hore-Belisha's resignation in January 1940 and seemed upset that he might be suspected of causing it. The problem which most urgently affected Gort in April and early May was his precise place in the allied chain of command. Uncertainties remained until the Germans invaded Belgium in the early hours of 10 May and the allies responded to the plea for assistance by implementing Plan D.

Commanding in the field, 1940–1941 Given Gort's temperament and thirst for action, his choice between the roles of a commander-in-chief at headquarters and a field commander actually fighting the battle from forward positions was a foregone conclusion. Taking Pownall and other senior staff officers with him, Gort immediately left general headquarters for a command post at Wahagnies, near Lille. The separation of the commander-in-chief from his GHQ for the critical phase of the campaign proved to be an administrative disaster because communications between the shifting command post and GHQ broke down almost completely. All reports of German movements, for example, were sent to the operations section remaining at GHQ but it was often impossible to pass the information to the command post. Montgomery later reflected that the distribution of staff duties between GHQ and the command post was amateur and lacking the professional touch. The verdict of the official historian was equally severe.

On 12 May General Billotte was appointed to co-ordinate the movements of the first group of armies (including the British and Belgian forces), but in the succeeding critical days he conspicuously failed to do so as the allies first advanced to the Dyle line and then retreated to the Franco-Belgian frontier while the German Panzer columns drove westward behind them to the channel coast.

British anxieties increased on 19 May when the Panzer advance severed the field force's line of communications with its bases in the Biscay ports. Pownall twice telephoned an uncomprehending War Office to warn that a retreat to the channel ports might be unavoidable. Unfortunately for Gort, Churchill and the war cabinet were seriously out of touch with fast-moving events and on the following day (20 May) the CIGS, Ironside, arrived at GHQ bringing orders that Gort was to march south-west towards Amiens to re-establish contact with the main French armies south of the narrow Panzer corridor. The CIGS was quickly persuaded that such a move was impossible.

On 21 May Gort ordered a small-scale counter-attack south of Arras to hold up the German advance. French participation in this operation was minimal but for a few hours it made encouraging progress even against SS units and Rommel's 7th Panzer division. Here was a tantalizing glimpse of what might have been had Gamelin retained a central reserve. Two days later Gort was obliged to withdraw the Arras garrison to prevent it from being cut off, but the French generals, notably Blanchard, interpreted this as an attempt to sabotage the counter-offensive which Gamelin—and now his successor Maxime Weygand—were planning to cut the Panzer corridor by a combined drive from north and south. Despite his waning faith in the French high command, Gort was still prepared to make two British divisions (5th and 50th) available for the northern counter-attack, but in view of the increasing pressure on his (and even more the Belgians') eastward-facing front he felt more and more convinced that the main effort must come from south of the corridor. In view of contemporary and subsequent French criticisms that Gort never seriously contemplated joining in a counter-attack, it is worth noting that Major-General Alan Brooke was dismayed at Gort's slowness to recognize the threat to his eastern flank where a Belgian collapse was imminent.

On the evening of 25 May Gort *did* heed Brooke's warning, moved the two available divisions to the threatened sector and, without consulting the French and in defiance of a war cabinet order, unilaterally cancelled his part in the projected counter-offensive. This was Gort's most critical decision during the campaign—perhaps in his whole career—and it was desperately uncongenial to him, the loyal ally and combative general *par excellence*. Had the French forces south of the Panzer corridor along the Somme been advancing, as was claimed at the time, Gort would have been charged with ruining the only hope of an allied counter-attack, but they were not. If any criticism may be levelled against Gort it is that he remained loyal for too long to the ineffectual French high command.

Recall, Gibraltar, and Malta Gort had made up his mind to stay with his troops at Dunkirk to face death or capture but Churchill ordered him to return to England and he did so on 1 June. He never entirely forgave this order, believing that he was being widely criticized for deserting his post for which the prime minister was to blame. This suspicion that he was being made a scapegoat was accentuated by an enforced delay in publishing his dispatches. He probably *was* justified in feeling that Dill and Brooke were cool, if not actually hostile, towards him since they left him to fret on the sidelines with the largely honorary appointment of inspector general of training.

In April 1941 Gort was made governor of Gibraltar. The appointment—usually a terminal one for senior officers—irked him, but there, at least, his passion for detail could be legitimately indulged, for example in getting the Rock's cavernous defences deepened and the air strip extended. In fact Churchill had not forgotten him or written him off. In November 1941 the prime minister toyed with the amazing idea of re-installing him as CIGS in place of the exhausted Dill, who was being posted to Washington; and in March 1942 he flirted with the notion—until dissuaded by Brooke—of appointing Gort to succeed Auchinleck in the Middle East command.

The change when it came (in May 1942, and for exactly one year) was less exalted but still important, namely governor of beleaguered Malta. The island was under relentless air attacks which had pounded the docks to rubble and blocked the harbour with sunken ships. An amphibious attack from nearby Sicily seemed imminent. Yet, with Rommel's final offensive about to begin, it was vital that Malta hold out as the base for attacks on axis convoys. Shortly after his arrival Gort helped to secure the safe arrival of a consignment of sixty Spitfires; then, by concentrating all available firepower Gort saved the supply ship *Welshman* by bringing down all the Stukas which attacked it. And, not least impressive, Gort supervised the distribution of scarce food and water supplies so successfully that at the height of the crisis 200,000 people were receiving rations each day. But Gort's outstanding achievement was to impress on the islanders his own indomitable fortitude and cheerfulness in adversity. He became immensely popular. Indeed the defence of Malta may be considered Gort's outstanding achievement. His reward was a belated promotion to field marshal.

Final appointment and assessment In 1944–5 Gort was briefly high commissioner and commander-in-chief in Palestine. When informed that his predecessor had been fired upon he characteristically remarked that it looked like being fun; but in reality he was terminally ill with cancer of the liver, and he had only just begun to gain the respect of both Arabs and Jews, and to reduce terrorist activities, when he was forced to return home. Apart from his daughter's happy marriage to a fellow grenadier and winner of the VC, William Sidney (later Lord de L'Isle and Dudley), Gort's private life had been unhappy; his marriage had failed; his elder daughter had died young; his only son had committed suicide in 1941; and at the end of his life he had no home of his own. Just before his death in Guy's Hospital on 31 March 1946, he was awarded an English viscountcy, but this was a doubtful asset since he had no heir and was too ill to take his seat in the House of Lords. He was buried at Penshurst Place, Kent.

Gort's early death and the absence of substantial private papers meant that—like Dill's—his reputation suffered an eclipse during the post-war 'battle of the memoirs' in which his severe critic, Montgomery, was so prominent. But Gort's positive qualities emerged strongly with the publication in 1972 of *Chief of Staff*, vol. 1, the diaries of his staunch admirer Pownall, and in the same year he was the subject of Colville's admirable—and on the whole admiring—biography (*Man of Valour*). In character he was upright and honourable, regulating his conduct by a strict code. Although not intelligent above the average of his peers, and surely promoted too early above his ceiling, Gort had qualities of steadfastness, resolution, courage, and loyalty which merit the appellation 'great British soldier'.   CYRIL FALLS, *rev.* BRIAN BOND

Sources J. R. Colville, *Man of valour: Field Marshal Lord Gort VC* (1972) • *Chief of staff: the diaries of Lieutenant-General Sir Henry Pownall,* ed. B. Bond, 1 (1972) • B. Bond, 'General Lord Gort', *Churchill's generals*, ed. J. Keegan (1991), 34–50 • R. J. Minney, *The private papers of Hore-Belisha* (1960) • B. Bond, *France and Belgium, 1939–1940* (1975) • L. F. Ellis, *The war in France and Flanders, 1939–1940* (1953) • Burke, *Peerage* (1959) • b. cert. • m. cert. • d. cert. • J. Kennedy, *The business of war: the war narrative of Major-General Sir John Kennedy*, ed. B. Fergusson (1957), 5 • *CGPLA Eng. & Wales* (1946)

Archives NRA, papers • PRO, corresp. relating to Malta and Palestine, CO 967/88–94 | CAC Cam., corresp. with Leslie Hore-Belisha • CUL, corresp. with Samuel Hoare • King's Lond., Liddell Hart C., corresp. with Sir B. H. Liddell Hart • NRA, priv. coll., letters to Colonel Dalrymple-Hamilton |FILM BFI NFTVA, documentary footage • BFI NFTVA, news footage

Likenesses W. Stoneman, two photographs, 1939, NPG • photograph, c.1939, Hult. Arch. • H. Carr, oils, c.1940, Cavalry and Guards Club, London • R. G. Eves, two oil paintings, 1940, IWM [*see illus.*] • E. Seago, oils, 1940, IWM • O. Birley, portrait, Cavalry and Guards Club, London • H. Carr, portrait, White's Club, London • Tom Tit [J. Rosciweski], pen-and-ink caricature, IWM

Wealth at death £173,236 0s. 7d.: probate, 19 Oct 1946, *CGPLA Eng. & Wales*

Verelst, Harmen (b. 1639x42, d. in or after 1691). *See under* Verelst, Simon Pieterszoon (*bap.* 1644, d. 1710x17).

Verelst, Harry (1734–1785), administrator in India, was born on 11 February 1734 in Hadbury, Worcester, the fifth of seven children of Robert Verelst and his wife, Elizabeth. Harry Verelst was brought up by his uncle, William *Verelst, a painter with influential connections, who managed to procure his nephew an appointment as writer on the East India Company's Bengal establishment. He arrived in Calcutta in 1749, then aged only fifteen. His first post of importance was his appointment in 1756 as chief of the company's factory at Lakshmipur. A few months later, after Siraj ud-Daula's attack on Calcutta, Verelst left his station for Falta, where the company's council had taken refuge. After the recapture of Calcutta, Verelst was again sent to Lakshmipur to resume his chiefship. On their way, Verelst and his party were imprisoned by Siraj ud-Daula's officers repudiating the treaty concluded between Clive and their master. Having spent two months in confinement, Verelst was released after the battle of Plassey. His chiefship at Lakshmipur was contested by William McGwire, who insisted on being appointed in Verelst's stead, supporting his demand with the company's order that only a member of the council should occupy that post. On finding his appointment overruled, Verelst returned to Calcutta. Soon after, in 1759, he was appointed to superintend the revenue collection in the Nadia district. He fulfilled this task to Clive's satisfaction and was sent to Burdwan with a similar mission later that year. In February 1760 he was called to Calcutta to take up his seat in the council. At the end of that year he was appointed to take charge of the company's affairs at Chittagong after the cession of that district to the East India Company by Mir Kasim.

As a member of the council, Verelst opposed Governor Henry Vansittart in his decision to depose Mir Jafar in favour of Mir Kasim. He deeply mistrusted Vansittart, and judged the latter's policy as 'the works of darkness' (Verelst to John Carnac, 27 Nov 1761, BL OIOC, MS Eur. F/128/5g), inspired only by private interest. At Chittagong,

Verelst was himself widely involved in private trade, including both inland trade (mainly in salt produced on the island of Sandwip) and seaborne country trade. For the latter purpose Verelst and his associates set up a wharf in nearby Bakarganj, from where a first schooner was launched in 1762.

In 1765 Verelst returned from Chittagong to take up his seat in the select committee under Clive's second governorship. Clive had come to appreciate Verelst's considerable administrative abilities during his first government, and had declared in 1764 that Verelst was one of those on whom he relied to reassert order in the company's Bengal establishment. From 1765 to 1766 Verelst's talents were put to good use at Burdwan, and later at Midnapore, where he supervised and reformed the revenue collection. Verelst became a loyal supporter of Clive and from 1766 onwards repeatedly acted as governor during Clive's absence or indisposition, and finally succeeded to the latter's position in January 1767.

As governor, Verelst firmly intended to pursue his predecessor's policy. But the authoritarian sway with which Clive had tried to suppress corruption and licentiousness among the Bengal company servants had made him many enemies. Fear and respect for Clive had kept them in abeyance until his departure, but Verelst did not inspire the same awe. Soon Verelst saw his policy and authority publicly attacked. Richard Smith, the commander of the company's Bengal army, sneered that Verelst thought 'Clive the greatest man that ever existed', and 'consequently all his systems infallible' (Smith to Robert Orme, 31 Aug 1768, BL OIOC, Orme MS 37). But Smith, a member of the select committee, was not the only man contesting Verelst's authority. William Bolts, a junior merchant who claimed to have been done great wrongs at the hands of Clive and Verelst, went to great lengths in publicly denouncing the supposed venality of their governments. His favourite target in Bengal was the governor himself. Back in Britain, in 1772, Verelst published his *View of the Rise, Progress and Present State of the English Government in Bengal*, defending his own and Clive's administrations, after a public attack was made on them by Bolts in his *Considerations on India Affairs* earlier in the same year.

Verelst was well aware of his meagre successes in imposing his authority on men who did not believe he had any. He never felt at ease in his elevated station and pressed his supporters at home to appoint his successor as soon as possible. As governor, he recognized the need for administrative reforms to put the company's government in Bengal on a more solid basis. On relinquishing his governorship, in December 1769, Verelst analysed the company's situation: 'The native government is now fallen, in the eye of the inhabitants, dependant on our own government … Our original constitution … must be enlarged in proportion, as our sphere of action is extended and our duty increased' (Verelst to John Cartier, 21 Dec 1769, BL OIOC, MS Eur. F/218/20). But he warned against an open avowal of sovereignty and advised that 'exteriors should be upheld as essentials' (ibid.), and that every order should carry the sanction of the native government. This staunch adherence to Clive's dual system, even when against his better judgement, is perhaps indicative of Verelst's incapacity to take decisive action where his intelligence clearly indicated that such was necessary.

Verelst was convinced that the people of Bengal should be governed according to their own laws. Acknowledging that the company itself was the source of all power in Bengal, Verelst realized that a thorough 'knowledge of the laws and customs of the country' was the *sine qua non* of the formulation of reforms to improve the administration of justice and thus to establish peace and order in Bengal. His scheme to send supervisors into the different parts of Bengal had, among other intentions, this object in view, and started a process of official information gathering on the country and the people the British were to rule for another 180 years.

Verelst returned to Britain in 1770. In Bengal he had had two illegitimate daughters and an illegitimate son with Sophia Yeandle. At least one of those children was in England by 1778. On 20 May 1771 Verelst married Ann, the rich and attractive daughter of Josias Wordsworth of Wadworth. They had six daughters and four sons. Soon after his return to Britain, Verelst was harassed by litigation started before the courts at Westminster on the instigation of William Bolts. The cases of two Armenians, formerly agents of Bolts, who accused Verelst of having abused his authority as governor in procuring their imprisonment on false grounds, created a stir in London. The cases went against him and Verelst was required to pay £9700 in damages. Though the East India Company would eventually indemnify him for this sum, he was at that time already in dire financial straits. In 1772 Verelst estimated his fortune at £142,711. Much of his fortune, however, was still in Bengal, where deteriorating economic circumstances after the great famine of 1770 severely endangered its recovery. In England, Verelst had stretched his fortune too far in buying the Aston estate, near Sheffield, from Lord Holdernesse for £49,800. In 1775 John Knott, Verelst's private secretary, volunteered to return to Bengal to recover his own and his employer's effects. On the return journey to Britain overland Knott died in the desert, and all papers and effects he carried with him were lost. Verelst's finances never recovered and in 1785 he fled to the continent to escape his creditors. He died on 24 October 1785 at Boulogne, and was buried at Minster in the Isle of Thanet.   WILLEM G. J. KUITERS

Sources W. G. J. Kuiters, 'Une société en transition: Bengale et les Britanniques de 1756 à 1774 vue à travers la biographie de William Bolts', PhD diss., EHESS, Paris, 1998 · BL OIOC, Verelst MSS, MS Eur. F/218 · BL OIOC, Clive MSS, MS Eur. G 37 · BL OIOC, Sutton Court MSS, MS Eur. F 128 · W. Bolts, *Considerations on India affairs, particularly respecting the present state of Bengal and its dependencies*, 2nd edn, 2 (1775) · W. Bolts, *Considerations on India affairs, particularly respecting the present state of Bengal and its dependencies* (1772) · [W. Irvine], 'Governor Verelst', *Bengal Past and Present*, 6 (1910), 177–8 · P. Sinha, *Calcutta in urban history* (1978), 198 [will of Sophia Yeandle]

Archives BL OIOC, corresp. and papers, MS Eur. F/218 · University of Minnesota, Minneapolis, Ames Library of South Asia, letterbooks | BL OIOC, corresp. with John Carnac, MS Eur. F/128 · BL OIOC, Sutton Court collection, MS Eur. F/128

Wealth at death Aston estate bought in 1777 for £49,800; financial affairs in great confusion at death: Verelst to Holdernesse, London 8 Nov 1777, BL OIOC, MS Eur. F/218/81, fol. 89

Verelst, John (*c*.1675–1734). *See under* Verelst, Simon Pieterszoon (*bap.* 1644, *d.* 1710x17).

Verelst, Simon Pieterszoon (*bap.* **1644**, *d.* **1710x17**), painter, was baptized in The Hague on 21 September 1644. He was the second son of Adriana van Gesel (*d.* before 1657) and Pieter Harmenszoon Verelst (*fl.* 1618–1668), originally from Dordrecht. Pieter had joined the painters' guild at The Hague in 1643: in 1663 Simon and his brother Harmen paid their first dues to the same guild. Simon was in London by 11 April 1669, when he met Pepys, who was entranced by one of his flower paintings ('a better picture I never saw in my whole life, and it is worth going twenty miles to see'; Pepys, 9.515). Early flower pieces by Verelst show that Pepys's praise was justified. De Lairesse singled him out as the finest flower painter of the seventeenth century, and Weyerman called him 'a painter in a thousand' (Weyerman, 248). Most of his best pictures, however, were made early in his career; the poor quality pigments he had to use in London did not improve his work. Nevertheless, he quickly established himself as the leading still-life specialist in London, and he also made portraits, with great financial (but middling artistic) success. He painted *inter alia* the duke of Buckingham, the duchess of Norfolk, the duchess of Portsmouth, Charles II, Nell Gwyn (several times, clothed and nude), James II, and Mary of Modena. When he married Ann Pember at St Mary's, Marylebone, on 2 December 1684, he was said to be the best-paid artist in London. This success was ended in the following year by an attack of 'frenzy'. The story of Verelst's madness and the state of laughable self-conceit which supposedly preceded it is often repeated in the literature, but this suspiciously entertaining tale owes its existence solely to Weyerman, whose trustworthiness is usually doubted by art historians. The behaviour they describe would today be thought symptomatic of bipolar affective disorder (manic depression). Before he lost his senses completely, it is said that Verelst stopped sleeping, gave up work, and went on long solitary walks; he then, apparently, bought a velvet cape, varnished his hat and shoes, and started calling himself the God of Flowers and King of Portrait-painters. In this state, he went to the palace of Whitehall, demanding that the king of England should come to speak with the King of Painters. The idea of Verelst varnishing his hat and shoes was taken by Weyerman from Karel van Mander's life of Joos van Cleef, and the rest of the tale may reasonably be doubted. However, Verelst does seem to have gone mad; about 1685, according to his brother-in-law, one Mr Rothwell junior:

> he shutt the doore & drew his Sword & swore he would kill me—I pulled off my Coate & I bid him not strike to hard—and I must he said bring my wife to him to whip her and bring 4 Rods with me—to whip my wife—he has beene distracted—he has run about the street in his shirt and cutt his feet—I never dust goe neere Varelst since I have seen him but never was in a Roome with him.   (minutes of the House of Lords, 5 Feb 1692)

The madness subsided but his days as a high-society portraitist were over. It seems that his marriage also ended: in 1692, when he appeared before the House of Lords as a witness in divorce proceedings between the duke and duchess of Norfolk, he was described as a bachelor. His testimony on that occasion was discounted, after Rothwell's evidence of his insanity. Weyerman claimed that his talents as a flower painter were also ruined by his madness. This is hard to assess, since no dated paintings are known between 1672 and 1709. One of the 1709 pictures is depressingly inept (ex Christies, London, 8 December 1995, lot 211) but another, a simple painting of a bunch of grapes (ex Christies, Amsterdam, 9 November 1998, lot 38), is worthy of his work in the 1670s. It seems, though, that Verelst's financial situation deteriorated; in 1692 he was 'lodged at Mr Cowell's, an Housekeeper' (minutes of the House of Lords) in Fleet Street, and about 1710, according to Weyerman, he was 'lodged, or rather chained in the galley, at a London art dealer named Lovejoy, resident in the Strand' (Weyerman, 250). Weyerman claimed that Verelst's work at this period was strikingly inept, with flowers grotesquely distorted in size and colouring, but this is probably an exaggeration. Another Dutchman, Allard de la Court, met the artist in June 1710, and wrote that he:

> asked me if I would like to see his art, [and said] that I would never have seen anything comparable in Holland or Italy, but when I saw the same it fell a long way short, it was badly painted. He nevertheless dared ask £100 for a small piece, a very bad flower piece.   (Roever, 71)

This is not the only contemporary testimony to suggest that Verelst was deluded about the quality of his late work. Vertue was told by Pieter Casteels that:

> Simon Verelst dyd at his house in Suffolk street near the haymarkett. he showd a historical picture he had been painting 20 years over & over at several times wherein (he sayd) was to be seen Raphael, Titian, Rubens and Vandyke in their several manners.   (Vertue, *Note books*, 1.42)

This passage of Vertue's notebooks was written in the second half of 1716 or the first half of 1717, so Verelst cannot have died in 1721, as is frequently claimed. The registers of St Martin-in-the-Fields and the parishes between Ludgate and Piccadilly do not appear to record his date of burial, unless he was the Simon Evret buried at St Martin's on 6 December 1713.

Verelst's elder brother, **Harmen Verelst** (*b.* 1639x42, *d.* in or after 1691), was a portrait painter. His birth date is deduced from information that his father was said to be a bachelor in 1638 and his younger sister, Helena, was baptized in January 1643. A later date in the range seems preferable, however, because Harmen Verelst enrolled in the St Luke's Guild in the same year as his younger brother, Simon. He married Cicilia Fene, a Venetian, in 1667 in Amsterdam, and worked between Amsterdam and The Hague until about 1678. He then travelled to Rome via Ljubljana, after which he spent three years in Vienna. He moved together with his family to London in 1683, perhaps fleeing the Turkish siege of Vienna in that year. He and Cicilia had at least five children: Peter, Adriana, John, Richard, and Lewis. Lewis, who died young in 1704, left a will which provides most of our evidence about the family members. Weyerman claimed that Harmen and Cicilia also had a son called Cornelis and a daughter called Maria; Lewis's will mentions neither. Cornelis may not have existed at all, while Maria (1680–1744), a portraitist known as Mrs Verelst, presumably (from her title) married into the family. Harmen's death date is uncertain; Vertue maintained that he died about 1700 and was buried in St Andrew's, Holborn, but he does not appear in the burial registers of that church between 1691 and 1704. His latest surviving dated work was made in 1691; Vertue claimed to have seen a work made in 1693. **John Verelst** (*c*.1675–1734), portrait painter, was probably the son of Harmen. Confusion arises because another John Verelst was father of two children in London in 1674 and 1682: this may have been Harmen's and Simon's brother, Johannes (*b*. 1648), whose profession is unknown. However, the painter John Verelst was most likely Harmen's son, as mentioned in the will of Lewis. His first surviving dated work was made in 1704. He and his wife, Anne, had at least seven children: Herman, Cicely, Adriana, George, James, Robert (father of Harry, governor of Bengal), and William *Verelst (*bap.* 1704, *d.* 1752): this latter was also a portrait painter. John was buried on 10 March 1734 in the parish of St Christopher-le-Stocks, London.   PAUL TAYLOR

Sources G. Veth, 'Aanteekeningen omtrent eenige Dordrechtse schilders XXXIX: Pieter Hermansz. Verelst en zijne zonen', *Oud Holland*, 14 (1896), 99–112 · J. C. Weyerman, *De levens-beschryvingen der Nederlandsche konst-schilders en konst-schilderessen*, 4 vols. (The Hague, 1729–69), vol. 3 · Vertue, *Note books*, 1–2 · N. de Roever, 'Een bezoek aan den ridder Adriaen van der Werff, kunstschilder, in 1710', *Oud Holland*, 5 (1887), 67–71 · MSS minutes of the House of Lords, 27 Dec 1690–26 Sept 1692 · G. de Lairesse, *Groot Schilderboek* (1707) · IGI · H. Walpole, *Anecdotes of painting in England: with some account of the principal artists*, ed. R. N. Wornum, new edn, 2 (1849) · F. Meijer, ed., *Catalogue of the Ward collection, Ashmolean Museum, Oxford* [forthcoming] · private information (2004) [F. Meijer] · P. Taylor, *Dutch flower painting, 1600–1750* (1996) [exhibition catalogue, Dulwich Picture Gallery, London, 3 July – 29 Sept 1996] · T. J. Broos, *Tussen zwart en ultramarijn: de levens van schilders beschreven door Jacob Campo Weyerman (1677–1747)* (1990) · F. Lewis, *Simon Pietersz. Verelst, 1644–1721* (1979) · will of Lewis Verelst, proved 8 Nov 1704, PRO, PROB 11/479, sig. 246 · will of John Verelst, proved 30 March 1734, PRO, PROB 11/664, sig. 76 · parish register, London, St Christopher-le-Stocks, 10 March 1734, GL [burial of John Verelst] · U. Lubej, 'Beiträge zu den Biographien der in der zweiten Hälfte des 17. Jahrhunderts in Krain wirkenden holländischen Maler', *Acta Historiae Artis Slovenica*, 2 (1997) · Pepys, *Diary*, 9.515

Verelst, William (*bap.* 1704, *d.* 1752), portrait painter, was baptized at St Martin-in-the-Fields, London, on 17 January 1704. He was the fifth of eight children of John *Verelst (*c*.1675–1734) [*see under* Verelst, Simon Pieterszoon (*bap.* 1644, *d.* 1710x17)], portraitist, and his wife, Anne. William Verelst was included in the *Dictionary of National Biography* in the article on Simon *Verelst under the name Willem Verelst and was erroneously described as the son of Cornelius Verelst. William presumably studied with his father; he was the executor of the latter's will, and his stylistic traits of clear profile, bright colour, and a slight gawkiness are close to his father's manner. Thieme and Becker identified him with the Guillaume Verelst who received payment for three paintings from members of the Rotterdam

wine traders' guild in 1729. Signed works appear from 1732 onwards. His most ambitious painting is the 35 figure group portrait *Representation of the audience given by the trustees for establishing the colony in Georgia in America, to Tomo Chachi Mico of Yamacran and his Indians on the 3rd day of July in the year of Our Lord 1734* (Winterthur Museum, Delaware). William's eldest brother, Herman (*bap.* 24 Jan 1693), was the accountant for the Georgia council, which probably explains why William was chosen as artist; although it seems noteworthy that John Verelst had painted portraits of four Native American chiefs who visited London in 1709. William Verelst's other work includes a few conversation pieces; *The Gough Family* of 1741 (priv. coll.) has received praise, its lively expressions, fresh colour, and beautifully rendered draperies masking its awkward perspective and anatomy. Among his portraits of individuals, that of John Dean (NPG) is of anecdotal interest: Dean was the sole survivor of a much-publicized shipwreck. The portrait of a woman identified (incorrectly) by an inscription as Eleanor Mytton (Sothebys, 13 April 1994), dated 1738, shows him at his best; her personable dog and the striking blue of her silk dress make for a very lively effect. A portrait allegedly of Tobias Smollett, and said to be signed and dated 1756 (Kerslake, 254), has presumably had its date misread, since Verelst was buried in the parish of St Christopher-le-Stocks, London, on 20 October 1752.
          PAUL TAYLOR

Sources parish register, St Christopher-le-Stocks, London [burial] · IGI · R. Jeffree, 'Verelst, William', *The dictionary of art*, ed. J. Turner (1996) · J. Kerslake, *National Portrait Gallery: early Georgian portraits*, 2 vols. (1977) · Thieme & Becker, *Allgemeines Lexikon* · artist's file, archive material, Courtauld Inst., Witt Library · Waterhouse, *18c painters* · will, PROB 11/664, sig. 76

Vergil, Polydore [Polidoro Virgili] (*c*.1470–1555), historian, was probably born at Fermignano, near Urbino, where his father, Giorgio di Antonio, owned a dispensary. He was the youngest of four sons. He is generally accepted as having been born about 1470 on the grounds that he was ordained priest some time before 20 December 1496, and the canonical age for ordination was twenty-five.

Family background and early writings There was a tradition of scholarship in the Virgili family. A grandfather, Antonio Virgilio, described as 'most learned in medicine and astrology' (Hay, 1), taught in the University of Paris. An older brother, Giovanni-Matteo, was a student of the philosopher Pietro Pomponazzi and himself taught philosophy at Ferrara and Padua. An uncle, Teseo Pinni, a clergyman and lawyer, wrote a book on vagabonds, *Speculum cerretanorum*, which was mentioned by Erasmus in his *Ecclesiastes* and published at Wittenberg in 1528 in an edition with a preface by Martin Luther. The family was armigerous: its arms, a laurel and two lizards, are discussed in Polydore's *De inventoribus rerum*, and a banner bearing them was recorded between 1540 and 1542 as hanging above the appropriate choir stall in Wells Cathedral, where he was archdeacon.

Vergil studied at the University of Padua, and possibly, although this is less secure, at Bologna under Filippo Beroaldo the elder, the author of an *Oratio proverbiorum*. In

1496 he published in Venice an enlarged edition of Niccolò Perotti's *Cornucopiae*, a work that in turn influenced his own first books, the *Proverbiorum libellus* (Venice, 1498) and *De inventoribus rerum* (Venice, 1499). The former, a collection of proverbs, was retitled *Adagiorum liber* in later editions after a minor controversy over the primacy of each man's work arose between Vergil and Erasmus, whose own *Adagia* were published two years later in 1500. Erasmus claimed to have published his *Adagia* several years before hearing Vergil's name, and as late as 1533 he still claimed (incorrectly) that his collection had been published before the latter's. The two men probably first met after Erasmus's second trip to England in 1505. They had many friends in common, exchanged many letters, and Erasmus later wrote that they had once laughed at table over their former rivalry. It is indeed significant that the two men were never seriously estranged by the dispute over their collections of adages. Vergil's collection, which was also the subject of a charge of literary theft by a more obscure humanist, Ludovico Gorgeri, went through frequent printings down to the seventeenth century, but its popularity, though considerable, was nevertheless far exceeded by that of his second book, the *De inventoribus rerum*.

In its first edition of 1499 *De inventoribus rerum* consisted of three books. Each chapter was devoted to a question of origins—the origin of the gods, the beginning of things, the creation of men, the origin of languages, down to the origins of prostitution, the printing press, and the first warm baths. Then in 1521 Vergil published an expanded version in eight books, in which the five new books treated principally religious questions. These additional books were already substantially complete by 1517, the date of their dedicatory letter. In his discussions of beginnings Vergil typically went through all the Latin and Greek authorities known to him, before proceeding to the earlier treatments of the relevant questions in the Old Testament. At Urbino he had at his disposal one of Europe's most impressive collections of Greek and Latin texts, enabling him to make *De inventoribus rerum* one of the new humanist encyclopaedias, a book which, like Raffaello Maffei's slightly later *Commentarii urbani* (Rome, 1508), attempted to bring together the new learning made available by the efforts of Renaissance humanists.

In *De inventoribus rerum* Vergil's most frequently cited source is the Bible, followed by Josephus and Eusebius, but in his search for beginnings he ranged over a vast number of writers. In many instances he also drew on his own experiences and those of his contemporaries, as when he described marital and baptismal customs, or the bonfires of Umbria, or (in the later books) the way the English kissed in greeting one another and the brevity of English widowhood. In its Latin format the work went through more than thirty editions in Vergil's lifetime, and altogether there were more than 100 editions when the numerous vernacular translations are included. His discussion in the last five books of the practice of Christian religion in his own day follows a generally Erasmian line.

He is critical of monks, attacks priestly celibacy, and criticizes the sale of indulgences at length. Martin Luther is mentioned twice, but not criticized. Consequently the book came in for searching scrutiny by the Catholic authorities, and in 1551, while its author was still alive, it was condemned by the Sorbonne. In 1564, when it was placed on the Trent index of prohibited books, it was said that the book had been 'expanded by the heretics' (Hay, 56 n.1); and an expurgated, approved version was published in Rome in 1576. An English 'translation' by Thomas Langley was published in 1546; however, this version omitted a full nine-tenths of the original text. An authoritative critical edition and translation was published by Brian Copenhaver in 2002; the translation by Beno Weiss and Louis Perez (1997) usefully distinguishes the passages suppressed by religious censors.

Servant of the papacy Although Vergil wrote his first two books at Urbino, little is known about his education or employment there. The *Proverbiorum libellus* was dedicated to Duke Guidobaldo da Montefeltro, *De inventoribus rerum* to Lodovico Odasio, who had been the duke's tutor. On the evidence of these dedications and of his considerable use of the ducal library, it has been suggested that Vergil was in the service of Duke Guidobaldo. Indeed it seems possible that the duke personally commissioned the *De inventoribus rerum*. The letters of a Venetian functionary in Ravenna, published in Sanudo's *Diarii*, mention a Polydore who was serving as secretary to Guidobaldo, a possible indicator of Vergil's position at Urbino; but since Sanudo dated these letters in 1503, when Vergil was already in England, his employment as ducal secretary cannot be regarded as certain.

The circumstances in which Vergil left Urbino to enter the service of Pope Alexander VI are not known. He is first recorded as a papal employee in 1502, when he was selected by one of Alexander VI's intimates, Adriano Castellesi da Corneto, to represent his interests in England. Castellesi had been collector of Peter's pence since 1490, and Vergil was sent to England as his subcollector. A Venetian ambassador, writing in 1502, described Castellesi as a 'hard and sinister man … much favored by the pontiff' (Paschini, 59), while another contemporary, Raffaello Maffei, called him Alexander's 'vicar in all things' (ibid., 61). An accomplice in Cesare Borgia's infamous slaughter of his enemies at Senigallia in January 1503, Castellesi was made cardinal priest of San Grisogono the following May. Thus Vergil was working as an agent of the Borgias during their seizure of his native Urbino from the Montefeltro in 1502–3.

When Vergil arrived as Castellesi's agent in England in 1502, he was received by Henry VII and 'ever after was entertained by him kindly', as he later wrote in the *Anglica historia* (Hay, 4). Already the author of two books, it seems likely that he was treated as a celebrity in an England that was eager for things Italian. Certainly he became well known to learned Englishmen—Erasmus listed Thomas More, Cuthbert Tunstall, Thomas Linacre, and William Latimer as among Vergil's English friends. Like More, Vergil belonged to Doctors' Commons, and he appears to have been on good terms with Colet's St Paul's School. One measure of Vergil's success in England is his accumulation of church benefices. In 1503 Sir Nicholas Griffin presented him to the living of Church Langton, Leicestershire; in 1507 he acquired prebends in Lincoln and Hereford cathedrals; in 1508 he became archdeacon of Wells and prebendary of Brent; in 1513 he was collated to the prebend of Oxgate in St Paul's. In 1504 he was charged with violating currency laws, but the case was regularly deferred until 1509, when he received a royal pardon.

Through his employer Castellesi, Vergil may have played a role in furthering ties between England and the restored Montefeltro court at Urbino. English relations with Urbino dated from the bestowal of the Order of the Garter on Duke Federigo da Montefeltro by Edward IV in 1474. With the death of Alexander VI on 18 August 1503 (after dinner at Castellesi's villa), followed shortly afterwards by that of Pius III on 18 October, and then by the election of Giuliano della Rovere, a deadly enemy of the Borgias, as Pope Julius II, Cardinal Castellesi found himself in a politically exposed position, so much so that Duke Guidobaldo of Urbino was able to put pressure on the cardinal to propose him to Henry VII for membership of the Order of the Garter. The ostensible purpose of his designation was to secure the support of the Montefeltro, who were related to the della Rovere, for Henry's quest for a papal dispensation that would permit Prince Henry to marry Katherine of Aragon. Henry VII concurred with the proposal, and Guidobaldo received the Garter in 1504 in Rome. Two years later, Count Baldassare Castiglione travelled to England to stand as proxy for Guidobaldo at the latter's formal installation. Castiglione almost certainly met Vergil, indeed, he probably lodged with him in London; Elias Ashmole, writing in the late seventeenth century, recorded that Castiglione stayed with one 'Paulus de Gygeles, the Pope's Vice-Collector' (Cartwright, 1.180), most likely a garbling or misreading of Polidorus de Virgiliis, who was indeed the 'Vice-Collector'. Vergil's personal copy of the later printed edition of the oration Castiglione composed for this occasion survives in the Vatican Library.

Vergil and English history Vergil is best known today for his *English History*, the *Anglica historia*. He had probably kept a journal and begun his research into English history soon after his arrival in 1502, but research for a full-scale history of England most likely began in 1506–7, encouraged by Henry VII. A first manuscript version of the *Anglica historia*, covering events to 1513, was completed in 1512–13 and is now preserved in the Vatican Library. This work was first published at Basel in 1534 by Johann Bebel, but in a version that only went down to 1509. This was followed by a much revised second edition of 1546, and by a third edition of 1555 that was again revised by the author and extended to 1538. True to the methods of the humanist historiography first developed by Leonardo Bruni in his early fifteenth-century *History of the Florentine People*, Vergil adopted a critical approach which required a comparison of the available sources before he constructed a single narrative of his own, one intended to be more accurate. In a

further imitation of Bruni and the historians of antiquity, he composed speeches of his own that he put into the mouths of historical personages, with the inevitable result that his accounts of events often read quite differently from those found in contemporary chronicles, giving rise to the famous and unfounded allegations by his critics that he had burnt older sources in order to hide his errors.

But although he frequently complained of a lack of documentation, Vergil was in fact able to compile an impressive array of sources. For his treatment of early Britain he used a wide array of classical authorities (for example Caesar, Tacitus, Pliny, and Strabo), many of which he probably consulted in the ducal library during a return visit to Urbino in 1514. For the post-Roman and later periods he relied especially on Gildas (whose *De excidio et conquestu Brittaniae* he discovered and published in 1525), Bede (whom he greatly admired), William of Malmesbury, Henry of Huntingdon, William of Newburgh, Roger of Howden, and Matthew Paris. For the later middle ages he used Ranulf Higden's *Polychronicon* and at least one version of the *Brut*, and he also drew extensively on Flavio Biondo, Bartolomeo Platina, Jean Froissart, Enguerrand de Monstrelet, and Robert Gaguin. He also used many documentary sources, including legal and heraldic material, along with the records of the office of collector of Peter's pence. A surviving letter to James IV of Scotland asks for the names and deeds of the Scottish kings. James refused to help, possibly because he thought Scottish history should be written by a Scot, but Gavin Douglas, bishop of Dunkeld, provided the requested information about 1522. An acute observer of his surroundings, Vergil also obtained a good deal of contemporary information from courtiers close to Henry VII.

Vergil frequently showed a sophisticated critical intelligence in his researches, for instance in his investigation of the languages spoken in Britain. His destructive analysis of Geoffrey of Monmouth, and in particular his denial of the historicity of King Arthur, resulted in his being attacked by the antiquarian John Leland, who attempted to prove Arthur's existence in the *Assertio inclytissimi Arturii regis Britanniae* (London, 1544). His ecclesiastical livings and prebends, his many friends in the English church, his work for the Peter's pence, and especially his Italian origins, also laid him open to attack from the more radical of the English reformers during the religious convulsions of the mid-sixteenth century. Although the protestant historian John Bale did not 'disprayse of his lernynge, (which I knowe to be verye excellent)', he still accused Vergil in 1544 of 'polutynge oure Englyshe chronicles most shamefullye with his Romishe lyes and other Italyshe beggerye' (Trimble, 38). Nearly a century later, in a Commons debate of 1628, when Vergil's history was cited as evidence that Cambridge was older than Oxford, the Oxonian Edward Littleton is said to have demanded, 'What have we to do with Polydore Vergil? One Vergil was a poet, the other a liar' (Woolf, 24). Yet notwithstanding these attacks, Vergil's treatment of the fifteenth and early sixteenth centuries, at least, remained authoritative down to the nineteenth century. From the wicked Richard III (largely echoed by Sir Thomas More, but all the more plausible in his villainy in Vergil's ostensibly impartial pages) down to the ambitious and arrogant Wolsey, 'Vergil's story has become part of the national myth' (*Anglica historia*, xxxix). Surprisingly, the *Anglica historia* still awaits a complete critical edition and modern translation, although the period down to 1485 is accessible in translations published by Henry Ellis (1844, 1846), while Denys Hay's fine edition covers the years 1485–1537.

Last years in England and Italy In 1508, while Vergil was just beginning work on the *Anglica historia*, Julius II deprived him of his subcollectorship of Peter's pence, conferring it instead on Pietro Griffo. Although Vergil's income from his benefices comfortably exceeded what he received as subcollector, he still made every effort to hold onto that office, and when Griffo arrived in England, Vergil refused to relinquish either the collectorship or its records and seals. Only after the pope sent a strong letter did Griffo obtain possession in 1509, but when he left England in 1512, Vergil took the office back, keeping it until 1515. In February 1514 Henry VIII wrote to Leo X to commend Vergil, who, he said, wished to visit his native land after twelve years' absence. Vergil duly travelled to Italy that year, visiting Rome first, where among other matters he discussed the issue of a cardinal's hat for Thomas Wolsey with his long-time patron, Cardinal Castellesi. He then proceeded to Urbino, where he paid a brother 600 florins to endow a chapel in the cathedral.

In 1515 Vergil returned to London, only to find out that Henry VIII had begun to support Andreas Ammonius in a campaign to replace Castellesi as collector of Peter's pence. Ammonius, who had come to England about 1505, and had been Henry's Latin secretary since 1511, arranged to have Vergil's correspondence with Castellesi intercepted. Some letters critical of Wolsey were found, and their author was thrown into the Tower of London, where he remained from April until the end of 1515. For a while, his imprisonment became a *cause célèbre*. Leo X, Cardinal Giulio de' Medici, and the University of Oxford all petitioned the king to release him. But only after Wolsey had been made a cardinal in September, and then lord chancellor in December, was he released, probably at the new cardinal's instance. But his imprisonment made Vergil a confirmed enemy of Wolsey, and undoubtedly gave extra animus to the attack on the latter that Vergil published in the third edition of his *Anglica historia*. Vergil also lost his subcollectorship, but he retained his ecclesiastical benefices. In 1516 Leo X and Castellesi summoned him to Rome, and afterwards he also visited Urbino again, before returning to England and his benefices before the end of 1517. After this crisis, and for the rest of his life, he managed to steer clear of political controversy.

In 1524 Vergil wrote a commentary on the Lord's prayer, with a prefatory letter to John Fisher, which was published in a combined edition of the *Proverbiorum libellus* and the *De inventoribus rerum* of 1525. In the latter year he

edited Gildas, collating a manuscript lent him by Cuthbert Tunstall with one of his own. A *Dialogus de prodigiis* followed in 1526–7, with a dedication (of 1530) to Francesco Maria della Rovere. Erasmus attempted to have this work published by Froben of Basel, but it did not appear until 1531, printed by Bebel. Erasmus dedicated an edition of some of John Chrysostom's sermons to Vergil, who himself completed a translation of Chrysostom's *Comparatio regis et monachi* in 1528; he published it in 1530. In June 1532 Vergil told Erasmus that he had been called back to Italy and that he was discussing the printing of the *Anglica historia* with Bebel. On 6 June 1533 he received licence to travel overseas with six horses and six servants, although he was still in London in August of that year, when he wrote the dedication to the first printed edition of the *Anglica historia*. He then travelled to the continent, stopping in Urbino to write his will, dated 1534, before returning to England that year. His last book, a collection of Latin *Dialogi*, was published by Isengrin in Basel in 1545, and in an Italian translation by Francesco Baldelli at Venice in 1550.

Vergil stayed out of England's religious conflicts. Though his religious sympathies seem likely to have been conservative, he signed the articles of 1536 which effectively repudiated the pope's efforts to summon a general council, and in 1547 he subscribed the declaration for communion in both kinds. His ecclesiastical duties did not interfere with his literary activities or participation in London social life. He lived in a house in St Paul's Churchyard that was described in 1522 as consisting of a hall, a parlour, three chambers, and four beds. From 1546 it appears to have been preparing to return home to Italy, since he resigned the archdeaconry of Wells at the end of that year. In 1550 he was licensed to return to Urbino without forfeiting the revenues from his offices, but he probably did not leave England until 1553. He died at Urbino on 18 April 1555, and was buried in the chapel he had endowed in the cathedral. His house in Urbino, which he had bequeathed to his brothers Giovanni-Francesco and Girolamo, belongs today to the University of Urbino.

WILLIAM J. CONNELL

Sources *The Anglica historia of Polydore Vergil, AD 1485–1537*, ed. and trans. D. Hay, CS, 3rd ser., 74 (1950) • *DNB* • J. P. Carley, 'Polydore Vergil and John Leland on King Arthur: the battle of the books', *Interpretations*, 15/2 (1984), 86–100 • J. Cartwright, *Baldassare Castiglione, the perfect courtier: his life and letters*, 2 vols. (1908) • F. V. Cespedes, 'The final book of Polydore Vergil's *Anglica historia*: persecution and the art of writing', *Viator*, 10 (1979), 375–96 • C. H. Clough, 'The relations between the English and Urbino courts, 1474–1508', *Studies in the Renaissance*, 14 (1967), 202–18 • C. H. Clough, 'Federigo Veterani, Polydore Vergil's *Anglica historia* and Baldassare Castiglione's *Epistola ad Henricum Angliae regem*', *EngHR*, 82 (1967), 772–83 • B. P. Copenhaver, 'The historiography of discovery in the Renaissance: the sources and composition of Polydore Vergil's *De inventoribus rerum* I–III', *Journal of the Warburg and Courtauld Institutes*, 41 (1978), 192–214 • B. P. Copenhaver, 'Polidoro Virgilio of Urbino', ed. P. G. Bietenholz and T. B. Deutscher, *Contemporaries of Erasmus*, 3 (1987), 397–99 • B. P. Copenhaver, 'The historiography of discovery in the Renaissance: the sources and composition of Polydore Vergil's *De inventoribus rebum* I–III', *Contemporaries of Erasmus*, ed. P. G. Bietenholz and T. B. Deutscher, 3 (1987), 397–9 • J. Ferguson, 'Notes on the work of Polydore Vergil, *De inventoribus rerum*',

Isis, 17 (1932) • T. S. Freeman, 'From Catiline to Richard III: the influence of classical histories on Polydore Vergil's *Anglica historia*', *Reconsidering the Renaissance*, ed. M. Di Cesare (1992), 191–214 • A. Gransden, *Historical writing in England*, 2 (1982) • G. Marc'hadour, review of Vergil, *Beginnings and discoveries*, trans. B. Weiss and L. C. Pérez, *Moreana*, 36/139–40 (1999), 117–28 • D. Hay, *Polydore Vergil: Renaissance historian and man of letters* (1952) • I. S. Leadam, 'Polydore Vergil in the English law courts', *TRHS*, new ser., 19 (1905), 288–94 • F. J. Levy, *Tudor historical thought* (1967) • P. Paschini, 'Adriano Castellesi cardinale di S. Grisogono', *Tre illustri prelati del Rinascimento* (1957), 43–130 • C. Ross, *Richard III* (1981) • R. Ruggeri, *Un amico di Erasmo: Polidoro Virgili* (1992) • R. Ruggeri, *Polidoro Virgili: un umanista europeo* (2000) • W. R. Trimble, 'Early Tudor historiography, 1485–1548', *Journal of the History of Ideas*, 11 (1950), 30–41 • E. A. Whitney and P. P. Cram, 'The will of Polydore Vergil', *TRHS*, 4th ser., 11 (1928), 117–36 • D. R. Woolf, *Reading history in early modern England* (2000)

Likenesses medallion in painted frieze of picture gallery, after 1816, Bodl. Oxf. • portrait, repro. in V. Andreas, *Imagines doctorum vivorum* (Antwerp, 1611), sig. B5v • portrait, repro. in J. Thane, *Supplement to the British autography* (London, [n.d.]) • portrait, repro. in A. Thevet, *Les vrais portraicts et vies des hommes illustres* (Paris, 1584), ii, f. 563

Verica (*fl. c.*AD 10–*c.*41). *See under* Roman Britain, British leaders in (*act.* 55 BC–AD 84).

Verity, Hedley (1905–1943), cricketer, was born at Welton Grove, Headingley, Leeds, on 18 May 1905, the eldest of three children and only son of Hedley Verity (1874–1945), coal merchant, and his wife, Edith Elwick (1873–1964), a Sunday school teacher. After attending Yeadon and Guiseley secondary school, he served a long cricket apprenticeship, playing for ten years in the Yorkshire and Lancashire leagues at Rawdon, Accrington, and Middleton. He was a professional player by the time of his marriage on 7 March 1929 to Kathleen Alice Metcalfe (1903–1957), a bookbinder, daughter of Frederick Metcalfe, sales agent, of Horsforth, Leeds. They had two sons.

In 1930 Verity followed Wilfrid Rhodes in Yorkshire's famed company of slow left-arm bowlers. Rhodes had held sway until his fifty-third year, and his dominance delayed Verity's début for the county until 21 May 1930, the year of Rhodes's retirement. In 1931, his first full season with Yorkshire, Verity was one of the five cricketers of the year in *Wisden*, chosen in recognition of bowling performances which included his feat of taking ten wickets in one innings against Warwickshire at Leeds on his twenty-sixth birthday. This was followed in 1932 by his record-breaking figures of 10 wickets for 10 runs, including the hat-trick, against Nottinghamshire. On seven other occasions for Yorkshire he took 9 wickets in an innings, helping the county to win the championship in seven of the ten seasons when he played for them.

Verity made his first test match appearance for England against New Zealand in July 1931. In his forty test match appearances, the last of which was against the West Indies at Lord's in June 1939, he took 144 wickets (at an average of 24.37). His most outstanding test match performance was against Australia at Lord's in June 1934, when he took 14 wickets for 80 runs on the third day, bringing about England's only victory over the Australians at Lord's in the twentieth century. His duels with Don Bradman stood out

above all else. He was one of the few bowlers who refused to be overawed by the cricketing genius, whom he dismissed on ten occasions. During the controversial 'bodyline' series to Australia in 1932–3 he forged a resolute unity with Douglas Jardine, the England captain, after whom he named his second son.

R. E. S. Wyatt, England's captain in 1934, commented:

> one of Verity's chief assets was his ability to make the ball lift on a wet wicket and bounce on a dry one. Batsmen frequently found themselves playing the ball in the air when they thought they had got well over the top of it. (Hill, 144)

His 'perching ball' brought the downfall of many rivals. According to Bill Bowes, a close friend and bowling partner, the essence of his art was a 'marvellous control of length' and a direction 'as straight as an arrow' (ibid.). He ran to the crease lightly and decisively over seven strides before delivering the ball at a pace quicker than most left-handers. He could contain batsmen, but was also devastating on helpful wickets. Jardine paid testimony to Verity's ability to place a field and bowl to it. During a decade dominated by batsmen, his ever present guile and acute brain brought a tally of 1956 wickets (average 14.90).

Verity presented a tall figure, with frank, friendly eyes, and a shy fearlessness. Nothing unsettled his dignified bearing; he showed a conspicuous absence of elation in victory, or disappointment in defeat. His conduct was in keeping with his reputation as a conscientious and disciplined professional, who practised a spartan regime. In the Second World War he proved as good a soldier as he was a cricketer. As a captain in the Green Howards he displayed courage of a high order in fierce action against German positions in Catania, Sicily. He sustained chest wounds from which he died, a prisoner of war, at the Italian military hospital at Caserta, near Naples, on 31 July 1943. He was buried in the military cemetery at Caserta, built and maintained by the Commonwealth War Graves Commission. A memorial match was played at Roundhay Park, Leeds, in 1944, the proceeds going to endow a hospital bed bearing Verity's name at Leeds General Infirmary. In the following year a benefit match between Yorkshire and Lancashire for Verity's dependants took place at Bradford. ALAN HILL

Sources A. Hill, *Hedley Verity: a portrait of a cricketer* (1986) • S. Davis, *Hedley Verity: prince with a piece of leather* (1952) • H. Verity, *Bowling 'em out* (1936) • W. A. T. Synge, *The story of the Green Howards, 1939–1945* (1952) • *DNB* • m. cert. • private information (2004)

Archives FILM BFI NFTVA, sports footage

Likenesses photographs, Hult. Arch. • portrait, priv. coll.

Wealth at death £3323 2s. 7d.: administration, 31 Dec 1943, *CGPLA Eng. & Wales*

Vermigli, Pietro Martire [Peter Martyr] (1499–1562), evangelical reformer, was born in Florence on 8 September 1499, the son of Stefano Vermigli (*c.*1456–*c.*1528) and Maria Fumantina (*d.* 1511). At his baptism he received the name Piero Mariano, possibly in honour of the contemporary Florentine preacher Fra Mariano Della Barba da Genazzano.

Education and early career Vermigli was the eldest of three surviving children; his sister Felicità Antonia and brother

Pietro Martire [Peter Martyr] **Vermigli** (1499–1562), by Hans Asper, 1560

Antonio Lorenzo Romulo were born on 31 July 1501 and 30 April 1504 respectively. His father, a shoemaker, was sufficiently prosperous to leave 200 scudi to the poor of Santa Maria Nuova in his will. Vermigli received his early education from his mother, who taught him Latin, after which he attended a school for the children of the Florentine nobility run by Marcello Virgilio Adriano, a chancellor of the republic and friend of Niccolò Machiavelli. In 1514—apparently against his father's will—he entered the monastery of San Bartolomeo at Fiesole, a house of the canons regular of St Augustine of the Lateran congregation. On completing his novitiate (probably in March 1518), he assumed the name Pietro Martire. Shortly afterwards he left Fiesole for Padua, where he attended the *Studio* and was received into the monastery of San Giovanni di Verdara. It was there that he taught himself Greek and acquired the Aristotelian training on which he was to base much of his work as a theologian. He also had contacts with Pietro Bembo's humanist circle, whose members included Reginald Pole and Marcantonio Flaminio.

Vermigli was ordained on 23 September 1525, and probably received his doctorate at about the same time. In April 1526 he was appointed a public preacher by the chapter-general of the Lateran congregation; he gave his first course of sermons in Brescia later that year. The next three years were spent preaching across northern and central Italy. Vermigli also lectured (on Homer as well as scripture) in the congregation's houses in Padua, Ravenna, Bologna, and Vercelli. In summer 1530 he took up the position of vicar to the monastery of San Giovanni in Monte in Bologna, where he began to study Hebrew with the assistance of a Jewish physician named Isaac.

Three years later the chapter-general elected him abbot of Spoleto, an appointment which he held until May 1536. In Spoleto Vermigli enhanced his reputation by successfully restoring discipline to the convents of San Matteo and La Stella. His reward was to be elected abbot to the house of San Pietro ad Aram in Naples (April 1537).

Controversy and conversion to protestantism In Naples Vermigli came into contact with the Spanish exile Juan de Valdés, who introduced him to the writings of the protestant reformers. According to his earliest biographer, Josias Simler, Vermigli at this time read Martin Bucer's *Enarrationes perpetuae in sacra quatuor evangelia* and *Sacrorum psalmorum libri quinque*, and Huldrych Zwingli's *De providentia Dei* and *De vera et falsa religione*. Under Valdés's tutelage Vermigli also embraced the key protestant tenet of justification by faith alone. The intellectual traffic was not all one-way: it has been suggested that Vermigli, for his part, was responsible for Valdés's adoption of a strict doctrine of predestination, derived ultimately from Gregorio di Rimini, whose works Vermigli had studied in Padua.

Vermigli's drift away from Catholic orthodoxy soon attracted attention. When, during a series of public lectures on the first epistle to the Corinthians delivered in late 1539, he failed to expound 1 Corinthians 3: 9–17 along traditional lines—as a proof-text for the doctrine of purgatory—the Theatines denounced him to the Spanish viceroy, Pedro de Toledo, who forbade his further preaching. Vermigli was able to have the ban overturned only after appealing to Rome.

The controversy did not check Vermigli's rise within the Lateran congregation, to which he was elected one of four visitors by a chapter-general in April 1540. The following year he was named prior of San Frediano at Lucca, a house in urgent need of reform. Vermigli responded to the challenge by converting San Frediano into a centre of biblical scholarship, aided by Paolo Lacizi, Celso Martinengo, and the former Jew Emmanuel Tremellius, who taught Latin, Greek, and Hebrew respectively. All three were later to convert to protestantism. Vermigli himself held public lectures on the Pauline epistles, winning a substantial following among the civic aristocracy. In recognition of his achievements, the chapter-general named him to a seven-strong disciplinary commission in May 1542.

However, Vermigli's position was compromised by the activities of some of his more enthusiastic followers, notably Costantino da Carrara, prior of Santa Maria di Fregionaia, who questioned the authority of the pope and church councils, and Girolamo da Pluvio, vicar of San Agostino, who went so far as to celebrate the eucharist according to protestant rites. Under pressure from the curia, the senate of Lucca instituted a crackdown on heretical literature, which had been circulating freely in the city, and imprisoned da Pluvio. On hearing that a warrant had been issued for his own arrest, Vermigli, who had been finding it increasingly difficult to perform his religious duties in good conscience, decided that his only option was to seek sanctuary in protestant territory. On 12 August 1542 he left Lucca with three of his fellow canons,

Lacizi, Teodosio Trebelli, and Giulio Santerenziano, who was to become his constant companion in exile. After conducting his first reformed Lord's supper (in Pisa), Vermigli fled via Florence, Ferrara, Verona, and Zürich to Basel. There he remained for some weeks in the hope of securing a teaching position at the university, but in mid-October he accepted an invitation to take up the chair of Old Testament at Strasbourg, which had been left vacant by the death of Wolfgang Capito.

In Strasbourg Vermigli formed a close association with Martin Bucer, the city's reformer, who taught alongside him at the college of St Thomas. His teaching duties consisted in the main of biblical exposition: between late 1542 and 1547 he lectured and presided over disputations on the minor prophets, Lamentations, Genesis, Exodus, and much of Leviticus, establishing himself in the first rank of continental reformed theologians. Unfortunately only the lectures on Lamentations and Genesis 1–42: 25 survive, although theses for disputation on the first three books of the Pentateuch were later included in editions of Vermigli's *Loci communes*. It was during this period that Vermigli perfected the method of biblical commentary that was to become his trademark: close textual exposition interspersed with so-called commonplaces (excursuses on specific doctrinal topics of relevance to the text under discussion). Although pre-eminently an academic theologian, Vermigli continued to take an active interest in the fate of the Reformation in Italy. One of his first acts in Strasbourg was to write to the evangelicals of Lucca setting out the reasons for his flight, and his first published work was an exposition of the apostles' creed in Italian (*Una semplice dichiaratione sopra gli XII articoli della fede christiana*, 1544).

The years in England Following the emperor Charles V's victory over the Schmalkaldic League at Mühlberg in April 1547 and the corresponding downturn of protestant fortunes in Germany, Vermigli's position in Strasbourg became precarious. However, in October he was invited to England by Thomas Cranmer, eager to attract continental protestant theologians to spearhead his drive for reform. Vermigli was accompanied to London by his fellow Italian Bernardino Ochino, who had received a similar invitation, and by the merchant John Abell. After spending the winter with Cranmer at Lambeth, he was appointed regius professor of divinity at Oxford, replacing Richard Smith (March 1548). There he undertook a major series of lectures on 1 Corinthians, in the course of which he condemned clerical celibacy and the doctrine of purgatory. The lectures proceeded smoothly until, commenting on 1 Corinthians 10: 16–17, Vermigli challenged the Catholic understanding of the eucharist. Led by his predecessor Smith, conservative members of the university demanded that Vermigli defend his views in a disputation, which was eventually fixed for 4 May 1549. Before it could be held, however, Smith fled, first to St Andrews and then to Louvain, from where he issued tracts attacking Vermigli's teaching on justification and religious vows. When Vermigli insisted that the disputation go ahead, it was rescheduled for 28 May; Smith was replaced as

spokesman for the Catholic party by William Tresham, a canon of Christ Church, William Chedsey, later president of Corpus Christi, and Morgan Phillips, principal of St Mary Hall. The outcome of the disputation, which took place over four days, was inconclusive, but it prompted Vermigli to publish the first systematic exposition of his eucharistic doctrine, the *Tractatio de sacramento eucharistiae* (1549), which appeared in an English translation the following year. In this work Vermigli weighed the competing Catholic, Lutheran, and 'Zwinglian' interpretations against the evidence of scripture and the fathers, rejecting all three in favour of his own conception of the eucharist as the vehicle for spiritual union with Christ. The Corinthians lectures that had given rise to the disputation in the first place were published by Christoph Froschauer in Zürich in 1551.

In July 1549 Vermigli was forced as a result of local disturbances accompanying the western rebellion to leave Oxford and seek refuge with Cranmer at Lambeth. Two of his sermons denouncing the rebels formed the basis for an address given by Cranmer at St Paul's on 21 July (Corpus Christi College, Cambridge, MS 102). Vermigli also influenced Cranmer's eucharistic thought; the archbishop's *Defence of the True and Catholic Doctrine of the Sacrament* (1550) makes considerable use of Theodoret, one of Vermigli's favourite church fathers, and of a manuscript of John Chrysostom's *Ad Caesarium monachum* which Vermigli had brought with him from Italy. The remaining years of Edward VI's reign saw Vermigli closely involved in English church politics; his intervention on the side of the church leadership was probably instrumental in persuading John Hooper to drop his opposition to the wearing of vestments in February 1551, for example. Even more significant was Vermigli's contribution to the reform of the liturgy. In late 1550 he and Martin Bucer were asked to suggest revisions to the 1549 prayer book. Although Vermigli's 'annotations' on the book do not survive, the general tenor of the revised liturgy is in keeping with his understanding of the sacrament, which emphasized the eucharistic action rather than the elements of bread and wine. The second exhortation to communion that was added to the 1552 prayer book is actually a translation of Vermigli's *Adhortatio ad coenam Domini mysticam*. Vermigli also participated in another of Cranmer's key projects, the reform of canon law. In October 1551 he was appointed to the commission of thirty-two scholars charged with this task, and over the winter of 1551–2 he helped produce the draft set of ecclesiastical laws later published by John Foxe as the *Reformatio legum ecclesiasticarum*. The manuscript copy of this text in the British Library contains marginal annotations in Vermigli's hand (BL, Harley MS 426.C). His influence has also been detected in the forty-two articles of 1553, especially in article 17, on predestination.

In Oxford, Vermigli began a course of lectures on Romans, published in 1558 as *In epistolam ad Romanos commentarii*. The work contains lengthy commonplaces on justification and predestination, directed against the

Catholic theologian Albert Pighius. However, he continued to encounter resistance in the religiously conservative university. On 20 January 1551 he was appointed first canon of Christ Church, but the local population reacted angrily when he attempted to bring his wife, Catherine Dammartin, a former nun from Metz whom he had married in 1545, into college. After the windows of his rooms, which looked out onto Fish Street, had been repeatedly smashed, Vermigli was forced to move to safer lodgings in the cloisters, where he built himself a study (demolished in March 1684). Following Mary's accession in July 1553, he was placed under house arrest, where he remained for six weeks until he was able to secure permission from the privy council to leave England. Once again he was received at Lambeth by Cranmer, who on 14 September advised him to flee to the continent. Some time after Vermigli's departure the body of his wife, who had died on 15 February 1553 and was buried in Christ Church Cathedral, was exhumed on the instructions of Cardinal Pole and placed on a dungheap. In 1558 the remains were reinterred in the cathedral, together with the relics of St Frithuswith.

Strasbourg and Zürich On 30 October 1553 Vermigli arrived back in Strasbourg, where the orthodox Lutheran party headed by Johann Marbach was now in the ascendant. In order that he might be allowed to resume teaching, Vermigli agreed to sign the Augsburg confession, but not the Wittenberg concord with its affirmation of the substantive presence of Christ in the eucharist. During his second Strasbourg period Vermigli lectured on the book of Judges and Aristotle's *Nicomachean Ethics*, while Girolamo Zanchi, a former protégé of his from San Frediano in Lucca, expounded the *Physics*. Among those attending Vermigli's lectures were numerous English exiles, including the future bishop of Salisbury John Jewel, who later accompanied him to Zürich; it is likely that they were the intended audience for the discussion of political questions, such as the right of resistance to tyranny, which dominates his Judges lectures. An English translation of part of those lectures was published as *A Treatise of the Cohabitacyon of the Faithfull with the Unfaithfull* by W. Rihel in 1555. Vermigli's links with the Marian exiles also extended to the English church at Frankfurt, which in August 1554 asked him to arbitrate in disputes over the use of the second Edwardian prayer book and the validity of Lutheran baptism.

In the face of increasing hostility from Marbach and the Strasbourg Lutherans, Vermigli accepted an invitation from Zürich to succeed Konrad Pellikan as professor of Old Testament (July 1556). There he was able to renew his friendship with Ochino, now minister to Zürich's Italian church, of which Vermigli was elected an elder. Between August 1556 and his death Vermigli lectured on 1–2 Samuel, 1 Kings and 2 Kings 1–11. His vigorous support for the doctrine of double predestination in these lectures brought him into conflict with his Erasmian colleague Theodore Bibliander, who defended the freedom of the will. The dispute was only settled by Bibliander's dismissal in February 1560, which some scholars have interpreted as a decisive moment in the theological transition of the Zürich church from Zwinglianism to Calvinism (Staedtke, 536). This was only one of several doctrinal controversies involving Vermigli during his final years. His continued interest in English affairs (evident also from his correspondence with John Jewel, Edmund Grindal, and Richard Cox, all bishops under Elizabeth, who repeatedly sought to entice him back to England) led him in 1559 to publish two polemical works against English Catholics: the *Defensio doctrinae veteris et apostolicae de sacrosancto eucharistiae sacramento*, a response to Stephen Gardiner's *Confutatio cavillationum*; and the *Defensio ad Riccardi Smythaei duos libellos de caelibatu*. The eucharistic tract, which was dedicated to Elizabeth I, runs to more than 800 pages and is widely regarded as the most comprehensive exposition of the reformed doctrine of the Lord's supper produced during this period.

Death and works The eucharist was again the main point at issue when, in September and October 1561, Vermigli attended the colloquy of Poissy as the representative of the Zürich church. There he was conspicuous in his opposition to any agreement between French Catholics and protestants that would have meant compromising the reformed position on the Lord's supper. Another focus of Vermigli's activity was Poland, whose reformed church was split over the doctrine of the mediator proposed by the Mantuan exile Francesco Stancaro. The Zürich church's official refutation of Stancaro's errors, the *Epistolae duae ad ecclesias polonicas* (1561) is sometimes attributed to Vermigli. Christology, with its implications for the doctrine of the eucharist, was also the theme of Vermigli's last published work, the *Dialogus de utraque in Christo natura* (1561), a refutation of the doctrine of ubiquity championed by the Lutheran theologian Johannes Brenz. A second work against Brenz was planned, but before it could be brought to fruition Vermigli fell ill of fever, and died in Zürich on 12 November 1562; he was buried in the cloisters of the Zürich Grossmünster. He was survived by his second wife, Caterina Merenda of Brescia whom he had married on 9 May 1559 and who later married the Locarnese merchant Ludovico Ronco, and by a posthumous daughter, Maria, who married first another Locarnese exile, Bernardo Zanino, and second Georg Ulrich, minister in Thalwil. A portrait of Vermigli, dated 1560 and painted by the Zürich artist Hans Asper, hangs in the National Portrait Gallery.

Before his death, Vermigli had published his Strasbourg lectures on Judges (*In librum Judicum commentarii*, 1561), but the task of editing his later works for publication fell mainly to the Zürich churchmen Josias Simler, Johannes Wolf, and Rudolf Gwalther. The lectures on the *Ethics* (*In primum, secundum, et initium tertii libri ethicorum Aristotelis ad Nicomachum … commentarius*) appeared in 1563, and were followed by the *Preces sacrae ex psalmis Davidis desumptae* (1564), a collection of prayers dating from Vermigli's first Strasbourg period; the lectures on 1–2 Samuel (*In duos libros Samuelis … commentarii*, 1564); the lectures on 1–2

Kings (*Melachim*, 1566); the lectures on Genesis (*In primum librum Mosis … commentarii*, 1569); and the lectures on Lamentations (*In Lamentationes … commentarium*, 1629). In 1576 the French minister in London, Robert Masson, published the first edition of the *Loci communes*, extracted from Vermigli's published commentaries and arranged according to a scheme based on Calvin's *Institutes*. Fourteen editions of the *Loci*, which subsequently included a selection of Vermigli's correspondence, sermons, and orations, appeared between 1576 and 1656. Vermigli's works appear to have been especially popular in England and in the English colonies in America. English translations of his commentaries on Romans and Judges, the *Loci*, the *Preces sacrae*, and the exposition of the apostles' creed were published during the later sixteenth century, and his commonplace 'On wine and drunkenness' was included in the Elizabethan Book of Homilies. Vermigli's reputation waned during the course of the seventeenth century, but he has recently become the focus of renewed scholarly interest, focusing on his achievements as an exegete and his contribution to the systematization of reformed doctrine in key areas such as predestination and, above all, the eucharist.   MARK TAPLIN

Sources J. Simler, *Oratio de vita et obitu viri optimi, praestantissimi theologi Petri Martyris Vermilii, sacrarum literarum in schola Tigurina professoris* (1563) • J. P. Donnelly and R. Kingdon, eds., *A bibliography of the works of Peter Martyr Vermigli* (1990) • P. McNair, *Peter Martyr in Italy: an anatomy of apostasy* (1967) • J. C. McLelland and G. E. Duffield, eds., *The life, early letters, and eucharistic writings of Peter Martyr* (1989) • J. C. McLelland, ed., *Peter Martyr Vermigli and Italian reform* (1980) • P. M. Vermigli, *Early writings*, ed. J. C. McLelland (1994) • J. P. Donnelly, *Calvinism and scholasticism in Vermigli's doctrine of man and grace* (1976) • S. Corda, *Veritas sacramenti: a study in Vermigli's doctrine of the Lord's supper* (1975) • R. Kingdon, ed., *The political thought of Peter Martyr Vermigli: selected texts and commentary* (1980) • J. C. McLelland, *The visible words of God: an exposition of the sacramental theology of Peter Martyr Vermigli, AD 1500–1562* (1957) • M. W. Anderson, *Peter Martyr Vermigli, a reformer in exile (1542–1562): a chronology of biblical writings in England and Europe* (1975) • C. Schmidt, *Peter Martyr Vermigli: Leben und ausgewählte Schriften* (1858) • K. Sturm, *Die Theologie Peter Martyr Vermiglis während seines ersten Aufenthalts in Strassburg, 1542–1547* (1971) • M. A. Overell, 'Peter Martyr in England, 1547–1553: an alternative view', *Sixteenth Century Journal*, 15 (1984), 87–104 • M. W. Anderson, 'Rhetoric and reality: Peter Martyr and the English Reformation', *Sixteenth Century Journal*, 19 (1988), 451–69 • A. Beesley, 'An unpublished source of the Book of Common Prayer: Peter Martyr Vermigli's *Adhortatio ad coenam Domini mysticam*', *Journal of Ecclesiastical History*, 19 (1968), 83–8 • J. Spalding, 'The *Reformatio legum ecclesiasticarum* of 1552 and the furthering of discipline in England', *Church History*, 39 (1970), 162–71 • G. C. Gorham, *Gleanings of a few scattered ears, during the period of the Reformation in England* (1857) • P. M. Vermigli, *Philosophical works*, ed. J. C. McLelland (1996) • F. James III, *Peter Martyr Vermigli and predestination: the Augustinian inheritance of an Italian reformer* (1998) • J. Staedtke, 'Der Zürcher Prädestinationsstreit von 1560', *Zwingliana*, 9 (1962), 536–46 • V. Vinay, 'Die Haltung Pier Martire Vermiglis gegenüber dem Bauernaufstand in Cornwall und Devonshire zur Zeit Eduards VI', *Wort und Welt* (1948), 277–88 • P. M. Vermigli, *Dialogue on the two natures of Christ*, ed. J. P. Donnelly (1995) • F. James III, 'Juan de Valdés before and after Peter Martyr Vermigli: the reception of *gemina praedestinatio* in Valdés's later thought', *Archiv für Reformationsgeschichte*, 83 (1992), 180–208 • F. James, 'A late medieval parallel in Reformation thought: *gemina praedestinatio* in Gregory of Rimini and Peter Martyr Vermigli', *Via*

Augustini: Augustine in the later middle ages, Renaissance, and Reformation, ed. H. Oberman and F. James (1991), 157–88 • D. MacCulloch, *Thomas Cranmer: a life* (1996) • P. M. Vermigli, *Sacred prayers drawn from the psalms of David*, ed. J. P. Donnelly (1996) • M. Di Gangi, *Peter Martyr Vermigli, 1499–1562: Renaissance man, Reformation master* (1993) • *DNB* • J. P. Donnelly, 'Italian influence on the development of Calvinist scholasticism', *Sixteenth Century Journal*, 7 (1976), 81–101 • J. C. McLelland, 'The reformed doctrine of predestination according to Peter Martyr', *Scottish Journal of Theology*, 8 (1955), 257–65 • M. W. Anderson, 'Peter Martyr, reformed theologian (1542–1562): his letters to Bullinger and Calvin', *Sixteenth Century Journal*, 4 (1973), 41–64 • M. W. Anderson, '*Vista Tigurina*: Peter Martyr and European reform (1556–1562)', *Harvard Theological Review*, 83 (1990), 181–206 • J. P. Donnelly, 'Three disputed Vermigli tracts', *Essays presented to Myron P. Gilmore*, ed. S. Bertelli and G. Ramakus (1978), 1, 37–46 • M. W. Anderson, 'Peter Martyr on Romans', *Scottish Journal of Theology*, 26 (1973), 401–20 • W. Hugelshofer, 'Zum Porträt des Petrus Martyr Vermilii', *Zwingliana*, 5 (1930), 127–9 • J. Thompson, 'The survival of allegorical argumentation in Peter Martyr Vermigli's Old Testament exegesis', *Biblical interpretation in the era of the Reformation: essays presented to David C. Steinmetz in honor of his sixtieth birthday* (1996), 255–71 • M. W. Anderson, 'Royal idolatry: Peter Martyr and the reformed tradition', *Archiv für Reformationsgeschichte*, 69 (1978), 157–201 • M. W. Anderson, 'Word and spirit in exile (1542–1561): the biblical writings of Peter Martyr Vermigli', *Journal of Ecclesiastical History*, 21 (1970), 193–201 • M. W. Anderson, 'Pietro Martire Vermigli on the scope and clarity of scripture', *Theologische Zeitschrift*, 30 (1974), 86–94 • P. M. Vermigli, *Life, letters and sermons*, ed. J. P. Donnelly (1999) • E. Campi, ed., *Peter Martyr Vermigli: humanism, republicanism, reformation* (2002)

Archives LPL, corresp., Selden MS 2010 | BL, Harley MS 426.C; Royal MS 17 C.v · CCC Cam., MS 102 · Zentralbibliothek, Zürich, MS Car 1.123

Likenesses H. Asper, oils, 1560, NPG [*see illus.*] • R. Houston, mezzotint, pubd 1759 (after unknown artist), BM, NPG • H. Hondius, line engraving, BM, NPG; repro. in S. Verheiden, *Praestantium aliquot theologorum* (The Hague, 1602) • Jos Murer, woodcut, repro. in J. Simler, *Oratio de vita … Petri Martyris Vermilii* (1563); repro. in T. Beza, *Icones* (1580)

Vermuyden, Sir Cornelius (1590–1677), drainage engineer, was born at St Maartensdijk, on the island of Tholen, Zealand, in the Dutch Republic, the son of Gillis Vermuyden and his wife, Sara, daughter of Cornelius Werckendet. The Vermuydens had lived in St Maartensdijk from the early fourteenth century, and Cornelius was brought up among drainage engineers. His mother came of a notable family in Zierikzee, capital of the neighbouring Isle of Schouwen, and her brother Lieven had been prominent in embanking, impoldering, and constructing the harbour of Zierikzee.

In England a general drainage bill had been discussed in parliament in 1585 to no effect, but from the 1590s Dutchmen competed with Englishmen in plans to drain the largest area of fen in the kingdom—the Great Level, around the Wash. The first scheme was devised by Humphrey Bradley, a Brabanter, in 1593; it was followed in 1606 by that of the so-called 'French contractors', Cornelius Verneuil (possibly French) and Cornelius Liens. Liens came from the same village as Vermuyden and the two families were related by marriage (the mother of Cornelius Liens was Phillipine, *née* Werckendet, great-aunt of Sara; later Cornelius Liens's brother, Joachim, married Cornelius Vermuyden's sister, Cornelia). Joachim Liens went to England in 1618 as a representative of the Dutch government, and he came close enough in court circles to be knighted by James I in 1619. When the king declared himself the undertaker of drainage in the Great Level in February 1621, it is probable that Liens had promised Dutch capital and expertise.

Cornelius Vermuyden arrived in England in 1621, after employment as a tax collector in his home town, and much later (in 1642) he declared that he had come by invitation to drain the Great Level; he did not say who had issued the invitation. Thereafter James I was diverted from the fen project and no progress was made. Liens put another drainage proposal to the king in 1622, this time naming Cornelius Vermuyden as his fellow undertaker, but that plan too was rejected. Still unemployed, Vermuyden was in close contact with Dutchmen in London, and in 1622 he was asked by the Essex sewer commissioners to repair, at a cost of £2000, a breach in the Thames bank at Dagenham and Havering, caused by recent storms. The commissioners complained of unsatisfactory work in February 1623, but Vermuyden claimed that he had spent £3600 and that the commissioners had paid him nothing.

At Rotherhithe on 6 November 1623 Vermuyden married Katherine, daughter of All-Saints Lapps (or Laps), a Dutch merchant in London. The Lapps were intermarried with the Croppenburghs, and Joos Croppenburgh was contracted in 1622 to drain flooded land in Erith, on the Kent bank of the Thames; he subsequently undertook land reclamation on Canvey Island, and in litigation in 1626 Vermuyden was named alongside Joos Croppenburgh in this work.

Events imply enduring royal favour towards Vermuyden: in 1623 he was engaged by James I to drain land in Windsor Park. In Hatfield Chase on the Yorkshire–Lincolnshire border, where the crown was principal landowner, James I ordered a survey in 1622, and when the local gentry pronounced against drainage he invited comment from Vermuyden, who gave a favourable opinion. James's death in 1625 frustrated immediate action, but on 24 May 1626 Charles I signed an agreement for Vermuyden to drain Hatfield Chase, the money being promised, it is thought, by Vermuyden's Dutch associates. Sir Robert Heath, newly appointed attorney-general, was almost certainly an influential ally of Vermuyden. Work was ordered to proceed briskly, but the king undertook first to conclude agreements with the local landowners and commoners, a task that was imperfectly performed.

Vermuyden brought workmen from the Netherlands, straightened river courses with artificial cuts, and towards the end of 1627 claimed the work complete. In July 1628 Vermuyden bought the manors of Hatfield Chase from the crown, and on 6 January 1629 he was knighted. The allotment of lands in payment began in 1628, but this unleashed complaints that land was inundated which had formerly been dry, and the commoners who had been granted their common rights for ever on the adjoining Isle of Axholme, on which Vermuyden's works encroached, put up bitter resistance. Violent clashes with the islanders and expensive litigation continued for years, but from 1630 Vermuyden disposed of his

lands there and withdrew. Blame for the enduring problems was not laid entirely at Vermuyden's door; Charles I had failed to anticipate and investigate the legal problems. But other ventures now beckoned, notably the Great Level drainage project which sprang to life in 1630. Vermuyden offered his own plan, and was contracted on 1 September 1629 to drain the area. But the contract did not proceed, perhaps because of local opposition to a foreigner (though Vermuyden had been naturalized in 1624) or perhaps because he could not raise the necessary capital. Instead, Francis, fourth earl of Bedford, was named the undertaker, his interest arising out of his ownership of an estate at Thorney; even so, Vermuyden became formally committed to the project as an 'adventurer' and was made the director of the works, effectively being the undertaker.

Completion of the drainage was promised within six years, and was so judged on 12 October 1637, Vermuyden having cut a new straight course for the Great Ouse River, called the Bedford River. The 95,000 acres in payment was about to be allotted to the adventurers when vigorous objections were made from all quarters. At this point Charles I announced himself as undertaker, and the investigating commission then pronounced the drainage incomplete and defective. In response Vermuyden put forward a fresh plan, entitled *A Discourse Touching the Draining of the Great Fennes* (1638, published 1642), extending the original objectives. The Bedford scheme had aimed to make 'summer ground'—land dry in summer—whereas the new objective was to make dry 'winter ground'. The larger plan now extended over land in six counties. Civil war delayed further action until 1649, when an act for the draining of the Great Level was passed—helped, it is thought, by the considerable influence of Oliver Cromwell.

Proceedings from 29 May 1649 until 5 April 1656 can be followed in the volumes of proceedings of the Bedford Level Corporation. The proposal to make Vermuyden director was highly contentious; the adventurers consulted other drainers with different ideas, including a Dutchman, Jan Barents Westerdyke, while Vermuyden refused to submit to their supervision, no doubt fearing that their intervention at some point would cut his work short. They for their part could not permit expenditure beyond a certain limit. Finally Vermuyden reached an agreement with the adventurers on 24 January 1650, accepting the conditions he had rejected in June 1649. The new work proceeded, and the drainage of 170,000 acres north-west of the Bedford River, the North and Middle levels, was declared complete on 24 March 1651, and the whole Level was finished on 17 February 1653. The condition of the North and Middle levels continued to be satisfactory, and, when visiting in 1657, William Dugdale saw rapeseed, wheat, and vegetables growing on the allotments of some adventurers. He was also told that sometimes during the draining 11,000 men had been at work. The condition of the South Level did not satisfy, and it remained imperfectly drained into the nineteenth century.

Vermuyden also dabbled in other ventures. In 1630 he

bought Malvern Chase, where a scheme to grow madder was briefly introduced, but he had sold the estate by 1637. Also in 1630 he bought Sedgmoor, which required drainage. He acquired an interest in the Wirksworth lead mines, in Derbyshire, in 1631, when Sir Robert Heath took possession and made Vermuyden a partner responsible for drainage. Vermuyden was continually indebted because of it, but his new sough drained deeper than before, and much lead was recovered. The work involved his sons Cornelius and John more than himself, for he put an agent in charge; nevertheless, two-thirds of the Dovegang mine still belonged to Vermuyden at his death. In 1653 he proposed a treaty of perpetual friendship between England and the Netherlands in a document, preserved in the Thurloe papers (Thurloe, *State papers*, 2.125–6), which was probably submitted to Cromwell. The plan to drain Sedgmoor was put before parliament in 1655, but it was rejected in December 1656 when the tenants and freeholders refused consent. During the civil war Vermuyden's sympathies probably lay with parliament, since Cromwell was his friend, and Colonel Cornelius Vermuyden, who fought at Marston Moor, is believed to have been his eldest son. Altogether he had thirteen children, of whom twelve were born in fourteen years; some married into worthy gentry families. After 1655 Vermuyden was described as a merchant, engaged in 'exchange, rechange, and chevissance', but otherwise he fades from the record until his death. He was buried at St Margaret's, Westminster, London, on 15 October 1677.

Vermuyden's writings convey the picture of an experienced, professional engineer. But contrary opinions on drainage strategies were inevitable, so he had many critics and opponents, and gathered a reputation for arrogance, ruthlessness, and obstinacy. A more balanced assessment results from weighing his sound decisions against mistakes and consequences that were unforeseeable; and although he was a complex figure, his significant role in the draining of the English fens cannot be disputed.

JOAN THIRSK

Sources L. E. Harris, *Vermuyden and the fens* (1953) • J. Korthals-Altes, *Sir Cornelius Vermuyden: the lifework of a great Anglo-Dutchman in land-reclamation and drainage* (1925) • B. E. Cracknell, *Canvey Island: the history of a marshland community* (1959) • F. N. Fisher, 'Sir Cornelius Vermuyden and the Dovegang lead mine', *Journal of the Derbyshire Archaeological and Natural History Society*, 72 (1952), 74–118 • M. Albright, 'The entrepreneurs of fendraining in England under James I and Charles I: an illustration of the uses of influence', *Explorations in Entrepreneurial History*, 8/2 (1955), 50–65 • *CSP dom.*, 1619–56 • J. D. Hughes, 'The drainage disputes in the Isle of Axholme and their connexion with the Leveller movement: a re-examination', *Lincolnshire Historian*, 2/1 (spring 1954), 13–45 • H. C. Darby, *The draining of the fens* (1940) • Thurloe, *State papers* • parish register (burial), Westminster, St Margaret's, 15 Oct 1677
Archives BL, Thomason Tracts • Cambs. AS, Bedford Level Corporation papers • East Riding of Yorkshire Archives Service, Beverley, corresp. and papers relating to drainage in West Riding of Yorkshire | East Riding of Yorkshire Archives Service, Beverley, Eustoft papers
Likenesses van Miereveldt, oils (of Vermuyden or Sir Philibert Vernatti), priv. coll.

Verne, Adela (1877–1952). *See under* Verne, Mathilde (1865–1936).

Verne, Alice Barbara (1868–1958). *See under* Verne, Mathilde (1865–1936).

Verne, Mathilde (1865–1936), pianist and piano teacher, was born on 25 May 1865 at 12 Portland Street, Southampton, the second daughter and fourth child of John Evangelist Wurm (c.1828–1892) and his wife, (Marie) Sophie Niggl (c.1838–c.1883). Her parents had come from Bavaria to Southampton about 1859 at the suggestion of Sophie's sister Josephine Herkomer, a music teacher there. J. E. Wurm became organist of the local Roman Catholic church and taught the piano, violin, and German in Hampshire schools, while Sophie gave music lessons at home. Of the ten children born to the couple (five girls and five boys), eight reached adulthood; of these, all four young women pursued music as a profession, largely at the urging of their mother, who gave them their first instruction. Mathilde, five years younger than her sister Mary *Wurm (1860–1938), was gifted but undisciplined; she was sent to boarding-school and subsequently had piano lessons from Franklin Taylor in London. Through the influence of A. J. Hipkins at Broadwood & Co., she was enabled to study for four years with Clara Schumann—a potent influence, as Mathilde later recalled: 'I owe everything to her' (Verne, 55).

Returning from Frankfurt, Mathilde established herself as a concert artist in London from 1887, making her début at the Saturday 'Popular' concerts at St James's Hall (in a Mendelssohn trio) with Wilma Norman-Néruda and Alfredo Piatti. She continued to appear at the 'Pops', and later in other chamber concerts at the Steinway, Aeolian, and Bechstein halls, while also making a name as a teacher, notably of well-placed amateurs who patronized her concerts and nourished her ambitions. Eager and self-confident, she made a trip to New York (playing with Theodore Thomas's orchestra), gave recitals (as Mathilde Wurm), and took charge of the keyboard training of her youngest sister, Adela [*see below*]. Late in 1893, making a fresh start after their father's death (and possibly with Adela's potential in view), she and her younger siblings changed their surname to Verne—an improvement on the English mispronunciation of their real name. Mathilde's peak as a soloist came in the mid-1890s, when her interpretations of Chopin received praise. She taught briefly at the Royal College of Music, and later made regular appearances under Henry Wood at the Queen's Hall Promenade Concerts from 1903 to 1907, and often at the Sunday afternoon concerts from 1908 to 1912. In this period she was valued for her Schumann, including the A minor piano concerto and *Papillons*. Thereafter she suffered from cramp; her public performances ceased except for occasional duo appearances with Adela and during a second visit to the USA, in 1926–7.

From about 1896 Adela Verne's platform success not only eclipsed Mathilde's but decided the older sister's course. She now basked in her role as Adela's instructor, taking her to play in Vienna, exploiting connections with

Paderewski to promote her, and developing plans, with her sister Alice, for a private school. In February 1909 the Mathilde Verne School of Pianoforte Playing opened at 194 Cromwell Road, South Kensington, and quickly gained attention with its student performances (some conducted by Artur Nikisch). Most notable was the stunning seven-year-old prodigy Solomon Cutner, later known simply as Solomon, whom Mathilde taught and shrewdly managed for five years (1910–15), transmitting the Clara Schumann tradition. Among other successful musicians passing through her hands—she claimed to have taught more than 1400 pupils—were Harold Samuel, Herbert Menges, and Moura Lympany. She also taught the young Elizabeth Bowes-Lyon (Queen Elizabeth, George VI's consort). The school survived, despite setbacks, until the early 1930s. Even longer lived were the Thursday 'Twelve O'Clocks', an innovatory series of chamber concerts, founded by Verne with the violinist Beatrice Langley, at the Aeolian Hall from 1907 to 1936. At the launch of her autobiography *Chords of Remembrance* (1936) Mathilde Verne gave her last performance; she died, unmarried, later the same evening, 4 June 1936, in the Savoy Hotel, Strand, London. The novel *Madame Sousatzka* by Bernice Rubens (1962; made into a film by John Schlesinger, 1988) is partly based on Verne's career.

Her younger sister **Alice Barbara Verne** (1868–1958), music teacher and composer, was born on 9 August 1868 at 12 Portland Street, Southampton, the third daughter and sixth child of John Evangelist and (Marie) Sophie Wurm. She sang and played the violin and hoped for a career as a singer of light opera but, partly through serious illness, turned to the piano, taking lessons from Marie Schumann in London. After accompanying her sisters on concert tours (Mathilde to New York, Adela to Australia), she married the amateur musician William Bredt. With a gift for teaching young children, Alice organized the junior department of Mathilde's piano school. Marked success led to its independence as the Children's College of Music and became a spur to Alice's own composing. Besides solo keyboard pieces and dances arranged for orchestra, she wrote a mass, *Phantasy Quartet* (c.1908), *Phantasy Quintet*, and *Phantasy Trio* (published 1910, winner of a Cobbett prize for its considerable charm), a bravura *Polacca* for piano and orchestra (originally for Solomon, c.1911), *Toy Suite* (for toy instruments and orchestra), and *Adagio for Strings* (1947). She died on 12 April 1958 at Fulham Hospital, Fulham.

By far the most celebrated of the sisters was the pianist **Adela Verne** (1877–1952). She was born Adeline Victorine Pauline Wurm on 27 February 1877, at 12 Portland Street, the fifth daughter and tenth child of John Evangelist and (Marie) Sophie Wurm. The youngest and arguably most gifted member of the family, she had her first piano lessons from her sister Alice. Marie Schumann wanted to take her as a child back to Frankfurt to study, but her father would not allow this; instead Adela attended schools in Southampton and Lymington (and Paris, briefly), and began serious lessons with her sister Mathilde. At the age of fourteen she made her London début at

one of the smaller Crystal Palace concerts, playing Tchaikovsky's B♭ minor piano concerto under August Manns; a short time later Paderewski heard her, sent an Erard piano to her school, and advised Mathilde to continue teaching her. Successful appearances at the Saturday 'Pops' and tours in Australia and Canada (one with Emma Albani) provided stimulating experience.

In mid-1896 Adela gave her first Queen's Hall recital, followed by many orchestral performances there over the next ten years, at the Saturday symphony concerts, the Sunday afternoon concerts, and the Promenade Concerts. A favourite of Henry Wood's, she appeared six times in the 1900 promenade season alone. Her repertory was impressive for one so young and physically slight—not only the Mendelssohn and Tchaikovsky piano concertos but also Saint-Saëns's second piano concerto and Franck's *Symphonic Variations*, the Grieg piano concerto, Beethoven's 'Emperor' concerto, and Brahms's second piano concerto (which she was first to play at the Promenades), besides Liszt's *Hungarian Fantasy* and Paderewski's *Fantasie polonaise*. She also played frequently in chamber concerts and toured at various times with Clara Butt, Mischa Elman, and Eugene Ysaÿe. Her effortless technique, power, and expressive range put her in the front rank of British pianists at this time, comparable with Fanny Davies. Some critics even placed her on a level with Teresa Carreño for grandeur and dignity.

Whether from an urge to see the world or to escape Mathilde's control, Adela soon undertook extensive foreign tours, alone and reportedly without the benefit of agents or advance advertising; she was still in her thirties. She visited Newfoundland, parts of Canada again, San Francisco, New York, Chicago, Buffalo (taking her first air flight), and Montreal; then later Mexico (where she survived an earthquake) and Cuba, Buenos Aires, and Chile (across the Andes on a mule), up to Lima and back to Buenos Aires (where she convalesced after contracting typhoid). Enthusiastically received everywhere, she returned to England soon after the outbreak of the First World War and helped at her sisters' school, also visiting Paderewski and his family in Switzerland for some months. In this period she seems to have been married to the singer Jean Vallier, and thereafter, in the 1920s when making Chicago her base, to Eustace Smith La Hare, a Canadian postal official. In 1932 she moved back to England and tried to re-establish her career. Adela Verne recorded some Chopin, Moritz Moszkowski, and Cuban dances, and in 1938 wrote a march for the queen (*Queen Elizabeth's March*, recorded by the band of the Grenadier Guards). But despite high-profile events at the Wigmore Hall, National Gallery, and elsewhere, and lingering respect in Britain for the romantic tradition she represented, she never regained her former prominence. She died at 67 Earls Court Square, London, on 4 February 1952. Her son, John Vallier (1921–1991), was himself an able pianist-composer.   LEANNE LANGLEY

Sources M. Verne, *Chords of remembrance* (1936) • D. D. K., 'Adela Verne: Soton born and world-famous', *Southern Evening Echo* [Southampton] (11 March 1960) • *The Times* (5 June 1936) • *The Times* (6 Feb

1952) • 'Wurm, Mary J. A.', *Riemann Musik Lexicon*, ed. W. Gurlitt, 12th edn, 3 vols. (1961) • b. certs. [Alice Verne, Adela Verne] • d. certs. [Alice Verne, Adela Verne] • *CGPLA Eng. & Wales* (1936)

Archives Royal College of Music, London, Department of Portraits and Performance History, concert programmes | SOUND BL NSA

Likenesses photographs, *c*.1909, repro. in Verne, *Chords of remembrance* • F. Lion, oils, 1925, Royal College of Music, London • photographs, *c*.1925

Wealth at death £262 19s. 5d.: probate, 13 July 1936, *CGPLA Eng. & Wales*

Vernet [*née* Cunningham; *other married name* Thornton], **Helen Monica Mabel** (1875/6–1956), bookmaker, was born in 1875 or 1876, but little else is known about her early life. She had a brief career as an actress, playing small parts, but this ended on her marriage, at the age of seventeen, to Spencer Thornton, a stockbroker. Influenced perhaps by her husband's occupation, Helen Thornton became a prolific gambler and quickly exhausted most of the £8000 left her by her father, who had died when she was still a child. The dissipation of her inheritance was accelerated when, following a serious illness which affected her lungs, she was advised by her doctor to spend more time in the open air: she opted to go racing several times a week. Her marriage to Thornton was annulled, possibly because his income proved insufficient for her needs, and she subsequently married another stockbroker, Robert Vernet.

In her early racing days Helen Thornton became aware that many women wished to bet in small amounts which bookmakers on Tattersall's rails were reluctant to accept. Entry to Tattersall's ring was more expensive than to normal enclosures and the bookmakers expected their customers to wager accordingly and not in denominations as low as 5 or 10s. During the 1918 racing season Mrs Vernet, as she had by then become, let it be known among her friends that she would accept bets of this order handed to her in writing. This was illegal, and as her clientele increased the professional bookmakers objected and had her warned off by racecourse officials.

However, Arthur Bendir, who had essentially established the bookmaking firm of Ladbrokes in 1902, saw the economic potential and publicity value of employing Helen Vernet as the first female licensed bookmaker on British racecourses. He was proved right and during her career with Ladbrokes, which began in 1919, she never earned less than £20,000 a year from her commission on gambling receipts. In 1928 she purchased a partnership in the firm. This was the year that the totalizator first came to British racing. It catered for the small-scale better but many gamblers still preferred the interaction with bookmakers, who offered character as well as negotiable odds. Mrs Vernet contrasted with the brash personalities of many of her male counterparts, being charming and extremely chic.

Helen Vernet's second marriage, coupled with her commission from bookmaking, allowed her to live in style in a succession of elegant, furnished London houses in Gray's Inn, Albany, and finally at 49 Eaton Place, Westminster. She also owned Cunningham Lodge at Hove where she installed her mother. She was fond of dancing and allegedly insisted that her clerks, who accompanied her to provincial meetings requiring overnight stays, should be both handsome and expert dancers. For holidays she favoured the Riviera where she could gamble in the casinos. She admitted to one weakness: a fondness for gigolos.

Helen Vernet continued with Ladbrokes until 1955, often in later years, as Parkinson's disease and arthritis took hold, being pushed to her position in a wheelchair by her 'bookmaker's runner' (or assistant), Alf Simmons. Her death, on 30 March 1956, at 49 Eaton Place, was from a combination of bronchial pneumonia and Parkinson's disease. Her estate was valued at £7573, £500 of which went to Alf Simmons. Five years after Helen Vernet died, betting shops were introduced to Britain: although they brought money to her old firm, she would not have appreciated their lack of glamour. WRAY VAMPLEW

Sources C. Ramsden, *Ladies in racing: sixteenth century to the present day* (1973) • R. Kaye and R. Peskett, *The Ladbrokes story* (1969) • *The Times* (31 March 1956) • *Ladbroke racing: a short history* (1995) • W. Vamplew, *The turf: a social and economic history of horse racing* (1976) • C. Chinn, *Better betting with a decent feller: bookmakers, betting and the British working class, 1750–1990* (1991) • d. cert. • *CGPLA Eng. & Wales* (1956)

Likenesses photograph (after Arion; formerly at Ganton House *c*. 1960–1966), repro. in Kaye and Peskett, *Ladbrokes story*

Wealth at death £7573 6s. 8d.: probate, 16 May 1956, *CGPLA Eng. & Wales*

Verneuil, John (1582/3–1647), librarian, was born in Bordeaux, France; his parents are unknown. He was educated at the protestant academy at Montauban, receiving an MA before he left for England as a religious refugee. On his arrival, he later explained, he had received a 'liberal maintenance' from Sir Thomas Leigh (*d.* 1626) of Stoneleigh, Warwickshire, and had 'belonged' to his grandson Thomas Leigh (1594/5–1671), later second baronet (*Tract of the Sovereign Judge of Controversies*, 1628, preface). Since Verneuil and the young Leigh matriculated from Magdalen College, Oxford, on the same day, 4 November 1608, when they were aged twenty-five and thirteen respectively, the probability is that Verneuil acted as under-tutor. He was admitted as a reader to the Bodleian Library on 31 January 1609.

According to Anthony Wood, once at Oxford Verneuil was assisted by, among others, the authorities of Magdalen College, but he does not appear in the college accounts. He may also have taught Henry Carey, later second earl of Monmouth, who was a fellow-commoner of Exeter College from 1611, and who graduated BA in 1613. In dedicating to Carey his French translation of Lewis Bayly's *Practise of Piety*, Verneuil speaks of 'un conte du temps que j'ai soustrait & desrobé de votre service' ('an account of the time which I have taken and snatched from your service'; *La pratique de piété*). Verneuil married Elizabeth Hill on 20 December 1612, in the church of St Peter-in-the-East, Oxford, and the baptisms, burials, and marriages of a number of their children appear in the parish registers.

It is not clear when Verneuil became underkeeper of the

Bodleian Library. A salary of £10 a year was paid to an unnamed officer from the resignation of Philip Price in 1613, but Verneuil is not mentioned in the library accounts until the year 1618/19, when he was paid for going to London to buy books. He made a number of such visits until the year 1631/2. The library's purchases were, no doubt, from the Stationers' Company's Latin stock shop in the grounds of Stationers' Hall. Later his and the librarian's visits became less frequent as the assiduity and efficiency of booksellers such as Henry Featherstone and Robert Martin increased.

In addition to his tutorial and library duties, Verneuil published translations from and into French. In the first category are his *Sermon Preached before the King's Majesty the 15th of June 1615* (1620) and *A Tract of the Sovereign Judge of Controversies in Matters of Religion* (1628), translations respectively of works by Pierre du Moulin and John Cameron; in the second category is his *La pratique de piété* (Geneva, 1625), Bayly's original having already run into fifteen editions in English, and *La descouverte de la cautelle du cœur de l'homme* (Geneva, 1634) from the work by Daniel Dyke. *La pratique de piété* was extremely successful, running to sixteen editions by 1700 and making a significant contribution to the sustenance of a common protestant culture in western Europe. Verneuil also published several supplements to the printed catalogues of the Bodleian Library. His MA from Montauban was incorporated at Oxford on 13 December 1625.

Elizabeth Verneuil died in 1634. Verneuil himself succumbed to illness in the winter of 1643–4—probably to plague in the overcrowded city of Oxford—and the library accounts note that he was then too weak to climb the library stairs. He died at his house in the Eastgate in September 1647, and was buried in the church of St Peter-in-the-East on 30 September. No will survives, but an (undated) inventory reveals that his goods and chattels were worth approximately £12 (Oxfordshire County Archives, 89/4/22). Wood's judgement was that by his death 'our public library lost an honest and useful servant, and his children a good father' (Wood, *Ath. Oxon.*, 3.222).

R. JULIAN ROBERTS

Sources W. D. Macray, *Annals of the Bodleian Library, Oxford*, 2nd edn (1890) · *Reg. Oxf.*, 2/2.302 · G. Hampshire, ed., *The Bodleian Library account book, 1613–1646* (1983) · Wood, *Ath. Oxon.*, new edn, 3.221 · parish register (death), Sept 1647, Oxford, St Peter-in-the-East · Bodl. Oxf., MS Wood E. 5, fol. 87v · Shakespeare Birthplace Trust RO, Stratford upon Avon, Leigh MSS · *DNB* · E. Haag and E. Haag, *La France protestante*, 10 vols. (Paris, 1846–59), vol. 9, p. 470
Wealth at death approx. £12: inventory, Oxfordshire County Archives, 89/4/22

Verney, Sir Edmund (1590–1642), courtier and politician, was born on 1 January 1590 in Drury Lane, London, the second son of Sir Edmund Verney (1535–1600), knight of Penley, Hertfordshire, and his third wife, Mary Blakeney (*d*. 1642). Sir Edmund's first well-documented ancestor, Sir Ralph Verney, a mercer, had been appointed lord mayor of London in 1465. Later the Verneys became courtiers through marriage and political alliances and in keeping with this tradition Sir Edmund became knight marshal

Sir Edmund Verney (1590–1642), by Sir Anthony Van Dyck, *c*.1636–40

and standard bearer to Charles I. In preparation for his career he studied briefly at St Alban Hall, Oxford, in 1603–4, visited the French and Italian courts, and toured battlefields in the Low Countries. In 1611 he was knighted and sent to Madrid. He returned 'an accomplished gentleman' (F. Verney, 1.70) and joined his uncle Francis as a member of Prince Henry's household. After Henry's early death, Verney, barely twenty-three, was appointed a gentleman of the privy chamber in young Prince Charles's household—a connection with the future king that engendered deep loyalty and caused later divisions within the Verney family.

On 14 December 1612 Verney married Margaret Denton (1594–1641); they had ten children who survived infancy. He received a £2300 portion and four years' room and board in return for a £400 jointure. The socially prominent Dentons of Hillesden, Buckinghamshire, lived near Middle Claydon, which the Verneys had owned since the 1460s. However, the Claydon estate was leased to a tenant, and Margaret and her children lived at Hillesden while Verney was attending court. His career as a courtier did not produce the expected financial benefits. Never an astute businessman, in 1620 he agreed to pay almost £4000 to secure the surrender of the lease on Middle Claydon, although it had only fifteen years to run. Prince Charles promised to pay £1000 per year for four years, but appears to have made only one £1000 payment, in 1623. Verney regained Claydon but 'thereby', he 'became much in depte' (Bruce, 135).

In 1622 Verney was made lieutenant of Whaddon Chase

and in 1623 he followed Prince Charles and Buckingham to Madrid where they were negotiating a Spanish match. There Verney proved himself an ardent protestant by protecting a dying Englishman from a Catholic priest. In addition he helped Prince Charles to extricate himself from the Spanish alliance, by providing him with a jewel paved with ten diamonds which the prince used as a gift. On his return to England he was elected MP for Buckingham borough in 1624. In 1625 he was elected for New Romney, one of the Cinque Ports, on the nomination of the duke of Buckingham, and he sat for Aylesbury in 1629, and for Chipping Wycombe in 1640 in the Short and Long parliaments.

When Charles became king Verney was appointed knight marshal for life with a £200 pension and responsibility to preserve order within 12 miles of the court. He and his deputies were to 'continually ride both in the day time and in the night, about our court' arresting anyone without proper credentials (Bruce, 115). He also had command of the Marshalsea prison and its profits. Throughout the 1630s he rode with the king on long journeys, which aggravated his sciatica and lameness, despite visits to Bath. In 1639 he delivered a message from the king to the Scottish army which led to a peace treaty. His court and political duties, however, required him mainly to be in London. Thus in 1634 he established himself in a great double house in Covent Garden Piazza with an annual rent of £160.

Verney's expenses continued to exceed the income paid to him by Charles I and his attempts to make money from patents, investments, and grants of offices ended in failure. His ventures included patents for hackney coaches and inspecting tobacco, investing in drainage projects in the fens, and buying confiscated Irish estates. He paid £1000 to the court of wards to marry his eldest son, Ralph *Verney (1613-1696), to an heiress, and in 1640 he lent the king another £1000. He hoped to provide for his family through a £400 annuity raised from the aulnage, a tax on sealing woollen yarn, but this proved disappointing. With only a life interest in his lands, he left Ralph saddled with debts: his younger sons and his unmarried daughters received only tiny annuities.

Verney's financial problems took place in the context of growing political unrest in parliament and the court. His life illustrates how families became divided during the civil wars and how individuals had to make painful choices between duty to family, religion, and king. 'Indeed the world now account[s] it policy', wrote Verney's daughter Cary, 'for the father to be one side and the son on the other' (Seventh Report, HMC, 440). Verney's younger sons, Henry, Edmund *Verney (1616-1649), and Thomas, served in the royalist army, whose standard their father bore, but at the same time, both Sir Edmund and his eldest son were deeply committed protestants, who disliked Laudian practices and desired simplicity in worship. They sat together in parliament and wore their hair long, but they voted in opposition to Charles I's wishes. 'The opinion, I see of the great ones most at the court', wrote Henry to his brother Ralph, 'is that my father and

you are all for the Parliament and not for the King' (Seventh Report, HMC, 440).

Verney admitted his predicament to a royalist friend:

> I do not like the quarrel, and do heartily wish that the King would yield and consent to what they desire, so that my conscience is only concerned in honour and in gratitude to follow my master. I have eaten his bread, and served him near thirty years, and will not do so base a thing as to forsake him; and choose rather to lose my life—which I am sure to do—to preserve and defend those things which are against my conscience to preserve and defend. (Gardiner, 1.5)

In explaining his motives he specified religious issues as the cause of his opposition to the king. 'I have no reverence for Bishops', he stated, 'for whom this quarrel subsists' (ibid., 1.5).

When civil war came Ralph Verney sided with parliament while his father raised the royalist standard at Nottingham in August 1642 and died on 23 October on the battlefield at Edgehill. Later a family story arose of how the standard was found clutched in his severed hand, although the body was never recovered. It was reported that Verney killed two men with his own hands and 'would nither put on armes or buff cote the day of battell' (F. Verney, 2.119), which implied a desire to die. Although these family tales cannot be proved, Sir Edmund was consistently described as a man 'of great courage and … confessedly valiant' (ibid., 1.72). Contemporaries confirm that his regiment bore the brunt of the action at Edgehill. He stood his ground at the head of the army and died in the service of the king. His sombre face can be seen at Claydon House in portraits by Van Dyck and others.

SUSAN E. WHYMAN

Sources Seventh report, HMC, 6 (1879), 433–509 [Sir Harry Verney] · J. Bruce, ed., Letters and papers of the Verney family down to the end of the year 1639, CS, 56 (1853) · F. P. Verney and M. M. Verney, Memoirs of the Verney family, 4 vols. (1892–9), vols. 1–2 · will, PRO, PROB 11/190, fols. 350–51 · S. Ranson, 'The Verney papers catalogued for the Claydon House Trust', 1994, Claydon House, Buckinghamshire · S. R. Gardiner, History of the great civil war, 1642–1649, 1–2 (1886–91) · P. Verney, The standard bearer: the story of Sir Edmund Verney (1963) · G. Lipscomb, The history and antiquities of the county of Buckingham, 4 vols. (1831–47) · VCH Buckinghamshire · H. Verney, The Verneys of Claydon (1968) · National Trust, Claydon House (1984) · Foster, Alum. Oxon. · The parish of St Paul, Covent Garden, Survey of London, 36 (1970), 74–5, 97, 370–77 · S. Whyman, Sociability and power in late Stuart England (1999)

Archives Claydon House, Buckinghamshire, papers, corresp. | BL · Bucks. RLSS · Dartmouth College, Hanover, New Hampshire · Princeton University, New Jersey

Likenesses A. Van Dyck, portrait, c.1636–1640, Claydon House, Buckinghamshire [see illus.] · A. Van Dyck, oils, c.1640, NPG · E. Marshall, bust, 1653, All Saints' Church, Middle Claydon, Buckinghamshire; repro. in Verney and Verney, eds., Memoirs, vol. 2, facing p. 126 · Rivers, stipple, NPG · A. Van Dyck, portrait, Claydon House, Buckinghamshire; repro. in Verney and Verney, eds., Memoirs, vol. 2, cover, frontispiece · oils, Stanford Hall, Leicestershire · portrait, Claydon House, Buckinghamshire; repro. in Verney and Verney, eds., Memoirs, vol. 1, cover, frontispiece

Wealth at death Middle Claydon estate value c.£2200, but debts c.£7700 and fixed expenses of £1470 (incl. £500 debt charge, interest charges, and annuities); six daughters hoped to receive £1000 portions, but received tiny annuities: J. Y. Broad, 'Gentry finances and the civil war: the case of the Buckinghamshire Verneys', Economic History Review, 2nd ser., 32 (1979), 189, 198; J. Y. Broad, 'Sir

Ralph Verney and his estates', DPhil diss., U. Oxf., 1973, 3, 214–17; Bucks. RLSS, D/X 2/27, Richard Grenville's notebook, c.1640; A. Johnson, 'Buckinghamshire 1640–1660', MA diss., U. Wales, Swansea, 1963, 8, 13, 15; Hunt. L., STTM 5/14, 'The value of each p[er]son's estate, 2 April 1660'; BL, Stowe MS 802, Richard Grenville's Buckinghamshire assessments, c.1637–1640

Verney, Sir Edmund (1616–1649), royalist army officer, was the third son of Sir Edmund *Verney (1590–1642) and his wife, Margaret Denton (1594–1641). Sir Ralph *Verney (1613–1696) was his eldest brother; his younger brother Henry was a royalist colonel. Edmund was educated at a private school in Gloucester, at Winchester College (1634–5), and then at Magdalen Hall, Oxford, where he matriculated on 22 January 1636. At Oxford he learned little and got into debt and into disgrace with his puritan tutor, Henry Wilkinson. In 1637 he went briefly to study under Mr Crowther, rector of Newton Blossomville, Buckinghamshire, formerly his eldest brother's Oxford tutor, who found that he 'understands not the very first grounds of logicke, or other university learning' but that he was willing and capable (F. P. Verney and M. M. Verney, 1.164).

Verney entered the army against the Scots as a volunteer in 1639 and joined his father in the royal army on the border. With the first money that he earned he paid off his Oxford creditors and, when the first bishops' war was over, he joined the army of the United Provinces in Flanders in Sir Thomas Culpepper's regiment. In winter quarters at Utrecht he studied Latin, French, and history seven or eight hours a day at the university. He had many disappointments about promotion, though Elizabeth, queen of Bohemia, did her best to help him. In 1640 he served again in the English army in the second bishops' war.

Verney sided with the king in the civil war, and suffered heavily for his loyalty; his pay as well as that of his men was constantly in arrears; the grief of his father's death at Edgehill was embittered by the sorrow and indignation he felt that his eldest brother, Ralph, should support the parliament; his portion invested in the aulnage, the family cloth inspection venture, was practically forfeited; and he suffered most of all from the mistakes he witnessed daily in the conduct of his own leaders.

Verney the professional soldier found service as an officer in Harcourt's regiment in the army sent from England to suppress the Irish rising in late 1641 and early 1642. In 1642–3 he served under the earl of Ormond in the savage wars against the confederates. 'The enemy runs from us wheresoever we meet them', he wrote, 'but if we chance to overtake them, we give no quarter, but all to the sword'. He sent the same report after the taking of Trim: 'after we put some four score men to the sword, but like valiant knights errant, gave quarter and liberty to all the women' (F. P. Verney and M. M. Verney, 2.135). He saw much action in Ireland, commanded at Rathcotty Castle, and was wounded at Rathconnel.

In November 1643 Verney returned from Ireland as a major of foot in Richard Gibson's regiment of foot, part of the army released for service in England by the cessation. He became a colonel in August 1644. He was knighted in 1643, and made lieutenant-governor of Chester; he served

during its two sieges, and was highly valued by Lord Byron and other commanders. After the surrender of Chester in 1646 Sir Edmund rejoined Ormond, to whom he had a personal loyalty, at Le Havre. Their portraits were painted in Paris by Egmont in 1648, as companion pictures. They returned to Ireland to take part in the last fierce struggle against Cromwell. Sir Edmund had been previously reconciled with his by now exiled brother. In the absence of a widow Ralph was to be the administrator of his dead younger brother's estate.

Ormond committed the command of his own regiment to his friend Verney, when he sent the best of his army with Sir Arthur Aston to reinforce the defenders of Drogheda. Sir Edmund wrote from the city (9 September 1649) earnestly begging Ormond to fall on the enemy's camp to make a diversion. He survived the horrors of the assault on 11 September, but the few who had escaped were sought out and killed in cold blood. Among these was Verney, killed three days after the fall of the town, while he was 'walkinge with Crumwell by way of protection'. 'One Ropier who is brother to the Lord Ropier, caled him aside in a pretence to speake with him, being formerly of acquaintance, and insteade of some frendly office wch Sir Ed: might expect from him, he barberously rann him throw wth a tuck' (F. P. Verney and M. M. Verney, 2.344–5). M. M. VERNEY, rev. SARAH E. TROMBLEY

Sources F. P. Verney and M. M. Verney, *Memoirs of the Verney family*, 4 vols. (1892–9), vols. 1–2 • P. R. Newman, *The old service: royalist regimental colonels and the civil war, 1642–1646* (1993) • P. R. Newman, *Royalist officers in England and Wales, 1642–1660: a biographical dictionary* (1981) • Foster, *Alum. Oxon.* • P. Verney, *The standard-bearer* (1963) • Clarendon, *Hist. rebellion* • J. Bruce, ed., *Letters and papers of the Verney family down to the end of the year 1639*, CS, 56 (1853) • S. R. Gardiner, *History of the Commonwealth and protectorate, 1649–1656*, 4 vols. (1894–1903), vol. 1 • S. R. Gardiner, *History of England from the accession of James I to the outbreak of the civil war*, new edn, 10 (1899) • H. D. Traill, *Social England*, 6 vols. (1893–7), vol. 4 • PRO, PROB 6/28, fol. 50r
Archives Claydon House, Buckinghamshire, corresp. and MSS; family MSS, 7/2–37
Likenesses Egmont, oils, 1648, Claydon House, Buckinghamshire; repro. in Verney and Verney, eds., *Memoirs*, vol. 2, facing p. 320

Verney, Sir Edmund Hope, third baronet (1838–1910). *See under* Verney, Margaret Maria, Lady Verney (1844–1930).

Verney, Ernest Basil (1894–1967), physiologist and pharmacologist, was born in Cardiff on 22 August 1894, the fourth son and fifth child of Frederick Palmer Verney, a farmer from Branston, north Devon, and his wife, Mary Ann née Burch, who came from Bradford, Somerset. Verney grew up on a farm at Hever, Kent, and in Tonbridge. His education began in 1904 at Judd School, Tonbridge, and in 1910 he obtained a leaving exhibition to Tonbridge School. He began on the classical side but transferred to the scientific, and was encouraged to take up medicine. He was awarded an exhibition in science at Downing College, Cambridge (1913). He gained a first class in part one of the natural sciences tripos (1916) and entered St Bartholomew's Hospital with the Schuster entrance scholarship in anatomy and physiology. Having qualified as MRCS and LRCP in April 1918, he joined the Royal Army Medical Corps as a regimental medical officer.

On demobilization in 1919 Verney began a year's house-physician appointment at St Bartholomew's and developed an interest in renal function. He then worked as house physician in the East London Hospital for Children (Shadwell). While working in Shadwell he met Ruth Eden Conway, the resident medical officer. They were married in 1923. She was the eldest daughter of Robert Seymour *Conway, Hulme professor of Latin in the University of Manchester, and his wife, Margaret Hall. They had two sons and a daughter.

While holding various clinical appointments, Verney obtained the MB BCh (Cantab., 1921) and the MRCP. In 1921 he opted for the academic side of medicine. E. H. Starling appointed him assistant in the department of physiology at University College, London. There Verney began fundamental work on renal physiology. In 1924 he became assistant in the medical unit at University College Hospital under the director, T. R. Elliot. During this period he held junior and fourth-year Beit memorial research fellowships. In 1926 he was appointed to the chair of pharmacology at University College. He became FRCP in 1928. In 1934 he moved to Cambridge, and in 1946 became first Sheild professor of pharmacology. In 1961 he retired as emeritus professor of pharmacology. He then held a personal chair for three years in Melbourne, Australia, after which he returned to live in Cambridge.

Verney's work was always meticulously planned. Much of it was on isolated organs, but his aim was to obtain results from animals in conditions which were as near normal as possible; that is, the animals should be healthy, contented, and, when possible, conscious. With colleagues he examined a number of factors responsible for regulating heart rate and blood pressure. Above all, Verney is remembered for his work on the kidney and on water balance. He showed clearly that water excretion was in part controlled by the hypothalamus and the posterior pituitary, that in conscious animals normal water diuresis followed renal denervation, and that there were central nervous osmoreceptors sensitive to changes in plasma osmotic pressure. He also studied the effects of exercise and emotion on renal function.

Verney had a lively and individual sense of humour. At times his comments were pungent. He was also a man of great kindness. He taught by example how much care must be taken in all details of experimental work. Verney carried on working very long hours despite a period of ill health involving two surgical operations. In committees his opinion was highly valued, as it always stemmed from careful preliminary study and thought.

Verney's abilities received wide recognition. In 1936 he was elected a fellow of the Royal Society. He gave a number of public lectures: the Goulstonian of the Royal College of Physicians (1929); the Sharpey-Schafer of the University of Edinburgh (1945); the Croonian of the Royal Society (1947); the Dunham of Harvard (1951); and the John Malet Purser of Trinity College, Dublin (1954). In addition he was elected an honorary fellow of Downing College (1961) and of the Hungarian and Finnish medical societies (1938 and 1949). He was awarded medals by the Royal College of Physicians (Baly medal) and by the universities of Liège and Ghent (1946 and 1948). He died in Addenbrooke's Hospital, Cambridge, on 19 August 1967, just before presentation of the Schmiedeberg-Plakette of the Deutsche Pharmakologische Gesellschaft.

MARY PICKFORD, *rev.*

Sources I. de B. Daly and L. M. Pickford, *Memoirs FRS*, 16 (1970), 523–42 · personal knowledge (1981) · *CGPLA Eng. & Wales* (1968) · **Archives** Wellcome L., corresp. and papers | Wellcome L., corresp. as editor of *Journal of Physiology* · **Likenesses** Bassano and Vandyk Studios, photograph, 1936, RS · W. Stoneman, photograph, 1936, RS · W. Sievers Ltd, photograph, repro. in Daly and Pickford, *Memoirs FRS* · **Wealth at death** £16,577: probate, 10 Jan 1968, *CGPLA Eng. & Wales*

Verney [née Nightingale], **Frances Parthenope**, **Lady Verney** (1819–1890), genealogist and author, was born on 19 April 1819 at Naples, the first among the two children of William Edward Nightingale, formerly Shore (1794–1874), and his wife, Frances (Fanny), née Smith (1789–1880). She and her sister, Florence *Nightingale, were given names after their birthplace, Parthenope being the Greek form of Naples.

After their three-year tour in Italy the Nightingales returned to Britain in 1821 and lived at Lea Hurst, Derbyshire, but from 1825 wintered at Embley Park, near Romsey, Hampshire, with visits to London. Parthe (also known as Pop) and Flo enjoyed visits from numerous cousins and distinguished guests, but Parthe was usually eclipsed by her prettier, strong-willed sister. They were educated at home by governesses, but from 1832 their father taught them Greek, Latin, German, French, Italian, history, and philosophy. Parthe was less scholarly than Florence, and turned to her socialite mother, Fanny. Nevertheless, she was fluent in French, acquired a lasting love of literature, and developed artistic talents allied to close observation of fauna and flora, later expressed in *Sketches from Nature with Pen and Pencil* (1877). Like Florence she benefited from the family continental tour (September 1837–spring 1839) and mingling in cultured circles in Italy and Paris.

To Florence's passionate friendships, rejected suitors, and alarming medical ambitions Parthe reacted with alternate submission and anger, adoration and jealousy. Later, like her mother, she was impressed by the official support for Florence's Crimean venture, and supported her work. On her return—as a celebrity—she guarded her sister's privacy. At Lea Hurst, Parthe was a devoted charitable visitor, closely observant of local life, stories, and dialect. Her latent talents blossomed when, on 24 June 1858, she married Florence's rejected suitor the handsome widower Sir Harry *Verney, formerly Calvert, second baronet (1801–1894), MP for Buckingham, supporter of liberal causes, and model landowner at Claydon House, Middle Claydon, Buckinghamshire. She soon made Claydon a salon for people of talent, and conscientiously visited tenants. Her marriage also released her energies as an author, with a gift for fiction and for social comment.

Lady Verney's novels, mostly set in the 1820s, present love stories in traditional societies, with close rendering of working-class occupations and regional dialects. The first three, published anonymously, were *Avenhoe* (1867), *Stone Edge* (1868), a story of Derbyshire farmers involving a tragic death, and *Lettice Lisle* (1870), which deals with Hampshire yeomen and smuggling. *Fernyhurst Court* (1871), 'an everyday story', is a middle-class romantic comedy, while *Llanaly Reefs* (1873) deals with Welsh seamen. In *The Grey Pool and other Stories* (1891) the title story depicts the grim life of bargees and poachers, while *Hasty Feet Sorrow Meet* is a remarkably realistic study of a Welsh strike, in which miners, mine owner, and union leader are all sympathetically portrayed.

The diverse articles collected in *Essays and Tales* (1891) show the same imaginative and critical gifts: 'Lady Verney's essays on dreams, on female education in France, on the dignity of labor, and on the decline of honorable dealing among the English commercial classes are the work of a first-class mind' (Mackerness, 136). Several publications expressed her strong views on landownership, as in *Cottier Owners, Little Tales and Peasant Properties* (1885). Drawing from her continental travels, first-hand enquiries, and official documents, she argued that the system of peasant patrimony, leading to tiny, scattered holdings, produces a life of grinding toil, poor returns, and brutal poverty. English farming, with its modern methods and machinery, she presented as more efficient, with the wage-earning labourer enjoying a better diet and culture. She contrasted peasant/aristocrat enmity with the English scene, where the 'big house' and park are 'the museum, entertainment ground and convalescent home of the neighbourhood' (*Cottier Owners*, 25). This thesis may be one-sided, but it reflected practice at Claydon, where large parties of schoolchildren came to spend a day in the park, and villagers gathered for tea, football, dancing, games, and fireworks. In these sociological tracts, which have in mind the problems of contemporary Ireland, she comes closest to her celebrated sister.

Lady Verney is best remembered, however, for her scholarly work at Claydon, seat of the Verneys for fourteen generations, where she 'threw herself into the congenial task of rescuing and renewing the interesting family relics which were falling into decay' (M. M. V., 'Memoir', xi). Portraits were restored and identified, furniture and carving installed, and gardens beautified. Above all she ordered the Verney family papers in the neglected long gallery, including letters (which amounted to no fewer than 30,000 up to the death of Sir Ralph in 1696), parchments, charters, account books, and rent rolls— papers merely sampled by Bruce in his Camden Society articles of 1845 and 1853. Drawing on this copious material, she first wrote *The House of Claydon and its Inhabitants, from 1480 to 1769* (repr. in *Essays and Tales*, 15–24). Then, contending with the painful arthritis which afflicted her in the 1880s, she completed volume 1 and drafted volume 2 of *Memoirs of the Verney Family during the Civil War* (1892). She was encouraged by the historian S. R. Gardiner, who wrote an introductory note for volume 1, and was helped by Sir Harry's daughter-in-law Margaret Maria *Verney, who continued the work. Parthenope delighted not only in the famous civil war heroes but also in 'the great stream of life of common people' (vol. 1, preface).

After a painful illness Lady Verney died on 12 May 1890 at Claydon House.   JOHN D. HAIGH

Sources M. M. V. [M. Verney], 'Memoir', in F. P. Verney, *Essays and tales* (1891), vii–xvi • E. D. Mackerness, 'Frances Parthenope, Lady Verney (1819–90)', *Journal of Modern History*, 30 (1958) • C. Woodham-Smith, *Florence Nightingale, 1820–1910* (1950) • S. R. Gardiner, 'Introductory note', in F. P. Verney, *Memoirs of the Verney family during the civil war*, 1 (1892), v–viii • F. P. Verney, 'Preface', *Memoirs of the Verney family during the civil war*, 1 (1892), ix–xvi • M. M. Verney, 'Preface', in F. P. Verney, *Memoirs of the Verney family during the civil war*, 2 (1892), v–vi • *The Times* (13 May 1890), 5 • *Claydon House*, National Trust (1981)
Archives Claydon House, Buckinghamshire, corresp. and papers | BL, corresp. with Florence Nightingale, Add. MS 45791 • UCL, letters to Sir Edwin Chadwick
Likenesses W. B. Richmond, portrait, 1869, Claydon House, Buckinghamshire; repro. in F. Parthenope, Lady Verney, *The grey pool and other stories* (1891), frontispiece
Wealth at death £46,410 2s. 6d.: probate, 7 July 1890, *CGPLA Eng. & Wales*

Verney, Sir Francis (1584–1615), pirate, was the elder son of Edmund Verney (1535–1600) of Penley, Hertfordshire, and Middle Claydon, Buckinghamshire, who was knighted in 1597 or 1598. Sir Edmund's first marriage had been childless and Francis's mother was his second wife, Audrey (1543–1588), daughter of William Gardner of Fulham and widow of Sir Peter Carew the younger. Shortly after her death Edmund Verney married Mary, daughter of William Blakeney of Sparham, Norfolk, and widow in turn of Geoffrey Turville of New Hall Park, Leicestershire, and William St Barbe of Ashington, Somerset. His father's remarriage had a radical effect on Francis Verney's future. It gave him a half-brother—Edmund *Verney (1590–1642), later famous as Charles I's standard-bearer slain at Edgehill—and in 1597 or 1598 (39 Elizabeth) their father obtained an act of parliament to divide his estates almost equally between his two sons and protect his widow's life interest in his estates. His father's remarriage also gave Francis a wife: in June 1599 he was married to Ursula St Barbe (1585–1668), his stepmother's daughter from her second marriage. The children were fourteen and twelve respectively, only just above the minimum legal age for marriage.

Verney matriculated at Trinity College, Oxford, aged fifteen, on 19 September 1600 and four years later, on 14 March 1604, he was knighted at the Tower of London. By then he was living in St Dunstan-in-the-West, London, where one of his servants was killed in a brawl. Verney was running up debts, and his uncle sought permission on his behalf from Robert Cecil to cut down timber to help pay off his creditors. However, when Francis himself made a similar request in March 1605 to 'fell certain timber growing upon his own land, which he might fell when he came to full age' his motive was not merely 'for the discharge of divers gentlemen that stood engaged' (*Salisbury MSS*, 17.115). Rather he was directly challenging the provision made by his father for his stepmother and younger half-brother at his expense. Lady Verney immediately complained that Francis had used Cecil's permission as a warrant to intrude on her jointure, carrying off her wood and destroying the rabbit warrens which she had leased out. The following year Francis took his campaign to parliament and in March 1606 sought to get the act of 39 Elizabeth overturned. The matter was quickly thrown out by the Commons: members could remember Sir Edmund's great efforts to get it passed and if it fell too many buyers' property rights would be at risk. Unhappily married and pursued by his creditors Francis Verney sold off his estates in the course of 1607 and 1608. During this period he journeyed to Jerusalem and back, where he acquired a pilgrim's staff inlaid with crosses.

By the end of 1608 Verney had left England for good. By the autumn of 1609 he was at Tunis: on 19 November the Venetian ambassador in London reported that the Levant Company was arming its Mediterranean ships against corsairs, 'who have recently been joined by a certain Francis Verney, an Englishman of very noble blood who has gone through a fortune of four thousand crowns a year' (*CSP Venice, 1607–10*, 386). A week later an Englishman in Madrid reported to a compatriot in Brussels that Verney had turned pirate. In May 1610 the Venetian ambassador reported again that some Venetian ships had been captured and their crew 'taken as slaves to Barbary'. Upon their release the sailors reported that Verney had lost some of his ships and that he was 'in great poverty and deeply in debt to the Turks' (*CSP Venice, 1607–10*, 481). In December the ambassador wrote that Verney was working closely with the pirate John Ward, that both had converted to Islam (as Arabic sources confirm about the latter), and that they had recently captured two ships sailing from Lisbon to Italy.

It is quite likely that Verney continued in his piracy until he was captured by a Sicilian galley. According to the Scottish traveller William Lithgow he was enslaved for two years, after which he was 'redeemed by an English Jesuit upon a promise of his conversion to the Christian faith' (*Rare Adventurs*, 228). On 25 August 1615 Verney entered the hospital of St Mary of Pity in Messina, Sicily, but died ten days later on 6 September 1615. He was buried by Lithgow who bewailed 'sorrowfully the miserable mutability of fortune, who from so great a birth had given him so mean a fortune' (ibid.). John Watchin, an English merchant, brought home to England relics of Verney's life in the Mediterranean: the pilgrim's staff, a purple Turkish robe, a turban, two pairs of Turkish slippers, and an enamelled ring. These are still kept at Claydon House, where there is also a fine portrait of Verney as a fashionable Jacobean gentleman. His widow was married again in 1619, to William Clark of Hitcham, Buckinghamshire, this time

directly against the wishes of the groom's father. The tradition of the Verney family—the family of his half-brother Edmund—remembered Francis as 'a great traveller' who 'fought several Duellos' (Verney, *Memoirs*, rev. edn, 1.48).

NABIL MATAR

Sources Foster, *Alum. Oxon.* • J. Bruce, ed., *Letters and papers of the Verney family down to the end of the year 1639*, CS, 56 (1853) • *CSP Venice, 1607–13* • *The rare adventurs and painful peregrinations of William Lithgow*, ed. G. Phelps (1974) • *Memorials of affairs of state in the reigns of Q. Elizabeth and K. James I, collected (chiefly) from the original papers of … Sir Ralph Winwood*, ed. E. Sawyer, 3 vols. (1725), vol. 3 • F. P. Verney and M. M. Verney, *Memoirs of the Verney family*, 4 vols. (1892–9), vol. 1 • F. P. Verney and M. M. Verney, *Memoirs of the Verney family during the seventeenth century*, 2nd edn, 4 vols. in 2 (1907), vol. 1 • *Calendar of the manuscripts of the most hon. the marquess of Salisbury*, 17, HMC, 9 (1938), 115 • *CSP dom., 1603–10*, 182
Archives Claydon House, Buckinghamshire, family papers
Likenesses attrib. D. Mitjens, portrait, Claydon House, Buckinghamshire

Verney [*formerly* Calvert], **Sir Harry**, **second baronet** (**1801–1894**), politician, was the son of General Sir Harry *Calvert, first baronet (*bap.* 1763, *d.* 1826), whose *Journals* he published in 1853, and his wife, Caroline (*d.* 1806), daughter of Thomas Hammersley. He was born on 8 September 1801 and educated at Harrow School; he then went to the Royal Military College, Sandhurst, where he was one of the earliest cadets (1818–19).

Calvert received his commission in the 31st foot, and was sent to Stuttgart at seventeen as attaché to Sir Brook Taylor's mission, with introductions to the old king's daughters, the queen of Württemberg and the electress of Hesse-Homburg, who entertained him kindly, as did King John of Saxony at Dresden. While abroad he perfected his French and German, and studied Italian. On his return in 1820 he joined the 7th fusiliers at Londonderry; he served also with the 72nd and 52nd regiments, and then entered the Grenadier Guards, where he became adjutant. He acted for a time as Sir Herbert Taylor's private secretary at the Horse Guards.

With the zeal to acquire knowledge which distinguished him throughout life, Calvert put himself to school again when he could obtain leave of absence from his military duties. In 1822 he studied with John Marriott (1780–1825), curate in charge of Broadclyst, to whom he became deeply attached; and while in Devon he laid the foundation of a lifelong friendship with Sir Thomas Acland and his family.

In 1826, after the death of his father, Calvert succeeded to the title. On the death of his cousin Mrs Verney of Claydon House, Buckinghamshire, he assumed the surname Verney in place of Calvert, by royal licence dated 23 March 1827. He found himself owner of an estate heavily burdened and long neglected, at a period of agricultural distress and widespread discontent; giving up his hopes of distinction as a soldier, he prepared to learn the new duties he had assumed with the name of Verney. Before he could settle down as a country squire, however, his father's old friend, Lord William Cavendish Bentinck, was made governor-general of Bengal, and Verney accepted

Sir Harry Verney, second baronet (1801–1894), by Frederick Richard Say [detail]

his offer to accompany him as military secretary; but, falling ill on the voyage out, he was left behind at Rio de Janeiro, and never rejoined his chief. He recovered his health by hunting with the Indians and riding wild horses on the pampas; he made a perilous journey across the snow-covered Andes, collected birds and insects, learned Spanish, and threw himself into the politics and wars of the small South American states, narrowly escaping death while helping to put down an insurrection at Santiago. At one time he took part in resisting some fresh claims of the papacy, which an Italian mission had been sent to assert. Years afterwards he was received at the Vatican by the once obscure young priest—by that time the pope—who had been employed in the mission, but Pius IX would allow no reference to the circumstances of their former meeting. After a year of romantic adventures, extending to Chile, Verney sailed round Cape Horn in the *Volage*, commanded by Michael Seymour, and returned to Claydon in 1829.

In 1835 Verney married Eliza, daughter of Sir George Hope, one of Nelson's captains at Trafalgar; they had four sons and three daughters. At Claydon he proved himself a model landlord. He drained and reclaimed the land, built and repaired cottages, founded schools, planted trees, and, by taking a much more active share in poor-law work and county business than was usual at that time among country squires, raised the tone of quarter sessions, and helped to give greater regularity and publicity to the proceedings. He knew George Stephenson, acquainted himself with the working of the new system of railroads, and,

with more foresight than his neighbours, he welcomed railways on his estate when other landowners were ordering their gamekeepers to warn off the surveyors, or to put an end to their operations by force.

When cholera broke out among the duck breeders of Aylesbury in 1832 and panic spread through the town, Sir Harry rendered energetic and fearless service to the sick and dying; later in 1832 he was at Paris during a far more terrible outbreak of cholera, and visited the hospitals. After these experiences he worked arduously to collect funds for a county hospital, the establishment of which at Aylesbury he considered one of the happiest events of his life. During a part of these busy years (1831, 1832, and 1833) Verney was studying at Downing College, Cambridge; being older than the other undergraduates, he lived chiefly with the fellows and tutors, and enjoyed the friendship of Adam Sedgwick and William Whewell.

On 10 December 1832 Verney was elected for Buckingham, for which he sat (with two short interruptions) for fifty-two years. A Liberal in politics, he was an ardent supporter of the abolition of the slave trade, and the repeal of the corn laws; he voted for factory legislation, the amendment of the criminal law, and the abolition of university tests, of Jewish disabilities, and of the paper duties; in later years he supported the disestablishment of the Irish church, the Elementary Education Act, the abolition of army purchase, and the successive measures for the extension of the franchise. He promoted the social reforms of Lord Shaftesbury, his old schoolfellow at Harrow and close friend; he was an active member of the Bible Society, the Church Missionary Society, and the Evangelical Alliance, and was able to render good service to the foreign protestant churches and pastors whom he loved to visit. In religious opinion he was of the old evangelical school, but his sympathies were broad.

An early member of the Royal Geographical Society, Verney had a remarkable knowledge of geography and a keen interest in every fresh discovery; he attended the Brussels conference on Africa in 1876, when King Leopold gave him his portrait, and afterwards kept up the acquaintance by correspondence. Verney was one of the founders of the Royal Agricultural Society; he attended its jubilee in 1888, when he was welcomed by the prince of Wales as the 'father' of the society. Verney's own political jubilee was celebrated at Buckingham in 1883 but the borough was disfranchised in 1885; he was then made a privy councillor.

Verney's first wife died in 1857. He at once married, in 1858, Frances Parthenope Nightingale (1819–1890) [*see* Verney, Frances Parthenope], elder daughter of William Edward Nightingale and sister of Florence Nightingale. It was under Verney's roof at Claydon that Florence Nightingale spent many of her bedridden years. Verney, who remained an active horseman to the last, died at Claydon, aged ninety-two, on 12 February 1894.

M. M. VERNEY, *rev.* H. C. G. MATTHEW

Sources *The Times* (13 Feb 1894) · *The Record* (16 Feb 1894) · F. P. Verney and M. M. Verney, eds., *Memorials of the Verney family*, 4 vols. (1892–9) · C. Hussey, 'Claydon House, Buckinghamshire, I', *Country*

Life, 112 (1952), 1278–81 · H. Verney, ed., *The Verneys of Claydon* (1969)

Archives Bodl. Oxf., letters · Claydon House, Buckinghamshire, corresp. and papers | BL, corresp. with W. E. Gladstone, Add. MSS 44353–44785 · BL, corresp. with Florence Nightingale, Add. MS 45791 · Bucks. RLSS, corresp. with first Baron Cottesloe · Bucks. RLSS, letters to Dr John Lee relating to county infirmary · HLHRO, corresp. with J. G. Shaw-Lefevre · Hunt. L., letters to Grenville family · W. Sussex RO, letters to duke of Richmond

Likenesses G. Hayter, group portrait, oils (*The House of Commons, 1833*), NPG · G. Hayter, study; formerly at Claydon House, Buckinghamshire · H. A. Pegram, bronze bas-relief, Middle Claydon church · G. Richmond, portrait, Buckinghamshire Health Authority, Aylesbury · W. B. Richmond, portrait, Claydon House, Buckinghamshire · F. R. Say, portrait; Christies, 4 Aug 1950, lot 33 [*see illus.*] · Spy [L. Ward], chromolithograph caricature, NPG; repro. in *VF* (15 July 1882) · F. J. Williamson, bust, Middle Claydon church

Wealth at death £25,643 14*s*. 11*d*.: resworn probate, Oct 1895, *CGPLA Eng. & Wales* (1894)

Verney, John, first Viscount Fermanagh (1640–1717), merchant and landowner, was born on 5 November 1640, second son of Sir Ralph *Verney MP, first baronet (1613–1696), of Middle Claydon, Buckinghamshire, and Mary Blacknall (1616–1650), heir of John Blacknall of Abingdon, Berkshire. At the age of seven John joined his family in Blois, France, in exile from the civil war. Because Sir Ralph feared any taint of popery, John was taught by protestant tutors. Although he never saw himself as a scholar, his life in France exposed him to continental codes of civility and politeness. He penned beautiful letters under the tutelage of Claudius Mauger, the author of epistolary manuals. John later owned works by Descartes, Montaigne, and Cervantes, as well as classical and religious books.

When the family returned to England in 1653, Verney studied at the Barn Elmes School with James Fleetwood, later bishop of Worcester. After it was closed by the authorities, John entered Samuel Turberville's school in Kensington. He reluctantly mastered writing, grammar, and 'an indiferent Latine', but he was mainly interested in business. 'One must have some living now adayes', he wrote. 'I doe veryly thinke that I am a great deale fitter to bee [in] some trade than to bee a la[w]yer' (Verney, *Memoirs*, 3.360, 367). In June 1659 Sir Ralph sent John to Mr Rich's school, where he received a commercial education and learned merchants' accounts.

On 31 December 1659 Sir Ralph paid £400 and signed a £1000 bond to apprentice John Verney to Sir Gabriel Roberts (1635–1715), a Levant Company merchant. John hoped that his career would be 'noe less satisfactory' to his father 'then if I had beene an Inns of Court Gentleman'. 'I never delighted in … any thing else soe much as I doe in this trade', he wrote, and 'in hearing of Business both inland and outland' (Verney, *Memoirs*, 3.374). John now spent his days in Sir Gabriel's warehouse learning to weigh and measure silk.

Finally, on 31 April 1662, Verney sailed on the *Dover Merchant* to Iskenderun, the port of Aleppo. There he joined the Levant Company and lived with other English merchants in their own khan. After six years of struggle with little capital or connections, on 28 July 1668 he received the company's liberty to trade for his own account. He eventually amassed a fortune large enough to set himself up as a London merchant. In 1674, when he returned to England, he claimed a fortune of £6000.

In London John Verney obtained his freedom of the Levant Company on 15 December 1674 and of the Vintners' Company on 21 November 1674, where he rose to liveryman and junior warden. He avoided holding office in the corporation of London, but served on tax commissions and grand juries. He was a governor of the Bridewell and Bethlem hospitals and a governor of the Royal Africa Company in 1679–81, 1686–8, 1691–2, and 1696–7. John regularly sent English cloths to the Levant in return for silk and other imports.

On 27 May 1680 John married Elizabeth Palmer (1664–1686), daughter of Ralph Palmer of Little Chelsea. On 10 July 1692 he married, secondly, Mary Lawley (1661–1694), daughter of Sir Francis Lawley, baronet, and after her death he wed, on 8 April 1697, Elizabeth Baker (1678–1736), daughter of Daniel Baker, a London haberdasher. Their three portions injected £9500 into the Verney estate. John had four children, all with his first wife, Elizabeth: Elizabeth, a spinster; Margaret, who married Sir Thomas Cave; Mary, who married Colonel John Lovett; and Ralph, who married Catherine Paschall of Great Baddow, Essex. His children's eighteenth-century alliances with landed families contrasted with John's own seventeenth-century marriages to three London women, whose fathers profited from business affairs.

After his first marriage, John Verney chose not to live with his City colleagues. He moved outside the walls to Hatton Garden, 'that being in the middle between the Exchange and Westminster' (Verney to John Lovett, 17 March 1706, Verney MS M/636, 53). He enjoyed a varied social life in the West End with his Verney relatives as well as with City friends from the Exchange. In the 1670s he frequented coffee houses from Tom's to Garraway's and sampled services at the French church and a presbyterian meeting-house. He also enjoyed the sermons of Dr John Tillotson and Dr Edward Stillingfleet. During the exclusion crisis he was present at parliament and at anti-papist spectacles. At the time of the Popish Plot he attended state trials and amassed a large pamphlet collection, now at Cambridge University Library. As the century waned, Verney shed his early sympathies for dissent and became immersed in high-church and tory party politics.

By 1690, however, the early deaths of Verney's elder brother, Edmund, and Edmund's two young sons unexpectedly made John his father's heir. John continued some trading as late as 1692, but he shifted assets into new investment alternatives, including £1900 in government funds from 1690 to 1693 and a further £5400 from 1696 to 1702. He also invested in the East India Company, Million Bank, and traded Bank of England stock and exchequer bills.

In September 1696 Verney succeeded his father as second baronet. He developed an intense interest in his lineage and spent countless hours annotating family letters.

With the help of the antiquarian Browne Willis, he compiled a directory of baronets. He immediately plunged into Buckinghamshire politics, standing for the county seat in 1696, 1698, and 1701, and for Buckingham in 1698. With little local support, he failed in each attempt. However, his candidacy helped the tory leader, William Cheyne, with whom John formed a valuable alliance. Queen Anne created John Viscount Fermanagh and Baron Verney of Belturbet, Ireland, on 16 June 1703, probably at Cheyne's behest.

From 1701 to 1709 Verney refused to meddle in parliamentary elections, but built a strong local interest as a justice of the peace and deputy lieutenant. In 1710 Dr John Cockman summarized John's transformation from London merchant to tory politician: 'He lives now at an extravagant rate and gains ground in these parts' (Cockman to Arthur Charlett, 16 Sept 1710, MS Ballard 21, fol. 123).

In 1710, at the age of seventy, Fermanagh stood for the county seat as a tory. He took first place with 2161 votes and spent almost £800. Plagued by gout, stone, and deafness, his activity was restricted. But he was a member of the October Club and dined at the Fountain tavern in the Strand. His name appeared on several lists as a tory in 1710 and 1712.

In 1713, with the help of his third wife, Elizabeth Baker, Fermanagh again won the county seat with 2018 votes. In contrast to Sir Ralph's day, mobs of revellers filled Claydon House with 'the noise of either drums, trumpet, haut boy, pipes, or fiddles and some days 400 guests' (John Verney to Ralph Verney, 8 Jan 1713, Verney MS M/636, 55). His expenses were almost £500, and he also won a safe seat at Amersham.

Fermanagh's refusal to stand again in 1715 was one of the factors leading to a whig–tory compromise in which one candidate from each party stood for the county seat. Although his excuse was old age, John 'did not think himself kindly us'd last time in relation to Amersham', which in 1713 had not been given to his son, Ralph (E. Fermanagh, to William Cheyne, 21 Sept 1714, Cheyne MSS, Ellesmere MS 10705).

In 1715 Fermanagh stood for Amersham unopposed. Although his name appeared on a list of Jacobite supporters, John's whig brother-in-law Daniel Baker considered him a loyal tory: 'You have too good an estate and are too much a Protestant and lover of the country than to embark in any such wicked design as to bring in the Pretender' (Daniel Baker to John Verney, 24 Dec 1715, Verney MS M/636, 55). One of Fermanagh's last acts was to vote against the Septennial Bill. He died at Claydon on 23 June 1717 and was buried at Middle Claydon church. His son, Ralph, inherited a healthy estate and his father's Amersham seat. It was Fermanagh's successful transition from Levant Company merchant to tory politician that enabled future generations of Verneys to marry heiresses and become land buyers. SUSAN E. WHYMAN

Sources S. Whyman, *Sociability and power in late-Stuart England: the cultural worlds of the Verneys, 1660–1720* (1999) • S. Whyman, 'Land and trade revisited: the case of John Verney, London merchant and baronet, 1660–1720', *London Journal*, 22/1 (1997), 16–32 • BL, Verney MS M/636 (1–60) [microfilm] • S. Ranson, 'The Verney papers catalogued for the Claydon House Trust', 1994, Claydon House, Buckinghamshire • J. Broad, 'Sir John Verney and Buckinghamshire elections, 1689–1715', *BIHR*, 56 (1983), 195–204 • M. M. Verney, *Memoirs of the Verney family*, another edn, 3–4 (1899) • M. M. Verney, ed., *Verney letters of the eighteenth century*, 2 vols. (1930) • M. Motley, 'Educating the English gentleman abroad: the Verney family in seventeenth-century France and Holland', *History of Education*, 23 (1994), 243–56 • PRO, PROB 11/558, fols. 364–5 • poll books, Buckinghamshire, Bucks. RLSS, D/C/3/61, D/X 933, D/MH/40/1, PB/17/1, D/FR/128/11 [1685, 1700–01, 1702, 1710, 1713, 1722] • Verney collection of Popish Plot pamphlets, CUL, MS Sel 2.114–26 • Levant Company court of assistants' minutes, 1660–1706, PRO, SP 105/152–156 • Hatton Garden assessments, 1692–3, 1693–4, Corporation of London Record Office, MS 83, fol. 7; MS 42, fol. 3 • Vintners' Company court minutes, 1669–82, GL, Guildhall MS 15201/5 • Vintners' Company, warden's account books, GL, MS 15333/5–6 • Royal Africa Company, court of assistants' meetings, 1664–1713, PRO, T70/76–88 • Royal Africa Company, General court minutes, 1671–1720, PRO, T70/100–101 • Exchequer receipt books, 1690–1717, PRO, E401/1985–2040 • Bodl. Oxf., MS Ballard 21 • Hunt. L., Cheyne papers, Ellesmere MSS 10440–11146 • HoP, *Commons, 1715–54*

Archives BL, letters [microfilm] • Bucks. RLSS, letters to John Baker • Claydon House, Buckinghamshire, papers • CUL, Popish Plot pamphlets, Sel 2.114–26 • Dartmouth College, Hanover, New Hampshire • Princeton University, New Jersey

Likenesses attrib. T. Murray, portrait, priv. coll.; repro. in Whyman, *Sociability and power* • G. Van Soest, portrait, Claydon House, Buckinghamshire; repro. in Verney, *Memoirs*, vol. 3, p. 351 • portrait, Claydon House, Buckinghamshire; repro. in Verney, *Memoirs*, vol. 4, facing p. 160

Verney, John (1699–1741), judge, was born at Brasted in Kent on 23 October 1699, the fifth son of George Verney, twelfth Baron Willoughby de Broke (1661–1728), of Compton Verney, Warwickshire, and his wife, Margaret (d. 1729), the daughter and heir of Sir John Heath (1614–1691) of Brasted, Kent. He matriculated at New College, Oxford, in 1714, but the need to provide for himself, being a younger son in an impoverished aristocratic family, led him towards a career in law, and accordingly the following year he was admitted a student at the Middle Temple. He received his call to the bar *ex gratia* in 1721, and was soon seeking to improve his range of contacts and clients through entry into parliament. At the general election the next year he obtained a borough seat at Downton, Wiltshire, through the offices of his brother-in-law Anthony Duncombe (later first Baron Feversham).

Following his family's politics Verney initially featured in the Commons as a tory, speaking against Sir Robert Walpole's ministry in January 1724. His tory connections were extended in significant new directions when on 16 September that year he married Abigail (d. 1760), the only daughter of Edward *Harley (the auditor) of Eywood, Herefordshire, whose brother had been Queen Anne's lord treasurer, Robert Harley, earl of Oxford. The marriage produced a son and a daughter. The political views of his in-laws, however, were not enough to prevent him from taking the vocationally more advantageous step of joining ranks with the government's whig supporters, a transition which he successfully accomplished by January 1726. Walpole, finding in him a quick and willing spokesman for the government, appointed him in November to a junior position on the Welsh bench as second justice on the Brecon circuit.

Thus, still in his mid-twenties, Verney was widely regarded as a rising figure in his profession; one acquaintance, commenting at this time on his immense industry, wrote that he 'was so immersed in the law that it is impossible to get a word about anything else out of him' (BL, Add. MS 70400). In July 1727 he was made a king's counsel, and in the year following became a bencher at Lincoln's Inn. At the general election in the summer of 1727 he engaged in a tough campaign at Radnor, formerly an electoral stronghold of his Harley in-laws, and within his judicial province. Despite support from the duke of Chandos, who was steward of the local manors, he was defeated but was returned once more at Downton. He continued to cut a prominent figure on the government side in the Commons, though not always with aplomb; on one occasion he 'very ridiculously' exposed his ignorance of fiscal matters and was 'lashed' by the City MP Sir John Barnard (*Portland MSS*, 8.458). In May 1729 he was included in a clutch of appointments to the royal household, accepting the post of attorney-general to Queen Caroline, which he held until her death in 1737. He resigned from the Welsh bench in May 1732 owing to ill health, but in December 1733 resumed his career by taking office as chief justice of Chester with a salary of £730. He chose not to stand again at the election the following year.

Verney's strong public-spiritedness is indicated by the senior role he assumed during these years in such bodies as the commission for building new churches in London, Dr Radcliffe's trust, and the corporation for the sons of the clergy. Eager for further advancement, he lost no time in applying to Lord Chancellor Hardwicke for the mastership of the rolls upon the death of its aged incumbent, Sir Joseph Jekyll, on 19 August 1738, claiming that this had been the summit of his ambitions for some time. Verney was not Hardwicke's immediate choice, however, but when the post was turned down by the solicitor-general, John Strange, the appointment of Verney was decided before the month had closed. Formally taking office on 9 October, he was sworn of the privy council on 12 October. Within a few years, however, Verney's performance of his duties had become badly hindered by worsening attacks of gout, and prolonged absences from chancery proceedings compelled him early in 1741 to offer Hardwicke his resignation. He was re-elected to parliament for Downton at the May election as part of his plan to pursue a less arduous public career, but his death, 'universally regretted', occurred on 5 August before a successor at the rolls could be found. He was buried near his seat at Compton Verney, Warwickshire. His only son, John, succeeded his father's elder brother in 1752 as the fourteenth Baron Willoughby. Verney was survived by his wife.   A. A. HANHAM

Sources Foss, *Judges*, 8.176–7 • HoP, *Commons, 1715–54*, 1.381; 2.451–2, 495–6 • W. R. Williams, *The history of the great sessions in Wales, 1542–1830* (privately printed, Brecon, 1899), 46 • Sainty, *King's counsel*, 92 • GEC, *Peerage*, new edn, 12/2.695, 697 • Sainty, *Judges*, 151 • BL, Add. MS 35586, fols. 73, 87, 329 • John Wainwright to second earl of Oxford, 15 Feb 1726, BL, Add. MS 70400 [unfoliated] • will, 1741, PRO, PROB 11/711/215 • Foster, *Alum. Oxon.* • *The manuscripts of his grace the duke of Portland*, 10 vols., HMC, 29 (1891–1931), vol. 8

Likenesses Ramsay, portrait, Compton Verney, Warwickshire • G. Vertue, line engraving (after A. Ramsay), BM, NPG • oils, Middle Temple, London

Wealth at death estates at Compton and Brasted; rectory, parsonage, and other lands at Otford, Kent: will, 1741, PRO, PROB 11/711/215

Verney, Sir John, second baronet (1913–1993), artist and writer, was born on 30 September 1913 at 12 Connaught Place, London, the elder son and first of three children of Sir Ralph Verney, first baronet (1879–1959), public servant, and his wife, Janette Cheveria Hamilton Walker (b. 1889), an heiress from Sydney, Australia. A great-grandson of Sir Harry *Verney MP (1801–1894), he spent part of his childhood in India. His father was military secretary (1916–21) to Lord Chelmsford, the viceroy, and then secretary to the speaker of the House of Commons (1921–55), receiving a baronetcy in 1946.

While a pupil at Eton College John Verney began to do comic drawings in the style of Heath Robinson and submitted some unsuccessfully to *Punch*. The thought of becoming an artist already appealed to him, but he chose to study history at Christ Church, Oxford (1932–5), where he finished with a third-class degree. He then trained for a year at the Architectural Association, London, before entering the film industry and working as an assistant director with Charles Laughton and Robert Donat. Contemporary art and literature were his main interests, however, and it was partly to combat his own introspectiveness that he joined the North Somersetshire yeomanry. On 29 March 1939 he married (Jeanie) Lucinda Musgrave (b. 1916/17), known as Jan, gave up his job in film, and moved to Chelsea having resolved to paint.

Called up in September 1939, Lieutenant Verney served initially in Palestine. He took part in the invasion of Syria in 1941 and the western desert campaign in 1942 before volunteering for the Special Air Service (SAS). 'Operation Swann' parachuted him into Sardinia in July 1943 to blow up German aircraft. When captured, he escaped from a train and rejoined the Eighth Army after three months in the Abruzzi mountains. Bouts of malaria thereafter did not prevent his fighting in France and Germany as a major in the Royal Armoured Corps. He received the Military Cross (1944) and the Légion d'honneur (1945).

Verney returned to painting after his demobilization in November 1945. His work was diverse, as he experimented with the abstract, surreal, and figurative manners, and used oils, watercolour, and gouache. His love for English domestic architecture was manifest in his townscapes, but many of his most striking pictures showed characteristic touches of the fantastic, mischievous, and absurd. Always keen on decorating his frames, he later painted all sorts of secondhand furniture: fanciful visions of the garden of Eden on a wardrobe, for instance, or the rape of the Sabine women on a table-top. He exhibited—diffidently—every two years or so at such galleries as the Leicester, Redfern, and New Grafton in London. Illustrating for children provided him with some steady income.

Verney drew more than a hundred cover-pictures and much else for *Collins' Magazine for Boys and Girls*, a monthly founded in 1948 and renamed the *Young Elizabethan* in 1955, which he briefly edited in 1961–2. His sketchy pen and ink drawings, likened to those of Edward Ardizzone, illustrated several books by Gillian Avery, Anthony Buckeridge, and others. Working in the converted stable of his home, Runwick House, on the outskirts of Farnham, Surrey, he enjoyed being surrounded by his seven children—two boys and five girls. The premature death of his elder son, Julian (1940–1948), was the worst trauma of his life.

By the time he became second baronet in February 1959, Sir John Verney had gained a reputation as a writer, based on *Going to the Wars* (1955), a vivid account of his years in the army which subtly blended humour and seriousness. Critics judged it one of the finest personal memoirs of the Second World War by a British serviceman. He described his return to Italy in peacetime in *A Dinner of Herbs* (1966). He wrote two semi-autobiographical novels, *Every Advantage* (1961) and *Fine Day for a Picnic* (1968), but more successful were his children's books (with drawings by himself), including *Friday's Tunnel* (1959), *February's Road* (1961), *The Mad King of Chichiboo* (1963), and *ismo* (1964).

A desire to conserve historic local buildings led Verney to help found the Farnham Trust in 1968, when he won election to Farnham urban district council as an independent. For a noted humorist, Sir John could seem melancholy and remote on first acquaintance: a slight man with a grandly upper-class voice, who wore a shabby old overcoat and battered hat and rode a rusty bicycle. However, his superficial air of world-weariness was in large part a droll disguise. He took great delight in good company, irreverent wit, and sheer nonsense. From 1965 his comic inventiveness found an outlet in the *Dodo-Pad*—an annual 'combined memo-doodle-engage-diary-message-ment book', ostensibly compiled by a Lord Dodo of Doodle, that came pre-defaced with odd proverbs, silly cartoons, and snippets of useless information. It sold over 30,000 copies per year at its peak in the 1970s.

In 1977 Verney moved to the White House, Clare, Suffolk, where he continued to paint and write and also served as chairman of the Gainsborough Museum at Sudbury in the early 1980s. He died there on 2 February 1993.

JASON TOMES

Sources *Daily Telegraph* (5 Feb 1993) · *The Times* (5 Feb 1993) · *The Independent* (4 Feb 1993) · *The Guardian* (15 Feb 1993) · J. Verney, *Going to the wars* (1955) · A. Horne, *The dictionary of 20th century British book illustrators* (1994) · B. Peppin and L. Micklethwaite, *Dictionary of British book illustrators: the twentieth century* (1983) · b. cert. · m. cert. · d. cert.
Wealth at death £175,156: probate, 30 June 1993, CGPLA Eng. & Wales

Verney, John Henry Peyto, twentieth Baron Willoughby de Broke (1896–1986), horse-racing administrator and air force officer, was born on 21 May 1896 at Compton Verney, Warwickshire, the only child of Richard Greville *Verney, nineteenth Baron Willoughby de Broke (1869–1923), and

his wife, Marie Frances Lisette (*d.* 1941), fourth and youngest daughter of Charles Hanbury of Belmont, Hertfordshire. Educated at Eton College until July 1914, he entered the Royal Military College, Sandhurst, and was commissioned in the 17th lancers in 1915. After a brief period at the cavalry training regiment in Ireland he joined his regiment in France later that year and served at the front in France continuously until the end of the war. In November 1918 he was wounded and awarded the MC for gallantry in action in the final breakthrough. He then went to Bombay as aide-de-camp to Sir George Ambrose Lloyd, governor of Bombay, from 1920 to 1922. After serving as adjutant to the Warwickshire yeomanry in 1922–5 Verney left the army in 1925.

In 1923 Verney had succeeded to the barony (and become *de jure* heir-general to the barony of Latimer). He spent the next few years as an amateur rider on the turf and as master of the Warwickshire foxhounds. He learned to fly in 1926, and was a well-known figure at air rallies. On 4 October 1933 he married Rachel Bourchier Wrey (1911–1991), only child of Sir Robert Bourchier Sherard Wrey, eleventh baronet. They had a son, Leopold David Verney (*b.* 1938), who succeeded as twenty-first baron, and a daughter, Susan Geraldine. In 1936 Willoughby de Broke formed the 605 (County of Warwick) squadron, Auxiliary Air Force, acting as its commander. He was removed as commanding officer in 1940 before the battle of Britain on account of his age and the conversion of the squadron to Spitfires. He served in the battle of Britain as a wing commander on the staff at fighter headquarters, Stanmore. He was awarded the AFC in 1941 and then was promoted to group captain and made assistant director (1941–4) and later director (1945–6) of public relations at the Air Ministry.

Elected to the Jockey Club in 1941, Willoughby de Broke became senior steward in 1946 and 1956. He reshaped racing for the post-war era and introduced the still camera for race results and later the film camera for race supervision. In his latter period as senior steward he was responsible for all negotiations for the Betting Bill of 1958, leading the Jockey Club representation and initiating race sponsorship by private firms. Subsequently he was concerned mainly with racecourse administration and was chairman of Birmingham, Cheltenham, and Wolverhampton racecourses, all of which he managed successfully.

The Verney family originally had an extensive estate of upwards of 13,000 acres in south Warwickshire. It was good strong land, fertile enough to produce good crops of corn and for fattening bullocks. The family had always lived up to their income and it had been necessary to sell some land after the eighteenth baron's death. When the nineteenth baron died death duties were onerous after the First World War, and agricultural income (and therefore rents) had collapsed. As a result the Compton Verney mansion and most of the agricultural land had to be sold to pay death duties on the nineteenth baron's estate. Willoughby de Broke therefore moved first to Woodley House, a large house in Kineton on the Wellesbourne road, and subsequently to Fox Cottage on the outskirts of Kineton.

A further drain on the Verney finances was the St Martin's Theatre, purchased by the nineteenth baron in 1916 at the height of the wartime entertainment boom, which failed to provide a profitable income during the depression. It was not until refurbishment after the end of the Second World War that it was sold on for a satisfactory figure. Accordingly, Willoughby de Broke always struggled to maintain his preferred standard of living and at the same time to provide for his family. As a result the family Zoffany was sold for more than £3 million, which enabled the current family settlements to be extended.

Willoughby de Broke was a highly intelligent, active man with a wide range of interests. He became lord lieutenant of Warwickshire in 1939 and held that office until he retired in 1967. He was an energetic local leader and was much concerned with the establishment of Warwick University and the rebuilding of Coventry Cathedral. His wife provided the firm base from which he could operate his manifold interests—wine, the theatre, aviation, racecourse administration, and running his small string of racehorses under the Jockey Club and National Hunt rules. A very good and amusing speaker, fluent in French, his annual speech at the Prix de L'Arc de Triomphe dinner was an event that was eagerly awaited on both sides of the channel. He was admired by all shades of party politics in his county and he was able to count on the support of both town and country when Birmingham and Coventry were still a part of the county of Warwick. His old age was spent mostly in London and by the time he was eighty-seven he needed full-time nursing. He died in a London nursing home on 25 May 1986, just four days after his ninetieth birthday, which he had set his heart on achieving. He was buried on 29 May among his ancestors at Chesterton.

WILLIAM DUGDALE

Sources Burke, *Peerage* (1953) · Burke, *Peerage* (1956) · Burke, *Peerage* (1963) · Burke, *Peerage* (2000) · Burke, *Gen. GB* (1914) · Kelly, *Handbk* (1965) · Kelly, *Handbk* (1972) · *The Times* (28 May 1986) · Richard, nineteenth Baron Willoughby de Broke, *The passing years* (1924) · R. Bearman, ed., *Compton Verney: a history of the house and its owners* (2000) · minutes of stewards and proceedings of members, 1941–80, Jockey Club, 42 Portman Square, London [esp. 1946 and 1956] · *Sporting Life* (28 May 1986) · Shakespeare Birthplace Trust RO, Stratford upon Avon, Verney family papers · personal knowledge (2004) · private information (2004) [Leopold David Verney, son and twenty-first baron; daughter] · R. Mortimer, R. Onslow, and P. Willett, *Biographical encyclopedia of British flat racing* (1978) · *WW* (1982)

Archives Shakespeare Birthplace Trust RO, Stratford upon Avon
Likenesses double portrait, photograph, 1922 (with Henry Hoare), Hult. Arch. · photograph, Jockey Club, Newmarket
Wealth at death £1,147,000: probate, 1987, *CGPLA Eng. & Wales*

Verney [née Hay Williams], **Margaret Maria**, **Lady Verney** (1844–1930), historian and promoter of higher education in Wales, was born at 66 Lower Grosvenor Street, London, on 3 December 1844, the elder daughter and coheir of Sir John Hay Williams, second baronet (1794–1859), of Bodelwyddan, co. Flint, and his wife, Lady Sarah Elizabeth Pitt Amherst (bap. 1801, d. 1876), only daughter of William *Amherst, first Earl Amherst of Arracan. On the death of

Margaret Maria Verney, Lady Verney (1844–1930), by Sir William Blake Richmond, 1869

Sir John Hay Williams in 1859 his family retired to Rhianva (later spelt Rhianfa), a house which he had built for them on the Menai Strait in Anglesey.

On 14 January 1868 Margaret Hay Williams married **Edmund Hope Verney** (1838–1910), the son of Sir Harry *Verney, formerly Calvert, second baronet (1801–1894), and his wife, Eliza, née Hope (d. 1857); they had one son, Sir Harry Calvert Williams Verney (1881–1974), and three daughters. Born on 6 April 1838 and educated at Harrow School, Edmund Verney had become a captain in the Royal Navy, and had been decorated for service in the Crimea and in the Indian revolt. His personal account of the latter was published as *The Shannon's Brigade in India* (1862); this, and his detailed letters home to his father, formed the basis for his great-nephew Ralph Verney's subsequent account of the mutiny *The Devil's Wind* (1956). Edmund Verney afterwards served on the Pacific seaboard of Canada (1862–5), where he found 'the country more interesting than the people' (Pritchard, 33); his letters home have been published as *The Vancouver Island Letters of Edmund*

Hope Verney, edited by Allan Pritchard (1996), and some of the artefacts he brought home are in the British Museum. Afterwards he commanded a vessel stationed off west Africa, and retired from active service in 1872, having been partially disabled in a shooting accident on the family's Buckinghamshire estate three years earlier. He represented Brixton on the first London county council and served as member of parliament for North Buckinghamshire, 1885–6 and 1889–91. A Gladstonian Liberal and a supporter of Irish home rule, he wrote a tract against imperial expansion, *Four Years of Protest in the Transvaal* (1881). His public career ended abruptly with his expulsion from the House of Commons in May 1891 following his conviction at the central criminal court on a charge of conspiring to procure for a criminal purpose an under-age girl, one Nellie Maud Baskett. He was sentenced to a year in prison. This was a notable and very public fall for one who had been noted for his piety, and who listed 'collector of early editions of the Bible' among his recreations in *Who's Who*. He succeeded to the baronetcy in 1894 on the death of his father (he and Lady Verney already resided partly at the family home at Claydon, Buckinghamshire), and died after a short illness on 8 May 1910.

Lady Verney, in the meantime, had divided her time and interest between her Buckinghamshire and Anglesey homes. In both localities she took an active interest in the community, especially in education and nursing. She served on the rural school boards, was co-opted to the Buckinghamshire county education committee, and originated the association for the loan of pictures to schools; later she started a similar scheme for Anglesey. In Wales her activities extended to higher education in connection with the University College of North Wales at Bangor; she was an original member of the court of governors, and a memorial scholarship in her name was set up shortly after her death. She was a member of the University of Wales court (afterwards the council) from 1894 to 1922, and she continued thereafter to represent that body on the court of the National Library of Wales and on the Bangor council. In 1919 she was appointed junior deputy chancellor of the university, and received the honorary degree of LLD. As a convinced Liberal, Lady Verney worked enthusiastically for her husband and son in their election campaigns. Throughout her life she showed indomitable industry and real breadth of view, well supported by unfailing courage, patience, and humour.

Lady Verney's principal achievement, however, lay in the literary work which she took up as an amateur and completed as an acknowledged authority. She continued the work begun by Frances Parthenope *Verney, the sister of Florence Nightingale and second wife of Sir Harry Verney, who had first discovered the historical value of the seventeenth- and eighteenth-century letters, diaries, and accounts preserved at Claydon House. Her illustrated history of the Verney family down to 1650 was completed for the press by Margaret Maria Verney as volumes 1 and 2 of *Memoirs of the Verney Family*, with a preface by S. R. Gardiner, in 1892. These were followed by volume 3 (1650–60) in 1894, and by volume 4 (1660–96) in 1899, which were

entirely her own work. The Claydon manuscripts, including over 30,000 letters dated before 1700, with drafts and copies of answers, required elaborate arrangement and comparison. The work attracted so much attention that a thoroughly revised reissue in two volumes appeared in 1904, and there were subsequent editions in 1925 and 1971.

In addition to contributions about the Verneys to magazines and the six articles she wrote for the *Dictionary of National Biography*, Lady Verney published a short *Memoir of Sir Henry Cunningham* (1923), and a textbook of county history, *Bucks. Biographies* (1912), for use in elementary schools. Later she returned to the family papers, and just before her death (1930) saw through the press two supplementary volumes, the first of which dealt with the correspondence of John Verney, Viscount Fermanagh (1696–1717), and the second with that of the two earls Verney (1717–91). Her editions of the Verney papers remain useful, though her selection of material, being informed by the historiographical preferences of the time, favoured public events over private and family concerns. It is the wealth of domestic detail that has attracted more recent scholars to base further work on the archive.

Lady Verney died at Rhianfa on 7 October 1930 and was buried on 10 October at nearby Llandegfan. The memorial tablet placed in Middle Claydon church in 1936 recalls her as 'steadfast in faith and unwearied in work … diligent as the historian of Claydon'.

H. E. D. BLAKISTON, rev. H. J. SPENCER

Sources *In memory of Margaret Maria, Lady Verney* (1930) • private information (1937) • personal knowledge (1937) • b. cert. • m. cert. • d. cert. • Burke, *Peerage* (1859); (1959); (1999) • *The Times* (10 May 1930); (8 Oct 1930); (11 Oct 1930); (4 Dec 1930) • *WWBMP*, vol. 2 [Capt. Edmund Hope Verney] • *WWW*, 1897–1915 [Verney, Sir Edmund Hope] • A. Pritchard, ed., *The Vancouver Island letters of Edmund Hope Verney* (1996) • memorial inscription, Middle Claydon church, Buckinghamshire • *Claydon House*, National Trust (1999)

Archives Claydon House [NT], Buckinghamshire, corresp., journals, and literary papers

Likenesses W. B. Richmond, oils, 1869, Claydon House, Buckinghamshire [*see illus.*] • photograph

Wealth at death £6974 12s. 1d.—save and except settled land: probate, 26 March 1931, *CGPLA Eng. & Wales*

Verney, Sir Ralph, first baronet (1613–1696), landowner and politician, was born on 9 November 1613 at Hillesden, Buckinghamshire, the son of Sir Edmund *Verney (1590–1642) and his wife, Margaret Denton (1594–1641). When Ralph was fifteen years old Sir Edmund paid £1000 to the court of wards to obtain a decree that permitted his son's marriage to Mary Blacknall (1616–1650), sole heir of John Blacknall, a wealthy Abingdon lawyer. Despite the protests of Mary's family, and the fact that at thirteen she was under legal age, she married Ralph on 31 May 1629. Attempts to get her to repudiate the marriage failed, and she brought the Verneys estates including Abingdon and Wasing in Berkshire and Preston Crowmarsh and Fifield in Oxfordshire. The couple lived apart until 1631, when Mary settled at the Verneys' Buckinghamshire seat at Middle Claydon. For two years Ralph spent college terms 20 miles away at Magdalen Hall, Oxford, where he formed ties with sons of important puritan families. He studied astronomy, arts, and Latin, but apparently not Greek, and spent 3–4 hours a day on logic and divinity with his tutor, John Crowther.

The couple had only two surviving children, Edmund (1636–1688) and John *Verney (1640–1717). After 1634 Verney's family lived part of each year in Covent Garden, London, with his father. Yet Verney always felt more natural giving country hospitality and he abhorred court compliment. He also became immersed in business affairs at an early age. He managed the Verneys' estates and finances and acted as trustee for friends.

Verney had deep feelings about his family's importance, and saved every scrap of paper, founding perhaps the largest consecutive family correspondence for seventeenth-century England. His prudent, conscientious nature and attention to detail showed most clearly in his methodical preservation of his papers, which remain at Claydon House. An ardent bibliophile, he also amassed many books and pamphlets, especially religious tracts. He was deeply interested in the theology and practice of the Church of England, and his own faith was tinged with a puritanical piety expressed in strict outward observance. Thus he refused to hire a gardener until he discovered whether he was 'married or popish or phanatical or takes tobacco' (Verney MSS, Ralph Verney/John Verney, 14 July 1679, BL, M/636 [33]).

In 1640 Verney represented Aylesbury in the Short and Long Parliaments, and was knighted in 1641. As he sat next to his father he secretly recorded his impressions, which may be read in *Notes of Proceedings in the Long Parliament*, published in 1845. As a young man with parliamentary sympathies, his position was difficult. His father was knight-marshal and standard bearer to Charles I, and he died at Edgehill in 1642 fighting for the king. Ralph Verney's younger brothers also served in the royalist army. At first he supported parliament, which caused grief to his family. However, he soon became disenchanted with political and religious radicalism, and in 1643 he refused to sign the solemn league and covenant, which pledged its signatories to religious reform and the removal of episcopacy. Moreover, the Verney estates were under financial strain, and Claydon House was located amid military positions. Rising taxes, decreasing rents, and the disruption of war combined to make his financial situation precarious.

Verney withdrew from parliamentary work in the summer of 1643, and fled to France in November, using the alias Ralph Smith. Prior to his flight he obtained letters of protection from both parliament and the royalists, and placed his property in trust. In 1645 he was expelled from parliament for absenting himself from his duties. It was, he confessed, 'one of the greatest and most inexpressible afflictions that ever yet befel me, for which my soul shall mourn in secret' (Gardiner, 2.23).

Verney's voluntary exile took him to Paris, Rouen, and then Blois. His decision to leave England was probably motivated by a combination of deep religious principles, loyalty to the traditional Church of England, his unstable finances, and the threat of sequestration. This indeed took place in October 1646, owing to a flawed trust deed. Sequestration was lifted only in 1648, when his wife, Mary, journeyed to England and lobbied friends in parliament. She died soon after her successful intervention, in May 1650.

Verney returned to England in 1653, but he was briefly imprisoned as a royalist suspect in 1655 and was fined in 1656. He had inherited an estate worth about £2200 per annum, but he had debts of £7700, fixed expenses of £1470, and responsibility for nine brothers and sisters. Rebuilding the Verney estate became a lifelong obsession. To obtain needed cash he sold all but a tiny portion of his late wife's dower lands. But he doggedly kept his Claydon estate intact through frugal living and debt consolidation at low rates. He avoided the court, improved his estate, and cleared it of debts.

After the Restoration Verney regained his county offices in the magistracy and lieutenancy and accepted a baronetcy in 1661. He did not re-enter parliament, however, until the 1680s—representing Buckingham in 1681, 1685, and 1689. His later religious and political views were grounded in his desire for peace and moderation after a life marred by sectarian feuding. The books that he gave to his sons reflected the midstream of religious thought: Jeremy Taylor's *The Rule and Exercises of Holy Living* (1658) and *The Rule and Exercises of Holy Dying* (1663), and Allestree's *The Whole Duty of Man* (1668). He also kept a stock of prayer books written by Dr Thomas Tenison to give as gifts to friends. He refused to take sides during the exclusion crisis, and only when the bishops and the church were threatened by James II did he finally back the revolution of 1688. Although he was a firm supporter of the crown he maintained a country independence and low-church sympathies.

Verney's enemies called him a 'trimmer', yet his trimming grew out of strength not weakness, and he commanded immense local respect. During elections in the 1680s he refused to treat the Buckingham populace, but he later contributed to their town hall, a decision of consequence in securing a successful outcome in the fiercely contested 1685 election. In 1686 he was removed from the county bench, and in 1688 from the lieutenancy, after he refused all three questions put by James II's agents concerning the repeal of the penal laws and Test Act. Yet in the Convention Parliament he voted for agreeing that the throne was not vacant, and subsequently appeared on several blacklists. In the 1690s he spent most of the year in Lincoln's Inn Fields, London. He died at Middle Claydon on 24 September 1696 aged eighty-two, leaving a healthy estate to his younger son, John, a London merchant, and was buried at Middle Claydon church. His family pride is reflected in the monument he erected at Claydon, with busts of his parents, his wife, and himself.

SUSAN E. WHYMAN

Sources S. Whyman, *Sociability and power in late-Stuart England: the cultural worlds of the Verneys, 1660–1720* (1999) · J. Broad, 'Sir Ralph Verney and his estates, 1630–1696', DPhil diss., U. Oxf., 1973 · S. Ranson, 'The Verney papers catalogued for the Claydon House Trust', 1994, Claydon House, Buckinghamshire · F. P. Verney and

M. M. Verney, *Memoirs of the Verney family*, 4 vols. (1892–9) · BL, Verney MS M/636 (1–60) [microfilm] · PRO, PROB 11/460, fol. 73 · *Seventh report*, HMC, 6 (1879) [Sir Harry Verney] · J. Bruce, ed., *Letters and papers of the Verney family down to the end of the year 1639*, CS, 56 (1853) · J. Bruce, ed., *Verney papers: notes of proceedings in the Long Parliament*, CS, 31 (1845) · J. Broad, 'Gentry finances and the civil war: the case of the Buckinghamshire Verneys', *Economic History Review*, 2nd ser., 32 (1979), 183–200 · M. Slater, *Family life in the seventeenth century: the Verneys of Claydon House* (1984) · S. Whyman, '"Paper visits": the post-Restoration letter as seen through the Verney archive', *Epistolary selves* (1999) · J. P. F. Broad, 'The Verneys and the sequestrators in the civil wars, 1642–1656', *Records of Buckinghamshire*, 27 (1985), 1–9 · L. Stone, 'The Verney tomb at Middle Claydon', *Records of Buckinghamshire*, 16 (1953–60), 67–82 · M. W. Helms, L. Naylor, and G. Jagger, 'Verney, Sir Ralph', HoP, *Commons, 1660–90* · S. R. Gardiner, *History of the great civil war, 1642–1649*, new edn, 2 (1893) · G. Lipscomb, *The history and antiquities of the county of Buckingham*, 4 vols. (1831–47) · W. Le Hardy and G. L. Reckitt, eds., *Calendar to the sessions records, county of Buckingham*, 1–4 (1933–51)
Archives Claydon House, Buckinghamshire, corresp. and MSS | Hunt. L., letters to Sir Richard Temple
Likenesses C. Johnson, oils, 1634, Claydon House, Buckinghamshire; repro. in Verney and Verney, eds., *Memoirs*, vol. 1 · E. Marshall, sculpture on family monument, 1653, All Saints' Church, Middle Claydon, Buckinghamshire; repro. in Verney and Verney, eds., *Memoirs*, vol. 3 · P. Lely, oils, *c.*1680, Claydon House, Buckinghamshire; repro. in Verney and Verney, eds., *Memoirs*, vol. 4
Wealth at death In 1688 Middle Claydon estate valued at £1078, with fixed expenses of £266 (debts and annuities); Sir Ralph also controlled son's East Claydon estate, valued at £1300 in 1688 with debts and annuities of £390 (this estate however reverted to the Abels of East Claydon); Sir Ralph had not expanded estate but cleared it of major debts and sold off other estates except Wasing, Berkshire: Broad, 'Gentry finances and the civil war', 198; Broad, 'Sir Ralph Verney and his estates, 1630–1696', 214–17

Verney, Ralph, second Earl Verney (1714–1791), politician, was born on 1 February 1714, the second son of Ralph Verney, first Earl Verney (1683–1752), landowner of Middle Claydon, Buckinghamshire, and his wife, Catherine (*d.* 1748), daughter of Henry Paschall of Baddow Hall, Essex. He was educated at Brentford, Middlesex, from 1721 and entered the Middle Temple in 1729. He was admitted fellow-commoner of Christ's College, Cambridge, on 20 April 1733, and graduated MA in 1735. His elder brother, John (1711–1737), died on 3 June 1737, leaving a widow, Mary, *née* Nicholson (*d.* 1789), with an unborn child. Ralph was therefore confirmed as heir to the family title and estates and styled Lord Fermanagh only when his sister-in-law gave birth to a daughter, Mary (1737–1810), on 21 October 1737. On 11 September 1740 he married Mary (1716–1791), daughter and coheir of Henry Herring, of Egham, Surrey, a London merchant and director of the Bank of England, but the couple were childless. As one of the largest landowners in Buckinghamshire, Verney inherited a substantial fortune, to which was added a wedding dowry in excess of £40,000. 'A man of great plainness' (*GM*, 61/1, 1791, 383), he ultimately squandered this wealth through ruinous extravagance, injudicious business dealings, and an absurd generosity that also destroyed his parliamentary interest.

Shortly after his father's death, on 4 October 1752, Verney embarked upon lavish improvements to Claydon House, designed to outshine the palace constructed at Stowe by his Buckinghamshire rivals, the Grenvilles, and thus make Claydon the political and cultural centre of the county. A new wing, with a suite of rococo rooms by Luke Lightfoot, was added, and work was begun on a domed rotunda and great ballroom, designed by Sir Thomas Robinson, but these were unfinished at Verney's death and were demolished in 1792. By 1770 Verney was laying out the gardens with trees and plants obtained from the Southern Netherlands. He also collected books, pictures, and works of art for Claydon and sought further fame as a patron of literature to add to the pleasure he derived from his election as FRS on 20 April 1758. In his heyday he cut a magnificent figure:

> Lavish in his personal expenses, and fond of show, he was one of the last of the English nobility who, to the splendour of a gorgeous equipage, attached musicians constantly attendant upon him, not only on state occasions but in his journeys and visits: a brace of tall negroes with silver French horns behind his coach and six, perpetually making a noise. (Lipscomb, 1.183–4)

Verney also spent profusely on politics. The first earl had built up a strong interest at Wendover and on 17 January 1753 Verney returned himself as MP for the borough, which he represented until 1761. He was a regular government supporter in the Commons and placed one seat at Wendover at the duke of Newcastle's disposal in both 1754 and 1761. In 1761 he used the second seat to bring in his cousin Major Verney Lovett (1705–1771). Meanwhile, he contested Great Bedwyn, Wiltshire, where he had been building up an interest since his purchase of the manor of Stock in 1752. However, he was soundly defeated by Lord Bruce's interest and came in instead for the Welsh borough of Carmarthen, where he paid £2000 to secure his return.

Verney, disappointed by his failure to obtain any patronage from Newcastle, remained a government supporter after Newcastle's resignation in 1762. On 9 December he seconded the address on the peace preliminaries on behalf of the Bute ministry. On 9 April 1763, the day after Bute's resignation, he set out his credentials for a British peerage in a letter to Henry Fox: 'My fortune is above £10,000 per annum … my own personal attachment to Government has been sincere, constant, and uniform … and … I have expended very large sums in several elections without obtaining, or indeed asking to this time, any favour whatever' (Bute MSS). On 29 April 1763 he similarly approached Grenville: 'My whole life', he wrote, 'has shown how much I have been inclined to forward the business of the Crown' (Smith, 2.49–50). Though Verney was offered no assurances he remained loyal to Grenville's administration when it was being run hard in the Commons over general warrants. The solitary exception to this record was his speech in favour of repealing the cider excise on 31 January 1764.

When Rockingham replaced Grenville at the Treasury in July 1765 he unexpectedly chose William Burke, a protégé of Verney, as under-secretary of state to Henry Conway. Verney was also rewarded by his appointment as a privy councillor on 22 November 1765, an unusual distinction for one who held no office. He brought in Edmund

Burke, William's relation, for Wendover on 23 December 1765. Meanwhile, Verney had been buying up the independent burgages at Great Bedwyn and even offered to buy out Lord Bruce. To retrieve control Bruce agreed to pay Verney 18,000 guineas and to bring in William Burke on 16 June 1766 for the existing vacancy.

Verney followed Rockingham into opposition in 1766. After his long experience of unrequited political support, the marquess's act of recognition had given him a lasting sense of gratitude. On 18 August 1767 Edmund Burke confirmed to Rockingham that Verney's interest was 'always at the service of the cause' (*Correspondence*, 1.322). For the next sixteen years Verney voted consistently with the party, although he almost never addressed the Commons. At the general election of 1768, when many of the Buckinghamshire country gentlemen signalled their unwillingness to accept the predominance of the Grenvilles, Verney was returned unopposed as one of the knights of the shire, a position he had long coveted. With Bruce's agreement William Burke was once more given one of the Great Bedwyn seats, while Verney again returned Edmund at Wendover. However, he unexpectedly lost control of the other seat through what Edmund later considered 'our own egregious neglects' (to Charles O'Hara, 9 Aug 1770, *Correspondence*, 2.148). Verney allowed his tenants to live rent free provided that they voted for his nominees, but he had reputedly become so easy-going about this arrangement that a secret understanding had been established by 'Mr. Atkins, a considerable lace manufacturer' (Oldfield, 1.40) in favour of Sir Robert Darling. Verney subsequently endeavoured to tighten up control at Wendover by ejecting voters from their houses and reinstating them only after extracting 'a promise of good behaviour in future' (Oldfield, 1.41). This allowed him to return his friend Joseph Bullock there unopposed in 1770 following Darling's death that year.

Verney's financial affairs were now deteriorating, but the lavish expenditure on Claydon was only partly to blame. His speculative purchases of West Indian lands fell heavily in value, an enterprising venture for the manufacture of French cambrics at Winchelsea backfired, and the initial success of his shareholding in the Ranelagh Gardens on the Thames was not sustained. Far worse were his incautious personal transactions in East India stock and his utterly reckless sense of generosity to the Burkes that financed similar speculations by William. Disaster now struck. The first great crash in East India stock in 1769 turned envisaged fortunes into ruinous losses, which the Burkes could not make good to Verney, whose own risk taking cost him dear. Still more catastrophic were the speculations on the Amsterdam market in which Verney and William Burke ran up an accumulated liability of £47,000 that fell entirely on the earl. By the general election of 1774 Verney's circumstances had brought him to virtual political impotence. There was no realistic prospect of making arrangements for William Burke's continuation at Great Bedwyn, and he was obliged to ask Edmund to find another constituency to allow him to sell

his seats at Wendover. Edmund, who successfully contested Bristol, readily understood. As he explained to Rockingham on 18 September 1774: 'He will, indeed he must, have those to stand for Wendover who can bear the charge which that borough is to him' (*Correspondence*, 3.33). None the less, he lamented 'the necessity which drives him to abandon the distinguished courses of disinterestedness and friendship, that has hitherto actuated him' (ibid., 3.33). Meanwhile Verney was somewhat fortuitously returned again unopposed for Buckinghamshire because of the last minute withdrawal for financial reasons of Richard Lowndes, whom Temple had hoped to run alongside his nephew and heir George Grenville jun. Despite a deteriorating relationship with the Grenville party, both sides were content for another uncontested county election in 1780 when Verney and Thomas Grenville were both returned. Verney again sold both his seats at Wendover which were filled without opposition.

The formation of the second Rockingham administration in March 1782 and the prominent appointments given to the Burkes temporarily gave Verney renewed hope. Yet nothing was done for Verney despite his loyal record over the preceding sixteen years. After Shelburne succeeded at the Treasury in July 1782 Verney distanced himself from Burke and signalled his support for the new minister. He then threw in his lot with the Fox–North coalition and voted for parliamentary reform on 7 May 1783 and for Fox's East India Bill on 27 November 1783. These changing political allegiances were largely motivated by Verney's desperation to hold his seat in order to protect himself from his creditors. His situation was now so poor that in 1783 he had been forced to sue Edmund Burke in chancery for a £6000 loan made in 1769. In the absence of any bond Verney failed to establish his claim. It seems likely that his capital had been swallowed up in William Burke's financial collapse. He did hold £20,000 in bonds against William, but the true debt was far in excess of this figure. In addition, he had a claim against Richard Burke for about £19,000, while Edmund was also estimated to owe £11,000. However, despite his distress, Verney 'would never rack up his tenants in their rents' (*GM*, 61/1, 1791, 383).

At the 1784 general election Verney was narrowly defeated by a Pittite candidate and petitioned in vain. He also failed at Wendover, having temporarily lost control of the borough and, deprived of parliamentary immunity from debt, fled his creditors to France. Such was his personal popularity, nevertheless, that a Buckinghamshire Independent Club was formed to give him political support, of which a committee of trustees and lawyers dealt with his debts, Wendover being sold in 1788.

At the general election of 1790 Verney, who had returned quietly from France, was elected for the county without opposition but at this moment of triumph the bailiffs were put in at Claydon, which they rapidly cleared. Local tradition states that a stable boy later found the septuagenarian earl wandering forlornly in the shuttered rooms of the empty, unfinished house. The boy fed and cared for his old master and concealed him for weeks in the house. Verney's confusion and gloom were exacerbated on 20 January 1791 when the countess died suddenly at their house in Curzon Street, Mayfair; she was buried at Middle Claydon on 4 February. Verney himself reportedly only eluded his creditors by escaping in his wife's hearse. The countess had borne her misfortunes 'with the greatest magnanimity, and readily parted with her money, and even her jewels, at times when Lord V. was pressed' (*GM*, 61/1, 1791, 383). Verney survived her by only a few weeks. He died at Curzon Street on 31 March 1791 still owing £115,731 5*s*. 8*d*. He was buried in the family vault at Middle Claydon on 8 April.

On his death Verney's titles became extinct. The family estates passed to his niece Mary, who on Pitt's recommendation was created Baroness Fermanagh of Ireland on 13 June 1792. Her uncle had held out for the full £20,000 plus interest owed to him by William Burke, but Richard Burke now agreed to pay her an immediate £5250 as composition with a vague agreement for a further £5000 four years later. This was unfulfilled and the baroness's lawyers unsuccessfully pursued William until his death in 1798. When she died unmarried on 15 November 1810 Lady Fermanagh bequeathed all her estates to her maternal half-sister Catherine (*née* Calvert, *d*. 1820), directing her husband, the Revd Robert Wright (*d*. 1827), to take the name and bear the arms of Verney.

PATRICK WOODLAND

Sources J. Brooke, 'Verney, Ralph', HoP, *Commons, 1754–90* · *The correspondence of Edmund Burke*, ed. T. W. Copeland and others, 10 vols. (1958–78), vols. 1–5 · M. M. Verney, ed., *Verney letters of the eighteenth century*, 2 vols. (1930), vol. 2 · *GM*, 1st ser., 61 (1791), 94, 383 · GEC, *Peerage*, new edn, 5.295–7 · J. Burke and J. B. Burke, *A genealogical and heraldic history of the extinct and dormant baronetcies of England, Ireland, and Scotland* (1838), 544–5 · G. Lipscomb, *The history and antiquities of the county of Buckingham*, 4 vols. (1831–47) · S. Ayling, *Edmund Burke: his life and opinions* (1988) · R. S. Lea, 'Verney, Ralph', HoP, *Commons, 1715–54* · D. R. Fisher, 'Verney, Ralph', HoP, *Commons, 1790–1885* · Cardiff City Library, Bute MSS · NMM, Sandwich MSS · *The Grenville papers: being the correspondence of Richard Grenville … and … George Grenville*, ed. W. J. Smith, 4 vols. (1852–3) · T. H. B. Oldfield, *The representative history of Great Britain and Ireland*, 6 vols. (1816) · *The last journals of Horace Walpole*, ed. Dr Doran, rev. A. F. Steuart, 2 vols. (1910) · R. W. Davis, *Political change and continuity, 1760–1885: a Buckinghamshire study* (1972) · Venn, *Alum. Cant.* · F. O'Gorman, *The rise of party in England: the Rockingham whigs, 1760–1782* (1975) · J. K. Fowler, *Records of old times* (1898), 62–3 · *VCH Buckinghamshire*, 4.34 · *Buckinghamshire*, Pevsner (1960), 206–9 · R. Fedden and R. Joekes, eds., *The National Trust guide*, 2nd edn (1977) · DNB · will, PRO, PROB 11/1205, sig. 258

Archives Claydon House, Buckinghamshire, MSS, (S)1–7

Likenesses two portraits, repro. in Verney, *Verney letters*, vol. 2

Wealth at death £115,731 5*s*. 8*d*.—owed; Claydon House inherited by niece; named wife as principal beneficiary, with minor bequests to servants and friends, but the countess predeceased him; Mary Verney, niece, granted possessions as next of kin: Ayling, *Edmund Burke*, 122; will, PRO, PROB 11/1205, sig. 258

Verney, Richard, eleventh Baron Willoughby de Broke (1622–1711), politician, was born on 28 January 1622 at Kingston, Warwickshire, the third of five children of Sir Greville Verney (1585/6–1642) and his wife, Katherine (1590/91–1657), daughter of Sir Robert Southwell and his wife, Elizabeth Howard, daughter of the first earl of Nottingham. Together with his younger brother George, he

was admitted to Jesus College, Cambridge, on 30 March 1640.

Verney and his family were neutral during the civil war, though with sufficient royalist sympathies to be assessed at £3500 by the committee for the advance of money. The Verneys were an old and wealthy Warwickshire family and though as a younger son Richard did not inherit much property at his father's death in 1642, he was able to purchase an estate at Allexton, Leicestershire, in 1652, which was valued at £1000 per annum in 1660. Shortly before this he married Mary Pretyman (*bap*. 1631, *d*. 1663), daughter of the royalist Sir John Pretyman of Lodington, Leicestershire, and his wife, Elizabeth Turpin. After Mary's death Verney married Frances, daughter and heir of Thomas Dove of Upton, Northamptonshire. Some time in the 1670s he moved to Belton, Rutland, and, at the death of his great-nephew William, on 23 August 1683, he inherited the principal Verney family estate at Compton Verney, Warwickshire.

With strong court support Verney was elected to parliament from Warwickshire in 1685, despite opposition from the whig Sir Richard Newdigate. He was knighted on 1 April 1685 after presenting a loyal address from his county to James II. He was 'discreetly absent' (*VCH Leicestershire*, 2.120) in 1687 when the questions were presented regarding the repeal of the Test Act and penal laws, and he was temporarily removed from office as a JP. Verney was elected from Warwickshire to the Convention Parliament and voted with the bulk of his fellow tories against declaring the throne vacant and making William and Mary king and queen. He was not returned to parliament in 1690.

At the prompting of his son John, Verney petitioned the House of Lords on 11 December 1694 to be formally recognized as Baron Brooke, tracing his claim to an individual writ of summons to the Lords received in 1491 by his ancestor Sir Robert Willoughby. Several objections were raised against this claim, including that an individual writ of summons in the fifteenth century did not automatically create a peerage; that if it did, it could not descend through a female line, as Verney's claim did; and that, even if it could so descend, the claim was extinguished first when it fell into abeyance and even more when Willoughby's direct heir, Sir Fulke Greville (1554–1628), was created Baron Brooke of Beauchamps Court on 29 January 1621. The current Baron Brooke especially objected to Verney's claiming the barony of Brooke, which may have influenced the Lords to reject his petition.

The following year Verney renewed his petition but this time, to appease Baron Brooke, claimed the title of Baron Willoughby de Broke. Despite the protest of some peers that the issue had already been decided the upper house voted to hear the case again. Verney's petition was approved on 13 February 1696 and he took his seat as Baron Willoughby de Broke on 27 February, at which time he signed the association in defence of William III. The pedigree submitted by Verney was published and the case became an important precedent for the inheritance of peerages.

In the Lords, Willoughby de Broke was a solid though

usually silent tory, opposing the Fenwick attainder bill, supporting bills against occasional conformity, and voting against the impeachment of Henry Sacheverell. He was more active in local affairs, including participating in election strategy meetings of Warwickshire tories. He served as justice of the peace in Warwickshire from 1660 to his death in 1711, as well as sheriff (1683–4) and deputy lord lieutenant (1686–7, 1689–1711) of that county and sheriff (1681–2) and deputy lord lieutenant (1682–8) of Rutland. He helped Sir William Dugdale in preparing his *Antiquities of Warwickshire* by drawing some local maps and monuments. Both Dugdale and the Rutland historian James Wright praised Verney as 'a true lover of Antiquities' (Wright, 22). Verney died on the night of 28 July 1711 at Compton Verney and was buried in the chapel there. He was survived by his second wife.

Verney's eldest son, John (1652–1707), was MP for Leicestershire in 1685 and again from 1695 to 1707, except for the last parliament of William III; his second son, George (1661–1728), became dean of Windsor and succeeded his father as Baron Willoughby de Broke. A third son, Thomas, a merchant, died in 1681 and a daughter, Mary, married Samuel Davenport of Calveley, Cheshire. From his second marriage Verney had a son, Richard, who died unmarried in 1698, and a daughter, Diana, who married Sir Charles Shuckburgh.   ROBERT J. FRANKLE

Sources HoP, *Commons, 1660–90*, vol. 3 · GEC, *Peerage*, new edn · *The manuscripts of the House of Lords*, new ser., 12 vols. (1900–77), vol. 1 · W. Dugdale, *The antiquities of Warwickshire illustrated*, rev. W. Thomas, 2nd edn, 2 vols. (1730) · J. Nichols, *The history and antiquities of the county of Leicester*, 3/1 (1800) · J. Wright, *The history and antiquities of the county of Rutland* (1684) · VCH *Leicestershire*, vol. 2 · VCH *Warwickshire*, vol. 5 · VCH *Rutland*, vol. 2 · *The life, diary, and correspondence of Sir William Dugdale*, ed. W. Hamper (1827) · Venn, *Alum. Cant.*
Wealth at death property at Compton Verney in Warwickshire, Belton in Rutland, and Ravensthorp in Northamptonshire, and probably elsewhere as well

Verney, Richard, thirteenth Baron Willoughby de Broke (1693–1752), poet and political writer, was the fourth of five sons of George, twelfth Baron Willoughby de Broke (1661–1728), and his wife, Margaret (d. 1729), daughter of Sir John Heath of Brasted, Kent. Verney's grandfather Richard *Verney (1622–1711) claimed the title of Lord Willoughby de Broke as a descendant of the second baron, and this was recognized in 1696, when he became the eleventh baron. Richard Verney was educated at Rugby School from 1699 before going to New College, Oxford, matriculating on 30 August 1711. His adult life was troubled by financial and matrimonial difficulties, possibly because his responsibilities were unexpected, his three elder brothers having died.

On 12 April 1717 Verney married Penelope Packe (*bap.* 1699), at St Martin-in-the-Fields, Westminster. In July the following year, after a violent quarrel with his father, he was disinherited and banished from Compton Verney, the family home in Warwickshire. Though he was later given an annuity, the estate was passed to his younger brother, John. On 31 August 1718 his first wife died. By 1720 he married Margaret or Elizabeth Walker or Williams (1702–

1767), daughter of Nehemiah of Newport, Wales, a seamstress of Bristol. Their only child, George, died in infancy. This second marriage did not last beyond 1732. He took his seat in the House of Lords on the death of his father.

In 1727 Verney wrote *The Craftsman Answered*, an essay in support of Sir Robert Walpole. His poem *Dances Out of State* (1733) led Pope to comment critically on him in *The Dunciad* (1735), and of his *Poem on the Safe Arrival of the Prince of Orange* (1733) Horace Walpole wrote '[the verses] are so ridiculously unlike measure, and the man was so mad and so poor, that I determine not to mention them' (Walpole, *Corr.*, 16.21). Walpole did, however, include Verney's poem in his *Royal and Noble Authors* (1758).

Though Verney contested his father's will, he was denied access to Compton Verney, and leased Farewell Hall, Staffordshire, seriously in debt. His wife refused to join him there. In 1736 he made off with Mrs Stiff, the wife of a stocking weaver, and in 1741 he assumed the title of earl of Carrick in Scotland, though he was entitled only to the barony of Kincleven. He died on 11 August 1752 and was succeeded in the title by his nephew John Verney (1738–1816).   F. D. A. BURNS

Sources GEC, *Peerage* · Foster, *Alum. Oxon.* · *Debrett's Peerage* (1995) · W. Dugdale, *The antiquities of Warwickshire illustrated*, rev. W. Thomas, 2nd edn, 1 (1730), 565–72 · *Manuscripts of the earl of Egmont: diary of Viscount Percival, afterwards first earl of Egmont*, 3 vols., HMC, 63 (1920–23), vol. 2, p. 218 · R. Bearman, 'The history of the Verney family', Shakespeare Birthplace Trust RO, Stratford upon Avon, typescript 20–22 · Shakespeare Birthplace Trust RO, Stratford upon Avon, DR 98/1326a–1327a, 1440, 1649/22–31, 42, 1658 · G. Tyack, *Warwickshire country houses* (1994), 64–70 · *Daily Advertiser* [London] (6 Feb 1741) · J. Nichols, *The history and antiquities of the county of Leicester*, 3/1 (1800), 361 · A. Pope, *The Dunciad*, ed. J. Sutherland (1943), vol. 5 of *The Twickenham edition of the poems of Alexander Pope*, ed. J. Butt (1939–69), 93 · D. F. Foxon, *English verse, 1701–1750: a catalogue of separately printed poems with notes on contemporary collected editions*, 1 (1975), v28–v30
Archives Shakespeare Birthplace Trust RO, Stratford upon Avon, family MSS
Wealth at death £300 annuity from his father begun in 1720; third assigned to second wife in 1734 when separation became permanent

Verney, Richard Greville, nineteenth Baron Willoughby de Broke (1869–1923), politician and fox-hunter, was born in London on 29 March 1869, the eldest son among the six children of Henry Verney, eighteenth Baron Willoughby de Broke (1844–1902), landowner, and his wife, Geraldine (1847–1894), the eldest daughter of James Hugh Smith Barry, of Marbury Hall, Cheshire.

Warwickshire landowner and fox-hunter In 1883 the Verney estates covered 18,145 acres, with over 12,000 acres in Warwickshire and sizeable holdings in another half-dozen counties besides. The agricultural depression of the late nineteenth century obliged Henry Verney to let the family seat, Compton Verney, near Stratford upon Avon, while the democratizing effects of the third Reform Act (1884) challenged the influence that he and other landowners traditionally exercised over county politics. His son and heir, Richard Greville Verney, felt the 'vertical breeze of political and economic upheaval' throughout his adult life (Verney, *The Sport of our Ancestors*, 16).

Verney, known to his family and friends as Grev, was educated at Eton College (1883–8) and at New College, Oxford (1888–92). He was sent to New College in the hope that he would take a degree and not spend all his time hunting, as his father had done at Christ Church. The bursar at New College, Alfred Robinson, urged upon him 'the serious life of the reading man', and appealed to his sense of duty to 'race, class, family, Eton' (Verney, *The Passing Years*, 150). Verney was inspired by Robinson but pulled up short at the prospect of seven hours' reading a day, his thoughts turning to the Irish bay horse that awaited him in stables in Merton Street. At Oxford he discovered that 'every day could be turned into a half-holiday', and he enjoyed himself even more than he had done at Eton (ibid., 152). Cheerfully forsaking the life of the scholar for that of the sportsman, he ambled to a third class in law, graduating BA in 1892.

Verney was directed to no particular profession at Oxford, but in hunting, playing cricket, and driving a coach and four he was aware of acquiring 'very necessary accomplishments in the life that seemed to be indicated for me' (Verney, *The Passing Years*, 165). Brought up in a 'sound Tory household', he conscientiously discharged the obligations that went with his rank. In October 1891 he became a lieutenant in the Warwickshire yeomanry cavalry, of which his father was lieutenant-colonel commandant (1891–1900); he retired in 1910 with the rank of major. Father and son sat on Warwickshire county council and on Kineton parish council, and in 1895 Richard Verney was elected Conservative member of parliament for Rugby. On 2 July of that year he married Marie Frances Lisette (*d.* 1941), the youngest daughter of Charles Addington Hanbury, of Belmont, East Barnet, Hertfordshire. They had one son.

Verney was a witty and forceful speaker, his fluent oratory peppered with hunting metaphors. He took to the political platform with ease and frequently addressed public meetings on topics ranging from home rule to death duties. In the House of Commons, by contrast, he seldom spoke. He made a short maiden speech on agricultural rates, on 28 April 1896, in which he stressed the paramount importance of British farming and the need for protection from foreign competition. But his depiction of landowners as an impoverished class left James Stuart, the radical member for Shoreditch, Hoxton, unconvinced. The poor in east London had a far greater claim, Stuart argued, to the tax relief that Verney wished to dole out to gentleman farmers. The exchange reveals one of the major fault-lines in the political landscape that Verney came to inhabit: 'A Radical', he once observed, 'was a person whose motto was "Down with everything"' (Verney, *The Passing Years*, 167).

Verney retired from the Commons in 1900 and in that year became master of the Warwickshire foxhounds, a post famously held by his father and grandfather before him. He wrote passionately about the sport, and in his elegant memoirs, *The Passing Years* (1924), lamented the damage done to the English countryside by roads and railways. He regarded the hunting of his youth as the twilight of a golden era that ended with the economic decline of the landed classes. When writing in the early 1920s he reflected that of all the generations into which he would have liked to have been born, that of his grandfather (*b.* 1810) would have been best. He would have reached seventy just before the agricultural depression set in and would have been untroubled by the democracy that disturbed the mind of his son and grandson and reacted 'so hideously upon the nation at large' (Verney, *The Passing Years*, 1–2). In his view there were no times so good—for the man born to independence, land, position, influence in the Warwickshire vale—than the period from 1850 to 1880.

Verney's most successful day as master involved two exhilarating chases across the Warwickshire countryside: 'both foxes were of the good old wild travelling breed who put up a stout fight against a pack of foxhounds which in those days was second to none in England' (Verney, *The Passing Years*, 207). He was obliged to add that it was a pack bred by his father and not by himself. Moral objections did not then threaten the sport but Verney anticipated the arguments later used to defend it. He considered it a mistake not to accept outright that all field sports involved some animal suffering but believed that hunters answered an 'instinct of pursuit' shared by all humanity. And for the true sportsman the attraction lay in the hunt, not the kill. He viewed with repugnance the hunting of rare species such as tigers.

Diehard peer After his father's death in December 1902, Verney succeeded to the title as nineteenth Baron Willoughby de Broke, and after the Liberal landslide in the general election of January 1906 he resumed a political role. In order to counteract the huge Liberal majority in the House of Commons the Unionist Party deployed its even greater majority in the House of Lords. Willoughby de Broke was a willing participant in the mobilization of the 'backwoodsmen', which saw important Liberal bills killed off in the upper chamber. He brought to politics the same sportiveness that he displayed on the hunting field. One of the first gatherings of the backwoodsmen—to oppose the Licensing Bill in 1908—brought together men who shared his own sporting predilections. Most of them had never spoken in the House of Lords before. Although he was 'not a man of high abilities', Willoughby de Broke's political value to the diehards was soon evident: he 'possessed an attractive personality, a real political flair, experience of the House of Commons, unbounded energy, and a marked talent for forcible and humorous platform oratory'. As a result his influence exceeded what his intellectual ability might have suggested (Lord Newton, *Lord Lansdowne: a Biography*, 1929, 424).

In spring 1909 the government regained the political initiative with a budget that provided for naval building and old-age pensions while shifting the burden of taxation to the landed classes. Four new land taxes encountered especially violent opposition from Unionists, and Willoughby de Broke never wavered from his view that the budget was 'a revolution' (*Hansard 5L*, 4.782). In the House of Lords on 22 November 1909 he sided with the majority in urging rejection.

In taking this constitutionally dubious step the Unionist peers laid themselves open to the charge that they were putting their vested interests before the welfare of the people: 'The order of battle,' Willoughby de Broke later wrote, 'was now fairly set for a campaign of class warfare' (Verney, *The Sport of our Ancestors*, 1). He blamed the chancellor, David Lloyd George, for instigating this; to the cry of 'peers against people' the Liberals won a narrow election victory in January 1910. This settled the issue of the budget, and battle moved on to the government's plans for abolishing the veto power of the upper chamber. Willoughby de Broke, who emerged as a central figure in the Unionist resistance, worked with Leo Maxse of the *National Review* to publicize the case against the Parliament Bill. He considered the party leadership lacking in spirit, and in October 1910 founded the Reveille group, with Henry Page Croft, 'to rouse the Unionist party without forsaking Unionist principles' (Phillips, 'Lord Willoughby de Broke', 207–8).

On 21 July 1911 the Unionist leaders recommended abstention in any division on the Parliament Bill. It was a tactical withdrawal rather than an outright surrender, but to Willoughby de Broke it was quite simply defeat with dishonour. Determined to continue the fight, he joined the 'diehard' group that gathered under the leadership of the octogenarian earl of Halsbury, and with F. E. Smith he became a joint secretary of the committee formed to co-ordinate diehard opposition. So effective was this lobby that when the House of Lords divided on the night of 10 August the outcome was genuinely in doubt; the bill was carried by the narrow margin of seventeen votes. After this defeat Willoughby de Broke's disenchantment with the Unionist leadership was complete, and he agitated for the creation of a new party. Friends urged him, however, to remain within the ranks, and from there he helped to organize resistance to the government's third Irish Home Rule Bill.

The enactment of home rule, previously blocked by the Unionist majority in the upper chamber, was made possible by the Parliament Act (1911). In his memoirs Willoughby de Broke confessed to 'an uneasy feeling' that his party should have let the budget of 1909 pass and should have 'lain in wait' for home rule instead (Verney, *The Passing Years*, 255). Unlike many diehards he had no personal economic interest in Ireland; his motivation was political and ideological. He regarded maintenance of the union as the defining principle of his party: 'As far as I am concerned it is not an Ulster question; it is a question of the union or separation' (*Hansard 5L*, 14.926). Denied a constitutional failsafe in the House of Lords, the diehards took their fight to the towns and counties of England, adopting methods that overtly challenged parliamentary authority. Willoughby de Broke was prepared to fight—quite literally—for Ulster.

In March 1913 Willoughby de Broke founded the 'British League for the Support of Ulster and the Union'; by November it had 10,000 volunteers trained for military action. He reasoned that the stronger the opposition to home rule the more likely it was that the issue would be put to a general election; 'but if that means of settlement is denied to us then we must fall back on the only other means at our disposal' (*Hansard 5L*, 14.921). His meaning was made clearer in a circular letter to Unionist peers in February 1914, which was also signed by lords Stanhope, Ampthill, and Arran: 'The real alternative to Civil War is a Dissolution of Parliament' (Phillips, *The Diehards*, 153). The diehard resistance helped to delay settlement of the home-rule question until the outbreak of European war in August 1914. When it was taken up afterwards most politicians accepted the inevitability of home-rule in some form, but not Willoughby de Broke, who remained a diehard to the last.

First World War and afterwards During the war Willoughby de Broke served as major, and from 1916 as lieutenant-colonel commandant, of the Warwickshire yeomanry 2nd line regiment. In July 1917 he was again involved in abortive plans to create a new political party, a reflection of his chronic disillusionment with the Unionist leadership and his opposition to the Lloyd George coalition government. Before the war he had stated the case for a rejuvenated toryism in articles for the *National Review*, where he advocated 'constructive social reform' (Phillips, *The Diehards*, 156). He regarded this as essential for the improvement of the race, and was a 'devoted and outspoken eugenicist' (ibid., 109). He published several articles on eugenics and was a friend of C. W. Saleeby, the founder of the Eugenics Society. The same concern for the health of the nation underlay his support for women's suffrage, which he supported in the House of Lords in May 1914 in a reasoned and well-informed speech. He was generous towards the militants, attributing their worst excesses to the fact that parliament and the national press had for so long deliberately ignored the suffrage issue. He reaffirmed his support during the debate on the Representation of the People Bill, on 10 January 1918, in which he called for immediate action: 'The delay is one of the things which has caused so much bitterness among women throughout the country. It is jam tomorrow, but never jam today' (*Hansard 5L*, 27.508). He attributed many social ills, in particular the labour unrest before the war, to the rise of self-made plutocrats, supplanting the paternalistic hereditary governing class.

Willoughby de Broke's last days were spent in uneasy reflection, writing his memoirs. His widow recalled how the task of recording his memory of what he saw as a vanished county society 'became almost an obsession with him' in the last year of his life (Verney, *The Passing Years*, xiv–xv). He took his account up to autumn 1910, and intended the final chapter to be on the proper relationship between landowner and dependants, with an appeal to the new owners of country estates to respect the traditional ways of the countryside as they were understood by those born to them. It was a distressing subject for him; in September 1921 he had been forced to sell the Compton Verney estate, including the house and almost 6000 acres, to Joseph Watson, a soap-maker. In a bitter irony Watson was later distinguished with a peerage from Lloyd George. Willoughby de Broke died on 16 December 1923 at his London home, 23 Gilbert Street, Grosvenor Square, after a short illness, and was buried at Compton Verney on 20 December. He was survived by his wife and by his son, John Henry Peyto *Verney, who succeeded him as twentieth Baron Willoughby de Broke.

To those who did not know him Willoughby de Broke appeared flippant, the archetypal fox-hunting, reactionary peer. Those close to him, however, recognized a serious and imaginative man. Unashamedly partisan, he nevertheless saw two sides to every question and respected the passion of his adversaries. He defended the hereditary principle, whether applied 'to Peers or ... to foxhounds', but also advocated service to the state as the ultimate determinant of rank: 'In the new Toryism, each man and woman will be known not by *who* they are, but by *what* they are' (Phillips, *The Diehards*, 156). Looking back he regretted many of the changes that England had undergone in his lifetime, and some of the tactics of his party before the war, which had left 'the hereditary peerage, with all its advantages and imperfections ... to manoeuvre in the open field'. The outcome was a political Agincourt, but armed with courage and conviction Willoughby de Broke had battled on (Verney, *The Passing Years*, 244).

MARK POTTLE

Sources R. G. Verney, *The passing years* (1924) • R. G. Verney, ed., *The sport of our ancestors* (1921) • Hansard 5L, 4, cols. 775–82; 14, cols. 920–30; 16, cols. 82–90; 42, cols. 458–63; 27, cols. 504–8 • Hansard 4, 40, cols. 28–30 • *WWW* • GEC, *Peerage* • earl of Rosslyn, *My gamble with life* (1928) • G. D. Phillips, *The diehards* (1979) • G. D. Phillips, 'Lord Willoughby de Broke and the politics of radical toryism, 1909–1914', *Journal of British Studies*, 20 (1980) • D. Cannadine, *Decline and fall of the British aristocracy* (1992) • G. R. Searle, *Corruption in British politics, 1895–1930* (1987) • A. Adonis, *Making aristocracy work: the peerage and the political system in Britain, 1884–1914* (1993)
Archives HLRO, political corresp. | HLRO, letters to R. D. Blumenfeld • HLRO, corresp. with Andrew Bonar Law • PRO NIre., corresp. with E. H. Carson • Shakespeare Birthplace Trust RO, Stratford upon Avon, letters to C. W. Saleeby
Likenesses Bassano, photographs, 1898, NPG • photograph, 1910, repro. in Verney, *Passing years*, facing p. 204 • photograph, 1919, repro. in Verney, *Passing years*, facing p. 274 • Spy [L. Ward], watercolour caricature, NPG; repro. in *VF* (23 Nov 1905)
Wealth at death £156,066 9s. 5d.: administration with will, 20 Feb 1924, *CGPLA Eng. & Wales*

Vernon. For this title name *see* individual entries under Vernon; *see also* Warren, George John, fifth Baron Vernon (1803–1866).

Vernon family (*per.* 1411–1515), gentry, was long established in the north midlands when **Sir Richard Vernon** (1389/90–1451) became speaker of the Commons in 1426. Coming of age in 1411, Vernon inherited an impressive array of properties acquired by his forebears, partly through advantageous marriages. At their heart lay manors in the Peak District and Derwent valley in Derbyshire, centred on Haddon Hall, whose chapel and hall were substantially rebuilt by Richard. The family maintained a secondary residence at Harlaston in east Staffordshire, held the hereditary forestership of Macclesfield Forest in Cheshire, possessed estates in another five English counties, from Westmorland to Buckinghamshire, and also held five manors in south Wales. From his greatuncle, Sir Fulk Pembridge, Richard inherited the lordship

of Tong Castle, Shropshire, and the manor of Aylestone, Leicestershire. In 1411 he helped Sir Fulk's widow, Isabel Lingen, secure the elevation of Tong parish church into a collegiate establishment, with an almshouse and school. Isabel was also Richard's mother-in-law, his wife, Benedicta, being her daughter by a previous marriage to Sir John Ludlow of Stokesay, Shropshire. Tong College subsequently became a family mausoleum for the Vernons.

As well as providing the manpower when necessary for political power, the Vernon estates yielded in the mid-fifteenth century an estimated annual income of £210. Falling rents were offset by the profits of Derbyshire lead mining and by the maintenance of large herds of sheep and cattle. Richard Vernon's wealth and power were also supplemented by offices, leases, and annuities arising from his links with magnate families. He obtained from John Mowbray, third duke of Norfolk, the stewardship of the latter's Derbyshire estates, close by several Vernon manors, and by 1440 he had become simultaneously a retainer of both the earl of Stafford (afterwards duke of Buckingham) and of William, Lord Ferrers of Chartley. But his most important links, as a result of his principal manors being held of the honour of Tutbury, were with the region's greatest territorial power, the crown's duchy of Lancaster. Knighted by December 1417, Vernon rose to an eminence surpassing that of his ancestors. In Staffordshire he was twice sheriff (1416–17 and 1427–8) and represented the county in parliament in 1419.

Not until the reign of Henry VI, however, did Richard Vernon's office holding in Derbyshire reflect his territorial status there. In 1423 he secured what became a lifelong seat on the county's peace commission, and represented Derbyshire in the parliaments of 1422, 1426 (when he was speaker), and 1433. In seven of the eleven parliaments between 1432 and 1451 a Vernon sat for Derbyshire, either Sir Richard or one of his three (of at least six) sons. Sheriff of Derbyshire and Nottinghamshire (1424–6), Vernon also consolidated his family's territorial power through offices held of the duchy of Lancaster. The most important of these, the stewardship and constableship of the High Peak, he first obtained in 1424. In 1438 he converted this grant to one in survivorship to himself and his son Fulk (d. 1449), who was soon to become an esquire in the royal household. Supported by an extensive network of retainers, tenants, and 'well-wishers', he deserved the epithet bestowed upon one of his sixteenth-century descendants, the 'king of the Peak'.

Sir Richard's magnate and court connections procured for the Vernons several important offices and grants in the 1430s and 1440s. He was a deputy justiciar of south Wales (1431–c.1438) under James, Lord Audley, and by 1445 was serving as knight steward in the court of the constable (Buckingham) and the marshal (Norfolk). He surely owed his position as treasurer of Calais (1445–51), as well as the keepership of his son Fulk of nearby Hammes Castle, to Buckingham, constable of Calais from 1442 to 1450. In June 1450 he acquired a life grant of the shrievalty of Pembroke, then in the king's hands, and a year later surrendered it in favour of his son John. The local authority of the Vernons did not go unchallenged, however, and in the 1440s started to come under pressure. In 1440 Sir Richard had to answer charges of intimidation and extortion, by himself and his deputies, in his High Peak stewardship. There were clashes over pasture rights with the Gresleys and legal disputes over the Pembridge inheritance. Lord Ferrers himself pursued a claim to Tong, which was settled by arbitration. Vernon's dubious claims to estates held by Isabel Lingen led to his engaging in lengthy legal and extra-legal manoeuvres, which in 1450 culminated in his forcibly seizing the valuable Staffordshire manor of Kibblestone.

Sir Richard died in August 1451, but many of his disputes were inherited by his eldest surviving son, **Sir William** [i] **Vernon** (c.1420–1467). Saddled with his father's debts, especially those arising from the latter's treasurership of Calais, William's position was gravely weakened by the loss of duchy offices and also by the rapid rise to local prominence of Walter Blount, who used his association with Queen Margaret to obtain the stewardship of the High Peak, which was part of her dower, and replaced the Vernons in parliament as the near permanent knight of the shire for Derbyshire. It was as a consequence of their rivalry with Blount that in May 1454 Sir William and three other Vernons joined in the coalition of forces responsible for one of the period's most memorable acts of gentry disorder, the assault on Blount's property and servants at Derby and Elvaston.

The violence, which was part of an escalating feud between Sir Nicholas Longford, an associate of the Vernons, and the Blounts and their relatives, the Shirleys, was accompanied by acts of defiance against the sheriff of Derbyshire and Nottinghamshire, Sir John Gresley, another adversary of the Vernons. This was also a direct challenge to the authority of the duke of York, recently installed as protector of the realm during Henry VI's insanity. York led a commission of oyer and terminer to investigate the affray, whereupon the duke of Buckingham, who in spite of his ostensible regional pre-eminence had hitherto generally failed to exercise effective leadership in the north midlands, now resumed his links with the Vernons. In August Sir William was retained for life by Buckingham and the latter's eldest son, Humphrey, Lord Stafford (d. 1458); perhaps as a result Vernon was returned to parliament in 1455 as a knight of the shire for Staffordshire, and later (May 1460) was appointed a JP in that county after serving two terms (1455–6 and 1457–8) on the Derbyshire bench. Not surprisingly, by the late 1450s Vernon had followed Buckingham into the ranks of York's enemies, while Blount committed himself to York and the Nevilles.

It is not clear whether the Vernons took part in any of the battles of 1459–61, but William was nominated to two anti-Yorkist commissions, along with Buckingham and John Talbot, second earl of Shrewsbury, both among the Lancastrians killed at Northampton in 1460. In the months following Edward IV's victory at Towton, Walter Blount (ennobled as Lord Mountjoy in 1465) headed commissions to arrest two of Sir William's brothers and

bring them to Westminster. In December 1461, however, Vernon received a general pardon, and made his peace with the new regime. He strove to shore up his family's damaged fortunes, feeing fellow gentry in Warwickshire and Staffordshire, while resuming a militant defence of his rights in Derbyshire against real or imagined wrongs. Violence followed by arbitration enabled him to regain the stewardship of the Mowbray lands. But a series of confrontations with the followers of Henry, Lord Grey of Codnor (himself a retainer of William, Lord Hastings), culminated in November 1467, five months after William Vernon's death, in the murder of his brother Roger at the hands of Grey's men—a notorious crime which probably inspired the statute of 1468 against retaining.

William [i] Vernon had gone some way towards recovering his family's position, retaining some disputed estates and purchasing additional properties. In 1467 he secured a Derbyshire seat in parliament for his son William [ii]. And while his second wife, Margaret Pipe, like his mother, was of gentry stock, his son and heir, **Sir Henry Vernon** (c.1445–1515), made an aristocratic marriage to Anne, sister of John Talbot, third earl of Shrewsbury. Henry did not become a knight for another twenty years, but he showed an unmistakable appreciation of his wife's status when he instructed his executors to build a sumptuous tomb at Tong for his wife and himself, 'the better and the more honorable for the bloode that my wyff is comyn of' (PRO, PROB 11/18, fol. 66r). In the meantime the Vernons obtained Shrewsbury's support against Grey during the judicial inquiry occasioned by Roger's murder. They also formed links with the duke of Clarence, who was granted the honours of Tutbury and the High Peak in 1464, and who restored the stewardship of the latter to Henry Vernon.

But although Vernon followed Shrewsbury in supporting Clarence and the earl of Warwick in the rebellion that led to the readeption of Henry VI in 1470, and was a member of the Derbyshire and Staffordshire peace commissions of 1469–71, his support fell short of a willingness to take up arms. When Edward IV landed in Yorkshire to reclaim the crown in March 1471, Vernon was prepared to provide Clarence with information concerning the king's movements, but otherwise played a waiting game. Orders and appeals from both Clarence and Warwick—the latter in the oft-quoted plaintive postscript, 'Henry I pray you fayle not now as ever I may do for you' (Rutland MSS, 1, 4)—alike fell on deaf ears. Vernon's wariness paid off when Clarence made peace with the king, and the battles of Barnet and Tewkesbury restored Edward to the throne. Presumably Vernon then answered Edward's peremptory summons, to bring his forces to meet the king at Coventry.

Having secured a general pardon in 1472, Henry Vernon was reinstated on the Derbyshire bench, remaining a member almost continuously for the rest of his life. This did not prevent his and his family's continuing to engage in bouts of violent self-help. As Clarence began his fall from grace, Vernon forged increasingly close ties both with the king (by 1474 he had become a member of the royal household as an esquire of the body) and with Lord Hastings, increasingly the dominant power in the north midlands on the king's behalf. He attended the parliament of 1478 as MP for Derbyshire, and there assented to Clarence's condemnation. In June 1483 he was summoned to the planned coronation of Edward V, there to receive knighthood. When Richard III's usurpation put paid to both ceremonies, Vernon nevertheless retained his household position, served on commissions, and even received a life annuity from the Tutbury revenues from the beleaguered monarch. In August 1485, however, he ignored Richard's demand for support against Henry Tudor, and was subsequently quick to establish links with the new dynasty. Sir Henry fought for Henry VII at Stoke in 1487, and against the Cornish rising of 1497.

Once more an esquire of the body, Henry Vernon was at last knighted in November 1489, when the king's first-born, Arthur, was created prince of Wales. In 1492 he became the prince's governor and controller of his household. A JP in six counties besides Derbyshire, he represented that county in the parliament of 1491–2, and doubtless on other occasions. He was frequently appointed to commissions in the midlands and west country. By 1500, now a knight of the body, Vernon had become a member of an influential midlands circle of courtiers that included George Talbot, fourth earl of Shrewsbury, William Blount, second Lord Mountjoy, and Sir Henry Willoughby of Wollaton. The Vernon–Talbot connection was especially close, for Sir Henry's brother Ralph had married Margaret, another daughter of John *Talbot, the second earl. The Vernons made peace with families that had once been their foes, with the Gresleys and Shirleys as well as the Blounts. The marriage of Anne Vernon to Sir Ralph Shirley provided a link to Lady Margaret Beaufort—there survives a book of hours that Lady Margaret gave to Anne, with a signed inscription. Other marriages were less exalted but no less profitable. The double marriage of Sir Henry's sons Thomas and Humphrey to their cousins, the granddaughters of Sir Richard Ludlow of Stokesay, brought extensive Shropshire properties to the Vernons.

The Vernons benefited from the economic upswing of the later fifteenth century. It has been calculated that by 1500 the annual value of their estates was over £600. Once more, however, they faced a challenge to their position in their 'home country', above all from the Savages of Cheshire, members of which family held the stewardship of the High Peak for much of Henry VII's reign [see Savage family (per. c.1369–1528)]. When the Vernons and the Savages took opposite sides in a series of interlocking conflicts in the north midlands and north-west, the judicial powers of the stewardship were employed in 1494 to harass Vernon tenants. The Vernons themselves continued to employ physical and legal intimidation, the most spectacular example of which was the abduction in 1502 of the heiress Margaret Kebell, and her forced marriage to Roger Vernon, Sir Henry's heir apparent. Although Roger may have already joined his father in the royal household, this did not prevent Henry VII from employing his accustomed fiscal tyranny to control a regional élite. He forced the Vernons to sue for expensive pardons, backed by performance bonds. Roger's pardon in 1503 cost 400 marks, while Sir Henry only obtained his pardon in 1507 for the sum of £900. In his will of 1515 he complained about this fine, and called for the restitution of the £500 he had so far paid. He specifically referred to the testimony of Sir Edmund Dudley, the king's financial agent, who had confessed that Vernon 'was to sore delt wthall' (Harrison, 88).

Sir Henry nevertheless continued to receive signs of royal favour. Sheriff of Derbyshire and Nottinghamshire in 1503–4, he was chosen as a member of the escort that accompanied the king's daughter to her Scottish marriage in 1503, while in 1507 he finally received a life grant of the Peak stewardship and related offices. Still a knight of the body under the young Henry VIII, he seems to have retired to the midlands, his service on the peace commissions reduced to a permanent place on those of Derbyshire, Staffordshire, and Shropshire. Indeed, his attention was increasingly given to his interests in the latter county, where he rebuilt Tong Castle in brick, and planned the construction of the Vernon chapel in the college there. Roger Vernon was dead by 1509, and when Sir Henry died in 1515 his heir was his second son, Richard, who outlived his father by only two years. Richard's son George Vernon (d. 1565) was the last member of this powerful gentry family, now fittingly commemorated by the chapel at Tong and the splendours of Haddon Hall. The Vernon arms were argent fretty sable.   JOSEPH A. NIGOTA

Sources S. M. Wright, *The Derbyshire gentry in the fifteenth century*, Derbyshire RS, 8 (1983) · C. Rawcliffe, 'Vernon, Sir Richard', HoP, *Commons, 1386–1421*, 4.712–17 · H. Castor, 'The duchy of Lancaster in the Lancastrian polity, 1399–1461', PhD diss., U. Cam., 1993 · C. Carpenter, *Locality and polity: a study of Warwickshire landed society, 1401–1499* (1992) · H. Castor, '"Walter Blount was gone to serve traytours": the sack of Elvaston and the politics of the north midlands in 1454', *Midland History*, 19 (1994), 21–39 · J. S. Roskell, 'Sir Richard Vernon of Haddon, speaker in the parliament of Leicester, 1426', *Parliament and politics in late medieval England*, 3 (1983), 265–75 · *The manuscripts of his grace the duke of Rutland*, 4 vols., HMC, 24 (1888–1905) · G. Wrottesley, ed., 'Extracts from the plea rolls', *Collections for a history of Staffordshire*, William Salt Archaeological Society, 15, 17, new ser. 3, 4, 6 (1894–1903) · *Chancery records* · *LP Henry VIII*, vols. 1–2 · *CIPM*, 19, nos. 583–4 · I. H. Jeayes, ed., *Descriptive catalogue of Derbyshire charters* (1906) · R. Horrox and P. W. Hammond, eds., *British Library Harleian manuscript 433*, 4 vols. (1979–83) · C. J. Harrison, 'The petition of Edmund Dudley', *EngHR*, 87 (1972), 82–99 · chancery, inquisitions post mortem, PRO, Henry VI, C139/145/8; Edward IV, C140/24/24; Henry VIII, C142/30/73 · probate act books, PRO, PROB 8/5, fols. 182–182v · will, PRO, PROB 11/18, sig. 9 · E. W. Ives, '"Against taking awaye of women": the inception and operation of the Abduction Act of 1487', *Wealth and power in Tudor England: essays presented to S. T. Bindoff*, ed. E. W. Ives, R. J. Knecht, and J. J. Scarisbrick (1978), 21–44 · D. A. L. Morgan, 'The king's affinity in the polity of Yorkist England', *TRHS*, 5th ser., 23 (1973), 1–25 · R. Somerville, *History of the duchy of Lancaster, 1265–1603* (1953) · J. C. Wedgwood and A. D. Holt, *History of parliament … 1439–1509*, 2 vols. (1936–8) · M. A. Hicks, 'The 1468 Statute of Livery', *Historical Research*, 64 (1991), 15–28 · H. J. H. Garratt and C. Rawcliffe, *Derbyshire feet of fines, 1323–1546*, Derbyshire RS, 11 (1985) · W. H. Dunham jun., *Lord Hastings' indentured retainers, 1461–1483* (1955) · I. Rowney, 'Arbitration in gentry disputes of the later middle ages', *Midland History*, 7 (1982), 367–76 · C. Rawcliffe, *The Staffords, earls of*

Stafford and dukes of Buckingham, 1394–1521, Cambridge Studies in Medieval Life and Thought, 3rd ser., 11 (1978) · M. K. Jones and M. G. Underwood, *The king's mother: Lady Margaret Beaufort, countess of Richmond and Derby* (1992) · *Derbyshire*, Pevsner (1978) · *The Anglica historia of Polydore Vergil, AD 1485–1537*, ed. and trans. D. Hay, CS, 3rd ser., 74 (1950) · *VCH Shropshire*, vol. 2 · E. Acheson, *A gentry community: Leicestershire in the fifteenth century: c.1422–c.1485* (1992) · G. Griffiths, *A history of Tong, Shropshire*, 2nd edn (1894) · A. Cameron, 'Sir Henry Willoughby of Wollaton', *Transactions of the Thoroton Society*, 74 (1970), 10–21 · C. Rawcliffe, 'The great lord as peacekeeper: arbitration by English noblemen and their councils in the later middle ages', *Law and social change in British history*, ed. J. A. Guy and H. G. Beale (1984), 34–54 · E. W. Ives, 'Crime, sanctuary, and royal authority under Henry VIII: the exemplary sufferings of the Savage family', *On the laws and customs of England*, ed. M. S. Arnold, T. A. Green, S. A. Scully, and S. D. White (1981), 296–320 · C. Carpenter, *The Wars of the Roses: politics and the constitution in England, c.1437–1509* (1997) · I. Jeayes, ed., *Descriptive catalogue of the charters and muniments of the Gresley family* (1906) · M. A. Hicks, 'Lord Hastings' indentured retainers', *Richard III and his rivals: magnates and their motives in the Wars of the Roses* (1991), 229–46 · *Report on manuscripts in various collections*, 8 vols., HMC, 55 (1901–14), vol. 2 · *The itinerary of John Leland in or about the years 1535–1543*, ed. L. Toulmin Smith, 11 pts in 5 vols. (1906–10) · J. P. Earwaker, *East Cheshire: past and present, or, A history of the hundred of Macclesfield*, 2 vols. (1877–80) · S. Shaw, *The history and antiquities of Staffordshire*, 2 vols. (1798–1801); reprint edn (1979) · J. Nichols, *The history and antiquities of the county of Leicester*, 4 vols. (1795–1815); facs. edn (1971) · *Shropshire*, Pevsner (1958) · R. A. Griffiths and R. S. Thomas, *The principality of Wales in the later middle ages: the structure and personnel of government*, 1: *South Wales, 1277–1536* (1972) · *VCH Staffordshire*, vol. 14 · J. C. Wedgwood, 'Staffordshire parliamentary history [1]', *Collections for a history of Staffordshire*, William Salt Archaeological Society, 3rd ser. (1917 [i.e. 1919]) · L. Drucker, ed., *Warwickshire feet of fines*, 3, Dugdale Society, 18 (1943) · W. A. Shaw, *The knights of England*, 2 vols. (1906) · HoP, *Commons, 1386–1421* · H. Castor, *The king, the crown, and the duchy of Lancaster* (2000)

Archives Belvoir Castle, Leicestershire, Duke of Rutland MSS · BL, Wolley MSS · Derbys. RO, Vernon of Sudbury MSS · PRO, deeds, legal records **Likenesses** alabaster effigies on monument, 1430–70 (Richard Vernon; with Lady Benedicta Vernon), Tong church, Shropshire · brass effigies on monument, 1430–70 (William Vernon; with Lady Margaret Vernon), Tong church, Shropshire · stone effigies on monument, 1500–40 (Henry Vernon; with Lady Anne Vernon), Tong church, Shropshire **Wealth at death** substantial; Sir Richard's landed estate c.£159, Sir William's c.£171; both excl. various estates: C 139/145/8 (1451); C 139/55/34 (1454); C 140/24/24 (1467); Wright, *Derbyshire gentry*, 7 · Sir Henry's return: PRO, C142/30/73 (1515) · Sir Richard's land wealth est. over £210 p.a.: Rawcliffe, 'Sir Richard Vernon', 714 · gross value of most Vernon property c.£612, 1500: Wright, *Derbyshire gentry*, 8 · income augmented by annuities and profits from stock farming, mining interests, office-holding · Sir William left 2000 marks (over-optimistically?) toward four daughters' marriages: will, PRO, PROB 8/5, fol. 182r · extensive money, jewels, plate, clothes, household furnishings, ore, animals (incl. 700 sheep): Sir Henry's will, PRO, PROB 11/18, fols. 66r–67v

Vernon, Augustus Henry, sixth Baron Vernon (1829–1883). *See under* Warren, George John, fifth Baron Vernon (1803–1866).

Vernon, Edward (1684–1757), naval officer, was born in Westminster on 12 November 1684, the second son of James *Vernon (*bap.* 1646, *d.* 1727), later editor of the *London Gazette*, and Mary Buck (*d.* 1715). James Vernon had been private secretary to the duke of Monmouth (1672–83) and after the revolution of 1688 he became under-

Edward Vernon (1684–1757), by Thomas Gainsborough, c.1753

secretary and later secretary of state (1697–1702) to William III. Between 1692 and 1700 Edward attended Westminster School, where he studied mathematics and astronomy and became proficient in Greek and Latin.

Early career On 10 May 1700 Vernon was entered as a volunteer in the *Shrewsbury* under Captain Benjamin Hoskins. The *Shrewsbury* was the flagship of Admiral Sir George Rooke, who took an Anglo-Dutch squadron to the sound to provide limited assistance to the Swedes in a dispute with Denmark. On 4 March 1701 Vernon moved to the *Ipswich* and shortly afterwards to the *Boyne*, which formed part of the expeditionary force under Rooke and the duke of Ormond sent to capture Cadiz in 1702. In September 1702 Rooke appointed Vernon third lieutenant on the *Lennox* and Vernon stayed with the *Lennox* on a variety of convoy duties during 1703, including a visit to Smyrna with the Levant trade.

On his return to England in March 1704 Vernon took up a commission as fifth lieutenant of Admiral Sir Cloudesley Shovell's flagship, the *Barfleur*, in which he sailed to the Mediterranean. Vernon remained with Shovell throughout 1704, and was with him on the *Barfleur* at the battle of Malaga (13 August). He returned to England with Shovell, and when Shovell succeeded Rooke as admiral of the fleet Vernon stayed with him as fourth and then third lieutenant of Shovell's new flagship, the *Britannia*, in December 1704. Shovell returned to the Mediterranean in the summer of 1705 and Vernon was present at the capture of Barcelona (28 September).

On 22 January 1706 Vernon was given his first command, the *Dolphin*, a small fifth rate of twenty-eight guns then at

Sheerness under orders for the West Indies. Before Vernon could get her rigged and stored he was transferred to the *Rye* (32 guns) on 2 February and sent with dispatches for Shovell and the Earl Rivers at Lisbon. They had sailed into the Mediterranean to join the allied force under the earl of Galway in Valencia before Vernon arrived. Vice-Admiral Sir George Byng was in command at Lisbon and Vernon was sent cruising down to Gibraltar. When Shovell returned to Lisbon and decided to take the fleet back into the Mediterranean to execute Marlborough's plan to attack Toulon, Vernon was left at Lisbon, but in May he joined the allied fleet at Alicante and sailed with it towards Toulon. On 30 June the *Rye* was one of the ships ordered to assist the allied crossing of the River Var by bombarding the French positions on the west bank. On the following day Vernon was present at the landings intended to distract the French from the main crossing. He continued cruising and escort duties until the autumn, when he was ordered back to England. During the passage Shovell's flagship, the *Association*, and several other ships were lost off the Isles of Scilly.

On 7 November 1707 Vernon was given command of the *Jersey* (50 guns) at Woolwich, which he prepared for sea. In February 1708 the *Jersey* sailed with Sir George Byng's squadron to the French coast to watch a large French force at Dunkirk, thought to be designed for an expedition to Scotland. In March Vernon was with the fleet that pursued the expeditionary force of Claude, comte de Forbin-Gardanne, to Scotland and, although he took no part in the battle, he helped secure the only prize of that affair, the French warship the *Salisbury* (50 guns). After this action Vernon was sent south with some of the French prisoners. He was already under orders to proceed to Jamaica to reinforce Commodore Charles Wager's squadron and he was ordered to take as many supernumeraries as he could to reinforce Wager. Vernon arrived at Port Royal on 6 September 1708 and spent the next year with Wager's squadron, cruising. He observed the Spaniards' failure to challenge the British at sea. In October 1708 he had his first sight of Cartagena de las Indias, the great city of the *galeones*, the treasure ships, where Wager had won a spectacular, if not very profitable, victory back in May.

In September 1709 Vernon sailed for England, and he delivered the *Jersey* to the Deptford Dockyard officers on 17 December. Throughout the first half of 1710 he commanded the *Jersey* on a range of duties in the channel and then went back to the West Indies, arriving at Port Royal in December. He remained on that station until March 1712, when he was ordered home again. For the next two years Vernon remained unemployed as the prospect of imminent peace and, possibly, his whig credentials militated against him.

On 2 March 1715 Vernon was given command of the *Assistance* (50 guns), a two-year-old ship then at Sheerness. After fitting and manning his ship in the spring he spent the summer on duties in the channel and the North Sea. By early 1716 he was the most senior captain in the downs and had command of that station in the absence of a flag officer. In July 1716 he was ordered to take the new British

ambassador's equipage to Constantinople. The ambassador, Edward Wortley Montagu, was then at Vienna. He was to join Vernon at Leghorn for the final leg of the journey. The departing ambassador, Sir Robert Sutton, would return with Vernon from Constantinople. The voyage involved a number of diplomatic complexities regarding the status of British warships in Ottoman waters and a further difficulty was caused by the ministry taking the opportunity to carry the envoy from Tripoli back to Port Mahon. After a few diplomatic exchanges, partly arising from the fact that the envoy wanted to travel by land across France, Vernon finally sailed in late October. During a terrible storm in the straits the sea broke through the stern, drove in the bulkhead of the state room, and smashed all the windows. Three days later, on 6 March 1717, the envoy was finally put ashore at Port Mahon. Vernon sailed on to Genoa, where he learned that Wortley Montagu would go to Constantinople by land. While at Leghorn, concerting plans to proceed to the Dardanelles, Vernon also took up the matter of Venetian impressment of British sailors directly with the grand duke of Tuscany at Pisa. Vernon's progress to Constantinople went smoothly and by careful preparation he avoided potential diplomatic difficulty on his return journey through the straits. He landed Sutton at Toulon and sailed on to Cadiz, where once more he took up the matter of detaining British seamen with the local authorities, before returning to England in October.

War with Spain broke out in December 1718, and Vernon's next commission, on 11 March 1719, was to the *Mary* (60 guns), attached to the earl of Berkeley's squadron at Portsmouth. On 15 May Vernon was appointed commander-in-chief of his majesty's ships at Jamaica and he hoisted his broad pennant on 24 July. On 4 October 1719 he arrived at Port Royal. During the remainder of the year Vernon cruised around the north coast of Jamaica and the Windward passage, protecting the homeward-bound trade. In March 1720 Vernon cruised up to Havana, chasing Spanish ships. On 20 March he sighted three Spanish sail in line. Followed closely by the *Ludlow Castle* he bore up to meet them. With a strong breeze and the weather gauge he found that he could not use his lower tier of guns effectively in his first pass and tacked to pass again to leeward, but in the battle the *Ludlow Castle* lost her foretop mast and fell out to leeward. Vernon followed to protect her stern as the Spaniards prepared to attack. Vernon took in sail to meet them and this display induced the Spaniards to break off and make a course for Havana. The rest of his time at Jamaica was relatively uneventful and he sailed for England in June 1721. Throughout Vernon's time in the West Indies the Spaniards had not shown much appetite for a fight.

Politics and national celebrity In England Vernon stood for one of the parliamentary seats at Penryn, Cornwall, in the 1722 general election. The precise relationship between the Vernons and Penryn is unclear. His father, James, had stood for this small borough, and won the seat three times in 1695, 1705, and 1708. The chief political interest was held by Hugh Boscawen, first Viscount Falmouth, who was the government's main political manager in Cornwall. With this support Vernon was returned unopposed and in this parliament Vernon spoke and voted with the ministry.

In April 1726 Vernon was appointed to command the new seventy-gun third rate, *Grafton*, in a squadron under Admiral Sir Charles Wager, sailing for the Baltic to counter a potential Russian threat to the peace there. He remained in command of the *Grafton* when the squadron returned to Britain and in 1727 he was sent back to the Baltic with another squadron under Sir John Norris. On 19 June, at Copenhagen, news arrived of the death of George I. Vernon was relieved of his command and sent back to England with a loyal address from the fleet.

At the general election Vernon was re-elected for Penryn, but his interventions, in committee and on the floor of the Commons, grew increasingly hostile to the ministry. In January 1729, during the debate on the address, Vernon made his famous, heated accusation that the death of Admiral Francis Hosier and the decimation of his fleet in the West Indies during 1726 could have been avoided had the ministry not ordered Hosier to blockade the Spanish treasure fleet. His experience of the Spaniards indicated that a blockade was unnecessary. Porto Bello, the staging post of Spanish silver from Panama to Havana, could have been taken easily with three hundred men. His strong views, passionate speech, and accusatory style became a feature of his parliamentary work. According to the earl of Egmont, Vernon was so passionate in his views about the French fortifications at Dunkirk that during the debate on 12 February 1730 'He brought up the Pope, the Devil, the Jesuits, the seamen, etc., so that the House had not patience to attend him, though he was not taken down. He quite lost his temper and made himself hoarse again' (*Egmont Diary*, 1.43–4). In 1732 his inflammatory rhetoric earned him a rebuke from the speaker and an accusation from one of the targets of his criticism, Sir John Eyles, that he hid behind parliamentary privilege.

On 15 July 1729 Vernon married Sarah (1699–1756), daughter of the prosperous Rochester brewer Thomas Best, which gave him opportunities in local Kent politics. His marriage, and the death of his father in January 1727, may have secured his financial position. He had purchased an estate at Nacton, near Ipswich in Suffolk. However, his political position at Penryn was looking increasingly fragile. His disillusion with Walpole's ministry and the replacement of Lord Falmouth as government election manager in Cornwall undermined his position. In the 1734 election he lost Penryn and was also defeated in his local borough, Ipswich.

For the next few years Vernon played the role of a Suffolk country gentleman, but when in December 1738 war with Spain over the depredations of the *garda costas* began to appear more likely, he approached Sir Charles Wager, the first lord of the Admiralty, for a command. His experience of the West Indies, his proven abilities in command, and the fact that no serving senior officer could be induced to take the appointment led to Vernon being promoted vice-admiral of the blue and given command of the West Indies squadron in July 1739. He sailed for Jamaica in July and arrived at Port Royal in October. He had a clear idea of how he wished to conduct operations there. Nineteen days after arriving at Port Royal he wrote to the secretary of state, the duke of Newcastle, about the prospect of capturing Spanish colonies. He knew Havana would be a great prize, but his best advice was to 'lay aside all thoughts of such expensive land expeditions as all the advantages may be better and cheaper procured by keeping a strong superiority at Sea in these seas' (Vernon to Newcastle, 31 Oct 1739, PRO, SP 42/85, fols. 29–30). Porto Bello, 'the only mart for all the Wealth of Peru to come to Europe' (ibid., fol. 31), was his objective and on 5 November 1739 he sailed to attack the little town. On 20 November he attacked the forts with his six warships and by the next day the town was in his hands. Vernon had left England as expectations of an easy victory against Spain were growing. War had been declared on 19 October and news of Vernon's victory arrived in March 1740 as a confirmation of public expectations. The rejoicing went far beyond the usual celebrations of victory. Vernon became a national hero almost overnight. Both houses of parliament voted their thanks and the City of London made him a freeman. Addresses of congratulations came to the king from across the country. His popular appeal was immense. Medals, pottery, road names, and public house signs bore the name Vernon or Porto Bello and his birthday became a day of celebration across the country. The ministry had already decided that a major expedition would be sent to the West Indies to bring Spain to peace by taking and holding some of her important colonies. The ministry hoped that Havana, the 'key to all America' (BL, Add. MS 32694, fol. 33), would be the objective, but left the final decision to the council of war under the joint command of Vernon and the army commander, Lord Cathcart.

Failure in the West Indies Vernon had destroyed the fortifications at Porto Bello, but otherwise left the town unharmed. It was now open to British traders. During March 1740 Vernon went to Cartagena de las Indias. He bombarded the city, but found it impossible to assault with his ships. He conceded to Newcastle that 3000 troops would have enabled him to capture the place and he would be prepared for the future, as he informed the secretary of state, 'I know now as much of the avenues to their harbours as they do themselves' (9 May 1740, PRO, SP 42/85, fol. 204). Vernon had also learned that the rolling seas and poor ground made the waters off Cartagena a dangerous anchorage. He sailed up to Porto Bello for repairs, then on to the little fortified port of Chagres. After two days the fort surrendered. It was destroyed and the town was left open to trade. While he was at Porto Bello news reached Vernon that the intended expedition was definitely coming out.

Over the summer of 1740 Vernon's concerns grew. He was short of naval stores and seamen. News that Spanish and French squadrons were on their way to the West Indies was worrying. Although France was neutral, the behaviour of the French governor on St Domingue suggested to

Vernon that France was bent on assisting the Spaniards. He decided to husband his forces at Port Royal, refusing to risk damage or to be drawn to leeward. Vernon's experience of the Caribbean and his concerns made him determined that the expeditionary force would serve as he intended. It would not go to Havana, but to Cartagena, which he believed the troops could rapidly take before they were reduced by disease. The city lay to windward of Jamaica so that they could return rapidly to the island if threatened by Spanish or French attacks.

The expeditionary force arrived in January 1741. Cathcart had died on the voyage and the army of about 8500 British and American troops was commanded by Major-General Thomas Wentworth. The naval escort, commanded by Vice-Admiral Sir Chaloner Ogle, brought Vernon's squadron up to thirty-three ships of the line. Although this fleet made the Franco-Spanish threat less worrying, Vernon was saddled with another serious problem. The Caribbean provided barely enough seamen to replace losses on his small squadron. This vast fleet would soon be losing, through disease and desertion, seamen that could not be replaced. The army was the only adequate source of manpower.

Although nominally equals in command, Wentworth deferred to Vernon's experience in the opening months of operations. He provided troops to help man the ships and concurred in the attack upon Cartagena. During the attack relations became strained as Vernon pressed Wentworth forward, making ill-considered accusations about inaction and incompetence within the army. When the army finally reached San Lazar, the final fortification before Cartagena, Vernon again urged Wentworth to press on and, contrary to the opinion of his council of war, Wentworth accepted Vernon's demand to assault the fort. The action on 10 April 1741 was a disaster. Both officers realized that a reduction of this last obstacle was impossible before disease, which was beginning to take a hold, reduced the army's capability. Vernon would not put his seamen ashore to suffer the same fate. The reports that were sent to London glossed over many of the issues raised by this operation, as the expeditionary force quietly returned to Jamaica.

The next objective was to be Santiago on the southern coast of Cuba. Vernon knew that a direct attack from the sea was difficult and was determined to land the army to the east. Unfortunately he did not tell Wentworth and from the beginning of this attack relations between the two services deteriorated. As Vernon urged the army to push on through difficult terrain and manipulated the information he allowed Wentworth to have, he was also acutely aware of how the news of failure would be received in London. His dispatches to London had always been very full, and he started to enclose carefully selected items of his correspondence with Wentworth. The dispatches themselves began to contain complaints and criticisms of the general. Wentworth's correspondence was, by comparison, brief and sometimes ambiguous. It was not until much later that Wentworth's enclosures began to shed much light on the campaign. Vernon also asked

his brother James to publish an account of Wentworth's incompetence, and in the summer of 1741 Captain Charles Knowles, a close colleague of Vernon, was sent home. Knowles was probably the author of a pamphlet, *An Account of the Expedition to Cartagena*, circulated in manuscript in London later that year, which was extremely hostile to the army. The campaign on Cuba ended in December 1741 with relations between the two services at an extremely low ebb.

A final attempt was made to attack Panama with a reinforcement of 2000 troops that arrived. Vernon was unenthusiastic given the rumours of French squadrons going to the West Indies, but it was a favourite scheme of the governor of Jamaica, Edward Trelawney, and Wentworth was determined to do something significant with the reinforcements before they wasted with disease. Trelawney and Wentworth forced the operation on Vernon with the same disastrous effect as Vernon's earlier pressure had created. Vernon did not follow the agreed plan so news got through to the Spaniards to defend the inland passes. He refused to allow the transports to concentrate before appearing off the town. With the army spread out across the sea from Cartagena to Porto Bello, the operation was called off. The last weeks of the operation were spent with minor expeditions to the island of Roatan and to Georgia. By September the army had ceased to exist as a military force and the troops were largely split up on the warships. Vernon was, at last, effectively commander-in-chief, but on 23 September orders arrived to return to England. Vernon sailed on 19 October, arriving off St David's Head on 26 December 1742.

Later career Vernon found his public popularity largely intact. His success at Porto Bello, his exposure of the shortcomings of Walpole's foreign policy, coupled with his earlier stand against the ministry, ensured Vernon's rise as a symbol of liberty and patriotic whig opposition to what many saw as a corrupt and out-of-touch administration. In the 1741 general election he had been chosen for Penryn, Rochester, and Ipswich. He had also been put up at London, Westminster, and Portsmouth, but ministerial disquiet over such numerous nominations led to support being withheld in these seats. Vernon chose to sit for Ipswich, a seat which he held from then until his death. He had a half-hour audience with George II, during which he pressed the king on the need to keep a force superior to the enemy at sea. According to his brother James, 'the King bore the lecture pretty well', but Vernon found his reward was not what he might have hoped (BL, Add. MS 40794, fol. 28). Unlike Wentworth, who was dispatched to Flanders to command a division, Vernon found himself unemployed and passed over in promotion. Vernon's hostility was directed at the first lord, the earl of Winchilsea. During 1744 he published his correspondence relating to the expedition, together with the selected enclosures. He also published his correspondence with the secretary to the Admiralty, Thomas Corbett, concerning the poor design of British ships, which Vernon claimed was the responsibility of the surveyor of the navy, Sir Jacob Acworth. He continued to comment upon many naval matters in the Commons, in print, and in letters to the Admiralty. Indeed his public profile, his acknowledged experience, his outspoken 'country' stance, and his attempts, laced with his usual invective, to have a select committee inquire into Acworth's conduct, made him highly unpopular at the Admiralty at a time when it was struggling to contain the operational and political problems of the early months of open war with France.

In December 1744 Winchilsea was replaced by the duke of Bedford as first lord of the Admiralty and on 23 April 1745 Vernon was promoted admiral of the white. Bedford had a high regard for Vernon's expertise and corresponded with him on the strategic situation in the West Indies and Europe. It was this habit of corresponding with such freedom that made Vernon both valuable and dangerous. His criticisms of the disposition of the western squadron during 1745 focused attention on a policy of concentration that George Anson put to such good effect during 1746–7. On 28 July 1745 Vernon was appointed to command the western squadron, but on 8 August he transferred to the downs, where the latest intelligence suggested French invasion forces were assembling to support the Jacobite rising in Scotland. He kept a close watch on the Flanders coast throughout the late summer and autumn of 1745, but became involved in a frustrating correspondence with the Admiralty over the size of his squadron and the limits of his command, which, in late November, became heated over the right to appoint warrant officers. The dispute rumbled on through December as Vernon made dispositions to resist a possible French invasion. Finally, on 26 December 1745, Vernon was ordered to hand over command to Vice-Admiral William Martin, who had travelled from Plymouth to join Vernon's squadron.

By mid-March 1746 copies of Vernon's correspondence with the Admiralty during the previous year were in print under the titles *Seasonable Advice from an Honest Sailor* and *A Specimen of Naked Truth from a British Sailor*. When called before the Admiralty for a meeting under Bedford's chairmanship on 9 April he refused to confirm or deny that he was responsible for the publication of the correspondence, asserting that he had been badly treated and that the publication was a private matter on which he was not obliged to answer. Bedford laid the matter before the king, who ordered that Vernon be struck off the flag list on 11 April.

Character and final years   Vernon remained politically active. He spoke on the naval officers' petition against making half-pay officers subject to martial law on 24 February 1749 and in the address of thanks in November of that year. He chaired the parliamentary committee on the herring fishery and helped to establish the Society of Free British Fishery. His great contribution was as an enthusiastic advocate for the maritime economy and defence. Throughout his pamphlets and speeches the major theme of an overwhelmingly powerful navy, based on good ship design, the humane encouragement of seamen to man the fleet, and the development of the maritime economy, is constantly repeated. His determined defence of liberty, country politics, and blue water strategy were a neat encapsulation of whig patriotism. His influence was based partly on his flamboyant style, but largely on the professional respect in which he was held. Until the fall of Louisbourg in the summer of 1745 Vernon had achieved the greatest maritime victories of the war. Although he never tried his ideas in battle he added to the signal commands in 1739 to create greater tactical flexibility in the line of battle. As a trenchant critic of naval officers who apparently failed in their duty he was in tune with current public concern, and he was not prepared to put long-standing friendship before a strict inquiry. On 10 April 1745 Vernon's vote to include Admiral Thomas Mathews in the Commons petition to George II to court-martial the admirals and six captains involved in the battle of Toulon was an important factor in his old friend's eventual disgrace. However, his political weight gradually diminished. His behaviour in 1745 was highly questionable. Anson eclipsed Vernon's achievements by his circumnavigation (1740–44) and the great victory off Finisterre in May 1747. Anson's political weight and professionalism dominated the later 1740s. In January 1748 Vernon published *Original Letters to an Honest Sailor*, being copies of several letters from political figures to him since 1739. It caused his enemies a little concern at first, but passed without serious repercussions. By 1756 Vernon had largely retired from public life. His three children had all died and his wife died on 9 May of that year. He died at Nacton on 30 October 1757 and was buried in St Martin's Church, Nacton, on 6 November.   RICHARD HARDING

Sources   personal papers of Edward Vernon, BL, Add. MSS 40804–40850 · E. Vernon, personal papers, NMM, VER 1/1–5 · E. Vernon, letters to the Best family, Medway Archives and Local Studies Centre, Rochester, Kent, Best MS U480 · memoirs of James Vernon, jun., BL, Add. MS 40794 · official correspondence of Vice-Admiral Vernon, PRO, SP 42/85 (1739–40); SP 42/90 (1741); SP 42/92 (1742) · parliamentary journal of Philip Yorke, BL, Add. MS 35337 · papers relating to the expedition to Cartagena, 1740–42, PRO, CO 5/41–2 · Vernon's correspondence with the admiralty, PRO, Adm 1/233 (Jamaica) · captain's letters, PRO, Adm 1/2624 (1698–1729), Adm 1/2625 (1730–1750) · captain's logs, PRO, Adm 51/254 (Dolphin); Adm 51/4327 (Rye); Adm 1/4118 (Assistance); Adm 51/582 (Mary); Adm 51/407 (Grafton) · commission and warrant books, PRO, Adm 6/6–13 · admiral's journal, PRO, Adm 50/27 · Walpole, *Corr.*, vols. 9, 17–19 · H. Walpole, *Memoirs of the reign of King George the Second*, ed. Lord Holland, 2nd edn, 3 vols. (1847) · *Manuscripts of the earl of Egmont: diary of Viscount Percival, afterwards first earl of Egmont*, 3 vols., HMC, 63 (1920–23) · Cornwall RO, Tremayne papers, T1918/3 [Penryn elections, 1705–41 and 1747–81] · J. Charnock, ed., *Biographia navalis*, 3 (1795), 349–74 · [C. Knowles], *An account of the expedition to Cartagena* (1743) · [E. Vernon], *Original papers relating to the expedition to Carthagena, Cuba and Panama* (1744) · [E. Vernon], *Admiral V----n's opinion upon the present state of the British navy* (1744) · [E. Vernon], *A specimen of naked truth from a British sailor: a sincere well-wisher to the honour and prosperity of the present royal family and his country* (1746) · [E. Vernon], *Seasonable advice from an honest sailor to whom it might have concerned, for the service of the C---n and C-----y* (1746) · [E. Vernon], *Original letters to an honest sailor* (1748) · E. Cruickshanks, 'Vernon, Edward', HoP, *Commons, 1715–54* · N. Rogers, *Whigs and cities: popular politics in the age of Walpole and Pitt* (1989) · K. Wilson, 'Empire, trade, and popular politics in mid-Hanoverian England: the case of Admiral Vernon', *Past and Present*, 121 (1988), 74–109 · W. F. Vernon, *Memorial of Admiral Vernon* (1861) · *IGI* · *Old Westminsters*, vol. 2

Archives BL, corresp. and papers, Add. MSS 40771–40850 · L. Cong., corresp. and papers relating to West Indies · Medway Archives and Local Studies Centre, Rochester, Kent, letters, some describing operations at Porto Bello and Carthagena · NMM, corresp. and papers, VER 1/1–5 · PRO · Royal Naval Museum, Portsmouth, instructions **Likenesses** J. Faber junior, mezzotint, 1740 (after T. Bardwell), BM, NPG · C. Philips, oils, 1743, NMM · T. Gainsborough, oils, c.1753, NPG [see illus.] · J. M. Rysbrack, bust on monument, c.1753, Westminster Abbey · G. Bockman, mezzotint (after G. Hansoon), BM · L. F. Roubiliac, bust, NMM · attrib. J. M. Rysbrack, marble bust, NMM · attrib. J. M. Rysbrack, marble bust, Sudbury Hall, Derbyshire · A. N. Sanders, mezzotint (after T. Gainsborough), BM, NPG · medals, BM

Vernon, Sir Edward (1723–1794), naval officer, was born on 30 October 1723, the fourth son of Henry Vernon (1663–1732), a politician, of Hilton, Staffordshire, and Penelope (d. 1726), daughter and coheir of Robert Phillips of Newton Regis, Warwickshire. Richard *Vernon was Edward's younger brother and Admiral Edward *Vernon (1684–1757) a distant relation. He entered the Royal Naval Academy at Portsmouth in November 1735, where he remained for three years and three months. He was then appointed a volunteer per order to the *Portland*, which had as its captain John Byng, whom he followed to the *Sunderland*, one of the fleet off Cadiz, and in the Mediterranean under Rear-Admiral Nicholas Haddock.

In 1742 Vernon was in the *Sutherland*, still in the Mediterranean, and he passed his examination on 3 March 1743. On 4 April he was promoted lieutenant of the sloop *Granada*, and in June 1743 he was appointed to the *Berwick*, then commissioned by Captain Edward Hawke, with whom he went out to the Mediterranean and was present in the action off Toulon on 11 February 1744. He was promoted commander of the sloop *Baltimore* on 5 December 1747, and captain of the *Mermaid* on 3 April 1753. In May 1755 he was appointed to the *Lyme* (20 guns) which was attached to the fleet in the Bay of Biscay during 1755–6, and in 1757 he was sent out to the Mediterranean with Admiral Henry Osborn. In November of the following year he was moved into the *St Albans* (64 guns), one of the fleet with Admiral Edward Boscawen when he defeated and destroyed the French fleet on 18–19 August 1759. Between 1760 and 1762 he commanded the *Revenge* under both Hawke and Boscawen in the Bay of Biscay.

After peace in 1763 Vernon was for some time captain of the *Kent*, flagship of Vice-Admiral Thomas Pye at Plymouth. In 1770 he successively commanded the guardships *Yarmouth* and *Bellona* at Portsmouth, and from March 1771, the *Barfleur*, Admiral Pye's flagship. Vernon was knighted by George II during a review of the fleet in June 1773. He remained in the *Barfleur* with Sir James Douglas until May 1775 when he was appointed to the *Ramillies* as commodore and commander-in-chief at the Nore. In May 1776 he became commander-in-chief in the East Indies, and went out with his broad pennant in the *Ripon* (60 guns) accompanied by only two small frigates and a corvette. When war with France broke out in 1778, Parker supposed his ships would come under attack from a superior French force. However, a similar sense of

limited capability also curbed French action. An indecisive action off Pondicherry on 10 August led to the French squadron's retiring permanently to Mauritius.

Vernon, who was promoted rear-admiral on 19 March 1779, returned to England early in 1781. He had no further service in the navy, but in the spring and summer of 1785 he attracted some notice by making a couple of balloon ascents from Tottenham Court Road, London, descending the first time at Horsham and the second at Colchester. Vernon became vice-admiral on 24 September 1787 and admiral on 12 April 1794; he died a few weeks later on 16 June 1794. After his death his arrears of pay were collected by his widow, Hannah, about whom no further details are known.   J. K. LAUGHTON, rev. NICHOLAS TRACY

Sources J. Charnock, ed., *Biographia navalis*, 6 vols. (1794–8) · D. Syrett and R. L. DiNardo, *The commissioned sea officers of the Royal Navy, 1660–1815*, rev. edn, Occasional Publications of the Navy RS, 1 (1994) · HoP, *Commons, 1715–54*
Archives NMM, papers, VER/2
Likenesses attrib. F. Hayman, oils, c.1755, NMM · plaster medallion, 1785 (after J. Tassie), Scot. NPG · H. Singleton, oils, c.1791, NMM

Vernon, Edward Venables-. *See* Harcourt, Edward (1757–1847).

Vernon, Francis (bap. 1637, d. 1677), traveller and diplomat, was born in London near Charing Cross and was baptized at St Martin-in-the-Fields on 18 January 1637, the elder son of Francis Vernon (d. 1647) and his wife, Anne (formerly Welby), daughter of George Smithes, a goldsmith in London; James *Vernon (bap. 1646, d. 1727) was his younger brother. He attended Westminster School between 1649 and 1654 and matriculated at Christ Church, Oxford, on 10 November 1654. He graduated BA on 28 January 1658 and proceeded MA on 17 July 1660. One of the leading scholars at Christ Church was the orientalist Edward Pococke, with whom Vernon later corresponded. It was probably Pococke who encouraged him to develop an interest in the Orient. After graduating Vernon spent several years on the move in Europe, and at one stage was captured by pirates. By March 1667 he was in Rome, an account of which he wrote for his mother. He was back in Oxford later in the year, when he composed a poem, printed with the title *Oxonium poema*, dealing with Oxford and its academic and student life.

Doubtless because of his 'great knowledge in many sciences and languages' (Rigaud, 2.243), the government decided to send Vernon on a diplomatic mission. He was initially selected to go to Sweden with the earl of Carlisle, but the decision was altered and he was sent instead to Paris in March 1669 with the embassy of Ralph Montagu. He remained in France until March 1672, apart from two brief visits to England in 1670 and 1671. His diplomatic duties were limited, most political correspondence of the embassy being conducted by his colleague, William Perwich. Vernon's chief responsibility was to keep track of the movement of British visitors, report to London any noteworthy incidents in which they were involved (crime and court cases being the most common), and render to well-connected travellers such assistance as they might require.

Vernon also made a point of mixing with scientists in Paris, and it is in this sphere that he was most prominent. He came to know members of the recently founded Academy of Sciences (1666), including Carcavy, Picard, Pecquet, Borelly, and Duhamel (who considered him a 'fort honneste homme, et tres capable'; *Correspondence of Henry Oldenburg*, 7.33); but he was especially close to Jean-Dominique (Giandomenico) Cassini and Christiaan Huygens. With the latter he had many conversations, and he visited Huygens when the scientist fell dangerously ill in 1670. Vernon passed news of the academy, and of these and other scientists, to Henry Oldenburg, secretary of the Royal Society. Oldenburg valued Vernon's letters, not least because the Academy of Sciences kept its proceedings secret and had no formal relations with other scientific bodies. Knowing that he would keep Oldenburg informed, Huygens, Cassini, and others spoke to Vernon about meetings of the academy, and thanks in no small measure to Vernon's intermediary services, Oldenburg and the Royal Society were kept up to date with developments within it. Vernon sent them progress reports on the building of the Paris Observatory, whose design caused much controversy among astronomers in the academy. He also took a close interest in Picard's project to deduce the size of the earth by obtaining an improved estimate of a degree of meridian. Vernon transmitted to Hooke, on Picard's behalf, questions on pendulums. When Picard's *Mesure de la terre* came out in 1671 Vernon sent Oldenburg a long abstract of the book, which as yet was unavailable in London. Cassini regularly provided Vernon with the results of his observations, including his discovery of the star Japet in 1671. Cassini hoped to become a member of the Royal Society, an aspiration which Vernon brought to the attention of Oldenburg. In 1672 both Cassini and Vernon himself were elected. Other British scholars were in contact with Vernon. Pococke sent some of his works to the Sorbonne via Vernon, and the mathematician John Collins maintained a steady correspondence, paying tribute to his 'assistance and friendship … concern[ing] the advancement of learning and mathematics' (Rigaud, 1.139). Collins employed Vernon's good offices in arranging the purchase and transportation to England of mathematical and other scientific books published in France and Italy.

The Paris embassy was Vernon's only diplomatic posting. His political masters seem to have concluded, and perhaps he himself agreed, that diplomacy was not his forte. He now planned an ambitious journey which reflected the influence of Pococke: back through France to Italy, down the Dalmatian coast to Smyrna, and thence to Persia. He left England in 1673, proceeding at a leisurely pace. By January 1676 he had reached Smyrna, from where he sent a description of his travels to Oldenburg, who published it in the *Philosophical Transactions* (24 April 1676). From there he proceeded across Asia Minor to Persia, which he reached early in 1677. Here he met disaster. He apparently engaged in a quarrel with a group of Arabs at Esfahan and

was killed; he was buried two days later. One can presume that, had he completed his journey, he would have written more accounts for the *Philosophical Transactions*, and perhaps would have composed a comprehensive history of his travels, for this was an age when travel literature was in vogue. His premature death means that we possess only hints of what might have been.

DAVID J. STURDY

Sources *The correspondence of Henry Oldenburg*, ed. and trans. A. R. Hall and M. B. Hall, 13 vols. (1965–86), vols. 5–9 · S. P. Rigaud and S. J. Rigaud, eds., *Correspondence of scientific men of the seventeenth century*, 2 vols. (1841) · 'Mr Francis Vernon's letter, giving a short account of some of his observations in his travels from Venice through Istria, Dalmatia, Greece, and the archipelago, to Smyrna', *PTRS*, 11 (1676), 575–82 · *CSP dom.*, 1668–9; addenda, 1660–70; 1671 · PRO, SP 78 (foreign) France, 126–36 · letter from Vernon to his mother, 26 March 1667, BL, Harley MS 6444 · F. Vernon, journals of travels in Greece, RS, MS 73 · Foster, *Alum. Oxon.* · Wood, *Ath. Oxon.*, new edn · *N&Q*, 2nd ser., 7 (2 April 1859) · *N&Q*, 9th ser., 4 (1 July 1899) · *IGI*
Archives RS, journals of travels in Greece | BL, description of Rome, in a letter to his mother, Harley MS 6444 · PRO, SP 78 (foreign) France, 126–36 · RS, letters to Henry Oldenburg

Vernon, Sir George (*c.*1578–1639), judge, was the son of Sir Thomas Vernon of Haslington, Cheshire, and his wife, Dorothy, daughter of William Egerton of Betteley. Admitted to the Inner Temple from Clement's Inn in 1594, Vernon was called to the bar in 1603 and to the bench in 1619, and as autumn reader in 1621 read on the Statute of Westminster II, c. 5, 'de advocationibus'. Created serjeant-at-law and knighted in 1627, Vernon served as baron of the exchequer from 1627 and justice of the common pleas from 1631 until his death in 1639.

Vernon came from a wealthy and well-established Cheshire family. He married twice, first Alice, daughter of Sir George Booth, from whom he acquired Haslington Hall. His second marriage, to Sir George Corbet's daughter Jane, brought them a daughter, Muriel, who married Henry Vernon of Sudbury in Derbyshire. At the time of his death Vernon had built up extensive land holdings around Haslington and Church Coppenhall. Vernon's 'slandering' (*CSP dom.*, 1627, 437) of the exchequer at Chester in litigation against Sir Randle Crew led to his imprisonment by Star Chamber about 1612. Vernon served in the parliament of 1626, where he was nominated to three committees examining acts to resolve oath taking and property issues.

Under James I the sale of the coif by the king's ministers had become an 'open scandal' (Baker, 110), exacerbated, in the reign of Charles I, by the influence of the duke of Buckingham over judicial appointments. Vernon was created serjeant-at-law on 4 July 1627, with the public patronage of Sir Thomas Coventry and Sir Robert Heath, and baron of exchequer on 13 November. Sir Richard Hutton, who was concerned by the non-consultation of judges before Vernon's call, was unsure whether to believe if Vernon had, as 'generalment reported', paid up to £1500 to the countess of Denbigh for his promotion to the exchequer, but hoped he would 'prove un honest man' (CUL, Add. MS 6863, fols. 40v–41). Upon appointment to a judgeship in the court of common pleas on 8 May 1631, Vernon remarked that he had found the king's 'favor far above his deserts' (*Diary of Sir Richard Hutton*, 86)—but it appears that he took his legal duties seriously; Croke later described him as 'a man of great reading in Statute and Common Law, and of extraordinary memory' (Leach, 566).

After his creation as serjeant Vernon challenged the integrity of the provincial council at Chester, and also at York. In 1627 attempts by Vernon to remove litigation between himself and Sir Randolph Crew from the determination of Roger Downes, vice-chamberlain of Chester, were rejected by fellow judges. In 1633 Vernon clashed with Sir Thomas Wentworth while presiding over the northern assizes, leading Wentworth to complain that the dignity of the council at York had been slighted, but Vernon continued to ride the northern circuit until the year of his death.

Generally Vernon was a supporter of crown policy. As a judge he enforced the oath of allegiance, serving on the high commission in 1633. Offering brief opinion in *Hampden's case* (1637–8) on grounds of poor health, Vernon supported the king's right to ship money 'notwithstanding any act of parliament', suggesting 'that a statute derogatory from the prerogative doth not bind the king; and the king may dispense with any law in cases of necessity' (*State trials*, 3.1125)—comments which drew his judicial reputation into obloquy. Vernon died on 16 or 17 December 1639, and was buried on 18 December in Temple Church. His death prevented his prosecution by parliament, but he was fined posthumously for his actions.

D. X. POWELL

Sources W. R. Prest, *The rise of the barristers: a social history of the English bar, 1590–1640* (1986), 141 n. 31, 261–2, 399 · Baker, *Serjeants*, 64, 110, 184, 364, 376, 380, 439, 542 · R. Stewart-Brown, ed., *Cheshire inquisitions post mortem: Stuart period, 1603–1660*, 3, Lancashire and Cheshire RS, 91 (1938), 134–9 [inquisition for Sir George Vernon] · W. J. Jones, *Politics and the bench: the judges and the origins of the English civil war* (1971), 38–9, 139, 143 · *The diary of Sir Richard Hutton, 1614–1639*, ed. W. R. Prest, SeldS, suppl. ser., 9 (1991), xxviii, 71, 84–6, 109, 111 · *CSP dom.*, 1625–49 · *State trials*, 3.1125 · *Liber famelicus of Sir James Whitelocke, a judge of the court of king's bench in the reigns of James I and Charles I*, ed. J. Bruce, CS, old ser., 70 (1858), 108 · W. B. Bidwell and M. Jansson, eds., *Proceedings in parliament, 1626*, 2: *House of Commons* (1992), 20–21; 3: *House of Commons* (1992), 139, 340 · J. S. Cockburn, *A history of English assizes, 1558–1714* (1972), 271–2, 292 · *Reports of Sir George Croke, knight: formerly one of the justices of the courts of king's bench and common pleas*, ed. and trans. H. Grimston, 4th edn, ed. T. Leach, 4 vols. (1790–92), vol. 3, p. 565 · *APC, 1628–9*, 562 · *R. v. George archbishop of Canterbury and Pryst* (1634), Croke Car 354, 79 ER 910 · *Crew v. Vernon* (1627), Croke Car 97, 79 ER 686 · *Stone v. Newman* (1635), Croke Car 427–32, 79 ER 971 · *Pine's case* (1628), Croke Car 117, 79 ER 703 · *Blunden v. Baugh* (1633), Croke Car 302, 79 ER 864 · *Williams' case* (1628), Croke Car 126, 79 ER 711 · *Smart v. Easdale* (1630), Croke Car 199, 79 ER 775 · *Lord Brooke v. Lord Goring* (1630), Croke Car 197, 79 ER 773 · *Bradstock v. Scovell* (1636), Croke Car 434, 79 ER 977 · *Hinsley v. Wilkinson* (1634), Croke Car 387, 79 ER 938 · *Hobert and Stroud's case* (1631), Croke Car 209, 79 ER 784 · administration, PRO, PROB 6/17, fol. 88v · will, PRO, PROB 11/183, sig. 89
Archives BL, MS 6666, fol. 509 · BL, MS 6668, fol. 899 · BL, MS 6673, fol. 101 · BL, MS 6681d, fol. 277 · BL, MS 38816, fols. 5–255, 258–61 · BL, Add. Charters MS 6283 · BL, Harley MS 786, fol. 7 · BL, Lansdowne MS dcxvii · BL, Sloane MS 3933, fol. 208b · CUL, MS Dd.9.22, fol. 25r
Wealth at death £46 2s.: Prest, *The rise of the barristers*

Vernon, George (1637/8–1720), Church of England clergyman, was born in Bunbury, Cheshire; his parents are unknown, but he was apparently unrelated to the great local dynasties of that name. His date of birth is derived from his age at matriculation and from his statement made in a deposition in 1670 that he was then thirty-two. He was admitted a servitor at Brasenose College, Oxford, matriculating in March 1654, aged sixteen, graduating BA in October 1657, and proceeding MA in July 1660. He took holy orders and became chaplain of All Souls, Oxford. In 1663 he was appointed rector of Sarsden in Oxfordshire. Subsequently Vernon was presented to the rectory of St Lawrence's at Bourton on the Water, Gloucestershire, a wealthy living of which he purchased the advowson, and to which his family continued to present until 1682.

The parish had a troubled recent history: of Vernon's predecessors, Temple, its priest at the commencement of the civil war, 'had been involved in scandalous suits … and actively resisted sequestration', while his successor, Anthony Palmer, 'a prominent Congregationalist', was ejected at the Restoration (*VCH Gloucestershire*, 6.46). Thereafter, Bourton was a prominent centre for dissenters, both Catholic and protestant: figures for 1667–76 suggest that the parish contained 'a higher proportion and a far higher number of Protestant dissenters than anywhere else in Stow deanery' and that 'half the papists were … gathered there'. A John Dunce, possibly the rector of Condicote during the interregnum, was preaching at Bourton in 1667 and was granted a licence for a meeting there in 1672; the lord of the manor, Charles Trinder, was a prominent Roman Catholic who housed chaplains of his faith (ibid., 6.47). These remarkable local circumstances probably best explain the beleaguered and often vituperative tone of the series of writings in defence of the theological and legal foundations of Anglican intolerance that followed Vernon's appointment.

The first of these, the anonymous *A Letter to a Friend Concerning some of Dr Owen's Principles and Practices* (1670) had its origins in a local debate, being Vernon's response to a friend's cordial invitation to read the writings of the dissenter John Owen. With the title-page taking its epigraphs from St Paul and the continental scourge of Independents, the heresiologist Salmasius, Vernon established from the outset a plangent tone. The first half of the pamphlet comprises a fierce attack on Owen's credentials, 'dilating upon the perjuries and perfidious as well as seditious practices of your friend' (p. 40), including his reneging on a succession of oaths, breaking faith with both Oliver and Richard Cromwell and, more predictably, Edward Hyde, earl of Clarendon, to whom he is alleged to have given a false assurance that he would not keep conventicles. Vernon's immediate grounds for writing are perhaps discovered in a passage elaborating on the reasons for considering Owen a continuing public menace, in which he claims his campaigns to persuade magistrates to relax their vigilance against dissenters had enjoyed some success. In the second half of the pamphlet Vernon denounces those beliefs and practices, supposedly endorsed in Owen's writings, 'that manifestly tend to the ruin of Religion and Government'; namely, 'if God's providence permits a mischief his will approves it'; that 'Saints [that is, dissenters] keep fast their holiness in their sinning'; concluding with a scornful attack on 'the modern way of pretending to, and praying, by the Spirit' (sig. A2v). In a postscript, addressed to Samuel Parker, the author of the controversial defence of Anglican monopoly *Ecclesiastical Politie* (1670), Vernon championed the legal restrictions on dissenting preachers and teachers, professing firsthand knowledge of their recent seditious assemblies, reporting 'You cannot imagine how many of the *Country-Coridons ...* were preached out of *Allegiance*', surmising luridly 'nothing was wanting but a *Lambert* or *Ludlow*' (p. 65). The pamphlet concludes with 'an Independent Catechism', a parody of the form chosen by Owen in his celebrated rejoinder to the Socinian Thomas Biddle, which, at its climax, professes regicidal republicanism as an article of faith.

Vernon was answered in *An Expostulatory Letter to the Author of the Late Slanderous Libel Against Dr O[wen]* (1671); a collaborative enterprise, its preface written by an anonymous well-wisher and correspondent of the dissenter, the main essay by Owen himself. The preface detected a well-worn strategy behind the *ad hominem* attack: 'by ... wounding, as you think, his Reputation, to render, as you hope, his Excellent and Learned Writings, the less useful to the great Ends of Christianity' (p. 2). It concluded with a personal rebuke to Vernon 'who make your pastime in most Companies where you come, to deride and scoff at your Reverend Diocesan hope, his Excellent and Learned Writings' (p. 12). Owen dismissed the 'whole discourse [as] a railing Accusation' (p. 16) and criticized Vernon's 'malicious wresting and false Applications of the passages he hath quoted' (p. 19). Shrewdly, Owen roundly denounced his detractor's rehearsal of his conduct during the interregnum as an offence against the king's wishes as published in the Act of Oblivion.

Vernon's next publication, *Ataxiae obstaculum* (1678), was also born of local disputation, *'being an answer to certain queries, dispersed in some parts of Gloucestershire'*. These had been sent to a local clergyman several years before by Thomas Overbury, nephew to the poet, and a sympathizer with dissenters, whose plight the original paper addressed, seeking to demonstrate 'the unreasonableness, especially on Protestant Principles, of exercising Force and Compulsion in Religion' (Overbury, sig. A2r). The private correspondence apparently remained so until 1676, when Overbury heard of 'a weak and unashamed Parson's having taken them into the Pulpit with him', a provocative act, precipitating a vigorous debate, one consequence of which was that the paper's author found himself 'Prosecuted at the Assizes as Criminal' (ibid., sig. A2r). Vernon's preface is forthright in its endorsement of religious intolerance, declaring his aims to be 'first, to remove those false Pretences of Conscience ... the *Scape-Goat*, to bear all Iniquities' and to come to 'the Defence of

Magistrate's Power in matters of Religion' (Vernon, *Ataxiae obstaculum*, sig. A5r). Urging unity 'against the common Enemy of *Protestantism*', Vernon reflected on the number of '*Jesuited*-Priests' who had escaped prosecution, concluding daringly with a contemptuous allusion to the king's earlier declaration of indulgence, observing that the 'vigorous execution of one Law, would do more good than a Million of *Proclamations*' (ibid., sigs. A6v, A6r). Vernon conceded that his answer to the queries had little originality, the defence of the established church's intolerance having been justified 'ex abundanti' by scholars, but pleaded some merit for his writings in its purpose of informing 'the private Christian' (ibid., sig. A2v). It was perhaps this professed aim that secured the imprimatur of William Jane, bishop of London. Overbury bolstered his reply by drawing on the writings of the Caroline divine William Chillingworth. He invited the reader to examine the caustic tone of Vernon's writing, reflecting 'how little he hath complied with the Gentleman's desire, in returning a Candid and Christian Resolution to them' (Overbury, sig. C1r). He also recorded his astonishment that 'an Impudent Libeller should be Licens'd to reflect thus upon the Government' (ibid., sig. C3r).

Vernon's next project was a life of Peter Heylin. In 1681 he was the principal contributor to an unsatisfactory account that appeared prefaced to the Laudian controversialist's collected works. In the following year he published *The Life of the Learned and Reverend Dr Peter Heylyn* (1682), justifying its publication by presenting it as his original text before it had been marred by 'the indiscretion of some persons, and the forwardness and ostentation of others' (Vernon, 'To the reader'). One remarkable curiosity of its preface was the extraordinary accusation made against one of Heylin's sterner critics, the presbyterian divine Richard Baxter, alleging his participation in a civil war atrocity. Baxter, he claimed, having witnessed a soldier run through with his sword a wounded royalist on the battlefield, took 'the King's picture from his Neck; telling him ... That he was a Popish Rogue and that was his Crucifix' (Vernon, 'To the reader'). Vernon further reported that Baxter had recently returned the image, and quoted the affidavit of the alleged victim of the assault.

The controversy that ensued came, however, from an unexpected and embarrassing quarter: a fellow Anglican clergyman John Barnard, Heylin's son-in-law who, in 1683, published *Theologo-historicus, or, The True Life of ... Peter Heylin*, in order, the title-page announced, 'to correct the Errors, supply the Defects, and confute the Calumnies of a late Writer'. In his compendious preface Barnard revealed the troubled history of Vernon's 'lame and imperfect' biography and his eventual unwilling collaboration in the version that had prefaced the 1681 collection at the request of its importunate publisher, by whom he was given *carte blanche* to make whatever additions he judged fitting (Barnard, 3). In contrast to his own authorial partitioning of the revised papers, Barnard alleged Vernon's response was 'to fall upon them as a Lion rampant', injudiciously revising contributions until 'mangled and metamorphised' beyond recognition and passed off without due acknowledgement as though his own (ibid., 8, 10). The remainder of the preface comprises a severe critique of Vernon's work, which, with some justice, accuses him of padding out the work with copious extracts from his subject's writings. Barnard was equally censorious of the inclusion of biographical material he considered indecorous, singling out for particular odium Vernon's apologetic account of Heylin's clandestine marriage. According to Anthony Wood, Vernon circulated a manuscript defence, composed with one of the Heylins, which apportioned blame between the printer and Thomas Barlow, bishop of Norwich, in whose possession the manuscript had resided. It remained unpublished and so this unhappy episode brought an end to his literary pretensions.

Vernon served the rest of his days as a parish priest. He died in his rectory in Bourton on the Water on 17 December 1720 and was buried at St Lawrence's Church. The succession of his eldest son, Richard (1674–1752), as rector inaugurated a series of family appointments to the living, which continued up until the eve of the nineteenth century. Richard was succeeded by William Vernon, a pluralist, who held the living until 1780, and 'after little more than a year a fourth member of the family, Edward, whose presentation, it was hinted, was simonaical, and whose learning, morals, and previous career were attacked, became rector' (VCH Gloucestershire, 6.46). Vernon is commemorated by a monument on the north wall of the chancel, commissioned by his daughter Dorothy, inscribed to her parents (Vernon's wife was also called Dorothy, but nothing more is known of her) and two brothers, Richard and Charles (1679–1736), rector of St Paul's, Shadwell, in Middlesex.　　　　　　　　　　　　　D. A. BRUNTON

Sources VCH Gloucestershire, vol. 6 · Wood, Ath. Oxon., new edn, 4.606 · J. Barnard, 'A necessary vindication', in J. Barnard, Theologo-historicus, or, The true life of … Peter Heylin (1683) [preface] · [T. Overbury], Ratiocium vernaculum (1678) · G. Vernon, The life of the learned and reverend Dr Peter Heylyn (1682) · [C. B. Heberden], ed., Brasenose College register, 1509–1909, 2 vols., OHS, 55 (1909) · DNB · N&Q, 148 (1925), 223

Vernon, George John Warren. See Warren, George John, fifth Baron Vernon (1803–1866).

Vernon, Sir Henry (c.1445–1515). See under Vernon family (per. 1411–1515).

Vernon, Henry, sixth Baron Powys (1548–1606), landowner and peerage claimant, was born on Christmas day 1548, the elder son of Thomas Vernon (d. 1557), of Stokesay, Shropshire, and his wife, Dorothy Lovel. His grandfather Thomas's marriage to Anne Ludlow, a coheir to the estate founded in the late thirteenth century by the famous wool merchant Lawrence of Ludlow, led to Henry's inheriting substantial Shropshire properties, and also a claim to greater eminence in the barony of Powys, founded on the belief that his maternal great-grandmother Elizabeth, wife of John Ludlow, was the daughter of Richard Grey, first Baron Powys. The death of Edward Grey, the fourth baron, without a legitimate heir in 1551 had led to Henry Vernon's father and uncle suing in chancery for the Powys lands and title; Henry himself devoted most of his adult life to the same cause. The records of this extended lawsuit, along with the survival of personal papers, help to make him one of the best-documented men of his rank from the Elizabethan age.

Aged nine when his father died in 1557, Henry Vernon was probably given into the custody of his grandfather, who died in 1562. On 15 November 1564 his wardship and marriage were granted to the countess of Rutland. He entered the Middle Temple on 31 October 1568, and came of age on 25 December 1569. No later than September 1571 he had relaunched his father's bid to secure the barony of Powys. As far as the lands were concerned he faced the problem that the fourth baron had made a series of settlements entailing most of his estates on his illegitimate son Edward Grey. Vernon's response was undeniably imaginative, a bizarre story (which became ever more elaborate as time passed) that the last document had been quite literally signed and sealed posthumously, when conspirators acting for Grey had opened his father's coffin as it lay at Buildwas and manipulated the dead man's hand so as to obtain a signature and a seal on a blank sheet of parchment, on which a conveyance had then been drawn up. As well as discrediting Grey's claim Vernon also had to prove his own, by providing satisfactory evidence that his ancestor Elizabeth Ludlow had indeed been Richard Grey's daughter. His attempts to do so provoked counter-allegations of forgery, possibly justified—he was said to have tried to strengthen his case by adding inscriptions to family tombs.

Vernon enjoyed an early success about 1574 when he secured the manor of Pontesbury in the bench; but thereafter constant litigation, both at county assizes and in the Westminster courts, though it aroused strong feelings in the west midlands, and provoked two successive days of rioting at Bridgnorth in 1577, brought him little but frustration. Baron Burghley referred Vernon's claim to the heralds, who found nothing to support it. In 1578 the issue was farcically complicated when it transpired that important documents in the keeping of Sir John Throckmorton had been nibbled by mice and the missing words later written in, enabling Vernon to make further allegations of forgery on Grey's behalf. But though his negligence cost Throckmorton 1000 marks and led to one of his subordinates losing his post, their offence hardly affected the issue. Vernon persevered, however, and made his greatest effort in 1590 when he appealed directly to the queen for recognition of his title. Elizabeth referred the case to the justices while Vernon, hopeful of success, on 22 October 1590 signed a deed styling himself cousin and heir of the late Lord Powys. But the justices sent the case to Star Chamber, where it had already been heard several times, and Vernon's hopes faded.

Possibly to build up an estate appropriate to a peerage title, Vernon bought four Herefordshire manors, paying £5500 for them between 1578 and 1581. The move proved unfortunate, for the vendors were in debt to the crown and by 1582 the manors had been taken into the queen's hands, reducing Vernon to trying to lease them from the crown. The costs of litigation were substantial, as were those of a lavish lifestyle. His account books show that he expected to dress well, purchasing such finery as a damask cloak with a velvet collar and 'a new taffeta hat with a bugle band and a black sprig in it' as well as a brush for his beard (PRO, SP 46/59, fol. 262). He usually travelled with a page and a handful of liveried attendants, but on 24 September 1583 he had a retinue of twenty-four men as he waited at Bewdley for the earl of Leicester (who did not come). He spent money on jewellery, gifts to musicians and paupers, books (in 1576 he bought Richard Edwards's *Paradise of Dainty Devices* and an account of the Spanish destruction of Antwerp), and food, some of it exotic—on 15 February 1583 he spent 2*d.* on 'potata roots' (ibid., fol. 321). Inevitably he borrowed frequently, and was several times rumoured to be financially stretched. In 1584 it was claimed that he was 'greatly in debt bothe by statute and otherwise and had solde much of his lande', an allegation Vernon angrily denied, asserting that his estate was worth at least £100 'more than discended to him from his father or grandfather' (PRO, REQ 2/136/34).

Disaster struck just when Vernon made his greatest effort. By Michaelmas 1591 he was in the Fleet, having backed a bond of £2000 for his cousin Francis Curzon of Kedleston. Curzon failed to pay and his creditors descended on his surety. While in prison Vernon received visits from a woman named Ursula Tey who claimed to be his wife. She was rumoured to be married to another man, and the warden of the Fleet was ordered to ensure 'that she slypp not to him in the house at any tyme disguised in man's apparell, as yt is likely she will, being the woman she is suspected to be' (*APC, 1591*, 468–9). Late in 1592 Vernon obtained his release and subsequently married Ursula, but his fortunes never recovered. Overwhelmed by debts, in December 1596 he mortgaged Stokesay, subsequently obtaining the money to redeem the mortgage and pay his other debts by undertaking to sell the manor to Sir George Mainwaring. Vernon later tried to renege on the deal but on 11 July 1598 the sale went ahead, for £6000. In February 1597 he had sold Pontesbury for £1600 and a few days later conveyed Westbury, part of his inheritance, to his cousin Robert Vernon of Hodnet.

By March 1599 Vernon was living in the Savoy, London, whence he claimed that Mainwaring owed him £3000; perhaps it was to settle this claim that on 4 March 1600 Mainwaring agreed to pay Vernon and his wife an annuity of £240. It was not much on which to keep up appearances (Vernon pertinaciously styled himself Lord Powys) and fend off creditors, and in Trinity term following he was outlawed for a debt of £400. Ursula seems to have died at the end of 1605, and by the following summer Vernon was living in Stoke Newington. He died there on 28 July 1606, having made a nuncupative will a few hours earlier, leaving all his worldly goods to one Peter Brambile, possibly his landlord; with perhaps characteristic panache he had declared that 'if they were a kingdom they were too little' (PRO, PROB 11/110, no. 69). Litigation against Brambile by Vernon's next-of-kin John Curzon followed, unsuccessfully. In 1609 Robert Vernon allowed Edward Grey, son of

Henry Vernon's opponent, to buy him out of his claim to the Powys lands; claims to the barony resurfaced at intervals for centuries. HENRY SUMMERSON

Sources chancery, early chancery proceedings, PRO, C 1/1080, 1364, 1389 · chancery, court of chancery, pleadings series 1, PRO, C 2/Eliz/M9/56 · chancery, court of chancery, pleadings series 2, PRO, C 3/77/37 · chancery, court of chancery, pleadings, Mitford, PRO, C 8/634/11 · chancery, common law pleadings, rolls chapel series, PRO, C 43/4/6, 6/66 · chancery, miscellanea, transcripts of deeds and evidences, PRO, C 47/9/52/10 · chancery, inquisitions post mortem series 2, PRO, C 142/104 no. 70, 108 no. 119, 128 no. 82, 132 no. 15, 235 no. 94 · chancery, ancient deeds series C, PRO, C 146/8652, 8665, 9131 · court of common pleas, recovery rolls, PRO, CP 43/69m 39d · exchequer, depositions taken by commission, PRO, E 134/32 and 33 Eliz/Mich. 1 · exchequer, inquisitions post mortem series 2, PRO, E 150/871/2 · prerogative court of Canterbury, wills, PRO, PROB 11/110/69 · prerogative court of Canterbury, acts of court books, PRO, PROB 29/22 · court of requests, proceedings, PRO, REQ 2/136/34 · state papers domestic, Elizabeth I, PRO, SP 12/147/19 · state papers domestic, supplementary, PRO, SP 46/43, 59, 175 · star chamber, proceedings Elizabeth I, PRO, STAC/P 2/26; G 8/38; V 4/5; V 5/29; V 6/20; V 8/3; V 8/29; V 8/39; V 9/9 · court of wards and liveries, deeds and evidences, PRO, WARD 2/38/145/1 · star chamber, proceedings Elizabeth I, addenda, PRO, STAC 7/8/3 · BL, Add. MSS 21023, 30322 · BL, Lansdowne MSS 66, 109 · CUL, Add. MS 3888 · Coll. Arms, Vincent MS 99 · Craven deeds, Bodl. Oxf., vols. 66, 67 · CPR, 1563–6; 1572–5 · APC, 1587–8, 1590–91; 1591; 1592 · R. Flenley, ed., *Calendar of the register of the queen's majesty's council in the dominion and principality of Wales and the marches of the same* (1916) · H. A. C. Sturgess, ed., *Register of admissions to the Honourable Society of the Middle Temple, from the fifteenth century to the year 1944*, 1 (1949) · P. Williams, *The council in the marches of Wales under Elizabeth I* (1958) · W. Burson, 'The Kynaston family', *Transactions of the Shropshire Archaeological and Natural History Society*, 2nd ser., 6 (1894), 209–22 · H. Hall, 'Some notes on the Powis peerage case in the reign of Elizabeth', *The Genealogist*, new ser., 4 (1887), 47–9 · GEC, *Peerage*, vol. 6

Archives PRO, personal account books and notebooks, SP 46/59, 175

Vernon, James (*bap.* 1646, *d.* 1727), government official and politician, was baptized on 1 April 1646 at St Martin-in-the-Fields, Westminster, the second son of Francis Vernon (*d.* 1647), government official, of Covent Garden, Westminster, and his wife, Anne, daughter of George Smithies, goldsmith, of London, and widow of William Welby of Gedney, Lincolnshire. He was educated at Charterhouse School and, from 1662, Christ Church, Oxford, where he graduated BA in 1666 and MA in 1669. He soon came to the attention of Sir Joseph Williamson, under-secretary, and later secretary, of state, who employed Vernon as a collector of news and in March 1672 sent him on a secret mission into Flanders to interview the spy John Scott and to gather military, political, and naval intelligence. The same year, in June, Vernon went with Viscount Halifax as a secretary on the latter's mission to the French court. In 1672 Williamson also recommended Vernon as a private secretary to the earl of Sunderland, then at his ambassador's post in Paris. Sunderland was to thank Williamson 'in giving Mr Vernon leave to come to me, desiring very much to have one bred up under you and [in] whome you have a good opinion' (PRO, SP 78/135, fol. 57). In turn Vernon noted that 'my L[or]d … received me very kindly which I owe entirely to the good opinion you have pleased to create in him of me by your letters' (PRO, SP 78/135, fol. 76).

In 1673 Vernon became private secretary to Charles II's eldest illegitimate son, James Scott, duke of Monmouth, and was given a pension of £300 a year. In 1675, by a licence of 6 April, he married Mary (d. 1715), daughter of Sir John Buck, first baronet, of Hamby Grange, Lincolnshire. The couple lived in St Martin-in-the-Fields and had two sons and two daughters. Both sons followed their father in the service of the state: the elder, James, was a government official, and the younger, Edward *Vernon (1684–1757), became an admiral. Vernon's wealth and position increased further with the death of his elder brother, Francis *Vernon, in 1677, and in the same year he met Godfrey Kneller and became his patron. Kneller painted Vernon's portrait, and in return Vernon paid the rent on a house in Durham Yard for Kneller. In addition Vernon profitably introduced the artist to Monmouth. Kneller was grateful and noted that Vernon could 'introduce [me] to courtiers, for I take him for an honest and most charming gentleman, as all who know him say' (BL, Add. MS 4277, fol. 104).

As Monmouth's secretary Vernon served with the duke in Scotland and Flanders and was given a seat in parliament as his client. His relationship with Monmouth was close; it was alleged that it was Vernon who erased the word 'natural' from Monmouth's patent for the post of commander-in-chief in 1674, which identified Monmouth as Charles II's 'natural son'. While in Flanders with the duke Vernon kept a journal of the campaign of 1678 which was meant to illuminate his patron's noble deeds. In the campaign against the Scottish covenanters in 1679 Vernon remained ever close to the duke and was later satirized as one of Monmouth's creatures and a possible evil counsellor. He sat for Cambridge University in the first parliament of 1679 and voted for the bill to exclude the duke of York from the succession. Vernon later became uncomfortable with Monmouth's politics, expressing the wish to Edmund Warcup that 'M[onmouth] would leave the party and return to [the] K[ing]' ('Journals of Edmund Warcup', 256). He did not, however, leave Monmouth's service until the duke went into exile for a second time in 1684. A warrant was issued for Vernon's arrest in June 1685 during Monmouth's rebellion. A whig 'collaborator' in 1688, he went over to William's service by late December. He donated £1500 to the new regime.

Vernon was subsequently employed on the *London Gazette* and then served as an under-secretary, or more correctly a private secretary, to the earl of Shrewsbury, secretary of state for the south, from February 1689 to June 1690. He then performed a similar task for Sir John Trenchard, and also served in Flanders as a collector of news from March 1693 to March 1694, until Shrewsbury's return to office from March 1694 until December 1697. In 1693 he was appointed a commissioner of prizes, a post he held until 1705. Vernon's work in the secretary's office was conscientious and professional. Although he was not an

innovative bureaucrat, he was one of the new administrators who were engineering a revolution in government. Indeed it was probably he, rather than the increasingly absent Shrewsbury, who really ran affairs in the office. The lords justices appointed Vernon as their secretary during their meetings while William III was on campaign and Vernon was effectively acting as *de facto* southern secretary during Shrewsbury's absence. He was prominent in the investigations into the assassination plot of 1696, ensuring the charges made by Fenwick against Godolphin, Shrewsbury, Marlborough, and Russell were placed under a suitable veil of obscurity.

Shrewsbury's frequent moral and physical collapses and Sunderland's wrangling with the junto lords eventually led to the crisis of 1697 when, through Sunderland's influence, Vernon was, reluctantly he said, bounced upstairs to the post of northern secretary of state on 2 December in place of Sir William Trumbull. Before his appointment Vernon wrote to Shrewsbury that:

> You are coming into a strange intricacy. My Lord Chamberlain [Sunderland] in some companies, declares for my Lord Wharton, and knows there is no such thing intended. My lord Wharton shews a willingness to accept it, and, at the bottom, has no mind to it … One you know [Vernon himself] is secretly designed for secretary, and he is utterly incapable of it. (*Letters Illustrative*, 1.431)

Shrewsbury's fellow secretary Trumbull had in fact already complained of being slighted and swindled by Vernon in his work, and although Vernon tended to portray himself as a mere official lost in the world of grasping high politics, he was as keenly ambitious as any other later seventeenth-century politician. Despite tearful protests that he had never wanted the post in the first place Vernon seized the seals with alacrity when they were offered.

Vernon clung on to high office for some six years but he was not, however, a policy maker. He was in reality one of the 'little men … such as were framed for a dependence on a premier minister' (*Letters Illustrative*, 2.359). He was often kept in ignorance as to the king's intentions in foreign affairs and as one satire put it, 'Vernon's by all men believed a meer Tool' (Lord and others, 6.222). Vernon also sat in parliament as a court whig for Penryn from 1695 to 1698, for Westminster from 1698 to December 1701, and for Penryn again from 1705 to 1710. He claimed in May 1699 that 'No man has ever had so little conversation with the Tories as myself' (*Letters from James Vernon*, letter 183, 13 May 1699).

Vernon became sole secretary of state from December 1698 to May 1699. When the earl of Jersey was appointed in May 1699 Vernon went into the northern province out of choice, claiming that without rank or ambition he would be exposed to envy should he be placed as senior secretary. It may also be significant that negotiations with France, part of the southern secretary's brief, were also at a delicate stage. With Jersey's dismissal in June 1700 Vernon did take the southern post, but he was able to exchange once more in 1702. He had some part in the formation of the two partition treaties: he was confronted with the terms of the document in the first instance and told to sound out the leading whig responses. In the second case he was merely directed to prepare a commission authorizing the plenipotentiaries with the names left blank. Vernon escaped impeachment, although undoubtedly involved, because it was well known that his role was more of a clerk than a maker of policy and he eagerly produced incriminating documents to a parliament with bigger prey in its sight.

Vernon finally left the secretary's office on 1 May 1702 claiming that he was 'too obnoxious to the [Tory] party to be continued' (*Letters Illustrative*, 3.222). His whig sympathies did not help his case, despite his still-diligent administrative capacity. It was then falsely rumoured that he was to go to Venice as envoy-extraordinary. To compensate him, however, Vernon was given an annual pension of £1000 and his arrears were paid. He was also made teller in the exchequer, a sinecure post which he lost in 1710 on the victory of the tories. Ultimately Vernon seems to have been relieved that his administrative burden had finally been laid down: 'I please myself with the satisfaction I shall find in retirement, and the conversation of honest old authors' and that it was 'infinitely preferable to the bustle of secretaryship' (*Letters Illustrative*, 3.222–9). He was a commissioner of the privy seal in 1716 but thereafter lived in retirement in Watford in Hertfordshire until his death on 31 January 1727, aged eighty-one. He was buried in Watford parish church.

One contemporary thought that Vernon had 'many good qualities, some of which one would not expect under so rough an outside' (*Letters Illustrative*, 3.233). Ultimately Vernon was a functional man of government and business rather than a politician or statesman of the first order. Gifted in the administrative field, his earlier career had given him a number of opportunities which he ably exploited, and his voluminous correspondence bears testament to his involvement in much of the complex politics of the 1690s.   ALAN MARSHALL

Sources PRO, SP 78/135, fols. 57–76 · *Letters illustrative of the reign of William III from 1696 to 1708 addressed to the duke of Shrewsbury by James Vernon*, ed. G. P. R. James, 3 vols. (1841) · *Letters from James Vernon to the duke of Shrewsbury, 1696–1708, from the Shrewsbury papers in Boughton House, Northamptonshire*, ed. D. Rubini (1980) [microform] · J. Child, 'Monmouth and the army in Flanders', *Journal of the Society for Army Historical Research*, 52 (1974), 3–12 · M. A. Thomson, *The secretary of state, 1681–1782* (1968) · J. P. Kenyon, *Robert Spencer, earl of Sunderland, 1641–1702* (1958) · J. N. P. Watson, *Captain-general and rebel chief: the life of James, duke of Monmouth* (1979) · J. C. Sainty, ed., *Officials of the secretaries of state, 1660–1782* (1973) · Vertue, *Note books*, vol. 1 · 'The journals of Edmund Warcup, 1676–84', ed. K. G. Feiling and F. R. D. Needham, *EngHR*, 40 (1925), 235–60 · BL, Add. MS 4277 · G. de F. Lord and others, eds., *Poems on affairs of state: Augustan satirical verse, 1660–1714*, 7 vols. (1963–75), vols. 6–7 · *Eleventh report*, HMC (1887) · *Twelfth report*, HMC (1890) · *Thirteenth report*, HMC (1892) · *Fourteenth report*, HMC (1896) · will, PRO, PROB 11/614, fols. 61–3 · IGI · J. P. Ferris, 'Vernon, James', HoP, *Commons, 1660–90*
Archives BL, corresp. and papers, Add. MSS 4199, 4202, 40771–40850 | BL, corresp. with William Blathwayt, Add. MS 34348; Egerton MS 920 · BL, corresp. with Sir William Dutton Colt, Add. MS 34096 · BL, letters to John Ellis, Add. MSS 28879–28900, *passim* · BL, corresp. with Lord Lexington, Add. MS 46527 · BL, corresp. with Lord Portland, Add. MS 29592 [copies] · BL, corresp. with Lord Portland and Sir Joseph Williamson, Add. MS 69955 · BL, corresp. with Sir Robert Southwell, Add. MS 34335 · CKS, corresp. with Alexander Stanhope · Glos. RO, letters to Sir George Rooke · Longleat House, Wiltshire, corresp. with Matthew Prior · NMM, letters to Edward Vernon, VER/1/1 · Northants. RO, corresp. with duke of Shrewsbury · PRO, corresp. with George Stepney, SP 105/54, 60, 82 · U. Nott. L., corresp. with Lord Portland · Yale U., Beinecke L., letters to William Blathwayt
Likenesses G. Kneller, oils, 1677, NPG, Beningbrough Hall · studio of G. Kneller, oils, 1677, NPG · F. Hayman, oils, Phoenix Art Museum, Arizona
Wealth at death £5880 (some sums in investments in Bank of England or out as loans): will, PRO, PROB 11/614, fols. 61–3

Vernon, Jane Henrietta. *See* Poitier, Jane Henrietta (*b.* 1736, *d.* in or after 1788).

Vernon, Joseph (*c.*1738–1782), singer and actor, was born in Coventry illegitimately and grew up in the Coventry charity school. He became a choirboy at St Paul's Cathedral, London, where William Savage was master of the choristers. While still a choirboy he made his Drury Lane début, on 26 December 1750, as Puck in the pantomime *Queen Mab*. He also performed that season in T. A. Arne's *Alfred*, Shakespeare's *Romeo and Juliet*, and Boyce's *The Shepherd's Lottery*. He continued to perform at Drury Lane after his voice broke and he became a tenor. On 27 June 1755 he married Jane *Poitier (*b.* 1736), another singer at Drury Lane. At least one of them was under age. The wedding took place at the Savoy Chapel, whose clergy mistakenly thought they were exempt from the provisions of Hardwicke's Marriage Act of 1754. The marriage was annulled and both the officiating chaplain and the curate, Tate Wilkinson's father, John, were sentenced to transportation to America. Vernon testified against them. On 27 September, and on several later occasions, Vernon was hissed off the Drury Lane stage for his role in the affair. Tate Wilkinson gave a detailed, though naturally biased, version of the episode: his father died on the voyage.

Vernon spent much of the following six years on the Dublin stage. In 1759 he is said to have witnessed a murder but was paid by the murderer's father not to testify. He returned occasionally to Drury Lane, until on 21 September 1762 he became once again a regular member of the company. He took leading roles in many of the new operas, including most of those by Dibdin, and Rush's *The Royal Shepherd*. He also acted in plays, including some by Shakespeare. When Sheridan and Linley took over Drury Lane from Garrick in 1776 he was past his best as a singer, but nevertheless took the title role in Linley's first opera, *Selima and Azor*. He made his final appearance on 9 October 1781.

On 8 January 1773 Vernon married Margaret Richardson. He was a freemason, a member of the grand lodge, in the 1770s.

Contemporary critics indicate that Vernon's acting remained strong throughout his career but his singing voice weakened with age. Quoting *The Theatrical Biography* of 1772, Genest states:

it is seldom found that a good actor is a good singer—Vernon stands an exception to that rule; for tho' he now only lives in point of voice upon the echo of his former reputation, he *was* excellent in both. (Genest, 6.220)

Vernon composed several songs and ballads, mostly for use in stage works in which he performed. He wrote the best-known version of Feste's epilogue in *Twelfth Night*, 'When that I was and a little tiny boy'.

He died on 19 March 1782 in Lambeth of a lingering illness, and the administration of his effects was granted to his widow, Margaret. He was buried at St Martin-in-the-Fields, London.

JANE GIRDHAM

Sources G. W. Stone, ed., *The London stage, 1660–1800*, pt 4: 1747–1776 (1962) · Highfill, Burnim & Langhans, *BDA* · R. Fiske, *English theatre music in the eighteenth century*, 2nd edn (1986) · T. Wilkinson, *Memoirs of his own life*, 4 vols. (1790), vol. 1, pp. 78–81 · *GM*, 1st ser., 52 (1782), 151 · PCC administration grant, 15 April 1782, PRO, PROB 6/158, fol. 230v · J. Burn, *The Fleet registers: comprising the history of Fleet marriages* (1834), 139–41 · Genest, *Eng. stage* · S. McVeigh, *Concert life in London from Mozart to Haydn* (1993), 187 · Mr Dibdin [C. Dibdin], *A complete history of the English stage*, 5 (privately printed, London, [1800]), 365 · J. Boaden, *Memoirs of Mrs Siddons*, 1 (1827), 262 · C. Dibdin, *The professional life of Mr. Dibdin* (1803), 2.55 · T. J. Walsh, *Opera in Dublin, 1705–1797: the social scene* (1973) · *New Grove*
Likenesses engraving, pubd 1776 (as Macheath) · G. Carter, group portrait, c.1782 (*The apotheosis of Garrick*; with contemporary actors), Royal Shakespeare Theatre, Stratford upon Avon · J. Caldwell and S. Smith, line engraving, pubd 1783 (*Immortality of Garrick*; after G. Carter), BM · J. Roberts, coloured drawing, on vellum (as Thurio in *The two gentlemen of Verona*), BM; engraved copy, repro. in J. Bell, *Bell's British theatre* (1777); Christies, 27 March 1793 [Bell collection] · J. Roberts, engraving (as Macheath in *The beggar's opera*), repro. in J. Bell, *Bell's British theatre* (1777); Christies, 27 March 1793 · J. Roberts, pencil drawing (in character), Harvard TC · Thornthwaite, engraving (as Macheath; after J. Roberts) · engraving (as Cymon), repro. in *Vocal Magazine* (1778) · engraving (as Hawthorn in *Love in a village*), repro. in J. Gay, *The beggar's opera* (1777) · pencil and watercolour drawing (as Cymon in *Cymon*), Garr. Club · prints, BM, NPG

Vernon, Philip Ewart (1905–1987), educational psychologist and university teacher, was born on 6 June 1905 in Oxford, the second of three children and the elder son of Horace Middleton Vernon, physiologist and fellow of Magdalen College, Oxford, and his wife, Katherine Dorothea, daughter of the Revd William Ewart, of Bishop Cannings, Wiltshire. He was educated at the Dragon School in Oxford, Oundle School, and St John's College, Cambridge, where he graduated with first-class honours in physics, chemistry, and physiology in 1926 (natural sciences tripos, part one) and in 1927 with a first in psychology (moral sciences tripos, part two). He then completed a PhD on the psychology of musical appreciation. Vernon was a good amateur musician, possessing perfect pitch and able to play the piano, oboe, organ, and horn.

While a research student at St John's College in 1927, Vernon won a Rockefeller fellowship for study in America. In 1929 he worked at Yale on personality assessment and spent a year at Harvard with Gordon Allport. From 1931 to 1933 he was a research and teaching fellow at St John's, which he left to work as a child psychologist at the Maudsley Hospital, London. There he gained important practical experience, which infused his work. In 1935 he was appointed head of the department of psychology in the

Jordanhill Training Centre, Glasgow, which trained teachers. In 1938 he became head of Glasgow University's department of psychology. He remained there until 1947, working also at the War Office and Admiralty on personnel selection. In 1949 he was appointed to the professorship of educational psychology in the Institute of Education, University of London. He retired from that post in 1968 to take up a professorship of educational psychology in the University of Calgary, Alberta, Canada, from which he retired officially in 1975.

Vernon was an outstanding educational psychologist, who specialized in psychometrics, the measurement of human abilities and personality. His work was notable for his exceptional ability to synthesize in a balanced and fair-minded manner large quantities of apparently disparate findings. In addition, the clarity of his writing enabled generations of students, in both education and psychology, to understand the statistical problems and complexities which render mental measurement such a difficult subject for many teachers.

In the field of human abilities Vernon synthesized two apparently opposing views, those of the British psychologists, who stressed the importance of a single general factor of ability, and the Americans, who thought that there were a number of separate human abilities. He showed that a hierarchical ordering of abilities with a broad general reasoning factor and important group factors such as verbal and spatial ability would fit the results. He also attempted to elucidate the environmental and genetic factors underlying general intelligence and his argument that there was a considerable genetic determination is generally accepted in the light of more recent data.

Unlike many psychometrists, Vernon believed that psychological findings should be applied to real-life situations. His writing was aimed at teachers and educationists in the hope that high standards of measurement would be employed in education—always, it should be noted, for the good of the children. During the Second World War his work for the War Office on officer selection hugely improved selection procedures. In 1949 he published, with J. B. Parry, *Personnel Selection in the British Forces*. Among his other books were *The Measurement of Abilities* (1940), *Personality Tests and Assessments* (1953), *Intelligence and Cultural Environment* (1969), and *Intelligence: Heredity and Environment* (1979).

Vernon was made an honorary DSc of the University of London and was a fellow of the American Psychological Association, life fellow of the Canadian Psychological Association, and honorary fellow of the British Psychological Society, of which he was the president in 1954–5. In 1980 he received an honorary degree of LLD from the University of Calgary.

Vernon was a shy and highly introverted person who rarely seemed to relax. He was a tall man with an impressive demeanour and an almost military bearing. Like his books he appeared to be supremely rational, although he was human enough not to abandon smoking despite the respiratory problems which first led him to Calgary. His choice of psychology may well have been influenced by his father, who abandoned his fellowship at Oxford to alleviate the conditions of factory workers and who effectively became an industrial psychologist. His older sister, Magdalen Vernon, also became a professor of psychology, at Reading University.

In 1938 Vernon married a schoolteacher, Annie Craig, daughter of Robert Gray, a solicitor. In 1946 she met an early death through ill health and in 1947 he married Dorothy Anne Fairley, an educational psychologist and daughter of William Alexander Lawson, a civil and marine engineer. They had one child, Philip Anthony, a specialist in human intelligence. Vernon died of cancer in Calgary, Alberta, on 28 July 1987.　　　　　　　PAUL KLINE, rev.

Sources *Bulletin of the British Psychological Society*, 40 (1987) · *The Times* (30 July 1987) · *The Independent* (7 Aug 1987) · personal knowledge (1996)
Likenesses photograph, repro. in *The Independent*

Vernon, Sir Richard (1389/90–1451). *See under* Vernon family (*per.* 1411–1515).

Vernon, Richard (1726–1800), horse-racing entrepreneur and politician, was born on 18 June 1726 and baptized on the same day in Shaveshill, Staffordshire, the fifth son of the seven children of Henry Vernon (1663–1732), MP for Hilton, Staffordshire, and his wife Penelope Phillips (*d.* 1726), daughter and coheir of Robert Phillips of Newton Regis, Warwickshire. Two of his elder brothers were Henry Vernon (1718–1765), who became MP for Lichfield and then Newcastle under Lyme, and Admiral Sir Edward *Vernon (1723–1794).

After travelling in Italy and France in 1743, Vernon was appointed ensign in the 1st regiment of Horse Guards on 22 November 1744. He was promoted lieutenant and captain on 12 January 1747, but resigned on 30 October 1751 in order to enter politics. He attached himself to John Russell, fourth duke of Bedford, and acted as his second secretary when Bedford was lord lieutenant of Ireland. He was returned to parliament on 10 December 1754 for the duke's borough of Tavistock, and, as member for Bedford in the succeeding parliament, was appointed in April 1764 a clerk comptroller of the household. He was re-elected for the same constituency in the next parliament (1768–74), and sat for Okehampton from 1774 to 1780, and for Newcastle under Lyme from 1784 to 1790. There is no evidence that he ever spoke in the Commons during the thirty-six years he sat as an MP in the chamber.

It was on the turf, and not in the army or in parliament, that Vernon made a name for himself. As early as 4 June 1751 the betting book at the old White's Club records a wager between Lord March and 'Capt. Richard Vernon, *alias* Fox *alias* Jubilee Dicky'. Vernon was blackballed at the new club the following year on account of his closeness to Bedford, although he was 'a very inoffensive, good-humoured young fellow, who lives in the strongest intimacy with all the fashionable young men' (H. Walpole to Sir Horatio Mann, 2 Feb 1752, Walpole, 20.301). On 15 February 1759 he married at St George's, Bloomsbury, Evelyn Fitzpatrick, countess of Upper Ossory (*bap.* 1724, *d.* 1763), widow of John Fitzpatrick, first earl of Upper Ossory, and

sixth daughter of John Leveson-*Gower, first Earl Gower, and his first wife, Evelyn Pierrepont. She was also the sister of the duchess of Bedford. They had three daughters; she died only four years after their marriage on 12 April 1763 at Montauban, France, where she was buried.

After moving to Newmarket, Vernon entered a racing partnership with Lord March, afterwards the fourth duke of Queensberry, commonly known as Old Q. Thomas Holcroft the dramatist, who was for two and a half years in his stables, thought Vernon 'a gentleman of acute notoriety on the turf'. By means of betting and breeding horses Vernon converted 'a slender patrimony of three thousand pounds into a fortune of a hundred thousand' before quitting the turf as an owner (*Memoirs of … Holcroft*, 1.91, 117, 165).

Vernon, who was one of the original members of the Jockey Club, bred and owned a large number of horses. The Vernon Arabian, sire of the dam of Emigrant, winner of the July Stakes in 1796, was owned if not imported by him; and Diomed, winner of the first Derby, came from his stables. He also ran horses for many years, and in 1758 himself rode in a gentleman-jockey race at Newmarket. In 1753 he won one of the two Jockey Club plates, and in 1768 carried off the first Jockey Club challenge cup with Marquis, son of the Godolphin Arabian. At the first Craven meeting (1771) he won the stakes with Pantaloon against a field of thirteen; and his three-year-old Fame by that sire ran second for the first Oaks on 14 May 1779. In 1787 he won the Oaks with Annette (by Eclipse).

Vernon was one of those who began the running of yearlings at Newmarket. In 1791, when the conduct of Chifney, the prince of Wales's jockey, had been criticized by the club but upheld by his master, Old Dick Vernon (as he was called) was reported to have said that the prince, having the best horses and the best jockey, was 'best off the turf'. The Jockey Club were his tenants at the old coffee-room at Newmarket. The ground lease was purchased by him in 1771, and bought by the stewards on its expiration sixty years later.

Vernon was an innovative horticulturist and is credited with the introduction of fruit-forcing. His peaches at Newmarket were famous. His sporting traditions were carried on by his nephew, Henry Hilton, whose name appears in the first official list of the Jockey Club, published in 1835.

Vernon died at Newmarket on 16 September 1800. Of his daughters, who are frequently mentioned in Horace Walpole's letters, the eldest, Henrietta, married in 1776 George Greville, second earl of Warwick. The second, Caroline, who shared her father's love for horse-racing, married the wit Robert Percy *Smith (Bobus Smith), and was the mother of Robert Vernon Smith, Lord Lyveden, who edited Walpole's correspondence with his grandmother, the countess of Ossory.

G. LE G. NORGATE, rev. J.-M. ALTER

Sources L. B. Namier, 'Vernon, Richard', HoP, *Commons, 1754–90* · R. Black, *The Jockey Club and its founders, in three periods* (1891) · W. B. Boulton, *The history of White's*, 2 (1892), 22 · L. H. Curzon, *A mirror of the turf, or, The machinery of horse-racing revealed* (1892), 27, 118 · L. H. Curzon [J. G. Bertram], *The blue ribbon of the turf: a chronicle of the race* *for the Derby* (1890), 229, 234, 239, 245–6 · J. R. Robinson, '*Old Q*': *a memoir of William Douglas, fourth duke of Queensberry* (1895), 37–8 · *Memoirs of the late Thomas Holcroft*, ed. W. Hazlitt, 1 (1816), 91, 117, 165 · Walpole, *Corr.* · J. C. Whyte, *History of the British turf*, 1 (1840) · Burke, *Gen. GB* (1858) · *GM*, 1st ser., 29 (1759), 94 · *GM*, 1st ser., 70 (1800), 909 · *IGI* · J. Ingamells, ed., *A dictionary of British and Irish travellers in Italy, 1701–1800* (1997)

Vernon, Robert (1774/5–1849), art collector and patron, was the son of William Vernon (*d.* 1801) and his wife, Mary. His father was a hackneyman in Mount Street, Berkeley Square, London, from 1793 until his death in December 1801, when his estate was valued at £3350; Vernon took over and greatly expanded the business. By 1812 he had a collection of English historical portraits and old masters, some of which he sold at a loss in 1831. By 1826 he was collecting modern British pictures, and in 1832 he leased 50 Pall Mall, which from 1843 he opened to the public. The adjacent property housed the *Art Union*, founded in 1839 and edited by S. C. Hall, who puffed Vernon's pictures, the right to reproduce which was granted to the journal by Vernon. Indeed, reproductions of Vernon's paintings became a mainstay of that journal.

On 22 December 1847 a selection of Vernon's collection—157 pictures (all British except one), eight sculptures, and one watercolour—made by the National Gallery was vested in its trustees. One picture depicted the home of Sir John Fleming Leicester, who had anticipated Vernon's idea of a public collection of modern British art, as too had Sir Francis Chantrey. Vernon, however, was the first to realize it. About 1830, together with Chantrey and J. M. W. Turner, Vernon had planned bequests to galleries and of money (£70,000 in Vernon's case) for the benefit of artists. However, he finally made a family friend, Leicester Viney Smith (1798–1860), his heir. Vernon died unmarried at 50 Pall Mall on 22 May 1849 and was buried at Ardington parish church, Berkshire, where he is commemorated by a bust by William Behnes (he had purchased Ardington House in 1839). Smith took the name Vernon in 1850 and inherited the money intended to assist struggling painters.

George Jones, who had advised Vernon on his purchases, deprecated this change and also the gift of the collection before a room was built for it at the National Gallery. There it was squeezed into the lower floor in 1848, before being moved to Marlborough House in 1850, to South Kensington in 1859, and back to the National Gallery in 1876. Following the National Gallery Act of 1883 the collection was no longer shown together in its own rooms as Vernon had wished (he had declined the suggestion of John Sheepshanks that their gifts be merged). His nephew Vernon Heath (1820–1895), who had been his secretary from 1841, wrote in 1894 that, had Vernon foreseen its fate, he would never have made his gift. Most of it is now in the Tate collection; six works belong to the National Portrait Gallery and nine have perished. 'A strange, singular man' (Heath, *Recollections*, 1), latterly wracked by gout, Vernon was not a popular figure. His gift, received ecstatically in 1847, was soon and has remained unappreciated, despite including such significant examples of

nineteenth-century British art as Turner's *The Dogano, San Giorgio, Citella, from the Steps of the Europa* (1842; Tate collection), the first work from his collection to hang in the National Gallery, and Edwin Landseer's virtuoso performance *King Charles Spaniels* (1845; Tate collection).

SELBY WHITTINGHAM

Sources R. Hamlyn, *Robert Vernon's gift: British art for the nation, 1847* (1993) [exhibition catalogue, Tate Gallery, London, 16 March – 31 Oct 1993] · V. Heath, *Vernon Heath's recollections* (1892), 1–31, 341–54 · S. Whittingham, 'Vernon's gift, integrity's loss', *Modern Painters*, 6/2 (1993), 70–2 · *GM*, 2nd ser., 32 (1849), 98–9 · D. S. Macleod, *Art and the Victorian middle class: money and the making of cultural identity* (1996), 484–5 · *Art Union*, 9 (1847), 365–72 · G. Jones, *Sir Francis Chantrey, R.A.: recollections of his life, practice, and opinions* (1849), 207–9 · R. N. Wornum, 'The Vernon Gallery', *Art Journal*, 11 (1849), 1–3 · *The Athenaeum* (16 June 1849), 626 · S. C. Hall, *Retrospect of a long life: from 1815 to 1883*, 2 (1883), 502–3 · 'Mr Vernon's pictures', *Literary Gazette* (30 April 1831), 283–4 · V. Heath, 'The Vernon collection', *The Times* (24 Aug 1894), 3f [see also letter in same column] · V. Heath, 'The Vernon collection', *The Times* (29 Aug 1894), 6b [see also letter in same column] · monument, Ardington parish church, Berkshire · Balliol Oxf., Jenkyns MSS

Archives Balliol Oxf., corresp. and MSS

Likenesses W. Bradley, oils, 1827 · H. W. Pickersgill, oils, 1846, Tate collection · G. Jones and H. Collen, oils, 1848 (after Pickersgill), NPG · W. Behnes, marble bust, 1849–50, Tate collection · W. Behnes, medallion, 1850, repro. in *ILN*, 15 (1849), 15 · W. Behnes, marble bust, Ardington parish church, Berkshire

Wealth at death will, PRO, PROB 11/2095 · sales of works of art for fairly modest sums in 1849 and 1877 · properties of Ardington and Pall Mall

Vernon, Robert [*formerly* Robert Vernon Smith], **first Baron Lyveden** (1800–1873), politician, was the only surviving son of Robert Percy *Smith (Bobus Smith) (1770–1845), whose *Early Writings* he edited (1850), and the nephew of Sydney Smith. His mother was Caroline Maria, daughter of Richard Vernon, MP for Tavistock. He was born on 23 February 1800 in Guilford Street, London, and named Robert Vernon Smith. Having spent several years at Eton College, he matriculated from Christ Church, Oxford, on 2 February 1819, graduating BA (second class in classics) in 1822; in the same year he became a student of the Inner Temple, but was never called to the bar. Smith married, on 15 July 1823, Emma Mary Wilson (*d.* 1882), the illegitimate daughter of John, second earl of Upper Ossory, and a minor; she brought substantial estates to her husband.

Smith was attracted by a political career, and was chosen at a by-election for Tralee in June 1829; he was re-elected the following year. From 1831 to 1859 he was whig MP for Northampton; he was a whig whip from 1830 to 1834. In Melbourne's second ministry he was joint secretary to the Board of Control for the affairs of India (April 1835 to September 1839), and then under-secretary of state for war and the colonies until September 1841; he was sworn of the privy council on 21 August 1841. Russell did not give him a post in 1846, but he joined the government as secretary for war three weeks before it fell in February 1852. He was not given office in the Aberdeen coalition, despite whig protests. On 28 June 1859 he was created Baron Lyveden, and was given permission by royal licence to use the surname Vernon. Under Palmerston he was president of the Board of Control, with a seat in the cabinet, from February 1855 to March 1858, during the period of the Indian mutiny.

Lyveden was for many years a metropolitan commissioner in lunacy. He had his country seat at Farming Woods, near Thrapston, Northamptonshire, of which county he was a deputy lieutenant. He was a cool, observant man of the world, a steady if rather weak-willed whig who benefited from Palmerston's premiership. He was made a GCB on 13 July 1872, and died at home on 10 November 1873.

W. R. WILLIAMS, rev. H. C. G. MATTHEW

Sources GEC, *Peerage* · Boase, *Mod. Eng. biog.* · J. B. Conacher, *The Aberdeen coalition, 1852–1855* (1968)
Archives BL OIOC, corresp. as president of Board of Control, MS Eur. F 231 · NL Scot., letters to second Lord Panmure · Northants. RO, corresp. with J. C. Gotch · PRO, corresp. with Lord John Russell · U. Southampton L., letters to Lord Palmerston
Likenesses M. Noble, marble effigy, 1876, St Andrew's Church, Brigstock, Northamptonshire · G. Hayter, group portrait, oils (*The House of Commons, 1833*), NPG
Wealth at death under £250,000: probate, 6 Jan 1874, CGPLA Eng. & Wales

Vernon, Thomas (1654–1721), law reporter and politician, was born on 25 November 1654, the only son of Richard Vernon (*c.*1615–1679), a clergyman, of Hanbury Hall, Worcestershire, and Jane Carter (*d.* 1697). He was admitted to the Middle Temple on 11 May 1672 and called to the bar on 20 May 1679. He was licensed on 5 January 1680 to marry Mary (*d.* 1733), one of the many daughters of Sir Anthony *Keck of Bell Yard in Chancery Lane, the pre-eminent chancery counsel of his day. This match could only have furthered Vernon's career, as he in turn became a leading practitioner in chancery cases. With judicious investment of his earnings Vernon was able to build up a substantial country estate in the neighbourhood of Hanbury in Worcestershire. Between 1685 and 1717 he spent £62,000 on land, mainly in Worcestershire, and erected a new house at Hanbury which he began to build about 1710. The concomitant of this wealth was increased social prestige and political power. By 1707 he was engaged in Worcestershire politics on the whig side, and in 1715 he was elected knight of the shire. In the House of Commons he supported the government, apart from voting against the Peerage Bill, which may have been a sign of family ambition, despite having no children.

Vernon may have been financially stretched by his estate-building for he returned to the law. Lord Cobham described to Alexander Pope 'Counsellor Vernon retiring to enjoy himself with £5,000, a year which he had got, and returning to Chancery to get a little more when he could not speak so loud as to be heard' (*DNB*). However, in 1720 he was still very active in chancery, standing thirteenth in the list of most busy practitioners. Vernon died on 5 or 6 February 1721 and was buried in Hanbury church, where a monument was erected to his memory. His wife survived him until 6 July 1733.

Ironically, Vernon's will was the subject of some contention in chancery, a dispute arising over the fate of his manuscript notes on chancery cases between 1681 and 1719. His widow claimed them as part of the 'household goods and furniture' which she had been left; the trustees claimed them as part of the residuary estate, as they had been left 'the residue of my personal estate'; and the heir, Bowater Vernon, claimed them as the guardian of the reputation of the testator. Lord Chancellor Macclesfield decided the case by retaining the manuscripts in order to have them printed under the court's direction without making any profit. Under the direction of Macclesfield and then Lord King they were published as *Cases argued and adjudged in the high court of chancery, published from the manuscripts of Thomas Vernon* in 1726–8 under the editorship of William Melmoth, the elder, and William Peere Williams. This edition was found to be so full of errors and discrepancies that, at the suggestion of Lord Eldon, a new and far superior edition was brought out in 1806–7 by John Raithby. A further edition appeared in 1828.

STUART HANDLEY

Sources HoP, *Commons, 1715–54*, 2.499 · W. R. Williams, *The parliamentary history of the county of Worcester* (privately printed, Hereford, 1897), 57 · T. Nash, *Collections for the history of Worcestershire*, 1 (1781), 548–50 · will, PRO, PROB 11/579, sig. 61 · D. Lemmings, *Gentlemen and barristers: the inns of court and the English bar, 1680–1730* (1990), 158, 160, 188, 191 · D. Lemmings, *Professors of the law* (2000), 353 · G. Holmes, *Augustan England* (1982) · H. A. C. Sturgess, ed., *Register of admissions to the Honourable Society of the Middle Temple, from the fifteenth century to the year 1944*, 1 (1949), 185 · A. Boyer, *The political state of Great Britain*, 36 (1728), 100 · J. L. Chester and J. Foster, eds., *London marriage licences, 1521–1869* (1887), 1386 · DNB
Archives Worcs. RO, MSS
Likenesses C. Horsnaile, effigy on monument, 1721, Hanbury church, Worcestershire · G. Vertue, line engraving (after G. Kneller), BM, NPG; repro. in *The reports of Sir Peyton Ventris*, 4th edn

Vernon, Thomas (*bap.* 1824, *d.* 1872), engraver, was born in Staffordshire and baptized at Skelton, Staffordshire, on 7 November 1824, the son of George Vernon and his wife, Hannah, *née* Simpson. He is said to have trained in Paris before returning to settle in London and study with the engraver Peter Lightfoot. Like his master, Vernon concentrated on line engraving, but, although he was highly skilled, his choice of such a narrow medium and the fact that he was rarely employed by the book trade meant that he struggled throughout his career. It was no doubt in search of security that he visited America, and worked as a bank note engraver in New York during a stay which appears to have lasted from 1863 to 1865. Vernon exhibited seven engravings at the Royal Academy between 1857 and 1867, three portraits and four history subjects.

Many of Vernon's most important plates were published by Henry Graves, and these included his two earliest exhibits at the academy in 1857: *The Infant Amazon: a Portrait of Princess Helena*, after Franz Winterhalter, and *The Virgin and Child*, after William Dyce. Both works came from Queen Victoria's private collection and were published, together with two other subjects, in Samuel Carter Hall's *The Royal Gallery of Art* (1857–8). Graves was also responsible for commissioning other prints after modern artists, such as *The First Born*, after Charles West Cope (1865) and *Olivia Unveiling*, after Charles Robert Leslie (1863). The other outlet for Vernon's modern subjects was the *Art Journal*, which reproduced a number of his works, among them *The Infant Bacchus*, after Martin Archer Shee.

Vernon's works after old masters encompassed a wide range of periods, and he showed engravings at the Royal Academy after Rubens's *Portrait of his Wife* and Murillo's *Pool at Bethesda*. Of the earlier masters, he also exhibited *Abundance*, after Jan Van Eyck, as well as working on an Arundel Society print after Fra Angelico's *Saint Matthew* from the chapel of Nicholas V in the Vatican.

Vernon was elected a member of the Graphic Society in 1867. He died on 23 January 1872. Examples of his work are in the print rooms at the British Museum and the Victoria and Albert Museum, London. GREG SMITH

Sources R. K. Engen, *Dictionary of Victorian engravers, print publishers and their works* (1979) · B. Hunnisett, *An illustrated dictionary of British steel engravers*, new edn (1989), 95 · *Art Journal*, 34 (1872), 75 · Graves, *RA exhibitors* · *IGI*

Vernon, Sir William (*c*.1420–1467). *See under* Vernon family (*per.* 1411–1515).

Véron, Jean (*d.* 1563), religious writer and translator and Church of England clergyman, was probably born at or near Sens, for he called himself 'senonoys'; nothing is known about his date of birth or about his family or private life. No record of Véron's life in France has been found, but it has been suggested that he may have attended the University of Orléans in 1534. He emigrated to England *c*.1536 and became a denizen in July 1544. By then he had been in the country for over eight years, living in Aldrichgate ward, and acting as a teacher of gentlemen's children. The record also states that he had been a student at Cambridge at some point during those eight years, but no evidence of his matriculation has come to light. Although there is no proof of his protestant faith until 1548, Véron probably left France for religious reasons, making him one of the first French protestant refugees in England. Perhaps because he had already been in the country so long Véron did not join the group of foreigners who formed their own French and Dutch Reformed congregations in 1550.

On 21 August 1551 Véron was ordained deacon by Nicholas Ridley, bishop of London. Eight days later he received priest's orders, and on 3 January 1553 he became the rector of St Alphage, Cripplegate. He did not flee to the continent upon the accession of the Catholic queen, Mary I; indeed, he was one of the 'seditious preachers' arrested by Marian authorities in the wake of a riot at St Paul's on 13 August 1553. It is unknown how he managed to escape execution. John Strype's puzzling reference to him as a 'confessor also under Queen Mary' suggests he may have temporarily converted to Catholicism (Strype, *Reformation*, 1/2.1) but there is no primary evidence to justify this claim. During Elizabeth's reign he became the vicar of St Martin Ludgate and Christ Church Greyfriars, and a prebendary of St Paul's. He preached regularly at St Paul's and Whitehall; Strype calls him a 'bold as well as eloquent man' (ibid., 1/1.200) and 'one of the eminentest preachers at this time' (ibid., 1/2.1). His boldness seems to have inspired enmity in the diarist Henry Machyn: Machyn was forced, on 23 November 1561, to kneel in front of Véron and ask his forgiveness for shouting out at a sermon that Véron kept a wench.

Throughout his career Véron translated and wrote books which advanced protestant belief and practice and criticized Catholicism, his intention being to instruct the 'rude and simple people' in the tenets of the new faith (preface to H. Bullinger, *An Holsome Antidotus or Counterpoysen, Agaynst … the Anabaptists*, 1548, sig. A4r–v). During the reign of Edward VI he was responsible for the publication of two tracts by Huldrych Zwingli, the leader of the Reformation in Zürich; three by Zwingli's successor, Heinrich Bullinger; a treatise of his own against the mass; and a compilation of patristic opinions on the Lord's supper. In the preface to Zwingli's *The Image of both Pastors* Véron makes explicit his hope that his 'little book' will serve as a temporary substitute for the lack of godly preaching in many parishes in England (preface to H. Zwingli, *The Image of both Pastors*, 1550, sig. B2v). In these works Véron not only made continental protestant doctrine available to English readers, but he also explained in his own words how and why the material was relevant to England.

In 1552 Véron issued a version of the French humanist Robert Étienne's French and Latin dictionary, adding English entries to make it a trilingual lexicon; this dictionary went through two more editions during the Elizabethan period. Also during Elizabeth's reign Véron published a series of dialogues in which Philalethes (lover of truth) leads Albion (England gone astray under Catholicism) back to protestant doctrine on predestination, purgatory, free will, justification by works, invocation of the saints, and clerical celibacy. The dialogue against purgatory is an English adaptation of several dialogues on the subject by the Calvinist author Pierre Viret; the rest of the dialogues appear to be original to Véron. In a humorous, highly persuasive style he asserted these protestant doctrines by attacking both Catholicism and Anabaptism, a tactic which had been successful for reformers on the continent and in England during the reign of Edward VI.

Véron died in London on 9 April 1563 and was buried the next day. It has been stated (*DNB*) that he was buried at St Paul's in an unmarked grave, but the evidence for this is unclear. John Awdelie wrote an epitaph in verse which praised the Frenchman's dedication to England and to the protestant faith. CARRIE EULER

Sources F. de Schickler, 'Le réfugié Jean Véron, collaborateur des réformateurs anglais, 1548–1562', *Bulletin Historique et Littéraire* [Société de l'Histoire du Protestantisme Français], 39 (1890), 437–46, 481–93 · P. Denis, 'Jean Veron: the first known French protestant in England', *Proceedings of the Huguenot Society*, 22 (1970–76), 257–63 · *STC, 1475–1640* · J. Strype, *The history of the life and acts of the most reverend father in God Edmund Grindal*, new edn (1821) · J. Strype, *Ecclesiastical memorials*, 3 vols. (1822) · J. Strype, *Annals of the Reformation and establishment of religion … during Queen Elizabeth's happy reign*, new edn, 4 vols. (1824) · J. Strype, *Memorials of the most reverend father in God Thomas Cranmer*, new edn, 2 vols. (1840) · G. Hennessy, *Novum repertorium ecclesiasticum parochiale Londinense, or, London diocesan clergy succession from the earliest time to the year 1898* (1898) · *The diary of Henry Machyn, citizen and merchant-tailor of London, from AD 1550 to AD 1563*, ed. J. G. Nichols, CS, 42 (1848) · *DNB* · *The acts and monuments of*

John Foxe, ed. S. R. Cattley, 8 vols. (1837–41) • E. Farr, ed., *Select poetry of the reign of Queen Elizabeth* (1845), 540 • *APC*, *1552–4*, 321 • W. Page, ed., *Letters of denization and acts of naturalization for aliens in England, 1509–1603*, Huguenot Society of London, 8 (1893) • R. E. G. Kirk and E. F. Kirk, eds., *Returns of aliens dwelling in the city and suburbs of London, from the reign of Henry VIII to that of James I*, Huguenot Society of London, 10/1 (1900)

Verral [Verrall], **William** (1715–1761), innkeeper and writer on cookery, was born on 10 April 1715, in Lewes, Sussex, the fifth of the eight sons (and one daughter) of Richard Verrall (*d.* 1737), master of the White Hart inn in Lewes from about 1724, and his wife, Sarah Mores (*d.* 1758). The family depended on the patronage of Thomas Pelham-Holles, first duke of Newcastle: William's father ran the inn, which had been converted from a Pelham family mansion; his eldest brother, Richard, managed a coffee house catering for the duke's political supporters; and after Richard's death in 1742 another brother, Henry, took over. Family members frequently petitioned the duke for places in the local surveyorship of windows, the customs, or the Post Office. After his father's death William was chosen to succeed him as master of the White Hart in 1738, after a period working in the ducal kitchens (probably at Newcastle House in London) under Newcastle's famous French cook, Pierre Clouet or Cloué. Despite Verral's assertion in his book concerning his several years' experience under Clouet, Newcastle's accounts suggest that he worked as an under-cook to the duke for only about two and a half years (BL, Add. MSS 33321, fol. 27; 33322, fol. 24). By August 1738 he was running the inn, for in that month he supplied suppers for two balls in Lewes for which Newcastle paid; similar payments were recorded in 1742, 1743, and 1744.

In the 1740s Verral seems to have prospered: in 1740 he applied to Newcastle for the position of Lewes postmaster and, although the place was already promised elsewhere, he did obtain the carriage of letters between Eastbourne and Lewes. In 1742 he contributed 3 guineas to the subscription for the building of a new hospital in the town, and in January 1745 his name headed the petition addressed to Sir Francis Poole by a number of Lewes tradesmen to protest against the prolonged quartering of a company of soldiers in the town. As a respected member of the community, Verral was a headborough for Lewes 1748–9, high constable in 1753–4, and served as an official again in 1756. But at some point in the late 1750s his prosperity declined, perhaps after the death of his first wife, Ann Botting, in 1757. They had married on 29 January 1745, and a daughter, Elizabeth, had been born in the same year. Verral may have turned to authorship in the hope of making money. His cookery book, *A Complete System of Cookery*, which appeared in 1759, was the result of his experience under Clouet, and the recipes offer an illuminating glimpse of French 'nouvelle cuisine', with its light, simple dishes, as it was practised in England in the 1730s and 1740s. Excellent though the recipes are, Verral's highly personal preface, with its satirical anecdotes of the rustic Sussex gentry, can have done nothing to endear the

book to its potential readers, and the first edition was also the last.

Verral's fortunes went from bad to worse: early in 1761 he appealed to Newcastle for help, and the duke recommended him to the justices of the peace of Middlesex as keeper of the house of correction. But, by February 1761, his furniture had been put up for auction, and in March he was declared bankrupt and was thus ineligible for the post. On 2 March he married Hannah Turner (*d.* 1765); he died later that month in Lewes, and was buried there on 26 March 1761 at St Michael's Church. Today Verral is remembered for his cookery book, one of the very few to give a true picture of French cookery in England in the middle of the eighteenth century. Verral's recipes are clear and well explained, with comments on the relative merits of French and English cookery, and on the success of particular dishes. Such a balanced discussion of the two cuisines is extremely rare among the mass of xenophobic comment which characterizes English cookery books of the period.   GILLY LEHMANN

Sources P. Lucas, 'The Verrall family of Lewes', *Sussex Archaeological Collections*, 58 (1916), 91–131 • C. Brent, 'Introduction', *William Verrall's cookery book*, ed. A. Haly (1988), 1–7 • V. Smith, ed., 'The town book of Lewes 1702–1837', *Publications of the Sussex Record Society*, 69 (1972–3) • BL, Newcastle MSS, Add. MS 33321, fols. 26v–27v • BL, Newcastle MSS, Add. MS 33322, fols. 9, 24, 44v • BL, Newcastle MSS, Add. MS 33137, fol. 529 • BL, Newcastle MSS, Add. MS 33158, fols. 27, 45 • BL, Newcastle MSS, Add. MS 32920, fol. 133 • Allibone, *Dict.* • W. Verral, *A complete system of cookery* (1759) • *IGI*
Archives BL, Newcastle MSS, Add. MS 32964, fol. 314; Add. MS 32704, fol. 22; Add. MS 32864, fol. 271
Wealth at death bankrupt: Lucas, 'The Verrall family'

Verrall, Arthur Woollgar (1851–1912), classical scholar, was born at Brighton on 5 February 1851, the eldest of a family of three brothers and two sisters. His father, Henry Verrall, was a well-known solicitor, for many years clerk to the Brighton magistrates; his mother was Anne Webb Woollgar. In October 1864 Arthur Verrall gained a scholarship at Wellington College, where he became a favourite pupil of the master, Edward White Benson, afterwards archbishop of Canterbury. In 1869 he was elected scholar of Trinity College, Cambridge. He had a distinguished undergraduate career: he was Pitt university scholar (1872), was bracketed second in the first class of the classical tripos (with T. E. Page) and was chancellor's medallist (1873), and became fellow of his college (1874). He was president of the union in 1873, and became a member of the Apostles. From 1873 to 1876 he lived in London, reading for the bar at Lincoln's Inn. He was called to the bar in 1876, having gained the Whewell scholarship for international law in 1875. In October 1877 he returned to Cambridge, where for thirty-four years he lectured at Trinity College, until 1911, when he was chosen to be the first King Edward VII professor of English literature. He was a tutor at Trinity from 1889 until 1899.

Verrall was an inspiring teacher, both as lecturer and as supervisor, with a particularly fine reading voice. He was one of the first classical scholars regularly to use modern literature in his exposition of ancient poetry, and to investigate Greek plays as examples of drama rather than simply as texts requiring emendation. Former pupils, including Professor F. M. Cornford and Sir Edward Marsh, remembered the excitement caused by his lectures and the ingenuity of the solutions he proposed to problems in the texts. Although Verrall's lectures achieved great popularity, his published works (which were chiefly on Greek tragedy, especially Euripides) received a mixed reception from other scholars and are no longer highly regarded. His interpretations of individual plays tended to be over-ingenious, and he was too ready to discount straightforward explanations in his search for what he believed to be hitherto undetected truth. He sought to show that Euripides was a 'rationalist' who did not believe in the Olympian gods, and that his plays were covert attacks on them, in which the real meaning was always hidden and only to be discovered by the most intelligent among the audience. Although such views on the intentions of the playwright and the reaction of the audience were influential on some later scholars, especially Gilbert Norwood, they are no longer generally accepted. Verrall edited several plays of Aeschylus and Euripides and produced studies of Latin authors including Horace, Martial, Statius, and Propertius. His approach to Greek drama is most clearly shown in his *Euripides the Rationalist* (1895) and *Essays on Four Plays of Euripides* (1905).

Verrall's work was not confined to classical authors: his Sidgwick lecture (1909), entitled 'The prose of Scott', and his Clark lectures (1909) on the Victorian poets proved very popular. On his appointment to the new chair of English literature in 1911 he delivered a series of lectures on Dryden, but he had suffered increasingly from arthritis for fourteen years, and had to be carried to and from the lecture room. He prepared, but never gave, a course on Macaulay.

In 1882 Verrall married Margaret de Gaudrion Merrifield [see Verrall, Margaret de Gaudrion (1857–1916)], daughter of Frederic Merrifield, barrister, with whom he had one surviving daughter, Helen. His wife became very interested in the supernatural and contributed several articles to the *Proceedings of the Society for Psychical Research*. Verrall himself was not a regular member of the society, which was started in 1882 by a group of fellows of Trinity, but was involved in some of his wife's experiments on automatic writing. Verrall died at his home, 5 Selwyn Gardens, Cambridge, on Waterloo day, or as he himself called it, 'Wellington College day', 18 June 1912, after a long illness, during which he bore his sufferings with unflinching courage and without complaint, and still managed to talk to intimate friends with alertness and something like his old vivacity.   RICHARD SMAIL

Sources A. W. Verrall, *Collected literary essays*, ed. M. A. Bayfield and J. D. Duff (1913) [with memoir by M. A. Bayfield, pp. ix–cii] • Venn, *Alum. Cant.* • A. N. Michelini, *Euripides and the tragic tradition* (1987), 11–19 • *CGPLA Eng. & Wales* (1912)
Archives BL, corresp. with Macmillans, Add. MS 55125 • King's AC Cam., letters to Oscar Browning • King's AC Cam., letters to John Maynard Keynes • U. Leeds, Brotherton L., letters to Edmund Gosse

Likenesses E. Kapp, drawing, Barber Institute of Fine Arts, Birmingham • W. Rothenstein, chalk drawing, FM Cam. • Tadell, oils, Trinity Cam. • print, BM
Wealth at death £16,207 4s. 3d.: resworn probate, 12 July 1912, *CGPLA Eng. & Wales*

Verrall [née Merrifield], **Margaret de Gaudrion** (1857–1916), university teacher and parapsychologist, was born on 21 December 1857 at 4 Dorset Gardens, Brighton, the first of two daughters of Frederic Merrifield (*b.* 1831, *d.* in or after 1912), barrister, and Maria Angélique de Gaudrion.

Margaret Merrifield went originally to Newnham Hall (as it then was), Cambridge, in 1875, intending to read political economy and moral sciences, but was persuaded by her close friend Jane Ellen Harrison to study classics. Although she had little grounding in Greek and Latin, she pursued them with considerable success aided by a natural talent for languages. She took second-class honours in the classics tripos in 1880 and was appointed classics lecturer at Newnham the same year. Her preferment to the post, ahead of Jane Harrison, the better qualified but more controversial candidate, caused Merrifield great misgivings. Harrison reports that Merrifield immediately visited her in London and 'literally stamped about the room, healing thereby her friend's hurt vanity' (Harrison, 378). Although Harrison describes her as 'never in spirit an Academic' (ibid.), she was a stimulating and confident teacher who assumed intellectual maturity on the part of her students and set high stylistic standards. As a colleague, she was efficient, accommodating, and reliable. On 17 June 1882 she married Arthur Woollgar *Verrall (1851–1912), classicist and later the first Edward VII professor of English literature; they had two daughters, one of whom died in infancy. After her marriage she continued to lecture and examine in classics at intervals up to the time of her death. Verrall was thus among the early group of middle-class women who did not feel that their own academic activity should be curtailed by marriage; she continued to teach, research, and write, sometimes in collaboration with her husband. She worked with him on the text of Pausanias for *The Mythology and Monuments of Ancient Athens* which she published jointly with Jane Harrison in 1890 and, after her husband's death in 1912, she edited his lectures on Dryden.

The bulk of Margaret Verrall's writing and most of her research work was concerned with parapsychology. She joined the Society for Psychical Research in 1889, although her interest in the subject had begun earlier. She had already recorded experiments in thought transference that she had tried with her five-year-old daughter Helen. She came to be regarded as one of the society's best observers and in possession of psychical powers herself. Her psychical experiences included the production of automatic writing and she produced hundreds of scripts from 1901 until her death. As a member of the society's reference committee from 1894, she reviewed all the papers submitted to the society for publication, making valuable criticisms and suggestions on their contents.

The Society for Psychical Research had been founded in

London in 1882 by two spiritualists who sought to attract to the society existing groups of psychical researchers, such as the Cambridge group led by Henry Sidgwick and Frederick Myers, and wherever possible top names in the scientific world and even among churchmen. Spiritualists and psychical researchers had distinct approaches to psychic phenomena, although both groups were driven by the loss of religious certainty that had defined man's place in the universe. Spiritualists, believing in life after death and the existence of spirits who communicated with the living, approached psychic 'events' in a positive frame of mind, while psychical researchers were more sceptical and brought greater critical judgement to bear on apparent evidence of spirit activity. This latter group, to which Margaret Verrall firmly belonged, was attracted by the possibility of proving immortality but also saw psychical research as a method of exploring the powers and scope of the human mind. Tensions developed between these groups and led to the withdrawal of spiritualists from the society.

Through the medium of suitable people, 'automatic' scripts were produced that were believed to convey messages from the spirits of identifiable people who had died. In some cases, these messages were received independently by a number of mediums and could only be interpreted when examined together. This phenomenon was known as 'cross-correspondences'. One prominent case that became known as the Palm Sunday scripts involved Margaret Verrall, her daughter, and the prominent Conservative parliamentarian Arthur Balfour. The scripts noted by the Verralls and two other mediums, one of whom was living in India, appeared to relate messages from a young woman whom Balfour had deeply loved and intended to marry, but who died of typhus on Palm Sunday 1875 before their official engagement could be announced. The case was held to be remarkable because of the private nature of the information, the independence of at least three of the mediums, and the geographical distance between them.

Although she had persuaded her to study classics, Jane Harrison recognized that Verrall had a scientific mind, describing her attitude to superstition among the ancient civilizations almost as 'physical shrinking and disgust', and understood her pursuit of psychic research as an attempt to establish scientific truths (Harrison, 53). Verrall was swayed by rational argument rather than emotion but could none the less hold violent prejudices in some matters and disliked the constant airing and debate of controversial subjects. She and her husband remained staunch Liberals without losing any friends at a time when Cambridge was still a tory stronghold and many Liberals had deserted Gladstone over home rule. Margaret Verrall died at her home, 5 Selwyn Gardens, Cambridge, of cancer on 2 July 1916, aged fifty-eight.

RITA McWILLIAMS TULLBERG

Sources Newnham College, Cambridge, register, 1.5 · J. E. Harrison, 'In memoriam Mrs A. W. Verrall', *Newnham College Letter* (1916), 53–63; repr. in *Proceedings of the Society for Psychical Research*, 29 (1916–18), 176–85 · E. M. Sidgwick, *Proceedings of the Society for Psychical Research*, 29 (1916–18), 170–76 · J. Oppenheim, *The other world: spiritualism and psychical research in England, 1850–1914* (1985) · b. cert. · d. cert. · *CGPLA Eng. & Wales* (1916)
Archives BL, letters to Blanche Athena Clough, Add. MS 72828, fols. 4–12, 14, 43–6, 118–21 · CUL, letters of F. Jenkinson, Add. MS 6463 · Trinity Cam., Salter MSS, 'automatic scripts' of Margaret Verrall and her daughter, Helen; notes and corresp. relating to scripts and 'cross-correspondences'; unpublished volumes of scripts by Verralls
Wealth at death £19,686 15s. 3d.: probate, 23 Sept 1916, *CGPLA Eng. & Wales*

Verrio, Antonio (*c*.1639–1707), decorative painter, was born in the Neapolitan city of Lecce, the son of Giovanni Lycien ('of Lecce'). (Verrio's early work *St Francis Appearing to Father Mastrilli* survives in the Convitto Nazionale, Lecce.) Verrio's early career took him to Naples, where he worked for the Jesuit college, and then to other Italian cities such as Florence, Rome, and Genoa. His artistic training is uncertain, but a local artist in Lecce, Giuseppe Verrio, may have been his uncle and first teacher. By 1655 he had married Massenzia Tornese. Although Verrio's first biographer, Bernardo De Dominici, stated that Verrio drowned in France, it is clear that he was living and working in Toulouse by 1666. By 3 July 1668 he was married to Françoise De Angeli, whose surname is recorded in the register at Toulouse Cathedral as 'dangely'. Verrio's gregarious personality seems to have made more of an impression on his biographer for this period, J. Malliot, than his painting; little information survives recording his work at this time. More importantly for his English career, by 1671 he was working in Paris, where during the following year he became a member of the Académie Royal de Peinture. It is thought that he worked at Versailles under Charles Le Brun and there learned to paint in the rich baroque style which helped to create the atmosphere of the court of Louis XIV.

Ralph Montagu, later first duke of Montagu, the English ambassador to the French court in Paris, persuaded Verrio to travel to England in 1672 to decorate the staircase and great room of Montagu House in London. Montagu introduced Verrio to his first significant patron, Henry Bennet, first Lord Arlington, for whom Verrio worked at Euston Hall, Suffolk, his country seat, and in London (at Arlington House, on the site later occupied by Buckingham House and Palace) in 1674. Charles II first encountered Verrio at Arlington House, and it was through Lord Montagu that he was given his first royal appointment as designer for the newly revived Mortlake tapestry works, of which Montagu was in charge from 1674. Verrio's first-known easel painting from his English period, a *Sea Triumph of Charles II* (Royal Collection), may date from this time, as it appears to have been painted with the royal appointment in mind. The first volume of Edward Croft-Murray's *Decorative Painting in England, 1537–1837* (1962) includes a catalogue of Verrio's works.

Verrio was denizened on 5 May 1675. He did not spend long at Mortlake and was soon engaged on a more significant commission, the redecoration of Hugh May's reconstructed north range of Windsor Castle, for which he was paid over £7000 in twelve years. This was to be his principal occupation from 1675 to 1684 and included the decoration of the king's chapel, St George's Hall, and around twenty ceilings and three staircases. The interiors he participated in creating at Windsor Castle for Charles II were among the finest baroque decorative schemes ever produced in Great Britain. Almost all of his work was destroyed by George IV's reconstruction of the castle (under Jeffry Wyatville) in the 1820s and 1830s, but visual sources convey an impression of his work at Windsor. Among these are three engravings of lost ceilings by Pierre Vanderbank and W. H. Pyne's aquatint views illustrated in his *Royal Residences* (1819), as well as the few fragments (notably the newly discovered portrait, still on its original plaster, of Charles II, from the ceiling of St George's Hall) that survive in the Royal Collection.

Verrio's treatment of the architectural spaces at Windsor (and his subsequent work) relied heavily upon Italian baroque models. The ceilings were painted as if open to a mythological sky, populated with historical figures or gods, often elaborately foreshortened. The space between the walls and ceilings, often conveniently coved at Windsor, was generally painted with a balustrade, or other architectural device, so as to manage the difficult transition between myth and reality. St George's Hall was decorated with subjects glorifying England's national saint and the Order of the Garter, while the king's chapel was dominated by a rendition of Christ healing the sick. In both spaces Verrio introduced a pattern for treating a huge expanse of wall which was accepted as the standard method of adorning staircases and large rooms for the next fifty years. The principal figural composition is set on a stage framed by a painted proscenium or screen, the columns of which support the false parapet or open dome surrounding the 'sky' on the ceiling. Thus the greater part of the architectural embellishment of the room is created by the ingenuity of the painter.

The sheer scale of the work at Windsor necessitated the employment of a large team of assistants, most of whom were French or Flemish. Of those listed in a warrant of 1678, the most significant was Louis Laguerre, who later had a successful career in England in his own right. The artists involved were often specialists, for instance Renée Cousin, a French gilder.

Verrio's undertaking at Windsor did not prevent his accepting the commission for a vast group portrait of the founders for the hall of Christ's Hospital. The piece, which was painted in oil on canvas in three sections, survives in the rebuilt mathematical school at Horsham, Sussex (as does a much reduced copy made for Samuel Pepys, now in the Yale Center for British Art, New Haven, Connecticut). The work progressed very slowly, partly because Charles II's death in 1685 meant that his portrait had to be replaced by that of James II as the principal figure in the composition. The final payment to Verrio took place in 1687. The work is best described as a baroque version of the traditional 'foundation picture'.

After his work on Hugh May's remodelled apartments at Windsor was complete, Verrio continued to receive royal commissions from James II, namely the decoration of Henry VIII's chapel at Windsor and the decoration of the chapel at Whitehall Palace, both for the Roman Catholic rite. In 1684 he was appointed chief painter to his majesty, at a salary of £200. Verrio was also known as a gardener, and it seems that he laid out the garden at Whitehall during this period, almost certainly using the principles established by Le Nôtre, which he would have seen in practice at Versailles. By 1686 Verrio had been made 'principal Gardiner & Surveyor to the King' (Vertue, *Note books*, 1.61) and had remodelled the gardens of St James's Palace, where he was living. Accounts describe him as a very sociable person, given to high living and entertaining in a lavish style. He was a member of the Society of Painters, an early artists' club. However, his time in London ended abruptly at the revolution of 1688, as his sympathies lay with the Jacobites and he refused to work for the new monarchy. In 1690 Françoise Verrio returned to France.

Verrio spent the next ten years or so in the country, mostly at Burghley House, Northamptonshire, and then at Chatsworth, Derbyshire. At the former he decorated six rooms and the staircase ceiling for John, fifth earl of Exeter, the most famous being the so-called Heaven Room, which depicts the capture of Mars and Venus in Vulcan's net. He was eventually persuaded to return to work for the crown, firstly back at Windsor. However, his major commission at this time was the decoration of Hampton Court Palace from 1701 onwards, where his work survives intact. There he decorated the entire interior of a small banqueting house by the river (the sketch for the ceiling is in the Victoria and Albert Museum), as well as the huge king's staircase and the queen's drawing room. Criticisms, particularly of the colouring, that have been levelled at these last works can be explained partly by Verrio's increasing loss of sight, which might have led to the accentuation of the least attractive elements in his paintings. He finished the last of these works in mid-1704, by which time he was almost completely blind.

Verrio retired on a royal pension of £200 a year. He died at his lodgings at Hampton Court on 15 June 1707, having made his will two days before. He made bequests to his two sons, John Baptist and Ffrancisco, and his two grandchildren, John Baptist and Mary. The 'Inventory of the Goods Chattels and Creditts of Anthony Verrio at his Lodgings at Hampton Court', which includes a valuation of these effects, made on 2 July 1707, provides a detailed account of the interior furnishings of his home (PRO, PROB 32/50/1).   KATHRYN BARRON

Sources E. Croft-Murray, *Decorative painting in England, 1537–1837*, 1 (1962), 50–60, 236–42 • Vertue, *Note books* • J. Barreau, 'Antonio Verrio à l'Hôtel Brûlart', *Revue de l'Art*, 122/4 (1998), 64–71 • J. Simon, *English baroque sketches* (1974) • *Burghley House Guide Book* (1985) • W. H. Pyne, *The history of the royal residences of Windsor Castle, St James's Palace, Carlton House, Kensington Palace, Hampton Court, Buckingham House and Frogmore* (1819), vol. 1: *Windsor Castle* • O. Millar, *The Tudor, Stuart and early Georgian pictures in the collection of her majesty the queen*, 2 vols. (1963), nos. 296–9 • J. D. Stewart, *Sir Godfrey Kneller and the English baroque portrait* (1983), 33–40 and no. 823 • P. J. Noon, *English portrait drawings and miniatures* (New Haven, CT, 1979), no. 17 [exhibition catalogue, Yale U. CBA, 5 Dec 1979 – 17 Feb

1980] • S. Brindle and B. Kerr, *Windsor revealed: new light on the history of the castle* (1997), 48–53 • will, PRO, PROB 11/495, sig. 155 • inventory of Verrio's personal estate, PRO, PROB 32/50/1

Archives Burghley House, Stamford, bills and receipts for clothes

Likenesses G. Kneller, oils, *c.*1690, Burghley House, Stamford • A. Verrio, self-portrait, oils, *c.*1700, NPG • A. Bannerman, line engraving, pubd 1762, BM, NPG; repro. in Walpole, *Anecdotes* (1762) • A. Verrio, self-portrait, King's Chapel, Windsor • A. Verrio, self-portrait; formerly at Thornham Hall, Suffolk • A. Verrio, self-portrait, sketch

Wealth at death 'household goods plate pictures and furniture': will, PRO, PROB 11/495, sig. 155; inventory, PRO, PROB 32/50/1

Verstegan [*formerly* Rowlands], **Richard** (1548x50–1640), writer and intelligence informant, was born in one of the east London liberties, probably between 1548 and 1550, the son of John Rowlands, a cooper, and grandson of Theodore Rowland Verstegan, a refugee from Gelderland; his father had adopted the patronym Rowlands as a more English-sounding name. In 1564 Verstegan was matriculated at Oxford under the name Richard Rowlaund, with Richard Vere and George Pettie, all being described as servants to Thomas Bernard, a canon of Christ Church. About 1569 he left the university without taking a degree, 'to avoid oaths' (Wood, *Ath. Oxon.*, 2.393). He returned to London to learn a trade, becoming a freeman of the Goldsmiths' Company in 1574.

Rowlands's *The Post of the World*, the first English guidebook to the continent, was printed in 1576 with a dedication to Sir Thomas Gresham. At the end of 1581 he secretly printed Thomas Alfield's account of Edmund Campion's execution (later reprinted in Paris, Lyons, and Milan) and had to flee the country. Abroad, he revived his ancestral surname. During the following five years he was active as a publicist in Paris, Rome, Rheims, and Antwerp, producing accounts of the executions of Catholics in England. The most famous, reprinted several times in Latin and in French, was the *Theatrum crudelitatum haereticorum nostri temporis* (Antwerp, 1587). He himself designed the plates, which were to influence the late mannerist representation of martyrdom in northern Europe. His first wife, about whom nothing is known, is mentioned in documents dating from 1585 and 1601. From 1586 to 1609 he was a pensioner of the king of Spain.

From March 1587 Verstegan lived in Antwerp. From 1590 until 1603 he worked as a publishing and intelligence agent for the superiors of the English mission, William Allen in Rome and Robert Persons in Spain. He maintained communications between them and the missionaries in England, arranged passports and the smuggling of books, bought books in Flanders for the seminaries in Spain, and oversaw the printing of numerous English Catholic works in Antwerp. He continued to write polemical and martyrological works, including, most importantly, answers to the 1591 proclamation against Jesuits and seminary priests. He also produced devotional translations (among them the first English translation of the Tridentine primer), religious verse, and a seminal work of Anglo-Saxon scholarship, the *Restitution of Decayed Intelligence in Antiquities* (1605), about which he corresponded

with Sir Robert Cotton. He edited or contributed to several of the political works generally attributed to Robert Persons. His writings in these years were a cause of great concern to the authorities in England, and did much to shape the perception of Queen Elizabeth's policies on the continent. In 1608 he provided the English verses in a multilingual edition of Otto van Veen's *Amorum emblemata*.

In 1610 he married his second wife, Catherina de Sauchy of Antwerp. When in 1612 measures were taken to protect the Flemish cloth industry a limited monopoly on the importation of undyed English cloth was granted to Verstegan, but diplomatic representations led to this licence's not being renewed the following year. In 1614 he was again working as a newswriter for the English Jesuits, and between 1615 and 1617 he travelled through the Netherlands for Manuel Sueyro, head of Spanish secret intelligence in the Low Countries. His last surviving intelligence letter, dated 1628, was addressed to Sir Robert Dudley.

From 1617 onwards Verstegan worked as a poet and journalist. His *Nederduytsche epigrammen* was printed in 1617. Over the following years this was followed by two more volumes of epigrams (one posthumous), volumes of characters modelled on those of Sir Thomas Overbury, a collection of satirical news reports, collections of anecdotes and 'witty replies', and serious works of political commentary and religious polemic, including a number of pamphlets in English on the Dutch and Bohemian risings and the Spanish match. The dedications and commendatory verses of these works show Verstegan to have had friendly contact with many of the leading figures of Flemish artistic and intellectual life. He was one of the earliest identifiable newspaper journalists, contributing satires, commentaries, and news reports to Abraham Verhoeven's *Nieuwe Tijdinghen* (Antwerp, 1619–29). Among the events on which he wrote for Verhoeven were the Synod of Dort, the Spanish match, the English parliaments of the 1620s, and the murder of the duke of Buckingham. Between 1617 and 1630 Verstegan was probably the most prolific vernacular writer in the Habsburg Netherlands. Apart from his political writings in support of Mary, queen of Scots and the Habsburgs, and his polemics against Calvinism, the main marks of Verstegan's writings are dry humour and a concern (also demonstrated by his Oxford contemporary George Pettie) to bring the standard of manners in northern Europe to the level set by the Italian humanists. On 26 February 1640 Verstegan made out his will, leaving his three houses and everything in them to his wife. He died soon afterwards, and was buried in the church of St Jacobus in Antwerp on 3 March 1640.

PAUL ARBLASTER

Sources payments of Verstegan's pension, Archivas Generales de Simancas, contaduría mayor de Cuentas, 2a época, 42 • A. F. Allison, 'A group of political tracts, 1621–1623, by Richard Verstegan', *Recusant History*, 18 (1986–7), 128–42 • P. Arblaster, 'Het wereldbeeld van Richard Verstegen (ca.1550–1640), een agent van de katholieke reformatie', licence diss., Leuven, 1994 • W. J. C. Buitendijk, 'Richard Verstegen als verteller en journalist', *De Nieuwe Taalgids*, 46 (1953) • P. H. Goepp, 'Verstegan's "Most ancient Saxon words"', *Philologica: the Malone anniversary studies*, ed. T. A.

Kirby and H. B. Woolf (1949) • S. C. Chew, 'Richard Verstegan and the *Amorum emblemata* of Otho Van Veen', *Huntington Library Quarterly*, 8 (1944–5), 192–9 • A. M. Crino, *Il duca di Northumbria in Toscana* [offprint from *English Miscellany*, 27–8] • D. A. Freedberg, 'The representation of martyrdoms during the early Counter-Reformation in Antwerp', *Burlington Magazine*, 118 (1976), 128–38 • A. J. Loomie, 'The authorship of "An advertisement written to a secretarie of M. L. treasurer of England"', *Renaissance News*, 15 (1962), 201–7 • A. G. Petti, 'A study of the life and writings of Richard Verstegan', MA diss., London, 1957 • *The letters and despatches of Richard Verstegan, c. 1550–1640*, ed. A. G. Petti, Catholic RS, 52 (1959) • A. G. Petti, 'A bibliography of the writings of Richard Verstegan (c.1550–1641)', *Recusant History*, 7 (1963–4), 82–103 • E. Rombauts, *Richard Verstegen, een polemist der Contra-Reformatie* (1933) • Wood, *Ath. Oxon.*, new edn, 2.392–6

Archives Stonyhurst College, Lancashire

Vertue, George (1684–1756), engraver and antiquary, was born in the parish of St Martin-in-the-Fields, London, on 17 November 1684, the eldest child of Roman Catholic parents, James Vertue (d. 1711) and Mary Carter (c.1663–1743). His mother had been a servant in the household of the duke of York (the future James II), and both parents were in service at the exiled court of James II. His father's later profession is unknown, though he is said to have been a tailor. Following what he described as 'proper schooling', Vertue was apprenticed on 25 March 1697 to a foreign-born silver engraver in London, probably the French silversmith Blaise Gentot. On Gentot's return to France around 1700, Vertue undertook private artistic study for two years before being apprenticed to the well-connected reproductive engraver Michael Vandergucht.

George Vertue (1684–1756), by Jonathan Richardson the elder, 1733

After seven years under Vandergucht, in 1709 Vertue set himself up as an independent engraver, producing a variety of work, notably reproductions of portraits by Sir Godfrey Kneller. From 1711 he continued his artistic education by attending the Great Queen Street Academy, run by Kneller. In 1715 he engraved that artist's portrait of the newly crowned George I on a large scale, and by Vertue's own account it was this work that established him. At this time Vertue was patronized by Heneage Finch, fifth earl of Winchilsea, and was receiving a number of individual prestigious commissions. In 1714 the lord mayor of London, Richard Hoare, engaged him to design and engrave a two-sheet print, *The View of the Charity Children in the Strand*, for a payment of £100. Two further well-paid projects, for a map of the British empire for the diplomat Henry Ferne and a reproduction of Holbein's painting of the Barber-Surgeons for that company, were aborted. But in 1717 Vertue was appointed the official engraver to the newly revived Society of Antiquaries. As engraver, a post he held until his death, he was responsible for engraving and printing all the images published under the society's auspices, collected as the *Vetusta monumenta*. This amounted to sixty-four projects, comprising some eighty-six separate plates. Although the plates remained the property of the society, this employment brought Vertue an average annual income of around £20, providing an unusual source of security for a professional engraver. In addition to the engraving work, Vertue undertook occasional duties such as attending the sale of John Talman's collection as the society's agent in 1727 and supplying 'a press

for holding prints' in 1754. Uniquely, he was also a fellow of the society, a privilege denied to the antiquaries' subsequent engravers, and so took an active part in scholarly activities, presenting a paper on the tomb of Edward the Confessor in 1731 (published in the first volume of *Archaeologia*, 1770) and describing the method of taking prints off medals to the society in 1746. Additionally, he frequently undertook private antiquarian commissions from members of the society.

Vertue's researches into the history of art in Britain began late in 1712 and occupied him for the rest of his life. Drawing on published and manuscript sources, as well as on his extensive travels around Britain, it would have been by far the most comprehensive account of the visual arts produced to date. But during his lifetime the most substantial published manifestations of his labours were his accounts of the works of Wenceslaus Hollar (1745) and of the medallist Thomas Simon (1753).

On 17 February 1720 Vertue married Margaret Evans (d. 1776), an event recorded by the artist in an etching (now in the Victoria and Albert Museum) showing the couple 'in the very Habits they were Married', posed before a wall adorned with his engravings. During the 1720s Vertue established himself as a leading figure in London's art circles: in 1724 he was made secretary of the Rose and Crown Club, and in 1726 he was elected one of the Virtuosi of St Luke, whose meetings he attended through to 1743. Probably through the influence of George Clarke of Christ Church, a keen patron of the artist, Vertue succeeded

Michael Burghers in 1727 as Oxford University engraver, taking on the responsibility for the engraving of the almanacs. The books were published by Oxford University Press and generally designed by a Mr Green or Greene of Oxford, but this post brought Vertue a handsome £50 a year through to 1751.

During the 1720s Vertue was very active as a book illustrator, notable projects being the illustrations for an edition of John Urry's *Works of Geoffrey Chaucer* (1721), Gerard Brandt's *History of the Reformation* (1720–23), and Edmund Waller's *Works* (1729). By the 1730s he tended instead to produce only portrait frontispieces for books. Thomas Dodd was able to list more than 120 separate portraits of this type produced between 1709 and 1756, and even this is demonstrably incomplete. Almost all were reproductions, although a handful were original designs by the artist, including the portraits of Edward Calamy that appeared in his *Sermons* (1722) and of Samuel Dale for his *Pharmacologia* (1737). Vertue's reputation in this field was such that puffs for new publications would often cite the presence of an engraved portrait by him as a selling point.

Vertue also established himself as a successful independent publisher of prints. In March 1726 he issued a printed sheet announcing the publication by subscription of 'The Effigies of Twelve of the Most Celebrated English Poets' (published 1726–9), an early example of such a commercial scheme. The idea was developed on a grander scale by the Knapton brothers with their *Heads of the Kings of England* (1733–6), for which Vertue was co-publisher and engraver. Vertue designed and engraved forty elaborate folio portrait reproductions and engraved twenty folio prints of royal monuments after designs by Gravelot. However, on the Knaptons' next project, the more extensive *Heads of Illustrious Persons* (1737–42), Vertue was employed on only nine plates before being dismissed for slowness, being displaced by the Flemish engraver Jacobus Houbraken. He continued to publish independently; the last two pages of his published account of the works of the medallist Thomas Simon (1753) lists more than a hundred prints 'Engraved, already Printed and Published' and available from him at his shop in Brownlow Street, Drury Lane. This includes groups of historical portraits, *Nine Historical Portraits* (1742–51) and the accompanying pamphlet by the artist, the twelve heads of poets, and many single portrait plates, together with antiquarian views and plans, depictions of curiosities, and maps.

Besides regular work for the Society of Antiquaries and the University of Oxford, and for the booksellers, Vertue received occasional commissions of a highly various nature. He produced the original design for the massive silver wine cooler commissioned by the banker and goldsmith Henry Jerningham in 1730–31 and executed by Charles Kandler and John Michael Rysbrack in 1731–4; engraved James Gibbs's designs for the Radcliffe Camera for the trustees of the library in 1737; and in 1748 was appointed by the office of the ordinance (whose comptroller was Charles Frederick, formerly director of the Society

of Antiquaries) to engrave the design of the royal fireworks that were to celebrate the peace of Aix-la-Chapelle in Green Park. The last commission was recorded in great detail by the engraver in a diary, which documents his frustration as an ambitious project involving a whole volume of large prints and text worth £500 to him was whittled down following delays to comprise only a single plate and the production of the tickets, at a charge of 20 guineas.

Vertue's autobiography, prepared as part of his history of British art, downplays the variety of his commercial printmaking activities in favour of his work as a draughtsman and antiquary in the employment of a series of prestigious patrons. During the 1720s and 1730s he enjoyed a sustained relationship with the earl of Oxford, for whom he drew and engraved and acted as an occasional art agent and touring companion. At the earl's death in 1741 Lady Oxford continued to patronize Vertue, engaging him to draw up an inventory of the Oxford collection and commissioning a number of prints. The earl's daughter, the duchess of Portland, employed him to engrave a series of plates of curiosities in her collection in the late 1740s. Frederick, prince of Wales, also employed Vertue extensively between 1749 and his death in 1751. For the prince, Vertue provided watercolours from stock, acted as an art adviser, and drew up manuscript catalogues of the royal collections. Most commonly, his work for élite patrons involved the production of private plates reproducing family portraits or monuments, for which the artist quoted a charge of 6 to 10 guineas in 1737. A detailed bill to the duke of Norfolk dated 1745–6 encapsulates the variety of his activities, among them charges for copying portraits of the duke's ancestors, drawing a 'lineal pedigree', and providing a volume of prints by Hollar. Only occasionally did he produce original portraits, such as the 1740 gilt watercolour of the third Baron Coleraine (British Museum) taken from life, which was created following a series of antiquarian tours with the baron during the 1730s.

Vertue's output as a printmaker was prodigious. His manuscript list of his own engravings (held in the Lewis Walpole Library) includes some 500 prints produced between 1708 and 1740 alone, and this is far from complete. He presumably employed assistants, although he mentions only one, Giles King. On several occasions he made up volumes of proofs of his own prints, created variously for James West in 1733, for the Bodleian Library in 1737, and for the earl of Oxford and for Thomas Frankland in 1740. By 1741 his history of British art was nearing a state of completion, and he even prepared a self-portrait to serve as a frontispiece, but the death of Oxford meant that the plan to publish was abandoned. Although suffering ill health, Vertue continued working into the 1750s, publishing his account of Thomas Simon (1753), producing frontispieces and plates, working on his notebooks, and preparing catalogues of the collections of Charles I, James II, and the duke of Buckingham (the first two were later published by Horace Walpole).

Vertue died on 24 July 1756 and was buried on 30 July in

Westminster Abbey. His will specified some £285 in cash payments to relatives and friends, in addition to the repayment of outstanding debts and mourning rings for nineteen individuals, among them the sculptor Rysbrack and the auctioneer Richard Ford. His remaining wealth was left to Margaret, which, according to Vertue's friend the antiquary William Cole, amounted to as much as £1000. His extensive collections of books, drawings, and prints were auctioned by Ford (as stipulated in his will) in sales running between 16 and 22 March 1757. Vertue's independently published antiquarian plates were acquired from his widow by the Society of Antiquaries and subsequently republished for members, while the rest remained with his widow and were distributed after her death by a sale at Langford's on 24–5 February 1777 (with John Boydell as the most extensive purchaser). The forty or more volumes of Vertue's notes on the history of art were purchased by Horace Walpole in 1758, who from September 1759 worked them up into what was published as his *Anecdotes of Painting in England* (1762–71). As transmitted by Walpole, and published in their original form by the Walpole Society in six volumes (1930–55), Vertue's *Note Books* have been a cornerstone of British art history, and have ensured that his memory survives. His reputation as an artist, however, went quickly into decline, suffering from a shift in taste that favoured the expressive potential of original printmaking over the assiduous and undeniably dry manner of his reproductions. Yet it was as both engraver and historian that he was celebrated by contemporaries, and it is the very variety of his professional activities and commercial enterprises that demonstrates most fully the vitality of the culture in which he operated.   MARTIN MYRONE

Sources Vertue, *Note books* · H. Walpole, *Anecdotes of painting in England: with some account of the principal artists*, ed. R. N. Wornum, new edn, 3 vols. (1849) · T. Dodd, 'Memoirs of English engravers', BL, Add. MS 33406 · G. Vertue, 'A collection of engraved prints', Yale U., Lewis Walpole Library, 49.3665 · treasurer's account book, 1718–38, S. Antiquaries, Lond. · I. Bignamini, 'George Vertue, art historian, and art institutions in London, 1689–1768', *Walpole Society*, 54 (1988), 1–148 · H. M. Petter, *The Oxford almanacks* (1974) · G. Vertue, *Medals, coins and great seals ... of Thomas Simon* (1753) · M. Myrone, 'Graphic antiquarianism in eighteenth century Britain: the career and reputation of George Vertue', *Producing the past*, ed. M. Myrone and L. Pelz (1999) · C. Whitfield, 'Balthassar Gerbier, Rubens and George Vertue', *Studies in the History of Art*, 5 (1973), 23–31 · J. Evans, *A history of the Society of Antiquaries* (1956) · A. Grimwade, 'The master of George Vertue', *Apollo*, 127 (1988), 83–9

Archives BL, accounts of tours with second Lord Oxford, Add. MSS 70434, 70437–70439 · BL, notebooks, memoranda, and travel journals, etc., Add. MSS 21111, 23068–23098 · BL, papers relating to his tours with Lord Oxford, loan 29 · Bodl. Oxf., topographical and antiquarian drawings · Yale U., Lewis Walpole Library, papers, incl. drawings | BL, letters to second Lord Oxford, Add. MS 70399 · Bodl. Oxf., letters to J. Murray

Likenesses J. Gibson, oils, 1715, S. Antiquaries, Lond. · G. Vertue, self-portrait, etching, 1720 (with wife), V&A · T. Gibson, oils, 1723, S. Antiquaries, Lond. · J. Richardson the elder, oils, 1733, NPG [*see illus.*] · G. Hamilton, group portrait, oils, 1735 (*A conversation of virtuosi ... at the Kings Armes*), NPG · J. Richardson the elder, drawing, 1735, S. Antiquaries, Lond. · attrib. G. Vertue, self-portrait?, pencil and chalk drawing, 1741, NPG · G. Vertue, self-portrait, drawing, 1741, BL · S. Bevan, ivory statuette, BM · W. Humphrey, etching (after G. Vertue), BM, NPG

Wealth at death £1500; plus collections of art and books: note by William Cole of subject leaving wife £1000, BL, Add. MS 5833, fol. 161v; will, PRO, PROB 11/824

Vertue, Robert (*d.* 1506), master mason, was the son of Adam Vertue (*fl.* 1475–1485), an ordinary working mason at Westminster Abbey and Eltham Palace. Robert's younger brother **William Vertue** (*d.* 1527) was also a master mason. Robert worked almost continuously as an ordinary mason on the nave of Westminster Abbey between 1475 and 1490. His standing must have risen greatly during the 1490s, for he is next recorded as the master mason for one of Henry VII's most important projects, the new riverside north range of Greenwich Palace, built in 1500–04 at a cost of £900. In 1501 and 1502 Robert was paid £100 for reconstructing the tower which contained the king's privy lodgings in the Tower of London.

In 1502 Robert was also involved in the rebuilding of St Mary-at-Hill, London, and in 1501–2 'V[e]rtu the mason', doubtless Robert, was paid for a new window in the master's lodging at St Antony's Hospital, also in London. Robert's architecturally most ambitious work was the vaulting in the new church of Bath Abbey, rebuilt from 1501. A letter of the patron, Oliver King, bishop of Bath and Wells, which was probably written in 1503, notes that at a meeting with Robert and William Vertue the brothers had assured him that by comparison with 'the vaute devised for the chancelle ... ther shal be noone so goodeley neither in england nor in france' (Westminster Abbey Muniment 16040). In fact the design, particularly of the aisle vaults, is notably less accomplished than that of the contemporary vaults in Henry VII's Chapel at Westminster. In 1506 Robert was one of three master masons responsible for drawing up an estimate for the stonework of Henry VII's tomb, and on 10 May of that year he witnessed the will of the designer of Henry VII's Chapel, Robert Janyns. The fact that Janyns and Robert Vertue both died in the summer of 1506 raises the possibility of a common cause: plague is perhaps the most likely.

Robert's will, proved on 12 December 1506, reveals that he was a citizen of London, that he was a parishioner of St Paul's, Canterbury, and that his wife was called Eleanor. They had two sons. The will's request for burial inside St Augustine's Abbey, Canterbury, and its bequests to monks of the abbey suggest that Robert was responsible for the major projects in hand there in 1506, the lady chapel and the bell-tower.

On 5 June 1506 William Vertue contracted jointly with the London master mason John Aylmer for the main vault and flying buttresses of the choir of St George's Chapel, Windsor. It is highly unlikely that William would have been put in charge of this work if either his brother or Robert Janyns had been alive and in good health. The design was to follow in most respects the recently constructed vault over the nave (almost certainly designed by Janyns) and the work was to be finished by Christmas 1508. A second contract of December 1511, undertaken by William alone, was for the completion of the lady chapel of St George's, specifically for its vault, its parapets, and the vault of its vestibule. Only the last two elements were ever executed. In 1512, together with the master carpenter Humphrey Coke, Vertue made a 'platt' (probably a complete set of drawings rather than just a plan) for each of the two main storeys of Corpus Christi College, Oxford, and in 1516 he participated in the devising of the plat for the west range of the inner court at Eton College. Since this second plat consisted of an entire paper book there can be no doubt that it encompassed much more than plans.

William Vertue had been king's chief mason from 28 July 1510, but on 12 September 1519 he received a new appointment to this office jointly with Henry Redman. Vertue's documented royal works, like those of Redman, must represent only a part of what he did for Henry VIII. They amount to no more than some alterations made to Woking Palace in 1512, the modest rebuilding of St Peter ad Vincula in the Tower of London in 1519–20, and a scheme for the adaptation of the Calais exchequer to provide lodgings for Francis I during his meeting with Henry VIII at the Field of Cloth of Gold in 1520. William Vertue's will is dated 15 March 1527, evidently the day of his death. In it he bequeaths property in Kingston upon Thames and desires burial in the parish church there, where his unnamed wife already lay.

That the most ambitious of William Vertue's documented works, those at St George's, Windsor, should have been stylistically wholly dependent on designs by Robert Janyns was almost inevitable, given that they were continuations of projects begun or continued by the latter. However, the picture is not very different if one takes account of the most important of the buildings whose design has been attributed to Vertue, the crossing vault at St George's (which bears the date 1528) and the two-storeyed cloister of St Stephen's Chapel in Westminster Palace, built c.1526–1529, for their emphasis on densely panelled surfaces enlivened by copious small-scale sculptured ornaments derives unmistakably from Janyns's chief work, Henry VII's Chapel.

Robert Vertue had two sons, William and **Robert Vertue** (*fl.* 1506–1555). The latter was the younger and held the post of master mason to Evesham Abbey at the time of its dissolution in 1539. He can probably be credited with all or most of the splendid series of works undertaken there by Abbot Clement Lichfield (1514–39). Those still extant are the detached bell-tower and the chantry chapels in the adjacent parish churches of St Lawrence and All Saints, the latter built before 1514 while Lichfield was prior. The chapels have richly decorated fan vaults heavily indebted to Robert Janyns's aisle and radiating chapel vaults in Henry VII's Chapel.

CHRISTOPHER WILSON

Sources J. Harvey and A. Oswald, *English mediaeval architects: a biographical dictionary down to 1550*, 2nd edn (1984) · H. M. Colvin and others, eds., *The history of the king's works*, 6 vols. (1963–82) · C. Wilson, 'The architect of Henry VII's chapel, Westminster Abbey', *The reign of Henry VII* [Harlaxton 1993], ed. B. Thompson (1995), 133–56 · J. H. Harvey, *Gothic England: a survey of national culture, 1300–1550* (1947), 183–6 [transcriptions of wills of Robert Vertue and William Vertue] · Westminster Abbey, Muniment 16040 · will of Robert Vertue (d. 1506) · will of William Vertue

Vertue, Robert (*fl.* 1506–1555). *See under* Vertue, Robert (d. 1506).

Vertue, William (d. 1527). *See under* Vertue, Robert (d. 1506).

Verulam. For this title name *see* Grimston, James Brabazon, fifth earl of Verulam (1910–1960).

Verzelini, Jacob (1522–1607), glass maker, was born in Venice, probably into a family already engaged in the glass trade; a brother, Nicholas (d. 1604), was active in Liège and London; another brother, Jasper, remained in Venice. Verzelini went to Antwerp about 1549. His marriage there in September 1556 to Elizabeth van Buren, daughter of a rich merchant, brought six children, and with this family he arrived in London in 1565, residing thereafter in the parish of St Olave, Hart Street. In 1571 Verzelini was recorded as a broker, probably trading with Antwerp, but in December 1574 he received a licence to set up a glasshouse and to manufacture drinking glasses as made in Murano. The glass, known as 'crystal', or 'façon de venise', was made from crushed flint and soda in the form of ashes imported from Spain, decoloured by the addition of manganese. A group of Venetians had arrived from Antwerp in 1549 to set up a crystal drinking-glass manufactory near Belsize Palace, north of London, but within a year or two all had left England. The import from Venice of vessels and mirrors of crystal for the luxury market represented for the government an unwelcome outflow of capital, and Verzelini's grant included the monopoly of manufacture for twenty-one years, with a general prohibition of imports of crystal wares.

The glasshouse was constructed within the premises formerly occupied by the Crutched Friars, in Hart Street, and manned by Italians and some Englishmen, to whom Verzelini's grant obliged him to teach this new craft. The shopkeepers who had hitherto imported glassware opposed Verzelini's monopoly, but to no avail; however, it may not have been coincidence that in the morning of 4 September 1575 his glasshouse was devastated by fire, fed by his adjacent store of firewood. Fortunately the fire was prevented from spreading by the outer stone walls. Verzelini operated a temporary glasshouse at Newgate, and rebuilt the Crutched Friars glasshouse, together with a spacious house for his family. He was granted denization on 26 November 1576, and shortly afterwards, in consideration of the damage at Crutched Friars, was granted a twenty-one-year lease allowing him to cut firewood on the royal estate of Kingswood, in Hampshire.

A succession of problems hit Verzelini in 1579. During the summer one of his servants brought charges that after three years of sexual abuse she had become pregnant by him. Having confessed, he was ordered to give 200 ells of canvas to the Bridewell Hospital poor and to have the child raised at his expense. Then Verzelini, who was not a freeman of the City and therefore prevented from trading with other 'foreigners', was penalized for selling to a trader from Leicester. He was ordered to demolish the glasshouse at Newgate when that at Crutched Friars was rebuilt, and he was ordered to shut down his furnaces in the winter, so as to spare some firewood for the citizenry. A demise of the Crutched Friars premises to Verzelini by Lord and Lady Lumley in 1586, for twenty-one years for a consideration of £200 and annual rent of £33 10s., mentions the great room enclosing the glasshouse, a hall or shop, with parlour and kitchen, a garden with further buildings, a house, a tennis court, and other buildings occupied by a third party.

It is often impossible to distinguish between crystalware produced in England and in the Low Countries at this time, but twelve pieces originating in England are ascribed to Verzelini, on the grounds that he had the monopoly at the time. Most are diamond-point engraved commemorative goblets created to celebrate a marriage or baptism. The British Museum has a clear cylindrical tankard, with decorated silver-gilt lid and base, made for Lord Burghley about 1572–4, and a goblet, inscribed '1577', the earliest dated example of any English glass. Two goblets, engraved respectively 'John Dier 1581' and 'RP MP', '1586 GOD SAVE QUYNE ELISABETH', are in the Victoria and Albert Museum. Others are in the Fitzwilliam Museum, Cambridge, the Birmingham Museum, and in the USA. The diamond-point engraved decoration, with foliage and animals, initials, and dates, is in a linear style with hatching, an Italian style which was then copied in England. The engraver was possibly Anthony de Lysle, a Frenchman resident in London who worked independently of Verzelini's workshop. Verzelini's output must have been considerable. He kept his glassworks in operation for over twenty-one years, creating a flourishing industry and a body of craftsmen trained in the Venetian tradition. It was also profitable, for he acquired property in nearby Mark Lane, and, over the years, estates in and around Downe, Kent, where he became lord of the manor.

Verzelini probably retired about 1590; his wife was naturalized that year, which would enable her to inherit land. The glasshouse was handed over to his sons Francis and Jacob. Meanwhile, however, a patent to make crystal was granted in February 1592 to Sir Jerome Bowers, soldier and courtier, as a reward for loyalty, to take effect on the termination of Verzelini's grant in 1595. Bowers had no knowledge of glass making, but he built a glasshouse in the former Blackfriars monastery and endeavoured to recruit Verzelini's Italian craftsmen. The feud between the Verzelinis and Bowers carried over into the courts with a victory for Bowers. The Crutched Friars glasshouse closed down, although Jacob and Elizabeth Verzelini continued to live there. Francis was imprisoned for ten years from 1598, his brother Jacob for a lesser period: the exact nature of their offences is not known.

Verzelini died at his house in Crutched Friars on 20 January 1607, and was buried, as he desired, at Downe Chapel on 3 February. His will, drawn up in 1604, benefited the poor in Christ's, St Bartholomew's, and St Thomas's hospitals, and his parishes of St Olave and Downe. One of his children had probably died young, but his daughters, Katherine (now dead), Elizabeth, and Mary, had all made good marriages; they and their children, and his sons, inherited the properties in Kent. His wife was chief beneficiary and executor, but before the will was proved she died, on 26 October 1607, and was likewise buried at Downe.   ANITA MCCONNELL

Sources A. Engel, 'In search of Jacob Verzelini', *Readings in Glass History*, 8 (1977), 29–50, 77–83 · A. Sutton and J. R. Sewell, 'Jacob Verzelini and the City of London', *Glass Technology*, 21 (1980), 190–92 · W. Buckley, *Diamond engraved glasses of the 16th century* (1929) · R. J. Charleston, *English glass and the glass used in England, circa 400–1940* (1984) · *CPR, 1572–5*, 543; *1575–8*, 249, 297 · R. Holinshed and others, eds., *The chronicles of England, Scotland and Ireland*, 2nd edn, ed. J. Hooker, 2 (1586), 156 · PRO, PROB 11/109, sig. 7 [will] · PRO, PROB 11/110, sig. 77 [will of Elizabeth Verzelini] · A. Gasparetto, 'Le relazioni fra Venezia e el Inghilterra nei secoli XVI e XVII e la loro influenza sulle forme vetrarie', *Vetro e Silicati*, 14/82 (1970), 16–20 · J. Wilson, 'Two early craftsmen', *Industry and enterprise*, Bromley Local History, 9 [1991], 21–5
Likenesses brass monument (with Elizabeth), Downe church, Kent
Wealth at death wealthy; extensive properties in London and Kent

Vescy [Vesci], **Eustace de** (1169/70–1216), baron, lord of Alnwick, Northumberland, the son of William de Vescy (d. 1183) and Burga, daughter of Robert (III) de *Stuteville, lord of Cottingham, Yorkshire, came of age in 1190. He was charged a relief of 1300 marks for his barony, which consisted of 36½ fees in Northumberland and Yorkshire. He married Margaret, the illegitimate daughter of *William the Lion, king of Scots, and half-sister of Alexander II of Scotland; at Richard I's second coronation on 17 April 1194 he witnessed a royal charter in favour of his father-in-law.

At the end of 1194 Vescy was at Chinon in France with Richard I. He was one of the guarantors of the treaty between John and Renaud, count of Boulogne, on 13 August 1199. In the same year, probably later, he was sent to William the Lion of Scotland to promise him satisfaction of his rights in England; he witnessed his homage on 22 November 1200, and on 10 April 1209 was sent to meet William the Lion on his visit to England. He served King John on his expedition to Ireland in the summer of 1210. In December 1207 Vescy was pardoned of a 300 mark amercement assessed in his plea against Richard de Umfraville concerning custody of an heir.

Accused along with Robert Fitzwalter of conspiring against John in August 1212, Vescy fled to Scotland. The tale of John's attempted seduction of his wife, and the trick played on him of substituting another woman in the royal bed, which first appears in William of Newburgh, is scarcely credible, and bears some resemblance to similar stories of the king's lecherous designs on others, for example, Robert Fitzwalter's daughter. Vescy was outlawed and his lands seized; but after John's submission to the pope he was forced to invite Vescy back on 27 May 1213, although orders were sent on the same day to cripple his power by destroying his castles at Alnwick and Malton. On 18 July 1213 he was one of the recipients of John's pledge to make restitution to those persons who had suffered damages during the interdict, and his lands were restored to him the next day. In 1213 Vescy was one of six northern barons who refused to participate in John's projected Poitevin expedition, and the next year he refused to pay scutage for the campaign. On 5 November 1214 Innocent III warned him to remain loyal to the king in his disputes with the barons. He was one of the most prominent of the northern barons who led the movement to impose Magna Carta on John. He was closely associated with another Yorkshire rebel, Robert de Ros (d. 1226/7), and both were among the twenty-five appointed to see Magna Carta carried out. He was one of nine barons whom the pope excommunicated by name in September 1215. On 3 May 1216 Vescy went to John seeking reconciliation. After Louis of France landed he accompanied Alexander II of Scotland on his way to do homage to the Capetian prince. On their way in late August 1216 they laid siege to Barnard Castle, co. Durham, belonging to Hugh de Balliol, and, approaching too near, Vescy was shot through the head by an arrow. His lands were confiscated and handed over to royal allies. He left a son, William (d. 1253), who came of age in 1226.   RALPH V. TURNER

Sources I. J. Sanders, *English baronies: a study of their origin and descent, 1086–1327* (1960) · Pipe rolls · Chancery records · *The letters of Pope Innocent III (1198–1216) concerning England and Wales*, ed. C. R. Cheney and M. G. Cheney (1967) · *Rogeri de Wendover liber qui dicitur flores historiarum*, ed. H. G. Hewlett, 3 vols., Rolls Series, [84] (1886–9) · *Memoriale fratris Walteri de Coventria / The historical collections of Walter of Coventry*, ed. W. Stubbs, 2 vols., Rolls Series, 58 (1872–3) · R. Howlett, ed., *Chronicles of the reigns of Stephen, Henry II, and Richard I*, 4 vols., Rolls Series, 82 (1884–9), vols. 1–2 · L. Landon, *The itinerary of King Richard I*, PRSoc., new ser., 13 (1935) · J. C. Holt, *Magna Carta*, 2nd edn (1992)

Vescy, John de (1244–1289), baron, was the eldest son of William de Vescy (d. 1253) and his second wife, Agnes, daughter of William de Ferrers, and the elder brother of William de *Vescy. According to the chronicler of Malton Priory, he was born on 18 July 1244. In 1253, on the death of his father in Gascony, he succeeded to the barony of Alnwick, Northumberland, besides Malton and considerable estates in Yorkshire. Henry III conferred his wardship and marriage on Peter of Savoy, Queen Eleanor's uncle, as a clear grant worth £625 p.a. According to the close rolls (1254), young Vescy was educated, with the Lord Edmund and Henry de Lacy, in the queen's household. Queen Eleanor and Peter of Savoy subsequently married him to their kinswoman Agnes of Saluzzo (d. c.1265). From May 1263 Vescy was (according to the chronicler Thomas Wykes) one of the noble 'boys' rebelling under the leadership of Simon de Montfort. His motives were unclear: Henry III had been personally kind to him, with several gifts to him and his mother. His Savoyard wife was devoted to him. Presumably Vescy was attracted by existing friendships with other rebellious royal wards, for instance Henry Hastings and Geoffrey de Lucy.

Vescy's main activity during the barons' war was fighting the king's supporters in the north. From October 1263 until the middle of 1264 he harassed the sheriff of Yorkshire. In December 1263 he was one of those barons listed as supporting the Montfortians' case at the mise of Amiens. However, it is not certain that he fought at Lewes, and he held no office under Montfort. He was summoned to Montfort's famous Model Parliament of 20 January 1265, which he may have attended (although he was still in the north on 9 January). He was due to attend the Dunstable tournament on 24 February 1265, and it is only from then that he seems to have been at court; he received grants in April and May. He was wounded and taken prisoner at Evesham, but was released and compounded for his estates after the dictum of Kenilworth. He may even have been saddled with a double fine. There is a Northumbrian legend that he took home with him to Alnwick, in bizarre northern fashion, one of Montfort's feet, which until the dissolution was preserved in the priory, shod with a silver shoe.

In 1267 Vescy rebelled again with some disinherited northern barons. However, early in the year Edward himself went north and forced him to submit, after taking Alnwick Castle by storm with the assistance of the men of Bamburgh. According to Wykes, the king's son treated him so leniently that ever after he was his devoted friend. Vescy was quickly reconciled, securing pardons for at least three retainers, and ransoming his lands from the count of St Pol for 3700 marks, most of which had been paid by Easter 1270. Unusually for ex-Montfortians he took the cross and attended Edward on crusade to Palestine, financed by the lease of manors and loans. The story that he helped lead Eleanor of Castile out when Edward was operated upon for his famous wound is now thought apocryphal, but he was growing in favour, and accompanied Edward to Gascony on his return to England.

From 1274 to 1276 Edward I made Vescy governor of Scarborough Castle. In 1275 he fought in the Scottish expedition which defeated Godred, king of Man. In early 1276 he went on pilgrimage to Santiago de Compostela but returned to attend parliament at the end of the year. He was now a trusted member of Edward I's inner circle (although the old tradition that he was the king's 'secretary' stems from a mistranslation). In August 1277 Vescy served in Wales and with Otho de Grandson led the substantial naval force which cut off Anglesey and helped bring Llywelyn of Wales to heel. In 1278 he was one of the ambassadors negotiating the marriage of the king's infant daughter, Margaret, to the duke of Brabant. In the following year, he adjudicated disputes between the king of Scots and the bishop of Durham. Vescy was sent in February 1282 with Antony (I) Bek to Aragon for the preliminary negotiations (ultimately unsuccessful) of a marriage between Alfonso, son of King Peter, and Edward's eldest daughter, Eleanor, and in August signed the contract as proxy at Huesca. Bek and Vescy then helped recruit Gascons for the renewed Welsh war. During that campaign Vescy again held the most important command of Anglesey with Otho de Grandson. In June 1285 he was sent with two others to negotiate the marriage between Edward's daughter, Elizabeth, and the son of the count of Holland. He accompanied Edward to Gascony from 1286 to 1289 and in 1287 assisted in the trial and dismissal of the seneschal, Jean de Grailly. Later in that year he again took part in negotiations with the king of Castile; he acted for a short while as Edward's hostage, and was treated with honour by the Castilians.

Vescy was married twice: first to Peter of Savoy's kinswoman Agnes, sister of Alice, countess of Lincoln, and daughter of Manfred III, marquess of Saluzzo. She died, presumably just after the battle of Evesham, for the Alnwick chronicler noted that it was 'of grief on hearing of the imprisonment of her lord' (Hartshorne, 2.5). She was buried with her sister at the Blackfriars, Pontefract. It must be significant that Vescy did not remarry for fourteen years. His second wife, whom he married in 1279 or 1280, was Isabel, sister of Henry de Beaumont (later earl of Buchan and lord of Man) and Louis de Beaumont (afterwards bishop of Durham). Vescy bargained with Queen Eleanor, his wife's kinswoman, to pay her £550 if the lady died childless. (Vescy's alleged marriage of 3 January 1279 to Marie de Lusignan, sister of Hugh XIII, count of La Marche, was merely an abortive prenuptial contract.)

Vescy patronized his family's foundation at Alnwick; additionally, in October 1286, he received a papal faculty to purchase the Friary of Penitence at Newcastle and founded there a house of the Sisters of St Clare. In the same year, he was granted an indult as 'a knight of the king' to have a portable altar for his household. Vescy died aged forty-four, childless, on 10 February 1289 at Montpellier, according to the Alnwick Abbey chronicler; he was buried at Alnwick Abbey, but his heart, as a mark of royal favour, was buried in 1290 with the hearts of Queen Eleanor and Prince Alfonso, in Blackfriars Church, London. His brother William succeeded to his estates. His widow was a prominent favourite of Edward II, and was specially banished by the ordinances of 1311, although she soon returned. She died just before 1 November 1334.

T. F. TOUT, rev. H. W. RIDGEWAY

Sources C. H. Hartshorne, *Memoirs illustrative of the history and antiquities of Northumberland*, 2 (1858), 5, 116 [Malton and Alnwick chronicles cited] · *Chancery records* · *Ann. mon.*, 2.365, 4.133, 197–8, 450, 455 · H. R. Luard, ed., *Flores historiarum*, 3 vols., Rolls Series, 95 (1890), vol. 3, p. 6 · W. Stubbs, ed., *Chronicles of the reigns of Edward I and Edward II*, 1, Rolls Series, 76 (1882), 99 · *CEPR letters*, 1.487, 490 · Rymer, *Foedera*, new edn, 1.1–2 · S. D. Lloyd, *English society and the crusade, 1216–1307* (1988), 108, 129–32, 194 · M. Prestwich, *Edward I* (1988), 79, 153, 180, 199, 305, 321–5 · J. E. Morris, *The Welsh wars of Edward I* (1901), 121, 187, 189–91

Vescy, William de, Lord Vescy (1245–1297), baron, was born on 19 September 1245, the second son of William de Vescy (d. 1253), lord of Alnwick, Northumberland, and of Agnes, the daughter of William de Ferrers and his wife, Sybil, one of the daughters of William (II) *Marshal, who divided his vast inheritance on the death of their brother Anselm. William senior died in 1253 and was succeeded by his eldest son, John de *Vescy, who died without heirs in 1289, leaving the family estate to the younger William, who was then forty-three years old. When his mother died in 1290 Vescy inherited a large portion of the county of Kildare in Ireland, as well as property in England. In middle age he became the head of an impressive patrimony in

England and Ireland and took on royal service commensurate with his new status.

As a younger son, William de Vescy only occasionally appears in royal records before his brother's death, and his early career clearly followed his brother's. John was an adherent of Simon de Montfort and was wounded and captured at Evesham on 4 August 1265. Like his brother, William supported the barons, and had attempted to hold Gloucester Castle against the Lord Edward earlier in June. After a further bout of rebelliousness in the north in 1267, John de Vescy became Edward's close companion, joined him on crusade in 1270–72, and, as his household knight, subsequently performed a variety of tasks, notably as a soldier and ambassador. In 1276 Edward pardoned the two brothers for depredations committed during the barons' wars, and William was given protection to go on a pilgrimage to Santiago de Compostela. William stood surety for John in a debt to the king, and in 1280 was described as one of his brother's household knights. In 1289, after his brother died, William was given custody of Scarborough Castle to hold on the same terms on which John had held it.

During the 1280s William de Vescy began to carve out a career for himself in royal service. He was summoned to perform military service in Wales in 1277, 1282, and again in 1283, and was summoned to parliaments and royal councils in 1283, 1288, and 1295, in consequence coming to be styled Lord Vescy. In 1285 Edward appointed him justice of the forest north of the Trent, and in 1290 named him one of his envoys to treat with the Scots. He also placed him on commissions of gaol delivery and oyer and terminer.

The year 1290 marked a new phase of Vescy's career, for Edward appointed him justiciar of Ireland, demonstrating how his inheritance there could divert Vescy's attention from his interests as a substantial landholder in the north of England. He had to step down as justice of the forest, and Edward immediately granted the office to Vescy's son, John. Vescy received his commission on 12 September, and landed in Ireland two months later on 11 November. Conditions in Ireland were very disturbed, so that besides the £500 allotted to him yearly to maintain him in his office, he was to receive an additional £500 in time of war. In fact Vescy incurred expenses at once for campaigning against the Irish and maintaining a force of Welsh retainers. In 1291 his attention turned briefly to Scotland. Not only was he summoned to serve in Scotland, but more importantly, after the death of Princess Margaret, he put in a claim to the throne of Scotland based on his descent from his grandmother Margaret, an illegitimate daughter of *William the Lion, king of Scots. His son, John, represented him in the process, but Vescy did not pursue the claim vigorously, and abandoned the effort just before Edward made his pronouncement on 17 November 1292.

Various disputes arising out of Vescy's overbearing conduct as justiciar and as lord of the liberty of Kildare demanded his attention in these years. In 1291 the abbot of St Thomas's, Dublin, accused Vescy and the other Marshal coheirs of unjustly impleading him in the court of the liberty. The case took a serious turn when Vescy went ahead and heard the plea anyway after the king had prohibited him from proceeding. Additional accusations, ranging from unjustly taking distresses, issuing prohibitions, proving weights and measures, and harassing officials, to falsely maintaining individuals in suits, were heard by king and council at the parliament at Westminster in October 1293. Edward ordered an inquiry, and the subsequent inquests conducted in March 1294 found Vescy and his men guilty of many transgressions.

The most sensational dispute involved John fitz Thomas Fitzgerald (d. 1316), lord of Offaly, who was Vescy's tenant. Tensions between them mounted to the point that the king intervened in 1293, and ordered Vescy to revoke a military summons that he had issued to raise an army to march on Offaly. Fitz Thomas lodged several of the accusations against Vescy heard in parliament in 1293. The following year Vescy accused fitz Thomas of defaming him before the king and council, by alleging that Vescy had tried to persuade him to enter into a sworn compact against the king. Fitz Thomas denied this accusation, but claimed that Vescy had said even more explosive things about the king, telling him that the Irish were a miserable people, but could be great lords and do without the king. If they knew Edward as well as he did, they would value him less for he was the most perverse and dastardly knight in the kingdom. And he recounted a story of Edward's conduct at Kenilworth during the barons' wars that showed him to be a coward. Outraged, Vescy denied the charges and offered to wage battle to prove his right. The king removed the case to England and ordered fitz Thomas and Vescy to appear before him on July 24. Vescy showed up, armed and ready for battle. Fitz Thomas did not appear, and the case was adjourned several times before it was finally nullified in parliament in 1295.

William de Vescy was removed as justiciar in 1294. Despite his record, Edward bore him no ill will, for Vescy was with the king in Wales in April 1295, was summoned to parliament in June, and was reappointed justice of the forest the following September. Indeed, Langtoft called him a 'prudent and wise knight' (*Chronicle of Pierre de Langtoft*, 2.231). Preparing for the campaign in Gascony of 1296, in October 1295 Vescy received permission to make a grant in mortmain to the prior and convent of Malton, while in December Edward promised that if Vescy died in Gascony he would charge his heirs for any outstanding debts.

Vescy was summoned to serve again in Gascony in 1297, but he died on 19 July. His wife was Isabel, the second daughter and coheir of Adam of Periton, of Ellington, Northumberland, and the widow of Robert of Welle, who had died in 1265. Their only son, John, died in Wales on 27 April 1295, and in his last years Vescy was much concerned with the inheritance of his estates. In 1296, therefore, he engaged in several transactions with Antony (I) Bek, bishop of Durham (d. 1311), to make his bastard son, another **William de Vescy** [*known as* Sir William de Vescy of Kildare], Lord Vescy (d. 1314), the inheritor of a number of his English estates. But in 1297 he surrendered the

county of Kildare and other Irish lands to the king, and received them back on condition that they would revert to the crown when he died. In return, Edward pardoned all debts and fines to the crown incurred by Vescy as justiciar of Ireland and justice of the forest, as well as the debts owed by his brother John. He was likewise pardoned for all legal actions against him from the time he was justiciar and justice.

After his father's death William of Kildare seems to have succeeded by stages to the lands entailed upon him by his father. He did homage for Caythorpe in Lincolnshire on 22 May 1298, and was summoned to serve in Scotland in 1300 as having lands worth more than £40 per annum in that county, but a petition from early in Edward II's reign, asking the king 'to enforce the covenants between the bishop of Durham and his father' (*CDS*, 3, no. 187), suggests that he was slow to obtain livery of his inheritance elsewhere. Later allegations that Bishop Bek defrauded William of the honour of Alnwick by selling it to Henry Percy have been shown to be baseless. In 1310 Vescy litigated against the widow of his half-brother, John de Vescy, for the Lincolnshire manor of Stapleford, claiming that his father had assigned it to her as dower with reversion to himself, but no judgment is recorded. None the less at the time of his death William held a number of manors in Yorkshire and Lincolnshire. He is recorded as a knight of Edward II's household, which may explain the summonses to parliament directed to him in 1313 and 1314; he is thus regarded as having become Lord Vescy in his own right. But it was as a retainer of the earl of Pembroke that he fought at Bannockburn, where he was killed on 24 June 1314. According to Dugdale he married Maud, widow of Thomas Neville of Cleatham, Lincolnshire, but this is unlikely. His heir was his distant cousin Gilbert Aton, who succeeded to all that was left of the Vescy inheritance.   SCOTT L. WAUGH

Sources GEC, *Peerage*, new edn, 12/2.281–5 · F. Palgrave, ed., *The parliamentary writs and writs of military summons*, 2 vols. in 4 (1827–34), vols. 1, 2/3 · *RotP* · *Chancery records* · Rymer, *Foedera*, new edn, vol. 4 · I. J. Sanders, *English baronies: a study of their origin and descent, 1086–1327* (1960), 103 · M. Prestwich, *Edward I* (1988), 353, 358, 461, 539 · A. J. Otway-Ruthven, *A history of medieval Ireland*, 2nd edn (1980), 150, 174, 209–12, 214 · C. H. Hartshorne, *Feudal and military antiquities of Northumberland and the Scottish borders*, 2 (1858) · *The chronicle of Pierre de Langtoft*, ed. T. Wright, 2 vols., Rolls Series, 47 (1866–8) · *Willelmi Rishanger ... chronica et annales*, ed. H. T. Riley, pt 2 of *Chronica monasterii S. Albani*, Rolls Series, 28 (1865) · *CDS*, 3, no. 187 · W. Dugdale, *The baronage of England*, 2 vols. (1675–6), vol. 1, p. 39 · F. W. Maitland, ed., *Years books of Edward II*, 3: *3 Edward II*, SeldS, 20 (1905), 4–9 · J. C. Davies, *The baronial opposition to Edward II* (1918), 221 · J. R. S. Phillips, *Aymer de Valence, earl of Pembroke, 1307–1324: baronial politics in the reign of Edward II* (1972), 75 · J. M. W. Bean, 'The Percies' acquisition of Alnwick', *Archaeologia Aeliana*, 4th ser., 32 (1954), 309–19

Vescy, William de, Lord Vescy (d. 1314). *See under* Vescy, William de, Lord Vescy (1245–1297).

Vesey, Elizabeth (c.1715–1791), literary hostess, was probably born in Ireland. She was the second daughter of Sir Thomas *Vesey, bt, bishop of Ossory (1668–1730), and his wife, Mary (d. 1746), daughter and heir of Denny Muschamp of Horsley, Surrey. The Veseys were an important

Elizabeth Vesey (c.1715–1791), by unknown artist, c.1770

Anglo-Irish family; Thomas's father, John, was archbishop of Tuam. Elizabeth was presumably educated at home; her correspondence suggests wide reading and at least some competence in French and Italian. She married William Handcock of Willbrook, co. Westmeath, before December 1731 when Mary Delany reported seeing them at a ball in Dublin. Handcock, who represented the borough of Fore in the Irish parliament, died in 1741. By early 1746 Elizabeth had married a wealthy cousin, Agmondesham Vesey (d. 1785) of Lucan, a member of the Irish parliament for Harristown, co. Kildare, and Kinsale, co. Cork. He also served as accountant-general of Ireland. Elizabeth had no children from either marriage.

The Veseys travelled frequently to England and by the 1760s their stays in Ireland were generally limited to the biennial meetings of parliament. In London they rented houses in Clarges Street and Bolton Row. In Ireland they lived at Lucan. Agmondesham Vesey, who fancied himself as an architect, improved his house there after his marriage, but between 1775 and 1777 he replaced it entirely with a correct Georgian mansion. Vesey was generally held to be an intellectual lightweight, always seeking to follow fashion. He was good company as a casual acquaintance but few valued his advice or friendship. He was also chronically unfaithful to his wife. Elizabeth Vesey maintained the façade of a successful marriage, nursed her husband during attacks of epilepsy, but depended for support upon a circle of female friends. Her domestic companion was a sister of her first husband. Miss Handcock (her first name is not known), who also assumed most of the duties of household management, was always acknowledged cordially by Vesey's correspondents, but she seems to

have stayed in the background on social occasions. Vesey's well-known friends included Mary Delany, whom she met in Ireland, Margaret, duchess of Portland, Elizabeth Montagu, Elizabeth Carter, Frances Burney, and Hannah More.

Vesey and Montagu seem to have met in the late 1740s. By the 1760s they were very close, sharing friends of both sexes and co-operating in establishing a salon where intelligent talk and witty repartee were more important than drink, politics, cards, or sexual encounters. They referred to their circle as the bluestocking philosophers. Vesey seems to have introduced this use of the term bluestocking, applying it to both men and women. The philosophy was put into action most effectively in her drawing-room; Vesey's charm and gifts as a hostess made her salon the most memorable of the group. In 1783 young Mary Hamilton wrote that at the Vesey house:

> one meets with a charming variety of society … the Learned, the witty, the old & young, the grave, gay, wise & unwise, the fine bred Man & the pert coxcomb; The elegant female, the chaste Matron, the severe prude, & the pert Miss, but be it remembered that you can run no *risque* in Mrs. Vesey's parties of meeting with those who have no claim to respect. (Anson and Anson, 132)

Hannah More's poem *Bas bleu* (1784) was written to commemorate such an assembly.

Vesey's success obviously depended on her personality. She was small in stature and retained her girlish beauty for many years. She seems to have been an incurable flirt, but her charm beguiled both men and women. Delany dubbed her Sylph, and her closest friends continued to call her that throughout her life. Like her friend Elizabeth Montagu she suffered from stomach complaints and other ills both real and imaginary. They frequently exchanged medications and medical advice. Vesey's surviving letters, found among those of her friends, reflect her restless flitting from one topic to another and her flights of fancy. They were treasured by such recipients as Elizabeth Carter who wrote that 'All your friends and correspondents receive the same delightful entertainment, and are equally charmed by your Letters, as they ever were; they breathe the same enchanting style which has ever marked what falls from your pen' (Pennington, 4.302). The modern reader, not knowing her in person, often finds Vesey's letters of less interest than those of other bluestockings. Despite her clerical forebears Vesey had no real religious convictions. This distressed many of her friends who believed her lack of belief made her more prey to the depression which afflicted her later years.

After 1782 the Vesey household did not return to Ireland. None of the principals was in good health, and by then Elizabeth Vesey feared she was losing both sight and hearing. Agmondesham Vesey died on 3 June 1785. His widow and her companion, Miss Handcock, were further distressed to find that neither was mentioned in his will. Their friends reported that Elizabeth had turned over all her funds to her husband at the time of their marriage; now all that remained was Vesey's jointure and Handcock's annuity which together brought in about

£800 a year. An added insult was the report that Agmondesham Vesey had left £1000 to his mistress. Some financial help was given to Vesey and Handcock by various relatives and in 1788 they moved to the Chelsea house of Vesey's cousin, Lord Cremorne. After her husband's death Vesey gave way to a tearful depression for some months. She reappeared briefly in society in 1787–8 but never again assumed the place she had previously held. Miss Handcock died in January 1789, leaving Vesey alone with her tears and her depression. She died in Chelsea early in 1791.

Any account of the bluestockings must include Vesey, although she is the most difficult to pin down. She left no literary remains, no mass of letters, and no autobiographical account. However, the brief success of the bluestocking philosophy probably owed more to her than to any of the other women usually identified with this group.   BARBARA BRANDON SCHNORRENBERG

Sources DNB · B. Rizzo, *Companions without vows: relationships among eighteenth-century British women* (1994) · S. Harcstark Myers, *The bluestocking circle: women, friendship, and the life of the mind in eighteenth-century England* (1990) · *The autobiography and correspondence of Mary Granville, Mrs Delany*, ed. Lady Llanover, 2nd ser., 3 vols. (1862) · *A series of letters between Mrs. Elizabeth Carter and Miss Catherine Talbot ... to which are added, letters from Mrs. Elizabeth Carter to Mrs. Vesey*, ed. M. Pennington, [2nd edn], 4 vols. (1809) · R. B. Johnson, ed., *Bluestocking letters* (1926) · *Mary Hamilton, afterwards Mrs John Dickenson, at court and at home: from letters and diaries, 1756 to 1816*, ed. E. Anson and F. Anson (1925)

Archives Hunt. L., letters to Elizabeth Montagu
Likenesses chalk drawing, c.1770, NPG [see illus.]

Vesey, John (1638–1716), Church of Ireland archbishop of Tuam, was born in Coleraine, co. Londonderry, on 10 March 1638, the eldest son of Thomas Vesey (c.1605–1669?), who held several livings in co. Londonderry. His mother was a daughter of another co. Londonderry clergyman, the Revd Gervaise Walker. According to Harris he was educated at Westminster School and then at Trinity College, Dublin, although the only reference to him in the college registers relates to a doctorate in divinity conferred in 1672. Harris also records somewhat circumspectly ('we are told') that Vesey was ordained by John Leslie, bishop of Raphoe, during Cromwell's lifetime, noting that this would have been before he reached the canonical age.

Although Thomas Vesey had continued to officiate during the interregnum, he emerged in 1660 as a leading supporter of the return of episcopacy. His son John was appointed chaplain to the Irish House of Commons in 1661, and in the same year was appointed by the crown to the livings of Ighturmurrow and Shandrum in the diocese of Cloyne. On 16 October 1662 John succeeded his father as archdeacon of Armagh; however Thomas Vesey resumed the office the following year. On 4 February 1667 the younger Vesey was collated as prebendary of Kilpeacon in the diocese of Limerick. The day before he had been presented to the deanery of Cork, where he was instituted on 4 November, and at the same time became treasurer of Cloyne. He became bishop of Limerick in 1673 (patent 11

January, consecrated 22 December), and in 1679 was promoted to the archbishopric of Tuam (patent 18 March, enthroned 16 May) and sworn of the privy council. He became warden of Galway in September 1684. In 1676 he published a life of Archbishop John Bramhall, prefixed to an edition of the archbishop's works. This included a sustained attack on Presbyterians for their rejection of the established church. Another publication, *A Sermon Preached at Clonmel, on Sunday the Sixteenth of September, 1683* (1683), attacked both Catholics and Presbyterians for their subversive doctrines.

In February 1689 Vesey left Ireland for England, having escaped from Tuam, by his own account, just days before the road 'became impassable by the multitude of skeinmen and half-pike men called now Raparies' (Mant, 1.748). He took with him his wife and four children, leaving six others behind. Although he claimed to have a licence for his absence, his goods were confiscated by the Jacobite authorities. He is reported to have supported himself by a lecturership worth £40 per annum, although he also drew up a list of donations, totalling some hundreds of pounds, which he received from sympathizers while in England. A sermon which he preached to the Irish in London on 23 October 1689 was subsequently published.

On his return to Ireland, Vesey preached before the lord lieutenant and both houses at the opening of the first Williamite parliament in Dublin, on 16 October 1692. His sermon was a careful restatement of traditional Anglican political values, insisting on the absolute necessity of civil government and the special status of monarchy 'as being a copy from the divine original', but also asserting the right of a people deprived of proper government 'immediately to apply the proper remedy, by filling the vacant throne by a free election, where they have power so to do; or peaceable submission to those who have a right without it' (*A Sermon Preached before his Excellency the Lord Lieutenant and the Two Houses of Parliament*, 1692, 12). In the reign of Queen Anne he used his control of the borough of Tuam to return two MPs for the tory party. He served as one of the lords justices between 4 February and 22 September 1713, and again between 7 February 1714 and the death of Queen Anne. Contemporaries were puzzled when in October 1713 a mob attacked Vesey's Dublin home and 'were for pulling the old prelate out of his house for a Whig' (*Correspondence of Jonathan Swift*, 1.394). The new whig regime that took power under George I kept Vesey in office as lord justice until September 1715, leading Lord Coningsby to protest that 'as he was certainly the most artful and dangerous man in the last commission, so is he much more so in the present' (PRO NIre., D638/145). But in fact he was by this time too ill to take an active part in government.

Vesey was an energetic builder and improver. The private residence he erected at Hollymount in co. Mayo was visited in 1756 by John Wesley, who reported that Vesey had 'built a neat commodious house on a little eminence, laid out fruit and flower gardens round it, brought a river to run through them, and encompassed the whole with walks and groves of stately trees' (*Journal*, 4.172). He also promoted the development of an estate village, as well as planting the surrounding area with protestant tenants and building a parish church dedicated to King Charles the martyr. Assessments of his performance as a bishop vary. In 1686 he was named as one of the many clergy forced to return to Ireland, in his case after an absence of three years, by the lord lieutenant's refusal to renew licences of absence. The reform-minded James Bonnell, in February 1692, expressed his fear that Vesey, by his 'smooth way', might obtain the archbishopric of Armagh: 'he is one of the nepotismo, and if he were primate, would perfect the ruin of the church' (CUL, Strype MS I, fol. 89v). His successor at Tuam, Edward Synge, wrote disparagingly of the state of the archdiocese as he inherited it (Gilbert Library, Dublin, MS 28, 90–94). Archbishop William King, likewise, criticized him for failing to honour a promise to waive his claim to a share in parochial tithes (the *quarta pars*) in exchange for being granted the wardenship of Galway (TCD, MS 2533, 176–81). A late twentieth-century assessment, however, dismisses these criticisms, pointing to Vesey's personal piety and support for charity schools, and suggesting that he should in fact be classed as a significant ecclesiastical reformer (Hayton, 133–4).

Vesey was married twice; his first wife was Rebecca Wilson, and his second Anne Muschamp, who survived him. His eldest son, Sir Thomas *Vesey (1672/3–1730), was bishop of Killaloe (1713–14) and of Ossory (1714–30). Archbishop Vesey died at Holymount on 28 March 1716 and was buried on the estate.   S. J. CONNOLLY

Sources NL Ire., de Vesci MSS · PRO NIre., de Vesci MSS, T 3738 · NA Ire., Sarsfield-Vesey MSS · H. Cotton, *Fasti ecclesiae Hibernicae*, 6 vols. (1845–78) · J. B. Leslie, ed., *Clergy of Connor: from Patrician times to the present day* (1993) · *The whole works of Sir James Ware concerning Ireland*, ed. and trans. W. Harris, rev. edn, 2 vols. in 3 (1764) · R. Mant, *History of the Church of Ireland*, 2 vols. (1840) · *The correspondence of Jonathan Swift*, ed. H. Williams, 5 vols. (1963–5) · J. Kelly, 'The politics of protestant ascendancy: county Galway, 1650–1832', *Galway history and society: interdisciplinary essays on the history of an Irish county*, ed. G. Moran and R. Gillespie (1996), 229–70 · D. W. Hayton, 'The high church party in the Irish Convocation, 1703–13', *Reading Swift*, ed. H. J. Real and H. Stöver-Leidig (1998), 117–40 · Burtchaell & Sadleir, *Alum. Dubl.*, 2nd edn · *The correspondence of Henry Hyde, earl of Clarendon, and of his brother Laurence Hyde, earl of Rochester*, ed. S. W. Singer, 2 vols. (1828) · *The journal of the Rev. John Wesley*, ed. N. Curnock and others, 8 vols. (1909–16) · GEC, *Peerage* · J. Lodge, *The peerage of Ireland*, rev. M. Archdall, rev. edn, 7 vols. (1789)
Archives NL Ire., de Vesci papers · NRA, priv. coll., corresp. and papers | NA Ire., Sarsfield-Vesey MSS · TCD, corresp. with William King

Vesey, Sir Thomas, first baronet (1672/3–1730), Church of Ireland bishop of Ossory, was born at Cork, the son of John *Vesey (1638–1716), successively dean of Cork, bishop of Limerick, and archbishop of Tuam, and his wife, Rebecca Wilson. His education began in Cork, was said to have continued at Eton College, and brought him to Christ Church, Oxford, whence he matriculated in July 1689, aged sixteen. The family fortunes having been depleted by the Jacobite revanche in Ireland, he was helped through university by the future archbishop William Wake. He graduated BA in 1693 and two years later became a fellow of Oriel

College. His father was already regarded as a notable nepotist and the fortunes of the family were further improved by Thomas Vesey's marriage, on 27 July 1698, to Mary (d. 1746), the only surviving daughter and heir of Denny Muschamp, muster-master-general of Ireland, and Elizabeth, daughter of Michael Boyle, the long-lived archbishop of Armagh; Vesey's stepmother had also been a Muschamp. Following this access of wealth Vesey was made a baronet on 28 September 1698. Also, in common with two of his half-brothers, he took holy orders, being ordained priest on 24 June 1700. His father immediately appointed him to the archdeaconry of Tuam, which he held in conjunction with two livings in the same diocese and the rectory of Drumcree in the diocese of Armagh. In 1703 the new lord lieutenant, the duke of Ormond, made him a chaplain, whereupon he resigned the archdeaconry. Ormond's patronage suggested tory leanings; these, together with assiduous courtship of the important in London, helped Vesey to the bishopric of Killaloe, where he was consecrated on 12 July 1713. In the following year, on 18 February 1714, he was translated to Ossory—convenient for Ormond's bailiwick of Kilkenny and for the bishop's recently acquired estate at Abbey Leix, Queen's county. Vesey and his wife devoted much energy and money to embellishing both house and grounds. They also spent long periods in London and at Bath.

George I's accession greatly diminished Vesey's influence and obliged him to be more circumspect in voicing his political opinions. He was still identified with the once powerful tory interest in Ireland. Despite the changed political climate he continued to appear at the Lords' sittings, particularly in 1719 and 1723–4, as one in a sizeable group of bishops who survived from Queen Anne's reign. Like his father he appointed close relatives to the more valuable livings within his diocese. His notoriety in this respect led to his being accused of ordaining 'debauchees and troopers' and incurred the disapproval of his superior, the more exacting Archbishop King of Dublin (Hunt. L., MS 143198–259, fol. 28; quoted in Pilkington, 2.372). Despite Vesey's laxity and worldly preoccupations, standards of residence, educational provision, and regularity of services improved under his episcopate. One contemporary regarded him as 'a well-bred gentleman as well as a good bishop' (*Whole Works of Sir James Ware*, 1.599). He died in Dublin on 6 August 1730 and was buried in St Anne's Church. His eldest son, Sir John Denny Vesey, inherited and further improved the Abbey Leix seat and was created Baron Knapton in 1750. His second daughter, Elizabeth *Vesey, married her cousin Agmondesham Vesey and became a celebrated literary hostess.

TOBY BARNARD

Sources NL Ire., de Vesci MSS, esp. 9/5 [journal of Archbishop John Vesey] · genealogy of the Veseys, NL Ire., department of manuscripts, MS 3100 · introduction to Sir Thomas Vesey MSS, NRA, priv. coll. · J. B. Leslie, *Ossory clergy and parishes* (1933) · J. Falvey, 'The Church of Ireland episcopate in the 18th century', MA diss., University College, Cork, 1995 · R. A. S. Macalister, 'Further Ossory letters', *Journal of the Royal Society of Antiquaries of Ireland*, 6th ser., 3 (1913) · *The whole works of Sir James Ware concerning*

Ireland, ed. and trans. W. Harris, rev. edn, 1 (1764), 598–9 · L. Pilking-
ton, *Memoirs of Laetitia Pilkington*, ed. A. C. Elias, 2 vols. (1997), 2.372 ·
DNB · GEC, *Baronetage* · IGI
Archives NRA, priv. coll., corresp. and papers | NL Ire., de Vesci
MSS, journal · TCD, corresp. with William King
Likenesses portrait, Abbey Leix, co. Laois · portrait (after
unknown portrait copy), bishop's palace, Kilkenny

Vespasian (AD 9–79). *See under* Roman emperors (*act.* 55 BC–
AD 410).

Vestey, Sir Edmund Hoyle, first baronet (1866–1953). *See
under* Vestey, William, first Baron Vestey (1859–1940).

Vestey, William, first Baron Vestey (1859–1940), industrialist and food importer, and his business partner, **Sir
Edmund Hoyle Vestey**, first baronet (1866–1953), were
both born in Liverpool. William was the eldest (*b.* 21 January 1859), and Edmund was the fifth child (*b.* 3 February
1866), of Samuel Vestey (1832–1902), a Yorkshireman and
provision merchant, and Hannah, *née* Utley (*d.* 1884). Samuel ran a business in Liverpool, buying and selling mainly
provisions imported from North America. Both William
and Edmund, after an education at the Liverpool Institute,
gained experience in the family business.

At the age of seventeen William was sent to the USA to
buy and ship home goods for his father. He established a
canning factory in Chicago, and purchased the cheaper
cuts of meat to make corned beef, which he shipped to Liverpool. This venture was successful, and the management
of the cannery was given to Edmund, who had joined the
firm in 1883. In 1890 William travelled to Argentina, and
decided to exploit the uses of refrigeration to preserve
foodstuffs. He began by shipping frozen partridges, and
later mutton and beef, from Argentina to Britain. William
was joined in this enterprise by Edmund, and in 1890 they
established the first cold store in Liverpool, which as the
Union Cold Storage Company was to become one of the
world's largest cold storage operations. They soon diversified into other products, using their extensive network of
cold stores to accommodate all types of perishable foodstuffs, and developed their supplies on a worldwide basis.
In 1906 they began to ship eggs, chickens, and other produce from China. The China trade led them into another
avenue of business, when they purchased two tramp
steamers in 1909, and converted them into refrigerated
ships. This was the beginning of the Blue Star Line, which
they registered, in 1911, with a capital of £100,000. In the
next five years they acquired five more ships, as well as a
butchery business, a chain of retail shops in Britain, and
small freezing works in Australia and New Zealand. This
set the pattern for the later growth of the Vestey empire—
a totally integrated business, with control of every link in
the chain of processing and distribution of food from producer to consumer.

A prominent part of the Vesteys' worldwide holdings
was the cattle-raising farms and ranches, which enabled
them to control supplies to their meat-packing and cold
storage plants. After 1915 Argentina became an important
base for their operations, especially when Britain's 1914
Finance Act with its high taxes made them tax exiles

William Vestey, first Baron Vestey (1859–1940), by Walter
Stoneman, 1924

there. While their business made large profits in the First
World War supplying the British army with meat, the Vesteys applied themselves energetically to their Argentinian
packing houses. They returned to Britain in 1919, when
William appeared before the royal commission on
income tax to argue the need for a return to the pre-1915
tax levels. Unable to convince the government of the validity of their case, in 1921 the Vesteys and their advisers
devised a complex and highly successful scheme which
not only satisfied their desire to live in Britain and avoid
paying any personal tax but also showed them to be as
innovative and pioneering in the field of tax avoidance as
in the food business. The greater part of the Vesteys' overseas empire was leased to their British company, Union
Cold Storage Ltd, for a yearly rent of £960,000, which was
used to set up a Paris trust fund. From the trust the money
flowed into the Western United Investment Company in
Britain, a Vestey holding company in which the family
held the management shares and controlling interest,
and thence, tax free, into the pockets of the Vestey
brothers. Once domiciled again in England, Edmund was
created a baronet in 1921, and the following year William
purchased a peerage from the Lloyd George government,
apparently for £25,000 (he had been made a baronet in
1913 for his role in making cheap food more widely available). The peerage evoked a letter of protest from George
V, who felt it wrong that a man who declined to pay
national taxes should be ennobled.

Edmund's first marriage in 1887 to Sarah Barker produced six children before they divorced in 1926. His second marriage was on 10 March 1926, to Ellen Soward (*d.* 1953).

The Vesteys' ownership of refrigerated ships increased so that by 1925 they had, in Blue Star, the largest refrigerated fleet in the world. In Britain they owned cold stores in several cities as well as 2365 retail butcher shops. The advantage of such an all-embracing organization for perishable commodities was that they could be held until prices were right, and once the chain of processing had started the arrival of further supplies could be controlled to avoid losses from overstocked markets. Their operations in Britain were managed from the Union Cold Storage Company Ltd, which by 1925 had a capital of £9,628,575. By 1933 the Union had an issued capital of £12 million. Despite the depression the Vesteys' business continued to expand, especially in Australia where in 1934 they took over the Anglis meat interests for £1.5 million.

William Vestey was married twice: first in 1882 to Sarah (*d.* 1923), daughter of George Ellis of Birkenhead; second on 9 August 1924 in New York to Evelene Brodstone (1875–1941), daughter of Norwegian emigrants to Superior, Nebraska. His second wife had joined the Vesteys' Chicago organization in 1895 as a secretary, and became a powerful figure in the enterprise as its international troubleshooter. Her help proved indispensable to the Vesteys in retaining their direct control over a multinational corporation which by William's death was conservatively valued at over £90 million. William's son and heir from his first marriage, Samuel (1882–1954), later joined Edmund in running the family business during the eventful post-war years. William died on 10 December 1940 at his home, Cleeve Cottage, Bulstrode Way, Gerrards Cross. His remains were buried at the parish church of St Peter Foley, Lancaster; his ashes were later re-interred in the Anglican cathedral in Liverpool. Edmund died, still chairman, on 18 November 1953, at St Bartholomew's Hospital, London, and his son, Ronald (*b.* 1898) assumed control of the business.   RICHARD PERREN

Sources R. Perren, 'Vestey, William, and Vestey, Sir Edmund Hoyle', *DBB* · P. Knightley, *The Vestey Affair* (1981) · S. G. Hanson, *Argentine meat and the British market* (1938) · 'Evidence', *Parl. papers* (1919), 23/1.450–55, Cmd 288-3 [royal commission on income tax] · 'Royal commission on food prices: first report', *Parl. papers* (1924–5), vol. 8, Cmd 2390 · *The Times* (12 Dec 1940) · *CGPLA Eng. & Wales* (1941) · d. cert. · *The Times* (20 Nov 1953) [Edmund Hoyle Vestey] · d. cert. [Edmund Hoyle Vestey] · *CGPLA Eng. & Wales* (1953) [Edmund Hoyle Vestey]
Likenesses W. Stoneman, photograph, 1924, NPG [*see illus.*] · photograph, repro. in Knightley, *Vestey affair* · photograph (with Edmund Hoyle Vestey), repro. in Knightley, *Vestey affair*
Wealth at death £261,514 10s. 8d.: probate, 13 June 1941, *CGPLA Eng. & Wales* · £175,082—Edmund Hoyle Vestey: probate, 1953, *CGPLA Eng. & Wales*

Vestris [*née* Bartolozzi; *other married name* Mathews], **Lucia Elizabeth** (1797–1856), actress and singer, was born on 2 March 1797, probably at 74 Dean Street, Soho, London. She was the granddaughter of the engraver Francesco *Bartolozzi and the first child of Gaetano Stefano Bartolozzi, a

Lucia Elizabeth Vestris (1797–1856), by Samuel Lover, c.1826 [as Mistress Ford in *The Merry Wives of Windsor*]

printseller, engraver, and drawing-master, and his wife, Theresa Jansen, the daughter of a dancing-master from Aix-la-Chapelle. Theresa, a pupil of Clementi, taught music herself and was regarded by Haydn, who dedicated five works to her, as one of London's leading pianists. The Bartolozzis' other child, Josephine, was born in 1807. Lucia probably learned Italian and French at home and was taught singing by masters including Domenico Corri, coach at the King's Theatre. On 28 January 1813 she married Armand Vestris (1787–1825), the third generation in a famous family of dancers of Italian origin; his father, Auguste, was for over thirty years *premier danseur* at the Paris Opéra. Armand was leading dancer at the King's Theatre, London, where in 1814 he became ballet-master.

Lucia Vestris made her début on 20 July 1815, under the stage name Madame Vestris, at her husband's benefit night in the title role in Peter Winter's *Il ratto di Proserpina*. She was greeted with approbation for her performance and especially for her beauty, and continued to appear that season and the next. For her joint benefit with her husband in the summer of 1816 she sang Susanna in *Le nozze di Figaro*. Peace having opened continental Europe to British travellers, and debts having driven Armand Vestris to leave England, his wife made her Paris début at the Théâtre des Italiens in December 1816. She did not return to England until 1819. Records of her life at this period are unreliable: it is said that she appeared at Paris theatres and sang in Naples. It may be safely assumed that she acquired further training and stage experience. There must also have been developments in her private life, since she returned to England in September 1819 without her husband, who died in Naples in 1825.

Madame Vestris was engaged by R. W. Elliston for his first Drury Lane season, and met critical approval for her French style. Contemporary opinion commends her mezzo-soprano voice, but it was not good enough to establish her as a leading singer in a period of great operatic performers. Instead she made a name for herself in the period 1820–30 as a scandalous beauty, a career launched by the *succès de scandale* of her famous breeches performance, the lead role in the musical burlesque *Giovanni in London* at Drury Lane in May 1820. The role had been created by Mrs Joe Gould in a very masculine style; Madame Vestris's appearances in breeches, while asserting her freedom, always also emphasized her femininity, showing off her fabulously perfect legs. For ten years she was ogled on stage and whispered about off, entertaining a series of lovers with whom she had profitable arrangements that supplemented her rising stage earnings to finance an extravagant lifestyle. Among these the most notable was the radical MP Thomas Duncombe, soon to take a leading part in the reform movement and sit on the 1832 parliamentary select committee whose remit was to reform the antiquated monopoly laws that prevented the legitimate growth of new theatres in London. Vestris's stage career now embraced other breeches roles (including Macheath, over which she fell out with John Anderson, her sister Josephine's husband-to-be) and light comedy acting. She was a fashionable star: she even acquired a signature tune when she introduced the song 'Cherry Ripe' into John Poole's *Paul Pry* at the Haymarket in 1825.

The major managements were eager for Madame Vestris's support. But London theatre was approaching a crisis point. Before the select committee on the state of the drama was called for, Covent Garden had bankrupted Charles Kemble and Vestris had joined the minor theatre rebellion as a manager as well as a performer. In December 1830 she leased the Olympic Theatre from John Scott, who had previously built the Sans Pareil Theatre for his daughter Jane. Both these new West End venues were granted annual licences by the lord chamberlain from 1807. Vestris held the burletta licence in her own name. It did not permit the 'classic' drama: all entertainments included music. The Olympic, a few steps from Drury Lane, held an audience only a third as large, but its potential was great. The old theatres had become unfashionable, and were obliged to mount lengthy and expensive bills to cater for their huge audience range. Vestris remodelled her theatre as a modern, feminine, and enjoyable alternative; well decorated, intimate, and tasteful, like a fashionable drawing-room, it attracted an enthusiastic audience. By avoiding the practice of disguising thin houses with free admissions, Madame Vestris segregated the auditorium reliably, defending sensitive patrons from mixing outside their class. She offered light musical pieces and farces, well mounted, often changed, pretty and undemanding, and made a point of finishing by 11 p.m. These apparently simple changes made her theatre fashionable. It attracted the *beau monde*, who amused

themselves there before moving on to their night pursuits. Aspiring City men and their families could join them, to see and be seen in fashionable company without taxing themselves intellectually, and get home early enough to be in the office next morning. The standard was reliable, the segregated auditorium offered no threats, and, since tipping was forbidden, there were no disconcerting demands for more money. Plain bills of the play, without the desperate hyperbole of the larger theatres, carried an air of quality and self-assurance that flattered the audience.

Behind the scenes Vestris copied the practices of the best French boulevard theatres, with fresh—sometimes innovative—scenery, good working conditions and contracts, and adequate rehearsal. She attracted loyal workers, including Planché, Liston, and Benjamin Webster, and regularly appeared herself, elaborately costumed and fêted in Planché's metatheatrical extravaganzas. While developing this formula she managed successfully from 1831 to 1839, during very difficult years in the theatre. Success brought her profit, but she continued to accept money from admirers, especially Duncombe, to meet her expenses. A large expense, for about four years from 1833, was an affair with Lord Edward Thynne (1807–1884), the reprobate son of the marquess of Bath. He and Madame Vestris's brother-in-law Anderson fleeced her by a series of fraudulent bill transactions that resulted in her bankruptcy in April 1837.

In the autumn of 1835 Vestris hired Charles James *Mathews (1803–1878) as a writer and actor. Brought up as a gentleman, Mathews was now eager to adopt his father's profession of comedian. He made a success at the Olympic, and of his meeting with Vestris; they developed a sophisticated, 'realistic' style of light comedy. On 18 July 1838 they married at Kensington church, having accepted a tour in America, under the management of Stephen Price, to repair their finances. The tour was not a success. There was a mismatch of expectations between audiences and performers, and neither the Olympic society comedies nor the aristocratic manners of the Mathewses were appreciated. They returned home in 1839. The Olympic, no longer the sole leader of fashion, was now heavily in debt. The couple took the bold step of leasing Covent Garden, a theatre large enough to pay the expenses of Vestris's high production values. Mathews was lessee, his wife manager. Despite the disapproval of Macready, Vestris's artistic practices transferred well, and her scrupulous preparation of texts, actors, and scenery was more effective in the revival of 'the national drama' than his hectoring bourgeois moralism had been. Released from the limitations of the burletta licence, for three seasons she staged classic high comedy and sought new comic writing, such as Boucicault's *London Assurance* (1841), and staged notable Shakespearian productions, including an excellent *Midsummer Night's Dream* (1840), the previously unrevived *Love's Labours Lost* (1839), and a *Merry Wives of Windsor* (1840) set in Shakespeare's time. Such a design decision was unique in a period when cumbersomely correct 'historical' settings for the plays were increasingly regarded as the only proper choice. But the huge expenses of the old theatre meant that there was little or no profit. Three previous managements had all finished bankrupt; Vestris did better than most, until she successfully brought out Adelaide Kemble in *Norma* (in 1841), and the singer's father, Charles, one of the proprietors, scented a personal opportunity and refused to renew their lease. Mathews declared bankruptcy in May 1842; it was perhaps some consolation that, despite Kemble's bad faith over his daughter, and his having unscrupulously appropriated all the new scenery built for Vestris, his management failed.

Macready, now leasing Drury Lane, maliciously hired Vestris and Mathews to disable them as competition, and insulted them by casting him in minor roles and billing her as a supporting player. They left and went to the Haymarket, where they did better, with Webster as manager. But Mathews was bankrupt again in December, pressed especially hard by the malignant Anderson. The couple entered into a period of unremitting work, between the Haymarket and provincial touring, to try to meet their debts. Then in 1847 they undertook a lease of the Lyceum. Their company included the writer and comedian Buckstone and Fanny Fitzwilliam. The theatre seated 1800, about 500 more than the Olympic, but Vestris worked to reproduce her previous success, beginning well with the Morton farce *Cox and Box*. Eleven more Planché extravaganzas followed, with scenery by William Beverley. In 1849, after an unexpected success with his translation *A Day of Reckoning*, G. H. Lewes was enrolled to bring modern French plays to the Lyceum. In these experimental plays Vestris and Mathews further developed their 'realistic' manner of acting, making a cool modern comedy style another of the Vestris innovations. The initial Lyceum team broke up under financial stress in 1853. Vestris took a farewell benefit with Mathews in July 1854, and retired, seriously ill. With good will from the public and assistance from professional friends Mathews continued to run Lyceum seasons until 1855 and to endure a punishing schedule of provincial tours: they were still deep in long-standing debts because Mathews had not renounced all personal liabilities in the 1842 bankruptcy. In July 1855 he was arrested in Preston, on tour, and imprisoned in Lancaster Castle; having finally been made completely bankrupt, he returned to London five days before Vestris died of cancer, on 8 August 1856. She was privately buried at Kensal Green cemetery.

Madame Vestris was born and bred in the international élite of art and entertainment. It is important in an understanding of her role in the development of the British stage to see her work in this European context, which valued virtuoso talent, ruthlessly perfected training, and the clear-sighted capacity to understand and to please a fashionable audience through perfect taste and unerring elegance. Her alert understanding of the theatre business made her aware of the need to innovate in order to manage the problems that beset the London stage. She found original solutions to a wide range of issues. Her management at the Olympic successfully negotiated the opposition between the antique practices of the theatre under

aristocratic patronage and rising middle-class aspiration and its self-definition through propriety. As a performer she exploited and at the same time minimized, excused, and made acceptable her sexual appeal and scandalous reputation. A similar sleight of hand enabled her to exploit her talent as stage manager and artistic director at three theatres, including Covent Garden, turning her femininity into an asset that connoted good taste and an acceptable luxury for the consumer rather than a threat from a woman usurping power. She has appealed in many ways to biographers, from contemporary pornographic scandal sheets to theatre historians of the twentieth century, who have presented her as a theatrical innovator while suggesting that she was reliant on the talents of male assistants. She is now beginning to be recognized, in scholarly work ranging from the gender politics of the theatre to Shakespearian production, as one of the most important practitioners of her generation in her own right.

JACKY BRATTON

Sources W. W. Appleton, *Madame Vestris and the London stage* (1974) · C. J. Williams, *Madame Vestris: a theatrical biography* (1973) · J. R. Planché, *Recollections and reflections*, rev. edn (1901) · G. J. Williams, *Our moonlight revels: 'A midsummer night's dream' in the theatre* (1997) · K. Fletcher, 'Planché, Vestris and the transvestite role: sexuality and gender in Victorian popular theatre', *Nineteenth Century Theatre*, 15 (1987), 9–33 · *The life and correspondence of Thomas Slingsby Duncombe*, ed. T. H. Duncombe, 2 vols. (1868) · E. Schafer, *MsDirecting Shakespeare: women direct Shakespeare* (1998) · G. Vandenhoff, *Leaves from an actor's notebook* (1860) · *Oxberry's Dramatic Biography*, 5/70 (1826) · [L. E. Vestris], *Memoirs of the public and private life, adventures and wonderful exploits of Madame Vestris* [1830] · m. cert. · d. cert. · *The Era* (17 Aug 1856) · Burke, *Peerage*

Likenesses hand-coloured etching, 1820 (as Don Giovanni), Theatre Museum, London · S. Lover, watercolour drawing, c.1826 (as Mistress Ford in *The merry wives of Windsor*), NPG [*see illus.*] · J. H. Lynch, hand-coloured lithograph caricature, music cover, 1826 (with John Liston), Theatre Museum, London · G. Clint, group portrait, engraving, pubd 1828 (in *Paul Pry*), V&A · T. Lupton, mezzotint, pubd 1828 (after cartoon by G. Clint), NPG · attrib. L. Sharpe, pencil and wash drawing, c.1828, Garr. Club · R. W. Buss, oils, 1833 (after G. Clint), Garr. Club · A. E. Chalon, oils, 1838, repro. in Williams, *Madame Vestris* · H. Robinson, etching, 1838 (after A. E. Chalon), Theatre Museum, London · A. E. Chalon, miniature, Royal Shakespeare Theatre, Stratford upon Avon · J. W. Childe, watercolour on ivory miniature, Garr. Club · M. Gauci, lithograph music cover (as Bavarian girl), Theatre Museum, London · Mayall, two cartes-de-visite, NPG · H. Singleton, chalk and watercolour drawing (as Zelmira), BM · hand-coloured engraving (as Apollo in *Midas*), Theatre Museum, London · prints, BM, NPG

Vetch, James (1789–1869), engineer, third son of Robert Vetch of Caponflat, Haddington, East Lothian, and his wife, Agnes Sharp, was born at Haddington on 13 May 1789. Educated at Haddington and Edinburgh, he entered the military college at Great Marlow, from where in 1805 he was transferred to the Royal Military Academy at Woolwich. He was employed on the trigonometrical survey at Oakingham, Berkshire (1806), until he was commissioned second lieutenant in the Royal Engineers in 1807. He was promoted lieutenant in 1808. After serving for three years at Chatham and Plymouth, he was sent in 1810 to Spain, where he served at the blockade of Cadiz and in the battle of Barossa on 5 March 1811, and was made the bearer of dispatches to Gibraltar. Vetch then went from Tangier to

Tetuan to report on the capabilities of the country to furnish engineer supplies. In 1812 he took part in the siege of Badajoz. He was promoted second captain in 1813, and returned to England the following year. For his services in the Peninsula he received the war medal with clasps for Barossa and Badajoz.

From 1814 to 1820 Vetch commanded a company of sappers and miners at Spike Island in Cork harbour and afterwards at Chatham. In 1819 he was appointed to the Ordnance Survey. After initial work on the Irish survey, he was employed from 1821 until 1823, with Thomas Drummond, Robert Kearsley Dawson, and Thomas Colby, on the triangulation of the Orkney and Shetland islands and of the western islands of Scotland. Their work virtually completed the primary triangulation of Great Britain by the survey, although a long gap caused by a concentration on the Irish survey meant that it was not finally completed until 1838–41.

Promotion being very slow, Vetch went on half pay on 11 March 1824, and, going to Mexico with John Rule, managed the silver mines of the English Compania de Real del Monte and of the Compania de Bolaños. He also worked for the Anglo-Mexican Association, and later the United Mexican Company. He returned to England in 1829, but again went to Mexico after his marriage on 2 February 1832, in London, to Alexandrina Ogilvie (d. 1853), daughter of Robert Auld of Edinburgh. They had ten children. He remained in Mexico until 1835 constructing roads in connection with the mines, organizing efficient systems of transport, and paving the way for the great expansion in mining in that country. Sir Henry Ward, the British envoy, in an official report, called attention to his services. Feeling the want of a good map, Vetch made astronomical and barometrical observations, measured several short baselines, and triangulated a large tract of country. His papers and maps from Mexico were presented after his death to the topographical department of the War Office. He presented a valuable collection of Mexican antiquities to the British Museum and in 1836 wrote a paper about them. Having returned to England, Vetch was resident engineer of the Birmingham and Gloucester Railway Company from 1836 to 1840 for the construction of one half of that line of railway.

In 1843 Vetch published an *Enquiry into the means of establishing a ship navigation between the Mediterranean and Red seas*, after having worked on the problem since 1839. The work ran through several editions and attracted much public attention, but the government, and especially Palmerston, opposed the plan as contrary to the political interests of the country. Twelve years later Ferdinand de Lesseps, a former French diplomat who is usually credited with being the inspiration behind the Suez Canal, which opened in 1869, published his scheme, printing Vetch's opinions as an appendix to his work.

In 1842 Vetch designed an effective system of sewerage for the borough of Leeds. In 1843 he and Sir Henry Thomas De la Beche prepared designs for the drainage of Windsor, and his designs for the drainage of Windsor Castle and parks and the purification of the Frogmore lakes were completed in 1847. Vetch was appointed one of the three commissioners to effect the Assessionable Manors of the Duchy of Cornwall Act of 1844. This reformed tenancy arrangements on the seventeen assessionable manors in the duchy in order to raise agricultural productivity. Vetch resided first at Devonport and then at Truro, and was commended when the commission's work was completed in 1846.

In 1844, 1845, and 1846 Vetch was examined before the tidal harbours and the harbours of refuge commissions, arguing for the advantages of using wrought-iron framework in the construction of piers and breakwaters. In July 1846 he was appointed consulting engineer to the Admiralty on all questions relating to the harbours, rivers, and navigable waters of the United Kingdom. In 1847 he was appointed to the new harbour conservancy board at the Admiralty, and in 1853 was appointed sole conservator of harbours. He published reports between 1847 and 1859 on several harbours in the United Kingdom. From 1849 to 1853 Vetch held the time-consuming honorary office of metropolitan commissioner of sewers. In 1849 he proposed an extended water supply for London, and in 1850 designed a system of drainage for Southwark. In 1858–9 he was a member of the royal commission on harbours of refuge.

Vetch retired from the Admiralty in 1863. He was elected a fellow of the Geological Society in 1818 and of the Royal Society in 1830, in which year he was a founder fellow of the Royal Geographical Society. He became an associate of the Institution of Civil Engineers in 1839 and a member of the Société Française de Statistique Universelle in 1852, and was a member of other learned bodies. He died on 7 December 1869 at Munster House, Fulham, and was buried in Highgate cemetery. Seven of his children survived him, including the Revd James Edward (d. 1870), Robert Hamilton, colonel, Royal Engineers, and William Francis, major-general, Royal Dublin Fusiliers. Vetch published many papers, mostly in connection with the engineering projects on which he was engaged, but also on other geographical and archaeological topics.

R. H. VETCH, *rev.* ELIZABETH BAIGENT

Sources *PRS* (1870) · *PICE*, 31 (1870–71), 255–62 · T. W. J. Connolly, *History of the royal sappers and miners*, 2nd edn, 2 vols. (1857) · W. Porter, *History of the corps of royal engineers*, 2 vols. (1889) · W. A. Seymour, ed., *A history of the Ordnance Survey* (1986) · C. Close, *The early years of the ordnance survey* (1926); repr. with introduction by J. B. Harley (1969) · C. R. Markham, *The fifty years' work of the Royal Geographical Society* (1881) · U. Texas, Alan and Lillie Probert MSS · *CGPLA Eng. & Wales* (1870)

Archives U. Texas, Alan and Lillie Probert MSS

Likenesses J. Munro, portrait; formerly in possession of eldest son, 1899

Wealth at death under £70,000: probate, 24 Nov 1870, *CGPLA Eng. & Wales*

Vetch, Samuel (1668–1732), army officer and colonial governor, was born in Edinburgh on 9 December 1668, the second son of the three children of William *Veitch (1640–1722), a Church of Scotland minister of Robertson, Lanarkshire, and Marion Fairlie (1639–1722) [see Veitch, Marion] from Edinburgh. In his childhood the family lived at Fallowlees, Northumberland, where William Veitch was minister, and from 1675 at Longhorsley. With his brother, also William (1667–1700), Samuel was educated at Utrecht where, aged fifteen, he had been sent to join his father who had been in exile since 1683 from the anti-covenanter policies of Charles II. Both brothers later joined the army of William of Orange and participated in the invasion of November 1688 as members of the Cameronians or 26th regiment of foot. They fought at Dunkeld (August 1689) and later in Flanders at the battles of Steenkerke (August 1692)—where William was wounded—and of Neerwinden (29 July 1693). Having returned to Dumfries in 1697, where his father was then minister, Vetch (who had achieved the rank of captain) and his brother volunteered for William Paterson's ill-fated expedition to establish a Scottish colony on the isthmus of Darien. They sailed for central America in July 1698 with 1200 men, Samuel having been elected as one of seven council members to govern the colony. Arriving in November, Vetch oversaw the establishment of a capital, 'New Edinburgh', before opposition from the English and Spanish led to the scheme's collapse and the island's abandonment in June 1699. Vetch and Paterson now sailed for New York. They were followed in September 1700 by William Vetch, who had headed another, equally disastrous, expedition earlier in that year; departing the island for the second time, in April, William died off Jamaica *en route* for New York.

On 20 December 1700 Samuel Vetch (who adopted this spelling of his name on arrival in America) married Margaret (d. 1763), daughter of Robert Livingstone, secretary for Indian affairs; the couple had three children, two of whom died in infancy. His marriage brought Vetch a comfortable place in New York society which he confirmed with his reputation for charismatic leadership, and a prosperous illegal trade with Canada. By 1705 he was living in Boston. There he began a new trade network under cover of a scheme for prisoner exchanges in which he acted as Governor Joseph Dudley's representative to the Canadian governor-general, Rigaud de Vaudreuil. It is probable that Dudley also expected Vetch to spy on Acadian defences and it was during this period that he gained a detailed knowledge of the navigation channels of the St Lawrence. However, in 1706 he was accused along with other Boston traders of simultaneously supplying the Acadians with arms at a time when Massachusetts traders faced frequent attacks from French-supported Indians. Tried by the Massachusetts general court, he was fined £200 but acquitted in September 1707 following the intervention of the privy council in London.

During 1708 Vetch travelled in Britain where he sought to convince Queen Anne to sponsor his dramatic plan for the conquest of French Canada, as set out in his detailed paper 'Canada survey'd', submitted in July of that year. The queen's approval granted, Vetch was promised a substantial invasion force together with a colonelcy and governorship of the new territory on its acquisition. Vetch now travelled to Massachusetts to gather support among colonial officials with the help of the former governor of

Virginia, Francis Nicholson (1655–1728). However, by October 1709, with considerable colonial forces gathered at Boston, it was clear that the required naval support would not be forthcoming from a British government already heavily committed to war in Europe. With the plan abandoned and Vetch discredited in colonial political circles, Nicholson renewed the call for assistance during a visit to London in 1710. The result was permission for a limited assault on Acadia (Nova Scotia) in which Vetch took the role of adjutant-general subordinate to Nicholson, the expedition's leader. The attack on the Acadian capital, Port Royal, proved successful against a small French garrison, and Vetch was appointed commander of the settlement now renamed Annapolis Royal. But the limits of the expedition's achievements quickly became apparent. By late 1710 Vetch had witnessed the departure of Nicholson and many of the colonial forces, and he spent his first severe winter surrounded by hostile French Canadians, with a garrison numbering fewer than 500 British marines and New England volunteers. In January 1711 he unsuccessfully sought reinforcements before the council of Massachusetts in Boston. His reputation for illicit trading preceded him and his energies were instead spent denying accusations of illegal exchanges with the local Indian population. Vetch returned to find his garrison further depleted while the French and Indians grew increasingly hostile to the British presence.

In June, Vetch was requested to join an expeditionary force of ten ships of the line and over thirty transports secured by Nicholson to undertake the original proposal set out three years earlier in 'Canada survey'd'. Vetch joined the force, led by Admiral Sir Hovenden Walker and Brigadier-General John Hill, at Boston and left for Quebec on 30 July in the role of commander of the New England forces. In view of his expert local knowledge Vetch was requested to navigate the fleet through the St Lawrence. Before he was able to do so, however, strong winds and poor visibility had scattered parts of the fleet among rocks on the northern shore of the Gulf of St Lawrence with the loss of eight ships and up to 900 men. Despite Vetch's calls to continue, the expeditionary force—running short of provisions, facing continued bad weather, and having also suffered the destruction of Hovenden's flagship—turned back. After reinforcing Annapolis Royal with troops from the failed expedition, Vetch returned to Boston from where during the winter of 1712 he continued to impress on Lord Oxford's tory administration the need for further assistance if the garrison were to be held. His cause was not helped when subordinates at Annapolis Royal—among them his deputy Thomas Caulfield—began their own correspondence with London in which they accused Vetch of malpractice, exploitation, and of planning the colony's destruction. In summer 1712 he returned to Annapolis Royal where he maintained control for another winter principally with the help of 200 Iroquois reinforcements organized by his father-in-law, Robert Livingstone. By this time Vetch had been replaced as governor by his former associate, and now adversary, Francis Nicholson. Though Vetch knew of the change (confirmed in London in October 1712), he remained in post until Nicholson's arrival in the following summer. The new governor made clear his intention of using Caulfield's complaints as the basis of a charge of maladministration against his predecessor. On 16 April 1714 Vetch left for England in an attempt to defend his conduct against earlier attacks and to seek financial reimbursement from Oxford's government.

However, Nicholson's governorship did not survive the change of administration following the Hanoverian succession. Vetch found a more sympathetic audience in the new whig government who dismissed Nicholson's and Caulfield's accusations as tory opportunism. In January 1715 he was reappointed as governor of Nova Scotia, though he did not return to Annapolis Royal, and only remained in post until August 1717, when he was succeeded by Richard Philipps (1661–1750), under whose command the colony at last acquired the resources and fortifications it required. Vetch was equally unsuccessful in establishing financial security for himself and his family, who joined him in England in 1717. His final years were spent pursuing a settlement (he requested £3000 per annum until employed) for his contribution to the establishment of Nova Scotia as a British colony between 1709 and 1715, and applying for vacant American governorships which he believed had been promised him by the government. Unsuccessful in all of his attempts, he was eventually imprisoned for debt at London's king's bench gaol, where he died on 30 April 1732; he was buried on 1 May at St George's, Southwark. He was survived by his wife, Margaret, who died in early to mid-1763, and his daughter, Alida (b. 1701), who married Samuel Bayard of New York, a nephew of Peter Stuyvesant, director-general of the New Netherland.

Samuel Vetch's contribution to the development of Britain's North American empire, if largely overlooked and under-appreciated during his lifetime, has since been recognized in favourable biographies by George Patterson (1885) and G. M. Waller (1960) which portray an innovative and dedicated imperial servant whose flair for commercial enterprise, if tarnishing his reputation during his lifetime, undoubtedly contributed to Canada's prosperity and importance to later British governments. A monument to Vetch was erected at Annapolis Royal's old fort in 1928. PHILIP CARTER

Sources G. M. Waller, *Samuel Vetch: colonial enterpriser* (1960) · G. Patterson, 'Hon. Samuel Vetch, first English governor', *Collections of the Nova Scotia Historical Society*, 4 (1885), 11–112 · J. C. Webster, *Samuel Vetch: an address on the occasion of the dedication of a monument* (1929) · G. M. Waller, 'Vetch, Samuel', *DCB*, vol. 2 · J. Bartlett Brebner, 'Vetch, Samuel', *DAB* · *DNB*
Archives Museum of the City of New York, letter-book | Franklin D. Roosevelt Library, New York, Livingston-Redmond MSS, corresp.
Likenesses oils, c.1705, Museum of the City of New York · P. Lely, portrait · engraving (after P. Lely), repro. in J. G. Wilson and J. Fiske, eds., *Appleton's Cyclopaedia of American biography*, rev. edn, 7 vols. (1887–1900) · portrait (in letter-book), Museum of the City of New York

Vettius Bolanus, Marcus (*d. c.*AD 93), Roman governor of Britain, could well have been a descendant of a Marcus Bolanus for whom Cicero wrote a letter of recommendation as 'a good, brave, and in every respect distinguished man' (Cicero, *Ad familiares*, xiii.77). The rare name Bolanus is found, together with that of Vettius, on an inscription at Mediolanum (Milan), and other Bolani are recorded there and in this region of Italy, which was presumably the governor's home. The family also had estates in Etruria, north of Rome. Bolanus had two sons, one with the same names as himself, the other called Crispinus, born in the late AD 70s and c.AD 80 respectively. Hence Bolanus evidently married late, as he himself was probably born between AD 20 and AD 30; he died c.AD 93.

Not much is known of his career before his governorship (AD 69–71), but Bolanus served as a legionary legate in Armenia in AD 62 in the campaign against the Parthians conducted by Gnaeus Domitius Corbulo. He then probably served as proconsul of Macedonia before holding the consulship in AD 66, or at least had strong links with that province, since a Macedonian who clearly owed his Roman citizenship to Bolanus, Marcus Vettius Philo, later left money in his will to celebrate Bolanus's birthday annually. In April AD 69 Bolanus was at Lugdunum (Lyons), where he had gone to greet the emperor Vitellius immediately after the latter's generals had defeated Otho in northern Italy. The governor of Britain, Trebellius Maximus, had just arrived, having been forced out of the province: the legionary legates, dissatisfied with Trebellius's sluggish and indecisive stance during the civil war, had stirred up the troops against the governor's 'greed and meanness' (Tacitus, *Histories*, i.60). Bolanus was selected to fill this difficult vacancy.

After a decade of inaction in the military field, there was now trouble on the northern frontier of the province. The Brigantes of the Pennines were at odds with their pro-Roman ruler Cartimandua, who was 'hated for her cruelty and lust', according to Tacitus (*Histories*, iii.45): she had divorced her anti-Roman husband Venutius and married his armour bearer. An added incentive to the anti-Roman party was provided by the fall of Nero and the ensuing civil war, not least because Vitellius had further diminished the province's garrison (already deprived of the crack fourteenth legion and eight cohorts of Batavians in AD 66) by withdrawing 8000 men from the other legions. Although Bolanus was allowed to take the fourteenth back to Britain, Vitellius soon demanded more troops. Bolanus temporized, because 'Britain was never peaceful enough' (ibid., ii.97); but substantial numbers of men from the British garrison were engaged in the civil war campaign in northern Italy in October AD 69. Besides this, the loyalties of his men were again divided, between Vitellius and Vespasian, with the second legion favouring the latter, its old commander from twenty-five years earlier. Thus Bolanus's room for manoeuvre was already limited when the crisis in the north broke out. He was able to rescue Cartimandua and fought several battles with mixed success, according to Tacitus's account in the *Agricola*, written in AD 98. But Venutius was left in control of the kingdom. Bolanus clearly had to refrain from further action until conditions were more favourable. At about this juncture, Julius Agricola took over command of the twentieth legion, replacing the turbulent Roscius Coelius, and fretted at his lack of opportunity for campaigning. Bolanus was replaced in AD 71, by Petillius Cerialis, who, with the garrison back to full strength, was able to launch an aggressive, forward policy in northern Britain.

Shortly after his return from Britain, in AD 73, Bolanus was honoured by Vespasian by being made a patrician and a little later became proconsul of Asia. Both items indicate that the man who had been appointed by Vespasian's enemy Vitellius had performed to the new emperor's satisfaction. Perhaps he had refused active support to Vitellius at a critical moment in AD 69. Three years before Tacitus wrote about Bolanus for the first time in the *Agricola*, the poet Statius had composed 180 hexameters in honour of Crispinus, the sixteen-year-old son of Bolanus; the latter had died shortly before. Crispinus was on the verge of beginning his own career, as a military tribune, and Statius recalled, as an inspiration for the young man, the martial deeds of Bolanus, which included capturing 'the breastplate of a British king' (Statius, v.2, 148–9). This can hardly be other than Venutius. At all events, Bolanus's successes may have been greater than is conveyed by Tacitus in his hostile version. Statius's poem also reveals that after the death of Bolanus, his widow had tried to poison Crispinus, who was probably as a consequence adopted into another family (the Clodii) and may be identified as the consul of 113, Gaius Clodius Crispinus. The elder son, Marcus Vettius Bolanus junior, was consul in 111.

A. R. BIRLEY

Sources Tacitus, *Agricola*, ed. and trans. M. Mutton (1914), 8, 16 · C. Tacitus, *The histories [and] the annals*, ed. and trans. C. H. Moore and J. Jackson, 1 (1925) · P. P. Statius, 'Silvae', *Statius*, ed. and trans. J. H. Mozley, 1 (1928) · A. R. Birley, *The fasti of Roman Britain* (1981)

Vevers, (Henry) Gwynne (1916–1988), marine biologist and intelligence officer, was born on 13 November 1916 at Girvan, Ayrshire, the elder son of Geoffrey Marr Vevers and Catherine Rigby, *née* Andrews, from Ayrshire. Gwynne Vevers's zoological and popularizing bent were dictated by his education and by his father's interests. Geoffrey Marr Vevers (1890–1970) was a helminthologist at the London School of Tropical Medicine and an honorary parasitologist at London Zoo from 1919; as superintendent of the zoo in 1921 he was instrumental in the acquisition of Whipsnade. As an avowed popularizer and as a communist fellow-traveller—he raised medical aid for the USSR during the Second World War and founded and edited the *Anglo-Soviet Journal*—Geoffrey Marr Vevers saw the distribution of knowledge as a duty. He was one of the first BBC television educators at Alexandra Palace and a contributor to *Children's Hour* in 1946–7.

Gwynne Vevers was a scholar at St Paul's School, where his collections of butterflies, mosses, and fossil brachiopods won him three Smee prizes. He gained a Kitchener scholarship and college exhibition to Magdalen College, Oxford, where he was tutored by J. Z. Young and Solly Zuckerman. In 1936, as an undergraduate, he collaborated

with James Fisher on a paper announcing a method for estimating the gannet population on the Scottish island of Ailsa Craig. He travelled to Greenland with the Oxford University Exploration Club in 1936 and to the Faeroes in 1937 to collect mouse and gannet statistics. From the Faeroes and Iceland in 1937–9 he reported to the naval intelligence division of the Admiralty on the German ships which were charting deep-water channels. So began Vevers's covert intelligence gathering, which was to last for several decades. His roving life as a zoologist proved perfect cover; even as late as 1970 he was being debriefed after a zoological trip to Rangoon.

From 1940 Vevers carried out wartime intelligence work for the RAF. He used aerial reconnaissance of the ice floes to determine the deep-water channels. When the German battleship *Bismarck* broke out of Bergen Fjord in May 1941 and sank HMS *Hood* off Iceland, Vevers predicted her position from his charts, and she was intercepted and sunk off Brest. For his work he was made a military MBE. He switched in 1943 to the Air Ministry, where with another zoologist, Wing Commander Frederick S. Russell, he assessed and distributed 'Ultra' ciphers after the British broke the encryptions of the German coding device Enigma. Towards the war's end he was in Germany, hunting down Reichsminister Rust, who committed suicide a few hours before Vevers caught up with him. Vevers was a gifted linguist: by 1945 he could deliver a speech in Russian to former prisoners of war. He spoke Norwegian and all the Scandinavian languages including Faeroese, and used his far-north posting to perfect his Icelandic at Reykjavík University.

After the war Russell became director of the Marine Biological Laboratory at Plymouth and brought Vevers in as bursar. Here from 1945 to 1955 he studied starfish and published on invertebrate pigments with Gilbert Kennedy. In 1949 he completed his Oxford DPhil on the effect of the female sex hormone oestrone; in this he showed that the plumage of the Amherst pheasant was a secondary sexual characteristic under hormonal control. At Plymouth, Vevers developed an underwater camera, which proved as useful in recording marine life around the Eddystone lighthouse as in searches for lost submarines by the US Navy. In 1954 came his first book, *The British Seashore*. Made assistant director of science in charge of the aquarium at London Zoo in 1955, he worked with Norman Millot on the pigmented eye-spots of echinoderms. This fascination with the hormonal and histochemical control of coloration led him to join up with his Savile Club friend Harold Munro Fox to write *The Nature of Animal Colours* (1960).

Amiable and unflappable, Vevers became a mainstay of Zoological Society meetings. He edited the *Journal of Zoology* and the *Zoological Record*, and as curator of the aquarium he introduced several novel exhibits, including the spectacular sea urchin *Diadema*. His administrative talents were in demand elsewhere: as zoological secretary and vice-president of the Linnean Society; on the Biological Council; at the Marine Biological Association and the Freshwater Biological Association; and as a trustee of the Savile Club.

Vevers was a very private person, yet he was also the perfect raconteur and this, with his interest in photography and sea life, made him an ideal natural-history presenter for the BBC unit in Bristol, which began its outside broadcasts in the early 1950s. He served on the science selection committee of the National Film Archive for over thirty years, and he appeared on Desmond Morris's *Zoo Time*. Vevers himself preferred the radio, and became a familiar wireless voice to the post-war generation.

Vevers's family life was very private indeed, and largely unknown to colleagues. He had four wives: he married Mary Brandt in 1942 (James Fisher, 1912–1970, was best man); (Pamela) Joyce Brigstocke on 9 September 1950 (he had with her a son, Geoffrey, in 1952); Winwood Reade in April 1969; and Barbara Oliver on 23 December 1974. He greatly enjoyed the company of women and there were a number of other, less formal liaisons.

Vevers was the oldest member of the Royal Society expedition to the Solomon Islands in 1965, and to the Cook Islands in 1969, to celebrate the bicentenary of Captain Cook's voyage. During the latter expedition he made a pidgin-English speech to the people of Aitutaku.

Vevers's writing was prolific: he produced nearly one hundred books and translations (from eight European languages). Most were popular: on birds, eggs, tracks, fish, animals of the Arctic and of Russia, the human body, the London Zoo, and aquariums. Twenty-four publishers kept him in commissions for thirty years, and he kept the natural world in sight for an increasingly urbanized population. Ultimately his children's books made him known worldwide. But he never would write his wartime memoirs, nor disclose his intelligence activity, despite the cajoling of publishers. He retired from the zoo in 1981 to his home, Wood's House, Bampton, Oxfordshire, where he died on 24 July 1988: he was cremated at Oxford on 1 August.   ADRIAN DESMOND

Sources S. Zuckerman, 'Dr Henry Gwynne Vevers', *Journal of Zoology*, 219 (1989), 527–31 [with select bibliography] • G. Y. Kennedy, 'Gwynne Vevers', *The Linnean*, 5/3 (1989), 40–43 • N. Millot, 'Dr Gwynne Vevers', *The Independent* (4 Aug 1988) • *Daily Telegraph* (27 July 1988) • *The Times* (27 July 1988) • private information (2004) • *Nature*, 226 (1970), 89 • A. J. E. C., 'G. M. Vevers', *BMJ* (31 Jan 1970), 309 • *The Times* (12 Jan 1970) • J. Todd, 'Geoffrey Marr Vevers', *Anglo-Soviet Journal*, 30/3 (1970), 62–5
Archives SOUND BBC Natural History Unit, Sound Archives
Likenesses photograph, repro. in Zuckerman, 'Dr Henry Gwynne Vevers', 531 • photograph (with Solly Zuckerman), repro. in Zuckerman, 'Dr Henry Gwynne Vevers', 531
Wealth at death £43,031: administration, 19 Feb 1990, CGPLA Eng. & Wales

Veysey [*formerly* Harman], **John** (*c*.1464–1554), bishop of Exeter, was the eldest son of William Harman (*d*. 1470) of Moor (or More) Hall, Sutton Coldfield, Warwickshire, and his wife, Joan (*d*. 1525), daughter of Henry Squier of Handsworth, Staffordshire. After an unknown schooling, he followed the arts course at Oxford in the early 1480s, took a BA degree, was admitted as a probationary fellow of Magdalen College on 27 July 1486, and became a full fellow one year later. He subsequently studied civil law, graduating as bachelor by 1489 and doctor by 1495. He left Magdalen in

1496, was presented to the rectory of Clifton Reynes in Buckinghamshire, and took holy orders as subdeacon, deacon, and priest between March 1497 and March 1498. His adoption of the surname Veysey dates from about this time, perhaps as a compliment to John Veysey (*d*. 1492), an Oxford graduate and London city rector, who came from the west midlands and whose will made bequests to Harman and to his brother.

After leaving Magdalen, Veysey enjoyed the patronage of John Arundell, bishop of his home diocese of Coventry and Lichfield, who gave him the rectory of Edgmond, Shropshire, in 1497, made him his vicar-general by 1498, and promoted him as archdeacon of Chester in 1499. When Arundell was translated to the see of Exeter in 1502, Veysey joined him there as bishop's chancellor and vicar-general, further receiving from him a canonry and prebend of Exeter Cathedral and the archdeaconry of Barnstaple, all in 1503. After Arundell's death in the following year, Veysey continued as vicar-general under his successor, Hugh Oldham, who collated him as precentor of the cathedral in 1508. He also received other benefices at various times, including the rectories of St Mary's on the Hill, Chester, in 1499 and Stoke in Teignhead, Devon, in 1504, the latter a crown appointment. In 1506 he exchanged the Chester rectory for a canonry of Salisbury Cathedral, with the prebend of Alton Borealis.

Veysey's high reputation by 1507 is shown by his election as president of Magdalen College on 20 January. He resigned on 30 April before his installation (perhaps through inability to hold the office along with his other benefices), but a majority of the college fellows still expressed a preference for him at a subsequent election. In October 1509 he was chosen as dean of Exeter Cathedral by its canons, after Henry VIII had attempted to impose an outsider—a circumstance that did not prevent his rise into royal favour. By 1514 he was dean of the Chapel Royal, and was made a canon and prebendary of St Stephen's Chapel, Westminster. In 1515 Henry presented him to the deaneries of St George's Chapel, Windsor, and Wolverhampton, and in 1518 to the rectory of Meifod, in Montgomeryshire. Veysey supported the crown against the bishops in 1515 during the disputes about jurisdiction which followed the death of Richard Hunne, and argued the right of secular judges to try clergy in criminal cases. In 1519 the king secured his appointment as bishop of Exeter. The papal provision was issued on 31 August, the temporalities of the see were granted on 4 November, and the archbishop of Canterbury consecrated him at Otford, Kent, on the 6th.

Veysey began his episcopate by organizing a visitation of his diocese in the winter of 1514–15. It was still in progress a year later and led to injunctions for the reform of the priories of Cornworthy in Devon and Tywardreath in Cornwall, and of the collegiate churches of Crediton and Ottery St Mary in Devon. Later, however, other concerns competed with his diocese for his attention. He became involved in diplomacy, accompanying the king to the Field of Cloth of Gold in 1520, welcoming the emperor Charles V to England in 1522, and greeting the pope's ambassador in 1524. In 1525 Henry made him president of the council of Wales and the marches, with the duty of supervising the household of Princess Mary (later Mary I), who was associated with the council as a royal representative. These duties often kept him in the marches, especially at Ludlow, until 1534, when, after being criticized for keeping poor order in Wales, he was replaced as president by Rowland Lee. He then returned to Devon and stayed there frequently until 1546. His episcopal register suggests that he ran his diocese efficiently, but without major initiatives or distinctive policies. Although he made a summary of the statutes of Exeter Cathedral, preserved in the register among material of 1541, this was mainly based on the legislation of previous bishops. He himself did little more than regulate the admission of residentiary canons and, at the request of the cathedral chapter, reduce from forty-six to thirty-six the number of days on which such canons had to reside each year.

The bishop was closely attached to his family and to his birthplace. He promoted his sisters' sons, John Gibbons (d. 1537) and William Leveson (d. 1582), to the chancellorship of Exeter Cathedral and, in Gibbons's case, to be his vicar-general. A third relative, William Veysey (d. c.1545), was made apparitor-general of the diocese, a fourth, Henry Squier (d. 1582), archdeacon of Barnstaple, and another connection, James Leveson, farmed the revenues of the church of Wolverhampton. Veysey was also a notable benefactor of Sutton Coldfield. In 1528 he secured for the town royal grants of corporate status and of the nearby free chase and park, in return for an annual rent of £58. He improved the parish church with new nave aisles, chancel chapels, organs, and a steeple. He gave a meadow to support fifteen poor widows and, between 1540 and 1543, endowed a free grammar school. He also built the moot hall and prison, laid out the market place, paved the town, gave pasturage in the chase to the local poor, erected fifty-one stone houses, and provided new bridges at Curdworth and Water Orton. Moor Hall was reconstituted as a brick house for his own residence, which passed after his death to John, the eldest son of his brother Hugh. He further attempted to establish the manufacture of Devonshire kerseys in Sutton, but this, according to his younger contemporary the Exeter historian John Hooker, 'in the end came to small effect' (Hooker, sigs. H2v–I1r).

Much that happened during the Reformation was probably unwelcome to Veysey. He issued an indulgence as late as 1536, and was rumoured to lack enthusiasm for change. His royal connections, however, kept him subservient to the crown, and he was dutiful in publicizing and enforcing its policies and edicts in his diocese, notably through a surviving set of injunctions in 1538. These are also noteworthy for instructing that children should be taught the Lord's prayer, Ave Maria, creed, and ten commandments either in English or in Cornish. Veysey complied, too, with requests from the royal court for leases of episcopal properties and, under Edward VI, demands for outright grants. As a result, the annual revenue of the bishopric of Exeter fell from £1566 in 1535 to a notional £500 in 1551. Serious unrest broke out in the diocese with the so-called western,

or 'prayer-book', rebellion of 1549, and two years later the octogenarian bishop received a royal command to resign, which he obeyed on 1 August 1551. He was succeeded as bishop by Miles Coverdale, a staunch protestant, and remained chiefly at Sutton, until the accession of Mary I in July 1553 led to Coverdale's deprivation and his own restoration, his register of acts resuming on 10 September. Although about ninety years old, he visited his palace at Exeter in November and stayed there for nearly two months before returning to Sutton, where he died at Moor Hall in 1554 'of a pang, going to his stoole yn the night tyme', according to Hooker (Exeter City Archives, book 51, fol. 351r). An inquisition post mortem, taken in Staffordshire, dated his death as 22 October, but his episcopal register gave the 23rd. He was buried in the north chancel chapel which he had built in Sutton church, beneath an effigy depicting him in mass vestments with mitre and pastoral staff. The effigy survives on a later tomb chest.

Hooker, a protestant writing in the reign of Elizabeth I, characterized Veysey as 'a very wor[l]dly wyse man and yn greate credyte with the king and counsell … He was as courtelyk [that is, courtly] a man as no man exceeded hym in any courtlyk behaviour'. Warwickshire tradition believed that he kept a retinue of 140 men in scarlet livery. His generosity is evident, as is his competence as an administrator, but he is less notable for originality or energy. Hooker (and some later writers) censured the grants of episcopal property which he made from the 1530s onwards. 'How well so ever he deserved of noble men and gentlemen, he deserved small commendation and thanckes of his church and bishopryk'. This does insufficient justice to the pressures faced by post-Reformation bishops, which made Veysey's actions virtually unavoidable.   NICHOLAS ORME

Sources episcopal register of John Veysey, Devon RO, Chanter XIV, XV, XVI, XVII · Emden, *Oxf.*, 3.1947–8 · W. Dugdale, *The antiquities of Warwickshire illustrated* (1656), 667–70 · D. H. Pill, 'The diocese of Exeter under Bishop Veysey', MA diss., University of Exeter, 1963 · *LP Henry VIII* · W. D. Macray, *A register of the members of St Mary Magdalen College, Oxford*, 8 vols. (1894–1915), vol. 1, pp. 110–13; vol. 4, pp. 179–80 · W. H. Frere and W. P. M. Kennedy, eds., *Visitation articles and injunctions of the period of the Reformation*, 2, Alcuin Club, Collections, 15 (1910), 61–4 · G. Oliver, *Lives of the bishops of Exeter, and a history of the cathedral* (1861), 471–6 · Devon RO, Exeter city archives, J. Hooker, book 51, fol. 351r · J. Hooker [J. Vowell], *A catalog of the bishops of Excester* (1584), sigs. H2v–I1r · *VCH Warwickshire*, 4.231–45
Archives Devon RO, episcopal register of Bishop Veysey, Chanter XIV–XVII
Likenesses painted effigy on tomb, Holy Trinity church, Sutton Coldfield, Warwickshire

Vézelay, Paule. *See* Williams, Marjorie Agnes Watson- (1892–1984).

Vezin, Hermann (1829–1910), actor, born in Philadelphia, Pennsylvania, on 2 March 1829, was the son of Charles Henri Vezin, a merchant of French origin, and his wife, Emilie Kalisky. His great-great-grandfather Pierre de Vezin married in the seventeenth century Marie Charlotte de Châteauneuf, an actress at the French theatre at Hanover; Rouget de Lisle, the composer of the 'Marseillaise', was one of the great-grandsons of this union. Hermann Vezin

Hermann Vezin (1829–1910), by Barraud, pubd 1891

was educated in Philadelphia, and entered Pennsylvania University in 1845. Intended for the law, he graduated BA in 1847 and MA in 1850. In 1848–9 he underwent in Berlin successful treatment for threatened eye trouble.

In 1850 Vezin travelled to England, and an introduction from Charles Kean secured him an engagement with John Langford Pritchard at the Theatre Royal, York. There, in the autumn of 1850, he made his first appearance on the stage, and played many minor Shakespearian parts supporting Charles and Ellen Kean, William Creswick, and G. V. Brooke. In the following year he fulfilled engagements at Southampton, Ryde, Guildford, Reading, and at the Theatre Royal, Edinburgh, where his roles included Young Norval in John Home's *Douglas*, Claude Melnotte in Bulwer-Lytton's *The Lady of Lyons*, and Richelieu.

In 1852 Charles Kean engaged Vezin for the Princess's Theatre in London, and he made his début on the London stage on 14 April 1852, as the Earl of Pembroke in *King John*. Minor parts in Shakespearian and contemporary plays followed. In royal command performances at Windsor Castle in 1853 Vezin appeared as Snare in *2 Henry IV*, and as the wounded officer in *Macbeth*.

On the termination of his engagement at the Princess's in 1853 Vezin returned for some four years to the provinces, and in 1857 he went to America, where he remained for two years. His first appearance there was on 7 September 1857, as St Pierre in *The Wife*, at the Walnut Street Theatre, Philadelphia. After returning to England in 1859 he undertook the management of the Surrey Theatre for six weeks, and opened there in June 1859 as Macbeth. He improved his reputation in such important parts as Hamlet, Richard III, Louis XI, Shylock, Othello, and King John.

Following a further tour in the provinces Vezin was engaged by Samuel Phelps for Sadler's Wells Theatre, where he opened in September 1860 as Orlando in *As You Like It*, and continued in various Shakespearian roles, including Aufidius, Bassanio, Mark Antony, and Romeo. At Windsor Castle, on 24 January 1861, he played De Mauprat in a command performance of Bulwer-Lytton's *Richelieu*.

Vezin was now widely recognized as an actor of talent in both high tragedy and comedy. Having been engaged by Edmund Falconer for the Lyceum Theatre, he made a great success as Harry Kavanagh in Falconer's *Peep o' Day* (November 1861), a part he played for more than 300 nights.

On 21 February 1863, at St Peter's Church, Eaton Square, Vezin married Mrs Charles Young, *née* Jane Elizabeth Thomson, an actress who subsequently performed as Jane Elizabeth (Eliza) *Vezin (1827–1902). She committed suicide in 1902. They had a son who also became an actor. Following a 'starring' tour with his wife in the provinces Vezin played, at the Princess's Theatre in January 1864, Don Caesar in *Donna Diana*, specially adapted for the actor and his wife by Westland Marston from Moreto's Spanish play *El Desden con el Desden*. Later he undertook three months' management at the Princess's Theatre, which proved an artistic success; he opened in July 1867 as James Harebell in W. G. Wills's *The Man o' Airlie*.

For the next twenty years Vezin played almost continuously leading parts at the chief London theatres in quality new or old pieces. He supported Samuel Phelps during 1874 in a series of revivals of old comedies, and the following year was Jaques in *As You Like It* and Benedick in *Much Ado about Nothing*. His Jaques proved a singularly fine performance, full of subtle irony, humour, and poetry. It subsequently contributed largely to the success of Marie Litton's revival of *As You Like It*, which ran for a hundred nights at the Imperial Theatre in 1880.

Under Chatterton's management of Drury Lane, Vezin played Macbeth to the Lady Macbeth of Geneviève Ward in 1876. In the same year, at the Crystal Palace, he took the part of Oedipus in a translation of Sophocles' *Oedipus at Colonos*, in which his declamatory powers showed to advantage. Among his numerous roles at various other London theatres, his performance as Sir Peter Teazle in *The School for Scandal* and his characters in Gilbert's comedies were successful, as was his rendering of the parts of Macduff and Macbeth, which he alternated with Charles Warner.

At Drury Lane Theatre in 1881 Vezin played Iago to the Othello of the American tragedian John McCullough. At the Grand Theatre, Islington, on 7 May 1886 he played, for the Shelley Society, Count Francesco Cenci in a single private performance of Shelley's tragedy *The Cenci*. He joined Henry Irving at the Lyceum Theatre in May 1888 as Coranto in the revival of A. C. Calmour's *The Amber Heart*. At the same theatre, in January 1889, owing to Irving's illness, he took the part of Macbeth with marked success.

From this time onward Vezin's appearances in London were few. He spent much of his time touring the provinces, and he gave occasional dramatic recitals at the St James's, St George's, and Steinway halls. He devoted himself mainly to teaching elocution. Among his later appearances in London he played, at the Opera Comique in 1891, in *Cousin Jack* and *Mrs MP*, two adaptations by himself of German farces; at Drury Lane Theatre, from September to December 1896, he was the Warden of Coolgardie in Eustace Leigh and Cyril Dare's *The Duchess of Coolgardie*, and Robespierre in George Grant and James Lisle's *The Kiss of Delilah*. At the Lyceum in 1897 he played Dr Primrose to the Olivia of Ellen Terry in W. G. Wills's *Olivia*, an adaptation of Goldsmith's *The Vicar of Wakefield*, and at the Strand Theatre on 2 May 1900 he was Fergus Crampton in Bernard Shaw's *You Never can Tell*. His final engagement was with Sir Herbert Tree at His Majesty's Theatre on 7 April 1909, when he appeared as Rowley in *The School for Scandal*. His health was then rapidly failing, and he relinquished his part before the run was over. After a career of nearly sixty years he died at his London home, 10 Lancaster Place, Strand, on 12 June 1910; in accordance with his instructions his body was cremated at Golders Green and his ashes were scattered.

A distinguished elocutionist, Vezin was probably the most scholarly and intellectual actor of his generation, although he never reached the height of the profession. His defect lay in a lack of emotional warmth and of personal magnetism. He was only 5 feet 5½ inches in height, and this was a disadvantage to him as an actor. He was an admirable instructor in elocution and acting, and many of his pupils attained prominence in their calling.

J. PARKER, rev. NILANJANA BANERJI

Sources *The Times* (14 June 1910) · C. E. Pascoe, ed., *The dramatic list*, 2nd edn (1880) · E. F. Edgett, 'Vezin, Hermann', *DAB* · T. A. Brown, *History of the American stage* (1870) · P. Hartnoll, ed., *The Oxford companion to the theatre* (1951); 2nd edn (1957); 3rd edn (1967) · *WWW* · B. Hunt and J. Parker, eds., *The green room book, or, Who's who on the stage* (1906–9) · *Era Almanack and Annual* (1897) · P. Hartnoll, ed., *The concise Oxford companion to the theatre* (1972) · E. Reid and H. Compton, eds., *The dramatic peerage* [1891]; rev. edn [1892] · Hall, *Dramatic ports.* · H. Morley, *The journal of a London playgoer from 1851 to 1866* (1866) · H. Morley, *The journal of a London playgoer, 1851–1866*, 2nd edn (1891) · *The Athenaeum* (Jan 1859) · *The Athenaeum* (18 June 1910), 743–4 · *Dramatic Year Book for … 1891* (1892) · J. Knight, *Theatrical notes* (1893) · J. Hollingshead, *Gaiety chronicles* (1898) · A. T. C. Pratt, ed., *People of the period: being a collection of the biographies of upwards of six thousand living celebrities*, 2 vols. (1897)

Archives Boston PL, letters · University of Bristol, corresp. and photographs

Likenesses Daily Mirror Studios, postcards, 1909, NPG · A. B., lithograph, NPG · Barraud, photograph, NPG; repro. in *Men and Women of the Day*, 4 (1891) [*see illus.*] · E. Matthews & Sons, lithograph, NPG · caricature, repro. in *Entr'acte* (7 Sept 1878) · caricature, repro. in *Entr'acte* (2 Sept 1876) · five prints, Harvard TC · photograph, BM; repro. in *The Theatre* (1878) · portrait, repro. in Hollingshead, *Gaiety chronicles*, 135

Wealth at death £137 7s. 6d.: probate, 28 June 1910, *CGPLA Eng. & Wales*

Vezin [*née* Thomson; *other married name* Young], **Jane Elizabeth** [Eliza] (1827–1902), actress, was born while her mother, the actress Peggy Cook, was on tour in England.

Jane Elizabeth Vezin (1827–1902), by L. Bertin

Her father was George Thomson, a merchant; her maternal grandfather was James Cook, a bass singer, and her mother's aunt was the actress Mrs West. At an early age Eliza accompanied her parents to Australia, and when she was eight, in Sydney, she earned the reputation of a child prodigy as a singer and dancer. In 1845 she was playing at the Victoria Theatre, Melbourne. On 6 June 1846, at Holy Trinity Church, Launceston, Tasmania, she was married to Charles Frederick Young (1819–1874), an eccentric, undisciplined, but versatile actor. She supported the well-known actor G. V. Brooke during his Australian tour of 1855, when she appeared with him as Beatrice in *Much Ado about Nothing*, Emilia in *Othello*, Pauline in *The Lady of Lyons*, and Lady Macbeth.

The Youngs returned to England with their daughter, and, as Mrs Charles Young, Eliza made her first appearance on the London stage under the management of Samuel Phelps, at Sadler's Wells Theatre, on 15 September 1857, playing Julia in *The Hunchback*. She was enthusiastically received. During the seasons of 1857 and 1858, when the bill changed two or three times a week, she performed most of the leading parts in Phelps's productions, making striking successes in a variety of roles, including Rosalind in *As You Like It*, Clara Douglas in *Money*, Portia, Desdemona, Fanny Stirling in *The Clandestine Marriage*, Cordelia, Mistress Ford in *The Merry Wives of Windsor*, Lydia Languish in *The Rivals*, Pauline in *The Lady of Lyons*, Lady Townly in *The Provoked Husband*, Viola in *Twelfth Night*, and Juliet.

During the summer vacation of 1858 Eliza Young had appeared at the Haymarket and Lyceum theatres, playing at the former house on 10 July, the last night of J. B. Buckstone's five years' continuous 'season', the Widow Belmour in A. Murphy's *The Way to Keep Him*. In March 1859 she was at the Lyceum under Benjamin Webster and Edmund Falconer. At the opening of the Princess's Theatre under the management of Augustus Harris senior (24 September), she played Amoret in John Oxenford's *Ivy Hall*, in which Henry Irving made his first appearance on the London stage. When Phelps reopened Sadler's Wells Theatre, under his sole management, on 8 September 1860, Mrs Young appeared as Rosalind, acting for the first time with Hermann Vezin, who appeared as Orlando. She remained with Phelps through the season of 1860–61, adding the parts of Miranda in *The Tempest* and Donna Violante in Susannah Centlivre's *The Wonder* to her repertory. Her chief engagement during 1861 was at the Haymarket Theatre, where on 30 September she played Portia to the Shylock of the American actor Edwin Booth, who then made his first appearance in London.

Her marriage to Young had broken down: he moved in with a dancer who bore his child, and in May 1862 Eliza obtained a divorce. On 21 February 1863, at St Peter's Church, Eaton Square, she was married to Hermann *Vezin (1829–1910), whom she immediately accompanied on a theatrical tour of the provinces. Afterwards she acted opposite him in Westland Marston's *Donna Diana*, at the Princess's Theatre (2 January 1864). On the tercentenary celebration of Shakespeare's birthday at Stratford upon Avon, in April 1864, she acted Rosalind. There followed a long engagement at Drury Lane Theatre, under F. B. Chatterton and Edmund Falconer, where she first appeared on 8 October 1864 as Desdemona, in a powerful cast which included Phelps as Othello and William Creswick as Iago. She repeated many of the chief parts she had already played at Sadler's Wells. She made a great hit as Marguerite in Bayle Bernard's *Faust* (20 October 1866). At the Princess's Theatre, on 22 August 1867, she gave a very beautiful performance of the part of Peg Woffington in Charles Reade's *Masks and Faces*. Again with Phelps at Drury Lane, during the season of 1867–8, she played Lady Macbeth (14 October 1867), Angiolina in Bayle Bernard's *The Doge of Venice* (2 November 1867), and Charlotte in Isaac Bickerstaff's *The Hypocrite* (1 February 1868).

Less important London engagements followed at the St James's Theatre. During March 1874 Eliza Vezin toured in the chief provincial cities with her own company, again playing parts of no great interest. At Drury Lane Theatre she reappeared under Chatterton as Lady Elizabeth in *Richard III* (Cibber's version; 23 September 1876), as Paulina in *The Winter's Tale*, with Charles Dillon (28 September 1878), and later in the season as Mrs Oakley in Colman's *The Jealous Wife*. She then joined the company at the Prince of Wales's Theatre in Tottenham Court Road, under the management of the Bancrofts, where she appeared on 27

September 1879 as Lady Deene in James Albery's *Duty*, an adaptation from Sardou's *Les bourgeois de Pont Arcy*. There followed an engagement at the Princess's with Edwin Booth in the season of 1880–81.

After playing Olga Strogoff in H. J. Byron's *Michael Strogoff* at the Adelphi (14 March 1881), Eliza Vezin fulfilled her last professional engagement at the St James's Theatre, under the management of Hare and Kendal, on 20 October 1883, when she gave an effective performance as Mrs Rogers in William Gillette and Frances Hodgson Burnett's *Young Folks' Ways*.

Mrs Vezin was a graceful and earnest actress, with a sweet and sympathetic voice, a great command of unaffected pathos, and an admirable elocution. Comedy as well as tragedy lay within her range, and from about 1858 to 1875 she had few rivals on the English stage in Shakespearian and poetical drama.

The death of her only daughter (from her first marriage) in 1901 unhinged her mind. At Margate, on 17 April 1902, she eluded her nurses, and flung herself from her bedroom window, with fatal result. She was buried at Highgate cemetery.   J. PARKER, *rev.* J. GILLILAND

Sources H. Morley, *The journal of a London playgoer from 1851 to 1866* (1866) · C. Scott, *The drama of yesterday and today*, 2 vols. (1899) · *AusDB* · *The Athenaeum* (26 April 1902), 540 · W. M. Phelps and J. Forbes-Robertson, *The life and life-work of Samuel Phelps* (1886) · H. B. Baker, *The London stage: its history and traditions from 1576 to 1888*, 2 vols. (1889) · *The life and reminiscences of E. L. Blanchard, with notes from the diary of Wm. Blanchard*, ed. C. W. Scott and C. Howard, 2 vols. (1891) · S. D'Amico, ed., *Enciclopedia dello spettacolo*, 11 vols. (Rome, 1954–68) · D. Cook, *Nights at the play* (1883) · B. Hunt, ed., *The green room book, or, Who's who on the stage* (1906) · F. Hays, *Women of the day: a biographical dictionary of notable contemporaries* (1885) · J. Knight, *Theatrical notes* (1893) · C. E. Pascoe, ed., *The dramatic list* (1879)

Likenesses L. Bertin, photograph, NPG [*see illus.*] · photographs, NPG · woodburytype carte-de-visite, NPG

Wealth at death £3329 14s. 1d.: probate, 14 May 1902, *CGPLA Eng. & Wales*

Vial de Sainbel [St Bel], **Charles Benoît** [*formerly* Benoît Vial] (**1750–1793**), veterinary surgeon, was an enigmatic figure about whose early life it is difficult to obtain many substantiated facts. Sainbel said that he was born at St Bel near Lyons, France, in 1753, and that he was orphaned at three years of age and subsequently cared for and educated by his guardian, M. de Flesseile, who, when Sainbel was sixteen, supported his education at the first veterinary school in the world, at Lyons, France. However, the veterinary school records show that he was born Benoît Vial on 28 or 29 January 1750, and that he entered the school when he was nineteen years old, on 6 August 1769, and that his education was provided 'at the expense of the town' (Pugh, 262).

The Lyons veterinary school was then under the directorship of Professor Pén and after two years of intensive study Sainbel was made a *conférencier assistant*, to a class of sixteen pupils, and at 'the end of his third year he was made an assistant surgeon and one of the public demonstrators' (Smith, 185). In 1774 an extensive epizootic raged among the horses in many provinces of France, and Sainbel was ordered to choose five students from the veterinary college at Lyons to accompany him in his provincial visits, and to assist in stopping the outbreak of disease. He accomplished his mission so satisfactorily that he returned with official testimonials of his skill. At this time Bourgelat, the inspector-general of the two royal veterinary schools in France, recommended Sainbel to Chabert, director of the Alfort veterinary school, where Sainbel was appointed junior assistant to the professor of anatomy. However, he soon quarrelled with his superiors and Bourgelat recorded that he was 'Renvoyé comme subject cabaleur, intrigant et détestable' (Pugh, 262).

Sainbel therefore left Paris and returned to Lyons, where he practised for some time as a veterinary physician and surgeon. He then moved to Montpellier and for five years held the post of professor of comparative anatomy at the medical school there. After the failure of his plan to establish a veterinary school at Montpellier he returned to Paris under the patronage of the prince of Lambesc, and was appointed one of the equerries to Louis XVI and chief of the manège at the academy of Lyons, posts which he retained for three years.

Sainbel came to England in June 1788, after being passed over for a promotion; he was provided with letters of introduction to Sir Joseph Banks, Samuel Simmons, and Daniel Layard from Dr Broussonet, the secretary of the Royal Agricultural Society of Paris. In the following September Sainbel published proposals for founding a veterinary school in England. The project was unsuccessful, and, after marrying an Englishwoman, Sainbel returned to Paris. He found that the revolution was impending in France, and he quickly came back to England, under the pretext of buying horses for the stud of his sovereign. His patrimonial estate of St Bel was confiscated during the revolution, and he was proscribed as an émigré.

On 27 February 1789 Sainbel was requested by Philip O'Kelly to dissect the body of the great racehorse Eclipse. He did so, and ultimately his essay on the proportions of Eclipse, published in 1791, brought him the highest reputation in some quarters as a veterinary anatomist. In October 1789 he tried, with no success, to give lectures in England on the veterinary art. It was at this time that he met Granville Penn (grandson of William Penn of Pennsylvania). Penn was very interested in improving the education of farriers and was a subscriber to the Odiham Agricultural Society's Farriary Fund. He re-examined Sainbel's proposals to found a veterinary school and together they issued the Plan for Establishing an Institution to Cultivate and Teach Veterinary Medicine (1790). Sainbel sent ten copies of the plan to the Odiham Agricultural Society and, as a result, he was elected an honorary member of the society in October 1790. By 1791 his plan had been adopted by the society and a London subcommittee had been formed to plan the establishment of a school there. A preliminary meeting of the subcommittee was held on 11 February 1791 at the Blenheim Coffee House in Bond Street, London, and on 18 February of the same year it was decided to form an institution to be called the London Veterinary College, funded by subscription, with Sainbel as professor.

For the next two years Sainbel 'was overworked and underpaid' (Pugh, 265). He drew up plans for the location, design, and running of the college, initiated a three-year plan of veterinary education, taught pupils, and examined the subscribers' horses. By May 1792 his salary had doubled but, according to Pugh, 'a sort of whispering campaign seems to have been carried out against him', led by James Huntingford, the college secretary (Pugh, 267). This led to Sainbel requesting that an examination of his character and ability as professor should be carried out. John Hunter, several eminent medical men, and lords Heathfield and Morton were asked to express their opinion of him in two reports. Sainbel was exonerated and Huntingford dismissed. Sainbel resumed work, but in August 1793 he became sick, possibly with glanders, and, despite the administrations of Dr Crawford and Dr Scott, he died on 21 August 1793. He was buried in the vault under the Savoy Chapel in the Strand. The college granted his widow an annuity of £50.

Sainbel may justly be looked upon as the founder of scientific veterinary practice in England. Hitherto, owing to the ignorance of any scientific understanding of animal diseases, the loss of animal life had been very great, and farriers had depended upon antiquated or empirical treatises such as those of Gervase Markham. Bracy Clark, one of Sainbel's students, writing in the Edinburgh Veterinary Review, gives us a good description of the man:

> His figure was well proportioned; of an open, manly countenance, and above the middle or standard size; his skin and complexion were a dark swarthy brown, with much dark black hair … his nostrils were particularly wide and swollen; his eyes very dark, not clear, hazel … he was polite and easy, and often disposed to etiquette and punctilio … in disposition he was highly jealous, and irascible and ever on the watch for an effront, which he would often imagine, where the smallest had not been intended. (Clark, 133–4)

It is reported that Sainbel spied on his pupils, and several were dismissed from the college because he believed they were critical of him. He appears to have had several enemies. Nevertheless, 'He lectured on the anatomy of the horse … in an ingenious and happy manner; his knowledge of medicine was confined … his prescriptions complicated and inelegant … he operated with considerable neatness in cases of surgery' (Clark, 133–4).

LINDA WARDEN

Sources F. Smith, *The early history of veterinary literature and its British development*, 4 vols. (1919–33); repr. (1976), vols. 2–3 · L. P. Pugh, *From farriery to veterinary medicine, 1785–1795* (1962) · L. P. Pugh, 'Vial de St Bel (1750–1793)', *British Veterinary Journal*, 118 (1962), 262–7 · B. Clark, 'Vial de St Bel', *Edinburgh Veterinary Review*, 3 (1861), 129–34 · *The Hippiatrist and Veterinary Journal* (1830), 5 · H. E. Carter, 'Modern veterinary education: the first 100 years', *Veterinary International*, 1 (1993), 28 · N. Gittins, 'Charles Vial de Sainbel sa vie—son oeuvre', diss., École Nationale Vétérinaire d'Alfort, 1984 · *Veterinary Record*, 3 (1891), 130 · 'Charles Vial de Sainbel', an unpublished brochure to mark the unveiling of a plaque to Vial de Sainbel, 1991 · R. Vines, *Veterinary and physiological essays* (1836) · private information (2004) · *Veterinary History* (summer 1985) [supplement to the St Bel plan dated 13 Dec 1790] · I. Pattison, *The British veterinary profession, 1741–1948*, [another edn] (1984) · *Sporting Magazine*, 1

(1792–3), 67, 161, 167–70, 225–7, 268 • E. Cotchin, *The Royal Veterinary College, London: a bicentenary history* (1990) • minute book, 1785–93, Royal Veterinary College, London • City Westm. AC • records, Veterinary School, Lyons

Likenesses W. Wood, portrait, priv. coll. • acrylic (after engraving by Leney; after portrait by W. Wood)

Vian, Sir Philip Louis (1894–1968), naval officer, was born in London on 15 June 1894, the son of Alsager Vian, secretary to a public company, and his wife, Ada Frances Renault. He was educated at Hillside School and the Royal Naval College at Osborne and Dartmouth. After the outbreak of the First World War, Vian was able to arrange a transfer to the new destroyer *Morning Star* which was present at the battle of Jutland. He was promoted lieutenant in 1916 and served in two other destroyers in turn, thus spending most of the war in small ships. After the war he specialized in gunnery and led the life of the peacetime navy, in which, however, he was already showing considerable ability. In 1929 he married Marjorie (*d.* 1973), daughter of Colonel David Price Haig; they had two daughters.

Vian was promoted commander in 1929, and in 1932 led a division of one of the Mediterranean destroyer flotillas; then, as a captain (1934), he was put in charge of a flotilla of reserve destroyers which was sent out to defend Malta during the Abyssinian crisis. In July 1936 the Spanish Civil War broke out and the ships of the first flotilla, to which Vian had transferred and which was on its way home to pay off, were diverted to Spanish ports. They spent a busy and rewarding period evacuating British subjects, exchanging refugees, and acting as a floating communications centre for the ambassador. Vian's clarity of thought, firm decisions, and astringent signals to Whitehall were outstanding.

Vian then had two years in command of the *Arethusa*, flagship of the 3rd cruiser squadron, where he gained experience of the Mediterranean side of the Spanish Civil War. In August 1939 his appointment to command a shore establishment was cancelled and he was sent to be captain of a flotilla of elderly destroyers from reserve which were to be based on Liverpool and used to escort Atlantic convoys. In the new year he was appointed to the fourth destroyer flotilla, consisting of the new and powerful Tribal-class destroyers which were working from Rosyth, escorting convoys to and from Scandinavia.

In February 1940 Vian in the *Cossack* led a force of one cruiser and four destroyers to the Norwegian coast and was then instructed to seize the German ship *Altmark* which was known to be carrying British merchant seamen prisoners. After a long search the *Altmark* was sighted in Norwegian territorial waters but quickly took refuge in Josing Fjord. After some polite but firm discussions with the officers commanding the two Norwegian torpedo boats which had been escorting the *Altmark* down the Leads, and following an interchange of signals with Whitehall, Vian took the *Cossack* into the fjord and sent a boarding party onto the German ship, which at the time was going astern out of the ice. After a scuffle with the enemy crew the boarding party rescued the 300 prisoners, whom the *Cossack* took home to receive a heroes' welcome. Normally Vian was not an above-average ship handler, but as always in an emergency his performance was immaculate.

During the Norwegian campaign in the spring of 1940 Vian, in the *Afridi*, was closely involved in many actions and his ship was eventually sunk by dive-bombers after evacuating troops from Namsos. In May he returned to the *Cossack* and the flotilla was based at Scapa during the summer until the peak danger period of invasion, when it transferred to Rosyth, where Vian spent much time exercising the tactics he would use on German landing-craft in the channel. In the autumn the flotilla went to Scapa and Vian led a successful night attack on a small German coastal convoy close to the Norwegian coast.

After a long and arduous winter, spent mostly in escorting large ships steaming fast in heavy seas, in May 1941 the flotilla was able to join in the attack on the battleship *Bismarck* whose steering had been crippled by aircraft from the *Ark Royal*. The destroyers, led by Vian, spent an exciting night in very heavy seas, shadowing and attacking the stricken battleship whose fire remained remarkably accurate. Next day, she was sunk by the heavy guns and torpedoes of the big ships.

In July 1941 Vian was specially promoted rear-admiral and left his command. He was sent on a flying visit to Russia to arrange for naval co-operation, but the task was made difficult by obstruction at every level. After reporting to Whitehall, he was appointed to force K at Scapa, the composition of which varied but which was normally led by the cruiser *Nigeria*. The force was sent to Spitsbergen to report on the situation there and also visited Bear Island where the weather reporting station was destroyed. In August 1941 the force returned to Spitsbergen to destroy the coalmining facilities, withdraw the Norwegian settlers, and evacuate the Russian colony to its own country. Thus started the first of the Russian convoys. On the return passage to Scapa, Vian took the *Nigeria* and the *Aurora* to attack a German naval force reported at the northern end of the Norwegian Leads. During one of the closest range actions of the war the *Nigeria* rammed and cut in half the German training cruiser *Bremse*.

In October 1941 Vian was flown through the Mediterranean to take command of the 15th cruiser squadron at Alexandria. There were few ships available and the enemy forces were greatly superior. The main British tasks were the sustenance of Malta and the prevention of supplies reaching the axis armies in north Africa. In December, Vian successfully bombarded Darnah, an enterprise not included in his operation orders. In the same month he took his first convoy to Malta and despite heavy air attacks succeeded in his objective; the Italian fleet which he sighted was luckily engaged in a similar operation to Africa.

In mid-February 1942 an operation to supply Malta ended in disaster, not one loaded merchant ship reaching the island; and in the following month Vian's flagship *Naiad* was sunk when he was escorting a cruiser and destroyer from Malta. Towards the end of the month three merchantmen set out for Malta with a strong escort of cruisers and destroyers under Vian's command. It met the Italian battle fleet consisting of a battleship, two 8 inch gun cruisers, a 6 inch gun cruiser, and a number of destroyers. By great bravery and brilliant tactics, the merchant ships remained unscathed from surface attack although enemy aircraft delivered some dangerous hits. In the end, one merchant ship arrived safely, a second was beached at Malta, and the third sunk. The action fully deserved the special message of congratulation from Churchill. During the next Malta convoy, in June, the situation in the desert was worse and even fewer aircraft were available to help. Combined threats by the Italian battle fleet, numerous aircraft, and some U-boats caused the recall of Vian's escorting forces, but two merchantmen reached Malta from the convoy which had approached from the west at the same time, so enabling the island to survive for a further two months, until the next convoy arrived.

In September 1942 Vian set out for home by air but his aircraft broke down in west Africa, where he contracted malaria. By April 1943 he was adjudged fit for shore service only and appointed to a post on the staff which was planning the invasion of Europe. But before he could take it up he was on his way back to the Mediterranean to take over an amphibious force whose commander had died in an air crash. He had two months to prepare for this new form of warfare and the successful assault on Sicily in July. In August, Vian was sent to command a squadron of small aircraft-carriers which were to provide fighter cover and tactical support for the invasion of Italy at Salerno in September. Although again he was new to this form of warfare, the squadron's performance was admirable and it was able to remain operating on station for longer than expected.

Immediately after the Salerno operations, Vian was informed that he was to be given the sea command of the allied navies engaged in the invasion of Normandy. Churchill's personal invitation to succeed Admiral Mountbatten (later Earl Mountbatten of Burma) as chief of combined operations he refused on the grounds that it would be a shore job. He spent two months in training Force J, one of the British amphibious forces. Plans for the naval command were revised and in January 1944 Vian was given command of the Eastern task force, the western force being commanded by an American. Vian had three British forces under him and, flying his flag in the cruiser *Scylla*, he spent a testing time during and after the initial invasion. He was next appointed to command the aircraft-carrier squadron which sailed on 19 November to join the British fleet to work with the Americans in the Pacific.

The British were, in comparison with the Americans, inexperienced in this form of warfare against the Japanese, particularly in the techniques of operating for long periods without a return to base for replenishment. Accordingly the task force made four attacks on oil refineries in Sumatra which offered useful practice. After a visit to Sydney, where the logistic arrangements were completed as far as possible, the task force sailed on 23 March 1945 to join the operations already in progress for the capture of Okinawa. Because of the comparative inexperience of the ships the task force was allotted a separate area in which to work and attacked with success a chain of islands used by the Japanese to reinforce Okinawa. Despite logistic difficulties due to the small and inadequate fleet train the fleet kept the sea for sixty-two days, broken only by eight days in harbour in the middle. Confidence was raised by the failure of the suicide bombers to penetrate the armoured decks of the British carriers which were able to operate very soon after a hit. On 25 May the fleet withdrew to Sydney for repairs and maintenance, sailing again on 23 June for further operations. This time Vian's task force 37 operated as an integral part of the vast American fleet and, despite potential difficulties over command, all went well. The British carriers attacked many targets on the Japanese homeland during this period but on 15 August all operations were cancelled because of the Japanese surrender. After goodwill visits in Australian and New Zealand waters Vian sailed for home and arrived in time to take part in the victory parade in London.

After the war Vian was fifth sea lord at the Admiralty, in charge of naval aviation (1946–8), but his essential qualities were not so suited to peacetime naval life. He was happier as commander-in-chief of the Home Fleet (1950–52) when in his flagship *Vanguard* he was able to go to sea. He retained a superb grasp of the tactical situation and his handling of the fleet was a joy to see. He had been promoted vice-admiral in 1945 and admiral in 1948 and on his retirement in 1952 he was specially promoted admiral of the fleet, a rank normally confined to first sea lords. This was fitting recognition of his remarkable service as a fighting sailor in the war in which no one else continued so long in combatant posts at sea without a break or had such an extensive geographical scope.

Vian's was a complex character which needed knowing well by his juniors if they were to retain his confidence, and his inherent shyness seemed to produce an offensive approach. But his loyalty to his seniors was complete, however much he disagreed with them, and this was not unusual. He had his faults: an apparent intolerance of officers who did not measure up to his high standards of efficiency and initiative, and resentment of any differences of opinion in public. He was then abrasive and sometimes abusive. But in private there was no more charming man, and no one with whom matters could more easily be discussed or even argued. His memoirs, *Action this Day* (1960), reveal the man who was so seldom seen in public. They are exceptionally modest, taking blame for failure or mistakes, while giving to others credit for victory or success.

Vian's fighting qualities were superb. He was full of the offensive spirit, which he communicated to those under him, but his juniors always knew that he would not take stupid risks. More than once he deferred some action because the odds were too great and he never hazarded his ships when little was to be gained. In battle he seemed to have an inborn instinct for the right decision and he was served by a devoted and competent staff. In harbour he insisted on the highest standards of cleanliness and smartness.

Vian was appointed to the DSO in 1940 with bars in 1940 and 1941. He was appointed KBE in 1942, CB and KCB in 1944, and GCB in 1952. He died at his home, Pitt House Farm, Ashford Hill, near Newbury, on 27 May 1968. There is a plaque in the crypt of St Paul's Cathedral near that of the man whom he admired more than any—Viscount Cunningham of Hyndhope.   PETER GRETTON, *rev.*

Sources P. Vian, *Action this day: a war memoir* (1960) · *The Times* (29 May 1968) · personal knowledge (1981) · S. W. Roskill, *The war at sea, 1939–1945*, 3 vols. in 4 (1954–61) · *WWW* · *CGPLA Eng. & Wales* (1968)
Archives FILM BFI NFTVA, news footage · IWM FVA, actuality footage · IWM FVA, news footage |SOUND IWM SA, oral history interviews
Likenesses W. Stoneman, photograph, 1942, NPG · O. Birley, oils, 1945–8, Royal Naval College, Greenwich · J. Pannett, chalk, 1967, NPG
Wealth at death £28,623: probate, 1 Aug 1968, *CGPLA Eng. & Wales*

Vicar of Hell, the. *See* Bryan, Sir Francis (*d.* 1550).

Vicars, Sir Arthur Edward (1862–1921), herald and genealogist, was born on 27 July 1862 at Holly Walk, Leamington Spa, Warwickshire, the youngest of the three sons (there were also two daughters) of Colonel William Henry Vicars (61st regiment) and Jane Mary (1821–1873), third daughter of Robert Gunn Cunningham, deputy lieutenant, of Mount Kennedy, co. Wicklow. His mother had previously been married to Peirce K. Mahoney (1817–1850) of Kilmorna in co. Kerry. She had three sons from her first marriage, and although Arthur Vicars was educated in England (at Magdalen College School, Oxford, and Bromsgrove School) he spent his holidays in Ireland at the country houses belonging to his half-brothers George and Peirce Mahony, and developed a longing to identify himself with the old Ireland that they represented.

Vicars developed an early interest in Irish heraldry and genealogy, and on 23 February 1893, at the age of only thirty, he was appointed to succeed Sir Bernard Burke as Ulster king of arms, registrar, and knight attendant of the Order of St Patrick. Honours quickly followed: he was created a knight bachelor in 1896, and appointed a CVO in 1900 and a KCVO in 1903.

Vicars contributed a number of articles to archaeological journals; was honorary secretary of the Kildare Archaeological Society from its foundation in 1891, a fellow of the Society of Antiquaries, and a governor of the National Library of Ireland; and produced an *Index to the Prerogative Wills of Ireland, 1536–1810*, published in 1897. But his name will be remembered not for his heraldic or literary studies but for the furore surrounding a single incident in the summer of 1907, which resulted in the abrupt termination of his career, his ignominious dismissal from office, and his death as an embittered recluse. The event has passed into history as the theft of the Irish crown jewels.

The 'crown jewels' comprised a jewelled star, a jewelled badge, and a partly jewelled gold and enamel badge of the Order of St Patrick, worn by the lord lieutenant of Ireland in his capacity as grand master of the order. Vicars was the official custodian of the jewels, which were kept in a safe in his office in Dublin Castle. On 6 July 1907 the crown jewels, five silver-gilt collars of the knights of St Patrick, and some personal family jewellery belonging to Vicars were discovered to be missing from their boxes in the safe, which showed no signs of being forced open. It was Vicars's misfortune that the theft occurred on the eve of a visit to Ireland by Edward VII, who had intended personally to invest a new knight of the order. The visit went ahead, but because of the theft of the knights' collars the investiture had to be cancelled. The king was furious and his anger did not diminish with the passing of time.

The event became a *cause célèbre* in Dublin, and attracted a number of rumours. The principal suspect was Francis Richard Shackleton (1876–1941), a member of Vicars's staff. Shackleton was a raffish and disreputable individual, who was acquainted with the duke of Argyll, husband of the king's sister, Princess Louise. Shackleton was on friendly terms with the duke's uncle, Lord Ronald Gower, and one unsubstantiated rumour alleged that Lord Ronald and his nephew were both involved in the theft. An undercurrent of gossip about the homosexuality of the protagonists added a *frisson* to the affair, and it was rumoured that the king was sufficiently alarmed to do everything possible to prevent any breath of scandal from touching his brother-in-law.

By 17 September 1907, with no sign of the jewels being recovered, the king was certain that Vicars should be removed from office. Although it was generally accepted that Vicars was not personally involved in the theft, it was probably perpetrated by a member of his staff, and as custodian of the jewels he was responsible. Furthermore, the safe in which the jewels were kept had been opened by a key and not by violence, and therefore Vicars must have been negligent in his care of the key. One of his contemporaries did remember him as 'a notoriously forgetful, casual sort of creature, nearly always late for his engagements' (H. Robinson, *Memories: Wise and Otherwise*, 1923, 221).

On 23 October Vicars was informed of his dismissal, but refused to go, and appealed for an official inquiry. The resulting viceregal commission, which met in January 1908, was a civil investigation into the conduct of Vicars as custodian of the jewels and not a criminal investigation into the theft. The commission based its judgment on the wording of the statutes of the Order of St Patrick, and concluded that Vicars did not exercise due vigilance or proper care as the custodian of the regalia. On 30 January 1908 he was informed that his appointment had been revoked.

The news came as a shattering blow to Vicars. He never accepted the possibility that he was in any way to blame for the theft, and his feeling of injustice lingered to the end of his life. He referred to his successor, Captain Nevile Wilkinson, as a 'usurper', and claimed that his career had been 'purposely shattered by a heartless government' (Bamford and Bankes, 187). In September 1911 he wrote: 'I was simply made a scapegoat … and Shackleton's wicked threats of a scandal (which were and are all bunkum and lies) were utilised to frighten the late King and make him hush it up' (ibid., 189).

The tragedy of Arthur Vicars was that he failed to understand the principal reason for his dismissal. He was not charged with theft of the jewels, but with dereliction of duty. Vicars was accused, not of being personally guilty, but of neglecting his ultimate responsibility for their safekeeping, and for that reason he was dismissed. He could see only that he was the victim of gross injustice. 'His privileged background and the good fortune of his early years probably nurtured Vicars' life-long and almost congenital capacity to ignore unpleasant and inconvenient facts' (Gaughan, 322). Angry and bitter, he went to live at Kilmorna House, 3 miles south-east of Listowel in co. Kerry, continuing to protest his innocence. In 1917 he married his old friend Gertrude Williford Wright (d. 1946), daughter of J. J. Wright MD of Campfield House, Malton, Yorkshire, and the move may have brought him some comfort in his last years. During the disturbances at the time of the partition of Ireland, the IRA had initiated a policy of burning the great country houses of Ireland. On 14 April 1921 Kilmorna House was surrounded by an armed group of men, who ordered the occupants to leave and then set fire to the house. Vicars was taken into the garden by three of the men and shot dead. Although the burning of houses was common, a shooting was rare; the reason was that he was said to be reporting local Sinn Féin activities to the security forces in Dublin and regularly entertained British troops whenever they were in the vicinity of Kilmorna.

The plaintive tone of Vicars's will demonstrated that his sense of grievance remained to the end:

> I might have had more to dispose of had it not been for the outrageous way in which I was treated by the Irish government over the loss of the Irish Crown Jewels in 1907, backed up by the late King Edward VII who I had always loyally and faithfully served, when I was made a scape goat … My whole life and work was ruined by this cruel misfortune and by the wickedly and blackguardly acts of the Irish government … I am unconscious of having done anyone wrong and my very misfortune arose from my being unsuspicious and trusting.   (Bamford and Bankes, 205)

Arthur Vicars was buried on 20 April 1921 in the churchyard of St Peter's Church, Leckhampton, near Cheltenham, Gloucestershire. Lady Vicars died at Clevedon, in Somerset, in 1946.   PETER GALLOWAY

Sources F. Bamford and V. Bankes, *Vicious circle* (1965) · P. Galloway, *The most illustrious order: the order of St Patrick and its knights* (1999) · *Kings, courts and society* (1930) · J. A. Gaughan, *Listowel and its vicinity*, 2nd edn (1974) · *The Times* (21 April 1921) · WWW · Burke, *Gen. Ire.* · b. cert.
Archives BL, corresp. and MSS relating to dismissal as Ulster king of arms, Add. MS 46065
Likenesses photograph, repro. in *Kings, courts and society* (1930), following p. 232

Vicars, Hedley Shafto Johnstone (1826–1855), army officer and evangelical, was born on 7 December 1826 in Mauritius, where his father, Richard Vicars (d. 1839), a captain in the Royal Engineers, was then stationed. After passing his examinations at the Royal Military Academy, Woolwich, he received a commission in the 97th regiment

on 22 December 1843, and in the following year proceeded to Corfu. On 6 November 1846 he obtained his lieutenancy. In 1848 his regiment was removed to Jamaica, and in 1851 to Canada. In November of that year he underwent an evangelical conversion which influenced the remainder of his life. He became a Sunday school teacher, visited the sick, and read the Bible and prayed with the men of his company, a most unusual proceeding at that time. In 1852 he became adjutant of his regiment. In May 1853 the regiment returned to England, and in August he resigned the adjutancy. He became a frequent attendant of meetings held at Exeter Hall, a centre of London evangelicalism, and an active member of the Soldiers' Friendly Society, besides holding frequent religious meetings with railway navvies. Before his regiment left England for the Crimea, early in 1854, it was reported that 'since Mr. Vicars became so good, he has steadied about four hundred men in the regiment'. At the Piraeus many men of the 97th died of cholera, and Vicars, while conducting the burial parties, took every opportunity of preaching to those at the graveside. On 3 November 1854 he was promoted to the rank of captain.

On 20 November 1854 Vicars landed in the Crimea, and, with his regiment, took part in the siege of Sevastopol. Here he continued his religious work, holding prayer meetings in his tent, visiting the sick in the hospitals, and carefully looking after his men. On the night of 22 March 1855, while he was in the trenches, the Russians made a sortie from Sevastopol, took the English by surprise, and drove them from their trenches. Vicars, keeping his men in hand, fired a volley into the enemy at twenty paces, and then, charging with the 97th, he drove the Russians back and regained possession of the trenches. He cut down two men with his own hand before he fell, bayoneted and shot through the right shoulder. He died shortly afterwards and was buried on the following day on the Vorontsov road, close to the milestone. In his dispatch on 6 April, Lord Raglan made special mention of Vicars's gallantry. Vicars became a posthumous hero, his deeds and his evangelicalism equally celebrated, notably in the best-seller by Catherine M. Marsh (published anonymously), *The Memorials of Captain Hedley Vicars* (1855). Evangelical meetings allowed Vicars to develop close relationships with private soldiers of a sort otherwise impossible in the class-stratified mid-Victorian army, and his example was for long an inspiration in the burgeoning military evangelical movement.   G. C. BOASE, rev. H. C. G. MATTHEW

Sources L. Taylor, *The story of Hedley Vicars* (1894) · H. V., *captain in H. M. 97th regiment* (1869) · *Walking with God before Sebastopol: reminiscences of the late Captain Vicars* (1855) · C. M. Marsh, *Memorials of Captain Hedley Vicars* (1856) · *Army List*
Likenesses portraits, repro. in Marsh, *Memorials of Captain Hedley Vicars* · portraits, repro. in Taylor, *Story of Hedley Vicars* · portraits, repro. in S. F. Harris, *Earnest young heroes* (1896)

Vicars, John (1580–1652), chronicler and poet, was probably born in London. Orphaned when young, he was brought up and educated on the charity of Christ's Hospital, London. As a penniless young man he was enabled by a stroke of providence (a lucky find, as he recalls in his will) to study for some time at Queen's College, Oxford, but not for long enough to graduate: he lamented that he was '(ah too soone) wained from the brests of my Sacred *Mother* the most famous University of Oxford'. He returned to Christ's Hospital as usher and remained there until old age, referring to himself as 'schoolmaster' in his will. He started writing translations, and his works show knowledge of Greek and Hebrew as well as of Latin. He published a translation of Virgil's *Aeneid* (1632). In his sixties when the civil war broke out, Vicars, a devout Calvinist and presbyterian, threw himself into the cause, heart and soul. His series of four chronicles, *Jehovah-Jireh, or, God in the Mount* (parts 1 and 2, 1644), *Gods Arke over-Topping the Waves* (1646), and *The Burning-Bush not Consumed* (1646), is an important source for historians. Although reluctant to concede any victories to the royalists, they provide many valuable details, being based on fresh eyewitness accounts; for example, he names his main informant for his account of the battle of Edgehill as Captain Nathaniel Fiennes, who fought in it. Vicars presents the parliamentarian commanders, particularly Sir Thomas Fairfax and the New Model Army, in a heroic light and stresses the role played by the tradesmen and apprentices of London. He compares Fairfax to Julius Caesar and praises his mercy after the battle of Marston Moor. He is scathing in his presentation of the royalists, and emphatic in asserting divine providence on the parliamentarian side. His description of the confusion caused by the wearing of a variety of colours on both sides belies popular anachronistic stereotypes. In *England's Worthies* (1647) Vicars wrote eulogies of Cromwell and the other parliamentary leaders.

Vicars's poems often comment on politics, for example, the Spanish match for Prince Charles and public jubilation when it failed. Despite believing, as Hill notes, that England was an elect nation (Vicars, *England's Hallelu-jah*, 1631), Vicars was essentially a militant protestant who wanted a confessional foreign policy. In *England's Remembrancer* (1641) he expressed solidarity with the Huguenots of La Rochelle, and advised Charles I to intervene on behalf of the protestants in the Thirty Years' War ('Thy royall Sisters poore Palatinate'). Apocalyptic beliefs, especially the papal Antichrist, abound in his works. His early translation in 1617 of Francis Herring's work as *Mischeefe's Mysterie*, recast in heroic couplets in 1641 as *The Quintessence of Cruelty*, is related to the apocalyptic comedies of Foxe and Dekker in its theology and its use of extended dialogue. Its allegory of the Whore of Rome spawning, with Pluto, a son, Treason, resembles Milton's allegory of Satan, Sin, and Death in book I of *Paradise Lost*. *The Quintessence of Cruelty* has a commendatory quatrain contributed by William Prynne, who addresses Vicars as 'his most affectionate, kind Friend'. It may have been Prynne's friendship which furthered Vicars's work as parliamentary propagandist.

Vicars married Jane, probably either Brackley or Stevens (his will refers to his 'most dearely beloved friend and brother Mr Thomas Birackley [sic]' and also to 'my most dearely beloved brother Mr Paul Stevens'). He had a son, John, who was ordained, and two daughters, Frances and

Hester. He died at Christ's Hospital on 12 April 1652, leaving bequests to it and to the poor of London and Witney in gratitude for the benevolence he felt he had received. He asked to be buried as near as possible to the school which had taken him in 'when my Father and mother forsooke me' and this was done. His gravestone in Christ Church Greyfriars was destroyed in the great fire of London.

JULIA GASPER

Sources will, PRO, PROB 11/221, sig. 66 · J. Vicars, 'Dedicatory epistle', in F. Herring, *Mischeefes mysterie, or, Treasons master-peece, the powder plot*, ed. and trans. J. Vicars (1617) · J. Vicars, 'Dedication', *England's hallelu-jah* (1631) · C. Hill, *The English Bible and the seventeenth-century revolution* (1993) · P. Christianson, *Reformers and Babylon: English apocalyptic visions from the Reformation to the eve of the civil war* (1978) · C. H. Firth, *Cromwell's army*, new edn (1992) · N. Smith, *Literature and revolution in England, 1640–1660* (1994) · *DNB*
Wealth at death bequests incl. £20 each to two daughters, 10s. to son, 20s. each to son's children, 20s. to the poor of Witney, 20s. to the poor of Christ Church parish, London, 10s. to former servant, 5s. to the maidservant of Christ's Hospital; residue, incl. seal and ring, to wife; excl. books bequeathed separately to friends and Christ's Hospital: will, 1652, PRO, PROB 11/221, sig. 66

Vicars, Thomas (1589–1638), theologian, was born and baptized in Carlisle, the eldest of the twelve children of William and Eve Vicars, and tells us he attended the school there. He matriculated from Queen's College, Oxford, on 19 June 1607; he graduated BA on 16 December 1611 and MA on 17 June 1615. He was elected chaplain on 7 July 1615 and fellow on 20 April 1616, and on 10 May 1622 was licensed to preach, receiving at the same time the degree of BD. In that year he married Anne, stepdaughter of a Carlisle man, George *Carleton (1557/8–1628), bishop of Llandaff, who on his translation to Chichester, also in 1622, presented Vicars to the vicarages of Cowfold and Cuckfield in Sussex. Carleton employed Vicars as his chaplain and in 1624 made him a prebendary of Chichester Cathedral. Vicars appears to have resided at Cuckfield, where the parish register records the baptism of five of his children; of these the only son, George, and the eldest girl, Anna (baptized on 26 July 1624), died before their first birthday.

In 1620 Vicars issued a translation from the Latin of Bartholomew Keckermann entitled *A Manuduction to Theologie*. The work was dedicated to the service and good of the church, to Lady Anne Neville (perhaps his wife's mother), and to 'The Lady Anne Fetiplace of Chilrey', Berkshire. In it he aimed 'to further the simplest of my countrymens growth in all godliness' (Fincham, 196). In 1624 he published *Astrologomania: the Madness of Astrologers*, addressed to his cousin Thomas Carleton of Carleton Hall in Cumberland, JP. The preface made clear his disbelief, 'whether it be a more artificial delusion, which satan worketh in the learned and great clerks of the world, or a more simple and gross kind of insinuation which he practiseth on the ruder and unlettered people', and cited a personal reason: during his school days at Carlisle, a 'cunning man' or 'wizard' visited the Vicars household while Thomas was entertaining a young schoolfriend. Having been persuaded to tell the fortunes of the two boys, he predicted that Thomas would become a scrivener and the other would be a preacher. 'Now it fell out, that my school fellow proved the scrivener, and I prove the preacher.' Vicars was buried at Cuckfield church on 29 August 1638.

STEPHEN WRIGHT

Sources W. Cooper, 'The parish of Cuckfield', *Sussex Archaeological Collections*, 45 (1902), 12–30 • W. Cooper, *History of the parish of Cuckfield* (1912) • K. Fincham, *Prelate as pastor: the episcopate of James I* (1990) • Wood, *Ath. Oxon.* • W. Renshaw, ed., *Registers of the parish of Cuckfield, Sussex, 1598–1699*, Sussex RS, 13 (1911) • *VCH Sussex*, vol. 2 • *Fasti Angl., 1541–1857*, [Chichester] • T. Vicars, *Astrologomania: the madness of astrologers* (1624)

Vicary, Thomas (*d.* 1561), surgeon, whose name is often written Vicars, Vikers, Vycars, and Vycary in contemporary records, was probably a native of Kent, and was a member of the Barbers' Company of London. In 1525 he was elected third warden. In 1528 he was upper warden, and in 1530 was elected master, to which annual office he was again elected in 1541, 1546, 1548, and 1557. His presence in London is, however, recorded as early as 1514, when he was licensed by the bishop of London to practise surgery within London and a 7 mile radius following the act of 3 Hen. VIII c. 11. At the same time he seems to have maintained a modest practice in Maidstone, and it was here in 1527, according to Clippingdale, that he successfully treated Henry VIII for a leg complaint, for which service he was appointed a royal surgeon at an annual salary of £20, his quarterly payment appearing for the first time at Christmas 1528. He married the sister of Thomas Dunkyn, a yeoman of St Leonard, Shoreditch; they had one son, William, who was admitted to the freedom of the company on 26 June 1547.

In 1530 Vicary obtained a promise of the reversion of the office of sergeant-surgeon to the king; he succeeded in 1536 and held the office, then worth £26 13s. 4d. a year, until his death. Further evidence of royal favour is shown in Holbein's painting of the king with members of the new Company of Barber–Surgeons of London, established by act of parliament in 1540, in which Vicary is depicted as receiving royal authority on behalf of the company in the form of a charter. He was probably active in securing new powers for the company under this act, among them the right to the bodies of four hanged felons yearly for dissection at quarterly anatomical lectures; he and other surgeon members of the company were certainly insistent on claiming the first body from Tyburn before the mayor's court in December of that year.

In 1546, on the grant of Henry VIII's second charter to St Bartholomew's Hospital, the city undertook the hospital's refitting, and Vicary was, on 29 September 1548, appointed a governor, and was reappointed each year until June 1552, when he was made 'one of the assistants of this house for the terme of his life' (minute book). On 2 October 1554 it was ordered that he should have the oversight of all such officers as be within the hospital, in the absence of the governors. He lived in the hospital, where his house was kept in repair by the governors, and he received an annual grant of livery of 'fyne newe collour' of 4 yards, at 12s. a yard. He was superior to William Cartar, Thomas Bailey, and George Vaughan, the first surgeons;

and his friendly relations with the two who survived him are shown by his bequest to Bailey of a gown of brown blue lined and faced with black budge, a cassock of black satin, his best plaister-box, a silver salvatory box, and all his silver instruments, and to George Vaughan of a doublet of crimson satin.

Vicary continued sergeant-surgeon to Edward VI and Elizabeth, and in 1554 he was appointed surgeon to Philip. In 1539 he had been granted a lease for twenty-one years of parts of the dissolved abbey of Boxley in Kent, the lands of which had been given to Sir Thomas Wyatt, and in 1542 he, with his son William, was appointed bailiff of the manor of Boxley, and received a regrant of the office from Philip and Mary in 1555. He bought a house and land in the same district.

In December 1547 Vicary married Alice Bucke of London, who survived him. He made his will on 27 January 1561 in St Bartholomew's Hospital, two days after treating Sir William Petre at Ingatestone Hall in Essex, and died at the end of that year. His will was proved on 7 April 1562. Besides bequests to his family and friends he left 1s. each to forty poor householders living within the hospital walls, and 10s. each to the chaplain, matron, steward, cook, and porter of St Bartholomew's. He alludes to his possession of the *Surgery* of Guido and of Vigo, and of other books, but mentions no work by himself. However *A Profitable Treatise of the Anatomie of Man's Body*, of which the earliest extant edition is of 1577, is stated on the title-page to have been compiled by him. It is dedicated to Sir Rouland Haiwarde, the president, and the governors, by William Clowes, William Beton, Richard Story, and Edward Bayly, surgeons to the hospital. The book was examined by Dr J. F. Payne (*BMJ*, 25 Jan 1896) and later by Sir Clement Price Thomas, among others, and is clearly an abbreviated version of a late fourteenth-century manuscript in English, which is itself based upon Lanfranc and Henri de Mondeville, with a few short additional passages. Its anatomy therefore belongs to the classical world of Galen and does not reflect the new ideas of writers such as Vesalius, which Vicary himself may have rejected. *A Profitable Treatise* was, however, the first anatomical textbook in English and could have been published both in memory of Vicary and for practical use by apprentices, few of whom knew Latin at that time. In many ways an obscure figure, Vicary is nevertheless an important one. Five times master of his company, a number never exceeded, and in 1555 its financial saviour by paying its debts, he brought stability to the practice of surgery in London and thus ensured the company's later eminence in the development of British surgery as a whole. The Thomas Vicary lecture has been delivered annually at the Royal College of Surgeons since 1919.

NORMAN MOORE, rev. I. G. MURRAY

Sources F. J. Furnivall and P. Furnivall, eds., *The anatomy of the body of man … with a life of Vicary*, EETS (1888) • S. Young, *The annals of the Barber–Surgeons of London: compiled from their records and other sources* (1890) • N. Moore, *The history of St Bartholomew's Hospital*, 2 vols. (1918) • N. Moore, 'Physicians and surgeons of St Bartholomew's Hospital before the time of Harvey', *St Bartholomew's Hospital Reports*, 18 (1882), 333–58 • C. P. Thomas, 'Vicary amongst his contemporaries', *Annals of the Royal College of Surgeons of England*, 30

(1962), 137–54 • G. G. Macdonald, 'General medical practice in the time of Thomas Vicary', *Annals of the Royal College of Surgeons of England*, 40 (1967), 3–21 • W. Clippingdale, medical court roll, 1922, RCS Eng. • R. R. James, 'The earliest list of surgeons to be licensed by the bishop of London', *Janus*, 41 (1937), 255–60 • G. Clark and A. M. Cooke, *A history of the Royal College of Physicians of London*, 1 (1964) • minute books, St Bartholomew's Hospital Archives • Court minutes and Freedom registers, Barbers' Company Archives • T. Tanner, *Notitia monastica, or, A short history of the religious houses in England and Wales* (1695)

Likenesses H. Holbein the younger, group portrait, cartoon, 1540–43, RCS Eng. • H. Holbein the younger, group portrait, oils, c.1541 (*Henry VIII and the barber surgeons*), Worshipful Company of Barbers, Barber-Surgeons Hall, Monkwell Square, London

Wealth at death approx. £200 in money as legacies; much valuable clothing; substantial value in Boxley estate

Viccars, John (*bap.* 1604, *d.* 1653?), orientalist, was baptized on 30 October 1604 at Treswell, Nottinghamshire, the second of four children of Gregory Viccars (*d.* after 1612), yeoman. He entered as pensioner at Christ's College, Cambridge, in July 1618, graduating BA in 1622. He was incorporated at Lincoln College, Oxford, on 24 February 1625 and proceeded MA on 28 March. By 1627 he was rector of St Mary's, Stamford, Lincolnshire, where he earned the enmity of some parishioners who in 1628 denounced him as a heretic. This led to his trial before Bishop Laud and others at the court of high commission in November 1631. He was convicted of keeping conventicles and of heresy and was sentenced to be removed from office, defrocked, and fined £100. Viccars spent several years in prison after, and possibly before, this trial, but in November 1635, after submitting and recanting, he was through the good graces of Laud restored to the ministry (though forbidden to serve at Stamford) and was forgiven the fine.

Soon after this Viccars embarked on extended scholarly travels in France and Italy. He examined manuscripts in Paris, Rome, Florence, Venice, and other Italian cities, and he consulted scholars such as Athanasius Kircher in Rome and learned Jews at Venice, Leghorn, Bologna, and elsewhere. The result of this was Viccars's sole publication, *Decapla in psalmos*, completed in 1638 and published in London in 1639, an erudite and voluminous commentary on all 150 psalms using ancient, medieval, and modern versions in ten different languages, including Hebrew, Syriac, and Arabic. Much of the commentary is extracted from rabbinical authors, but under the heading 'alius auctor' ('another author') Viccars provides his own remarks, which include, besides extensive classical quotations, sidelights on his travels with descriptions of monuments and eyewitness accounts of Vesuvius, the Alps, and other natural marvels. The book cost John and his younger brother Samuel much money for Syriac and Arabic types specially cast (the latter only the second Arabic font produced in England) and a fine engraving by Wenceslas Hollar for the title-page. *Decapla in psalmos* was dedicated to Laud and it was presumably as a reward that Viccars was presented to the rectory of South Fambridge, Essex, on 30 May 1640. However, his conversion to Laudian orthodoxy was soon overtaken by the civil war: among the accusations made against him before the Essex county

committee on 16 April 1644 was that he was a Roman priest, because he had been at Rome. He was sequestered and he perhaps never again held a benefice, for it is not certain whether the John Viccars who was instituted as rector of Battlesden, Bedfordshire, 5 May 1645, is the same man.

Viccars may have been living in London in 1652 when he was named by Brian Walton in the prospectus for the polyglot Bible as one of those to be employed in preparing the copies. However, it is likely that he died soon afterwards for there is no trace of his participation in the published work, which was issued between 1653 and 1657. The 'second edition' of *Decapla in psalmos* (1655) is simply the sheets of the 1639 edition reissued by a new publisher, omitting the dedication to Laud, and it may well be posthumous. Viccars was certainly dead by 1660 when a successor to him was appointed at South Fambridge. He seems never to have married, but through the two marriages of his elder sister, Helen, the second to the nonconformist minister Obadiah Grew, he became uncle to the physician Henry Sampson and the scientist Nehemiah Grew.

G. J. TOOMER

Sources J. Viccars, *Decapla in psalmos* (1639) • S. R. Gardiner, *Reports of cases in the courts of star chamber and high commission*, CS, 39 (1886), 198–238 • PRO, SP 16/203, fols. 39–42 • PRO, SP 16/261, fols. 1, 5, 15, 35, 71, 77, 142, 175, 183, 209, 295 • PRO, SP 62/119, fols. 69–75 • Wood, *Ath. Oxon.*, new edn, 2.657 • *Walker rev.*, 166 • J. Peile, *Biographical register of Christ's College, 1505–1905, and of the earlier foundation, God's House, 1448–1505*, ed. [J. A. Venn], 1 (1910), 324 • parish register, Treswell, 30 Oct 1604 [baptism] • G. J. Toomer, *Eastern wisedome and learning: the study of Arabic in seventeenth-century England* (1996), 75–7, 207–8 • H. J. Todd, *Memoirs of Brian Walton* (1821), 49 • BL, Add. MS Sloane 5829, fol. 83r • BL, Add. MS 15669, fol. 158v • BL, Add. MS 15670, fol. 137r • F. H. Blaydes, ed., *Bedfordshire Notes and Queries*, 2 (1889), 197 • Venn, *Alum. Cant.*, 1/3.301 • T. W. Davids, *Annals of evangelical nonconformity in Essex* (1863), 230 • *Thoroton's history of Nottinghamshire*, ed. J. Throsby, 2nd edn, 3 vols. (1790–96), vol. 3, p. 268 • H. Smith, *The ecclesiastical history of Essex under the Long Parliament and Commonwealth* [1933], 115 • W. A. Shaw, *A history of the English church during the civil wars and under the Commonwealth, 1640–1660*, 2 (1900), 379 • R. Newcourt, *Repertorium ecclesiasticum parochiale Londinense*, 2 (1710), 254

Vicious, Sid [*real name* Simon John Beverley; *formerly* Simon John Ritchie] (**1957–1979**), rock musician, was born on 10 May 1957 at Lewisham Hospital, London, the only child of John George Ritchie, a publisher's representative, and his wife, Anne Jeannette, *née* McDonald. His parents divorced, and his mother then married Chris Beverley; after the death of her second husband Anne retained his surname, as did her son.

Simon Beverley's childhood was dominated by frequent house moves around London, prompted by his mother's unstable personality. Poverty was a constant problem, but adversity strengthened their relationship. Acquaintances likened them to co-conspirators rather than parent and child. By his teenage years Simon was borrowing his mother's syringe to take amphetamine sulphate ('speed'). His heavily disrupted secondary education ended at a special-needs school in Stoke Newington when he was fifteen. A job in a textile factory followed, before he enrolled at Hackney technical college in 1973 to take a course in

Sid Vicious (1957–1979), by Ebet Roberts

photography. He was a fan of David Bowie, whom he emulated by dressing in an outlandish manner. The look drew him closer to his fellow student and old school friend John Lydon, and they lived together in various squats in London. The nickname Sid originated from this time, in homage to Lydon's pet hamster. Money was scarce, prompting Beverley to dabble in prostitution as a rent boy.

In 1976 Beverley became a leading figure in the punk rock scene that developed in London under the influence of Malcolm McLaren, proprietor of the clothes shop Sex in the King's Road, Chelsea. The pre-eminent punk band was the Sex Pistols, formed by McLaren in 1975 from customers of his shop; Lydon—renamed Johnny Rotten—was the group's lead singer. Punk music was basically structured and roughly produced, with lyrics detailing society's ills (rather than the traditional theme of love) and sung in an angry, shouting manner. Unable to play any musical instruments, Beverley became the group's most notorious fan and invented the 'pogo' dance—so-called because it involved jumping up and down. Encouraged by McLaren's desire for publicity, he called himself Sid Vicious and lived up to the name. At a Sex Pistols show in April 1976 he attacked a music journalist with a bicycle chain. In September he threw a glass during a concert and injured several people. He was subsequently found guilty of possessing an illegal weapon (a knife) and sentenced to a short spell at Ashford remand centre.

Sid Vicious's lasting imprisonment, however, was his new name: the naïve, fashion-obsessed teenager had assumed a new identity. The image consisted of spiked black hair, a snarling upper lip, and torn clothes held together by safety pins and 'bondage' straps. He also wore swastika T-shirts and armbands. The context for this deployment of Nazi insignia was mounting racial tension in Britain, exacerbated by rising unemployment. Vicious, however, was apathetic about politics: his aim was simply to shock. He was led by the clothes available in McLaren's shop, which in turn had been influenced by the popularity of the film *Cabaret* (1972). The film's depiction of Weimar decadence seemed apposite to disaffected youth during Britain's own crisis of governability in the mid-1970s. This *Zeitgeist* was subsequently captured by the Sex Pistols' first single, 'Anarchy in the UK', released in November 1976.

Punk's do-it-yourself ethic and contempt for traditional notions of musicianship encouraged Vicious to try to learn bass guitar. He played along to the first album by the Ramones but found even their three-chord structures difficult to master. His stage début was as a drummer for Suzie (later Siouxsie) and the Banshees on 20 September 1976. The performance consisted of a twenty-minute version of the Lord's prayer; they had rehearsed only once, as the intention was to make as horrible a racket as possible. That autumn he practised with a pool of punk musicians calling themselves the Flowers of Romance. He also tried writing lyrics. The results were either doom-laden or simply offensive—as in 'Belsen was a gas'.

In February 1977 a split occurred between the main songwriters in the Sex Pistols. Rotten, the lyricist, disliked the melodic inclinations of the bass guitarist, Glen Matlock, and so replaced him with Sid Vicious. During the course of the next year Vicious lived out punk's nihilistic inner core to the full but the band's output of new songs dried up; subsequent releases had mainly been written and recorded during the Matlock era. With pop stardom came groupies. Vicious was pursued by Nancy Spungen (1958–1978), daughter of a Philadelphia businessman, who came to Britain in early 1977. The two became inseparable, in large part because she introduced him to heroin. The relationship alienated Vicious from the other members of the band. None of them visited him when he was in hospital with hepatitis in April and May of that year.

The peak of the Sex Pistols' notoriety came in June 1977 with the release of 'God Save the Queen', timed to coincide with Elizabeth II's silver jubilee. Originally entitled 'No future' (after its refrain), the song equated deference to Britain's ruling institutions with being moronic. It reached number two in the charts and would have been number one but for the machinations of an embarrassed music industry. A chart-topping album, *Never Mind the Bollocks, Here's the Sex Pistols*, came out in October. Vicious helped to write two of the album's twelve tracks ('Holidays in the sun' and 'Bodies') but his rudimentary bass contributions were overdubbed by other members of the band. Nevertheless, his surly swagger in film footage from jubilee week helped define the group—and that summer—for posterity.

The band's notoriety made it difficult for them to play live dates, but Vicious relished the attention when they did (even though his guitar was usually unplugged from the amplifiers). Off stage his heroin addiction made him increasingly difficult to handle; it also made him a liability when the band toured America in January 1978. During shows he gashed himself to draw blood and in Texas he clubbed a member of the audience with his instrument, nearly causing a riot. At the end of the tour (17 January) Rotten left the band and Vicious became the Sex Pistols' front man. McLaren, meanwhile, was preoccupied with documenting the creation of the band on celluloid. The fictionalized account, *The Great Rock 'n' Roll Swindle*, was filmed mainly in 1978. Vicious sang three cover songs, Eddie Cochran's 'Something else' and 'C'mon everybody', plus Sinatra's 'My way' (a top ten single in June 1978). He also resurrected his own compositions.

Heroin abuse, meanwhile, began to take its toll. In August 1978 Vicious was jolted when a friend died of an overdose while sharing a bed with himself and Spungen—it was hours before they realized that he was dead. A month later the pair flew to New York to make a fresh start. They stayed at the Chelsea Hotel on West 23rd Street, a renowned residence for artists. To earn money, Vicious performed at local venues. On the morning of 11 October he woke to find Spungen dead in the bathroom with a knife wound to the stomach. He was arrested and, while in a confused state, admitted to stabbing her. Bail of $50,000 was put up by his record label on the 17th, allowing for his release. On 22 October he was admitted to Bellevue Hospital after a suicide attempt. After being discharged a few days later, he acquired a new girlfriend, Michelle Robinson. A nightclub fight in December resulted in his returning to custody until 1 February 1979. His mother flew to America on his release and they stayed the night with Robinson at her Greenwich Village apartment. In the early hours of 2 February, while the others were sleeping, Vicious took some heroin from his mother's purse and injected himself with what proved to be a lethal dose. He was cremated in New York on 7 February. His mother later scattered the ashes over Spungen's grave at the King David cemetery in Bensalem, Philadelphia.

Sid Vicious's death at twenty-one was worldwide news and instantly elevated him to the 'live fast, die young' hall of fame. Iconic status was ensured. At the Sex Pistols' peak, elements of the establishment regarded the band as a treasonous threat—best seen in Julian Temple's documentary film *The Filth and the Fury* (2000). But even then Vicious's contribution owed more to the fantasy of rock martyrdom than to any serious questioning of society's values. His drawn-out drug-induced demise turned punk rebellion into a revolt against the self. By 1979 punk was just another product and his death prompted one last surge of hype. The soundtrack to the *Swindle* film was rush-released that same month, though its cinema opening did not occur until May 1980. A single, 'Something else', came out at the end of February and sold nearly twice as many copies as 'God Save the Queen', but when the record company released the live album *Sid Sings* in December, few bought it. Vicious's obsessive relationship with Spungen proved a more enduring story and was the subject of the feature film *Sid and Nancy* (1986).

MICHAEL T. THORNHILL

Sources J. Savage, *England's dreaming* (2001) · J. Lydon, *Rotten: no Irish, no blacks, no dogs: the authorized autobiography of Johnny Rotten of the Sex Pistols* (1995) · G. Matlock, *I was a teenage Sex Pistol* (1990) · J. Temple, director, *The filth and the fury: a Sex Pistols film*, 2000 [film] · M. Gray, *The Clash: the return of the last gang in town* (2000) · A. Parker and K. Bateson, *Sid's way: the life and death of Sid Vicious* (1991) · G. Cole, *Sid and Nancy* (1986) · D. Dalton, *El Sid* (1998) · b. cert.
Archives FILM BFI NFTVA, *Arena*, 'Punk and the Pistols', BBC2, 20 Aug 1995 · BFI NFTVA, news footage · *The filth and the fury: a Sex Pistols film*, dir. J. Temple (2000) | SOUND BL NSA, interview recordings · BL NSA, performance recordings
Likenesses P. Kodick, print, 1977, NPG · photographs, c.1977–1978, Hult. Arch. · E. Roberts, photograph, Redferns Music Picture Library [*see illus.*] · photographs, repro. in A. Beverley, *The Sid Vicious family album* (1980)

Vick, Sir (Francis) Arthur (1911–1998), scientist and university administrator, was born on 5 June 1911 at Oakland, Fox Hollies Road, Acocks Green, Warwickshire, the son of Wallace Devonport Vick (*d.* 1952), toolmaker, and Clara, *née* Taylor (*d.* 1932). His father was employed in the manufacturing industries of the west midlands. Vick's education at Waverley grammar school in Birmingham gained him entry to the University of Birmingham, where he graduated in physics with honours in 1932; his mother, whose health had generally been poor, died the same year. Vick then embarked upon a research project in solid state physics, being awarded a Birmingham PhD in 1936 for his thesis, 'Absorbed layers of oxygen on tungsten and their effect on thermionic emission'.

Vick's employment began with an appointment in 1936 to University College, London, as an assistant lecturer in physics, in 1939 raised to lecturer grade. At the start of the Second World War in 1939 he was seconded into the Ministry of Supply as a research scientist; there he worked alongside many others who were to become famous in that crucial period when science served defence, among them Sir John Cockroft, who became the leader of the British atomic bomb team and the founding director of the Atomic Energy Research Establishment (AERE) at Harwell. Official reports show that the scope of Vick's wartime research included fuses for explosive devices, optical devices for photographing fast projectiles, illumination and visibility at night, and the motion of waves in shallow water. The ministry, evidently recognizing that organizational gift upon which his later reputation grew, appointed him an assistant director of research in charge of general physics. Another significant pointer was a paper he wrote in 1945 proposing the creation of an army physical laboratory, though this was not enacted. He was appointed OBE in 1945 for his wartime contribution in science to national defence.

On 11 October 1943 Vick married Elizabeth Dorothy

Story (1912–1989), whom he had met as a colleague at University College, London, in the 1930s and who at the time of their marriage also worked at the Ministry of Supply. Throughout their marriage she shared her husband's interest in the sciences and the arts. They had one daughter, Christine (b. 1950), who followed a scientific career with a PhD in botany from Liverpool University. Towards the end of the war, in 1944 Vick began a return to academic life as a part-time lecturer in the physics department at Manchester University; he became full-time in 1946 and was upgraded in 1947 to senior lecturer. The university's records show that in addition to his activities within physics, which included research into the solid state of matter, he was active in the broader academic life, interested in the arts and in taking a lead in reforming the teaching of physics nationally. Scientific publications based upon his research included 'Thermionic emission from oxide-coated cathodes' (*Nature*, 160, 1947) and 'Semiconductors and their applications' (*Nature*, 162, 1948).

Those who knew Vick to be an educational innovator were not surprised when he left Manchester in 1950 to become the vice-principal of the newly created University College of North Staffordshire at Keele. Here he assumed the office of acting principal for a year after the death of the principal, Lord Lindsay. The college was questioning the specialization of the conventional three-year honours degree and was the first to introduce a four-year course with a broader curriculum. Vick played a leading role in planning this major academic development. His connection with Sir John Cockroft was evident in 1953 when Cockroft opened new physics laboratories for the college. The success of the educational experiment was recognized nationally by the granting of full university status as Keele University in 1962.

However, it seems that the attraction of government research laboratories, where many of his friends and colleagues of the wartime years were now employed, became irresistible. In 1959 Vick was appointed deputy director of AERE Harwell, by then one of the world's leading research establishments. In 1960 he became director, an office he held until 1966. Those years signalled a transition for Harwell partly because of Vick's vision of postgraduate research institutes based within it and partly because the data from basic research for the nuclear electricity industry were becoming sufficient to meet the needs of the development engineers. Vick wanted to affiliate these institutes to the universities and thus utilize an expensively created national resource at Harwell for postgraduate education and research. This did happen eventually, but not in quite the way he had envisaged, maybe because some universities saw it as a threat to their ownership of an independent research function. But his ideas took root and Harwell later hived off several important activities into national laboratories on the adjacent site at Chilton effectively run by 'user' universities under the management of the research councils. That became the standard arrangement and access for university personnel to research facilities in astronomy, space, laser light, soft X-rays, and neutrons was maintained by those councils.

Harwell prospered under Vick's direction and a vitality of spirit among the staff was engendered by his own enthusiasm for winning knowledge through research. His interaction with the younger members of his staff was frequent, positive, and encouraging.

A man looking for a challenge in 1966 and skilled in diplomacy could hardly have done more than move into a vice-chancellorship, but Vick went to the limit by accepting this office at Queen's University of Belfast. By all accounts he was a brilliant vice-chancellor who managed to cope with the student radicalism that characterized all universities in the late 1960s; but in Belfast he did so in an explosive civil environment. He was greatly admired for being able to stay calm and logical and to keep sectarian violence off his campus. He was knighted in 1973 for his services to Northern Ireland and retired from Queen's in 1976 at the age of sixty-five.

As the university system expanded the population of graduates so did the voters' interest expand in its value and its cost. The relationship between vice-chancellors and the government became a hot zone of politics. Vick was a greatly respected figure on all sides and played a vital role in keeping the confidence of government officials in science and the universities. The list of influential committees on which he served is long; of special significance were his membership of the UK Atomic Energy Authority in 1964–6 and of the University Grants Committee in 1959–66, and his chairmanship of the Committee of Vice-Chancellors and Principals in 1971–2.

In 1976 Vick's role in universities transformed from leadership to governance as he became chairman of the council for Warwick University—a position he retained until 1990, though continuing in the office of pro-chancellor until 1992. During those sixteen years his wisdom helped Warwick to pre-eminence among the new universities of the 1960s, institutions in the creation of which he had had a major hand during his membership of the University Grants Committee thirty years earlier. It seems that he was somehow involved whenever bold innovative moves in government science and university education were afoot during his most creative half-century. His inspiring beliefs were in providing an education for all that was balanced in the arts and sciences and in enabling colleagues to develop their talents to the full. Sir Arthur died at his home, Fieldhead Cottage, Fieldhead Lane, Myton Road, Warwick, on 2 September 1998.

MICHAEL THOMPSON

Sources papers, 1987–98, U. Warwick Mod. RC, Sir Francis Arthur Vick papers · private information (2004) [Christine Vick, daughter] · b. cert. · m. cert. · d. cert. · *Debrett's People of today* (1998) · *The Independent* (17 Sept 1998)
Archives U. Warwick Mod. RC, corresp. and papers
Likenesses portrait, repro. in *The Independent*
Wealth at death £1,058,037—gross; £1,054,777—net: probate, 23 Dec 1998, *CGPLA Eng. & Wales*

Vickers, Albert (1838–1919). *See under* Vickers, Thomas Edward (1833–1915).

Vickers, Alfred (1786–1868). *See under* Vickers, Alfred Gomersal (1810–1837).

Vickers, Alfred Gomersal (1810–1837), marine painter, was born at Lambeth, London, on 21 April 1810 and baptized on 20 November 1811 at St Mary, Lambeth, the son of **Alfred Vickers** (1786–1868), landscape painter, and his wife, Mary Agnes. Born at St Mary, Newington, London, on 10 September 1786, Vickers senior exhibited numerous pictures of English scenery at the Royal Academy, from 1828 to 1868, as well as at the British Institution, and the Suffolk Street Gallery. He died on 20 November 1868. He is now best known for his river scenes, an example of which is in the Victoria and Albert Museum. The work of the father and son is often confused.

The son, Alfred Gomersal Vickers, who received instruction in art from his father, exhibited paintings in both oil and watercolours at the same galleries and at the New Society of Painters in Water Colours from 1827 until his death. He painted marine subjects, architecture, and figures. On 20 April 1833 he married Mary Liverseege. In the same year he was commissioned by Charles Heath to make sketches in Russia for publication. Steel-engravings from these and from many of his marine pieces appeared in the annuals (1835–7). His work indicates that Vickers used the opportunity of the commission to travel widely in Europe. Sketches of Turkish and Italian scenes are recorded, in addition to views of Poland, Germany, France, and the Low Countries. His talent, which surpassed that of his father, was beginning to obtain public recognition when he died on 12 January 1837 at his home, 20 Cumming Street, Pentonville, London. His pictures were sold at Christies on 16 February in the same year. Pencil and watercolour drawings by Vickers are in the Victoria and Albert Museum and the department of prints and drawings at the British Museum, London; the Williamson Art Gallery, Birkenhead; Birmingham City Art Gallery; the Fitzwilliam Museum, Cambridge; New Port Art Gallery; and York City Art Gallery.

CAMPBELL DODGSON, *rev.* PAUL A. COX

Sources Graves, *Artists* · Graves, *Brit. Inst.* · Graves, *RA exhibitors* · J. Johnson, ed., *Works exhibited at the Royal Society of British Artists, 1824–1893, and the New English Art Club, 1888–1917*, 2 vols. (1975) · Redgrave, *Artists* · Mallalieu, *Watercolour artists*, 2nd edn, vol. 1 · L. Lambourne and J. Hamilton, eds., *British watercolours in the Victoria and Albert Museum* (1980) · L. Binyon, *Catalogue of drawings by British artists and artists of foreign origin working in Great Britain*, 4 vols. (1898–1907) · *CGPLA Eng. & Wales* (1869) · IGI

Wealth at death under £100—Alfred Vickers: probate, 25 Feb 1869, *CGPLA Eng. & Wales*

Vickers, Sir (Charles) Geoffrey (1894–1982), lawyer and social theorist, was born on 13 October 1894 in Nottingham, the youngest child in the family of two sons and a daughter of Charles Henry Vickers, a lace maker, and his wife, Jessie Lomas. Educated at Oundle School, he gained an exhibition at Merton College, Oxford, and went there to study classics in 1913. When war came a year later he volunteered for service in the army, being gazetted as a second lieutenant in the Sherwood Foresters (7th Robin Hood battalion). He was soon engaged in battle in Flanders and on his twenty-first birthday in 1915 found himself the sole defender of a barricade under heavy attack. In this

Sir (Charles) Geoffrey Vickers (1894–1982), by Godfrey Argent, 1968

engagement he showed outstanding courage, for which he was awarded the VC.

The wounds incurred on this occasion consigned Vickers to hospital and convalescence for nearly a year. He then returned to France and was again in action in 1918, being awarded the Croix de Guerre. Leaving the army with the rank of major, he went back to Oxford for two terms and took a pass degree in French, European history, and law in 1919. After qualifying as a solicitor in 1923, he became a partner in the City firm of Slaughter and May in 1926, where he specialized in commercial finance, dealing often with its international ramifications. He enjoyed this work down to 1939 and was later to say that his career in law had been the one undoubted success in his life.

After the outbreak of the Second World War, Vickers joined his old regiment, but was quickly seconded to intelligence work. He went on a mission to South America and on his return in 1941 was put in charge of economic intelligence in the Ministry of Economic Warfare, later becoming deputy director-general. He remained on this work until the war ended and was knighted for his services in 1946. By then Vickers no longer wanted to return to private legal practice and welcomed the chance of joining the new National Coal Board as its legal adviser in late 1945, becoming board member in charge of personnel and training in 1948. His career as a public servant continued until retirement in 1955. Meanwhile he had become deeply involved in voluntary work in support of medical research, taking a close and informed interest in psychiatry and mental illness. He was an active chairman of the research committee of the Mental Health Research Fund from 1951 to 1967 and a member of the Medical Research Council between 1952 and 1960.

The years of retirement, which were to stretch over a quarter of a century, were in many respects the most absorbing of Vickers's life. It was then that he gained distinction as a writer on action and relationships in complex patterns of social organization—not that he was any stranger to writing. His literary impulses were always strong, being expressed early on in his First World War letters and unpublished diary as well as in plays and stories for children written in the 1920s, one of which, *The Secret of Tarbury Tor*, was published in 1925. He was also an indefatigable letter writer. Even before 1939 he had gained some reputation for his ideas on social and political questions and was from 1939 to 1942 a visiting fellow of Nuffield College, Oxford, then newly founded. But retirement gave him the chance to concentrate entirely on committing his ideas to paper. Between 1959 and 1980 eight books were published, five in Britain, three in North America. Posthumously two further books appeared, one of which he was still working on shortly before he died. Well over a hundred papers, articles, and lectures were also published, many of them in medical and psychiatric journals. Much of this material was later embodied in his books, most of which took shape in this way.

The problem which chiefly preoccupied Vickers was how individuals can best fulfil the requirements of social co-operation in conditions of accelerating economic and scientific change. He came to reject moral and economic individualism and argued that institutions are necessary conditions of satisfactory social co-existence. Influenced by Michael Polanyi he saw the achievement of an adequate understanding of institutions as an epistemological challenge: individuals have to grasp how their actions always involve the regulation of relationships with others, and this occurs only through the exercise of judgement. Consequently much of his work is devoted to the analysis of judgement in terms of what he called 'appreciative behaviour', the most notable contribution being made in *The Art of Judgement* (1965), a study of policy-making. Though appreciation and judgement express individual capacities, Vickers never saw the individual as isolated or sovereign, but rather as defined by the relationships he has. He believed that social institutions are best analysed in terms of systems and his published work, notably *Human Systems are Different* (1983), made far-reaching contributions to systems thinking in its applications to human society. These themes, refined, developed, and set within various organizational contexts, recur in all his mature works.

Yet in his later years Vickers was somewhat saddened by what he saw as a certain lack of interest in his ideas in Britain. His work was, however, taken up by the Open University Systems Group, where he became a regular contributor to seminars, and there were many psychologists and medical scientists who recognized his originality. In the USA and Canada his ideas were warmly received from the start and he became widely known through his frequent visits there. Among British social theorists Vickers was unusual in drawing extensively on those experimental sciences concerned with human behaviour, though he never regretted his own humanistic and historical education. The breadth of his reading and knowledge was remarkable, but his sensitivity to the English language enabled him to write about administrative behaviour and organizations with elegance and clarity, keeping footnotes to the minimum and always eschewing jargon. He

was that rare combination, a man of action who was also an original thinker.

In 1918 Vickers married Helen Tregoning, daughter of Arthur Henry Newton, a director of Winsor and Newton, makers of watercolour paints and brushes, of Bexhill, Sussex. A son and daughter were born in the early 1920s, but the marriage later broke down and was dissolved in 1934. In 1935 he married (Ethel) Ellen (d. 1972), daughter of Henry Richard B. Tweed, solicitor, of Laindon Frith, Billericay, Essex; they had one son. Active and full of intellectual curiosity to the end, Vickers died at Goring-on-Thames on 16 March 1982. As testimony to his abiding love of poetry a small volume of his poems, *Moods and Tenses*, was published privately in 1983.   NEVIL JOHNSON, *rev.*

Sources *The Times* (18 March 1982) · *The Times* (25 March 1982) · *The Times* (29 March 1982) · M. Blunden, 'Geoffrey Vickers: an intellectual journey', *The Vickers papers* (1984) · private information (1990) [Mrs R. B. Miller, daughter] · *CGPLA Eng. & Wales* (1982)
Archives King's Lond., Liddell Hart C., military diaries and corresp. [copies] · NRA, priv. coll., corresp. and papers | Bodl. Oxf., corresp. with Sir Alister Hardy
Likenesses G. Argent, photograph, 1968, NPG [*see illus.*]
Wealth at death £101,596: probate, 13 July 1982, *CGPLA Eng. & Wales*

Vickers, Joan Helen, Baroness Vickers (1907–1994), politician, was born in London on 3 June 1907, the eldest of three children of (Horace) Cecil Vickers (1882–1944), stockbroker, and his wife, Lilian Monro Lambert, *née* Grose (c.1881–1923). Her father, one of two senior partners in the London stock exchange firm Vickers da Costa, was Winston Churchill's stockbroker. She was educated at St Monica's College, Burgh Heath, Surrey, and at a finishing school in Paris. Her mother having died when she was a teenager, Joan was presented at court by Clementine Churchill. She was a brilliant equestrian and—riding side-saddle—performed with distinction both in England and Ireland; she came third in the women's section of the famous Dublin horse show. Meanwhile she trained as a Norland nurse, working at the Margaret Macdonald and Mary Middleton Hospital, Notting Hill, London. She seemed settled into the life of a glamorous, extrovert débutante, when suddenly she changed the course of her life. She did so under the influence of Winston Churchill. In August 1936 she went to see Churchill to ask his advice on how she could become a member of parliament. Churchill believed that women were not suited to be MPs but could serve a useful role in local government. He therefore wrote on her behalf to Sir George Hennessy, a vice-chairman of the Conservative Party with particular responsibility for local government affairs. 'She is a very clever young lady', ran Churchill's words; 'She is a brilliant horsewoman and an independent and attractive spinster. … She could pay her own expenses at a County Council election' (*The Times*, 25 May 1994). The following year, Vickers was elected as Conservative councillor for Norwood.

During the Second World War, Vickers served in the Red Cross and, towards its end (1944–5), in south-east Asia. For her assiduous work there she was appointed MBE. However, her desire to make a career in domestic politics

Joan Helen Vickers, Baroness Vickers (1907–1994), by Madame Yevonde, 1951–2

remained unsated, and at the war's end she returned to England to seek a Conservative parliamentary candidacy, ignoring Churchill's avuncular injunction that the House of Commons was not a suitable place for women. She gained the nomination for Poplar, but went down to defeat in the débâcle of the 1945 general election, whereupon she returned to Malaya, serving with the colonial service there until 1950.

In 1953 Vickers was chosen as the Conservative candidate for the supposedly safe Labour seat of Devonport, then held by one of the darlings of the Labour left, Michael Foot. Neither Foot nor her own party took her seriously. But, with that indomitable will that was to mark her whole political career, she campaigned incessantly, and emerged victorious from the 1955 election: Foot later observed that she was the only candidate he had ever known who had canvassed every household in a constituency. She was to hold the seat until 1974.

Vickers made an instant impact on the House of Commons. This was partly due to her appearance, but largely due to her expertise. She cut a striking figure: her hair was always blue-rinsed and she invariably wore a blue dress. These, she explained, were her tory colours. Later in life—as one of her relations observed—the blue rinse turned almost to purple. But what astonished the house most was her command of military argument. True, her constituency hosted a significant naval base, and she would be expected to pay lip service to its concerns. But she did much more. She became genuinely expert on all matters of defence policy. This astonished colleagues and political

enemies alike, not solely because she was a woman—though women in her day were not supposed to be capable of understanding military matters—but because, in appearance, she seemed to be the epitome of the strident and mindless Conservative matron. On one famous occasion, during the Nigerian civil war over Biafra, the normally affable tory chief whip, William Whitelaw, flung an ashtray at her during a meeting in his office; she moved her head and continued her discourse as she wanted to.

The word 'indomitable' could have been coined for Vickers. Even given her onerous parliamentary responsibilities she never—until towards the end of her life—neglected her social concerns, remaining active in the Red Cross and closely involved with charities working in south-east Asia: on one trip to Indonesia she even had a species of fish, hitherto thought to be extinct, named after her. She was also active in support of women's causes, serving, *inter alia*, as British representative on the United Nations Commission on the Status of Women. She was twice engaged, but never married. She was irrepressibly vivacious but invariably rejected her many suitors. She resisted the onset of old age, and once gave a series of prescriptions for avoiding its appearance. 'It is the whole body, not just the face that can keep one attractive … keep your feet in good order: this makes all the difference to the way you walk—your walk can often give away your age' (private information). To the end she retained a capacity to terrify ministers of the crown, not only with her knowledge of military matters but with her sheer spirit.

The end of Vickers's House of Commons career came at the general election of February 1974. The boundary commissioners had decreed that her constituency should be split, and she opted to stand for the section less likely to favour a Conservative candidate. She was defeated by David Owen. Later that year she was awarded a peerage. (She had already been made DBE in 1964.) 'It was a compensation', she said, 'a small compensation, but a compensation nonetheless' (*The Independent*, 25 May 1994). She continued to be active in politics in the House of Lords until nearly the end of her life. In 1982 she steered the Falklands Nationality Bill through the House of Lords, and the following year (after the Falklands War) she flew out at the invitation of the islanders, who accorded her a warm welcome. Latterly increasing frailty made it difficult for her to travel, and she retired to her father's cottage, the Manor House, East Chisenbury, near Pewsey, Wiltshire, where she died of bronchopneumonia on 23 May 1994. She left behind her a warm glow of affection and admiration for her achievements and her character. Although she never held ministerial office, she was widely recognized as one of the most formidable Conservative politicians of her age. She donated her body to medical research, and on 3 June 1997 her remains were buried in Enford churchyard, Wiltshire.   PATRICK COSGRAVE

Sources private MSS, priv. coll. [in the possession of Hugo Vickers] · *WWW*, 1991–5 · personal knowledge (2004) · private information (2004) [H. Vickers] · *The Times* (25 May 1994) · *The Independent* (25 May 1994) · M. Gilbert, *Churchill: a life* (1991)

Archives priv. coll., MSS | S O U N D BL NSA, Fawcett collection, 4 Feb 1991, C 468/006/01–02
Likenesses B. Ker-Seymer, photograph, 1930–39, repro. in *The Independent* · Madame Yevonde, photograph, 1951–2, NPG [*see illus.*] · photograph, 1968, repro. in *The Times* · photograph, 1986, repro. in *The Independent*
Wealth at death £482,918: probate, 9 Aug 1994, *CGPLA Eng. & Wales*

Vickers, Kenneth Hotham (1881–1958), historian and university administrator, was born on 22 May 1881 at Naburn, near York, where his father, the Revd Randall William Vickers, was then vicar. He was the youngest of a family of four, having a brother and two sisters. His mother, Emma Mary Davidson, was of Scottish descent. He was at school at Oundle until the age of fifteen, when, as a result of polio, he was left with a serious weakness in one arm and one leg. He faced this disability with great courage, to live a normal life full of activity. He had been a good cricketer at Oundle and retained a keen interest in the game. In spite of his leg he did much walking in Germany and eastern Europe. He spoke German well and liked the German people.

With the aid of private tuition Vickers gained an open scholarship in history at Exeter College, Oxford, matriculating in October 1900. Then, as later, he was a friendly, good-natured man who 'used to sing'. He just missed a first in the final history school (1904), but was twice *proxime accessit* for the Stanhope prize essay, college prizeman (1903), and *proxime accessit* for the Arnold prize (1906).

For three years (1905–8) Vickers was lecturer in history at University College, Bristol; he was also organizer and lecturer in London history for the London county council (1907–9), then tutor to the University of London joint committee for tutorial classes (1908–13). Extramural studies were developing rapidly and Vickers revealed himself as a teacher of great power and devotion. He attracted students to his voluntary classes and retained them year after year. He also gained experience in the organization of academic teaching, of great value to him later, and did much work for the Historical Association and similar bodies. He became a fellow of the Royal Historical Society in 1909. He married in 1911 Alice Margretha (d. 1948), youngest daughter of Dr Edward Crossman of Hambrook, Gloucestershire; they had two sons of whom one died in infancy.

During these years Vickers kept up his historical studies, publishing a biography of Humphrey, duke of Gloucester (1907), *England in the Later Middle Ages* (1913), and *A Short History of London* (1914). In 1913 he was elected professor of modern history in the University of Durham at Armstrong College, later the University of Newcastle. In 1922 he published volume 11 of the *Northumberland County History*.

In 1922 Vickers became principal of the University College of Southampton, and thereafter until his retirement in 1946 devoted himself to the task of developing the college to full university status. The provision of new buildings was a major need. When Vickers was appointed, the college consisted of two wings of brickwork united by a corridor with an arched roof, which he once described as its most notable architectural feature, and a number of wooden huts. The huts, which continued in use to some extent throughout Vickers's time, were a legacy of war, when the newly erected buildings, formally opened in June 1914, but not yet occupied, had been handed over for use as a hospital.

The new principal faced a heavy task: 'Throughout the twenty-four years during which I was responsible for the administration', Vickers wrote, 'there was no time when lack of money did not prove a serious obstacle.' The long succession of financial difficulties, the critical situations which arose, the appeals for money, only partially successful, and the timely aid of generous benefactors are set out in detail in the centenary history *The University of Southampton* (1962) by A. Temple Patterson.

Deficits of £2000 or £3000, mainly due to capital expenditure, in those days caused serious concern and even reduction of staff and equipment. As late as 1937, when a refectory and students' union building was planned at the modest cost of £10,000, the University Grants Committee undertook to make a grant of £8000 only on condition that the remaining £2000 was obtained from private donors. Vickers fought on and held fast to the principles he considered essential to a university. He stressed the importance of residence and of tutorial supervision of students and their self-government in many activities, and particularly strove to ensure that the academic body should have a large share in all matters of policy.

Much had been achieved by 1939. A new library of some distinction linked the two wings, science departments had been partly rehoused, and work had begun in some new and promising fields such as aeronautics. Halls of residence had been provided for men and women and further building was planned. Again the incidence of war suspended development and it was not until 1952, six years after Vickers retired, that his final aim was reached, when the University of Southampton was constituted by royal charter. In its rapid growth and expansion it retains much of Vickers's design, not least in its social and democratic quality. The university recognized its debt to him by conferring upon him an honorary LLD in 1953.

Vickers's career was characterized by a humane and liberal outlook owing much to deep religious conviction. In some autobiographical papers which he left, he recalled that the religious atmosphere of his home led him to fall naturally into accepting religion as the foundation of life and the guide to conduct. A churchman of high Anglican views, he was at the same time singularly free from bigotry or intolerance. 'In my opinion true Christianity teaches men to look at the other man's point of view and to feel that in the grace of God one has the power and the duty to practise charity in the true sense of the word'. This ideal, his devotion to his difficult task, his shrewdness of judgement, and his courage in the face of all obstacles and physical handicaps, enabled Vickers to carry his team with him through long years of effort, often of frustration and disappointment. 'He never allowed differences or controversy on policy to cut him off from his colleagues and always remained a genial member of the Senior Common Room' (*The Times*, 23 Sept 1958). Vickers died on 5 September 1958 at Southampton.

G. F. FORSEY, *rev.* MARK POTTLE

Sources *The Times* (6 Sept 1958) · *The Times* (23 Sept 1958) · personal knowledge (1971) · private information (1971) · *CGPLA Eng. & Wales* (1958)
Archives U. Southampton L., papers
Likenesses A. S. Hill, oils, 1971, U. Southampton L. · photograph, repro. in A. T. Patterson, *The University of Southampton* (1962), facing p. 143
Wealth at death £22,145 11s. 11d.: probate, 26 Nov 1958, *CGPLA Eng. & Wales*

Vickers, Thomas Edward [Tom] (1833–1915), steel maker and armaments manufacturer, was born on 9 July 1833 in Sheffield, the son of Edward Vickers (1804–1897) and his wife, Anne, *née* Naylor. His brother, **Albert Vickers** (1838–1919), was born on 16 September 1838, also in Sheffield. Their father was a miller who had launched the Vickers' steel-making dynasty in Sheffield in the 1820s; their mother was the daughter of a local steel maker. Tom attended Sheffield collegiate school and then received technical training in Germany, at Neuwied am Rhein; Albert was educated privately in Sheffield and then studied at Hameln an der Weser, Germany.

Tom (usually known as Colonel Tom because of his association with the local militia) had joined the business by the age of twenty-one. By then the family firm, known as Naylor Vickers, was one of the leading crucible steel makers in Sheffield, and Edward had firmly established the Vickers' name in the town's commercial and political life: he had served as the town's alderman and mayor, and was the first president of the Sheffield chamber of commerce. His sons did not maintain this involvement, but they were to take the family firm to new heights.

In 1860 Tom Vickers married Frances Mary Douglas (1841–1904), the only child of Joseph Douglas, a London surgeon; they had two sons and four daughters. For many years the family resided at Bolsover Hill, a large house on high ground to the north of Sheffield, where they lived a life of unostentatious luxury surrounded by eight servants. Later they moved to London, where Tom indulged his taste for ceramic art and frequented the leading chess clubs. In 1861 Albert Vickers married Helen Horton George (*d.* 1873) of Boston, Massachusetts; they had three children. After her death he married, in 1875, Edith Foster (*d.* 1909), daughter of John Foster of Maltby, near Sheffield; they had a son and two daughters.

Tom Vickers's arrival at Naylor Vickers coincided with a period of frenzied activity, as the firm shared in the heyday of the crucible steel trade. It rapidly outgrew its old site in Millsands and, beginning in 1863, under Vickers's direction, steel-making activity was transferred to the River Don works in the Brightside district of Sheffield. Utilizing German technology, he pioneered the manufacture of steel castings, still using the crucible process to produce cast-steel bells and railway wheels. The success of the business owed much to his leadership in the foundry, where he acquired a reputation as a tough individual who

Thomas Edward Vickers (1833–1915), by John Singer Sargent, *c.*1903

never knew when he was beaten. He was known to sleep at the works, when the occasion demanded. A series of patents dealing with the production of steel castings, particularly cast-steel tyres, and a paper read before the Institution of Mechanical Engineers in 1861, 'On the strength of steel containing different proportions of carbon', testified to his technical prowess. His innovations placed Naylor Vickers at the forefront of world steel making, and only German firms such as Krupp could compete in size or technology.

In 1867 the firm was incorporated as Vickers, Sons & Co. Ltd, with a capital of £155,000 split equally between the Vickers brothers and Ernst Benzon, their American agent, who became chairman until Tom Vickers succeeded him in 1873. The business then employed about a thousand men, ranking the firm third in Sheffield behind Charles Cammells and John Browns. By then Albert Vickers was also playing a significant part in the business. He had joined the firm in 1854, gaining experience in the American market, which he was to visit thirty-four times. The brothers complemented each other: Tom was the technologist, and Albert the salesman and strategist. Although equally autocratic by nature, Albert did not have Tom's technical knowledge, but was more daring and speculative, with the courage to back his business convictions. Handsome, commanding, having an easy way with customers, and familiar with other countries and their languages, 'Don Alberto', as he was sometimes known, was the perfect foil for his taciturn brother.

Vickers was rather slower to commit itself fully to the arms business than its rivals Browns, Cammells, and Firths. But by the late 1880s a fall in profits led to a marked shift towards the arms sector, which gathered pace towards 1900. In 1897 the Maxim Gun Company was acquired for £1.3 million, and in the same year the Naval Construction and Armaments Company was bought at the bargain price of £425,000. Four years later Vickers absorbed Wolseley cars, partly with an eye to manufacturing military vehicles. In 1902 Vickers again extended its empire to include a half-share in William Beardmore & Co., the Glasgow-based armour-plate and warship makers, and in 1906 a similar-sized holding in Whitehead & Co., the torpedo makers of Weymouth and Fiume, Croatia. After 1900 Vickers also developed an interest in submarine and aircraft manufacture and began creating foreign subsidiaries or holding companies in Spain, Italy, Japan, Russia, and Turkey. Vickers, Sons and Maxim, as it became known, was then in the unique position of being able not only to build a battleship but also to equip her with engines, fit her with armour, provide the necessary guns and shells, and, in fact, launch her from Barrow in Furness ready for immediate service. 'All this we can do without outside help', stated Tom Vickers (*Sheffield Daily Telegraph*, 20 Oct 1915). Significantly, by then the firm's head office had shifted to London. The brothers had turned the company into an integrated, though diverse, arms conglomerate, which vied with W. G. Armstrong as Britain's leading arsenal.

In 1909 Tom Vickers resigned as chairman, handing over to Albert, who held the post until 1918. By 1914 Vickers' issued share capital was almost £6 million, its workforce in the UK was 22,000, and its average annual profits since 1897 had been £589,391. Its growth continued unchecked during the First World War, when its products—battleships, naval guns, machine-guns, torpedoes, aircraft, and submarines—could be found in every theatre of war. By 1919 the company's £20 million issued capital meant that only Coats, Lever Brothers, and Imperial Tobacco surpassed it in capital size as a British industrial firm—though this was not entirely welcome to the old family members, who recognized that the company could no longer be under such close personal control. By the customary measures of business success, Tom and Albert Vickers had presided over a period of continuous growth; on the other hand, they might be criticized for becoming over-committed to armaments, which left Vickers with a legacy of problems which were to come home to roost when arms orders evaporated in the 1920s.

In his later years Tom Vickers was an aloof and patriarchal, though greatly respected, figure, who was used to deferential treatment from his shareholders, who

> soon came to realise that curiosity was a folly which could not be indulged in pleasantly while this man of iron occupied the chair. In time the enquiring shareholder became as extinct as the Dodo, and the annual meeting of Messrs Vickers was concentrated into a kind of lightning episode ... [of] four or five minutes.   (*Sheffield Daily Telegraph*, 20 Oct 1915)

The River Don works was his absorbing passion and he continued to visit it until only a few months before his death, when he was wheeled around it in a bath chair. His

technical achievements were recognized by the Howard Quinquennial prize from the Institution of Civil Engineers in 1907. Outside business, both Tom and Albert Vickers shunned publicity and disliked being photographed. Apart from chess, and a little shooting and fishing, Tom's only passion was drilling the Hallamshire volunteers, of which he was commanding officer from 1871 to 1899. A staunch Conservative, he also served as a magistrate, and as master cutler in 1872, and was created CB, civil division, in 1898. Albert's influence as armourer–statesman is evidenced by the award of several foreign decorations, such as the order of the Rising Sun in Japan.

Tom Vickers died at his home, 12 Stanhope Place, Hyde Park, London, on 19 October 1915 and was cremated at Golders Green, Middlesex. Albert Vickers died at Compton Place, Eastbourne, Sussex, on 12 July 1919 and was buried at Hascombe church, Surrey.

GEOFFREY TWEEDALE

Sources G. Tweedale, 'Vickers, Thomas Edward, and Vickers, Albert', *DBB* · G. Tweedale, *Giants of Sheffield steel* (1986) · G. Tweedale, *Sheffield steel and America: a century of commercial and technological interdependence, 1830–1930* (1987) · G. Tweedale, *Steel city: entrepreneurship, strategy, and technology in Sheffield, 1743–1993* (1995) · J. D. Scott, *Vickers: a history* (1962) · C. Trebilcock, *The Vickers brothers* (1977) · J. Hamilton, *The Misses Vickers: the centenary of the painting by John Singer Sargent* (1984) · *Sheffield Independent* (20 Oct 1915) · *Sheffield Independent* (14 July 1919) [Albert Vickers] · *Sheffield Daily Telegraph* (20 Oct 1915) · *Sheffield Daily Telegraph* (14 July 1919) [Albert Vickers] · d. cert. · *CGPLA Eng. & Wales* (1919) [Albert Vickers]

Archives CUL · Sheff. Arch. · Sheffield Central Library

Likenesses J. S. Sargent, oils, c.1903; Sothebys, New York, 11 March 1999, lot 93 [*see illus.*] · J. S. Sargent, double portrait, oils (Albert Vickers and his wife), Fine Arts Museum, San Francisco · photographs, presumed CUL; repro. in Tweedale, *Giants of Sheffield steel*

Wealth at death £117,347 13*s.* 3*d.*: probate, 19 Feb 1916, *CGPLA Eng. & Wales* · £886,584 19*s.* 6*d.*—Albert Vickers: probate, 9 Oct 1919, *CGPLA Eng. & Wales*

Vickery [Drysdale], **Alice** (1844–1929), physician and campaigner for women's rights, was baptized on 13 October 1844, the fifth child and second daughter of John Vickery (*d.* in or before 1871), of West Moor Farm, Swimbridge, Devon, and his wife, Frances Mary, *née* Leah (*d.* 1891). By 1851 the family had moved to Peckham, in London, where John Vickery followed the trade of piano maker and organ builder, leaving Alice Vickery behind at a local school.

By 1861 Alice Vickery had joined her family and was employed as a pupil teacher, probably at the secularist William Ellis endowed school in nearby Peckham Fields, Camberwell. In 1869 she began her quest for medical education at the Ladies' Medical College, a controversial establishment providing superior midwifery training for women. Here she met Charles Robert *Drysdale (1828/9–1907) [*see under* Drysdale, George], who became her companion and co-worker; both objected to the institution of marriage and they were never married. Alice Vickery gained her midwifery certificate in 1873, then registered with the British Pharmaceutical Society, which admitted women to courses and examinations, though not to membership. She is said to have been the first woman to pass the examination, probably after working as a dispenser, enabling her to describe herself as 'chemist and druggist'.

Since no British medical schools admitted women, Vickery went to France in 1873 to study medicine at the University of Paris. Her first son, Charles Vickery *Drysdale, was born in Paris in 1874. Although Vickery became proficient in French and published several translations over the years, she did not take her degree in Paris. The London Medical School for Women (LMSW) was inaugurated in 1874 and Vickery registered immediately, although she did not enter at that time. In 1877 her existing qualifications were refused recognition by the King and Queen's College of Physicians in Ireland, the first institution to admit women to medical licensing, and it was only then that she returned to London and entered the LMSW to complete her training.

In 1877 Vickery became involved in the trial of Charles Bradlaugh and Annie Besant on the grounds of obscenity for publishing Charles Knowlton's contraceptive handbook *The Fruits of Philosophy* (1877). Vickery was active in the subsequent formation of the Malthusian League, which accepted Malthus's law of population but believed that its corollary was the desirability of birth control, becoming one of the first vice-presidents and a member of its council. Her Malthusian activities, however, were initially curtailed through the intervention of the council of the LMSW, which was reluctant to be openly associated, via one of its students, with this scandalous body. She therefore withdrew from public association with the league until she had obtained the medical qualification for which she had been striving for so long, finally qualifying LKQCPI and LM in 1880.

Once qualified, Vickery practised as a doctor. Throughout the 1880s she also gave frequent lectures on Malthusianism, advancing birth control as an essential element for the emancipation of women. Her liaison with Drysdale continued, and their second son, George Vickery, was born about 1881 or 1882. However, the couple did not live together until 1895, when they moved to Dulwich and let it be assumed that they were married.

Alice Vickery was deeply involved in a number of enterprises critical of the late Victorian social norm. She was among the first few British women to obtain a medical qualification, though lacking the privileged background of other pioneers—although she must have had Charles Drysdale's financial, as well as moral and professional, support. She was a freethinker and secularist. She was active in the campaign against the Contagious Diseases Acts, and was an articulate advocate of the prudential limitation of the family. She appeared on public platforms and engaged in public debate. She lived out in her own life the objections which many contemporary feminists had to the institution of marriage.

In the 1890s Vickery became involved with the Legitimation League which was set up to protest against the legal penalties borne by the illegitimate but developed a far more wide-ranging agenda critical of existing sexual mores and suggesting remedies and alternatives. She condemned the existing legal position of women, and made sweeping suggestions for its improvement. During the same decade she joined the National Society for Women's Suffrage, later moving on to the more militant Women's Social and Political Union (WSPU), and then the Women's Freedom League which seceded from the WSPU in protest at the Pankhurst autocracy. She subscribed generously to the cause and participated in demonstrations but does not seem to have been a major figure in the political struggle, presumably regarding her work for birth control as her most significant contribution to women's emancipation, though it was a subject by no means universally approved of within the suffrage movement.

After Charles Drysdale's death Alice Vickery continued her work, both as a doctor and for the Malthusian League. About 1910 she was asked by Anna Martin, a welfare worker in Rotherhithe, London, to instruct local women in birth control methods, which she did privately and informally. New causes she took up were eugenics (she was an early member of the Eugenics Education Society), divorce law reform, and the international birth control movement.

In 1923 Vickery moved to Brighton to be near her elder son and his wife, and became an active president of the local branch of the Women's Freedom League, addressing a meeting only days before her death, at 13 Victoria Road, from pneumonia, on 12 January 1929.

LESLEY A. HALL

Sources M. Benn, *The predicaments of love* (1992) · L. Cong., manuscript division, Sanger MSS · *Medical Women's Federation Journal* (1929) · *The Shield* (1929) · d. cert. **Archives** L. Cong., Sanger MSS · Smith College, Northampton, Massachusetts, Sophia Smith collections **Wealth at death** £29,853 3s. 1d.: probate, 18 March 1929, CGPLA Eng. & Wales

Vickris, Richard (d. 1700), religious writer, was born in Bristol, the son of Hester (d. 1722?) and Robert Vickris (d. 1684) of that city. His father was a puritan merchant and local politician whose family came from Bewdley, Worcestershire. Like his own father, Richard Vickris the elder (d. 1668), sheriff in 1636, Robert Vickris was a prosperous merchant who served as master of the Merchant Venturers' Society. Both men opposed the growing Quaker presence in Bristol.

Richard Vickris received a gentleman's education. Probably following the example of his mother, who was a member of the Bristol Quaker meeting from at least 1669 or 1670, young Richard Vickris began an association with the Quakers. Aiming to rid him of his new beliefs, Robert Vickris sent his son to France. There he continued his education and encountered the ideas of Nicolas Malebranche, who had been employing a modified Cartesianism to formulate a 'search for truth'. The ideas that eventually found their way into Malebranche's *Recherche de la vérité* (1674) provided Vickris with a metaphysical explanation for the central Quaker tenet, the inner light of Christ. Consequently, Vickris left France intellectually as well as spiritually engaged with his beliefs.

After his return to England, Vickris married Elizabeth Bishop (1655–1724), daughter of Elizabeth Bishop, *née*

Canne (d. 1658), and the Bristol Quaker organizer and writer Captain George *Bishop (d. 1668). Their marriage, on 25 March 1672, took place at a Bristol Quaker meeting. Richard and Elizabeth Vickris left Bristol in 1684 and raised their eight or more children at Firgrove, the family estate at Chew Magna, Somerset. There Vickris hosted Quaker meetings, was involved in their administration and the enforcement of discipline, and opposed the schismatic William Rogers. He aided George Fox and William Penn to record Quaker history and 'sufferings'.

Before the Toleration Act of 1689 Vickris publicized the violence and persecution of Quakers that had increased under the prescription of the Restoration settlement. He was detained and fined on several occasions for attending Quaker meetings. Refusing to retract his beliefs and attend the services of the Church of England, he was made an example of when the authorities indicted him under the 1670 Conventicle Act (22 Chas. II c. 1) and subsequently tried him under the Elizabethan act of 35 Eliz. I c. 1, against recusants and sectaries, which carried the death penalty for those who refused to abjure their beliefs or depart the realm. This harsh action was instigated by the sheriff of Bristol in 1681–2, Sir John Knight, and may have been propelled by a fanatical hatred of Quakers so extreme that he had once threatened personally to hang Vickris's father-in-law for attending their meetings. Vickris was sentenced to death on 23 August 1684. He and his lawyer used a number of legal tactics to postpone any action that would curb his freedom. Backed by the substantial support of their co-religionists, and in particular of the influential William Penn (a friend of the family whose marriage certificate was to be witnessed by Vickris's brother-in-law Nathaniel *Wade), Elizabeth Vickris travelled to London and met James, duke of York. The duke used his influence and the case, removed for trial to London under a writ of habeas corpus because of alleged errors in the original indictment in October 1684, was quashed by Sir George Jeffreys the following month. Vickris was the only English Quaker who was threatened with the death penalty for his refusal to conform, though during the reign of Charles II some Baptists also faced death under the act of 35 Elizabeth (and at least 450 Quakers did actually die in disease-ridden gaols or from being beaten up by arresting officers). The Quakers' response to the Vickris case has been cited as a prime example of their legal sophistication in the later Stuart period. In December 1681, in an effort to reconcile Robert Vickris with his son, William Penn wrote an inspirational letter, commending Richard's father for 'the sincere love thou hast shown to thy son and his troubles' (Penn to Robert Vickris, 4 Oct 1681).

Vickris wrote several tracts which, in comparison with those of Quaker contemporaries, are notable for the moderation of their polemics. His most important work, *A Just Reprehension* (1691), counters the attack on the Quakers made by the Anglican clergyman John *Norris. Norris, the chief proponent of Malebranche's ideas in England, had dismissed the inner light as 'a gross notion'. Vickris died at Chew Magna in April 1700, leaving substantial holdings, including property in Chew Magna and Bristol and elsewhere in Somerset and Gloucestershire. His wife, Elizabeth, lived until 1724. A daughter married into the Dickinson family of Somerset, themselves wealthy members of the gentry, and continued the Quaker beliefs which remained in the family until at least the fourth decade of the eighteenth century.   MARYANN S. FEOLA

Sources *DNB* · C. Horle, 'Death of a felon: Richard Vickris and the Elizabethan Conventicle Act', *Quaker History*, 76 (1987), 95–107 · supplement of the quarterly meeting of Bristol and Somersetshire births, 1653–1784, Bristol RO, SF/R1/2 · quarterly meeting of Bristol and Somersetshire burials, 1651–1777, Bristol RO, SF/R1/6 · F. A. Wood, *Collections for a parochial history of Chew Magna* (1903) · J. Latimer, *The annals of Bristol in the seventeenth century* (1900) · J. Besse, *A collection of the sufferings of the people called Quakers*, 1 (1753) · R. Mortimer, ed., *Minute book of the men's meeting of the Society of Friends in Bristol*, Bristol RS, 26, 30 (1971–7) · P. McGrath, ed., *Records relating to the Society of Merchant Venturers of the city of Bristol in the seventeenth century*, Bristol RS, 17 (1951) · J. Smith, ed., *A descriptive catalogue of Friends' books*, 2 vols. (1867); suppl. (1893) · William Penn to Robert Vickris, 4 Oct 1681, Swarthmore College, Pennsylvania, Friends Historical Library, Penn MSS · 'Malebranche, Nicholas', *DSB*, vol. 9 · will, PRO, PROB 11/459

Archives Swarthmore College, Swarthmore, Pennsylvania, Friends Historical Library, W. Penn to Robert Vickris, 4 Oct 1681

Wealth at death substantial property at Chew Magna, Somerset, and Bristol, Gloucestershire: will, PRO, PROB 11/459; Wood, *Collections*

Vicky. See Weisz, Victor (1913–1966).

Victor, prince of Hohenlohe-Langenburg [known as Count Gleichen] (1833–1891), naval officer and sculptor, was the third and youngest son of Prince Ernst of Hohenlohe-Langenburg and his wife, Princess Feodore, the only daughter of Emich Charles, reigning prince of Leiningen, and his wife, Princess Victoria of Saxe-Coburg-Saalfeld, afterwards the duchess of Kent; his mother was half-sister to Queen Victoria. He was born Victor Ferdinand Franz Eugen Gustaf Adolf Constantin Friedrich at the castle of Langenburg in Württemberg, Germany, on 11 November 1833 and was sent to school at Dresden, from which he ran away. In 1848, through the interest of Queen Victoria, he entered the British navy as a midshipman on the *Powerful*. He then served in the *Cumberland*, the flagship of Admiral Sir George Seymour on the North American station. During the expedition to the Baltic in 1854 he was slightly wounded at Bomarsund. He was next appointed to the *St Jean d'Acre* off Sevastopol, and was afterwards transferred to the naval brigade and did duty in the trenches. As aide-de-camp to Sir Harry Keppel he was present at the battle of the Chernaya, and was distinguished for his bravery under fire.

In 1856 Prince Victor was appointed flag lieutenant to Sir Harry Keppel in China; he took a prominent part in the fighting and was recommended for the Victoria Cross. Repeated illness, however, undermined his constitution and prevented his earning fresh distinction in the navy, and he was compelled to retire on half pay in 1866. He was created KCB in January 1866, and was appointed by the queen to be governor and constable of Windsor Castle. On 26 January 1861 he married Laura Williamina, the youngest daughter of Admiral Sir George Francis Seymour. By an old German law Prince Victor's wife, not being of equal rank, was disqualified from using her husband's title. So Prince Victor assumed the title of Count Gleichen, the second title in the family, by which he was known for many years.

After he retired from the navy Count Gleichen devoted himself to an artistic career, for which he had considerable talent. Being fond of modelling, he studied for three years under William Theed. The loss of his fortune, the result of a bank failure, caused him to look to sculpture as a serious profession. He had been granted by Queen Victoria a suite of apartments in St James's Palace, where he set up a studio and entered into regular competition as a working sculptor. He made several imaginative groups as well as monuments and portrait busts. Some of the busts were considered very successful, notably those of the earl of Beaconsfield, the marquess of Salisbury, and Sir Harry Keppel. His most important work was a colossal statue of Alfred the Great, made for the main square of the town of Wantage. His success as a sculptor enabled him to build a small house near Ascot. In 1885 Count and Countess Gleichen were permitted by the queen to revert to the names of Prince and Princess Victor of Hohenlohe-Langenburg. In 1887 Prince Victor was promoted GCB and admiral on the retired list. He died at St James's Palace, London, on 31 December 1891. He was survived by his son, Count, later Major-General Lord, Albert Edward Wilfred Gleichen (1863–1937) of the Grenadier Guards—who served in the Sudan, South Africa, and the First World War—and three daughters, of whom the eldest, Lady Féodora *Gleichen (1861–1922), inherited her father's skill in sculpture.

L. H. Cust, rev. Andrew Lambert

Sources H. Keppel, *A sailor's life under four sovereigns*, 3 vols. (1899) • V. Stuart, *The beloved little admiral* (1967) • *The letters of Queen Victoria*, ed. A. C. Benson, Lord Esher [R. B. Brett], and G. E. Buckle, 9 vols. (1907–32) • E. Longford, *Victoria RI* (1964) • WWW
Likenesses F. R. Say, double portrait, 1856–7 (with Ernest, prince of Leiningen), Royal Collection; *see illus. in* Ernest (1830–1904) • C. Pellegrini, chromolithograph caricature, 1872, NPG • GO, chromolithograph caricature, NPG; repro. in *VF* (5 July 1884) • carte-de-visite, NPG
Wealth at death £10,129 8s. 8d.: probate, 19 Feb 1892, *CGPLA Eng. & Wales*

Victor, Benjamin (d. 1778), theatre manager and writer, began life as a barber 'within the liberties of Drury Lane', but from the first was drawn to the stage. In 1722 he was at Norwich for a term, possibly to establish a business in the sale of Norwich linen. That year, after he had been introduced to Richard Steele by the poet and dramatist Aaron Hill, he defended, in *An Epistle to Sir Richard Steele* (two editions, 1722), Steele's play *The Conscious Lovers* against the attacks of John Dennis. He married Mary Rooker (d. 1757) at Charterhouse Chapel, Finsbury, on 3 July 1722. In 1728 he was introduced to Barton Booth, and his *Memoirs of the Life of Barton Booth, Published by an Intimate Acquaintance* (1733) is one of the chief authorities on that actor's career.

After the arrival of Frederick, prince of Wales, in England in December 1728, Victor presented to him a congratulatory poem in the hope of obtaining a place in the prince's household, but was disappointed. The following year he composed a satire called *The Levée Haunter*, which looked for and gained the approval of Sir Robert Walpole. But Walpole was not much given to literary patronage, and Victor returned to the linen trade and established a business in Pall Mall. He experimented with acting, and played Polydore in Thomas Otway's *The Orphan* at Lincoln's Inn Fields on 18 April 1734, but does not seem to have acted again. Between 1734 and 1746 he made two visits to Ireland in order to extend his linen trade connections. The business did not prove profitable, however, and in January 1746 he resolved to give it up. On 11 October 1746 he settled with his family in Dublin as treasurer and deputy manager to Thomas Sheridan (1719–1788) at the theatre in Smock Alley.

From that year Victor wrote the birthday odes for the court of Dublin, and the duke of Dorset, when resigning the position of lord lieutenant in 1755, obtained permission to appoint him poet laureate of Ireland, with a pension of £50 per annum. Several of these painful productions are in his collections of 1776, and two of them, printed separately, are in the British Library. The theatre was for some years fairly successful, but about 1753 Sheridan was at odds with a portion of the theatregoing public, and for two years Victor and John Sowden, a principal actor in the company, took over its management. On 15 July 1755 Sheridan returned to Dublin, and Victor resumed his old position. After much discouragement and financial trouble the theatre was closed on 20 April 1759, and Victor returned to England, out of debt, but with little money at his command.

Between October 1758 and June 1759 Victor married his second wife, Penelope Wolseley (d. in or after 1794), the daughter of Sir William Wolseley, bt, and his mistress, Christina Horton, an actress. Victor had known Wolseley since 1729; Penelope had joined Sheridan's company at Smock Alley in February 1749, and acted as Penelope Danvers. In 1752 Victor drew up the articles for the marriage of Sir William to Ann Whitby. Whitby later claimed that the marriage had been forced upon her and that she was already married to John Robins. Victor wrote *The Widow of the Wood*, published in 1755, as an attack on Whitby and a defence of Wolseley; he was a witness for Wolseley when the latter sued for divorce on grounds of adultery, but Sir George Hay, the presiding judge, ruled that Ann Whitby had indeed already been married to John Robins, and so no divorce could be granted. Victor's book reached a second edition in 1769. Although it was written in support of Wolseley, it was said to be so offensive to members of the Wolseley family that they destroyed every copy of the narrative that they could obtain, but in the nineteenth century it was still to be found in catalogues of secondhand books.

Shortly after his return to England, Victor was appointed treasurer of the Theatre Royal, Drury Lane, a post which he retained until his death. In 1761 he published, in two volumes, the work for which he is chiefly remembered, *The history of the theatres of London and Dublin from the* year 1730, with an annual register of all plays performed at the theatres royal in London from 1712, and in 1771 he published a third volume, bringing the narrative down to that date. The second volume has much information on the lives of the chief actors from about 1710 to 1745, and the work retains its value at the beginning of the twenty-first century. Its egotism was so marked that Charles Churchill said 'Victor ego' should have been Victor's motto. Walley Chamberlain Oulton compiled in 1796 a continuation of the work in two volumes, bringing the record down to 1795, and in 1818, in three more volumes, he carried it on to 1817.

Victor published in 1776, with a dedication to David Garrick, three volumes of *Original Letters, Dramatic Pieces, and Poems*. The first volume preserved some interesting anecdotes, especially on Sir Richard Steele, and the second volume contained Victor's plays—*Altamira*, a tragedy; *Fatal Error*, a tragedy; *The Fortunate Peasant*, a comedy; and *The Sacrifice, or, Cupid's Vagaries*, a masque—all of which were unperformed. Victor also produced an adaptation of Shakespeare's *The Two Gentlemen of Verona*, which was given five times at Drury Lane in 1763.

Victor was living in Maiden Lane, Covent Garden, when he received a legacy of 50 guineas from Hester Booth. He died at his lodgings in Charles Street, Covent Garden, on 3 December 1778. His wife, Penelope, survived him, and was still receiving her pension of £100 per annum (granted 1763) in 1794.

W. P. COURTNEY, *rev.* DAVID GOLDTHORPE

Sources D. E. Baker, *Biographia dramatica, or, A companion to the playhouse*, rev. I. Reed, new edn, rev. S. Jones, 1 (1812), 726–7; 2 (1812), 21, 228, 245–6; 3 (1812), 52, 236 · B. Victor, *Original letters, dramatic pieces, and poems*, 3 vols. (1776) · private information (2004) [B. Rizzo] · *GM*, 1st ser., 48 (1778), 607 · 'Robins v. Wolseley', *Robins v. Wolseley* (1757), 2 Lee 421, 161 ER 391 · G. A. Aitken, *The life of Sir Richard Steele*, 2 vols. (1889), vol. 2, p. 285 · *The private correspondence of David Garrick*, ed. J. Boaden, 1 (1831), 16, 235; 2 (1832), 163, 235, 303 · *Fourth report*, HMC, 3 (1874), 281 · *The works of the late Aaron Hill*, 4 vols. (1753), vol. 2, pp. 115–19 · R. Simms, ed., *Bibliotheca Staffordiensis* (1894) · Highfill, Burnim & Langhans, *BDA*

Victoria, Princess [Princess Victoria of Saxe-Coburg-Saalfeld], **duchess of Kent** (1786–1861), mother of Queen Victoria, was the fourth daughter of Franz Friedrich Anton (Francis), duke of Saxe-Coburg-Saalfeld (*b.* 1750), and his wife, Augusta Caroline Sophia, the daughter of Count Reuss-Ebersdorf. She was born Victoria Mary Louisa at Coburg on 17 August 1786 and married, first, in 1803, Emich Charles, prince of Leiningen (*d.* 1814), with whom she had a son, Charles, and a daughter, Feodore, and second, *Edward, duke of Kent (1767–1820), the fourth son of *George III and Queen *Charlotte. They had one daughter, the future Queen *Victoria.

Widowed first in 1814, Victoria was persuaded by her brother Prince Leopold, the widower of Princess *Charlotte, George IV's heir, to marry Prince Edward and secure the English succession. They married at Coburg on 29 May 1818 (Lutheran rite) and at Kew Palace on 13 July. Although the duchess was pregnant, the couple lived abroad until

Princess Victoria, duchess of Kent (1786–1861), by Sir William Beechey, 1821 [with Princess Victoria]

just before the birth of Princess (Alexandrina) Victoria at Kensington Palace on 24 May 1819. Fortunately the sensible duchess brought with her Frau Siebold, a German doctor, and nursed her baby, though a wet-nurse was usually hired. Suddenly, on 23 January 1820, the duke died of pneumonia in Devon, leaving her in straits.

Money was not the only problem during the first eighteen years of the mother–daughter relationship with Princess Victoria. Parliament and Prince Leopold made necessary contributions. The main trouble was a bitter division in the duchess's household. Springing from fierce rivalries between Baroness Lehzen, Princess Victoria's beloved governess, and Sir John Ponsonby *Conroy, the duchess's major-domo, the schism developed into a tight domestic cabal known as the Kensington system. At its centre lay Conroy's ambition to run not only the mother's household but also the daughter's future court. Conroy played on the duchess's fears of the royal family. Would they not kidnap Victoria unless she was closely guarded? Accordingly she was kept away from her royal relatives and, until her accession, was made to sleep in her mother's bedroom. Queen Victoria criticized 'Mama' for limiting her close childhood friends to Feodore (who married abroad in 1828) and Conroy's daughters Victoire and Elizabeth Jane.

The diarist Charles Greville noticed Conroy's familiarities with the duchess, and thought they must be lovers. The duke of Wellington agreed. Lord Melbourne, the prime minister, told the speaker of the House of Commons: 'God, I don't like the man; there seems to be something odd about him' (Queen Victoria, journal, 29 April

1838). There was indeed something odd: Conroy cherished the illusion that his wife had royal blood, making them all semi-royal. But if Conroy did have a royal mistress, it was more likely to have been Princess Sophia, another inhabitant of Kensington Palace. She corresponded familiarly while Conroy managed—or mismanaged—her finances, as he did the duchess's. No lovers for the duchess.

Melbourne considered the duchess foolish and weak-minded; but she was pious. She would not let Victoria read a novel such as *Oliver Twist*. In her diary, studied by a deeply remorseful Queen Victoria after her death, the duchess expressed touching devotion to a child who had believed herself unloved and who took to calling the pair curtly in *her* diary Ma and JC. The duchess claimed that Conroy was useful because he organized tours to show Victoria to the people. Though these 'royal progresses' infuriated William IV, they educated the princess. Her mother hoped she would first reign as a minor (under eighteen) with herself as regent. But William survived until 20 June 1837, when his niece was over eighteen.

As the queen's mother, the duchess found her trials increased. Victoria quitted her bedroom; night fell on the duchess for nearly three gloomy years. After the coronation Queen Victoria kissed her aunt Queen Adelaide, but only shook her mother's hand. When Lady Flora Hastings, her mother's lady-in-waiting, was dying of a liver tumour, Victoria and Lehzen decided she was '*with child!*'—by JC (Queen Victoria, journal, 3 Feb 1839).

There was 'a schocking alternative' (Queen Victoria, journal, 17 April 1839) to life with Ma—marriage. On 10 February 1840 Victoria married the duchess's nephew Prince Albert of Saxe-Coburg and Gotha, Conroy and Lehzen were both tactfully ejected, and Queen Victoria entered her 'safe haven' (Longford, 165–6). The duchess spent twenty harmonious years at court and with her grandchildren, and was the first to spot that the newborn Prince Leopold was affected by an undiagnosed illness (in fact haemophilia). She died of cancer at Frogmore House, Windsor, on 16 March 1861 and, after temporary interment in St George's Chapel, Windsor, was buried in the Royal Mausoleum at Frogmore. Queen Victoria broke down with grief and guilt. Nine months later she lost her husband also.   ELIZABETH LONGFORD

Sources Queen Victoria, journal, Royal Arch. · *The letters of Queen Victoria*, ed. A. C. Benson, Lord Esher [R. B. Brett], and G. E. Buckle, 9 vols. (1907–32) · K. Hudson, '*Royal conflict': life of Sir J. Conroy* (1994) · Duchess of Kent, diary, Royal Arch., Kent papers · E. Longford, *Victoria RI* (1964) · M. Gillen, *The prince and his lady* (1970) · Duchess of Coburg, diary, 1818, Royal Arch., Kent papers · J. Roberts, *Royal artists: from Mary queen of Scots to the present day* (1987) · *DNB* · d. cert. · C. Zeeprat, *Prince Leopold* (1998)
Archives Royal Arch. | Balliol Oxf., letters to Sir Edward Conroy; letters to Sir John Conroy · BL, corresp. with Lord Aberdeen, Add. MS 43051 · BL, corresp. with Lord Holland, Add. MS 51524 · BL, corresp. with Sir Robert Peel, Add. MSS 40424–40553 *passim* · Flintshire RO, Hawarden, corresp. with duchess of Northumberland · Lambton Park, Chester-le-Street, Durham, letters to earl of Durham · NA Scot., letters to Sir Charles Augustus Murray · NRA, priv. coll., letters to Lord Conyngham · U. Durham L., archives and special collections, corresp. with Lord Grey · U. Nott. L., corresp. relating to education of Princess Victoria, 1845 · U. Southampton L., letters to Lord Palmerston
Likenesses P. Müller, portrait, 19th cent. (when princess of Saxe-Coburg-Gotha), Royal Collection · G. Dawes, oils, 1818, Royal Collection · Besnes, marble bust, 1819, Leighton House, London · W. Beechey, double portrait, oils, 1821 (with her daughter Victoria), Royal Collection [*see illus.*] · Doyle, chalk drawing, 1830, BM · W. Ross, oils, 1830–40, Royal Collection · R. Rothwell, oils, 1832?, Royal Collection · G. Hayter, oils, 1835, Royal Collection · F. Winterhalter, oils, 1843, Royal Collection · H. Selous, oils, 1851, Royal Collection · F. Winterhalter, two oils, 1857–61, Royal Collection · F. Say, oils, 1861, Royal Collection

Victoria (1819–1901), queen of the United Kingdom of Great Britain and Ireland, and empress of India, was born on 24 May 1819 at Kensington Palace, London. She was the only legitimate child of the fourth son of King George III, *Edward Augustus, duke of Kent (1767–1820), who in 1818 had abandoned Julie de St Laurent, his mistress of many years, in order to join his brothers in the attempt to provide an heir to the throne. His wife was a young widow: born Princess Victoire of Saxe-Coburg-Saalfeld (1786–1861) [*see* Victoria, Princess], she had married the prince of Leiningen, with whom she had two children, Prince Charles and Princess Feodore, before his death in 1814. Among the duchess's brothers were Ernest, duke of Saxe-Coburg-Saalfeld, who was the father of the future prince consort, and the future king of the Belgians *Leopold I (1790–1865), who had been the husband of Princess *Charlotte of Wales. Charlotte's death in 1817 had precipitated the efforts to produce a new heir for the throne. Unsubstantiated rumours that Victoria was not her father's child surface periodically.

Conflict with George IV Relationships between the duke and duchess of Kent and the court of King *George IV determined the character of the princess's early years. Tension between Kent and his eldest brother spilled over at the infant's baptism on 24 June 1819, when at the last moment the prince regent as godfather refused to allow her to be named Victoire Georgiana Alexandrina Charlotte Augusta after her mother and godparents, but he eventually agreed to Alexandrina Victoria (after her godfather, the tsar of Russia, and her mother). By December 1819 deteriorating relations with the regent and ever-increasing debts led Kent to leave London, and the court. Determined to stay in England because he was convinced that his daughter would inherit the throne, Kent took his family to a house in Sidmouth, Devon; there, most unexpectedly, he died on 23 January 1820, less than a week before his father. Under his will Alexandrina Victoria, now fifth in line to the throne, was left to the sole guardianship of her mother.

The duchess of Kent shared her late husband's conviction that their daughter would one day become queen, and was determined that she should be brought up as an English princess. Not a very wise woman (and widely regarded as a stupid foreigner), the duchess was greatly under the influence of the controller of her household and former equerry to the duke, Sir John *Conroy, first

Victoria (1819–1901), by Heinrich von Angeli, 1875

baronet. Conroy harboured great ambitions for himself and his family, and viewed the little princess as his route to power and influence. His advice reinforced the duchess's difficulties with the rest of the royal family, and they isolated Victoria from the morally contaminated court of her 'wicked uncles'. George IV initially refused to modify his dislike of Kent's widow; he did not regard Victoria as his eventual heir, for the duke of Clarence seemed likely to pre-empt her claim by producing a legitimate child. The king would not even help to relieve their disastrous finances, leaving them to the care of Prince Leopold, until parliament in 1825 made an annual grant to the princess as heir presumptive. Even when it became clear that Victoria was likely to inherit the throne, George showed little interest in the family; it was her half-sister, Feodore, who caught his attention (and was for a time spoken of as a possible bride for the aged king).

The duchess of Kent made something of a virtue of necessity, keeping Victoria away from the court even when relations defrosted slightly, thus ensuring that the public would not see Victoria as infected by the dissolute regime of the late Hanoverian monarchy. The king invited them to Windsor for the first time when Victoria was six; she retained a strong memory of the event, and recalled in 1872 that the king had taken her by the hand, saying 'Give me your little paw' (Letters, 1st ser., 1.16). He was persuaded

to permit his sister-in-law and niece to reside in apartments in Kensington Palace, and it was there that the princess spent her childhood.

Education of a princess Looking back on her childhood, Victoria often commented on how solitary she had been. True, the princess had little company of her own age: her half-sister, Feodore, was twelve years her senior (and married in 1828), and her only surviving cousins, Prince George of Cumberland and Prince George of Cambridge (Princess Mary of Cambridge was not born until 1833), were kept away from her. Sir John Conroy encouraged the duchess in isolating her daughter; his own daughters, Victoire and Elizabeth Jane, provided her only regular—and increasingly unwelcome—companionship. She amused herself instead with an extensive family of dolls and animals. Dash, a King Charles spaniel, a gift from Conroy to the duchess in 1833, was the first in a long line of beloved little dogs. Other carefully vetted children were occasionally brought to play with Victoria, but friendship was out of the question with a princess who from infancy had been given a firm sense of her high position (although not of her ultimate destiny). A much quoted anecdote has the princess tell a child about to play with her toys, 'You must not touch those, they are mine; and I may call you Jane, but you must not call me Victoria' (Longford, 28).

Although she lacked companionship, Victoria was never alone. From her birth she was surrounded by devoted attendants, servants, and teachers; she never walked downstairs without someone holding her hand, and famously she never slept alone until she succeeded to the throne; instead she shared a bed with her mother. Her earliest attendants were her nurse Mrs Brock (although most unusually for the time and her class she was not put to a wet-nurse but was fed by her mother), her mother's lady-in-waiting Baroness Späth, and Princess Feodore's governess, Louise *Lehzen. Lehzen, the daughter of a Lutheran pastor from Hanover, was among Victoria's most important formative influences, setting herself in opposition to Conroy and the duchess, whom she considered weak. Lehzen's ideal of a queen was Queen Elizabeth I, and she imbued in Victoria a sense of the importance of strength of will, elevating her natural obstinacy and stubbornness to a principle. Lehzen, who was the princess's constant preceptress until she came to the throne, would read to Victoria morning and evening, while she was being dressed or prepared for bed, thereby helping to instil the rigid work discipline which served Victoria well throughout her life.

Contrary to her own later recollections, Victoria's formal education began before she was four, when the Revd George *Davys (later bishop of Peterborough) became her tutor. From April 1823 he went regularly to Kensington Palace, where he taught Victoria the basic skills of literacy and numeracy, and gave religious instruction. Like that of most girls at this time, Victoria's early education was dominated by the writings of the evangelical moralist Mrs Trimmer, but with Davys and Lehzen she also studied history, geography, natural history, poetry, and (by 1828)

Latin. Despite her future destiny, Victoria never experienced the classical education that was the shared intellectual heritage of the men of the political classes: the requirements of femininity were not to be subordinated to the needs of the state. Nor was Victoria to be a Renaissance woman like Elizabeth I, educated to write poetry as well as to embroider, to muse philosophically as well as to direct the affairs of her family. Yet her education was thorough and intensive—by 1829 she was spending five hours a day, six days a week, in formal lessons—and it stood her in good stead. French, German, and Italian were added to her curriculum. (English was always spoken in Kensington Palace, despite the preponderance of German-speakers; Davys commented on the princess's German accent, which he helped to eradicate.) She began to study the 'female accomplishments' with a succession of tutors: playing the piano and singing with Mrs Mary Anderson and John Sale, painting and drawing with Richard Westall RA, and, with Madame Bourdin, dancing, in which she took a particular delight.

In 1830 the duchess of Kent invited the bishops of London and Lincoln to examine her daughter, and to comment on her education so far. The bishops' verdict was positive, and the duchess was publicly commended. Shortly after this examination the princess was allowed to learn of her probable future destiny. Keeping the information from her had been a kindness in the light of the uncertainty of the succession, and although some doubted whether she could have been as ignorant as was claimed, Victoria herself endorsed Lehzen's account of the way she was told. A genealogical table was inserted in her history book for her to study; 'I see I am nearer the throne than I thought … I will be good', she said. 'I cried much on learning it, and ever deplored the contingency', she commented later (Martin, 1.13).

Conroy and the 'Kensington system' After the examination Victoria's lessons were relieved by regular visits to the theatre and the opera. This latter was the princess's passion, and she now acquired her lifelong love of the bel canto operas of Bellini, Donizetti, and Rossini. She was even star-struck: the soprano Giulia Grisi always remained her ideal type of the singer, and she idolized the ballerina Marie Taglioni. Luigi Lablache, the bass baritone whom she first heard at a private recital in 1834, became the princess's singing teacher in 1836, beginning a relationship that lasted twenty years.

If Victoria's childhood resembled a moral and improving tale for young women, her teenage years approached melodrama. Victoria herself was the oppressed heroine, supported by her faithful retainer Lehzen, with the duchess of Kent as wicked (step)mother, the willing tool of Sir John Conroy, the 'Arch-Fiend'. Walk-on parts were played by the new king, William IV, as the choleric but kindly uncle, and the duke of Cumberland (the next heir) as the off-stage bogeyman. Victoria later recast her memories, painting her entire youth in gloomy colours and seeking to absolve her mother from all responsibility as, like herself, a victim of an all-powerful, all-malignant Conroy. Yet the duchess was no dupe, and concurred willingly in Conroy's actions: she was no less ambitious than he to wield the authority of her daughter's crown.

Conroy's influence had been tempered by the irregular but commanding presence of the duchess's brother Prince Leopold. Then in 1830 Leopold accepted the throne of Belgium. He remained in regular correspondence with both his sister and niece, but his absence enhanced the position of Conroy, whom Victoria came to loathe as 'the Monster and demon Incarnate' (Hudson, 153).

From 1830 onwards the duchess and Conroy implemented what was termed the 'Kensington system'. Their aim was to ensure that Victoria was totally dependent on them, and would not look to others for advice when she came to the throne. The duchess was appointed regent in the event of William IV dying before Victoria reached eighteen, and Conroy's aim was to get the princess to agree to appoint him her private secretary. There was thus a practical, political reason for keeping Victoria away from the court, where she might find other advisers, and away from society, in which she might find alternative sources of support. The Kensington system was, however, more than an exercise in ambition: the aim was to make Victoria herself popular and ensure the survival of the monarchy. The Britishness of her education and upbringing was to be stressed, while her youth and purity marked her out as the herald of a new future, distanced from the moral and political corruption of the British *ancien régime*.

Beginning in 1830, Conroy and the duchess staged a series of royal progresses (directly imitating those of Elizabeth I), ostensibly to show the princess some of the historic sites of her country but in practice to bring her before the public eye and to assert her position as the heir to the throne. They succeeded: large crowds gathered to see the princess wherever she was taken, local dignitaries presented loyal addresses, and, until the enraged William IV stepped in to prevent it, guns were fired in salute. Victoria herself became increasingly unhappy about these progresses, which became more frequent and exhausting as she neared her eighteenth birthday and William IV's health began to fail.

In 1835 Victoria became seriously ill at Ramsgate. While she was in her sickbed, Conroy unsuccessfully attempted to force her to sign a document making him her private secretary when she became queen. Conroy believed she could be bullied and hectored into compliance, while the duchess applied a none-too-subtle mixture of commands, threats, and emotional blackmail. In this they misread Victoria's character completely. Strong-willed, intelligent, emotionally sensitive, lonely, with a fierce temper kept firmly in check, the young Victoria had a deep sense of duty and obligation instilled in her by Lehzen, and also a profound sense of propriety. A feeling that she was a pawn in a game being played by Conroy, who did not even treat her with courtesy, aroused all the princess's stubborn hostility and enabled her to resist her mother's demands. A little kindness and consultation, together with an acknowledgement that she was not without power, always went a long way with Victoria.

William IV's court Victoria was not alone in her dislike for Conroy and the Kensington system. The most important opponent of Conroy and the duchess was the king himself. William IV and Queen Adelaide were fond of their niece, and in the 1820s had a better relationship with the duchess of Kent than most of the rest of the royal family. On coming to the throne, William acknowledged Victoria as his probable successor and approved the appointment of the duchess as her regent. He hoped that the princess would become a regular visitor to his court, and indeed on 24 February 1831 Victoria made her first appearance at her aunt's drawing-room (these were formal occasions at which ladies were presented and received at court; men were received at the levees). But the isolationism of the Kensington system demanded otherwise, and the duchess deeply offended the king by refusing to allow her daughter to attend his coronation. Further disputes about the composition of the princess's entourage followed, and the king ordered Conroy to leave Victoria's confirmation service at the Chapel Royal in St James's Palace on 30 July 1834. At a dinner in August 1836 William IV publicly insulted the duchess, who was sitting next to him, as he announced his intention to live another nine months solely to thwart her plans for a regency:

> I should then have the satisfaction of leaving the royal authority to the personal exercise of that young lady … and not in the hands of a person now near me, who is surrounded by evil advisers and who is herself incompetent to act with propriety in the station in which she would be placed. (Charlot, 68)

The king sought to free Victoria from Conroy and her mother when she came of age by offering her an independent income and household. The duchess of Kent dictated the refusal which Victoria sent, but the king recognized the mother's voice, and exonerated the princess from blame. On her eighteenth birthday, 24 May 1837, Victoria noted in the journal which she had kept since 1832, 'I shall from this day take the *firm* resolution to study with renewed assiduity, to keep my attention always on whatever I am about, and to strive to become every day less trifling and more fit for what, if Heaven wills it, I'm some day to be!' (*Girlhood*, 1.190). That evening she attended a ball at St James's before returning to Kensington through the thronged streets: 'the anxiety of the people to see poor stupid me was very great, and I must say I am quite touched by it, and feel proud which I always have done of my country and of the English nation' (ibid., 1.191). The king had not been at the ball, as he was ill in bed. Time was fast running out for the Kensington system.

Accession King William IV survived for another month, before finally succumbing on 20 June 1837. Lord Conyngham (the lord chamberlain) and William Howley (the archbishop of Canterbury) were dispatched at once to Kensington Palace to bring the news to the new queen. Victoria was summoned from her bed by her mother at six in the morning to receive them, which she did '(only in my dressing gown), and *alone*' (*Girlhood*, 1.196). That characteristic emphasis pointed to the total and immediate failure of the Kensington system as far as it concerned the ambitions of its progenitors: Conroy was immediately banished from the royal presence, and although the duchess was regularly called upon to attend her daughter in public, she was systematically excluded from all the new queen's decisions and counsels.

But in its wider aims the Kensington system bore instant fruit in the widespread popularity of the new queen. The hagiographical accounts of universal popular acclaim for Victoria were undoubtedly exaggerated: radicals, republicans, and the huge masses of the indifferent certainly did not see her as their saviour, or the monarchy as the guardian of British liberty. But, primed by the careful publicity of the previous years, the political classes were swept up in a fever of curiosity about the new queen, and for a few weeks her smallest actions were recorded, analysed, and discussed, and her public appearances were attended by vast, good-humoured crowds. Those who came into direct contact with the queen at this time had little but praise for her charm, her graciousness, her willingness to be happy, her sheer pleasure in her position, and even her appearance. Although the adjective 'lovely' was much in evidence, no one could seriously describe her as beautiful: with her lack of chin, her small mouth, and her rather prominent blue eyes, she bore a close resemblance to her unlovely Hanoverian forebears. The queen was constantly spoken of in diminutives at this time ('her little majesty', 'the little queen'), and even when fully grown she was only 4 feet 11 inches tall, and in extreme age lost several inches. She was also already tending towards the traditional stoutness of her family, although it took some years and nine children before she achieved her unmistakable 'pepper pot' silhouette. Her voice, on the other hand, was praised from the outset for its melodious quality: 'as sweet as a Virginia nightingale's', rhapsodized one American observer (E. Boykin, ed., *Victoria, Albert, and Mrs Stevenson*, 1957, 107).

Much play was made with the burdens of majesty heaped on the small shoulders of an inexperienced, unprotected girl. David Wilkie's painting *The First Council of Queen Victoria*, painted in 1837, contrasts the white-clad Victoria with the sombrely dressed, bewhiskered, elderly members of her government. The picture was inaccurate in several respects—Victoria was actually dressed in mourning for her uncle at the council on the first day of her reign—but the contrast between the masculine world of politics and the femininity of the queen was valid. It was not, however, Victoria's inexperience and fragility that impressed those present so much as her presence of mind, dignity, and courage.

Although curiosity about the queen was universal among the political classes, intense party factionalism meant that whigs and tories responded rather differently to the new reign. Seen from a long-term perspective, the monarchy's political power was slipping by comparison with that of parliament and the cabinet. But from the standpoint of the 1830s many of the precedents limiting the sovereign's power were recent and susceptible to challenge from a new monarch. The monarchy's patronage powers were considerable: a new reign might entail a new distribution. The whigs were in office in 1837, but had never had the real support of William IV. Victoria's accession offered them hope for the first time of receiving the active favour of the monarch, for the duchess of Kent and Sir John Conroy were known to support the whigs, and Victoria was supposed to have been raised a whig. The same facts caused the tories to despair: the support they had enjoyed from the monarch and their virtual monopoly on power since 1760 seemed to be at an end. The queen's intense and close relationship with her first prime minister, Lord Melbourne, lent credence to tory fears and whig hopes.

Learning to be queen: Lady Flora and the bedchamber crisis

Victoria herself greeted the news of her accession with the characteristic reflection that:

> I shall do my utmost to fulfil my duty towards my country; I am very young and perhaps in many, though not in all things, inexperienced, but I am sure, that very few have more real good will and more real desire to do what is fit and right than I have.   (*Girlhood*, 1.196)

Melbourne was with the queen by 9 a.m. on 20 June, and was informed that he was to remain prime minister. She found him sympathetic, her initial assessment of him as 'a very straightforward, honest, clever and good man' (ibid., 1.197) remained unchanged, and her attachment to him deepened with time. Melbourne's constant attendance on the queen and his obvious affection for her earned her the nickname Mrs Melbourne, but although their relationship had an air of romance about it, Melbourne was more father figure than potential lover. Despite his rather lurid past, Melbourne was in many respects the ideal minister, counsellor, and private secretary for the young queen; his scholarly mind and fund of learning supplied the theoretical and practical answers to her questions about her position, and his wide experience of aristocratic and royal society, men, women, and manners was invaluable for one who had lived as secluded a life as the queen. 'Lord M. says …' was a constant refrain in her journal until 1840.

Victoria was not a complete political innocent in 1837. Her first mentor was her uncle Leopold, who on her fourteenth birthday began her political education with a dissertation on the character necessary for a monarch in an era when 'the transition from sovereign power to *absolute want* has become as frequent as sudden' (*Letters*, 1st ser., 1.46): he urged her to spend some time each day in quiet reflection and self-examination, to avoid vanity and selfishness, and to distinguish carefully between the important and the trifling. Over the next four years he regularly discussed current (especially foreign) affairs with her and advised her about reading: history and historical memoirs would enable an isolated princess to learn about the world and thus avoid being imposed on by 'wicked and designing people, particularly at a period when party spirit runs so high' (ibid., 1.48). By 1837, when it was obvious that his niece's succession to the throne his wife had been born to occupy was close, Leopold's advice came thick and fast, and much of it had a lasting impact on Victoria. He

impressed on her the value of listening to the conversation of clever and informed people at dinners and social gatherings, of prudence and discretion, of support for the established church and generally conservative (though not tory) principles. Although Victoria occasionally resented the energetic interference of her uncle, Leopold gave her enough early guidance and backbone to take on her new position with something approaching equanimity. Moreover, in June 1837 he sent his own confidential adviser, Baron Christian *Stockmar, to act as a friend at court for the new queen; he remained there for fifteen months, until disquiet about foreigners' influence over the queen sent him back to Coburg.

Praised and admired in her reign's honeymoon months, Victoria blossomed in her new role and threw herself with energy into learning her profession, and into the novel social whirl of balls, theatre, opera, dinners, and confidential chats with the attentive Melbourne. For the first time in more than three generations Britain had a young monarch and a lively court. Victoria relished the contrast between her oppressed youth and her new position. The coronation was held on 28 June 1838, and, while much of the lengthy ceremonial was ineptly performed (the ancient Lord Rolle tripped and rolled down the steps when paying homage to the queen), the large crowds that turned out to see the queen were enthusiastic. 'Their good-humour and excessive loyalty was beyond everything, and I really cannot say *how* proud I feel to be the Queen of *such* a Nation', Victoria recorded in her journal (*Girlhood*, 1.357).

But the adulation did not last long. In accordance with tradition, the ministry of the day was responsible for forming the queen's household as well as her government, and Melbourne surrounded the queen exclusively with active whig partisans. Not only her officials and attendants but also the society which gathered at the court was dominated by the whig aristocracy. By the end of the first year of her reign the tories considered Victoria 'the queen of the whigs'. Attacks on the government began to include attacks on the queen; she came to view the tories as her enemies and clung even more closely to Melbourne.

The dangers of a party-political court surfaced in the Lady Flora *Hastings affair, which broke out in February 1839. The unmarried Lady Flora, the duchess of Kent's lady-in-waiting and a member of a prominent tory family, was suspected of being pregnant by Conroy. In fact, she was suffering from a tumour on her liver, and died in agony on 5 July. But before the nature of her illness became known, rumours flew about the court, medical examiners were called in, and the affair became public. The Hastings family fanned the flames of hostility towards the queen, who had not acted to quench the gossip or protect the reputation of Lady Flora. Victoria's popularity took a considerable blow—she was, after all, supposed to stand for a new, moral court, and the Lady Flora affair smacked of the old Hanoverian scandals—and she was hissed by two aristocratic ladies as she drove to Ascot on 7 June.

On 7 May 1839, in the midst of the Flora Hastings controversy, Melbourne resigned. Victoria responded with an 'agony of grief and despair' (Charlot, 141). He was not only her minister; he was her friend. The tories she considered her enemies, and she had a particular horror of the probable new prime minister, Sir Robert Peel, whose lack of social graces made the contrast with Melbourne unbearable. Melbourne's advice to the distraught queen was sound: she must accept the tories as her ministers and try to shed her dislike for Peel. She should safeguard her prerogatives, but be seen to be scrupulously fair. But he also put in her mind the idea that she might keep her household as it was, and when Peel requested changes among the ladies of her household, Victoria baulked. The ladies made a convenient sticking point for Victoria, but possibly also for Peel, who perhaps had less relish for the task of forming a minority government than his party supposed. The queen maintained that the ladies were domestic appointments, that they had no political influence, and that the precedents required no changes. Peel argued that the exclusively whig female court signalled that his government lacked the queen's confidence. If changes were not made, he could not form a government. 'Was Sir Robert so weak that *even* the ladies must be of his opinion?' (*Letters*, 1st ser., 1.209), asked the queen. Melbourne had stayed away from the palace during these negotiations, but Victoria had written him almost hourly accounts of events, and now she sent for him to tell him of Peel's demands. Melbourne called a cabinet meeting, which formally advised her to refuse changes to her household. (Here, if nowhere else, Melbourne acted unconstitutionally: until Peel declined the commission to form a government, Melbourne had no authority to advise the queen.) The attempt to form a tory ministry over, Victoria rejoiced in Melbourne's resumption of office, and in the retention of the ladies who were supporting her through the later, and most trying, stages of the Lady Flora affair.

The 'bedchamber crisis' has been ascribed to the hysterical tantrum of a young and inexperienced woman, but at the time some viewed it as an ill-omened attempt to reassert the political power of monarchy over ministers. In fact, it was something in between: the already overwrought Victoria certainly responded emotionally in this crisis, but in resisting her ministers she was testing the limits of her power. As it was obvious, even to Victoria, that the whigs could not be kept in power indefinitely, the principal result of the crisis was to confirm the widespread view that an unmarried girl on the throne was a loose cannon.

Marriage and motherhood Since marriage with a commoner was thought undesirable (though not, in Britain, illegal) the pool of Victoria's possible spouses was restricted to the protestant princes of Germany, the Netherlands, and Scandinavia, and (a remote possibility) the Orthodox princes of Russia. A great dynastic marriage was unnecessary, even unwanted: by 1840 uniting disparate countries by marriage between their hereditary rulers was a thing of the past. Possible consorts had been suggested for her since she was a tiny child, among them her cousins Prince George of Cambridge and Prince George of Cumberland. King Leopold had long ago determined to promote another Coburg alliance—between Victoria and her cousin Prince *Albert of Saxe-Coburg and Gotha (1819–1861)—and had been supervising the education of his motherless nephew as a potential consort.

Victoria was alerted to the intention, and Albert and his brother Ernest were brought to Britain in May 1836 to be scrutinized. Eager to frustrate the duchess of Kent's plans, King William IV favoured a match with Prince Alexander of Orange, and invited him to Britain with his brother also in May 1836, but he was not a success with Victoria, and nothing more was heard of that match. Albert, on the other hand, came with the blessing of Uncle Leopold, and Victoria was more or less determined to find him pleasing. His physical attractions did much to outweigh his tendency to fall asleep during evening parties, and the cousins kept up a correspondence over the next few years. But the engagement which Albert had been led to expect was slow to materialize. Once on the throne, Victoria relished her independence. Even the scandals of 1839 failed to persuade her that marriage was a solution to her difficulties. On 15 July (ten days after Lady Flora's death) she told Leopold that there was no prospect of her marrying Albert for at least two or three years: she had a '*great repugnance to change my present position*' (*Letters*, 1st ser., 1.224). A visit from the Coburg brothers was nevertheless scheduled for the autumn, and on 10 October they arrived at Windsor. Watching them arrive from the top of the stairs, Victoria fell in love. 'It was with some emotion that I beheld Albert—who is *beautiful*', she told her journal (*Girlhood*, 2.262). On 15 October she undertook the somewhat awkward task of proposing to Albert, saying 'it would make me *too happy* if he would consent to what I wished (to marry me)' (ibid., 2.268). Albert accepted.

Albert was far from a popular choice of consort. In some quarters he was viewed as a penniless foreign adventurer, coming to Britain to burden its taxpayers. Moreover, he was slightly younger than the queen, and part of the purpose of encouraging her marriage was to place the inexperienced, wilful girl under the tutelage of a more mature, masculine intellect. When the match was first raised with him, Melbourne objected on grounds of their consanguinity, adding 'Those Coburgs are not popular abroad; the Russians hate them.' But as Victoria herself pointed out, 'Who was there else?' (*Girlhood*, 2.153).

Marriage changed everything for Victoria. Before the wedding, on 10 February 1840 in the Chapel Royal at St James's Palace, she had been anxious to assert herself and her authority over her future husband. Albert was not permitted to select his own household (apart from a few personal retainers); his desire for an extended honeymoon in the country was rebuffed with a reminder that his wife had political duties in London; and in several ways Victoria made plain that politics were to be her preserve, not his. Within two years Albert had moved from wielding the blotting paper on Victoria's official letters to dictating their content. He also changed her preference for the gaieties of London society to one for the relative rural quiet of

Windsor, and was poised to remove from his wife's house-hold the long-serving Baroness Lehzen (whom he loathed and regarded as an evil, and countervailing, influence with his wife).

This transformation stemmed in part from Albert's determination to reshape his wife's character and to be the master in their relationship, and in part from Victoria embracing wholeheartedly the prevalent view of the correct relationship between the sexes, and especially between husband and wife: women were by nature infer-ior and dependent, and it was their duty to submit to and adore their husbands. Indeed, Victoria frequently expressed her regret at the unnatural order within her own household, in which the accident of her birth and position denied Albert his rightful place at the head of all her affairs. Not that a submissive role came entirely easily. She was used to having her own way, and her fiery temper fitted uneasily with Albert's chilly rationality. There were frequent scenes: Albert preferred to deal with an argu-ment by leaving the room, and the corridors could echo to the sound of his wife's fury. Victoria soon became accus-tomed to finding herself in the wrong, and blamed herself bitterly for disputing with her husband. For his part, Albert keenly felt the anomalies of his position, and deter-mined from the outset that although he could not offi-cially assume the male role at the head of his family's pub-lic affairs, he would be master in his own house.

Albert's dominance over Victoria became total; after his death she observed desolately that she had 'leant on him for all and everything—without whom I did nothing, moved not a finger, arranged not a print or photograph, didn't put on a gown or bonnet if he didn't approve it' (*Dearest Mama*, 23). This was the ideal of womanhood with a vengeance, and it was achieved by Albert breaking his wife's will. If she challenged him, he responded by threat-ening to withdraw his affection or even (on occasion) to withdraw entirely from the relationship; Victoria would respond with abject submission. Albert's patriarchy was thus achieved by treating his wife as a wilful child (in the evangelical tradition of child-rearing, the child's will had to be broken in order for it to be remade as a Christian): the 'Beloved Victoria' of his letters before their marriage soon became 'Dear Child' or 'Dear Good, Little One'. The fatherless Victoria all her life needed a strong, masculine figure to lean on. Albert was only too happy to oblige. But no doubts can be entertained about the depth of Victoria's passion for her husband. Albert made up for her child-hood; he became her moral guide and teacher as well as her lover, companion, friend. She idolized him, wor-shipped him, and sang his praises to all who would listen. He was 'my beloved Albert', an 'Angel' (constantly), a 'per-fect being' (*Letters*, 1st ser., 1.460), 'the purest and best of human beings' (ibid., 3.452). The strong-willed, stubborn, curious, sociable Victoria, whose character had been forged by the Kensington system, was transformed within years of her marriage (not without some difficulty and rebellion on her part) into a personally and intellectually submissive, almost reclusive wife by Albert's patriarchal insecurity. She loved him; she was diminished by him.

If the transformation of Albert's position owed much to his wife's temperament, it owed as much to her fertility. Within weeks of their marriage Victoria was dismayed to find herself pregnant. Although the queen was blessed with an iron constitution and her pregnancies were gener-ally physically easy, custom—and memories of the death of her cousin Princess Charlotte in childbirth—required that she be treated as an invalid for their duration. She also suffered severely from what was later termed post-natal depression after the births of several of her children. It was during the weeks before the birth of their first child that Albert established himself *de facto* as the queen's pri-vate secretary (she had no officially appointed private sec-retary until 1867), and as a powerful, even dominant, voice in court politics. *Victoria Adelaide was born on 21 November 1840; 'Never mind, the next will be a Prince', Victoria told her disappointed attendants (Weintraub, 149). It was: Albert Edward, prince of Wales [*see* Edward VII], was born on 9 November 1841 and was fol-lowed by *Alice (1843), *Alfred (1844), *Helena (1846), *Louise (1848), *Arthur (1850), *Leopold (1853), and *Bea-trice (1857). The queen suffered no miscarriage or still-birth, and all her children survived to adulthood, a situ-ation unusual even among the Victorian upper classes. During the birth of Prince Leopold the queen was given chloroform for the first time—'soothing, quieting & delightful beyond measure', said the queen (Longford, 234)—and put an end to the arguments about its general use. Victoria herself had been breastfed by her mother; her own children were promptly put out to wet-nurses. Victoria, who dreaded childbirth, recognized the political as much as the personal inconvenience of numerous off-spring. These were, after all, the 'hungry forties', and rad-ical opinion, which had commented unfavourably on Vic-toria's choice of a penniless husband, groaned at the bien-nial increases to her family.

Family values and the bourgeois monarchy The critics were in a minority. From the birth of the princess royal in 1840 the royal couple—now a royal family—were held up as an example of domestic felicity. The irony, however, was that although the Victorians placed a high premium on the role of the wife and mother in creating ideal family life, in the royal family this was Albert's province. Despite his inroads into Victoria's public life, both he and Victoria always remained uncomfortably aware that the 'natural order' was inverted, and that Victoria reigned sovereign, while Albert's position derived exclusively from his rela-tionship with her and, even more humiliatingly, from fathering the heir to the throne. They consciously took the decision that, in their home life at least, Albert would have the authority and rights of a traditional paterfamil-ias. Hence it was he, not Victoria, who (after some early arguments) was the dominant voice in determining how the children were educated and brought up, who oversaw the modernization of the royal household (managing ser-vants was usually a female job), and who romped in the nursery with his children. Victoria was by no means an archetypal Madonna-esque mamma, her world revolving around her children: she disliked small babies—'froglike', she thought—and children were a worry. Besides, they distracted her attention from Albert and, more importantly, they distracted Albert's attention from her. Being a wife ranked high above motherhood in Victoria's priorities, and she was jealous of anyone or anything that took his attention from her. She was lucky in Albert's utter uxoriousness: his care to avoid even the semblance of interest in other women pleased Victoria, while alienating him further from British aristocratic society and the royal household.

The apocryphal story of the lady in the audience at a performance of *Antony and Cleopatra* turning to her companion and saying 'How unlike, how very unlike the home life of our own dear Queen' represents something fundamental about the impact of royal domesticity. George IV and William IV in their private lives had been bywords for lechery and irregular marital affairs; Victoria and Albert were their diametric opposites. And as the sons of George III symbolized the excesses of aristocratic behaviour, so his granddaughter came to symbolize middle-class virtue, with her family life—notably painted by Landseer—at its heart. But although the queen shared some of the tastes and values of her most respectable subjects (Lord Salisbury later declared that if he knew what the queen thought about an issue, he knew what the middle classes would think), and although in later life her deliberate shunning of the more ostentatious trappings of royalty made it easy to think of her as a bourgeois widow at the head of the family firm, she was in fact *sui generis*, one of a kind. As Arthur Ponsonby put it, 'She bore no resemblance to an aristocratic English lady, she bore no resemblance to a wealthy middle-class Englishwoman, nor to any typical princess of a German court. ... she was simply without prefix or suffix "The Queen"' (Ponsonby, 70).

'A place of one's own': Osborne and Balmoral
Creating a suitable setting for this idyllic family life took up much royal energy in the 1840s and 1850s. Victoria had inherited three royal residences with the crown: Buckingham Palace, Windsor Castle, and the Brighton Pavilion. All had disadvantages: Albert disliked London life, which made him ill; at Windsor there were no private grounds (the public had admission to all the gardens and park, and the family were on constant display); and the Brighton Pavilion was hedged in by suburban development. Added to which, all three were, as crown property, under the control of the Office of Woods and Forests, which inhibited changes to the buildings that would make them suit their needs and taste. The need for a home of their own became pressing. The major role in imagining, designing, and executing the building of the royal houses most closely associated with Victoria—Balmoral Castle on Deeside in Aberdeenshire, and Osborne House, near Cowes on the Isle of Wight— was Albert's, with Victoria an uncritical admirer of his achievements. Albert's taste in matters architectural inevitably dominated: he, after all, had travelled, had been in Italy as well as his native Germany, while Victoria's experience, even of her own country, was limited to the tours Sir John Conroy had planned, and the childhood trips to the south coast for her health. In September 1842 the royal

couple made their first visit to Scotland, keeping great state in Edinburgh (but not on the scale of George IV's famous Scottish jaunt of 1822), and then visiting in slightly less state some grandees of the lowlands and southern highlands. It was, 'Albert says very German-looking' (*Leaves from the Journal*, 13). There could be no higher praise, and Victoria's love affair with Scotland, which long survived her husband, began.

A summer cruise around the south coast and across to France and Belgium in 1843 reminded Victoria of her pleasant seaside holidays as a child, and she and Albert began to look for a seaside retreat. The Osborne estate near Cowes on the Isle of Wight was for sale, and after a preliminary visit in October 1844 they completed the purchase in November 1845. Even before this, Albert began an ambitious programme of building, and he and Victoria visited Osborne seven times in 1845 to familiarize themselves with their new home and to oversee progress on the building site. An Italianate palace replaced the original eighteenth-century Osborne House with remarkable speed: the old house was demolished in May 1845, and Victoria and Albert moved in during September 1846, although the building was not complete until 1849. Victoria was delighted with it: it offered distance from the annoyances of London and politics, privacy, serenity, space for family life. More importantly, it was a 'place of *one's own*' (*Letters*, 1st ser., 2.41). And it was all Albert's work: 'I get fonder and fonder of it, one is so quiet here, and everything is of interest, it being so completely my beloved one's creation—his delight and pride', she wrote (Duchess of York, *Victoria and Albert: Life at Osborne House*, 1988, 117). Albert relaxed at Osborne, and occupied himself with estate improvement, building, and playing with the children while Victoria sketched and painted in watercolours and admired everything he did. Courtiers and ministers were less enamoured of the domestic idyll on the island: there was no room in Osborne for a large entourage, and staff and courtiers were out-housed around the estate, while ministers found the distance from London inconvenient for the execution of public business. But the royal couple found that even a few miles of sea were insufficient protection from the intrusions of the curious and the demands of their position: Scotland called them.

Victoria and Albert returned to Scotland in 1844 to stay with the duke and duchess of Atholl at Blair Castle, Perthshire, and again in 1847, this time as part of a yachting tour. Their pleasure was dimmed by wet weather, and on learning that the east coast, and Deeside in particular, had a better climate, Victoria and Albert decided to look there for a Scottish home. They purchased Balmoral, sight unseen, in August 1848 and rebuilt it between 1853 and 1855. Balmoral provided privacy in abundance and, for Victoria, a kind of freedom unavailable elsewhere: 'The Queen is running in and out of the house all day long, and often goes about alone, walks into the cottages and sits down and chats with the old women', Charles Greville reported (Charlot, 290). Victoria delighted in the frank conversation of the highlanders. Influenced by her love of

Walter Scott's novels, she saw highlanders as noble peasants, with none of the cringing servility, corrupted manners, and predatory impertinence of southerners. They seemed to stand outside the usual British class structure: she thought them a colourful feudal remnant rather than an agricultural proletariat, enjoyed their theatricality, and granted them a licence not permitted to any others of her subjects.

Victoria and Albert embraced Scottishness wholeheartedly. Balmoral was bedecked in tartan, the children were dressed in kilts, and the whole family took to highland pursuits. They made expeditions (some in transparent incognito) to local beauty spots, climbed and rode in the mountains, attended the local highland games, and rowed on the loch. Albert studied Gaelic, hunted, shot, and fished; Victoria followed, often taking her sketchbooks with her. When even Balmoral seemed too crowded, too urban, Victoria and Albert retreated to the remodelled shiels (stone huts), formerly used by the gillies, at Alt-na Giuthasach, some 5 miles from the castle, for greater solitude and simplicity. Solitude was relative: their party included a maid of honour, two maids, a valet, a footman, a cook, Albert's Jäger, and 'old John Gordon and his wife' (*Leaves from the Journal*, 112). The annual autumn train journey to Balmoral (Victoria first travelled by train in 1842) was eagerly awaited by the royal family; the royal household were less enthralled at the prospect of weeks of isolation in the chilly north, while the ministers required to be in attendance, far from Westminster, seldom comfortable, and often unwelcome, tended to greet news of their duty with dismay. But the convenience of politicians was of no interest to the queen: 'Really', she wrote, 'when one is so happy & blessed in one's home life, as I am, Politics (provided my country is safe) must take only a 2nd. place' (Longford, 184).

Moving on from Melbourne The fall of the Melbourne government in 1841 was a personal and political blow to the queen. Under Melbourne she had developed from an isolated, quietly rebellious child into an eager, imperious young woman. She had thoroughly established her independence from her mother and her mother's agents: by 1841 she was beginning to forgive the duchess of Kent for her childhood, and to establish a more amicable relationship with her. Albert's arrival at her side in 1840 ensured that the lessons of her early errors did not go unheeded: that gossip leads to slander, and too much fraternizing with courtiers endangered the dignity of the queen; and that while the ministry served at the queen's pleasure, the queen was to find her pleasure in accordance with the will of the electorate.

Even before the return of a tory majority in the House of Commons in September 1841, Melbourne began preparing the ground for his inevitable departure, offering sound advice to Victoria on her constitutional duty towards her ministers, of whatever political complexion. With Albert and Albert's private secretary, George Anson, Melbourne began a series of secret negotiations with Peel over the composition of the queen's household to avoid a repetition of the 'bedchamber crisis': the queen could not be seen to back down and remove her ladies at the demand of the prime minister, but Peel still needed to be able to show that the female household was not dominated by his enemies. It was arranged that three ladies would offer their resignations without being asked and would be replaced with less overtly political women, thereby saving face all round. But, despite the months of careful preparation, Victoria was desolated by Melbourne's departure, and Melbourne (similarly distressed) agreed to continue their correspondence. Although Melbourne's letters urged the queen to have confidence in Peel and to comply with the ministry, the correspondence was strictly unconstitutional, as it meant that the monarch was secretly receiving information and advice from the opponents of her ministers. Had it become widely known, the exchange would have amounted to a public declaration of her lack of confidence in her government. Despite intervention from Baron Stockmar the correspondence continued unabated through 1842, and diminished only when Melbourne's health collapsed and the queen thoroughly let go of the past.

The constitution, according to Stockmar, gave 'the Sovereign in his functions a deliberative part' (*Letters*, 1st ser., 1.352–3), that is to say, the queen's constitutional role was to reflect on the policies, persons, and practices of her ministers, and after due consideration to give her opinion to her ministers, expecting it to be heard and heeded. Her prerogatives were to be observed rigorously, and in return she would support her ministers publicly and endorse their decisions. Stockmar doubted whether the queen possessed the means to carry out this deliberative role, an assessment which belittled both Victoria's intellect and her character. Certainly the queen needed political advisers, yet the constitution hindered her from obtaining them, as theoretically the monarch should be advised only by her ministers, and particularly by her prime minister. From her ministers she would hear only one side of an argument, restricting her capacity to deliberate on the issues. If she could not receive advice from the opposition, where was she to turn? A king might expect his court to provide an additional source of political information, from among the lords-in-waiting with seats in parliament, and the great officers of his household, or from friends of his youth. This route was closed to Victoria because her closest attendants were all women and because after the 'bedchamber crisis' it became expedient to disengage the entire household from politics. And she had no friends from her childhood. Educated in isolation, and a girl to boot, she had no network of acquaintances in the political world and restricted contacts even with aristocratic society: when she came to make appointments to her household, she was forced to rely on hearsay accounts of the agreeable qualities of different ladies or, as time passed, to select her attendants from among the families of people already in her service. So the queen had a small pool of resources on which to draw: King Leopold and Stockmar, Albert and his secretary Anson, and ultimately her own judgement. Her judgement generally found that reliance on Albert in all political matters would produce the best results.

An account of Victoria's political opinions and actions from her marriage until Albert's death, then, is largely an account of Albert's. Slowed down by her frequent pregnancies and constrained by her acceptance of the inferiority of women's capabilities and her own education and intellect, she gave the function of deliberation to Albert. Fitted by sex, by temperament, and by training, Albert was king in all but name. 'Oh! if only I could make him king', Victoria exclaimed (Longford, 179). It was the one thing she could not do for him. The years between 1840 and 1861 have often been described as a period of 'dual monarchy': Albert took on the executive, deliberative role, while Victoria took the more dignified part (to use Bagehot's term) and provided legitimacy for Albert's executive. She worked hard at the official papers, discussing them with Albert every morning and corresponding with and interviewing her ministers (always with Albert present); but Albert often drafted the responses, which Victoria copied out to send. In 1850 Albert summed up his interpretation of his position to the duke of Wellington: he was 'the natural head of her family, superintendent of her household, manager of her private affairs, sole *confidential* adviser in politics, and only assistant in her communications with the officers of the Government, ... the private secretary of the sovereign and her permanent minister' (Martin, 2.260).

Unlike Melbourne, Albert was not subject to the vagaries of the electorate, and he had no political interests to serve that were not Victoria's. The monarchy, in Albert's and Stockmar's formulation, was to be politically neutral. Neutrality meant not taking sides in party-political disputes; it meant considering a question from all sides and promoting the national interest, not the short-term interests of political parties bent on gaining and retaining power. It did not mean forgoing a political function for the monarchy. If anything, it elevated the importance of the monarch's political voice: 'Is the sovereign not the natural guardian of the honour of his country, is he not *necessarily* a politician?', Albert reflected (Connell, 142). In the early Victorian state Albert was the politician in the royal family.

Victoria's conversion to Albert's way of thinking was nowhere clearer than in the transformation of her feelings about Sir Robert Peel, whose assumption of office in 1841 she had so dreaded. By 1845 his own resignation was a matter of profound regret, for he had become 'our worthy Peel ... a man of unbounded *loyalty, courage*, patriotism, and *high-mindedness*' (*Letters*, 1st ser., 2.75). Peel was a man after Albert's own heart: hard-working, earnest, reserved, dedicated. Through Albert's eyes Victoria came to see the merits of her prime minister, and, in his resignations over the corn laws in 1845 and 1846, recognized a disinterested service to herself and the nation that rose above the interests of party.

Above all, the domestic political agenda for Victoria and Albert was defined by a quest for political stability. Men and measures that upset the equilibrium of the country were to be deplored, and the highest praise they could heap on a minister was that he was 'safe'. A safe minister placed the needs of his country above the demands of party politics; a safe minister headed a government with a firm, controllable majority in the House of Commons, thus obviating the need for frequent, potentially tumultuous elections; a safe minister was considerate of Victoria's and Albert's feelings and position, and upheld the constitutional privileges of the monarchy.

All government business passed across Victoria's and Albert's desks; Albert's conscientiousness ensured that it all received due attention. Victoria involved herself wholeheartedly less often. The issues which caught her attention and seemed to her to be of paramount importance fell broadly into two categories: matters concerning British security and prestige, and matters concerning royal authority, prestige, and security. In the substantive domestic debates of the 1840s—over the corn laws, the effects of industrialization, the implications of organized working-class radicalism—she expressed little interest. Neither Lord Ashley's Ten Hours Act (which reduced working hours for women and children in factories) nor the agitations of the Chartists could expect sympathy from the queen. It was not that Victoria lacked compassion. She believed profoundly in the obligations of the rich towards the poor, and dispensed large sums in personal charity: between 1837 and 1871 she gave £8160 (nearly 15 per cent of her privy purse) annually to charities (Prochaska, 77), and the figure rose thereafter. But like most of the upper classes, she regarded charity as an individual, religious duty, not a matter for government or collective action, which could damage trade and industry. She used her position to encourage others to be charitable, and became patron of some 150 institutions. She periodically issued orders that ladies appearing at court should wear gowns of British manufacture, to support native industry, while the *bal costumé* of 12 May 1842 (at which the queen and prince appeared as King Edward III and Queen Philippa) was intended to provide work for the unemployed Spitalfields silk weavers. A regularly repeated calumny, that Victoria gave only £5 to the many appeals on behalf of the starving Irish during the famine years, is belied by the evidence: she headed one subscription list with a donation of £2000, made contributions to other projects brought to her attention by her ladies-in-waiting, and attended a charity performance at the opera as well as other fundraising events. But her sympathy with the sufferings of the Irish peasantry waned rapidly when they turned to political action to improve their lot, threatening the security of her realm. The agitation in Ireland and the murders of landlords in 1847–8, coinciding with the year of revolutions on the continent, filled Victoria with foreboding for the safety of her throne; the Chartists' Kennington Common meeting of 10 April 1848, though ultimately a damp squib, sent the royal family scurrying from London to the safety of the Isle of Wight.

'Provided my country is safe' Foreign affairs were Albert's greatest preoccupation, and he drew Victoria along with him. His vision was for Europe to be led by a united, liberal

Germany in alliance with Britain—constitutional monarchy triumphing over the despotic monarchies of Russia, Austria, and Prussia for the general good and in the interests of international peace. Ironically, it was with Britain's hereditary enemy, France, that Victoria and Albert developed their first ties in the 1840s. Their uncle Leopold had married a daughter of the Orléanist king of the French, Louis Philippe, in 1832, and it was essentially a family visit that Victoria and Albert paid to the French royal family at the Château d'Eu, near Cherbourg, in August 1843: it was the first time an English sovereign had visited the French sovereign since 1520, and Victoria's first journey abroad. Perhaps in consequence, Victoria was in 1844 visited by no fewer than three reigning sovereigns: the king of Saxony, Tsar Nicholas I of Russia, and Louis Philippe paying a reciprocal visit, the first such since 1356. The crown prince of Prussia also visited Windsor in 1844, and in 1845 Victoria made her first journey to Germany, to see Albert's homeland of Coburg and also to visit the Prussian court in Berlin. In consequence, Victoria came increasingly to feel herself part of an international brotherhood of monarchy. She and Albert felt that their personal ties with the ruling houses of Europe gave them a special knowledge and authority in foreign affairs, an opinion which brought them into regular conflict with Lord Palmerston, who in 1846 returned to the Foreign Office.

Palmerston took a thoroughgoing whig view of the relationship between crown and parliament, and had no time for the royal couple's inflated idea of their own role. For their part, Victoria and Albert found Palmerston's policies often rash and inflammatory, and they found his unpopularity in the courts and embassies of Europe personally embarrassing. His support for liberal, constitutional causes abroad and his hostility to French interests seemed to Victoria and Albert the very opposite of desirable—not least because they undermined the position of monarchs abroad—and his habits in the matter of the dispatches, which he often sent to the royal couple only after they had been sent abroad, were at best discourteous and at worst unconstitutional. While the queen repeatedly called on her prime minister, Lord John Russell, to dismiss Palmerston, and even threatened to do so herself, Palmerston, secure in popular approval and parliamentary ascendancy, carried on blithely, though he bowed to proprieties and pulled back from the brink of open confrontation with the queen. Great were the rejoicings at court in December 1851 when Palmerston brought about his own downfall by expressing support for the new emperor of France, Napoleon III, contrary to the government's stated policy of neutrality.

The high Victorian decade: war and rebellion Palmerston's fall crowned for Victoria a triumphant year which had been dominated by the realization of Albert's plans for the Great Exhibition. Her total faith in her husband's vision for the Crystal Palace in Hyde Park was triumphantly vindicated. The opening was, Victoria thought, 'the *greatest* day in our history, the *most beautiful* and *imposing* and *touching* spectacle ever seen' (*Letters*, 1st ser., 2.383); more importantly, it was a triumph for Albert, who at last

seemed to receive the popular acclaim his wife thought he deserved. Albert still had no official status in Britain, a situation the queen considered intolerable and which she regularly pressed her ministers to remedy, to no avail.

Two events overseas engaged Victoria in a way that no peacetime incident had: the war in the Crimea, and the mutiny in India in 1857. As the first troops departed for the Crimea in 1854, she became fervently martial in spirit. Regarding herself as head of the army, and the soldiers peculiarly her own, she watched countless soldiers depart, and when the navy set sail for the Baltic, she was aboard the royal yacht *Fairy* at Spithead: 'Navy and Nation were particularly pleased at *my leading them out*', she reported to King Leopold (*Letters*, 1st ser., 3.20). Victoria was not called on to be another Elizabeth, but she became engrossed in the distant war, seizing on dispatches and news, writing constant encouragement to her generals and to the widows of fallen officers, instigating the casting of the Crimean campaign medal, and bestowing it personally on hundreds of returning soldiers; the first such ceremony was on 18 May 1855. She helped to design the Victoria Cross, suggesting its famous motto, 'For Valour', and instituting it by royal warrant. More warlike, if that were possible, than her prime minister, Palmerston, she reluctantly acquiesced in the peace concluded in March 1856, recognizing that 'no *glory* could have been hoped for us' (ibid., 3.235) by continuing hostilities. She followed with interest and approval the activities of Florence Nightingale at Scutari, and presented her with a brooch on her return as a mark of approbation for her work among the soldiers 'whose sufferings you have had the *privilege* of alleviating in so merciful a manner' (ibid., 3.216). The queen herself visited countless wounded and sick soldiers on their return to Britain, and urged on the government the need to provide adequate hospital facilities. On 19 May 1856 she laid the foundation stone for the Royal Victoria Hospital, Netley, Hampshire, and for the rest of her life she took a keen interest in it, visiting it regularly.

The war also transformed Napoleon III into Britain's closest ally. An imperial visit to Britain in May 1855 convinced Victoria of the emperor's qualities; Empress Eugénie too met with her approbation, for Victoria admired beauty in other women. Victoria paid a reciprocal visit in August to her ally in Paris, where she was '*delighted, enchanted, amused* and *interested*, and think I never saw anything more *beautiful* and gay than Paris' (*Letters*, 1st ser., 3.172), and paid a visit of respect to the tomb of the first Napoleon. The visit sealed the alliance, and had longer-term importance as the origin of the prince of Wales's love of France which in a new century brought the entente cordiale.

The country had scarcely recovered from the Crimean War when news began filtering back to Britain of a mutiny by sepoys serving in the East India Company's army. Victoria was shocked by the accounts of the massacres: 'Altogether, the whole is so much more distressing than the Crimea—where there was *glory* and honourable warfare, and where the poor women and children were safe', she observed (*Letters*, 1st ser., 3.313). She received regular reports from the governor-general, Lord Canning, and from his wife, Charlotte, who had been one of her own ladies-in-waiting. The rebellion suppressed, the queen put herself firmly behind Canning's policy of relative clemency towards Indians not directly involved in the insurrection. Palmerston's government fell in February 1858, and it was Lord Derby's second short-lived ministry which brought India under direct British rule. Victoria required that the proclamation made in India to inform the people of the change should 'breathe feelings of generosity, benevolence, and religious feeling', and was especially insistent on the inclusion of a message of religious toleration (ibid., 3.379, 389).

The fluid state of party allegiances in the 1850s meant that changes in administration were relatively frequent (and threatened changes more so). The royal prerogative of appointing ministers had not yet fallen into abeyance, and Albert in particular was active in negotiating the formation of cabinets. Palmerston's return to cabinet office under Lord Aberdeen in December 1852 effectively set the limits on royal power. He could not be kept out of the cabinet, but he accepted the Home Office rather than the Foreign Office. This became a standard approach for Victoria: rather than objecting to an individual *tout court*, she would suggest he was inappropriate for a particular office. When Aberdeen's coalition government was brought down in January 1855, Albert unsuccessfully attempted to broker new coalitions with Derby or Russell at the head, but the royal couple were forced to concede defeat and ask Palmerston to form a government.

In the context of the Crimean War, Victoria became more sympathetic to Palmerston's aims and methods: his belligerent stance enhanced British (and Victoria's) prestige. With Clarendon as foreign secretary in the new ministry she had the additional reassurance that foreign affairs were in the hands of 'an able, sensible, impartial man' (Charlot, 367). Although Victoria and Albert softened their view of Palmerston during his period as prime minister, they attempted to prevent his return after the fall of Lord Derby's minority Conservative administration following the general election in June 1859. By then the European situation was critical, as Austrian rule in northern Italy came under challenge, and the court, fearing that Palmerston would be anti-Austrian, invited Granville to form a ministry. On Granville's failure to do so, Palmerston was unavoidable, as was Russell, his foreign secretary. Victoria and Albert subsequently expended much energy in mediating between Russell and Palmerston, and in insisting that Britain should not be drawn into war over Italian affairs.

An expanding family, 1841–1861 While politics, government, and foreign affairs dominated Victoria's and Albert's official, but largely unobserved, life, the affairs of their family dominated public perceptions of the royal couple. The public image of a domestic family enjoying bourgeois pursuits (albeit on a regal scale) belied the reality of the long periods of separation of the parents from their children, whose regular companions were tutors and governesses, as in most upper-class families. Victoria was not a cold, distant mother: like many mothers, she had mixed feelings towards her children. Once past babyhood, if they were attractive, moderately intelligent, and above all, well behaved, she responded well to them. She loved the idea of family life (which she had not herself experienced as a child), and was proud of her collective brood; individually, she could find them trying.

In Vicky, the princess royal, their eldest and most intellectually promising child, Victoria and particularly Albert felt a special interest, and the education of their eldest son, Albert Edward, the prince of Wales, was planned in minute detail. An inappropriate educational programme, unfavourable comparisons with his elder sister, and constant hectoring from both his parents drove the prince in precisely the direction his parents had sought to avoid. Victoria wanted Bertie, as he was known, to be the image of his upright, dutiful, morally austere, intellectual father, to become a model king, liberal, just, pure. Bertie, as soon as the opportunity presented itself, kicked over the traces and threw himself into a life of pleasure. Affie (Alfred), as the second son and heir presumptive to the dukedom of Saxe-Coburg and Gotha, also caused his parents concern, showing too much inclination to follow Bertie's example: wanting to be a sailor, he joined the navy at thirteen, and spent most of his formative years away from home. Alice, the third child, shared in some measure the interest bestowed on the elder children, but the children who followed later (Helena, Louise, Arthur, and Leopold) were unlikely to succeed to the throne, and were all too aware of their secondary importance, a position which, ironically, left their parents more freely affectionate towards them. Arthur was Victoria's favourite child, and Leopold, by virtue of his ill health, the most over-protected. Beatrice, the youngest and a bright, lively child, captured her mother's affection in a way the older children had not, and 'Baby' was indulged.

The relationship between Victoria and her eldest daughter became difficult as Vicky approached maturity. Her interests and tastes had been formed by her father, her intellectual skills were considerable, and she and Albert adored each other. Victoria felt excluded and threatened by the closeness of their relationship; Albert found his daughter more intelligent and sympathetic than his wife, and did not hesitate to scold Victoria in front of their children. Increasingly preoccupied with public affairs, he could not accept that Victoria sometimes needed his company and undivided attention. During her last pregnancy in 1856–7 the issue caused frequent disputes between them: Albert thought that with eight children his wife had sufficient resources and company, but Victoria did not find it easy to establish intimate relationships with young people, and, as she told her uncle, '*All* the numerous children are as *nothing* to me when he [Albert] *is away*' (*Letters*, 1st ser., 3.305).

It had long been Albert's hope that his eldest daughter should marry the heir to the Prussian throne, a project first officially mooted in 1851, when the prince and princess of Prussia visited the Great Exhibition with their son

Prince Frederick William (Fritz). The alliance was to rescue Prussia—and hence Germany and all Europe—from the dangers of 'Russian reaction and French licence' (Longford, 259). In September 1855 the 24-year-old prince arrived at Balmoral to ask for the hand of the princess royal, who had not yet celebrated her fifteenth birthday, or made her début in society. Victoria and Albert approved, but required that nothing be said to Vicky until after her confirmation (to be held after Easter 1856). Fritz would then be allowed to 'make her the proposal, which, however, I have little—indeed no—doubt she will gladly *accept*' (*Letters*, 1st ser., 3.187), Victoria exulted. The queen believed that love was a precondition of marriage and had strong reservations about child brides, but she wanted Albert's hopes fulfilled and was anxious lest Fritz should be unwilling to wait for Vicky to grow up. She was, however, persuaded of Fritz's virtues and, with her own experience in mind, expected her daughter to find the young man irresistible. Vicky herself expediently allowed herself to fall in love with her suitor. The planned delay was allowed to lapse within days, and on 29 September 1855 he proposed in form and was accepted, on the understanding that no marriage could take place until after Vicky's seventeenth birthday. It now became necessary that the princess royal be treated as an adult, despite her youth. The queen veered emotionally between sorrow at the premature ending of her eldest child's childhood and her impending initiation into the world of matrimony, pride in securing the ambitious match, and irritation that Vicky now shared the precious dinners with Albert that had often become the queen's only waking time alone with her husband.

It was in the context of her children's increasing maturity that Victoria raised once more the question of Albert's official status: as matters stood, he owed his position entirely to his wife, and in the event of her early death would have only such status as his son chose to give him. An attempt to have him made prince consort by act of parliament in 1854 soon foundered, and in 1856 Victoria again attempted to have his position confirmed, but without success. Giving up on the parliamentary route, on 25 June 1857 she conferred the title of prince consort on her husband by royal letters patent.

The princess royal's wedding took place at the Chapel Royal, St James's, on 25 January 1858, Victoria having firmly quashed any suggestion that the ceremony might take place in Berlin: 'Whatever may be the usual practice of Prussian Princes, it is not *every* day that one marries the eldest daughter of the Queen of England', she declared (*Letters*, 1st ser., 3.321). Once her daughter was safely in Berlin, and officially a woman rather than a girl, Victoria found herself able to enter into the sort of confidential relationship that had previously eluded her. Her eldest daughter received a regular barrage of letters, and the correspondence flourished for forty years, punctuated by infrequent visits. Indeed, so frequently did Victoria write in the first months of Vicky's marriage, with so many demands, instructions, criticisms, and admonitions, that Baron Stockmar (who was still offering advice from Coburg) warned Albert that she would make her daughter ill. Vicky, like her mother, had soon become pregnant and in January 1859 gave birth to her first son, Victoria's first grandchild, the future Kaiser Wilhelm II, known to his family as Willie. Unlike Victoria, Vicky loved babies and small children, and the queen regularly scolded her for spending too much time in the nursery. Breastfeeding too was a practice of which Victoria disapproved strongly for women in their position—'I hoped … she would give up nursing, as we Princesses had other duties to perform', she told one of her cousins (ibid., 3.350)—and it was to be a regular bone of contention with her daughters.

Others were leaving the schoolroom: in 1860 the prince of Wales made his first official solo tour, to Canada and the United States, where he was greeted with enthusiasm. Prince Alfred had already gone to sea in 1858. Princess Alice's future was settled in November 1860, when she became engaged to the rather stolid Prince Louis of Hesse, Victoria having taken advantage of Vicky's vantage point at the heart of protestant Europe to assess potential marriage partners for her other children. Vicky also vetted possible brides for the prince of Wales: 'God knows! where the young lady we want is to be found! Good looks, health, education, character, intellect and a good disposition we want; great rank and riches we do not', Victoria told her daughter (*Dearest Child*, 223). Eventually they settled on Alexandra of Denmark, although an alliance with Denmark was unfavourably regarded in Prussia. Victoria's family thus began the expansion which placed her direct descendants on ten European thrones and in dozens of other royal houses.

Victoria's and Albert's court Court life under Victoria and Albert also took on a decidedly domestic and rather dull tone. Ceremonial was performed punctiliously when required, but with little enjoyment, for example at state openings of parliament and at levees and drawing-rooms, where the queen received the bows and curtseys of men and women wishing to be admitted to high society. Balls and concerts were held at Buckingham Palace, and the queen frequently attended the theatre and especially the opera, for which she retained her early love. She also enjoyed visits to Astley's circus, and the American showman Phineas T. Barnum was invited to bring the diminutive 'General' Tom Thumb to the palace three times in 1844. Such diversions were a welcome relief for courtiers, who were otherwise condemned to weeks of inactivity, literally 'in waiting' for the queen to require their services. Evenings could hang very heavy. A maid of honour, Eleanor Stanley, wrote of the dullness of the hours after dinner: the queen sat at one table with her ladies-in-waiting and female visitors, making conversation, and the maids of honour sat at another working at embroidery, while the prince remained in another room talking with the men for some time. He and 'one or two big-wigs' would then join the queen until she retired at 10.30, whereupon 'the other gentlemen make a rush from the whist-table or from the other room, and we gladly bundle up our work, and all is over' (Erskine, 176).

For visiting potentates a more ceremonial and formal

programme of entertainments was devised, and courtiers were kept busy looking after their visiting counterparts. But Victoria's court was never glamorous and seldom sparkling. The queen was no fashion plate: the huge crinolines and poke bonnets of the 1840s and 1850s flattered few of their wearers, any more than the lurid colours they often chose. Victoria's dress sense was often the despair of the more fashion-conscious of her ladies and her dressers, especially when odious comparisons could be made between the queen and more elegant women. On the visit to France in 1843 Lady Canning was 'very much distressed to see our Queen appear in scarlet china crape [sic]' (V. Surtees, *Charlotte Canning*, 1975, 99); Victoria did not hesitate to wear it again, however, to receive Grand Duke Michael of Russia later in the year. Her shyness discouraged easy sociability, and conversation was often stilted because she would not initiate subjects about which she was ignorant.

Nothing contributed so much to the staid tenor of life at court as the regularity of court mourning. Victorian etiquette on mourning practices was rigorously prescriptive, and the correct degree of gloom for the passing of each of Victoria's and Albert's relations was observed, from complete black with no visitors or public appearances for three months for close relatives, to a day or two in 'slight mourning' for more distant connections. In 1852 the queen observed that she had been in mourning for nine months in every year for three or four years, and that since her marriage she had lost ten uncles and aunts. A lady-in-waiting was sorely tempted to ask 'And pray, Madam, how many more have you to lose?' (Erskine, 205). The toll of compulsory grief mounted through the 1850s: the duke of Wellington's death in 1852 was the cause of national mourning, while the court marked (among others) the deaths of Victoria's aunt the queen of Belgium in 1850, her uncle the king of Hanover in 1851, her half-brother Prince Charles of Leiningen in 1856, her cousin the duchess of Nemours (from complications after childbirth) in 1857, and the prince consort's stepmother in 1860. This was mere preparation for the mourning that was to come.

The year of desolation, 1861 The year 1861 began with a death in the family. The aged King Frederick William of Prussia died on 1 January, making Vicky and Fritz crown prince and princess of Prussia. In February Victoria and Albert celebrated their twenty-first wedding anniversary, 'a day which had brought us, and I may say the *world* at *large*, such incalculable blessings!' (*Letters*, 1st ser., 3.433). Then on 16 March the duchess of Kent died and Victoria suffered a nervous breakdown. Her relationship with the duchess, so tense during her teenage years, had been repaired by Albert, who had a firm idea of the appropriate relationship between a mother and daughter, and in old age the duchess had become beloved. Moreover, Victoria knew herself to be isolated by her position, and her mother was one of the few people with whom she could be open. Rumours about the queen's mental health flew about the courts of Europe, and it was with some difficulty

that Albert brought her back into her public role to meet the king of Sweden in August.

Later in August the royal couple visited Ireland, the expedition planned to coincide with Bertie's military training at the Curragh. Still dwelling on her mother's death, Victoria set off with Albert in September for Balmoral, where Albert had planned several of the big expeditions they so enjoyed in the highlands. At the end of October they returned to Windsor, where they were confronted with news of the deaths in rapid succession of two of the sons of one of their Coburg cousins, Pedro V of Portugal and his brother Ferdinand, and then a report from the hand of the watchful Stockmar that the prince of Wales had been involved in an affair with an 'actress', Nelly Clifden. Victoria and Albert were horrified, not least because negotiations were in train for the prince's marriage to Princess Alexandra of Denmark. Albert's health, which had been poor for some years (modern diagnosis suggests he had cancer of the stomach or bowel), deteriorated rapidly. He had been suffering from a cold which he could not shake off. Victoria, wrapped up in her own misery, did not take Albert's condition seriously, and on 9 December she was finding her husband's illness 'tiresome': 'I need not tell you *what* a trial it is to me' (*Letters*, 1st ser., 3.470–71). On 11 December she was still feeling more for the difficulty of her own position while Albert was out of action, until the first public bulletins about his health were issued, when the full seriousness of his condition—believed to be typhoid fever—burst upon her. After three days of failing hopes Albert died on 14 December surrounded by his family, Victoria kneeling at his side and holding his hand.

Mourning practices: seclusion and memorials The devastation Albert's death caused in his widow is the strongest evidence of his part in forming her character. That she loved him went without saying; but the dependence he had created in her left her unprotected and helpless at his death. Her prostration was total. In accordance with custom and her own preferences and feelings, Victoria plunged into deep mourning. The court was swathed in black clothing and crepe, and henceforth the thousands of letters from Victoria's pen were written on paper edged up to half an inch deep in black (leaving little space for the queen's angular handwriting), in black-trimmed envelopes, and sealed with black wax. It was customary also for the recently widowed to avoid public appearances, an embargo Victoria embraced with gloomy enthusiasm. To most of her subjects the queen's grief and her withdrawal from public and social life were natural, reasonable, and proper. It was only when her mourning exceeded the traditional period (which decreed one year of full mourning for a husband, followed by a second year of half-mourning and a lifetime of black gowns and white caps) that the disquiet already felt by the political élite became more widespread.

Victoria committed herself to Albert's memory: 'his wishes—*his* plans—about everything, *his* views about *every thing* are to be *my law*! And no *human power* will make me swerve from *what he* decided and wished' (*Letters*, 1st ser.,

3.606). The public initially sympathized. Statues were erected by public subscription in some twenty-five cities; hospitals, infirmaries, and museums were given his name; and national memorials to the prince consort were built in London, Edinburgh, Dublin, and Tenby. Victoria responded by leaving her seclusion to appear in public and open several of the memorials. Her own memorials to Albert included Ludwig Gruner's and A. J. Humbert's Romanesque mausoleum at Frogmore, where Albert's remains were eventually interred, and the remodelling of the Wolsey chapel in St George's Chapel, Windsor, by G. G. Scott as the Albert memorial chapel. At Balmoral Victoria raised a cairn to his memory and erected a huge statue of him, and sculptors, painters, and photographers were kept busy with her commissions for likenesses of her lost husband. She commissioned Theodore Martin to write her husband's life in five volumes; she prepared the materials for *The Early Years of HRH the Prince Consort* (1867), which appeared over the name of her equerry, General Charles Grey; the clerk to the privy council, Arthur Helps, was selected to edit a volume of the prince's speeches. Helps was also called on by the queen to edit and introduce *Leaves from a Journal of our Life in the Highlands* (1868), which Victoria published as a tribute to Albert and as a substitute for public appearances.

Victoria's grief was genuine, fuelled by the feeling that she, like the public, had been insufficiently grateful for Albert during his lifetime, and she kept it stoked by creating images not only of the lost beloved, but also of her own sorrow: she seldom showed herself to anyone outside her family circle and circumscribed household, but by having her image captured as she gazed lovingly at a bust of Albert, surrounded by her younger children, she constantly viewed herself as a tragic heroine. Albert's image was everywhere about her: a photograph of him on his deathbed hung over his pillow in every bed the queen slept in.

Victoria's mourning caused an almost complete cessation of her public appearances. She resumed her day-to-day duties of reading dispatches, and her interest in foreign affairs soon had her again involved, making inimitable marginal comments on Foreign Office and Colonial Office papers. But she was unwilling for a time personally to receive ministers, who were to communicate with her through General Charles Grey or Princess Alice. When the privy council met, the queen sat in one room, the councillors in another, with Arthur Helps, the secretary to the council, acting as intermediary. Her workload was reduced by an act passed in March 1862 relieving her of triple-signing all army commissions (though she later resumed the practice). The queen's gloomy behaviour at the prince of Wales's marriage to Princess Alexandra of Denmark in March 1863 attracted unfavourable comment: she did not attend the wedding breakfast, and watched the ceremony from a secluded vantage point, in unrelieved black. It was a nice distinction between Disraeli's view—that 'the presence of the imperial and widowed mother in her Gothic pavilion, watching everything with intense interest, seeing everything, though herself unseen, was deeply dramatic and even affecting' (Monypenny and Buckle, 4.397)—and the more general sense that the queen had been something of a wet blanket.

Royal opening of parliament had been willingly suspended in 1862, but by 1864 its absence was criticized, and not merely by the marginal or even radical press. On 1 April 1864 *The Times*'s leader—the choice of date allowing for a licence of comment otherwise impossible—constituted a sustained sermon to the queen on her failure to do her public duty, and feigned to assume her imminent return to public life. On 6 April the queen herself wrote to the paper, with ill-concealed anonymity, to deny that she was 'about to resume the place in society which she occupied before her great affliction'. With a lead from *The Times*, other papers followed. In 1866, seeking a dowry for the marriage of her third daughter, Princess Helena, Victoria opened parliament, but avoided other public appearances, such as royal levees and drawing-rooms, which were held on her behalf by the prince and princess of Wales. In general, however, she refused to let the prince come forward as an alternative; she both blamed him for indolence, and opposed his emergence as a replacement for herself.

The madness of Queen Victoria? Widowhood badly affected Victoria's character. Without Albert to urge self-control she gave in completely to her grief; her physical and mental health suffered, and her doctor Sir William Jenner provided medical authority for her incapacity to undertake public appearances. Nobody except Albert had ever had any power to make the queen do anything she found uncongenial; now, with the excuse of her great sorrow and her fragile health, her family and household spoke of 'the extreme difficulty there was in managing her or in the slightest degree contradicting her' (Kennedy, 189). Only the firmly held belief that she too would die soon and be reunited with Albert helped Victoria through the first years of her widowhood. Her convictions that the prince of Wales (whom she held responsible for Albert's death) was unfit for the throne and that monarchy was a sacred obligation prohibited abdication. As a result Victoria became profoundly selfish and self-centred, and her native stubbornness was given full play. Her world had revolved around Albert; now it would revolve around herself.

Beneath all the discussions about the queen's mourning were worries about madness. King George III had, after all, been her grandfather. His long illness was (probably wrongly) considered to have been insanity, and the behaviour of his sons, especially George IV, was widely viewed as (at best) eccentric. Fears of hereditary madness, of bad blood, dominated the Victorian imagination; moreover, women who transgressed the bounds of 'normal' femininity were liable to be labelled mad by a patriarchal establishment with an interest in maintaining the sexual status quo. Baron Stockmar had warned Albert of the possible instability of his wife, and successfully urged on him the need to contain Victoria's passionate temperament. Doctors too kept a constant vigil over Victoria's mental health, their prognostications of disaster given revived force by her regular postnatal depressions. After 1861 rumours of the queen's madness flourished, encouraged by her seclusion, and gossip about her state of mind filled the letters of concerned politicians. Well into the 1870s Lord Derby was commenting on her increasing peculiarities and supposing 'that she will be what her predecessors since George III inclusive have been, if her life extends to old age' (*Derby Diaries, 1869–1878*, ed. J. Vincent, 1994, 179). Fears of triggering outright madness contributed to the caution with which everyone approached the queen in the 1860s, and to their reluctance to contradict or thwart her. Suggestions of insanity were also a means of containing the perceived dangers of a woman on the throne who was still young but no longer under the appropriate control of a husband; they notably tailed off after the queen passed the menopause. Victoria could be temperamental, passionate, self-willed, opinionated, proud, selfish, obstinate, stubborn, and difficult, but she was not mad. Even after 1861, at the depths of her nervous prostration, she was simply very sad.

Mrs Brown Victoria's sense of isolation after Albert's death was not easily alleviated. She had always enjoyed male company, but the proprieties restricted her as a widow to the society of women. Her unmarried daughters were too young to provide her daily support, and although she clung tenaciously to some of her female household, especially the duchesses of Sutherland and Atholl, Lady Ely, and Lady Augusta Bruce, in their company she could never bring herself to forget that she was the queen and they her subjects. Parliament (which feared placing an adviser about the queen who was not accountable to the ministry) was unwilling to concede that the queen needed a private secretary until 1867, when Charles Grey, formerly Albert's private secretary, was appointed. He generally retained the queen's confidence despite making it clear, in his bluff way, that he thought her grief exaggerated.

In this desolate situation John *Brown (1826–1883), who had become a permanent feature of the queen's daily life by 1865, seemed to Victoria sympathetic and understanding. He had been a regular attendant on the royal couple in the highlands and hence had Albert's seal of approval. Brown's domineering approach to the queen (unthinkable and unacceptable to her courtiers and family) was unique, being made possible by his lowly social position. No minister or secretary could say to her 'Hoots, then wumman. Can ye no hold yerr head up?' (Longford, 325). The exact degree of intimacy between the queen and John Brown cannot now be known (there is no evidence of marriage, despite many rumours and press reports), but Brown certainly became for a time the chief focus of the queen's emotional life, thereby helping to wean her from grief for her dead husband. Brown was especially useful to her during the late 1860s and early 1870s, but he remained her chief personal attendant until his death in 1883. The queen's grief on this occasion was unconfined, and she erected a large obelisk at Balmoral and a granite seat at Osborne to his memory.

In 1884, using his diaries, the queen wrote a memoir of Brown intended for private circulation. As Sir Henry Ponsonby (who had become her private secretary in 1870) at once saw, the document could not but be of sensational interest. He persuaded the queen to delay printing the memoir, and, according to his son and biographer, 'the papers were destroyed' (Ponsonby, 147). The destruction (if indeed it took place) was perhaps in the long run misguided: it has been taken by the prurient as evidence of an affair between the queen and Brown that her courtiers and family were anxious to hush up, whereas the mere fact of its being written tends to support the innocence of the relationship, for Victoria would never have publicized an illicit affair. When the queen published *More Leaves from a Journal of a Life in the Highlands* (1884), she gave it a fulsome dedication to Brown (*Leaves* had been dedicated to Albert), with a conclusion specifically to his memory, remarking that 'he is daily, nay hourly, missed by me, whose lifelong gratitude he won by his constant care, attention, and devotion'.

Family affairs, affairs of state, 1861–1868 Victoria was soon drawn back to foreign affairs through the letters of her daughter Vicky: now crown princess of Germany, Vicky was an impotent witness to Bismarck's policy of uniting Germany through 'blood and iron'. With Albert's dearest hopes and plans for a liberal Germany unravelling fast, the queen had to acknowledge that her initial vow to follow his wishes and policy in everything was impossible to fulfil: by 1880 the world he had known had been completely transformed, and Victoria was wise enough to know he would not have tolerated many of the inevitable changes, 'which might have done him harm' (*Darling Child*, 239). The marriage of Princess Alice to Louis of Hesse in July 1862—'more like a funeral than a wedding', Victoria reported approvingly (ibid., 2.85)—took away the daughter on whom she had leant most after Albert's death, and a dispute arose between them in 1866, when Alice opposed the marriage of Princess Helena to Christian of Schleswig-Holstein-Augustenburg. That marriage also caused some ill feeling with the prince and princess of Wales, for it was arranged in the aftermath of the Prussian-Danish War, over Schleswig-Holstein. The Danish-born princess of Wales could seldom be brought to politeness to Prussians, which added to tensions in the family, and persuaded the queen to sanction the marriage in 1871 of Princess Louise to a commoner, the marquess of Lorne, heir to the dukedom of Argyll: 'Times have changed', she told the prince of Wales. '[G]reat foreign alliances are looked on as causes of trouble and anxiety, and are of no good' (*Letters*, 2nd ser., 1.632). It was the closest she came to criticizing Albert.

The death of Lord Palmerston in October 1865 forced Victoria to take a more active part in domestic politics. For the first time since 1840 she faced an important political interview alone, on the formation of the new ministry. She turned to Lord Russell to continue the administration; 'strange, but these politicians never refuse' was King Leopold's cynical observation (*Letters*, 2nd ser., 1.281). It was one of the old campaigner's last comments; he died on 10 December, leaving Victoria to mourn one 'who has ever been to me as a Father' (ibid., 1.287). In 1866, with war brewing between Prussia and Austria, Victoria wrote to Lord Derby to hope that he would raise 'no violent or factious opposition' (ibid., 1.330) to parliamentary reform which, under Russell, was once more a live issue. She attempted to keep Russell's ministry in office when it was defeated on its Reform Bill in June 1866, by appealing to its duty to maintain stability in the face of continental war, but to no avail. Derby formed the new government with Benjamin Disraeli as chancellor of the exchequer; Victoria found him 'amiable and clever, but … a strange man' (ibid., 1.379).

Disraeli succeeded Derby as prime minister in February 1868 and Victoria rapidly fell under his charm: 'he has always behaved extremely well to me, and has all the right feelings for a Minister towards the Sovereign', she told Vicky. He was, moreover, 'full of poetry, romance and chivalry' (*Your Dear Letter*, 176), qualities that had been sadly lacking in the queen's life in recent years. He enchanted the queen with references to her experience, wisdom, and abilities, declaring 'It will be his delight and duty to render the transaction of affairs as easy to your Majesty, as possible', and asking her guidance in 'the great affairs of state' (*Letters*, 2nd ser., 1.505). This was a very different sort of minister from any she had had before. Only Peel and Aberdeen had shown such 'care for my personal affairs or that respect and deference for me' (*Your Dear Letter*, 208), and they had never called her wise or sought her guidance. Disraeli's failure at the polls in November 1868 brought their promising relationship to a temporary end. Albert had thought Disraeli an adventurer, an unprincipled rogue. He had given his seal of approval instead to William Ewart Gladstone, the disciple of Peel and Aberdeen, but his widow did not renew it.

Ending seclusion: the first Gladstone ministry Victoria had encountered Gladstone regularly over the preceding twenty years; under Albert's guidance she admired his religious earnestness and his cleverness. Without Albert these virtues overbalanced into their opposites: she suspected him of 'humbug' (hypocrisy), and his cold intellectualism both intimidated and repelled her. Gladstone, like Albert, had a theoretical mind. Victoria's sharp intelligence was at its best with the concrete. Gladstone had twice resigned from government (in 1845 and again in 1855); on neither occasion had he been in disagreement with his colleagues, and on both occasions his explanation left the queen bewildered. Gladstone was not quite 'safe', a little 'strange'. Nor did his personal manner endear him to Victoria. He was a committed monarchist, with an almost religious reverence for the role of the queen, but he could never forget he was dealing with his sovereign, and while treating her as an intelligent mind, he never managed to absorb the advice of his wife, to treat her also as a woman. 'I cannot find him very agreeable, and he talks so very much', Victoria grumbled (*Your Dear Letter*, 248). One of the few things that united them was opposition to the growing movement for women's suffrage. Responding in 1870 to an anti-feminist pamphlet which Gladstone had forwarded to her, Victoria declared

'the strongest aversion for the *socalled & most erroneous* "Rights of Woman"' (P. Guedalla, ed., *The Queen and Mr Gladstone*, 1933, 1.221).

Gladstone's foremost aim in his first ministry was, as is well known, 'to pacify Ireland'. His second objective was to bring the queen out of her seclusion and to restore her place at the ceremonial head of government. Concerned about the queen's absence from public view, he had frequently discussed the subject with his closest contact at court, Harriet, duchess of Sutherland, mistress of the robes under successive whig ministries from 1837. The slow rise of a popular republican movement gained pace in the late 1860s (coupled with violent acts and threats from Irish Fenians), and Gladstone was concerned above all that the queen should not give it extra fuel by her invisibility. Those who did not have to deal with her on a regular basis sometimes thought his concern exaggerated. Lord Kimberley, for example, regretted her 'somewhat selfish seclusion', but considered that 'the nation will forgive a great deal in a woman, and besides she has many admirable qualities which go far to redeem some weaknesses' (E. Drus, ed., *A Journal of Events during the Gladstone Ministry, 1868–1874*, 1958, 26). But Gladstone's was not the only voice urging the queen to resume her public role, or warning of potential dangers if she did not. Her children—particularly the prince of Wales, who had a vested interest—periodically plucked up courage to hint that her actions were not best calculated to protect and enhance her throne; King Leopold had reminded her in 1864 that the British needed to see their rulers; a few of her courtiers, including Lady Augusta Stanley and the dean of Windsor, gently encouraged her to lessen her mourning.

Victoria felt bullied, beleaguered, and besieged. Everyone, she felt, was against her, no one understood—or cared about—her feelings and needs; she maintained, with some justification, that she worked extremely hard for the country, studying the huge quantities of official papers sent to her, corresponding with her ministers and attempting to keep national (rather than merely party) interests in their minds, continuing an extensive international correspondence with other courts in the effort to keep the peace, trying, above all, to live up to the standards Albert had set. What she would not do was that on which her ministers—Gladstone in particular, it seemed—set the greatest store. She would not appear in public to be stared at by curious crowds, she would not put off her mourning to wear the official regalia of her position, and she would not endure unnecessary ceremonial.

Gladstone's attempts to persuade the queen to reverse her policy failed almost completely for three years, and in the process he equally completely alienated her. His policies, too, Victoria found uncongenial, especially those on the army and Ireland. 'There is so little true feeling of loyalty in many of these clever radicals', she wrote. 'They would alter everything without being able to put better things in their place' (*Your Dear Letter*, 236). She was persuaded to abolish the purchase of army commissions by royal warrant, despite the opposition of her cousin the commander-in-chief, the duke of Cambridge: if nothing else, she was glad to exercise prerogative powers over the issue. The disestablishment of the Church of Ireland in 1869 touched on her prerogative as head of the Anglican church, and it was partly displeasure at the proposal which led her to decline to open parliament in person that year. Gladstone's plan to reform both the Irish Office and the frivolous habits of the prince of Wales by sending him to Dublin as viceroy met scornful rejection from the queen whenever the subject was raised.

Victoria rigorously shut the prince of Wales out from involvement in her political business. Instead, he and the princess of Wales threw themselves into the pleasure-loving world of aristocratic society, the very world against which Albert had sought to inoculate his family, and of which Victoria disapproved: 'The higher classes—especially the aristocracy ... —are so frivolous, pleasure-seeking, heartless, selfish, immoral and gambling that it makes one think ... of the days before the French Revolution', she wrote (*Your Dear Letter*, 165). Her son's excesses contributed to the growing anti-monarchical sentiment in British politics. When, in 1870, he was exposed as a licentious playboy during the notorious Mordaunt divorce case, the queen was isolated at Windsor, herself the subject of rumour and scandal at the height of the Brown affair.

Public criticism of the monarchy mounted through 1871, with the publication of a pamphlet, *What does she do with it?*, subjecting the queen's finances to scrutiny, and a speech by Sir Charles Dilke at Newcastle in November advocating a republican alternative. At the end of November the queen was recovering from several months' extreme ill health—her symptoms this time were physical, with abscesses on her arm, gout, and rheumatic pains and fever—when she received news that the prince of Wales had typhoid fever. His illness reached a crisis on the anniversary of the prince consort's death and, in the national rejoicing at his recovery, the republican moment was lost. Gladstone urged the value of a service of thanksgiving at St Paul's Cathedral; Victoria resisted energetically, but for once her prime minister prevailed, and on 27 February 1872 the queen drove in state through London, greeted by 'wonderful enthusiasm and astounding affectionate loyalty' (*Letters*, 2nd ser., 2.194). Two days later Arthur O'Connor thrust a pistol at the queen as she was returning to Buckingham Palace after a drive in her carriage but was seized by the faithful Brown before he could make his demand for the release of Fenian prisoners. Public sympathy for her was immense.

The thanksgiving of 1872 was a turning point for the monarchy, setting a precedent for the huge ceremonial functions of later years, and for Victoria herself, who was surprised and affected by the enthusiasm of her reception and gradually allowed herself to shed some of the adjuncts of misery which she had wrapped around herself. She still resisted opening parliament, and refused to alter her rigid schedule of visits to Scotland and the Isle of Wight, but she did agree to receive the shah of Persia in 1873 on a state visit and went so far as to wear the koh-i-noor diamond in brooch form to greet him. Public criticism ended almost overnight. From the nadir of 1871 Victoria's popularity increased year on year before reaching a virtual apotheosis in the jubilee years of 1887 and 1897.

Crown imperial: the second Disraeli ministry By the end of Gladstone's first ministry Victoria had finally discovered a political confidence which the long years of tutelage under Albert had subjugated and which, with a congenial prime minister, she was keen to bring into action. Her longevity, coupled with an accurate and detailed memory, became her principal political assets, which increased with time. She was the one constant feature of the nineteenth-century political scene, and this gave her voice much of its authority.

The success of the Conservatives at the polls in February 1874 brought Disraeli back into office, to the queen's delight. Having lost his wife in 1872, he was now more welcome than ever. On kissing hands as prime minister he said, 'I plight my troth to the kindest of *Mistresses*!' (*Letters*, 2nd ser., 2.322). It was the true beginning of a mutually beneficial partnership, which contained elements of both romance and farce. He frankly admitted to his use of flattery and recommended that for a royal audience 'you should lay it on with a trowel' (Longford, 401). Unlike Gladstone, Disraeli never forgot that he was addressing a woman as well as his sovereign; she, by turns, enjoyed the chivalric flirtation which perhaps more closely resembled her relationship with Melbourne than that with any man since her marriage. To Albert she had always been his 'gutes Frauchen' ('good little wife'), or 'beloved child'. He would never have thought of the fanciful name Disraeli bestowed on the queen, 'The Faery'; he would never have said, as Disraeli did, that '*whatever I wished should be done*, whatever his difficulties might be' (*Letters*, 2nd ser., 2.321). If there was something fantastical, even ridiculous, about a man of seventy with dyed black ringlets addressing a short, stout woman of over fifty in the language of Spenser's *Faerie Queene*, it was in itself a harmless enough amusement. The negative side of Disraeli's flowery compliments was that the queen's sense of her powers moved out of step with contemporary thinking on the monarch's role in the constitution: Lord Derby, whose hostility to the queen was veiled but not hidden, cautioned his chief against 'encouraging her in too large ideas of her personal power, and too great indifference to what the public expects' (Blake, 548). Disraeli too occasionally reminded the queen of the realities of their positions: 'Were he your Majesty's Grand Vizier, instead of your Majesty's Prime Minister, he should be content to pass his remaining years in accomplishing everything your Majesty wished; but, alas! it is not so' (*Letters*, 2nd ser., 2.385).

Victoria's alliance with Disraeli rested on more than personal attraction, however. In the changed circumstances of the European political scene of the late 1860s and 1870s, in which Bismarck's united Germany loomed large and the general European peace looked increasingly fragile, she was desperately concerned to maintain British prestige and power. She had witnessed the effects of war in the 1850s, and throughout the 1860s her family was shaken by the effects of Bismarck's wars, which placed her children on different sides of the conflicts. War, she concluded, was terrible; more terrible, however, would be the effect of a general European belief that Britain would not engage in warfare. Russia was her particular bugbear, despite cordial personal relations with the tsar and his family. She shared Disraeli's view that Russia posed a serious threat to British interests in India, and that Russian expansion into the Mediterranean, via a collapsing Turkey, was to be prevented at all costs. 'I have but one object', she wrote in 1877, 'the honour and dignity of this country' (*Darling Child*, 251). Disraeli's brand of Conservatism, with its forward foreign policy, seemed to her to share her perspective.

Disraeli, above all, had the measure of how to manage the queen: 'I never deny; I never contradict; I sometimes forget' (Longford, 403). Victoria rewarded his tact by opening parliament in person three times during his ministry (in 1876, 1877, and 1880), giving a public mark of approval to her prime minister. If Disraeli expected his vows of personal devotion and service to be understood strictly rhetorically, however, he was soon disabused. The queen had become increasingly concerned in the early 1870s at the rise of the ritualist party within the Church of England and its 'Romanising tendencies' (*Letters*, 2nd ser., 2.290). She was herself, by necessity and inclination, 'Protestant to the very *heart's core*' (ibid., 2.302): her personal preference was for extremely simple services, and she argued for greater unity among the different protestant churches. (She took communion at a Presbyterian service at Crathie kirk for the first time on 3 November 1873, having previously held back from scruple as to her position at the head of the episcopalian church.) In 1873 she began to badger Gladstone to bring in legislation to outlaw ritualist practices in the Church of England, knowing him to be high-church and believing him to be a ritualist sympathizer, if not actually a secret Romanist. Disraeli was less able to withstand her onslaught, and the Public Worship Regulation Act of 1874 owed much to her pressure.

The Royal Titles Act of 1876 was also close to Victoria's heart, and caused Disraeli considerable political difficulties. Since 1858, when Britain assumed direct control of the territories formerly managed by the East India Company, the queen had been spoken of informally as the empress of India. Victoria was now delighted by Disraeli's proposal that 'empress of India' be added to her formal style, although she was keen to point out that it would make no difference to her style in Britain, believing the title was 'best understood in the East, but which Great Britain (which *is an Empire*) never has acknowledged to be higher than King or Queen' (*Letters*, 2nd ser., 2.450–51). She denied it strongly, but the fact that the unified Germany now had an emperor (and her daughter would one day be empress) and that her second son, Alfred, had married into the Russian imperial family in 1873 also weighed with her, as issues of precedence and rank arose: the senior monarch of Europe, she would not allow her family to be belittled as Albert had been by rank-conscious foreigners.

She found the outcry against the new title incomprehensible, dismissing Liberal objections as mere party factionalism: her relationship with Lord Granville (who had formerly been the acceptable face of the Gladstonian administration) never recovered from his publicly stated opposition. She was proclaimed empress of India on 1 January 1877 at a spectacular durbar at Delhi, stage-managed by the viceroy, Lord Lytton, and the same day signed herself for the first time 'Victoria R & I' ('Victoria regina et imperatrix', Victoria, queen and empress). It was intended that she should use the new designation only in her dealings with India, but she soon made it her usual style.

It was in Victoria's response to the crisis in the Balkans in the later 1870s that Disraeli reaped as he had sown, as the queen sought to drive him to an ever more interventionist policy. Evading her private secretary, Henry Ponsonby (who had succeeded Grey in 1870), who was a whig and whom she unjustly suspected of disloyalty to her prime minister, she bombarded Disraeli with letters, telegrams, and memoranda. She initially sympathized with the Christians in the Balkans in 1876 (the victims of the 'Bulgarian atrocities') but, as the question increasingly focused on the fact that it was the Russian rather than the British government that acted to protect them, Victoria became passionately engaged in keeping her government up to the mark in opposing Russian action against Turkey. Between April 1877 and February 1878 she five times threatened abdication if Beaconsfield (as Disraeli became in 1876) did not hold firm, and she encouraged her prime minister to force the resignations of Lord Carnarvon and Lord Derby, leaders of the conciliatory group in the cabinet. By treating policy as a game of flirtatious verbiage, Beaconsfield encouraged the queen in her enthusiasms, although in the long run all her frenetic activity had little impact on the course of events.

Outside Europe, Beaconsfield's active imperialism gave his sovereign two wars, the Anglo-Zulu War and the Second Anglo-Afghan War, and embroiled the country inextricably in imperial expansion. Prestige was no longer a purely European matter, and Victoria endorsed his policy enthusiastically, fully accepting that 'If *we* are to *maintain* our position as a *first-rate* Power—and of that *no one* … can doubt, we must … be *prepared* for *attacks* and *wars*, somewhere or *other*, CONTINUALLY' (*Letters*, 2nd ser., 3.37–8). It has been pointed out that 'there was not a single year in Queen Victoria's long reign in which somewhere in the world her soldiers were not fighting for her and for her empire' (B. Farwell, *Queen Victoria's Little Wars*, 1973, 1). With the European powers competing to acquire colonial empires, more and more of those conflicts and actions took place in Africa, and Victoria's interest in the colonies (which had been rather lukewarm until now) became intense. She supported Beaconsfield's policies publicly and privately, and sent a telegram of sympathy and encouragement to the commanding general in South Africa after the defeat of the British at the hands of the Zulu at Isandlwana in January 1879. Her commitment to the empire remained unshaken even after the death in battle of the prince imperial, son of the deposed Napoleon III, later in the same war, and the disastrous loss of the mission to Afghanistan in September 1879. Victoria viewed her empire as benignly civilizing: 'the Native Sovereigns CANNOT maintain their authority … It is not for aggrandisement, but to prevent war and bloodshed that we must do this [that is, take possession]', she told Beaconsfield (*Letters*, 2nd ser., 3.43).

When Beaconsfield asked for a dissolution of parliament in March 1880, Victoria hoped that 'the Government will do well in the elections' (*Beloved Mama*, 71); she did not delay her planned visit to Darmstadt for the confirmation of Alice's daughters and to Baden-Baden, where she received Beaconsfield's telegram announcing the defeat of his ministry: 'The Queen cannot deny she (Liberal as she has ever been, but never Radical or democratic) thinks it a great calamity for the country and the peace of Europe!' (*Letters*, 2nd ser., 3.73).

Victoria's dramatic transformation from the glumly dutiful, nearly invisible 'widow of Windsor' into this dynamically engaged, energetic interventionist owed much to her personal relationship with Disraeli, and also something to the experience of 1871–2. But more, perhaps, was owed to a radical shift within Victoria herself. Her personality had been re-formed by Albert after 1840 and it underwent a kind of disintegration after his death. By the 1870s Victoria's personality had reasserted itself, and characteristics that had been sublimated for almost thirty years reasserted themselves: the Victoria of 1837–41 was easily recognizable in the Victoria of 1876–86. The queen was sixty-one in 1880; she had now reigned alone for almost as long as her dual monarchy with Albert had lasted. The violence of her feelings on Gladstone's return to office and the continual struggles with him over the next fifteen years showed just how thin was the veneer of impartiality and self-control that Albert had placed over her natural inclinations after 1840.

Grandmother of Europe   By relaxing her seclusion Victoria reduced one of the major sources of tension with her elder children. Not that all was plain sailing: the prince of Wales remained irredeemably frivolous and worldly (although his mother was now more willing to admit and praise his good qualities); Alfred (created duke of Edinburgh in 1866) was safely married to Grand Duchess Marie of Russia after some years of alarm, but he was indiscreet politically and the queen worried about his connections with his in-laws. Victoria's relationships with her married daughters also fluctuated, especially over their regular childbearing. Even with Vicky there were periodic coolnesses, sometimes over politics, but more often over her 'inconsiderate' habit of visiting the queen with a large suite of courtiers. The death of Princess Alice from diphtheria in 1878 on the anniversary of the prince consort's death was the first breach in the family circle (excepting a few tiny children, victims of the high infant mortality rate which even royalty could not escape); the queen mourned the 'precious child who stood by me and upheld me seventeen years ago' (*Beloved Mama*, 30), but was not prostrated as the crown princess feared.

As Victoria's youngest son, Leopold (created duke of Albany in 1881), grew up he resented the restrictions the queen placed around him: constantly anxious over his health, she attempted to keep him away from the social life of his brother and refused to allow him to take up a career. From 1876 she used him as an unofficial private secretary (part of her method of evading Ponsonby), and even gave him keys to the dispatch boxes, a privilege she denied her heir until much later. He was permitted to marry Princess Helen of Waldeck-Pyrmont in 1882—'such a risk and experiment', the queen thought (*Beloved Mama*, 111). His death in March 1884 from complications of the epilepsy and haemophilia which had restricted his life was 'an awful blow' (ibid., 162–3). Princess Beatrice, the youngest child, was brought up to be the daughter at home, the prop and mainstay of her mother. 'She is like a sunbeam in the house and also like a dove, an angel of peace who brings it wherever she goes and who is my greatest comfort', Victoria wrote (*Darling Child*, 290). Marriage was never to be mentioned in front of her, but in 1884 she met Prince Henry of Battenberg and fell in love. The queen was horrified at first, but was eventually induced to consent on condition that Beatrice and Henry (or Liko, as the family called him) should always live with her. Only Arthur, duke of Connaught (so created in 1874), always her favourite son, gave the queen unalloyed pleasure, making a successful career in the army and marrying the suitable Princess Louise of Prussia in 1878.

The inevitable result of the marriages of all Victoria's offspring was the proliferation of grandchildren (thirty-four survived childhood) and, before long, great-grandchildren: Victoria was a grandmother at thirty-nine and a great-grandmother at sixty. Only Princess Louise remained childless, for even Leopold had fathered two children in the two years of his marriage, his son being born posthumously. Victoria still found babies a bore, and the size of her family was a continual source of grumbling: 'when they come at the rate of three a year it becomes a cause of mere anxiety for my own children and of no great interest', she told the crown princess, who had just produced her fourth daughter and eighth child (*Darling Child*, 40). Sons in particular were a problem—'I think many Princes a great misfortune—for they are in one another's and almost everybody's way' (ibid.). But as they put aside babyhood, she interested herself minutely in the details of their upbringing and in the arrangement of their marriages. The five surviving motherless Hesse children spent a lot of time in Britain with their grandmother, while Beatrice's four children grew up in the household of 'Grandmamma Queen'. The grandchild who consumed most of Victoria's attention was not the heir presumptive to her own throne, the prince of Wales's eldest son, Albert Victor (who should perhaps have worried her more; his early death in 1892 saved Britain the embarrassment of a barely literate monarch implicated in numerous carefully hushed-up scandals), or his brother George, later King George V. Rather, it was Vicky's eldest son, William, who from an early age was taught by his paternal grandfather to despise his parents and particularly his British mother: endless concern flowed between the two Victorias about the future German Kaiser, who idolized his grandmother while absorbing Bismarck's lessons about British perfidy.

Court and household Victoria's court never went out of mourning after 1861; her ladies-in-waiting (many of whom were themselves widows) joined the queen in perpetual black silk, but the younger maids of honour wore white, grey, mauve, or purple (except when another death put them back into black). Equally immutable was the queen's routine: Christmas and the new year were spent at Osborne, then the early part of the year was spent at Windsor, with a few days in London. She went to Balmoral in time for her birthday in May, then returned to Windsor in June, before spending most of July and August at Osborne. Late in August she would go back to Balmoral; she would remain there until November, when she returned to Windsor, before leaving for Osborne as soon as the anniversary of the prince consort's death had passed. Little was allowed to interfere with this regime, a source of constant disquiet to her ministers. Despite improved travel facilities and the invention of the telegraph, the queen in Scotland was inconveniently inaccessible, especially after 1868, when she built a villa, the Glassalt Shiel, at the end of Loch Muick, to which she regularly retreated. Inevitably, with so many people kept in close confinement jostling (in however restrained a fashion) for the ear of the queen, the court itself became a hotbed of petty feuds, trivial disagreements blown up into full-scale 'rows', misunderstandings transformed into ill feeling. The all-pervasive influence of John Brown did not help; nor did the queen's habit of indirect communication. Rather than confront people directly, she preferred to make her feelings known through little notes or through intermediaries; when the messenger was Brown or some other lesser mortal and the recipient one of her children, tempers often flared.

After Brown's death in 1883 the atmosphere lightened somewhat. The marriage of Princess Beatrice brought a cheerful, easy-going masculine presence into the queen's family, and Victoria permitted the gloom to be lifted by a little sedate liveliness: amateur theatricals enlivened the court periodically, and the tableaux vivants of which the Victorians were so fond were produced. The queen never went to a theatre after 1861, but in 1881 the prince of Wales persuaded her to attend a command performance of F. C. Burnand's *The Colonel* at his highland residence Abergeldie Castle. The experiment was a success, and in 1887 Victoria had the Kendals brought to Osborne to perform; thereafter command performances at Balmoral and Windsor enabled the queen to see the great performers of the day, from Henry Irving and Ellen Terry to Eleanora Duse and Sarah Bernhardt (who performed for the queen during a visit to Cimiez in 1897).

In the second half of her reign Victoria's court attracted little public attention. Other than her private secretary, Ponsonby (a model of discretion), her principal courtiers were elderly women: pre-eminent among the ladies-in-waiting were Jane, marchioness of Ely; Jane, Lady Churchill; and Anne, duchess of Atholl. Harriet Phipps (daughter of her keeper of the privy purse, Sir Charles Phipps) and Horatia Stopford were originally maids of honour, but in time became permanent bedchamber women. They acted as personal secretaries and assistants to the queen, who bullied them unmercifully: they read to her and dealt with her private and personal correspondence. In the 1890s they were joined by Marie Mallet. Victoria had always valued her physicians: Sir William Jenner was consulted on matters beyond mere health, and in 1881 she appointed James Reid, a young Scottish doctor, as her personal physician. In the 1890s (after Henry of Battenberg's death) Reid in some measure took the place Brown had occupied, both in the queen's esteem and in managing the household. But unlike Brown, Reid was almost universally popular: he could smooth over difficulties with a jest.

From the 1870s the queen's court almost exclusively comprised Conservatives and Unionists. Sir Henry Ponsonby was the single exception, and he alone of the courtiers recognized the dangers of the queen's being surrounded by associates of a uniform political stripe, especially when that stripe belonged to the opposition. 'Incessant sneers or conversation against a policy always damages', he remarked (Ponsonby, 154), concluding that Sir Robert Peel had been right to insist on changing the ladies of the household with the ministry. 'Perhaps', he added, 'now it does not really matter whether the Queen dislikes them [her ministers] or not' (ibid.). Gladstone's second ministry put that question to the test.

Victoria rampant: the second Gladstone ministry Victoria had greeted Gladstone's electoral defeat in 1874 with ill-concealed glee. She quoted Palmerston's assessment that Gladstone was 'a very dangerous man', and went on to catalogue his failings: 'so very arrogant, tyrannical and obstinate, with no knowledge of the world or human nature … a fanatic in religion … and much want of *égard* towards my feelings … make him a very dangerous and unsatisfactory Premier' (*Darling Child*, 130). His retirement as leader of the Liberal Party in 1875 raised her hopes that she would not have to deal with him again, but she was sadly disappointed, for the 'Bulgarian atrocities' brought him out of retirement in 1876. In September 1876 Victoria found his campaign 'incomprehensible', and considered him 'most mischievous—though I believe unintentionally so' (ibid., 222). Ten days later the qualifier had gone: he was 'most reprehensible and mischievous', deliberately making the government's task more difficult (ibid., 223). In February 1877 he was 'that half madman Mr Gladstone' (ibid., 242), and by May 'that madman Gladstone' (ibid., 251). Her hope that the tories would return from the polls in 1880 'stronger than ever' was misplaced. Furious at what she considered the demagoguery of Gladstone's Midlothian campaigns of 1879–80 and anxious above all to exclude him from the premiership, she went to considerable lengths to find an alternative, inviting first Lord Hartington and then Lord Granville to form the administration. The effect of her intervention was to strengthen

Gladstone's position, as the weakness of the potential alternative Liberal leaders was exposed.

The queen had boxed herself into a dangerous corner, for she faced at least several years of Liberal government with a large majority, having made her commitment to the policies of the Conservative Party transparent by her demeanour and her remarks to her courtiers. Mary Ponsonby, the wife of the queen's private secretary and herself a formidable intelligence, reflected in 1878 that 'Dizzy has worked the idea of personal government to its logical conclusion', an idea planted by Stockmar and Albert, who had 'kept the thing between bounds, but they established the superstition in the Queen's mind about her own prerogative', which could be exploited by an unscrupulous minister. She concluded that:

> If there comes a real collision between the Queen and the House of Commons … it is quite possible she would turn restive, *dorlotède* [coddled] as she has been by Dizzy's high sounding platitudes, and then her reign will end in a fiasco. (M. Ponsonby, ed., *Mary Ponsonby*, 1927, 144–5)

It was a perceptive analysis: Victoria was fortunate that Gladstone, Granville, and Rosebery—the chief ministers concerned—were careful to hide the full extent of her hostility even from the Liberal cabinet. Moreover, it was the Liberal Party, and especially its leadership, which was vital to the queen in the matter of royal finances, and she was fortunate that Gladstone did not use the issue to extract a quid pro quo.

The queen—always low-church in her opinions—approved of some Liberal measures, such as the Burials Bill (1880), which allowed dissenters to use Anglican graveyards, and the Deceased Wife's Sister Bill (1883); but on questions of foreign, defence, south African, and Irish policy there were constant confrontations and friction, especially when Beaconsfield's policy in the Near East was threatened. A row over the paragraph in the queen's speech in January 1881 on the evacuation of Kandahar in Afghanistan made a tetchy start. The queen disliked most aspects of the government's Irish legislation, and particularly its land legislation, on which she had an inside source: the father-in-law of her daughter Louise, the duke of Argyll, who resigned from the cabinet in March 1881 over the Irish Land Bill. Argyll's resignation was followed in April 1881 by Beaconsfield's death. The queen had continued her correspondence with her former prime minister on political and personal matters after Beaconsfield went out of office, Victoria preferring to hear his account of proceedings in the House of Lords to that provided by her ministers. 'I look always to *you* for ultimate help', she assured him in September 1880 (*Letters*, 2nd ser., 3.143). The queen's various tributes to her former prime minister attracted much attention. (Beaconsfield on his deathbed remarked, when offered a royal visit, 'No, it is better not. She would only ask me to take a message to Albert' (Blake, 747).) These two events increased Victoria's political isolation, the second much more than the first, for Argyll differed sharply from her on Indian and Near Eastern policy, and, though the queen saw him as her last '*independent* and true friend' in the Gladstone cabinet, he was never quite

the source of Liberal cabinet leaks for which she hoped. A rare moment of conciliation occurred in the autumn of 1884, when the queen encouraged a compromise between the Commons, which had passed a Representation of the People Bill, and the Lords, which declined to proceed with it without an accompanying measure of redistribution, which the government said would be its next legislative measure. The queen thought the Lords right, but feared the consequences of a popular movement against them, which might revive the republicanism of the early 1870s. How far the queen's mediation was significant is disputed, but her intentions were clear: 'I have worked very hard to try and bring about a meeting of the two sides in which I have succeeded so that they may try and come to an agreement upon these difficult questions of reform' (5 Nov 1884, *Beloved Mama*, 170–71).

Victoria was incensed by the Gladstone government's handling of the Sudanese question in 1883–5, when General Gordon met his death at Khartoum before Wolseley's relief expedition reached him: 'We were just too late as we always are—it is I, who have, as the Head of the Nation, to bear the humiliation'. She believed Gladstone 'will be forever branded with the blood of Gordon that heroic man' (*Beloved Mama*, 182–3), and she publicized her fury at the government with a rebuke unprecedented and unrepeated in the history of the British constitutional monarchy: she telegraphed *en clair* (that is, not in code, thus ensuring immediate leaks to the press) to Granville, Hartington, and Gladstone: 'These news from Khartoum are frightful, and to think that all this might have been prevented and many precious lives saved by earlier action is too frightful' (*Letters*, 2nd ser., 3.597). Popular though this view may have been, its public expression was scarcely in keeping with the queen's obligation to support her ministers, and contrasted markedly with Victoria's public affirmation of confidence in the authorities after the battle of Isandlwana in January 1879.

Home rule and Unionism The Irish question and the relationship of Ireland to the other constituent parts of the United Kingdom were a central issue of Victoria's reign. It did not attract her early enthusiasm. Even so, encouraged by Albert, she visited the country more than her prime ministers, who went as such only twice: Russell in 1848, and Gladstone for a morning in 1880. The queen visited Dublin (creating the prince of Wales earl of Dublin) and Belfast in September 1849. She visited Dublin again in August–September 1851 and in September 1861, on this occasion venturing as far as Killarney. But these were visits which presupposed Ireland to be a place of danger. There was to be no Irish Balmoral, and after Albert's death the visits ceased until the very end of her reign, when, on her own initiative, she visited Dublin in April 1900. In the interim she refused all suggestions (chiefly, but not exclusively, proposals from Gladstone) that there be a royal residence and a regular royal presence in Ireland.

The queen, who was personally moved by the murder of Lord Frederick Cavendish in Dublin in May 1882, had no sympathy for those ministers who met the Land League of the early 1880s with anything other than coercion. She quickly and perceptively sensed the significance of the cabinet's change of direction in the spring of 1882. She felt she had been pressured by the cabinet into agreeing to the release of Charles Stewart Parnell in May 1882, and she thought Gladstone's policy of releasing prisoners disastrous, Joseph Chamberlain an 'evil genius', the home-rulers 'dreadful'. She complained to the prince of Wales about her 'dreadfully Radical Government which contains many thinly-veiled *Republicans*—and the way they have truckled to the Home Rulers—as well as the utter disregard of all my opinions which after 45 years of experience ought to be considered', and she blamed Hartington for failing to take office in 1880 and thus leaving her with 'this most dangerous man [Gladstone]' (*Letters*, 2nd ser., 3.298–9). She encouraged the prince to speak to Liberal ministers who might support her views: that she had to request her son to do this showed the extent of her alienation from her cabinet.

In the great political crisis of 1885–6, when Gladstone introduced a Government of Ireland Bill to provide for home rule together with a further Land Bill, and the Liberal Party split in consequence, the queen was an enthusiastic protagonist on the Unionist side, and not a passive spectator as she had been when the tories split over free trade in 1846. The queen, predicting a Conservative defeat in the election of November 1885 and dreading the return of Gladstone, tried to prepare the ground for G. J. Goschen to lead a coalition. Victoria opened parliament on 21 January 1886, the last occasion on which she did so. When Salisbury's government was defeated in the debate on the queen's speech, she refused to accept his resignation in 'an almost incoherent outpouring of protest and dismay' (G. Cecil, *Life of Robert, Marquis of Salisbury*, 3, 1931, 290). When Goschen declined the queen's commission, Ponsonby avoided a dangerous crisis by going immediately to Gladstone, though it was after midnight, and successfully gained the queen's objective of having Rosebery made foreign secretary. Throughout Gladstone's third government, which fell in June 1886 when the Home Rule Bill was defeated in the Commons, the queen sent Lord Salisbury copies of all Gladstone's important letters to her, and some of her replies to him (Longford, 485). Melbourne's legacy on this unconstitutional practice had cast a long shadow. The tories were thus exceptionally well placed to engineer the Liberal split which was Salisbury's chief objective during Gladstone's attempt to achieve an Irish constitutional settlement. She even went so far as to ask Salisbury, the leader of the opposition, to let her know if she should refuse the prime minister a dissolution, should he ask for it (as Gladstone did, following the defeat of his bill).

It is easy to characterize Victoria's position during this her most politically active decade as political partisanship, pure and simple. Undeniably, she lent all the support she could to Disraeli and to Lord Salisbury, and hindered as far as possible the radical agenda of Gladstone's successive ministries. The constitutional rights of the monarch, as expressed by Walter Bagehot in *The English Constitution* (a volume Victoria did not read and would not have approved if she had), to be consulted, to encourage, and to warn, were interpreted by the queen as the rights 'to instruct, to abuse, and to hector' (Matthew, 2.260). And yet Victoria did not see herself as partisan—which had been Albert's great lesson—or even as Conservative. She considered herself a liberal constitutional monarch; it was Gladstone who had abandoned liberalism for radicalism or even democracy, Gladstone who threatened the constitutional arrangements of the country, Gladstone who took issues of national significance, security, or prestige and made party-political capital out of them. Disraeli had persuaded her that she herself stood for the national interest; by making the monarchy an important element of tory democracy, he had allied his party with the queen. Now she was convinced that 'all moderate, loyal and *really patriotic* men, who have the safety and well-being of the Empire and Throne at heart, and who wish to save them from destruction' had a duty to 'rise above party and be true patriots!' (*Letters*, 2nd ser., 3.712–13). Her views were reinforced by her narrow reading of the press, for she relied on two Conservative papers, the *Morning Post* and the *St James's Gazette*. The queen was thus a proponent of the notions that Conservatism was not an ideology, that radicalism was incompatible with patriotism, and that her own views reflected, by definition, the national interest.

Salisbury, Rosebery, and the late Victorian state Salisbury treated the queen much more along Gladstonian than along Disraelian lines, but they were largely at one on major political questions, and certainly so over Ireland. Salisbury defeated the queen over the appointment of Randall Davidson as bishop of Rochester in 1891, but the dispute was a personal one, with the queen wishing to retain Davidson as dean of Windsor, where he played an important role in her spiritual life and in advising on ecclesiastical appointments.

Victoria's aversion to ceremonial continued unabated. It owed much to her dislike of show and to her shyness, while the six attempts to assassinate or assault her during her reign gave substance to her fears about public appearances. Despite the decline of republicanism, she never felt entirely secure in her position, and did not take the allegiance of the poor for granted. Her concern for their welfare—manifested in the later phase of her reign by her support for the Sunday opening of museums, housing reform, and public works schemes for the unemployed—combined feelings of stewardship towards her subjects with a desire to pacify the potentially unruly.

The queen was with difficulty brought to participate in the jubilee celebrations of her coronation. Though there had been some further signs of political and press complaint at her behaviour in 1886, in 1887 the golden jubilee celebrations went off with apparent popular enthusiasm. It was the first of those gatherings of royalties *en masse* which, either for such celebrations or for funerals, were a marked feature of the years before 1914, and it provided a splendid stage on which to display Victoria as the grandmother of Europe. The procession to the service of thanksgiving in Westminster Abbey on 21 June featured royalties from throughout Europe, several Indian princes, the queen of Hawaii, and princes from Japan, Persia, and Siam. The queen's refusal to wear the crown and robes of state—she wore a bonnet laced with diamonds in the simple landau coach—emphasized the public role she chose for herself in her final years: the 'widow of Windsor', her simplicity elevating her above even the majestic trappings of royalty. Though Joseph Chamberlain objected that her visit to Birmingham was insufficiently accompanied by royal paraphernalia, this was a rare complaint. Victoria's self-presentation as a simple, apolitical old lady, remote from wealth and power, was one which the public relished (and contrasted with the flamboyant, etiquette-ridden, politically active monarchies of continental Europe). The jubilee service was followed by a series of tiring events. On 24 June the queen issued a letter of thanks to the nation. The celebrations concluded with army and navy reviews at Aldershot and Spithead respectively, and with a great variety of deputations and presentations. Victoria did not usually on such occasions make speeches, but she often said a few words of thanks, in a clear and audible voice.

When the Unionists lost the general election of 1892, the queen hoped to give public notice of her wish to avoid a fourth Gladstone premiership by sending for Lord Rosebery. Ponsonby dissuaded her from this, and Gladstone formed a government. The queen was careful to make it clear, at least to Ponsonby, that she disliked sending for Gladstone, '(not because she has any personal dislike to him) [but] as she utterly loathes his very dangerous politics' (Ponsonby, 217). In the *Court Circular* she announced that she accepted Salisbury's resignation 'with regret'. Gladstone's last ministry was a miserable episode on both sides, ending with the aged premier unable to extract a promise from his sovereign that she would treat confidentially his plans for retirement. When he did retire, in March 1894, the queen did not ask his advice about a successor. (Constitutional lore is unclear whether she should have done so. When Derby resigned in somewhat analogous circumstances in 1868 Disraeli's succession was already a matter of common agreement; the queen did not directly ask Derby's advice at the time of resignation, though, unlike the more scrupulous Gladstone, he offered it anyway.) The queen sounded out Salisbury about the possibility of another minority Conservative-led government, and then turned to Rosebery (rather than Sir William Harcourt), whom she had long championed among the Liberals. Ignoring a letter from him offering his usual series of objections to taking office, the queen invited Rosebery to form a government, which he agreed to do. Rosebery's skilful letters and his widowed status promised a revival of a Disraelian relationship, but his government soon resigned, in June 1895, following defeat in the Commons.

Victoria turned happily to Salisbury, 'who has so faithfully served her before' (*Letters*, 3rd ser., 2.523), and Salisbury's third premiership saw out her reign. This was the nineteenth occasion (ignoring abortive attempts and failed resignations) on which Victoria had played the monarch's role in initiating a new government, and Salisbury was the last of her ten prime ministers. In her late seventies she was inevitably growing tired, although a challenge to British prestige could still draw out one of her inimitable rebukes. When her grandson Kaiser Wilhelm congratulated the president of the Transvaal on foiling the Jameson raid in January 1896 in the so-called Kruger telegram, she fired off a letter regretting his actions, 'as your Grandmother to whom you have always shown so much affection and of whose example you have always spoken with so much respect' (*Letters*, 3rd ser., 3.8); his explanations she found 'lame and illogical' (ibid., 18). The illness and death of Sir Henry Ponsonby in 1895 marked a major change in the queen's household; he was replaced by his two assistants Fleetwood Edwards and Arthur Bigge.

The aged queen: diamond jubilee The greatest sadness of Victoria's later years was the death of her first son-in-law in 1888, a mere ninety-eight days after he had succeeded his father as German emperor. All Albert's hopes for creating a liberal Germany under the guidance of Vicky and Fritz crashed to the ground, and Vicky's son Willie became emperor and set Germany on the path that led eventually to war with his mother's homeland in 1914. For once the queen acknowledged a grief greater than her own when Albert died: 'You are far more sorely tried than me. I had not the agony of seeing another fill the place of my angel husband which I always felt I could not have borne' (*Darling Child*, 72). More grief followed in January 1892, when the prince of Wales's eldest son, Albert Victor, duke of Clarence, died shortly after becoming engaged to Princess May of Teck. Victoria approved unequivocally when Princess May became engaged instead to Clarence's brother George. The death of Prince Henry of Battenberg in 1896 was a still greater blow: chafing somewhat under the restrictions of living under his mother-in-law's roof, Beatrice's husband had persuaded the queen to allow him to serve in the Asante expedition, but he caught a fever and died on a hospital ship. 'My heart aches for my darling child, who is so resigned and submissive', Victoria wrote (*Letters*, 3rd ser., 3.26). The tone of restrained jollity which had come into the royal household with Beatrice's marriage never really returned, although the queen was generally serene and often cheerful. She was surrounded now by a circle of devoted women courtiers whose veneration of the 'poor dear Queen' made her comfortable.

The Indian princes who had attended the jubilee celebrations in 1887 had captured Victoria's imagination, and she was delighted to acquire two Indian servants of her own. The first of many, they attended the queen in Indian dress, adding an exotic touch to the humdrum household. The queen was, for her time and place, remarkably free from racial prejudice: she had

> a very strong feeling (and she has few stronger) that the natives and coloured races should be treated with every kindness and affection, as brothers, not—as alas! Englishmen too often do—as totally different beings to ourselves, fit only to be crushed and shot down. (*Letters*, 2nd ser., 2.361)

One of the original pair of servants, Abdul Karim, soon made it clear that he was no mere domestic: he had been a *munshi*, or clerk, in India, and the queen soon promoted him to teach her Hindustani. The munshi, as he was known, was the last recipient of the queen's passionate devotion to her servants: in her eyes he could do no wrong. The household and her own children, on the other hand, greeted this newly ascendant servant with the horror that had formerly been reserved for John Brown. He became a constant source of friction, with the queen insisting that he be treated as a member of the household rather than as a servant, while the household—who did not on the whole share the queen's liberal views towards people of other races—abominated him. They accused him of spying, of unduly influencing the queen in favour of Muslim rather than Hindu Indians, of feathering his own nest at the queen's expense. Most heinous of all, they found out that his father was not the respectable surgeon he had claimed, but an apothecary at the gaol at Agra: Indians of good birth could be tolerated, but the household felt they were being asked to dine with their servants. Rows over the munshi punctuated the queen's last years. Politics aside, the queen's interests were now those of the very elderly: her family, her health, her memories of the past, and her expectation of reunion with Albert, so long delayed.

On 23 September 1896 the queen noted in her journal that 'To-day is the day on which I have reigned longer, by a day, than any English sovereign' (*Letters*, 3rd ser., 3.79). She rejected suggestions that the event be marked by any public ceremony, asking that they be put off 'until I had completed the sixty years next June'. Victoria had long since stopped expecting to die any moment: at seventy-seven she fully expected still to occupy her throne a year later. The sixtieth anniversary of her accession (20 June 1897) was celebrated in a service of thanksgiving in St George's Chapel, Windsor, with her family around her. The golden jubilee had been celebrated ten years earlier by the royal families of Europe; the queen had deprecated the cost and the difficulties of housing so many of her royal relations at one time, and refused to do so again. The colonial secretary, Joseph Chamberlain, was credited with the idea of turning the jubilee into a celebration of empire: colonial premiers and their wives would not have to be put up in the royal palaces, and their invitation would be a compliment to the colonies they represented.

The public celebration of the diamond jubilee took place on 22 June: the queen was driven in procession in an open carriage through the streets of London to St Paul's Cathedral, where a brief outdoor service was held. One German princess expressed horror: 'after 60 years Reign, to thank God in the Street!!!' (J. Pope-Hennessy, *Queen Mary*, 1959, 335), but it was a popular and pragmatic solution for the queen, whose lameness would have made leaving and re-entering her carriage in public an undignified matter. The return journey took the queen over London Bridge and along the Borough Road, allowing many of her poorer subjects the chance of a glimpse of her. They were 'just as enthusiastic and orderly as elsewhere', she

remarked (*Letters*, 3rd ser., 3.176). Thus the queen who hated pomp and ceremony inaugurated the practice of large-scale royal ceremonial which defined the twentieth-century monarchy.

The end of an era, 1898–1901 Victoria's powers were fading by 1898. Confined to a wheelchair, her eyesight giving out, her digestion troubled, and her memory occasionally lapsing, she looked set for a gentle decline into senility, a possible regency, and death. She was saved from this ignominy by the worsening of relations between Britain and Germany, by the outbreak of the Second South African War, and by her own determination. The Kaiser's deep ambivalence towards his British heritage kept him personally respectful towards his grandmother, but his bellicosity worried her deeply: in 1898 she was moved to send a messenger to the leading newspaper editors, asking them to moderate their tone towards Germany, in hopes that it would be reciprocated (in fact, Wilhelm interpreted the milder tone which prevailed for a time as a sign of weakness). She celebrated the victory at Omdurman and the retaking of Khartoum in September: Gordon was avenged at last. Gordon's destroyer, her old enemy Gladstone, had died in May; crippled by her absolute honesty, she could not bring herself to offer a public tribute of regret. She was worried by the Dreyfus affair, and when Dreyfus was convicted afresh in September 1899 sent *en clair* telegrams to Salisbury and her ambassador in France deploring 'this monstrous horrible sentence against this poor martyr Dreyfus' (Weintraub, 603). She was excoriated in the French right-wing press.

Rising tensions in southern Africa occupied Victoria throughout the summer of 1899, and the declaration of war in October gave her a new lease of life. She inspected troops from her wheelchair, visited the sick and injured as they returned to Britain, and at Christmas gave a tin of chocolate to each soldier serving in the field. She corresponded supportively with her army commanders (she never undermined morale in the field by criticizing the often disastrous conduct of the war), but regularly berated her ministers about the inefficiency of the bureaucracy of war and particularly the medical provision for the sick and wounded, which in many ways had not improved since the Crimean War. During 'black week' (10–15 December 1899), when the British suffered a series of devastating reverses, she famously rebuked the downhearted A. J. Balfour with the positively Elizabethan declaration 'Please understand that there is no one depressed in *this* house; we are not interested in the possibilities of defeat; they do not exist' (Weintraub, 611). To mark the seriousness of the situation the queen broke with her previously inflexible routine, and instead of leaving Windsor after the anniversary of Albert's death to spend Christmas at Osborne, she remained at Windsor. She told Marie Mallet, 'After the Prince Consort's death I wished to die, but *now* I wish to live and do what I can for my country and those I love' (*Life with Queen Victoria*, 213).

The reliefs of Kimberley and Ladysmith in February 1900 were cause for celebration, and the queen thanked the City of London (which had raised and financed a regiment for the war) by making an official visit in March. The streets thronged with enthusiastic and loyal subjects: while Victoria reigned, the empire was yet safe. But Britain was deeply unpopular in Europe, not just in Germany, where Wilhelm used the war to fan hatred of his mother's country, but also in France and Italy, and the aged and increasingly enfeebled Victoria was savagely caricatured as an imperial tyrant. The political climate made her annual visit to the French riviera unwise, and instead, inspired by the Irish troops relieving Ladysmith, she went to Ireland. The visit was her own idea: 'I must honestly confess it is *not* entirely to please the Irish, but partly because I expect to enjoy myself', she said (*Life with Queen Victoria*, 192). Security was tight for her three-week stay at Viceregal Lodge in Dublin, and the queen saw only cheerful crowds of well-wishers.

During 1900, as the war in south Africa dragged on, Victoria's health declined rapidly. She had trouble sleeping at night and staying awake during the day. Her appetite, once so enormous, was gone, and she was able to eat only infrequently. And, with the powers of its linchpin fading, the structures of court life began disintegrating as well. But the queen still saw her ministers, still read (or had read aloud to her) the official papers, still fired off her regular hail of letters to her widespread family, politicians, her army officers, and representatives overseas, although now they were usually dictated to her daughters Princess Helena and Princess Beatrice. Victoria's second son, Affie, the duke of Edinburgh and duke of Coburg, died from cancer of the throat on 31 July; Empress Frederick was dying slowly and in excruciating pain from spinal cancer (although she outlived her mother by six months); and on 27 October Victoria's grandson Prince Christian Victor (Christle), son of Princess Helena, died from enteric fever on his way home from south Africa, where he had been serving with the army. This death brought the queen back from Balmoral to Windsor, where she remained for the annual service at Frogmore mausoleum on 14 December before going to Osborne for Christmas. It was an unfestive occasion, despite the presence of children and grandchildren, the gloom deepened by the death—in waiting to the last—of Jane, Lady Churchill, on Christmas day. Lady Churchill was the last of the queen's ladies from Albert's time (Lady Ely had died in 1890, the duchess of Atholl in 1898), and Victoria wept over her passing.

The court circular continued to state that the queen drove out daily, but this was often a polite fiction intended to disguise Victoria's decline. She could no longer write in her journal, but dictated entries to her granddaughter 'Thora' (Princess Helena Victoria); after 13 January 1901 even this stopped, and the record which had begun in 1832 was ended. Her last, characteristic order, on 15 January, was that the ambassador in Berlin should decline an honour offered him by the Kaiser. Joseph Chamberlain was the last minister to have an audience with her, on 11 January, but he tactfully withdrew as it was obviously beyond the queen's strength. On 16 January she did not get up, and

she never left her bed again. On 19 January a bulletin about the queen's health was issued for the first time, and her family began gathering at Osborne. On 21 January the prince of Wales arrived, with his brother Arthur, duke of Connaught, and his nephew Kaiser Wilhelm, who had rushed from Berlin on hearing the news. The queen slept, rousing herself to ask for her Pomeranian dog, and to wonder whether the prince of Wales should be told she was ill. Her son was at her side, and she seemed to recognize him; her last audible word was 'Bertie'. After lunch the family again gathered at her bedside, while the vicar of Whippingham, and Randall Davidson, now bishop of Winchester and still the queen's favourite clergyman, prayed aloud. Davidson recited Newman's 'Lead, kindly light'; whether she heard or not, it was a fitting accompaniment:

> So long Thy power hath blest me, sure it still
> Will lead me on,
> O'er moor and fen, o'er crag and torrent, till
> The night is gone.
> And with the morn those Angel voices smile,
> Which I have loved long since, and lost awhile.

At Osborne House, at half past six in the evening of 22 January 1901, in her eighty-second year and the sixty-fourth year of her reign, Victoria died.

Funeral Lytton Strachey captured perfectly the sense of dismay which swept the country as news of Victoria's failing health was announced:

> It appeared as if some monstrous reversal of the course of nature was about to take place. The vast majority of her subjects had never known a time when Queen Victoria had not been reigning over them. She had become an indissoluble part of their whole scheme of things, and that they were about to lose her appeared a scarcely possible thought. (*Queen Victoria*, 1921, 309)

Victoria had left detailed instructions about her funeral: her cousin Princess Mary, duchess of Teck, had died in 1897 without leaving a will, and the queen had immediately set her own wishes on paper. Despite her commitment to the forms of personal mourning, the queen hated 'black funerals', and decreed that her own was to be white and gold. She was proud of being a soldier's daughter and the head of the armed forces, and hers was to be a military funeral, her coffin to be pulled on a gun carriage by eight horses. Under no circumstances was her body to be embalmed. In addition to these general commands she had also written a set of instructions 'for my Dressers to be opened directly after my death and to be always taken about and kept by the one who may be travelling with me' (M. Reid, *Ask Sir James*, 1989, 215), which were kept secret from her family, and contained a list of items which were to be placed in her coffin.

There was considerable flurry over the arrangements, as Victoria's household—now superseded by that of the new king—sought to carry out their last duties to the queen. With Victoria lying on her bed in a white gown, surrounded by flowers, covered by her wedding veil, Albert's deathbed portrait hung above her head, her last portraits were taken, by Emile Fuchs, Hubert von Herkomer, and an unknown photographer (possibly Reid). On 25 January the queen's body was placed inside the first of the three coffins she had ordered (made locally after some confusion with the undertakers, Bantings). Beneath her, her dressers and doctor, Sir James Reid, had arranged Prince Albert's dressing gown and a cloak worked for him by their long-dead second daughter, Princess Alice, a plaster cast of Prince Albert's hand, mementoes of virtually every member of her extended family, her servants, and friends, including an array of shawls and handkerchiefs, framed photographs, lockets, and bracelets, and a sprig of heather from Balmoral. Once the family had left the room, Sir James placed a photograph of John Brown and a lock of his hair in the queen's left hand; among the rings she was wearing was the wedding ring of Brown's mother, which he had given to the queen in 1883. The coffin was sealed in the presence of the male members of the royal family, and was brought downstairs to lie in state in a temporary *chapelle ardente*, which more usually served as the dining-room.

On 1 February the queen's body (now encased in a triple coffin of oak, lead, and more oak, weighing half a ton) was placed on a gun carriage and taken to Cowes, where the royal yacht *Alberta* was waiting. Accompanied by Lady Lytton and the Hon. Harriet Phipps, two of her ladies-in-waiting, the queen's body made its last voyage across the Solent, between two rows of battleships and cruisers, one comprising thirty ships from the British navy, the other vessels sent in tribute from Germany, France, Portugal, and Japan, firing minute guns to mark her passing. The coffin remained overnight on the *Alberta* before proceeding to London on the following day by train. From Victoria Station the cortège moved along streets hung with purple cloth and white satin bows, the lampposts adorned with evergreen wreaths (provided by the activity of a volunteer ladies' committee), and through parks packed sixty deep with silent, black-clad crowds, to Paddington Station, where it joined the royal train to Windsor. At Windsor the coffin was placed once more on a gun carriage, but a horse shied and broke the traces, so the coffin was pulled by a guard of sailors to St George's Chapel, where the short funeral service was held. The coffin remained in the Albert memorial chapel until 4 February, when it was taken to the mausoleum at Frogmore, and, in a ceremony witnessed only by her family, Victoria was laid to rest with Albert. The Marochetti effigy of the queen which had been made at the same time as that of the prince consort had been found (after some difficulty), walled up in a store-room in Windsor, and was placed over the tomb.

The queen and the later Victorian constitution To the last the queen remained a very active and fertile element of the working constitution. She had safeguarded her prerogative jealously and zealously, and handed over to her son a monarchy much more engaged in the day-to-day working of the government than was apparent to her subjects. Indeed, given the democratization of politics which occurred during her reign, the royal prerogative was much less altered than might have been expected. It cannot be said that this was the result of the queen's skill, for she had by her partisan behaviour placed the monarchy in

considerable danger, to the extent that she had been warned by Gladstone about the serious long-term dangers to the monarchy of the partisan unionism of the court:

> At the present juncture, the views of Your Majesty's actual advisers, although now supported by a majority of the people (to say nothing of the people of the Colonies, and the English-speaking race at large), are hardly at all represented, and as Mr Gladstone believes, are imperfectly known, in the powerful social circles with which Your Majesty has ordinary personal intercourse. (*Letters*, 3rd ser., 2.172)

Through the loyalty and reticence of political leaders on both sides this issue was largely kept out of public discussion, and the Liberals brought forward no plan for the reform of the monarchy during the queen's reign. The concentration of radical critics on royal finances in the early 1870s produced only superficial discussion, for the issue was not really the financing of the monarchy but the role of the royal family in national life. Partisanship on the part of the monarch was, of course, nothing new; what was new was that the monarch could no longer give effect to partisan views. However much the queen might loathe Liberal governments led by Gladstone, even she did not think that she had the power to prevent them. The removal, before the start of her reign, of crown electoral control through rotten boroughs, and the consolidation of the political parties after the uncertainties of the mid-century, meant that the role of the monarch in making ministries was at best confined, except in very unusual circumstances, to a choice of personalities, and even then, as the queen found in 1880 and on other occasions, the political process rather than her will was ultimately decisive.

In the second half of her reign, it was only in 1895—the choice of Rosebery—that the queen's will was decisive, and even then only because the Liberals did not object, preferring Rosebery to W. V. Harcourt. In her later years the queen's partisan behaviour was in fact unnecessary, for the objectives of unionism, at least in the short term, were achieved by Lord Salisbury and Joseph Chamberlain; the queen's violent anti-Liberalism in fact could only endanger rather than aid their objectives. The queen was fortunate also in the forbearance of her successor, who handled his mother tactfully; the prince of Wales did not press himself forward, even when, at fifty-one, he experienced the humiliation of the queen's refusing Gladstone's suggestion that he should regularly see copies of the cabinet papers that were sent to the monarch.

For her part, Queen Victoria's sense of duty and pertinacity did much to maintain the monarchy in the working constitution. Her willingness to read every paper put before her, her speed in spotting when a paper which should have been sent to her had been withheld, her tenacity with respect to appointments, whether ecclesiastical, military, political, or diplomatic, and her long experience and encyclopaedic knowledge of European dynastic politics meant that she retained the respect of her premiers, most of whom were of high intellectual calibre, even when they differed from her. Disraeli's treatment of the queen as his 'Faery' creates a highly misleading view of this tough-minded, resourceful woman who, though she disliked political life, learned the tricks of its trade and knew how to anticipate the manoeuvres of its practitioners. The queen was very rarely taken by surprise by any political development, though her correspondence is often larded with such words as 'alarm' and 'shock', and those who dealt with her knew they had little chance of getting round her by sleight of hand. One result of this was that she often called forth from ministers memoranda on policy matters which were their most cogent statements of the case.

Victoria acted boldly in the pursuit of her own objectives, and was never embarrassed. Her appointment of Liberal secretaries, Grey and Ponsonby, was a sensible arrangement for dealing with the party with which she was most likely to be in dispute, but it placed an extra weight on her, for it meant that she had to formulate her views without much reference to her secretary, the person with whom, after the death of Albert, confidential political discussion most naturally occurred. The queen, in effect, relied on Ponsonby to allow her to form a view and then to see that her view was presented in as acceptable a form as possible to her ministers; Ponsonby became adept at delaying letters and suggesting alternative, less combative ways of expressing points. The queen, while feeling that she should express her views as if she was directly responsible for policy, also realized the impracticability of that position and relied on Ponsonby to reconcile the two; this he was stoically successful in doing. The queen did not see herself as partisan, since her view of politics, like that of many Conservatives, defined the national interest in terms of her own views. For her, unionism was self-evidently right.

Victoria was not a willing agent in the development of the modern British constitutional monarchy; but it began to form itself around her during her reign even so. The prerogatives she left to a monarch who was willing to be active publicly as well as privately were, however, considerable, as her son's forays into foreign policy were soon to show. In 1837 Victoria had inherited a tarnished crown, its powers waning, its popularity sinking. She left it to her son in 1901 restored and renewed, but fundamentally altered. Victoria had felt it her duty to engage actively with ministers in the business of government; her successors enjoyed less in the way of political authority. Ironically, it was as ceremonial figureheads and model families that Britain's monarchs reigned in the twentieth century. Victoria had been the last Hanoverian.

Reputation There can be few lives more monumentally documented than that of Queen Victoria. It was a process she began herself, for the habit of journal-keeping was instilled in her at an early age. She left her journal to her daughter Beatrice in her will, and the princess religiously transcribed those portions she thought fit for posterity and destroyed the originals, but even the bowdlerized journal is an invaluable source for historians. She was a prolific writer of letters, personal and political, vast numbers of which have survived. Her official life brought her into contact with politicians, diplomatists, soldiers, churchmen, foreign royalties, visiting dignitaries, artists,

writers, musicians, actors, scientists—anybody with any pretensions to importance in Victorian Britain crossed her path at some time or other. She was, moreover, an object of great curiosity to virtually everybody who met her, many of whom recorded their impressions and experiences. Even restricting the search to printed sources, it is possible to find Victoria's views on a huge range of subjects and her impressions of the people she met. She was also one of the most painted, sculpted, drawn, caricatured, and photographed people of her day: from the watercolour sketch made by Paul Fischer in 1819 to the photograph taken on her deathbed there were few incidents and relationships in her life which were not captured in visual form.

Biographies of the queen began appearing early in her reign. Among the first was Agnes Strickland's *Queen Victoria from her Birth to her Bridal* (1840), which the queen informed the author was wildly inaccurate; the volume was withdrawn. At the time of her jubilees many accounts of her life appeared, often in the form of salutary and improving tales for children; her son-in-law the marquess of Lorne produced one of the earliest commemorative volumes after her death, *V. R. I.: Her Life and Empire* (1901). The timing of the queen's death was inconvenient for the editors of the *Dictionary of National Biography*: the intended end date had been 1900. An additional volume was hastily added, the 93,000 words on the late queen being written by the second editor, Sidney Lee, and subsequently published separately.

Lee's *Queen Victoria* was the first full biography to appear, and the only one not to benefit from the publication of the *Letters of Queen Victoria*, the first series of which appeared in 1907, edited by Lord Esher and A. C. Benson; it covered the queen's life from her birth until the death of the prince consort. (In 1912 Esher edited the two-volume *Girlhood of Queen Victoria*, which contained valuable extracts from her early, uncut journal.) The *Letters of Queen Victoria* (two subsequent series were published in 1926–8 and 1930–32, edited by G. E. Buckle) provides the basis for every student of Victoria to whom the Royal Archives are inaccessible. While the letters do not present a 'warts and all' image of the queen, they are surprisingly frank in their portrayal of the queen's political role and private opinions: as Frank Hardie pointed out in *The Political Influence of Queen Victoria, 1861–1901* (1935), the queen had so successfully projected the public image of a charming old lady, benignly and impartially presiding over the welfare of her nation, that readers were surprised, even shocked, to discover how far she had taken an active—and sometimes obstructive—role in political affairs. The Gladstone family were so distressed by the *Letters* that they arranged to publish the correspondence between the queen and Gladstone; this showed rather more clearly both the prime minister's side of the story and how far the queen used her position to hinder his ministries.

Lytton Strachey's biography (1921) disappoints readers expecting a Bloomsbury attack: his Victoria is rather sympathetically portrayed in her 'vitality, conscientiousness, pride, and simplicity' (Strachey, *Queen Victoria*, 1921, 306).

Of the modern biographies of Victoria, Lady Longford's (1964) remains indispensable: based on a close reading of the extensive archival sources, including Princess Beatrice's transcript of the journal, her *Victoria R. I.* is a rounded life, which perceptively integrates the political with the personal.

Few people are truly legends in their own lifetimes: Victoria was one such, and her mythic status increased with the passage of time. Her image continues to surround us: few towns in Britain are without a statue of Victoria, a Victoria park, hospital, theatre, hall, or museum, or a street named for her. Despite the disintegration of the British empire, statues of Victoria remain in place in former colonies from India to the Bahamas, New Zealand to Canada, South Africa to Singapore. The most conspicuously removed statue of the queen was that which stood in Dublin; dismantled after independence, it was eventually given to the people of Australia and stands in Sydney. The ubiquity of the stern, matriarchal Victoria in public sculpture ingrained the image of the queen as an unsmiling prude on the general consciousness. Victoria felt it undignified and unqueenly to be painted or photographed smiling: a rare photograph of her smile captured by Charles Knight in 1898 reveals the transformation. The chilling put-down 'We are not amused' is perhaps the best-known 'fact' about the queen, although its provenance is unclear. Victoria's determination to present a regal face to posterity thus did her a great disservice, for a readiness to be pleased, and indeed amused, was one of her more endearing characteristics. She had a tendency towards the lachrymose, but there were many genuine causes for grief in her life. Nor was she a prude, as the published letters to her daughter Empress Frederick reveal, but she did have a great sense of modesty: even at eighty she held her fan in front of her face when speaking of a *risqué* play to a man— 'delightfully young, modest and naive!' commented an observer (*Life with Queen Victoria*, 170). She could be rude, dictatorial, selfish (especially in old age); she was also shy, honest, and humble in the face of virtue in others and in the sight of the God who she fervently believed watched over her and her country.

After the First World War, and Lytton Strachey's assaults on the preceding generation, 'Victorian' came to mean hypocritical, mealy-mouthed, prudish; the adjectives multiplied, and attached themselves to Victoria's own reputation, in defiance of the evidence. For a long time the Victorians were widely misunderstood: their closeness in time made it difficult to comprehend just how different they were from their successors. Earnestness can easily look like cant to an unsympathetic audience; moral certitude looks like hypocrisy when failure to meet high standards rather than the attempt to do so is taken as the measure. In her sincerity, her enthusiasms, her effort to do her duty, Victoria was truly Victorian: the age rightly bears her name.

H. C. G. MATTHEW and K. D. REYNOLDS

Sources VICTORIA'S LETTERS AND WRITINGS *The letters of Queen Victoria*, ed. A. C. Benson, Lord Esher [R. B. Brett], and G. E. Buckle, 9 vols. (1907–32) · *The girlhood of Queen Victoria: a selection from her majesty's diaries between the years 1832 and 1840*, ed. Viscount Esher [R. B. Brett], 2 vols. (1912) · *Dearest child: letters between Queen Victoria and the princess royal, 1858–1861*, ed. R. Fulford (1964) · *Dearest mama: letters between Queen Victoria and the crown princess of Prussia, 1861–1864*, ed. R. Fulford (1968) · *Your dear letter: private correspondence of Queen Victoria and the crown princess of Prussia, 1865–1871*, ed. R. Fulford (1971) · *Darling child: private correspondence of Queen Victoria and the crown princess of Prussia, 1871–1878*, ed. R. Fulford (1976) · *Beloved mama: letters between Queen Victoria and the German crown princess, 1878–1885*, ed. R. Fulford (1976) · *Beloved and darling child: last letters between Queen Victoria and her eldest daughter, 1886–1901*, ed. A. Ramm (1990) · Queen Victoria, *Leaves from the journal of our life in the highlands*, ed. A. Helps (1868) · Queen Victoria, *More leaves from the journal of a life in the highlands, from 1862 to 1882* (1884) · T. Martin, *The life of … the prince consort*, 5 vols. (1875–80) · B. Connell, ed., *Regina v Palmerston* (1962) · P. Guedalla, *The queen and Mr Gladstone*, 2 vols. (1933)

BIOGRAPHIES E. Longford, *Victoria RI* (1964) · S. Weintraub, *Victoria: biography of a queen* (1988) · M. Charlot, *Victoria: the young queen* (1991) · C. Woodham-Smith, *Queen Victoria: her life and times, 1: 1819–1861* (1972) · W. Arnstein, *Victoria* [forthcoming] · L. Strachey, *Queen Victoria* (1921)

STUDIES L. Vallone, *Becoming Victoria* (2001) · M. Warner, *Queen Victoria's sketchbook* (1979–81) · K. Hudson, *A royal conflict* (1994) · D. Thompson, *Queen Victoria: gender and power* (1990) · G. Rowell, *Queen Victoria goes to the theatre* (1978) · F. Prochaska, *Royal bounty: the making of a welfare monarchy* (1995) · F. Hardie, *The political influence of Queen Victoria* (1935) · W. Kuhn, *Democratic royalism* (1996) · R. Williams, *The contentious crown* (1997) · A. Munich, *Queen Victoria's secrets* (1996) · A. Ponsonby, *Sir Henry Ponsonby: his life from his letters* (1942) · *Life with Queen Victoria: Marie Mallet's letters from court, 1887–1901*, ed. V. Mallet (1968) · Mrs S. Erskine, *Twenty years at court* (1916) · H. C. G. Matthew, *Gladstone*, 2 vols. (1986–95) · R. Blake, *Disraeli* (1966) · W. F. Monypenny and G. E. Buckle, *The life of Benjamin Disraeli*, 6 vols. (1910–20) · M. Reid, *Ask Sir James* (1989) · T. Aronson, *Grandmama of Europe* (1973) · L. Mitchell, *Lord Melbourne* (1997) · R. Lamont-Brown, *John Brown: Queen Victoria's highland servant* (2000) · A. L. Kennedy, *My dear duchess* (1956)

Archives BL, album consolativum on death of Prince Albert, Add. MSS 62089–62090 · Hunt. L., letters · NL Scot., corresp. · Royal Arch., political and personal corresp. and papers · V&A NAL, notebook in the shape of a cross used by Victoria as a child | Balliol Oxf., letters to Marie Mallet · Balliol Oxf., letters to Jonathan Peel · BL, corresp. with Arthur James Balfour, Add. MS 49683, *passim* · BL, corresp. with W. E. Gladstone, loan 73 · BL, letters to Lady Holland, Add. MS 52113 · BL, corresp. with Lord Holland, Add. MS 51524 · BL, corresp. with Sir Stafford Northcote, Add. MS 50013 · BL, corresp. with Sir Robert Peel, Add. MSS 40303, 40432–40441 · BL, corresp. with Lord Ripon, Add. MSS 40864–40877 · BL OIOC, corresp. with J. C. Hobhouse, MS Eur. F 213 · Blair Castle, Perthshire · Bodl. Oxf., corresp. with Benjamin Disraeli · Bodl. Oxf., corresp. with Sir William Harcourt · Borth. Inst., corresp. with Lord Halifax · Chatsworth House, Derbyshire, letters to Lord Hartington · Glos. RO, corresp. with Sir M. Hicks Beach · Hants. RO, corresp. with third earl of Malmesbury · Hatfield House, Hertfordshire, corresp. with Lord Salisbury · Hove Central Library, Sussex, letters to Lord Wolseley · LPL, corresp. with Randall Thomas Davidson, archbishop of Canterbury · LPL, corresp. with A. C. Tait · Lpool RO, letters to fourteenth earl of Derby · McGill University, Montreal, McLennan Library, letters to Lord Hardinge · N. Yorks. CRO, letters to Lady Downe · NA Scot., letters to marquess of Breadalbane · NA Scot., letters to sixth duchess of Buccleuch · NA Scot., corresp. with Lord Panmure · NAM, corresp. with Lord Raglan · NAM, letters to Earl Roberts · NL Scot., corresp. with Lord Rosebery · NL Wales, letters to Sir John Williams, her physician · NRA, priv. coll., letters to duchess of Roxburghe · NRA, priv. coll., letters to first duke of Westminster · PRO, corresp. with Hugh Childers and Gladstone · PRO, corresp. with Lord Ellenborough, PRO 30/12 · PRO, corresp. with second Earl Granville, PRO 30/29 · PRO, letters to Lord Kitchener, PRO 30/57; WO 159 · PRO NIre., corresp. with Lord Dufferin · PRO NIre., notes to General Charles Grey · St Deiniol's Library, Hawarden, Flintshire, corresp. with Catherine Gladstone · Staffs. RO, letters to duchess of Sutherland · Suffolk RO, Bury St Edmunds, letters to seventh duke of Grafton · Suffolk RO, Ipswich · U. Birm. L., corresp. with Joseph Chamberlain · U. Durham L., corresp. with third Earl Grey · U. Durham L., corresp. with General Charles Grey · U. Nott. L., corresp. with duke of Newcastle · U. Southampton L., corresp. with Lord Palmerston · U. Southampton L., letters to duke of Wellington · W. H. Smith Archive Ltd, corresp. with W. H. Smith · W. Sussex RO, letters to duke of Richmond · Warks. CRO, letters to Sir Alexander George Woodford · Wilts. & Swindon RO, corresp. with Sidney Herbert and Sir Michael Herbert

Likenesses P. Fischer, watercolour sketch, 1819, Royal Collection · W. Beechey, double portrait, oils, 1821 (with her mother), Royal Collection; *see illus. in* Victoria, Princess, duchess of Kent (1786–1861) · G. Hayter, oils, 1833, Belgian royal collection · D. Wilkie, group portrait, oils, 1837 (*The first council of Queen Victoria*), Royal Collection · G. Hayter, oils, 1838, Royal Collection · T. Sully, oils, 1838, priv. coll.; copy, 1838, Wallace Collection, London · F. Chantrey, marble bust, 1839, Royal Collection; replica, 1841, NPG · E. Landseer, 1840–45 (*Windsor Castle in modern times*), Royal Collection · F. X. Winterhalter, oils, 1842, Royal Collection · F. X. Winterhalter, oils, 1843, Royal Collection · F. X. Winterhalter, oils, 1843 (informal portrait), Royal Collection · F. X. Winterhalter, double portrait, 1846 (with the prince of Wales), Royal Collection · T. Thornycroft, plaster statue, in or before 1851; *see illus. in* Thornycroft, Thomas (1815–1885) · E. Landseer, oils, 1865 (*Queen Victoria at Osborne*), Royal Collection · W. & D. Downey, photograph, 1868 (with John Brown), NPG; *see illus. in* Brown, John (1826–1883) · H. von Angeli, oils, 1875, Royal Collection [*see illus.*] · J. E. Boehm, bronze statue, 1887, near Windsor Castle · Princess Louise, marble statue, 1893, Kensington Gardens, London · C. Knight, albumen cabinet card, 1898, NPG · H. von Angeli, oils, 1899, Royal Collection · H. von Herkomer, watercolour, 1901 (deathbed portrait), Royal Collection · bromide print, 1901 (deathbed photograph), NPG · J. Hughes, statue, unveiled 1908, Queen Victoria Building, Town Hall Place, Sydney, Australia · T. Brock and A. Webb, statue, 1911 (The Victoria Monument), The Mall, London · G. Hayter, oil sketch (for portrait of 1833, Belgian royal collection), Royal Collection

Victoria, princess royal (1840–1901), German empress, consort of Frederick III, was born Victoria Adelaide Mary Louisa at Buckingham Palace, London, at 1.50 p.m. on 21 November 1840, the eldest of the nine children of Queen *Victoria and Prince *Albert. She was her father's favourite child and not unlike him in her clear mind, faith in logical argument, and intellectual, artistic, and scientific interests. Her father paid great attention to her education and to that of the next child, the future Edward VII: she responded, whereas he rebelled. A French governess, Mme Charlier, gave her fluent French, in addition to the German and English she naturally spoke. Her much loved English governess, Miss Hildyard (a parson's daughter, known as Tilla), gave her wide general reading. She never lost the respect for learning and scholars or the power of concentration which her education gave her. She was taught music, drawing, and watercolour painting, and performed with some skill in all.

In 1855, at the age of fourteen, Victoria was engaged to be married to Prince Frederick William of Prussia (1831–1888). They had first met when he was the guest of Queen Victoria for the Great Exhibition of 1851. He was again the

Victoria, princess royal (1840–1901), by James Russell & Sons

queen's guest when, with their parents' consent, he proposed. The engagement was not made public until April 1856, since during the Crimean War Prussia was inclined to Russia. The engagement was lengthy, all parties agreeing that the wedding should be preceded by Victoria's seventeenth birthday. The princess royal was confirmed before her marriage, which eventually took place in the Chapel Royal, St James's Palace, on 25 January 1858.

After two days at Windsor Castle, Victoria (known as Vicky) and Frederick (known as Fritz) moved to Berlin, where they lived at first in the gloomy Old Schloss. Friedrich Wilhelm IV was in seclusion; his son Wilhelm (later Kaiser Wilhelm I) was regent and with his wife, Augusta, had a stiff, formal, and elderly court and exercised what Vicky called an oppressive tyranny over the young couple. She never came to like Berlin, and always felt the need to avoid intimacies in a circle given to gossip and petty squabbling. She found the city without artistic or scientific life and socially dull. From 1859 they lived at the palace at Charlottenburg or in the New Palace in Unter den Linden, and at the New Palace at Potsdam. Later they could retreat to Bornstedt where Fritz had a farm. Their first child, William (later Kaiser Wilhelm II), was born on 27 January 1859, after an extremely difficult delivery. A fall during the princess's pregnancy was believed to have been the cause of the damage to the child's left arm, which, despite desperate efforts at a cure, remained shorter than the right. There were to be seven more children: Charlotte, born on 24 July 1860; Henry, born on 14 August 1862, who had a naval career; Sigismund, born in November 1864, who died of meningitis on 18 June 1866; Victoria (Moretta), born on 12 April 1866; Waldemar, born on 10 February 1868, who died from diphtheria on 27 March 1879; Sophie, born on 14 June 1870; and lastly Margaret (Mossy), born on 2 May 1872.

The crown princess (so called after her husband became heir to the Prussian throne in 1861) conformed comfortably with the Church of England or with the Evangelische Kirche in Germany, though she disliked the narrow Hofprediger (whom she thought cliquish in Berlin), and particularly the antisemitic Dr Adolf Stocker. The tedium of long, unoccupied days in Berlin was relieved by lectures, enjoyed by both husband and wife, on electricity (she liked electric light and installed it where she could), German history, and literature. They both liked Shakespeare and Sir Walter Scott, and Fritz read Goethe's *Faust* aloud to his wife. They read current English and German novels, as well as philosophic writers. Late in 1859 Vicky began to sculpt and to paint in oils, which she did off and on for the rest of her life.

The 1860s were dominated by three wars—of 1864 with Denmark, of 1866 with Austria, and of 1870–71 with France. The crown princess was much alone while her husband served in the field, with some distinction. She was active in work for the Red Cross and in helping to find care for the sick and wounded (she was knitting socks for the British soldiers in South Africa even during her last illness). She and Fritz founded the Friedrichsheim hospital and she continued to visit it after his death, as she had visited the Roman Catholic hospital of St Hedwig in Berlin earlier. She was active in founding schools, libraries, and hospitals and in relieving the poor in the neighbourhood of her several homes. She worked to raise money for the Frauen Groschen Verein ('Women's farthing league'), the oldest charitable society in Berlin. She furthered the education of women, patronized painters, and visited exhibitions of their work. She herself made a notable collection of medals and another of books on Charles I. She had a special love of Handel's music, and the society which she helped to found in 1894 to further its performance and study bore her name. In any local disaster she was active in relieving the homeless or injured, as in the floods of 1891. She visited Florence Nightingale and shared her objections to the starting of a nurses' register. She patronized Dr Koch (who isolated the tuberculosis bacillus) and helped to spread knowledge of his work. As late as 1896 she was patron of the International Amateur Photographic Exhibition in Berlin.

The crown prince and princess became the centre of a liberal constitutional circle in Prussia, which brought them increasingly into conflict with the chancellor, Bismarck. This added to Vicky's alienation from William, her eldest son, who was wilful and inconsiderate, and showed no signs of affection for his mother. He found support in his sister Charlotte who, on 18 February 1878, married Prince Bernhardt of Saxe-Meiningen and gained a measure of independence. Prince Henry, because of his affection for Charlotte, sided with them, and Bismarck, for his own purposes, encouraged the children's openly shown preference for their grandparents over their parents.

In the 1880s the conflict with Bismarck intensified and took a personal form over the engagement of the crown princess's daughter, Victoria (Moretta), with Alexander (Sandro) of Battenberg. They had met in 1879 when she was thirteen, and in 1885 she accepted his proposal. This love match was successfully opposed by Bismarck and the German emperor and empress on political grounds, and William used their opposition as an excuse to be disagreeable to his sister and mother. A climax was reached in the crown princess's difficulties with her eldest son in 1887. Queen Victoria was reluctant to invite him to her jubilee celebrations, but the crown princess persuaded her otherwise. All the queen's skill was needed to prevent William from putting himself too much forward and to prevent his offending the prince of Wales, which he did annually when he visited his grandmother at Osborne during the Cowes regatta.

In February 1887, the crown prince had begun to show signs of the cancer of the throat which was to kill him in the following year. The disputes between the doctors over the malignancy of the disease, and the appropriate treatment for the heir to the aged emperor (who was ninety), spilled over into national rivalry when a British specialist, Morell Mackenzie, advised against operating. Although Bismarck had supported both Mackenzie's consultation and his recommendation, the crown princess's 'English prejudice' was held responsible in Germany for Bergmann's failure to operate. Other doctors were called in; six German doctors had advised by the end.

Meanwhile, it was arranged that the crown prince and princess should attend Queen Victoria's jubilee, staying at Norwood in south London. After the celebrations (21–22 June 1887) and treatment in Mackenzie's London clinic, Fritz stayed at Braemar (where his health appeared to improve) while his wife visited friends in Devon. They returned to Germany on 30 August and were in Baveno and then San Remo from November 1887 to March 1888. The dispute was now whether, given Wilhelm I's age, they should or should not return to Germany. There was even intrigue for their son William to bypass his father and succeed to the throne immediately Wilhelm I died. The operation on Fritz was deferred until 9 February 1888, when a tracheotomy was successfully performed by Dr Bramann (Bergmann's assistant) in San Remo.

On 9 March Wilhelm I died. The new emperor and empress travelled to Berlin, where they arrived on 11 March. Fritz showed great energy, issuing a proclamation and writing to Bismarck asking him to remain as chancellor; by 13 March he was back in bed. In mid-April Queen Victoria visited them at Charlottenburg, and on 24 May Prince Henry married Irene of Hesse, Princess *Alice's daughter. On 15 June 1888 Frederick died. The grief of the Empress Frederick (as she chose to be known) imitated in intensity that of her mother in 1861, and was strengthened by her bitterness at the lost opportunity for Germany: 'We wished to see her strong and great, not only with the sword, but in all that was righteous, in culture, in progress and in liberty ... We had treasured up much experience! Bitterly, hardly bought!!!—that is now all wasted' (Ponsonby, 320).

Wilhelm II's hostility to his parents was undiminished by the death of his father, whose memory he set about obliterating. He caused Professor Geffcken, who published extracts from the emperor Frederick's Franco-Prussian War journal, to be arraigned for high treason in October 1888; the case collapsed, but it increased Vicky's distress, as did the discovery of an unopened letter from Fritz concerning his funeral arrangements.

Otherwise the empress's life was quiet and the public feeling against her died away gradually. She was able to build for herself 'a comfortable and independent country house to end my days in', to exercise a large hospitality 'with nothing ugly' about her, and with many up-to-date devices, including the telephone. Called Friedrichshof, the house was on land at Kronberg, a small estate with a ruined castle that Wilhelm II gave her, and was largely paid for by a legacy of 5 million francs from the duchesse de Galliera. It was finished, and the grounds laid out, by 1894.

On 27 October 1889 Princess Sophie married, at Athens, the future King Constantine of Greece, and thenceforward the Empress Frederick had a new interest: she visited Greece frequently; Greek antiquities and Greek politics absorbed her; and she was the source of views and information about Macedonia and Crete and the settlement of Balkan disputes. Despite a row with Wilhelm II over Sophie's reception into the Greek Orthodox church, the Empress Frederick was able to indulge her pleasure in her Greek grandchildren without further turmoil. She similarly acted as surrogate mother to Henry's wife, Irene, whose own mother had died in 1878. But chiefly she enjoyed her yearly visits to England, where she advised her mother on the repair of monuments in Westminster Abbey and on the arrangement of pictures at Buckingham Palace and Osborne. She was, of course, present at the diamond jubilee in 1897. Nearly every year she was able to spend a month or two in 'the south', as she called the Mediterranean, or in the Tyrol. In January 1890 her youngest daughter, Mossy, married Frederick Charles of Hesse, and she soon had another set of grandchildren. In 1890 Bismarck fell and, though the increases in the army and the spread of socialism worried the empress, she welcomed the lessening of domestic tension.

The empress did not share Victoria's dislike of Gladstone and defended him against the queen, though not agreeing with his Irish policy. After one stiff audience with the queen, Gladstone had found the empress lingering in the corridor outside and they exchanged more relaxed words. He noted: 'she talked abundant Liberalism of a deep-rooted kind' (Gladstone, *Diaries*, 16 July 1881). She agreed with him over the Armenian massacres in 1895,

regretting Wilhelm II's colonial and naval policy and support for Turkey. Though still suffering 'wounds and stabs', she knew now that her son had no application or power of adhering to a policy and so took his incursions into her quiet life more calmly. Nevertheless, after his foolish telegram to President Kruger in 1896 she was powerless to lessen the increasing political hostility between Germany and Britain. She regarded Dreyfus as the innocent victim of the French army and ultramontane extremism. Over China and the Boxer riots in 1898 she thought Wilhelm II had simply gone too far in self-assertion and, though she would have liked a British–American–German alliance, knew it was an impossible ideal. She followed with intense British patriotism developments in both the Sudan and the Transvaal, and her feelings during the Second South African War were entirely predictable.

While staying at Dalmeny with Lord Rosebery in October–November 1898 the Empress Frederick had an attack of giddiness and thenceforward cancer was suspected. One surviving letter refers to the diagnosis of something 'incurable' and another of 29 January 1899 to her mother referred to 'the evil which cannot be cured'. But she wrote about her health on a separate sheet in her letters, so that it could be destroyed. For public consumption her illness was described as lumbago. She followed the advice of Sir Francis Laking and Sir James Reid, with long spells in bed, whether at Friedrichshof or on the Riviera. She outlived her mother by six months only, dying at Friedrichshof on 5 August 1901. By her own direction she was buried by the side of her husband at the Friedenskirche, Potsdam.

Brought up by Prince Albert to lead Germany into the paths of liberalism and constitutionalism, the Empress Frederick was thwarted by the longevity of one emperor and the early death of another. Her genuinely liberal instincts and intellectual interests found no resonance with her son, who, encouraged by Bismarck, rejected her influence and led Germany along an entirely different route from that envisaged at his mother's engagement in 1855. Devoted to her native country, which she believed to exemplify liberal virtue, she was regarded with deep suspicion in a Germany which took praise of other nations as criticism of itself. Hostility to 'die Engländerin' long survived her death: Frederick Ponsonby observed that she had been 'calumniated, abandoned and distrusted and even hated' in Germany for twenty-five years after her death. His edition of some of her letters (which she had given him to smuggle out of Germany only months before her death) was published in 1928, and began the rehabilitation of her reputation. This was taken further by the edition of the correspondence between her and her mother, begun by Roger Fulford and completed by Agatha Ramm.

AGATHA RAMM

Sources F. Ponsonby, *Letters of the Empress Frederick* (1928) • *Dearest child: letters between Queen Victoria and the princess royal, 1858–1861*, ed. R. Fulford (1964) • *Dearest mama: letters between Queen Victoria and the crown princess of Prussia, 1861–1864*, ed. R. Fulford (1968) • *Your dear letter: private correspondence of Queen Victoria and the crown princess of Prussia, 1865–1871*, ed. R. Fulford (1971) • *Darling child: private correspondence of Queen Victoria and the crown princess of Prussia, 1871–1878*, ed. R. Fulford (1976) • *Beloved mama: private correspondence of Queen*

Victoria and the German crown princess, 1878–1885, ed. R. Fulford (1981) • *Beloved and darling child: last letters between Queen Victoria and her eldest daughter, 1886–1901*, ed. A. Ramm (1990) • J. C. G. Rohl, *Kaiser Wilhelm II* (1989) • Gladstone, *Diaries* • Queen Victoria, journal, Royal Arch.

Archives Royal Arch. • Schloss Fasanerie, Fulda, Germany, Archiv der Hessischen Hausstiftung | BL, letters to Bishop Carpenter, Add. MS 46721 • BL, corresp. with Florence Nightingale, Add. MS 45750 • BL OIOC, letters to Lord and Lady Napier, MS Eur. F 114 • CCC Cam., letters to Lady Derby • LUL, corresp. with Sir Edwin Chadwick • N. Yorks. CRO, letters to Lady Downe • NL Scot., corresp. with Lord Rosebery

Likenesses E. Landseer, oils, 1841, Royal Collection • R. J. Lane, lithograph, 1841 (after W. C. Ross), BM, NPG • C. R. Leslie, group portrait, oils, 1841 (*Christening of the princess royal*), Royal Collection • E. Wolff, marble bust, 1841, Royal Collection • Queen Victoria, drawing, 1841–2, Royal Collection • W. C. Ross, two miniatures, 1841–50, Royal Collection • F. Grant, double portrait, oils, 1842 (with prince of Wales), Royal Collection • F. Grant, group portrait, oils, 1842, Royal Collection • G. Hayter, drawing, 1842, Royal Collection • T. M. Joy, double portrait, oils, 1842 (with prince of Wales), Royal Collection • E. Landseer, drawing, 1842, Royal Collection • E. Landseer, oils, 1842, Royal Collection • E. Landseer, two group portraits, oils, 1842, Royal Collection • H. Robinson, stipple, pubd 1842 (after W. C. Ross), BM • F. X. Winterhalter, oils, 1842, Royal Collection • F. X. Winterhalter, group portrait, oils, 1843 (*Reception of Queen Victoria and Prince Albert by Louis Phillipe at the Chateau d'Eu*), Musée de Versailles • J. Lucas, oils, 1844, Royal Collection • F. X. Winterhalter, double portrait, oils, c.1844 (with prince of Wales), Royal Collection • M. Thornycroft, marble bust, 1846, Royal Collection • F. X. Winterhalter, two group portraits, oils, 1846–9, Royal Collection • H. J. Stewart, group portrait, pencil and watercolour drawing, 1849 (study for *The landing of Queen Victoria at Dumbarton in 1847*), Scot. NPG • F. X. Winterhalter, double portrait, watercolour drawing, 1850 (with Princess Alice), Royal Collection • H. C. Selous, group portrait, oils, 1851 (*The opening of the Crystal Palace*), V&A • F. X. Winterhalter, oils, 1851, Royal Collection • R. J. Lane, lithograph, pubd 1855 (after F. X. Winterhalter), NPG • E. M. Ward, two group portraits, oils, 1855, Royal Collection • H. Watkins, albumen print, 1855–9, NPG • C. L. Müller, oils, 1856, Royal Collection • F. X. Winterhalter, oil sketch, 1856, Schloss Friedrichshof, Germany • F. X. Winterhalter, oils, 1857, Royal Collection • H. Hagen, marble bust, c.1858, Royal Collection • J. Phillip, group portrait, oils, 1858 (*The marriage of the princess royal*), Royal Collection • H. von Angeli, portrait, 1860 • A. Graefle, oils, c.1860, Royal Collection • H. C. Heath, miniature, c.1860 (after A. Hahnisch), Royal Collection • A. Menzel, group portrait, oils, 1861 (*Coronation of Wilhelm I at Königsberg*), Staatliche Schlosser und Gärten, Sanssouci, Potsdam • F. X. Winterhalter, group portrait, oils, 1862, Royal Collection • W. P. Frith, group portrait, oils, 1863 (*The marriage of the prince of Wales*), Royal Collection • J. C. Horsley, group portrait, oils, 1865, RSA • S. Durant, marble medallion, 1866, Royal Collection; small related ormolu medallion, NPG • F. X. Winterhalter, oils, 1867, Royal Collection • H. von Angeli, oils, 1876, Royal Collection • S. P. Hall, group portrait, oils, 1879 (*The marriage of the duke of Connaught*), Royal Collection • H. von Angeli, oils, 1880, Staatliche Schlosser und Gärten, Sanssouci, Potsdam • H. von Angeli, oils, 1882, Wallace collection, London • A. von Werner, group portrait, watercolour, 1882 (*The baptism of Crown Prince Wilhelm*), Staatliche Schlosser und Gärten, Potsdam • L. Tuxen, group portrait, oils, 1887 (*The royal family at the time of the jubilee*), Royal Collection • Lehngraff, miniature, c.1888 (after photograph), Royal Collection • A. von Werner, group portrait, oils, 1888 (*Opening of the Reichstag under Wilhelm II*), Staatliche Schlosser und Gärten, Potsdam • H. von Angeli, oils, 1893, Schloss Friedrichshof, Germany • J. Mordechi, oils, c.1900 (after photograph), NPG • T. A. Voight, photograph, 1900 • J. B. Hunt, stipple (after A. Hunt), BM, NPG; repro. in *Ladies' Companion* (1853) • E. Landseer, group portrait, oils

(*The queen sketching at Loch Laggan with the prince of Wales and the princess royal*), Royal Collection • R. J. Lane, lithograph (after W. C. Ross; after sketch by Queen Victoria, 1841), BM, NPG • Nemo [C. de Grimm], chromolithograph caricature, NPG; repro. in *VF* (7 June 1884) • J. Russell & Sons, photograph, NPG [*see illus.*] • photographs, Royal Collection • photographs, V&A • prints (after photographs), BM, NPG

Victoria, Princess (1868–1935), was born Victoria Alexandra Olga Mary on 6 July 1868 at Marlborough House, London, the fourth of the six children of Albert *Edward (1841–1910) and *Alexandra (1844–1925), prince and princess of Wales. Her father became King Edward VII; her mother was the daughter of King Christian IX and Queen Louise of Denmark. Princess Victoria (known familiarly as Toria) was educated at home with her two sisters. She was a lively, naughty child, who became an intelligent, attractive woman, tall and elegant, with large expressive eyes. Although sensitive and reserved, she had a great sense of fun and was good company, lacking any affectation or grandeur. She enjoyed bicycling and horse-riding, designed her own bookbindings, loved reading, music, and dancing, and was a very enthusiastic amateur photographer, who compiled many albums and took part in Kodak exhibitions. The princess was also fond of pets; some of her favourites were dogs, including Sam, Mac, and Punchie. Dovey was a tame dove which she kept for six years and which used to accompany her on holiday, travelling in a little basket.

Princess Victoria had strong family feelings; these embraced more distant relatives, and she was particularly fond of her cousins from the Russian and Greek royal families. One of the most important people in her life was her brother *George V (1865–1936); they were devoted to one another, and shared a sense of humour and a similar outlook. When she died the king commented 'How I shall miss her & our daily talks on the telephone. No one had a sister like her' (Gore, 436). His own health deteriorated from this time and he died only a month later. For Princess Victoria the importance of the relationship with her brother might have made it difficult for her to accept his wife, no matter who she had been. As it was, she was not greatly in sympathy with Queen Mary, whom she once referred to as being 'deadly dull' (Pope-Hennessy, 279), a feeling which was increased by their differences in character, education, and interests.

Princess Victoria loved her parents dearly, and this feeling was fully reciprocated. She became 'the good angel' of the family who was indispensable to the king and queen, accompanying them on visits and official engagements and generally helping to make their lives easier. But this was achieved only by suppressing her own inclinations, and her life as an adult unmarried daughter at home was not always easy. If she had wanted to marry a prince of equal rank, such as her cousin King Christian X of Denmark, her parents would have been happy to agree, but they were less willing to consider an alliance with, for example, a British commoner. The princess would not hear of marrying her cousin, and refused to marry anyone except for love, but those whom she might have chosen were barred to her, which left this area of her life apparently sad and unfulfilled. After her father's death she lived in the shadow of Queen Alexandra, who was by then elderly, often depressed, and almost stone-deaf. Princess Victoria longed for greater independence, but lacked the stamina and perhaps the self-interest for open rebellion; moreover, she saw it as her duty to care for her mother. Nevertheless, she was always grateful for the occasional holiday and is reported as saying 'Thank God you can take my place now for a while' (De Stoeckl, 161) to a friend who was going to stay with Queen Alexandra at one of these times. But when, in 1920, she and the princess royal had to deputize for their mother on Alexandra Rose day, she wrote in one of her albums that it had been 'horrible without Mama' (Princess Victoria's photograph album, 1919–22, 18, Royal Archives, RPC 03/0114).

The frustrations of this kind of existence undermined Princess Victoria's health, which had never been robust. Although by nature kind, generous, and unselfish, she gained a reputation for being sometimes sharp-tongued and difficult. Once, on impulse, she said to her doctor 'Can you realise what it means to have always driven with your back to the horses?' (Lord Dawson to George V, 2 Dec 1935, Royal Archives, GV/AA 57/10)—metaphorically describing a life spent putting others first and having to bear any consequent discomfort. As a result she was always sympathetic to those in distress, but she had an unfortunate way of showing it. She once visited the Harrogate Infirmary with a friend, taking presents for all the elderly inmates. A number of smiling old ladies were waiting to meet her, but the princess proceeded to sympathize so heartily with them on their plight that she left them sobbing and discontented. She preferred facing unhappiness rather than pretending that it did not exist, and at the time of King Edward VII's last illness was one of the few people who admitted that he was dying and insisted that public bulletins on his health should reflect this.

Queen Alexandra died in 1925 and Princess Victoria set up home at Coppins, Iver, in Buckinghamshire, where she lived until her death, enjoying music and gardening and taking a keen interest in local matters. She was much in sympathy with young people, and among those for whom she felt a special affection were Beatrice Harrison, the cellist, and her sisters, also musicians. They had spent a holiday on the Sandringham estate in 1918, at the princess's invitation, and she wrote afterwards to thank them:

> for giving me the time of my life! in actually playing with an orchestra with real live artists!! I *never* thought it could come to pass … Music is so *wonderful* so *helpful* & I have *longed* to be able to play, or produce in some way the sounds *I feel &* *understand.* (Harrison Sisters' Trust, archives, 6 Oct 1918)

As a skilled amateur pianist, she recorded two works by Elgar with the Harrisons in 1928. Her other friends included the Musgrave family, with whom she sometimes stayed (Lady Musgrave was a lifelong friend who was also the princess's lady-in-waiting), the widowed fifth earl of Rosebery, and Violet Vivian, formerly a maid of honour to Queen Alexandra, whose garden at Cestyll, near Cemais

Bay, the princess helped to design. Princess Victoria died on 3 December 1935 at Coppins and was interred in the royal burial-ground at Frogmore on 8 January 1936.

FRANCES DIMOND

Sources *The Times* (4 Dec 1935) • G. Battiscombe, *Queen Alexandra* (1969) • private information (2004) • T. Conway, *Cestyll garden* (Nuclear Electric plc, 1992) • J. Pope-Hennessy, *Queen Mary* (1959) • B. Harrison, *The cello and the nightingales*, ed. P. Cleveland-Peck (1985) • correspondence, Royal Arch. • Royal Arch., Royal Photograph Collection • J. Gore, *King George V: a personal memoir* (1941) • Agnes, Baroness de Stoeckl, *Not all vanity* (1950)

Archives Royal Arch., incl. Royal Photograph Collection | PRO NIre., letters to Lady Antrim • Royal College of Music, London, Harrison Sisters' Trust, archives | FILM BFI NFTVA, current affairs footage • BFI NFTVA, news footage • British Movietone News Limited, East Barnet • Reuter's Television Library, London | SOUND Symposium Records, East Barnet

Likenesses K. W. F. Bauerle, oils, 1871, Royal Collection • H. M. Thornycroft, double portrait, marble statue, 1877 (with her sister Princess Maud), Royal Collection • H. von Angeli, oils, 1878, Royal Collection • S. P. Hall, group portrait, oils, 1883 (*Daughters of Edward VII*), NPG • L. Tuxen, group portrait, oils, 1887 (*The royal family at the time of the jubilee*), Royal Collection • C. J. Turrell, miniature, 1890, Royal Collection • L. Tuxen, group portrait, oils, 1893 (*Marriage of King George and Queen Mary*), Royal Collection • E. Hughes, oils, 1896, Royal Collection • L. Tuxen, group portrait, oils, 1896 (*Marriage of Princess Maud and Prince Charles of Denmark*), Royal Collection • L. Alma-Tadema, drawing, 1897, Royal Collection • P. A. de Laszlo, oils, 1907, NPG • L. Charles, photograph, 1909, Royal Photograph Collection • A. Broom, photographs, NPG • Byrne & Co., photographs, NPG • W. & D. Downey, photographs, NPG • R. Milne, photographs, NPG • J. Russell & Sons, photographs, NPG • photographs, Royal Photograph Collection • photographs, PRO • portraits, Royal Collection

Wealth at death £237,455 18s. 9d.: probate, 11 March 1936, CGPLA Eng. & Wales

Victoria Alexandra Alice Mary. *See* Mary, princess royal (1897–1965).

Victoria Eugénie Julia Ena. *See* Ena, princess of Battenberg (1887–1969).

Victoria, Vesta [*real name* Victoria Lawrence] (1873–1951), music-hall entertainer, was born on 26 November 1873 at 8 Ebenezer Place, Holbeck, Yorkshire, the daughter of Joseph Lawrence, machine smith, and his wife, Emma, *née* Thompson. Her father was also a 'blackface' performer with the sobriquet the Upside-Down Comedian, who specialized in singing while standing on his head, and she appeared with him at the age of four. Her first professional appearance was as Little Victoria at the Cambridge Music-Hall on 22 October 1883. By the age of nineteen, as Vesta Victoria, she was topping bills in both British music-halls and American vaudeville (she toured the USA for six years) and had developed an inventive, not-so-dumb-blonde stage persona, a prototype to be further explored by comedians such as Gracie Allen and Marilyn Monroe. With dreamy, fair good looks she could put over a song with a surface innocence that was regularly subverted by an underlying intelligence hinted at by the richness and depth of her voice; it was never quite clear whether or not she was as naïve as her songs suggested. Her earliest successes were both knowing and childlike: 'Daddy wouldn't

Vesta Victoria (1873–1951), by Langfier

buy me a bow-wow', a major success in 1893, or 'Our lodger's such a nice young man', in which a young girl describes the way he kisses all the females of the family ''cos Papa was away'.

Later Vesta Victoria developed a more complex and ironic comedy, which was largely grounded upon the inventive songwriting skills of Harry Pether and Fred Leigh. Their work for her built up into a series of wry comments on the progress of love and marriage in a lifetime. 'Waiting at the Church' in 1906, about a bride left at the altar by a groom who sends a note to say 'Can't get away to marry you today—my wife won't let me', was perhaps her best-known song. Its cheerful tune echoed the refusal of her stage persona to be crushed: she might be treated badly, but she remained able to laugh at herself. 'Poor John' in 1907 used the same combination of sadness and survival in a story of a girl being looked over by her future mother-in-law, 'boiling with aggravation' as the old woman mutters, 'Poor John! Poor John!' As matters came to a head, Victoria showed some spirit:

> Then all at once she gave a sigh and cried, 'O Lor'
> I wonder what on earth he wants to marry for?'
> That was quite enough—up my temper flew
> Says I, 'Perhaps it's so that he can get away from you.'

The pressures on women to get married were summed up by the song 'Some would marry anything with trousers on'; Victoria wryly sang of the various consequences that might ensue from desperation—the disillusion of finding out that a man is not, after all, free, in 'I've told his missus all about him', or the galling situation of losing the man of her dreams to her mother—'And now I have to call him Father.' She was equally pessimistic about her prospects as a working girl: in one song she portrayed an artist's model, complaining that 'It's all right in the summer time.' Victoria's complete 'marriage' sequence of songs concluded with her as the widow of a 'chilly man'—in, it was implied by her tone of voice, more than one sense of the word—dreamily reflecting that 'I hope and trust there's a nice warm fire where my old man has gone.'

Vesta Victoria's special talent was to clown about such disappointments while retaining an essential self-confidence. The audience laughed at her, only to find that they were in fact laughing with her. Although she never shirked unbecoming or tatty costumes when a role demanded it, on the whole her clothes were elegant and her sexual attractiveness was to the fore even when she ruefully narrated the latest betrayal; she generally included some non-comic songs such as Tabrar's ballad 'All in a Day' or the still well-known 'Comin' thro' the rye', which not only showed her voice to advantage, but stressed her distance from her 'unsuccessful' persona and underlined the control she exercised over the stage.

Vesta Victoria's own marriage in 1912 to the actor Herbert Edward (or W. G. H.) Terry ended in divorce in 1926. She had at least one daughter. Victoria retired in 1918 but made a successful comeback in 1929 with Fred Collins's road show *Vaudeville Past and Present*, and in 1931–2 she toured with other veterans such as Wilkie Bard and Harry Champion in Lew Lake's *Stars that Never Failed to Shine*. Her material allowed her to assume a variety of ages, so that she could bring her gently satirical edge to her stories of a woman's lot throughout a long career. In 1944, Columbia Pictures brought out the film *Cover Girl*, which included a dream sequence in which Rita Hayworth travelled back in time to become her own theatrical grandmother and sang several Vesta Victoria hits. The writers, Pether and Leigh, did not appear in the credits. This reflects, perhaps, not so much Hollywood carelessness as the place of these songs in the popular imagination; Victoria had made them seem a natural product of her generation, spontaneous and authorless. Victoria's last appearance was in the finale of the royal variety show of 1932 at the London Palladium. She died from breast cancer at St Columba's Hospital, Hampstead, on 7 April 1951.   FRANCES GRAY

Sources R. Busby, *British music hall: an illustrated who's who from 1850 to the present day* (1976) · B. Green, ed., *The last empires: a music hall companion* (1986) · H. C. Newton, *Idols of the halls* (1975) · *The Times* (9 April 1951) · *Who was who in the theatre, 1912–1976*, 4 vols. (1978) · b. cert. · d. cert.

Archives SOUND BL NSA, performance recordings

Likenesses Langfier, photograph, priv. coll. [*see illus.*]

Wealth at death £15,631 17s. 5d.: probate, 15 Jan 1952, *CGPLA Eng. & Wales*

Victorinus (*fl.* 400). *See under* Roman officials (*act.* AD 43–410).

Vidal, Alexander Thomas Emeric (1792–1863), naval officer and hydrographer, was the youngest of the three sons (there was also a daughter) of Emeric Vidal, a naval officer who served as secretary to three distinguished admirals (Sir Robert Kingsmill, Sir John Ross, and Robert Duff), and his wife, Jane Essex. The Vidals came originally from the Basque country. Vidal entered the Royal Navy as a first-class volunteer on the *Illustrious* in 1803. On 22 May 1807 he joined the Royal Naval College in Portsmouth for eighteen months, after which, as a midshipman, he served in the *Lavinia* in the Mediterranean and north Atlantic for more than three years.

In 1814 Vidal sailed in the *Conway* for the North American station, and later was detached to work under Captain W. F. Owen on a survey of the Canadian Great Lakes. Here he learned surveying, and on 6 February 1815 was promoted lieutenant. When Captain Owen commissioned the ship-sloop *Leven* (24 guns) and the brig *Barracouta* (10 guns) in 1821 for his survey of the east coast of Africa, Vidal was appointed first lieutenant in the *Leven*. When the *Barracouta*'s captain died in 1823 Vidal was placed in command and confirmed in the rank of commander from 15 May 1823. Two years later, when Owen brought his ships home, Vidal was advanced to captain (4 October 1825).

In the summer of 1830, as a consequence of a number of reports and unsuccessful searches for Aitkin's Rock, which was said to lie about 70 miles off the north-west coast of Ireland, two ten-gun brigs were placed under Vidal's orders to make a final search. In three months the area covered by the several reports was closely examined and this potential danger to shipping erased from the charts.

In December 1835 Vidal sailed in command of the converted bomb-vessel *Aetna* with twelve chronometers to measure the meridian distances from the Cape Verde Islands to a number of places on the west coast of Africa, and afterwards to carry out surveys of the coast. It was unpopular but useful work, which he completed despite ill health. From 1841 to 1846, closely associated with the authorities in Lisbon, he surveyed the Azores in the *Styx*. He was a fellow of the Royal Geographical Society and contributed papers on hydrographic matters to its journal. He became rear-admiral on 27 January 1854 and vice-admiral on 17 June 1859. He published a chart of the Salvage Islands, thirteen charts of the Cape Verde Islands, a chart of the coast of England, and one of Vidal Bank off the north-west coast of England.

In October 1839, in Canada, Vidal married Sarah Antoinette (d. June 1843), the daughter of Henry Veicht of Madeira; they had two sons, one of whom died at an early age and the other, Beaufort, became a general in the Canadian army. Vidal died at 13 Sion Hill, Clifton, Gloucestershire, on 5 February 1863. Several features in the different parts of the world he surveyed bear his name, notably Cape Vidal on the east coast of Africa.

G. S. RITCHIE, *rev.*

Sources G. S. Ritchie, *The Admiralty chart: British naval hydrography in the nineteenth century* (1967) · D. Syrett and R. L. DiNardo, *The commissioned sea officers of the Royal Navy, 1660–1815*, rev. edn, Occasional Publications of the Navy RS, 1 (1994) · *GM*, 3rd ser., 14 (1863), 396 · O'Byrne, *Naval biog. dict.* · L. S. Dawson, *Memoirs of hydrography* (1885) · Hydrographic Office archives · family letters, priv. coll.
Wealth at death under £2000: probate, 7 May 1863, *CGPLA Eng. & Wales*

Vidal [*née* Johnson], **Mary Theresa** (1815–1873), novelist, was born at Torrington, Devon, on 25 July 1815, the eldest child of William Charles Johnson, curate of Torrington, and his wife, Mary Theresa Furse, whose mother, Elizabeth Johnson, was the sister of Sir Joshua *Reynolds. She had three sisters and two brothers, one of whom Charles Wellington Johnson (later Furse), became archdeacon of Westminster. Her other brother, William Johnson *Cory, became a poet and a tutor at Eton College.

Brought up and educated at Torrington, on 25 April 1835, at Ideford, Mary Theresa Johnson married the Revd Francis Vidal (1805–1884), curate of Torrington. After some time at Exeter gaol where Francis was chaplain, ambitions for better fortune—and apparent health problems—led the young couple, with their three small sons, to emigrate to Australia. They arrived in Sydney on the *Earl Grey* on 25 February 1840. The new experiences of their lives at Penrith and Denham Court, New South Wales, where Francis Vidal continued his ministry, spurred Vidal to write and generated her most important, her Australian, fiction: *Tales for the Bush* (1844), *The Cabramatta Store* (1850), and *Bengala, or, Some Time Ago* (1860). Her most substantial novel with an English setting was *Ellen Raymond* (1859). In 1845 the Vidals returned to England. Here Francis succeeded Vidal's brother William as tutor at Eton College after Cory's dismissal, this most English of institutions thus becoming the unlikely site of Vidal's colonial writing.

Mary Vidal's Australian works and nine English novels and novellas are Victorian romances marked by their lively observation and a Christian didacticism severe enough to disrupt their worldly sense of injustice. The interesting sub-plot of *Bengala* exposes an upper-class conduct which harshly betrays all convict aspiration to civilized life.

Mary and Francis Vidal had six sons and one daughter; the writer Faith Compton Mackenzie (d. 1960) was their granddaughter. Mary Vidal died of meningitis on 19 November 1873 at the vicarage, Sutton, Suffolk.

ELIZABETH LAWSON

Sources introduction, M. T. Vidal, *Bengala, or, Some time ago*, ed. S. McKernan (1990) · F. C. Mackenzie, *William Cory: a biography* (1950) · F. C. Mackenzie, *As much as I dare* (1938)
Archives Eton, William Cory MSS · NL Aus., letters to her brothers
Likenesses M. T. Vidal?, self-portrait, oils, 1840–49, NL Aus.

Vidal, Robert Studley (1770–1841), antiquary, was the son of Robert Studley Vidal (d. 1796) of Exeter, formerly a solicitor in London. He was called to the bar at the Middle Temple on 22 August 1795. He had antiquarian tastes, and communicated two papers on trial by ordeal and on the site of Kenwith Castle, Devon, to the Society of Antiquaries through his friend Henry Wansey: they were published in *Archaeologia*, volume 15. His chief work was the translation of J. L. von Mosheim, *Commentaries on the Affairs of the Christians before the Time of Constantine*. The first two volumes were published in 1813, but the third did not appear until 1835. In the intervening years Vidal prepared the third edition of Charles Watkins's *A Treatise on Copyholds*, published in 1821, and the fifth edition of Sir Geoffrey Gilbert's *The Law of Tenure*, published in 1824. His projected edition of Ralph Cudworth's *The Intellectual System of the Universe* (1678) was not published. Vidal formed a valuable collection of coins and medals, which was sold by Leigh and Sotheby on 18 June 1842 after his death. He kept a pack of harriers at Cornborough, near Bideford, Devon. He died there at his home, Cornborough House, on 21 November 1841. By his will he founded two scholarships of £20 a year each at St John's College, Cambridge, which were charged upon his manor of Abbotsham.

CAMPBELL DODGSON, *rev.* JOANNE POTIER

Sources GM, 2nd ser., 17 (1842), 114 • GM, 2nd ser., 19 (1843), 208 • private information (2004) [M. Underwood, archivist, St John Cam.] • H. A. C. Sturgess, ed., *Register of admissions to the Honourable Society of the Middle Temple, from the fifteenth century to the year 1944*, 2 (1949), 413 • J. Hutchinson, ed., *A catalogue of notable Middle Templars: with brief biographical notices* (1902), 249–50
Archives Devon RO, letter-book, notebooks, notes, sale bills of collections | BL, corresp. with John Brand, Add. MS 41313

Vidler, William (1758–1816), Universalist minister and Unitarian preacher, was born on 4 May 1758 at Battle, Sussex, the tenth and last child of John Vidler (*d.* 1780) and Elizabeth Bowling. He was apprenticed to his father, a stonemason, a trade for which, as an asthmatic, he was hardly suited. When George Gilbert came to Battle in 1776 an independent Calvinist church was organized. Vidler joined and started preaching. He seems to have received some training with Mr Nairne, vicar of Godshill, Isle of Wight, from 1777 to 1778. After he was persuaded of the correctness of believer's baptism and baptized by Mr Purdy of Rye (January 1780), the Battle church re-established itself as a Particular Baptist church. Although Vidler, called to be its minister, was still working as a stonemason, the number of members rose from 15 to 150. They took over and pulled down the disused Presbyterian meeting-house and built a new one, which left them £160 in debt.

Vidler offered to travel afield to collect funds. At the same time he took the opportunity to test the doubts which the Universalist Elhanan Winchester's *Dialogues on the Universal Restoration* had raised for him. After meeting John Ryland and Andrew Fuller in Northampton, he continued into Lincolnshire, where Winchester had followers among the General Baptists. He returned to Battle a convinced believer in the universal restoration of all humankind. This provoked the withdrawal of a minority of the church; while the majority remained they were eventually expelled from the local Particular Baptist association.

Vidler fortified his allegiance with Winchester, and in 1794 he became Winchester's assistant at Parliament Court Chapel, London, and then, in 1796, his successor. With John Teulon, Vidler opened a bookshop, first in the Strand and then in High Holborn. They started a periodical, the *Universalists' Miscellany* (from 1805 the *Monthly Repository*), among whose readers was the Unitarian missionary Richard Wright. Wright became Vidler's friend and convinced him of the truth of Unitarianism. This divided the Parliament Court congregation, which in turn divided the General Baptist assembly when Parliament Court joined in 1803.

Vidler ardently promoted both Universalist and Unitarian views. He was associated with a number of new Universalist and Unitarian societies at Northiam, Rye, Steyning, Reading, and Boston, and in 'the North Marches of Lincolnshire'. He co-founded, with Richard Wright, the Unitarian Evangelical Society (1804) and the Unitarian Fund (1806) (from 1825 the British and Foreign Unitarian Association, and from 1928 the general assembly of Unitarian and Free Christian Churches). Their evangelical fervour did much to transform the conservative rational dissent of the eighteenth century into the more vigorous Unitarianism of the nineteenth. Meanwhile Parliament Court Chapel (from 1824 South Place Chapel, Finsbury) became the South Place Ethical Society (from 1927 at Conway Hall, Red Lion Square, London).

Vidler published *God's Love to his Creatures* (1799), in which he held that God's love extends to animals; *Letters to Mr. Fuller on the Universal Restoration* (1803); and new editions of Paul Siegvolk's *The Everlasting Gospel* (1795) and Winchester's *Dialogues on the Universal Restoration with a Memoir of its Author* (4th edn, 1799). He was also associated with Nathaniel Scarlett's *A Translation of the New Testament from the Original Greek* (1798).

On 7 September 1780 Vidler had married Charity Sweetingham (*c.*1752–1808), daughter of William Sweetingham of Battle. They had five children, three of whom survived him—a daughter, who married William Smith, the Parliament Court organist; Ebenezer, a sailor; and William (*d.* 24 March 1861), missioner at Chapel Street Domestic Mission, London.

Vidler was excessively large and always booked two seats when travelling. While returning to London from Wisbech in 1808 to see his dying wife, the post-chaise in which he was travelling fell down a steep bank. Never fully recovering from the accident, he delivered his sermons from then on sitting down. He died on 23 August 1816 at his home in Spencer Street, Northampton Square, London. He was buried on 28 August in the graveyard of the Unitarian chapel at Hackney.

ALEXANDER GORDON, *rev.* ANDREW M. HILL

Sources 'Memoir of the late Rev. W. Vidler', *Monthly Repository*, 12 (1817), 65–72, 129–36, 193–200 • R. Wright, *Monthly Repository*, 12 (1817), 1–4 • F. W. Butt-Thompson, 'William Vidler', *Baptist Quarterly*, 17 (1957–8), 3–9
Archives E. Sussex RO, church books of Baptist church, NU3/1–2 • South Place Ethical Society, Conway Hall, London, minutes of Parliament Court Chapel
Likenesses J. Partridge, stipple (after T. Millichap), BM; repro. in *Monthly Repository*, 12 (1817), frontispiece • B. Reading, portrait

(after R. Williams), repro. in *Universalists' Miscellany*, 1 (1797), frontispiece

Vidyasagar, Iswarchandra (1820–1891), social reformer and Sanskrit scholar, the eldest son of Thakurdas Bandyopadhyay and Bhagavati Devi, was born on 26 September 1820 in the village of Birsimha, Midnapore district, Bengal. The name Vidyasagar is actually an academic title, conferred on him in 1839 when he passed the examination in Hindu law from Sanskrit College, Calcutta.

His ancestors on both sides were Sanskrit scholars, but his father was penurious at the time of Iswarchandra's birth. Father and son walked to Calcutta in 1828. The latter was admitted to Sanskrit College in 1829, where he proved to be a student of extraordinary merit and mastered several branches of Sanskritic learning over a period of twelve years, during which time he married Dinamayi Bhattacharya. He left the college in 1841 and was appointed head pandit at Fort William College, Calcutta, in the same year. There he also studied English and Sanskrit. He was appointed assistant secretary of Sanskrit College in 1846, but resigned the following year when his proposals for reform were turned down. He accepted the chair of Sanskrit at the same college in 1851, and became its principal in the next year. As principal he carried out extensive reforms, especially in the curriculum, which now emphasized a knowledge of English as well as Western logic and mathematics. Convinced that the traditional Sanskritic systems of *darsana* (systems of thought and speculation described inaccurately as Indian philosophy) were erroneous, he wanted to create a body of scholars trained in Sanskritic as well as Western learning, who would interpret Western thought to the Indian literati.

Iswarchandra is counted among the creators of modern Bengali prose. As an educationist, he wrote a number of books in Bengali, including the Bengali primer, *Barnaparichay*, which is still used to introduce Bengali children to their mother tongue. His other works intended for children include *Bodhoday*, *Kathamala*, and *Charitabhali*. The last of these, based on Webster's *Biographies*, contains improving tales of high achievement drawn from the life stories of eminent Europeans. His prose works include several adaptations from the Sanskrit classics: *Betalpanchavimsati* (a collection of twenty-five tales), *Sakuntala*, and *Sitar banabas* (1874). While he drew extensively upon Sanskrit for his vocabulary, his style marked a distinct break with the older tradition of highly florid Sanskritic diction. In addition he edited a number of Sanskrit texts, including Kalidasa's *Raghuvamsam*, *Meghadutam*, and *Kumarasambhavam*, Bhavabhuti's *Uttararamacharita*, and the philosophical compendium *Sarvadarsanasamgraha*.

Iswarchandra played a courageous role, and one for which he is remembered, in the movement for social reform, especially the agitation in favour of permitting the remarriage of widows among caste Hindus. He published his first tract arguing that such remarriage was sanctioned by the Hindu scriptures in 1854, he impoverished himself by sponsoring such marriages, and he got his own son, Narayanchandra, to marry a widow, defying orthodox convention. He established the Hindu Family Annuity Fund to help Hindus in distress. His other attempt at social reform, demanding the prohibition of polygamy, was not successful. His tracts on the subject, written in a popular style, were among the finest satirical writings of the period.

He was also among the pioneers of women's education in Bengal, and, as a government-appointed special inspector of schools, he established twenty model schools in a period of six months, as well as a normal school for the training of teachers. By 1858 there were 1300 students in the girls' schools he had established. He also took over the Calcutta Training School in 1864: renamed Hindu Metropolitan Institution, the college was entirely run by Indian teachers and administrators.

Iswarchandra is best remembered in his own country as a man of unbending moral courage and for his fabled generosity. People who benefited from his secret charity were probably thousands in number. Among these beneficiaries was the wayward poet Michael Madhusudan Datta. Embittered by the ingratitude of those he had helped and the hostility of the orthodox, Iswarchandra spent his latter years among the aboriginal Santals. He died in Calcutta on 29 July 1891.   TAPAN RAYCHAUDHURI

Sources S. Sengupta and A. Basu, eds., *Samsad Bangali charitabhidhan* (1975) · B. Sazkas, *Vidavagas* (1895)
Archives Calcutta, Bangiya Sahitya Parishad · National Archives of India, New Delhi
Likenesses bust, College Square, Calcutta · portrait, National Library of India, Calcutta · portrait, Calcutta, Bangiya Sahitya Parishad

Vieuxpont [Veteri Ponte, Vipont], **Robert de** (d. 1228), administrator and magnate, came of a family that took its name from Vieuxpont-en-Auge (Calvados) in Normandy. He was the younger son of William de Vieuxpont (d. in or before 1203), who became an important Anglo-Scottish landowner, and his wife, Maud de Morville (d. c.1210), whose father Hugh (in 1170 one of the assassins of Thomas Becket) forfeited the barony of Westmorland in 1173. Robert's elder brother, Ivo, inherited their father's estates in Northamptonshire and Northumberland, while Robert had entered royal service by 1195, and was custodian of the honours of Peverel, Higham Ferrers, and Tickhill in the latter years of Richard I's reign. But he achieved much greater eminence under John. At first he was principally employed in Normandy, especially as a paymaster of troops and director of military works, including those on Rouen Castle, and in 1203 he became *bailli* of the Roumois. His services were rewarded by the grant of Vieuxpont itself, formerly held by an uncle who had joined the French, and also by grants in England. In February 1203 he was given custody of the castles of Appleby and Brough, to which the lordship of Westmorland was added a month later; then in October 1203 custody during pleasure was changed to a grant in fee simple, for the service of four knights, and Vieuxpont had become one of the leading barons in northern England. He was also to be given a number of valuable wardships, while his wife, Idonea, the daughter of John de Builli, whom he married before June

1213, brought him lands in Bedfordshire and a claim to the Yorkshire honour of Tickhill.

After leaving Normandy with John in December 1203 Vieuxpont was in frequent attendance on the king until the end of 1205, when he became increasingly involved in northern administration. In October 1204 he became sheriff of Nottinghamshire and Derbyshire, and so had control of the strategically important castle of Nottingham, which was also a major repository for royal treasure—11,000 marks were sent there from Winchester in July 1207—and thus a base for the king's authority. Employed in 1206 as a justice and assessor of tallage in the northern counties, in 1207 he was given custody of the see of York, and in April 1208 custody of that of Durham. His manifold responsibilities may have been more than he could handle, since at the end of 1208 he had to proffer 4000 marks for royal 'grace and favour', and undertake to submit a number of delayed accounts. But he was pardoned 3000 marks of his fine, and though he ceased to be sheriff of Nottingham he continued to be prominent in John's service. He held Durham until 1210, and in the following year was employed in Wales, as the king's lieutenant in Powys. His loyalty to John brought him the accolade of a place in Roger of Wendover's list of that king's evil counsellors, and John himself acknowledged Vieuxpont's reliability by temporarily placing his second son, Richard, and his niece Eleanor in his custody. He also continued to handle substantial sums of royal money—in May 1213 he and Henry of Braybrooke received 30,000 marks from the king's treasure. He accompanied John to France in 1214, and in the civil war that broke out in the autumn of 1215 was one of the principal defenders of royal castles and interests in Yorkshire. In January 1216, moreover, he was entrusted with the custody of Cumberland and Carlisle Castle. He also had important interests of his own to defend in the north-west. His acquisition of Westmorland had been followed by an accumulation of estates in the region, including one on which he built a castle at Brougham, in order to defend his lordship against attack from the north—the constable of Scotland, Alan of Galloway, had a claim to Westmorland through his mother, Helen de Morville, and occupied the lordship for a year when the Scots overran English Cumbria in 1216.

Vieuxpont fought for the young Henry III at Lincoln in 1217, but gave much trouble in the years that followed. He was said by Wendover to have continued to plunder after peace had been made, but greater difficulties arose from his claim to Tickhill, which was disputed by Alice, countess of Eu. In order to appease him for the time being the regency government, which had reappointed him sheriff of Cumberland in September 1217, conceded in the following year that he should hold that office without accounting for the profits of office until justice had been done on his claim to Tickhill. In the event he held Cumberland until 1222, without accounting for any issues at all. Having dislodged Alan of Galloway from Westmorland, he was by far the greatest figure in the north-west, which he governed with a heavy hand—there were complaints over his administration of the royal forest in 1220 and 1225, and

he quarrelled with William of Lancaster, lord of Kendal, over suits to Westmorland county court. He was not always fractious, however, and served as a justice itinerant in Yorkshire and Northumberland in 1218–19. In 1222 the dispute over Tickhill was settled; Vieuxpont abandoned his claim to the honour, settling instead for six and a half knights' fees and £100 in cash. A further consequence was that he immediately lost his shrievalty of Cumberland, and with it yearly revenues of nearly £300. He may have been discontented, since at the end of 1223 he was one of the adversaries of the justiciar, Hubert de Burgh, protesting against the resumption of royal castles and sheriffdoms. But he had been reconciled to the government by February 1225, when he attested the reissue of Magna Carta, and in 1226–7 headed a judicial eyre in Yorkshire. Although Vieuxpont was a benefactor to the Cumbrian monasteries of St Bees and Shap, in 1227 he bequeathed his body, along with his estate at Wycombe in Buckinghamshire, to the knights templar. The bequest itself, and the fact that its witnesses included a doctor, point to failing health, and by 1 February 1228 he was dead, probably very recently. He left a son and a daughter. The latter, Christian, he married to his ward, Thomas, son of William of Greystoke, the heir to the barony of Greystoke in Cumberland. His son and heir, John, died in 1241, his grandson, another Robert, in 1264. Divided between this younger Robert's daughters, the Vieuxpont inheritance was finally reassembled by the Cliffords, to form the basis of one of the greatest, and longest-lasting, northern lordships.

HENRY SUMMERSON

Sources *Chancery records* (RC) · *Chancery records* · *Pipe rolls, 7 Richard I – 17 John* · H. C. M. Lyte, ed., *Liber feodorum: the book of fees*, 1 (1920) · T. D. Hardy, ed., *Rotuli Normanniae*, RC (1835) · *Curia regis rolls preserved in the Public Record Office* (1922–), vols. 9, 11 · T. Stapleton, ed., *Magni rotuli scaccarii Normanniae sub regibus Angliae*, 2, Society of Antiquaries of London Occasional Papers (1844) · J. Parker, ed., *Feet of fines for the county of York*, 3: *from 1218 to 1231*, Yorkshire Archaeological Society, 62 (1921), 42–3 · Bodl. Oxf., MS Dodsworth 70, 83 · J. C. Holt, *The northerners: a study in the reign of King John* (1961) · D. A. Carpenter, *The minority of Henry III* (1990) · K. J. Stringer, 'Periphery and core in thirteenth-century Scotland: Alan, son of Roland, lord of Galloway and constable of Scotland', *Medieval Scotland: crown, lordship and community: essays presented to G. W. S. Barrow*, ed. A. Grant and K. J. Stringer (1993), 82–113 · H. Summerson, M. Trueman, and S. Harrison, *Brougham Castle, Cumbria* (1998) · I. J. Sanders, *English baronies: a study of their origin and descent, 1086–1327* (1960) · H. M. Colvin, *The white canons in England* (1951) · *Rogeri de Wendover liber qui dicitur flores historiarum*, ed. H. G. Hewlett, 3 vols., Rolls Series, [84] (1886–9) · *CPR, 1232–47*, 284 · T. D. Hardy, ed., *Rotuli litterarum clausarum*, RC, 1 (1833), 136 · *Calendar of the charter rolls*, 6 vols., PRO (1903–27), vol. 1, p. 77

Wealth at death very wealthy; wardship of son valued (presumably conservatively) at £400 p.a. in 1241: *CPR* · tenure of Cumberland valued at nearly £300 p.a. extra

Vigani, John Francis [*formerly* Giovanni Francesco Vigani] (*c.*1650–1713), chemist, was born in or near Verona. No record of his early life in the area remains, and there is no evidence of his having a degree or licence or following a regular course of study. However, he did travel extensively in Italy, France, Spain, the Netherlands, and England. As a wandering scholar he studied medicine and pharmacy, and collected plants and minerals. In 1671 he was in Parma, where he saw a quack swallow snake poison. In September 1682 he settled in England, at Newark-on-Trent, but it is likely that he had already been in London for some time. It was probably about this time that Vigani married. He and his wife, Elizabeth (d. 1711), later had two daughters, Frances (bap. 22 Jan 1683) and Jane (bap. 7 March 1864).

In 1682, Vigani's *Medulla chemiae* was printed in Danzig, bearing an undated dedication to a gentleman from the Low Countries, one Joannes de Waal, 'Toparcha in Ankeveen', whom the author extolled for his generous patronage. The book, being a small collection of chemical processes, contains references to the chemical work of Jean Baptiste van Helmont, Robert Boyle, Sylvius, and Otto Tachenius. Vigani clearly adopted a corpuscular theory of matter and rejected the chemical theory of the three principles (sulphur, mercury, and salt). In 1683 Vigani published the second, enlarged, edition of his work, with the title of *Medulla chymiae*, which he dedicated to William, earl of Devon, Philip, earl of Chesterfield, and Thomas, Viscount Fauconberg. Prefixed to the work was a letter to the author signed 'T. R.', possibly the initials of his correspondent Dr Robson. The letter, dated London, 10 September 1682, eulogized Vigani for adhering to Boyle's corpuscular philosophy as well as for ruling out the three principles and the related, obscure terminology. In the preface the author briefly outlined the theoretical foundation to his chemical work: 'the world', he wrote, 'is concreted of atoms of various figures, with the innate qualities of motion, figure, magnitude and place'. The remainder of the work deals with the analysis of some substances, such as vitriol, urine, common salt, and nitre, describes the preparation of a number of chemical medicines, and includes three plates, depicting furnaces and vessels, by Vigani and his friend J. Troutbeck of Cambridge. The *Acta Eruditorum* for 1684 published a laudatory review of this edition of Vigani's *Medulla*, which was subsequently reprinted with additions in 1685, 1693, and 1718. The *Medulla* was conceived of as a guide to performing experiments in chemical courses, rather than as a textbook.

Vigani started teaching chemistry in Cambridge in 1682 or 1683, independently of any university or college connection, to apothecaries and medical students, but continued to live in Newark. In a letter to Dr John Covell, master of Christ's College, of 2 August 1692, he wrote that he had been invited to write a treatise on chemistry, the preparation of which he had carried on for several years, but that was never published. From 1696 to 1704 Vigani was associated with St Catharine's College, and from 1704 he lectured in Queens' College cloisters (both chemistry and materia medica), where he had a laboratory with a remarkable number of drugs, which were purchased at the expense of the college. In 1707 Bentley built a laboratory for him at Trinity. Surviving notes of his course of chemistry show that he lectured there from November 1707, and it is likely that he taught regularly for several years. There is, however, no evidence that he was a member of any college in Cambridge. In February 1703 the senate conferred on him the title of honorary professor of chemistry in the University of Cambridge. As no stipend was paid to him, he depended entirely on student fees and opened his lectures to the public. He also had a laboratory in Newark, where he carried on some experiments. His surviving lectures on materia medica and chemical courses cover a wider range of subjects than his published work. In them Vigani did not confine himself with practical instructions, but also made a number of observations on medical and chemical topics. He adhered to the acid/alkali theory and explained fevers as the outcome of an exceeding acidity of human blood.

Vigani's knowledge and skill in chemistry were recognized by his contemporaries. Among his students were William Stukeley, Stephen Hales, and Abraham de la Pryme, the latter of whom described him as 'a learned chemist ... but a drunken fellow' (*The Diary of Abraham de la Pryme*, Surtees Society publication no. 54, 1870, 24–5). Vigani was one of Newton's few friends in Cambridge. They used to have conversations on chemical subjects, but Newton, who possessed a copy of the 1683 edition of Vigani's *Medulla*, broke with him when Vigani told him an improper story about a nun. Vigani corresponded with Robert Boyle in 1682 (two letters from Vigani to Boyle are recorded, but they are no longer extant), and with Roger Cotes in 1708.

Vigani's will was made on 19 July 1712. It was proved in the exchequer court of York by the oath of Frances Phisick, the sole executrix and legatee, on 13 June 1713, and the contents of his laboratory were valued for probate at £20. Vigani died in February 1713 at Newark, where he was buried on 26 February at the church of St Mary Magdalen.

ANTONIO CLERICUZIO

Sources J. Ferguson, notes on Vigani, CUL · E. Saville Peck, 'John Francis Vigani, first professor of chemistry in the University of Cambridge ... and his materia medica cabinet in the library of Queens' College', *Proceedings of the Cambridge Antiquarian Society*, 34 (1932–3), 34–49 · L. J. M. Coleby, 'John Francis Vigani', *Annals of Science*, 8 (1952), 46–60 · R. T. Gunter, *Early science in Cambridge* (1937), 221–6, 238, 333 · J. F. Vigani, *Medulla chemiae* (Danzig, 1682) · J. F. Vigani, *Medulla chymiae*, another edn (London, 1683) · J. Ferguson, ed., *Bibliotheca chemica*, 2 vols. (1906) · A. Guerrini, 'Chemistry teaching at Oxford and Cambridge', *Alchemy and chemistry in the 16th and 17th centuries*, ed. P. Rattansi and A. Clericuzio (1994), 183–99 · S. Maffei, *Verona illustrata*, 2 (1721) · *DSB* · parish register (burial), 18 Dec 1711 and 26 Feb 1713, Newark-on-Trent, St Mary Magdalen
Archives BL, Add. MSS 22910, 4276 · CUL · Gon. & Caius Cam. · Harvard U. · Queens' College, Cambridge | U. Glas. L., Ferguson MSS
Wealth at death £136 10s.: Ferguson MSS, U. Glas. L.

Viger, Denis-Benjamin (1774–1861), politician in Canada, born at Montreal on 19 August 1774, was the only son of Denis Viger (b. 1741), a businessman and member of the house of assembly, and his wife, Périne-Charles (d. 1823), the second daughter of François-Pierre Cherrier. He was educated at the Collège de Montréal, and, after serving articles (1794–9), was called to the bar on 9 March 1799, where he soon became distinguished. On 21 November 1808 he married Marie-Amable (d. 1854), the daughter of Pierre Fortier. Their one child, a daughter, died in infancy.

Viger entered the assembly as member for Montreal in 1808, and, being a cousin of Louis-Joseph Papineau, espoused the popular side. In 1809 he issued a pamphlet urging in the interests of Great Britain that the manners and institutions of the French Canadians should be preserved. When the Anglo-American War of 1812–14 broke out he was promoted captain in the militia; he served until the end of the war. From 1810 to 1814 Viger represented the county of Leinster in the legislature, and from 1827 to 1830 that of Kent. In 1828 he was chosen by the legislature as one of three delegates to proceed to Westminster as the exponent of their grievances. In 1830 he became a member of the legislative council, and in 1831 was again sent to England as the legislature's agent. He remained there until 1834, and was joined at times by other colonial leaders, including William Lyon Mackenzie. During the rebellions of 1837 and 1838 he played an obscure role in financing radical newspapers, and on 4 November 1838 he was arrested for seditious articles published in one of these. Having declined bail, he was kept in prison for nineteen months.

In 1841, when the two Canadas were united, Viger entered the new parliament as member for Richelieu county, and in 1845 was elected member for Trois Rivières. He denounced the union because it did not respect representation by population and restricted the use of French. However, when in 1843 the Liberals resigned, Viger, who appreciated the statesmanship of Sir Charles Metcalfe's policy and had supported him in his quarrel with the ministry, was sworn in as president of the council (12 December 1843). He was virtually head of the administration until 2 September 1844. The French Canadians, however, failed to understand his motives, and owing to the general dissatisfaction he was forced to resign in June 1846. On 25 February 1848 he was again called to the upper house; but, tired of political struggles, he did not attend. In 1858 his seat was declared vacant. He died at Montreal on 13 February 1861. Viger Square and Viger Garden in Montreal were named after him.   C. A. Harris, rev. Jacques Monet

Sources F. Ouellet and A. Lefort, 'Viger, Denis-Benjamin', *DCB*, vol. 9 · F. Hincks, *Reminiscences of his public life* (1884) · F. Ouellet, 'Denis-Benjamin Viger et le problème de l'annexion', *Bulletin des Recherches Historiques*, 57 (1951), 195–205 · J. M. S. Careless, *The union of the Canadas: the growth of Canadian institutions, 1841–1857* (1967) · J. Monet, *The last cannon shot* (1969)
Archives NA Canada | Archives du Séminaire du Québec, Fonds Viger-Verreau · Archives Nationales du Québec, Papineau–Bourassa MSS
Likenesses B. Sulte, repro. in *Histoire des Canadiens français*, 4 (1882), 104
Wealth at death considered one of Montreal's wealthiest people; owned much property in town; profited from wife's considerable inheritance (after 1842); inherited fortune from businessman father (building contractor, exporter of potash)

Viger, Jacques (1787–1858), author and surveyor, only surviving child of Jacques Viger (d. 1798) and Amaranthe Prévost, was born in Montreal, Canada, on 7 May 1787 into an influential family circle. Denis-Benjamin Viger and Louis-

Joseph Papineau were among his cousins. He studied at the Collège Saint-Raphaël (1799–1808) before leaving to undertake editorial work on *Le Canadien* (1808–9). On 17 November 1808 he married Marie-Marguerite, *née* La Corne, widow of Major John Lennox, and daughter of the Chevalier de St Luc. They had three children, all of whom died in infancy. The marriage brought Viger money from the Lennox estate and stepdaughters from his wife's first marriage. In 1810 he began his scholarly writing with a book on Canadian neologisms which, however, was not published until 1909–10. He served in the Anglo-American War of 1812–14, as a lieutenant and then captain, and by 1829 was lieutenant-colonel of the Montreal 3rd militia battalion, having kept his interest in military matters.

Meanwhile, in 1813 Viger had become surveyor of roads and bridges in Montreal. This post involved him in some early town planning, and in 1817 and 1837 he had town directories of Montreal compiled to help in his work. In 1825 he became census commissioner and by requiring information over and above that demanded by census legislation he compiled a set of returns which form a valuable historical source and of which he compiled a summary. It has been suggested that he collaborated with Joseph Bouchette in drawing the first map of the city or by contributing to his topographical works, but the evidence seems slight. Although he failed in his attempts to achieve a range of public offices, he was mayor of Montreal from 1833 to 1836, helped by his influential political connections. During his time as mayor he had drained a marshy suburb of the city which had been badly hit by the cholera epidemic of 1832, but his term was marred by controversy; in 1836 he lost his post as mayor and in 1840 that of surveyor of roads.

Viger is best known as a local historian and antiquary, although most of his writing remained unpublished. His chief work is his unpublished 43-volume 'Ma saberdache', begun in 1808, of which the first thirty volumes included material which could be used for the history of the Canadas; the latter volumes were a miscellany of notes and documents relating to events in which he himself had taken part. He was also a keen collector of books and materials related to Canadian history. In 1858 he was a founder and first president of the Société Historique de Montréal. He was well connected in influential Roman Catholic church circles and used with pride his title of commander of the papal order of St Gregory the Great, awarded in 1855. Viger died in Montreal on 12 December 1858. Although he and his notes and compilations were much consulted in his lifetime, he had rather little lasting influence because his works were mainly unpublished and, although now accessible in the archives of the Séminaire de Québec, long remained in the private possession of his family. His most important work is now judged to be his 1825 census material.

Elizabeth Baigent

Sources J. C. Robert, 'Viger, Jacques', *DCB*, vol. 8 · F. X. Grondin, *Jacques Viger* (1942) · V. Morin, 'Esquisse biographique de Jacques Viger', *Proceedings and Transactions of the Royal Society of Canada*, 3rd ser., 32 (1938), section 1, pp. 183–90

Vigfússon, Gúðbrandur (1827–1889), scholar of Icelandic literature, was born on 13 March 1827 in Galtadalur, Dalasýsla, western Iceland. He was the son of Vigfús Gíslason, of an old and respected Icelandic family, and Halldóra Gísladóttir. He was brought up by his foster-mother and great-aunt Kristín Vigfúsdóttir, to whom, as he thankfully recorded in his last days, he owed not only that he became a man of letters, but almost everything. He received his early education in the house of his cousin, a clergyman, who prepared him for the Latin high school of Bessastaðir; he studied there, moving with the school to Reykjavík. In 1849 he left the school, and Iceland, for Copenhagen University, which he entered in 1850, holding a bursary at Regentsen College. He was appointed stipendiarius under the Arnamagnæan trustees, and worked in the Arnamagnæan Library, under the patronage of Jón Sigurðsson, leader of the Icelandic independence movement. It was this work that made him familiar with every vellum and paper copy of the classic and popular Icelandic and Old Scandinavian literature, and gave him the material for his future research. For fourteen years he led a life of research interrupted by two visits to Iceland (the second in 1858) and tours in Germany (during which he called on Jakob Grimm) and Norway. His superb travelogue recounting the last tour was published in 1855 by Jón Sigurðsson in the Icelandic journal he edited.

Vigfússon's first printed piece of scholarship was *Tímatál* (written between October 1854 and April 1855), a complete chronology of the whole body of classic Icelandic literature, which has not been entirely superseded by subsequent scholarship. His work on editing the sagas began with *Biskupa sögur* in 1858. In 1860 followed *Bárðar saga* and *Forn sögur* (in partnership with Theodur Möbius), and in 1864 *Eyrbyggja saga*. In 1868 he finished eight years' work in co-operation with Carl Richard Unger, and published the last volume of his edition of *Flateyjarbók*. The prefaces to these editions opened a new era of Icelandic scholarship, in which historical method and the results of modern philology were applied with a view to elucidating the whole history of classic Scandinavian literature. During these years Vigfússon's chief friends were H. Larpent (the translator of *Tartuffe*), K. Dahlenborg, Konrad Maurer, Möbius, Unger, and Jón Árnason. For Árnason he sought out folk-tales in Iceland, and he wrote a preface for Árnason's collection, which is still of significance in Icelandic folklore. In 1858 Vigfússon became engaged to the daughter of an important local government official in Dalasýsla, an engagement which foundered on the long wait for him to take his final examination. Eventually Elínborg Kristjánsdóttir married another. Vigfússon never married.

In 1864 Vigfússon was approached by Sir George Webbe Dasent, who had been entrusted by the representatives of Richard Cleasby with the task of completing and printing an Icelandic–English dictionary, on which that scholar had been engaged until his death. Konráð Gíslason had been supposedly engaged on the work for nearly twenty years, but the heirs, foreseeing no speedy conclusion, asked Dasent to find someone else. Dasent persuaded Vigfússon to come to London and take up the work. The Oxford University Press, largely at the instigation of the dean of Christ Church, H. G. Liddell, agreed to publish the book, and, after some months in London, Vigfússon moved to Oxford in 1866, where he resided until his death. Without transcribers or assistants, with the help of his own collections of Fritzner's *Icelandic–Danish Dictionary*, then appearing in fascicles, and a miserably inadequate mass of materials supplied by Cleasby's Copenhagen employees, Vigfússon finished the *Oxford Icelandic–English Dictionary* in 1873. During its progress he had the advantage of being able to consult Liddell, whose practical knowledge of lexicography was unrivalled. Liddell obtained for him an honorary MA (1871) and common-room rights at Christ Church. The dictionary was generally well received, though Dasent's insistence on retaining Cleasby's name in the most prominent position on the title-page caused his estrangement from Vigfússon.

Vigfússon made many firm English friends, though his laborious life left him little time. And, despite his 'weird but imposing personality', he built up a devoted group of students, including W. P. Ker, John Sephton, Charles Plummer, W. A. Craigie, and Joseph Wright. It was during this period that Vigfússon became embroiled in a major feud with Britain's other prominent Icelandic scholar, Eiríkur Magnússon, over a new translation of the Bible into Icelandic.

In 1874–5 Vigfússon went to Copenhagen and to Stockholm to make transcripts for the Rolls Series editions of *Orkneyinga Saga* and *Hákonar saga*, and discovered a fuller text of part of the former than had before been known to exist. These appeared with prefaces in 1887. The next three years, 1875–8, were occupied with *Sturlunga saga* (1878), to which was affixed a complete literary history of old northern literature, with a full account of the extant manuscript material. Unfortunately *Sturlunga saga* 'fell foul of factors as banal as excessive cost price, hopeless advertising and total absence of reviews' (Wawn, 836). Scarcely a copy reached Iceland, while the prohibitive cost limited purchasers in Scandinavia.

In 1879 Vigfússon brought out an *Icelandic Prose Reader*. In 1883 the *Corpus poeticum boreale* appeared; although, after the dictionary, this represents Vigfússon's most lasting memorial, the *Corpus*—'so vast, so full of delights, so unbelievably unreliable' (Dronke, 93)—was innocent of new philological methodology, and today remains a quarry for ideas rather than a model for a text. The *Grimm Centenary Papers* (1886), containing many of Vigfússon's most original thoughts on Norse history and Germanic literature, may be considered as an appendix to the *Corpus*. He also wrote several papers in the Oxford Philological Society's *Transactions*, in the Philological Society's *Transactions*, and in the *English Historical Review*, on philological and historical subjects.

From 1866 to 1889 Vigfússon was occupied with his edition of the *Landnáma-bóc*, and with the duties of his readership, for he had been appointed reader in Icelandic in the

University of Oxford in 1884, a position created for him at the instigation of Liddell and York Powell. He was centenary doctor of Uppsala in 1877, and he received the order of the Dannebrog in 1885. He had a long stay in Copenhagen, working at the Arnamagnæan Icelandic manuscripts. In 1886 he went to the Isle of Man, and published in the *Manx Note Book* his readings of the runic monuments there. In the autumn of 1888 he fell victim to cancer, and he died on 31 January 1889 at the Sarah Acland Home, Wellington Square, Oxford; he was buried on 3 February at St Sepulchre's cemetery in a ceremony attended by every notable philologist in Oxford. *Origines Islandicae*, on which he was working until his death, and which York Powell was supposed to complete, was published by the press after the latter's death with a hasty list of corrigenda by W. A. Craigie, but otherwise in a lamentably error-ridden condition.　　　　F. Y. POWELL, *rev.* CAROLYNE LARRINGTON

Sources B. S. Benedikz, 'Guðbrandur Vigfússon: a biographical sketch', *Úr Dölum Til Dala*, ed. R. McTurk and A. Wawn, 11 (1989), 11–34 • U. M. Dronke, Gudbrander Vigfússon centenary lecture, May 1989 • U. M. Dronke, 'The scope of the *Corpus poeticum boreale*', *Úr Dölum Til Dala*, ed. R. McTurk and A. Wawn, 11 (1989), 93–111 • J. Þorkelsson, 'Guðbrandur Vigfússon', *Andvari*, 19 (1894), 1–43 • A. Wawn, 'Brass-brained rivalries: the birth and death of Sturlunga Saga in Victorian Britain', *Samtíðarsögur / The contemporary sagas: the Ninth International Saga Conference preprints* [Akureyri 1994], 2 (Reykjavík, 1994)
Archives Bodl. Oxf., papers • faculty of English language and literature, U. Oxf., personal accounts and notes • U. Lpool, Sydney Jones Library, biographical papers
Likenesses H. M. Paget, oils, 1888, English Faculty Library, Oxford • photograph, repro. in Þorkelsson, 'Guðbrandur Vigfússon'
Wealth at death £328 1s. 8d.: probate, 22 Feb 1889, CGPLA Eng. & Wales

Vigne, Godfrey Thomas (1801–1863), traveller, eldest son of Thomas Vigne of Walthamstow, Essex, was born on 1 September 1801. He entered Harrow School in 1817, was admitted a student of Lincoln's Inn on 23 December 1818, and was called to the bar in 1824. In 1831 he travelled in the United States of America and Canada, publishing an account of his journey in 1832, entitled *Six Months in America*. In the same year he left Southampton for India, on 16 October, and, after passing through Persia, spent the next seven years travelling north-west of India. He visited Kashmir, Ladakh, and other parts of central Asia, besides travelling through Afghanistan, where he had several interviews with the emir, Dost Mohammed. Vigne was described by Boase as the first Englishman to visit Kabul. The Scot Alexander Burnes, described by Dost Mohammed as the first Englishman he had met, had reached Kabul in the spring of 1832. Vigne described his travels in *A Personal Narrative of a Visit to Ghuzni, Kabul, and Afghanistan* (1840) and *Travels in Kashmir* (1842). These two books give a valuable view of northern and western India before the establishment of British supremacy. The former was reprinted in 1982 and 1986, the latter in 1981.

In the years after 1852 Vigne visited the West Indies, Mexico, Nicaragua, and the United States. He died unmarried, at The Oaks, Woodford, Essex, on 12 July 1863, while preparing for the press his *Travels in Mexico and South America* (1863). He was neither 'a professional author nor a commissioned tourist'. He travelled for amusement; as his will was proved at 'under £12,000' it is clear he did not write for money, and, despite having visited some strategically extremely important areas, he seems to have had no ulterior political motives.

　　　　E. I. CARLYLE, *rev.* ELIZABETH BAIGENT

Sources GM, 3rd ser., 15 (1863), 250 • R. Courtenay Welch, ed., *The Harrow School register, 1801–93* (1894) • W. P. Baildon, ed., *The records of the Honorable Society of Lincoln's Inn: the black books*, 1–4 (1897–1902) • Boase, *Mod. Eng. biog.* • P. Hopkirk, *The great game: on secret service in high Asia* (1990) • CGPLA Eng. & Wales (1863)
Wealth at death under £12,000: resworn probate, 14 Aug 1863, CGPLA Eng. & Wales

Vignoles, Charles Blacker (1793–1875), civil engineer, was born on 31 May 1793 at Woodbrook, co. Wexford, the only child of Charles Henry Vignoles (*d.* 1794), a descendant of a Huguenot military family serving in Ireland, and Camilla (1764?–1794), youngest daughter of Charles *Hutton. His father was a captain in the 43rd or Monmouthshire regiment of foot, which was sent out to the West Indies; he was wounded and taken prisoner at the storming of Pointe-à-Pitre in Guadeloupe in 1794. Soon afterwards he and Camilla died of yellow fever.

Charles Vignoles was brought to England by an uncle, and raised by his grandfather. When eighteen months old Vignoles was gazetted as an ensign on half pay in his father's regiment, a common method of compensating deceased officers' families. He was educated at the Royal Military Academy at Woolwich, where his grandfather taught, but since his grandfather favoured a legal career he was articled to a proctor in Doctors' Commons for seven years. How long he remained is not known, but in 1813 he rowed with his grandfather, possibly over his decision to give up law, and left home. This breach was never healed.

In November 1813 Vignoles was transferred to the York chasseurs, and soon afterwards was at Sandhurst as a private pupil of Thomas Leybourn, one of the college lecturers. Leybourn was guardian of Mary Griffiths (*d.* 1834), eldest daughter of a Welsh gentleman farmer, and Charles and Mary became secretly engaged. Assisted by the duke of Kent, Vignoles was commissioned in the 1st or Royal Scots regiment in January 1814. He was present at Bergen-op-Zoom in March, and was then in Canada for eight months. In October 1815 he was made lieutenant and posted to Scotland, and from April 1816 until May 1817 was aide-de-camp to General Sir Thomas Brisbane at Valenciennes, where he produced comparative tables of French and English weights and measures for the duke of Wellington.

Put on half pay in May 1816 and with no private means, Vignoles had to seek his livelihood elsewhere, although he did not leave the army until 1833. After returning to England, he married Mary at Alverstoke, Hampshire, on 13 July 1817, and set sail for America, intending to serve with Simón Bolívar, but by the end of 1817 he was at Charleston, South Carolina, as assistant to the state civil engineer. In 1821 he became city surveyor at St Augustine, Florida, and in 1823 published a map of Florida. Severe financial problems and news of his grandfather's death persuaded him to return to England in early 1823.

Vignoles worked as a surveyor and wrote articles for the *Encyclopaedia Metropolitana*, becoming assistant to James Walker, engineer of the London Commercial Docks. By mid-1824 he had his own office in Hatton Garden, with three pupil assistants. In 1825 he was hired by George Rennie (1791–1866) and Sir John Rennie (1794–1874) to survey a railway between London and Brighton, and a new Liverpool and Manchester line, after parliament had rejected George Stephenson's original scheme. Vignoles moved north and made Liverpool his base for the next fifteen years. His legal training made him a good parliamentary witness, a factor in the success of the second Liverpool and Manchester Railway Bill, and it brought much similar work subsequently. He was employed as Stephenson's assistant, but a clash of personalities made him resign in January 1827 after disagreements over measurements for Edge Hill Tunnel. Marc Brunel offered Vignoles a post as resident engineer on the Thames Tunnel, but the offer was withdrawn when Brunel realized he could appoint his son Isambard to the post. Vignoles subsequently spent a year in the Isle of Man, surveying government property. He was then recommended by Brunel to straighten the northern section of the Oxford Canal, but fell out with Brunel, after criticizing work on the breached Thames Tunnel and submitting new proposals, which were rejected in June 1830. In 1829 Vignoles was involved in the locomotive trials at Rainhill, working with John Braithwaite and John Ericsson on the *Novelty*. In 1830 he and Ericsson patented a method of ascending steep inclines on railways (no. 5995). Vignoles also advocated a flat-bottomed rail which would bear directly on sleepers without any chair, but despite occasional trials the rail was never adopted in Britain. On the continent it was, and in Germany and France it was named after him.

During the 1830s Vignoles surveyed and constructed numerous English railways, especially in Lancashire, and also worked in Ireland, France, and Germany. Between 1832 and 1834 he worked on Ireland's first railway, the Dublin and Kingstown Railway, and between 1836 and 1838 he was engineer to the royal commission on railways in Ireland. At the end of the decade financial problems almost ruined him. In 1835 he had surveyed the proposed Sheffield, Ashton under Lyne, and Manchester Railway, and he became the resident engineer. Problems arose with raising the necessary finance, so Vignoles, with the blessing of the company directors, bought many depreciated shares in the names of friends and relatives, on the understanding that they were trustees for himself and that no calls would be made on them. This manoeuvre allowed work to commence, but financial difficulties meant that the directors later insisted that calls be met, leaving Vignoles with a bill for £14,000 he could not meet.

He fought the decision, but had to resign. He did recover and pay these debts, but the next three years were difficult. He became professor of civil engineering at University College, London, advocated and built atmospheric railways, and reported on railways in the German kingdom of Württemberg. Then the 'railway mania' of 1844–6 brought him much work.

Vignoles had no spectacular engineering achievement to his credit, but in 1846 he was employed to construct the Kiev Bridge in Ukraine, a suspension bridge over 1½ miles long, which brought him fame. In 1847 he moved to Ukraine and lived there until the bridge was completed in 1853. During these years Vignoles paid several visits to England, and on 16 June 1849 married Elizabeth Hodge (*d*. 1880) at St Martin-in-the-Fields, his first wife, Mary, having died on 17 December 1834. After Russia, Vignoles was involved in some English projects, but his main work lay abroad: the Frankfurt, Wiesbaden, and Cologne Railway; the Western Railway in Switzerland; the Bahia and San Francisco Railway in Brazil; and the Tudela and Bilbao Railway in Spain. In 1863 he retired, and in 1867 acquired a house at Hythe, near Southampton, where he became a country gentleman and JP. He still visited London frequently, actively participating in several scientific societies. On his return from one such visit he suffered a stroke and died four days later, at his home, Villa Amalthea, Hythe, Hampshire, on 17 November 1875. He was buried in Brompton cemetery, London, on 23 November. From his first marriage there were seven children, five of whom reached adulthood. Three of his sons—Charles Francis Fernando, Hutton, and Henry—became engineers, although mental problems forced Charles to retire early. Another son, Olinthus John, became a minister of the Church of England and wrote a biography of his father, published in 1889.

Vignoles joined the Institution of Civil Engineers on 10 April 1827, and became president in December 1869. He became a fellow of the Royal Astronomical Society on 9 January 1829. Bad weather spoiled his view of a total solar eclipse near Kiev, but while building a Spanish railway he entertained a government astronomical expedition and in 1860 published his observations of this solar eclipse, and in 1870 was part of another government expedition to observe a solar eclipse. He became a fellow of the Royal Society on 7 June 1855, was a founder member of the Photographic Society of London, served in 1855 as a member of the royal commission on the Ordnance Survey, and was connected with the Royal Irish Academy and the Royal Institution. K. R. FAIRCLOUGH

Sources K. H. Vignoles, *Charles Blacker Vignoles: romantic engineer* (1982) • O. J. Vignoles, *Life of Charles Blacker Vignoles* (1889) • *ILN* (5 Feb 1876), 143 • presidential address, *PICE*, 29 (1869–70), 272–321 • *PICE*, 43 (1875–6), 306–11 • *The Times* (19 Nov 1875) • *CGPLA Eng. & Wales* (1875) • R. E. Carlson, *The Liverpool and Manchester railway project, 1821–1823* (1969)

Archives BL, journals, corresp., and accounts, Add. MSS 34528–34536, 35071, 58203–58206 • BL OIOC, papers relating to Indian railways, MS Eur. D 162 • Inst. CE, unpublished manuscript reports • Inst. CE, notebook and photographs relating to Bahia

Railway, Brazil · Portsmouth City RO, corresp. · Portsmouth Museums and Records Service, corresp. and papers **Likenesses** portrait, repro. in Vignoles, *Life of Charles Blacker Vignoles* · stipple, NPG · three portraits, repro. in Vignoles, *Charles Blacker Vignoles* · wood-engraving, repro. in *ILN* (11 Dec 1875), 581 · woodcut, NPG; repro. in *The Builder* (1870) **Wealth at death** under £60,000: probate, 22 Dec 1875, *CGPLA Eng. & Wales*

Vigor [*other married names* Ward, Rondeau], **Jane** (1699–1783), travel writer, was probably the daughter of the Revd Edward Goodwin of Rawmarsh Hall, Yorkshire, and Jane Wainwright. Her father had a considerable fortune, which his daughter inherited on the death of her brother. In 1728, probably shortly after this event, she was married to Thomas Ward (son of Sir Edward *Ward, former chief baron of the exchequer), and accompanied him to St Petersburg on his appointment that year to the post of consul-general to Russia and agent of the Russia Company. He died suddenly in February 1731 and was succeeded by his secretary, Claudius Rondeau, the son of a French protestant who had settled in England, who swiftly married his predecessor's widow on 23 November 1731. Rondeau served the British government effectively, and managed to reconcile the bickering factions within the Russia Company at St Petersburg. However, he was a delicate man and died in October 1739, and his widow, who had also been suffering from ill health, returned to England. Empress Anna, 'having a particular benevolence towards the said Widow', sent her home with a letter of recommendation to George II, requesting his 'consolation in the melancholy Station she is in' (PRO, SP 102/50). Mrs Rondeau seems not to have needed this support, however, since she was accompanied on her voyage home by William Vigor (*d*. 1767), a merchant and a Quaker, whom she married in 1740.

Thereafter Mrs Vigor's life seems to have been lived quietly at Taplow and Windsor until the publication in 1775 of *Letters from a Lady who Resided some Years in Russia, to her Friend in England*. John Nichols states that 'she was in a manner obliged to publish, to prevent a spurious and incorrect copy from being obtruded on the world' (Nichols, *Lit. anecdotes*, 3.209). Although anonymous, the authorship of the *Letters* was at once widely known. They were favourably reviewed and translated into German, French, and Dutch by 1776. A second English edition (corrected) was printed in 1777. Mrs Vigor featured as a character in a fictionalized series entitled *Letters from Henrietta to Morvina. Interspersed with Anecdotes, Historical and Amusing*, which also plagiarized her work and was therefore greeted with critical derision on its publication in 1779. In 1784 (after Mrs Vigor's death the preceding year) was published *Eleven Additional Letters from Russia*, 'found among her papers since her decease' (p. v), with a short biographical preface and some historical notes. These letters date from her earliest years at St Petersburg as Mrs Ward. They are more personally revealing than the letters she had herself published, but, like the earlier ones, they offer a unique eyewitness account of imperial and expatriate society at St Petersburg. She makes sophisticated use of the epistolary form, constructing a playful relationship with her female correspondent not unlike that between Anna Howe and Clarissa in Richardson's novel. Contemporary reviewers praised especially the *Letters'* anecdotes of courtly occasions (such as the marriage and death of Peter II), and of aristocratic intrigue and romance. The *Monthly Review* pronounced the *Letters* 'agreeably written, somewhat in the lively manner of Lady Montagu' (*Monthly Review*, Sept 1775, 211).

Mrs Vigor seems not to have had children (her will makes provision for a servant and for the daughter of a local labourer). William Vigor died in October 1767, and she survived him until her own death at Windsor on 6 September 1783. She was buried beside him in the churchyard at Taplow. John Nichols recalls that having 'lived much in the world, and being well acquainted with books, her conversation was the delight of all who had the pleasure of knowing her', and reports that her loss was 'severely felt by the neighbouring poor, amongst whom she was constantly searching after proper objects for the exertion of her charity and benevolence' (Nichols, *Lit. anecdotes*, 3.209). Another Englishwoman resident in St Petersburg during the 1730s, the governess Elizabeth Justice, observed of Mrs Rondeau that she was 'a fine woman; very tall, and perfectly genteel', and 'in all her answers, even to her inferiors, she shows the greatest condescension, and most obliging temper' (Justice, 40).

KATHERINE TURNER

Sources *GM*, 1st ser., 53 (1783), 806 · A. G. Cross, *By the banks of the Neva: chapters from the lives and careers of the British in eighteenth-century Russia* (1997) · L. Leowenson, 'Lady Rondeau's letters from Russia', *Slavonic and East European Review*, 35 (1956–7), 399–408 · Blain, Clements & Grundy, *Feminist comp.*, 1114 · will, PRO, PROB 11/1108, sig. 488 [Jane Vigor] · J. Vigor, *Eleven additional letters from Russia, in the reign of Peter II* (1784) · [J. Vigor], *Letters from a lady who resided some years in Russia, to her friend in England. With historical notes* (1775) · Nichols, *Lit. anecdotes*, 3.209 · E. Justice, *A voyage to Russia* (1739) · *Monthly Review*, 53 (1775), 211 · will, PRO, PROB 11/933, sig. 393 [William Vigor] **Wealth at death** £500 in assets: will, PRO, PROB 11/1108, sig. 488

Vigors, Nicholas Aylward (1785/6–1840), zoological administrator and quinarian, was born at Old Leighlin, co. Carlow, Ireland, the son of Nicholas Aylward Vigors (1755–1828) and his first wife, Catherine, daughter of Solomon Richards of Soulsborough, co. Wexford. He entered Trinity College, Oxford, in 1803, and was also admitted a student at Lincoln's Inn in 1806. Leaving Oxford in 1809, after preparing for publication *An Inquiry into the Nature and Extent of Poetick Licence* (1810), he purchased an ensigncy in the Grenadier Guards. He was severely wounded during the Peninsular War in 1811. Invalided home, he left the army and returned to Oxford, graduating BA in 1817.

As a wealthy gentleman Vigors devoted himself to ornithology and entomology, becoming a fellow of the Linnean Society in 1819. It was here that his gifts as a reforming administrator and systematist became apparent. He reacted against the Linnean's botanical emphasis, slow publication rate, and old methodology, and (with W. S. MacLeay, J. F. Stephens, Adrian Howarth, and others) formed the semi-autonomous Zoological Club on 27

November 1822. It became a forum for the zoological careerists at the hub of an expanding maritime nation and for methodological dissidents (Vigors was a quinarian) rebelling against Linnaean systematics. It also set the trend for enthusiast-driven societies, being less formal and socially stratified, and it prepared the way for more regional autonomy of scientific disciplines. While still in the Linnean orbit, the club had its own by-laws (drawn up by Vigors and others), electoral procedures, subscriptions, and fast publication in its own cheap house organ, the *Zoological Journal* (1824–34), which allowed free taxonomic discussion.

By the mid-1820s Vigors was the leading quinarian, arguing for a geometric ordering of species, orders, and families into sets of five bounded by a circle, a system pioneered by William MacLeay (1792–1865). The general minutes testify that Vigors, the secretary of the club and its last chairman in 1828–9, was the real power. He exhibited specimens and circular charts, and steered discussions towards quinarian explanations. Quinarianism provided a strong heuristic and led to his overhaul of avian classification in 'Observations on the natural affinities that connect the orders and families of birds', read at the club in 1824 and published in 1825. Vigors wrote on birds, mammals, and insects in the *Zoological Journal* and in 1827 became its principal editor until the journal closed in 1834.

Vigors was elected a fellow of the Royal Society in February 1826. By then his discomfort at an increasingly restrictive Linnean Society was apparent. As a result the Zoological Club's personnel slid readily into managerial positions at the new Zoological Society. It was Vigors, with Joseph Sabine and Sir Stamford Raffles, who drew up the prospectus for the Zoological Society in February 1826, and it was founded in April, with Vigors as its first secretary. He was joined by E. T. Bennett, his Zoological Club assistant, as vice-secretary in 1827.

Vigors's organizational flair was again apparent. The Zoological Society minutes show that he, Sabine, and Lord Auckland were the driving force in the early years. Vigors's careerists, interested in systematic science and a vocation from imperial gains, staffed the society's museum in Bruton Street, Mayfair. However, they were often at odds with the aristocrats, who, as the titular heads of the promenading gardens, saw the zoo's role as a game park, to provide exotic delicacies for the nobleman's table. Vigors donated his preserved birds to the museum, as well as display cases and cabinets of insects. He bought collections at auction and catalogued the museum's birds and mammals. Bruton Street became a repository for specimens gathered during surveying voyages. Captain Phillip Parker King of the *Beagle* had Vigors examine his birds, and it was Vigors who described the birds of the American north-west from Captain Frederick Beechey's voyage in the *Blossom*. Vigors's forty-odd papers (some co-authored with Thomas Horsfield) covered a wide ornithological range and introduced many new species.

The zoological gardens, according to Humphry Davy's original plan, were to exhibit animals of the colonies and assert London's global pre-eminence. Vigors's zoology too spoke of imperial pride and he sparked a rash of anti-Gallic papers from the Bruton Street careerists. The former grenadier, who had seen war with France, insisted that her Napoleonic days of appropriating nature were over. However, his domineering style alienated outsiders, not least the prickly William Swainson, who accused Vigors of bureaucratic dictatorship.

On the death of his father in 1828 Vigors succeeded to the family estate in co. Carlow, although he spent the scientific season at his house in Chester Terrace, Regent's Park. He was created an honorary DCL by Oxford University on 4 July 1832. On 15 December 1832 he entered the reformed parliament as the member for Carlow, resigning as secretary of the Zoological Society in 1833. He was an extreme Liberal and usually voted with the radicals. He rarely spoke in the house, but he was a key radical witness before the 1836 parliamentary select committee on the British Museum, where he deplored the lack of scientifically trained commoners among the titled trustees and wanted a professional board appointed by the learned societies. In the management of science, Vigors proved himself a critical transitional figure in the move towards the hegemony of gentlemanly specialism over aristocratic interest. He lost the seat of Carlow (where he was deputy lieutenant) in 1835, but was returned in 1837, and he represented this constituency until his death at his home, Chester Terrace, Regent's Park, on 26 October 1840. He was buried in the nave of Old Leighlin Cathedral. Vigors did not marry but was survived by a son, Ferdinand Vigors (*b.* 1814/15) who went to Trinity College, Oxford, in 1833.   ADRIAN DESMOND

Sources 'Nicholas Aylward Vigors', *Proceedings of the Linnean Society of London*, 1 (1838–48), 106–7 · *GM*, 2nd ser., 14 (1840), 659–60 · A. Desmond, 'The making of institutional zoology in London, 1822–1836', *History of Science*, 23 (1985), 153–85, 223–50 · Linn. Soc., Zoological Club papers · minutes of council, Zoological Society of London · 'Select committee on … the British Museum', *Parl. papers* (1836), vol. 10, no. 440 · Burke, *Gen. GB* (1858)
Archives Linn. Soc., letters to William Swainson · Royal Museum, Edinburgh, letters to Sir William Jardine · UCL, letters to Society for the Diffusion of Useful Knowledge
Likenesses G. Hayter, group portrait, oils (*The House of Commons, 1833*), NPG
Wealth at death inherited family estate in Old Leighlin, co. Carlow, Ireland

Vile, William (1714/15–1767), furniture maker, was probably born in Somerset, where the name is common. Support for a west-country origin is provided by Vile's will, in which he left money to his Humphrey cousins at South Petherton and Middle Lambrook. (Vile's father's will may have been among the twenty-four Vile wills proved in the Taunton archdeaconry, but all of them were destroyed in Second World War air raids on Exeter.) Vile's tombstone inscription in the Wandsworth Huguenot cemetery states that he died in 1767 aged fifty-two years and from this record his birth date has been calculated. In the late 1730s he married Sarah (*b.* 1709/10); her surname may have been Strickland, as there are bequests to several Strickland nephews and nieces in Vile's will. His wife's Christian name was recorded when their son, William Waldron Vile, was baptized at St Paul's Church, Covent Garden, on 2 June 1740; she died in 1782 and was buried alongside her husband.

Education, partnership, and early commissions Apprentices were normally put to learn a trade at the age of fourteen years, but the first notice of Vile's affiliation to furniture making was in 1749: on 10 August he wrote on behalf of 'My Master', the maker William Hallett senior (1707–1781), to George Selwyn. The letter suggests that, in view of Vile's marriage, and the birth of his son in 1740, and his needing a job, he probably continued to serve Hallett as a journeyman. By 1749 he was in any case well trained and no longer an apprentice. Soon afterwards he seemed to be hankering after setting up his own furniture making firm.

To set up in business required money and there is evidence to suggest that Vile and his new partner, John *Cobb (c.1715–1778), turned to Hallett for this. First, the rate books show them establishing premises in London in 1751 in the New Street ward of St Martin-in-the-Fields. By 1752 they were paying rent on four premises—they were next door to Hallett's own premises—but by 1755 the latter's property was taken over by Cobb. Hallett married successfully in 1756 and, significantly, from this year his bank account at the Royal Bank of Scotland, Drummond's branch, London, shows cash paid in from Vile and Cobb, almost monthly, in amounts of £150 to £300. A receipt of 1758 shows various payments from the partners (whose own accounts were at the same bank) totalling £3219; in 1761 there were four further substantial payments, adding up to £2350. It was this intermeshed practical form of financial backing which allowed the partnership to flourish, although there is no reason to think that Cobb, from his training as an upholsterer, looked solely after this side of the business. Either partner received payment, and applied it to their common good.

The furniture that Vile made in partnership with Cobb was done between about 1751 and 1764. In these busy years the two partners took on as apprentices Thomas Plaistowe on 23 December 1752 and John Daniel on 27 February 1753. Their parents were charged the high premiums of £60 and £63 respectively.

The first commission to which Vile's name has been attached was work in 1752–3 for Anthony Chute at The Vyne, Hampshire. The bills, for some £222, cover the whole range of furnishing provision: carpeting, festoon curtains, beds, bedding, neat mahogany chairs stuffed under linen covers, even a stand for Chute's hardstone cabinet, corner and other tables, a walnut bureau, and other minor items such as bellows and hearth brushes. The accepted role for furniture makers then included inventory listing, and sometimes the conduct of funerals. The making of coffins, and their equipping, was a morbid duty of furniture makers to families who had used their service in other ways. When Anthony Chute died in 1754, Vile at least took an inventory of effects, assisted by the London auctioneer John Prestage.

Commissions in the early 1750s were plentiful. Making

most of their furniture of mahogany, and assisted now by Samuel Reynolds, who in 1753 had transferred his services from William Hallett senior to Vile and Cobb, the partners worked for the fourth duke of Beaufort providing furniture for Badminton House, Gloucestershire; the second duke of Cleveland of 19 St James's Square, London; Sir William Proctor in Bruton Street, London; and Caroline, Lady Bridges. The reference in the Bridges bill to a mahogany dressing table with cutwork sides is of interest in view of Vile's later use of this style in the early 1760s. It resembled a complex array of thin horizontal and vertical timbers in precise geometrical formation, investing the sides and back of the object with a filigree quality almost unknown before. The firm's fire insurance valuation was first recorded in 1752 (Sun register 95, no. 129677, Guildhall Library, London), for three houses, warehouses, and workshops, but with a valuable stock of timber and mirror glass this was increased by 1755 to £6000.

The middle years In an advertisement in the *Public Advertiser* (20 May 1754) Vile and Cobb had announced themselves as 'Messrs Vile & Cobb's Cabinet and Upholstery Warehouse, the corner of St. Martin's Lane, Long Acre'. Neither partner is known to have issued published designs, although they probably made some use of those issued by their contemporary and near neighbour Thomas Chippendale senior (1718–1779) who had issued the first edition of his *The Gentleman and Cabinet-Maker's Director* in 1754. One of the most important eighteenth-century country houses, Holkham Hall, Norfolk, was ready for furnishing in the 1750s. Its owner, Thomas Coke, earl of Leicester, built the Palladian-style house from 1734, and the work was continued after his death in 1759 by his widow. The earl paid £8 to Vile on 3 May 1755 for a 'Pattern Chair like the Duke of Devonshire's'. This was a recognized activity—to make furniture, or indeed parts of buildings, after a pattern seen elsewhere. Vile, as an accomplished craftsman, was also able to provide the earl with a domed bed and all its accoutrements, fabric, fringes, and mattresses, the latter at an extra cost of £4 15s.

There were at least eleven other known commissions in hand in the high years of the firm's activity prior to 1760. These were all for private owners, and none was more supportive than George William, sixth earl of Coventry (1722–1809). The earl patronized several leading furniture makers during his fifty or so years of buying. He had to furnish both a Worcestershire house, Croome Court, and a London house at 29 Piccadilly. Inheriting his title in 1751, he set about rebuilding the Jacobean Croome Court and furnishing it from 1757 onwards. He left the main task of its interior design from about 1760 to the architect Robert Adam (1728–1792), and to Adam's group of reliable craftsmen, including Vile and Cobb. They were, however, involved from a few years earlier, in 1757, and Vile worked on until his retirement in 1764, with his partner continuing to work for the earl until 1773. Their various bills in the Croome estate office have been listed and some of the furniture itself, together with that of other makers, is still in the possession of family descendants. Much has since moved to other locations—for example, a pair of looking-glasses and pier-tables, supplied by Vile and Cobb in 1760 for £173 and £33 12s. respectively, is now at Temple Newsam House, Leeds. In June 1763 the library at Croome Court was embellished with two pedimented breakfront bookcases, made to correspond with the Ionic frame of the room's Venetian window. Adam supplied the detailed drawings for Vile and Cobb to work to, and they charged £260 for their work which included two men working for 226 days at the house taking down old bookcases and putting up the new ones. The applied carving in the bookcase pilasters was entrusted to the carver Sefferin Alken (*fl.* 1744–1783), who was also employed again on carving a clothes press. This last was supplied by Vile and Cobb in 1764, but after Vile's retirement Cobb charged a further £129 on 26 February 1766 for changing the press into a pair of cabinets. These bookcases and cabinets are now in the Victoria and Albert Museum, London. From the late 1750s the firm, with plenty of work, had been employing the furniture makers William France senior (*c.*1734–1773) and John Bradburne (*fl.* 1750–1781), and they were presumably responsible for much of the finer carved work on some of the pieces made in these years.

Royal service, 1761–1764 After receiving the royal warrant on 5 January 1761 which confirmed Vile and his partner as 'Joint Upholsterers in Ordinary to His Majesty's Great Wardrobe' (PRO, LC 5/57) their names started to appear regularly in accounts, firstly for the quarter ending Lady day (25 March) 1761. All their relevant bills are in the bill books of the great wardrobe (PRO, LC 9/306–10), the organization responsible for the embellishment of royal palaces. They made much of their new position, soon providing George III and his wife, Queen Charlotte, with several pieces of furniture. An important medal cabinet, started in 1760 for the king, now only survives in the form of its two end-cabinets. The central part connecting the ends probably consisted of drawers and folio shelves. Vile charged in 1761 for '3 Difft pieces of work fited in Bet. the Legs of His Majesty's Grand Medal Case with Carved Doors & Ends and a New Sub plinth to Do on a Frame, £80' (PRO, LC 9/306). The two end-cabinets have been described in detail (Shrub), and are in the collections, respectively, of the Victoria and Albert Museum, London, and the Metropolitan Museum of Art, New York. Despite being but part of the whole they are very impressive in appearance.

In 1761 Vile also made a superb mahogany bureau-cabinet for Queen Charlotte's apartments. It was invoiced at £71 in March 1762, and included similar cutwork sides to the dressing table provided to Lady Bridges in 1753. The cutwork is a feature of at least three other secretaire cabinets. Two of these were made for Robert D'Arcy, fourth earl of Holdernesse, secretary of state from 1751 to 1761. It is a form that has gone through the salerooms frequently, but a good example of 'handsome cuttwork', as it appears in accounts, may be found on the secretaire acquired by Noel Terry in 1964, and now part of the collection he bequeathed to Fairfax House, Castlegate, York, where it is on permanent display.

Perhaps the two finest items made by Vile for Queen Charlotte (and still in the Royal Collection) are her jewel cabinet and a fine bookcase, both dated to 1761. The first has a mahogany frame with its front ends and top inlaid with ivory, and is further embellished with veneers of several exotic woods—olive, padouk, amboyna, tulip, and rosewood. The hinged top is inlaid with the royal arms, and a concealed catch secures this. It can only be opened when the doors are also open. Therein is a nest of eight drawers and a further drawer, secured by a lock. It cost £138 10s. in 1762 and has often been illustrated. Queen Charlotte's jewels were celebrated and were purchased by George III from his uncle. The bookcase, always credited to Vile, has been similarly illustrated, but the bill for it needs explanation. The bookcase, as at present, does not have one of the distinctive features described in the bill: 'one side of this is all in one Door that opens from Top to bottom and serves for the Door that goes into the Water Closet within the Bed Chamber' (PRO, LC 9/308). The entry implies that the bookcase was made for the queen's bedroom on the north-west corner of Buckingham House. A closet was in the north-east corner of the room, to the left of the queen's bed, and it could be expected that the bookcase showed some evidence of this opening. None has been found. When the bookcase was exhibited in an exhibition held at the queen's gallery, Buckingham Palace, in 1990 ('A royal miscellany', no. 2), it was noted that a possible explanation might lie in a subsequent payment of £31 in 1767, to John Bradburne. With his partner, William France senior, Bradburne had succeeded Vile and Cobb in royal service and remedial tasks lay therefore with them. With the payment there is an entry which reads, 'A New Mahogany Book Press made out of the Water Closet which was one Part a Book Press, the other part a Passage Door, but now the Whole Front is made into one Press' (PRO, LC 9/314). It was, if this explanation is correct, a careful transformation of Vile's work.

One of the most unusual tasks Vile was entrusted with in 1763 by his royal patrons was to amend a mahogany organ case which had been made about 1735, probably by Benjamin Goodison. He was to refashion it to form a cabinet and did this at a charge of £57. This involved putting the whole on a mahogany plinth and ornamenting it with 'Ovals of Laurels and other Carved Ornaments & Carved Mouldings' (PRO, LC 9/308, 310). The ovals had appeared on pieces made in the Hallett shop. Vile, from his years there, carried forward the idea and their presence is usually some indication of his involvement, given a correct date and, hopefully, some documentation. The resulting piece in the Royal Collection has been illustrated both in its early and later states. Finally, among much else, a small item for which £5 5s. was charged in 1764 (PRO, LC 9/293) was the carcass of a large shaped toilet-table, made from mahogany. The serpentine shape of this can be discerned beneath the fabric 'toylette' in the painting by Johan Zoffany, *Queen Charlotte with her Two Eldest Sons* (1764; Royal Collection).

On 31 May 1763 the master of the great wardrobe, Francis, Baron le Despencer, had nominated William France senior to succeed Vile and Cobb in royal service, and in the following June a similar concession was granted to France's partner, John Bradburne (PRO, LC 5/57). No reason was given for Vile's discharge, but it is known that he 'retired' at the age of forty-nine years, made his will, and was dead three years later. So he was probably unfit for health reasons to carry on his trade, and there seems no reason to attribute his discharge from service to overcharging. Some overcharging by his firm had occurred—in the first quarter of 1763 there was a deduction of £75 for work in the 'New Japan Room' of the queen's house, the total being reduced from £858 18s. to £783 18s. (PRO, LC 9/308). Vile had also been guilty of overcharging Lord Folkestone in 1760 (Coleridge, *Chippendale*), but this was a common trait among craftsmen, and was usually due more to faulty calculation than to dishonesty. There is no doubt that Vile and his partner were competent at what they had done over some fourteen years, and Cobb's success in trade in later years presages what the two of them might have accomplished had Vile not been sickly in health, forcing his early retirement.

Will and death With ever-present thoughts of his mortality thrust upon him, Vile compiled his will in August 1763. He bequeathed to his wife, Sarah, two houses then in his own possession at Battersea Hill, his household furniture, and a sum of £300. There were bequests to his nephews John and William Strickland, and £20 each to his workmen Samuel Reynolds, John Bradburne, and William Eversley. He owned that he had not made any calculations in respect of his partnership with John Cobb, and left the settlement of this to his two executors, William Hallett senior and the London upholsterer and cabinet maker Charles Smith (*fl.* 1763–1767). They were to make such allowances to Cobb as they thought proper, and to invest the remainder of the estate so that his wife could receive £25 a year in her lifetime, and at her death this was to pass to a named list of nieces and nephews. Wills often have later codicils added, and Vile's was no exception. On 9 November 1764 the £20 he had left to his three workmen was only to be paid them if they were still in Vile's employment at his death. This excluded Bradburne, who had taken up royal service at Vile's discharge, and the £20 went instead to Mrs Vile. Reynolds continued with Vile and Cobb, not only appearing as a friend to testify to his knowledge of Vile when the will was proved on 23 September 1767, but also serving John Cobb in later years. Of Eversley nothing further is known. The cause of Vile's death on 21 August 1767 in Battersea is likewise unknown.

It was established by Tessa Murdoch that Vile was buried in the Huguenot cemetery at Wandsworth, although neither he nor his wife is known to have any Huguenot connection. The inscription on his chest tomb is now almost illegible, but was, fortunately, transcribed in 1885. It reads: 'In memory of William Vile, Gent., of St. John's Place Battersea who died August 21st, 1767 Aged 52 years. Also the body of Mrs Sarah Vile, his Wife, who died June the 17th, 1782, Aged 72 years'.   GEOFFREY BEARD

Sources G. Beard, 'William Vile again', *Furniture History*, 11 (1975), 113–15 · G. Beard and C. Gilbert, eds., *Dictionary of English furniture makers, 1660–1840* (1986) · A. Coleridge, 'English furniture supplied for Croome Court', *Apollo*, 151 (Feb 2000), 4–19 · D. Shrub, 'The Vile problem', *Victoria and Albert Museum Bulletin*, 1 (4 Oct 1965), 26–35 · R. Edwards, *Dictionary of English furniture*, 2nd edn, 3 vols. (1954) · C. Gilbert, *Furniture at Temple Newsam House and Lotherton Hall*, 1–3 (1978–98) · H. C. Smith, *Buckingham Palace* (1931) · A. Coleridge, *Chippendale and his contemporaries* (1968) · J. T. Squire, 'The Huguenots at Wandsworth', *Proceedings of the Huguenot Society*, 1 (1885–6), 229–42, 261–312 · will, PRO, PROB 11/932, fol. 327 · S. Fisher, ed., *Harleian Society parish registers*, 27 (1938) · E. A. Fry, ed., *Taunton wills, 1577–1799* (1912) · PRO, Croome Court MSS, Earl's Croome estate office, LC 9/308; LC 9/310, 17 Feb 1762 · tombstone, Huguenot cemetery, Wandsworth, London · City Westm. AC, F 527 · Sun register 95, GL, no. 147043 · Hants. RO, M57, 630–31, 646 · Shakespeare Birthplace Trust RO, Stratford upon Avon, Leigh MS DR18/5 · weekly departmental accounts, 3 May 1755, Holkham Hall, Norfolk, Holkham MSS · G. Beard, 'Decorators and furniture makers at Croome Court', *Furniture History*, 29 (1993), 88–110

Villareal, Kitty da Costa. *See* Mellish, Catherine Rachel (1710–1747).

Villettes, William Anne (1754–1808), army officer, born at Bern, Switzerland, on 14 June 1754, was the second son of Arthur Villettes (1701–1776), diplomatist. His family, who were Huguenot, had left France and settled in England after the revocation of the Edict of Nantes. His father, who was British plenipotentiary at Turin, and afterwards in the Helvetic cantons, retired to Bath, where he died. Villettes was educated at Claverton School, Bath, and St Andrews University; intended for the bar, he completed two or three terms at Lincoln's Inn. But he was set on a military life, and his father granted him his wish and obtained for him a cornetcy in the 10th light dragoons on 19 December 1775. He was promoted lieutenant in the regiment on 25 December 1778 and captain on 22 January 1782. On 24 December 1787 he was promoted to a majority in the 12th light dragoons.

For part of the earlier period of his service in the army Villettes served as aide-de-camp and military secretary to General Sir William Pitt, commanding the forces in Ireland. On 30 July 1791 he was promoted lieutenant-colonel of the 69th foot, and he commanded that regiment during the siege of Toulon, where his good services were acknowledged by General Charles O'Hara and his successor, General David Dundas; here he commanded a mixed force of British and Neapolitan troops, and defended, until ordered to withdraw, the key position of Les Sablettes.

Villettes was next engaged in the conquest of Corsica, in 1794. He commanded a force of 1200 soldiers which landed from the fleet, and, with Nelson, then captain of the *Agamemnon* and 250 naval gunners, was entrusted with the siege of Bastia. Admiral Lord Hood bore testimony to his good services, and Nelson described him as 'a most excellent officer' (*Dispatches and Letters*, 1.393). On the surrender of Bastia on 9 May 1794 Villettes was appointed governor of the town and gazetted colonel from 21 August 1795. In June 1796 he led a punitive expedition, accompanied by Sir Gilbert Elliot, the viceroy, to crush a rebellion in central Corsica, but was not permitted to finish the task, as Elliot conceded the rebels' demands. Ill health compelled his return to England, but on 30 November 1796 he was appointed a brigadier-general with a force sent to Portugal under Sir Charles Stuart. On 23 March 1797 he was transferred from the lieutenant-colonelcy of the 69th foot to that of the 1st dragoon guards, and was shortly afterwards made comptroller of the household to the duke of Kent.

On 18 June 1798 Villettes was promoted major-general. In 1799 he was sent to Corfu to raise a corps of Albanians—a mission that proved impracticable. The following year he was posted to Malta as second in command to General Pigot. He succeeded the latter in 1801. On 25 July 1802 he took over from General Fox as commander-in-chief in the Mediterranean. In the meantime he was made colonel of a newly raised regiment of foot from 12 April 1799, and on 28 March 1801 was appointed colonel commandant of a newly raised battalion of the 4th King's Own (disbanded on 24 May 1802). He served in Malta until 1807, exhibiting great tact and firmness during a sometimes difficult period. He had to face the unpopularity caused by the explosion of a powder magazine in the city of Vittoriosa, and to suppress a mutiny in Froberg's regiment in 1807. He raised the Royal regiment of Malta, and was appointed its colonel on 7 December 1804. On 30 October 1805 he was promoted lieutenant-general.

Although he was recalled to England in 1807 to join Cathcart's expedition to the Baltic, Villettes arrived too late to participate, but on 7 November he was appointed lieutenant-governor and commander of the forces in Jamaica, with the local rank of general. On 4 January 1808 he was appointed colonel of the 64th foot. While on a tour of inspection in the island in July 1808 he fell ill with yellow fever, and he died, unmarried, on 13 July 1808 at Union. He was buried with military honours in the parish of Halfway Tree, near Kingston, and a monument was erected to his memory in Westminster Abbey. He had proved to be one of the most popular and capable commanders in the British army, his favourite maxim always being '*Suaviter in modo, fortiter in re*' (Bowdler, 11).

ROBERT HOLDEN, *rev.* DESMOND GREGORY

Sources T. Bowdler, *A short view of the life and character of Lt. Gen. Villettes* (1815) · *GM*, 1st ser., 78 (1808), 852 · *GM*, 1st ser., 79 (1809), 297, 301, 798 · Fortescue, *Brit. army*, vol. 4 · D. Gregory, *The ungovernable rock: a history of the Anglo-Corsican kingdom and its role in Britain's Mediterranean strategy during the revolutionary war (1793–1797)* (1985) · D. Gregory, *Malta, Britain and the European powers, 1793–1815* (1996) · G. C. Dempsey, 'Mutiny at Malta: the revolt of Froberg's regiment, April 1807', *Journal of the Society for Army Historical Research*, 67 (1989), 16–27 · *The dispatches and letters of Vice-Admiral Lord Viscount Nelson*, ed. N. H. Nicolas, 7 vols. (1844–6), vol. 1

Archives BL, Lowe MSS, Add. MSS 20107, 20162, 20189 · BL, letters to Lord Nelson, Add. MSS 34904–34928 · NL Scot., corresp. with Hugh Elliot · NL Scot., letters to first earl of Minto · PRO, Colonial Office records, CO 158/6, 12, 15 · PRO, Foreign Office records, FO 20/11 · PRO, War Office records, WO 1/293

Likenesses C. Heath, stipple, BM; repro. in Bowdler, *A short view*

Villiers, Barbara. *See* Palmer, Barbara, countess of Castlemaine and *suo jure* duchess of Cleveland (*bap.* 1640, d. 1709).

Villiers, Charles Amherst (1900–1991), engineer and portrait painter, was born in London on 9 December 1900, the

Charles Amherst Villiers (1900–1991), by unknown photographer [detail]

second child and elder son in the family of two sons and two daughters of Ernest Amherst Villiers (1863–1923), Liberal MP for Brighton from 1906 to 1910, and his wife, the Hon. Elaine Augusta Guest, third daughter of Ivor Bertie Guest, first Baron Wimborne. His father, who was descended from Thomas Villiers, first earl of Clarendon (of the second creation), was the nephew of William Amhurst Tyssen-Amherst, first Baron Amherst of Hackney. His mother was a cousin of Winston Churchill. His formal education began at Oundle School, where he first developed a passion for engineering, particularly propulsion systems for motor cars and aircraft. During the First World War, with the help of his headmaster at Oundle, H. W. Sanderson, he was apprenticed to the Royal Aircraft Factory at Farnborough. He was on the point of being commissioned into the Royal Flying Corps when armistice was declared in November 1918. In 1919 he entered Cambridge, where he read physics.

Villiers's first appointment after Cambridge was with the Armstrong-Whitworth Development Company in Coventry, where he stayed until 1922 before joining Raymond Mays, founder of ERA cars and later of BRM, whom he had met at university. Villiers successfully modified the camshafts of two 1.5 litre Brescia Bugatti cars which Mays had acquired, enabling them to out-perform larger-engined vehicles. This attracted the attention of Ettore Bugatti, who invited Villiers to spend six months at his works at Molsheim in eastern France. This was an important period in the enhancement of Villiers's reputation, since a number of his ideas were incorporated into

Bugatti cars to enable them to achieve higher r.p.m. During the 1920s Villiers established himself as a leading authority on superchargers and was much in demand as a consulting engineer of high reputation. Commissions by Raymond Mays and others enabled him to supercharge some of the leading motor cars of the day, from the 1.5 litre AC to the 7.7 litre Rolls-Royce. He also worked on Malcolm Campbell's Bluebird car, powered by a 24 litre Napier Lion aero-engine, which Campbell used in his successful attempt on the land speed record at Daytona Beach. Perhaps one of Villiers's most notable successes was his work on the supercharger of the four-cylinder Bentley engine. Although it never won a race, the 'Blower Bentley' achieved outstanding performances at Brooklands and Le Mans and was driven to second place by Sir Henry Birkin in the French grand prix of 1930. The flamboyant reputation of the famous 'Bentley Boys' of this period owed much to Villiers's engineering skill. On 30 July 1932 he married Marietta Strakosch, also known as Maya de Lisle (b. 1893/4), widow of George Strakosch, and daughter of Georges Mungovich, financier. There were no children of the marriage.

Villiers's interest in flying was evident as early as 1918 when the armistice ended his plans to join the Royal Flying Corps. He founded his own aero-engine company in the 1920s but this failed to grow as he concentrated on motor vehicle development. In 1935, however, he joined the newly formed Straight Corporation where, among other things, he designed and built an advanced light aero-engine (named the Maya de Lisle, after his wife), which he tested himself in a company monoplane. During the Second World War he delivered bomber and fighter aircraft from the factories to their RAF squadrons, as a member of the RAF transport auxiliary. In his spare time he designed a heavy bomber capable of flying non-stop round the world, but this aeroplane was never built.

In 1943 Villiers was recruited by the Canadian Car and Foundry Company, which manufactured Hurricanes in Montreal, to lead its research division. After the war he moved to the United States. He remained there for the next twenty years, becoming an American citizen. His first marriage having ended in divorce, in 1946 he married Juanita Lorraine (Nita) Brown (d. 1968), daughter of Charles Brown, of Minneapolis. They had a son, Charles, and a daughter, Jane. In 1948 Villiers became president of the Rocket Society. His many projects during this period included rocket-powered spacecraft and satellite communications for the United States Aircraft Corporation, Boeing, and Douglas Aircraft at Santa Monica. This latter work was followed by six years of research with Bendix-Aviation-Eclipse and at the University of California.

Villiers returned to England in 1965 to resume his work on the technical enhancement of motor car engines, working with Peter Berthon on the 1.5 litre BRM engine, and with Graham Hill on the Cosworth. However, his engineering work soon lapsed as he became passionately devoted to portrait painting. His subjects included Graham Hill, Cardinal Spellman, and Pope John Paul II. A portrait of Ian Fleming was used on a *James Bond* cover.

Some of Villiers's projects, including a Mars landing, never came to fruition, while the efficacy of others was questioned. Nevertheless, he was an engineer and inventor of truly outstanding range and talent. He was said to hold deep religious convictions and in later life tended towards the mystical. He died of cancer at his home, 46a Holland Street, Kensington, London, on 12 December 1991. He was survived by the son and daughter of his second marriage.   DAVID THOMS

Sources *The Independent* (28 Jan 1992) · *The Times* (31 Jan 1992) · K. Richardson and C. N. O'Gallagher, *The British motor industry, 1896–1939* (1977) · W. O. Bentley, *W.O.: an autobiography* (1958) · T. P. Newcomb and R. T. Spurr, *A technical history of the motor car* (1989) · Burke, *Peerage* · m. cert., 1932 · d. cert.
Likenesses photograph, repro. in *The Independent* · photograph, repro. in *The Times* [*see illus.*]
Wealth at death £253,000: probate, 16 March 1992, *CGPLA Eng. & Wales*

Villiers, Sir Charles English Hyde (1912–1992), merchant banker, was born on 14 August 1912 at 21 Ampthill Square, St Pancras, London, the only son and the older of the two children of Algernon Hyde Villiers (1886–1917), a stockbroker, grandson of the fourth earl of Clarendon, and his wife, Beatrice Eleanor (c.1891–1978), daughter of Herbert Woodfield *Paul MP. His father was killed in action in November 1917, and his mother later married Walter Durant Gibbs, fourth Baron Aldenham, and had two more sons.

Charles Villiers was educated at Eton College, and after working for a few months as assistant to the Revd 'Tubby' Clayton, founder of Toc H, he spent two years working for the merchant bank Glyn Mills before going to New College, Oxford, in 1933 to read philosophy, politics, and economics, graduating with a second in 1936. He returned to Glyn Mills, and on 9 June 1938 he married Pamela Constance Flower (1913/14–1943), daughter of Major John Flower: she died, with the child, at the birth of their second son on 17 October 1943.

After the outbreak of the Second World War Villiers fought at Dunkirk with the Grenadier Guards, and was later transferred to the Special Operations Executive. In 1944 he was parachuted into Austria and Yugoslavia, where he helped to organize the Yugoslav resistance: in 1970 the Yugoslav government awarded him the Order of the People in recognition of this. By the end of the war he had reached the rank of lieutenant-colonel. On 1 October 1946 Villiers remarried: his second wife was Countess Marie José de la Barre d'Erquelinnes (b. 1915/16), daughter of Count Henri de la Barre d'Erquelinnes of Jurbise, Belgium: they had two daughters. After the war he returned to banking, joining Helbert Wagg & Co., and specialized in corporate finance. He was made a partner in 1948, and when the bank merged with J. Henry Schroder & Co. in 1960 to become Schroder Wagg, Villiers became a managing director.

In 1968 Villiers was appointed managing director of the Industrial Reorganization Corporation (IRC), set up by the Labour government in 1966 under the chairmanship of Sir Frank Kearton to rationalize industries and promote mergers, in order to improve the international competitiveness of British industry. Villiers was very successful in handling these delicate negotiations, and the IRC usually achieved the result it wanted, including the merger of GEC and English Electric and the creation of British Nuclear Design and Construction in 1968, and British United Trawlers in 1969. When the IRC was wound up in 1971 he returned to merchant banking as chairman of Guinness Mahon & Co. Ltd. He also served as chairman of the Northern Ireland Finance Corporation from 1972 to 1973. He was knighted in 1975 for services to industry.

Villiers succeeded Sir Monty Finniston as chairman of the British Steel Corporation (BSC) in 1976, and spent four difficult years trying to rationalize the steel industry and ensure its survival at a time when BSC's markets were crumbling, and the crisis in the steel industry was deepening. He embarked on a programme of closures, and clashed with the select committee on nationalized industries in November 1977 when he refused to disclose details of his plans to steer BSC through the crisis. In March 1978 his strategy for the future, 'The road to viability', which abandoned the ten-year development strategy adopted in 1973, was presented to parliament; by then he was about to announce losses of £443 million for 1977–8. He agreed to delay financial reconstruction until BSC broke even, which in June 1979 he predicted would be in March 1980, and continued closing loss-making plants—eleven steelworks altogether. But Sir Keith Joseph, the new secretary of state for industry, announced that the government would not finance BSC losses after March 1980. BSC was still losing £1 million a day, and after Villiers closed the Consett steelworks in November 1979, with the loss of 4000 jobs, and announced a further 52,000 redundancies, and a pay rise of only 2 per cent, at a time when the rate of inflation was 17 per cent, union opposition to the reduction in the size of the steel industry culminated in a three-month national steel strike, starting in January 1980. The strike cost BSC over £200 million, and led steel-using industries to switch permanently to imported steel.

Villiers's strategy began to work under his successor, Ian Macgregor, appointed in 1980 after the strike ended, but only when the government, realizing that BSC might be forced into liquidation, reversed its stand and pumped billions of pounds of public money into the company to ensure its survival with a view to future privatization. Until 1989 Villiers remained chairman of BSC (Industry) Ltd, the subsidiary set up to encourage new industries to move into former steel-making areas, to provide jobs for former steelworkers. Villiers published *Start Again Britain* (1984), an analysis of the problems facing British industry. His interests included Anglo-American relations, and in 1985 he set up the British American project for the successor generation. He was a trustee of the Royal Opera House, and chairman of the Theatre Royal, Windsor. He died from cancer on 22 January 1992 at his home, Blacknest House, Sunninghill, Ascot, Berkshire.

ANNE PIMLOTT BAKER

Sources G. F. Dudley and J. J. Richardson, *Politics and steel in Britain, 1967–1988 ... the life and times of the British Steel Corporation* (1990) · D. Hague and G. Wilkinson, *The I.R.C.—an experiment in industrial intervention. A history of the Industrial Reorganisation Corporation* (1983) · *The Times* (23 Jan 1992) · *The Independent* (24 Jan 1992) · Burke, *Peerage* (1999) · *WW* · b. cert. · m. certs. · d. cert.
Archives CAC Cam., papers
Likenesses Wesley, photograph, 1976, Hult. Arch. · photograph, repro. in *The Times* · photograph, repro. in *The Independent*
Wealth at death £638,692: probate, 6 May 1992, *CGPLA Eng. & Wales*

Villiers, Charles Pelham (1802–1898), politician, was born on 3 January 1802 in Grosvenor Street, London, the third son of George Villiers (1759–1827) and his wife, Theresa Parker (1775–1855), the only daughter of John, first Baron Boringdon, and his second wife, Theresa, daughter of Thomas, first Lord Grantham. His sister was Lady (Maria) Theresa *Lewis (1803–1865). His grandfather was Thomas *Villiers, first earl of Clarendon. With the Parker and Villiers families later co-residing at Kent House, Knightsbridge, Villiers was brought up in a lively political home, where Canning was a frequent visitor. With his elder brothers, George William Frederick *Villiers and Thomas Hyde *Villiers, he attended the Kensington school of Thomas Wright Hill before going to East India College, Haileybury, Hertfordshire, with India beckoning as a career. As a result of poor health, he went instead to St John's College, Cambridge, matriculating in Michaelmas term 1820, graduating BA in 1824, and proceeding MA in 1827. He presided over the union in 1822 with Macaulay, Howick (third Earl Grey), W. M. Praed, and Charles Austin among his circle. In 1823 he entered Lincoln's Inn, and qualified for the bar in 1827.

The law was to prove Villiers's main financial stay until the late 1850s but these early years also permanently marked his political vision. At Haileybury he had been taught by Thomas Malthus and Sir James Mackintosh; in London he heard John McCulloch lecture, and with his brothers, he was soon deeply involved in a number of 'March of Mind' societies, discussing issues such as population, the poor law, and Owenite co-operation. This brought him into touch with the Benthamites and J. S. Mill but Villiers, unlike his brothers, acquired increasingly radical political views. However, it was as a liberal tory inspired by Huskisson that he contested Hull in 1826, reputedly on the cry of 'Cheap Bread', the theme that would shape his life. While George had become a commissioner of customs in 1823, and Hyde had been elected for Hedon in 1826, Charles, considered by some the most brilliant, if also the most difficult, of the brothers, took the western circuit and served as secretary to the master of the rolls in 1830. In 1832 his intellectual interests were well suited to his appointment as an assistant poor-law commissioner, investigating the midland and western counties, and he also acquired at first hand a knowledge of London's slums. Villiers became a convinced supporter of the new poor law, for whose administration he would later be responsible. In 1833 he was appointed examiner of witnesses in the court of chancery, a well-paid if relatively onerous post which he held until 1852. This gave him sufficient financial security to sustain his political career, for

Charles Pelham Villiers (1802–1898), by William Walker, c.1865

Villiers now became an extremely forceful advocate in parliament of free trade, renewing his motion for repeal of the corn laws in April and May 1840, but also bolstering the cause by his part in the highly influential select committee on import duties, nominally chaired by Joseph Hume, whose work Villiers in effect took over. As the spokesman for the radical extra-parliamentary movement, and a seeming rebel to his class, Villiers was placed in a difficult position with regard to the whigs, as they showed a growing readiness to support freer but not completely free trade, and his conspicuous advocacy of total repeal cost him many personal and political friendships.

With the return of an even stronger protectionist majority in the election of 1841 (only 90 voted for Villiers's repeal motion in 1842, compared with 177 in 1840), Villiers was increasingly identified with the Anti-Corn Law League, performing 'a manly part' in its out-of-doors work (A. Prentice, *History of the Anti-Corn Law League*, 1853, 2.101). His annual motions were important not so much for the recruits they made as for the opportunity to rehearse, with growing sophistication, the case for total repeal. These set pieces focused a national debate, allowing the Anti-Corn Law League to orchestrate its campaigns and exert pressure upon parliament in a way that would slowly erode the protectionist majority. Villiers, however, by no means always agreed with the tactics of the league and found more palatable the milder views of James Wilson, with whom he struck up a strong friendship and whom he assisted in setting up *The Economist* in 1843. With the return to parliament of the league's leader Cobden in 1841, Villiers gradually ceded the leadership of the free trade party, especially as Cobden, and later Bright, rose into talented and inspiring political orators. As a result, when the corn laws were finally repealed in 1846, Villiers and his friends felt that his pioneering role was not given sufficient due, and Cobden himself recognized 'I have trod upon his heels, nay, almost trampled him down, in a race where he was once the sole man on the course' (*Free Trade Speeches*, 1.lxvii). However, Villiers did not bear grudges. He formed a lasting political rapport with Bright, and his outwardly successful alliance with the league was confirmed by his election for South Lancashire in 1847. Claiming poverty, Villiers sensibly stuck to Wolverhampton, and was to remain its MP until his death, forming the longest continuous link between MP and constituency in nineteenth- and twentieth-century Britain.

After 1846 Villiers was never to recapture the political limelight that he had hitherto enjoyed, especially as Lord John Russell—for whom the Villiers family were never true whigs—declined to give him an important office in 1846 (although he was considered as governor of Bombay, until vetoed by the East India Company). He remained a strong radical, urging further parliamentary reform and especially the ballot, but he also became embroiled in the feud between Edwin Chadwick and the Villiers and Lewis families over the administration of the new poor law following the Andover workhouse scandal. In 1852 he once more acted with the Manchester school, urging in the debate that closed the corn law issue that repeal should be

otherwise he was largely dependent upon an income generously allowed him by his elder brother (and subsequently by his heir). He also dabbled in the stock market and was for many years a director of the General Life Assurance Company.

Villiers entered parliament for Wolverhampton in 1835, for while his association with the new poor law proved a handicap, Wolverhampton was primarily a strong centre of opposition to the corn laws, led by its MPs Richard Fryer and William Wolryche Whitmore. Villiers formed a successful constituency partnership with the Liverpool merchant Thomas Thornely, standing as a free-trader and radical, and acting with the philosophical radicals in parliament. Above all, he readily took up opposition to the corn laws as his parliamentary métier, working with the London Anti-Corn Law Association and in 1836 seconding William Clay's motion for a fixed duty of 10s. on corn. At the election of 1837 in Wolverhampton Villiers pledged himself to move for total repeal, which he did for the first time on 15 March 1838. By this time other cities had also become active in the movement against the corn laws, and with the formation of the Manchester Anti-Corn Law Association in September 1838, Villiers was soon the parliamentary pivot of the free-trade movement, ready to co-ordinate action with the provinces. Having banqueted in Manchester in January 1839, he urged that its anti-cornlaw campaigners be heard at the bar of the house in February, and in March, prompting a lengthy debate, proposed for the second time total repeal of the corn laws.

recognized as 'wise, just, and beneficial'. On this occasion Palmerston's milder resolution won the day, and Villiers was later distanced from his league allies, believing for example that the Anglo-French commercial treaty of 1860 was a breach of the unilateral free trade principles of 1846; by 1861 Cobden noted 'I seem to feel as if we had never a thought in common, instead of our having been seven years in constant correspondence' (Cobden to Bright, 14 Oct 1861, BL, Add. MS 43651, fol. 262).

In 1852, after his 'eighteenth year of unrequited toil in that House' (Villiers to Cobden, 27 Dec 1852, Cobden MSS, 10, W. Sussex RO), Villiers's career took a new turn as he eventually achieved significant (and well-paid) office under Aberdeen, that of judge-advocate-general, a position he also held under Palmerston (1855–8). In 1853–4 Villiers also chaired an important select committee on public houses, which proved a benchmark in subsequent debate. Its report was considered too 'free-trading' by a growing band of temperance critics but Villiers, who had no great faith in governments making men moral, rejected undue restrictions on drink until rational recreation was available for the working classes. In the 1850s Villiers enjoyed considerable influence in the Commons from his radical past, was very much a fixture in London society, and was extremely well-informed politically, 'always sensible, unprejudiced and the most satisfactory person to talk to', according to the Whig diarist Greville (L. Strachey and R. Fulford, *The Greville Memoirs, 1814–1860*, 1938, 7.351). His eventual appointment to the cabinet as president of the poor-law board in 1859 considerably strengthened Palmerston's first 'liberal' government, while providing for Villiers a post at last fully commensurate with his interests and talent.

For, as his legal career had shown, Villiers had a capacity for drudgery, and ably served by officials, especially Sir John Lambert and Sir Robert Rawlinson, his tenure at the poor-law board was marked by the most important series of reforms since 1834. First, the crisis in poor relief in London in the winter of 1860–61 led to Villiers setting up a select committee, which he chaired over three parliamentary sessions and whose evidence led ultimately to the Union Chargeability Act of 1865. This act, still described by Beatrice and Sydney Webb in 1929 as 'the latest measure substantially changing the Poor Law' (*English Poor Law History*, 3.431), made the union, not the parish, the unit of financial responsibility, a reform of vital importance in London but one that also helped to undermine the negligence of landlords in closed rural parishes. Second, the report of the committee set in train a series of reforms in London's poor-law relief, with the extension of the board's authority over committees set up under local acts, the establishment of a common fund for relief of the casual poor, and the equalization of metropolitan poor rates. These reforms, in the pipeline under Villiers, were largely embodied in the Metropolitan Poor Law Act of 1867. Villiers, open to persuasion by Florence Nightingale, also began important steps for the reform of nursing within the poor law. Third, Villiers's association with Lancashire was renewed when the poor law proved unequal to the

demands placed on it by the cotton famine of 1861–5. Villiers met this crisis in a remarkably flexible manner, foreshadowing the Union Chargeability Act by allowing parishes to seek union or even county-wide support and by allowing unions to raise loans. More innovatively, the Public Works (Manufacturing Districts) Act (1863) fostered job-creating public health schemes, which although by no means equal to the extent of unemployment had important multiplier effects on the local economy. Interestingly, Villiers refused to encourage emigration schemes but did eventually relax the labour test for poor relief. Finally, Villiers was responsible for a variety of other measures, including the Union Assessment Act of 1862 (giving power to assess rates to committees, not underqualified overseers), and the irremovability of paupers after one year's residence, and he prepared the ground for the poor-law board to become a permanent part of the machinery of government. Villiers's administrative pragmatism combined with political nous did much to give shape to the poor law into the twentieth century.

Villiers's contribution to the poor law was therefore a notable, if unsung, success, belying his reputation as a political weathercock, more interested in gossip than policy-making. He also played an important part in further parliamentary reform, for it fell to his board to prepare the electoral statistics upon which the reform bills of the 1860s were based. Villiers guardedly supported an extensive measure, ultimately preferring the claims of democracy to those of plutocracy, for while he always had a strong confidence in aristocratic rule, he was far more critical of Mammon than of the masses.

After the second Reform Act, Villiers's political career withered, partly overshadowed by the greater stature of his brother the earl of Clarendon but most probably because of the antipathy between Villiers and 'the old devil' Gladstone. For while Gladstone and Villiers shared a common acquaintance with the reformed prostitute Laura Thistlethwayte (at whose salon they often met), Gladstone had often been the butt of Villiers's caustic wit, and in 1868 he omitted Villiers from his cabinet, ostensibly on the ground that two brothers could not sit in the cabinet (as they had previously done in those of Palmerston and Russell). Villiers's later mark therefore was confined to his chairmanship in 1871 of the select committee on conventual and monastic institutions, where he had little truck with the anti-Catholic prejudices of Charles Newdegate and whose report paradoxically pointed towards the further removal of Catholic disabilities. Villiers remained a frequent attender at the Political Economy Club (to which he had been elected in 1847), a pillar of the Reform Club, and a noted social personality, ill-dressed but witty, informed, civilized, at times mischievous, well loved in his family circle, and widely popular outside it. He declined a peerage in 1885.

Villiers by the late 1870s had in fact become more important as a political symbol than as an active participant in the house, a position recognized by the erecting of a statue to him in Wolverhampton in 1879, an unusual honour for a living politician. Against the background of the fair-trade movement too, Villiers's past career was celebrated by the publication of his *Free Trade Speeches*, an edition prepared by Agnes Lambert, the daughter of Sir John. Her projected biography of Villiers was never published. Villiers also remained a conscientious, if absentee, local MP, keeping closely in touch with constituency activists and making the issue of redistribution in Wolverhampton the subject of his last speech in the House of Commons in 1885. In 1886 he supported the Liberal Unionists, distrusting the leadership of Gladstone, an abiding antagonism still strongly voiced in the 1890s. 'Father of the House', Villiers was re-elected in 1892 and 1895 but rarely attended the Commons save to vote against home rule. On the jubilee of the repeal of the corn laws in 1896 he was presented with a commemorative address by the Cobden Club and replied with a lucid defence of free trade since 1846 but was too ill to attend the celebrations. In his declining years, frail but alert, he retained a lively interest in politics, observing the operation of parish councils and the rise of the Independent Labour Party, supporting women's suffrage, reading the newspapers thoroughly, and maintaining an extensive correspondence. For the last thirty years of his life Villiers, who had never married, was looked after by his housekeeper, Maria Walsh. He died of a severe cold, following his ninety-sixth birthday celebrations, on 16 January 1898 at his home, 50 Cadogan Place, London. He was buried at Kensal Green on 20 January.

Villiers left a large hoard of papers and a considerable personal fortune. His vast correspondence was reputedly destroyed by his housekeeper, to whom he had bequeathed it. His wealth, over £350,000, occasioned surprise and a minor political outcry. For he had received (and carefully guarded from Gladstonian frugality) a pension of £2000 p.a. on the grounds of income insufficient to sustain his former cabinet rank, lamenting on leaving office in 1866 'I have always been unlucky and I am worse off now than when I began thirty-one years ago' (Villiers to Mrs Anne Graham, July 1866, BL, Add. MS 48214). His change of fortune may have been largely due to the legacy he received in 1880 from a family friend, Catherine Mellish, which included a life interest in a 2000 acre Hertfordshire estate (Hamels Park), sold in 1884 to the textile bleacher H. S. Cross.   A. C. HOWE

Sources *The free trade speeches of the Right Hon Charles Pelham Villiers*, ed. A member of the Cobden Club [A. Lambert], 2 vols. (1883) · W. O. Henderson, 'Charles Pelham Villiers', *History*, new ser., 37 (1952), 25–39 · Thornely MSS, BLPES, R SR 1094 · W. Sussex RO, Cobden papers · BL, Bright MSS · BLPES, Villiers MSS · BL, Florence Nightingale MSS · Bodl. Oxf., Clarendon MSS · T. Mackay, *A history of the English poor law*, 3: *From 1834 to the present time* (1899) · *The Times* (15 Jan 1898) · *The Times* (17 Jan 1898) · *The Times* (21 Jan 1898) · *Wolverhampton Chronicle* (19 Jan 1898) · *Wolverhampton Chronicle* (22 Jan 1898) · *Hansard* · W. L. Arnstein, *Protestant vs Catholic in mid-Victorian England: Mr Newdegate and the nuns* (1982) · [E. C. Whitehurst], 'Charles Pelham Villiers and the repeal of the corn laws', *Westminster Review*, 120 (1883), 110–51 · Venn, *Alum. Cant.*
Archives BLPES, corresp. and papers · U. Birm. L., letters | BL, corresp. with John Bright, Add. MS 43386 · BL, letters to Richard Cobden, Add. MS 43662 · BL, corresp. with W. E. Gladstone, Add. MSS 44370–44788, *passim* · BL, letters to Mrs A. P. C. Graham, Add. MS 48214 · BL, corresp. with Florence Nightingale, Add. MS 45787 · Bodl. Oxf., corresp. with Lord Kimberley · Man. CL, Manchester Archives and Local Studies, letters to J. B. Smith · PRO, corresp. with Lord John Russell, 30/22 · U. Nott. L., letters to duke of Newcastle · U. Southampton L., corresp. with Lord Palmerston · W. Sussex RO, letters to Richard Cobden; letters to F. A. Maxse · Wolverhampton Archives and Local Studies, letters to William McIlwraith
Likenesses S. W. Reynolds junior, mezzotint, pubd 1844 (after C. Duval), BM, NPG · S. Bellin, group portrait, mixed engraving, pubd 1850 (*Meeting of the council of the Anti-Corn Law League*; after J. R. Herbert), BM, NPG · W. Walker, photograph, c.1865, NPG [*see illus.*] · W. Theed, marble statue, 1879, Wolverhampton, Staffordshire · A. Cope, oils, exh. RA 1885, Reform Club, London · statue, 1899, Manchester Free-Trade Hall · J. H. Lynch, lithograph (after daguerreotype), NPG · cartoon, repro. in *VF* (31 Aug 1872)
Wealth at death £355,557 17s. 4d.: resworn probate, Dec 1898, *CGPLA Eng. & Wales*

Villiers, Christopher, first earl of Anglesey (d. 1630), courtier, was the third son of Sir George *Villiers (c.1544–1606) [*see under* Villiers, Sir Edward] of Brooksby, Leicestershire, and his second wife, Mary Beaumont (c.1570–1632), later countess of Buckingham in her own right. John *Villiers, Viscount Purbeck, and George *Villiers, first duke of Buckingham, were his brothers and Sir Edward *Villiers was his half-brother. Christopher, though 'an unattractive and unintelligent' youth (*DNB*), shared the good fortune of the family consequent upon the rise of his brother George. In February 1617 he was appointed gentleman of the bedchamber to James I (though not sworn until January 1618), and on 7 March following he was granted an annuity of £200 a year. In December 1617 Sir Robert Naunton, who had no sons, was appointed secretary of state on condition that he made Villiers his heir; the latter consequently received lands worth £500 a year. He was also promised £800 a year out of the monopoly for gold and silver thread, but actually received only £150 during the whole of its existence. In addition to these sources he received considerable sums from the patent for ale houses, and his malpractices in this connection formed the subject of charges against him in parliament, which were, however, abandoned. In 1620 it was said that Villiers was in line for the office of master of the robes, which would have secured his place at court, and his access to its bounty.

Villiers's next step was to secure a suitable heiress as a wife; ineffectual suit was made first for the only daughter of Sir Sebastian Harvey, lord mayor of London, and then for Elizabeth Norris, daughter of the earl of Berkshire. He eventually married Elizabeth (d. 1662), daughter of Thomas Sheldon of Howley, Leicestershire. On 23 March 1623 he was created Baron Villiers of Daventry and earl of Anglesey, the patent passing on 18 April. His mediocre abilities prevented his employment in any important position, and he himself acknowledged to his brother the duke that 'his want of preferment proceeded from his own unworthiness rather than from the duke's unwillingness' (*CSP dom.*, 1627–8, 327). His weakness appears to have been alcohol, and in 1625 it was rumoured that he had been 'banished the court … the king saying he would have no drunkards of his chamber' (GEC, *Peerage*, 1.132n.). On 6

December 1628 he was appointed keeper of Hampton Court, and on 4 March 1629 of Bushey Park. About the same time he was said to have purchased the reversion of the office of chancellor of the exchequer from Edward Barrett, Lord Newburgh. He died on 3 April 1630 at Windsor, and was buried on 12 April in St George's Chapel. His widow married Benjamin Weston in 1641. Villiers's only son, Charles (d. 1661), succeeded as second earl of Anglesey. On 25 April 1648 he married Mary, widow of his cousin William Villiers, Viscount Grandison, and mother of Barbara Villiers. He died childless and was buried at St Martin-in-the-Fields, London, on 4 February 1661. His honours became extinct, and the estates passed to his sister Anne, widow of Thomas Savile, earl of Sussex.

A. F. POLLARD, rev. SEAN KELSEY

Sources DNB · CSP dom., 1611–31 · GEC, Peerage, new edn, 1.132–3; 3.389–90 · G. E. Aylmer, The king's servants: the civil service of Charles I, 1625–1642 (1961) · A. Davies, Dictionary of British portraiture, 1 (1979) · D. E. Doyle, The official baronetage of England (1886)
Likenesses group portrait, oils, 1628, Royal Collection · G. Honthorst, engraving (after G. Honthorst), repro. in Doyle, Official baronetage, 1.46 · G. Honthorst, oils

Villiers, Sir Edward (c.1585–1626), government official and administrator, was the second son of Sir George Villiers and his first wife, Audrey (d. 1587), daughter and heir of William Saunders of Harrington, Northamptonshire. **Sir George Villiers** (c.1544–1606) came of a family which had been settled at Brooksby in Leicestershire from at least 1235. A prosperous sheep farmer, he was the eldest son of William Villiers and Colett, daughter and heir of Richard Clarke of Willoughby, Warwickshire, and widow of Richard Beaumont of Coleorton, Leicestershire. He served as sheriff of Leicestershire in 1591–2, was knighted in 1593, and represented his county in parliament from 1604 until his death on 4 January 1606. He had four daughters from his first marriage and two sons, the eldest of whom, Sir William, obtained a baronetcy in 1619. Sir George's second marriage, about 1590, was to his beautiful but penniless first cousin by the half-blood, Mary (c.1570–1632), daughter of Anthony Beaumont of Glenfield, Leicestershire, with whom he had four children: John *Villiers, Viscount Purbeck; George *Villiers, first duke of Buckingham; Christopher *Villiers, first earl of Anglesey; and Susan Villiers, who married William Feilding, first earl of Denbigh. Sir George's widow was created countess of Buckingham for life on 1 July 1618, and had two more husbands: first Sir William Rayner and then Sir Thomas Compton.

Edward Villiers matriculated as a fellow-commoner from Queens' College, Cambridge, in 1601. About 1612 he married Barbara, one of the daughters of Sir John St John of Lydiard Tregoze in Wiltshire, with whom he had ten children. A captain and muster master in the Leicestershire militia by 1614, in the following year he resigned his positions after a scandal involving regimental funds. His fortunes were dramatically transformed by the rise to royal favour of his younger half-brother, George. Soon after George Villiers was ennobled, Edward was knighted

(7 September 1616), and on 23 December 1617 he became master of the mint at the behest of his brother, who was by then earl of Buckingham. He held this lucrative office, which was thought to be worth between £1500 and £2000 per annum, until August 1619, after which time he shared its duties with another man. At various times between 1618 and 1622 he was tipped to become comptroller of the household, master of the wardrobe, master of the jewel house, and even lord deputy of Ireland, but further preferment temporarily eluded him.

By the early 1620s Villiers was settled in Dean's Close, Westminster, but he also purchased the manor of Baggrave, in his native Leicestershire, for which in October 1620 he paid £6900. He was well able to afford such a sum, for in addition to the income from his office he ruthlessly exploited his kinship with Buckingham for financial gain. For example, in 1620–21 the Irish magnate Richard Boyle paid him £4500 for the earldom of Cork and a viscountcy for his eldest son. Villiers also invested heavily in several projects, most notably the farm for the sole manufacture of gold and silver thread. He sank £4000 into this scheme, for which he derived an annual return of at least £500. This valuable source of income was threatened in August 1619 when several silkmen refused to enter into bonds promising to give over their trade. Villiers urged that they be imprisoned to which the attorney-general, Sir Henry Yelverton, agreed, fearing that to refuse would incur the anger of Buckingham. In November 1620 Villiers persuaded the lord chief justice, Sir Henry Montague, to pay Buckingham £20,000 for the lord treasurer's staff and a peerage. Buckingham was so pleased at this valuable service that he arranged for Villiers and his sons by his wife, Barbara, to be allowed to inherit the title of Viscount Grandison, which on 3 January 1621 was bestowed upon Barbara's childless uncle, Sir Oliver St John.

Villiers was elected to parliament for Westminster in December 1620, undoubtedly on the interest of Buckingham, the borough's high steward, but in the following month he was sent to the Palatinate bearing James I's message of support for his son-in-law, the beleaguered elector, Frederick V. During his absence Villiers was denounced in the Commons for his part in imprisoning those silkmen who had earlier refused to enter into bond. News of this development reached him while he was abroad, and it was only with the greatest reluctance that he crossed the channel. On his return Buckingham advised him not to take his Commons seat until the House of Lords had exonerated him from any ill-dealings. Villiers accordingly delayed his entrance until after Yelverton and the patentees had been examined, but he failed to wait until he was formally cleared and entered the house prematurely on 2 May, prompting calls for him to be ejected. Rather than suffer such an indignity, he withdrew voluntarily. The Commons were finally notified that he had been cleared on 4 June, but on this day parliament adjourned for the summer, so he could not resume his seat until it reassembled in November. In September he was again sent to the Elector Frederick to persuade him to disarm his forces and leave the Dutch army, which he had joined. On his return to England in the following month Villiers reported that his mission had succeeded and that Frederick had agreed to renounce the throne of Bohemia in return for the restoration of the upper Palatinate.

Villiers's financial interests had been damaged by the king's cancellation of the gold and silver thread patent following the parliamentary outcry in 1621. For this reason, in 1622 Buckingham procured for him a 21-year lease of the import duties on gold and silver thread. However, in order to secure this grant Villiers was first required to surrender his co-mastership of the mint. He eventually did this in July 1623, but by then the grant on the import duties had been undermined by the erection of a company of goldwiredrawers. He therefore persuaded the king to grant him office as joint warden of the mint, which was not as lucrative as his previous position, and an annuity of £500. Moreover, he also coerced the new Goldwiredrawers' Company to pay him an additional annuity. Despite these generous arrangements, he resented the new company, and in March 1624, having been once again elected to parliament for Westminster, he helped thwart the Goldwiredrawers' attempt to obtain statutory recognition of their charter, although his call to suppress the indigenous manufacture of gold and silver thread went unheeded.

In April 1625 Villiers and his departmental colleagues were joined in commission to execute the office of master of the mint after the previous incumbent was dismissed. By this time, however, he was no longer much interested in the mint, as he had been promised appointment as lord president of Munster. His letters patent were sealed on 27 May 1625, and orders were given to allow him a lump sum of £3000 as a reward for his former services. He was also granted 500 acres of the Forest of Dean for industrial exploitation. Before leaving England he sold Baggrave and sat in parliament for a third time as member for Westminster. He reached Waterford in October and, lacking an official residence, rented the college of Youghal from the earl of Cork. Early in the new year he endeavoured to billet and clothe survivors of the ill-fated Cadiz expedition whose ships had put in to Youghal. In June 1626 he complained that he had 'shipwrecked' his own credit in this service. On 2 September he fell sick at Youghal, possibly from dysentery contracted from those he had sought to assist. He died in the early hours of the morning on the 7th and was buried the following day in the newly built chapel at Youghal. By the terms of his will, drafted on 31 August 1625, he entrusted his estate and the settlement of his debts, which were substantial, to his widow, as his eight surviving children were under age. His eldest son, William, succeeded Sir Oliver St John as second Viscount Grandison in 1630; he was father of Barbara Villiers, duchess of Cleveland. Sir Edward's second and third sons, John and George, succeeded as third and fourth viscounts Grandison; a fourth son, Sir Edward, was father of Edward Villiers, first earl of Jersey. Villiers's widow died in 1672.

ANDREW THRUSH

Sources 'Villiers, Edward', 'Villiers, George', HoP, *Commons* [drafts] • *CSP dom.*, 1603–26; 1663–4, 611 • *CSP Ire.*, 1625–32 • *CSP Venice*, 1621–3 • J. Morrin, ed., *Calendar of the patent and close rolls of chancery in Ireland, of the reign of Charles I* (1863) • W. Notestein, F. H. Relf, and H. Simpson, eds., *Commons debates, 1621*, 7 vols. (1935) • *JHC*, 1 (1547–1628), 726 • *The letters of John Chamberlain*, ed. N. E. McClure, 2 (1939) • *The Lismore papers*, ed. A. B. Grosart, 10 vols. in 2 series (privately printed, London, 1886–8) • [T. Birch and R. F. Williams], eds., *The court and times of James the First*, 2 (1848), 119 • *Fourth report*, HMC, 3 (1874), 285 • PRO, SO3/6 and SO3/7 • CKS, U269/1/ON1531 • PRO, PROB 11/151, fol. 162v • PRO, PROB 11/340, fols. 57–8 • PRO, C66 [patent rolls] • City Westm. AC, E151, E152 • A. M. Burke, ed., *Memorials of St Margaret's Church, Westminster* (1914) • J. Lodge, *The peerage of Ireland*, 2 (1754), 94 • GEC, *Peerage* • Venn, *Alum. Cant.* • V. Treadwell, *Buckingham and Ireland, 1616–28: a study in Anglo-Irish politics* (1998) • T. Cogswell, *Home divisions: aristocracy, the state and provincial conflict* (1998), 88 • DNB
Likenesses portrait, Lydiard Tregoze, Wiltshire
Wealth at death heavily indebted: *CSP dom.*, 1663–4, 611

Villiers, Edward, first earl of Jersey (1655?–1711), politician, was the eldest son of Sir Edward Villiers (1620–1689), knight marshal, and his first wife, Frances (1630–1677), youngest daughter of Theophilus Howard, second earl of Suffolk. Villiers entered St John's College, Cambridge, on 17 March 1671, aged sixteen. Villiers's father was very much a courtier and in 1676 Villiers obtained the reversion of his father's post as knight marshal. Together with his sister Elizabeth *Villiers (who may later have become William III's mistress), Villiers accompanied Princess Mary to the Netherlands in 1677 on the occasion of her marriage to William of Orange. On 8 December 1681 Villiers was licensed to marry Barbara (1662/3–1735), daughter of William Chiffinch, keeper of the backstairs to Charles II. Villiers returned with William in 1688 and was soon a favourite of the new court. He became Queen Mary's master of horse in February 1689 and succeeded his father in July. On 20 March 1691 he was created Baron Villiers of Hoo and Viscount Villiers of Dartford. He was made ranger of Hyde Park in 1693, a post he kept until February 1702. However, the death of Queen Mary on 28 December 1694 made his office as master of the horse redundant.

Villiers was then employed as a diplomat, being named on 17–18 May 1695 as envoy-extraordinary to the states general of the United Provinces and arriving in Rotterdam on 8 July. On 26 February 1697 he was made envoy-extraordinary and -plenipotentiary to the peace conference at Ryswick, and at the suggestion of the earl of Sunderland he was made a lord justice of Ireland in April 1697. His Catholic wife may have caused Villiers problems in this regard, but he did not leave the United Provinces until November of that year. Before his return he was created, on 13 October 1697, earl of Jersey and was made a privy councillor on 25 November 1697. On 26 July 1698 he was made ambassador-extraordinary to France, and arrived in Paris on 11 September 1698; he spent part of November and December in the Netherlands, and returned from France on 26 May 1699.

Although a nominal tory, Jersey was primarily a courtier, and moreover a friend of the new court favourite the earl of Albemarle. This no doubt smoothed his appointment on 13 May 1699 as secretary of state for the southern department, taking the senior secretaryship even though he was technically junior to James Vernon. As befitted his new office he was named a lord justice in June 1699, when William III was away on the continent during the summer. Jersey was also a signatory of the second partition treaty, even though he and Albemarle intrigued against it, possibly because he was not included in most of the negotiations. Jersey was also now one of the key ministerial servants in the House of Lords and acted as a conduit of information for the king. Thus, when the houses became deadlocked over the resumption of Irish forfeited estates in April 1700 it was Jersey whom Henry Boyle sought out to communicate with the king, and Jersey who lobbied peers to avoid the loss of the bill (which included the land tax) and back down over amending the bill. In June 1700 he exchanged his secretaryship for the post of lord chamberlain. In May–June 1701 Jersey came under attack from whigs seeking to defend their colleagues under threat of impeachment for their role in the partition treaty, but his affinity with the new tory ministry protected him, and Speaker Harley ruled an attempt to impeach him as out of order. This did not prevent his voting on 17 June 1701 against the acquittal of Lord Somers.

Jersey retained his office as lord chamberlain following the accession of Queen Anne in March 1702, but his relations with the queen were somewhat frosty, probably owing to the perceived slights suffered by the queen when Princess Anne after she had come into conflict with her sister and retired from court in February 1692. As it was, his son lost a lucrative post as teller of the exchequer. In fact Jersey was one of many tory politicians in office at the beginning of Anne's reign. However, he was also critical of the military strategy of the duke of Marlborough and by June 1703 he was described as one of those who 'does not do the Queen that service they ought to do' (Snyder, 1.202). He voted in favour of both the first and second occasional conformity bills in 1703. His dismissal in April 1704 for persistently obstructing the policies of Godolphin and Marlborough brought protests from the earl of Nottingham and a personal justification from Jersey to the queen as he was reported to be 'extremely surprised, not being conscious of any crime of omission or commission that might deserve such a disgrace' (ibid., 1.284n.).

Jersey joined the tories in opposition. When a tory propagandist in *The Memorial of the Church of England* cast aspersions on Marlborough's and Godolphin's commitment to the church, Marlborough laughed at the idea of Jersey as a pillar of the church given that he 'would have been a Quaker or any other religion that might have pleased the late king' (Snyder, 1.475). He was omitted from the privy council following the union with Scotland in 1707. Jersey voted on 20 March 1710 in favour of a lenient punishment following the impeachment of Dr Sacheverell. The new ministry formed under Robert Harley later in 1710 would have liked to employ Jersey, possibly in the Admiralty, but this proposal foundered on the queen's obstinate refusal to employ him on the grounds that he

was a Jacobite. Jersey certainly had good links in the diplomatic community and among the Catholics to act as a secret agent in Harley's peace strategy, as it was Jersey who met with Gaultier and thus initiated the process which ended at Utrecht. The death of the duke of Newcastle in July 1711 presented a suitable opportunity to reward Jersey with the post of lord privy seal, aided by Jersey's disavowal of his Jacobitism in a letter to Harley. Unfortunately on the morning of 26 August, the day his appointment was to be made public, he collapsed at his house near St James's and died of a 'gout in his stomach or apoplexy, or both' (Swift, 345). He was in his fifty-sixth year.

Jersey was buried on 4 September in Westminster Abbey. Macky's comment was that 'he hath gone through all the great offices of the kingdom with a very ordinary understanding' (GEC, *Peerage*). Jersey died in debt and his wife sold what she could and fled to France with her youngest son, Henry. This caused considerable embarrassment to Jersey's heir, William, and was made worse by her Catholicism and Jacobitism, which saw him created a Jacobite peer. She died in Paris on 22 July 1735.

Jersey's eldest son and successor, **William Villiers**, second earl of Jersey (*c*.1682–1721), politician, was known as Viscount Villiers from 1697 to 1711. Villiers entered Queens' College, Cambridge, in 1699, and graduated MA in 1700. He was appointed teller of the exchequer in 1701, but on the accession of Queen Anne in 1702 exchanged the post for a pension. On 22 March 1705, at Hampstead, he married Judith Herne (*d*. 1732), daughter of Frederick Herne, a London merchant. They had two sons, William, later third earl of Jersey (*d*. 1769), and Thomas *Villiers, later first earl of Clarendon (1709–1786), and a daughter, Barbara. Both Lord and Lady Villiers gained reputations for extramarital affairs. In May 1705 he was elected member of parliament for Kent, but his performance was criticized and he did not seek re-election in 1708. He succeeded his father as earl of Jersey in 1711, and supported the Oxford ministry in the Lords. He remained a tory following the fall of Oxford and the accession of George I. His mother's overt Jacobitism led him to be arrested on suspicion of treason in 1715; he was created earl of Jersey in the Jacobite peerage by the Stuart pretender, 'James III', in 1716. He was in Paris on grounds of ill health in 1718, and died at Castlethorpe, Buckinghamshire, on 13 July 1721, and was buried on 23 July at Westerham, Kent, near the family home of Squerries. He left his wife, Judith, 'having refused to settle her lands on her children, and for other sufficient reasons not proper to be mentioned here' (GEC, *Peerage*, 7.89), one shilling. STUART HANDLEY

Sources GEC, *Peerage* · D. B. Horn, ed., *British diplomatic representatives, 1689–1789*, CS, 3rd ser., 46 (1932), 12, 110, 156 · J. L. Chester, ed., *The marriage, baptismal, and burial registers of the collegiate church or abbey of St Peter, Westminster*, Harleian Society, 10 (1876), 192, 223, 272–3 · H. Horwitz, *Parliament, policy and politics in the reign of William III* (1977) · G. S. Holmes, *British politics in the age of Anne*, rev. edn (1987) · E. Gregg, *Queen Anne* (1980) · *The Marlborough–Godolphin correspondence*, ed. H. L. Snyder, 3 vols. (1975) · M. E. Villiers, *Records of* the family of Villiers, earls of Jersey (1924), 11–16 • J. Swift, *Journal to Stella*, ed. H. Williams, 2 vols. (1948); repr. (1974), 345 • G. M. Trevelyan, 'The "Jersey" period of the negotiations leading to the treaty of Utrecht', *EngHR*, 49 (1934), 100–05 • N. Luttrell, *A brief historical relation of state affairs from September 1678 to April 1714*, 6 vols. (1857) • D. Szechi, *Jacobitism and tory politics, 1710–1714* (1984), 182–4 • M. A. Thomson, *The secretaries of state, 1681–1782* (1968)

Archives LMA, MSS | BL, letters to Lord Albermarle, Add. MS 63630 • BL, letters to Lord Lexington, Add. MS 46536 • BL, corresp. with J. Vernon, Add. MSS 40771–40774 • Boston PL, letters to William Blathwayt • CKS, corresp. with Alexander Stanhope • LMA, papers and corresp. with Matthew Prior • Longleat House, Wiltshire, corresp. with Matthew Prior • Northants. RO, corresp. with duke of Shrewsbury • Staffs. RO, letters to Lord Dartmouth • Surrey HC, letters to Edward Nicholas • U. Nott. L., corresp. with Lord Portland

Likenesses H. Rigaud, oils, *c.*1698–1701, St John Cam. • T. Athlone, wash drawing, AM Oxf. • G. Kneller, portrait, Middleton Park, Oxfordshire • Rygault, portrait, Middleton Park, Oxfordshire • oils (as young man), St John Cam.

Wealth at death unknown, but died in debt

Villiers [*married name* Hamilton], **Elizabeth**, **countess of Orkney** (*c.*1657–1733), presumed mistress of William III, was the eldest daughter of Sir Edward Villiers (1620–1689) of Richmond, Surrey, knight marshal of England. Her mother, Frances (1630–1677), was the daughter of Theophilus Howard, second earl of Suffolk, and governess to princesses Mary and Anne. Upon Princess Mary's marriage to William of Orange [*see* William III and II] in 1677 Villiers accompanied her to The Hague. In 1685 rumours about Villiers's intimacy with Mary's husband reached the ears of James II's ambassador Bevil Skelton, who (it was said) sought to drive a wedge between the prince and princess of Orange. As a result, Villiers was expelled from the royal household, along with the servants and chaplain who had conveyed the gossip. Villiers none the less maintained some sort of relationship with William until Mary's death in 1694, when, according to William Whiston, Archbishop Tenison persuaded the widowed king to break off all contact with her. On 25 November 1695 Villiers married the distinguished soldier Lord George *Hamilton (*bap.* 1666, *d.* 1737), who was created earl of Orkney five and a half weeks later. They had several children, among them Frances Lumley-*Saunderson.

Villiers's status as William's mistress was commonly enough regarded as fact in the eighteenth century for Horace Walpole to repeat the story that Catherine Sedley, upon meeting Elizabeth Villiers and the duchess of Portsmouth in a drawing-room at Windsor, cried 'God! who would have thought that we three royal whores should meet *here*' (Walpole, 33.529). But unlike the mistresses of Charles II, she attracted little public comment in William's lifetime. The king was more commonly satirized by his enemies as a sodomite rather than a heterosexual adulterer, while his supporters would not jeopardize the politically useful image of the royal couple as models of conjugal love and moral probity.

Villiers did receive unwelcome public attention during William's reign as a result of the king's gift to her of lands in Ireland formerly belonging to James II. In 1699 the

Elizabeth Villiers [Hamilton], **countess of Orkney** (*c.*1657–1733), by Sir Godfrey Kneller, 1698

commissioners appointed by parliament to investigate the fate of the Irish lands forfeited by Jacobites gratuitously included in their report a final paragraph estimating that the countess of Orkney's property was worth £26,000, a figure which the government claimed was grossly exaggerated by the 'country' party in order to embarrass the king. The lands were then resumed to public use, but Villiers may have been compensated for her loss by payments of £13,000 out of secret service funds in 1701 and 1702. Her lasting contribution to Ireland (or to English interests therein) was the generous endowment of a school at Middletown, Cork, in 1709.

Villiers has often been portrayed as a political intriguer, but evidence of her role is elusive. She doubtless politicked actively to protect her Irish lands. But of her alleged part in Marlborough's fall from favour in 1692 there is little proof beyond the duchess of Marlborough's remark that 'Mrs. Villiers … was my implacable enemy' (*Marlborough–Godolphin Correspondence*, 41). The story that Villiers deliberately promoted Arnold Joost van Keppel, who became earl of Albemarle, in William's affections in order to undermine the power of her hated brother-in-law William *Bentinck, earl of Portland, is perhaps substantiated by a letter of Charles Montagu to Shrewsbury reporting that 'my lord W[harton] has been framing a new scheme, in concert with a fair lady, to make my Lord Albemarle the minister' (Coxe, 533). Her most well-documented political act was her attempt, carried out with great charm but no immediate success, to persuade the earl of Shrewsbury to become secretary of state in 1693–4. The friendship between Villiers and Shrewsbury continued, at least intermittently: in 1710 Godolphin warned Marlborough that '[Orkney's] lady and [Shrewsbury] are all one, and both of them extremely meddling, and 'tis hard to determine which is the greater politician' (Snyder, 3.1497).

As Godolphin's letter suggests, Lady Orkney's loyalties in Anne's reign were not rigid. Her letters to Harley, although they hardly substantiate Swift's claim that 'her advice [was] asked and followed in the most important affairs of state' (*Correspondence of Jonathan Swift*, 5.224), suggest she was sympathetic to Harley's goals and eager to cultivate his favour. Yet, she was also spotted in the company of Harley's enemy the duchess of Marlborough, offering 'a health to her and all that's for the Duke's interest, and total destruction to those that are not for it' (*Portland MSS*, 4.542). It is likely that she kept a foot in each camp.

In the Hanoverian era Lady Orkney remained in the social orbit of the court, hosting both George I and George II at her estate at Cliefden in south Buckinghamshire, on the Thames near Maidenhead. When she appeared at the coronation of George II in 1727 her physical appearance, never regarded as her best asset, was mocked by Mary Wortley Montagu, who gleefully described her 'mixture of fat and wrinkles … considerable pair of bubbys a good deal withered, a great belly that preceded her … the inimitable roll of her eyes, and her grey hair which by good fortune stood directly upright' (*Complete Letters*, 2.85–6). She died on 19 April 1733 in Albemarle Street, London, and was buried at Taplow, Buckinghamshire, six days later. Her eldest daughter inherited the Orkney title.

Like many women of her generation, Villiers expressed herself primarily in conversation rather than writing. Observers as different as Jonathan Swift, who considered her 'the wisest woman I ever saw' (Swift, *Journal to Stella*, 2.558), and the duchess of Marlborough agreed that she was an exceptionally good talker. Only a few of her letters survive. They suggest personal warmth, an interest (though not powerful influence) in politics, and an appealing lack of self-importance. It is a pity there are not more of them; in the absence of a written record, Villiers will remain someone about whom much is said and little known.   RACHEL WEIL

Sources GEC, *Peerage*, new edn · G. de F. Lord and others, eds., *Poems on affairs of state: Augustan satirical verse, 1660–1714*, 7 vols. (1963–75), vols. 5–6 · *The Marlborough–Godolphin correspondence*, ed. H. L. Snyder, 3 vols. (1975) · T. B. Macaulay, *The history of England from the accession of James II*, new edn, ed. C. H. Firth, 6 vols. (1913–15), vol. 6 · [N. Hooke], *An account of the conduct of the dowager duchess of Marlborough … in a letter from herself to my lord* (1742) · *The manuscripts of his grace the duke of Portland*, 10 vols., HMC, 29 (1891–1931), vols. 4–5 · *Report on the manuscripts of his grace the duke of Buccleuch and Queensberry … preserved at Montagu House*, 3 vols. in 4, HMC, 45 (1899–1926), vol. 2 · *Report on the manuscripts of the earl of Denbigh, part V*, HMC, 68 (1911) · Walpole, *Corr.* · *Letters to and from Henrietta countess of Suffolk*, ed. J. W. Croker, 2 vols. (1824) · *The complete letters of Lady Mary Wortley Montagu*, ed. R. Halsband, 2 (1966) · *A biographical history of England, from the revolution to the end of George I's reign: being a continuation of the Rev. J. Granger's work*, ed. M. Noble, 3 vols. (1806) · *Private and original correspondence of Charles Talbot, duke of Shrewsbury*, ed. W. Coxe (1821) · *Letters illustrative of the reign of William III from 1696 to 1708 addressed to the duke of Shrewsbury by James Vernon*, ed. G. P. R. James, 3 vols. (1841) · G. J. Wolseley, *The life of John, duke of Marlborough*, 2 vols. (1894) · H. van der Zee and B. van der Zee, *William and Mary* (1973) · W. Whiston, *Memoirs of the life and writings of Mr William Whiston: containing memoirs of several of his friends also*, 2nd edn, 2 vols. (1753) · J. H. Jesse, *The court of England from the revolution in 1688 to the death of George II*, 3 vols. (1843) · N. A. Robb, *William of Orange: a personal portrait*, 2 vols. (1966) · F. Harris, *A passion for government: the life of Sarah, duchess of Marlborough* (1991) · J. Swift, *Journal to Stella*, ed. H. Williams, 2 vols. (1948) · *The correspondence of Jonathan Swift*, ed. H. Williams, 5 vols. (1963–5) · *Jus regium, or, The king's right to grant forfeitures* (1701) · *Report of the commissioners appointed by parliament to enquire into the Irish forfeitures … 1699* (1700) · C. Smith, *The ancient and present state of the county and city of Cork*, new edn, 2 vols. (1815) · Cobbett, *Parl. hist.*, vol. 5 · *DNB*
Archives BL, Portland MSS, Harley papers · BL, letters to and relating to Betty Villiers, Add. MS 69286
Likenesses G. Kneller, portrait, 1698; Sothebys, 9 July 1969, lot 16 [*see illus.*] · G. Kneller, portrait, priv. coll. · P. Lely, portrait, priv. coll.

Villiers [*née* Twysden], **Frances, countess of Jersey (1753–1821)**, royal mistress and courtier, was born on 25 February 1753 at Raphoe, Donegal, the only daughter (posthumous) of Philip Twysden (1713–1752), bishop of Raphoe, and his second wife, Frances, daughter of Thomas Carter of Robertstown and Rathnally, co. Meath, and his wife, Mary. Her father was descended from the Twysdens of Roydon Hall, in East Peckham, a long-established Kentish family. At his death he was bankrupt. On 26 March 1770 Frances married George Bussy *Villiers, fourth earl of Jersey (1735–1805), extra lord of the bedchamber, of Middleton Park, Middleton Stoney, Oxfordshire, at the house of her stepfather, Colonel James Johnstone, in St Martin-in-the-Fields, London. The couple had at least seven daughters and three sons, including the fox-hunter George *Villiers (1773–1859) [*see under* Villiers, Sarah Sophia Child-], who succeeded to the earldom.

From the mid-1770s Lady Jersey was closely associated with the whig Georgiana, duchess of Devonshire, and the 'Devonshire House circle'. She was intelligent and witty, and in 1777 Richard Brinsley Sheridan satirized her (and Lady Melbourne) as the venomous Lady Sneerwell in *The School for Scandal*. With Georgiana she campaigned for Charles James Fox at the famous 1784 Westminster election. In 1782 she had attracted the amorous attentions of *George, prince of Wales (1762–1830): 'If he is in love with me I cannot help it', she remarked. 'It is impossible for anyone to give another less encouragement than I have' (BL, Hickleton MS A1.2.7). However, during the spring of 1793 she embarked on an affair with him. She was a noted coquette and her other lovers included Frederick *Howard, fifth earl of Carlisle (1748–1825); Georgiana's husband, William *Cavendish, fifth duke of Devonshire (1748–1811); and the diplomat and clerk to the privy council, William Augustus Fawkener (1747–1811), who was said to be the father of one of her daughters (*Diaries of Sylvester Douglas*, 1.88–9). Yet she remained close to her husband, and genuinely grieved when he died. In spite of her affairs, he had been her 'constant companion'. She told Georgiana's sister, Lady Bessborough, 'when all the world deserted her', Villiers had continued to show her

Frances Villiers, countess of Jersey (1753–1821), by John Hoppner, *c.*1795

'undiminish'd and unremitting kindness' (*Lord Granville Leveson Gower*, 2.109).

During 1794 Lady Jersey encouraged the prince of Wales to marry his German cousin Caroline of Brunswick, and in 1795 she was appointed as one of the future princess's ladies of the bedchamber. Her motives for encouraging the marriage puzzled contemporaries, but presumably she wanted to embarrass the prince's 'unofficial' wife, Mrs Fitzherbert. From the first she ridiculed the princess's rough naivety. Lady Jersey was late for her arrival at Greenwich on 4 April, and she censured her costume. When the prince was condemned for immuring the princess in Carlton House, Lady Jersey shared in his unpopularity. 'I thought Lady Jersey was as cunning as a serpent, though not quite as harmless as a dove', remarked Lady Palmerston, prophetically, during May. 'She must feel like her cousin Robespierre (for I am sure they are related) and that ere long she may not be murdered but she will be driven from society' (Connell, 319).

During the spring of 1796 Caroline of Brunswick pressed the prince to have Lady Jersey removed from Carlton House, and she became the subject of an extraordinary private correspondence. Caroline's letters infuriated the prince, who denied that Lady Jersey was his mistress. At the same time she also became the target of a virulent newspaper campaign accusing her of stealing compromising letters from Caroline to her mother, which had been entrusted to her care by Caroline's English tutor, Francis Randolph, and of passing them to the queen, who appears to have favoured her. Day after day she became increasingly vulnerable: a mob forced her to abandon her house

in Pall Mall for her daughter Anne's in Berkeley Square, and in the streets she was hissed and insulted. On 29 June she proffered her resignation. She would have resigned her place far earlier, she told the princess, had not the prince insisted that the step would be regarded as a 'confirmation of every absurd & abominable falsehood'. However, the time had now arrived when she could 'with propriety, withdraw from such persecution & injustice, with the conscious satisfaction of *knowing*' that she had given the 'strongest proofs' of her duty to the royal family (Add. MS 27915, fol. 26). Lord Jersey attempted to defend his wife's reputation from the charge of stealing Caroline's letters, but the matter was never satisfactorily cleared up, and in some circles Lady Jersey remained *persona non grata*. During July 1796 she was burnt in effigy at Brighton. Her life was 'intolerable to endure and more than insipid to describe', she told her friend Edward Jerningham, and her nights were 'sleepless and weary' (Bettany, 247–8). Afterwards she escaped London for Bognor Rocks. The prince arrived in September, and the couple made plans to spend Christmas at Critchell House, near Wimborne Minster. Meanwhile, the prince settled her and her husband in a house in Warwick Street, adjoining Carlton House, which provoked another furore.

During the summer of 1798 the first observable cracks began to appear in Lady Jersey's relationship with the prince; he had an affair with Elizabeth Fox, a former mistress of Lord Egremont, and there was talk of a reconciliation with Mrs Fitzherbert. Determined to separate from her amicably, the prince sent Edward Jerningham, his private secretary Colonel John McMahon, and other friends to negotiate with her. However, Lady Jersey was reluctant to be cast off, and it was not until 1799 that the relationship was unambiguously ended. During the summer of 1799 she moved out of Warwick Street into Stratford Place, and in December there was mention of a settlement. Finally, in January 1800, her husband was dismissed from his position as the prince's master of the horse (a position which he had held since 1795), and she went abroad. On returning to London, she resolved to 'plague' the prince, and they never re-established their former intimacy.

Subsequently Lady Jersey suffered financial problems, and in 1802 her husband was threatened with imprisonment. The earl's death on 22 August 1805 left her without a 'sufficient income to support [her] rank', and during 1811 McMahon encouraged her to apply for a pension. However, the request was ill-received, and she was distressed to appear 'in the disgraceful shape of a beggar!' (*Letters of George IV*, 1.216–17). Her son the fifth earl of Jersey raised her jointure from £1100 to £3500 per annum and paid off her debts 'at different times' (*Creevey Papers*, 368), but her attempts to economize appear to have been unavailing. She died at Cheltenham on 25 July 1821 and was buried in the family vault at Middleton Stoney. Shortly afterwards her papers, including 'great abundance' of letters from George IV, were burned by her executor, Lord Clarendon (ibid., 367).

Lady Jersey was a scintillating society woman, a heady

mix of charm, beauty, and sarcasm. Lady Bessborough once remarked that she could not be happy 'without a rival to trouble and torment' (*Lord Granville Leveson Gower*, 1.359), and clearly she was a practised intrigante. Yet there was also a softer side to her character; she was much concerned with the welfare of her children, and she could be charitable. She relished sophistication and wit, and even her worst enemies acknowledged her intelligence. Her personal attractions were widely admired: Horace Walpole described them as superior to those of the duchess of Devonshire (Walpole, *Corr.*, 25.411); in her prime, she was thin, *soignée*, and elegant. Although the satirists made much of the fact that she was already a grandmother when she began her affair with the prince, even in old age she never straitened her urge to dazzle and sparkle. In 1816 she reportedly said, 'It were better to go to Hell at once than live to be old & ugly' (Farington, *Diary*, 14.4912).

MARTIN J. LEVY

Sources *The correspondence of George, prince of Wales, 1770–1812*, ed. A. Aspinall, 8 vols. (1963–71) · *Georgiana: extracts from the correspondence of Georgiana, duchess of Devonshire*, ed. E. Ponsonby, earl of Bessborough [1955] · C. Hibbert, *George IV*, 1: *Prince of Wales* (1972) · A. Foreman, *Georgiana, duchess of Devonshire* (1998) · M. J. Levy, *The mistresses of King George IV* (1996) · L. Bettany, ed., *Edward Jerningham and his friends: a series of eighteenth century letters* (1919) · Farington, *Diary* · Walpole, *Corr.* · *Lord Granville Leveson Gower: private correspondence, 1781–1821*, ed. Castalia, Countess Granville [C. R. Leveson-Gower], 2nd edn, 2 vols. (1916) · B. Connell, *Portrait of a whig peer* (1957) · *The letters of King George IV, 1812–1830*, ed. A. Aspinall, 3 vols. (1938) · *The diaries of Sylvester Douglas (Lord Glenbervie)*, ed. F. Bickley, 2 vols. (1928) · *The Creevey papers*, ed. H. Maxwell, 3rd edn (1905); repr. (1906) · BL, Hickleton MS A1.2.7 · BL, Add. MS 27915, fol. 26 · *The family of Twysden and Twisden: their history and archives from an original by Sir John Ramskill Twisden*, ed. C. H. Dudley Ward (1939) · G. Villiers, *The correspondence between the earl and countess of Jersey, and the Rev. Dr. Randolph, upon the subject of some letters belonging to H. R. H. the princess of Wales* (1796) · *GM*, 1st ser., 91/2 (1821), 180
Archives BL · Chatsworth House, Derbyshire · LMA · Royal Arch.
Likenesses J. Hoppner, oils, *c*.1795, priv. coll. [*see illus.*] · T. Watson, engraving (after portrait by D. Gardner, 1774), BM
Wealth at death straitened finances: *Creevey papers*, ed. Maxwell

Villiers, François Hüet (1772–1813), painter, was the second son of Jean-Baptiste-Marie Hüet, a French artist, and his wife, Marie-Geneviève, *née* Chevalier. He was born in Paris on 12 or 14 January 1772, and studied under his father. According to Foskett 'He enlisted in 1792 and took up painting professionally on leaving the army' (Foskett, 572). He exhibited portraits at the Paris Salon in 1799, 1800, and 1801, and then settled in London, adopting the name Villiers, from the village of Villiers-sur-Orge where his father owned land. His name appears as both Hüet-Villiers and Villiers-Hüet. He was a versatile artist, drawing landscapes, animals, and architecture, but excelled in his portraits in miniature on ivory, alabaster, and marble, and in larger size in oils and chalk. He was appointed in 1805 miniature painter to the duke and duchess of York, his portraits of whom were engraved, as were also those of Louis XVIII (he was painter to the king of France), the duke and duchess of Angoulême, the duc d'Enghien, and Mrs Quentin. Villiers painted portraits of many actresses and other ladies in mythological character and his *Hebe* was

very popular and frequently engraved. His miniature of the opera singer Angelica Carulani (1806) is in the Victoria and Albert Museum. He exhibited largely at the Royal Academy and other exhibitions from 1803, when he exhibited a self-portrait, until his death, and was a member of the Associated Artists in Water-Colours from 1807 to 1812. He published two sets of etchings: *Rudiments of Cattle* (1805) and *Rudiments of Trees* (1806–7), and made the drawings for some of the plates in R. Ackermann's *History of the Abbey Church of St Peter's Westminster, its Antiquities and Monuments* (1812; letterpress by William Combe). Villiers died at his home in Great Marlborough Street, London, on 28 July 1813, apparently unmarried, and was buried on 1 August in St Pancras churchyard. Examples of Villiers's work in miniature are in the Victoria and Albert Museum, London; the Ashmolean Museum, Oxford; the Royal Collection; and the Musée Condé, Chantilly. At Westminster Abbey are volumes containing drawings by Villiers.

F. M. O'DONOGHUE, *rev.* JOHN-PAUL STONARD

Sources Redgrave, *Artists* · B. Stewart and M. Cutten, *The dictionary of portrait painters in Britain up to 1920* (1997) · Bénézit, *Dict.* · G. Meissner, ed., *Allgemeines Künstlerlexikon: die bildenden Künstler aller Zeiten und Völker*, [new edn, 34 vols.] (Leipzig and Munich, 1983–) · J. Turner, ed., *The dictionary of art*, 34 vols. (1996) · C. Gabillot, *Les Hüet, Jean-Baptiste et ses trois fils* (1892) · D. Foskett, *Miniatures: dictionary and guide* (1987) · *GM*, 1st ser., 83/2 (1813), 197

Villiers, Sir George (*c*.1544–1606). *See under* Villiers, Sir Edward (*c*.1585–1626).

Villiers, George, first duke of Buckingham (1592–1628), royal favourite, was born at Brooksby Hall, Leicestershire, on 28 August 1592. He was the second son of Sir George *Villiers (*c*.1544–1606) [*see under* Villiers, Sir Edward] and his second wife, Mary (*c*.1570–1632), daughter of Anthony Beaumont of Glenfield, also in Leicestershire; he was the brother of John *Villiers, first Viscount Purbeck (1591?–1658), and Christopher *Villiers, earl of Anglesey (*d*. 1630), and the half-brother of Sir Edward *Villiers (*c*.1585–1626).

Early years and rise to favour At ten years of age George Villiers was sent to school at Billesdon, 9 miles south-east of Brooksby, where the vicar, Anthony Cade, had established a reputation for himself as a good teacher. He respected Cade and later acted as his patron, but he was not a natural scholar. He excelled in skills such as dancing, fencing, and riding, and since these were combined with exceptional good looks and charm of manner he was well equipped for life as a courtier. After the death of Sir George Villiers in January 1606 his upbringing became the responsibility of his mother, with whom he enjoyed a loving but stormy relationship. She had no links with courtly circles, but after a brief second marriage she made the acquaintance of Sir Thomas Compton, who was to become her third husband. As the son of a peer and the brother of the future earl of Northampton, Compton had the connections that Mary Villiers lacked, and it was through his agency that Villiers and his elder brother, John Villiers, secured privy council passes in 1609 'to repair unto the parts beyond the seas, to gain experience' (BL, Add. MS 11402, fol. 147*v*).

The two brothers were abroad for some three years,

George Villiers, first duke of Buckingham (1592–1628), by Sir
Peter Paul Rubens, c.1625

spending the last part of that time in Angers, which had
an academy renowned as a finishing school for young
gentlemen. When Villiers returned to England in 1611 he
made his way to London, where he met Sir John Graham, a
gentleman of the king's privy chamber, who advised him
to seek his fortune at court and acted as his mentor and
promoter. It was probably no coincidence that in August
1614 Villiers was at Apethorpe, the Northamptonshire
seat of Sir Anthony Mildmay, when James I came to stay.
The king was known to be susceptible to the charms of
good-looking young men, particularly those whose manners had been polished in France, and Villiers made a good
impression. However, his scope for further advancement
was limited by the fact that the king already had an established favourite, Robert Carr, recently created earl of Somerset. Carr blocked a proposal to appoint Villiers a gentleman of the king's bedchamber, but he could not prevent
his rival being given the post of cupbearer, which entailed
waiting on the king at table. James appreciated the fact
that Villiers, who had been carefully groomed by Sir John
Graham, was well informed about public affairs and
openly praised him for the quality of his conversation.

Somerset had recently married Frances Howard, after
she had been divorced from her first husband, the earl of
Essex. This brought him firmly within the orbit of the
influential Howard family, whose members were in
general supportive of James's policy of friendship with
Catholic Spain, and who were opposed by a protestant
grouping, led by George Abbot, archbishop of Canterbury,
and William Herbert, earl of Pembroke. Despairing of any

change in James's policy while the Howards were in the
ascendant, Abbot and Pembroke took up Villiers and used
him as an instrument to bring about Somerset's downfall—to be followed, they hoped, by that of the Howard
connection. Their efforts were crowned with success in
April 1615, when Villiers was not only appointed gentleman of the bedchamber but was also knighted by James
and given an annual pension of £1000. Later that year, in
August, he and the king occupied the same bed at Farnham Castle, where the king was on progress. Sharing a bed
was not uncommon in the early seventeenth century, and
did not necessarily imply physical intimacy. Yet there was
every indication that the relationship between the king
and Villiers had entered a new phase, and that the days of
Somerset's favour were numbered.

Early in 1616 Somerset and his wife were found guilty of
the murder of Sir Thomas Overbury, formerly Somerset's
close friend and adviser, and although James saved their
lives he ordered them to be imprisoned in the Tower of
London. With Somerset removed from the scene the way
was now open to Villiers, and in January 1616 James made
him master of the horse—a prestigious post which Somerset had long sought but never attained. A few months
later, in April 1616, James appointed Villiers to the Order
of the Garter, and on 27 August, the eve of his favourite's
birthday, he created him Baron Whaddon of Whaddon
and Viscount Villiers. Villiers declined James's offer of the
Sherborne estate, which had previously belonged to Somerset, on the grounds that he did not wish to build his fortunes upon the ruins of his predecessor's, but he agreed to
accept crown lands with the equivalent value of £30,000.
He also benefited from Somerset's fall in that the king
secured for him the office of chief clerk for the enrolment
of pleas in the court of king's bench, worth some £4000 a
year.

James continued to delight in the company of his new
favourite, whom he called affectionately Steenie, a diminutive of Stephen, since St Stephen, according to the Bible,
had a face like an angel. On 6 January 1617—the customary
time for new year's gifts—James elevated Viscount
Villiers to the earldom of Buckingham, and in the following month he was sworn of the privy council. Just under a
year later, on 1 January 1618, James created Buckingham a
marquess. The king made no secret of his feelings for his
favourite. On the contrary, in September 1617 he declared
before his privy councillors that 'he loved the Earl of Buckingham more than any other man' and that they should
not regard this as a defect in his nature. After all, 'Jesus
Christ had done the same as he was doing … for Christ had
his John and he had his George' (*Documentos ineditos para la
historia de España*, 1936–45, 1.101–2).

James took it for granted that his favourites would
marry, and encouraged Buckingham to ask for the hand of
Lady Katherine Manners [see MacDonnell, Katherine,
duchess of Buckingham (1603?–1649)], whose father, the
earl of Rutland, ruled the roost in the part of the world
where Buckingham had grown up. Katherine was an heiress, which no doubt carried weight with Buckingham, but

was far from being a beauty. She was also a Roman Catholic, like her convert father. James would not hear of his favourite marrying a Catholic, and instructed one of his chaplains, John Williams, to persuade Katherine to give up her faith. After a long struggle Katherine did so, and it was Williams who carried out the private marriage service at Lumley House, near Tower Hill, on 16 May 1620. Katherine brought with her a dowry of £10,000 as well as lands worth some £5000 a year, but the marriage was not merely one of convenience. Buckingham loved his wife, and as for Katherine, she told him in 1623 that 'never woman was so happy as I am, for never was there so kind a husband as you are' (Goodman, 2.309–14). They had four children. First, in March 1622, came Mary [see Villiers, Mary, duchess of Lennox and Richmond (1622–1685)], named after Buckingham's mother. Next, in November 1625, was a son, baptized Charles in honour of the new king, but he died before he was two years old. A second son, George *Villiers (1628–1687), was born in January 1628 and in due course succeeded his father as duke of Buckingham. A third son, Francis (1629–1648), who inherited his father's striking good looks, was born in April 1629, by which time Buckingham was dead, but he was killed in July 1648 while fighting for the king in the civil war.

Property, patronage, and office   At the time of his creation as Baron Whaddon, Buckingham had been presented by the king with estates in Buckinghamshire which had come to the crown by forfeit. He was now a landowner in the county from which he drew his titles, but he was eager to acquire property in his native Leicestershire. In 1617 he purchased an estate at Dalby from his former neighbour Sir Edward Noel, and shortly after his marriage he bought Burley on the Hill, in the adjoining county of Rutland. Burley cost him £28,000, and more money was needed as he transformed the existing mansion to suit his own tastes. Burley, however, was too far removed from London to be used regularly, so in July 1622 he bought the Elizabethan mansion of New Hall, just outside Chelmsford in Essex, for £20,000. He also acquired a substantial house at Wanstead, in Essex, from Mountjoy Blount, for whom he procured an Irish baronage.

Although he had official lodgings in the royal palace of Whitehall, Buckingham felt the need for a London residence of his own and in 1621 persuaded the fallen Bacon to hand over York (later Buckingham) House, on the Thames. At the same time he purchased Wallingford House, which had an enviable position overlooking St James's Park. It was worth a great deal more than the £3000 he paid for it, but Viscount Wallingford, the previous owner, was the brother-in-law of Frances Howard, and as part of the bargain Buckingham secured the release of Somerset and Frances from their long imprisonment. The final addition to his London properties came in 1626, when he used the opportunity provided by Cranfield's impeachment to acquire from him the great house at Chelsea which had once belonged to Sir Thomas More. Wallingford House remained Buckingham's principal London home, where his wife and children lived. York House was used mainly for official functions, and for the display of the magnificent collection of pictures which he built up. His adviser on artistic matters was the architect Sir Balthasar Gerbier, who told him in 1625 that

> sometimes when I am contemplating the treasure of rarities which your excellency has in so short a time amassed, I cannot but feel astonishment in the midst of my joy; for out of all the amateurs and princes and kings there is not one who has collected in forty years as many pictures as your excellency has collected in five!   (Goodman, 2.369–76)

Buckingham admired Italian painters, particularly the Venetians. When he was in Spain in 1623 he was so impressed by Titian's portrait of Charles V on horseback that he had a copy made, to be hung in the great hall at York House. He subsequently commissioned an equestrian portrait of himself from Rubens, whom he regarded as the greatest living artist. Buckingham did not confine his collecting activities to paintings. He also acquired sculptures, books, and manuscripts. Like many of his contemporaries he was fascinated by unusual objects from all over the world, made available by the expansion of European commerce, and he assembled a major collection. He was assisted in this by his gardener, John Tradescant, who subsequently established one of the earliest museums in England.

Buckingham spent at least £100,000 on purchasing properties and renovating them, which was far more than he had available from his own resources. In addition to a royal pension of £1000 a year he made £1300 out of a grant of 3d. in the pound on the trade of alien merchants, and £4000 from the clerkship of the king's bench. His estates brought him in £3000 in rents, and other miscellaneous payments raised his 'open' income to about £14,000. He was also in receipt of a concealed income from such things as monopoly grants, 'gifts' in return for patronage, and the profits of acting as the king's agent for the sale of titles and offices, all of which brought in a minimum of £6000 a year. Buckingham, then, had a total income of £20,000, and quite possibly a good deal more, but the demands on his purse were considerable. His income probably did not cover his regular expenditure; it certainly could not have coped with the cost of buying land and houses. He resorted to borrowing, and James was so alarmed about the scale of this that he turned for help to Buckingham's client Lionel Cranfield, whom he had created earl of Middlesex and appointed lord treasurer. A number of complicated transactions took place, involving the surrender to the crown of certain properties belonging to the favourite, and Buckingham was saved from insolvency, but only at considerable cost to the royal exchequer (BL, Trumbull Alphabetical MSS, XVIII, 82).

Although Buckingham paid £30,000 for the Dalby estate this may have been below its market value, for Sir Edward Noel received a baronage in addition to the purchase money. The sale of titles had started before Buckingham appeared on the political scene, but he turned it into a lucrative business. As a result, the eighty-one peerages existent in December 1615 had increased to 126 by the time of his death. The crown profited from the sale of both honours and offices, but the major beneficiary was Buckingham. He specialized in selling Irish titles, and may have been responsible for the creation of a new order of Irish baronets in 1619. He seems to have regarded Ireland as virtually his own preserve, set aside for plunder by the Villiers kin and connection, and his operations there, conducted mainly for financial gain, were subversive of the established government. Taken together with his involvement in the shady underworld of monopolists, financiers, and projectors in early Stuart England, they explain why he became for many members of the political nation the embodiment of corruption.

Buckingham was also blamed for securing titles and offices for his many relatives, though the initiative in this was probably taken by James. His immediate kindred were the first to profit from the king's bounty. His mother was given the title of countess of Buckingham in 1618. His elder brother, John, was appointed groom of the bedchamber in 1616, and elevated to the peerage as Viscount Purbeck in 1619. Christopher Villiers, the favourite's younger brother, became a gentleman of the bedchamber in 1617 and subsequently master of the robes. However, he had to wait until 1623 before being created earl of Anglesey. Buckingham's sister, Susan, had long been married to William Feilding, a Warwickshire gentleman, but as a consequence of her brother's rise to favour her husband became master of the wardrobe and earl of Denbigh. Edward Villiers, Buckingham's half-brother, was knighted in 1616 and subsequently appointed master of the mint and comptroller of the court of wards. At the very end of James's reign he was given the additional office of president of Munster. Edward Villiers married a niece of Sir Oliver St John, for whom Buckingham secured the major post of lord deputy of Ireland. The rapid rise of Buckingham's kindred provoked hostile comment, but a good deal of this arose from envy and it should not be assumed that his actions ran counter to prevailing conventions. When defending himself against impeachment charges in 1626 Buckingham argued that he would have deserved condemnation by 'all generous minds if, being in such favour with his master, he had minded only his own advancement and had neglected those who were nearest unto him' (*JHL*, 3.662).

While Buckingham was to become the major distributor of royal patronage in Jacobean England he never obtained a monopoly—except in the negative sense that he could usually block the promotion of those of whom he disapproved. When the king, as was usually the case, had no strong opinions on an appointment, Buckingham's choice was likely to prevail. If, however, the king chose to intervene directly, the favourite had no choice but to acquiesce. In 1619, for example, James chose Sir George Calvert as secretary of state, ignoring Buckingham's candidates. Similarly, in 1621, when a new lord keeper was needed to replace Sir Francis Bacon, the king disregarded Buckingham's recommendations and selected John Williams, at that time dean of Westminster. Buckingham immediately set about bringing Williams within his circle of influence, showing a typical capacity for making the best of a situation that was not of his own devising.

Patrons expected to be rewarded by their clients, and Buckingham was no exception. Gifts of money, plate, and works of art were significant additions to both his wealth and his prestige, but this does not mean that he was prompted solely by considerations of profit when he advanced the claims of one of his clients. Among the most prominent of these was Sir Francis Bacon, who resented the fact that despite his exceptional talents he had not attained high office. No sooner did Buckingham appear on the scene than Bacon appointed himself as the new favourite's guide and mentor, and, as a consequence, his career at last took off. In 1616 he was made a privy councillor, and in the following year he achieved his ambition of becoming lord keeper—the office which his father had held under Elizabeth. Another of Buckingham's clients who well merited the advancement the favourite procured for him was Lionel Cranfield, a successful merchant turned financier and government adviser. Cranfield, as James later told parliament,

> was an instrument, under Buckingham, for reformation of the household, the navy and the exchequer, Buckingham setting him on and taking upon himself the envy of all the officers; and he himself many a time protested unto me that he had not been able to do me any service in the ministerial part if Buckingham had not backed him in it. (*JHL*, 3.344)

Naval affairs were the responsibility of the lord admiral, Charles Howard, earl of Nottingham. He had won renown when he commanded the English fleet against the Armada, but by 1618 he was over eighty and no longer in control of the principal officers of the navy, who had become bywords for corruption. Buckingham had been informed about the true state of the navy by Cranfield, and was eager to demonstrate that although he had come to prominence on account of his looks he could be of real service to the crown. His lack of seagoing experience was not a major impediment, since the lord admiral's job was mainly administrative. What was needed, apart from good advisers, was energy, commitment, and the support of the king, and on all these counts he was well qualified. This was the logic behind his appointment as lord admiral in January 1619. He decided that the principal officers of the navy should no longer run it as they saw fit. Instead, he transferred responsibility to the reform commissioners, who brought about a steady improvement. When Buckingham became lord admiral the amount spent on the navy exceeded £50,000 a year. By 1624 this figure had been cut to £30,000, yet the number of seaworthy ships had gone up from twenty-three to thirty-five. Officers' pay was increased in 1618, and that for ordinary sailors in 1624. All in all his administration of the navy in the years of peace that lasted until near the end of James's reign was effective and successful. However, the war years were to show that underlying weaknesses remained.

International crisis and the 1621 parliament James gloried in the name of peacemaker, but the prospects of maintaining peace in Europe became markedly worse after 1619, when his son-in-law, Frederick, the elector palatine, who had rashly accepted the offer of the Bohemian crown, was driven out of Prague by forces acting in the name of Ferdinand, the deposed king of Bohemia and now holy Roman emperor. Frederick and his wife, Elizabeth, could not simply return to the Palatinate because Spanish forces had occupied the area on the left bank of the Rhine while the army of the Catholic League was advancing along the right bank. Buckingham was said to be an ardent advocate of the palatine's cause, and strongly approved of James's decision to send a volunteer force to the Palatinate to garrison a number of key towns. His initial enthusiasm cooled as a result of a clash with Frederick's ambassador, who rejected his nomination of Sir Edward Cecil as commander of this force, but he nevertheless contributed the large sum of £5000 to the voluntary benevolence which James authorized as a means of financing it.

The benevolence was at best a short-term palliative. For more substantial support a parliament was necessary, and James summoned one to meet in January 1621. Apart from the short-lived Addled Parliament of 1614 this was the first meeting for eleven years, and the Commons were certain to seize the opportunity to make known to the king the grievances of which their constituents complained. The principal grievance concerned the abuse of monopolies. These were licences, or patents, either sold or given by the crown, granting the patentees the sole right to engage in a specific activity. Buckingham was not a monopolist himself, but he had secured a number of grants for members of his family. The most notorious of these was the patent for regulating inns, which had been acquired by Sir Giles Mompesson, the brother-in-law of Sir Edward Villiers, on the understanding that the profits—mainly gained from extortion—would be shared with Sir Edward and Christopher Villiers. Another monopoly in which Sir Edward was involved was that for the manufacture of gold and silver thread. Before the session opened Buckingham had been advised by Bacon to 'put off the envy of these things (which I think in themselves bear no great fruit) and rather take the thanks for ceasing them than the note for maintaining them' (*Works of Francis Bacon*, 14.148–9). The advice was timely, for no sooner had parliament opened than the Commons mounted an attack upon Mompesson, who was one of its members. Mompesson appealed to Buckingham for help, but promptly went into hiding, thereby implicitly acknowledging his guilt. Attention then turned to the role of Sir Edward and Christopher Villiers, but Buckingham warded off criticism of himself by assuring members of both houses that if his two brothers were guilty of malpractice 'he would not protect them; but we should see that the same father who begot them that were the offenders begot a third that would get them to be punished' (W. Notestein and others, eds., *Commons Debates, 1621*, 7 vols., 1935, 2.212).

Buckingham's insistence that he, like James, had been misled by the spurious claims of monopoly seekers switched the attention of the Commons to the referees whom the king appointed to scrutinize all projected patents and report on whether they were in accordance with law and for the public good. Among the principal referees was Bacon, now lord chancellor, and the Commons' investigations revealed that he had taken bribes. They transmitted this information to the Lords and called on them to take appropriate action. Bacon, who had retired to his sickbed, appealed to Buckingham, whom he described as 'my anchor in these floods' (*Works of Francis Bacon*, 14.225), but although the favourite made repeated visits to his mentor he did not intervene on his behalf. In the event, Bacon acknowledged his guilt and was sentenced by the Lords to loss of office, imprisonment, and a heavy fine. Buckingham was the only member of the upper house to vote in Bacon's favour.

Further problems for Buckingham arose when the Lords questioned the attorney-general, Sir Henry Yelverton, about the heavy-handed way in which he had enforced the patent for gold and silver thread. Yelverton responded by throwing all the blame upon Sir Edward and Christopher Villiers and claiming that 'my lord of Buckingham was ever at his majesty's hand, ready upon every occasion to hew me down'. He added that 'if my lord of Buckingham had but read the articles exhibited in this place against Hugh Spencer, and had known the danger of placing and displacing officers about a king, he would not have pursued me with such bitterness' (*JHL*, 3.121). The house was shocked by the comparison of Buckingham with the Despensers, the hated favourites of Edward II, and James even more so. 'If he Spencer', said the king, 'I Edward II ... I had rather be no king than such a one as King Edward II' (*Camden Miscellany*, 20, CS, 3rd ser., 83, 1953, 33). It may be that Buckingham's enemies in the upper house had planned to use Yelverton as an instrument to procure his downfall, but if so they overplayed their hand. The Lords, to whom James had remitted Yelverton's judgment, had no choice but to find him guilty and sentence him to fines and imprisonment—though Buckingham immediately remitted the fine of 5000 marks which had been imposed for the slur upon his honour.

Buckingham had been a regular attender in the Lords during the first session of the 1621 parliament, but was rarely present in the second, which opened in November 1621, since the king demanded his company in the hunting field. A decisive moment in the debates came when Sir George Goring, acting on Buckingham's instructions, suggested that the Commons should draw up a petition to the king proposing that if the Spaniards intensified the fighting in Germany by continuing to assist the emperor, James should announce his readiness to redress the balance by entering the conflict. The Commons followed Goring's suggestion, but extended its terms by asking that the prince of Wales should be married to a protestant. This infuriated James, who was engaged in delicate negotiations for Charles to marry a Spanish princess. His angry response to the Commons' petition set in train a course of events that led to the abrupt dissolution of parliament. Many people accused Buckingham of bringing this about in order to prevent further attacks upon himself, and in particular to blunt the effectiveness of the commission of inquiry into the governance of Ireland which James, at

Cranfield's prompting, had agreed to set up. Buckingham was virtually the sole channel of communication between the king at Newmarket and parliament and the privy council in London, and could conceivably have limited the amount of information that James received, and encouraged him to take a hard line with the Commons. But James was never merely a cipher. He had strong opinions of his own, not least upon the role of the Commons, and it may well be that Buckingham was acting as the executant of the king's policy rather than pursuing his private interests. Goring's motion could have been an attempt on James's part to strengthen his hand in the negotiations with Spain by demonstrating the strength of popular feeling on the palatine issue. If this was his intention, then his anger against the Commons is understandable, for by 'misreading' his message they transformed it into something that was, from the king's point of view, counterproductive. On this issue, as on a number of others, the surviving evidence is inconclusive.

The Spanish match and the road to war, 1623–1625 James was convinced that the best hope for restoring Frederick to the Palatinate lay in co-operation with Spain, and was therefore anxious to conclude the long-drawn-out negotiations for his son's marriage. John Digby, his ambassador at the court of Philip IV, sent back optimistic reports, but these failed to dispel suspicions that the Spanish ministers were not acting in good faith. In order to clarify the situation James dispatched Endymion Porter to Madrid. Porter was a member of Buckingham's household and a relative by marriage; more to the point, he had been brought up in Spain and spoke the language fluently. When he returned to England in January 1623 Porter gave assurances that negotiations for both the marriage and the restoration of the Palatinate were well advanced. However, he revealed to Buckingham his suspicion that the count of Olivares, Philip IV's chief minister, was opposed to both projects. This news was unwelcome to Prince Charles, who was in his twenty-third year and eager to be married, and he may have been the author of the plan to make an unannounced journey overland to Spain, since, by arriving in person in Madrid, he would compel Philip and Olivares to reveal their true intentions. If this interpretation is correct, the prince would have turned to Buckingham for assistance in winning James's consent. James did eventually agree, but only on condition that Buckingham accompanied his son. Buckingham and Charles set out for Paris, disguised and under assumed names, on 18 February 1623, and on 7 March they arrived at Digby's house in Madrid.

The prince and Buckingham spent the next six months in Spain, and in the course of firsthand encounters with Philip IV and his ministers Buckingham was made aware that their principal objective was the maintenance and increase of Habsburg power in Europe, with little regard to English interests. The Spaniards demanded further concessions on the treatment of English Catholics before they would agree to the marriage, and Olivares believed that the prince would have been prepared to accept these, had it not been for Buckingham's countervailing pressure.

Relations between the two favourites deteriorated, and in one of his letters home Buckingham blamed 'the foolery of the Conde of Olivares' for the failure to complete the negotiations. He accused the Spaniards of 'first delaying us as long as possibly they can. Then, when things are concluded of, they thrust in new particulars, in hope they will pass, out of our desire to make haste' (BL, Harley MS 6987, fol. 107). The articles of marriage were eventually drawn up and accepted by both sides, but the Spaniards refused to allow the infanta to leave until a papal dispensation had arrived. They were hoping that the prince would stay on, while Buckingham returned home, but by this time even Charles was distrustful of the Spaniards' promises, especially since there had been no agreement on their part to assist in the recovery of the Palatinate. Buckingham and the prince therefore decided to leave Madrid at the end of August 1623 and to make their way to Santander, where an English fleet awaited them.

Buckingham had taken a risk by absenting himself from England, and in particular from James, for so long a period. Even before he left there had been talk of the king's increasing fondness for Cranfield's brother-in-law, Arthur Brett, and Buckingham ensured that the young man was sent into temporary exile. Yet James remained as attached as ever to his favourite. He delighted in the frequent letters—beginning with 'Dear Dad and Gossip' and signed by 'Your humble slave and dog'—which Buckingham wrote on behalf of himself and the prince, and responded with his own to 'My sweet boys'. One of James's letters, sent in May, informed Buckingham that he was now a duke, and Buckingham wrote a fulsome reply thanking the king for the way in which he had 'filled a consuming purse, given me fair houses, more land than I am worthy of to maintain both me and them, [and] filled my coffers so full with patents of honour that my shoulder cannot bear more' (BL, Harley MS 6987, fol. 153). James longed for the return of his 'dear venturous knights' (G. P. V. Akrigg, ed., *Letters of King James VI & I*, 1984, 388) and when the two young men reached Royston on 6 October the warmth of his reception was unmistakable. Yet Buckingham was no longer the uncritical executant of royal policy that he had been before the Spanish journey, nor was Prince Charles. James complained that when the prince set out for Spain he had been

> as well affected to that nation as heart could desire, and as well disposed as any son in Europe; but now he was strangely carried away with rash and youthful counsels and followed the humour of Buckingham, who had he knew not how many devils within him since that journey. (*Cabala*, 276)

The prince had returned without his bride, though negotiations for the marriage had not yet been formally broken off, and Buckingham was convinced that the expansion of Habsburg power was a threat to England as well as other states, and would have to be resisted. He was clearly envisaging war with Spain, but he needed the support of parliament, not simply to win over the ever-hesitant James but also to rally public opinion behind his policy and ensure financial backing for it. As the first step towards a parliament he gave a report on his negotiations to a cabinet-council of leading ministers, but these were divided in their response. Even those who were eager for a change of course found it hard to accept that a man who had been so closely identified with the king's pro-Spanish stance had really changed his spots. Buckingham would probably not have secured majority support if he had been acting alone. However, with Prince Charles firmly behind him he succeeded in doing so, and James thereupon agreed to summon the parliament which began its session in February 1624.

Buckingham had prepared the way for a constructive meeting by making conciliatory gestures towards his principal opponents in the Lords and establishing close contacts with his former critics in the Commons. He also addressed a meeting of both houses, giving them a detailed account of all that happened during the time that he and the prince had spent in Spain, and making plain his belief that it was futile and dangerous to rely upon Spanish promises. He ended by calling on the assembled members to decide whether they should advise James to continue the negotiations with Spain or 'to trust in his own strength and to stand upon his own feet' (Rushworth, 1.125). Buckingham would have liked parliament to make a speedy vote of supply, not simply to enable the fleet to be set out but, even more important, to show James that his subjects could be trusted to support him if he took a firm line against Spain. However, James, like Buckingham, was a hostage to his former attitudes, and members of parliament had good reason for fearing that any moneys they voted would be frittered away. Conversely, James had been taught by experience that parliaments were generous in their promises of assistance but unforthcoming when it came to putting them into effect. Years of mutual distrust could not be swept away overnight, particularly since there was no agreement over policy objectives. Buckingham, like most members of parliament, wanted a sea war against Spain. James, on the other hand, was thinking in terms of a limited military campaign in the Palatinate. He had not broken off his contacts with the Spanish envoys in England and still hoped to secure a resolution of the crisis through diplomacy.

Buckingham could not openly advocate a sea war against Spain for fear of alienating the king. At the same time he could not confine himself to pressing for military action in the Palatinate, since this would have lost him support in parliament. He therefore pursued a deliberately ambiguous policy, encouraging all the parties involved to feel that he was advancing their interests and playing down the significance of any differences that became apparent. His assumption was that once war was in progress the course of events would dictate appropriate responses. However, the path to war proved to be tortuous, and by acting as the link figure between the king and parliament Buckingham was in constant danger of losing the confidence of both. His frequent visits to court served to keep James in line, but only at the cost of straining personal relations, as was shown when the king accused him of using 'cruel, Catonic words' (BL, Harley MS 6987, fol. 196). Meanwhile, the Spanish envoys were mounting a propaganda campaign against the duke, alleging that he intended to keep James permanently in the country while he took over the reins of government himself. The sudden reappearance on the scene of Arthur Brett was another alarm signal. Buckingham had already lost patience with Brett's brother-in-law, Lionel Cranfield, earl of Middlesex, for opposing war with Spain on financial grounds, and also for continuing his efforts to combat corruption— much of it linked with the Villiers connection—in Ireland. The favourite now struck back by instigating the lord treasurer's impeachment in April 1624. Middlesex's cost-cutting measures, while benefiting the crown, had alienated all those who profited from James's largesse, and his abrasive manner had won him few friends. Overthrowing Middlesex was therefore calculated to increase Buckingham's popularity at the same time as it removed a threat to his policies and position.

By April 1624 Buckingham had persuaded the Commons to give the first reading to a subsidy bill in return for a formal assurance, which he delivered to both houses, that the king had broken off negotiations with Spain. He had also persuaded James to receive the mercenary commander, Count Mansfeld, who had offered his services for the recovery of the Palatinate. At the same time Buckingham, despite the lack of parliamentary funding, had set on foot preparations for a naval expedition against the Spaniards, in which he invited the Dutch to join. The conflicting pressures upon him contributed to a breakdown in his health, but although this removed him for some six weeks from his central role, it had the advantage of restoring his position with James. The king came to see him frequently, sent gifts of fruit, and gave repeated assurances that he loved and trusted him as much as ever. Buckingham was profuse in his thanks to his sovereign, whom he described as 'my purveyor, my goodfellow, my physician, my maker, my friend, my father, my all' (NL Scot., Denmilne MSS 33.1.7, vol. 22, 79).

When he returned to court in mid-June 1624 Buckingham concentrated on concluding an alliance with France, to be cemented by a marriage between Prince Charles and Louis XIII's sister, Henrietta Maria. Negotiations, which began in early April, had been proceeding smoothly, but in June 1624 Louis dismissed his chief minister and replaced him by Cardinal Richelieu, who insisted that no marriage could take place unless James gave a formal promise to relax the persecution of English Catholics. James's immediate reaction was hostile, but Buckingham, working hand in glove with the French ambassador, persuaded him to make a constructive response. The area for compromise was limited by the fact that Prince Charles had given an undertaking in the House of Lords that the terms of a French marriage, if ever it came about, would include no concessions to the recusants at home. This was circumvented when James, under pressure from Buckingham, agreed to give the written assurance that Richelieu required, but only on condition that it should not be included in the formal marriage treaty. In the French negotiations, as with those he had earlier conducted between the king and parliament, Buckingham was working on the assumption that the essential first step was to get the parties committed. Half-truths and ambiguities were part of the price that had to be paid to bring this about, but the pressure of events—or so he hoped—would make these irrelevant by forcing the constituent parts of the anti-Habsburg alliance into ever closer co-operation. This gamble might have paid off had the initial operations been successful. In the event, failure led to accusations of bad faith against Buckingham, who had been the architect of the strategy.

The first fruits of Anglo-French co-operation consisted in an expedition to the Palatinate under the command of Mansfeld. England was to provide 10,000 infantry, while 3000 cavalry were to come from France. If Buckingham had been a free agent, as his enemies assumed, the expedition would have had a reasonable chance of success, but James insisted on imposing conditions that prompted the French to draw back. Mutual distrust led to last-minute changes of plan which effectively sabotaged Mansfeld's expedition. His troops were held so long on board ship, waiting for agreement on where they should go, that infection set in and they died like flies. Matters were no better when the survivors arrived in the Netherlands, for the winter quarters provided for them were inadequate and food supplies exiguous. News of the disintegration of Mansfeld's army had a profound effect upon English public opinion, and responsibility for the failure was firmly pinned upon Buckingham.

The death of James I in March 1625 could have entailed the end of Buckingham's influence, for history had few examples of favour being transferred from a reigning monarch to his successor. However, during the journey to Spain in 1623 the relationship between Buckingham and the prince of Wales had developed into a deep friendship, and one of Charles's first actions after he ascended the throne was to assure the duke that his favour would continue into the new reign. It might have been better for Charles if he had not done so, for Buckingham was now the object of suspicion and even hatred among the king's subjects, but Charles saw no reason to dispense with the services of a man he trusted and who shared his own views on how to respond to the crisis in Europe. A key element in their strategy was to cement the alliance with France, and Buckingham hoped to do this when he went to Paris in May 1625. The official purpose of his visit was to bring back the king's bride, Henrietta Maria, but he took the opportunity to hold discussions with Richelieu designed to commit France to an anti-Habsburg league. The timing of his initiative was unfortunate, for the Huguenots of La Rochelle, alarmed by the accession to power of a man they regarded as a hardline Catholic, had taken up arms in self-defence. Richelieu regarded it as axiomatic that as long as the Huguenots were in revolt against Louis's authority France could not risk foreign entanglements. He therefore declined to enter into any new engagements of the sort that Buckingham wanted. The duke was not only disappointed; he also had to consider the possibility that Richelieu, as might be expected

from a churchman, put religious before political considerations and was more inclined to *détente* with Catholic Spain than alliance with protestant England. If this were the case, then Richelieu would have to be removed from power. The cardinal had many enemies at court, not least the queen, Anne of Austria, to whom Buckingham expressed his devotion in ways that some observers believed exceeded the bounds of decorum. Louis's anger when he heard reports of this became another thread in the tangled skein of Anglo-French relations.

Cadiz and Ré expeditions, 1625–1627 When Charles opened his first parliament in June 1625 he assumed that its members, thankful for the accession of a ruler who shared their desire for active involvement in the European war, would make a generous grant of supply. However, he gave them no indication of how much money was needed, and left to their own devices the Commons granted a mere two subsidies. When Buckingham heard of this he urged his friends and clients in the lower house to push for more, and instructed Sir John Coke, his principal adviser on naval matters, to provide the Commons with a detailed account of the government's financial needs. The Commons refused to enlarge upon their grant, yet money was urgently required for Mansfeld, who was still in the field—though his army now consisted mainly of German mercenaries—and for the king's uncle, Christian IV of Denmark, who was ready to invade north Germany. The greatest need of all was for the fleet which Buckingham was assembling to attack the Spanish coast. The Dutch had already agreed to join in the expedition, but if its departure was delayed until the autumn, when the weather worsened, its prospects of success would be diminished.

Buckingham was insistent that parliament should be recalled for a second session, this time to Oxford, since plague had broken out in London. Charles agreed, and the two houses reassembled at the beginning of August. Although on this occasion they were given full particulars of the king's requirements it became clear when debate opened in the Commons that members had no confidence in Buckingham and were unwilling to finance his strategy. The duke decided to use the tactics that had succeeded so well in 1624 by appearing in person before the two houses and publicly rebutting the complaints made against him. On this occasion, however, he did not succeed in winning over his critics, who now claimed that he was responsible for everything that had gone wrong. The king therefore decided to cut his losses, and on 12 August 1625 he dissolved parliament.

Buckingham had originally planned to lead the expedition against Spain himself, but his health was still far from robust, and he was engaged in negotiations for the formal establishment of an anti-Habsburg alliance that demanded his presence elsewhere. He therefore appointed Sir Edward Cecil, a soldier with long experience fighting for the Dutch, as commander. Charles had raised loans from the City and international financiers to set out the expedition, but shortage of money remained a major problem, and continued delays undid much of the work already done. The expedition was not ready to sail until early October, by which time the weather was deteriorating. Despite suffering storm damage in the Bay of Biscay, it managed to reach the Bay of Cadiz, but a half-hearted attempt to assault the town turned into farce when the soldiers stumbled across wine vats and broke them open to quench their thirst. Cecil's army was transformed into a drunken rabble, incapable of fighting, and he had no alternative but to re-embark it and sail for home. Food and water were now running short and infection had set in. Both soldiers and sailors were in such bad shape that the journey back to England was a nightmare, and when the ships at last straggled into harbour their crews looked like skeletons. Among those who witnessed this inglorious return was Sir John Eliot, and in the 1626 parliament he expressed a sense of outrage, focused on Buckingham, which was widely felt: 'our honour is ruined, our ships are sunk, our men perished, not by the sword, not by an enemy, not by chance, but … by those we trust' (Eliot, 1.155).

While the Cadiz expedition was making its way home Buckingham was in The Hague to sign a treaty with Danish and Dutch representatives which committed their respective countries to joint military action for the restoration of the Palatinate and the containment of Habsburg power. He hoped that France would join the alliance, but the situation was complicated, as always, by the Huguenot revolt. In late 1624, when France had been planning an attack upon Genoa, which was a Spanish satellite, Louis had asked the Dutch and the English to lend warships to blockade the port. Both states made a positive response, but after the outbreak of the Huguenot revolt there were fears that the ships might be used against La Rochelle. The Dutch could do little about this, for they had already handed over their vessels, but Buckingham engaged in delaying tactics until assured that peace had been concluded between Louis and the rebels. This assurance proved incorrect, but because of their late arrival the English vessels, unlike the Dutch, played only a minor part in the naval engagement in early September in which the Huguenot fleet was virtually destroyed. This did not prevent Buckingham's detractors from asserting that he had connived with the French to defeat the Huguenots instead of defending them, as a good protestant ought to have done.

Buckingham was eager to see the dispute between Louis and the Huguenots resolved, for, as he told the French ambassador, it was impeding the creation of 'a great union of all the states which are apprehensive about the power of Spain' (PRO, Baschet transcripts, 31/3, bundle 62, fol. 159v). He therefore dispatched two trusted envoys, the earl of Holland and Sir Dudley Carleton, to France to try to reconcile the warring parties. This they succeeded in doing in January 1626, and he was hopeful that Richelieu would now commit France to the objectives of the Hague treaty, even if he preferred to remain outside the formal alliance. Holland and Carleton were given assurances to this effect, yet while Richelieu was talking about a forthcoming military campaign in Italy, he was secretly negotiating a settlement with Spain which would restore peace to the Peninsula. When news of this leaked out it revived all the earlier doubts about the cardinal's exact intentions and made it imperative to consider the possibility of concerted action to remove Richelieu from power.

Since any action would require money the king summoned parliament to meet in February 1626. Before it did so Buckingham called a conference at York House to discuss the vexed question of Arminianism. The Arminians, who formed a minority high-church group within the Church of England, were regarded by the non-Arminian majority as crypto-Catholics. It was widely assumed that Buckingham—whose mother and father-in-law, as well as many of his friends, were Catholic—was himself an Arminian sympathizer, and he was under pressure from his critics to make his position plain. There was no doubt that if he aligned himself with the anti-Arminians, his relationship with parliament would improve, and the York House conference, which took place on 11 and 17 February 1626, provided an appropriate opportunity. The key question was whether he would support the anti-Arminians' proposal that the established church should adopt the articles drawn up by the Synod of Dort, held in the Netherlands in 1619, which formally condemned the principal Arminian positions. In the event, Buckingham—who was aware that the king inclined towards the Arminians— refused to do so, and although the York House conference ended inconclusively it left Buckingham exposed to the wrath of the anti-Arminians who dominated the House of Commons.

Parliament met under the shadow of the failed Cadiz expedition, and the Commons set up a committee to identify the causes of the evils by which the state was afflicted and to propose remedies. The committee decided that Buckingham was the principal cause and that he should therefore be impeached. In the charges presented to the Lords on 8 May 1626, he was accused of holding too many offices; of delivering English ships into French hands for use against the Huguenots; of selling honours and offices; of procuring titles for his kindred; and, finally, of poisoning James I. In his reply to the charges, which he made on 8 June, Buckingham acknowledged that he had been 'raised to honour and fortunes … beyond my merit' but insisted that 'what I have wanted in sufficiency and experience … I have endeavoured to supply by care and industry'. He dealt with the charges one by one, giving his version of disputed issues, and ended with the assertion that 'his love and duty to his country have restrained him and preserved him (he hopeth) from running into heinous and high misdemeanours and crimes' (JHL, 3.656, 663).

Impeachment was a legal process, dependent upon proof, but there was no clear evidence of either criminal intent or activity in Buckingham's case. The attack on the favourite was essentially political, and was aimed at removing him from the king's counsels. But Charles saw no reason to abandon him, especially since, as the king had already made plain, 'he hath not meddled or done anything concerning the public or commonwealth but by special directions and appointment, and as my servant' (Rushworth, 1.217). Far from deserting Buckingham he exerted all his influence to ensure that the duke acquired yet another prestigious office, namely the chancellorship of Cambridge University, in June 1626. Charles believed the attack upon the favourite was really aimed at himself and monarchical rule in England. Rather than allow the impeachment to continue its course before the Lords, who could no longer be relied upon to throw out the charges, he dissolved parliament.

Before the dissolution the Commons had decided, in principle and as a quid pro quo for Buckingham's dismissal, to vote three subsidies. Charles and his councillors now decided to raise the equivalent amount by means of a forced loan. This would enable the king to continue supporting his allies in the anti-Habsburg league. Buckingham was more than ever convinced that the key to success for the league was to be found in Paris, but there was continuing uncertainty about the true nature of French intentions. Richelieu's decision to assume responsibility for naval matters and begin construction of a powerful French fleet implied a threat to England of which Buckingham, as lord admiral, was particularly conscious. Of more immediate concern was the French seizure of the entire English wine fleet, lying in harbour at Bordeaux in late 1626, in retaliation for the English capture of French vessels accused of trading with Spain. Buckingham riposted by sending a fleet under the command of one of his best captains, John Pennington, to cruise up and down the French coast and 'intercept and take … all French, Dunkirkers' and Spanish ships and goods as shall come out of the Low Countries for the use of the French king' (BL, Add. MS 37817, fol. 31v).

As evidence of Richelieu's apparent untrustworthiness mounted, Buckingham became convinced that the cardinal must be overthrown. He planned to achieve this by fusing the discontents of peripheral states such as Savoy and Lorraine with those of the Huguenots and the French nobility, who deeply resented Richelieu's monopoly of power. Knitting together these various elements was a complex operation, and nothing effective would be accomplished without a clear lead from England. Buckingham planned to provide this by a combined naval and military expedition to the island of Ré, off La Rochelle. The capture of Ré would inhibit French attempts to blockade the Huguenot stronghold and also enable reinforcements to be sent in if Richelieu launched a direct attack. More important, it would be a major blow to Richelieu's reputation and weaken his hold on power.

Charles I's financial position had eased as the proceeds of the forced loan came in, especially as these were supplemented by the sale of goods and ships taken by Pennington. As a consequence the expedition which Buckingham assembled was far better prepared than that for Cadiz. The fleet arrived off the south-eastern tip of Ré on 12 July 1627 and the troops were successfully landed, although they suffered losses from attacks by enemy cavalry. Five days later the army reached St Martin, the main town on the island, and invested the citadel into which the French defenders had withdrawn. By the end of September the garrison was close to capitulation, and one of the leading Huguenot nobles, the duke of Rohan, subsequently gave his opinion that if the citadel had fallen 'there was every possibility of a great change in the face of affairs' (*Mémoires Du Duc de Rohan*, 1675, 207). However, Richelieu, who had taken personal charge of the French forces on the nearby mainland, dispatched a convoy of small ships which slipped through the English blockading fleet and brought supplies to the starving garrison. There was no prospect now of a swift victory for Buckingham's army, and his officers advised him to withdraw from Ré before the onset of winter, particularly since the reinforcements sent from England had been too little and too late. Buckingham made one last attempt to capture the citadel, this time by storming it, but his troops were beaten off by the defenders. He then gave the order to retreat, but the way to the ships was blocked by French forces sent over from the mainland. The English had to fight their way through, and suffered heavy casualties. Buckingham's army numbered nearly 8000 when it set out for Ré, but only 3000 returned to Portsmouth in November 1627.

1628 parliament and assassination The failure of the Ré expedition made Buckingham even more unpopular, if such a thing was possible, and anonymous ballads spread the message that 'These things have lost our honour, men surmise: Thy treachery, neglect and cowardice' (Fairholt, 24). He was also held responsible for actions such as the levying of the forced loan, the imprisonment of resisters, and compulsory billeting of troops that seemed to threaten fundamental English liberties. Yet Charles, who blamed himself for not ensuring the timely dispatch of supplies and reinforcements to Ré, had no intention of abandoning either Buckingham or the policies which they had jointly formulated. The immediate need was to secure the English coast against privateers and enemy forces, and in February 1628 the lord admiral ordered the construction of ten pinnaces 'of extraordinarily good sail … and with the most advantage as may be for sailing and rowing' (PRO, SP 16, 94, 37). He also ended the reign of the navy commissioners, whom he blamed for the failure to cope with the demands of wartime, and restored control to the principal officers. Changes in administrative structures, however, could not compensate for the crippling shortage of money. Only parliament could provide the solution, but Charles was reluctant to summon one unless he had some assurance that it would not renew the attack upon Buckingham. However, there was by now a general recognition that disharmony between the king and his subjects had reached dangerous heights and that some sort of reconciliation must be attempted. It was against this background that the king sent out writs for his third parliament, which met on 17 March 1628.

In response to detailed expositions of the government's policy the Commons decided, in principle, to offer the king five subsidies, worth over a quarter of a million pounds. Charles welcomed this as a positive step, but the offer was conditional on his acceptance of a petition of right, confirming English liberties. Debates on the wording lasted until early June, and Buckingham spent much of this time trying to persuade the Lords that a clause explicitly confirming the king's prerogative powers should be inserted. However, his influence had been diminished by the retreat from Ré and the subsequent failure of an expedition to La Rochelle, sent out under the command of his brother-in-law, the earl of Denbigh. In the end the Lords agreed to go along with the Commons, and Buckingham accepted their decision. He was now involved in preparations for another expedition, to be led by himself, but these were hamstrung by the continuing shortage of money, and nothing would be forthcoming until the petition had passed through all its stages. This process was virtually completed by 2 June, when the king gave his response, but since it was not in the traditional form it deprived the petition of its quasi-statutory status. The Commons blamed Buckingham for Charles's equivocal reply, and although the king tried to assuage their anxieties by summoning both houses before him and ordering the conventional response to a petition of right to be read, he could not stop them from renewing the attack upon the favourite. In the remonstrance which the Commons presented to Charles on 17 June 1628 they called on him to consider 'whether, in respect the said Duke hath so abused his power, it be safe for your majesty and your kingdom to continue him either in his great offices or in his place of nearness and counsel about your sacred person' (Rushworth, 1.626). Charles had already declared that he was fully persuaded of Buckingham's innocence, 'as well by his own certain knowledge as by the proofs in the cause' (ibid.), and on 26 June 1628 he put an end to further proceedings by bringing the session to a close.

The expedition which Buckingham was now planning included a number of fireships packed with explosives, designed to blow gaps in the floating palisade which the French had constructed to cut off the seaward approaches to La Rochelle. The fleet was assembling at Portsmouth, but the duke remained in London until late July, since his presence was essential if the vital supplies and munitions were to be dispatched on time. Writing to Secretary Conway, who was with the king at Portsmouth, on 6 August, he complained that 'I find nothing of more difficulty and uncertainty than the preparations here for this service of Rochelle. Every man saith he hath all things ready, and yet all remains as it were at a stand' (PRO, SP 16, 112, 32). Shortage of money remained, as always, an intractable problem, and Buckingham was frequently distracted from his principal task by hungry sailors who thronged round his house and coach, demanding relief. The duke caused a proclamation to be set up in the Royal Exchange, reminding the sailors that

> I have done more for you than ever my predecessors did. I procured the increase of your pay to a third part more than it was. I have parted with mine own money to pay you, and engaged all mine own estate for your satisfaction. (Bodl. Oxf., MS Tanner 276, 114)

His commitment to the Huguenot cause did not make him any more popular. The passions aroused by the debates in the Commons had created a climate of barely suppressed violence, and while he provided bodyguards for his own safety he could not protect his associates. These included the astrologer John Lambe, whom he had frequently consulted. On 13 June, the day before the Commons formally adopted the remonstrance against the favourite, Lambe was set upon by a London mob who taunted him with being 'the Duke's devil' and hacked him to death. 'And shortly after', as Rushworth records,

> so high was the rage of people that they would ordinarily utter these words:
> 'Let Charles and George do what they can,
> The Duke shall die like Doctor Lambe.'
> (Rushworth, 1.618)

Before leaving town Buckingham took steps to strengthen his position by rewarding his friends and extending an olive branch to his enemies. The earl of Marlborough, who had succeeded Cranfield as lord treasurer, was replaced by Sir Richard Weston, one of the duke's clients. At the same time Buckingham gave up the lord wardenship of the Cinque Ports, which he had purchased in 1624 in order to complement his authority as lord admiral, to a close friend, the second earl of Suffolk. The bishop of Lincoln, John Williams, and the earl of Arundel, both of them opponents of the duke, were invited to York House and given a warm reception, while one of the duke's most outspoken critics in the lower house, Sir Thomas Wentworth, was created a baron.

Buckingham arrived at Portsmouth, where the expedition was assembling, on 14 August, and established his headquarters at The Greyhound inn, near the dockyard. He kept in close touch with Charles, who had taken up residence at Southwick House, just outside the town. It was while he was preparing to ride over to the king, on 23 August, that Buckingham met his death. He went down into the hall of the inn, which was, as usual, crowded with people, and while he was talking to one of his colonels he was suddenly stabbed through the left breast. The assassin escaped in the confusion but later gave himself up. He was John Felton, a professional soldier who had served under Buckingham in Ré and blamed him for lack of promotion and indebtedness. However, as he later explained, it was 'reading the remonstrance of the House of Parliament' that convinced him that by 'killing the Duke he should do his country great service' (Bodl. Oxf., MS Rawl. B 183, 191).

Buckingham's corpse was carried back to London by coach, appropriately escorted, and lay in state at Wallingford House while preparations were made for the funeral. This took place at night on 18 September, and he was given his final resting place in Henry VII's chapel in Westminster Abbey, where, in 1634, his widow set up a tomb with effigies of herself and her husband by Hubert Le Sueur. In the following year she married Randal MacDonnell, second earl and first marquess of Antrim. Another monument was erected in Portsmouth parish church (later Portsmouth Cathedral) by Buckingham's sister, Susan, countess of Denbigh.

Before leaving for Ré, Buckingham had drawn up a will.

The greater part of his estate went to his widow and his son, the second duke, but there were also bequests to relatives and to members of his household. It was not easy to honour these, for he died heavily in debt, with many of his lands mortgaged. His wealth had derived from the crown, but he had spent much of it in the king's service, and although Charles I appointed a special commission to try to sort out the dead duke's finances it was unable to clarify them beyond a certain point. The debts seem to have been paid off, presumably with Charles's assistance, within two years, but probate was not finally granted until March 1635.

Assessment Buckingham was vilified during his lifetime, and historians have, in general, echoed the opinions of his contemporaries. One of the main charges against him, that of corruption, is clearly valid. He used his position to build up his power and wealth and was unscrupulous about the methods he and his associates employed. Because he was royal favourite the scale of his operations surpassed that of his contemporaries, but the quantitative difference should not be taken as implying a qualitative one. In early Stuart England there was a general assumption that the holding of public office opened the way to personal enrichment. The distinction between acceptable and unacceptable conduct was hazy, and varied with persons and circumstances. Buckingham has been linked with a decline in public morality, but there is no clear evidence that standards were slipping in James's reign. Moreover, if they were, the primary responsibility was the king's.

Another charge against the duke is that he was essentially a playboy, who took from the state but gave nothing back. This is far from the case. His administration of the navy was effective, and the mounting of both the Cadiz and Ré expeditions would have been impossible without his personal involvement. He used his own money and the credit he could command to fill the gaps left by the shortage of public funds, and he chose as his assistants men such as Sir John Coke and Edward Nicholas who were dedicated to the state's service.

Buckingham has been accused of allowing personal considerations, such as his dislike of Olivares and Richelieu, to determine his attitude towards foreign powers in and after 1623, and of engaging England in unnecessary wars, conducted without due regard to the resources available. Yet there are good grounds for arguing that he had a clearer perception of the power struggle in Europe, and of how England should react to this, than most of his critics. The house of Austria, under the leadership of Philip IV and the emperor Ferdinand, was expanding its authority and, in the process, imposing an intolerant Catholicism on large parts of Europe. This was a threat to all non-Habsburg states, both protestant and Catholic, and the Hague league which he brought into existence was an appropriate response.

Buckingham was correct in his assumption that the adhesion of France to the league was essential, if it was to succeed in its aims, and although it is clear, with hindsight, that he misread Richelieu, he was not alone in this respect. During his first years as Louis XIII's principal minister the cardinal cultivated ambiguity as a means of winning support. Only once he felt secure in office did he reveal himself as a determined opponent of Spain. It was Buckingham's misfortune that his attempts to bind France into the anti-Habsburg league coincided with this period of uncertainty in French politics—a confusion compounded by the Huguenot revolt, which Charles and Buckingham felt bound to support, even though it held back France from participating in operations against the common enemy.

It is true that Buckingham did not match his aims with his resources, but had he postponed action until assured of parliamentary support he would never have acted at all. The political nation wanted England to intervene effectively in the Thirty Years' War, but its representatives in the Commons showed no understanding of the true costs involved or any willingness to vote the requisite sums. Given this situation, the best response, as James I instinctively understood, was to do nothing, but inaction at such a critical juncture diminished the prestige of the monarchy and raised doubts about its commitment to the protestant cause. Buckingham attempted to give the political nation what it demanded and showed that the administrative system of the *ancien régime* could be goaded into activity as long as he was there to exert the necessary pressure. His assumption was that if only he could get England fully committed to the war, the country would unite behind the king and give him the moral and financial support he needed. This turned out to be a miscalculation and he became a scapegoat instead of a hero. Since part of the function of a favourite was to shield the monarch from blame for the actions of his government, Buckingham's fate was not inappropriate. ROGER LOCKYER

Sources BL, Harley MS 6987 • PRO, state papers domestic, SP 14; SP 16 • PRO, state papers Holland, SP 84 • BL, Trumbull MSS • Warks. CRO, Denbigh papers • Archivo General de Simancas, Spain, MSS sección estado • Archives du Ministère des Affaires Étrangères, Paris, Archives Diplomatiques M.D. • *The works of Francis Bacon*, ed. J. Spedding, R. L. Ellis, and D. D. Heath, 14 vols. (1857–74), vol. 14 • J. Rushworth, *Historical collections*, new edn, 1 (1721) • *Cabala, sive, Scrinia sacra: mysteries of state and government in letters of illustrious persons*, 3rd edn (1691) • [T. Birch and R. F. Williams], eds., *The court and times of Charles the First*, 2 vols. (1848) • *The letters of John Chamberlain*, ed. N. E. McClure, 2 vols. (1939) • J. Eliot, *Negotium posterorum*, ed. A. B. Grosart, 2 vols. (1881) • F. W. Fairholt, ed., *Poems and songs relating to George Villiers, duke of Buckingham*, Percy Society (1850) • *The Fortescue papers*, ed. S. R. Gardiner, CS, new ser., 1 (1871) • G. Goodman, *The court of King James the First*, ed. J. S. Brewer, 2 vols. (1839) • J. Hacket, *Scrinia reserata: a memorial offer'd to the great deservings of John Williams*, 2 pts (1693) • F. Francisco de Jesus, *El hecho de los tratados del matrimonio pretendido por el principe de Gales con la serenissima infante de España, María / Narrative of the Spanish marriage treaty*, ed. and trans. S. R. Gardiner, CS, 101 (1869) • Lord Herbert of Cherbury, *The expedition to the Isle of Rhé*, Philobiblon Society (1860) • S. R. Gardiner, ed., *Documents illustrating the impeachment of the duke of Buckingham in 1626*, CS, new ser., 45 (1889) • *A journal of all the proceedings of the duke of Buckingham, his grace, in the Isle of Ree* (1627) • JHL, 3 (1620–28) • W. B. Bidwell and M. Jansson, eds., *Proceedings in parliament, 1626*, 1: *House of Lords* (1991) • R. C. Johnson and others, eds., *Proceedings in parliament, 1628*, 5 (1983) • F. Osborne, 'Osborne's traditional memoires', *Secret history of the court of James the First*, ed. W. Scott, 1 (1811), 1–297 • E. W. Harcourt, ed., *The life of the renowned*

Doctor Preston, writ by his pupil, Master Thomas Ball, D.D., minister of Northampton, in the year 1628 (1885) · J. Nichols, The progresses, processions, and magnificent festivities of King James I, his royal consort, family and court, 4 vols. (1828) · The letters of Peter Paul Rubens, ed. and trans. R. S. Magurn (1955) · The manuscripts of Henry Duncan Skrine, esq. Salvetti correspondence, HMC, 16 (1887) · [A. Weldon], The court and character of King James (1650) · A. Wilson, 'The life and reign of James I, King of Great Britain', A complete history of England: with the lives of all the kings and queens thereof, ed. [W. Kennett, J. Hughes, and J. Strype], 2nd edn, 2 (1719), 661–792 · H. Wotton, 'The life and death of George Villiers, duke of Buckingham', Reliquiae Wottonianae, 3rd edn (1672), 207–38 · H. Wotton, 'Of Robert Devereux, earl of Essex, and George Villiers, duke of Buckingham', Reliquiae Wottonianae, 3rd edn (1672), 161–83 · S. R. Gardiner, History of England from the accession of James I to the outbreak of the civil war, 2–6 (1883–4) · R. Lockyer, Buckingham: the life and political career of George Villiers, first duke of Buckingham, 1592–1628 (1981) · A. P. McGowan, 'The Royal Navy under the first duke of Buckingham', PhD diss., U. Lond., 1971 · M. Prestwich, Cranfield: politics and profits under the early Stuarts (1966) · R. E. Ruigh, The parliament of 1624: politics and foreign policy (1971) · C. Russell, Parliaments and English politics, 1621–1629 (1979) · V. Treadwell, Buckingham and Ireland, 1616–28: a study in Anglo-Irish politics (1998)

Archives Berks. RO, corresp. · BL, Harley MSS, corresp. and papers · BL, letter-books, Add. MS 11309; Egerton MS 860 · Bodl. Oxf., financial papers · CUL, household account book; speeches and papers · Herts. ALS, papers relating to impeachment · HLRO, papers relating to impeachment and parliament · Leics. RO, commissions and papers · LPL, corresp. · NA Scot., corresp. · NL Scot., papers relating to impeachment · NRA, priv. coll., material relating to expenditures · S. Antiquaries, Lond., corresp. · Sheff. Arch., papers relating to impeachment | BL, Sloane, Royal, King's MSS, letters and papers · Bodl. Oxf., MSS Tanner, corresp. · CKS, corresp. with Lionel Cranfield · Hunt. L., letters to Temple family **Likenesses** attrib. W. Larkin, portrait, c.1616, NPG · S. de Passe, line engraving, 1617, BM · B. Gerbier, miniature, 1618, Syon House, Brentford · D. Mytens, portrait, c.1620–1622, Royal Collection · portrait, c.1623 (after B. Gerbier?), Palace of Westminster, London; on loan from Clarendon collection · M. J. van Miereveldt, portrait, c.1625, Lamport Hall, Northamptonshire · P. P. Rubens, chalk drawing, 1625, Albertina, Vienna · P. P. Rubens, portrait, c.1625, Palazzo Pitti, Florence [see illus.] · P. P. Rubens, sketch, 1625, Kimbell Art Museum, Fort Worth, Texas · D. Mytens, portrait, 1626, Euston Hall, Suffolk · group portrait, oils, 1628 (Family of the duke of Buckingham), Royal Collection; version, NPG · H. Le Sueur, tomb effigy, in or before 1634, Westminster Abbey, London · C. Turner, mezzotint, pubd 1810 (after C. Johnson), BM, NPG · Black and Hopwood, aquatint, pubd 1812 (after MacKenzie), NPG · attrib. B. Gerbier, portrait, NMM · W. Marshall, line engraving (after unknown artist), BM, NPG · portrait (after D. Mytens), Royal Collection

Villiers, George, second duke of Buckingham (1628–

1687), politician and wit, was born on 30 January 1628 at Wallingford House, Westminster, the third child of George *Villiers, first duke of Buckingham (1592–1628), courtier and royal favourite, and Lady Katherine Manners (later Katherine *MacDonnell, 1603?–1649), eldest daughter of the earl of Rutland. His elder brother, Charles, died in infancy. Following the murder of their father in 1628 Buckingham and his posthumous younger brother, Lord Francis Villiers, were brought up with the king's children in the royal nursery at Richmond. In 1636 Buckingham was placed under the joint guardianship of the earls of Rutland and Newcastle. In 1641 he was sent up to Trinity College, Cambridge, and was admitted to the degree of MA on 5 March 1642.

George Villiers, second duke of Buckingham (1628–1687), by John Michael Wright, 1669

Divided loyalties, 1642–1661 Buckingham's youth prevented his taking part in the military campaigns of the civil war, but he and Francis did attend the siege of Lichfield Close in April 1643. Parliament reacted by sequestering the lands and movable goods of the two brothers (10 February 1644). That same year the boys' interests were placed in the hands of Algernon Percy, the parliamentarian earl of Northumberland, and William Aylesbury, a royalist whose father had served the first duke. In 1646 Aylesbury took the two boys on a continental tour to complete their education: 'I was not thought of age sufficient to beare armes' said Buckingham later (BL, Add. MS 18979, fol. 286) while Northumberland lobbied parliament to have the sequestered goods returned. On 4 October 1647 the Commons lifted the sequestration order. Despite this, the two Villiers boys took up royalist arms in the second civil war, apparently emboldened by the Commons' reported insulting of the first duke. They joined the earls of Holland and Peterborough for action in Surrey. Parliament, with advance intelligence of their movements, secured all the strategic local outposts, and on 7 July 1648 Francis Villiers was killed in a skirmish near Kingston. Three days later Buckingham and Holland were intercepted at St Neots in Huntingdonshire; Holland was captured, while Buckingham escaped to the continent.

The execution of Charles I on 30 January 1649 prompted many royalists to abandon the cause and compound for their confiscated estates, and Buckingham was no different. In April he approached parliament through his aristocratic sympathizers, Northumberland, Pembroke, and Denbigh, but could not accept the 'base submissions' required of him (O. Ogle and others, ed., Calendar of the

Clarendon State Papers Preserved in the Bodleian Library, 5 vols., 1869–70, 2.7). Instead, he joined the future Charles II's court in exile, quickly establishing himself among the pragmatists who were urging the prince to form an alliance with the Scottish presbyterians. His advance in royal favour was both rapid and tangible. On 19 September 1649 he was created a knight of the Garter; on 25 January 1650 he was commissioned to raise and supply troops on the continent, and on 6 April was sworn to the privy council. Accompanying Charles to Scotland, he attached himself to their presbyterian host, the marquess of Argyll, and that way survived the Scots' purge of the royal household. In February 1651 a royalist–presbyterian army was mobilized, top-heavy in senior officers appointed to satisfy rival factions, in which Buckingham was commissioned to lead the English royalists. He was, nevertheless, dismayed to find that the Scot David Leslie outranked him, and although he, like Charles, escaped to the continent after the crushing defeat at Worcester (3 September 1651), the snub appears to have soured relations between the boyhood friends for many years to come.

Barred from royal counsels, and with his financial credit exhausted, Buckingham's career now took a bewildering switchback course, glimpsed briefly and intermittently in the censorious correspondence of senior royalists-in-exile such as Hyde and Nicholas, and in the intelligence reports of Cromwell's agents. For the next five years he was variously reported as having made his peace with Cromwell, spying for Cromwell, and co-ordinating an ambitious scheme to unite France, the papacy, royalists, and republicans in the overthrow of the protectorate. In 1657, having the previous year failed in an attempt to reconcile himself with Charles, Buckingham returned to England and paid suit to Mary Fairfax (1638–1704), daughter and sole heir of Thomas, Lord Fairfax, the parliamentarian general. Mary, smitten with the duke, broke off her engagement to the earl of Chesterfield, and Buckingham and Mary were married on 15 September at Bolton Percy in Yorkshire. As Fairfax had been granted the major portion of the duke's confiscated estates, the marriage was a blatantly opportunist move to secure his inheritance. Because the Fairfax family were known to be in contact with royalist agents Cromwell feared subterfuge, and ordered Buckingham's arrest. The following spring this was commuted to house arrest, and when in August he broke this, he was placed in the Tower. Brian Fairfax later suggested that only Cromwell's death, on 3 September, prevented the duke's execution (BL, Harleian MS 6862, fol. 10), but no such warrant was issued, and it is most unlikely that the protector would have alienated Fairfax in this way. The duke was released on 21 February 1659, Fairfax standing security of £20,000.

The council now allowed Buckingham to retire to Fairfax's Nunappleton estate in Yorkshire. He was thus able to join the force that Fairfax raised in January 1660, an action which facilitated General Monck's unchallenged passage to London. Even so, Buckingham received no more than a royal pardon at the Restoration, and achieved the distinction of being the only former privy councillor still alive not to be resworn to the new council. He attended parliament regularly throughout the summer of 1660, concerned as he was with his petition, presented on 13 June, for the recovery of his estate. Early the following year he made overtures to Lord Chancellor Hyde (later created earl of Clarendon), who replied soothingly. Charles had also relaxed his hostility, perhaps through the agency of his latest mistress, Buckingham's young cousin Barbara Palmer (*née* Villiers). As a result, he was admitted as a gentleman of the bedchamber in August 1661, and on 30 October was sworn in as lord lieutenant of the West Riding.

The courtier, 1661–1667 The West Riding lieutenancy had attached to it more deputies than any other county, and therefore promised Buckingham extensive local patronage. Within months he had created a loyal clientele of youngish, politically inexperienced deputies, among whom Sir Thomas Osborne (later earl of Danby) and George Savile (later marquess of Halifax) were to advance farthest. He also lobbied for the presidency of the council of the north, the regional court whose reconstitution after the Restoration was widely predicted. However, the rival candidature of Lord Strafford split opinion both in Whitehall and the north, and Charles seems to have decided that the renewal of the court was not worth the factionalism it created. The duke was readmitted to the privy council on 28 April 1662. He was not, though, appointed to any important conciliar committees and made only a token appearance throughout the first few years of his membership. Nor, at this stage, was he active in the House of Lords, excepting the debates upon the Uniformity Bill in early 1662, when he opposed Clarendon's proviso allowing the king to dispense with the act in order to exempt individual ministers from observing certain rites. He was studiously ambivalent when, in July 1663, the earl of Bristol attempted to impeach Clarendon. Instead, he entertained the court with impersonations of the ageing lord chancellor, and tried to anticipate a shift in the king's romantic liaisons by sponsoring Frances Stuart as a rival to his cousin (now countess of Castlemaine). Frances, although fascinated by Buckingham's skill in building castles of playing cards, proved too virtuous to oblige his wider plan.

The duke's first real chance to advertise his abilities, and to expunge the republican taint that his return to England in 1657 had created, occurred in autumn 1663, when news reached London of a major republican conspiracy in Yorkshire. The duke journeyed to York, and requested a commission to raise a horse regiment. This was unduly alarmist, since government spies had already infiltrated the claques, but three rabble-like gatherings of dissidents did take place on 12 October, and this appeared to vindicate his caution. He was instructed to oversee the prosecution of the ringleaders, and some twenty men were hanged in Yorkshire early the following year. The Anglo-Dutch War represented another opportunity for him to display his martial prowess. In April 1665 he joined the fleet, but quarrelled with York and Sandwich and was ordered ashore. He felt the humiliation keenly: 'I have soe long accustomed to bee ill used, that I may very well begin to thinke that I deserve noe better, and that it is high time for me to leave off the persuing of those things that I have had soe little success in' (Bodl. Oxf., MS Carte 34, fols. 160–61). He retired from political life completely for the next few months, not once attending the autumn 1665 session of parliament.

In 1666 Buckingham fell in love with Anna-Maria Brudenell, countess of Shrewsbury, a society beauty who had already acquired a reputation as a *femme fatale*. 'I would take a wager she might have a man killed for her every day, and she would only hold her head the higher for it' was Count Grammont's observation (A. Hamilton, *Memoirs of Count Grammont*, 2 vols., 1908, 2.3). Their affair was to have tragic consequences, but in the first instance it seems to have reawakened Buckingham's taste for political intrigue. On 5 October, two weeks into the new parliamentary session, he took his seat in the Lords and introduced a 'wild motion' that those guilty of embezzling public funds be executed for treason (Pepys). Thereafter, he attended Westminster with unusual assiduity, was named to all the most important standing committees, and chaired several inter-house conferences. Meanwhile, he courted aggrieved and energetic MPs in the Commons, notably Sir Richard Temple, Sir Edward Seymour, Sir Robert Howard, and William Garway. These men filibustered debates on supply for the king, challenged a ruling made by Clarendon in his legal capacity as lord chancellor, and promoted a bill to ban the import of Irish cattle, passage of which would undermine the government's Irish administration and deprive the king of customs duties. Buckingham was its leading sponsor in the Lords, where tempers flared. On 25 October Lord Ossory, son of the lord lieutenant of Ireland, challenged him to a duel for insulting his countrymen ('whoever was against the bill had either an Irish interest or an Irish understanding'); both were sent briefly to the Tower to cool off (Bodl. Oxf., MS Carte 35, fols. 109, 111, 115, 117; JHL, 12.18–20, 22). Charles now lost his patience with Buckingham and ordered the intelligence services to collect incriminating evidence against him. On 25 February 1667 a warrant for the duke's arrest was issued on the grounds that he had both encouraged seamen to mutiny and had commissioned a horoscope of the king's birth—a treasonable offence, since it presupposed the encompassing of the king's death. Buckingham went into hiding, while Whitehall learned that many 'thought his crime small, or none at all' (*CSP dom.*, 1667, 11). In early summer 1667 the devastating Dutch raid along the Medway damaged the government's standing beyond repair, achieving in a few hours what Buckingham and his allies had laboured over throughout the winter. Confident now that the government would not press charges, he emerged from hiding. He was conveyed to the Tower in June 1667, in what became a triumphal procession—dining as he did at a tavern before a crowd of applauding onlookers. He was released in the following month after a perfunctory interrogation that he treated with contempt. Pepys called his enlargement 'one of the strangest instances of the fool's play with which all public things

are done in this age' (Pepys, 8.342). On 23 September Buckingham was restored to the privy council and the bedchamber.

The minister, 1667–1674 In restoring him to favour Charles was effectively inviting Buckingham to employ his populist talents on the government's behalf. Thus, ten days into the new parliamentary session the duke's allies in the Commons impeached the now dismissed Clarendon. When the issue came before the Lords, Buckingham led the protest (20 November) at the house's decision not to commit the earl upon an unspecified charge of treason. It was rumoured that Charles would break the legal deadlock by proroguing parliament and trying the earl before a court of twenty-four selected peers, presided over by Buckingham. Although it is unlikely that the duke, who had no legal expertise, would have chaired such a court, the threat was sufficiently real for Clarendon to take ship and flee to France.

Buckingham did not himself gain high office from Clarendon's disgrace: he lacked administrative experience and was probably content to operate in a more casual advisory role. His position was, nevertheless, formalized over the next nine months. On 2 November 1667 he was recommissioned as lord lieutenant of the West Riding. More important, on 31 January 1668 he was added to the committee for foreign affairs, an inner cabinet that met weekly on Mondays to debate the most sensitive policy matters. Finally, in the summer he bought from the duke of Albemarle, for the colossal sum of £20,000, the post of master of the horse, a position with sentimental value, since his father had held the post half a century earlier. The duke's security in royal affections is also suggested by his immunity from prosecution and disgrace following his duel, on 16 January 1668, with his cuckold, the earl of Shrewsbury. The status of the combatants, the number who fought (three on each side), and the bloody outcome (one killed, one seriously wounded) combined to make it the most notorious duel of the reign. The affair embarrassed the government on the eve of a fresh parliamentary session. As Pepys sarcastically put it, 'This will make the world think that the king hath good councillors about him' (Pepys, 9.27). But it did not deflect business. Charles pardoned the duellists (27 January), and parliament made no reference to the episode until 18 March, when Shrewsbury, wounded and bedridden, died. Buckingham responded by moving the countess into one of his London residences, Wallingford House.

All the same the duke's efforts to manage parliament in 1668 were strikingly unsuccessful. His attempt to introduce legislation on behalf of protestant nonconformists—his client Sir Richard Temple terming it a policy 'by which the presbyterians are absolutely gained and the nation satisfied' (BL, Stowe MS 304, fol. 88*v*)—was a serious misreading of the mood at Westminster. In the Lords, senior churchmen spoke against the rumoured bills to such effect that none was presented. The duke absented himself from Westminster for much of the second half of the session, and when he returned, on 21 April, it was to drive on a jurisdictional dispute between the two houses in the hope of wrecking a session that had turned against him. For the next few years he consistently urged Charles to dismiss the assembly. When supply was eventually voted, on 2 May 1668, Charles was bemused to see that it was Clarendon's friends, not Buckingham's, who had forwarded his business most effectively.

Buckingham was excluded from the secret negotiations that led to the secret treaty of Dover (22 May 1670). This committed Charles to war with the Dutch, and to declare himself Roman Catholic, in return for a French subsidy, an undertaking by France not to attack Spain, and a suspension of Louis XIV's shipbuilding programme. In July 1670 Charles sent Buckingham to Versailles to treat with Louis XIV for an 'official' alliance. The resulting treaty (21 December) omitted the Catholic clause, and was signed by all the principal cabinet officers: Clifford, Arlington, Buckingham, Ashley, and Lauderdale (whose combined initials provide the resonant but misleading acronym 'the Cabal'). Buckingham rarely attended Westminster during the 1671 session of parliament. His illegitimate child with the countess of Shrewsbury died in infancy, and was buried in the Villiers family vault at Westminster Abbey on 12 March 1671 (which caused an outcry). In the summer he diligently and successfully canvassed to be chancellor of Cambridge University (11 May). His main concern, as ever, was to cover himself in military glory. In January 1672 he pressed for the war with the Dutch to be started with an unprovoked attack on Cadzand. On the outbreak of war he took a small vessel and joined the fleet, but, as in 1665, was swiftly recalled. His commission to lead a regiment of foot (19 June) was some compensation.

There is some evidence that Buckingham was now alerted to the existence of the secret treaty by the duke of York (W. D. Christie, *A Life of Anthony Ashley Cooper, First Earl of Shaftesbury, 1621–83*, 2 vols., 1871, 2.85–6). To placate him Charles attached Buckingham to the embassy to The Hague (June 1672), which achieved the limited goal of ensuring that William of Orange did not detach either ally. The sluggish war effort and the unparliamentary nature of Charles's declaration of indulgence (1672) provoked great unity of opposition within parliament when it reconvened in February 1673. According to Burnet, Buckingham advised Charles to use the military to eject the recalcitrant MPs (*Bishop Burnet's History of my Own Time*, pt 2, *The Reign of Charles II*, ed. O. Airy, 2 vols., 1897–1900, 2.11). The duke was commissioned lieutenant-general on 13 May 1673, junior only to York and Prince Rupert. However, his association with increasingly unpopular policies undermined his recruitment activities that summer. To distance himself from charges of popery he took the sacrament in 'almost all' the West Riding churches (W. D. Christie, ed., *Letters Addressed to Sir Joseph Williamson ... 1673–4*, 2 vols., CS, new ser., 1874, 1.25, 57–8), but was still short of men when the army mustered at Blackheath in July. When a Huguenot count was promoted above him he refused to serve.

Aware now of his exclusion from influence Buckingham turned to mischief-making. In November it was reported that he sought censure in parliament, if only to gain a platform from which to incriminate Arlington: 'contented to loose an eye himself to leave his enemie none' (W. D. Christie, ed., *Letters Addressed to Sir Joseph Williamson ... 1673–4*, 2 vols., CS, new ser., 2.62). At the same time he took the precaution of obtaining a royal pardon for all offences committed up to the present (granted 19 November). On the opening day of the new session, 7 January 1674, the young earl of Shrewsbury's family petitioned against the 'wicked and scandalous life' led by Buckingham and the countess of Shrewsbury (*JHL*, 12.599). The house ordered him not to converse with or cohabit with the countess on pain of a £10,000 fine. Correctly fearing a Commons address for his removal, which, unlike an impeachment charge, would give him no opportunity to defend himself, the duke requested, and was granted, permission to address the house himself. His cryptic, evasive, and frivolous defence impressed no one, and after two days' debate the Commons duly addressed Charles for the duke's removal from all his employments, and from his presence and councils forever. Charles agreed.

Opposition and retirement, 1674–1687 Even before he had been officially dismissed Buckingham was noted as having joined a cabal of disgruntled peers who met at the presbyterian Lord Holles's house. On 21 April 1675, after a year of retirement, he joined Shaftesbury and twenty-one other peers in protesting that the government's non-resisting bill encroached upon the privileges of the house. The bishops, bloc voters for the bill, were ridiculed by Buckingham in a speech of 'eloquent and well placed nonsense' (A. Marvell, *The Poems and Letters of Andrew Marvell*, ed. H. M. Margoliouth, 3rd edn, 2 vols., 1971, 2.341–3). In November 1675 the duke delivered a short speech to the Lords asking leave to introduce a private bill advocating toleration for protestant dissenters. This was both a reply to Charles's request, made at the start of the session, that ways be found to secure the protestant religion, and a declaration of solidarity with government critics. The bill was never presented as Charles prorogued the session on 22 November, but the gesture had been made.

In 1676 the duke divided his time between the new country mansion he was building at Cliveden, near Maidenhead, and the City of London, where he was involved in corporation politics. On 4 October Whitehall received intelligence that Buckingham and the Leveller John Wildman had drunk a health to a new parliament, 'and to all the honest men of it who would give the king no money' (*CSP dom.*, 1676–7, 352). The king's decision not to call parliament in 1676 determined Buckingham's next move. On the opening day of the next session, 15 February 1677, he delivered a long speech arguing that the prorogation had *ipso facto* rendered parliament dissolved, since there existed two unrepealed medieval statutes decreeing that a parliament be called at least every twelve months. 'Statutes are not like women, for they are not one jot the worse for being old', he explained to their lordships (Phipps, 104–12). Despite its wit and ingenuity, the speech was a major tactical blunder. The campaign was never likely to commend itself to the Commons for the simple reason that MPs, unlike peers, would have the expense and uncertainty of re-election. Accordingly, the Commons voted not to debate the issue. In the Lords, Buckingham and his fellow dissolutionists (Shaftesbury, Salisbury, and Wharton) were required to seek the pardon of the house, and, when they refused, were sent to the Tower (16 February). As in 1667, the intelligence service collected evidence of Buckingham's subversion, but the duke's courtier friends, Middlesex, Rochester, and Nell Gwyn, together, surprisingly, with Lord Treasurer Danby (BL, Add. MS 28051, fol. 41), persuaded Charles to relax the duke's confinement; on 5 August 1677 he obtained a full release.

For the next few years Buckingham was a marginal figure, dependent upon payments from the French government, who thought him a usefully popular figure in London. The Popish Plot allegations of 1678 briefly revived his parliamentary career. On 28 October 1678, shortly after the mysterious death of Sir Edmund Godfrey, the London JP who had taken Titus Oates's depositions, Buckingham suggested a special subcommittee to investigate the supposed murder, and proceeded to nominate government critics such as Shaftesbury, Halifax, and Winchester to sit alongside him on it. The duke was subsequently invited to manage important inter-house conferences upon the security of the realm and the protestant religion. The following year his scope for action was circumscribed by a complicated vendetta with his former client, Danby, and was absent from Westminster for almost the entire session of the new parliament, which met in early March 1679. In August and September he electioneered on behalf of whig candidates in areas where he possessed land and influence, thereby earning a dressing down from the king (Bodl. Oxf., MS Carte 228, fol. 121). Next, he was accused of sodomy—an increasingly common political charge, as it carried the same penalty as for treason, and therefore allowed the crown to dispose of the defendant's estate should the prosecution succeed. In May 1680 a grand jury brought a verdict of *ignoramus*, after which Buckingham successfully sued his accusers, who included the spy–adventurer Colonel Blood, for libel.

Ill health prevented Buckingham from attending the much prorogued parliament until 22 November 1680. It is a measure of his diminishing sway that he survived the tory *revanche* of 1681–5. Only when James II succeeded Charles in 1685 did Buckingham return to public life. He attended almost every day of the new session of parliament, and published a religious tract implicitly advocating toleration for Roman Catholics as well as for protestants. He spent the last two years of his life in retirement on his Yorkshire estates, dying on 16 April 1687 of a chill caught on the hunting field—not, as Pope had it, in 'the worst inn's worst room' (*Moral Essays*, epistle 3, 1.299), but in the house of a tenant at Kirkby Moorside. On 7 June he was interred in the Villiers family vault in St George's Chapel, Westminster Abbey.

Estates and finances Legend has it that Buckingham died a bankrupt, having frittered away a splendid inheritance: 'In squandring wealth was his peculiar art' (J. Dryden, *Absalom and Achitophel*, line 559, printed in G. de F. Lord and others, *Poems on Affairs of State: Augustan Satirical Verse, 1660–1714*, 7 vols., 1963–75, 2.455–93). His inheritance was indeed splendid, comprising as it did major estates in Yorkshire, Buckinghamshire, Rutland, Leicestershire, and Lincolnshire, large properties in Essex and Herefordshire, two London mansions (York House and Chelsea House), and an enormous art collection, the paintings in which were valued by parliament in 1645 at £20,000. The estate was dismantled by parliament in April 1650. Fairfax was the chief beneficiary, gaining York House and most of the Rutland and Yorkshire holdings; the rest of the duke's lands were put up for sale on 16 July 1651. Buckingham's marriage to Mary Fairfax in 1657 had made him joint heir to all the lands granted to Fairfax, and in summer 1660 he regained his inheritance by parliamentary petition.

A survey of his English lands, drawn up in 1668, showed an annual rental of £19,306 18s. 6d. In the 1660s his policy was to sell his outlying, hard to administer properties and mortgage the rest to secure large-scale loans. This allowed him to meet extraordinary expenditure such as the mastership of the horse (£20,000 in 1668), and the building of the Cliveden estate in the 1670s. His principal creditor was the duke of Albemarle, who loaned a massive £40,000 before his death in 1670. By 1671 nearly all Buckingham's estate was under mortgage, some properties three or four times over. In August 1671 he created a freehold trust to administer the estate and retain all profits in return for an annual allowance of £5000, an arrangement which persisted until the death in 1704 of his widow, Mary. Contemporaries assumed that this abdication of responsibility revealed the duke's financial plight, but there is reason to suppose that it was no more than a legal device to protect the estate from escheating to the crown should Buckingham be prosecuted for treason (Melton, 307–13). Had the duke fathered an heir he might have shown more respect for landed wealth, as opposed to monetary wealth; as it was, he died both without heir and intestate, obliging the trustees to alienate the remainder of his estate.

Friends and associates Buckingham enjoyed the loyalty and affection of a wide and talented circle of friends, thanks largely to his own social and conversational gifts. 'He was the finest gentleman of person and wit I think I ever saw', wrote Sir John Reresby (*The Memoirs of Sir John Reresby*, ed. A. Browning, 1940, 40). The duke's boyhood governor, the earl of Newcastle, was a strong influence, for Buckingham soon came to share Newcastle's enthusiasm for plays, poetry, music, and scientific inquiry. Grammont held that Buckingham had a fine singing voice, while Pepys thought his 'musique' the 'best in towne' (Pepys, 9.13). The duke's scientific interests grew out of his belief in empiricism and rational thought. He was a fellow of the Royal Society (1661–85), installed a laboratory in Wallingford House, and even had one fitted in his chambers when he was sent to the Tower in 1677. His efforts to convert flint glass into high quality glass yielded a successful glass making factory at Vauxhall. He also attended an astrological discussion group run by John Digby, and it was at one of these that he met the lawyer-cum-astrologer

John Heydon, whose horoscope drafting was to embarrass Buckingham so severely in 1667.

The duke's intellectual household was ornamented by liberal Anglican scholars such as Martin Clifford (author of *A Treatise of Humane Reason*, 1672) and Thomas Sprat (propagandist for the Royal Society and later bishop of Rochester). Clifford was a friend from Buckingham's undergraduate days at Cambridge; in the early 1660s he was acting as the duke's accountant, and became a trustee of his estate in 1675. Sprat's career pursued a similar path: he entered the duke's service soon after the Restoration as a chaplain, and like Clifford was a trustee of the duke's estate. He was one of the first men to be told of Buckingham's death in 1687. In drafts of the duke's will that were never formalized Clifford and Sprat were both beneficiaries, as was Sir Charles Wolseley, the former Cromwellian courtier who in 1668 wrote a pamphlet advocating liberty of conscience. In contrast to contemporary rumour Buckingham did not patronize nonconformist ministers to any great extent. His close epistolary friendship, in the last few years of his life, with the Quaker William Penn was altogether different, since Penn, as the confidant of James II, was effectively the patron in the relationship. On the other hand, the duke had a natural affinity for the political *demi-monde*. In the 1650s he consorted with the Levellers John Lilburne, Edward Sexby, and John Wildman, the Irish Jesuit Peter Talbot, and the Catholic convert Ellis Leighton. The association with Wildman and Leighton endured into the 1680s. Leighton had a gift for diplomatic intrigue and became the duke's agent in the latter's various dealings with the French government, while Wildman combined a flair for radical solutions with a sound business brain. He became a trustee for the duke's estate in 1675, and was almost certainly the duke's point of contact with London radicals such as Slingsby Bethel and Francis Jenks in the late 1670s.

Socially the duke felt most at home with sophisticated but politically unambitious courtier wits such as John Wilmot, earl of Rochester, Charles Sackville, earl of Dorset, Sir George Etherege, and Sir Charles Sedley. Rochester helped secure Buckingham's release from the Tower in 1677, and they spent much of the summer and autumn together. As an undergraduate at Cambridge, Buckingham befriended the poet Abraham Cowley, ten years his senior, and the two were sufficiently close for Cowley to act as best man to Buckingham in 1657. After the Restoration he employed Cowley as a bailiff on his manor at Garrendon, and when Cowley died, in 1667, put up a large sum of money for an elaborate iron and stone memorial. The satirist Samuel Butler, author of *Hudibras*, was part of the duke's entourage in France in 1670, and became his secretary when Buckingham returned to Cambridge University as chancellor. The duke was also friendly with Charles de Saint-Evremond, with whom he collaborated in a court play, *Sir Politic Would-Be* (1662), and, through Saint-Evremond, with the poet Edmund Waller. Finally, the duke had an acquaintance with the playwright William Wycherley, for in 1672 he made him a lieutenant in the regiment he never got to lead.

Writings Buckingham's literary reputation was sewn soon after the Restoration and was embroidered by a series of editions and miscellanies published in the hundred years or so after his death. The first, *Miscellaneous Works, Written by his Grace George, Late Duke of Buckingham*, edited by T. Brown, appeared in 1704. Subsequent editions by other editors followed in 1705, 1715, 1752, 1754, and 1775. These eighteenth-century collections exploited Buckingham's name to introduce readers to writings by a variety of Restoration wits: most of the items printed were not in fact written by him. He then suffered two hundred years of editorial neglect, until in 1985 Christine Phipps produced an edition of his non-dramatic works.

The duke's principal literary claim to attention is his satire upon contemporary heroic drama, *The Rehearsal*, which showed how well his gift for caricature and mimicry translated to both stage and page. The play was several years in the writing, and was apparently a collaborative effort with Martin Clifford, Thomas Sprat, and Samuel Butler. When eventually it was first performed, at the Theatre Royal, Drury Lane, on 7 December 1671, it exhibited both literary targets (Dryden) and political (Arlington). *The Rehearsal* was immediately popular, being published five times in his own lifetime, and performed nearly three hundred times until 1777, during which its lead role (Bayes) was taken by the greatest actors of the day such as Colley Cibber and David Garrick. The appearance in 1779 of an even better satire, Sheridan's *The Critic*, effectively ended its run, but *The Rehearsal* retains its importance as the pioneer of a tradition of dramatic burlesque upon the English stage.

The Chances was Buckingham's adaptation of John Fletcher's comedy of the same name. This was probably the play that Pepys saw in early 1667. The text was published in 1682, at the time of its next performance. A slightly bowdlerized version was revived by Garrick in 1773, and performed eleven times that season. It was playing as recently as 1962, with Laurence Olivier in the role of Don John. The play's endurance is not surprising, for most critics agree that it far surpasses Fletcher's original. Even Dryden praised Buckingham's comic enrichment of the character of Don John. *The Restoration, or, Right will Take Place* was Buckingham's adaptation of Beaumont's and Fletcher's *Philaster*, and was aimed at his sometime political ally, Shaftesbury. It is unclear whether or not the play was performed. Buckingham is also credited as being co-author, with Sir Robert Howard, of *The Country Gentleman* (1669). In fact, the duke's contribution came after the play was substantially complete, and helped to render it unperformable: he inserted a buffoon of a character, Sir Cautious Trouble-All, who was clearly modelled upon the naval treasurer, Sir William Coventry. Coventry heard of the impertinence and challenged Buckingham to a duel, whereupon he was deprived of his office. The play, which was due to open on 27 February 1669, was halted and its text was not discovered and identified until the 1960s. An edition edited by Scouten and Hume was published in 1976.

Except for the poems written into his commonplace book (Phipps, 163–227), no holograph manuscripts of Buckingham's poetry survive, and the dozen or so pieces generally ascribed to him (Phipps, 141–53) are not especially distinguished. The commonplace book also contains squibs, aphorisms, gnomic couplets, lampoons of political opponents such as Clarendon and Dryden, and an unfinished play.

The duke's prose works (Phipps, 81–137) carried a political purpose, or at least allowed him to turn political resentment to a creative end. *The Battle of Sedgmoor*, written in July 1685, was a one-act farce directed against the earl of Feversham, the French-born general of the royalist forces at the battle. Several of the duke's parliamentary speeches were printed (1668, 1674, 1675, and 1677). Of these, his November 1675 speech, requesting leave to introduce a toleration bill, was perhaps the most influential: it was published with a speech of Shaftesbury's in a single pamphlet, sold well in the London coffee houses, and attracted comment in the provinces. *A letter to Sir Thomas Osborn … upon the reading of a book called 'The present interest of England stated'* (1672) was written to justify the Anglo-Dutch War. It took the form of a reply to a pamphlet of Slingsby Bethel's published the year before, and argued that since the Dutch were England's greatest commercial rivals, they were also her natural enemies in war. *To Mr Martin Clifford on his Humane Reason* (1672) proclaimed Buckingham's faith in 'reason, and the interpretation of Scripture'. It could have been an oblique criticism of the declaration of indulgence, promulgated that same year, for in the essay Buckingham explicitly excluded Roman Catholics from his proposed toleration. By contrast, *A Short Discourse upon the Reasonableness of Man's Having a Religion, or Worship of God* (1685), implicitly embraces the desirability of toleration for Catholics: there was no mention of 'protestants', only 'Christians'. The paper was apparently written at the behest of Buckingham's Quaker friend William Penn, with the specific aim of currying favour with the new king, the Roman Catholic James II. Theologically lightweight, it nevertheless provoked a lively controversy among theologians, to which Buckingham contributed a brief, humorous defence, *The duke of Buckingham's letter to the unknown author of … A short answer to the duke of Buckingham's paper* (1685). The hoped-for return to court was not, however, forthcoming.

Buckingham's career reveals both the possibilities and limitations of friendship with the king. Charles II usually forgave his indiscretions, but from their first falling out, at Worcester in 1651, he never really trusted him. As a result, the duke's political and military ambitions were constantly thwarted. His status as the leading non-royal peer, and his genuine talents for friendship and intrigue, made him a powerful and inspiring patron: his clientele was the most diversely brilliant and loyal of the period, and an apt reflection of his own broadminded intellect. His satirical gifts brought him sporadic popularity at court, in parliament, and on the streets of the capital. They also shaped his best writing. Ultimately, however,

the man who had been brought up with two future kings of England expected more. Buckingham died an embittered man.   BRUCE YARDLEY

Sources State papers in the reign of Charles II, PRO, SP29 · Transcripts of the French ambassadors' dispatches, 1663–81, PRO, 31/3/111–39 · Papers relating to Buckingham's imprisonments in the Tower, 1667, 1677, BL, Add. MS 27872 · Buckingham's accounts, 1662–70, GL, MS 15818; MSS 1993, 15613 · Ormonde correspondence, 1660–82, Bodl. Oxf., MSS Carte 31–9 · Fairfax correspondence, 1625–88, BL, Add. MS 18979 · Clarendon correspondence, 1654–67, Bodl. Oxf., MSS Clarendon 49, 58–60, 70–87 · *The life of Edward, earl of Clarendon … written by himself*, 2 vols. (1857) · *JHL*, 11–15 (1660–96) · Pepys, *Diary* · *The Nicholas papers*, ed. G. F. Warner, 4 vols., CS, new ser., 40, 50, 57, 3rd ser., 31 (1886–1920) · *Buckingham, public and private man: the prose, poems and commonplace book of George Villiers, second duke of Buckingham, 1628–1687*, ed. C. Phipps (1985) · F. T. Melton, 'A rake refinanced: the fortune of George Villiers, 2nd Duke of Buckingham, 1628–85', *Huntington Library Quarterly*, 51 (1988), 297–318 · B. Yardley, 'George Villiers, second duke of Buckingham, and the politics of toleration', *Huntington Library Quarterly*, 55 (1992), 317–37 · Second duke of Buckingham [G. Villiers], *The rehearsal*, ed. D. E. L. Crane (1976) · Second duke of Buckingham [G. Villiers] and R. Howard, *The country gentleman: a 'lost' play and its background*, ed. A. H. Scouten and R. E. Hume (1976) · A. Mizener, 'George Villiers, 2nd Duke of Buckingham: his life, and a canon of his works', PhD diss., University of Princeton, 1934 · J. P. Fowler, '*The chances*, adapted by George Villiers, 2nd Duke of Buckingham, from the comedy by John Fletcher', PhD diss., U. Birm., 1978–9 · Brian Fairfax's life of Buckingham, BL, Harleian MS 6862 · R. Lockyer, *Buckingham: the life and political career of George Villiers, first duke of Buckingham, 1592–1628* (1981) · duke's bailiffs' accounts, Bucks. RLSS, D 135 · *GM*, 1st ser., 56 (1786), 203–4

Archives BL, inventory of pictures, jewels, etc., left to Buckingham, Add. MS 18914 · BL, letter-book · BL, papers and corresp., mainly relating to his imprisonment, Add. MS 27872 · Bodl. Oxf., MSS Eng. lett. · Bucks. RLSS, estate corresp. and business ledgers · Chatsworth House, Derbyshire, letter-book · Folger, business MSS · GL, accounts · GL, estate MSS and accounts · Guildford Muniment Room, business ledgers · HLRO, papers relating to parliamentary disputes and concerning protestant dissenters · Leeds Central Library, corresp. · Leics. RO, legal papers relating to his debts · LMA, commonplace book · NL Wales, vouchers and accounts relating to personal expenses · PRO NIre., MSS relating to lands in Ireland, MSS 1A-40-40/41 | BL, newsletters to Sir Willoughby Aston, Add. MS 36916 · BL, Danby MSS, Add. MSS 28042–28051 · BL, Nicholas MSS, Egerton MSS 2537–2539, 2543 · BL, Sir Richard Temple's political collections, Stowe MS 304 · Bodl. Oxf., Clarendon corresp. · Bodl. Oxf., Ormond corresp. · Hist. Soc. Penn., Penn MSS · HLRO, main MSS and committee minutes · Leeds Central Library, Mexborough MSS, Reresby corresp. · NA Scot., Penn corresp. · PRO, state papers in the reign of Charles II, SP 29 · PRO, French ambassadors' dispatches, 31/3/111–139 [transcripts] · PRO, registers of the privy council, PC 2/54–74 · W. Yorks. AS, Leeds, letters to Sir H. Slingsby and Sir T. Slingsby · Yale U., Osborn collection MSS

Likenesses G. van Honthorst, group portrait, oils, 1628 (*Family of the duke of Buckingham*), Royal Collection; version, NPG · A. Van Dyck, double portrait, oils, 1635 (with his brother Francis), Royal Collection · portrait, c.1642, Cliveden, Buckinghamshire · attrib. H. Gascars, oils, c.1665, Longleat House, Wiltshire · J. M. Wright, oils, 1669, priv. coll. [see illus.] · P. Lely, oils, c.1675, NPG · R. White, line engraving, pubd 1679, BM, NPG · R. Dunkarton, mezzotint, pubd 1814 (after A. Van Dyck), BM, NPG · I. Beckett, mezzotint (after S. Verelst), BM, NPG · engravings, repro. in [T. Evans], ed., *The works of … George Villiers, duke of Buckingham*, 2 vols. (1775) · line engraving, NPG

Wealth at death estate value c.£19,000 p.a. in late 1660s; freehold trust established 1671 (renegotiated 1673 and 1675)

exchanged control of estate for £5000 p.a. pension; lands sold after death to settle debts

Villiers, George, Lord Villiers (1773–1859). *See under* Villiers, Sarah Sophia Child-, countess of Jersey (1785–1867).

Villiers, George Bussy, fourth earl of Jersey (1735–1805), courtier, was born on 9 June 1735 and baptized on 6 July at St George's, Hanover Square, London, the second but only surviving son of William Villiers, third earl of Jersey (*d.* 1769), and Anne (*d.* 1762), daughter of Scrope Egerton, first duke of Bridgewater, and widow of Wriothesley Russell, third duke of Bedford. Styled Viscount Villiers from 1742, he was educated at home by his tutor, the future poet laureate William Whitehead, and then from 1754 to 1756 he and Lord Nuneham toured Germany, Switzerland, and Italy, Whitehead acting as tutor to both young men. In 1756 he succeeded his uncle Thomas Villiers as MP for Tamworth, a seat he retained until 1765. He then sat first as MP for Aldborough, Yorkshire (1765–8), and later for Dover from 1768 until his elevation to the peerage on his father's death on 28 August 1769. A close friend of the duke of Grafton, he followed his political lead in both the Commons and Lords. He first held office as a lord of the Admiralty in the duke of Newcastle's ministry from 1761 but was dismissed in autumn 1762 for voting against Lord Bute's peace preliminaries. He returned to office as vice-chamberlain in Rockingham's ministry in 1765, and held a succession of court posts until 1800, apart from during the period 1777–82 when he was in opposition. He was sworn of the privy council on 11 July 1765 and was elected a fellow of the Society of Antiquaries in 1787.

In the month that Villiers took his seat in the Lords as fourth earl of Jersey and seventh Viscount Grandison he married, on 26 March 1770, Frances (1753–1821) [*see* Villiers, Frances], daughter of Philip Twysden, bishop of Raphoe, and Frances Carter. They had at least ten children but his wife was notoriously unfaithful and had a string of affairs, the most significant of which was her liaison with the prince of Wales from 1793. It was undoubtedly through her influence that Jersey was appointed master of the horse to the prince of Wales in 1795 and after she had fallen out of favour in 1799, Jersey was dismissed from his post in January 1800. At court Jersey gained a reputation as a fop and was noted for his ostentatious etiquette that bordered on sycophancy; Elizabeth Montagu dubbed him 'the Prince of Maccaronies'.

Jersey died suddenly, probably from a heart attack, on 22 August 1805 while walking with his eldest son, George *Villiers [*see under* Villiers, Sarah Sophia Childs-], near his son's house, Prospect Lodge, in Tunbridge Wells. He was buried at the family seat, Middleton Stoney, and was survived by his wife.   H. E. MAXWELL, *rev.* M. J. MERCER

Sources J. Brooke, 'Villiers, George Bussy', HoP, *Commons, 1754–90* • GEC, *Peerage* • *GM*, 1st ser., 43 (1773), 412 • J. Ingamells, ed., *A dictionary of British and Irish travellers in Italy, 1701–1800* (1997)
Archives LMA, grand tour diary, notebook and letters, accounts | BL, letters to George Grenville, Add. MS 57814 • BL, corresp. with duke of Newcastle, Add. MSS 32942, fols. 412, 438; 32945, fol. 131; 32949, fol. 189; 32972, fols. 151, 164; 32980, fol. 70;

33069, fol. 107 • BL, letters to Georgiana, Countess Spencer and to second Earl Spencer, pp. 2, 11 • BL, establishment book of prince of Wales signed by Villiers, Add. MS 44843, fols. 1, 8*v* • NRA, priv. coll., letters to Lord Shelburne • U. Nott. L., letters to third duke of Portland
Likenesses N. Dance, oils, 1770, Althorp, Northamptonshire • J. S. Copley, group portrait, oils (*The collapse of the earl of Chatham in the House of Lords, 7 July 1778*), Tate collection; [on loan to NPG]

Villiers, George Child-. *See* Villiers, George, Lord Villiers (1773–1859), *under* Villiers, Sarah Sophia Child-, countess of Jersey (1785–1867).

Villiers, George Herbert Hyde, sixth earl of Clarendon (1877–1955), public servant and courtier, was born on 7 June 1877 at 31 Upper Brook Street, London, the only son and elder child of Edward Hyde Villiers (1846–1914), fifth earl of Clarendon of the second creation, and his first wife, Lady Caroline Elizabeth Agar (*d.* 1894), eldest daughter of the third earl of Normanton. His father, a Liberal Unionist peer, was lord-in-waiting (1895–1901) to Queen Victoria and lord chamberlain (1901–5) to King Edward VII. The family seat was The Grove, Watford, Hertfordshire.

Bertie Villiers bore the courtesy title of Lord Hyde from birth. His education at Eton (1891–3) came to a premature close after he fell down a flight of stone stairs running for a fagmaster's call. A broken hip kept him in hospital for eighteen months and left him with a permanent limp. Previously a promising athlete, he later excelled at shooting, billiards, and golf despite his disability. At the time, however, his disappointed father took his name off the list of candidates for Marylebone Cricket Club, the Royal Horse Guards, and Oxford University.

In 1902 Lord Hyde went to Dublin as extra aide-de-camp to the lord lieutenant of Ireland, Lord Dudley. He returned to London three years later to marry (Adeline) Verena Ishbel (1886–1963), second daughter of the late Herbert Haldane Somers Cocks and sister of the sixth Baron Somers, at Trinity Church, Sloane Square, on 5 August 1905. They soon had a son and daughter (and a second son followed in 1916), but old Lord Clarendon insisted that the couple live with him at The Grove, where he carried on subjecting Bertie to austere parental discipline. Lord Hyde was deputy lieutenant of Hertfordshire from 1909. To escape from his father, in 1911 he emigrated to Canada with his wife and children (and Lord Somers) to run a fruit farm near Toronto.

After inheriting his earldom on 2 October 1914, Clarendon lived once again in England. He owned about 500 acres of land in Hertfordshire and Warwickshire (including the ruins of Kenilworth Castle), and latterly derived additional income as a director of the English Insurance Company, the General Electric Company, and Barclays Bank. Unfit for active service during the First World War, he nevertheless joined the Hertfordshire volunteer regiment and served as temporary lieutenant-colonel and county commandant (1916–20). In 1922 he was mayor of Watford before forsaking his ancestral home for Pitt House, Hampstead.

Clarendon had taken his seat in the House of Lords on 2

February 1915, but after moving the loyal address in 1916 he did not speak there again for over five years. The Primrose League elected him as its chancellor in May 1919, however, and he emerged as a Conservative politician when appointed a government whip on 4 April 1921, with the sinecure of lord-in-waiting to King George V. He assisted by speaking on bills that emanated from the Ministry of Labour. The replacement of the coalition by a Conservative administration in October 1922 was followed by his promotion to chief whip in the Lords and captain of the Honourable Corps of Gentlemen-at-Arms, which post he held until June 1925 (with a break in 1924 when Labour was in office).

After the dominions division of the Colonial Office was turned into a separate Dominions Office, Clarendon entered the public eye as its first parliamentary under-secretary of state from 5 August 1925, serving under Leo Amery. His platform speeches on imperial themes were conventional enough: moral ties signified more than legal commitments, he explained, after the dominions refused to ratify the Locarno guarantee treaty. He belonged to the southern Irish loyalists' claims committee and chaired the overseas settlement committee (much being made of his personal experience of migration). A tour of Canada in August–September 1926 enabled him to survey the progress of the group system of settlement. By then he knew that he would be leaving his post in December to become first chairman of the board of governors of the newly chartered British Broadcasting Corporation (BBC). His only substantial political speech thereafter was an appeal to the Baldwin government in December 1928 to grasp the nettle of House of Lords reform.

Clarendon took up his duties as BBC chairman on 1 January 1927, having been recommended by Lord Wolmer to the director-general, Sir John Reith, as a nice man who would not interfere. However, Reith had already found him too docile *vis-à-vis* the government during negotiations about the royal charter. Their relationship might yet have worked had it not been for the presence of Ethel Snowden on the board of governors. The wife of Labour MP Philip Snowden, she aspired to a very active role indeed, and she and Reith were soon at daggers drawn, with Clarendon impotent to restrain them. Despite viewing Mrs Snowden as a wretched nuisance, after being pushed from pillar to post the chairman came down on her side in 1929 in a tussle over the ill-defined respective powers of the director-general and the board. Reith called Clarendon a spineless dolt; Clarendon likened Reith to Mussolini. The prime minister, Ramsay MacDonald, announced in February 1930 that the earl was leaving the BBC in order to become governor-general of South Africa (ten months later).

Since the Imperial Conference in 1926 had recognized equality of status between Great Britain and the dominions, the government of South Africa argued that the next governor-general should be appointed on its own advice. The new constitutional relationship had still to be formalized by the statute of Westminster (1931), however, so a compromise had been reached: the South African leader

J. B. M. Hertzog, who had met Clarendon in 1926 and judged him acceptable, was allowed to submit his name in December 1929, though MacDonald officially advised the king to approve. The fact that Hertzog had effectively selected Clarendon may have muted Afrikaner hostility towards the monarchy. Furthermore, this governor-general differed from his predecessors in Pretoria by serving solely as representative of the crown; a high commissioner dealt with intergovernmental relations.

Having been made a privy councillor and GCMG, Clarendon arrived in Cape Town in January 1931. The economic slump soon followed, and Hertzog's National Party ministry began to crumble after South Africa left the gold standard in December 1932. The governor-general praised J. C. Smuts for agreeing to a coalition in February 1933, and the subsequent fusion of the two main political parties, accompanied by a gradual revival of trade, produced a period of relative harmony between the English-speaking and Afrikaner communities. In these circumstances, Clarendon performed his ceremonial functions with success. Spontaneous tact, a strong sense of duty, and a modicum of Afrikaans saw him through. His term of office was extended by two years in 1935, when the death of his son, Lord Hyde (1906–1935), in a shooting accident caused him much sadness. The Order of the Garter awaited him on his return to England in March 1937.

On 3 July 1938 Clarendon succeeded the second earl of Cromer as lord chamberlain of the household to King George VI. Grand royal occasions were less frequent than usual during his fourteen years in charge of them because of the Second World War and austerity, though the conflict did give rise to a large number of investitures. At these, the lord chamberlain announced the names of recipients of honours (or their next of kin, for posthumous awards), and Clarendon did so in a resonant sympathetic voice. He looked suitably dignified, with deep-set, slightly hooded eyes and a bushy moustache rather greyer than his hair. Appointed GCVO in 1939, he was *ex officio* chancellor of the Royal Victorian Order and also chancellor of the venerable order of St John of Jerusalem (1938–46) and the Order of St Michael and St George (1942–55).

Charity work took much of Clarendon's time during the war, when the king made St James's Palace the headquarters of the British Red Cross and St John's War Organization. He supervised parcels for prisoners of war and turned his own country house (Kyre Park, near Tenbury, Worcestershire) into a convalescent home. Another duty of the lord chamberlain was theatrical censorship. Perhaps the play on which he found it most difficult to rule was *Follow my Leader* by Terence Rattigan, a burlesque of Nazi Germany kept off the stage in 1938–9 for fear of reaction in Berlin. Issues of morality and taste never caused Clarendon any soul-searching: he applied existing criteria with a predictability that theatre managers found convenient. He refused to licence only seventy-nine plays—a comparatively low figure, yet there were fewer submissions in wartime. Dismayed by the proliferation of dirty jokes and nude posing, Clarendon held a conference in April 1940 to stress the need for stricter monitoring of revue and nightclub acts: naked women should be motionless and expressionless. He sometimes went incognito to watch dubious shows, but theatre staff easily recognized the gentleman with a stick and round wire glasses who invariably lit up a cigar in defiance of the 'no smoking' signs. Post-war calls to lift the total ban on homosexuality as a stage theme left him unmoved.

Lord Clarendon retired in October 1952, having been warned of the long periods of standing that the coronation of the new queen would entail. The customary final honour of the Royal Victorian Chain was awarded him. He died at his London home, 8 Chelsea Square, on 13 December 1955, when the earldom passed to his grandson. Clarendon's career demonstrated what could be attained in the mid-twentieth century by a good-natured and public-spirited aristocrat of unremarkable abilities.

JASON TOMES

Sources DNB · *The Times* (14 Dec 1955) · *The Reith diaries*, ed. C. Stuart (1975) · J. Johnston, *The lord chamberlain's blue pencil* (1990) · R. Lacour-Gayet, *A history of South Africa* (1977) · *Hansard 5L* · N. de Jongh, *Politics, prudery, & perversions: the censorship of the English stage, 1901–1968* (2000) · A. Briggs, *Governing the BBC* (1979) · A. Boyle, *Only the wind will listen: Reith of the BBC* (1972) · GEC, *Peerage*

Archives NRA, papers | PRO, Dominions Office records | FILM BFI NFTVA, current affairs footage · BFI NFTVA, documentary footage · BFI NFTVA, news footage

Likenesses photograph, *c.*1899, NPG · W. Stoneman, photograph, 1917, NPG · W. Stoneman, photograph, 1930, NPG · W. Stoneman, photograph, 1943, NPG · R. de Maistre, oils, 1949, Royal Commonwealth Society, London; repro. in Johnston, *Lord chamberlain's blue pencil*, 148 · G. Belcher, sketch, repro. in *Punch* (5 Jan 1927) · O. Birley, portrait; known to be in Pretoria in 1971 · M. Guion, portrait; known to be in family's possession in 1971 · photograph, repro. in Briggs, *Governing the BBC*

Wealth at death £28,685 4s. 9d.—and £139,435 in settled land: probate, 1956, CGPLA Eng. & Wales

Villiers, George William Frederick, fourth earl of Clarendon (1800–1870), politician, was born in Upper Grosvenor Street, London, on 26 January 1800, the eldest son of George Villiers (1759–1827), third son of the first earl, and his wife, Theresa (1775–1855), daughter of John Parker, first Lord Boringdon. Thomas Hyde *Villiers and Charles Pelham *Villiers, politicians, and Henry Montagu *Villiers, bishop, were his younger brothers. His father, Pittite MP for Warwick from 1792 to 1801, supported a numerous family on the income from a string of sinecures bestowed in the classical eighteenth-century fashion on the cadet of a house whose wealth was not equal to its rank. His mother was the dominant influence on her children; her strength of character, understanding of the world, and ready wit compensated for the weakness and misfortunes of her husband as a gentleman farmer. The younger George Villiers was educated at Christ's Hospital, probably as the private pupil of a master and not on the foundation, and at St John's College, Cambridge, matriculating in Michaelmas 1816 and graduating MA in 1820.

Necessity and ambition, 1820–1833 '... the learning of languages is the only thing I have any turn for', wrote the undergraduate Villiers to his only sister, Theresa [see Lewis, (Maria) Theresa], who, after the death of her first

George William Frederick Villiers, fourth earl of Clarendon (1800–1870), by Sir Francis Grant, 1843

husband, T. H. Villiers Lister, a minor literary figure, married her brother's future cabinet colleague, George Cornewall Lewis (Maxwell, 1.17). She was the sibling closest to him, the recipient of a stream of affectionate, revealing letters. A subvention from his uncle John, the third earl, enabled Villiers to enter diplomacy as an unpaid attaché at St Petersburg; but anxiety to provide for himself and assist his family led him to describe his otherwise agreeable years in Russia (1820–23) as 'wasted ... I [am] ... unable to make or improve acquaintances that may be useful to one' (ibid., 34). The warm friendship of his ambassador, Sir Charles Bagot, the patronage of George Canning, his father's friend, parental links with the court, and George IV's pleasure when shown one of his amusing, apparently well informed letters, combined to raise Villiers to a commissionership of customs—a dramatic change of fortune still possible in the last years of the unreformed parliament. Financially secure for life, he shouldered his dead father's responsibilities and his debts. Over nearly ten years (1824–33) he proved an able administrator with a talent for pleasing his political masters. Sent to Ireland in 1827–9 to effect a departmental reorganization, he became close to the cautious liberalizing viceroy of the day, Lord Anglesey. This experience on the eve of Catholic emancipation confirmed the Canningite toryism that made him a supporter of parliamentary reform and Lord Grey's ministry, in which his brother Hyde (d. 1832), to whose heavy election expenses he contributed, held minor office. Like many other reformers, he was alarmed by the spread of what he regarded as subversive ideas and by the violence of the popular agitation. Together with his friend Charles Greville, the diarist, he attempted to start a newspaper which they thought of calling the *Anti-Radical*, but failed to raise the money for the venture (*Greville Memoirs*, 2.94–5). His partisanship, and a successful commercial mission to France (1831) undertaken jointly with the Benthamite John Bowring, commended Villiers to Palmerston, another Canningite, who appointed him minister to Spain (August 1833). Although they were not always on the best of terms, Villiers never ceased to feel grateful to Palmerston: 'when I was a commissioner of customs and miserable at so passing my life but too poor to resign, he made me minister at Madrid … and from that moment I got on' (Kennedy, 135). He had put security first: now he was free to pursue ambition.

Minister plenipotentiary to Spain, 1833–1839 Villiers was young for his important post. He replaced a tory, recalled as unsympathetic to Spanish liberalism. Palmerston set great store by his policy of integrating Spain and Portugal with the western entente of Britain and Louis Philippe's France; Villiers was his instrument in circumstances considerably more difficult than the British foreign secretary realized. Palmerston's success in concluding the Quadruple Alliance of 1834 did not, as Villiers hoped, overawe the reactionary Carlist rebels against the succession of the infant Isabella II and the regency of her mother, Queen Maria Cristina, Ferdinand VII's widow identified with the Spanish liberals. The First Carlist War (1833–40) involved Villiers in an incessant struggle to save the liberal regime from collapse under the strain of military defeat, factional strife, and disordered finances. His task was the harder because direct British assistance was limited to the deployment of warships and the landing of a few marines. The British Legion of volunteers paid in arrears by the Spanish government and commanded by the radical soldier and MP de Lacy Evans was a doubtful military asset. 'The affairs of the Legion almost drive me mad', confessed Villiers as he wrestled with its problems, which included, at times, a reluctance to face the enemy (*Palmerston: Private Correspondence*, 631). Anglo-French co-operation in Spain, of which much had been expected, quickly gave way to rivalry for influence. In his private letters to Palmerston, Villiers raged against the 'selfish and inhuman policy' he ascribed to the French king (ibid., 758). The British minister played a significant, and occasionally crucial, part in ensuring the survival of the regime. He saw quite clearly that the Spanish people were indifferent or hostile to liberal institutions which he believed essential to their well-being. He would have preferred to administer his political medicines 'in small doses and well disguised or they will all be *brought up*', but the pressures of the time were too great (ibid., 227).

Villiers backed Juan Mendizabal, recalled from exile in London, the one politician with the intelligence and the will to make the liberal revolution succeed. Villiers persuaded the regent to make him prime minister in January 1836, although well aware of his weaknesses—'good intentions enough to lay down the whole of Hell with new pavement' (*Palmerston: Private Correspondence*, 363). The nationalization of monastic property that followed was a

turning point, giving purchasers a vested interest in defeating the Carlists. In Palmerstonian mode, Villiers had no qualms about interfering in Spain's internal affairs. The liberals' eventual victory in the civil war owed something to his relentless badgering of the politicians in Madrid, who neglected to pay and equip their armies.

Spain was the making of Villiers. While the fruits of his commercial and financial diplomacy were disappointing for British exporters and investors in Spanish bonds, he had acquired a considerable reputation at home, where whigs and radicals took a proprietary interest in Spanish liberalism. His published letters from Madrid reflect the personal charm, restless energy, and talent for intrigue characteristic of him. Soon fluent in Spanish, the handsome British minister was a popular figure in the society of the Spanish capital, especially with the ladies. His Edwardian biographer records that when the countess de Montijo was asked whether her daughter Eugénie, the future empress of the French, was really Villiers's child, she replied, after a pause for thought, 'Les dates ne correspondent pas' (Maxwell, 2.91).

The cabinet and whig politics, 1839–1847 '… an independent income—that's the only wish I have', wrote Villiers in 1837, a wish granted when he succeeded his uncle as the fourth earl of Clarendon (22 December 1838) and the owner of some 2000 acres in Hertfordshire and Warwickshire (Maxwell, 1.139). He was then about to propose, through his sister Theresa, to Lady Catherine Barham (*d.* 1874), the wealthy widow of John Foster Barham and daughter of Walter James Grimston, first earl of Verulam, whom he married on 4 June 1839. Not a love match on either side, it was nevertheless a happy marriage from which six children were born. Lady Clarendon was neither beautiful nor brilliant, but she understood her clever husband and supported his political career. He craved 'the interest of business and the excitement of responsibility … indispensable to me' (ibid., 157). Before he left Madrid he was offered first the post of governor-in-chief of British North America in succession to Lord Durham (February 1839) and on his return political office outside the cabinet, as master of the Royal Mint. Urged on by Charles Greville, he held out for a seat in the cabinet, which he secured as lord privy seal (privy council, 3 January 1840). Tory as well as Liberal newspapers approved of the appointment. Clarendon said of himself in later years that 'allegiance to party is the only strong political feeling I have', but Lord John Russell, the guardian of the whig tradition, sometimes questioned his loyalty to it (ibid., 2.319; Mandler, 101). The new recruit had, and retained, a Canningite fondness for the idea of coalition. He soon came into conflict with his old patron, Palmerston, over the latter's policy in the Near East. Clarendon, and others, objected to Britain's combination with the conservative powers in defence of the Ottoman empire against France and her protégé, Mehmet Ali, the ruler of Egypt. Lacking Palmerston's nerve, he protested at the risk of war in the midst of an economic recession: 'it would almost amount to national ruin' (Maxwell, 1.190). Palmerston got his way by threatening resignation, and was triumphantly vindicated by the outcome of his diplomacy in the Straits convention (1841). Behind a confident exterior, Clarendon was a cautious politician at home and abroad. Largely for that reason, he was not as reactionary as he often seemed in private. On the formation of the next whig government (1846), led by Russell, in which Clarendon was president of the Board of Trade, he pressed his colleagues to adopt 'a *middle class* policy' and to reconstruct a party he described as 'nearly effete' by taking in selected Peelites and Cobden, to whom overtures were made. The plebeian electorate cared about nothing except 'taxes, trade and peace', a Cobdenite formula (ibid., 1.265, 267, 273).

Viceroy of Ireland, 1847–1852 When he followed Lord Bessborough as viceroy in May 1847, Clarendon spoke of the 'sacrifice and … misfortune' which the post involved for him personally; but he was really 'in a great fright' that it would go to someone else (*Greville Memoirs*, 5.449). A member of the Political Economy Club (elected 1833) in his days as a commissioner of customs, he was eager to distinguish himself in the tremendous crisis of the great famine in Ireland; an immense task of social reconstruction faced her rulers. Beset by a host of problems, he struggled to do more than maintain order and let economic forces do their work. His efforts to extract additional funds for relief operations from the Treasury ran up against 'that harsh Trevelyanism', the doctrine of Sir Charles Trevelyan, the department's assistant secretary, that Irish expenditure should as far as possible fall upon Irish property-owners. '*Ireland cannot be left to her own resources*', argued Clarendon in one letter after another on that theme (MSS Clarendon, Irish letter-books, 31 Dec 1849, 23 Oct 1847). His remonstrances met with limited success: he was even less successful with plans for land banks on the Prussian model and a rather stronger government bill to compensate tenants for the little capital and intensive labour sunk in their holdings. He pointed in vain to advice from some of the Catholic hierarchy that this modicum of legal security for peasant occupiers would 'do more than anything else to … knock Repeal [of the Union] on the head' (ibid., 26 Oct 1847).

Want, starvation, and disease acting on endemic nationalist and agrarian unrest quickly drove Clarendon into repressive measures which he knew to be 'essentially bad'. The savagery of rural violence, compared with the weakness of political agitation by Old and Young Ireland, convinced him that 'whether the pretext be repeal of the union or separation from England … war against property is the object both of priest and peasant' (MSS Clarendon, box 81, 5 Nov 1847; Irish letter-books, 26 Nov 1847). With Russell, he devised a scheme for detaching the Catholic clergy from their popular sympathies by means of a state endowment; the probable outcry in protestant Britain ruled it out. The cabinet killed off their proposals for resettling Irish emigrants in the colonies. Clarendon was left to hope that the massive unaided emigration and the forced sale of landed property under the Encumbered Estates Act

(1849) would somehow effect the regeneration of the economy and society. The viceroyalty enhanced Clarendon's reputation. It confirmed him and his countrymen in the reassuring belief that Ireland's ills, social and political, were, at bottom, due to the character of the people: 'The real Celt is … almost incapable … of foreseeing the consequences of his own acts … He will … rather plot than work … sooner starve … than prosper by industry' (ibid., Irish letter-books, 10 June 1848). His name is not kept in benediction by the descendants, in Ireland and the Irish diaspora, of those whom he so described.

Foreign secretary, 1852–1858, and 'candid friend', 1858–1864 Clarendon's ill-concealed ambition was to step into Palmerston's shoes at the Foreign Office. Throughout the life of the ministry to which they belonged, he complained of his old patron's diplomacy as 'mischievous and disgraceful', setting all Europe against Britain (Maxwell, 1.330). When Russell finally dismissed his too independent foreign secretary in December 1851, Clarendon was the cabinet's preferred successor but Russell chose to take his protestations at face value—'Heaven knows I never coveted *any* office, and much less his'—and appointed Lord Granville (ibid., 336). Charles Greville thought his friend was afraid of Palmerston, easily the most popular politician of the day.

After Palmerston had brought down Russell in February 1852, Clarendon reached the Foreign Office in Lord Aberdeen's coalition of Peelites and whigs formed at the end of 1852. Regarded as a safe choice, because he was not Palmerston, who consented to go to the Home Office, Clarendon came down on Palmerston's side against Aberdeen when Britain and France moved towards war with Russia in defence of the Ottoman empire. At his suggestion Palmerston was invited to join the inner cabinet that endeavoured to frame policy. Inevitably, the former foreign secretary dominated the small group of ministers and handled Clarendon with skill and unfailing good humour. Palmerston had public opinion, increasingly warlike, behind him, while Clarendon lamented that 'the newspapers now render the business of government almost impossible' (Maxwell, 2.30). Palmerston always insisted that more resolute diplomacy could have averted the Crimean War. Clarendon's letters show that he was 'in a state of muddle and hesitation' (Taylor, 53, n. 4). His heart was not in the ensuing conflict (March 1854–April 1856); he anticipated a 'monster catastrophe' (Maxwell, 2.50). On the collapse of Aberdeen's ministry in January 1855, he was mentioned as a possible premier, but Queen Victoria and her husband, with whom he was a favourite, nevertheless observed that he lacked the necessary courage (*Letters of Queen Victoria*, 1st ser., 3.86).

Retained at the Foreign Office in Palmerston's first administration, Clarendon made a better foreign secretary under a prime minister who decided policy for him. He was genuinely fearful of revolution in the violent, if passing, storm of criticism that assailed aristocratic government after the administrative and military failures of the first Crimean winter. Defeatist until the fall of Sevastopol—'our prospects at home and abroad are as little cheering as our worst enemy could desire' (Steele, 'Palmerston's foreign policy', 66)—he was frightened by Palmerston's effective tactic to prevent the French, tired of war, from diluting the terms of peace: the intimation that Britain would fight on alone, if need be. '… we should have had all Europe against us at once, and the United States … soon', Clarendon told his brother-in-law Cornewall Lewis, conjuring up an improbable combination. He was uneasy when the British fleet was deployed in the Black Sea to enforce the peace: 'Palmerston is for acting rather more strongly than I am, but not much' (ibid.). Yet if he lacked the nerve that is a requisite of statesmanship, he was an accomplished diplomat, and won high praise for his technical performance at the congress of Paris (February–April 1856). Palmerston's oversight of the execution of policy, as distinct from its formulation, was galling: 'it was nonsense to write to me what Russia should be told and what Russia ought to do, &c' (ibid., 67).

Clarendon's caution where powerful countries were concerned did not prevent him from frequently denouncing the pusillanimity and turpitude of others. He was scathing about 'our cowardly public' for its indifference to the encroachments of the United States upon British interests in Central America. In the Far East he was bellicose: the restraints of international law did not apply, he contended, to dealings with 'barbarous states' like the Chinese and Japanese empires (Steele, 'Palmerston's foreign policy', 69; Steele, *Palmerston and Liberalism*, 58). The Indian mutiny, which broke out during the second (1856–8) of the wars to open China more widely to Western trade, made him sharply critical of Palmerston for underestimating the magnitude of the revolt, and its implications for Britain's position among the great powers. Mismanagement of the Indian crisis was his ostensible reason for turning against Palmerston after his ministry was overthrown in February 1858 on the Conspiracy to Murder Bill, a legislative gesture of appeasement to the French emperor, following a British-based attempt upon his life. Clarendon had fully supported the bill, but he believed, like many others, in Palmerston's political extinction on the sudden end of his government.

Clarendon had long been uncomfortable with Palmerstonian hostility to Austria in Italy and friendship for Sardinia, although he was strongly anti-papal and had censured misrule in the pope's dominions and Naples at the Paris congress. Clarendon grew less liberal with age, telling Palmerston that Britain would be unwise in the light of the Indian uprising to encourage Napoleon III in his plans for an Italian federation once Austria had been beaten: 'if we are to engage in a crusade for oppressed nationalities, it is a comparison we should make privately to ourselves … the Austrians cannot be more hated than we are' (Steele, 'Palmerston's foreign policy', 68). These sentiments, and Russell's wish to take that department for himself, cost Clarendon the Foreign Office on the formation of Palmerston's second administration in June 1859; 'we would have felt so sure with Lord Clarendon',

wrote the queen regretfully (ibid.). He declined to fill any other post, and cast himself in the role of the ministry's candid friend until in April 1864 he entered the cabinet as chancellor of the duchy of Lancaster. Always an influential figure in whig circles and now close to the tories, especially after his daughter Constance married Lord Derby's younger son in 1863, he was undoubtedly useful to a government with a small majority, and it was the stronger for his return.

Last years at the Foreign Office, 1865–1866, 1868–1870, and domestic politics As chancellor of the duchy, Clarendon was enlisted to help Palmerston and Russell in the last stages of the struggle over Schleswig-Holstein, in which Britain's diplomatic support failed to save for Denmark even a part of the territories she had disputed with the German powers. On Palmerston's death in October 1865, he succeeded to the Foreign Office under Russell's premiership. From the start of the new administration he was nervous of his leader's long-standing commitment to another instalment of parliamentary reform: 'I dread the advance of democracy', he had written in 1850 (MSS Clarendon, box 81, 27 February). Acquiescing in the Reform Bill of 1866, which he thought went too far, he was in politicians' minds as prime minister at the head of a ministry of tories and conservative Liberals when the bill was the undoing of Russell. Though he disliked and feared the coming man among the Liberals, Gladstone, as 'a far more sincere Republican than Bright' (*Greville Memoirs*, 7.459), his party allegiance was too strong to be broken, and he refused to continue at the Foreign Office in Derby's minority government (June 1866). He viewed with dismay the tory Reform Bill that conceded household suffrage in the boroughs, calling Disraeli's tactics 'Hebrew thimble-rigging' (Maxwell, 2.333). Gladstone rewarded his reluctant loyalty to a changing Liberalism with his third, and final, spell as foreign secretary.

This time, the widowed Queen Victoria strongly objected to Clarendon at the Foreign Office, saying that he was the only minister who had ever been impertinent to her. The old court favourite had forfeited her esteem by openly contemptuous references to Germany's princes and peoples over the years leading up to national unification. By his own account, Victoria 'gave it him pretty sharply, telling him he forgot the stock she came of' (Maxwell, 2.353, 282). Perhaps more importantly, he had also amused himself by gossiping about her relations with John Brown. Gladstone was, however, pledged to reappointing Clarendon, and pointed out that by then he was the only candidate whose name carried some weight in the chancelleries of Europe (*Selection*, ed. Vincent, 64; Gladstone, *Diaries*, 6.641–2, 645). Clarendon took an Erastian view of the Vatican Council in 1870, but his hostility to infallibility was cautious (too much so for Gladstone). He was believed to have a significant influence with Napoleon III, which he used in 1869–70 to resist the drift to war between France and Prussia. While he lacked the element of idealism in Gladstone's thinking on foreign policy, he was quite as convinced of the need for peace and for European co-operation to that end which stopped short of adding to existing treaty obligations. Without optimism he worked, unsuccessfully, to secure a measure of Franco-Prussian disarmament. He did succeed in lowering the tension between the two powers: Bismarck later remarked that, had he lived, Clarendon might have averted the war that destroyed Napoleon III's France and completed German unity (Maxwell, 366).

A want of 'popular fibre' Gladstone described Clarendon as the pleasantest colleague he had ever had. The first of Gladstone's Irish Land Acts in 1870, thoroughly distasteful to the former viceroy in its unprecedented invasion of landlord rights, did not lead to the resignation of which he freely talked. 'He is always a tall talker', wrote Granville; 'His normal state is a passion for office' (Ramm, 1.6). These weaknesses were well known to his contemporaries. Never an MP or a parliamentary candidate, he was not hardened to the rough and tumble of political life, remaining the talented, hard-working official of his formative years. His alarm about the Irish Land Bill as the precursor of a general attack on his class in the United Kingdom tends to confirm what a *Times* editorial (4 July 1870) said of him after his death. It spoke of his want of 'popular fibre', and suggested that he probably understood foreign rulers and ministers better than his own countrymen.

A cultured man, Clarendon broke Spanish law, when minister at Madrid, in exporting paintings by the country's masters for his private collection (*Palmerston: Private Correspondence*, 676). Out of office in the early 1860s, he chaired the eponymous royal commission on the ancient public schools, and showed himself, in that context, a judicious modernizer. But his principal recreation was gossip, the stuff of an enormous correspondence with colleagues, family, and friends; he was one of Charles Greville's best sources. As a letter-writer and conversationalist, he was exceptionally lively and amusing, though prone to considerable exaggeration. If he often excited the disapproval of the serious-minded, he was the kindest of men, a devoted father and brother. His wife tolerated an *amitié amoureuse* with Queen Sophia, wife of William III of the Netherlands and a frequent visitor to England (*Selection*, ed. Vincent, 63, 27, 406). Two great ladies in London society—Mary, marchioness of Salisbury, later countess of Derby, and the young duchess of Manchester, wife of the seventh duke—were among his other correspondents. There are very few allusions to personal religious beliefs in all his letters. He professed to detest evangelicals, but his brother Montagu was a noted evangelical prelate. Clarendon was 'no sceptic ... [I] believe in the resurrection of man and his admission to paradise' (Maxwell, 2.362). The worldliness fought with a Victorian ethic. His working habits at the Foreign Office depict the man: accustomed to spending the day in talk, he compensated by toiling over his papers far into the night, one of the first recorded chain-smokers of the cigarettes he had learned to like in Spain.

Clarendon died suddenly on 27 June 1870 at his London house, 1 Grosvenor Crescent, just before the outbreak of the Franco-Prussian War, and was buried in a cemetery near his country house, The Grove, on the outskirts of Watford on 2 July. His honours included the Garter (23 March 1849); he refused a marquessate after the congress of Paris, pleading insufficient means to support the dignity. The earldom passed to his second and eldest surviving son, Edward, Lord Hyde (d. 1905), lord chamberlain in unionist governments (1900–05).   DAVID STEELE

Sources Bodl. Oxf., Clarendon MSS · H. E. Maxwell, *Life and letters of George William Frederick, fourth earl of Clarendon*, 2 vols. (1913) · *The Greville memoirs, 1814–1860*, ed. L. Strachey and R. Fulford, 8 vols. (1938) · *Palmerston*, ed. R. Bullen and F. Strong, 1: *Private correspondence with Sir George Villiers ... as minister to Spain, 1833–1837* (1985) · A. L. Kennedy, ed., *My dear duchess: social and political letters to the duchess of Manchester, 1858–1869* (1956) · E. D. Steele, *Palmerston and liberalism, 1855–1865* (1991) · R. D. Edwards and T. D. Williams, *The great famine: studies in Irish history, 1845–52* (1956) · J. B. Conacher, *The Aberdeen coalition, 1852–1855* (1968) · J. B. Conacher, *Britain and the Crimea, 1855–56* (1987) · P. Mandler, *Aristocratic government in the age of reform: whigs and liberals, 1830–1852* (1990) · D. E. D. Beales, *England and Italy, 1859–60* (1961) · R. Millman, *British foreign policy and the coming of the Franco-Prussian War* (1965) · E. D. Steele, 'Palmerston's foreign policy and foreign secretaries', *British foreign policy and foreign secretaries*, ed. K. M. Wilson (1987), 25–84 · E. D. Steele, *Irish land and British politics: tenant-right and nationality, 1865–1870* (1974) · *Disraeli, Derby and the conservative party: journals and memoirs of Edward Henry, Lord Stanley, 1849–1869*, ed. J. R. Vincent (1978) · *A selection from the diaries of Edward Henry Stanley, 15th earl of Derby (1826–93), between March 1869 and September 1878*, ed. J. R. Vincent, CS, 5th ser., 4 (1994) · Gladstone, *Diaries*, vols. 5–7 · M. Cowling, *1867: Disraeli, Gladstone and revolution* (1967) · *The political correspondence of Mr Gladstone and Lord Granville, 1868–1876*, ed. A. Ramm, 2 vols., CS, 3rd ser., 81–2 (1952) · A. J. P. Taylor, *The struggle for mastery in Europe, 1848–1918* (1954) · *The letters of Queen Victoria*, ed. A. C. Benson and Lord Esher [R. B. Brett], 3 vols., 1st ser. (1907) · K. Weigand, *Österreich, die Westmächte und das europäische Staatensystem nach dem Krimkrieg, 1856–1859* (1997) · GEC, *Peerage* · *The Times* (4 July 1870)

Archives Bodl. Oxf., corresp. and papers · PRO, corresp., FO 361 | Balliol Oxf., corresp. with Sir Robert Morier · BL, Aberdeen MSS · BL, corresp. with W. E. Gladstone, Add. MSS 44133–44134 · BL, letters to Mrs A. P. C. Graham, Add. MS 48214 · BL, corresp. with Lord and Lady Holland, Add. MS 51617 · BL, corresp. with Lord Holland, Add. MS 51208 · BL, corresp. with A. H. Layard, Add. MSS 38960–39135, *passim* · BL, letters to Sir Charles Napier, Add. MSS 40023–40041, *passim* · BL, corresp. with Lord Westmorland, M/509/1, 517/1, 3, 518/1–2, 527/3 [microfilm] · BL, corresp. with Lord Wodehouse, Add. MSS 46692–46694 · BLPES, letters to Charles Villiers · Bodl. Oxf., corresp. with Sir John Crompton · Bodl. Oxf., letters to Charles Ellis · Bodl. Oxf., letters to Sir William Harcourt · Bodl. Oxf., corresp. with Lord Kimberley · Bodl. Oxf., letters from Villiers and his wife to Lady Theresa Lewis and Sir Thomas Lister · Bodl. Oxf., letters to James Wilson · Borth. Inst., corresp. with Sir Charles Wood · CCC Cam., letters to Madame Grahame · CKS, corresp. with Lady Westmorland · Duke U., Perkins L., letters to James Wilson · Durham RO, letters to Lord and Lady Londonderry · Harrowby Manuscript Trust, Sandon Hall, Staffordshire, letters to Lord Harrowby · Harvard U., Houghton L., letters to Sir John Bowring · Indiana University, Bloomington, Lilly Library, corresp. with Sir Robert Ker Porter and Jane Porter · JRL, letters to Lord Lyttelton · LPL, corresp. with A. C. Tait · Lpool RO, letters to fourteenth earl of Derby · NA Scot., corresp. with Sir Charles Murray · NA Scot., corresp. with Lord Panmure · NAM, corresp. with Lord Raglan · New Brunswick Museum, corresp. with Sir William Williams · NL Scot., corresp., incl. with Lord Rutherfurd · Norfolk RO, corresp. with Sir Henry Lytton Bulwer · NRA, priv. coll., corresp. with John Hamilton · NRA, priv. coll., letters to Lord Napier in Washington · PRO, corresp. with Stratford Canning, FO 352 · PRO, corresp. with Lord Cowley, FO 519 · PRO, corresp. with

Lord Granville, PRO 30/29 · PRO, letters to Lord Hammond, FO 391 · PRO, letters to Lord William Hervey, FO 528 · PRO, letters to Lord John Russell, PRO 30/22 · PRO, corresp. with Odo Russell, FO 918 · PRO NIre., letters to duke of Leinster · Royal Arch., Melbourne MSS · St Deiniol's Library, Hawarden, corresp. with duke of Newcastle · TCD, letters to Robert Carew · TCD, corresp. with Sir Philip Crompton · TCD, corresp. with Lord Donoughmore · Trinity Cam., letters to Lord Houghton · U. Durham L., corresp. with third Earl Grey · U. Nott. L., corresp. with Sir Andrew Buchanan · U. Nott. L., corresp. with duke of Newcastle · U. Southampton L., Broadlands MSS · U. Southampton L., corresp. with Lord Palmerston · W. Yorks. AS, Leeds, letters to Lord Clanricarde · Wilts. & Swindon RO, corresp. with Sidney Herbert · Woburn Abbey, Bedfordshire, letters to duke of Bedford · Woburn Abbey, Bedfordshire, letters to Lord George William Russell

Likenesses F. Grant, portrait, 1843, priv. coll. [*see illus.*] · W. Walker, mezzotint, pubd 1847 (after F. Grant), BM, NPG · J. Bell, marble statue, 1874, Gov. Art Coll. · E. Desmaisons, lithograph, BM · A. E. Dyer, oils (after S. C. Smith, 1861), Shire Hall, Hertford · J. Gilbert, group portrait, pencil and wash (*The coalition ministry*, 1854), NPG · W. Holl, stipple (after G. Richmond), BM · C. Hutchins, lithograph (after E. Hayes), BM · G. Sanders, two mezzotints (after C. Smith), BM · J. Sant, oils, Gov. Art Coll. · C. Silvy, carte-de-visite, NPG · W. Walker & Sons, carte-de-visite, NPG · J. Watkins, carte-de-visite, NPG

Wealth at death under £250,000: probate, 3 Aug 1870, *CGPLA Eng. & Wales*

Villiers, Henry Montagu (1813–1861), bishop of Carlisle and of Durham, was born in London on 4 January 1813. He was the fifth son of George Villiers (1759–1827) and his wife, Theresa (1775–1855), only daughter of John Parker, first Baron Boringdon. George William Frederick *Villiers, the fourth earl of Clarendon and foreign secretary, was his eldest brother. Nothing is known of Villiers's early education. He entered Christ Church, Oxford, in 1830 and held a studentship there, graduating BA in 1834 and MA in 1837. He was awarded an Oxford DD in 1856. On 30 January 1837 he married Amelia Maria (1815–1871), eldest daughter of William Hulton of Hulton Park, Lancashire, and they had a family of two sons and four daughters.

Villiers was ordained deacon in 1836 and became curate of Deane, Bolton-le-Moors, Lancashire; on being ordained priest in 1837 he became the vicar of St Nicholas's, Kenilworth, Warwickshire. In 1841 the lord chancellor (Lord Lyndhurst) gave him the wealthy rectory of St George's, Bloomsbury, London, and in 1847 he became a canon residentiary of St Paul's Cathedral. In the 1840s he was described in a document prepared for J. T. Delane, the editor of *The Times*, as perhaps 'the most influential clergyman in London' (Bodl. Oxf., MS Add. c. 290).

Shortly after ordination Villiers became an evangelical through a fellow curate, and on moving to Kenilworth was converted to Calvinism and premillennialism through William 'Millennial' Marsh. From 1842 Villiers held annual Lent lectures on the second coming of Christ. A large, diverse congregation was attracted by his sermons, many of which were published. His *Balls and Theatres, or, The Duty of Reproving the Works of Darkness* was published in 1846 and achieved a fourth edition in the same year. He also gave lectures under the auspices of the Young Men's Christian Association and the Church of England Young

Henry Montagu Villiers (1813–1861), by Cundall & Downes

Men's Society. A hard-working and able parish administrator, he had a team of curates and made use of lay workers and London City Missioners, and worked in close harmony with nonconformists.

Villiers was consecrated bishop of Carlisle in April 1856, the first of Lord Palmerston's episcopal appointments. Having authority over an enlarged diocese, he unified the ancient diocese of Carlisle with that of the northernmost part of the Chester diocese. He encouraged the appointment of Francis Close as the dean of Carlisle and the two men worked together in promoting the evangelical cause throughout the diocese. His diocesan appointments of archdeacons and rural deans were not, however, partisan.

Villiers encouraged greater personal piety among his clergy and raised the academic standard for those entering the diocese. But as the majority of livings were poor it was difficult to retain able clergy. He exercised discipline over drunken clergy, three of whom were dismissed. He encouraged monthly communion services and took pains over his confirmation services, and began the practice of confirming candidates from the English chapels in Scotland. He travelled extensively throughout his diocese and was also in demand elsewhere as a speaker. In 1857 he preached the first of a series of sermons to the working classes in Exeter Hall. Villiers was keen to improve elementary education in his diocese, in which he was supported by the activity of the philanthropist George Moore.

Villiers was little involved in the politics of the day and rarely spoke in the House of Lords. With Lord Shaftesbury he was active in the London Society for Promoting Christianity amongst the Jews.

He was translated to Durham in 1860 and began his work in earnest. However, in the following summer he became ill; he died within a fortnight on 9 August 1861 in Auckland Castle, Bishop Auckland, and was buried in the chapel there. His wife and family were left in financial difficulties and Amelia and her three unmarried daughters were given grace-and-favour accommodation at Hampton Court Palace. His eldest son, Henry Montagu Villiers (1841–1908), became vicar of St Paul's, Knightsbridge.

The last six months of Villiers's life were blighted by the Cheese affair, and it may well have contributed to his early death. Edward Cheese (d. 1886) married Villiers's daughter Amy Maria in 1860. In February 1861 Villiers appointed his new son-in-law, bishop and domestic chaplain to the lucrative living of Haughton-le-Skerne, near Darlington. *The Guardian* accused Villiers of gross nepotism. He became the target of wounding criticism and was the subject of a cartoon in *Punch* (9 March 1861). Although he contemplated resignation, his friends encouraged him to remain as bishop. Bishop A. C. Tait saw him in a different light, as 'a man of rare charm and full of friendship' (E. H. Thomson, *Life and Letters of William Thomson*, 1919, 53).   A. F. MUNDEN

Sources *The Times* (10 Aug 1861) · *The Times* (19 Aug 1861) · *Punch*, 40 (1861), 101 · A. F. Munden, 'The first Palmerston bishop: Henry Montagu Villiers, bishop of Carlisle, 1856–1860 and bishop of Durham, 1860–1861', *Northern History*, 26 (1990), 186–206 · A. F. Munden, 'Early evangelicals in mid-Warwickshire', *Warwickshire History*, 8/4 (1991–2), 118–30 · *DNB*

Likenesses W. J. Edwards, stipple, pubd 1856 (after G. Richmond), NPG · C. Baugniet, lithograph, BM · W. Berwick, Auckland Castle, co. Durham · Cundall & Downes, carte-de-visite, NPG [*see illus.*] · D. J. Pound, stipple and line engraving (after photograph by Mayall), NPG; repro. in D. J. Pound, *Drawing room portrait gallery of eminent personages* · G. Richmond, pastel drawing, Auckland Castle, co. Durham

Wealth at death under £20,000: probate, 7 Sept 1861, *CGPLA Eng. & Wales*

Villiers, James Michael Hyde (1933–1998), actor, was born on 29 September 1933 at 1A Devonshire Terrace, London, the son of Eric Hyde Villiers, a retired brandy distiller, and his wife, Joan Ankaret Talbot. He was educated at Abberley Hall preparatory school, Worcestershire, where he became stage-struck, and at Wellington College, Berkshire. He trained for the stage at the Royal Academy of Dramatic Art and made his professional début at the summer theatre, Frinton, as William Blore in Agatha Christie's *Ten Little Niggers* (1953). His first London appearance was at the Prince's in *Toad of Toad Hall* (1954) with the Shakespeare Memorial Company. In 1955 he joined the Old Vic, where he played such parts as Trebonius in *Julius Caesar*, Antenor in *Troilus and Cressida*, and Bushy in *Richard II*. The last two he also played on the company's North American tour (1956–7), when he made his New York début in *Richard II* at the Winter Garden. While spending a year with the English Stage Company at the Royal Court,

he appeared in Nigel Dennis's religious satire *The Making of Moo* (1957).

Villiers, who claimed descent from George Villiers, duke of Buckingham, and kinship with the earl of Clarendon, quickly became a distinctive character actor. His aristocratic demeanour and plummy accent made him instantly recognizable and much in demand at a time when it was fashionable for actors to have regional accents or a rough edge; not far beneath the surface was a haughty disdain, a supercilious arrogance which usually lent itself to dislikeable characters, some merely ironic or sardonic, others decidedly chilling. His essential good nature, though, ensured that life was enjoyed as fully off the stage as on it.

In 1960 Villiers appeared in the melodrama *Tomorrow—with Pictures* at the Lyric, Hammersmith, before transferring to the Duke of York's, but subsequent stage roles in the decade were usually lighter, such as Frederick Knott's *Write me a Murder* (1962) at the Lyric, *Everybody Loves Opal* (1964), and Brigid Brophy's *The Burglar* (1967), both at the Vaudeville. He was, though, becoming more visible in films and on television. His film début, a bit part in *Carry on Sergeant* (1958), was followed by Tony Richardson's *The Entertainer* (1960), an unlikely heroic part in *The Clue of the New Pin* (1961), and a string of roles in films which epitomized the 1960s, including three for director Joseph Losey—*The Damned* (1961), *Eva* (1962), and *King and Country* (1964)—two Agatha Christie films—*Murder at the Gallop* (1963) and *The Alphabet Murders* (1966)—Clive Donner's *Nothing but the Best* (1964), Roman Polanski's *Repulsion* (1965), *The Nanny* (1965), as the father opposite Bette Davis, Michael Winner's *You Must be Joking!* and Bryan Forbes's *The Wrong Box* (both 1966), as well as *Otley* (1969), by Dick Clement and Ian La Frenais. He made numerous television appearances, especially in plays—*The Siege of Manchester* (1965), *A Piece of Resistance* (1966), and *The Fantasist* (1967)—and was a notable Charles II, to whom he bore more than a passing resemblance, in the series *The First Churchills* (1969). On 20 August 1966 Villiers married Patricia Nora Donovan (b. 1942/3), a solicitor's assistant, daughter of William Victor Donovan, a retired RAF officer; they divorced in 1984.

The high point in Villiers's stage career was as Victor Prynne in John Gielgud's revival of Noël Coward's *Private Lives* (1974) at the Queen's, opposite Maggie Smith and Robert Stephens; some critics felt he improved on Laurence Olivier's original. Villiers played Belcredi in Pirandello's *Henry IV* (1974) at Her Majesty's opposite Rex Harrison, and later that year appeared at the Oxford festival as the Earl of Warwick in G. B. Shaw's *Saint Joan* and, with an excellent comic performance, in André Roussin's *The Little Hut*; the latter transferred to the Duke of York's. He played Sir Ralph Bonnington in Shaw's *The Doctor's Dilemma* (1975) at the Mermaid, and was in an unlikely combination at the Old Vic, *The White Devil* and *The Ghost Train* (1976). He also enjoyed himself as both Mr Darling and Captain Hook in *Peter Pan* (1979) at the Shaftesbury. Among his later roles were Lord Thurlow in *The Madness of*

George III (1991) at the National and Mr Brownlow in the hit revival of *Oliver!* at the Palladium (1994).

Through the 1970s and 1980s Villiers remained just as busy on small and large screen, 'enjoying to the full the advantages of the character actor, who often proves more durable than the leads in whose shadows he often lurks' (*The Times*). His many television appearances included *Lady Windermere's Fan* and *The Millionairess* (both 1972) and *Pygmalion* (1973), as Professor Higgins, and in the two mini-series *Fortunes of War* (1987) and *Hemingway* (1988). He was excellent as the prime minister's sad brother in *House of Cards* (1990); a final role was as Buster Foxe in Anthony Powell's *A Dance to the Music of Time* (1997). His films included *Blood from the Mummy's Tomb* (1971), *The Ruling Class* (1972), with long-time friend Peter O'Toole, *Joseph Andrews* (1977), *Saint Jack* (1979), *For your Eyes Only* (1981), *Under the Volcano* (1984), *Scandal* (1989), *Let him have it* (1991), and, his last, *The Tichborne Claimant* (1998).

Villiers was married again, on 30 July 1994, to Lucinda Claire Noelle (Lucy) Jex (*b.* 1959/60), a secretary, daughter of Alan Jex, a retired pilot. Away from acting he was a keen follower of cricket and football. He died on 18 January 1998 of cancer at Arundel Hospital, Sussex. His wife survived him.   ROBERT SHARP

Sources *The Times* (12 Feb 1998) · *The Independent* (21 Jan 1998) · *Daily Telegraph* (22 Jan 1998) · *The Guardian* (30 Jan 1998) · www.uk. imdb.com, 17 Nov 2001 · I. Herbert, ed., *Who's who in the theatre*, 1 (1981) · b. cert. · m. certs. · d. cert.
Likenesses group photograph, 1964, Hult. Arch. · photograph, repro. in *The Times*
Wealth at death £183,499: probate, 11 March 1998, *CGPLA Eng. & Wales*

Villiers, John, Viscount Purbeck (1591?–1658), courtier, was the eldest son of Sir George *Villiers (*c.*1544–1606) [*see under* Villiers, Sir Edward] and his second wife, Mary (*c.*1570–1632), daughter of Anthony Beaumont of Glenfield, Leicestershire. His two younger brothers were George *Villiers, the future duke of Buckingham (1592–1628), and Christopher *Villiers, the future earl of Anglesey (*d.* 1630). Nothing is known of his education, but in 1602 his brother George went to school at Billesdon, Leicestershire, where Anthony Cade was the master, and Villiers may well have preceded him.

In May 1609 Villiers's mother was able to procure a pass via her future third husband, Sir Thomas Compton, to enable Villiers and his brother George to travel abroad. Three years were spent at places such as Blois and Angers before the brothers returned in 1612–13. By the beginning of 1616 George Villiers had begun his meteoric rise to power and influence, and he was not averse to advancing his elder brother. On 30 June 1616 John Villiers was knighted, and he soon became groom of the bedchamber and master of the robes to Prince Charles (the future Charles I). When the king conferred the earldom of Buckingham on George in January 1617, it was entailed upon his elder brother should the new earl die without male heirs.

Villiers married on 29 September 1617 Frances (1599–1645), daughter of Sir Edward *Coke and his second wife,

Lady Elizabeth Cecil [*see* Hatton, Elizabeth], widow of Sir William Hatton (and therefore known as Lady Hatton). For Coke this was a marriage intended to form an alliance with the Villiers family, and so regain royal favour. For Villiers the attractiveness of the match was more material: as Lady Hatton put it, her daughter 'is heir to the mother to a fortune not much inferior to any unmarried heir of England' (*Letters of John Holles*, 2.185). Lady Hatton was opposed to the marriage, and hid her daughter at Oatlands, near Hampton Court. Coke then forcibly took possession of his daughter, who seems to have reconciled herself to the match knowing that 'it will be a means of the King's favour to my father', and because Villiers was 'not to be misliked; his fortune is very good; a gentleman well born' (Lockyer, 43). The marriage was conducted by the bishop of Winchester at Hampton Court, in the presence of the king, the queen, and Prince Charles.

Lady Hatton appears to have accepted the match, but when it came to bestowing some of her fortune, inherited from her late husband, on to the couple, she prevaricated, and it is not known how much was eventually settled upon them. It was in anticipation of some of the Hatton property on the Isle of Purbeck, Dorset, being settled on Villiers that James I on 19 July 1619 created him Baron Stoke and Viscount Purbeck. In 1620 Purbeck and his wife were abroad, visiting Spa; this was possibly an early indication of the need to find a cure for his ill health. By this date he was exhibiting signs of mental instability, which took the form of several days of uncontrolled behaviour, before he subsided in a 'dull fit', which allowed him to be calmed down. In October 1622 Purbeck was at Compton to recover from 'his fit', and Lady Purbeck was living elsewhere and enjoying financial support from Buckingham.

On 19 October 1624 Lady Purbeck gave birth to a son, Robert. The father was rumoured to be Sir Robert Howard, a younger son of the earl of Suffolk. Buckingham was outraged, given that at this date he was without an heir himself and the child stood to inherit his titles and honours. Both Lady Purbeck and Howard protested their innocence and were ordered to appear before the court of high commission on 5 March 1625. Purbeck himself accompanied Buckingham on his embassy to the Netherlands later in 1625. A second hearing before the court of high commission took place on 19 November 1627, when Lady Purbeck was found guilty of adultery, fined, and ordered to undertake a public penance. This she avoided by taking refuge in the Savoy, and she then escaped to live with her father. After Coke's death in 1634 she returned to London, but for fear of renewed prosecution she fled to France with Howard, before returning in the early 1640s. She was buried on 4 June 1645.

Following the death of Buckingham in 1628, Purbeck appears to have been put under royal protection. A letter survives from 1632 which enjoins a strict regimen for Purbeck, now a patient at the home of Dr Cudiman: no tobacco or wine, nor any visitors apart from those who came with him out of the country. At some point after 1645 Purbeck was married for a second time, to Elizabeth

(d. 1696), daughter of Sir William Slingsby of Kippax, Yorkshire, and the widow of Colonel Chichester Fortescue of Dromiskin, Ireland. Purbeck made his will on 29 August 1655, making his wife executrix. In December 1655 he petitioned for lodgings at Somerset House, but these were refused. His death was reported on 26 February 1658 by two of Secretary Nicholas's Parisian correspondents, but another source reported his death on 18 February 1658 at Charlton, near Greenwich, Kent. Robert *Danvers (1624–1674), either his son or the illegitimate son of his wife, fought for the king, married the daughter of a regicide, became a presbyterian, and died a Catholic in France.

STUART HANDLEY

Sources GEC, *Peerage* · R. Lockyer, *Buckingham: the life and political career of George Villiers, first duke of Buckingham, 1592–1628* (1981) · C. D. Bowen, *The lion and the throne* (1957) · PRO, PROB 11/274/129, fol. 185r · BL, Egerton MS 2552, fol. 25v · *Letters of John Holles, 1587–1637*, ed. P. R. Seddon, 2, Thoroton Society Record Series, 35 (1983), 31, 35–6 · F. Villiers, *The curious case of Lady Purbeck* (1909) · T. Birch, *The court and times of James the First*, 2 vols. (1848) · W. D. Macray, ed., *Beaumont papers* (1884), 34–5 · *The manuscripts of his grace the duke of Rutland*, 4 vols., HMC, 24 (1888–1905), vol. 1, pp. 467–8 · CSP dom., 1655–6, 81; 1657–8, 306
Likenesses group portrait, oils, 1628 (*The family of the duke of Buckingham*), Royal Collection

Villiers [Danvers], **John**, styled third earl of Buckingham (*c.*1677–1723), peerage claimant, was born about 1677, the only surviving son of Robert Villiers or Danvers, styled third Viscount Purbeck (*c.*1656–1684), and his wife, Margaret Maccarty (d. 1698), the widow of Charles Maccarty, third Viscount Muskerry, and the daughter of Ulick Bourke, marquess of Clanricarde. His grandfather was the adventurer Robert *Danvers, regarded as the illegitimate son of Frances Coke, the wife of John Villiers, Viscount Purbeck. His father had called himself third Viscount Purbeck, despite the fact that his claim to succeed to that dignity had been disallowed by the House of Lords in 1678 on the grounds of Robert Danvers's illegitimacy. Robert Villiers had left England heavily in debt, and was killed at a duel at Liège in April 1684. His widow subsequently married the notorious rake Robert *Feilding.

John Villiers, styled fourth Viscount Purbeck from the death of his father, was educated at Eton College, 'from whence he entered into the debaucheries of the town, and associated himself with the gamesters of it' (Sterry, 345). On 16 April 1687, on the death of his grandfather's supposed first cousin George Villiers, second duke of Buckingham, he became (if his grandfather's illegitimacy was set aside) third earl of Buckingham under the terms of a patent issued by James I to the first duke in 1617. On 23 November 1699 he married Frances (d. before 1730), the widow of George Heneage of Lincolnshire and the daughter of a clergyman called Moyser, 'a person of a dissolute abandoned character but of a large jointure' (ibid.). She may have been Frances Moiser, the daughter of George Moiser, baptized at St Michael's, New Malton, Yorkshire, on 23 December 1677. They had two daughters, Mary (d. 1703) and Elizabeth (*c.*1701–1786), and a son, John, styled Lord Villiers (1707–1710?).

Villiers is first recorded using the title earl of Buckingham in a petition to the House of Lords on 16 May 1702, but he did not make a formal claim to the earldom until April 1709, nor did the Lords then take any notice of his appeal. In 1720 he unsuccessfully petitioned George I for the title. He died at Dancer's Hill, South Mimms, Middlesex, on 10 August 1723, and was buried at South Mimms on 18 August as Lord Buckingham. His claims were adopted by his first cousin George Villiers (1690–1748), vicar of Chalgrove, Oxfordshire, but he did not press them beyond issuing a thin pamphlet, *The Case of George Villiers*, in 1723. On the death of this clergyman's son, George, vicar of Frodsham, Cheshire, on 24 June 1774, this claim to the earldom of Buckingham became extinct.

THOMAS SECCOMBE, rev. MATTHEW KILBURN

Sources 'Buckingham', GEC, *Peerage*, new edn · 'Purbeck', GEC, *Peerage*, new edn · W. Sterry, ed., *The Eton College register, 1441–1698* (1943), 345 · J. B. Burke, *Vicissitudes of families* (1883) · N. H. Nicholas, *The historic peerage of England*, rev. W. Courthope (1857) · T. C. Banks, *The dormant and extinct baronage of England* (1807) · J. Burke, *The patrician*, 6 vols. (1846–8), 2.96 · *The case of George Villiers* (1723)

Villiers, John Charles, third earl of Clarendon (1757–1838), politician, was born on 14 November 1757, the second son of Thomas *Villiers, first earl of Clarendon of the second creation (1709–1786), diplomatist and politician, and Lady Charlotte Capel (1721–1790), eldest surviving daughter of William *Capel, third earl of Essex, and Jane Hyde. He was educated at Eton College (1766–74) and at St John's College, Cambridge; he graduated MA in 1776 and LLD on 30 April 1838. At Cambridge he met and became friends with William Pitt the younger. He entered Lincoln's Inn in 1774 and was called to the bar on 22 June 1779. On 6 February 1782 he was made joint king's counsel in the duchy court of Lancaster by his father, then chancellor of the court.

In January 1784 Villiers was brought into parliament for the pocket borough of Old Sarum by Thomas Pitt, Lord Camelford, at the request of William Pitt. Villiers voted consistently with the administration and was rewarded with several court appointments. He became surveyor of woods south of the Trent on 29 July 1786, and comptroller of the king's household, and was sworn of the privy council on 19 February 1787. In February 1790 he was made a commissioner of the Board of Trade and left his post in the household to accept the sinecure of warden and chief justice in eyre north of the Trent, which brought him an income of £2250 per annum. In the same year he was returned for Dartmouth, which he continued to represent until 1802. He did not make his mark as a debater in parliament but was known as 'a mere courtier, famous for telling interminable stories' (*Diaries*, ed. Jackson, 2.302). The *Rolliad* described him as 'Villiers, comely with the flaxen hair' and, together with Wraxall, regarded him as the "Nereus" of Pitt's forces' (*Memoirs of … Wraxall*, 5.112).

On 5 January 1791, at her father's house in Savile Row, Villiers married his first cousin, Maria Eleanor Forbes (1756/7–1838), the younger twin daughter and coheir of Admiral John *Forbes (1714–1796) and Lady Mary Capel, daughter of the third earl of Essex. Following the outbreak of war with France, he volunteered to use the income from his sinecure to help raise a regiment of fencible cavalry, to which he was appointed colonel on 14 March 1794. He remained a staunch supporter of Pitt during Addington's administration and was returned on Lady Sutherland's interest for Tain burghs at the general election in 1802. He succeeded as first protonotary of common pleas in the county palatine of Lancaster in 1804, a reversionary sinecure that required him to seek re-election to parliament, which he did, though not without some demur. Pitt's return to office with Addington, which Villiers strongly disapproved of, led him to break formally with Pitt on 10 February 1805 and he gave up his seat in May 1805.

Villiers returned to the Commons as MP for Queensborough in 1807 and, to general astonishment, was chosen by Canning to be envoy to the Portuguese court in 1808. Arriving in Lisbon in November 1808, he did not relish his diplomatic role and asked to be recalled in September 1809, although he did not leave until February 1810. He seems, however, to have established a reasonable relationship with both Wellington and Wellesley and afterwards felt confident to offer advice on policy in the Peninsula. On the death of his elder brother, Thomas, unmarried, on 7 March 1824, Villiers succeeded to the earldom. Thereafter he took little part in political life apart from voting with the whigs in the upper house, and devoted himself to religious and charitable works.

Clarendon died suddenly at his home, Walmer Terrace, Deal, on 22 December 1838, nine months after his wife's death on 18 March, and was buried in Watford on 29 December. Their only child, Mary Harriet, had died unmarried on 20 January 1835 and so he was succeeded by his nephew George William Frederick *Villiers as fourth earl of Clarendon.   W. R. WILLIAMS, rev. S. J. SKEDD

Sources GEC, Peerage · 'Villiers, John Charles', HoP, Commons · The historical and the posthumous memoirs of Sir Nathaniel William Wraxall, 1772–1784, ed. H. B. Wheatley, 5 vols. (1884) · The diaries and letters of Sir George Jackson, ed. Lady Jackson, 2 vols. (1872) · GM, 2nd ser., 11 (1839), 207–8 · R. A. Austen-Leigh, ed., The Eton College register, 1753–1790 (1921), 536
Archives BL, corresp. with Bishop Butler, Add. MSS 34585–34590, passim · BL, letters to Sir Arthur Paget, Add. MS 48407 · BL, corresp. with Lord Wellesley, Add. MSS 37286–37312, passim · NA Scot., letters to Alexander Ross, GD2/152 · PRO, letters to William Pitt, PRO 30/8 · Royal Military Academy, Sandhurst, letters to General Le Marchant

Villiers, John Henry de, first Baron de Villiers (1842–1914), judge in South Africa, was of Huguenot descent and was born at Paarl, Cape Colony, on 15 June 1842. He was the second son of Carel Christiaan de Villiers, government land surveyor, of Paarl, and his wife, Dorothea Elizabeth Retief, also of Paarl. Educated at the South African College, Cape Town (1853–61), he went next to Utrecht, intending perhaps to prepare for a clerical career. He read widely in literature, philosophy, and history, and transferred in 1862 to Berlin University. But in June 1863, overcome by vocational doubts, he entered the Inner Temple,

John Henry de Villiers, first Baron de Villiers (1842–1914), by unknown photographer

London, to train for the bar, qualifying in November 1865. Early in 1866 he began to practise at the Cape bar. In 1871 he married Aletta Johanna (d. 1922), daughter of Jan Pieter Jordaan, a wine farmer, of Worcester, Cape Colony. They had two sons and two daughters. From June 1867 he sat as a member of the house of assembly for Worcester, advocating, inter alia, the withdrawal of state aid from the churches, and the institution of responsible government in Cape Colony, hoping thereby to thwart eastern Cape separatism. In 1872 he became attorney-general in the ministry of John Charles Molteno, but, at the urgent request of the premier and of William Porter, he resigned in December 1873 to become chief justice. Though now a judge, he never lost touch with legislation and politics. He presided over several key commissions, notably the Cape federal commission (1873), the education commission (1880), and the diamond laws commission (1887) and was ex officio president of the legislative council.

De Villiers was deeply concerned with, and had a major impact on, wider southern African affairs. He worked for regional federation, trying to arrange this with President J. H. Brand of the Orange Free State in 1871. In 1877 they actually agreed upon a scheme, which would have been submitted to the high commissioner, Sir Bartle Frere, but for Sir Theophilus Shepstone's annexation of Transvaal. In 1881 he was a member of the royal commission which drew up the Pretoria convention. He had already been knighted in 1877, and he was now created KCMG (1882).

In 1888 and 1895 de Villiers was invited to stand for the Orange Free State presidency and, in 1893, at the instance of Cecil Rhodes, he agreed to take office as prime minister of Cape Colony; but Rhodes suddenly re-formed his cabinet without him. De Villiers offered his services again in 1896 and 1902, but on both occasions the premiership was offered to J. G. Sprigg, who accepted. In 1894 de Villiers went to the Ottawa colonial conference to further Rhodes's schemes of intercolonial preference and communications. Personally he was on good terms with Rhodes, and with the high commissioners Sir Hercules Robinson and Sir Henry Loch, but, like Loch, he feared the use to which Rhodes might put his wide and indefinite powers, and he began to turn against him early in 1894. After the Jameson raid (January 1896), de Villiers successfully urged President Kruger to show mercy to his prisoners; and early in 1897 he unsuccessfully mediated between Kruger and his chief justice, J. G. Kotze, over the power claimed by some of the judges to test the validity of laws by the touchstone of the *grondwet* (constitution). For some time de Villiers had tried to form a South African court of appeal as a step towards federation, and in 1886 had urged the inclusion of colonial judges in the privy council. He was himself sworn in, as the first colonial judge to take his seat on the judicial committee, in July 1897, though he was unable to attend regularly.

During 1899, in spite of failing health, de Villiers worked hard for peace. He lay dangerously ill for many weeks in England and on the Riviera in 1901, during the Second South African War, but he recovered and helped to block the proposed suspension of the Cape constitution in 1902. By 1906 he was again promoting federation, and from 1907 kept in close touch with J. X. Merriman, the Cape premier, and General Smuts. A visit to Canada as representative of the four South African colonies at the Canadian tercentenary now persuaded him that union was better than federation. On his return, he was unanimously elected president of the national convention, and as such he personally conducted the negotiations with the imperial government on the future of the protectorates. In the convention itself he presided over the plenary sessions and most of the committees, thanks to the confidence he inspired, sometimes securing the adoption of motions which, put forward by anyone else, would have been rejected. He also headed the drafting committee which finalized the Union of South Africa Bill, prior to its passage through the British parliament. For this he was created baron, with the title de Villiers of Wynberg. He returned home to become first chief justice of the union (1910). In 1912, and again in July 1914, he was acting governor-general. He died quickly, of pneumonia, at Pretoria, on 2 September 1914 and was buried at Woltemade cemetery, Maitland, on 7 September. He was succeeded as second baron by his elder son, Charles Percy (b. 1871).

De Villiers was relatively tall, lean, and active, a man of immense dignity relieved by a kindly spirit and dry humour. He 'had a square face, blunt features, firm jaw, long thin nose, close-shut mouth, deep-sunk eyes, while from his cheeks hung thin Dundreary weepers which later spread under his chin like a white crescent moon' (*DSAB*). He enjoyed hunting and fishing, loved dogs, kept bees, and his enthusiasm for fruit farming embraced viticulture, and citrus and deciduous fruit. His chief claim to fame, however, is as a judge. Other South African judges may have been more learned in the letter of the law, but none understood its spirit so well. It was sometimes said that at times he dispensed 'de Villiers's law' (and some of his judgments were reversed on one or two points after his death), but despite his speed in reaching decisions, his judgments were only questioned by the privy council four times. Over the course of forty-one years he dispensed justice fearlessly, without respect of persons, on a great variety of subjects, notably those which—like his decisions in *In re Kok and Balie* (1879) and *Sigcawu's case* (1895)—went right to the core of individual liberty. He outshone the Cape, and outlived judges of his own generation.

De Villiers's desire to see the consolidation of Southern African judiciaries into a single system grew *pari passu* with the political unification of the subcontinent, drawing the coastal and inland states closer together. Besides the supreme court in Cape Town, there were by 1882 five similar courts in South Africa under four separate legislatures, unchecked by a common court of appeal. Their law and practice were fundamentally the same, but divergences necessarily occurred. These divergences were checked by the fact that the Cape supplied many of the judges to the other courts, and by the growing prestige of de Villiers. Even so the law of the colony was in a state of confusion. The criminal law had become practically English. But the Roman-Dutch civil law was being Anglicized in a haphazard manner, partly owing to the influence of de Villiers himself. He has been criticized for consulting too narrow a range of authorities and applying English precedents sometimes with inconsiderate haste, as in the matter of water rights (*DSAB*). The marriage of English and Roman-Dutch law, however, which had begun to take place from the early years of British rule, was achieved piecemeal in the longer term, and perhaps owes more to de Villiers than to any other single man. It later spread from the borders of the South Africa of 1873 northward to the Zambezi.   E. A. WALKER, *rev.* T. R. H. DAVENPORT

Sources E. A. Walker, *Lord de Villiers and his times: South Africa, 1842–1914* (1925) • E. Kahn, 'De Villiers, Johan Hendrik (John Henry), Lord de Villiers, first Baron de Villiers of Wynberg', *DSAB* • *Minutes of proceedings … of the South African National Convention* (Cape Town, 1911) • L. M. Thompson, *The unification of South Africa, 1902–1910* (1960) • *Selections from the correspondence of J. X. Merriman*, ed. P. Lewsen, 4 vols. (1960–69) • J. S. Marais, *The fall of Kruger's republic* (1961) • D. M. Schreuder, *Gladstone and Kruger* (1969) • J. G. Kotzé, *Biographical memoirs and reminiscences*, 2 vols. (1933–54) • P. A. Molteno, *The life and times of Sir John Charles Molteno*, 2 vols. (1900) • *Selections from the Smuts papers*, ed. W. K. Hancock and J. van der Poel, 7 vols. (1966–73), vols. 1–4 • will, South African Library, Cape Town, De Villiers MSS

Archives National Library of South Africa, Cape Town | BL, corresp. with Lord Gladstone, Add. MSS 46069–46075, *passim* • Bodl. Oxf., corresp. with Lord Selborne • National Library of South Africa, Cape Town, J. Rose Innes MSS • National Library of South Africa, Cape Town, J. X. Merriman MSS • University of Cape Town, Winifred de Villiers MSS

Likenesses E. Roworth, group portrait (the National Convention), Parliament, Cape Town, South Africa • E. Roworth, portrait,

University of Cape Town, South Africa · P. Tennyson-Cole, portrait, Parliament, Cape Town, South Africa · bust, University of Cape Town, South Africa · cartoon, University of Cape Town, South Africa · marble bust, Parliament, Cape Town, South Africa · photograph, repro. in Walker, *Lord de Villiers*, frontispiece [*see illus.*] · photograph, University of Cape Town, South Africa · wood-engraving (after photograph by Gribble), NPG

Villiers, Margaret Elizabeth Child- [*née* Margaret Elizabeth Leigh], **countess of Jersey** (1849–1945), political hostess and philanthropist, was born on 29 October 1849 at Stoneleigh Abbey, Warwickshire, the eldest daughter of William Henry Leigh, second Baron Leigh (1824–1905) and his wife, Lady Caroline Amelia Grosvenor (*d.* 1906), daughter of Richard *Grosvenor, the second marquess of Westminster. On 19 September 1872 she married Victor Albert George Child-*Villiers, seventh earl of Jersey (1845–1915). They had two sons and four daughters, of whom the eldest daughter died in infancy and the elder son and third daughter both predeceased their mother. At Middleton Park, Oxfordshire, and Osterley Park near Isleworth, the Jerseys were notable hosts to political society. The countess rapidly exchanged the Liberal politics of her father's household for the Conservatism (and later Unionism) of her husband, regularly attending debates in the House of Lords. She accompanied her husband to New South Wales from 1891 to 1893 when he was governor there.

A committed imperialist, Lady Jersey travelled widely and entertained many international visitors at Osterley. In 1901 she assisted in the formation of the Victoria League, which aimed to strengthen ties between England and the colonies; she was president of this organization for twenty-six years. She took a prominent part in the Primrose League. An active opponent of women's suffrage, she chaired the inaugural meeting of the Women's National Anti-Suffrage League in 1908, and later served as deputy president of the mixed-sex National League for Opposing Women's Suffrage, of which Lord Cromer was president. Despite her opposition to the formal representation of women, the countess was herself a public speaker of note, and tenacious of the influence of women within the NLOWS.

Lady Jersey took an active interest in the welfare of children, great numbers of whom from London schools she entertained at Osterley; and she was president of the Children's Happy Evenings Association from its foundation in 1894 until the war of 1914–18. She was a magistrate at the children's court, and also a governor of Charterhouse School. Lord Jersey died in 1915, and she moved to Montagu Square in London. She published her autobiography in 1922, and also wrote many articles on travel for the *Nineteenth Century* and other reviews, and a number of children's plays and stories.

Lady Jersey was made CBE in 1920 for work with the Red Cross, and DBE in 1927. She died at Middleton Park on 22 May 1945, in her ninety-sixth year, and was buried in the churchyard at All Saints, Middleton Stoney.

DUNSANY, rev. K. D. REYNOLDS

Sources M. E. Child-Villiers, *Fifty one years of Victorian life* (1922) · V. Powell, *Margaret, countess of Jersey: a biography* (1978) · B. Harrison, *Separate spheres: the opposition to women's suffrage in Britain* (1978) ·

Margaret Elizabeth Child-Villiers, countess of Jersey (1849–1945), by Ellis Roberts

L. Walker, 'Party political women: a comparative study of liberal women and the Primrose League, 1890–1914', *Equal or different: women's politics, 1800–1914*, ed. J. Rendall (1987), 165–91 · GEC, *Peerage* · *The Times* (23 May 1945) · Viscountess Milner [V. G. M. Milner], *My picture gallery, 1868–1901* [1951]

Archives LMA, corresp. and papers | U. Birm., corresp. with Joseph Chamberlain, JC/5 · Yale U., Beinecke L., letters to Locker-Lampsons

Likenesses R. Rothwell, portrait, 1858 · L. Desanges, portrait, 1878 · H. J. Brooks, oils, 1889 (*Private view of the Old Masters Exhibition, Royal Academy, 1888*), NPG · E. Roberts, drawing, priv. coll. [*see illus.*] · lithograph (after L. Desanges), NPG; repro. in *Whitchall Review* (25 Oct 1879) · portraits, repro. in Powell, *Margaret, countess of Jersey*

Wealth at death £27,803 16*s.* 2*d.*: probate, 7 Aug 1945, *CGPLA Eng. & Wales*

Villiers [*married name* Stuart], **Mary, duchess of Lennox and Richmond** (1622–1685), courtier, was born at Wallingford House, London, in March 1622, and baptized at St Martin-in-the-Fields on 30 March, the eldest child and only daughter of George *Villiers, marquess (later duke) of Buckingham (1592–1628), and his wife, Lady Katherine (1603?–1649) [*see* MacDonnell, Katherine], daughter of Francis *Manners, sixth earl of Rutland. In her childhood Mall (as she was then commonly known) moved in favoured court circles. James I, who was her godfather, allowed her free access to the privy quarters, frequently cuddled her, and called her his 'little grandchild' (Lockyer, 152). Her father's privileged status led to early plans for an arranged marriage. A projected alliance with the heir of the elector palatine having failed, in 1626, as part of Buckingham's political reconciliation with William Herbert, earl of Pembroke, she was betrothed to Pembroke's nephew Charles Herbert, Lord Herbert of Shurland (1619–

Mary Villiers, duchess of Lennox and Richmond (1622–1685),
by Sir Anthony Van Dyck, c.1637 [as St Agnes]

1636), eldest surviving son of Philip *Herbert (1584–1650) (who succeeded his brother to the earldom in 1630) and his first wife, Lady Susan de Vere. On 27 August 1627 her father obtained a patent granting his daughter the dukedom of Buckingham should he die without sons, but the subsequent birth of her two younger brothers voided this. After Buckingham was murdered in 1628, her mother declared herself a Catholic, and Lady Mary's guardianship was entrusted to the Herbert family.

Lady Mary continued to spend much of her time at court, and she participated in masques from 1630. At Michaelmas 1634 she played Sabrina in John Milton's *Comus* at Ludlow Castle, an appearance later acknowledged by Samuel Butler in *Hudibras*. On one occasion she was carried to an unsuspecting Charles I in a hamper, gaining in consequence the nickname Butterfly or Papillon. She married Lord Herbert on 8 January 1635 in the royal closet at Whitehall, an event celebrated in verse by William Davenant and marked by a drama from Henry Killigrew, published in 1638 as *The Conspiracy*. Herbert soon left with his younger brother Philip to travel abroad, and in January 1636 died of smallpox in Florence, evoking from Philip Massinger the elegy *Sero, sed serio*. On 3 August 1637, bringing with her a dowry of £20,000, Lady Mary was married by Archbishop William Laud at Lambeth to the king's cousin James *Stuart, fourth duke of Lennox (1612–1655) (from 1641 first duke of Richmond), son of Esmé

*Stuart, third duke of Lennox, and Katherine Clifton, Baroness Clifton. The couple had a house at Cobham Hall, Kent, but also remained prominent at court, where the duchess's beauty was celebrated in verse and prose; numerous portraits include several by Anthony Van Dyck.

After the outbreak of the civil war Duchess Mary joined the queen in Holland, returning early in 1643. Gossip that she 'had used beating up of quarters … too frequently with Prince Rupert' (P. Morrah, *Prince Rupert of the Rhine*, 1976) points to a romance between the two that year. At a late stage of the war, in April 1646, she obtained a pass to visit London to consult the physician Theodore Mayerne. In July 1648 her brother Lord Francis Villiers was killed in a skirmish, and elegies on his death by Andrew Marvell and others coupled her name with his. On the morning of Charles I's execution, in January 1649, the king found his father's watch which Lady Mary had played with as an infant, and as his last bequest had it sent to her.

Duchess Mary had two children, a son, Esmé, born in London on 2 November 1649, and a daughter, Mary, born in July 1651. On the death of her husband on 30 March 1655 she found herself in debt and set out for France, where she became involved in royalist intrigues. Her son died in Paris on 10 August 1660, and was buried on 4 September in Westminster Abbey. It was probably at this point that the duchess returned to England. In December de Bartet, a French agent in England, wrote to Cardinal Mazarin, following a visit to her house, that she was the most 'rejouissante' (amusing) woman in the world (PRO, PRO 31/3/108, fols. 124–5). Although going then to court de Bartet gave Charles II the news that he had just been instrumental in securing Duchess Mary's conversion to Catholicism, the king had responded positively to the agent's request that she be repaid £40,000 jacobus owed her by the crown and had proposed the three meet privately to discuss potential royal brides. In March 1662 she was appointed a lady of the bedchamber to the queen dowager, Henrietta Maria, and on 30 April a privy seal was issued for £20,000 in full repayment of the debts owing to her and to her husband by Charles I, but the following year she was still in financial difficulties. Before 26 November 1664 she married Colonel Thomas Howard (d. 1678), known as Northern Tom Howard, who was lieutenant of the yeomen of the guard and younger brother of Charles Howard, first earl of Carlisle. It seems that she remained in England when Henrietta Maria returned to France in June 1665, and was in London in the spring of 1667 to plead for a pardon for her brother the second duke of Buckingham, then in hiding after political dissidence. She finally departed for France that October. Once there she apparently played a part in the intrigue surrounding negotiations between Charles II and his sister Henriette Anne, duchess of Orléans: French diplomatic correspondence reported in March 1669 that Duchess Mary had told Buckingham (now rehabilitated) of Henrietta Anne's distrust of him in a letter whose diction was 'very confused' and 'corresponded to the spirit of the lady' (PRO, PRO 31/3/121, fols. 70–72). She was still a member of the queen dowager's entourage when the latter died at Colombes in August.

By 1674 Duchess Mary had been granted a pension of £1000 a year for life. Her daughter Mary, who had married Lord Richard *Butler (1639–1686), later first earl of Arran, had died in July 1668; Thomas Howard died in the summer of 1678. Little is known of her last years, although she has recently been advanced as one of several possible identifications of 'Ephelia', whose verse circulated between 1679 and 1682. The duchess of Richmond, as she continued to be known, died in November 1685 and was buried on 28 November in the Richmond tomb in Westminster Abbey, with her second and third husbands and her son, and near to her father.

FREDA HAST

Sources Burke, *Peerage* · R. Lockyer, *Buckingham: the life and political career of George Villiers, first duke of Buckingham, 1592–1628* (1981) · S. Butler, *Hudibras*, ed. J. Wilders (1967), pt 1, canto 2 · W. A. H. C. Gardner [Lady Burghclere], *George Villiers, second duke of Buckingham, 1628–1687: a study in the history of the Restoration* (1903) · PRO, PRO 31/3/108, fols. 124–5; 31/3/112, fols. 186–7; 31/3/121, fols. 70–72 · W. A. Shaw, ed., *Calendar of treasury books*, [33 vols. in 64], PRO (1904–69) · *CSP dom.* · *Archaeologia Cantiana*, 12 (1878) · M. C. La Motte [Countess d'Aulnoy], *Memoirs of the court of England in 1675*, ed. G. D. Gilbert (1927) · *Calendar of the Clarendon state papers preserved in the Bodleian Library*, ed. O. Ogle and others, 5 vols. (1869–1970), vols. 4–5 · T. Herbert, *Memoirs of the last two years of the reign of King Charles I* · [T. Birch and R. F. Williams], eds., *The court and times of Charles the First*, 2 vols. (1848) · Pepys, *Diary*, 11 vols. (1971), 3.68. 8.330–31 · R. Davies, *The greatest house at Chelsey* (1914) · J. Donovan, 'The Key to Hudibras and Cleveland's *The character of a London diurnall*', *N&Q*, 218 (1973), 175–6 · *ESTC* [online; 'Ephelia' records] · M. Mulvihill, letter, *TLS* (1 Sept 2000)

Likenesses A. Van Dyck, oils, *c*.1637, Royal Collection [*see illus.*] · attrib. J. Honthorst, group portrait, oils, Hampton Court, Surrey · A. Van Dyck, group portrait, oils, Gov. Art Coll. · A. Van Dyck, group portrait, oils, Wilton House, Wiltshire · A. Van Dyck, oils, North Carolina Museum of Art, Raleigh · effigy (father's tomb), Westminster Abbey · oils, Rousham House, Oxfordshire

Villiers, Robert. *See* Danvers, Robert (1624–1674).

Villiers, Sarah Sophia Child- [*née* Lady Sarah Sophia Fane], **countess of Jersey** (1785–1867), political hostess, was born on 4 March 1785, the second child and eldest of the three daughters of John *Fane, tenth earl of Westmorland (1759–1841), and his first wife, Sarah Anne (1764–1793), daughter and sole heir of Robert *Child of Osterley Park, Middlesex. Under the terms of her grandfather's will Lady Sarah was the heir to the great Child's Bank fortune, which brought her an income estimated at some £60,000 a year, and Osterley Park, Middlesex. The immensity of her fortune influenced her character: one less well-endowed young woman found her frightening: 'she is so completely a *maitresse femme* (very naturally, from her immense fortune which always made her superior to everybody she ever lived among) that I feel overpowered by her somehow' (Wyndham, 34–5). Lady Sarah was inevitably much sought after as a bride: Lady Harriet Cavendish observed three suitors (Lord Villiers, Tom Sheridan, and Lord Granville Leveson-Gower) at one house party alone. 'Perhaps', opined Lady Harriet, 'they would not object to sharing her affections, but I doubt whether the division of the rest of their acquisition would

Sarah Sophia Child-Villiers, countess of Jersey (1785–1867), by James Holmes, 1834

be borne as quietly' (*Hary-O*, 66). It was **George Villiers** [*later* George Child-Villiers], Lord Villiers (1773–1859), who caught the heiress; she married him in London on 23 May 1804.

Villiers, who was born on 19 August 1773, was the elder son of George Bussy *Villiers, fourth earl of Jersey (1735–1805), and his notorious wife, Frances *Villiers (1753–1821), daughter of Philip Twysden, bishop of Raphoe, and mistress of the prince of Wales. Educated at Harrow School and St John's College, Cambridge, he succeeded as fifth earl of Jersey the year after his marriage, and took the additional surname Child in 1812. Jersey had nothing of the flamboyance of his wife, and he accepted her activities with complacency. He was a keen foxhunter: Nimrod, in his *Crack Riders of England*, referred to him as 'not only one of the hardest, boldest, and most judicious, but perhaps the most elegant rider to hounds the world ever saw' (*DNB*). He was also a dedicated supporter of horse racing, breeding and training his own horses at Middleton Park, Oxfordshire: among his successes were Cobweb, who won the Oaks in 1824, and three Derby winners: Middleton (1825), Mameluke (1827), and Bay Middleton (1836). He played no active part in politics, but served as lord chamberlain to William IV in the Wellington and Peel ministries of 1830 and 1834–5, and as master of the horse to Queen Victoria, under Peel in 1841–6 and Derby in 1852.

After some anxiety about her failure to become pregnant early in her marriage, Lady Jersey bore eight children, one of whom died in infancy. But childbearing interfered little with her career as one of the most prominent hostesses and social figures of her generation. She entertained in London at 38 Berkeley Square, at Osterley, and at Middleton, and her houses became centres for the whig party. With her friends, enemies, rivals, and almost exact contemporaries Emily, Lady Cowper and the Russian ambassadress, Princess Lieven, she was one of the lady patronesses of the exclusive Almack's club at Willis's Rooms, and as such exerted huge social influence. Dark-haired and attractive, her volubility was such that she earned the nickname 'Silence' and the ridicule of her detractors, and exhausted even her friends: Lady Granville found her 'remarkably amiable from being more silent than usual' (*Hary-O*, 127). Creevey compared her to a mechanical musical bird:

> She begins to sing at eleven o'clock, and, with the interval of the hour she retires to her cage to rest, she sings till 12 at night without a moment's interruption. ... Of the *merits* of her songs I say nothing until we meet.   (Maxwell, 296)

More disturbing to the comfort of her friends, however, was her habit of self-dramatization, of excesses of romantic feeling and sensibility, and her perpetual enjoyment of the role of tragedy queen. This romanticism prompted Lady Jersey to become a supporter of Byron during his troubles in 1814–15, and she offered him a refuge at Middleton.

Like many women of her class and generation Lady Jersey had pronounced political views and did not hesitate to express them, and for some years she was an important whig. Brougham commented in 1816 that 'Lady Jersey's absence is very bad for the party. ... Her great influence in society was always honestly and heartily exerted with her usual excellence of disposition' (Maxwell, 259–60). Her love of being at the centre of attention, perhaps, as much as conviction led her to take up the unfashionable cause of Queen Caroline when George IV was seeking to divorce her: she championed the queen with such frenzied fervour that her friends began to doubt her reason. By the end of the 1820s, however, Sarah Jersey had aligned herself with the tories: Wellington and Peel became her great heroes, and in the 1830s and 1840s her parties were held on behalf of the opponents of reform. She fancied herself the confidante of the duke—who mistrusted her discretion, and was once heard to mutter 'What damned nonsense Lady Jersey talks!' (ibid., 574)—and her family was linked to Peel's by the marriage of her eldest son to Peel's daughter. Her influence waned considerably in the 1840s, when new faces, such as the duchess of Sutherland, supplanted the older woman, and the marriage of her rival Lady Cowper to Lord Palmerston in 1839 cast her into the shade as a political hostess.

There was more to Sarah Jersey than the society hostess. Somewhat incongruously, she was the owner and senior partner of Child's Bank, and kept a desk in the office. She was an active partner, and did not delegate her responsibilities to her husband or other men. She also took great interest in the people who lived on the Jersey estates, especially in Oxfordshire, and set up and financed a number of schools for the benefit of the tenants and labourers. As her

own children grew up, they were a source of mixed anxiety and pride. The eldest surviving son was in poor health, and his wife was notoriously unfaithful; the second son died in 1837, and the fourth, Francis, was a wastrel whose early death in 1862 was perhaps a mercy. Lady Jersey arranged an ambitious match for her eldest daughter, Lady Sarah Villiers, with the Austrian Prince Nicholas Esterházy. Although the engagement was announced in 1836, the wedding did not happen until 1842, as the Esterházys sought to extricate themselves from a match that (to the status-conscious Austrians) was tainted by associations with trade. The princess died in 1853. The second daughter, Lady Clementina, who was a constant companion to her mother and well known in society, died unmarried in 1858, and the third daughter, Lady Adela, died in 1860, having scandalized her family by eloping with a Captain Ibbetson.

Lord Jersey died at 38 Berkeley Square, London, on 3 October 1859 and was buried at Middleton Stoney. Three weeks later he was followed to the grave by his eldest son, whose own son succeeded as seventh earl of Jersey. Sarah Jersey disdained the excesses of Victorian mourning and continued to entertain, receiving visitors every evening into the 1860s. Her sister-in-law, Lady Westmorland, described her in 1863 as 'still brilliant, talkative, gay, and beautiful, always dressed in the latest fashion in sky blue or rose colour, with flowers in her (own) hair, which is not grey. ... She has kept her sight, hearing, and memory, without any change' (*Correspondence of Priscilla, Countess of Westmorland*, 445). After a decline of a few weeks Sarah, Lady Jersey died on 26 January 1867 at 38 Berkeley Square, and was buried at Middleton Stoney. Her will aroused some curiosity, but it was uncontroversial. Most of the property went to the seventh earl, with generous provision made for her other grandchildren. Henry Greville considered that

> It was her great zest and gaiety, rather than her cleverness, which constituted her power of attracting remarkable men, many of whom I have seen listen with the greatest complacency to what they would have considered to be egregious nonsense had it emanated from less charming lips. (*Diary of Henry Greville*, 4.309–10, 4 Feb 1867)

Lady Jersey's foibles lent themselves to caricature, and she featured in Disraeli's novels as Zenobia and Lady St Julians, and as Lady Augusta in Lady Caroline Lamb's *Glenarvon*. In her youth she was a beauty and much painted. Mrs Mee included her among her series of miniatures of court beauties for the prince regent in 1814, but he rejected it; Byron wrote her a 'condolatory address' on the occasion.

K. D. REYNOLDS

Sources Burke, *Peerage* (1901) · DNB · J. S. Lewis, *In the family way* (1986) · K. D. Reynolds, *Aristocratic women and political society in Victorian Britain* (1998) · *The Creevey papers*, ed. H. Maxwell, 3rd edn (1905) · Margaret, countess of Jersey, *Records of the family of Villiers* (1922) · Lady Enfield, memoir, in *Leaves from the diary of Henry Greville*, ed. A. H. F. Byng, countess of Strafford, 4 vols. (1883–1905) · *Hary-O: the letters of Lady Harriet Cavendish, 1796–1809*, ed. G. Leveson-Gower and I. Palmer (1940) · Mrs Hugh Wyndham, *The correspondence of Sarah Lady Lyttelton* (1912) · *The correspondence of Priscilla, countess of Westmorland*, ed. R. Weigall (1909) · V. Powell, *Margaret, countess of Jersey: a biography* (1978) · *The Lieven–Palmerston correspondence,*

1828–1856, ed. and trans. Lord Sudley [A. P. J. C. J. Gore] (1943) · K. Bourne, *Palmerston: the early years, 1784–1841* (1982) · P. Clarke, 'Child & Co: three hundred years at no 1 Fleet Street', *Three Banks Review*, 98 (1973), 40–48 · *The private letters of Princess Lieven to Prince Metternich, 1820–1826*, ed. P. Quennell (1937) · IGI · d. cert. · *CGPLA Eng. & Wales* (1869) · *CGPLA Eng. & Wales* (1859) [George Child-Villiers]

Archives LMA, corresp. and papers | Balliol Oxf., letters to Lady Alice Peel · BL, corresp. with Lord Holland, Add. MS 51729 · BL, corresp. with Prince Lieven and Princess Lieven, Add. MSS 47287–47297, 47374, 47402 · BL, corresp. with Sir Arthur Paget, Add. MSS 48406, 48416 · Suffolk RO, Bury St Edmunds, letters to Lord Bristol · U. Durham L., letters to second Earl Grey

Likenesses T. Lawrence, portrait, c.1807, priv. coll. · G. Hayter, pencil and watercolour drawing, 1819, NPG · J. Holmes, portrait, 1834, priv. coll. [*see illus.*] · Gerard, portrait, priv. coll. · Hoppner, portrait, priv. coll. · H. Mayes, engravings · Romney, portrait (as a child), priv. coll.

Wealth at death under £300,000: probate, 22 May 1867, *CGPLA Eng. & Wales* · under £30,000—George Child-Villiers: resworn probate, Jan 1861, *CGPLA Eng. & Wales* (1859)

Villiers, Susan Alice (1863–1945), nurse, was born on 6 September 1863 at Chase Vale, Edmonton, Middlesex, the eighth of the nine children of John Fitzpatrick Villiers (1815/16–1874), barrister-at-law of Gray's Inn, and his wife, Mary Ann(e) (*bap.* 1825, *d.* 1899), daughter of William Sharp, a farmer of Upwell, Cambridgeshire, and his wife, Mary. The product of a middle class family, she was privately educated. However, the death of her father in 1874 appears to have strained the family's finances. By 1892 she was twenty-eight and perhaps regarded as a confirmed spinster; it was therefore appropriate for her to support herself in a career suitable to her station in life. In May that year she commenced three years of general nurse training at St Bartholomew's Hospital, London. Probably because of her social class she began as a special probationer. However, in November 1892 she became an ordinary probationer, which enabled her to benefit from a wider range of experience. She qualified in April 1895 and was appointed staff nurse at Bart's in May, working in that capacity until she resigned in March 1896.

Various factors are likely to have influenced Susan Villiers's decision to specialize in fever nursing. Infectious diseases were still rife, although mortality rates were mostly declining. The growth of fever (or isolation) hospitals necessitated large numbers of nurses who required leadership. Susan Villiers's comprehensive nurse training, which included work on a diphtheria ward, gave her an insight into the skilled care necessary. She may also have been influenced by her matron at Bart's, Isla Stewart, who believed that employment with the Metropolitan Asylums Board was the best possible school for matrons. She herself had been matron of two asylums board institutions, a tented smallpox camp at Darenth, Dartford, Kent (1885–6), and the Eastern Fever Hospital, Homerton, East London (1886–7). Susan Villiers therefore knew that there was tremendous potential for advancement in asylums board hospitals, and it was within their large fever institutions in London that she spent her whole career and became a leader of the fever nurses. She went on to hold appointments as night superintendent at the South Eastern Hospital (1896–9) and assistant matron at the

Brook Hospital (1899–1901) before becoming matron at the Fountain Hospital (1901–10), the Park Hospital (1910–13), and the South Western Hospital (1913–27).

Between 1861 and 1891, 353 new public isolation hospitals were created in England and Wales. Although they varied tremendously in size, they experienced comparable problems of recruitment and retention of nurses. The main solution to this was seen as fever nurse training. A few hospitals had established courses, but they varied in length, content, and clinical experience. This led to the recognition that standardization was necessary. Susan Villiers was a key figure in fever nurse training from 1908 to 1937. In June 1908 she was appointed to the first council of the Fever Nurses' Association, a new body established in January 1908 to provide a unified system of fever nurse training in British hospitals approved by the association. Moreover, she was determined to ensure the rights of fever nurse members in their conditions of work, and in obtaining special recognition for those with both fever and general training under state registration. She was in an ideal position to implement the association scheme after its approval by the asylums board in July 1909. Following the Nurses Registration Act, 1919, the General Nursing Council for England and Wales was established. A general register of nurses was opened in which she was the seventh entry, while the supplementary register of fever nurses records her name as the 60th entry. As the fever nurse representative to the council, 1920–37, she served on various committees and contributed to its decision to adopt the association scheme virtually unchanged.

Susan Villiers's commitments were wide ranging. She was one of three representatives of the Matrons' Council of Great Britain and Ireland to the National Council of Women of Great Britain, where she served on the public health sectional committee (1926–7). She became a member of the British College of Nursing in 1926. This new organization was established on 29 April that year by Mrs Bedford Fenwick, matron of Bart's (1881–7) and the chief protagonist of state registration. It was intended to be a rival to the College of Nursing set up in 1916; both had similar educational and professional aims. Although not a militant feminist, Susan Villiers quietly supported the interests and rights of women. In 1927, for instance, she represented the British College of Nursing in support of equal suffrage at the National Union of Societies for Equal Citizenship, formerly the National Union of Women's Suffrage Societies. She was a serene, dignified, ladylike person with a charming manner. By conviction she was an Anglican. In 1935 she became the superior of the Guild of St Barnabas, an Anglican organization which gave spiritual support to nurses.

In retirement Susan Villiers, who remained unmarried, lived first at Stevenage, Hertfordshire, where she was a county magistrate for Stevenage petty sessional division. Towards the end of her life she moved to Little Nutcombe, Portsmouth Road, Shottermill, Hindhead, Surrey, where she died on 29 March 1945. She was buried on 3 April at St Alban's Church, Hindhead. A very well attended requiem mass on 12 April at St Alban the Martyr, Holborn, London, was organized by the Guild of St Barnabas—a celebration of her life's work and particularly of her contribution to fever nursing.   MARGARET R. CURRIE

Sources b. cert. · d. cert. · d. cert. [John Fitzpatrick Villiers, father] · d. cert. [Mary Anne Villiers, mother] · parish register, Winchmore Hill, St Paul, 20 Dec 1863 [baptism] · parish register, Upwell [Mary Ann(e) Sharp, mother], 25 Sept 1825 [baptism] · census returns, 1881, 1901 · census returns, 1861 [John Fitzpatrick Villiers, father] · J. Foster, *The register of admissions to Gray's Inn, 1521–1889, together with the register of marriages in Gray's Inn chapel, 1695–1754* (privately printed, London, 1889), 461, 487 · matron's report book on probationers, St Bartholomew's Hospital, London, MO 54/2, p. 195 · register of probationer nurses, St Bartholomew's Hospital, London, MO 53/1, p. 54 · register of nurses, St Bartholomew's Hospital, London, MO 52, p. 58 · 'League news', 1900, St Bartholomew's Hospital, London, SL 6 · 'League news', 1901, St Bartholomew's Hospital, London, SL 6 · 'League news', 1910, St Bartholomew's Hospital, London, SL 6 · 'League news', 1914, St Bartholomew's Hospital, London, SL 6 · 'League news', 1927, St Bartholomew's Hospital, London, SL 6 · 'League news', 1936, St Bartholomew's Hospital, London, SL 6 · Metropolitan Asylums Board, minutes and staff registers, LMA · minutes, 18 Dec 1926, British College of Nursing, pp. 1–2 · minutes, 26 Feb 1927, British College of Nursing, pp. 1–2 · *Handbook of the National Council of Women of Great Britain* (1926–7), 27, 28, 50, 95 · *Misericordia* [Guild of St Barnabas], 54 (1935), 88 · letter of sympathy to Queen Mary, *Misericordia* [Guild of St Barnabas], 55 (1936) · *Misericordia* [Guild of St Barnabas], 64/683 (1945), 3 · 'The general register of nurses', PRO, DT 10/57, entry no. 7, date of registration 30 Sept 1921 · 'The supplementary register of fever nurses', PRO, DT 10/173, no. 1: entry no. 60, date of registration 17 March 1922 · *British Journal of Nursing*, 40 (1908), 70 · *British Journal of Nursing*, 41 (1908), 30 · *British Journal of Nursing*, 43 (1909), 158 · *British Journal of Nursing*, 93 (1945), 41 · *Kelly's directory for Hertfordshire* (1933), 253 · *The Times* (31 March 1945) · E. R. D. Bendall and E. Raybould, *A history of the General Nursing Council for England and Wales* (1969) · G. M. Ayers, *England's first state hospitals and the Metropolitan Asylums Board, 1867–1930* (1971) · M. R. Currie, 'The rise and demise of fever nursing', *International History of Nursing Journal*, 3/1 (1997), 5–19 · S. McGann, *The battle of the nurses: a study of eight women who influenced the development of professional nursing, 1880–1930* (1992) · B. Abel-Smith, *A history of the nursing profession* (1960)
Likenesses portrait, c.1927, repro. in *British Journal of Nursing*, 93/2121 (April 1945), 41
Wealth at death £10,723 0s. 4d.: probate, 6 June 1945, *CGPLA Eng. & Wales*

Villiers, Thomas, first earl of Clarendon (1709–1786),

diplomatist, was the second son of William *Villiers, second earl of Jersey (c.1682–1721) [see under Villiers, Edward, first earl of Jersey], and his wife, Judith (d. 1735), daughter and heir of Frederick Herne, a wealthy London merchant. He was educated at Eton College (1725), and matriculated from Queens' College, Cambridge, in 1728, but left the university without a degree. After making a grand tour to France and Italy in 1733–4, he entered the diplomatic service.

Early in 1738 Villiers was sent as envoy-extraordinary to the court of Augustus III, elector of Saxony and king of Poland, residing in both Dresden and Warsaw from 23 May 1738 to December 1742. From 1742 to 1743 he served as minister-plenipotentiary to Augustus in his capacity as elector of Saxony. From mid-January to mid-March 1743 he was envoy at Vienna, from where he was sent to a number of imperial cities. In July 1743 he was reporting from

Hanau on the progress of the War of the Austrian Succession. In September of the following year he returned to Poland, where Augustus had taken refuge on being driven out of Saxony by Frederick the Great. In November 1745 Frederick instructed his minister to make proposals for peace with Saxony through the medium of Villiers. Carlyle judged that Villiers showed himself 'really diligent, reasonable, loyal; doing his very best now and afterwards; but has no success at all' (Carlyle, 6.109). He followed Augustus in his flight to Prague, and continued his efforts there without success until Frederick's victory at Kesselsdorf on 12 December 1745 rendered Augustus more amenable. Villiers made several journeys between Prague and Berlin during the negotiations, and peace was eventually signed on Christmas day 1745. These efforts gained for Villiers Frederick's good opinion, and on 3 January 1746 he was appointed resident minister at Berlin, where he resided from 22 February to 5 September 1746. Horace Walpole, however, attributed Frederick's liking for Villiers to his dislike of men of ability: '[Villiers] has, you know, been very much *gazetted*, and had his letters to the king of Prussia printed, but he is a very silly fellow' (Walpole, *Corr.*, 20.17).

In February 1748 Villiers retired from the diplomatic service and devoted himself to home politics. He had been returned to parliament for Tamworth on 3 July 1747, in spite of his confession to Walpole that he did not understand elections, and on 24 December 1748 he was made a lord of the Admiralty in Henry Pelham's administration. He was re-elected for Tamworth on 18 April 1754, but vacated the seat on his creation, on 3 June 1756, as Baron Hyde of Hindon. He had married, on 30 March 1752, Lady Charlotte (1721–1790), third but eldest surviving daughter of William *Capel, third earl of Essex (1697–1743), and coheir of his first wife, Lady Jane Hyde (d. 1724), daughter of Henry Hyde, fourth and last earl of Clarendon of the first creation. They had three sons and one daughter. The second son was the politician John Charles *Villiers, third earl of Clarendon.

On 2 September 1763 Hyde was sworn of the privy council, and on the 10th he was appointed joint postmaster-general in Grenville's administration. He was chancellor of the duchy of Lancaster from 14 June 1771 to 1782, during Lord North's administration. On 14 June 1776 he was created earl of Clarendon of the second creation, and on 16 July 1782 obtained license to add to his arms the royal eagle of Prussia, for Frederick III had created him a count of that kingdom. In 1783 he joined the opposition to Pitt's administration.

Clarendon died at Watford on 11 December 1786, and was buried there on the 20th. He was succeeded in the title by his eldest son, Thomas (1753–1824).

                              A. F. POLLARD, *rev.* R. D. E. EAGLES

Sources GEC, *Peerage* · Venn, *Alum. Cant.* · D. B. Horn, ed., *British diplomatic representatives, 1689–1789*, CS, 3rd ser., 46 (1932) · Walpole, *Corr.* · H. Walpole, *Memoirs of the reign of King George the Second*, ed. Lord Holland, 2nd edn, 3 vols. (1847), vol. 1, p. 450; vol. 2, p. 202; vol. 3, p. 111 · R. R. Sedgwick, 'Villiers, Hon. Thomas', HoP, *Commons, 1715–54* · L. B. Namier, 'Villiers, Hon. Thomas', HoP, *Commons, 1754–90* · H. Walpole, *Memoirs of the reign of King George the Third*, ed.

G. F. R. Barker, 4 vols. (1894), vol. 1, p. 235; vol. 4, p. 217 • Frederick II, *Œuvres*, ed. J. D. E. Preuss, 30 vols. (1846–57) • T. Carlyle, *History of Friedrich II of Prussia, called Frederick the Great*, new edn, 6 vols. (1858–65) • J. Ingamells, ed., *A dictionary of British and Irish travellers in Italy, 1701–1800* (1997), 969

Archives BL, Egerton MSS 2685–2693 • BL, Add. MSS 22530, 23801–23824 • Bodl. Oxf., corresp. and papers | BL, corresp. with Lord Grenville, Add. MS 57814 • BL, corresp. with duke of Newcastle, Add. MSS 32705–33090, *passim* • BL, letters to Sir Thomas Robinson, Add. MSS 23801–23824, *passim* • BL, letters to Lord Stair, Lord Hardwicke, etc., Add. MSS 35452–35455, 35607–35657, *passim* • BL, letters to Tyrawley, Add. MS 23631 • Christ Church Oxf., corresp. with Sir Richard Browne • LMA, letters to Lord Jersey • NRA, priv. coll., letters to Sir Robert Atkyns • NRA, priv. coll., corresp. with Lord Grandison • NRA, priv. coll., letters to Lord Shelburne

Likenesses attrib. E. Seeman junior, oils, *c*.1740, Gov. Art Coll. • C. Bestland, stipple, pubd 1803 (after T. Hudson), BM; repro. in G. O. Cambridge, ed., *The works of Richard Owen Cambridge* (1803) • engraving (after portrait by T. Hudson), repro. in J. E. Doyle, *The official baronage of England: showing the succession dignitries, and offices of every peer from 1066 to 1885*, 3 vols. (1886)

Villiers, Thomas Hyde (1801–1832), politician, born on 27 January 1801, was the second son of George Villiers (1759–1827), who married, on 17 April 1798, Theresa (1775–1855), only daughter of John Parker, first Baron Boringdon. Villiers's father died at Kent House, Knightsbridge, on 21 March 1827; his mother survived until 1855. Three of Thomas's brothers were G. W. F. *Villiers, C. P. *Villiers, and H. M. *Villiers.

Villiers was educated at home and very imperfectly. He was then sent with his eldest brother, George, to St John's College, Cambridge, and, keenly conscious of his own defects, set to work to repair the loss of time. At Cambridge he mixed with Charles Austin, Edward Strutt, John Romilly, T. B. Macaulay, and other young men of ability and advanced opinions, several of them influenced by the views of Jeremy Bentham. In 1822 he graduated BA, and in 1825 MA. After taking his degree in 1822 he entered the Colonial Office, where early in 1824 Sir Henry Taylor (1800–1866) became his subordinate and then his close friend.

The brothers lived during their earlier years with their parents in part of Kent House at Knightsbridge, but from 1825 Thomas Villiers and Taylor shared a house in Suffolk Street. In that year, Villiers joined a debating club called the Academics, where several of his college friends, and J. S. Mill, discussed politics and economics. His chief speech, an hour long, on colonization 'made some noise, procured him a compliment and an invitation from the chancellor of the exchequer' (*Correspondence of Henry Taylor*, 6–7). Not long afterwards Villiers abandoned the government service to embark on politics. His chief source of income from that date until his acceptance of office arose from the agencies for Berbice and Newfoundland (*Hansard* 3, 5, 1831, 283–7).

At the general election in June 1826 Villiers was elected for Hedon in Yorkshire, and sat until the dissolution in 1830. In 1830 and 1831 he sat, respectively, for Wootton Bassett, Wiltshire (a family borough), and Bletchingley,

and voted for the Reform Bill in all its stages. Villiers travelled in Ireland in 1828 with the object of informing himself on Irish affairs, and set out his views in long letters to Taylor. A letter written by him in February 1829 was shown to R. L. Sheil, who thereupon brought about the suppression of the Catholic Association. In 1831 Villiers suggested the formation of the royal commission on the poor law, and helped in its preliminary inquiries. On 18 May 1831 he became secretary to the Board of Control under Charles Grant (afterwards Lord Glenelg). On 22 August 1831 he made a long speech in the House of Commons on the Methuen treaty with Portugal (*Hansard* 3, 6, 1831, 437–9). The committees on Indian affairs, whose labours formed the basis of subsequent legislation, were organized by Villiers, with the assistance of Lord Althorp. The question of the renewal of the charter to the East India Company, which came up for consideration at this time, demanded all his faculties, and official work weighed heavily. On 2 November 1831 Villiers and Taylor entered as students at Lincoln's Inn.

At the time of his death Villiers was a candidate for the constituency of Penryn and Falmouth in Cornwall, and had a promising political career. After three months' suffering from an abscess in the head, he died, unmarried, on 3 December 1832 at Carclew, the seat of Sir Charles Lemon, near Penryn, where he was staying. A monument was placed to his memory in Mylor church. Villiers possessed 'indefatigable industry and a clear understanding, set off by pleasing address and considerable powers of speaking'. It was a scheme of his to give 'parliamentary seats, without votes, to persons holding certain offices' (*Correspondence of Henry Taylor*, 196).

W. P. COURTNEY, *rev.* H. C. G. MATTHEW

Sources H. Taylor, *Autobiography*, 2 vols. (1885) • *Correspondence of Henry Taylor*, ed. E. Dowden (1888) • J. S. Mill, *Autobiography* (1873) • *GM*, 1st ser., 103/1 (1833)

Archives Bodl. Oxf., political papers

Villiers, Victor Albert George Child-, seventh earl of Jersey (1845–1915), colonial governor, was born on 20 March 1845 at Berkeley Square, London, the eldest son of George Augustus Frederic Child-Villiers, sixth earl of Jersey (1808–1859), and his wife, Julia (d. 1893), the eldest daughter of Sir Robert *Peel, second baronet and prime minister. He was educated at Eton College and Balliol College, Oxford, and succeeded to his father's titles at the age of fourteen. On 19 September 1872 he married Margaret Elizabeth (1849–1945) [see Villiers, Margaret Elizabeth Child-], the daughter of William Henry, second Baron Leigh of Stoneleigh. They had two sons and four daughters. His wife was undoubtedly a more effective political activist and speaker than Jersey, and was prominent in the Conservative Victoria and Primrose leagues.

Jersey served as a lord-in-waiting to Queen Victoria between 1875 and 1877, and in 1889 became paymaster-general in the Salisbury government. He was appointed governor of New South Wales in 1890 and arrived in Sydney in January 1891. Apparently he soon found the post less stimulating than he had imagined, and to be largely of a 'social character' (Cunneen). Two months after his arrival the premier, Sir Henry Parkes, noted: 'I could hardly tell you how our new governor is getting on. I see little of him, and he seems to be very much occupied with his own family' (Martin, 401). Jersey remained in post only until November 1892, resigning on the grounds of 'pressing business affairs' (Cunneen). Although a 'strong Conservative' (*Sydney Morning Herald*, 2 June 1915), upon his return to England he was appointed by the Rosebery government as representative at the Ottawa colonial conference.

Jersey was an active freemason, being senior grand warden of England. He was involved in many athletic pursuits in his younger days, and also frequented race meetings, where he built up large debts. In 1885 he was compelled to sell the library collection at his home, Osterley Park, Isleworth, Middlesex, raising £13,000. He was knighted in 1890 and appointed GCB in 1900. From 1903 to 1905 he acted as New South Wales agent-general in London. Incapacitated by a stroke in 1909, he died six years later, on 31 May 1915, at his home, Osterley Park, and was buried on 4 June at All Saints' Church, Middleton Stoney, Oxfordshire.   MARC BRODIE

Sources *The Times* (1 June 1915), 10 · *Sydney Morning Herald* (2 June 1915), 10 · C. Cunneen, *AusDB* · Burke, *Peerage* · A. W. Martin, *Henry Parkes: a biography* (1980) · *DNB* · GEC, *Peerage*
Archives LMA, corresp. and papers · NL Aus., corresp. relating to New South Wales | BL, corresp. with Lord Ripon, Add. MS 43560
Likenesses F. Sargent, pencil drawing, 1870–79, NPG · H. J. Brooks, group portrait, oils (*Private view of the Old Masters Exhibition, Royal Academy, 1888*), NPG · oils (after W. W. Ouless, 1909), Oxfordshire County Council

Villiers, William, second earl of Jersey (*c.*1682–1721). *See under* Villiers, Edward, first earl of Jersey (1655?–1711).

Villula, John de. *See* Tours, John of (*d.* 1122).

Vilvain, Robert (*bap.* 1576, *d.* 1663), physician and philanthropist, was born in the parish of All Hallows, Goldsmith Street, Exeter, and baptized in its church on 17 March 1576. He was the son of Peter Vilvain (*d.* 1602), steward of Exeter in 1579, and his wife, Ann (*d.* 1616). Robert received his early education at Exeter and matriculated from Exeter College, Oxford, on 22 February 1594, aged eighteen. He graduated BA on 9 May 1597 and MA on 11 July 1600. On 30 June 1599 he was elected to a Devonian fellowship of his college, which he held until 30 June 1611.

Vilvain began to practise medicine about 1600, and on 20 June 1611 took the Oxford degrees of BM and DM. He was incorporated at Cambridge in 1608, and with these further degrees was reincorporated in 1612. From this date he practised with great success in his native city, where he spent the rest of his life. His wife, Ellenor, second daughter of Thomas Hinson of Tavistock, who married Anne, daughter of Sir William Spring of Pakenham, Suffolk, was buried at All Hallows, Exeter, on 7 December 1622. Their only child, Thomas, matriculated at Exeter College, Oxford, on 8 April 1636, aged sixteen, graduated BCL on 7 March 1642, and died unmarried on 20 May 1651. Ten epicedial distichs composed on his death are in his father's *Enchiridium epigrammatum* (1654), leaf 185.

In 1640 Vilvain was one of twelve doctors—five in theology, four in medicine, and three in law—living in Exeter. His epigram on them, the English translation, and a list of their names are printed in Richard Izacke's *Antiquities of the City of Exeter* (1723, 156). Thomas Fuller (1608–1661), when he visited Exeter, was delighted by some rare manuscripts in Vilvain's library and his museum of natural curiosities. Vilvain's benefactions to his native city and his college were numerous and costly. He gave £20 towards the cost of the new buildings at Exeter College about 1624, and he founded at the college in 1637 four exhibitions of £32 each per annum, to be paid through the rector and sub-rector. For the free school at St John's Hospital, Exeter, he gave a tenement in Paris Street without the east gate of Exeter, and he erected new buildings within the hospital at a cost of about £600.

On Vilvain's motion the corporation of Exeter in December 1657 allowed the lady chapel in the cathedral to be fitted up as a library, and the valuable collection of books then at St John's Hospital, which had previously formed the cathedral library, to be moved there. Vilvain defrayed the cost of the alterations in the lady chapel, and the care of the library was entrusted to him. The books remained there until 1820. With Vilvain's charitable benefactions and decreasing strength there came a loss of income; the preface to his *Enchiridium epigrammatum* refers to his ruined fortune. Between 17 April and 4 November 1662 there are frequent references in the state papers (domestic series) to the lease to him from 1647 by the dean and chapter of Exeter of the manor of Staverton, which he 'deserves to forfeit for ill-carriage during the late distractions'.

'In his younger days Vilvain was esteemed a very good poet, orator, and disputant, and, in his elder, as eminent for divinity as his proper faculty', but what should have been his most productive years were not fruitful and his writings are 'nothing but scraps, whimseys, and dotages of old age' (Wood, *Athenæ Oxon.*, ed. Bliss, 3.631–3).

Vilvain died on 21 February 1663 and was buried in the north aisle of the choir of Exeter Cathedral, where a stone marks his resting place; a mural tablet to his memory was placed on the north side of the entrance to the lady chapel, but was later taken to St James's chantry.   W. P. COURTNEY, rev. MICHAEL BEVAN

Sources R. Polwhele, *The history of Devonshire*, 3 vols. (1793–1806), vol. 2 · Foster, *Alum. Oxon.* · G. Oliver, *The history of the city of Exeter* (1861) · C. W. Boase, ed., *Registrum Collegii Exoniensis*, new edn, OHS, 27 (1894) · J. E. Bailey, *The life of Thomas Fuller, D.D.* (1874) · R. Izacke and S. Izacke, *Remarkable antiquities of the city of Exeter*, 2nd edn (1724) · R. Izacke, *An alphabetical register of divers person, who … have given tenements, rents, annuities, and monies, toward the relief of the poor of the county of Devon, and city of Exon* (1736) · *Notes and Gleanings*, 1 (1888), 187 · *Notes and Gleanings*, 2 (1889), 166 · *Notes and Gleanings*, 3 (1890), 6 · J. Maclean and W. C. Heane, eds., *The visitation of the county of Gloucester taken in the year 1623*, Harleian Society, 21 (1885) · W. Cotton and H. Woollcombe, *Gleanings from the municipal and cathedral records relative to the history of … Exeter* (1877) · private information (1899) · C. Worthy, *The history of the suburbs of Exeter* (1892) · *DNB*

Vinaver, Eugène [Yevgeny Maksimovich Vinaver] (1899–1979), literary scholar, was born on 18 June 1899 in St Petersburg, Russia, the son of Maksim Moiseyevich Vinaver (1863–1926), lawyer and politician. His father was a member of the first national Duma, and, following the 1917 revolution, minister of foreign relations in the regional government in the Crimea, committed to the establishment of democratic government in Russia. The family emigrated to Paris in 1919 (Wieczynski, 42.108). Eugène Vinaver shared his father's ideals, publishing his unfinished history of the Crimean government, including documents gathered from other surviving members of that government (1928). The family took French citizenship, which Eugène kept all his life, serving as an attaché in the cultural section of the Comité de la France Libre (1940) and as *délégué culturel* of the French embassy in London (1946).

Eugène Vinaver studied at the University of Paris, preparing a doctorate under Alfred Jeanroy and Joseph Bédier. His thesis, *Le roman de Tristan et Iseut dans l'œuvre de Thomas Malory* (1925), introduced what were to be the predominant themes of his academic career: the aesthetic and textual relationships between the French and English Arthurian romances. The significance of the comparatist approach, a relativist not an absolutist assessment of aesthetic qualities linked to a search for a clear understanding of textual meaning in evolving historical contexts, remained his permanent philosophy, reappearing in his *Discours de réception* as a foreign member of the Belgian Académie Royale de Langue et Littérature Françaises (1961) and his presidential address to the Modern Humanities Research Association (1966).

While working on his doctoral thesis Vinaver's dual interest in English and French literature had led him to spend two years at Lincoln College, Oxford (1921–2), completing a BLitt, and it was in England, at Oxford, and then Manchester, that he was to spend the rest of his teaching career. He was a fellow of Lincoln College and lecturer (1924–8) then reader in French at Oxford (1928–33); he became professor of French language and literature at Manchester University in 1933. While there he met Alice Elizabeth Malet Vaudrey (b. 1919) (generally known as Elizabeth, and to friends as Betty), daughter of Hugh John Kenelm Vaudrey, solicitor, whom he married on 23 September 1939; they had one son. He remained in Manchester until his retirement in 1966, when he became professor emeritus. He was honorary fellow of Lincoln College, Oxford (from 1959), honorary professor at the universities of Hull and Kent (both from 1977), corresponding fellow of the British Academy (from 1972), and of the Medieval Academy of America (from 1973). In addition he was visiting professor at five universities and received honorary degrees from another five. He was president of the Society for the Study of Mediaeval Language and Literature (1939–48), the Modern Language Association (1961), the Modern Humanities Research Association (1966), and the International Arthurian Society (1966–9), laureate of the Académie Française (1971), and chevalier of the Légion d'honneur (1959).

Eugène Vinaver (1899–1979), by Lotte Meitner-Graf, pubd 1965

Vinaver's scholarly range was vast, encompassing in a bibliography containing nearly one hundred items, many of them major books, French and English medieval literature and the French classics, notably Racine. His discovery and publication of Racine's own notes on Aristotle's *Poetics* (1944) had almost as profound an effect on studies of French neo-classical tragedy as did his edition of Malory on studies in medieval English literature (Delbouille and others, 4–5). Vinaver was working on a new edition of *Le Morte d'Arthur*, when the Winchester manuscript of Malory was discovered (F. Whitehead and others, vi–viii). Vinaver's conviction, based on textual evidence, was that Malory had never intended to produce a unified work, only a series of translated adaptations from disparate French sources. He therefore published his edition of the manuscript as *The Works of Sir Thomas Malory* (1947). Although his views raised immediate and persistent controversy, Vinaver never changed his fundamental view of the nature of Malory's text (Gaines, 40–41). The Folio Society, London, used selections from Vinaver's *Malory* to constitute the story of *Lancelot and Guinevere* (1953), and issued the whole *Works of Sir Thomas Malory* (1982), both in modernized language (Gaines, 44, 69). Since Vinaver's edition is also the basis for a very large number of translations into foreign languages it would not be an exaggeration to say that he 'has done no less than to present Malory to the world' (Gaines, 42).

Although Vinaver could allow temporary considerations to mar his judgement of others, as with his unfairly harsh criticism of H. Oskar Sommer during the Second

World War, a judgement he modified after the war (Gaines, 26), Vinaver was renowned for his warmth, generosity, and enthusiasm in encouraging others. This emerges in the work of Professor Barry Gaines, to whom Vinaver gave his library and archive shortly before his death (Gaines, x), and in many letters written by John Steinbeck, who consulted Vinaver extensively while composing his own adaptation of Malory, *The Acts of King Arthur*, noting particularly Vinaver's 'simplicity, clarity, generosity [and] enthusiasm' (Steinbeck and Wallsten, 557). These qualities were still apparent at the Exeter conference of the International Arthurian Society (1975): speaking with only a few slides to guide him, and illustrating textual points from manuscripts, small and physically frail though exuding energy, he gave an illuminating paper on the relationships of the French *Mort Artu* and two different Middle English versions of the story.

Vinaver was always an instigator and innovator, founding the periodicals *Arthuriana* (1928)—which became *Medium Ævum* (1930)—and, with others, *French Studies* (1947), and two series for Manchester University Press (French Classics and Les Ouvrages de l'Esprit). He was the prime mover in founding the International Arthurian Society (1948), the British branch of which established the Vinaver Trust in 1980 to be a permanent memorial to him. In retirement he lived at 20 Fordwith Road, Sturry, Canterbury, Kent, and at 4 rue des Eaux, Paris, France. He died in the Kent and Canterbury Hospital on 21 July 1979 of malignant lymphoma, survived by his wife, Elizabeth, and their son; he was buried at Sturry.   PHILIP E. BENNETT

Sources J. L. Wieczynski, ed., *The modern encyclopedia of Russian and Soviet history*, 42 (1986), 108 · M. M. Vinaver, *Nashe pravitel'stvo: Kryskiia vospominaniia, 1918–1919* (1928) · M. Delbouille, E. Vinaver, and D. De Rougemont, *Tristan et Iseut à travers les temps* (Brussels, 1961) · *Form and meaning in medieval romance* (1966) [presidential address by E. Vinaver to the Modern Humanities Research Association] · F. Whitehead, A. H. Diverrès, and F. E. Sutcliffe, eds., *Medieval miscellany presented to Eugène Vinaver by pupils, colleagues, and friends* (1965) · B. Gaines, *Sir Thomas Malory: an anecdotal bibliography of editions, 1485–1985* (1990) · E. Steinbeck and R. Wallsten, eds., *Steinbeck: a life in letters* (1975) · A. H. Diverrès, 'Eugène Vinaver, 1899–1979', *Bulletin Bibliographique de la Société Internationale Arthurienne*, 32 (1980), 297–300 · *WW* · m. cert. · d. cert.
Archives JRL, letters to *Manchester Guardian*
Likenesses L. Meitner-Graf, photograph, pubd 1965, priv. coll. [*see illus.*]

Vince, Samuel (1749–1821), mathematician and astronomer, was born at Fressingfield, Suffolk, on 6 April 1749, the youngest son of John Vince, a bricklayer, and his wife, Ann. He worked with his father until he was about twelve, when the Revd Warnes noticed him sitting reading beside his hod. Warnes lent him books and eventually sent him to Mr Tilney's school at Harleston, Norfolk, where he acted as assistant teacher. In 1768 Vince's early competence in mathematics allowed him to propose one, and answer ten, of the serious mathematical problems regularly set in the *Ladies' Diary*. With financial help from Dr Samuel Cooper of Great Yarmouth, he briefly attended St Paul's School, London, from where in 1771 he was admitted sizar at Gonville and Caius College, Cambridge; he graduated in 1775 as senior wrangler and first Smith's

prizeman. He was a member of the Hyson Club, established by the wranglers of 1757. His contemporary Gilbert Wakefield recalled Vince as 'an accomplished mathematician [and] an amiable man … rewarded with no preferment adequate to his reasonable pretentions' (*Memoirs of the Life*, 137). Vince migrated to Sidney Sussex College, where he proceeded MA in 1778; he continued to reside at least partly in Cambridge.

In 1780 Vince married Mary, daughter of Thomas Paris; she survived him, with their only child, Samuel Berney Vince (1781–1845), later vicar of Ringwood, Hampshire. Having taken orders, Vince was presented in 1784 to the rectory of Kirby Bedon, Norfolk, which he occupied for two years before handing over to a curate and moving to the vicarage of South Creek, Norfolk, in 1786. He was presented to the prebend of Melton Ross with Scamblesby, Lincolnshire, in 1803, and in 1809 to the archdeaconry of Bedford.

During these years Vince published books of a religious nature and others dealing with astronomy and mathematics. He was one of the last representatives of the English synthetical school. His textbooks were used in the university and ran through several editions. He also communicated several papers to the Royal Society: the first to be published, 'An investigation of the principle of progressive and rotatory motion' (*PTRS*, 70, 1780, 546–77), gained him the society's Copley medal. He was elected fellow of the Royal Society on 22 June 1786. He followed with a series of papers on the summation of infinite series, and delivered several Bakerian lectures: between 1794 and 1797 on aspects of fluid rotation and of bodies rotating in fluids, in 1798 on an unusual horizontal refraction of the air, and in 1804 on the hypotheses of gravitation. He contributed the last volume, dealing with fluxions, hydrostatics, and astronomy, to James Wood's four-volume digest of university lectures entitled *The Principles of Mathematical and Natural Philosophy* (1793–9).

On the death of Anthony Shepherd (1721–1796), Vince was appointed to succeed him as Plumian professor of astronomy and experimental philosophy at Cambridge, and he held the post until his death. His masterly and best-known work, *A Complete System of Astronomy* (3 vols., 1797–1808), appeared in a second enlarged edition in 1814–23. Professor John Playfair asserted in the *Edinburgh Review* of June 1809 that the tables collected in the third volume marked 'a great epoch in astronomical science'. At some time prior to 1811 Vince retired to Ramsgate, Kent, where he died on 28 November 1821.   ANITA MCCONNELL

Sources J. Venn and others, eds., *Biographical history of Gonville and Caius College*, 2: *1713–1897* (1898), 90 · *Memoirs of the life of Gilbert Wakefield*, ed. J. T. Rutt and A. Wainewright, 2 vols. (1804), vol. 1, p. 137 · E. H. Kinder, *Kirby Bedon* (1924) · *Cambridge Chronicle and Journal* (7 Dec 1821), 3b · *GM*, 1st ser., 87/2 (1817) · 'Athenae Suffolkensis', BL, Add. MS 19167, fol. 201 · W. Beloe, *The sexagenarian, or, The recollections of a literary life*, ed. [T. Rennell], 1 (1817), 38 · *GM*, 1st ser., 91/2 (1821), 643 · *N&Q*, 9th ser., 4 (4 Nov 1899) · will, PRO, PROB 11/1651, sig. 695 · *Report on the adjudication of the Copley, Romford and Royal medals, and appointment of the Bakerian, Croonian and Fairchild lecturers* (1834)

Archives CUL, corresp., treatises, and notes | RAS, letters to William Herschel
Likenesses R. Cooper, stipple, pubd 1821 (after drawing by T. Wageman, 1821), BM, NPG

Vincent, Augustine (c.1584–1626), herald and antiquary, was born presumably at Wellingborough or Finedon, Northamptonshire, the third and youngest son of William Vincent (d. 1618) and his wife, Elizabeth, daughter of John Mabbott of Walgrave, merchant of the staple. Nothing is known of his education. About 1599 he obtained a post in charge of records in the Tower of London, where he was probably simply a clerk but acquired a reputation as an antiquary. On 30 June 1614 he married Elizabeth (d. 1667), third daughter of Francis Primecourt of Canterbury. In 1616 he was given the position of Rouge Rose pursuivant-extraordinary in the College of Arms, almost certainly through the influence of his friend William Camden, who had been made Clarenceux king of arms in 1597. In spite of criticism of the practice from opponents resentful of Camden's promotion, the king of arms made use of Vincent as his deputy in heraldic visitations, alone in Northamptonshire and Rutland in 1618–19, with others in Warwickshire and Leicestershire in 1619 and in Surrey and Shropshire in 1623. Vincent played a prominent part in the celebrated public quarrel between Camden and Ralph Brooke, York herald, contributing, in defence of Camden, *A discoverie of errours in the first edition of the catalogue of nobility published by Ralphe Brooke* (1622), essentially a reprint of Brooke's book, in sections, with hostile comments after each. The dispute is notable for the way in which both sides made critical use of original source materials: while Brooke utilized the evidence of armorial bearings on tombs, Vincent employed his expert knowledge of the public records, something of an innovation in the scholarly argument of the day.

Over the years Vincent accumulated a very significant reference collection of heraldic and genealogical manuscript material, regarded as the most important collection attributable to a single herald at the College of Arms. It consists of 260 volumes, many of which were written by himself. In his *Discoverie of Errours* Vincent announced his intention to produce a 'Baronage of England' and a 'Lives of all the knights of the Garter' (foreshadowing William Dugdale), and that he was pursuing this as an active project is shown by the existence of a volume by him with 396 pages of peers' pedigrees, with painted arms. As he observed to Sir Robert Cotton, 'I find the further I go in that labour the further I am to seeke, yet it shall not discourage me' (Nicholas, 75).

Vincent's further intention was to write a county history for Northamptonshire. His collection of manuscripts contains a substantial body of Northamptonshire material; he is known to have collected information about armorial bearings in the county during his visitation. The papers accumulated by the Northamptonshire antiquary John Bridges in preparation for his own *History of Northamptonshire* include a copy of a list of headings under which Vincent intended to systematically consider his Northamptonshire material. Like many other contemporary antiquaries, however, overwhelmed by notes, Vincent did not manage to publish his work. None the less, his material was offered to, and made use of by, William Burton for his *Description of Leicestershire* (1622), William Dugdale, and John Weever for his *Ancient Funerall Monuments* (1631). Weever was particularly grateful for Vincent's help and encouragement, symptomatic of a general tendency to share the fruits of research within antiquarian circles. In Vincent's case, the circle also included John Selden.

Vincent's position within the College of Arms was regularized in May 1621 when he became Rouge Croix pursuivant; in June 1624 he became Windsor herald. He died on 11 January 1626 and was buried on 14 January at St Benet Paul's Wharf, London. His widow married, before 30 November 1630, Eusebius Catesby of Castor, Northamptonshire; she died on 6 August 1667.

Vincent's son John (1618–1671) was also interested in genealogical and antiquarian matters, although not possessing the scholarly abilities of his father. He took over his father's manuscript collections and made additions to them, finishing, but not managing to publish, the work on the baronage. When he died he bequeathed the collection to his patron, Ralph Sheldon of Beoley, Worcestershire, who left them to the College of Arms in 1684.

A. E. BROWN

Sources N. H. Nicholas, *Memoir of Augustine Vincent* (1827) · M. Noble, *A history of the College of Arms* (1805) · Bodl. Oxf., MSS Wood B. 7, D. 6 · L. Campbell and F. Steer, *A catalogue of manuscripts in the College of Arms collections*, 1 (1988), 233–5 · J. Nichols, *The history and antiquities of the county of Leicester*, 4/2 (1811), 933 · J. Weever, *Ancient funerall monuments* (1631) · W. C. Metcalfe, ed., *The visitations of Northamptonshire made in 1564 and 1618–19* (1887), 111–12 · W. Burton, *The description of Leicestershire* (1622), iii · G. Parry, *The trophies of time: English antiquarians of the seventeenth century* (1995) · D. R. Woolf, *The idea of history in early Stuart England* (1990)
Archives Bodl. Oxf., notes relating to College of Arms, catalogue of knights, and notes on early Chancery records · Coll. Arms, collections, incl. pedigrees, extracts from records, visitation papers, and armorial and genealogical case papers · Folger, armorial and treatise on baronies by writ · W. Yorks. AS, Leeds, treatise on nobility and precedence | BL, letter to William Camden, Faust E1 fol. 147 · BL, letter to Sir Robert Cotton, Jul CIII 379

Vincent, Charles (*fl.* 1777–1795). *See under* Vincent, Richard (1697×1701?–1783).

Vincent, Edgar, Viscount D'Abernon (1857–1941), financier and diplomatist, was born on 19 August 1857, at Slinfold, Sussex, youngest child of Frederick Vincent (1798–1883), rector of Slinfold, 1844–68, who succeeded as eleventh baronet in 1880, and his second wife, Maria Copley (d. 1899), daughter of Robert Herries Young. He had two half-brothers, three half-sisters, and four brothers. He was educated at a preparatory school at Frant Green and at Eton College, where he made a successful Derby book at the age of about fourteen. After attending a military crammer at Storrington, he passed as head of the examination list to become a student dragoman (interpreter) at Constantinople. Although he did not accept the appointment, his success was proof of his linguistic brilliance. He was joint

Edgar Vincent, Viscount D'Abernon (1857–1941), by John Singer Sargent, 1906

author of a *Handbook to Modern Greek* (1879) and with his publisher George Macmillan initiated the Society for the Promotion of Hellenic Studies.

Vincent was commissioned in the Coldstream Guards in 1877. During this period he helped his brother C. E. Howard *Vincent to draft a report on police procedure which had such impact that in 1878 the latter was appointed director of criminal investigation at Scotland Yard. While a subaltern stationed in Ireland, he corresponded about terrorism there with E. W. Hamilton, private secretary of the prime minister, W. E. Gladstone. In 1880, through his friendship with the Gladstone family, he was appointed private secretary to Lord Edmond Petty-Fitzmaurice, British commissioner for Eastern Roumelia under the treaty of Berlin.

Levantine diplomacy and finance Vincent resigned his commission in October 1882 to become British, Belgian, and Dutch representative on the council of the Ottoman public debt administration at Constantinople. He swiftly became an adept in the complexities of financial diplomacy. In March 1883 he was promoted to the presidency of this council, but was transferred in November to become financial adviser to the Egyptian government. Recommending him for this post, G. J. Goschen wrote, 'He grapples with a subject very rapidly, has a very quick understanding and plenty of courage … his energy almost approaches restlessness' (G. J. Goschen to E. Baring, 25 Oct 1883; PRO, FO 633/7). For five years Vincent worked with vigour and ingenuity to save Egyptian state finances from

insolvency. He was fertile in expedients and merciless in enforcing economies. He undertook political initiatives and administrative reforms, introduced a new coinage, and instigated a tariff agreement with Greece on tobacco. To his colleague Alfred Milner he seemed 'not only a strong man, but one whose natural inclination, encouraged by success, has always led him to play a decidedly forward game' (Milner, 87). He was appointed KCMG in 1887, aged thirty.

In 1889 Vincent returned to Constantinople as governor of the Imperial Ottoman Bank, in which French investors held the majority of shares. He insisted on great latitude of initiative and action before accepting this appointment. At first he was a consummate success. He surrounded himself with able men to whom he was a model chief. He was *au mieux* with the sultan. He delighted in the Levant, and its high intrigues, though he perhaps despised Levantines. He played a strong hand in all the games of financiers and concession-hunters that he chose to join. Yet he was unable to curb the sultan's extravagance, and his own claims to prudence were travestied by his love of gambling.

Vincent visited South Africa on two occasions in the early 1890s, and in 1895 promoted the Eastern Investment Company, registered in London and using Turkish and other capital to deal in South African shares. At the same time he involved the Ottoman Bank in large risky operations in South African mining shares on the European bourses. This aroused a speculative frenzy in Constantinople, where tens of thousands of people, some of them very poor, plunged into South African mining shares, often with money loaned by the bank for that purpose. The culmination was a run on the Ottoman Bank late in 1895, followed by a crash in values, an international panic, and the ruin of a multitude. Vincent personally made a fortune, but had set a fatal example of speculation among his staff, and the bank felt compelled to pay the stock exchange debts of its junior employees. He was heavily condemned.

On the island of Prinkipo in the Bosphorus Vincent had caused to be built a large, neglected hotel which was known as 'Vincent's Folly' and stood as a constant, visible reminder of his failures; but a more decisive crisis occurred in August 1896. The bank having partly financed the suppression of the recent Armenian and Cretan rebellions, a gang of armed Armenian desperadoes seized control of its headquarters at Galata. Vincent clambered over a roof to an adjoining building to escape being taken hostage or shot. This incident, which played a part in the circumstances that led to the massacre of at least 5000 Armenians in Constantinople alone, doubtless influenced his decision to leave the Levant in 1897.

Return to Britain Vincent settled in Surrey at Esher Place, a large hilltop mansion in the French style built for him in 1895–8 by G. T. Robinson and Achille Duchêne, with a sunken garden by Lutyens. There he entertained generously and housed his collection of pictures. On 24 September 1890 he had married Lady Helen Venetia Duncombe

(1866–1954), second daughter of the first earl of Feversham. They were childless. She was a cosmopolitan beauty, who for many years owned a palace on the Grand Canal at Venice, and was described tartly by Lutyens as 'a lovely Easter egg with nothing inside, terribly dilettante and altogether superficial' (Percy and Ridley, 117). As Margot Asquith classed Vincent among 'the four best looking men I ever saw' (Bonham Carter, 129), and Sir Colin Scott-Moncrieff judged him as 'beautiful … like a son of the gods' (Hollings, 157), they made a resplendent, seductive couple, although Vincent's extramarital affairs earned him the nickname the 'Piccadilly Stallion'. He was tall, imposing, gracious, vivid, and amusing, and spoke with sportsmen, artists, capitalists, and duchesses on their own level. The selfishness of his behaviour in Constantinople was soon varnished with the romance of a character from Dumas or Stendhal: J. E. B. Seely gossiped that Vincent had 'escaped over the roofs at Constantinople with a document in his pocket which subsequently brought him half a million pounds' (Taylor, 255).

Vincent was elected Conservative MP for Exeter in a by-election of November 1899 and held the seat until January 1906. He was more a personal follower of A. J. Balfour than a true Conservative, and never an effective speaker in the Commons: an administrator rather than a legislator, his instincts were too emollient for oratorical battle, and he was too reasonable not to see all sides of all questions. Although flattered with predictions from his friends that he would be chancellor of the exchequer, political office eluded him. Eventually his opposition to tariff protection led to his unsuccessful parliamentary candidature for Colchester as a Liberal in December 1910. He proved as hardy and impervious to political disappointment as to bad investments. In July 1914 he was raised to the peerage as Baron D'Abernon of Esher, at the recommendation of Asquith, who wrote of him two months later, 'Edgar is a curious study—fine intelligence, undeniable charm, and the simulation of bigness without quite the reality' (Brock and Brock, 240). Asquith had previously approved his appointment in 1912 as chairman of the royal commission on imperial trade and the natural resources of the British dominions. Its final report in 1917 recommended the formation of an imperial development board, though its deliberations had been partly overtaken by the effects of the war. D'Abernon was also chairman in 1915–20 of the central control board (liquor traffic) and joint author of the central control board's manifesto *Alcohol: its Action on the Human Organism* (1918). He argued for increased taxes on alcoholic liquor as a measure for national health. Within eighteen months of the board's formation, 'drunkenness had diminished by one-half; within three years—aided by restriction of quantity—it had diminished by more than 80 per cent on the pre-war convictions' (E. Vincent, 'Preface' to H. M. Vernon, *The Alcohol Problem*, 1928, vi–vii). The mortality attributable to alcoholic causes diminished by three-fifths in the twenty years after the administration of this board. D'Abernon was promoted GCMG in 1917.

Vincent continued his business speculations: as one example, he formed a company in 1912 to make commercial fuel out of peat and half-ruined the Balfour family by his advice to invest in it. He remained a gambler both at cards and on the turf. He served as chairman of the Thoroughbred Horse Breeders' Association (1917–32) and was a member of the Racecourse Betting Control Board in 1928–32.

Ambassador to Germany In June 1920 D'Abernon was appointed first ambassador to the German republic and was sworn of the privy council. Lady Cunard falsely claimed responsibility for the appointment, but there is little doubt that his position in society promoted his selection and that Lord Curzon wished to rehabilitate an old friend. D'Abernon's knowledge of currency and economics was indubitably greater than that of anyone in the foreign service. Before reaching Berlin he went in July 1920 to Poland as the leader of a special mission intended to urge on Marshal Pilsudski's government an armistice in its war with the Bolsheviks. The red armies were routed in their advance on Warsaw in August, chiefly by the strategic advice of the French Marshal Weygand, but partly from the steadying effects of D'Abernon, who had telegraphed to Curzon asking for the immediate dispatch of a Franco-British expeditionary force of at least 20,000 men. This episode is described in D'Abernon's *The Eighteenth Decisive Battle of the World: Warsaw 1920* (1931). In its immediate aftermath the prime minister, Lloyd George, was described as evincing 'blind admiration and hero worship of D'Abernon' (Gilbert, 215).

D'Abernon in Berlin sought the conciliation of Germany with its former enemies despite a sombre, menacing background of mutual fear and rancour. Personally he was a success with most German leaders, but was distrusted by the French, whose press remembered the débâcle in 1895 and challenged his probity in terms that were disharmonious. He recognized from the outset that the settlement of Germany's obligation to pay war reparations was impossible until the Weimar leaders had secured currency stability and budget equilibrium. 'It is good to have D'Abernon here', Charles Repington noted in Berlin in 1921. 'He is known as "the doctor of sick finance" … very active and quick at things and has vast experience … He is also a man of the world, and that means more, in every profession, than people admit' (Repington, 269). D'Abernon set out to quell the war spirit. 'I have no extravagant belief in anyone, but incline to the maxim that you make people better by treating them with consideration and confidence', he noted in his journal on 10 July 1925 (*Ambassador of Peace*, 3.175). Although any other course would have been warmongering, some contemporaries saw in his diplomacy the roots of appeasement. His embassy in the Wilhelmstrasse became an important centre of discussion for German leaders.

The early years of D'Abernon's ambassadorship were marked by a succession of conferences. The French government made formidable demands on the Weimar republic for the payment of war reparations, and were more disposed to menaces, sanctions, and compulsion than the British. The divergences between the British and French became irreconcilable by late 1922, and in January 1923 French and Belgian troops occupied the Ruhr and completed Germany's economic ruin. As he was not a professional diplomat, and had no career to consider, D'Abernon took risks that others would not have dared. He said and wrote what he thought rather than what the Foreign Office wished; if his policy of magnanimity and patience was not always supported in London, his fine judgement ensured that he was never repudiated, and he therefore maintained Berlin's trust. He was the ultimate author of the stringent internal measures by which a stabilized currency was achieved and was crucial to the Dawes settlement in 1924, involving the evacuation of the Ruhr and the restoration of German financial stability. This inaugurated a less tense phase in D'Abernon's ambassadorship. French anxieties about national security, which were the next obstacle to European pacification, were assuaged by the Locarno agreement of 1925, whereby Britain guaranteed the Franco-German frontier against aggression by either nation. Both the idea for the Locarno policy, and its essential preliminaries, were initiated by D'Abernon. This treaty was followed after vexing delays by the admission of Germany into the League of Nations in September 1926. In this too D'Abernon played a central part. He relinquished his ambassadorship in October 1926 and left Berlin amid rich demonstrations of gratitude. In the 1930s he would remark that the Dawes plan, the Locarno treaty, and other measures had each occurred at least three years too late.

Retirement In the year of his diplomatic retirement D'Abernon was created GCB and elevated to a viscountcy. His candid Berlin journals, entitled *An Ambassador of Peace*, were published in three volumes (1929–31). These books reveal a shrewd, temperate, ironic man surviving the pelting of political storms with patience and optimism. His prose, like his conversation, was aphoristic and only occasionally sententious. It is charmingly displayed in his *Portraits and Appreciations* (1931). His trenchant judgements on public issues are represented in *The Economic Crisis: its Causes and the Cure* (1930), *Foreign Policy* (1930), and *The Path to Recovery* (1931). In addition to Esher Place, the D'Abernons lived during the 1930s in Arlington Street in London and rented palaces in Rome.

D'Abernon remained active in public life until the late 1930s. He led a successful British economic mission to Argentina and Brazil in 1929. He was chairman of the royal commission on national museums and public galleries (1927–37) and subsequently of the standing commission. He was a trustee of the National Gallery from 1907 and later of the Tate Gallery, although increasingly handicapped by deafness and in decline after 1935. He served as chairman of the Industrial Fatigue Research Board in 1926 and of the Medical Research Council in 1929–34. He was president of the National Institute of Industrial Psychology, the Lawn Tennis Association (1927–32), and (to his pride) the Royal Statistical Society (1927). His reputation as

an economic expert is indicated by the choice of him, together with J. M. Keynes and Sir Josiah Stamp, to broadcast on the slump for the American CBS network in 1931. In 1927 he was made honorary LLD by Manchester University, and in 1934 he was elected FRS.

After the death of several nephews and brothers, D'Abernon succeeded as sixteenth baronet in 1936. He died from hypostatic pneumonia and paralysis agitans on 1 November 1941 at 13 New Church Road, Hove, when all his titles became extinct. His wife, who had trained as an anaesthetist and served in France during the First World War, died in 1954.

In the Near East and Berlin D'Abernon seldom hesitated long over perplexities. He respected, and even savoured, certain types of ethical anomaly, but disliked challenges to the rules of his social set. He was tolerant and unsentimental in his judgements, supple and generous in his conduct, resilient and versatile in his public activities. He had a magnificent ability to enjoy every moment of his life. Gambling was his vulnerable point. R. G. Vansittart wrote:

> D'Abernon was handsome, brilliantly intelligent, financier, scholar, as good judge of a horse as of a picture, white-bearded as an acute Father Christmas with something more than an eye for a pretty girl, excellent company, one of those Britons who contrive to be cosmopolitan in culture and insular in outlook; he was in fact almost everything but great. (Vansittart, 253)

RICHARD DAVENPORT-HINES

Sources R. P. T. Davenport-Hines, *Speculators and patriots* (1986) · PRO, FO 633/7 · Lord Milner, *The English in Egypt* (1907) · *The letters of Edwin Lutyens to his wife Lady Emily*, ed. C. Percy and J. Ridley (1985), 117 · M. Asquith, *The autobiography of Margot Asquith*, 2 vols. (1920–22); repr. in 1 vol. with introduction by M. Bonham Carter (1962) · M. A. Hollings, *The life of Sir Colin Scott-Moncrieffe* (1917) · F. Stevenson, *Lloyd George: a diary*, ed. A. J. P. Taylor (1971), 255 · *H. H. Asquith: letters to Venetia Stanley*, ed. M. Brock and E. Brock (1982), 240 · M. Gilbert, *Sir Horace Rumbold* (1973), 215 · C. À Court Repington, *After the war* (1922), 269 · C. V. Balsan, *The glitter and the gold* (1953), 111–12 · Lord Vansittart [R. G. Vansittart], *The mist procession: the autobiography of Lord Vansittart* (1958), 253 · H. Nicolson, *Friday mornings* (1944), 21–4 · DNB · *The diaries of Cynthia Gladwyn*, ed. M. Jebb (1995) · m. cert. · d. cert. · E. Vincent, Viscount D'Abernon, *An ambassador of peace*, 3: *The years of recovery: January 1924 – October 1926* (1930), 175

Archives BL, corresp. and papers, Add. MSS 48922–48962 · NA Scot., extracts from diary as ambassador in Berlin · PRO, extracts from diary as ambassador in Berlin with corresp., FO 794/11 | Barlow Rand Archives, Johannesburg, Eastern Investment Company MSS · BL, W. E. Gladstone and E. W. Hamilton MSS · BL OIOC, letters to Lord Curzon with diaries, nos. 1014–1017 · Bodl. Oxf., letters to Lady Edward Cecil · Herts. ALS, letters to Lady Desborough · HLRO, corresp. with J. C. C. Davidson, incl. Berlin diary extracts · HLRO, corresp. with David Lloyd George |SOUND BBC WAC

Likenesses C. E. Hallé, oils, c.1886 · Bassano, photographs, 1895, NPG · F. von Lenbach, oils, 1901 · B. Stone, two photographs, 1901, NPG · G. C. Beresford, two photographs, 1903–15, NPG · J. S. Sargent, portrait, 1906; Christies, 22 Nov 1994, lot 136 [see illus.] · W. Stoneman, photograph, 1917, NPG · A. McEvoy, oils, c.1919 · A. John, oils, 1922–32, Tate collection · F. Dodd, pencil drawing, 1930–39 · M. Beerbohm, caricature drawing, 1931, Indiana University, Bloomington, Lilly Library · A. O'Conor, bronze bust, 1934, Tate collection · F. Dodd, oils · Spy [L. Ward], chromolithograph caricature, NPG; repro. in *VF* (20 April 1899) · photographs, Hult.

Arch. • photographs, repro. in Vincent, *Ambassador of peace* • photographs, repro. in Davenport-Hines, *Speculators and patriots* **Wealth at death** £75,640 12s. 10d.: probate, 12 Dec 1941, CGPLA *Eng. & Wales*

Vincent, George (1796–1832), landscape painter, was born in the parish of St John Timberhill, Norwich, and baptized there on 27 June 1796, the son of James Vincent (1756–1834), worsted weaver and shawl manufacturer, and his first wife, Mary Freeman (d. c.1800). Vincent was educated at Norwich grammar school, where fellow pupils were John Berney Crome and James Stark. As a small boy he was 'always fond of drawing with charcoal' (*Eastern Daily Press*, 20 Jan 1885), and about 1811 he was articled to the Norwich school artist John Crome (1768–1821). In the same year he exhibited with the Norwich Society of Artists and continued to contribute fairly regularly until 1831. He also exhibited in London with the Royal Academy (1814–23), the British Institution (1815–31), the Society of Painters in Water Colours (1818–29), and the Society of British Artists (1824–30) as well as in Manchester and Glasgow. In 1816 he accompanied John Berney Crome and Benjamin Steel (who later married John Crome's daughter) to Paris. Vincent suffered from seasickness: 'They had a charming voyage over, Vincent belshing as loud as the steam packet, much to the discomfiture of some of the other passengers' (John Crome to James Stark, January 1816 [1817?], BL, Add. MS 43830, fol. 73). Soon after he probably painted *Rouen* (c.1817; Norwich Castle Museum and Art Gallery), the only continental subject known by Vincent. By 1818 he had moved to London and was living at 86 Newman Street, close to his Norwich friends James Stark and Joseph Clover (1779–1853). About this time Clover painted Vincent's portrait, to which Vincent added the landscape background (c.1818; Norwich Castle Museum and Art Gallery). Referring to the portrait, a Norwich newspaper reported: 'Mr [Alfred] Stannard says of him that his face was disfigured by small-pox, and that he was a very plain man. As to the latter point, we hardly think the recollection is confirmed by the portrait' (*Eastern Daily Press*, 20 Jan 1885).

In 1819 Vincent toured Scotland, and in the following year exhibited with the British Institution the large canvas *View of Edinburgh from the Calton Hill, Evening* (Royal Bank of Scotland, London). Other Scottish subjects followed at intervals. His exhibited works won critical acclaim in Norwich and London, and in 1820 Sir John Leicester bought Vincent's painting *London, from the Surrey Side of Waterloo Bridge* for his collection at Tabley House, Cheshire. In 1822 Vincent married the daughter of a Dr Cugnoni, wrongly believing her to be a woman of property. They moved to a grand house in Kentish Town, London. By 1824 he appears to have been heavily in debt. This was presumably the cause of the 'folly' that alienated him from his father and cut him off from his Norwich friends. Much of what is known of this period of his life is recorded in a series of letters written by Vincent from 26 Upper Thornhaugh Street, Bedford Square, London, to William Davey, a neighbour of Stark in Norwich, dated between 1824 and 1827 (BL, Add. MS 37030, fols. 1–20). On 27 July 1824 he

wrote bitterly: 'so much infamy has been unjustly levelled at me, by those whose duty it was to protect, that I am not astonished a man, like my father, should express himself with severity upon my past folly', adding 'from the sufferings my mind experiences my stay in this world will not be for a very long duration'. Subsequent letters written during 1824 reveal Davey helping Vincent to sell paintings in Norwich at low prices. It was to no avail, because on 27 December 1824 Vincent wrote 'I am at this moment and have been for three weeks a prisoner in the Fleet … I can paint small pictures here but not any of size.' He begged Davey that apart from Stark, no one should know of his whereabouts, particularly his father. During his imprisonment he was allowed out with a keeper to visit Stark in Norwich. He was discharged eventually in February 1827.

In the years surrounding these events, Vincent nevertheless produced some of his finest work, for example the large panoramic painting *A Distant View of Pevensey Bay, the Landing Place of King William the Conqueror* (1824; Norwich Castle Museum and Art Gallery), probably his most ambitious work, and *Trowse Meadows, Near Norwich* (1828; Norwich Castle Museum and Art Gallery). Vincent was the most accomplished of Crome's pupils, and in a short career produced a remarkable body of work. It shows a range of subjects and compositions with a breadth of handling and harmony of colour that exceeds that of his Norwich school contemporaries. Crome's influence is evident, and the crowded incident of Vincent's paintings of Great Yarmouth, for example *Dutch Fair on Yarmouth Beach* (1821; Great Yarmouth Museum) may be compared with similar compositions by Crome. Many of Vincent's landscapes are of Norfolk, including views on the River Yare, while others are the result of visits around Britain. He often signed his work with a conjoined GV and dated some in the 1820s. Few drawings by him exist, but of his etched work twelve etchings dated between 1820 and 1827 and one mezzotint (all British Museum) are known. His work is well represented in the collection at Norwich Castle Museum and Art Gallery. Following his release from the Fleet, he received some commissions, including one from James Wadmore for another large canvas, *Greenwich Hospital from the River* (1827). Although he continued to exhibit his work until 1831, nothing further is known of him until an obituary appeared in the Norwich press: 'Died lately at Bath, in his 36th year, Mr George Vincent, artist—' (*Norwich Mercury*, 14 April 1832).

CAMPBELL DODGSON, rev. NORMA WATT

Sources W. F. Dickes, *The Norwich school of painting: being a full account of the Norwich exhibitions, the lives of the painters, the lists of their respective exhibits, and descriptions of the pictures* [1906] • Rajnai Norwich Artists archive • BL, Reeve collection • H. A. E. Day, *East Anglian painters*, 3 vols. (1967–9), vol. 2 • *Norwich Mercury* (14 April 1832) • *The exhibition of the Royal Academy* (1818–22) [exhibition catalogues] • Norwich Society of Artists catalogues (1811–31) • *Catalogue of the works of British artists in the gallery of the British Institution* (1815–31) [exhibition catalogues, British Institution] • letters to William Davey, BL, Add. MS 37030

Archives BL, letters to William Davey, Add. MS 37030 • BL, Reeve collection

Likenesses J. Jackson, watercolour drawing, *c.*1816, NPG · J. Clover, oils, *c.*1818, Norwich Castle Museum and Art Gallery

Vincent, Henry (1813–1878), radical, was the eldest son of Thomas Vincent (*d.* 1829), a gold- and silversmith. He was born on 10 May 1813 at 145 High Holborn, London. When the family business failed in 1821, the Vincents moved to Hull. Henry received little schooling, though he was an avid reader. In 1828 he was apprenticed to a printer. During his apprenticeship, his early interest in radical politics ripened into activism with his election as vice-president of a local Paineite discussion group and as a member of the Hull Political Union. Upon the completion of his apprenticeship in 1833, Vincent's uncle helped him obtain a position at Spottiswoode's, the king's printers, in London.

In 1836 Vincent became involved with a dispute at Spottiswoode's and left the firm with about sixty other employees. About this time his mother inherited an independent income, which freed Vincent of family responsibilities (his father had died in 1829, leaving a widow and six children). Vincent became more deeply involved in radical circles and in 1836 joined the London Working Men's Association. He became a very successful lecturer and travelled extensively promoting the People's Charter. His greatest impact was in the west country and south Wales. His oratorical skills led to his selection as the chief speaker at the great Chartist meeting held in London in the autumn of 1838. So remarkable was his command over an audience that he was called by Sir William Molesworth 'the Demosthenes of the new movement'.

In December 1838 Vincent further contributed to the Chartist cause through the founding of a weekly newspaper, *The Western Vindicator*. His lecturing and writing activities were brought to an abrupt halt when he was arrested on 7 May 1839 at his house in Cromer Street, London. The warrant from the Newport magistrates charged him with having participated in 'a riotous assemblage' held in that town on 19 April 1839. He was taken to Bow Street, charged, and committed to Monmouth gaol to stand trial at the ensuing assizes. So great was the tumult outside the court that the mayor was obliged to read the Riot Act. The trial took place on 2 August 1839 before Sir Edward Hall Alderson, baron of the exchequer. Serjeant Thomas Noon Talfourd conducted the case for the crown, and John Arthur Roebuck that for the defence. Roebuck showed clearly from the admissions of the chief witnesses for the prosecution that Vincent had told the people to disperse quietly and to keep the peace. Vincent, however, was found guilty and sentenced to twelve calendar months' imprisonment. He applied for the use of books and writing materials but was refused all but religious books. On 9 August 1839 Lord Brougham brought Vincent's case to the attention of the House of Lords. Vincent, though found guilty of a misdemeanour on one count only, was treated as a felon. Lord Melbourne was forced to promise an inquiry. The intense feeling among the Welsh miners about Vincent's treatment in prison helped spark an armed rising of the Chartists in south Wales. On the morning of 4 November 1839 large crowds, estimated variously at from eight thousand to twenty thousand,

Henry Vincent (1813–1878), by Henry John Whitlock

marched towards Newport, where they came into collision with the military. Ten of the rioters were killed and about fifty wounded. Frost, their leader, was arrested that night, with Williams and Jones, leaders of other divisions which had not reached the town in time for the riot. In March 1840 Vincent (along with Edwards) was tried a second time at Monmouth for 'having conspired together with John Frost to subvert the constituted authorities, and alter by force the constitution of the country'. A second count charged the men with having uttered seditious language. Again Serjeant Talfourd conducted the prosecution. Vincent having been dissatisfied with Roebuck's conduct of the defence at his first trial, now decided to defend himself. He did so with such skill and persuasion that the Monmouthshire jury, while finding both prisoners guilty, recommended clemency for him. He was sentenced to twelve months' imprisonment. Talfourd was so impressed by Vincent's defence that he indicated his regrets at having undertaken the case for the prosecution and became involved in the efforts to obtain better conditions for Vincent. His efforts, along with those of Francis Place and Thomas Slingsby Duncombe, and others, resulted in his transfer from Milbank penitentiary to Oakham gaol. There he did much to improve his education in French, history, and political economy with Place's help. On 31 January 1841 Vincent obtained a remission of the sentence through the help of John Cleave, a printer and bookseller in Fleet Street.

After his release Vincent married Lucy Chappell, daughter of John Cleave, at the register office, St Luke's, Chelsea, on 27 February 1841. They settled in Bath, where Vincent resumed lecturing and publishing *The Vindicator*. Following his time in prison, he espoused a more moderate political philosophy. He associated himself with teetotal Chartism and Joseph Sturge's Complete Suffrage Union. In July 1841 he stood as a radical candidate for Banbury in the first of what was to be a long list of unsuccessful attempts to gain a parliamentary seat: Ipswich (1842, 1847), Tavistock (1843), Kilmarnock (1844), Plymouth (1846), and York (1848, 1852).

Afterwards, he lectured on a number of social and historical questions. Among his topics were 'The constitutional history of parliaments', 'Home life: its duties and its pleasures', 'The philosophy of true manliness', 'Cromwell and the men, principles, and times of the Commonwealth', and 'Human brotherhood'. In these later years he also spoke out in favour of popular education, free trade, and religious tolerance. In 1848 he lectured for the Peace Society. Vincent's own religious sympathies were with the Society of Friends, though he was never formally received into membership. In addition to his public lectures, Vincent frequently conducted services on Sundays in free church chapels as a lay preacher. His strong advocacy of the north in the American Civil War made him a welcome visitor when he arrived in the United States. He made lecturing tours in September 1866, October 1867, the winter of 1869, and again in the winter of 1875–6. On all these occasions he was enthusiastically received. His lecturing career drew to a close following a tour of the north of England in late 1878. Arriving home from Barrow in Furness, he endured three weeks of illness and died on 29 December 1878 at his house, 74 Gaisford Street, London. He was survived by his wife and several children.

ALBERT NICHOLSON, *rev.* EILEEN GROTH LYON

Sources W. Dorling, *Henry Vincent* (1879) · R. G. Gammage, *The history of the Chartist movement, from its commencement down to the present time* (1854) · B. Harrison, 'Vincent, Henry', *DLB*, vol. 1 · *CGPLA Eng. & Wales* (1879)

Archives Labour History Archive and Study Centre, Manchester, corresp. with John Minikin

Likenesses H. J. Whitlock, photograph, NPG [*see illus.*] · photograph, repro. in Dorling, *Henry Vincent*

Wealth at death under £450: probate, 6 Feb 1879, *CGPLA Eng. & Wales*

Vincent, Sir (Charles Edward) Howard (1849–1908), politician and police administrator, born at Slinfold, Sussex, on 31 May 1849, was the second and eldest surviving son of the five sons of Sir Frederick Vincent, eleventh baronet (1798–1883), rector of Slinfold and prebendary of Chichester Cathedral, and his second wife, Maria Copley (*d.* 1899), daughter of Robert Young of Auchenskeoch. His father was succeeded in the baronetcy by William, the eldest son of his first marriage. Of Vincent's younger brothers, Claude (1853–1907) was under-secretary of the public works department in India and Edgar *Vincent was created Viscount D'Abernon in 1914.

Howard Vincent, one of whose godfathers was Cardinal

Sir (Charles Edward) Howard Vincent (1849–1908), by James Russell & Sons

H. E. Manning, then archdeacon of Chichester, was a delicate child; in adult life, however, his activity and vitality were exceptional. He made little mark as a pupil at Westminster School, but being sent to travel in France and Germany he acquired an interest in foreign languages. In 1866, while in Dresden, he witnessed some aspects of the Austro-Prussian War. In November that year he entered Sandhurst, and in 1868 was commissioned in the Royal Welch Fusiliers. He made a brief visit to Italy in 1870 to learn the language, and later that year sought permission to act as a correspondent covering the Franco-Prussian War. Permission was denied; however, in 1871, as a correspondent of the *Daily Telegraph*, he travelled to Berlin. After carrying dispatches for Lord Bloomfield, the British ambassador, he went on to Russia to study both the language and its military organization. In 1872 he began his indefatigable publishing career, first with a translation of the warnings sent to France by the French military attaché in Berlin, but ignored by the minister of war, and second with a guide to military geography and reconnoitring. Although only a young subaltern he was also soon writing in service magazines and lecturing at the Royal United Service Institution. In 1872 he travelled to Ireland with his regiment. Once there, much of his time was spent in hunting and private theatricals, but he also addressed political meetings expressing broadly Liberal views on the Irish question. The next year he resigned his lieutenant's commission and, on 3 May, enrolled as a student at the Inner Temple. Excursions to Russia and Turkey in the course of

1873 and 1874 extended his range of languages as well as his knowledge of the politics of the Near East; the inevitable publications followed rapidly. During 1874–5 he served as a captain in the Berkshire militia, and from 1875 to 1878 was lieutenant-colonel of the central London rangers. While holding the latter post he studied and published on volunteer organization, and promoted a series of conferences designed to secure more generous treatment from the government. The climax of his military career came between 1884 and 1904 when he was colonel-commandant of the Queen's Westminster volunteers.

Vincent was called to the bar on 20 January 1876, and joined the south-eastern circuit in the Probate, Divorce, and Admiralty Division of the High Court. Almost immediately he produced a book on the law of criticism and libel, but he never fully devoted himself to legal practice. On the outbreak of the Russo-Turkish War he went, as a representative of the *Daily Telegraph*, to report on the Russian army. The Russians were suspicious of him, possibly because of his knowledge of their language, and there was a fear that he sympathized with the Turks; he was refused permission to go with the army and there was no appeal.

In 1877 Vincent entered himself as a student of the Paris *faculté de droit* and made his own investigation of the Parisian police. That same year the 'turf fraud' scandal led to the dismissal of several leading officers of the detective branch of the London Metropolitan Police and a commission was appointed to investigate the branch. Vincent presented the commission with a succinct, but thorough, description of the Paris detective system; this, in turn, recommended him to the home secretary, R. A. Cross, and brought about his appointment in 1878 to the newly created post of director of criminal investigation at Scotland Yard. Over the next six years Vincent set out to reform and reorganize the detective department, a task made especially arduous by the Fenian outrages of the early 1880s. While at Scotland Yard he formed plans for the reform of criminals and the aid of discharged prisoners. From 1880 to 1883 he was chairman of the Metropolitan and City Police Orphanage. He published on legal and police matters, notably, in 1882, *A Police Code and Manual of Criminal Law*, which remained a basic textbook for police forces in both Britain and the empire until well into the following century. From 1883 he edited the *Police Gazette*, the official journal containing information and descriptions of wanted offenders and details of lost or stolen property. His interest in detective work was abiding, and he bequeathed 100 guineas for an annual prize, the Howard Vincent cup, for the most meritorious piece of work in connection with the detection of crime. In the midst of his busy schedule, on 26 October 1882, he married Ethel Gwendoline, daughter and coheir of George *Moffatt MP, of Goodrich Court, Hertfordshire, with whom he had a daughter, Vera.

Much as the job with the Metropolitan Police interested him, Vincent soon recognized that it offered little chance of advancement. In 1883 he resolved to resign and enter politics, though his resignation was deferred for a year.

While he had toyed with Liberalism, Vincent was not particularly committed to any political party. However, a tour round the world following his departure from Scotland Yard fostered in him an ardent faith in imperialism and protection. He was adopted as Conservative candidate for Central Sheffield, and at the general election in November 1885 he defeated Samuel Plimsoll by 1149 votes. He was to represent the constituency until his death, being re-elected five times: three times after a contest in July 1886, July 1892, and January 1906, and twice unopposed in 1895 and 1900. Soon after entering parliament he joined the London county council, on which he served from 1889 to 1896. Vincent showed the same industry as a politician that he had demonstrated earlier in his career. He was soon a prominent organizer of the party, becoming chairman of the National Union of Conservative Associations in 1895, chairman of the publication committee of the Conservative Party in 1896, and, in 1901, vice-chairman of the grand council of the Primrose League. He was a hard-working back-bencher, but was very much his own man, often asking questions which discomforted the party leadership. Probably as a consequence, he was never invited to join an administration. Nevertheless, he had a remarkable success in converting private measures of his own or his friends' devising into statutes. In particular he played a key role in acts dealing with the probation of first offenders (1887), saving life at sea, merchandise marks (1887), alien immigration (1905), and the appointment of a public trustee (1906). The last of these took many years of labour and lobbying, and Vincent regarded its passage as his chief political achievement. He was best-known in the Commons for his advocacy of protection, even when tariff reform was not part of official Conservative policy. He strongly urged the principle of colonial preference, and to this end, in 1891, he founded the United Empire Trade League and acted thenceforth as its honorary secretary.

Vincent, who was made CB in 1885, was knighted in 1896. In 1898 he attended as British delegate the conference at Rome on the treatment of anarchists, and was made KCMG for his services. When the Second South African War broke out in 1899 Sir Howard busily helped to form and equip volunteer contingents. His selection for the command of the infantry of the City Imperial Volunteers in South Africa was, to his disappointment, cancelled because of a heart problem. But he went to South Africa as a private observer, and his lay services there led to the award of the Second South African War medal and the appointment as aide-de-camp to the king. In 1901 he served as chairman of a departmental inquiry on the Irish constabulary and the Dublin police.

Sir Howard had been troubled by a cough since his youth, and over the years was given several warnings about his heart. Failing health towards the close of 1907 led him to spend some time in the family villa at Cannes. He came back to England for his daughter's wedding early in 1908, but on his return to France he died suddenly of heart failure at Menton on 7 April 1908. He was buried on 9 April at Cannes.   REGINALD LUCAS, *rev.* CLIVE EMSLEY

Sources S. H. Jeyes and F. D. How, *The life of Sir Howard Vincent* (1912) • S. Petrow, *Policing morals: the Metropolitan Police and the home office, 1870–1914* (1994) • *The Times* (8 April 1908) • *The Times* (9 April 1908) • *The Times* (10 April 1908) • *The Times* (11 April 1908) • *The Times* (19 May 1908) • m. cert. • Burke, *Peerage*
Archives BL, corresp. with Lord Carnarvon, Add. MS 60822 • Bodl. Oxf., memoranda and corresp., some with Sir William Harcourt • CUL, letters to Lord Hardinge • Sheff. Arch., letters to Sheffield chamber of commerce
Likenesses B. Stone, photographs, 1897–1901, NPG • J. Russell & Sons, photograph, repro. in Jeyes and How, *Life of Sir Howard Vincent*, frontispiece [*see illus.*] • Spy [L. Ward], watercolour study for a caricature, NPG; repro. in *VF* (22 Dec 1883) • portraits, repro. in Jeyes and How, *Life of Sir Howard Vincent*
Wealth at death £64,680 0s. 6d.: probate, 15 May 1908, CGPLA Eng. & Wales

Vincent [*née* Burchell; *other married name* Mills], **Isabella** (**1734/5–1802**), singer, is said to have been a milkmaid on the Surrey estate of the proprietor of Vauxhall Pleasure Gardens, Jonathan Tyers, who gave her a musical education and introduced her at Vauxhall in 1751. In September the *Universal Magazine* printed 'Young Colin was the bonniest swain' as sung there by Miss Burchell. She sang at the gardens for ten summers and her name appears on songs by Thomas Augustine Arne, John and James Worgan, Samuel Howard, and Rayner Taylor. On 25 August 1755 she married the violinist and kettledrummer Richard Vincent (*d.* 1766), the leader of the orchestra at Vauxhall, and their daughter Elizabeth was born in 1757. Two other daughters, born in 1760 and 1763, died in infancy.

In October 1759 Covent Garden theatre scored a huge success with a production of John Gay's *The Beggar's Opera*, with Charlotte Brent as Polly. Brent was a pupil of Arne, and her brilliantly ornamented singing of the role caused a sensation. Isabella Vincent was pretty with a sweet 'English' voice, while Charlotte Brent was plain, and in the summer of 1760 they both sang at Vauxhall. In June the *British Magazine* published 'A parallel between Mrs. Vincent and Miss Brent', which claimed that Mrs Vincent sang with more ease and grace, but that the lower part of her voice was much finer than the upper, and her songs were less musically interesting than Miss Brent's. The conclusion was that 'she who sung last always sung best' (*British Magazine*, 1760, 348–50). That autumn Garrick mounted *The Beggar's Opera* at Drury Lane with Mrs Vincent as Polly, her first stage role, and for a few days the two theatres repeated the piece on alternate nights. Charles Churchill, charmed by her modesty and virtue, much preferred Vincent:

> She laughs at paltry arts, and scorns parade:
> Nature through her is by reflection shewn,
> Whilst Gay once more knows Polly for his own.
> (*Poetical Works*, 1.48)

And the *Smithfield Rosciad* (p. 22) echoed these sentiments:

> … the shade of Gay enraptur'd smil'd,
> Calling her *Polly*, and his own sweet child.

Mrs Vincent remained at Drury Lane, singing incidental music and taking a few roles in musical afterpieces, including Zaida in Garrick's *The Enchanter*, with music by J. C. Smith. In 1764–5 she sang in two new English 'serious operas', *Almena* and *Pharnaces*. She played Polly every season, but was no actress. In 1763 she was Helena in *A Midsummer Night's Dream*, with the fifth act omitted and extra airs inserted; the prompter noted in his diary that the piece was murdered by the 'singing speakers', with Palmer and Mrs Vincent 'beyond description bad' (Stone, 1021). According to *Thespis* (1766), although she could 'warble sweetly thro' some trifling airs', her singing was 'mindless' (Kelly, 34). Moved by 'melody's divinest strains', *Anti-Thespis* (p. 15) dismissed this as spite and malice.

Richard Vincent died on 28 August 1766, and Isabella was beginning to look too old for Polly, a role she played only once in her final season, on 27 May 1767. From 1764 to 1767 she sang in the summer at Marylebone Gardens under the management of Thomas Lowe, her first Macheath, and it was there that she was heard by John Mills (*c.*1722–1811), a merchant navy captain in the service of the East India Company and a survivor of the Black Hole of Calcutta. They were married on 24 October 1767 and travelled to India with her daughter early the following year. Their son John Wedderburn Samuel Thomas Mills was baptized in Calcutta in March 1769 and was buried there that July. The family apparently left Calcutta before the birth of Alfred *Mills (1776–1833), who became a successful book illustrator. Isabella Mills died on 9 June 1802 at her home in Hampstead Road, London, and was buried on 15 June in St Pancras old churchyard, where her epitaph mourned a singer whose

> simple notes could strike the heart,
> Beyond the utmost skill of labour'd art.
> (Cansick, 83)

OLIVE BALDWIN and THELMA WILSON

Sources G. W. Stone, ed., *The London stage, 1660–1800*, pt 4: *1747–1776* (1962) • parish register, St Paul, Covent Garden • parish register, the Queen's Chapel of the Savoy • parish register, the Mission Church, Calcutta, BL OIOC • parish register, Old St Pancras • L. Baillie and R. Balchin, eds., *The catalogue of printed music in the British Library to 1980*, 62 vols. (1981–7) • P. R. Broemel, 'Biographical sketches of Captain John Mills and Mrs. Isabella Mills', 1924, City Westm. AC, envelope B/MIL • 'A parallel between Mrs. Vincent and Miss Brent', *British Magazine* (1760), 348–50 • *The poetical works of Charles Churchill*, ed. W. Tooke, 1 (1804) • *Smithfield Rosciad* (1763) • H. Kelly, *Thespis, or, A critical examination into the merits of all the principal performers belonging to Drury-Lane Theatre* (1766) • *Anti-Thespis* (1767) • *European Magazine and London Review*, 41 (1802) • *GM*, 1st ser., 72 (1802) • M. Sands, *The eighteenth-century pleasure gardens of Marylebone, 1737–1777* (1987) • W. Wroth and A. E. Wroth, *The London pleasure gardens of the eighteenth century* (1896) • H. E. Busteed, *Echoes from old Calcutta*, 4th edn (1908) • T. W., 'History of the stage', *Monthly Mirror* (1801), 341–6 • F. T. Cansick, *A collection of curious and interesting epitaphs*, 1 (1869)
Likenesses J. R. Smith, mezzotint, pubd 1786 (after miniature by G. Engleheart, 1780), BM • tracing, repro. in G. C. Williamson and H. L. D. Engleheart, *George Engleheart* (1902)

Vincent, James (*bap.* 1718?, *d.* 1749). *See under* Vincent, Richard (1697x1701?–1783).

Vincent, James Edmund (**1857–1909**), journalist and author, born on 17 November 1857 at St Anne's, Bethesda, Caernarvonshire, was the eldest son of James Crawley Vincent (1827–1869), perpetual curate there, and later vicar of Llanbeblig with Caernarfon, where his devoted service during the cholera epidemic of 1867 led to his death, and his wife, Grace Elizabeth, daughter of William Johnson, rector of Llanfaethlu, Anglesey. Sir Hugh Corbet Vincent (1862–1931), who became a solicitor in Bangor, and Sir William Henry Hoare Vincent (1866–1941), who had a distinguished career in the Indian Civil Service, were his younger brothers. His grandfather, James Vincent Vincent, was dean of Bangor (1862–76). In 1870 he was elected to scholarships both at Eton and Winchester colleges, and attended the latter. In 1876 he won a junior studentship at Christ Church, Oxford. He gained a second class in classical moderations in 1878 and a third class in the final classical school in 1880, when he graduated BA.

Vincent entered the Inner Temple in April 1881, and was called to the bar in January 1884. He married on 12 August 1884 Mary Alexandra, second daughter of Silas Kemball Cook, governor of the Seamen's Hospital, Greenwich, with whom he had two daughters. He practised as a barrister on the north Wales circuit, and was also a reporter for the *Law Times* in the bankruptcy department of the Queen's Bench Division from 1884 to 1889. In 1890 he was appointed chancellor of the diocese of Bangor.

By this date, though, Vincent had already begun to devote more attention to journalism than to the law. He joined the staff of *The Times* in 1886 and for the greater part of his life was the principal descriptive reporter of the paper. He had particular experience of covering industrial matters, and reported on many of the major strikes and lock-outs of the period. In 1901, as special correspondent, Vincent accompanied King George V, then duke of Cornwall and York, on his colonial tour, and later he wrote on motoring. From 1894, after W. E. Henley's retirement, to 1897 he edited the *National Observer*, and from 1897 to 1901 *Country Life*. He was a lover of country pursuits, and enjoyed sailing, shooting, fishing, and otter hunting.

Vincent did much work outside newspapers. He contributed occasionally to the *Quarterly Review* and the *Cornhill Magazine*. In 1885, having been a keen footballer in his youth, he collaborated with Montague Shearman in *Football*, a volume in the Historical Sporting series. In 1889 he published a substantial pamphlet, *Tenancy in Wales*, a reply to *Landlordism in Wales* (1887) by Adfyfr, the chosen name of Thomas John Hughes, the Welsh Liberal and nationalist polemical writer. Vincent gave an overview of the circumstances of the agrarian agitation in *The Land Question in North Wales* (1896), which further defined the landowners' point of view. He later acted as an adviser to the landlords in preparing evidence for the royal commission on Welsh land (1893–6). But his best literary work was in biography and topography. His *Life of the Duke of Clarence* (1893) was written by authority, while *From Cradle to Crown* (1902) was a profusely illustrated popular account of the life of Edward VII, reissued in 1910 as *The Life of Edward the Seventh*. Other biographical studies were *John Nixon: Pioneer of the Steam Coal Trade in South Wales* (1900) and *The Memories of Sir Llewelyn Turner* (1903); Turner was his father's friend and co-worker in north Wales.

After buying Lime Close, Drayton, a house near Abingdon, Vincent developed an antiquary's interest in the district, and in 1906 he wrote *Highways and Byways in Berkshire*.

He later contributed the historical surveys in W. T. Pike's *Berks, Bucks, and Bedfordshire in the Twentieth Century* (1907), and wrote *Hertfordshire in the Twentieth Century* (1908) and *Through East Anglia in a Motor-Car* (1907), a lively record of travel. He was at work upon his *Story of the Thames* (1909) when he died; it was published posthumously by his wife. Vincent died of pleurisy at a nursing home, at 99 Cromwell Road, South Kensington, London, on 18 July 1909, and was buried in Brookwood cemetery. He was survived by his wife. A brass memorial tablet, with Latin inscription, was placed in Bangor Cathedral on St Thomas's day, 1910.

G. LE G. NORGATE, *rev.* MARK POTTLE

Sources *The Times* (19 July 1909) • *The Times* (22 July 1909) • *The Times* (23 Aug 1909) • *Wales Chronicle* (23 Dec 1900) • *Wales Chronicle* (23 July 1909) • J. B. Wainewright, ed., *Winchester College, 1836–1906: a register* (1907) • Foster, *Alum. Oxon.* • *The Wykehamist* (21 Dec 1909) • private information (1912) • 'Vincent family', *DWB* • *Wellesley index* • K. O. Morgan, *Rebirth of a nation: Wales, 1880–1980* (1981) • CGPLA *Eng. & Wales* (1909)
Archives News Int. RO, papers
Wealth at death £574 4*s.* 10*d.*: probate, 18 Aug 1909, CGPLA *Eng. & Wales*

Vincent, John (1591–1646). *See under* Vincent, Nathaniel (1637/8–1697).

Vincent, John Painter (1776–1852), surgeon, was born at Newbury, Berkshire, the son of Osman Vincent, silk merchant and banker in Newbury, who lived at nearby Donnington. Richard Budd *Vincent, naval captain, was his elder brother. John Vincent was apprenticed in 1793 to William Long, who was surgeon to Christ's Hospital and assistant surgeon to St Bartholomew's Hospital. While an apprentice he attended Leigh Hunt, then a boy at Christ's Hospital, who said that Vincent 'was dark, like a West Indian, and I used to think him handsome' (Hunt, 141). Vincent became a member of the Company of Surgeons on 20 March 1800, and of the newly incorporated Royal College of Surgeons two days later. He was assistant surgeon to St Bartholomew's Hospital from 1807, succeeding William Long and taking over his house in Lincoln's Inn Fields. He was full surgeon from 1816. Vincent married Maria, daughter of Samuel Parke of Kensington, on 28 May 1812; they had six children, of whom three sons survived him. One became a barrister, and two became clergymen. His wife died in October 1824, and he then married Elizabeth Mary Williams, who survived him.

At the Royal College of Surgeons Vincent was a member of the council (from 1822), a member of the court of examiners (1825–51), Hunterian orator (1829), vice-president (1830, 1831, 1838, and 1839), and president (1832 and 1840). He was not in favour of establishing fellowships, but was one of the original 300 elected in 1843.

'Old Vinco' was popular with the students. He always walked to the hospital, 'shuffling along with short steps, his hands never in his pockets, never behind him, but always clasped in front, as if ready to do handy work. He was very careful of his hands, and well he might be, for they were his best instruments' (Plarr, 462). Vincent was an 'able practical surgeon, shrewd in diagnosis … he never taught in the school—never even, I think, gave a clinical lecture … disposed to avoid operations, unless obviously necessary' (ibid., 462). He wrote little, but published his Hunterian oration in 1829, and a work on surgical practice, in 1847.

Vincent fell ill and resigned as surgeon to St Bartholomew's in 1847; he was made a governor of the hospital, but he kept his college offices until 1851. He died at Woodlands Manor, near Wrotham and Sevenoaks, Kent, on 17 July 1852, and was buried in the church he had built at Woodlands, where his youngest son was perpetual curate.　　　D'A. POWER, rev. JEAN LOUDON

Sources Medical Times and Gazette (24 July 1852), 101–2 • V. G. Plarr, Plarr's Lives of the fellows of the Royal College of Surgeons of England, rev. D'A. Power, 2 vols. (1930) • The Lancet (24 July 1852), 91–2 • L. Hunt, The autobiography of Leigh Hunt, with reminiscences of friends and contemporaries, 3 vols. (1850), 140–41 • private information (1899) • P. J. Wallis and R. V. Wallis, Eighteenth century medics, 2nd edn (1988)
Likenesses E. U. Eddis, oils, c.1850; at St Bartholomew's Hospital in 1899

Vincent, Nathaniel (1637/8–1697), nonconformist minister, was the third son of **John Vincent** (1590/91–1646), heir of Thomas Vincent of Northill, Cornwall, and younger brother of Thomas *Vincent (1634–1678). John matriculated from New College, Oxford, on 15 December 1609, and became a student at Lincoln's Inn in 1612. He was first beneficed in Cornwall, but was ejected from several positions in various parts of the country. After arriving in London in 1642, he was nominated by the committee of the Westminster assembly to the rich rectory of Sedgefield, co. Durham, and instituted in 1644, but died in 1646. His widow, Sarah Vincent, petitioned on 1 November 1656 and in April 1657 for £60 which her husband had lent to the parliament.

Nathaniel was registered at Oxford as a chorister on 18 October 1648, aged ten. He matriculated from Corpus Christi College on 28 March 1655, graduated BA from Christ Church on 13 March 1656, proceeded MA on 11 June 1657, and returned as chaplain to Corpus Christi College. He was appointed by Cromwell as one of the first fellows of Durham College, but never lived there. About 1658, aged twenty, he was preaching at Pulborough, Sussex, and the following year he was ordained and presented to the rectory of Langley Marish, Buckinghamshire.

After his ejection in August 1662, Vincent served for three years as chaplain to Sir Henry Blount and his wife, Hester, at Tittenhanger, Hertfordshire. Here, as he later recalled, 'the world was presented to me in the gayest dress: your house large, and bravely furnished; your gardens delightful; your park and walks hardly to be matched; your table abundantly and sumptuously furnished' (Vincent, The Spirit of Prayer, A2r–v). According to Edmund Calamy, soon after the great fire in 1666 he went to London, where he preached to large crowds among the ruins of the city. In 1669 he was reported to be preaching at Wraysbury and Colnbrook in Buckinghamshire to '2 or 300 none of any quality, the most considerable is one Slocombe a mercer. They say they will uphold their conventicle in spite of the King or Bishop' (Gordon, 161). But in that year he was also active in London, at Farthing Alley,

and in the Southwark parishes of St Saviour, where he preached a sermon published as The Day of Grace (1669), and St Olave, where, 'in a house built on purpose' shortly after the great fire, he 'catechiseth the people and baptizeth children some privately some publicly in his conventicle' (ibid.), although periodically soldiers arrived to prevent his preaching. In the early summer of 1670 Vincent married Anna, whose other name is unknown.

That July Vincent was arrested by soldiers who 'rudely pulled him out of the pulpit by the hair of the head, after they had planted four muskets at the four corners of his pulpit', but 'as they were carrying him through the narrow alley adjoining, the multitude crowded in between him and the soldiers, and rescued him'. However, within a few weeks he was recaptured and soon sent to the Marshalsea in Southwark, 'where the great number of people that came to visit him gave offence', so the prisoner 'was hurried away' (Calamy, Continuation, 1.137–8). His removal to the Gatehouse, Westminster, would have remained secret had not an acquaintance observed it by chance. On 28 September the council granted his wife's petition to visit him, as he was suffering from fever. Towards the end of November Anna petitioned for permission to attend her husband with a nurse, and for a physician to be admitted, 'he having been taken dangerously ill' (CSP dom., addenda, 1660–70, 546). His book A Covert from the Storm was written in the Gatehouse, 'during his close confinement, when few could come at him but his God' (title-page). The date of Vincent's release is unclear, but Joseph Williamson noted on 31 December 1671 that he was again preaching in Farthing Alley and was 'very followed' (CSP dom., addenda, 1660–85, 341). Vincent was licensed as a presbyterian teacher there on 2 April 1672, following the receipt of a letter in his favour from his sister's husband, James Inness. Vincent's The Morning Exercise Against Popery (1675) included sermons from other nonconformist ministers, but he continued to publish extensively on his own account. Works on conversion were complemented by The Little Childes Catechism (1679) and several funeral sermons.

In December 1681, according to the official record, Vincent's meeting-house was visited 'by three justices with constables and other officers'; he refused to obey their order to stop preaching, 'but proceeded in his discourse, till the noise was so great he could not well be heard' (CSP dom., 1680–81, 640). When the meeting broke up, the justices took a note of the names of those who were known and then departed. However, this account appears to do less than full justice to the incident. As the justices discovered, the meeting-house had both many exits and many peep-holes from which to view visitors: 'when the justices commanded his audience to disperse, they were drowned out with hymn-singing while the preacher made his escape' (Greaves, 92). On 4 January 1683 Oliver Heywood kept a solemn fast with Vincent at his meeting-house. The following Wednesday Vincent appeared at the quarter sessions at Dorking, Surrey, far from his Southwark friends, charged with conventicling under the statute of 35 Elizabeth. He was sentenced to three months in gaol, to be followed by banishment. Heywood took leave of him in the Marshalsea on 29 January 1683, but on Vincent's petition the privy council ordered on 14 February that a writ of error be issued by the attorney-general, returnable in the king's bench, and after the expenditure of £200, and many delays in which he was unable to secure a hearing, news reached Heywood on 26 May that Vincent was 'cleared in open court the solicitor saying there was more faults in the indictment than in the man, and so threw it out blessed be God' (*Autobiography*, 89). In the aftermath of the duke of Monmouth's rebellion, some time before 26 January 1686 Vincent was arrested at Exeter on charges of involvement, and sent for by the king.

Apparently for some time an admirer of Richard Baxter, in 1691 Vincent published *An Elegy* upon his death. After 1689 he had been less troubled by official harassment, but in 1692 sixty members of his church departed to join the congregation of Richard Fincher at Unicorn Yard, in Southwark. This 'made a deeper impression upon his Spirit, than any of the Troubles he had met with for Nonconformity' (Wilson, 306). Also in 1692, he was nominated, but declined to serve, as a manager of the common fund of presbyterians and Independents. This may have been due to the illness which also gave rise to his *A Present for such as have been Sick ...* (1693). In November 1695 he preached a funeral sermon for Edward Laurence, a fellow minister, published as *The Perfect Man Described* (1696). He was living at St Giles, Holborn, when he signed his will on 1 February 1697, and died suddenly on 22 June, aged fifty-eight, leaving a widow, Anna, a son, Nathaniel, and daughters Mary, Elizabeth, Hannah, and Judith. He was buried at Bunhill Fields. The funeral sermon was preached by Nathaniel Taylor, who provides evidence that the congregation had been plagued with contention even after the defections to Fincher. He recalled the deceased pastor's 'great zeal against bold intruders into the work of the ministry', who 'begin to swarm among us', warning against false friends whose aim was 'the tearing and dividing you in pieces' (Taylor, 25, 28). Taylor recalled of Vincent that 'His compassion to the poor was great, to whom he gave alms and holy advice at the same time' (ibid., 26). Anthony Wood's assessment of Vincent was also (and more surprisingly) positive: 'He was of smarter, more brisk, and florid parts than most of his dull and sluggish fraternity can reasonably pretend to; of a facetious and jolly humour, and a considerable scholar' (Wood, *Ath. Oxon.*, 4.617).   STEPHEN WRIGHT

Sources Calamy rev. • E. Calamy, *A continuation of the account of the ministers ... who were ejected and silenced after the Restoration in 1660*, 2 vols. (1727), vol. 1 • G. L. Turner, ed., *Original records of early nonconformity under persecution and indulgence*, 1 (1911) • W. Wilson, *The history and antiquities of the dissenting churches and meeting houses in London, Westminster and Southwark*, 4 vols. (1808–14), vol. 4 • M. Burrows, ed., *The register of the visitors of the University of Oxford, from AD 1647 to AD 1658*, CS, new ser., 29 (1881) • A. Gordon, ed., *Freedom after ejection: a review (1690–1692) of presbyterian and congregational nonconformity in England and Wales* (1917) • CSP dom., 1660–81; addenda, 1660–85 • E. Calamy, ed., *An abridgement of Mr. Baxter's history of his life and times, with an account of the ministers, &c., who were ejected after the Restauration of King Charles II*, 2nd edn, 2 vols. (1713) • N. Taylor, *A funeral sermon, occasioned by the sudden death of the Reverend Mr Nathanael Vincent, late minister of the gospel in Southwark* (1697) • *The Rev. Oliver Heywood ... his autobiography, diaries, anecdote and event books*, ed. J. H. Turner, 4 (1885) • R. L. Greaves, *Secrets of the kingdom: British radicals from the Popish Plot to the revolution of 1688–89* (1992) • will, GL, Peculiar of the dean and chapter of St Paul's, MS 25626/9, fols. 148–9 • Wood, *Ath. Oxon.*, new edn, 4 • N. Vincent, *The spirit of prayer, or, A discourse* (1677) • N. Vincent, *A present for such as have been sick and are recovered* (1693) • *The life and times of Anthony Wood*, ed. A. Clark, 2, OHS, 21 (1892) • *Report on the manuscripts of the marquis of Downshire*, 6 vols. in 7, HMC, 75 (1924–95)

Likenesses R. White, line engraving, 1681, BM, NPG • oils, DWL

Vincent, Philip

Vincent, Philip (*bap.* 1600?), author, may have been the Philip Vincent baptized on 23 November 1600 at Frisby in the parish of Conisborough, Yorkshire, the second son of Richard Vincent (*d.* 1617), a lawyer, and his wife, Elizabeth, daughter of Thomas Rokeby of Hotham in the same county. This would make him the grandson of Richard Vincent, army officer and younger son of the family of Vincent of Braywell, Yorkshire. This Philip Vincent was educated at Peterhouse, Cambridge, and in 1625 was presented by Sir Francis Vincent to the rectory of Stoke D'Abernon in Surrey, which he resigned on 17 August 1629. At the church of St Bartholomew-the-Great, London, on 17 March 1625 he married Frances, daughter of Sir Christopher Hedon of Baconthorpe, Norfolk, and widow of Henry Draper of Bromley, Kent. They had three sons before her death on 30 November 1630.

Vincent produced two known works, which appear to have come from his travels. The first, *The lamentations of Germany, wherein, as in a glasse, we may behold her miserable condition, composed by Dr Vincent, Theo.*, was signed P. Vencent, and appeared in London in 1638. The account describes his travels in Germany from 1633 to 1635, during which he was besieged in Heidelberg by the Spaniards. His accounts describe the horrors of the scene in great detail, graphically depicting the hardships of the inhabitants and the abuses of the soldiers.

Vincent's second work, *A True Relation of the Late Battell Fought in New England and the Salvages*, also first appeared in London in 1638, and was signed P. Vincentius. The author states he had previously visited Guiana and describes the New England scene with such detail that he received his information either at first hand or from a reliable second-hand source. The account describes the 1637 war between the New England colonists and the Pequot Indians, whom Vincent describes as 'a stately warlike people, which have been terrible to their neighbours, and troublesome to the English'. Manipulated by the Pequot's Amerindian rivals, Connecticut sent an ultimatum demanding that the Pequot become a tributary. Not surprisingly, the powerful Pequot refused and braced for war. Vincent's account describes the destruction of the second largest Pequot village in May 1637. The Connecticut-led force of some ninety colonists, seventy Amerindians under the command of the Mohegan leader Uncas and 500 Narragansett warriors caught the village by surprise. Defended fiercely by 150 warriors, the colonists and their Amerindian allies feared that the delay in taking the village would allow the main Pequot force to engage them. The Connecticut commander, John Mason, ordered that the village be burned and the survivors killed. Despite his vivid detail of the action and estimate of 'not less that 700 slaine or taken prisoners', Vincent did not hesitate to endorse the slaughter, remarking that 'sever justice must now then take place'. The colonists lost only sixteen men. When the main Pequot force arrived, they were demoralized by the scene, and surrendered in large numbers. The destruction of the Pequot marked the rise of Connecticut and the changing face of colonial–Amerindian warfare to conflicts of total destruction and extermination. Nothing more is known of Vincent.   TROY O. BICKHAM

Sources DNB · *The lamentations of Germany, wherein, as in a glasse, we may behold her miserable condition, composed by Dr Vincent* (1638) · P. Vincentius [P. Vincent], *A true relation of the late battell fought in New England and the Salvages* (1638) · I. K. Steele, *Warpaths: invasions of North America* (1994), 91–5 · V. F. Voight, *Uncas: sachem of the wolf people* (1963) · A. A. Cave, *The Pequot war* (1996) · *IGI*

Vincent, Richard (1697x1701?–1783), musician, was born probably in London and may have been the Richard Vincent baptized at St Martin-in-the-Fields on 27 June 1697, the son of Richard and Elizabeth Vincent, although this conflicts with his age at death stated by the *Gentleman's Magazine*, which would suggest a birth date of 1700 or 1701. He was the first of a family of musicians active in London, mainly in the Covent Garden area, during the eighteenth century. Some confusion has arisen and persisted owing to the number of musicians referred to simply as Mr Vincent in contemporary records. By February 1720 he was a member of the opera band at the Academy of Music, playing the bassoon for an annual salary of £40. He had joined the king's musick by 1 April 1724. On 12 December 1737, at the church of St Benet Paul's Wharf, he married Elizabeth Bincks (sometimes Binks; c.1708–1792?), a young actress who had made her début at Lincoln's Inn Fields in 1729 and acted at the Covent Garden Theatre in the 1730s (she was probably the daughter of the Mrs Bincks who was a dresser at Covent Garden from 1735 to 1740). Billed as Mrs Vincent from January 1738, Elizabeth continued with her acting career in Dublin and at Covent Garden into the 1770s, by which time she was considered past her best. Her address for benefit tickets between 1750 and 1752 was the Cock and Turk's Head in Bedford Street. At least three of the couple's children joined the acting or musical professions. Richard Vincent was an original subscriber to the declaration of trust that established the Royal Society of Musicians in August 1739. His brother Thomas and his brother's sons Thomas and James [see below] were also subscribers at this time. Richard also performed on the harpsichord in a number of concerts and composed songs, and at some point he joined the Covent Garden orchestra as an oboist. He may have been the Mr Vincent paid 5s. per night in 1767–8. Burney refers to him as being 'for more than thirty years the principal hautbois at Covent-garden' (Burney, *Hist. mus.*, 2.1011), and he was living in the Little Piazza, Covent Garden, in 1769. At the time of his death on 10 August 1783 at Tottenham Court Road, London, he was described as 'the oldest Musician belonging to Covent-

garden playhouse and to Vauxhall-gardens, who enjoyed, till the last year of his life, a remarkable flow of spirits' (*GM*). This obituary notice makes no mention of a widow, although it is thought that his wife survived him.

One of Vincent's sons, **Richard Vincent** (d. 1766), musician, lived in the Covent Garden area. Known primarily as a violinist and drummer, he became a member of the Royal Society of Musicians on 5 January 1752 and was leading the band at Vauxhall Gardens at the time of his marriage in 1755. On 25 August at St Paul's, Covent Garden, he married the singer and actress Isabella Burchell [see Vincent, Isabella]. They had at least three daughters, according to the registers of St Paul's: Elizabeth (who possibly became the actress Mrs Ferguson), Sophia, and Penelope Louisa, the latter two dying in childhood. Vincent was living in King Street, Covent Garden, in 1763. He died in London on 28 August 1766 and was buried at St Paul's, Covent Garden, on 31 August. His will, which places him in the parish of St Marylebone, was made on 25 August 1766 and left all of his estate, unspecified, to his widow, Isabella.

Another son (possibly the youngest) of Richard Vincent senior, **Charles Vincent** (*fl.* 1777–1795), acted at the Drury Lane Theatre in 1777 and joined Tate Wilkinson's company at Wakefield in September of that year. However, by 1795 he was curate of St John's in Leeds and a schoolmaster. A Miss Vincent (*fl.* 1762–1771), probably a daughter of Richard and Elizabeth Vincent, made her début at Covent Garden at the latter's benefit on 16 April 1762 and performed there during 1767–8. There was also Sarah, who is described as the illegitimate daughter of 'Richard Vincent, Sr' and whose baptism (30 April 1758) is recorded in the registers of St Paul's. A Richard Vincent, with a wife named Isabella and five children baptized at St Paul's, Covent Garden, in the 1740s, and whose will was proved on 2 August 1783, may have been related.

The brother of Richard Vincent senior, **Thomas Vincent** (*bap.* 1693?, *d.* 1751?), possibly the son of Richard and Elizabeth Vincent baptized on 22 January 1693 at St Martin-in-the-Fields, played the bassoon in the guards for many years, composed music for the Lincoln's Inn Fields Theatre, and probably contributed some music for some dances published in 1721. Besides subscribing to the Royal Society of Musicians, he served on the first board of governors. The list of the king's musick features the name Thomas Vincent regularly between 1727 and 1750, although some of these instances probably refer to his son. Vincent died probably in late 1751, as his will was proved on 13 January 1752. The sole executor and administrator was the same son, **Thomas Vincent** (c.1720–1783), oboist and composer, who was born in London about 1720 and may have been one of the Thomas Vincents baptized at St Martin-in-the-Fields on 28 October 1720 and 11 August 1723, both the sons of Thomas and Elizabeth Vincent. He became a very successful performer. His family connections no doubt assisted him in acquiring Giuseppe Sammartini as his teacher. Hawkins noted that Thomas junior was known to have possessed most of his teacher's 'excellencies' in 'a very eminent degree', at a time when oboists were 'greatly superior to any that can be remembered before the arrival of Martini in England' (Hawkins, 2.895). He appeared at events including the annual spring concerts given at the King's Theatre for the benefit of the Royal Society of Musicians (1743–68), the annual Foundling Hospital *Messiah* in 1754 and 1758, and the Covent Garden and Drury Lane oratorios during the 1750s, and he was concerto soloist at the Lock Hospital on 29 February 1764. Vincent also published a number of works during this period, including six solos (1748), *A Sett [sic] of Familiar Lessons for the Harpsichord* (1755), and songs (1760?). He was a member of the king's musick during the 1760s (while living at Brook Green, Hammersmith), although he may have gained this position much earlier, and may have appeared at the Dublin Rotunda in 1770. In 1764–5 Vincent joined Peter Crawford and John Gordon in the management of opera at the King's Theatre, but the venture ended in 1769 with the loss of a considerable sum of money. The will of a John Gowland (proved 23 August 1776), described as Vincent's assignee, shows Vincent to have been deeply in debt, as he was paying his entire salary of £40 as a royal musician, and his additional income as the king's barber, to Gowland; income was then to pass to a bookseller in New Bond Street, James Robson, who, after taking his own costs, was to transfer the sum to Vincent's wife, Penelope, for as long as she lived. Vincent was not to receive the money until after her death. Burney suggests happier times, when Vincent, an experienced professor and 'long a favourite on the hautbois', had 'been in great favour with the prince of Wales', presumably George III's father Frederick, and 'had acquired a considerable sum of money in his profession, which he augmented by marriage' (Burney, *Hist. mus.*, 2.870). Vincent died in 1783, probably on 10 May. An oboist, Thomas Vincent (*fl.* 1784?–1795), may have been his son and may have appeared in the Handel commemoration (1784) and been a member of the king's musick in 1793 and 1795.

The younger Thomas Vincent's brother **James Vincent** (*bap.* 1718?, *d.* 1749), who may have been the James, son of Thomas and Elizabeth Vincent, baptized at St Martin-in-the-Fields on 18 March 1718, was an organist in London, holding posts (with John Stanley) at the Inner Temple Church and also at St Luke's, Old Street. He also published compositions, including a few songs which appeared mainly during the 1730s and 1740s. Burney described him as 'a brilliant performer' who 'died young' (Burney, *Hist. mus.*, 2.870). He died in London on 6 October 1749.

DAVID J. GOLBY

Sources Highfill, Burnim & Langhans, *BDA* · C. Hogwood and J. K. Page, 'Vincent, Thomas', *New Grove*, 2nd edn · Burney, *Hist. mus.*, new edn, 2.870, 1011 · J. Hawkins, *A general history of the science and practice of music*, new edn, 2 (1853), 895 · *GM*, 1st ser., 53 (1783), 717 · P. R. Broemel, 'Biographical sketches of Isabella Mills and Captain John Mills', MS, 1924, Marylebone Public Library, London
Wealth at death all to widow; Richard Vincent jun.: will, mentioned in Highfill, Burnim & Langhans, *BDA*

Vincent, Richard (*d.* 1766). *See under* Vincent, Richard (1697×1701?–1783).

Vincent, Richard Budd (1770?–1831), naval officer, was born at Newbury, Berkshire, where his father, Osman Vincent, was a silk merchant and banker. John Painter *Vincent was his brother. Richard entered the navy in 1781 on the *Britannia*, flagship of Vice-Admiral Samuel Barrington, and was present at the relief of Gibraltar and the encounter with the allied fleet off Cape Spartel in October 1782. He was, after the peace, for three years in the *Salisbury* on the Newfoundland station, served for four years in the channel, and on 3 November 1790 was promoted lieutenant. In 1793 he went to the Mediterranean in the *Terrible*, was present at the Toulon operations, and in 1794 on the coast of Corsica. In October 1794 he was moved into the *Victory*, Lord Hood's flagship, then understood to be the prelude to certain promotion. But in April 1795 Hood was summarily ordered to strike his flag, and Vincent's chance was gone. It did not come again until 29 April 1802, when, after seven years' continuous service, mostly in the North Sea, he was promoted commander, and three weeks later was appointed to the *Arrow*, one of a class of sloops built and armed on a plan proposed by Samuel Bentham. She carried twenty-eight 32-pounder carronades, an armament heavier, in the weight of shot, than that of any frigate then afloat, but effective at only very short range. After nearly a year's anti-smuggling service in the channel, she was paid off on 28 February 1803, and recommissioned the next day, again by Vincent, for the Mediterranean, where for the next two years she was mostly engaged in convoying the trade up the Adriatic and around the Greek archipelago.

By the end of 1804 the *Arrow* was in need of a thorough repair; many of her timbers were rotten, and a survey at Malta decided that she was too weak to heave down; she must go home to be docked. She was accordingly ordered, with the bomb-vessel *Acheron* in company, to take charge of the homeward-bound trade. They sailed from Malta towards the end of January, and on 3 February were seen and chased between Algiers and Cape Ténès by two French frigates, the *Incorruptible* (38 guns) and *Hortense* (40 guns), the only two ships of Villeneuve's squadron which had continued at sea when the squadron itself was driven back by bad weather on 21 January. Between these and the convoy Vincent interposed the *Arrow* and the *Acheron*, hoping that he might at least be able to give the merchant ships time to escape. At about 7.30 on the morning of 4 February the French frigates brought them to action, and captured both after a brilliant defence of nearly two hours. Armed only with carronades the two vessels were outranged in a one-sided battle. The *Arrow* sank almost immediately afterwards, before all her men could be removed; the *Acheron* was set on fire and destroyed. The merchant ships had meanwhile escaped to the westward, and only three of them were captured. Officers and men were taken to Cartagena, whence in May they were sent in a cartel brig to Gibraltar. They arrived in England early in June. The court martial on Vincent, on 17 June, honourably acquitted him, and praised his conduct.

Two days after the trial Vincent was advanced to post

rank by a commission dated 8 April, and on 3 July the committee of the Patriotic Fund awarded him a sword of the value of £100, and a piece of plate of the same value. Four years later the merchants of Malta presented him with a handsome service of plate. In May 1806 he was appointed to the *Brilliant* (28 guns) on the Irish station, but in October he was obliged by ill health to resign the command, nor was he able to accept any further employment until March 1808, when he was appointed to the frigate *Cambrian* in the Mediterranean. From her he moved into the *Hind* (28 guns), but in September 1808, being at Malta, he complied with the request of Sir Alexander John Ball to assist him in the duties of the port as captain of the *Trident* (64 guns). With Ball and his successors, he remained in the *Trident* until December 1815, when he was appointed to the *Aquilon* (32 guns), in which he returned to England in April 1816. He was made a CB in June 1815. He had no further service and died at Deal, Kent, on 18 August 1831.

J. K. LAUGHTON, rev. ANDREW LAMBERT

Sources W. P. Gosset, *The lost ships of the Royal Navy, 1793–1900* (1986) · J. Marshall, *Royal naval biography*, 2/2 (1825), 912–29 · W. James, *The naval history of Great Britain, from the declaration of war by France, in February 1793, to the accession of George IV, in January 1820*, [2nd edn], 6 vols. (1826), vol. 4 · *GM*, 1st ser., 101/2 (1831), 469 · 'Biographical memoir of Captain Richard Budd Vincent', *Naval Chronicle*, 17 (1807), 265–304

Archives BL, letters to Nelson, Add. MSS 34920–34930, 34977 *passim*

Likenesses H. R. Cook, stipple, pubd 1807, NPG · portrait, repro. in 'Biographical memoir', 265

Vincent, Thomas [T. V.] (1634–1678), clergyman and ejected minister, was born in May 1634 in Hertford (where he was baptized on 18 October), the son of John *Vincent (1590/91–1646) [*see under* Vincent, Nathaniel]. The name of Vincent's mother is uncertain: John's widow Sarah petitioned in 1656 for repayment of loans that he had made to parliament but she may have been a second wife. His father was a puritan clergyman whose lack of conformity led to his being harried by the ecclesiastical authorities. Indeed, Thomas's childhood was unsettled, his father being 'so harrassed, and forc'd upon so many Removes for his Nonconformity' that, Calamy claimed, Vincent and his many siblings were each born in different counties (Calamy, *Continuation*, 1.30). Thomas's younger brother Nathaniel *Vincent became a Presbyterian minister.

Vincent was educated first at Westminster School, and then at Felsted School, Great Dunmow, Essex, the latter a strongly puritan institution under the mastership of Martin Holbeach. Admitted to Christ Church, Oxford, in 1648, he matriculated in February 1651, graduating BA in March 1652, and MA in June 1654. At this point, exceptionally for a junior member, he was elected catechist. He subsequently became chaplain to Robert Sidney, second earl of Leicester, and in 1656 was incorporated into the University of Cambridge. No surviving evidence indicates Vincent's formal ordination. In July 1657 he was nevertheless appointed rector by sequestration of St Mary Magdalen, Milk Street, London. Ejected in 1662 under the Act of Uniformity, he assisted Thomas Doolittle for the next few

years at his nonconformist academy in Bunhill Fields, continuing to preach privately and opportunistically. Vincent's address at this time is unknown; he was certainly living in Spitalfields in 1671–2.

Upon the outbreak of the plague in 1665 Vincent was among a number of silenced nonconformists who emerged, as conforming ministers fled the city, to attend to the congregations they left behind. Vincent preached in churches throughout London and, undeterred by the risk of infection, ministered to the sick and dying in their homes. 'Void of all fear of death' (Neal, 451), he won interdenominational respect; his sermons also accumulated a multitudinous following, their peculiar intensity honed by the extreme circumstances. His printed meditation on the plague, *Gods Terrible Voice in the City* (1667), ran to sixteen editions within just eight years.

After 1665 Vincent preached more openly without licence, and was thus regarded with suspicion by the Restoration authorities. He had gathered together a congregation, for which a large meeting-house, seating 500, was built in 1669 in Hand Alley, off Bishopsgate Street. This meeting-house was allegedly among those seized by conformists who had lost their own churches to the fire of 1666; while Vincent reclaimed his premises, he remained subject to harassment and prosecution, and in 1672 was fined £20 for preaching. He was nevertheless granted a licence under the declaration of indulgence in 1672, and ministered to a devoted congregation until his death. Throughout his final decade he published a number of writings, most notably the popular *Explicatory Catechism* (1673). While his works were predominantly doctrinal and devotional, he also published polemical challenges to William Penn and William Sherlock. Towards the end of his life he moved to Hoxton, Middlesex.

There are few extant details of Vincent's immediate family. At some point he married, and with his wife, Mary, who survived him, had at least four children. He died on 15 October 1678 in Hoxton, and was buried on 27 October at the church of St Giles Cripplegate. His funeral sermon, subsequently published, was preached by Samuel Slater. Vincent was apparently of comfortable means at the time of his death, leaving property and assets of unknown value to his family, and a number of monetary gifts to individual beneficiaries and the parish poor. While no visual likeness survives of him, a clear impression of his character and reputation emerges from the many eulogistic sketches of his life. A formidably eloquent and learned man, who reputedly knew the entire New Testament and Psalms by heart, Vincent was at once selfless and single-minded in his ministry, his 'Zeal and Diligence' (*Reliquiae Baxterianae*, 3.95) unwavering in the face of both plague and persecution. He does indeed seem, as Slater states, to have been 'freely willing to venture his life for the salvation of souls' (Slater, 41). BETH LYNCH

Sources W. Wilson, *The history and antiquities of the dissenting churches and meeting houses in London, Westminster and Southwark*, 4 vols. (1808–14), vol. 2 · S. Slater, *Vincentius Redidivus: a funeral sermon, preached Octob. 27. 1678* (1679) · *Calamy rev.* · *Reliquiae Baxterianae, or, Mr Richard Baxter's narrative of the most memorable passages of his life*

and times, ed. M. Sylvester, 1 vol. in 3 pts (1696) · E. Calamy, A continuation of the account of the ministers … who were ejected and silenced after
the Restoration in 1660, 2 vols. (1727) · G. L. Turner, ed., Original records
of early nonconformity under persecution and indulgence, 3 vols. (1911–
14) · CSP dom., 1671–2 · Wing, STC · Wood, Ath. Oxon., new edn,
3.1174 · Wood, Ath. Oxon.: Fasti (1815) · Foster, Alum. Oxon. · D. Neal,
The history of the puritans or protestant nonconformists, ed. J. Toulmin,
new edn, 5 vols. (1822) · N. H. Keeble, The literary culture of nonconformity in later seventeenth-century England (1987) · T. V. [T. Vin-
cent], Gods terrible voice in the city (1667) · Schools in eastern England,
Independent Schools Information Service (East) (1998–9) · PRO,
PROB 11/361, sig. 168 [fols. 329v–330r] · DNB · IGI
Wealth at death left property to wife and children and money to
named individuals and parish poor: will, 1679, PRO, PROB 11/361,
sig. 168

Vincent, Thomas (bap. 1693?, d. 1751?). See under Vincent,
Richard (1697x1701?–1783).

Vincent, Thomas (c.1720–1783). See under Vincent, Richard
(1697x1701?–1783).

Vincent, William (1739–1815), dean of Westminster and
classical scholar, was born in the City of London on 2
November 1739, the fifth and youngest son of Giles Vincent of Lime Street ward and his wife, Sarah, daughter of
Thomas Holloway of Newnham Murren, Oxfordshire. His
father pursued the business of a packer and Portugal merchant, though the latter business was devastated by the
Lisbon earthquake of 1755, which also killed William's
eldest brother.

Vincent was admitted to Westminster School in September 1748 and became a king's scholar in 1753. He
remained associated with Westminster until his death
and was only absent from its precincts during his years at
Cambridge, where he entered Trinity College in June 1757.
He was elected to a scholarship in April 1758, matriculated
the same year, and graduated BA in 1761, MA in 1764, and
BD and DD in 1776. In 1762 he was elected to a fellowship
but in the same year he returned to Westminster School as
usher, or assistant master. He was ordained deacon on 19
December 1762 and priest on 22 September 1765.

In 1771 Vincent succeeded Pierson Lloyd as under-
master at Westminster and was also appointed chaplain
to the king. On 15 August at St Margaret's, Westminster,
he married Hannah (bap. 1735, d. 1807), fourth daughter of
George Wyatt, chief clerk of the vote office in the House of
Commons, and his wife, Hannah. They had three children: William St Andrew (1772–1849), who became a clergyman; George-Giles (1774–1859), who was appointed chapter clerk and registrar of Westminster Abbey in 1803; and
Hannah-Elizabeth (1776–1777).

In 1778 Vincent succeeded Samuel Smith as headmaster
of Westminster School. In the same year he was appointed
vicar of Longdon, in Worcestershire, but soon resigned
that living to become rector of All Hallows-the-Great, in
the City of London. He was appointed sub-almoner to the
king in 1784, was president of Sion College in 1798, and
acted as prolocutor of the lower house of convocation in
1802, 1806, and 1807.

In 1792, when alarm at the potential consequences of

William Vincent (1739–1815), by Henry Edridge, 1809

the French Revolution was at its height, Vincent preached
at St Margaret's, Westminster, for the benefit of the Grey
Coat Hospital, a Westminster charity school. The sermon,
in which he defended both the prevailing social order and
the constitution, reflected his strongly held tory views,
and the major part of it was published by the Patriotic
Association in a print-run of 20,000 copies.

Vincent was installed as a prebendary of Westminster
on 21 April 1801. He consequently retired from his teaching at Westminster School but not before responding vigorously to accusations by Thomas Rennell, master of the
Temple, and Thomas Lewis O'Beirne, bishop of Meath,
that religious education was being neglected in the public
schools. A pamphlet entitled A Defence of Public Education
(1801), in which Vincent refuted the allegations by drawing on his intimate knowledge of the curriculum at Westminster, occasioned some controversy and ran to three
editions. It was the only one of his works from which he
ever benefited financially (the profits were good-
humouredly presented to his wife) and his subsequent
installation as dean of Westminster on 7 August 1803
appears to have resulted from it.

In 1805 Vincent obtained the living of St John's, Westminster, in the gift of the dean and chapter, and resigned
his incumbency at All Hallows-the-Great. After two years
he exchanged St John's for another of the dean and chapter's livings, the rectory of Islip, in Oxfordshire, thereby
obtaining a country residence which he much enjoyed
and where he regularly stayed. He attended diligently to
parochial business, enquired into the antiquities of the
parish, and repaired and enlarged the dilapidated rectory.

Islip also brought him into close proximity with Oxford University, where he preached the annual sermon for the benefit of the Radcliffe Infirmary in July 1808.

The first fruits of Vincent's classical scholarship was *De legione Manliana quaestio ex Livio desumta* (1793), in which by means of an ingenious emendation he reconciled the seemingly contradictory accounts of Polybius and Livy respecting the Roman legion. This solution to a problem that had long perplexed classical scholars was well received both at home and on the continent. Two further pamphlets quickly followed, *The Origination of the Greek Verb: an Hypothesis* (1794) and *The Greek Verb Analysed: an Hypothesis* (1795), both concerned with the development of the Greek language and the inflection of its verbs. These works Vincent was required to defend against charges of plagiarism, conclusions of a similar nature having appeared in the *Encyclopaedia Britannica* about the same time. His views did not succeed in holding their ground.

Vincent's chief study, however, was ancient geography and commerce, and his scholarly reputation rests on two major works. *The Voyage of Nearchus from the Indus to the Euphrates* (1797) is a commentary on an expedition recorded by Arrian of Nicomedia in his *Indica* that Vincent termed 'the first event of general importance to mankind in the history of navigation' (*The Voyage of Nearchus*, 1.1). The voyage was conceived by Alexander the Great, about whom Vincent wrote with an admiration unusual for the time. His commentary drew on a wide range of sources and he was assisted by Samuel Horsley, dean of Westminster, who loaned two astronomical treatises, and by Alexander Dalrymple, hydrographer to the Admiralty, who prepared charts for him. More unusually for the period he made use of oral evidence from those who had recently visited the regions concerned. The subject was pursued further in *The Periplus of the Erythraean Sea*, issued in two parts, in 1800 and 1805, respectively. He argued against the prevailing view that this too was the work of Arrian, attributing it instead to an unidentified Alexandrian merchant of the first or second century BC.

In 1807 these erudite commentaries were brought together as a second edition (in two volumes) under the title *The Commerce and Navigation of the Ancients in the Indian Ocean*. The whole work was dedicated to Lord Sidmouth (to whom Vincent owed his promotion to the Westminster deanery), though the original dedication of each individual part to George III was retained. Vincent's own copy, annotated with his manuscript notes, survives in the library at Westminster Abbey. English translations of the original Greek texts of the *Voyage of Nearchus* and *The Periplus* followed in 1809.

Vincent also published a number of other pamphlets and contributed articles on a range of geographical and classical subjects to the *Classical Journal*, the *Gentleman's Magazine*, and the *British Critic*. Through the columns of the last of these he participated in the debates concerning the existence of Troy and the historical veracity of the Trojan War. A volume entitled *Sermons on Faith, Doctrines, and Public Duties* was published posthumously in 1817 by Vincent's eldest son and prefaced with a biographical account by his friend Robert Nares, archdeacon of Stafford. A second volume of sermons appeared in 1836.

At Westminster Abbey Vincent's most pressing task was the much needed restoration of Henry VII's lady chapel, but when a serious fire broke out in the roof of the lantern in July 1803 resources had to be directed instead to immediate and expensive repairs in the north transept. Under Vincent's leadership the dean and chapter successfully petitioned the House of Commons for public money to support the repair of the chapel, and between 1807 and 1822 a series of grants totalling more than £42,000 was received. Work proceeded under the direction of Thomas Gayfere and Benjamin Wyatt, and though the supervising parliamentary committee tried hard to restrict repairs to those that were necessary for the security of the building Vincent resisted by simply ordering the work to continue.

Although as a master at Westminster School Vincent reputedly resembled Richard Busby in his love for the rod, in other respects he was warm-hearted by nature, wearing his erudition lightly and with modesty. With the learned he was 'ready to enquire and to communicate' and with the ignorant 'so very indulgent, that they hardly suspected their infirmity' (Nares, xix). Generous in spirit, as exemplified when, on his advancement as dean, he quickly obtained a living for the curate who had been his assistant at All Hallows-the-Great for twenty-two years, he was a zealous patron of the Society of Schoolmasters, even though its formation post-dated his own departure from that profession.

From an early age weakness of the eyes had prevented Vincent from reading or writing by artificial light but in other respects he had a robust constitution, in spite of taking very little exercise. He died, aged seventy-six, at the deanery, Westminster, on 21 December 1815, after a short illness of the stomach, and was buried in St Benedict's chapel in Westminster Abbey on 29 December. Mural monuments in the south transept (by unknown artists), with inscriptions composed by Vincent, commemorate both himself and his wife. His name is perpetuated by Vincent Square, which through his influence was preserved as a playing field for Westminster School.

TONY TROWLES

Sources R. Nares, 'Life of the author', in W. Vincent, *Sermons on faith, doctrines, and public duties* (1817) · E. Carpenter, ed., *A house of kings: the history of Westminster Abbey* (1966) · J. L. Chester, ed., *The marriage, baptismal, and burial registers of the collegiate church or abbey of St Peter, Westminster*, Harleian Society, 10 (1876) · J. Sargeaunt, *Annals of Westminster School* (1898) · Venn, *Alum. Cant.* · G. F. R. Barker and A. H. Stenning, eds., *The Westminster School register from 1764 to 1883* (1892) · *DNB*

Archives BL, Add. MSS · Westminster Abbey, muniments

Likenesses H. Edridge, pencil and watercolour, 1809, NPG [*see illus.*] · C. Picat, stipple, pubd 1810 (after H. Edridge), BM, NPG; repro. in *Contemporary portraits* · G. P. Harding, watercolour (after W. Owen), NPG · H. Meyer, stipple (after W. Owen), BM, NPG; repro. in W. Combe, *The history of the abbey church of St Peter's, Westminster, its antiquities and monuments*, 2 vols. (1812) · W. Owen, oils, the deanery, Westminster Abbey · J. Stow, engraving (after G. P. Harding),

Westminster Abbey · C. Turner, engraving (after H. Howard), Westminster Abbey · oils, the deanery, Westminster Abbey
Wealth at death approx. £1000; plus goods and chattels: will, PRO, PROB 11/1576

Viner, Charles (*bap.* 1678, *d.* 1756), legal writer and university benefactor, was born in Salisbury and baptized there at St Mary's Church, on 3 November 1678, the son of Charles Viner (*fl.* 1660–1711) and his wife, Mary. His father was a prosperous draper, and perhaps a kinsman of Sir Robert Vyner, goldsmith and lord mayor of London. He matriculated at Hart Hall, Oxford, in 1695, but left without taking a degree. In 1699 he married the fifteen-year-old Ralegh Weekes (1684–1761) of Gloucester, a descendant of Sir Walter Ralegh. They lived together at Aldershot, Hampshire, until Viner's death.

Viner entered the Middle Temple in 1700, and although he was never called to the bar he kept chambers in King's Bench Walk, Temple, from where he gave occasional legal advice. His real interest, however, was more in the literature of the law than in its practice. He began to collect notes of recently decided cases in 1703, but devoted the greater part of his life to the exhaustive arrangement of existing legal materials under alphabetical headings, based on the works of his predecessors Robert Brooke and Henry Rolle. His *General abridgment of law and equity: alphabetically digested under proper titles, with notes and references to the whole* was published in 23 volumes between 1742 and 1757 (the final volume posthumously). This was printed, reputedly under Viner's direction at his own home, on paper watermarked with his monogram, published by him personally, and the earlier volumes sold from his chambers in the Temple. Though unwieldy to use, it was the most comprehensive attempt to render accessible the legal materials printed before his time, and it remains an invaluable key to these works. An *Alphabetical Index* to the work was published by Robert Kelham in 1758, and incorporated into the second edition of the *Abridgment* (1791–4).

From the early 1740s Viner had it in mind to leave his estate to support the study of the common law in the University of Oxford, and he was encouraged in this by the university. He died at Aldershot on 5 June 1756; on his death Oxford received almost the whole of his estate, valued at £12,000, to endow a professorship of the common law—whose first holder was Sir William Blackstone—together with fellowships and scholarships. The Vinerian foundation formed the bedrock of common law studies at Oxford. Viner's correspondence reveals him as an irritable, at times exasperating, man, with a marked antipathy towards lawyers, booksellers, and printers. He was the most generous academic benefactor of the University of Oxford in the eighteenth century.

DAVID IBBETSON

Sources Bodl. Oxf., MSS Viner · Oxf. UA, Viner deposit · Bodl. Oxf., MSS Gough, Oxford 96 (14)–(42) · W. S. Holdsworth, 'Charles Viner and the abridgments of English law', *Law Quarterly Review*, 39 (1923), 17–45, esp. 17 · D. J. Ibbetson, 'Charles Viner', in J. A. Bush and A. Wijffels, *Learning the law: teaching and the transmission of law in England, 1150–1900* (1999) · Foster, *Alum. Oxon.* · H. Wigan, *Wiltshire Notes and Queries*, 1 (1893–5), 576 · *GM*, 1st ser., 26 (1756), 314 · *DNB* ·

R. Benson and H. Hatcher, *The history of modern Wiltshire*, ed. R. C. Hoare, 6 (1843) · *IGI*
Archives Bodl. Oxf., corresp. and papers
Wealth at death approx. £12,000: U. Oxf., Viner Deposit

Viner, Sir Robert. *See* Vyner, Sir Robert, baronet (1631–1688).

Viner, Sir Thomas. *See* Vyner, Sir Thomas, first baronet (1588–1665).

Viner, William Letton (1790–1867), organist and composer, was born at Bath on 14 May 1790. He studied under Charles Wesley (1757–1834), and in 1820 became organist of St Michael's, Bath. While at Bath he wrote an overture for *Rob Roy*, which though very popular and constantly performed at the theatre there, was never published. He became better known for the religious music that he later published. In December 1835, on the recommendation of Samuel Sebastian Wesley, he was appointed organist of St Mary's Chapelry, Penzance, where he remained until he went to America in 1859.

Viner was a prolific composer of church music, organ music, and songs, and was the author of the hymn tune 'Helston' or 'Kingston', sometimes described as an ancient Cornish melody. He edited *One Hundred Psalm and Hymn Tunes in Score* (1838), *A Useful Selection from the most Approved Psalms* (1846), and *The Chanter's Companion* (1857). He was also an excellent teacher of the organ, harp, and piano. He died at Westfield, Massachusetts, on 24 July 1867.

F. G. EDWARDS, *rev.* NILANJANA BANERJI

Sources Grove, *Dict. mus.* · Brown & Stratton, *Brit. mus.* · [J. S. Sainsbury], ed., *A dictionary of musicians*, 2 vols. (1824) · D. Baptie, *A handbook of musical biography* (1883)

Vines, Richard (1597/8–1651), colonist in America and the West Indies, was born in London. Nothing is known about his parents and very little about his early years, and his date of birth is derived from his statement that he was fifty in 1648, when he witnessed a will. Some time before 1630 Sir Ferdinando Gorges dispatched Vines to explore lands claimed by Gorges in New England. Vines lived for a time in London, where his son was born in 1626, but he had migrated to North America by the summer of 1630. He settled near the Saco River, and spent a decade and a half in Maine as an agent and deputy governor for Gorges. A leading promoter of colonization, Gorges held a series of grants from the British crown capped by a charter for the province of Maine in 1639. An operator of a trading post and a large landowner, Vines also explored the province he helped to govern. Although a frequent correspondent with Massachusetts Bay governor John Winthrop, Vines remained a conforming member of the Church of England. His biggest challenge was defending the Gorges' interests against the claims of George Cleeve, an agent for Sir Alexander Rigby, a member of parliament who had secured the title to lands within territory granted to Gorges. Because his own property was within the tract claimed by Rigby, Vines decided to leave Maine when it appeared that a parliamentary inquiry which began in 1643 would rule in Rigby's favour. Parliament did so in 1646, but by then he had sold his lands and had sailed for the English colony of Barbados. On that prosperous sugar-producing island he acquired about 50 acres. By summer 1647 he could report that he was making a profit from the cultivation of tobacco and cotton and from his medical practice. Within four years he was able to make the transition to sugar cultivation. This modestly successful planter died on the island on 19 April 1651 and was buried in St Michael's Church. His wife, Joane, and four children, named Richard, Margaret, Elizabeth, and Joan, survived him. Although he spent his last six years in the West Indies, Vines's most notable contribution was in the early development of Maine. LARRY GRAGG

Sources *The Winthrop papers*, ed. W. C. Ford and others, 4–5 (1944–9) · R. C. Anderson, ed., *The great migration begins: immigrants to New England, 1620–1633*, 3 (Boston, MA, 1995) · will, 1651, Barbados Archives, RB6/11, 473 · G. B. Roberts, ed., *English origins of New England families*, 3 (1985) · *The journal of John Winthrop, 1630–1649*, ed. R. S. Dunn, J. Savage, and L. Yeandle (1996) · L. F. Stock, ed., *Proceedings and debates of the British parliaments respecting North America*, 1: *1542–1688* (1924) · J. G. Wilson and J. Fiske, eds., *Appleton's cyclopaedia of American biography*, 6 (1889)

Wealth at death 50 acres in Barbados; bequests of 11,000 pounds of sugar, and £200: will, Barbados Archives, RB6/11, 473

Vines, Richard (1599/1600–1656), Church of England clergyman, was born at Blaston, Leicestershire; his parents' names are unknown. In 1619 he matriculated sizar from Magdalene College, Cambridge, where he was an excellent Greek scholar, and he graduated BA in 1623 and proceeded MA in 1627. He was ordained deacon and priest at Peterborough on 23 and 24 May 1624. That year he became schoolmaster at Hinckley, Leicestershire, and married Katherine (*d.* in or after 1656), daughter of Humphrey Adderley of Weddington, Warwickshire, and granddaughter of Humphrey *Adderley (1512–1598). He was schoolmaster until 11 March 1628 when he was presented by his father-in-law to the rectory of Weddington, and on 10 June 1630 to the neighbouring rectory of Caldecote. When Thomas Jacombe preached Vines's funeral sermon twenty-six years later he had this comment on his schoolmastering phase: 'let this be no disparagement' [how else could it have been taken?], he could instance but 'rare instruments of Gods glory in the Church of Christ, who began with that employment' (Jacombe, 39). In that funeral sermon Jacombe alluded to two common criticisms that were levelled at Vines: that he was restless and covetous. Since he held both his livings, worth together £80 a year, while the parish register at Hinckley shows that he was still living there in 1640 and, in addition, conducted a well-attended fortnightly lecture at Nuneaton, these early career moves may have been the foundation of the later criticisms. However, at the time Vines was well regarded among the godly of Warwickshire and was, for instance, a close friend of the theologian George Abbot, stepson of the militant puritan William Purefoy of Caldecote.

When the civil war broke out Vines left Hinckley and was presented as one of the 'orthodox divines' to be consulted by parliament 'touching the reformation of church government and liturgie'. Another sign of his rising status was the frequency of invitations from the Long Parliament for him to preach to them. They liked his message: a warning against liberalism to popery which could be a 'Trojan horse' (*Calebs Integrity*, 1646, preached on 30 Nov 1642); a readiness (like Luther) to take on the sects even if they could be mobilized as allies against the Catholics (*The Impostures of Seducing Teachers*, 1656, preached on 23 April 1644); a dismay at religion's being debased into 'a kind of Philosophy of Opinions' (*The Posture of Davids Spirit*, 1656, preached on 22 Oct 1644); and a plea to Independent ministers to break with the sects (*The Authour, Nature, and Danger of Heresie*, 1662, preached on 10 March 1646). They may also have liked the way that the message was delivered. The fast sermons are, in general, by their nature ephemeral, but some of Vines's phrases were made to last. In the latter sermon, for instance, he has this striking observation: 'to make conscience the final judge of actions, is to wipe out the hand-writing of the Word of God' (*The Authour, Nature, and Danger of Heresie*, 45). There is also a certain equivocation, of having it both ways. Thus in the same sermon he does not condemn Calvin for the execution of Servetus, but quotes approvingly Calvin's comment that Servetus 'might have saved his life had he been but modest'. Still, it would have been better to have fought heresy by light, not fire—leave the fire to the papists. Papists can join Jews, Turks, and other heretics by being given the right to live in the kingdom, but it is another matter to allow them liberty to trade, and open up shops, for the purpose of disseminating their 'destructive' ideas (ibid., 48, 50).

From 1643, having been ejected from his livings, Vines joined other puritan exiles (including Cornelius Burges and Richard Baxter) in Coventry, and established a daily lecture there at St Michael's. He was nominated a member of the Westminster assembly of divines by the ordinance of 12 June 1643, was sent up to London, and was placed in the rectory of St Clement Danes; it was later alleged that he preached there only when the assembly was in session. One of his parishioners was the earl of Essex. Vines's funeral oration for him on 22 October 1646 was later published as *The Hearse of the Renowned*. His respect for the godly magistrate comes out in his tribute to Essex: 'he was a Justice that would scatter the drunkards from the Ale-bench' (*The Hearse of the Renowned*, 15). Death for Vines was not the great leveller. True, we rot equally in the grave, and yet 'honour will follow after worth and merit even into its grave'. Again the gift for the striking phrase comes out in his claim that 'we do not buy up the carkasse of every Cole-ship with that respect as that of Drakes was' (ibid., 16). This is more than a conventional defence of hierarchy; it is also a defence of the funeral sermon. Like other English puritans he championed the funeral sermon as a genre for education; the Scottish presbyterians shunned it because they knew that it elevated personal merit above the insight that all of us rot in the grave equally—and deserve to do so.

Vines's contributions to debate in the Westminster assembly are well brought out in the minutes. Vines defended on 13 September 1643 the right of a colleague

(Cornelius Burges) to sit in the assembly, even though he had opposed the solemn league and covenant. A day later he expressed his worries about an over-rigid Calvinism, which might fall short of full-scale antinomianism but which could be equally dangerous. Although he made common cause with a like-minded ecumenical spirit in the Independent minister Philip Nye, he nevertheless reminded him that agreement had to be rooted 'in things that are well not only in terms and notions'. But the role of his Scottish presbyterian colleagues was equally firmly circumscribed: 'counsellors', not 'dictators' ('Minutes of the Westminster assembly', 1, 1.238*v*). Like his Erastian colleague John Selden he was sceptical of divine-right claims from any quarter—episcopalian or presbyterian. The claims made for the Hebrew Sanhedrin were a 'fiction', he said on 13 December 1643 (ibid., 1, 2.268*v*). Vines's own position in that assembly came under scrutiny on 8 July 1644. He had been sought for the mastership of Pembroke College, Cambridge. The debate focused on whether he should be forced to leave Coventry by a parliamentary ordinance, even though he was reluctant to take up the Cambridge job. The presbyterian minister Herbert Palmer, commented: 'I have not heard any piece of newes that troubles me more than this' (ibid., 2.155*v*). In the event Vines showed administrative flair in his mastership of Pembroke College and his reputation in the assembly itself continued to rise.

It was a mark of colleagues' esteem that Vines was placed on the parliamentary 'committee of accommodation' on 13 September 1644, and was chosen as chairman a week later of the acting subcommittee. Although himself episcopally ordained, he defended the validity of ordination by presbyterians while simultaneously deflating the excessive claims for 'a classical presbytery' from the Scots ('Minutes of the Westminster assembly', 2.43). He was one of the assisting divines at the Uxbridge conference (30 January–18 February 1645). He resigned St Clement Danes on being presented to the rectory of Walton, Hertfordshire, on 22 May 1645. He was placed on the assembly's committee (12 May 1645) for drafting the confession of faith produced in 1647. He recalled that time in a letter years later to Richard Baxter, arguing justly that his compromise proposals then had avoided the overemphasis on works which was to bring so much criticism on Baxter's head. That criticism had focused on Baxter's first published work, *The Aphorismes of Justification* (1649), which he had (perhaps brashly) dedicated to Vines and Anthony Burgess. Burgess was so incensed by it that he wrote against it. Baxter claimed, in contrast, that 'Mr Vines wrote to me applaudingly of it' (*Reliquiae Baxterianae*, 1.107). The actual letter is more opaque than that would indicate. Vines repeats a list of current criticisms that Baxter had gone soft on Arminianism under the cover of the honest reporter, using the phrase 'This is said'. He even said that it draws 'too near Socinianisme' in places (Keeble and Nuttall, 1.58).

Nevertheless, Vines and Baxter were puritans who could work with 'moderate' episcopalians (that is, those who did not subscribe to Laudian *jure divino* claims for the office). Baxter, Vines, and Cornelius Burges were among a group of ministers and parliamentarians who had met twice a week in the early 1640s and who were 'not one for total abolishing of all, or any, but usurped Episcopacy' (Keeble and Nuttall, 1.409). Vines had sympathized with Burges's scruples about taking the covenant. Vines had his own scruples about the selling of church lands. Vines told Baxter that this was sacrilege (of interest to Burges, who had purchased Wells deanery and part of the cathedral estates). He explained to Baxter on 21 July 1649 that was why 'I could not maintain the cause as on the parliamentary side' with reference to the debate between the parliamentary commissioners and Charles I on this issue at Newport, Isle of Wight, in 1648. At those crucial last-ditch negotiations for monarchy Vines struck up a personal rapport with the king. It is significant that, on the morning of the king's execution, Vines was one of the puritan divines who proffered religious services to Charles.

It was logical then that Vines declined the engagement in 1649; in 1650 it cost him his mastership of Pembroke and the rectory of Walton. It was, perhaps, less logical that Baxter joined him on this issue. They debated the matter together by letter, and both thought that the Commonwealth was constitutionally improper. But there is a personal quality to Vines's support for monarchy which is lacking in Baxter's position. This is well brought out many years later. At the turn of the century Thomas Carte was trying to kill off the rumours—and he blamed Baxter principally for purveying them—that Charles I had been mixed up in a popish plot. He then played his master-card: 'you may remember the character which Mr. Vines after the Treaty in the Isle of Wight gave the King to Mr. Gilbert the Presbyterian of Coventry … Of all the Kings of Israel and Judah there was none like him' (Bodl. Oxf., MS Carte 223, fols. 276–7).

These sentiments did not hold Vines back for long. In 1650 the parishioners of St Lawrence Jewry called him to be their minister, and he was invited to hold the living. The parishioners rebuilt the vicarage-house for him at a cost of £500; a few years later his stipend was £180 per annum. With his propensity to acquire offices, he was also chosen as one of the weekly lecturers at St Michael Cornhill. Baxter later recalled an occasion when he preached at St Lawrence Jewry to a church so packed that 'Mr. Vines himself was fain to get up into the Pulpit, and sit behind me, and I to stand between his legs' (*Reliquiae Baxterianae*, 1.111–12).

Vines and Baxter had a common hero in Archbishop James Ussher, whose 1641 scheme for a 'reduced episcopacy' was pressed in the 1650s by both men. When Baxter recommended to the tireless ecumenist John Durie the setting up of a committee of four each of 'Episcopalian', 'Presbyterian', 'Independent', and 'Erastian' groups, he placed Vines in the presbyterian camp (Ussher in the episcopalian). Baxter (substituting for Ussher) and Vines were among the ministers assisting the committee of ten to advise Cromwell on articles 36–38 of the 'Instrument of government'. After Ussher's death Vines recommended

Bishop Ralph Brownrig of Exeter to Baxter as his likely spiritual heir, but Brownrig was less flexible than Ussher and Baxter by then was himself moving to Cromwellian sympathies which would have shocked Vines.

But Vines himself had died by then, at the age of fifty-six; he was survived by his wife and buried at St Lawrence Jewry. As Jacombe in his funeral sermon put it pithily: on 4 February 1656 'Vines died suddenly. He went well to bed, slept and died.' Jacombe deplored a contemporary cheap shot: 'since extempore prayer, more extempore death' (Jacombe, 43). Baxter read his death differently. By dying so soon after administering the sacrament of the Lord's supper, Vines had joined that select band for whom mortality struck 'in the midst of some holy exercise' (Keeble and Nuttall, 1.204).

In another way Vines's was an appropriate end. The last work that he published was *A treatise of the institution, right administration and receiving of the sacrament of the Lords supper* (1656). He took on in debate the Erastian lawyer, William Prynne, who had argued that qualifications for admission to communion were over-rigorous. Vines disagreed: he argued that it was better that those who could should be elevated to the ordinance than that the ordinance should be lowered to them (free admission). Vines's treatise had been approved by Baxter. Yet Vines's line of defence was that discipline was necessary when the help of the civil magistrate was withdrawn. Thus the church under a heathen emperor (or no emperor at all), had no other way of 'self-preservation from scandals of members, but purging them out'. The alternative way of preventing scandal—a partnership between church and magistrate—was what Baxter urged in his *Holy Commonwealth* of 1659. At the time of Vines's death such a hypothesis would have been unthinkable for either man and—given Vines's feelings for monarch and monarchy—would have gone on being unthinkable for Vines. But when Baxter consulted three divines before publishing his Confession in 1654, such was then their unity that (Baxter said) none of them wanted him to change a word of it. Baxter brought the three together (in execrable verse) in his final obituary tribute to Vines:

If but three such in all our times
as USHER, GATAKER and VINES.
(*A Treatise of … the Lords Supper*, 1656, preface)

WILLIAM LAMONT

Sources Venn, *Alum. Cant.* · T. Jacombe, *Enoch's walk* (1657) · E. M. Thompson, 'Minutes of the Westminster Assembly of Divines', U. Edin., New Coll. · *Calendar of the correspondence of Richard Baxter*, ed. N. H. Keeble and G. F. Nuttall, 1 (1991) · *Reliquiae Baxterianae, or, Mr Richard Baxter's narrative of the most memorable passages of his life and times*, ed. M. Sylvester, 1 vol. in 3 pts (1696) · A. Hughes, *Politics, society and civil war in Warwickshire, 1620–1660* (1987) · Tai Liu, *Puritan London: a study of religion and society in the City parishes* (1986) · *Walker rev.*, 45, 46, 365 · will, PRO, PROB 6/32, fol. 83v

Archives DWL, Baxter corresp.

Wealth at death see will, PRO, PROB 6/32, fol. 83v

Vines, Sydney Howard (1849–1934), botanist, was born on 31 December 1849 at Ealing, the only child of William Reynolds Vines, a schoolmaster turned businessman, and his wife, Jessie Robertson. For part of his early life he lived in Paraguay where his father had a sheep ranch. His formal education began at a Moravian school in Germany, where he acquired a command of the language, and was concluded at Dr Dawes's school at Surbiton. Under paternal persuasion Vines began in 1869 a medical course at Guy's Hospital, but he disliked certain aspects of the work and, influenced by Michael Foster at Cambridge, decided to specialize in physiology, reading for a London science degree. In 1872 he won an entrance scholarship at Christ's College, Cambridge; the following year he took his London BSc with first class honours and in December 1875 was placed first in the natural sciences tripos at Cambridge.

In 1874 Vines met W. T. Thiselton-Dyer, who invited him to help during the summer sessions of 1875 and 1876 with the botanical practical classes he taught for intending schoolteachers at the Royal School of Mines, South Kensington. The following year Vines worked under Thiselton-Dyer at Kew, and in 1876 in the newly built Jodrell Laboratory there, was the first to extract active principles from water in the pitchers of the carnivorous *Nepenthes*. Meantime, Vines was also elected to a fellowship and lectureship in botany, a move which displeased his parents, at Christ's. It was his practical acquaintance with his subject matter that made his presentation a revelation, for botany as generally taught then was little more than the study of flowers from books. There was no laboratory work and Vines, wishing to gain further experience before he organized such courses, spent the summer of 1877 working with Julius von Sachs at Würzburg. During the following Michaelmas term laboratory work was started at Cambridge in a room lent by Foster and equipped with microscopes and apparatus bought at Vines's own expense. In 1879 and 1880 he worked in Heinrich de Bary's mycological laboratory in Strasbourg, but moved on to Würzburg once more, to work with D. H. Scott. In 1879 he was awarded the DSc by the University of London; in 1880 he translated Karl Prantl's *Lehrbuch der Botanik* as *Elementary Botany* and in 1881 teaching room was allotted to him at the Cambridge Botanic Garden. In 1882 he brought out the second English edition of Sachs's *Lehrbuch der Botanik nach dem gegenwärtigen Stand der Wissenshaft* as the *Textbook of Botany*. In the following year he was made a reader and in 1885 he was elected FRS at the early age of thirty-five. On 30 December 1884 he married Agnes Bertha, eldest daughter of Walter Woodcock Perry, brewer, of Chelmsford. They had two sons, of whom the elder, Walter Sherard, became professor of English language and literature at University College, Hull, and a daughter. In 1886 he published his own *Lectures on the Physiology of Plants* and by the next year a building large enough to take classes of up to a hundred had been provided for him. His more notable pupils included F. O. Bower, with whom he wrote *A Course of Practical Instruction in Botany* (1885), Percy Groom, Reynolds Green, F. W. Oliver, Ethel Sargent, and Edith Saunders. Vines was full of enthusiasm, ready to repeat his practical classes two or three times because of limitation of space, and prepared to work the whole night through, if need be, lecturing, teaching, translating, and writing. Such efforts may have overtaxed his strength and laid the foundations of ill health that influenced his subsequent long life.

Vines was elected to the Sherardian professorship at Oxford (including a fellowship at Magdalen College) in 1888, with the further responsibilities of a botanical garden and a herbarium. By contrast with Cambridge, he presided over the Oxford science department which had least success in attracting students, there being only seven botany graduates between 1886 and 1900. According to A. E. Gunther, Vines 'put more undergraduates off botany and careers in botany than any other Sherardian professor in history' (Howarth) and was alleged to be prejudiced against taking women. However, the department was cramped at the Oxford Botanic Garden, Acland's proposal to move it to near the University Museum having failed. Vines was also at odds with his brilliant demonstrator, A. H. Church, and had, moreover, to be careful of his health. His public reply to Ruskin's accusation of science's being inimical to art 'was [by comparison] a limp and feeble affair' (Allen, 183). Facilities for research did not exist, and it was not until twenty-three years later that Vines was able to secure any considerable addition to the laboratory. Other Oxford science professors had similar difficulties, largely because the attractive tripos at Cambridge (1881) siphoned off suitable students and Cambridge's funding arrangements were more favourable to science. Although Vines argued against the narrow specialization of Oxford in the 1890s, by 1897 he was fighting for botany against the tendency to convert the university into a 'technical school', in this case referring to a 'threatening school of agriculture'. None the less the school of forestry was founded in his time. The energy which he had displayed at Cambridge seemed to have been sapped at Oxford and, except for his period of office as president of the Linnean Society (1900–04), notable for the decision to admit women to fellowship in 1903, he was rarely seen by his contemporaries. Devoting himself increasingly to his own garden, at Headington Hill, and the Ashmolean Natural History Society, he did not go to congresses—illness prevented him from attending the British Association meeting of 1900 when he was president of the botanical section—and he became almost a legendary figure. He retired in 1919 and shortly afterwards went to live at Exmouth.

Vines had an acquisitive and critical rather than a constructive mind, presenting lectures without definite conclusions. He was not an experimenter, and although he contributed an important series of papers on proteolytic enzymes in plants, literary work appealed to him more strongly than laboratory experimentation. He found pleasure in the historical treasures of the Oxford department and collaborated with George Claridge Druce in books on the Dillenian (1907) and Morisonian (1914) herbaria. None the less, in carrying through the programme advocated by Thiselton-Dyer, in turn inspired by T. H. Huxley, for the study of plants as living organisms, Vines had already established the 'new botany', where A. W. Henfrey had failed twenty-five years before. By 1900 the influence of those men who had brought the German approach to biology to Britain had permeated all the country's teaching institutions. Vines was one of the group of botanists whose memorial to the Clarendon Press led to the foundation of the *Annals of Botany* in 1887, and he edited that journal from 1887 to 1899.

In 1897 Vines was elected an honorary fellow of his Cambridge college. He had been an honorary fellow of the University of London since 1892. By his contemporaries and friends he was regarded as a man of exceptional ability with social charm, wide interests, and an appreciation of music. Although not a mountaineer, he regularly visited the Engadine and took a delight in alpine botany. He died at Langstone, Exmouth, on 4 April 1934 and was buried in Exmouth. T. G. B. OSBORN, *rev.* D. J. MABBERLEY

Sources A. B. R., *Obits. FRS*, 1 (1932–5), 185–8 · A. B. Rendle, 'Sydney Howard Vines', *Proceedings of the Linnean Society of London*, 146th session (1933–4) · *Journal of Botany, British and Foreign*, 72 (1934), 139–41 · J. Reynolds Green, *A history of botany in the United Kingdom* (1914) · F. O. Bower, *Sixty years of botany in Britain (1875–1935)* (1938) · *Bulletin of Miscellaneous Information* [RBG Kew] (1934) · S. H. Vines, 'Reminiscences of German botanical laboratories in the 'seventies and 'eighties of the last century, 1', *New Phytologist*, 24 (1925), 1–8 · *The Times* (6 April 1934) · *Nature*, 133 (1934), 675–7 · private information (1934) · J. Howarth, 'Science education in late-Victorian Oxford: a curious case of failure?', *EngHR*, 102 (1987), 334–71 · J. Gilmour, *British botanists* (1944) · S. M. Walters, *The shaping of Cambridge botany* (1981) · B. E. Juniper and others, *The carnivorous plants* (1989) · H. M. Clokie, *An account of the herbaria of the department of botany in the University of Oxford* (1964) · F. A. Stafleu and R. S. Cowan, *Taxonomic literature: a selective guide*, 2nd edn, 6, Regnum Vegetabile, 115 (1986) · D. J. Mabberley, 'The Oxford Botanical Museum and its fate', *Oxford Plant Systematics*, 3 (1995), 15–16 · D. E. Allen, *The naturalist in Britain: a social history* (1976) · Venn, *Alum. Cant.*

Archives Bodl. Oxf., lectures, catalogues, and papers · CUL, corresp. | Oxf. U. Mus. NH, letters and postcards to Sir E. B. Poulton · U. Leeds, Brotherton L., letters to Sir E. W. Gosse

Likenesses J. Collier, oils, 1905, Linn. Soc.; repro. in Bower, *Sixty years*, facing p. 51 · Elliott & Fry, photograph, Christ's College, Cambridge

Wealth at death £4382 7s. 6d.: resworn probate, 29 May 1934, *CGPLA Eng. & Wales*

Vining family (*per.* 1807–1915), actors, flourished in London during the nineteenth century. The common ancestors were Charles Vining, a silversmith in Kirby Street, Hatton Garden, and his wife, Mary. They had eight children, all of whom were connected with the theatre. The Miss E. Vining (*fl.* 1798–1806) who appears in the records at Drury Lane as a dancer and singer was probably one of them. **Frederick Vining** (*bap.* 1790, *d.* 1871), a son, appeared as Young Norval at Gravesend in 1807, afterwards remaining on the Gravesend, Worthing, Hythe, and Brighton circuit. In 1809 he played Durimel in *The Point of Honour* at Bath, and subsequently played at Norwich. On 17 September 1813 he made his London début at Covent Garden as Frederick in *The Poor Gentleman*; other parts there included Harry Dornton in *The Road to Ruin*, and the original Count Frederick Friberg in *The Miller and his Men*. On 2 March 1814 he married Marian Jemima Bew, an actress, who died from breast cancer on 17 June 1853 at the age of sixty-one. A daughter, Marian, was baptized in Ipswich in 1817. In 1821 Frederick Vining was back in Bath, where, among other roles, he was the first Tressilian in *Kenilworth*.

In 1823 he opened at the Haymarket as Young Rapid in *A Cure for the Heartache*, and went on to play many more characters in comedy at that theatre, at which he was also stage manager for a short time. He died at Camberwell House Lunatic Asylum, Camberwell, on 2 June 1871.

There appear to have been two actresses called Fanny Vining. **Fanny Elizabeth** [Fanny Ellen] **Vining** (*d.* 1869) was Frederick's daughter, and married Charles Gill (1796/7–1869), actor and theatre manager, on 5 July 1843; they had a daughter, Ellen Marian Eva Gill, baptized in Colchester in 1845. This Miss Vining acted with Charles Kean and William Macready, and with Mrs Warner at the Marylebone Theatre. She apparently died in the same year as her husband, 1869. Another **Fanny Elizabeth Vining** (1829–1891?) was born in London on 17 July 1829, the daughter of Charles Frederick Vining and a Miss Johnstone. It seems unlikely that this is the same Fanny Vining, for she would not have been fourteen years old on her marriage to Gill, and the marriage certificate declares them both to be of full age. It seems probable that this is the Fanny Vining (whose relationship to the other Vinings is not clear) who married Edward (or Edgar) Loomis Davenport (1816–1877), an American actor, in January 1849, and died in 1891. It is likely that the Miss Fanny Vining who appeared with Alfred Wigan's company at the Olympic in 1849 in a production of *The Two Gentlemen of Verona* was the one who married Davenport, whom she accompanied to New York, and appeared with him in leading roles until his death. They had nine children, six of whom had careers on the stage, principally in the United States, most successfully Fanny Lily Gipsy Davenport (1850–1898), who had her own company, and Harry George Bryant Davenport (1866–1949), who, in 1912, became one of the first movie actors. Fanny Elizabeth Vining's sister, Adele (*d.* 1893), married Charles Steyne, and was the mother of E. T. Steyne (*d.* 1912), the manager and producer.

James Vining (1795–1870) was another son of Charles and Mary Vining. He first appeared on the London stage at Covent Garden on 3 October 1828 as Tybalt in *Romeo and Juliet*. He also played the prince of Wales in *1 Henry IV*, Raymond in *Raymond and Agnes*, and appeared with Madame Vestris at the Olympic in 1831. Most appreciated in the parts of lovers and fops, he gave his last performance at the Lyceum on 30 January 1860 as Dr Manette in Tom Taylor's adaptation of *A Tale of Two Cities*. The success of his career may be gauged by the proving of his will at under £6000 in 1870, following his death on 27 June that year at his home, 25 St John's Park, Upper Holloway, London. He left a widow, Caroline, *née* Johnes (1801/2–1876), whom he had married on 27 May 1823, and at least one son, **George James Vining** (1824–1875), who also enjoyed a successful career on the stage. George James was educated at St Peter's Grammar School in Eaton Square, London, and subsequently in France, and spent six years working in a bank before making his professional theatrical début in Newmarket on 4 December 1845 as Hamlet. In Jersey he met Macready (in whose company James Vining had been) and played with him in Bath and Bristol. He then joined

Mary Amelia Warner for her opening season at the Marylebone Theatre, making his London début there as Florizel in *The Winter's Tale* (20 August 1847). On 31 August 1850 he married Sarah Mary Vertigan Stubbs (*b.* in or before 1828/9). In 1853 he was with Alfred Wigan at the Olympic, where he was the first Captain Hawksley in Tom Taylor's *Still Waters Run Deep*. In 1856 he created the part of Frank Lauriston in *Stay at Home*, an adaptation by Slingsby Lawrence of *Un mari qui se dérange*, and in 1857 created the part of Charles in *Daddy Hardacre*, an adaptation of *La fille de l'avare*. When the Olympic management of Robson and Emden opened in August 1857 he spoke a prologue, and remained at that theatre for some years, creating numerous roles in farces and comedies, especially those of Tom Taylor and John Oxenford. He was initially stage manager for the winter season of 1861–2 at the St James's Theatre, but when Alfred Wigan withdrew as manager Vining took over. In January 1862 he appeared there as the hero in *Self-Made*, his own adaptation of *Le chevalier de St Georges*. His management ended in September, when he joined Charles Fechter's company at the Lyceum. Vining's most popular creation was Badger the detective in Dion Boucicault's *The Streets of London*, which he first played on 1 August 1864 at the Princess's Theatre. He had taken on the lease of the Princess's in 1863, and continued to act there until he went bankrupt in November 1869, being discharged the following February. He was very successful in portraying Count Fosco in Wilkie Collins's *The Woman in White* at the Olympic in October 1871. A good actor of the second rank, George Vining died at the Great Western Hotel, Reading, on 17 December 1875.

The **William Vining** (*bap.* 1783, *d.* 1861) who made his first appearance at Drury Lane in 1819 was the eldest brother of Frederick and James Vining and was baptized on 20 October 1783 at St Bartholomew-the-Great, West Smithfield. His wife, **Mary Gossop Vining** (1795/6–1868), made her stage reputation playing the first Amy Robsart in *Kenilworth* at Covent Garden on 8 March 1821, and, four days later, Lady Anne to Macready's Richard III. She had enjoyed considerable popularity at Bath in 1813–14, and was later to be celebrated for her portrayals of Meg Merrilies and Helen Macgregor. She died on 20 January 1868 aged seventy-two. It is not clear whether before her marriage she was the Miss Johannet or Johannot who first appeared as a theatrical dancer. William Vining died at their home, 77 Arlington Street, Camden Town, London, on 21 November 1861. Henry Vining (*bap.* 1789) was another of the Vining brothers; his wife, Amelia Quantrell (1803/4–1874), whom he married in 1828, was also an actress and survived him. Their daughter, Matilda Charlotte (*bap.* 1831, *d.* 1915), enjoyed a long and successful career in the theatre under the name Mrs John Wood [see Wood, Matilda Charlotte]. Matilda's daughter and granddaughter, Florence Wood and Molly Lumley, also had theatrical careers which brought the dynasty into the twentieth century. Other Vinings who appeared on the Victorian stage included Arthur (*d.* 1895) and his wife, Rosa Bella (*d.* 1876), who performed in the music-halls.

K. D. REYNOLDS

Sources *DNB* · Highfill, Burnim & Langhans, *BDA* · *IGI* · *The Era* (1870–98) · *Era Almanack and Annual* (1869–96) · *The life and reminiscences of E. L. Blanchard, with notes from the diary of Wm. Blanchard*, ed. C. W. Scott and C. Howard, 2 vols. (1891) · Genest, *Eng. stage* · Macready's reminiscences, and selections from his diaries and letters, ed. F. Pollock, 1 (1875) · *Oxberry's Dramatic Biography* · *Theatrical Times* (4 Nov 1848), 423–4 · J. Parker, ed., *Who's who in the theatre*, 6th edn (1930) · *CGPLA Eng. & Wales* (1870) · m. cert. [Fanny Ellen Vining] · m. cert. [George James Vining] · d. cert. [Marian Jemima Vining] · d. cert. [William Vining] · d. cert. [Mary Gossop Vining] · d. cert. [Charles Gill] · d. cert. [James Vining] · d. cert. [Frederick Vining] · d. cert. [Amelia Vining] · d. cert. [George Vining] · d. cert. [Caroline Vining] · d. cert. [Matilda Charlotte Wood]

Likenesses Southwell Bros., carte-de-visite (George James Vining as Mercutio in *Romeo and Juliet*), NPG · portrait (Frederick Vining), repro. in *Theatrical Times* · prints (George James Vining), Harvard TC

Wealth at death under £6000—James Vining: probate, 25 July 1870, *CGPLA Eng. & Wales*

Vining, Fanny Elizabeth (*d.* 1869). *See under* Vining family (*per.* 1807–1915).

Vining, Fanny Elizabeth (1829–1891?). *See under* Vining family (*per.* 1807–1915).

Vining, Frederick (*bap.* 1790, *d.* 1871). *See under* Vining family (*per.* 1807–1915).

Vining, George James (1824–1875). *See under* Vining family (*per.* 1807–1915).

Vining, James (1795–1870). *See under* Vining family (*per.* 1807–1915).

Vining, Mary Gossop (1795/6–1868). *See under* Vining family (*per.* 1807–1915).

Vining, William (*bap.* 1783, *d.* 1861). *See under* Vining family (*per.* 1807–1915).

Vinnianus. *See* Findbarr moccu Fiatach (*d.* 579) *under* Ulster, saints of (*act. c.*400–*c.*650).

Vinogradoff, Sir Paul Gavrilovitch [Pavel Gavriilovich Vinogradov] (1854–1925), historian and jurist, was born in Kostroma, Russia, about 200 miles north-east of Moscow, on 18 November/1 December 1854. His father, Gavriil Kiprianovich Vinogradov (*d.* 1885), was a teacher at the Kostroma Gymnasium, who soon afterwards became director of a prominent boys' school in Moscow and, in 1866, the founding director of a group of five girls' schools there. His mother, Yelena Pavlovna (*d.* 1918), was the daughter of General Pavel Kobelov, who had fought in the Anglo-American War of 1812–14. It was she who was the main influence on her son and encouraged him to follow an academic rather than a military career. After attending the public *Gymnasium* Vinogradoff entered Moscow University at the age of sixteen, and concentrated his studies on history under Vasily Klyuchevsky. On graduating in 1875, he won a scholarship to study in Berlin under the jurist Theodor Mommsen and the historian of old German law Heinrich Brunner. In 1876 he published his first paper, in German, on old German customary law, the product of his participation in Brunner's seminar. On his return to Moscow he lectured at the university and decided that his

Sir Paul Gavrilovitch Vinogradoff (1854–1925), by Lafayette, 1913

next field of research should be the origin of feudalism, which had previously been studied mainly in the Frankish setting. Vinogradoff opted for the origin of feudal relations in Lombard Italy, spent much time in Italian libraries, and in 1881 published the results (in Russian) as a dissertation for his master's degree.

Vinogradoff next turned to the feudal land law in England, where the volume of surviving records exceeded that in other Western countries. In 1883 he first visited England, where he studied in the Public Record Office and also met leading historical scholars, such as Sir Henry Maine, Sir Frederick Pollock, Frederic Seebohm, and especially Frederic William Maitland. In a letter to *The Athenaeum* of 19 July 1884 Vinogradoff called attention to a manuscript in the British Museum, which contained a collection of cases for the reign of Henry III that appeared to have been compiled for the use of Bracton when writing his famous treatise. It excited the interest of Maitland, who edited it as *Bracton's Note Book* (1887). In the preface Maitland marvelled that a Russian scholar, 'in a few weeks learned, as it seems to me, more about Bracton's text than any Englishman has known since Selden died'.

Vinogradoff's work on English feudal institutions won him his Moscow doctorate, and was published in Russian in 1887 and in English, under the title *Villainage in England: Essays in English Mediaeval History*, in 1892. In the preface he explained that his interest in the subject had been aroused by Russia's relatively recent 'social revolution of the peasant emancipation' and the hope that modern Russia could learn from the way Western societies had coped with similar social movements in earlier periods. In 1893, in the *English Historical Review*, he demonstrated that the Anglo-Saxon word *folcland* did not mean, as was the generally held view, land owned by the people but rather land held under folk-right, or unwritten custom.

In 1887, after three years as extraordinary professor, Vinogradoff was made full professor of history in the University of Moscow. His main aim was to form a school of historians trained in the methods of Western scholarship, but he was also concerned with the progress of general education in Russia. He became chairman of the education committee of the Moscow municipal duma, and personally wrote elementary textbooks of history for use in schools. As a liberal, however, he found it intolerable that the increasingly reactionary government should interfere in the life of the university and expect professors to act as state agents. During this period he extended the field of his research to cover Scandinavian antiquities, and mastered Old Norse with the same linguistic ease that had enabled him to acquire German, French, English, and Italian. In 1897, on a visit to Norway, he met Louise, the widowed daughter of Judge A. Stang of Arendal and of an Englishwoman, Isabel Mary Newbold. They were married on 29 May 1897; their daughter Helen was born in 1898 and their son Igor in 1901.

Although his reputation as a scholar and teacher was growing, Vinogradoff could not avoid politics. When a scheme he proposed to improve relations between the university authorities and the students was rejected by the minister, he decided to leave. In December 1901, with a large crowd of students attending the railway station to see him off, he and his wife and children left Moscow for England. In 1903 the Corpus chair of jurisprudence in the University of Oxford became vacant and Vinogradoff, although not formally a lawyer, was unanimously elected. The professor's remit was described as 'the History of Laws and the Comparative Jurisprudence of different nations', which exactly fitted his interests. His inaugural lecture was devoted to the teaching of Sir Henry Maine, the founder of the comparative method in law and the first holder of the chair.

Vinogradoff's Oxford lectures to undergraduates were rather over the heads of his students, who found it difficult both to understand his accent and to see how the content related to the examinations. On the other hand, he made a profound impact on graduates, mainly through his introduction of the continental-style seminar. In his hands this was highly structured and even had its own library (the Maitland Library). It made heavy demands on those who enrolled, usually about a dozen. They received a specially printed volume of basic sources, mainly cases from the year-books, to illustrate, for example, the history of English land law. The members of the seminar took turns to analyse and report on a case. 'The Professor' introduced the topic and from time to time would make a magisterial pronouncement. Formal minutes were taken. The seminar was welcomed as a course in scientific method, especially by the younger history dons, burdened with routine teaching. Many of the seminar's fruits were published in the Oxford Studies in Social and Legal History, which Vinogradoff edited from 1909.

In 1905 Vinogradoff was elected a fellow of the British Academy; he later became editor of its Records of English Economic and Social History. He co-edited (with F. Morgan) the first volume, *The Survey of the Honour of Denbigh, 1334*, which appeared in 1914. In 1905 he published *The Growth of the Manor*. Instead of following the prevailing fashion of a detailed study of a particular provincial area, he preferred to attempt a synthesis of 'the general features of the English mediaeval system' as a whole, from the Celtic period onwards. He explained this preference as appropriate for a foreigner, but in fact he liked generalization and could make apposite comparisons with French and German analogues to the manor. In the preface he praised Maitland's critical studies of particular institutions, and continued:

> But in some cases people with a hopeful turn of mind may venture on reconstruction where his subtle scepticism has dissolved; and perhaps in the end we may get a better insight into historical peculiarities of thought and social arrangement.

Maitland's death in 1906 affected Vinogradoff greatly. In 1908 he succeeded Maitland as joint literary director of the Selden Society (with Sir Frederick Pollock); he remained in office until 1920. With L. Ehrlich he edited two volumes of the *Year Books of 6 Edward II* for the society.

In 1908 *English Society in the Eleventh Century* appeared. Based on the Domesday inquest, it concentrated on the 'terminological and institutional' aspects of the subject rather than 'the statistical and topographical'. Vinogradoff contributed the chapters on feudalism in the *Cambridge Medieval History* (1911–36) and wrote two short 'popular' books. *Roman Law in Medieval Europe* (1909) was based on lectures he gave in the University of London. He described it as 'a ghost story', since it dealt 'with the second life of Roman law after the demise of the body in which it first saw the light' (*Roman Law in Medieval Europe*, 4). It covers the so-called 'barbarian codes', the revival of the study of Justinian's *corpus juris* in Bologna, and the diffusion of Bolognese learning in England, France, and Germany; it is still widely quoted. The second book, *Common Sense in Law* (1914), was rather less successful. It dealt with the nature of legal rules and tried to show that the basic ideas of law, although expressed in technical language, were actually expressions of common sense.

Vinogradoff enjoyed Oxford but did not break his ties with Russia, where his mother and sisters remained. He paid regular visits there and kept in touch with liberal reformers. Since his obligations in Oxford required only two terms' teaching each year, he was able to accept a regular visiting professorship at his old university of Moscow and lectured there from 1908 to 1911. Once again, however, he had to resign on account of governmental interference. He loved travel and in 1913 visited India and gave a lecture, 'Tribal law', in Calcutta. In the same year he presided over the legal history section of the International Congress of Historical Sciences in London and edited its proceedings as *Essays in Legal History* (1913). The outbreak of war in 1914 and the alliance of Russia with the democratic powers gave him encouragement. On 14 September 1914 he wrote to *The Times*, 'The war is indeed our *Befreiungskrieg*. The Slavs must have their chance in the history of the world and the date of their coming of age will mark a new departure in the growth of civilization.' He was in Moscow in 1915, 1916, and 1917, working to improve mutual understanding between Russia and Britain. In 1915 he published *Selfgovernment in Russia*. In 1917 he received a knighthood for these services. The success of the Bolsheviks, however, was a shock which hurt him greatly. In January 1918 he renounced his Russian nationality and became a British subject.

Vinogradoff spent 1923–4 in the United States, where he had first taught in 1907. He was now working on what he intended to be his *magnum opus*, an ambitious work in four volumes called *Outlines of Historical Jurisprudence*, which sought, in the manner of Maine, to trace the growth of legal science. He envisaged six stages. The first three purport to be universal, the law being based on the type of society: totemistic, where there is no technical law; tribal, where law is discovered in the sense of the community and declared by a chief; and civic, where law is that of a city-state, such as in ancient Greece. Two volumes, with an introduction to jurisprudence and covering these stages, appeared in 1920 and 1922. The remaining three stages were, he admitted, restricted to the evolution of legal ideas within the circle of European civilization: medieval, an ingenious amalgam of canon law and feudal law; individualistic, where the law gives the maximum scope to individual freedom; and socialistic, which gives more attention to social forces. The volumes covering these stages were unfinished at his death. Most of his important articles, together with a bibliography of his publications, appeared in his posthumous *Collected Papers* (2 vols., 1928), which were edited by his widow.

In 1925 Vinogradoff was given a dinner at All Souls, at which he was presented with his portrait by Henry Lamb. In his reply he identified the 'three guiding stars' of his intellectual formation: the Russian Klyuchevsky, the German Mommsen, and the Englishman Maitland. In the same year Vinogradoff was invited to Paris to receive an honorary doctorate. At a reception in his honour he caught a cold, which developed into pneumonia, from which he died on 19 December. After a funeral service at the Russian church in Paris, his body was cremated and his ashes buried on 24 December in Holywell cemetery in Oxford. The inscription on his tomb was chosen by himself: *Hospitae Britanniae gratus advena* ('a grateful foreigner to his host Britannia').　　　　　　　　　　PETER STEIN

Sources *DNB* · H. A. L. Fisher, 'Memoir', *Collected papers of Paul Vinogradoff*, ed. L. Vinogradoff, 2 vols. (1928) · F. de Zulueta, 'Paul Vinogradoff, 1854–1925', *Law Quarterly Review*, 42 (1926), 202–11 · W. S. Holdsworth, 'Professor Sir Paul Vinogradoff, 1854–1925', *PBA*, 11 (1924–5), 486–501 · W. S. Holdsworth and B. Pares, *Slavonic Review*, 4 (1926), 529–51 · F. M. Powicke, 'Sir Paul Vinogradoff', *EngHR*, 41 (1926), 236–43 · *CGPLA Eng. & Wales* (1926)
Archives Harvard U., law school, MSS
Likenesses Lafayette, photograph, 1913, NPG [*see illus.*] · E. Walker, photogravure, 1913 (after Lafayette), NPG · W. Stoneman, photograph, 1918, NPG · H. Lamb, oils, *c.*1925, Examination Schools, Oxford
Wealth at death £5187 18*s.* 1*d.*: probate, 14 May 1926, *CGPLA Eng. & Wales*

Vinsauf, Geoffrey of [*called* Galfridus Anglicus] (*fl.* **1208–1213**), poet and teacher of grammar and rhetoric, also called Anglicus, is best-known as the author of the *Poetria*

nova ('The new poetics'), the single most successful textbook on rhetorical composition written during the middle ages. It is not known what his name means. What little is known about his life comes chiefly from the *Poetria nova* and a shorter poem, *Causa Magistri Gaufredi Vinesauf*, preserved in Glasgow University Library, Hunterian MS V.8.14. An Englishman, he studied at Paris and perhaps also at Bologna. While teaching at Northampton, he became involved in a legal dispute with his rival Robert, who had been his friend at Paris. When Bishop Adam of St Asaph (1175–81) ruled against him, Geoffrey wrote the *Causa* to tell the archbishop of Canterbury his side of the story and appeal for help. He dedicated the *Poetria nova* to Innocent III, during whose pontificate he had visited Rome in the English king's service. The king in question was John, and if the plea for reconciliation with which the *Poetria nova* concludes is addressed to Innocent III, then the work must have taken its final shape between 1208, when England was placed under papal interdict, and 1213, when Pope Innocent was reconciled with King John. Nothing is known about Geoffrey's life after this date.

In addition to the *Poetria nova* Geoffrey almost certainly composed two prose treatises on rhetorical composition—*Documentum de modo et arte dictandi et versificandi* and *Summa de coloribus rhetoricis*—and a number of shorter poems. All of these works have been printed by Faral (*Arts poétiques*; Manuscrit 511), and many of the short poems by Harbert (*Thirteenth-Century Anthology*). The *Documentum* survives in two versions, preserved in some twenty English manuscripts. The shorter version, printed by Faral, is probably authentic; the longer and still unprinted version is either the work of a later author or else underwent interpolation after Geoffrey's death. Geoffrey may also be the author of a *Summa de arte dictandi* (1188–90), written at Bologna and printed by Licitra.

None of Geoffrey's other works approached the *Poetria nova* in popularity. It is preserved in nearly 200 manuscripts from all parts of Europe, and many copies are provided with glosses or accompanied by full-scale commentaries. The commentaries indicate that an important source of its appeal was the fact that it was not only about the art of poetry but also an example of that art, a poem of 2116 hexameter lines. In this respect it resembled one of its two main sources, Horace's *Ars poetica*, also known as the 'old poetics'. What made Geoffrey's 'poetics' new was in part its equal reliance on the pseudo-Ciceronian *Rhetorica ad Herennium*, often called the 'new rhetoric'. The five canons of rhetoric—invention, arrangement, style, memory, and delivery—provide the poem's structure, with arrangement (mainly the varieties of artificial order) and style (techniques for amplifying and abbreviating the subject matter, difficult and easy ornament, and so on) receiving fullest treatment. Concise yet comprehensive, the *Poetria nova* combines the essentials of grammatical and rhetorical instruction, offering precepts equally applicable to the composition of prose and verse. The prose *Documentum* covers most of the same and a few additional subjects, but without the economy, inventiveness, and technical virtuosity that made the *Poetria nova* so popular.

For at least three centuries Geoffrey of Vinsauf was considered the supreme authority on the art of poetry. Chaucer adopted his metaphor of poetic invention (*Poetria nova*, trans. Nims, 43ff) in *Troylus and Cryseyde* and mentioned him by name when parodying his rhetorical lament for the death of Richard I (ibid., 368ff.) in 'The Nun's Priest's Tale'. His influence outlived the middle ages: as late as 1489 Erasmus rated his value to students of poetry on a par with that of Cicero, Quintilian, and Horace. In modern times he is read by students of medieval literature rather than by apprentice poets, but his fame is sufficient to have justified three separate translations of the *Poetria nova* and one of the *Documentum*. MARTIN CAMARGO

Sources E. Faral, *Les arts poétiques du XIIe et du XIIIe siècle* (Pariss, 1924) [edn of works] · B. Harbert, ed., *A thirteenth-century anthology of rhetorical poems: Glasgow MS. Hunterian V. 8. 14.* (1975) · E. Faral, 'Le manuscrit 511 du "Hunterian Museum" de Glasgow', *Studi Medievali*, new ser., 9 (1936), 18–121 · V. Licitra, 'La *Summa de arte dictandi* di Maestro Goffredo', *Studi Medievali*, 3rd ser., 7 (1966), 865–913 · Geoffrey of Vinsauf, *Poetria nova*, trans. M. F. Nims (1967) · E. A. Gallo, *The 'Poetria nova' and its sources in early rhetorical doctrine* (1971) · J. B. Kopp, trans., 'The new poetics', *Three medieval rhetorical arts*, ed. J. J. Murphy (1971), 27–108 · *Geoffrey of Vinsauf: Documentum de modo et arte dictandi et versificandi*, trans. R. P. Parr (1968) · D. Kelly, *The arts of poetry and prose*, Typologie des Sources du Moyen Age Occidental, 59 (1991) · M. C. Woods, *An early commentary on the 'Poetria nova' of Geoffrey of Vinsauf* (1985) · E. Gallo, 'The *Poetria nova* of Geoffrey of Vinsauf', *Medieval eloquence*, ed. J. J. Murphy (1978), 68–84 · J. J. Murphy, *Rhetoric in the middle ages* (1974), esp. 169–73 · M. Camargo, 'Toward a comprehensive art of written discourse: Geoffrey of Vinsauf and the *Ars dictaminis*', *Rhetorica*, 6 (1988), 167–94 · H. G. Richardson, 'The schools of Northampton in the twelfth century', *EngHR*, 56 (1941), 595–605 · P. Klopsch, *Einführung in die Dichtungslehren des lateinischen Mittelalters* (1980), esp. 127–38
Archives U. Glas., Hunterian MS V.8.14

Vint, Mary. See Say, Mary (1739/40–1832).

Vint, William (1768–1834), Congregational minister, was born at High Thrunton, near Whittingham, Northumberland, on 1 November 1768, the son of John Vint. He was educated at Alnmouth and at the grammar school of Warrenford. At about the age of fifteen he began to study theology at Northowram Academy with Samuel Walker, minister at Northowram. He soon gained fame as a preacher, and on 25 December 1790 was appointed minister at Idle in Yorkshire.

In 1795 the academy at Northowram was dissolved, and several of the students were temporarily placed with Vint for theological instruction. It was felt, however, that more permanent arrangements should be made, and, chiefly through the exertions of Edward Hanson of London, a regular academy was founded at Idle in 1800. Initially Vint worked as sole tutor, and had only four students, but his energy and reputation led the establishment to grow and prosper. On 21 June 1826 it received the name of Airedale Independent College. Vint continued to direct it until his last illness. On 5 March 1834 the college moved to Undercliffe, near Bradford.

Besides acting as tutor to Airedale College, Vint continued minister of Idle until his death. He married, on 17 June 1795, Sarah Sharp (*d.* 1855) of Idle, with whom he had six sons and two daughters. A printing press was established at Idle in 1824 under the management of his brother, John Vint, at which some seventeen of William's publications were printed. Besides sermons, he was the author of two works on the millennium, and the editor of a five-volume *Life and Works of Oliver Heywood* (1825–7), a hymn book (1834), and three selections of discourses, *The Suffering Christian's Companion* (1830), *The Active Christian's Companion* (1830), and *The Privileged Christian's Companion* (1830). William Vint died in Idle on 13 March 1834, and was buried in the graveyard of his chapel.

E. I. CARLYLE, *rev.* J. M. V. QUINN

Sources J. H. Turner, *Nonconformity in Idle with the history of Airedale College* (1876) · private information (1899) · *IGI*
Likenesses Fry, stipple, pubd 1819, NPG · H. Meyer, portrait, repro. in Turner, *Nonconformity in Idle with the history of Airedale College* · Richardson, stipple, BM; repro. in *Evangelical Magazine* (1819) · portrait, Yorkshire United College, Bradford

Violante [Larini], **Signora** (1682–1741), rope-dancer and theatre company manager, was for some sixteen years from 1720 onwards a celebrity on the stages of London, Bristol, Dublin, Cork, and Edinburgh. Much is unknown or uncertain about this popular entertainer. Contemporary advertisements and reviews describe her as Italian, as does Chetwood, while Molloy, followed by Dunbar, speak of her as French. Neither are her married or maiden names certain, for both she and her husband, the rope-slider Signor Violante, are sometimes named Larini in newspaper accounts. However, by 1730 she was a prominent enough figure for Jonathan Swift to use her as a vehicle for satire in his *A Vindication of his Excellency Lord C[artere]t*.

Signora Violante's first appearances on the London stage, between March and June 1720, were with a French *commedia* troupe at both the King's and the Lincoln's Inn Fields theatres. Alongside her pantomime roles, her speciality rope-dancing entranced spectators and inspired those in the gods to shower her with coins, as a poem from *Oxoniensis* of 6 June 1720 describes at length. In 1726 she reappeared in London with an Italian *commedia* troupe playing Colombina at the Haymarket Theatre from March to May. She remained in London after the troupe had left and appeared at regular intervals at the Haymarket rope-dancing with flags, or with someone mounted on her shoulders or tied to each foot. She also performed in a booth at Southwark fair. Emboldened by her success, she formed a company and took over the Haymarket for some seventy performances between 2 November 1726 and 28 April 1727. Pantomimes, dances, tumbling, and rope-dancing formed the company's repertory, and Violante's two young daughters feature in accounts of performances (though it is not possible to distinguish which of the two was the Rosina Violante who married the dancer George Richard Estcourt Luppino, forebear of the Lupino family of English performers and designers).

After touring to Dublin, Edinburgh, and possibly Paris during the summer of 1727, Signora Violante reopened at the Haymarket with what she announced to be a new company and played regularly between 23 October and 6 May 1728. In February a pantomime entitled *The Rivals*, in which Violante played the role of Colombina, was added to the repertory. Her company performed this pantomime in Bristol during the summer, where it is also recorded that her husband slid on a rope from St Vincent's rocks to the other side of the river before a vast crowd of spectators.

There is only one record of Violante performing in London during the following season (at the Haymarket on 28 April 1729). However, this was a benefit performance by command of the prince of Wales, and it seems unlikely that she did not perform at other times during that season. By the end of the year she had taken her company to Ireland, where, besides performing in Dublin at Smock Alley and in Cork during the summer of 1730, she opened a booth theatre in Dublin, first in Dame Street (1730–31) and later in George's Lane (1733–4). Her company at this time included Charles Lalaize, a French dancing-master, William 'Harlequin' Phillips, and her two daughters, aged nine and thirteen. She began to attract a number of children to her company. Among these was a girl whom she had observed carrying water from the Liffey to her mother's wash-house. Signora Violante's 'discovery' and subsequent coaching of the young Peg Woffington is perhaps the action for which she is most remembered. She directed her 'Lilliputians' in a version of *The Beggar's Opera*, in which Woffington played Macheath. After ninety-six performances in Dublin the production was taken to London, where it opened at the Haymarket on 4 September 1732.

Information concerning Violante, after the end of the Haymarket engagement on 20 September, is sparse. She returned to Dublin and opened a new booth theatre. In the winter of 1734 she performed in Norwich, and later she was in Ipswich. By the end of 1735 she was in Edinburgh, where she founded a dancing-school and lived until her death there, probably in June 1741.

LESLIE DU S. READ

Sources Highfill, Burnim & Langhans, *BDA* · J. C. Greene and G. L. H. Clark, *The Dublin stage, 1720–1745: a calendar of plays, entertainments, and afterpieces* (1993) · *Memoirs of the celebrated Mrs Woffington*, 2nd edn (1760) · W. R. Chetwood, *A general history of the stage, from its origin in Greece to the present time* (1749) · J. F. Molloy, *The life and adventures of Peg Woffington*, 2 vols. (1884) · J. Dunbar, *Peg Woffington and her world* (1968) · J. Swift, *A vindication of his excellency Lord C[ar-tere]t* (1730) · *Scots Magazine*, 3 (1741), 279 · J. Parker, ed., *Who's who in the theatre*, 11th edn (1952)
Archives BL, Latreille MSS, transcription of advertisements, playbills, and records of performances

Violante, Pauline [*real name* Selina Young] (*b.* **1840/41**), tightrope walker, was the second of the two daughters of Elizabeth Wild, actress, and a bandsman named Young. Her parents acted with Old Wild's, a company of travelling players from Yorkshire, but had left to marry by 1830. Trained as an acrobat, Selina Young performed at Bury with Samuel Wild's company in 1853 as 'Pauline Violante, the first tight-rope dancer in the world'. In 1858 she became the first artist to cross a high wire at the Crystal Palace.

G. Van Hare (*b.* 1815), manager of the Alhambra, renamed Young the Female Blondin in 1861. She amazed audiences by ascending a telegraph wire stretched from the stage to the roof. Edward Tyrrel Smith (1804–1877) contracted her to walk a tightrope across the Thames from Battersea Bridge to the Cremorne Gardens. Dressed in Albanian national costume, she made her attempt on 12 August 1861, watched by 20,000 spectators. Although a poorly weighted wire forced her to abandon her crossing, she succeeded in a second effort the following Monday.

During her career Young crossed the high rope in several dangerous ways: in a suit of armour, in a sack, and pushing a wheelbarrow. She had imitators using the same pseudonym, notably Madame Genieve (Selina Powell, with whom she is sometimes confused), who, eight months pregnant, was killed falling from a rope at Aston Park in July 1863.

Young's career came to a violent conclusion on 14 August 1862 at Highbury Barn. As she crossed the wire amid a spectacular firework display, she stumbled and fell 50 feet to the gravel below, fracturing her left leg and shoulder. Attended by several doctors who happened to be dining nearby, she was taken to St Bartholomew's Hospital the following morning, emerging from Queen's ward on 24 October. Newspapers reported that she had urged surgeons to amputate the useless leg, which was 3 inches shorter than the other.

On 1 November 1862 an appeal was launched on Young's behalf by Felix Joseph (1840–1892) and Sarah Ann Hughes, Young's aunt, the widow of Edwin Hughes (1813–1867), circus proprietor. Joseph stressed that Young's career had provided support for her aged father and invalid sister (her mother had died some years previously). A total of £300 was collected, allowing them to set up as shopkeepers. In 1864 she married Charles Greaves jun., and kept an inn in Surrey. Selina Young died in obscurity, her passing unrecorded by the press.

MATTHEW SWEET

Sources G. L. Banks, *Blondin: his life and performances* (1862) · *Dean's new moveable book of Leotard, Blondin as the ape, female Blondin, etc.* [1862] · K. Wilson, *Everybody's heard of Blondin* (1990) · 'The Female Blondin', *The Times* (13 Aug 1861) · 'The female Blondin', *Daily Telegraph* (13 Aug 1861) · 'Frightful accident to the "Female Blondin"', *Daily News* (16 Aug 1862) · 'Accident to a rope walker', *The Times* (16 Aug 1862) · 'The female Blondin', *Daily Telegraph* (27 Oct 1862) · 'The Female Blondin', *The Times* (28 Oct 1862) · 'Appeal for the Female Blondin', *The Times* (1 Nov 1862) · 'Female Blondin donations', *The Times* (6 Nov 1862) · 'Female Blondin donations', *The Times* (10 Dec 1862) · J. M. Turner, *Victorian arena: the performers* (1995), vol. 1 of *A dictionary of British circus biography* · *The original, complete … story of 'Old Wild's' …: a nursery of strolling players and the celebrities who appeared there, being the reminiscences of its chief and last proprietor, Sam Wild*, ed. Trim [W. B. Megson] (1888) · G. Van Hare, *Fifty years of a showman's life, or, The life and travels of Van Hare* (1888) · W. W. Wroth, *Cremorne and the later London gardens* (1907) · engraving, 1861, Bodl. Oxf., John Johnson collection
Archives Bodl. Oxf., John Johnson collection
Likenesses coloured engraving, 1861, Bodl. Oxf., John Johnson collection · engraving, 1861, Bodl. Oxf., John Johnson collection · engraving on poster, 1861, Central Library, Hull, Theatre Poster collection

Violet, Pierre-Noël (1749–1819), miniature painter, was born in Flanders. He became a member of the Académie des Arts in Lille, in 1782, before moving to Paris, where he exhibited at the Salon de la Correspondance in 1782 and in 1787, and where he published his *Traité élémentaire de l'art de peindre en miniature* (1788). Although he had been miniature painter to Louis XVI, Violet joined the revolutionary committee in Paris before resigning and settling in London as an émigré in 1790. Forced at first to make a living by teaching watercolour painting and dancing, Violet soon established a successful practice as a miniaturist, exhibiting at the Royal Academy, and at the Society of Artists from 1790 to 1819. In this he may have been assisted by the circulation, by his friend Bartolozzi, of engravings of his portraits of Louis XVI and Marie Antoinette (1790), and of George IV when prince of Wales (1791).

Violet and his wife, Marguerite Becret (d. 1841), whom he married in or before 1771, had two daughters, Maria (1794–1868), later Mrs James Brook Pulham, a miniaturist who exhibited at the Royal Academy (1808–11), and Cecilia (1797–1880), who married the miniaturist Louis Ferrière. Violet died at his home, 1 Charlotte Street, Fitzroy Square, London, on 9 December 1819 and was buried at St Pancras Old Church. Examples of his work are in the British Museum and the Victoria and Albert Museum, London; the Walker Art Gallery, Liverpool; and the Louvre Museum, Paris. V. REMINGTON

Sources F. L. Bruel, 'Pierre Noël Violet (1749–1819): un miniaturiste de l'émigration', *Gazette des Beaux-Arts*, 4th ser., 6 (1911), 19–44 · F.-L. Bruel, 'Catalogue de l'oeuvre peint, dessiné et gravé de Pierre-Noël Violet (1749–1819)', *Archives de l'Art Français*, 1 (1907), 367–408 · *GM*, 1st ser., 89/2 (1819), 571 · P. Jean-Richard, *Inventaire des miniatures sur ivoire conservées au cabinet des dessins Musée du Louvre et Musée d'Orsay* (Paris, 1994), 299–300 · D. Foskett, *Miniatures: dictionary and guide* (1987), 354, 669 · B. S. Long, *British miniaturists* (1929), 449 · L. R. Schidlof, *The miniature in Europe in the 16th, 17th, 18th, and 19th centuries*, 2 (1964), 854–5 · Graves, *RA exhibitors* · G. C. Williamson, *The history of portrait miniatures*, 1 (1904), 195
Likenesses P.-N. Violet, self-portrait?, engraving, 1788, repro. in P.-N. Violet, *Traité élémentaire de l'art de peindre en miniature* (1788) · F. Bartolozzi, drawing, 1796, repro. in Bruel, 'Pierre Noël Violet', 31 · double portrait, drawing, 1796 (with his daughter Maria), repro. in Bruel, 'Pierre Noël Violet', 37 · J. Bouilliard, miniature, 1797, repro. in Bruel, 'Pierre Noël Violet', 19 · P.-N. Violet, engraving, 1806, repro. in Bruel, 'Pierre Noël Violet', facing p. 40

Violet, Thomas (d. 1662/3), goldsmith and writer on trade, registered his earliest goldsmith's mark in 1627 and came to the notice of James I when Sir Edward Coke, then secretary to the privy council, found that he had been playing the money market by exchanging English silver coin for French gold. Violet professed surprise at being thus 'discovered', claiming that his activities were well known. He was imprisoned, but as his account books showed that he had made a profit, thereby enriching the country, he was pardoned, the king demanding £2000 as his share of this profit.

At this time there was a considerable traffic in coinage; goldsmiths and refiners were buying up overweight coins, leaving lightweight and clipped coin in circulation. The heavy coins were illegally exported, to circulate freely in France and Germany, or melted down for sale to the gold and silver wire-drawers, with whom Violet was closely connected. After his release Violet turned informer, a task he undertook with gusto, hiring agents at home and abroad to examine the books of merchants and traders, and ships' documents, and bringing numerous cases of alleged illegal export of coin to the Star Chamber. Successful prosecutions brought large fines to the state treasure; these, according to Violet, were subsequently misspent by Cromwell on the parliamentarian armies.

On being pardoned for his own misdeeds, Violet endeavoured to make his peace with the Goldsmiths' Company, of which he was at that time a warden, saying that his accusations were made under duress; at the same time, he paid £1500 for the post of surveyor to the gold and silver wire-drawers. His duties were to inspect the wire which was made up into braids and lace for the extensive luxury trade, and he instituted a system of assaying each skein and sealing it with the craftsman's mark. He found that much of this wire was only a copper core lightly plated. He was empowered to confiscate such substandard wire, and he prosecuted many of the tradesmen involved with a zeal which brought him many enemies, among them Bradbourn, the queen's silk-man, though he wisely dropped proceedings in that case. He also sought to prosecute John Wollaston, a wealthy goldsmith and parliamentarian, who afterwards seized the opportunity to take his revenge on Violet. Between 1635 and 1640 Violet was involved in the attempts to set up the Wyre-drawers' Company, in the face of Goldsmiths' Company opposition.

In the autumn of 1643 Violet, an admitted royalist, was recruited by Sir Basil Brooke, a Catholic who was endeavouring to win over the City to Charles's cause. Lord General Essex gave him a parliamentary pass to collect a letter from the king at Oxford for delivery to Wollaston, then lord mayor, and the common council of the City of London. On delivering it Violet was immediately arrested, charged with high treason, and in January 1644 committed to the Tower. His estates in Essex and Shropshire were sequestered, and bonds relating to the Shropshire property were seized from his sister. Officers went to his mother's house and took away various bills and bonds belonging to him, his business papers, and a document wherein the king acknowledged Violet's expenses of £19,068 in respect of the Star Chamber prosecutions.

Violet was closely confined for 928 days without trial, being obliged to borrow at interest £800 for his subsistence; he was not released until 1652, when at some expense he regained possession of some of the confiscated bonds. He did not recover his post as surveyor of gold and silver wire, but, on successfully charging Wollaston with defrauding the king of revenue, was appointed to succeed him as melter at the Royal Mint. Violet later petitioned Richard Cromwell to mint farthing tokens, promising that a part of the profits should go to benefit maimed soldiers, but before this project materialized there was a change of government and all was forgotten. While in prison Violet had begun to set down his ideas for reviving trade. He supposed that the prosperity of certain foreign ports flowed from their equal treatment of merchants and traders of all nations, and their reduction of customs duties, and he urged that free ports should be established in England, which by drawing in cheap and plentiful raw materials, would benefit the working class.

In 1652–3 Violet again investigated illegal transport of coin, accusing the masters of the ships *Samson*, *Salvador*, and *George* of seeking to export silver. He claimed to have borrowed a further £675 to pursue his enquiries and to have refused a bribe from the Spanish ambassador to concede that the silver belonged to various merchants in the Spanish Netherlands, and to drop charges. The owners of the vessels were prosecuted in the court of admiralty and the value of the recovered bullion was over £300,000, but again Violet was unable to recoup his outlay. Over the years, he published numerous letters from himself and his supporters, also tracts, and narratives, seeking to defend himself from accusations of perfidy and to recover his seized assets and outlays, yet continuing to lay accusations against the wire-drawers, goldsmiths, and refiners, and all those who in his view deprived the nation of its rightful wealth by exporting gold and silver.

These attacks inevitably drew responses, the most virulent of which was published anonymously in 1660, entitled *The Great Treppaner of England*. Its author said of 'Thomas Violet, a name too sweet for so foule a carkass' that

> his birth was at sea ... ingendred between a poor Dutch Fidler and a Moorish woman. How he came into England without the help of the Devil, or even got into the repute to be intrusted in any man's service as an Apprentice, and to become a member of this famous City of London, I am altogether ignorant.

These statements were said to be sworn, but are otherwise unsubstantiated. Certainly Violet's own writings, though prolix and much given to flowery metaphor, are not those of an ill-educated man.

It is not known if Violet was married or what his relationship was with the William Violet mentioned in connection with his sequestered Essex estate. It seems possible that he died in debt, or at least without assets; his nuncupative will was proved in 1663.

ANITA McCONNELL

Sources W. S. Prideaux, *Memorials of the Goldsmiths' Company*, 1 (1896), 161, 174–5 • H. Stewart, *History of the Worshipful Company of Gold and Silver Wyre-drawers* (1891) • E. Glover, *The gold and silver wyre-drawers* (1979) • *A remonstrance and declaration of the young men and apprentices of the city of London: to the Rt Hon the Lord Mayor, court of aldermen, and Common-councell of the same* (1647) • *The great treppaner of England* (1660) • E. Bagshaw, *A true and perfect narrative of the differences between Mr Busby and Mr Bagshawe* (1659) • J. Snelling, *View of the copper coin and coinage of England* (1766), 35 • S. R. Gardiner, *History of the great civil war, 1642–1649*, new edn, 1 (1893); repr. (1965), 269 • T. Violet, *Mysteries and secrets of trade and mint-affairs* (1653) • BL, Add. MS 33924, fol. 40 • BL, Add. MS 39222, fols. 32–3

Viotti, Giovanni Battista (1755–1824), musician, was born in Fontanetto da Po, Piedmont, Italy, on 12 May 1755, possibly the illegitimate son of Antonio Viotti, a blacksmith and amateur horn player, and Maria Magdelena Milano. His early instruction may have come from his father and, when he was eleven, from Giovanni, a lutenist in Fontanetto. Viotti's talents were discovered while he was playing at a church festival at Strambino in 1766. He impressed a bishop who was present and who recommended him as a companion to the young Alfonso dal Pozzo, prince of Cisterna. They travelled to Turin, where Viotti came to the attention of Colgnetti, a musician at the royal court of Sardinia-Piedmont; he persuaded the prince's father, the marchese di Vogliera, to take responsibility for Viotti's welfare and further education. After tuition with Antonio Celoniat, Viotti studied with Gaetano Pugnani, the principal exponent of the school of violin playing begun by Arcangelo Corelli; Pugnani returned from London in 1770 to become first violinist in the king's music at Turin.

After five years (1775–80) at the back of the first violins in the orchestra of the royal chapel in Turin, Viotti embarked on a concert tour with Pugnani. From early 1780 they travelled to Switzerland, Dresden, and on to Berlin, where his first publication, a concerto in A (now known as no. 3) was published in 1781. From there they visited (via Warsaw) St Petersburg, then returned to Berlin towards the end of 1781. It was now important for Viotti to establish himself in his own right, and he made the journey to Paris alone.

Viotti's remarkably successful début at the Concert Spirituel took place on 17 March 1782, following which he remained in great demand and in high critical esteem for the next year and a half. He then turned his back on public performance for a time and was appointed Queen Marie Antoinette's accompanist at Versailles, with a life pension of £150, in January 1784. In the following year, while living with his friend the musician Luigi Cherubini, Viotti held private academies on Sunday mornings for fellow musicians, which often featured his own latest compositions. With the patronage of Louis-Stanislas-Xavier, comte de Provence, brother of Louis XVI, Viotti built in 1788 the Théâtre de Monsieur (later the Théâtre Feydeau), which he ran to great effect. Following the revolution the Théâtre de Monsieur closed, and Viotti moved opera performances to the Théâtre de la Foire St Germain, but they proved less successful there.

Viotti's Parisian period had been immensely productive and influential, but his close association with the court came to threaten not only his livelihood but also his life, and to escape the hostility of the Jacobins he abandoned Paris for London, arriving in July 1792. He established himself as a teacher, but once again made his greatest impact as a performer. His début at Johann Peter Salomon's Hanover Square concert on 7 February 1793, playing his twenty-first violin concerto, was a huge success, and he became the primary violinist of the series for two seasons. He returned briefly to Paris in July 1793, on the death of his mother, before going back to London (via Switzerland, Germany, and Flanders) in December. He was living at 34 Wells Street, Oxford Street, in 1794. Viotti came into contact with Haydn about this time, playing at his benefit concerts in 1794 and 1795. He also became musical director and a performer at the new opera concerts in 1795 and managed Italian opera at the King's Theatre during the 1794–5 season. The connection with the King's endured (his salary was £300 during 1795–6), and he took Wilhelm Cramer's position as leader and director of the orchestra in 1797. Often to be found performing in the homes of the social élite, he enjoyed an assured position as the foremost violinist in London.

Viotti's fortunes, however, took a distinct turn for the worse soon afterwards. On 20 February 1798 he was replaced as leader at the King's Theatre by Salomon, and, suspected of Jacobin activity, he was ordered to leave Great Britain the following month. Despite his written protestations to the contrary and the flimsy evidence, amounting to little more than that he still had correspondents in France, the order stood. He stayed in Schenfeldt, near Hamburg, for a year and a half, the guest of the Chinnery family, musical English friends from London. Viotti continued to work during this difficult period, publishing a set of duos, op. 5, dedicated to William Chinnery, and teaching; his pupils included the influential German music teacher Friedrich Wilhelm Pixis.

In July 1799 he left Germany, and he returned to London at some time before 1801. Viotti had been involved with the wine trade before his exile, and this became his primary focus on his return, although he continued to compose and publish new works and perform privately. The Chinnery family remained close friends, and he was often a guest performer at Gilwell, their country house near Stewardstone in Epping Forest, Essex. There were also visits to Paris in 1802 and 1814, and he was a founder member of the London Philharmonic Society in 1813, although his performances for that body were infrequent. The London-born Nicolas Mori, the first violin professor at the Royal Academy of Music, was a pupil of Viotti about this time.

Viotti's wine business folded in 1818, and Paris apparently offered more possibilities for continuing his musical career and repaying some of his debts. His former patron, the comte de Provence, was now Louis XVIII. A performance of one of his own concertos at a reception held in his honour was received enthusiastically, and he was appointed director of the Paris Opéra on 1 November 1819 with an annual salary of 12,000 francs. Once again his good fortune was curtailed. This time the assassination of the king's nephew Charles-Ferdinand, duc de Berri, at the Opéra shortly afterwards (while Viotti was visiting London) created severe difficulties for the company and its director. Viotti finally resigned in November 1821, and, despite his enduring directorship of the Italian theatre in Paris, his financial predicament continued. He made his will in Paris (13 March 1822) and travelled to London in the following year to stay with his old friends the Chinnery family at 17 Montague Street and then at 5 Upper Berkeley Street, Portman Square. He died there on the morning of 3 March 1824, and may have been buried at Stewardstone. He left two violins, a fine 1712 example by Antonio Stradivari, used by Viotti until his death, and a Klotz that once belonged to Mrs Chinnery.

Viotti's will and other documents reveal that his debts (by his own estimation, 80,000 francs and 800 francs to Mrs Chinnery and his brother André respectively) and 'bitter regrets of neglected talent' (White, 'Viotti') played heavily on his mind during the final period of his life. Despite this inner torment, contemporary accounts and visual representations depict him as physically attractive with a strong, endearing, and refined personality. His personal attributes, integrity, and talents allowed him to rise from humble origins to the highest echelons of musical and social circles in Italy, France, and England. His suspected Jacobin sympathies and a few questionable career decisions did not prevent him from becoming a hugely important and influential figure whose legacy endured through pupils, protégés, and their writings. Viotti was an innovator, bridging the gap between the Italian and Franco-Belgian (modern) traditions of violin playing, although this also meant that he was denied the relative security offered to earlier court musicians and to the travelling virtuosos of the following era. His ten 'London' concertos combine elements of Haydn's symphonic writing with the qualities of the violin model of Stradivari and the bow developed by Tourte, paving the way for the violin concertos of Beethoven and Brahms. He was sufficiently accomplished as a musician and a virtuoso to develop violin technique and the genre of the violin concerto in general at a time when expressive ideals were in a crucial state of transition. However, modernism and virtuosity were never to be at the expense of lyricism, refinement, and beauty of tone, and these were priorities appreciated by English critics and connoisseurs in particular. Viotti, and later Louis Spohr, represented these qualities in the eyes of the English well into the nineteenth century.

Viotti was a prolific composer, mainly for his own instrument. Autographs, sketches, and fragments of his work survive at the Conservatoire National de Musique, Paris, the British Library, and the Conservatorio di Musica Luigi Cherubini, Florence. An increasing number of recordings of his works, in particular the concertos, reflected the ongoing reassessment of their importance and quality at the end of the twentieth century.

DAVID J. GOLBY

Sources C. White, 'Viotti, Giovanni Battista', *New Grove*, 2nd edn [incl. list of works] • C. White, *From Vivaldi to Viotti: a history of the early classical violin concerto* (1992) • Highfill, Burnim & Langhans, *BDA* • R. Stowell, 'Viotti's 'London' concertos (nos. 20–29): progressive or retrospective?', *Music in eighteenth-century Britain*, ed. D. W. Jones (2000), 282–98 • D. J. Golby, 'Violin pedagogy in England during the first half of the nineteenth century, or, *The incompleat tutor for the violin*', *Nineteenth-century British music studies*, ed. B. Zon, 1 (1999), 88–104

Archives Powerhouse Museum, Sydney, corresp. with Chinnery family, patrons of the arts

Likenesses Flatters, bust, 1813 • Peuvrier, bronze medal, 1824, Royal College of Music, London • G. Chinnery, drawing, probably Royal College of Music, London; repro. in *The Connoisseur* (Nov 1911), 160 • Lambert, engraving (after P. Guérin), repro. in Highfill, Burnim & Langhans, *BDA*, 185 • A. V. Lebrun, portrait, repro. in *The Connoisseur* (Nov 1911), 152 • Mayer, engraving (after J. Trossarelli), repro. in Highfill, Burnim & Langhans, *BDA*, 187 • pen and ink, and wash drawing, BM; repro. in C. White, 'Viotti, Giovanni Battista'

Wealth at death over 80,000 francs in debt: Highfill, Burnim & Langhans, *BDA*

Virgili, Polidoro. *See* Vergil, Polydore (*c*.1470–1555).

Virgilius [St Virgilius] (*d*. **784**), bishop of Salzburg, was almost certainly born an Irishman. Both an anonymous verse epitaph and a poem by his younger contemporary, Alcuin, refer to his Irish origin, but nothing is known of his career before he appears in Francia.

Continental career Virgilius is first attested on the continent in or shortly after 743. The earliest account of his career, in the *Conversio Bagoariorum et Carantanorum*, written in 870 or 871, places him at the court at Quierzy of the Carolingian Pippin III, then mayor of the palace, though effective ruler, of the Frankish kingdom. He won the confidence of Pippin and was sent *c*.745 to Bavaria, apparently with the approval of Odilo, duke of the Bavarians, despite the tense relationship between the two rulers. After the death of John, bishop of Salzburg and abbot of the monastery of St Peter there, in June 746 or 747, Virgilius became abbot-bishop, although he was not consecrated until late 748 or 749. Virgilius may have advised Pippin on issues of canon law, and may also have had a role in procuring the sanction of Pope Zacharias for Pippin's usurpation of the kingship of the Franks, and for the anointing ceremony which followed it. While he was supported by the Bavarian dukes, Virgilius maintained links with the Frankish court and is believed to have worked closely with Fulrad, abbot of St Denis and chaplain to the Carolingian kings. Close connections between Salzburg and St Denis are suggested by the script in use at Salzburg, which resembles that of St Denis, and the style of Salzburg Cathedral, commenced in 767, as well as by the entry concerning Fulrad in the *Liber confraternitatum* of St Peter's, which was begun during the year preceding Virgilius's death.

Initially, Virgilius performed only the duties of abbot at Salzburg, handing over the episcopal functions to his compatriot Dubdagrecus (Dub-dá-chrích), who later became abbot of the monastery of Chiemsee. Virgilius spent the years following his consecration consolidating the role of the diocese and, above all, organizing missions to Carinthia and Pannonia (approximately, modern Austria and western Hungary). Among the missionaries whom he sent there, Dupliterus (Dub-Littir) certainly, and Modestus possibly, had also come from Ireland, perhaps with Virgilius.

During the early years of his career, Virgilius had an uneasy relationship with the papal legate, St Boniface (*d*. 754). From the correspondence between Boniface and the pope we learn that Boniface objected to the decision of Virgilius and his companion Sidonius not to rebaptize those who had been christened by a priest in Bavaria with the incorrect formula 'baptizo te in nomine patria et filia et spiritus sancti' (literally, 'I baptize you in the name fatherland and daughter and of the Holy Spirit'. Zacharias took Virgilius's side, and rebuked Boniface for his ignorance of canon law on the matter. The pope was more favourable to Boniface in a letter of 1 May 748, in which he replied to the latter's complaint that Virgilius propagated the heretical doctrine of the antipodes, which claimed that people lived on the other side of the earth, and that

there were another sun and moon there. Virgilius and Sidonius were summoned to the pope, and Boniface empowered to call a synod and excommunicate Virgilius if the accusations could be substantiated. It would seem that Virgilius was vindicated, since no further references to the controversy exist, and he was consecrated bishop shortly after the date of the letter. Virgilius's long career came to an end with his death on 27 November 784, his feast day.

In spite of his undoubted high standing, attested by his participation in synods and his involvement with the Bavarian dukes in legal transactions, both as witness and as defender of the rights of the church of Salzburg, Virgilius was forgotten at his episcopal church until his body was discovered there in 1181. His remains were then translated and his life written. In 1233 efforts to secure his canonization were successful, making him one of the few Irish saints recognized by the church.

The Irish background Since the seventeenth century Virgilius has been sometimes identified with Fergil, abbot of the Irish monastery of Aghaboe (Laois). Since the *Liber confraternitatum* of St Peter's at Salzburg includes a list of the abbots of Iona from Columba to Sléibíne (*d*. 767), there was clearly some connection between Virgilius's see and Iona, and the repeated mention of Cainnech, the patron saint of Aghaboe, in the eighth-century life of Columba of Iona might provide a possible link between Virgilius and Aghaboe via Iona. In its entry for the year 784, the seventeenth-century compilation known as the annals of the four masters is explicit: 'Feirghil, i.e. the Geometer, abbot of Achadh Bó, died in Germany, in the thirteenth year of his bishopric'. The accuracy of the year of Virgilius's death given here, and the nature of the added information, could mean that the seventeenth-century compilers were responsible for the identification themselves, especially since the annals of Ulster give the obit of Feirgil of Aghaboe under the year 789 (almost certainly a contemporary entry), and report no connection with Germany. It has also been thought that Virgilius could be identified with Fergil, *vir sanctus* and son of Mael Dúin, who appears in the twelfth-century Rawlinson genealogies as a descendant of Loegaire, one of the many sons of the mythical Irish king Níall Noígíallach (Níall 'of the Nine Hostages'), which would place his lineage in a branch of the southern Uí Néill in Meath.

Literary and artistic activity at Virgilius's Salzburg While no work in Virgilius's own hand is extant, various texts betray his influence. The confraternity book, still in the library of St Peter's Abbey in Salzburg, was commenced just before he died in 784. The contents of this monumental work, comprising the names of many hundreds for whose souls the monks at Salzburg offered prayers, show the extent of the connections which Virgilius enjoyed. Palaeographical details in this and other Salzburg manuscripts also point to the scribes' Irish training or use of Irish exemplars. Copies of works such as *De locis sanctis* by Adomnán of Iona, penitentials, and a litany in a prayer book later preserved at the monastery of Fleury, testify to an interest in Irish texts at Salzburg even after the death of Virgilius. He is also credited with having commissioned the first Salzburg annals and the original life of Rupert, patron of Salzburg, whose translation from Worms he instigated. The so-called 'Rupertus-Kreuz' (processional cross) may have been made for this occasion. The famous 'Tassilo chalice', now at the monastery of Kremsmünster in Austria, which is named after Odilo's successor as duke of the Bavarians (d. 788) and displays both Irish and Northumbrian characteristics, may also have been used in Virgilius's cathedral.

Scholars have also proposed that Virgilius was the author of a cosmography, written under the pseudonym Aethicus Ister, and supposedly devised as a retort to his old adversary, Boniface. Although some traces of Irish influence in the text may point to the circle around Virgilius, his authorship has yet to be proven.

DAGMAR Ó RIAIN-RAEDEL

Sources J. F. Kenney, *The sources for the early history of Ireland* (1929) · H. Dopsch and R. Juffinger, eds., *Virgil von Salzburg: Missionar and Gelehrter* (1985) · *Das Verbrüderungsbuch von St Peter in Salzburg: vollständige Faksimile-Ausgabe im Originalformat*, ed. K. Forstner (Graz, 1974) · M. Tangl, ed., *Die Briefe des heiligen Bonifatius und Lullus*, MGH Epistolae Selectae, 1 (Berlin, 1916), nos. 68, 80 · H. Wolfram, ed., *Conversio Bagoariorum et Carantanorum* (Vienna, 1979) · *AFM*, 2nd edn · H. Wolfram, 'Virgil of St Peter's at Salzburg', *Irland und die Christenheit*, ed. P. Ní Chatháin and M. Richter (1987), 415–20 · 'Aethicus Ister', *Cosmographia*, ed. M. W. Herren [forthcoming] · M. A. O'Brien, ed., *Corpus genealogiarum Hiberniae* (Dublin, 1962) [genealogies from Bod., MS Rawlinson B. 502, fol. 144 g 56]

Virgno (d. 623). *See under* Iona, abbots of (act. 563–927).

Virtue, George (1794–1868). *See under* Virtue, James Sprent (1829–1892).

Virtue, James Sprent (1829–1892), publisher, was born on 18 May 1829 at 26 Ivy Lane, Paternoster Row, London, the second of six children. His father, **George Virtue** (1794–1868), publisher, was born on 20 April 1794 in Polwarth, Berwickshire, the third son of Robert Virtue, cart-hirer, and his wife, Hellen McDougal. He married Helen Sprent on 25 May 1826, having established himself at Ivy Lane, London, in the 'numbers trade', selling extensive works in parts by subscription. His first major success was Alexander Fletcher's *Guide to Family Devotion* (1834) but it was as a publisher of illustrated books, employing the best artists and engravers, that he made his reputation. A series of steel-engraved topographical books, many illustrated by W. H. Bartlett, sold widely at home and abroad, notably William Beattie's *Switzerland* (2 vols., 1836). As the market for expensive 'view books' declined during the 1840s, George Virtue turned his attention to art publishing. In 1848 he acquired the moribund *Art Union* and transformed it into the lavishly illustrated *Art Journal*, which did much to promote the art of the engraver and raise standards of public taste. It was to prove one of the nineteenth century's most important art periodicals and has been an invaluable source of information for art historians of the period. At this time Virtue entered into partnership with Arthur Hall & Co. and founded his own printing works at 294 City Road, London. The firm became self-sufficient in printing, engraving, and bookbinding, and provided such services for other publishers. He was active in the City of London as a deputy for Farringdon Within, a member of the court of the Stationers' Company and a director of the Great Central Gas Consumers' Company. An attack of paralysis in 1855 led to his retirement from business to Oatlands Park, Surrey. He died on 8 December 1868 of an apoplectic fit while dining at 7 Porchester Square, London, home of his son-in-law James Cotter Morison, and was buried at St Mary's, Walton-on-Thames, on 14 December 1868. His wife survived him.

At the age of fourteen James Virtue was apprenticed to his father and in 1848 was sent to the New York branch of the business. By 1851 he was head of a firm with offices across North America. Apart from a visit to London in 1850 to be admitted a liveryman of the Stationers' Company, he remained in the United States until 1855, when he returned to England to succeed his father. Under his proprietorship the *Art Journal* continued to prosper, distinguished by series of engravings of important collections such as the *Royal Gallery* (1855–61) and the *Turner Gallery* (1860–65), illustrated catalogues of international exhibitions, and monographs on contemporary artists. In 1862 the partnership with Hall was dissolved and Virtue established a second company with his elder brother George Henry at 1 Amen Corner, London. This closed after the latter's death in 1866 and the following year Virtue founded the monthly magazine *St Paul's* with Anthony Trollope as editor. However it failed to meet commercial expectations and in May 1869 was transferred to Strahan & Co., where Virtue acted as printer and chief creditor. He eventually took control of the firm's management and in 1873, with Strahan's other creditors, formed the partnership Virtue, Spalding and Daldy. Two years later the firm became a limited company with Virtue as major shareholder and chairman of the board.

Following his father's example, Virtue continued to publish illustrated books of distinction, particularly editions of the Bible, Shakespeare, and topographical works. However, his commitment to expensive production standards led to periodic financial problems and a difficult legacy for his successors. Virtue married Jane Elizabeth Shirreff (b. 1841/2) on 20 November 1867; she eventually survived him. A keen sportsman, he became a founder member of the London Rowing Club in 1856, serving as treasurer and vice-president. For several years he donated the annual prize of a sculler's boat for novice rowers. He died of heart disease on 29 March 1892 at his London home, 3 Prince's Mansions, Victoria Street, and was buried on 2 April at St Mary's, Walton-on-Thames.

G. C. BOASE, rev. J. P. HOPSON

Sources private information (1899) [Herbert Virtue] · private information (2004) [Michael Virtue] · E. C. Worman, 'George Virtue and the British "numbers" game', *AB Bookman's Weekly* (15 June 1987), 2646–57 · P. T. Srebrnik, 'Trollope, James Virtue, and "Saint Paul's Magazine"', *Nineteenth Century Fiction*, 37/3 (1982), 443–63 · H. Curwen, *A history of booksellers, the old and the new* (1873) · *Register and Magazine of Biography* (Feb 1869) · *Art Journal*, new ser., 12 (1892) · *The Bookseller* (6 April 1892) · *Stationery Trades Journal* (30 April 1892) · *The Times* (7 April 1892) · B. Hunnisett, *Steel engraved* *book illustration in England* (1980) · *London, Provincial and Colonial Press News* (Feb 1886), 15–16 · *'Art Journal': a short history* (1906) · J. Sutherland, 'Trollope and St. Paul's, 1866–70', *Anthony Trollope*, ed. A. Bareham (1980), 116–37 · board of trade, companies registration office, company file, 1875, PRO, BT 31/2141/9875 · m. cert. [James Sprent Virtue] · bap. reg. Scot. [George Virtue] · m. cert. [George Virtue]

Archives Bodl. Oxf., Anthony Trollope MSS, Don. c. 9 · RS Friends, Lond., Bernard Barton MSS [George Virtue]
Likenesses H. Watkins, photograph, *c*.1850 (George Virtue), priv. coll.; repro. in Worman, 'George Virtue and the British "numbers" game', 2646
Wealth at death £9722 0s. 2d.: probate, 30 April 1892, *CGPLA Eng. & Wales*

Vischer, Sir Hanns (1876–1945), educationist, was born at Basel, Switzerland, on 14 September 1876, the third of five children of Adolf Eberhard Vischer (1839–1902), a prosperous Swiss silk merchant, and his wife, Carolina Rosalia (Rosalie) Sarasin. His father was a deeply committed evangelical Christian and an Anglophile, sentiments which his son Hanns fully shared. Educated first at the Humanistisches Gymnasium in Basel, Vischer then went on to St Lawrence College at Ramsgate, Kent. He read modern languages at Emmanuel College, Cambridge, graduating BA in 1899. His early rowing experience on the Rhine got him into the first boat crew: a contemporary recalled the courage, gaiety, and charm of 'Swissy'.

From childhood Vischer had been attracted by the idea of Africa, and he spent his last long vacation from Cambridge studying Hausa in Tripoli. He also undertook a medical course at a Swiss hospital. After a year studying theology at Ridley Hall in Cambridge, he sailed for Nigeria in November 1900 as a lay missionary with the Church Missionary Society. He spent a year at Loko on the Benue River, but resigned from his post in 1902. He informed the society that in order to keep in touch with the country where he felt 'lies the work of my life' (Parkinson, 7) he had applied for British nationality and also for a place in the British colonial service. He successfully obtained both, and in 1903 joined Sir Frederick Lugard's staff in Northern Nigeria. Appointed resident at Bornu in 1905, he spent much of these early years having to live down 'the objections to employing him which his name at first excited' (ibid.). A keen linguist, he became proficient not only in Hausa, but also in Arabic and a number of other local languages.

Keen to learn more about the peoples of the region, Vischer obtained permission to return from leave via an ancient slave trading route. His subsequent journey from Tripoli across the Sahara to Lake Chad between July and December 1906 proved to be a memorable experience, and in 1910 he published *Across the Sahara*, an account of the journey illustrated with his own sketches. As well as describing the colourful characters he met, he collected much useful information about this neglected region; and the book was given much publicity in the *Illustrated London News* and elsewhere.

In 1908 Vischer was seconded to take charge of educational work in the Muslim emirates—a field which he was thereafter to make his own during a long and successful career. In 1910 he was appointed the first director of education in Northern Nigeria. His initial objectives were to open a government school at Kano for training teachers, and to institute a school to provide technical instruction in local agriculture and crafts. He also organized a class for the sons of local chiefs, to familiarize them with European teaching, and to foster good relations within the emirates. He set to work with what Marjorie Perham later described as 'enthusiastic idealism' (Parkinson, 9). After studying what was being done in the Sudan and elsewhere in the region, and despite his evangelical background, Vischer sought to adapt Western educational ideas to local African values and traditions.

On 31 January 1911 Vischer married Isabelle von Tscharner (1884–1963) from Bern; they had four sons. Isabelle shared his love for the Hausa, and between 1912 and 1914 they lived in 'a large, rambling mud-brick house … surrounded by examples of local arts and crafts' (Parkinson, 11). A popular figure among the Hausa, Vischer became known as Dan Hausa ('son of Hausa'). During this period he built up an ethnographic collection that he later presented to the Basel Museum für Völkerkunde, run by an uncle.

Vischer's educational work in Nigeria was unfortunately cut short by the onset of the First World War, but his achievements, though modest, were enlightened, and provided a model for later expansion. Between 1915 and 1919 he served in military intelligence, and from May 1917 was based in Bern with the rank of major. Because of ill health and a desire to be with his young family, however, he chose not to return to the colonial service after the war, but sought other employment in Britain. In 1923 he was approached by J. H. Oldham, the influential secretary of the International Missionary Council, with a view to becoming secretary of the newly established advisory committee on native education in tropical Africa. Vischer's blend of colonial service and commitment to the cause of educational progress in Africa, allied to his linguistic ability in European and African languages, made this an ideal appointment. The committee's role was expanded in 1929 to cover education in the colonies, and Vischer then shared the workload with a joint secretary, Arthur Mayhew. Part of Vischer's role was to provide the committee with up-to-date information on conditions in Africa, and to keep in touch with educational authorities throughout the continent. Through his wide contacts and travels during the following two decades Vischer was able to promote his educational ideals. He played an important role in the investigation carried out by the committee that resulted in the report *The Place of the Vernacular in Native Education* (1927). He made important recommendations for the recruitment, training, and selection of education officers; and he also tried to organize support and hostels for African students studying in Britain.

A skilled linguist himself, Vischer was instrumental in the foundation of the International Institute of African Languages and Culture in 1926, and served as its honorary secretary-general until 1945. In this role he worked closely with scholars and missionaries on projects that aimed to transform oral African languages into literate ones. In particular, he played a key role in running the institute's bureau, which produced textbooks for African schools and a quarterly journal, *Africa*. He himself continued to write and speak about comparative colonial education and Hausa linguistics. From 1931 he helped organize a series of pioneering social and anthropological studies in Africa, funded by the Rockefeller Institute. His concern was not so much academic as social, writing that 'if we are to be true to our ideal these studies must further a practical and human cause, the progress of the African' (Parkinson, 28).

With the onset of the Second World War, Vischer again served in intelligence. He nevertheless ensured the institute's survival, and it resumed full working from 1 January 1943. During the war he worked for the department of propaganda to enemy countries, and served as its liaison officer with MI6. In addition he broadcast in Hausa, French, and English on the BBC West Africa Service on a variety of subjects ranging from Britain's allies to the colour bar, 'a subject about which he had strong feelings' (Parkinson, 37). He was made a CMG in 1936, and knighted in 1941. Early in 1945 Vischer was invited to Paris to meet the new French minister for the colonies, but unfortunately caught a chill which led to pneumonia. He returned to Britain, and died at his home, Tykeford Lodge, Newport Pagnell, Buckinghamshire, on 19 February 1945.

Vischer devoted his life to the progress of education in Africa. With his cosmopolitan background and strong sympathy with African culture, he made an important contribution to the evolution of British educational policy. As Sir Ralph Furse wrote, 'Hanns was unique. So was his contribution to the modern colonial story' (Parkinson, 1). STEPHAN WINKLER

Sources 'Sir Hanns Vischer: an authority on Nigeria', *The Times* (24 Feb 1945) • F. Lugard, *The Times* (6 March 1945) • G. J. F. Tomlinson, 'Sir Hanns Vischer', *Nature*, 155 (1945), 446 • R. D. Furse, *Aucuparius: recollections of a recruiting officer* (1962) • S. F. Graham, 'A history of education in relation to the development of the protectorate of Northern Nigeria, 1900–1919, with special reference to the work of Hanns Vischer', PhD diss., U. Lond., 1955 • S. F. Graham, *Government and mission education in Northern Nigeria, 1900–1919, with special reference to the work of Hanns Vischer* (1961) • R. Heussler, *The British in Northern Nigeria* (1968) • A. Kober, 'Bürger dreier Welten: Erinnerungen an Hanns Vischer', *Schweizerische Illustrierte Zeitung* (16 May 1945) • A. Kober, 'Bürger dreier Welten: Erinnerungen an Hanns Vischer', *Schweizerische Illustrierte Zeitung* (23 May 1945) • A. Kober, 'Bürger dreier Welten: Erinnerungen an Hanns Vischer', *Schweizerische Illustrierte Zeitung* (30 May 1945) • M. Perham, *Lugard*, 2: *The years of authority, 1898–1945* (1960) • S. Sivonen, *White-collar or hoe handle: African education under British colonial policy, 1920–1945* (1995) • C. Whitehead, 'Education in British colonial dependencies, 1919–39: a re-appraisal', *Comparative Education*, 17 (1981), 71–80 • C. Whitehead, 'The advisory committee on education in the [British, S.W] colonies, 1924–1961', *Paedagogica Historica*, 27 (1991), 385–417 • S. F. G. Parkinson, 'Sir Hanns Vischer, champion of African cultures: a portrait of an adviser on colonial education', *Education Research and Perspectives*, 25 (June 1998), 1–45 • *CGPLA Eng. & Wales* (1945)
Archives priv. coll. | Bodl. RH, corresp. with Lord Lugard • Bodl. RH, Perham MSS

Likenesses photograph, repro. in Kober, 'Bürger dreier Welten' • photograph, repro. in Graham, *Government and mission education in Northern Nigeria*
Wealth at death £2529 3s. 1d.: probate, 30 April 1945, *CGPLA Eng. & Wales*

Vismes, Louis de (1720–1776), diplomatist, was born on 25 September 1720, the third of eight sons of Philippe de Vismes, a Huguenot refugee from Normandy, and Marianne de la Majanes, who married on 26 July 1716. He was educated at Westminster School and matriculated from Christ Church, Oxford, on 22 June 1739. After graduating BA (1743) and proceeding MA (1746) he was ordained deacon but does not appear to have gained preferment in the church. In summer 1753 he travelled to Padua with William Nassau de Zuylestein, fourth earl of Rochford, and in 1758 he returned to Italy as tutor to Sir Wyndham Knatchbull-Wyndham (1737–1763). By April 1759 they were in Venice, where the following month they parted company on good terms. De Vismes had been recommended to the British ambassador in Florence, Horace Mann, by William Pitt as 'a Gentleman of much worth' (Ingamells, 295), and in January 1765, when he was in Madrid, he was appointed secretary to his former travelling companion, Rochford, by then ambassador to the Spanish court. He took charge of the embassy when Rochford departed in 1766, and left Madrid in November 1767.

De Vismes was posted to St Petersburg as secretary in March 1768 and arrived in June; he was headed for the embassy there until the arrival of the new ambassador, Lord Cathcart. Although in December 1769 de Vismes was appointed minister to the imperial diet at Ratisbon, he principally resided at Munich during his four years in the post. He succeeded Sir John Goodricke as envoy-extraordinary at Stockholm, where he arrived on 15 March 1774. He reputedly lived in some poverty and, according to Lady Minto, 'had no secretary, contenting himself with a boy who understood no language but his own, merely to copy for him'. Frederick the Great had a high regard for de Vismes and awarded him the honour of bearing the Prussian eagle as a crest.

De Vismes, who was unmarried, died in Stockholm on 4 September 1776. ROBERT HARRISON, *rev.* S. J. SKEDD

Sources D. B. Horn, *British diplomatic representatives, 1689–1789* (1932) • Burke, *Peerage* (1857), 1117–18 • Foster, *Alum. Oxon.* • J. Ingamells, ed., *A dictionary of British and Irish travellers in Italy, 1701–1800* (1997), 295 • *Old Westminsters* • countess of Minto [E. E. E. Elliot-Murray-Kynynmound], *Memoir of Hugh Elliot* (1868)
Archives BL, corresp. with R. Gunning, Add. MSS 2696–2703 • priv. coll., letters to Charles, ninth Lord Cathcart
Likenesses A. R. Mengs, drawing, 1759 • portrait, Christ Church Oxf.

Vitelli, Cornelio (*d.* in or before **1554**), humanist scholar, was among the first Italians to show in person to Oxford the levels reached in rhetoric and philology by the Italian Renaissance. By his own account a native of Cortona, Vitelli may have studied in Bologna and in Rome under Francesco Filelfo, Domizio Calderini, and perhaps Nicolò Perotti. Vitelli's first work may be his letter, or *Commentariolus* (probably of 1473), to Perotti on the elder Pliny. It was printed with Perotti's commentary in Venice about 1482 as well as in the Aldine (1499) and some early sixteenth-century editions of Perotti's *Cornucopiae*. In late August 1474 Federigo da Montefeltro was created a papal duke; probably hoping for patronage, Vitelli eulogized the creation in a Latin epigram. In 1478 he was certainly tutoring the son of Paolo Leoni of Padua. Within three years he was acting as tutor to the sons of Venetian patricians, and in 1481 gave a course of lectures, perhaps at the studium of Padua, perhaps in Venice. Vitelli attacked the scholarship of Giorgio Merula, professor of eloquence in Venice. His *Defensio Plinii et Calderini*, first printed at Venice in 1481–2 along with his tractate on Roman time measurement, was dedicated to Ermolao Barbaro the elder; his third essay in Plinian controversy, *Enarratiuncula in C. Plinium*, which seems to belong to this phase of his career, was first printed with Marino Becichemo's Pliny commentaries (Paris, 1519).

Vitelli's polemic against Merula led to his securing the latter's post, which was probably its intention. From May 1483 he served the Venetian republic as state rhetorician, being replaced in that position by Giorgio Valla towards the end of 1484. From about January 1485 he was praelector of New College, Oxford, a position he occupied for two years, during which he taught Latin and Greek in Oxford; William Grocyn and Thomas Linacre may have been his pupils. It was most likely in 1486 that he made the Latin oration to which Thomas Chaundler is reported by Leland as having responded.

From 1 February 1487 to the end of January 1488 Vitelli held the chair of poetics at Louvain. In the summer of 1488 he was in Paris, where he met two fellow Italian humanists, Giovanni Balbi and Publio Fausto Andrelini, and was authorized with them on 5 September 1489 to lecture publicly on the poets. Becoming involved in verse controversy in Balbi's interest against Andrelini, Vitelli lost Balbi's favour also. He left Paris at the end of 1489 or the beginning of 1490, and appears to have gone first to London, where he failed to win royal patronage by joining Giovanni Gigli, Bernard André, and Pietro Carmeliano in deriding the French humanist and ambassador Robert Gaguin, who had been successively his friend and rival in Paris. From autumn 1490 to summer 1492 Vitelli rented a room in Exeter College, as Grocyn did from 1491 to 1493. Competition for pupils from Grocyn may have been the reason for Vitelli's leaving Oxford, which he seems to have done in late summer 1492. In 1490 he ate Christmas lunch with the vice-president of Magdalen College, and he may have dined in New College in 1492.

Thereafter little can be said of Vitelli. He may have been the *cortonese* to whom Constantino d'Andrea hoped to give pleasure by his Italian *Disticha Catonis*, published in Venice *c*.1493–4, and it is also possible that he tried to support himself by teaching in Florence. By 9 February 1508, however, he had become rector of Sant'Antimo in the diocese of Arezzo; he still held the benefice in 1525, and may have done so until 1554.

The only work Vitelli wrote in England that is extant is his poem against Gaguin. A Greek epigram by Poliziano (*d*. 1494) may be directed against him. No English or Scottish contemporary author mentions him, though he had a later reputation here for verbal fluency and as a teacher: André, about 1500, calls him the most eloquent of orators, and Polydore Vergil, after 1514, says that he was nobly born and Oxford's first instructor in good letters. In 1528 Erasmus refers dismissively to him among the ruck of Ciceronians.   J. B. TRAPP

Sources Emden, *Oxf.*, 3.1950–51 · C. H. Clough, 'Thomas Linacre, Cornelio Vitelli, and humanistic studies at Oxford', *Essays on the life and works of Thomas Linacre, c.1460–1524*, ed. F. Maddison, M. Pelling, and C. Webster (1977), 10–23 · C. H. Clough, 'New light on Cornelio Vitelli and humanistic studies at Oxford University in the late fifteenth century', *The Ricardian*, 12 (2000), 94–119 · G. Tournoy, 'Cornelio Vitelli', *Contemporaries of Erasmus: a biographical register*, ed. P. G. Bietenholz and T. B. Deutscher, 3 (1987), 404–5 · R. Weiss, *Humanism in England during the fifteenth century*, 3rd edn (1967), 6, 136, 173–4, 200 · P. O. Kristeller, *Iter Italicum*, 7 vols. (1963–97), vol. 2, nos. 22, 53; cf. 18, 63, 285, 286; vol. 3, no. 109a · C. G. Nauert, 'Caius Plinius Secundus', *Catalogus translationum et commentariorum / Medieval and renaissance Latin translations and commentaries*, ed. F. E. Cranz and P. O. Kristeller, 4 (1980), 295–422, esp. 329–32 · J. I. Catto, 'Scholars and studies in Renaissance Oxford', *Hist. U. Oxf. 2: Late med. Oxf.*, 769–84 · W. Nelson, *John Skelton, laureate* (1939); repr. (1964), 24–9 · B. André, *Historia regis Henrici septimi*, ed. J. Gairdner, Rolls Series, 10 (1858), 56 · *The Anglica historia of Polydore Vergil, AD 1485–1537*, ed. and trans. D. Hay, CS, 3rd ser., 74 (1950), 147 · D. Erasmus, '"The Ciceronianus": a dialogue on the ideal Latin style: *Dialogus Ciceronius*', trans. B. I. Knott, *Literary and educational writings, 6*, ed. A. H. T. Levi (1986), vol. 28 of *Collected works of Erasmus*, ed. W. K. Ferguson and others (1974–), 323–448, esp. 418 · *Gesamtkatalog der Wiegendrucke* (1925), no. 6374

Vittels [Vitell], **Christopher** (*fl.* 1543–1579), religious separatist leader, was thought by John Rogers, a later adversary, to have originated in Delft, Netherlands, where he was in 1543. At some point he joined the Family of Love, a mystical religious fellowship founded in Amsterdam and Emden by 'H. N.' (Hendrick Niclaes) during the 1540s. He was resident in Southwark, London, as early as 1551, and his wife, of whom nothing is known, was still living there in 1579. He was a joiner by trade, though he is also listed in one source as a merchant who operated between England and the Low Countries. He was an elusive and charismatic figure, capable of remaining almost invisible to his enemies while generating and sustaining an enthusiastic English following. The sources available to the biographer are usually hostile in tone.

During the middle decades of the century Vittels belonged to the radical religious underworld. His theology appears, at this stage, to have been loosely defined, but it included the following beliefs: that the true godly did not sin; that infant baptism was invalid; that the pope was not Antichrist; and, last, that God and Christ were not equal. He also believed that spiritual dissenters could, with a clear conscience, attend officially prescribed church services of which they disapproved. Vittels participated in a heated debate on some of these points at a Colchester tavern in 1555. A witness later recalled that Vittels had, on this occasion, also spoken of his intention to promote 'the doctrine of a man, who lived … beyond the seas an holy life and an upright conversation' (Wilkinson, fols. 3v–A1r). This was presumably a reference to Niclaes, whose teachings came to dominate the remainder of

Vittels's shadowy life. Although in 1559 his opinions on the inequality of God and Christ led him to be called before the bishop of London, Edmund Grindal, at Paul's Cross, and to a possible public recantation, he was not silenced.

During the 1560s and 1570s Vittels emerged as the leading member in England of Niclaes's sect, travelling the country and building a dedicated and secretive discipleship for Niclaes that may have extended to a thousand men and women. In 1574–5 Vittels put his bilingual skills to use in an ambitious scheme to translate, reprint, and distribute the works of his mentor. Eighteen of these were printed in Cologne, bearing titles such as *Terra pacis*, *Evangelium regni*, and *The prophetie of the spirit of love*. The books were soon on their way to England in an operation that Vittels almost certainly masterminded. It was at this point, not surprisingly, that members of the Family of Love began to attract hostile attention from English magistrates and authors. The group's devotion to a foreign, self-proclaimed messiah with an allegorical attitude to scripture caused considerable anxiety in England. Niclaes taught that individuals who committed themselves to him could become 'godded with god', or inwardly transformed to the point at which their sins ceased or became meaningless. Between 1574 and 1580, a number of 'confessions' were extracted from Familists in Cambridgeshire, the Isle of Ely, and Devon, and at the court of Elizabeth I. Vittels proved typically slippery during these years, and does not seem to have been captured or examined.

The first known reference to Vittels in print appeared in Stephen Batman's *The golden booke of the leaden goddes* (1577), where he was described uncharitably as 'one altogether unlearned, savinge that he is somwhat erroniously, Bewitched'. This was merely a foretaste of the invective that Vittels was to encounter in 1578–9. John Rogers, about whom very little is known, was a particularly animated adversary, and deeply frustrated by Vittels's activities:

> What travell he hath taken, howe he hath trudged from countrie to countrie, and howe he will not once move his speech, if any learned or godly persons, that hath any true knowledge of the worde be present, is very wel known: but among the simple he is peerelesse, and in deede, the oldest Elder of our English Familie, amongst whome he hath his maintenance. (Rogers, *The Displaying*, fol. D3r–v)

Other prominent anti-familists included two Cambridge graduates, William Wilkinson, who later became chancellor of the diocese of Salisbury, and John Knewstub, a prominent puritan who was minister of Cockfield, Suffolk, in 1579.

Rogers, Wilkinson, and Knewstub led the assault on the Family of Love in these years. The fellowship became the subject of privy council discussions, parliamentary debates, several books, and a royal proclamation. Still Vittels remained at large, and secretly delivered to Rogers a robust written defence of his beliefs and behaviour. Rogers printed it, with his own angry responses, in *An answere unto a wicked and infamous libel* (1579). Pressure upon the Family was maintained into 1581, when it somewhat

mysteriously eased. It appears that members of the Family at court successfully convinced some of the highest authorities that the danger was not as serious as had been suggested. By this date Vittels, who had evaded his enemies even when they were in the ascendancy, had disappeared and becomes virtually untraceable.

CHRISTOPHER MARSH

Sources *The displaying of an horrible secte of … heretiques … the familie of love, with the lives of their authours* [i.e. D. Joris and H. Niclas] … *newely set foorth by J. R[ogers]: whereunto is added certeine letters sent from the same family*, ed. J. Rogers and S. Bateman, another edn (1579) · J. Rogers, *An answere unto a wicked and infamous libel* (1579) · W. Wilkinson, *A confutation of certaine articles* (1579) · J. Knewstub, *A confutation of monstrous and horrible heresies* (1579) · S. Batman, *The golden booke of the leaden goddes* (1577) · C. W. Marsh, *The Family of Love in English society, 1550–1630* (1994) · A. Hamilton, *The Family of Love* (1981) · J. W. Martin, 'Christopher Vitel: an Elizabethan mechanick preacher', *Sixteenth Century Journal*, 10/2 (1979), 15–22

Vivares, Francis (1709–1780), landscape engraver, was born on 11 July 1709 in St Jean-du-Bruel, north of Montpellier, the third son of Jean Vivares, who abjured his protestant faith to remain in France. At two years old Francis was sent to Geneva and then, aged eighteen, to London. According to George Vertue, who noted details of Vivares's career in 1741, his 'profession was originally a Taylor—this he was brought up to did follow to mans estate, and in London was a Master Taylor faild—or broke went away to Paris' (Vertue, *Note books*, 6.195). In France Vivares studied drawing and etching; he then returned to London where in the 1730s he worked in the Marlborough Street studio of the Venetian painter Jacopo Amigoni. The Swiss engraver Joseph Wagner lived with Amigoni and published his paintings, and Vivares presumably assisted Wagner with some of the prints that he engraved between 1733 and 1738. In 1739 Wagner and Amigoni left for Venice where Wagner established a print shop and published one set of prints signed by Vivares.

In 1739 the Huguenot printseller James Regnier published a drawing book designed and engraved by Vivares. By this time Vivares had married Anne Charieux (d. 1744?), and in September 1739 their first child, Marie, was born. Their sons Jacques and Jean followed in 1742 and 1743 and in 1743 Vivares stood godfather to the son of his close friend John Rocque at the Huguenot church of Spring Gardens. In 1740 he had begun to work for Arthur Pond and Charles Knapton, who were publishing an influential series of prints of picturesque landscapes by Gaspar Poussin, Claude, and other seventeenth-century masters, copied from paintings in British collections. Vivares undertook twelve of their earliest prints for 3 guineas a plate. His next association was with the landscape painter and printseller Thomas Smith of Derby. Fifteen large prints by Vivares after paintings by Thomas Smith were published between 1743 and 1749. In 1745 Vertue, who spoke of the pair as joint 'undertakers' (or publishers), noted '4 Views done at Derby of Dunington Cliffe Anchor church Hopping Mill Ware & Lym Park by Smith & Vivares' (Vertue, *Note books*, 6.201). It seems likely that this pioneering set of picturesque English scenes was literally 'done' at Derby, for in September 1744 his son Thomas Vivares [*see below*] was baptized in that town. Francis was the only parent named and it is possible that Anne died in childbirth.

Francis Vivares took Peter Benazech as his apprentice in 1746, by which time he was probably back in London. He had married a woman named Elizabeth by spring 1748; their child David was baptized at St Anne's, Soho, in December. By March 1749, when he launched a subscription for his first solo publication, Vivares was established at the Golden Head in Porter Street, Leicester Fields. By 1752 he had a print shop in Newport Street, near Long Acre, and he remained in this house (subsequently numbered 13 Great Newport Street) until his death. Here he sold 'all sorts of Italian, French and Flemish Prints of the best Masters' as well as prints by himself and his pupils. In 1755 he took a second apprentice, William Hebert and, on 31 January, a third wife, Susanna Parker (d. 1792). With her he had at least three children of whom the eldest, Elizabeth, proved to be a gifted artist. Vivares was elected a fellow of the Society of Artists but he only exhibited in 1766 and 1768. His children did extremely well in the competitions held by the Society for the Encouragement of Arts, Manufactures, and Commerce, with Thomas, Mary, Francis junior, and Elizabeth all winning prizes for drawing or engraving. Theirs must have been a family business in the fullest sense. By the 1760s it was thriving. Vivares published drawing books, books of ornament, and swags and borders for use in print rooms, as well as his own landscape engravings. These were very highly esteemed and his prints were collected by contemporary connoisseurs (a two-volume œuvre compiled by Viscount Fitzwilliam survives in the Fitzwilliam Museum, Cambridge, for instance). He usually published a pair of major landscapes every year. Vivares was widely considered to be the best engraver of Claude, but he also interpreted a number of modern painters including George Smith of Chichester, Thomas Gainsborough, and the Venetian visitor Francesco Zuccarelli (a connection probably owed to Vivares's acquaintance with Wagner, Zuccarelli's publisher in Venice).

When the poet Thomas Gray visited the picturesque landscapes of northern England in 1769, he noted that 'at the alehouse where I dined, in Malham, Vivares the landscape painter, had lodged for a week or more'. Vivares had published two prints after his own drawings of scenes around Malham in 1753, but it is possible that Gray was not mistaken about Vivares's occupation and that he painted landscapes as well. Nicholas Thomas Dall, who was the scene painter at Covent Garden Theatre, lodged with Vivares from 1764 to 1770, during which time he exhibited many northern views. In June 1763 Vivares visited the German engraver Johann Georg Wille in Paris: 'c'est un fort brave homme. Je l'aime', wrote Wille. A few months later Vivares supplied Wille with some English-made copper plates and burins. He visited Wille again in 1776 with his wife, 'et nous les avons vus avec plaisir'. Vivares continued to work until his death on 26 November 1780. A part of his stock of prints was sold by auction on 25 October 1781. The print on which Vivares had been working when he died, *The Enchanted Castle* after Claude, was completed for his widow by William Woollett. Susanna Vivares had probably always run the shop and she continued to sell and publish prints from Newport Street until her death in 1792.

Thomas Vivares (*bap.* 1744), designer and landscape engraver, the son of Francis Vivares, was baptized at All Saints' Church, Derby, on 4 September 1744. He may have been named after Thomas Smith of Derby, with whom his father was collaborating at the time of his birth. He was trained as an engraver by his father and between 1760 and 1766 won a succession of prizes for drawing or engraving from the Society for the Encouragement of Arts, Manufactures, and Commerce. He exhibited drawings and engravings with the Free Society in 1764 and 1782 and with the Society of Artists in 1782. He married first Hannah Allen on 18 June 1783 and second Sally Lucas on 1 January 1786, both at St Pancras Old Church. Some of his working life was spent in Paris, where he engraved landscapes after P. Royer and Adrian Zingg. TIMOTHY CLAYTON

Sources Vertue, *Note books*, 6.195–7, 199–204 · administration, Francis Vivares, PRO, PROB 6/156, fol. 319*v* · will of Susan Vivares, PRO, PROB 11/1224, sig. 537 · *Registre des églises de la Savoye de Spring Gardens et des Grecs*, Huguenot Society, 26 (1922) · parish register, St Anne's, Soho, City Westm. AC · parish register, All Saints, Derby, Derbys. RO · GL, Sun Insurance Office, MS 11936, policies 448223, 497868 · *GM*, 1st ser., 50 (1780), 590 · E. Miller, 'Landscape prints by Francis Vivares', *Print Quarterly*, 9 (1992), 272–81 · H. Vivarez, *Pro domo mea: un artiste graveur au XVIIIe siècle, François Vivares; un artiste en ferronerie au XVIIIe siècle, Jean Vivarais* (Lille, 1904) · Graves, *Soc. Artists* · L. Lippincott, *Selling art in Georgian London: the rise of Arthur Pond* (1983) · L. Lippincott, 'Arthur Pond's journal ... 1734–1750', *Walpole Society*, 54 (1988), 220–333 · *Mémoires et journal de Jean-Georges Wille*, ed. G. Duplessis, 2 vols. (1857) · T. Clayton, *The English print, 1688–1802* (1997) · T. Friedman, 'Two eighteenth-century catalogues of ornamental pattern books', *Furniture History*, 11 (1975), 66–75 · C. Archer, 'Festoons of flowers ... for fitting up print rooms', *Apollo*, 130 (1989), 386–91 · M. Snodin and E. Moncrieff, eds., *Rococo: art and design in Hogarth's England* (1984) [exhibition catalogue, V&A, 16 May – 30 Sept 1984] · *IGI*

Archives Bibliothèque Nationale, Paris · BM · FM Cam. · V&A
Likenesses F. Vivares & J. Caldwall, self-portrait, line engraving, pubd 1776, BM, V&A

Vivares, Thomas (*bap.* 1744). *See under* Vivares, Francis (1709–1780).

Vivekananda [*known as* Swami Vivekananda; *formerly* Narendranath Datta] (1863–1902), Hindu religious leader, was born on 12 January 1863 in Calcutta and named Narendranath Datta. His family were Kayasthas, a writer caste traditionally employed in government service. His father, Vishwanath Datta (d. 1884), a successful lawyer, and his mother, Bhuvaneshwari, ensured that their son received the education necessary for a professional career in British-ruled India. At the age of fifteen he attended a mission school and in 1880 he entered Presidency College, Calcutta. In 1884 he graduated BA, in the second division, and went on to study law at the Metropolitan Institution, completing his studies there in 1886. He also attended the Scottish Church College in Calcutta. However, his life was not to follow the path for which his education had been intended to prepare him.

Like many educated young Indian men at this time he

Vivekananda (1863–1902), by unknown photographer

Swami Vivekananda, a name suitable for a Hindu ascetic. He accepted the suggestion, and it is by this name that he is best-known.

From this time he became one of the most influential Hindu thinkers and publicists at a time of religious ferment and reconstruction in India, presenting Hinduism in India and abroad as a highly significant world religion, equal to other religious traditions such as Christianity or Islam. He argued, in the face of Western condemnation of India and of Hindu tradition, that India was a deeply spiritual land, in contrast to the materialistic West; and that Hinduism was a noble and ancient religion. Compared with the great historical diversity of religious traditions in Hindu society, he preached Vedanta as the core or gospel of Hinduism as a world faith; and he also broke new ground by arguing the centrality of social service in the truly spiritual Hindu life. Both these aspects of his teaching made him a compelling figure at home and abroad.

Vivekananda sailed from Bombay in May 1893 to attend the World Parliament of Religions in Chicago. He addressed the conference at the Chicago Art Institute on its opening day, 11 September, and eight days later read a paper on Hinduism. A forceful speaker and a striking figure, he made a dramatic impression on the audience and provoked considerable comment in the American press, including a piece in the *New York Herald* which commented how foolish it was to send Christian missionaries to the home of Hinduism. After the conference Vivekananda toured the United States, lecturing and writing extensively. He focused on four themes: bhakti yoga (the path of devotion), jnana yoga (the path of knowledge), raja yoga (the path of action), and the question of class. He gained many devotees, who would form the North American core of his religious movement. Two early disciples, initiated through the traditional rituals of *sanyas* and given Hindu names, were Marie Ibusie (Swami Abhayananda) and Leon Landsberge (Swami Kripananda).

He remained in the United States until September 1895, when he was invited to London by the theosophists Henrietta Müller and E. T. Sturdy. In London he followed another intense schedule of lecturing and teaching, which met with similar success to his American tour; on 22 October 1895 he gave a public lecture at Prince's Hall, Piccadilly. In December he returned to the United States, where in January 1896 he established the Vedanta Society of New York, under the presidency of one of his disciples, Francis H. Legget. Another disciple, Miss Waldo, took the name Swami Haridasi, and taught raja yoga. Vivekananda returned to lecturing, and attempted to formalize the rituals and organization of the monastery in India through his extensive correspondence with the monks there. Back in London in April, he sent his fellow monks a letter containing a constitution for the monastery.

In January 1897 Vivekananda returned to Calcutta, where he pushed for greater organization and a higher degree of discipline among his followers. On 1 May he established the Ramakrishna mission, for both monks and laity, an organization which was to be devoted to

joined the Brahmo Samaj, a rationalist organization that sought to reform Hinduism, and in 1881 he met, for the first time, the Hindu ascetic Ramakrishna Paramahansa. Initially he showed little interest in the swami, but gradually grew closer to him and to his teachings. Throughout his time at college his interest in religion grew and he became a freemason in 1884. His ties with Swami Ramakrishna strengthened, especially after the death of Narendranath's father on 25 February 1884. He became a regular attender at the Dakshineshwar Temple where Ramakrishna taught, and he lost interest in institutional education and a professional career, although he completed his courses. The swami had attracted a group of young men who had for the most part been educated in English-speaking schools, and when he fell ill in October 1885 this group of disciples, including Narendranath, brought him to Calcutta where they nursed him until his death on 16 August 1886. The following month the group dispersed.

In December 1886 Narendranath located a dilapidated house at Baranagar, near the River Ganges, which became a crude monastery dedicated to Ramakrishna's teachings, for himself and four others, until November 1891 when with the financial support of some Hindu princes they moved to a superior lodging at Alambazar. The following year, while visiting sacred sites on the western coast, he met the raja of Khetri, who urged him to take the name social service. He sought a direct application of the spiritual life to the problems of the world; his legacy to Hinduism was the addition of social action to spiritual experience. Shortly afterwards he instituted a famine relief fund, and in the same year the mission opened a Ramakrishna ashrama at Sagachhi, and founded an orphanage. In 1898 a 7 acre tract of land along the Ganges to the north of Calcutta was purchased, and became the site of the Belur Math (monastery). Vivekananda encouraged the publication of a Bengali-language fortnightly paper, *Ubodhan*, as the voice of the movement; its first issue was published on 14 January 1899. Having brought a degree of order to the evolving organization, he turned his attention once more to the West.

In June 1899 Vivekananda departed once more for the United States, via London. He spent four months in 1900 in California, where he established the Shanti Ashrama on 160 acres of land in Santa Clara donated by a supporter, Minnie Block. He visited San Francisco, and sent Swami Turyananda with twelve disciples to direct the work of inaugurating the ashrama. When he returned to New York his programme was curtailed by ill health. In August he attended the Congress of Religion in Paris, after which he embarked on a tour of Europe, visited Cairo, and finally returned to Belur Math on 9 December 1900. This proved to be his last overseas journey.

Vivekananda devoted himself to placing the math and the mission on a firm legal and organizational footing, transferring the management of all land and buildings owned by the math and mission to a president and board of trustees. He then resigned the presidency; in February 1901 the board of trustees elected Swami Brahmananda president, leaving Vivekananda free of organizational responsibilities. He set off on a pilgrimage through East Bengal and Assam, but poor health forced him to settle at the Belur Math, where he died on 4 July 1902.

Vivekananda left behind a vigorous and growing movement both in India and in the West. In the West it emphasized doctrine and worship based on his interpretation of Ramakrishna's teaching. In India there were two interrelated goals: religious devotion and social service. Both within and beyond this religious milieu Vivekananda left a heroic and popular image of an Indian who had affirmed the spiritual superiority of Hinduism at the very source of material power, and amid persistent condemnation of Hinduism by Western missionaries and writers. He initiated the long and continuing succession of swamis, gurus, and maharishis who have sought to offer their own interpretations of Hinduism as a cure for the ills of wealthy but materialistic Western societies. KENNETH W. JONES

Sources Swami Jyotirangananda, *Vivekananda: a comprehensive study* (1993) · *The life of Swami Vivekananda*, 4th edn (1965) · Swami Gambhirananda, *History of the Ramakrishna Math and mission* (1957) · J. N. Farquhar, *Modern religious movements in India* (1915); repr. (1919) · K. W. Jones, *Socio-religious movements in British India* (1989) · Swami Vivekananda, *Complete works of Swami Vivekananda* (1963–6)
Likenesses photograph, repro. in *The life of the Swami Vivekananda by his eastern and western disciples* (1912), vol. 1 [see illus.] · portrait, repro. in Farquhar, *Modern religious movements in India*, facing p. 195

Wealth at death no estate at time of death; all property turned over to the Ramakrishna Math and mission prior to his death

Vives, Juan Luis (1492/3–1540), scholar, was born in Valencia, Spain, on 6 March 1492, according to the traditional dating as inscribed on his tombstone, although recently published records of the Inquisition would indicate early 1493. He was born into a family of *converso* Jews of Valencia who were forced to convert to Christianity after the uprisings of 1391 in that city. His father, Lluís Vives Valeriola (1463–1524), was a well-to-do cloth merchant. His mother, Blanquina March Almenara (1473–1508), was of a family of jurists and notaries from Gandía.

Education and early career Vives must have been raised as a Christian but it seems quite probable that his parents and many of his relatives secretly observed certain religious practices of Judaism, of which the young Vives could not have been unaware. The persecution and execution of many members of his family and his *converso* origins remained a determining psychological factor throughout his life. As far as can be ascertained, his training in Latin both in primary school and at university was of the traditional kind, not yet influenced by the reforms instituted by Elio Antonio de Nebrija at Salamanca. At the estudi general of Valencia, formally elevated to the rank of university in 1500 by the Borgia pope Alexander VI, a native of neighbouring Játiva, he would have taken two years of grammar and three years of arts.

In 1509, the year following his mother's death, Vives set out for Paris to complete his studies. There he joined many other students from Spain, especially Aragon, enrolled in the faculties of arts and theology. As was the practice at Paris at this time, the young Vives took courses at different colleges, probably beginning his studies under the Aragonese logician Juan Dolz de Castellar at the college of Lisieux. He must also have attended at the lessons of Nicolas Bérault, who had come to Paris from Orléans and taught the classical authors at the College of La Marche. During these years the French humanist was giving lectures on authors not usually included in the arts curriculum, such as Quintilian, Juvenal, and Suetonius. These consisted of close readings of the classical texts with ample historical, mythological, and geographical commentary. It seems very likely that Vives was inspired by these examples to give his own lectures on authors and works that were the subjects of Bérault's lectures, such as Cicero's *De legibus* and Francesco Filelfo's encyclopaedic work, the *Convivia*. At the Collège de Montaigu, Vives studied under the Aragonese Gaspar Lax de Sariñena, master of the intricacies of terminist logic, and Jan Dullaert of Ghent, commentator on the *Physics* of Aristotle and interested also in astronomy. Among Vives's early writings published in Paris is a *praelectio* on the *Poeticon astronomicon* of pseudo-Hyginus and a brief life of Dullaert, who died at a very young age. During these Parisian years Vives published an impressive number of *praelectiones* and dialogues on Christian themes in Roman dress, chief of which was a depiction of Christ's victory over death in the form of a Roman triumph.

Bruges and Louvain From 1512 Vives divided his time between Paris and Bruges, where there was a flourishing Jewish community. He was the guest of a relative of his from Valencia, Bernardo Valdaura, whose daughter Margarita (1505–1552) he married on 26 May 1524. In 1514 he left Paris definitively for the Low Countries, where he gave private lessons in Bruges and Louvain. One of his pupils there was the young Guillaume de Croy, nephew of the powerful lord of Chièvres, who at the age of eighteen became bishop of Cambrai and at nineteen cardinal-archbishop of Toledo and primate of Spain. Through the patronage of his young ward Vives was licensed by special privilege to give public lectures at the University of Louvain without being on the official roster. Vives dedicated to him a book of meditations on the seven penitential psalms, which provide early evidence of the exceptional learning of the Spanish humanist. Besides the Septuagint and Vulgate version of the Psalms he makes reference to a 'Chaldean' (that is Aramaic) version made by a certain Jonathan, son of Abenuziel. Even in these religious pieces Vives made use of a florid declamatory style that was to characterize his later writings. At Louvain he made contacts with members of Erasmus's circle, Marcus Laurinus and Jan van Fevijn, and with Frans van Cranevelt, member of the grand council of Malines, who became his most trusted friend. That Vives had attained a position of some authority at the court of Charles I is made evident in a letter of 13 November 1516 from the magistrates of the city of Valencia to Vives—whom they address as 'most learned gentleman and philosopher, Master Luis Vives, resident at the royal court' (Vives, 116–18)—in which they seek his intercession with the king concerning the affairs of the university.

Vives must have made the personal acquaintance of Erasmus as early as October 1516, when Erasmus was resident in Brussels and referred to Vives as one with whom he was on quite familiar terms. By 1519 Erasmus was so impressed with his younger contemporary's learning that he wrote an effusive letter of praise to Juan de la Parra, personal physician of Archduke Ferdinand of Austria, brother of Charles V, recommending Vives as a tutor for the archduke. Vives chose not to desert his pupil, Guillaume de Croy, but in compensation dedicated a work to Ferdinand, the *Sullan Declamations*, an exercise in deliberative oratory and political philosophy, which once again drew extraordinary praise both from Erasmus and Thomas More. In this Louvain period Vives wrote several other works, including a short piece on the origins of philosophy, a piquant fable on man, which is a subtle parody of Pico della Mirandola's *Oration on the Dignity of Man*, and a commentary on Cicero's *Dream of Scipio*, preceded by a delightful dream of his own that ushers in the more serious discussion.

The most important work to issue from Vives's pen at this time was the *In pseudodialecticos*, a spirited attack against the Parisian doctors at whose feet he had once sat. It is a brilliant diatribe, all the more effective, as Erasmus wrote to Thomas More soon after its publication, since 'No one is better fitted to break the serried ranks of the sophists, in whose army he has served so long' (*Correspondence*, 7.295). As Erasmus had done before him in *The Praise of Folly*, Vives singles out for ridicule the absurd Latin used by the dialecticians, incomprehensible to all but themselves. He promises that one day he will demonstrate, not by argument but by deed, that all the arts can be communicated in normal speech without the use of jargon, as indeed he was to do in his monumental work on education, the *De disciplinis*. Vives insists that too much time is dedicated to the study of logic, a subject that should be learned not for its own sake but as a tool and support of the other arts.

Vives returned to Paris a few months later in the company of Guillaume de Croy and on his return was able to report to Erasmus that he was given a friendly reception by the very people who had been the object of his satire. It was during this visit that he met for the first time the foremost French humanist, Guillaume Budé, with whom he had already been in frequent correspondence, and with whom he retained friendly relations until the end of his life. Amid this newly won fame and success Vives suffered a serious set-back when his young patron fell from his horse and was killed on 11 January 1521. This turn of events left him in a state of great depression. He became ill and retired to Bruges, where he gradually recuperated. For several months he had to cease work on the formidable scholarly task Erasmus had set him: a commentary on St Augustine's *City of God*, which would form part of the complete edition of Augustine that Erasmus was preparing for Froben. The newly discovered letters of Vives to Cranevelt reveal that in his present quandary Vives was anxious to meet with Thomas More during his impending visit to the prinsenhof in Bruges in the company of Cardinal Wolsey. The meeting, arranged by Vives's good friend Cranevelt, would prove to be of great significance for Vives's future career. In the summer of 1522 he finally completed the commentary on Augustine at the cost of great physical and mental fatigue, but Erasmus was displeased with its excessive length and poor sales at the Frankfurt fair. The relations between the two humanists became noticeably strained after this. He dedicated the work to Henry VIII in a very florid preface, in which he exalts him above all the kings of the earth and congratulates him on the *Defence of the Seven Sacraments*, which had just appeared. The acknowledgement from the palace of Greenwich was polite and appreciative.

Vives continued to give lessons at the University of Louvain at this time and to tutor private students, among whom were some notable English scholars: Nicholas Wotton, Giles Wallop, William Thale, and the physician John Clement. In May 1522 he was offered the prestigious chair of Latin philology at the University of Alcalá, to succeed the famous Antonio de Nebrija. There is no indication of his response until a year later in letters written both to Erasmus and Cranevelt: he announces his intention to set out for Spain by way of England, since the land journey through France was rendered impossible by the hostilities raging there. Before his departure for England he wrote the first of his pacifist essays, an open letter to the newly elected pope, Adrian VI, who was from Utrecht. Vives was emboldened to write such a letter since he had been a good friend of Adrian Florensz when he was vice-chancellor of the University of Louvain. It is a plea for peace among Christian nations and for the peaceful solution of religious controversies, in which regard he urges the pope to call a general council of the church. Vives has no sympathy with the subtle distinctions made by theologians concerning the just and the unjust war but accounts all wars among brothers, united by the bond of baptism, as iniquitous and criminal. During these decisive months Vives was plagued by news concerning the fortunes of his family in Spain. In a letter of 4 January 1523 to Cranevelt he laments the death of his only brother, Jaime, and the pitiful conditions of his father, charged by the Inquisition of clandestine Judaizing. Vives often refers to the hated tribunal by the veiled term *Fortuna*. In the face of these disastrous events he took for himself as a motto a phrase from Seneca: *Sine querela* ('Without complaint'). Vives's worst fears were realized: his father was delivered to the secular arm and burnt at the stake on 6 September 1524. Vives never did return to Spain but must have felt great anguish over his powerlessness to help his family.

England   Vives departed for England on 18 March 1523, and immediately won favour with Cardinal Wolsey, who appointed him his reader in humanity at Oxford in succession to Thomas Lupset; he delivered his lectures in Corpus Christi College. There is extant a fragment of a letter of his to Wolsey, in which he says that he has assigned to the students philosophical questions that elicit more pleasant as well as more fruitful debate, and has rid them of many corrupt opinions regarding dialectics. In the first year of his tenure the king and queen, breaking a long tradition of the English crown, entered the city of Oxford to pay him a visit. This event is recorded with some exaggeration in Brian Twyne's *Antiquitatis academiae Oxoniensis apologia* of 1608. Vives also received a royal invitation to spend the Christmas and Epiphany holidays at Windsor Castle.

Vives quickly made the acquaintance of all the famous English humanists of the day: Cuthbert Tunstall, William Linacre, William Latimer, and John Fisher, and was a frequent visitor at the home of Thomas More in Chelsea. At court Vives also exercised great influence in the role of friend and spiritual counsellor of Queen Katherine and tutor to Princess Mary. At the behest of the queen, Vives had begun a long treatise on the *Education of a Christian Woman* while still in Bruges. It was ready for publication in April 1523 but did not appear until the following year. It was translated into English by Richard Hyrde, a tutor in More's household, under More's personal supervision. The work enjoyed enormous popularity in England and became the prototype of various conduct books for women during the Tudor period. For Princess Mary, Vives also wrote a practical plan of study and a collection of spiritual mottoes and devices entitled *Satellitium animi*, or *Escort of the Soul*, a predecessor to the popular emblem books of the later sixteenth century. This pamphlet was followed by yet another instructional book, the *Introduction to Wisdom*, directed toward a wider audience.

Vives now turned from educational to political writing in an impressive series of works on affairs of state. In homage to the cardinal he produced translations of two famous speeches of the Greek orator Isocrates: his address to the Areopagus and his speech to Nicocles, both on the subject of government. The next work was a brief letter he wrote from Bruges to John Longland, bishop of Lincoln and confessor to the king. As in the letter to Adrian VI, he continually refers to Europe as a political entity and begs the bishop's intercession in the interests of peace. He has heard, he says, that even the ignorant savages in the New World honour a man of peace. He returned to England in September 1524 to resume his duties there but sailed back to Bruges in the following spring after an outbreak of plague. Just before his departure Vives addressed an earnest appeal to Henry VIII asking him to seek the release of François I, who had been captured by the imperial forces at the battle of Pavia and was held prisoner in Madrid. He exhorts the king and the emperor to make moderate and magnanimous use of their victory and refrain from devastating the most flourishing realm of Christendom.

A few months after the battle of Mohács in 1526, in which the Turkish forces of Sulayman the Magnificent defeated the Hungarians, Vives wrote a dialogue of the dead in the style of the Greek satirist Lucian. Mythological figures in Hades discuss the present European conflicts and their precedents both in more recent history and in antiquity. It is an ironic commentary on the disunification of Christian leaders in the face of the Turkish menace. In the same year Vives wrote a treatise, *On the Relief of the Poor*, solicited by the magistrates of the city of Bruges through their ambassador to England, Lodewijk van Praet. It addressed the thorny problem of poverty and beggars with concrete proposals to the civil authorities on how to remedy it. It is regarded as a very important document in the history of social welfare. His enlightened attitude, imbued with the principles of Christian charity, was far in advance of his time.

In February 1526 Vives was again in England (his frequent crossings prompted Erasmus to call him an 'amphibious animal'), apparently still intent on persuading Henry to intervene on the side of peace. As the king's Great Matter became more and more complicated, Vives had no choice but to side with the queen, incurring Henry's and Wolsey's great displeasure. Through the machinations of the latter he was placed under house arrest from 25 February to 1 April 1528—together with the Spanish ambassador in London, Iñigo de Mendoza, who was suspected of transmitting messages to Pope Clement VII and to the emperor. Upon his release Vives returned to Bruges but it seems that he was called back to England by the queen, together with two jurists from Flanders to counsel her. When Vives refused to defend her in the trial at Blackfriars before the papal legates, knowing that it would be a farce, she dismissed him and cut off his pension. So ended Vives's career in England. Actually, at the request of Wolsey, Vives had previously sent a rather long legal and theological opinion to the king some time in 1528, which for one reason or another did not reach him and which is no longer extant. Vives refers to this document in a letter he wrote to the king three years later and sent him another exemplar. He expresses his continued devotion and good wishes to the royal pair for the brief span of life that remains to them. He also gives some very sound advice to the king about the uncertainty that will surround the possible succession of a male heir from another marriage.

Bruges and Breda: Vives's final years With both royal pensions discontinued Vives was left in penurious conditions. He remained for the most part in Bruges with occasional trips to Louvain, Brussels, Antwerp, and Malines. During this last part of his life (1528–40), an extraordinary number of lengthy and important works poured from the pen of Juan Luis Vives. In 1532 he began to receive a pension from the emperor Charles V, which, he records, sufficed for half of his living expenses. In 1537 he became preceptor to Mencía de Mendoza, the wife of the duke of Nassau, and resided for a time at the ducal castle in Breda in North Brabant. Having failed in his mission of peace with Henry, Vives turned to Charles V in a long treatise entitled *On Concord and Discord in the Human Race* (1529). In the dedicatory epistle Vives congratulates the emperor on his imminent trip to Italy, where he would be signatory to the treaty of Cambrai. He reiterates his appeal to leaders of the Christian world to rise above national interests and unite in the face of the common enemy. Discord is the monster that devours the human species. This was followed by a complementary piece, *De pacificatione*, addressed to the Spanish grand inquisitor, Alonso Manrique, a fellow *converso* and a defender of Erasmists in Spain.

Vives's *magnum opus*, the *De disciplinis*, an encyclopaedic survey of education in all its aspects, was published by the printer Michael Hillen in Antwerp in 1531. It was dedicated to João III, king of Portugal, a patron of the new learning. The first book gives the reasons for the corruption of learning, mostly to be attributed to the excessive importance given to dialectics by the scholastic philosophers. The second book is a complete reorganization of teaching and curricula at every level, embracing the entire domain of knowledge. Vives would have the child begin to learn through the observation of nature—astronomy, geography, zoology, botany, even husbandry and gardening. Trades and crafts could be learned by visiting the workshops of the tradesmen. University education would begin with many years of intensive training in language and literature, chiefly Latin, then Greek, but not to the exclusion of the vernacular languages. Next would come rhetoric, dialectical reasoning, and lastly mathematics, to be followed by formal professional training in medicine and jurisprudence, the latter requiring a profound knowledge of history and moral philosophy. In the third book Vives concentrates on philosophy and gives a terse critique of individual classical, medieval, and

humanist authors. The final goal of education is both practical and spiritual, the application of learning to the contemporary world and the acquisition of virtue.

The *De disciplinis* is a landmark in the history of education, which had great influence on such writers as Rabelais, Montaigne, Melanchthon, Comenius, and Descartes. Many other works followed, the most important of which is his *De anima et vita* (1538), loosely derived from Aristotle's treatise on this subject. Rather than define the soul, Vives investigates its operations and functions. His shrewd observations on the passions or emotions earned him the title of father of modern psychology from nineteenth-century historians of philosophy. Vives's final work, *On the Truth of the Christian Faith*, a Christian apologetic in the form of a dialogue between Christians, Jews, and Muslims, was published posthumously by his friend Cranevelt. Worn out by his scholarly labours and suffering from kidney afflictions and the gout, he died on 6 May 1540 at Bruges, and was buried there in the church of St Donatian, now destroyed.

Vives's works enjoyed great popularity throughout the sixteenth century and innumerable editions, both in Latin and in translation, were printed by the great publishing houses of Antwerp, Basel, Lyons, Paris, and Venice. His pedagogical innovations had great influence on English writers on education such as Roger Ascham, Thomas Elyot, and Richard Mulcaster. Numerous editions of his popular Latin dialogues for schoolboys, the *Exercitatio linguae Latinae*, were published in England. Tudor prayer manuals and devotional works borrowed heavily from Vives's *Preces et meditationes diurnae* (1535) and books like John Bradford's *Private Prayers and Meditations* (1559) and Richard Day's *Book of Christian Prayers* (1578), based on Vives's devotional writings, achieved great popularity in protestant circles. Interest in Vives waned in the next two centuries but was revived again at the end of the nineteenth century and continues with great vigour at the present day, especially in Belgium and Spain. Juan Luis Vives is a towering figure of the Renaissance, a man of immense learning, integrity, and originality, whose worth has yet to be fully estimated.

CHARLES FANTAZZI

Sources J. A. Majensius, 'Joannis Ludovici Vivis Valentini vita', in *Joannis Ludovici Vivis Valentini opera omnia*, ed. J. A. Majensius, 1 (Drôme, 1782), 1–220 · H. de Vocht, *Literae virorum eruditorum ad Fr. Craneveldium* (1928) · J. IJsewijn, D. Sacré, and G. Tournoy, *Literae ad Craneveldium Balduinianae humanistica Iovaniensia*, 41–4 (1992–5) · Enrique González y González, *Joan Lluís Vives de la escolástica al humanismo* (1987) · C. Noreña, *Juan Luis Vives* (1970) · A. Bonilla y San Martín, *Luis Vives y la filosofía del Renacimiento* (1903) · J. L. Vives, *Epistolario*, ed. J. Jiménez Delgado (1978) · M. Pinta Llorente and J. M. de Palacio, *Procesos inquisitoriales contra la familia judía de J. L. Vives* (1964) · *LP Henry VIII*, vol. 4 · *The correspondence of Erasmus*, ed. and trans. R. A. B. Mynors and others, 22 vols. (1974–94), vols. 1–12 · T. Fowler, *The history of Corpus Christi College*, OHS, 25 (1893) · G. Tournoy and others, *Vives te Leuven* (1993)

Likenesses F. Gaulle, engraving, c.1567, NPG; repro. in Tournoy and others, *Vives te Leuven* · R. Boissard, engraving, c.1587, NPG; repro. in Tournoy and others, *Vives te Leuven* · E. de Boulonois, line engraving, repro. in J. J. Boissard, *Bibliotheca chalcographica*, new edn, 1 (Frankfurt, 1650) · portrait, repro. in A. M. Salazar, *Iconografía de J. L. Vives* (1953)

Vivian, Charles Crespigny, second Baron Vivian (1808–1886). *See under* Vivian, Hussey Crespigny, third Baron Vivian (1834–1893).

Vivian, Henry Harvey (1868–1930), promoter of co-partnership and politician, was born on 20 April 1868 at Moor Cross, Cornwood, Devon, the son of William Henry Vivian, a carpenter on Lord Blatchford's estate, and his wife, Mary Ann Norris. He was educated at Cornwood national school, and after serving an apprenticeship to a Plymouth carpenter went to work in London. There he became active in trade-union affairs and was elected president of the Pimlico branch of the Amalgamated Society of Carpenters and Joiners. Vivian saw at first hand the damaging effects of industrial strife and experienced the many hardships faced by working people. In response he turned not to socialism but to co-partnership, an offshoot of the nineteenth-century co-operative movement.

Whereas the co-operative movement distributed any surplus in the form of a dividend to consumers, the co-partnership movement gave primacy to the rights of the wage earners themselves. In a co-partnership concern the workers were assured the right to become shareholders; to share in profits; and to participate in management decisions. In 1884 the Labour Association was formed to promote co-partnership, and Vivian later became friendly with two of its leading figures, Edward Owen Greening and Thomas Blandford. In 1890, at twenty-two, he was appointed its secretary. In addition to his administrative duties he lectured about co-partnership at industrial and educational gatherings, and advised workers on setting up co-partnership enterprises. His evidence before the royal commission on labour in January 1893 represents a clear statement of the contemporary co-partnership position. He was also the founding editor, in 1894, of the journal *Labour Copartnership*. By 1901 there were more than one hundred co-partnership societies in existence with a turnover approaching £3 million. This success was in large measure a reflection of Vivian's work as secretary. He retired in 1909 but served as honorary secretary of the Labour Co-partnership Association (as it had become) during 1909–10, and remained on the executive committee until his death.

In 1891 Vivian established General Builders Ltd, a co-partnership enterprise that aimed to provide its members with employment and housing. By 1897 there were sixteen London branches with 800 individual members, but in spite of this growth no steps had been taken towards providing housing. A stimulus came with the publication in 1898 of Ebenezer Howard's influential *Tomorrow: a Peaceful Path to Real Reform*, which encouraged the development of 'garden cities' on co-operative lines. Early in 1901 Vivian was asked to discuss a co-partnership housing scheme with a group of Ealing-based workers, several of whom were members of the local branch of General Builders Ltd. The outcome was Brentham Garden Suburb, the pioneer co-partnership suburb.

Vivian explained his ideas at a meeting in the Haven Arms off Ealing Broadway on 16 February 1901. Somewhat against the wishes of the Ealing group he favoured communal rather than individual ownership. He envisioned a community of like-minded individuals who would say 'This estate is ours', rather than 'This house is mine'. On 6 March another meeting led to the establishment of Ealing Tenants Ltd on the co-partnership basis suggested by Vivian, its first chairman. It promised the workers involved 'better homes without destroying their industrial mobility' (Brentham Society, 8). Then, and later, Vivian glossed over the serious financial difficulties faced by the company in its early days. Help came from a variety of sources, including the Amalgamated Society of Railway Servants, through the agency of Vivian's friend and political ally Fred Maddison.

Ealing Tenants Ltd benefited its members both by profit-sharing and by the application of the most progressive principles of town planning. A farmland site was purchased, and within a matter of years Brentham Garden Suburb had been created. It had many of the features of Ebenezer Howard's garden city ideal, with a social institute offering a library, games, and lectures, as well as tennis courts and a bowling green. There were plenty of large gardens, and the limit of ten to twelve houses per acre meant the retention of open spaces. It was the product of a fusion between the garden city movement and co-partnership: 'Without garden city planning Brentham might have looked like any other suburb. But without co-partnership, Brentham would never have been founded at all' (Reid, 15).

In 1907 Vivian became chairman of Co-partnership Tenants Ltd, which advised new tenant societies and served the emerging garden suburbs in a wholesale capacity. Large parts of Letchworth garden city and Hampstead Garden Suburb were developed by Co-partnership Tenants Ltd and subsidiary companies. Vivian was also associated with garden city and garden suburb projects at Birmingham, Derwentwater, Manchester, and Wolverhampton. When Ealing Tenants Ltd came under the auspices of Co-partnership Tenants Ltd members of the latter company were given votes in the affairs of the former. It meant a departure from the original concept of co-partnership in Ealing and bitter disputes subsequently arose because of this. Vivian, however, was committed to the growth of Co-partnership Tenants, and by the outbreak of war in 1914 the company had more than £300,000 in shares and loan stock. Of the thirty co-partnership housing societies then in existence, and which together were responsible for some 7000 houses nationwide, fourteen were affiliated to Co-partnership Tenants.

Brentham was essentially a local initiative, but Vivian was quick to see its wider significance. He invited local and national politicians to view the site, and at one of the early public meetings of Ealing Tenants Ltd the prominent American radical Henry Demarest Lloyd was present. Lloyd was greatly impressed by the Ealing experiment and its obvious applicability in other countries. In 1910 Vivian visited Canada at the invitation of the governor-general, Albert Henry George Grey, fourth Earl Grey, to discuss town planning and housing development. He returned there in 1912 at the invitation of Grey's successor, Arthur, duke of Connaught. By this time there was an International Garden Cities and Town Planning Association, and garden city and suburb associations were appearing across Europe.

In politics Vivian was a free-trade Liberal and a disciple of John Stuart Mill. At the general election of 1906, standing as a Lib–Lab, he won Birkenhead. The Lib–Lab members were known as the trade union group in parliament, but Vivian and his Lib–Lab colleague Fred Maddison were no longer active in trade-union affairs. Both were consequently marginalized and they became 'notorious for their anti-socialist activities' (Clegg, Fox, and Thompson, 391). In 1907 they were censured by the Trades Union Congress for opposing the successful Labour Party candidate at the Jarrow by-election. And in 1908 they opposed the Lib–Lab decision to join the Labour Party. They also secured the defeat at the second reading on 13 March 1908 of the Unemployed Workmen Bill. Introduced by a Labour member and known as the 'Right to Work Bill', the measure proposed a national network of unemployment committees to provide work or relief for the unemployed. John Burns ridiculed the measure as impractical and was strongly supported by Vivian, who argued that it 'would destroy the character, the self-reliance, and the moral fibre' of the workforce (Hansard 4, 186, 1908, 48).

At the general election of January 1910 Vivian held Birkenhead by 144 votes, but he lost the seat to the Conservative in the December general election. After this Vivian stood as a Liberal. In his brief time in parliament he was a member of the royal commission on canals and waterways, the select committee on housing and town planning, and the departmental committee on accidents in factories and workshops. He also helped to draft the 1909 Housing and Town Planning Act. In November 1911 he was narrowly defeated in the Somerset South by-election. At Edmonton in December 1918, standing as an Asquithian Liberal, he came third, but at Northampton in November 1922 he lost his deposit in a contest won by a Lloyd George Liberal. He won Totnes, Devon, by a narrow margin in December 1923, but lost to the Conservative in October 1924. This was his last parliamentary contest, although he afterwards remained active in the Hornsey Liberal Association.

After the First World War, Vivian became an enthusiastic supporter of the League of Nations and he was chairman of his local branch of the League of Nations Union in Hornsey. He remained on the committee of Ealing Tenants Ltd until his death. He died at his home, The Limes, Crouch End Hill, Middlesex, on 30 May 1930, and was survived by his wife, Harriet Helen Vivian, and a daughter, Barbara. Vivian wrote extensively on the co-partnership movement and particularly its application to housing development. He was a skilful publicist and a passionate speaker, wholly committed to the co-partnership cause.

John Burns, opening a new recreation ground at Brentham in June 1908, described him as a 'practical mystic' (Reid, 104).   MARK POTTLE

Sources *DLB* · A. Reid, *Brentham: a history of the pioneer garden suburb, 1901–2001* (2000) · *The Times* (31 May 1930), 14b · *WWBMP* · *WWW* · *Hansard 4* (1908), vol. 186 · *The pioneer co-partnership suburb*, Brentham Society (2000) · J. W. R. Adam, *Modern town and country planning* (1952) · A. Bonner, *British co-operation* (1961) · H. A. Clegg, A. Fox, and A. F. Thompson, *A history of British trade unions since 1889*, 1 (1964) · P. Rowland, *The last liberal governments: the promised land, 1905–1910* (1968) · F. W. S. Craig, *British parliamentary election results, 1885–1918* (1974) · b. cert. · d. cert. · *CGPLA Eng. & Wales* (1930)
Wealth at death £17,275 14s. 8d.: probate, 25 July 1930, *CGPLA Eng. & Wales*

Vivian, Henry Hussey, first Baron Swansea (1821–1894),

industrialist and politician, was born on 6 July 1821 at Singleton, Swansea, the eldest son of John Henry *Vivian (1785–1855), industrialist and politician, and his wife, Sarah, *née* Jones (d. c.1885). Richard Hussey Vivian, first Baron Vivian, was his uncle. He was educated at Eton College from about 1832 until 1840, and in 1838 went to Germany and France to study languages and metallurgy. When in France, Vivian shared lodgings for a time with Friedrich Engels. He went up to Trinity College, Cambridge, in 1840. In 1842 he entered the family business as a partner, taking charge of the Liverpool office of Vivian & Sons, which dealt with the export trade. In 1845 he was appointed manager of the Hafod smelting works in Swansea, of which he took full control following the death of his father in 1855. Under his influence Swansea became 'the metallurgical centre of the world'.

Vivian married three times. His first marriage, on 15 April 1847, was to Jessie Dalrymple, daughter of Ambrose Goddard, MP for Swindon. She died on 28 February 1848, shortly after the birth of their son, Ernest Ambrose. His second marriage, on 14 July 1853, was to Caroline Elizabeth (Flora), daughter of Sir Montague John Cholmely MP, and granddaughter of the duke of St Albans. She became crippled by illness after giving birth to their son, John Aubrey, and died on 25 January 1868. He married his third wife, Averil Beaumont (c.1840–c.1935), on 10 November 1870. She was twenty years his junior and the daughter of Captain Richard Beaumont and granddaughter of Godfrey, third Lord Macdonald. They had two sons, Henry Hussey and Odo Richard, and four daughters, Violet Averil, Averil, Alberta, and Alexandra.

As a businessman Vivian was an innovator, taking out several patents for improved metallurgical processes, and was largely responsible for the continued expansion of Vivian & Sons and the diversification of their interests. He was involved with introducing the manufacture of zinc in the 1840s. The firm began to extract gold from auriferous copper ores using Plattner's process in 1850 and silver from argentiferous copper ores in 1856. This same year they also began smelting nickel and cobalt. In 1883 a separate company, H. H. Vivian & Co., was established for nickel and cobalt smelting. In 1864 Vivian & Sons introduced Gerstenhöfer furnaces, which facilitated the recovery of sulphur for the manufacture of sulphuric acid, which was used by the firm to manufacture chemical fertilizers and pesticides. This innovation also received favourable publicity because of the reduced emission of the polluting 'copper smoke'. In 1871 the firm erected works at White Rock, near Swansea, to treat poor silver-lead ores. The business became a limited liability company on 12 February 1883 under the style H. H. Vivian & Co. with Vivian as its chairman. Vivian also played an active role in the Second Copper Trade Association, a secret cartel of copper smelters which operated from 1844 until 1867.

A man of remarkable energy and business capacity, Vivian's activities extended beyond metallurgy. As a coal owner he was involved in negotiating a settlement of the 1875 miners' strike, by which the sliding scale of linking wages to price fluctuations was introduced into the south Wales mining industry. He was also one of the chief promoters of the Rhondda and Swansea Bay Railway, which linked the coal mines of the Rhondda valley to the port of Swansea.

Vivian was elected Liberal MP for Truro in 1852, joining his father in the House of Commons. Following the death of his father, he was elected MP for Glamorgan in 1857 and for the Swansea District in 1885. In parliament he served on the exchequer loan commission in 1861, the channel tunnel committee in 1882–3, the committee to establish an imperial institute, and the royal commission on tithe redemption. Although a supporter of Gladstone, Vivian openly disagreed with his leader over aspects of the Home Rule Bill, which apparently prevented him from accepting the chancellorship of the duchy of Lancaster in 1886. He also consistently voted in favour of disestablishment in Wales while a staunch member of the Church of England. Throughout his long parliamentary career he was a frequent speaker in the Commons. Locally, Vivian was a trustee of the Swansea Harbour Board, and was elected the first chairman of the newly formed Glamorgan county council in 1889.

Like his father, Vivian maintained a strong interest in education, and together they were responsible for Vivian & Sons opening a school in Sketty. He became the first treasurer of the newly founded University College of South Wales and Monmouthshire in 1884, and was later its vice president, and he was involved in the founding of a technical school in Swansea, which opened after his death in 1895. He was a fellow of the Geological Society, twice president of the Royal Institution of South Wales, and president of the Cambrian Archaeological Association from 1861 to 1862.

In later life Vivian devoted less time to the business and more to leisure interests. He frequently visited his house in Scotland for shooting holidays, and sailed on his yacht. He also farmed at Parc le Breos in the Gower, and was well-known locally as a stock-breeder. Vivian's lack of involvement may have contributed to the decline of the family business, and especially the firm's failure in a mining venture in Sudbury, Canada, though towards the end of the century British non-ferrous metal manufacturers faced increasing international competition.

Vivian was created a baronet on 13 May 1882 on the recommendation of Gladstone in recognition of his long public service, and elevated to the peerage, also by Gladstone, as Baron Swansea on 9 June 1893. He was made a freeman of Swansea in the same year. Vivian died suddenly of heart failure at Singleton on 28 November 1894 shortly after returning from America; he was buried in Sketty churchyard, near Swansea, on 3 December. He was survived by his wife.

W. R. WILLIAMS, *rev.* EDMUND NEWELL

Sources R. A. Griffiths, *Singleton Abbey and the Vivians of Swansea* (1988) · S. Vivian, *The story of the Vivians* (1989) · A. Stewart, *Family tapestry* (1961) · R. R. Toomey, *Vivian and Sons, 1809–1924: a study of the firm in the copper and related industries* (1985) · G. W. Roderick, 'South Wales industrialists and the theory of gentrification', *Transactions of the Honourable Society of Cymmrodorion* (1987), 65–83, 78–9 · *Cardiff Times* (1 Dec 1894) · *Cardiff Times* (8 Dec 1894) · *South Wales Daily Post* (30 Nov 1894)
Archives NL Wales, corresp., diaries, and papers · U. Wales, Swansea · West Glamorgan Area RO | BL, letters to W. E. Gladstone, Add. MSS 44411–44518
Likenesses M. Hanhart, lithograph, 1883, NMG Wales · Spy [L. Ward], chromolithograph cartoon, NPG; repro. in *VF* (*c*.5 June 1886) · statue, Swansea
Wealth at death £215,032 17s. 11d.: double probate, June 1896, *CGPLA Eng. & Wales* (1895)

Vivian, Hussey Crespigny, third Baron Vivian (1834–1893), diplomatist, born in Connaught Place, London, on 19 June 1834, was the eldest son of Charles Crespigny Vivian, second Baron Vivian, and his first wife, Arabella (*d.* 1837), daughter of John Middleton Scott of Ballygannon, co. Wicklow.

The father, **Charles Crespigny Vivian**, second Baron Vivian (1808–1886), son of Richard Hussey *Vivian, first Baron Vivian (1775–1842), and his first wife, Eliza Champion de Crespigny (*d.* 1831), was born at Truro on 24 December 1808, and educated at Eton College. He became cornet in the 7th hussars in 1825, and was subsequently promoted lieutenant (1826), captain (1829), and major (12 August 1834), after which he retired. He represented Bodmin in parliament from 1835 to 1842, when he succeeded to the title. He was appointed special deputy warden of the stannaries in 1852 and lord lieutenant of Cornwall in 1856, resigning the latter office in 1877. He died at Ventnor on 24 April 1886 and was buried at Glynn, leaving six sons and three daughters by his two wives: Arabella, *née* Scott, whom he married on 2 July 1833 and who died on 26 January 1837, and Mary Elizabeth, *née* Panton, whom he married on 21 September 1841. Tall, with a large nose and a monocle, he was known as 'Hook and Eye'. His widow died aged eighty-two on 23 January 1907.

Also educated at Eton College, the eldest son, Hussey Vivian, was appointed a clerk in the Foreign Office on 18 November 1851. He was attached to several important special missions, accompanying the earl of Clarendon to Paris in 1856 and the earl of Breadalbane to Berlin in 1861. In 1864 he was sent to Athens with the draft treaty for the annexation of the Ionian Islands to Greece. He became senior clerk in the Foreign Office on 3 July 1869. In 1873 he was appointed acting agent and consul-general at Alexandria, and the following year was transferred to Bucharest.

He was again appointed to Egypt in 1876; while there he was made CB.

Vivian was appointed resident minister to the Swiss confederation in 1879, and two years afterwards was raised to the rank of envoy-extraordinary and minister-plenipotentiary to Denmark. He was sent to Brussels with the same rank in 1884, and during his time there was made KCMG. He succeeded to his father's title on 24 April 1886 and was politically a Liberal. He was appointed British plenipotentiary to the slave-trade conference held at Brussels in 1889, and for his services was made GCMG. On 1 January 1892 he was appointed ambassador in Rome, where he remained until his death, from pneumonia, at the British embassy on 21 October 1893. At his funeral in Rome on the 25th the prince of Naples followed on foot with Lord Vivian's son.

Vivian was a conscientious but not a brilliant diplomatist. 'He was certainly much fonder of horses than of chanceries … but he was a man who could always be relied on in an emergency' (The Times, 23 Oct 1893). He was elected a fellow of the Royal Geographical Society in 1872. He married, on 8 June 1876, Louisa Alice (d. 3 April 1926), daughter of Robert George Duff of Ryde; they had three daughters and one son, George, who succeeded to the title. Their daughter Dorothy Maud (d. 1939) was maid of honour to Queen Victoria and Queen Alexandra and in 1905 married Douglas Haig (1861–1928), later first Earl Haig.

E. L. Radford, rev. H. C. G. Matthew

Sources The Times (23 Oct 1893) · FO List (1893) · Boase, Mod. Eng. biog.
Archives Lincs. Arch., corresp. with his wife and other family letters · St Ant. Oxf., Middle East Centre, corresp. | Lpool RO, corresp. with fifteenth earl of Derby
Likenesses Lock & Whitfield, carte-de-visite, NPG
Wealth at death £6534 15s. 9d.: probate, 7 Feb 1894, CGPLA Eng. & Wales

Vivian, John (1750–1826), mining and copper-smelting entrepreneur, was born on 9 January 1750 in Cornwood, Devon, the eldest of four sons of Thomas Vivian, vicar of Cornwood and writer on religion and science, and his wife, Mary, daughter of John Hussey, barrister, and sister of John Hussey, solicitor-general. He was educated at Truro grammar school and in France. When aged twenty-four he married Betsy (d. 1816), daughter of Richard Cranch, vicar of St Clements, near Truro, and granddaughter of Richard Peters, from whom she inherited a part of his considerable estate. From a reportedly very large family they had three surviving sons, Richard Hussey *Vivian, John Henry *Vivian, and Thomas, and a daughter, Lucy.

In contrast to two of his brothers, who became fellows of Exeter College, Oxford, Vivian was involved in business at an early age. He was a wine and lime merchant in partnership with William McCarmick in Truro until 1777. He began his involvement in the metal industry acting as agent in Cornwall for the copper smelter Thomas Williams and the Cheadle Brass and Wire Company, purchasing copper ore from the mines in the county on their behalf and arranging for its shipment to their smelting

works in south Wales. He diversified his interests by acquiring shares in a number of mines, and became a partner in a firm supplying mining materials and in the Miners' Bank of Truro. Such was his involvement in the industry that he was called as a witness by the 1779 parliamentary committee on the state of the copper mines and copper trade. With Matthew Boulton, Vivian was instrumental in establishing the Cornish Metal Company in 1785, which sought to buy the entire output of Cornish mines and break the smelting companies' hold over the market for copper ore. He acted as deputy governor of the company, which proved unsuccessful and was wound up in 1792.

With high levels of demand for copper during the Napoleonic wars, Vivian turned his attention to smelting copper, perhaps also with the intention of developing a family business for his sons. Without the financial resources or technical expertise to establish his own works, in 1800 he became a partner of the Cheadle Brass and Wire Company, whose works were in Pen-clawdd, south Wales. He withdrew his interest from this company in 1808 and in the following year established his own smelting works at Hafod, north of Swansea, going into partnership with his sons Richard Hussey and John Henry. Vivian & Sons soon established itself as a major manufacturer of copper and by 1820 was the second largest producer of copper in Britain, accounting for about 17 per cent of national output. By 1811 Vivian had returned to Cornwall to handle the purchase and sales of copper ore in Truro, corresponding weekly with John Henry, who managed the Hafod works.

As well as his business activities, Vivian was a justice of the peace, high sheriff of Cornwall, vice-warden of the stannaries from 1817 until his death, and master of Fourbarrow hunt for forty years. Although highly respected, especially in Cornwall, his daughter-in-law Sarah later recalled that he had never been on sufficiently good terms with anyone to allow of them going into his room without knocking. Vivian died in Truro on 7 December 1826, from injuries sustained eleven weeks earlier in a hunting accident.

Edmund Newell

Sources R. A. Griffiths, Singleton Abbey and the Vivians of Swansea (1988) · S. Vivian, The story of the Vivians (1989) · A. Stewart, Family tapestry (1961) · R. R. Toomey, Vivian and Sons, 1809–1924: a study of the firm in the copper and related industries (1985) · Royal Cornwall Gazette (9 Dec 1826) · Devon RO
Archives NL Wales · U. Wales, Swansea · West Glamorgan Area RO
Likenesses portrait, NL Wales

Vivian, John Henry (1785–1855), industrialist and politician, was born on 9 August 1785 in Truro, the second surviving son of John *Vivian (1750–1826), mining and copper-smelting entrepreneur, and his wife, Betsy, née Cranch (d. 1816). He was educated at Truro grammar school and Lostwithiel School, and at the age of sixteen went to Germany to study languages. In 1803 he became a student at the Mining Institute of the University of Freiberg as a pupil of the geologist Abraham Werner. In 1806, at the age of twenty-one, he was appointed manager of the Pen-clawdd copper-smelting works of the Cheadle Brass and Wire Company in south Wales, in which his father was a partner. In 1809 he became a partner of Vivian & Sons, together with his father and brother Richard Hussey *Vivian, and was appointed manager of its Hafod works in Swansea.

In 1816 Vivian married Sarah Jones (d. c.1885), daughter of Arthur Jones of The Priory, Reigate, Surrey. They had nine children, who were brought up in the family home, Marino, near Swansea, which was greatly extended and remodelled in a Gothic style and later renamed Singleton Abbey.

While Richard Hussey Vivian pursued a military career, and as his father became less involved in the direct running of the firm, John Henry Vivian devoted himself to the development of the family business. He was involved in a secret cartel of copper smelters, which operated in the 1820s to control the price of copper. He applied his technical knowledge of smelting to improve production methods and was largely responsible for the growth of Vivian & Sons into one of the major firms in the industry, developing Hafod into a works town known as 'Vivian's Town' or 'Trevivian'. In 1835 the firm diversified into zinc smelting and shipping; in 1838 the firm acquired the Margam copper works from the English Copper Company; and in 1839 Vivian founded the Swansea Coal Company, both to supply his smelting works and to trade independently. In 1842 Vivian & Sons began to manufacture 'Yellow Metal', an alloy of copper and zinc. Following the death of Richard Hussey Vivian the same year, Vivian bought out his late brother's estate to retain family control of the firm.

Vivian took particular interest in the atmospheric pollution or 'copper smoke' problems associated with copper smelting, and during the 1820s employed Michael Faraday and Richard Phillips to develop a means of reducing the emission of pollutants. The firm was also involved in several court cases concerning pollution from smelting works.

Vivian had strong interests in science and education. In 1818 he established a select reading society in Swansea with his friend the industrialist Lewis Weston Dillwyn, and in 1835 they were founder members of the Philosophical and Literary Society, which later became the Royal Institution of South Wales. Vivian was the institution's first vice-president. His published account of the 'Welsh process' of copper smelting and his scientific interest in copper production led to his being elected a fellow of the Royal Society in 1823. He was also an early member of the Geological Society and a founder member of the Cambrian Archaeological Association in 1846. Vivian enjoyed travelling and in 1815 met the exiled Napoleon Bonaparte on Elba while dressed in the uniform of the Cornish militia, in which he served. An account of their conversation was later published.

Though apparently shy and a poor public speaker, Vivian was involved in public affairs. He became deputy lieutenant for Glamorgan in 1820, high sheriff in 1827, and as a whig was elected MP for Swansea in 1832. Described as an assiduous worker on committees, he remained in parliament until his death. Through his political involvement, he was instrumental in establishing in Cornwall in 1830 the newspaper the *West Briton* to counter the tory *Royal Cornwall Gazette*. He served as a justice of the peace, and, as a trustee of Swansea Harbour Board, he was involved in the major development of the town's port facilities. Vivian contributed to many charitable causes in the Swansea district and, with his son Henry Hussey *Vivian, established an Anglican church and school house in Sketty.

Vivian died at Singleton Abbey, Swansea, on 10 February 1855 and was survived by his wife. EDMUND NEWELL

Sources R. A. Griffiths, *Singleton Abbey and the Vivians of Swansea* (1988) · S. Vivian, *The story of the Vivians* (1989) · A. Stewart, *Family tapestry* (1961) · R. R. Toomey, *Vivian and Sons, 1809–1924: a study of the firm in the copper and related industries* (1985) · *The Cambrian* (16 Feb 1855)
Archives NL Wales, corresp. and papers · U. Wales, Swansea · West Glamorgan Area RO
Likenesses J. H. Lynch, engraving, 1855, University College, Swansea

Vivian, Richard Hussey, first Baron Vivian (1775–1842),

Vivian, Richard Hussey, first Baron Vivian (1775–1842), army officer, was born in Truro on 28 July 1775, the eldest son of John *Vivian (1750–1826) of Truro, vice-warden of the stannaries, and Betsy (d. 1816), only daughter and coheir of Richard Cranch, vicar of St Clement's Church, near Truro. Reportedly John and Betsy Vivian had thirty-two children; among the few who survived was Richard's brother John Henry *Vivian. Richard received the name Hussey from his grandmother, a sister of Richard Hussey of Okehampton, attorney-general and MP for St Michael's. After attending Truro grammar school under Dr Cardew, a school in Lostwithiel, Harrow School, and Exeter College, Oxford (matriculated March 1790), where he spent only two terms, Vivian went in 1791 to France to learn the language. In 1793 he was articled to Jonathan Elford, a solicitor at Devonport, but he preferred a military career, and an ensign's commission in the 20th foot was procured for him on 31 July 1793. He did not join the regiment, and on 20 October he was promoted lieutenant in an independent company of foot; he exchanged into the 54th foot on 30 October.

At war in the Low Countries Vivian was promoted captain in the 28th foot on 7 May 1794, and joined Lord Moira's reinforcements for the duke of York's army in Flanders, disembarking at Ostend in June. He took part in the operations ending in York's withdrawal to Antwerp and the concentration at the end of July of his whole force at Breda for the defence of the Netherlands. He was in hot fighting at Nijmegen at the end of October, and after its evacuation and the return of York to England, he was in the action at Thiel under General Dundas in December, and at Geldermalsen under Lord Cathcart in severe weather early in January 1795, when his regiment greatly distinguished itself.

Vivian returned to England in June 1795, and was stationed at Gosport. He embarked with his regiment in the autumn in the expedition under Sir Ralph Abercromby,

Richard Hussey Vivian, first Baron Vivian (1775–1842), by
William Salter, 1837–40

but after some weeks at sea his transport was driven back
by the weather, and in August 1796 he accompanied his
regiment to Gibraltar. In August 1798 he exchanged into
the 7th light dragoons, with which he took part in the
expedition to The Helder, sailing from Deal on 13 August
1799 with the first division of the British army under Abercromby. He was present at the battles of Bergen on 19 September and 2 October, and at the battle of Alkmaar on 6
October. In December he returned to England with his
regiment. On 9 March 1800 he was promoted major, and
on 20 September 1804 lieutenant-colonel in the 25th light
dragoons; he did not join the regiment, however, and on 1
December he exchanged back into the 7th light dragoons.

The Peninsular War In October 1808 Vivian sailed in command of the 7th light dragoons for Spain; after disembarking at Corunna in the following month he joined the army
under Sir David Baird. On 5 December he marched with
the rest of the cavalry under Lord Paget from Astorga and
on 10 December he joined Sir John Moore at Toro. In the
retreat to Corunna, Vivian was frequently engaged, as his
regiment formed the rearguard from Astorga to Corunna.
On one occasion during the retreat Vivian, accompanied
by only one non-commissioned officer, collected some
600 infantry stragglers who had been attacked by French
cavalry, formed them up, and repulsed the enemy; for this
he received the thanks of Paget and Moore, who witnessed his success. After the battle of Corunna (16 January
1809) Vivian embarked with the army for England. He was

awarded the gold medal for the actions of Sahagun and
Benavente.

Having recruited its losses in the Corunna campaign,
Vivian's regiment was sent to Ireland in 1810. While there
he was promoted colonel in the army (20 February 1812)
following appointment as aide-de-camp to the prince
regent (March 1811). In March 1812 he was appointed
equerry to the prince. In the spring of 1813 he returned
with his regiment to England, and in August he sailed
with it for Spain, landing towards the end of the month at
Bilbao. In September he joined Lord Edward Somerset's
brigade at Olite. He was present at the battle of the Nivelle
on 10 November, and was later made a colonel on the staff
to command a cavalry brigade (consisting of the 10th and
14th light dragoons) of Hill's division, which was posted
between Usterits and Cambo on the River Nive. Vivian was
in command of Hill's cavalry at the passage of the Nive on
9 December and in the fighting that took place on the succeeding days, and in the battle of St Pierre on 13
December.

On 1 January 1814 Vivian was transferred to the command of the cavalry brigade of General Alten's division
(consisting of the 18th light dragoons and the German
hussars) at Hasparren. He advanced with the army in the
middle of February, attacked the enemy at the Gave de
Pau on 23 February, and took part in the battle of Orthez
on 27 February, where his brigade was with the 4th and
7th divisions on the height of St Boës. His conduct in this
battle gained the approbation of Sir William Carr Beresford, and he was awarded a clasp to his gold Peninsula
medal.

On 12 March Vivian entered Bordeaux; soon afterwards
he joined Wellington in his advance on Toulouse. On 8
April he attacked a superior force of cavalry at Crois d'Or-
ade, took about 100 prisoners, and gained possession of an
important bridge over the Ers. During the action Vivian
was wounded. When the 18th light dragoons returned to
England the officers presented Vivian with a sword of
honour. Vivian's severe wound prevented him from taking further part in the campaign, and he returned to England in June, having been promoted major-general on 4
June. In January 1815 Vivian was made a KCB (military division). His promotion severed his connection with the 7th
hussars, and the officers presented him with a valuable
piece of plate. He was shortly afterwards appointed to the
command of the Sussex military district, with his headquarters at Brighton.

Waterloo and afterwards On 16 April 1815 Vivian embarked
to take command of a cavalry brigade (7th, 10th, and 18th
light dragoons) under Lord Uxbridge in Wellington's army
in Belgium. He arrived on 3 May at Ninove, where his brigade was assembled. Towards the end of May the 7th hussars were transferred from Vivian's to Sir C. Grant's brigade and replaced by the 12th hussars of the King's German Legion. On 13 June Vivian, having personally
ascertained that the French were concentrating, reported
it to headquarters. On 15 June he was at the duchess of
Richmond's ball at Brussels; he left to march on Enghien
and thence to Quatre Bras, where he arrived after a 40

mile march over bad roads just too late to assist in defeating the French attack. On 17 June Vivian's brigade assisted to cover on the left the British retreat to Waterloo, encountering a tremendous rainstorm which, however, relieved them of some pressure from the enemy. Having bivouacked in the vicinity of the forest of Soignies on the night of 17 June, his brigade was drawn up next morning in rear of the Wavre Road. It suffered little until towards the close of the last attack, as the ground on the left was such that the cavalry could not advance.

About six o'clock in the evening, ascertaining that the cavalry in the centre had suffered severely, Vivian moved his brigade from the left to the right centre of the British line, arriving most opportunely as Bonaparte was making his last and most desperate efforts. Wheeling his brigade into line close in rear of the infantry, Vivian was ready to charge directly they had retreated through his intervals. Lord Edward Somerset, with the remnant of the two heavy cavalry brigades (some 200 out of 2000), retired through Vivian's brigade, which was then for about half an hour exposed to a hot fire of shot, shell, and musketry. The presence, however, of Vivian's brigade, which was shortly afterwards followed by the brigade of Sir John Ormsby Vandeleur, inspired the infantry with fresh confidence. On the repulse of Bonaparte's two huge columns of attack by the fire of the allies, Vivian led his brigade to attack the French reserves posted close to La Belle Alliance. He charged with the 10th light dragoons (the 18th being in support and the King's German Legion in reserve), and as soon as the 10th were well mixed up with the enemy and the French making off, he galloped to the 18th. Vivian was attacked by a cuirassier, but he gave him a thrust in the neck with his left hand (his right hand was in a sling from his Peninsula wound), and his little German orderly cut the man off his horse. With the 18th light dragoons he charged the second body of cuirassiers and chasseurs, defeating them, and taking fourteen guns which had been firing at them during the movement. He then ordered the 10th to charge an infantry square, which was gallantly done, the French being cut down in their ranks, and Count Lobau, who commanded an army corps, taken prisoner. The pursuit lasted as long as it was possible to see, and Vivian bivouacked for the night at Hilaincourt.

For his services at Waterloo, Vivian, who was mentioned in dispatches, received the thanks of parliament, a KH (1816), and Austrian and Russian orders. During the occupation of France he was with his brigade in Picardy. He returned to England with the army in 1818, and was for a short time unemployed. On the disbandment of the 18th hussars on 10 September 1821 the soldiers presented him with a silver trumpet and banner purchased with part of the prize money for horses captured by the brigade at Waterloo. This trumpet was presented by the second Lord Vivian to the new regiment of 18th hussars in September 1880.

Political career and final years In 1819 Vivian was sent first to Newcastle upon Tyne because of disturbances which had occurred there, and later to Glasgow, where serious riots were expected. In 1820 he was elected a whig MP for

Truro, a town he continued to represent until 1825, and from 1825 until 20 July 1830 he was inspector-general of cavalry. On 22 June 1827 he was promoted lieutenant-general, and on the following day he received the colonelcy of the 12th or Prince of Wales's Royal lancers. From 1826 until 1831 he was MP for Windsor. He was a frequent speaker in the House of Commons, especially on military subjects. In January 1828 he was created a baronet. From 1 July 1831 until 1836 he was commander of the forces in Ireland; on taking up this appointment he retired temporarily from parliament, and was given the GCH. From 1830 to 1837 he was groom of the bedchamber to William IV, and from 1832 to 1834 he was again MP for Truro. In June 1834 he was awarded an Oxford DCL. In 1835 he declined the position of secretary at war. On 4 May 1835 he succeeded General Sir George Murray as master-general of the ordnance, and was sworn of the British privy council; he had become a member of the Irish privy council in 1831. Vivian's first marriage, on 14 September 1804, was to Eliza (d. June 1831), daughter of Philip Champion de Crespigny of Aldeburgh, Suffolk; they had daughters and two sons. His second marriage, on 10 October 1833, was to Letitia (d. January 1885), third daughter of the Revd James Agnew Webster of Ashford, co. Longford; they had one daughter.

On 29 January 1837 Vivian was transferred from the colonelcy of the 12th lancers to that of the 1st (Royal) Dragoons, and on 30 May he was given the GCB (military division). In this year he was returned to parliament as member for East Cornwall; he continued to represent it until August 1841, when he was created a peer as Baron Vivian, and took his seat in the upper house. Vivian died suddenly from 'aneurism of the heart' (GEC, *Peerage*, 2.290) at Baden-Baden on 20 August 1842. He was buried in the family vault in St Mary's, Truro, and a cenotaph of white marble was erected in the church.

Vivian was survived by his second wife. His sons from his first marriage were Charles Crespigny *Vivian [see under* Vivian, Hussey Crespigny, third Baron Vivian] and John Cranch Walker (d. 1879), captain, 11th hussars, MP for Truro, and permanent under-secretary of state for war. Vivian also had an illegitimate son, Sir Robert John Hussey *Vivian.

                 R. H. VETCH, *rev.* JAMES LUNT

Sources R. Cannon, ed., *Historical record of the seventh, or the queen's own regiment of hussars* (1842) · *Reminiscences of William Verner, 7th hussars*, ed. R. W. Verner (1965) · R. H. Vivian, 'Autobiographical memoir', in W. Scott, *Letters addressed to R. Polwhele*, ed. R. Polwhele (1832), 69–79 [Dublin, 9 March 1832] · C. H. Vivian, *Richard Hussey Vivian: a memoir* (1897) · *GM*, 2nd ser., 18 (1842), 542–4 · *Colburn's United Service Magazine*, 3 (1847), 145 · GEC, *Peerage* · J. M. Brereton, *The 7th queen's own hussars* (1975) · W. F. P. Napier, *History of the war in the Peninsula and in the south of France*, 3 vols. (1882) · *Selections from the dispatches and general orders of Field Marshall the duke of Wellington*, ed. J. Gurwood, new edn (1851)

Archives NAM, letter-books, diaries, military order books · NL Wales, corresp. | BL, corresp. with Captain Siborne, Add. MSS 34703–34707 · Lpool RO, letters to Lord Stanley · U. Durham L., corresp. with Henry George, third Earl Grey · U. Southampton L., corresp. with Lord Palmerston · W. Sussex RO, letters to duke of Richmond

Likenesses W. Salter, oils, 1837–40, NPG [*see illus.*] · J. Brown, stipple, pubd 1840, BM · G. Hayter, group portrait, oils (*The House of Commons, 1833*), NPG · Meyer, mezzotint (after portrait by Shee) ·

W. Salter, group portrait, oils (*The Waterloo Banquet at Apsley House*), Wellington Museum, London; oil study, NPG • Shee, portrait

Vivian, Sir Robert John Hussey (1802–1887), army officer, was born at Arundel, Sussex, an illegitimate son of Richard Hussey *Vivian, first Baron Vivian (1775–1842). He was brought up as one of the family, and was educated at Dr Burney's academy, Gosport, and on the continent, in part at Beauvais and Dresden. He entered the Madras army as ensign on 12 June 1819, was immediately promoted lieutenant, and served in the 10th native infantry until 1824. That year he was posted to the 18th Madras native infantry for service in Burma under Sir Archibald Campbell.

Vivian took part in the capture of Rangoon in May 1824, was made adjutant of the battalion on 4 June, and fought in several actions between 1824 and 1826 including the battle of Pagan (9 February 1826). He was promoted captain on 1 August 1825. At the end of the war he resigned the adjutancy, and went home on leave.

When Vivian returned to India in July 1827 he was appointed assistant adjutant-general of the Nagpur subsidiary force, and in May 1830 was transferred in a similar capacity to the light field division of the Hyderabad subsidiary force at Jalna. After nearly four years' furlough at home he resumed this appointment until his promotion to major on 9 December 1836. On 18 January 1837 he took command at Madras of a battalion of the 10th Madras native infantry, and shortly after accompanied it to Belgaum. In February 1841 he captured Fort Napani and received the thanks of Sir Robert Dick, the commander-in-chief, and of the governor in council at Bombay.

On 15 October 1841 Vivian was promoted lieutenant-colonel, and on 5 January 1843 was posted to the 1st Madras European regiment (later the Royal Dublin Fusiliers). From 1844 to 1847 he was on furlough, marrying in 1846 Emma (*d.* 1887), widow of Captain Gordon of the Madras army. On his return to India he commanded several native infantry regiments in succession. On 14 August 1849 he was appointed adjutant-general of the Madras army. He was promoted brevet colonel on 15 September 1851, and resigned as adjutant-general in August 1853.

Vivian returned to England in January 1854, and on 28 November was promoted major-general. In 1855 he became a director of the East India Company. Several British officers served with the Turkish army in the Crimea, among them Vivian, who was the most senior. He held the Turkish rank of lieutenant-general after joining on 25 May 1855, and during the winter of 1855–6 he occupied the Kerch peninsula with his troops. He received the thanks of the government and the first class of the Turkish order of the Mejidiye. While commanding the Turkish contingent Vivian clashed with Major-General W. F. Beatson, who was commanding bashi-bazouks. Beatson, an East India Company officer, went home angry, subsequently bringing an action against Vivian, which Vivian won.

On 22 January 1857 Vivian was made KCB, and on 21 September 1858 he was appointed a member of the new Council of India. On 30 September 1862 he was given the colonelcy of the Royal Dublin Fusiliers, was promoted lieutenant-general on 24 October 1862, and general on 22 November 1870. He was made GCB on 20 May 1871. He retired from the army in 1877 and died on 3 May that year at his residence, 10 Eaton Gardens, Hove, Sussex, his wife having died four days earlier.

R. H. VETCH, *rev.* JAMES LUNT

Sources Hart's Army List • Burke, *Gen. GB* (1887) • A. W. Kinglake, *The invasion of the Crimea*, [new edn], 9 vols. (1877–88) • Major-General Vivian [R. J. H. Vivian], *Narrative of circumstances which led to Major-General Beatson being relieved of the command of the Turkish irregular cavalry* (1860) • W. B. F. Laurie, *Sketches of some distinguished Anglo-Indians* (1875) • Fortescue, *Brit. army*, vol. 12 • Walford, *County families* (1875) • *Dod's Peerage* (1858) • CGPLA Eng. & Wales (1887)
Archives NAM, personal family and estate papers | NA Scot., letters to Lord Panmure • NAM, letters to William Codrington
Likenesses D. J. Pound, stipple (after photograph by J. Watkins), BM, NPG; repro. in *Illustrated News of the World*
Wealth at death £30,967 8s. 9d.: probate, 1 June 1887, CGPLA Eng. & Wales

Vivian, Valentine Patrick Terrell (1886–1969), intelligence officer, was born in Kensington on 17 March 1886, one of four sons and five daughters of (Thomas) Comley Vivian, a portrait painter of 80 Warwick Gardens, and his wife, Elizabeth Baly Farquhar (*b.* 1846). Comley Vivian exhibited at the Society (later Royal Society) of British Artists in 1874–5 and at the Royal Academy between 1877 and 1892. Valentine Vivian's mother, the daughter of William Farquhar, inventor and chronometer maker, was a miniaturist and, later, portrait painter who exhibited at the Royal Academy under her maiden name between 1867 and 1871, and under her married (and widowed) name between 1886 and 1918.

Like his elder brother Percy (Sylvanus Percival (1880–1958), registrar-general 1921–45, knighted 1937) Vivian was educated at St Paul's School, where he was a foundation scholar in classics; he left in 1905. Intended for a curatorship at the Victoria and Albert Museum, he went instead to India, in 1906, and joined the Indian police in the Punjab. In 1910, still in the Punjab, he was transferred to the small provincial criminal intelligence staff, under a deputy inspector-general, that had been established as a result of Sir Andrew Fraser's police commission of 1903. Vivian served in the Punjab until 1914 and, while there, married, on 14 November 1911, Mary Primrose (1890–1971), daughter of the Venerable Edmund John Warlow, archdeacon of Lahore. They had a son and a daughter.

In 1914 Vivian was appointed to the government of India's central department of criminal intelligence in Simla, as an assistant director. The department, established in 1904 as one of Curzon's reforms, co-ordinated but did not direct the work of the provincial departments of criminal intelligence. It also took an interest in seditious activity outside India. Vivian saw active service in the Indian army in Palestine and Turkey in 1918–19. He was mentioned in dispatches and appointed OBE in 1918.

By 1920 Vivian was holding an ostensibly military intelligence appointment as a major at the headquarters of the general officer commanding, allied forces, Constantinople. His post was in fact jointly sponsored by the government of India, anxious about the threat of pan-Islamism,

Valentine Patrick
Terrell Vivian
(1886–1969), by
unknown
photographer
[detail]

and by the section of the War Office known as MI1c, a label for Mansfield Cumming's Secret Service Bureau, about to become the Secret Intelligence Service (SIS). Vivian became actively involved in the latter's operations to gain intelligence on Soviet subversive activity in Turkey and Persia. His work must have been sufficiently successful to catch Cumming's eye, for he was promoted CBE in 1923, the year in which he joined SIS, one of the last officers to be personally appointed by Cumming. In his later career he was often referred to by his initials, V. V.

Reluctant to stay overseas after so long abroad, Vivian undertook a short tour of duty with the Allied Control Commission in Cologne and then returned to SIS headquarters in 1925 as head (and for many years the only officer) of section V (counter-espionage). As early as 1921 SIS had circulated annual reports on 'Bolshevism, Chinese communism and anarchism'. Under Vivian section V concentrated upon the subversive aspects of Soviet communism, in particular the clandestine activities of the Comintern. He was ideally suited to this task both by experience and temperament and brought to his post habits of meticulous casework and attention to detail acquired in India. The professional experience of Constantinople had also given him first-hand knowledge of Soviet clandestine activity. The mental discipline of a classical education may also have helped.

Later, in 1933, when Johann Heinrich deGraff (known as Jonny), a Comintern agent, offered his services to Frank Foley, the SIS representative in Berlin, Vivian was dispatched by Admiral Sinclair, Cumming's successor, to oversee the handling of the case. As deGraff moved to Manchuria, then to Shanghai, and finally to Brazil he kept Vivian, his case officer, abreast of Comintern activity. Thus by 1938 the British government was completely informed about the internal effect of Stalin's purges on the leadership of the Comintern. Furthermore deGraff's intelligence had also substantially contributed to the failure of the Comintern's 1935 armed conspiracy (orchestrated by deGraff and led by Luis Carlos Pestes) to overthrow the government of President Vargas in Brazil. This was a major success, both for SIS and for Vivian personally.

In 1939 Vivian, now fifty-three and more accustomed to

a small service run on a shoestring, handed over the expanding section V to Felix Cowgill. Thus the successes of the war-time section V, based upon the exploitation of German intelligence service communications, were achieved under Cowgill, some of whose junior officers failed to recognize Vivian's role in securing the survival of the section and the relevance of its counter-intelligence experience between the wars. Vivian was promoted to the uneasy triumvirate at the top of SIS as nominal deputy to Sinclair's successor, Sir Stewart Menzies. The other member was the acerbic Claude Dansey, cheese to Vivian's chalk and no believer in counter-intelligence.

Vivian did not have a second good war. His CMG (1947) came long after Foley's (1941) and was eclipsed by Dansey's knighthood. He retired, finally, in 1951, after a number of anomalous appointments in security policy. It is ironical that he retired just at the time that the Soviet Union had resumed its position as SIS's major opponent. The policy of attacking its intelligence apparatus, rooted in Vivian's pre-war penetration of the Comintern, led to considerable success, though it took a decade or more to re-acquire his experience and skills. In this sense Vivian was a man ahead of his time.

Vivian, in his old age, did not escape the controversy that surrounded the treachery of (Harold) 'Kim' Philby. He was attacked, with cruel hindsight, for fostering Philby's SIS career. He had known the father, St John Philby, as a self-opinionated assistant commissioner in the Punjab, and his wife had been a childhood friend of St John Philby's wife, Dora. He had thus taken an avuncular interest in the young Philby. But the defects of attitude and approach within SIS that failed to recognize the flaws in Philby or to detect their consequences were as much systemic as personal. Nevertheless the effect on Vivian made an already reserved personality more austere.

Valentine Vivian died at the War Memorial Hospital, Milford-on-Sea, on 15 April 1969. His son, John Michael Comley Vivian (1917–1979), was a member of the diplomatic service.   A. O. BLISHEN

Sources private information (2004) [H. Clerk; S. Kirkham] · R. J. Popplewell, 'British intelligence and Indian subversion: the surveillance of Indian revolutionaries in India and abroad, 1904–1920', PhD diss., U. Cam., 1988 · SIS report of 10 Aug 1921, BL OIOC, L/P&V/12/45 · SIS report of 11 June 1938, BL OIOC, L/P&V/12/144 · R. Cecil, 'Five of six at war: section V of MI6', *Intelligence and National Security*, 9/2 (1994), 345–53 · M. Smith, *Foley: the spy who saved 10,000 Jews* (1999) · *CGPLA Eng. & Wales* (1969) · *WW* (1962) · b. cert. · m. cert., BL OIOC, N/I/377/323 · d. cert.
Likenesses T. C. Vivian, oils, *c*.1894, priv. coll. · photograph, *c*.1910, repro. in C. Andrew, *Secret service* (1985) · photograph, BL OIOC [*see illus.*]
Wealth at death £9174: probate, 27 July 1969, *CGPLA Eng. & Wales*

Vizard, William (1774–1859), lawyer, born in Dursley, Gloucestershire, was the second of the six sons and four daughters of William Vizard (*d*. 1807) and his wife, Ann (*née* Phelps). Both the Vizard and the Phelps families had been well-established landowning families in Gloucestershire for a century or more. William Vizard senior was a solicitor, practising in Dursley. Two sons were articled to him and joined the Dursley firm, while William was sent to London after completing his education at school in Gloucester.

In 1790 Vizard was articled to Thomas Lewis of 12 Gray's Inn Square. Five years later he was admitted a solicitor and in 1797 he established his own practice at 7 Holborn Court. Thomas Creevey, a barrister then practising in the court of chancery, had chambers in the same building. Creevey had connections with the whig party and he became a personal client of Vizard, providing him with introductions to prominent whig lawyers and politicians, including Henry (later Lord) Brougham.

Brougham was to be a most significant influence in Vizard's life, as a client, a friend, and a patron. From 1807 until 1812 the two worked together as counsel and solicitor, presenting the case in parliament, on behalf of the merchants of Liverpool and Manchester, for the repeal of the 1807 orders in council.

Vizard soon became closely involved in whig politics. In 1812 he accompanied the distinguished whig lawyer Samuel Romilly to Bristol to seek election there—unsuccessfully in the event—and from then on he was active in the whig party machine.

In 1811 Vizard married Mary Hodges and, leasing some 30 acres of land in Dulwich from Dulwich College, he commissioned the building of Kingswood Lodge (later known as Kingswood House) where the Vizard family lived until 1831. The Vizards had two sons: William, educated at Eton College and Trinity College, Cambridge, who became a barrister and later registrar in the court of bankruptcy; and Henry Brougham, educated at Blackheath School and Trinity College, Cambridge, who became a clergyman. There were also two daughters, Frances and Caroline, the latter named after a significant client.

At some point between 1811 and 1813 Vizard was, at Brougham's suggestion, appointed solicitor to Caroline, then princess of Wales. Estranged from the prince regent, Caroline spent the years between 1814 and 1820 travelling in Europe. Vizard's work for her did not become onerous until she returned to London in June 1820 when her husband succeeded to the throne, following the death of George III in January that year.

Determined that she should not be queen, the new king, George IV, instructed the government to introduce to parliament a bill of pains and penalties to dissolve the marriage. It was Vizard's task to organize the queen's defence during the second reading of the bill in the House of Lords—known as the trial of Queen Caroline—which took place between August and November 1820. Vizard himself announced the government's withdrawal of the bill from the balcony of the House of Lords to the crowd supporting the queen. Caroline's death in August 1821 ended three years of intensive activity on her behalf by Vizard, who continued for some time to be occupied with settling her estate for her executors.

Vizard's connections with Caroline and the whigs brought him many aristocratic and wealthy clients for

whom he conducted much litigation in the court of chancery. His expertise in the court's proceedings was recognized in 1824 when he gave extensive evidence to the commission investigating the court and the delays for which it was then notorious. In the 1830s he came to be regarded similarly as an expert on parliamentary practice, particularly the committee procedures for private bills.

When Henry Brougham became lord chancellor in 1830, Vizard was appointed to his private office as secretary of bankrupts, the first solicitor ever to hold the office. Surviving evidence (in the Brougham papers) suggests that he played a significant role in the reform of the bankruptcy system carried out by Brougham. Vizard continued to hold the post of secretary of bankrupts in succeeding whig administrations, from 1835 to 1841 and from 1846 to 1852. He was also, for a time, solicitor to the secretary of state for the Home Office, combining all these official appointments with a large professional practice.

'Great zeal, promptitude and ability' were the qualities attributed to Vizard by his obituarist (in the *Solicitors' Journal*) and it seems that he was also not lacking in business sense. In the 1830s he bought the Hoyland Hall estate, near Sheffield, from the earl of Mulgrave (a whig associate and a friend) and in the 1840s Vizard was instrumental in the development there of the Hoyland Silkstone colliery. In 1831 he sold the family's Dulwich home and bought a house and estate at Little Faringdon, Oxfordshire. After the death of his first wife in 1833, he married his second wife, Mary Cipriani, who outlived him; there was one child, a daughter named Anne, of this marriage. Vizard was professionally active until the early 1850s, managing his practice and being involved with the early development of the Law Society. In retirement he enjoyed country pursuits until his death at Little Faringdon on 15 January 1859. He was buried in his home town, Dursley, nominated through his influence in 1832 as the returning place for MPs for West Gloucestershire. The firm he founded continues to practise in London. JUDY SLINN

Sources J. Slinn, *The history of Vizards* (1997) · *Solicitors' Journal*, 3 (1858–9), 313 [obit., repr. from *Bristol Mercury*] · UCL, Brougham MSS · Royal Arch. · A. Aspinall, ed., *Three early nineteenth-century diaries* (1952) [extracts from Le Marchant, E. J. Littleton, Baron Hatherton, and E. Law, earl of Ellenborough] · *The Creevey Papers*, ed. J. Gore, rev. edn (1963); repr. (1970) · A. K. Clayton, 'Platts Common, William Vizard and the Hoyland Silkstone', *Transactions of the Hunter Archaeological Society*, 9/1 (1964) · H. P. Brougham, *The life and times of Henry, Lord Brougham*, ed. W. Brougham, 3 vols. (1871) · Dulwich Society, *Kingswood* (1985) · *CGPLA Eng. & Wales* (1859)
Archives Royal Arch., Queen Caroline MSS · UCL, letters to James Brougham
Likenesses portrait, Law Society, London
Wealth at death under £40,000: resworn probate, May 1861, *CGPLA Eng. & Wales* (1859)

Vizetelly, Frank (1830–1883?). *See under* Vizetelly, Henry Richard (1820–1894).

Vizetelly, Henry Richard (1820–1894), journalist and publisher, was born in London on 30 July 1820 and baptized at St Botolph without Bishopsgate. He was the son and

Henry Richard Vizetelly (1820–1894), by unknown photographer, 1863

grandson of printers who were members of the Stationers' Company. According to family tradition they were descended from a Venetian named Vizzetelli who settled in England towards the end of the seventeenth century. His father was James Henry Vizetelly (d. c.1838), a printer and engraver, and his mother was Mary Anne, née Vaughan, of Cheshire. From 1831 to 1835 he was taught by a Mr Wyburn at a 'classical and commercial academy' at Chislehurst. He was then apprenticed to the wood-engraver George William Bonnar. After Bonnar's death the following year he became a pupil of John Orrin Smith, another wood-engraver, and was formally apprenticed to his father at Stationers' Hall. He engraved several of John Leech's first successful drawings, *Paris Originals*, for *Bell's Life* and sold sketches of the coronation of Queen Victoria to *Bell's Life* and *The Observer*. In 1841, after coming of age, he became a partner in the printing and engraving business established by his elder brother James Thomas (1817–1897) in Peterborough Court, London. The next year, inspired by the potential benefits to the business of a weekly newspaper 'more or less filled with engravings', he assisted Herbert Ingram in founding the *Illustrated London News*, for which he wrote the prospectus. Less than twelve months later, in partnership with Andrew Spottiswoode, the queen's printer, the two Vizetelly brothers set up their own weekly paper, the *Pictorial Times*. The literary staff

included the *Punch* luminaries Douglas Jerrold, Mark Lemon, and Thackeray. Vizetelly sold his share to Spottiswoode at the end of 1844, ostensibly in order to devote himself to the expanding business of Vizetelly Brothers as printers, engravers, and publishers. The firm's most notable successes were achieved in the early 1850s, with engravings for David Bogue's editions of a number of Longfellow's poems and for the fifty or so volumes of the National Illustrated Library, published by Ingram, and with the publication of the first British edition of Harriet Beecher Stowe's *Uncle Tom's Cabin* in partnership with Salisbury and Clarke. In 1848 Vizetelly established a short-lived illustrated weekly magazine, the *Puppet Show*, and in 1849 he scored a critical and commercial coup as an author with a fictitious diary, *Four Months among the Goldfinders of Alta California*, published by Bogue, that was almost universally assumed to be authentic.

When the newspaper stamp was abolished in 1855 Vizetelly, again in partnership with Bogue, launched by far the most successful of his journals, the *Illustrated Times*, a two-penny weekly. Attracting the services of Frederick Greenwood, Robert Brough, Edmund Yates, George Augustus Sala, James Hannay, and many other up-and-coming journalists, it for a while boasted a circulation of over 200,000, double that of the *Illustrated London News*; Vizetelly claimed to have made a clear profit of £1200 from the engravings for a single issue devoted to the marriage of the princess royal in January 1858. Herbert Ingram, still the proprietor of the *Illustrated London News*, reacted to the competition from the new paper by purchasing a one-third share in 1857 and buying Vizetelly out two years later for more than £4000, but retaining him as editor for a further five years on an annual salary of £800. In May 1858 Vizetelly had started a penny weekly, the *Welcome Guest*, edited by Sala and Brough, but after losing £2000 or £3000 on this he sold it to John Maxwell, also in 1859. Despite the undoubted profitability of many of his undertakings, Vizetelly's stock of capital may have been depleted by gambling and bohemian pleasures, in which he associated for some years with Sala, the acknowledged 'king' of literary Bohemia. Sala's *Make your Game* (1860) presented a fictionalized account of their costly excursion to the roulette tables of Homburg in the autumn of 1858.

From 1865, when the *Illustrated Times* ceased publication, until the end of 1877 Vizetelly lived in Paris. For the first five years he was Paris correspondent and general representative on the continent of the *Illustrated London News*, with a salary of £800 per year, and he remained on the paper's staff for some time afterwards. He also contributed articles to the *Pall Mall Gazette*, *All the Year Round*, and *Once a Week*. He published *The Story of the Diamond Necklace*, based on Carlyle's well-known historical essay 'The Diamond Necklace', in two volumes in 1867, and a free translation of *The Man in the Iron Mask* in 1870. During the siege of Paris in 1870 both he and his seventeen-year-old son Ernest Alfred (1853–1922) were transformed into war correspondents, dispatching their sketches of the beleaguered city to the *Illustrated London News* by 'balloon-post';

to ensure that at least one would reach its destination, several photographs of each were sent by successive posts. Vizetelly subsequently retreated to England for a time, but his son, who remained in France throughout the war, was created a chevalier of the Légion d'honneur for the gallantry he displayed. He later collaborated with his father on a two-volume account of the siege, *Paris in Peril* (1882), and accompanied him on many of his assignments as the special correspondent of the *Illustrated London News* in various parts of Europe after the war. One of these, to Berlin in 1872, bore fruit in the book *Berlin under the New Empire* (2 vols., 1879). Both father and son made themselves authorities on wine during their long residence in France, Henry Vizetelly producing four monographs on the subject between 1875 and 1880 and serving as a wine juror at the Vienna Exhibition of 1873 and the Paris Exhibition of 1878.

On his return to England in 1878 Vizetelly resumed his old business of publishing after a break of nearly a quarter of a century. Apart from relatively innocuous books by old friends such as Sala, the output of his new firm, Vizetelly & Co., consisted chiefly of translations of French and Russian novelists, including Flaubert, Daudet, Dostoyevsky, and Tolstoy. Many of them affronted Victorian notions of propriety, which Vizetelly also challenged explicitly by publishing George Moore's *Literature at Nurse, or, Circulating Morals: a Polemic on Victorian Censorship* (1885), and by issuing cheap unexpurgated editions of The Best Plays of the Old Dramatists (the Mermaid Series). But it was above all his publication, between 1884 and 1888, of translations of seventeen novels by Emile Zola that brought him notoriety for the first time in his life and turned him into a reluctant martyr, one of the early heroes of the fight against oppressive literary censorship which culminated in the lifting of the ban on *Lady Chatterley's Lover* in 1960. On 31 October 1888 he was fined £100 for publishing *The Soil*, a translation of *La terre*, which the solicitor-general Sir Edward Clarke branded a work of 'bestial obscenity'. To avoid a heavier penalty Vizetelly, on his counsel's advice, had pleaded guilty and promised to withdraw all his Zola translations from sale, although only a few weeks earlier he had issued a pamphlet, *Extracts Principally from English Classics*, to demonstrate that suppressing Zola's works would logically entail 'bowdlerising ... the greatest Works in English Literature' (BL, private case 29a.45). By 30 May 1889 he had released the offending translations, minimally expurgated by his son Ernest, and was back in court. This time, again pleading guilty on counsel's advice, he was sentenced to three months' imprisonment and forfeited bail of £200. *The Times* interpreted his plea of guilty as an admission that profit had been his only motive. By now he was sixty-nine and neither his health nor his finances recovered in the few years of life remaining to him after he had served his sentence. He died at Heatherlands, Farnham, on 1 January 1894. Just before his death he had the satisfaction of reading that Sir Edward Clarke's successor as solicitor-general, Sir Charles Russell, had led the applause for Zola when he read a paper at a meeting of the Institute of Journalists in September 1893.

Vizetelly had married Ellen Elizabeth, *née* Pollard, the daughter of John Pollard MD, on 30 March 1844; she died about 1857. On 6 February 1861 he had married Elizabeth Ann, *née* Ansell, of Brompton, who died in 1874. The well-known author and lexicographer Frank Horace Vizetelly (1864–1938) was a child of his second marriage. Two of the sons of his first marriage, not only Ernest Alfred but also Edward Henry (1847–1903), won some fame as war correspondents, as did one of the sons of his elder brother James, Montague Vizetelly (1846–1897). But in this sphere the best-known member of the family was Henry's youngest brother, **Frank Vizetelly** (1830–1883?), journalist, who was born at 76 Fleet Street, London, on 26 September 1830, educated at Boulogne, along with Gustave Doré and Blanchard Jerrold, and first employed by Henry on the *Illustrated Times*, of which he became Paris correspondent until his appointment as editor of *Le Monde Illustré* in 1857. Having returned to England in 1859 he served as war correspondent first for the *Illustrated Times*, then for the *Illustrated London News*, and later for other papers. He reported on the battle of Solferino (1859), Garibaldi's Sicilian and Neapolitan campaigns (1860), the American Civil War, the Austro-Prussian War of 1866, and the Carlist uprising in Spain in the 1870s. Finally, on 4 November 1883, he disappeared in the Sudan, near Kashgil, while covering the fighting between an Egyptian army under the command of William Hicks (Hicks Pasha) and the forces of the Mahdi. His name appears on a memorial to war correspondents in the crypt of St Paul's Cathedral.

THOMAS SECCOMBE, rev. P. D. EDWARDS

Sources H. Vizetelly, *Glances back through seventy years: autobiographical and other reminiscences*, 2 vols. (1893) • *The life and adventures of George Augustus Sala*, 2 vols. (1895) • *The Times* (1 Nov 1888) • *The Times* (31 May 1889) • *The Times* (2 Jan 1894) • F. L. Bullard, *Famous war correspondents* (1914) • E. H. Yates, *Edmund Yates: his recollections and experiences*, 2 vols. (1884) • Boase, *Mod. Eng. biog.* • *WWW, 1916–28* • *WWW, 1929–40* • d. cert. • m. certs.
Likenesses photograph, 1863, NPG [*see illus.*] • wood-engraving (after portrait?), BM; repro. in *ILN* (14 May 1892), 580

Vizir Ali (d. 1817). *See under* Oudh, nawab wazirs of (act. 1754–1814).

Voce, William (1909–1984), cricketer, was born at Annesley Woodhouse, Nottinghamshire, on 8 August 1909, the eldest of six children (four daughters and two sons) of Henry Voce, coalminer, of Annesley Woodhouse, and his wife, Kate Leatherland. He was educated at Annesley Woodhouse School to the age of thirteen, when, on the death of his father, he assumed responsibility for the family and went to work in the local colliery.

Fred Barratt (1894–1947), the Nottinghamshire and England fast bowler, saw the young Voce playing casual local cricket and was sufficiently impressed to recommend him to Nottinghamshire, who took him on the county staff before his sixteenth birthday. Voce's main ability was as a left-arm bowler, in several different styles at varying periods of his career. Like most lads, he aspired to bowl fast but, on joining the Nottinghamshire staff, under guidance, he bowled orthodox finger-spin from round the wicket well enough to be given a trial for the first eleven in

June 1927. Still short of his eighteenth birthday, he took five wickets for 36 in the first Gloucestershire innings: and with thirty-six wickets at 27.16 retained his place in the Nottinghamshire side which finished as runners-up in the county championship. In the following season, however, he changed to fast left-arm round-the-wicket swing, with some success. Then, in 1929, top of the Nottinghamshire bowling with 107 wickets at 16.03, when the team won the county championship, he was the leading pace bowler in the national averages. In that year (on 5 September) he married Elsie Emma Soar (b. 1907/8), of Hucknall, Nottinghamshire, daughter of William Soar, a labourer; they had one son, who died in childhood, and a daughter.

Some experts regretted Voce's change of bowling method, believing he might have become a great slow left-armer. On the other hand, tall and immensely strongly built, he was probably the finest left-arm fast bowler in the world in the 1930s. He was, too, a forcing right-hand batsman who in 1933 scored 1020 runs; while his powerful, loose left arm made him a valuable and accurate thrower from the deep field.

Voce's penetrative county bowling partnership with Harold Larwood led to them being selected for the unfancied MCC team which D. R. Jardine took to Australia in 1932–3. They were the main instruments of a strategy which employed fast leg theory directed particularly against Donald Bradman, whom Jardine regarded, correctly, as the likeliest Australian match-winner. In this tactic Voce bowled fast left-arm over the wicket, took six wickets in the first test match, which England won, and five in the second, which they lost. He was injured for the third test, missed the fourth, and took three in the fifth; England won by four to one what became known as the 'bodyline' series. The repercussions of those matches were such that Jardine, Larwood, and Voce did not play in the tests of 1934 with Australia. Larwood and Voce, too, declared themselves unavailable for tests in 1935.

In 1936, however, Voce made himself available; he played once against India, and went with G. O. Allen's 1936–7 MCC party to Australia. He reverted to fast left-arm round the wicket and reached his bowling peak. In the first test he took six for 41 in the first innings; in the second, after rain, he took the first three Australian wickets—O'Brien, Bradman, and McCabe—for one run (in all, four for 16). England won. Voce had seven for 76 in the second test, which England also won, and five for 169 in the third, which they lost. Unfit, and picked against the captain's wish for the fourth test, Voce took one for 135; in the fifth he took three for 123. England lost both tests, and the rubber with them.

Immediately after the Second World War, Voce's four for 7 in a test trial took him again to Australia, in 1946–7. Now, though, he was thirty-seven and a knee injury had robbed his bowling of its fire. Unsuccessful in his two tests, in 1947 he reverted to slow left-arm spin and in June retired from county cricket. Strong-looking, dark, and ruggedly handsome, he became a valuable and popular coach for Nottinghamshire and the MCC. He was one of the few major England cricketers who played often against Australia—in his case eleven times—but never once in England. Altogether he made twenty-seven test appearances, in which he took 98 wickets at 27.88; in all cricket, he took 1558 wickets at 23.08 and made 7583 runs (with four centuries) at 19.19. Voce died in the university hospital at Nottingham on 6 June 1984.

JOHN ARLOTT, rev.

Sources private information (2004) · personal knowledge (2004) · *The Times* (7 June 1984) · *The Times* (18 June 1984) · b. cert. · m. cert. · *CGPLA Eng. & Wales* (1984)
Archives FILM BFI NFTVA, sports footage
Wealth at death under £40,000: probate, 26 July 1984, *CGPLA Eng. & Wales*

Voelcker, (John Christopher) Augustus (1822–1884), agricultural chemist, was born on 24 September 1822 at Frankfurt am Main, the fifth son (in a family of seven sons and one daughter) of Frederick Adolphus Voelcker, a Frankfurt merchant. His father died in 1833 and early ill health postponed the commencement of his formal schooling until the age of twelve. However, with the energy which Voelcker evinced throughout his career, by the age of sixteen he was sufficiently well educated to gain employment as a pharmacist's assistant at Frankfurt; in 1842 he was appointed as a manager of a pharmacy business at Schaffhausen. In 1844 he entered the University of Göttingen where he studied chemistry under Professor Wöhler; he also attended Liebig's influential lectures at Giessen. He was awarded the degree of doctor of philosophy at Göttingen in 1846, the subject of his doctoral dissertation being the composition of tortoiseshell. He then investigated compounds of manganese and other metals and published the results of his laboratory experiments in German and Dutch scientific periodicals. Wöhler recommended him to Professor Gerrit Jan Mulder at Utrecht; Voelcker became an assistant and aided him in the preparation of *Chemische Untersuchungen* (1852). Mulder was much interested in the study of physiological chemistry, especially in its relation to vegetable and animal production, and this work had a considerable influence on Voelcker's later career.

In February 1847 Voelcker went to Edinburgh as assistant to J. F. W. Johnston, then chemist to the Agricultural Chemistry Society of Scotland. He lectured on Johnston's behalf at Durham University, a remarkable transition for a native German speaker. There was scarcely a trace of a foreign idiom in his writing, which was noted for its clarity, although this facility can have been gained only by great determination. While in Scotland he formed a close friendship with George Wilson (1818–1859), the regius professor of technology at Edinburgh. It was at this time that he first came into contact with farmers and their agricultural requirements.

In August 1849 Voelcker was appointed professor of chemistry at the Royal Agricultural College, Cirencester (founded in 1844), where he began a series of field experiments and extensive laboratory investigations. In 1852 he married Susanna Wilhelm of Frankfurt; they had four sons and a daughter. The eldest son, George, died at the age of twenty-three in 1876 from diphtheria contracted while training in hospital as a medical student. In 1855 Voelcker was appointed consulting chemist to the Royal Bath and West Society and two years later he gained the same position at the Royal Agricultural Society of England.

Voelcker left Cirencester for London in 1863 and commenced private practice as a consulting chemist at a laboratory which he established in Salisbury Square. His advice was in constant demand on technical and legal inquiries, especially those in connection with sewage, water and gas supply, river pollution, and agricultural holdings. He was one of the jurors of the international exhibition of 1862, of the fisheries exhibition of 1883, and of the health exhibition of 1884. In 1870 he was elected a fellow of the Royal Society. He was one of the founders and an early vice-president of the Institute of Chemistry of Great Britain and Ireland, established in 1877.

It was through his work for the Royal Agricultural Society of England that Voelcker made his greatest mark. Every half-yearly volume of the society's *Journal* between 1857 and 1884 contains one or more of his extensive contributions. He carried out a large range of agricultural investigations for the society and, between 1865 and 1884, completed 13,068 chemical analyses for its members. At a time when farmers were often sold substandard or adulterated samples of fertilizers or feeding-stuffs the publication of Voelcker's impartial and meticulous analyses—which on occasion led to litigation—was an important way in which quality guarantees could be achieved. The high regard in which he was held in the agricultural community was marked by his election to the chairmanship of the London Farmers' Club in 1875; no man, it was said, 'ever more happily united "Science with Practice"' (*Farmer's Magazine*).

Voelcker's experimental work and writings on agricultural chemistry were marked by analytical precision and thoroughness. Although he did not write a comprehensive textbook and made no revolutionary discoveries, his work on the composition of farmyard manures and fertilizers, soil processes, the feeding of animals, milk, and dairy practice contributed significant increments of knowledge to agricultural science.

Voelcker took a considerable interest in religious movements and was an active participant in the affairs of the British and Foreign Bible Society. He died of heart disease on 5 December 1884 at his London home, 39 Argyll Road, Kensington. Two of his sons, John Augustus and William, continued the consulting practice that he had established. The former also succeeded him as the Royal Agricultural Society of England's consulting chemist and occupied the position until 1938. Indeed, a member of the Voelcker family continued to act in that capacity until 1976—an outstanding example of family continuity in professional service.   NICHOLAS GODDARD

Sources *Farmer's Magazine*, 3rd ser., 34 (1868) • J. H. Gilbert, *Journal of the Royal Agricultural Society of England*, 2nd ser., 21 (1885), 308–21 • *Bell's Weekly Messenger* (8 Dec 1884) • *Mark Lane Express* (8 Dec 1884) • *Agricultural Gazette* (8 Dec 1884) • E. J. Russell, *A history of agricultural science in Great Britain, 1620–1954* (1966) • N. Goddard, *Harvests of change: the Royal Agricultural Society of England, 1838–1988* (1988), 96–9
Likenesses J. B. Hunt, stipple, pubd 1869 (after photograph), NPG • engraving (after photograph), repro. in *Farmer's Magazine*
Wealth at death £84,320 10s. 8d.: probate, 13 March 1885, CGPLA Eng. & Wales

Voerst, Robert van (1597–1636), engraver, was born in Deventer, Holland, on 8 September 1597. He was taught engraving by Crispijn de Passe the elder in Utrecht, and was a fellow pupil with Joachim von Sandrart in the Utrecht Academy in 1625–6. He had arrived in London by 1627, when he engraved a portrait of the earl of Lindsey, after a painting by Georg Geldorp. Since all his early English prints are after Geldorp, it is reasonable to conclude that it was Geldorp, whose father had been a close associate of de Passe in Cologne, who brought him to London.

By 1630 Voerst had begun to work for the London publisher William Webb, for whom he made a series of at least five plates, including one of Philip Herbert, the future fourth earl of Pembroke. His breakthrough came the following year, when Charles I commissioned him to engrave Gerrit van Honthorst's portrait of his sister Elizabeth of Bohemia; the link was probably through Pembroke. The success of this led to a sequence of important commissions. For Pembroke he engraved a large plate of the third earl, his recently deceased brother, while for Charles he engraved the emperor Otho, one of the set of the twelve Caesars by Titian that had been purchased from Mantua in 1628. The plates of this and of Elizabeth are both recorded in van der Doort's inventory of Charles's collection.

Voerst's greatest work followed in 1634, when he engraved on a large scale the double portrait of Charles and Henrietta Maria painted two years earlier, shortly after Van Dyck's arrival in London. This is a masterpiece, and explains why Voerst was the only engraver working in London with whom Van Dyck was willing to collaborate; none of the numerous other painted portraits of English sitters was engraved in London during Van Dyck's lifetime. The plate was published by Voerst himself with a royal privilege, and must be linked with his appointment as engraver to the king, a position that was newly created for him, probably in 1635. Voerst was working on another large plate after a marble bust of Charles when he died, a victim of the plague of 1636.

About thirty plates by Voerst are known, all made in London and all portraits, as well as a set of twenty-one animal pattern sheets that was posthumously reissued by Crispijn de Passe. At least seven plates were made for Van Dyck, and were intended to form part of the series of portraits now known as the *Iconography* (*c*.1632–1644), although only four were in fact included in the first edition. Among them was Voerst's own portrait, showing him holding a rolled-up sheet of paper, engraved after a drawing by Van Dyck that is now in the Louvre. In 1635 the eighteen-year-old Gerard ter Borch, his sister's stepson, came to work in Voerst's studio in London, and made a portrait drawing of the engraver that is now in the Rijksmuseum.   ANTONY GRIFFITHS

Sources F. G. Waller, *Biographisch woordenboek van Noord Nederland-sche graveurs* (1938), 347 · J. von Sandrart, *Teutsche Academie der edelen Bau-Bild und Mahlerey-Künste* (1675), 2.360 · PRO, LC3/33 · C. Schuckmann, *Hollstein's Dutch and Flemish etchings, engravings and woodcuts, c. 1450–1700*, ed. D. de Hoop Scheffer, 41 (1992), 239–68 · A. Griffiths and R. A. Gerard, *The print in Stuart Britain, 1603–1689* (1998), 81–8 [exhibition catalogue, BM, 8 May – 20 Sept 1998] · 'Abraham van der Doort's catalogue of the collections of Charles I', ed. O. Millar, *Walpole Society*, 37 (1958–60), 148
Archives PRO, LC3/33
Likenesses G. ter Borch, drawing, 1635, Rijksmuseum, Amsterdam · A. Van Dyck, drawing, Louvre · R. van Voerst, line engraving (after A. Van Dyck), BM; repro. in *Centum icones* (1645)

Vogel, Sir Julius (1835–1899), premier of New Zealand, was born on 24 February 1835 in London, the second of three children and the elder son of Albert Leopold Vogel, a Dutch Christian, and his wife, Phoebe, the daughter of Alexander and Sophia Isaac. His mother's Jewish merchant family had lived in England from at least the mid-eighteenth century. His father was estranged from the family after the birth of the third child, and, after his younger brother died in 1841, he moved with his mother and his sister, Frances, into the large, comfortable Isaac home in New Cross Road, south London. His education was typical of the commercial middle class. Until the age of eleven he was taught by governesses at home. This was followed by a year at the junior school of University College in Gower Street, two years boarding at a Jewish school in Ramsgate, and a final year back at Gower Street. In 1850 he joined the family firm, already overstocked with uncles and cousins, only too aware that his future as a young clerk was precarious. The death of his mother in August 1851 determined that he would have to seek his fortune elsewhere, and he began to attend lectures at the newly opened Government School of Mines in London. A year later, with some expertise in assaying, he sailed for the Victorian goldfields.

Vogel was only seventeen when he arrived in Melbourne. He first set up as an assayer, and then went into goldfield storekeeping and gold purchasing. By mid-1854 he was based in Maryborough and travelled to the nearby goldfields with pharmaceuticals and other supplies. Two years later he pitched his tent in the main street of Dunolly and became a journalist. He began by contributing articles to the Melbourne *Argus* and then became editor of the Dunolly *Advertiser*. His career in newspapers collapsed with the decline of the goldfields in 1861, and he stood for a seat in the Victorian parliament. After being heavily defeated, he left for Otago, New Zealand, where gold discoveries had recently been reported.

Vogel settled in Dunedin, and in November 1861 became co-founder and editor of the *Otago Daily Times*, New Zealand's first daily newspaper. With a staff including Ebenezer Fox, later secretary to the cabinet, and Benjamin Farjeon, a future novelist, *The Times* became the leading newspaper in the largest and wealthiest town in the country. Vogel used it as a springboard first into community affairs and then into local politics. In June 1863 he was elected to the Otago provincial council and in November

1866 he became head of the provincial executive, occupying the post of provincial treasurer until May 1869.

Election to the provincial council was followed in September 1863 by victory in a by-election to the house of representatives. In parliament Vogel quickly demonstrated his outspoken, argumentative nature and his financial ability. When William Fox took over the leadership of government in June 1869, he recruited Vogel as his colonial treasurer.

On 19 March 1867 Vogel married Mary, the daughter of William and Emily Clayton, his Dunedin neighbours. William Clayton was a highly regarded architect. Mary Clayton was eighteen at the time of her marriage, a seemingly quiet but forceful young woman who bore four children between 1868 and 1875, and strongly supported her husband's political and social ambitions. Vogel adored her, as he did his sister who came to live with them, and always attempted to provide his family with the material comforts and domestic warmth that he felt he had missed through his youth and early career.

The Vogels had planned to move to Auckland after the parliamentary session of 1869, and Vogel had arranged to become editor of the *Southern Cross*, having lost his control of *The Times* in 1868. The colonial treasurership ended this plan, although he did for a while own the *Cross*. Vogel won Auckland constituencies in the elections of 1871 and 1875, but henceforth was never really settled in New Zealand. The family lived in Wellington during the parliamentary sessions but spent long periods out of the country on political business until Vogel's appointment to London in 1876. Although he returned to New Zealand on business in 1882–3 and was back in politics between 1884 and 1888, most of the rest of his life after 1876 was spent in England.

Vogel was at the height of his political powers in the first half of the 1870s. As a representative of Otago on the South Island, he had viewed the wars of the 1860s between Europeans and Maori as a northern matter. He had then advocated that the South Island separate from the North to pursue its economic development unencumbered by the disruption of fighting and war debts. However, by 1869 he recognized that European control and progress required a unified colony, increased migration and settlement, and a modern transport and communications infrastructure. His financial statement of 1870 revived the colonizing creed of rapid progress through public expenditure by outlining a ten-year plan for government-financed and -managed immigration and public works. During the following years 'Vogelism' brought more than 100,000 immigrants into the colony to settle on the land and work in construction and domestic service, and provided the country with a network of roads, railways, and bridges. Vogel became the dominant figure in politics. When the provincial governments, previously responsible for settlement and development, created political difficulties for the operation of his policy, he proposed the abolition of the provincial councils in the North Island. By 1875 parliament had agreed that all the provincial councils should go, making the central government supreme. Vogel held at various stages the offices of colonial treasurer, postmaster-general, commissioner of customs, telegraph commissioner, and minister of immigration. He was premier from April 1873 until July 1875 and then again from February to August 1876.

Vogel recognized that New Zealand needed to increase its exports, and he worked to establish trade with Australia, the United States, and the Pacific islands. He spent many months in Australia, and visited the United States to negotiate steamship services to New Zealand. He also arranged contracts to link New Zealand and Australia by cable. He returned to England on political and financial missions in 1871 and 1874–5, assisted in raising loans for the colony, and discussed defence and British policy in the Pacific. In 1872 he was rewarded with a CMG and, in 1875, a KCMG.

In August 1876, with the country on the verge of a financial recession and his own political support much eroded, Vogel resigned the premiership and accepted appointment as agent-general in London. He was in poor health and finances, and intended to use the colonial appointment to establish a career in business or politics in England. In the 1880 general election he stood as a Conservative for the borough of Penryn and Falmouth and shared in the party's massive defeat. His official duties provided him with valuable contacts, but when his private financial interests began to conflict with those of the government he was required to resign.

Vogel spent the early 1880s promoting a range of speculative land, electricity, railway, and telecommunication companies. All were high risk and under capitalized and damaged his business reputation. In 1884 he returned to New Zealand and, hoping to save one of his companies through government intervention, contested a seat in parliament. The country, suffering badly from depressed export prices and government retrenchment, welcomed him back. He took a seat in the house as member for Christchurch North and became colonial treasurer in a government led by Robert Stout. Unable to effect a financial recovery, this government was thrown out of office in 1887. Vogel retained his seat and was leader of the opposition for a year. However, after the 1888 parliamentary session the Vogels returned to England for good.

Although he believed that he had given the best years of his life to New Zealand, Vogel's real commitment was to the notion of a Greater Britain. He envisaged New Zealand as the Britain of the south seas and pursued colonial expansion in the Pacific, urging Britain to annex strategic and potential trading partners among the islands. He was an early advocate of imperial federation, and supported a federal parliament and collective responsibility exercised by states bound in an indissoluble union.

Vogel published some thirty or more articles on the politics of New Zealand and the empire, most of which appeared in the *Nineteenth Century* and the *Fortnightly Review*. He edited the 1875 *Official New Zealand Handbook* and in 1889 published a novel, *Anno Domini, or, Woman's Destiny*.

The latter prophesied a united Anglo-American empire, ruled by women and free of poverty.

Rather short in stature, Vogel was portly, even as a young man. His bachelor period on the goldfields gave him a penchant for pipes and cigars, alcohol, and oysters, which took their toll on his health. By his forties he suffered from gout and by the 1880s could barely walk. He wore big woollen slippers, travelled with a wheelchair, and always needed assistance. His increasing deafness made his participation in parliamentary debate difficult. Lines of pain are etched on his face in later photographs.

Perhaps because of the rejections of childhood and youth, Vogel cherished an overwhelming desire for public success and recognition. He was an extrovert, impulsive, generous, and headstrong. Some of his contemporaries were repelled by his brash abuses of political power and his disregard for propriety, while they also recognized his ability and personal charm. Few could separate the man from his policies, and his reputation fluctuated with economic cycles. He was often blamed for the severity of the 1880s depression, and then, in the late 1890s, was seen as the man who had provided the country with the infrastructure necessary for an export-led recovery. The Keynesian view that depression could be cured by government expenditure cast Vogel as a visionary economic thinker.

Vogel's life ended in disappointment and poverty. Confined to a book-lined room in his home, Hillersdon, in East Molesey, Surrey, from the early 1890s, he worried over his family and their future. In 1893 his second son was killed in action against the Matabele (Ndebele). Mary Vogel was so concerned by his depression and financial worries that she turned to New Zealand friends for help. In his last years the New Zealand government provided him with a small sinecure. He died at home of a heart attack on 12 March 1899 and was buried three days later at the Jewish cemetery at Willesden.   RAEWYN DALZIEL

Sources R. Dalziel, *Julius Vogel, business politician* (1986) · R. M. Burdon, *The life and times of Sir Julius Vogel* (1948) · d. cert.
Archives NL NZ, Turnbull L. | Canterbury University, Christchurch, New Zealand, Hall MSS · NL NZ, Turnbull L., Hall MSS · NL NZ, Turnbull L., McLean MSS · NL NZ, Turnbull L., Stout MSS
Likenesses photograph, 1866, NL NZ, Turnbull L. · photograph, 1871, NL NZ, Turnbull L. · photograph, 1876–9, NL NZ, Turnbull L. · photograph, 1880–89, NL NZ, Turnbull L. · wood-engraving, NPG; repro. in *ILN* (3 July 1875)
Wealth at death £178 5s. 9d.: probate, 31 May 1899, CGPLA Eng. & Wales

Voigt, Frederick Augustus (1892–1957), journalist and author, was born on 9 May 1892 in Hampstead, London, the fourth of the five children of Ludwig Reinhard Voigt, a wine merchant, and his wife, Helene Mathilde Elizabeth Hoffmann. His family originated from Germany, where both of his parents had been born. He was educated at Haberdashers' Aske's School, Hampstead, and at Birkbeck College, London. In 1915 he obtained a first-class honours degree in modern languages from London University. In the following year he was called up and served for nearly three years in the army, two of them on the western front.

After demobilization he turned his diaries and letters into one of the earliest war books, *Combed Out* (1920).

In May 1919 Voigt joined the staff of the *Manchester Guardian* under the editorship of C. P. Scott, and in February 1920 he was sent to Germany, where he first worked as assistant to J. G. Hamilton. Shortly after his arrival he got an immediate impression of the grave dangers arising out of the unstable political situation of the Weimar republic. While reporting on the communist uprising in the Ruhr area after the Kapp putsch he was arrested and maltreated by Free Corps men.

After Hamilton's removal Voigt found himself on his own as the main correspondent of his paper in Berlin. In his political outlook a typical left-wing journalist of the inter-war years, he had excellent contacts to a number of prominent representatives of the German left. These connections enabled him to make his sensational disclosures about the hitherto secret collaboration of the Reichswehr with Soviet military authorities which sparked off a major government crisis in Germany in December 1926. Though based in Berlin, he covered many trouble spots in central and eastern Europe. His special endeavour was directed towards the public exposure of political repression and terror. Especially famous became his merciless description of the ruthless 'pacification' of Ukraine by the Polish Pilsudski regime in 1930.

Voigt was one of the first foreign correspondents to draw public attention to the true nature of national socialism. As early as 1930 he had come to regard Hitler's movement as a fundamental threat to European civilization. For obscure reasons he was transferred from Berlin to Paris a few weeks before Hitler became chancellor on 30 January 1933. Nevertheless German affairs remained at the centre of his journalistic work throughout the 1930s. With the willing support of German émigrés and a Swiss agent he built up a confidential news network providing him with authentic material about Hitler's regime. This 'German service' of the *Guardian* soon became a highly reputable source of reliable information about Nazi Germany.

Voigt's transfer from Paris to London in September 1934 did not stop this anti-Nazi engagement. His new position as the first diplomatic correspondent of his paper carried a wide range of duties. But it also brought better access to various diplomatic sources. He now became a confidant of Vansittart, the influential permanent under-secretary at the Foreign Office. Even the troubles of his private life could not affect his commitment to what he regarded as his journalistic duty. In 1935 he was divorced by his first wife, Margaret Lola Goldsmith, whom he had married in 1926. She was the daughter of Bernard Goldsmith, an American businessman, and was herself a writer; Voigt had collaborated with her in writing a biography, *Hindenburg* (1930). In 1935 he married Janka, daughter of Oskar Radnitz, formerly wife of Johannes Heinrich Dransmann, with whom he had one daughter. This marriage was dissolved, and in 1944 he married Annie Rachel, daughter of the Revd Hugh Frederic Bennet.

Meanwhile Voigt had begun to reverse his entire view of life and politics. In 1933 he was deeply disillusioned with the German left, which he charged with having capitulated ignominiously to Hitler's onslaught. On the other hand he came to regard Christianity as the only effective counter-force against the overwhelming power of a regime founded on a pseudo-religious ideology. As a consequence he veered away from the scientific materialism of his earlier years to a deeply Christian attitude. Influenced in part by Karl Barth's theology, he began to see national socialism itself as an essentially anti-Christian phenomenon. This theological view is fully though not very systematically worked out in *Unto Caesar*, Voigt's most important book on current affairs, which he brought out in April 1938. Marxism and national socialism are presented here as competing variants of a novel phenomenon, as revolutionary secular religions arising from the arrogant endeavour of man to transform religious promises directly into worldly reality.

Voigt's political reorientation led to a gradual estrangement from the positions for which the *Manchester Guardian* stood. His time-consuming job as the paper's diplomatic correspondent did not prevent him from taking on the editorship of the Conservative monthly the *Nineteenth Century and After* in 1938, a position he kept until 1946. In January 1940 Voigt left the *Guardian* to join the department of propaganda in enemy countries, where he served for a while as German adviser to Britain's psychological warfare effort.

At the end of the war Voigt was a prominent representative of a current of political thinking which George Orwell polemically but aptly called neo-toryism (*Collected Essays, Journalism and Letters*, 3, 1970, 422). As expounded in *Pax Britannica* (1949), Voigt regarded the maintenance of British imperial power as an indispensable precondition for a stable international peace. He followed events in south-eastern Europe with particular interest. Between 1946 and 1950 he visited Greece several times to study the communist revolutionary threat on the spot. The fruit of these journeys was another study on international affairs entitled *The Greek Sedition* (1949).

In his remaining days Voigt was a frequent contributor to various periodicals. Seeing himself as a Conservative writer in the tradition of Burke, he was mainly concerned with the deeply pernicious influence of utopian thinking culminating in the revolutionary ideologies of his time. In his heyday Voigt was a celebrity among the British foreign correspondents. Owing to his incorruptible veracity and his philosophical and theological erudition, he was better able than most of his contemporaries to face the stark reality of the newly established terroristic regimes in Europe. His main work *Unto Caesar* must be seen as a pioneering study on the nature and the similarities of totalitarian ideologies. By comprehending Marxism and national socialism as genuinely religious phenomena Voigt introduced an interpretative concept which figures prominently in some later theories of totalitarianism.

Voigt's fragile appearance could easily obscure the fact that he was a man of immense moral and physical courage. His articles were written and their content collected with complete disregard for public opinion and his own safety. Burning sincerity and heroic idealism were indeed constant traits running through all his radical changes of philosophy. Voigt died in hospital in Guildford, Surrey, on 7 January 1957.　　　　　　　　　　　MARKUS HUTTNER

Sources DNB · Manchester Guardian (9 Jan 1957) · The Times (9 Jan 1957) · M. Huttner, Totalitarismus und säkulare Religionen (1999) · M. Huttner, Britische Presse und nationalsozialistischer Kirchenkampf (1995) · F. R. Gannon, The British press and Germany, 1936–1939 (1971) · D. Ayerst, Guardian: biography of a newspaper (1971) · R. Cockett, Twilight of truth (1989) · C. Pütter, 'Deutsche Emigranten und britische Propaganda', Exil in Großbritannien, ed. G. Hirschfeld (1983), 106–37 · R. Albrecht, 'F. A. Voigts Deutschlandberichte im Manchester Guardian (1930–1935)', Publizistik, 31 (1986), 108–17 · A. Schwarz, Die Reise ins Dritte Reich (1993) · priv. coll., F. A. Voigt's MSS · JRL, Manchester Guardian Archive, foreign correspondence · private information (2004)

Archives NRA, priv. coll., papers | Bodl. Oxf., letters to Lady Milner · CAC Cam., corresp. with M. Belgion · JRL, Manchester Guardian Archive, letters to Manchester Guardian

Likenesses photograph, NPG; repro. in Cockett, Twilight of truth, following p. 118

Vokes, Frederick Mortimer (1846–1888), actor and dancer, the son of Frederick Vokes, master of the wardrobe at the Surrey Theatre, and his wife, Sarah Jane, née Godden, was born in London on 22 January 1846. He made his first appearance at the Surrey in 1854, as the boy in the farce *Seeing Wright*. Vokes and his two sisters Jessie and Victoria, subsequently joined by a third sister, Rosina, and by Walter Fawdon, who assumed the name of Vokes on joining the company, became known as the Vokes children, a name which they afterwards changed to the Vokes family. They made their joint début on 26 December 1861 at Howard's Operetta House, Edinburgh. After playing at the Alhambra, they returned for six years to provincial theatres and music halls. In December 1868 the family made a great sensation at the Lyceum in the pantomime *Humpty Dumpty*. It led to their engagement for the pantomime at Drury Lane, at which house the entire family appeared for the next ten years, playing always in the burlesque introduction and often in the harlequinade. In February 1870, in a farce at Drury Lane given by the Vokeses called *Phoebus's Fix*, Frederick Vokes sang a song by E. L. Blanchard, 'The Man on Wires'. The same year he visited Paris, but had to leave on account of the Franco-Prussian War. In August 1875 *The Belles of the Kitchen*, a fanciful sketch that had previously been given at the Alhambra, was performed at the Adelphi with great success. In June 1876 the family produced at the same house Blanchard's *Bunch of Berries*, an altered version of which they presented at Brighton in April 1880. After the retirement of Rosina Vokes on her marriage, Frederick played with the remaining members of the family at the Aquarium Theatre in *The Rough Diamond* and *Fun in a Fog* in April 1879. The last appearance of the family in the Drury Lane pantomime was Christmas 1879. Most of its members were in the pantomime at Covent Garden in 1880. Vokes married Bella, the daughter of Thomas William Moore of the Moore and Burgess minstrels. She played occasionally as one of the family, particularly as a replacement for Rosina. Vokes made more than one visit with his sisters to the United States and Canada. In 1888 he was compelled by illness to forgo his engagements, and on 3 June he died of paralysis at the house of his sister Victoria. He was a fair comedian, a good dancer, and a wonderful pantomimist. With the rest of the Vokes family he was buried in Brompton cemetery.

Victoria Rosaline Sarah Vokes (1850/1853–1894), actress, sister of Frederick Mortimer Vokes, was born in London. She appeared at the Surrey under Creswick as Geneviève in *The Avalanche* when scarcely two years old. She continued to share with her sisters all the child parts undertaken by the Vokes family, and became very popular as Albert in *William Tell* and the duke of York in *Richard III*; she played the latter part at the St James's Theatre with Barry Sullivan. Besides taking part in the performances of her family, she played, in February 1871 at Drury Lane, Amy Robsart in *Kenilworth*, owing to the illness of Lilian Adelaide Neilson. She had a good voice and sang effectively. Her performances in *The Belles of the Kitchen* and as Margery in *The Rough Diamond* were humorous and spirited. In November 1890 she appeared at the Shaftesbury, with a company organized by herself, in *My Lady Help*, a comedietta by Arthur Macklin. She died on 2 December 1894 at 16 Blenheim Road, Marylebone, London.

Another sister, **Jessie Catherine Biddulph Vokes** (1851–1884), played juvenile parts at the Surrey, as Teddy in *Dred, or, The Dismal Swamp* and Florence in *The Dumb Savoyard*. Most popular were her roles of Mamillius in *The Winter's Tale* at Sadler's Wells and the prince of Wales in *Richard III*, performed with Barry Sullivan at the St James's. She shared the fortunes of her family, with whom she played in Edinburgh, London, Paris, and America. She was a sprightly and accomplished dancer and an acceptable actress. She died at 16 London Road, Marylebone, London, on 4 August 1884, and her death contributed to the break up of the family.

A third sister, **(Theodocia) Rosina Vokes** (1854–1894), was born on 18 October 1854. She was the youngest, sprightliest, and most popular member of the Vokes family, and made her first public appearance at the Alhambra in *The Belles of the Kitchen*. With the rest of her family she took part in the performance of *Humpty Dumpty* at the Lyceum on 26 December 1868. The following Christmas she appeared under Chatterton at Drury Lane in the pantomime in which, in the small part of Fatima, she acquired a reputation for vivacity and witchery, which strengthened with each succeeding year. With her family she played at the Châtelet in Paris until the approach of the German army compelled them to take to flight. At Drury Lane, in February 1870, she was Albert to the William Tell of Thomas King in Sheridan Knowles's *William Tell*. On 10 March 1877 she married Cecil Clay, the author of *A Pantomime Rehearsal* and the brother of Frederick Clay, the composer of light operas. She then retired from the English stage. In October 1885, however, she was invited to America with her husband, and took over with her a small theatrical company, including Brandon Thomas, Weedon Grossmith, and other actors subsequently well known, and played in light comedy and burlesque. For nine consecutive years she made a tour of the principal cities of the United States and Canada, playing in G. W. Godfrey's *The Parvenu*, A. W. Pinero's *The Schoolmistress*, Grundy's *The Milliner's Bill*, and in *The Circus Rider, Maid Marian*, and *A Pantomime Rehearsal*. Her last tour was completed in 1893, and she died at Babbacombe, Torquay, on 27 January 1894. She had remarkable gifts in light comedy and in burlesque. Though the Vokeses all died young, their father lived to the age of seventy-four, dying on 4 June 1890, and their mother survived them all, living until 8 February 1897.

JOSEPH KNIGHT, *rev.* NILANJANA BANERJI

Sources C. E. Pascoe, ed., *The dramatic list*, 2nd edn (1880) · *The life and reminiscences of E. L. Blanchard, with notes from the diary of Wm. Blanchard*, ed. C. W. Scott and C. Howard, 2 vols. (1891) · P. Hartnoll, ed., *The Oxford companion to the theatre* (1951); 2nd edn (1957); 3rd edn (1967) · P. Hartnoll, ed., *The concise Oxford companion to the theatre* (1972) · Hall, *Dramatic ports.* · d. cert. [Victoria Vokes] · d. cert. [Jessie Catherine Biddulph Vokes] · b. cert. [Rosina Vokes]
Likenesses print (Vokes, Jessie Catherine Biddulph), Harvard TC · prints (Vokes, Victoria), Harvard TC · wood-engraving, NPG; repro. in *ILN* (13 Jan 1877) · woodburytype carte-de-visite, NPG · woodcut (Vokes, Rosina), repro. in *Harper's Weekly*, 38 (1894)
Wealth at death £3034 15s. od.—Jessie Catherine Biddulph Vokes: probate, 25 Nov 1884, *CGPLA Eng. & Wales*

Vokes, Jessie Catherine Biddulph (1851–1884). *See under* Vokes, Frederick Mortimer (1846–1888).

Vokes, (Theodocia) Rosina (1854–1894). *See under* Vokes, Frederick Mortimer (1846–1888).

Vokes, Victoria Rosaline Sarah (1850/1853–1894). *See under* Vokes, Frederick Mortimer (1846–1888).

Vokins [*née* Bunce], **Joan** (*d.* 1690), Quaker preacher and traveller, was the daughter of Thomas Bunce (*d.* 1682?), a yeoman farmer of Charney Bassett, Berkshire. Joan and her husband, Richard Vokins, a yeoman farmer of West Challow, Berkshire, had two sons and four daughters; one son predeceased her. Her first child was born in 1654, suggesting that she herself was probably born about 1630.

In 1663 Oliver Sansom, husband of her younger sister Jane, declared himself a Quaker and converted Joan Vokins along with the rest of his and his wife's families. Vokins became one of the leaders of the Quakers of north Berkshire, and an assiduous attender at the monthly meetings where administrative matters were discussed. The women's meetings in the Vale of the White Horse, which Vokins and Jane Sansom dominated, became a personal commitment. Such meetings came under attack in 1678 from supporters of the Wilkinson–Storey schism, which aimed to move the Quakers towards conventional nonconformist respectability, and in particular to abolish the women's meetings. Vokins participated in a stormy conference in Reading to ensure their continuance.

About this time, Vokins felt herself called to undertake a visit to the American colonies, to which many Quakers were emigrating. After arriving in New York in May 1680 she began a comprehensive tour in which she preached, attended meetings, set up new local Quaker organizations, and joined in actions against a heretical Quaker

sect, the 'ranters'. She returned to New York in late summer in the expectation of returning to England, but was inspired to go to Barbados instead. It was the hurricane season, and she found herself making an impromptu tour of the Caribbean islands, at the mercy of winds and the availability of shipping. She had no doubt expected to reach Barbados by December, in time for a meeting which was to discuss the Wilkinson–Storey controversy, but arrived too late. In Barbados she worked tirelessly, holding two or three meetings each day and preaching to both white and black people. She arrived back in Dover in June 1681 and prolonged her preaching tour with another three weeks in Kent before returning home. Another major journey, in 1686, took her to Ireland. How these journeys were organized and financed remains obscure.

In line with Quaker ideology, Vokins saw herself as a servant, even a soldier, obedient unconditionally to the commands of the indwelling Christ. These commands came to her perception direct and unmediated. The tasks with which she would be entrusted might be difficult, but prophetic inspiration and providential occurrences would ensure success. She was particularly chosen because her own bodily weakness and insignificance emphasized the divine power which worked through her. In fact, her achievements are all the more noteworthy in that she was permanently in poor health, sometimes bedridden, and often in pain. During her American journey she was dependent on female companions met by chance and apparently persuaded to remain with her; on one occasion she had to be carried into a meeting where she was to preach. What she sought above all in her religion was an emotional communion with other believers, especially with fellow members of the women's meetings, and a feeling of the presence of the holy spirit among them.

Vokins died on 22 July 1690 in Reading, having fallen ill on her way home from a meeting in London. Her husband survived her. Her writings were edited by Oliver Sansom into a volume of standard Quaker hagiography under the title *God's Mighty Power Magnified* (1691).

MANFRED BROD

Sources J. Vokins, *God's mighty power magnified*, ed. O. Sansom (1691) · Vale of the White Horse, Quaker women's meetings, Oxon. RO · O. Sansom, *An account of many remarkable passages of the life of Oliver Sansom* (1710) · T. Crisp, *Babel's builders unmasking themselves* (1681) · A. J. Worrall, *Quakers in the colonial northeast* (1980) · R. M. Jones, *The Quakers in the American colonies*, new edn (1923) · Berks. RO, Quaker records · V. M. Howse, *West Challow, a parish record* (1985), 72

Voltaire. *See* Arouet, François-Marie (1694–1778).

Volusene, Florence. *See* Wilson, Florence (*d.* in or after 1551).

Von. For names including this prefix (also von der) *see under* the substantive element of the name; for example, for Emilie von Berlepsch *see* Berlepsch, Emilie von.

Vonier, Martin [*name in religion* Anscar] (1875–1938), theologian and abbot of Buckfast, was born on 11 November 1875 at Ringschnait, near Biberach-an-der-Riss, a Swabian township of the state of Württemberg (Germany), one of fourteen children of Theodulf Vonier, farmer and owner of a brickworks, and his wife, Agatha. The family were migrants from the Tyrol and convinced Catholics. Being born on the feast of St Martin he was baptized with the saint's name. When Vonier was a few years old the family moved to Rissegg, another small village near Biberach; he attended the village school and began to serve mass. In 1888 he was one of six local boys recruited for the monastery of St Mary at Buckfast, Devon. This consisted of a secular house and some ruins, the remains of the Cistercian abbey dissolved in 1539, which had been acquired in 1882 for the exiled monks of La Pierre-qui-Vire (Yonne). It was assumed that the French monks would eventually be able to return, so two German members of the community suggested that their home area, Swabia, where there were no monasteries, would be a good source of vocations; a small school (alumnate) was established for German boys in 1884. The new recruits were first sent to the college of the Holy Ghost Fathers at Beauvais for a year, to learn French, the working language of Buckfast until 1898; soon Vonier was more fluent in French and English than German. Vonier arrived at Buckfast in August 1889 and, after four years in the alumnate, entered the noviciate (12 May 1893), being given the name Anscar.

On 2 July 1894 Vonier made his simple monastic vows and began studies in philosophy and theology. Because of his obvious ability he was made assistant to the novice master and, after solemn profession (11 July 1897) and ordination to the priesthood (17 December 1898), was sent to the Benedictine Collegio Sant' Anselmo in Rome. There he completed a doctorate in philosophy in one year, with a thesis 'De infinito'. In 1902 Buckfast, an independent priory from 1899 and now with very few French monks, was raised to the status of an abbey (although still a member of the French province of the Cassinese Congregation of Primitive Observance); the first abbot was Boniface Natter, the German monk who had recruited Vonier. In 1905, after serving as master of the alumnate and procurator at Buckfast, Vonier was appointed for a five-year term as professor of philosophy at Sant' Anselmo. At the end of the first year Abbot Natter invited Vonier to accompany him for the visitation of a French province monastery in Argentina; they met at Barcelona and embarked on the *Sirio*. The next day (4 August 1906) the ship ran onto rocks off Cabo Palos and sank with nearly 300 drowned, including Natter. Vonier returned to Buckfast and on 14 September was elected abbot for life; he was thirty and the youngest abbot in the order.

Soon after his abbatial blessing Vonier announced that he would rebuild the great abbey church on the medieval foundations, which had gradually been excavated. This was an act of faith because the community had no money for the project. The work had to be done by the monks themselves, although only one was a trained mason, the materials being acquired as donations came in. On 5 January 1907 the abbot laid the first stone, with a more formal and public laying of a foundation stone by the bishop of Plymouth on 2 July. The spectacle of these largely foreign monks building their church over the next thirty years

stirred popular interest in a way that the boarding-schools and parishes of the English Benedictines had never done. Buckfast became a destination for inquisitive holiday-makers from Torquay and Paignton, the beginnings of a ministry to tourists which is still the major work of the community. Part of the abbey church was opened for worship in 1922 and the solemn consecration followed on 25 August 1932; Pius XI appointed Cardinal Bourne as his legate to preside over the occasion and conferred on Vonier the privilege of wearing the *cappa magna*. The tower was completed later, the final scaffolding being removed a few days before his death.

One of the major crises in Vonier's abbacy came at the outbreak of war in 1914. He was visiting Austria and was arrested as a British subject; only the intervention of the Vatican prevented his detention for the duration. However, when he reached Buckfast in October the problem was reversed. Out of almost forty monks two thirds were German subjects; only the abbot and one other had been naturalized. There was pressure for these enemy aliens to be interned in a concentration camp, but Vonier was able to negotiate a settlement whereby the Germans were confined to the abbey grounds, a ban which was enforced until September 1919. Thus monastic life and the rebuilding continued undisturbed.

The greatest testimony to Vonier's leadership is that he held together a community comprising English, French, and Germans at this time. The war meant the closing of the alumnate for German boys but Vonier worked hard to attract British vocations, so that the community doubled during his abbacy to over sixty. He modified the excessive austerity of the French tradition, enhanced the beauty of the liturgy, and improved the monastic buildings. Although he was an autocrat whose refusal of a request was beyond discussion, he explained himself to his monks in frequent conferences and sermons. In 1938 he took Buckfast into the English province of the congregation, paving the way for its eventual transfer to the English Benedictine congregation.

If the abbey and community of Buckfast is Vonier's enduring memorial, he was known in his own time as a theologian and preacher. He was much in demand as a preacher on special occasions and he saw this as a spiritual echo of the material rebuilding which he had initiated. Between 1913 and 1937 he published fifteen books. Some of these began as talks to his monks, as retreats, or as articles in the *Buckfast Abbey Chronicle*. Their style is uneven, mainly because they were dictated and not revised, but they were popular and were often translated. The two major influences on his thought were St Paul and St Thomas Aquinas, both of whom he saw as preachers. He had a strong sense of the divinity of Christ at a time when there was more academic interest in his humanity, and this led to an optimistic view of the church and the vocation of the lay Christian. Phrases such as 'the whole People of God are anointed in the Spirit of God' (*Collected Works*, 2.121) were advanced for the times, and on occasion he was advised not to publish lectures; yet if his works are not much read today, it is because his ideas were largely endorsed by the Second Vatican Council and are now taken for granted. His most enduring work was *A Key to the Doctrine of the Eucharist* (1925) in which he approached the dispute about the nature of the sacrifice of the mass through St Thomas's sacramental theology; ecumenical dialogue revived interest in it towards the end of the twentieth century.

In late October 1938 Vonier left Buckfast to preach in London, Manchester, and Liverpool before giving retreats in French at Ligugé and Paris. Finally he travelled to Rome for a lecture at a missionary conference. He returned exhausted on 6 December but rose from his sickbed to preside at a solemn profession. On 26 December, after receiving communion early in the morning, he fell asleep. By eight o'clock he had suffered a coronary thrombosis and died. Abbot Vonier was buried at the north side of the high altar at Buckfast Abbey four days later.

AUGUSTINE CLARK

Sources E. Graf, *Anscar Vonier: abbot of Buckfast* (1957) · 'In memoriam: Abbot Vonier, 1875–1938', *Buckfast Abbey Chronicle*, 9/1 (1939) · J. Stéphan, *Buckfast Abbey: a short history and guide* (1970) · *The collected works of Abbot Vonier*, ed. B. Fehrenbacher, 3 vols. (1952–3) · *Buckfast Parish Magazine* (1920) · *Chimes* (1921–30) · *Buckfast Abbey Chronicle* (1931–70) · R. Gazeau, 'Dom Anscar Vonier (1875–1938), abbé de Buckfast', *Revue Mabillon*, 50 (1961), 285–99 · *CGPLA Eng. & Wales* (1939)
Archives Ste Scholastique, Dourgue, France, letters to the abbess
Likenesses photographs, 1906, Buckfast Abbey; repro. in *Buckfast Abbey Chronicle* · B. Elkan, bronze memorial tablet with effigy, 1938, Buckfast Abbey church · S. Elwes, oils, 1938, Buckfast Abbey church · bust, Buckfast Abbey

Voorst, John Van (1804–1898), natural history publisher, was born on 15 February 1804 at Highbury, Middlesex, the son of John and Elizabeth Van Voorst; the family was of Dutch descent but had been settled in England for several generations. Apprenticed to Richard Nicholls of Wakefield from 1820 to 1826 before joining the old publishing house of Longman, Green, Orme, Hurst & Co., Van Voorst commenced publishing at 3 (afterwards 1) Paternoster Row, London, in 1833. His list of titles began with illustrated reprints, the earliest notable being Gray's *Elegy in a Country Church-Yard* and Goldsmith's *Vicar of Wakefield*, before moving on to the specialized sphere of natural history works. Among his illustrators were John Constable, William Mulready, Richard Westall, and Edwin Landseer, all of the Royal Academy, together with Copley Fielding, George Cattermole, W. Dickes, John Thompson, Sam Williams, Stothard, and DeWint.

Van Voorst was not afraid to take risks in the cause of science. With his intense interest and knowledge of scientific practice he published many zoological and botanical treatises in English which have become classical works. An acquaintance of T. H. Huxley and friend of Richard Thomas Lowe, his name became synonymous with good quality printing combined with fine illustrations. He printed works of natural history ranging from the well known, such as Yarrell's *British Fishes* and Gosse's *Naturalist's Rambles*, to less pretentious popular works such as the treatises *Earthworm and Housefly* and the *Honey Bee*, by Samuelson and Hicks. He published at least one work by each of the foremost nineteenth-century naturalists except Darwin, the quality of his publications attracting the likes of Thomas Bell, Philip Henry Gosse, George Johnston, Edward Forbes, Frederick Apthorp Paley, Edward Newman, Charles Spence Bate, John Obediah Westwood, Richard Owen, and David Thomas Ansted, among many others. A list of works dated 1871 comprised 224 current titles of books or learned journals of which 63 per cent were on the subject of natural history.

An astute businessman, Van Voorst successfully used Dickens's ploy of issuing works in regular parts or classified and sold in sets, as in the sixty-two volumes of *The Natural History of the British Islands*; in later years he innovatively experimented with the use of photographs mounted on the page, as in Courtauld's *Ferns of the British Isles*. He was appointed bookseller to the Zoological Society in 1837 and published *The Ibis* from 1865. Elected a fellow of the Linnean Society on 15 March 1853, he was also a founding fellow of the Royal Microscopical Society, which was established on 20 December 1839, later holding the rank of senior fellow for many years.

Van Voorst's main attributes were that of pioneer publisher, a benefactor of biological and related literature, and in associating and establishing artistic execution with science. The realization that beautiful illustration by eminent artists and engravers enhanced learned books of good quality, sold at a reasonable price, kept Van Voorst at the top of his profession for sixty years. Retiring from business in December 1886 without son or heir, he passed on his business to his assistants Messrs Gurney and Jackson. An active retirement enabled Van Voorst still to maintain his interest in the next generation of naturalists until his death at Utrecht House, Clapham Park, London, on 24 July 1898 at the grand age of ninety-four.

GILL PARSONS

Sources *Proceedings of the Linnean Society of London* (1898–9), 61–2 · transactions of the society, *Journal of the Royal Microscopical Society* (1899), 122 · Boase, *Mod. Eng. biog.* · *The Athenaeum* (30 July 1898), 159, 161–2 · R. B. Williams, 'John Van Voorst: patron publisher of Victorian natural history', *Private Library*, 4th ser., 6 (1988), 5–12 · *Nature*, 58 (1898), 299 · *The Times* (27 July 1898), 10b · parish register (baptism), 15 March 1804, Islington, St Mary
Archives Bath Royal Literary and Scientific Institution, letters to Leonard Blomefield · Bodl. Oxf., corresp. with Sir J. G. Wilkinson · NHM, letters; corresp. with Sir Richard Owen and William Clift
Wealth at death £165,645 3s. 6d.: probate, 19 Sept 1898, *CGPLA Eng. & Wales*

Vorhaus, Bernard (1904–2000), film director, was born on 25 December 1904 at 160 East 80th Street, New York city, the youngest of the four children of Louis Vorhaus, a lawyer born near Cracow, Galicia, and his wife, Joanna, *née* Cohn. The family was comfortably off; but good fortune did nothing to dull Vorhaus's concern for social justice. He was first introduced to films as a child by his eldest sister Amy, who had sold several scenarios for production at the Fort Lee Studios, New Jersey, in the 1910s. The young Bernard gathered film scraps from the studio floor, spliced them together, and ran the jumble through his toy projector, entranced. It was the beginning of one of the twentieth century's more unusual film careers, shaped variously by bad luck, good luck, quirks of history, and his own considerable talent.

Vorhaus's early education in New York city took place at a private school run by the Ethical Society, and at De Witt Clinton High School. At Harvard University he studied law, and was expected to follow his father's profession. Vorhaus bargained for a chance to try his luck in films, and won. He moved to Hollywood as a scenario writer, working at first for Columbia Pictures, and usefully observing directors at work. He also learned the pain of ghostwriting a box office hit, *Seventh Heaven* (1927), without being able to bask in its success. Further misfortune arrived in 1928 when he co-directed *Sunlight*, a silent dramatic short lost from sight in the excitement of talking pictures. Afterwards Vorhaus took a holiday in England, and stayed for eight years. The bedlam of sound films gave him a niche as production supervisor for British Sound-Film Productions. When the company collapsed Vorhaus gathered enough resources to make his first independent feature, *On Thin Ice*, in 1932.

By the terms of the Cinematograph Films Act of 1927 the British film industry was required to generate a set quota of products. The lowliest, cheapest products became known as 'quota quickies', easy to make badly. Working mostly for Julius Hagen at Twickenham Studios, Vorhaus soon acquired a high reputation in the field, and proved that inventive direction could turn the most unpromising script from dialogue with pictures tacked on into a genuine film. In films like *Crime on the Hill* (1933) and *The Ghost Camera* (1933), the latter edited by the young David Lean, he approached the crime thriller genre with an outsider's fresh eye. Vorhaus's greatest British achievement was *The Last Journey* (1935), a taut melodrama set on a train hurtling toward destruction at the hands of a driver inflamed by jealousy. On 6 November 1933 he married Welsh-born Esther Olwen (Hetty) Davies (1909–1997), the daughter of David Gwilym Davies, musician. They had two children, David (*b.* 1942) and Gwynneth (1946–1996). After their marriage Hetty trained as a film editor, worked as a dialogue editor on Vorhaus's films, and campaigned vigorously for left-wing causes.

In 1937, with recession facing the British industry, Vorhaus accepted an offer from Herbert J. Yates, head of Republic Pictures. Artistically, his return to America was not very fruitful. He found the Hollywood assembly line restrictive. He compounded his troubles by avoiding subjects he could do well, like mystery thrillers, in favour of unsuitable material. Vorhaus's own political beliefs sharpened during the Spanish Civil War, but as fascism advanced in Europe he made only trivial films. One, *Fisherman's Wharf* (1939), featured the child star Bobby Breen and a performing seal. The compensation was Hollywood's busy anti-fascist scene and the friendship of other left-wing film makers.

During the Second World War, Vorhaus worked in

America's air force and signal corps film units. His assignments included documenting the Yalta and Potsdam conferences, though after American relations with Russia deteriorated Washington abandoned the resulting film. Vorhaus found it hard to re-establish himself in civilian life. The melodrama *The Spiritualist* (1948), a triumph of style over content, remains the best of his post-war American films.

Fretting at factory production methods, Vorhaus moved to New York to make an earnest independent film about juvenile delinquency, *So Young so Bad* (1950). Two other films followed in Europe. But luck was now running against him: after being named as a communist by Edward Dmytryk in 1951 during the House Un-American Activities Committee hearings, Vorhaus decided to lie low with his family in England. For safety's sake he chose not to pursue film work. He took architecture classes, and developed Domar Properties, a house conversion company in London, working with mild satisfaction but losing all touch with the film industry. He acquired British citizenship in the 1960s during the Vietnam War.

In retirement during the 1980s Vorhaus's quiet life changed when David Lean singled him out in an interview as the British director who had most impressed him in the 1930s. Intrigued, the British Film Institute located Vorhaus, still living in London, screened his surviving films, and paved the way for a heartening rediscovery of the man and his career. Though he voiced regret that he had not fought harder to stay in the film business, Vorhaus displayed remarkably little bitterness about his life's twists and turns. Kindly and modest, he kept lively in body and mind well into advanced old age. In his eighties only the danger of broken bones made him give up his passion for skiing. He died in London on 23 November 2000, shortly before the publication of his autobiography, *Saved from Oblivion*.   GEOFF BROWN

Sources B. Vorhaus, *Saved from oblivion: an autobiography* (2000) · G. Brown, 'Money for speed: the British films of Bernard Vorhaus', *The unknown 1930s*, ed. J. Richards (1998), 181–99 · G. Brown, 'Vorhaus: a director rediscovered', *Sight and Sound*, 56/1 (1986–7), 40–43 · *The Independent* (24 Nov 2000) · *The Times* (27 Nov 2000) · *The Guardian* (15 Dec 2000) · personal knowledge (2004) · private information (2004) · m. cert. · *The Guardian* (4 Oct 1997) [Esther Vorhaus]

Archives FILM BFI NFTVA

Vorteporius (*fl. c.*540), king of the Demetae, whom Gildas in his *De excidio Britanniae* calls 'tyrant of the Demetae' (Gildas, cap. 31), is probably the Voteporix commemorated in a bilingual (Latin and Irish) inscription formerly at Castelldwyran in the west of Carmarthenshire in the heartland of early medieval Dyfed. The form of the name in the Irish inscription would fit a sixth-century date, while the traditional date of *c.*540 for Gildas's *De excidio Britanniae* is unlikely to be far out. The Latin, in square capitals, runs as follows:

MEMORIA
VOTEPORIGIS
PROTICTORIS
(Nash-Williams, no. 138)

This is usually translated 'The memorial of Voteporix

"protector"'. The Irish inscription on the same stone contains only the name and is in the ogham alphabet: Votecorigas. The person commemorated was, therefore, known both by a British name and by its Irish cognate. The Irish version of the name suggests that he belonged to the Irish settlers in Dyfed; this is corroborated by the appearance of forms of the name Voteporix in, first, an Old Irish text about the migration of the Déssi (the people whose name is preserved in the baronies of Decies in Waterford) and, second, in Old Welsh genealogies of the mid-tenth century. Both the Irish and the Welsh versions of the pedigree of the kings of Dyfed agree with Gildas, however, in inserting an 'r' into the name (Gildas has the name in the vocative, Vortipori—'O Vortiporius'). Gildas's tyrant was, according to him, the wicked son of a good father, namely, if the pedigree is reliable, Aircol (Agricola). The father is described as king; here, then, as elsewhere, Gildas was using 'tyrant' of a king of evil conduct rather than of a ruler who took power by a coup. As with his other wicked tyrants, Vortiporius had distinguished himself by vicious conduct both domestic and familial: killing male kinsmen and having sexual intercourse with his own daughter.

Solutions of the problem posed by different forms of the name start from the title used in the inscription, *protector*. In the later Roman empire the term *protector* was used for one of the two corps of élite bodyguard troops (*domestici* and *protectores*). Typically the *protectores* served as staff officers and were likely to receive high military office as the next step in their careers. The term remained in use in the successor states, as in a Burgundian inscription:

HARIULFUS PROTECTOR DOMESITICUS EILIUS [filius] HANHAUALDI REGALIS GENTIS BURGUNDIONUM (Le Blant, *Nouveau recueil des Inscriptions de la Gaule*, no. 38)

Here both titles, *protector* and *domesticus*, are used, making it doubly clear that the reference is to the Roman institution. On the other hand, the name Voteporix has the literal meaning 'Refuge-King', and this has led Celticists to wonder whether the Latin title might not be a gloss on the name, or, on the other hand, whether the name might not, in origin, have been a title corresponding to the Latin *protector*. Some knowledge of the title *protector* seems to have come down to the tenth-century compiler of the Harleian genealogies: he inserts the title some generations above his Guortepir in the pedigree of the Dyfed kings.

The two most likely solutions to this entangled problem begin, in the first case, from the suggestion that the form with 'r' is a deformation of the form without 'r'—Vortipori of Votepori—and, in the second case, from the proposal that the two names stood for different but related men, both belonging to the royal kindred of the Demetae (compare Hariulf, a member of the Burgundian Gibichung dynasty). The first explanation has to face the difficulty that a supposedly deformed version of the name was the one recorded in the genealogies; the second has to meet the objection that the Old Welsh genealogy suggests that its Guortepir (with an 'r') was connected with the title *protector* (as in the inscription, which does not have 'r').

The first explanation sees the two names as standing for the one person; according to it, the person commemorated in the inscription was indeed Gildas's Vortiporius. For the second they were not the same person, but rather kinsmen.   T. M. CHARLES-EDWARDS

Sources Gildas, 'De excidio et conquestu Britanniae', *Gildas: 'The ruin of Britain', and other works*, ed. and trans. M. Winterbottom (1978) · P. C. Bartrum, ed., *Early Welsh genealogical tracts* (1966), 4, 9–10 · V. E. Nash-Williams, *The early Christian monuments of Wales* (1950) · E. Le Blant, *Inscriptions chrétiennes de la Gaule* (1856), 2, no. 606 · E. Le Blant, *Nouveau recueil des inscriptions de la Gaule* (1892), no. 38 · *Cassiodori senatoris variae*, ed. T. Mommsen, MGH Auctores Antiquissimi, 12 (Berlin, 1894), 348 · P. Mac Cana, 'Votepori', *BBCS*, 19 (1960–62), 116–17 · C. Thomas, *And shall these mute stones speak? Post-Roman inscriptions in western Britain* (1994), esp. 77–84 · A. H. M. Jones, *The later Roman empire* (1964), 53–4, 597, 636–40 · E. P. Hamp, 'Voteporigis Protictoris', *Studia Celtica*, 30 (1996), 293

Vorticists (*act.* 1914–1919), group of artists and writers, were conceived as British art's independent alternative to French cubism, Italian futurism, and German expressionism. The word 'vorticism' was coined by the poet and critic Ezra *Pound (1885–1972) early in 1914, and he explained in the vorticists' magazine *Blast* that:

> the vortex is the point of maximum energy. It represents, in mechanics, the greatest efficiency. We use the words 'greatest efficiency' in the precise sense—as they would be used in a text book of Mechanics. (E. Pound, 'Vortex Pound', *Blast*, 1, 1914, 153)

The most substantial and active vorticist artists were Edward Alexander *Wadsworth (1889–1949), Henri Gaudier-*Brzeska (1891–1915), and William Patrick *Roberts (1895–1980). Gaudier-Brzeska and Roberts contributed written material to *Blast* as well as illustrations of their work, and in 1914–15 the sturdy Roberts executed some of the most impressive vorticist drawings and watercolours. Pound also contributed essays to *Blast*, and played a crucial part in supporting and defining the vorticist movement as a critic. But (Percy) Wyndham *Lewis (1882–1957) was the dominant vorticist, performing a multi-faceted role as editor, artist, critic, and writer of fiction.

The arrival of vorticism was announced with great gusto, wit, and belligerence in the first issue of *Blast* (July 1914), edited by Lewis. Aggressive, cheeky, and wildly uninhibited, its opening manifestos set out to attack a wide range of targets. England was blasted first, 'from politeness', and its climate cursed 'for its sins and infections, dismal symbol, set round our bodies, of effeminate lout within' (*Blast*, 1, 1914, 11). Vorticism was self-consciously virile in character, and wanted to wage war on the legacy of the Victorian era. Lewis and his friends aimed at freeing England from the stifling influence of the past, and their magazine shouted: 'Blast years 1837 to 1900' (ibid., 18). They used laughter 'like a bomb', in order to discredit the forces which prevented England, and English art in particular, from realizing its full potential. The vorticist manifesto maintained that 'we are Primitive Mercenaries in the Modern World ... a movement towards art and imagination could burst up here, from this lump of compressed life, with more force than anywhere else' (ibid., 30, 32).

The list of signatures at the end of the movement's rumbustious group manifesto included eleven names. But not all of them were closely involved with vorticism itself. Richard *Aldington (1892–1962), who had collaborated with Pound in the poetic imagist movement, was a writer with only a marginal commitment to the vorticist aesthetic. Malcolm Arbuthnot (1874–1967), an innovatory photographer who had organized a post-impressionist exhibition in Liverpool in 1913 and met Wyndham Lewis the following year at the Rebel Art Centre, London, never made vorticist photographs. Alvin Langdon *Coburn (1882–1966) performed that role in 1916–17 when he invented vortography with Pound, but his signature did not appear in the *Blast* manifesto. The other nine names were all directly caught up in the vorticist cause: of these Gaudier-Brzeska, Lewis, Pound, Roberts, and Wadsworth are noticed elsewhere. The remaining members: Lawrence Atkinson, Jessica Dismorr, Cuthbert Hamilton, and Helen Saunders are noticed below.

Lawrence Atkinson (1873–1931), artist, writer, and musician, was born on 27 January 1873 at 10 Leamington Street, Chorlton upon Medlock, Lancashire, the son of Leonard William Atkinson, a salesman of cotton goods, and his wife, Mary, *née* Barnes. After attending Bowden College, Chester, he studied singing and music at Berlin and Paris, which he then taught in Liverpool and London, and gave concert performances. Self-taught as an artist, he first exhibited at the Allied Artists' Association in 1913,

and moved from fauvism to vorticism when he joined Lewis's Rebel Art Centre in 1914. After appearing in the 'Invited to Show' section of the 'First Exhibition of the Vorticist Group' at the Doré Gallery, London, in 1915, he published a book of poems called *Aura*. A solo exhibition of his painting and carving was held at the Eldar Gallery, London, in 1921, and that year his sculpture *L'oiseau* gained the grand prix at the Milan Exhibition. In later life he concentrated on sculpture, executing some remarkably abstract carvings. Atkinson died on 21 September 1931 in the American Hospital, Paris. He had been living at the Villa les Topares, Cannes. Examples of his work are in the Tate collection, including *The Lake* (pen and watercolour, *c*.1915–1920).

Cuthbert Francis Hamilton (1884–1958), artist, was born on 15 February 1884 in India, the son of a judge. After studying at the Slade School of Fine Art from 1899 to 1903 (about the same time as Wyndham Lewis), he taught art at Clifton College, Bristol (1907–10). Though he played a more minor role in the vorticist movement, he collaborated with Lewis on his decorations for Madame Strindberg's Cabaret Theatre Club in 1912, having previously been involved in the avant-garde cabaret club the Cave of the Golden Calf, decorated with murals and sculpture by Jacob Epstein, Eric Gill, Charles Ginner, Spencer Gore, and Wyndham Lewis. The art critic Roger Fry included Hamilton in the last month of the 'Second Post-Impressionist Exhibition' held in London in 1912, and he joined the Omega Workshops designing furniture and interiors in the summer of 1913. But Hamilton joined

Vorticists (*act.* 1914–1919), by William Roberts, 1961–2 [*The Vorticists at the Restaurant de la Tour Eiffel, Spring 1915*; seated (left to right) Cuthbert Hamilton, Ezra Pound, William Roberts, Wyndham Lewis, Frederick Etchells, and Edward Wadsworth; standing (left to right) Jessie Dismorr and Helen Saunders, with the waiter and proprietor]

Lewis in storming out of Omega later that year, and contributed to the 'Post-Impressionist and Futurist Exhibition' in the autumn. Then, having been included in the 'Cubist Room' section of a 'Camden Town Group and Others' exhibition at Brighton, Hamilton joined the Rebel Art Centre and contributed an explosive, mechanistic illustration called *Group* to the first issue of *Blast*. He did not contribute to the vorticist exhibition in 1915, but rejoined the vorticists in 1920 when they exhibited together for the last time in Group X at the Mansard Gallery, London. One of Hamilton's few surviving works, his vigorous *Reconstruction*, is in the Tate collection. In later years he turned to pottery and sculpture, founding the Yeoman Potteries. Hamilton died on 5 January 1958 at his home, Shelleys, High Street, Cookham, Berkshire.

The two women associated with the vorticist movement are more substantial artists than Hamilton. **Jessica** [Jessie] **Stewart Dismorr** (1885–1939) was born on 2 March 1885 at Hillcrest Lodge, West Hill, Gravesend, Kent, the daughter of John Stewart Dismorr, a colonial merchant, and his wife, Mary Ann Rebecca, *née* Clowes. She attended the Slade School of Fine Art in 1902–3 before studying painting under Jean Metzinger, J. D. Fergusson, A. Dunoyer de Segonzac, and J.-E. Blanche at the Atelier La Palette, Paris, from 1910 to 1913. There she became a fauviste, and contributed to several issues of *Rhythm* magazine. Dismorr exhibited with S. J. Peploe and Fergusson at the Stafford Gallery, London, in 1912, and at the Salon d'Automne the following year. At about this time she met Wyndham Lewis and by 1814 had become an ardent member of the Rebel Art Centre. By the time she signed the vorticist manifesto Dismorr was working in a strongly abstract style. Her work was illustrated in the second issue of *Blast* (1915), where her writings were also published. The girder-like forms of her *Abstract Composition* (1914–15; Tate collection) are suggestive of

the new machinery that wields the chain of muscles fitted
   beneath
my close coat of skin.
(Dismorr, 'Monologue', *Blast*, 2, 1915)

She showed in the vorticist exhibition in London in 1915, after which she left to carry out war work in France. Her work was included at the vorticist exhibition in New York in 1917, and her first solo exhibition was held at the Mayor Gallery, London, in 1925; the following year she was elected to the London Group and the Seven and Five Society. Her involvement with the avant-garde continued throughout her life: during the 1930s she exhibited with the Association Abstraction–Creation, and in 1937 contributed to *Axis* magazine. At the end of her life Dismorr was living at 17 Willoughby Road, London. She committed suicide by hanging herself at 21 St Edmund's Terrace, St Marylebone, London, on 29 August 1939.

Dismorr's friend **Helen Beatrice Saunders** (1885–1963) was born on 4 April 1885 at 10 Addison Road, Bedford Park, Chiswick, London, the daughter of Alfred Robert Henry Saunders, a solicitor, and his wife, Annie, *née* Daley. After being educated at home, Saunders studied at the Central School of Arts and Crafts and at the Slade School of Fine

Art (1906–7), and exhibited with the Friday Club in 1912. By then her interest in post-impressionism was evident, and she showed her work at the Allied Artists' Association in 1912 and 1913. One of the first in Britain to work in a non-figurative style, Saunders reached her most extreme stage as a painter in 1914 when she exhibited at the Whitechapel Art Gallery's 'Twentieth Century Art' exhibition and joined the Rebel Art Centre. Like Dismorr, she contributed a poem as well as an illustration to the second issue of *Blast*, and was included in the vorticist exhibitions in London and New York. But she came closest to Lewis when together they painted murals in the Vorticist Room at the Restaurant de la Tour Eiffel, Percy Street, London. At the end of her life Saunders was living at 39 Gray's Inn Road, Holborn, London. Following her accidental death by gas poisoning on new year's day, 1963, three of her works—*Monochrome Abstract Composition* (c.1915), *Abstract Composition in Blue and Yellow* (c.1915), and *Abstract Multicoloured* (c.1915)—were that year presented to the Tate Gallery in memory of her sister by Ethel M. Saunders.

The list of signatures in *Blast* excluded several artists whose work had much in common with the vorticists. Frederick *Etchells (1886–1973) certainly executed paintings and drawings which can confidently be described as vorticist. Jacob *Epstein's (1880–1959) *Rock Drill* (1913–16; Tate collection) put many vorticist ideas into compelling sculptural form. But he was almost as determined to distance himself from vorticism as David *Bomberg (1890–1957), who adamantly rejected Lewis's invitation to contribute to *Blast*. Bomberg also refused advances from the Italian writer and theorist Filippo Marinetti, who only succeeded in attracting the loyalty of one English artist: Christopher Nevinson (1889–1946).

Most of the artists associated with the vorticist movement had previously been impressed by Marinetti and the Italian futurists, who first exhibited in London at the Sackville Gallery in March 1912. The vorticists sympathized with Marinetti's call for an art directly expressive of the new machine age, and they also admired the Italian leader's dynamic ebullience as a performer of his own poetry. But by 1914 they had begun to resent Marinetti's attempts to enlist them as members of the futurist movement. Pound, who had become dissatisfied with his earlier commitment to the imagist movement in poetry, was eager to involve himself with a new group. So was Wyndham Lewis, who explained his conception of the vortex by telling a friend to think 'at once of a whirlpool … At the heart of the whirlpool is a great silent place where all the energy is concentrated. And there, at the point of concentration, is the Vorticist' (D. Goldring, *South Lodge*, 1943, 65).

The stillness of the 'great silent place' was far removed from Italian futurism, which preferred to rhapsodize about the machine age and convey its excitement through blurred, multiple images stressing the exhilaration of movement. Vorticisim valued energy, too, and Ezra Pound defined the vortex as 'a radiant node or cluster … from which, and through which, and into which, ideas are constantly rushing' (E. Pound, 'Vorticism', *Fortnightly Review*, 1 Sept 1914). But the vorticists preferred to define single forms rather than embrace flux, vagueness, and rapid motion. A vorticist picture is often explosive in its implications, using diagonal forms redolent of pistons and girders which reach out towards the edges of the composition. Alongside this restless energy, though, there is a counter-emphasis on firm, clear-cut forms, often enclosed by strongly defined contours. The vorticists were fascinated by the modern world, and wanted to incorporate its mechanistic structures in their work. But they tempered this enthusiasm with a cool, hard awareness of the machine age's impersonal harshness. They knew how dehumanized the modern urban world could be, and they saw no reason to echo the ecstatic romanticism of Marinetti's attitude towards twentieth-century dynamism.

The vorticists wanted to place this 'modern world' at the very centre of their work. They filled their pictures with what *Blast* described as the 'forms of machinery, Factories, new and vaster buildings, bridges and works'. But they had no desire to depict the world in too representational a style. Lewis criticized the futurists for 'their careful choice of motor omnibuses, cars, aeroplanes, etc.' (W. Lewis, *Blast*, 1, 1914, 144) and declared that 'the Automobilist pictures were too "picturesque", melodramatic and spectacular, besides being undigested and naturalistic to a fault' (ibid.). Cubism, which had also influenced many of the vorticists at an early stage in their careers, was likewise criticized. Lewis announced that Picasso's cubist sculpture 'no longer so much interprets, as definitely makes, nature (and "dead" nature at that)' (ibid., 140).

The vorticists believed that their intentions could best be conveyed by a more abstract language. Not because they regarded total abstraction as a desirable end in itself: the vorticists thought that the machine age demanded a severely simplified, hard, bare approach. *Blast* proclaimed that machinery 'sweeps away the doctrines of a narrow and pedantic Realism at one stroke' (W. Lewis, *Blast*, 1, 1914, 39), enabling the vorticists to develop a language which contained many layers of reference. A vorticist picture can therefore be read in several different but equally legitimate ways. It might be seen as a map, a vision, an aerial view of the earth, a diagram, a blueprint for a machine, or a distillation of an urban scene with buildings and robot-like figures. All these possibilities were contained in a single image, and Lewis had no desire to restrict them in any way. He wanted vorticism to be richly allusive even as it refined and simplified its formal vocabulary. In 1915 he explained that the vorticist work of art should be 'a hallucination or dream (which all the highest art has always been) with a mathematic of its own' (W. Lewis, 'Note', *The First Exhibition of the Vorticist Group*, 1915, exhibition catalogue, Doré Galleries, London).

Despite the rivalries within the group, vorticism stood a good chance of establishing itself as a major force. So indeed it did, but only for a short time. A few weeks after *Blast* was published, the First World War erupted. The militancy of vorticism was rapidly overtaken by the outright militarism of a call-to-arms. So the vorticists had little

more than a year to develop their ideas. They enjoyed boisterous evenings at the Restaurant de la Tour Eiffel where Vorticist Room murals by Lewis and Saunders made an appropriately clangorous impact. The meetings were commemorated, nearly half a century later, in Roberts's monumental painting *The Vorticists at the Restaurant de la Tour Eiffel, Spring 1915* (Tate collection). That year, which saw the first vorticist exhibition and the first issue of *Blast*, Lewis claimed in the magazine that 'we have subscribers in the Khyber Pass, and subscribers in Santa Fé' (W. Lewis, *Blast*, 2, 1915, 7), but Gaudier-Brzeska had already been killed fighting at the front. He was widely mourned by other members of the movement, and by 1916 most of the vorticists were fighting in France.

Left at home, Pound persuaded the major American collector John Quinn to purchase vorticist work on a grand scale, and stage an 'Exhibition of the Vorticists' at the Penguin Club, New York, in 1917. But when the vorticists returned from the war, they soon discovered that the world had changed irrevocably. They could not recapture the pre-war context of heady experimentation, in a cultural climate dominated by the need for a 'return to order'. By 1920, despite Lewis's stillborn attempt to launch a third issue of *Blast*, the movement had ceased to exist.

RICHARD CORK

Sources W. C. Wees, *Vorticism and the English avant-garde* (1972) · R. Cork, *Vorticism and its allies* (1974) [exhibition catalogue, Hayward Gallery, London, 27 March – 2 June 1974] · R. Cork, *Vorticism and abstract art in the first machine age*, 2 vols. (1975–6) · G.-G. Lemaire, ed., *Pour un temps: Wyndham Lewis et le vorticisme* (Paris, 1982) [exhibition catalogue, Centre Georges Pompidou, Paris] · ICSAC Cahier, 8/9 (1988) [Vorticism issue, ed. A. Wilson] · K. Orchard, ed., *BLAST: Vortizismus, die erste Avantgarde in England, 1914–18* (Hanover and Munich, [1996]) [exhibition catalogue, Sprengel Museum, Hanover, 18 Aug 1996 – 3 Nov 1996, and Haus der Kunst, Munich, 15 Nov 1996 – 26 Jan 1997] · b. certs. [Atkinson, Dismorr, Saunders] · CGPLA Eng. & Wales (1931) [Lawrence Atkinson] · d. certs. [Dismorr, Hamilton, Saunders] · CGPLA Eng. & Wales (1963) [Helen Beatrice Saunders] · CGPLA Eng. & Wales (1958) [Cuthbert Francis Hamilton] · H. Shipp, *The New Art: a study of the principles of non-representational art and their application to the work of Lawrence Atkinson* (1922)

Likenesses W. Roberts, group portrait, oils, 1961–2 (*The Vorticists at the Restaurant de la Tour Eiffel, spring 1915*), Tate collection [*see illus.*]

Wealth at death £46 10s. 0d.—Lawrence Atkinson: probate, 10 Nov 1931, CGPLA Eng. & Wales · £15,192—Helen Beatrice Saunders: probate, 11 March 1963, CGPLA Eng. & Wales · £1323 19s. 0d.—Cuthbert Francis Hamilton: administration, 7 March 1958, CGPLA Eng. & Wales

Vortigern [Gwrtheyrn] (*fl.* **5th cent.**), ruler in Britain, came to be regarded as responsible for inviting the Anglo-Saxons into Britain. The significance of this role was such that accounts of Vortigern became largely legendary at an early date, and are probably historically unreliable. It seems reasonable to assume that he was some sort of administrative or military overlord of the southern *civitates* of Britain in the fifth century. That he was wholly or largely responsible for the *adventus Saxonum*, as later tradition would have it, is perhaps more difficult to accept, though it seems possible that he had some connection with early English mercenaries or settlers. Writing a century after the events he describes, Gildas states in chapter 23 of his *De excidio Britanniae* that the Britons convened a council (*consilium*) to determine how best to counter barbarian incursions from the north, and that the councillors and the *superbus tyrannus* ('proud tyrant') agreed to invite 'Saxon' mercenaries to fight on their behalf and in return gave them the eastern side of Britain. Some manuscripts of the *De excidio* explicitly name this 'proud tyrant' as Vortigernus or Gurthigernus; and, while it is not clear whether the name was included in the authorial text, the identification with Vortigern is strengthened by the fact that the Old Welsh form Guortigern meant 'high king', suggesting the phrase *superbus tyrannus* was a typical piece of Gildasian onomastic word play.

It should be stressed that Gildas offers no absolute chronology for these events. While, with the benefit of hindsight, Gildas thought the decision to hire the Saxon mercenaries was an error, in fact it reflects a policy also followed on the continent by other late-Roman leaders, such as Aëtius, and was probably regarded as less erroneous by contemporaries. Archaeology suggests the presence of Germanic mercenaries in fifth-century Britain. Most subsequent accounts of Vortigern are derived ultimately from that of Gildas but add increasing layers of legendary and (no doubt) unhistorical details. The earliest definite named references to him occur in the works of Bede, where Vertigernus or Vurtigernus—synchronized with the emperors Martian and Valentinian III (449–50)—is styled king (*rex*), and his invitation is linked with the settlement in Kent of Hengist and his son Oeric (or brother Horsa). Subsequently, the Anglo-Saxon Chronicle records for 449 that Hengist and Horsa arrived at Ebbsfleet, Kent, at the invitation of Wyrtgeorn, king of the Britons, to fight the Picts; but that in 455 they fought against him at Aylesford, Kent, where Horsa fell. Here, it can be seen how Vortigern had become an essential element in the origin-legend of the kingdom of Kent.

By the early ninth century the Welsh had gathered additional legendary material around the figure of Vortigern, bringing him into conflict with both St Germanus and Ambrosius Aurelianus. The *Historia Brittonum*, once attributed to Nennius, which also drew upon the English accounts, credits Vortigern with four sons: Vortimer, who for a time is said to have fought against the English; Cadeyn; Pasgen, said to have ruled the kingdoms of Buellt and Gwrtheyrnion; and lastly, St Faustus (fathered by Vortigern on his own daughter), who founded a monastery at Riez in France. The same source gives three different accounts of his death, including one in which he is burnt to death through the prayers of Germanus, and names his father as Vitalis. Welsh genealogies, of highly dubious value, record Severa, 'daughter of Maximus the king', as his wife. Furthermore, it seems Vortigern acquired the role of ancestor for some early medieval Welsh dynasties. The fragmentary 'pillar of Elise (or Eliseg)', erected in the first half of the ninth century by Cyngen ap Cadell, seems to connect Guarthigirn with the origin of the kingdom of

Powys, contrary to the genealogical derivation from Cadell Deyrnllug. That a Welsh dynasty should associate its origins with the figure held responsible for the arrival of the Anglo-Saxons is perhaps surprising, and it is possible that rather there are two different individuals who became identified because of the common personal name Vortigern. Alternatively, it may have been Vortigern's bad reputation which compelled the rulers of Powys to claim a different ancestor. Either way, it seems unlikely that such legendary material can be employed to further illuminate Gildas's account of the 'proud tyrant'. It did, however, make a contribution to the long and circumstantial narrative of Vortigern's life and death which was much later provided by Geoffrey of Monmouth.

DAVID E. THORNTON

Sources Gildas: 'The ruin of Britain', and other works, ed. and trans. M. Winterbottom (1978), chap. 23 • Bede, *Hist. eccl.*, 1.15; 2.5 • Bede, *Opera de temporibus*, ed. C. W. Jones, Medieval Academy of America, 41 (1943) • *ASC* • T. Mommsen, ed., *Chronica minora saec. IV. V. VI. VII.*, 3, MGH Auctores Antiquissimi, 13 (Berlin, 1898) • Nennius, 'British history' and 'The Welsh annals', ed. and trans. J. Morris (1980) • P. C. Bartrum, ed., *Early Welsh genealogical tracts* (1966) • D. N. Dumville, *Histories and pseudo-histories of the insular middle ages* (1990) • D. P. Kirby, 'Vortigern', *BBCS*, 23 (1968–70), 37–59 • J. N. L. Myres, *The English settlements* (1986)

Vosenius (*fl. c.*AD 10). *See under* Roman Britain, British leaders in (*act.* 55 BC–AD 84).

Voss, Jane [*alias* Jane Roberts] (*d.* **1684**), highwaywoman and thief, reputedly was born in St Giles-in-the-Fields in London. *The German Princess Revived, or, The London Jilt* (1684), the only contemporary full-length biography of Jenny, as she was known, appears to be a highly sensationalized and romanticized account of her life and no evidence has emerged to support its claims for her early life before she reached London. It suggests that by the age of fifteen she had run away from home to join a gang of travelling Gypsies who operated around Guildford and that within a year she was a 'Crafts-Mistress in the Art of Deceit' and a gang leader. It further claims that, deciding to strike out for herself, she took up highway robbery in the west of England with a lover. She is described, having adopted male disguise, as fearless on the road, bravely presenting her pistols to her intended victims during numerous robberies.

Central to this biography of Jenny is a comic, slightly prurient, and highly improbable set piece. Jenny having been gaoled in Wiltshire for horse-stealing, the gaoler's wife, it seems, fell in love with her (while she was still in male disguise) and offered to help her to escape in exchange for sexual favours. Under cover of darkness it was Jenny's lover who kept her side of the bargain for her and ensured that the satiated gaoler's wife would engineer her escape. She then made for London, leaving her highwayman lover to the gallows and the duped gaoler's wife to her husband's wrath.

In London, so *The German Princess Revived* claims, Jenny became a skilled confidence trickster and pickpocket, a view corroborated by Samuel Smith, the ordinary of Newgate, in his account of her final months in Newgate gaol, from March to December 1684. She was known to work with prominent gang leaders to whom she offered her advice and expertise as a practised thief. She was particularly intimate with Thomas Sadler and was involved in his most famous crime, the theft of the lord chancellor's mace in 1677. She may even have seduced Sadler from his trade as a bricklayer, for a biography of Sadler, entitled *Sadler's Memoirs* (1677), claims that 'a lewd woman in St Gileses' first introduced him to a gang of thieves. It is true that Jenny had numerous lovers; Samuel Smith claimed that seven persons who passed as her husband were eventually executed, while *The German Princess Revived* claimed that the number of 'reputed Husbands or friends' executed was nearer eighteen. Certainly Francis Robinson, who was executed on 23 May 1684 for burglary and was in Newgate with Jenny at the time of her final condemnation, called her his wife and begged Smith to reform her.

Samuel Smith gives the most detailed account of Jenny's final months. She was condemned on 10 April 1684 for the theft of a silver tankard on 19 March. She was reprieved when midwives testified that she was pregnant, and she used her extra time to try to obtain a pardon. However she had already been in Newgate over twelve times—there is a reference in Elizabeth Cellier's account of conditions in Newgate to a Jane Voss being imprisoned there in July 1667—and she had also been transported and condemned to die on several previous occasions. Thus when she proved not to be pregnant her former sentence was reinstated, and she was executed at Tyburn on 19 December 1684.   BARBARA WHITE

Sources *The German princess revived, or, The London jilt: being a true account of the life and death of Jenney Voss, who after she had been transported for being concerned with Sadler about eight years past in stealing my lord chancellors mace, and several times since convicted of repeated fellonies was executed on Friday the 19th of December, 1684, at Tyburn. Published from her own confession* (1684) · [S. Smith], *A true account of the behaviour, confessions, and last dying words, of Capt. James Watts, Capt. Peter Barnwell, Daniel D'Coiner alias Walker, Richard Jones, and Jane Voss alias Roberts, who were executed at Tyburn, on the 19th of December 1684. for robbing on the high way, high treason, murther, and fellony, etc.* (1684) · B. White, 'Jenny Voss: the fantasy of female criminality', *Writing and fantasy*, ed. C. Sullivan and B. White (1999) · H. Weber, 'Rakes, rogues, and the empire of misrule', *Huntington Library Quarterly*, 47 (1984) · *A true account of the prisoners executed at Tyburn on Friday the 23d of May 1684. With their behaviour in Newgate, since their receiving sentence at the Old-Bayly and dying confessions at the place of execution* (1684) · *Sadler's memoirs, or, The history of the life and death of that famous thief Thomas Sadler. Giving a true account of his being fifteen times in the gaol of Newgate, and a relation of his most notorious pranks in city and countrey. With a particular description of the manner of his robbing the lord high chancellour of England; for which he was condemned to dye, and executed at Tyburn on Fryday the sixteenth of March, 1677* (1677) · 'A brief account of the tyrannical barbarism inflicted on the kings prisoners in his majesties gaol of Newgate', *Malice defeated, or, A brief relation of the accusation and deliverance of Elizabeth Cellier, wherein her proceedings both before and during her confinement, are particularly related, and the mystery of the meal-tub fully discovered. Together with an abstract of her arraignment and tryal, written by her self, for the satisfaction of all lovers of undisguized truth* (1680)

Vossius, Gerardus Joannes (1577–1649), humanist scholar and author, was born in Heidelberg, Germany, probably in March or April 1577, the son of Joannes Vossius (Alopecius; 1549–1585), Calvinistic minister, and Cornelia Van Buel (*d.* 1584). In his autobiography and correspondence Vossius mentions that he was born in early spring, without giving a precise date. His parents came from Roermond, a city in the south of the Netherlands. After completing his theology studies at Heidelberg his father, then a merchant, became minister of a congregation in the vicinity of that city in 1573. After serving his office in the Palatinate he was then called to serve in Leimuyden, the Netherlands, in Veurne, Flanders, and finally in Dordrecht, the Netherlands, where Gerardus's mother died in 1584. His father married Anna Fransdochter de Witt, but died soon after. Gerardus attended the Latin school in Dordrecht and enrolled at Leiden University in 1595 as student on a grant in the Collegium Theologicum. In 1598 he obtained the degree of MA. He went on to study theology and also lectured in physics at the university.

Dordrecht In April 1600 Vossius broke off his theology studies to become vice-rector of the Latin school in Dordrecht. Soon he became rector of the school, which flourished under his guidance. In February 1602 he married Elisabeth Van den Corput (1578–1606), the daughter of a Dordrecht clergyman. They had three children, of whom only the youngest, Joannes (1606–1636), survived. Elisabeth died on 12 February 1606, and on 28 August 1607 Vossius married Elisabeth Junius (1585–1659), daughter of the Leiden professor in theology Franciscus Junius. Five more children were born in Dordrecht: Franciscus (1608–1645), Antonius (1609–1610), Matthaeus (1611–1646), Dionysius (1612–1633), and Cornelia (1613–1638). As a student, Vossius had been adding to his father's library and he continued to do so in Dordrecht, and eventually acquired a large collection. A catalogue which he kept until 1630 has survived as well as a little notebook in which he recorded loans in later years. In 1606 he published his first substantial work, the *Oratoriarum institutionum libri sex* ('Lectures in eloquence'), a compendium summarizing all that had been published on rhetoric until the present time.

Leiden During the twelve-year truce (1609–21) between the Netherlands and Spain, a fierce controversy broke out in the Dutch Reformed church between remonstrants and counter-remonstrants, respectively advocates of a more liberal interpretation of predestination theology and those who clung to the strict Calvinistic theology of divine predestination. Interwoven with this church conflict was a political conflict between the stadholder and the regents on the limitations of their power. The well-known scholar and diplomat Hugo Grotius invited Vossius to participate in this controversy, and from 1613 the two men were in busy correspondence. When Vossius was approached to fill the chair in theology at the Gymnasium Illustre in Steinfurt, Germany, Grotius procured him the post of regent of the Leiden Theological College in June 1615. The job proved a difficult one as the college was the training ground for future ministers for the church. Vossius himself steered a middle course in the theological conflict of those years and also tried to persuade his students to follow his example. But he nevertheless openly championed the cause of the remonstrants, who had been unjustly charged with Pelagian heresies by their opponents, with the publication of his study *Historia Pelagianismi*.

In 1618 the conflicts in the republic reached a critical stage. Stadholder Maurits took harsh measures, and had his foremost political opponents (among whom was Grotius) imprisoned. A national synod, held at Dordrecht, passed censure on the remonstrants. Vossius followed these events with an anxious mind. He tried not to issue provocative statements, but could not prevent his students from taking sides in the conflict. He did support his imprisoned friend Grotius and saw to it that he was regularly supplied with cases filled with books; Grotius in fact escaped prison in one of those cases in March 1621. But would Vossius himself escape unscathed? In Leiden a committee had been installed for the removal from the university of teachers and students who had supported the remonstrants. Vossius was dismissed as regent of the Collegium Theologicum, but he was allowed to continue as unofficial member of the academic community. His publications and the stand he had taken as regent had made him suspicious in the eyes of the now all-powerful counter-remonstrants, though apparently there were insufficient grounds for official censure. However, even after his dismissal, Vossius continued to be harassed by the church. Again and again in his career he had to defend himself against certain passages in his church-historical works.

Fortunately Vossius was protected by the university board, which was averse to the church's interfering with its staff. Thus in November 1620 Vossius was allowed to lecture at the Collegium Oratorium, and in 1621 he published a *Rhetorica contracta* ('A brief course in eloquence'). In November 1622 he was completely rehabilitated and appointed professor in eloquence and history. He enjoyed great esteem as professor, and was given a variety of responsibilities. When he was offered a chair in history at Cambridge in 1625, the curators of Leiden University made the counter-offer of the vacant chair in Greek language and literature in order to retain him. Vossius was also commissioned to refute Cardinal Baronius's monumental Catholic historiography. There were in addition ordinary executive chores: the educational reform of the Latin schools was particularly time-consuming, but as part of a committee of Leiden professors Vossius formulated an entirely new curriculum and edited new textbooks.

While in Leiden, Vossius revised the old grammatical textbooks of Ludolphus Lithocomus and Nicolaus Clenardus for Latin and Greek, and his own *Rhetorica contracta* for rhetoric. He also wrote elementary textbooks, such as the *Elementa rhetorica* ('The first principles of rhetoric'), which together with the *Latina grammatica* remained in use in Dutch schools through the nineteenth century. In the same period Vossius also published important scholarly works, such as his *Ars historica* ('The science of history') in 1623 and the two lexicons of Latin and Greek historiographers in 1623 and 1627. His publications and his many pupils made him a much valued figure in the republic of letters. As the years progressed his correspondence grew: 1296 letters are known to have been written by him, and at least 2092 letters were addressed to him. Scholarly correspondence with students and scholars all over Europe forms a large part. Faithful letter writers included Hugo Grotius in France, Joannes Meursius in Denmark, Erycius Puteanus in Louvain, and the theologians Ludovicus Crocius and Matthias Martinius in Germany.

Relations with England Vossius had been informed by two English representatives at the Dordrecht national synod in 1618 that he had built a reputation for himself in England with his study on Pelagianism. There was considerable interest in his work in the circles of high-churchmen. Vossius for his part appreciated the Church of England because he felt that it remained close to the early church. Gradually the number of English friends and admirers grew. William Laud, later to become archbishop of Canterbury, especially exerted himself on Vossius's behalf, partly because the latter looked after Laud's interests in the Netherlands. Laud procured Vossius's son Joannes a fellowship in Cambridge and a prebend for Vossius senior in Canterbury. During the final months of 1629 Vossius was in England, where he was received by Charles I and was installed as a canon.

Vossius had several connections in England. In 1624 Fulke Greville, Lord Brooke, offered him a chair in history in Cambridge. Vossius also entertained good relations with the English ambassadors in the Netherlands Sir Dudley Carleton and Sir William Boswell. James Ussher, archbishop of Armagh, and Vossius were in correspondence on the subject of their joint interest in church antiquity. Mericus Casaubon, fellow canon at Canterbury, maintained Vossius's interests there. Edward Herbert, Lord Cherbury, contacted Vossius in connection with his book *De religione gentilium* ('The religion of the pagans'). Vossius was also in correspondence with the linguist Thomas Farnaby. For Vossius, England had thus become a second home. The civil war, which wrecked so much that was dear to him and ended in regicide, was to afflict him so deeply that he fell seriously ill as a result.

Amsterdam and final years In May 1631 Vossius exchanged Leiden for Amsterdam to lay the foundation for the Athenaeum Illustre, later the University of Amsterdam, as professor in history and political science. On 8 January 1632 Vossius officially opened the new educational institute with an inaugural lecture 'De historiae utilitate' ('On the usefulness of history'). The athenaeum was then not yet a fully-fledged university, and was intended mainly to prepare matriculants of the Latin schools for the academic curriculum, but it soon became an important scholarly centre in its own right. During his time in Amsterdam, Vossius managed to publish some important works. In 1635 he brought out his monumental Latin grammar, the *Aristarchus, sive, De arte grammatica libri septem*. Another impressive work was his *Theologia gentilis* ('The knowledge of God among the pagans'), a brilliant and exhaustive summary of everything published on the subject of the natural phenomena that had led many to a belief in a creator. A very modern study on three old creeds was his *Dissertationes tres de tribus symbolis* of 1642. His last two major publications were the book on errors in Latin usage, *De vitiis sermonis* of 1645, and the *Poeticae institutiones* ('Lessons in the poetical art') of 1647.

When Vossius came to Amsterdam he was the proud father of eight thriving and promising children: in addition to the five children born in Dordrecht, they were Isaac *Vossius (1618–1689), Gerardus (1619–1640), and Joanna (1623–1640), all three of whom were born in Leiden. A few of the sons had already drawn attention to themselves with their scholarly publications, but the years in Amsterdam, which had started out so full of promise, were to become a period of intense sorrow. In 1633 the highly talented Dionysius died, and in the years that followed all but one of Vossius's children died (the last, Matthaeus, in 1646, leaving his parents two grandchildren). Isaac, the only child to survive his parents, accepted a post at the Swedish court and left his parental home in 1648. For Vossius himself, old and in ill health from a variety of causes, including a kidney complaint, the end came at home, Oudezijds Achterburgwal, after a brief and painful sickbed, on 17 March 1649. He was buried in the Nieuwe Kerk, Amsterdam, on 22 March.

Legacy Elisabeth Vossius, who survived her husband by ten years, settled the estate. Vossius's large library was sold to Queen Kristina of Sweden. A number of his works were published posthumously, such as a book on the various academic disciplines (1650), a lexicon of Latin and Greek poets from antiquity (1654), and a large etymological dictionary of the Latin language (1662). Thanks to the efforts of his son Isaac and grandson Gerardus Joannes (1645–1717), the thousands of letters written by and to Vossius were preserved and are now to be found in libraries in Oxford, London, and Amsterdam. The last-named also became the depository of the many collections of Vossius's scholarly manuscripts. In 1690 Paulus Colomesius in London published some thousand letters in *Gerardi Joannis Vossii et clarorum virorum ad eum epistolae* ('Letters by G. J. Vossius and by famous men written to him'). At the turn of the century Vossius's collected works were issued in Amsterdam in six folio volumes.

After that, silence ruled. Vossius was one of the last of the great savants from the era of scholarly humanism and after him scholarship took a different direction. Organizing the rich heritage of the past was replaced by experimentation and progression, in search of new knowledge. Vossius, the great representative of late humanism, was the last one to stand in that older tradition. As an exceptionally erudite systematician, he summarized in concise manuals the achievements of the past. He was not a revolutionary thinker, though he did point the way to new methods for research for the future. Instead he was content that after him others would improve on his work. Serviceability was the cornerstone of his character: it was the

driving force behind his scholarly work, and also prompted him to be ready for all who required his help. Next to his all-encompassing erudition, it was for this that he was justly admired by his contemporaries.

C. S. M. RADEMAKER

Sources G. J. Vossius, autobiography, University Library of Amsterdam, MS RK III A 34 · G. J. Vossius, *Opera in sex tomos divisa* (Amsterdam, 1695–1701) · *Gerardi Joannis Vossii et clarorum virorum ad eum epistolae*, ed. P. Colomesius (1690) · I. G. de Crane, *Oratio de Vossiorum Iuniorumque familie* (Groningen, 1821) · C. S. M. Rademaker, *Life and work of Gerardus Joannes Vossius (1577–1649)* (Assen, 1981) · C. S. M. Rademaker, *Leven en werk van Gerardus Joannes Vossius (1577–1649)* (Hilversum, 1999) · G. A. C. van der Lem and C. S. M. Rademaker, *Inventory of the correspondence of Gerardus Joannes Vossius (1577–1649)* (Assen-Maastricht, 1993) · F. F. Blok, *Isaac Vossius and his circle: his life until his farewell to Queen Christina of Sweden (1618–1655)* (Groningen, 2000) · C. S. M. Rademaker, 'Gerardus Joannes Vossius and his English correspondents', *Lias*, 19 (1992), 173–213 **Archives** BL, Harley MSS · Bodl. Oxf., corresp. · University of Amsterdam, handschriften Remonstrantse Kerk **Likenesses** D. Bailly, pen drawing, 1624, Rijksprentenkabinet, Amsterdam; repro. in J. Meursius, *Athenae Batavae* (1625) · D. Bailly, oils, c.1625, Remonstrant Community, Amsterdam · attrib. D. Bailly, oils, 1630, University of Amsterdam · J. von Sandrart, oils, c.1641, University of Amsterdam · A. Blooteling, line engraving (after von Sandrart, 1641), V&A; repro. in G. J. Vossius, *Theologia gentilis* (1641) · T. Matham, engraving (after von Sandrart, 1641), Rijksprentenkabinet, Amsterdam · T. Matham?, line engraving, NPG · G. Vertue?, line engraving, NPG

Vossius, Isaac (1618–1689), philologist and author, was born in the Collegium Theologicum in Leiden, the eighth of the nine children of Gerardus Joannes *Vossius (1577–1649), a professor, and his second wife, Elisabeth Junius (1585–1659), daughter of Franciscus Junius sen. (1545–1602). In May 1631 Gerardus Vossius and his family moved to Amsterdam. Together with his younger brother Gerardus, Isaac was educated at home by his gifted elder brother Dionysius and by private tutors. A talented and precocious student, he was able to assist the poet Joost van den Vondel in 1639 with the latter's translation of Sophocles' *Electra*. In November 1632 the French scholar Claude Saumaise (Claudius Salmasius) was invited by the curators of the university to settle in Leiden; five years later, in 1637, he was to take Isaac under his wing. Isaac never studied at the University of Leiden; he confined himself to his philological studies under Saumaise's personal tutelage. Stimulated and aided by his mentor, Isaac in 1639 produced an edition of a Greek text, the *Periplus* by the Greek geographer Scylax (fourth century BC), with a Latin translation and notes. Early in 1640 his edition of M. Junianius Justinus appeared with the Leiden Elzeviers.

Travels In April 1641 Isaac Vossius set off on his *peregrinatio*. First he went to England, where in London the presence of his uncle Franciscus Junius, librarian of Thomas Howard, earl of Arundel, stood him in good stead. While he was there he also met Patrick Young, librarian of the Royal Library, and James Ussher, archbishop of Armagh and primate of Ireland. After a brief visit to Cambridge, Vossius crossed for France, where he arrived in Dieppe on 14 August 1641. In Rouen he met the jurist Claude Sarrau, *parlementaire* to the *parlement* of Paris, and in Paris he presented himself to Hugo Grotius. Vossius was often to be found in the Cabinet Dupuy, where hosts Pierre and Jacques Dupuy daily welcomed scholars from Paris and elsewhere. He must have made the acquaintance of most of the regular visitors there during the three months he spent in Paris in 1641: Ismael Boulliau, the philologist-mathematician, the philosopher Pierre Gassendi, the bibliophile Jean de Cordes, the jurist Jerôme Bignon, Henri de Valois, François Guyet, and Gilles Ménage. On his travels, apart from associating with other scholars, Vossius spent most of his time in libraries, collating and copying manuscripts of classical texts, preferably Greek *inedita*. Vossius left Paris for Italy in November 1641. Four months later he arrived in Florence where he began working in the Biblioteca Laurentiana towards the end of February 1642. It was there that he copied Arrian's *Ars tactica* partly for the benefit of Saumaise, who had been commissioned by Stadholder Frederick Henry to write his *Militia Romana*, a work on military tactics. Later, during a second stay in Florence, Vossius also copied for Saumaise an extensive work on the same subject by Urbicius (both works are in the Codex Mediceus LV, 4). He furthermore copied an important manuscript containing the authentic text of Ignatius, to which James Ussher in London had directed his attention.

Vossius next visited Naples and its surroundings where he spent about two weeks, finding the city too beautiful to spend much time on study; from there he went to Rome about June 1642, where he worked mostly in the Barberiniana and in the Vaticana. In September 1642 Vossius returned to Florence, and at the end of December he travelled to Venice and to Padua, where he visited Gaspare Scioppio a few times. Although Venice did not have much to offer to a scholar, he stayed there some five weeks, during which time he also relished the famous carnival. He left Venice in March 1643 and barely managed to reach Milan, where he lay seriously ill for some time, as a result of which he was only able to work in the Biblioteca Ambrosiana for a limited time.

Vossius was back in Paris in July 1643. Soon he was staying in the home of Grotius, where he replaced Grotius's secretary Coenraad van Beuningen, who returned to Amsterdam. A year later, in August 1644, much to Grotius's regret, he left Paris to go home again, though not before first picking up a licentiate in law at Orléans in June. He travelled home via Caen in order to make the acquaintance of the learned theologian Samuel Bochart.

From October 1644 until December 1648 Vossius lived in the parental home in Amsterdam. In March 1646 his elder brother Matthaeus, historian to the provinces of Holland and Zeeland, died. Isaac succeeded his brother in this post in the same year and completed part 4 of the latter's *Annales*. The title 'historian' Vossius came to regard more and more as an honorary title with an attendant allowance. Vossius now had the time to sort out and work up the material he had acquired on his travels. In 1646 he brought out with Blaeu in Amsterdam his edition of the letters of Ignatius as they had been transmitted in the Codex Mediceus LVII, 7. (He had never delivered the transcript of this manuscript in the Laurentiana to Ussher as

Ussher had hoped.) Interest in this new edition was great, as the letters of Ignatius formed an important document, to which both Roman Catholics and Anglicans appealed to vindicate the early Christian nature of episcopacy in the contemporary debate on the presbyterian and episcopal church order. The protestant party tended to believe that the Ignatius epistles had been forged. Vossius convincingly defended the authenticity of the letters edited by him in a private polemic with the French theologian David Blondel. Contemporary and later philologists had much to say against the text of Vossius's edition. Vossius was not an outstanding textual critic: he copied and collated too hastily. When John Pearson later collected material for a new edition of the Ignatius letters he had the text of Vossius's edition—on the latter's own advice—compared once more with that of the Codex Mediceus LVII, 7, in Florence.

Stockholm In summer 1648, while on a brief tour of the Southern Netherlands, Vossius received an invitation on behalf of Queen Kristina to present himself at the Stockholm court. Should Vossius wish to remain in Stockholm, the queen would consider which duties to confer on him at court, as he was known not to wish to hold any professorship. Vossius arrived in Stockholm on Sunday 21 March 1649; the next morning he was received by Kristina. During his audience with her Isaac addressed her in Latin; she answered him in Dutch.

Kristina and Vossius got on rather well together. Like the queen, Vossius was quick and witty in conversation, something which is borne out by a great many testimonies of people who knew him personally. On 28 May 1649 Kristina signed an order accepting her 'beloved, esteemed and highly learned Isaac Vossius' into her service against an annual salary of 2000 riksdaler. With it he became Kristina's Greek tutor, succeeding Johannes Freinshemius.

The queen's library in the palace was continually enriched with war booty. In May 1649 for instance the art collections and books and manuscripts from the Hradčin in Prague arrived in Stockholm. Kristina also bought private libraries: after Grotius's death (he had died on his way back from Sweden, having been summoned there by Kristina) she bought his library from his widow, Maria van Reigersberch, for 24,000 guilders. In the meantime Vossius's father Gerardus Joannes had died on 17 March 1649. Isaac turned down the offer of succeeding his father at the Athenaeum Illustre in Amsterdam. His father's vast library he sold to Kristina for 20,000 guilders. Gerardus Vossius's library was placed separately in the royal library and remained under his son's supervision. Isaac's own library, too, was brought to Stockholm from Amsterdam. He did not place his library in his own room, but had it put separately in the court library so that the queen, too, might freely consult it. According to Isaac it was a fine library, not lacking in any classical author and counting more than 500 manuscripts. It was not, however, his entire library; he had left a collection of manuscripts at home.

In spite of the many affairs of state demanding her attention, Kristina still managed to reserve time for her studies, but to the disadvantage of her health. In spring 1650 she fell seriously ill, and recovery was slow. This illness put an end forever to the period in which Kristina under Vossius's guidance studied regularly and intensively, a period which lasted roughly from April 1649 to April 1650. But the expansion of her library continued through acquisitions of libraries and transcriptions of *inedita* of mainly Neoplatonic texts. During his travels Vossius had seen and noted down many *inedita* in libraries. He knew where to find Neoplatonic texts which had not yet been published and had them copied for her. Vossius also assisted the queen with her reading of these texts. In 1650 a Swedish copyist, Petrus Nicolai Rezander, was sent to Paris to copy Greek *inedita*. In summer that same year, Vossius himself also travelled to Paris to purchase manuscripts and printed books for the royal library. From Alexandre Petau he bought a proportion of his manuscripts—probably around 2000—for 40,000 livres.

A month after his return to Stockholm in September 1650 Vossius was appointed librarian. Freinshemius was reappointed *professor eloquentiae* in Uppsala; a year later he requested and was granted honourable discharge and received permission to return to his native Germany. As it was Kristina's wish that the printed books should receive more attention than before, it was decided that Vossius should continue to look after the department of manuscripts, but that somebody else should be in charge of the printed books. For this post Vossius recommended Gabriel Naudé, whom he had first met in 1643.

The Amsterdam rabbi Menasseh Ben Israel was a friend of the Vossius family. Unlike Isaac's father, who not only had a high personal regard for Menasseh but also esteemed his great learning, Isaac Vossius did not rate him very highly as a scholar: he considered Menasseh's views to be too speculative. In 1650 Menasseh came into contact with Queen Kristina through the diplomat Michel le Blon, who acted as her agent in Amsterdam. Menasseh requested le Blon to send the queen a copy of each of the works he had written. After consultation with royal librarian Isaac Vossius, Menasseh furthermore sent a collection of Hebrew books for the royal library. This collection, which the rabbi had valued at 900 guilders, fell into the wrong hands in Stockholm. Menasseh received not a single response nor any payment from the queen, and being a man of little means got into difficulties as a result. Isaac Vossius eventually paid Menasseh 900 guilders out of his private funds, an amount which he hoped to recover from the queen. In 1655 Menasseh dedicated his *Piedra gloriosa* to Vossius, as a token of gratitude for the generosities received from the Vossius family.

Among the foreign scholars whom Isaac Vossius had brought to the queen's attention were Nicolas Heinsius and Claude Saumaise. Both had been invited by the queen to come to Stockholm, but Saumaise greatly resented it that Vossius had recommended his enemy Nicolas Heinsius to the queen. As a result, he and Vossius became embroiled forever. Heinsius entered the queen's service about the beginning of March 1650, but when Saumaise arrived in Stockholm at the end of August, the queen granted him permission to be of service to her elsewhere, in Italy, buying books. Saumaise left Stockholm again for Leiden on about 9 September 1651. Earlier, in October 1649, René Descartes had arrived in Stockholm by royal invitation, though prompted by the French envoy Pierre Chanut. The queen turned out to have little affinity with the Cartesian philosophy, while the French philosopher for his part had scant appreciation for the Greek which Vossius taught her. Descartes died in Stockholm on 11 February 1650, probably of a form of influenza.

Another arrival from Strasbourg, as Freinshemius before him, was Johannes Boeclerus. He accepted a professorship in Uppsala in May 1649, but soon came into open conflict with his colleagues and students. About July 1650 he took refuge in Stockholm, where in obedience to the queen's wishes he stayed until the beginning of 1652, when he was allowed to return to Strasbourg. From the beginning of September 1650 until that time, Vossius and Boeclerus were thrown together in Stockholm. Boeclerus disliked Vossius; virtually all accusations of theft of books and atheism levelled against Vossius find their origin in the slanders of Boeclerus and his friend Herman Conring, professor in Helmstedt.

Amsterdam At the end of January 1652 Vossius received permission to go to Amsterdam on leave. While in Holland he came into open conflict with Saumaise, who passed one of Vossius's seasoned letters to him on to Queen Kristina. On 4 May 1652 the unsuspecting Vossius returned from Amsterdam to Stockholm. At the Swedish border near Halmstad, Vossius was denied entrance by a messenger of the queen in retribution for his insulting behaviour towards Saumaise. His exile in Amsterdam lasted until the middle of August 1653, during which time he prepared an edition of Catullus containing text and commentary (this edition appeared in England only in 1684).

In August 1652 Vossius's close friend Coenraad van Beuningen was sent to Sweden by the states general as a special envoy. He was to keep the exiled Vossius informed about the events at the court in Stockholm. Like his friend, van Beuningen was a libertine, but one who opposed atheists. He informed Vossius about the then most offensive form of libertinism, atheism in the true sense of the word, to which Queen Kristina and Bourdelot had abandoned themselves. For Vossius this news was remarkable enough to pass on to Nicolas Heinsius almost verbatim.

Meanwhile Kristina had sent for Gabriel Naudé from Paris to replace Isaac Vossius. When Naudé arrived about the middle of September 1652, the library was reasonably ordered and usable. But then the queen had the rooms of the library vacated to afford accommodation to some ladies. All books were heaped together in one large room; the private library of Vossius and that of his father, which until then had been placed separately, became absorbed in the chaos of the large royal library.

Naudé and Bochart left Stockholm in June 1653. Naudé died on his way home. Pierre Bourdelot also left Sweden that same month, while Du Fresne alone remained behind at the queen's request. She had imparted to Du Fresne her decision to abdicate, and entrusted him with the task of secretly selecting collections from the royal library and the royal art collection which she wanted to take with her abroad following her abdication. At the same time she recalled Vossius to Stockholm, where he arrived about the middle of September 1653. Kristina allowed him to select a collection of books from the royal library as a first compensation for the loss of his own library and salaries due. This collection arrived in Amsterdam in two shipments, and included the *Codex Argenteus*, published by his uncle Franciscus Junius in 1665, as well as Hugo Grotius's *Historia Gotthorum*, which Vossius published with Louis Elzevier in 1655. Vossius left Stockholm together with van Beuningen in June 1654, before Kristina's abdication in Uppsala. In Amsterdam he was to await her further orders.

About the middle of August 1654 Kristina, then in Antwerp, sent for Vossius. He brought order to the collection of books which had arrived there packed in sixty large cases. Two catalogues were compiled under his guidance: the first containing the printed books and one category of manuscripts, the second catalogue exclusively manuscripts. They are kept in the Vaticana in one manuscript (Codex Vaticanus Latinus 8171, fols. 1r–171r; fols. 174–404r). This library was transported to Rome, where Kristina eventually settled. She would have been happy to take with her her librarian; Vossius, however, preferred to take his leave of her. This he did in September 1655; they were never to meet in person again thereafter. In 1655 Vossius moved to The Hague, where he lived together with his mother Elisabeth Junius and his uncle Franciscus Junius jun.

Vossius now turned his attention to chronology. As the basis of his scheme he took the chronology of the Septuagint, the ancient Greek translation of the Old Testament, which differed in its chronology from the Hebrew original. In 1659 he published *Dissertatio de vera aetate mundi, qua ostenditur natale mundi tempus annis minimum 1440 vulgarem aeram anticipare*. A defence of the original Hebrew text and computation was at once undertaken by George Horn, whose treatise elicited *I. Vossii castigationes ad scriptum G. Hornii*. Other tracts on the same subject followed, and the views of Vossius were further contested by Bircherod in his *Lumen historiae sacrae veteris* (1687), and by John Milner in his *Defence of Ussher Against Cary and Vossius*. Vossius returned to the subject in his *De Septuaginta interpretibus eorum que translatione et chronologia dissertationes* (1661, appendix 1663; new edition 1665). Hulsius proceeded to vindicate the Hebrew text in his *Authentia S. textus Hebraei*, while Schook (followed in 1663 by Schotanus, and much later by Patrick Cockburn) attacked his theory of a local and partial deluge in *Diatriba qua probatur Noachi diluvium toti terrarum orbi incubuisse* (1662). The Royal Society, to whom Vossius sent several communications, thought highly of him; he was elected a fellow on 20 April 1664. The society's secretary, Henry Oldenburg, included him 'among the most ingenious and famous philosophers' (*Correspondence*, 6.423). Among his more scientific tracts were *De lucis naturae et proprietate* (1662), in which he attacked Descartes' ideas on the nature of light, *De motu marium et ventorum liber* (1663), and *De Nili et aliorum fluminum origine* (1666).

De motu attracted considerable attention among his contemporaries. With the growing importance of maritime trade and exploration there was considerable speculation about the cause of tides. Vossius rejected the influence of moon, stars, or occult forces, arguing that the sun's heat was the single cause of tides, winds, and ocean currents. He explained that between the tropics the tides followed the sun, and winds blew in the same direction. But the continents formed a barrier to this movement and so the water was deflected north and south, which accounted for the ocean currents. The high tide on the side of the earth opposite the sun was the result of water rushing in to fill the hollow caused by the rise elsewhere. He explained that tides occurred 48 minutes later each day due to the lag following the rise, and that the same afface accounted for the bi-monthly maximum. In *De lucis* he relied on the readings of the mercury barometer to assess the likely height of the atmosphere, and he concluded *De motu* with a brief argument on its usefulness to predict storms at sea. In *De Nili* he attributed the Nile floods to the rains in Ethiopia, a controversial idea at a time when it was believed that there was insufficient rainfall on the continents to account for river flow. Archibald Lovel's translation of *De motu* as *A Treatise Concerning the Motion of the Seas and Winds* (1677) was intended to make Vossius's text available to a wider seagoing and mercantile community.

In 1666 and 1669 Vossius saw through the press the amusing collection of table talk called *Scaligerana*, and the similar collection entitled *Perroniana, sive, Excerpta ex ore Cardinalis Perronii*. In the early 1660s Vossius spent a good deal of time in Geneva and Paris, and in 1663 he received from the French king a handsome 'gratification', and a flattering letter alluding to his own and his father's services to learning. It was in Paris that Vossius first met Charles de Saint-Évremond, the famous man of society, sceptic, and soldier. Saint-Évremond sent enthusiastic reports of their meetings in his correspondence. In 1671 he wrote to François, mareschal de Créqui: 'I know one of the most learned men in Europe, of whom one may learn a thousand things, curious or profound; in whom, nevertheless, you will find a foolish credulity in every thing extraordinary, fabulous, or exceeding belief' (Katz, 156).

London In 1670 the states of Holland finally refused to pay Vossius his salary as historian to the provinces of Holland and Zeeland (he had written nothing on the subject during the previous twenty years in the post). Offended at their lack of understanding, Vossius went to England in 1670 as a protégé of John Pearson, master of Trinity College, Cambridge, and later bishop of Chester. Their common interest was the vindication of the authenticity of the 'Eusebian' epistles of Ignatius, in opposition to the views of Daillé, Saumaise, and Blondel, and when Pearson's *Vindiciae* appeared at Cambridge in 1672, *Isaaci Vossii epistolae duae* formed an appendix, together with his *Responsio ad Blondellum*. What is perhaps the most original of Vossius's works appeared anonymously at Oxford in 1673, under the title *De poematum cantu et viribus rythmi*, dedicated to Lord Arlington. The author retraces the ancient alliance between poetry and music, and insists on a strict adherence to the rules of prosody as opposed to the intuitive method.

Having previously embraced Anglicanism as most congenial to his beliefs (and doubts) Vossius was created DCL at Oxford on 16 September 1670 and was presented by Charles II to a vacant prebend in the royal chapel of Windsor (he was installed on 12 May 1673, in place of Thomas Viner). He was now frequently to be seen about the court. Evelyn met him at the lord chamberlain's at supper with the bishop of Rochester, at the houses of other prelates, and at Monmouth House. But it was not until 1675 and the arrival of the duchess of Mazarin in London that Vossius gained entry to the sort of intellectual centre he had known in Sweden. Saint-Évremond visited the duchess at Windsor, St James's, or her house at Chelsea almost every day, and Vossius frequently attended with him. It was frequently observed of him that he knew all the languages of Europe, but did not speak one well, and that he was intimately acquainted with the manners and characters of all ages but his own. His style was held to be too disputatious, and his epithets were thought too erudite for the drawing-room. Mazarin's circle was known for freethinking, and anecdotes about Vossius's own scepticism, such as his habitual reading of Ovid during services, circulated widely. Yet he was by no means free from credulity, and Charles II echoed Saint-Évremond's opinion when he remarked that Vossius would believe anything, if only it were not in the Bible.

Vossius next turned his attention to the highly controversial subject of the sibylline oracles, in *I. Vossii de sibyllinis aliisque quae Christi natalem praecessere oraculis* (1679). The oracles were ancient Greek prophetic verses which were thought to have predicted the coming of Christ, and thus provided a link between the biblical and classical worlds. The status of the verses—whether true prophecies or forgeries of Greek or early Christian origin—was much debated, and Vossius's conclusion that they were of ancient Jewish origin met with great hostility. Along with his controversial championing of the Septuagint over the Hebrew Bible (the latter was deemed infallible in England, as in other protestant countries), this work consolidated his reputation as a thorough, and in some cases, dangerous sceptic. He was answered first by Reiskius's *Exercitationes* (1688), and later by Fontenelle; meanwhile his position on the chronology of the Septuagint was being challenged by Richard Simon (*R. Simonis opuscula critica adversus I. Vossium*, 1685).

In 1685 Vossius published *Variarum observationum liber*, which contained a dissertation of interest, 'De triremium et liburnicarum constructione', which Graevius inserted in the twelfth volume of his *Thesaurus antiquitatum Romanorum*, a treatise, 'De origine et progressu pulveris bellici', and another opuscule, 'De antiquae Romae magnitudine'. Throughout this work Vossius gave free rein to his capricious imagination and to his love of paradox. He passes an extravagant eulogy on the Chinese civilization, and tries to prove that the population of Rome was 14 million, and that its area was twenty times greater than that of Paris and London combined. (He also introduces some flattering remarks about Charles II and on the country of his adoption, but his alleged depreciation of the size of London elicited several replies, notably *London Bigger than Old Rome Demonstrated … Against Vossius, by De Souligné*, 1701 and 1710.) Evelyn, who was delighted with their ingenuity, mentions several other short works, notably one 'Peritachyploia', on the subject of tacking in navigation, which was never published; he was also greatly diverted by a note of Vossius on a certain harmony which was produced in the East by the snapping of drivers' whips (Evelyn to Pepys, 23 September 1685).

Among the labours of Vossius's last years were some annotations on the works of his father, particularly the *Etymologicon*. Some corrections by him were included in the 1695 edition of Anacreon, 'Variae lectiones ex notulis I. Vossii' appeared in the Lucretius of 1725, and some notes by him were embodied in the edition of Hesychius of Alexandria, published at Leiden in 1746. He also made some notes on Arrian, which were included in the large edition of 1842.

Vossius fell ill during winter 1688–9. According to the story told by Des Maizeaux and Nicéron, he obstinately refused to conform to the usages of religion and receive the sacrament until two of his fellow canons urged that if not for the good of his soul he should comply for the honour of the chapter. He died at Windsor on 21 February 1689 and was buried there in St George's Chapel.

According to Wood, Vossius had accumulated 'the best private library, as it was then supposed, in the whole world' (Wood, *Ath. Oxon.*, 3rd edn, 2.323). It included 762 manuscripts which his enemies described as 'spoils'. A catalogue of these was drawn up by Paul Colomiès; £3000 was offered by the University of Oxford for the library in September 1710, but on 10 October it was sold to Leiden for 36,000 florins. Evelyn bitterly deplored the loss to the country. 'Where are our rich men?' he asked. 'Will the Nepotismo never be satisfied?' (*Diary and Correspondence*, 3.306, 308). Some of Vossius's correspondence, included in the d'Orville collection, was purchased by the Bodleian in 1805. The same library has the 'Codex Vossianus', a Latin psalter of the tenth century, in Anglo-Saxon characters. The British Museum has a Greek Testament (1620, fol.), with manuscript notes and readings by Vossius. Most of his books were included in the *Index librorum prohibitorum*, some of them, it is said, against the advice of Mabillon, the usual referee in such matters between 1680 and 1705. Vossius's correspondence with Heinsius comprises the third volume of the *Sylloges epistolarum* of Burmannus (1727), and other letters to the same correspondent are in the British Library (Add. MS 5158).

THOMAS SECCOMBE, rev. F. F. BLOK

Sources F. F. Blok, *Isaac Vossius and his circle: his life until his farewell to Queen Christina of Sweden, 1618–1655* (Groningen, 2000) · F. F. Blok, *Contributions to the history of Isaac Vossius's library* (1974) · J.-G. de Chauffepié, *Nouveau dictionnaire historique et critique, pour servir de* supplément ou de continuation au dictionnaire historique et critique de M. Bayle (Amsterdam, 1750–56), 4.614–31 • S. de Vries, 'Isaac Vossius', Nieuw Nederlandsch biografisch woordenboek, 1 (1911), col. 1519–25 • D. S. Katz, 'Isaac Vossius and the English biblical critics, 1670–1689' • Y. H. Rogge, 'De reis van Isaac Vossius (1641–1645)', Oud Holland, 18 (1900), 3–20 • F. S. de Vrieze, 'Academic relations between Sweden and Holland', Leiden University in the seventeenth century: an exchange of learning (Leiden, 1975), 344–65 • H. van de Waal, 'Rembrandts Radierungen der Piedra gloriosa des Menasseh ben Israel', Imprimatur, ein Jahrbuch für Bücherfreunde, 12 (1954–5), 52–60 • A. K. Offenberg, 'Some remarks regarding six autograph letters by Menasseh ben Israel in the Amsterdam University Library', Menasseh ben Israel and his world, ed. Y. Kaplan (Leiden, 1989), 191–8 • H. Wieselgren, Drottning Kristinas bibliotek och bibliotekarier före hennes bosättning i Rome (Stockholm, 1901) • P. C. Molhuysen, Geschiedenis der Universiteits-Bibliotheek te Leiden (Leiden, 1905), 28–33 • J. Bignami Odier, 'Le fonds de la reine à la Bibliothèque Vaticane', Collectanea Vaticana in honorem Anselmi M. Card. Albareda a Bibliotheca Apostolica edita (Vatican, 1962), 159–89 • E. Hulshoff Pol, 'The library', Leiden University in the seventeenth century: an exchange of learning (Leiden, 1975), 442, 444 • Diary and correspondence of John Evelyn, ed. W. Bray, new edn, ed. [J. Forster], 4 vols. (1850–52) • Catalogus variorum et exquisitissimorum librorum Gerardi Ioannis Vossii, quorum auctio habebitur in aedibus Petri Leffen bibliopolae sub signo Phoenicis [die mercurii 4 Octobris] Anno 1656 (Leiden, 1656) • C. Callmer, Catalogus codicum manuscriptorum bibliothecae regiae Holmiensis c. annum MDLC ductum et auspicio Isaaci Vossii conscriptus; Suecice et Britanice praefatus editionem indicibus auctam curavit Christian Callmer (Stockholm, 1971) • K. A. de Meyïer, Codices Vossiani Graeci et miscellanei (Leiden, 1955) • K. A. de Meyïer, Codices Vossiani Latini, 4 vols. (Leiden, 1973–84) • P. C. Boeren, Codices Vossiani chymici (Leiden, 1975) • A. C. Balsem, 'Libri omissi' italiani del cinquecento provenienti dalla biblioteca di Isaac Vossius ora nella biblioteca della Rijksuniversiteit di Leida (Leiden, 1994) • A. Grape, Magnus Gabriel De la Gardie, Isaac Vossius och Codex Argenteus (Uppsala, 1927) • D. J. H. ter Horst, Isaac Vossius en Salmasius: een episode uit de 17de-eeuwsche geleerdengeschiedenis (The Hague, 1938) • Wood, Ath. Oxon., new edn • Foster, Alum. Oxon. • GM, 1st ser., 66 (1796), 717 • M. B. Deacon, introduction, in I. Vossius, A treatise concerning the motion of the seas and winds; together with, De motu marium et ventorum, facs. edn (1993) • T. Birch, The history of the Royal Society of London, 4 vols. (1756–7); repr. with introduction by A. R. Hall (1968) • The correspondence of Henry Oldenburg, ed. and trans. A. R. Hall and M. B. Hall, 13 vols. (1965–86) • D. Burger, 'Two dissertations on the tides in the seventeenth century', Janus, 46 (1957), 41–5

Archives Bibliotheek der Rijksuniversiteit, Leiden, Netherlands, Latin, Greek, and alchemical MSS • BL, corresp., Harley MSS 7012–7013 • BL, letters, Add. MS 5158 • Bodl. Oxf., corresp. and papers • University of Amsterdam, corresp. • University of Leiden, corresp.

Vowell, John. See Hooker, John (c.1527–1601).

Voyce, (Anthony) Thomas (1897–1980), rugby player, was born on 18 May 1897 at Gloucester, the only son and the sixth of seven children of Thomas Voyce, stevedore, of Gloucester, whose family came from the village of Ashleworth, and his wife, Anne Hackney, also of Gloucester. He was educated at the national school, Gloucester, and while he was there he was capped for England in 1911 as a schoolboy international rugby player. He was also a chorister at Gloucester Cathedral. Even though under age, he joined the army as a private at the outbreak of war in 1914 and served in the Gloucestershire regiment in France. While there, he contracted peritonitis and was repatriated for an operation. He thus missed the first battle of the Somme. Subsequently, he went to the Royal Military College, Sandhurst, at the same time as Prince Henry of Gloucester and was commissioned into the Royal West Kent regiment. He was severely wounded in his right eye by a shell-burst in France in 1917. The wound left him with permanently impaired vision, but despite the handicap he took up rugby football again and played for the army and Blackheath.

After the war Voyce returned to captain Gloucester and Gloucestershire and also played for Cheltenham, Richmond, the Barbarians, England, and the British Lions. He won twenty-seven consecutive caps for England between 1920 and 1926, and under the captaincy of W. Wavell Wakefield contributed a great deal to one of the most successful periods in England's rugby union history. Before the days of Wakefield and Voyce forward specialization was almost unheard of, but Voyce, at wing forward, and Wakefield, at number eight, pioneered the basis of the loose forward game as it was later played. Voyce toured South Africa with the British Lions in 1924, and represented Gloucestershire on the Rugby Football Union from 1931 until he became its president in 1960–61. He was appointed OBE in 1962 for his services to the National Playing Fields Association, to various hospital authorities in Gloucestershire, to the National Savings movement, and to the St John Ambulance Brigade. He was also chairman of the Ministry of Pensions in Gloucestershire.

Voyce was a man of rich character: a hard man who played, as one of his contemporaries put it, 'like a pirate coming over the side of a ship with a knife in his mouth. The only difference was that Tom didn't need a black patch over one eye. He couldn't see out of it in any case.' His interests were wide-ranging. Apart from his public work, he played golf to a single-figure handicap and was an ardent salmon and trout fisherman. He also collected antique clocks and at one stage had seven grandfather clocks in his house in Gloucester.

In 1926, his last year of international rugby, Voyce married Hilda (Pat), daughter of Joseph Weekes King, farmer, of Berkeley, Gloucestershire; they had a son and a daughter. Voyce died at his home, 21 Tewkesbury Road, Gloucester, on 22 January 1980.   JOHN REASON, rev.

Sources personal knowledge (1986) • private information (1986) • The Times (4 Feb 1980) • CGPLA Eng. & Wales (1980)

Wealth at death £62,430: probate, 24 March 1980, CGPLA Eng. & Wales

Voyle, Mary. See Manning, Rosemary Joy (1911–1988).

Voynich [née Boole], **Ethel Lilian** [Lily; E. L. V.] (1864–1960), novelist, translator, and musician, was born on 11 May 1864 at Lichfield Cottage, Blackrock, Ballintemple, near Cork, the youngest daughter of the mathematician and logician George *Boole (1815–1864) and his wife, Mary *Boole, née Everest (1832–1916), niece of Sir George Everest after whom the mountain is named. Soon left a widow, the gifted but eccentric Mary Boole took her five young daughters to London, where she worked as a librarian at Queen's College, managed a student hostel, taught mathematics, and wrote about impossible philosophies.

Lily Boole was a sensitive child, with searching eyes and a head of golden hair. She early showed a gift for music and a love of poetry. At the age of eight she developed erysipelas and was sent to an uncle in Lancashire, who treated her harshly but ensured her progress on the piano; she also spent periods in Ireland and Cornwall. Of a religious but romantic disposition, she was fascinated by Lamennais and Mazzini (in imitation of whom she wore black, in mourning for the world). In 1882 she received a small inheritance which enabled her to study piano for three years at the Hochschule der Musik in Berlin; she then lived in Paris for a while. She returned to England an atheist and radical, eager to view nihilism in Russia. She sought introductions from émigrés including Prince P. A. Kropotkin and Stepniak (Sergey Kravchinsky), whose *Underground Russia* (1883) had been a revelation to her. Stepniak taught her enough Russian to travel about his country meaningfully in 1887–9, which she did while teaching English and music and living on the fringe of revolutionary circles.

In 1890 the Society of Friends of Russian Freedom was founded in London and Stepniak became editor of its journal, *Free Russia*. Lily Boole joined the committee and laboured tirelessly, translating Russian tales as well as works by Stepniak himself; he considered her an outstanding translator and introduced her *Stories from Garshin* (1893) and *The Humour of Russia* (1895). Through him she had meanwhile met and then married in the summer of 1892 the colourful Polish refugee Wilfrid Michael Voynich or Habdank-Wojnicz (1865–1930), who helped create the Russian Free Press Fund. E. L. V. (as she was now commonly called) worked energetically for this, holding her own in debate with volatile male revolutionaries. Some thought her domineering, but many recognized the talent soon to find expression in *The Gadfly* (1897). The idea for this novel had crystallized at the Louvre in 1885 in front of a portrait of a young man in black, by the sixteenth-century Florentine painter Franciabigio, a reproduction of which E. L. V. cherished until her death. She researched the historical background in Florence in the summer of 1895. Although she maintained her only direct models for *The Gadfly* to be Lamennais (for Montanelli) and Kropotkin's comrade Charlotte Wilson (for Gemma), it is said that she went to Italy with a lover, Sigmund Rosenblum—the future spy Sidney Reilly—and used him in the delineation of her hero.

The Gadfly, an evocation of the Risorgimento, has a delirious, Dostoyevskian intensity. Its plot is melodramatic and its language sentimental, but it derives astonishing moral power from its clear statement of right and wrong. It proved popular with socialists, especially in Russia, where it was translated in 1898. Shaw safeguarded E. L. V.'s dramatic rights by producing it as a play; Conrad claimed to hate it; Lawrence pronounced it excellent but disliked its treatment of pain. The lack of authorial tact in *The Gadfly* is actually its strength, because offset by triumphant historical reality; by contrast, E. L. V.'s fiercely anti-clerical *Jack Raymond* (1901) and *Olive Latham* (1904), novels of undeniable passion and power, do appear to wallow in man's beastliness to man, and morbidity is seen also in *An*

Interrupted Friendship (1910), which reverted to the subject and character of the Gadfly.

Wilfrid Voynich lost interest in revolution and became a successful rare-book dealer. During the First World War he shifted from London to New York; E. L. V. followed only in 1920, having stayed behind to do social work with the Quakers. In the United States she devoted herself to music, for which she said her writings had been only a prelude. She translated (1931) *Chopin's Letters*, adding an idiosyncratic preface; taught piano and composition; and wrote much music of her own, mostly circulated privately, including part-songs, motets, the oratorio *Babylon*, and the cantatas *Epitaph in Ballad Form* and *The Submerged City*.

During the Second World War, Ethel Voynich returned briefly to her Gadfly with the novel *Put off thy Shoes* (1945). *The Gadfly* itself was meanwhile becoming an icon of communism: it was translated into eighteen languages of the USSR and operas were based on it, as well as the celebrated film with music by Shostakovich; Soviet readers ranked its author among the world's great novelists. Only in 1955, quite by chance, was she made aware of this, but she soon received Soviet royalties, then a mark of exceptional regard. *The Gadfly* was revived in the English-speaking world, Bertrand Russell declaring it one of the most exciting novels he had ever read.

Ethel Lilian Voynich died of pneumonia during the night of 27 July 1960 at Apartment 17, London Terrace, 450 West 24th Street, New York, where she had resided for much of her thirty years' widowhood.

PATRICK WADDINGTON

Sources Ye. A. Taratuta, *Etel'Lilian Voynich: sud'ba pisatelya i sud'ba knigi* (1960–64) • D. MacHale, *George Boole: his life and work* (1985) • E. L. Voynich, 'Autobiographical notes', in E. L. Voynich, *The gadfly* (1964), 321–6 • A. Kettle, 'E. L. Voynich: a forgotten English novelist', *Essays in Criticism*, 7/2 (April 1957), 163–74 • R. B. Lockhart, *Ace of spies: the incredible story of Sidney Reilly* (1967) • A. Fremantle, 'Return of the Gadfly', *Commonweal*, 74/7 (12 May 1961), 167–71 • D. Senese, *S. M. Stepniak-Kravchinskii: the London years* (1987) • E. M. Sowerby, *Rare people and rare books* (1967) • *Tea and anarchy! The Bloomsbury diary of Olive Garnett, 1890–1893*, ed. B. C. Johnson (1989) • *Olive and Stepniak: the Bloomsbury diary of Olive Garnett, 1893–1895*, ed. B. C. Johnson (1993) • W. L. Courtney, 'Mrs Voynich', in W. L. Courtney, *The feminine note in fiction* (1904), 159–77 • T. Szamuely, 'The gadfly and the spy', *The Spectator* (17 May 1968), 665 • *IGI* • *New York Times* (29 July 1960), 25

Likenesses two photographs, c.1883–1890, repro. in MacHale, *George Boole*, 255, 271 • two photographs, 1888–1958, repro. in Taratuta, *Etel'Lilian Voynich*, facing pp. 48, 192 • two photographs, 1898–1944, repro. in Voynich, *Izbrannyye proizvedeniya*, 1 (1958), frontispiece, and 2 (1958), frontispiece • photograph, 1945, repro. in *New York Times*, 25

Voysey, Annesley (c.1794–1839). *See under* Voysey, Charles (1828–1912).

Voysey, Charles (1828–1912), theistic preacher, was born in London on 18 March 1828, the youngest son of **Annesley Voysey** (c.1794–1839) and his wife, Mary, daughter of Thomas Green. His father, the son of Henry Voysey and Ann Maria Annesley, *née* Ellison, was a direct descendant of John Wesley's sister, Susannah Ellison, and a noted

Charles Voysey (1828–1912), by unknown photographer, 1868?

architect. He was reputedly responsible for the first purpose-built office building in London, constructed *c*.1823 in Clement's Lane. He afterwards emigrated to Jamaica, where he died of fever on 5 August 1839. Charles Voysey passed from Stockwell grammar school to St Edmund Hall, Oxford, where he matriculated in 1847 and graduated in 1851, when he was ordained and appointed to the curacy of Hessle, Hull. In 1852 he married Frances Maria, daughter of Robert Edlin, partner in the banking firm Herries, Farquhar & Co. They had six daughters and four sons, the eldest being Charles Francis Annesley *Voysey (1857–1941), the architect.

In 1858 Charles Voysey was appointed incumbent of St Andrew's, Craigton, Jamaica. After eighteen months he returned to England and, through A. P. Stanley's influence, obtained a curacy at Great Yarmouth, but six months later, in 1861, was appointed curate at St Mark's, Whitechapel. He was ejected from the curacy after preaching a sermon in which he denied the doctrine of eternal punishment. He was recommended in 1863 by the bishop of London, A. C. Tait, to the curacy of St Mark's, Victoria Docks, under Dr Henry Boyd, later of Hertford College, Oxford. Soon he became curate of Healaugh, near Tadcaster, and in 1864 became its vicar.

Voysey began his career as a religious reformer by the publication, in 1864, of a sermon *Is Every Statement in the Bible about our Heavenly Father Strictly True?*. It was withdrawn by Voysey after three editions when another clergyman involved in its production was censured. In 1865 he began the monthly publication of his sermons under the title *The Sling and the Stone*, which continued for six years. His sermons continued to be published after 1871, upwards of 1,250,000 copies being produced. His preaching and writing were denounced for unorthodoxy, and in 1869 he was required to appear before the chancellor's court of the diocese of York, where judgment was given against him. He appealed to the privy council and conducted his own defence, but the York chancellor's decision was upheld on 11 February 1871, and sentence of deprivation of his living was pronounced, to be rescinded if within a week Voysey expressly and unreservedly retracted the errors of which he had been convicted. This he refused to do. Before the judgment Voysey had begun to hold services in London at St George's Hall, Langham Place, to which he attracted a number of sympathizers, pledged to support the Voysey Establishment Fund. He thus started a movement which eventually took shape as an independent religious denomination under the name of the Theistic church. In 1885 he established for his followers a regular place of worship in Swallow Street, Piccadilly, where he continued to hold services for nearly thirty years. An observer of one of his services found it most remarkable for its similarity to the form of service of the Anglican church.

Voysey's ultimate theological position amounted to the rejection of the creeds, biblical inspiration, the sacramental system, and the divinity of Christ, and his teaching was the inculcation of a pure theism, without any miraculous element. He was an attractive preacher, courageous and sincere in challenging doctrines which he believed to be erroneous, and he undoubtedly had a profound influence in deepening the religious sense of his followers, among whom was Anne Besant. He was one of the founders of the Cremation Society of England, and for twenty-five years a member of the executive council of the Homes for Inebriates. In politics he was an ardent Unionist. He died at his home, Annesley Lodge, Platts Lane, Hampstead, on 20 July 1912. He was succeeded at Swallow Street by Walter Walsh, but within a short time two separate congregations were formed, one retaining the name of the Theistic church, the other adopting that of the Free Religious Movement. The Swallow Street building was closed in 1913 and shortly afterwards demolished.

DUDLEY WRIGHT, *rev.* K. D. REYNOLDS

Sources private knowledge (1927) · personal information (1927) · *Men and women of the time* (1899) · *Men of the time* (1875) · Foster, *Alum. Oxon.* · *WWW* · A. Taylor, *Annie Besant: a biography* (1992) · C. M. Davies, *Heterodox London, or, Phases of free thought in the metropolis*, 1 (1874), 274–310 · *CGPLA Eng. & Wales* (1912) · 'Voysey, Annesley', Colvin, *Archs.*

Archives BL, letters to W. E. Gladstone, Add. MSS 44449–44524 · Harris Man. Oxf., letters to Thomas Allsop · LPL, corresp. with A. C. Tait and related papers

Likenesses photograph, 1868?, NPG [*see illus.*] · H. J. Whitlock, carte-de-visite, NPG · chromolithograph caricature, NPG; repro. in *VF* (21 Oct 1871)

Wealth at death £7047 3s. 6d.: resworn probate, 17 Aug 1912, *CGPLA Eng. & Wales*

Voysey, Charles Francis Annesley (1857–1941), architect and designer, was born in Hessle, near Hull, on 28 May 1857, the third child and eldest son of the six daughters and four sons of the Revd Charles *Voysey (1828–1912) and his wife, Frances Maria, *née* Edlin. His father was expelled from the Church of England in 1871 for heretical doctrines and then founded the Theistic church. The experience of his father's ecclesiastical trials, which became a national *cause célèbre* when he was a young adolescent, instilled in the young Voysey a romantic admiration for the martyr's plight. He regarded his architectural philosophy as an extension of his father's teaching and throughout his career the uncompromising clarity and reforming simplicity of his work were inseparable from a profound belief in heredity. Voysey could trace his ancestry back to John Wesley, whose sister was his great-great-great-grandmother, and he delighted in a physical resemblance to Wesley: in later life he modelled for a portrait of him.

Voysey was educated at home until the family moved to London in 1871, when he was sent, for two years, to Dulwich College. His academic work was undistinguished and, believing himself to be the dunce of the family, he later claimed to have become an architect because it was the only profession for which one did not need to pass any examinations. His grandfather Annesley *Voysey (c.1794–1839) [*see under* Voysey, Charles] had been an architect. From 1874 to 1879 Voysey was a pupil of John Pollard Seddon, an architect of the Gothic revival. After a brief period as an assistant in Saxon Snell's office he became 'an improver' in the office of George Devey, whose practice consisted mainly of large country houses.

Voysey commenced practice on his own account in London in 1881. In 1885 he married Mary Maria, daughter of Henry Evans, of Torquay; they had two sons, one of whom became an architect, and one daughter. His first commission for a house was not executed until 1888 and during his early years in practice his income was dependent upon wallpaper and textile designs. He is reputed to have learned the art of pattern design from Arthur Heygate Mackmurdo and initially he was better known as a decorative designer than as an architect. In 1896 *The Studio* magazine claimed that the name Voysey had become to wallpaper what Wellington was to the boot. Throughout his career Voysey was acutely aware of the advantages of good publicity. A speculative design for a cottage, published in *The Architect* in 1888, attracted his first client for The Cottage at Bishop's Itchington, Warwickshire, and he commissioned photographs of his newly completed houses and interiors which were then published in British, American, and German magazines. He was a regular exhibitor at the Royal Academy, where he showed watercolour perspectives of his buildings, and he exhibited furniture, decorative designs, and domestic objects as well as photographs of his buildings with the Arts and Crafts Exhibition Society in London.

Early published drawings describe a stylistic debt to the picturesque, half-timbered buildings of R. Norman Shaw

Charles Francis Annesley Voysey (1857–1941), by Harold Speed, 1905

and Devey. Voysey's individuality as an architect, however, and the distinctive 'Voysey style' were founded on a rational and artistic interpretation of the modern country cottage. His standard prescription for domestic design resulted in long, low houses with plain roughcast walls, buttresses at the angles, grey or green slate roofs of steep pitch with gables, small low leaded windows with square stone mullions and dressings, and tapered chimney pots. Voysey designed every detail of his houses and by 1895 hinges terminating in heart motifs, elongated handles, and ventilator grilles depicting birds and berries—all wrought or cast to his designs—were specified as standard for his houses. His buildings were extremely simple and, although they were not particularly cheap, their economic plans, solid workmanship, and their use of good-quality materials earned them a reputation for good value. In his rejection of the elaborate quasi-Elizabethan style affected by Devey, Shaw, and Sir Ernest George, Voysey may certainly be described as the originator of a new movement; moreover, he was the mentor of Charles Rennie Mackintosh, W. M. Dudok, and J. J. P. Oud, usually acclaimed as pioneers.

Between 1890 and 1914 Voysey enjoyed an extensive domestic practice, and his methods of design had a considerable vogue abroad, enhanced by the publication between 1900 and 1905 of books by Hermann Muthesius in German. Among the many country houses built by him during this period are: Walnut Tree Farm at Castlemorton, Worcestershire; Perrycroft at Colwall, Herefordshire; Lowicks at Frensham in Surrey; Hill Close at Studland Bay in Dorset; Greyfriars House at Puttenham in Surrey;

Norney at Shackleford in Surrey; New Place at Haslemere in Surrey; Moorcrag and Broadleys, both at Windermere in Westmorland; Spade House (for H. G. Wells) at Sandgate in Kent; his own house, The Orchard, at Chorleywood in Hertfordshire; The Pastures at North Luffenham in Rutland; Holly Mount at Knotty Green in Buckinghamshire; The Homestead at Frinton-on-Sea in Essex; Littleholme at Kendal, Westmorland; and Brooke End at Henley in Arden in Warwickshire.

He also produced designs for houses in Egypt and Massachusetts. In Chelsea he erected town houses in Hans Road and numerous studios for artists. Other work included inns at Elmesthorpe and at Stetchworth, near Newmarket, a cottage hospital near Beaworthy in Devon, an extension to Sanderson's factory at Chiswick, and office interiors throughout Britain for the Essex and Suffolk Equitable Insurance Society. Occasionally he submitted designs in competition for public buildings, but none was successful. All through his active career he was a hard worker and a confirmed individualist. He conducted his practice on somewhat old-fashioned lines, doing most of the work himself and relying for the rest mainly upon pupils. He published only one book, *Individuality* (1915), and a pamphlet, *Reason as a Basis of Art* (1906).

The outbreak of the First World War virtually extinguished Voysey's practice but it had already begun to decline by 1906. His condemnation of the classical and neo-Georgian architectural styles which became fashionable around the turn of the century, on the grounds that they were un-English, lost him potential clients. His refusal to compromise his own artistic ideals in order to comply with the wishes of his patrons may have contributed to his eclipse. Whatever the cause, he ceased to figure prominently in English architecture, although he continued to submit designs to competitions and he executed a few war memorials. He was out of harmony with the general body of his profession until his last years, being opposed to the registration of architects and to the system of education favoured by the Royal Institute of British Architects, but he was elected a fellow of that body in 1929 and was awarded the royal gold medal for architecture in 1940. For many years he was a zealous member of the Art Workers' Guild, of which he was master in 1924. Late in life he was granted a civil-list pension.

From 1917 Voysey chose to live alone in a service flat in St James's Street, and spent most of his days at the Arts Club not far away, where he had many friends. Somewhat below the middle height, he never played games or read novels, but he was fond of company and enjoyed an argument. Intellectually he was an artist rather than a scholar. Voysey died at his home, Park House, Winchester, on 12 February 1941.

M. S. BRIGGS, rev. WENDY HITCHMOUGH

Sources *The Times* (13 Feb 1941) • H. Robertson, *RIBA Journal*, 48 (1940–41), 88 • N. Pevsner, 'Charles F. Annesley Voysey, 1858–1941', *ArchR*, 89 (1941), 112–13 • B. Oliver, *The Builder*, 160 (1941), 197 • R. Donat, 'Uncle Charles', *Architect's Journal* (20 March 1941), 193–4 • private information (1959) • personal knowledge (1959) • *CGPLA Eng. & Wales* (1941) • W. Hitchmough, *C. F. A. Voysey* (1995)

Archives CKS, drawings of Kent buildings • RIBA BAL, register, address book, and papers; personal papers • RIBA BAL, architectural and natural history sketches and drawings • V&A, drawings; furniture designs | BL, corresp. with Sir Sydney Cockerell, Add. MS 52757 • RIBA BAL, drawings for 'Dallas' in Belfast • V&A, corresp. with Sir James Morton • William Morris Gallery, London, letters to A. H. Mackmurdo

Likenesses H. Speed, chalk drawing, 1896, NPG • H. Speed, oils, 1905, NPG [*see illus.*] • G. M. Frampton, oils, 1924, Art Workers' Guild, London • S. P. Hall, group portrait, chalk and wash (*The St John's Wood Arts Club, 1895*), NPG • W. L. Hankey, portrait, Arts Club, London

Wealth at death £1474 16*s.* 4*d.*: probate, 26 March 1941, *CGPLA Eng. & Wales*

Voysey, Henry Wesley (1791–1824), geologist and surveyor, was born in Salisbury, the son of a Baptist minister, Henry Voysey, and his wife, Ann Maria Annesley (*née* Ellison). He was the brother of the architect Annesley Voysey (*c.*1794–1839) and had two sisters, Mary Ellison and Francis Martha. His early life is known only from written accounts by his contemporary the orientalist H. H. Wilson. He is said to have studied medicine in both Edinburgh and Aberdeen and to have shown an aptitude for natural history, particularly geology. He seems to have acquired an interest in geology through Professor Robert Jameson (1774–1854) and later John MacCulloch, whom he accompanied on a Hebridean journey about 1813.

Voysey served as a hospital assistant in the 59th regiment of foot from May 1815, and is believed to have served in the Waterloo campaign of that summer and subsequently in the army of occupation in Paris, where he learned French. He went to the Cape of Good Hope with a detachment of his regiment in 1816, and made the acquaintance of Tom Sheridan. While he was at the Cape it is said that Voysey was persuaded to go to India by an official of the Bengal establishment of the East India Company. In Calcutta, Voysey became known for his literary and scientific aptitude (he studied Hindi and Sanskrit). He met Colonel William Lambton of the trigonometrical survey of India in Calcutta and joined the survey as geologist at Hyderabad on 15 December 1818. While with the survey he retained a military attachment, first to the 46th regiment of foot (from July 1819) and later to the 1st of foot (March 1821).

Voysey made numerous journeys in India while working for the survey, during which he collected geological specimens at the trigonometrical stations and made the first geological map of part of peninsular India. The first of these journeys with the trigonometrical survey, in November 1818, was in the company of Colonel Lambton and George Everest. Other important journeys for the survey took place in 1819. Some details of these expeditions were given posthumously in the *Journal of the Asiatic Society of Bengal* (13, 1844, 853–62; 19, 1850, 189–212). It was on these trips that Voysey contracted the fever that later ended his life. His work and observations allowed him to compile his 'Report on the geology of Hyderabad', which appeared in two parts in the *Journal of the Asiatic Society of Bengal* (2, 1833, 298–305; 392–405). Working expeditions with the survey continued, but in November 1820 Voysey was sent on sick leave to Madras. Posthumous accounts of this journey, on which he visited the diamond workings at Banganapalle in the Golconda, appeared in *Asiatic Researches* (15, 1825, 120–25). These travels allowed him to augment his geological map of central India. By February 1822 he was based with Lambton at Ellichpur and his geological observations continued. Agra and the Nagpur area were visited and Voysey's posthumous paper on the building stones of the Taj Mahal (*Asiatic Researches*, 15, 1825, 429–35) originated during this period.

Voysey's financial position was never secure and, being nominally on the strength of a British army regiment, he did not receive the full salary from the survey, and was ineligible for regimental and survey promotion. Everest and Lambton had each made representations about his pay and allowances to the East India Company government with only partial success. In pursuit of his claim Voysey felt compelled to visit Calcutta at the end of 1822. His financial position deteriorated further after he was put on regimental half pay in 1823 and in January 1824 he felt compelled to resign from the survey. He set out from Ellichpur for Calcutta on 6 January in order to return to England. He died (intestate) of 'jungle fever' on the way, at Sulkia Ghat, Howrah, on about 19 April 1824.

The bulk of Voysey's geological specimens collected at the survey trigonometrical points came into the possession of the Asiatic Society of Bengal through Voysey's friends in Calcutta H. H. Wilson, Henry Piddington, James Franklin (1783–1834), and James Prinsep. These officials were also responsible for the posthumous publication of his journals. In 1854 Piddington sent representative geological specimens from Voysey's collection to the company's India Museum in London. The company was taken over by the crown in the late 1850s and subsequently many of this museum's collections were acquired by the British Museum (1879). Thus Voysey's specimens were transferred to the Natural History Museum, London, which houses the natural history departments of the original British Museum. Others of Voysey's geological specimens were given to his brother, Annesley Voysey, who gave them to the Geological Society of London. The British Museum acquired this collection in 1911 and these specimens are also housed in the Natural History Museum.

Voysey's claim to fame rests on his having prepared the first geological map of peninsular India. This was apparently handed to the East India Company authorities on 8 August 1821 and sent to London. In 1842 Henry Piddington in Calcutta asked for a copy as it contained 'almost the only existing materials we have for a geological sketch map of much of part of India' (*Journal of the Asiatic Society of Bengal*, 11, 1842, 892), and a reply was sent from London on 1 November 1843 indicating that a copy was being returned. However, when preparing in 1951 for celebrations of the centenary of the Geological Survey in India, Colonel R. H. Phillimore RE (1879–1964) reported that he could not find it in Calcutta (*Historical Records of the Survey of India*, 3, 1954, 510). Enquiries in London in the 1980s were equally sterile. D. T. MOORE

Sources R. H. Phillimore, ed., *Historical records of the survey of India*, 5 vols. (1945–58) · D. T. Moore, 'New light on the life and Indian geological work of H. W. Voysey (1791–1824)', *Archives of Natural History*, 12 (1985), 107–34 · L. Lewis, *Wesleyan Methodist Magazine*, 64 (1841), 240–41 · [H. H. Wilson], 'Memoir of the late Mr. H. W. Voysey', *Asiatic Journal*, 18 (1824), 590–93 · Bengal wills, BL OIOC · E. W. Groves and D. T. Moore, 'Some plants noted by H. W. Voysey (1791–1824) in India, about 1820', *Archives of Natural History*, 13 (1986), 9–10 · Southlands College, Wimbledon, Methodist Archives · J. Keay, *The great arc: the dramatic tale of how India was mapped and Everest was named* (2000)

Archives NHM, department of mineralogy, specimens | Geodetic Survey of India Archives, Dehra Dun, India

Vratz, Christopher (*d.* 1682). *See under* Königsmark, Karl Johann, Count Königsmark in the Swedish nobility (1659–1686).

Vulliamy family (*per. c.*1730–1886), clock- and watchmakers, was founded in London by **(François) Justin Vulliamy** (*bap.* 1712, *d.* 1797), a Swiss watchmaker, son of a pastor at Gingins in the Pays de Vaud, who moved to London in the 1730s to study English watchmaking, particularly, it is believed, the cylinder escapement recently developed by George Graham. By the late 1730s Justin was associated with **Benjamin Gray** (1676/7–1764), a leading watchmaker, it is believed, in St James's Street, who was noted for making fine repeating watches and pedometers. On 12 July 1741, Vulliamy married Gray's daughter Mary (1707–1783); they had four children, Jane (*b.* 1743), Benjamin (1747–1811), Lewis (1749–1822), and Mary (*b.* 1750).

In 1742 Gray was appointed watchmaker in ordinary to George II and Vulliamy, who became Gray's partner at about this time, was closely associated with these duties, though there is no evidence that he himself ever held the royal warrant. In 1752, the business moved to 75 (later renumbered 68) Pall Mall, where it remained for the next hundred years. The partnership continued to produce the high quality watches which had made Gray's reputation, as well as a number of clocks, chiefly of conventional type but including an advanced regulator using John Harrison's 'grasshopper' escapement, which was given to the Society of Antiquaries by Benjamin Lewis Vulliamy in 1848.

After Gray's death on 1 February 1764 Vulliamy continued to produce expensive watches for his fashionable clients as well as cheaper watches to be sold under fictitious names, as his successors were to do. He also made clocks and a number of fine barometers. Although Vulliamy was not as concerned with the search for greater precision in timekeeping as some of his contemporaries, his reputation was sufficiently high for the board of longitude to select him as possible replacement for one of the three watchmakers asked to assess Harrison's revolutionary marine timekeeper H4 in 1765. Gray had lost his royal warrant to George Lindsay on the accession of George III in 1760, but Vulliamy was able to maintain close connections with the horologically minded new king, supplying him with a regulator and a 'follower' clock for timing astronomical observations for the private observatory which the king built at Kew to observe the transit of Venus in 1769. Vulliamy and his elder son, Benjamin, assisted with these observations.

The 1760s also saw Justin Vulliamy increasingly active outside the business. In 1762 he took a leading role in founding the Église Helvétique, or Swiss protestant church, in London, becoming president of its *consistoire* or governing body; in 1766, with other Swiss émigrés, he helped to found a French-speaking lodge of freemasons. Such social activities strengthened Vulliamy's connections within London's large French-speaking community of expatriate merchants and craftsmen, connections which were further reinforced by the apprenticeship of his younger son, Lewis, to the Huguenot merchant John Daniel Lucadou in 1764. Lewis was later to marry one of Lucadou's daughters and this, like the marriage in 1779 of Justin's elder son Benjamin to Sarah de Gingins (1758–1841), natural daughter and heir to the English property of a Swiss officer formerly in the East India Company's service, placed the Vulliamys firmly within the more prosperous ranks of this expatriate community. Justin Vulliamy's wife, Mary, died in 1783 and he died at Kensington on 1 December 1797, leaving his share of the business to his elder son and partner, Benjamin.

Benjamin Vulliamy (1747–1811) had assumed the daily running of the firm many years earlier, possibly in the late 1770s. He was born in St James's on 27 August 1747 and trained in the family business. It is not certain when he became a full partner but he was appointed clockmaker to the king (a post distinct from that of watchmaker, held by his grandfather) as early as 1772. He further developed the firm's contacts with the court, the evident competence of his work allowing him to survive a major reduction in civil list posts in 1782, subject to agreeing to look after the crown's turret clocks—a condition which, under his successor, was to lead to the firm's involvement in turret clock design and construction. However, Benjamin's own horological interests lay in other directions. The market for astronomical clocks such as those made by the Vulliamys for the king was clearly limited. On the other hand, their core business of high quality watches was increasingly threatened by illegal imports of cheaper foreign watches. Attempts at control by the Clockmakers' Company, stimulated by Vulliamy and other leading watchmakers who became honorary freemen in 1781 for this purpose, proved ineffective. Benjamin therefore decided to move into the market for expensive, ornamental, clocks, hitherto dominated by French makers. Not only did this fit the firm's existing clientele but it also suited Benjamin's own artistic tastes (shown as early as 1758 when, as a child, he had won a prize for drawing from the Society of Arts). During the 1780s he began to produce a series of clocks in the latest neo-classical style which were to establish the firm as the leading British producer of ornamental clocks. This expanded during the 1790s into the production of ornamental objects in ormolu, bronze, and marble, such as candelabra and chimney pieces. Under the patronage of wealthy connoisseurs like the prince of Wales and stimulated by the wars which made

French luxury products more difficult to obtain, the supply of such *objets d'art* became, for a time, more important to the Vulliamys than their traditional business of clock- and watchmaking. Unfortunately, this concentration on very expensive luxury articles made the firm vulnerable to delays in payment by its major customers. By 1807 Benjamin Vulliamy was having to borrow money to sustain the business and his problems were compounded by the collapse of his bankers, Devaynes & Co., in 1810. The confusion in his financial affairs was unresolved at his death in 1811, preventing a proper settlement of his personal estate.

Given these problems in his final years, it is not surprising that Benjamin's second son, Justin Theodore, should later describe him as 'too much a gentleman to make a good tradesman', a judgement which may appear to fit the rather refined figure shown in the portrait of Benjamin Vulliamy owned by the Clockmakers' Company, but which is misleading if applied to the earlier stages of his career. Nearer the truth was Justin Theodore's further comment that his father had been a 'clever, unsociable man'. Although Benjamin succeeded his father as president of the Swiss church in London, he was certainly less active in the institutions with which he was associated than either his father or his sons, and seems to have been an essentially private man. Nevertheless, he possessed an enquiring mind and was acquainted with scientific and industrial leaders like Sir Joseph Banks and Matthew Boulton. His inventiveness led him in such varied directions as patenting improved methods of harnessing and suspending two-wheeled carriages in 1792; and sinking what is said to have been the first artesian well in Britain in 1794, an achievement which he reported to the Royal Society in 1797. The well was on the Norland estate in Kensington, which he had bought with his brother, Lewis, in 1792. Originally Benjamin had the farm while Lewis, a prosperous sugar refiner, occupied the main house and its extensive grounds. However, Benjamin later reunited the estate (valued at £13,000 in 1806), and Norland House became his main home from about 1800 until his death in 1811. This, combined with bouts of ill health, meant that the running of the Pall Mall business was increasingly entrusted to Benjamin's eldest son, Benjamin Lewis [see below], assisted by his second son, Justin Theodore [see below], though Benjamin undoubtedly retained an active interest and must take much of the responsibility for the difficulties which the business experienced in these years.

In spite of his financial problems, the business which Benjamin left to his successors on his death on Christmas day 1811 was much larger than under his predecessors, with net profits approaching £1900 per year. He also left property in stocks and land worth about £30,000. In default of a comprehensive will, the main beneficiary was Benjamin Lewis, who inherited the whole of the Norland estate (which was soon let), as well as a share of his father's personal wealth. He also took control of the business, with Justin Theodore as junior partner. Benjamin and Sarah's other surviving children—Mary (*b.* 1781),

Lewis *Vulliamy (1791–1871), Frances (*b.* 1801), and Frederick (1803–1892)—fared relatively badly in the disposition of their father's estate and this led to protracted legal disputes within the family which were not finally concluded until after Benjamin Lewis's death in 1854. None of these younger children joined the family business: Lewis became a successful architect and Frederick entered a bank, while Mary married first a naval captain, C. W. Boys RN (*d.* 1809), and subsequently a barrister, W. V. Hellyer, and Frances married the Revd Frederick Neale.

Benjamin Lewis Vulliamy (1780–1854), who succeeded his father as head of the firm and clockmaker to the king, was born on 25 January 1780, probably at 75 Pall Mall. Although his formal education is unknown, he evidently received a thorough training in both the theoretical and practical aspects of the business. By 1800 he was already helping to run the firm and after he became a partner in 1801 his involvement rapidly increased, so there was little immediate change in the firm's direction when he took over in 1811. He was assisted from 1810 by his younger brother **Justin Theodore Vulliamy** (1787–1870), who took on much of the administrative work, but problems in working with his domineering older brother led Justin to leave the partnership in 1821. In 1822 Justin became residuary legatee of his uncle Lewis Vulliamy's estate and in 1824 moved to Normandy, where he established a factory for spinning woollen yarn.

During the later years of the regency and the reign of George IV, the steady expansion of government and the rebuilding of central London brought about a gradual shift in the Vulliamy firm's output from the production of expensive decorative objects for private customers to the supply of larger numbers of well made but more austere clocks for the new public institutions. This trend was most pronounced in its growing involvement in producing turret clocks, a field in which Benjamin Lewis Vulliamy became an acknowledged expert and in which he introduced a number of practical improvements, such as the two second pendulum with very heavy bob used on the clock supplied to the Plymouth victualling yard in 1831. In 1844, at the request of his friend the architect Sir Charles Barry, he drew up the original specifications for the great clock for the new houses of parliament. His subsequent failure to secure the contract was attributed by Vulliamy to unfair influences; and being, as Manby's obituary was to note, 'fearless in the expression of his opinion of any deviation from the right path', he reacted by publishing much of the relevant correspondence in 1848 in order to demonstrate the rectitude of his own actions. Several of his other publications were also on the subject of public clocks, though he had earlier contributed to the article on watches in Rees's *Cyclopaedia* (1819).

Unlike his father, Benjamin Lewis Vulliamy played a major role in the Clockmakers' Company, of which he was made free in 1809, serving as master five times and fighting strongly on behalf of the declining London trade. He showed a pioneering interest in the early history of the industry and was active in building up the company's museum and library, although his methods of restoration, while typical of his time, have subsequently given him a largely unjustified reputation as a destroyer of his predecessors' work. Apart from business matters, he had an unusually wide range of artistic, scientific, and technical interests, and was a fellow of the Royal Astronomical, Geographical, and Zoological societies and an associate of the Institution of Civil Engineers, to which he left his important horological library. He married Frances Moulton Stiles, daughter of George Stiles, on 3 January 1815; they had three children, Benjamin Lewis (1815–1895), **George John Vulliamy** (1817–1886), and Lucy Sarah Frances (1819–1872), none of whom joined the family firm. The occupation of Benjamin Lewis junior is not known but he was in financial difficulties and living in Rome when his father died; George became an architect and civil engineer; and Lucy married the cleric and schoolmaster S. J. Rigaud, son of Benjamin Lewis Vulliamy's friend, the Oxford professor of astronomy S. P. Rigaud.

With Benjamin Lewis Vulliamy's death from bronchitis at 68 Pall Mall on 8 January 1854, the firm came to an end. Much of the equipment was left to Vulliamy's leading craftsmen, the Jump family, who set up their own business in Bond Street, London, but the goodwill was bought by another leading London clockmaker, Charles Frodsham, who subsequently obtained Vulliamy's post as superintendent of the royal clocks at Buckingham Palace.

George John Vulliamy was born on 19 May 1817, educated at Westminster School from 1826 to 1833, then articled to Joseph Bramah & Sons, engineers. In July 1836 he entered the office of his father's friend Sir Charles Barry, leaving in 1841 to travel through France, Italy (where he made drawings for Henry Gally Knight's *Ecclesiastical Architecture of Italy*, 1842–4), Greece, Asia Minor, and Egypt. Returning to England in 1843, he commenced practice as an architect, briefly assisting his uncle, the architect Lewis Vulliamy, on Dorchester House. Among the buildings for which George John Vulliamy was responsible were a mansion at Dyffryn, Monmouthshire, the Swiss church in Endell Street, Westminster, and St Mary, Greenhithe, in Kent. He was a fellow and member of council of the Royal Institute of British Architects, a member, and for a time secretary, of the Royal Archaeological Institute, and he exhibited at the Royal Academy in 1838 and 1845. On 2 April 1851 Vulliamy married Eliza King (*née* Umfreville); they had five children.

Elected superintending architect to the Metropolitan Board of Works in March 1861, Vulliamy thereafter devoted all his time to this work, designing various buildings, several fire-brigade stations, and the pedestal and sphinxes for Cleopatra's needle on the Embankment. He resigned in 1886 due to ill health and died at his home, Ingress House, Greenhithe, on 12 November 1886; he was buried on 17 November at Stone, near Dartford.

ROGER SMITH

Sources S. Benson Beevers, 'Benjamin Gray', *Antiquarian Horology and the Proceedings of the Antiquarian Horological Society*, 1 (1953–6),

76-7 • S. Benson Beevers, 'Francis Justin Vulliamy', *Antiquarian Horology and the Proceedings of the Antiquarian Horological Society*, 1 (1953–6), 142–5 • S. Benson Beevers, 'Benjamin Vulliamy', *Antiquarian Horology and the Proceedings of the Antiquarian Horological Society*, 2 (1956–9), 31–3, 37 • S. Benson Beevers, 'Benjamin Lewis Vulliamy', *Antiquarian Horology and the Proceedings of the Antiquarian Horological Society*, 1 (1953–6), 15–16 • S. Benson Beevers, notes on Vulliamy family, GL, MS 29186 • *Vulliamy v. Noble*, 1810–19; *Vulliamy v. Vulliamy*, 1845–55; *Gray v. Egerton*, 1707, PRO, chancery papers • PCC suit, *Vulliamy v. Vulliamy*, 1822, PRO • C. M. Manby, 'Memoir of Benjamin Lewis Vulliamy', *Annual Report of the Institution of Civil Engineers* (1854–5) • *GM*, 2nd ser., 41 (1854), 325 [obit. of Benjamin Lewis Vulliamy] • *DNB* • E. Bunt, 'An eighteenth century watchmaker and his day book', *Antiquarian Horology and the Proceedings of the Antiquarian Horological Society*, 8 (1972–4) [Benjamin Gray] • C. Jagger, *Royal clocks* (1983) • Archives Cantonales Vaudoises, Switzerland, Eb. 61/1, 339 • R. Smith, 'Benjamin Vulliamy's painted satinwood clocks and pedestals', *Apollo*, 141 (June 1995) • R. Smith, 'Benjamin Vulliamy's library, a collection of neo-classical design sources', *Burlington Magazine*, 141 (1999) • records of the Swiss church, Endell Street, London • parish registers, St Mary Abbot, Kensington, 1741–64 • parish register, St Martin-in-the-Fields, 22 June 1707 [baptism, Mary Gray] • parish registers, St James's Westminster, 1758–1854 • register of Leicester Fields Chapel, PRO, RG 4/4585, 20 Sept 1747 [baptism, Benjamin Vulliamy] • d. cert. [Benjamin Lewis Vulliamy] • d. cert. [Sarah Vulliamy] • will of Benjamin Gray, PRO, PROB 11/895, fols. 362–3 • will of François Justin Vulliamy, PRO, PROB 11/1301, fols. 177–8 • will of Benjamin Vulliamy, PRO, PROB 11/1529, fol. 376 • will of Benjamin Lewis Vulliamy, PRO, PROB 11/2188, fols. 401–4 • private information (2004) [family]
Archives British Horological Institute, Upton Hall, Nottinghamshire, papers | BM, clocks and watches • GL, Clockmakers' Company Museum, clocks and watches • GL, Clockmakers' Company papers • PRO, chancery papers, *Vulliamy v. Noble*, 1810–19; *Vulliamy v. Vulliamy*, 1845–55 • Royal Collection, clocks and watches • V&A, clocks and watches
Likenesses oils, *c*.1740 (Benjamin Gray), GL, Clockmakers' Company Museum • oils, *c*.1740 (Justin Vulliamy), GL, Clockmakers' Company Museum • oils, *c*.1790 (Benjamin Vulliamy), GL, Clockmakers' Company Museum • W. F. Wainwright, watercolour drawing, 1838 (Benjamin Lewis Vulliamy), repro. in F. J. Britten, *Old clocks and watches and their makers*, 5th edn (1922), 376; priv. coll. • R. C. Lucas, wax cameo, *c*.1850 (Benjamin Lewis Vulliamy), GL, Clockmakers' Company Museum
Wealth at death under £10,000—personal estate; Justin Vulliamy: PRO, will, death duty registers • over £30,000 incl. real estate; Benjamin Vulliamy: will, PRO, PROB 11/1529, sig. 49, death duty registers • approx. £20,000; Benjamin Lewis Vulliamy: will, PRO, PROB 11/2188, sig. 250, death duty registers • under £20,000—effects; Justin Theodore Vulliamy: PRO, will, death duty registers

Vulliamy, Benjamin (1747–1811). *See under* Vulliamy family (*per. c.*1730–1886).

Vulliamy, Benjamin Lewis (1780–1854). *See under* Vulliamy family (*per. c.*1730–1886).

Vulliamy, George John (1817–1886). *See under* Vulliamy family (*per. c.*1730–1886).

Vulliamy, (François) Justin (bap. 1712, d. 1797). *See under* Vulliamy family (*per. c.*1730–1886).

Vulliamy, Justin Theodore (1787–1870). *See under* Vulliamy family (*per. c.*1730–1886).

Vulliamy, Lewis (1791–1871), architect, was born on 15 March 1791 at 68 Pall Mall, London, the third son of Benjamin *Vulliamy (1747–1811) [*see under* Vulliamy family], clockmaker, and Sarah de Gingins (1758–1841); Benjamin

Lewis *Vulliamy (1780–1854) [*see under* Vulliamy family] was his eldest brother. Articled at the age of sixteen to Robert Smirke, Vulliamy entered the Royal Academy Schools in March 1809 and won the silver medal in 1810 and the gold medal in 1813 with a design for a nobleman's country mansion. On leaving Smirke's office in 1814 he commenced his own practice: one of his first commissions, obtained in 1815 through a family recommendation, was to oversee the repair and enlargement of Syston Park in Lincolnshire for Sir John Heyford Thorold, bt. Vulliamy was to add a notable library wing there in 1822–4. In 1818 he was awarded the Royal Academy's travelling studentship, which enabled him to spend four years on the continent, chiefly in Italy, although he also ventured as far as Greece and Asia Minor. His study of classical and Renaissance buildings, together with an equal familiarity with English domestic architecture, formed a firm foundation for his subsequent career as a country house architect.

On his return to England Vulliamy established himself in London at 361 Oxford Street and in 1822 submitted as his first entry to the Royal Academy a 'design for the court of a palace' (Graves, *RA exhibitors*, 8.94). His commissions were initially rather more humble, and included speculative housing in Tavistock Square and Gordon (later Endsleigh) Place in Bloomsbury in 1827. Vulliamy's very considerable output was itemized in *The Builder* in 1871, an account which was based on a list drawn up by the architect himself. He established a reputation for his Gothic churches, such as St Bartholomew's, Sydenham (1826–31), St Barnabas's, Addison Road, Kensington (1828–9), St Michael's, Highgate (1830–32; design exhibited at the Royal Academy, 1831), and Christ Church, Woburn Square (1831–3; design exhibited at the Royal Academy, 1833; dem.). Other churches built by Vulliamy were: at Wardle, Worsthorne, at Burnley (Holy Trinity, Accrington Lane), and at Habergam Eaves, all in Lancashire; St Paul's, Burslem, and Christ Church, Cobridge, in Staffordshire; Christ Church, Todmorden, Yorkshire; and in Dorset, Norfolk, and elsewhere. He was also responsible for works at Rochester Cathedral in the mid-1840s. Vulliamy's non-Gothic churches included the Norman Glasbury church in Brecknockshire (1836–7), and the Italianate All Saints', Ennismore Gardens, Westminster (1848–9).

Vulliamy was also responsible for a number of diverse public buildings across the country, including a grandstand at Wolverhampton racecourse (1828), the Epping union workhouse (1837), and the Lock Hospital, Paddington (1842–9). His most prestigious London commissions were the Law Society's premises in Chancery Lane (1828–32), with later additions; designs exhibited at the Royal Academy in 1830 and 1832; and the re-fronting of the Royal Institution in Albemarle Street in 1838, to which he added a screen of giant Corinthian half-columns (designs exhibited at the Royal Academy in 1837 and 1838). On 16 January 1838 Vulliamy married Elizabeth Anne, only child of Frederick Papendiek, vicar of Morden, Surrey; they had four sons and a daughter.

Vulliamy is best remembered for his domestic work. A

number of Lincolnshire commissions followed on from his work at Syston Park, including Boothby Pagnell Hall (1825), and he was soon engaged across the country carrying out alterations to gentlemen's seats, besides designing numerous rectories. Vulliamy's mastery of classical, Gothic, Renaissance, and Tudor idioms enabled him to respond to the period's eclectic requirements. His most important patron was the multi-millionaire Robert Stayner Holford, who in 1839 engaged Vulliamy to carry out work at his Gloucestershire seat at Westonbirt. Having commenced with alterations to the extant house he was subsequently commissioned to design a totally new house in an opulent English Renaissance idiom; this was commenced in 1864 and was unfinished at Vulliamy's death. Westonbirt was one of Vulliamy's two most important works. The other was Holford's London residence: Dorchester House, on Park Lane. This replaced John Vardy's house of the 1750s and was completed in 1857. It was a massive palazzo based on Peruzzi's Villa Farnesina, with a magnificent staircase and sumptuous internal decoration by Alfred Stevens. Until it was demolished in 1929 to make way for the eponymous hotel, Dorchester House was one of the grandest residences of Victorian London.

Vulliamy's extremely successful career was 'due equally to his ability and his industry … He was well known to be peculiar in his notions, and many odd anecdotes are related of him' (The Builder, 142). His best-known pupil was Owen Jones; his nephew George Vulliamy assisted him on Dorchester House. Never regarded among the first rank of architects, he was, with Charles Barry, one of the outstanding practitioners of the Italianate style in early Victorian England. Vulliamy published two works: The Bridge of the SSa. Trinita, over the Arno at Florence (1822) and Examples of ornamental sculpture in architecture, drawn from the originals in Greece, Asia Minor, and Italy in the years 1818, 1819, 1820, 1821 (1823). His drawings of the castle at Newcastle were published in Vetusta monumenta vol. 5 (1835) as plates 10–18. He died at his house on Clapham Common on 4 January 1871: despite having suffered from chronic bronchitis for several years, he worked until the end. He left an estate valued at about £60,000. ROGER BOWDLER

Sources Colvin, Archs. · DNB · The Builder, 29 (1871), 142 [incl. list of works] · J. Lees-Milne, 'Westonbirt House, Gloucestershire [pts 1–2]', Country Life, 151 (1972), 1226–9, 1310–13 · Graves, RA exhibitors · CGPLA Eng. & Wales (1871)
Archives RIBA BAL, corresp. and office papers | Durham RO, letters to Lady Londonderry and her agent · RIBA BAL, drawings collection, biography file
Wealth at death under £60,000: probate, 3 Feb 1871, CGPLA Eng. & Wales

Vyner [Viner], **Sir Robert**, baronet (1631–1688), goldsmith and banker, was born in Warwick, the third son of William Vyner and his second wife, Susannah, née Fulwood. The Vyner family belonged to what their seventeenth-century contemporaries often called 'the middling sort', and their story illustrates the extent of social mobility: William's eldest son remained in the country and does not seem to have changed his status or radically improved his fortunes; the second son, Thomas, made a career in the church and ended his days as a doctor of divinity and dean of Gloucester. Robert was apprenticed to his father's half-brother Thomas *Vyner (1588–1665) in 1646. He became free of the Goldsmiths' Company and his step-uncle's partner in 1656; a third member of the partnership conveniently died soon after this and Robert took over his share. He was involved in public finance under the protectorate, but on account of his relative youth less prominently so than his step-uncle. A year after Charles II's return he became the king's goldsmith supplying the royal jewel house (a branch of the royal household) over the next twenty-four years. In this way he must have enjoyed opportunities for patronage, being, through his office, in a position to commission silver plate and other gold- and silverware from master craftsmen in the Goldsmiths' Company. On the death of his step-uncle, Sir Thomas, in 1665, Vyner assumed sole control of the banking house, then at the Vine in Lombard Street, which had to be relocated after the great fire a year later. In addition he was made an overseer of Sir Thomas's will, but within eighteen months the latter's younger son and sole executor in turn died; Sir Robert then became executor of both their wills and was also effectively the heir to his cousin's estate. His wealth must have been very considerably increased as a result of this. During the years that followed, he came to be the crown's largest single individual creditor and one of the country's largest-scale private bankers. He suffered a liquidity crisis in 1667–8 because of the crown's growing indebtedness at the end of the Second Anglo-Dutch War; he made desperate appeals both to the king and to the leading minister of the time, Lord Arlington, the senior secretary of state, but it seems more likely that it was Edward Backwell who came to his help, returning his assistance provided two years earlier. By this time Vyner was one of the commissioners and farmers of the customs, and also the power behind the syndicate farming the unpopular hearth tax.

Having weathered one crisis Vyner appears to have gone on increasing his advances to the crown, these presumably much exceeding any credit balance on the private deposits in his hands. The only fragmentary ledger of his banking transactions known to exist covers three weeks beginning a few days after the great fire in September 1666, and it obviously cannot be taken as representative of his banking activities over a longer period. None the less a few facts stand out: his clients included the other goldsmith–bankers who were to be involved with him in the so-called 'Stop of the exchequer' just over five years later. These apart, the largest individual transactions recorded were with the famous firm of scriveners, Robert Clayton and John Morris, and with the excise farmers, but all manner of men, from Arlington himself to those of modest circumstances, dealt with him. The amount of cash left in hand at the end of each day's dealing varied greatly, from under £2000 to nearly £13,000, the average figure being just below £5000 and the median £3858.

Like bankers in all ages, the London goldsmiths aimed to charge higher rates of interest to borrowers than they themselves had to pay to depositors; likewise, to make use of the overall credit balance in their hands at any given time to make further loans or to invest in other projects. Again, as with all banks, this depended on confidence in their creditworthiness and on their not suffering either unexpected major withdrawals or unanticipated large-scale defaulting by 'bad' debtors. Lending to English monarchs, as to other rulers and governments, had always been a risky business. For Vyner and his contemporaries the risks were much increased as a consequence of the system of Treasury orders and assignments devised by Sir George Downing and implemented from 1665 to 1666. This attempt to establish a system of short-term royal paper credit was a success, but not in the precise way which Downing and the politicians who backed him had intended. They had hoped that large numbers of reasonably affluent private individuals would lend money to the crown on the security of hypothecated future revenues—secured initially on parliamentary taxes, and latterly also on the crown's ordinary or 'regular' income from customs, excise, and the hearth money. In practice, however, most such lenders rapidly reassigned their orders for repayment to one or more of the goldsmith–bankers, whose exposure thus grew indirectly as well as by their own direct advances to the crown. So when the king's inner circle of advisers persuaded him to avert a general bankruptcy while preparing for the Third Anglo-Dutch War, by the Stop of the exchequer in December 1671 – January 1672, they were hit disproportionately hard. It is not the case that all issues of money were suddenly cut off: that would have been royal bankruptcy indeed. Some payments were actually made to Vyner immediately following the Stop. None the less the cessation of all hypothecated payments on orders either assigned or reassigned, initially for one year and later extended to two years, cut the ground from under the bankers and imperilled them with their own creditors. In the first series of calculations of how much was owing by the crown to individuals or syndicates among the goldsmiths, Vyner's total was omitted, presumably being too complicated to work out in the time available, but when these debts were first refunded in 1674 by establishing a 6 per cent annual payment (of the capital sums owing in January 1672 plus the interest which had accrued since then), he was reckoned to be owed over £400,000. This was a truly colossal sum for that date, equivalent to well over one-third of the total amount owing to all the bankers, or—to give another measure of comparison—more than one-third of the total annual income supposedly settled on Charles II by parliament in 1660–61 but not in fact attained (war taxation apart) until well into the 1670s. It was equivalent to the yield of five pre-civil war parliamentary subsidies, or to the entire unprecedented, once-for-all grant made to Charles I in 1641–2, levied on the whole of England and Wales.

It is remarkable that Vyner remained technically solvent until 1684, though his surviving papers show him borrowing on bond like any other impecunious character of the day: under this system the debtor and/or his securities committed themselves to pay twice (or nearly twice) the sum being borrowed if this was not repaid by a fixed date,

usually, though not invariably, one year ahead. The king, or rather his ministers, tried to get the letters patent under the great seal (originally of 1674, revised in 1677) for the 6 per cent repayment by annuity turned into an act of parliament in 1678, in order to put the bankers' own provisions for the repayment of their respective creditors beyond the possibility of challenge in the courts; but deadlock between the two houses prevented this. In his first general attempt to settle with his creditors made in 1681 Vyner offered to pay four-fifths of what he owed them by instalments out of the king's annuity to him; the remaining one-fifth was to be found out of his own estate within one year. By 1684 it appears that about 40 out of the original 158 creditors had agreed to this and the offer had still not been implemented. It seems to have been these forty who shared the costs of the proceedings leading to the commission of bankruptcy which was issued against him in that year. How much had been extracted from his estate by the time of his death in 1688 is not clear; the crown's annuity was then stopped, but pressure for a final settlement evidently continued, for in 1699, fifteen years after his bankruptcy and eleven after his death, a private act of parliament (modelled on that passed for Backwell's creditors the year before) was at last passed; under its terms, if two-thirds of the creditors, in numbers and in the value of their claims, agreed to settle, the minority would have to accept the same conditions or else forfeit any claim on the estate thereafter—an interesting use of statute to override or prevent ordinary legal process at either equity or common law.

Vyner was knighted in 1665; he was created a baronet in 1666, the year in which he also became an alderman. He was high sheriff of London in 1667, having to obtain a special pardon on account of his formal responsibility for the escape from one of the city prisons of a convicted counterfeiter of the royal seal. Notwithstanding the crash of 1672, he was chosen as lord mayor in 1674, and—according to oral tradition—entertained the king with embarrassing conviviality. He undertook more than one confidential mission overseas, on the crown's behalf, in order, so it was said, to evade his creditors at home. In 1665 he married Mary Hyde (d. 1675), daughter of John Whitchurch of Walton, Buckinghamshire, and widow of Sir Thomas Hyde, bt, a wealthy Hertfordshire landowner (not related to the earl of Clarendon or the other Wiltshire Hydes); she was said to have brought him a very large additional fortune during her lifetime.

What became Vyner's country seat, the mansion house of Swakeleys near Ickenham, Middlesex, had been built in the 1630s by a future royalist lord mayor. It was inherited by one of his daughters, who married the republican politician Sir James Harrington, bt, who added embellishments to the interior of the house. Although he was attainted, imprisoned, and degraded to plain Mr Harrington after the Restoration, his wife somehow retained this property, which was bought by Vyner in 1665, presumably with his own wife's marriage portion. The daughter of her first marriage, Bridget Hyde, was also a considerable heiress. In January 1675, during his mayoralty, Vyner became a trustee to enforce the proposed marriage settlement between her and Peregrine Osborne, Lord Dunblane, second son of the lord treasurer, the earl of Danby. This became an extraordinary and embarrassing *cause célèbre*. The bride was held to have already entered into a form of marriage, at the age of twelve, with a plebeian relative. The courts took until 1682–3 to reach a final decision, the rival claimant to Bridget Hyde's hand (and fortune) having even then, it was said, to be bought out by the father-in-law to be, though by then Danby himself was in the Tower and Vyner on the eve of his own bankruptcy. Meanwhile, his wife having died on new year's day 1675, Vyner's step-daughter was living with him at Swakeleys when she was abducted at pistol-point by a gang headed by a minor functionary of the royal bedchamber acting on behalf of Dunblane's rival, the girl's alleged husband. She was rescued in east London and restored to her stepfather's care, but just as the length of the matrimonial case reflects on the legal system, so the virtual pardon of the page of honour involved seems a reflection on Charles II's way of conducting business, almost reminiscent of his relations with the notorious Colonel Thomas Blood. A further legal agreement between Vyner and Danby survives from 1680. While there is some evidence of their relations having been strained at times, the whole affair emphasizes that Vyner moved in court circles to an extent which marked him out from the other goldsmiths—indeed, from most other financiers and merchants of his day. The only child of his own marriage, Charles Vyner (1667–88), predeceased him by a few months, Vyner according to hearsay dying of a broken heart in consequence of this loss. He died at Windsor on 2 September 1688 and was buried at St Mary Woolnoth in the City of London on the 16th.

His son's death caused Vyner to make a new will. All his properties and possessions were to be sold by his executors to the best possible advantage. Out of the proceeds his creditors were to receive 30 per cent of what he owed them, provided they accepted this offer and remained bound by it; the other 70 per cent owing to them was then secured on the 6 per cent annuity, payable to him out of the excise revenue until the king's debt to him was fully discharged. Out of the overplus on the estate, however much or little that might turn out to be, one-quarter was reserved to his executors—his nephew Thomas, son of the late dean of Gloucester, and Francis Millington, his one-time business partner and fellow customs commissioner; of the remaining three-quarters, £100 was reserved for each of his two nephews, the sons of his eldest brother (the stay-at-home Warwickshire branch of the family), while each of the four great London hospitals was to receive one-tenth (that is, three-fortieths of the total); the residuary legatees in equal shares were his four nieces and his other two nephews. Any legatee going to law with the executors was automatically to forfeit the whole of her or his share. Assuming that the terms of the will were observed, this explains how the residue of the estate descended through the dean's son, Thomas, and negates the claim by a latter-day descendant of Vyner's elder brother that their line had been cheated of their inheritance; if the terms of the will were not carried out, then this must remain an open question. It was the dean's grandson who became the owner of Swakeleys, which was later sold in order to enlarge the estate in Lincolnshire, where this branch of the family was very well established during the eighteenth century and into the nineteenth. Their descendants then moved from Gautby in Lincolnshire to Newby Hall in the West Riding of Yorkshire later in the nineteenth century. The family's funeral monuments remained at Gautby, whither they had been removed from the City; the famous equestrian statue, originally commissioned for the king of Poland whose agents were unable to pay for it and which was then bought by Vyner, who had it shipped back to England and altered to represent Charles II, having been removed from the City during the eighteenth century and then erected at Gautby, was taken to Newby when the family moved there.

Sir Robert's place in the long-term development of banking is hard to assess. In one sense he was obviously the forerunner of those financiers of the 1680s and 1690s who made possible the establishment of the Bank of England and the national debt. It might equally be argued that the Stop of the exchequer, into which the crown was tempted by the vulnerability of Vyner and the other goldsmiths, served to delay such changes by twenty years. Whichever view is preferred, there can be no doubt of his pre-eminence as a financier of the Restoration era.

G. E. AYLMER

Sources CSP dom., 1660–80 · J. M. S. Brooke and A. W. C. Hallen, eds., *The transcript of the registers of … St Mary Woolnoth and St Mary Woolnoth Haw … 1538 to 1760* (1886) · A. B. Beaven, ed., *The aldermen of the City of London, temp. Henry III–[1912]*, 2 vols. (1908–13) · A. Browning, *Thomas Osborne, earl of Danby and duke of Leeds, 1632–1712*, 3 vols. (1944–51) · *London: north-west*, Pevsner (1991) · C. D. Chandaman, *The English public revenue, 1660–1688* (1975) · D. K. Clark, 'A Restoration goldsmith-banking house: the Vine on Lombard Street', *Essays in modern English history in honor of Wilbur Cortez Abbott* (1941), 3–47; facs. edn (1971) · GEC, *Baronetage* · A. Heal, ed., *The London goldsmiths, 1200–1800: a record of the names and addresses of the craftsmen, their shop-signs and trade-cards* (1935); facs. edn (1972) · J. K. Horsefield, 'The "stop of the exchequer" revisited', *Economic History Review*, 2nd ser., 35 (1982), 511–28 · Pepys, *Diary* · D. Mitchell, 'Innovation and the transfer of skill in the goldsmiths' trade in Restoration London', *Goldsmiths, silversmiths and bankers: innovation and the transfer of skill, 1550 to 1750* [London 1993], ed. D. Mitchell (1995), 5–22 · G. O. Nichols, 'English government borrowing, 1660–1688', *Journal of British Studies*, 10/2 (1970–71), 83–104 · S. F. Quinn, 'Banking before the bank: London's unregulated goldsmith-bankers, 1660–1694', PhD diss., University of Illinois, 1994 · S. Quinn, 'Balances and goldsmith-bankers: the co-ordination and control of inter-banker clearing in seventeenth-century London', *Goldsmiths, silversmiths and bankers: innovation and the transfer of skill, 1550 to 1750* [London 1993], ed. D. Mitchell (1995), 53–76 · R. D. Richards, *The early history of banking in England* (1929) · H. G. Roseveare, 'The advancement of the king's credit, 1660–1672: a study in economic, political and administrative history based mainly on the career of Sir George Downing, knight and baronet', PhD diss., U. Cam., 1962 · H. G. Roseveare, *Government, financial policy and the money markets in late 17th-century England* (1926); later pubn (Italy, 1981) · H. Roseveare, *The financial revolution, 1660–1760* (1991) · W. A. Shaw, ed., *Calendar of treasury books*, 1–9, PRO (1904–31) [incl. introductions by W. A. Shaw] · J. R. Woodhead, *The rulers of London, 1660–1689* (1965) · DNB

Archives HLRO, box 17, no. 628; 11 William III, no. 19 • PRO, estate papers, C.107/112 • PRO, exchequer of receipt, E.403/2510, 3034; E.406/16–19 • PRO, lord chamberlain's department, L.C.5/107 • V&A NAL, statement, warrant, and receipt relating to work done for James II • W. Yorks. AS, Leeds, corresp. and papers | BL, Add. MSS • Royal Bank of Scotland, London, Edward Backwell MSS, Backwell's ledgers, EB.1/1–9 and 2
Likenesses J. M. Wright, group portrait, oils, 1673, NPG • group portrait, oils, 1673 (after J. M. Wright), Newby Hall, North Yorkshire • W. Faithorne, line engraving, BM, NPG • oils (after J. Riley), Goldsmiths Hall

Sir Thomas Vyner, first baronet (1588–1665), by unknown artist

Vyner [Viner], **Sir Thomas**, first baronet (1588–1665), goldsmith and banker, was born on 15 December 1588 at North Cerney in Gloucestershire, the son of Thomas Vyner, of a Warwickshire family, and his second wife, Anne. The younger Thomas was apprenticed in London, first to his half-sister's husband, Samuel Moore, of the Goldsmiths' Company, in 1601 and then to William Terry in 1604, taking his freedom in 1611. He first came to notice in 1624, when he obtained a reversion to the comptrollership of the mint—an appropriate investment for someone with his qualifications, though he never took up this office. In 1639 he sold £79 worth of plate to Edward Nicholas, the future royalist secretary of state, but his political sympathies are better indicated by his having advanced £100 for the parliamentarian army under the earl of Essex in October 1643. He was one of the contractors appointed to manage the sale of bishops' lands in 1646, and he was named to various London committees in the years following the civil war. His allegiances have been described as those of a political presbyterian in the years 1646–8. His attitude towards the Commonwealth seems equivocal: he became an alderman of the City of London in 1646 and remained one until 1660. He served as high sheriff of the City of London in 1648–9 but certainly achieved greater prominence under the Cromwellian protectorate (1654–9) after the repeal of the engagement, the republican loyalty oath which expressed explicit approval of the abolition of monarchy and House of Lords and implicit support for the regicide. Even so, in December 1649 he was asked by the council of state to collect Spanish pieces of eight and to meet the admiralty committee if his other commitments permitted, and the next day he offered 7000 ryals at 4s 10d. each, pointing out that he could have asked for and received more than this. In 1652 he gave security for the settlement of his penal fine by the Catholic peer Lord Petre; but this was less a pointer to religious sympathy than a disguised way of obtaining the equivalent of a bond or mortgage. He was elected lord mayor of London in 1653–4 and was knighted by the protector at his inauguration in February 1654.

In 1623 Vyner had acted as a co-treasurer or accountant for the money received from the Dutch East India Company as compensation for the Amboyna massacre, to be paid to the victims if they were still alive or, more likely, to their heirs and executors. He served in the same capacity for the funds raised to relieve various groups of persecuted European protestants, and he was involved in the transmission of captured Spanish bullion to the mint for coinage. He may also have acted as a banker for private individuals. His apprentices during the 1630s and 1640s included Edward Backwell, who was acting as a financier in his own right by the 1650s, and his own step-nephew Robert *Vyner (1631–1688), who entered into an informal partnership with him in 1656.

Sir Thomas was married three times. His first wife was Anne, daughter of Richard Parsons of London, a merchant; they had five daughters, including Elizabeth who married Sir Henry Pickering, another Cromwellian knight who became a Restoration baronet, and Rebecca who married Sir Richard Piggott, a tax farmer and successor to his wife's stepbrother as an office-holder in chancery. Vyner's second wife was Honor Humble (d. 1656?), daughter of George Humble, of London, citizen and stationer; their two sons were George Vyner (d. 1673) and Thomas Vyner (d. c.1666). His third, who survived him, was Alice, widow of Alderman John Perryn; they had no children.

There is little evidence of the activities of Thomas and Robert Vyner between the fall of Richard Cromwell and the Restoration. Along with all other Cromwellian titles, Sir Thomas's knighthood automatically lapsed with the return of monarchy in 1660, but within nine weeks he was reknighted by Charles II, though he did not recover his place as an alderman, which he lost to another returned royalist. In 1661 he petitioned unsuccessfully for the office of king's goldsmith. He was made a baronet on 18 June 1661 and despite his age took an active part in providing cash and credit for the government of the restored monarchy. On 11 May 1665 he died at his country house in Hackney (then a suburban village), Middlesex, and Samuel Pepys attended his funeral at St Mary Woolnoth in the City on 1 June. Sir Thomas certainly helped to lay the foundations for the achievements of later seventeenth-century goldsmith–bankers, notably his own apprentices Edward Backwell and Robert Vyner.

At his death Vyner had already established himself as a landed gentleman besides having had a house and an office in the City. He was perhaps fortunate in not having lived to see the effects of the plague, the great fire, and the naval disasters in 1667 at the end of the Dutch War. The arrangements at his death were a little unusual. The baronetcy passed to his son, Sir George Vyner, who was married to Abigail, daughter and coheir of Sir John Lawrence. George was also a member of the Goldsmiths' Company and, according to one authority, was acting as a banker around 1670; but he does not seem to have been very prominent as such, having by then established himself as a landed gentleman, as intended by his father. As required by the custom of the City, after payment of Sir Thomas's debts the residue was to be divided into three equal shares: one to his two sons, one to his wife, and the third, about £7000, to charities and other named legatees. All his real property in Middlesex and Essex was to go to Sir George for his lifetime, then to his heir apparent, Sir Thomas's grandson, and then to the grandson's heirs, in default of which to Sir Thomas's second son, Thomas, a minor office-holder in chancery, and his heirs. Sir George was required within two years to lay out a further £7000 on additional landed property; if he failed to do so, the bond for that amount entered into by his brother Thomas and his cousin Sir Robert (by an indenture of 1663) was to be forfeit to Thomas. If Sir Thomas's wife outlived him, she was to be paid £4330 by instalments, according to the marriage agreement made between them in 1658. This sum and a further £2500 which was to be paid by Sir George to his younger brother (in addition to an outright legacy of £2000 for Thomas) were both secured on part of the existing Essex property. To effect these complicated arrangements, the younger son was made sole executor, with two of Sir Thomas Vyner's sons-in-law and his step-nephew Sir Robert (here called 'cousin') as overseers of the will. The omission of the elder son is very striking. In the event Thomas, the executor, died only about a year and a half after his father, having made over his interest in the estate and the executorship to Sir Robert, who had already assumed sole control of the banking business at the Vine in Lombard Street (temporarily relocated after the great fire). Sir George died in 1673. When his son, Sir Thomas, third baronet, died under age and without heirs ten years later, the baronetage became extinct.

G. E. AYLMER

Sources CSP dom., 1624; 1639–64 · M. A. E. Green, ed., *Calendar of the proceedings of the committee for compounding … 1643–1660*, 3, PRO (1891) · M. A. E. Green, ed., *Calendar of the proceedings of the committee for advance of money, 1642–1656*, 1, PRO (1888) · C. H. Firth and R. S. Rait, eds., *Acts and ordinances of the interregnum, 1642–1660*, 3 vols. (1911) · W. A. Shaw, ed., *Calendar of treasury books*, 1, PRO (1904) · J. M. S. Brooke and A. W. C. Hallen, eds., *The transcript of the registers of … St Mary Woolnoth and St Mary Woolnoth Haw … 1538 to 1760* (1886) · M. Ashley, *Financial and commercial policy under the Cromwellian protectorate*, 2nd edn (1962) · R. Ashton, *The crown and the money market, 1603–1640* (1960) · A. B. Beaven, ed., *The aldermen of the City of London, temp. Henry III–[1912]*, 2 vols. (1908–13) · R. Brenner, *Merchants and revolution: commercial change, political conflict, and London's overseas traders, 1550–1653* (1993) · D. K. Clark, 'A Restoration goldsmith-banking house: The Vine on Lombard Street', *Essays in modern English history in honor of Wilbur Cortez Abbott* (1941), 3–47; facs. edn (1971) · GEC, *Baronetage* · A. Heal, ed., *The London goldsmiths, 1200–1800: a record of the names and addresses of the craftsmen, their shop-signs and trade-cards* (1935); facs. edn (1972) · R. D. Richards, *The early history of banking in England* (1929) · J. R. Woodhead, *The rulers of London, 1660–1689* (1965) · D. Mitchell, 'Innovation and the transfer of skill in the goldsmiths' trade in Restoration London', *Goldsmiths, silversmiths and bankers: innovation and the transfer of skill, 1550 to 1750* [London 1993], ed. D. Mitchell (1995), 5–22 · DNB · *The obituary of Richard Smyth … being a catalogue of all such persons as he knew in their life*, ed. H. Ellis, CS, 44 (1849), 42, 63 · PRO, PROB 11/316, sig. 55

Archives W. Yorks. AS, Leeds, Newby Hall MSS | BL, Add. MSS 4184, 4197, 5489

Likenesses funeral monument, All Saints Church, Gautby, Lincolnshire · oils, NPG [*see illus.*] · oils, second version, Goldsmiths' Hall, London

Vynne, Eleanora Mary Susanna [Nora] (1870?–1914), journalist and political activist, was the daughter of Charles Vynne, a chemical manufacturer. The Vynnes were an old Norfolk family, corn merchants based around Swaffham and Narborough, many of whom became active members of the Baptist church. They joined forces with another local Baptist family, the Everetts, and Vynne and Everett became a major agricultural supplier in the area.

Nora's family moved away from East Anglia, probably to Scotland, during her childhood. She was educated at home and her youthful artistic talent won her prizes, but she started her working life as a teacher in Peterhead, Aberdeenshire. When her father died she moved to London and immediately started contributing to a variety of newspapers and magazines, including *The Speaker*, *Sketch*, *Gentlewoman*, and *Winter's Weekly*. She published her first volume of short stories at the age of twenty-three. *The Blind Artist's Pictures* (1893) was dedicated to John Strange Winter, a pseudonym for Mrs Arthur Stannard, founding editor of *Winter's Weekly*, 'to whose kindly help and encouragement' Vynne said she owed much. Winter, who was the influential president of the Writer's Club in Fleet Street, published Vynne's stories in her first issues, including one on the front cover with a portrait of the author.

This book was an immediate success and won Vynne excellent reviews. J. M. Barrie described the short stories as the best he had ever read. A year later she published a second collection, *Honey of Aloes and Other Stories*, and in 1895 brought out her first full-length novel, *A Man and his Womankind*, a story of three women, including a journalist, who sacrifice their own lives to protect one man.

In September 1896 Vynne initiated a postal school of journalism, which ran until January 1898, in the columns of *Atalanta*. For 10s. a year subscribers were entitled to compete in monthly competitions and have their efforts criticized by Miss Vynne, who directed their studies and gave practical advice and counselling. This included a warning to women against 'indulging your own emotion instead of rousing the emotion of your readers'. But she also advised 'spelling need not trouble you, compositors can all spell'. Prize winners of the school were awarded an Oxford scholarship of £20.

By the age of thirty Vynne was contributing articles to a

variety of journals and giving lectures, and her growing reputation as a feminist and political writer led to her being invited in 1903 by the Committee of the Freedom of Labour Defence to write, with Helen Blackburn, *Women under the Factory Act*. In it she advised women to stick to the law in case employers decided to hire fewer women, but added:

> lest their obedience to law should be mistaken for approval of it, let all women who find restrictions cause them loss or inconvenience and all women who claim to enjoy the liberty men would certainly refuse to give up—namely the liberty to earn extra money—consult with each other and lodge protests.

Vynne worked for the weekly tabloid *Women's Tribune* from its first issue in May 1906, writing chiefly about homeworking and the sweated industries, until it folded later that year. Within two months she had resurrected the paper under a new title—*Women and Progress*—and become joint editor with Lady Frances Balfour. Both papers were based on the assumption that all intelligent, tax-paying women desired equal rights of citizenship with male citizens, but they were not primarily suffrage journals: housing reform, temperance reform, and poor-law reform were all considered urgent needs as well. Vynne urged moderation in demanding the suffrage, arguing that an age limit was acceptable as long as it was the same for both sexes. Girls who should forfeit the right to vote included those 'who have been found guilty of any fraud or dishonesty, cruelty, or neglect of responsibilities voluntarily undertaken' (*Women and Progress*, 2 Nov 1906). Vynne herself described the paper as 'a high-class women's journal dealing with all the questions of the day and chronicling, impartially, all women's movements'. It lasted until June 1914, when it ran out of funds, ironically just as circulation was rising, advertisements coming in, and many of her readers promising to help by becoming shareholders.

Vynne wrote a number of other books: *The Pieces of Silver* (1911); a light romance entitled *So it is with the Damsel* (1913); *The Priest's Marriage* (1899; repr. 1911); and a series of one-act plays which were put on in the provinces, as well as a five-act play produced by the Play Actors. She was a member of the Institute of Journalists and the Society of Women Journalists as well as the Writer's Club, where on one occasion a fellow member described her short stories as 'brilliant' (White). She never married, and died on 18 February 1914 at 3 Cambridge Lodge Villas, Mare Street, Hackney, London, from breast cancer.

ANNE M. SEBBA

Sources WWW · *Women and Progress* (2 Nov 1906) · *Atalanta* (1897–8) · F. Hunter, 'Women in British journalism', *The encyclopedia of the British press, 1422–1992*, ed. D. Griffiths (1992), 686–90 · parish register (baptism), Swaffham parish church, Swaffham, Norfolk · *Winter's Weekly* (May 1891–1895) · F. Hunter, 'Girl reporters', Conference paper for Research Society for Victorian Periodicals, 1992 · F. White, *A fire in the kitchen: the autobiography of a cook* (1938) · Society of Women Journalists database · *Buchan Observer* (18 April 1893) · d. cert.
Archives Jarrold publishers, Norwich, archives

Likenesses Messrs Martin & Swallow, photograph, repro. in *Winter's Weekly*, 11/49 (5 March 1892)

Vyse, Richard (1746–1825). *See under* Vyse, Richard William Howard (1784–1853).

Vyse, Richard William Howard (1784–1853), army officer and Egyptologist, born on 25 July 1784, was the only son of General Richard Vyse and his second wife, Anne (only surviving daughter and heir of Field Marshal Sir George *Howard), whom he married on 20 May 1780.

The father, **Richard Vyse** (1746–1825), army officer, born at Lichfield on 11 July 1746, was the younger son of William Vyse (1710–1770), canon residentiary and treasurer of Lichfield, and younger brother of William Vyse (1741–1816), canon residentiary and chancellor of Lichfield. His mother, Catherine, was daughter of Richard *Smalbroke, bishop of Lichfield. He was appointed cornet in the 5th dragoons on 13 February 1763. He attained the brevet rank of colonel on 7 January 1781, received the command of the 1st dragoon guards on 28 May 1784, and during the Revolutionary War served in Flanders in command of a brigade under the duke of York. He distinguished himself on several occasions, particularly at the battle of Le Cateau on 25 April 1794, where, at the head of two brigades of heavy cavalry, he significantly contributed to the victory, and at the evacuation of Ostend, which he superintended on 1 July. Vyse was promoted major-general on 2 October 1794, and lieutenant-general on 1 January 1801. In 1799 he became the duke of Cumberland's comptroller. Frustrated in attempting to further his military career, he became MP for Beverley in 1806; he supported Cumberland and his faction, but made way for his son in 1807. He became general on 1 January 1812, and died at Lichfield on 30 May 1825.

His son, Richard William, assumed the additional name of Howard by royal sign manual, dated 14 September 1812, on inheriting the estates of Boughton and Pitsford in Northamptonshire through his maternal grandmother, Lucy, daughter of Thomas Wentworth, second earl of Strafford. Vyse entered the army as cornet in the 1st dragoons on 5 May 1800, and was promoted lieutenant in the 15th dragoons on 17 June 1801 and captain on 29 June 1802. In 1809 he acted as aide-de-camp to his father on the staff of the Yorkshire district, and on 5 July 1810 received the honorary degree of DCL from Oxford University. He married, on 13 November 1810, Frances, second daughter of Henry Hesketh of Newton, Cheshire. They had eight sons and two daughters. Like his father, he enjoyed the duke of Cumberland's patronage, being his equerry 1813–37. He attained the brevet rank of major on 4 June 1813, and was made captain in the 87th foot on 31 August 1815 and in the 2nd Life Guards on 5 July 1816; he was appointed major in the 1st West India regiment on 4 January 1819, and in the 2nd Life Guards on 4 February in the same year. On 13 May he attained the brevet rank of lieutenant-colonel, and was placed on half pay on 10 September 1825. On 10 January 1837 he was raised to the rank of colonel, and on 9 November 1846 to that of major-general.

Vyse was returned to parliament for Beverley on 8 May

1807. He voted against Catholic emancipation and parliamentary reform. In October 1812 he was elected MP for Honiton in Devon, which he retained until the dissolution of 1818. In 1824 he was high sheriff for Buckinghamshire.

In 1835 Vyse visited Egypt and Syria, and became very interested in the excavations being undertaken at Giza. He then spent over a year excavating and exploring the pyramids. In January 1837 he obtained the assistance of John Shae Perring, and, although he returned to England in August, he provided the funds for Perring's subsequent explorations to the south of Giza and at Abu Roash. The researches of Vyse and Perring were important in surveying and measuring the pyramids. Vyse published *Operations Carried on at the Pyramids of Gizeh in 1837* (2 vols., 1840), followed in 1842 by a third supplemental volume devoted to Perring's researches at Abu Roash. Vyse died at Stoke Poges, Buckinghamshire, on 8 June 1853.

E. I. CARLYLE, rev. H. C. G. MATTHEW

Sources *GM*, 1st ser., 95/2 (1825), 180 · *GM*, 2nd ser., 40 (1853), 200 · HoP, *Commons* · Burke, *Gen. GB*
Archives Bucks. RLSS, letters to his father; journal of his travels in Middle East

Vyvyan, Jennifer Brigit (1925–1974), singer, was born on 13 March 1925 at St Ives, Granville Road, Broadstairs, Kent, the daughter of Captain Cecil Albert Vyvyan, formerly of the Royal Engineers, and his wife, Brigit Maria Stokes. She was educated at St Paul's Girls' School and at Talbot Heath, Bournemouth, before training at the Royal Academy; there she took piano as her first study, gained an LRAM in performance, and was also awarded a teaching diploma in singing. She went on to have singing lessons with Roy Henderson, and after winning a Boise Foundation travelling scholarship she was able to study with Fernando Carpi and to travel to Milan and Rome. When she won first prize at the Concours International in Geneva in 1951 she was the first British singer to do so. In the same year she created the role of the Matron in Brian Easdale's opera *The Sleeping Children* at Cheltenham. Her first big success in the opera house was as Constanze in Mozart's *Die Entführung aus dem Serail* at Sadler's Wells in 1952, followed by the role of Donna Anna in *Don Giovanni* in the same season.

Jennifer Vyvyan had already made her operatic début in 1948, as Jenny Diver in Benjamin Britten's version of John Gay's *The Beggar's Opera*, performed by the English Opera Group in Cambridge, and she was to appear in many more Britten operas. At Covent Garden on 8 June 1953 she sang the part of Lady Penelope Rich in the first performance of Britten's *Gloriana*, written to celebrate the coronation, and did so again in many future productions. Britten was so attracted by her voice and her dramatic gifts that he created three more parts for her: the governess in *The Turn of the Screw*, first performed at La Fenice as part of the Venice Festival in 1954; Tytania in *A Midsummer Night's Dream* at Aldeburgh in 1960; and Mrs Julian in *Owen Wingrave*, commissioned for television and first broadcast in May 1971. She also appeared as Female Chorus in *The Rape of Lucretia*, and at various different times as Nancy, Miss Wordsworth, and Lady Billows in *Albert Herring*, in performances by the English Opera Group. She created roles in three operas by

Malcolm Williamson: the countess de Serindan in *The Violins of Saint-Jacques* (1966) at Sadler's Wells, Agnes in *The Growing Castle* (1968) at Dinefwr Castle, and a series of comedy roles in *Lucky-Peter's Journey* (1969) at the Coliseum, London. She sang at Glyndebourne, where she took the role of Electra in *Idomeneo* in 1953, and made frequent appearances with the Handel Opera Society. She sang again at the Aldeburgh Festival in 1972 in Schumann's *Scenes from Goethe's Faust*, conducted by Britten.

But Jennifer Vyvyan did not confine herself to opera. She sang in choral works, including Britten's *Spring Symphony* and *War Requiem*, Beethoven's ninth symphony, and Bach's St Matthew passion and St John passion. She took part in the first performance of *The Beatitudes*, the cantata written by Sir Arthur Bliss for the opening of the new Coventry Cathedral in 1962 but first performed in Coventry Theatre. She gave song recitals, and broadcast frequently.

Vyvyan was well known internationally. She went on a concert tour of South Africa and Southern Rhodesia in 1958, and made her first visit to the United States in 1963, when she sang in four performances of Britten's *Spring Symphony* with the New York Philharmonic Orchestra. She was also one of the group of British musicians led by Sir Arthur Bliss on a British Council tour of the Soviet Union in April 1956. Her recordings included *The Turn of the Screw* and Purcell's *The Fairy Queen*.

On 2 March 1962 Jennifer Vyvyan married Leon Crown (b. 1920/21), a chartered accountant, with whom she had one son. She died, suddenly, on 5 April 1974 at her home, 59 Fitzjohn's Avenue, Hampstead, London.

ANNE PIMLOTT BAKER

Sources *The Times* (6 April 1974) · *New Grove*, 2nd edn · *WW* · b. cert. · m. cert. · d. cert.
Archives FILM BBC TV, *Owen Wingrave*, May 1971 | SOUND BBC Sound Archives
Likenesses photograph, repro. in D. Mitchell, *Benjamin Britten: a pictorial biography* (1978), no. 263
Wealth at death £19,244: probate, 27 Nov 1974, CGPLA Eng. & Wales

Vyvyan, Sir Richard, first baronet (1613–1665), politician and local administrator, was the eldest son and heir of Sir Francis Vyvyan (d. 1635) of Trelowarren, Mawgan in Meneage, Cornwall, and his second wife, Loveday, daughter of John Connock of Treworgy, St Cleer, in the same county. His father was governor of St Mawes Castle from 1603 until 1632, when he was removed for embezzlement. Vyvyan matriculated from Exeter College, Oxford, on 20 June 1631, graduating BA the same day. He entered the Middle Temple in November 1631, reigning as prince in the Christmas masque of 1635, but was not called to the bar. Knighted on 1 March 1636, in October of that year he married Mary, daughter of James Bulteel of Barnstaple. They had six daughters and two sons. Vyvyan represented Penryn in the Short Parliament of 1640, and Tregony in the Long Parliament until he was disabled for royalism in January 1644.

In late September 1642, during the Truro mayoral elections, Vyvyan arrived at the town hall urging the outgoing mayor to call out the trained bands for the king. Upon the mayor's refusal Vyvyan appealed to the crowd outside, since 'they know not what unlawfull Assemblies were gathered in many parts of the County to the danger of their lives, their wives, and children, if they came not out to assist the Sheriffe and Justices' (*New News from Cornwall*, 1642, 1). The new mayor duly released the town arms, and the following day the trained bands were sent out for the king.

On 14 November 1642 Charles I issued a commission to Vyvyan to coin plate into money and to pay it over to Sir Ralph Hopton. On 3 January 1644 the king issued a further commission to Vyvyan to erect a royalist mint at Exeter, but Vyvyan's two surviving account books for the mint show that he had moved the mint to Exeter in September 1643, immediately after the capture of the city. He remained there almost continuously from September 1643 to April 1646, with two notable exceptions. On 27 January 1644 he attended the Oxford parliament, and he was created a DCL by the university the following month. In August 1644 he followed the king in his campaign against Essex in Cornwall, and on 12 February 1645 was created a baronet for his services to the royal cause.

In November 1642 Hopton had commissioned Vyvyan to erect a fort on Dennis Head, at the mouth of the Helford River. Building work began in spring 1643. On 19 February 1644 the king issued a commission authorizing Vyvyan to complete the fort, and to establish a garrison of one lieutenant, one master gunner, five other gunmen, one porter, and forty rank and file. Vyvyan paid for the erection of the fort and maintained it for eighteen months at his own expense, at a total cost of £1350. After the fort's surrender to Fairfax on 18 March 1646 Vyvyan spent a further £2055 10s. on arrears of pay.

Vyvyan was in Exeter when the city fell and on 9 April 1646 was named in the articles for the surrender of the city. On 20 June 1646 he begged to compound for his delinquency, and on 8 October his fine was fixed at £600. It was also agreed that his goods in Exeter and stock in Cornwall, seized contrary to the terms of the treaty of Exeter, should be restored, but the local committees did not comply. It was only after Fairfax's intervention that, on 3 April 1648, parliament remitted £300, the second half of Vyvyan's fine, in compensation for the loss of his goods. On 11 May 1649 Vyvyan accepted this final discharge of his estate, estimating that he had spent nearly £10,000 in the king's cause.

Nothing is known of Vyvyan's activities during the interregnum. However, he celebrated the Restoration in 1660 by erecting two granite pillars at Trelowarren, and his former services were rewarded with the governorship of St Mawes Castle and appointment as gentleman of the king's privy chamber. He was returned as the member for St Mawes in 1663 and served the constituency until his death on 3 November 1665. He was buried, as he had requested, 'without any Pompe or extraordinary cost or expense' (will), on 10 November at Mawgan in Meneage. His wife survived him, and his eldest son, Vyell (*bap.* 1634, *d.* 1697), succeeded to the baronetcy.   ANNE DUFFIN

Sources M. Coate, *Cornwall in the great civil war and interregnum, 1642–1660* (1933) • Cornwall RO, Vyvyan papers, 5 • J. L. Vivian and H. H. Drake, eds., *The visitation of the county of Cornwall in the year 1620*, Harleian Society, 9 (1874) • Keeler, *Long Parliament* • A. Duffin, *Faction and faith: politics and religion of the Cornish gentry before the civil war* (1996) • *New news from Cornwall* (1642) • will, PRO, PROB 11/322, fols. 253–255v • E. Cruickshanks, 'Vyvyan, Sir Richard', HoP, *Commons, 1660–90*, 3.646

Archives Cornwall RO, letters, appointments, warrants • NRA, priv. coll., accounts as county treasurer | Cornwall RO, letters, etc. to Lewis Tremayne

Likenesses portrait, Trelowarren, Cornwall; repro. in Coate, *Cornwall in the great civil war*, 4–5

Wealth at death see will, PRO, PROB 11/322, fols. 253–255v

Vyvyan, Sir Richard Rawlinson, eighth baronet (1800–1879), politician and philosopher, was born on 6 June 1800 at the family home at Trelowarren, in the parish of Mawgan in Meneage, Cornwall, the eldest of seven children of Sir Vyell Vyvyan, seventh baronet (*bap.* 1767, *d.* 1820), and his wife, Mary Hutton (1777–1812), only daughter of Thomas Hutton Rawlinson of Lancaster. Vyvyan was educated at Harrow School from 1813 to 1816 or 1817 and matriculated at Christ Church, Oxford, on 22 May 1818 but he did not proceed to a degree. Upon his father's death on 27 January 1820 he succeeded to the title and estates of Trelowarren and in September that year became lieutenant-colonel commandant of the Cornwall yeomanry cavalry.

Vyvyan's political career commenced in 1825 when, at a by-election on 27 January, he was returned to parliament for the county of Cornwall; he was re-elected in 1826 and 1830. 'Although unswerving in his attachment to the principles of toryism, he was far from being a subservient supporter of his party' (*Annual Register*, 212). He disapproved of the concession of Roman Catholic emancipation, and early in 1830 announced his intention of weakening the Wellington administration as much as possible. In that year he was a member of the select committee on the East India Company's charter. In the previous October he had explained his views to Palmerston, and invited him to lead the House of Commons in a tory administration without the duke of Wellington, but with the inclusion of a few young Liberals. He voted for Sir Henry Parnell's motion for referring the civil list to a select committee, which caused the resignation of the Wellington ministry, but he and the other high tories would not support the new whig ministry. Although Vyvyan recognized the need for change in the electoral system he strongly opposed the Reform Bill. On its second reading on 21 March 1831 he was put forward by the tories as their spokesman to move that it should be postponed for six months. When the boom of cannon announced the approach of William IV to dissolve parliament on 22 April 1831 Vyvyan was engaged in moving the rejection of the Reform Bill so vehemently that it was only 'by pulling him down by the skirts of his coat' that he was compelled to take a seat (*Annual Register*, 212). He was then at the height of his fame and had a well-earned reputation for eloquence.

A severe contest for the representation of the county of Cornwall ensued. However, after the poll had been open for five days Vyvyan and his tory colleague Lord Valletort lost to their whig opponents, Mr Pendarves and Sir Charles Lemon (Courtney, 408–10). Vyvyan became MP for Okehampton in Devon on 14 July 1831. At this time he purchased the ruins of its old castle as he was the rightful heir to the ancient but dormant barony of Courtenay of Okehampton. However, Vyvyan never attempted to revive the title in his favour. At the general elections in December 1832 and February 1835 he was returned, after expensive victories, for the city of Bristol, but he did not seek re-election in 1837. After the Reform Bill his interest in politics seems to have declined, and he spoke little, though he strenuously opposed the third reading of the Municipal Corporations Bill. From 1837 to 1841 he was without a seat, and in 1840 became high sheriff for Cornwall. At the general election on 1 July 1841 he was returned for Helston, a few miles from Trelowarren, and he continued to sit for it until 1857. A protectionist, opposing free trade doctrines and the introduction of income tax, he addressed, in June 1842, a letter on the subject to his constituents pointing out the pitfalls of the commercial and financial policy of Sir Robert Peel's administration. Macaulay, in July 1843, wrote of the tory party as split into three or more factions, one being represented by Vyvyan and the *Morning Post*. Vyvyan continued to oppose reform and voted against Peel on the repeal of the corn laws and against Disraeli's budget of 1852.

Vyvyan was a philosopher and a metaphysician. His scientific writings commenced in 1825 when he printed for private circulation *An Essay on Arithmo-Physiology*, which purported to be 'A Chronological Classification of Organised Matter'. In 1826 he was elected a fellow of the Royal Society. Vyvyan was engaged for many years with Dr Charles T. Pearce of Durleston Park, Swanage, in scientific experiments and research on light, heat, and magnetism. He purchased a section of the library of M. Libri which formed a part of his 'most choice library' (H. N. Pym, ed., *Memories of Old Friends: Journals and Letters of Caroline Fox*, 1882, 1.26). Vyvyan also published several letters and speeches. His letter to the magistrates of Berkshire on their practice of consigning prisoners to solitary confinement before trial, and ordering them to be disguised by masks, passed into a second edition in 1845. His account of the 'fogou', or cave, at Halligey, Trelowarren, is in the *Journal of the Royal Institute of Cornwall* (1885), 8.256–8. Unpublished writings include night journals in Italian kept by Vyvyan from 1841 to 1846 and the outline of a Maratha novel about the fortunes of an attendant in a foreign country.

As a metaphysician he published a volume entitled *Psychology, or, A Review of the Arguments in Proof of the Existence and Immortality of the Animal Soul*, but it was recalled immediately after publication. Two volumes on metaphysical subjects, entitled the 'Harmony of the universe' (1842) and 'Harmony of the comprehensible world' (1845), were written but never published. Nevertheless, perhaps by private drafts and discussion, his views and activity were sufficient to make him a suspect as author of *Vestiges of the Natural History of Creation* (1845).

After 1857 Vyvyan lived in complete retirement until his death at Trelowarren on 15 August 1879. He was buried in the family vault in the north-west corner of Mawgan in Meneage church on 21 August. In the event of his death not taking place at Trelowarren, Vyvyan had made provision in his will to be buried at Kensal Green cemetery close to his friends Mr Broderip and Robert Browne; the will also ensured that his domestic servants and paid agents would receive one year's salary after his death. Vyvyan never married and was succeeded by a nephew, the Revd Vyell Donnithorne Vyvyan, the son of his brother Vyell Francis Vyvyan.   W. P. COURTNEY, *rev.* RITA M. GIBBS

Sources Cornwall RO, Vyvyan papers, DD.V · *Annual Register* (1879), 212 · E. R. Vyvyan, 'The ancient barony of Courtenay of Okehampton', *N&Q*, 5th ser., 9 (1878), 296 · E. R. Vyvyan, letter, *N&Q*, 7th ser., 4 (1887), 235 · C. T. Pearce, letter, *N&Q*, 5th ser., 12 (1879), 357 · R. Vyvyan, *A letter from Sir Richard Vyvyan, … to his constituents: upon the commercial and financial policy of Sir Robert Peel's administration* (1842) · W. P. Courtney, *The parliamentary representation of Cornwall to 1832* (1889) · *The Reform Act, 1832: the correspondence of the late Earl Grey with His Majesty King William IV and with Sir Herbert Taylor*, ed. Henry, Earl Grey, 2 vols. (1867) · G. O. Trevelyan, *The life and letters of Lord Macaulay*, 1 (1876) · Boase & Courtney, *Bibl. Corn.*, vols. 2–3 · *Debrett's Peerage* (1887) · Foster, *Alum. Oxon.* · *CGPLA Eng. & Wales* (1879)

Archives BL, letters · Cornwall RO, corresp. and papers, philosophical journals, and literary MSS | BL, letters to Sir Richard Owen, Add. MS 39954 · Bodl. Oxf., letters to S. L. Giffard · Devon RO, letters to Sir Thomas Dyke Acland, 1148M

Wealth at death under £18,000: resworn administration with will, Jan 1882, *CGPLA Eng. & Wales* (1879)

W. H. [Mr W. H.] (*fl.* 1609), dedicatee of William Shakespeare's sonnets, is one of the most elusive figures in literary history. He appears in the epigraph which follows the title-page of *Shake-Speares Sonnets*, published in 1609: 'To. the. onlie. begetter. of. / these. insuing. sonnets. / Mr. W. H. all. happinesse. / and. that. eternitie. / promised. / by. / our. ever-living. poet. / wisheth. / the. well-wishing. / adventurer. in. / setting. / forth. / T. T.'. There is general agreement that T. T. is the publisher, Thomas Thorpe, but the identity of Mr W. H. has been a matter of widespread and sometimes bitter dispute.

Many commentators have assumed that 'begetter' in the epigraph means 'inspirer', and thus that Mr W. H. is the young man addressed in the sonnets. This interpretation was first elaborated in 1780 by Edmond Malone, who favoured Thomas Tyrwhitt's suggestion, based on a pun on 'hue' in Sonnet 20, that the initials stand for William Hughes. Various young men of this name (some probably apocryphal) were suggested over the next century or more, culminating in Oscar Wilde's fictionalized boy actor Willie Hughes, but none gained much following. Numerous similar candidates have also come and gone, including Shakespeare's brother-in-law William Hart, supposed patron William Hammond, and innkeeper's son William Holgate. Leslie Hotson's book-length argument in 1964 for law student William Hatcliffe made few converts, partly because it relies on an improbably early dating of the sonnets.

The two most popular candidates within the 'inspirer' camp, based on the assumption that W. H. was an aristocratic patron of Shakespeare, have been Henry Wriothesley, third earl of Southampton (dedicatee of *Venus and*

Adonis and *The Rape of Lucrece*), and William Herbert, third earl of Pembroke (co-dedicatee of the first folio of Shakespeare's plays). Southampton was first proposed as the youth of the sonnets in 1817, but not until 1836 did Gottlob Regis further suggest that he was also Mr W. H., with his initials reversed. Four years earlier, in 1832, James Boaden had first proposed Pembroke as the youth, using the earl's initials, W. H., as one of his arguments. Countless commentators since then have argued for Southampton or Pembroke as the youth, with many (but not all) further identifying their candidate with Mr W. H. By the latter half of the twentieth century, supporters of Southampton as W. H. had dwindled, but major editions of the sonnets by Wilson (1966) and Duncan-Jones (1997) still argued for Pembroke as both the youth and as Mr W. H.

Opposed to the 'inspirer' camp are those who interpret 'begetter' as 'procurer', or the person who obtained the manuscript of the sonnets for Thorpe. This interpretation was first advanced in 1799 by Chalmers (who proposed no specific candidate) and has gained numerous adherents, many of whom accept Southampton or Pembroke as the youth but doubt that Thorpe would have addressed a nobleman so informally. Thus Sidney Lee argued in the *Dictionary of National Biography*, and in his extremely popular 1898 biography of Shakespeare, that W. H. was Thorpe's fellow stationer William Hall. After enjoying a vogue in the early twentieth century, Lee's theory faded under the scrutiny of sceptics.

Another popular 'procurer' candidate has been Southampton's stepfather Sir William Hervey, or Harvey, who was widowed in 1607 and remarried in 1608 (thus the 'eternitie' promised by the epigraph). This theory, obviously acceptable only to supporters of Southampton as the youth, was notably promoted by Fleay in the nineteenth century and by Southampton's biographer Stopes in the twentieth. It was vigorously defended as late as 1973 by A. L. Rowse, but at the time of writing has few active adherents. Various relatives of Shakespeare with the appropriate initials (William Hart, William Hall, William Hathaway) have also been proposed as 'procurers', but none have gained significant acceptance.

Yet another school of thought holds that Mr W. H. is William Shakespeare. Barnstorff first suggested in 1860 that the initials stand for 'William Himself' and that Shakespeare wrote the sonnets to his own genius, while Brae (1877) and von Kralik (1907) argued that 'onlie begetter' meant 'sole author', and suggested that 'W. H.' was a misprint for 'W. S.' or 'W. SH.' (that is, William Shakespeare). Despite occasional sympathetic notice, such theories were largely ignored for most of the twentieth century because of the unquestioned assumption that the 'ever-living poet' must be Shakespeare. However, in 1987 Foster breathed new life into the misprint theory by showing that 'begetter' in early modern book dedications meant 'author' with virtually no exceptions, and that misprinted initials were not uncommon. He further suggested that 'our ever-living poet' is God: the Creator as eternal poet was a common metaphor, 'ever-living' was a conventional epithet for God, and 'eternity', or eternal life, could only be promised by God in contemporary usage.

Foster's solution has been viewed with cautious acceptance by some critics, and with more scepticism by others. Many others have been unwilling to accept any of these solutions, preferring to view Thorpe's epigraph as a possibly insoluble riddle. Rollins wrote in 1944 that Mr W. H. 'has caused the spilling of more ink, the utterance of more futile words, than almost any other personage or problem' of the sonnets, and he may have been correct to predict that 'there is not the slightest likelihood that the mystery surrounding his initials will ever be dispelled in a fashion satisfactory to a majority of critics, editors and commentators' (*Sonnets*, ed. Rollins, 22.166).

DAVID KATHMAN

Sources W. Shakespeare, *The sonnets*, ed. H. E. Rollins, 2 (1944), 166–241 · D. Foster, 'Master W. H., R. I. P.', *Publications of the Modern Language Association of America*, 102 (1987), 42–54 · O. Wilde, 'The portrait of Mr. W. H.', *Blackwood*, 146 (1889), 1–21 · L. Hotson, *Mr. W. H.* (1964) · E. Malone, *Supplement to the edition of Shakespeare's plays published in 1778 by Samuel Johnson and George Steevens* (1780), 579 · J. Boaden, 'On the sonnets of Shakespeare', *GM*, 1st ser., 102/2 (1832), 217–21, 308–14, 407 · G. Regis, *Shakespeare-Almanach* (1836), 247–50 · J. D. Wilson, introduction, in W. Shakespeare, *The sonnets*, ed. J. D. Wilson (1966), lxxxviii–cviii · K. Duncan-Jones, introduction, in *Shakespeare's sonnets*, ed. K. Duncan-Jones (1997), 1–105, esp. 1–69 · G. Chalmers, *A supplemental apology for believers in the Shakespeare-papers* (1799), 52 · *DNB* · S. Lee, *A life of William Shakespeare* (1898) · F. G. Fleay, *A chronicle history of the life and work of William Shakespeare* (1886), 62 · C. C. Stopes, *The life of Henry, third earl of Southampton, Shakespeare's patron* (1922), 343–4 · A. L. Rowse, *Shakespeare the man* (1973) · D. Barnstorff, *A key to Shakespeare's sonnets*, trans. T. J. Graham (1860–62) · A. E. Brae, 'Shakespeare's sonnets', *Lippincott's*, 19 (1877), 761–2 · R. von Kralik, 'Shakespeare-Studien: Shakespeares epische und lyrische Dichtungen', *Die Kultur*, 8 (1907), 385–92

Waad [Wade], **Armagil** (*c.*1510–1568), government official, was stated in his grant of arms in 1547 to be a native of the northern parts of England. His date of birth is deduced from his date of graduation and may err by several years. The address he gave at his graduation was Kilnsey, near Coniston, in the West Riding of Yorkshire, where no other Wades are known at this early date. However, there were many others nearby at Leeds, Bolton upon Dearne, and at Aldingham, where one William Wade was assessed at £10 5s. in 1524. Although not apparently armigerous, William and subsequent Aldingham Wades were the wealthiest of the Yorkshire family, all of whom appear to have been materially prosperous. All those Wades from this area recorded from 1522 in a dozen wills, numerous fines, and deeds seem to boil down to no more than two enduring dynasties and may indeed all have been interrelated. Richard Wade of Bolton upon Dearne mentioned that his son Richard Wade was studying at Cambridge in 1522. Given how well these wills crossmatch, it is surprising that none of them even mentions Armagil, an unusual name. Perhaps he had already left home and lost contact with his Yorkshire kin. Is it possible that he had changed his name to Armagil, perhaps at university? In short, it seems unlikely that Armagil hailed from the lowest ranks of society: it was most probably education locally and family support that enabled him to study at Oxford University, where he graduated BA in 1532, perhaps at Magdalen College, and he may have studied at an inn of court. He seems to have been an adventurous young man. It was presumably by unrecorded foreign travel that he developed his later proficiency in both French and Spanish. The notion that a Holderness childhood introduced him to the sea is speculative and unlikely; however, Armagil was among thirty young gentlemen from the inns of court and chancery who voyaged for six months in 1536 (April–October) with Captain Hore's two vessels to Cape Breton, Newfoundland, and Penguin Island in what is now Canada. With 'divers others of great account' Armagil Waad embarked from Gravesend on the second ship, the *Minion*. The crew were reduced by shortage of food to eating herbs and roots and even perhaps to cannibalism. Had they not captured a well-provisioned French ship, they would have perished. Returning to St Ives, the survivors were fêted all the way to London. Waad was not the captain or even an officer. Hence he did not deserve the title 'the English Columbus' which his son, as family aggrandizement, posthumously bestowed upon him and which earned him inclusion in the *Dictionary of National Biography*. Any narrative that Waad may have written is lost; William Butt's surviving account is extremely cursory.

There is also no supporting evidence that it was Sir Richard Gresham, the post-dissolution lord of Kilnsey, who recommended Waad to Henry VIII, but it definitely was Henry, Lord Maltravers, deputy of Calais and later earl of Arundel, who proposed him as assistant clerk of the council at Calais in 1540 and further recommended him to the French secretaryship there in 1543. By then Waad had married, at the church of St Leonard Eastcheap on 29 May 1541, Alice (d. 1557/8), daughter of the London tradesman Richard Patten (d. 1536) and widow of Thomas Searle, another Londoner. She had numerous offspring with Waad, and she also brought him London connections—two merchants wrote warmly of him—and no doubt the resources on which he founded his career. He was appointed a customer of Calais in 1545. He was replaced in 1546, when he proceeded to London, where he reported to Secretary of State Paget. Next year he became one of the four clerks of the privy council, all of whom secured seats in the parliament of 1547: Waad's seat at Chipping Wycombe, Buckinghamshire, may have been arranged by John, Lord Russell. A grant of arms in the same year confirmed his genteel status. Initially supernumerary and unpaid, Waad was formally appointed third clerk of the privy council in 1548 at 50 marks a year and chief clerk in 1551 on a salary of £50; an annuity of 200 marks for services to Henry VIII and Edward VI was added in 1550. Among several responsible services was that of deputy clerk of parliaments, in which capacity he four times read out the commission of prorogation. He seems to have been committed to the Edwardian regime, both its protestant and socially reformist character, penning a celebration of Protector Somerset's victorious return from Scotland in 1548, which was printed by his brother-in-law William Patten, and nine lines of Latin verse in *Lives and Deaths*

of the Two Brothers Henry and Charles Brandon [Dukes of] of Suffolk by Thomas Wilson, who died in 1551.

The accession of Mary Tudor seems to have resulted in Waad's dismissal, most probably on religious grounds, and his annuity was reduced to a still substantial £100: he was pardoned on 3 November 1553. Despite composing an elaborate unpublished treatise entitled 'The distresses of the commonwealth, with the means to remedy them', which was submitted to the government and remains among the state papers, Waad was not restored to his clerkship on Elizabeth's accession, but was employed instead in various *ad hoc* capacities. He was sent to the duke of Holstein in 1559 to negotiate about commercial relations; to Rye in Sussex in 1562 to muster 600 men for service at Le Havre and to collect information on Huguenot plans; and to the Tower in 1566 to examine Cornelius de Lannoy, an alchemist who had failed to manufacture gold for the queen's service. There survive several reports dated at Somerset House from Armagil Waad to the secretary of state Sir William Cecil. The previous year he had secured a thirty-year monopoly of making sulphur and growing plants for oil (linseed) for cloth manufacture. On a number of occasions Waad advised Cecil on the use of new patents to provide monopolies for new industrial processes.

Although only briefly in government service and never in a senior capacity, Waad evidently made his fortune. His marriages and his annuity must have helped. Waad also seems to have had an eye for commercial possibilities and surely dealt on a large scale, since in 1555 he was summoned to account for £800 paid to him by the London skinner and Calais stapler Alderman Sir Andrew Judde. As late as 1565 he was advocating his brother-in-law Marbury as a supplier of French wines to the queen's household: it is not clear which of his brothers-in-law was meant. Described in 1553 as of London and Soulbury, Buckinghamshire, where the connection has not been traced, Waad was granted Milton Grange in Oxfordshire in 1554, and in 1557 was assigned the lease of the manor of Belsize in Hampstead, Middlesex, a property of the dean and chapter of St Paul's, where he was resident when his first wife died and which was named as his address in his pardon of 1559. He was named to the commission of the peace for Middlesex from 1561, and served as a commissioner for the benevolence for the rebuilding of St Paul's in 1564 and as a commissioner of sewers in 1564 for Kent and Sussex. He had secured by royal grant a substantial area (several thousand acres) of salt marshes near Lydd in 1562. Following his first wife's death, he had married almost at once Anne, *née* Marbury, widow of Edward Bradley (d. 1558), a London haberdasher from the same social circle as his first wife. She already had two young daughters whom Waad remembered in his will. According to his epitaph, his two wives Alice and Anne between them had with him no fewer than twenty children, fourteen of whom predeceased him: all the survivors were offspring of his first wife. Waad had amassed a considerable estate by his death, when he held the rectory of Horton Kirkby, Kent, the leases of Belsize and of Lowden in Kentish Town,

Middlesex, his own house in London, tenements in Golding Lane, and chambers at Gray's Inn that he himself had constructed. It is a measure of how far he had come that 100 marks was assigned as portion for his unmarried daughter Joyce: other daughters unprovided for in his will were presumably already married, even perhaps Anne, to whom he gave nothing because of her disobedience. Waad died at Belsize on 20 June 1568 and was buried in the chancel of Hampstead church. It was his eldest son with his first wife, Sir William *Waad, also clerk of the privy council, who proudly concocted his epitaph on the elaborate alabaster monument, now lost, in Hampstead church. In his will Waad acknowledged his godson Armagil Corkoram, on whom he had presumably bestowed his name. A much later descendant, Armengilda Wade, evidently took her name from him in recognition of his role in establishing their family.   MICHAEL HICKS

Sources DNB · HoP, Commons, 1509–58, 3.531–2 · R. Hakluyt, *The principal navigations, voyages, traffiques and discoveries of the English nation*, 8, Hakluyt Society, extra ser., 8 (1904), 3 · CPR, 1547–69 · J. Foster and W. H. Rylands, eds., *Grantees of arms named in docquets and patents to the end of the seventeenth century*, Harleian Society, 66 (1915) · R. W. Hoyle, ed., *Early Tudor Craven: subsidies and assessments, 1510–1547*, Yorkshire Archaeological Society, record ser., 145 (1987) · *Calendar of the manuscripts of the most hon. the marquis of Salisbury*, 1, HMC, 9 (1883) · VCH Buckinghamshire, vol. 3 · VCH Middlesex, vol. 9 · VCH Yorkshire, vol. 3 · R. Cooke, *Visitation of London, 1568*, ed. H. Stanford London and S. W. Rawlins, [new edn], 2 vols. in one, Harleian Society, 109–10 (1963) · [T. Wilson], *Vita et obitus duorum fratrum Suffolciensium, Henrici et Caroli Brandoni* (1551) · PRO, PROB 11/52, sig. 6 · Borth. Inst., Archbishop of York probate registers, 11 and 13 · parish register, St Leonard Eastcheap, GL · epitaph, Hampstead church, Middlesex

Waad, Sir William (1546–1623), diplomat and administrator, was the son and heir of Armagil *Waad (*d.* 1568), clerk of the privy council, and his first wife, Alice Patten (*d.* 1557/8). He attended Gray's Inn in 1571. Waad's entrée to Elizabethan officialdom was his father's old friend and patron, William Cecil, who provided support, patronage, and, by 1572, a place in his household for the young William. In return for Cecil's help, which included the vicarage of Hynton, Chester, and sponsorship of his continental travels in the 1570s, Waad gave unstinting allegiance to the Cecilian faction. While he travelled, he functioned as a key correspondent of the lord treasurer. He visited most of Europe, including a long stay in Italy, and then became for a time in 1576–7 a part of Sir William Paulet's embassy at Paris. In what capacity he served is indeterminable, but he seemed to have had a quasi-secretarial role. Later, at Sir Henry Cobham's insistence, Waad joined Cobham's residency in Paris, where he served from 1580 to 1581 as the ambassador's contact with the French court and did 'accomplements' with other ambassadors for Cobham. It was ideal diplomatic training. But while Paulet had praised the younger man's 'discretion, honesty and many good parts', Cobham was less eulogistic—there was seemingly a personality conflict between them—and Waad, though he stayed in Paris, separated himself from the entourage (*CSP for.*, 11, no. 1162; 15.133). He did, however, continue both to gather intelligence for the government and to pursue schemes involving the various Portuguese

pretenders, an interest that earlier contacts had cultivated. He was to remain a key Elizabethan gatherer of foreign intelligence throughout the reign.

Languages, including French, Italian, and Latin, extensive travel abroad, associations with serving ambassadors, and an apparent negotiating skill led to repeated employment overseas for Waad. It was as an independent diplomatic agent that he served Elizabeth most distinguishedly and certainly most arduously. His key assignments were about as unpalatable as any in the reign. In 1584, for instance, he was the one designated to go to Spain to explain to King Philip why his ambassador, Bernardino de Mendoza, had been expelled from England. Not only was Waad treated with scant courtesy in Madrid, but the Spanish king, perhaps in retaliation for Elizabeth's two-year isolation of Mendoza in London, refused Waad an audience. Instead, Philip's secretary, Idiaquez, requested the envoy's letters to his master, which Waad refused to surrender except in person to the king. The king arbitrarily resolved the impasse by immediately issuing Waad his return passport. With this curt dismissal the ambassador left, having been prevented from explaining Mendoza's machinations, Elizabeth's great forbearance in the face of the Spaniard's provocative actions, and the English desire to preserve amity with Spain. As had often been the case before, the king gave as his excuse for refusing audience that he wanted nothing to do with an ambassador reputed to be a 'great heretic, being a Puritan, even worse than a Calvinist' (*CSP Venice*, 7, no. 87). The religious characterization of Waad, judging from his will, seems entirely accurate. It was, at any rate, such mutual intolerance, the breakdown of communications, and the continuation of what could only be characterized as diplomatic warfare that led ultimately to more open hostilities.

In January 1587 Waad travelled as a special ambassador to France to explain to the French court why Mary, queen of Scots, had just been executed. Again, it was a trying mission. Waad, however, was as sound a choice as any: he was familiar with France, and he had been the one sent by Elizabeth to Chartley to seize Queen Mary's papers, which contained the ultimate proof on which her conviction was based. He thus had inside information about the case and could be uniquely persuasive in his presentation. He did in fact mute French objections to this treatment of a former French queen by demonstrating that Mary had unequivocally, in her last years, cast her lot with Spain. A secondary aspect of his mission—to resolve mutual shipping seizures—saw some progress. Thus what began as another diplomatic fiasco—the ambassador was barred from court, and blamed for harsh feelings engendered by the unwelcome news he bore—ended on a modestly successful official note for the English. Waad was personally misused on his return journey by the Catholic duc d'Aumale, who detained him and seized his letters, diplomatic immunity notwithstanding.

Waad had substantial preparation for his challenging diplomatic assignments. Besides touring the continent in the 1570s and his service with the English legation in Paris, he performed several minor diplomatic chores. He was joined, in June 1581, by Lord Willoughby in a mission to bestow the Garter on the Danish king. In this embassy he was but a minor functionary and the ambassador's mouthpiece, commuting frequently between the Danish court and the ambassador's lodgings to settle various points of disagreement before the investiture ceremony on 14 August. In April 1583, now a clerk of the privy council through the joint sponsorship of Burghley and Walsingham (whose secretary he had briefly been in 1581), Waad went to Vienna to protest at the withdrawal of English trade privileges by the Hanse towns. He was received most courteously by the imperial court, but the mission was fruitless, apparently both because the emperor considered the dispute beyond his jurisdiction and because of German distaste for the English Merchant Adventurers. In yet another mission, in March 1585, Waad required of the French king the surrender of the English conspirator, Thomas Morgan, whose treasons in England made him a much sought felon. He received kind words from Henry III, but the king apparently did not return Morgan. For his efforts, Waad was beaten by Catholic sympathizers in France during his return journey to England, again in contravention of international law.

A potentially much more important assignment had been proposed in early 1580, immediately after the death of Cardinal Henry of Portugal, which had thrown open the question of the Portuguese succession. While Waad's official instructions exist, there is no evidence that he ever undertook this mission to the two pretenders to the throne, the duke of Braganza and Dom Antonio. Waad nevertheless continued his involvement with Portuguese affairs throughout the rest of his life, especially schemes involving Dom Antonio, and he became in fact the recognized Elizabethan expert on the area, succeeding Thomas Wilson in that role.

In all Waad conducted four independent missions, but this aspect of his career concluded after 1587. He remained at home, where his clerkship increasingly involved him in the pursuit of dissidents and subversives. He became the terror of the English recusants, and particularly of the foreign Jesuits sent into England. 'Lord Chief Justice Popham is in circuit', a Mr Cordale commented in 1595, 'but William Waad keeps the papists in line' (*CSP dom.*, *1598–1601*, 253). His was the unsavoury but diligently executed task of ferreting out and then examining, often under torture, men suspected of treasonous intent. No major conspiracy after 1585—whether the Lopez plot, the Babington plot, the Essex rebellion, the trial of Ralegh, the Gunpowder Plot, the Main plot, the Bye plot, or others—failed in some way to involve his investigations. He was also involved with many rather more minor interrogations and committees of inquiry.

Besides serving as something of the English counterpart to the Spanish grand inquisitor, Waad also had responsibilities for provisioning the English army in the Low Countries and in Ireland. Here he was the successor of his diplomatic colleague, Sir Thomas Wilkes, but soon found himself involved in massive controversy over both alleged speculation and incompetence. As with almost any Elizabethan official, Waad claimed, in 1593, that the Cecilian connection had borne little fruit and that his official services were negligibly rewarded; but a variety of farms, grants, and licences associated with his name argue otherwise. Probably his most notable patent was the monopoly to manufacture sulphur, brimstone, and oil. Certainly his wealth in an inflationary age would suggest that the niggardly Elizabethan reward system had not unduly slighted him.

Waad served in parliament for the duchy of Lancaster boroughs of Aldeburgh (1585), Thetford (1589), and Preston (1601), and he also represented the Cornish borough of West Looe in 1604, undoubtedly all through the influence either of the Cecil faction or Walsingham. He made little mark on parliamentary proceedings. He was also a justice of the peace for both Middlesex, from 1591, probably until his death, and Kent, by 1592, and served on various county commissions.

Strongly allied with Robert Cecil, and indispensable to the government as an intelligencer and in his covert operations, Waad remained active when King James acceded to the throne. Knighted almost immediately (20 May 1603) after the king arrived in England, he also received, in a particularly apt appointment, the lieutenancy of the Tower. In this capacity he continued to pursue interrogations, and was, perhaps most famously, the gaoler of Sir Walter Ralegh, with whom he had repeated misunderstandings. In 1613, however, having lost Cecilian protection when Salisbury died the previous year, and in the face of the attacks of the many enemies his past activities had earned, Waad was forced to surrender his position. The charge against him, probably specious, was that he had both embezzled jewels belonging to his charge, Lady Arabella Stuart, and that he had allowed too much freedom while guarding her. He retired thereafter to the patrimonial Belsize House in Hampstead to pursue his private interests, which, like his father's, included a sizeable interest in the New World. He was, for instance, a member of the governing council for the Virginia Company and an investor in the purchase of the island of Bermuda.

Despite Waad's prominent involvement in state affairs, his personality—hard-edged and querulous as it must have been to pursue his interrogation tasks so successfully and repeatedly—precluded him from attaining anything more than modest stature in the realm. In his correspondence he is certainly periodically at odds with various colleagues, and the enemies, some well placed in the realm, that his interrogations created may be imagined. He nevertheless profited by his activities, and in a moralistic will giving clear evidence of his puritan inclinations he left a sizeable estate to his son James (a godson of the king) and to his second wife, Anne, whom he married probably in 1599, a daughter of Sir Humphrey Browne. He had previously married, in 1586, another Anne (d. 1589), a daughter of Owen Waller of London. He died in October 1623 at Battles Hall in Essex, another of his estates, and was buried in nearby Maunden church, where his noteworthy tomb was restored in the late nineteenth century.

GARY M. BELL

Sources R. C. Barnett, *Place, profit and power: a study of the servants of William Cecil, Elizabethan statesman* (1969) · S. T. Bindoff and others, *Elizabethan government* (1961) · T. Birch, *Memoirs of the reign of Queen Elizabeth*, 1 (1754) · N. M. Fuidge, 'Waad, William', HoP, *Commons, 1558–1603*, 3.560–62 · J. Hurtsfield, *The queen's wards* (1958) · F. Pollard, *EngHR*, 38 (1923), 56 · W. Phillimore, *An index to bills of privy signet* (1890) · C. Read, *Lord Burghley and Queen Elizabeth* (1960) · R. B. Wernham, *Before the Armada: the growth of English foreign policy, 1485–1588* (1966) · *APC, 1585–1614* · *Memorials of affairs of state in the reigns of Q. Elizabeth and K. James I, collected (chiefly) from the original papers of … Sir Ralph Winwood*, ed. E. Sawyer, 3 vols. (1725) · *CSP dom., 1598–1601; 1619–23; addenda, 1580–1625* · *CSP for., 1575–1586* · *CSP Spain, 1525–9* · *CSP Venice, 1581–91* · *Report on the manuscripts of the marquis of Downshire*, 6 vols. in 7, HMC, 75 (1924–95), vol. 4 · *Calendar of the manuscripts of Major-General Lord Sackville*, 2 vols., HMC, 80 (1940–66), vol. 1 · *Calendar of the manuscripts of the most hon. the marquis of Salisbury*, 24 vols., HMC, 9 (1883–1976), vols. 2, 4–9, 12, 15, 17 · PRO, SP 70/148, fol. 14; E 403/2559, fol. 252; E 403/2425, fol. 47; SP 12/103, fol. 72 · will, PRO, PROB 11/142, sig. 116 · BL, Lansdowne MSS 10, fol. 207; 22, fol. 78; 23, fol. 172; 58, fol. 174; 114, fols. 104 ff. · *DNB*
Archives Magd. Oxf., family MSS | Magd. Oxf., S. C. Wade MSS
Likenesses line engraving, BM, NPG
Wealth at death extensive estates: will, PRO, PROB 11/142, sig. 116

Waagen, Gustav Friedrich (1794–1868), museum director and art historian, was born on 11 February 1794 in Hamburg, Germany, the second son of the painter Christian Friedrich Heinrich Waagen (*b.* 1750) and his wife, Johanna Louise Alberti (*d.* 1807). He was educated at the universities of Breslau (1815–18) and Heidelberg (1818–19). In 1822 he published his dissertation on Hubert and Jan van Eyck which has been described as the first ever art historical monograph. In 1830 he was appointed director of the new Königliche Gemäldegalerie (the royal gallery) in Berlin. In the following year he married Blandine von Seehausen (1811–1880); they had three daughters.

Waagen's European renown was based initially on his arrangement of the pictures in the royal gallery. His method for visually structuring the displays in Berlin built upon the principles of historicism, drawing on documentation and scholarship to demonstrate the development of painting. But although Waagen held that the visual arts should serve to edify and cultivate their audience he did not ignore the purely aesthetic pleasures of viewing. While his systematic presentation of artworks in the gallery attracted the attention of continental connoisseurs, his new catalogues of the old masters in the leading museums and private collections of Europe were of still more interest to the expanding art world. Unhappy with Prussian bureaucracy, Waagen applied constantly for leave to go abroad on study tours, and published bulky volumes on the picture galleries of Germany, France, Italy, the Netherlands, Belgium, Austria, Spain, and England. Britain, in particular, recurred in his itinerary: he visited the country in 1835, 1850, 1851, 1854, 1856, 1857, 1862, and 1867. In addition to contributions to reviews and magazines—in particular his stream of articles for the *Art Journal*—in which he often expounded his educational and art historical principles, Dr Waagen, as he was known, was a constant presence and influence in the English art world. He sat on parliamentary committees, offering advice on the

Gustav Friedrich Waagen (1794–1868), by unknown engraver (after Ludwig Knaus, 1855)

reorganization of the National Gallery, formed friendships with Charles Eastlake and John Murray, helped to arrange the Manchester Art Treasures Exhibition in 1857, and visited every important collection in the country. 'No Englishman has seen as much as he has', Theophile Thoré wrote in 1857 (T. Thoré, *Trésors de l'Art en Angleterre*, 1857, 19). He was closely associated with his countryman the prince consort, who reputedly wished to see Waagen appointed director of the National Gallery; in 1854, he catalogued a collection of primitives which Albert had just purchased from Prince Ludwig-Kraft-Ernst von Oetingen Wallerstein.

So extended was Waagen's influence that for at least twenty years he was the first foreign authority to be consulted on many artistic matters. His authority in Britain was founded in particular on two books: *Works of Art and Artists in England* (3 vols., trans. H. E. Lloyd, 1838) and the revised and enlarged version of his *Treasures of Art in Great Britain* (4 vols., trans. Lady Eastlake, 1854–7). The former is a strange mixture of travel writing and dry accounts of the major collections of old masters, written in an informal tone and offering picturesque insight into English society in 1835. Waagen was highly appreciative of all things English, praising the women, gardens, weather, education system, and even the comfortable beds in the inns of his host country. Describing the art collection of Lord Ashburton, he opined that 'nobody enjoys life in so noble and varied a manner as Englishmen of the higher classes of society, who, together with wealth, have the advantage of extensive general knowledge' (G. F. Waagen, *Works of Art and Artists in England*, 1838, 2.265). His English associates returned this good opinion: Lady Eastlake, somewhat patronizingly, described Waagen as 'a most intelligent, clever, witty old gentleman, full of mimicry and drollery and more well-bred than most Germans' (E. Eastlake, *Journals and Correspondence of Lady Eastlake*, ed. C. E. Smith, 1895, 1.249). *Treasures of Art in Great Britain*—an entirely different work from the *Works of Art*—was a straightforward catalogue of the 200 most important collections of the country, the most complete survey ever made.

Waagen's publications highlighted the hitherto unknown wealth of the private collections of Great Britain, while his application of the new techniques of German art historical studies and museology revolutionized British practice. In England technical expertise was vigorously promoted by the visits of Waagen and his compatriot Johann David Passavant. Waagen was the first to question many of the legendary and optimistic attributions of pictures in the private collections of the British aristocracy: his *Treasures of Art* is still used in auction rooms today to establish a painting's provenance and quality. Through his detailed study of British collections, his desire to enlighten a nation which he considered in need of education in art historical matters, his fluent advocacy of the seriousness of the fine arts and their economic and social importance, Waagen shaped the development of public provision for the arts in Britain to a greater extent than any of his peers. Not all his ideas were found congenial by the British and the positivist aspects of his art criticism were often challenged. But the flowering of museums and exhibitions, national and local, in Britain in the 1850s and 1860s must to a great extent be ascribed to his energy and imagination, as well as to his ability to gain acceptance among the British ruling classes in a way that he never achieved in his native Prussia. Waagen died on 15 July 1868, while visiting Copenhagen. He was buried on 27 July in the Assistenz-Friedhof, Copenhagen.

FLORIAN ILLIES

Sources I. Geismeier and others, *Jahrbuch der Berliner Museen*, 37 (1995) [bibliography] · A. Wolfmann, *G. F. Waagen, eine biographische Skizze* (1875), 1–52 · F. Haskell, 'The growth of British art history and its debts to Europe', *PBA*, 74 (1988), 203–24 · F. Illies, 'Waagen, Prinz Albert und die Manchester Art Treasures Exhibition von 1857', *Künstlerische Beziehungen zwischen England und Deutschland in der viktorianischen Epoche / Art in Britain and Germany in the age of Queen Victoria and Prince Albert*, ed. F. Bosbach and F. Büttner (Munich, 1998), 131–46 · C. Stowe, 'Making private collections public: G. F. Waagen and the Royal Museum in Berlin', *Journal of the History of Collections*, 10 (1998), 61–74 · F. Herrmann, 'Dr. Waagen's *Works of art and artists in England*', *The Connoisseur*, 161 (1966), 173–7 · D. Robertson, *Sir Charles Eastlake and the Victorian art world* (1978) · W. Waetzoldt, *Deutsche Kunsthistoriker*, 2 vols. (1921–4) · G. Bickendorf, *Der Beginn der Kunstgeschichtsschreibung unter dem Paradigma "Geschichte"* (Worms, 1985) · U. Finke, 'The art-treasures-exhibition', *Art and architecture in Victorian Manchester*, ed. J. H. G. Archer (1985), 102–26 · private information (2004) [Egil Skall, Staatarchiv Copenhagen]
Archives Geheimes Staatsarchiv Preussischer Kulturbesitz, Berlin, I. HA. Rep 76, Ve Sekt 15 · John Murray, London, archives · Staatliche Museen zu Berlin, Zentralarchiv, Handakte Waagen, MSS, I/GG 35
Likenesses L. H. Waagen, oils, 1812, Staatliche Museen, Berlin · L. Knaus, oils, 1855, Staatliche Museen, Berlin · J. Frantz, bust, 1860, Staatliche Museen, Berlin · F. Krüger, pen and watercolour drawing, Staatliche Museen, Berlin · F. Villot, pencil drawing, priv. coll. · engraving (after L. Knaus, 1855), BM, department of prints and drawings [*see illus.*]

Waban (*c*.1600–*c*.1684), Native American leader, was born about 1600. By 1630 American Indians near Massachusetts Bay had been devastated by European epidemics and raids by neighbouring tribes, and readily accepted the settlement of puritan colonists in Shawmut. Waban was then a counsellor in Nonantum, 10 miles to the west, married to the daughter of a neighbouring *sachem* (leader). He had higher ambitions, later confessing that 'I wished to be a witch, I wished to be a Sachem' (Eliot, *Further Account*, 231). Like other natives, he was impressed by European technologies and how the English seemed unaffected by the terrible diseases that decimated his people. Thus he was primed when John Eliot came to preach at his village in October 1646. Waban gave the minister his eldest son to be raised in an English family, and his wigwam for the minister's meetings.

Waban's influence grew along with Eliot's audiences. A few years later they obtained land for Natick, the mission town which became the cornerstone of the Bay Colony's missionary programme, with the first Indian Congregational church and a school for Indian ministers and teachers. By 1655 Waban had become Natick's leader and helped direct the growing Christian Indian network. Native teachers and preachers extended his power—and that of John Eliot and the Bay Colony—throughout the region. As this network grew, however, it (and the colonists) drew increasing opposition from other natives, including *sachems* such as the Wampanoags' Metacom (or King Philip), worried about the political implications of the Bay Colony's missionary and land purchase efforts.

By the spring of 1675 war loomed. Twice Waban warned that Metacom 'intended some mischief shortly to the English and Christian Indians'. King Philip's War began in July and rapidly engulfed the entire region. In October Waban and all other 'friendly' Indians were forced by panicked colonists to a desolate island in Boston harbour. There they faced terrible conditions. By spring many died and Waban was seriously ill. Luckily, the war had turned for the English, and he and his people were released in late May. In the wake of the war Natick became the largest Indian community in the Massachusetts Bay Colony, although it no longer lay at the centre of the network of mission towns. In the 1680s Waban led an exhausting but largely successful fight against the illicit sale of Nipmuc lands west of Natick. He remained a ruler in the town until his death about 1684. His son Thomas would inherit his role as Natick's political and cultural broker with the English. One of the first Native Americans in New England to embrace the puritan gospel, Waban's fortunes, like those of the missionary programme, were shattered by

King Philip's War. His career represents the temporarily successful but ultimately frustrated effort by some Indians to ride the initial wave of the colonial invasion.

DANIEL R. MANDELL

Sources H. von Lonkhuyzen, 'A reappraisal of the praying Indians: acculturation, conversion, and identity at Natick, Massachusetts, 1646–1730', *New England Quarterly*, 63 (1990), 396–428 · J. Eliot, *The day-breaking, if not the sun-rising of the gospel with the Indians in New England* (1647), 381–4 · D. Gookin, *Historical collections of the Indians in New England* (1792), 141–226 · D. Gookin, *An historical account of the doings and sufferings of the Christian Indians* (1836), 429–534 · J. Eliot, *A further account of the progress of the gospel* (1660), 231 · D. Mandell, '"Standing by his father": Thomas Waban of Natick, circa1630–1722', *Northeastern Indian lives, 1630–1816*, ed. R. Grumet (1996), 166–92 · D. Mandell, *Behind the frontier: Indians in eighteenth-century eastern Massachusetts* (1996), 12–44 · N. Salisbury, 'Red puritans: the "praying Indians" of Massachusetts Bay and John Eliot', *William and Mary Quarterly*, 32 (1975), 27–54 · deeds, Middlesex county, Massachusetts

Wace (*b.* after **1100**, *d.* **1174×83**), historian and poet, was born soon after 1100 on Jersey. Some have considered Wace to have been of noble birth, following a suggestion by Gaston Paris that Toustain, chamberlain of Duke Robert (I) of Normandy, was Wace's maternal grandfather; this has not been substantiated, nor has the misnomer Robert Wace, which dates back to the eighteenth century. According to autobiographical passages in his last work, the *Roman de Rou* (*c.*1160–74), Wace was taken to Caen as a young boy for religious training. He continued his studies in the Île-de-France, later returning to Caen where he devoted himself to a literary career; in the *Rou*, he refers to himself as a *clerc lisant* (a reading or teaching cleric), a role whose definition has generated debate among scholars. Although none of the *sirventes* (lyric poems, often of a satiric or political nature) which Wace says that he wrote appears to survive, three saints' lives are extant from the earlier part of his career: the *Vie de Sainte Marguerite* (*c.*1130–40), the *Conception Nostre Dame* (*c.*1130–40, but probably after the *Marguerite*), and the *Vie de Saint Nicolas* (*c.*1150).

In 1155, Wace completed the *Roman de Brut*, the oldest extant Old French chronicle of the early kings of Britain. Although Wace called the 14,866 line *Brut* a translation, it is more than a translation of a single work. Based largely on the vulgate and first variant versions of Geoffrey of Monmouth's *Historia regum Britanniae* (*c.*1138), the *Roman de Brut* contains material from oral sources and possibly from other written sources as well, including the earliest extant reference to King Arthur's round table. In his Middle English adaptation of Wace's *Brut* (*c.*1200), Layamon reports that Wace offered the *Roman de Brut* to Eleanor of Aquitaine, consort of Henry II; however, no other evidence has yet been found to support Layamon's claim.

Wace's chronicle of the Norman dukes which he dedicated to Eleanor of Aquitaine and Henry II, the *Roman de Rou* ('The Romance of Rollo'), was less popular than his Arthurian chronicle, less stylistically homogeneous, but more synthetic and original. In the *Rou*, Wace drew on Latin sources, including the Norman histories of William of Jumièges, William of Poitiers, and Dudo of St Quentin,

and the English histories of William of Malmesbury and Eadmer of Canterbury, as well as on oral sources. Unlike Wace's *Brut* and the saints' lives which are continuous narratives in octosyllabic rhymed couplets, the *Roman de Rou* contains four parts, the first two in alexandrines and the last two in octosyllables. The first part, known as the *Chronique ascendante des ducs de Normandie* (315 lines), traces the projected scope of the history in reverse chronological order, from Henry II back to Rollo; the second (4425 lines) describes the founding of the duchy by Rollo, and the history of the early dukes to the peace of 965; the third (11,440 lines) continues the narrative from 965 to the imprisonment of Robert Curthose by his brother, Henry I, following the battle of Tinchebrai in 1106. The fourth part (750 lines), dedicated to the career of the pirate Hasting, is thought to have been the first draft of the poem, later abandoned, and not part of the final poem as Wace intended. Early in the third part of the *Rou*, Wace records Henry II's gift of a prebend in Bayeux, which he may have received in payment for the *Brut* or as incentive to work on the *Rou*; documentary evidence suggests that Wace received the prebend between 1165 and 1169. At the end of the *Rou*, Wace reports that the monarch had grown less generous, and that he was removing Wace's commission in favour of a poet named Maistre Beneeit, most often identified as Benoît de Ste Maure, author of the *Roman de Troie* (*c.*1160) and the *Chronique des ducs de Normandie* (*c.*1174–80). The transfer may have taken place in or around 1174, since the last recorded event in the *Chronique ascendante* can be dated to 1174, but Henry II's son, Henry, the Young King (*d.* 1183), is mentioned as still alive.

Wace played an important role in the development of the French language through his use of an especially large and varied vocabulary and in the development of Old French narrative, primarily Arthurian romance.

JEAN BLACKER

Sources Wace, *Life of St Nicholas*, ed. M. Crawford (1923) · Wace, *La vie de Sainte Marguerite*, ed. E. A. Francis (1932) · E. du Méril, 'La vie et les ouvrages de Wace', *Études sur quelques points d'archéologie* (1862), 214–72 · H.-E. Keller, *Étude descriptive sur le vocabulaire de Wace* (1953) · B. Woledge, 'Notes on Wace's vocabulary', *Modern Language Review*, 46 (1951), 16–30 · J. Blacker, *The faces of time: portrayal of the past in Old French and Latin historical narrative of the Anglo-Norman regnum* (1994) · R. W. Leckie jun., *The passage of dominion: Geoffrey of Monmouth and the periodization of insular history in the twelfth century* (1980) · W. R. Schirmer and U. Broich, *Studien zum literarischen Patronat im England des 12. Jahrhunderts* (1962) · M. Pelan, *L'influence du 'Brut' de Wace sur les romanciers français de son temps* (1931) · M. D. Legge, 'Cleric lisant', *Modern Language Review*, 47 (1952), 554–6 · M. D. Legge, *Anglo-Norman literature and its background* (1963) · G. Paris, 'Sur un épisode d'Aimeri de Narbonne', *Romania* (1880), 515–46 [at 526–7] · *Le 'Roman de Rou' de Wace*, ed. A. J. Holden, 3 vols. (Paris, 1970–73) · *Le 'Roman de Brut' de Wace*, ed. I. Arnold, 2 vols. (Paris, 1938–40) · Wace, *Vie de Sainte Marguerite*, ed. H.-E. Keller (1990) · Wace, *Conception Nostre Dame*, ed. W. R. Ashford (1933) · Wace, *Vie de Saint Nicolas*, ed. E. Ronsjö (1942) · Wace, *The Roman de Rou*, trans. G. S. Burgess (St Helier, 2002) [text of A. J. Holden with notes by G. S. Burgess and E. A. van Houts] · *Wace's Roman de Brut: a history of the British*, ed. and trans. J. Weiss (1999) · E. Baumgartner and I. Short, eds. and trans., *La geste du roi Arthur: selon le Roman de Brut de Wace et l'Historia regum Britanniae de Geoffroy de Monmouth* (1993) · I. Arnold and M. Pelan, *La partie arthurienne du Roman de Brut* (1962)

Archives Bibliothèque Nationale, Paris, MSS • BL, MSS

Wace, Alan John Bayard (1879–1957), archaeologist, was born at 4 Camden Place, Cambridge, on 13 July 1879, the second son of Frederic Charles Wace (1836–1893), a mathematics don at St John's College, and his wife, Fanny, elder daughter of John Campbell Bayard, formerly of the 96th regiment, of Gwernydd, Aberriw, Montgomeryshire. The Bayards were descended from a well-known New York family. Frederic Wace played an active role in the life of both the university and city of Cambridge; he served as the first don to be mayor of Cambridge (1890–91). Following his death in January 1893, the family moved to Shrewsbury; Wace followed his brother Emeric to Shrewsbury School, and in 1898 was head of the school. Unlike his father and brother, who attended St John's College, Cambridge, Wace read for the classical tripos at Pembroke College, Cambridge, where he held a scholarship (matriculating in 1898). He obtained a first class in part one (1901), though the elation was marred by the death of his brother Emeric just before the results were posted. At the suggestion of Wace's tutor, R. A. Neil, just days before Neil's death, Wace decided to study classical archaeology for part two, for which he obtained a first class with distinction (1902). His contemporaries included Richard M. Dawkins and Percy Ure, both of whom were to continue their interest in the archaeology of the Greek world.

The British Schools at Athens and Rome At Cambridge Wace was influenced by Charles Waldstein (later Walston), Slade professor of fine arts, and William Ridgeway, Disney professor of archaeology. The former would provide interest in Greek, and in particular Hellenistic, sculpture, the latter in Bronze Age Greece. Ridgeway's *The Early Age of Greece* (1901) had just appeared; Wace later wrote the preface for the posthumous second volume (1931). Wace was awarded a Prendergast studentship and admitted as a student at the British School at Athens for the 1902–3 session: Robert Carr Bosanquet was director, Marcus N. Tod the assistant director. His research project for the year was on Hellenistic Greek sculpture; part of this was published as 'Apollo seated on the Omphalos' in the *Annual of the British School at Athens* (1902–3).

Wace's first year at the British School at Athens coincided with the admission of Louisa Pesel (d. 1947) as an associate of the school. Pesel, as the director of the Royal Hellenic School of Needlework, may have introduced Wace to Greek textiles, though Bosanquet, too, was a collector. Wace subsequently prepared for an exhibition of Greek textiles in the Fitzwilliam Museum, Cambridge, *Catalogue of a Collection of Modern Greek Embroideries* (1905), and in the summer of 1906 he toured the southern Sporades, then part of the Ottoman empire, with Richard Dawkins, 'studying the conditions of modern life as well as the ancient remains, and collecting information about local styles of embroidery' (*Annual Report of the British School at Athens*, 1905–6, 484). Wace and Dawkins collaborated on a study, 'Greek embroideries', for the *Burlington Magazine* (1914). On the eve of the First World War Wace helped to write the *Catalogue of a Collection of Old Embroideries of the*

Greek Islands and Turkey (1914) with William M. T. Lawrence, for the winter exhibition at the Burlington Fine Arts Club; over half the loans were from the collections of Wace and Dawkins.

In 1903, holding a Craven studentship, Wace started the year at the British School at Rome where Henry Stuart-Jones was the newly appointed director, and Thomas Ashby the assistant director. This initiated a pattern for the next few years: Wace would spend the autumn at the British School at Rome, and the spring and summer excavating in Greece. Stuart-Jones had an interest in ancient sculpture, and had initiated a project to study the collections in the city of Rome. In 1904 Wace was elected a fellow of Pembroke College, Cambridge, a post he held until 1913. Following a British government grant to the British School at Rome, Wace was appointed librarian specifically to work on the catalogue of the sculpture collections for the 1905–6 session. Thomas Ashby was *de facto* acting director, with Wace as his assistant (a title which he used in the *Annual Report of the British School at Athens*). Although Wace applied for the directorship in spring 1906, Ashby was appointed; Wace was offered the assistant directorship, but declined it. However, he continued to work on the sculpture project alongside Henry Stuart-Jones, and in 1909 Wace was considered as a possible future director to succeed Ashby, whose contract was due to expire in 1911; but this was not to be. Wace's contribution to the field of sculpture included studies on Turin in the *Journal of Hellenic Studies* (1906), and the Palazzo Spada in *The Papers of the British School at Rome* (1910), as well as a contribution on Roman portraits in H. Stuart-Jones, *A Catalogue of the Ancient Sculptures Preserved in the Municipal Collections of Rome, 1: The Sculptures of the Museo Capitolino* (1912).

In Greece Wace was involved in the British School's work in Laconia as well as developing his own excavations and survey in Thessaly. The British School at Athens had up to this point been involved with the excavation of prehistoric sites, notably at Phylakopi on Melos, and at Palaikastro on Crete. However, as Bosanquet's directorship came to an end, it was decided to initiate a campaign at the historic mainland site of Sparta, which it was thought would attract more financial support through the creation of the Laconian Excavation Fund; a topographical survey of Laconia was also started. Wace (with an initial interest in the sculpture) and Tod prepared *A Catalogue of the Sparta Museum* (1906). In 1905 Wace joined his first dig, working with F. W. Hasluck, the librarian of the British School, at Geraki in Laconia. Wace was also involved in the main British School excavations at Sparta, with particular responsibility for the Roman remains at the Arapissa at Sparta as well as the city wall along the Eurotas. In 1906 Robert Carr Bosanquet indicated that he was to resign as director of the British School at Athens to take up a chair in the University of Liverpool. Wace was one of the three short-listed candidates, and was considered 'a competent and keen worker and capable of extracting work from others' (minutes of the British School at Athens, 1906). However, Dawkins, Wace's Cambridge contemporary, though senior in age, was selected.

In June 1907, once the Sparta excavations had been completed, Wace and a Cambridge student, John P. Droop (1882–1963), joined forces to excavate at Theotokou in Thessaly. Once the Theotokou excavation was over they went to search for potential new sites, 'maghoula-hunting' (Droop, 32), identifying Zerélia, to which they returned in June 1908 along with the Oxford-educated Maurice S. Thompson supported by the Cambridge University Worts fund. Droop was to recall his work with Wace: 'Enquiry often gave us the direction, and we tramped the plain until we came to them [maghoulas], when the sherds and stone implements that we picked up gave a good indication of what lay beneath' (ibid., 33). Some of these sherds and stone artefacts were presented by Wace to the Fitzwilliam Museum, Cambridge, in 1907, 1908, and 1909. Wace and Thompson continued their work in Thessaly, culminating in their *Prehistoric Thessaly* (1912). Arnold Toynbee recorded the exploits of Wace and Thompson when he came out to the school for the academic year 1911–12:

> They hunted together like a couple of hounds; and, like hounds on the scent, they were indifferent, while chasing their quarry, to heat, cold, hunger, or exposure to the elements. They set one an exacting standard of physical endurance. (Toynbee, 22)

Wace and Thompson collaborated on the study of the Vlachs in northern Greece, especially in the community of Samarina, which appeared as *The Nomads of the Balkans: an Account of Life and Customs among the Vlachs of Northern Pindus* (1914). Further work in the region was restricted by the outbreak of the First Balkan War in 1912.

Visits to Athens also gave Wace an opportunity to visit major sculptural collections as well as excavations in Greece and the Ottoman empire. By the summer of 1903 he was acting as secretary to Professor Ernest Gardner's tours in Greece, a complement to Wilhelm Dörpfeld's *Reisen*. Members of the British School at Athens had been involved in a survey of Byzantine churches in Constantinople sponsored by the Byzantine Research Fund and under the direction of Professor Alexander van Millingen, who had been studying the city since the late nineteenth century. Wace contributed to the study of Walter S. George, *The Church of Saint Eirene at Constantinople* (1913) and, with the architectural student Ramsay Traquair (who had been working in Laconia), collaborated on a study of the base of the obelisk of Theodosius (*Journal of Hellenic Studies*, 1909).

Director of the British School at Athens In 1912 Wace was appointed as lecturer in ancient history and archaeology at the University of St Andrews. However, following Dawkins's decision to resign as director of the British School at Athens in 1914, Wace was appointed as his replacement with Hasluck as his assistant director. The outbreak of the First World War disrupted Wace's own work, and restricted the number of visitors to Athens. An exception, in spring 1915, was the Australian V. Gordon Childe, then a postgraduate student in Oxford, who made a short trip to Greece to study prehistoric 'Minyan' pottery.

During the 1915–16 session Wace was seconded to the British legation, initially as director of relief for British refugees from Turkey, and the British School became a hostel for those involved in its work. In autumn 1915 Compton Mackenzie described his encounter with Wace:

> a delightful combination of great scholarship and humour, a worldly humour too and not in the least pedagogic … a tall slim man full of nervous energy, with a fresh complexion and an extraordinarily merry pair of light blue eyes. (Mackenzie, 194)

Wace, who was in part responsible for encipherment and decipherment at the legation, devised the idea of a passport control in winter 1915 to stop the relatively free movement of spies between Egypt and Greece. Mackenzie observed that 'from it sprang the whole of that great system of passport control round the world which made life hideous for travellers during the war, continued to do so for so long afterward, and has not yet been relaxed' (ibid., 208). Wace continued his studies, though largely confined to Athens. The British School was not allowed to dig during these war years, but he joined Carl Blegen (1887–1971), then secretary of the American School of Classical Studies at Athens, on the excavation of the prehistoric site of Korakou near Corinth during 1915 and 1916. Their shared interest in the archaeology of mainland Greece during the Bronze Age, derived from a study of pre-Late Bronze Age finds in the National Museum in Athens, brought about a challenge, published in the *Annual of the British School at Athens* (1916–17, 1917–18), to the view expressed by Arthur Evans and Duncan Mackenzie from the Knossos excavations that Crete had dominated the mainland. Their work created tensions and was dismissed by Mackenzie as 'all schoolboy archaeology and so naïve!' (Mackenzie to Evans, 30 Oct 1920, Evans MSS). Yet even this research was to be curtailed. In December 1916 French and British forces landed at Piraeus against the background of the growing split between the supporters of King Constantine and the prime minister, Eleftherios Venizelos. This unwise move led to the evacuation of British personnel from Athens, and Wace, along with members of the legation, was quartered aboard the *Abbasieh*, positioned in the Strait of Salamis, for the following winter. The staff were eventually allowed to return to Athens, and Wace continued his work at the legation until November 1919, when his contract as director of the British School was renewed for a further three years. His international reputation drew a number of foreign students, notably Axel Boethius and J. E. Hondius, to the British School. During this period Wace helped with the creation of the Museum of Decorative Art (since 1958, the Museum of Greek Popular Art) in Monastiraki, Athens.

In spring 1920 Wace initiated a series of excavations at Mycenae with the support of Evans, who perhaps hoped that they would shed further light on the relationship between the Greek mainland and Crete. The concession had been ceded personally to Wace by Christos Tsountas on behalf of the Archaeological Society of Athens. The results from the excavations were not to Evans's liking: he launched an attack on Wace in the *Times Literary Supplement* (15 July 1920, 454). These excavations, conducted with Blegen, continued until 1923; they were notable for the participation of female students from the British School, especially Winifred Lamb, honorary keeper of Greek antiquities at the Fitzwilliam Museum, Cambridge. The work was published in the *Annual of the British School at Athens* (1919–20, 1921-2/1922–3) and *Archaeologia* (1933). Alongside these excavations, Wace was involved with the work of the American School under Blegen at Zygouries, which lay between Corinth and Mycenae.

After Wace had spent ten years in Athens the committee of the British School at Athens decided not to re-appoint him as director in 1923; he was succeeded by Arthur Woodward, his assistant director, who initiated new excavations at Sparta in spring 1924. Wace did not return to excavate in Greece until summer 1939. Rebuffed, it seemed, by the British, Wace accepted the first of several invitations to lecture in North America as the Vanuxem lecturer at Princeton (1923), and as the Norton lecturer for the Archaeological Institute of America (1923–4). He was even invited to excavate for the University of Pennsylvania Museum at Beth Shean in 1925, but he declined. Tensions between Evans and Wace continued, and in spring 1924 Evans launched another attack on Wace in *The Times* (8 April 1924, 10). Yet it was Wace, rather than Evans, who was invited to write the chapters on Aegean civilization for the *Cambridge Ancient History* (vol. 1, 1923, and vol. 2, 1924).

The Victoria and Albert Museum Wace was offered the position of Mediterranean section curator at the University of Pennsylvania Museum in 1924, but had to decline it owing to family commitments in Britain, following the death of his brother-in-law. His interest in Greek and Anatolian embroideries gave him sufficient experience to accept, in 1924, the post of deputy keeper in the department of textiles at the Victoria and Albert Museum, where he had already been involved with the organization of its collection; he had donated sixty-two pieces of Greek embroidery in 1919. On 20 June 1925, at St Albans, Wace married Helen Pence (1892–1982), daughter of Professor W. D. Pence of Evanston, Illinois, USA, and a former student at the American Academy in Rome. They had met at Mycenae in June 1922 and were engaged during an island cruise in May the following year on a yacht chartered by the American George D. Pratt; three American archaeologists on the cruise, Blegen, Bert Hodge Hill, and Leicester Holland, had been accompanied by their future brides, Elizabeth Pierce, Ida Thallon, and Louise Adams, respectively.

Following his move to London, Wace broadened his interest in textiles to include other periods and areas. He wrote the preface for *Practical canvas embroidery: a handbook with diagrams and scale drawings taken from XVIIth century samplers and other sources* (1929) by his old friend Louisa Pesel, now president of the Embroiderers' Guild, and his work with E. A. B. Barnard on Sheldon tapestry weavers was published in *Archaeologia* (1928). He produced a number of catalogues on the collection of the Victoria and Albert Museum, notably *Catalogue of Algerian Embroideries* (1935) and (with Leigh Ashton) *Brief Guide to Persian Embroideries* (1929). With his wife, he prepared the *Catalogue of Loan Exhibition of English Decorative Art at Lansdowne House* (1929). During the 1930s he worked on a study of Flemish military tapestries, though the publication, *The Marlborough tapestries at Blenheim Palace and their relation to other military tapestries of the War of the Spanish Succession* (1968) did not appear until long after his death. He himself owned a fine collection of Greek embroideries which was placed on loan with Liverpool Museum (now the National Museums and Galleries on Merseyside) after the Second World War and subsequently sold to the museum.

In 1925 Wace sold ninety pieces from his collection to George Hewitt Myers, founder of the Textile Museum in Washington, DC. Wace prepared the catalogue, *Old Embroideries of the Greek Islands from the Collection of George Hewitt Myers* (1928). Wace also assisted Beatrice Lindell Cook with a study of the collection of textiles which had been acquired by her husband Frank in Egypt, where he represented his family firm of Cook's Tours. This was published as *Mediterranean and Near Eastern Embroideries from the Collection of Mrs F. H. Cook* (1935). Part of the Cook collection was later acquired by the St Louis Art Museum, and Wace gave a lecture at the opening of the collection in March 1953.

Professorships in Cambridge and Alexandria In 1926 Sydney Cockerell and Winifred Lamb invited Wace to prepare a monograph on a Cretan marble 'goddess' which had just been acquired (with the support of Evans) by the Fitzwilliam Museum, Cambridge. This appeared as *A Cretan Statuette in the Fitzwilliam Museum: a Study in Minoan Costume* (1927). Sadly the acquisition attracted much criticism and came under suspicion of being a forgery. One of the few other associations with Bronze Age archaeology was in 1933 when Wace joined Blegen during the renewed excavation of Troy. They also planned a joint work, *Helladica*, which was never published. The retirement of Arthur B. Cook in 1934 left a vacancy for the Laurence chair in Cambridge, and Wace was elected. His choice of subject for his inaugural lecture, *An Approach to Greek Sculpture* (1935), took him back to his early interests. He held this chair, along with a fellowship at Pembroke College, until he retired in 1944; he was made an honorary fellow of Pembroke in 1951.

Early in 1939 Wace was the Armstrong lecturer in Toronto. He celebrated his sixtieth birthday by returning to Greece to resume excavating at Mycenae. A celebratory lunch was held in the tholos tomb, the Treasury of Atreus, attended by leading Greek, American, and German scholars. With war looming, Wace helped at the National Museum in Athens to store the finds. He ostensibly joined the staff of the British legation, though he was probably working for MI6, known as the inter-services liaison department. After the fall of Athens in spring 1941, he was evacuated to Cairo where he was in charge of the department preparing identity documents for Special Operations Executive agents operating in Greece. Before the battle of Alamein (1942) he was temporarily evacuated to Jerusalem, where John H. Iliffe, director of the Palestine

Archaeological Museum, arranged for Wace's manuscript of Mycenae to be prepared for publication. In 1944, realizing that he would be unable to return to Cambridge owing to the war, Wace resigned the Laurence chair and, with the encouragement of the British Council, accepted the chair of classics and archaeology at the Farouk I University at Alexandria. He was able to pursue his earlier interest in the archaeology of the Hellenistic world. This included the excavation of Kom al-Dikka, the presumed site of the tomb of Alexander the Great, as well as the study *Hermopolis Magna, Ashmunein: the Ptolemaic Sanctuary and the Basilica* (1959), published posthumously. He also organized, with Étienne Drioton, an exhibition of Coptic art in Cairo (1944), and was elected an officer of the patriarchal order of St Mark the Evangelist, Alexandria (1952).

With the ending of the war, Wace was able to return to his interest in Bronze Age Greece. As a member of the Institute of Advanced Study in Princeton in 1948 he completed *Mycenae: an Archaeological History and Guide* (1949). The Greek civil war ended in October 1949, and the following year he resumed excavations at Mycenae. Wace celebrated fifty years in archaeology in 1951 and was presented with a special volume of the *Annual of the British School at Athens* (vol. 46). In 1952 he discovered Linear B tablets which complemented Blegen's own finds at Pylos in 1939; in 1952 Michael Ventris was to announce the decipherment of the script. Wace was dismissed by the Egyptian government from the chair in Alexandria in 1952, following an incident in the Suez Canal, and he took up residence on Cyprus. Excavations at Mycenae continued until 1955, interspersed with annual visits to Princeton, and with further study seasons at Mycenae in 1956 and 1957. In July 1957 the Mycenaean Room at the National Museum in Athens was reopened.

Wace's contribution to archaeology was recognized by the award of honorary degrees of LittD from the universities of Amsterdam (1932) and of Pennsylvania (1940), of LLD from the University of Liverpool (1935), and of DLitt from the University of Cambridge (1951), and his election as a fellow of the Society of Antiquaries of London, and a fellow of the British Academy (1947). He was an honorary member of the Archaeological Institute of America, the Archaeological Society of Athens, and the Royal Society of Archaeology of Alexandria, and vice-president of the British School at Athens and the Society for the Promotion of Hellenic Studies. He was a recipient of the Petrie medal for distinguished work in archaeology (1953).

For some years Wace suffered from a heart condition. In spring 1957 he suffered a heart attack; his health deteriorated over the summer (though he was able to work on the Mycenae finds in Nauplion), and he died in Athens from a heart attack on 9 November 1957. He was buried in the protestant section of the First Cemetery in Athens. Frank H. Stubbings completed his *Companion to Homer* (1962), a work which had been planned in 1939. His widow separately published some of his fictional essays in *Greece Untrodden* (1964).   DAVID GILL

Sources *The Times* (11 Nov 1957) • F. H. Stubbings, 'Alan John Bayard Wace, 1879–1957', *PBA*, 44 (1958), 263–80 • C. W. Blegen, 'Alan

John Bayard Wace (1879–1957)', *American Philosophical Society Yearbook* (1958), 162–71 • S. Hood, 'Alan John Bayard Wace', *Gnomon*, 30 (1958), 158–9 • C. Zerner, 'Alan John Bayard Wace and Carl William Blegen: a friendship in the realms of bronze', *Wace and Blegen* [Athens 1989], ed. C. Zerner (1993) • R. Hood, *Faces of archaeology in Greece: caricatures by Piet de Jong* (1998) • H. Waterhouse, *The British School at Athens: the first hundred years*, British School at Athens, suppl. vol. 19 (1986) • T. P. Wiseman, *A short history of the British School at Rome* (1990) • H. Waterhouse, 'Bibliography, 1903–1950', *Annual of the British School at Athens*, 46 (1951), 232–43 • H. Waterhouse, 'A. J. B. Wace: supplementary bibliography', *Annual of the British School at Athens*, 63 (1968), 327–9 • A. J. Toynbee, *Experiences* (1969) • N. Momigliano, *Duncan Mackenzie: a cautious canny highlander and the palace of Minos at Knossos* (1999) • K. Butcher and D. W. J. Gill, 'The director, the dealer, the goddess and her champions: the acquisition of the Fitzwilliam goddess', *American Journal of Archaeology*, 97 (1993), 383–401 • C. Mackenzie, *First Athenian memories* (1931) • R. Koehl, 'A letter from Evans to Droop on the "problem" of Wace', *Classical Journal*, 86 (1990), 45–52 • J. K. Papadopoulos, 'The correspondence of A. J. B. Wace in the library of the Australian Archaeological Institute at Athens', *Annual of the British School at Athens*, 88 (1993), 337–52 • E. B. French, 'In the tracks of the British School in Laconia', *Travellers and officials in the Peloponnese: descriptions-reports-statistics. In honour of Sir Steven Runciman* (Monemvasia, 1994), 297–302 • R. Taylor, *Embroidery of the Greek islands and Epirus* (Brooklyn, NY, 1998) • J. P. Droop, *Archaeological excavation*, Cambridge Archaeological and Ethnological Series (1915) • A. Beevor, *Crete: the battle and resistance* (1992) • private information (2004) [E. French, daughter]

Archives FM Cam., antiquities • Pembroke Cam., notebooks, mainly relating to Greece • priv. coll., papers • SOAS, papers relating to Kom-Ed-Dik excavation • U. Cam., Museum of Classical Archaeology, antiquities | AM Oxf., Evans archive • Bodl. Oxf., letters to O. G. S. Crawford • Bodl. Oxf., corresp. with J. L. Myres • Emmanuel College, Cambridge, letters to R. M. Dawkins • U. Birm., Mycenae archive

Likenesses P. de Jong, caricature on cartridge paper, *c.*1920, repro. in Hood, *Faces of archaeology*; priv. coll. • photograph, repro. in Stubbings, 'Alan John Bayard Wace'

Wace, Henry (1836–1924), dean of Canterbury, was born in Islington, London, on 10 December 1836, the eldest son and second child in a family of twelve children of the Revd Richard Henry Wace (d. 1893) and his wife, Eulielia, daughter of Charles Grey. His earliest education was at home, in Islington, until 1842, and then at Goring-on-Thames, Berkshire, but in February 1848 he was sent to Marlborough College, transferring to Rugby School in August 1850. In 1853 he entered King's College, London, living as a pupil with the church historian the Revd Charles Hole. He matriculated at Trinity College, Oxford, in May 1856, but shortly afterwards won a scholarship at Brasenose College. He was secretary of the Union Society in 1857, and in 1858 he obtained a first class in mathematical moderations, graduated BA in 1860 with second classes in *literae humaniores* and mathematical Greats, and proceeded MA in 1873. He returned to King's College as an evening-class lecturer in history from 1860 until 1862.

Wace was ordained deacon in 1861 and priest the following year, becoming curate at St Luke's, Berwick Street, London (1861–3), and then at St James's, Piccadilly (1863–9), and rapidly earning a reputation as a striking and forceful preacher. On 15 August 1863, at Limpsfield, Surrey, he married his second cousin Elizabeth (d. 1893), eldest daughter of Henry Arnett, with whom he had four sons.

Henry Wace (1836–1924), by William Logsdail, exh. RA 1912

The same year Wace contributed a letter to *The Times* protesting against the treatment of Bishop J. W. Colenso, and this attracted the attention of the editor, J. T. Delane, who was impressed by his terse and vigorous style of writing. As a result he invited Wace to become a writer of leading articles, a position which he held for twenty years, and in which he displayed an ability to produce copy on any topic at short notice. Wace was appointed lecturer at Grosvenor Chapel, South Audley Street, London (1870–72), and successively chaplain (1872–80) and preacher (1880–96) of Lincoln's Inn. He delivered the Boyle lectures in London in 1874–5, published as *Christianity and Morality* (1876), and the Bampton lectures at Oxford in 1879, published as *The Foundations of Faith* (1880). On several occasions from 1878 onwards he was select preacher at Oxford and Cambridge. He was awarded a BD (1882) and DD (1883) by Oxford University, and an honorary DD (1882) by the University of Edinburgh.

Wace resumed his connection with King's College, London, in 1875 on his appointment to the professorship of ecclesiastical history. He was joint editor with William Smith (1813–1893) of the *Dictionary of Christian biography, literature, sects and doctrines during the first eight centuries* (4 vols., 1877–87), and with Philip Schaff of the second series of the *Nicene and Post-Nicene Fathers* (14 vols., 1890–1900). In 1883 he became principal of King's College, to which he gave strong and able leadership at a time when it was struggling to survive. Wace took a leading part in the ultimately unsuccessful campaign to unite King's College, University College, and Gresham College into one university, and when in 1894–6 the government withdrew its

grant to King's because it was a denominational institution he opposed the relaxation of its religious requirements to meet this objection. Despite his onerous duties as principal of King's College he continued to lecture and write on theological topics, publishing among other books *The Gospel and its Witnesses* (1883) and, in response to T. H. Huxley, *Christianity and Agnosticism* (1895). He also edited with C. A. Buchheim a selection of Luther's works (1883; rev. edn, 1896). In 1894, after the death of his first wife in the previous year, he married Cornelia Gertrude (*d.* 1925), daughter of the German scholar Dr Leonard Schmitz and formerly vice-principal of the ladies' department of King's College, who outlived him by almost a year.

In 1881 Wace was made a prebendary of St Paul's Cathedral, and from 1883 until 1903 he was examining chaplain to successive archbishops of Canterbury E. W. Benson and Frederick Temple. He was also appointed honorary chaplain to Queen Victoria (1884–9) and chaplain-in-ordinary (1889–1901), and subsequently honorary chaplain to Edward VII (1901–3). Although his nomination to the benefice of St Michael, Cornhill, in 1896 enabled him to recover a strong constitution overstrained by hard work, his wide-ranging activities continued unabated.

Wace was by now well known as an effective administrator, a protestant churchman of deep scholarship, and a stout champion of the Reformation settlement. Increasingly he was called upon to serve on the councils and committees of Anglican organizations, often as president or chairman, where his gifts of courtesy, tact, fairness, and humour won the confidence of many whose opinions differed from his own. In 1900, and again in 1901, he was asked to chair round-table conferences at Fulham Palace organized by successive bishops of London (Mandell Creighton and A. F. Winnington-Ingram) to discuss the controversial issues surrounding holy communion, confession, and absolution. Around the turn of the century he became more closely identified with evangelicals because he shared their hostility to ritualism and destructive biblical criticism, and these concerns found expression in such works as *The Sacrifice of Christ* (1898), *The Bible and Modern Investigation* (1903), and *Principles of the Reformation* (1910). In 1902 a conference of clergy under his chairmanship passed resolutions asking the bishops to make a public declaration in support of the virgin birth and physical resurrection of Christ. In 1905 he led a broadly based deputation to Lambeth Palace to urge that only the generally accepted usages of the first six centuries of the church should be adhered to. This petition attracted the signatures of more than 4000 clergy.

Belated recognition of Wace's gifts and ability came in 1903 when he succeeded F. W. Farrar as dean of Canterbury. He found the work there congenial: he raised more than £30,000 towards the repair of the cathedral's fabric; he was heavily involved in educational and hospital work in the city; his robust sermons and addresses inspired and strengthened many, especially during the First World War; and his popularity was such that on the occasion of his eighty-fifth birthday in 1921 he was presented with the freedom of the city. As dean, Wace became for the first time a member of the convocation of Canterbury, and he soon made his mark in that assembly as a vigorous debater and outspoken opponent of theological and liturgical innovations, particularly the high-church attempts to revise the Book of Common Prayer.

Until almost the end of his long life there was no diminution in Wace's faculties or slackening in his many-faceted activities. He continued to publish books and pamphlets, often based on his sermons and addresses, and to contribute regularly to newspapers and religious journals, and he remained a prominent figure in many evangelical organizations. In 1919 he allied himself with Dr Darwell Stone, the Anglo-Catholic principal of Pusey House, in opposing the appointment of the liberal Hensley Henson to the bishopric of Hereford. And in 1922 he was a principal founder (and vice-president in 1923–4) of the Bible Churchmen's Missionary Society, which was established when a group broke away from the Church Missionary Society in order to reassert traditional evangelical doctrines. However, if in the public arena he was generally regarded as a keen and combative controversialist, in private life he was admired as a witty and attractive conversationalist and a charming host. Following a traffic accident in London, Wace died at the deanery in Canterbury on 9 January 1924 and was buried three days later in the cloister garth of Canterbury Cathedral.

STEPHEN GREGORY

Sources Crockford (1924) · *The Guardian* (11 Jan 1924) · J. S. Reynolds, *The evangelicals at Oxford, 1735–1871: a record of an unchronicled movement*, [2nd edn] (1975) · F. J. C. Hearnshaw, *The centenary history of King's College, London, 1828–1928* (1929) · W. G. Johnson, 'Dean Wace', *The Churchman*, new ser., 38 (1924), 95–101 · P. Collinson, P. N. Ramsay, and M. Sparks, eds., *A history of Canterbury Cathedral* (1995) · Foster, *Alum. Oxon.* · *The Times* (10 Jan 1924) · A. I. Dasent, *John Thadeus Delane*, 2 vols. (1908) · G. K. A. Bell, *Randall Davidson, archbishop of Canterbury*, 3rd edn (1952) · D. W. Bebbington, *Evangelicalism in modern Britain: a history from the 1730s to the 1980s* (1989) · *The Guardian* (18 Jan 1924) · L. W. James, ed., *Marlborough College register: 1843–1952*, 9th edn (1952) · G. A. Solly, ed., *Rugby School register*, rev. edn, 1: *April 1675 – October 1857* (1933) · W. S. Hooton and J. S. Wright, *The first twenty-five years of the Bible Churchmen's Missionary Society* (1947) · Crockford (1893) · *Clergy List* (1842) · *Clergy List* (1843) · *DNB* · *IGI*
Archives King's Lond., papers relating to King's College, London | BL, letters to C. C. Osborne, Add. MS 46408 · CUL, letters to B. F. Westcott · Durham Cath. CL, letters to J. B. Lightfoot · LPL, corresp. with E. W. Benson · LPL, letters to A. C. Tait · LPL, corresp. with Frederick Temple · U. Birm. L., letters to R. W. Dale
Likenesses photograph, 1883–97, repro. in Hearnshaw, *Centenary history of King's College, London* · W. Logsdail, oils, 1903, deanery, Canterbury · W. Logsdail, portrait, exh. RA 1912, NPG [*see illus.*] · photograph, repro. in Hooton and Wright, *First twenty-five years of the Bible Churchmen's Missionary Society*
Wealth at death £22,329 2s. 5d.: probate, 15 March 1924, *CGPLA Eng. & Wales*

Wadd, William (1776–1829), surgeon, the eldest son of Charlotte and Solomon Wadd (d. 1821), a surgeon who had lived and practised for more than half a century in Basinghall Street, London, was born on 21 June 1776. He entered Merchant Taylors' School late in 1784 and then served as apprentice to James Earle in 1797, becoming one of the privileged class of surgeon's pupils at St Bartholomew's Hospital. He was admitted a member of the Royal College of Surgeons on 18 December 1801, and set up practice in the West End of London. On 5 July 1806 he married Caroline Mackenzie. They had two children.

Wadd was a member of the council of the Royal College of Surgeons in 1824, and he was appointed a member of the court of examiners in succession to John Abernethy on 3 August 1829. He was appointed one of the surgeons-extraordinary to the prince regent on 19 August 1817, and surgeon-extraordinary to George IV on 30 March 1821.

Wadd was killed on 29 August 1829 when he jumped from a runaway carriage on the road from Killarney to Mitchelstown, while he was on holiday in Ireland. At the time of his death he was a fellow of the Linnean Society and an associate of the Société de Médecine of Paris. His wife survived him.

A man of high talents, Wadd had a rich fund of anecdotes. He was an excellent draughtsman, and his etchings were so skilled that he illustrated all his works himself. Wadd was the author of several medical texts, including *Comments on Corpulency, Lineaments of Leanness, Mems on Diet and Dietetics* (1829), which is illustrated by his own caricature etchings. He is, however, best known for *Nugae chirurgicae, or, A biographical miscellany illustrative of a collection of professional portraits* (1824). The nucleus of the collection of portraits was presented to him about 1814 by Henry Fauntleroy, the banker, who was hanged for forgery. The catalogue is arranged under two alphabets—one of anecdotal biographies, the other of memorabilia. It is interesting reading but contains many errors. Both *Nugae canorae, or, Epitaphian mementoes* (in stone-cutters' verse) *of the Medici family, by Unus Quorum* (1827) and *Mems, Maxims, and Memoirs* (1827) contain a miscellany of things medical, and of the history of medicine and surgery in England.

D'A. POWER, *rev.* KAYE BAGSHAW

Sources GM, 1st ser., 99/2 (1829), 562 · private information (1899) · C. J. Robinson, ed., *A register of the scholars admitted into Merchant Taylors' School, from AD 1562 to 1874*, 2 vols. (1882–3) · *IGI*
Likenesses J. Jackson, oils, RCS Eng.

Waddell, Helen Jane (1889–1965), writer and translator, was born on 31 May 1889 at 25 Nakano-Cho, Azabu, Tokyo, the youngest child in the family of eight sons and two daughters of the Revd Hugh Waddell (1840–1901) and his wife, Jane Martin (1850–1892), of Banbridge, co. Down. Helen's father was a missionary, and both parents inherited a long tradition of service to the United Presbyterian church in Scotland. Jane Waddell became ill, and after returning with her children to Belfast in 1892, died in that year when Helen was two. Hugh married his cousin Martha Waddell in the following year, and took the family back to Japan in 1896. Ill health caused him to return with them in 1900 to Ulster, where he died in 1901.

Helen Waddell was educated at Victoria College (1900–07), and after a year of private study, at Queen's University, Belfast, where under Professor Gregory Smith she graduated BA with first-class honours in English in 1911, and MA by thesis ('John Milton the epicurist') in 1912. Her dissertation was examined by George E. B. Saintsbury, who remained an inspiring friend and courtly correspondent until his death in 1933. Though she found her stepmother uncongenial, she dutifully stayed with her in Ulster until Martha's death in 1920. During these years she published *Lyrics from the Chinese* (reprinted seven times between 1913 and 1938) and devotional Bible stories later collected in *Stories from Holy Writ* (1949), as well as articles and reviews. She also wrote a play, *The Spoiled Buddha* (published 1919), which was performed in 1915 in Belfast with her brother Samuel (who became well known in Dublin as actor and playwright) in the chief role. During this period she became an ardent home ruler, bitterly critical of the politics of Sir Edward Carson.

Helen Waddell was thirty-one when in 1920 she went up to Somerville College, Oxford, registering for a research degree but never submitting her dissertation. There she renewed contact with her childhood friend Maude Clarke, and was befriended by the Homeric archaeologist Helen Lorimer. At the invitation of St Hilda's Hall she delivered a successful course of lectures on medieval mime, but her first acquaintance with the *Carmina burana* determined the course of her life's work on medieval Latin lyric and medieval humanism. After five terms at Oxford she moved without reluctance in June 1922 to London. After failing to secure various university posts and turning down the headship of Victoria College, she taught for a year at Bedford College, London, in 1922–3.

The influence of Saintsbury helped Waddell to win the award of a Susette Taylor travelling scholarship from Lady Margaret Hall, which allowed her two years' study in Paris in 1923–4. There she perfected her French, learned some German, and above all attained familiarity with the most important poetry of the fourth to the twelfth centuries. Enid Starkie became a friend at this time. Waddell returned to London in December 1924, and in 1926 delivered a course of lectures at Lady Margaret Hall entitled 'The wandering scholars' to crowded audiences; she had complemented her wide reading in Paris with further study at the British Museum, by which time she had read through the entire 217 volumes of the *Patrologia Latina*.

In the years following her return Waddell published a stream of works which took the academic and literary worlds by storm. *The Wandering Scholars* (1927), which was reprinted three times within a year and for which she was awarded the A. C. Benson silver medal by the Royal Society of Literature, remains an indispensable introduction for students embarking on medieval Latin studies. This published research provided a historical frame for her creative translations in *Medieval Latin Lyrics* (1929). These two classic works demonstrate a combination of qualities which explain the fascination which she exercised over a wide public: the phenomenal breadth of her reading, the vivid historical imagination with which she brings an Ausonius or Alcuin or Abelard to life, and the compelling command over language evident in both her poetic translations and her descriptive prose. She was never an exact Latin scholar (G. G. Coulton was an inveterate and carping critic who seems to have blocked her election as fellow of the British Academy), but she converted this limitation into an advantage. Though often failing to reproduce exactly what was said, she created original poems which none the less uncannily mirror the moods of the originals. In an unpublished paper on translation, she emphasizes the basic truth that 'the plant must spring again from its seed, or it will bear no flower'; with Fitzgerald, she believed 'better a live sparrow than a stuffed eagle'.

Perhaps Waddell's greatest creative achievement was her novel *Peter Abelard* (1933), which was reprinted fifteen times within a year, and has been translated into nine languages, an authentic evocation of the worlds of twelfth-century Paris and Brittany. This was followed by *The Desert Fathers* (1936), a translation of selections from Rosweyd's celebrated edition of *Vitae patrum* (1615), to which she prefaced a characteristically perceptive and enthusiastic introduction. Earlier, despite the demands of her editorial job at Constables which she accepted after publication of *The Wandering Scholars*, she found time to edit *A Book of Medieval Latin for Schools* (1931, frequently reprinted). In that same year she edited Cole's *My Journey to Paris in the Year 1765*, translated *Manon Lescaut*, and wrote a play about its author, *The Abbé Prévost*. In 1934 she collected and published translated stories from the Latin called *Beasts and Saints*.

During the thirties Waddell was overwhelmed with demands to lecture to learned societies. She received honorary degrees from Durham (1932), Belfast (1934), Columbia (1935), and St Andrews (1936). She was made a member of the Royal Irish Academy (1932) and a corresponding fellow of the Medieval Academy of America (1937). Through her books and her engaging personality she gained the friendship of such disparate literary figures as George William Russell (AE), Max Beerbohm, Charles Morgan, George Bernard Shaw, and Siegfried Sassoon. She breakfasted with Stanley Baldwin and corresponded regularly with him. She lunched with Queen Mary and later (during the Second World War) with General de Gaulle, who had asked her to translate his speech delivered at Tunis in June 1943 to galvanize the Americans to decisive action.

After the appearance of *Peter Abelard*, Waddell planned to write a sequel in two further books, but this and her life's ambition to publish a study of John of Salisbury were thwarted by the onset of the Second World War. Her duties at Constables, where she now assumed the assistant editorship of the *Nineteenth Century* under F. A. Voigt, her passionate and time-devouring patriotism, and the domestic distractions of a large house in Primrose Hill Road, where her ageing publisher became a permanent resident (her tendency to conduct platonic love affairs with older men like Gregory Smith and George Saintsbury extended to Otto Kyllmann), left her little leisure for sustained writing. The occasional translations which she essayed have been gathered by Dame Felicitas Corrigan in *More Latin Lyrics from Virgil to Milton*.

These pressures, accentuated by a near escape from a German 'doodle-bug' in 1944 and by further bomb damage to her house in the following year, took a heavy toll of Waddell's nervous energy, and she began to suffer from intermittent amnesia.

An invitation from the University of Glasgow to deliver the W. P. Ker lecture stimulated her to resume her intellectual activities, but this was to be Waddell's last sustained contribution. Published as *Poetry in the Dark Ages* (1948), it retraverses the areas of *The Wandering Scholars* which might best have inspired post-war Britain seeking to build the new Troy. By the early 1950s she was increasingly gripped by mental paralysis, and for some years before her death she was oblivious to her surroundings. She died at the Whittington Hospital, in Highgate, London, on 5 March 1965, and was buried at Magherally, co. Down. She had never married.   P. G. WALSH

Sources F. Corrigan, *Helen Waddell: a biography* (1986) · M. Blackett, *The mark of the maker: a portrait of Helen Waddell* (1973) · C. Nesbitt, *A little love and good company* (1975) · F. Corrigan, *More Latin lyrics from Virgil to Milton* (1976) · private information (2004) [family] · *CGPLA Eng. & Wales* (1965)
Archives CUL, corresp. · PRO NIre., letters · Queen's University, Belfast, letters · Stanbrook Abbey, Worcestershire, corresp. and literary MSS | Bodl. Oxf., letters to R. Roberts and his wife · Bucks. RLSS, corresp. with T. Roscoe · Kilmacrew House, Banbridge, co. Down, letters · NL Wales, corresp. with T. Jones · PRO NIre., letters to Lady Londonderry
Likenesses G. Henry, two portraits, Kilmacrew House, Banbridge, co. Down; repro. in Corrigan, *More Latin lyrics* · H. Sticht, portraits, repro. in Corrigan, *Helen Waddell*
Wealth at death £5348: probate, 6 July 1965, *CGPLA Eng. & Wales*

Waddell, Hope Masterton (1804–1895), missionary, was born on 14 November 1804 at Monaghan, Ireland, the son of Susan Hope and her husband, the son of Alexander Waddell, a leader of volunteers and representative at the Dungannon Convention of 1782. On both sides he was descended from long-established Ulster Presbyterian families; his mother was a descendant of Charles Masterton (*fl.* 1722), a Presbyterian secessionist divine. Waddell grew up in the secessionist congregation at Cahans, co. Monaghan. From an early age he was interested in a career in the ministry but a speech impediment led him in 1821 to become apprenticed to a druggist and general merchant in Dublin.

In 1822 Waddell decided to study for the ministry and ended his apprenticeship. He was accepted by the Scottish Missionary Society (SMS) as a missionary candidate in 1825, and in 1827 he entered United Secession Hall, Edinburgh. In 1829 he was ordained by the Edinburgh presbytery of the United Secession church. In the autumn of the same year he married Jessie Simpson (*d.* 1894), daughter of Robert Simpson, a builder, of Edinburgh. They had four children of their own, two of whom survived childhood, and adopted a fifth.

In 1829 the SMS sent Waddell, accompanied by his wife, to Jamaica, where he was to work for the next sixteen years. He selected Cornwall, in the north-west of the island, as the centre of his labours; by the time he left Jamaica in 1845 the congregation at his church, Mount Zion, had reached some 700 members. The situation facing Waddell and his colleagues was brought into sharp focus by the slave rising of December 1831, whose causes, the authorities claimed, lay with missionary, and more

particularly Baptist, teaching. Waddell and other missionaries faced calls for their expulsion and several chapels were attacked in the reaction that followed. Thereafter the issue confronting the Presbyterian missionaries was the transition to the ending of slavery. Waddell and others encouraged the establishment of 'free villages' around mission stations and churches where ex-slaves could remain together under pastoral influence.

From the late 1830s discussions took place within the Jamaican presbytery on establishing a mission to Africa. Letters were sent to the rulers of Creek Town and Duke Town, the major towns of Old Calabar (Calabar), west Africa, and following favourable replies the decision was taken to send a mission led by Waddell. The mission was adopted by the Secession church (from 1847 the United Presbyterian church).

Waddell, accompanied by Jamaican assistants, arrived in Old Calabar in 1846. His wife joined him in 1849. The mission was initially established in Duke Town but when more missionaries arrived in 1847 Waddell made Creek Town his base. He built a close relationship with its ruler, King Eyo Honesty II, and used his influence against the infanticide of twins, polygamy, and human sacrifice, achieving some success; he made agreements to abolish human sacrifice and to build a settlement for twins and their mothers. Yet the relationship with Eyo was not without tension, notably over the issue of polygamy, the role of the mission as an asylum for escaped slaves—though Waddell in practice was prepared to tolerate slave holding—and mission attempts to move inland.

Education was central to Waddell's work. He taught regularly in the mission school and stressed the need for practical education and for teaching in English. He remained cautious about accepting converts for the church, wishing for a small, dedicated group of members. When in 1853 the first converts for the mission, all from Creek Town, were baptized while he was absent in Scotland, it was to precipitate a split between Waddell and some of his colleagues. Further clashes became apparent during the mid-1850s and reflected deeper divisions over the running of the mission.

In 1858 Waddell left Old Calabar on the grounds of ill health, though clearly differences with his colleagues were involved. He left recognized as the founder of the mission, and his contribution was marked by the creation in 1895 of the Hope Waddell Institute, one of Nigeria's leading educational establishments. Waddell returned to Ireland and settled in Dublin, where he helped to establish a missionary congregation. In 1864 he inherited the Kilmore estate, co. Monaghan, from his maternal uncle. He died a widower at his home, 4 St James Terrace, Clonskeagh, Dublin, on 18 April 1895, and was buried in the Mount Jerome cemetery on 23 April.   MARTIN LYNN

Sources H. M. Waddell, *29 years in the West Indies and central Africa: a review of missionary work and adventure, 1829–58* (1863) · *United Presbyterian Church Missionary Record* (1 June 1895), 156–9 · H. Goldie, *Calabar and its mission* (1901) · D. M. McFarlan, *Calabar: the Church of Scotland Mission, 1846–1946* (1946) · G. Johnston, *Of God and Maxim guns: presbyterianism in Nigeria, 1846–1966* (1988) · W. Mackelvie, *Annals and statistics of the United Presbyterian church*, ed. W. Blair and

D. Young (1873) • *Orthodox Presbyterian*, 1 (Dec 1829), 97 • R. H. Boyd, *Couriers of the dawn* (1938) • M. Turner, *Slaves and missionaries: the disintegration of Jamaican slave society, 1787–1834* (1982) • P. Wright, *Knibb 'the notorious' slaves' missionary, 1803–45* (1973) • J. F. A. Ajayi, *Christian missions in Nigeria, 1841–1891* (1965) • E. U. Aye, *Presbyterianism in Nigeria* (1987)

Archives NL Scot.

Likenesses photographs, 1846–93, repro. in *United Presbyterian Church Missionary Record*, 156–7 • D. Macnee, portrait, Church of Scotland World Mission Office, 121 George Street, Edinburgh • T. North, photograph, repro. in Goldie, *Calabar and its mission*, 70–71 • photograph, repro. in Boyd, *Couriers of the dawn*, 14

Wealth at death £9844 2s. od.: Irish probate sealed in London, 22 Aug 1895, *CGPLA Eng. & Wales*

Waddell, Lawrence Augustine (1854–1938), army medical officer and orientalist, was born at Cumbernauld, Dunbartonshire, on 29 May 1854, the son of Thomas Clement Waddell DD, schoolmaster and author, and his wife, Jean, youngest daughter of John Chapman, of Banton, Stirlingshire. At an unknown date his second forename changed to Austine. From a private school he entered the University of Glasgow, where in 1878 he graduated (MB MCh) with the highest honours. After being resident surgeon in the Western Infirmary, Glasgow, he entered the Indian Medical Service in 1880. For ten years from 1885 he was assistant sanitary commissioner and from 1888 to 1895 he was medical officer for the Darjeeling district. From 1896 for six years he was professor of chemistry and pathology in the Calcutta Medical College, and for four years editor of the *Indian Medical Gazette*. He accompanied military operations in Burma (1886–7), Chitral (1895), Peking (Beijing) (1900), and the Mahsud blockade (1901–2), and won military decorations on each occasion. In 1903 he served with the Malakand expeditionary force. His scientific publications include a memoir 'Are venomous snakes auto-toxic' (*Scientific Memoirs by Medical Officers of the Army of India*, 1889), and an article 'Birds of Sikkim' (*Sikkim Gazette*, 1893).

Interest in Buddhism, first perhaps kindled by his time in Burma, led to Waddell's explorations of sites in the founder's country, in particular of the ancient capital, Pataliputra, the Palibothra of the Greeks, and the identification of Buddha's birthplace, on the Nepal border; also in the course of his military services on the north-western frontier he acquired material for papers on the early 'Indo-Grecian' Buddhist art of Gandhara.

Visits to Darjeeling from 1884 and Waddell's subsequent official connection with the district, besides resulting in a descriptive work, *Among the Himalayas* (1899), drew him to the study of Tibet and Tibetan Buddhism, concerning which he contributed numerous papers to orientalist journals and published a highly substantial and valuable treatise, entitled *The Buddhism of Tibet, or, Lamaism* (1894; 2nd edn, 1934). As chief medical officer accompanying the Tibetan expedition of 1904, and with a special commission, he superintended the official collections of literature and art, which were later distributed, together with one private collection of his own, to libraries in Calcutta, London, Oxford, and Cambridge. He published in 1905 *Lhasa and its Mysteries*. On his return to England he was

from 1906 to 1908 professor of Tibetan at University College, London. His retirement to Scotland was marked, until about 1915, by contributions to European journals and encyclopaedias, continuing his studies of Buddhism and Tibet. He listed his recreations as painting and photography.

In 1917 Waddell began to display interest in a new field, that of ancient relations of India to the Mesopotamian world. This led to large volumes such as *Indo-Sumerian Seals Deciphered* (1925) and a theory of an 'Aryan' origin of the Sumerian and Egyptian civilizations, and, more generally, of the 'Aryans' as *The Makers of Civilization in Race and History* (1929) and the ultimate source of *The British Edda Reconstructed from Mediaeval MSS* (1930). These works, containing much painstaking research and impressive to many, did not win the approval of experts.

Waddell received in 1895 the honorary degree of LLD from the University of Glasgow. He was made a CIE (1901) and a CB (1904). He married in 1895 Amy Louise Reeves; they had a son, who was killed in the First World War, and a daughter. Waddell died at Craigmore, Rothesay, where he had been latterly settled, on 19 September 1938.

F. W. THOMAS, *rev.* SCHUYLER JONES

Sources *Glasgow Herald* (20 Sept 1938) • F. W. Thomas, 'Colonel L. A. Waddell', *Journal of the Royal Asiatic Society of Great Britain and Ireland* (1939), 499–504 • personal knowledge (1949) • *WWW* • *CCI* (1939)

Wealth at death £1249 12s. 11d.: confirmation, 9 Jan 1939, *CCI*

Waddell, Peter Hately (1817–1891), Presbyterian minister and author, son of James Waddell of Balquhatston, Stirlingshire, and his wife, Alice Hately, was born at Balquhatston House, Slamannan, on 19 May 1817. His father soon afterwards disposed of the property and moved to Glasgow, and Waddell was educated at the high school and the university in Glasgow. He was a probationer for ordination at the time of the Disruption in 1843, and joined those who soon formed the Free Church of Scotland, outlining his thoughts in his *Orthodoxy is not Evangelism* (1843) and several other pamphlets published that year. Having been licensed as a preacher, in 1843 he was ordained as minister of Rhynie, Aberdeenshire, and in the following year he moved to Girvan, Ayrshire, to the pastorate of a small Free Church congregation. In 1845, while at Girvan, he married Helen Halcro Wardlaw, second daughter of Walter Wardlaw, a Glasgow merchant and descendant of Ebenezer Erskine, founder of the Secessionist church in Scotland. They had four sons and two daughters.

Waddell's attachment to the Free Church was loosened when he found that its members intended to retain in their entirety the rigid doctrinal definitions contained in the Westminster confession of faith. When in 1847 he refused to subscribe to the confession his licence was withdrawn. Waddell then founded an independent chapel at Girvan called the Church of the Future, whose objectives he defined in a pamphlet with the same title (1861). His *Sojourn of a Sceptic in the Land of Darkness and Uncertainty* (1847) is a somewhat tedious allegory modelled on *The Pilgrim's Progress*. Many of his congregation left the Free

Church and joined him. Waddell remained at Girvan until 1862, when he went to Glasgow and began preaching in the city hall as an independent minister. He soon gathered a large congregation, and in 1870 a church was erected for him in East Howard Street. Financial difficulties led to the abandonment of this building, and Waddell once more gathered a congregation by preaching in the Trades Hall. In 1888, encouraged by friends and adherents, he joined the Church of Scotland.

Waddell was an orator of very exceptional power. In his early years his lectures in London and in Scottish cities had attracted much attention. His skill as a dialectician was displayed in a series of lectures on Renan's *Vie de Jésus* delivered in Glasgow City Hall before large audiences in 1863, and afterwards published. His profound admiration for Robert Burns led to his issuing a new edition of the poems, with an elaborate criticism (2 vols., 1867–9). He presided at the meeting held in Burns's cottage on 25 January 1859 to celebrate the centenary of the poet's birth, and then delivered an impassioned eulogy on Burns. His chief historical work was a volume entitled *Ossian and the Clyde, Fingal in Ireland, Oscar in Iceland, or, Ossian Historical and Authentic* (1875), in which he sought to confirm the authenticity of the Ossianic poems by the identification of topographical references that could not have been known to James Macpherson when he edited Ossian in the eighteenth century. His book was an important stimulus to the Celtic revival at the end of the nineteenth century. Waddell also contributed a remarkable series of letters to a Glasgow journal on Ptolemy's map of Egypt, arguing that the discoveries of Speke and Grant had been foreshadowed by the classical geographer. He took a keen interest in educational matters, and was a member of the first two school boards in Glasgow. His most original contribution to literature was a translation of the Psalms of David from the Hebrew into the Scottish language, under the title *The Psalms: frae Hebrew intil Scottis* (1871). This work was followed in 1879 by a similar translation of Isaiah. He also wrote a verse tragedy, *Behold the Man* (1872). Between 1882 and 1885 he edited a people's edition of Walter Scott's Waverley novels with notes and an introduction. Advancing years compelled Waddell to retire from the ministry in October 1890, and he then began to make selections from his published works to form a volume. The task was not completed when he died at 9 Ashton Terrace, Dowanhill, Glasgow, on 5 May 1891.

The Waddells' third son, **Peter Hately Waddell** (1854–1922), was born at Girvan on 15 June 1854 and was educated at the high school and university in Glasgow, matriculating in 1870 and graduating MA in 1877. He was tutor to the family of Dr Fergus, an oculist in Glasgow, and was licensed by the presbytery of Glasgow in 1878. In 1879 he was called to be minister of Whitekirk and Tyninghame. He married, on 4 July 1882, Elizabeth (d. 1924), daughter of John Watson Laidlay, of Seacliff near Whitekirk, and his wife, Ellen. He was a well-known preacher and something of a humorist. Unusually among the Scottish clergy he was a keen Wagnerian, and in 1894 published *The Parsifal of*

Richard Wagner at Bayreuth. He also published several works of theology. He died on 22 November 1922 at Whitekirk.　　　　　H. C. G. MATTHEW

Sources *Glasgow Herald* (6 May 1891) · J. C. Gibson, *Peter Hately Waddell* (1925) · *Fasti Scot.* · bap. reg. Scot.
Wealth at death £785 18s.: confirmation, 23 July 1891, *CCI*

Waddell, Peter Hately (1854–1922). *See under* Waddell, Peter Hately (1817–1891).

Waddilove, Lewis Edgar (1914–2000), social reformer, was born on 5 September 1914 at 67 Wellington Avenue, Southend-on-Sea, the son of Alfred Waddilove, railway clerk, and his wife, Edith Emily, *née* Javens. He was born into a strong Quaker tradition and was educated at Westcliffe High School, Southend. Although he later received a number of honorary degrees, he never took one himself. After leaving school, Lewis Waddilove studied for the diploma of public administration at the University of London and worked for the education department of the London county council from 1936 to 1938. He moved to the Ministry of Health to work on its wartime evacuation scheme until 1943. He was a committed pacifist, and spent his military service (1943–5) with the Friends Ambulance Unit in the Middle East; colleagues found him to be courageous as well as meticulous. On 9 November 1940 he married (Cissie) Louise Power (1914/15–1967), with whom he had a son, Trevor, and a daughter, Pamela.

In 1946 Waddilove was appointed director of the Joseph Rowntree Memorial Trust (known as the Joseph Rowntree Foundation from 1990). The trust was established in 1904 with a substantial endowment from the Quaker businessman Joseph Rowntree, and its affairs had been guided by Rowntree himself, his son, Seebohm Rowntree, and other family members. Lewis Waddilove was the first paid director and held the post until 1979. When he joined the trust its work concentrated on the development and management of the garden village of New Earswick, to the north of York. Under Lewis Waddilove's guidance, the organization divided into a registered housing association on the one side (the Joseph Rowntree Housing Trust), which continued with pioneering projects of housing and care provision, and an endowed charitable trust (the Joseph Rowntree Memorial Trust), which could pursue the founder's desire to 'search out the underlying causes of weakness or evil in the community, rather than of remedying their superficial manifestations'. The memorial trust supported programmes of research on the themes of housing, poverty, the reform of social services, and other social policy issues.

The housing origins of the trust led to Lewis Waddilove's becoming a founder trustee both of the British Churches Housing Trust (which promoted church-based housing associations) in 1964 and then of Shelter in 1966 where he was later to take the chair (1970–72). He chaired the National Federation of Housing Associations (subsequently the National Housing Federation) for all but three years of the period between 1965 and 1979. He served on the board of the Housing Corporation from 1972 to 1983, collaborating closely with the corporation's chairman, Lord Goodman, for the influential years before and after the Housing Act 1974; he was deputy chairman of the corporation from 1978 to 1983. Lewis Waddilove also served on major inquiries into housing issues in the 1960s and 1970s, including the Milner Holland committee on housing in Greater London (1963–5). In these many contexts, he was able to influence housing policy formulation for over thirty years, supported by the research output from his trust. He was also involved in a range of other social policy issues and chaired the Personal Social Services Council, the BBC/Independent Broadcasting Authority central appeals advisory committee, and the coal-mining subsidence compensation review committee. The 1984 Waddilove report on this issue was largely reflected in the 1991 Coal Mining Subsidence Act.

In 1973, at the request of Sir Keith Joseph, secretary of state for health and social services, Lewis Waddilove expanded the work of the trust by accepting responsibility for distributing grants to families with severely disabled children, in the wake of the thalidomide drug scandal.

Waddilove's involvement in the Society of Friends continued throughout his working life. In 1967 he chaired the fourth World Conference of Friends in North Carolina. On 21 January 1969, he married Maureen Piper (b. 1928/9), a commercial planning officer.

In the city of York he was a magistrate and chaired the York City Charities (1957–65 and 1972–88) and the York University Council (1977–87). He was a long-standing governor of three major Quaker schools: Leighton Park School, Reading, for nearly twenty years, until 1972, and the two Quaker schools in York, The Mount and Bootham, for a similar period. He was appointed OBE in 1965 and CBE in 1978.

As well as numerous articles in professional journals, Waddilove published two books: *One Man's Vision* (1954) and *Private Philanthropy and Public Welfare* (1983), which documented the development of Joseph Rowntree's legacy and gave Waddilove a platform from which to propound his views on housing policy.

Waddilove's influence flowed from his mode of operation, whether with community groups and residents on council estates, or with government ministers. He was always quiet, courteous, and unassuming but he was also intellectually rigorous and tenacious in carrying forward rational argument. Beneath this he had an engaging sense of humour, and—despite his immaculate appearance and establishment contacts—held powerful views on the empowerment of citizens and the inherent value of every individual. He championed the idea of housing co-operatives and was critical of local authority housing, where he felt tenants were often powerless. To the end, he remained a tenant himself in one of the Joseph Rowntree Housing Trust's properties in New Earswick.

Much of his twenty-five years of retirement was spent in continuing and concluding his voluntary and civic commitments. A stroke in 1997 affected his eyesight and his speech. But he remained alert, and able to offer profoundly helpful guidance to others. He died in York District Hospital on 21 August 2000, and was cremated in York on 25 August. He was survived by his second wife.

BEST

Sources WW (1996) · 'Lewis Waddilove—the PSSC's modest radical', *Social Work Today*, 8/43 (9 Aug 1997), 5–6 · *The Times* (22 Aug 2000) · *The Guardian* (23 Aug 2000) · b. cert. · m. certs. · d. cert. · personal knowledge (2004)

Likenesses photograph, repro. in *The Times* · photograph, repro. in *The Guardian*

Waddilove, Robert Darley (1736–1828), dean of Ripon, was born on 5 November 1736, the son of Abel Darley of Boroughbridge in the West Riding of Yorkshire, who moved later to Scoreby in the East Riding. He was educated at Westminster School and Clare College, Cambridge, where he was admitted as a pensioner on 6 January 1755, before graduating BA (sixth optime) in 1759 and proceeding MA in 1762. Darley was academically able but, standing in line to inherit landed property at Boroughbridge from his uncle Robert Waddilove (1698–1762), president of Bernard's Inn, he was not considered for a fellowship on graduation. Instead, having taken holy orders (deacon, 1759) Darley began a career in the church's parochial ministry. He was curate at Winwick, Northamptonshire, from 1759 to 1760, then moved to be curate of Wotton and Abinger in Surrey (to 1766) in the gift of the Evelyn family, and finally curate of Ockham from 1766 to 1771. Meanwhile, he had succeeded his uncle in 1762 and had adopted his surname from as early as the previous year, according to Wotton parish registers. It may have caused him to consider following his uncle's example and switch from the church to the law. Waddilove, as he was now known, was admitted to the Middle Temple on 25 March 1766, but went no further in a legal career. Instead, he was instituted on 2 March 1767 to the perpetual curacy of Whitby by Archbishop Drummond of York. The move raised his income and status and induced him to stay in the ministry.

Waddilove's frustrations in the 1760s were partly due to lack of a patron. That want was supplied by Thomas, second Baron Grantham, of Newby Park, near Boroughbridge, who was British ambassador to Spain from 1771 to 1779 and took Waddilove with him as embassy chaplain. This was the most exciting point in Waddilove's career. His scholarly gifts flowered and he also contentedly acted as an antiquarian courier for several British friends. He had access to the library of the Escorial, where he collated the manuscript of Strabo for Thomas Falconer's edition (2 vols., 1807), and obtained much useful information for William Robertson's *History of America* (1777), despite what Waddilove called 'the Difficulty of getting for him any really useful information in this country' (Waddilove to Frederick Robinson, 8 Nov 1776, Lucas MSS, L30/15/66/5). Waddilove also wrote remarks on the pictures in the Spanish royal collection formerly owned by Charles I of England, translated A. R. Mengs's *Essay on Painting* (2 vols., 1796), and was a friend of the Abbé Bayer, preceptor to the eldest son of Carlos III.

Robert Darley Waddilove (1736–1828), by William James Ward, pubd 1827 (after George Marshall)

While in Spain, Waddilove exchanged Whitby for the vicarage of Topcliffe (and the curacy of adjacent Dishforth) in 1774, and appointed himself rector of Cherry Burton on 9 March 1775, both in Yorkshire. He held both until death. Once back in England, Waddilove married on 3 April 1781 Anne Hope (1746/7–1797), daughter of Sir Ludovick Grant of Grant, seventh baronet. He also obtained additional ecclesiastical preferment. On 25 July 1780 he was collated prebendary, canon residentiary, and treasurer of Ripon, positions he retained on the vote of the chapter after Dean Francis Wanley's return from the continent the next year. In 1782 Waddilove was appointed prebendary of York (prebend of Osbaldwick, exchanged for Wistow in 1783), and archdeacon of the East Riding in 1786. He acted as chaplain for Archbishop Drummond from 1775 and was reappointed in that post to Archbishop Markham. Waddilove finally secured for himself the deanery of Ripon following Dr Wanley's death in July 1791. Grantham's premature death in 1786 deprived Waddilove of his main patron. He thereafter looked to Thomas, Lord Pelham (later second earl of Chichester) and the first earl of Malmesbury (Grantham's relation by marriage) for support when required, but it was insufficient to achieve exchanging the deanery of Ripon for the more lucrative equivalent at York in 1802. He was awarded the Lambeth LLD by Archbishop Moore in 1804.

Waddilove was an energetic, dedicated dean. Ripon Minster was well maintained during his long involvement in its affairs, in part a reflection of his own antiquarian learning. In 1775 he was elected FSA, and he contributed several papers to Archaeologia; An Historical and Descriptive Account of Ripon Minster, his most important work of scholarship, appeared in 1810. The dean was an active magistrate in the liberty of Ripon from 1771 to his death, and was a popular figure in local society. He was president of the Society for the Relief of the North Riding Clergy and gave generously to several other charities, as well as from his own funds increasing the endowments of parishes either in his own gift or that of the Ripon chapter. His wife died on 21 May 1797, aged fifty. Waddilove died at the deanery, Ripon, on 18 April 1828, leaving a large family. He bequeathed to the library of York Minster a magnificent copy of Falconer's edition of Strabo and the rare work Bibliotheca arábica del Escurial.   NIGEL ASTON

Sources *GM*, 1st ser., 51 (1781), 193 · *GM*, 1st ser., 52 (1782), 96 · *GM*, 1st ser., 99/1 (1829), 90 · Venn, *Alum. Cant.* · H. I. Longden, *Northamptonshire and Rutland clergy from 1500*, ed. P. I. King and others, 16 vols. in 6, Northamptonshire RS (1938–52), vol. 14, p. 103 · GEC, *Peerage* · *Fasti Angl., 1541–1857*, [York] · [J. T. Fowler], ed., *Memorials of the church of SS Peter and Wilfrid, Ripon*, 2, SurtS, 78 (1886), 274–6, 311 · L. Smith, *The story of Ripon Minster* (1914), 237–48 · A. Chadwick, *Ripon liberty: law and order over the last 300 years* (1986) · Nichols, *Illustrations* · *N&Q*, 9th ser., 4 (1899), 5 · will, Borth. Inst., probate register 178 [R. D. Waddilove], fols. 384–7 · Beds. & Luton ARS, Lucas MS L30/15/66/5

Archives Beds. & Luton ARS, Lucas MSS, L30/13/26; L30/14/116; L30/14/289 | Beds. & Luton ARS, corresp. with Lord Grantham; corresp. with Frederick Robinson · BL, Pelham MSS, Add. MS 33099 · Bodl. Oxf., MSS 38144, fols. 199–200; 41552, fol. 90; 40510, fols. 193–7; 42079, fols. 250–51 · Hants. RO, Malmesbury MSS, 9M73/137; 194; 572; 573/1–5 · Plymouth and West Devon RO, Robinson MSS, 1259/1/71; 1259/2/328, 563, 627, 630

Likenesses W. J. Ward, mezzotint, pubd 1827 (after G. Marshall), BM, NPG [*see illus.*]

Wealth at death £4000: will, 1828, Borth. Inst., probate register 178, fols. 384–7

Wadding, Luke [*name in religion* Francis] (1588–1657), Roman Catholic priest and historian, was born in Waterford, Ireland, on 16 October 1588 and baptized on 18 October, St Luke's day.

Family background Wadding was the eleventh of fourteen children of Walter Wadding (d. 1602), merchant, and Anastasia Lombard (d. 1602). The family, originally from Wexford, had land near Tramore Bay and a tomb in the Franciscan friary in Waterford; they were Old English, and three of them became mayors of the city in Luke's time. Other forms of the surname are Waddy and Wotton. Luke is sometimes confused with his first cousin, Luke Wadding SJ (d. 1651) of Salamanca, and with Luke *Wadding, bishop of Ferns from 1683 or 1684 to 1687. His brother Ambrose became a Jesuit lecturer, as did his first cousins Peter *Wadding and Michael Wadding, the latter being better known in Mexico as Miguel Godínez. Other famous relatives included six bishops, Peter Lombard (Armagh, 1601–25), Thomas Walsh (Cashel, 1626–54), David Rothe (Ossory, 1618–50), John Roche (Ferns, 1624–36), Patrick Comerford (Waterford, 1629–52), and Nicholas French (Ferns, 1645–78). The Jesuit Peter Sherlock, rector of Irish colleges in Spain, and Andrew Wyse, grand prior of the knights of Malta, were also related to Wadding. Two of his nephews, Francis Harold and Bonaventure Baron, followed him into the Franciscans; the former became his biographer and

Luke Wadding (1588–1657), by Carlo Maratti, c.1653

successor as chronicler of the order, while the latter (brother of the lawyer Geoffrey, an important envoy for the confederate Catholics) was a lecturer and writer of copious output.

Education and early works There is some confusion about Wadding's early teachers. Peter White in Kilkenny (c.1560s) was too early; a Mrs Barden, a Father Dermot O'Callaghan, and fugitive priests have been suggested; another possibility is John Flahy, that 'famous and very fortunate schoolmaster' in Waterford, 'to whom especially the province of Munster is beholden for good breeding' (Comerford, 19). Wadding himself said that his father watched over his Catholic training and his education; and Harold recorded that Luke's brother Matthew tutored him in elementary logic and physics, and that he received a good grounding in Latin (the language of the family prayer book, the *Pius Quintus*), and could write Latin when he was thirteen. Later he learned Hebrew and Greek, and quickly became fluent in Portuguese, Spanish (Castilian), and Italian. A poem in Irish, eight lines in honour of Nicolaus Claudius Fabricius Peyresius, was published in Rome in 1638, but this may be a translation by another friar in St Isidore's of a short eulogy in Latin by Wadding.

Luke's parents died in 1602—his mother of the plague, and she was not buried in the family grave. The following year Matthew, a merchant, brought Luke to Lisbon and placed him with his cousins under the Jesuits in the Irish College, where he continued his studies for six months. He left it to join the Franciscans in September 1604 at the friary of the Immaculate Conception, Matozinhos, near Porto. He was given the name Francis in religion, and sometimes used the title Luke of St Francis. He made his profession on 23 September 1605; he studied the philosophy of Duns Scotus and his school for two years at Leiria, and theology first at Lisbon and then, from 1609, at the University of Coimbra under various professors including the Jesuit Francisco Suárez. He had begun to edit the writings of St Francis of Assisi when he was ordained in Vizeu in 1613. He preached in Portuguese and Spanish, and compiled two manuscript volumes of quotations from the Bible, the fathers, and others. His talents attracted attention, and the vicar-general of the Franciscans, Antonio de Trejo, brought him to the Franciscan province of St James in Spain, of which he became a member. He studied Hebrew in Alba de Tormes, and taught theology at León and at the University of Salamanca while he was director of the Franciscan students and chaplain to the Poor Clares. In 1614 he was asked to publish the summa of cases of conscience by the Franciscan Manoel Rodrigues, and in 1618 the spiritual talks of the Franciscan Luis de Miranda. When the Salamanca friary was redecorated for the general chapter of 1618, he provided 268 lines of Latin verse for a long series of paintings there of Franciscan popes, cardinals, martyrs, and writers, which were published later. Here it can be added that he did not write the Christmas poem (two verses) repeatedly attributed to him; it is from a Wexford carol collected or written by Father William Devereux (d. 1771).

Work for the Spanish delegation Antonio de Trejo became a bishop in July 1618, and as King Philip III's special *orator* was sent to Rome to plead before Pope Paul V for the defining of the doctrine of the immaculate conception of Mary, 'in order to remedy the grave scandals [concerning the doctrine] which were threatening the public peace of his kingdom' (Balić, 474); he took Wadding with him as his theologian and secretary. They arrived on 17 December 1618 and stayed with Cardinal Gabriel de Trejo, the bishop's brother. Wadding moved to the friary of San Pietro in Montorio in Trastevere, where Hugh O'Neill, earl of Tyrone, had been buried in 1616 beside his son, the baron of Dungannon, and his brothers-in-law, Ruairi and Cathbharr O'Donnell. Through the Franciscans in Spain and Rome the Old English Wadding made contact with Old Irish persons and ideas. He was asked to save the writings of Angelo del Paz (d. 1596), who had lived in San Pietro, and, with the help of Anthony Hickey, edited some of his scripture commentaries in 1623–8; he was to follow Angelo's example as a fervent Franciscan, writer, editor, and founder of a library. Wadding moved between the friary in Trastevere and the head house at Aracoeli, and finally to San Isidoro (see below). His collection of discussions, orations, and reports for the *legatio* of Philip III and Philip IV to Paul V and Gregory XV he sent privately to Florence Conry in Louvain; but it was printed there without Luke's permission in 1624, and a folio edition appeared in Antwerp in 1641. This work established his fame in Rome; and about it Charles Balić OFM wrote, 'side by side with his [Wadding's] tenacity, there stand out his profound theological learning, his vast erudition, his prudence, and his uncommon tact' (ibid., 475). Wadding continued to work for this ongoing commission, and much later (when illness had restricted his activities) published three further volumes in Rome, *Immaculatae conceptioni B. Mariae virginis non adversari eius mortem corporalem* (1655), *De redemptione B. Mariae virginis* (1656), and *De baptismo B. Mariae virginis* (1656).

Such work in speculative theology entailed the study of scripture, and Wadding knew Hebrew. In 1621 he edited by papal request four large volumes of concordances of the Hebrew Bible by Friar Marius (*d.* 1620) from Cajazzo, with whom he had lived. This entailed his making special printing arrangements at Aracoeli, and writing under various pseudonyms all the preliminary articles. In 1624 Wadding enlarged and edited a Latin concordance of the Bible (concerned with virtues and vices) then attributed to St Anthony of Padua but in fact the work of several Franciscans (Kleinhans). He appended to it a *Promptuarium sacrae scripturae*, a preachers' aid, by an anonymous Irish Franciscan. His work for the Spanish delegation also entailed a study of the teaching of John Duns Scotus. Eager to free him from the ignominious title of 'dunce' and the myths repeated by the Dominican Abraham Bzowski (Bzovius), Wadding began to prepare an edition of the Scotsman's writings, with an account of his life that included a tactful discussion of the question of his country of origin and commentaries by other Irish friars (see below). Written in twelve tomes, some in two parts, it was eventually published in sixteen volumes in 1639. Collecting everything that was thought to be by St Francis, Wadding had the first edition of his works printed at Antwerp in 1623. It included commentaries and a preface wherein Wadding explained what inspired the work: his resolve to answer the attacks of others on the saint and his followers as ignorant and unlettered men. This explains, too, his two printed refutations of Augustinian theories about St Francis; it explains his labours on the writings of Scotus and on his *magnum opus*, the *Annales minorum*, a history of the Franciscan order from 1208 to 1540, in eight folio volumes (1625–54), begun when he was in the friary of San Pietro in Montorio, and compiled from material gathered also by Bartolomeo Cimarelli, Jakob Pohl, and others. His collection of papal bulls appended to each volume inspired the *Bullarium Franciscanum*. It explains, too, his very useful *Scriptores ordinis minorum*, with a list of martyrs (1650), and his books and essays on Franciscans, as well as work in progress on the general chapters, rules, and constitutions of the order, and the contents of old Franciscan libraries. As he said: 'My research-work [on St Francis] intensified my purpose, while the joy at what I found aroused the desire to find still more' (Mooney, 'Writings of Father Luke Wadding'). His *B. P. Francisci Assisiatis opuscula* appeared in many small editions.

Foundation of St Isidore's College As the Franciscans were then being persecuted in Ireland, Wadding wished to set up a house for Irish candidates in Rome. The minister-general asked him to make use of a new Spanish Franciscan foundation, an unfinished and debt-laden friary and church (between Ludovisi and Barberini properties) dedicated to the recently canonized farmer St Isidore of Madrid (1622), to whom King Philip III was devoted. Wadding took responsibility for the building in June 1625, and it is presumed that he became a member of the Irish Franciscan province about this time. With the help of his generous neighbours and others, he completed the church, and over the years famous artists such as Carlo Maratti, Pier Naldini, Andrea Sacchi, and Gianlorenzo Bernini decorated its side-chapels for wealthy patrons. The friary became a house of prayer as well as a famous school. There the students defended theses in philosophy and theology in the presence of distinguished guests, cardinals, and even a pope, Innocent X, in 1649. Many of them went on to lecture on Scotist philosophy and theology in Franciscan and other schools throughout Europe.

There, too, the students of the Irish College attended lectures from 1628 to 1635. The cardinal protector of Ireland (from 1623), Ludovico Ludovisi, nephew of Pope Gregory XV, having taken the advice of Luke Wadding and John Roche (then made bishop of Ferns), had begun to provide for six students chosen by Wadding. They first attended the Collegio Romano under the Jesuits, whom the cardinal favoured. Then a house was rented for them across the street from St Isidore's so that they could attend lectures there. It was referred to in some early account books as the seminary of St Patrick (other Irish colleges on the continent were dedicated to him), and was also known as the Collegium Ludovisianum. The cardinal, who died in 1632, supplied the necessary ongoing financial support, which was doubled in his will and a large vineyard with fruit trees in Castel Gandolfo donated; but his testament revealed that he wanted the education of the students to be in the hands of the experienced Jesuits. This was a blow to Wadding, who had inspired the project and drawn up the statutes for the college, and was its first president. He contested the provision with the support of the cardinal's brother, Prince Ludovisi, but the case went against him, and the ruling in favour of the Jesuits came into effect in January 1635. Wadding was consulted about the problems involved in founding Irish friaries in Prague and Wielun (Poland); in 1648 he was instrumental in having erected necessary accommodation at the head friary (Aracoeli) for the Franciscan representatives of some northern European provinces of the order, including Ireland; and in the year before his death he was given permission to make his final foundation, a noviciate house for the Irish friars, attached to the church of Santa Maria del Piano at Capranica, north of Rome, near Viterbo. Apart from visits to Umbria and Naples in particular, it seems that Wadding stayed mostly in Rome. It was at Viterbo in 1656 that he arranged for the printing of *De oculo morali*, moral and spiritual applications for prelates and others of the current scientific knowledge of the eye. Wadding tried hard to prove that the author was the Franciscan John of Wales, but it is now attributed to Pierre de Limoges (Petrus de Seperia, known to Wadding as La Cepiera). He had already printed in Rome in 1655 a combined *Florilegium de vita et dictis illustrium philosophorum et breviloquium de sapientia sanctorum* by the same author. About two dozen of Wadding's works were published, and about six more prepared for the press; besides these he had planned to edit further works by Angelo del Paz and John of Wales, a history of episcopal sees, and the lives of six recent popes and the cardinals they had appointed.

There is some evidence for a Carmelite influence on Wadding's spirituality. In 1637 he published a book on the life and deeds of Blessed Peter Thomas of Aquitaine (d. 1366), a Carmelite patriarch of Constantinople; in his preface he explained the Franciscan connections that had induced him to print it, 'out of gratitude for the most holy order, which I venerate highly'. In Spain Wadding had studied Hebrew at Alba de Tormes where Teresa of Avila, who reformed the Carmelites, had died in 1582, only six years before Wadding was born. She was canonized in 1622 together with Isidore of Madrid, the patron of the church taken over by Wadding, which had been founded by Alcantarine Franciscans in 1621. Peter of Alcantara, counsellor to Teresa, had been beatified in that same year (he had died on the feast of St Luke). Wadding would have been impressed by the ceremonies; thirty-five years later his attendance at a sermon in honour of Blessed Peter brought on pneumonia and his death. He left an annotated notebook that contains spiritual exercises based on a Discalced Carmelite source.

Church and politics Wadding was a much respected consultant to some Roman congregations and commissions, and he planned to edit selected material from such sources. By the early 1630s archbishops and bishops in Ireland were seeking his help in the matter of appointments to vacant sees and other offices. The Holy Office and the Congregation for the Propagation of the Faith (founded in 1622) consulted him on matters relating to the church there; in 1634 on recovering some of the places in the Holy Land; in 1637–9 on the theological problems of missionaries in China; in 1640 on an Armenian union with the Holy See; and in 1644 on a revision of the Arabic Bible and the ritual of the Greek church. He assisted the Congregation for Rites in the reform of the breviary ordered by Pope Urban VIII in 1629, compiling new readings when he could, and taking the opportunity to have the feast of St Patrick inserted into the calendar for the universal church. As a consultor for the Holy Office and the Congregation of the Index he was involved in the controversy concerning the doctrine of grace, opposing the Jesuit leniency; but he failed to detect the denial of free will in Cornelius Jansen's *Augustinus*, and thought that the propositions taken from it could be given an orthodox interpretation, but he accepted their condemnation. In his writings he appears 'an upright and unbiassed man' (Ceyssens).

Nevertheless Wadding was bitterly attacked, even by a minister-general of his order. From the beginnings of the Irish College in Rome the perpetual dissensions between Old Irish and Old English arose among the students. After the death of Cardinal Ludovisi in 1632 a list of complaints against Wadding was sent to the new cardinal protector of Ireland by a disgruntled person in Rome (possibly a Jesuit student from Connaught), who claimed some backing, but whose statements were suspect. He said that for about four years Wadding had been practically the only one in the city supplying information for appointments in Ireland even though he had been out of the country since he was a child ('ab infantia fere'); and that he favoured his own province (Munster) and class (Old English merchants), and impeded the applications made for other candidates, even by the earls of Tyrone and Tyrconnell 'who had fought against Queen Isabella of England for nearly twenty years'! He asked that a special inquiry be made into the abuses that he listed by the secretary of the Congregation for the Propagation of the Faith, Francesco Ingoli, who, incidentally, knew Wadding very well; it seems that nothing came of the request (Jennings, 'Miscellaneous documents', 184–7). Twenty years later the old brew of rivalries boiled over again, and a previous friend of Wadding's, the Franciscan Pedro Manero, who had become minister-general, complained bitterly to the king of Spain about his activities in 1653–4 which were thought to be pro-French and anti-Irish. The Spaniards had lost influence in Rome and the French party was predominant. The Old Irish clung to the dream of Spanish help for Ireland, while the Old English there favoured the French connection with the king of England. Internal Franciscan politics, Irish and European, were mixed into the brew, and Wadding had to drink a bitter draught of provincial jealousies. In 1654 a clique wanted him out of St Isidore's, and Francis Magruairk poured out his venom in a memorial presented to the king of Spain in the autumn of 1656. He said that Wadding, the Barberini, and others in Rome were to blame for the Cromwellian devastation in Ireland; that Wadding had been a secret agent of the marquess of Ormond, and had got Old English bishops appointed; that the money he collected went not to the Old Irish but to English Youngs, Dutch Harolds, and Jewish Waddings; that he possessed diabolical powers and succeeded where others failed in driving the Irish out of Ireland. Magruairk exhorted King Philip IV to make a name for himself by attacking the Barberini, Mazarin, and Wadding; he accused his fellow friar of ambition, hypocrisy, and calumny, of being harsh and unjust, of refusing to obey the pope, and of causing the deaths of certain persons. In 1665 it was reported that Magruairk had 'died a heretic in Dublin' (Mooney, 'Was Wadding a patriotic Irishman?' and 'Father Francis Magruairck').

Wadding had done his best to help the Catholic cause in the war years from 1641, when neither the Spanish king, nor the French, nor the popes Urban VIII and Innocent X wanted to intervene overtly. The Thirty Years' War was still on, and the great powers were watching each other warily. Then the Old Irish rebelled, and the Act of Adventurers of 24 February 1642 branded all Irish Catholics rebels, and forced the Old English and Old Irish to unite at Kilkenny on 24 October. Even before the confederate Catholics there appointed him agent and procurator in Rome and Italy in December 1642, Wadding put pressure on pope, princes, and others to support his people. He saw the need for sending someone from Rome to get accurate information, to unite the Catholics, and co-ordinate their efforts. He got Pope Urban to send the Oratorian Pierfrancesco Scarampi as special envoy in July 1643, bringing money and arms. Wadding was so highly thought of in Europe that the confederates wished to see him made a cardinal (he blocked that), and votes were cast for him in the papal conclave of 1644. He persuaded the new pope, Innocent X, to send a well-briefed nuncio to Ireland, Archbishop Giovanni Battista Rinuccini, in October 1645. Wadding had earlier helped Owen Roe O'Neill, Thomas Preston, and other Irish officers on the continent to go to Ireland with arms and men; and after the victory at Benburb in 1646, he sent from St Isidore's, by Dionisio Massari, the sword of Hugh O'Neill, earl of Tyrone, to Owen Roe. Others took offence at what was said about this, and Ormond somehow got the sword. It is because of the relatively small amount of money and arms obtained for the confederates in those years that Wadding was called a gun-running priest. But he was caught in the cross-fire between the Irish Catholics, who were split over the question of a foreign protector, and again over the truce of 1643 and 1646 that did not guarantee freedom of religion and conscience, and over the Inchiquin treaty (1648). Wadding was accused of being an Ormondist; the marquess of Ormond (representative of the embattled Charles I) had in fact written to him, as had Queen Henrietta Maria, expecting him to side with the Old English friars who, urged on by Ormond, sought separation from the Old Irish in a divided Franciscan Ireland. For Wadding the important thing was concord among the friars. He tried to pour oil on a very troubled sea, a veritable storm of conflicting interests, English and Irish, French and Roman, Catholic and protestant, clerical and lay. In the end he was bypassed in Rome, and some influential men on the scene held conflicting views about him. The Capuchin Francis Lavalin Nugent (Old English) thought him too Irish; while the pro-Irish nuncio Rinuccini suspected Wadding of turning against him. It was true that he realized how divisive the nuncio's excommunication of the Ormondist Catholics could be; but in May 1649 the friar wrote to congratulate the cardinal on his safe return from Ireland, and said among other things:

> I confess that every time I hear mention of that infamous peace and the way of acting of that country, or even recall it to my mind, I am ashamed, and regret that I was born among such a people.

Was he thinking of his Old English heritage? Wadding said he would not be sorry to see them punished by God, if he did not fear 'it might mean the complete extirpation of the Catholic religion' (Mooney, 'Was Wadding a patriotic Irishman?', 53). Three months later Ireland was struck by the plague in the west and by Cromwell in the east; the Waddings in Waterford lost their lands and were banished to Connaught. It is clear that Wadding was working only for the Catholic religion in Ireland, not for a party; there were Catholics on both sides of the political divide (which was not always strictly Old English versus Old Irish). Wadding wanted to keep them united, and he paid the price of the man in the middle, being attacked by both. He was replaced as guardian of St Isidore's by an ungrateful Paul King, whom he had once ransomed from pirates, one of

the Aracoelitani (Irish friars at Aracoeli) who fought to oust Wadding.

Assessment, later years, and death Wadding's life's work was, of course, in the service of the Franciscan order, as an observant religious, a lecturer in theology and preacher, a guardian (four or five times) of a student house with all its problems of administration and discipline, a vice-procurator (1633–4) and vice-commissary of the order (1645); he avoided becoming a definitor or a minister-general. Wadding is best-known as a historian and chronicler, a collector of manuscripts and books, a writer, and an editor of Franciscan texts. He was urged to write an ecclesiastical history of Ireland, but the sources were beyond him, and his confrères in Ireland and Louvain were trying to bring them to light. When one takes into account as well his constant work for Roman congregations and voluminous correspondence, one can understand why he was compared with the mythical Briareus of the Hundred Hands; he himself had applied that name to another indefatigable worker for the church, Anselm the younger, bishop of Lucca (1071–86), friend of Pope Gregory VII, whose life and minor spiritual works he published in 1657 as a model for prelates; it was dedicated to Cardinal Marco Antonio Franciotto, a former bishop of Lucca, to whom he felt particularly bound and had already dedicated his *Scriptores*. Wadding was not alone; he had helpers, learned companions, and paid copyists, such as Jean Claude Thierry from Besançon. John Punch helped with the works of John Duns Scotus, and good use was made as well of the earlier commentaries by Maurice O'Fehily and Hugh MacCaughwell. Most notably Anthony Hickey (d. 1641), one of the best theologians in Rome at that time, joined his confrère in his labours for the immaculate conception, for the revision of the breviary, for the church in the East, and for the honour of Scotus. Wadding's nephew Francis Harold was at hand to assist him, especially in his last years. Wadding needed all the help he could get; Harold recorded that sickness laid him low for a total of two months in every year. From his student days in Lisbon he suffered at times from severe headaches and vomiting; he had chronic nasal problems and bronchitis, but the worst pain of all for him was not being able to get on with his work. We are told he was of medium height and had fair hair. A portrait (now in Killiney, co. Dublin), dated 1645, when he was fifty-seven, shows him round-faced, almost clean-shaven, with a shiny pate; not at all like the ascetic, bearded Father Luke seen in later portraits by Ribera (disputed) and Maratti. When he was sixty-three Wadding became very ill, and was not expected to live. Thereafter, for the last seven years of his life, he was unable to go out without transport; but he continued to write and to meet people. He probably met the young Oliver Plunket, who was ordained on 1 January 1654 in Rome by an Irish Franciscan, Anthony MacGeoghegan, bishop of Clonmacnoise; Plunket had been ten years in Rome by the time of Luke Wadding's death. In his last illness he was visited several times by Pope Alexander VII, by cardinals, princes, prelates, and courtiers. As famous for sanctity as for learning (*Acta sanctorum*, Maii, 3.546), Wadding died at St Isidore's Friary, Rome, at 10 a.m. on Sunday 18 November 1657. An autopsy revealed diseased lungs, one kidney destroyed, a large gallstone, and an enlarged heart. In view of his many painful illnesses, the amount of work he did was most remarkable. It was said of him, 'No man ever served so successfully and so faithfully so many causes with so few resources' (see McClean, *Bethlehem*, 11). Wadding was buried in St Anthony's chapel in St Isidore's three days later, when the church was filled to overflowing. A Dominican preached the funeral oration, and Wadding's epitaph was written by a lawyer friend, Hercule Ronconio. A new tomb was erected in 1890, but the remains were later placed in the crypt. So well known worldwide was the name of Luke Wadding that, about two years after his death, an Irishman condemned to death in Mexico, wishing to make a good impression on his judges, claimed to be related to him. The man was William Lamport from Wexford, whose extraordinary escapades probably gave rise to the story of Zorro. IGNATIUS FENNESSY

Sources G. Aiazzi, *Nunziatura in Irlanda di Monsignor Gio. Battista Rinuccini* (Florence, 1844) · A. F. Allison and D. M. Rogers, eds., *The contemporary printed literature of the English Counter-Reformation between 1558 and 1640*, 1 (1989) · C. Balić, 'Wadding the Scotist', *Father Luke Wadding: commemorative volume*, ed. Franciscan Fathers dún Mhuire, Killiney (1957) · F. Casolini, *Luca Wadding OFM, l'annalista dei Francescani* (1936) · L. Ceyssens, 'Florence Conry, Hugh de Burgo, Luke Wadding, and Jansenism', *Father Luke Wadding: commemorative volume*, ed. Franciscan Fathers dún Mhuire, Killiney (1957) · G. Cleary, *Father Luke Wadding and St Isidore's College, Rome* (1925) · P. C. [P. Comerford], *The inquisition of a sermon ... in February 1617 etc. by Richard Daborn* (1644) · J. de Castro, 'Primera parte de el Arbol chronologico de la santa provincia de Santiago' (1722), *Cronicas Franciscanas de España*, ed. O. Gómez Parente, 1 (1976) · M. de Castro, 'Wadding and the Iberian peninsula', *Father Luke Wadding: commemorative volume*, ed. Franciscan Fathers dún Mhuire, Killiney (1957) · *History of the Irish confederation and the war in Ireland ... by Richard Bellings*, ed. J. T. Gilbert, 7 vols. (1882–91), vol. 7 · F. Haroldus, *Vita Fratris Lucae Waddingi*, 3rd edn (1931) · B. Jennings, 'Miscellaneous documents—I. 1588-1634', *Archivium Hibernicum*, 12 (1946) · B. Jennings, *Wadding papers, 1614-1638* (1958) · A. Kleinhans, 'De concondantiis biblicis S. Antonio Patavino, aliisque fratribus minoribus saec. XII attributis', *Antonianum*, 6 (1931) · 'Letters of Owen Roe O'Neill', *Journal of Ardagh and Clonmacnoise Antiquarian Society*, 1/5 (1935) · P. Logan, 'The medical history of Father Luke Wadding, OFM', *Journal of the Irish Medical Association*, 40/240 (1957) · C. Ó Maonaigh, 'Uaidín Gaelach', *Feasta* (Sept 1957) · L. McClean, ed., *Bethlehem: a sixth Franciscan book at Christmas* (1957) [to commemorate the Luke Wadding tercentenary] · C. Mhág Craith, *Dán na mBráthar Mionúr*, 2 (1980) · B. Millett, 'Guide to material for a biography of Fr Luke Wadding', *Father Luke Wadding: commemorative volume*, ed. Franciscan Fathers dún Mhuire, Killiney (1957) · B. Millett, 'Irish Scotists at St Isidore's College, Rome, in the seventeenth century', *De doctrina Ioannis Duns Scoti* (1968) · B. Millett, 'The archives of St Isidore's College, Rome', *Archivium Hibernicum*, 40 (1985) · C. Mooney, 'Was Wadding a patriotic Irishman?', *Father Luke Wadding: commemorative volume*, ed. Franciscan Fathers dún Mhuire, Killiney (1957) · C. Mooney, 'Father Francis Magruairck, OFM', *Seanchas Ardmhacha*, 2/2 (1957) · C. Mooney, 'The letters of Luke Wadding', *Irish Ecclesiastical Record*, 88 (1957) · C. Mooney, 'The writings of Father Luke Wadding, OFM', *Franciscan Studies* (1958) · *DNB* · J. H. Sbaralea, *Supplementum ... ad scriptores*, 2 (1921) · L. Waddingus, *Scriptores ordinis minorum*, new edn (1906) · L. Waddingus, *Annales minorum*, 3rd edn, 1 (1931) · G. B. Balducci,

Cenni storici sul santuario e convento della Madonna del Piano in Capranica (1924) · J. C. Beckett, 'The confederation of Kilkenny revisited', *Historical Studies*, 2 (1959) · S. Bertelli, 'Francesco nell'erudizione ecclesiastica: da Cesare Baronio a Luka Wadding, editore di Francesco e storico del Francescanesimo primitivo', *L'immagine di Francesco nella storiografia dell'umanesimo all'Ottocento* (1983) · F. J. Bigger, 'The Irish in Rome in the seventeenth century', *Ulster Journal of Archaeology*, 5/3 (1899) · M. J. Brenan, *An ecclesiastical history of Ireland*, new edn (1864) · L. Brophy, 'The first Irish ambassador, Father Luke Wadding', *Capuchin Annual* (1958) · M. Browne, *Commemorative sermon preached in the church of St Isidore, Rome* (1957) · *Report on Franciscan manuscripts preserved at the convent, Merchants' Quay, Dublin*, HMC, 65 (1906) · J. Campbell, 'Escrits et paroles de S. François d'après les opuscules de Wadding', *Franziscanische Studien*, 47 (1965) · C. Cannarozzi, 'Una fonte degli Annali del Waddingo ... fra Mariano da Firenze', *Studi Francescani*, 27 (1930) · J. L. Casway, *Owen Roe O'Neill and the struggle for Catholic Ireland* (1984) · A. Chiappini, *Annales Minorum*, 30 (1951) · A. Clarke, *The graces, 1625–41* (1968) · A. Clarke, *The Old English in Ireland, 1625–1642* (1966) · G. Cleary, 'Wadding, Luke', *The Catholic encyclopedia*, 15 (1912) · G. Cleary, 'Father Luke Wadding's work for the education of the Irish clergy', *Blessed Oliver Plunket: historical studies* (1937) · A. Coleman, 'An Irish friar and an Irish protestant theory', *Irish Ecclesiastical Record*, 20 (1906) · *Collegiorum S. Isidori de urbe et S. Mariae de Plano Capranicae FF. minorum recollectorum Hiberniae fundatio a P. Waddingo* (1892) · P. Conlan, *St. Isidore's College Rome* (1982) · P. Conlan, *St Isidore's* (1989) [brochure] · P. Conlan, 'The Luke Wadding quadricentennial', *Franciscan College Annual* [Multyfarnham] (1990) · P. Conlan, 'Foundation of St Isidore's College in Rome', *St Anthony Brief*, 60/6 (2000) · J. Corboy, 'The Waddings—an illustrious Irish family', *Irish Monthly*, 71 (1943) · T. Corcoran, 'An Irish tercentenary: St Isidore's, Rome', *Studies* (1926) · P. J. Corish, 'Father Luke Wadding and the Irish nation', *Irish Ecclesiastical Record* (1957) · P. J. Corish, *The origins of Catholic nationalism* (1968), vol. 3/8 of *A history of Irish Catholicism* · P. J. Corish, 'Ormond, Rinuccini, and the confederates, 1645-9', *A new history of Ireland*, ed. T. W. Moody and others, 3: *Early modern Ireland, 1534–1691* (1976), 317–35 · A. Corna, 'Alcune lettere inedite del P. Luca Vadingo a Pier Maria Campi', *Bollettino Storico Piacentino*, 5 (1910) · E. R. De Brewer, '1625 or 1925?', *Catholic Bulletin*, 15 (1925) [review article] · M. Gonçalves da Costa, ed., *Fontes inéditas Portuguesas para a história de Irlanda* (Braga, 1981) · A. Daly, *S. Isidoro* (Rome, [n.d.]) · W. B. Doyle, 'Wadding and the nuncio', *Assisi* (Nov 1939); (Jan 1940) · I. Fennessy, 'Patrick Roche of Kinsale and St Patrick's College, Rome', *Cork Historical and Archaeological Society Journal*, 100 (1995) · I. Fennessy, 'The B manuscripts in the Franciscan Library Killiney', *Dún Mhuire, Killiney, 1945-95*, ed. B. Millett and A. Lynch (1995) · I. Fennessy, 'Printed items among the Wadding papers', *Collectanea Hibernica*, 39 and 40 (1997–8) · I. Fennessy, 'More printed items from the Wadding papers', *Collectanea Hibernica*, 41 (1999) · I. Fennessy, 'Who was Luke Wadding?', *Franciscan College Annual* [Multyfarnham] [forthcoming] · E. B. Fitzmaurice, 'Irish Franciscans and the immaculate conception', *Drogheda Independent* (1905) · U. Flanagan, *Luke Wadding*, 1957 [an address delivered at University College, Cork] · A. Gemelli, 'Luca Wadding e una editione dei suoi Annales', *Vita e Pensiero*, 22 (1931) · A. Gemelli, *Il Francescanesimo*, 2nd edn (1933) · A. Gemelli, *The Franciscan message to the world*, ed. and trans. H. L. Hughes (1934) · J. T. Gilbert, ed., *A contemporary history of affairs in Ireland from 1641 to 1652*, 3 vols. (1879–80) · T. Gogarty, 'A word on behalf of three great Irish men', *Catholic Bulletin*, 4 (July 1914) · S. Gori, 'Le lettere inedite di Luca Wadding ad Antonio Carraciolo e la riforma liturgica di Urbano VIII', *Archivum Franciscanum Historicum*, 73 (1966) · J. Hanly, *Letters of St Oliver Plunkett* (1979) · E. Hogan, 'Worthies of Waterford and Tipperary', *Journal of the Waterford and South-East of Ireland Archaeological Society*, 3 (1898) · *Holinshed's chronicles of England, Scotland and Ireland*, ed. H. Ellis, 6 (1808) · M. J. Hynes, *The mission of Rinuccini in Ireland: nuncio extraordinary to Ireland, 1645–1649* (Dublin, 1932) · B. Jennings, 'Some correspondence of Father Luke Wadding, OFM', *Collectanea Hibernica*, 2 (1959) · B. Jennings, 'Theses defended at St. Isidore's College, Rome, 1631–1649', *Collectanea Hibernica*, 2 (1959) • B. Jennings, *Wild Geese in Spanish Flanders, 1582–1700* (1964) • C. Lennon, *Richard Stanihurst the Dubliner* (1981) • E. Longpré, 'La philosophie de B. Duns Scot', *Etudes Franciscaines*, 34 (1922) • D. McCarthy, ed., *Collections on Irish church history from the MSS of the late V. Rev. Laurence F. Renehan*, 1 (1861) • L. McClean, *Father Luke Wadding, Irishman and Franciscan: a tercentenary tribute* (1956) • P. Mac Fhionnlaighe, 'A plea for a great forgotten Irishman', *Catholic Bulletin*, 6 (1916) • T. D'Arcy McGee, *The Irish writers of the seventeenth century* (1863) • C. P. Meehan, *The rise and fall of the Irish Franciscan monasteries*, 5th edn (1877) • C. P. Meehan, *The confederation of Kilkenny*, new edn (1882) • C. P. Meehan, *The fate and fortunes of Hugh O'Neill, earl of Tyrone, and Rory O'Donel, earl of Tyrconnel*, 3rd edn (1886) • B. Millett, *The Irish Franciscans, 1651–1665* (1964) • B. Millett, 'Wadding, Luke', *New Catholic encyclopedia*, 14 (1966) • B. Millett, 'Irish literature in Latin, 1550–1700', *A new history of Ireland*, ed. T. W. Moody and others, 3: *Early modern Ireland, 1534–1691* (1976), 561–86 • B. Millett, 'Wadding, Luke, OFM', *Dictionary of Irish Biography* [forthcoming] • C. Mooney, 'A day in the life of Luke Wadding', *Franciscan College Annual* (1957) • C. Mooney, 'Father Luke Wadding, the man and the religious', *Assisi*, 19 (1957) • C. Mooney, 'Father Luke Wadding, the last years', *Assisi*, 19 (1957) • C. Mooney, 'The Franciscans in Waterford', *Journal of the Cork Historical and Archaeological Society*, 54 (1964) • F. Morales, 'Un Wadding en la Nueva España de siglo xviii', *Archivum Franciscanum Historicum*, 87 (1994) • H. Morgan, 'Wadding, Luke', *The Oxford companion to Irish history*, ed. S. J. Connolly (1999) • G. Morris, *'Neath alien skies* (1969) • S. Ní Chinnéide, 'Luke Wadding, 1588–1657: tercentenary lecture', *Journal of the Galway Archaeological and Historical Society*, 26 (1954–6) • M. O'Connell, 'Wadding (Luc)', *Dictionnaire de spiritualité*, 16 (1994) • J. R. O'Connell, *Irish Catholic* (7 May 1910) [report on a lecture on Luke Wadding] • B. O'Ferrall and D. O'Connell, *Commentarius Rinuccinianus de sedis apostolicae legatione ad foederatos Hiberniae Catholicos per annos 1645–1649*, ed. J. Kavanagh, 6 vols., IMC (1932–49) • T. O hAnnracháin, 'Vatican diplomacy and the mission of Rinuccini to Ireland', *Archivium Hibernicum*, 48 (1993) • T. O hAnnracháin, 'Far from terra firma: the mission of Gianbattista Rinuccini to Ireland, 1645–49', PhD diss., 2 vols., European University Institute, Florence, 1995 • T. O hAnnracháin, 'Though heretics and politicians misdoubt their good zeal: political ideology and Catholicism in early modern Ireland', *Political thought in seventeenth century Ireland: kingdom or colony?*, ed. J. Ohlmeyer (2000) • T. O hAnnracháin, 'Disrupted and disruptive: continental influence on the confederate Catholics of Ireland', *The Stuart kingdoms in the seventeenth century*, ed. A. I. Macinnes and J. Ohlmeyer (2002) • P. Sella, *Leone X e la definitiva divisione dell' ordine dei Minori (OMin.): la bolla 'Ite vos' (29 Maggio 1517)* (Rome, 2001) [Wadding on the final division of the order of Friars Minor] • M. O'Reilly and R. Brennan, *Lives of Irish martyrs and confessors* (1882) • J. O'Shea, *The life of Father Luke Wadding, founder of St. Isidore's College, Rome* (1885) • B. Pandžić, 'Gli Annales minorum del P. Luca Wadding', *Studi Francescani*, 54/3–4 (1957) • B. Pandžić, 'Gli Annales minorum del P. Luca Wadding', *Archivum Franciscanum Historicum*, 70 (1977) • E. Pásztor, 'Luca Wadding, editore della Vita Anselmi episcopi Lucensis', *Archivum Franciscanum Historicum*, 54 (1961) • J. Pou y Martí, 'Embajadas de Félipe III a Roma, pidiendo la definición de la concepción de Maria', *Archivo Ibero-Americano* (1935) • P. Power, *Waterford saints and scholars: 17th century* (1920) • H. Quinn, *St Isidore's church and college of the Irish Franciscans, Rome* (1949) • H. Quinn, 'Sosta Irlandese', *Ecclesia*, 9/2 (1950) • J. Ranson, 'The Kilmore carols', *The Past: the Organ of the Uí Cinsealaigh Historical Society*, 5 (1949) • G. Ryan, 'Zorro of Wexford', *The Past: the Organ of the Uí Cinsealaigh Historical Society*, 22 (2000) • *Sant'Isidoro: sommario della storia delle costruzioni e dei restauri* (1889) • *Statuta collegii S. Isidori FF. Hibernorum S. Francisci Recollectorum de urbe ex constitutionibus a P. Luca Waddingo factis* (1885) • B. Share, *Irish lives* (1971) • J. J. Silke, 'The Irish abroad, 1534–1691', *A new history of Ireland*, ed. T. W. Moody and others, 3: *Early modern Ireland, 1534–1691* (1976), 587–633 • W. P. Treacy, *Irish scholars of the penal days* (New York, [n.d.]) • F. Troncarelli, 'The man behind the mask of Zorro', *History Ireland*, 9/3 (2001) • A Viewer, 'From the hill tops', *Catholic Bulletin*, 26 (1936) • C. de Villiers, 'Petrus Thomas', *Bibliotheca Carmelitana*, ed. G. Wessels (1927) • T. Wall, 'Parnassus in Waterford (apropos of Latin proses)', *Irish Ecclesiastical Record* (1947) • J. Ware, *The history of the writers of Ireland*, ed. W. Harris (1764) • R. Welch, ed., *The Oxford companion to Irish literature* (1996)

Archives Bibliotheca Nazionale di Napoli, Italy, papers • Franciscan Library, Killiney, co. Dublin, Ireland, papers • La Landiana, Piacenza, Italy, letters • St Isidore's College, Rome, papers

Likenesses oils, 1645, Franciscan Friary, Killiney, co. Dublin • C. Maratti, oils, c.1652, St Isidore's, Rome • C. Maratti, portrait, c.1653; Sothebys, 8 July 1981, lot 21 [*see illus.*] • E. di Como, fresco, 1672, St Isidore's, Rome • F. W. Burton, drawing, 1845, repro. in *Celtic Society Journal* • A. Simington, portrait, c.1949, priv. coll. • U. Bruni, marble bust, 1957, St Isidore's, Rome, Irish College, Rome, Gormanston College, co. Meath • G. Hayes, bronze statue, 1957, Waterford • attrib. J. Ribera, oils, NG Ire. • G. Valet, line engraving (after C. Maratti), BM

Wadding, Luke (1631–1687), Roman Catholic bishop of Ferns, was born in the town of Wexford, the son of Walter Wadding and Mary Sinnott. His father was a younger son of a landed family settled at nearby Ballycogley since the twelfth century. By the 1630s the townspeople of Wexford, with very few exceptions, had opted for the Catholic Counter-Reformation, and the Wadding family were prominent in the affairs of the confederate Catholics during the 1640s.

However, on 11 October 1649 the town was stormed by Oliver Cromwell; the army ran amok and there was much loss of life and damage to property. Two years later, on 7 October 1651, Wadding was, in his own words, 'banished' and went into exile (Corish, 51). He studied at the University of Paris, was ordained priest, and taught for some time in Paris in some capacity. In 1667 his name was among those put forward for the presidency of the Irish College in Louvain. The next year, 1668, the bishop of Ferns, Nicholas French, in exile and with little prospect of returning to Ireland, named Wadding his vicar-general. Wadding returned to Ireland and settled in New Ross. Bishop French's hopes of returning steadily declined, and Wadding was appointed coadjutor bishop on 6 May 1671. He accepted the nomination, but French agreed that the consecration might be deferred until after his own death. Shortly afterwards Wadding moved to Wexford.

The town still bore scars of the sack of 1649. It was controlled by an exclusively protestant corporation, but many of the former Roman Catholic merchants had returned. Their presence had to be at least connived at if economic life was to be carried on, and it appears that in some respects relations were quite good. Certainly Wadding was on good terms with many protestants as he set about rebuilding his own Catholic community. He began a series of parish registers that are the oldest extant in the Roman Catholic church in Ireland, and he recorded many details in a personal notebook, which survives. Pride of place in this was given to listing his library of about 700 works, ranging from the standard theology and spirituality of the Counter-Reformation to the English metaphysical poets.

In 1684 Wadding published in Ghent *A Small Garland of*

Pious and Godly Songs for the Solace of his Friends in their Afflictions; a popular work, it was to be reprinted a number of times during the eighteenth century. It included a collection of Christmas carols, reflecting a local tradition ranging from before the Reformation to the present day. His notebook also details his efforts to furnish the chapel that the protestant corporation allowed him to build in 1684 and the house that he acquired in the same year.

When the Popish Plot had erupted in September 1678 it was inevitable that Wadding should have been indicted. He escaped conviction, however, because he had good friends among the protestant community and because he could plead in all honesty that he was neither a bishop nor a vicar-general, this office having lapsed on Bishop French's death in Ghent on 13 August 1678. Wadding was soon under pressure not to defer his consecration any longer, but it was only prudent to be cautious for a time. No record of episcopal consecration survives but it took place some time in 1683 or 1684. After the accession of James II he attended the first of the provincial synods held by Archbishop Russell of Dublin in July 1685. Like the other bishops, he received a pension from the king, in his case £150 a year, but he did not live long to enjoy it. That his health began to fail is clear from a number of entries in his notebook dated 1687 detailing the disposition of his possessions after his death. He died in Wexford in December 1687 and was buried in the chapel of the Franciscan friary there.   PATRICK J. CORISH

Sources C. Murphy, '"Immensity confined": Luke Waddinge, bishop of Ferns', *Journal of the Wexford Historical Society*, 12 (1988–9), 4–22 • P. J. Corish, ed., 'Bishop Wadding's notebook', *Archivium Hibernicum*, 29 (1970), 49–114 • 'The ancient inheritance of the Waddings', NL Ire., MS 5193 • L. F. Renehan, *Collections on Irish church history*, ed. D. McCarthy, 2 (1874), 22–9 • C. Rafferty, 'The Roman Catholic parish registers of Wexford town from 1672', *Journal of the Wexford Historical Society*, 15 (1994–5), 102–14 • T. Wall, ed., *The Christmas songs of Luke Wadding* (1960) • J. Ranson, 'The Kilmore carols', *The Past*, 5 (1949), 61–102 • D. E. Muirithe, *The Wexford carols* (1982) • W. H. Grattan-Flood, *History of the diocese of Ferns* (1916), 217 • P. F. Moran, ed., *Spicilegium Ossoriense*, 2 (1878), 264–5 • B. Millett, ed., 'Calendar of volume 2 (1669–71) of the *Scritture riferite nei congressi, Irlanda* in Propaganda archives [pt 2]', *Collectanea Hibernica*, 17 (1975), 17–68, 45, 52–3 • B. Millett, ed., 'Calendar of volume 3 (1672–5) of the *Scrittore riferite nei congressi, Irlanda* in Propaganda archives [pt 1]', *Collectanea Hibernica*, 18–19 (1976–7), 40–71, esp. 51, 54–5 • B. Millett, ed., 'Catalogue of Irish material in vols. 370 and 371 of the *Scritture riferite originali nelle congregazioni generali* in Propaganda archives', *Collectanea Hibernica*, 27–8 (1985–6), 44–85, esp. 69 **Archives** Franciscan Library, Killiney, co. Dublin, personal memorandum book, MS J5 **Wealth at death** modest: Corish, ed., 'Bishop Wadding's notebook'

Wadding, Peter (1583–1644), Jesuit and theologian, was born at Waterford in Ireland, the son of Thomas Wadding and Mary Walsh (*d.* before 1601). Both parents belonged to prominent Roman Catholic families of whom many members entered religious orders. Five of Peter Wadding's brothers and many of his cousins were ordained priests, mostly Franciscans or Jesuits, among whom was his cousin, the well-known Franciscan Luke Wadding, later founder of St Isidore's College, Rome. Thomas Walsh,

archbishop of Cashel from 1626 to 1654, was related to Peter Wadding on his mother's side.

Wadding studied humanities for seven years in Ireland, probably at the local grammar school in Waterford, before he left for the continent, where he studied for some time at the Irish College, Douai. He entered the Jesuit noviciate on 24 October 1601 at Tournai. There he studied and subsequently taught theology, philosophy, poetry, and rhetoric. On 18 October 1609 he was ordained priest. In 1611 one of his superiors described him as

> a man of remarkable talent, judgment and virtue, and fit for all offices in the Society; he will be a good preacher, and good superior, and he is gifted with conversational powers. As he is a man of great promise, it seems desirable that he should complete his theological studies at Louvain, before he is sent to Ireland or destined for anything else.   (Hogan, 183ff.)

There were several requests from Ireland for his return, but his superiors decided otherwise and he continued his studies at Louvain, where he became professor of theology in 1615. He also taught for some time at the Jesuit college at Antwerp. He was certainly active in Antwerp in 1621, when he had a public dispute about theological questions regarding predestination and grace with the Dutch Arminian Simon Biscop or Episcopius. A Latin manuscript relating to this dispute is preserved in the Bodleian Library. An account of it was later published in Dutch under protestant auspices as *Twee brieven van den gelerden Peter Wading in sijn leven Jesuit tot Antwerpen* (1649).

Wadding continued to work at Louvain until 1629 when he was transferred to Prague. There he became chancellor of the Fernandean Academy, a university newly founded by the Jesuits next to the old Karl or Caroline University. His position involved him in disputes with the archbishop of Prague and the Franciscans concerning the authority of conferring degrees and the relations between the two universities. The correspondence between the cousins Luke and Peter Wadding illustrates the resulting conflict between Irish Jesuits and Franciscans. While at Prague, Peter Wadding wrote, besides several minor treatises, *Tractatus de incarnatione*, a solid theological work of more than 600 pages. It was published at Antwerp in 1636.

In 1641 the general of the society decided to move Wadding in view of controversies relating to the university chancellorship. In July 1641 he left for Graz, where he also became chancellor of the university and the first professor of canon law. He died there on 13 September 1644.

J. BLOM and F. BLOM

Sources E. Hogan, 'Worthies of Waterford and Tipperary. 2. Father Peter Wadding', *Journal of the Waterford and South-East of Ireland Archaeological Society*, 3/14 (Oct 1897), 183–201 • H. Foley, ed., *Records of the English province of the Society of Jesus*, 7 (1882–3), 799 • A. F. Allison and D. M. Rogers, eds., *The contemporary printed literature of the English Counter-Reformation between 1558 and 1640*, 1 (1989), 175–6 • Bodl. Oxf., MS Mus. e.114 • B. Jennings, ed., 'Documents of the Irish Franciscan college at Prague', *Archivium Hibernicum*, 9 (1942), 173–294 • Epistolae generalium, Anglia, Roman Archives of the Society of Jesus, Rome, 57, 61, 64, 68, 196 • Archives de l'Etat, Brussels, Tournay diary MSS, n. 1016, fol. 418 • *Father Luke Wadding: commemorative volume*, ed. Franciscan Fathers dún Mhuire, Killiney

(1957) · B. Jennings, ed., *Wild geese in Spanish Flanders, 1582–1700*, IMC (1964)

Waddington, Charles (1796–1858), army officer, fifth son of William Waddington of Walkeringham, Nottinghamshire, and his wife, Grace Valentine, daughter of Henry Sykes of London, was born at 124 Sloane Street, Brompton, London, on 24 October 1796. After Addiscombe College he was commissioned second lieutenant in the Bombay Engineers on 3 April 1813, and arrived in India on 22 May 1814. He accompanied Colonel Kennedy's force to the Konkan, and his services at the assaults of Madanghar (80 miles south-east of Bombay) and of Jamba were favourably mentioned (general orders, 15 February 1818). Towards the end of 1819 he went home on furlough, and was promoted lieutenant on 16 November 1820.

In 1822 Waddington married Anne Rebecca, daughter of John Pinchard of Taunton, Somerset, and they had six sons and two daughters; she survived him. Their eldest son, William (b. 1823), colonel in the Bombay staff corps, served in Persia (1856–7), and became JP for Wiltshire. Another son, Thomas (b. 1827), was major-general of the Bombay staff corps.

On his return to India in 1823 Waddington acted as executive engineer at Baroda. He was promoted captain on 29 July 1825, and appointed in October executive engineer of the Baroda subsidiary force. In November 1827 he was moved to Bombay as civil engineer at the presidency, and in August 1828 acted also as superintending engineer. He was appointed to the command of the engineer corps and to take charge of the Engineer Institution in October 1830. In September 1834 he commanded the engineers at Sirur, returning to the presidency as superintending engineer in January 1835.

On 28 June 1838 Waddington was promoted major, and in May 1839 was appointed superintending engineer of the southern provinces. In September 1841 he went to Sind as commanding engineer. He accompanied Major-General Richard England in his march through the Bolan Pass in the autumn of 1842, and was mentioned in dispatches. On 4 November 1842 he was appointed commanding engineer in Baluchistan as well as Sind. He accompanied Sir Charles Napier as commanding engineer of his force in the celebrated march of 82 miles from Dijikote on 6 January 1843 to Imamgarh, where they arrived on 12 January. Instructed to demolish the fort, Waddington fired his mines on 15 January. He himself lit the fuses of three mines, and was bending over the train of one when his assistant called upon him to run as the other mines were about to explode. But he deliberately ensured that the fuse was well alight before he walked away amid a storm of bursting mines. Napier mentioned him in his dispatch of 22 January 1843 for his bravery. He called it a grand action, but advised Waddington that he would have done better to appreciate his own worth and reserve his heroism for an occasion where it might turn the crisis of a war.

Waddington took part in the battle of Miani on 17 February 1843, where he acted as aide-de-camp to Napier, and was mentioned in dispatches. He was also at the battle of Hyderabad, or Dabo, on 24 March, and was again mentioned in dispatches. He was promoted brevet lieutenant-colonel and made a CB for his services in Sind.

After a furlough in England, Waddington was employed in special duty at Poona until October 1847, when he was appointed superintending and executive engineer at Aden, altered to chief engineer in April 1851. He was promoted colonel on 24 November 1853, and major-general on 28 November 1854. On 4 May 1854 he was appointed chief engineer in the public works department, Bombay, and his services in preparing the Persian expedition received official acknowledgement. In November 1857 he was appointed to the command in Sind. He contributed to the *Professional Papers of the Corps of Royal Engineers*. In September 1858 he was compelled by ill health to leave India, and he died at Cox's Hotel, 55 Jermyn Street, St James, London, on 22 November of that year.

R. H. VETCH, *rev.* M. G. M. JONES

Sources BL OIOC · dispatches · H. M. Vibart, *Addiscombe: its heroes and men of note* (1894) · Kelly, *Handbk* · Royal Engineers' records · private information (1899) · Boase, *Mod. Eng. biog.* · *CGPLA Eng. & Wales* (1859)

Wealth at death under £6000: probate, 16 Feb 1859, *CGPLA Eng. & Wales*

Waddington, Conrad Hal (1905–1975), geneticist and embryologist, was born in Evesham on 8 November 1905, the only son and elder child of Hal Waddington, a tea planter, and his wife, Mary Ellen Warner, who both came from long established Quaker families. Not only were they first cousins but so also were Mary Ellen's parents. Waddington spent his early years in India where his father was a tea planter in Madras. He returned to England at the age of four to live first with an aunt and uncle in the shadow of Bredon Hill, and then with his grandmother in Evesham. She and an elderly member of the Quaker meeting in Evesham, a Dr Doeg, were the main influences on him as a child. He describes the latter as 'almost the last surviving real … scientist. By that I mean that he reckoned to deal with the whole of science' (cited in Robertson, 576).

From his preparatory school, Aymestrey House, Malvern Link, Waddington won a scholarship to Clifton College, followed by another to Sidney Sussex College, Cambridge, where he took a first class in part two of the natural sciences tripos in geology (1926). He chose geology 'because it seemed that becoming an oil geologist would be a good way of earning a living' (cited in Robertson, 578). However, his interests were many sided and he held at the same time an 1851 studentship in palaeontology and an Arnold Gerstenberg studentship in philosophy (1927). Gradually his interests moved towards evolutionary biology and genetics, partly due to the influence of his friend Gregory Bateson, son of William Bateson, who introduced genetics into Britain. Waddington worked for two years on the systematics of fossil ammonites but preferred to study living organisms and he published on the genetics of germination in stocks (1929) and a mathematical paper on genetics with J. B. S. Haldane (1931). In 1926 Waddington married Cecil Elizabeth (Lass), daughter of Cecil

Henry Lascelles, sixth son of the fourth earl of Harewood. The couple had one son, Jake. In these early graduate years, Waddington, who was heavily built but light on his feet, was squire of the Cambridge Morris Men. He led the group on several tours and is said to have collected several morris dances which would otherwise have disappeared.

By 1930 Waddington had become interested in the work of Hans Spemann who had demonstrated induction in amphibia, that is, the ability of one group of cells in the embryo to influence the development of adjacent cells. Experimental grafts could lead to the development of a whole new nervous system. In 1930 Waddington approached Honor B. Fell, the director of the Strangeways Research Laboratory, Cambridge, with the aim of using chick embryos to study induction. His skills in operating on embryos were immediately evident and he soon demonstrated induction in the chick. He was a fellow of Christ's College, Cambridge, from 1934 to 1945.

Waddington's first marriage was dissolved in 1936. In the same year, on 8 August, he married (Margaret) Justin Blanco White (b. 1911/12), daughter of George Rivers Blanco White, recorder of Croydon. She was an architect, and through her Waddington's social circle grew to include figures from the contemporary arts, including Henry Moore, Ben Nicolson, Walter Gropius, and Laszlo Moholy-Nagy. Two daughters were born: Caroline became a social anthropologist, Dusa a mathematician.

In the mid-1930s Waddington, in collaboration with Joseph Needham, tried to identify the chemical nature of the inducing signal (work for which he was awarded the first Albert Brachet prize in 1936). He developed a number of concepts in relation to induction, the most significant being that of competence, which refers to the period during which cells can respond to an inducing signal. This interest eventually petered out, partly due to the coming of the Second World War and partly because it was discovered that many substances could mimic some of the properties of inducers.

Waddington was among the first in Britain to try to bring together embryology and genetics. He strongly supported the views of the American geneticist T. H. Morgan and stated that the fundamental agents that brought about embryonic development were the genes, and that the only satisfactory theory of embryology must be a theory of how the activities of genes were controlled. He summarized his views in his book *Organisers and Genes* (1940). He here defined epigenetics as the causal analysis of development and introduced a visual analogy of developmental pathways—the epigenetic landscape down which a developmental ball could run, being guided by the hills and valleys.

Waddington joined the operational research section at RAF Coastal Command during the war. In 1947 he was appointed to the chair of animal genetics at Edinburgh, which he combined with a post of geneticist for the Agricultural Research Council. He found there in 1947 an almost empty laboratory in which he created one of the largest genetics departments in the world. In addition to the animal breeding group, there were units with diverse financial support devoted to mutagenesis, protozoan genetics, and radiation mutagenesis in small animals. Waddington himself returned to his main interest in evolution and development. His book *The Principles of Embryology* (1956) was an essential text for a whole generation of young developmental biologists.

Waddington was convinced that the evolution of organisms must be regarded as the evolution of developmental systems. In this area he is particularly well known for his ideas on genetic assimilation and canalization which are summarized in *The Strategy of the Genes* (1957). Canalization is the buffering of developmental pathways, so that if development is perturbed slightly it will nevertheless regulate back to normality. Genetic assimilation refers to the situation in which an organism has a genetically determined adaptive response to an external stimulus, the response then becoming established in the population in the absence of the external stimulus. He reported some remarkable experiments on the fruit fly *Drosophila* that supported these ideas.

Waddington played a major role in the organization of the International Biological Programme and it supported his four influential meetings on theoretical biology held in Bellagio, Italy. These brought together for the first time a diverse group of theoreticians and opened up new ways of thinking about development. The French mathematician René Thom tried, for example, to apply the mathematical concepts of catastrophe theory to developmental processes. Waddington was influenced by the philosopher Whitehead and was not persuaded that attempts to reduce biology to precise statements about molecules were the only true path to understanding. He remained interested in the arts and in philosophy and among his publications in 1969 was *Behind Appearance*, a study of modern art, in which he drew parallels between art and science. In 1972 he contributed to the Gifford lectures 'The nature of mind'. He tried to apply ideas about evolution to ethical issues. The fact that we are animals capable of thinking about ethics was for him itself a product of evolution. He argued that an examination of the direction of evolution could provide us with the criteria from which we could judge whether any ethical system was fulfilling its function. In his last years he was much interested in the future of human society and was a founder member of the Club of Rome.

Waddington became bald at the age of twenty-one and this, coupled with his erudition, caused many people to think that he was much older than he actually was. His interests remained wide-ranging and he loved both the visual arts and jazz. He was elected a fellow of the Royal Society in 1947 and of the Royal Society of Edinburgh, in 1948. He was appointed CBE in 1958. He held honorary degrees from Montreal (1958), Trinity College, Dublin (1965), Prague (1966), Aberdeen (1966), Geneva (1968), and Cincinnati (1971). Waddington died on 26 September 1975 outside his Edinburgh home, Newington Cottage, 15 Blacket Place. He was survived by his wife.

ALAN ROBERTSON, *rev.* L. WOLPERT

Sources A. Robertson, *Memoirs FRS*, 23 (1977), 575–622 · *WWW* · *CCI* (1976) · m. cert. (1936)
Archives Bodl. Oxf., corresp. with C. D. Darlington · Rice University, Houston, Texas, Woodson Research Center, corresp. with Sir Julian Huxley · RS, corresp. with Sir F. C. Bawden
Likenesses photograph, repro. in Robertson, *Memoirs FRS*
Wealth at death £31,419.60: confirmation, 12 Jan 1976, *CCI*

Waddington, Edward (1670/71–1731), bishop of Chichester, was born in London. He was a scholar of Eton College, and was admitted to King's College, Cambridge, in 1687. He was a fellow at King's from 1691, and proceeded BA in 1692, MA in 1695, and DD in 1710. He was a fellow of Eton from 1720, and was, by all accounts, a very generous benefactor, bequeathing his entire library (valued at £2000) to the college at his death. He was presented by the crown to the living of Wexham, near Eton, in Buckinghamshire, in 1702, and was the incumbent of All-Hallows-the-Great, Thames Street, London, from 1712 to 1726. He became chaplain to Henry Compton, the bishop of London, and then, in 1717, to George I. In 1724 he succeeded Thomas Bowers as bishop of Chichester, a position he held until his death. He is said to have found the bishop's palace in very poor condition, and set about renovating it at his own cost. Waddington married Frances, daughter of Jonathan Newey of Worcestershire, who predeceased him in 1728; they had no children.

Waddington seems to have walked a very narrow path between low- and high-churchman. He was a zealous protestant, like his patron, Bishop Compton, and was firmly committed to the Hanoverians as well as to the duke of Newcastle's whig interest in Sussex. There is an anecdote told about him that he was such a partisan of the Hanoverians that, when George II acceded to the throne, Waddington provided the gunpowder for the celebrations in Chichester at his own expense and had a kite flown from the spire of the cathedral. He seems, in addition, to have created a stir in Chichester Cathedral with his whig determination to wrestle the tory dean and chapter into submission (Curtis, 13–16). But he also had the religious sensibilities of a high-churchman. In a sermon preached in the House of Lords on 30 January 1729 he decried the regicide of the martyr Charles I (without, it should be added, overstressing the king's piety or prerogative), and blamed puritan religion because its 'enthusiasm' (ungoverned religious zeal) had so carried away the murderers and warped their sensibilities that they were able to commit the heinous crime. This was an indictment, in his mind, against dissent, because dissenters were all subject to 'enthusiasm'. Further, he vigorously advocated punishing deists and freethinkers, and objected when anyone maintained that they should be tolerated or treated humanely. Toleration was not one of Waddington's virtues. A number of his sermons were published between 1718 and 1729. He died in Chichester on 7 September 1731 and was buried in Chichester Cathedral.   J. S. CHAMBERLAIN

Sources L. P. Curtis, *Chichester towers* (1966), 12–16, 18, 63 · J. S. Chamberlain, *Accommodating high churchmen: the clergy of Sussex, 1700–1745* (1997), 73, 87, 88, 128 · *A biographical history of England, from the revolution to the end of George I's reign: being a continuation of the Rev. J. Granger's work*, ed. M. Noble, 3 (1806), 92–3 · A. Kippis, 'The life of Dr. Nathaniel Lardner', *The works of Nathaniel Lardner, D.D.* (1838), 1.x, lxvi–lxviii · Christ Church Oxf., ArchW. Epist. 10, fol. 66 · PRO, SP 36, vol. 7, fols. 57–8 · PRO, SP 36, vol. 4, fols. 14–17 · Venn, *Alum. Cant.*, 1/4.307 · W. Sterry, ed., *The Eton College register, 1441–1698* (1943) · *DNB*
Likenesses H. Winstanley, oils, 1730, King's Cam. · J. Faber junior, mezzotint (after H. Winstanley), BM, NPG · portrait, bishop's palace, Chichester

Waddington, George (1793–1869), traveller and church historian, son of George Waddington (*bap.* 1753, *d.* 1824), vicar of Tuxford, Nottinghamshire, and his wife, Anne, youngest daughter of Peter Dollond [see under Dollond family], optician, was born at Tuxford on 7 September 1793. He had a younger brother and two younger sisters. His paternal grandfather was Joshua Waddington (1710–1780), also a clergyman, and the family was long established in the Halifax area. Waddington was educated at Gainsborough School, at Charterhouse from 1808 to 1811, and then at Trinity College, Cambridge, where he matriculated in 1811 and was admitted scholar in 1812. His career at the university was distinguished. He was Browne medallist in 1811 and 1814, Davies's university scholar in 1813, and chancellor's English medallist in 1813. He graduated BA in 1815, being senior optime in the mathematical tripos and the first chancellor's medallist, and in 1816 he was member's prizeman. He was admitted minor fellow of Trinity College, Cambridge, in 1817, and major fellow in 1818; he proceeded MA in 1818.

Waddington turned to travel in the east and in 1822, in conjunction with the Revd Barnard Hanbury, published *Journal of a Visit to some Parts of Ethiopia* describing a journey from Wadi Halfa to Merawe and back and illustrated by Waddington. This included some entertaining adventures on a journey which took them further up the Nile than Burckhardt had reached and resulted in the publication of some useful maps and the presentation of some valuable artefacts to the Fitzwilliam Museum in Cambridge. Waddington's *Visit to Greece in 1823 and 1824* (1825) passed into a second edition in the same year after having been well reviewed. In 1829 he published *The present condition and prospects of the Greek or oriental church, with some letters written from the convent of the Strophades*. The letters were addressed to 'T.', probably Connop Thirlwall, his contemporary at school and at college.

About 1826 Waddington was ordained. His college presented him to the perpetual curacy of St Mary the Great, Cambridge, on 1 February 1833, and to the vicarage of Masham and Kirkby Malzeard in Yorkshire on 17 June 1834. On 1 October 1834 he was appointed commissary and official of the prebend of Masham and did valuable work in the parish, improving secular and Sunday schools, founding a library, and commuting tithes. From 1833 to 1841 he was prebendary of Chichester Cathedral. He was installed dean of Durham on 25 September 1840, graduating DD from Durham in that year. His attentions to the cathedral fabric were intended to encourage people into the church, although some were later regretted. An ardent Liberal, he was active in local politics. Although he opposed the appointment of outsiders to examine the state of Durham University, he was ready to give money for the improvement of teaching there, became warden of the university in 1862, and oversaw several important reforms.

Waddington died, unmarried and widely mourned, at Durham on 20 July 1869, and on 23 July was buried on the north side of the cathedral yard. He was a rich man, his will being proved at 'under £60,000', and was a generous subscriber to charities and individuals. He left the cathedral library a small but good collection of Greek vases. In 1870, in memory of him and his brother Horatio (1799–1867), his sisters Anne and Clara founded the Waddington classical scholarship at Cambridge. His best-known works were those on ecclesiastical history, especially *History of the Church from the Earliest Ages to the Reformation* (2 vols., 1833) and *History of the Reformation on the Continent* (3 vols., 1841). Each got mixed reviews, as was unsurprising in such wide-ranging texts.

A founder member of the Athenaeum in 1824, Waddington 'could never have been fairly charged with any tendency to asceticism, but rather the reverse' (Klottrup, 3). His dinners were abundant and convivial and he enjoyed asking Puseyite undergraduates to dine on Ash Wednesday. He was a keen advocate of education for children and adults and gave generously to support local schools. Jovial and well intentioned, he was long remembered in Durham with affection.

W. P. COURTNEY, rev. ELIZABETH BAIGENT

Sources A. Klottrup, *George Waddington, dean of Durham* (1990) · Boase, *Mod. Eng. biog.* · C. Knight, ed., *The English cyclopaedia: biography*, 6 vols. (1856–8) [suppl. (1872)] · Venn, *Alum. Cant.* · *CGPLA Eng. & Wales* (1869) · private information (1899, 1994) · Allibone, *Dict.*
Archives UCL, letters to Society for the Diffusion of Useful Knowledge
Likenesses F. R. Say, portrait, 1850, Durham Cath. CL · J. E. Jones, marble bust, 1858, Durham Cath. CL · C. Burlinson, portrait, c.1868, Prior's Hall, Durham · cartoon, Durham Cath. CL · line drawing, repro. in C. M. Carlton, *History of the charities in the city of Durham* (1872) · photographs, Durham Cath. CL
Wealth at death under £60,000: probate, 30 Aug 1869, *CGPLA Eng. & Wales*

Waddington, John (1810–1880), Congregational minister and historian, born at Leeds on 10 December 1810, was the son of George and Elizabeth Waddington. As a boy he was deeply religious and began to preach at the age of fifteen. He trained for the ministry at Airedale College under William Vint from 1830 to 1833 and was ordained and inducted as minister of the Congregational church in Orchard Street, Stockport, on 23 May 1833: here he pioneered the introduction of Sunday schools to his own and other Congregational churches. He also assisted in a government inquiry into distress in the town which had been hard hit in the 'hungry forties': a blue book followed. In 1846 Waddington moved to Union Street Chapel, Southwark, which was then in dire straits and faced with possible dissolution. The crisis was overcome, and in 1864 a new building was opened as a memorial to the Pilgrim Fathers, some of whom had come from this historic church. These associations stimulated Waddington's interest in church history, especially that of his own

denomination, to which he now gave thirty years' intensive study. In 1854 he published *John Penry, the Pilgrim Martyr*, and in 1861 a larger work on Congregational martyrs. In 1862 an essay on Congregational church history from the Reformation to 1662 won him a special prize from the Congregational Union. In 1866 he wrote the history of his own church, and in 1869 he began his great five-volume *Congregational History* which was completed in 1880. For this he received an honorary DD from the University of Williamstown, USA. The *History* relates chronologically the story of English Congregationalism from 1200 to the author's own day, the last volume dealing with the 1850–80 period. Though now largely redundant it was a pioneering venture and served as a source book for a generation or more of Congregational historians.

Apart from his historical works Waddington wrote *Emmaus, or, Communion with the Saviour at Eventide* (1846), *The American Crisis in Relation to Slavery* (1862), *The Track of the Hidden Church* (1863), and a number of smaller works. He also edited Josiah Basset's autobiography, *The Life of a Vagrant* (1850). Waddington was a rather shy and self-effacing man, nervous and intense in speech. Apart from his work as a historian he was not prominent within his denomination. He died at his house in Surrey Square, Old Kent Road, London, on 24 September 1880. He was apparently unmarried.

E. I. CARLYLE, rev. IAN SELLERS

Sources *Congregational Year Book* (1881) · B. Senior, *A hundred years at Surrey Chapel* (1892) · W. M. Field, *A Southwark ship, a Southwark church* (1950) · D. Godfrey, *Clink: the story of a forgotten church* (1966) · *Congregational Year Book* (1880)
Likenesses J. Cochran, stipple (after photograph), NPG
Wealth at death under £3000: probate, 5 Oct 1880, *CGPLA Eng. & Wales*

Waddington, Mary King [née Mary Alsop King] (c.1833–1923), observer of British society, was born in New York, the youngest of the four daughters and one son of Charles King (1789–1867), president of Columbia College, New York, and his second wife, Henrietta Liston Low. She had seven half-brothers and half-sisters. Her grandfather was Rufus *King, the second US minister to the court of St James (1796–1806). She was educated in America, and travelled with her family in Europe after the civil war. Following the death of her father, in 1871 she went with her mother and sisters to live in France, where on 10 November 1874 she married, as his second wife, **William Henry Waddington** (1826–1894). They had a son, Francis. Waddington's grandfather was an English cotton manufacturer and banker who had become a French citizen. Waddington, born on 11 December 1826 at St Rémy sur Avre, Eure-et-Loire, was the son of Thomas Waddington (1792–1869) and Janet Mackintosh Colin Chisholm (d. 1890), and was educated at Rugby School and Trinity College, Cambridge, where he rowed for the university in the first boat race in 1849. On returning to France, Waddington took up a political career, was elected to the national assembly, and in 1873 became minister of public instruction. In 1876 he was elected a senator, resuming the same portfolio. In December 1877 he became minister of foreign affairs, in which capacity he attended the Congress of Berlin in 1878. He served as prime minister in 1879, and, having declined ambassadorial appointment in 1880, in May 1883 he attended the coronation of Alexander III in Moscow as ambassador-extraordinary. On his return to France he was appointed ambassador to the court of St James, which appointment he held for ten years. Waddington was a keen student of numismatics and published widely on the subject; his collection of coins is in the Bibliothèque Nationale, Paris. Mary Gladstone, visiting Paris in 1879, described Waddington as 'very English in appearance and manner, reticent but not the kind of reticence that implies volumes, in fact rather dull', but she liked his wife, 'a lively, sensible American' (*Mary Gladstone*, 176).

Mary King Waddington stands out among the many diplomatic wives who spent time in Britain on account of the vivid letters she wrote to her sisters, selections of which she published as *Letters of a Diplomat's Wife* (1903). The value of her account lies in the freshness of her eye: the routines and rituals of upper-class London society were new to her and her correspondents, and she provides a wealth of detail that English writers, familiar with the social round, took for granted. She had found the immense ceremonial and rigid etiquette of the Russian coronation fascinating, 'like some old mediaeval picture', and contrasted it with the simplicity of Queen Victoria's court. The twice-republican Mary Waddington thought Victoria 'a wonderful woman and a wonderful Queen' (Waddington, 372), but continued to be amused at the way the English considered London 'the great centre of the world', and that life there 'spoils one for everything else' (Waddington, 389). The Waddingtons returned to Paris in April 1893, where William died on 13 January 1894. Mary Waddington returned to England in 1900, when she was at Cowes and had a final interview with the queen. On this occasion, she also called on the former Empress Eugénie, who was living out her long exile in England: they had never met before, as William Waddington 'was in such violent opposition always to the Empire' (Waddington, 393).

Madame Waddington published her letters from Russia and Britain in 1903, and followed it with *Italian Letters of a Diplomat's Wife* (1905), and *Chateau and Country Life in France* (1908). In 1914 she published her recollections of *My First Years as a Frenchwoman. My War Diary*, an account of the first months of the First World War in France, was published by Scribners in New York in 1917 and by John Murray in London in 1918. She died in France on 30 June 1923.

K. D. REYNOLDS

Sources M. K. Waddington, *Letters of a diplomat's wife* (1903) · Burke, *Gen. GB* (1937) · *IGI* · *Mary Gladstone (Mrs Drew): her diaries and letters*, ed. L. Masterman (1930) · Venn, *Alum. Cant.* · E. L. Lach, 'King, Charles', *ANB*

Likenesses A. Bryan, pen-and-ink drawing (William Henry Waddington), NPG · César, Paris, photograph (William Henry Waddington), repro. in Waddington, *Letters* · Russell & Son, photograph (William Henry Waddington), repro. in Waddington, *Letters* · drawing, repro. in Waddington, *Letters*

Waddington, Samuel Ferrand (*b.* 1759, *d.* in or after 1820), radical, born at Walkeringham, Nottinghamshire,

was educated at a German university and trained for a life in commerce. He engaged in the hop trade, and resided near Tonbridge, Kent. On the outbreak of the French Revolution he strongly espoused the cause of the republicans, and in 1795 was chairman of several meetings in London held for the purpose of petitioning the crown and parliament to make peace with France. In consequence of his views he was expelled from the Surrey troop of light horse. In 1796 he attacked Edmund Burke in a pamphlet, *Remarks on Mr Burke's two letters 'on the proposals for peace with the regicide Directory of France'*, censuring him for applying the term 'regicide' to the Directory. In 1800 he was brought to trial for forestalling hops, having purchased a large number of hop-grounds with a view to controlling the price of their produce. He was found guilty, fined £500, and sentenced to one month's imprisonment. Waddington wrote a number of pamphlets regarding his trial, as well as writing on more general political and commercial matters. Labelled by satirists as Little Waddington on account of his being only 4 feet 2 inches tall, he lived in Southwark and in Kent until 1812, the year of his last known publication, *An Address to the People of the United Kingdom*, which he wrote under the pseudonym Algernon Sydney. He was a member of the Union for Parliamentary Reform, set up in the same year, the later Committee of Two Hundred, and stood trial in 1820 for his support of the soldiers who mutinied during the Queen Caroline affair. Details of Waddington's death are unknown.

E. I. CARLYLE, *rev.* STEPHEN M. LEE

Sources [J. Watkins and F. Shoberl], *A biographical dictionary of the living authors of Great Britain and Ireland* (1816) · J. A. Hone, *For the cause of truth: radicalism in London, 1796–1821* (1982)

Waddington, William Henry (1826–1894). *See under* Waddington, Mary King (*c.*1833–1923).

Wade, Arthur Savage (*bap.* 1787, *d.* 1845), Chartist and Church of England clergyman, was baptized on 19 September 1787 at St Mary's, Warwick, the second son of Charles Gregory Wade, an attorney and leading Warwick tory, and his wife, Susanna, *née* Savage. Educated at the town's grammar school, Wade served briefly as a naval midshipman before entering St John's College, Cambridge, in 1806. Graduating in 1810, he was presented by Warwick corporation to the living of St Nicholas in the borough in 1811. This he held until his death. Influenced by Samuel Parr (the 'whig Dr Johnson'), minister of nearby Hatton, Wade became latitudinarian in theology and a moderate radical. In 1821 he was among a borough deputation presenting a loyal address to Queen Caroline (whose chaplains Parr headed). He supported emancipation of dissenters and Catholics and on four occasions nominated the successful whig parliamentary candidate at the borough hustings. In 1831 Wade convened a county meeting to press for parliamentary reform which marked an important stage in the evolution of the Birmingham Political Union (BPU). He was elected to the union's council shortly after.

In November 1831 Wade moved to London. He was soon

involved in co-operation and labour exchanges and took a leading role in supporting the Derby spinners and Tolpuddle labourers. Within the National Union of the Working Classes (NUWC) Wade opposed military flogging, the new poor law, and emigration, and supported Irish home rule and the reform of theatre licensing. Profits from the sale of his sermon *A Voice from the Church* went to those imprisoned under the laws against unstamped newspapers. In October 1832, with Henry Hunt, Wade led a NUWC delegation to Birmingham to initiate the Midland Union of the Working Classes. Their impact was such that Henry Hetherington dubbed them the Castor and Pollux of radicalism. The BPU, however, sought to expel Wade. In his most important political statement (*Poor Man's Guardian*, 17 Nov 1832) Wade replied that he 'would feel proud to be ostracised': he now believed the interests of property and labour were irreconcilable and a separate workers' reform movement was thus inevitable. He gravitated naturally to the Grand National Consolidated Trades' Union and, as its chaplain, led with Robert Owen the great Tolpuddle demonstration of 21 April 1834: 'he was dressed in full canonicals, and wore the red badge of a Doctor of Divinity, which corresponded with the Union badge' (*Pioneer*, 26 April 1834). The episode widened Wade's notoriety: *The Times* pronounced him 'half-witted' (24 April 1834) and he was formally forbidden to preach by his bishop. Owen's journal *The Crisis* retorted, 'Dr Wade's is the true Christianity' (3 May 1834).

Wade was energetic in the metropolitan organizations that developed into Chartism: the Great (Marylebone) Radical Association, the Central National Association, the Universal Suffrage Club, and particularly the London Working Men's Association (LWMA). In May 1838 he was sent by the LWMA to present the People's Charter to a mass gathering on Glasgow Green and represented the association at the Birmingham demonstration in August, both pivotal moments in the emergence of Chartism as a national movement. In his person, Wade bridged middle and working classes, the midlands and London, and his reputation for class-based radicalism, at a time when many Chartists were suspicious of both the BPU and LWMA, made him a useful ally in O'Connor's bid to unite the movement. In September Wade, like O'Connor, spoke at a mass meeting in Westminster Palace Yard. Wade's presentation of fraternal greetings from Parisian workers (the LWMA had recently sent him to France to publicize the Charter) was an early harbinger of Chartist internationalism.

Wade represented Nottingham at the national convention (and led its opening prayers). He was among those delegates whose mail was intercepted by the government; but Wade proved a resolute opponent of physical force, resigning on the issue from the convention after seven weeks. This inevitably diminished his role within Chartism, though he presented its principal petitions supporting the Newport prisoners to Queen Victoria in February 1840. He initially supported the Complete Suffrage Union, attending its inaugural conference at Birmingham in April 1842. However, delegated by Tower Hamlets to a second conference in December, Wade spoke to support Lovett's and O'Connor's resolution that the title of the Charter must be retained. He also supported Lovett's National Association and Place's Metropolitan Parliamentary Reform Association. Wade's last recorded political commitment was as chairman of a dinner organized by the London trades in honour of Thomas Slingsby Duncombe in February 1845. He died of apoplexy in a tailor's shop on Regent Street, London, on 17 November 1845. It appears that he was never married; his sole beneficiary and executrix by the terms of his will was a woman named Mary Anne, whose surname is uncertain but whose father came from East Dereham, Norfolk.

Wade 'was a short thick-set man, and walked rather lame' (*GM*). This enhanced a corpulent appearance, which was commented upon as frequently as the 'full canonicals' worn at the 1834 Tolpuddle demonstration. That event sealed Wade's reputation among critics and admirers alike, but has diverted attention from his broader radical career assisting a national movement to cohere in the formative years of Chartism. It would be fallacious to claim that his prominence derived purely from ability. As a clergyman and Cambridge DD (conferred in 1825), Wade was a sought-after member of committees and platform parties; but his conversion to a class-based political analysis in the early 1830s was genuine. 'He was proud to be a link between the poorer and the richer classes of society; and if his poorer brethren were to fall, he would rather perish with them than flourish with the rich' (*The Crisis*, 28 April 1832).   MALCOLM CHASE

Sources *Pioneer, or, Grand National Consolidated Trades' Union Magazine* (28 Dec 1833); (29 March 1834); (12 April 1834); (26 April 1834); (3 May 1834); (24 May 1834) • *The Crisis* (14 April 1832); (28 April 1832); (14 July 1832); (21 July 1832); (22 Sept 1832); (29 Sept 1832); (17 Nov 1832); (12 Jan 1833); (1 Feb 1834); (29 March 1834); (5 April 1834); (3 May 1834) • *Poor Man's Guardian* (24 Dec 1831); (26 June 1832); (30 June–14 July 1832); (29 Sept–6 Oct 1832); (20 Oct–17 Nov 1832); (26 Jan 1833); (31 Dec 1833); (15 March 1834); (29 March 1834); (26 April 1834); (24 May 1834) • *Northern Star* (8 Feb 1845) • *The Times* (24 April 1834) • *The Times* (20 Nov 1845) • *GM*, 2nd ser., 25 (1846), 210–11 • T. H. Lloyd, 'Dr Wade and the working classes', *Midland History*, 2 (1973–4) • A. S. Wade, *A voice from the church* (1832) • R. G. Gammage, *History of the Chartist movement, 1837–1854*, new edn (1894) • C. Flick, *The Birmingham Political Union* (1978) • I. Prothero, *Artisans and politics in early 19th-century London* (1979) • parish register, Warwick, St Mary, 19 Sept 1787 [baptism] • Venn, *Alum. Cant.*

Likenesses B. R. Haydon, sketch, 1832?, Birmingham Museums and Art Gallery • H. Mayer, engraving, 1834; copy, Warks. CRO

Wealth at death property; effects; money; shares in Cornish mines; valued for probate duty at £1000: *GM*, 211

Wade, Sir Claude Martine (1794–1861), army officer in the East India Company, son of Lieutenant-Colonel Joseph Wade (*d.* 12 Sept 1807), Bengal army, from Ireland, and his wife, Maria Anne (1774/5–1863), eldest daughter of Lieutenant-Colonel Robert Ross RM, was born in Bengal on 3 April 1794. He was named after General Claude Martine, the French soldier of fortune, a friend of his father. Wade was appointed a cadet in the Bengal service in 1809, and immediately went to India. On arrival he joined the institution at Barasat, near Calcutta, where cadets were

Sir Claude Martine Wade (1794–1861), by unknown engraver

instructed in Indian languages and military duties. After the shortest possible period—six months—Wade passed out, receiving the sword of honour.

After serving with the 1st battalion 15th regiment of native infantry as a cadet, Wade was commissioned ensign in the 45th regiment of native infantry on 20 July 1812. With the 45th he served in 1813 in a field force on the Gwalior frontier, and was afterwards stationed at the cantonment of Kunch. Through the unhealthiness of the station he presently found himself in command of his own corps and of a detachment of artillery and acquitted himself successfully.

Wade was promoted lieutenant on 21 October 1815, and served during that year in operations caused by aggressive movements of the forces of Sindhia and Holkar against Bhopal, which was friendly to the British government. From 1816 to 1819 he served in the Pindari campaigns, being also employed with the 5th division, under General Sir J. W. Adams, at the siege and capture of the fortified town of Chanda. At the end of hostilities in 1819 he was stationed at Lucknow.

In 1820–21 Wade officiated as brigade-major to the troops in Oudh, and in 1822 he was deputed on political duty to Calcutta, as bearer of a letter from the king of Oudh to the governor-general. He was next appointed an extra assistant in the office of the surveyor-general of India, and completed the examination, arrangement, and analysis of the many maps and surveys long accumulated

there. So satisfied was the governor-general, Lord Hastings, with his performance that he wanted to appoint him to the political department, and recommended him to his temporary successor, John Adam.

Adam appointed Wade on 28 February 1823 to the office of political assistant at Ludhiana, an important post as there was no regular British representative in the Punjab proper and from Ludhiana, in British-controlled territory, were maintained British relations with Maharaja Ranjit Singh (1780–1839), ruler of the powerful Lahore-based Sikh Punjab state with its Westernized army. Wade's principal duty was at first the charge of Shah Shuja-ul-Mulk, the exiled ruler of Afghanistan. Shortly after his appointment important negotiations devolved on him, as the alarm and excitement caused in India by the ill success of British early operations in Burma endangered the northern frontier. Ranjit Singh, then at the height of his power, suspended his operations against the Afghans, and, assembling his whole force about Lahore, was apparently ready to avail himself of any British reverse by joining the insurgent raja of Bharatpur and other rulers disaffected from the British government. Wade, promoted captain on 13 May 1825, was in constant communication with Ranjit Singh throughout this critical period, and gradually succeeded in convincing him of the power and sincerity of the British government. In 1826 the end of the First Anglo-Burmese War and the capture of Bharatpur convinced Ranjit of British ascendancy; and in 1827 Wade conducted a complimentary mission from Ranjit Singh to the governor-general, Lord Amherst, who in return sent presents by Wade's hand to the court of Amritsar. Amherst shortly afterwards (autumn of 1827) entrusted him with responsibility for dealings with Ranjit. Wade did this for seventeen years, and was largely instrumental in maintaining harmony between the British and the Sikh governments; he gained Ranjit's confidence such as to be permitted freely to visit the Punjab at a time when it was closed to British officials. Wade was a short, fat man fond of eating and sleeping; prickly, capable, and knowledgeable, he became an acknowledged expert on the Punjab and Afghanistan, and influential in shaping British policy in the north-west. In 1831 he was instructed to correspond directly with the governor-general, and in 1832 was given the title of political agent, Ludhiana. He was instrumental in arranging the historic interview at Rupar in October 1832 between Ranjit Singh and Lord William Henry Cavendish-Bentinck, an important event.

In 1833 Wade mishandled and delayed negotiations for Bentinck with Ranjit, who was very suspicious, on the Indus navigation: an agreement was signed in August 1833. He built up a network of unofficial agents in Tibet, Peshawar, Kabul, Kandahar, Herat, and Bahawalpur, and in 1835 was put in charge of all political relations with Lahore and the states beyond the Indus. In 1837 he advised Lord Auckland to give priority to alliance with the Punjab rather than with Afghanistan. The success of Wade's diplomatic dealings with Ranjit Singh was repeatedly officially acknowledged by governors-general, but he received no other official reward. However, he was probably corrupt and gained illicitly.

Wade opposed the policy of uniting Afghanistan, arguing that it would 'play into the hands of our rivals and … deprive ourselves … of the powerful means which we have in reserve of controlling the present rulers of Afghanistan' (Macrory, 66–7). However, the determination of the British government to depose Amir Dost Muhammad Khan from Afghanistan and to replace him by the exiled shah, Shuja-ul-Mulk, gave Wade his opportunity. The main advance of the invading army on Kabul was to be made through the Bolan Pass, and thence through southern Afghanistan; but it was decided to make a converging attack through the Punjab and the Khyber Pass. This subsidiary movement was entrusted to Wade, who was promoted major on 28 June 1838, and was given the local rank of lieutenant-colonel, 'while serving beyond the Indus', on 29 September of the same year. Arriving at Peshawar, his base, in March 1839, he set to work energetically to collect and organize an army, and negotiate with the various Afridi groups of the Khyber region, whom it was desired to propitiate. Wade was assisted by a small but capable staff of eleven officers, of whom the most distinguished were Lieutenant Frederick Mackeson, Dr Percival Barton Lord, and Lieutenant Joseph Davey Cunningham. He first attempted to win over the Afridis, but, though partially successful, he eventually found it impossible to satisfy the greed of all parties, and was obliged to try to force the Khyber Pass. His troops were most unpromising as regards discipline, though individually of good fighting material. They consisted of 5000 Punjabi Muslims from Ranjit Singh's regular army, about 4000 of Shah Shuja's untrustworthy Afghan levies (led by Shazadeh Muhammad Timur), and 380 of the company's regular troops.

The object of Wade's operations being to aid the advance of the army of the Indus by compelling Dost Muhammad Khan to divide his forces, it was necessary to penetrate the Khyber Pass as early as possible. So he attacked Fort Ali Masjid on 22 July 1839, little over four months from when the formation of his force was begun. The fall of Ghazni compelled Dost Muhammad to recall his son Muhammad Akbar Khan from Jalalabad, and thus deprived the Afridis of Afghan assistance. Despite the enemy's numerical superiority, Wade captured Ali Masjid after four days' fighting; and, distributing his Afghan levies in positions commanding the road to Kabul, he continued his march to the Afghan capital, which he shortly afterwards entered unopposed at the head of the Sikh contingent. For his success Wade was promoted lieutenant-colonel, and awarded a knighthood (11 December 1839), a CB on the same day, and the Durani order (1st class). Lord Auckland stated in an official dispatch that 'it was not upon record that the celebrated Khaibar Pass had ever previously been forced'.

After the fall of Kabul and the flight of Dost Muhammad Khan, Wade returned to resume his political duties in India, and soon after, at the beginning of 1840, was removed from his Ludhiana post at the request of the Sikhs, who complained of his behaviour. From 31 March 1840 until his retirement on 1 May 1844 he was resident at Indore, an important post. During his service in Malwa, Wade, among other achievements, effected the settlement of the Bhil people, who at that period gave much trouble; and throughout his long political employment he was successful in dealing peacefully with the most turbulent peoples.

When he left India Wade had served continuously there since 1809, longer than any of his contemporaries except Lord Metcalfe. Wade married at Bath on 7 August 1845 Jane Selina, eldest daughter of Captain Thomas Nicholl (1796–1842), Bengal horse artillery, distinguished by his gallant services in Afghanistan, and killed in action in the Jagdalak Pass on 12 January 1842, during the disastrous retreat from Kabul.

From his retirement on the Isle of Wight, in 1848 Wade opposed British annexation of the Punjab. He was promoted colonel on 28 November 1854. He died at 16 Queen Square, Bath, on 21 October 1861. His widow married in 1864 Dr Edward Deane MacDermot of Bath. His only son, Claude FitzRoy Wade (1849–1917), was a Middle Temple barrister and associate of the north-eastern circuit.

H. W. PEARSE, rev. ROGER T. STEARN

Sources J. W. Kaye, *History of the war in Afghanistan*, 2 vols. (1851) · Sir Claude Wade MSS · M. E. Yapp, *Strategies of British India: Britain, Iran and Afghanistan, 1798–1850* (1980) · P. Macrory, *Signal catastrophe: the story of a disastrous retreat from Kabul, 1842* (1966; repr. as *Kabul catastrophe* (1986) · parliamentary MSS and official gazettes (various) · *GM*, 3rd ser., 11 (1861) · Burke, *Gen. Ire.* (1958) · V. C. P. Hodson, *List of officers of the Bengal army, 1758–1834*, 3 (1946) · V. C. P. Hodson, *List of officers of the Bengal army, 1758–1834*, 4 (1947) · P. Moon, *The British conquest and dominion of India* (1989) · Boase, *Mod. Eng. biog.* · *Dod's Peerage* (1858–78)

Archives NAM, letters and documents

Likenesses engraving, AM Oxf. [*see illus.*]

Wealth at death under £20,000: probate, 21 Dec 1861, *CGPLA Eng. & Wales*

Wade, George (1673–1748), army officer and road builder, was the third son of Jerome Wade of Kilavally, co. Westmeath, whose father, William Wade, had served as a major under Cromwell. Wade's first commission, dated 26 December 1690, was as ensign in Captain Richard Trevanion's company of the earl of Bath's regiment. At that time the regiment was based in the Channel Islands, but in spring 1691 it transferred to Flanders as William III concentrated his troops to confront Louis XIV in the Low Countries. On 24 July / 3 August 1692 Wade's regiment participated in the bloody action at Steenkerke, and helped to cover the retreat of the Anglo-Dutch army; it subsequently joined the attack upon the Lines of Lys in July 1693. Wade rose rapidly within his regiment during this period of active service and heavy casualties: he was promoted lieutenant on 10 February 1693, captain-lieutenant in what was now Sir Bevil Granville's regiment on 19 April 1694, and on 13 June 1695 gained the captaincy of the élite grenadier company.

War of the Spanish Succession Wade returned to England at the peace of Ryswick, but when a fresh war with France he commanded the 3rd brigade of British infantry which encountered fierce fighting and suffered accordingly. Wade none the less evaded capture to join Galway at Alcira, and was sent to England with dispatches. On 1 January 1708 Wade was promoted brigadier-general in the British army, and returned to Spain in the spring.

Wade's record as a competent and courageous officer led to his selection as second in command to General James Stanhope in the expedition to Minorca which sailed from Barcelona in September 1708. At the siege of Fort St Philip, the strongpoint guarding the harbour of Port Mahon, Wade led one of the storming parties, captured the outer defences, and subsequently negotiated the fort's capitulation. The entire island soon after submitted, to become a valuable British base in the Mediterranean. Wade was granted the honour of returning home with the news of Minorca's reduction; in 1709 he received a flattering letter from 'Charles III', the allies' candidate for the Spanish throne, and the rank of major-general while serving in Spain. Wade returned to Portugal, remaining there until 1710, when he rejoined Stanhope in Spain and was given the command of a brigade of infantry. On 9/20 August Wade participated in the overwhelming victory over the forces of Philip V at Saragossa; the battle avenged Almanza, but failed to stave off ultimate allied defeat in the dismal Peninsular campaign.

The Commons and the ''Fifteen' Wade was sent home for reinforcements and in 1711 was serving in England on the subcommittee of the board of general officers. With the accession of George I, Wade's prospects improved dramatically. He was promoted major-general on 3 October 1714, and a month later was appointed commander of the forces in Ireland. It is unclear whether Wade actually took up his new post. A staunch whig, he was returned to parliament for Hindon, Wiltshire, on 25 January 1715. When rebellion broke out later that year, Wade was placed at the head of two regiments of dragoons and sent to overawe the potential Jacobite stronghold of Bath. The veteran Wade proved an effective enforcer for the Hanoverian regime; his efforts unearthed eleven chests of weapons and ammunition, four artillery pieces, and moulds to cast more—an impressive haul which indicated that the west country Jacobites enjoyed the potential, if not the inclination, for insurrection. Wade soon consolidated his reputation for counter-insurgency work; two years later he was instrumental in foiling a Jacobite conspiracy to purchase military assistance from Sweden. The intrigue centred upon Charles XII's ambassador, Count Gyllenborg. It was Wade who led the troops responsible for arresting the count, searching his house, and securing incriminating papers. Wade's zeal did not go unrecognized: on 19 March 1717 George I gave him the colonelcy of the regiment that subsequently became the 3rd dragoon guards. When Spanish support for the Jacobite rising in Scotland prompted a British reprisal against Vigo in September 1719, Wade was appointed second in command to Richard Temple, Viscount Cobham. The expedition proved a complete success. Vigo surrendered, and in October Pontevedra was taken by Wade, who destroyed the

George Wade (1673–1748), by Jean Baptiste van Loo

erupted in 1702, his corps revisited the familiar battle-fields of Flanders. The regiment was once again heavily engaged, fighting at Nijmegen and during the sieges of Kaiserswerth, Venloo, and Ruremond. In the autumn of 1702 Captain Wade served at the siege of Liège where his grenadiers distinguished themselves by storming the citadel, reckoned to be one of the region's strongest fortifications. In March 1703 Wade was promoted major, and in August of the same year served at the siege and capture of Huy; that October he succeeded to the lieutenant-colonelcy of his regiment. Having established his reputation during a decade of fighting in Flanders, Wade now volunteered for service with the British contingent bound for Portugal under the earl of Galway. Galway's influence gained Wade the staff appointment of adjutant-general, with the brevet rank of colonel, on 27 August 1704. In the spring of 1705 Galway laid siege to the frontier town of Valencia d'Alcantara, which was captured by assault on 27 April / 8 May. Officers slain during the attack included Robert Duncanson, colonel of the regiment later numbered the 33rd foot, and the vacant colonelcy was bestowed on Wade. In April 1706 Wade was wounded at the siege of Alcantara but continued to serve on Galway's staff, accompanying the allied forces on their triumphal entry into Madrid on 16/27 June. After remaining at the capital for more than a month, Galway's army retreated to Valencia. Wade's combat leadership was once again apparent in the fighting withdrawal; with two infantry battalions he repulsed a superior force of cavalry at Vila Nova. When the allied army was defeated by Bourbon troops under the duke of Berwick at Almanza on 14/25 April 1707, Wade emerged from the disaster with an enhanced reputation:

arsenal after salvaging the most valuable armaments and munitions.

In 1722 Wade was elected MP for Bath and continued to represent the borough until his death. He established an impregnable political position in the city; indeed in 1734 he achieved the unequalled feat of polling all thirty votes. The general's dominance stemmed from several factors—the personal prestige acquired during his anti-Jacobite investigations of 1715, a philanthropic concern for local causes, and his alliance with the city's powerful postmaster and quarry owner, Ralph Allen, 'the man of Bath'; the frequently quoted story that Allen married Wade's illegitimate daughter appears to be a myth.

The 'military ways' Wade's record as a vigorous soldier with an aptitude for intelligence work may have influenced his appointment in 1724 to reconnoitre the Scottish highlands and observe their strength and resources. Wade found the district in 'a state of Anarchy and Confusion' (Allardyce, 1.137). Blood feuds, blackmail, and cattle rustling were rife; more worryingly for national security, efforts to disarm the highlands in the wake of the 'Fifteen had proved so ineffective that the pro-Jacobite clans were now better equipped for rebellion than ever before. Wade's report of 1724, and a scheme presented to George I in the following year, recommended a programme of reforms to redress the situation: these included establishing companies of loyal highlanders capable of policing the rugged region; improving communications; building new barracks; and repairing existing fortresses. These proposals gained Wade the post of commander of the forces in north Britain, an appointment he held until 1740. While en route to the highlands in the summer of 1725, he was obliged to quell disturbances in Glasgow, where attempts to enforce the malt tax had triggered serious rioting; he concentrated sufficient troops to arrest the ringleaders and restore order. In the highlands Wade's measures were implemented with considerable success: in a second report, made to George II in 1727, he described how the 'Disarming [of] the Highlands was happily Executed without Resistance or Bloodshed' (ibid., 159). The general's improvements included the construction of a road stretching 60 miles from Inverness to Fort William through the heart of the highlands; he believed that further 'military ways' would provide crucial links with troops in the lowlands, so discouraging future uprisings. In the decade after 1725 Wade's 'highwaymen'—gangs of soldiers given double pay for their labours—toiled to build more than 240 miles of road, and some thirty bridges, including the spectacular five-arch crossing of the Tay at Aberfeldy. Wade's road-making programme was a remarkable feat of civil engineering, yet its strategic role proved ambiguous: ironically the general's fine roads merely served to expedite the movements of the Jacobite forces in 1745–6.

During his sojourn in Scotland Wade continued to accumulate honours. He was promoted lieutenant-general on 7 March 1727, and when three regiments of dragoons were raised that summer to reinforce the troops in Scotland Wade gained the colonelcy of one of them. In

1732 he was awarded the sinecure government of Berwick and Holy Island, followed in 1733 by appointment to the governorships of forts William, Augustus, and George. On 2 July 1739 Wade was promoted general of horse, and in 1742 was sworn of the privy council and became lieutenant-general of the ordnance.

Field command and the ''Forty-Five' These honours were crowned on 14 December 1743 when Wade received a field marshal's baton and command of the British forces in Flanders. The appointment followed the resignation of the earl of Stair; for Wade, who had never before commanded an army in the field, it was to prove a poisoned chalice. His return to Flanders yielded no victories to set beside those of his youth; indeed, in the opinion of one modern commentator the operations of 1744 proved 'one of the dingiest campaigns ever waged by British arms and nourished by British gold' (Whitworth, 84). Wade's contingent was required to co-operate with the Austrian and Dutch forces under the duc d'Aremberg and the prince of Nassau. Ranged against these uneasy allies was a powerful French army commanded by the most able general of the day, Maurice de Saxe. When the allies finally took the field in May 1744 they lacked both unified command and common objectives. Saxe reacted with decision: within weeks the French reduced Menin, Ypres, and Furnes. In July, when Prince Charles of Lorraine invaded Alsace, so obliging Louis XV to divert troops from Flanders, George II urged Wade to exploit the situation by mounting an offensive. An advance towards Lille was eventually organized, but subsequently stalled amid logistical problems and acrimonious councils of war. In October Wade made a successful application for leave to return to England. The field marshal had provided a convenient scapegoat for the allies' dismal showing: in fairness to Wade, who was now aged over seventy and in poor health, his performance had been hampered by obstructive colleagues and the unsettling interference of Lord Stair. Accepting Wade's resignation in March 1745, the secretary of state, Lord Harrington, assured him that George II expressed 'the most perfect Satisfaction' in his services (Parker, 114). The king demonstrated his continuing confidence in Wade by appointing him commander-in-chief in England.

On the outbreak of the Jacobite rising in Scotland Wade headed the military committee responsible for deciding the government's response to the crisis. It was agreed that Wade should march north with thirteen battalions of foot, including a large contingent of foreign troops. By the end of October 1745 Wade's force had arrived at Newcastle upon Tyne, which was considered the most likely objective for the army of Charles Edward Stuart, the Young Pretender. Contrary to expectations, the Jacobites sidestepped Wade, opting for a western route to Carlisle, which they besieged. At Newcastle Wade faced problems controlling his heterogeneous command, half of which consisted of unenthusiastic Swiss, Dutch, and German auxiliaries. When he finally began his march on 16 November it was already too late: his sickly and dispirited troops made slow progress over bad roads in appalling weather conditions. Encountering heavy snow, Wade's jaded men slogged on as far as Hexham, only to learn that Carlisle had already fallen. After a day of rest Wade and his army retraced their laborious steps, arriving back in Newcastle on 22 November. Wade had retired in the belief that the Jacobites would not risk a further advance into England; once again he was proved wrong as they proceeded unopposed into Lancashire. By the end of the month the duke of Cumberland had been ordered to counter the threat; he was to co-ordinate operations with Wade, but if the two armies met, the duke would assume command. Cumberland was alarmed by the field marshal's sluggish progress south and urged the duke of Newcastle to replace 'grandmother Wade' with a more dynamic general (McLynn, 123). Wade had failed to catch the swift-moving highland army on its southward march; more alarming was his inability to intercept the Jacobites on their subsequent retreat from Derby. Indeed, when Wade reached Wakefield on 10 December, he learned that the highlanders were at least three days ahead of him. Detaching his cavalry in the hope of blocking Prince Charles's route to Preston, Wade returned to Newcastle with the slow-moving infantry.

Cumberland was appointed commander-in-chief for the coming pursuit of the Jacobite army into Scotland; Wade, who had already registered a plea that his age rendered him unfit for further campaigning, now retired from active service. In 1746 he presided over the court martial that considered the actions of Sir John Cope during the operations that culminated in disaster at Prestonpans; the tribunal exonerated Cope of any blame. Wade's own conduct of his final campaign prompted fierce contemporary criticism, and modern scholars have been scarcely less damning in their verdicts. The most careful account of the campaign finds it 'incredible' that Wade's 'extraordinarily lacklustre performance' did not lead to *his* court martial (McLynn, 197). However, in Lord George Murray, Wade found himself pitted against an exceptionally gifted opponent who also outmanoeuvred Cumberland; in addition Wade's inability to maintain the momentum of a harsh winter campaign says more about George II's misguided penchant for superannuated generals than the deficiencies of a sickly 72-year-old who should have been enjoying a well-earned retirement.

Conclusions A competent brigadier, Wade lacked the ability to command an army in the field. In his prime he had none the less proved himself a brave soldier and diligent servant of the crown; these valuable qualities did not go unrecognized. Recording his death, one popular journal chose to forget his poor showing during 1744–5, instead emphasizing the faithful service through which 'he rose under four succeeding princes to the highest honours of his profession' (*GM*, 139). Wade died on 14 March 1748 at his house in Abbey Churchyard, Bath, aged seventy-five and 'worth above 100,000 l' (ibid.). As the numerous surviving portraits of Wade testify, he was keen to perpetuate his own memory; by his will, dated 1 June 1747, he left £500 for a monument to himself in either Bath or Westminster Abbey. His memorial was erected at Westminster, where he was buried. The sculptor Roubiliac considered Wade's memorial to be 'his best work'; he wept upon observing that it had been placed too high to be appreciated. Unmarried, Wade left most of his substantial estate to his four children—William (sometimes identified as William *Wade (1734/5–1809)), John, Jane, and Emilia; he also provided generously for the widow and children of his brother William, canon of Windsor.

STEPHEN BRUMWELL

Sources J. B. Salmond, *Wade in Scotland* (1934) · J. Allardyce, ed., *Historical papers relating to the Jacobite period, 1699–1750*, 1, New Spalding Club, 14 (1895) · J. C. R. Childs, *The Nine Years' War and the British army, 1688–1697: the operations in the Low Countries* (1991) · W. M. Parker, 'Wade's campaign in Flanders', *Army Quarterly*, 86 (1963), 106–14 · F. J. McLynn, *The Jacobite army in England, 1745: the final campaign* (1983) · *GM*, 1st ser., 18 (1748), 139 · G. M. Trevelyan, *England under Queen Anne*, 3 vols. (1930–34) · R. S. Neale, *Bath, 1680–1850: a social history, or, A valley of pleasure, yet a sink of iniquity* (1981) · B. Lenman, *The Jacobite clans of the Great Glen* (1984) · A. Parnell, *The war of the succession in Spain during the reign of Queen Anne, 1702–1711* (1888); repr. (1905) · W. Taylor, *The military roads in Scotland* (1976) · R. S. Lea, 'Wade, George', HoP, *Commons, 1715–54* · R. Whitworth, *Field Marshal Lord Ligonier: a story of the British army, 1702–1770* (1958) · *DNB* · B. Boyce, *The benevolent man: a life of Ralph Allen of Bath* (1967), 20

Archives Bodl. Oxf., letter-book · NL Scot., letter-books and papers; corresp.; reports; military maps | BL, letters to duke of Newcastle, Add. MSS 32703, fol. 389; 32704, fol. 347; 32708, fol. 140 · BL, Hardwicke MSS, corresp. and papers, Add. MSS 35354; 35890, fol. 298; 35893, fols. 100–136; 36251, fol. 51 · BL, corresp. with Lord Carteret, Add. MS 22538 · BL, orders 1726–1727, Add. MS 23671, fols. 1–19 · BL, King's MSS, 100–103 · CKS, corresp. with James Stanhope · NA Scot., miscellaneous gifts and deposits; papers relating to service in Flanders and Scotland, GD 1 · NL Scot., letter-book and letters to Henry Pelham and Lord Townshend

Likenesses J. van Diest, oils, *c*.1731, NPG · attrib. J. van Diest, oils, *c*.1731–1736, Scot. NPG · J. Faber junior, mezzotint, 1736 (after van Diest), BM, NPG · L. F. Roubiliac, relief portrait medallion on monument, 1746, Westminster Abbey · G. Scharf, pencil drawing, 1911 (after J. B. van Loo), NPG · A. van Haecken, pencil and chalk drawing (after J. Vanderbank), Scot. NPG · J. B. van Loo, oils, United Service Club, London [*see illus.*] · pencil and charcoal drawing, NPG

Wealth at death over £100,000: *GM*

Wade, George Edward (1853–1933), sculptor, the youngest of six sons of the Revd Nugent Wade, rector of St Anne's Church, Soho, London, and later canon of Bristol, and his wife, Louisa, was born on 2 March 1853 and baptized in St Anne's on 17 April. He was educated at Charterhouse School, Surrey (1863–5), and later in Switzerland, becoming an intelligent scholar and good linguist with keen interests in cricket, fishing, and shooting. However, while reading for the bar, his health broke down and, following a period of recuperation in Italy and without formal art training, he took up painting, and an art patron, Sir Coutts Lindsay, provided him with a studio in London. Then in his mid-thirties and not entirely happy with his pictures, he turned to sculpture and was almost immediately successful with work in the round. His first exhibits at the Royal Academy were, in 1889, a bronze bust of Lieutenant-Colonel Myles Sandys MP; in 1890 a terracotta bust of his father; a terracotta statuette of a grenadier guard—his most popular work—of which a copy in bronze was purchased by Queen Victoria and one hundred others by the regiment; and a bronze statuette *Il Penseroso* (one of a pair) which was also sold in large numbers. In 1889 he married Isabella Mary Josephine (Ella), eldest daughter of Lieutenant-General John Mackenzie Macintyre, Royal Artillery, of Fortrose, Ross-shire; they had two daughters.

Wade then took over the studio of Sir J. Edgar Boehm and in 1891 his bust of the Polish pianist Ignacy Paderewski was so appreciated that 500 reproductions of it were ordered for the American market alone. Throughout his career he continued with a series of busts of well-known personalities such as W. E. Gladstone, and General William Booth of the Salvation Army, and appealing statuettes such as *Aphrodite* (marble, exh. RA, 1891), *The Dancer*, and *St George and the Dragon* (bronze, exh. RA, 1892). However, more of his time was taken up with monumental sculpture, such as the colossal bronze statue of the duke of Connaught for Hong Kong (exh. RA, 1892); those of Queen Victoria for Allahabad, India, and Colombo, Ceylon; William Rose Mansfield, first Baron Sandhurst, for Bombay; a Cameron highlander for Inverness; and Sir John A. MacDonald for the Canadian cities of Montreal, Quebec, and Hamilton and Kingston, Ontario. One of his largest commissions was the Second South African War memorial in Pietermaritzburg, Natal, a composition in marble and bronze surmounted by a winged figure; and he produced, among others, statues of Edward VII and Queen Alexandra, the equestrian statues of the maharaja Sir Chandra Shamshere Yung for Nepal and the first Earl Haig for the esplanade outside Edinburgh Castle, and a children's fountain for the Women's World Temperance Association, a replica of which was placed in Temple Gardens, London.

With so many commitments it is understandable that Wade ceased rather early in his career to show his work in public exhibitions, but he still found time to pursue other interests. In the early days of aviation he made designs for aeroplanes and, later in life, took up golf and planned houses for himself and his friends in Berkshire. The popularity of his sculpture was probably due not only to the fact that it was always comprehensible but that it was both ennobling and restrained in equal measure. In portraiture he obtained at the same time a good likeness, much appreciated by the sitters and their families, and, in these works and in his more fanciful subjects, he engendered feelings of respect and admiration. It might be argued by some that his approach was too prosaic, but it would perhaps be more true to say that he cloaked classical ideals in the trappings of his own environment. His last major work was a war memorial in Stourbridge, Worcestershire, unveiled in 1931. He died at his home, 30 Hyde Park Street, London, on 5 February 1933.

S. C. HUTCHISON, *rev.*

Sources *The Times* (6 Feb 1933) · private information (1993) · d. cert. · *WWW* · [R. L. Arrowsmith], ed., *Charterhouse register, June 1769–May 1872* (1964) · Graves, *RA exhibitors* · IGI
Archives Tate collection, corresp., sketches, and papers

Wade, John (*d.* in or before **1668?**), parliamentarian army officer and ironmaster, was a native of the Forest of Dean in Gloucestershire. He hailed from Little Dean according to one eminent local historian, but nothing is known of his family background.

Wade served parliament in the civil war, rising to the rank of major. In late 1649 or early 1650 he co-authored a pamphlet with three others. This argued that the ironworks which some local parliamentarian soldiers had taken over after they had been confiscated from the courtier–ironmaster Sir John Winter should be demolished, on the grounds that they were ruining the Forest of Dean's potential as a nursery for naval timber. On 1 January 1650 the Rump appointed the four as conservators of Dean, ordering them to prevent timber trees being felled and to suppress the ironworks by 10 February. In July 1650 Wade was named a JP for Gloucestershire and he appeared at quarter sessions in most years up to 1658. In 1651 he became deputy to the governor of the Gloucester garrison, Sir William Constable. He was also named to the local militia and assessment committees. Wade was presumably a member of a gathered church, for local congregations named him one of three men notable for their 'godlynesse, zeale, faithfulnesse, wisdome, justice and tendernesse' (Nickolls, 125–6) when suggesting candidates for the nominated parliament of 1653. However, he was not chosen.

In that year the Commonwealth regime, desperately short of ordnance and shot, reversed its earlier decision about the ironworks. On 27 August 1653 it commissioned Wade to head a project in the Forest of Dean to make iron using 'dotard' wood for charcoal and supply the navy from the best timber. His own views had also changed, and he enthusiastically advocated the complementary nature of ironmaking and forest management. Over the next seven years he rebuilt furnaces and forges and dealt with JPs and other ironmasters. He also worked, first with a timber purveyor, then also with a shipwright from August 1656, then from June 1657 with the shipwright alone, in supplying timber and both building and repairing ships. Despite frequent money shortages, bureaucratic delays, and resistance from the riotous poor of the forest the project was highly successful. Wade proved himself 'able, honest and hardworking … a first-class administrator' (Hammersley, 226). Audits showed that the project generated 3750 tons of pig iron, 770 tons of bar iron, and 700 tons of shot, achieving a profit of £12,000 on turnover of £41,000. It also supplied 50,000 treenails, 300 tons of timber, and a ship, the *Forester*, which left the stocks in September 1657.

In February 1655 Wade was among ten Gloucestershire JPs most active in preparing to fight the Penruddock rebels. By 16 June 1655 he was one of three local deputies to Major-General Disbrowe, as well as an active decimation commissioner. Disbrowe wrote to Cromwell on 29 December 1655 saying that he hoped the rumours that Wade was to be removed from the governance of the Isle of Man were untrue, since Wade was 'a faithfull person and exceeding usefull to your highness and the Commonwealth' (Thurloe, *State papers*, 3.360). On 30 July 1659 Wade was named lieutenant-colonel to Mitchell's regiment, and he took part in the suppression of Colonel Edward Massey's attempted uprising in Gloucestershire. From August he and John Crofts had sole charge of the county militia, reporting directly to the council of state. However, he had been fighting an uphill battle against local opposition to his project ever since a major increase in disorder had erupted in April 1659. On 13 April 1660 he asked to be relieved of his post, complaining bitterly about the 'horrid wastes and spoils' committed with impunity by rioters (CSP dom., 1659–60, 413). This was done two weeks later.

The Restoration regime's decision to abandon the state ironworks in Dean, although continuing to build ships (another ship, the *Princess*, was ready for launch in May 1660), left Wade redundant. However, he continued to hold traditional forest posts and in 1662 he served on a commission that vainly recommended continuing direct management. Wade last appears in the records on 21 December 1665. He may have been dead by June 1668, when he was not listed among the verderers and regarders of Dean. However, if, as seems likely, he was the same man as the Major John Wade of The Wicke, Arlingham, Gloucestershire, whose 'wife' Anne, formerly Lane, died there in 1678 and was buried in Bristol, he may still have been alive and resident in either place. If this identification is correct, he had at least three sons, including Nathaniel *Wade. ANDREW WARMINGTON

Sources CSP dom., 1650–60 · G. F. Hammersley, 'The history of the iron industry in the Forest of Dean region, 1562–1660', PhD diss., U. Lond., 1972 · C. E. Hart, *Royal forest* (1960) · A. R. Warmington, *Civil war, interregnum and Restoration in Gloucestershire, 1640–1672* (1997) · *Original letters and papers of state addressed to Oliver Cromwell ... found among the political collections of Mr John Milton*, ed. J. Nickolls (1743) · Thurloe, *State papers* · W. A. Shaw, ed., *Calendar of treasury books*, 1, PRO (1904)

Archives PRO, letters to navy and admiralty commissioners in state papers, domestic, SP 18

Wade, John (1788–1875), radical author, was born in London, where he wrote his way out of obscurity. Nothing is known about his parents. Indeed, the only ascertainable fact about his early life was that he worked for over a decade as a journeyman wool-sorter.

Wade embarked on a career in journalism with the encouragement of metropolitan radicals such as Francis Place. He started out by editing the short-lived, one-penny *Gorgon* (1818–19), but is chiefly notable for his compilation of several versions of *The Black Book, or, Corruption Unmasked!* (first published in cheap instalments in 1819, in book form the following year, then in a supplement in 1823, and in revised editions in 1831, 1832, and 1835), of which over 50,000 copies were sold. Its pages formed a far more accessible utilitarian critique of élite parasitism than anything to be found in the writings of his hero, Jeremy Bentham. The point behind this thick compendium was to draw attention to every conceivable abuse within the 'borough-mongering system'. Singling out the alleged depredations of church pluralists, government sinecurists, aristocratic pensioners, and virtually anyone else connected to the political power structure through money or interest, Wade sought to convince his readers

that the only way to transform the central administration from a tax-plundering instrument of the well connected to an instrument of the people's will was through radical parliamentary reform.

At first glance Wade seems to bear little resemblance to the greatest spokesmen for 'plebeian' radicalism in the years after Waterloo, William Cobbett and Henry Hunt. Indeed, he castigated them as demagogues. For their part, Cobbett and Hunt certainly did not share Wade's commitment to political economy, his Malthusianism, or his faith in the political virtue of the industrial middle classes. But all three were fixated on the ways in which a tax structure which had evolved over a quarter-century of virtually uninterrupted warfare had allegedly transferred vast sums of money from the pockets of the people to those of state parasites, and all three tended to exaggerate their plain-spoken allegations. Thus while there was a good deal of truth in Wade's charges of corruption, he often relied on outdated information in order to convey the impression that official 'abuses' cost the British taxpayer far more than they actually did. He simply ignored recent Pittite reforms of the administrative system, such as the reduction of sinecure offices and unmerited pensions, in order to cast the Pittites and their ilk in the worst possible light.

While Wade's portrayal of the governing élite was not especially accurate, it was certainly influential; for it was strictly as a chronicler of war-related corruption that Wade was known to a truly broad audience. Thus one Durham observer lamented that the instalments of the *Black Book* had an 'almost unlimited circulation' thanks to 'their cheapness, and the familiar style in which they are written'. Indeed, they were 'to be found', along with copies of T. J. Wooler's *Black Dwarf*, 'in the hat band of almost every pitman you meet' (J. Buddle to H. Philpotts, 25 Oct 1819, PRO, HO42/197, fol. 682). The legal authorities were concerned enough about the popularity of the cheap numbers of the *Black Book* to briefly contemplate prosecuting some of them for seditious libel (Sir Robert Gifford and Sir John Singleton Copley to Lord Sidmouth, 31 July 1820, PRO, Treasury Solicitor's MSS, 11/155/473).

Wade steered an easier course for the rest of his career because the political tide had moved in his direction. In his subsequent books and pamphlets, most notably the *History of the Middle and Working Classes* (1833), *British History, Chronologically Arranged* (1839), and *Glances at the Times, and Reform Government* (1840), as well as in his leader writing for Robert Stephen Rintoul's *Spectator*, Wade advocated ideas which found a comfortable home below the gangway in the early Victorian House of Commons: gradual constitutional reform, free trade, and an informal alliance of the 'productive' classes against aristocratic drones. Indeed, the advocacy of such ideas became so inoffensive that in 1862 they won for the impecunious Wade, erstwhile assailant of the civil list, a £50 pension. He died at 5 Hans Terrace, Chelsea, on 29 September 1875, and was buried in Kensal Green cemetery on 2 October.

PHILIP HARLING

Sources DNB · P. Harling, 'Rethinking "old corruption"', *Past and Present*, 147 (1995), 127–58 · R. E. Zegger, 'Wade, John', *BDMBR*, vol. 1 · *The Times* (28 Oct 1875) · *The Athenaeum* (23 Oct 1875), 544 · K. Gilmartin, *Print politics: the press and radical opposition in early nineteenth-century England* (1996), 16–17, 152–3 · E. P. Thompson, *The making of the English working class* (1963), 769–74 · W. D. Rubinstein, 'The end of "old corruption" in Britain, 1780–1860', *Past and Present*, 101 (1983), 55–86 · d. cert.
Archives BL, Francis Place collection

Wade, John Francis (1711/12–1786), plainchant scholar, is a figure about whose origins nothing certain is known. He, or his father, may have been a cloth merchant called John Wade, who converted to Roman Catholicism in the early 1730s, as noted by Archbishop Blackburn in his 1735 visitation to York. He was probably educated at the Dominican College at Bornhem in Flanders between 1731 and 1734; this affiliation is confirmed by his inclusion in the college lists of members of the Confraternity of the Rosary. It is clear that subsequently he spent most of his time in London.

Wade is most widely known in connection with the popular Christmas carol 'Adeste fideles', which he is said to have composed. He was much more significant, however, as a plainchant scribe and publisher of liturgical books for use in the Roman Catholic church. These undertakings, in combination with the extensive influence his manuscripts exerted on the revival of English choral worship in the late eighteenth and nineteenth centuries, have rightfully earned him the title of 'father of the English plainchant revival'. His plainchant manuscripts are exquisite examples of the art of illumination and calligraphy; small hand-held manuscripts were written primarily for use by aristocratic Catholics resident in London, or at ancestral homes elsewhere, while larger, choir-size books were produced for the choirs of the foreign embassy chapels in London. In both formats his manuscripts included graduals, antiphonals, *cantus diversi*, psalters, vesperals, offices, and masses for the dead, and a *Bona mors* handbook. The originals date from 1737 to 1774 and manuscript copies of many of them have survived and are located in university and monastic libraries in Britain and the USA.

Something of Wade's political outlook emerges through examination of the conscious proximity in which he often placed liturgical texts and Jacobite typographical ornaments. A clear case of this appears in one of his printed books, *The Evening Office of the Church* (1773), in which an engraving of Charles Edward Stuart, replete with cross imagery, is found opposite the text of 'Vexilla regis' ('Behold the royal ensigns'), unmistakably casting Charles Edward as the 'Christ the King' figure who will save English Catholics and restore the Stuart throne. 'Adeste fideles', which first appears in the Wade manuscript *Modus intonandi gloria patri* (1750), preserved at Glasgow University Library, is similarly deported in a number of later Wade manuscripts. It is evident from this that 'Adeste fideles', like 'Vexilla regis', had acquired a Jacobite subtext through the medium of Wade's manuscripts. Whether it was conceived originally in these terms is not known. Wade's printed liturgical books also bear this mark in their inclusion of Jacobite prayers, an aspect in

which Wade appears to be alone among contemporary publishers of Catholic books. His early influence is found in the letters of Samuel Wesley and in the first publications of Vincent Novello, and throughout a vast number of subsequent nineteenth-century books. Wade died on 16 August 1786; according to his obituary in the *Laity's Directory* he was seventy-five. BENNETT MITCHELL ZON

Sources B. M. Zon, 'Plainchant in the eighteenth-century Roman Catholic church in England, 1737–1834: an examination of surviving printed and manuscript sources, with particular reference to the work of John F. Wade', DPhil diss., U. Oxf., 1993 · B. M. Zon, *The English plainchant revival* (1999) · *Laity's Directory* (1787)

Wade, Joseph Augustine (1800/01–1845), composer, was born in Dublin. Earlier accounts usually gave his date of birth as about 1796, but the register of his death suggests that it was 1801. His father is said to have been a dairyman near Thomas Street, Dublin. He was a schoolfellow of Richard Robert Madden at Chaigneau's academy, Usher Street, Dublin, from about 1814 to 1816. Wade claimed to have been a student at Trinity College, Dublin, to have been a junior clerk in the Irish record office, and to have studied anatomy at the Irish College of Surgeons; but none of the records of these institutions bear any traces of his name, though in later years he may, with William Rooke, have found employment in the record office. Equal uncertainty surrounds his early musical education; he was probably self-taught. He left Dublin and about 1818 married a lady of fortune, a Miss Kelly of Garnaville, near Athlone, but he soon became tired of her. On his return to Dublin he is said to have acquired considerable skill as an anatomist and surgeon. Surgery was, however, soon abandoned, and Wade became a poet and musician, publishing, about 1818, *A Series of Select Airs*. Sir John Andrew Stevenson, recognizing his great gift of melody, advised Wade to apply for the university chair of music, dormant since 1774 after the resignation of Lord Mornington, but the matter fell through.

Wade migrated in 1821 to London, where he became conductor of the opera at the King's Theatre during Monck Mason's regime. His first significant success in London was his oratorio *The Prophecy*, from Pope's *Messiah*, which was produced at Covent Garden Theatre on 24 March 1824. His opera *The Two Houses of Granada*, of which he wrote both words and music, was first performed at Drury Lane on 31 October 1826, with John Braham as Don Carlos; two of its numbers, the duet 'I've wandered in dreams' and the song 'Love was Once a Little Boy', became popular favourites. In 1826 Wade composed and published his most successful song, a setting of his own text 'Meet me by moonlight alone', which enjoyed extraordinary popularity. It had the good fortune to be further immortalized by the witty Father Prout in *Fraser's Magazine* (October 1834, 480), in a French poem: 'Viens au bosquet, ce soir, sans témoin, Dans le vallon, au clair de la lune'. Two further operas, *The Convent Belles* (on which he collaborated with William Hawes), produced at the Adelphi on 8 July 1833, and *The Pupil of da Vinci*, given at St James's Theatre on 30 November 1839, made little impression.

A man of remarkable gifts and acquirements as a writer of lyrics, a composer, a violinist, and a journalist witty and quick in perception, Wade became increasingly indolent and self-indulgent. He drank to excess, and latterly became an opium addict. For the last few years of his life he was largely forgotten. He did some editorial work for the music publishers Chappell & Co. at a salary of £300 a year, and in that capacity, with William Crotch and George Alexander Macfarren, he harmonized some of the airs of W. Chappell's *Popular Music of the Olden Time*, originally published in 1838 as *A Collection of National English Airs*. From early 1829, for a while, he provided reviews of Italian opera in London for *The Athenaeum*, in which he showed his independence by chastising the other London critics for their disparagement of Rossini; he also contributed to *Bentley's Miscellany* and the *Illustrated London News*, but he could never be relied upon. He compiled *The Handbook for the Pianoforte* (1844), which he dedicated to Liszt, and apparently left a history of music in manuscript. He died penniless, in a state of mental derangement, at his lodgings, 450 (or 340) Strand, on 15 July 1845. His first forename appears in the death registers at Somerset House as Joseph (not John, as he sometimes signed himself), and his surname as Ward. His first wife having died childless, Wade lived with another woman, and at his death a subscription was raised for his presumed widow and her two destitute children. Wade's character may be best summarized in the words of the Revd John Richardson:

A wise man in theory and a fool in practice. A vigorous intellect; planning everything, performing nothing. Always in difficulties, having the means at hand to extricate himself from their annoyance, yet too apathetic to arouse himself to an effort; content to dream away his time in any occupation but that which the requisitions of the occasion demanded.

F. G. EDWARDS, rev. CLIVE BROWN

Sources *Musical World* (14 Aug 1845), 385–6 · *Musical World* (16 Oct 1845), 501 · J. Richardson, *Recollections* (1855), 1.231 · N&Q, 4th ser., 2 (1868), 440, 520 · N&Q, 4th ser., 3 (1869), 114, 205, 245, 294–5 · *MT*, 39 (1898), 597 · T. Fenner, *Opera in London: views of the press, 1785–1830* (1994), 45 · d. cert.

Wade, Nathaniel (*d.* 1718), lawyer and conspirator, was the third son of John *Wade (*d.* in or before 1668?) of The Wicke, Arlingham, Gloucestershire, a Cromwellian army officer usually identified as the sometime governor of the Isle of Man during the protectorate. His mother, Anne (formerly Lane), died on 19 May 1678 and was buried at St Stephen's, Bristol. Pursuing a career in the law, Wade was admitted to New Inn on 11 June 1678, transferred to the Middle Temple on 15 June 1681, and was called to the bar on 26 May 1682.

In the 1670s and early 1680s Wade and his brother William, a grocer, were active in dissenting circles in Bristol, often protecting and defending fellow nonconformists. In August 1680 Wade, then awaiting trial at the Wells assizes, was described as guilty of seditious and disloyal practices for the past three years. He was supposedly the ringleader of a company of about sixty sectarians that practised armed drills. He was also convicted and fined for resisting a justice who was disturbing a conventicle. In London Nathaniel was friendly with Green Ribbon Club whigs and for a time resided in Soho Square with fellow club members Richard Nelthorpe and Colonel John Rumsey. Not surprisingly, in 1682 he was brought into the whig conspiracy later known as the Rye House Plot. Wade later declared that he had had nothing to do with the plot to assassinate the royal brothers Charles II and the Catholic James, duke of York, but was only involved in a planned insurrection for the redressing of grievances and to have Monmouth, 'the Protestant Duke', declared prince of Wales. Wade was present at a meeting of conspirators in October 1682, at which the earl of Shaftesbury urged a group of whig leaders, among them William, Lord Russell, Lord Howard of Escrick, and Lord Grey of Werk, as well as a lower cabal of conspirators including John Ayloffe, Robert West, Major John Wildman, Richard Rumbold, and Thomas Walcott, to initiate a rising. Shaftesbury imagined, Wade later stated, 'that he had many thousands at his devotion in an hour's warning' (Wigfield, *The Monmouth Rebellion*, 153). Shortly after this meeting Shaftesbury took refuge in Amsterdam and Wade returned to Bristol; he felt that he and his friends had been abused by the hesitancy and 'unconstancy' of the 'great men and their little resolution to execute what they had resolved' (ibid., 153–4). He did, however, remain in contact with fellow conspirators in London and brought his brother William and the Bristol merchant James Holloway in on the planned insurrection.

In the winter of 1682 Wade was back in London and was informed by Colonel Rumsey of the plot to assassinate the king and his brother at Rye House mill. Wade supposedly refused to take part. The plans of the whig plotters were exposed in June 1683. Members of the lower cabal met one last time, and Wade proposed that they immediately muster what men they could and lead a rising 'here or in the west to die like men than be hanged like dogs' (*State trials*, 9.409). But Colonel Rumsey declared that the situation was hopeless, and they finally decided that they should go their separate ways. On 23 June a royal proclamation was issued for the arrest of Wade, Rumsey, Nelthorpe, Rumbold, and others. Wade and Nelthorpe escaped abroad and lived for a time with the regicide Colonel Edmund Ludow in Switzerland.

In the spring of 1684 Wade was in Holland serving as an intermediary between the duke of Monmouth and Archibald Campbell, ninth earl of Argyll. Following the death of Charles II Argyll and Monmouth agreed to co-ordinate their invasions. On 2 May Argyll set sail for Scotland, and Monmouth and his tiny band of eighty-three men followed three weeks later, landing at Lyme Regis on 11 June. Wade commanded the Red regiment and saw action at Bridport, where he proved himself a courageous commander. At the battle of Sedgemoor on 5 July Wade's battalion was routed and he fled the field. With fifty other men he rode to Ilfracombe, where they seized a coastal vessel only to be forced ashore by two frigates. Wade fled alone to Brendon Devon, where he was shot in the back trying to avoid capture.

Despite his notoriety, Wade was allowed to turn king's

evidence. At Windsor Castle and then Newgate, where he was held prisoner, he made a complete confession of his activities beginning with the dissolution of the Oxford parliament and continuing up to his capture. Wade's confession, which is not in his handwriting and, as he was recovering from a near fatal wound, was probably dictated, remains one of the best sources for Monmouth's rebellion. Although Wade was supposed to reveal names, he stated that 'all the persons I can positively charge to have been concerned in it are either outlawed, dead or executed' (Wigfield, *The Monmouth Rebellion*, 149). James's administration probably learned very little from Wade's confession, and at the trial of Lord Delamere in January 1686 he was only able to offer 'hearsay' evidence, but nevertheless he was granted a full pardon in May 1686. In 1687 he married Anne (d. 1735/6), widow of Samuel Davies, daughter of Robert Vickris, a Bristol merchant, and sister of Richard *Vickris. Anne was a Quaker and defied the wishes of the Bristol Friends' meeting in marrying Wade, who attended the Independent Church of Christ congregation, which met at Castle Green, Broadmead, Bristol. They had at least three children and in the 1690s owned two houses, in St Leonard's and St Augustine's parishes, Bristol. In January 1688, as part of James's efforts to court his former enemies, whigs and dissenters, Wade was sent to Bristol and appointed town clerk. In October that year, on the eve of the revolution of 1688, Wade lost his position when the corporation was ousted. Out of loyalty to James II Wade did not join the prince of Orange's army in November 1688.

Wade remained active in local politics, supporting whig-dominated initiatives such as the creation of the Bristol corporation of the poor in 1696; helping to set up the Bristol workhouse; and becoming a guardian of the poor for St Ewen's parish from 1696 for twelve years, and deputy governor in 1704–5. He was also a member of the Bristol Society for the Reformation of Manners, active between 1700 and 1705. Their mission was to assist the local authorities in 'discouraging of Prophaneness and Debauchery' by 'discovering disorderly houses' and by the 'taking up of offenders and carrying them before magistrates' (Barry and Morgan, 15). In 1701 Wade petitioned parliament, hoping to have the attainder against Monmouth's followers reversed. In 1709 he commanded the Bristol militia against the Kingswood colliers who rioted against high food prices. He died in 1718 and was buried on 14 March in Redcross Street burial-ground, Bristol.

MELINDA ZOOK

Sources BL, Harley MS 6845 · E. Ralph and M. E. Williams, eds., *The inhabitants of Bristol, 1696*, Bristol RS, 25 (1968), 48, 100 · J. Latimer, *The annals of Bristol* (1900) · E. B. Underhill, ed., *The records of the Church of Christ, meeting in Broadmead, Bristol, 1640–1687* (1847) · S. Seyer, *Memoirs of Bristol* (1823) · CSP dom., 1677–8, 391; 1679–80, 597–8; 1683–4, 24–6; 1684–5, 18; 1685, 311, 312, 349, 394; 1686–7, 143 · *State trials*, vol. 9 · *Report on the manuscripts of the late Reginald Rawdon Hastings*, 4 vols., HMC, 78 (1928–47), vol. 4, p. 307 · Greaves & Zaller, *BDBR* · N. Luttrell, *A brief historical relation of state affairs from September 1678 to April 1714*, 6 vols. (1857), vol. 1 · *Bishop Burnet's History*, 1.630 · G. Roberts, *The life, progresses and rebellion of James duke of Monmouth*, 1 (1844), 252 · *The autobiography of Sir John Bramston*, ed. [Lord Braybrooke], CS, 32 (1845) · R. Clifton, *The last popular rebellion* (1984) · W. M. Wigfield, *The Monmouth rebels, 1685*, Somerset RS, 79 (1985), 178–9 · J. Barry and K. Morgan, *Reformation and revival in eighteenth-century Bristol*, Bristol RS, 45 (1994) · H. A. C. Sturgess, ed., *Register of admissions to the Honourable Society of the Middle Temple, from the fifteenth century to the year 1944*, 3 vols. (1949) · W. M. Wigfield, *The Monmouth rebellion: a social history* (1980) · R. Mortimer, ed., *Minute book of the men's meeting of the Society of Friends in Bristol*, Bristol RS, 26 (1971), 218 · R. Mortimer, ed., *Minute book of the men's meeting of the Society of Friends in Bristol*, Bristol RS, 30 (1977), 9–10

Wade, Thomas (1805–1875), poet and playwright, was born in Woodbridge, Suffolk, the son of Searles Wade of Woodbridge. Nothing is known of Wade's education or childhood—indeed, biographical evidence on Wade is peculiarly sparse—but he emerged on the literary scene in 1825 with a volume of poems entitled *Tasso and the Sisters … Poems*, which included a preface dated December 1824. Dialogues of blank verse characterize the volume, which tends toward the dramatic, but the centrepiece of the work, 'The Nuptials of Juno', owes a lyric debt to Shelley, a debt which was to pervade Wade's writing. At this early phase of his career Wade turned from poetry to drama, and in this both luck and charisma were with him. Moving now in London's dramatic circles, Wade found a useful patron in Charles Kemble, of the eminent early nineteenth-century acting family and at that time manager of the Theatre Royal, Covent Garden. Kemble's theatre was in dire financial straits—it was in the possession of bailiffs during the 1829–30 season—and, in this desperate situation, the timing was right for an untried dramatic talent such as Wade's. Wade's first effort, *Woman's Love, or, The Triumph of Patience*, later to be known as *Duke Andrea*, was mounted in December 1829, with Kemble acting the lead role; a fairly simple melodrama based on the Griselda story, the play was a minor success, and was published under its original title in 1829. Wade's next effort, *The Phrenologists*, a farce based on the then popular pseudo-science, was performed at Covent Garden in January of 1830 and published that same year.

Wade's next foray into drama was a defining moment in his career, and put to the test the Shelleyan liberalism that seems to have energized him. Called *The Jew of Arragon, or, The Hebrew Queen*, Wade's play told the story of a thirteenth-century Spanish king whose love for a Jewish noblewoman leads to a popular insurrection against the Jewish population of Aragon. A thinly veiled political parable, it is an impassioned plea for civil liberties for British Jews. The play was powerfully backed—Charles Kemble again took the lead role, with his equally renowned daughter Fanny playing the Hebrew queen, Rachel—but its début, on 20 October 1830 at Covent Garden, was a disaster. *The Times* reported (21 October 1830) the 'very loud disapprobation' and hisses of the audience, and Fanny Kemble, years later, was to recall the evening as her one professional failure. Wade, however, seems not to have been daunted by the play's reception; Fanny Kemble, in her *Record of a Girlhood*, remembers his composure, and quotes his remark to her father: 'Never mind for me, Mr.

Kemble; I'll do better another time' (Kemble, 306). Indeed, Wade published the play in 1830, with a defiant dedication entitled 'To the Jews of England' and with the passages censored by the deputy play licenser restored and in capitals.

Despite his courage, however, Wade seems not to have enjoyed 'another time' in the drama. He left behind two unacted plays: *Elfrida*, of which no copy exists, and *King Henry II*, which remains only in manuscript form. At this point Wade seems to have returned to verse, his Shelleyan politics converted into Shelleyan poetics. His most important collection of poetry, entitled *Mundi et cordis, de rebus sempiternis et temporalis: carmina* (1835), is an uneven mixture of political verse, including stanzas on the Reform Bill and on Shelley's death, and finely wrought nature lyrics such as 'The Coming of Night' and 'The Winter Shore'. Lacking Shelley's gift for formal experimentation, Wade found the confines of the sonnet congenial, and much of his later work is in that form. His subsequent works include *The Contention of Death and Love*, *Helena*, and *The Shadow Seeker*, all published in 1837.

In this period Wade married the pianist and widow Lucy Bridgman, *née* Eager (d. 1882), and shortly afterward left poetry for journalism, briefly editing *Bell's Weekly Messenger*. When this financial venture failed, Wade retired to Jersey, where he edited the *British Press* and continued to produce verse, including a number of sonnets and an unpublished translation of Dante's *Inferno*, until 1871. Throughout his career, whether in his poetry, his dramatic productions, or his journalistic work, Wade's writing is fired by a reformist zeal and progressive temper, an energy which was inspired by Shelley, who to the last remained Wade's ideal. Wade died in Jersey on 19 September 1875.   NICHOLAS DAMES

Sources H. B. Forman, 'Thomas Wade: the poet and his surroundings', *Literary anecdotes of the nineteenth century*, ed. W. R. Nicoll and T. J. Wise, 1 (1895), 43–67 • F. A. Kemble, *Record of a girlhood*, 3 vols. (1878) • 'Covent Garden', *The Times* (21 Oct 1830) • H. Bloom, *The visionary company: a reading of English romantic poetry* (1961) • A. Nicoll, *A history of English drama, 1660–1900*, 6 vols. (1952–9) • *The nineteenth century: 1* (1915), vol. 12 of *The Cambridge history of English literature*, ed. A. W. Ward and A. R. Waller (1907–27) • *DNB*

Wade, Sir Thomas Francis (1818–1895), diplomatist and Sinologist, was born on 25 August 1818 in London, the eldest son of Colonel Thomas Wade (d. 1846) and his wife, Anne, daughter of William Smythe. In his youth Wade accompanied his father on military postings to Mauritius and southern Africa, and in 1832 he was sent to Harrow School. He went to Trinity College, Cambridge, in 1837, but left after a year when his father bought him a commission in the 81st regiment of foot. In 1839 he exchanged into the 42nd highlanders, with whom he served in Ireland and Corfu. He was promoted lieutenant in 1841 and exchanged into the 98th regiment of foot, which was then bound for China to fight in the First Opium War. Always interested in languages and foreign cultures, Wade began to study Chinese on the long voyage to Hong Kong. After a short period of military action in China Wade fell ill with

Sir Thomas Francis Wade (1818–1895), by unknown engraver, pubd 1895 (after Eveleen Myers)

malaria and during his convalescence was made interpreter to the Hong Kong garrison (1843). After a period of sick leave in Britain, Wade was appointed interpreter in Cantonese to the supreme court of Hong Kong in 1845, and in 1846 he became assistant Chinese secretary to Sir John Davis, then superintendent of trade. Another bout of malaria returned him to Britain, after which he became vice-consul at Shanghai in 1852, and in 1855 was appointed Chinese secretary in Hong Kong, in which position he was responsible for the student interpreters' language studies. Apart from brief visits to Britain, Wade remained in China until his retirement in 1883. On one of his visits to England he married, on 28 July 1868, Amelia Herschel (d. 1926), daughter of the physicist and astronomer Sir John F. W. *Herschel. It was a happy marriage, and produced four sons, one of whom died in the Second South African War.

Wade's diplomatic career was successful, if controversial. His rise in the service depended on his knowledge of the Chinese language, not diplomatic skills. As vice-consul in Shanghai in 1854 he assisted Sir Rutherford Alcock with the negotiations that led to the creation of the Maritime Customs Service, which collected customs duties for the Chinese government, then being besieged by the Taiping insurgents. Wade himself served as its first inspector, a role later taken over with great success by Sir Robert Hart. Lord Elgin also made use of Wade's linguistic abilities during the Second Opium War (1856–60). Together with Horatio Nelson Lay, and under Elgin's supervision, Wade did the actual work of negotiating the treaty of Tientsin (Tianjin) (1858), which secured the right of residence of foreign diplomats in Peking (Beijing), opened the Yangtze (Yangzi) River to foreign trade, and obtained for foreigners the right of travel under passport throughout China. In 1861 he was on the staff of the first British legation in Peking, and was twice acting chargé d'affaires there (1864–5 and 1869–71). Wade was likewise involved in the negotiations undertaken by Alcock in 1867–9. The Alcock convention was ratified in Peking, but ultimately was rejected in London, principally because of English merchants' opposition to acquiescence in the continued levying of *likin*, or transit dues, in China.

In 1871 Wade was appointed minister-plenipotentiary to Peking. In this role he strove to improve Sino-British relations, but ultimately could not prevent their deterioration; his own peppery temperament probably contributed to the situation. While in principle he was opposed to the use of force, and hoped to see China modernize and become an equal partner in diplomatic relations, he ended up threatening and bullying the Chinese negotiators. There were three significant incidents during his tenure of office: the audience question, the Formosa (Taiwan) crisis, and the Margary affair. Wade was insistent that the Guangxu emperor receive the diplomatic corps when he came of age in 1872. Chinese refusals were seen by Wade and others as attempts to maintain the old tribute system and as a refusal to meet on equal terms (the treaty of Tientsin had explicitly stated that foreign diplomats would no longer be obliged to perform the *kowtow* to the emperor; this would be the first time that they had to honour the treaty terms). During the negotiations that dragged on between 1871 and 1873, Wade lectured and hectored the Chinese at length. The eventual audience, which took place on 29 June 1873, was a cursory affair, which left all sides frustrated. Wade played a more positive role in the Formosa crisis of 1874. When the Japanese invaded Formosa in reprisal for injuries suffered by Japanese fishermen, Wade acted as mediator, resulting in the payment of an indemnity by the Chinese and the withdrawal of Japan from Formosa. While the settlement advertised China's weakness, the agreement averted a war at that time. In 1875 Wade seized upon the Margary affair to attempt a broad settlement of issues in Sino-British diplomatic relations. A British vice-consul, Augustus Raymond Margary, had been sent up the Yangtze River to meet an expedition led by Colonel Horace A. Browne which had set out to travel from Burma into Yunnan province in south-west China. Although the mission had been sanctioned by the Chinese government, Margary was murdered and the Browne expedition attacked by guerrillas in Yunnan. Wade was instructed to gain redress from the Chinese, but was quick to broaden his demands to involve questions of diplomatic protocol in Peking, trade, travel, and taxes, as well as an investigation of the murder and an indemnity for Margary's family. Taking his cue from Japanese conduct during the Formosa crisis and from Lord Elgin's style of operation, Wade threatened force, sounded uncompromising, and withdrew the legation to Shanghai. Despite appearances, H. B. Morse suggested that Wade's move was less the result of a desire to break off diplomatic relations in preparation for war than of a wish to be at the end of a telegraph line to London. Robert Hart, who as inspector of customs was officially in the service of China, but who was also a long-standing dining partner of Wade's, was sent to Shanghai to mollify Wade. Negotiations began in 1876 in Chefoo (Yantai) between Wade and Li Hongzhang, the Chinese plenipotentiary who was assisted by Hart. The Chefoo convention of September 1876 settled the Margary affair, obtaining Chinese approval for frontier trade between Burma and

China, and arranging for a mission of apology to London, which was to become the first resident Chinese legation abroad. Agreement was also reached on protocol and diplomatic etiquette in Peking, and a number of legal issues in cases which involved both Chinese and foreigners were settled. The convention opened up five further ports for trade, and secured the simultaneous collection of import and *likin* taxes at the treaty ports. None the less, because Wade had agreed to the raising of taxes on opium and the continued imposition of *likin* taxes outside the treaty ports, the convention ran into opposition in London, and was finally ratified in modified form in 1885. During further negotiations in Peking, Wade angered diplomatic colleagues of other countries as well as Chinese interlocutors. He had also made enemies in the Foreign Office; in 1882 he was recalled to London and retired the following year. Elements of the Chefoo convention continued to be effective in Sino-British relations until the fall of the Ch'ing dynasty in 1912.

Wade's real love was not diplomacy, but the study of the Chinese language. The system of transliteration of Mandarin which he developed and which was modified by H. A. Giles (known as Wade–Giles) was the standard for English speakers for more than a century until the development of pinyin. He periodically sought to retire from the diplomatic service in order to extend his scholarly studies, but failed to do so. He nevertheless produced a number of books on China and Chinese, including the first standard texts on Chinese language, *Wen-chien tzu-ehr Chi: a Series of Papers Selected as Specimens of Documentary Chinese* (1867) and *Yu-Yen tzu-ehr Chi: a Progressive Course of Colloquial Chinese* (1867). A charter member of the Asia Society in Hong Kong, he wrote important articles on the Chinese army and Chinese government. In 1888 he became the first professor of Chinese at Cambridge University, but published no more and had no students. An avid collector of Chinese books from his earliest days in China, he donated his library to Cambridge University Library. Containing most of the classic works of Chinese philosophy, history, geography, and literature, the Wade collection laid crucial foundations for the serious study of China in Britain.

Wade, who was made KCB in 1875 and GCMG in 1889, died on 31 July 1895 at his home, 5 Salisbury Villas, Station Road, Cambridge. Contemporary colleagues and observers such as Robert Hart and H. B. Morse describe Wade as an intelligent and hard-working man, whose tendency to throw tantrums made him his own worst enemy. Like Hart, he was a Victorian modernizer, hoping to instruct both Chinese and British officials in the ways of progress, and using his office for this end. Unlike Hart, however, his frequent offerings of advice and admonition were prone to cause offence. If he did want in some ways to conduct negotiations on a basis of equality, ultimately he did not resist the temptation to appeal to Britain's superior military power to implement his understanding of how China should develop, and how Sino-British relations should be structured. Yet Wade's interest in China was passionate, and he was firmly convinced that knowledge of the language and sensitivity to Chinese culture were essential to Sino-British relations.   HANS J. VAN DE VEN

Sources J. C. Cooley, *T. F. Wade in China: pioneer in global diplomacy, 1842–1882* (1981) • H. B. Morse, *The international relations of the Chinese empire*, 3 vols. (1918) • *The I.G. in Peking: letters of Robert Hart, 1868–1907*, ed. J. K. Fairbank, K. F. Bruner, and E. M. Matheson (1975) • J. Hevia, 'An imperial nomad and the Great Game', *Late Imperial China*, 16/2 (1995), 1–22 • P. D. Coates, *The China consuls: British consular officers, 1843–1943* (1988) • m. cert. • d. cert.
Archives CUL, notes on Chinese affairs • SOAS, notes on Cantonese | CUL, letters to R. S. Gundry • Lpool RO, corresp. with Lord Derby • PRO, letters to Lord Hammond, FO 391
Likenesses wood-engraving (after photograph by E. Myers), NPG; repro. in *ILN* (10 Aug 1895) [*see illus.*]
Wealth at death £23,333 19s. 6d.: probate, 14 Oct 1895, *CGPLA Eng. & Wales*

Wade, Walter (*c.*1740–1825), surgeon, physician, and botanist, was the son of John Wade (*d.* 1799), a Dublin apothecary (a descendant of Henry Wade of Clonebraney, co. Meath, Ireland) and his wife, Katherine. He was probably educated in Dublin, and was then apprenticed to a surgeon. By 1776 he was in practice as a surgeon and man-midwife in Bolton Street, Dublin, and from 1781 in Capel Street where his father had his pharmacy. On 25 July 1777 ten of Dublin's most eminent physicians, including Dr Edward Hill and Sir Nathaniel Barry, signed a testimonial (MSS, University of St Andrews muniments) recommending that he merited a 'Diploma to Practice physick' because they either had 'certain proofs of [his] capacity, skill and attention in his attendance on many persons committed to his care in the medical line' or had 'reason to believe him a person of medical experience'. On 27 June 1786 the senate of the University of St Andrews agreed to confer on him the degree of doctor of medicine on the basis of this nine-year-old testimonial. On 30 October that year, and on the following 23 April, he was examined by the King and Queen's College of Physicians in Ireland, after which he was admitted a licentiate.

From the late 1780s Wade became prominent as a botanist, not a difficult achievement as there were few botanists active in Ireland at the time. He was an active member of the Experimental Society of Dublin for the Improvement of Natural Knowledge. In 1787 he tried unsuccessfully to publish by subscription *Flora Dubliniensis*, a handsome, illustrated work modelled on William Curtis's *Flora Londinensis* (1775?–1798). During 1789 he advertised public lectures in his Capel Street house on midwifery and on botany.

On 9 February 1790 a petition from Wade was presented to the Irish House of Commons by the solicitor-general, John Toler, 'that the Establishment of a Publick Botanical Garden in this City, or its Environs, on an enlarged plan, would be of the greatest National Advantage' (Wade). With the powerful support of the speaker, John Foster, Wade's scheme succeeded when, after much delay, on 25 March 1795 the Dublin Society's Botanic Gardens were founded at Glasnevin. Wade had assiduously cultivated the Dublin Society, ingratiating himself by presenting

various botanical manuscripts, and was elected an honorary member in 1792. He was invited to undertake the layout of the new garden, and in 1796 was elected the society's professor of botany. He remained in control of the gardens until his death.

Wade held other positions simultaneously, including physician to the Dublin General Dispensary and lecturer in botany at the Royal College of Surgeons. He failed on two occasions (1800, 1809) to obtain the chair of botany in the University of Dublin. He was ambitious, and careful to maintain the patronage he enjoyed from John Foster (1740–1828), who was a skilful politician and a passionate gardener. The first of Wade's publications, *Catalogus systematicus plantarum indigenarum in comitatu Dublinensi* (1794), was dedicated to Foster, who was to eulogize his protégé as 'a man of great worth, zeal and knowledge … no man could excel him in his perfect knowledge [of botany]' (Foster to Dublin Society, 7 Nov 1825, Belfast RO, Foster/Massereine MSS). On the other hand, Erinensis (Dr Peter Hennis Green) jibed that Professor Wade was 'an old-fashioned *prig* … an old coxcomb' (Erinensis, 255). Wade was elected an associate of the Linnean Society of London (1792), a member of the Royal Irish Academy (1811), a fellow of the Royal Society of London (1811), and an honorary fellow of the Royal College of Physicians of Ireland (1811). He was deputy grand master of the Grand Lodge of Free and Accepted Masons of Ireland (1794–9).

Wade visited various parts of Ireland in search of plants: in 1796 and 1805 he was in co. Kerry, and during 1801 in Connemara where he discovered pipewort (*Eriocaulon aquaticum*). His published works include the earliest catalogues of the plants cultivated in the botanic gardens, two sets of lecture notes on grasses (1808), an English edition of François Michaux's treatise on oaks (1809), and a monograph on willows (1811).

Wade married Mary Chambers (1733/4–1831), a Quaker, in 1781; she was disowned by the Society of Friends for marrying a man 'not of our Society' (Nelson and McCracken, 23). The couple had no children. He died at Dublin on 25 July 1825, at which time he was described by a contemporary as an octogenarian.

E. CHARLES NELSON

Sources E. C. Nelson and E. M. McCracken, *The brightest jewel: a history of the National Botanic Gardens, Glasnevin, Dublin* (1987) • E. C. Nelson, 'A select annotated bibliography of the National Botanic Gardens, Glasnevin, Dublin', *Glasra: contributions from the National Botanic Gardens, Glasnevin*, 5 (1981), 1–20 • M. Fallon, ed., *The sketches of Erinensis: selections of Irish medical satire, 1824–1836* (1979) • J. H. Lepper and P. Crossle, *History of the Grand Lodge of Free and Accepted Masons of Ireland* (1925), 309–13, 434–5 • E. C. Nelson, 'Walter Wade's "Flora Dublinensis" — an enigmatic Irish botanical publication', *Long Room*, 20–21 (1980), 16–20 • E. C. Nelson, 'Dr Walter Wade of Dublin; a missing portrait found', *Archives of Natural History*, 14 (1987), 110–11 • E. C. Nelson, *Archives of Natural History*, 10 (1981–2), 538 • Erinensis, 'Dr Litton … the Glasnevin Botanic Garden', *The Lancet* (16 May 1835), 253–8 • W. Wade, *The memorial* [1790]
Archives Linn. Soc., letters to Sir James Smith • National Botanic Gardens, Dublin, specimens • PRO NIre., corresp. with John Foster

Wade, William (1734/5–1809), master of ceremonies, though often identified as the illegitimate son or nephew of Field Marshal George *Wade (1673–1748), was more probably his great-nephew and the grandson of George's brother William Wade (1670–1732), canon of St George's Chapel, Windsor. He was educated at Westminster School and later joined the army, becoming a captain in the 73rd regiment. On 16 December 1760, aged twenty-five, he married Katherine (d. 1787), the daughter of the prosperous Henry Gore of Leatherhead, at St Anne's, Soho, Westminster; thereafter his newly acquired wealth allowed him to abandon his military career. Between 1722 and 1748 George Wade had been MP for Bath, and it was here that William was elected master of ceremonies by the town's company in 1769.

Wade's appointment ended an ugly interlude in the hitherto largely polite history of the resort. Following the death of Richard 'Beau' Nash, Bath's premier master of ceremonies, the town's corporation had struggled to find a suitable replacement. Nash's immediate successors, Jacques Colet and Samuel Derrick, had been criticized by would-be rivals who, with Derrick's death in March 1769, began a heated competition to secure the post. The resulting 'Bath contest' ended in a violent confrontation between supporters of the competing parties, one Mr Plomer and William Brereton (1723–1813), who both claimed the office. From this confusion Wade emerged as a compromise candidate, having 'the good fortune to please all parties and to restore perfect harmony to the city' (*The Original Bath Guide*, 1811, 100). His term began with a ball on 18 April 1769, and shortly afterwards he was presented with a medallion symbolizing the qualities of the office: harmony, gentility, and civic responsibility. At some point in his career as master of ceremonies Wade became known as 'the Bath Adonis'. Certainly Thomas Gainsborough's magnificent portrait (1770–71) depicts a commanding gentleman—mature, tall, handsome, and refined—satisfyingly distinct from the elderly Colet and the diminutive Derrick. To a later observer he was, quite simply, 'the *immaculate* Captain *Wade*' (*Bath Chronicle*, 25 Sept 1777). Through his stewardship, which was praised for its 'polite attention, ease, and elegance of manners' (*The Original Bath Guide*, 100), Wade restored some of the respect for the role of master of ceremonies as established by Nash. He also supervised the building of the New Assembly Rooms—at £20,000 the town's most expensive eighteenth-century structure—which marked a significant shift in the centre of polite Bath from the lower spa of Nash's day to the higher ground near John Wood's Circus. Gainsborough's portrait now hangs in the Octagonal Room of the new assembly; there, from September 1771, Wade officiated for six years. In addition he continued to supervise at Gyde's, an existing set of rooms in the lower town, which was now required to compete for trade in an increasingly aggressive entertainment market. Wade's dual stewardship sat awkwardly with this new spirit of competition. In 1774 relations broke down between the committee of the lower rooms, who sought to divide the market and conserve the social cohesion of Nash's day, and that of the upper rooms, who claimed their right to maximize profits, even if this meant superseding Wade's independence and city-wide authority.

In July 1777 Wade resigned as master of ceremonies after being named in the divorce proceedings of Elizabeth Eustatia, *née* Bassett (d. 1812), and John Hooke Campbell. The news appeared to confirm the Adonis's reputation for womanizing, an identity often associated with the role of master. However, some, like the dramatist Samuel Foote, dismissed any allegation of widespread philandering, Wade being in his opinion 'unfit for that office, since he is so bashful as to be ashamed of an amour' (*Town and Country Magazine*, Nov 1777, 9.599). Certainly, Wade's attachment to Elizabeth Campbell outlasted the scandal, and following the death in 1787 of his first wife, Katherine (with whom he had five children), the couple married on 30 June 1787 at St Marylebone, London. In an attempt to avoid the conflict of interests which had dogged Wade's mastership, the office was now divided between two candidates, William Brereton and William Dawson, who managed the lower and upper assembly rooms respectively. Like Nash and Derrick at Tunbridge Wells, Wade had held the post at Bath with that of another town, in this case Brighton. On leaving Bath, he became full-time master of ceremonies at the Sussex resort, where he remained until his death at his residence in New Street on 16 March 1809.

PHILIP CARTER

Sources S. Sloman, '"The immaculate Capt. Wade": "Arbiter Elegantiae"', *Gainsborough's House Review* (1993–4), 46–61 · S. Sloman, *Gainsborough in Bath* (2002) · R. S. Neale, *Bath: a social history, 1680–1850* (1981) · T. Fawcett, *Bath entertain'd* (1995) · *GM*, 1st ser., 79 (1809), 285 · *The Bath contest* (1769) · will, PRO, PROB 11/1510, fol. 226 · *IGI*
Likenesses T. Gainsborough, oils, 1770–71, Bath Assembly Rooms

Wade, Sir Willoughby Francis (1827–1906), physician, was born on 31 August 1827 at Bray, co. Wicklow, Ireland, the eldest son of Edward Michael Wade (d. 1867), who was for many years vicar of Holy Trinity Church, Derby, and his wife (*née* Fox), the daughter of an Irish judge. One of his ancestors was Field Marshal George Wade, the military engineer. Sir Thomas Francis Wade, who was British ambassador to China and professor of Chinese at Cambridge University, was a cousin. Wade's early education was at Brighton. He entered Rugby School on 13 August 1842, and Trinity College, Dublin, where he matriculated in arts as well as medicine on 2 December 1844; he graduated BA in 1849 and MB in 1851. After a short spell studying in Paris he was apprenticed to Douglas Fox, a surgeon in Derby. Wade also took up an appointment as house physician and medical tutor at Birmingham General Hospital. He qualified as a licentiate in midwifery in Dublin, and as MRCS in London, both in 1851. He was also admitted MRCP in London in 1859, and FRCP in 1872.

In 1855 Wade began to practise on his own account in Birmingham. Although 'constitutionally too indolent to work persistently at his profession' (*BMJ*, 9 June 1906, 1380), his practice, which for many years was based at 24 Temple Row, Birmingham, attracted a large number of patients. He left the general hospital in 1857 to become physician to Birmingham General Dispensary and, in 1860, to the Queen's Hospital. In the early 1860s he was promoted senior physician to the Queen's Hospital and appointed professor of medicine at Queen's College. In 1865 he returned to the General Hospital as physician, relinquishing his posts at Queen's and all systematic teaching activity. He remained on the staff of the General Hospital until 1892, for his last seven years as senior physician. Between 1892 and 1898 he continued in practice while serving as consulting physician to the General Hospital. In the course of his career Wade held several other medical posts in the west midlands. He was also co-proprietor of Burman House private lunatic asylum at Henley in Arden. On 4 February 1880, comparatively late in life, Wade married his cousin, Augusta Frances, daughter of Sir John Power of Kilfane, co. Kilkenny. The marriage was childless.

Wade had a long and distinguished connection with the British Medical Association at a time when its wealth, membership, and influence were growing rapidly. He emerged as an influential figure in the 1860s, at which time Birmingham was its centre of power. He became a member of council in 1864, a position he retained for more than three decades. In 1868 he joined the association's powerful committee of council. His other positions were as chairman of the scientific grants committee (1880–84), treasurer (1881–4), and president (1890–91). In 1878, at the anniversary meeting in Bath, he proposed the motion which led to women doctors being denied membership of the association. In 1882, when the association met at Worcester in its jubilee year, he read the address in medicine. He contributed to the reform of the association's constitution in the 1880s, and to its efforts to obtain the Medical Act 1886. The last BMA meeting Wade attended was at Carlisle, in 1896, on which occasion he proposed further reform of the association's constitution. In the same year he received a knighthood and an honorary MD degree from Dublin.

One of Wade's main professional interests was the development of medical science. In 1883, as chairman of the scientific grants committee, he successfully proposed that the BMA should finance scientific research scholarships. In his presidential address at the association's annual meeting in Birmingham, he pointed out the inadequacy of the scientific training received by medical students. His analysis drew widespread attention and favourable comment, from Thomas Huxley and Herbert Spencer among others. Wade himself lacked the 'quality of mind that makes advances in science' (*BMJ*, 9 June 1906, 1380), though he was the first to record the presence of albuminuria in diphtheria. Aside from a few articles and pamphlets he wrote little, his most substantial publication being *On Gout as a Peripheral Neurosis* (1893), fifty-nine pages long. In 1884 he contributed 'On the liver and its difficulties' to the Birmingham health lectures. In 1896 he delivered the

Ingleby lectures at Queen's College, Birmingham, taking as his title 'Some functional disorders of females'.

Wade possessed a powerful physique, and though affable and hospitable he could be belligerent in presenting his views. He lacked effectiveness as a speaker but was renowned for his sound judgement and fairness. He was a Liberal Unionist in politics. Although he played no active political role, his wife was prominent in the Birmingham Women's Liberal Unionist Association. Aside from his medical interests Wade served as a JP for Warwickshire. Keenly interested in music, he served on the committee of the Birmingham Music Festival and as chairman of the orchestral committee. He retired from medical practice in 1898 and moved initially to Bournemouth, and then, in the interests of Lady Wade's health, to Villa Monforte, Maianao, near Florence. During his last years he made a special study of crime in Italy, contributing several papers on the subject to the *Rassegna Nazionale*. In 1905, again to safeguard his wife's health, he sold the villa and moved to Rome, taking an apartment at via Torino 153. Soon after arriving his own health broke down; following a few months' illness he died at his home in Rome on 28 May 1906. His wife survived him.   P. W. J. BARTRIP

Sources *BMJ* (9 June 1906), 1379–80 · *The Lancet* (16 June 1906), 1722, 1725–6 · *Birmingham Daily Post* (5 June 1906) · *DNB* · Munk, *Roll* · P. W. J. Bartrip, *Themselves writ large: the British Medical Association, 1832–1966* (1996) · A. T. C. Pratt, ed., *People of the period: being a collection of the biographies of upwards of six thousand living celebrities*, 2 vols. (1897) · *The Lancet* (24 June 1905), 1734 · Burtchaell & Sadleir, *Alum. Dubl.* · m. cert. · d. cert.
Likenesses photograph, repro. in *BMJ*

Wadeson, Anthony (*bap.* 1573), playwright, was baptized on 1 March 1573 in the parish of St Peter-at-Arches, Lincoln, the son of James Wadeson (*d.* 1593), blacksmith. Contrary to the speculation of Eccles, Anthony's father was not the James Wadeson who was rector of Custlerworth, Lincolnshire, in 1576, nor the James Wadeson who was at Cambridge between 1578 and 1586. On 15 October 1590 Anthony Wadeson of Lincolnshire, 'pleb. fil.', matriculated at Magdalen College, Oxford. However, he never received a degree, possibly because his education was interrupted by the death of his father in early 1593. James Wadeson's nuncupative will, made on 20 January, left his entire modest estate to Anthony's elder brother Edward (*b.* 1568).

At some point during the 1590s Wadeson made his way to London and became involved in the theatre, writing plays for Philip Henslowe. In June and July 1601 Henslowe lent Wadeson a total of 30s. for a play in progress for the Lord Admiral's Men called 'The Honorable Lyfe of the Humorous Earle of Gloster, with his Conquest of Portugall' (Foakes and Rickert, 165). This play does not survive and may not have been completed, but it was probably a sequel to the anonymous play *Look About You*, also written for the Lord Admiral's Men and printed in 1600. This historical comedy is one of the half-dozen 'Robin Hood' plays written for the Admiral's Men about this time, in which the folk hero Robert, earl of Huntington, is a central character. The witty earl of Gloucester also plays a prominent role, and promises at the end to go 'with an exceedinge zeale to Portingale' (L4r) and free it from the Moors, suggesting the title of Wadeson's play. If Wadeson wrote the sequel, he may have written the original, though Henry Chettle is perhaps a more likely candidate. In July and September 1602 Henslowe lent money to 'Antony the poet' for a play called 'The Widow's Charm' (Foakes and Rickert, 205). This may be Wadeson, but a more likely candidate is Anthony Munday, also writing for Henslowe at the time. Wadeson may be the A. W. who contributed several poems to Francis Davison's *Poetical Rhapsody* (1602).

There is no evidence that Wadeson ever married, but he did have at least one illegitimate child. On 26 January 1600, 'Hellen, daughter of Anthony Wadson, base born of [blank] Slee' was baptized at St Giles Cripplegate, and two days later, 'Ellen the daughter of Anthony Weadson' was buried at St Mary Magdalen, Bermondsey (Eccles, 123). Wadeson is not traceable after 1602; he may have died soon after, or he may have eventually returned to Lincolnshire. DAVID KATHMAN

Sources Henslowe's diary, ed. R. A. Foakes and R. T. Rickert (1961) · M. Eccles, *Brief lives: Tudor and Stuart authors* (1982), 123 · Foster, *Alum. Oxon.* · *IGI* · will of James Wadeson, Lincolnshire consistory court, 1593, 333r · *Look about you* (1600); facs. edn, ed. J. Farmer (1912) · H. D. Sykes, 'The dramatic work of Henry Chettle, V: *Look about you*', *N&Q*, 12th ser., 12 (1923), 324–7
Archives Dulwich College, London, Henslowe MSS, receipt for 20s. in Wadeson's hand, with signature, fol. 85 of Henslowe's diary, Henslowe MS VII

Wadeson, Richard (1826–1885), army officer, was born at Gaythorse, near Lancaster, on 31 July 1826. On 17 November 1843 he enlisted at Plymouth in the 75th (Stirlingshire) regiment (later 1st battalion, Gordon Highlanders). He was promoted corporal on 27 August 1846 and sergeant on 7 November 1848, and went to India in 1849. He was promoted regimental sergeant-major on 24 February 1854. Then the Indian mutiny broke out. The 75th made forced marches from Kasauli in the Himalayas to Ambala where, in May, it was part of the force ordered to Delhi, then held by the mutineers. On 2 June 1857 Wadeson was commissioned ensign in the regiment, without purchase, and was promoted lieutenant on 19 September. He served with the regiment throughout the mutiny campaign, including the battle of Badli-ki-sarai and at the siege of Delhi, after which he was mentioned in dispatches, and awarded the Victoria Cross. He was with the regiment and was wounded at the assault of Delhi on 14 September 1857.

On 11 March 1859 he was appointed adjutant of the regiment, which position he retained until promoted captain on 9 December 1864. He was with the 75th during the Fenian disturbances of 1866–7, and served in Gibraltar, Singapore, Hong Kong, Mauritius, and the Cape, until promoted major on 11 July 1872. In 1873 the 75th returned home, and was quartered in England and Ireland, and there, on 18 December 1875, he was promoted to the command of the regiment, which he held at home and in the Channel Islands until his promotion to a brevet colonelcy on 18 December 1880. On 26 March 1881 he was appointed major and lieutenant-governor of the Royal Hospital,

Chelsea, London, where he died on 24 January 1885, survived by his widow, Susan. He was buried with military honours at Brompton cemetery.

ROBERT HOLDEN, *rev.* M. G. M. JONES

Sources *Army List* · records 75th regimental district · *Guide to Chelsea Hospital* · T. E. Toomey, *Heroes of the Victoria Cross* (1895) · *The register of the Victoria cross* (1981); rev. edn (1988); 3rd edn (1997) · Boase, *Mod. Eng. biog.* · *CGPLA Eng. & Wales* (1885)
Likenesses Maull & Fox, photograph, repro. in Toomey, *Heroes of the Victoria cross* · engraving, repro. in *ILN*, 76 (1885), 178 · photograph, repro. in *The Register of the Victoria cross* · portrait, repro. in Toomey, *Heroes of the Victoria cross*, 105
Wealth at death £530 8s. 5d.: probate, 13 Feb 1885, *CGPLA Eng. & Wales*

Wadham [*née* Petre], **Dorothy** (1534/5–1618), founder of Wadham College, Oxford, was the second and eldest surviving child of Sir William *Petre (1505/6–1572), then a civil and canon lawyer in the service of the crown, and of his wife, Gertrude (d. 1541), daughter of Sir John Tyrrell; a portrait of her at Wadham College gives her age as sixty in 1595. Her mother died on 28 May 1541, and Dorothy was thereafter brought up by Petre's second wife, Anne, also a Tyrrell by her first marriage. Petre was to be a principal secretary to Henry VIII, Edward VI, and Queen Mary from 1544 to 1557. Dorothy was presumably educated at home at Ingatestone Hall, Essex. A younger sister was sent away to service in a great lady's household, but if this was also Dorothy's experience, there is no record of it. In her old age she wrote a firm English hand, and apparently understood Latin. On 3 September 1555 she married Nicholas *Wadham (1531/2–1609), gentleman, at St Botolph, Aldersgate, London; the wedding was a sumptuous one, with a good deal spent on clothes and jewellery.

Little is known of the next fifty years of Dorothy Wadham's life. The Wadhams lived at the family seat at Merrifield, near Ilton, Somerset. They had no children. The Petre connection probably strengthened their inclination to Catholicism. In 1612–13 Dorothy, then a widow, suffered the confiscation of her armoury as a suspected recusant, but in 1615 she was granted a formal pardon for offences under the 1593 act 'against Popish recusants'. Yet there is no hint of Catholic sympathies in Dorothy's will, or in her letters to her brother, John, Lord Petre, whom she habitually commends 'to the protection of the Almighty'. Nor did any such leanings prevent friendly relations with protestant gentry and clergy.

Dorothy's father had virtually refounded Exeter College in Oxford, and it is possible that the idea of founding an Oxford college came from Dorothy. However, she always professed to be acting solely to fulfil her husband's intention, 'for it would greatly offend my conscience to violate any jot of my husband's will' (Briggs, 64). Nicholas Wadham, however, left a confused situation following his death on 20 October 1609. Dorothy was his sole executor, charged with using the money he had put aside 'for such uses and purposes' as he had 'requested her and she hath assented to' (Wadham College muniments, 10/1/1). On the other hand, on his deathbed he had summoned the sometime surveyor of the ordnance and Essex conspirator, Sir John Davis, to confer about his plans with Dorothy and the

Dorothy Wadham (1534/5–1618), by unknown artist, 1595

Wadhams' two men of business; Davis induced Nicholas to sign an 'instrument' naming him as jointly responsible with Dorothy for carrying out the design. Davis's involvement threatened the whole scheme. He was a convicted traitor because of his role in the Essex conspiracy, and a recusant. Discussion on a bill for his restitution in blood in the 1610 parliament revealed that he still refused the Church of England sacrament. He may also have wished to subsume the Wadham foundation in his *alma mater*, Gloucester Hall, rather than, as Nicholas Wadham probably intended, taking over the assets of Gloucester Hall for the new college.

A month after Wadham's death Dorothy was writing to Lord Treasurer Salisbury angrily denying Davis's accusation that she had no intention of proceeding with her husband's project. An offer was made to Gloucester Hall but, probably to Dorothy's relief, was turned down by the principal unless he became head of the new college. There is no record of any offer, as Wadham had indicated, for an arrangement with Jesus College. Dorothy's agents identified a site for the college in February 1610, and an architect, William Arnold, was appointed. A letter from the king induced Oxford city council to lower its asking price. A collusive suit in chancery resulted in July 1610 in the establishment of a trust which excluded Davis. Dorothy's brother Lord Petre was important in mobilizing this support at Westminster, but Dorothy firmly rejected Petre's offer to take over the responsibility 'which my dear husband so solely and absolutely trusted me with' (Briggs, 62). On 20 December 1610 Wadham College received its royal letter patent. Statutes were drafted and approved by Dorothy in 1612, and the building was opened and the college

formally instituted in April the next year. Dorothy had carried through a formidable task quickly and completely. She also added some £7270 of her own to her husband's contribution of £19,200.

The appointment of warden, fellows, and scholars, and even on occasion of the college cook, remained in Dorothy's hands, conveyed in a series of letters to 'my college' from Edge Manor, the Wadham dower house in Branscombe, Devon. They were written by John Arnold, her man of business, but signed by her, as were successive drafts of the statutes. She was anxious that these should be amended in the light of experience before she died, confessing that 'my experience in such matters is but small', and sending some drafts in English for translation into Latin (*Letters of Dorothy Wadham*, letters 18, 19). She never visited the college, whether from infirmity, or because of the travel restrictions imposed on recusants, and depended a good deal on Arnold. However, she retained a clear view of her mission in carrying out what she claimed, perhaps too modestly, to be her husband's design. She died on 16 May 1618, at Edge and was taken to Merrifield to be buried on 16 June with her husband in St Mary's Church, Ilminster.   C. S. L. DAVIES

Sources C. S. L. Davies, 'A woman in the public sphere: Dorothy Wadham and the foundation of Wadham College, Oxford', *EngHR*, 118 (2003) • T. G. Jackson, *Wadham College, Oxford* (1893) • *The letters of Dorothy Wadham, 1609–1618*, ed. R. B. Gardiner (1904) • N. Briggs, 'The foundation of Wadham College, Oxford', *Oxoniensia*, 21 (1956), 61–81 • F. G. Emmison, *Tudor secretary: Sir William Petre at court and home* (1961) • L. Stone, 'The original endowment of Wadham College', *Wadham College Gazette*, 146 (1959), 118–19 • A. C. Edwards, *John Petre* (1975) • muniments, Wadham College, Oxford, 10/1/2 [Dorothy Wadham's will] • muniments, Wadham College, Oxford, 10/1/1 [Nicholas Wadham's will] • E. R. Forster, ed., *Proceedings in parliament, 1610*, 1 (1966), 40, 60–63, 205–7; 2 (1966), 368
Archives Wadham College, Oxford, corresp. relating to the college • Wadham College, Oxford, letters to first and second Baron Petre [photocopies] | Essex RO, Chelmsford, corresp.
Likenesses portrait, 1595, Petworth House, West Sussex [*see illus.*] • follower of Custodis, oil on wood (aged about sixty), priv. coll. • carved statue, Wadham College, Oxford • funerary brass, St Mary's Church, Ilminster, Somerset
Wealth at death gave £7270 cash to Wadham College, Oxford, between 1609 and 1618; left *c*.£1000 cash disbursements; also plate, jewels; income in widowhood presumably derived from land held in trust for her, value £400 p.a.; total estate from Nicholas seemingly £22,200: Stone, 'Original endowment of Wadham College'; Briggs, 'Foundation of Wadham College', 78–9; will, muniments, Wadham College, 10/1/2

Wadham, Sir John (*d.* 1412), justice, was probably a native of Devon, though his background is obscure. Having entered upon a legal career, he is first recorded in 1367, as an attorney at Westminster, and prospered sufficiently to be returned to parliament as a burgess for Exeter in 1379. In January 1383 he was ordered to become a serjeant-at-law, and thereafter appeared regularly in the central courts as a pleader. In 1384 he was in receipt of livery from Edward Courtenay, earl of Devon, for whom he acted as a feoffee in the following year. A JP for Devon for the first time in 1384, he was a commissioner of array there in 1385, and was subsequently appointed to judicial commissions, and to be a justice of assize and gaol delivery, in many southern and midland counties. By June 1387 he had become a king's serjeant. The purge of the judiciary by the lords appellant in the following year provided Wadham with further opportunities for advancement. On 20 May 1389 he was one of three new justices appointed to the court of common pleas, receiving an annual fee of 50 marks as well as the usual salary of £40. For as long as he held this office he was invariably among the justices summoned to parliament, and seven times acted as a trier of petitions.

The profits of success soon became apparent. Between 1384 and 1386 Wadham acquired the Dorset manor of Haydon. Following the exile of Sir John Carey in 1388, Wadham and his friend and fellow justice William Hankeford were able for £400 to buy Carey's estates at Hardington Mandeville, Chilton Cantelo, Merrifield, and Trent in Somerset. Other acquisitions included the manors of Harberton and Silverton, and half the manor of Lustleigh, all in Devon. Perhaps his rise prompted resentment, for in 1392 he fell foul of his former employer, the earl of Devon, who sent word to Wadham while he conducted a gaol delivery in Exeter, 'that he should sit more uprightly without partiality than he had at the last session' (Leadam and Baldwin, 77–81). The earl had to plead for the king's grace, and Wadham remained in favour, active as a justice both at Westminster and in the localities, regularly named as a commissioner, and appointed to the bench in counties as far apart as Devon and the North Riding of Yorkshire. By September 1397 he had been knighted. Even if Wadham did not always act upon his commissions, the demands of the king's business must have been considerable, and perhaps it is not surprising that on 10 May 1398 he should have been discharged from the common pleas at his own request and at once withdrew from an assize circuit in south-east England. For his good service Wadham was granted £20 a year for life.

For the rest of his life Wadham was largely concerned with his affairs in the south-west, where he seems mainly to have resided at Merrifield. He was, however, returned as a knight of the shire for Devon in 1401, and he continued to be appointed to the county bench for Devon until 1408 and for Somerset until May 1410. In December 1407 he was appointed to investigate the sensitive issue of oppressions by royal officials in Somerset, but otherwise he withdrew from public business almost entirely. Provision for the descent of his estates to his wife and sons had been largely completed in 1397, but in 1404 he added to his earlier arrangements. Wadham drew up his will on 12 March 1411. It shows that he was a wealthy man, with a fine collection of plate, and enough cash (£835 in all) to allow him to bequeath £100 each to his wife, three of his sons, William, John, and Thomas, and his three daughters, Joan, Elizabeth, and Margery, who married John *Stourton, first Baron Stourton [see under Stourton family]. A fourth son, Walter, who was a priest, received only £40. Other bequests were less generous. William Hankeford received a silver cup with a cover, but Wadham's sister Cicely was left only £5, and his niece Agnes just 13s. 4d. A variety of small sums, and in one case ten sheep, were

left to London friaries, local churches and roads, neighbours, friends, and servants. 40 marks were set aside for prayers for the testator's soul, but with the evident hope that the four chaplains stipulated for could be hired for less. Wadham died on 27 July 1412, leaving lands valued at £115 per annum. He had married twice. His first wife, Maud, and his eldest son, Robert, both predeceased him; before 1385 he had married his second wife, Joan Wrothesley, who outlived her husband. HENRY SUMMERSON

Sources HoP, *Commons, 1386–1421*, 3.727–9 · *Chancery records* · Baker, *Serjeants* · Sainty, *Judges* · *RotP*, vol. 3 · I. S. Leadam and J. F. Baldwin, eds., *Select cases before the king's council, 1243–1482*, SeldS, 35 (1918), 77–81 · M. S. Arnold, ed., *Select cases of trespass from the king's courts, 1307–1399*, 2; SeldS, 103 (1987) · E. Green, ed., *Pedes finium, commonly called, feet of fines, for the county of Somerset*, Somerset RS, 17: *Edward III to Richard II, 1347–1399* (1902) · E. Green, ed., *Pedes finium, commonly called, feet of fines for the county of Somerset*, Somerset RS, 22: *Henry IV to Henry VI, 1399–1460* (1906) · *Calendar of the … commissions on the dorses of the patent rolls: Richard II*, PRO (1977) · F. W. Weaver, ed., *Somerset medieval wills*, 1, Somerset RS, 16 (1901), 52–5 · *CIPM*, 19, nos. 982–5

Wealth at death £115 lands valued p.a.; £835 total of cash bequests in will: HoP, *Commons, 1386–1421*, 3.729

Wadham, Nicholas (1531/2–1609), benefactor of Wadham College, Oxford, was probably born at the family seat, Merrifield, near Ilton, Somerset, the only son of John Wadham (d. 1578) and his wife, Joan (d. 1583), daughter of John Tregarthin and widow of John Kellaway. The Wadhams had been at Edge Manor, Branscombe, in south Devon since the late fourteenth century. Sir John Wadham (d. 1412), justice of the common pleas, acquired extensive properties in Devon and Somerset, augmented through the fifteenth century by a series of marriages to heiresses. Nicholas Wadham's grandfather Sir Nicholas (d. 1542) was at various times sheriff of Somerset and Dorset, of Devon, and of Wiltshire. Sir Nicholas's youngest son, also Nicholas (d. 1551), was a member of Thomas Cromwell's household, subsequently holding court office as a gentleman pensioner, and commanding troops in Boulogne from 1544. John Wadham was less prominent than his father, but was sheriff of Somerset and Dorset in 1556–7 and retained a place on the Somerset commission of the peace until his death in 1578.

A brief biography, written before 1637, has Wadham attending Corpus Christi College, Oxford, as a commoner ('commensalis'), evidently not taking a degree. He may also have lodged with the civil lawyer John Kennall, subsequently canon of Christ Church; Kennall was presented to the Wadham benefice of Silverton, Devon, in 1583, and eventually died a Catholic. The same biography has Wadham briefly at court ('vitam Aulicam aliquantisper ingressus est'). He is almost certainly the Nicholas Wadham of Brimpton, Somerset, admitted to the Inner Temple on 9 March 1553 'on the pledge of Richard Baker', shortly to be his brother-in-law. Baker was married to Catherine Tyrell, a stepdaughter of Sir William *Petre, principal secretary to the king. Petre, of Devon origins, a protégé and colleague of Thomas Cromwell, must have known the Wadhams. On 3 September 1555 Nicholas Wadham married Petre's eldest daughter, Dorothy

Nicholas Wadham (1531/2–1609), by unknown artist, 1595

(1534/5–1618), at St Botolph, Aldersgate [see Wadham, Dorothy].

In spite of these court connections Wadham opted for a country life. Almost immediately after the marriage Sir Giles Strangways, married to Nicholas's sister Joan, made over his wardenship of Roche forest in Somerset to be held jointly with him. Wadham and his wife lived with his parents, and under their shadow, until his father died in 1578, at which point his mother moved to the dower house at Edge. Wadham was then appointed to the commission of the peace and to other minor commissions in Somerset. He appears as executor and overseer in the wills of other Somerset gentlemen. Only two personal letters have come to light: one is from Sir Amias Paulet, ambassador in France in 1577, remarking that Wadham was unlikely 'to be envious of our French news' and thanking him for his efforts about the leasing of Paulet's park (Ogle, 48–9); the other is to John Talbot of Grafton, married to Dorothy's sister Katherine—again Wadham had used his good offices in negotiating a lease.

Wadham was a shrewd property manager. By his death he had added lands worth at least £800 per annum to his inherited estate, worth some £3000 per annum, making him 'among the fifty or so richest men in England, and well up in the peerage class' (Stone, 118–19). He was renowned for his hospitality and maintained a magnificent household at Merrifield. Following his father's example, he arranged in his will for a full heraldic funeral, costing £500, and for alms to be distributed widely over the county. His old-fashioned views may help explain his Catholic inclinations, as do his wife's connections. After his death Thomas Moore, a Roman Catholic priest, described him as 'an ancient schismatic', implying that he

attended Church of England worship. However, Wadham evidently generated suspicion. Some time between 1593 and 1596 he was removed from the commission of the peace; at about the same time he began to cede his rights of ecclesiastical presentation to others. (The 'Master Wadham' involved in 1597 in tracking an escaped priest may be his cousin Edward.) He seems never to have been convicted of recusancy, but came close in 1608 when the privy council ordered a 'stay of proceedings' against both Wadhams on that charge. Thomas Moore claimed him as 'dying a Catholic' (Questier, 63).

Nevertheless, Wadham maintained good relations with his protestant neighbours. John Carpenter, the incumbent of Branscombe, dedicated his *Contemplations; for the Institution of Children in the Christian Religion* (1601) to him, remarking on his 'gentle affability with all persons' and his material generosity rather than on any spiritual qualities. Wadham was probably responsible for the fine oak gallery at Branscombe church. The later story that he intended to found a college for English Catholics at Venice seems improbable, if only because the illegality and impracticality of such an action is at odds with Wadham's character. Childless, and with his inheritance due to pass to the children of his three sisters, Wadham was determined to use the additional wealth he had accumulated to perpetuate his name. In 1606 he founded an almshouse at Ilton for eight poor people. He had been setting money aside for the foundation of a college at Oxford for some time, but nothing was put on paper and Wadham's contradictory instructions on his deathbed were to sow confusion, ably resolved by his widow. His contribution was restricted to the financial, amounting to a munificent £19,000. Wadham died at Merrifield on 20 October 1609, aged seventy-seven, and was buried in the Wadham family chapel at St Mary's Church, Ilminster on 21 November.

C. S. L. Davies

Sources C. S. L. Davies, 'A woman in the public sphere: Dorothy Wadham and the foundation of Wadham College, Oxford', *EngHR*, 118 (2003) • T. G. Jackson, *Wadham College, Oxford* (1893) • N. Briggs, 'The foundation of Wadham College, Oxford', *Oxoniensia*, 21 (1956), 61–81 • L. Stone, 'The original endowment of Wadham College', *Wadham College Gazette*, 146 (1959), 118–19 • W. Wyndham, 'The Wadhams and Merifield', *Somerset Archaeological and Natural History Society*, 4th ser., 20 (1935), 1–10 • O. Ogle, ed., *The letter book of Sir Amias Poulet*, Roxburghe Club, 84 (1866), 48–9 • *Genealogical collections illustrating the history of the Roman Catholic families of England: based on the Lawson manuscript*, ed. J. J. Howard, H. F. Burke, and H. S. Hughes, 1 (privately printed, London, 1887) • M. C. Questier, *Newsletters from the archpresbyterate of George Birkhead*, CS, 5th ser., 12 (1998) • will, Wadham College muniments, 10/1/1 • letter from Nicholas Wadham to John Talbot, BL, Add. MS 46457, fol. 99 • F. W. Weaver, ed., *Somerset incumbents* (privately printed, Bristol, 1889) • G. Oliver, *Ecclesiastical antiquities in Devon*, 1 (1840), 87–91 • BL, Add. MS 11402, fol. 135b • PRO, SP 13/Case F/11 • R. Branscombe, *A guide to the church of St. Winifrid Branscombe* (1998), 26–7

Likenesses oils, 1595, Petworth House, West Sussex [see illus.] • carved statue, 1613, Wadham College, Oxford • funerary brass, 1618, St Mary's Church, Ilminster, Somerset • J. Faber senior, mezzotint (after unknown artist), BM, NPG • mezzotint, BM, NPG • oils, versions, Wadham College, Oxford • silver medal, BM

Wealth at death inherited estate to heirs est. £3000 p.a. (£60,000 capital); cash and lands to Wadham College, Oxford, £19,200; money and rent to Dorothy Wadham allegedly £22,200; total therefore £100,000: Stone, 'Original endowment of Wadham College'

Wadia family (*per.* *c.*1730–1893), shipbuilders in India, were Parsi shipwrights, famed for the excellence of their teak ships, and employed by the East India Company in the Bombay dockyard. The first family member to work for the company was **Lowjee Nusserwanjee Wadia** (*c.*1700–1774), who was born at Siganpur, near Surat. Already an esteemed Surat shipbuilder, he moved in 1736 at the request of the Bombay council. Little is known of his antecedents except that he was of good family. His children married well and he was appointed to the Parsi *panchayat* and was loaned Rs 1000 by the government to complete his house. In August 1740, on the death of the English master carpenter, Lowjee replaced him, and from 1764 was referred to as master builder. The mid-eighteenth century saw an increase in shipbuilding to counter Maratha aggression at sea. Lowjee chose the site of the first dry docks to be built in the East, which during the French wars were of paramount importance in keeping the fleet at sea, earning the gratitude of successive admirals. Lowjee built about fifteen ships (nine for private merchants). The second award of a silver rule convinced him, he wrote, that his fifty years were approved as 'good and faithful'; he hoped that 'the encouragement shown by the Hon. Company be continued to my sons' (Wadia, *Bombay Dockyard*, 153). Lowjee was twice married, first to Dinbai, daughter of Bachajee Davar (with whom he had no children), and, second, to Hirabai, daughter of Nowrojee Rutlongee (*d.* 1792), with whom he had at least two sons. Lowjee died at Bombay on 3 July 1774, 'leaving no property than his dwelling house and … Rs 20,000 in cash' (*A Memorial*, 22).

As he had hoped, Lowjee was succeeded by his two sons **Maneckjee Lowjee Wadia** (1720–1792) and **Bomanjee Lowjee Wadia** (1722–1790), who jointly held the post of master builder. By them about nineteen ships were built (fourteen for private merchants; some later transferred to the Royal Navy). In 1783 Admiral Sir Edward Hughes gave them gold medals, and on his recommendation the family was awarded 40 *morahs* of *batty* (rice) grounds at Parel, not finally confirmed until 1795. Both were widely respected men of outstanding integrity. In December 1775 Bomanjee was struck by a British officer, Thomas Troubridge, for insisting that a carpenter, flogged for stealing nails, should have been brought before a JP. Bomanjee's threat to resign prompted all the workmen to leave the dockyard, the dispute only being settled on appeal to Admiral Hughes. Maneckjee, who married Ruttonbai (*d.* 1809), daughter of Sapurjee Gursetjee, died in Bombay on 8 April 1792; Bomanjee, who married Hamabai (*d.* 1789), daughter of Dhunjee Hatoojee, died on 25 April 1790.

In 1792 their respective sons, Framjee Maneckjee Wadia (1749–1804) and **Jamsetjee Bomanjee Wadia** (*c.*1754–1821) succeeded jointly. Framjee's eldest son, Rustomjee Maneckjee (1766–1812), was, from 1801, in charge of the Mazagon dockyard. Rustomjee's second son, Dhunjibhoy Rustomjee (1799–1854) was also a master builder with a distinguished career in Cochin and Calcutta before, in

1837, being appointed head of Mogul Dock, Mazagon (P. & O.'s first Indian dock) until his death. At his death on 15 December 1804 Framjee Maneckjee 'left not a rupee' for the support of his widow, Gulbai (*d.* 1826), daughter of Bomanjee Lowjee, and family (Money, 7). While at Bombay his brother Jamsetjee faced an official inquiry into the suitability of the builder who purchased teak supplies from Gujarat and Malabar. The inquiry not only exonerated him but revealed to the company the benefit of his principled management. (He was said, for example, to have thrown his shoe at a timber merchant who proffered a bribe.) Jamsetjee's portrait (1812) by Edward Nash, editor of the *Bombay Gazette*, depicts him wearing the white robes of the Parsi shipwright, a rule tucked into his sash. He spoke and wrote English perfectly. On 30 May 1802 Admiral Sir Thomas Troubridge, his father's former assailant, wrote to Jamsetjee pledging 'that you will build a 74 gun ship … that will be a pattern to an English builder' (ibid., 11). This was the first ship built for the Royal Navy outside England. In all, five 74-guns, including the much admired *Minden* (1810), were built together with an 84-gun battleship, a sloop, and five frigates. Five ships of over 1200 tons were also built for the company's China trade, in addition to Bengal pilot vessels and private ships. The appearance in England of the *Marquis Cornwallis*, a frigate built for the Bombay marine, sold to the Royal Navy in 1804, won Jamsetjee the support of the Navy Board, which later presented him with a silver cup. A man of spirit, he revealed to friends that the ship went to the British sporting the following motto below her waterline: 'This ship built by a d—d Black Fellow 1800' (Wadia, *The Bombay Dockyard*, 191). A further example of his craftsmanship, the *Foudroyant*, formerly the *Trincomalee* (built in 1817) can still be seen at Hartlepool. Despite praise from the Navy Board, Jamsetjee, unlike his brothers Pestonjee Bomanjee (1758–1816), an associate of Bruce Fawcett & Co., and Hormajee Bomanjee (1766–1816), partner and lifelong friend of Charles Forbes, did not achieve great wealth from his work. Married to Mithibai (*d.* 1827), daughter of Cowasjee Cursetjee Mody, Jamsetjee died on 31 August 1821.

He was succeeded by his eldest son, **Nowrojee Jamsetjee Wadia** (1774–1860), who was born in Bombay on 11 September 1774. He was considered to have 'more science than his father … his drafts have very great merit … [he] testifies the greatest desire to visit the English Yards, but his father cannot spare him' (Graham, 44). In a fifty-year career Nowrojee built four 84-gun warships, two frigates, and about thirty-five vessels for the Bombay marine, some of them steamers as well as vessels for private merchants including opium clippers. He also constructed the 411-ton *Hugh Lindsay* (1829), Bombay's first steamship. Realizing that Bombay could not match European advances in technology, Nowrojee arranged for his son and nephew to visit the English yards at the same time as his cousin, the engineer Ardesir Cursetjee Wadia. The government granting no pensions, he introduced the Dockyard Artisans' Pension Fund. He was married three times: first to Soonabaiom (*d.* 1812), daughter of Pestonjee Bomanjee; second to Manickbai (*d.* 1831), daughter of Bunjorjee Nanabhai Davar, and lastly to Ruttonbai (*d.* 1876), daughter of Jeeranjee Nusseurajee. He was highly esteemed; on his death, at Bombay on 1 November 1860, flags on the ships were flown at half-mast. Nowrojee was described in obituaries as 'plain and unpretending in his habits' (*Telegraph and Courier*, 5 Nov 1860).

The last ship of the line built by the family (in 1848) was supervised by Nowrojee's nephew Cursetjee Rustomjee Wadia (1788–1863), who was born on 1 October 1788, the son of Rustomjee Maneckjee (1766–1812). Cursetjee retired with pension in 1857 (dying on 29 April 1863) and was succeeded by his cousin Jahangir Nowrojee Wadia (1821–1866), who was born on 6 March 1821, the son of Nowrojee Jamsetjee. By the mid-nineteenth century the decline in shipbuilding, the demise of the company and the Indian navy, and determination to employ European builders was discouraging Parsis from training as shipwrights. At Jahangir's early death at Bombay on 21 February 1866 the last of Lowjee Nusserwanjee's descendants employed in the yard was Jamsetjee Dhunjeebhoy (1829–1893), who was born on 13 March 1829, the son of Dhunjeebhoy Rustomjee (1799–1854). On his retirement as 'constructor' in 1885 (the post of master shipbuilder having been abolished in 1883) he was rewarded with 300 acres, the third government grant of land to the family in Bombay. Jamsetjee died on 12 September 1893 and was survived by his wife, Mehorbai, daughter of Dossabhoy Merwajee, until her death in February 1913.

ANNE BULLEY

Sources R. A. Wadia, *The Bombay dockyard* (Bombay, 1957) · R. A. Wadia, *Scions of Lowjee Wadia* (Bombay, 1964) · F. Dosabhai, *The Parsees, their history, manners, customs and religion* (1884) · W. T. Money, *Observations on the expediency of ship-building at Bombay* (1811) · J. Phipps, *A collection of papers relative to shipbuilding in India* (Calcutta, 1840) · *A memorial, descendants and representatives of Monachjee Lowjee and Bomanjee Lowjee deceased relative to the revocation and an exemption from taxes enjoyed by the Lowjee family* (Bombay, 1840) · J. N. Wadia and H. Merwanjee, *Journal of a residence in Great Britain and Ireland* (1841) · W. Kirk, 'Shipbuilding in southern Asian ports', *Mariner's Mirror*, 19 (1933), 460 · M. Graham, *A journal of a residence in India* (1812) · W. Milburn, *Oriental commerce*, 2 vols. (1813), vol. 1, p. 17 · B. Lubbock, *The opium clippers* (1933)
Likenesses E. Nash, drawing, 1812 (Jamsetjee Bomanjee), NMM · Indian paintings (Nowrojee Jamsetjee; Maneckjee Lowjee; Framjee Maneckjee), priv. coll.; repro. in Wadia, *Scions of Lowjee Wadia* · photographs (Cursetjee Rustomjee; Jehangir Nowrojee; Jamsetjee Dhunjeebhoy), repro. in Wadia, *Scions of Lowjee Wadia*
Wealth at death Three grants of land over the space of 150 years in Bombay to Lowjee descendants: R. A. Wadia, *Scions of Lowjee Wadia* (Bombay, 1964); R. A. Wadia, *The Bombay dockyard* (Bombay, 1957)

Wadia, Bomanjee Lowjee (1722–1790). *See under* Wadia family (*per. c.*1730–1893).

Wadia, Jamsetjee Bomanjee (*c.*1754–1821). *See under* Wadia family (*per. c.*1730–1893).

Wadia, Lowjee Nusserwanjee (*c.*1700–1774). *See under* Wadia family (*per. c.*1730–1893).

Wadia, Maneckjee Lowjee (1720–1792). *See under* Wadia family (*per. c.*1730–1893).

Wadia, Nowrojee Jamsetjee (1774–1860). *See under* Wadia family (*per. c.*1730–1893).

Wadmore, James (1782–1853), art collector, was born on 4 October 1782 in Hampstead Road, London, the son of James Wadmore, who worked in the stamp office. He was educated at a school near Greta Bridge, Yorkshire, and joined his father in the stamp office, but resigned this position in order to become a land surveyor. After an apprenticeship to a land surveyor in Highgate, he set up on his own in Lisson Grove.

Wadmore began to collect pictures; his first important purchase was Richard Westall's *Hagar and Ishmael*. In 1815 he inherited a fortune from an uncle. The following year he moved to 40 Chapel Street, Marylebone, where he collected pictures by modern English artists including Turner, David Wilkie, and Thomas Webster, and by old masters; he also built up a good collection of English watercolours, as well as prints, books, and manuscripts.

Wadmore moved to Upper Clapton late in life, and died there at his home, 1 Sheldon Villas, on 24 December 1853. He was buried in Highgate cemetery. After his death his collection of 186 pictures was sold at Christies, but only three of the seventy-five old masters fetched high prices; these included Carracci's *Virgin and Child with the Figure of St Roch* and Gerrit Dow's *Jewish Bride*. His collection of English pictures included George Vincent's *View of Greenwich Hospital from Blackwall Reach*, and three Turners—*Cologne*, *Harbour of Dieppe*, and *Guard Ship at the Nore*—which fetched over 5000 guineas.

CAMPBELL DODGSON, *rev.* ANNE PIMLOTT BAKER

Sources Boase, *Mod. Eng. biog.* · *GM*, 2nd ser., 42 (1854), 85–7

Wadsworth, Alfred Powell (1891–1956), journalist and economic historian, was born at Rochdale on 26 May 1891, the elder son of John William Wadsworth, master tailor, and his wife, Jane Seeley. From Cronkeyshaw School he won a scholarship to the higher-grade school in Fleece Street, later known as the Central School. At fourteen he started as a copyholder in the reading-room of the *Rochdale Observer*. The editor, W. W. Hadley, promoted him to junior reporter two years later and trained him in accuracy and newspaper ethics, lessons which remained with him all his life. A zest for knowledge prompted Wadsworth to join as its youngest member the first tutorial class organized by the Workers' Educational Association, then a young venture with a doubtful future. The class was arranged at Rochdale under R. H. Tawney. Wadsworth developed an eager interest in the economic and social features of British history. While taking a full share of a young reporter's routine duties, he began to specialize in local industrial affairs, and in the paper's monthly literary supplement conducted a notes and queries department to save local antiquarian lore in danger of being lost.

In 1917, already an accomplished craftsman with rapid and accurate shorthand, Wadsworth joined the staff of the *Manchester Guardian*. He won distinction when in 1920 he went to Ireland to report the 'troubles'. An investigation of Black and Tan outrages earned him the warm approval of his editor, C. P. Scott, who promoted him to be labour correspondent. In this capacity he wrote occasional leaders on industrial and labour subjects, and reported fairly and sympathetically in the years of industrial unrest culminating in the general strike of 1926. He held this post for about sixteen years while organized labour was growing in strength and stature and sharpening some of its methods. He married in 1922 Alice Lillian (d. 1955), daughter of Handel Ormerod, coal merchant, of Rochdale; they had one daughter.

On the death of E. T. Scott, C. P. Scott's son, in 1932 Wadsworth became a general economic and political leader writer, but continued to attend the annual conferences of the Labour Party and Trades Union Congress until 1936. He became an assistant editor in 1940 and in 1944 succeeded W. P. Crozier as editor. The circumstances were not propitious. Owing to shortage of staff under war conditions Wadsworth had not been able to take a night off (except on a Saturday) for many months. He now had to write a leader every night, and sometimes two, while maintaining a minutely critical oversight of the paper, without the editorial support that he would have had in peacetime. He worked with a speed and sureness of judgement which impressed all his colleagues.

With the coming of peace the paper only slowly recovered its pre-war fullness. Like its rivals, it was still cramped by newsprint restrictions. It had among provincial papers, though, unrivalled authority as a national and international influence, and Wadsworth chose to concentrate on this dimension rather than on spacious treatment of northern affairs. The policy was found to be justified when the government restraint on newspaper sales ended and the demand for the *Manchester Guardian* rose significantly, the sales increasing each time the newsprint ration was adjusted. Under Wadsworth's editorship they rose from 72,527 a day to 168,773. In September 1952 news appeared on the front page for the first time, an important step in the evolution of the paper from a local to a national.

Wadsworth made his political power felt in the general election of 1945. Although he admired Winston Churchill as the greatest living Englishman, he openly attacked him in his leaders, believing that 'nothing could be worse than another House of Commons in which the Tory party was all-powerful'. He expected a close result in this election, and for this reason advocated electoral accommodation between the Liberals and Labour, though his affinities were certainly with the latter. When Labour won its emphatic victory, he hailed it as the 'Silent Revolution'. In the following five years he gave Labour discriminating support, at times expressing disappointment with its actions. But his long experience with the unions gave him a sympathetic understanding of the Labour Party, even when he criticized its faults. Perhaps his greatest achievement in these years was to rally the intellectual left behind Ernest Bevin's foreign policy, and away from appeasement of Russia. Intellectually he had much in

common with Liberalism, for which the *Manchester Guardian* had done so much, but during his editorship the official link between the paper and the Liberal Party was broken. In the 1950 election Wadsworth was accused of impartial ferocity towards all the party programmes, and in 1951 his dissatisfaction with Labour increased. 'For the next few years at any rate,' he wrote, 'a Churchill Government is, it seems to us, the lesser evil.' It was not that he began to be won over to Conservatism, but rather that he rejected the confrontational politics of 'Bevanism'. He wanted the left to find a settled philosophy again and to reconcile its idealism with the changed economic status of the country.

Besides being a vigilant and outspoken editor, in the C. P. Scott tradition, and creator of the post-war *Guardian*, Wadsworth made his name as an economic historian. Stimulated by Professor George Unwin, he collaborated with Julia Mann (then principal of St Hilda's College, Oxford) in *The Cotton Trade and Industrial Lancashire, 1600–1790* (1931), a masterpiece of enlightening scholarship; it was reprinted in 1967 and 1999. With R. S. Fitton he wrote *The Strutts and the Arkwrights, 1758–1830* (1958). Papers for such bodies as the Rochdale Literary and Scientific Society and the Manchester Statistical Society were the outcome of patient research. The University of Manchester conferred upon Wadsworth the honorary degree of MA in 1933 and of LLD in 1955. He was a governor of the John Rylands Library, Manchester, a visiting fellow of Nuffield College, Oxford, and an enthusiastic member of the International Press Institute.

In an autobiographical note written in 1951 Wadsworth attempted his own epitaph: 'Though journalism was his life Wadsworth would have preferred to be known as an historian' (Ayerst, 614). He saw the life of his day with a historian's perspective. His writing was like the man—straightforward, quick in getting to the point, unpretentious. Though modest in demeanour—'a small, plump, soft-spoken, twinkling man'—he stood out as a strong personality in the sudden crises of a newspaper office, when his firm judgement gave confidence to all his colleagues. Both as an editor and as a man he was an uncompromising opponent of tyranny, whether from the right or the left, and an ardent defender of individual liberty.

Wadsworth had a strong constitution and for most of his life worked twelve hours a day, six days a week. But in 1955–6 he contracted what appeared to be an obscure viral disease; this proved to be incurable, and five days after his official retirement he died at his home, 30 Old Broadway, Withington, Manchester, on 4 November 1956. The issue of the *Manchester Guardian* that carried news of his death told also of the Soviet suppression of the Hungarian revolution, and the Anglo-French preparations for the invasion of Egypt: it was for a day such as this that Wadsworth had done so much to equip the paper as an influential voice of liberal dissent.

LINTON ANDREWS, *rev.* MARK POTTLE

Sources *Manchester Guardian* (31 Oct 1956) · *Manchester Guardian* (5 Nov 1956) · T. S. Matthews, *The sugar pill: an essay on newspapers* (1957) · personal knowledge (1971) · S. E. Koss, *The rise and fall of the*

political press in Britain, 2 (1984) · D. Ayerst, *Guardian: biography of a newspaper* (1971) · *CGPLA Eng. & Wales* (1957)
Archives JRL, corresp. and papers relating to *Manchester Guardian* · JRL, historical collections
Likenesses D. Low, cartoon, repro. in Ayerst, *Guardian* · B. Lundquist, caricature, pen drawing, repro. in Ayerst, *Guardian* · photograph, repro. in Ayerst, *Guardian*
Wealth at death £9280 13s. 10d.: probate, 15 Jan 1957, *CGPLA Eng. & Wales*

Wadsworth, Edward Alexander (1889–1949), painter and printmaker, was born at Cleckheaton, Yorkshire, on 9 October 1889, the only son of Fred Wadsworth (*d.* 1921), a worsted-spinning industrialist whose father, Elymas, had established both Broomfield Mill and the firm E. Wadsworth & Sons. His mother, Hannah, *née* Smith (*d.* 1889), who also came from a family of worsted spinners and was an amateur painter, died of puerperal fever soon after giving birth to Edward. After schooling in Edinburgh at Fettes College, he left for a year in Munich (1906–7)—the cosmopolitan, stimulating Munich of Kandinsky and the magazine *Simplizissimus*—to learn machine draughtsmanship and the German language. These skills were intended for business purposes, but at the Knirr School of Art he experimented with printing, woodcutting, painting, and non-technical drawing. At concerts and the opera he developed a love and knowledge of music. No longer a provincial, and clashing with his father's strong wish that he should succeed him in 'Waddie's Mill', Edward decided to become a painter. In 1908 he went to Bradford School of Art, from where he won a scholarship to the Slade School of Fine Art, London, which he attended from 1909 to 1912. He won first prizes for landscape in 1910 and for figure painting in 1911. On 8 April 1912 he married a violinist, Fanny Mary, daughter of George Eveleigh, banker, of Horncastle, Lincolnshire.

Wadsworth was an artist who could operate on any scale. He painted a large mural in the De La Warr pavilion, Bexhill, Sussex, and he designed the initial letters used by T. E. Lawrence in his *Seven Pillars of Wisdom*. Wadsworth's reputation is based firstly on his pioneering early work as a member of the radical *Vorticists, followed by his advanced abstract paintings of 1930–33; secondly on his Black Country drawings (1919–20); and thirdly on his distinctive tempera paintings of 1922–9 and 1934–44. These evoke the light and ambience of the sea, while tending to exclude large expanses of the sea itself.

On leaving the Slade, where the teaching had been firmly traditional, Wadsworth moved forward rapidly. First fauvism, then Cézanne influenced him, and in 1914 he was called upon to support an English 'futurist manifesto'. Having met Wyndham Lewis, he joined the vorticist group and translated Kandinsky's 'Über das Geistige in der Kunst' for the first issue in 1914 of the magazine *BLAST*. Many of his paintings of this period have been lost, but his series of inventive, striking yet intricate woodcuts of 1914–18 survive in private and public collections, including the British Museum. Wadsworth served with the Royal Naval Volunteer Reserve in the First World War as an intelligence officer on the Greek island of Mudros. Later he was employed on dazzle camouflage. The National Gallery of Canada owns his large oil on canvas *Dazzle-Ships in Drydock at Liverpool* (1919).

In 1920 the Leicester Galleries gave Wadsworth a one-man show. The catalogue introduction was by Arnold Bennett. Wadsworth's angular but legible ink and wash images of Black Country furnaces, quarries, and outlandish slag heaps were acclaimed. In 1921 his father died, leaving him wealthy. Turning his back on the industrial north, he indulged his love of seaside environments in the south of England and the Mediterranean. His first visit to Italy was in 1923. He discovered the medium of tempera as practised by such masters as Giotto, Gozzoli, Fra Angelico, and Cimabue, and he avoided oil paint from then on. Between 1923 and 1929 he produced a superb series of tempera paintings of ports and little seaside harbours. They were first classical, then rococo in style. A group of sophisticated magic realist marine still-life paintings followed. *Fruits de mer* (1926) is in the collection of the Stedelijk Museum, Amsterdam; *Regalia* (1928) was bought by the Tate Gallery.

Between 1930 and 1933 Wadsworth was again in the vanguard of abstraction, joining the international group Abstraction-Création and Paul Nash's more diverse ginger group Unit One. In 1934 he returned to his maritime subject matter. In 1936 he completed two large paintings for the smoking rooms of the ocean liner *Queen Mary*. Because of family connections in Germany he did not become an official war artist, but he accepted election as an associate of the Royal Academy in 1944, not without the heart-searching of a one-time radical. His final more abstract work (1945–9) sometimes shows the influence of Fernand Léger.

Wadsworth was a technical perfectionist who loved to consult books on painting technique, from Cennino Cennini's *Il libro dell' arte* (*c*.1300) to Hilaire Hiler's *Notes on the Technique of Painting* (1934). Having lived and exhibited in Paris in the 1920s, he was unusually alert to developments on the continent. He maintained that he strove for 'joy, tenderness and strength' in his work, above all. In 1929 he moved from London to Dairy Farm (later Dairy House), Maresfield, Sussex. His studio there remained the disciplined centre of his professional life, but he could be convivial, despite a reserved nature. He had many stimulating, distinguished English and foreign friends, mostly fellow artists, who contributed to a stylish, lively social life. He was kind and generous and there could be a twinkle under his dark, shaggy, and somewhat forbidding eyebrows. He was a conscientious letter writer. Powerful, beautiful cars were important to him. Wadsworth died at 29 Cleveland Gardens, Bayswater, London, on 21 June 1949, survived by his wife. One of their devoted daughters died at the age of nine; the other, Barbara, wrote his biography.   MARK GLAZEBROOK

Sources B. Wadsworth, *Edward Wadsworth: a painter's life* (1989) · *A genius of industrial England: Edward Wadsworth, 1889–1949* (1990) [exhibition catalogue, Bradford and London, 12 Oct 1989 – 22 April 1990] · *Edward Wadsworth, 1889–1949: paintings, drawings and prints* (1974) [exhibition catalogue, P. and D. Colnaghi & Co. Ltd, London, 16 July – 16 Aug 1974] · J. Rothenstein, *Modern English painters: Lewis to Moore* (1956) · G. Waldemar, M. Sevier, and O. Zadkine, *Edward*

Wadsworth (Anvers, 1933) · A. Bennett, *Edward Wadsworth: the Black Country* (1920) · M. Glazebrook, *Edward Wadsworth: paintings from the 1920s* (1982) [exhibition catalogue, Mayor Gallery, London, 1982] · *CGPLA Eng. & Wales* (1949) · will, Principal Registry of the Family Division, London, probate department

Archives Tate collection, corresp. with Richard Eurich · Tate collection, letters to Lincoln Jenkins

Likenesses E. Wadsworth, self-portrait, oils, 1911, priv. coll. · A. Allinson, pen and ink, *c.*1914 (*The futurist Wadsworth*), priv. coll. · A. L. Coburn, photogravure, 1916, NPG · W. Lewis, chalk drawing, 1920, Pembroke College, Oxford · photograph, 1936, Hult. Arch. · E. Wadsworth, self-portrait, tempera, 1937–8, priv. coll. · W. Roberts, group portrait, oils, 1961–2 (*The Vorticists at the Restaurant de la Tour Eiffel, spring 1915*), Tate collection; *see illus. in* Vorticists (*act.* 1914–1919)

Wealth at death £17,406 2s. 6d.: probate (limited), 1949/51, resworn (limited)

Wadsworth, James (*c.*1572–1623), Church of England clergyman and Roman Catholic convert, matriculated at Cambridge in 1586 as a scholar of Emmanuel College, where he was a friend and contemporary of William Bedell. He graduated BA in 1590, MA in 1593, and BD in 1600. After ordination, in June 1596, he served as vicar of Tharston, Suffolk, before being appointed rector of Pakesfield (1598–1603) and vicar of Cotton and Great Thornton (1600–07). He also served as chaplain to Bishop Redman of Norwich. He and his wife, Susannah, whom he married in Suffolk, had four children, the youngest of whom was born in 1604. In May 1605 he was appointed chaplain to Sir Charles Cornwallis on his embassy to Spain. In a letter to Bedell he later claimed that his religious views had been unsettled for three or four years before his departure, and his allegiance to the Church of England was further shaken in the course of controversy with English Jesuits at Valladolid. In August 1605 he left the embassy for Salamanca, where he was received into the Roman Catholic church. After a period of theological study at the University of Alcalá de Henares he was granted a pension by the Spanish crown and given employment by the Inquisition. Wadsworth also converted his brother Paul, or Seth, who emigrated to Spain and was appointed consul of the English speaking community at Sanlúcar de Barrameda in 1612. Wadsworth's emotive translation into Spanish of the parliamentary statutes enacted in the wake of the Gunpowder Plot, published in Madrid, gave offence to the British ambassador and embarrassed the Spanish authorities.

Wadsworth's wife, two sons, and two daughters joined him in Spain in 1610. From 1610 to 1620 he kept up a friendly theological debate with William Bedell, who published their correspondence after Wadsworth's death. At Madrid he was tutor in English to the infanta Maria, for whom he may have prepared *Grammar Spanish and English*, published at London in 1622. His unpublished correspondence from 1618 with Sir Robert Phelips provides information about Prince Charles's visit to Madrid in 1623 and his negotiations for the Spanish match. Wadsworth died of consumption on 30 November 1623 and was buried in Madrid. According to the records of the English College, Madrid, his widow Susannah, was still living at Madrid in

1632. Their younger son James *Wadsworth became a government informer who betrayed many of his former Roman Catholic brethren. Wadsworth's apologia, *The Contrition of a Protestant Preacher*, a meditation on Psalm 50, was published posthumously at St Omer in 1625.

G. MARTIN MURPHY

Sources J. W. Stoye, *English travellers abroad, 1604–1667*, rev. edn (1989) · J. Wadsworth, *The English Spanish pilgrime* (1629); facs. edn (1970), 1–5 · *English polemics at the Spanish court: Joseph Creswell's 'Letter to the ambassador from England'*, ed. A. J. Loomie (1993) · A. Loomie, 'Thomas James, the English consul of Andalucia', *Recusant History*, 11 (1971–2), 165–78 · *Third report*, HMC, 2 (1872), appx, pp. 282–4 · G. Burnet, *Life of William Bedell* (1736) · *A true relation of the life and death of … William Bedell*, ed. T. W. Jones, CS, new ser., 4 (1872) · *Memorials of affairs of state in the reigns of Q. Elizabeth and K. James I, collected (chiefly) from the original papers of … Sir Ralph Winwood*, ed. E. Sawyer, 3 vols. (1725), vol. 2, pp. 109, 131, 136 · Venn, *Alum. Cant.*

Archives Som. ARS, letters to Sir Robert Phelips

Wadsworth, James [*pseud.* Diego de Vadesfoote] (*b.* 1604), writer and government official, was the second son and youngest child of James *Wadsworth (*c.*1572–1623), vicar of Tharston, Suffolk, and his wife, Susannah. His father departed for Spain in 1605 as chaplain to the ambassador but left the embassy when he became a Catholic, and after 1610 his wife and children joined him in Andalusia. James the younger attended schools in Spain until 1618, when he entered the Jesuit English College at St Omer in Artois. After four years alongside the sons of English recusants, he joined other former students in a voyage from Calais to Sanlúcar. On 16 August 1622 they were captured by the Dutch, who transferred them to a Hamburg merchant ship headed southward. On 3 September they were captured by Moroccan pirates and held at Salé, near Rabat, until a ransom was pledged for their release and, finally, on 14 November the group reached Seville. Later in 1623 Wadsworth was asked to be an interpreter for courtiers in Prince Charles's entourage in Madrid.

Following the death of Wadsworth's father on 30 November 1623, his older brother, Hugh, and his mother lived on his father's pension, while his two sisters entered convents: Katherine at Lisbon in the Bridgettines, and Mary at Cambrai in the Benedictines. James was granted by Philip IV a captain's commission in the army of Flanders, although he had slight interest in a career on a battlefield, but he enjoyed the use of the title of captain. Late in 1625 he returned to England where he publicly denounced popery and offered his services as a spy to the privy council. Sent to Paris and later Calais, his performance was not successful, for he was imprisoned in both cities. Eventually Wadsworth settled down in London, where he wrote a memoir of his escapades that appeared in 1629 as *The English Spanish Pilgrime, or, A New Discoverie of Spanish Popery and Jesuitical Strategems*. Its popularity led to a second printing in 1630, and for its third he wrote a new prelude called *Further Observations* …. Here he was eager to establish his protestant credentials by warning of the dangers of Spain and St Omer and to dwell on his success with the pirates at Salé in contrast to the Jesuits in Seville. A manuscript by William Atkins, of the original group on the voyage from St Omer, was printed with original evidence to contradict Wadsworth only in 1994. He ended the year 1630 with two new English translations. From an unknown Italian original he produced an essay entitled *The Present State of Spayne* and a French text by Jacques Gaultier appeared in English as *Miles gloriosus, the Spanish Bragadacio*.

For over two decades Wadsworth was a pursuivant, or messenger, of the court of high commission and the privy council. Armed with their warrants, he arrested for a fee recusants and priests, several of whom he knew from his years overseas with Catholic students. In 1635 he was summoned to answer charges of corrupt practices before the high commission but escaped conviction. His petitions for reimbursement by the crown give examples of his activities. In 1634 he sought the costs of 'bringing jesuits and papists to conviction' (*CSP dom.*, 1633–4, 319). In August and October 1643, Captain Wadsworth and two other messengers submitted their expenses for the 'priests indicted and attainted at the Old Bailey since 22 July 1640' (*Fifth Report*, HMC, 102, 109). He produced two more translations in 1640–41: *On the Nature and Quality of Chocolate* from an original by Antonio Colmenero and, under a pseudonym of Diego de Vadesfoote, a guide to the fairs of Europe called *The European Mercury*. However, the fees of a pursuivant attracted him still. In December 1642 his testimony convicted his schoolmate at St Omer, the Jesuit Thomas Holland. He appeared at several other trials, including that of another Jesuit, Henry Morse, in January 1645.

After the civil war the role of the pursuivants declined, so that a contemporary royalist observed an impoverished Wadsworth in 1656 to be a 'renegade, proselyte, turncote of any religion' who lived in Westminster as a 'common Hackney to the basest catchpole Bayliffs' (Sanderson, 491). The date of his death is unknown.   A. J. LOOMIE

Sources 'William Atkins, "A relation of the journey from St. Omers to Seville, 1622"', ed. M. Murphy, *Camden miscellany*, XXXII, CS, 5th ser., 3 (1994), 195–288 · M. Havran, *The Catholics in Caroline England* (1962) · H. Foley, ed., *Records of the English province of the Society of Jesus*, 1–5 (1875–9) · *STC, 1475–1640* · *Fifth report*, HMC, 4 (1876) [House of Lords] · G. Holt, *St Omers and Bruges colleges, 1593–1773: a biographical dictionary*, Catholic RS, 69 (1979) · B. Camm, 'An apostate at St. Omer, 1618–22', *The Month*, 94 (1899), 162–70 · *CSP dom.*, 1628–34 · W. Sanderson, *A compleat history of the lives and reigns of Mary queen of Scotland and of her son and successor James the Sixth* (1656)

Wadsworth, Thomas (1630–1676), nonconformist minister and religious writer, was born in the parish of St Saviour's, Southwark, on 15 December 1630, the son of Thomas Wadsworth, who was a friend of Samuel Bolton, master of Christ's College, Cambridge, and lecturer at St Saviour's. Wadsworth attended school in Southwark, where he was taught by a Mr Woodward. On 22 June 1647 he was admitted as a pensioner to Christ's College, Cambridge, with a Mr Harrison and then William Owtram as his tutor. He graduated BA in 1651 and proceeded MA in 1654. He was elected a fellow of Christ's before Christmas 1652, but resigned his fellowship to take up the position of minister to St Mary's parish, Newington Butts, Surrey, to which he was appointed on 16 February 1653. He was

ordained by the eighth London classis in the church of St Mary Axe.

Young and inexperienced, Wadsworth wrote to Richard Baxter asking for his advice. Baxter later wrote that he 'had long much communication by Letters' with Wadsworth 'before I ever saw his face' (Baxter, foreword, sig. A4). Wadsworth organized his ministry along lines suggested by Baxter: 'with prayers and tears, not only publickly, but from one house to another, I have beseeched you to be reconciled unto God' (*Exhortation*, sig. A3). According to Baxter, to Wadsworth's:

> constant Publick Preaching he added this work of *Personal* and Family Instruction; not only to visit the sick, but to teach and Exhort his Flock in health, to prepare for death, *and work out their Salvation*, To Catechize them, and help them understand the words, and to get down the sweetness and power of the matter upon their hearts.   (Baxter, foreword, sig. A7v)

Wadsworth even 'hired another to help in that work; gave Bibles to the poor People of his Parish, and expended … his Estate on these Works' (*Reliquiae Baxterianae*, 3.95).

Wadsworth published several expanded sermons and treatises, beginning in 1660 with *A Serious Exhortation to an Holy Life*. The same year, however, on 29 September, he was forced to resign the living at St Mary's in favour of James Meggs, who had been sequestered by parliament on 20 June 1643, although he did retain a Saturday morning lectureship at St Antholin's, as well as a Monday evening lectureship at St Margaret's, New Fish Street Hill. On 29 January 1662 he was chosen by the parishioners of St Laurence Pountney in London to fill the perpetual curacy that was in their patronage, but was ejected when the Act of Uniformity came into effect on 24 August 1662. Wadsworth's first wife, whose name is unknown but who was a younger daughter of Henry Hastings from Newington Butts, died during childbirth on 13 October 1661. In November 1663 he married Margaret (d. 1668), daughter of Henry Gibs from Bristol, and widow of Thomas Sharp, a London merchant. Margaret had a son named Thomas from her previous marriage, but she and Wadsworth had no surviving children.

'His health calling him to abide most in the Country', Wadsworth moved to Theobalds in the parish of Cheshunt, Hertfordshire, where he preached privately to a congregation of dissenters (Baxter, foreword, sig. B4). At the request of members of his former parish in Southwark he also quietly gathered a congregation there which met in Globe Alley. Wadsworth divided his time between these two congregations, but took no salary from either, living instead off his own income. He owned lands and properties in Hertingfordbury, Hertfordshire, and Pickle Herring Stairs, Globe Alley, and Deadman's Place, all in Southwark. He was also active in raising money to support the families of ejected ministers.

During the plague of 1665 Wadsworth continued to minister in the London area, and after the fire of 1666 a timber meeting-house was built for his congregation in Deadman's Place. He resumed publishing with *The Immortality of the Soul* and *Faith's Triumphs over the Fear of Death*, both in 1670, and *Separation yet No Schism* (1675). His wife Margaret died on 3 January 1668, and in 1671 he married Anna, daughter of Colonel Markham; they had two sons, Thomas and Nathaniel, and two daughters, Anna and Hester. After Charles II's indulgence of 1672, Wadsworth was licensed on 1 May 1672 to be 'a Presbyterian Teacher' in Jonathan Pritman's house in Theobalds, which was also licensed as a 'Presbyterian Meeting-place' (Urwick, 509).

Several weeks before his death Wadsworth moved from Theobalds back to his house at Pickle Herring Stairs in Southwark. He had suffered for some time from kidney and bladder stones, and was in poor health and constant pain. He died on 29 October 1676 and was buried at St Olave's, Southwark, on 6 November; his wife, Anna, survived him. His funeral sermon was preached by his Theobalds assistant, Robert Bragge, and published as *The Life and Death of the Godly Man* (1676). Several of Wadsworth's works were published posthumously including *Mr. Thomas Wadsworth's Last Warning to Secure Sinners* (1677), *Wadsworth's Remains* (1680), and *A Serious Exhortation unto Self-Examination* (1687).

ALEXANDER GORDON, rev. J. WILLIAM BLACK

Sources Calamy rev. • J. Peile, *Biographical register of Christ's College, 1505–1905, and of the earlier foundation, God's House, 1448–1505*, ed. [J. A. Venn], 1 (1910) • *Walker rev.* • R. Baxter, foreword, in *Mr. Thomas Wadsworth's last warning to secure sinners* (1677) • T. Wadsworth, *A serious exhortation to an holy life* (1660) • *Reliquiae Baxterianae, or, Mr Richard Baxter's narrative of the most memorable passages of his life and times*, ed. M. Sylvester, 1 vol. in 3 pts (1696) • W. Urwick, *Nonconformity in Hertfordshire* (1884) • will, PRO, PROB 11/352, fol. 147 • R. Bragge, *The life and death of the godly man* (1676) • S. Clark [S. Clarke], *The lives of sundry eminent persons in this later age* (1683) • *Calendar of the correspondence of Richard Baxter*, ed. N. H. Keeble and G. F. Nuttall, 2 vols. (1991) • W. Wilson, *The history and antiquities of the dissenting churches and meeting houses in London, Westminster and Southwark*, 4 vols. (1808–14)
Likenesses R. White, line engraving, BM, NPG; repro. in *Wadsworth's remains* (1680) • oils, DWL • oils, Christ's College, Cambridge
Wealth at death £35 in cash bequests; also lands, tenements, and apartments in Hertingfordbury, Hertfordshire; lease of house and wharf at Pickle Herring Stairs, Southwark; several tracts of land and a number of houses in Globe Alley, Southwark; also land and several houses in Deadman's Place, Southwark; also plate left to children: will, PRO, PROB 11/352, fol. 147

Waern, Morton (*fl.* 1754–1756). *See under* Industrial spies (*act. c.*1700–*c.*1800).

Wafer, Lionel (*d.* 1705), surgeon and buccaneer, may have been of Huguenot descent. His knowledge of Gaelic, and a boyhood spent in Scotland and Ireland, may indicate that his father was a Scottish soldier quartered in Ireland, or that the family was one of those 'planted' in Ireland by James I or Oliver Cromwell. Wafer claimed to have been 'very young' (Wafer, 1) when, in 1677, he embarked as surgeon's assistant on the *Great Anne*, an East India Company vessel. After transferring into the *Bombay Merchant* at Sumatra he visited Borneo before returning to England in March 1679. A month later Wafer left for Jamaica to visit his brother; he worked briefly as a surgeon in Port Royal before joining the privateer Captain Edmund Cook. Cook joined a squadron of buccaneering vessels at Golden Island, and it was here that Wafer first met William Dampier. On 5 April 1680 he disembarked as part of a force of some 330 buccaneers who intended to cross the Isthmus of Darien and raid Panama. On entering the Bay of Panama the buccaneers, led by Captain Bartholomew Sharpe, seized several armed vessels, and broke out along the Pacific coast from Costa Rica to southern Chile in search of prizes.

On 17 April 1681, dissatisfied with Sharpe's leadership, Wafer, Dampier, and fifty-two others defected near the Isle of Plate and travelled nearly 600 miles, in three open boats, to reach the coast of Panama. On 5 May, during their subsequent return march overland, Wafer injured his leg when some gunpowder was accidentally ignited. Four days later a slave stole his medicines, his gun, and all his money, and Wafer 'was left among the wild Indians' (Wafer, sig. A3).

The Cuna Indians cured Wafer's injury, and he in turn practised 'Physick and Phlebotomy'. After four months it became clear that the Indians intended Wafer to marry among them. On the pretext of travelling to England to fetch hunting dogs, and promising to return, Wafer escaped to the Atlantic coast where he boarded a French vessel commanded by Captain Tristian. Dampier, and others with whom he had defected, were on the vessel but none of them recognized the surgeon. 'I sat a while cringing upon my Hams among the *Indians*, after their Fashion', he writes in his journal 'painted as they were, and all naked but only about the Waist, and with my Nose-piece' (Wafer, 41–2).

After cruising in the Caribbean with Captain Yanky, Wafer sailed with John Cook in the *Revenge* to Chesapeake Bay, arriving in April 1683. On 23 August he and Dampier sailed from Virginia for the South Sea under Cook, and later, when off Sierra Leone, they transferred into a prize renamed the *Batchelor's Delight*. From 19 March 1684 they kept company with the *Nicholas* and in May they became the first English crews to visit the Galápagos Islands. In October the *Batchelor's Delight* (Captain Eaton) joined the *Cygnet* (Captain Swan), and both crews collaborated in an assault on Paita on 2 November. News of the imminent arrival of the silver fleet at Panama prompted both vessels to join nearly 1000 French and English buccaneers assembled at the Pearl Islands, in February 1685. Here Wafer participated in an indecisive action against a superior Spanish fleet at the end of May.

The *Batchelor's Delight* left the Bay of Panama in July 1685, and cruised north to Cocos Island, south to the Galápagos Islands, and south again to Juan Fernandez, where she spent Christmas 1686. In the autumn of 1687, having replenished once more at the Galápagos, the buccaneers rounded the Horn. As the ship sailed northwards towards the Caribbean, Wafer transferred to a vessel bound for Pennsylvania. After a brief stay in Philadelphia he and two others made for Point Comfort in Virginia where Wafer intended to settle.

On 22 June 1688 Wafer and his companions were arrested by Captain Simon Rowe, commanding officer of HMS *Dumbarton*, as they crossed Chesapeake Bay in a small boat. They were imprisoned in Jamestown on suspicion of piracy. Wafer declared he had been a trader in the West Indies for seven years. He denied stoutly ever having been a privateer and he signed his depositions 'Delawafer'. His defence was weakened, however, by the inventory of his effects taken at the time of his arrest, which included thirty-seven silver plates, some silver lace, and three bags of Spanish money marked with his initials, containing about 1100 dollars. Despite calls by Lord Sutherland of the council of trade and plantation for Wafer to be prosecuted, he was released in September 1689, whereupon he returned to England after an absence of nearly eleven years. In March 1692 it was agreed that Wafer's property should be restored to him, but a royal order withheld £300, plus a quarter of the amount still in Jamestown. The moneys forfeited may have been applied to the building of the College of William and Mary in Williamsburg, Virginia. In November 1693 the council of Virginia invited creditors to come forward, perhaps indicating that full restitution had still not taken place at that date.

In England Wafer established himself as the foremost authority on the Darien isthmus. Dampier deferred to Wafer for descriptions of Darien, claiming he 'is better able to do it than any man that I know' (Dampier, 24). On 2 July 1697, following Dampier's recommendation, Wafer was interviewed by John Locke and the other commissioners of the council of trade and plantation concerning Darien and the projected Scots' colony. Wafer's knowledge of Darien was also sought by the directors of the Darien Company, and the advice he gave them almost certainly influenced the siting of the disastrous Scots' colony in 1698.

Wafer was invited to visit the company's directors in Edinburgh in the spring of 1698. He travelled to Scotland as Mr Brown of London, and stayed with Andrew Fletcher of Saltoun where he met the directors before removing to a secret garret in Edinburgh. Having been engaged by the company, Wafer ordered his affairs in preparation for a voyage to Darien, but a mysterious breach dissolved these plans. In the same year he provided the duke of Leeds with a report on the key ports along America's Pacific rim which might be seized from Spain if they remained shut to foreign traders. His analysis of the strategic and commercial advantages of securing the Chilean ports of Coquimbo and Valdivia, for English vessels rounding the Horn, bears striking resemblance to a scheme Daniel Defoe was to lay before Robert Harley in July 1711.

Lionel Wafer is best known today as the author of *A New Voyage and Description of the Isthmus of America* (1699), a work which retains interest for modern anthropologists because of its detailed descriptions of Darien and the Cuna Indians. In dedicating the second edition (1704) to the duke of Marlborough, Wafer stressed the feasibility of English settlement in Darien, despite the Scots' disaster. A popular figure among the buccaneers, Wafer was a resilient man of unquestionable intelligence, who may have enjoyed connections with the Royal Society after his return to England. Between 1699 and his death in 1705 he lived in London.   JAMES WILLIAM KELLY

Sources BL, Add. MS 33054, Wafer · L. Wafer, *A new voyage and description of the Isthmus of America* (1699) · Basil Ringrose's journal, BL, Sloane MS 3820 · W. Dampier, *A new voyage round the world* (1697) · W. Hacke, ed., *A collection of original voyages* (1699) · B. Ringrose, *Bucaniers of America: the second volume, containing the dangerous voyage and bold attempts of Captain Bartholomew Sharp and others* (1685) · L. E. E. Joyce, 'Introduction', in L. Wafer, *A new voyage and description of the Isthmus of America*, ed. L. E. E. Joyce (1934), xi–lxvii · G. Williams, *The great South Sea: English voyages and encounters, 1570–1750* (1997) · P. T. Bradley, 'Sharp and company: the first of the buccaneers, 1679–82', *The lure of Peru: maritime intrusion into the south sea, 1598–1701* (1989), 103–28 · D. Howse and N. J. W. Thrower, eds., *A buccaneer's atlas: Basil Ringrose's atlas, Basil Ringrose's South Sea waggoner* (Berkeley, CA, 1992) · P. Edwards, *The story of the voyage* (1994) · P. K. Kemp and C. Lloyd, *The brethren of the coast* (1960) · J. Masefield, *On the Spanish main, or, Some English forays on the isthmus of Darien* (1906) · G. Williams, '"The inexhaustible fountain of gold"': English projects and ventures in the south seas, 1670–1750', *Perspectives of empire: essays presented to Gerald S. Graham*, ed. J. E. Flint and G. Williams (1973), 27–52
Archives BL, Add. MS 33054 · BL, Sloane MSS

Wager, Sir Charles (1666–1743), naval officer and politician, was born at Rochester, Kent (not West Looe as is sometimes reported), after the death on 24 February 1666 of his father, Captain Charles Wager (*b.* 1630), who had started life as a boatswain in the merchant service and had become a lieutenant, then a captain, in the navy of the Commonwealth. His paternal grandfather was John Wager (*d.* 1656) of St Margaret's, Rochester, who became a mariner after migrating from Charlton Kings, Cheltenham. Wager's mother was Prudence (*b.* 1640/41), daughter of Vice-Admiral William Goodson, who had come into the Commonwealth navy as captain of a merchant ship converted to a warship and became a renowned officer. With ample justification Wager remarked in 1731, 'On both sides I am related to the navy' (Coxe, 3.116).

Wager's father had promptly accepted the Restoration. He commanded the *Yarmouth* in the fleet that brought Charles II to England and quickly proved to be a capable, trustworthy, well-liked officer of the Royal Navy. Two years after the elder Wager's death, Samuel Pepys heard a friend who had been at Tangier contrast his conduct with that of others who had served in the Strait of Gibraltar, remarking, as Pepys noted, 'that above all Englishmen that ever was there, there never was any man that behaved himself like poor Charles Wager, whom the very Moores do mention with teares sometimes' (Pepys, *Diary*, 9.137). After her husband's death, Wager's mother married a Quaker, Alexander Parker, a London merchant. There was already an older sister, Prudence, and the marriage produced six more children. With his father dead and his maternal grandfather severed from the navy in 1660 (Goodson's radicalism was indelible), young Charles lacked the usual professional advantages of his parentage.

Wager was apprenticed to a Quaker merchant captain of New England named John Hull, son of Tristram and Blanche Hull, both Quakers, of Barnstable, Massachusetts. Tristram was a sea captain and substantial citizen and John operated a transatlantic shipping service and eventually settled in Rhode Island. Wager's mother was a witness when John Hull married Alice Teddeman in the London Quaker Meeting in 1684. When Dr Teddeman Hull, their oldest son, visited London in 1742 he had a letter of introduction from Governor Richard Ward of Rhode Island which stated that he was 'the son of Captain John Hull, late of this colony, under whom Sir Charles Wager was educated' (Kimball, 1.215). There is clear evidence that the mature Wager continued to care about the Hull family, but how much time he spent in New England as a boy is not known.

Lieutenant, captain, and commodore, 1689–1709 The earliest record of Wager's naval service is his listing as lieutenant of the frigate *Foresight* on 1 August 1689. By 1691 he had become first lieutenant of the *Dreadnought* (64 guns). On 8 December that year he married Martha Earning (*b.* 1664x6, *d.* 1748), daughter of Anthony Earning, a Commonwealth navy captain who went into the East India Company's service after 1660 and died while captain of the *George* in the Indian Ocean. Wager was in the *Britannia*, Admiral Edward Russell's flagship, in 1692, took part in the battle of Barfleur, and was made post captain on 7 June.

The year 1693 saw Wager in command of the *Samuel and Henry* (44 guns), in which he convoyed the New England trade. He was captain of the *Newcastle* (48 guns) in 1694, and in 1695, after a month in the *Mary*, he was re-assigned to the *Woolwich* (54 guns). In early March 1696 the *Woolwich* was watching Dunkirk against a rumoured invasion. A month later Wager moved to the *Greenwich* (50 guns) and commanded a small squadron for convoying the tobacco trade home from the Chesapeake. He stayed in the *Greenwich* until she was paid off in late 1699. Finally, on half pay, he lived at Kilminorth near West Looe (in the Watergate cottages near the river), a place where he had already established his family by June 1699 when the ship was under repair at Plymouth. He immediately became a freeman of that borough. As he informed the Admiralty in June 1700, his residence was only 'about ten miles from his Majesty's Yard at Plymouth' and he could 'be at London in four or five days, if required' (PRO, ADM 1/2637–8).

Evidently Wager was eager for employment and eight months later, in February 1701, he was appointed to the *Medway* (64 guns). In the mobilization of January 1702 he was assigned to the *Hampton Court* (70 guns) and remained her captain for the next five years. He commanded a squadron of four of the line and two frigates that cruised between Cape Barfleur and the Isle of Batz in early 1703. Later that year he went to the Mediterranean and in October he came under the command of Admiral George Byng (later Lord Torrington). The occasion having arisen for renegotiating England's treaty with the dey of Algiers, captains Wager and John Baker were the men Byng sent ashore to carry out negotiations and witness the signing. Going again to the Mediterranean in 1704, Wager was with the fleet under Sir George Rooke that captured Gibraltar. The *Hampton Court* was on detached service and missed the battle off Malaga, but she was present at the capture of

Barcelona in 1705. After wintering with Sir John Leake's squadron at Lisbon, Wager took part in the relief of Barcelona and the winning over of Ibiza and Majorca before returning home with Leake in late 1706.

As a senior captain who had commanded detached squadrons Wager was a logical choice for the West Indies command. Appointed in January 1707, he left Spithead in the *Expedition* (70 guns) on 28 March and reached Jamaica on 22 June. A French squadron under Admiral Ducasse was known to be coming from Europe, and Wager's initial deployments were designed to gain intelligence of its arrival and protect trade. He learned in December that Ducasse had gone to Havana, far to leeward; thus the French squadron (ten of the line) could neither surprise Jamaica nor shield the galleons at the isthmus, and if those galleons were to follow their usual practice of returning to Cartagena before proceeding to Havana, Wager would have a chance to intercept them after they loaded Peruvian silver at Portobello. The *Expedition*, *Kingston* (60 guns), and *Portland* (50 guns) plus a fireship left Port Royal in time to attain, on 23 May 1708, a position about 36 miles west of Cartagena.

Five days later seventeen ships appeared to the southwest. Most proved to be armed; the broadsides of the three largest matched those of Wager's squadron. A shift of wind direction prevented the Spanish from steering for Cartagena. Though forced to tack to the northward, they did not try to flee; rather, they formed a loose line of battle under easy sail: the admiral in the *San Josef* (64 guns) in the centre; the vice-admiral, also in a 64-gun ship, in the rear; and the rear-admiral in the *Santa Cruz* (50 guns) in the van, the large warships spaced about half a mile apart with armed merchant ships in between. The Spanish admiral evidently did not believe that the small British squadron would dare oppose this force.

Wager, however, did not hesitate. He ordered the *Kingston* to attack the vice-admiral and the *Portland* to attack the rear-admiral. The former closed sluggishly and the latter held back while Wager bore down on the admiral. The *Expedition*'s guns roared just as the sun was setting and the fighting continued as darkness fell. Suddenly, an hour and a half into the engagement, the *San Josef* blew up. She sank instantly, carrying the admiral, officers, passengers, and crew—almost 700 in all—to the bottom along with most of the registered silver. Less than half a pistol shot away, Wager's ship was showered with large planks and fiery splinters, but the greatest hazard came from the wash of the blast when it flooded through the gun ports. As the crew feverishly put out fires and worked the pumps, the Spanish squadron scattered; the moon had not yet risen, but Wager could discern the shadow shape of a large ship not far off and steered for it. It was the *Santa Cruz*. His first broadside blasted through her stern and took down the mizzen yards. Unable to manoeuvre and observing that the other British men-of-war had been drawn by the gunfire, the Spanish rear-admiral surrendered. Total British losses were six killed and eleven wounded, all in the *Expedition*. The *Santa Cruz* carried a great deal of unregistered treasure, the property of passengers and private merchants.

Wager's flagship, having suffered damage, taken aboard 300 prisoners, and supplied a prize crew for the *Santa Cruz*, was unable to act against the remaining Spanish ships. He expected that they would turn back towards Cartagena, and just before sunrise he saw them. He signalled the *Kingston* and *Portland* to chase, a signal he had to repeat when, to his consternation, they broke off. The Spanish vice-admiral barely managed to find refuge in shoal waters. Back at Port Royal, Wager convened a court martial that deprived both captains, Timothy Bridges and Edward Windsor, of their commands. The Spanish authorities were so shocked by the attack that for the rest of the war Peruvian silver had to be transported in more difficult ways.

Wager returned to England a rich man. He also came home a rear-admiral, the promotion having occurred by seniority on 19 November 1707. His wealth stemmed chiefly from the silver on the captured galleon, its value estimated at over £60,000, but also from his flag share of other prizes taken in the West Indies. Nevertheless Wager gained the merchants' praise for his conduct in protecting their trade. The action against the galleons made him a hero and he was knighted on 8 December 1709. At Portsmouth he was nominated for a by-election to parliament and was elected on 23 January 1710.

Admiral and diplomat Notwithstanding the tory landslide Wager was re-elected at Portsmouth in 1710, but the tory-dominated house overturned the result on petition. As a firm whig he could no longer expect an important command. Having spent all but two of the last twenty years in sea service and now possessing fame and fortune, he was prepared to spend the rest of his life ashore. There is no record of his residing again at Kilminorth though he served as MP for West Looe from 1713 to 1715.

Two days after Queen Anne died Wager was ordered to take charge of the ships at Portsmouth, and in December 1714 he was ordered to go out to the Strait of Gibraltar and assume command of the Mediterranean Fleet. Instead he opted for civil employment ashore; he became comptroller of the navy, at the head of the Navy Board. In January 1715 he was once again elected MP for Portsmouth. Three years later, in March 1718, he moved to the Board of Admiralty, where he remained until almost the end of his life; his tenure on that board, twenty-four consecutive years, was longer than anyone else's in the eighteenth century. In 1720 Wager leased Hollybush, a stately brick house, evidently rebuilt in the Queen Anne style (demolished 1884) and situated at the south-east corner of Parson's Green, Fulham. He spent twenty-two years there and seems to have loved the place. He remained on the list of admirals and advanced by seniority. Except for a moment in 1722 when he was appointed to take a squadron to Lisbon (the mission was cancelled), he did not hoist his flag until 1726.

Wager then began a period of intensive sea service. He commanded a large battle fleet sent to the Baltic to protect Sweden and Denmark from the threat of a recently mobilized Russian fleet. Stopping first at Copenhagen, he met with the court and completed arrangements for co-operation with the Danish navy. His report of 30 April 1726 evoked a glowing response from the secretary of state, Viscount Townshend:

> his Majesty has commanded me to let you know from Him, that he was before persuaded you was a very good Admiral, but he now sees that you are likewise an able Minister. All the answers you gave to the questions proposed to you at the Conference with the Danish Council were extremely right. (PRO, SP 42/81, fol. 47)

After calling on the Swedish court, Wager took his twenty ships of the line to Reval. He had orders to engage and destroy the Russian fleet if it came out. A frustrated and angry tsarina felt compelled to demobilize it instead. To reassure Sweden the British fleet stayed at Reval all summer, losing many men to sickness, and did not enter the Thames until 1 November.

Within less than two months Wager was ordered back to sea; his destination was Gibraltar, against which the Spanish were preparing a siege. He arrived on 2 February 1727 with six ships of the line, two cruisers, two bomb-vessels, and additional troops for the garrison. The fleet helped cover the land approaches (Wager ordered two frigates and a bomb-vessel to 'the back of the Hill') and ensured resupply. Britain and Spain were undoubtedly at war. At one point in early May there was a furious artillery exchange, but usually the actions were cautious and desultory. It was chiefly a naval war, with prizes taken. The main burden was borne by Francis Hosier's fleet in the Caribbean, which suffered losses to tropical disease while successfully accomplishing its mission of preventing the galleons from leaving Cartagena. The Spanish king, destitute of the silver needed for his diplomatic commitments, agreed to a cessation of arms in mid-June, but gave no indication of actually yielding. Finally, in early March 1728, Spain agreed to a convention and Wager's fleet could be ordered home; he arrived on 9 April after sixteen months abroad.

Wager resumed his regular attendance at the Admiralty board, but in May 1729 he was ordered to take command of thirty-three ships, which were soon joined by fourteen Dutch. This huge squadron never left Spithead and was popularly ridiculed as the 'stay-at-home fleet'. It was assembled because the court of Spain was acting as if the convention meant nothing and France, though an ally in this matter, was doing nothing about it. Parliament was dangerously impatient. The fleet remained in readiness until it was learned that Spain would sign a firm treaty.

Wager's next and last deployment as a fleet commander arose from provisions of that treaty (signed at Seville on 9 November 1729). It confirmed the Spanish queen's title to certain parts of Italy, which she assigned to her son, Don Carlos; a right to install Spanish garrisons was also obtained. It seemed advisable to have a strong British fleet alongside the Spanish when the troops were to be landed at Leghorn. With Wager's flag in the *Namur* (90 guns), the British fleet entered Cadiz Bay on 1 August 1731, and after many grand entertainments and reciprocating invitations, moved into the Mediterranean. The mission at Leghorn was accomplished without incident but only after much delay, so Wager did not get back to England until 10 December 1731. Upon arrival he reported his sense of 'pleasure to have a success where doubtful' (PRO, SP 42/82, fol. 395). Thus, for one brief moment this man who had blasted and captured galleons, whose thoughts had been and would continue to be focused on strategies for crushing the Spaniards, had done them good service, with cordiality reigning on both sides.

Between April 1726 and December 1731 Wager had spent as many months flying his flag as he spent ashore. The missions he was asked to execute all involved diplomatic discretion as well as strategic acumen. In 1732, in a letter to a Gloucestershire acquaintance from the Admiralty office, he remarked that for many years he had been inclined to retire. 'But', he continued,

I have been sent on several expeditions (not by my own choice), wherein I have succeeded so well, as to have the King's approbation, and very like may be put, in case of a Vacancy, at the head of this Board. (*Gloucestershire Notes and Queries*, 1, 1881, 120)

Evidently he believed that his elevation, if it occurred, would stem from his successes as a fleet commander and diplomat, not his long experience in naval administration.

First lord, 1733–1742 When Lord Torrington died in January 1733, Under-Secretary Delafaye reported to a colleague: 'Every body looks upon Sir Charles Wager as the person who will now be at the head of the affairs of the navy; as indeed I may say he has been for some time' (Coxe, 3.128). It seems that Wager's administrative knowledge and talent did matter. The official appointment as first lord was dated 21 June 1733. He was popular enough to be nominated and elected MP for Westminster in 1734.

Besides administrative capacity, Wager brought some important assets to the office. His character as a trusted senior admiral tended to subdue the incipient factions of the officer corps. The most prominent example of his candid professionalism was the strong plea he made to the leading ministers in December 1738 that Edward Vernon should be given the West Indies command, notwithstanding his unrelenting opposition in parliament. Wager was also a 'Parliament man', as he described himself to Sir Robert Walpole (Cholmondeley [Houghton] MS, 1881). In him Walpole had a staunchly loyal (they were personal friends as well as closely co-operating ministers of state) spokesman in the House of Commons who was well liked, well informed, and widely trusted; it was an advantage that Wager was not made a peer. Finally, no other first lord of the eighteenth century had so comprehensive a knowledge of maritime geography, seaborne commerce, and colonial circumstances. It seems that when anyone in government needed an opinion touching these subjects Wager was asked. Many of his responses, most of them written in his own hand, have survived (Vernon–Wager MSS); he was, in effect, a one-man bureau of maritime intelligence.

Wager's reputation has suffered from a profoundly mistaken idea that the navy was then at a low ebb. In reality its numerical preponderance over other navies was greater than at any other time in the century, and its dockyard facilities, overseas bases (Wager was much involved in the development of new bases in the Caribbean), victualling organization, and central co-ordination were by far the most elaborate and advanced. Although British warship design was inferior to French in some respects, the real problem was an insufficiency of the versatile and seaworthy 60-gun ships, a class that Wager's Admiralty had chosen to augment during the 1730s but, as wartime experience would show, not aggressively enough.

The great unsolved problem was manning. In May 1731 Wager had remarked:

we have no difficulty but in getting men; ... our Country being such a free Country, that every man does what he pleases: by reason of which, this Nation will be lossd [*sic*] one time or other, if it wont admit of a remedy. (PRO, SP 42/82, fol. 137)

Upon the outbreak of war the problem rapidly grew severe, and Wager, strongly encouraged by Admiral Sir John Norris, pressed for legislative measures; the government introduced bills to facilitate naval manning and Walpole supported them, but parliament would not pass anything meaningful.

The strategy for defeating Spain, insisted upon by the duke of Newcastle, called for capturing a major objective in the West Indies, and thus a large fleet and army had to be sent to a region where tropical diseases were rife. Wager was not confident; he feared complications, and well knew the price of delay in that climate. He preferred strategies that could frustrate Spanish silver shipments while employing smaller forces. His favourite was to threaten the Peruvian coast from the 'South Sea'. The famous voyage of Commodore George Anson, who sailed from England in 1740, was a result of Wager's advocacy.

The assault on Cartagena failed mainly because the forces succumbed to disease. Even before the expedition left England disease took its toll; the typhus epidemic of 1740—the worst of the century—ravaged newly recruited seamen and spread through the fleet, seriously aggravating the manning problem and delaying departure. The profound disappointment of a public that had never doubted success was played upon by the fervid opposition to Walpole, and eventually (though not in the eighteenth century) Wager's reputation was injured.

Claims that Wager had grown too old for his responsibilities can neither be proved nor disproved, but may be doubted. A captain who attended the great debate of 13 February 1741 on whether to petition the king to remove Walpole from office observed: 'Sir Charles Wager is as Hearty as I ever knew Him, spoke in the motion ... at four in the morning, tho He had been there from seven the morning before'. On that occasion Wager issued a challenge, saying that if there were any mismanagements 'in the Office of Admiralty, He & the rest of the Board ought to answer it at their own peril, & not Sir Robert' (BL, Egerton MS 2529, fol. 122). He was fit enough to command the king's channel crossings in 1740 and 1741. (Wager's decision to turn back to Holland on a stormy night in December 1736 had probably saved the whole entourage.) Rumours that he was inattentive may be offset by his record of steady attendance at the board, cabinet meetings, in parliament, and by much else.

The king's insistence on having Wager see him across the water in May 1741 was unfortunate politically because the voyage coincided with the Westminster election. Wager was still popular and his presence during the polling might have prevented the surprise nomination of Edward Vernon (who, in the West Indies, knew nothing about it and later apologized to Wager). As it happened the bailiff pre-emptively closed the poll, thus provoking a riot and inviting a challenge. The fiasco, which culminated in a voiding of the election on a very close vote in the House of Commons, contributed notably to Walpole's loss of parliamentary control. The year 1741 also witnessed some key strategic failures and in January 1742 Wager offered to resign as first lord. The king refused, but very soon after (11 February) his resignation was accepted when it became clear that Walpole was arranging to leave office.

Final year and character In December 1742 Wager was appointed treasurer of the navy, a handsome sinecure which served as a pension. He remained in parliament, having been elected for West Looe. He was reportedly living at Stanley House, Chelsea, when he died, peacefully, on 24 May 1743. Francis Gashry, long his right-hand man of business, arranged the monument in Westminster Abbey, and he was buried in the north cross of the abbey on 30 May. His chief heir was Charles Bolton, son of his sister, Prudence. His widow, Martha, was executor. They had no children, but numerous relatives, many stemming from his half-sisters, all of whom he is said to have helped financially or by appropriate patronage recommendations. Yet Wager was also known for spreading his generosity very widely, to individuals in need as well as philanthropic organizations.

When Wager died Horace Walpole observed that he had 'left the fairest character' (Walpole, *Corr.*, 2.245–6), a judgement supported by every scrap of surviving evidence. A remembrance recorded many years later by Arthur Onslow, the respected speaker of the Commons, remains highly instructive:

> He was of the most gentle and humane disposition I ever knew, and spent almost the whole he got in generous acts of charity and compassion. I had a long and intimate acquaintance with him, and have seen where his temper has been tried by much provocation, but I never saw him discomposed. He had a very good understanding, great plainness of manners, and a steadiness of courage that no danger could daunt, with the same calmness in it that he shewed in the most ordinary acts of his life. He was indeed a person of most extraordinary worth, and the world bore him a respect that was due to it. His father was a captain of a man of war before the restoration, and very likely after that: but dying when this son was young, and the mother marrying a Quaker, he was bred up among that people; by which he acquired the simplicity of his manners, and had much of their fashion in his speech as well as carriage. And all this, with his particular roughness of countenance, made the

softness of his nature still more pleasing, because unexpected at first.   (*Bishop Burnet's History*, 5.390)

Lady Wager died on 7 April 1748 and was buried next to him, in the north cross of Westminster Abbey.

DANIEL A. BAUGH

Sources D. A. Baugh, 'Sir Charles Wager', *Precursors of Nelson: British admirals of the eighteenth century*, ed. P. Le Fevre and R. Harding (2000), 101–26 · T. Lediard, *The naval history of England*, 2 vols. (1735) · PRO, SP 42/81–83 · E. Cruickshanks, 'Wager, Charles', HoP, *Commons, 1715–54* · L. Cong., manuscript division, Vernon–Wager MSS, Peter Force collection · J. L. Chester, ed., *The marriage, baptismal, and burial registers of the collegiate church or abbey of St Peter, Westminster*, Harleian Society, 10 (1876) · J. O. Austin, *The genealogical dictionary of Rhode Island: comprising three generations of settlers who came before 1690* (1887) · *Bishop Burnet's History* · *Manuscripts of the earl of Egmont: diary of Viscount Percival, afterwards first earl of Egmont*, 3 vols., HMC, 63 (1920–23) · W. Coxe, *Memoirs of the life and administration of Sir Robert Walpole, earl of Orford*, 3 vols. (1798) · CUL, Cholmondeley (Houghton) MSS, 1784, 1786, 1807, 1881 · J. F. Chance, *The alliance of Hanover* (1923) · G. S. Kimball, ed., *The correspondence of the colonial governors of Rhode Island, 1723–1775*, 2 vols. (1902–3) · [E. Vernon], *Some letters to an honest sailor* (1746) · B. Capp, *Cromwell's navy: the fleet and the English revolution, 1648–1660* (1989) · J. D. Davies, *Gentlemen and tarpaulins: the officers and men of the Restoration navy* (1991)
Archives BL, corresp. and papers, Add. MSS 19028–19031 · BL, official corresp., King's MSS 57–59 · L. Cong., corresp. and papers | BL, corresp. with duke of Newcastle, Add. MSS 32688–32992 · CUL, Cholmondeley (Houghton) MSS, letters to Walpole · CUL, letters to Sir Robert Walpole · L. Cong., Vernon–Wager MSS, Peter Force collection · NMM, corresp. with Edward Vernon · NRA, priv. coll., letters to first Earl Waldegrave
Likenesses G. Kneller, oils, 1710, NMM · T. Gibson, oils, *c.*1731, NMM · J. Faber junior, mezzotint, 1732 (after T. Gibson, *c.*1731), BM, NPG · P. Scheemakers, relief medallion on monument, 1743, Westminster Abbey · J. Landseer, line engraving, pubd 1805 (after T. Gibson), NPG · Dahl, portrait · White, engraving · I. Wood, portrait
Wealth at death very wealthy, though much given away to charity; wife inherited a manor near Kilminorth: Cruickshanks, 'Wager, Charles'

Wager, Lawrence Rickard [Bill] (1904–1965), geologist and explorer, was born on 5 February 1904 at Batley, Yorkshire, elder son of Morton Ethelred Wager (1871–1939), headmaster of Hebden Bridge secondary school, and his wife, Adelina, *née* Rickard (1876–1916). Wager attended his father's school and Leeds grammar school. He proceeded to Pembroke College, Cambridge, and took a first class in the natural sciences tripos (part one, 1925; part two, geology, 1926). Elected to a Goldsmiths' Company research studentship he undertook research at Cambridge until 1929 when he was appointed lecturer in the geology department at Reading University.

During the next ten years Wager carried out extensive explorations in east Greenland; he overwintered there as a member of Gino Watkins's British Arctic air route expedition in 1930–31. He was a member of the Scoresby Sound committee's second east Greenland expedition under Ejnar Mikkelsen in 1932, and, from July 1935 until August 1936, he led his own British east Greenland expedition. It was during these expeditions that Wager commenced his classic studies of the Skaergaard layered basic igneous intrusion, work later to be extended in the field during his east Greenland geological expedition in the summer of 1953.

Lawrence Rickard Wager (1904–1965), by Walter Stoneman

An outstanding mountaineer and climber, Wager was chosen to join the 1933 Everest expedition, led by Hugh Ruttledge. With Percy Wyn-Harris, he reached a height of some 28,000 feet in the final attempt to reach the summit without the use of extra oxygen. On 12 October 1934 he married Phyllis Margaret (*b.* 1912), daughter of Edgar Worthington, secretary of the Institution of Mechanical Engineers. She was his constant partner, and accompanied him on his 1935–6 Greenland expedition. They had two sons and three daughters, forming a very close-knit family.

After distinguished war service as squadron leader in the photographic interpretation section of the Royal Air Force, a position which entailed some duty in Arctic Russia, Wager was appointed in 1944 to the chair of geology at Durham in succession to Arthur Holmes. He was elected FRS in 1946 and in 1950 moved to the chair at Oxford where he created an outstanding research department and was a professorial fellow of University College.

Wager's work with various collaborators on the Skaergaard intrusion is characterized by an attention to fine detail that has ensured its place as a keystone of petrological thought, enshrined in a lengthy memoir (with W. A. Deer) in *Meddelelser om Grønland* (1939), and supplemented by many subsequent published papers. The extension to other cases of principles established in his Skaergaard work culminated in the publication (with G. M.

Brown) of his book *Layered Igneous Rocks* in 1967, shortly after his death. While more recent opinion might assign a lesser role to convection currents in the formation of layered intrusions than Wager envisaged, he was beginning to think in terms of convective circulation within the earth as a mechanism for continental drift, a process in which he believed at a time when adherence to Alfred Wegener's hypothesis was unfashionable. Sadly, he did not live to see the full development of the plate-tectonics paradigm. The time dimension in geology fascinated Wager and he set up in Oxford the first laboratory in Britain concerned with isotope geochemistry and radiometric age determination.

As a teacher Wager exerted a profound influence through his research students, who became imbued with his enthusiasms and high standards. As a formal lecturer he was less effective, but few ever took greater pains in the preparation of their material.

Bill Wager was one of the finest geological thinkers of his generation and his influence upon his science was deep and lasting. He became concerned about scientific publication in his fields and was the driving force behind the establishment of the journals *Geochimica et Cosmochimica Acta* in 1950 and *Journal of Petrology* in 1960. He was also active in promoting international collaboration in the geological sciences. A Wager medal, awarded quadrennially, was instituted in his memory by the International Association of Volcanology and Chemistry of the Earth's Interior. The full breadth of Wager's geological expertise was apparent only to those who worked closely with him in research or on scientific committees. He was a single-minded and exacting team leader; it was not always easy to work with him but the experience was uniquely rewarding. He set the highest standards and maintained them himself; honesty and straightforwardness were equally important in both his personal and scientific life. Wager's work was recognized by the award of the Lyell fund (1939), the Bigsby medal (1945), the Lyell medal (1962), all from the Geological Society of London, and the Spendiarov prize from the International Geological Congress (1948). For his achievements in exploration Wager received the Polar medal (1933) and the Mungo Park medal of the Royal Scottish Geographical Society (1936).

In appearance, Wager was short and stocky, with an upright bearing and elegance of movement, and he had a beautiful speaking voice. In manner he was modest yet confident; shy and reserved with those he knew less than well but displaying warmth, humanity, and understanding towards those privileged to be counted his close friends. He was proud of his Yorkshire roots and the family enjoyed time at their farmhouse, Sawyersgarth, in Littondale, Yorkshire, where Wager did much of his thinking and writing, away from the distractions of his Oxford department. He died suddenly, at 63 Whitehall Court, while visiting London on 20 November 1965. Following cremation at Oxford his ashes were scattered at Sawyersgarth.   E. A. VINCENT

Sources J. Hargreaves, *L. R. Wager, a life, 1904–1965* (1991) · E. A. Vincent, *Geology and mineralogy at Oxford, 1860–1986* (1994) · *The Times*

(22 Nov 1965) • W. A. Deer, *Memoirs FRS*, 13 (1967), 359–85 • personal knowledge (2004) • private information (2004) • *CGPLA Eng. & Wales* (1966)

Archives Oxf. U. Mus. NH, corresp. and papers; geological specimens, scientific MSS, and corresp.; research notes and papers • priv. coll., field notebooks and expedition diaries **Likenesses** W. Stoneman, photograph, RS [*see illus.*] • photographs, priv. coll.; repro. in Hargreaves, *L. R. Wager* **Wealth at death** £9477: probate, 1 March 1966, *CGPLA Eng. & Wales*

Wager, Lewis (*d.* 1562), playwright, is of unknown origins. He first appears as a Franciscan friar in the Oxford convent, where he became a subdeacon on 21 July 1521. On 24 March 1536 he received a special dispensation to wear the habit of a Franciscan beneath the garb of a secular priest; two years later, the houses of the friars in Oxford were suppressed. Some time before 1538 the Church of England clergyman and playwright William *Wager (1537/8?–1591) was born, who may very probably have been Wager's son. On 5 April 1560 Wager became rector of the parish of St James Garlickhythe, London. He died over two years later, and was buried on 18 July 1562 in his parish. His property was assigned to his widow, Elenore.

The only work which is certainly by Wager, *A new enterlude … of the life and repentaunce of Marie Magdalene, not onlie godlie, learned and fruitefull, but also well furnished with pleasaunt myrth and pastime, very delectable for those which shall hear or reade the same*, was entered in the Stationers' register late in 1566 by John Charlewood, who printed it in 1566 and 1567. The play, doubled for four actors, was acted at the universities, and was influenced by Calvin's 'Institutes'. The Stationers' register attributed the fragmentary interlude 'The Cruel Debtor', entered about March 1566, to Wager (without forename), but this may be the William Wager who is thought to be his son. PETER HAPPÉ

Sources G. Hennessy, *Novum repertorium ecclesiasticum parochiale Londinense, or, London diocesan clergy succession from the earliest time to the year 1898* (1898), 248 • Emden, *Oxf.*, vol. 4 • M. Eccles, *Brief lives: Tudor and Stuart authors* (1982), 123–4 • W. H. Phelps, 'The date of Lewis Wager's death', *N&Q*, 223 (1978), 420–21 • P. W. White, 'Lewis Wager's *The life and repentaunce of Marie Magdalene* and John Calvin', *N&Q*, 226 (1981), 508–12 • W. W. Greg, *A bibliography of the English printed drama to the Restoration*, 4 vols. (1939–59) • Arber, *Regs. Stationers* • P. W. White, *Reformation biblical drama in England* (1992) • P. Happé, 'The protestant adaptation of the saint play', *The saint play in medieval Europe*, ed. C. Davidson (1986), 205–40

Wager, William (1537/8?–1591), Church of England clergyman and playwright, was probably born in 1537 or 1538 (in 1579 he testified in chancery that he was '41 yeres and upwardes'), and was almost certainly the son of the playwright Lewis *Wager (*d.* 1562). Although Greg and Chambers refused to accept that W. Wager of two title-pages was necessarily the same person as William Wager, the circumstantial evidence remains persuasive.

Of Wager's education nothing is known. Eccles suggests that, given Wager's strong protestantism, he may have studied abroad during Mary's reign. On 26 October 1562 he married Ellen Godson at St James Garlickhythe, London (where Lewis Wager had been rector). By January 1567 four children had been baptized in the parish, of whom

two boys can be traced: Edward at Magdalene College, Cambridge, and Thomas at St John's College, Oxford.

Wager became rector of St Benet Gracechurch on 22 July 1567. He also held the living at St Michael Queenhithe, and the rectory of Cradley in Herefordshire. He was licensed to preach, as a lecturer, in any London parish from 6 May 1579, at a stipend of £8 per annum, and was known for his strong protestantism—his 'hot words' and anti-papist attacks (Seaver, 80, 209). This is a link with the plays which can be attributed to him.

The two plays bearing the name W. Wager are polemical protestant interludes. *Enough is as Good as a Feast* shows the tragic, but sinful, downfall of Worldly Man, an extortioner who dies refusing grace. It was doubled for seven actors, and influenced by Tyndale and Latimer. It has seventy-four lines in common with the anonymous *Trial of Treasure* (1567), and is valued as developing the conventional form of the interlude. Further experimentation continued with *The Longer thou Livest the More Fool thou art*, entered in the Stationers' register in April 1569. It was arranged for performance by four actors and was especially enlivened by the musical fool, Moros, who at one point sings 'the foot of many songs as fools were wont'.

In public affairs, Wager earned praise for his preaching and was active in pastoral care. In 1569 John Sturgeon, haberdasher, bequeathed him and his churchwardens an annuity of 40s. In 1573 he was appointed a governor of the queen's new grammar school at Barnet, and two years later he is found hearing petitions from inmates of three London prisons. His achievements suggest he was the 'Master Wager' who joined two wardens of the Stationers' Company on 4 September 1589 to receive the entry of a ballad on the assassination of Henry III of France (Arber, *Regs. Stationers*, 2.530). He was buried at St Benet's on 29 March 1591.

Two fragments of a play called 'The Cruel Debtor', entered in the Stationers' register about March 1566 as by Wager, have survived, but as there is no forename in the record, the play may be the work of either William or Lewis (who had died in 1562). A further play attributed to W. Wager, *Tis Good Sleeping in a Whole Skin*, was said to have been burnt by William Warburton's cook in the eighteenth century. Greg has demonstrated that the former attribution of *Tom Tyler* and *The History of the Trial of Chivalry* go back to a palpable error by Edward Phillips in 1675 (Greg, 'Dramatic bibliographers', 325–7). Wager's reputation as a dramatist is now based upon the two extant lively and challenging polemical interludes which have appeal as vigorous examples of their genre, and which were, no doubt, acceptable, as well as contributory, to the expanding protestant culture of their time. PETER HAPPÉ

Sources M. Eccles, 'William Wager and his plays', *English Languages Notes*, 18 (1981), 258–61 • G. Hennessy, *Novum repertorium ecclesiasticum parochiale Londinense, or, London diocesan clergy succession from the earliest time to the year 1898* (1898), 248 • W. W. Greg, *A bibliography of the English printed drama to the Restoration*, 4 vols. (1939–59) • W. W. Greg, 'Dramatic bibliographers', *Malone Society Collections*, 1/4–5 (1911), 324–40 • P. S. Seaver, *The puritan lectureships: the politics of religious dissent, 1560–1662* (1970) • W. W. Greg, *Licensers for the press, &c. to 1640: a biographical index based mainly on Arber's 'Transcript of the* registers of the Company of Stationers', new ser., 10 (1962), 93 · Arber, *Regs. Stationers* · E. K. Chambers, *The Elizabethan stage*, 4 vols. (1923) · Venn, *Alum. Cant.* · Foster, *Alum. Oxon.*, 1500–1714 [Thomas Wager] · W. C. Hazlitt, *Hand-book to the popular, poetical and dramatic literature of Great Britain* (1867), 637 · STC, 1475–1640 · R. R. Sharpe, ed., *Calendar of wills proved and enrolled in the court of husting, London, AD 1258 – AD 1688*, 2 (1890), 684

Wagg, Alfred Ralph (1877–1969), merchant banker, was born on 14 March 1877 at 40 Bryanston Square, London, the youngest of the six children of stockbroker Arthur Wagg (1842–1919) and his wife, Mathilde, *née* Merton. Alfred Wagg was educated at Ashdown House preparatory school in Brighton, and at Eton College. Of Jewish origin, his parents were without strong religious convictions and raised no objections to his becoming a practising Anglican as a schoolboy. Wagg left school with the ambition of joining the Foreign Office, and he spent 1894–5 learning French and German in Versailles and Frankfurt. In 1896 he went to King's College, Cambridge, where he studied medieval and modern languages, without much application, and received a third-class honours degree. Abandoning the idea of a career as a diplomat, he joined the family firm, stockbrokers Helbert, Wagg & Co.; he became a member of the stock exchange in 1901, and a partner of the firm in 1903.

Helbert, Wagg & Co. had been formed in 1848 by John Helbert (1785–1861) and his nephew John Wagg (1793–1878), who was Alfred's grandfather. For many years it acted as principal broker to the leading merchant bankers, Rothschilds, the Waggs being relatives of the Rothschilds. Helbert and Wagg both retired in 1857, and in 1866 John Wagg's son Arthur became senior partner; he was joined by his brother Edward (1843–1933), a barrister, in 1870. Arthur possessed excellent social connections, essential for a successful nineteenth-century stockbroker, but Edward, a bachelor who divided his time between the City, his club, and the grouse moor, provided the firm's driving force and was probably a model for Alfred. Arthur remained a partner until his death, and Edward was the first chairman of Helbert, Wagg & Co. Ltd, as the business became from 1919, until he was succeeded by Alfred in 1922.

About the turn of the century, the Rothschild connection waned and Edward and Alfred developed new businesses, focusing on the distribution and arbitrage of international securities, and especially on new issues on behalf of British corporate clients. Helbert Wagg became an important if not a leading firm, though the simultaneous resignation of their stock-exchange memberships by all of its partners on 6 December 1912 caused a minor sensation. The reason was that new rules enforcing single capacity and fixed commissions threatened to hamper the firm's activities as an issuing house. A further factor may have been personal pique, stemming from the defeat of Alfred Wagg, a leader of the opposition to the reforms, in the crucial election to the committee of general purposes.

The issuing boom of 1913–14 kept Helbert Wagg very busy and produced exceptional profits for the tyro issuing house. But with the outbreak of the First World War this business came to a halt, necessitating the development of other activities. Alfred Wagg, now the only active partner, took a variety of initiatives and successfully built up a substantial operation dealing in Treasury bills and gilts. He covered the firm's costs, a not inconsiderable achievement, during the war years of 1914–18, producing a profit of £19.

After the war Wagg recruited a new and talented team of senior executives. Spurred by the generous profit-sharing scheme he devised in 1919, they made the firm a leader in foreign exchange, corporate finance, and investment management. Junior personnel were also well-motivated, receiving the best wage-rates in the City and some of the most munificent benefits: a pioneering pension scheme, three weeks' paid holiday, and a summer garden party.

Motivator, mediator, and ambassador were the roles Alfred Wagg played as chairman of Helbert Wagg from 1922 to 1954. He had impressive social and business contacts and held many outside directorships, and he sat on the boards of the Provident Mutual Life Assurance Association and of the bus operator Thomas Tilling. He became a firm friend of Montagu Norman, governor of the Bank of England, following an episode when they clashed, in 1922. Norman was attempting through informal influence to reserve the London capital market for British borrowers. Learning that Wagg was proposing to make an issue for a French client, Norman summoned Wagg to see him and told him that he would be very displeased if the loan proceeded. Wagg replied that having given his word, he intended to honour his commitment. The loan went ahead. In fact, the governor was impressed by his integrity, and a few weeks later Wagg was astonished to be informed by Norman that he wished Helbert Wagg to handle his personal investments.

The revival of the firm after the Second World War was led by Lionel Fraser, deputy chairman and chief executive from 1946. With Wagg's active interest, Fraser recruited a new generation of executives who took the firm forward. In 1954 Fraser succeeded Wagg as chairman. Although in retirement, Wagg continued to attend the office on Thursdays and was consulted on major matters, notably the sale of the firm to Schroders in 1959 to create a stronger integrated business. Despite his reservations, the deal went ahead.

Wagg never married, but he was a caring and paternalistic figure towards his employees. However, the staff of Helbert Wagg were not the only beneficiaries of his generosity; he was also a supporter of boys' clubs, especially the Eton Manor Boys' Club, a patrician 'mission' in London's impoverished East End, in which he took an active interest from 1907. In 1928, Wagg purchased 100 acres of Ashdown Forest, Sussex, called the Isle of Thorns, which was presented to the club along with a clubhouse and laid-out playing fields. To the town of East Grinstead he donated East Court, a large house and estate. He supported numerous charitable causes and served as the honorary treasurer of the Guinea Pig Club, an organization established to assist the rehabilitation of members of the armed forces who had been disfigured by burns. He was made a commander of the British empire in 1957, at the time of his eightieth birthday, in recognition of his charitable endeavours.

A colleague described Alfred Wagg as 'a tall, pale man, of ascetic appearance, with the kindest pair of eyes I have ever seen' (Jones, 2). He sported a small moustache, smoked a pipe, and felt most comfortable in tweeds. In demeanour he was quiet and self-effacing, and he had enormous charm and a delicious sense of humour. A clubbable man, Alfred Wagg was a popular member of Brooks. He died at his home, The Hermitage, East Grinstead, Sussex, on 30 May 1969.   RICHARD ROBERTS

Sources A. Wagg, autobiography (c.1858) [Schroder Archive, London] · R. Roberts, *Schroders: merchants and bankers* (1992) · L. Jones, 'The one and only Alfred Wagg', *Wagtail* [house magazine of Helbert Wagg & Co.] (1955), 2 · d. cert. · b. cert.

Archives SOUND BL NSA, recordings

Waggett, Philip Napier (1862–1939), Church of England clergyman and scholar, was born at 4 Stanley Terrace, Kensington, London, on 27 February 1862, the third of the four sons of John Waggett, a distinguished London physician, and his wife, Florence Blechynden Whitchurch, who was descended from nonjuring ancestors. His younger brother, Ernest, followed his father's profession and became a distinguished surgeon. Waggett was educated at Charterhouse School and at Christ Church, Oxford, where, as an exhibitioner, he was awarded a first class in natural science (1884) and, after a year's work, a second class in theology (1885). At Oxford he was influenced by such theologians as Charles Gore, E. S. Talbot, Francis Paget, and H. S. Holland. The last regarded Waggett as the quickest brain he had known. Waggett was impressed by *Lux mundi* (1889), edited by Gore, which showed how the Catholic faith was compatible with modern knowledge, including science. The reconciliation of science and theology was to be one of the themes of Waggett's ministry.

Waggett was ordained deacon in 1885 and priest in 1886. Drawn like very many of the young Anglo-Catholic clergy of the time to work in the slums, he joined the staff of Henry Luke Paget, later bishop of Chester, at Christ Church Mission, Poplar, and accompanied him in 1887 to St Pancras parish church. In 1889 Waggett accepted the headship of the Charterhouse Mission in Southwark, where he proved a keen and tireless parish worker, and launched an appeal to old Carthusians and others for money to build a gymnasium, church, and meetingrooms. The evangelical bishop of Rochester, A. W. Thorold, heartily disliked the ritualism of his Anglo-Catholic clergy, but was won over by the brilliance of Waggett's conversation. In 1892 Waggett, believing he needed a simpler life under obedience, joined the Anglican religious order the Society of St John the Evangelist at Cowley in Oxford. Four years later he was sent to South Africa as priest in charge of St Philip's Mission, Cape Town. After three years he returned to England. He was given charge of his community's new work in London and raised money to build an impressive new house near Westminster Abbey for the society. He became well-known as a preacher, missioner, scholar, and retreat conductor.

In 1911 Waggett was made head of St Anselm's House, an unsuccessful attempt to establish an Anglo-Catholic centre in Cambridge. On the outbreak of the First World War in 1914 he immediately offered himself as a chaplain in the army. These years as an army chaplain were probably the happiest of his life: he was twice mentioned in dispatches, and in 1918 he was sent to Palestine as a political officer to improve relations between the various factions.

In 1920 Waggett delivered the Hulsean lectures at Cambridge (he had been appointed lecturer for 1914–15) and, after going to India with the Mission of Help in 1922–3, he became lecturer at the General Theological Seminary in New York in 1924. At home he had been elected a proctor in convocation for the diocese of Oxford in 1922. Over the years his unremitting pastoral and scholarly work resulted in periods of exhaustion and illness. In 1927 his community allowed him to accept the living of Great St Mary's, Cambridge, but by now, at sixty-five, he was physically a broken man, and he failed to exercise the influence in the university which had been expected. So, when he resigned in 1930, he retired to spend most of the nine remaining years of his life at Cowley, unable to take any part in the services and easily wearied by the visits of the friends whom he cherished. He died in Ardmore Nursing Home at Parkstone, Dorset, where he had been living with his sisters, on 4 July 1939. He was buried in the churchyard of Cowley St John, Oxford.

In 1921 Oxford University gave Waggett the honorary degree of DD. Before the First World War he published two notable books: *The Heart of Jesus* (1902), a series of Holy Week sermons, and *The Scientific Temper in Religion* (1905), an expression of his quest for a synthesis between theology and science. He was one of the most gifted figures in what may be called the third period of the Catholic revival in the Church of England. But he was also a bridgebuilder between traditions—he said that the best expression of the Catholic doctrine of the sacrifice of the mass was the evangelical hymn 'Rock of Ages'. He was a scientist, a theologian, a philosopher, a notable preacher, and a monk, but also a brilliant and witty conversationalist with a love of paradox.

SIDNEY DARK, *rev.* ALAN WILKINSON

Sources J. Nias, *Flame from an Oxford cloister: the life and writings of Philip Napier Waggett* (1961) · *The Times* (6 July 1939) · personal knowledge (1949) · private information (1949) · *CGPLA Eng. & Wales* (1939)

Archives Society of St John the Evangelist, 22 Great College Street, London SW18 3QD, corresp., notes on Psalms | BL, letters to G. K. Chesterton, Add. MS 73241 · Borth. Inst., corresp. with second Viscount Halifax

Wealth at death £1204 12s. 4d.: probate, 23 Aug 1939, *CGPLA Eng. & Wales*

Waghorn, Martin (d. 1787), naval officer, from Deptford, had probably already been some years in the navy when, on 2 May 1756, he married Ann Marriott, at St Thomas's Church, Portsmouth; they had at least four children. On 16 December 1762 he was commissioned lieutenant on the

Manila by Vice-Admiral Sir Samuel Cornish. This ship was one of the prizes taken after the British capture of Manila from Spain. In August 1763 he was appointed, again by Cornish, second lieutenant of the frigate *Liverpool*, and in her he returned to England.

Waghorn was put on half pay in November 1764 and during the long period which ensued before his next Royal Navy lieutenancy he served as first mate in the East India Company's *Ponsborne* and *Lioness*, on four voyages to India and China between 1768 and 1777. On 19 March 1778 he was appointed third lieutenant of the *Victory*, then fitting for the flag of Admiral Augustus Keppel; Waghorn became second lieutenant on 29 April, and then, on 13 May, second lieutenant of the *Prince George*. He returned to the *Victory*, as sixth lieutenant, on 16 February 1779, and remained with her until 15 August 1781, when he obtained his first command, the sloop *Fly*. On 6 April 1782 Waghorn was promoted captain of the *Royal George* (100 guns), in which Richard Kempenfelt, who may have known him in the East Indies, and was now a rear-admiral, hoisted his flag.

On 29 August 1782 the *Royal George* capsized and sank at Spithead while heeled to replace a blocked seacock. Waghorn, two lieutenants, and 330 men were saved, but his son William—a midshipman on board—was drowned, along with Admiral Kempenfelt, over 400 crewmen, and 360 women and children. Waghorn was exonerated by the court martial held on 7 September, it being concluded that there had been a structural failure in the ship's 'old and rotten' frame. However, it now seems that she was simply swamped through her open larboard lower gun ports, through which large rum casks were being loaded; there was a failure of communication and of supervision by the officers; and the procedure should never have been attempted in the first place. For all this, Waghorn must share much of the blame with the admiral.

From September 1783 to July 1785 Waghorn was captain of Commodore Sir John Lindsay's flagship, *Trusty*, in the Mediterranean. He died on 17 December 1787, at Dover Place in Surrey, and was survived by at least two of his children: one daughter who died on 19 December 1798, and Eliza, who on 3 June 1799 married Captain Henry *Blackwood (1770–1832).   RANDOLPH COCK

Sources PRO, ADM 6/20, 21 · Waghorn's court martial, PRO, ADM 1/5321 · *GM*, 1st ser., 52 (1782) · *GM*, 1st ser., 57 (1787) · *N&Q*, 165 (1933), 458 · R. Cook, '"The finest invention in the world": the Royal Navy's early trials of copper sheathing, 1708–1770', *Mariner's Mirror*, 87 (2001), 446–59 · R. F. Johnson, *The Royal George* (1971) · D. London, 'Mutiny in the public eye: the role of newspapers in the Spithead mutiny', PhD diss., U. Lond., 2001
Archives PRO, commission and warrant books, ADM 6/20, 21

Waghorn, Thomas (1800–1850), naval officer and self-publicist, the only son of Thomas Waghorn, a butcher, and his wife (*née* Stedman), was born in Rochester, Kent, on 20 July 1800. He entered the navy in 1812 as a midshipman and left in 1817 before completing the six years required to qualify as a lieutenant. He settled in Calcutta in 1819, was employed as second mate in the Bengal pilot service in 1823, and for the next two years took part in the

Thomas Waghorn (1800–1850), by Sir George Hayter

First Anglo-Burmese War (1824–6). Although noted for his extraordinary energy and keenness, he was not promoted.

Developments in marine technology in the 1820s enabled vessels to make short sea voyages by steam: this aroused great interest in India, and rival 'steam committees' were set up to find the best route to England. Waghorn saw that there was money in the new technology, and, despite the failure of Calcutta's experiment round the Cape of Good Hope in 1826 and his own lack of experience in steam shipping, he went twice (1827–8 and 1828–9) to England to seek patronage for another attempt on the Cape route, but he failed to extract any money for what an official called his 'wild scheme'. He returned to Calcutta via Egypt and the Red Sea, and landed in Bombay to find that the *Hugh Lindsay*, a steam warship built there and commanded by Captain J. H. Wilson, had just started on her first voyage (1830) between Bombay and Suez. The shorter overland route via the Red Sea was successfully demonstrated but Waghorn's mind remained fixed on the Cape route until 1831, when he travelled to London again. After driving to distraction every official in sight both in the government and in the East India Company, he resigned from that company after one of his many uncontrollable and sometimes violent displays of temper. He then completed his training as a midshipman, but was not promoted to lieutenant. Meanwhile, the *Hugh Lindsay* continued to make voyages with a few important passengers aboard. Wilson escorted them to and from Suez and Cairo or Alexandria, and dispatched mails that were speedily conveyed by camels driven by Bedouin to the relevant port. In Egypt in 1833 Waghorn heard what Wilson was doing and decided to become a private courier himself. Here he showed that he lived in a fantasy world in which he could do anything and everything. In a pamphlet he claimed that he had opened the Red Sea route and could run up and down it throughout the year—including the period of the south-west monsoon—in a single small vessel. In fact, however, the first time he set foot on a steamer in the Red Sea was two years later, when he went aboard the *Hugh Lindsay* to meet Wilson, but he never made a voyage in that vessel.

In December 1834 Waghorn married Harriet Martin, a Kent farmer's daughter, at Old Snodland church, Kent; they had no children. Two years later he bought The Lodge, a gentleman's residence in Snodland, and mortgaged it. In 1835 Smith Elder & Co., traders in the East and Waghorn's publishers, allowed him to base his courier business in their premises at 65 Cornhill, London.

Waghorn was adept at keeping his name in the public eye. Helped by people more educated than himself, he produced a number of pamphlets (1831–48) in which he heckled his dedicatees, always high-ranking aristocrats or prominent politicians, and offered useless advice. His evidence to the two select committees on steam communication to India (1834 and 1837) revealed his extraordinary ideas and gross ignorance. As a choice example, he maintained that he had surveyed the whole of the Cape and Red Sea routes by 'an eye sketch'. His appointment in 1837 as deputy agent in Egypt lasted only three months because of an explosive argument with his senior. Extending his private letter business into a passenger agency, he set up a partnership with George Wheatley at the Overland register office, 71 Cornhill. As more travellers chose to go overland to India, there were opportunities for entrepreneurs to facilitate the crossing. Waghorn tried to compete with the established Hill & Co. but instead was forced to merge with them by the arrival of the Peninsular and Oriental Steam Navigation Company (P. & O.). Having engaged Waghorn as a sub-agent and seen his ways, P. & O. paid him up in 1842, the year he was given the rank of lieutenant by the Admiralty. Never able to stay in the same place for long, he left Egypt for England in 1843, ill, almost certainly bankrupt and 'perfectly shattered by the fatigues and excitement he had undergone' (Wheatley, 353). He now announced, falsely, that he was responsible for 'promoting and achieving the Overland Route to India three years before the route was taken up' (T. Waghorn, 'Acceleration of Mails (once a fortnight) between England and the East Indies', BL, MS 1393, fol. 4) by the British government and the East India Company.

In the last years of his life Waghorn was involved with the Austrian Lloyd Steam Navigation Company. It engaged him to make trial journeys to promote Trieste as a better mail port than Marseilles and to compete with P. & O. His journeys were closely charted by *The Times* (1846), but publicity and enthusiasm did not convince the Admiralty that Ostend–Trieste was better than Calais–Marseilles for conveyance of mails. The Treasury refused to pay more than £4000 towards the cost of these expensive trials, which left Waghorn with a debt of £2000 added to those he had already incurred, and his public appeals failed to relieve him of all his troubles. Asked to convene a meeting in London to campaign for steam to Australia and to pave the way for the India and Australia Steam Packet Company, which would soon be formed by bankers, merchants, and Austrian Lloyd, Waghorn widened his fantasy world by telling his audience that his object was to have 'the honour of opening [the Australian] line in my own person as I first did the Indian one' (*Morning Advertiser*, 3). His name appeared on the company's share lists in spite of his debts until the company's disappearance.

In 1847, still working for Austrian Lloyd, Waghorn tried to persuade the Austrian government to build a railway between Trieste and Ostend. Lord Palmerston, who took an interest in this project because it would give British industrialists access to a huge German market, found that for political reasons Prince Metternich, the Austrian chancellor, was willing but other ministers objected both to British engineers and to the line Waghorn was pressing upon them. By this time Waghorn was worn out. P. & O. gave him a free ticket to Calcutta to enable him to wind up his affairs. He died on 7 January 1850 at Golden Terrace, Pentonville, London.

Restless, hyperactive, crude, with ambitions far above his ability to achieve them, Waghorn was kept alive in the popular mind by chance. In the week of his death 'the moving Diorama of the Overland Route to India' was on show in Regent Street and attracted many visitors. The pictures confirmed Egypt as Britain's high road to India, and Waghorn's imaginary exploits served as symbols for Britain's expanding empire. Later, in 1884, the burghers of Rochester commemorated his 'achievements', but, apart from the terms 'pioneer' and 'originator', the real celebration was about Britain's recent triumph, the occupation of Egypt (1882). Whether liar or simpleton, Waghorn had played no more than a minute off-stage part.

FREDA HARCOURT

Sources J. H. Wilson, *Facts connected with the origin and progress of steam communication between India and England* (1850) · M. Sankey, *Care of Mr Waghorn: a biography*, special ser. (1964) · G. Wheatley, 'Some account of the late Lt. Waghorn, RN, the originator of the overland route', *Bentley's Miscellany*, 27 (1850), 349–57 · G. Smith, 'The life and labour of Lt. Waghorn', *Household Words* (17 Aug 1850), 494–500 · G. M. Smith, 'In the early forties', *Cornhill Magazine*, [3rd] ser., 9 (1900), 577–85, esp. 577–9 · P. E. Clunn, *Lt Waghorn, RN, pioneer of the overland route to India* (1894), 2–14 · 'Select committee on steam navigation to India', *Parl. papers* (1834), 14.389, no. 478 · 'Select committee on steam communication with India', *Parl. papers* (1837), 6.361, no. 539 · PRO, FO 7/329, 334, 336, 337–9 · PRO, FO 120/204 · PRO, Post 29/26, 27 · PRO, CO 201/410 · PRO, BT 1/463/464 · *The Times* (18 April 1846), 6 · *The Times* (Aug–Dec 1846) · *Morning Advertiser* (18 April 1846), 3 · *Cheltenham and Rochester Observer*, 1 (March 1884), 5 · 1840–47, NMM, P. & O. MSS · *DNB*

Archives NRA, letters and ships' logbooks

Likenesses Day & Haghe, lithograph, pubd 1837 (after C. Baxter), NPG · H. H. Armstead, monument, 1888, Chatham, Kent · G. B. Black, lithograph (after Sabatier), NPG · G. Hayter, oils, NPG [*see illus.*]

Wealth at death £200: Sankey, *Biography*

Wagner, **Sir Anthony Richard** (1908–1995), herald, was born on 6 September 1908 at 90 Queen's Gate, South Kensington, London, the elder child and only son of Orlando Henry Wagner (1867–1956), schoolmaster, and his wife, Monica (1878–1970), daughter of George Edward Bell, vicar of Henley in Arden, Warwickshire. He was educated at his father's private day school for young boys, in Queen's Gate, and after the First World War at Beaudesert Park, Minchinhampton, Gloucestershire. In 1921 he won a king's scholarship to Eton College, which he later saw as the pivotal event in his life, though he always believed his schoolmaster father to have been his best teacher. Eton implanted in him a love of old buildings and a keen sense of tradition and ceremonial; he was school captain in 1925–6. From there he went as a Robin Hollway scholar to Balliol College, Oxford, where he met the medieval historian V. H. Galbraith, who was to become a lifelong friend.

From an early age Wagner was fascinated by family trees, copying out the pedigrees of various royal houses of Europe and learning them by heart. In the library at Eton he discovered many books on heraldry and genealogy. Having graduated with a third-class degree in *literae humaniores* in 1931 he entered the College of Arms as Portcullis pursuivant, the start of a long and distinguished career as an officer of arms. During the Second World War he worked as a temporary civil servant, first in the War Office (1939–43) and then in the Ministry of Town and Country Planning (1943–6), where he was private secretary to the minister, William Shepherd Morrison (1944–5). Later he helped to set up the historic buildings section (1945–6), writing the guidelines on the listing of buildings; he subsequently served as a member of the advisory committee on buildings of special architectural or historic interest (1947–66). In 1946 he returned full-time to the College of Arms, having been promoted Richmond herald in 1943. In 1961 he became Garter principal king of arms and was promoted KCVO, having been made CVO in 1953. He retired as Garter in 1978, at the traditional age of seventy, though he was never convinced by this rule; on his retirement he was made a KCB and took on the less demanding position of Clarenceux king of arms, which he held for life, despite the onset of blindness in 1984. On 26 February 1953 he married Gillian Mary Millicent (b. 1927), eldest daughter of Major Henry Archibald Roger Graham, an officer in the Grenadier Guards. She was a distinguished public servant and authority on social care, and was appointed OBE in 1977 and DBE in 1994. They had two sons, Roger Henry Melchior and Mark Anthony, and a daughter, Lucy Elizabeth Millicent.

As a junior pursuivant Wagner led the procession at George V's funeral, and as Garter he was responsible (under the duke of Norfolk) for the state funeral of Winston Churchill in 1965 and the investiture of the prince of Wales in 1969. He engaged in a number of long-term projects. From 1940 until his death he was general editor of the Society of Antiquaries' *Dictionary of British Arms*, the first volume of which appeared in 1992. He also launched a project to list and describe the existing English medieval rolls of arms, contributing the first volume in 1950, and

Sir Anthony Richard Wagner (1908–1995), by Elliott & Fry, 1952

initiated the cataloguing of the college manuscripts, beginning with his own *Records and Collections of the College of Arms* (1952). He was the founder and first director of the Heralds' Museum (1978–83), which displayed some of the college's heraldic treasures. He also established the College of Arms Trust, thus helping to put the college on a sound financial footing.

Wagner's greatest legacy, however, was his wide-ranging and knowledgeable work on heraldry and genealogy, which did much to ensure their acceptance as valuable tools for the study of history as well as being subjects worthy of serious academic study in their own right. His *English Genealogy* (1960) and *Pedigree and Progress* (1975) greatly added to the understanding of English social mobility. *Heralds and Heraldry in the Middle Ages* (1939) was an early seminal study drawing upon numerous primary sources, and his much larger *Heralds of England* (1967) became the standard work on the subject. In 1957 he was awarded the Oxford degree of DLitt in recognition of his prolific and scholarly publications. He also built up a fine collection of heraldic manuscripts, including several medieval rolls of arms.

Wagner was a tall man who learned to carry himself well in heraldic tabard. He was donnish and shy, sometimes appearing aloof to acquaintances who did not know him well. He disliked having to make speeches or leading ceremonies. His financial acumen, though serving the college well, was not always appreciated by all, but he generously supported those whom he felt were genuinely interested in genealogy and heraldry. He was conservative in outlook and a strong supporter of the hereditary principle. He was fond of the institutions and organizations to which he was attached, such as the Society of Antiquaries, the Chelsea Society, the Georgian Group, and various London clubs; he was particularly pleased to be made an honorary fellow of Balliol in 1979. He died in London on 5 May 1995 and was survived by his wife, Gillian, and their three children. The oration at his funeral service in St Benet Paul's Wharf, opposite the College of Arms, was given by his old friend Enoch Powell. Following a secondary service in the parish church he was buried at Aldeburgh on 12 May 1995. An engraved memorial (one of a series to past Garters) was later installed in St Benet's.   ADRIAN AILES

Sources A. Wagner, *A herald's world* (1988) · H. Chesshyre and A. Ailes, *Heralds of today: a biographical list of the officers of the College of Arms, London, 1987–2001* (2001) · *WWW, 1991–5* · Wagner pedigree, Coll. Arms, Norfolk MS 42 · E. Lemon, ed., *The Balliol College register, 1916–1967*, 4th edn (privately printed, Oxford, 1969) · policy of appointing Garter, 1961, PRO, HO 286/47 · P. Howard, 'The king who stands out from the pack', *The Times* (4 Nov 1981) · *The Times* (11 May 1995) · *The Independent* (10 May 1995) · *The Independent* (16 May 1995) · *Daily Telegraph* (10 May 1995) · *Society of Antiquaries annual report: proceedings* (1996) · private information (2004) [Gillian Wagner, wife]
Archives Bodl. Oxf., corresp. and papers · S. Antiquaries, Lond., notes and papers | Helmingham Hall, Stowmarket, corresp. relating to Tollemache armorial · PRO NIre., letters to Lady Brookeborough · W. Sussex RO, corresp. with Oswald Barron, incl. article on heraldry | FILM BFI NFTVA
Likenesses H. Riviere, oils, 1925–6, Eton, provost's lodge; repro. in Wagner, *A herald's world* · Elliott & Fry, photograph, 1952, NPG [*see illus.*] · photograph, 1961, repro. in *The Independent* (10 May 1995) · photograph, c.1970, repro. in Wagner, *A herald's world* · photograph, 1970, repro. in *Daily Telegraph* · H. D. Marsh, silhouette, 1974, repro. in P. Begent and H. Chesshyre, *The most noble order of the Garter: 650 years* (1999), 143 · H. A. Freeth, oils, c.1979, Coll. Arms · H. Riviere, group portrait, oils (with officers), Coll. Arms; repro. in Wagner, *A herald's world* · photograph, repro. in *The Times*
Wealth at death £760,001: probate, 4 Oct 1995, *CGPLA Eng. & Wales*

Wagner, Arthur Douglas (1824–1902), Church of England clergyman, was born on 13 June 1824 at Park Hill, Windsor; he was the only child of Henry Michell Wagner (1792–1870), clerk in holy orders, and his first wife, Elizabeth Harriott (1797–1829), daughter of the Revd William Douglas, vicar of Gillingham in Dorset, chancellor of Salisbury Cathedral, and canon of Westminster. Wagner's father was tutor to the sons of the first duke of Wellington until his appointment to the vicarage of Brighton and West Blatchington in Sussex, to which he was inducted on 30 July 1824. Wagner was educated at Eton College (1835–42) and at Trinity College, Cambridge (1842–6), where he took an honours degree in mathematics. He was ordained deacon in 1848 and priest in 1849, serving as curate to his father, who, between 1846 and 1849, built the new church of St Paul at Brighton. Henry Wagner intended that St Paul's should be served by his son, who was appointed its first perpetual curate in January 1850. Wagner's father was a pre-Tractarian high-churchman and Wagner himself was strongly influenced by the Tractarian movement. The new church of St Paul was designed by one of the leading Tractarian architects, Richard Cromwell Carpenter,

and it was the first church in Brighton at which an advanced ritual, including eventually the use of vestments and incense, was adopted. Wagner remained at St Paul's for the whole of his ministry, becoming its first vicar when a parish was assigned to the church in 1873.

In 1855 Wagner founded a sisterhood in connection with St Paul's, the Community of the Blessed Virgin Mary. Wagner and the sisterhood became the source of controversy in 1865 when Constance Kent, who was a nurse at the home for the reclamation of prostitutes established by the community, was tried for the murder, some five years earlier, of her half-brother. She had voluntarily admitted to the murder after having made a sacramental act of confession to Wagner, who at the trial refused to answer questions relating to this confession. Public meetings were organized in Brighton to protest against Wagner's actions, and he was assaulted in the street.

Wagner never married. He continued to live at Brighton vicarage until his father's death in 1870, when he moved into the neighbouring house, Belvedere, which he had inherited from his aunt Mary Ann Wagner in 1868. He used his wealth to carry on the tradition established by his father by building four further churches in Brighton: St Mary Magdalene (1862), the Annunciation (1864), the vast and austere St Bartholomew, in Ann Street (1874), and St Martin (1875). In 1873 he purchased Totease Hall at Buxted in Sussex, in which parish he erected a new church between 1885 and 1886. Altogether Wagner is estimated to have spent some £70,000 during his lifetime on financing churches, schools, and even houses for his poorer parishioners.

Wagner lived an ascetic life, though in later life he became extremely stout; he was looked after by his two unmarried cousins, Elizabeth and Fanny Coombe. His only luxuries were the purchase of books and manuscripts. After his death the sale of his library, which totalled 12,000 volumes, took three days. He was not considered a good preacher and published very little: *Parochial Sermons Bearing on the Subjects of the Day* (1855), *Reasons for Disobeying on Principle* (1874), *Christ or Caesar: an Open Letter to the Archbishop of Canterbury* (1874), and *Christ or Caesar, Part II: a Letter to the Lord Bishop of Chichester* (1877). The last three pamphlets were attacks on the Public Worship Regulation Act and the courts created by it for suppressing illegal ritual in the Church of England. Although Wagner used illegal ritual at St Paul's in Brighton, no attempt was ever made to prosecute him under the provisions of the act. His brand of ritualism became popularly known as the 'London, Brighton, and South Coast Religion'.

By 1896 Wagner was in failing health and mentally incapable of administering his own affairs; his parish was run by curates. Attempts were made to persuade him to resign but they were unsuccessful. After six years of further decline he died on 14 January 1902 at his house, Belvedere, and was buried four days later, wearing full eucharistic vestments, at Lewes Road cemetery in Brighton. Large congregations attended the requiem masses said for him at all the churches in Brighton which he had helped to establish, and 3000 people attended the interment. Part of his estate, valued at £49,907 15s. 6d., was used to provide endowments for the churches and the sisterhood that he had founded in his lifetime.   NIGEL YATES

Sources A. Wagner and A. Dale, *The Wagners of Brighton* (1983) · E. P. Hennock, 'The Anglo-Catholics and church extension in Victorian Brighton', *Studies in Sussex church history*, ed. M. J. Kitch (1981), 173–88 · W. N. Yates, 'Bells and smells: London, Brighton and south coast religion reconsidered', *Southern History*, 5 (1983), 122–53 · N. Yates, *Anglican ritualism in Victorian Britain, 1830–1910* (1999) · H. H. Maughan, *Wagner of Brighton* (1949) · J. S. Reed, *Glorious battle: the cultural politics of Victorian Anglo-Catholicism* (1996) · P. F. Anson, *The call of the cloister: religious communities and kindred bodies in the Anglican communion*, rev. edn (1964) · J. Bentley, *Ritualism and politics in Victorian Britain* (1978) · D. R. Elleray, *The Victorian churches of Sussex* (1981) · A. Dale, *Brighton churches* (1989)
Archives E. Sussex RO, parish records of St Paul's, Brighton, PAR 276/7/1; PAR 276/12/1
Likenesses photographs (as young man and in old age), repro. in Wagner and Dale, *Wagners of Brighton*, pls. 11a, 11b
Wealth at death £49,907 15s. 6d.: Wagner and Dale, *Wagners of Brighton*, 133

Wagstaff, Harold (1891–1939), rugby player, was born on 19 May 1891 in Underbank, Holmfirth, Yorkshire, the son of Andrew Wagstaff, a painter's labourer, and his wife, Hannah, *née* Rhodes (1858/9–1904), of Rochdale. After playing junior rugby for his native village team Underbank, he signed for Huddersfield of the Northern Union for 5 gold sovereigns and played his first senior game at Bramley on 10 November 1906, when he scored a try in a 28–11 victory. He was aged only fifteen years and 175 days. He continued to play for Huddersfield until 1925, and became club captain in 1911.

Wagstaff's time with Huddersfield saw the creation of a side immortalized as 'the team of all the talents'. During his career Huddersfield won the challenge cup three times, the championship three times, the Yorkshire cup six times, and the Yorkshire league championship six times. In the season of 1914–15 he led them to the famous all four cups clean sweep, a feat emulated only by Hunslet in 1907–8 and Swinton in 1927–8.

Wagstaff was ideally built for the centre at 5 feet 11 inches and about 12 stone 8 pounds. He was strong and possessed a fine swerve but was never regarded as quick. His supreme gift was as a playmaker and strategist. He revolutionized the game by adhering to the principle that possession was sacrosanct: kicking was a last resort. In combination with Jim Davies, the Huddersfield stand-off, Wagstaff invented the standing pass manoeuvre following scrums. As a result he took terrific buffetings on his left side but the movement brought his team shoals of tries. Mystified opponents described the subterfuge as 'scientific obstruction'.

On 17 October 1908 Wagstaff entered the arena of representative rugby when he won the first of fifteen caps for Yorkshire. At seventeen years and 141 days he is believed to be the youngest recipient of a county cap. Within another three months he became the youngest international player in history when he figured in England's 14–9 victory over Australia on 2 January 1909 on his home ground, Fartown. Between 1909 and 1923 he played in twenty-three international and test matches, the majority as captain.

In 1914 Wagstaff was selected as captain of the Great Britain touring party to Australasia. That Ashes series was one of the most controversial in history, with the Australian authorities, despite British protests, deciding to play all three tests within one week. The decider at Sydney on 27 June has been enshrined in the game's annals as 'the Rorke's Drift test', in remembrance of a heroic action by a small British force against a Zulu army in 1879. An already depleted British team suffered a series of injuries in the match which reduced them from thirteen men to ten. Almost miraculously Wagstaff led his team to a 14–6 triumph and regained the Ashes. It was unquestionably his finest hour.

Wagstaff again captained the Lions in Australasia in 1920, when the Ashes were retained, and was in charge for a third consecutive series victory in England in 1921–2. His last test match, at Salford on 14 January 1922, a 6–0 victory over the Kangaroos, was regarded as one of the most strenuous games ever played. At its conclusion Wagstaff was carried from the field by the crowd, minus his jersey, which had been ripped to shreds by idolatrous souvenir-hunters.

Wagstaff was the most revered and influential player in Northern Union (later rugby league) football in the first quarter of the twentieth century. To contemporary observers he seemed to embody all the virtues to which sportsmen should aspire. First and foremost he was a centre three-quarter of such consummate skills that he earned the title the Prince of Centres. Yet he was more than merely the greatest player of his generation. He bore himself with dignity, was renowned for his sense of fair play, was the catalyst for new playing methods, and became the most successful and inspirational captain of his era at both club and representative levels.

Wagstaff served in the Royal Army Service Corps as a motor driver in the First World War. On 4 January 1915 he married Ann Battye, daughter of Wilson Battye, of Arrundon, Cartworth, Holmfirth. They had one son, Robert. Wagstaff was the licensee of the Royal Swan Hotel, Westgate, Huddersfield, when on 19 July 1939 he died of cardiac failure and acute gastroenteritis at the Trinity Street Nursing Home, Huddersfield. He was buried three days later in Holmfirth cemetery. His wife survived him.

ROBERT GATE

Sources *Sports Post* [Leeds] (9 Feb 1935–4 May 1936) · V. A. S. Beanland, *Great games and great players: some thoughts and recollections of a sports journalist* (1945) · A. N. Gaulton, 'This was a player!', *Rugby League Review*, 90 (1950), 4–6 · b. cert. · d. cert. · CGPLA Eng. & Wales (1939)
Likenesses photograph, 1913, repro. in *The book of British sporting heroes*, ed. J. Huntington-Whiteley (1998) [exhibition catalogue, NPG, 16 Oct 1998–24 Jan 1999]; priv. coll.
Wealth at death £3502 10s. 9d.: administration, 11 Sept 1939, CGPLA Eng. & Wales

Wagstaffe, John (c.1633–1677), writer on witchcraft, was born in Cheapside, London, the son of John Wagstaffe of London; his mother's name may have been Elizabeth. He was educated at St Paul's School and went up to Oriel College, Oxford, as a Pauline exhibitioner in 1649; he matriculated in 1650, graduated BA in 1653, and proceeded MA in 1656. In 1660 he contributed a Greek poem and a Latin acrostic to the volume of verses published at Oxford to celebrate the Restoration. He incorporated at Cambridge in 1668. On the death of an uncle, who died without male children, Wagstaffe inherited his estate at Hasland, Derbyshire; he never married.

Wagstaffe's first book, entitled *Historical reflections on the bishop of Rome, chiefly discovering those events of humane affaires which most advanced the papal usurpation*, published in 1660, gave a rather cynical account of the means by which papal hegemony was achieved at the expense of the susceptible barbarians in the early middle ages. His most famous work was his *The Question of Witchcraft Debated* (1669; 2nd edn, 1671). This offered a robust critique of the belief in witchcraft, appealing to reason and invoking sarcasm to make his case that the power of witches was illusory. The thrust of his case was threefold: '1. That the opinion of Witchcraft is not to be found in Scripture. 2. That Politique interest hath founded it on fables. 3. That those fables discover themselves to be so, by their impossibility' (pp. 144–5). Echoing the theme of his earlier *Reflections*, he took the view that witch beliefs had been consciously embroidered by the clergy as a means of self-aggrandizement; in his view such priestly manipulation capitalized on the fact that 'all men have fear implanted in them by nature, the very strongest of all their passions' (p. 125), a notion almost certainly derived from Hobbes. In making his case he took a confident and iconoclastic line, appealing to 'any sober unbiased person; especially if he be of such ingenuity, as to have freed himself from a slavish subjection, unto those prejudicial opinions, which Custome and education, do with too much Tyranny impose' (p. 147). Moreover, alluding to the empirical evidence by which such store was set by contemporary defenders of witch beliefs like Joseph Glanvill, he argued: 'it is far more easie, and far more rational to believe, that witnesses are lyars and perjured persons, than it is to believe; that an old Woman can turn her self, or any body else into a Cat' (p. 146).

Wagstaffe's book was attacked by one R. T. in a book entitled *The Opinion of Witchcraft Vindicated* (1670), and by the veteran scholar Meric Casaubon in his *Of Credulity and Incredulity; in Things Divine & Spiritual* (1670), both of whom asserted a more traditional view of the subject. The result was that in 1671 Wagstaffe brought out a greatly extended second edition of his book. In it he elaborated his case and, in his preface, defended himself against the 'ridiculous slander' that he was an 'atheist' (sig. A2), which evidently owed much to contemporary anxieties about the corrolaries of sadducism—scepticism about witchcraft—though it is also understandable in the light of Wagstaffe's iconoclasm and his somewhat deistic religious views.

The importance of Wagstaffe's work as one of the very few open attacks on witch beliefs in its period is illustrated by the fact that it was twice reprinted in the early eighteenth century, first in 1712 as part of the controversy over the conviction as a witch and subsequent pardoning of Jane Wenham and then in 1736 in connection with the repeal of the Witchcraft Act; in each case it provided the sole exposition of a strongly sceptical viewpoint. It was also translated into German in 1711.

Apart from the notoriety associated with this book, relatively little is known about Wagstaffe's life. A few personal details come from Anthony Wood, who notes that he was 'a little crooked man, and of a despicable presence'; indeed, he looked 'like a little wizard', and his book on witchcraft accordingly caused mirth among the wits at Oxford. He died, according to Wood, aged forty-four or thereabouts, in London at his lodgings in Holborn, opposite Chancery Lane, on 2 September 1677, 'in a manner distracted, occasion'd by a deep conceit of his own parts, and by a continual bibbing of strong and high tasted liquors' (Wood, *Ath. Oxon.*, 3.1114). He was buried in the Guildhall chapel, City of London.   MICHAEL HUNTER

Sources M. Hunter, 'The witchcraft controversy and the nature of free-thought in Restoration England: John Wagstaffe's *The question of witchcraft debated* (1669)', *Science and the shape of orthodoxy: intellectual change in late seventeenth-century Britain* (1995), 286–307 · Wood, *Ath. Oxon.*, new edn, 3.1113 · J. Wagstaffe, *The question of witchcraft debated* (1671) · M. McDonnell, ed., *The registers of St Paul's School, 1509–1748* (privately printed, London, 1977), 198 · Foster, *Alum. Oxon.* · BL, Add. MS 6670, fol. 132

Wagstaffe, Sir Joseph (*bap.* **1611?**, *d.* **1666/7**), royalist army officer, was probably baptized on 13 August 1611 at Harbury, Warwickshire, and was probably the seventh and youngest son of Richard Wagstaffe (*b.* 1574) of Harbury, and his wife, Anne, daughter of John Hanslap of Stonythorpe in the same county. Thomas *Wagstaffe the nonjuror and William *Wagstaffe, physician, were relatives of Joseph Wagstaffe.

Wagstaffe's early life is obscure, but at the beginning of 1642 he was a major in an Irish regiment in the service of France. In June 1642 he became lieutenant-colonel in the army destined by the parliament for the recovery of Ireland, and in the following autumn he held the same rank in John Hampden's regiment of foot in the earl of Essex's army. Taken prisoner by the royalists in January 1643, he changed sides and accepted a commission to raise a regiment for the king. He was wounded at the recapture of Lichfield Close by Prince Rupert's forces in the spring of 1643. Subsequently he was major-general of foot under Prince Maurice in the west of England, was knighted at Crediton on 27 or 28 July 1644, and distinguished himself by his soldierly retreat in the disastrous battle of Langport. In September 1648 he was placed under arrest on suspicion of plotting an uprising, but he escaped from confinement at Peterhouse prison, London, almost as soon as he arrived. At some point thereafter he fled to the continent.

Wagstaffe returned in 1655 when the western royalists asked for him to be their leader in their part of an intended national rising against Cromwell, he being well known to them and generally beloved. Clarendon characterizes him as fitted:

rather for execution than counsel, a stout man who looked not far before him, yet he had a great companionableness in his nature, which exceedingly prevailed with those who in the intermission of fighting loved to spend their time in jollity and mirth.

Despite the collapse of the conspiracy in other parts of the country on 8 March, Wagstaffe, with about 200 Wiltshire royalists, optimistic expectations of nationwide insurrection, and assistance from France, entered Salisbury early on 12 March 1655, and proclaimed Charles II.

The judges on circuit and sheriff were seized in their beds, and Wagstaffe thought of hanging them as a seasonable example, but was prevented by the opposition of Colonel Penruddock and the country gentlemen. After leaving Salisbury with about 400 men, the royalists marched into Dorset, but gained few recruits on their way. When they entered Somerset their numbers began to diminish, and the few who remained were taken or dispersed by Captain Unton Croke at South Molton on the night of 14 March. Wagstaffe himself escaped all the searches made after him, and was back in Flanders by July. He survived the Restoration, petitioned for the reversion of an office which he did not obtain, and received a small grant of some of the late king's goods in 1662. He died between July 1666, when his will (which makes no mention of a wife or children) was written, and 12 February 1667, when it was proved. His place of burial is unknown.

C. H. FIRTH, *rev.* SEAN KELSEY

Sources W. Camden, *The visitation of the county of Warwick in the year 1619*, ed. J. Fetherston, Harleian Society, 12 (1877), 289 · *Calendar of the Clarendon state papers preserved in the Bodleian Library*, ed. O. Ogle and others, 5 vols. (1869–1970), vol. 1, pp. 222, 263, 290; vol. 5, p. 42 · E. Peacock, *The army lists of the roundheads and cavaliers* (1874), 12, 46, 70 · *Diary of the marches of the royal army during the great civil war, kept by Richard Symonds*, ed. C. E. Long, CS, old ser., 74 (1859), 2, 54 · R. Bulstrode, *Memoirs and reflections upon the reign of King Charles the 1st and K. Charles the IInd* (1721) · Clarendon, *Hist. rebellion*, 5.373–9 · *CSP Ire.*, 1642–59, 200 · *CSP dom.*, 1648–9, 261, 263, 271; 1655, 99, 245; 1660–61, 288; 1661–2, 535 · *The Nicholas papers*, ed. G. F. Warner, 4 vols., CS, new ser., 40, 50, 57, 3rd ser., 31 (1886–1920). 2.240, 243, 259, 261–2 · C. H. Firth, 'Cromwell and the insurrection of 1655 [pt 1]', *EngHR*, 3 (1888), 323–50 · P. R. Newman, *Royalist officers in England and Wales, 1642–1660: a biographical dictionary* (1981) · W. A. Shaw, *The knights of England*, 2 vols. (1906) · IGI · will, PRO, PROB 11/323, sig. 32 · A. H. Woolrych, *Penruddock's rising, 1655*, Historical Association, general ser., 29 (1955)

Wagstaffe, Thomas (1645–1712), bishop of the nonjuring Church of England, was the son of Thomas Wagstaffe of Binley, Warwickshire, and his wife, Anne Avery of Bishop's Itchington in the same county. He was born either at Binley on 13 February or at Stafford two days later. He studied at Charterhouse School, London, before matriculating at Pembroke College, Cambridge, on 14 May 1660. He then migrated to New Inn Hall, Oxford, on 14 March 1663, graduated BA in 1664, and proceeded MA in 1667. He was ordained deacon by John Hacket, bishop of Lichfield, on 6 June 1669 and priest five months later, on 19 November, by Joseph Henshaw of Peterborough. Henshaw subsequently appointed him rector of Martinsthorpe, Rutland. Made chancellor and canon of Lichfield on 6 December 1684, the following year he was presented by Henry Compton, bishop of London, to the rectory of the united parishes of St Margaret Pattens and St Gabriel Fenchurch.

During this period of advancement Wagstaffe published several sermons which were explicit statements of his tory Anglican loyalism. Those preached at Stowe, Buckinghamshire, in 1683 and at St Margaret Pattens in 1685 were the thanksgiving day sermons for the failure of the Rye House plot and the Monmouth rising. His defence of the Church of England at the Guildhall in November 1684 branded its critics as 'Rebels, Schismatics, Seditious, Turbulent, and unquiet' (T. Wagstaffe, *A Sermon Preached before the Right Honourable the Lord Mayor … at the Guild-Hall Chappel on November the 23d. 1684*, 1685, 29). The sermon that he delivered at St Mary-le-Bow on 24 November 1687 was more eirenic in tone. Its text, 'Be ye all of one mind, having compassion', exhorting his hearers to the spiritual virtues of Christian unity and charity, was no doubt apposite to its audience—the annual feast for Warwickshire men living in London. But it was also the cry of a committed Anglican now urging a common protestant front against the threat posed by James II's Catholicizing policies. Protestant disunity was both shameful in itself and provided ammunition to the common Romish enemy: 'We must cease our Dissentions, and be as Good and Peaceable as our Principles. This will effectually answer all the clamors of our Adversaries, and do our Religion more right than all the Arguments of its Friends' (T. Wagstaffe, *A Sermon Preached at a Meeting of the Natives and Inhabitants of the County of Warwick … Novemb. 24. 1687*, 1688, 25). Their philanthropy, he added, amply disproved the charge that protestants had come to neglect the Christian obligation of charity when they abandoned belief in salvation by good works.

Wagstaffe married Martha Broughton of St Margaret's, Westminster, by licence dated 4 February 1686. They had several children, including a son, Thomas *Wagstaffe (1692–1770), who like his father became a leading member of the nonjuring community and served as an Anglican chaplain to the exiled Stuart court at Rome. A daughter married his kinsman, William *Wagstaffe, who became a well-known physician at St Bartholomew's Hospital and a fellow of the Royal College of Physicians.

Wagstaffe continued in his ecclesiastical positions until he was deprived in 1690 for refusing the oaths to William and Mary. Having studied medicine before taking orders, Wagstaffe now supported his family by taking up the practice of medicine in London, allegedly visiting his patients in full canonical attire. He also became a leading participant in the nascent nonjuring community in London, serving as an adviser and possibly as a physician to the deprived archbishop of Canterbury, William Sancroft. Having attended to the deprived archbishop before his death, Wagstaffe published an intimate account of Sancroft's last years and his death entitled *A letter out of Suffolk to a friend in London giving some account of the late sickness and death of Dr. William Sancroft, late lord archbishop of Canterbury* (1694). There he gave an account of the archbishop's deportment and faith during his forced retirement, noting that contrary to rumour that Sancroft received pastoral care and the sacraments from conforming clergy, Sancroft received these only from nonjurors such as himself.

Sancroft never accepted his deprivation, believing that the government had acted illegally and that his successor at Canterbury was an illegitimate usurper, thereby setting the stage for the continuation of the nonjuring separation. He granted to William Lloyd, the deprived bishop of Norwich, his metropolitan authority, which included the right to consecrate bishops for the nonjuring line. Therefore, with his primate's sanction, Lloyd and fellow nonjuring bishops Francis Turner of Ely and Thomas White of Peterborough looked to the interregnum for precedent in continuing the succession. Noting that the ageing Laudian bishops had conferred with the exiled Charles II and had gained his permission to continue the historic succession just before the Restoration intervened and made the action unnecessary, Lloyd sent George Hickes to obtain permission from James II to continue the nonjuring line. With approval from the exiled king, the bishops took advantage of Henry VIII's act, setting up two suffragan sees for the diocese of Norwich; they decided to fill these seemingly empty sees, which allowed them to continue the succession but avoid the problem of setting up rival sees. The purpose of continuing the nonjuring line was to offer the established church a pure church to return to when the cause of the schism had been resolved. While Hickes was nominated by Sancroft to fill the see of Thetford, Lloyd nominated Wagstaffe to the see of Ipswich, making them the only nonjuring bishops to fill titular sees. The two men were consecrated on 24 February 1694 by Lloyd, Turner, and White at the home of William Gifford at Southgate, Middlesex.

Although he agreed to his consecration, Wagstaffe did not exercise his episcopal prerogatives, and refrained from participating in any ordinations. He none the less remained active in nonjuring affairs, writing in defence of the movement and helping to raise funds to support impoverished nonjuror clergy. For this activity he was arrested and appeared before the privy council, together with bishops Ken, White, and Lloyd and the nonjuror clergyman Nathaniel Spinckes. Released by order of the council on 23 May 1696, Wagstaffe, whose connections and medical practice provided him with sufficient income to support his family, remained actively involved in the effort to provide financial support for his less fortunate colleagues.

Although he was not a prolific writer, Wagstaffe did write several short works and pamphlets in support of the Stuart dynasty and in defence of the nonjuring and Jacobite cause. A strong Stuart supporter and proponent of the principle of divine-right monarchy, he believed that former colleagues, such as William Sherlock, had acted inconsistently with the principles of the Church of England by taking the oath of allegiance to William and Mary, whom he considered usurpers of James II's proper title. His strong belief in divine-right monarchy is given voice in *An answer to a late pamphlet entitled 'Obedience and submission to the present government' demonstrated from Bishop Overall's convocation book* (1690), in which he responded to an anonymous pamphlet that charged the nonjurors, such as Sherlock, with 'ignorance and malice' for 'reproaching those of the Church of England, who have taken the Oaths with deserting their principles'. He responded that it was indeed a malicious thing to be deprived of one's livings for keeping to principle (Wagstaffe, *Answer*, 1). Wagstaffe sought to show that the principal doctrines found in Bishop John Overall's convocation book included passive obedience and non-resistance. Thus, the principles of the Church of England insisted that once a government was settled it should be obeyed, therefore, subjects should 'obey their lawful governors, and upon no account whatsoever to resist them' (ibid., 21).

Wagstaffe's most notable work was his defence of Charles I's authorship of the *Eikon basilike*, entitled *A vindication of King Charles the Martyr; proving that his majesty was the author of Eikōn basilikē* (1691, 1697, 1711), and his later *Defense of the vindication of King Charles the Martyr; justifying his majesty's title to Eikōn basilikē* (1699). In the controversy that re-emerged shortly after the revolution of 1688 over the book's true author, his was one of those tory and Jacobite voices that maintained it had been written by the martyr-king against the whig attribution of John Gauden.

True to his reluctance to exercise his episcopal authority, Wagstaffe refused to perform any episcopal consecrations when George Hickes sought his assistance, first in December 1711 and then in February 1712, in continuing the endangered nonjuring succession after William Lloyd's and Thomas Ken's return to the established church removed the last of the English bishops consecrated before the schism. Wagstaffe rebuffed his colleague, claiming that age and illness, along with distance from London, prevented him from complying. He also told Hickes that he believed this venture

> to be impracticable, that it has no foundation to stand on, but that the least opposition that will or hereafter be made to it cannot fail, but it must sink under it and come to nothing, and that consequently we shall destroy and irrecoverably defeat what is designed to be built up. (Yould, 402)

With Wagstaffe's refusal to act, Hickes finally turned to the nonjuring Scottish bishops for assistance and continued the nonjuring succession by consecrating Jeremy Collier, Samuel Hawes, and Nathaniel Spinckes.

In his later years, though retaining a London house in Charterhouse Yard, Wagstaffe had returned to Binley, where he continued his writing. It was there that he died on 17 October 1712 and was buried three days later. He was survived by his wife, Martha, and six children. The announcement of his death in the *Postboy* spoke of him as:

> a man of extraordinary judgment, exemplary piety, and unusual learning; and had he not had the misfortune to dissent from the established government by not taking the oaths, as he had all the qualities of a great divine, and a

governor of the Church, so he would have filled deservedly some of the highest stations in it. (Overton, 114)

The great whig historian Lord Macaulay called Wagstaffe and Hickes 'two fierce and uncompromising nonjurors' (Macaulay, 4.2008). Though there was a bitter barb in his comment—he had just mocked Wagstaffe's providentialist reading of the death of Mary II in December 1694, which drew close parallels in the timing of the turns in her descent to the grave with the timing of her betrayed father's loss of his throne in December 1688—Macaulay also recognized Wagstaffe to be 'a writer whom the Jacobite schismatics justly regarded as one of their ablest chiefs' (ibid., 5.2472). ROBERT D. CORNWALL

Sources Foster, *Alum. Oxon.* • Venn, *Alum. Cant.*, 1/4 • J. H. Overton, *The nonjurors: their lives, principles, and writings* (1902) • Nichols, *Lit. anecdotes* • A. Chalmers, ed., *The general biographical dictionary*, new edn, 32 vols. (1812–17) • Allibone, *Dict.* • P. A. Knachel, ed., *Eikon basilike* (1966) • G. M. Yould, 'The origins and transformation of the nonjuror schism', PhD diss., U. Hull, 1979 • *Fasti Angl.* (Hardy), vol. 1 • T. B. Macaulay, *The history of England from the accession of James II*, new edn, ed. C. H. Firth, 6 vols. (1913–15), vols. 4–5 • *IGI* • E. H. Plumptre, *The life of Thomas Ken*, 2nd edn (1890) • J. Kettlewell, *The works of John Kettlewell*, 2 vols. (1719), vol. 1 • will, PRO, PROB 11/530, sig. 224

Archives Episcopal Church of Scotland Theological College, Edinburgh, papers of Scottish Episcopal College

Wealth at death £100 p.a. to wife from rent: will, PRO, PROB 11/530, sig. 224

Wagstaffe, Thomas (1692–1770), clergyman of the nonjuring Church of England and theologian, was the son of Thomas *Wagstaffe (1645–1712), bishop of the nonjuring Church of England, and Martha Broughton (*fl.* 1687–1692). He was probably educated at home by his father, and became a well-read divine and classical scholar. A superior Latinist, he could speak seven languages besides English, and was an able scholar in Hebrew, Arabic, and Syrian. He was ordained deacon in 1718 and priest on 25 April 1719 by the nonjuror Bishop Jeremy Collier at Roger Laurence's chapel in London. He served the nonjuror community as the keeper of records, succeeding Thomas Deacon. In that capacity he drew up a bibliographical list of tracts concerning the usages controversy within the nonjuror movement. Wagstaffe took over Deacon's congregation at Dunstan's Court, Fleet Street, London, in 1722, serving there for ten years. During that period he acted as London representative for the primus of the usager party, Thomas Brett.

Wagstaffe formed, with his fellow usagers Laurence, Deacon, Francis Peck, John Rutter, and Samuel Jebb, a block that pushed usager party leaders Collier and Brett to emphasize the essential nature of the four usages—the mixed chalice, invocation of the Holy Spirit, oblation, and prayers for the dead—and to break communion with the nonusages party. He contributed several works to the usages controversy, including *The Necessity of an Alteration* (1718) and *The Reasonableness and Necessity of some Practices of the Reformation of the Church of England* (1720). Wagstaffe carried on a debate with Samuel Drake in Latin over the necessity of a mixed chalice containing both water and

wine. In 1719 Drake denounced the practice in a Cambridge University sermon, *Vino eucharistico aqua necessario admiscenda*. Wagstaffe's rejoinder of the same title (1719) led to Drake's 1721 response, *Ad Thomam Wagstaffe*, to which Wagstaffe responded in 1725 with his *Responsionis ad concionem vindiciae*.

Despite his insistence on the essential nature of the usages, Wagstaffe reluctantly agreed to the reunion of the two parties engineered by Thomas Brett and George Smith in 1732. Nevertheless, he criticized the concordat for abandoning the theological foundations of the usages, and believed that the abandonment of their communion office would lead to greater decline in the nonjuror movement's congregations, his included. Yet he did not feel comfortable with the party of Archibald Campbell and Thomas Deacon that continued to hold the essentialist position. Before leaving Dunstan's Court he warned his congregation not to secede to Campbell, whom he charged with holding heretical doctrines concerning hell.

The discomfort with the concordat and the tension with Brett over his remarks concerning Campbell led Wagstaffe to withdraw from active involvement in the movement. His congregation at Dunstan's Court disappeared and he refused to take over the Scroop's Court congregation. In the spring of 1734 Wagstaffe left England for the continent. He joined the Stuart court in Rome, where he served as the Anglican chaplain to James III (James Stuart) and then to his son, Charles Edward. He lived in Rome very simply and spent his time in scholarly pursuits, producing a manuscript detailing the Greek manuscripts of St Paul's epistles held in the Vatican and Cardinal Barberini libraries, which was given to Sion College.

Wagstaffe died on 3 December 1770 in Rome, where he was buried, respected by the Stuart court and the people of Rome who knew him. At his death he was described as a 'fine, wel-bred old gentleman', who was a pious and sincere Christian, whom the people of Rome 'were wont to say that had he not been a Heretic, he ought to have been canonized' (Overton, 338). ROBERT D. CORNWALL

Sources H. Broxap, *The later nonjurors* (1924) • J. H. Overton, *The nonjurors: their lives, principles, and writings* (New York, 1903) • H. Broxap, *A biography of Thomas Deacon* (1911) • R. Cornwall, 'The later nonjurors and the theological basis of the usages controversy', *Anglican Theological Review*, 75 (1993), 166–86 • Foster, *Alum. Oxon.* • A. Chalmers, ed., *The general biographical dictionary*, new edn, 32 vols. (1812–17)

Archives Bodl. Oxf., corresp. | Bodl. Oxf., Brett MSS

Wagstaffe, William (1683/4–1725), physician and satirist, was born at Cublington, Buckinghamshire, the only son of the Revd Thomas Wagstaffe, rector of Cublington. He was related to the Wagstaffes of Knightcote in Warwickshire, and was a relation of Sir Joseph Wagstaffe. He went to school in Northampton, and in 1700 entered Lincoln College, Oxford, where he graduated BA (1704) and MA (1707).

In 1707 Wagstaffe moved to London, where his relative the Revd Thomas *Wagstaffe (1645–1712) was a nonjuror, one of the Church of England clergy who refused to swear allegiance to William and Mary and who were deprived of

a living. Although unlicensed, Thomas Wagstaffe practised physic without interference from the College of
Physicians. William Wagstaffe acquired a taste for medical studies, and he also married Thomas Wagstaffe's
daughter. She died soon afterwards and he married, secondly, the daughter of Charles *Bernard, surgeon to St
Bartholomew's Hospital. Wagstaffe graduated BM and DM
at Oxford in 1714; he was elected a fellow of the College of
Physicians in 1718, and was a censor in 1720. He was
elected a fellow of the Royal Society in 1718. A reader in
anatomy to the barber–surgeons since 1715, he was
elected physician to St Bartholomew's Hospital in 1720, on
the death of Salisbury Cade. He wrote 'A letter showing
the danger and uncertainty of inoculating the small pox'
(1722), and edited James Drake's anatomical manual.

Wagstaffe's *Miscellaneous Works* (1725) contains a biographical preface, suggesting that Henry Levett, a physician at St Bartholomew's, was its author. The pieces had
appeared separately and it was thought by Dilke and Sir
Henry Craik that Swift might have been their author,
though the Revd Whitwell Elwin did not agree. The various pieces ridicule the praise of Chevy Chase in *The Spectator* (nos. 70 and 74), and they attack Benjamin Hoadly,
Marlborough, John Woodward, and Richard Steele, who
credited Swift with this piece. Wagstaffe had no personal
enmity against Steele, whom he did not know by sight.
Daniel Turner, who had met Wagstaffe in consultation,
praised his honesty and good nature. Wagstaffe was also a
friend of John Freind, and may have met Swift at Charles
Bernard's. He approved of Henry Sacheverell, and was a
high-churchman and a hater of the whigs.

Wagstaffe was a lover of good company but, spending
more time in society than in study, he became impoverished and, in consequence, melancholy. The weight upon
his spirits led to illness from which a contemporary said
he 'might have recovered if he had unburdened his mind
to some who had a more than ordinary value for him'
(Nichols, 324). In March 1725 he obtained formal leave of
absence from St Bartholomew's, and went to Bath for his
health. He died there on 5 May 1725.

NORMAN MOORE, *rev.* JEAN LOUDON

Sources W. Wagstaffe, *Miscellaneous works of Dr William Wagstaffe*,
2nd edn (1726) · Foster, *Alum. Oxon.* · Munk, *Roll* · N. Moore, letter,
The Athenaeum (10 June 1882), 731 · C. Creighton, *A history of epidemics in Britain*, 2nd edn, 2 (1965), 478–9 · D. Turner, *The ancient physician's legacy impartially surveyed* (1733), 2 · Nichols, *Lit. anecdotes*,
1.323–7 · J. Swift, *The journal to Stella: together with other writings relating to Stella and Vanessa* (1904) · C. W. Dilke, ed., *The papers of a critic:
selected writings by Charles Wentworth Dilke*, 2 vols. (1875) · H. Craik,
Life of Jonathan Swift (1882), chap. 11 · W. Elwin, *Some XVIII century
men of letters*, ed. W. Elwin, 2 vols. (1902) · G. A. Aitken, *The life of Sir
Richard Steele*, 2 vols. (1889), vol. 1, p. 415
Likenesses copper engraving (*Mr Toby*), repro. in Wagstaffe, *Miscellaneous works of Dr. William Wagstaffe*, frontispiece

Wailes, Reginald [Rex] (**1901–1986**), engineer, was born at
Hadley Wood, Middlesex, on 6 March 1901, the elder son of
Reginald Percy Wailes and his wife, Florence. Though baptized Reginald, he used Rex as his first name. He was educated at Oundle School where his enthusiasm for history
won him the school prize in that subject. From school he
proceeded to an apprenticeship with Robey & Co. of Lincoln as a precursor to his employment in the family firm
of George Wailes & Co. in London. This firm had been
founded by his grandfather and was employed in the
manufacture of castings, machinery, and equipment. The
nearby University College was a major customer, ordering
items for research projects, and machinery, and several
models were made for the Science Museum.

Wailes joined George Wailes & Co. in 1924, became manager in 1940, and continued to manage the firm until 1960
when it was compulsorily closed for the widening of the
Euston Road. The company had a good reputation for
sound and careful workmanship, and during the Second
World War was busy with wartime production. In 1930 he
married Enid Berridge, a professional violinist; they had
two daughters. He served as an associate member of the
council of the Institution of Mechanical Engineers from
1934 until 1937, when he became a fellow.

Wailes is best known for his authoritative work on
windmills. When he was with Robey & Co. he received a
request from K. J. Tarrant for information about Lincolnshire windmills, and because of his work on the subject
was invited in 1925 to join the Newcomen Society for the
Study of the History of Engineering and Technology. During his long membership of this society he presented
forty-three papers of which all but three were devoted to
windmills. Two of his books—*Windmills in England* (1948)
and *The English Windmill* (1954)—are models of his careful
study of the way in which windmills have come into being
and have developed over the centuries. The Newcomen
Society honoured him by making him its president from
1953 to 1955 and by electing him as an honorary member
in 1977. As a committee member in the society's earlier
years he was responsible for much of its sound development.

In 1929 the Society for the Protection of Ancient Buildings was persuaded by the national press to add windmills
to its working brief and Wailes was invited to assist as the
honorary technical adviser on windmills. Two years later
the windmill section came into being and since 1946 has
been the wind and watermill section. Wailes was made
president of the section in 1978 having served on its committee since its inception.

When Wailes retired on the closure of the family firm
he became consultant to the Industrial Monuments Survey, firstly under the Council for British Archaeology but,
after 1969, under the aegis of the then Ministry of Public
Building and Works. He was made OBE in the new year's
honours list in 1974. He also contributed to international
work on windmills. He attended the first symposium of
the International Molinological Society in 1965 and presented papers to the first four symposia. He supervised the
reconstruction of the windmill at colonial Williamsburg
in Virginia and advised on the watermill at Sleepy Hollow
on the Hudson River.

Rex Wailes was admired for the care with which he
encouraged others working in the same field, and in many
instances helped to train them. His courtesy, humour, and
love of music were strong elements in his relationship

with all who knew him. He died at Davidge Cottage, Knotty Green, Beaconsfield, where he had lived throughout his married life, on 7 January 1986. He was survived by his wife.   J. KENNETH MAJOR

Sources J. K. Major, *Rex Wailes: an appreciation of his work* (1989) · *Transactions* [Newcomen Society], 57 (1985–6), 188 · J. K. Major and J. Boyes, 'Rex Wailes: a bibliography', *Transactions* [Newcomen Society], 57 (1985–6), 189–91 · R. Wailes, 'The work of the windmill section of the SPAB, London, England', *Transactions of the second International Molinological Society symposium* (1969), 'Bibliographic notes' · d. cert.
Archives Royal Commission on the Historic Monuments of England, photographic negatives and prints · Sci. Mus. | FILM East Anglian Film Archive, "And Now They Rest" (1938) [supervised by Rex Wailes, an important short film documentary]
Wealth at death £89,358: probate, 23 April 1986, *CGPLA Eng. & Wales*

Wain, John Barrington (1925–1994), writer and poet, was born at 44 James Street, Stoke-on-Trent, on 14 March 1925, the son of Arnold Wain, a dentist, and Annie, *née* Turner. He had an elder sister, Margaret, and a young brother, Noel. In 1928 the family moved to a house in Penkull overlooking the Staffordshire countryside. He attended Newcastle under Lyme high school. Unfit to go into the armed forces, Wain went up to St John's College, Oxford, in 1943 where he read English. His principal tutor was C. S. Lewis. He published his first verse in *Mandrake*, a literary magazine founded by himself. His first critical essays were published in *Cherwell* and *Mandrake*. He occasionally acted, on one occasion playing Claudio in an Oxford University Dramatic Society production, directed by Nevill Coghill, of *Measure for Measure*. Richard Burton was Angelo in the production.

Wain took a first in finals in 1946 and held a Fereday research fellowship at St John's. At Oxford he met Kingsley Amis and Philip Larkin, and attended meetings of the Inklings. On 4 July 1947 he married Marianne Uffenheimer (*b.* 1923/4). That year he became a lecturer in English at the University of Reading, where his colleagues included D. J. Gordon and Frank Kermode. Wain's poems appeared in the limited edition *Mixed Feelings* in 1951, his first collection. It takes its title from Auden's remark: 'Poetry … might be defined as the clear expression of mixed feelings' and contemporary themes are on view: 'When it comes' is about 'the burning instant' of the atomic bomb, and speaks of global destruction as 'when it comes', not 'if it comes'. His first novel, *Hurry on Down* (1953), following the picaresque career, after reading history at Oxbridge, of Charles Lumley, caused considerable interest, since it voiced the sceptical and irreverent attitudes of the post-war generation in a similar vein to Kingsley Amis's *Lucky Jim* (1954). Wain's extremely prolific career as a scholar and critic ran alongside his imaginative productions, and each fed into the other. An early scholarly work was *Contemporary Reviews of Romantic Poetry* (1953).

Wain is associated with the Movement, a group of nine poets (never a tightly constituted group), published in D. J. Enright's collection *Poets of the 1950s* (1955) and Robert Conquest's anthology *New Lines* (1956). The Movement poems

John Barrington Wain (1925–1994), by Mark Gerson, 1958

were sceptical, middle-brow, ironical, common-sensical, and suspicious of Romantic excess, in reaction to the obscurity and posturing of the surrealists and the apocalyptic poets. They often employed strictly disciplined forms, such as *terza rima* and *villanelle*. *Living in the Present*, another novel, was published in 1955, the year Wain gave up full-time university teaching. It was followed in 1956 by his second collection of poetry, *A Word Carved on a Sill*, which took its title from Robert Graves's 'Yet love survives, a word carved on a sill.' It was inevitable that when the term Angry Young Men was coined by G. Fearon in the *Daily Telegraph* in October 1957 John Wain should be included in their number, although they never formed a tightly constituted group. Wain contributed an essay to Tom Maschler's *Declarations* (1957), which was a kind of 'angry' manifesto. His novel *The Contenders* (1958) portrays the clash between the artist Robert Lamb and the industrialist Ned Roper, both of whom come from the same provincial town. It is told from the point of view of Joe Shaw, who is critical of the metropolitan way of life.

Divorced from Marianne Uffenheimer in 1956, Wain married Eirian Mary James (1920/21–1988), deputy director of the recorded sound department of the British Council, on 1 January 1960. They had three sons and lived mainly in Wolvercote, Oxford, also spending time at Eirian's cottage in north Wales.

Wain's foray into the theatre in 1960 was not successful. He was commissioned by John Osborne and Tony Richardson to write a play and presented them with *The Take-over Bid* about a restaurant owner, Tony Orsolini, who resists the attempts of his competitors to take over his café. It was not accepted, perhaps because of its didactic antisocialism. In *Weep before God*, the 1961 poetry collection, we see Wain breaking away from some Movement elements, perhaps as a result of his visits to America in 1957 and 1958–9. His novel *Strike the Father Dead* (1962) draws on the passionate interest in jazz cultivated by Wain and his circle as it focuses on a young man called Jeremy who runs away from school and becomes a jazz pianist in low London dives during the Second World War. Yet from the collection *Wildtrack* (1965) onwards, Wain continued to separate himself from the restrictions of the Movement influences to cover the 'inward-looking Night-self' and the 'outward-looking Day-self'. The novel *The Smaller Sky* (1967), a version of Melville's *Bartleby the Scrivener*, is a study of Arthur Geary, who wishes to evade the pressures of modern living.

Wain always kept one foot in academia, lecturing in universities in France, Canada, and the United States. In 1971–2 he held the post of fellow in creative arts at Brasenose College, Oxford, and in 1973 he succeeded John Jones as professor of poetry at Oxford. His lectures were popular and included critiques of Auden, Larkin, Emily Dickinson, and Edward Thomas, among others. A selection of these lectures, accompanied by a narrative of his life as professor, was printed in *Professing Poetry* (1977). Wain also lectured on radio and television.

In 1973 Wain edited *Johnson as Critic*, anticipating his most distinguished scholarly work, *Samuel Johnson: a Biography* (1974), which won the James Tait Black memorial prize. He had a special understanding of Johnson; as a north-midlander and as someone who regarded himself as a man of letters in the broadest sense, he brought unique insights to bear on the biography. His *Poems, 1949–79* appeared in 1981 while in the following year he published *Mid-Week Period Return*, a sequence describing a train journey from Oxford to Stoke-on-Trent. John Betjeman, of whom Wain had been adversely critical earlier, is the presiding genius. *Young Shoulders* (1982), based on an earlier unsuccessful play, *Spade*, won the 1982 Whitbread prize.

Wain was appointed CBE in 1984 and made an honorary fellow of St John's College, Oxford, in 1985. *Dear Shadows: Portraits from Memory* (1986) was the second of his two autobiographical works—the first being *Sprightly Running* (1962). Here Wain presents pen-portraits of some of his contemporaries, including C. S. Lewis, E. H. W. Meyerstein, Donald MacKinnon, Charles Williams, Nevill Coghill, Marshall McLuhan, Robert Lowell, Ezra Pound, and Bill Coleman. His last collection of poems, *Open Country*, appeared in 1987.

Wain's wife Eirian died on 1 June 1988. On 17 May 1989 he married an art teacher, Patricia Ann Adams (*b.* 1942/3), only daughter of R. F. Dunn, and the editor of *With a Poet's Eye* (1986).

Wain's final novels made up the Oxford trilogy *Where the Rivers Meet* (1988–94). Following the careers of a don, Peter Leonard, and his brother Brian, who works for Morris Motors, it surveys both Oxfords, the 'town' and the 'gown', between 1930 and the early 1950s. Although none of his subsequent fiction ever had the *éclat* of his first novel, *Hurry on Down*, it has been respected and admired. A feature running through the *oeuvre* is the narrative voice—often common sense, often opinionated, sometimes hectoring and angry, sometimes facetious, sometimes sentimental—which bears a strong resemblance to Wain's.

Wain's radio dramas were more successful than his plays for the theatre, in particular the triology *The Mathematical Triangle*, written in collaboration with Laszlo Solymar, fellow in engineering at Brasenose. Broadcast in November and December 1991, the three plays dramatize the lives of Anaxagoras, Archimedes, and Hypatia.

On 10 July 1994 Bruce Purchase performed Wain's one-man show, *Johnson is Leaving*. This play portraying Samuel Johnson at the end of his life was, appropriately, Wain's swansong.

After suffering from diabetes and gradually failing sight, John Wain died of a brain haemorrhage at the John Radcliffe Hospital in Oxford on 24 May 1994, his wife Patricia surviving him. His ashes were scattered by the River Thames, Oxford.   BERNARD RICHARDS

Sources D. Gerard, *John Wain: a bibliography* (1987) · I. Hamilton, ed., *The Oxford companion to twentieth-century poetry in English* (1994) · E. Hatziolou, *John Wain: a man of letters* (1997) · B. Morrison, *The Movement: English poetry and fiction of the 1950s* (1980) · b. cert. · m. certs.
Archives Indiana University, Bloomington, letters and writings · Ransom HRC, corresp. and papers · U. Edin. L., papers | Georgetown University, Washington, DC, letters to Elizabeth Jennings · Loughborough University, letters to John Lucas · NL Wales, corresp. with Emyr Humphreys · U. Edin. L., corresp. with Philip Larkin and others
Likenesses M. Gerson, photograph, 1958, NPG [*see illus.*]

Wain, Louis William

Wain, Louis William (1860–1939), artist, was born on 5 August 1860 in St John's Street, Clerkenwell, London, the eldest child of William Matthew Wain (1825–1880), a textile trader and embroiderer of Leek, Staffordshire. His mother, Felicia Marie (Julie Felicie) Boiteux (*d.* 1910), came from Paris. He was educated first at the Orchard Street foundation school, Hackney, in London's East End and then in 1873 at St Joseph's Academy, Kennington, where he remained until 1876.

Although interested in a possible career in music, Wain decided in 1877 to enrol at the West London School of Art, where in 1881 he became assistant master. His first drawing to be published appeared in the Christmas 1881 issue of the *Illustrated, Sporting and Dramatic News*. In 1882 he was offered a staff job on the magazine and at the same time he fell in love with Emily Marie Richardson (1850/51–1887), a governess employed in the Wain household. She was the daughter of Thomas Richardson, a fruiterer. They were married on 30 January 1884 in St Mary's Chapel, Hampstead, and in the same year went to live at 42 Englands Lane, Hampstead. Soon afterwards, as Wain subsequently wrote, an addition was made to the household: a black and white kitten christened Peter. He was to be a great comfort to Emily who had been found to have breast cancer soon after their marriage. Louis would sit with his wife drawing the cat from every angle. Emily pressed him to show his drawings to his editor. In 1884 her persistence paid off; Sir William Ingram, the proprietor of the *Illustrated London News*, agreed to publish the drawings of Peter. It was this black and white cat and his antics that first brought Wain public acclaim. The publication of these drawings in *Madame Tabby's Establishment* (1886) under the pen-name Kari brought the recognition Emily wanted for her husband. He became known affectionately as 'the man who drew cats'.

Wain's pleasure in his new-found fame was short lived, as Emily died childless and in great pain in January 1887. Greatly affected by his wife's death, the young widower withdrew more and more into himself but without succumbing to grief. Accompanied by his one intimate friend, 'Peter the Great', he moved to New Cavendish Street. Although he produced many drawings for the *Illustrated London News* from 1888 to 1890 the definitive Louis Wain cat did not materialize until the Christmas issue of 1890 when the artist's transition to drawing humanized figures began with elegant cats in evening dress, sporting monocles and cigars. The British public loved them and the name Louis Wain became a household word. His drawings of cats appeared in various publications including: *The Idler* (January 1896), the *Ludgate Magazine* (April 1897), *The Captain* (December 1901), and the *Arts Realm* (1907). With so much of his work in circulation, however, it became difficult for him to sell further work. His subsequent decline can be attributed to shyness and a total lack of business acumen. He sold his drawings outright without negotiating fees or royalties. Finding himself in debt, he decided to go to America, where he worked for the Hearst newspaper group drawing a comic strip for three years (1907–10). On the death of his mother Wain returned to England, living first at Westgate-on-Sea, Kent, and then in Kilburn, London. He designed futuristic pottery and became interested in breeding spotted cats. In 1891 he had become president of the National Cat Club.

A humorist, a serious man, a worried man, and finally a mentally unbalanced man, Wain developed a persecution complex and became suspicious of his sisters, finally attacking one. This led to him being certified insane on 16 June 1924 and taken to the paupers' ward of Springfield Hospital, Tooting (the Middlesex county asylum). Here he remained for a year until the journalist and bookshop owner Dan Rider found him and publicized his plight. A fund was started and even the prime minister, Ramsay MacDonald, took a personal interest in him which resulted in Wain being transferred to Bethlem Hospital (now the Imperial War Museum). The novelist H. G. Wells stated that 'English cats that do not look like Louis Wain cats are ashamed of themselves' (his words were read by the actor Robert Lorraine in a broadcast by BBC's 2LO station on 27 August 1925). At Bethlem he was given his own room and supplied with art materials with the result that an exhibition of his work was held in London at the Twenty One Gallery in October/November 1925. Many of the drawings and watercolours of this rediscovered celebrity were undoubtedly disturbed and regarded as manifestations of schizophrenia. (Examples are included in the Guttman–Maclay collection at the Institute of Psychiatry, Maudsley Hospital, Denmark Hill.) In May 1930 he was moved to Napsbury Hospital near St Albans. The buildings were set in spacious gardens and became the background for many of his watercolours. The last exhibition held during his lifetime took place in June 1937 at Clarendon House, Clifford Street, London. In November 1936 Wain

suffered a stroke and became bedridden. He died in Napsbury Hospital on 4 July 1939, and was buried on 6 July with his father and sisters Caroline and Josephine in Kensal Green cemetery, close to the grave of his friend the humorous artist Phil May (1864–1903). A comprehensive exhibition of his work was held at the Victoria and Albert Museum, London, in 1972–3.

During his lifetime Wain illustrated more than two hundred books, many written by himself. Other publications in which his illustrations appeared from 1891 to 1913 included the *Illustrated London News*, *Boy's Own Paper*, and *Chatterbox*. Sixteen Louis Wain annuals appeared from 1901 to 1913. His postcards were published by more than forty publishers including Raphael Tuck and Valentine & Sons. They were also published in America, Holland, France, Germany, and Spain. Wain produced much publicity material for many advertisers including De Benkelaer biscuits, Jackson's hats and boots, Jackson's of Piccadilly tea, the Mazawattee tea company, and Castile soap. In 1916 he was approached by the pioneer filmmaker H. D. Wood who asked him to draw an animated cartoon entitled *Pussyfoot*. The venture was not a success.

MICHAEL PARKIN

Sources R. Dale, *Louis Wain* (1991) · M. Parkin, *Louis Wain's cats* (1983) · C. C. Delulio and D. Ross, *Especially cats: Louis Wain's humorous postcards* (1965) · B. Reade, *Louis Wain* (1972) [exhibition catalogue, V&A] · b. cert. · m. cert. · d. cert.
Archives priv. coll., reference MSS collection · V&A, MSS

Wainewright, Thomas Griffiths [*pseuds.* Janus Weathercock, Cornelius van Vinkbooms] (**1794–1847**), painter, writer on art, and putative poisoner, was born probably on 4 October 1794, the son of Thomas Wainewright (*d.* in or before 1803) of Sloane Street, in the parish of St Luke, Chelsea, London, and his wife, Ann (1773–1794), daughter of Ralph *Griffiths (1720?–1803), founder and editor of the *Monthly Review*, and his second wife, Elizabeth, *née* Clark. His parents had married by special licence at St Nicholas's, Chiswick, on 13 December 1792. Thomas Wainewright senior was the second son of the twelve children of Robert Wainewright, a solicitor of Gray's Inn who lived in Hatton Garden. Though their father was a Unitarian, several of the elder Thomas Wainewright's brothers became Church of England clergymen, while others followed him into the legal profession. After their marriage Thomas and Ann Wainewright lived with her father at his home, Linden House, Turnham Green, Chiswick, where Wainewright probably was born. His mother died at his birth and his father died while he was still a child, before June 1803, when his grandfather Ralph Griffiths made his will. Ralph Griffiths, to whom Wainewright owed his second name and by whom he was brought up after being orphaned, left his grandson annuities of about £200 (the interest on a sum settled on his mother on her marriage and a further sum paid to his trustees on the death of his father) but no further capital or property, the bulk of which he left to his widow and the son from his first marriage, George Edward Griffiths, to whom he also left the proprietorship of the *Monthly Review* and the responsibility of taking care of Wainewright, his half-sister's child.

Early life: artist and writer Wainewright was educated at Charles Burney's school in Greenwich. His talent for drawing the likenesses of his friends and masters led to his apprenticeship at the age of nineteen to his kinsman the fashionable portrait painter Thomas *Phillips. He made a copy (City of Nottingham Museums, Newstead Abbey collections) of his master's celebrated portrait of Lord Byron (1813; priv. coll.). Boredom and 'giddiness', however, led him 'to postpone the pencil to the sword' (Hazlitt, 305). A brief spell (from April 1814 to May 1815) as an ensign in the Bedfordshire regiment of foot (more notable in the early nineteenth century for the glamour of its uniform than for any form of active service) induced in Wainewright a deep depression. From this manifestation of the instability that was to underlie his future behaviour he was gradually restored to health by the care of 'a most delicately affectioned and unwearied (though young and fragile) nurse' and the healing power of Wordsworth's poetry (ibid., 306). On 13 November 1817 at St Martin-in-the-Fields, Trafalgar Square, he married his 'fragile nurse', Eliza Frances Ward, daughter of the first marriage of Mrs Abercromby, a widow who lived at Mortlake.

Following his recovery Wainewright began to contribute to the *London Magazine* under the pseudonyms Janus Weathercock and Cornelius van Vinkbooms. Under the editorship of John Scott, between 1821 and 1823 he regularly contributed 'Sentimentalities on the Fine Arts' and 'Dogmas for dilettantes', written in a fluent but facetious style. W. C. Hazlitt's attribution to Wainewright—in his introduction to *Essays and Criticisms of Thomas Griffiths Wainewright* (1880)—of articles published under the pseudonym Egomet Bonmot has recently been challenged by Marc Vaulbert de Chantilly. In his last contribution to the magazine, 'Janus Weatherbound, or, The Weathercock Steadfast for Lack of Oil', Wainewright 'admitted the tawdry articles signed J. W. and C. V. V.' (Hazlitt, 304). Wainewright's connection with the magazine brought him into contact with Thomas Hood, Allan Cunningham, William Hazlitt, Thomas de Quincey, and Charles Lamb, who wrote of him as 'their best stay, kind, light-hearted Wainewright' (ibid., xxx). W. C. Hazlitt acknowledged that 'the literary criticisms of Wainewright are unquestionably the offspring of an acute and cultivated mind' (ibid., xxiv). Though many of his contemporaries wrote under a pseudonym in journals and magazines, Wainewright's literary guises, stylistically in keeping with T. N. Talfourd's description of him as 'a young man on the bright side of thirty, with an undress military air and the conversation of a smart, clever, lively, heartless, voluptuous coxcomb' (ibid., xxiii), may provide an indication of a deeper fragmentation of his personality. Within his reviews the two-faced Janus sometimes speaks directly to the more seriously minded van Vinkbooms, and vice versa, thereby creating a further level of literary 'deception'. Though they remained fairly thin disguises, these literary personae provided Wainewright with opportunities to explore a variety of identities.

Known to have assisted in the compilation of exhibition catalogues at Somerset House, and to have contemplated the publication of 'An Art Novel' and two works on the various schools of painting, from 1821 to 1825 Wainewright was also an exhibitor at the Royal Academy. The titles of his exhibited works record their risqué subject matter; they include 'Subject from the Romance of Undine, chap. VI'; 'Paris in the Chamber of Helen: "There Jove-loved Hector Entered"'; 'An Attempt from the Undine of de la Motte Fougué [*sic*]: "By degrees, outward terrors joined to inward misgivings, to punish Bertalda's passion for the husband of her friend"'; and 'The Milk-Maid's Song: "Come live with me and be my love"' (Graves, *RA Exhibitors*, 8.99). Talfourd commented that Wainewright's drawings of women were 'voluptuous, trembling on the borders of the indelicate' (Curling, 89). The British Museum holds a sepia drawing of his that confirms that his treatment of this subject, though not devoid of skill, was coarse. His interest in erotic images he explored with fellow artists Henry Fuseli and Theodore von Holst; the latter sold many of his 'private' drawings to the prince of Wales (later George IV).

Connections: forger and putative poisoner Of his circle of literary and artistic friends and patrons Wainewright stated that 'his pen and brush introduced him to the notice and friendship of men whose fame is European' (Blair, 263). Among these were Fuseli ('the god of his idolatry'), Stothard, Westall, Sir Thomas Lawrence, and Flaxman (Hazlitt, xix). His occasional work as a reviewer and artist, together with some art dealing, slightly increased his income; this derived mainly from the annuity from his grandfather but was not sufficient to sustain the lifestyle that he enjoyed from 1821 to 1828 in luxuriously furnished rented apartments at 49 Great Marlborough Street (formerly inhabited by the actress Sarah Siddons), where he formed a collection of prints and maiolica and entertained extravagantly. His guests included Lamb, Sir David Wilkie, William Macready, Charles Wentworth Dilke, Talfourd, and B. W. Procter (Barry Cornwall), who described Mrs Wainewright as 'a sharp-eyed, self-possessed woman dressed in showy, flimsy finery' (Curling, 218). Under mounting financial pressure Wainewright, in the names of his trustees, forged the signatures on a power of attorney instructing the Bank of England to pay him part of the capital sum on which, under the terms of his grandfather's will, he was entitled to the interest alone. According to Andrew Motion the forgery took place in 1822, ten days 'after the £5,000 Navy 5 per cent stock, which TGW had inherited from his grandfather, was converted to £5,250 New 4 per cent Annuities on 5 July 1822' (Motion, 129). On that occasion Wainewright fraudulently obtained £2250 and then 'committed a second forgery on 17 May 1823, and collected the remaining £3000' (ibid.).

Again financially embarrassed, in 1828 Wainewright and his wife went to live with his uncle George Edward Griffiths, who had remained a bachelor, at Linden House, Chiswick. When Griffiths died, suddenly and intestate, on 16 January 1828, aged about fifty-six, his estate passed to Wainewright as his next of kin. On 4 June at St Nicholas's, Chiswick, Wainewright's son was baptized Griffiths Wainewright, after his recently deceased great-uncle (the gap of eleven years between his parents' marriage and the boy's baptism has led some commentators to suggest that he may have been illegitimate). Over the same period Wainewright's mother-in-law, Mrs Abercromby, and his wife's two half-sisters Helen Frances Phoebe (b. 1809) and Madalina Rosa Hibernia (Madeleine; b. 1810) also came to live at Linden House. Apart from the house itself, however, the value of George Griffiths's estate had amounted to about £5000—not enough to pay off all Wainewright's debts and maintain the property and his extended family—and he entered into precipitous loan arrangements with a number of creditors. Under a warrant of attorney he owed £610 to a Mr Sharpus, to whom in July 1830 he granted a bill of sale for the furniture and effects of Linden House. Both the warrant and the bill were dated 21 December 1830. The house and estate he mortgaged to a moneylender to whom he was already heavily in debt.

In March 1830 Wainewright, with his wife, persuaded her half-sister Helen Abercromby (of whom Wainewright made a portrait drawing; repr. Hazlitt, facing p. 29) to insure her life for two sums, of £2000 and £3000. Mrs Abercromby objected to further policies being taken out on her daughter's life, but in August of that year she herself died a sudden and agonizing death in Linden House. Further policies were taken out in Helen's name; her life was insured, in total for £18,000, with six different insurance companies. In each case Wainewright paid the premium. On 12 December the family moved to lodgings at 12 Conduit Street, London, where on the following day Helen made a will naming her sister Madeleine legatee and Wainewright executor. On 21 December, the day that Wainewright's bills fell due, Helen Abercromby died, aged twenty-one. Her symptoms, as recalled by the family nurse, Sarah Handcock, and the servant Harriet Grattan, were identical to those of her mother, but in contrast to her mother's sudden death Helen's condition, which led to dizziness, vomiting, loss of sight, and convulsions, had worsened over several days. Dr Charles Locock (who later attended Queen Victoria at the births of her children) had attended Helen in her illness and performed an autopsy on the day after her death. He observed some irritation to the stomach but attributed her death to the ill effects of a gastric chill and an indigestible supper of oysters and beer that Helen had consumed a few days before she died. At that date the means to detect strychnine as a cause of death had not been established, and her case is of interest in the history of toxicology. The suspicious circumstances of her death led the insurance companies to withhold payment, and Wainewright filed a bill in chancery to recover £3000 from one insurance company, the Imperial, before leaving for the continent. Mrs Wainewright, the boy Griffiths, and Madeleine Abercromby meanwhile went to live in Pimlico.

In 1835 Wainewright's suit against the Imperial insurance company came before Mr Justice Abinger in the court of the exchequer. The judge directed the jury not to consider whether murder had been committed. They could not agree a verdict and the case went to a second trial, when the jury found for the defendants on the ground of concealment by Miss Abercromby. Throughout this period Wainewright had remained in France, where he had spent some months in prison in Paris; on his arrest the French police had found him to be carrying strychnine. In June 1837 he returned to London, even though in 1835 the Bank of England had discovered the forgery that he had committed over ten years earlier and had issued a warrant for his arrest. He was recognized by Forrester, a City runner, and arrested. On 5 July 1837 he at first pleaded not guilty to five indictments at the Old Bailey but then, after hearing that the Imperial would not press the three capital charges if he pleaded guilty to the two small charges, he changed his plea accordingly. He was sentenced by the recorder to transportation to Van Diemen's Land for life. Though strongly suspected, no charge of murder was ever brought against him. The anecdote, referred to by Oscar Wilde, that Wainewright confessed to killing Helen because she had such thick ankles, while supported by visual evidence in his drawings of women that he was fascinated by their ankles, remains unconfirmed by a first-hand confessional document. (Various sources mention that Wainewright left a diary but this has not come to light.) While in Newgate awaiting transportation he was recognized by Macready, who was visiting the prison with John Forster and Charles Dickens.

Transportation, death, and reputation Sent out on the convict ship *Susan*, Wainewright arrived in Hobart on 21 November 1837. He worked on the roads in a chain gang and later transferred from the prisoners' barracks to Hobart Hospital, where he worked on the wards. Following a decline in his health he was relieved of some duties and allowed to paint portraits of hospital staff, local officials, and members of their families. His portraits of women tend to show slender, smooth-haired, doe-eyed sitters in a hard outline resembling a fashion plate. Examples of these are in the Art Gallery of South Australia, Adelaide, and the National Gallery of Australia, Canberra. A self-portrait drawing that he made in the 1840s (repr. Curling, frontispiece) shows him almost full-face, with long, thinning, receding hair and a dark moustache. His eyebrows are sharply arched over deep-set eyes that do not confront the viewer directly but look away to one side. A dark line over the bridge of his nose gives the impression of a frown. His shirt is open at the neck and the collar of his jacket turned up in a slightly Byronic fashion. The drawing is inscribed, perhaps in Wainewright's hand, 'Head of a *Convict*, very characteristic of *low cunning & x revenge*!'. In April 1844 he fulsomely petitioned the governor of Van Diemen's Land, Sir John Eardley-Wilmot, for a ticket-of-leave. This was refused but he was granted a probation pass, and in November his name was announced in the Hobart *Gazette* as one that would go forward to Queen Victoria for a conditional pardon (Motion, 277). In December 1845 his ticket-of-leave was granted. Wainewright died, of apoplexy, in St Mary's Hospital, Hobart, on 17 August 1847.

A gentlemanly education, literary and artistic skills, and a cultivated taste for objects of high aesthetic quality, combined with the capacity for criminal acts including forgery and, apparently, poisoning, have made Waine-wright an intriguing subject for fiction and biography; examples of the former include Edward Bulwer Lytton's *Lucretia, or, The Children of the Night* (1846), Dickens's *Hunted Down*, and Hal Porter's *The Tilted Cross* (1961). Melodramatic newspaper and magazine accounts of Wainewright that appeared after his death coloured later studies and biographical accounts such as those included in Talfourd's *Final Memorials of Charles Lamb* (1848); Walter Thornbury's *Old Stories Re-told* (1870); A. G. Allen's account in Thomas Seccombe's *Twelve Bad Men* (1894); B. W. Procter's *An Autobiographical Fragment* (1877); Oscar Wilde's essay 'Pen, Pencil and Poison: a Study in Green', in the *Fortnightly Review* (1889); and W. C. Hazlitt's biographical essay in his collection of Wainewright's essays and criticisms (1880). In *Janus Weathercock* (1938) Jonathan Curling set out to distinguish between the facts of Wainewright's existence and the layers of speculation and story-telling that have subsequently embellished accounts of his life. His conscientious use of primary sources corrected many errors but introduced others, and further records have subsequently come to light. Perceiving difficulties in the use of 'orthodox biographical methods' in recovering Wainewright's history, Andrew Motion experimented in *Wainewright the Poisoner* (2000) with 'a mixture of different forms—some imaginative, some factual' (pp. xvi, xviii). Although not 'designed to "correct" [Wainewright's] Confession in any consistent way' (Motion, xviii) the notes at the end of each chapter contain unreliable information that undermines their usefulness in establishing the facts of Wainewright's existence. The recent discovery of further documents relating to Wainewright means that he continues to be the subject of biographical investigation.

ANNETTE PEACH

Sources J. Curling, *Janus Weathercock: the life of Thomas Griffiths Wainewright, 1794–1847* (1938) · W. C. Hazlitt, *Essays and criticisms by Thomas Wainewright now first collected, with some account of the author* (1880) · M. Vaulbert de Chantilly, *Wainewright the poisoner: an example of Andrew Motion's 'high scholarship'* (privately printed, 2000) · A. Motion, *Wainewright the poisoner* (2000) · M. Vaulbert de Chantilly, ed., *'Some passages' in the life, &c. of Egomet Bonmot, Esq. ... ascribed to Thomas Griffiths Wainewright, but probably the work of Edward Gandy* (2000) · Graves, *RA exhibitors* · A. Peach, 'Portraits of Byron', *Walpole Society*, 62 (2000), 1–144 · D. Blair, '"Janus Weathercock": a curiosity of literature', *N&Q*, 3rd ser., 10 (1866), 263–4 · P. Hammond, 'Thomas Griffiths Wainewright', *Brentford and Chiswick Local History Society Journal*, 7 (1998), 5–11 · private information (2004) [Peter Hammond] · photographs, sale catalogues, NPG, Heinz Archive and Library · 'Wainewright, Thomas', *AusDB* · bishops' transcripts of Chiswick parish registers, LMA · E. Wagner, 'Crossing the border between fact and fantasy', *The Times* (17 Feb 2000), 40 · J. Ezard, 'Fact vies with fiction in pursuit of the classic English poisoner', *The Guardian* (26 Feb 2000), 3 · *DNB* · IGI

Likenesses photograph, *c.*1843 (after T. G. Wainewright), BM, NPG · T. G. Wainewright, self-portrait, repro. in Curling, *Janus Weathercock*, frontispiece

Wainwright family (*per. c.*1750–1825), musicians, were active in north-west England in the eighteenth and early nineteenth centuries. It is difficult to identify individuals precisely as biographical evidence is often anecdotal, and contemporary accounts may only refer to 'Mr' or 'Miss' Wainwright.

John Wainwright (*bap.* 1723, *d.* 1767/8) was baptized at St Mary the Virgin, Stockport, Cheshire, on 14 April 1723, the son of John Wainwright (*d.* 1766), and his wife, Mary Heginbothom (*d.* 1767). The family probably lived at 58 Churchgate, Stockport, and John senior, a joiner, was occasionally employed at St Mary's. The younger John's education is unrecorded. He is described as organist of St Mary's on a memorial plaque erected in 1903 but no evidence of this appointment exists. On 30 December 1746 he married Anne Clarkson (*bap.* 1725, *d.* in or after 1781) at St Peter's, Blackley, north of Manchester, although she too came from Stockport. They had moved to Pool Court, Manchester, by 1748, when their first child, Robert, was baptized at Manchester collegiate church, now the cathedral. John Wainwright's occupation is given as 'Musick Master' in the church register. On 19 October 1749, according to the records of the court leet, a John Wainwright (there may have been another in Manchester at this time) was appointed scavenger for 'St Anns Square and the Streets Adjacent' (*The Court Leet Records of Manchester*, 7, 1888, 180). Newspaper references to 'Mr Wainwright' suggest that he also performed locally as an organist, conductor, and perhaps violinist. John Wainwright is famous as the composer of the Christmas hymn 'Christians awake', to words by John Byrom. Apparently on Christmas eve 1750, Byrom recorded in shorthand in his pocket book, 'The singing boys with Mr Wainwright came here and sang "Christians Awake"' (W. Shaw, 186). The tune was published by Caleb Ashworth (1761) as 'Mortram, old 50th Psalm Tune' and by Wainwright in *A Collection of Psalm Tunes, Anthems, Hymns and Chants* (1766) under the title 'A Hymn for Christmas Day': today it is usually called 'Yorkshire' or 'Stockport'. Although Wainwright is described as organist of the collegiate church at Manchester on the title-page of his *Collection*, he was not officially appointed organist and instructor of the choristers until 12 May 1767. He died in Manchester and was buried at St Mary the Virgin, Stockport, on 28 January 1768. In 1908 part of his gravestone was discovered supporting a greenhouse in a local garden: it seems that it was destroyed when the church steeple was blown up with gunpowder in 1810.

Robert Wainwright (*bap.* 1748, *d.* 1782) was baptized at Manchester collegiate church on 17 September 1748, the first child of John Wainwright (*d.* 1767/1768). He was elected chorister at Manchester collegiate church on 25 June 1759. After his father's death he was appointed organist, instructor of the choristers, and 'singing man' at Manchester collegiate church on 18 February 1768. He matriculated from Magdalen College, Oxford, on 18 April 1774, and received the degrees of BMus and DMus from the university on 29 April 1774. He married Mary Woodworth (*bap.* 1754, *d.* 1778) at Manchester collegiate church on 12 January 1775, and on 1 March of the same year he was elected organist at St Peter's, Liverpool. According to Edward Miller, he applied for the post of organist at Halifax parish church in 1776, but the builder of the new organ, John Snetzler, thought he played too fast: 'Te tevil, te tevil, he run over te keys like von cat; he vill not give my piphes room to shpeak' (W. Shaw, 187). William Herschel, later the well-known astronomer, was appointed instead. Like his father, John, Robert Wainwright conducted performances of Handel's oratorios throughout north-west England. He is said to have sold the copyright of his own oratorio *The Fall of Egypt* (now lost) for £1000, and his setting of Dryden's *Ode on St Cecilia's Day* was performed at a Liverpool music festival. Some collections of his chamber music are still extant, but they are rarely performed today. He died in Liverpool on 15 July 1782.

Richard Wainwright (*bap.* 1757, *d.* 1825) was baptized at St Ann's, Manchester, on 8 July 1757, the third son of John Wainwright (*d.* 1767/1768). He became a chorister at Manchester collegiate church on 6 January 1768, and probably became organist and instructor of the choristers at some time after 1775 when his brother Robert moved to Liverpool. There is no specific record of his appointment, and the collegiate records state that 'Dr Wainwright' was organist in the annual audit of 23 December 1776, but this is perhaps an error; Richard Wainwright was listed in the 1777 audit. In 1780 he composed music for a grand Christmas pantomime, *The Lancashire Witches, or, Harlequin Everywhere*, performed at the Theatre Royal, Manchester, and he later wrote a celebrated glee, 'Life's a Bumper', and *A Collection of Hymns … for the Children of the Liverpool Blue Coat Hospital* (1812). He was also apparently a cellist at the Manchester Gentlemen's Concerts, and may have been both the Mr Wainwright who led many local performances of Handel's oratorios as first violinist, and the one who at the Liverpool and Manchester music festivals between 1784 and 1789 variously played in the orchestra, played the organ, and conducted. He reputedly eloped with Jane Marriott (*bap.* 1765, *d.* 1794), a young lady from a boarding-school in Prestwich. They subsequently married at Manchester collegiate church on 5 November 1781, and their first child, John, was baptized on 25 March 1782 at St Peter's, Liverpool, where, on 4 September 1782, Richard again succeeded his brother Robert as organist. He resigned this post in October 1804, and moved to Preston where he became organist of the parish church, probably until 1810. He was never organist of St James's, Toxteth Park, Liverpool, contrary to some accounts. He was reinstated at St Peter's in 1812 and died at St Anne Street, Liverpool, on 20 August 1825.

Other musical members of the family include **William Wainwright** (*bap.* 1736?, *d.* 1797), who is supposed to have been a son of John (*d.* 1767/1768), although no baptismal record exists, and he could equally have been his brother, as a William, son of John and Mary Wainwright, was baptized at St Mary the Virgin, Stockport, on 9 May 1736. William Wainwright was an excellent double bass player, sang at Manchester collegiate church, and ran a music shop with William Sudlow at the sign of the Violin and Flutes in Hanging Ditch, Manchester, between about 1780 and 1795. He was buried at St Mary the Virgin, Stockport, on 5 July 1797, and the church records describe him as an organist. Richard Wainwright, baptized at St Mary's, Stockport, on 19 January 1729, was certainly a brother of

John Wainwright. He was elected a singing man at Manchester collegiate church on 27 December 1753, and remained there until his death. He was buried at St Mary's, Stockport, on 2 January 1759. Some sources also mention a Samuel Wainwright, who may have been the S. Wainwright for whom a benefit concert was held at Stockport in 1757. Another benefit concert, for 'Miss Wainwright, Organist', was held in 1765 (G. Shaw, 142). She may have been the organist at St Mary's, Stockport, who according to the parish accounts of 1781 received 'her salary' of 10 guineas (churchwarden's accounts, St Mary's, Stockport, Ches. & Chester ALSS, 3435/8/4, vol. 2, p. 4).

SALLY DRAGE

Sources T. M. Griffith, unpubd paper to be read before the Lancashire and Cheshire Antiquarian Society, 1972, Man. CL, Manchester Archives and Local Studies, C26/1/1 • H. W. Shaw, *The succession of organists of the Chapel Royal and the cathedrals of England and Wales from c.1538* (1991), 186–9 • G. Shaw, ed., *Annals of Oldham and district* [n.d.], vol. 2, pp. 112–239 • H. Heginbotham, *Stockport: ancient and modern* (1892), 365–6 • G. R. Axon, 'John Wainwright—musician', *Cheshire Life* (Dec 1950), 33–4 • B. St. J. B. Joule, 'Music and musicians in Manchester', *Manchester City News* (7 Dec 1878), 231–2 • 'John Wainwright', *Cheshire Notes and Queries*, 9 (1904), 221–2 • parish register, Cheshire, Stockport, St Mary the Virgin, 14 April 1723 [baptism: John Wainwright junior]; 31 Jan 1725 [baptism: Ann Clarkson]; 9 May 1736 [baptism: William Wainwright]; 22 June 1766 [burial: John Wainwright senior]; 24 Aug 1767 [burial: Mary Heginbothom]; 28 Jan 1768 [burial: John Wainwright junior]; 5 July 1797 [burial: William Wainwright] • parish register, Lancashire, Blackley, St Peter, 30 Dec 1746 [marriage: John Wainwright junior] • parish register, Manchester, St Ann, 8 July 1757 [baptism: Richard Wainwright] • parish register, Lancashire, Manchester collegiate church, 17 Sep 1748 [baptism: Robert Wainwright] • *GM*, 1st ser., 95/2 (1825), 286 • J. Adkins, *Preston parish church: its organists, choir and organs, 1574–1915* (Preston, 1915)

Archives Man. CL, Manchester Archives and Local Studies, C26/1/1

Wainwright, Alfred (1907–1991), walker and writer, was born on 17 January 1907 at 331 Audley Range, Blackburn, Lancashire, the fourth and last child of Albert Wainwright (*b.* 1870), a stonemason, and his wife, Emily, *née* Woodcock (1873–1942), daughter of an ironmonger. Although baptized Alfred, he never used his first name, and preferred to be known as A. Wainwright or A. W., which is how he became known to millions of Lake District lovers for his walking books. If asked what the A. stood for, he replied 'it isn't for Aloysius, if that's what you're thinking' (*The Independent*, 22 Jan 1991). He was brought up in a terraced house, surrounded by cotton mills belching out their smoke and mill girls clip-clopping in their clogs along the cobblestones to work. His father was not always in work, partly because of his drinking problem, and the family suffered periods of poverty. Wainwright went to Blakey Moor higher elementary school, Blackburn, but left at the age of thirteen in 1920 to begin work as an office boy at Blackburn town hall. After three years he became a clerk in the borough treasurer's department, where it was pointed out to him that he would never be promoted unless he had passed the appropriate professional exams. For most of the next seven years he studied accountancy by correspondence and evening classes, before eventually qualifying as a municipal accountant. In any spare time he

Alfred Wainwright (1907–1991), by Nicholas A. Read

followed the fortunes of Blackburn Rovers, and later helped to found their supporters' club in 1939.

Wainwright's first visit to the Lake District was in 1930, at the age of twenty-three. This was rather late, in some ways, as rambling in Lakeland had become very popular with young men from industrial Lancashire. In *Ex-Fellwanderer* (1987) he described his first impressions on looking over Lake Windermere: 'It was a moment of magic, a revelation so unexpected that I stood transfixed, unable to believe my eyes. Those few hours on Orrest Head cast a spell which changed my life.' From then on he spent his leisure time walking, either locally in Lancashire or on visits to Lakeland, determined to find a job there if he could. He managed it in 1941, when he joined the borough treasurer's department in Kendal, taking a drop in salary. Meanwhile he had married Ruth Holden (1909–1985), a cotton weaver and daughter of William Holden, at Furthergate Congregational Church, Blackburn, on 24 December 1931. They had one son, Peter (1933–1998). According to Wainwright, it very soon became an unhappy marriage. Rather unfairly, he felt his wife had not kept pace with his rising professional status and that he had little in common with her. They kept up appearances in view of his august municipal position—he became borough treasurer of Kendal in 1948—but at home they hardly talked to each other.

Wainwright's passion for walking became even more intense once he moved to Lakeland, partly to escape from his unhappy home life. In 1952 he began the self-created task of walking every fell in Lakeland and recording his walks, with pen-and-ink drawings, for his own amusement, so he said, to read by his fireside when he was too old to walk. He divided Lakeland into seven regions and took thirteen years over the project, climbing 214 fells,

travelling on foot or by public transport from his Kendal home. He never learned to drive a car. On completing the first book, he decided to publish it himself. He wanted his own handwriting, his own drawings, his own page layouts to be reproduced the way he had done them, without an ounce of printer's type. *The Eastern Fells*, the first in his Pictorial Guides to the Lakeland Fells, came out in 1955 and the final one, *The Western Fells*, was published in 1966. The early editions of the first five books in the series had the name of a colleague, Henry Marshall (borough librarian of Kendal), as the publisher. Later they were all published by the *Westmorland Gazette*.

Wainwright retired as borough treasurer of Kendal in 1967 and threw himself into writing and walking full-time. In all he published fifty-nine books on walking, in Wales and Scotland as well as Lakeland. The Pictorial Guides were the best-known and best-loved, along with *Pennine Way Companion* (1968), and *A Coast to Coast Walk* (1973). By 1985 over 1 million of his Pictorial Guides had been sold—yet Wainwright had given no interviews, done no publicity or signing session, and no biographical details ever appeared on his guidebooks. He was appointed MBE in 1966. His first marriage was dissolved in 1968 and on 10 March 1970 he married Betty McNally (*b.* 1922), a state-enrolled nurse, and daughter of John Hayes, public works contractor. Her first marriage had also been dissolved. They had twenty years of an exceedingly happy marriage together.

Wainwright was 6 feet 3 inches tall and burly, with thick hair which originally was carrot red, much to his embarrassment as a young man. Even when, in later years, his hair had turned a more distinguished white, Betty, his second wife, always referred to him as Red. He avoided all publicity until the 1980s, when his devotion to Animal Rescue Cumbria—an animal refuge which he and Betty had helped to set up, and to which he was very soon giving away almost all his royalties—led him to agree to a series of walking programmes for BBC television with Eric Robson. These turned him, aged eighty, into a national figure. He also did a series of glossy photographic walking books for Michael Joseph, in order to help the same charity. He was not naturally sociable, disliked public occasions, and could be gruff and short with strangers, but on paper, and in private, he was amusing and engaging. His Pictorial Guides were considered little masterpieces—philosophical strolls rather than mere guidebooks, with his own personal feelings and observations, written and drawn by a master craftsman. Wainwright died at the Westmorland County Hospital, Kendal, on 20 January 1991, of cardiac failure. He was cremated at Kendal four days later, and his ashes were scattered on Hay Stacks, above Buttermere, one of his favourite fells. In *Fellwanderer* (1966) he wrote: 'If you dear readers should get a bit of grit in your boots as you are crossing Haystacks in the years to come, please treat it with respect. It might be me.'

HUNTER DAVIES

Sources H. Davies, *Wainwright* (1995) · A. Wainwright, *Fellwanderer: the story behind the guide books* (1966) · A. Wainwright, *Ex-fellwanderer: a thanksgiving* (1987) · *The Times* (22 Jan 1991) · *The*

Independent (22 Jan 1991) · Wainwright's MSS and family documents · private information (2004) · personal knowledge (2004) · b. cert. · m. certs. · d. cert.

Archives priv. coll. | Cumbria AS, Kendal, papers and drawings relating to Lakeland Fells · Kendal Museum, Kendal, Cumbria | FILM BBC TV series, 1986 – available as five videos · Border TV – last TV interview with him, 27/1/1991 | SOUND *Desert island discs*, BBC Radio 4, 4/9/1988 [one of few radio interviews he ever gave]

Likenesses N. A. Read, photograph, NPG [*see illus.*] · photograph, repro. in *The Times* · photograph, repro. in *The Independent* · photographs, repro. in Davies, *Wainwright*, following pp. 52 and 292

Wealth at death under £234,316: probate, 8 March 1991, CGPLA Eng. & Wales

Wainwright, John (*bap.* 1723, *d.* 1767/8). *See under* Wainwright family (*per.* c.1750–1825).

Wainwright, Richard (*bap.* 1757, *d.* 1825). *See under* Wainwright family (*per.* c.1750–1825).

Wainwright, Robert (*bap.* 1748, *d.* 1782). *See under* Wainwright family (*per.* c.1750–1825).

Wainwright, William (*bap.* 1736?, *d.* 1797). *See under* Wainwright family (*per.* c.1750–1825).

Waismann, Friedrich (1896–1959), philosopher, was born on 21 March 1896 in Vienna, the son of Leopold Waismann (*d.* 1931), a manufacturer of hardware who was a naturalized Austrian of Russian origin, and his wife, Clara Schwarz (*d.* 1929). Having taken his *Matura* in 1917 as an external applicant, he entered Vienna University as a foreign student of Russian nationality. He took a degree in physics in 1922. In 1937 he received a doctorate for his philosophical publications.

From 1922 to 1936 Waismann had a precarious career under the patronage of Moritz Schlick, professor of philosophy and founder of the Vienna circle. He taught at the Volkshochschule, from 1929 he was librarian of the philosophy faculty, and he gave private tuition. Throughout he served as Schlick's unofficial assistant, running his graduate seminar.

Realizing that the conception of logic presented in the *Tractatus logico-philosophicus* was of fundamental importance to logical empiricism, Schlick made contact with Ludwig Wittgenstein in 1927. Schlick came to envisage a more accessible presentation of Wittgenstein's ideas, and assigned this task to Waismann. From 1928 Waismann's efforts centred on gathering and expounding Wittgenstein's ideas under Schlick's general supervision. Waismann acted as the spokesman for Wittgenstein's point of view (notably at the Second Congress for Scientific Philosophy at Königsberg in September 1930). Within the Vienna circle, Waismann sided with Schlick, who represented the conservative wing, against the radicals headed by Otto Neurath. The conservatives wanted the work of the circle to be politically neutral and to focus on the analysis of logic, mathematics, and the natural sciences, whereas the radicals urged active political engagement along Marxist lines, and directed attention to the social sciences. This split led to intellectual conflict and personal animosity.

From shorthand notes of conversations with Wittgenstein, supplemented by dictations and typescripts, Waismann wrote lectures and articles on Wittgenstein's conception of mathematics, his view of logic, and his treatment of identity and probability. The culmination was to be a systematic presentation of his ideas on logic, language, and philosophy. Advertised in 1930 under the title *Logik, Sprache, Philosophie*, this book was to be the initial volume in the series Schriften zur Wissenschaftlichen Weltauffassung (the series envisaged as a systematic exposition of the philosophy of the Vienna circle). Schlick wanted the book to give a perspicuous account of the conception of logic presented in the *Tractatus*, since he regarded that conception as the basis of logical empiricism. The project generated tension with Wittgenstein. He worried about its misrepresenting his current, rapidly evolving position. As a consequence he decided in 1932 to become co-author with Waismann, but then withdrew from co-authorship in 1934, promising to Schlick to continue to assist Waismann in the project.

Deprivation of the librarianship and Schlick's murder in 1936 made Waismann's position untenable. He desperately needed to publish to obtain a secure post. He compiled a collection of Schlick's later papers (*Gesammelte Aufsätze*, 1938). He completed *Einführung in das mathematische Denken* (1936), which developed some of Wittgenstein's leading ideas into an overview of the nature of mathematics. He signed a contract with Springer in October 1936 to publish *Logik, Sprache, Philosophie*. Although it was finished in 1937, the text remained unpublished (probably because of the *Anschluss*). A second attempt to publish it in the Netherlands was frustrated by the outbreak of war.

Waismann went temporarily to Cambridge in October 1937. One term's funding was extended to two, whereupon the *Anschluss* made him a permanent refugee. This created awkwardness when Wittgenstein himself returned to Cambridge from leave in Norway, since Waismann's lectures, based on his own two completed texts, expounded Wittgenstein's earlier ideas. Wittgenstein did nothing to soften the difficulties, allegedly banning his students from attending Waismann's lectures. Waismann felt bitter and depressed.

In February 1940 Waismann moved to Oxford, where he remained permanently apart from a brief period of internment (as an enemy alien) at Paignton, Devon, from 22 July to 3 October 1940. Supported by funding for refugees and grants from Magdalen and All Souls colleges, he gave miscellaneous lectures. Eventually he became lecturer in the philosophy of science and mathematics in 1946, then successively senior lecturer (1948) and reader (1950) in the philosophy of mathematics, and finally reader in the philosophy of science in 1955. He took British nationality in 1950, and he was elected a fellow of the British Academy in July 1955.

Waismann had close contact with some leading Oxford

philosophers—especially Henry Price, Isaiah Berlin, Stuart Hampshire, Herbert Hart, and Gilbert Ryle. His lectures and classes were a focus of excitement. One seminar saw the first exposition by J. L. Austin of his doctrine of performative utterances. Having, like Ryle, 'learned much from Wittgenstein', Waismann played a leading role in the post-war transformation of logical empiricism into 'Oxford philosophy'. In this way he was a protagonist in both main developments within analytic philosophy in his lifetime.

Outside Oxford, Waismann's reputation rested on three papers, subsequently reprinted in *How I See Philosophy* (ed. R. Harré, 1968). 'Verifiability' (1945) suggested modifications of the principle of verification to accommodate the essential indeterminacy of symbolism ('open texture'). This influential doctrine (prominent in Hart's legal theory) is that no empirical concept can be so precisely defined as to exclude all possible doubt about how it is to be applied in bizarre circumstances. 'Language-strata' (1953) explored the 'loose' logical relations between different domains of discourse (for example, between psychological concepts and descriptions of behaviour). 'How I see philosophy' (1956) distinguished philosophical arguments from demonstrations of theses, instead illustrating how to treat philosophical problems on the model of psychoanalysis: the patient must be led to acknowledge his own difficulties and to view things in new ways.

All this work shows ambivalence towards Wittgenstein, deep indebtedness together with critical distance. Waismann built much on ideas that Wittgenstein later discarded (especially the concept of a 'hypothesis'), and he directed Wittgenstein's method of clarifying 'the grammar of our language' primarily to investigating changes in mathematical and scientific concepts where appeals to everyday use played no role.

There are major posthumous publications. Transcriptions of shorthand notes of Wittgenstein's conversations with Waismann and Schlick in 1929–32 were published in 1967 as *Ludwig Wittgenstein and the Vienna Circle*. Some later dictations and early drafts for *Logik, Sprache, Philosophie* were being prepared for publication at the end of the twentieth century. An English translation of that book was completed in 1939, at least partly by Margaret (Ramsey) Paul, but it was first published only in 1965 under the title *The Principles of Linguistic Philosophy*. This was presented (and misunderstood) as a secondhand rehash of Wittgenstein's work rather than the precipitate of seven years of co-authorship and collaboration. A reconstruction of the original German text appeared in 1970, with a fuller and more accurate account of its origins.

Other publications include *Philosophical Papers* (1977); *Lectures on the Philosophy of Mathematics* (1982), which was reconstructed from notes and manuscripts; and *Wille und Motiv* (1988; translated as *Ethics and Will*, 1994). Much remains unpublished: a book on the concept of causality, some early lectures and drafts of parts of *Logik, Sprache, Philosophie*, and a quantity of poems and aphorisms.

Waismann's wife, Hermine Antscherl (born in Vienna in 1894), whom he married in 1929, committed suicide in 1943. So too, nine years later, did his only son, Thomas (born in Vienna in 1935). Waismann died at the Radcliffe Infirmary, Oxford, on 4 November 1959.

GORDON BAKER

Sources S. Hampshire, 'Friedrich Waismann, 1896–1959', *PBA*, 46 (1960), 309–17 · *The Times* (6 Nov 1959) · PRO, Home Office MSS · Oxf. UA · G. P. Baker, 'Verehrung und Verkehrung: Waismann and Wittgenstein', *Wittgenstein: sources and perspectives*, ed. G. F. Luckhardt (1979), 243–85 · G. P. Baker, 'Preface', in F. Waismann, *The principles of linguistic philosophy*, 2nd edn (1995), xi–xxiii · R. Monk, *Ludwig Wittgenstein: the duty of genius* (1990), 282–327 · private information (2004) · d. cert. · *CGPLA Eng. & Wales* (1960)
Archives Bodl. Oxf., MSS
Wealth at death £2370 11s.: probate, 15 Jan 1960, *CGPLA Eng. & Wales*

Wait, Daniel Guildford (1789/90–1850), Hebrew scholar, was the son of Daniel Wait of Bristol, and his wife, of whom little is known. He matriculated from University College, Oxford, on 20 October 1809, and later moved to St John's College, Cambridge, where he graduated LLB in 1819 and LLD in 1824. He appears to have become a close friend of the organist Samuel Wesley (1766–1837) while in Cambridge. He was ordained as curate in Pucklechurch, near Bristol, and on 12 March 1819 became rector at Blagdon in Somerset.

Wait's first scholarly contribution was his *Defence of a Critique of the Hebrew Word Nachash* (1811), in which he defended the conclusion that Eve was deceived by a serpent and not by an ape, as Adam Clarke had suggested in the *Classical, Biblical, and Oriental Journal*. His most important work, however, was *Jewish, Oriental, and Classical Antiquities*, which appeared in 1823. He also translated the New Testament from the German of Leonard Van Hug into English, though his translation was superseded by that of Moses Stuart in 1836. Wait was essentially a comparatist, comparing Jewish scriptures with the New Testament, and looking at the influence of Hebrew texts on non-Christian philosophers. In addition he published sermons and psalms, and edited *Repertorium Theologicum* (1829), of which only one edition was printed.

Wait died, unmarried, at the rectory, Blagdon, on 30 September 1850.   E. I. CARLYLE, *rev.* SINÉAD AGNEW

Sources Foster, *Alum. Oxon.* · *GM*, 2nd ser., 33 (1850), 669 · J. Foster, ed., *Index ecclesiasticus, or, Alphabetical lists of all ecclesiastical dignitaries in England and Wales since the Reformation* (1890), 181 · [J. Watkins and F. Shoberl], *A biographical dictionary of the living authors of Great Britain and Ireland* (1816) · Allibone, *Dict.*

Waite, Arthur Edward (1857–1942), mystic and historian of occultism, was born on 2 October 1857 at Brooklyn, New York, the son of Charles Frederick Waite, an American merchant marine captain of Lyme in Connecticut, and his common-law wife, Emma Lovell, whose family were involved in the East India trade. In 1858 Captain Waite died at sea, shortly before the birth of a second child, Frederica. Unhappy in New England, Emma Lovell took her children back to England where, rejected by her family, she raised them in the northern suburbs of London in a genteel poverty alleviated by fervent devotion to the Roman Catholic church to which she had turned for

Arthur Edward Waite (1857–1942), by Alvin Langdon Coburn, 1921

solace. Sacramental Christianity was to remain a profound influence on Waite's mature thought, but such orthodoxy as he professed was lost in the trauma of his sister's death in 1874 which led him away from the church and towards spiritualism. This he rejected as a creed but it served to introduce him, by turns, to theosophy, to alchemy, and to the work of the French occultist Eliphas Levi (Alphonse Louis Constant; 1810–1875). However, it was not these aspects of the 'occult revival' (the term now applied to the mid-nineteenth century reawakening of educated interest in alchemy, magic, and other aspects of occultism that had previously been treated with ridicule) which were the principal influences on Waite. His thought and writing were largely moulded by the conflicts and tensions of his private life, beginning with his unacknowledged illegitimacy.

As he completed his two terms at St Charles's College, Bayswater—the only formal education he ever received—and passed out of adolescence, Waite turned briefly to ideas of the priesthood. Such vocation as he may have had, however, did not include a call to celibacy and he took up instead his always precarious literary career. As a poet he met with little success but his early studies of the various occult sciences and *The Mysteries of Magic* (1886), which he translated from Levi's original, all show the critical acumen that would become the hallmark of his mature writing. They also illustrate his ambivalent attitude to occultism in general. Further conflict entered his life in 1888 through an unhappy marriage, on 7 January, to Ada Alice

Lakeman (1867–1924), the sister of Dora, Waite's first and only love; Dora married, also unhappily, the Revd Granville Stuart-Menteath. If not materially, Waite undoubtedly psychologically neglected his wife and daughter, Sybil (*b.* 1888), as he turned inward towards his esoteric studies. These bore immediate fruit and the 1890s were Waite's most prolific decade with ten books, fifteen works edited or translated, and the first independent journal in this field, the *Unknown World*, to his credit.

Waite also entered, in January 1891, the hermetic order of the Golden Dawn which enabled him to indulge in ceremonial without the constraints of Catholic orthodoxy. However, he was never truly an occultist: in all his work he presented himself as a non-denominational mystic, seeking to propagate what he termed the 'secret tradition'—a knowledge, preserved down the ages, of the way by which man can be spiritually regenerated and attain divine Union, or 'realization in God'. It is ironic that the works in which he clearly expresses this are not those by which he is known. If his most important works of the 1890s were his editions of alchemical texts, issued between 1892 and 1896, the most popular was *Transcendental Magic* (1896), his translation of Levi's *Dogme et rituel de l'haute magie*. Similarly the collections of poems he published in the Edwardian era, *A Book of Mystery and Vision* (1902) and *Strange Houses of Sleep* (1906), are now forgotten, while *The Pictorial Key to the Tarot* (1910) and the pack of cards designed under his supervision by Pamela Colman Smith became, as they remain, the most popular pack ever published. They were followed by another commercially successful work, the contents of which were anathema to Waite: *The Book of Ceremonial Magic* (1911).

Other strings remained to be added to Waite's bow. In 1901 he became a freemason and rapidly entered every masonic order open to him as a part of his quest for yet further aspects of the secret tradition. He wrote now on the French mystic Louis Claude de Saint-Martin; on the Hebrew cabbala; on the Holy Grail; on the Rosicrucians; on freemasonry; and yet more on alchemy. As part of his active life in esoteric circles he played a prominent part in the tribulations of the Golden Dawn and helped to found the Alchemical Society, while in the everyday world he weaned Arthur Machen away from despair and back to a productive career.

Waite's own career was now crystallizing. For nine years, from 1899 to 1907, he was a manager for Horlicks, the malted milk company, but from 1908 onwards he depended solely on income from his writing. London proved to be an increasingly uncongenial setting for the journalism that had become an essential supplement to books that were never financially rewarding; *The Way of Divine Union* (1915), his finest work, sold badly (and is now virtually unknown), and he decided to move. Eventually, in 1919, he moved to Ramsgate from where he returned only to arrange contracts and to oversee the offshoot of the Golden Dawn that he had created in 1915. The long-suffering Ada Waite died in 1924 but her death had little effect on his work, and on 15 August 1933 he married Mary

Broadbent Schofield (b. 1885), who had been his unpaid secretary for ten years.

Waite's final years were taken up with completing his studies of the secret tradition: *The Brotherhood of the Rosy Cross* (1924), *The Secret Tradition in Alchemy* (1926), *The Holy Kabbalah* (1929), and *The Holy Grail* (1933), are the new or revised works on which his reputation largely rests. His last book was his autobiography, *Shadows of Life and Thought* (1938), and although it reveals little enough of his outer life it contains within it the clearest statement of his own beliefs. Waite died at Gordon House, Bridge, near Canterbury, on 19 May 1942, unnoticed in death as in life, and was buried at Bishopsbourne, Kent.

It is ironic that works of lesser importance in Waite's own eyes—his translations of Levi's work and the brilliantly innovative tarot cards designed under his guidance—have ensured that his influence is still felt in the 'New Age' movement, a movement that embodies all that Waite rejected in occultism. This effect of his work is balanced, however, by its influence in varying degrees on writers as diverse as W. B. Yeats, Charles Williams, Arthur Machen, Evelyn Underhill, and T. S. Eliot, and in the wider field of the history of ideas. Through his critical and historical studies of occultism in all its forms, and even more by his carefully edited alchemical texts, Waite brought order out of the chaos of the occult revival and enabled the study of both the history and content of 'rejected knowledge' to become academically acceptable. It is the growing awareness of his importance in this field that has finally brought him the wider acclaim he always deserved.   R. A. GILBERT

Sources A. E. Waite, diary, 1902–3, 1909–10, 1912–13, 1915–42, priv. coll. [Gilbert collection, Bristol] · A. E. Waite, *Shadows of life and thought* (1938) · R. A. Gilbert, *A. E. Waite: magician of many parts* (1987) · E. Howe, *The magicians of the Golden Dawn* (1972) · private information (2004) · m. certs. · d. cert. · personal knowledge (2004)
Archives priv. coll., Waite MSS · Societas Rosicruciana in Anglia, London, high council library
Likenesses photographs, c.1880–1938, priv. coll. · J. B. Trinick, pencil drawing, 1920, repro. in A. E. Waite, *A new encyclopaedia of freemasonry* (1921) · A. L. Coburn, photograph, 1921, priv. coll. · A. L. Coburn, photograph, 1921, NPG [see illus.] · E. O. Hoppé, photographs, 1927, priv. coll.
Wealth at death £4667 4s. 3d.: probate, 12 Oct 1942, CGPLA Eng. & Wales

Waite, Thomas (fl. 1634–1668), parliamentarian army officer and regicide, was probably the eldest son of Henry Waite of Wymondham, Leicestershire. Thomas Waite was admitted to Gray's Inn on 5 March 1634, and may have been the Thomas Waite appointed king's receiver for the counties of Warwick and Leicester for 1640–41. Waite sided with parliament at the outbreak of civil war. By spring 1643 he held a captaincy from Lord Grey of Groby and was stationed with Sir Edward Hartop at Rockingham Castle, Northamptonshire. In December 1643 he raided royalist quarters at Waltham on the Wolds, Leicestershire, and defeated the royalists based at Belvoir Castle at Sproxton Heath in the same county. He was soon commissioned colonel of horse and governor of Rutland.

In July 1644, while serving as governor of Burghley House, Northamptonshire, Waite became involved in a dispute with Lord Grey; articles were framed by Rutland gentlemen to suspend him from his governorship, while counter-petitions were presented in his favour. On 11 August 1645 parliament discharged him from further attendance upon the case and he returned to Burghley. However, the dispute lingered and on 14 October the committee of both kingdoms feared that, with the king nearby, unrest within the garrison might undermine its strength. The dispute was revived on 27 November and Waite was called to attend the House of Commons again on 3 December. The case was still being heard in June 1646. Nevertheless Waite was elected county MP for Rutland in July 1646, and on 9 January 1647 the House of Commons ordered that £2166 be paid him out of Rutland's delinquency fines.

On 4 June 1648 Waite was dispatched from Leicester by Lord Grey with a commission to proceed with martial law to quell a royalist uprising around Peterborough and Stamford. Pursuing the insurgents to Woodcroft House, Waite's forces stormed the building on 6 June and killed the royalist leader, Dr Michael Hudson, for which Waite received parliament's thanks on 8 June. At the end of August, under the command of Lord Grey, Waite participated in the pursuit and capture of the duke of Hamilton, relating the affair to the House of Commons on 28 August 1648. He was among the witnesses at Hamilton's subsequent trial, where Hugh Peter openly accused him of lying over whether Hamilton had surrendered to Grey's or John Lambert's forces. Although not personally excluded, he disapproved of Pride's Purge and withdrew from the House of Commons on 13 December 1648. He returned to his estates, and later alleged that he suppressed republican petitions there before the threat of sequestration compelled him to return to London on 25 January 1649. Named to the high court of justice, he attended only three meetings, but was among the last of the signatories of the king's death warrant [see also Regicides].

On 5 March 1650 Waite was appointed commander-in-chief of the Rutland militia's cavalry, but three years later, with the dissolution of the Rump Parliament, he retired from state affairs, and endeavoured to recover his wartime losses. On 31 July 1650, with over £400 still due to him, parliament had authorized his purchase of the duke of Buckingham's Rutland estates. On 13 March 1654 Waite's tenants at Hambleton petitioned the council of state complaining of Waite's doubling their rents, diverting their water supply, violating an earlier agreement by enclosing their commons, and endeavouring to evict eighty families.

Waite did not return to the House of Commons until 1659, and was excepted from the Restoration's Act of General Pardon and Oblivion on 9 June 1660. Four days later he obeyed the proclamation summoning the regicides to surrender themselves. He was brought to trial on 10 October 1660; pleading not guilty, he claimed that he had been tricked into attending court on 27 January 1649 by a note he thought had come from Lord Grey, but which had actually been sent by Oliver Cromwell and Henry Ireton. He claimed that he attended on 29 January only after he received assurances that the king would not be executed, and that Cromwell overpowered his objections, demanding 'These that are gone in shall set their hands, I will have their hands now' (Fraser, 287). Waite's absence from the house during much of December and January 1648–9 supports the case that he was a reluctant regicide.

Nevertheless, Waite was found guilty and condemned to death. However, on 28 August 1660, because he had surrendered, his name was included on the list of those whose execution was not to take place without a special act of parliament. An act to accomplish this was passed by the House of Commons in January 1662, and Waite was summoned to the bar of the House of Lords on 7 February 1662 to plead for his life. He pointed out, quite truthfully, that he had no part in establishing the high court, but his contention that he was 'forced by Cromwell to signe a writing not knowing what was conteyned therein' (*Seventh Report*, HMC, 167) remains unconvincing. The act was eventually dropped and his life was consequently spared, but he spent the rest of his life in prison while his wife, Jane, unsuccessfully appealed for his release, pleading her own ill health and the burden of her five children. He remained a prisoner in Jersey, where he was ordered to be committed to the old castle on 13 February 1668. No will survives and the eventual date of his death is not known.

ANDREW J. HOPPER

Sources Greaves & Zaller, *BDBR* · *DNB* · *JHC*, 2–8 (1640–67) · *JHL*, 7–11 (1644–66) · *Seventh report*, HMC, 6 (1879), 1–182 [House of Lords] · *The manuscripts of his grace the duke of Portland*, 10 vols., HMC, 29 (1891–1931), vol. 1 · D. Underdown, *Pride's Purge: politics in the puritan revolution* (1971) · M. Noble, *The lives of the English regicides*, 2 (1798) · *CSP dom.*, 1640–68 · A. Fraser, *Cromwell, our chief of men* (1973) · F. Peck, ed., *Desiderata curiosa*, new edn, 2 vols. in 1 (1779) · J. Foster, *The register of admissions to Gray's Inn, 1521–1889, together with the register of marriages in Gray's Inn chapel, 1695–1754* (privately printed, London, 1889)

Archives BL, Heath and Verney papers, Egerton MSS 2986, fols. 216, 290, 291; 2978, fol. 19

Wealth at death negligible; estates confiscated

Waithman, Robert (1764–1833), political reformer, was born at Wrexham, Denbighshire, Wales, the son of John Waithman (d. 1764), a joiner, of Bersham, and Mary Roberts, who married on 29 January 1761. When Robert was only four months old, his father died; in September 1776 his mother married Thomas Mires, a furnaceman, of Bersham. At an early age Waithman was placed under the instruction of a Mr Moore by his uncle, before moving to Reading about the year 1778 where he worked as a shop assistant and then to London where he was apprenticed in the trade of a linen draper. In 1786 he opened his own store at the south end of Fleet Market, later moving his business to other premises at the corner of Fleet Street and New Bridge Street from which he reportedly amassed a considerable fortune by the time of his retirement. On 14 July 1797 he married his first cousin, Mary Davis (1761–1827), of Red Lion Street, Holborn, with whom he had several sons.

The outbreak of the French Revolution aroused Waithman's interest in politics and he honed his oratorical skills about 1792 as a frequenter of a debating society at Founders' Hall in Lothbury, in the City. His first real taste of politics came as a liveryman of the Framework Knitters' Company when he was elected as a common councilman for the ward of Farringdon Without in December 1795, although his public career had begun on 23 January 1795 when he seconded a successful motion at a common hall against the war with France. Maintaining his position on peace, a petition for an end to the revolutionary war presented by Waithman was approved by the livery on 19 February 1800 and he published his arguments in the same year as a pamphlet entitled *War proved to be the cause of the present scarcity, and enormous high price of every article of consumption, with the only radical remedies*. About this time, Waithman was involved in founding the Society of the Independent Livery of London, along with a number of prominent common councilmen and liverymen of the City of London as well as Thomas Hardy, the founder of the London Corresponding Society. The Independent Livery emerged as a significant lobbying group in City politics, championing the cause of the people at a time of high prices, pushing for a petition campaign against the war and for parliamentary reform, and seeking a repeal of income tax. Waithman was an influential member of the Independent Livery, frequently voicing his ideas on reform at this level, although he was unsuccessful in 1802 when he campaigned as parliamentary candidate for the organization.

Waithman carried his reformist ideas further in 1805 when he proposed at a common hall that a petition be presented to parliament for an inquiry into fiscal management, successfully carrying a petition to parliament on this issue three years later as well as an address to George III for an investigation into the convention of Cintra. In 1808 he also published a *Letter to the Governors of Christ's Hospital*, which revealed that places in the school were being reserved for children of wealthy parents, in exchange for political patronage, rather than being left vacant for those with lower incomes. Within a year he had called for complete parliamentary reform and on 6 June 1810 he carried a motion to petition the House of Commons on the issue of political representation. He regularly supported radical occasions and dinner meetings; he was among a group of over 1200 people which assembled at a reformist dinner held in the Crown and Anchor tavern on 1 May 1809. Later that year he attended the anniversary dinner commemorating the acquittals at the treason trials of 1794 and at much the same time he became acquainted with the freethinking banker–brewer Timothy Brown, and with William Cobbett through a subscription committee for Gwyllym Lloyd Wardle. For six years, between 1809 and 1814, he was also convener of annual dinners of a group known as the Livery of London, Friends of the Constitutional Reform of Parliament, and one of his speeches to the common council on electoral reform and the management of public money was published in 1817.

Despite his public reformist stance, Waithman made

sure that he distanced himself from more radical elements of the reform movement during the Regency years. As such he conducted a running battle against the active Spencean movement, engaged himself in a prolonged confrontation with Henry Hunt, and disengaged himself from the philosophical tenets of Robert Owen. He did, nevertheless, openly support issues associated with the liberty of the press at a time when radical publicists such as Thomas Wooler, William Hone, and Richard Carlile faced prosecution. On 29 December 1817 he attended a dinner at the City of London tavern to celebrate 'trial by jury and liberty of the press' and he participated in opening a subscription for the embattled William Hone.

With his success as a City politician, Waithman also acquired an interest in parliamentary politics. After two abortive campaigns in the early nineteenth century, he contested the 1812 election as a candidate for the City of London but was defeated. Six years later, however, he was voted as one of the four City representatives, defeating the tory candidate, Sir William Curtis. Making his début in parliament on 25 January 1819, Waithman advocated a revision of the criminal code and a notable speech on parliamentary reform made on 1 July of that year was published in 1823. Soon after his election, in July 1818, he was chosen as alderman for his ward of Farringdon Without, replacing the deceased Sir Charles Price, but failed to regain his parliamentary seat in 1820. Despite this loss and his failure in 1831 to be elected city chamberlain, Waithman was successful, during the intervening years, in attaining the post of sheriff of London and Middlesex in 1820–21, during which time he sided with the popular radicals in support of Queen Caroline; he was re-elected to parliament in 1826 and retained his seat at the elections of 1830, 1831, and 1832. Moreover, he served as lord mayor of London between 1823 and 1824, a term of office satirized by his political opponents in *Maxims of Robert, Lord Waithman, Somewhile Chief Magistrate of London* (1824).

Throughout his political career, Waithman was a consistent advocate of peace, triennial parliaments, and an extension of the suffrage to taxpaying householders as well as a vocal anti-cornlaw campaigner. These sentiments alienated him from more conservative whigs and the tories stigmatized him as something of a rabble-rouser. By contrast, popular radicals such as William Cobbett and Henry Hunt, Waithman's long-time adversary, thought his reform programme was too moderate in not calling for annual parliaments and universal suffrage. Waithman's distance from most members of the radical fraternity is exemplified by the view expressed by Samuel Bamford, who, in recalling his introduction to Waithman about 1820, described him as 'a dissatisfied, bilious looking man. He had recently experienced some provoking opposition in the city, and seemed as if both mind and manners were soured. I had no desire to meet him again' (Bamford, 232). Most contemporaries, however, would have agreed with the assessment of Waithman's career offered by *The Times* newspaper on the occasion of his death:

The magistracy of London has thus been deprived of one of its most respectable members, and the city of one of its most upright representatives. ... His natural parts, his political integrity, his consistency of conduct, and the energy and perseverance with which he performed his duties, placed him far above the common run of persons whose reputation is gained by their oratorical displays at meetings of the Common Council. (*The Times*, 7 Feb 1833, 3)

Waithman died, at the age of seventy, on 6 February 1833 at his house in Woburn Place, London. Eight days later, an impressive cortège of twenty-seven carriages proceeded from the Guildhall to the church of St Bride, Fleet Street, where Waithman was buried. To perpetuate his memory, Waithman Street in London was named in his honour and a subscription was raised by the St Bride's Society to set up an obelisk as a testimonial to his political importance. The obelisk was erected in June 1833 at the southern end of Farringdon Street, opposite the site of Waithman's first shop, and following relocation to Bartholomew Close in 1951 it was resited in Salisbury Square in 1972 where it now stands.   MICHAEL T. DAVIS

Sources DNB · J. R. Dinwiddy, '"The patriotic linen-draper": Robert Waithman and the revival of radicalism in the City of London, 1795–1818', *BIHR*, 46 (1973), 72–94 · CLRO, biographical notes file · information file, Robert Waithman, CLRO · *The Times* (7 Feb 1833), 3 · *The Times* (20 Feb 1833), 5 · *GM*, 1st ser., 103/1 (1833), 179–80 · S. Bamford, *Passages in the life of a radical*, ed. W. H. Chaloner, new edn, 2 vols. (1967) · J. A. Hone, *For the cause of truth: radicalism in London, 1796–1821* (1982) · *Annual Register* (1833)

Likenesses R. Dighton, caricature, coloured etching, pubd 1818, BM, NPG, V&A · R. Cooper, stipple, 1821 (after portrait by C. Holroyd), BM, NPG; repro. in *Aurora Borealis* (1821) · E. Scriven, stipple, pubd 1821 (after W. Patten), BM, NPG · W. Patten, oils, Guildhall Art Gallery, London · C. S. Taylor, stipple, BM, NPG; repro. in *European Magazine* (1823)

Wealth at death amassed a considerable fortune: *DNB* · died in poverty: *The Times* (20 Feb 1833)

Wake, Sir Isaac (1580/81–1632), diplomat and political commentator, was the second son of Arthur Wake (*c*.1543–1596), master of St John's Hospital, Northampton, and canon of Christ Church, Oxford, and his wife, Christian (*d.* 1609), daughter of Sir William Wigston of Wolston, Warwickshire. His father had also been rector of Great Billing, Northamptonshire, from 1566 to 1573, when he was deprived of all his livings for nonconformity; he retired to Jersey for a period, but by 1576 had regained his positions at Oxford and Northampton. His elder son, Abraham, baptized at Wolston on 5 July 1577, was admitted to Christ Church early in 1593, and was soon joined by Isaac, who matriculated on 25 May, aged twelve. By this time the family was probably resident in Oxford: following his death on 12 July 1596 Arthur was buried in the choir at Christ Church. Still relatively young Isaac graduated BA on 23 July 1597, and the following year was elected a fellow of Merton College.

Early career and social circle Under the wardenship of Sir Henry Savile, Merton enjoyed vigorous direction and a lively fellowship, and the college both nurtured Wake's talents and provided patrons and friends. Older colleagues included Thomas Horne and Savile's kinsman Henry Wilkinson (1566–1647), who married Wake's sister

Sarah, perhaps before 1601, when he became rector of Waddesdon, Buckinghamshire. Wake proceeded MA on 22 February 1603 and in 1604 became public orator to the university, a post he officially retained until 1621; his admission on 14 February 1604 to the Middle Temple, where his elder brother was a barrister, was evidently honorary. Anthony Wood learned from sources at Merton that Wake 'had his pen more at command in the Latin, English and French tongue than any of his time in the university' and 'that his speaking was majestic' (Wood, *Ath. Oxon.*, 2.539). On King James's visit to Oxford in August 1605 he delivered an oration in Christ Church which later appeared with a description of the entertainment as *Rex platonicus* (1607), dedicated to Henry, prince of Wales. His funeral oration for the Mertonian Greek scholar and biblicist John Rainolds, given on 27 May 1607, was first published in 1608. Although the king is said to have found the accomplished Ciceronian style of Wake's delivery soporific, he rewarded him on 3 July 1607 with the reversion of the keepership of Ewelme Hospital, Oxfordshire.

In 1609 Wake obtained leave to go to France and Italy; by the end of the year he was living in Venice. When in 1610 Savile's stepson-in-law, Sir Dudley Carleton, a near contemporary of Wake at Christ Church, was appointed ambassador to Venice, Horne became his chaplain and Wake his secretary. Drawn, like Carleton, into Savile's projected edition of Chrysostom, on 2 February 1612 Wake was commissioned to make a collation with a manuscript in Venice and on 27 March Merton granted him three further years' residence abroad. None the less in October/ November he was dispatched to England by Carleton to renew contact with the latter's patrons and to press his case for promotion. While in Oxford in March 1613 Wake delivered the funeral oration for another Mertonian, Sir Thomas Bodley, published later that year.

By mid-April 1613 Wake was back in Venice, having left behind a good impression. Thus when Carleton's longed for transfer to The Hague was announced in the summer of 1614 Wake was named as official agent until the new ambassador, Henry Wotton, arrived. His grasp of Italian was evidently better than Carleton's and the gratification he expressed to the Venetian senate at his posting to a city where in five years he had never received anything but kindness seems more than mere diplomatic politeness. When the reshuffle was delayed so that Carleton could negotiate a peace settlement between Spain and Savoy events worked further to Wake's advantage. Sent again to England by Carleton in spring 1615 he took the opportunity to cultivate his own patrons: his letter-book reveals that these included Archbishop George Abbot, Sir Horace Vere, and the lord chamberlain, to whom he acknowledged himself 'to be wholy apiece of your creacon' and 'the worke of your owne hands' (BL, Add. MS 18639, fol. 9*v*). Within a few days of his arrival in London he was appointed to succeed Albertus Morton as English agent in the Savoyard capital, Turin. Arriving back in Italy in midsummer he assisted Carleton with the successful conclusion of the peace of Asti, but when the latter was finally recalled in September they parted company with some coolness: Carleton's wife and sister apparently found Wake's industry officious or interfering, although he assured several correspondents that he had been 'a meere cifre' (ibid., fols. 8*r*, 18*v*).

Residency at Turin The residency at Turin proved the most significant period of Wake's career. Initially, following the treaty, life in this third rank posting was dull, 'after a storme quite becalmed with peace and quiett, which to active Spiritts is as tedious as warre is dangerous' (BL, Add. MS 18639, fol. 19*v*), and on 20 August he wrote to Carleton requesting the forwarding of his books, 'there being as greate a scarcity of that commodity here, as there is plenty of it at Venice' (ibid., 38*v*). But soon the routine work of protecting and scrutinizing passing British merchants and travellers was overtaken by higher profile diplomatic activity. Wake's intellectual and professional powers became engaged by the complex political relations of the north Italian states and their neighbours in the Swiss Confederation, and his religious sympathies were awakened by the plight of beleaguered protestants in the area; both became lifelong concerns. In January 1616 he accompanied the Savoyard representative Gabaleoni to Bern as arbitrator in negotiations for an alliance between the two states. After what seemed to him an 'endlesse labyrinth' (BL, Add. MS 18640, fol. 45*v*) of intricate mediation involving many interested parties, the treaty concluded in June 1617 represented a triumph. Previous attempts by Henri IV and others to broker a mutual defence pact had foundered on rival claims to the Pays de Vaud, conquered by Bern in 1536, but in return for carefully calculated promises of money and troops, Savoy now renounced its interest in the protestant territory on the far side of Lake Geneva. Wake's posthumously published *A Three-Fold Help to Political Observations* (1655) attributed the untying of 'this Gordian knot' (p. 21) to the pious genius of James I, but his letters to secretary of state Robert Naunton reveal much of the initiative as his own.

Duke Charles Emanuel of Savoy, whose priority had become the security of his territories in the French Alps and Italian valleys, regularly traversed by Spanish soldiers *en route* between Genoa and the Franche Comté, was well pleased with Wake. John Pory, who visited Turin, reported to John Chamberlain early in 1618 that he kept 'a port and table … more like an ambassador than an Agent, and that he is in such favor with the Duke that he will do nothing without him' (*Letters of John Chamberlain*, 2.139). In a deteriorating international situation Wake became indispensable to others too: strategically placed, he negotiated with Bern and other states the passage of Count Mansfelt's antiimperialist mercenaries over alpine passes; when from June 1618 Savoy sent subsidies to James I's son-in-law Frederick, elector palatine, his proximity to the duke also gained importance back home. Wake himself built close relations with Mansfelt and Frederick, which shaped his later perspectives. Recalled for consultation he left Turin in late October/early November 1618, delegating business to his nephew, almost certainly the young John Wilkinson. Well received in Paris and London he was promised the succession to Wotton at the Venice embassy and knighted by the king from his sickbed at Royston on 10 April 1619. At Royston he developed or renewed contact with one of his most powerful patrons, James Hay, Viscount Doncaster, James's extraordinary ambassador. His subsequent letters to Doncaster (from 1622 earl of Carlisle), with those to William Trumbull, agent at Brussels and in the 'confraternitye in his Majesties service' (BL, Add. MS 72320, fol. 73) and his regular dispatches to successive secretaries of state, form a three-tier commentary on international relations at this period.

Wake returned to Savoy in May 1619 via Brussels and Heidelberg, where he was delegated to confer with the princes of the German protestant union. Despite encountering 'many crocodiles' (BL, Egerton MS 2592, fol. 59) on his way down the Rhine, as he reported in his briefing to Doncaster, who was to follow him, he gained the princes' trust and commissions to press their case for assistance from Savoy. Once in Turin Wake tackled the difficult tasks of holding the duke to his protestant alliance when French marriage and imperial marriages were offered for his son, the prince of Piedmont, and his daughter, and of curbing his ambitions to control Geneva. Wake also found time for an unsuccessful bid for a fellowship at Merton for his nephew Wilkinson, now back in Oxford, and to become deeply interested in the fate of the Grisons (Graubünden). This area, sandwiched between the Swiss Confederation and Austria, encompassed the Valtelline and two vital alpine passes which gave Spanish military access to Lake Constance and to south Bavaria and Bohemia. John Chamberlain, one of Wake's regular correspondents, confessed to Carleton that he had never before heard of it, but, as Venetian observers noted, Wake was not only moved by the plight of persecuted Waldenses and protestants there, but also perceived that the Grisons' fate was an acid test of Spanish and papal power, the outcome of which was of critical concern for all of western Europe. If through their inaction and division the Swiss and their potential allies, 'those people who stand in the centre of Europe to serve the interests of all', allowed the Grisons to fall, the Spaniards, 'the enemies of liberty, from whom a universal domination is preparing' (CSP Venice, 1619–21, 342), would then take not only Italy but also Germany.

Marriage, promotion, and the parliament of 1624 In February 1622 Wake suffered a set-back when his attempt to succeed Savile as warden of Merton failed, despite backing from the prince of Wales. The visitor, Archbishop Abbot, protested in a letter of 26 February that, as his conscience and the world knew, he wished Wake 'all the good that may bee in my power' (BL, Stowe MS 176, fol. 221), but he bowed to Savile's and the fellowship's desire to appoint Nathaniel Brent, another former secretary to Carleton who had resettled in England. By the summer, as he explained to Carlisle, Wake was pressed by the financial difficulties that beset diplomats: 'the Exchequer hath been lockt up against mee, almost three yeares' (BL, Egerton MS 2595, fol. 98). However, that summer rumours of his imminent promotion to Venice revived. Early in 1623 he obtained leave to return home; inevitably delayed

he arrived in London in November. Here, before 6 December, with 'a very hansome and pithie collation' made by his brother-in-law Henry Wilkinson, he was contracted to marry his 'sweet-heart' and Chamberlain's 'auncient valentine' (Letters of John Chamberlain, 2.495), Anna Bray (b. before 1593?, d. 1642), stepdaughter of secretary of state Sir Edward Conway. The wedding took place on 18 December, after the arrival of the bride's uncle, Sir Horace Vere. As Chamberlain observed, it had been a long courtship: Wake had written to Anna in terms of close friendship in 1615. The daughter of Dorothy Tracy (d. 1612) and her first husband, Edward Bray of Great Barrington, Gloucestershire, Anna seems to have spent part of her youth in the households of her kinsman, Sir Thomas Tracy (acknowledged by Wake as a patron in 1615), and of an aunt, perhaps Lady Vere. Wake's poverty and uncertain future, and the bride's delicate health, seem the most likely explanations for the delay; he had been comfortably fixed in her pious family circle.

In January 1624 Wake was finally named ambassador to Venice. As Chamberlain informed Carleton, he had a 'large commission for all Italie, and to kepe agents in Piemont, Switzerland, … among the Grisons, and elsewhere as he shall find fit for the king's service'; he was 'to be a kind of ambassador paramount, or like an archbishop to many suffragans' (Letters of John Chamberlain, 2.540). By the end of the month he had been chosen with secretary of state Sir George Calvert as member for Oxford University in the parliament that met in February. There he argued for the war against Spain on which his commission largely rested. Like Carlisle and Sir Robert Anstruther he lingered in London as long as possible to await the upshot, and left only as the session ended. His wife was to follow at leisure.

Embassy at Venice The embassy at Venice began auspiciously enough. Venetians noted approvingly his close link with the secretary, Conway, and his own local knowledge, reassuring behaviour and sympathy for their interests. Wake, 'your magnifico of Venice' (Letters of John Chamberlain, 2.467), knew how to play the part. However, ultimately he proved little more successful than his predecessors. Like them he had constant financial worries and fretted over maintaining goodwill at court: Conway was not always communicative and Carlisle, on his travels, was often elusive, although a visit from the latter's son Doncaster allowed Wake to gain favour through his careful attentions to the young man. When his friend Trumbull gained preferment in England he asked him wistfully to 'remember mee sometimes when you are in your kingdom' (BL, Add. MS 72323); later he sent one of his secretaries, Peter Moreton, to court to report back. There were problems too in Venice. Lady Wake disliked the local diet and, succumbing to a serious illness, nearly died in autumn 1627. Although Wake followed the practice of Carleton and Wotton in escaping frequently to the congenial university town of Padua, he also spent such prolonged periods in Savoy (including his first six months of embassy from July to December 1624) that the Venetians concluded, wrongly but damagingly, that he was a creature of the duke. Wake in turn concluded that papalist factions were gaining the upper hand over 'patriots' in the republic, to the detriment of his mission.

Wake's official aim, verified with Conway in May 1625, was to secure the restoration of the palatinate. This involved continued liaison with Bern, Zürich, and Geneva, and justified his commitment to the Valtelline. In the unfolding tragedy of violent suppression there, graphically described to Conway in 1627 and 1628, he increasingly came to see the conspiratorial hand of France alongside that of Spain, and linked it to Cardinal Richelieu's plot with the pope for 'the extirpation of all the Protestants in France' (BL, Add. MS 34311, fol. 108v). As he saw it, 'the balance of power in Europe' (ibid., 241v) lay in Charles I's hands: a particularly frank expression of 'private conceits' to Carlisle on 17 March 1629 urged his patron to move the king to act. Protestants must 'hereafter relye wholye upon the protestation of God … accounting for true friends none but those of our owne Religion' (ibid., fol. 292v).

Embassy in France and legacy By this time frustration had led Wake to leave Venice permanently for Savoy, and recurrent ill health had driven his wife home, but enforced inactivity while others attempted flawed peace negotiations with France continued to irk him. He wrote to Carlisle on 23 April 1629 that 'wee have had here much to do, & have done nothing: our business proved like the sheering of a Hogg' (BL, Add. MS 34311, fol. 316). Following the conclusion of peace and months of rumours, in January 1630 he received letters of credence as ambassador to France, a promotion. There was much scepticism about the likely effectiveness of this well-known opponent of French foreign policy, and thus much uncertainty through that year as he lingered, detained in Savoy by unfinished business. It was only after an outbreak of plague had removed thirteen of his household and replacements had been dispatched from England that he arrived in Paris in March 1631, only to place his household in quarantine. Further delays in gaining audiences with Louis XIII and Richelieu and the gulf between English and French objectives in Germany contributed to a general lack of progress. However, although Conway's death in January 1631 had removed a vital line of communication he was once again on good terms with Carleton (now Viscount Dorchester and secretary of state), who shared his perspectives. When Dorchester also died, on 15 February 1632, Wake enlisted Carlisle to argue his case to succeed as secretary, but this reward eluded him. He died suddenly in Paris of a fever on 10 June (31 May os). His body was escorted to Dover, where it arrived on 6 July (os) and was buried in the castle chapel, the funeral sermon being given by the minister, John Reading, who had known him at Oxford.

Wake left his wife in straitened circumstances. An undated petition to the king from 'your Majesties poore handmaide in all humilitie casting her selfe downe at the feete of good Josia the king of Juda' supplicated for a pension and payment of arrears of expenses promised to the widow of a man 'knowne for abilities, honestie, and integritie to his Maister, to be a man of a Thowsand' (BL, Egerton MS 2597, fol. 112). Assisted by William Weld of Addle Street, London, an old friend of her husband, she obtained a £200 annuity from her half-brother Edward, second Viscount Conway, but was still short of money and entangled in a Star Chamber suit in February 1636. John Wilkinson also experienced difficulty in getting 'recompense' for the 'choice collection of papers' bequeathed him by Wake, '(being all he had to leave to his nearest kinsman)' (CSP dom., 1634–5, 525), which he had delivered up to the secretary of state Sir John Coke. In addition to his letter-books Wake had also accumulated notes of speeches and treaties of the 1620s in which he and Carleton were involved. It is not clear who edited for publication *Divine meditations … whereto is adjoyned, a determination of … whether men ought to kneele at the receipt of the holy communion and an essay of friendship* (1641) or *A Three-Fold Help to Political Observations* (1655). The latter, consisting of 'three discourses' 'concerning the thirteen cantons of the Helveticall League', 'declaring the state of Italy, as stood … about the year 1625' and 'touching the King of Sweden in his wars in Germany' testifies to the scope of his interests and to his taste for careful political observation and analysis, played out against a strong protestant faith.

VIVIENNE LARMINIE

Sources Wake's diplomatic letter-books, BL, Add. MSS 18639, 18640, 34310–34311 · Carlisle correspondence, BL, Egerton MSS 2592–2597 · Trumbull MSS, BL, Add. MSS 72320–72323 · Moreton correspondence, BL, Add. MS 33935 · papers relating to diplomatic missions, BL, Add. MS 48047 · CSP dom., 1603–37 · CSP Venice, 1613–32 · *The letters of John Chamberlain*, ed. N. E. McClure, 2 vols. (1939) · *Dudley Carleton to John Chamberlain, 1603–1624: Jacobean letters*, ed. M. Lee (1972) · Foster, *Alum. Oxon.* · Wood, *Ath. Oxon.*, new edn, 2.539–41 · H. I. Longden, *Northamptonshire and Rutland clergy from 1500*, ed. P. I. King and others, 16 vols. in 6, Northamptonshire RS (1938–52), vol. 14, p. 113 · GEC, *Peerage* · H. A. C. Sturgess, ed., *Register of admissions to the Honourable Society of the Middle Temple, from the fifteenth century to the year 1944*, 1 (1949), 73, 83 · *Hist. U. Oxf.* 4: *17th-cent. Oxf.*, 198, 649–51 · [T. Birch and R. F. Williams], eds., *The court and times of Charles the First*, 2 vols. (1848) · J. Stoye, *English travellers abroad, 1604–1667*, 2nd edn (1989) · T. Cogswell, *The blessed revolution: English politics and the coming of war, 1621–1624* (1989) · L. J. Reeve, *Charles I and the road to personal rule* (1989) · O. Barron, ed., *Northamptonshire families* (1906), 325–6

Archives Alnwick Castle, Northumberland, letter-book while ambassador in Paris · BL, letter-books and diplomatic papers, Add. MSS 18639–18642, 34310–34311, 48047 · BL, letters, Add. MS 33935 · BL, letters and papers, Stowe MS 135 · BL, papers, Add. MSS · LPL, letter-book while ambassador to France | Arundel Castle, West Sussex, letters to earl of Arundel · BL, letters to James Hay, earl of Carlisle, Egerton MSS 2592–2597 · BL, letters to William Trumbull, Add. MSS 72320–72323 · LPL, letters to Secretary Murray and others, letters to Lord Dorchester and others

Wake, Joan (1884–1974), historian and archivist, was born on 29 February 1884 at Courteenhall, the Wake family home in Northamptonshire, the fifth of the six children of Sir Herwald Craufurd Wake, twelfth baronet (1852–1916), and his wife, Catherine St Aubyn (1852–1944). She was educated by governesses and tutors at Courteenhall and at an early age developed an interest in music, learning to play the piano and organ.

It was not until Joan Wake was nearly thirty that she became acutely aware of the deficiencies in her formal education. In 1913 she enrolled at the London School of Economics for a two-year part-time course in palaeography and diplomatic and medieval economic history, where she was inspired by her tutor, Hubert Hall, and the young Eileen Power. At the sessional examination in July 1915 she gained first place. Any hope of further research was temporarily abandoned because of the First World War, when assisting the war effort took priority. After serving as a clerk at a Cambridgeshire hospital, she became honorary secretary of the Northamptonshire District Nursing Association from 1916 to 1919. Her travels throughout the county made her aware of the rich historical material which was available, much of it being lost to the salvage campaigns.

Two events in 1915 set Wake on the path of her future historical investigations. She began copying early charters from the private collection of her near neighbour Sir Thomas Fermor-Hesketh at Easton Neston, and she was introduced by friends to Frank Stenton, professor of modern history at University College, Reading. Stenton encouraged her to continue copying records in private custody and to produce the results in local monographs. The Lincoln Record Society had been instituted in 1910 and Stenton encouraged Wake to establish another in her native county. With great energy and perseverance she obtained the support of leading town and county people for this project. The Northamptonshire Record Society came into being on 10 December 1920. It differed from the Lincoln Record Society in that one of its prime aims was to accumulate a collection of documents relating to the county which students could consult. Joan Wake became the society's first honorary secretary, and held the post for forty-three years (1920–63).

To build up the record collection, Wake tirelessly visited stately homes in Northamptonshire and elsewhere to which she had an entrée, as well as the premises of solicitors, business people, and tradespeople. Her appearance changed little over the years. She was stockily and heavily built, with a determined jaw. Clothes were of little interest to her, though she always carried her best hat in a box on her motor cycle, and later in her small car, for visits to the grander houses. The record rooms of the society were opened at County Hall in 1930 but were housed in temporary accommodation during the Second World War. The burden of the society was becoming too much for one person, and in 1952 the custody of the records became a county responsibility.

A new home was needed for the record office and the record society; this was provided by Delapre Abbey, a medieval building on the outskirts of Northampton which was threatened with demolition by the borough council unless sufficient funds were raised to save it. Joan Wake took charge of the operation and brought the enterprise to a successful conclusion. In May 1959 Delapre became the headquarters of the Northamptonshire Record Office and the Northamptonshire Record Society.

Wake's own contribution to historical scholarship was impressive. Besides being general editor of the record society's series publications (1924–65), she edited a number of volumes herself. These include *Quarter Sessions Records of the County of Northampton, 1630, 1657, 1657–8* (1924), *The Montagu Muster Book, 1602–1623* (1935), and *The Letters of Daniel Eaton to the Third Earl of Cardigan, 1725–1732* (1971). She was also editor of the society's journal, *Northamptonshire Past and Present* (1948–60), and wrote many articles and pamphlets. Her major work, *The Brudenells of Deene*, was published in 1953. In 1937 she rented Green Farm, Cosgrove, Northamptonshire, and in 1955 moved to one of the two houses which she had inherited, 11 Charlbury Road, Oxford. She never married. She was awarded an honorary MA by Oxford University (1953) and an honorary LittD by Leicester University (1959), and she was made CBE (1960). Joan Wake died in a Northamptonshire nursing home on 15 January 1974 and was buried at Courteenhall church on 20 January. In many ways she was a pioneer of English local history writing based on archival sources. Her lifelong campaign for the preservation of local records in written, oral, or photographic form, to be made available to students, led to the establishment of a national network of county record offices.

PETER GORDON

Sources P. Gordon, *The Wakes of Northamptonshire* (1992), 298–335 · G. Isham, *Northamptonshire Past and Present*, 5 (1973–7), 157–60 · R. Eady, 'The published works of Joan Wake', *Northamptonshire Past and Present*, 5 (1973–7), 162–5 · P. I. King, *Journal of the Society of Archivists*, 5 (1974–7), 144–8 · K. Major, *Archives*, 12 (1975–6), 28–9 · *Mercury and Herald* (17 Jan 1974)

Archives Northants. RO, notes and papers relating to T. Cowper; notes relating to her introduction to an edition of Daniel Eaton's letters | Bodl. Oxf., account of her first meeting with Dame Edith Sitwell, 1911 · U. Reading L., letters to Sir Frank Stenton and Lady Stenton

Likenesses Mrs A. Harris, portrait, 1963, Northamptonshire Record Society, Wootton Hall, Northampton

Wealth at death £62,054: probate, 18 April 1974, *CGPLA Eng. & Wales*

Wake, Thomas, second Lord Wake (1298–1349), nobleman, was the son and heir of John, first Lord Wake (1268–1300), and Joan (d. 1309), who was probably the daughter of Sir John Fitzbernard of Kingsdown, Kent. He was born about 20 March 1298. After the death of his father his lands and marriage fell into the custody of the crown and various of his estates were granted in wardship to his mother, Henry de Lacy, earl of Lincoln, Piers Gaveston, earl of Cornwall, and Queen Isabella, wife of Edward II. He married, before 9 October 1316, without the king's permission, Blanche, daughter of Henry of Lancaster, later earl of Leicester and Lancaster; Edward II, who had been hoping to organize a match with Joan, daughter of the deceased Gaveston, was initially angered at this breach of his rights and fined Wake £1000. However, on 6 June 1317 the king, at the request of Wake's father-in-law, showed Thomas favour by allowing him to take seisin of his estates while still under age. Although Wake supported actions against the Despensers and had to be instructed not to attend the meeting of the king's baronial opponents summoned by his wife's uncle Thomas, earl of Lancaster, at Doncaster in November 1321, he appears to have remained loyal to the king during and after the civil war of 1322. In 1325 he was referred to as 'the king's cousin' (*CDS*, 3, no. 859); the marriage of his sister, Margaret, to Edward II's half-brother, Edmund, earl of Kent, in the same year, established a further link with the royal house.

Wake held lands in Lincolnshire, where his family had long been established at Bourne, but he also inherited important estates in Yorkshire, especially in and around Cottingham. In addition he had extensive landed interests in Westmorland and Cumberland: the castle of Liddel in the latter county was regarded as his *caput honoris*. Consequently he was much involved in the Scottish wars of Edward II and Edward III. He was regularly summoned to serve against the Scots between 1318 and 1323. He was expected to take forty men to the campaign of 1318, and although he was absent from Edward II's unsuccessful siege of Berwick in 1319, he again sent troops. In April 1323, when negotiations were under way for a thirteen-year truce, he was one of several English noblemen sent to Scotland to act as hostages for the Scots' ambassador, the earl of Moray. In December 1324 he was also summoned to serve in Aquitaine with John de Warenne, earl of Surrey (*d.* 1347), during the war of St Sardos.

By March 1326 the first signs of political disaffection became evident when Wake was reported to have disobeyed a summons to attend the king's council. It is not clear whether Wake was influenced by his father-in-law, by his own political judgement of the Despensers, or by his personal grievances against a regime which, by coming to terms with the Scots, had effectively deprived him of certain ancestral lands and rights north of the border. Whatever the case, Wake clearly supported the invasion of England by Queen Isabella and her lover, Roger Mortimer, in September 1326. He joined Isabella and Mortimer at Gloucester and was one of the barons who agreed on 25 October at Bristol that the king's eldest son should be made keeper of the realm. The benefits of office soon followed. Wake was justice of the forests south of the Trent from 10 November 1326 to May 1328 and keeper of the Tower of London from 9 December 1326 to April 1328; he was also appointed keeper of Hertford Castle on 9 December 1326. In the parliament that met at Westminster in January 1327 he was appointed as one of the members of a council set up under the presidency of his father-in-law to guide the administration of the realm during the youth of the new king, Edward III. It is possible that he also held the office of king's chamberlain for a short period during the early stages of the new reign.

Isabella and Mortimer owed much to the support of the northern barons, and it is not surprising that they quickly determined to launch a campaign against the Scots. Wake responded in person to the feudal summons issued on 5 April 1327 and served on the ensuing ill-fated expedition. He was appointed a commissioner to treat with the Scots in the resulting peace negotiations. However, the treaty made at Edinburgh and confirmed by the parliament of Northampton in 1328 was a humiliating admission of English defeat and particularly irksome to Wake and the other disinherited, since it made no specific provision for the restitution of their lands in Scotland. These personal grievances, coupled with Roger Mortimer's rapid and alarming rise to power, explain why Wake joined Henry of Lancaster in refusing to attend the parliament of Salisbury in October 1328 and acted as his father-in-law's spokesman in meetings of the discontented barons at London in December. On 29 December the king announced his intention of moving against this mounting opposition, but promised to pardon all those who submitted before 7 January. Wake joined Lancaster and others in declaring that they would not proceed against the king, but this was to no avail and on 16 January the escheators were ordered to seize the estates of the rebels. About the same time the Lancastrian party was forced to submit near Bedford; Wake was allowed seisin of his lands by orders issued on 20 February, but only on condition that he bound himself to pay the enormous sum of 15,000 marks. A year later Wake was accused of complicity in the supposed conspiracy of his brother-in-law the earl of Kent, had his lands confiscated again, and was forced to flee to France. He remained in exile until after Mortimer's fall from power and Edward III's assumption of authority in October 1330. Thereafter the king was quick to restore him to favour: Wake was summoned home, formally pardoned, had his estates restored under orders of 9 December 1330, and his unpaid fine remitted on 12 December. Finally, on 30 December 1330, Edward III demanded restitution of Wake's Scottish lands from David II, a demand repeated, though to no avail, in February 1331 and April 1332. Wake's appointment as keeper of the Channel Islands from 18 October 1331 to 3 February 1333 was another mark of Edward's confidence in his ability and loyalty: Wake was frequently referred to as the king's kinsman in instruments of Edward III.

In 1332 Henry Beaumont organized a campaign against the Scots on behalf of the disinherited and achieved a notable victory at Dupplin Moor. Wake's support for this enterprise is indicated by a petition he addressed to Edward III before 22 April, which declared his refusal to be bound by the treaty of Edinburgh until such time as he was restored to his Scottish lands. He was prevented from participating in the Dupplin Moor campaign by a violent feud with the abbot of Crowland. However, he took part in at least some of the later expeditions launched by Edward III against the Scots. He was summoned to the campaign of 1333 and was one of the witnesses to the letters patent of 12 June 1334 by which Edward Balliol, the English-backed claimant to the throne of Scotland, handed over sovereignty of the lowland shires to the king of England. In September 1337 he also led a twelve-day foray from Carlisle into Scotland. At the same time, however, he became increasingly involved in the diplomatic and defensive strategies that preceded the outbreak of the Hundred Years' War. In 1335 he was sent to France with the bishop of Norwich and others to discuss Anglo-French tensions and the projected crusade. Wake was part of a group of northern lords who remained in England after the king's departure for the continent in the summer of 1338 to defend the Scottish march and assist in the government of the realm. Wake became a particularly prominent member of the domestic administration after the king's brief return to England in the spring of 1340. He was appointed to the committees set up in the parliament of March–May 1340 to investigate the king's finances and to receive petitions and prepare legislation. In April he was pardoned all his debts to the crown and was appointed one of the assessors in the city of London for the new tax of a ninth granted in parliament. On 28 May he was selected as a member of the council appointed to run the country under the titular regency of Edward, duke of Cornwall, when the king once more left for the Low Countries.

A late fourteenth-century St Albans chronicle claims that Wake was imprisoned by the king on the latter's unexpected return to England in December 1340 (*Chronicon Angliae*, 10). However, no other source mentions Wake's name among the list of ministers dismissed and/ or imprisoned during this political crisis, and it seems unlikely that Wake was treated in this way. In fact, he was appointed on 12 December to inquire into grievances brought against the king's ministers and was a member of the judicial commission set up in East Anglia to hear accusations of corruption against the local agents of the crown. The real focus of the king's wrath was John Stratford, archbishop of Canterbury. Although there is no evidence of Wake's response to the king's decision to exclude Stratford from the parliament of April–May 1341, Wake was one of the members of the lords' committee subsequently set up to hear Edward's charges against the archbishop; he also served on the legislative committee of 1341.

Wake remained active in public life during the 1340s. He was a trier of petitions in the parliaments of 1341, 1344, 1346, and January 1348. In November and December 1342 he was asked to serve with the king in Brittany; later in the same year he received wages for keeping the northern march for three months with two knights and eighteen esquires. In February 1346 his castle of Liddel was besieged and his lands seized by Sir William Douglas, but in April 1346 he was excused from going north to fight on the grounds of ill health. Liddel Castle was captured by the Scots shortly before the battle of Neville's Cross later in the same year and its keeper, Sir Walter Selby, was put to death.

Wake died on 30 or 31 May 1349; although the cause of death was not specified, his demise coincided with the first outbreak of bubonic plague in England. He was buried at his own foundation of Haltemprice Priory, Yorkshire. Wake had demonstrated his personal piety by planning, and presumably undertaking, a pilgrimage to Santiago de Compostela in 1341–2, and throughout his career he had shown a particularly keen interest in the religious orders. He had founded the Franciscan house at Ware, Hertfordshire, in 1338 and had planned to establish a house for the Crutched Friars at Kirkby Moorside, Yorkshire, in 1347–8, though nothing came of the latter plan.

His proposal to alienate lands for the foundation of a religious house for an unspecified order at Great Harrowden, Northamptonshire, in 1338 also proved abortive, as did his declared intention of c.1345 to establish a house of Dominican nuns in England. The failure of these schemes may be explained at least in part by lack of resources: Wake was often in debt, and in 1334 he was even accused of appropriating the chapel at Pontefract that contained the shrine of the unofficial saint, Thomas of Lancaster, in order to lay claim to the offerings made there. His principal foundation was therefore his first: namely a house of Augustinian canons, licensed in 1320 and first established in 1322 at Cottingham, Yorkshire, by members of the Augustinian priory of Bourne, Lincolnshire. In 1325 Wake obtained a licence from the pope, John XXII, allowing him to transfer this community to a more convenient location, and in January 1326 the canons moved to the nearby site of Haltemprice. The house, dedicated to the Virgin and Holy Cross, was intended to have a full quota of thirteen canons, but only three were recorded in 1328–9; the numbers had risen to nine by 1381.

Thomas Wake left no children, and the Wake estates and barony passed via his sister Margaret to the earls of Kent and thence to the Holland family. His widow, Blanche, was involved in an acrimonious and violent quarrel with Thomas de Lisle, bishop of Ely, as a result of a land dispute between two of their servants. In the parliament of November 1355 Lady Wake appealed directly to Edward III for assistance, and the king announced that he was taking the matter into his own hands. He ordered the immediate seizure of the bishop's temporalities, and although his ministers successfully opposed this on the grounds that it contravened one of his own statutes of 1340, a judgment against Lisle in the king's bench in October 1356 gave Edward the legal basis he needed in order to confiscate the episcopal estates. The whole business suggests very close personal and family ties between Edward III and his cousin Lady Wake from which the latter's husband had undoubtedly benefited in his lifetime. Blanche herself died shortly before 12 July 1380 and was buried at the Franciscan convent at Stamford, Lincolnshire.

W. M. ORMROD

Sources GEC, *Peerage* · *Chancery records* · *CDS* · [T. Walsingham], *Chronicon Angliae, ab anno Domini 1328 usque ad annum 1388*, ed. E. M. Thompson, Rolls Series, 64 (1874) · W. Stubbs, ed., *Chronicles of the reigns of Edward I and Edward II*, 2 vols., Rolls Series, 76 (1882–3) · *Adae Murimuth continuatio chronicarum. Robertus de Avesbury de gestis mirabilibus regis Edwardi tertii*, ed. E. M. Thompson, Rolls Series, 93 (1889) · Tout, *Admin. hist.* · J. Stevenson, ed., *Chronicon de Lanercost, 1201–1346*, Bannatyne Club, 65 (1839) · D. Knowles and R. N. Hadcock, *Medieval religious houses, England and Wales*, new edn (1971) · G. A. Holmes, 'The rebellion of the earl of Lancaster, 1328–9', *BIHR*, 28 (1955), 84–9 · R. Nicholson, *Edward III and the Scots: the formative years of a military career, 1327–1335* (1965) · J. Aberth, 'Crime and justice under Edward III: the case of Thomas de Lisle', *EngHR*, 107 (1992), 283–301

Wake, William (1657–1737), archbishop of Canterbury, was born on 26 January 1657 at Blandford Forum, Dorset, the son of Colonel William Wake (1628–1705), a royalist army officer, and his wife, Amie, the daughter of Edward

William Wake (1657–1737), by Thomas Hill, c.1720–25

Cutler. The Wake family was staunchly royalist: William's father, who was involved in John Penruddock's uprising, his grandfather, and his uncle were all imprisoned on numerous occasions for their loyalty to Charles I and Charles II. Just before his sixth birthday the young William entered Blandford Free School under Mr Welstead. On Welstead's resignation he moved to a private school which was opened at Iwerne by Mr Curgenven, the former usher of the free school, returning to Blandford when Curgenven was appointed headmaster. From Blandford he went to Oxford, where he matriculated as a commoner at Christ Church on 28 February 1673. Securing the favour of John Fell, the influential dean, Wake was admitted as a student (an equivalent post to fellow in other colleges) on 12 July 1675, before proceeding BA on 26 October 1676 and MA on 29 June 1679. Despite the wishes of his father that he return to Dorset and become a farmer, he was ordained deacon by Fell, at that time bishop of Oxford, on 25 September 1681 and was priested on 12 March the following year. Shortly afterwards he was appointed one of the four lecturers at St Martin's Church, Carfax, Oxford.

Paris and London Fell influenced Wake's career decisively once more, recommending him to Richard Graham, Viscount Preston, as chaplain for his embassy to France. Wake served in Paris from June 1682 until September 1685, cultivating a wide acquaintance among both the French Catholic clergy and the Huguenots. There were elements of Catholicism that appealed to him—their 'Monastic way of living … The beauty and Ornaments of their Churches; The solemnity of their Service; Their Care and decency in the performance of it'. At the same time

life in France confirmed him in many of the common protestant objections to that religion—its 'plain, and notorious Idolatry', its denial of the right of private judgement, Latin services, 'Halfe Communion', the papal supremacy, and its 'narrow and uncharitable Spirit, in Confining Salvation only to their Own Church & Party' (Christ Church, MS 541A, pp. 10–11). Wake's personal experiences of Catholicism led him to compose his first major publication, *An Exposition of the Doctrine of the Church of England*, which was a reply to Bishop Bossuet's *Exposition de la doctrine de l'église catholique*. This engagement with the leading French controversialist won Wake applause from many leading churchmen. At the core of the pamphlet was a defence of the doctrine of the Church of England on those points where it differed from the Church of Rome. He dealt first with the adoration of saints and images and the doctrine of justification, before devoting long sections to the sacraments and to the authority of scripture, tradition, and the church. He summarized the position of the Church of England as one based on the twin principles of scripture and the practice of the primitive church, arguing that, while he and Bossuet were agreed on 'what is *most necessary*'—belief in God, in Christ, and in the same creeds—they were separated by the innovations of the Church of Rome (*Exposition*, 87).

The *Exposition* was written in France, but it was published only after Wake's return to England, in 1686, the year after James II's accession. Inevitably, its appearance propelled him to the forefront of the Catholic controversy generated by the new king's policies. Over the next two years he produced a sequence of polemical pamphlets, all of which concentrated on the theological differences between the Church of England and the Church of Rome—*A Discourse of the Holy Eucharist* (1687), *Two Discourses of Purgatory and Prayers for the Dead* (1687), and *A Discourse Concerning the Nature of Idolatry* (1688)—and also two catalogues of the tracts produced during the controversy. Gilbert Burnet, indeed, saw Wake as the most important of the many clergymen who rallied to the church's defence in these years (*Bishop Burnet's History*, 3.105). During this time Wake secured the friendship of a number of prominent London clergy, including Thomas Tenison and William Clagett. The recommendation of the former gained him appointment as afternoon lecturer at St Anne's, Soho, while, on the death of the latter in March 1688, the benchers of Gray's Inn elected him as their preacher, despite the opposition of the court. In the summer of 1688 he acted as secretary to the commission established by Archbishop Sancroft to consider liturgical revision as a means of comprehending moderate dissenters within the Church of England. On 1 October 1688 he married Etheldreda (d. 1731), the daughter of Sir William Howell of Illington, Norfolk. The marriage was performed by another friend, Thomas Sharp, the future archbishop of York, emphasizing the extent to which Wake was at the centre of the powerful group of London clergy co-ordinating the clerical opposition to James II's policies.

Wake's prominence during James II's reign surely entitled him to major preferment after the revolution.

That he did not receive it might be explained by Thomas Hearne's claim that 'he was of nonjuring Principles' (*Remarks*, 8.287). In fact, he had no problems in accepting the government of William and Mary, and at the beginning of their reign he was rewarded with a royal chaplaincy, the deputy clerkship of the closet, and a canonry of Christ Church. But the position he adopted at the revolution was a moderate one: unlike many, he had no doubts about the legitimacy of James Francis Edward, prince of Wales, and, while he took the oaths himself, he disliked their imposition on others. Consequently, he took no part in the nonjuring controversy and refused to accept any preferments vacated by the deprivation of nonjurors. Thus he declined the deanery of Worcester, the bishopric of Bath and Wells, and the bishopric of Norwich, while simultaneously feeling piqued at not being offered the deanery of St Paul's or the deanery of Canterbury. His *nolo episcopari* created 'an intire Coldnesse' (Christ Church, MS 541 A, p. 43) between him and Archbishop John Tillotson and prevented further offers.

Before his death William Clagett had tried to moderate Wake's polemical inclinations, warning him that such work 'took us off from other, and better, thoughts' (Christ Church, MS 541A, p. 20). It was advice that Wake took to heart. Over the next few years he avoided participation not only in the nonjuring controversy but also in the allegiance and trinitarian controversies. He had already established a reputation as a 'pious & excellent Preacher' (Evelyn, *Diary*, 4.543), but, from this time, his published sermons, apart from a few delivered on special occasions such as fast days, concentrated on pastoral topics. The piety which they revealed was 'unemotional and rational', emphasizing the 'truth and reasonableness of Christian belief and … the prudential wisdom of its practice' (Sykes, 1.54). Wake also threw himself into practical pastoral work as the rector of St James's, Westminster, to which he was appointed in 1695, having declined an offer of the same living in 1692 on the grounds of ill health. He established a weekly catechism and increased the frequency of daily prayers to four times in the parish church and twice in King Street Chapel. The most concrete outcome of his ministry at St James's was his catechetical treatise, first published in 1699 under the title *The Principles of the Christian Religion Explained*. This quickly established itself as one of the most popular of the longer catechisms, intended for the instruction of more advanced pupils, and it continued to be used through the eighteenth century. Alongside his commitment to pastoral work, Wake hankered after a life of scholarly retreat. During a period of convalescence after illness he produced a translation of the *Genuine Epistles of the Apostolic Fathers*, which was published in 1693. Although reprinted twice, this was not a work of original scholarship but of popularization, making available to English readers texts which helped to demonstrate that the Church of England 'in all respects comes the nearest up to the *primitive pattern* of any Christian Church at this Day in the World' (*Genuine Epistles*, vi).

The appearance of Francis Atterbury's *Letter to a Convocation Man* in 1697 once more drew Wake into controversy.

Prompted to investigate further the history of convocation, Wake was then encouraged by Archbishop Tenison to publish his findings. The central point of his *Authority of Christian Princes*, which appeared at the end of 1697, was that Atterbury had failed to recognize the crucial distinction between a parliamentary convocation and an ecclesiastical synod. By controverting Atterbury's parallel between parliament and convocation, Wake was able to undermine the case for restoring a sitting convocation, a conclusion which brought down on him the fury of the tory clergy. This criticism prompted him to publish the *Appeal to All True Members of the Church of England* (1698), in which he defended what he saw as the traditional Anglican doctrine of the royal supremacy. Ironically, given his dislike of controversy, this pamphlet was written in a tone of which even some of his friends disapproved, Edmund Gibson lamenting 'the provocation given' (Bodl. Oxf., Ballard MS 6, fol. 13) to the clergy desiring a convocation. Atterbury's reply, *The Rights, Powers and Privileges of an English Convocation* (1700), attacked Wake's scholarship and knowledge of the constitution. Wake's response was magisterial, a folio volume of over 860 pages entitled *The State of the Church and Clergy of England*. Based on exhaustive historical research, it quickly established itself as the definitive account of the history of English synods since Anglo-Saxon times and is recognized as a 'complete demolition' of Atterbury's work (Sykes, 1.115). By the time *The State of the Church and Clergy* appeared in 1703, however, the ministry had conceded a sitting convocation and the debate had moved on. Wake played no further role in the convocation controversy, but his exchange with Atterbury had established him as the hero of the whig clergy.

It was, therefore, no surprise that the commissioners for ecclesiastical preferments offered Wake the bishopric of Bristol in April 1700. Once more he refused, professing himself content with his life as rector of St James's and bridling at hints from Bishop Burnet that he could expect no further offers of preferment. Archbishop Tenison was angered by Wake's behaviour, clearly feeling that he was putting his own interests before 'his duty to the Church' (Christ Church, MS 541A, p. 50). But a breach between the two was avoided, and in November 1701 Wake accepted nomination to the deanery of Exeter, though he was again irritated by the court's insistence that he resign his canonry of Christ Church. Over the next four years, however, it appears that he continued to devote most of his energies to his parish. He resided little in Exeter, and he certainly did not play the active part in the proceedings of convocation which might have been expected of one of the leading whig clergy in the lower house.

Bishop of Lincoln In 1705 the whig interest at court was again strengthening after a period of tory dominance, and shortly after the death of James Gardiner, bishop of Lincoln, Tenison approached Wake with the offer of the bishopric of Oxford. On this occasion Wake accepted, as he did a week later when he was offered Lincoln instead. According to his own account he had two reasons for this change of mind. First, he received the consent of his dying father, and, second, he was concerned that, if he refused, political manoeuvrings at court might force Tenison to accept the nomination of someone 'very unacceptable, if not unfit' (Jones, 124). As it was, lobbying by other factions, both whig and tory, delayed Wake's promotion until the summer. He was nominated on 16 July and consecrated on 21 October, and he took up residence at the episcopal palace at Buckden, Lincolnshire. Throughout the next decade he was constantly at the centre of the influential group of whig clerics around Tenison, and he met regularly with leading whig politicians such as John, Baron Somers, and Charles Spencer, third earl of Sunderland. He attended both the House of Lords and convocation regularly, and he made a powerful and effective speech defending toleration during the trial of Henry Sacheverell in 1710; he also used his influence within the diocese of Lincoln to support whig candidates in parliamentary elections. None the less, despite the highly charged atmosphere of the latter years of Anne's reign, Wake avoided the kind of polemical pamphleteering on behalf of the whig cause that had characterized his involvement in the convocation controversy.

If Wake performed the political duties of his new office conscientiously, he was no less energetic in his oversight of his diocese, which was the largest in the country, stretching from the Humber to the Thames and containing more than a thousand parishes. Indeed, he was a model of the new breed of post-revolutionary bishops, who were adapting to problems facing the Church of England in the conditions of *de facto* religious pluralism brought about by the Toleration Act of 1689. Like many of his colleagues, he placed fresh emphasis on effective episcopal oversight and the diligent performance of their pastoral responsibilities by bishops and clergy alike. He conducted ordinations regularly at least four times a year, he carefully supervised the examination of ordinands, he held regular triennial visitations (though his last, in 1715, was carried out by commissioners), and he confirmed vast numbers of people, more than 18,000 during the 1712 visitation tour alone. It was in the conduct of visitations that Wake revealed himself at his most innovative, shifting the emphasis away from the judicial towards the pastoral. At each of his visitations he circulated a series of written queries to all the parish clergy, which supplemented the traditional articles sent to churchwardens. The aim of these queries was to give the bishop a variety of information about the parish and its people, the provision of services, and the state of charities. The answers were extracted into a *speculum*, or diocese book, which provided the bishop with a manual for his administration of the diocese. Wake's practice was continued by his successor at Lincoln, Edmund Gibson, and rapidly spread through the church to become the model for eighteenth-century episcopal visitations.

The same commitment to pastoral work was demonstrated by Wake after his confirmation as archbishop of Canterbury on 16 January 1716. Visitations were conducted regularly, in 1716, 1720, 1724, and 1728, following the practice developed at Lincoln. After 1719 Wake himself ordained clergy intending to serve within the diocese, in contrast to most seventeenth-century archbishops who had asked other bishops to ordain them on letters dimissory. Moreover, he continued the efforts of his predecessors to reform standards of clerical practice within the province. In 1716 he issued a circular letter containing instructions for bishops and clergy to tighten up on the admission of ministers to the church and to ensure that curates had an adequate maintenance. In 1724 he issued similar directions to ensure the decency of the administration of the rite of confirmation, and in addition he secured a royal letter to enforce the residence of royal chaplains who were also cathedral prebendaries.

Archbishop of Canterbury Wake's appointment as archbishop was warmly welcomed by many clerical whigs, who saw him as the natural successor to Tenison. Gibson commented that 'his intire interest in the prince and Princess, with his free Access to the King, and the benefit of speaking French fluently, seem to bid fair for a speedy establishm[en]t of all things upon the right foot' (Bodl. Oxf., MS Add. A. 269, p. 52). In fact, Wake was a less natural ally for the whigs than was apparent at the beginning of George I's reign. The bitterness of the convocation controversy had pushed him into the whig camp, and during the last years of Anne's reign he firmly believed that the protestant succession, and thus the church itself, was being threatened by the policies of her tory ministry. But he was still the same man who had refused to accept preferments vacated by nonjurors, and even at the time of the Jacobite rising in 1715 he found himself at a loss how to reassure clergy who believed that the church was in danger under the whig administration. The first public evidence of tension occurred in June 1716 when the Select Vestries Bill came before the House of Lords. This bill, intended to reform the abuses of close vestries in London, reflected the inclinations of anti-clerical whigs by including provisions which would have removed clergymen from participation in parish government and excluded churchwardens from the new vestries. Wake launched such a powerful attack on this measure that he persuaded Lord Chancellor Cowper to admit that 'there was not one Sound part in its whole Composition' and to abandon his support of it, thereby ensuring its defeat (Christ Church, Arch. W.Epist. 7, fol. 125). At least as significant as his triumph in the Lords, however, were the facts that Wake had been forced to oppose a government-sponsored measure publicly rather than privately and that his efforts won him the applause of many tory clergy.

The appointment in April 1717 of the Sunderland–Stanhope ministry, which was committed to a more liberal religious policy, highlighted the gulf that was developing between Wake and the government. In the same month Benjamin Hoadly's sermon, *The Kingdom of Christ*, appeared, provoking a storm of controversy about his extreme latitudinarian views, which seemed to call into question not merely the authority of, but even the need for, a visible church. Privately, Wake was incensed by the actions of the bishop of Bangor and his allies, and he denounced those 'pastors, bishops, who destroy with their own hands the Church in which they minister'. In particular, he singled out the threat from 'a set of Latitudinarian writers' who attacked clerical subscription as a form of ecclesiastical tyranny and were 'enemies … to the most fundamental articles' of the faith (Sykes, 2.150). But he found that he had little support from the new ministry, which, on 8 May, informed the primate that convocation was to be prorogued in order to shield Hoadly from the threat of synodical censure. Wake was left fuming about the way in which ministers put 'their politicall interests' above the 'Service of God, & his Church' (TCD, MS 1995–2008/1815).

Some of Wake's clerical allies, who liked to describe themselves as 'Church Whigs', blamed the archbishop for a lack of leadership. Gibson urged him to attend court more often, reminding him of Tenison's advice that 'tho' he could do noe great good … yet he could hinder mischief' (Christ Church, Arch. W.Epist. 20, fol. 437). But there was probably little Wake could have done to influence the religious policy of the ministry, which was committed to legislating in favour of the protestant dissenters. Over the next eighteen months debate focused on the issue of the repeal of the Test Act. Wake, like all the moderate whig bishops, was resolutely opposed to such a measure, regarding the act as an essential bulwark of the constitutional position of the Church of England and a necessary accompaniment to the toleration. By the end of 1717, however, divisions were opening up between Wake and some of his former allies, notably bishops Edmund Gibson, John Hough, and Lancelot Blackburne. The latter group came to accept the ministry's arguments that some concession had to be made to dissent for political reasons, and they were prepared to support the repeal of the Occasional Conformity and Schism Acts. This group was also becoming concerned about Wake's growing contacts with tory bishops such as George Smalridge and Thomas Manningham, and they feared that he was abandoning the 'clear Church whig bottom' adopted by his predecessor (University of St Andrews Library, MS 5219).

Wake, however, would not countenance even this more limited measure. What is puzzling is why. After all, throughout Anne's reign both clerical and lay whigs had generally opposed tory attempts to outlaw the practice of occasional conformity, and Wake himself had entered his protest against the passage of the Schism Act in 1714. The key to his behaviour seems to lie in changing circumstances. Whereas before 1714 the Occasional Conformity and Schism Acts were seen as paving the way for further erosion of the freedoms granted to dissenters by the Toleration Act of 1689, by 1717 Wake regarded their repeal as a prelude to further concessions to dissent by a ministry hostile to the established church. Thus, when the legislation finally came before the House of Lords in December 1718, the archbishop again found himself leading the opposition to a piece of ministerial legislation which he denounced as an assault on one of the 'Outworks' of the ecclesiastical constitution (Christ Church, Arch. W. Epist., 8/87). This debate, however, revealed the gulf dividing Wake from the ministry and the court much more starkly

than the Select Vestries Bill. Not only was his opposition ineffective, but he also found that his support on the bench of bishops came primarily from the tories, and he was deeply hurt by what he saw as the desertion of his former whig allies, bitterly denouncing them as 'betrayers of the Church' (Bodl. Oxf., Add. MS A. 269, pp. 73–4).

Policy differences lay at the heart of Wake's exclusion from government counsels at the end of the 1710s, but they do not entirely explain it. First, his character made him an awkward colleague. There was, at times, an imperiousness about his utterances and a sensitivity to criticism which inclined him to treat differences of opinion as personal slights. Second, his only close confidant among the whig leadership was Earl Cowper, himself a slightly marginal figure who resigned in April 1718. The ministers most involved in ecclesiastical affairs, lords Townshend and Sunderland, knew Bishop Charles Trimnell far better and were often inclined to turn for advice to him and, increasingly, to Edmund Gibson, the young and politically astute bishop of Lincoln. Third, Wake became embroiled in the split at court between George I and the prince of Wales (afterwards George II). He had always been close to the prince and, especially, the princess (afterwards Queen Caroline), the latter of whom was widely credited with securing the archbishopric for him. When the prince of Wales was instructed to leave St James's in November 1717, Wake continued to wait on the prince and princess at Leicester House, in defiance of the king's instructions. It was hardly a course of action calculated to increase his influence at court.

From 1719 Wake was 'pretty much in disgrace' (Herts. ALS, D/EP F62, fols. 90–91) at court and politically marginalized. There were occasional bursts of activity, but these served merely to emphasize how little influence he possessed. In 1721 he was involved in attempts to pass the Blasphemy Bill, a misleadingly named attempt to combat Arianism by reinforcing the provisions for clerical subscription. In the following year, supported only by John Potter among the whig bishops, he opposed the passage of the Quaker Affirmation Act. In 1724 he did at least find support from most of his episcopal colleagues in a protest against masquerades. But by this time, as one observer noted, he was playing almost no part in 'Eccl[esiastical] affairs' (BL, Lansdowne MS 1018, fol. 9). In 1727 the archbishop did have some hopes that his influence would revive when George I died and Caroline, his old patron, became queen. However, within a few weeks it became clear that both Robert Walpole and his 'pope', Bishop Gibson, had survived the change of regime, and Wake retired once more to Lambeth.

The churches abroad Wake stands out among eighteenth-century archbishops of Canterbury for his commitment to correspondence and engagement with the churches in Europe. Like many whig churchmen of the post-revolutionary era he expressed a strong commitment to the ideal of protestant union, both at home and with the reformed churches abroad. In large part this was an expression of his fear of the threat from Catholicism—even after the flight of James II, he continued to interpret events such as the Nine Years' War as a struggle to defend 'the *Protestant Religion*' against Louis XIV's efforts 'to root out the very memory of it from off the Earth' (*Sermon Preached in the Parish Church*, 13). Importantly, he believed that protestants were already united 'in a *common profession of the same Faith*', that what separated them were only differences over inessentials, and he thus saw no reason why they 'should not also be united in the same *common Worship* of God' (*Exhortation to Mutual Charity and Union*, 26).

The elevation of Wake to the primacy was warmly welcomed by many foreign protestants, including Gottfried Wilhelm Leibniz in Hanover, Daniel Ernst Jablonski in Berlin, Jean Le Clerc in Amsterdam, and Samuel Turrettini in Geneva. The new archbishop sought to build on these contacts, and he developed an extensive correspondence with leading protestants throughout Europe. Among the more important initiatives that resulted were the formal authorization of intercommunion with the church in Zürich and a series of interventions attempting to reconcile differences among the Swiss churches. Most notable, however, was his involvement, along with Jablonski, whom he had first met at Oxford in 1680, in efforts to bring about a union between the Lutheran and Calvinist churches in Germany. Jablonski, the religious counsellor to Frederick William I of Prussia, believed that the Church of England could act as a formal mediator in negotiations, and Wake responded positively to the suggestion, beginning a correspondence that lasted from 1717 to 1725. Ultimately, the initiative came to nothing, undermined as much as anything by inertia and political differences between the courts of Hanover and Prussia. But confessional distinctions were also a powerful force impeding moves towards union, a fact revealed clearly even by Wake himself, who, despite his belief that differences in inessentials were no barrier to union, could still complain to a foreign correspondent that 'there is no dogma more inimical to piety' than the Calvinist doctrine of predestination (Sykes, 2.59).

Wake was unusual among eighteenth-century Anglicans in his commitment to engagement with foreign protestants; even more remarkable were his contacts with French Catholics. In February 1718 he responded favourably to overtures from Ellies Du Pin, a theologian of Jansenist sympathies at the Sorbonne, about a possible union between the Church of England and the Gallican church. However, what emerges clearly from the ensuing correspondence, much of which was carried on through William Beauvoir, the chaplain in Paris, is that Wake did not envisage a full union, but merely some form of intercommunion. Moreover, any agreement would have to be preceded by a breach between the Gallican church and the papacy. In retrospect, even this aim was clearly unrealistic. Both Wake and Du Pin were looking for doctrinal concessions, which the other party was unlikely to make. Wake, indeed, does not seem to have grasped that the differences between Gallican clergy and the papacy did not imply any dissatisfaction with those points of Catholic

doctrine, such as transubstantiation, which were so offensive to protestants. In fact, no formal negotiations ever took place. Wake was nettled by the refusal of Cardinal de Noailles, the archbishop of Paris, to become involved, but Noailles's behaviour emphasizes the fact that Du Pin's initiative was essentially a personal one, on behalf of himself and a few professors at the Sorbonne, which had no support from either the French government or the ecclesiastical hierarchy. Finally, early in 1719, an abrupt end was put to the exchanges when the French secretary of state seized Du Pin's papers.

None the less, Wake did continue to correspond regularly with two other French clergymen, Piers de Girardin, another professor at the Sorbonne, and Pierre Le Courayer. The correspondence with Le Courayer, which began in 1721, is of particular note, as it reveals that Wake gave considerable assistance to Le Courayer in the preparation of his *Dissertation sur la validité des ordinations des Anglois* and then in the defence of that work after its publication in 1723. Wake clearly remained committed to the ideal of intercommunion, and he believed that could be advanced by convincing Gallicans that the Church of England enjoyed an unbroken episcopal succession. Significantly, however, he offered little help to Le Courayer in defending his discussion of the sacrificial character of the mass and in his attempts to reconcile the Book of Common Prayer and Thirty-Nine Articles to Roman teaching. On these issues, his attitude was that the Gallican church had to accept the position of the Church of England. Yet that was not going to happen—these were precisely the issues which led to episcopal censures of Le Courayer in August 1727 and prompted his flight to England.

Last years Politically marginalized after 1719, Wake lived in semi-retirement at Lambeth and focused his attentions increasingly on preparation for the next life. He himself called his existence 'almost a monastic life' (Thomson, 2.85), which was not an inappropriate description of a regime which included divine service four times a day within his household. He continued to discharge the business of his diocese, he corresponded actively with his foreign friends, and he roused himself to organize the order of service for the coronation of George II and Queen Caroline in 1727, but he had been prone to illness throughout his life, and there is little doubt that his strength was declining. He performed his last visitation of his diocese in 1728 and carried out his last ordination in person in September 1730. That year he suffered a serious illness, prompting satires about the race to succeed him as archbishop, and on 15 April 1731 his wife died. In the following year he was experiencing severe difficulties in writing and he consecrated his last bishop—thereafter all consecrations were carried out by commission. By this time Wake was relying heavily on his son-in-law John *Lynch (1697–1760) in the administration of his diocese and as secretary. Lynch had married Mary, the sixth and youngest of Wake's daughters. As the only clergyman among the archbishop's immediate family—the elder five daughters, Amy, Etheldred, Hester, Dorothy, and Magdalen, had all married gentlemen—he accumulated some of the best preferments in his gift. Even in an age that accepted the responsibility of public figures to provide for their families, Lynch's extensive pluralism became a subject of some scandal in Wake's declining years; the most vivid of numerous attacks was a satire depicting him as an ass loaded with preferments. Wake died at Lambeth on 24 January 1737 and was buried on 9 February alongside his wife in the south chancel of Croydon parish church. The *Gentleman's Magazine* estimated that he left 'upwards of £100,000', and among his bequests were £1000 for the charity school in his native Blandford (*GM*, 1st ser., 7, 1737, 61).

Wake was a distinguished historian. His *State of the Church and Clergy of England* was widely regarded as the definitive account of English synods well into the twentieth century, while his researches enabled Le Courayer to provide an account of the consecrations of Archbishop Parker and Bishop Barlow, a crucial episode in the defence of the validity of Anglican orders, to which modern historians have been able to add little. He was also an innovative, reforming bishop, who established the model for eighteenth-century episcopal visitations. To contemporaries, however, he was probably most admired for that part of his career which he valued least, namely his work as a controversialist, first against popery in James II's reign and later in the convocation controversy. His role in the convocation controversy, and the attacks upon him by the 'high flying' clergy who supported Atterbury, ensured that he became identified with the whigs and the church party around Archbishop Tenison. Other things also drew Wake to the whigs and their low-church allies during the reigns of William and Anne. He was a strong supporter of the Toleration Act of 1689, he adopted an eirenic approach to foreign protestants, he condemned those clergy who denounced lay baptism as invalid, and, in characteristically low-church fashion, he believed that the Thirty-Nine Articles were framed so that 'they may, without an equivocation, have more senses that one fairly put upon them' (Sykes, 2.32–3). But the party labels of this period tend to obscure rather than reveal Wake's churchmanship, as other elements of his thought were more characteristic of high-churchmen. He was attracted to the beauty and solemnity of Catholic worship, he could appreciate the religious value of monasteries and nunneries, he could sympathize with the stand taken by the nonjurors, he placed considerable emphasis on the value of antiquity and tradition in elucidating Christian doctrine, and, despite his commitment to the principle of toleration, he could still regard English dissenters as 'a buisy, indefatigable generation' (TCD, MSS 1995–2008/1929). It is not surprising that he was an uncomfortable ally for whig ministries after the Hanoverian succession.

Since Wake's death it is probably the enterprise that was closest to his own heart, his work for church union, that has attracted most attention. In the eighteenth century his correspondence with the Gallican church was seen as treading 'upon the heels of Popery' by latitudinarians such as Francis Blackburne, who believed that there had been 'few such renegadoes to' the principles of protestantism (Nichols, *Lit. anecdotes*, 3.12). Wake did not lack defenders, but from the mid-nineteenth century assessments have become more consistently positive as Anglican interest in dialogue with other churches has increased. Norman Sykes is typical of modern opinion in regarding his ecumenical work as 'the most outstanding of his achievements' (Sykes, 2.267). But the fact that he was accorded a two-volume biography by the leading twentieth-century scholar of the eighteenth-century church, the only Georgian bishop to be so honoured, tells us at least as much about the priorities of the modern Church of England as about its history in the decades after the revolution of 1688. Ultimately the singling out of Wake's foreign correspondence for special attention—it occupies one-third of Sykes's biography—is unconvincing. As W. R. Ward has suggested, it is necessary to locate that correspondence in the context of Wake's other concerns in the years after the Hanoverian succession. The search for church union should not be regarded as a precursor of the ecumenical movement of the twentieth century. Rather, it was another means of shoring up the church's defences in response to the threats from Arianism and Socinianism, from latitudinarianism among the clergy and from the liberal religious policies of some whig politicians.

STEPHEN TAYLOR

Sources N. Sykes, *William Wake, archbishop of Canterbury, 1657–1737*, 2 vols. (1957) · W. Wake, correspondence, Christ Church Oxf., Wake MSS Arch. W. Epist. · W. Wake, autobiography, Christ Church Oxf., MS 541A · W. Wake, *An exposition of the doctrine of the Church of England, in the several articles proposed by Monsieur de Meaux, late bishop of Condom, in his exposition of the doctrine of the Catholick church* (1686) · *Bishop Burnet's History* · *Remarks and collections of Thomas Hearne*, ed. C. E. Doble and others, 11 vols., OHS, 2, 7, 13, 34, 42–3, 48, 50, 65, 67, 72 (1885–1921) · Evelyn, *Diary* · W. Wake, ed., *The genuine epistles of the apostolic fathers*, 2nd edn (1710) · E. Gibson and A. Charlett, correspondence, Bodl. Oxf., MS Ballard 6 · C. Jones, 'The politics and the financial costs of an episcopal appointment in the early eighteenth century: the promotion of William Wake to the bishopric of Lincoln in 1705', *Huntington Library Quarterly*, 53 (1990), 119–29 · Gibson–Nicolson correspondence, Bodl. Oxf., MS Add. A. 269 · TCD, King MSS 1995–2008 · Herts. ALS, Cowper papers, D/EP F62 · BL, Reynolds–Kennett corresp., Lansdowne MS 1018 · W. Wake, *A sermon preached in the parish church of St James Westminster, April xvith 1696, being the day of thanksgiving for the preservation of his majesty's person from the late horrid and barbarous conspiracy* (1696) · W. Wake, *An exhortation to mutual charity and union among protestants, a sermon preach'd before the king and queen at Hampton-Court, May 21 1689* (1689) · K. Thomson, *Memoirs of Viscountess Sundon, mistress of the robes to Queen Caroline*, 2 vols. (1847) · *GM*, 1st ser., 7 (1737), 61 · Nichols, *Lit. anecdotes*, vol. 3 · W. R. Ward, *The protestant evangelical awakening* (1992) · I. Green, *The Christian's ABC: catechisms and catechizing in England, c.1530–1740* (1996) · G. Holmes, *The trial of Doctor Sacheverell* (1973) · W. Wake, *His grace the archbishop of Canterbury's letter to the right reverend the lords bishops of his province, Westminster, June 5, 1716* (1716) · 'Ent'ring book', DWL, Morrice MS Q · S. Taylor, '"Dr Codex" and the whig "pope": Edmund Gibson, bishop of Lincoln and London, 1716–1748', *Lords of parliament: studies, 1714–1914*, ed. R. W. Davis (1995), 9–28 · *The London diaries of William Nicolson, bishop of Carlisle, 1702–1718*, ed. C. Jones and G. Holmes (1985) · *William Wake's Gallican correspondence and related documents, 1716–1731*, ed. L. Adams, 7 vols. (1988–93) · U. St Andr. L., Gibson MSS · N. Sykes, 'Archbishop Wake and the whig party, 1716–1723: a study in incompatibility of temperament', *Cambridge Historical Journal*, 8 (1944–6), 93–112 · E. B. Fryde and others, eds., *Handbook of British chronology*, 3rd edn, Royal Historical Society Guides and Handbooks, 2 (1986)

Archives BL, abstract of register, Add. MSS 6106–6107 · Canterbury Cathedral, archives, notebook containing account of incumbents and churches, incl. personal remarks, in Kent, Essex, Lancashire, and London · Christ Church Oxf., autobiography, MS 541A · Christ Church Oxf., corresp. and papers · Cornwall RO, letters, PB8/5–8 · LPL, autobiographical papers and journal [copies] · LPL, corresp. and papers relating to gift of MSS to Christ Church, Oxford · LPL, diary, MS 1770 | Öffentliche Bibliothek der Universität in Basel, MS Fr. Gr. 111; MS Ki Ar. 26b · Bibliothèque Publique et Universitaire, Geneva, MS Inventaire 1569, collection J. A. Turrettini; corresp., TAN-ZWI; corresp. Ecclésiastique XXXIX, MS Inv. 440 · BL, corresp. with White Kennett, Lansdowne MS 1016 · BL, Blenheim papers, letters to Lord Sunderland, Add. MS 61612 · Bodl. Oxf., corresp. with Arthur Charlett, MS Ballard 3 · Bodl. Oxf., letters to Browne Willis · Herts. ALS, letters to first Earl Cowper and Countess Cowper, D/EP · LPL, corresp. with William Beauvoir, MS 1552 · LPL, letters to David Wilkins · PRO NIre., corresp. with William Nicolson [copies] · Staatsarchiv, Bern, B. 111. 98 · Staatsarchiv des Kantons Zürich, E. 11.432; A. 222. 3, 4 · TCD, corresp. with William King, MSS 1995–2008 · V&A NAL, corresp. with William Nicolson and Lady Sundon [copies] · Zentralbibliothek, Zürich, MS H. 293

Likenesses T. Gibson, oils, *c*.1715–1720, Christ Church Oxf.; copy, St James's Church, Piccadilly · T. Hill, oils, *c*.1720–1725, NPG [*see illus.*] · oils, *c*.1730, NPG · J. Ellis, oils, 1732 · I. Whood, oils, 1736, LPL · J. Dassies, silver and copper medal, BM · J. Faber junior, mezzotint (after J. Ellis), BM, NPG · M. Vandergucht, line engraving (after unknown artist), NPG · G. White, mezzotint (after T. Gibson), BM, NPG

Wealth at death over £100,000: *GM*, 61; will, 1737, PRO, PROB 11/687, sig. 51

Wakefeld, Robert. See Wakefield, Robert (d. 1537/8).

Wakefeld, Thomas. See Wakefield, Thomas (d. 1575).

Wakefield, Arthur (1799–1843). *See under* Wakefield, William Hayward (1801–1848).

Wakefield, Charles Cheers, first Viscount Wakefield (1859–1941), oil industrialist and philanthropist, was born in Liverpool on 12 December 1859, the fourth and youngest son (there were no daughters) of John Wakefield, a customs official, and his wife, Mary, daughter of William Cheers, of Manchester. After schooling at Liverpool Institute, he declined to follow his father into a safe civil-service job and instead joined a Liverpool oil-broking firm. Later he moved to the London office of an American petroleum company, where he was soon appointed manager for the British empire, a post which took him on several journeys round the world. His book, *Future Trade in the Far East* (1896), gained him a fellowship of the Royal Geographical Society. On 17 February 1888 Wakefield married Sarah Frances (d. 1950), daughter of William Graham, bookkeeper of Wavertree, Liverpool. They had no children.

In 1899 Wakefield set up his own firm in London, C. C. Wakefield & Co., which dealt in lubricating oil and equipment; and in the following decade he concentrated mainly on providing lubricants for British and overseas

railways resisting the temptation to diversify into other oil products. On the administrative side, he was aided by his brother-in-law, Walter Graham, as well as managers who came with him from the American company and decided to stay permanently. Their aptitude and loyalty gave him the freedom to seek office in the City of London. In 1904 he was elected to the court of common council. He served as sheriff in 1907–8, and later became alderman. He was knighted in 1908.

Meanwhile, the rapid growth of the motor car market in Britain was creating new opportunities for the firm. Wakefield introduced Wakefield Motor Oil, subtitled in 1912 the Castrol brand, since one aromatic ingredient was castor oil. Once having overtaken rival firms, none of which was yet taking automobile lubrication seriously, the company pursued two characteristic policies: of massive and often topical advertising, and of advanced research at its Liverpool blending plant. An additional plant was built at Hayes, Middlesex, in 1925. The conquest of the air furnished a particular challenge: in 1909 Wakefield launched the Castrol R brand, an aircraft lubricant which remained fluid at high-altitude temperatures as low as −32 °C. That year the first British racing event for aeroplanes took place at Doncaster; the engines of all the winning machines were lubricated by Castrol R.

The First World War was the first conflict in which the internal combustion engine came to play a vital part. Castrol R received an almost unique testimonial—which the firm eagerly seized on—when the Kaiser's chief of staff admitted to the Kaiser that the British had discovered the secret of a non-freezing aircraft lubricant, which the Germans had been seeking for months. In a different area, the widespread mechanization of British farming, to combat the U-boat threat to food supplies, led to the introduction of Agricastrol in 1917. Despite all his wartime commitments, Wakefield served as lord mayor of London in 1915–16. He energetically promoted recruiting drives and war charities, and visited the western front and the Grand Fleet at Scapa Flow. He received a baronetcy in 1917 and two years later was appointed CBE.

In 1918 C. C. Wakefield & Co. was registered as a private company, with capital of £250,000. Owning most of the shares, Wakefield as governing director (he never called himself chairman) left decisions of detail to his managers but intervened with effect when necessary. During the inter-war period, world records were regularly being broken by (mainly British) cars, motor cycles, speedboats, and aircraft; virtually all used one of the Castrol range of lubricants. To exploit the publicity thus engendered, the company raised its advertising outlay from £41,000 in 1923 to £300,000 in 1938, one-third of which was spent in the press. Newspapers often left display advertisements open to the last moment, so as to record the previous day's triumphs. On the research side, the knowledge gained from all these events helped the company's scientists to develop ever more advanced types of oil, and new brands emerged such as Patent Castrol for cars, in 1935, and the new lighter oils of 1938. Between 1923 and 1939 annual sales grew threefold to £1,760,000; profits rose even faster, from £75,000 to £250,000.

Between the wars Wakefield received a total of over £3 million from his company in dividends and salary; as a childless man he devoted the bulk of this sum to an impressive range of good causes. In the City of London, for example, he was a generous donor to the Guildhall Library and Art Gallery. He furthered the work of psychiatric treatment by acting as president and benefactor of the Bethlem and Bridewell Royal hospitals and the Mental Aftercare Association. St Thomas's and St Bartholomew's hospitals and the National Children's Home and Orphanage likewise benefited from his time and money. He endowed research at the Imperial Institute and was patron of many flying clubs around the world. On the cultural side, in 1918 he endowed the British Academy lectures to mark the tercentenary of Sir Walter Ralegh; he donated books and relics to the Dickens fellowship; and he anonymously assisted the British Museum in its purchase of the Codex Sinaiticus. Among the objects from Britain's heritage which he presented to the nation were the Armada jewel, papers of Sir Isaac Newton, Lord Nelson's personal logbook, and the Mint collection. He was created Baron Wakefield in 1930 and advanced to a viscountcy in 1934, and he was appointed GCVO in 1936.

Wakefield was below average height, with a large head and a square and stocky build; he later discarded the handlebar moustache of his younger days. His deliberate manner of speaking showed just a trace of his Liverpool origins; after an unsuccessful early debating performance, he never gave impromptu addresses but always read from a prepared script. In London he dressed in a morning coat and top hat, though he subsequently replaced the latter with a bowler. His conduct towards others was as formal and gentlemanly as his attire. Rigorously prompt and thorough himself, he sternly discounted a lame excuse, but was patient, kindly, and solicitous for the well-being of friends and associates, and the beneficiaries of his public acts.

His success could be attributed to a combination of foresight, courage, and flair. For a businessman, he had an unusually well-developed sense of obligation to the state as a guardian of society: he settled his tax bills without fuss or delay and strongly disapproved of covenants to avoid income tax on charitable donations. These principles of conduct he had adopted from a Wesleyan minister in his home town, and his stance on religion was benevolent and undogmatic. As lord mayor he floated the idea of calling a conference at the Mansion House to settle all religious differences and lay the foundations of a single great British church. This ingenious notion foundered on the indifference of the respective denominational leaders. He thereafter immersed himself in freemasonry, of which he was an ardent member, wanting its tenets to become the basis of ethics in the City of London.

Wakefield remained active in business until a month before he died, on 15 January 1941, at his home, Ashwell Lodge, Furzefield Road, Beaconsfield, Buckinghamshire. He was buried at Hythe in Kent, from which he had taken his title; when receiving the town's freedom in 1930, he had admitted to finding peace, health, and friendship there. He was survived by his wife and left £776,220.

T. A. B. CORLEY

Sources *The Times* (16 Jan 1941) · GEC, *Peerage* · H. Begbie, *The proud citizen* (1917) · L. Sultan, 'The Castrol story', Burmah Castrol plc, Swindon · Castrol Ltd, *Wheels, wings and water* (1974) · *Journal of the Royal Society of Arts*, 89 (1940–41), 210–11 · Burke, *Peerage* · *Debrett's Peerage* (1937) · WWW
Archives Burmah Castrol plc, Swindon, archives of Castrol Ltd · National Motor Museum, corresp. | FILM BFI NFTVA, news footage | SOUND BL NSA, current affairs recording
Likenesses J. Lavery, oils, exh. RA 1916, Hythe town hall, Kent · O. Birley, oils, 1932; formerly at Royal Aero Club, Piccadilly, London [c/o crown commissioners] · O. Birley, oils, 1943, Bethlem Royal Hospital, Beckenham, Kent · F. E. Beresford, oils, Worshipful Company of Haberdashers, London · photographs, Burmah Castrol House, Swindon, Castrol Ltd archives
Wealth at death £776,220 18s. 0d.: probate, 27 Feb 1941, CGPLA Eng. & Wales

Wakefield, Daniel (1776–1846), barrister and writer on political economy, was born in the spring of 1776, in Tottenham, Middlesex. He was the youngest of three children in the family of Edward Wakefield (1750–1826), merchant, and his wife, the writer Priscilla *Wakefield (1750–1832), daughter of Daniel Bell. Daniel Wakefield's elder brother was Edward *Wakefield; Edward Gibbon *Wakefield was his nephew. Wakefield was privately educated by scholars of some eminence. One tutor, Stewart Kyd, was later tried for high treason with Horne Tooke. His commitment to Quakerism, despite the influence of his mother, was not strong and he abandoned it for the Church of England at a relatively young age, partly in the hope of qualifying for employment with the government. In 1798 he did gain a part-time post in the naval pay office; but the wage was poor and he despaired of further advancement. Other attention-seeking schemes included pamphlets on political economy, urging poorly conceived reforms of the public finance system. Expensive schemes for the reclamation of Irish bogs similarly proved unrewarding. In 1799 he published the most important of his works, *An Essay of Political Economy*, an inquiry into the various French schools of writing on value.

On 9 February 1802 Wakefield became a student of Lincoln's Inn. His commitment to the legal profession must, however, be doubted as various distractions, riotous living, and, according to his mother, unsuitable company prevented much headway. An ill-advised marriage on 3 June 1805 to Isabella Mackie, an adventuress and swindler, followed. It dragged him into a morass of debt and fraud that almost ended in bankruptcy and emigration. Remarkably, his legal career was not destroyed and he was called to the bar on 2 May 1807. A sullied reputation and an inadequate knowledge of the law, however, meant that clients were not plentiful and his financial dependence upon his parents and brother continued. Attempts to annul the marriage failed; then, in August 1813, Isabella committed suicide by taking poison. On 11 November that year Wakefield married Elizabeth Kilgour. Neither marriage produced children. Poverty had made him a diligent student and the past six years had not been wasted. With his newly acquired respectability and demonstrable skill, his practice flourished. He became known as one of the ablest equity draftsmen of his day and was often consulted in major cases. He was elected bencher of Lincoln's Inn on 15 January 1835, having become king's counsel during the previous Michaelmas vacation. His most famous brief was, perhaps, *Attwood v. Small*. The dispute concerned the sale of an ironworks whose price was over £1 million. It was appealed to the House of Lords in 1838 and his successful argument won him a considerable reputation, a silk gown from the lord chancellor, and £5000 from the grateful John Attwood.

Towards the end of his career, Wakefield became known for his philanthropy. At times, he refused payment for briefs and returned fees to clients in distress. His eminence was recognized by his involvement in the administration of the inn and in the planning and construction of the new hall. His country residence was at Hare Hatch, near Twyford, Berkshire, where he was magistrate and deputy lieutenant. Wakefield died suddenly on 19 July 1846, in London, while taking a shower. He was buried on 23 July 1846 in the crypt of Lincoln's Inn chapel.

DAVID J. MOSS

Sources GM, 2nd ser., 26 (1846), 323–4 · *Morning Post* (23 July 1846) · Ward, *Men of the reign* · DNB · private information (2004) · register and records, Lincoln's Inn, London, 11, 9, 122
Archives priv. coll.
Likenesses F. C. Lewis, stipple (after engraving by A. Wivell), BM, NPG
Wealth at death £1500: will

Wakefield, Edward (1774–1854), philanthropist, land agent, and writer on political economy, was born in Tottenham, Middlesex. He was the elder son of Edward Wakefield (1750–1826), merchant, and the writer Priscilla *Wakefield (1750–1832), daughter of Daniel Bell. Daniel *Wakefield was his younger brother. Edward, described by his nurse as 'born to make hearts ache', always had many female admirers. His first marriage was to 'the most beautiful girl in Essex', Susanna Crash, a farmer's daughter of Felsted in Essex, on 3 October 1790. They had ten children, of whom seven were boys; their eldest son was Edward Gibbon *Wakefield, and their fourth was William Hayward *Wakefield. Susanna died in 1817 and six years later, under mysterious circumstances, Edward married Frances Davies, daughter of David Davies, headmaster of Macclesfield grammar school. The marriage, solemnized in Paris on 3 August 1823, was not announced to either family, and Frances remained in her father's house for four years.

Brought up a Quaker, Wakefield was privately educated and spent much of his youth at the farm of John Gurney, an uncle, in Earlham, near Norwich. Shortly after his first marriage, he decided to become a gentleman farmer: obtaining first by purchase, Romford Lodge, and secondly by lease, Burnham Wyck, Essex. Both enterprises failed badly and the latter was sold at a considerable loss. However, he had become friends with many of the innovating and influential farmers in the area, including Squire Coke, Lord Petre, the duke of Bedford, and C. C. Western.

A short, financially unrewarding period at the naval arsenal, Northfleet, followed. He ceased attending Quaker meetings and became loosely affiliated to the Church of England in the hope of winning a more lucrative government post. For the next few years, while his family lived in Bury St Edmunds, he spent his time educating himself by visiting prisons (Elizabeth Fry was a cousin) and workhouses, and by travel, including an extended visit to Ireland. Despite a continuing lack of success in his business affairs, his friends considered him to be particularly knowledgeable about economics. He gave evidence to parliamentary committees on sugar imports (1808), bullion (1810), and agricultural depression (1821). There is some suggestion that he was consulted by William Pitt about Ireland and that he advised Henry Dundas, first Viscount Melville, when president of the Board of Trade. In 1808 John Foster, afterwards Lord Oriel, chancellor of the exchequer for Ireland, persuaded him to return to Ireland and write a book about that country's rural economy. The subsequent two-volume work, *Ireland, Statistical and Political*, published in 1812, was described by John Ramsay McCulloch as 'the best and most complete work on Ireland since Arthur Young's tour' (DNB). Although it does contain some inaccuracies and has a distinctly Malthusian tone, its candour, intelligent analysis, and relatively unbiased perspective have ensured that it remains a valuable source for Irish historians.

In 1814, on the strength of his newly acquired reputation and the contacts made some fifteen years earlier, Wakefield opened one of the first land agencies in the country at 42 Pall Mall. He was soon occupied traversing the country, from Cornwall to Yorkshire, acting as the agent for, among others, David Ricardo, and as manager/adviser for several large landowners. As an adjunct to his estate management activities he engaged in the sale and purchase of parliamentary rotten boroughs, and did well at this secretive trade. His Irish book also provided an introduction into Benthamite and whig/radical circles in London. He formed close friendships with Francis Place, John Mill, and Henry Brougham. Two philanthropic causes, education and the condition and ill-treatment of lunatic asylum patients, attracted most of his attention. In the former case Wakefield strongly supported Joseph Lancaster's educational theories, introducing him to a number of wealthy patrons among whom, he later claimed, was George III. He helped organize several Lancastrian schools in London and cleverly manipulated public opinion to raise funds. His use of large public meetings, set agendas, and planted questions from the audience to create the right atmosphere was particularly sophisticated. For the latter cause, several visits to the lunatic asylum of Bethlem in 1814 and orchestrated publicity led to some celebrated evidence to a parliamentary inquiry in 1816.

Wakefield stood as a tory candidate for Reading in the general election of June 1826, but a scandal involving his son's abduction escapade, in which his wife was involved, seems to have caused his retirement on the third day of the poll. In the 1830s and 1840s he became a warm advocate of Edward Gibbon Wakefield's colonization schemes, writing many letters to newspapers and lobbying the cabinet. Financial problems eventually resurfaced and, facing bankruptcy proceedings, he was forced to flee the country in the early 1840s. With the help of a loan from Lord Ashburton he lived comfortably for some years in Blois, France, where he managed a silk factory. Eventually the debts were paid and he returned to England. Wakefield died on 18 May 1854 in Knightsbridge and is buried in Kensal Green cemetery.   DAVID J. MOSS

Sources Boase, *Mod. Eng. biog.* · R. H. I. Palgrave, ed., *Dictionary of political economy*, 3 vols. (1894–9) · P. Bloomfield, *Edward Gibbon Wakefield: builder of the British Commonwealth* (1961) · *DNB*
Archives NRA, corresp. and papers · priv. coll. | BL, Peel MSS · BL, letters to Arthur Young, Francis Place, and others · CUL, Ricardo MSS · PRO NIre., Foster/Massereene MSS · PRO NIre., letters to Lord Oriel · UCL, letters to James Brougham
Likenesses portrait, priv. coll.

Wakefield, Edward Gibbon (1796–1862), promoter of colonization, was born on 20 March 1796 in London. He was the second child and eldest son of Edward *Wakefield (1774–1854), philanthropist, land agent, and writer on economics, and Susanna, *née* Crash (d. 1817), a farmer's daughter from Felsted, Essex. His middle name was taken from his great-grandmother, Isabella Gibbon, a relative of the historian. The Wakefields were an old Quaker family, originally from Kendal in Westmorland. The family moved almost immediately after his birth to Essex, farming first at Romford then at Burnham Wyck. Financial problems and the serious illness of Susanna led to Edward Gibbon being sent to his grandmother in Tottenham. Priscilla *Wakefield, a devout Quaker, was not impressed by her eldest grandson, a boy with 'an inflexible and pertinacious temper'. During the next five years Edward was expelled from three schools, Mr Haigh's school in Tottenham, Westminster School, and Edinburgh high school, for fighting and disobedience. His uncle, Daniel *Wakefield, succeeded in having him admitted to Gray's Inn on 5 October 1813, but there is no evidence that he ever studied law. His father, who had been absent during much of his son's childhood, had to admit that, at seventeen, he had become incorrigible. Fortunately, Edward became acquainted with the Hon. William Noel Hill, the British envoy at Turin and son of Lord Berwick. He spent the winter of 1814–15 in Turin as Hill's secretary. In the summer he temporarily left Hill's employ to enjoy life as a king's messenger, travelling on several occasions to Paris. The first sign of an above average mind at last emerged with the publication in *The Statesman* of his acute observations on the Bourbon restoration celebrations in that city.

Marriage and imprisonment After wintering again with Hill in Turin, Wakefield returned with his employer to a house in Princes Street, off Hanover Square, London. Opposite lived a widow, Mrs E. A. Pattle, and her daughter, Eliza, a ward of chancery. Thomas Charles Pattle, a rich Canton merchant, had died in Macao the year before. Edward, recognizing the opportunity, wooed the seventeen-year-old heiress without the knowledge of her

Edward Gibbon Wakefield (1796–1862), by unknown artist, *c.*1820

mother or uncles. On 13 June 1816 Wakefield eloped with Eliza, and the couple were married on 27 July in Edinburgh. The lord chancellor became involved, but following the intervention of several influential people, including Hill, the marriage was grudgingly accepted. A Church of England ceremony on 10 August and an immediate income of £600 a year out of the Pattle estate to maintain his wife sealed the affair. Eliza was to gain a further £30,000 on her twenty-first birthday and further sums were to accrue when obligations to other members of the family were satisfied. The gamble had succeeded and Wakefield's financial future was assured. For the next four years he was attached to the Hon. Algernon Percy, undersecretary at the British delegation in Turin, but spent more time with Hill, who was now in Genoa. A daughter, Susan Priscilla (known as Nina), was born on 4 December 1817 in Genoa (she died on 12 February 1836 of consumption). In 1820 the Wakefields returned to England where, on 25 June, a second child, Edward Jerningham [*see below*], was born. Eliza died ten days later, before she was twenty-one, of complications from the birth. In consequence, the £30,000 remained with the Pattles. For the next few years Wakefield travelled, spending much of his time in Paris.

Despite being relatively wealthy from the proceeds of the chancery settlement, Wakefield's ambition, a seat in the Commons, demanded more. On 7 March 1826, with the connivance of his brother William *Wakefield and his stepmother, Frances, he abducted an heiress, Ellen Turner, from her boarding-school near Liverpool. She was fifteen and the daughter of William Turner of Shrigley, a wealthy Cheshire manufacturer. Told that her father was dangerously ill, Ellen was bundled into a coach and taken to Gretna Green. A second lie, that her father's fortune depended on marriage to Wakefield, persuaded her to agree to a marriage ceremony. They were caught by angry relatives at Calais, *en route* for Paris. William had already been arrested and, on his return to England in May, Edward was committed to Lancaster Castle. The trial was heard on 23 March 1827. Found guilty, the brothers were sentenced to three years apiece; William served his in Lancaster Castle, Edward languished in Newgate. An act of parliament was needed to annul the marriage because, according to Scottish law, it had been perfectly legal despite the fact it had not been consummated. The case had attracted immense attention, and the reputations of the brothers appeared for ever blighted.

Prison life was difficult but not impossible for Edward. His children lodged nearby and made frequent visits; moreover, he enjoyed the ministrations of a procession of relatives including Elizabeth Fry. Imprisonment proved, ironically, to be Wakefield's salvation. Given the time for reflection, he began the transition from vain and arrogant gadfly to serious student of society and its ills, although he remained arrogant and ill-tempered. Part of his time was spent talking to prisoners and discussing the usefulness of imprisonment and, in particular, capital punishment. His ideas were later published in *Facts Relating to the Punishment of Death in the Metropolis* (1831) and in evidence to the select committee on secondary punishments (1831). In both he condemned the use of capital punishment for all but the most serious crimes, and sought to emphasize the certainty of punishment as the deterrent rather than the harshness of the penalty. His other occupation, a corollary of his studies on the causes of crime, was to devise a programme of systematic colonization.

Between August and October 1829 the *Morning Chronicle* published in instalments Wakefield's *Letter from Sydney*. In the newspaper no author was credited, but when it was reprinted as a book, *Letter from Sydney, the Principal Town of Australasia*, in 1830, Robert Gouger, with whom Wakefield had corresponded while in Newgate, was credited as editor. Wakefield also published a pamphlet, *Sketch of a Proposal for Colonising Australia*. These brilliantly imaginative pieces—the first was written from the point of view of a settler (although Wakefield himself had never been to Australia)—offered a plan, based on six principles, to overcome the problems of over-population identified by Malthus. Colonies, he wrote, were unprofitable because they suffered from a scarcity of labour, the reverse of the situation in Britain. Emigration must therefore be encouraged. The plan's first principle demanded that land be sold for a 'sufficient price'. The proceeds of the sale and a land tax were to be used to provide the transportation of labourers to the colonies 'free of cost'. These people should be both men and women from all classes of society, not convicts or slaves, and should govern themselves at the earliest opportunity, under a viceroy. The weakest part of the plan lay in its definition of 'sufficient price'. Wakefield understood that it should not be placed too high. Ideally, it needed to be high enough so that labour

was available to capital, but sufficiently low to allow labourers to acquire their own land after four or five years. Wakefield tended to put the price on the high side and the plan suffered criticism as a result.

The National Colonisation Society In May 1830 Wakefield was released from prison and began his campaign to win public acceptance of his ideas by forming the National Colonisation Society. Among the early members were Robert Gouger (a future colonial secretary in South Australia), Robert Rintoul (editor of *The Spectator*), Charles Buller, and John Stuart Mill. Sir William Molesworth joined in 1833. Other notable members were Colonel Torrens, W. W. Whitmore, and William Hutt. Jeremy Bentham was also won over and offered some useful advice. The group's first success came when Lord Howick, son and heir of Lord Grey, the prime minister, read the *Letters* and persuaded Lord Goderich, the secretary for war and colonies, to pass the Ripon regulations in January 1831. These ordered the abandonment of the free grant of land in New South Wales and its replacement by the sale of waste land at not less than 5s. an acre. Two months later Wakefield gave evidence to the select committee on secondary punishments (1831) and cautiously emphasized the need to end the system of transportation. His intent was the creation of a colony in Australia that would not rely on convicts for labour. Taking advantage of favourable reviews, he and Buller then formed the South Australia Land Company. Various plans were proposed to Goderich but all were rejected, the last as a result of its overly enthusiastic endorsement of responsible government for the settlers. Wakefield was not disheartened and continued the pressure by publishing *England and America* in 1833. It added to the debate by urging the benefits of high wages, in Britain as in America, and recommended the repeal of the corn laws, the first step on the road to free trade. By this date Wakefield had become a confirmed disciple of Adam Smith and published an edited version of the *Wealth of Nations*, in four volumes, between 1835 and 1839. The extensive commentaries that accompany each chapter clearly outline his thinking as he sought to create a model post-enlightenment society. A new joint-stock company, the South Australia Association, was formed and a fresh enabling bill was introduced in the Commons. Further recruits to the cause included George Grote, Henry George Ward, and, at one remove, the duke of Wellington. After several rewrites, the South Australia Bill became law on 15 August 1834. The plan was essentially Wakefield's land scheme, including no convicts and self-government when the population reached 50,000. At this point, to his chagrin, he was pushed aside and virtually ignored as Gouger and others prepared to administer the new act. As might be expected, Wakefield thereupon found fault with most of their decisions: he considered the list of commissioners, chosen in 1835, to administer the colony unimpressive and the price set for the new land too low. Nine ships left England with the first settlers between 22 February and 23 July 1836. Wakefield, distressed by the death of his daughter, had intended to travel with them despite his grievances, but changed his mind at the last moment. The vision of a colony in a new country, New Zealand, over which he might gain more control now commanded his attention.

New Zealand and Canada Two rival committees competed to determine the future of New Zealand. The select committee on Aborigines met first, in July 1835, and was dominated by Thomas Fowell Buxton and spokesmen for the missionaries already resident in the country. The second, the committee on the disposal of lands in the British colonies, did not meet until June 1836. Wakefield, described in the prime of life as 'of middle stature, fair complexion, fine skin, fine intellectual forehead, apparently of fixed and decisive character', dominated it. Over three days of testimony Wakefield spent some time discussing the true meaning of self-government, particularly in connection with Canada. But his primary thrust was the reiteration of the need for systematic colonization as a means of relieving over-population. His clear and often spellbinding rhetoric won many friends and led to the creation, on 22 May 1837, of the New Zealand Association, under the chairmanship of Francis Baring. Its hopes were, however, quickly blighted as the select committee on Aborigines reported that it was opposed to all colonization in the south sea islands. Their opposition, coupled with renewed doubts about the legislative implications, ended with the defeat of the association's bill in the Commons in June 1838. Wakefield had anticipated defeat and had already left to join Lord Durham in Canada.

Durham, involved in the failed New Zealand Company of 1825, had been recruited by Wakefield for the association on his return from Russia in July 1837. They had become friends and, before leaving to take up his position as governor-general and high commissioner of all North American colonies after the suspension of the constitution, Durham asked Wakefield to join his staff. On arrival he discovered that Lord Glenelg, secretary for the colonies, had denied him an official position. Durham, however, gave him the job of chief commissioner of crown lands, Charles Buller's nominal title. Upper and Lower Canada were in uproar, the mission was not a success, and against Wakefield's advice Durham soon resigned. His *Report on the Affairs of North America*, finished in January 1839, recommended that the two Canadas be united with an elected assembly whose powers approximated the British parliament. Durham was reluctant to submit the report to the Commons, but Wakefield forced his hand by leaking it to *The Times*. Wakefield's contribution to the final version is debated, but Durham admitted to paying close attention to his advice. A popular epigram, coined from a jibe by Lord Brougham, put it crudely: 'Wakefield thought it, Buller wrote it, Durham signed it.' Before leaving Canada on 20 October 1838 Wakefield also completed his report on land and emigration. Attached to the report as Appendix B, it sought to apply his colonization system to British North America.

Wakefield returned to Canada on three occasions. In 1841 he arrived in May as agent for the North American Colonial Association of Ireland. It planned to provide immigrants and encourage economic growth by building a canal through the seigneurie of Beauharnois, near Montreal; that it was a 'horrid swindle' was the first response of the governor-general, Lord Sydenham. This visit was brief, but he was back again in December and co-operated with the new governor-general, Sir Charles Bagot, in encouraging the government to include the French Canadians within the new constitution, through letters to the *Colonial Gazette*. His participation in Canadian politics was further enhanced by his election to the assembly in November 1842 as the member for Beauharnois. His primary objective was to steer the canal and land project through the house; he reputedly made £20,000 from his work for the association between 1841 and 1844. But his interest in politics generally led, reputedly, to a role as secret adviser to Sir Charles Metcalfe, Bagot's successor, in December 1843. They enjoyed an excellent relationship, attested by the publication by Wakefield of two tributes to Metcalfe, a pamphlet entitled *A View of Sir Charles Metcalfe's Government of Canada* (1843) and an article, 'Sir Charles Metcalfe in Canada', in *Fisher's Colonial Magazine* (1843). The latter is remarkable for its affirmation of his belief in the merit of a relatively narrow definition of responsible government, and a forecast that the colonial future lay in what might, in modern terms, be described as a commonwealth of nations. News of the death of his brother Arthur *Wakefield [see under Wakefield, William Hayward] at Wairau in New Zealand brought him back to England.

The failure of the New Zealand Association's bill in 1838 had been followed by the creation of a land company built on his old association, on a colonization society formed by City of London interests, and on the 1825 company. The new company was determined to establish a colony with or without the government's blessing. Wakefield led the planning, and in May 1839 the *Tory* left Plymouth for New Zealand under the leadership of his brother William and his son Edward, with instructions to seize as much land as possible to force the government's hand. Wakefield stayed in London seeking support. He gave evidence to the parliamentary committee on New Zealand in 1840, used the *Colonial Gazette* to attack the Church Missionary Society's obstructionist tactics, and lobbied tirelessly for official blessing. The government refused to listen and had already, in a fit of concern for the Maori and in fear of French intentions, dispatched Captain Hobson to persuade the chiefs to accept British sovereignty. For some time there was the spectre of confrontation as William Wakefield's purchases on behalf of the company were in danger of being disallowed. The next five years were a mix of euphoria and despair, as successive governments attempted to deal with the colonies and their own perceptions of sovereignty, alternately giving and withholding favour. The death of Arthur Wakefield in 1843 at the hands of the Maori, for example, was greeted unsympathetically by the colonial secretary, Lord Stanley. Wakefield again gave evidence to a parliamentary committee in 1844 and kept up his pressure for greater legislative responsibility. On 18 August 1846 he suffered a stroke, and for some weeks it was thought he would die. A long period of convalescence was required and others took over the direction of the company. He resigned from it in 1849.

Wakefield wrote *A View of the Art of Colonisation* (1849) while resting at Château Mabile, near Boulogne, France. This rather disorganized work, in part an attack on past enemies, including Sir James Stephen and Lord Grey, proposed the establishment of colonies formed by different religious groups, in the manner of the seventeenth-century New England colonies in North America. The practical outcome of the idea to provide greater coherence for a colony and, incidentally, overcome missionary opposition, was a Church of England settlement at Canterbury, New Zealand. A second tactic was the creation, with the help of Charles Bowyer Adderley, of a new pressure group, the Society for the Reform of Colonial Government. The Canterbury Association, formed with the help of Lord Lyttelton and John Robert Godley, gained a charter in October 1849. Wakefield, after organizing several groups of settlers and steering the colony's constitution through parliament in 1852, himself landed in Port Lyttelton on 2 February 1853. Election in August to both the Wellington provincial council and the general assembly as member for the Hutt district followed. But his popularity declined when he became the confidential adviser to the acting governor, Colonel Robert Henry Wynyard, and seemed to be supporting a delay in the movement towards responsible government. The excitement proved too much and he suffered another breakdown in December 1854. He lingered a further seven years, dying on 16 May 1862 at Wellington, without making a will. He was buried in the Sydney Street cemetery, Wellington; the inscription merely provides his name, date of death, and age.

Wakefield irrevocably altered the temper and style of the British empire in the nineteenth century. He brought to the subject a spark of imaginative genius, the vision of systematic colonization, and joined it to a far-sighted emphasis on the merits of colonial self-government. As Thornton Hunt wrote in Wakefield's obituary in the *Daily Telegraph*: 'administrative and constructive reform [in the empire] can scarcely be traced to the single hand of any other man'. In his lifetime his qualities were often overlooked: only in his close family was he able to inspire affection and loyalty. Critics pointed out that his New Zealand and South Australia colonies were small-scale endeavours, soon lost in the tide of nineteenth-century mass emigration. Others remembered his ill-temper, impatience, and reputation as an unscrupulous schemer. These judgements unfairly devalue his contributions and have led to the absence of suitable memorials in both South Australia and New Zealand.

His only son, **Edward Jerningham Wakefield** (1820–1879), settler in New Zealand, was born on 25 June 1820 in London. He received an unorthodox education, partly on the continent, partly in Newgate prison, and partly at Bruce Castle School, Tottenham. The castle curriculum was unusual in its emphasis on science and mathematics and its provision of a measure of student self-government. He attended King's College, London, 1836–8,

before travelling, as his father's secretary, to Canada. The next year he sailed with his uncle to New Zealand to establish the Wakefield colony and remained there until reprimanded by Governor Fitzroy in 1844. According to his critics, most of his time had been spent in debauchery. His diary of these years, *Adventure in New Zealand*, and the accompanying *Illustrations* were published in 1845, timed to coincide with the New Zealand Company's campaign against the Colonial Office. It is well written and offers perceptive commentary on the flora and fauna of the islands as well as the Maori. The observations on the settlers and government are, as might be expected, heavily biased. Four years later he again departed for New Zealand with the Canterbury settlers, leaving behind large debts. The political contributions of this intelligent but unstable man were few: he was elected for a Canterbury constituency in 1854 and was member of the executive council from August to September of that year, being elected again to the house of representatives in 1876. He married Ellen Roe, the daughter of a Wellington printer, on 3 October 1863, and had three daughters. Alcoholism destroyed the marriage and he died in distressed circumstances on 3 March 1879.   DAVID J. MOSS

Sources P. Bloomfield, *Edward Gibbon Wakefield: builder of the British Commonwealth* (1961) · R. Garnett, *Edward Gibbon Wakefield: the colonisation of South Australia and New Zealand* (1898) · A. J. Harrop, *The amazing career of Edward Gibbon Wakefield* (1928) · I. O'Connor, *Edward Gibbon Wakefield: the man himself* (1929) · M. F. Lloyd Prichard, ed., *The collected works of Edward Gibbon Wakefield* (1968) · *Daily Telegraph* (18 Aug 1862) · U. Macdonnell, 'Gibbon Wakefield in Canada', *Bulletin of the Department of History and Political and Economic Science* [Queen's University, Kingston, Ontario] (1925) · H. T. Manning, 'E. G. Wakefield and the Beauharnois Canal', *Canadian Historical Review*, 48 (1967), 1–25 · J. Stevens, ed., *The London journal of Edward Jerningham Wakefield, 1845–6* (1972) · Burke, *Peerage* · priv. coll., Wakefield MSS · private information (2004) · E. Olssen, 'Mr Wakefield and New Zealand as an experiment in post-Enlightenment experimental practice', *New Zealand Journal of History*, 31 (1997), 197–218
Archives Bibliothèque Nationale, Paris, papers relating to T. B. Bond · BL, family corresp., Add. MS 35261 · Canterbury Museum, official and personal corresp. · Christchurch Museum, Christchurch, New Zealand · Essex RO, legal corresp. and papers · Mitchell L., NSW, corresp. and papers · NL NZ, Turnbull L. · priv. coll. · Wellington Public Library, New Zealand | BL, Allom MSS · BL, Place MSS · Canterbury Museum, corresp. with J. R. Godley · NL NZ, Turnbull L., letters to Lord Durham · NL NZ, Turnbull L., letters to James Fitzgerald · NL NZ, Turnbull L., letters to Lord Lyttelton · Wellington Public Library, New Zealand, Allom MSS
Likenesses miniature, *c*.1820, NPG [*see illus.*] · B. Holl, engraving, 1826 (after A. Wivell), Mitchell L., NSW · E. J. Collins, oils, 1850, Christchurch Museum, New Zealand · J. Durham, marble bust, 1875, Gov. Art Coll. · portrait, NL NZ, Turnbull L.
Wealth at death under £500

Wakefield, Edward Jerningham (1820–1879). *See under* Wakefield, Edward Gibbon (1796–1862).

Wakefield, Felix (1807–1875). *See under* Wakefield, William Hayward (1801–1848).

Wakefield, Gilbert (1756–1801), biblical scholar and religious controversialist, born on 22 February 1756 in the parsonage-house of St Nicholas's, Nottingham, was the third son of George Wakefield (1720–1776), rector of that

Gilbert Wakefield (1756–1801), by Robert Dunkarton, pubd 1802 (after William Artaud, exh. RA 1802)

parish and later vicar of Richmond and Kingston, and his wife, Elizabeth (1721–1800), whose grandfather had been twice mayor of Nottingham. From infancy, Wakefield showed a remarkable aptitude for learning, but his early education was erratic: passed from master to master, he made considerable progress after enrolling at the free school of Kingston in 1770. There he was among the last to study with Richard Wooddeson, who had counted George Steevens, Edward Gibbon, and William Hayley among his scholars.

In April 1772 Wakefield entered Jesus College, Cambridge, having obtained a Marsden scholarship, established 'for the son of a living clergyman, born at Nottingham, both of which conditions were united in me' (*Memoirs of the Life*, 1.62). As was customary, he divided his studies between mathematics and classics, preferring the latter, but applying himself to the former 'with all the assiduity that I could bear' (ibid., 1.83). When not engaged in formal study, he taught himself Hebrew, played cricket and fished, published a volume of Latin verse (1776), and befriended Robert Tyrwhitt and John Jebb (who also inclined to Unitarian views). He received his BA in January 1776, second wrangler and second chancellor medallist in classics. In April of that year he was elected fellow of his college.

Wakefield spent the years of his fellowship dedicated to biblical studies, acquiring several oriental languages as he did so. In 1778 he was ordained deacon, in spite of growing doubts about matters of doctrine and scruples about the practice of subscription to the Thirty-Nine Articles (several Jesuans, including Tyrwhitt, had recently resigned

their fellowships over this practice). It was, he later wrote, 'the most disingenuous action of my whole life; utterly incapable of palliation or apology' (*Memoirs of the Life*, 1.121). His clerical life lasted just over a year: he served as curate in Stockport, Cheshire, under a Mr Watson, then successively at St Peter's and St Paul's in Liverpool, all the while hoping to find employment as a schoolmaster. In Liverpool he crusaded against the slave trade and British privateering, and denounced both practices from the pulpit, angering many parishioners. This was the first sign of the political activism that was to characterize his later life.

On 23 March 1779 Wakefield married Anne Watson (*d.* 1819), the niece of his rector in Stockport. The couple had five sons and two daughters. Wakefield gave up his fellowship on marrying, and shortly afterwards he resigned his curacy as well because of doctrinal differences. Wakefield's study of scripture had led him to reject the doctrines of the Trinity and incarnation. Yet he embraced the teachings of Jesus Christ, whom he regarded as the greatest moral philosopher, sent by God to redeem mankind. Chief among these teachings was the mandate to love one another, and the corollary to it was service to the poor, respect for individual liberty, and the pursuit of peace. Initially he was opposed to all but defensive war, and later became a total pacifist. Although technically a dissenter or Unitarian, Wakefield never associated himself with any sect or congregation, being averse to most forms of worship.

In the summer of 1779 Wakefield accepted an appointment as classical tutor at Warrington Academy, the prominent dissenting academy where Joseph Priestley had taught, and where John Aikin was tutor of divinity and William Enfield tutor of philosophy. The years at Warrington were the happiest of his life. There he began a lifelong friendship with the Aikin family (his beloved daughter Anne later married Charles Aikin), established valuable connections with wealthy dissenters, and was encouraged to pursue his theological enquiries. These began to appear, in pamphlet form, in 1781. Essays on baptism and inspiration gained him notoriety as a controversialist, while his *New Translation of the First Epistle of Paul to the Thessalonians* (1781) announced his intention to produce a new translation of the New Testament, a project completed a decade later. The following year saw the publication of his first book-length work, *A new translation of the gospel of St Matthew, with notes critical, philological, and explanatory* (1782). This work aimed to follow the idiom and phraseology of the original as closely as possible, and to apply the principles of classical philology to study of the Bible. It is an interesting early example of historical criticism, but Wakefield's denunciations of Anglican doctrine and the American War of Independence made even his friends uncomfortable, and made him the object of ridicule in the periodical press. When Warrington Academy failed in 1783, Wakefield's outspokenness was thought to have been a partial cause; the next year, when his *Enquiry into the opinions of the Christian writers of the three first centuries concerning the person of Jesus Christ* (1784) sold poorly, he ceased publication on theological subjects for several years.

After leaving Warrington in 1783, Wakefield resided briefly at Bramcote, near Nottingham, and at Richmond, in Surrey, before settling in Nottingham in 1784, where he 'had three or four pupils on very handsome terms' (*Memoirs of the Life*, 1.270). Over the next two years, a pain in the left shoulder 'harasst me beyond measure' (ibid., 277) so that he lost all but one of his pupils and was able to write little: an edition of the poetry of Thomas Gray appeared in 1786, and of Virgil's *Georgics*, published by Cambridge University Press, in 1788. Cambridge also published his *Silva critica*, the first volume of which appeared in 1789. The *Silva*, one of Wakefield's most important works, was intended to demonstrate 'the union of theological and classical learning … thus promoting in the world at the same time a profitable heathenism … and a rational theology' (ibid., 1.293). Unlike his earlier theological works, the *Silva* was well received in both Anglican and dissenting circles; it was completed in five volumes in 1795.

A new dissenting college had been established in 1786, eventually located at Hackney, and its founders, including the radical minister Richard Price, invited Wakefield to become classical tutor. He accepted, moving to Hackney in 1790. The appointment was not without controversy: Price and Priestley were initially opposed, ostensibly because of Wakefield's refusal to attend Christian worship. Wakefield himself was hesitant because he felt that the college's requirements in classical philology were insufficient for understanding scripture. A year later he resigned, defending himself in *An Enquiry into the Expediency and Propriety of Public or Social Worship*, where he argued that there was no gospel authority for public worship. This pamphlet was satirized in the Pittite press and sparked a public debate among liberal dissenters, to which Priestley, Anna Barbauld, and Mary Hays all contributed. Wakefield's *Memoirs* (1792) was a product of this debate, designed as an apologia for his opinions and actions.

After resigning from Hackney College, Wakefield could no longer support himself as a private tutor, and began publishing at an astonishing rate. His translation of the New Testament was published in 1792 and went through several editions, including one in Cambridge, Massachusetts. *Evidences of Christianity*, a work of apologetics, appeared the next year. Companion editions of Horace (1794) and Virgil (1796), an edition, with extensive commentary, of selected Greek tragedies (2 vols., 1794), an edition of Moschus and Bion (1795), an annotated edition of Alexander Pope's Homer (12 vols., 1796), and, finally, his massive three-volume edition of Lucretius (1796–7), published at his own expense and dedicated to Charles James Fox, established Wakefield as one of the two leading British scholars of his time, the other being Richard Porson. Unlike Porson, however, Wakefield was excessively fond of emendation, always worked in great haste, and rarely took time for revision. Thus, although his critical remarks can show considerable brilliance and an unusual awareness of continental advances in scholarship (Wakefield seems to have been among the first Englishmen to promulgate F. A. Wolf's conclusions about Homer), his work is riddled with errors and was largely dismissed by the British Academy within a few years of his death.

Wakefield also achieved notoriety as a political controversialist for his attacks on the Pitt government. He had come to believe that true Christian morality and Pittite policy were wholly incompatible, and that any church promoting such policy was the Antichrist. In the French Revolution, wrote John Aikin, the son of his colleague at Warrington, Wakefield saw 'the undoubted commencement of a better order of things, in which rational liberty, equitable policy, and pure religion, would finally become triumphant' (Aikin, 1.208), and was appalled by British attempts to subvert its progress. Of the several pamphlets he wrote on this subject, most notable were *The Spirit of Christianity Compared with the Spirit of the Times in Great Britain* (1794), which influenced S. T. Coleridge, and *A Reply to the Letter of Edmund Burke, Esq., to a Noble Lord* (1796), both of which went through three editions. But Wakefield could be as vehement against Tom Paine as against Burke, and in two pamphlets (1794 and 1796) attacked the deism of *The Age of Reason* with such spirit that Pittite reviewers had to blink in wonder. These pamphlets circulated internationally, especially in America. Wakefield further incurred the displeasure of the government by organizing contributions for the defendants in the treason trials of 1794, and by defending William Frend against the charges brought against him by Cambridge University for publishing the pamphlet *Peace and Union*. Wakefield's defence of Frend caused the university press to withdraw support from the *Silva critica*, and its last two volumes were published in London at Tyrwhitt's expense.

By 1798 the prime minister, William Pitt (1759–1806), fearing a French invasion, had decided to silence political opposition, and Wakefield unluckily provided the occasion. In January of that year Richard Watson, bishop of Llandaff, published *An Address to the People of Great Britain*, supporting Pitt's proposal for an income tax. Wakefield responded in *A Reply to some Parts of the Bishop of Landaff's Address*, a pamphlet 'never written over twice, and … finished … in the compass of a single day' (*Memoirs of the Life*, 2.117). In it, he argued that the government had provoked war with France, and that this policy had so hurt the British poor that, if the French were to invade, they would be unlikely to meet with resistance.

> For alas! the ground-floor of this grand and stable edifice, where myself, and my mess-mates of the swinish multitude, were regaling ourselves, as well as existing circumstances would possibly admit, on our cheese-parings and candles' ends; our ground-floor, I say, is sunk for ever in damps and darkness; only to make, forsooth! a more firm foundation for our aristocratical and prelatical superiors. (*Reply to the Bishop of Landaff's Address*, 16)

For this pamphlet Wakefield, together with his publisher and booksellers (including Joseph Johnson), were indicted on an information and convicted. Their convictions, thought Charles James Fox, meant that liberty of the press was dead. At the trial Wakefield eschewed the offer of legal assistance from the radical Scottish lawyer Henry Erskine (1746–1817) and represented his own case, casting himself as a latter-day Socrates or Jesus. Henry Crabb Robinson, who witnessed the event, wrote that 'his delivery of his own defence must have been one of the most gratifying treats which a person of taste or sensibility could enjoy. His simplicity quite apostolic, his courage purely heroic' (*Henry Crabb Robinson*, 1.36–7). Upon conviction, Wakefield was sentenced to two years' confinement in Dorchester gaol and a fine of £500. A fund was established to support his family, and £5000 was raised almost immediately, largely from Foxite whigs and liberal dissenters. Wakefield, who was never rich, remarked that he owed his fortune to his majesty's attorney-general (*Memoirs of the Life*, 2.156).

In prison, Wakefield became a celebrity among the politically disaffected. Fox, the duke of Bedford, and Lord Holland all visited him in his cell and took measures to ease his conditions. The friendship with Fox was especially rewarding, as the two had corresponded for several years, chiefly about classical literature. Wakefield led Fox to a new discovery about the dating of Lycophron, explained and defended his theories about the Homeric poems, and chided Fox gently about the evils of hunting and the virtues of vegetarianism. But, despite celebrity, the prison years were disheartening: in the first year Wakefield's mother died; in the second he suffered a recurrence of the debilitating shoulder ailment, spent much of his time attending to capital prisoners, and, just before his release, lost his youngest child to illness. Although he completed a translation of essays by Dio Chrysostom (1800), and a short work on Greek metres (*Noctes carceriana*, 1801), his main project, a Greek-English dictionary, was abandoned for lack of public interest, and a scholarly controversy with Porson grew increasingly mean-spirited.

Wakefield was released from prison on 29 May 1801 and returned to Hackney. It was at this time that William Artaud painted a large oil portrait of him, later housed at Dr Williams's Library, London. It shows a keen-eyed scholar at work in his study, a pamphlet open on the desk before him, the large folios of his Lucretius in the shadows. Wakefield barely lived to see the finished work: in late August he showed the first signs of typhus fever, and by 1 September was delirious. He died on 9 September 1801 at Hackney, in the company of family and close friends, having refused all medical assistance. Survivors included his wife and five of his children. The body was borne with great ceremony through the streets of London and interred on 18 September at St Mary Magdalene's, Richmond, where his brother, Thomas, was vicar. A tablet to Wakefield's memory hangs on the south wall of the church, erected by his brother. He was memorialized in prose by John Aikin, and in Latin and English elegies by Lucy Aikin, George Dyer, and Alexander Geddes. Three years later J. T. Rutt and A. Wainewright issued their two-volume *Memoirs* of Wakefield, which remains the standard account of his life.   BRUCE E. GRAVER

Sources *Memoirs of the life of Gilbert Wakefield*, ed. J. T. Rutt and A. Wainewright, 2 vols. (1804) • J. Aikin, 'Memoir of Gilbert Wakefield', *Memoir of John Aikin*, ed. L. Aikin, 2 vols. (1823) • *GM*, 1st ser., 71 (1801), 866 • A. Gray, memorandum, Jesus College, Cambridge • Venn, *Alum. Cant.* • *Henry Crabb Robinson on books and their writers*, ed. E. J. Morley, 3 vols. (1938) • *The correspondence of the late Gilbert Wakefield, BA, with the late Right Honourable Charles James Fox in the years 1796–1801, chiefly, on subjects of classical literature* (1813)
Archives Harvard U. | BL, letters to Lord Holland, Add. MS 44992 • BL, letters to William Russell, Add. MS 44992 • DWL, letters to William Frend • Jesus College, Cambridge, Jesuan collection
Likenesses J. Downman, chalk drawing, 1778, FM Cam. • J. Gillray, caricature, 1798, repro. in *The Anti-Jacobin Review and Magazine* (Aug 1798) • W. Artaud, oils, exh. RA 1802, DWL • R. Dunkarton, mezzotint, pubd 1802 (after W. Artaud, exh. RA 1802), BM, NPG [*see illus.*] • W. Say, mezzotint, 1804 (after W. Artaud, exh. RA 1802), BM, NPG; repro. in Rutt and Wainewright, eds., *Memoirs* • lithograph, c.1870 (after the destroyed Armytage mural in DWL), DWL; repro. in E. Morley, *The life and times of Henry Crabb Robinson* (1935) • R. Laurie, mezzotint (after unknown artist), BM, NPG • W. Ridley, stipple (after Green), BM, NPG; repro. in *Monthly Mirror* (1798)
Wealth at death at time of conviction (1799), friends and supporters collected £5000 for family; extensive library auctioned within a year of death: *Memoirs of the life of Gilbert Wakefield*, ed. Rutt and Wainewright

Wakefield, Gordon Stevens (1921–2000), Methodist minister and scholar, was born on 15 January 1921 at 42 Gainsborough Road, Crewe, the only child of Ernest Wakefield (b. c.1877), a metal machinist in the railway works there, and his wife, Lucy Spooner (b. c.1881), a housekeeper. Both parents were devout Methodists; Ernest was a society steward and trustee, Lucy a 'class' leader. Both loved literature and music, and had Roman Catholic friends. As a small child Gordon's health was poor, and he suffered from rheumatic fever, which had a lasting effect. He was an avid reader and would act out scenes from *Pilgrim's Progress*. Later he won a scholarship to Crewe County Secondary School, where he excelled at English and history and in 1939 won a Hulme Hall exhibition to read history at Manchester University, but his parents could not afford to send him there.

Wakefield began preaching at sixteen and was an accredited lay-preacher at nineteen. He was rejected as unfit for military service in 1939, and was accepted as a candidate for the Methodist ministry in 1940, although his training was delayed by the war. About this time he began, but did not complete, a philosophy course at Manchester University. His wartime jobs included that of an investigating officer at the Assistance Board. In 1944 he was appointed a pre-collegiate probationary minister at Edgware, and in 1946 was sent to Wesley House, Cambridge, to study theology under the theologian and church historian Robert Newton Flew, an ecumenist whom he greatly admired. He was later commissioned to write Flew's biography, which appeared in 1971.

Wakefield's first ministerial appointment was at Woodstock, on the Oxford Methodist circuit. While at Woodstock he married, on 2 July 1949, Beryl Dimes (b. 1930/31), who was a lifelong support in his work. They had a son, Adrian, and three daughters: Helen, Pamela, and Penny. Wakefield came to love Oxford; he read for a BLitt degree,

Gordon Stevens Wakefield (1921–2000), by unknown photographer [detail]

writing on puritan devotion, and gave the Fernley–Hartley lecture on the subject, which led to the publication of his *Puritan Devotion* (1957). Described in his preface as 'a modest effort towards ecumenical understanding' (p. viii), it became a minor classic.

Wakefield's gifts as a preacher, a sympathetic listener, and an ecumenist of wide sympathies were all shown in his subsequent ministries at Stockport (five years), Gosforth (Newcastle upon Tyne; four years), and Bristol (two years). His evident literary gifts led to his appointment in 1963 as Methodist connexional editor responsible for the Epworth Press, where his books included *Unity at the Local Level* (1965), *Methodist Devotion* (1966), and *The Life of the Spirit in the World of Today* (1969). He worked alongside John Bowden at the Student Christian Movement (SCM) Press and Noel Davey at the SPCK. He further developed his liturgical and ecumenical interests, worked on commissions and committees that transformed Methodist worship through the service book of 1975, and belonged to the influential Joint Liturgical Group from 1966 to 1994. Wakefield was steeped in English literature and knew the Catholic mystics and the great Anglicans and Methodists, interests that found expression in his sermons—delivered in his melodious voice—and in his extempore prayers. He was a select preacher at both Oxford (1971, 1982) and Cambridge (1988).

From 1971 to 1979 Wakefield was chairman of the Manchester and Stockport Methodist District, where he was not always at ease, finding the disciplinary aspects of his role in dealing with fellow ministers uncongenial. He was happier as a conductor of retreats. He firmly supported women's ordination. A notable and demanding undertaking was his completion of the theological work *Crucifixion–Resurrection*, on which E. C. Hoskins had worked until his death, in 1937, and which Wakefield's associate Noel Davey had continued but not completed at his own death, in 1973. At some personal cost Wakefield brought the work to a fit state for publication in 1981.

In 1979 Wakefield began the greatest and most congenial period of his ministry, when he was appointed the first non-Anglican principal of the ecumenical theological Queen's College in Birmingham, formed ten years earlier by amalgamating the Anglican Queen's and the Methodist Handsworth colleges. There his pastoral concern for ordinands, and his scholarship, were exercised to the full, and his charm, wit, and gifts as a raconteur and innocent ecclesiastical gossip flourished. At Queen's he edited the SCM *Dictionary of Spirituality* (1983), for which he wrote nearly sixty articles himself, and published *The Liturgy of St John* (1985). He was president of the Methodist Retreat Group, the Methodist Sacramental Fellowship, and the Ecumenical Society of the Blessed Virgin Mary, gaining the respect of Anglican, Roman Catholic, and Orthodox leaders. He was well acquainted with many Anglican bishops, including archbishops Michael Ramsay and Robert Runcie (for whom he is reputed to have written sermons). Runcie awarded him a Lambeth DD in 1986.

On his retirement from Queen's, in 1987, Wakefield moved to Lichfield, where he frequently preached in the cathedral and kept in touch with the Methodist circuit. He listed his leisure interests in *Who's Who* as 'watching and talking cricket' and 'churches and cathedrals'. In 1988–9 he was chaplain at the Methodist Westminster College, Oxford, and from 1989 to 1992 director of the Alister Hardy Centre for Research into Religious Experience. He wrote *An Outline of Christian Worship* (1998), *Methodist Spirituality* (1999), and two biographies—*John Wesley* (1990) and *Bunyan the Christian* (1992)—as well as obituaries of prominent Methodists for the *Daily Telegraph* and sermons for the *Methodist Recorder*. Over his career he wrote for many journals, including a series in the *Expository Times*, on modern English poets.

Wakefield died at his home, 56 Wissage Road, Lichfield, on 11 September 2000, and his funeral was held in Lichfield Cathedral on 18 September. He was survived by his wife and four children. He was described by a fellow Methodist as 'the greatest of contemporary Methodism's scholar saints' (*The Independent*), and also as 'one of the great ecumenists of the 20th Century' (*The Times*).

JOHN D. HAIGH

Sources *The Times* (15 Sept 2000) · *The Independent* (15 Sept 2000) · *Daily Telegraph* (29 Sept 2000) · *The Guardian* (20 Sept 2000) · *WW* (2000) · G. Wakefield, *Bunyan the Christian* (1992), ix–x, 1 · b. cert. · m. cert. · d. cert.
Likenesses photograph, repro. in *Daily Telegraph* · photograph, News International Syndication, London [see illus.]

Wakefield, Henry (c.1335–1395), administrator and bishop of Worcester, was from the West Riding of Yorkshire, probably from a family of modest account. His spinster sister, Alice, lived with him and was his principal legatee. Other kinsfolk included at least one other sister, the brothers John and Thomas Sneynton, Cecily Sneynton, John Thomas, and Eleanor and Joanne, daughters of Agnes. He also had 'poor relations' in Aton in Pickering in 1395. He was a royal clerk, probably by July 1359, certainly by 1361. Exhibiting nothing more than competence, he became keeper of the great wardrobe on 27 June 1369, at the time when Edward III, and hence his court and government, were lapsing into passivity.

In such circumstances Wakefield, like others well placed, could direct royal patronage in the church towards himself without doing much in return: the treasurership of St Paul's Cathedral (1369–75), the archdeaconry of Northampton (1371–2), the prestigious archdeaconry of Canterbury (1374–5), and much else. Wakefield even secured election to the small but immensely rich see of Ely in June 1373, but such was the disarray round the old king that Edward III also nominated his confessor, John Woodruff. Pope Gregory XI chose Thomas Arundel, the twenty-year-old son of Richard (II) Fitzalan, earl of Arundel, and a future archbishop of Canterbury. Undoubtedly this proved the right decision, if for the wrong reasons. On 12 September 1375 the pope awarded Wakefield the lesser see of Worcester, his share of the spoils carved out between royal and papal envoys at the concordat of Bruges; this superseded an election by the chapter of their prior, supposedly confirmed by the king.

Wakefield received the temporalities on 14 October 1375, and was consecrated in Hatfield on the 28th. According to scandal, his promotion also dashed the hopes of John Wyclif, who thereupon took the road to heterodoxy in his disappointment: this cannot be more than a fragment of the story. Wakefield was a court creature, and only a draught animal at that. Still, after the court had been rocked by the impeachments and accusations of corruption made in the Good Parliament of 1376, John of Gaunt, duke of Lancaster, led a vicious counter-attack against the critics, and on 11 January 1377 put in Wakefield as treasurer of the realm, an uncompromising and unconvincing choice. As soon as Edward III died (Wakefield being an executor of his will) and a general reconciliation was mooted to look after the young Richard II, Wakefield was replaced (19 July 1377). He retired from public life (or, just as likely, was not invited to continue in it).

Although he attended parliaments regularly enough, Wakefield spent his last twenty years running his diocese with the same competent mediocrity by which he had acquired it. None the less, his deathbed will is a surprisingly sensitive and austere statement, with an unusual concentration of his goods upon the sick and poor, especially those among his own tenants, and 'particularly those who have been hurt by me' (Marett). Though his kin, servants, and three former benefices were remembered dutifully enough, there is nothing of the wider political world where he had made his fortune, scarcely more of his own diocese or even of the cathedral itself, before whose pulpit he sought burial. He died the day after he made his will, 11 March 1395.　　　R. G. DAVIES, rev.

Sources W. P. Marett, ed., *A calendar of the register of Henry Wakefield, bishop of Worcester, 1375–95*, Worcestershire Historical Society, new ser., 7 (1972) · R. G. Davies, 'The episcopate in England and Wales, 1375–1443', PhD diss., University of Manchester, 1974 · R. G. Davies, 'The episcopal appointments in England and Wales of 1375', *Mediaeval Studies*, 44 (1982), 306–32

Wakefield, John of (*fl.* 1294/5), schoolman and medical writer, was presumably a Yorkshireman, but is recorded with certainty only at Oxford. He may have been the John de Wakerfeld who with other northern clerks was involved in a brawl with clerks from the Welsh marches on 29 April 1285. But he can be identified with greater conviction as the Master John of Wakefield who in 1294/5 was one of the university's assessors of disputed rents in the parish of St Peter-in-the-East. His works survive in two manuscripts, both now in the library of Gonville and Caius College, Cambridge. In MS 344/540, a collection of works on grammar and logic written in what even M. R. James describes as 'a hideously contracted hand' (James, 1.387), and which probably originated in a student's notebook, a report of lectures found at folios 264–277v shows Wakefield to have been one of the many members of the Oxford arts faculty who commented on the first book of Aristotle's *Physics* in the years on either side of 1300.

Greater interest, however, attaches to Wakefield's treatise on fevers, found with other medical tracts in MS 407/413, folios 80–91v. Conventionally based on humoral theory, its reticence with regard to sources (just two references to Avicenna) gives a misleading impression of originality, for other authorities, above all Galen, are paraphrased without acknowledgement. But although the tract is written entirely in Latin, perhaps suggesting that it was composed with a university readership in mind, its approach is by no means narrowly academic. Meticulously defining the various types of fever in terms of their symptoms, Wakefield several times advises the doctor to make careful examination of the patient, perhaps by inspecting the tongue or urine, or by taking the pulse, or simply by questioning. Treatment may be by control of diet, the use of baths and sweats to open the pores, the application of poultices and electuaries, even the placing of sweet-smelling flowers and herbs round the bed. Laxatives might be employed, but there is surprisingly little reference to bleeding, and then only to cupping. The herbs and spices to be used are seldom very recherché—nothing more exotic than ginger, sugar-cane, and sandalwood—and the nearest Wakefield comes to the conventional practice of varying the ingredients of his medicines according to the social rank of the patient, is a comment that wine may be given to the person who is used to it, and then only in moderate quantities. Not without reason does the explicit of his treatise describe it as a 'most noble' work.

There is no reason to suppose that Oxford's John of Wakefield had any connection with his contemporary and namesake, the John the Leech who was active as a doctor on the Yorkshire manor of Wakefield in the years around 1300. This other John, who was dead by November 1306, and members of his household (including a son, also John), made regular appearances in the manor court, usually charged with offences against the by-laws.

HENRY SUMMERSON

Sources Gon. & Caius Cam., MSS 344/540, 407/413 · T. Hunt, *Popular medicine in thirteenth-century England: introduction and texts* (1990) · *Healing and society in mediaeval England: a middle English translation of the pharmaceutical writings of Gilbertus Anglicus*, ed. F. M. Getz (1991) · H. E. Salter, ed., *A cartulary of the Hospital of St John the Baptist*, 3, OHS, 69 (1917), 39 · *Snappe's formulary and other records*, ed. H. E. Salter, OHS, 80 (1924), 287–8 · J. C. Russell, 'Dictionary of writers of thirteenth century England', *BIHR*, special suppl., 3 (1936) [whole issue], esp. 54 • M. R. James, *A descriptive catalogue of the manuscripts in the library of Gonville and Caius College*, 2 vols. (1907–8), 387–8, 472–4 • C. Rawcliffe, *Medicine and society in later medieval England* (1995) • P. O. Lewry, 'Grammar, logic and rhetoric, 1220–1320', *Hist. U. Oxf.* 1: *Early Oxf. schools*, 401–33 • J. North, 'Natural philosophy in late medieval Oxford', *Hist. U. Oxf.* 2: *Late med. Oxf.*, 65–102 **Archives** Gon. & Caius Cam., MSS 344/540, 407/413

Wakefield, Peter of

Wakefield, Peter of (*d.* 1213), hermit, was a simple unlettered man, living on a diet of bread and water and with a popular reputation as a prophet. According to Higden:

> Christ appeared to this Peter twice at York and once at Pontefract, in the likeness of a child between the hands of the priest, inspiring him and saying 'Peace, peace, peace' and taught him many things, which afterwards he showed to bishops and people of evil life.

In the latter part of 1212—probably on his northern journey of that year—King John heard that the hermit had prophesied that by the following Ascension day, 23 May 1213, the crown would have been transferred from him and his line. Summoned to the king's presence, Peter maintained his conviction of the veracity of his prophecy, adding that were it not true the king could do with him as he pleased.

John committed the prophet to William de Harcourt to be kept in chains at Corfe until the truth of his words should be proved. The prophecy, which is said to have spread even to France, was very generally believed, or at least feared, and the king himself, as the day approached, was evidently nervous. Matthew Paris asserts that this fear hastened John's submission to the papal nuncio, Pandulf, which was completed by the act of homage on the eve of Ascension day 1213. John celebrated the Ascension in state, but some now claimed that the prophecy referred to the calendar anniversary of the king's coronation, Ascension day (27 May) 1199. When this passed, the king ordered Peter, together with his son, to be dragged by horses to Wareham and there hanged.

The story is significant as an illustration of popular opinion in regard to John's act of submission to the pope. The chroniclers are fairly unanimous in declaring that Peter's famous prophecy had indeed been fulfilled, though in a sense other than had been expected.

It is possible that behind Peter's prophecy was a more directly political cause. In 1209 John de Lacy, heir to the honour of Pontefract, was in treasonable correspondence with Philip II of France and was clearly viewed with suspicion by King John when he inherited the honour in 1211; once freed from his heavy relief payments John de Lacy joined the northern rebels in the spring of 1215. Wittingly or not, as the prominent local holy man, Peter may have been a spokesman for rebellion.

ALICE M. COOKE, *rev.* J. R. WHITEHEAD

Sources Paris, *Chron.*, vol. 2 • *Memoriale fratris Walteri de Coventria / The historical collections of Walter of Coventry*, ed. W. Stubbs, 2, Rolls Series, 58 (1873) • *Radulphi de Coggeshall chronicon Anglicanum*, ed. J. Stevenson, Rolls Series, 66 (1875) • *Ann. mon.*, vols. 1–4 • H. R. Luard, ed., *Flores historiarum*, 3 vols., Rolls Series, 95 (1890), vol. 2 • *Polychronicon Ranulphi Higden monachi Cestrensis*, ed. C. Babington and J. R. Lumby, 9 vols., Rolls Series, 41 (1865–86), vol. 8, p.193 • A. Gransden, ed. and trans., *The chronicle of Bury St Edmunds, 1212–1301* [1964] • S. Painter, *The reign of King John* (1949) • J. C. Holt, *The northerners: a study in the reign of King John* (1961) • M. Rubin, *Corpus Christi* (1991)

Wakefield, Priscilla

Wakefield [*née* Bell]**, Priscilla** (1750–1832), author and philanthropist, was born on 20 November 1750 in Tottenham, Middlesex, the eldest of six children of Catherine Barclay (1727–1784) and Daniel Bell (1726–1802), coal merchant. She was a great-granddaughter of the Quaker martyr Robert Barclay, author of *An Apology for the True Christian Divinity*; the maternal 'Barclay blood' was said to have produced many strong women with force of character. Priscilla was raised in Stamford Hill, Tottenham High Cross, a semi-rural and prosperous Quaker centre 4 miles north of London. Educated at home under maternal supervision she learned Latin and Greek and, as the eldest daughter, she helped to teach her sisters; her brother recalled that they were considered 'a knot of clever women' (Bell, 40). On 3 January 1771, aged twenty, Priscilla married Edward Wakefield (1749–1826), a merchant from a Quaker family with Irish connections. He inherited a business from his father in London, where he and Priscilla lived from 1771 to 1796. During that time three children were born to them: Isabella (1773–1841), Edward *Wakefield (1774–1854), and Daniel *Wakefield (1776–1846). Having returned to Tottenham High Cross in 1796 the family lived at Ship Yard, in the High Street, for the next two decades. Grandchildren lived with them at various times, including Edward Gibbon *Wakefield. When scant family finances and health matters forced Priscilla and Edward to move in 1812 they found a haven near their daughter, Isabella Head, in Ipswich, Suffolk.

Wakefield wrote seventeen books, principally moral tales, introductory works of natural history, and travelogues. She was well known as an author for the rising generation at a time when the developing field of children's literature offered welcome opportunities to women. Her career began in the early 1790s, when she was more than forty years old and her husband's business was in difficulty; by the end of 1798 she had four books in print. Financial need and legal costs from the unhappy marital entanglements of both her sons led her to put pen to paper for the next twenty years. Proud of the fruits of her own industry she continued writing even when immediate business pressures eased. A busy writer who learned on the job, she published first with Elizabeth Newbery and Joseph Johnson, and then extensively with the Quaker firm of Darton and Harvey; many of her books also appeared in American editions.

Wakefield succeeded because she produced improving and didactic works of non-fiction that middle-class parents were choosing to buy. Unlike Romantic writings that celebrated imagination and fantasy Wakefield's books have a deliberate moral tone, are filled with information, and focus on real-life experiences in the present day. Characteristically they have a family setting and promote a new-style progressive pedagogy based in domestic conversations; mothers often teach their own children, and girls receive attention as much as boys. Wakefield's books were meant for reading in the home schoolroom but also for leisure. She shaped several age-specific miscellanies that most widely known, however, as a pioneering travel writer for young readers. *The Juvenile Travellers* (1801; 19th edn, 1850) initiated a series of six books about an English family journeying around Europe to promote the general improvement of their children. Wakefield was only an armchair traveller but she did her research, cites sources, and includes maps. *A Family Tour through the British Empire* (1804; 15th edn, 1840) is replete with geographical details about England, Scotland, Ireland, and Wales. Other books take the young people of the Middleton family around London and to America, Canada, Africa, and Asia.

Personally and politically Wakefield shied away from radicalism but she advocated reform in many areas of public and private life. Her books contain extended criticisms of the slave trade and cruelty to animals; letters to magazines weigh in on social topics such as the plight of apprentices and equal wages for women and men. Wakefield believed that education was the key to the improvement of individuals and society. In *Reflections on the Present Condition of the Female Sex* (1798; 2nd edn, 1817), her one book for an adult audience, she called for more educational and occupational opportunities for women. Advocating economic self-sufficiency she offered practical and vocational suggestions, such as establishing institutions to train teachers and encouraging women to be farmers. Wakefield did not contest the division of society into social classes; she directed her ideas about female improvement to women of the nobility, the middle classes, and the labouring poor. Nor did she contest gendered ideas about the 'female character'. She wrote:

> There are many branches of science, as well as useful occupations, in which women may employ their time and their talents, beneficially to themselves and to the community, without destroying the peculiar characteristic of their sex, or exceeding the most exact limits of modesty and decorum.   (P. Wakefield, *Reflections*, 8–9)

Nevertheless she worked hard to make the benefits of education available to all and was disappointed that a reviewer of *Reflections* thought her ideas applied only to women. Like Mary Wollstonecraft she believed that improvements in education and employment opportunities for women brought benefits to men as well.

The Friendly spirit of usefulness and social service that characterizes Wakefield's writing was evident in her philanthropic work on behalf of children, women, and the poor. Starting in 1791 she organized maternity charities to cover expenses for midwives and provide bags of linen to lying-in women. She supported the educational system of Quaker Joseph Lancaster for teaching reading and writing to the labouring poor, and regularly visited a school for the daughters of poor parishioners. In October 1798 she established a female benefit club at Tottenham High Cross to give pensions to the labouring poor at the age of sixty-five; honorary members paid 12s. annually and benefited members paid 6d. or more monthly, depending on their age. In that same year she formed a penny bank, into which children deposited 'any sum above one penny'. She also established a 'frugality bank' to encourage deposits from labourers and servants; the bank received sums

Priscilla Wakefield (1750–1832), by James Thomson, pubd 1818 (after Thomas Charles Wageman)

combined moral tales and substantive knowledge. In *Mental Improvement, or, The Beauties and Wonders of Nature and Art* (3 vols., 1794–7; 13th edn, 1828) children from the ages of nine to sixteen have evening conversations with their parents that serve as 'rational amusements' and exemplify moderation, diligence, and toleration. In 'Conversation 12' the father says, 'Endeavour, children, to increase your stock of useful knowledge daily, by attention to everything you see and hear' (p. 94). Their topics for discussion include whales, sugar, slavery, glassmaking, and woollen manufacture. Wakefield continued this successful and popular format in other books. *Domestic Recreation, or, Dialogues Illustrative of Natural and Scientific Subjects* (1805) features a mother and her daughters talking about such topics as the human eye, rainbows, and sea anemones. When the daughters wonder how to spend their time one rainy evening mother replies: 'None but the idle need want employment: there is always a great variety of pursuits, that are both useful and agreeable, for those who are disposed to fill their leisure properly' (p. 96).

Wakefield also wrote expository natural history books that are part of the Enlightenment history of disseminating science to new audiences. *An Introduction to Botany* (1796) is an account of Linnaean botany in the form of letters between sisters; in print until 1841 it was adapted for the American market and translated into French. Wakefield continued that successful format in *An Introduction to the Natural History and Classification of Insects* (1816). She was above 1s. and gave 5 per cent interest for every 20s. held for one year. Because these philanthropic projects gave practical form to ideas that had been circulating in England at that time Wakefield can be considered the founder of the first English savings bank. In 1847 her son Edward organized a campaign to erect a monument to her as a founder of savings banks.

Priscilla Wakefield was a lifelong Quaker but disagreed with some Quaker habits of dress, language, and behaviour. 'True religion is of sterling value', she wrote in her journal for 27 June 1799, 'but I long to be set free from the slavish shackles of the prejudices of my infancy and the false lights of enthusiasm'. She was spunky and resilient, and loved theatre and dancing. An engraved portrait shows a small woman with a lively and direct gaze. Oral tradition records that when their house caught fire her husband, who was given to 'hysterics' in times of stress, fled to a corner in tears and she, 'with her usual energy', organized the rescue efforts.

Illness, increasing lameness, invalidism, and widowhood characterized the final years of Wakefield's long life. She died at her daughter's home, Albion Hill, Carr Street, in Ipswich, on 12 September 1832 and was buried on 20 September in the Quaker burial-ground of the New Meeting-House in Ipswich. ANN B. SHTEIR

Sources notebooks and letters, priv. coll. • Lady Georgiana Chapman, 'Life of Priscilla Wakefield', [n.d.], priv. coll. [typescript] • W. Robinson, *The history and antiquities of the parish of Tottenham High Cross, in the county of Middlesex*, 2nd edn, 2 vols. (1840) • journals, 1796–1816, RS Friends, Lond., Mews papers [photocopies] • P. Wakefield, *Mental improvement*, ed. A. B. Shteir (1995) • J. Bell, 'Memoirs of the Bell family', 1851, priv. coll. • *Ladies' Monthly Museum* (Aug 1818), 60–64 • [T. Bernard], *The reports of the Society for Bettering the Condition and Increasing the Comforts of the Poor*, 4 vols. (1798–1805) • 'Letters on erecting a monument to the founder of savings banks', June–Aug 1847, RS Friends, Lond., Hazel Mews papers • register of London and Middlesex births, 1720–1830, RS Friends, Lond. • *DNB* • Tottenham Monthly Meetings, burials 1727–1837
Archives priv. coll., documents • RS Friends, Lond., Hazel Mews MSS, journals and letters, Temp. MSS 284/2/21, 1–2 [photocopies]
Likenesses F. Wheatley, group portrait, oils, c.1774, Castle Museum, Norwich • J. Thomson, stipple, pubd 1818 (after T. C. Wageman), NPG [*see illus.*] • engraving (after portrait by Wageman), repro. in *Ladies' Monthly Museum*

Wakefield [née Brewin], **Rebecca** (1844–1873), missionary wife, was born in Mountsorrel, Leicestershire, on 19 August 1844, the only daughter and youngest of four children born to Simeon Brewin (*d.* 1857), a hosier and draper and Methodist local preacher, and his wife, Rebecca (1802/3–1862), daughter of Richard Wale, baker, of Mountsorrel, and herself active in local Methodist and temperance activities, and a role model for her daughter. Theirs was a close-knit, middle-class Methodist community. By 1857 Rebecca Brewin had lost two brothers, and she experienced a new religious commitment. By 1861, at seventeen, after attending school in Mountsorrel and in Loughborough, she became mistress of a school for 'young ladies'. After the death of her father and mother, she left the school in 1864 and moved to Birmingham to live with an aunt. In the same year she received a letter

from her childhood friend John Mitchel, a missionary in Ceylon; he proposed marriage and she accepted, believing that she must redouble her efforts in the service of God. She was twenty, with dark brown hair and eyes, 'above the average height, well formed, and inclining to stoutness' (Brewin, *Memoirs*, 22).

Wherever she lived, Rebecca taught Sunday school and actively joined in other church-related activities. Late in 1865 she lost both her aunt and her fiancé, who died of cholera in Ceylon, and went to live with her remaining brother Robert Brewin, a Methodist minister. In 1867 they moved to Plumstead, near Woolwich, and in 1868 to Louth, Lincolnshire. She met Thomas Wakefield (1836–1902) in May 1869 at the annual assembly of the United Methodist Free Churches Missionary Society. A pioneer missionary in east Africa, he had established a station at Ribe, among the Nyika north of Mombasa. They married on 2 December 1869 and left England on 24 February 1870.

Their storm-tossed voyage to Zanzibar took ninety-seven days in a small sailing ship and the discomfort was aggravated by Rebecca's pregnancy; their daughter, Helena Rebecca (Nellie), was born at Zanzibar on 16 October 1870. The Wakefields moved to Ribe to a two-room stone house and Rebecca took up her duties as a missionary wife. She taught the women sewing, led the singing at services, and occasionally taught the boys as well. Like other Europeans she met, she complained about Arab and African laziness and thievery. Yet she was truly distressed that British missionaries were not allowed to aid escaped slaves. She suffered periodic bouts of fever, and disastrous household losses wreaked by ants and rats that ate their way through books, clothing, and the mission's piano. Outside, night-prowling leopards scavenged their fowl and goats. In March 1873 Sir Bartle Frere visited Ribe on a government mission. His servants cooked for the thirteen officers of his party; Rebecca, again pregnant, fed his escort of fifty soldiers. Grave illness followed the birth of the Wakefields' son Bertie on 8 June 1873, and Rebecca died on 16 July, four days after she lost her son. They were buried together in the cemetery at the Ribe missionary station.

For Rebecca Wakefield growing up in an earnest religious environment made the choice of being a missionary wife a desirable challenge. To preach the gospel to the 'heathen' was an exciting religious adventure for women as well as for men. When she died at twenty-nine, she was experienced as a worker in the field, dispensing medicine daily, planning Christian festivals, and self-consciously providing a model for Christian womanhood. Her brother Robert Brewin turned her graphic letters home into her memorial, *Memoirs of Rebecca Wakefield, wife of the Rev. T. Wakefield, United Methodist Free Churches missionary in eastern Africa* (1876). DOROTHY O. HELLY

Sources R. Brewin, *Memoirs of Mrs. Rebecca Wakefield, wife of the Rev. T. Wakefield, United Methodist Free Churches missionary in eastern Africa*, 2nd edn (1879) • E. S. Wakefield, *Thomas Wakefield: missionary and geographical pioneer in east equatorial Africa*, 2nd edn (1904) • B. Wolstenholme, *Not dear to themselves* (1994) • *Welcome Words: a magazine* *of Religious Literature and Missionary Information* (1881-6) [ed. R. Brewin] • R. Brewin, *The martyrs of Golbanti, or, Missionary heroism illustrated in the lives of Rev. John and Mrs Houghton of east Africa* (1886) • C. Hall, 'Missionary stories: gender and ethnicity in England in the 1830s and 1840s', *White, male, and middle class: explorations in feminism and theory* (1992), 205–54 • J. Rowbotham, '"Soldiers of Christ"? Images of female missionaries in late nineteenth-century Britain: issues of heroism and martyrdom', *Gender and History*, 12/1 (April 2000), 82–106

Likenesses engraving, *c*.1869, repro. in Brewin, *Memoirs of Mrs. Rebecca Wakefield*, frontispiece

Wakefield [Wakefeld], **Robert** (*d.* 1537/8), Hebraist, was born in Yorkshire, probably to an influential Pontefract family; Thomas *Wakefield was his brother. Nothing is known about his early life. He was admitted BA at the University of Cambridge on 9 June 1514, determining in arts in the following year. On 14 July 1516 he was elected to a fellowship of Clare College, Cambridge, and by 1518 he was already a friend of John Fisher, bishop of Rochester, to whom he taught Hebrew. On 16 November of that year he matriculated at the University of Louvain, where he acquired an MA degree which was incorporated at Cambridge in the following year. He then lectured in Hebrew at the trilingual college in Louvain between 1 August and 1 December 1519. In the same year or that following he became a fellow of Fisher's Cambridge foundation, St John's College, receiving a stipend there which was to continue until 1528. In 1520 or 1521 he was probably the 'Mr Wakefield' who acted as a guarantor on behalf of Cambridge University for John Siberch's new Cambridge press.

Fisher granted Wakefield permission to go abroad again for the study of Hebrew. Probably during this period he taught in Paris and, while in Hagenau, he was invited to take up an appointment as lecturer in Hebrew at Tübingen, in succession to Johannes Reuchlin, the leading Christian Hebraist of his age; he did so in August 1522. Shortly afterwards he was known to Erasmus, who reported positively on his teaching to John Fisher. His lectures (at a salary of 104 florins per annum, which Erasmus thought generous, and including elementary Arabic and Aramaic as well) were so highly valued that the University of Tübingen wrote to Fisher, and Archduke Ferdinand of Austria wrote to Henry VIII, asking for the postponement of his return to Cambridge. This return took place, however, in 1523, when he was made Cambridge's first salaried lecturer in Hebrew, paid for by the king. By 1526–7 he was receiving a half-yearly wage of 56s. 8d. from the crown.

Wakefield delivered his famous inaugural oration at Cambridge entitled 'Oratio de laudibus & utilitate trium linguarum Arabicae, Chaldaicae & Hebraicae' in April of 1524. The 'Oratio' was printed, probably after extensive revision, in 1528 or early 1529, by Wynkyn de Worde, in the changed circumstances generated by Henry VIII's desire to annul his marriage to Katherine of Aragon and marry Anne Boleyn. In 1527 Wakefield had been teaching Hebrew to Richard Pace in the Bridgettine house at Syon. From this period of study emerged both Pace's *Praefatio in Ecclesiasten recognitum ad Hebraicam veritatem* (1527?) and

Wakefield's own *Paraphrasis in librum Koheleth* (1528?), a summary of the Hebrew text of Ecclesiastes. It was at this time that Pace recommended Wakefield to the king, because of potential advantages which might accrue to the royal argument for the divorce from an examination of the Hebrew texts of scripture. In connection with the Henrician cause Wakefield had dealings with the royal servants Edward Foxe and John Stokesley, in whose home he stayed for some time, and also had an audience with the king. It must also be in the context of Henry VIII's 'great matter' that, as he claims in the *Oratio*, Wakefield taught Hebrew to James Boleyn, Anne's uncle, and to Reginald Pole, who was sent to him for this purpose by Henry VIII.

All of this involved a fairly rapid change of allegiance for Wakefield, who, as the client of Bishop Fisher, Katherine of Aragon's leading intellectual advocate, had originally opposed Henry's case, later a matter of some embarrassment to Wakefield. The publication of the *Oratio* is therefore closely connected to the royal campaign to secure an annulment of the marriage. Its wide-ranging and uncompromising case for the superiority of Hebrew to the other ancient languages, and especially the value of Hebrew for Christian theologians, was particularly apt for the king at this moment, when Wakefield was using precisely these special linguistic skills—rare as they were in the England of his time—to argue the royal case against Fisher, which he did more exactly in a series of closely related treatises which were central to the debates on the divorce. Some of these are now lost; one in manuscript (BL, Cotton MS, Otho C x, fols. 184r–198r) demonstrates Henry's reliance on the Hebrew version of scripture from the outset of his campaign in 1527, and introduces to the debate the important issue of whether the marriage of Henry's late brother, Arthur, to Katherine had been consummated; and two were published after much revision as part of the royal campaign at a latter stage in its development. *Kotser codicis*, which was printed by Thomas Berthelet in 1534, contains a dedicatory letter to Anne Boleyn's father, Thomas, and another letter justifying Wakefield's behaviour to Bishop Fisher, and was part of a larger treatise in favour of Henry's case. *Syntagma de Hebreorum codicum incorruptione* (printed by Wynkyn de Worde, also in 1534) contains, besides two other items, a defence of the Hebrew Bible against the charge that the Jews had corrupted its text to reduce its Christological significance, and an untitled treatise on the divorce. In this work Wakefield's attitude to Fisher had noticeably hardened, and his tone towards his former patron is scornful. As a result of Wakefield's initiative in the divorce campaign, more Christian and Jewish Hebrew scholars from Venice were brought in on the king's side in 1530.

Despite brief remarks in his works on the value of learning Hebrew in order to dispute with Jews and convert them (not likely to be a persuasive justification for studying the language in a country which officially had no Jewish population), as well as on Jewish wickedness, and on the unreliability of the Talmud, Wakefield displays considerable reverence for Jewish writers of the middle ages, especially Abraham ibn Ezra, David Kimchi, Maimonides, Nachmanides, and Rashi. He also believed that the biblical Hebrews were the originators of every art and science which were often claimed for the ancient Greeks, and that Hebrew is God's own language. These positions make him sympathetic to Jewish experience in a period when Christian condemnations of Jews habitually crossed intellectual and ideological divides. Some of this stems from having absorbed, less critically than a number of his northern humanist contemporaries, the cabbalistic interests of such Renaissance figures as Giovanni Pico della Mirandola and Johannes Reuchlin, whose works he cites. More pronounced in Wakefield's writings, however, is the orthodox Christian humanist's and grammarian's case for Hebrew: no Christian theologian can reach an authentic comprehension of the Old Testament without studying it in its original language; and the same goes for the Greek New Testament, which contains many words derived from Hebrew. Christian scholastics, not Jews, are the most common objects of Wakefield's attacks, the church fathers his most frequent Christian allies; Lorenzo Valla's Greek philology is preferred over Pico's Hebrew scholarship which, according to Wakefield, was seriously flawed. In the *Oratio* there are related cases for doubting the divine authority of the Vulgate and Septuagint and for the value of studying Arabic and Aramaic. The latter leads him in turn to strong condemnation of Luther's linguistic and therefore exegetical abilities. Since Wakefield's treatise 'On faith and works'—if it was indeed by him—is no longer extant, we must assume in the light of his criticism of Luther that he remained a Catholic, albeit one who came to accept the royal ecclesiastical supremacy.

Clearly not all of Wakefield's writings are available to us, and his private library can only be imagined. Although many of the works attributed to him by the contemporary bibliographer John Bale were in fact by Robertus Britannus of Arras, Bale does mention an 'Institutiones Hebraicas' which is probably one of the Hebrew works which Wakefield, as he claims in the *Oratio*, hoped to publish when the printer developed more Hebrew type. In Archduke Ferdinand's letter to Henry VIII of 1523 it is stated that Wakefield took some of his works to be published to the Hagenau printing house of Thomas Anshelm. In the *Syntagma* Wakefield denounces Richard Collier, former Carthusian and vicar in Sittingbourne, for stealing from his home many rare Hebrew, Aramaic, Latin, Greek, and Arabic books, including his own 'Lexicon Chaldaicum', as well as the Koran, works by Avicenna, and Adam Easton's fourteenth-century Latin translation of the Hebrew Bible. According to John Leland, however, Wakefield himself pilfered from Ramsey Abbey a Hebrew dictionary which had been written by one of the abbey's early fifteenth-century monks, Laurence Holbeach. Wakefield was an admirer of the Hebrew printer Daniel Bomberg and probably owned some of his works. A number of Hebrew books belonging to his younger brother Thomas survive, and may have been given to him by Robert.

Wakefield's change of allegiance from Fisher and Katherine of Aragon to the king and Anne Boleyn had a major impact on his income and career. By the end of 1528 he was being paid a quarterly wage of 100s. by the treasurer of the king's chamber; in the following year he became regius praelector of Hebrew at Oxford at a salary of £6 13s. 4d.—his inaugural oration is printed in the *Syntagma*, together with a letter from Oxford University thanking the king for his appointment. On 18 July 1532 he was made a canon and prebendary of Henry VIII College, about three months after the incorporation at Oxford of his Cambridge bachelorship in theology. He complained, however, that for seven years his annual salary of £20 had been denied him due to an unnamed enemy who has plausibly been identified as Edward Foxe, whom Wakefield believed to be envious of him; Thomas and Anne Boleyn seem to have helped him recover the money owing, which by about 1533 amounted to more than £100.

Wakefield's students and admirers represent a diverse and influential group, including, by his own testimony, Thomas Hurskey, master of the Gilbertines, John Taylor, master of the rolls, John Stokesley, bishop of London, William Frisel, prior of the Rochester Cathedral chapter, William Tait, canon of Windsor and York, Thomas Lovell, canon of Bath and Wells, and Kaspar Amman, prior of the Augustinian house in Lauingen, Germany. We know from other evidence that he probably taught John Bale, the civil lawyer John Oliver, and the Liège humanist Paschasius Berselius. Through his teaching, publications, and influence with the king, he was the pioneering figure in the establishment of Hebrew study in Tudor England. One of the chief interests of Wakefield's life and writings is in demonstrating in a particularly well-documented fashion the opportunities offered to scholars and to new fields of scholarly endeavour by Henry VIII's divorce, as well as the intellectual conflicts, crises of loyalties, and ruptures of friendship and patronage this could engender.

In the final years of his life Wakefield seems to have gravitated away from Oxford, residing around 1534 in Moorgate. His will, naming his brother Thomas as his executor, was dated 8 October 1537 and was proved in London on 13 May of the following year. His place of burial is not known. JONATHAN WOOLFSON

Sources R. Wakefield, *On the three languages*, ed. and trans. G. L. Jones (1989) · R. Wakefield, *Kotser codicis* (1534) · R. Wakefield, *Syntagma de Hebreorum codicum incorruptione* (1534) · R. Rex, *The theology of John Fisher* (1991) · R. Rex, 'The earliest use of Hebrew in books printed in England: dating some works of Richard Pace and Robert Wakefield', *Transactions of the Cambridge Bibliographical Society*, 9 (1986–90), 517–25 · Emden, *Oxf.*, vol. 4 · H. de Vocht, *History of the foundation and the rise of the Collegium Trilingue Lovaniense, 1517–1550*, 4 vols. (1951–5) · *Opus epistolarum Des. Erasmi Roterodami*, ed. P. S. Allen and others, 12 vols. (1906–58) · Bale, *Cat.* · *Commentarii de scriptoribus Britannicis, auctore Joanne Lelando*, ed. A. Hall, 2 (1709), 452 · will, PRO, PROB 11/27, fols. 127–8

Archives BL, treatise on divorce of Henry VIII, Cotton MS, Otho C x

Wealth at death see will, PRO, PROB 11/27, fols. 127–8

Wakefield [Wakefeld], **Thomas** (*d.* **1575**), Hebraist, was born at Pontefract, Yorkshire. His brother was the renowned Hebrew scholar Robert *Wakefield. In a marginal note in one of the books in his library he records that he was twice married and that he fathered nine children, but he does not name his wives. He was educated at Cambridge, where he graduated BA in 1523. He is presumed to be the Wakefield granted leave of absence with pay from St John's College by John Fisher in 1523 so that he could continue his studies abroad. Writing to the master of St John's, Fisher expresses the hope that by going 'beyond the sea' Wakefield would become 'the more expolite and perfect in the tongue of Hebrew' and on his return would be able 'to perfect others in the same learning and do honour both to your college and to the whole realm' (Baker, 1.358). Of his subsequent career nothing is known until he was elected to the newly created regius chair of Hebrew on 9 November 1540, which carried with it membership of Trinity College. He was buried at Chesterton, near Cambridge, on 24 April 1575. His second wife, also buried at Chesterton, predeceased him in December 1570.

Wakefield held the endowed chair in name but not in practice until his death. Though others were appointed to teach Hebrew between 1549 and 1553, and again between 1569 and 1575, his competence as a linguist was not in doubt. It is probable that he was disqualified from teaching because of his adherence to Roman Catholicism. His place was taken by a succession of religious refugees from the continent, notably Paul Fagius, Immanuel Tremellius, Anthony Chevallier, and Philip Bignon. However, there is little direct proof of his knowledge of Hebrew, for as far as is known he published nothing. His one extant work is an examination of phrases in the New Testament which have an obvious Hebrew background: *Locutiones seu phrases in novo testamento, quae videntur secundum proprietates linguae Hebraeae*. Dated 1544, it is dedicated to Henry VIII and preserved in manuscript in the British Library. The only other clue to his Hebrew scholarship is to be found in the marginalia of the books he inherited from his brother Robert (*d.* 1537), some of which are now in Lambeth Palace Library. His copy of Felix Pratensis's Latin psalter, a translation from the Hebrew original, is heavily annotated. In the margin of Sebastian Muenster's Hebrew version of the gospel of Matthew, he identifies the source of the translator's note on a particular word as David Kimchi's *Book of Roots*. While Reuchlin's *De arte cabbalistica* was also on his shelves, it is not as well-thumbed as the Hebrew version of *The Book of Joseph Ben Gorion*. His close perusal of the first three chapters of this latter work indicate considerable competence in post-biblical Hebrew and familiarity with the relevant texts. It would appear that Wakefield's Hebrew books were no mere ornaments. They were read and studied by one who was able to appreciate their contents.

G. LLOYD JONES

Sources Cooper, *Ath. Cantab.*, 1.337–8 • J. B. Mullinger, *The University of Cambridge*, 2 (1884), 416–17 • T. Baker, *History of the college of St John the Evangelist, Cambridge*, ed. J. E. B. Mayor, 1 (1869), 358 • J. W. Clarke, *Endowments of the University of Cambridge* (1904), 156 • S. R. Maitland, *A list of some of the early printed books in the archiepiscopal library at Lambeth* (1843), 354ff. • *CSP dom.*, 1547–80 • G. Lloyd Jones, *The discovery of Hebrew in Tudor England: a third language* (1983), 193–4, 203ff.

Wakefield, (William) Wavell, Baron Wakefield of Kendal (1898–1983), sportsman and politician, was born on 10 March 1898 at Beckenham, Kent, the eldest of four sons (there were no daughters) of Roger William Wakefield (1865–1958), a medical practitioner in Beckenham, and his wife, Ethel Mary (*d.* 1960), daughter of John Frederick Knott, of Buxton, in Derbyshire. He was educated at the Craig preparatory school, Windermere, and at Sedbergh School, which he left in 1916 to serve in the Royal Naval Air Service and later in the Royal Air Force. On 19 November 1919 he married Rowena Doris (*d.* 1981), daughter of Llewellyn Lewis, medical practitioner; they had three daughters. Wakefield went to Pembroke College, Cambridge, in 1921, on the first RAF course arranged at the university, and took a BA degree in engineering (1923). He was a tremendous enthusiast in everything he did, and he was already an England rugby international when he went to Cambridge. He won two blues and was captain of the university in his second year. Typically, he discarded the traditional selection procedures in that year, and combed the colleges for talent. He took players from obscurity, moved them into different positions, and moulded them into such an effective team that they beat Oxford, the hot favourites, by what was then a record score. He went on to win thirty-one caps for England, which remained a record for forty-two years.

Wakefield retired from the RAF as a flight lieutenant in 1923, having reached the rank of captain in his wartime service and having been mentioned in dispatches. On leaving the RAF he joined Boots, the chemists, and qualified as a pharmaceutical chemist during his four years with the firm. In those years he established himself as one of the great players of rugby union football and as one of the best-known Englishmen of his time. He played cricket for the MCC and was also an exceptionally gifted athlete. He won the RAF 440 yards championship, and in sprint training at Cambridge he was fast enough to extend Harold Abrahams, who went on to win the gold medal for the 100 metres in the 1924 Olympic games. That speed, then unusual in such a big man, enabled Wakefield to transform forward play in rugby football, and such was his enquiring mind and innovative nature that he was in the forefront of introducing specialization to the various forward positions. With his white scrum cap laced firmly on his fair hair and round his strong, open face, he played for England for eight years and captained his country to the most successful period in its rugby history since the breakaway of the northern clubs which formed the Rugby League in 1892. Wakefield was elected to the Rugby Football Union while he was still a player, and he went on to become president in 1950–51 and to represent England on the international rugby football board. He maintained an active interest in skiing and water-skiing throughout his life. He won the Kandahar gold and became president of the Ski Club of Great Britain. In the summer months he was fond of water-skiing and sub-aqua diving in his beloved Lake District, where he lived and where he had some of his family banking and business interests. After he left the RAF he continued flying as a pilot in the reserve

(William) Wavell Wakefield, Baron Wakefield of Kendal (1898–1983), by unknown photographer, 1923

and in 1939 was recalled to active service for flying duties. He was then transferred to the Air Ministry as parliamentary private secretary and in 1942 was made director of the Air Training Corps.

Wakefield stood unsuccessfully for parliament in a by-election at Swindon in 1934, but a year later, at the general election, he won the seat for the Conservatives. In 1945 he left Swindon and won Marylebone. He held that seat until 1963, when he was created a baron. He had been knighted for public services in 1944. He served on the committees of the YMCA and the National Playing Fields Association; he was president of various manufacturing and transport associations, and was an active member of the governing body of Sedbergh School. He also held a wide range of company directorships, including those of Rediffusion Ltd, Skyways Engineering, and the Portman Building Society. Wakefield died in Kendal on 12 August 1983. The barony became extinct.   JOHN REASON, *rev.*

Sources personal knowledge (1990) · private information (1990) [Wakefield family] · *The Times* (16 Aug 1983) · Burke, *Peerage* (1967) · *CGPLA Eng. & Wales* (1983)
Archives Museum of Rugby, Twickenham, papers | FILM BFI NFTVA, news footage
Likenesses photographs, 1923–7, Hult. Arch. [*see illus.*]
Wealth at death £204,797: probate, 5 Oct 1983, *CGPLA Eng. & Wales*

Wakefield, William Hayward (1801–1848), colonist in New Zealand, was born at Burnham, Essex, on 8 August 1801, the fifth of the ten children of Edward *Wakefield (1774–1854), a farmer, and his wife, Susanna Crash (*d.* 1817). He was educated at Haigh's School, Tottenham, Middlesex, and was later attached to the British embassy in Turin. On 23 March 1826, in Paris, he married Emily Elizabeth, the daughter of Sir John Shelley Sidney. For assisting his brother Edward Gibbon *Wakefield in the abduction of Ellen Turner in 1826 he was sentenced in 1827 to three years' imprisonment in Lancaster Castle. Emily died on 12 August 1827; a daughter, Emily Charlotte, had been born in February that year. From 1832 to 1834 Wakefield served in the Portuguese army, where he was made a knight of the order of the Tower and Sword. He then joined the British Auxiliary Legion of Spain, and in

1837 attained the rank of colonel. He commanded the 1st regiment of lancers in 1836–7 and the 3rd legion in 1837–8. For distinguished service he was created a knight of the order of San Fernando.

In May 1839 Wakefield sailed in the *Tory* to New Zealand as the leader of the New Zealand Land Company's preliminary expedition. On 27 September he purchased the site for the company's settlement at Port Nicholson (Wellington harbour), and by 8 November had bought large areas on both sides of Cook Strait. In all, he acquired nominally about 20 million acres from the Maori in exchange for goods such as muskets, umbrellas, and Jews' harps. Acting on the express directions of the company, he reserved a tenth of his purchases for the Maori chiefs. These transactions, and the departure of the first emigrant ships in September 1839, took place before Britain had assumed sovereignty over New Zealand. Realizing the immigrants would lack British protection, the company appointed a committee, with Wakefield as president, to maintain order in the new settlement. The committee functioned after the settlers arrived in early 1840, but following the signing of the treaty of Waitangi on 6 February that year Lieutenant-Governor Hobson began acquiring sovereignty for the crown from the Maori chiefs. On hearing of the committee's activities on 21 May he immediately proclaimed sovereignty over the whole country, and on 23 May declared the committee illegal.

Meanwhile, the validity of the company's land purchases was being questioned. According to the system of Maori land tenure, any transfer of territory required the express and public sanction of every member of the tribe, including those temporarily absent. In his haste to acquire land, Wakefield had on occasions ignored this condition, which rendered his title invalid according to Maori custom. Moreover, on 14 January 1840 Hobson's superior, Sir George Gipps, had issued a proclamation announcing that commissioners would be appointed to investigate past purchases of Maori land. A commissioner from Britain began investigating the company's claims in 1842. At Wakefield's suggestion it was agreed that the commissioner would also decide where compensation was due to the Maori. Wakefield none the less obstructed the investigations until 1843, when tension over land in the Wairau district led to a tragic clash between Maori and a group of Nelson settlers. During the investigations it became clear that Wakefield's principal interpreter had had difficulty translating the deeds of purchase and that many Maori had not understood the implications of the transactions. In 1845 the company's entitlement was cut to 266,400 acres and the Maori were awarded £3500 compensation.

The land problem affected race relations and political life in the company's settlements for some years. In March 1847 the *Wellington Independent* strongly attacked the company's land policy, sparking off a duel between Wakefield and the editor, Isaac Earl Featherston. After Featherston had fired and missed, Wakefield fired into the air, commenting that he would not kill a man with seven daughters.

Wakefield was a member of the general legislative council of New Zealand in 1841. As the company's principal agent he supervised the settlements at Wellington, Wanganui, Nelson, and New Plymouth, and investigated sites for the New Edinburgh settlement at Otago. A connoisseur of cigars, cheroots, and continental wines, he was regarded by contemporaries as a shrewd negotiator and a competent administrator. Called 'Wideawake' by the Maori, he was known among the colonists for his reticence: no one knew what he really thought or meant to do. He died of apoplexy in Wellington on 19 September 1848, and was buried on 22 September in the city's Bolton Street cemetery. He was survived by his daughter, who in 1846 had married Edward William Stafford, a future premier of New Zealand.

William Hayward Wakefield's elder brother, **Arthur Wakefield** (1799–1843), colonist in New Zealand, was born at Burnham on 19 November 1799 and entered the navy in 1810. He served at Batavia, and in the Atlantic and Mediterranean, and rose to the rank of captain. In 1841 he became agent for the New Zealand Company's projected Nelson settlement. After selecting the site in November, he set about establishing the settlement. As he required more land for the growing number of settlers he sent surveyors to the Wairau district, Marlborough, in April 1843. The company's claim to the land was disputed by the Maori chiefs Te Rauparaha and Te Rangihaeata and was awaiting investigation by the land commissioner. Upset by interference with the survey, Wakefield attempted to arrest the chiefs on 17 June. In the fighting which broke out at Tuamarina that day about six Maori and twenty-two Europeans, including Wakefield, were killed. He was buried there on 23 June.

William Hayward and Arthur's younger brother, **Felix Wakefield** (1807–1875), engineer, born in Norfolk, married about 1830, in France, Marie Felicie Eliza Bailli, with whom he had nine children. In the early 1830s he became superintendent of public works in Van Diemen's Land. After returning to England in 1847, he assisted his brother Edward Gibbon Wakefield in his colonizing schemes. His report *Colonial Surveying with a View to the Disposal of Waste Land*, prepared for the New Zealand Company, was published in 1849. He joined the Canterbury settlement in New Zealand in 1851 and farmed near Christchurch. In 1854 he became principal superintendent of the Army Works Corps in the Crimea, with the rank of lieutenant-colonel, and built the railway from Balaklava to Sevastopol. Following his return to New Zealand in 1863 he was secretary to the government agent on the Otago goldfields from 1867 to 1870. A keen horticulturist, he published *The Gardener's Chronicle for New Zealand* (1870). He died at Sumner, Canterbury, on 23 December 1875, and was buried on 26 December in Christchurch cemetery.

E. I. CARLYLE, rev. DIANA BEAGLEHOLE

Sources *Parl. papers* (1841–54) [papers referring to New Zealand] · P. Burns, *Fatal success: a history of the New Zealand Company* (1989) · J. Millar, *Early Victorian New Zealand: a study of racial tensions and social attitudes, 1839–1852* (1958) · J. C. Beaglehole, *Captain Hobson and the New Zealand Company: a study in colonial administration* (1928) · R. M. Allan, *Nelson: a history of early settlement* (1965) · R. Tonk, '"A difficult and complicated question": the New Zealand Company's Wellington, Port Nicholson claim', *The making of Wellington, 1800–1914*, ed. D. Hamer and R. Nicholls (1990), 35–59 · G. W. Rusden, *History of New Zealand*, 1 (1883) · D. M. Beaglehole, 'Political leadership in Wellington, 1839–1853', *The making of Wellington, 1800–1914*, ed. D. Hamer and R. Nicholls (1990), 165–93 · P. Mennell, *The dictionary of Australasian biography* (1892) · E. J. Wakefield, *Adventure in New Zealand, from 1839 to 1844*, 2 vols. (1845) · I. O'Connor, *Edward Gibbon Wakefield: the man himself* (1929) · A. H. McLintock, *Crown colony government in New Zealand* (1958) · W. H. Wakefield, private notebook, priv. coll. · A. H. McLintock, ed., *An encyclopaedia of New Zealand*, 3 vols. (1966) · d. cert. · *DNZB* · P. Temple, 'New Zealand: a family business', *Edward Gibbon Wakefield and the colonial dream: a reconsideration*, ed. P. Temple (1997), 15

Archives NL NZ, Turnbull L.

Likenesses engraving?, 1826?, repro. in O'Connor, *Edward Gibbon Wakefield* (1928) · C. Heaphy, watercolour, 1839, NL NZ, Turnbull L. · miniature (Arthur Wakefield), repro. in O'Connor, *Edward Gibbon Wakefield*

Wakeford, John (1859–1930), Church of England clergyman, was born on 26 October 1859 at 21 Claremont Terrace, Prince of Wales Road, Kentish Town, the second son (one of eight surviving children) of William Wakeford, then a Metropolitan Police sergeant and afterwards police superintendent of Devonport dockyards, and his wife, Catherine Crocker. His chief education was acquired on the streets of Devonport and by private study. Despite his social and educational disadvantages he was ordained, and in 1885 was appointed curate of West Alvington, Devon. His ardour and zeal found fulfilment as an itinerant rural missioner in the dioceses of Exeter and Chichester (1886–93). Wakeford married, in 1893, Evelyn Mary, daughter of John Worthington, rector of Northlew and a member of the brewing family. They had a son and daughter.

At W. E. Gladstone's recommendation Wakeford was appointed in 1893 as vicar of the poor, sprawling parish of St Margaret's, Anfield, where the *Liverpool Review* reported 'his intense vitality, his volcanic energy, his fire, his earnestness, his enthusiasm' (Treherne, 53). Though he enjoyed the confidence of his congregation, outsiders demonstrated against his high-church practices, which included masses and confessionals. In 1899–1904 he was calumnied by militant Protestant agitators led by George Wise (1856–1917), pastor of the Protestant Reformers' Church in Liverpool, who claimed that ritualism corrupted women: 'weak feminine minds are readily led astray by theatricalism' (Treherne, 59). Wakeford was involved in two libel actions.

Wakeford became BD at Durham (1901), passed his intermediate law examinations at London University (1902), lectured in pastoral theology at King's College, London (1911–12), and published numerous devotional and doctrinal writings. He was appointed canon and precentor of Lincoln (1912), archdeacon of Stow (1913), and vicar of Kirkstead (1914) by Bishop Edward Lee Hicks, who respected 'his powers of physical endurance, of memory and observation, of spiritual instruction and mystical exposition', but regretted his tactlessness and 'peremptory handling of what he thought laxity among the clergy'

(Fowler, 246). There were many malicious intrigues in the cathedral chapter, and Wakeford had a powerful adversary in the dean, T. C. Fry.

In February 1921 Wakeford was found guilty by Lincoln consistory court on charges of adultery at the Bull Hotel, Peterborough, on 14–16 March and 2 April 1920. The evidence against him had been collected by a detective hired by the Revd C. Thomas Moore, who detested Wakeford and had himself appeared before a consistory court in 1915 on a charge of immorality instigated by Wakeford. Moore acted in concert with his friend the Revd Herbert Worthington, Wakeford's brother-in-law and enemy. The Lincoln hearings were both ill-managed and unjust. Though the testimony against Wakeford seemed strong, he insisted that the most damaging witnesses had been suborned. Afterwards, much of the incriminating evidence proved nugatory: there was tampering with the hotel registration book, for example, and an apparently guilty remark attributed to Wakeford by the hotel staff was, in fact, uttered as a joke by another guest, Edmund Blunden, who became a strong and reasoned supporter of Wakeford. The case aroused intense public excitement. However, the judicial committee of the privy council to which Wakeford appealed in April 1921 was unable to accept his theory of an elaborate conspiracy (perhaps because this would have required police corruption). Wakeford was deprived of his preferments but not (according to precedent) of his holy orders. He conducted a platform campaign across the country, supported by Horatio Bottomley, who saw the case as an opportunity to revive the popularity of his *John Bull* newspaper. Wakeford was bankrupted in 1924 by continuing legal costs. He lived on the proceeds of his wife's poultry farming at Biggin Hill until he was committed in March 1928 to Barming Heath Asylum, Maidstone, Kent, where he died of heart failure on 13 February 1930. He was buried in Cudham churchyard.   RICHARD DAVENPORT-HINES

Sources *The Times* (14 Feb 1930) · *The Times* (5 Feb 1921) · *The Times* (7 Feb 1921) · *The Times* (8 April 1921) · *The Times* (9 April 1921) · *The Times* (12 April 1921) · *The Times* (13 April 1921) · *The Times* (15 April 1921) · *The Times* (16 April 1921) · *The Times* (19 April 1921) · *The Times* (27 April 1921) · J. E. Treherne, *Dangerous precincts: the mystery of the Wakeford case* (1987) · E. Blunden, 'The case for the archdeacon', *Nation and the Athenaeum* (30 April 1921), 161, 164–5 · I. Colvin, *The life of Lord Carson*, 3 (1936), 393–9 · J. Wakeford, *Not peace but a sword* (privately printed, Biggin Hill, 1925) · R. Hanbury, *The Wakeford appeal, a defence of the archdeacon* (1921) · W. C. Pilley, *The mystery of the Wakeford case* (1922) · M. L. T., *Was Archdeacon Wakeford impersonated?* (1922) · J. H. Fowler, *The life and letters of Edward Lee Hicks* (1922) · b. cert. · Burke, *Gen. GB* · A. Bennett, *Journals, 1911–1921*, ed. N. Flower (1932), 287

Archives Lincs. Arch., list of case papers for Wakeford's consistory court trial | FILM *The girl in the cathedral*, Gaumont film of 1921

Likenesses portraits, *c.*1910–1921, repro. in Treherne, *Dangerous precincts*, facing pp. 49, 129; p. 52 and p. 88

Wakeman, Sir George, baronet (*b.* 1627), physician, the son of Edward Wakeman (1592–1659), barrister, of Beckford, Gloucestershire, and his wife, Mary (*d.* 1676), daughter of Richard Cotton of Warblington, Sussex, was born in Hampshire on 20 October 1627. He had at least five brothers and an unknown number of sisters. Wakeman belonged to a Roman Catholic family and was educated at home before being sent in 1642 to the English Jesuit school at St Omer in Spanish Flanders. After five years of studying rhetoric at St Omer, Wakeman, together with his brother Edward, entered the English College at Rome, where he remained until 1650. On joining the college, he claimed he was the son of 'noble Catholic Parents, impoverished by the evilness of the times and of the soldiery' (Kenny). He was at this time undecided about his career. On leaving Rome he went to Padua, and from there may have gone to Paris to study medicine. On his return to England about 1658 he became involved in a plot against the protector, and was imprisoned until the eve of the Restoration. In 1661 Wakeman was created a baronet by Charles II, though it seems that the patent was never sealed.

The first trace of Wakeman's professional activity is in August 1668, when he appears to have been attending Sir Joseph Williamson. He seems to have owed his appointment some two years later as physician-in-ordinary to Catherine of Braganza mainly to the fact that he enjoyed the best repute of any Roman Catholic physician in England. In their perjured *Narrative* of the Popish Plot of 1678 Titus Oates and Israel Tonge declared that Wakeman had been offered £10,000 to poison Charles II. It was pointed out that he could easily effect this through the agency of the queen. Wakeman, however, obstinately refused the task, and held out until £15,000 was offered. The temptation then, according to the *Narrative*, proved too strong; he attended the Jesuit consult on 30 August 1678, received a large sum of money on account; and, with the promise of the further reward of a post as physician-general in the army, he agreed to poison the king. Wakeman was a man of high reputation, and from the first the charge against him was repugnant to many. John Evelyn wrote in his diary that he was 'well acquainted' with the physician and took 'him to be a worthy gentleman abhorring such a fact' (*Diary of John Evelyn*, 2.351). The government, too, was reluctant to allow any steps to be taken against him. But after their successes in the trials of the early part of 1679, the whig leaders were eager to continue the pursuit of the 'plotters', knowing that a successful prosecution of Wakeman would almost certainly incriminate the queen. The government was forced to yield to the pressure. Both parties felt that the trial would be a test one, and it proved to be a turning point in the Popish Plot episode.

Wakeman was indicted for high treason at the Old Bailey on 18 July 1679, the case being tried by Lord Chief Justice Scroggs. With Wakeman were arraigned three Benedictine monks, William Marshal, William Rumley, and James Corker. The chief witnesses for the prosecution were William Bedloe and Oates. The latter swore he had seen the paper appointing Wakeman to be physician-general and also his receipt for £5000 (on account of the £15,000), though it was elicited from Oates in the course of the proceedings that he was incapable at the time in question of identifying either Wakeman's person or his handwriting. Wakeman objected that Oates's accusation was based entirely on hearsay, and brought evidence to prove that incriminating documents produced in the case were forgeries. He pointed out the absurdity that a man in his position would take into his confidence a person such as Bedloe, who swore that Wakeman had been on intimate terms with him. He also drew attention to his family's loyalty to the crown. Not only had he himself been imprisoned because he was 'suspected to be a favorer of the Royal Party' and had 'conspired with Captain Lucy and several others to attempt something for his majesties Restauration' but his brother Richard had raised a troop of cavalry for the king and his father 'hath suffer'd very much to the value of Eighteen thousand Pounds and more for the Royal Family' (*Tryals*, 60). Scroggs commented severely on the character of the evidence, and the jury, after asking if they might find the prisoners guilty of misprision of treason, and being told they could not, found all the prisoners not guilty.

Charles II is said to have wept with joy at the outcome (Hutton, 378), which caused a good deal of surprise, not least because it was the first acquittal of any of those tried for their involvement in the 'plot'. Narcissus Luttrell wrote of the judge's conduct of the trial that it was 'worth takeing notice off and compareing the tryalls of Mr. Coleman and this about sir George Wakeman together, and you will find the lord chief justice Scrogs to be infinitely chang'd from what he was in Colemans tryall, even in the same things' (Luttrell, 1.18). The effect of the acquittal was considerable in dealing a direct blow at the 'plot' and the credibility of its sponsors, and at the same time it freed the queen from suspicion. On the day following the trial the Portuguese ambassador called and thanked Scroggs.

A few days later, Wakeman went to Windsor to see the king and queen, and soon after left for Brussels. The verdict was supported in a pamphlet of *Some Observations upon the Late Tryals by Tom Ticklefoot* (1679); but this was answered in a similar production, entitled *The Tickler Tickled* (1679), and there is little doubt that the verdict was unpopular. It was openly said that Scroggs had been bribed, while Bedloe and Oates complained bitterly of the treatment they had received in the summing-up. Scroggs was ridiculed in *A Letter from Paris from Sir George Wakeman to his Friend Sir W. S.* (1681). The jury was termed an 'ungodly' one, and the people, said Luttrell, 'murmur very much'. It is noteworthy that in the course of evidence given at subsequent trials, Oates entirely ignored the verdict, and continued to speak of the bribe offered to and accepted by Wakeman.

Wakeman was back in London before 1685, when he was seen by Evelyn at Lady Tuke's; and he had the satisfaction of giving evidence against Titus Oates on 8 May 1685, on the occasion of his first trial for perjury. Nothing is known of his further career.

THOMAS SECCOMBE, *rev.* MICHAEL BEVAN

Sources G. Holt, *St Omers and Bruges colleges, 1593–1773: a biographical dictionary*, Catholic RS, 69 (1979) · A. Kenny, ed., *The responsa scholarum of the English College, Rome*, 2, Catholic RS, 55 (1963) · *The tryals of Sir George Wakeman* (1679) · *Bishop Burnet's History of his own time*, ed. G. Burnet and T. Burnet, 2 vols. (1724–34) · J. Kenyon, *The Popish Plot* (1972) · J. P. Kenyon, 'The acquittal of Sir George Wakeman: 18 July 1679', HJ, 14 (1971), 693–708 · *State trials* · J. W. Bund, *A selection of cases from the state trials*, 2 vols. (1879–82) · T. Ticklefoot [F. Smith], *Some observations upon the late tryals of Sir George Wakeman, Corker and Marshal* (1679) · M. Mason, *The tickler tickled* (1679) [pseud.] · N. Luttrell, *A brief historical relation of state affairs from September 1678 to April 1714*, 6 vols. (1857) · L. Eachard, *The history of England*, 3 vols. (1707–18) · Burke, *Gen. GB* · *Diary of John Evelyn*, ed. W. Bray, new edn, ed. H. B. Wheatley, 4 vols. (1879) · J. Lingard, *The history of England*, 5th edn, 10 vols. (1849) · L. von Ranke, *A history of England, principally in the seventeeth century*, 6 vols. (1875) · *The autobiography of Sir John Bramston*, ed. [Lord Braybrooke], CS, 32 (1845) · T. Seccombe, ed., *Lives of twelve bad men: original studies of eminent scoundrels by various hands* (1894) · A. Strickland and [E. Strickland], *Lives of the queens of England*, 5 (1840) · H. Irving, *Life of Judge Jeffreys* (1898) · R. Hutton, *Charles the Second: king of England, Scotland and Ireland* (1989); pbk edn (1991)

Wakeman [*alias* Wiche], **John** (*d.* 1549), abbot of Tewkesbury and bishop of Gloucester, was probably born in Worcestershire. He was educated at Oxford, where he supplicated for the degree of BTh in 1511. He had been ordained acolyte in 1501, deacon in 1503, and priest in 1504, but otherwise little is known about him before he entered Tewkesbury Abbey in 1531. In all likelihood he had been a Benedictine monk for some time, since he soon became prior and was elected abbot on 27 April 1534. This was a turbulent time for monasticism in England, and impending religious change would be the main challenge facing the new abbot. On 31 March 1534, just a month before he gained royal assent to his election, Wakeman joined with others attending a meeting of convocation in subscribing to the royal supremacy, and in August 1535 Cromwell's commissioners arrived to 'peruse the inventory, appropriations and other muniments' of Tewkesbury Abbey (*LP Henry VIII*, 9.3). Five and a half years later the information gained during that visit would facilitate the surrender of that house.

In the intervening years Wakeman seems to have done all in his power to mitigate the possible future damage to his community and to his own career. His election as abbot, however, seems to have been the subject of some concern since he subsequently expressed his gratitude to both Thomas Cromwell and Sir William Kingston, constable of the Tower and a prominent figure among the Gloucestershire gentry, for their support. Wakeman sent Kingston a letter of thanks, but he gave Cromwell a gelding and £5 towards the purchase of a saddle. Wakeman then had the opportunity to demonstrate his loyalty to the king by receiving Henry VIII and Anne Boleyn during their progress through Gloucestershire in the summer of 1535. In the end, however, John Wakeman was not able to prevent the dissolution of his monastery, and he surrendered the abbey to Cromwell's commissioners on 9 January 1540. His ecclesiastical career was none the less to continue. On 3 September 1541 the diocese of Gloucester was established, with John Wakeman as its first bishop. Perhaps his efforts to ingratiate himself had been a success, or quite possibly his administrative experience and knowledge of the region made him the best candidate.

To some scholars it appears that Wakeman was given the bishopric as something of a 'retirement package', perhaps in thanks for some perceived loyalty during the tumultuous 1530s. In any event he repaid the king for his appointment by dutifully conforming to the changing official religious policies of Henry's last years, and by visiting his diocese on a regular basis. None the less, Wakeman's episcopate was less energetic than those of either his predecessors, Hugh Latimer and John Bell, in the diocese of Worcester, or his successor, John Hooper, in the diocese of Gloucester. Bishop Wakeman did conduct the requisite visitations, but there is no evidence of vigour. Perhaps he was a 'time-server', merely going through the motions and occupying the office of bishop to fund his retirement, or maybe his actions reflected the apparent ambiguity in official religion during that portion of Henry's reign. However, his performance as bishop can be read in another way. He was the first bishop of a new and very poor diocese. It may have taken some time to establish the ecclesiastical structure needed to administer the see effectively. Early in Edward VI's reign Wakeman conducted a more thorough visitation, perhaps owing to the increased clarity of religious policy under Protector Somerset. On the other hand, the difference may have been a result of the establishment over the previous seven years of a more effective diocesan administrative structure. In either case, the later visitation still fell far short of the standards set by Latimer or Bell, and Wakeman seems to have continued to turn a blind eye to traditional practices which he was supposed to discourage as harmful, even though they were not explicitly forbidden.

Focusing on Wakeman's episcopal administration, however, may misrepresent his role in the religious life of mid-Tudor England. Thomas Cranmer valued his learning sufficiently to ask him to participate in the project to create a new English translation of the Bible, and he was one of nine bishops chosen to 'attend upon the conduct of … [Henry VIII's] corps' during the king's funeral (Strype, 2/2, 291). John Wakeman's own death came in Forthampton, Gloucestershire, on 6 December 1549, nearly three years after Henry's, and he was probably buried in a small private chapel there. He had drawn up his will on 30 July that year, appointing as his executors his brothers Thomas and Richard, and making bequests to three nephews and a niece, as well as to servants. He also left 20 nobles to one Thomas Poyner, a student at Magdalen College, Oxford. Wakeman died a dutiful member of the English ecclesiastical hierarchy, but although he was careful to bequeath his soul to the Trinity alone, he was definitely not a proponent of evangelical reform.

CAROLINE LITZENBERGER

Sources BL, Cotton MSS, appx 9, fols. 2–10 · *DNB* · Foster, *Alum. Oxon.* · Furney, 'History of Gloucester', Glos. RO, D327 · Hockaday abstracts, chronological, 1535–49, Gloucester Public Library · Glos. RO, Gloucester diocese, vols. 2, 4 · Glos. RO, Furney MS B · *VCH Gloucestershire* · register of Archbishop Cranmer, LPL · *LP Henry VIII* · D. MacCulloch, *Thomas Cranmer: a life* (1996) · A. Douglas and P. Greenfield, eds., *Records of early English drama: Cumberland, Westmorland, Gloucestershire* (1986) · J. Strype, *Ecclesiastical memorials*, 3 vols. (1822), vol. 2 · *Gloucestershire*, Pevsner · Emden, *Oxf.*, 4.600 · G. Baskerville, 'Some ecclesiastical wills', *Transactions of the Bristol and Gloucestershire Archaeological Society*, 52 (1930), 281–93, esp. 290–92

Archives Glos. RO · Gloucester Public Library
Wealth at death see will, PRO, PROB 11/32, fols. 343v–344

Wakering, John (d. 1425), administrator and bishop of Norwich, was from Great Wakering, Essex, where he provided for prayers for the souls of his parents and brothers. While he had poor relations there, two other kinsmen served as master of St Bartholomew's Hospital, Smithfield, which had the patronage of Great Wakering church. The bishop's own first preferment was St Benet Sherehog.

On 13 April 1380 a chaplain named John Wakering was pardoned his outlawry after failing to appear in the London hustings court on a charge of illegal retaining. However, the certain career of the bishop can only be traced from 1392 when he was already a senior member of the administration of John of Gaunt, duke of Lancaster. In March of that year Wakering appears as deputy to the chancellor of the duchy of Lancaster. He was chancellor of the county palatine by 4 August 1395, and probably even a year earlier, while in 1394–5 he held also the privy seal of the duchy. He then began to work for the king as well. First termed a royal clerk in October 1394, he was a master in chancery in 1395 and acted as a receiver of petitions for Gascony in both parliaments in 1397. However, when the king banished Gaunt's heir, Henry Bolingbroke, in 1398, Wakering was naturally appointed on 8 October as one of the attorneys to care for the exile's interests. Richard reneged on this agreement when Gaunt died, and confiscated the duchy and county palatine.

When Henry Bolingbroke took the throne, his longstanding confidence in Wakering was demonstrated at once. On 15 October 1399 Wakering was reappointed as chancellor of the county palatine, a post he still held in February 1403 and probably retained until March 1405, and from 25 November 1402 he was also paid as chancellor of the duchy. Between 1400 and 1402, moreover, he acted as a duchy attorney in chancery, of which he was still a master. On 2 March 1405 the king brought him wholly into the royal administration as keeper of the rolls of chancery, an office he would hold for ten years.

Wakering's ecclesiastical preferments had been augmented steadily by Gaunt and Bolingbroke, the rectory of Orpington, Kent, being the one he remembered especially on his deathbed, but on 10 March 1409 he was granted no less than the archdeaconry of Canterbury by the crown. Although he was admitted promptly to the confraternity of Christ Church, Canterbury, and could offer the cathedral useful connections in its legal and other administrative dealings with the crown, his inevitable absence from his responsibilities as archdeacon (which were considerable) is unattractive. This archdeaconry, at least, was usually provided with a full-time occupier. Wakering's regular duties in chancery engaged him in such occasional work as acting as proctor for various ecclesiastical bodies and prelates in parliaments between 1404 and 1416, acting as a receiver of petitions for England there in May 1413 and April and December 1414, deputizing for the dean of St Martin's-le-Grand, London, in January 1411, and acting three times as custodian of the great seal (19–31 January 1410, 10/12–20 June 1411, and 20 December 1411–17 January 1412) while the king and prince of Wales contested for control of the chancellorship and government.

On his accession Henry V was content to continue Wakering in office, even while dismissing those who had served his father in the greatest offices. Wakering was granted letters of attorney on 8 October 1413 because he was going abroad, but nothing more is known of this proposed journey. On 3 June 1415 Wakering was appointed as keeper of the privy seal to succeed John Prophete, who had himself served nine years in that office. Unlike his seven immediate predecessors, Prophete had not obtained a bishopric, by his own account because he refused to intrigue for one. Wakering, by contrast, had instant success. The king's close friend Richard Courtenay, bishop of Norwich, died at the siege of Harfleur at the age of thirty-three. The monks were given licence to elect on 3 November 1415, and royal assent to their choice of Wakering (no doubt by nomination from the crown) was given on 24 November. The Council of Constance was then in session, and on the following day the crown wrote to the papal curia, as being located there, to signify the choice of Wakering. However, John XXIII had been deposed, Gregory XII had resigned, and Benedict XIII was an unrecognized renegade. After some hesitation, the king wrote on 7 April 1416 to the archbishop of Canterbury, instructing him to confirm Wakering's position; Chichele did so on 27 May, and the temporalities were restored on the same day. Wakering was consecrated in St Paul's Cathedral on 31 May. He thus became the first bishop in England for seventy years not to be papally provided to his see. Looked at in another way, he was to be the last non-graduate 'civil servant', of a kind so familiar in the previous century, to achieve episcopacy.

Wakering resigned as keeper of the privy seal on 7 July 1416, but not in order to turn to diocesan life. On 20 July he was appointed as a royal delegate to the Council of Constance where Henry V intended to strengthen the English presence substantially, and also to rein in Bishop Robert Hallum's reforming enthusiasm by making him share the leadership of the delegation with four bishops who had risen through the royal administration and would serve the king's will. Wakering did not return to England until about February 1418, and only in the following month did he finally enter his diocese.

Wakering held no more offices of state, but he did continue to be used as a councillor, and still more so after being appointed to the council of regency for the infant Henry VI on 9 December 1422. It has been assumed that this made him a gross absentee from his diocese, but his register proves otherwise; he was a vigorous commuter and managed to spend most of his time in his see. Until March 1419 he chose Hoxne, Suffolk, as his base, making

tours of primary visitation in May and September–October 1418. Thereafter he lived almost entirely at Bishopthorpe; his career had quite probably given him a distaste for administration by wagon train. Indeed, his handling of his diocese seems exactly as might be predicted from his career: competent and uneventful. This should, however, be contrasted with the unsavoury feuds with Norwich Cathedral and city, and with the town of Lynn, which his two predecessors sustained; it would be surprising if Wakering simply found peace by lethargy. It must be noted that in the valleys south-east of Norwich towards Lowestoft lived scores of Lollards whom Wakering's successor, William Alnwick, had no difficulty scouring out in 1428–31. Wakering accepted the compurgation in July 1424 of the chaplain, Hugh Pye of Loddon, Norfolk, who was to prove a leading figure in this sectarian network, and of two other men whose kin were to prove implicated. He delved no further. On the other hand, Alnwick only acted with vigour when the archbishop told him to.

Wakering returned to Bishopthorpe from his last trip to London in early March 1425. His will (29 March) was predictably long and meticulous, and carefully remembered his earlier benefices, his family, and his servants. He had a collection of his own sermons to bequeath. There is, however, more than this to Wakering's final thoughts. Throughout the will there is persistent attention to paupers, not so much for those at his own funeral (for whom he left just 20 marks), but notably in his own properties, past benefices, and especially those in hospitals and across his diocese, these last being left no less than 1000 marks. Furthermore, the bishop recalled the celebrated aphorism of St Augustine of Hippo that funerals were more a solace for the living than help to the dead, and asked for unpompous rites on the day of his death, but 1000 masses on that same day if possible. Wakering died on 9 April 1425. He had, of course, arranged his burial site, tomb chest (still extant, though without its brass), and chantry in the cathedral, on the south side of the presbytery by that of the founder.   R. G. DAVIES

Sources Wakeryng's register, Norfolk RO, Reg/4/8 · E. F. Jacob, ed., *The register of Henry Chichele, archbishop of Canterbury, 1414–1443*, 2, CYS, 42 (1937), 311–14 [will] · R. Somerville, *History of the duchy of Lancaster, 1265–1603* (1953) · R. G. Davies, 'The episcopate in England and Wales, 1375–1443', PhD diss., University of Manchester, 1974, 3. ccxciii–v · I. Atherton and others, eds., *Norwich Cathedral: church, city and diocese, 1096–1996* (1996)
Archives Norfolk RO [register]

Wakley, Thomas (1795–1862), medical journalist and politician, was born on 11 July 1795 at Land Farm, Membury, Devon, the youngest son in the family of eleven children of Henry Wakley (1750–1842), a prosperous farmer, and his wife, Mary, née Minifie. He went to good grammar schools at Chard and Honiton, and at the age of ten was sent to Calcutta on a ship captained by a family friend. Although he never spoke of his experiences at sea, they probably affected his later campaigns against flogging and brutality in the armed forces. He returned to school, possibly at Wiveliscombe, Somerset, until he was apprenticed from the age of fifteen to a succession of medical

Thomas Wakley (1795–1862), by Sir Edwin Landseer

practitioners: an apothecary in Taunton, a surgeon in Beaminster, and Mr Phelps, his brother-in-law and a surgeon in Henley-on-Thames.

Surgeon and medical journalist In 1815 Wakley went to London to complete his medical education. He remained primarily in the metropolis for the rest of his life. He enrolled as a pupil at the united hospitals of St Thomas's and Guy's, and also studied at the private anatomy school in nearby Webb Street run by Richard and Edward Grainger. He qualified for membership in the Royal College of Surgeons in 1817 and set up a private practice in the City, living in Gerard's Hall, Basing Lane. Two years later his prospective father-in-law, Joseph Goodchild, a wealthy lead merchant from Hendon, helped him purchase a fashionable practice in the West End and a fifteen-room house at 5 Argyll Street, near Oxford Circus. On 5 February 1820 he and Elizabeth Goodchild (1799–1857) were married at St James's, Piccadilly. He seemed set fair for the comfortable life of a successful London practitioner. Six months later, his life was in complete disarray.

On 27 August 1820 Wakley was assaulted in his own home. He had had a headache and had applied leeches to his temple, wrapping his head in a tourniquet. A man knocked on his door and asked him to see a former patient of his and then requested a glass of cider. When Wakley went to the basement to fetch it, the man apparently admitted some masked companions. They knocked Wakley unconscious with a blow to his head, the tourniquet probably saving his life, and kicked and stabbed him. When he came to, the house was on fire. He escaped through the roof light, but the house and its wedding contents, which were heavily insured, were destroyed. The insurance company suspected Wakley of deliberate arson and refused to compensate him.

The incident attracted much attention in the newspapers. Although the assailants were never identified, it was suggested that they were members of a radical political gang whose leader, Arthur Thistlewood, and four associates had been executed in May 1820. Wakley was rumoured to have been the anonymous surgeon who had beheaded the victims after hanging. There is suggestive evidence that the Newgate beheader was actually a hospital porter and body snatcher named Parker, but the assault and fire forced Wakley and his bride to find another house in less genteel Norfolk Street, off the Strand. Wakley took the insurance company to court, where in June 1821 he obtained full compensation and costs.

His recuperation and the legal entanglement disrupted Wakley's medical practice, which among the poorer folk around Norfolk Street was in any case less lucrative. His wife expected more, and apparently suggested that he consider abandoning medicine for another career. At about the same time, he acquired the friendship of William Cobbett, the radical journalist, writer, and reformer. A visit in 1823 by Dr Walter Channing, a Boston physician and one of the founders of the *New England Journal of Medicine and Surgery* (1812), also prodded Wakley to consider establishing his own weekly journal in London. Channing may even have helped fund *The Lancet*, first published on Sunday 5 October 1823. It was Wakley, however, who made this journal what it was, and the journal was the making of him.

Wakley chose the title of his periodical carefully. As he pointed out, a lancet was not just a surgical instrument for cutting out the dross, it was also an arched window, for letting in light. It was successful from the very first issue, almost a quarter of which was devoted to a lecture by Sir Astley Cooper, London's leading surgeon, and a consultant at Guy's Hospital. The early issues were edited anonymously, although Cooper suspected Wakley and had his suspicions confirmed by going to Wakley's house disguised as a patient and discovering his former pupil correcting proofs.

Three features help explain the journal's immediate and continuing impact. First, it was published weekly, which allowed it to carry news of topical interest, to foster a correspondence column, and to encourage readers to anticipate its publication each week. Although *The Lancet* spawned other rival medical weeklies, in 1823 no other British medical periodical appeared more frequently than monthly, and several of them were irregular. This in effect allowed Wakley quickly to dominate the field.

Second, Wakley always aimed his journal at a wide audience. As a former general practitioner himself, he identified with the rank and file of the medical profession. Didactic lectures by eminent London teachers dominated the early volumes, which offered medical students and others the substance of these lectures without the necessity of paying the requisite fees. Initially, these were reproduced without the permission of the lecturer,

Wakley or one of his collaborators attending and taking down the spoken words, usually in shorthand. Cooper had permitted the publication of his lectures, but John Abernethy, senior surgeon at St Bartholomew's Hospital, objected to seeing his own in print, grammatical infelicities and all, and took Wakley to court in December 1824. Initially Abernethy's injunction was denied, but a second application, in June 1825, was upheld, only to be overturned on Wakley's appeal in November, on the grounds that public lectures delivered in a public place were for the public good and therefore were public property. Wakley's version of these legal proceedings was fully and colourfully reported in *The Lancet*. Eventually, medical teachers began to co-operate with Wakley, delivering copy of their lectures for reproduction in the journal.

In addition to publishing lectures by prominent teachers, Wakley also hoped to increase circulation in the early issues with general news items, including theatre reviews and a chess puzzle, two of his own passionate interests. *The Lancet* soon establishing itself, these non-medical features disappeared, as Wakley concentrated on a third successful ambition, using his journal to catalyse medical reform. He has been described as an improbable radical, but he retained his radicalism throughout his adult life. Reform was always top of his agenda, even after he became assimilated into the British establishment.

The first few volumes of *The Lancet* sought medical change through an aggressive, bombastic style. In the editorials and articles in his journal, Wakley assaulted nepotism, complacency, and secrecy within medicine. He campaigned for hospitals to make public their cumulative statistics of treatments and cures, and a series of articles, entitled 'Hole and corner surgery', exposed to ridicule surgeons who had bungled operations. A fatal lithotomy operation carried out in 1828 by Bransby Cooper, Sir Ashley's nephew, attracted much attention, especially after Cooper sued Wakley for libel. Wakley defended his own case and although he lost the legal battle, Cooper was awarded only token damages, which with costs were paid by public subscription. Characteristically, Wakley and Cooper became friends in later life. Wakley made frequent appearances in court during the decade, defending himself against libel charges brought by the surgeon Frederick Tyrell and Roderick Macleod, editor of the *London Medical and Physical Journal*. Wakley himself obtained libel damages from James Johnson, editor of the *Medico-Chirurgical Journal*, for the latter's malicious reference to the fire which had destroyed Wakley's house.

Wakley also attempted to open up to greater democracy the medical corporations, especially the Royal College of Surgeons, of which he was a rank-and-file member. The college's council was a closed, self-perpetuating oligarchy, whose members ran the college, approved each other's anatomy and surgery courses as obligatory for medical students wishing to obtain the college's qualification, and collected the lucrative fees for examining these new recruits. In a series of meetings, all of them animated and some of them violent, Wakley sought to put pressure on the college to reform itself, in addition to petitioning parliament to revoke the college's charter. The surgeons proved resistant to rapid change, especially as some of Wakley's earlier supporters, such as William Lawrence, began to modify their demands as they themselves achieved positions on the college's council. Significantly, Wakley himself was never elected to the fellowship of the college, created in 1843 partially as a means of expanding the number of doctors who could participate in running the affairs of the Royal College of Surgeons.

During the 1830s Wakley also attempted to create a radical alternative to the older medical corporations. His proposed London College of Medicine would have provided the basis of a universal medical qualification for general practitioners and consultants alike. He envisioned it as overseeing and improving educational and examination standards within medicine, an issue to which Wakley continued to devote much energy, both through his journal and, after 1835, as a member of parliament. The London College of Medicine never got beyond the blueprint stage.

Wakley continued to use his journal to publicize other medical and social issues that he wished to see reformed. These included the system of poor relief and its medical services, the adulteration of foods, public health, medical quackery, and flogging and other forms of corporal punishment in the armed forces. His strategies became more subtle than the blockbuster tactics of the early *Lancet*, and also more effective. A number of individuals helped Wakley conduct his journal. These included J. F. Clarke, William Lawrence, William Cobbett, and, before Wakley exposed his mesmeric experiments on two young female mediums, John Elliotson. He was not always liked, but he was admired by many, including Charles Dickens, William Thackeray, Henry Brougham, and others outside the medical profession. He was in effect the first full-time medical journalist who demonstrated how powerful the medical press could be.

Member of parliament Medical politics infused *The Lancet* from the very beginning, and by the time of the Reform Act of 1832, Wakley had acquired a substantial reputation. He published from 2 January 1831 until late in 1832 a political weekly called *The Ballot*. This both reflected his wider political interests and more actively involved him in the radical political scene surrounding the debates about extending the franchise and reforming parliament. He also realized that his own ambitions had a better chance of being achieved with him inside parliament rather than simply as a critic of it. With Cobbett's backing, he agreed to stand as an independent radical for Finsbury, London, in the first general election after the Reform Act, in December 1832. Although his own financial situation necessitated a low-key campaign, he made a creditable showing, which encouraged him to stand again in 1834. He was successful in his third attempt, in January 1835. In June that year he made a great impression in the House of Commons with an impassioned speech on behalf of six Dorset labourers (the 'Tolpuddle martyrs') sentenced to transportation for combining to resist the reduction of their wages. Shortly after entering parliament, he published from 23 April to 22 May 1836 another short-lived political periodical, *A Voice from the Commons*. He remained a popular and conscientious member for Finsbury until ill health forced his retirement in 1852.

Wakley had consistently campaigned for parliament as an independently minded citizen who wished to extend the franchise, facilitate local democracy, increase parliamentary accountability, and reduce the rates. He was true to his word, and although he obviously took matters of medical reform most seriously, he participated in a wide range of parliamentary matters, attending sittings regularly and voting in the majority of divisions. His early speeches were usually brief, but he developed sufficient oratorical skills to bring himself into national notice. He addressed many of the leading questions of the day, including the reform of the law courts, prison and workhouse conditions, taxation, the state of the railways, church reform, copyright law, and Chartism.

Inevitably, however, medical matters preoccupied Wakley. With Henry Warburton and others, he helped draft and comment on the successive medical acts that were debated in parliament through the late 1830s and 1840s. These were eventually to culminate in the Medical Act of 1858, which legally defined the medical practitioner, and created the Medical Register and a professional regulatory body, the General Medical Council. Although Wakley had by then retired from parliament, the act disappointed him in perpetuating the variety of medical educational and licensing bodies, and in its failure to address directly the issue of quackery. It embodied a public recognition of professionalism within medicine, however, a subject always near the top of Wakley's agenda.

Wakley had earlier been successful in helping shape several pieces of medically related legislation. The Medical Witnesses Act of 1837, which gave coroners more power in requiring doctors to assist at inquests, also mandated payment for their professional services. He was much concerned with the public health implications of burial-grounds and with the Public Health Act of 1848. He used both his position in parliament and his journal to publicize the scandals in the Andover workhouse, and the death, following flogging, of a young private named Frederick John White in 1846. In the 1850s he created through *The Lancet* an Analytical Sanitary Commission, whose work exposed extensive adulteration of many foods and drinks and led to regulatory legislation beginning in 1860.

Coroner for West Middlesex In addition to editing a weekly journal and representing Finsbury constituency in parliament, Wakley found the time and energy to offer himself for election as coroner in 1830. Lawyers had traditionally occupied this ancient post; Wakley was the first medical man to seek it. Unsuccessful at first, he was elected coroner for West Middlesex in 1839, a position he held until his death. It was his sixth campaign of the decade (four for parliament as well as the earlier one for the coronership), but Wakley was easily elected in 1839 on a platform of

extending the powers of the office, investigating every case of suspicious death in the large and populous district, and of publicly exposing crime whenever he found it. This he subsequently did, finding his position more powerful as a result of the Medical Witnesses Act that he had helped push through parliament.

Wakley's insistence that determining the cause of a sudden or suspicious death was essentially a medical matter brought him into conflict with magistrates and their clerks. His determination to hold inquests on every appropriate occasion, and to pay his medical witnesses, meant that his expenses were much greater than those of his predecessors. However, a parliamentary committee of 1840 supported Wakley's view of the office. The use of deputy coroners was also queried early in Wakley's tenure of office, as was his right to commit individuals determined during the course of his coroner's inquest to have been guilty of murder. He also ran foul of workhouse officials by insisting that accidental or violent deaths of inmates should also be subject to coroner's inquests, which in several instances revealed negligence or maltreatment. Since Wakley and his journal had ever been critical of the new poor laws of 1834, and their medical provisions, neither Wakley's energetic use of his coroner's powers, nor the publicity he gave scandals in *The Lancet*, endeared him to officialdom. He believed that the health of incarcerated paupers would improve were the poor-law infirmaries to be better provisioned, and poor-law medical officers given more power, status, and income.

Industrial accidents and railway injuries and deaths provided another highly contentious arena for Wakley's enterprise. He was able to use the ancient law of deodand to impose fines on employers or industrialists found guilty of causing death through negligence until the Deodants Abolition Act of 1846 abolished this possibility; although it was accompanied by a Fatal Accidents Act, tighter legislation relating to industrial accidents and injuries was not passed until after Wakley's death.

Above all, Wakley used his coroner's office as a platform to campaign for medical coroners as a matter of course. He was accused of being self-serving, but the stance was entirely consistent with his more general belief that doctors were undervalued, and that collective professional advancement was the way forward. He sought less to denigrate medical élites than to raise the rank and file, through improvements in education, better conditions of employment, and more social respect.

Personal life Despite his personal historical visibility and the continuing importance of the journal he founded, Wakley remains enigmatic. He was ever indignant at social or political injustice, and he never lost his concern for the plight of the ordinary individual. He hated cant and humbug, which endeared him to Charles Dickens. At the same time he was personally ambitious, with a highly developed sense of his own worth. He maintained a home in Bedford Street, London, and an estate, Harefield Park, and entertained lavishly, even while remaining abstemious himself. He seemed addicted to the rough and tumble of turbulent public life, but he remained a devoted family man. A lifelong radical, he was also an active Anglican. His wife's death in 1857 affected him deeply. A daughter died young, but he was intensely proud and supportive of his three sons. Two of these, Thomas Henry *Wakley (1821–1907) and James Goodchild Wakley (1827–1886), followed him into medical journalism, continuing *The Lancet* as a family business until the twentieth century. The middle son, Henry Membury, became a barrister and deputized for his father as a coroner.

Wakley was a large man with enormous energy, who routinely worked sixteen-hour days. In his early life he acquired fame as an accomplished boxer. In 1851, following a strenuous day involving seven inquests and attendance at the House of Commons until midnight, he was found unconscious outside the *Lancet* office, where he had gone to continue working. This episode convinced Wakley to slow down, and although he left parliament, he retained the coronership and *The Lancet*, which his sons joined him in editing. Their take-over was probably gradual, and Wakley retained the official editorship until his death.

In the late 1850s Wakley enjoyed a brief period of better health, and he contemplated running again for parliament. However, in late 1860, signs of active pulmonary tuberculosis supervened. He spent the winter of 1861–2 in Madeira, where his lungs began to heal. He had made arrangements to return to England, but on 11 May 1862 he slipped on the beach, the haemoptysis recurred, and he died on 16 May. His embalmed body was brought back for burial beside his wife and daughter in Kensal Green cemetery on 14 June.   W. F. BYNUM

Sources S. S. Sprigge, *The life and times of Thomas Wakley* (1897) · J. Hostettler, *Thomas Wakley: an improbable radical* (1993) · E. Sherrington, 'Thomas Wakley and reform', DPhil diss., U. Oxf., 1973 · C. Brook, *Thomas Wakley* (1962) · M. Bostetter, 'The journalism of Thomas Wakley', *Innovators and preachers*, ed. J. Wiener (1985) · J. Loudon and I. Loudon, 'Medicine, politics and the medical periodical, 1800–50', *Medical journals and medical knowledge: historical essays*, ed. W. F. Bynum, S. Lock, and M. Porter (1992) · J. F. Clarke, *Autobiographical recollections of the medical profession* (1874) · I. Loudon, *Medical care and the general practitioner, 1750–1850* (1986)
Archives BL, Place papers, Add. MSS · UCL, Brougham papers
Likenesses W. H. Egleton, stipple, pubd 1840 (after K. Meadows), BM, NPG; repro. in Sprigge, *Life and times* · J. Doyle, caricatures, BM · E. Landseer, oils, The Lancet, London [*see illus.*] · G. E. Madeley, lithograph, NPG

Wakley, Thomas (1851–1909), medical journalist, the only son of Thomas Henry *Wakley (1821–1907), and his wife, Harriette Anne, *née* Blake, was born at 33 Guilford Street, London, on 10 July 1851. He was educated at Westminster School from 1865 to 1870 and represented his school at both cricket and football; he also won the quarter mile, and was awarded a leaving scholarship in classics. At Trinity College, Cambridge, he studied medicine, but passed only the first MB examination. His path to qualifying in medicine was delayed by what was probably a fracture in the base of the skull sustained in a bicycle accident shortly after coming down from Cambridge; this left him with a permanent weakness of his right eye. He resumed his medical studies at St Thomas's Hospital, London, after six

years, and qualified LRCP in 1883. Immediately afterwards he joined his uncle, James Wakley, at *The Lancet*, and he worked under his editorship for three years until James's death in 1886. Thereafter he became joint editor with his father, Thomas, until the latter's death in 1907, when he became sole editor. He was thus the fourth and last Wakley to edit the journal in a dynasty that lasted from 1823 until 1909, when he died and was succeeded by Squire Sprigge, who had written a biography of the first Thomas Wakley.

The adjectives that occur most frequently in tributes to Wakley are quiet, unassuming, and fair. Apart from obituary notices, he seems to have written little in the journal, though he regularly used his editorial pen to remove potentially wounding phrases from the writings of others. Unlike his grandfather and uncle, he was on good terms with the staff of the *British Medical Journal*, co-operating with them in friendly rivalry, and he served as chairman of the International Association of the Medical Press at both of its meetings in London.

Wakley was a talented amateur actor, an enthusiastic freemason, and a fellow of the Royal Numismatic Society. At his death he had almost completed a catalogue of his collection of British and colonial crown pieces. He published privately *The Log of the Wyvern*, recording boating trips up the Thames undertaken with his cousin. Seemingly a lifelong bachelor, he lived in his father's house until he married on 8 August 1903 Gladys Muriel (*b.* 1878/9), daughter of Norman Barron, a solicitor; their son was also named Thomas. Wakley died of hepatitis at his home, 16 Hyde Park Gate, London, on 5 March 1909, and on 10 March his ashes were interred at Putney Vale cemetery. He was survived by his wife.   STEPHEN LOCK

Sources DNB · *The Lancet* (13 March 1909), 857, 772, 800–04 · BMJ (13 March 1909), 697–8 · Venn, *Alum. Cant.* · *Old Westminsters*, 2.956 · b. cert. · m. cert. · d. cert. · *CGPLA Eng. & Wales* (1909)
Likenesses photograph, repro. in BMJ, 697 · photograph, repro. in *The Lancet*, 803
Wealth at death £25,136 12s.: resworn probate, 1 June 1909, *CGPLA Eng. & Wales*

Wakley, Thomas Henry (1821–1907), journal editor and surgeon, eldest of the three sons of Thomas *Wakley (1795–1862) and his wife, Elizabeth, *née* Goodchild (*d.* 1857), was born in London on 21 March 1821. He never used his second Christian name, partly, it is said, out of reverence for his father, who was proprietor of the medical journal *The Lancet*, and partly because a younger brother also had the same name. After being educated privately he went up briefly to Wadham College, Oxford, but the University of London apparently appealed more to his liberal views (and perhaps those of his father as well), so that he changed to University College, London, at the same time electing to study medicine and abandoning his original thoughts of entering the church. His father also believed that medical education was better in Paris than in London, so he went there for part of his studies, also choosing to study music and singing under Garcia and Ronconi (which many years later stood him in good stead when in 1903 he composed a wedding march for a cousin).

Wakley qualified MRCS in 1845 and was elected assistant surgeon to the Royal Free Hospital, London, three years later; he became FRCS in 1849 (and was senior fellow of the college at the time of his death). As a surgeon he invented a urethral dilator and popularized the use of glycerine in treating inflammation of the outer ear passages. Though he wrote little, he contributed an article on diseases of the joints to a dictionary of practical surgery. In 1850 he married Harriette Anne, third daughter of Francis Radford Blake, of Rickmansworth. She survived him, with a son, Thomas *Wakley (1851–1909), and a daughter, Amy Florence.

In 1857 his father made Wakley and his youngest brother, James Goodchild Wakley, part proprietors of *The Lancet*, with a share in the management. Five years later the father died and James Wakley became editor of the journal, with Thomas maintaining an active interest in it. Nevertheless, at this time he was in great demand as a surgeon all over the country, and he spent much of his time travelling to operate on patients in their own homes, many of whom came, in the words of one obituary, from the highest ranks in society.

The Lancet, founded in 1823, was the leading weekly medical journal, crusading and combative in pressing for medical reforms such as attacking incompetence, nepotism, the conditions in workhouse infirmaries, and those conducive to cholera. In 1866 the rival *BMJ* 'poached' the *Lancet's* Ernest A. Hart (1835–1898), who had been denied his aspiration to be co-editor. As co-editor at the *BMJ* Hart was largely responsible for its gaining pre-eminence in the last third of the century. Until his death in 1886 James Wakley, the principal editor, lived in 'open hatred' with Hart (Bartrip, 64). Meanwhile, Thomas Wakley had retired from surgery in 1882, though he continued to consult and work as a journalist until 1886, when he necessarily became joint editor of *The Lancet* with his son Thomas. The younger Thomas then restored relationships with the *BMJ* to friendly rivalry.

In 1895 the two Wakleys commissioned Squire Sprigge, who was to become editor himself in 1909, to write an official biography of the elder Thomas Wakley, the founder of the journal. There are no detailed accounts of Thomas Henry Wakley's contribution as editor, but he seems above all to have been efficient, fairminded, and emollient where his father (and his brother James, who was a noted boxer with a warm temper) would have been vitriolic. For many years he spent the winter in Brighton, but he was renowned for arriving promptly at *The Lancet* offices by 10 a.m., even on Saturdays. He was also particularly concerned about doctors who fell on hard times and started *The Lancet* relief fund, helped to direct the Hospital Saturday Fund, and donated £1000 of *Lancet* funds to Epsom College for the education of the sons of doctors.

Wakley's energy was unbounded. A fine runner in his youth, he hunted until his seventies and was fond of salmon fishing, particularly in Ireland. He died at his house, 5 Queen's Gate, Kensington, London, on 5 April 1907, and was cremated at Golders Green, Middlesex, five days later. STEPHEN LOCK

Sources *DNB* · *The Lancet* (13 April 1907), 1025, 1048–53 · *BMJ* (13 April 1907), 903–4 · P. Bartrip, *Mirror of medicine: a history of the British Medical Journal* (1990)
Likenesses photograph, repro. in *The Lancet*, 1053
Wealth at death £525 15s. 0d.: probate, 4 June 1907, CGPLA Eng. & Wales

Walbran, John Richard (1817–1869), antiquary, son of John and Elizabeth Walbran, was born at Ripon, Yorkshire, on 24 December 1817, and educated near by at Whixley. After leaving school he became assistant to his father, an iron merchant, before entering business as a wine merchant in Ripon. His antiquarian interests led to his becoming local secretary of the British Archaeological Institute, which he addressed in 1846 'On the necessity of clearing out the conventual church of Fountains'. Publication of the paper resulted in excavations at Fountains Abbey, carried out under his personal direction, which marked the beginning of the modern archaeological study of that important site. Walbran also studied the documentary sources, publishing the first volume of *The Memorials of the Abbey of St. Mary of Fountains* for the Surtees Society in 1864. This was followed by a second, posthumous volume completed by James Raine in 1878. The first volume of another uncompleted work, his *History of Gainford, Durham*, was published in 1851 with the support and assistance of his friend William Harrison, printer, of Ripon. Walbran embarked on other substantial local antiquarian studies, but did not see them to completion. He did, however, have success as a writer of popular guides of a scholarly type. His *Guide to Ripon*, which included Harrogate and the abbeys of Fountains and Bolton, was published in 1844 and went through nine editions, under various titles, during his lifetime. He also shared the contemporary taste for the picturesque, publishing *A Summer's Day at Bolton Abbey* in 1847, which combined his antiquarian knowledge and a sensitive evocation of the landscape, complete with quotations from Wordsworth.

Walbran married, on 3 September 1849, Jane, daughter of Richard Nicholson of Ripon, solicitor and left two sons, the elder of whom, Francis Marmaduke Walbran of Leeds, was the author of works on angling. Walbran was elected FSA on 12 January 1854, and in 1856 and 1857 was mayor of Ripon. In April 1868 he was struck with paralysis, and died on 7 April 1869. He was buried in Holy Trinity churchyard, Ripon. After his death his manuscripts were purchased by Edward Akroyd of Halifax, and deposited at York Minster Library. WILLIAM JOSEPH SHEILS

Sources J. Raine, preface, in J. R. Walbran, *Memorials of the abbey of St Mary of Fountains*, 2, SurtS, 67 (1878) · E. Peacock, 'Memoir', in J. R. Walbran, *Guide to Ripon*, 11th edn (1875) · m. cert.
Archives Borth. Inst., notebooks of extracts mainly relating to Yorkshire monastic houses · U. Durham L., notes for 'Antiquities of Gainford' · W. Yorks. AS, Leeds, transcripts, notes, etc. relating to Fountains Abbey charters · York Minster Library, genealogical and heraldic MSS | Bodl. Oxf., corresp. with Sir Thomas Phillipps
Likenesses engraving, repro. in Peacock, 'Memoir'

Walbrook [*formerly* Wohlbrück], (**Adolf Wilhelm**) **Anton** (1896–1967), actor, was born in Vienna, Austria, on 19 November 1896, the son of Adolf Wohlbrück, a circus clown from Hamburg, and his Austrian wife, Gisela Rosa Cohn. Brought up in a show-business environment, he could also trace his ancestry back through several generations of performers to his great-great-grandfather, an eighteenth-century actor named Gottfried Wohlbrück. He was educated initially at a Catholic convent school in Klosterneuburg, near Vienna, then at a Berlin *Gymnasium*, where he took the 'Abitur'. A scholarship enabled him to enrol at the acting school recently founded in Berlin by Max Reinhardt, who subsequently recruited him for his company at the Deutsches Theater, but Wohlbrück's five-year contract was soon interrupted by military service. Commissioned as lieutenant in a regiment of guards during the First World War, he was taken prisoner in France and whiled away captivity by organizing a drama group which gave performances and poetry recitals to fellow inmates of the prisoner of war camp.

After demobilization Wohlbrück returned to the stage in a production of Dumas *fils*'s play *La dame aux camélias* at the Munich Schauspielhaus, and then furthered his career through successive engagements at Otto Falckenberg's Munich Kammerspiele, at other provincial theatres in Dresden and Düsseldorf, and from 1930 at the Barnowsky-Bühne in Berlin. At the same time he was slowly acquiring a reputation in the German-language cinema: having made his screen début in Vienna as early as 1915 in *Marionetten*, he appeared in occasional silent films during the 1920s, but rose to prominence with the advent of sound, when his smooth, cultured voice, allied to a boulevardier's sophistication, soon made him a popular leading man—as in *Salto mortale* (1931, as Robbie), *Walzerkrieg* (1933, as Johann Strauss), and *Viktor und Viktoria* (1933, as Robert, the doting English gentleman), among others. In 1934 the success achieved by Willi Forst's *Maskerade* brought Wohlbrück international recognition and a lucrative contract with UFA Studios, where he went on to make *Régine* (1934), *Zigeunerbaron*, *Der Student von Prag* (both 1935), and a lavish Franco-German co-production based on Jules Verne's novel *Michel Strogoff* (also known as *Der Kurier des Zaren*, 1936), followed by another multinationally financed project, Miklos Farkas's *Port Arthur* (also known as *I Give my Life*, or, *Orders from Tokyo*, 1936), made in German, Czech, French, and English versions.

It was Wohlbrück's starring role as Michael Strogoff that allowed him to side-step an increasingly threatening situation in Germany and the impending *Anschluss* of Austria. His Jewish blood rendered him vulnerable to professional annihilation, if not worse, but the film's purchase by RKO Pictures for release in the United States led to an invitation to California from Pandro Berman, and he was able to leave a Berlin gripped with nationalist fervour by the Olympic games of 1936. In Hollywood he re-shot dialogue sequences with an English-speaking cast, having his name changed to Anton Walbrook for the purpose, and the film was re-issued in 1937 as *The Soldier and the Lady*. Unhappy in America, he re-crossed the Atlantic to co-star (as Prince Albert) opposite Anna Neagle in Herbert Wilcox's *Victoria the Great* (1937) and *Sixty Glorious Years* (1938), and promptly set aside part of his earnings to assist less fortunate Jewish performers and help them and their families to escape from Nazi Germany.

Walbrook settled in London and remained in Britain throughout the Second World War, appearing in a succession of leading film roles: as the bigamous husband in *Gaslight* (Thorold Dickinson, 1940), the Polish concert pianist–RAF pilot in *Dangerous Moonlight* (Brian Desmond Hurst, 1941), a German-speaking Canadian settler in *49th Parallel* (Michael Powell and Emeric Pressburger, 1941), an aristocratic Prussian officer in *The Life and Death of Colonel Blimp* (Powell and Pressburger, 1943), and a Czech resistance fighter in *The Man from Morocco* (Max Greene, 1945). His now-confident command of English also enabled him to get established on the London stage: he made his début there as Otto, the artist, in the British première of Noël Coward's *Design for Living* (Haymarket, January 1939), following this with a sensitive, deeply felt portrayal of Kurt Müller, the Jewish fugitive, in Lillian Hellman's *Watch on the Rhine* (Aldwych, April 1942), and a nicely judged comic performance as Michael Fox in Frederick Lonsdale's brittle tale, *Another Love Story* (Phoenix, December 1944).

Although Walbrook became a naturalized British subject in January 1947 and maintained a home in London, his working life took on a distinctly nomadic character after the war. While continuing to appear occasionally in the West End—as Hjalmar Ekdal in Henrik Ibsen's *The Wild Duck* (St Martin's Theatre, November 1948), as Hugo Möbius, the fortune-hunting philanderer in Walter Hasenclever's *Man of Distinction* (Princes Theatre, October 1957), as Han van Maasdijk, the artist–forger in *Masterpiece* by Larry Ward and Gordon Russell (Royalty Theatre, January 1961), and, with hereditary adaptability and instinctive timing, as a non-singer in two musicals, Irving Berlin's *Call me Madam* (Coliseum, March 1952) and *Wedding in Paris* (Hippodrome, April 1954)—he acted extensively in Germany. His first post-war engagement there was with Gustaf Gründgens's company at the Düsseldorf Schauspielhaus in 1951, and he later worked in Stuttgart, Hamburg, and at the Renaissance-Theater in Berlin. In the cinema his career was no less international and impressively polyglot. Not only did he star in three further British films, two of them for Powell and Pressburger—*The Red Shoes* (1948, as Boris Lermontov, the ruthless ballet impresario) and *Oh, Rosalinda!* (1955, as Dr Falke)—and one for Dickinson, *The Queen of Spades* (1948, as Herman Suvotin), but he also made a similar number in France: *La ronde* (1950, as the world-weary, gently ironic *meneur du jeu*) and *Lola Montès* (1955, as Ludwig I of Bavaria) for Max Ophüls, and *L'affaire Maurizius* (1954, as Grégoire Warenne) for Julien Duvivier. He also played major roles in two films by American directors working in Britain—as Bishop Cauchon in Otto Preminger's *Saint Joan* (1957) and a sardonic Major Esterhazy in José Ferrer's account of the Dreyfus affair, *I Accuse* (1958)—and two in Austria, Joe May's *König für eine Nacht* (1950) and E. E. Reinert's *Wien tanzt* (1951), as well as several for German television. It was during one of his many return visits to Germany that he suffered a fatal heart attack: in March 1967 he collapsed on stage during a performance of Coward's *A Song at Twilight* at the Kleine-Komödie in Munich, and died a few months later, on 9 August, in Garatshausen, on the Starnberger See. His body was brought back to London and lies buried in Hampstead cemetery, close to his former home in Frognal.

The sheer resilience that sustained Walbrook's career inevitably overshadows any of his individual achievements, which, while not spectacular, were occasionally memorable. At all times there was a quality of restraint about his acting which radiated inner authority, even aloofness, no less than surface charm; a soft, measured tone of voice, capable of intensity without resort to histrionics, and a handsome appearance, maturing gracefully from matinee-idol good looks into stern, moustached elegance, combined to powerful effect, and translated easily from stage to screen. Off screen, though friends found him engaging, he could display the arrogance of the egocentric star or the secretive reserve of the rootless émigré who never married. But for British audiences who lived through the war years, he was the quintessentially civilized continental, whose urbane demeanour and exotic accent represented the acceptable face of 'foreignness' at a time when their country lay beleaguered and Europe ravaged by armed conflict. DONALD ROY

Sources *The Times* (10 Aug 1967), 1, 8 · *Who was who in the theatre, 1912–1976*, 4 vols. (1978), vol. 4 · A. L. Unterburger, ed., *International dictionary of films and filmmakers, 3: actors and actresses*, 3rd edn (1997) · E. M. Truitt, *Who was who on screen*, 3rd edn (1983) · D. Shipman, *The great movie stars*, 2nd rev. edn, 1: *The golden years* (1989) · D. Thomson, *A biographical dictionary of the cinema*, rev. edn (1980) · H.-M. Bock, ed., *Cinegraph: Lexikon zum deutschsprachigen Film*, [7 vols.] (1984–) · L. Maltin, ed., *Leonard Maltin's movie encyclopedia* (1994) · E. Katz, *The international film encyclopaedia* (1980) · WWW, 1961–70 · www.geocities.com/plorre/anton.html, 13 Nov 2001 · B. McFarlane, ed., *An autobiography of British cinema* (1997) · D. Quinlan, *Quinlan's film stars*, 4th edn (1996) · J. Walker, ed., *Halliwell's film-goer's companion*, 10th edn (1993) · R. Bean, ed., *Films and Filming* (March 1978) · K. Loup, *Die Wohlbrücks: eine deutsche Theaterfamilie* (Düsseldorf, 1975) · W. Holl, *Das Buch von Adolf Wohlbrück* (Berlin, 1935)

Archives U. Texas

Likenesses photographs, 1937–48, Hult. Arch. · Radio Pictures, photograph, *c*.1939, repro. in *Play Pictorial* (July 1939), p. 9 · photograph, 1942, repro. in *Theatre World* (June 1942), cover · photograph, 1948, repro. in Unterburger, *International dictionary*, p. 1245 · photograph, 1949, repro. in *Theatre World* (Feb 1949), p. 21 · photograph (as a young man), repro. in www.geocities.com/plorre/anton.html · photograph, repro. in Quinlan, *Quinlan's film stars*, p. 480

Wealth at death £9733: probate, 1967, *CGPLA Eng. & Wales*

Walburg [St Walburg, Walburga] (*c*.710–779?), abbess of Heidenheim, was born in Wessex *c*.710. She was the sister of *Willibald and *Winnebald and probably a kinswoman of Leoba. Walburg inherited the Benedictine monastery of Heidenheim in southern Germany from Winnebald, its founder, in 761, and brought a group of nuns, including Hugeburc, to the foundation with her. Heidenheim thus became the only double monastery established on the continent by the Anglo-Saxon mission. Walburg was in Germany already, probably summoned by Boniface, perhaps with Leoba, to the mission field in the early 740s. The abbess encouraged Hugeburc to compose the lives of Walburg's two brothers and in particular Hugeburc drew on Walburg's own report of the miracles accompanying the death of Winnebald.

There is no life of Walburg; Wolfhard von Herriede's *Miracula S. Waldburgis Monheimensia*, composed *c*.899, is the earliest attempt at a biography, but Wolfhard knew little about his subject's early life and so depicts Walburg as a stereotypical model nun and abbess. Walburg died on 25 February, probably in 779. The body was translated to Eichstätt on 21 September, probably in 879, marking the official recognition of her cult. Her relics were taken in 893 to Monheim, where a miracle-working oil still exudes from her shrine. The saint has become conflated with a female fertility figure, banisher of the spirits of winter, in southern German superstition: on Walpurgisnacht, the eve before May day (the anniversary of Walburg's canonization), witches dance and evil spirits roam abroad.

CAROLYNE LARRINGTON

Sources A. Bauch, ed. and trans., *Quellen zur Geschichte der Diözese Eichstätt, 2: Ein bayerisches Mirakelbuch aus der Karolingerzeit* (Eichstätt, 1979) · A. Bauch, ed. and trans., *Quellen zur Geschichte der Diözese Eichstätt, 1: Biographien der Gründungszeit* (Eichstätt, 1962) · C. H. Talbot, ed. and trans., *The Anglo-Saxon missionaries in Germany* (1954) · O. Engels, 'Die Vita Willibalds und die Anfänge des Bistums Eichstätts', *Der Heilige Willibald, Klosterbischof oder Bistumsgründer?*, ed. H. Dickerhof, E. Reiter, and S. Weinfurter (1990), 171–98 · H. Bächtold-Stäubli, *Handwörterbuch des Deutschen Aberglaubens*, 5 (1932–3), cols. 1542–7 · M. Mengs, *Schrifttum zum Leben und zur Verehrung der Eichstättischen Diözesanheiliger* (1987) · *Acta sanctorum: Februarius*, 3 (Antwerp, 1658), 523–42

Walcher, earl of Northumbria (d. 1080), bishop of Durham, was the Lotharingian priest chosen by William the Conqueror to succeed in 1071 to the troubled see of Durham, following William's harrying of the north in 1069 and 1070 and the rebellion and outlawing of the previous bishop, the Anglo-Saxon Æthelwine. In the tenth and eleventh centuries Lotharingia was prominent as a centre of ecclesiastical reform and Walcher was not the first of his contemporaries to join the English episcopacy; he was preceded, for example, by Duduc of Wells (1033–1061?) and Giso of Wells (1061?–1088). Nothing is known of Walcher's background except that he was a clerk at Liège when William invited him to come to Durham.

In 1071 Walcher began his journey to the embattled north complete with bodyguard, accompanied as far as York, according to the principal source, Symeon of Durham, by the housecarl Eilaf and 'many other leading men'. From York he was escorted to Durham by the Northumbrian earl, Gospatric. The next year, 1072, William the Conqueror, in a further attempt to break rebel networks in the north dismissed Gospatric, appointing Waltheof of Huntingdon in his place. Waltheof had local ties but at the same time was bound by marriage to William and initially at least was prepared to work with Walcher. Symeon gives a picture of their beleaguered co-operation: the Conqueror had built a castle at Durham 'where the bishop might keep himself and his people safe from the attacks of assailants. Bishop Walcher and earl Waltheof were very friendly and accommodating to each other; so that he, sitting together with the bishop in the synod of priests, humbly and obediently carried out whatever the bishop decreed for the reformation of Christianity in his earldom' (Sym. Dur., *Opera*, vol. 2, s.a. 1072). Recent excavations give some indication of how formidable Walcher's castle really was. The moat was at least 19 yards wide, 164 yards long, and 6 yards deep. In the building no expense seems to have been spared; William I had given Walcher an estate at Waltham, Essex, and it is likely that he used its revenues to further the castle's construction.

Symeon's rosy picture notwithstanding, within three years of Walcher's arrival Waltheof had joined a rebellion against the Conqueror which was to cost him his life. The earldom was now given to Walcher. The office required, to use Symeon's words, skill 'in difficult affairs'; how far Walcher possessed this it is hard to tell. According to Symeon, Walcher was 'a man worthily beloved by all for the honesty of his life and the sobriety and gentleness of his nature; yet he too displeased the natives by permitting his followers unrestrainedly to do whatever they pleased, nor did he check them when they acted wrongfully. Moreover, his archdeacon [Leobwine] swept away from the church many of its ornaments and much of its money and distributed them among his own friends and relations' (Sym. Dur., *Opera*, vol. 1, c. 58).

It is around archdeacon Leobwine that the final drama of Walcher's life centres. Leobwine, so Symeon relates, had become jealous of the place in Walcher's affection and counsels of Ligulf, a local nobleman without whose advice Walcher would not carry out the greater matters of secular business. In 1080, on Leobwine's orders, Ligulf and most of his family were slain in their beds. The murder was laid at the door of Walcher, perpetrated as it had been, not only by the plotting of his archdeacon, but also by the complicity of his deputy and his knights. Despite protestations of innocence Walcher could therefore neither expect, nor did he receive, any mercy. On 14 May 1080, at Gateshead, where they had gone for an alleged peace meeting, he, his entourage—a hundred French and Flemish according to the Anglo-Saxon Chronicle—and Leobwine were killed. Walcher thus became the tenth Northumbrian earl since 993 to have met a violent end. Murky though the details are, it is clear that behind his death lay a history of feud that pre-dated not only his own accession to power but also the conquest itself. According to John of Worcester, Walcher's murderer was Eadwulf Rus, a man who came from the same house as Ligulf's widow (the house of Bamburgh) and who had scores of his own to settle; his father had been killed by Tostig, the earl Edward the Confessor had imposed on Northumbria in 1064. William the Conqueror's reprisals to the deaths at Gateshead were both savage and decisive. Northumbria was once again ruthlessly harried and terrorized and a new castle—the Newcastle of the future—built on the site of Walcher's murder.

As a bishop, Walcher's career was not, however, simply dominated by the politics that beset his earldom. In his insistence that his cathedral clergy should sing canonical rather than monastic offices he may have shown himself to be unsympathetic to the traditions of his see but against this can be offset his encouragement of the revival of Northumbrian monasticism. In the early 1070s a small band of monks from Evesham and Winchcombe, fired by their reading of Bede's *Historia ecclesiastica*, had set off to the north to recreate the way of life of the first Anglo-Saxon monks. Their arrival was welcomed by Walcher who gave them first Bede's monastery at Jarrow to repair and resettle and then, after their successful establishment of a community there, the Anglo-Saxon foundation of Whitby. Melrose, in Scotland, was their next destination but Walcher, under pain of excommunication, recalled the monks who had gone there so they would remain in Northumbria and restore the other Bedan monastery of Wearmouth. Under Walcher's protection, according to Symeon, monasticism, destroyed two hundred years earlier by viking incursions, could now flourish again; 'like a loving father' Walcher frequently visited the monks and 'liberally bestowed upon them whatever they required' (Sym. Dur., *Opera*, vol. 1, c. 57). Had he lived, he had plans to introduce a monastic community into his cathedral to act as the guardians of St Cuthbert's shrine and to himself become a monk. At his death, it was the monks of Jarrow who came to fetch his body. The buildings of Jarrow erected during Walcher's episcopacy can be associated stylistically with Lotharingian models and it has been suggested that Walcher may have employed in Northumbria masons from his homeland. There would seem to be no doubt that Walcher's commitment to the cause of monastic reform was both deep and of long standing; this would not, of course, have precluded, but rather strengthened, his appreciation that if Norman power was ever to become acceptable in the north it would only be through the intercession and veneration of local saints and shrines.

Walcher was buried in his cathedral; but under the circumstances it was, to Symeon of Durham, 'a funeral less honourable than became a bishop' (Sym. Dur., *Opera*, vol. 1, c. 59).   HENRIETTA LEYSER

Sources Symeon of Durham, *Opera* • John of Worcester, *Chron.* • *ASC*, s.a. 1080 [text E] • W. E. Kapelle, *The Norman conquest of the north: the region and its transformation, 1000–1135* (1979) • C. J. Morris, *Marriage and murder in eleventh-century Northumbria: a study of De obsessione Dunelmi*, Borthwick Papers, 82 (1992) • V. Ortenberg, *The English church and the continent in the tenth and eleventh centuries* (1992) • D. W. Rollason, M. Harvey, and M. Prestwich, eds., *Anglo-Norman Durham* (1994)

Walcot, Humphrey (1586–1650). *See under* Walcot, Sir Thomas (1629–1685).

Walcot, Sir Thomas (1629–1685), judge and politician, was the second of the three sons of **Humphrey Walcot** (1586–1650) of Walcot, Shropshire, and Anne (*d.* 1675), daughter of Thomas Docwra of Putteridge, Hertfordshire. Humphrey Walcot, presumably the son and heir of Humphrey Walcot (*d.* 1616?), matriculated from Clare College, Cambridge, at Easter 1604. He was receiver of Shropshire in 1625 and high sheriff in 1634. Thomas was born at Walcot on 6 August 1629. He entered Trinity College, Cambridge, on 16 May 1646 and the Middle Temple on 12 November 1647, being called to the bar on 25 November 1653. By that date his father, a distinguished royalist, had died, on 2 June 1650. In 1655 he seems to have come into possession of Bitterley Court, Shropshire, which he made his home. He married, on 10 December 1663, Mary (d. 1695), daughter of Sir Adam Littleton, first baronet, of Stoke St Milborough, Shropshire. They had one child, Thomas, who died as an infant, and the lack of an heir may account for Walcot's decision to sell Bitterley to his elder brother, John, in 1672, on condition that he could retain it as a residence until his death.

Walcot's first important judicial appointment came on 15 February 1662, when he was made attorney-general of Denbighshire and Montgomeryshire. In the same year he became a freeman of Ludlow. In 1671 he became recorder of Bewdley, Worcestershire, a post he held until his death, and on 11 November 1671 he became a bencher of the Middle Temple. In April 1676 Walcot was appointed second justice of the north Wales circuit and a member of the council in the marches of Wales. As a Welsh judgeship did not preclude a Westminster legal practice, he continued to pursue his career as a barrister in London. Walcot was elected to parliament for Ludlow on 23 September 1679. He was created a serjeant-at-law in May 1680, his patrons being his brother-in-law, Sir Thomas Littleton, second baronet, and the lord chief justice of common pleas, Sir Francis North. On 21 November 1681 Walcot was knighted and became chief justice of north Wales, which he retained until his appointment as a judge in king's bench on 22 October 1683. In the interim, on 19 July 1683 he had been granted the king's licence to act as a justice of assize in his native county *non obstante statuto*. The earl of Danby described him as 'much at the devotion' of the duke of York, and he presided over the trials of Thomas Rosewell, Titus Oates, Algernon Sidney, and Sir Thomas Armstrong. Walcot was reappointed to the bench on the accession of James II, but he died in York on 6 September 1685 and was buried on the 8th at Bitterley. Litigation from Armstrong's widow revealed that Walcot had died intestate and insolvent. His widow was buried at Ludlow on 1 December 1695.

STUART HANDLEY

Sources HoP, *Commons, 1660–90*, 3.648–9 · J. R. Burton, *Some collections towards the history of the family of Walcot of Walcot, and afterwards Bitterley Court, Shropshire* (1930), 50–63 · Sainty, *Judges*, 34 · Baker, *Serjeants*, 447, 542 · W. R. Williams, *The history of the great sessions in Wales, 1542–1830* (privately printed, Brecon, 1899), 105–6 · H. A. C. Sturgess, ed., *Register of admissions to the Honourable Society of the Middle Temple, from the fifteenth century to the year 1944*, 1 (1949), 145 · Venn, *Alum. Cant.* [see also Humphrey Walcott] · *The manuscripts of the earl of Buckinghamshire, the earl of Lindsey … and James Round*, HMC, 38 (1895), 439 · J. R. Burton, 'The sequestration papers of Humphrey Walcot', *Transactions of the Shropshire Archaeological and Natural History Society*, 3rd ser., 5 (1905), 303–48, esp. 335–6 · *State trials*, 10.151, 1197 · BL, Add. MS 29743, fols. 60, 67 · *DNB*
Wealth at death see HoP, *Commons, 1660–90*, vol. 3, p. 649

Walcot, William (1874–1943), architect and artist, was born at Lustdorf, near Odessa, Kherson, Russia, on 11 March 1874 os, the elder son of Enoch Shannon (1854–

William Walcot (1874–1943), by John Caswall Smith, pubd 1919

1895), known as Frank Walcot, a travelling merchant, and his wife, Catherine (1853–1940), daughter of Gottlieb Reichert, a Russo-German steppe farmer. Highly cosmopolitan in origins, education, and professional life, Walcot was famed in turn-of-the-century Russia for his buildings and applied arts. In this context Diaghilev described him in 1903 as one of 'the Moscow celebrities'. Through the 1920s and 1930s, in Britain, Europe, and America, he was renowned as an outstanding etcher and then as 'the greatest British architectural draughtsman of the twentieth century' (Stamp). A heavily religious education having left him avowedly pagan in his outlook, he was deeply learned in the culture and architecture of antiquity. His greatest artistic fame and concomitant wealth derived from his etched modern cityscapes and visualizations of daily life in the temples and palaces of ancient Rome and Egypt. Like his watercolours, these were characterized by a superb but often unorthodox technique which gave his subjects extraordinary spontaneity.

Walcot was sent to school in Amiens and Paris in the 1880s. On returning to Odessa at the age of seventeen he was launched on his architectural career by the city architect, Alexander Bernardazzi. He studied under Leonti (Louis) Benois at the Imperial Academy of Fine Arts, St Petersburg, from 1895 to 1897, when he obtained his certificate for practice and moved to Moscow. His principal architectural works there were the elevations of the Hotel

Metropol (1898–1902), and several progressive and original private villas (1899–1902). Closely involved with the artistic circle of the great Russian industrialist and Maecenas, Savva Mamontov, he was also known for architectural ironwork, ceramics, and furniture, and for his energetic contributions to exhibiting and publicizing 'the new architecture'.

Some time during this period Walcot married an Irish governess, Margaret Ann O'Neill (1874–1904). When her life was threatened by consumption the couple went to England, where she died in 1904. He remained there and his artistic talents became his livelihood. The Fine Art Society sent Walcot to Venice and Rome and exhibited the resulting watercolours in 1909. Numerous exhibitions followed in London and Edinburgh, which also included etchings and oils. The London firm H. C. Dickins became his publishers and in 1919 produced a book of his architectural etchings and watercolours.

In the arts and crafts tradition, Walcot continued to work in diverse media. His activities included architectural perspectives, exhibited annually at the Royal Academy from about 1908–1910, the design and illustration of luxury editions of Flaubert (*Salammbô* and *Hérodias*) for Les Éditions d'Art Devambez, Paris, and a major tapestry for Swansea Guildhall.

Always an elegant and gracious figure, Walcot's talents and the current fashion for collecting etchings (notably in the USA) enabled him to live in great affluence and style. He had houses in Oxford and Antibes, and studios in London and Rome that were famed for his hospitality. Apart from an elegant building at 61 St James's Street, London (1933), he did not practise architecture, but his perspectives for others had an animation that was highly sought after. His presentation series of 1913 for Lutyens's New Delhi, for instance, were outstanding for their evocation of the Indian heat and environment.

In 1913 Walcot became a member of the Royal Society of British Artists and in 1916 an associate of the Royal Society of Painter-Etchers and Engravers. He was an associate of the British School at Rome and in 1922 was elected a fellow of the Royal Institute of British Architects. On 5 December 1911 he married Alice Maria Wheelan (c.1877–1963), with whom he had two daughters. From 1926 his partner was Ada Grace (Margot) Chamberlain (1901–1987), with whom he had a further daughter and a son.

During the early part of the Second World War both Walcot's London studios were bombed and he moved with his family to the estate of his friend Frank Brangwyn in Ditchling, Sussex. In 1940 he was awarded a civil-list pension for his services to British art. By then he was working in Patrick Abercrombie's team for the replanning of London, which produced the County of London Plan in 1943. Depressed by the strains of war and fading eyesight, Walcot died after falling from a window at St George's Nursing Home, Hurstpierpoint, on 21 May 1943. He was cremated at Brighton.

CATHERINE COOKE and POLLY WALCOT STEWART

Sources Central State Historical Archive of Russia, St Petersburg · M. C. Salaman, ed., *Architectural water-colours and etchings of W. Walcot* (1919) · private information (2004) [Benjamin Bather, Michael Walcot, Polly Walcot Stewart: genealogical research] · Historico-Architectural Archive of GlavAPU (Chief Architectural and Planning Administration), Moscow · M. C. Salaman, ed., *William Walcot, R.E.* (1927) · T. Lingard, *William Walcot, 1874–1943: artist-architect* (1986) [exhibition catalogue] · P. W. Stewart, 'William Walcot: etcher and architect', *Printmakers' Journal*, no. 11 (Jan 1990), 31–4 · P. Abercrombie, *The County of London Plan, 1943* (1944) · S. Diaghilev, 'Moskovskiia novosti', *Mir Iskusstva*, no. 3 (1903), 8–10 · G. Stamp, *The great perspectivists* (1982), 139 · baptism certificate, English church, Odessa, Russia · m. cert. [Alice Maria Wheelan] · d. cert. · b. cert. [Enoch Shannon (Frank Walcot)] · d. cert. [Catherine Walcot] · b. cert. [Margaret Ann O'Neill] · d. cert. [Ada Grace Chamberlain]

Archives Central State Historical Archive of Russia, St Petersburg, Delo Kantseliarii Imperatorskoi Akademii Khudozhestv, Val'kot, Vil'iam Frantsevich · RIBA | Historico-Architectural Archive of GlavAPU, Moscow · Pushkin Museum of Fine Arts, Moscow · Shchusev State Research Museum of Architecture, Moscow

Likenesses R. Gibbings, woodcut, 1921, repro. in *The Studio*, 84/353 (Aug 1922), 88; priv. coll. · J. C. Smith, photograph, repro. in Salaman, ed., *Architectural water-colours* [*see illus.*] · W. Walcot, self-portrait, dry-point etching, repro. in *Bookman's Journal and Print Collector*, 5/3 (Dec 1921), 77 · photograph, repro. in Stewart, 'William Walcot'

Wealth at death £1877 16s. 8d.: probate, 13 Sept 1943, *CGPLA Eng. & Wales*

Walcott, John (1754–1831), naturalist, was born on 8 August 1754, probably in Cork, where he was baptized, the eldest son of John Walcott and Mary Yeamans. He lived in England with his father between 1756 and 1766. The family owned estates at Croagh, near Limerick, and lived off the rents of these estates, in some style. The elder John Walcott died in 1776 in Bath, leaving evidence of a wide range of bookish interests in both natural history and geology. He had been elected a fellow of the Society of Arts in 1766. His son inherited his scholarly interests and remained in Bath between 1776 and 1783. He was an early disciple of Carolus Linnaeus (1707–1778), and inspired by Linnaeus's death, he published a never completed *Flora Britannica … Taken from Linnaeus's Systema naturae*, in fourteen monthly parts in Bath between 1778 and 1779. His book *Description and Figures of Petrifactions Found in Quarries, Gravel Pits etc Near Bath* followed in 1779. This contained the first illustrations of the commonest fossils to be found around Bath, later known as the cradle of English geology from the work there of William Smith (1769–1839), who was to acknowledge his debt to Walcott. One of the fossils so well illustrated in Walcott's *Description*, showing its internal spiralia, was named *Spiriferina walcotti* by James Sowerby in 1822.

Walcott was twice married. On 21 November 1777 he married Anne Lloyd, who died in 1782. On 15 November 1783 he married Dorothy Mary Lyons (1759–1832). There were children from both marriages.

Bath, during the period that Walcott lived there, was a hive of intellectual activity. In 1779 Walcott, already a member of the Bath Agricultural Society, became a founder member of the first Bath Philosophical Society. He moved to nearby Bathford in 1783, and adopted a highly peripatetic lifestyle, moving round the country renting (often large and impressive) houses to live in. By

1784 he was at West Teignmouth in Devon. Here he planned, and certainly commenced, a work on British fishes, for which he made over one hundred drawings during his stay in Devon in 1784 and 1785. This was never published probably because of the too limited sales of his earlier books. He lived in Chelsea, London, from 1787 to 1788. Here he published his third book, *The figures, description and history of exotic animals, comprised under the classes Amphibia and Pisces of Linnaeus,* in two parts in 1788. His final book, in two volumes, *Synopsis of British Birds,* appeared between 1789 and 1792 when he was based at Greenwich. Here he remained until 1802, although he seems to have taken little further interest in natural history, apart from subscribing to new books. He lived in Bristol between 1803 and 1819, in Southampton in 1819 and 1820, and at Highnam Court, Gloucestershire, from 1821 to 1827. By 1829 he had returned to Bathwick and he died in Great Pulteney Street, Bath, on 5 February 1831.

Walcott had led a very private life. He changed his name to Sympson in 1819 on the death of a cousin, but seems soon to have reverted to using his original name. He was a devoted member of the Countess of Huntingdon's Connexion in Bath and later joined the Wesleyan Methodists. His other devotion, to natural history, is best proved by the forenames given to some of his many children, such as Scopoli, Linnaeus, and Ray.   H. S. TORRENS

Sources G. Godwin, 'Walcott family of Croagh, co. Limerick', *N&Q,* 8th ser., 9 (1896), 383 · H. S. Torrens, 'Geological communication in the Bath area in the last half of the eighteenth century', in L. J. Jordanova and R. Porter, *Images of the earth* (1979), 219–21 · C. E. Jackson, *Bird etchings: the illustrators and their books, 1655–1855* (1985) · B. Henrey, *British botanical and horticultural literature before 1800,* 3 (1975), 132–3, 141 · H. S. Torrens, *Newsletter of the Geological Curators Group,* 1/6 (1976), 291–3 [fate of the Walcott geological collection] · Burke, *Gen. GB* (1879) · A. J. Turner, *Science and music in eighteenth-century Bath* (1977), 93–4
Archives NHM, drawings of fish, butterflies, flowering plants, ferns, mammals, reptiles, crustacea, and other invertebrates | BL, Mackenzie E. C. Walcott collection, Add. MS 29743
Likenesses engraving, repro. in Jackson, *Bird etchings*; priv. coll.

Walcott, Mackenzie Edward Charles (1821–1880), ecclesiologist, born at Walcot, Bath, on 15 December 1821, was the only son of Admiral John Edward Walcott (1790–1868), MP for Christchurch in the four parliaments from 1859 to 1868. His mother was Charlotte Anne (1796–1863), daughter of Colonel John Nelley. Entered at Winchester College in 1837, Walcott matriculated from Exeter College, Oxford, in 1840. He graduated BA in 1844, taking a third class in classics, and proceeded MA in 1847 and BD in 1866. He was ordained deacon in 1844 and priest in 1845. His first curacy was at Enfield, Middlesex (1845–7); he was then curate of St Margaret's, Westminster, from 1847 to 1850, and of St James's, Westminster, from 1850 to 1853. On 20 July 1852 he married Roseanne Elizabeth, second daughter of Major Frederick Brownlow and niece of Lord Lurgan, at St James's Church, Piccadilly. In 1861 he was domestic chaplain to his relative Lord Lyons, and assistant minister of Berkeley Chapel, Mayfair, London, and from 1867 to 1870 he held the post of minister at that chapel. In 1863 he was appointed precentor (with the prebend of

Oving) of Chichester Cathedral, and held that preferment until his death. Always at work on antiquarian and ecclesiological subjects, he was elected FSA on 10 January 1861. He died on 22 December 1880 at 58 Belgrave Road, London, and was buried in Brompton cemetery. He left no children.

Walcott contributed articles on his favourite topics to numerous magazines and to the transactions of the learned societies, and he was one of the oldest contributors to *Notes and Queries.* His works mainly comprised historical accounts and guides to the English cathedrals and other ecclesiastical buildings in the British Isles. His account of *William of Wykeham and his Colleges* (1852) was the first of several works on the early constitutions of ecclesiastical foundations. He contributed to the Revd Henry Thompson's collection *Original Ballads* (1850) and an article entitled 'Cathedral reform' to the Revd Orby Shipley's *Church and the World* (1866). He presented to the British Museum manuscript materials for a history of cathedrals and conventual foundations in England.

W. P. COURTNEY, *rev.* TRIONA ADAMS

Sources Boase, *Mod. Eng. biog.* · *Men of the time* (1875) · *N&Q,* 6th ser., 3 (1881), 20 · P. Barrett, *Barchester: English cathedral life in the nineteenth century* (1993)
Archives BL, collections for history of Chichester Cathedral and annals of Exeter College, Add. MSS 30265–30266 · BL, collections relating to church architecture and history, Add. MSS 24632, 24966, 29534, 29540–29542, 29720–29727, 29741–29743, 31362–31382 · S. Antiquaries, Lond., collection relating to St Albans Abbey
Wealth at death under £25,000: probate, 11 Jan 1881, CGPLA Eng. & Wales

Walcott, Mary (*b.* 1674/5). *See under* Salem witches and their accusers (*act.* 1692).

Walcott, Thomas (*c.*1625–1683), conspirator, was a native of Warwickshire and (according to Roger Boyle, earl of Orrery, who knew him from the 1650s) a relative of Edmund Ludlow. His father became a settler in Ireland, and the memory of 1641 was to burn itself into Walcott's political identity. In 1672 he was to recall to his interrogators, 'how the Irish Papists had in 1641 murdered his father, and turned all his children a-begging, whereof he being one and a spectator, he believed their principles were the same now as then' (*CSP dom.,* 1672–3, 152–3).

Walcott served in Cromwell's army in Ireland in the 1650s, possibly initially in Henry Ingoldsby's regiment of dragoons, certainly as a captain-lieutenant in Edmund Ludlow's regiment of horse, for he acted as Ludlow's agent in obtaining land for troopers' arrears upon its disbandment in 1655. He commanded a troop of horse in the brigade dispatched to England in August 1659, and though he had supported the reinstatement of the Rump Parliament, he was arrested by Daniel Redman, its new commander. General Monck permitted Walcott to return to his family and estate in Ireland, 'supposing (as affaires were) he could doe less hurte there than in England', according to Ludlow's account (Ludlow, 86). Ludlow speaks approvingly of his former officer and possible kinsman in *A Voyce from the Watch Tower*: Captain Walcott was 'an honest and faithfull officer of the Irish brigade, having gained an interest in the officers and souldiers by his sincere deportement and good conduct'; he was 'a faithfull servant of the Comonwealth' (ibid., 85, 177).

By May 1660 Walcott was back in England and on 22 May he appeared at the bar of the House of Commons to accuse the Irish Catholic Sir Edward Fitzharris of having told him in Westminster Hall 'that the Irish were the King's best subjects, and that they would have their lands againe' (Ludlow, 177). Perhaps he had returned to England with Sir John Clotworthy, who had gone over in March to represent the interests of the Irish adventurers and the soldiers settled in Ireland: when Walcott went to the Commons to accuse Fitzharris and a Mr Johnson, he was accompanied by Clotworthy. Indeed, Walcott's information seems to have played its part in the declarations by the Commons two days later that all Irish rebels and papists in England were to depart and that no Irish Catholics were to disturb the possession of any English protestant in Ireland except by due course of law until parliament had decided the future of such properties.

The Restoration brought Walcott incarceration in Dublin Castle on suspicion of having been Charles I's executioner, but he was acquitted. About 1661 he sold his property and went to London, but had returned by early 1663. Following the disclosure of the Dublin plot early that year, Orrery, who had already required him to be bound over in £1000 for his good behaviour, sent him to Dublin for interrogation. In early 1666 Thomas Blood recruited Walcott for the abortive Liverpool plot, allegedly placing him in charge of Clare and Limerick. In November 1672 Walcott was again accused of conspiring to seize Limerick. Reportedly, he intended to acquire weapons from the Netherlands and had a declaration calling for the Long Parliament's return and the abolition of popery, prelacy, and the hearth tax. He was arrested, upon which he vividly described his panic at the thought of a new Irish rising and implied his fear of the king's pro-Catholic intentions, for otherwise, 'If the king would stand neuter, he doubted not but we were able to beat them into the sea' (*CSP dom.*, 1672–3, 153). Walcott was sent to England and confined in the Tower of London on 8 February 1673, notwithstanding his professions of innocence and his assertion that the English monarchy was the best in the world. In May 1673 the earl of Essex, the lord lieutenant, who deemed Walcott 'a great man with the Anabaptist Partie here', thought he would be useful as an informer against dissidents in Ireland, but nothing came of this (BL, Stowe MS 213, fol. 196r). After his release, the date of which is uncertain, Walcott returned to Limerick and his estate in co. Clare, which was now worth approximately £800 per annum.

Walcott returned to England in June 1682 at the invitation of the earl of Shaftesbury, to whom he had been introduced by William, Lord Howard of Escrick. Walcott would later admit that the earl had enlisted him in his proposed insurrection. In October 1682 the barrister Robert West, as he subsequently confessed, learned about Shaftesbury's plans from Walcott, who invited West to draft a manifesto. When Shaftesbury fled to the Netherlands in November 1682 he was accompanied by Walcott and the minister Robert Ferguson. After returning to England in February 1683 Walcott and Ferguson participated in the cabal that included Colonel John Rumsey and the whig attorneys Richard Nelthorpe and Richard Goodenough. This group plotted to assassinate Charles and James at the Rye House, near Hoddesdon, Hertfordshire. According to West, Walcott agreed to lead the party that would attack the royal guards, though Walcott later insisted he had opposed assassination. He admitted attending three or four meetings of the cabal, at which they asserted that their 'liberties and properties as English men … were … violated' (Walcott, 2). After the Rye House scheme collapsed, Walcott participated in meetings to plan a general insurrection.

When the plotters learned that Josiah Keeling had disclosed the conspiracy to the government, eight of them met at Walcott's house on 18 June 1683, but he opted not to flee overseas because he suffered from gout. Walcott, said West, 'comforted himself with a prophetick faith, saying he was perswaded that God would yet deliver the Nation but did not approve of the Instruments who had at present undertaken it' (BL, Add. MS 38847, fol. 119v). Arrested on 8 July, he was the first person tried, probably because he had been involved with both Shaftesbury and West, and had sent a letter to Sir Leoline Jenkins offering a full confession in return for a pardon. Although he had effectively admitted his involvement, he pleaded not guilty when a pardon was not forthcoming. West, Rumsey, Keeling, and Zachary Bourne testified against him. Denouncing their credibility, Walcott insisted that he was guilty only of misprision of treason. Found guilty of treason, he was hanged, drawn, and quartered at Tyburn on 20 July. His son John received permission to bury the body, but the head was affixed to Aldersgate.

Walcott, described as 'a very stout man' in 1672, was depicted as a tall, rather slender man with a dark complexion eleven years later (PRO, SP 63/332/47; SP 29/429/32). Although a Baptist, he once referred to himself as 'being for the Congregational way' (PRO, SP 63/332/47, 53.1). Michael Boyle, archbishop of Dublin, deemed him 'a very considerable person under the usurper [Cromwell] and a by-got in his perswasions' (PRO, SP 63/332/49); in fact, he was a man whose convictions prompted him to risk his estate and ultimately his life to save England and Ireland from the perceived threat posed by James and Catholicism.

RICHARD L. GREAVES

Sources T. Walcott, *A true copy of a paper writen by Capt. Tho. Walcott* (1683) · PRO, SP 29/425–429, 437; 63/332, 333, 335 · BL, Stowe MSS 200, 201, 213 · BL, Lansdowne MS 1152 · BL, Add. MSS 35520; 38847 · [T. Sprat], *Copies of the informations and original papers relating to the proof of the horrid conspiracy against the late king, his present majesty and the government*, 3rd edn (1685) · *State trials*, vol. 9 · R. L. Greaves, *Secrets of the kingdom: British radicals from the Popish Plot to the revolution of 1688–89* (1992) · R. L. Greaves, *Enemies under his feet: radicals and nonconformists in Britain, 1664–1677* (1990) · E. Ludlow, *A voyce from the watch tower*, ed. A. B. Worden, CS, 4th ser., 21 (1978) · *Execution and confession … of Capt. Thomas Walcot …* (1683) · Bodl. Oxf., MS Carte 219 · C. H. Firth and G. Davies, *The regimental history of*

Cromwell's army, 2 vols. (1940) · *JHC*, 8 (1660–67), 41–2, 44 · N. Luttrell, *A brief historical relation of state affairs from September 1678 to April 1714*, 1 (1857), 270
Archives BL, Add. MSS 35520; 38847 · BL, Egerton MS 3327 · BL, Lansdowne MS 1152 · BL, Stowe MSS 200, 201, 213 · Bodl. Oxf., MS Carte 219 · PRO, SP 29/425–429, 437; 63/332, 333, 335 · U. Nott., MS PwV95

Waldby, Robert (*c*.1335–1397), archbishop of York, is generally accepted as having come from Yorkshire. His ordination as priest in 1362 suggests a birth date of the mid-1330s, at the latest. He was related to the preaching friar John Waldby (*d*. 1372), probably as nephew or cousin rather than brother (as has been claimed). Of his early life nothing is known. He took orders, from acolyte to priest, in ordinations in York diocese between March 1361 and March 1362, when he was already an Augustinian friar. His epitaph links him with their house at Tickhill, but the ordination lists assign him to York. He is assumed to have attended the studium at Oxford, and (because he is called 'Tholosanus' in 1382) to have moved on to Toulouse, possibly in accordance with Pope Urban V's instructions to the Augustinian friars in 1365 to send some of their students there. In 1383 he appears as both master of theology and *sacre theologie professor*; his epitaph also suggests legal education, and (unless mistranscribed) that he knew medicine.

Waldby's early administrative career is obscure, but probably focused on Aquitaine and service to Edward, the Black Prince (*d*. 1376). Later, on 1 April 1383, he was named among envoys to Aragon. On 20 August 1389 he was appointed keeper of the seal for the seneschal of Aquitaine, a post he still held in 1390. (The suggestion that he was chancellor of Aquitaine by 1389 seems to be based on a misreading.) This bureaucratic activity was rewarded on 4 June 1386, when Pope Urban VI (*r*. 1378–89) made him bishop of Aire (not Sodor, as sometimes erroneously reported) by provision, his title sometimes being extended to Aire and St Quittière. Gascony had remained loyal to the Roman line of popes in the great schism, while most of France accepted the antipopes of Avignon. Aire was not a wealthy see; from 1388 Waldby supplemented his resources by acquiring the farm of various alien priories, whose endowments had been seized by the crown during the French wars. On 14 November 1390 he was translated to Dublin. He showed no anxiety to visit his new archbishopric, and on 30 October 1391 received royal permission to absent himself from Ireland for life. Although appointed chancellor of Ireland in February 1392 (the nomination being repeated in July), he remained an absentee; indeed, he is several times recorded as attending the king's continual council in the early months of that year. In March 1394 he received further permission to stay in England; but later that year joined Richard II's expedition to Ireland, and he briefly had custody of the Irish great seal in 1395. That year he was again involved in diplomatic activity, among the envoys to Charles VI of France whose negotiations resulted in Richard II's marriage to Isabella of France.

On 3 November 1395 Waldby was again translated, to Chichester. This was presumably to give greater access to Richard II, although Thomas Walsingham suggested additional advantages: the move entailed a drop in status, from archbishop to bishop, but Chichester was worth more than Dublin. Just under twelve months later he was moved once more, being provided on 5 October 1396 to succeed Thomas Arundel, who had been translated to Canterbury, as archbishop of York. The St Albans chroniclers report that his appointment was against the wishes of all the York clergy; but their veracity cannot be tested. A hostile verse does, however, hint at simony. As far as is known, he never visited York. The diocesan government was conducted solely by vicars-general, whose register is the sole survivor of the many Waldby's career must have generated (a register of his York *acta extra diocesim* never returned there). He died on 27 December 1397, probably in London (although the Kirkstall chronicler places his death at Gloucester, of a diseased shin bone), and certainly in financial difficulties. As a mark of royal favour he was accorded burial in Westminster Abbey, in the chapel of St Edmund and St Thomas the Martyr, where his funerary brass still exists.

Waldby was an active academic and campaigner against heresy. Bale ascribes to him several works that reflect his academic and theological careers: four books of lectures on the *Sentences*, a book of *quaestiones ordinariae*, a book of quodlibets, a book of sermons for the year, and (potentially most interesting of all) a volume *Contra Wiclevistas*, with 'alia plura' (Bale). None of these is now known to exist. In 1382 he was among the theologians at the Earthquake Council at Blackfriars which condemned ideas extracted from the works of Wyclif; and in 1392 he participated in the Council of Stamford. In 1391 he and other Irish bishops were given powers to arrest heretical preachers, although this may have been directed against preaching in support of the antipope Clement VII (*r*. 1378–94) rather than doctrinal deviation. His benefaction to support the rebuilding of the chapel of University College, Oxford, was commemorated in a window inscription that survived until a later seventeenth-century rebuilding.

From the late 1380s Waldby's career was tied to his association with Richard II. The epitaph description of him as *medicus* has led to assertions that he was the king's personal physician. This seems unlikely: he clearly had other qualities that recommended him to Richard. Although praised by the historian of the York archbishops, Waldby remains a rather shadowy figure. Confusion with John Waldby has led to exaggeration of his intellectual activity; conversely, the apparent loss of all of his own works makes it extremely difficult to render a complete and accurate assessment of his contribution to church life in the latter part of the fourteenth century.

R. N. SWANSON

Sources *Chancery records* · *CEPR letters*, vols. 3–4 · F. X. Roth, *The English Austin friars, 1249–1538*, 2 vols. (1961–6) · A. Gwynn, *The English Austin friars in the time of Wyclif* (1940) · E. Perroy, *L'Angleterre et le* *grand schisme d'occident* (Paris, 1933) • Reg. 11, Borth. Inst. • [T. Netter], *Fasciculi zizaniorum magistri Johannis Wyclif cum tritico*, ed. W. W. Shirley, Rolls Series, 5 (1858) • J. Raine, ed., *The historians of the church of York and its archbishops*, 2, Rolls Series, 71 (1886) • D. M. Smith, ed., *A calendar of the register of Robert Waldby, archbishop of York*, 1397, 2 (1974) • *The diplomatic correspondence of Richard II*, ed. E. Perroy, CS, 3rd ser., 48 (1933) • J. Taylor, ed., *The Kirkstall Abbey chronicles*, Thoresby Society, 42 (1952) • *Johannis de Trokelowe et Henrici de Blaneforde ... chronica et annales*, ed. H. T. Riley, pt 3 of *Chronica monasterii S. Albani*, Rolls Series, 28 (1866)

Archives Borth. Inst., register 11

Likenesses brass effigy, 1360–1440, Westminster Abbey, London

Wealth at death died in financial difficulty: *CPR*; *Calendar of the fine rolls*

Waldeby [Waldby], **John** (*d.* after **1372**), Augustinian friar and preacher, was probably a relative of two other Augustinian friars of York, Simon Waldby, resident there in 1349, and Robert Waldby, resident in 1361 and later archbishop of York (*d.* 1397). Originating perhaps at Waldeby near Hull, he was at the Lincoln convent when he was ordained acolyte in 1334, and must have read theology at Oxford in the 1340s, becoming doctor of theology before 1354. In the latter years he was licensed to hear confessions in York for two years. At that time too he evidently visited the prior of Tynemouth, Thomas de la Mare, later abbot of St Albans (*d.* 1396), to whom he dedicated a collection of sermons written for the Tynemouth monks. He was first in the delegation of the English province of his order to the general chapter at Perugia in 1354, and vicar of the province in 1359. Some time later, and most likely in 1366, he was prior provincial. He probably died shortly after 1372; the statement in a fifteenth-century manuscript of his homilies on the Pater noster that he died at York in 1393 appears to be without support.

Waldeby was a notable preacher whose collections of homilies enjoyed some currency. His twelve homilies on the apostles' creed were revised, perhaps shortly after 1354, for the monks of Tynemouth at the request of Abbot de la Mare. He also wrote seven on the Pater noster and five on Ave Maria; a collection of Sunday sermons, *Novum opus dominicale*, completed in 1365; and a further collection of sermons for feast days, *Novum opus de sanctis*, which is not extant. A commentary on the Apocalypse was extant about 1426, when it was cited by another preacher, Alexander Carpenter, and four other works were recorded in 1372 in the catalogue of the Austin friars' library at York: *Exhortacio monachi ad parentes suos*, *Tractatus super xii psalmos penitentiales*, *Repertorium*, and *Misericordias domini*. The last may be *De Dei misericordia*, attributed to Richard Rolle. He was also named by its translator as the author of the lost Latin original of *Speculum vitae*, a meditation in English verse by William Nassington (*d.* 1354). Waldeby's sermons are undoubtedly those of a theologian, but he made a conscious effort to simplify their message for the laity, and to play down the importance of learning. Devotion to the Virgin Mary was a central theme in his teaching, together with meditation on the humanity and sufferings of Christ. Through this affective piety, characteristic of the friars, he came to an idea of the contemplative art as a practice open to the laity similar to that of his contemporary Richard Rolle (*d.* 1349), and the latter's successors Walter Hilton (*d.* 1396) and the author of the *Cloud of Unknowing*.

JEREMY CATTO

Sources Sunday homilies, Bodl. Oxf., MS Laud misc. 77 • homilies on the creed, Pater noster and Ave Maria, Bodl. Oxf., MS Laud misc. 296 • 'Speculum vitae', BL, Harley MS 45 • De Dei misericordia', Magd. Oxf., MS lat. 71 • K. W. Humphreys, ed., 'Austin friars: York', *The friars' libraries*, ed. K. W. Humphreys (1990), 11–154 • Bale, *Index*, 261–2 • Tanner, *Bibl. Brit.-Hib.*, 745–6 • A. Gwynn, *The English Austin friars in the time of Wyclif* (1940) • F. X. Roth, *The English Austin friars, 1249–1538*, 2 vols. (1961–6) • M. J. Morrin, *John Waldeby O.S.A.* (1975) • B. Hackett, *William Flete, OSA, and Catherine of Siena*, ed. J. E. Rotelle (1992) • Emden, *Oxf.*, 3.1957–8 • G. R. Owst, *Preaching in medieval England* (1926), 65–6

Archives Bodl. Oxf., MS Laud misc. 296 • Bodl. Oxf., MS Laud misc. 77 | BL, Harley MS 45 • Magd. Oxf., MS lat. 71

Waldef [Waltheof] (*c*.**1095–1159**), abbot of Melrose, was the second son of *Maud, also called Matilda (*d.* 1131) [*see under* David I], eldest daughter of *Waltheof (*d.* 1076), and her first husband, Simon (I) de *Senlis, earl of Northampton and Huntingdon (*d.* 1111×13). Maud's second marriage, to David, earl of Huntingdon, the future *David I, king of Scots, produced one child, *Henry (*d.* 1152). The outlines of Waldef's career are clear, if imprecise. At their father's death, Waldef, his elder brother, Simon (II) de *Senlis, and his sister Matilda were not yet of marriageable age. His mother's second marriage brought Waldef into David's comital and then royal household, together with the much younger Ailred of Rievaulx (*d.* 1167) and Henry, but there were differences: Henry was witnessing charters by the age of six (*c*.1120) and Ailred early achieved household office. Waldef, however, was still simply 'the son of the queen' *c*.1126–1131, and witnessed only once in David's reign. About 1128–1131 Waldef entered the remote Yorkshire house of Augustinian canons at Nostell (founded between 1113 and 1122) to escape, it was said, David's plan to make him a bishop. He quickly achieved minor office there, and then was made prior of Augustinian Kirkham, founded *c*.1122 by Walter Espec. On the death of Archbishop Thurstan of York in 1140, Waldef was the first to be proposed as his successor. Rejected by Stephen because of his relationship to David, Waldef figures prominently among those opposing the election of William Fitzherbert (*d.* 1154). In 1143, however, he abandoned his allies, house, and office to join the Cistercians at Rievaulx. In 1148 he was appointed abbot of Melrose (founded 1136), daughter house of Rievaulx. He died there on 3 August 1159, having refused, it is said, episcopal preferment.

Waldef's burial at Melrose was followed by miracles, a popular cult, demonstrations of incorruption at the opening of his tomb in 1170 and 1206, and a campaign for his canonization. Jocelin of Furness's life (*Acta sanctorum*, Aug, 1) is virtually the only source. It was commissioned by Patrick, tenth abbot of Melrose (1206–7), and completed by 1214. There had been an earlier, lapsed process for canonization, and an earlier, now lost, life by Everard, Waldef's companion at Kirkham and Melrose. Jocelin, who never knew Waldef, used Everard as his principal source to demonstrate the abbot's sanctity: the Bollandists later accepted Waldef's miracles and cult, but rejected his canonization (he has never been officially canonized). Jocelin's apologetic life is inevitably misleading. While Waldef associated with the great figures in the northern regular revival, he cannot be ranked with them. His spirituality was homely and his advancement was the consequence of his connections. The flight to Nostell was a fiction. David had early, strong, and continuing connections with Nostell; he was the associate of Thurstan and of Espec, who founded Kirkham and Rievaulx, and himself founded Melrose. Clearly the partner in Thurstan's policies, David had his own objectives in church and state as well, and Waldef's career is indicative here. So too, perhaps, is that of Ailred, like Waldef sent to Yorkshire, to become another apparently unexpected recruit to an Espec foundation. In life, Waldef was, according to Jocelin, an approachable and familiar spiritual father, but he was also the instrument of his stepfather's ambitions.

DEREK BAKER

Sources Jocelin of Furness, 'Vita sancti Waldeni', *Acta sanctorum: Augustus*, 1 (Antwerp, 1733), 241–77 · *The life of Ailred of Rievaulx by Walter Daniel*, ed. and trans. M. Powicke (1950) · A. C. Lawrie, ed., *Early Scottish charters prior to AD 1153* (1905) · G. W. S. Barrow, ed., *Regesta regum Scottorum*, 1 (1960) · D. Knowles, *The monastic order in England*, 2nd edn (1963) · D. Baker, 'Legend and reality: the case of Waldef of Melrose', *Church, society and politics*, ed. J. Bulloch, SCH, 12 (1975), 59–82 · D. Baker, 'Patronage in the early twelfth century: Walter Espec, Kirkham, and Rievaulx', *Traditio, Krisis, Renovatio aus theologischer Sicht: Festschrift Winfried Zeller*, ed. B. Jaspert and others (Marburg, 1976) · D. Baker, 'San Bernardo e l'elezione di York', *Atti del Convegno di Studi su San Bernardo di Chiaravalle, 1974* (1975) · D. Baker, 'A nursery of saints: St Margaret of Scotland reconsidered', *Medieval women*, ed. D. Baker, SCH, Subsidia, 1 (1978) · G. W. S. Barrow, *The kingdom of the Scots: government, church and society from the eleventh to the fourteenth century* (1973)

Waldegrave. For this title name *see* individual entries under Waldegrave; *see also* Fortescue, Frances Elizabeth Anne Parkinson- [Frances Elizabeth Anne Waldegrave, Countess Waldegrave] (1821–1879).

Waldegrave, Sir Edward (1516/17–1561), courtier and administrator, was the eldest son of John Waldegrave and his wife, Laura (*d.* in or after 1545), daughter of John Rochester, and the grandson of Sir Edward Waldegrave of Bures, Suffolk. His father died in 1543, and two years later he succeeded his grandfather in the family estates. In 1546 he bought the manor of Borley, Essex, which was to become his principal residence. In religion and politics he had strong conservative connections through his marriage (before 1551) to Frances (1518/19–1599), the daughter of Sir Edward Neville of Addington, Kent, who was executed with the Poles and Courtenays in 1539, and through his uncle Sir Robert Rochester, a member of Princess Mary's household. By 1549 Waldegrave had joined his uncle in Mary's household, and by 1551 he had become one of her inner circle of servants. In August of that year, along with Rochester and Sir Francis Englefield, he was summoned before the privy council and ordered to terminate the celebration of mass in Mary's household. When they reported the order to Mary, she refused to obey, sending them back to the council with a letter to

Edward VI. Ordered to go back with a second order, the three men refused to obey and were sent first to the Fleet and then to the Tower. Following an attack of ague and the intercession of his wife, Waldegrave was removed to a house nearby and then his own home until his final release on 24 April 1552. As a member of Mary's household and a landholder in Suffolk he was among those who arranged her successful escape to the safety of Kenninghall and Framlingham during the succession crisis of July 1553. His advice to her during those perilous days was rewarded with a seat on her council, the keepership of the great wardrobe, and a knighthood.

An active member of the council and trusted adviser, Waldegrave allied himself with the conservatives led by Stephen Gardiner, and, perhaps due to his wife's influence, he soon outdid his uncle in opposition to the queen's Spanish match. He argued forcefully against the marriage on the grounds that it would cause a war with France, but was unable to persuade the queen. Once it was clear that Mary could not be moved, most of her councillors, including his uncle, acquiesced, but Waldegrave did not. He continued his support for Edward Courtenay as the queen's consort, and Renard, the Spanish ambassador, reported that he and Sir Edward Hastings had joined the opponents of the marriage to Philip in the Commons. According to rumour, Waldegrave considered leaving the queen's service, and he remained close to Courtenay until Wyatt's rebellion finally ruled him out as a possible husband for Mary. Renard continued to regard him with suspicion, and erroneously suspected that Waldegrave's support for the Catholic restoration and Cardinal Pole's early return to England were all part of a plot to prevent the marriage. Earlier Rochester had advised Renard against offering his nephew a monetary reward from Philip, but after the marriage he accepted a pension of 500 crowns.

Waldegrave attended the council on a regular basis and served on numerous committees and commissions. In 1557 he replaced his uncle as chancellor of the duchies of Cornwall and Lancaster, and in 1558 he served on the council of finance. In her will Mary named him one of her six assistant executors. He also sat in four of Mary's five parliaments, representing Wiltshire in 1553, even though he was not a major property holder in that county, and Somerset, where he was accumulating manors, in both parliaments of 1554. In 1558, after his uncle's death, he was a knight of the shire for Essex. Robert Wingfield dedicated his account of the 1553 succession crisis to Waldegrave, describing him as 'modest' and a man noted for his 'good fellowship' (MacCulloch, 252), but his religious conservatism did not recommend him to Elizabeth I and his career at court ended. He did not accept the religious settlement of 1559, and in April 1561 he and his wife, who had been one of Mary's gentlewomen, were indicted at Brentwood, Essex, on charges of hearing mass and harbouring priests. Waldegrave died in the Tower on 1 September 1561, aged forty-four, and was buried at St Peter ad Vincula, Tower Green, two days later. His widow later erected a monument to him in Borley parish church. A committed opponent of the Elizabethan settlement, in

1565 Frances was questioned after two of their daughters tried to escape to the continent, where no doubt it was intended they should receive a Catholic education. Later Waldegraves persisted in recusancy until the eighteenth century.   ANN WEIKEL

Sources D. MacCulloch, 'The *Vita Mariae Angliae Reginae* of Robert Wingfield of Brantham', *Camden miscellany, XXVIII*, CS, 4th ser., 29 (1984), 181–301 · D. MacCulloch, *Suffolk and the Tudors: politics and religion in an English county, 1500–1600* (1986), 45, 49 · A. I. Doyle, 'Borley and the Waldegraves in the sixteenth century', *Transactions of the Essex Archaeological Society*, new ser., 24 (1951), 17–31 · Burke, *Peerage* (1930) · D. Loades, *Mary Tudor: a life* (1989), 353, 355–6, 379 · D. Loades, *The reign of Mary Tudor: politics, government and religion in England, 1553–58*, 2nd edn (1991), 18, 24, 36–7, 42, 52, 55, 104, 195, 200, 211, 247, 324–5, 388, 392, 401 · W. R. Trimble, *The Catholic laity in Elizabethan England, 1558–1603* (1964), 18–19, 39 · J. G. Nichols, ed., *Narratives of the days of the Reformation*, CS, old ser., 77 (1859), 135–76, 152 · R. Somerville, *History of the duchy of Lancaster, 1265–1603* (1953), 395 · HoP, *Commons, 1509–58*, 3.7, 534–5 · CSP Spain, 1553–8, esp. 1553, 236, 310, 312, 322, 349, 382, 399, 431–2, 443–5, 471 [for opposition to marriage] · APC, 1550–70 · CPR, 1547–58 · DNB · will, PRO, PROB 11/44, sig. 29 · *The diary of Henry Machyn, citizen and merchant-taylor of London, from AD 1550 to AD 1563*, ed. J. G. Nichols, CS, 42 (1848), 266 · P. Morant, *The history and antiquities of the county of Essex*, 1 (1768), 24 · H. Foley, ed., *Records of the English province of the Society of Jesus*, 5 (1879), 382 · BL, Harley MS 897 · PRO, state papers domestic, Elizabeth I, SP 12/16/49 (1–2), 50 (1, 3); SP 12/17/13, 19; SP 12/18/7; SP 12/19/9, 39
Archives PRO, SP 12/16/49 (1–2), 50 (1, 3); SP 12/17/13, 19; SP 12/18/7; SP 12/19/9, 39
Wealth at death see PRO, PROB 11/44, sig. 29

Waldegrave, Frances Elizabeth Anne. *See* Fortescue, Frances Elizabeth Anne Parkinson- (1821–1879).

Waldegrave, George Granville, second Baron Radstock (1786–1857), naval officer, eldest son of William *Waldegrave, first Baron Radstock (1753–1825), and his wife, Cornelia (1762/3–1839), second daughter of David Van Lennep, of the Dutch factory at Smyrna, was born in London on 24 September 1786. In 1794 his name was placed on the books of the *Courageux*, commanded by his father, but he seems to have first gone to sea in 1798 in the *Agincourt*, his father's flagship at Newfoundland. After eight years' service, on 16 February 1807, he was made captain. From 1807 to 1811 he commanded the *Thames* (32 guns), in the Mediterranean, and from 1811 to 1815 the *Volontaire* in the Mediterranean, and afterwards on the north coast of Spain. During these eight years he was almost constantly engaged in attacking the enemy's coasting trade, in destroying coast batteries, or in cutting out and destroying armed vessels. After paying off the *Volontaire* (38 guns), he had no further service. On 4 June 1815 he was made a CB.

Waldegrave married, on 7 August 1823, Esther Caroline (1800–1874), youngest daughter of John Puget of Totteridge, Hertfordshire, a director of the Bank of England; they had one son and two daughters. On 20 August 1825 he succeeded his father as Lord Radstock. From September 1831 to November 1841 he was naval aide-de-camp to the monarch, and on 23 November 1841 was made rear-admiral. He became vice-admiral on 1 July 1851.

During his last forty years Radstock was active in the administration of naval charities, promoted the study of the French wars, and formed a valuable collection of books and pamphlets on naval history. This was presented by his widow, Esther, Lady Radstock, to the library of the Royal United Service Institution. Radstock was a tory, with strongly held views on naval subjects, shown by his commissioning a new biography of Earl Howe, to refute whig aspersions in Edward Brenton's *Naval History of Great Britain*.

Radstock died on 11 May 1857 at 26 Portland Place, London, and was buried in Highgate cemetery. He was succeeded by his son, Granville Augustus William *Waldegrave, third Baron Radstock (1833–1913), lay evangelist and philanthropist, who visited India, 'distributing Bibles among the natives in memory of Queen Victoria' (*Annual Register*, 1913, 122).   J. K. LAUGHTON, *rev.* ANDREW LAMBERT

Sources Royal United Services Institute, London, Radstock Bequest · D. Syrett and R. L. DiNardo, *The commissioned sea officers of the Royal Navy, 1660–1815*, rev. edn, Occasional Publications of the Navy RS, 1 (1994) · O'Byrne, *Naval biog. dict.* · GEC, *Peerage* · GM, 3rd ser., 2 (1857), 731–2 · *Annual Register* (1913), pt 2, p. 122
Archives NMM, logbooks, order books, corresp., and papers · Royal United Services Institution, London | Balliol Oxf., letters to Morier family
Likenesses F. Holl, stipple, pubd 1848 (after G. Richmond), BM, NPG

Waldegrave, Granville Augustus William, third Baron Radstock (1833–1913), philanthropist and evangelist, was born in London on 10 April 1833, only son of George Granville *Waldegrave, second Baron Radstock (1786–1857), and Esther Caroline (1800–1874), daughter of John Puget, a director of the Bank of England of Huguenot descent. Educated at Harrow School (1846–51) and Balliol College, Oxford (1851–4), he served as an army officer towards the close of the Crimean War. On 11 May 1857 he succeeded to the title, and on 16 July 1858 he married Susan (1833–1892), youngest daughter of John Hales Calcraft, MP for Wareham, Dorset, and Lady Caroline Montagu, daughter of the fifth duke of Manchester. They had three sons: Granville, fourth Baron Radstock; John, a barrister, who died of dysentery in 1901 during the Second South African War; and Montagu, fifth baron. They also had five daughters.

After experiencing a religious awakening while recovering from fever in the Crimea, Waldegrave devoted his time and wealth to philanthropic and evangelistic work, even giving up command of the battalion of the West Middlesex volunteers, which he had recruited and trained, in order to free more time.

Though retaining his connections with the Church of England, Radstock did not identify himself exclusively with any specific denomination, describing himself as belonging to 'the Church of England inclusively' (Trotter, 31). After acquiring Mayfield House in Woolston, near Southampton, in 1889 he attended the parish church but also associated with the (Plymouth) Brethren group then meeting at Oswald Lodge, Woolston.

Radstock became involved in the revivalist network that flourished in the 1860s and 1870s, distributing tracts as he rode in Rotten Row, holding meetings in his home in Bryanston Square, London, and preaching at evangelistic meetings around the country. He combined concern for the spiritual welfare of those of his own social class with compassion for the disadvantaged. In 1884 he built Eccleston Hall as a centre for Christian activities in Belgravia, London, frequently preaching there himself. He also established lodging houses and hostels for women and immigrants, and frequently evangelized in London's East End.

Radstock's most spectacular work was done overseas. He visited eleven countries in Europe, India (seven times), and the USA. As a result of meeting members of the Russian nobility in Paris he was invited to Russia in 1874, where he made a national impact. Religious meetings were held in some forty aristocratic homes, including those of princesses Lieven and Gagarin, counts Korff (the lord chamberlain) and Bobrinsky, and the town and country homes of Colonel Pashkov, colonel of the guard. Subsequent visits were made in 1875–6 and 1878. Following Radstock's exclusion from Russia in 1878 the movement he had initiated was led by Pashkov, and became known as Pashkovism. It combined belief in justification by faith with social service to the poor and, as one of the 'Baptist' movements, was to play a part in the human rights movement in Soviet Russia. Similar visits to Finland, Sweden, Denmark, and the Netherlands were less remarkable in their effects.

A Russian writer described him as 'large and tall, an imposing figure. A square head, framed with a crown of wispy blond hair, short, red side-whiskers, a clear and somewhat benevolent look, an almost habitual smile illuminated his face'. Radstock died at the Hôtel d'Jéna, Paris, on 8 December 1913 after a heart attack, and was buried in the churchyard of Weston parish church, Southampton.

HAROLD H. ROWDON

Sources D. Fountain, *Lord Radstock and the Russian awakening* (1988) · E. Heier, *Religious schism in the Russian aristocracy, 1860–1900: Radstockism and Pashkovism* (1970) · Mrs E. Trotter, *Lord Radstock: an interpretation and a record* (1914) · GEC, *Peerage*
Archives U. Birm. L., corresp. with V. A. Pashkov; account of his first visit to St Petersburg
Wealth at death £64,604: probate, 16 Feb 1914, *CGPLA Eng. & Wales*

Waldegrave, Henry, first Baron Waldegrave (1661–1690). *See under* Waldegrave, James, first Earl Waldegrave (1684–1741).

Waldegrave, James, first Earl Waldegrave (1684–1741), diplomatist and politician, was the eldest son of Lady Henrietta Fitzjames (1666/7–1730), the eldest illegitimate daughter of James, duke of York (later King *James II), and Arabella *Churchill, the sister of John Churchill, later first duke of Marlborough. His father was **Henry Waldegrave**, first Baron Waldegrave (1661–1690), a court official, the son of Sir Charles Waldegrave, third baronet (d. 1684), and Helen Englefield. Henry and Henrietta married on 29 November 1683, and in January 1686 Henry was created Baron Waldegrave of Chewton by his father-in-law, James II. A year later he was made comptroller of the royal household. From a staunchly Roman Catholic family, Henry was a zealous supporter of the king. In November 1688 he went as his envoy to France and remained there in

James Waldegrave, first Earl Waldegrave (1684–1741), by Gustaf Lundberg, c.1738–40

exile, still as comptroller, until his death at Châteauvieux, St Germain-en-Laye, aged only twenty-eight, on 24 January 1690. He was survived by his wife, Henrietta, who later married Pierce *Butler, third Viscount Galmoye and Jacobite earl of Newcastle; she died, aged sixty-three, on 3 April 1730.

James, named after his royal grandfather, inherited the barony as a child, and was groomed to follow his father's path. He received a Catholic education in France, in the household of his uncle James *Fitzjames, duke of Berwick, and at the Jesuit college of La Flèche in Anjou. His education was finished by a residence in Florence, at the court of Grand Duke Cosimo III, between 1704 and 1706. In May 1714 James married Mary Webb (1695/6–1719), the second daughter of the nonjuring Jacobite Sir John Webb, bt, of Hatherop in Gloucestershire. In March the following year they had a son, James *Waldegrave, later second Earl Waldegrave, who was followed by two brothers, both born in Ghent and both named John, the first died within a day of his birth. They seemed set to perpetuate a recusant dynasty.

Conversion and early political career Waldegrave, however, broke sharply with this tradition after his young wife died giving birth to a daughter, Henrietta, on 22 January 1719. He was prominent among the Catholic peers and gentry who negotiated to create for patriotic Catholics a *modus vivendi* with the Hanoverian regime. These talks had failed by December 1719, and Waldegrave now chose Hanover and a public career over Catholicism. On 12 February 1722 he declared himself a protestant, swore the oaths of allegiance to the crown, and took his seat in the House of Lords. His abjuration, which scandalized his family and connections, brought him the reward of a bedchamber post in George I's household in June 1723. Lord Townshend, along with Horace and Robert Walpole, seem to have seen Waldegrave as a promising colleague. Genteel, worldly, and pleasure-loving, he also had a great capacity for the intensive bursts of work and correspondence that punctuated a diplomat's life. His French education and intimate Jacobite connections were also potential assets. He remained on intimate terms with his uncle Berwick, a significant figure at the court of Louis XV, for whom even the elder Horace Walpole while at the Paris embassy acquired a 'particular attachment & freindship' (Walpole to Waldegrave, 13 June 1734, os, Waldegrave MSS). Late in August 1725 he was given credentials for a mission of compliment to Louis XV on his marriage. He arrived in Paris in mid-September and left once more a month later, having had, as Horace Walpole briskly said, 'no preparation to make besides a Suit of Cloaths' (Walpole to Newcastle, 4 Sept 1725 NS, Waldegrave MSS). He was assured by Townshend that this employment would be 'an Earnest of further favours to you from his Maty. which I shall be always desirous to promote' (25 Aug 1725, BL, Add. MS 46856, fol. 160v).

A full diplomatic appointment did not follow until May 1727, when Waldegrave was appointed ambassador-extraordinary and plenipotentiary to the emperor, to sign the preliminaries of peace. He was obliged to seize the opportunity and hurry away, leaving his 'private affairs in the greatest confusion', and relying heavily on the help of Townshend (Waldegrave to Townshend, 5 July 1727 NS, Waldegrave MSS). Waldegrave reached Paris on 14 June 1727 NS, with instructions to go no further than Strasbourg until he was assured of a welcome in Vienna. These orders were overtaken by the death of George I on 11 June, when all appointments were plunged into uncertainty. Not only his ministerial friends but also his mother lobbied energetically on Waldegrave's behalf 'at a time when all the world was pushing for themselves or for those they had the most concern for' (Waldegrave to Townshend, 19 Nov 1727 NS, Waldegrave MSS). In the event, although he lost his bedchamber post, in exchange for which he received only a promise of a future governorship of Barbados, Waldegrave was repeatedly assured by Horace Walpole that the new king and queen spoke highly of him. He was directed to remain for the time being at Paris, and began his diplomatic career by acting together with Walpole in the embassy there. He at once began cultivating informants in a way that was to characterize his later tenure of the Paris embassy. It was here that he met Montesquieu, a friend of Berwick and soon a friend and dining companion of his own. In this city of diversion and intrigue, he also earned the dubious tribute of being known as a man of pleasure. In December 1727 he had already taken a formal leave of the French king, but when Walpole was needed in parliament he had Waldegrave placed in charge of affairs in Paris, from 22 January to 17 March 1728. Waldegrave was trusted and valued, and his conduct of the embassy was approved at home, but he was not yet truly established in his diplomatic career. Indeed, his position was highly tentative, George II having agreed to send him to Vienna only if the emperor nominated a minister of equal rank to come to Britain. On Cardinal Fleury's pressing to have Waldegrave sent to Vienna to exchange the ratifications, George II ordered him to go, 'out of regard to the Cardinal, and to facilitate the Conclusion of this Affair'. However, he was to present his full credentials only if an imperial ambassador was named, 'that it may appear you were sent to Vienna for that purpose only, and that His Maty. had not made too great an Advance towards the Emperor' (Newcastle to Waldegrave, 15 Feb 1728, BL, Add. MS 32754, fols. 303–4).

Waldegrave travelled in company with Montesquieu, arriving on 25 April in Vienna, where he was in fact able to present his credentials in form as ambassador. Waldegrave's assurances of the British ministry's support and goodwill for the empire secured the ratification of the preliminary articles of peace with Britain and France, and laid the ground of the better relations secured during the mission of his successor, Thomas Robinson. As throughout his service, Waldegrave's 'prudent and judicious Conduct' was praised by the king, along with his 'Attention & Diligence to give exact Accounts of what passes' (Townshend to Waldegrave, 23 Aug, 18 Oct 1728, Waldegrave MSS). Eager to keep himself in his royal master's eye, he obtained permission to attend the king in Hanover in summer 1729. His success in a strained and distrustful situation was rewarded on 13 September 1729, when he was created Viscount Chewton of Chewton and first Earl Waldegrave. In April 1730, when Townshend resigned from the ministry, Waldegrave was given the prestigious Paris embassy, although the appointment was at first kept secret. Horace Walpole suggested the appointment, acting on a recommendation from Berwick, though Newcastle was not slow to claim a share of the credit. Soon afterwards Waldegrave was given leave to return to England to attend to his family concerns, and Robinson was moved from Paris to take charge of affairs in Vienna. Waldegrave's personal business at home arose from the fact that his mother, Lady Henrietta, died intestate on 3 April 1730 and his grandmother Arabella a few days later. In effect, and despite the fact that he did not actually go back to England after all, this compassionate leave was the end of Waldegrave's Vienna mission, and he went to Paris, arriving on 21 June 1730 NS. Townshend had ordered Waldegrave not to take a formal leave at Vienna, and, in order not to arouse suspicion that he did not intend to return, he had to shoulder the expense of keeping a full 'family' there for some months, even when he had actually taken up his duties at Paris.

Ambassador to Paris In his new post Waldegrave met at first with suspicion and hostility from Cardinal Fleury and, especially, from the *garde des sceaux*, Germain Louis de Chauvelin. His task was to secure a general peace despite bitter European divisions and, if possible, to negotiate a new 'treaty of equilibre' while preventing France from using it to dominate affairs and redistribute territories. Waldegrave's standing with George II was so high at this time that his bedchamber post was restored by the king in October 1730, unsolicited by and even unknown to the Walpoles. Paris was a crucial diplomatic centre for the exiled Stuart court, and from the outset Waldegrave closely followed Jacobite affairs, assiduously cultivating spies and diplomatic analysts such as the 'Sicilian abbés', Caracciolo and Platania. In February 1731 he had the tricky diplomatic task of informing Fleury that Britain had conducted peace negotiations with the emperor without concerting plans with the French. He pleased George II by skilfully mollifying the French cardinal, and by promptly sending his servant to Madrid to contradict false reports, spread by the Spanish minister in Paris, about the British negotiation.

Working urbanely but persistently to build a personal relationship with Fleury and to persuade him of British goodwill, Waldegrave at the same time was forthright in countering the blustering antagonism of Chauvelin. He won the approval of the king for showing 'a Spirit becoming an English Ambassador' (Newcastle to Waldegrave, 9 Dec 1731, BL, Add. MS 32775, fol. 277r). Horace Walpole, however, frequently urged Waldegrave to give a sharper edge to his 'complaisance & good nature'. He deplored 'that *supplesse* wch is so natural to you, and makes you all things to all men, wch is always agreable to those you talk to, but is not always profitable or usefull on all occasions for ye publick interest' (28 March 1734, Waldegrave MSS). The ambassador's suavity and address, though, enabled him to take into his pay the needy and extravagant François Bussy, who had known Waldegrave in Vienna, and who now transcribed Chauvelin's letters. In October 1734 the king authorized Waldegrave to attempt this 'Affair of the greatest Consequence' (Newcastle to Waldegrave, 24 Oct 1734, BL, Add. MS 32786, fol. 59), which could have been seriously embarrassing if Bussy had refused, and divulged the approach. By the following summer, Bussy (code-named 101) was in Waldegrave's pay, and he continued to supply the British ministry with information and diplomatic evaluations until the outbreak of war between the two countries ten years later.

Sir Robert Walpole's refusal to enter the War of the Polish Succession made it hard for any British diplomatist to influence Fleury's successful treaty making and reshaping of power relationships at the end of the conflict, and it was probably only Horace Walpole's customary impatience that led him to blame the French advantage on Waldegrave's 'supple & mild temper' (Walpole to Lord Harrington, 2 Oct 1735 NS, Weston MSS, vol. 2). In October 1736 a great stroke of luck gave Waldegrave direct proof of Chauvelin's Jacobite dealings, when the French minister in error handed him a letter from James Edward Stuart, the Pretender, urging France to take the lead in a pro-Stuart alliance with the emperor. It gave him a lever to use against Chauvelin himself, but also allowed him, without betraying Chauvelin, to confront Fleury about France's encouragement of the Pretender. Queen Caroline praised Waldegrave's 'great Prudence and Discretion' in making

the most effective use of this diplomatic windfall (Newcastle to Waldegrave, 8 Oct 1736, BL, Add. MS 32793, fol. 26). The incident stirred the regency council at home, and Walpole urged that only Britain's inclusion in a general renewal of treaties could scotch Jacobite intrigues overseas and popular disorders at home.

Notwithstanding his success in Paris, Waldegrave complained of the usual tendency of ministers to forget their absent friends. A preferment promised in 1731 for his chaplain and secretary Anthony Thompson had still not materialized six years later, and Waldegrave declared that to neglect Thompson, who had been with him since 1722, looked like a reproach to himself. His discontent was soon soothed with the promise of a Garter. At the French court, his favoured standing was shown when Louis XV invited Waldegrave to a day's hunting and made him a generous present of game, the first instance of such complaisance to a foreign ambassador, and much talked of at court. From February to late April 1738 he was on leave in England, and witnessed the popular agitation over Spanish depredations. While there, in February, he received the blue ribbon of a knight of the Garter.

Waldegrave's well-placed informants continued to bring diplomatic benefits, as when he secured early notice of an intended double marriage alliance between France and Spain, and later detected a new French agent, Silhouette, opening a ciphered correspondence with the British opposition. Waldegrave drew on Walpole directly for the funds that kept open these valuable channels. Bussy, however, became ever greedier, while the quality of his intelligence varied greatly. As the prospect approached of a war with Spain, and perhaps France also, Waldegrave dared not dispense with 101's information, but he registered increasing exasperation with his demands: 'surely' as he put it to the duke of Newcastle on 29 January 1739 NS, 'there is not a more brazen-faced wretch' (BL, Add. MS 32800, fol. 54). He had to place a further spy, Guyot, to check on Bussy's reports. The Franco-Spanish rapprochement and prospect of war strengthened doubts at home about the value of such a very amiable and obliging ambassador at the French court. Horace Walpole senior once again murmured, in a letter to Robert Trevor, that 'his Lordship's credit has, I'm afraid, arisen from nothing else but because his Eminence [Fleury] found him too easy, and tractable' (28 April 1739 NS, *Buckinghamshire MSS*, 28).

Final years Increasingly troubled with asthmatic symptoms, Waldegrave was in any case less able to perform his functions. In the dangerous state of European affairs, Newcastle feared that Waldegrave's disorder was obstructing business more than the ambassador himself realized, and he secretly approached Anthony Thompson to supplement the official dispatches. Thompson confirmed that his superior was indeed very ill, the physicians divided over both causes and cure. In early October 1740 Waldegrave begged leave to return to breathe his native air, and to consult physicians whom he could trust. He complained of experiencing asthma and convulsions on any exertion. He returned to London, leaving Thompson in charge of affairs in Paris, a post which he retained until his recall in 1744 on the eve of war with France. Waldegrave's own diplomatic career was over, and the air of England did not in the event restore his health. In November Waldegrave was in London, gravely ill and dropsical. He took himself to the house he had built in the 1720s at Navestock, Essex, where he died on 11 April 1741 and was buried seven days later.

Waldegrave, with his Catholic, Jacobite, and freemasonry connections, was a risky choice of ambassador to the court of France, and in 1742 one of the articles of Walpole's attempted impeachment charged him with placing a nephew of the Pretender in that post. English suspicions were always likely to revive when events drew attention to his Catholic background, as friends in the ministry reminded him. He found the truth of this in 1732, when he brought his sons over to have them under his eye and complete their education in Paris. He was obliged vigorously to counter rumours, fostered not least by his ambitious secretary of embassy Thomas Pelham, that he intended to bring them up in his old faith. On balance, however, the Hanoverian regime benefited from his relationships in Jacobite circles, and his intimate knowledge of their outlook and beliefs. His courtesy and noble demeanour secured acceptance in the élite world of the French court, and his shrewd judgement and diplomatic skills may be seen in the quality of his ambassadorial letters. Thompson, succeeding him as chargé, had neither the flair of his master nor even the same caution in dealing with the Jacobites. Very soon after Waldegrave left, Thompson conversed freely with one of the Pretender's leading correspondents, giving him a detailed breakdown of the diplomatic analyses of 'those Lord Waldegrave most depended upon' (George Robinson to James Edward Stuart, 14 Nov 1740 NS, Royal Archives, Windsor Castle, Stuart MS 228, 129). By contrast, Waldegrave's own discretion and his judicious and sceptical evaluations of French intentions and the characters of the ministers and diplomats in Paris were of great value to his country, and his correspondence was both thoughtful and professional. He seems never to have wavered in his allegiance to the house of Hanover or in the protestant religious principles that he adopted. No surviving evidence supports the pious Catholic story, preserved at third hand into the following century, that on his deathbed Waldegrave put his hand on the tongue that had abjured his religion and cried: 'This bit of red rag has been my damnation' (G. Oliver, *Collections illustrating the history of the Catholic religion in the counties of Cornwall, Devon, Dorset, Somerset, Wilts, and Gloucester*, 1857, 69–70).

PHILIP WOODFINE

Sources DNB · Countess Waldegrave, 'Waldegrave family history, part 2', 1975 · Waldegrave MSS, Chewton House, Chewton Mendip, Somerset · BL, Add. MSS 43441, 46856, 32750, 32754, 32767, 32768, 32771, 32775, 32786, 32788, 32793, 32795, 32797, 32800, 32801, 32802 · Yale U., Lewis Walpole Library, Weston MS vol. 2 · CUL, Cholmondeley (Houghton) correspondence, 2706 · PRO, SP 78/219, 223, 224 · *The manuscripts of the earl of Buckinghamshire, the earl of Lindsey ... and James Round*, HMC, 38 (1895) · Royal Arch., Stuart papers, 228 · *The memoirs and speeches of James, 2nd Earl Waldegrave, 1742–1763*, ed. J. C. D. Clark (1988) · John, Lord Hervey, *Some materials towards memoirs of the reign of King George II*, ed. R. Sedgwick, 3 vols. (1931) · W. Coxe, *Memoirs of the life and administration of Sir Robert Walpole, earl of Orford*, 3 vols. (1798) · D. B. Horn, ed., *British diplomatic representatives, 1689–1789*, CS, 3rd ser., 46 (1932) · P. Woodfine, *Britannia's glories: the Walpole ministry and the 1739 war with Spain* (1998)

Archives BL, Add. MSS 32687–33085, corresp. · Chewton House, Chewton Mendip, Somerset, corresp. and papers · NRA, priv. coll., corresp. and papers · PRO, SP 78/219, 223, 224 | BL, letters to third earl of Essex, Add. MSS 2732–2803 · BL, corresp. with duke of Newcastle, Benjamin Keene, and others, Add. MSS 32687–33085 · BL, letters to Thomas Robinson, Add. MSS 23780–23803 · CUL, letters to Sir Robert Walpole

Likenesses attrib. A. Soldi, portrait, c.1738, Chewton House, Somerset · G. Lundberg, pastels, c.1738–1740, NPG [see illus.] · miniature, Chewton House, Somerset

Waldegrave, James, second Earl Waldegrave (1715–1763), courtier and politician, was born on 4 March 1715, the eldest of the three sons of James *Waldegrave, second Baron and first Earl Waldegrave (1684–1741), of Navestock, Essex, and his wife, Mary (1695/6–1719), the second daughter of Sir John Webb of Hatherop, Gloucestershire. The name is often spelt Waldgrave or Walgrave, evidence of its pronunciation. The Waldegraves were a Catholic family, with a Jacobite tradition, and the first baron died in exile in 1690 at the Stuart court of St Germain. The second baron, who had a Catholic wife and a Jacobite father-in-law, renounced this religious and political allegiance of his family about 1722, but these antecedents sometimes haunted his son. Conversion to the Church of England opened the path to political advancement. In 1723 the second baron was appointed a lord of the bedchamber, a post he held until his death in 1741, and one that gave him access to the sovereign. The £1000 salary was welcome, for in the reign of George I the combined income of the Waldegrave estates, Navestock and Borley in Essex and Chewton in Somerset, was under £3000. He served as ambassador to Vienna from 1728 to 1730, and then at Paris until 1740. Among his rewards were the titles in 1729 of Earl Waldegrave and Viscount Chewton, the latter being used as a courtesy title by his son James, who left Eton College in 1732 to assist his father in the Paris embassy, soon as his confidential secretary.

James succeeded to his father's titles and estates on 11 April 1741 and took his seat in the Lords thirteen days later. He followed in his father's steps as a courtier, and George II evidently took to the young second earl, appointing him a lord of the bedchamber in 1743. 'It looks as if it was His Majesty's own doing', the duke of Newcastle, accustomed to dispense patronage, informed a disappointed applicant (McCann, 132). Waldegrave held the post until 1752, taking his turn at personal attendance on the sovereign. In parliament he sided with the Pelham ministry, refusing an invitation to join the Leicester House opposition of Frederick, prince of Wales. Waldegrave preferred social life to politics, White's Club to Westminster; however, he combined with his delight in eating and gambling an interest in literature and philosophy, Montesquieu being a favourite author. In the 1750s he had to abandon pleasure for politics, and even wrote memoirs that form a chief historical source for the period; first published in 1821, they reappeared in a scholarly edition of 1988. George II had plans for Waldegrave, and vainly sought to make him ambassador to Paris, like his father, so as to qualify him to be secretary of state. The prime minister, Henry Pelham, and his brother the duke of Newcastle thought him unsuitable for high office. The earl, wrote Pelham in 1751, was:

> as good-natured, worthy and sensible a man as any in the kingdom, but totally surrendered to his pleasure; and I believe that mankind, and no one more so than himself, would be surprised to see him in such an office. (*Memoirs and Speeches*, 49)

The death of the prince of Wales that year enabled the king to do something for Waldegrave, for the duchy of Cornwall reverted to the crown. On 18 April 1751 George II appointed Waldegrave lord warden of the stannaries, a post, worth £450 a year, connected with the tin mines and with much patronage in Cornwall. The next year he was given a far more significant post, governor to the new young prince of Wales. After Lord Harcourt resigned it several others refused before Waldegrave accepted that onerous post, one that brought him membership of the privy council but involved much anxiety and attention. He gave up his comfortable bedchamber place for one of only the same salary. Contrary to some reports he did so willingly. Newcastle was the intermediary because, as Waldegrave noted, 'his Majesty did not chuse to speak to me himself, that I might be at full liberty to either accept or refuse as I liked best' (*Memoirs and Speeches*, 57 n. 179). He was governor of the future George III as the prince grew from fourteen to eighteen. The princess dowager in 1753 had 'a very good opinion of him, that he was very well bred, very complaisant, and attentive, etc., and the children liked him extremely' (*Political Journal of … Dodington*, 202).

Waldegrave's friendly character and enjoyment of royal favour made him an obvious political broker in the crises of the mid-1750s. In 1754 he helped Newcastle to secure the support of Henry Fox for the ministry he formed on Pelham's death. But he was obviously the ministry's man at Leicester House, and he fell out of favour there when the prince's court went into opposition at the end of 1755. A decision had to be made when the prince came of legal age on his eighteenth birthday, 4 June 1756, for the post of prince's governor would then lapse. George II pushed for Waldegrave to be head of the prince's household as his groom of the stole, but the prince wanted his mother's friend Lord Bute. Waldegrave escaped from a difficult situation by securing royal permission to resign from the prince's household: he also gave up his post of lord warden of the stannaries. He was offered and refused an Irish pension, but accepted the reversion of a lucrative tellership of the exchequer, which fell in during February 1757. Waldegrave gained revenge on his foes at Leicester House by fanning current rumours about an illicit relationship between Bute and the princess dowager, a scandal that persisted into the next century, being zealously retailed by Waldegrave's friend Horace Walpole. It was probably resentment at Waldegrave's role in this respect that

caused George III to recall him in 1804 as 'a depraved worthless man' (*Memoirs and Speeches*, 53).

As the confidant of George II, Waldegrave was the intermediary in the prolonged negotiations of 1757 preceding the formation of the Pitt–Newcastle coalition ministry. He was the conduit of correspondence between the king, Newcastle, and Fox. When matters seemed to have reached an impasse, with Newcastle insisting on the inclusion of Pitt, whom George II detested, Waldegrave himself agreed on 8 June to be first lord of the Treasury in a ministry wherein Fox would be the leading figure: since he never formally took up the appointment, however, he cannot be listed among British prime ministers, and the *Dictionary of National Biography* errs in stating he was 'premier' for five days. On 11 June he advised George II to accept Pitt, and he quit politics for social life, being rewarded for his services on 30 June with the Garter. Waldegrave now found time to get married, and Horace Walpole claimed the credit for the match. The bride was Walpole's niece *Maria (bap.* 1736, *d.* 1807) [see under William Henry, Prince], the second illegitimate daughter of Sir Edward Walpole and Dorothy Clements. 'A month ago', Horace wrote on 11 April 1759, 'I was told he liked her—does he?—I jumbled them together, and he has already proposed. For character and credit, he is the first match in England—for beauty, I think she is' (*Letters of Horace Walpole*, 4.254). The marriage took place on 15 May 1759, the bride at twenty-two being half the age of the groom. Three daughters were born, but politics soon obtruded on the domestic bliss at Navestock.

When George II died on 25 October 1760 Waldegrave was one of the few men closely acquainted with the new monarch, and eased his embarrassment at his first privy council by chatting to him. George III evidently did not at this time harbour any grudge against his former governor. Soon the king planned to enlist Waldegrave's support for the peace terms negotiated by the Bute ministry in 1762, and Fox was sent to enquire whether he would attend cabinet if asked. 'The Earl, who had been bred a courtier, who was of too gentle manners for opposition', Horace Walpole wrote, 'desired time to consider.' He consulted the duke of Cumberland, the king's uncle and Bute's enemy, and then 'wrote to Fox to desire the proposal might not be made to him' (Walpole, *Memoirs*, 1.155–6). But he approved the peace terms, and told Cumberland, 'as to opposition in general, I may oppose measures which I think wrong. But I shall never enter into engagements with any factions' (BL, Add. MS 51380, fol. 107). He spoke for the peace on 9 December.

When in March 1763 Bute's decision to resign led to the planning of a new ministry, Waldegrave was again considered for high office. Fox put him forward as 'a man of strict honour, will go through what he engages in without any indiscretion, has great firmness, with great gentleness of manner, is by his friends both respected and beloved, has few enemies, and no view to popularity' (Fitzmaurice, 1.143). But George III dismissed the suggestion, writing that 'he would fairly be but a chip in the porrige' (*Letters … to Lord Bute*, 199). Waldegrave opposed the Bute ministry in the Lords debate of 28 March on the cider tax. Yet the very next day Fox, who had earlier proposed Waldegrave to Bute as lord lieutenant of Ireland, vainly offered him the ambassadorship to Paris. Death then suddenly put an end to all such ideas. On 30 March Waldegrave contracted smallpox, against which he had not been inoculated when young, as 'the eldest son and weakly' (*Letters of Horace Walpole*, 5.303). He died at Albemarle Street, London, on 8 April, to the consternation and dismay of high society, after dedicated nursing by his wife, whose uncle Horace Walpole was astonished 'to see so much beauty sincerely devoted to a man so unlovely in his person' (ibid., 5.297). He was buried in Navestock church. His estate produced only £2300 a year, but out of his tellership income he had saved enough to endow his three daughters with about £8000 each, and they later married well. His widow was married secretly in 1766 to the king's younger brother, the duke of Gloucester, and died on 22 August 1807.

Waldegrave's titles and estates passed to his only surviving brother, **John Waldegrave**, third Earl Waldegrave (1718–1784), army officer and courtier. Born on 28 April 1718 at Ghent, he also left Eton in 1732 for Paris. 'My youngest would never be a scholar', wrote his father (*Memoirs and Speeches*, 30), and so John entered the army in 1735. Like his brother he was a member of White's Club and enjoyed a busy social life. In 1751 'by the intrigues of the Earl of Sandwich', so Horace Walpole wrote, 'Colonel John Waldegrave stole Lord Gower's daughter' (ibid., 41). His bride, against her father's wishes, was Elizabeth Leveson-Gower (1724–1784), the fifth daughter of the first Earl Gower; they had two sons, including William *Waldegrave, first Baron Radstock, and two daughters. This was a valuable political connection, for the duchess of Bedford was his wife's sister. But the Waldegraves were first and foremost courtiers, and John was appointed a groom of the bedchamber in 1747, with a salary of £500, a post he retained, into the reign of George III, until his peerage in 1763. In 1747 he was also appointed aide-de-camp to the duke of Cumberland and brought into the House of Commons for the government borough of Orford. In 1754 he transferred to the Gower borough of Newcastle under Lyme, which he represented until his elevation to the Lords. None of this prevented John Waldegrave enjoying a successful military career: he served in the wars of 1740–48 and 1756–63, rising steadily in rank from ensign in 1735 to major-general in 1757. He was the British hero at the battle of Minden on 1 August 1759, where his success in leading the British infantry against the French cavalry was the crucial factor in the famous victory. His wife boasted to Bedford on 4 August, 'Mr Waldegrave is not only adored by the army, but by all the country' (*Memoirs and Speeches*, 86). His rewards included promotion to lieutenant-general, a colonelcy in the dragoon guards, and in 1760 appointment as governor of Plymouth. Made a full general in 1772, he took offence when in 1770 secretary at war Lord Barrington told the House of Commons that there was no military officer fit to be appointed army commander-in-chief. Waldegrave retired from active service when the end of the Seven Years' War coincided with his peerage. He voted with the Bedford party in the Lords, as against the repeal of the Stamp Act in 1766, but always with government after they returned to office in 1767—apart from the Fox–North coalition. He died on 22 October 1784, suddenly of apoplexy at an inn near Reading, and was buried at Navestock on 30 October.

PETER D. G. THOMAS

Sources *The memoirs and speeches of James, 2nd Earl Waldegrave, 1742–1763*, ed. J. C. D. Clark (1988) · *The correspondence of the dukes of Richmond and Newcastle, 1724–1750*, ed. T. J. McCann, Sussex RS, 73 (1984) · *The political journal of George Bubb Dodington*, ed. J. Carswell and L. A. Dralle (1965) · *The letters of Horace Walpole, fourth earl of Orford*, ed. P. Toynbee, 16 vols. (1903–5) · H. Walpole, *Memoirs of the reign of King George the Third*, ed. G. F. R. Barker, 4 vols. (1894) · *Life of William, earl of Shelburne … with extracts from his papers and correspondence*, ed. E. G. P. Fitzmaurice, 2nd edn, 2 vols. (1912) · *Letters from George III to Lord Bute, 1756–1766*, ed. R. Sedgwick (1939) · J. C. D. Clark, *The dynamics of change: the crisis of the 1750s and English party systems* (1982) · Fortescue, *Brit. army* · J. Brooke, 'Waldegrave, Hon. John', HoP, *Commons, 1754–90* · GEC, *Peerage* · *DNB* · Burke, *Peerage*
Archives Chewton House, Somerset, MSS · NRA, priv. coll., memoirs | BL, corresp. with Lord Holland, Add. MS 51380 · BL, corresp. with duke of Newcastle and others, Add. MSS 32724–32923
Likenesses J. Thomson, stipple, pubd 1821 (after J. Reynolds), NPG · J. Macardell, mezzotint (after J. Reynolds), BM, NPG · J. Reynolds, portrait, priv. coll.; repro. in Clarke, ed., *Memoirs and speeches*
Wealth at death £2300 rental; cash capital *c*.£25,000: *Memoirs and speeches of James Waldegrave*, ed. Clark, 100

Waldegrave, John, third Earl Waldegrave (1718–1784). *See under* Waldegrave, James, second Earl Waldegrave (1715–1763).

Waldegrave, Maria (*bap.* 1736, *d.* 1807). *See* Maria, duchess of Gloucester and Edinburgh, *under* William Henry, Prince, first duke of Gloucester and Edinburgh (1743–1805).

Waldegrave, Sir Richard (*c*.1338–1410), courtier and speaker of the House of Commons, was the son of Sir Richard Waldegrave of Brant Broughton, Lincolnshire, who was knight of the shire for Lincolnshire in 1335, and died late in 1339. A minor at his father's death, the younger Richard Waldegrave eventually succeeded to the Lincolnshire estates and to family lands at Walgrave, Northamptonshire. About 1363 he secured further lands, and entry into Suffolk society, by marrying Joan, widow of Sir Robert Bures, who brought him substantial estates in Suffolk, Essex, and other counties. As a young man Waldegrave served in the household of William and Humphrey (IX) de Bohun, successive earls of Northampton, and during the 1360s he fought in France, Italy, and Prussia under Bohun leadership; in 1365 he was knighted during a campaign against the Turks. His association with the Bohuns led to his forming friendships which would be important in his later political career. Waldegrave first represented Suffolk in the Commons in 1376, and was to sit in parliament on a further eleven occasions between then and 1390. In 1377 he became a knight of the king's household, where Guy, Lord Brian, a former associate of the Bohuns, was the newly appointed chamberlain. During the next fifteen years Waldegrave retained political influence partly through his links to other men who had been connected with the Bohuns, supporters both of Richard II and his opponents.

In June 1381 Waldegrave's life and property came under threat in Suffolk following the outbreak of the peasants' revolt. He may have been targeted due to his appointment to a commission investigating poll tax evasions in that county four months earlier. This experience probably influenced his term as speaker of the Commons after his election to that office in November 1381. On 18 November, when the house was divided over rescinding earlier royal concessions to the rebels, Waldegrave asked to be excused from the speakership. When his request was refused he demanded a repudiation of the Commons' 'charge' for the session, and spoke perceptively of the causes of the rising. Waldegrave's attempted resignation may have been due to a reluctance to voice the Commons' criticisms of the administration; certainly his analysis of the origins of the rising drew attention to the faults of the royal household, and also emphasized the obstruction of justice in the furtherance of their disputes by magnates and gentry.

In the politically turbulent 1380s and 1390s Waldegrave became increasingly closely attached to the court, and he accompanied Richard II on his Scottish campaign of 1385, though he also continued to maintain links with some of the king's opponents. His appointment to the royal council in 1393 marked the high point of his association with Richard II. But the king's actions against his former opponents during the first session of the parliament of 1397–8 led to Waldegrave's distancing himself from the royal cause, and in November 1397 he left the king's council, after obtaining a general pardon and letters of exemption from service in royal office. His departure from the council proved timely; unlike Richard II's more infamous councillors Waldegrave was to retain influence after their master was deposed in 1399, though after 1400 he was less active in government. The contrast between his 1404 confirmation of exemption from office, and the grant of this privilege in 1397, illustrates Waldegrave's altered fortunes, for the later confirmation represented essentially a peaceable and self-imposed withdrawal from government, due to old age. Waldegrave died on 2 May 1410 and was buried later that month in the parish church of Bures St Mary, Suffolk. He was survived by a son.

MAX SATCHELL

Sources HoP, *Commons*

Waldegrave, Robert (c.1554–1603/4), printer, was the son of Richard Waldegrave, yeoman, of Blackley, Worcestershire. He was apprenticed to William Griffith, stationer, of London, for eight years, starting on 24 June 1568, by which date his father was dead. Waldegrave would have gained his freedom by 1576, a year for which the Stationers' Company records have been lost, but the first record of him as a licensee occurs on 17 June 1578, when he was licensed to publish a book of prayers, *The Castle for the Soule*, printed for him by Thomas Dawson in the same year. This first licence was a taste of what was to come during a long career of printing and publishing religious and theological texts.

Waldegrave printed in London for ten years, mostly at premises 'Without Temple Bar in the Strand', near Somerset House, although in 1583 he was briefly located at Foster Lane and in the late 1580s occasionally published at The Crane in St Paul's Churchyard. His device was a swan within an oval medallion. Although printing overtly until 1588, he quickly gained a reputation as a printer of puritan material. Books by dissenting English clergymen, such as Dudley Fenner, Laurence Chaderton, and the leading presbyterian John Field were printed by Waldegrave, as were editions of Luther, Calvin, and Knox. According to later anonymous tracts printed by Waldegrave, he was imprisoned twice in the 1580s in the White Lion prison at Southwark, the longest spell being one of twenty weeks in 1586–7 (a date sometimes confused with autumn 1588 when he was clearly at liberty). In fact there is no supporting evidence for the longer imprisonment, and it must be remembered that Waldegrave had a taste for dramatic propaganda. None the less he was despised and pursued by the episcopacy in England, and Thomas Cooper, bishop of Winchester, described him as 'a notorious disobedient and godelesse person' (Cooper, 41). Clerical influence in Star Chamber secured a decree in February 1588 aimed at ending his press activity. On 16 April the officers of the Stationers' Company entered his premises and confiscated his press and most, though not all, of his type, along with anonymous copies of John Udall's *The State of the Churche of England Laid Open* … (otherwise known as *Diotrephes*), a tract extremely offensive to the bishops. A month later the books were burnt and his printing materials destroyed, but Waldegrave himself retreated underground and avoided arrest.

Even before these events Waldegrave had decided to begin covert printing activity and he received encouragement from the puritan John Penry. In May–June 1588 Waldegrave and Penry took sanctuary at the East Molesey home of Mrs Elizabeth Crane, the widow of Anthony Crane, master of the queen's household, conveniently sited near John Udall's parish in Kingston upon Thames. There Waldegrave printed anonymously some tracts by Penry and Udall and also in October the first mocking pamphlet under the pseudonym Martin *Marprelate, Penry's *Oh Read over D. John Bridges* (known as *The Epistle*). As the officers of the Stationers' Company began searching the area, in November Waldegrave, his family, and materials moved to Northamptonshire and to the home of the puritan supporter Sir Richard Knightley at Fawsley. There Waldegrave disguised himself as Knightley's clerk and printed *The Epitome*. However, to keep ahead of the authorities, at the turn of the year the press was again on the move, this time to the house of another sympathetic patron, John Hales of Coventry. There in March 1589 Waldegrave's last Marprelate tract *Hay any Worke for Cooper* was printed, and it reveals much bitterness at his treatment by the authorities. Then, either out of fear of arrest or because he tired of tactics now disowned by some puritans, Waldegrave abandoned Marprelate activity in spring 1589, leaving it to some lesser printers who would not be so lucky in avoiding authority. Subsequently Waldegrave is known to have arrived in Scotland by the spring of 1590, but the intervening period is something of a mystery. He may have gone briefly to Devon and more likely on to La Rochelle in France, where he may have printed books by Penry and Job Throckmorton. Penry himself reported Waldegrave in La Rochelle in May 1589. The fact that puritan activists at this time tended to leave false trails to protect themselves from arrest makes it difficult to be certain of his movements. None the less the fact that Waldegrave was awarded a printing licence in Edinburgh in March 1590 confirms that he was by then in Scotland.

Long before he arrived in Scotland Waldegrave had direct and indirect contacts with that country. Both Penry and Udall had strong Scottish associations, Penry joining Waldegrave in Scottish exile in 1589. Moreover Waldegrave had earlier printed for the Scottish reformed church, including Knox's confession of faith in 1581. When he came to Scotland he was welcomed as the first printer of the puritan *Booke of the Forme of Common Prayer* (1584–5), a book banned by the English Star Chamber. But Waldegrave impressed James VI as well as the kirk, and on 9 October 1590 he was appointed to the vacant position of king's printer and came under royal protection. Over the next thirteen years, at an undiscovered Edinburgh address, he printed over 100 works, making him the most prolific Scottish printer of the sixteenth century. His 'puritan' output did not cease overnight and he produced two anonymous editions by Penry (1590) and openly printed the works of committed Scottish presbyterians like John Davidson and James Melville. As well as the writings of puritans and presbyterians, Waldegrave published William Welwood's *The Sea-Law of Scotland* (1590), the earliest British book of maritime jurisprudence, John Napier's popular millenarian work *A Plaine Discovery of the Whole Revelation of Saint John* (1593), and much else. His press is best known, however, as the mouthpiece of the major works of King James: his *Poetical Exercises* (1591), *Daemonologie* (1597, reprinted 1600), *The Trew Law* (1598), and *Basilikon doron* (1599, reprinted 1603).

Waldegrave's 'pirated editions', such as Sir Philip Sidney's *Arcadia* (1599), were not pirates in the Scottish market. Nevertheless, these editions were resented by the Stationers' Company, just as his Edinburgh-produced puritan tracts were by the English government. Both types of production were subject to confiscation when they crossed into England. In general Waldegrave introduced a measure of Anglicization to the Scottish press, both in language and manners, such as the greater incidence of printed dedications. He suffered little government interference in Scotland, though King James was angered by some of Davidson's views. None the less, in February 1597 Waldegrave was charged with 'tressonabill imprenting' an act of parliament (Pitcairn, 2.2). He was, indeed, the only Scottish printer to be tried for treason. Waldegrave's

crime was to print, without permission, a version of the so-called Golden Acts of 1592 authorizing presbyterianism, and in a form too embarrassing for the increasingly Erastian regime of 1597. He was found guilty by the high court of justiciary, but the charge was set aside when it was found that a clerk of register had furnished him with the act.

Leaving his wife to continue printing in Edinburgh, in 1603 Waldegrave followed King James to London. This was a return he had hoped for during all his years in Scotland, but it was to be brief. He obtained a licence with the Stationers' Company in June that year, but had died by February 1604. The following month his widow sold certain of his Scottish printing privileges to Thomas Finlason, who also took possession of Waldegrave's printing materials. His office of royal printer, held for life only, reverted to the crown. In spite of generalized information conveyed by the Marprelate pamphlets very little is known in detail about his family. Presumably he married his wife Mary c.1580, as they had six children before they came to Scotland. A seventh child, Robert, was born in Edinburgh in September 1596. No will and testament has survived and his place of burial is unknown.   A. J. MANN

Sources Arber, *Regs. Stationers*, 1.372, 528–9; 2.490; 3.237 · NA Scot., PS.1 (privy seal) 61, 58v; 75, fol. 127 · R. Pitcairn, ed., *Ancient criminal trials in Scotland*, 2, Bannatyne Club, 42 (1833), pt 1, pp. 2–3, 14–17 · R. Dickson and J. P. Edmond, *Annals of Scottish printing from the introduction of the art in 1507 to the beginning of the seventeenth century* (1890), 394–474 · old parish register, Edinburgh, NA Scot., OPR 685.1 · K. S. van Eerde, 'Robert Waldegrave: the printer as agent and link between sixteenth-century England and Scotland', *Renaissance Quarterly*, 34/1 (1981), 40–78 · T. Cooper, 'An admonition to the people of England', *The Marprelate tracts, 1588, 1589*, ed. W. Pierce (1911), 41–3 [1589] · E. Arber, ed., *An introductory sketch to the Martin Marprelate controversy, 1588–1590* (1908) · W. Pierce, *An historical introduction to the Marprelate tracts* (1908) · M. A. Bald, 'The Anglicisation of Scottish printing', *SHR*, 23 (1925–6), 107–15 · F. S. Ferguson, 'Relations between London and Edinburgh printers and stationers—1640', *The Library*, 4th ser., 8 (1927–8), 183–4 · H. G. Aldis and others, *A dictionary of printers and booksellers in England, Scotland and Ireland, and of foreign printers of English books, 1557–1640*, ed. R. B. McKerrow (1910)

Waldegrave, Samuel (1817–1869), bishop of Carlisle, was born at Cardington, Bedfordshire, on 13 September 1817, the second son of William Waldegrave, eighth Earl Waldegrave (1788–1859), and his first wife, Elizabeth (d. 1843), daughter of Samuel *Whitbread. Elizabeth Waldegrave was an evangelical and led her son, at an early age, to faith in Christ. He was educated at Cheam School under Charles Mayo, an evangelical, before entering Balliol College, Oxford, in 1835. His tutor, A. C. Tait, cared for him during a serious illness, becoming a lifelong friend. After obtaining first-class honours in classics and mathematics he graduated BA in 1839 and MA in 1842. He was elected to a fellowship of All Souls College in 1839. He remained in Oxford, and was public examiner in mathematics between 1842 and 1844.

Waldegrave was ordained deacon in 1842 and priest in 1843, serving as curate of the working-class parish of St Ebbe's, Oxford, where, in conjunction with his fellow curates Charles Thomas Baring and Edward Arthur Litton, he promoted the erection of Holy Trinity, which opened as a district church in 1844. In that year he was appointed to the All Souls living of Barford St Martin, Wiltshire. After relinquishing his fellowship he married in 1845 Jane Ann (*d.* 1877), daughter of Francis Pym of The Hasells, Bedfordshire; they had two children. At Barford his views brought him into conflict with the bishop of Salisbury (Walter Kerr Hamilton).

In 1854 Waldegrave delivered the Bampton lectures at Oxford, in which he countered the popularly held premillennialist view of the second coming of Christ (a literal belief in the 1000 years predicted in Revelation 20) with a powerful presentation of the amillennialist (non-literal) position. The eight lectures were published in 1855 as *New Testament millenniarianism, or, The kingdom and coming of Christ as taught by himself and his apostles.* Waldegrave regarded premillennialism as unscriptural, a 'bewitching phantasy' which needed to be refuted.

Palmerston appointed Waldegrave a canon residentiary of Salisbury Cathedral in 1857, and then bishop of Carlisle in 1860. Waldegrave built on the work of his predecessor (H. M. Villiers), and spent much of his time in diocesan administration and securing the position of the evangelical party in his diocese. He appointed evangelicals as archdeacons and attracted a number of evangelicals into the diocese, supporting the patronage work of Alfred Peache. He was the first bishop to ordain men from the London College of Divinity. Waldegrave was particularly vigilant over the selection, examination, and ordination of ordinands, and like Villiers tried to improve the academic quality of the candidates. He was also concerned about the housing and salary of his clergy, a particular problem in a diocese where half of the livings were valued at under £100 a year. The Carlisle Diocesan Church and Parsonage and Benefice Augmentation Society (founded in 1862) raised money from local sources as well as obtaining grants from the ecclesiastical commissioners. His aristocratic connections were used to good effect; Angela Burdett-Coutts, the duke of Westminster, and Waldegrave's stepmother, Sarah, the Countess Waldegrave, gave financial support to church building in the diocese.

Waldegrave and Francis Close were united in their opposition to the English Church Union, an Anglo-Catholic body in Barrow in Furness. Waldegrave erected an evangelical church to counter the union's activities, and in his third charge (1867) made a strong attack upon ritualism. Although not a frequent speaker in the House of Lords, he supported Lord Shaftesbury's efforts to legislate against extreme ritualism and vigorously defended the law of Sunday observance. Waldegrave was a gentle, quiet-spoken, sensitive, devout, and hard-working bishop, held in high regard by his evangelical contemporaries. J. C. Ryle described him as a man 'of rare gifts and graces' (S. Waldegrave, *Christ the True Altar*, 1870, vi).

In December 1868, exhausted, Waldegrave developed a brain tumour. During his prolonged illness the diocese was in the hands of Bishop David Anderson, the vicar of Christ Church, Clifton, Bristol. Waldegrave died at Rose Castle, Carlisle, on 1 October 1869 and was buried in the graveyard of Carlisle Cathedral. A monument was erected to his memory in the cathedral in 1872. He left a son, Samuel Edmund Waldegrave (1856–1907), rector of Oborne, Dorset, and a daughter, Elizabeth Janet (1858–1890), who married Richard Reginald Fawkes, vicar of Spondon, Derbyshire.   A. F. MUNDEN

Sources *The Times* (4 Oct 1869) · *Carlisle Journal* (5 Oct 1869) · E. Peel, *Cheam School from 1645* (1974) · J. S. Reynolds, *The evangelicals at Oxford, 1735–1871: a record of an unchronicled movement*, [2nd edn] (1975) · *DNB*
Archives Cumbria AS · NRA, priv. coll., corresp. and papers | LPL, letters to Lady Burdett-Coutts · LPL, corresp. with Roundell Palmer · LPL, letters to A. C. Tait
Likenesses J. Adams-Acton, monument, 1872, Carlisle Cathedral · J. Cochran, stipple (after photograph by Maull & Fox), NPG · T. Rodger, carte-de-visite, NPG
Wealth at death under £20,000: probate, 19 Nov 1869, *CGPLA Eng. & Wales*

Waldegrave, Sir William (1636?–1701), physician, was perhaps a son of Sir Henry Waldegrave, second baronet (1598–1658), the grandfather of the first Lord Waldegrave; he was apparently closely connected with this branch of the family. He received the degree of doctor of medicine at Padua on 12 March 1659, and was admitted an honorary fellow of the College of Physicians, London, in December 1664. He was created a fellow of the college by the charter of James II in 1686, but does not appear to have been admitted as such at the *comitia majora extraordinaria* of 12 April 1687, which was specially convened for the reception of the charter and the admission of those who were thereby constituted fellows.

In 1689 Waldegrave was one of the seven fellows named by the college to the House of Lords as being 'criminals or reputed criminals' (apparently Jacobites, Cook, 217). He was one of the physicians to Queen Mary of Modena and was hastily summoned, along with Sir Charles Scarburgh, to the queen in 1688, shortly before the birth of the prince of Wales, when she was in danger of miscarrying. Waldegrave was knighted by her bedside on 10 June 1688, shortly after the delivery of James Edward. He accompanied the queen and the prince on their flight to France, being at that time called first physician to the prince. He was a member of the exiled court and was appointed first physician to the king in 1695. He was married to Elizabeth Ronchi (the queen's almoner or confessor was named Giacomo Ronchi), who, in 1698, was described as a lady of the bedchamber to the queen. She was presumably also the Madam Walgrave who was one of her bedchamber women in 1684 and died at St Germain aged fifty in 1706. Waldegrave mentions no children in his will. He was described by Roger North as 'a prodigy of an arch-lutanist' (North, 123). Waldegrave died, aged sixty-five, in the old château at St Germain about June 1701, and was buried on 9 July.   MICHAEL BEVAN

Sources *DNB* · Munk, *Roll* · Burke, *Peerage* (1931) · H. J. Cook, *The decline of the old medical regime in Stuart London* (1986), 217 · C. E. Lart, ed., *The parochial registers of Saint Germain-en-Laye: Jacobite extracts of births, marriages, and deaths*, 2 vols. (1910–12) · Marquise Campana de Cavelli, ed., *Les derniers Stuarts à Saint-Germain en Laye*, 2 vols. (Paris, 1871) · E. Grew and M. S. Grew, *English court in exile: James II at*

St Germain (1911) · R. North, *Memoirs of musick*, ed. E. F. Rimbault (1846) · *LondG* (11 June 1688)

Waldegrave, William, first Baron Radstock (1753–1825), naval officer, was born on 9 July 1753 in Kensington, London, second of the two sons and two daughters of John *Waldegrave, third Earl Waldegrave (1718–1784), general and MP [*see under* Waldegrave, James, second Earl Waldegrave], and his wife, Lady Elizabeth Leveson-Gower (1724–1784), daughter of the first Earl Gower and Evelyn Pierrepoint. On 17 May 1766, after seven years at Eton College (1759–65), he joined the *Jersey* (60 guns), flagship of Commodore Richard Spry, commander-in-chief, Mediterranean. Waldegrave's three years in her were broken by nine months' leave in England. He returned home in the *Dorsetshire* (70 guns) and in August 1769 sailed in the frigate *Quebec* (Captain Francis Reynolds) for the West Indies where he served for three years, including a year in the sloop *Spy* and eight months in the *Montagu* (60 guns), flagship of Rear-Admiral Robert Man; in her he returned home as a lieutenant (promoted 1 August 1772). In January 1773 he joined the *Portland* (50 guns), and sailed again for the West Indies where he transferred to *Princess Amelia* (80 guns), before returning to England in September.

In March 1774 Waldegrave was appointed first lieutenant of the *Medway* (60 guns), Mediterranean flagship of Rear-Admiral Man who promoted him to commander on 23 June 1775 with command of the sloop *Zephyr*. Less than a year later he was promoted captain (30 May 1776) and in August assumed command of the *Rippon* (60 guns). Despite his mother's instruction to Lord Sandwich that her son should not be sent to the East Indies, Waldegrave sailed for that destination in September in the *Rippon*, flagship of the commander-in-chief, Commodore Sir Edward Vernon. After fifteen months Waldegrave's health broke down, obliging him to return home.

Waldegrave commissioned the frigate *Pomona* in September 1778, sailed for the West Indies, and in January 1779 captured the *Cumberland*, a large and troublesome American privateer, and four other prizes before transferring in June to the larger frigate *La Prudente* and returning to England. In July 1780 *La Prudente*, belatedly assisted by the frigate *Licorne*, captured the large French frigate *Capricieuse* after a four-hour battle in the Bay of Biscay, taking over 200 prisoners of war; so shattered was the *Capricieuse* after her gallant resistance that Waldegrave was obliged to burn her. In April 1781 *La Prudente* was at Admiral Darby's relief of Gibraltar—'Waldegrave is a very attentive good officer' (Darby to Sandwich, 20 June 1781, Barnes and Owen, 4.46)—and in December he was at the capture by a squadron under Rear-Admiral Richard Kempenfelt of twenty sail of a French convoy in the Bay of Biscay. In March 1782 Waldegrave transferred to the frigate *Phaeton*, in Howe's fleet which in October again relieved Gibraltar.

Waldegrave paid off the *Phaeton* at the peace in April 1783 and was unemployed until 1790. He travelled widely for his health, and at Smyrna on 28 December 1785 he married Cornelia Jacoba (1762/3–1839), daughter of David Van Lennep, chief of the Dutch factory. They had three sons (two of them became naval officers, including George Granville *Waldegrave, second Baron Radstock) and four daughters. He returned to England in 1786 and commanded the *Majestic* (74 guns) for three weeks during the Spanish armament of 1790.

On the outbreak of war in 1793 Waldegrave commissioned the *Courageux* (74 guns) and sailed to the Mediterranean. After the occupation of Toulon that August Lord Hood sent him home with dispatches, travelling by frigate to Barcelona, overland to Corunna, and by sea to Falmouth. He rejoined the fleet via the Netherlands, Germany, and Italy with orders for Hood. After promotion to rear-admiral on 4 July 1794 he returned home and from May 1795 commanded a small squadron in the channel. On 1 June 1795 he was promoted vice-admiral and in November he returned to the Mediterranean in the *Barfleur* (98 guns) to join the fleet under Sir John Jervis (later earl of St Vincent) whom he did not please: 'Vice-Admiral Waldegrave is so very troublesome to me', Jervis wrote to the first lord, 'that I must request Your Lordship to remove him to some other service' (letter of 29 July 1796, Corbett, 2.43). Nevertheless Waldegrave remained to take part, as third in command, at the battle of Cape St Vincent on St Valentine's day 1797. The second and fourth in command were made baronets, an honour Waldegrave declined, the rank being junior to his own as the son of an earl.

Waldegrave returned to England in April 1797 before embarking for Newfoundland where for the next three years he was governor and commander-in-chief and, according to an early history of the colony, he 'rendered his administration remarkable by his zeal for the public welfare' (Bonnycastle, 1.138–9). On 27 December 1800 Waldegrave was created Baron Radstock in the Irish peerage; he was promoted admiral on 29 April 1802, but had no further employment. On 2 January 1815 he was created GCB. His speedy promotion to flag-rank in twenty-eight years compared with, say, Collingwood (thirty-eight years) illustrates the advantage of influence as an earl's son.

Waldegrave died of apoplexy in Portland Place, London, on 20 August 1825. He was buried on 26 August in Navestock church, Essex, where there is a memorial to him with a portrayal of his gold medal for Cape St Vincent.

Not only the earl of St Vincent found Radstock difficult. Barham when first lord found him 'unreasonable' when seeking an appointment for his son (letter to Lord Collingwood, 12 Dec 1805, *Letters and Papers of … Barham*, 3.348); and one of his officers in the *Barfleur* remarked on his 'very distant manner to the officers of the ship who were not desirous of the day of invitation to his table' (letter of 13 Jan 1803, Farington, *Diary*, 5.1960).   C. H. H. OWEN

Sources *DNB* · captains' letters, PRO, Admiralty documents, ADM 1 · passing certificate, PRO, Admiralty documents, ADM 6/87 · ships' muster books, PRO, Admiralty documents, ADM 36 · captains' logs, PRO, Admiralty documents, ADM 51 · *GM*, 1st ser., 95/2 (1825), 272–5 · *GM*, 2nd ser., 12 (1839) · *Naval Chronicle*, 10 (1803), 265–83 · J. Marshall, *Royal naval biography*, 1 (1823), 56–63 · Farington, *Diary*, vol. 5 · R. H. Bonnycastle, *Newfoundland in 1842*, 2 vols.

(1842) • *Private papers of George, second Earl Spencer*, ed. J. S. Corbett and H. W. Richmond, 2, Navy RS, 48 (1924) • *Letters and papers of Charles, Lord Barham*, ed. J. K. Laughton, 3, Navy RS, 39 (1911) • *The private papers of John, earl of Sandwich*, ed. G. R. Barnes and J. H. Owen, 4, Navy RS, 78 (1938) • Burke, *Peerage* • memorial, Essex, Navestock church • R. A. Austen-Leigh, ed., *The Eton College register, 1753–1790* (1921)

Archives BL, dispatches as agent of the raja of Tanjore, Add. MS 39856 • NMM, corresp. and papers • Yale U., Lewis Walpole Library, account of mission to Tunis | Balliol Oxf., letters to the Morier family • BL, letters to Lord Aberdeen, Add. MS 43229, fols. 190–205 • BL, letters to J. Clare, Egerton MSS 2245–2250, *passim* • BL, Melville MSS, Add. MS 38257 • Hunt. L., letters to Grenville family • NMM, letters to Lord Nelson • NRA, priv. coll., letters to Countess Waldegrave

Likenesses G. Romney, oils, 1781, priv. coll. • J. Northcote, portrait, 1783 • J. Northcote, portrait, 1803 • Ridley, stipple, pubd 1803 (after J. Northcote), NPG • Worthington and Parker, group portrait, line engraving, pubd 1803 (*Commemoration of the 14th February 1797*; after *Naval victories* by R. Smirke), BM, NPG • F. W. Wilkin, watercolour drawing, 1810 • bust, *c.*1818, priv. coll. • G. Hayter, oils, 1820 • T. Landseer, line engraving, pubd 1820 (after G. Hayter), BM, NPG • C. Wilkin, stipple (after F. W. Wilkin), BM, NPG; repro. in *Contemporary portraits* (1810) • engraving (after G. Hayter), NMM • engraving (after F. W. Wilkin), NMM • engraving (after J. Northcote), repro. in *Naval Chronicle*

Wealth at death £80,000: *GM*, 1st ser., 95/2 (1825), 648

Walden [Waleden], **Sir Humphrey** (*d.* **1330/31**), administrator, probably took his name from Walden in Essex. Nothing is known of his parentage. Recorded as a king's clerk on 8 February 1290, he had earlier entered the service of Eleanor of Castile, perhaps in the late 1270s, acting as her bailiff in several counties, and being entrusted with the administration of her lands after her death. He served Edward I, too, primarily as an administrator of estates; in 1295, for instance, he was the keeper of Stogursey Castle and Cannington hundred in Somerset, from 30 January 1302 to 4 February 1303 he had custody of the see of Worcester, while between 8 June 1306 and 26 March 1307 he was custodian of the archbishopric of Canterbury. Following Edward I's second marriage, to Margaret of France, in 1299, he served the latter as he had served Queen Eleanor, being recorded early in 1305 as keeper of the queen's gold and receiver of the farms and issues of her lands. In 1304 he was an assessor of tallage in Cambridgeshire, Huntingdonshire, Hertfordshire, and Essex. Two years later, on 19 October 1306, he was appointed a baron of the exchequer, taking the oath on 7 November following. Walden certainly acted as a baron in the remaining months of Edward I's reign, but equally certainly left that office early in the next reign. There is no evidence that he was disgraced, and his leaving the exchequer should probably be linked to the protection he received on 1 December 1307 to cover an anticipated journey to France with Queen Margaret.

Walden remained in Queen Margaret's service at least until 1314, and he also became the earl of Hereford's steward. Although he was sometimes referred to as a clerk, there is no evidence that he took even minor orders. By 25 March 1310 he had been knighted, and he was appointed to a number of oyer and terminer commissions, most often in Essex. It was probably Margaret's death, on 18 February 1318, that brought Walden back into central government. A household knight in the year 1319–20, his experience as an estate administrator made him increasingly useful to Edward II. On 31 March 1320 he was summoned to attend the king, 'to give his counsel upon certain of the king's affairs, whereof the king believes he can be informed by him' (*CClR, 1318–1323*, 226); less than a month later, on 26 April, Walden was appointed steward of a number of royal estates, for whose revenues he was to account directly to the king's chamber. Four years later, on 8 March 1324, the number of estates was significantly increased, and Walden acquired a colleague. In the meantime he was also involved in the administration of lands forfeited by opponents of Edward II's regime, and was close enough to the king to have heard allegations against supporters of Roger Mortimer in Edward's own presence in 1323. His links with an unpopular government may have had repercussions for Walden, who in July 1322 complained of having been assaulted in both Hertfordshire and Surrey. But they brought him further office, for on 18 June 1324 he was again appointed a baron of the exchequer. His appointment formed part of a scheme for reform of the exchequer involving its division into two departments, northern and southern—Walden worked in the latter. He was active in the exchequer until at least 6 July 1326, but although he was among the justices and exchequer barons summoned to the parliament of January 1327 at which Edward II was deposed, he did not act as a baron thereafter. He did not otherwise suffer from the change of regime, and on 28 March 1330 was appointed a commissioner of oyer and terminer in Essex. He had died by 8 April 1331. Many of his lands, which were concentrated in Essex, were held for life only. There is no evidence that he married; his heir was his nephew, Andrew Walden.

HENRY SUMMERSON

Sources Chancery records • *RotP*, 1.398 • *Registrum Hamonis Hethe, diocesis Roffensis, AD 1319–1352*, ed. C. Johnson, 1, CYS, 48 (1948), 274, 290–91, 303–6 • F. Palgrave, ed., *The parliamentary writs and writs of military summons*, 2 vols. in 4 (1827–34), vol. 2/1, p. 351; vol. 2/2, appx, pp. 244–6 • T. Madox, *The history and antiquities of the exchequer of the kings of England* (1711), 577, 579, 584 • J. C. Parsons, *Eleanor of Castile: queen and society in thirteenth-century England* (1995) • J. C. Davies, *The baronial opposition to Edward II* (1918) • T. F. Tout, *The place of the reign of Edward II in English history: based upon the Ford lectures delivered in the University of Oxford in 1913*, rev. H. Johnstone, 2nd edn (1936) • *VCH Essex*, vol. 4 • *Calendar of the fine rolls*, PRO, 4 (1913), 256 • *CIPM*, 7, no. 340 • *CPR, 1307–13*, 554–5

Wealth at death over £21 3s. 10½d.: *Calendar of the fine rolls*, 256

Walden, Roger (*d.* **1406**), administrator, archbishop of Canterbury, and bishop of London, was from Walden (later Saffron Walden), Essex, and disdained by some contemporaries as of low birth, possibly the son of a butcher. While this may have been the family's trade, they could still have been, and do appear, quite prosperous and of standing.

Family background and early administrative career The Waldens certainly had close associations with St Bartholomew's Priory, Smithfield, where two branches of the family actually had homes within the close and to which the bishop left the manors of Tottenham, Middlesex, and Dedham, Essex, if his brother had no male heirs. Indeed, this brother, John Walden esquire (d. 1417), married Idonea Lovetoft (d. 1425) and had just two daughters. He may have been only a half-brother to the bishop, for Isabelle Walden, who was living with John in 1400, was said to be only stepmother to the bishop. The surname was common around London and Essex: Sir Alexander Walden, for example, had a brother John in 1394–5; it might well be possible to construct an extended pedigree from intensive research. There was a later suggestion that the bishop himself married in early life and even had a son, but there is no contemporary evidence for this, especially not in the bishop's will. Walden did not attend university, and, despite his evident administrative talent, critics such as Thomas Walsingham derided his lack of academic education.

Walden had entered royal service as a clerk before 6 September 1371, when he was presented to the rectory of St Helier, Jersey. He may, therefore, already have been serving in the Channel Islands, although in 1376 he was appointed as attorney in England for Robert Ferrour, who was going to Ireland. On 26 August 1378 he was appointed as attorney in the Channel Islands for various persons staying in England, while on 8 December 1379 he had a writ of protection as he set out for Jersey with Sir Hugh Calveley, warden of the islands. On 15 March 1382 he had custody of the estates of Sir Reginald Carteret on Jersey during the minority of the heir. About 1383–4 he was formally entitled *locum tenens seu deputatus* (deputy warden) of the Channel Islands. On 24 June 1386 he was ordered to secure the king's share from five recently captured Castilian ships, and on 5 May 1387 he paid over £100 for the *St John*, a similar capture.

Promotion in government Given Walden's special favour from Richard II later, caution must be applied to the reasons for his considerable career enhancement which began in 1387. Hitherto lightly endowed, he became archdeacon of Winchester by royal grant on 22 July 1387, and dean of St Martin's-le-Grand on 21 January 1390, enjoying the income without doing the work in both cases. There followed five rectories and six prebends, most held concurrently, in the next seven years. However, he was, as Adam Usk was to grumble later, 'better versed in military matters and the ways of the world than in church affairs or learning' (*Chronicle of Adam of Usk*, 81–3). From 20 March 1387 he was treasurer of Calais, presumably by appointment of the controversial commission appointed in 1386 to supervise the king's affairs; this position he still held on 21 October 1391, resigning before October 1393. He became, besides, captain of the march of Calais from 6 October 1387 to 10 October 1391. He had added the bailiwick of Guînes by 1 February 1390. All in all, he had become a powerful administrator in a key sphere at a very sensitive time, and gained the confidence of both the king and his critics. Being necessarily away from the centre so much probably helped him to avoid faction. He is to be found included in negotiations with France and Flanders throughout.

Walden acted as proctor for Bishop Thomas Brantingham of Exeter in parliament in January 1393, and for the chapter of Exeter in the concurrent convocation (so perhaps too in parliament). This shows he was in England at the time, and possibly even free of his various posts across the channel. He became king's secretary by 16 October 1393, but it has never been established that he held his Calais offices until that time or, indeed, when exactly he did join the king, who had not been allowed a secretary since 1387. Richard II's confidence in him cannot be doubted. Walden went with the king on his expedition to Ireland in 1394, returning with messages to the council in early January 1395. He was nominated by the king for the see of Exeter in that month, but this was in contradiction to a crown nomination already made of the keeper of the privy seal, Edmund Stafford, which the chapter and pope stood by. At least Walden secured Stafford's deanship of York in August (resigning his archdeaconry). The keeping of Portchester Castle, Hampshire, granted to him on 12 May 1395 and jointly with his brother John on 1 February 1397, was profitable as well as responsible work; it was forfeited in September 1399.

On 25 September 1395 Walden became treasurer of the realm, retaining the position until 22 January 1398. In a mild flirtation with ecclesiastical matters, he had joint custody of Beaulieu Abbey from 16 March 1397 to settle disputes in the house, and on 12 April 1397 he, Archbishop Thomas Arundel, and bishops Stafford and Richard Medford (Salisbury) were appointed to hear a dispute between the bishop and cathedral of Norwich, a predictably tortuous business, given the personalities involved, which still engaged him on 1 March 1399. This business was the only sign that he was seen as appropriate to the weightiest matters of the church.

Archbishop of Canterbury On 25 September 1397 Richard II banished Archbishop Arundel from the realm as party to the supposed treason of his brother, the earl of Arundel, and others, both in 1386–8 and recently. By 8 November Boniface IX had agreed to translate Arundel to the schismatic see of St Andrews and provide Walden to Canterbury. On 21 January 1398 Walden received the temporalities, with effect from 25 September previous. He was consecrated on 3 February and enthroned on 24 March. There had been no immediate promotion to Canterbury since 1349. 'Modest, pious and courteous' though he was, 'practical and sensible in his conversation' (*Chronicle of Adam of Usk*, 81), Walden's career had been extremely secular, with almost literally no experience of church matters, and not even a formal academic qualification amid an episcopal bench bristling with doctorates. 'He rose by leaps and bounds, far too hastily in fact' (*Chronicle of Adam of Usk*, 83). It is very hard to see his appointment as a wise one by the king, especially in such controversial circumstances. There is no sign that Richard had tried but failed to entice any more senior figure to fill the office (but nor is there evidence, it should be said, that the pope had any qualms);

presumably Richard was determined to stifle any objections from the English church to his treatment of Arundel or other actions in its direction, but he was being supremely optimistic if he thought Walden could enjoy credibility. The new archbishop was present at Coventry in September 1398, to witness the king's halting of the Mowbray–Bolingbroke duel, and was named as a supervisor of the wills of John of Gaunt, duke of Lancaster (3 February 1399), and of the king himself (16 April).

There was no time to discover how Walden intended to approach his unexpected primacy, although despite the absence of a register it can be discovered from various sources that he spent all the time he could in his diocese. He was arrested in Westminster by the London authorities in August 1399, once they heard of Richard II's capture by Henry Bolingbroke. Arundel, who was with Bolingbroke, had resumed as archbishop *de facto* as soon as they invaded England, and formally from 1 October. Walden's possessions were distrained in Arundel's favour forthwith, the return of stolen goods as it were. Walden himself was placed rather surprisingly in the friendly custody of William Colchester, abbot of Westminster, through whom he apparently became associated with the conspiracy leading to the 'Epiphany plot' in 1400. He was committed to the Tower of London on 10 January and put on trial shortly after the 28th; he pleaded privilege as a consecrated bishop, but this was denied and apparently he was found guilty on 4 February. However, he was then freed immediately and even acquitted by the crown, being granted full restitution of his property as early as 23 February. On 12 July 1400 the king even granted him two tuns of Gascony wine a year. He probably took up residence in London.

It can only be supposed that, although he had made an improbable archbishop, Walden's previous administrative career had been an honest and respected one, that his elevation to Canterbury was seen as an involuntary submission to Richard's determined mood in 1397, that he personally had not been an intimate or political crony of the disgraced king, and that it was his misfortune, not fault, if even his gaoler fell under suspicion of treason. Certainly, Archbishop Arundel bore him no ill will, as indeed he may generally have been instrumental in the forgiving attitude of the dynasty to those several bishops embarrassingly close to the late king who would by recent practice have suffered seriously for it.

Bishop of London Walden's last episode, however, is the most curious. He was apparently the king's choice for the see of Rochester in 1404, as too of Arundel once the archbishop's first-choice candidate had declined his election. However, Boniface IX translated Richard Young, replacing him at Bangor with an adherent of Owain Glyn Dŵr. Unsurprisingly, the king blocked this. Then Bishop Robert Braybrooke of London died on 28 August 1404. Arundel certainly urged the king to promote Robert Hallum, his own principal officer, claiming later (not very convincingly) that he was unaware that Henry IV wanted to make a nomination. Of course he did, and Thomas Langley, his keeper of the privy seal, soon to become chancellor, was

elected on 10 October 1404. Yet on 10 December Walden was provided by the new pope, Innocent VII. This infuriated the king, who came to listen to stories that Arundel and Hallum had swung behind Walden in curial machinations to frustrate Langley. Hallum himself had to go to Rome to have the pope declare their innocence. Things hung fire for six months. Then everything changed on 8 June 1405. The king executed Archbishop Richard Scrope of York as a traitor in arms. Arundel was appalled by the canonical consequences of the king's deed, which had been perpetrated in open contradiction of his own urgent advice. Henry was defiant, not only defending himself but wanting Langley to have York. However, he realized that all possible had to be done to minimize the pope's reaction to the execution. On 24 June Walden was allowed to have London. He made his profession to the archbishop five days later, and was enthroned the next day.

Thereafter, Walden took with interest to this, his native diocese. Indeed, he even had the energy to be at Worcester with the king in October, probably helping to receive (or perhaps deliver) clerical and lay subsidies. It was sudden sickness, not old age, that obliged him to make his will at Much Hadham, Hertfordshire, on 31 December. He died on either 9 or, more probably, 11 January 1406. John Prophete described in a private letter his lying-out in St Bartholomew's and the procession to All Saints' Chapel in St Paul's Cathedral for the interment on 14 January and, having himself uncovered the bishop's face, how much better he looked than in life. He added that Walden, whom he had known well for over twenty years, had never bemoaned his bad times or gorged in his good ones. Arundel added his own tribute to Walden's honesty of life and his thought for his priestly duties. Even Usk was to agree that he had been a pleasant and popular participant in public life. This perhaps is the key to what might otherwise, from just official records, seem a characterless and partisan career. R. G. DAVIES

Sources R. G. Davies, 'The episcopate in England and Wales, 1375–1443', PhD diss., University of Manchester, 1974, 3.ccc–ccciii • E. A. Webb, *The records of St Bartholomew's Priory and of the church and parish of St Bartholomew the Great, West Smithfield*, 1 (1921), 186–94 • register for London, GL, MS 9531/4, fols. 4v–20v • register of Thomas Arundel, LPL, vol. 1, fols. 227–8 [will] • *The chronicle of Adam Usk, 1377–1421*, ed. and trans. C. Given-Wilson, OMT (1997) • BL, Harley MSS, MS 431 [John Prophete's letter-book], fol. 97v • J. B. Sheppard, ed., *Literae Cantuarienses: the letter books of the monastery of Christ Church, Canterbury*, 3, Rolls Series, 85 (1889), 98–9
Archives GL, MS 9531/4, fols. 4v–20v

Walderne [Waldron], **Richard** (*bap.* 1616, *d.* 1689), merchant and politician in America, was born in Alcester, Warwickshire, son of William Walderne (*bap.* 1577, *d.* 1636) and Catherine Raven, and baptized on 6 January 1616. Around 1638, as a married man in his early twenties, he migrated with his wife to Boston, having made a preliminary visit to New England in 1635. His wife's name is unknown.

Walderne's interests came to focus very quickly on the rich timber resources of New Hampshire. By 1640 he was living in Dover, where he soon became a leading landowner and one of the most influential men in the community. By the 1660s, having served frequently as a selectman of Dover and as a deputy to the Massachusetts general court and having expanded his commercial interests and contacts, he was probably the richest man in the region of the Piscataqua River, which had come under the jurisdiction of Massachusetts in 1641. About 1663, having been widowed the previous year, he married Anne Scammon, who died in 1685. With her and with his first wife, he had at least ten children.

During King Philip's War (1675–6) Walderne commanded all the Massachusetts militia north of the Merrimack River, retaining the rank of major and command of New Hampshire forces even after the separation of New Hampshire from Massachusetts in 1679. When the crown decreed that New Hampshire should be a distinct province, he was a member of the first province council, and after the death of President John Cutt in April 1681, he served briefly as acting president of the province until January 1682. His most conspicuous political role after that was as leader of the opposition to the hereditary claims of Robert Mason, heir to the first proprietor of New Hampshire, which if successful would have deprived Walderne and his fellow great landowners of their own principal source of wealth.

Walderne's life ended abruptly in Dover, New Hampshire, during the night of 27/28 June 1689 near the beginning of King William's War, when he was tortured to death by American Indians in revenge for an act of betrayal during a supposedly friendly 'field day', or mock battle, back in 1676. He was buried in Dover.

CHARLES E. CLARK

Sources J. Belknap, *The history of New-Hampshire*, 3 vols. (1784–92) · J. Savage, *A genealogical dictionary of the first settlers of New England*, 4 vols. (1860–62), vol. 4 · D. E. van Deventer, *The emergence of provincial New Hampshire* (1976) · J. R. Daniell, *Colonial New Hampshire: a history* (1981) · A. H. Quint, 'Genealogical items relating to the early settlers of Dover, NH', *New England Historical and Genealogical Register*, 9 (1855), 55–8 · *CSP col.*, vols. 5, 10–11, 13 · C. E. Clark, 'Walderne, Richard', *ANB* · H. G. Somerby, 'Pedigree of Waldron', *New England Historical and Genealogical Register*, 8 (1854), 78 · private information (2004) [R. Whitehouse]

Waldhere [Wealdhere] (*fl.* 694–704/5), bishop of the East Saxons, often (later) called bishop of London, must have been appointed between 688, when Bishop Earconwald, named as an adviser in the law code of Ine (688–726), was still in office, and 694. In that year, Bede relates, Waldhere gave the religious habit to Sebbi, king of the East Saxons, who brought to him a large sum of money for the poor and, later in the same year, asked that Waldhere be one of only three people present at his deathbed.

Surviving extracts from later copies of apparently genuine charters show that grantors to Waldhere included Æthelred, king of the Mercians (675–704) and Offa, who was among the kings of the East Saxons at some time after Sebbi. Some doubt hangs over another of these grants, authorized by Cenred, king of the Mercians, and dated 701—Cenred did not succeed until 704. The only grant to Waldhere for which there is a full text, made in 704 by

Swæfred, king of the East Saxons, and one Pæogthath, is known only from a document whose artificial hand, of uncertain date, raises doubts about its authenticity.

In 704 or 705 Waldhere wrote a letter to Berhtwald, archbishop of Canterbury, which is both the earliest letter on parchment to survive in the original anywhere in Europe and the earliest closely datable example of the script known as insular minuscule. The tie which originally closed it, indicated by a gap between two words in the address on the dorse, was no guarantee that no one would open it. When Waldhere explained to Berhtwald that he was communicating in writing to preserve confidentiality, he must have expected that his messenger would be unable to read the letter—an indication, perhaps, of the exclusivity of Latin at the time. The same desire for secrecy meant that he could not have employed a scribe: the letter is therefore in Waldhere's own hand. The bishop could write well, the high standard of his Latin probably owing much to the influence of continental figures like Berhtwald's predecessor, Archbishop Theodore (d. 690).

The letter sought Berhtwald's advice on a critical problem for Waldhere: he had been called upon to help resolve apparently long-running disputes between the king of the West Saxons (Ine, not named here) and the rulers of the East Saxons (also not named, probably Sigeheard and Swæfred); but a synod in the previous year had forbidden the bishops to communicate with the West Saxons while the latter failed to carry out Berhtwald's decree on the consecration of bishops. While the letter implies that the West Saxons had been the aggressors, it is significant that both parties were trying to settle their disputes by negotiation. Although the precise points at issue between the East and West Saxon rulers are obscure, this evidence for negotiation between them corrects the emphasis of other sources which devote themselves entirely to the East Saxons' relations with the powerful Mercian kings. The letter reveals the high status of bishops in secular politics and their role as acceptable mediators: both parties had agreed to assemble at a meeting at Brentford on 15 October and had promised to observe the conditions of the pact agreed between Waldhere and the bishop of the West Saxons.

But most striking is Waldhere's deference to his metropolitan, Berhtwald, whom he addressed as 'ruling the government of all Britain' (*totius Brettaniae gubernacula regenti*; Birch, no. 115, p. 169; *English Historical Documents*, 1.729), a valuable confirmation of the pre-eminence which the see at Canterbury had attained by this time. Waldhere had not attended a meeting called by Cenred of Mercia about the reconciliation of a certain Ælfthryth because he had not known the archbishop's views on the matter. He told Berhtwald that he wished to 'remain ever of the same opinion as you'. Waldhere was clearly anxious to abide by the decree of the archbishop on the consecration of West Saxon bishops—probably a reference to the division of the West Saxon diocese. Since the letter envisages only one West Saxon bishop, the enactment of this division in 705 following the death of Bishop Hædde provides its *terminus ante quem*. It is also the last reference to Waldhere.

The probably genuine witness list to an otherwise spurious charter indicates that his successor, Ingwald, was in place by 716.
MARIOS COSTAMBEYS

Sources P. Chaplais, 'The letter from Bishop Wealdhere of London to Archbishop Brihtwold of Canterbury: the earliest original "letter close" extant in the west', *Essays in medieval diplomacy and administration* (1981), 3–23 · A. Bruckner and R. Marichal, eds., *Chartae Latinae antiquiores: facsimile edition of the Latin charters prior to the ninth century*, pt 3: *British Museum, London* (Olten, 1963), 188 · Bede, *Hist. eccl.*, 4.11 · *AS chart.*, S 65, 1783, 1784, 1785 · *English historical documents*, 1, ed. D. Whitelock (1955) · W. de G. Birch, ed., *Cartularium Saxonicum*, 4 vols. (1885–99) · C. Cubitt, *Anglo-Saxon church councils, c.650–c.850* (1995)

Waldie, Charlotte Ann. *See* Eaton, Charlotte Anne (1788–1859).

Waldman, Ronald Hartley (1914–1978), television executive, was born at 32 Gore Road, South Hackney, London, on 13 May 1914, the second of three sons of Michael Ernest Waldman, chief clerk with a firm of wholesale merchants supplying mineral water, and his wife, Bloema Greenberg. Born into a Jewish family, he grew up in London. Waldman was educated at Owen's School and Pembroke College, Oxford, where he graduated BA in history and was a member of the Oxford University Dramatic Society.

Waldman learned his craft as an actor and a producer with the Brighton Repertory Company and he wrote and composed theatrical reviews. He joined the BBC in 1938 as a variety producer and under the tutelage of Harry S. Pepper he became skilled in the creation of such radio programmes as *Monday Night at Seven* (later *Monday Night at Eight*). His voice became familiar through 'Puzzle corner', a popular part of the programme. His career was interrupted by the Second World War: he served in the RAF and produced variety shows for the armed services. He returned to BBC radio in 1945 and moved to BBC television in 1950. On 23 February 1953 Waldman married an actress, Lana (1930/31–1998), daughter of Sydney Morris, a skirt manufacturer. They had a son.

Waldman joined in the BBC television pioneering days at Alexandra Palace when television was the junior partner to radio. By the time competition arrived on 22 September 1955 in the shape of ITV, Waldman, now head of light entertainment, was responsible for 450 programmes a year. There were variety programmes like *Café Continental*, *This is Show Business* with Vic Oliver (Sir Winston Churchill's son-in-law), and *Face the Music* with Henry Hall. Comedy programmes starred Arthur Askey, Benny Hill, Frankie Howerd, Norman Wisdom, and Terry-Thomas. Panel programmes made household names of Gilbert Harding, Barbara Kelly, and Eamonn Andrews.

Within the television service light entertainment was not as highly regarded as drama and current affairs; but as Waldman welded his producers into a firmer unit, more programmes became successful, some outstandingly so. His visits to the United States taught him that the foundation of good programmes was to build series. He recruited the best comedy writers like Frank Muir and Denis Norden, who wrote *Whacko* for Jimmy Edwards, and he

ensured that *Hancock's Half Hour*, starring Tony Hancock and written by Ray Galton and Alan Simpson, was transferred triumphantly from radio to television. His support for the writers ensured that they stayed loyal to the BBC.

Among other successful programmes launched during Waldman's time were such landmarks in the television schedule as *The Billy Cotton Band Show*, *Dixon of Dock Green* with Jack Warner, and *This is your Life*. After the twenty-first anniversary of BBC television in November 1957, Waldman summed up his role: 'This is Our Life … to entertain 95 per cent of the people 95 per cent of the time' (Briggs, 4.139).

After more than seven years of leading light entertainment Waldman was appointed in 1958 to a new post dealing with buying, making, and selling telefilms. His energy and vitality, coupled with a shrewd business sense, led to a growing role for the BBC as an exporter of programmes. Waldman was well regarded as a BBC ambassador: he was a man of medium height, a warm smile, and always well dressed. He was promoted to general manager, TV Enterprises, in 1961 and was congratulated by the director-general, Hugh Carleton Greene, for his tenacity and cheerfulness in a pioneering task.

Waldman made his final career switch in 1963 when he was asked to head the British Commonwealth International Newsfilm Agency (BCINA). This was a BBC venture which brought together like-minded public service broadcasters from Australia, Canada, and New Zealand (and in addition the Rank Organization) to create a company which would bring about the fast flow of film (later videotapes) covering news events around the world. After an uncertain start BCINA became VisNews, and when the world-wide news agency Reuters joined, success followed. Waldman was a hands-on managing director and when he retired, aged sixty, in 1974, he had laid the foundations of a major international company that was to become Reuters Television.

Waldman died from cancer, aged sixty-three, at his home, 60 Wolsey Road, Moor Park, Rickmansworth, Hertfordshire, on 10 March 1978. He was survived by his wife and son, Simon (who also worked for BBC television, in the news department).
PAUL FOX

Sources A. Briggs, *The history of broadcasting in the United Kingdom*, 4 vols. (1961–79) · private information (2004) [Simon Waldman, son] · b. cert. · m. cert. · d. cert. · *The Times* (11 March 1978)
Archives BBC WAC | FILM BFI NFTVA, performance footage | SOUND BL NSA, performance recording · IWM SA, performance recording
Wealth at death £74,183: probate, 22 June 1978, *CGPLA Eng. & Wales*

Waldock, Sir (Claud) Humphrey Meredith (1904–1981), jurist and international lawyer, was born on 13 August 1904 in Colombo, Ceylon, the fourth son in the family of four sons and one daughter of Frederic William Waldock, tea planter, and his wife, Lizzie Kyd Souter. He was educated at Uppingham School and at Brasenose College, Oxford, where he represented the university at hockey and played cricket for his college. He obtained second classes in classical honour moderations (1925), jurisprudence (1927), and in the degree of BCL (1928). His professional career began modestly, and there is a measure of uncertainty in the beginnings. He was called to the bar by Gray's Inn in 1928, and practised for a while on the midland circuit. However, in 1930 election to a tutorial fellowship at Brasenose drew him away from practice.

The Second World War not only interrupted his academic career but helped to point Waldock away from his interest in land law and equity and towards public international law. In the war years he joined a branch of the Admiralty called military branch I, of which he became the head, attaining the grade of principal assistant secretary in 1944. The work involved the Royal Navy's foreign relations at a time when relations with neutrals and the war at sea generated difficult issues during the critical early phases of the war, issues which were of concern at the highest level of government.

Although Waldock left his duties at the Admiralty in 1945, the experience had marked him out as a man to be relied upon when the stakes were high, and in 1946 he became the United Kingdom member of the commission of experts for the investigation of the Italo-Yugoslav boundary, at a time when the Trieste question was very prominent.

By 1947 the pattern for the future was established. In that year Waldock was elected to the Chichele chair of public international law at Oxford, and combined his university duties with a specialist practice at the bar. He appeared as counsel in leading cases before the International Court of Justice, and provided expert advice to his own and numerous other governments. In 1951 he accompanied the United Nations secretary-general, Dag Hammarskjöld, on a difficult mission to China at a critical point in the Korean War.

Waldock's contribution to books about his subject was modest but by no means insignificant. In 1963 he produced an edition of *The Law of Nations* by J. L. Brierly. He also wrote a remarkable 'general course' at the Hague Academy of International Law (*Recueil des cours*, 1962). The latter evidenced his exceptional ability to apply the positivist method to the world of post-colonial diversity and his readiness to assess new trends in state practice objectively. His legal method was always empirical and, though he was not blind to its influence, he did not favour theory.

In the last twenty years of his life Waldock's particular qualities, including his capacity to influence his colleagues, and penchant for hard work carefully done, produced a career which combined personal success with a conspicuous fruitfulness for the practice of the rule of law. The great contributions were to be in the codification of the law and in the field of international adjudication.

Waldock's contribution to codification resulted from his role, in the international law commission, as special rapporteur on the law of treaties, and, subsequently, as expert consultant at the United Nations conference on the law of treaties held at Vienna in 1968 and 1969. His role in the field of adjudication began with his membership of

the European Commission of Human Rights (1954–61) at a pioneer stage of its activity, and he was president for six years. In 1966 he was elected a judge of the European Court of Human Rights and became president in 1971. In 1973 Waldock laid down his practice and his various offices, not without reluctance, on his election to the International Court of Justice. To no one's surprise, he became president of the court in 1979; he died in office. As a judge he was recognized for what he was, a model of integrity and careful work, attracting the considerable respect of his colleagues.

Apart from Waldock's role in the drafting committees of the International Court, and the publications noted earlier, his principal published work comprises his six reports on the law of treaties prepared for the international law commission, which remain as a major source of the law of treaties. This aside, his other major contribution to the law of nations was institutional and exemplary. He was dedicated to the practical science of the peaceful settlement of disputes between states, and the high standards, and the ability to solve difficult problems, he brought to the sphere of adjudication and arbitration provide an example which will be long remembered.

Waldock enjoyed a very happy home life and his beloved wife, Beattie, was a great source of strength. She was Ethel Beatrice (*d.* 1981), the daughter of James Herbert Williams, shipowner, of the Black Diamond Line, of Wellington, New Zealand. They were married in 1934 and had a son and a daughter. Beattie predeceased her husband.

Waldock had a quiet manner but was a loyal friend and readily inspired confidence among colleagues: hence his gravitation towards the presidency of any institution of which he was a member. He was a loyal servant of the institutions with which he was associated, and was a bencher of Gray's Inn (1956) and, in 1971, its treasurer. He was appointed OBE (1942) and CMG (1946), became KC (1951), and was knighted (1961). Waldock died at The Hague on 15 August 1981.   IAN BROWNLIE, rev.

Sources *The Times* (18 Aug 1981) · *The Times* (24 Aug 1981) · G. Fitzmaurice, *Graya: A Magazine for Members of Gray's Inn* (1981) · I. Brownlie, *British Year Book of International Law*, 54 (1983), 7 · personal knowledge (1990) · *CGPLA Eng. & Wales* (1981) · F. Vallat, *Graya: A Magazine for Members of Gray's Inn* (1981)

Wealth at death £253,588: probate, 16 Oct 1981, *CGPLA Eng. & Wales*

Waldric [Gaudry] (*d.* 1112), administrator and bishop of Laon, had a short but adventurous career. Henry I, on his accession in 1100, after making William Rufus's chancellor, William Giffard, bishop of Winchester, and his replacement, Roger, bishop of Salisbury, promoted towards the end of 1102 a household clerk, Waldric, whose background is unknown. His possession, however, when bishop, of an 'Ethiopian' slave named John could mean that he had crusaded in 1096. As chancellor Waldric attested over sixty royal acts, but he was certainly also a soldier after his master's heart. On 27–28 September 1106, clad in mail and taking his place among the knights, he fought in Henry's army at Tinchebrai against the king's elder brother, Duke Robert of Normandy, and took Robert prisoner—an act of immense value to Henry, for it gave him the duchy.

Waldric's reward, however, took a strange form. During the winter he secured election to the French bishopric of Laon, a city with some Norman and English ties, but prized by the Capetian kings. The canons, for long without a bishop because of disputed elections, asked Henry at Rouen for Waldric, as they believed that he was enormously rich. The king saw some advantage in the move. The clerk was hastily ordained subdeacon, made a canon of Rouen, and dispatched to Laon. The city's chief distinction at this time was the cathedral school under Master Anselm and his brother Ralf, men of immense reputation in Western Christendom, who inevitably opposed Waldric's election. But at Langres in February and March 1107 Pope Paschal II upheld the election, although Guibert, abbot of nearby Nogent-sous-Coucy, who was in the episcopal delegation, thought that the insufficiently educated candidate performed poorly. He reported that at his consecration the prognosticon was, 'Yea, a sword shall pierce through thy own soul' (Luke 2: 35). Waldric took with him to Laon his brother Rorigo, whom Guibert considered an 'obscene lecher' (*Patrologia Latina*, 156); and he also took, or welcomed, the sons of his successor as Henry's chancellor, Ranulf, so that they could attend Anselm's school under the tutorship of William de Corbeil, the future archbishop of Canterbury. Guibert, who considered Waldric wonderfully erratic in speech and behaviour, and unconventional in dress, wrote at length about his deplorable character and misdeeds.

The views of the monk are naturally prejudiced. Waldric was addicted to practical jokes and pranks. He loved to talk of soldiering, hawks, and hounds, a habit he had acquired in England. He was unscrupulous in his search for money. The finances of the cathedral and city were in a parlous state. The great treasure that he had wickedly gathered and taken to Laon was soon squandered; and he returned to England with Master Anselm in search of more. He also debased the coinage. Rival powers in the city were, however, his main problem. Waldric and his archdeacons were implicated in the murder, by Rorigo, of Gerard, the city's castellan, on 31 December 1109, while he was at prayer in the cathedral. As a result the bishop was driven out of Laon. A visit to Rome and, after an unsuccessful military assault on the city, a bribe to Louis VI secured his restoration. Even more threatening was the ambition of the citizens, rich from the wine trade, to form a commune, that is to say, obtain self-government. In his typically Anglo-Norman opposition to this revolutionary movement, Waldric was at first supported by his archdeacons, and usually by the local garrison and nobility. And he could hope for help from the king, although Louis normally favoured the higher bidder. During Waldric's absence in England the citizens obtained their commune. The bishop retaliated by having one of its leaders blinded by his black servant. For this crime Waldric was suspended by the pope, and it required another visit to Paschal to secure his restoration.

At Easter 1112 matters came to a head. On 18 April Waldric entertained Louis in his palace and bought the suppression of the commune. A week later, on 25 April, the citizens revolted. In the afternoon, while Waldric was engaged in financial business, an armed mob surged through the cathedral and burst into the episcopal palace. The nobles went to the bishop's rescue, but the castellan, who had snatched up only a spear and a shield, was the first casualty. Waldric, taking a cloak from a servant, fled to the church's treasury, where he hid in a small storeroom. His pursuers called him approbrious names—'forkbearer' (*furcifer*) and Isengrin, the name of the wolf in the fable of Reynard the Fox. He was betrayed by one of his servants; and the rioters dragged him out and stood him up in the alley in the close, outside the house of Godfrey the chaplain. A man named Bernard des Bruyères sliced off the top of his head with an axe; a second stroke brought him to his knees; and he expired under a hail of blows. Another man hacked off his finger to get his episcopal ring. Many nobles also were killed. The cathedral, several churches, and the canons' houses were set on fire. Everything was looted. In the end Master Anselm ordered the bishop's naked corpse to be covered by a cloth, and carried to the church of St Vincent outside the walls, where, probably the same day, he was given an ignoble burial.

Waldric's unsuitability for the episcopal office was aggravated by the conditions he inherited. But the success claimed by Guibert for the next bishop, Bartholomew, probably owed something to Waldric. Authoritarian opposition to urban communes was general. Waldric's attitude, if not his violence, was acceptable to Paschal, and also to Abbot Suger, Louis VI's panegyrist. The townsfolk, Suger wrote, did not shrink from laying hands on the Lord's anointed and killing the venerable bishop, the defender of the church, most cruelly. What especially outraged him was the exposure of Waldric's naked body to the beasts and birds, and the mutilation. Louis VI as punishment withheld granting a commune until 1128, and then, at a stiff price, something short of their aspirations.

FRANK BARLOW

Sources Guibertus, 'De vita sua', *Patrologia Latina*, 156 (1853), 911–31, 963–5 · Suger, abbot of St Denis, *Vie de Louis VI le Gros*, ed. and trans. H. Waquet (Paris, 1929), 177–9 · Ordericus Vitalis, *Eccl. hist.*, vol. 6 · H. W. C. Davis, 'Waldric, the chancellor of Henry I', *EngHR*, 26 (1911), 84–9 · J. Dunbabin, *France in the making, 843–1180* (1985), 268–70 · F. Barlow, *The English church, 1066–1154: a history of the Anglo-Norman church* (1979), 248–9 · *Reg. RAN*, vol. 2

Waldron, Francis Godolphin (*bap.* 1743, *d.* 1818), actor and playwright, was probably the Francis Godolphin Wallderan baptized on 30 November 1743 at St Peter's, Liverpool, the son of George Wallderan. Nothing further is known about his family circumstances. An early nineteenth-century source suggests that he was apprenticed to the woodcarver Hayworth (the uncle of Samuel De Wilde, who later painted his portrait in character). He acted at Edinburgh in 1766 and 1769, when he also appeared in Richmond, Surrey. Garrick then engaged him for the 1769–70 season at Drury Lane, where he stayed as a player of secondary roles, often in comedy, until 1796. On his London début, as Scrub in George Farquhar's *The Beaux' Stratagem*, the Drury Lane prompter William Hopkins commented on his 'mean figure' and 'a small impediment in his speaking' (Highfill, Burnim & Langhans, *BDA*, 15.202). Waldron's lisp seems to have limited his professional success, and his roles in some plays that are still revived are a fair indication of his status: Justice Shallow in *The Merry Wives of Windsor*, Corin in *As You Like It*, the Second Grave Digger in *Hamlet*, and The Beggar in *The Beggar's Opera*. The *Biographia dramatica* described him as 'an actor of very useful, rather than splendid talents'.

Little is known about Waldron's actress wife, even her name. They were presumably married by 1770, when their son Francis Waldron was baptized on 18 September; a second son, George, was baptized on 18 August 1771 and became an actor. After 1788 Waldron was estranged from his wife and set up house with Sarah *Harlowe (1765–1852), a much younger actress, with whom he had four children.

Despite his limitations as an actor, Waldron was usually well employed during the summer months: he returned to Edinburgh and Richmond in 1770, and was at Birmingham in 1774 (he was there again in 1797, 1799, and 1800). At Drury Lane in 1774 he was one of the committee that established the Drury Lane Theatrical Fund, a pension scheme for old and ill theatrical personnel. Waldron first tried to acquire the lease of the Richmond theatre in 1776 but failed to raise the total required, despite appealing to Garrick for help. He lost the considerable sum of £722 that he had paid as a deposit, but was acting at Richmond again in 1777 and 1778, when he also appeared in Brighton (as he did in 1791). He did acquire the Richmond lease in 1778 and managed seasons there until 1783 (also taking the company to Windsor); he appeared at Richmond as late as 1790. Waldron also ran a company at Hammersmith in 1785 and 1786, when he played more substantial characters, wisely eschewing heroic roles for eccentric parts such as Old Hardcastle in Oliver Goldsmith's *She Stoops to Conquer*, Shylock, and Polonius.

In 1793 Waldron joined the Haymarket summer company, working mainly as prompter but playing a number of small parts such as Erpingham in *Henry V*, Tubal in *The Merchant of Venice*, and Lucianus in *Hamlet*. He stayed at the Haymarket until 1805 but also worked at Drury Lane again from 1800. In 1806 he claimed a pension from the Drury Lane fund that he had helped to establish, although he made a few appearances at the Haymarket and in Brighton in 1807.

Waldron developed a second, albeit undistinguished, string to his bow as a playwright from relatively early on in his career. His first comedy, *The Maid of Kent* (played for his benefit at Drury Lane, 17 May 1773; revised as *'Tis a Wise Child Knows its Father*, 1795), was based on a story in number 123 of *The Spectator* and was described by the *Covent Garden Magazine* (May 1773) as 'the hasty production of an unskilful writer'. None of Waldron's theatrical works was particularly successful: *The Prodigal* (adapted from Aaron

Hill's *The Fatal Extravagance*) achieved twelve performances at the Haymarket in 1793–4, but *Heigho for a Husband* (also known as *The Imitation, or, The Female Fortune Hunters* and, originally, as *The Belle's Stratagem*) was his most performed play. A lively romantic comedy inspired by Farquhar's *The Beaux' Stratagem*, but substituting two young women for Aimwell and Archer, its general approach is faintly redolent of *She Stoops to Conquer*, another play that acknowledges its intertextual debt to Farquhar. Stock characters and stock situations are handled deftly and the dialogue is well crafted.

Waldron's strong literary and antiquarian interests were manifested in his completion of Ben Jonson's *The Sad Shepherd* (1783) and in editions of John Downes's *Roscius Anglicanus* (1789), Chaucer's *Troilus and Criseyde* (1796), and Thomas Lodge's *Rosalynde* (1802). His *The Virgin Queen*, an unperformed sequel to *The Tempest*, published in 1797, is generally regarded as one of the worst pieces of drama inspired by Shakespeare. However, according to the *Authentic Memoirs of the Green Room* it was intended as a contribution to the Ireland Shakespeare forgeries controversy, aiming 'to expose the vile and well-known forgeries practised on the public by the pretended discovery of certain manuscript plays' by imitating Shakespeare's style and thereby demonstrating that 'the forgeries in question are not entitled, even on the plea of *ingenuity*, to the praise so inconsiderately bestowed upon them' (Roach). Waldron was also co-author, with Charles Dibdin, of *A Compendious History of the English Stage* (1802).

Waldron died in March 1818 at his home in Orange Street, Red Lion Square, London. He left all his property (in a will made in 1805) to Sarah Harlowe and their four children.   TREVOR R. GRIFFITHS

Sources D. E. Baker, *Biographia dramatica, or, A companion to the playhouse*, rev. I. Reed, new edn, rev. S. Jones, 3 vols. in 4 (1812) • [J. Roach], *Authentic memoirs of the green-room* [1814] • Highfill, Burnim & Langhans, *BDA* • G. W. Stone, ed., *The London stage, 1660–1800*, pt 4: *1747–1776* (1962) • *Covent Garden Magazine* (May 1773) • *GM*, 1st ser., 88/1 (1818), 283-4 • C. B. Hogan, ed., *The London stage, 1660–1800*, pt 5: *1776–1800* (1968)
Archives Hunt. L., Larpent MSS
Likenesses W. N. Gardiner, stipple, pubd 1788 (as Sir Christopher Hatton in *The Critic*; after S. Harding), NPG • S. Harding, portrait, 1788 • S. De Wilde, group portrait, 1803 (with Mrs Henry in *All the world's a stage*), National Theatre, London • F. Wheatley, portrait, Man. City Gall.

Waldron, George (1689/90–1726x31), antiquary, was the son of Francis Waldron of London who was descended from an ancient Essex family. He attended Felsted School and on 7 May 1706 he matriculated from Queen's College, Oxford, when he was stated to be 'aged 16'. On 28 November 1711, at St James's Church, Clerkenwell, he married Theodosia Clift (*d.* in or after 1731). Most of the information about his later life comes from snippets in his published works.

Waldron lived in adult life on the Isle of Man, where he acted as commissioner from the British government to watch and report on shipping in an attempt to stop Dutch, Irish, and East India vessels unloading their cargoes on Man, later to be smuggled into Britain, thus escaping

British excise duties. In 1726 Waldron wrote and published his *Description of the Isle of Man*, which is of particular note for its retelling of the legends and folklore of the island. Waldron was the earliest author to record the traditional tales of the fishermen and country people of Man, though he rendered them in standard English without the characteristic expressions used by Manx people. He had lived on the island for nearly twenty years and evidently took pleasure in Manx culture, though he says little about the island's topography or geography. Waldron died in England in or before 1731, just after he had obtained a new deputation from the British government and just before his *Compleat Works in Verse and Prose* (1731) was printed for the 'widow and orphans'. The dedication to William O'Brien, earl of Inchiquin, is signed by Theodosia Waldron. The first part contains 'Miscellany poems' and the second consists of 'Tracts, political and historical' and includes Waldron's main work, *A Description of the Isle of Man*, detailed above. His *Description* was reprinted in 1744, with a new edition in 1780, and in a scholarly edition with an introductory notice and notes by the Manx antiquary William Harrison (1802–1884) for the publications of the Manx Society (vol. 11, 1865). Sir Walter Scott made extensive use of Waldron's *Description* while writing *Peveril of the Peak*, and transferred long extracts from it to his notes to that romance. He described Waldron's work as 'a huge mine, in which I have attempted to discover some specimens of spar, if I cannot find treasure' (*DNB*). Waldron also published various speeches and poems declaring his loyalty to the Hanoverian succession.

ELIZABETH BAIGENT

Sources G. Waldron, *A description of the Isle of Man*, ed. W. Harrison, Manx Society (1865) · administration, PRO, PROB 6/107, fol. 202*r* · *DNB* · Foster, *Alum. Oxon.* · *IGI*
Wealth at death see administration, PRO, PROB 6/107, fol. 202*r*

Waldron, Richard (1694–1753), lawyer and politician in America, was born on 21 February 1694 in Portsmouth, New Hampshire, the first of six children of Colonel Richard Waldron (1650–1730), a leading New Hampshire politician and merchant, and his second wife, Eleanor Vaughan (1670–1727), daughter of William Vaughan of Portsmouth and his wife, Margaret, *née* Cutt. His childhood was spent on the Piscataqua frontier where American Indian warfare, chaotic politics, and proprietary threats to his father's extensive estate led him to adopt the Congregationalist and pro-Massachusetts economic and political orientations of his father. Educated at Harvard College, Waldron graduated BA (1711) and MA (1714) with training in the law. He returned to New Hampshire, and Governor Thomas Dudley appointed him clerk of the New Hampshire council as a favour to Waldron's father, a post which he held from 1715–30. With his clerk's salary and his law practice, Waldron moved to Portsmouth where he married Elizabeth Westbrook (1701–1758) on 31 December 1718, and joined Portsmouth's north-side Congregational church in 1720.

As clerk of the council Waldron witnessed a political coup, undertaken by Samuel Penhallow and John Wentworth with the support of Governor Samuel Shute, that removed all his relatives, including his father and uncle, from their political positions between 1716 and 1718. The next decade saw the gradual consolidation of power by what was known as the Wentworth 'clan'. Frustrated and vengeful, Waldron, though small of stature, spent the next thirty-five years seeking to return himself, his family, and his allies to positions of political prominence at a time of significant economic and social change in the colony. Portsmouth emerged as the economic and political centre of the colony; its merchants became the controlling group in the colony's politics; a new Anglican church came to dominate modes of religious worship among the élite; and issues of land and boundaries with Massachusetts led to vexatious controversies.

Waldron's best opportunity occurred unexpectedly, when Jonathan Belcher, a kinsman whose favourite sister had been married to Waldron's uncle, was appointed governor of Massachusetts and New Hampshire in 1730. Waldron convinced Belcher to help him remove the Wentworth 'clan' from positions of authority in the province. Belcher appointed Waldron to the New Hampshire council and as a justice of the peace, a judge of the court of common pleas, and secretary of the colony. Waldron then found allies among the inland towns who sought local meetings of the province courts, and who feared the domination of the Wentworths and their Portsmouth merchant allies. For the next eleven years Waldron was the central figure in New Hampshire government. By the mid-1730s he was also a judge of probate and the colony's naval officer. But the Wentworth faction fought back in every way it could, and Waldron and New Hampshire endured intense political conflict during these years. By the early 1730s the 'clan' had gained control of the assembly, while the Belcher–Waldron alliance controlled the council and executive activities. This struggle for power had a lasting impact on New Hampshire as, during its course, Wentworth's supporters founded an Anglican church in the colony to win friends in Britain against Belcher. Critics of Belcher and Waldron also revived a forty-year-old boundary dispute between Massachusetts and New Hampshire, to discredit the governor and to enlarge New Hampshire's boundaries so that the British might consider it financially able to support a governor separate from Massachusetts.

Waldron, almost single-handedly, attempted to thwart the 'clan's' varied efforts, but by late 1741 he had lost on all counts. Perhaps his finest effort was the 1740 council petition to the crown defending Belcher's administration, including an attachment, signed by 650 men, requesting that New Hampshire be made a part of Massachusetts. While Waldron and his allies favoured the reactionary vision of a Congregational New Hampshire as part of a larger New England with Boston as its capital, this proposal contradicted the values of Benning Wentworth, his followers, and the Portsmouth merchant community who sought autonomy from Massachusetts. By 1741 the consequences of this factional discord included significantly larger boundaries for New Hampshire, a new Anglican church, and its own governor. The first incumbent,

Benning Wentworth, stripped Waldron of his public offices and restored the Wentworth faction's authority in New Hampshire politics, which it held until the American War of Independence. By provoking a desperate and successful opposition during the 1730s, Waldron's revenge had helped bring about what he abhorred.

Waldron's personal life had fluctuations as well. His father died in November 1730, leaving him his extensive property in Dover and Portsmouth. Six of his eight children died; his home in Portsmouth burnt down twice; and his father-in-law declared bankruptcy and lost the Portsmouth farm that Waldron managed. Despite this in the late 1740s he possessed a farm on the Portsmouth plains, a £20,000 Portsmouth estate, an extensive Dover lumber-milling estate, and 5000 acres of land in western townships. He was active in town and church affairs, and in 1750 participated in the establishment of Portsmouth's first library society. At the same time he remained intensely ambitious politically, scheming ineffectually until his death to regain his lost authority.

Waldron's last chance occurred during the late 1740s, after Governor Wentworth, seeking funding for a controversial western fort, unilaterally authorized several western towns to send representatives to the assembly. The action provoked a power struggle between Wentworth and the assembly. Waldron got himself elected to the assembly in 1748 and was elected its speaker, only to be disapproved by the governor. This action further inflamed the assembly, to the point where it refused to do any public business until the governor surrendered on these two points. For three years the government was at an impasse. In 1752, however, Wentworth received a special instruction from the crown upholding his decisions on both issues, providing him with a complete victory and a strengthening of crown prerogatives over the assembly. Again, Waldron's actions had brought lasting and unwelcome consequences in New Hampshire politics. Waldron became ill, retired from public life, and died, at a house on the plains of Portsmouth, of unknown causes on 23 August 1753. He was buried in Portsmouth.

DAVID E. VAN DEVENTER

Sources D. E. Van Deventer, 'Waldron, Richard (1694–1753)', *ANB* • New Hampshire Historical Society, Concord, New Hampshire, Waldron MSS, 2 vols. • New Hampshire Historical Society, Concord, New Hampshire, Belcher MSS, 3 vols. • Mass. Hist. Soc., Belcher MSS • New Hampshire State Library, Concord, New Hampshire, Portsmouth town records • PRO, Colonial Office MSS, class 5, vols. 880–969 • N. Bouton and others, eds., *Provincial and state papers: documents and records relating to the province of New Hampshire*, 40 vols. (1867–1943), vols. 2–6, 9, 17–19, 29 • *CSP col.*, vols. 1, 5, 7, 9–45 • *Collections of the Massachusetts Historical Society*, 6th ser., 6–7 (1893–4) [*The Belcher papers*, vols. 1–2] • *Collections of the Massachusetts Historical Society*, 6th ser., 10 (1899) [*The Pepperrell papers*] • D. E. Van Deventer, *The emergence of provincial New Hampshire, 1623–1741* (1976) • C. K. Shipton, *Sibley's Harvard graduates: biographical sketches of graduates of Harvard University*, 17 vols. (1873–1975), vol. 5, pp. 653–7 • M. C. Batinski, *Jonathan Belcher, colonial governor* (1996) • J. R. Daniell, *Colonial New Hampshire: a history* (1981) • J. A. Schutz, *William Shirley: king's governor of Massachusetts* (1961) • C. E. Clark, *The eastern frontier: the settlement of northern New England, 1610–1763* (1970) • C. H. C. Howard, *Genealogy of the Cutts family* (1892) • S. Noyes, C. T. Libby, and W. G. Davis, *Genealogical dictionary of Maine and New Hampshire*, 5 vols. (Portland, ME, 1928–39); repr. (Baltimore, MA, 1972); repr. (Baltimore, MA, 1983) • New Hampshire State Library, Concord, New Hampshire, Dover town records

Archives New Hampshire Historical Society, MSS • New Hampshire State Archives, Concord, corresp. • New York Historical Society, MSS | Mass. Hist. Soc., Belcher papers • Mass. Hist. Soc., Belknap papers • New Hampshire Historical Society, Belcher MSS • New Hampshire State Library, Concord, Portsmouth town records, MSS • PRO, Colonial Office papers, class 5, vols. 880–969

Waldstein, Charles. *See* Walston, Sir Charles (1856–1927).

Wale, Sir Charles (1763–1845), army officer, was born on 5 August 1763, the second son of Thomas Wale (1701–1796) of Shelford, Cambridgeshire, and his wife, Louisa Rudolphina, daughter of Nicholas Rahten of Lüneburg, Hanover. The family claimed descent from Walter de Wahul, recorded in Domesday Book as a landholder in Northamptonshire. Several members of the family acted as sheriff of that county. A Sir Thomas Wale was knight of the Garter in Edward III's reign, and another Thomas was killed at Agincourt in 1415. A branch of the family migrated to Ireland late in the twelfth century and founded Walestown. The branch to which Sir Charles belonged acquired Shelford in the seventeenth century. His father, Thomas Wale, an eighteenth-century squire, kept a notebook, extracts from which were printed by the Revd H. J. Wale in *My Grandfather's Pocket-Book* (1883).

Charles Wale was sent up to London in 1778 to learn arithmetic and fencing. In September 1779, much against his father's wish, he accepted a commission in a regiment which was then being raised by Colonel Keating, the 88th foot. He went out with it to Jamaica, but on 13 April 1780 his father purchased him ('cost £150') a lieutenancy in the 97th which went to Gibraltar with Admiral Darby's fleet in April 1781, and served throughout the latter part of the defence.

Wale obtained a company in the 12th foot on 25 June 1783, but was placed on half pay soon afterwards. On 23 May 1786 he exchanged to the 46th, and served with it in Ireland and the Channel Islands. He married in 1793 and retired on half pay, becoming adjutant of the Cambridgeshire militia on 4 December. On 1 March 1794 he was made major, and on 1 January 1798 lieutenant-colonel in the army. He returned to full pay on 6 August 1799 as captain in the 20th, and served with it in the expedition to The Helder in the autumn. On 16 January 1800 he was promoted major in the 85th, and on 9 October to lieutenant-colonel of the 67th. He joined it in Jamaica, and brought it home at the end of 1801. In 1805 he went out with it to Bengal, but returned to England and exchanged to the 66th on 16 June 1808.

Wale did not serve long with the 66th. He had been made colonel on 25 April 1808, and in March 1809 he was appointed a brigadier-general in the West Indies. He commanded the reserve in the expedition under Sir George Beckwith, which took Guadeloupe in February 1810, and was wounded in the action of 3 February. On 4 June 1811 he was promoted major-general, and on 21 February 1812 was appointed governor of Martinique, and remained so until it was restored to France in 1815. He was made KCB on 2

January 1815, promoted lieutenant-general on 19 July 1821, and general on 28 June 1838, and made colonel of the 33rd foot on 25 February 1831. In politics he was 'of the high Conservative party' (*GM*).

Wale was three times married: first, in 1793, to Louisa, daughter of the Revd Castel Sherrard of Huntington; second, in 1803, to Isabella, daughter of the Revd Thomas Johnson of Stockton-on-Tees; third, in 1815, to Henrietta, daughter of the Revd Thomas Brent of Croscombe, Somerset. Wale died at Shelford, Cambridgeshire, on 19 March 1845. He was survived by his third wife, seven sons, and five daughters.

Wale's eighth son, **Frederick Wale** (1822–1858), army officer in the East India Company, entered the East India Company's service in 1840, and was posted to the 48th Bengal native infantry on 9 January 1841; lieutenant 23 February 1842, captain 1 October 1852. He was appointed brigade major at Peshawar on 19 August 1853, and was serving there when his regiment mutinied at Lucknow in May 1857. He took command of the 1st Sikh irregular cavalry (known as 'Wale's horse'), and served in the relief of Lucknow, and in the siege and capture of it in March 1858. His unit formed part of the 2nd cavalry brigade, and the brigadier reported that Wale 'showed on all occasions great zeal in command of his regiment, and on 21 March led it most successfully in pursuit of the enemy till he was shot' (*London Gazette*, 21 May 1858). Lord Roberts wrote that he was 'a gallant officer' (Roberts, 227). He had married Adelaide, daughter of Edward Prest of York; they had two daughters.   E. M. LLOYD, rev. ROGER T. STEARN

Sources *GM*, 2nd ser., 23 (1845) · H. J. Wale, *My grandfather's pocketbook* (1883) · T. C. W. Blanning, *The French revolutionary wars, 1787–1802* (1996) · Lord Roberts [F. S. Roberts], *Forty-one years in India*, 31st edn (1900) · Boase, *Mod. Eng. biog.*

Archives Cambs. AS, papers as governor of Martinique | BL, letters to third earl of Hardwicke, Add. MSS 35643–35757 *passim* · NL Scot., letters to Sir A. F. I. Cochrane

Wale, Frederick (1822–1858). *See under* Wale, Sir Charles (1763–1845).

Wale, Samuel (1721?–1786), painter and book illustrator, is said to have been born in Yarmouth, Norfolk, possibly on 25 April 1721, the son of Samuel and Margaret Wale. His background is obscure, however, and certain sources give his place of birth as London. Apart from producing a handful of oil paintings, he is chiefly remembered as one of the most prolific book illustrators of the eighteenth century and as a founder Royal Academician. He was apparently apprenticed to a goldsmith in 1735 and is said to have gone on to study drawing at the St Martin's Lane Academy. He reportedly painted decorative designs for ceilings (although none survive) and tradesmen's signs, and in the 1740s he presented three views of London hospitals to the Foundling Hospital, where they still remain. Possibly also in the 1740s he painted a historical scene in oils of the Norfolk insurrectionary Robert Kett: entitled *Under the Oak of Reformation at his Camp on Mousehold Heath, Norwich*, it is now in the Norwich Castle Museum. About 1751 Wale designed a series of prints of Vauxhall Pleasure Gardens, including a rococo *General View of Vauxhall Gardens*,

engraved by Johann Sebastian Müller (copy in the Victoria and Albert Museum).

Wale's chief occupation throughout his career was book illustration, and he produced designs for more than 100 publications. Unlike many of his contemporaries, he chose not to engrave his own designs, preferring to pass them on to engravers such as Charles Grignion. Although this may have reduced Wale's profit (designers were given one-off payments while engravers were paid for the time spent on the work), it had the effect of distancing him from the mechanical part of the trade and increasing his output. Despite often producing schematic designs (on at least one occasion, too—when illustrating Thomas Percy's *Reliques of Ancient English Poetry* (3 vols., 1765)—he worked to the author's direction), Wale's range was broad. His *œuvre* included dense allegorical work for the *Oxford Almanack* in 1753 and 1755 (original drawings are in the Ashmolean Museum, Oxford); extensive religious illustrations (for instance, for *The Liturgy of the Church of England*, 1755, and J. Fleetwood's *Christian's Dictionary*, 1775); and graphic illustrations of violent crime for John Cooke's *The Tyburn Chronicle* (4 vols., 1768) and *The Newgate Calendar* (5 vols., 1773). Many of Wale's original drawings, usually in pen, ink, and wash, for the latter two publications survive in the British Museum, the Victoria and Albert Museum, Nottingham Castle Museum, and the Tate's Oppé Collection.

Wale was an active participant in every major effort of the mid-eighteenth century to establish an academy of the arts in London. In 1749 he assisted the architect John Gwynn with his *Proposals for Erecting a Public Academy*, and in 1755 both men were involved in an early abortive effort to found such an institution. In 1759 Wale was on the committee of artists chaired by Francis Hayman which successfully made an approach to the Society for the Encouragement of Arts, Manufactures, and Commerce to request the use of their rooms to mount the first major exhibition of contemporary art in Britain. When the artists split after the first exhibition in 1760, Wale exhibited with the breakaway Society of Artists of Great Britain, and produced a vignette of *The Genius of Painting, Sculpture, and Architecture Relieving the Distressed* for the catalogue of their 1761 exhibition. Other than in 1765, Wale exhibited at the Society of Artists every year until 1768, when he was among the twenty-two artists who petitioned the king to found a royal academy. After the foundation of the academy he was appointed as the first professor of perspective, on 17 December 1768. According to Edward Edwards, Wale possessed 'a good deal of science in the accessary parts of his art' (Edwards, 116), and he had demonstrated his skill in architectural drawing in the designs which he published with Gwynn for the decoration of St Paul's Cathedral in 1752: these were engraved by Edward Rooker, and a 1755 print from the series is held in the Victoria and Albert Museum. As a professor, Wale delivered six lectures a year for an annual salary of £30, and he remained in the post for the rest of his life, despite reportedly being a very timid and diffident lecturer.

At both the Society of Artists and the Royal Academy,

Wale showed 'stained drawings' (pen and wash), including original designs for book illustration, and designs for 'an altar-piece for a gothic chapel'. Over half of his exhibited works were scenes of British history, including *The Widow of Sir John Grey Petitioning Edward IV* (exh. Society of Artists, 1760) and *King Alfred Making a Code of Laws* (exh. RA, 1771); both were engraved by Grignion for Thomas Mortimer's *New History of England* (1764–6). Wale was probably the most prolific illustrator of native historical scenes in the eighteenth century: although many designs were repeated in several historical texts, he produced more than 150 different designs for works such as Rapin-Thoyras's *History of England* (vol. 5, 1744–7), Mortimer's *New History of England*, and W. H. Mountague's *New and Universal History of England* (2 vols., c.1771). The artist was described as 'the celebrated Wale' on title-pages, and his narrative scenes of dramatic and sometimes obscure episodes in British history enlivened what were sometimes mediocre and derivative texts. His work appears to have influenced senior academicians such as Benjamin West, whose painting of *Oliver Cromwell Dissolving the Long Parliament* (exh. RA, 1783; Montclair Art Museum, New Jersey) is compositionally very similar to Wale's illustration of the same scene for Mortimer's *New History of England*.

In 1778 Wale suffered a paralytic stroke and became the first recipient of the Royal Academy's benefit fund for artist members incapable of work. He continued to serve as professor of perspective, but because of ill health was allowed to deliver his lectures from home. In 1782 he was also given the post of librarian of the Royal Academy, which he held until his death, on 6 February 1786 at his home, Little Court, Castle Street, Leicester Fields. Wale was apparently unmarried and childless and left his copperplates, prints, and belongings to his friend John Gwynn, with whom he shared his house, and his nurse, Mrs Mary Gurpin. He was buried in St Martin-in-the-Fields.   M. G. SULLIVAN

Sources H. A. Hammelmann, 'Eighteenth century English illustrators: Samuel Wale', *Book Collector*, 1 (1952), 150–65 · H. Hammelmann, *Book illustrators in eighteenth-century England*, ed. T. S. R. Boase (1975), 89–96 · M. G. Sullivan, 'Historiography and visual culture in Britain, 1660–1783', PhD diss., U. Leeds, 1998, 256–78 · E. Edwards, *Anecdotes of painters* (1808); facs. edn (1970), 116–18 · W. Sandby, *The history of the Royal Academy of Arts*, 1 (1862), 86–7 · Redgrave, *Artists* · DNB · 'Samuel Wale: Ket the Tanner', *Gazette des Beaux-Arts*, 6th ser., 91 (1978), suppl. 68 · J. Turner, ed., *The dictionary of art*, 34 vols. (1996) · S. C. Hutchison, *The history of the Royal Academy, 1768–1968* (1968), 44, 45, 47, 62, 232 · E. Croft-Murray, *Decorative painting in England, 1537–1837*, 2 (1970), 290 · D. B. Brown, *Catalogue of the collection of drawings in the Ashmolean Museum*, 4 (1982), 642–4 · T. Percy, letter to S. Wale, Harvard U., Houghton L., Percy MSS · Graves, *Soc. Artists*

Archives RA, Society of Artists of Great Britain MSS · RA, minutes of the Royal Academy

Likenesses J. Zoffany, group portrait, oils, 1771–2 (*The academicians of the Royal Academy, 1772*), Royal Collection · Earlom, engraving, pubd 2 Aug 1773 (after Zoffany, 1771–2), Royal Collection

Wealth at death copperplates, prints, pictures, furniture etc. to John Gwynn; later codicil left half belongings to nurse: will, cited Hammelmann, *Book illustrators*, 90

Waleden, Humphrey de. *See* Walden, Sir Humphrey (d. 1330/31).

Waleran [Waleran de Beaumont], **count of Meulan and earl of Worcester** (1104–1166), magnate and soldier, was the son of Robert de *Beaumont, count of Meulan and earl of Leicester (d. 1118), and Isabel (d. 1147), daughter of Hugues, count of Vermandois. Waleran was born one of twins, according to Orderic Vitalis. He was named Waleran after the first count of Meulan, his great-grandfather. That he was the elder twin is probable because he later had the marriage of his sisters and he inherited the marriage portion of his mother at Elbeuf in Normandy. Waleran and his younger twin, *Robert (II), earl of Leicester, were under age when their father died in 1118. They passed into royal wardship and their lands in England and Normandy into the hands of their stepfather, William (II) de *Warenne, earl of Surrey, and Nigel d'Aubigny, assisted by Morin du Pin, the late Count Robert's steward, and Ralph, his butler. The twins were kept at court, and appeared in Henry I's entourage at Gisors in 1119, when the king incited them to debate philosophy with the cardinals accompanying Calixtus II. They were knighted and came of age in 1120, before October. Waleran succeeded to Meulan, a small but strategically important county on the Seine above the Norman frontier, and also had his father's great Norman honours of Beaumont, Pont Audemer, and Brionne. In England he acquired properties to the value of £140 in Dorset and Winchester. After an initial stay in Meulan in 1120, Waleran appears to have remained with the curia of Henry I.

Late in 1122, however, perhaps moved in part by a desire for military glory, Waleran became implicated in the Norman plot contrived by Amaury, count of Évreux, in favour of William Clito, the son of Robert Curthose. But Henry I was forewarned, and in December 1123 captured Waleran's stronghold at Pont Audemer after a short siege, while on 25 March 1124 Waleran himself, with many of his knights, was taken prisoner after a battle with royal troops at Bourgthéroulde. He remained in captivity, first in Normandy and later in England, until he was received back into royal favour in the summer of 1129. Until the end of the reign Waleran faithfully attended the royal curia in England and Normandy, and he and his twin brother were at the king's side when he died on 1 December 1135. Waleran seems to have come to terms quickly with Stephen's seizure of the throne, although it is unlikely that he was in England for the coronation. He had, however, received grants from the new king before the Easter court of 1136, when most magnates made their submission, and was specially singled out for royal favour, being betrothed to the king's daughter, Matilda, who died in infancy. At this time he may have received Worcester, Droitwich, and the royal demesne in Worcestershire. After Easter 1136 Waleran was sent to Normandy to take charge of its defence against Geoffrey, count of Anjou, and the Empress Matilda. This he successfully accomplished, repulsing Angevin raids and defeating internal rebellion in a battle near Acquigny on 3 October. He welcomed Stephen to a largely pacified duchy in spring 1137, and was rewarded with custody of the county of Évreux, and a grant of the *vicomté* of the city.

Waleran's influence in central Normandy was by now unchallengeable, and he felt secure enough to return with the king to England in November 1137, whereupon he was sent to repulse a Scots invasion of the north, which he accomplished by the relief of Wark Castle. But in May 1138 he was back, dealing with new outbreaks in Normandy. After further successes, accomplished with aid from France, Waleran devastated the Norman estates of his principal adversary, the earl of Gloucester, and ended the stubborn rebellion of the Tosny family. Late in 1138 Waleran returned once more to Stephen in England, and at this time received investiture as earl of Worcester, an event he apparently marked by the foundation of a large Cistercian abbey at Bordesley in November. There is evidence that his next mission was to lead a large embassy to the Christmas court of Louis VII at or near Paris, to confirm the alliance Stephen had made earlier with Louis VI and perhaps begin negotiations to marry Louis's sister Constance to Eustace, son of King Stephen. He returned to England about Easter 1139. Unchallengeable at the head of a great aristocratic party, Waleran engineered the downfall of his rival, Bishop Roger of Salisbury, in June, obtaining the replacement of Roger's son as chancellor by his own cousin, Philip de Harcourt. The outbreak of civil war in England late in 1139 made Waleran the principal target of Angevin supporters. Robert, earl of Gloucester, devastated his city of Worcester on 7 November 1139. Taking this as a personal insult, Waleran revenged it by the sack of Tewkesbury and the wasting of the Vale of Evesham in early spring 1140, saying, as he returned to Worcester, that he had never carried out so great a pillage in England or Normandy.

Waleran's influence over King Stephen was effectively ended by the battle of Lincoln on 2 February 1141. Although Waleran escaped capture, and carried on the royalist fight for some months after the battle, he had surrendered to the empress before September, being threatened with the loss of his Norman lands by Geoffrey of Anjou's invasion of central Normandy. The surrender did not materially lessen his possessions, for Worcester was confirmed to him, as were his Norman possessions; he even added to them by marriage to Agnes, daughter of the late Count Amaury of Évreux, late in 1141 or early in 1142. She brought him Norman estates and the honour of Gournay, east of Paris. However, according to Robert de Torigni, Geoffrey of Anjou never trusted him. Waleran led the Anglo-Norman contingent that accompanied Louis VII on the second crusade (1147–8). It seems to be from this point that he began a dangerous flirtation with the Capetians, to enhance his uncertain position in Normandy. In 1153 his capture was engineered by Henry Plantagenet, acting with Robert de Montfort, Waleran's nephew (whom Waleran had dispossessed of Montfort-sur-Risle). The count also lost his English earldom at this time. Waleran remained thereafter an outsider to the court of Henry II, and vulnerable in any warfare between Henry and Louis VII, with whom he kept up a friendship.

In 1160 Waleran sided with Louis in a campaign fought in the Vexin, and as a result lost his Norman lands and castles. These had been restored by July 1162, but Waleran's active career ended with this disaster. He fell ill in the spring of 1166, and entered as a monk the ancestral abbey of Préaux, where he died on 9 or 10 April. He was buried there next to his father, below the chapter house floor. He was succeeded in his lands by his son, Count Robert, except at Gournay, which remained to his widow, Countess Agnes, and passed successively to his younger sons Amaury and Roger de Meulan. He left three other sons, and married one daughter to Geoffrey de Mayenne, and another to William (I) de Beauchamp of Elmley (d. 1170). Like his twin brother, Waleran was a literate man, a writer of letters and, according to Geoffrey of Monmouth, of Latin verse. He was a friend of the Cistercian pope Eugenius III, and a generous patron of the order; he founded Bordesley (1138) and (in response to a vow) Le Valasse in Normandy (1150)—both unfortunately abstracted from his advocacy by the Empress Matilda. He had a deserved reputation for liberality and loyalty to his followers. His less attractive traits lay in a purposeless acquisitiveness and heedless brutality which did not fit him for the role of viceroy and statesman into which he thrust himself.

DAVID CROUCH

Sources Ordericus Vitalis, *Eccl. hist.* • R. Howlett, ed., *Chronicles of the reigns of Stephen, Henry II, and Richard I*, 4, Rolls Series, 82 (1889) • F. Sommènil, ed., *Chronicon Valassense* (Rouen, 1868) • *The chronicle of John of Worcester, 1118–1140*, ed. J. R. H. Weaver (1908) • William of Malmesbury, *The Historia novella*, ed. and trans. K. R. Potter (1955) • Symeon of Durham, *Opera* • E. Houth, 'Galeran II, comte de Meulan', *Bulletin Philologique et Historique* (1961), 627–82 • G. H. White, 'The career of Waleran, count of Meulan and earl of Worcester', *TRHS*, 4th ser., 17 (1934), 19–48 • D. Crouch, *The Beaumont twins: the roots and branches of power in the twelfth century*, Cambridge Studies in Medieval Life and Thought, 4th ser., 1 (1986) • E. King, 'Waleran, count of Meulan, earl of Worcester', *Tradition and change: essays in honour of Marjorie Chibnall*, ed. D. Greenway, C. Holdsworth, and J. Sayers (1985), 165–81

Walerand, Robert (*d.* 1273), administrator, was the eldest son of William Walerand of Whaddon in Wiltshire, and Isabel, daughter of Roger de Berkeley of Dursley, Gloucestershire, by her second marriage. He had two brothers: William, who married the elder daughter and coheir of Hugh of Kilpeck, Herefordshire, and John, a clerk, who joined Robert in the king's service in the 1250s. 'Maud, sister of Robert Walerand' entered Romsey Abbey near Robert's bailiwick in the New Forest in 1253, and may be the Alice Walerand who became abbess in 1268. Another Alice, Robert's half-sister by his mother's first marriage, was the mother of Alan de *Plugenet.

By 1242–3 Robert Walerand had already succeeded to his patrimony at Whaddon, part of the Domesday barony of Walerand the Huntsman, whose descendants had often held the New Forest and the Forest of Clarendon in fee. The family's tradition of forest service and connections with the southern marches of Wales set the pattern of Walerand's early years as a royal servant. In 1243 he appears as the knight of the marcher baron, William (II) de Cantilupe, steward of the king's household. In 1244 he was granted 20 marks annually at the exchequer for his maintenance, and commissioned to take four crossbows from the Tower of London to the castle of Cardigan. On the death of Anselm, the last Marshal earl of Pembroke, in 1245 he was made custodian of his lands in west Wales, including the castle of Pembroke. From 1246 to 1250 he was also keeper of Gloucester Castle and sheriff of Gloucestershire; in 1247 he was made custodian of the bishopric of St David's; from August 1248 to February 1254 he held the castles of Carmarthen and Cardigan, for the strengthening of which he was commissioned to extract regular payments from the abbot of Strata Florida; and from August 1250 to May 1251 he was warden of Lundy island. He was commissioned to settle disputes between marcher lords, to stop English and Welsh landlords from harbouring malefactors from the other nation, and to hear forest pleas, special assizes, and pleas of trespass in western counties. In the 1250s his forest responsibilities widened: by June 1253 he held the stewardship of the New Forest in fee; in November 1255 he was made keeper of the Forest of Dean and constable of St Briavels Castle for five years; and in September 1256 he was appointed steward of the king's forests south of Trent and to exercise all the duties of justice of the forest, with a stipend of 100 marks a year.

Walerand was unique in his many-sided service to the king. By 1256 he had also been for five years a steward of the household. In 1253 and 1254 he was with Henry III in Gascony, where he was surety for the king's agreements with Gascon lords and merchants, and witnessed many royal grants immediately after the king's family and any earls present. Then in March 1254 Henry accepted the papal offer of the crown of Sicily for his second son, Edmund, and began to use Walerand on the business that helped to precipitate the barons' war. The chroniclers describe how the steward and Peter d'Aigueblanche, bishop of Hereford (d. 1268), tricked English bishops and abbots into adding their seals to blank charters on which large sums of money could be entered at Rome, in order to persuade the pope that Henry was in a position to finance his Sicilian ambitions. Matthew Paris represents Richard, earl of Cornwall, as bitterly rebuking the bishop and the steward in a parliament at Westminster in October 1255 for 'so wickedly persuading the king to subvert the kingdom' (Paris, *Chron.*, 5.521). In the following year Walerand was given custody of all vacant bishoprics and abbacies so as to raise money for the 'Sicilian business'. Between August 1255 and the spring of 1257 he was also engaged on missions with Richard de Clare, earl of Gloucester, Simon de Montfort, earl of Leicester, John Mansel, and others to Scotland, to the princes of Germany, and to the king of France. He was one of the king's four chief ministers who in June 1257 entered into a bond for the repayment of the king's debts to Montfort, the extraordinary terms of which accepted that they should be excommunicated in case of default. In the same month he was ordered to levy 1000 marks from the vacant bishopric of Ely to repay the king's debt to Prince Edward. The money was actually received from the late bishop's executors by John Walerand, 'the king's clerk', and sent to Robert, who was in Wales with Edward on campaign. It was in this year that

Robert's brother William obtained half of Hugh of Kilpeck's barony, including the manor and castle of Kilpeck and the keepership of the Hay of Hereford. By December 1259 these had passed to Robert, who may have purchased them in 1257 when he married Matilda, daughter and heir of Ralph Russell of Derham, Gloucestershire.

It was Robert Walerand who 'swore on the king's soul' in May 1258 that the state of the realm should be reformed as the magnates demanded (Sanders, 74). At the beginning of the reform he was given custody of Salisbury Castle, commissioned to seize for the king's use the treasure of Henry's expelled half-brothers, and attended Hugh Bigod, the baronial justiciar, on eyre at Winchester. In July 1259 he was probably appointed to fill a vacancy in the council of fifteen, which committed Edward's castle of Bristol to him. But on his departure to France with the king in November 1259, he was replaced as steward of the forests south of Trent by a baronial partisan, and Edward took Bristol away from him. Walerand was busy at this time in negotiations for a settlement of Montfort's grievances over the dower of his wife, Eleanor, Henry's sister, which were holding up the conclusion of a treaty between the kings of England and France, and for the maintenance by Louis IX of 300 knights in Henry's service. In April 1260 he was sent back to England with the chancellor, Henry Wingham, and John Balliol (d. 1269) to declare Henry's 'state and intentions' and prepare for his return, which heralded a worsening of relations with the baronial leaders. The mayor and citizens of London were instructed to admit to the city only such as Walerand and Philip Basset should tell them, and Walerand became, with Mansel and Peter of Savoy, one of Henry's chief advisers at the Tower of London as the king made his move to shake off the regime of the provisions. This involved for Walerand appointment in July 1261 to the strategic sheriffdom of Kent and custody of the castles of Rochester and Canterbury; to membership with Basset, the justiciar, and Walter of Merton, the chancellor, of a commission with the task of choosing new sheriffs generally; and to the wardenship of the Cinque Ports and the custody of the castles of Dover, Ludgershall, and Marlborough. In July 1262 Walerand again accompanied Henry to France. For a time in September he had custody of the king's seal when many of Henry's entourage at St Germain were laid low by plague. But on 10 October the justiciar and his 'bachelors' in England were instructed to give unhesitating faith to Robert Walerand over the message he was bringing from the king, which was perhaps in connection with the threat of Llywelyn ap Gruffudd to break the truce that Walerand had sworn to on the king's behalf in 1260.

In the event it was Simon de Montfort who brought general war in June 1263, his partisans first seizing Aigueblanche in his own cathedral, then Walerand's castle of Kilpeck and the towns of the marches from Bristol to Shrewsbury. In the following month, as Montfort closed on London, Walerand appeared in the company of Edward when the prince sought to gain control of the king's treasure at the Temple. His old association with Aigueblanche in extorting money for the 'Sicilian business' still figured prominently in the barons' case as it was presented to King Louis in January 1264. But he recovered his lands on renewing his oath to the provisions, and was able to re-establish himself in the marches and lead Edward's castellans to redeem the situation when King Henry and his son were captured at the battle of Lewes on 14 May. After the defeat and death of Montfort at Evesham in August 1265 Walerand allegedly proposed the disinheritance of those who had fought against the king, and imposed a huge fine on the city of London. But he was one of the authors of the dictum of Kenilworth which provided in October 1266 'for the state of the realm especially in the matter of the disinherited' (Sanders, 319). In his remaining years he continued to attest royal writs, serve on special assizes, and negotiate truces with the Welsh. In 1269 he was again in Paris with Edward to make arrangements with King Louis for a crusade, and he was one of the five, headed by Richard of Cornwall, appointed in 1270 to look after the prince's interests while he was away. In this role he was soon replaced by Robert Burnell, the future chancellor of King Edward, and he died in late January or early February 1273, before the new king's return.

Royal service brought Walerand extensive properties, some in Ireland, others (notably Hugh de Neville's borough of Stogursey in Somerset) from the disinherited. But he had no children, and his heir was his brother William's seventeen-year-old son, Robert, an idiot for whom Walerand was reputed to have secured the royal ordinance that removed the overlord's rights of wardship in such a case and transferred the safeguarding of the idiot's interests to the king. In fact, long before his death, Walerand had enfeoffed his half-sister's son, the staunch royalist Alan (II) de Plugenet, with the castle and manor of Kilpeck and the family lands in Wiltshire, taking them back as life tenancies.   ALAN HARDING

Sources CIPM, 2, nos. 6, 7, 89 · H. C. M. Lyte and others, eds., *Liber feodorum: the book of fees*, 3 vols. (1920–31) · *Chancery records* · VCH *Wiltshire*, vol. 2 · Paris, *Chron.*, 5.511, 521 · *Ann. mon.*, vols. 3–4 · R. F. Treharne and I. J. Sanders, eds., *Documents of the baronial movement of reform and rebellion, 1258–1267* (1973) · F. M. Nichols, ed., *Britton*, 1 (1865), 243 · F. Pollock and F. W. Maitland, *The history of English law before the time of Edward I*, 2 vols. (1898), 1.481
Wealth at death see CIPM, 2, no. 6

Wales. For this title name *see* Joan, *suo jure* countess of Kent, and princess of Wales and of Aquitaine (c.1328–1385); Edward, prince of Wales and of Aquitaine (1330–1376); Edward, prince of Wales (1453–1471); Edward, prince of Wales (1474x6–1484); Arthur, prince of Wales (1486–1502); Henry Frederick, prince of Wales (1594–1612); Frederick Lewis, prince of Wales (1707–1751); Augusta, princess of Wales (1719–1772); Diana, princess of Wales (1961–1997).

Wales, James (1747–1795), portrait painter and archaeological draughtsman, was born in Peterhead, Aberdeenshire. He moved early in his life to Aberdeen, where he was educated at Marischal College. It was there that he also began painting modest portraits on tin plates. Apparently self-taught, Wales benefited from the early patronage of Francis Peacock in Aberdeen. By 1783 Wales had moved to London, where he exhibited two portraits at the Society of Artists, with the catalogue recording his address as Little St Martin's Lane. Wales exhibited one more portrait at the Society of Artists in 1791 and three paintings at the Royal Academy between 1788 and 1789, but stiff competition encouraged him to seek employment in India. He applied to the East India Company for permission to work in Bombay in 1790, was granted permission on 5 January 1791, and arrived in Bombay on 15 July of the same year. Wales left his wife, Margaret (d. 1795), and their daughters in Hampstead, Middlesex, although he soon encouraged them to go to Bombay after learning of his six-year-old daughter's death in 1792. Wales's family arrived in India some time in 1793, but Margaret died in childbirth in May 1795, leaving the artist to provide for five daughters.

While Bombay was a smaller and less affluent market than Calcutta or Madras for a British painter, Wales was fortunate enough to meet Sir Charles Warre Malet, the resident at the Maratha court in Poona from 1786 to 1797. In addition to painting portraits for Malet, Wales painted a number of remarkable portraits of the Maratha chiefs and their ministers. The most impressive surviving example is a group portrait, *Madhu Rao Narayan, the Maratha peshwa with Nana Fadnavis and Attendants* (1792; Royal Asiatic Society, London). Unfortunately, the subsequent Anglo-Maratha wars of 1803–5 and 1817–18 encouraged the destruction of many of Wales's Indian portraits.

In March 1793 Wales met the artists Thomas and William Daniell, who encouraged him to continue his detailed drawings of Indian caves and temples. On a 1795 drawing expedition to the Kanheri caves, Wales became ill and was carried back to Bombay, where he died on 18 November. The majority of Wales's work would have been lost or forgotten had it not been for the diligence of his friend and patron Charles Warre Malet. On 16 September 1799 Malet married Wales's eldest daughter, Susanna, in England, and in 1800 he published twelve of Wales's views of Bombay. Wales's most ambitious undertaking was a series of studies begun in 1792 for a history painting depicting Malet's negotiations for a British treaty with the Marathas. Malet made these studies available to Thomas Daniell, who exhibited the finished work at the Royal Academy in 1805 under the title *Sir C. Malet, bart., the British resident at Poonah, in the year 1790 concluding a treaty in the durbar with Souae Madarow the peshwa or prince of the Mahratta empire* (priv. coll.). A collection of Wales's drawings is in the collection of the Yale Center for British Art, New Haven, Connecticut.

J. L. CAW, rev. DOUGLAS FORDHAM

Sources M. Archer, *India and British portraiture, 1770–1825* (1979) · Graves, *Soc. Artists*
Archives Yale U. CBA, 'A collection of manuscripts, diaries and notebooks', Wales MSS, vols. 1–6 | BM, Whitley papers, 1616

Wales, John of [John Wallensis] (d. 1285), Franciscan friar and theologian, was born in north Wales and graduated in theology from Oxford, before joining the Franciscans in 1258. He belonged to the custody of Worcester, which included north Wales. He was sixth lector to the Oxford

Franciscans, from 1259 to 1262, and it can be deduced from his works that he spent the early to mid-1260s living and writing in Oxford, before transferring to Paris in the late 1260s. He was certainly in Paris by June 1270, as a sermon of this date survives. There are no references to John's activities during the 1270s, but his abundant works show that he spent most of his time writing, while his sources indicate that he did this in Paris. During the years 1281–3, John was one of two Franciscan regent masters of theology in Paris, and three of the sermons he preached there have survived. In this period John left Paris for long enough to travel to Wales twice as Archbishop Pecham's ambassador to Llywelyn ap Gruffudd—he made trips in October and November of 1282. From 1283 to 1285 he was still based in Paris, as part of the commission appointed to examine the works of Peter John Olivi, a Provençal friar suspected of heresy. John died in 1285, before the commission had completed its task, and was buried in Paris.

John of Wales was a remarkably prolific writer. Some twenty surviving works are now accepted as his. They range from sermons and biblical commentaries to pastoral handbooks of various kinds. The body of work as a whole was extremely popular from the late thirteenth until the mid-sixteenth century. Over 450 manuscripts of John's works survive, and fourteen early printed editions of various texts appeared between 1472 and 1550.

The pastoral handbooks were by far the most popular of John's works. They are remarkable particularly for the wide variety of texts that John quoted to help educate his readers. His fascination with the ancient world led him to seek out an extraordinary range of sources, some extremely rarely cited in his time. His use of more than fifty classical authors establishes him as a major classicizing writer for the thirteenth and fourteenth centuries, and he seems to have been an important link between the classical interests of Robert Grosseteste (d. 1253) and the wider classicizing tendencies of many fourteenth-century English friars. In particular, John was one of the first medieval writers to quote from a full text of the *Noctes Atticae* of Aulus Gellius, doing much to spread and popularize knowledge of this author.

The four best known of John's works were his *Breviloquium de virtutibus antiquorum principum et philosophorum* (151 manuscripts survive, and 5 early printed editions), *Communiloquium, sive, Summa collationum* (144 manuscripts survive, and 10 printed editions), *Compendiloquium de vita illustrium philosophorum* (27 manuscripts survive, and 3 early printed editions), and *Breviloquium de sapientia sanctorum* (23 manuscripts and 5 early printed editions). These four works have many stylistic similarities and seem to have been written as a group between the mid-1260s and the early 1270s, the first two predating 1270–72, and the latter two postdating this.

The *Breviloquium de virtutibus* relates to the group of works on virtue produced in the later thirteenth century, and to the *Fürstenspiegel* or volumes of advice to princes. John was unusual in his inclusion of philosophers, a theme popular at the time but usually treated separately.

This, with the inclusion of many lively classical tales, does much to explain the work's success and popularity. Apart from the many manuscripts and early printed editions, this work spawned at least ten separate translations and abridgements in five different languages.

John's greatest work, in size as in popularity, was his *Communiloquium*. Written between *c.*1265 and 1269–72, it is a vast handbook for preachers, crammed with extracts from a wide variety of sources. It deals primarily with the state and its ruler, with shorter sections on various divisions of society. John had a clear concept of the state (*respublica*) as a separate entity, and reveals distinct ideas about the need of every individual to support the state and to obey its laws—rulers included. John says that if a king does not rule properly, he is no longer a king but rather a tyrant, and that it is no crime to kill a tyrant. The dating of *Communiloquium* to the mid- to late 1260s, a time of conflict and civil war in Italy, Germany, and England, made these comments highly topical. The later parts of *Communiloquium* comment at length upon contemporary society: husbands and wives, children and education, masters and servants, merchants and farmers, churchmen of all kinds. The work was extraordinarily popular, and its vast compass and selection of exciting tales must partly explain this, but the evidence of textual use indicates that for the readers, as for the writer, the political content was the real meat of the volume.

John's more conventional works were rather less popular. Even so, the *Legiloquium*, *Moniloquium*, *Summa iustitiae*, *De poenitentia*, *Ars praedicandi*, and *Ordinarium vitae religiosae* each survives in between sixteen and forty-four manuscripts—still substantial numbers for handbooks of this period. John's *Postilla in Apocalypsim* was also popular (thirty-seven manuscripts), more so than his various series of sermons. John of Wales's posthumous influence was immense. His works were quoted from Oxford sermons of the 1290s to an English political tract of the 1430s, while Chaucer made considerable use of *Communiloquium* in his *Canterbury Tales*, notably in the general prologue and in the tales of the wife of Bath, the summoner, and the pardoner. John's writings were owned and used in every country in medieval Europe, and were translated into the vernaculars of England, France, Spain, and Italy.

JENNY SWANSON

Sources J. Swanson, *John of Wales: a study of the works and ideas of a thirteenth century friar* (1989)

Wales, Owen of. See Owen of Wales (*d.* 1378).

Wales, William (*bap.* 1734, *d.* 1798), astronomer and mathematician, was baptized at Warmfield in the West Riding of Yorkshire on 1 March 1734, the son of John Wales, of humble circumstances. He is said to have 'walked to London with a Mr Holroyd … Plumber to George 3rd' (*Journals*, 885). Nothing is known of his early years or education, but by the early 1760s he was no mean mathematician, and contributed to the *Ladies' Diary*, a journal specializing in advanced mathematical problems. On 5 September 1765, at Greenwich, he married Mary, the youngest sister of a fellow Yorkshireman, Charles Green, who had recently been assistant at the Royal Observatory. Through Green he met Nevil Maskelyne, the new astronomer royal, who in 1766 commissioned Wales to assist in computations for the first few issues of the *Nautical Almanac*.

In 1767 Wales told the council of the Royal Society that he was willing to go abroad to observe the forthcoming transit of Venus but would prefer a warm climate. In the event, he sailed with Joseph Dymond (Maskelyne's assistant from 1765 to 1766) in May 1768, over-wintered at the Churchill River on the north-west coast of Hudson's Bay with temperatures down to -43 °F, successfully observed the transit in June 1769, and reached London again in October.

In 1771 plans were being made for Captain Cook to go on a second voyage of discovery in the southern hemisphere, the main object of which was to prove or disprove the existence of a great southern continent in temperate latitudes. On 14 December 1771 the board of longitude appointed Wales and William Bayly to go as astronomers, in the *Resolution* (Captain Cook) and *Adventure* (Captain Furneaux) respectively, 'to make Nautical & Astronomical Observations, and to perform other Services tending to the Improvement of Geography & Navigation' (*Journals*, 724). Wales took as his 'servant' George Gilpin (d. 1810), who was to be Maskelyne's assistant at Greenwich (1776–81) and clerk to the Royal Society (1783–1809), and was to succeed Wales as secretary of the board of longitude (1799–1810); he married Lydia Green, a niece of Mrs Wales, in 1781. One of the important secondary objects of the voyage was the trying-out of the new longitude timekeepers; Larcum Kendall's copy of Harrison's prizewinner was one of two taken by Wales.

The two sloops sailed together from Plymouth on 13 July 1772. During the *Resolution's* three-year voyage around the world, twenty-one months of which were spent in the Pacific, Cook came to rely heavily on Wales for all matters astronomical and navigational—for ascertaining geographical position, for making scientific observations ashore and afloat, for instructing junior officers. 'For Mr Wales, whose abilities is equal to his assiduity, lost no one observation that could possibly be obtained', wrote Cook in his journal in November 1774 off New Zealand, continuing: 'Even the situation of such Islands as we past without touching at are by means of Mr Kendalls Watch determined with almost equal accuracy' (*Journals*, 580). The *Resolution* reached Spithead on 30 July 1775.

In the same year Wales was appointed master of the Royal Mathematical School (RMS) within Christ's Hospital, founded by Charles II in 1673 specifically to train boys in navigation to become ships' officers. One of his first tasks was to curb the rowdy behaviour of the RMS boys, older than most others in the school, whose loutish behaviour by 1775 had become a byword. Within a very few years discipline was restored. Charles Lamb, a pupil, described him as a severe but genial man with 'a perpetual fund of humour, a constant glee about him, which,

heightened by an inveterate provincialism of north-country dialect, absolutely took away the sting from his severities' (Lamb, 30). During the Gordon riots of 1780, Wales single-handedly dissuaded rioting prisoners newly freed from Newgate prison from entering Christ's Hospital and looting it because they considered it papist.

Wales was elected fellow of the Royal Society in November 1776. On behalf of the board of longitude he edited his own and Bayly's observations taken on Cook's 1772–5 voyage (published 1777); the observations taken on the 1764–71 voyages of Byron, Wallis, Carteret, and Cook (1788); and *Tables Requisite to be Used with the Nautical Ephemeris* (with Maskelyne, 1781, 1802). On his own behalf he published new editions of John Robertson's *Elements of Navigation* (1780, 1796); his own *An Inquiry into the Present State of Population* (1781); and *Method of Finding Longitude at Sea by Time-Keepers* (1794, 1800). He was appointed secretary of the board of longitude in December 1795.

Wales died in Christ's Hospital (where he was subsequently buried) on 29 December 1798, leaving his wife, Mary, and five children, the eldest of whom, Sarah, married Arthur William Trollope, headmaster of Christ's Hospital from 1799 to 1826.

E. I. CARLYLE, rev. DEREK HOWSE

Sources private information (2004) · CUL, Board of Longitude MSS, RGO 14, vols. 5 and 6 · W. Wales and J. Dymond, 'Astronomical observations made at Prince of Wales's Fort', *PTRS*, 59 (1769), 467–88 · W. Wales, 'Journal of a voyage to Churchill River', *PTRS*, 60 (1770), 100–36 · 'Observations on the state of the air, winds and weather, etc. made at Prince of Wales's fort', *PTRS*, 60 (1770), 137–78 · W. Wales, 'Observations on the solar eclipse', *PTRS*, 68 (1778), 1013–18 · W. Wales, 'Hints relating to the use which may be made of the tables of natural and logarithmic sines, tangents, etc.', *PTRS*, 71 (1781), 454–78 · *The journals of Captain James Cook*, ed. J. C. Beaglehole, 2, Hakluyt Society, 35 (1961); repr. (1969) · W. Trollope, *A history of the royal foundation of Christ's Hospital* (1834), 94–5, 128 · C. Lamb, 'On Christ's Hospital, and the character of the Christ's Hospital boys', *Christ's Hospital: recollections of Lamb, Coleridge, and Leigh Hunt*, ed. R. Brimley Johnson (1896), 30 · council minutes, 1767, RS

Archives CUL, logbook and observations, RGO 14/58 and 59 · Mitchell L., NSW, journal 1773-4, Safe PH 18/4 · RS, miscellaneous papers

Likenesses J. Russell, pastel, 1794, Christ's Hospital collection, Horsham, Sussex

Waley [*formerly* Schloss], **Arthur David** (1889–1966), translator of Chinese and Japanese literature, was born at Tunbridge Wells on 19 August 1889, the second of the three sons of David Frederick *Schloss (1850–1912), economist and Fabian socialist, and his wife, Rachel Sophia, daughter of Jacob *Waley, legal writer and professor of political economy. His elder brother was Sir (Sigismund) David *Waley, authority on international finance. The family adopted Jacob Waley's surname in 1914, in what is assumed to have been a response to anti-German sentiment at the onset of the First World War.

Arthur Waley was brought up in Wimbledon and sent to Rugby School (1903–6), where he shone as a classical scholar and won an open scholarship at King's College, Cambridge, while still under seventeen. He spent a year in

Arthur David Waley (1889–1966), by Rex Whistler, c.1928–38

France before going up to the university in 1907; he obtained a first class in part one of the classical tripos in 1910 but had to abandon Cambridge when he developed diminished sight in one eye. He rested, and travelled on the continent, becoming fluent in Spanish and German.

Although Waley had got to know Sydney Cockerell at Cambridge, it was through Oswald Sickert, a brother of the painter, that he was led to consider a career in the British Museum. Sickert was one of a group of friends, mostly museum staff or researchers in the library, who met regularly for lunch in the years before 1914 at the Vienna Café in New Oxford Street; Laurence Binyon was also one of the regulars. In June 1913, supported by Sickert and Cockerell, Waley started working in the newly formed sub-department of oriental prints and drawings under its first head, Binyon. His task was to make a rational index of the Chinese and Japanese painters represented in the museum collection; he immediately started to teach himself Chinese and Japanese. He had no formal instruction, but by 1916 was privately printing his first fifty-two translations of Chinese poems, and in 1917–18 he added others in the first numbers of the *Bulletin* of the newly established School of Oriental Studies, and in the *New Statesman* and the *Little Review*. By 1918 he had completed enough translations of poems, mainly by writers of the classic Tang period, to have a volume entitled *A Hundred and Seventy Chinese Poems* accepted for publication, largely on account of a perceptive review in the *Times Literary Supplement* of the 1917 *Bulletin* poems. In 1919 Stanley

Unwin became his publisher and remained his constant friend and admirer.

From his sixteen years at the museum Waley's only official publications were the index of Chinese artists (1922), the first in the West; and a catalogue (1931) of the paintings recovered from Tunhuang (Dunhuang) by Sir Aurel Stein and subsequently divided between the government of India and the British Museum. *An Introduction to the Study of Chinese Painting* (1923) was a by-product of his unpublished notes on the national collection and its relation to the great tradition of Chinese painting. He also set in order and described the museum's Japanese books with woodcut illustrations and its large collection of Japanese paintings. He retired from the museum on the last day of 1929 because he had been told that he ought to spend his winters abroad. Waley had started to ski as early as 1911 and liked to get away into the mountains whenever he could, generally to Austria or Norway and not to the regular runs but as a lone figure on the high snow slopes.

Waley's largest translation, and probably the one for which he was best-known during his lifetime, was of the *Genji Monogatari* by Murasaki Shikibu, the late tenth-century classical novelist of Japan. The first volume appeared in 1925; the sixth volume did not appear until 1933. This was not the first of Waley's Japanese translations, for it had been preceded by two volumes of classic poetry, selections from the *Uta* (1919) and *No* plays (1921). In these he was more concerned with the resonances of the Japanese language, whereas in the *Genji* he aimed rather at an interpretation of the sensibility and wit of the closed society of the Heian court, voiced in the idiomatic English of his day. Inevitably this shows signs of dating as the idiom itself becomes remote, and a less exuberant version (by Edward G. Seidensticker, 1976) took its place.

Waley continued through life as a creative translator of Chinese poetry. His use of 'sprung rhythm' to convey in the English mode the shape of Chinese verse forms differs from that of Gerard Manley Hopkins: in place of urgent acceleration it evokes the clear phrasing of the flute, an instrument he liked to play. But Waley's systematic engagement with China over the last thirty years of his life took him far beyond poetry. He revisited the early thinkers (*The Way and its Power*, 1934; *The Analects of Confucius*, 1938; *Three Ways of Thought in Ancient China*, 1939), explored the lives of sympathetic writers and divines (Bo Juyi, 1949; Li Bo, 1950; *The Real Tripitaka*, 1952; Yuan Mei, 1956), and discovered the bright colours of vernacular literature (*Monkey*, 1942; *Ballads and stories from Tunhuang*, 1960). These books all speak with the same clear but intimate voice; their readers find that a distant and alien world grows subtly close to their own.

Waley moved with the smooth grace of the skier, his gesture was courtly in salutation, but more characteristic was the attentive, withdrawn pose of his finely profiled head with its sensitive but severe mouth. His voice was high-pitched but quiet and unchanging, so as to seem conversational in a lecture, academic in conversation. In later life he had a slight stoop which accentuated his ascetic appearance. He enjoyed meeting sympathetic people and hearing their conversation but never spoke himself unless he had something to say; he expected the same restraint in others. His forty years' attachment to Beryl de Zoete (d. 1962), anthropologist and interpreter of Eastern dance forms, brought out the depth of feeling and tenderness of which he was capable.

As a scholar Waley aimed always to express Chinese and Japanese thought and sensibility at their most profound levels, with the highest standard of accuracy of meaning, in a way that would not be possible again because of the growth of professional specialization. He was always a lone figure in his work, though he was not remote from the mood of his times. Although he never travelled to east Asia and did not seek to confront the contemporary societies of China or Japan, he was scathingly critical of the attitude to their great cultures displayed by the West in the world in which he grew up: hence his scorn for the older generation of Sinologists and his hatred of imperialism, as shown in *The Opium War through Chinese Eyes* (1958).

For over forty years Waley lived in Bloomsbury, mostly in Gordon Square. Although he had many connections with the Bloomsbury group of artists and writers, he was never a member of a clique, and his friendships with the Stracheys, the Keyneses, and with Roger Fry dated from his Cambridge days. He was elected an honorary fellow of King's in 1945 but was not often seen there. Other honours also came to him late: election to the British Academy in 1945, the queen's medal for poetry in 1953, CBE in 1952, and CH in 1956. Aberdeen and Oxford universities awarded him honorary doctorates. After Beryl de Zoete's death in 1962 he went to live in Highgate where he was looked after by Alison Grant Robinson, an old friend from New Zealand, who was formerly married to Hugh Ferguson Robinson. He married her a month before his death at his home, 50 Southwood Lane, Highgate, from cancer of the spine on 27 June 1966.

A volume of appreciation and an anthology of Waley's writings was edited by Ivan Morris, under the title *Madly Singing in the Mountains* (1970), a phrase taken from a poem by Bo Juyi which Waley had translated in 1917 and chosen because of its 'joyfulness'. For Waley the work of a translator was 'made to the measure of his own tastes and sensibilities' (I. Morris, ed., *Madly Singing in the Mountains*, 1970, 158). He sought to make his translations works of art, aiming at literature rather than philology. In this he was successful. BASIL GRAY, *rev.* GLEN DUDBRIDGE

Sources A. D. Waley, introduction, *A hundred and seventy Chinese poems*, new edn (1962) · I. Morris, ed., *Madly singing in the mountains* (1970) · *The Times* (28 June 1966) · L. P. Wilkinson, *King's College Annual Report* (1966) · personal knowledge (1981) · private information (1981) · A. Waley, *A half of two lives* (1982)
Archives King's AC Cam., papers and family papers relating to him; further papers | Rutgers University, New Brunswick, corresp., literary MSS, and papers | Dartington Hall, Totnes, letters to Leonard Elmhirst · Harvard University, Center for Italian Renaissance Studies, near Florence, Italy, letters to Bernard Berenson · McMaster University, Hamilton, Ontario, corresp. with Bertrand Russell | SOUND BL NSA, 'Conversation', P76R BD1, P114R BD1 · BL NSA, 'He never went to China', T2409W C1 · BL NSA, 'Hunter of beautiful words', B1610/1 · BL NSA, performance recordings
Likenesses R. Whistler, pencil drawing, *c.*1928–1938, NPG [*see illus.*] · W. Stoneman, photograph, 1946, NPG · C. Beaton, photograph, 1956, NPG · M. Ayrton, pencil drawing, 1957, King's Cam. · R. Strachey, oils, NPG
Wealth at death £152,998: administration, 1966, *CGPLA Eng. & Wales*

Waley [*formerly* Schloss], **Sir** (**Sigismund**) **David** (1887–1962), civil servant, was born in London on 19 March 1887, the eldest of the three sons of David Frederick *Schloss (1850–1912), Board of Trade official and writer on economic and social matters, and his wife, Rachel Sophia, the daughter of Jacob Waley. Throughout his life he was known to friends and colleagues as Sigi, but in 1914 he assumed the surname of Waley, as did his brother Arthur David *Waley. He was educated at Rugby School, where he was head boy, and at Balliol College, Oxford; he obtained a first class in both classical honour moderations (1908) and *literae humaniores* (1910). He held scholarships at both Rugby and Balliol.

It was the classic preparation for a career in the public service, which Schloss duly joined in 1910, in circumstances characteristic of the man. In order to sit the civil service examination, he had to cross the English Channel. The passage was stormy; when he arrived in London he was prostrated by seasickness. But he presented himself at the appropriate place on the following morning; when the results were made known, he had achieved first place. The physical hardiness and the single-minded determination which this incident epitomizes remained with him for the rest of his career. He was assigned to the Treasury, where he followed another Balliol man, appointed in the previous year, Frederick Leith-Ross, with whom he worked closely on external finance between the wars. He was in the Treasury barely long enough to take his first step on the ladder of promotion—by becoming private secretary in 1915 to Edwin Montagu, the financial secretary (of whom he later wrote a sympathetic biography, published in 1964)—when he enlisted in August 1916 and served as a second lieutenant in the 22nd battalion, London regiment.

In the course of his subsequent service in the army Waley (as he had now become) was seriously wounded and was awarded the MC in October 1918. He never spoke of this period of his early adult life; but its effect on his naturally sensitive nature was always clear in the reluctance with which he brought himself to contemplate pain and suffering and the vehement conviction with which he maintained that deliberate cruelty was perhaps the worst of all human sins. On 18 November 1918 he married Ruth Ellen, daughter of Montefiore Simon Waley, stockbroker, and his wife, Florence, daughter of Samuel Montagu (later Lord Swaythling) and sister of Edwin Montagu. They had two sons.

After the war Waley returned to the Treasury and replaced John Maynard Keynes in Paris for the last days of the peace conference. Thus began a satisfying and challenging career in the Treasury division dealing with overseas finance. For some time after 1918 it was permissible to hope that the world might really be rebuilt on more rational and less selfish foundations. At the Paris peace conference in 1919 and the Lausanne conference in 1922–3 Waley devoted all his formidable intellectual powers to guiding his political leaders, with wisdom and humanity, through the maze of problems generated by reparations, war debts, and the financial reconstruction of Europe under the League of Nations. The young high-flyers of the inter-war Treasury such as Waley were given interesting and demanding tasks rather than accelerated promotion, and his progress through the ranks was solid, but unspectacular. He became assistant secretary in 1924 and the principal assistant secretary in overseas finance in 1931. In the 1930s his internationalism—in common with that of most Treasury officials—was tempered by the need to nurture Britain's domestic recovery and to avoid currency and international financial commitments that might lead to higher interest rates in London. But when the clouds began to gather again, he redirected his attention and his energy to husbanding Britain's resources of gold and foreign exchange for the long haul which he knew lay ahead and reorganizing the administrative structure of the overseas finance division to take a new and unprecedented strain.

When Sir Frederick Phillips became the British Treasury representative in Washington in 1940, Waley succeeded him as the under-secretary in charge of home and overseas finance. His interest in home finance was, however, extremely limited and in 1942 he returned to exclusive charge of overseas finance. His achievements were impressive. He did more than anyone to ensure that Britain's wartime exchange controls were not merely effective but were administered with common sense and humanity—not least towards those countries whose people were Britain's allies but whose territories were occupied by her enemies. His diplomatic and problem-solving abilities were also evident in the friendly but sometimes difficult negotiations with the US treasury over financial support for the UK war effort and the preparations for a new post-war international settlement. Indeed he was a key member of the British delegation to Washington in September 1943 that tackled two explosive questions: the coverage of the lend-lease scheme and the reconciliation of British and American plans for post-war international finance. He manifested the same combination of qualities when, towards the end of 1944, he was sent to Athens to advise on the economic reconstruction of Greece after the German forces had withdrawn. At the end of the war he was fully stretched, attending the Potsdam and Moscow conferences, grappling once again with the familiar problems of reparations and inter-allied debts and, a little later in Washington, helping to bring into fruition those cornerstones of post-war world economic expansion, the International Monetary Fund and the International Bank for Reconstruction and Development. Indeed, in 1946, shortly before retirement, he was promoted to Treasury third secretary.

Even in the 1930s Waley was a familiar figure in the world of international finance. He was instantly recognizable—a small, dark man, with alert eyes flashing though gold-rimmed spectacles over a little beak of a nose. He was tough and wiry in build, but modest and unassuming in manner, and was often seen with head cocked slightly on one side and an impish smile on his face. He had no great respect for established reputations; and he made short work of pretentious nonsense. But his penetrating intellect was married to a shrewd sense of the feasible. His mind moved so quickly and often obliquely that he appeared to some observers to cut corners and side-step obstacles in a way that could be interpreted as superficial and rushed. Those who worked more closely with him recognized that the darting speed with which he operated was simply the reflection of a restless intellectual vitality, which had to explore every avenue and overturn every stone.

It was Waley's nature to do business by personal exchange of views rather than through the written word; and, by comparison with senior colleagues, he left comparatively thin pickings on the Treasury files for subsequent researchers. His minutes and memoranda were concise, but always penetrating and occasionally sharp. In part, this reflected the personalities and structure of the Treasury between the ends of the two world wars. It boasted a series of excellent draftsmen with a keen interest in international financial problems and a mission to show how finely balanced were their policy recommendations. There were also external experts, such as Keynes and Sir Hubert Henderson, equally ready to supply closely reasoned advice. But even when he became the head of overseas finance Waley remained the man for succinct, clear, and practical advice. But he was by no means an anti-intellectual. He grasped the new ideas in domestic economic policy, which were associated with Keynes and came to the fore in Whitehall in the 1940s, more securely and sympathetically than other senior Treasury officials. Typically, he was much less committed to deeply entrenched Treasury shibboleths—the need for eventual restoration of the gold standard in the 1930s and the defence of the balanced budget principle in the 1940s—than any in the upper echelons of the department. He was more intellectually consistent and committed than colleagues might have imagined. He was appointed CB in 1933 and KCMG in 1943.

When Waley retired in 1948 he embarked on a new life with zest and vigour. He joined the boards of several City companies; was active in the work of an international charity for deprived children; was treasurer of the British Epilepsy Association; and became the chairman of the Furniture Development Council (1949–57), the Sadler's Wells Trust, and the Mercury Theatre Trust. The last of these gave him particular pleasure. Although not a maker of music himself, he delighted in music made by others; and the Ballet Rambert, controlled by the Mercury Theatre Trust, greatly enhanced the happiness of his later years. In return he brought to it, as to every enterprise in which he took part, invaluable gifts of common sense, enthusiasm, and simple, unaffected lightness of heart. He died at 26 Wolverton Avenue, Kingston upon Thames, Surrey, on 4 January 1962; he was survived by his wife.

TREND, rev. ALAN BOOTH

Sources *The Times* (5 Jan 1962) · *The Times* (9 Jan 1962) · personal knowledge (1981) · private information (1981) · treasury registered files, PRO · *The collected writings of John Maynard Keynes*, ed. D. Moggridge and E. Johnson, 30 vols. (1971–89), vols. 16, 23, 25–7 · G. C. Peden, *The treasury and British public policy, 1906–1959* (2000) · *Imperial Calendar and Civil Service List* · CGPLA Eng. & Wales (1962)
Likenesses photograph, priv. coll.
Wealth at death £14,023 15s. 6d.: probate, 16 March 1962, CGPLA Eng. & Wales

Waley, Jacob (1818–1873), barrister and Anglo-Jewish community leader, was the elder son of Solomon Jacob Waley (d. 1864), of London, and his wife, Rachel Hort. Simon *Waley, pianist and composer, was his brother. Educated in London at Mr Neumegen's school in Highgate and at University College, in 1839 he graduated BA at the University of London, coming top of his year in both mathematics and classics, a feat which earned him a gold medal. His initial ambition was to practise as a solicitor, but after a year he determined on a career at the bar, and entered Lincoln's Inn, where he became a pupil of Lord Justice Rolt; he was called to the bar on 21 November 1842, one of the earliest professing Jews to achieve this distinction. On 28 July 1847, in a ceremony conducted by the chief rabbi, Dr Nathan Adler, Waley married Matilda, third daughter of Joseph Salomons and his wife, Rebecca, sister of Sir Moses Montefiore. There were several children of the marriage, including Julia *Cohen (1853–1917). Another daughter, Rachel Sophia, married the economist and Fabian socialist David Frederick *Schloss; their children included Arthur *Waley and Sir David *Waley.

Waley specialized in conveyancing, becoming in time one of the most respected conveyancers of his day. Although conveyancers rarely appeared in court, he was several times summoned in cases of particular difficulty and acted as conveyancing counsel for the Bedford estates. In collaboration with T. C. and C. D. Wright he edited Davidson's *Precedents and Forms in Conveyancing* (5 vols., London, 1855–65). In 1870 he was appointed one of the conveyancing counsel of the court of chancery. He had previously, in 1867, served as a member of the royal commission on the transfer of land; the legislation on this subject, approved by parliament in 1874, was based substantially upon his opinions.

Waley was a stereotypical 'emancipated' Jew, one of the generation of British Jews who took full advantage of the atmosphere of tolerance and civic equality which characterized the Victorian age. He was an expert in political economy, acting as examiner in this subject for the University of London; in 1853 he was appointed professor of political economy at University College, London, a post he was compelled to resign some thirteen years later owing to pressure of other work. He was also, until his death, joint secretary of the Political Economy Club.

A nephew by marriage of both Sir Moses Montefiore and Sir David *Salomons, Waley was centrally placed within 'the cousinhood' which ruled Anglo-Jewry in the nineteenth century, and he played a substantial part in its communal affairs. He was one of the originators of the scheme (approved by parliament in 1870) to amalgamate the major Ashkenazi (German-speaking) synagogues in London to form one United Synagogue, whose constitution he drafted. The following year he helped to found the Anglo-Jewish Association—a sort of Anglo-Jewish ministry of foreign affairs—and became its first president. He was also president of the Jews' Orphan Asylum and a member of the council of Jews' College, London, which was established in 1859 as a training centre for the Anglo-Jewish ministry. He was prominent in the Hebrew Literary Society and in the Jewish Board of Guardians. He took much interest in the treatment of Jews abroad and in 1872 wrote a brief preface to *The Jews of Roumania*, published by the Anglo-Jewish Association, in protest against the persecution of Jews in that country.

Waley died of liver disease at his home, 20 Wimpole Street, London, on 19 June 1873, and was buried in the United Synagogue's West Ham cemetery. He was survived by his wife. It was a measure of the communal esteem in which he was held that the funeral was attended by both Sir Moses Montefiore and Sir Francis Goldsmid, lay leaders respectively of the Orthodox and Reform Jewish communities in Britain, and by Chief Rabbi Adler.

GEOFFREY ALDERMAN

Sources DNB · *Jewish Chronicle* (23 June 1873) · *Jewish Chronicle* (27 June 1873) · *Jewish Chronicle* (4 July 1873) · *Law Times* (12 July 1873) · CGPLA Eng. & Wales (1873) · m. cert. · d. cert.
Archives UCL, lecture notes
Wealth at death under £50,000: probate, 9 July 1873, CGPLA Eng. & Wales

Waley, Julia Matilda. *See* Cohen, Julia Matilda (1853–1917).

Waley, Simon Waley (1827–1875), composer and banker, was born on 23 August 1827 at Stockwell, London, the younger son of Solomon Jacob Waley (d. 1864) and his wife, Rachel Hort; Jacob *Waley (1818–1873) was his elder brother. He became a prominent member of the London stock exchange, with offices at 2 Angel Court from 1858 to 1873, and at 13 Copthall Street from 1873 to 1875, and a leading figure in the Jewish community during the period of the emancipation of the Jews from civil disabilities. He was very interested in international traffic, and at the age of sixteen he wrote his first letter on the subject to the *Railway Times*. He contributed at length to the correspondence columns of *The Times* under the signature W. London, advocating Boulogne as the postal route between England and Europe, and he sent a series of letters on 'A tour in Auvergne' to the *Daily News* in 1858, which were later incorporated into John Murray's *Handbook for Travellers in France*.

Waley was a highly gifted musician as well as a shrewd man of business. He began to compose before he was eleven years old, and many of his childhood compositions showed great promise. His first published work, *L'arpeggio*, a piano study, appeared in 1848. He had piano lessons from Ignaz Moscheles, William Sterndale Bennett, and George Alexander Osborne, and lessons in theory and composition from William Horsley and Bernhard Molique. In addition to being a brilliant pianist—he performed regularly at concerts of the Amateur Musical Society conducted by Henry Leslie—Waley was a prolific composer. His published compositions include a piano concerto (op. 16), two piano trios, in B♭ and G minor (op. 15 and op. 20), marches and caprices for piano, and many songs, including 'Angels' voices' and 'Sing on, sing on, ye little birds'. He also wrote orchestral pieces, which were not published. One of his finest works is a setting of Psalms 117 and 118 for the synagogue service.

Waley married Anna, the daughter of P. J. Salomons, and they had eight children. He died at his home, 22 Devonshire Place, Marylebone, London, on 30 December 1875, and was buried at the Jewish cemetery, Ball's Pond.

F. G. EDWARDS, *rev.* ANNE PIMLOTT BAKER

Sources Grove, *Dict. mus.* · Boase, *Mod. Eng. biog.* · Brown & Stratton, *Brit. mus.* · *Jewish Chronicle* (7 Jan 1876) · *Jewish Chronicle* (21 Jan 1876) · private information (1899)
Wealth at death under £80,000: probate, 12 Jan 1876, *CGPLA Eng. & Wales*

Waleys, Henry le (*d.* 1302), merchant and mayor of London, may have originated at Chepstow, Monmouthshire, but moved to London with other members of his family, including his brother Walter, who also became active in the city. Like many London merchants of his day Henry le Waleys dealt in a variety of goods, importing hides in 1267, and trading in cloth at St Ives fair in 1287. But he made his fortune as a vintner, dealing in exceptionally large quantities (300 tuns of St Émilion wine in 1284), and importing wine directly from Gascony. He came to be styled 'king's merchant', selling wine to the royal household from 1252 until the early 1280s, with sales whose yearly value averaged about £100. This interest in the wine trade explains his involvement in an unsuccessful attempt to reduce brokers' charges on wine, and he was later accused by the men of other towns of having restricted to city freemen the right to sell wine in London during his mayoralty. Prosperity brought social advancement, which his marriage confirmed; his wife, Joan, daughter of William of Haddestock and Avice of Basing, and granddaughter of Adam of Basing (mayor of London 1251–2), belonged to a family prominent in London since the early twelfth century. At his death he had property scattered all over London, including a house called Le Hales near London Bridge and a large mansion in Stepney, where a great council summoned by the king met in March 1299. He also owned property in Berwick and Boston, as well as the manor of Beckenham in Kent, and land in several other counties, including Somerset.

Waleys was one of the leading figures in the government of London in the late thirteenth century. After an unsuccessful attempt to become bailiff in 1265, he was alderman of Cordwainer ward from 1269 to 1294, sheriff in 1270–71, and mayor in 1273–4, 1281–4, and 1298–9. He represented London on several occasions, going to Paris in 1274 to consult with Edward I on his approaching coronation, and attending the Shrewsbury parliament of 1283. His first term as mayor was marked by action against former supporters of Simon de Montfort; in January 1274 he secured the annulment of the charters which Walter Hervey, who had dominated the city in the late 1260s, had granted to the craft guilds, and later engineered Hervey's final exclusion from public life. But his policy went far beyond the defence of traditional and vested interests. As mayor Waleys directed inquiries into and promulgated ordinances on various trades, including masons and carpenters, but above all those concerned with victualling—he was clearly well aware of the connection between public order and the food supply. In his first mayoralty he had new vessels provided for the official and public measurement of corn, and in his second introduced the practice of dragging bakers convicted of fraud through the city streets on a hurdle. He was also responsible for ordinances creating a watch and keeping a check on strangers, while in 1283 he had a new prison, the Tun, built on Cornhill for curfew breakers and men caught in fornication. He expanded the paving of city streets in the direction of Westminster, and was instrumental in extending the wall of the city near Blackfriars. In 1282 he took decisive action towards the repair and maintenance of London Bridge by setting up a trust to finance it: the trust consisted of a new market for the victualling trades to the north of St Mary Woolchurch, known as The Stocks, and a housing development next to St Paul's Churchyard, on which Waleys later attempted to speculate for his own profit. He may also have had a role in the creation of the London Puy about 1300. His policies were backed by Edward I, but were unpopular with some Londoners, who considered that the city's franchise was being infringed, and in October 1284 Waleys lost the mayoralty. The government of the city was taken into the king's hand shortly afterwards, and the Londoners had to wait for a reversal of royal policy until 1297, when that year's political crisis led to the restoration of the city's liberties, along with the abolition of the Tun and of Waleys's edicts for the corn trade. In April 1298 the mayoralty was restored, and the Londoners elected Waleys, although he appears to have resigned his aldermanry four years earlier. The election was intended to placate the king, and Waleys was not re-elected the following year, but disappeared thereafter from the city's governing circle.

Waleys had already benefited from royal favour during the reign of Henry III, even though his record during the barons' wars was ambivalent. His connections with the court, and with Edmund, earl of Cornwall (*d.* 1300), in particular, enabled him to obtain exemption for life from all royal levies in 1266, and from being put on assizes and made sheriff against his will in 1267. He may have been knighted by the king in 1281; in 1283 he was given the wardship of John de Neville by the queen mother, Eleanor of Provence, and her cousin Amadeus, count of Savoy. He was also a friend of the chancellor, Robert Burnell (*d.* 1292). The inevitable corollary of royal favour was royal service. Waleys was nominated to a number of judicial commissions, and in the 1280s may have been involved in the works at Westminster. In 1284, along with Gregory of Ruxley (d. 1291) and Itier d'Angoulême, he was appointed to enforce edicts on the clipping and falsification of money. He was several times employed by Edward I on commissions for town planning, for instance at New Winchelsea in November 1281, while in January 1297 he was advising Edward on the rebuilding and development of Berwick. Waleys also frequently went abroad, on his own business or in the king's service. In 1275 he was appointed mayor of Bordeaux, but Waleys, unable to govern a city divided by internal strife, had to resign in the autumn of the same year. In July 1284 he was appointed farmer of the revenues of six Gascon bastides (planned new towns), while in February 1286 he represented the king's interests in court at Rouen. He also either had interests of his own in Ireland, or was active there in the king's service in 1294. Moreover, Edward employed him in his Scottish wars, in October 1297 commissioning him to levy 1000 men in Worcestershire.

Henry le Waleys died in London on 29 June 1302, and his will was proved in the court of husting on 16 July following. A patron of the mendicant orders, he was buried on 5 July in the church of the London Minoresses outside Aldgate, and was also a benefactor of the city's Franciscans, building the nave of their church, giving timber for its altars, and leaving them a large legacy. His son, Augustine Uxbridge, became keeper of the exchange under Edward II, and married Margaret, the sister of Richard Conduit. Waleys had another son, Henry, mentioned in 1276, who probably predeceased his father.

FRÉDÉRIQUE LACHAUD

Sources CLRO · Chancery records · G. A. Williams, Medieval London: from commune to capital (1963) · W. Stubbs, ed., 'Annales Londonienses', Chronicles of the reigns of Edward I and Edward II, 1, Rolls Series, 76 (1882), 1–251 · T. Stapleton, ed., De antiquis legibus liber: cronica majorum et vicecomitum Londoniarum, CS, 34 (1846) · Y. Renouard, ed., Bordeaux sous les rois d'Angleterre (1965) · N. Beresford, New towns of the middle ages: town plantation in England, Wales and Gascony (1967) · A. B. Beaven, ed., The aldermen of the City of London, temp. Henry III–[1912], 2 vols. (1908–13) · C. L. Kingsford, The Grey friars of London, British Society of Franciscan Studies, 6 (1915) · E. Wedemeyer Moore, The fairs of medieval England: an introductory study (1985) · M. D. Lobel, ed., The British atlas of historic towns, 3 (1989) · J. Stow, A survey of London, rev. edn (1603); repr. with introduction by C. L. Kingsford as A survey of London, 2 vols. (1908); repr. with addns (1971) · DNB · A. F. Sutton, 'Merchants, music and social harmony: the London Puy and its French and London contexts, circa 1300', London Journal, 17 (1992), 1–16

Waleys [Wallensis], **Thomas** (fl. 1318–1349), Dominican friar and theologian, joined the Dominican order in his youth and by 1318 was a bachelor of theology at Oxford. A three-year dispute between the university and the Dominicans prevented him from lecturing on the Sentences. This has customarily been referred to 1311–14, but Waleys is explicit that the dispute that affected him was heard before John XXII (r. 1316–34), so it must have been the second one, in 1317–20. Since it was only in December 1320 that the Dominicans were ready to accept a settlement, Waleys cannot have started lecturing on the Sentences until 1321, so he can hardly have incepted as DD before 1323. In 1326 he was sent as lector to San Domenico, Bologna, since the pope wanted Benedetto da Como, who had been appointed, to go instead on a mission to the Greeks. The general chapter of 1327 attests Waleys's participation, as lector of Bologna, in a consultation on a point of Dominican law. In 1331 Richard Winkley, later provincial of England, was sent to Bologna, and Waleys became chaplain to the Dominican Cardinal Matteo Rosso Orsini in Avignon.

Waleys's surviving academic works, which include Moralitates on the Old Testament and commentaries on part of the psalter and on books 1–10 of De civitate Dei, show him to have been an observant and witty man, with a growing interest in classical antiquity, fostered particularly by the access to rare books that his time in Bologna and Avignon provided. In Beryl Smalley's judgement, his attitude to the classics was more objective and less moralizing than that of his contemporary Petrarch. Learning to approach his texts 'as a scholar, who has collated manuscripts and collected variants', Waleys 'steeped himself in primary sources and he gave exact references' (Smalley, 98, 100). As a teacher and preacher he was never afraid to speak his mind. In Italy he engaged in active polemic against the Franciscan views on poverty condemned by John XXII in 1323; he once went to Arezzo and personally broke up a gathering of allegedly heretical Franciscans. In Avignon, on 3 January 1333, he ventured to combine in one sermon a denunciation of several recognizably Franciscan 'heresies' and a long refutation of the pope's own controversial theory about the beatific vision, especially as expounded by Cardinal Annibaldo da Ceccano. Neither the pope nor the Franciscans were explicitly named, but Waleys's clerical audience would have taken the point. At the end of the sermon he was carried away by his theme, as he admitted later, and made the unpremeditated claim that it was the hope of winning prompt success for their petitions at the papal court that most moved people to support the pope's theory of the beatific vision.

Within days Waleys was summoned before the local inquisitor, the Franciscan Guillaume de Montrond, who had him imprisoned. His position on the beatific vision was not challenged, but six propositions from his sermon were denounced as heretical. The affair became a cause célèbre, arousing intense interest in Paris; the French king himself followed it closely. Most people saw the hand of the pope in what had happened, but Waleys was more aware of the role of his Franciscan enemies, particularly Walter Chatton (d. 1343/4), and complained that he was being unfairly and dishonestly harassed. During a long lull in the proceedings against him he managed to smuggle out of his prison a further contribution to the debate sparked off by the pope's ideas on the beatific vision, a treatise De temporibus et momentis in which he elaborated on his most original theory, of the simultaneity of resurrection and judgement, and incidentally denounced as heretical a view that Chatton had propounded in a sermon. Waleys had eloquent supporters, including the master of the Sacred Palace, Armand de Belvézer, who denied that he was guilty of any heresy; but his enemies were lined up against him. The non-schismatic Franciscans were naturally keen to show their loyalty to John XXII, and in any case they had theological reasons for finding the latter's views on the beatific vision more congenial than the Dominicans did; and the successive committees of masters called to discuss Waleys, while excluding those likely to be sympathetic to him, included outspoken supporters of the pope's theory, such as John Lutterell (d. 1335), who had incidentally been chancellor of Oxford during the dispute of 1317–20 and represented the university against the Dominicans.

On 12 October Waleys appealed to the pope and was soon transferred to the papal prison. In February and March 1334 he appeared before a commission headed by two cardinals. After that the case seems to have lapsed without a verdict. Waleys was freed in August, but not allowed to leave Avignon. After his release he presumably took up residence in the Dominican priory. He did not return to Matteo Rosso Orsini's household, but he evidently remained on good terms with him. In 1336 Matteo's 27-year-old nephew, Tebaldo, was made archbishop of Palermo and he seems to have asked Waleys's advice about preaching. His reply was the readable and sensible *De modo et forma praedicandi*, in which he stresses content rather than style or form. His own recent experiences appear to have left him unperturbed: he advises Tebaldo that, although a preacher should not cause unnecessary offence, if the good of church or state requires it he must be fearless in his denunciation of wrongdoing. It has been argued that *De modo* was written after Waleys's return to England, but he cites something that happened 'in my country', which means he was writing outside England, and the dedication suggests that Tebaldo was still fairly new to his pastoral responsibilities; the second part of the treatise, a set of Advent sermons, is not necessarily based on the Sarum lectionary, as has been alleged, since the Dominican lectionary contained exactly the same readings. *De modo* was followed by another preachers' aid composed for Tebaldo, an alphabetic collection of patristic *sententiae* culled from the corpus of canon law, entitled *Campus florum*, and that seems to be the last thing Waleys wrote.

Probably after Clement VI became pope in 1342, Waleys was allowed to return to Oxford, where he made friends with a secular priest who was studying there, Lambert Poulshot. In 1349 he petitioned the pope to give his friend a benefice. Describing himself as 'broken by old age and struck down with paralysis' (Emden, *Oxf.*, 3. 1961), Waleys says that Lambert, from sheer kindness, is looking after him; otherwise he would be entirely destitute. Evidently the black death had left the Dominican community unable to cope. It is not known when Waleys died.

SIMON TUGWELL

Sources E. Panella, *Scriptores ordinis praedicatorum medii aevi*, 4 (Rome, 1993), 401–8 • Emden, *Oxf.*, 3.1961–2 • B. Smalley, *English friars and antiquity in the early fourteenth century* (1960), 75–108 • M. Dykmans, 'À propos de Jean XXII et Benoît XII: la libération de Thomas Waleys', *Archivum Historiae Pontificiae*, 7 (1969), 115–30 • T. M. Charland, *Artes praedicandi: contribution à l'histoire de la rhétorique au moyen âge* (Paris, 1936), 94–5, 325–403 • T. Kaeppeli, *Le procès contre Thomas Waleys O.P.* (1936) • C. Trottmann, *La vision béatifique: des disputes scolastiques à sa définition par Benoît XII* (1995) • *CEPR letters*, 2.167, 199 • H. Rashdall, 'The Friars Preachers v. the University', *Collectanea: second series*, ed. M. Burrows, OHS, 16 (1890), 193–273 • T. Kaeppeli, 'Benedetto di Asinago da Como († 1339)', *Archivum Fratrum Praedicatorum*, 11 (1941), 83–94 • M. O'Carroll, 'The lectionary for the proper of the year in the Dominican and Franciscan rites of the thirteenth century', *Archivum Fratrum Praedicatorum*, 49 (1979), 85 • S. Tugwell, 'Thomas Waleys: a few details', *Dominican History Newsletter*, 5 (1996), 108–10 • B. M. Reichert, ed., *Acta capitulorum generalium ordinis praedicatorum*, 2 (Rome, 1899), 166, 175–6

Walford, Cornelius (1827–1885), writer on insurance, was born at 79 Curtain Road, Shoreditch, London, on 2 April 1827, the eldest of five sons of the naturalist Cornelius Walford (d. 1883) of Park House Farm, near Coggeshall, Essex, and Mary Amelia Osborn, of Pentonville, London. He was educated at Felsted School, Essex. After working as a solicitor's clerk at Witham, Essex, and then as a local journalist, Walford qualified as a barrister in 1860 at the Middle Temple, but found his métier as an insurance inspector and agent, initially at Witham. He became a director of the East London Bank in 1862, and also undertook the management of the ailing Unity Fire and Life Association. Four years later he was elected to the board of the Accident Insurance Company, and remained a director until his death. Walford made the first of many visits to the USA in 1861, and this led to a number of North American connections: he founded the Colonial Assurance Corporation in 1867, and from 1870 managed the European business of the New York Insurance Company.

By that time Walford was established as an authoritative writer on insurance and actuarial affairs. He published anonymously in 1857 his *Insurance Guide and Handbook*, and this was widely pirated in the USA; it had large sales, and the second edition carried his name. His *Insurance Year Book* appeared in 1870, but his great work was the *Insurance Cyclopaedia*, six volumes of which appeared between 1871 and 1880. In addition to giving a definitive account of Victorian professional practice, Walford discussed the pioneers of the insurance industry. He also wrote the majority of the articles in the *Dictionary of National Biography* about actuaries and insurance men. An active historian, he also published studies of guilds (1879), the Hanseatic League (1881), fairs, plagues, and the effects of famine.

Walford was an associate and then a fellow of the Institute of Actuaries, and was on the council of the Statistical Society. A lifelong interest in shorthand led in 1881 to his becoming president of the newly founded Shorthand Society. In December 1884 he was awarded the Samuel Brown prize of the Institute of Actuaries for his paper on the history of life insurance. Married three times, Walford was the father of three sons and six daughters. He died at his house at 86 Belsize Park Gardens, London, on 28 September 1885 and was buried on 3 October in Brookwood cemetery, Woking; he was survived by his third wife, Laura Walford. W. P. COURTNEY, *rev.* ROBERT BROWN

Sources E. Walford, *In memoriam: Bro. Cornelius Walford* (privately printed, London, 1887) · Dr Westby-Gibson, 'Memoir', *Shorthand* (Nov 1885) · *Biograph and Review*, 3 (1880), 161–4 · *Booklore*, 12 (Nov 1885), 177 · Boase, *Mod. Eng. biog.* · *N&Q*, 6th ser., 12 (1885), 280 · private information (1899) · *CGPLA Eng. & Wales* (1886)
Likenesses portrait, repro. in Walford, *In memoriam*
Wealth at death £11,689 2s. 6d.: probate, 11 Feb 1886, *CGPLA Eng. & Wales*

Edward Walford (1823–1897), by Barraud, pubd 1897

Walford, Edward (1823–1897), writer and compiler of reference works, was born on 3 February 1823 at Hatfield Place, near Chelmsford, Essex, the eldest son of William Walford (d. 1855) of Hatfield Peverel, rector of St Runwald's, Colchester, and his second wife, Mary Ann, daughter of Henry Hutton, rector of Beaumont, Essex, and granddaughter of Sir William *Pepperrell. He was educated at Hackney Church of England school and Charterhouse School where, in 1840–41, he won a Latin hexameter gold medal. He gained an open scholarship at Balliol College, Oxford, in 1841 and in 1843 won the chancellor's prize for Latin verse. He graduated BA (third class) in 1845 and MA two years later. At Balliol with Matthew Arnold, Walford was made deacon in 1847 and ordained priest by Bishop Samuel Wilberforce in 1848, gaining the Denyer theological prize in both years.

Walford spent a year as assistant master at Tonbridge School, then moved to Clifton, near Bristol, and London, preparing private pupils for Oxford, publishing Latin and Greek grammars, and writing theological books. In Clifton, on 8 August 1847, he married Mary Holmes Gray (1824/5–1851). A daughter, Mary Louisa (later Mrs Colin Campbell Wyllie), was born in 1848. Walford had joined the Roman Catholic communion as a lay member by 1852, and married Julia Mary Christina Talbot (1822–1895), the daughter of Admiral Sir John *Talbot, on 3 February 1852. The eight years from 1853 saw the birth of their children; Julia Marion (later Mrs Philip Conron), Edith (later Mrs Frederick Waddy), and Ethel were born in Clifton, and Alice (1857–1870) was born in Westminster, and Edward and Philip in Hampstead.

In 1855 Walford had started his long career in biographic journalism when he compiled the first editions of the annuals *Hardwicke's Shilling Baronetage and Knightage*, *Hardwicke's Shilling Peerage*, *Hardwicke's Shilling House of Commons*, and *Hardwicke's titles of courtesy containing an alphabetical list of all those members of titled families whose names do not fall within the scope of peerage, baronetage or knightage*. Taken as a whole this series detailed the 'top ten thousand' of Victorian society. In 1860 he compiled the first edition of his comprehensive *County Families of Great Britain* which was published annually for sixty years. In 1860 the Walford family moved into a substantial Georgian house at 17 Church Row, Hampstead, from where, for some twenty-six years, Edward wrote, edited, and compiled his biographical, topographical, and antiquarian books and his articles for a range of magazines and newspapers.

In 1858 Walford started contributing to Charles Knight's *Cyclopaedia*, but his forte was producing biographies at short notice, his 192-page biography of the prince consort arriving on the streets within twenty-two days of Albert's death in 1862. He produced similar biographies of others including Palmerston, Louis Napoleon, and Disraeli. Moving into periodical journalism, Walford became sub-editor and then editor of *Once a Week* (1859–65). He edited the *Gentleman's Magazine* in 1866 and strongly objected to the proprietor Joseph Hatton's decision to change the character of that magazine. Walford resigned and started his own *Register and Magazine of Biography*, but this failed within a year. Writing as Londoniana he then concentrated on topographic articles for *The Times* and leading periodicals. In 1874–6 Walford edited Charles Knight's six-volume *London*, so he was the natural choice of the publisher Cassell & Co. when Walter Thornbury, the author of its *Old and New London*, died in 1876 having written only the first two volumes. Walford completed the final four volumes of what became the standard popular work describing the history and growth of the metropolis. Originally published in monthly parts in 1873–8, this lavishly illustrated series was frequently updated and reissued, as was Walford's equally successful two-volume *Greater London* (1882–3). A 1968 overview of publications on London noted: 'for light bedside reading these books are admirable; they were obviously produced for the beginner who did not want his text cluttered with learned references' (Rubinstein, 124). But their popularity continues, and both series remain available in London reference libraries.

Within months of moving to Hampstead, Walford returned to the Church of England, but in 1870 he reverted to the Roman Catholic faith, resigning his holy orders in 1886. In the 1880s Walford edited the new journal *The Antiquary*, but he was soon engaged in another acrimonious dispute with his proprietor, Elliot Stock, over the latter's treatment of him, and both protagonists published their case in the dispute. Walford retired from his journalistic duties in 1886 although he continued writing legal obituaries for *The Times* until 1891 and contributed to *Notes and Queries* until the month of his death. Walford retired to Ventnor, Isle of Wight, in 1891, was awarded a civil-list pension for his literary work in 1892, then continued his literary output by compiling the eight-volume

Windsor Peerage (1890–97). In his *'Patient Griselda' and other Poems* (1894), which contains a good likeness of himself, Walford included acerbic verses satirizing his former proprietor Elliot Stock and calling him Ellicott Skinflint. A journalist contemporary of Walford's annotated his copy of *Patient Griselda* by assessing his former Hampstead neighbour as 'part author of *Old and New London* … a very cantankerous sort of man, always quarrelling' (Woolven, 25).

After years of illness and at the age of seventy-four, Walford died of a stroke in Ventnor on 20 November 1897. He was buried at Holy Trinity, Ventnor, on 24 November. Although it was reported that he had finally returned to the Church of England, his grave is in the Catholic area of the churchyard. He was a fellow of the Royal Historical Society, a member of the Royal Archaeological Institute and of the Genealogical Society, and was a council member of the Society for Preserving the Memorials of the Dead. The British Library catalogue lists some eighty-seven books written, compiled, or edited by the industrious Edward Walford.   ROBIN WOOLVEN

Sources DNB · R. Woolven, 'The industrious Edward Walford — Church Row's cantankerous compiler', *Camden History Review* (1994), 21–5 · *The Times* (23 Nov 1897) · *The Times* (24 Nov 1897) · *The Times* (25 Nov 1897) · collected MSS on the Walford family, *c.*1926, Society of Genealogists, London · Crockford (1824) · Crockford (1860) [and some subsequent edns] · *Converts to Rome* [various edns, held at Westminster Cathedral Library] · manuscript annotation by E. E. Newton (*c.* 1900) in his copy of Walford's *'Patient Griselda'*, Camden Libraries · E. Walford, *'Patient Griselda' and other poems* (1894) · private information (2004) [Ventnor, Isle of Wight, Local History Group; Major Walford-White; local studies library staff in Guildford, St Albans, Ryde, Isle of Wight, and Camden] · S. Rubinstein, *Historians of London* (1968) · *CGPLA Eng. & Wales* (1898) · *London Directory* (1847–91)
Archives NL Scot., Blackwood MSS, corresp.
Likenesses Barraud, photograph, pubd 1897, NPG [*see illus.*] · engraving (after photograph?), repro. in Walford, *'Patient Griselda'*, frontispiece
Wealth at death £9801 10s. 6d.: probate, 28 Jan 1898, *CGPLA Eng. & Wales*

Walford [*née* Colquhoun], **Lucy Bethia** (1845–1915), novelist and artist, was born on 17 April 1845 at 11 Brighton Crescent, Portobello, Edinburgh, the seventh child of Frances Sara Fuller Maitland (1813–1877), poet and hymn writer, and John *Colquhoun (1805–1885) of Luss, Dunbartonshire, a sportsman, naturalist, author of *The Moor and the Loch*, and former military officer. Her paternal grandfather was Sir James Colquhoun, baronet, and her grandmother was Lady Janet *Colquhoun (1781–1846), a religious writer. Other family connections included her aunt, the evangelical novelist Catherine Sinclair (1800–1864). Lucy Colquhoun led a privileged childhood, spending summers either at her mother's family home near Henley-on-Thames, Oxfordshire, at the highland family seat at Rossdhu, Dunbartonshire, or in touring the Western Isles. Educated at home by German governesses, she began reading avidly at an early age and was strongly influenced by the works of Charlotte Yonge, Susan Ferrier, and, in later

years, Jane Austen—influences reflected in her subsequent writing. In 1855 the family moved to 6 Eton Terrace in Edinburgh, but dissatisfaction with the accommodation prompted a move shortly after to 1 Royal Terrace. Here the family entertained members of Edinburgh society, including the painter Noël Paton, who encouraged Lucy Colquhoun to take up painting. Success came in 1868 when she exhibited work at the annual Royal Scottish Academy exhibition, a practice she continued for several years following. About this time she also began writing secretly and her first short piece was published in May 1869 in the *Sunday Magazine*. In June of that year she married Alfred Saunders Walford (*d.* 1907), magistrate, of Cranbrook Hall, Ilford, Essex, and they moved to London; they had two sons and five daughters.

In 1874, after many years of work, Lucy Walford published her first novel, *Mr Smith: a Part of his Life*, with the Edinburgh firm William Blackwood & Son. A light-hearted treatment of domestic life, it proved a great success and was admired by Queen Victoria, to whom she was presented at Buckingham Palace a year or so later as a consequence. Coventry Patmore also admired it, and he praised her in the *St James Gazette* as the equal of Thomas Hardy. Her subsequent works continued in the same vein and included *Pauline* (1877), *The Baby's Grandmother* (1884), *Cousins* (1885), *Stiff Necked Generation* (1889), and *The Havoc of a Smile* (1890). Her last novel, *David and Jonathan on the Riviera*, was published in 1914. She also wrote extensively for various London journals, including *The World*, and from 1889 to 1893 served as the London correspondent for the New York-based publication *The Critic*. By the time of her death on 11 May 1915 at her London home, 17 Warwick Square, Pimlico, Lucy Walford had published more than forty-five books, including two memoirs, *Recollections of a Scottish Novelist* (1910) and *Memories of Victorian London* (1912).   DAVID FINKELSTEIN

Sources L. B. Walford, *Recollections of a Scottish novelist* (1910); [new edn] (1984) · Blain, Clements & Grundy, *Feminist comp.* · Boase, *Mod. Eng. biog.* · *CGPLA Eng. & Wales* (1915) · WWW
Archives NL Scot., Blackwood MSS · Waddesdon Manor, Buckinghamshire, Kyllin archive
Likenesses etchings, Waddesdon Manor, Buckinghamshire · photographs, Waddesdon Manor, Buckinghamshire
Wealth at death £2993 17s. 10d.: probate, 29 July 1915, *CGPLA Eng. & Wales*

Walford, Thomas (1752–1833), antiquary, born on 14 September 1752, was the only son of Thomas Walford (*d.* 1756) of Whitley, near Birdbrook in Essex, and his wife, Elizabeth Spurgeon (*d.* 1789) of Linton in Cambridgeshire. He was an officer in the Essex militia in 1777, and was appointed deputy lieutenant of the county in 1778. In March 1797 he became a captain in the provisional cavalry, and the following May he was promoted major. In February 1788 he was elected a fellow of the Society of Antiquaries, in October 1797 a fellow of the Linnean Society, in 1814 a member of the Geological Society, and in 1825 a fellow. In 1818 he published *The Scientific Tourist through England, Wales, and Scotland*. In this he described the principal objects of antiquity, art, science, and the picturesque in Great Britain, under the county headings. The work was too comprehensive to be exhaustive, and its value varied with Walford's personal knowledge of the places he describes.

Walford died, apparently unmarried, at Whitley on 6 August 1833, and was buried at Birdbrook parish church. He published several papers in *Archaeologia*, *Vetusta monumenta*, and *Transactions of the Linnean Society* and left several manuscripts, including a history of Birdbrook in Essex and another of Clare in Sussex.

E. I. CARLYLE, *rev.* J. A. MARCHAND

Sources *GM*, 1st ser., 103/1 (1833), 469 · T. Wright, *The history and topography of the county of Essex*, 1 (1836), 611 · will, PRO, PROB 11/1822, sig. 608

Wealth at death £7400 left to sister; £2500 left to servants; funds to executors for erection of memorial statue in church at Birdbrook: will, PRO, PROB 11/1822, fols. 58v–59r

Walkden, Alexander George, Baron Walkden (1873–1951), trade unionist and politician, was born in Hornsey, London, on 11 May 1873, the second of the nine children of Charles Henry Scrivener Walkden, an accountant with the Great Northern Railway, and his wife, Harriet Rogers. He was educated at the Merchant Taylors' School, Ashwell, Hertfordshire. In 1898 he married Jennie (*d.* 1934), daughter of Jesse Wilson, clothier and director of a brickworks at Market Rasen; they had three daughters.

In 1889 Walkden began work as a clerk on the Great Northern Railway, subsequently becoming a freight representative at Nottingham and, in 1905, goods agent at Fletton near Peterborough. A convinced trade unionist, he had joined the Railway Clerks' Association (RCA) on its formation in 1897. He served as secretary and then chairman of the powerful Nottingham branch before his move to Fletton, and was instrumental in persuading a conference in 1898 not to wind up the union, which was then in severe difficulties. He served on the national executive from 1899 to 1904, and became a Labour member of Nottingham council in 1905.

At the May 1905 RCA conference Walkden easily beat off rivals to be elected the union's general secretary, a post he held until his retirement in May 1936. He brought to his new task an attractive personality, determination, courage, imagination, enthusiasm, and boundless energy. His aim was that railway clerks could and should become as good trade unionists as any other workers. But although the RCA now had 4000 members, its future was far from clear. Funds were almost depleted and morale low, and the railway companies still refused to recognize the union. Some companies had no salary scales, working hours varied between different companies and offices, and companies often expected clerks to act as strikebreakers. For many years Walkden (widely known as A. G.) worked tremendously hard, with most of his evenings and weekends being given to union service.

Walkden's achievements were numerous. First, the union grew. Its membership rose to 19,151 in 1910 and 29,394 by the end of 1914. By 1918 it had 71,500 members, representing about 93 per cent of the railways' salaried staff. This figure then fell back somewhat, but by 1936 the RCA, with around 60,000 members, was probably the strongest white-collar union in Britain. Second, he was a keen and successful defender of the RCA's independence. The Amalgamated Society of Railway Servants and its successor, the National Union of Railwaymen, made periodic attempts to unite all the railway unions (as in 1908, 1917–18, and 1932), but each time Walkden was able to head off pressure for fusion. He also saw off the threat from a rival 'non-political' union, the Railway Salaried Staffs' Association. Formed in 1928, it had ceased to exist two years later.

Third, Walkden's great object was achieved in February 1919 when, after the threat of a strike, official recognition of the union as a negotiating body was conceded by the railway companies. The negotiations which followed led to the introduction of a national agreement with standard minimum conditions covering all railways. Collected together in one green-covered book, they represented the ultimate outcome of Walkden's efforts. He seldom referred to it as other than the 'Bible of the RCA'.

Finally, Walkden was a leading figure in pressing for the nationalization of Britain's railways. He was mainly responsible for drafting a National Transport Services Bill in 1918, and in 1929 he submitted an impressive sixty-paragraph memorandum to the royal commission on transport. Both of these foreshadowed much of the transport legislation of the post-war Labour government; significantly, he was later to be responsible for the passage through the House of Lords of the bill which nationalized the railways.

The wider labour movement also made its claims upon Walkden. He was a member of the general council of the Trades Union Congress from its creation in 1921 until his retirement in 1936. Although a moderate, he played a significant role in preparations for the general strike of 1926 and supported the calling of the strike. However, he was one of the first to see that it was unlikely to succeed, and as his own members began to drift back to work he was one of those keenest to see the dispute brought to an end. He later supported the attempts at industrial conciliation represented by the Mond–Turner talks of 1928–9. However, he was no 'soft touch': along with other railway union leaders he ordered his members back out on strike in May 1926 once it became clear that the companies were trying to enforce less favourable wages and conditions on the returning workers. He also made determined attempts to secure the reinstatement of victimized individual members. The limits of his moderation were also seen in 1931, when he was part of the five-man general council deputation which finally told the Labour cabinet that its proposed package of spending cuts was not acceptable to the TUC. In 1932–3 he served as TUC chairman. His trade union activities spread also to the international field through his membership of the International Transport Workers' Federation.

Walkden's contribution on the political side of the movement was less substantial but still significant. He was one of the leaders of the movement to get the RCA to affiliate to the Labour Party; this was achieved in 1911. In 1912 he became the RCA-sponsored Labour candidate for West Wolverhampton, but he was defeated there three times between 1918 and 1922. Defeat in a Lancashire constituency (Heywood and Radcliffe) followed in 1924. In 1929 he finally won, at Bristol South, but was defeated in 1931. However, he was elected for the same constituency in 1935 and retained the seat until his retirement in June 1945, when he was created Baron Walkden. In his first spell as an MP he made very few contributions to debate. Relieved of union concerns after 1936, though, he became more active and spoke on a wide range of issues, although with the railways remaining the most significant. Between 1943 and 1945 he served on the administrative committee of the Parliamentary Labour Party. From August 1945 to July 1949 he was captain of the king's bodyguard of the yeomen of the guard and government second whip in the House of Lords.

Walkden was an excellent speaker and writer, and a shrewd negotiator. His cleverness showed through in debate; he was at his rhetorical best when 'fighting back'. Contemporaries saw him as a man of great personal charm with a twinkle in his eyes, but one who had an iron will when he thought an injustice was being committed. Physically he was a small, bearded man, but he had a deep voice and a disarming throaty chuckle, which was at its best when deriding opposition.

Brought up in the country by a father who wrote on small-holdings for William Morris's *Commonweal*, A. G. always remained a countryman at heart. He liked the theatre and the cinema, and was particularly fond of Gilbert and Sullivan and Garbo. He had a profound knowledge of trees, birds, and flowers. As a hobby, he bred some of the best old English gamecocks in Britain.

On Walkden's retirement in 1936 an RCA collection raised £1150; but with a typical gesture he asked for the money to be used to endow a men's ward at Manor House Hospital, Golders Green, and to provide books for the library of Ruskin College, Oxford. Although in 1951 the RCA changed its name to the Transport Salaried Staffs' Association, recognizing the expanded interests of the union, its registered office was named Walkden House. He died at Holloway Sanatorium, Virginia Water, Egham, Surrey, on 25 April 1951, and the barony became extinct.

ANDREW THORPE

Sources DNB · A. Tranter, 'Walkden, Alexander George', *DLB*, vol. 5 · P. S. Bagwell, *The railwaymen: the history of the National Union of Railwaymen*, [1] (1963) · H. A. Clegg, A. Fox, and A. F. Thompson, *A history of British trade unions since 1889*, 3 vols. (1964–94) · D. Lockwood, *The blackcoated worker* (1958) · A. R. Griffin and C. P. Griffin, 'The non-political trade union movement', *Essays in labour history, 1918–1939*, ed. A. Briggs and J. Saville (1977), 133–62 · WWW
Archives U. Warwick Mod. RC, Transport Salaried Staffs' Association MSS · U. Warwick Mod. RC, Trades Union Congress MSS
Likenesses E. J. Clack, bronze bust, Transport Salaried Staffs' Association, Walkden House, London · photographs, Transport Salaried Staffs' Association, Walkden House, London
Wealth at death £346 19s. 2d.: administration, 25 Sept 1951, *CGPLA Eng. & Wales*

Walkden, Peter (1684–1769), Presbyterian minister and diarist, was born at Flixton, near Manchester, on 16 October 1684. Nothing is known of his parents. He was educated at a village school, then from 1706 at the academy of James Coningham, minister of the Presbyterian chapel at Manchester. From 1 May 1709 he served as pastor at Garsdale, Yorkshire. At the end of 1711 he became minister of two congregations at Newton in Bowland, Yorkshire, and Hesketh Lane, near Chipping, in a poor and sparsely inhabited part of rural Lancashire. He remained there until 1738, when he moved to Holcombe, near Bury, in the same county. In 1744 he was appointed to the pastorate of the Old Tabernacle, Stockport, Cheshire.

Walkden's diary for the years 1725, 1729, and 1730 presents a vivid picture of the hard life of a poor country minister. Passages from his correspondence and commonplace books have been printed, as well as most of the extant part of his diary.

Walkden was twice married: his first wife died in December 1715. One of his wives was named Margaret Woodworth, and he had eight children. Walkden died at Stockport on 5 November 1769, and is buried in his chapel there. One of his four sons, Henry, followed him in the Presbyterian ministry and wrote a Latin epitaph for his tomb. Henry is said to have been educated in London, but after a promising start, 'some immoral conduct occasioned his dismissal' from a congregation at Tintwistle, Cheshire (Nightingale, 1.228). He died at Clitheroe, Lancashire, in 1795. Peter Walkden's daughter Catherine married William Fogg, and was the mother of the Revd Peter Walkden Fogg of Ormskirk, Lancashire, and grandmother of Henry Fogg, also minister there for sixty-four years.

C. W. SUTTON, *rev.* JIM BENEDICT

Sources *Rev. Peter Walkden's diary and early nonconformist baptisms*, ed. G. A. Foster (1996) · *Extracts from the diary of Rev. Peter Walkden*, ed. W. Dobson (1866) · J. Bromley, 'The rural life of a Lancashire minister 150 years ago', *Transactions of the Historic Society of Lancashire and Cheshire*, 32 (1879–80), 117–42 [see also vols. 36–7] · B. Nightingale, *Lancashire nonconformity*, 6 vols. [1890–93], vols. 1–2 · H. Heginbotham, *Stockport: ancient and modern*, 2 vols. (1882–92) · E. Baines and W. R. Whatton, *The history of the county palatine and duchy of Lancaster*, rev. edn, ed. J. Harland and B. Herford, 2 (1870), 2.98 · M. R. Watts, *The dissenters: from the Reformation to the French Revolution* (1978), 327
Archives Ches. & Chester ALSS, diary, CR 678

Walkelin (d. 1098), bishop of Winchester, was one of the Conqueror's chaplains but the claim that he was his kinsman is unsubstantiated. William of Malmesbury tells a story of Archbishop Maurilius of Rouen being concerned with his early career; hence Walkelin the future bishop is probably to be identified with the Walkelin, canon of Rouen, who attests a charter of Maurilius, dated to between 1055 and 1066, in favour of Chartres. Following the deposition of the pluralist Stigand by the papal legate, c.11 April 1070, Walkelin was appointed by the king to the see of Winchester, to which he was consecrated on 30 May by the legate Ermenfrid. Immediately on entering office, Bishop Walkelin sought to replace the monks in his cathedral by canons. This would seem to suggest that he realized the true nature of the problem for a contemporary bishop in that most English of institutions, the monastic cathedral: that is, how to pay the household if the resources of the church were in the main directed to the support of monks. Initially he obtained the support of the king, as well as that of most of his colleagues, for this tactic. His good relations with the Conqueror are evident from the story related by the Winchester annalist, in which William, having granted to Walkelin as much timber as he could take from the wood of Hempage in three days and nights, allowed himself to be appeased after the bishop, with the help of many carpenters, had cut down the entire wood. However, Lanfranc, appointed archbishop of Canterbury later in 1070, successfully resisted this policy. A somewhat embittered narrative of Bishop Walkelin's deeds is placed in the mouth of his successor, Bishop William Giffard, and recorded in the St Swithun's Priory cartulary. Walkelin is said to have divided the goods of the see between himself and the convent and to have appropriated 300 librates of the monks' share of the land for his grandiose building plans, as well as the patronage of all the priory's churches for these same purposes.

Walkelin's principal monument is his building work, for no written material issued in his name appears to survive. His was the decision to destroy the Old Minster church in Winchester, the principal church of Anglo-Saxon Wessex (if not of England in its entirety), and to replace it with the vast Norman cathedral, much of which survives today. The plan was huge in contemporary terms: with a length of almost 180 yards, Walkelin's Winchester was rivalled only by the Cluny III of St Hugh. The work began in 1079 or 1080; the Winchester annalist claimed that the new church was consecrated and the monks took possession of it on 8 April 1093 but the evidence of modern archaeology is that only the eastern portion of the church, and possibly the crossing, could have been completed by then, the remainder not being finished until c.1122, under Walkelin's successor, William Giffard.

Under Rufus, Walkelin remained involved in politics in the royal service—in 1097, shortly before his death, he was appointed regent along with Ranulf Flambard (d. 1128) when the king left England. He continued to attest royal charters, as would be expected while Winchester and the crown-wearing ceremony there at Christmas remained an important manifestation of royal authority. When the dispute between the archbishop of Canterbury and the king concerning papal authority first arose, Walkelin was one of the bishops who tried to persuade Anselm not to pursue his demands for leave to visit Rome. On the occasion of the consecration of Battle Abbey (11 February 1094) he obtained permission for St Giles's Fair, one of the five or six great fairs of medieval England, a major source of wealth for the see and crucial for the economic development of his cathedral city in the twelfth century. Little or no evidence survives on which to base an assessment of Walkelin's career as a diocesan. It is known that he consulted Ernulf of Rochester, an acknowledged expert on canon law, when in difficulty on a point of marriage law. The text of Ernulf's reply, in which it is made

clear that Walkelin's point was originally raised in discussion at Canterbury, and not in writing, still survives. In April 1095 the monks of Bury St Edmunds, doubtless to the chagrin of his colleague Hermann, the bishop of Thetford, called in Walkelin to officiate at the translation of the bones of their patron saint. Following this event Bishop Walkelin issued an indulgence, which proved extremely popular.

Walkelin made his brother Symeon prior of St Swithun's Cathedral Priory, and as such, the latter was doubtless a great assistance to him in his dealings with his monks. The narrative of Walkelin's deeds purporting to be issued by William Giffard stresses that it was this link which made the division of the goods of the see a practical proposition. In 1093 Symeon became abbot of Ely. Walkelin's nephew, Gerard, who also began his career in the church of Rouen, was successively bishop of Hereford and archbishop of York. Walkelin died on 3 January 1098.

M. J. FRANKLIN

Sources [H. Wharton], ed., *Anglia sacra*, 2 vols. (1691) · *Willelmi Malmesbiriensis monachi de gestis pontificum Anglorum libri quinque*, ed. N. E. S. A. Hamilton, Rolls Series, 52 (1870) · D. S. Spear, 'Les chanoines de la cathédrale de Rouen pendant la période ducale', *Annales de Normandie*, 41 (1991), 135–76 · B. Guérard, ed., *Cartulaire de l'abbaye de saint-Père de Chartres*, 2 vols. (1840) · D. Whitelock, M. Brett, and C. N. L. Brooke, eds., *Councils and synods with other documents relating to the English church, 871–1204*, 2 (1981) · *Ann. mon.*, vol. 2 · *Eadmeri Historia novorum in Anglia*, ed. M. Rule, Rolls Series, 81 (1884) · M. J. Franklin, ed., *Winchester, 1070–1204*, English Episcopal Acta, 8 (1993) · M. Biddle, ed., *Winchester in the early middle ages: an edition and discussion of the Winton Domesday*, Winchester Studies, 1 (1976) · D. Keene and A. R. Rumble, *Survey of medieval Winchester*, 2, Winchester Studies, 2 (1985) · *Reg. RAN*, vol. 2 · *Patrologia Latina*, 163 (1854) · T. Arnold, ed., *Memorials of St Edmund's Abbey*, 3 vols., Rolls Series, 96 (1890–96) · D. Knowles, C. N. L. Brooke, and V. C. M. London, eds., *The heads of religious houses, England and Wales*, 1: 940–1216 (1972) · J. Crook, 'The Romanesque east arm and crypt of Winchester Cathedral', *Journal of the British Archaeological Association*, 142 (1989), 1–36 · John of Worcester, *Chron.*

Walker family (*per.* 1741–1833), iron, steel, and lead manufacturers, came to prominence with Jonathan, Samuel, and Aaron Walker, the three sons of **Joseph Walker** (1673–1729), nailmaker and farmer, of Grenoside, in the parish of Ecclesfield, 5 miles north of Sheffield, and his second wife, Ann Hargreaves (d. 1741); there were also three daughters. Following their marriage in 1710 Joseph and Ann lived at Hollin House, Hill Top, Grenoside, and some time after 1722 they moved a short distance to Stubbing House, though they continued to lease Hollin House and two cottages in Grenoside. Joseph Walker was one of the numerous nailmakers who lived and worked in the countryside immediately north of the cutlery-manufacturing district centred on Sheffield. The mining and smelting of iron there were centuries old, and industries were now slowly adapting from charcoal fuel to the use of coke. South Yorkshire was also becoming a centre for the manufacture of steel in cementation furnaces and in the new crucible furnaces pioneered by Benjamin Huntsman. Joseph Walker died at Grenoside on 21 December 1729.

Aaron Walker (1718–1777) was born at Hollin House on

19 February 1718. The youngest son of Joseph and Ann, he began to experiment with metal founding in the spring of 1741 with his step-cousin John Crawshaw in a smithy at Grenoside, but met with 'bad success'. At this time he worked on local farms, mowing hay and shearing sheep. He married Rhoda, the daughter of Bartholomew Wood, and they had a son and a daughter. An obituary in the firm's records noted: 'He had the internal management of the casting and steel trade, in which he certainly exhibited more ingenuity than patience' (John, 13). He died at Masbrough on 28 January 1777.

His brother **Samuel Walker** (1715–1782) was born on 15 November 1715, also at Hollin House. The second son of Joseph and Ann, he became the master at Grenoside endowed school, but supplemented his living by land surveying and making sundials. On 18 March 1742 he married Mary (d. 1793), the daughter of Thomas Sykes; they had four sons and three daughters. In the autumn of 1741 he and Aaron built an air furnace (a reverberatory furnace) in the nailer's smithy at the rear of Samuel's cottage in Grenoside. They were successful in remelting pig iron and scrap cast-iron, and in casting pots. In 1745, as the business expanded, Samuel resigned his teaching post, and the following year he and Aaron moved a few miles to Masbrough, alongside the newly navigable River Don at Rotherham, where they built a casting house.

Jonathan Walker (1710–1778), the eldest son of Joseph and Ann, was also born at Hollin House, Grenoside, on 8 July 1710. He became a partner in his brothers' ironworks on their move to Masbrough in 1746; he was in charge of transport and continued to manage the farms, in which 'he always evinced the greatest caution and prudence' (John, 14). He had a son and two daughters by his first wife, Sarah Platt, but no children by his second wife, Elizabeth Hodgkinson. He died at Grenoside on 5 August 1778 and was buried in Ecclesfield parish churchyard.

The three brothers entered a partnership with John Booth, a nail chapman, and in 1748 built a cementation steel furnace at Masbrough. A similar furnace was erected at Grenoside in 1749–50. By 1787 the Walkers had five cementation steel furnaces at Masbrough, though the production of iron products remained their chief concern. The Masbrough site was expanded in 1753–6 by the purchase of adjacent property at the Yellands and in 1757–9 by leases of the Holmes estate. In 1766 they built their first crucible steel furnace, at Yellands. The business was boosted by government orders for cannon (some of which can still be seen in the city of Quebec), obtained through the patronage of the local landowner, Charles Watson-Wentworth, second marquess of Rockingham, when he was prime minister. The Walkers' business expanded rapidly and they became the leading ironmasters in the north, concentrating on cast and bar iron, as well as sheet, slit iron, tin plate, and many articles of wrought iron. Their fame spread when they built bridges at Yarm and Sunderland. The Southwark Bridge gave them a national reputation.

In 1778 Samuel Walker, in partnership with Richard Fishwick and Archer Ward of Hull, began a white lead manufacturing business at Elswick, near Newcastle upon Tyne. Samuel Walker provided most of the capital, while his partners contributed business and practical expertise. Rising prices for lead encouraged many others to enter this trade about this time. Samuel died at Masbrough on 12 May 1782, and his four sons succeeded him as partners. They opened premises at London (1785), new works at Derby (1792) and Chester (1800), and a warehouse at Liverpool (1801–2).

An obituary of Samuel Walker noted that he was 'of a thoughtful, serious disposition, and seldom indulged himself in levity or in any kind of dissipation' (John, vii). Samuel and Aaron were early converts to Methodism, and about 1758 led the Calvinistic split from the Rotherham Methodist meeting. They built a meeting-house at Masbrough in 1762 and (later) a family mausoleum. In 1795 Jonathan's son, also Jonathan, founded an Independent college at Masbrough to train students for the ministry; the college proved influential in the evangelical revival in the north.

The next generation of Walkers continued to run the metal businesses, but were regarded as gentlemen. They served as justices of the peace and lived in grand new houses, some of which were designed by John Carr of York. Jonathan's son, Jonathan Walker (1756/7–1807), of Ferham House, Rotherham, JP, married his cousin Mary, Samuel's eldest daughter. The line ended with their son, Jonathan Walker of Ferham (1781–1842). Aaron's only son, John Walker, left the firm in 1783 and is thought to have died in Russia without issue. Samuel's four sons were Samuel (1742–1792), Joshua (1750–1815), Joseph (1752–1801), and Thomas (1756–1828). They married into families with similar industrial and nonconformist backgrounds; and Joseph Walker's second son married the daughter of Samuel Walker Parker, who in 1802 had been admitted into the lead partnership (which then became known as Walkers, Parker, & Co.).

In 1833, after a period of uncertain trade and a quarrel among the partners, the Walkers' iron and steel partnership was dissolved. Some capital was invested in a Rotherham bank, but the family gradually moved away from south Yorkshire. The lead trade continued to prove far more lucrative. All the male descendants of the first Samuel Walker owned shares in the lead business and some were actively involved in the business, but most preferred to live as country gentlemen. Nevertheless, the firm's archives show members of the family being trained in metallurgy in Saxony in the 1850s and investigating new lead manufacturing processes in the USA in the 1870s. The managing partners at the firm's various works were still in the 1870s being drawn exclusively from the Walker family. The Walkers only finally withdrew from the lead trade in 1893 after a lengthy dispute between the partners.

The Walkers are a classic example of a family of humble origins who rose rapidly in society through the ingenuity and hard work of the first generation and whose later members gradually withdrew from trade to live as landed gentry. Samuel, Aaron, and Jonathan Walker established an iron-founding business in the period when coke was replacing charcoal as fuel, and they soon diversified into the manufacture of both cementation steel and the new crucible steel. They rank alongside the firm established by Benjamin Huntsman in the transformation of the south Yorkshire heavy metal industries in the second half of the eighteenth century. Samuel, the gloomy genius who was mainly responsible for the firm's success, also established a successful lead business in north-eastern England. His numerous descendants became accepted as country gentry in various parts of the north and north midlands.

DAVID HEY

Sources A. H. John, ed., *Minutes relating to Messrs. Samuel Walker & Co. Rotherham, ironfounders and steel refiners, 1741–1829, and Messrs Walker Parker & Co. lead manufacturers, 1788–1893* (1951) · D. G. Hey, 'The nailmaking background of the Walkers and the Booths', *Transactions of the Hunter Archaeological Society*, 10/1 (1971), 31–6 · J. Guest, *Yorkshire. Historic notices of Rotherham: ecclesiastical, collegiate, and civil* (1879) · C. Morley, *The Walkers of Masbrough: a re-examination* (privately published, Sheffield, 1996)
Likenesses portrait (Samuel Walker), Clifton House Museum, Rotherham

Walker, Aaron (1718–1777). *See under* Walker family (*per.* 1741–1833).

Walker, Adam (1730/31–1821), itinerant lecturer and writer, was born at Patterdale, Westmorland, into the numerous family of a woollen manufacturer. Neither the exact date of his birth nor the identity of his parents is known. Walker left school barely able to read but persevered alone to achieve a general education. He developed a considerable mechanical skill, constructing models of the milling machinery employed locally for fulling, grinding, and papermaking. At the age of fifteen he became assistant master at Ledham School in the West Riding of Yorkshire, and at eighteen he was appointed writing master and accountant at Macclesfield Free School, where he studied mathematics and issued his first publication, *A System of Family Bookkeeping, with a Ready Ruled Book* (1758). From 1762 to 1766 he ran a school in Manchester, teaching a range of commercial and polite subjects appropriate to the city's needs. He speculated unsuccessfully in trade, and gave lectures on astronomy.

Walker was probably married by this time. He and his wife, Eleanor, were living at Kirkland, Westmorland, at the time of the birth of their eldest son, **William Walker** (*bap.* 1766, *d.* 1816). A second son, Adam John Walker (1769/70–1839), was born in Newry, co. Armagh, and the youngest, **Deane Franklin Walker** (1778–1865), in York. There was also a daughter, Eliza, who married Benjamin Gibson of Gosport.

In 1766 Walker bought the apparatus of the itinerant lecturer William Griffis, gave up schoolmastering, advertised his lectures in various local papers, and took to the road. He wrote the first of several extremely successful tracts: his *Analysis of a Course of Lectures on Natural and Experimental Philosophy* was first published at Kendal in 1766, and under the editorship of his sons reached its twentieth edition in 1827. Walker travelled through the north of England and southern Scotland, then spent four

years in Ireland, before settling in York. Like most itinerant lecturers, Walker captured the attention of his audiences by his demonstrations. One of the most spectacular exhibits was his eidouranion, a transparent orrery, which stood the Walker family in good stead for fifty years. Walker's mechanical skill enabled him to invent and build a simple cometarium which demonstrated Kepler's first two laws of planetary motion. He was a friend of James Ferguson (*d.* 1777), one of the best-known itinerant lecturers, and on Ferguson's death acquired his eclipsareon to demonstrate the nature of eclipses, and came to give lectures in London in 1778–9. This venture was successful, and in 1781 he moved his home to George Street, Hanover Square.

Although now based in London, Walker continued to travel. In northern towns artisans flocked to his lectures on mechanics. He was friendly with most of the eminent industrialists and scientists making up the Lunar Society, and dined with Matthew Boulton. In London he filled the Theatre Royal, Haymarket, with a staged performance of his new eidouranion. His demonstration was accompanied by the heavenly music of the coelestina, a mechanical harpsichord producing continuous sound, which Walker had patented in 1772. In his *Epitome of Astronomy* (1782), Walker announced himself lecturer to the duke of Gloucester; this tract went through thirty editions by 1824. A visit to Paris in 1785 led him to publish his views on aspects of French life; he was similarly inspired by a tour of Flanders, Germany, France and Italy, on which he commented in 1790. He lectured at the public schools of Eton, Westminster, Winchester, St Paul's, and Rugby. Between lectures Walker put his hand to improvements to various machines, a method of thermo-ventilation (patented in 1786), and plans for a rotating light which he helped to erect on St Agnes in the Isles of Scilly in 1790. He died at Richmond, Surrey, on 11 February 1821, and was buried in the family vault at Hayes, Middlesex, on 16 February, where a monument commemorated him as 'the inventor of the Eidouranion'.

William Walker was baptized on 26 June 1766 at Kendal. Educated at Eton College as king's scholar, 1778–80, he gave his first lecture at Newbury with his father, when only sixteen. He continued this profession until his death on 14 March 1816 at the Manor House, Hayes, Middlesex; he left a widow, Elizabeth, and four young children, all of whom died shortly afterwards from consumption. He was buried at Hayes, and commemorated alongside his father as astronomical lecturer.

Adam John Walker was educated at the Royal Grammar School, Lancaster, then at the University of Cambridge, where he graduated BA in 1791 and MA in 1794. He served as rector and vicar of parishes on the Welsh border. He was vicar of Bishopstone at the time of his death, on 1 January 1839.

Deane Franklin Walker, born at York on 24 March 1778, continued his father's custom of lecturing at public schools and giving theatrical performances on the London stage during the winter season. He was also responsible for the later editions of his father's books. He married

Ellenora, daughter of Thomas Normansell; a son and three daughters survived his death at Upper Tooting, Surrey, on 10 May 1865.

E. I. CARLYLE, *rev.* ANITA MCCONNELL

Sources J. R. Millburn, *Wheelwright of the heavens: the life and work of James Ferguson* (1988) · *GM*, 1st ser., 91/1 (1821), 182–3 · *GM*, 1st ser., 86/1 (1816), 374 · *York Chronicle* (19 Feb 1773) · H. C. King, *Geared to the stars: the evolution of planetariums, orreries and astronomical clocks* (1978), 309–15 · *GM*, 3rd ser., 19 (1865), 113 · R. A. Austen-Leigh, ed., *The Eton College register, 1753–1790* (1921), 540–41 · *GM*, 2nd ser., 11 (1839), 216 · A. Murray, ed., *A biographical register of the Royal Grammar School, Lancaster* (privately printed, Lancaster, *c.*1955), pt 1, p. 15
Likenesses plaster medallion, 1795 (after A. J. Tassie), Scot. NPG · H. Humphrey, etching, pubd 1796, NPG · S. Drummond, stipple, NPG, BM; repro. in *European Magazine* (1792) · G. Romney, group portrait, oils, NPG

Walker, Alexander (1764–1831), army officer in the East India Company, born on 12 May 1764, was the eldest son of William Walker (1737–1771), minister of Collessie in Fife, and his wife, Margaret (*d.* 1810), daughter of Patrick Manderston, an Edinburgh merchant. Appointed an East India Company cadet in 1780, he went to India in the same ship as the physician Helenus Scott, with whom he formed a lifelong friendship. On 21 November 1782 he became an ensign, and that year served in the campaign under Brigadier-General Richard Mathews directed against Haidar Ali's forts on the coast of Malabar. He was present with the 8th battalion at Mangalore during the siege by Tipu, and offered himself as a hostage on the surrender of the fortress on 30 January 1784. In recompense for the danger he incurred he received the pay and allowance of captain from the Bombay government while in the enemy's hands.

In December 1785 Walker commanded a Bombay government expedition to establish a military and commercial port on the north-west coast of America, from where the Chinese obtained furs. After exploring in 1786 as far north as 62°, however, and remaining a while at Nootka Sound, the enterprise was abandoned.

Walker rejoined the grenadier battalion in garrison at Bombay. On 9 January 1788 he received a lieutenancy, and in 1790 served under Colonel James Hartley as adjutant of the line in the expedition sent to the relief of the raja of Travancore. In 1791 he served under General Sir Robert Abercromby as adjutant of the 10th native infantry during the campaign against Tipu. After the conclusion of the war a special commission was nominated to regulate the affairs of the province of Malabar, and Walker was appointed an assistant. In this capacity he showed ability, became known to the Indian authorities, and received the thanks of Marquess Wellesley. When the commander-in-chief of the Bombay army, General James Stuart, proceeded to Malabar, Walker became his military secretary with the brevet rank of captain. On 6 September 1797 he attained the regimental rank of captain, and in the same year was appointed quartermaster-general of the Bombay army, which gave him the official rank of major. In 1798 he became deputy auditor-general. He took part in the last

war against Tipu, and was present at the battle of Seedaseer in 1799 and at the siege of Seringapatam. At the request of Sir Arthur Wellesley, he was selected, on account of his knowledge of the country, to attend the commanding officer in Mysore and Malabar.

In 1800 Walker was dispatched to Gujarat by the Bombay government with a view to tranquillizing the Maratha states in that neighbourhood. His reforms were hotly opposed at Baroda by the indigenous officials, who were interested in corruption. The discontent culminated in 1801 in the insurrection of Malhar Rao, the chief of Kurree. Walker took the field, but, being without sufficient force, could do little until reinforced by Colonel Sir William Clarke, who on 30 April 1802 defeated Malhar Rao under the walls of Kurree. In June, Walker was appointed political resident at Baroda at the court of the guikwar, and in this capacity succeeded in establishing an orderly administration. On 18 December 1803 he attained the regimental rank of major, and in 1805 gained the approbation of the East India Company by negotiating a defensive alliance with the guikwar. In 1807 he restored order in the district of Kathiawar, and with the support of Jonathan Duncan (1756–1811), governor of Bombay, suppressed infanticide. On 3 September 1808 he attained the rank of lieutenant-colonel, and in 1809, after he had embarked for England, he was recalled to Gujarat to repel an invasion by Futtee Singh, the ruler of Cutch. Order was restored by his exertions, and in 1810 he proceeded to England.

On 12 July 1811 Walker married Barbara (*d.* 1831), daughter of Sir James Montgomery, baronet, of Stanhope, Peeblesshire. They had two sons: Sir William Stuart Walker KCB, who succeeded to the estate of Bowland in Edinburgh and Selkirk, which his father had purchased in 1809; and James Scott Walker, captain in the 88th regiment.

In 1812 Walker retired from the service. In 1822 he was appointed, with the rank of brigadier-general, governor of St Helena, then under the East India Company. An active administrator, he improved agriculture and horticulture by establishing farming and gardening societies, founded schools and libraries, and introduced the culture of silkworms. Soon after retiring he died at Edinburgh on 5 March 1831. While in India, Alexander Walker formed a valuable collection of Arabic, Persian, and Sanskrit manuscripts, which was presented by his son Sir William in 1845 to the Bodleian Library.

E. I. CARLYLE, *rev.* M. G. M. JONES

Sources *Annual Biography and Obituary*, 16 (1832), 24–50 · *GM*, 1st ser., 101/1 (1831), 466–8 · J. G. Duff, *History of the Mahrattas*, 3rd edn (1873), 562, 563, 626 · Dodwell [E. Dodwell] and Miles [J. S. Miles], eds., *Alphabetical list of the officers of the Indian army: with the dates of their respective promotion, retirement, resignation, or death … from the year 1760 to the year … 1837* (1838) · Burke, *Gen. GB*
Archives BL OIOC, corresp., MS Eur. C 198 [copies] · NL Scot., personal and family corresp. and papers, MSS 13601–14193 | W. Sussex RO, letters to duke of Richmond

Walker, Alexander (1779–1852), writer on anatomy and physiology, was born at Edinburgh on 20 December 1779. He studied at the Edinburgh medical school, but there is no evidence that he completed a degree in either anatomy or surgery. He received instruction in anatomy from John Barclay at Edinburgh, but when he was twenty years old he left Scotland for London to pursue his interest in anatomy under the direction of John Abernethy at St Bartholomew's medical school. Walker was a middle-class radical, a polemicist, and an eccentric, and his intellectual formation was of the late Scottish Enlightenment with its commitment to the development of a science of 'man'. He attracted attention at Abernethy's school for the precise, mathematical nature of his anatomical instruction, but he was forced to leave for pointing out a dissecting error made by Abernethy during one of his lectures. John Struthers, a friend and colleague, explained: 'What position he had occupied at St Bart's, or in Abernethy's class, I am unaware, but the incident of the nerve being tied instead of the artery (on the dead subject), and Mr Walker's giving offence and having to leave there, in consequence of pointing it out, I have on good authority' (Struthers, 77).

After retiring to Edinburgh for a short period of time, Walker returned to London in 1808 and was listed as a lecturer in the 'Extra-Academical School of Medicine and Surgery'. There he delivered medical lectures at the Lyceum and lectures 'on general and particular science' at the assembly rooms. His subsequent career was mainly literary, though he described himself as a 'lecturer in anatomy and physiology' committed to the popularization of science. Besides contributions to newspapers, reviews, and magazines (notably a series of articles on science and art for the *Literary Gazette* and *Archives of Universal Science*), he published fourteen books, including two scientific works on the nervous system in 1834 and 1839, and a popular trilogy, *Woman*, in 1836, 1838, and 1839, which was reprinted in several editions in England and the United States during the nineteenth century. As early as 1809 Walker suggested that the roots of the spinal nerves had different functions—that the anterior root determined the sensory function whereas the dorsal root determined the motor function—but the subsequent experiments of François Magendie and Charles Bell proved that though correct in his initial assertion, he had attributed the wrong functions to the wrong roots. In separate studies, Magendie and Bell demonstrated that the anterior root determined the motor function and the dorsal root determined the sensory one. Throughout his life Walker persisted in his belief that Magendie and Bell had 'borrowed and inverted' his great discovery, stealing the credit and misinterpreting the facts (Walker, iii). He defended his position in two works, *The Nervous System* (1834) and *Documents and Dates of Modern Discoveries in the Nervous System* (1839), and it is ironic that the latter work actually makes Bell's own claim to priority over Magendie (in *The Idea of a New Anatomy of the Brain*, 1811) available to the public for the first time. Walker's work on physiognomy was published as *Physiognomy, Founded on Physiology* (1834).

Walker's most successful work was *Beauty* (1836), the first volume of his trilogy on *Woman*—which also included *Intermarriage* (1838) and *Woman* (1839)—in which he applied the scientific disciplines of anatomy and physiology to the female form. Drawing on the work of such notable theoreticians of beauty as Leonardo da Vinci, Johann Joachim Winckelmann, Joseph Hume, William Hogarth, and Edmund Burke, *Beauty* foreshadowed Walter Pater's work *The Renaissance* (1870). Yet according to Walker, accounts of the 'mystical and delusive' character of female beauty should be replaced by the division of the human figure into a hierarchical structure with three major sections: the feet and legs (the locomotive organs); the trunk (the nutritive or vital organs); and the head (the mental organs). Two further works on the same theme—*Female Beauty* (1837) and *Exercises for Ladies* (1837)—were published under the authorship of Mrs A. Walker and Donald Walker respectively, but (though it is known that Walker was married at some point) it is generally thought that he wrote these works himself. He returned to Edinburgh in 1842 in failing health and died on 6 December 1852.   LUCY HARTLEY

Sources A. Walker, ed., *Documents and dates of modern discoveries in the nervous system* (1973) · J. Struthers, *Historical sketch of the Edinburgh Anatomical School* (1867) · *DSB*

Walker, Sir Alexander (1869–1950), whisky blender and industrialist, was born on 22 March 1869 at Wallace Bank, Kilmarnock, the third and youngest son of Alexander Walker, chairman of John Walker & Sons, and his wife, Isabella (*née* McKemmie). Educated at Ayr Academy he subsequently had a legal training as well as a trade apprenticeship with Robertson and Baxter Ltd, wine and spirit merchants of Glasgow. In 1888 he joined the family business, one of the largest and oldest blending houses, and two years later was elected to the board. In 1895 he married Rosaline, daughter of Arthur S. Josling of Arkley, Hertfordshire; they had two sons and two daughters.

In 1908 Walker commissioned the artist Tom Brown to portray his grandfather, the original Johnnie Walker, in a sketch for advertisements; in different forms it continues in use today. In 1913 Walker became joint managing director of John Walker & Sons. He worked for the Ministry of Munitions during the First World War, was a member of the munitions disposal board, and was knighted in 1920 for his wartime service. When Walkers became a public company in 1923 Sir Alexander became chairman, and when two years later the firm merged with the Distillers Company Ltd (DCL), along with Buchanan–Dewar Ltd, he was elected to the board of DCL.

Walker was renowned for his independent views on trade matters, especially when he attempted, unsuccessfully, to persuade the royal commission on whisky (1908–9) that whisky should be made from a mash containing not less than 30 per cent of malted barley and that blended whisky should contain at least 50 per cent malt whisky. At the royal commission on licensing (1931) he rejected the view that the trade should refrain from exporting to the USA during prohibition. His independence, and the need to consult other family members, prolonged the negotiations leading to the amalgamation

Sir Alexander Walker (1869–1950), by Walter Stoneman, 1931

with DCL in 1925, much to the irritation of the other parties.

As one of DCL's younger and more dynamic directors Walker played a prominent role in the group's development. With a declining demand for whisky and gin, DCL moved into the production of industrial alcohol and solvents and via this into a range of organic chemicals. Many complex problems accompanied diversification. These included DCL's relations with much larger competing firms like ICI and I. G. Farben; the large capital investment which was required; and a highly unsettled technology in which the choice of raw material lay between molasses, where DCL had invested heavily, oil, where petroleum producers were firmly ensconced, and coal, the only domestically produced raw material. The most sensitive issue was the appropriate form of organization, because the capital for diversification had to come from DCL's potable activities. This meant that diversification required the approval of the blenders, the dominant group on the board, and not all were prepared to take a long-term view of the chemical business. Several blenders saw diversification as a short-term insurance policy which could be discarded when the potable spirits market recovered. Ranged against them were those who had built the chemical business and wanted DCL to adopt a divisional structure, splitting it into two divisions, whisky and industrial.

When, in 1931, DCL's chairman was absent through illness a small finance and executive committee was established as a temporary expedient. Walker was a member

and argued successfully for greater centralized control. The new management structure in 1935 rejected the divisional approach and established a management committee in which each member controlled a group of subsidiary companies and departments. Walker took charge of research and development and many of the chemical interests. His chairmanship of the management committee (from 1937 to 1939) saw DCL move into the marketing of finished products in addition to the production of raw materials and intermediates. DCL negotiated a 'spheres of interest' agreement with ICI and initiated joint research with the Royal Dutch Shell and Anglo-Iranian Oil companies for synthetic alcohol production. Joint ventures with the British government for the production of strategically important chemicals were also started well before the outbreak of war.

Walker's great contribution was his perception of the problems accompanying DCL's late entry into chemicals, especially his desire to avoid 'encirclement', a situation where DCL did not control the markets for chemical products. Although his technical knowledge sometimes fell short of what the technical staff desired, his presence on the research and development committee reassured the blenders and, in the context of the 1930s, he bridged the gulf between potable and non-potable activities. Later in 1967, DCL was to dispose of much of its industrial division to British Petroleum.

Walker had many other interests. He was a member of the Ayrshire Electricity Board, chairman of the Ayrshire gas supply committee, and chairman of a Board of Trade investigation into the feasibility of a gas grid for the west of Scotland, as well as holding several directorships. A trustee of C. K. Marr's bequest for the erection of a further education college at Troon, he became chairman of the governors of Marr College when it opened in 1934. Walker gifted land to the burgh and promoted the Troon bathing pool. In 1944 he donated £10,000 to the town council for a centre for the treatment of rheumatism. He was rewarded in 1946 for his services to the town with the freedom of Troon, the first person to receive this honour. By then he was the only survivor of the nine commissioners appointed to govern the burgh when it was formed in 1896. Predeceased by his wife in 1948, Walker died at Piersland, Troon, on 13 May 1950 from a coronary thrombosis.

RONALD B. WEIR

Sources R. B. Weir, 'The development of the distilling industry in Scotland in the nineteenth and early twentieth centuries', PhD diss., Edinburgh, 1974, vol. 2, pp. 494–526 · R. B. Weir, *The history of the Distillers Company, 1877–1939* (1995) · T. Boyd, 'History of the house of Walker', *DCL Gazette* (April 1930), 57–63; (July 1930), 117–24; (Oct 1930), 174–8 [in United Distillers archive, Leven, Fife] · R. Wilson, *Scotch: the formative years* (1970) · R. B. Weir, 'Walker, Sir Alexander', *DSBB* · d. cert.
Archives United Distillers, Leven, Fife, John Walker & Sons Ltd archive
Likenesses W. Stoneman, photograph, 1931, NPG [*see illus.*] · photograph, repro. in Boyd, 'History of the house of Walker', 62
Wealth at death £521,203 12s. 11d.: confirmation, 22 June 1950, *CCI*

Walker, Alice (1900–1982), literary scholar, was born on 8 December 1900 at 97 Dover Street, Crumpsall, Manchester, the daughter of George Edward Walker, then of independent means and later a solicitor, and Mary Alice Walker, née Cort. From 1912 she attended Blackburn High School for Girls and passed the University of London matriculation examination in 1919. She took her BA with first-class honours from Royal Holloway College in 1923, receiving the George Smith studentship for graduate studies, and in May 1926 she was passed as PhD in the faculty of arts with a thesis on the works of Thomas Lodge (1558?–1625). In October she entered Girton College, Cambridge, on a Jex-Blake scholarship, intending to work towards a four-volume edition of Lodge's works, and was awarded a University of London postgraduate scholarship for travel and research during 1927–8. After research at Coimbra, Lisbon, Madrid, and Rome, she received a three-year appointment as assistant lecturer in English at Royal Holloway College (1928–31). Thenceforth, until her return to the college in 1939 as librarian, she lived with friends or with her parents at 49 Denmark Road, Churchtown, Southport Lancashire.

Walker published her first article in 1932 in the *Review of English Studies* and this was followed by some forty reviews in this publication, founded and then edited by R. B. McKerrow. Her first book, *The Life of Thomas Lodge* (1933), also appeared at this time, published by Sidgwick and Jackson, the firm of which McKerrow was a director. Her second book (1934) was an edition of Puttenham's *Arte of English Poesie*, published collaboratively with Gladys Doidge Willock, her long-standing friend, head of the English department and later professor at Royal Holloway College. In the same year she published her first article on Shakespeare and was employed by McKerrow to assist with the Oxford Old-Spelling Shakespeare for the Clarendon Press, which had been delayed by his illness. McKerrow accounted her 'the ideal person to help me with the job' (Oxford University Press Archives, CP/ED/000018, 2/5/36), considering her accurate beyond his own standards. On McKerrow's death in 1940 two volumes of Shakespeare's early plays were close to publication and work on another was advanced. Although the press was disposed to ask Walker to carry on the edition, it appears to have been suspended during the Second World War and abandoned in 1948.

In 1939, already with 'a wide reputation for bibliographical scholarship' (*College Letter*, 1940, 14), Walker was appointed librarian at Royal Holloway College and was quickly involved in the fortunes of Janet R. Bacon (principal from 1935 to 1944) who appointed her principal's secretary and registrar in 1941. When Bacon resigned because of ill health in 1944, Walker also resigned and retired with her friend to Welcombe, near Bideford, Devon; they later lived in Bude, Cornwall, and in Oxford.

During the war Walker had published only the 'Summary of periodical literature' in the *Review of English Studies*. After six years' private study intended to complete McKerrow's edition, in 1950 she began to publish a remarkable series of articles on Shakespeare's text, and in 1952 to review Arden and New Variorum editions of Shakespeare's works and Malone Society facsimiles for the *Review*. Her next book, *Textual Problems of the First Folio* (1953, in J. Dover Wilson's Shakespeare Problems series), for which she was awarded the 1954 British Academy's Rose Mary Crawshay prize, preceded five successive textual articles in Fredson Bowers's *Studies in Bibliography*. These works revealed her as the most acute and challenging textual critic of the decade, her work innovatively conspicuous for the attention given to the influence of compositors on the transmission of texts.

After publishing *Othello* and *Troilus and Cressida* in Dover Wilson's new Cambridge Shakespeare (both 1957), Walker was urged to apply for the Oxford readership in textual criticism vacated by Herbert Davis, though she expected that she was 'much too old to be considered unless a stop-gap is wanted' (A. Walker to D. Davin, November 1959). Nevertheless, the appointment would facilitate her work on the Oxford Old-Spelling edition which had been revived in 1952, albeit on a different plan, with the appointment of G. I. Duthie as editor; applying for the readership in December 1959, Walker listed herself as Duthie's co-editor. She was appointed reader for seven years with effect from Michaelmas term 1960, and was elected professorial fellow of St Hilda's College in November 1962. The Clarendon Press announced *Coriolanus* in 1964 as the first volume of the Oxford edition but only proofs survive. In 1965, when applying for sabbatical leave, she noted that her increasing teaching load had put her own work (the edition) 'shockingly in arrears' (University of Oxford Archives FA 9/2/910; board minutes DL 19.1.65). Following her appointment, other than her British Academy annual Shakespeare lecture (1960), two short reviews, and a quatercentenary article in the *Times Literary Supplement* (1964), she did not publish until the year of her death. She retired in September 1968, having spent much of Michaelmas term 1967 and Hilary term 1968 in Bude recovering from a broken pelvis. She was created reader emeritus in 1972 and died unmarried, of cancer of the liver, on 14 October 1982 at Plymouth Hospital. Her last article appeared posthumously in the *Review of English Studies*.

Described in 1997 as 'the most important female editor in the twentieth century' (Thompson, 85), Walker never managed to publish the editions which her long involvement with Shakespeare promised. Her dominant interest during the last forty years of her life lay in the textual problems which must be resolved before a work can be edited. Her most notable contribution was to identify the effects of compositors—the neglected agents of textual transmission—and to indicate how their influence could be studied. She was the senior member of the triumvirate including Fredson Bowers and Charlton Hinman which made compositorial analysis the distinctive editorial tool of the second half of the twentieth century. She was acute in criticism, direct and trenchant in conversation, and, at Oxford, solicitous for the well-being of her students.

T. H. HOWARD-HILL

Sources U. Oxf., summary of EL/5, closed personal file · Oxford University registry, Oxf. UA, FA 9/2/910 · LUL, ULL/NJ/nj/sf, 4/9/97 · Oxford University Press, archives, CP/ED/000018 · Egham, *College Letter*, 1926-47, Royal Holloway College, Egham, Surrey, RF/132/7 [college paper] · C. Bingham, *The history of Royal Holloway College, 1886-1986* (1987) · A. Thompson, 'Feminist theory and the editing of Shakespeare', *The margins of the text*, ed. D. C. Greetham (1997), 83-103 · T. H. Howard-Hill, 'Alice Walker', *Twentieth-century British book collectors and bibliographers*, ed. W. Baker and K. Womack, DLitB, 201 (1999), 297-305 · b. cert. · d. cert.
Archives Royal Holloway College, Egham, Surrey, papers
Wealth at death £84,833: probate, 13 Dec 1982, *CGPLA Eng. & Wales*

Walker, Sir Andrew Barclay, first baronet (1824-1893), brewer and benefactor, was born at Auchinflower, Ayrshire, on 15 December 1824, the second son of Peter Walker (1795-1879) of the Fort brewery, Ayr, and his wife, Mary (d. 1846), eldest daughter of Arthur Carlaw of Ayr. He was educated at Ayr Academy and at the Liverpool Institute. On completion of his education Walker was taken into partnership in the brewing business by his father, who had established a small brewery in Ray Street, near St Paul's Square in Liverpool. The business expanded rapidly and in 1846 a new brewery was opened in Warrington, where the family already had two breweries. In 1877 another brewery was opened in Burton upon Trent to specialize in the brewing of high-quality bitter ales under the title of A. B. Walker & Sons. On the death of his father in 1879 Walker became sole proprietor of the Warrington breweries and in 1890 the firm converted to a limited liability company, 'Peter Walker & Son Warrington & Burton Ltd', with Walker as the first chairman. Walker also acquired a number of colliery properties in Ayrshire and south Wales from which he derived a large income.

Walker entered the Liverpool city council in 1867. He was elected alderman in 1871, served the office of mayor in 1873-4 and 1876-7, and was high sheriff of Lancashire in 1886. At a cost in excess of £50,000 he built the Walker Art Gallery which was opened and presented to the town in September 1877. In 1886 he provided £20,000 for the building of engineering laboratories in connection with the Liverpool University College which was opened in 1889. He also contributed other large sums to charity and art and literature in Liverpool throughout his life. To the village of Gateacre, near Liverpool, he gave a village green and an institute, library, and reading-room. In recognition of his public services he was knighted on 12 December 1877, and created baronet on 12 February 1886. In 1884, for approximately £250,000, he purchased Osmaston Manor in Derbyshire, with furniture, model village, and estate. As a mariner he owned a famous steam yacht called the *Cuhona* on which he entertained several members of the royal family, including the prince of Wales.

In November 1889 Walker resigned from his position as alderman on the city council because of ill health. In recognition of his service to the city, Liverpool made him its first honorary freeman in January 1890, and in December the same year he was presented with his portrait by W. Q. Orchardson RA.

Walker was twice married. His first wife, whom he married in 1853, was Eliza, daughter of John Reid of Limekilns, Fife; they had six sons and two daughters. She died on 20 March 1882, and on 11 October 1887 he married the Hon. Maude (b. 1861/2), second daughter of Haughton Charles Okeover of Okeover Hall, Staffordshire, whose title derived from her having been a maid of honour to Queen Victoria. Walker died at his residence, Gateacre Grange, Little Woolton, Lancashire, on 27 February 1893, leaving personalty valued at £2,876,781 18s. 10d., besides much freehold property. He was survived by his second wife and was succeeded in the baronetcy by his eldest son, Peter Carlaw Walker (1854-1915), who also took over control of the family firm and lived at Osmaston.

C. W. SUTTON, rev. FIONA WOOD

Sources *Manchester Guardian* (28 Feb 1893) · B. G. Orchard, *Liverpool's legion of honour* (1893) · *Liverpool Pulpit*, 4, no. 36 (Jan 1895) · *Walker's Warrington ales*, P. Walker & Son Ltd [1900], 12-18 · *ILN* (4 March 1893) · Burke, *Peerage* · d. cert.
Archives Allied Domecq, Burton upon Trent, P. Walker & Son, records of brewery company · Merseyside RO, Liverpool, financial and business papers · Walker Art Gallery, Liverpool
Likenesses oils, c.1891 (after W. Q. Orchardson), Walker Art Gallery, Liverpool · Lib [L. Prosperi], chromolithograph caricature, NPG; repro. in *VF* (7 June 1890) · W. Q. Orchardson, portrait, Lpool RO · oils, Walker Art Gallery, Liverpool · photographs and prints, Lpool RO · portrait, repro. in *ILN*, 266 · sculpture, Walker Art Gallery, Liverpool
Wealth at death £2,876,781 18s. 10d.: probate, 28 March 1893, *CGPLA Eng. & Wales*

Walker, Anne (1631-1660×67), educational benefactor, was baptized on 17 April 1631 at Charlbury, Oxfordshire, the posthumous only child of James Walker (d. 1631), a wealthy yeoman, and Anne (née Evans). Her mother married again—her new husband's name was William Pitchford—and moved to London where at some point Anne joined her. Nothing is known of Anne's life before 1660 except that she became a committed puritan: she omitted the word 'saint' from the titles of all the parishes mentioned in her will made on 20 March 1660. The will which is very detailed, also indicates that she had a wide circle of family and friends particularly in the London mercantile community, probably sharing puritan sympathies. They included four presbyterian clergymen—James Nalton of St Leonard, Foster Lane, Samuel Clark of St Benet Fink, William Blackmore of St Peter Cornhill, and Richard Adams of St Mildred, Bread Street—all of whom were ejected in 1662, and an uncle in Dort in the Netherlands. Anne had inherited land and property in Shotswell, Warwickshire, and Cropredy, Oxfordshire, with an annual value of £60. In Charlbury, although there was a schoolhouse which had been in use at one time, there was no endowment to pay a master's salary. Her will stipulated that as soon as the town had made the building fit for a school, her mother and uncle, Richard Eyans, should give her property to the principal and fellows of Brasenose College, Oxford. The fellows should choose a member of the college to be schoolmaster at a salary of £40. A further £10 was to maintain two poor boys from the school to study at Brasenose and another £10 was for the college's own use.

The date of Anne's death, in London, is unknown. Her will was proved by her mother Anne Pitchford on 8 May 1667. In 1675 Charlbury leased the schoolhouse to Richard Eyans, who drew up the statutes for a grammar school. Later it met in the manor house until 1837, when a new building was erected. It closed in 1911 but the endowment, the Charlbury Exhibition Foundation, survived, providing financial assistance for students in higher education.

JOAN A. DILS

Sources will, PRO, PROB 11/324, fols. 114r–118r • VCH Oxfordshire, 1.466; 10.155 • Oxfordshire Archives, MSS D. D. par Charlbury b.1 and c.1 • Oxfordshire Archives, MS wills Oxon. 70/3/35 [will of James Walker] • Calamy rev., 2, 59, 119, 360
Wealth at death messuage, tenement, and five yardlands at Shotwell, Warwickshire, and two closes at Cropredy, value £60 p.a.; cash bequests and annuities value at least £145: will, PRO, PROB 11/324, fols. 114r–118r

Walker, Anne (b. c.1864). See under Graham, Andrew (1815–1908).

Walker, Annie Purcell, Lady Walker (1871–1950). See under Walker, Sir James (1863–1935).

Walker, Anthony (bap. 1622, d. 1692), clergyman, was baptized on 2 April 1622 at Conington, Cambridgeshire, the son of William Walker (fl. 1610–1660), a clergyman. While it is possible that his mother was Mary Bois (bap. 1599, d. 1638), daughter of the biblical scholar John *Bois, of whom Walker wrote a brief life, it is more likely that she was his stepmother. Smith suggests she and Walker married in 1618, but a date of 1629 has also been recorded. Walker was educated in Ely, and (from 1638) at St John's College, Cambridge, from where he graduated BA in 1642 and MA in 1645. He was incorporated at Oxford in 1657. Ordained in 1644, Walker was appointed as tutor to the stepdaughter of John Gauden in the same year, and Walker also assisted Gauden in his parochial duties at Bocking, Essex. About 1647 Walker became domestic chaplain to the principal patron of East Anglian puritanism, Robert Rich, earl of Warwick, at Lees, Essex. He was intimate with Mary Rich, who described him as 'Good natured' and an 'Ingenious persone' (BL, Add. MS 27357, fols. 22–3). In 1650 Walker was appointed rector of Fyfield, Essex, a living in the disposal of the Rich family. He continued as a spiritual mainstay of the Rich household, providing fellowship and funeral sermons when required. On 22 July 1650 Walker married Elizabeth Sadler [see Walker, Elizabeth (1623–1690)], with whom he had eleven children, all of whom predeceased him. Walker edited her vivid autobiography as The Holy Life of Mrs. Elizabeth Walker (1690).

Walker welcomed the Restoration, his first published work being a sermon on the occasion. He petitioned Charles II to enable him to receive the degree of DD from Cambridge, from which he had been debarred during the interregnum. In 1662 he conformed to the Act of Uniformity, and he remained as incumbent of Fyfield until his death. Additionally he was perpetual curate of St Mary

Aldermanbury, London, from 1664 to 1666, and from 1690 to 1691. Owing to the poor health of his wife he became a regular visitor to Tunbridge Wells, where he appears to have occasionally preached. Two of these sermons were published in his Fax fonte accensa (1684), which also included meditations 'for the use of those who attend the Mineral Waters' (Fax fonte accensa, sig. A9r). In 1685 Walker suffered some form of persecution for ten days, perhaps on political grounds: he obliquely refers to being the victim of 'spightful Malice' (Holy Life of Mrs. Elizabeth Walker, 133). Palgrave alleges that Walker was imprisoned at Tilbury. Walker concurred with the revolution of 1688–9, seeing it as an opportunity for national reformation, as he suggested in The True Interest of Nations Impartially Stated, his Chelmsford assize sermon of 1691. Elizabeth Walker died on 23 February 1690 and on 21 September of the following year Walker married Margaret Masham (d. 1730) of Oates, Essex, possibly the sister-in-law of Damaris Masham. Walker was dead by 18 April 1692, and was probably buried on that date at Fyfield. He endowed the village with several charities. Josiah Woodward, another spiritual reformer of the 1690s, preached his funeral sermon at Fyfield on 18 April.

Of his eleven published works Walker is remembered for A True Account of the Author of a Book Entituled Eikon basilike (1692). Here he defended himself from Richard Hollingworth, who had attacked Walker for his belief that it was John Gauden, rather than Charles I, who was author of the Eikon basilike. Walker reiterated his claim, and told how Gauden had discussed the work with him and had claimed that the royal family knew about Gauden's role in the work's composition. Gauden also showed Walker the manuscript, which Walker himself claimed to have delivered to be printed in London in December 1648. The True Account ignited a pamphlet war which raged throughout the 1690s, but Walker himself took no further part in it, having died while the True Account was in publication.

HANNAH SMITH

Sources H. Smith, Essex Review, 44 (1935), 156–72 • F. F. Madan, A new bibliography of the Eikon basilike of King Charles the First (1950) • A. Walker, The holy life of Mrs. Elizabeth Walker (1690) • B. Donagan, 'The clerical patronage of Robert Rich, second earl of Warwick, 1619–1642', Proceedings of the American Philosophical Society, 120 (1976), 388–419 • C. Fell Smith, Mary Rich, countess of Warwick (1625–1678): her family and friends (1901) • BL, M. Rich MSS, diaries, meditations, and autobiography, Add. MSS 27351–27358 • Walker rev. • M. E. Palgrave, Mary Rich, countess of Warwick (1625–1678) (1901) • Venn, Alum. Cant., 1/4.315 • J. E. B. Mayor, ed., Admissions to the College of St John the Evangelist in the University of Cambridge, pts 1–2: Jan 1629/30 – July 1715 (1882–93), 39 • CSP dom., 1661–2, 582 • F. Peck, ed., Desiderata curiosa, 1 (1732), bk 8, pp. 36–58 • will, PRO, PROB 11/410, sig. 137 • J. L. Chester and J. Foster, eds., London marriage licences, 1521–1869 (1887), 1399 • A. Walker, A true account of the author of a book entituled Eikon basilike (1692) • J. Woodward, A sermon preached on the 18th of April 1692 at the funeral of the reverend Dr Anthony Walker (1692) • parish register, Conington, Cambridgeshire, Cambs. AS, 2 April 1622 [baptism] • parish register, High Laver, Essex, July 1730 [burial, Margaret Walker] • parish register, Boxworth, Cambs. AS, May 1599 [baptism; Mary Bois] • parish register, Boxworth, Cambs. AS, May 1629 [marriage; Mary Bois and William Walker]
Archives Essex RO, Chelmsford, legal papers, parish registers

Wealth at death see will, PRO, PROB 11/410, sig. 137

Walker, Anthony (1726–1765), etcher and engraver, was born at Thirsk, Yorkshire, and baptized there on 19 March 1726, the son of John Walker (d. 1763), an exciseman; he was apparently the sixth son in a family of ten children. Having been apprenticed in the Goldsmiths' Company to the London engraver and printseller John Tinney on 2 May 1740, he became free of the company on 5 April 1753. During this period he also studied at the St Martin's Lane Academy.

Walker was one of the most gifted engravers of the period, known for topographical views, religious and genre subjects, portraits, and book illustrations. Individual plates were exhibited at the Society of Artists from 1760 onwards, and he produced a number of fine large-scale prints for the publisher John Boydell, sometimes in collaboration with William Woollett. Walker's technique was heavily reliant on etching rather than pure engraving, a means that gave his work its characteristic fluidity of line. It was not a technique, however, which produced plates capable of prolonged use, and his work is best judged from the earliest impressions that may be found. Walker also has claims as an original artist, and he designed original frontispieces and illustrations of great verve and style. His illustrations for Tobias Smollett's *The Life and Adventures of Sir Launcelot Greaves*, serialized in the *British Magazine* (1760–61), are believed to be the earliest magazine illustrations for any serialized novel.

Working from premises originally in Great Kirby Street and by 1763 at the corner of Nevils Court, Fetter Lane, Walker numbered among his apprentices Joseph Ryland, Thomas Cook, and Joseph Collyer. Little record survives of his personal life and character. Horace Walpole, who admired his work, expressed exasperation at Walker's reluctance to tackle more ambitious subjects. Walker's reported response, that 'he had got fame enough' (*Letters*, 6.19), although considered 'shameful' by Walpole, may equally have been expressive of any emotion from an innate modesty to an irritation at being told his business by a man of leisure. Walker died at Kensington, London, on 9 May 1765 and was buried in the parish churchyard. Administration of his estate was granted to his widow, Mary Walker, of whom nothing further is known.

William Walker (bap. 1729, d. 1793), engraver, the younger brother of Anthony Walker and the seventh son in the family, was baptized at Thirsk on 4 December 1729. After serving an apprenticeship with a dyer he went to London and was trained by his brother. He was a gifted artist responsible for a wide variety of engraved portraits, historical scenes, and views, including landscapes after Paul Sandby, and his neat work graced many of the most handsome illustrated books of the period. Like his brother, he engraved larger plates for Boydell, but this connection was discontinued when Walker returned a painting which he considered obscene. He was the inventor of the 'rebiting' technique much employed by Woollett, who claimed never to complete a plate without

a renewal of gratitude. Walker was noted for his serene temperament and the domestic felicity of his marriage of thirty-four years. His final years were spent in seclusion and he died at his house in Rosoman Street, Clerkenwell, on 18 February 1793.

John Walker (fl. 1784–1802), engraver, the only son of William Walker, was responsible for *The Copper-Plate Magazine, or, Monthly Cabinet of Picturesque Prints* (1792–1802), a much esteemed compilation which he engraved and published and which gave employment to the young J. M. W. Turner. Walker had learned his craft under his father, with whom he frequently worked in collaboration.

LAURENCE WORMS

Sources H. A. Hammelmann, 'Anthony Walker: a gifted engraver and illustrator', *The Connoisseur*, 168 (1968), 167–74 • H. Hammelmann, *Book illustrators in eighteenth-century England*, ed. T. S. R. Boase (1975) • *GM*, 1st ser., 63 (1793), 189, 279 • parish register, Thirsk, N. Yorks. CRO • binding book, Company of Goldsmiths' archives, Goldsmiths' Hall, London, 6.292 • *The letters of Horace Walpole, fourth earl of Orford*, ed. P. Toynbee, 6 (1904), 19 • I. Maxted, *The London book trades, 1775–1800: a preliminary checklist of members* (1977) • D. F. McKenzie, ed., *Stationers' Company apprentices*, [3]: 1701–1800 (1978) • grant of administration, PRO, PROB 6/141, fol. 315
Wealth at death see administration, PRO, PROB 6/141, fol. 315

Walker, Sir (George) Augustus (1912–1986), air force officer, was born in West Garforth, near Leeds, on 24 August 1912, the son of George Henry Walker, a consulting engineer, and his wife, Josephine Robertson, *née* Rolph. Educated at St Bees School, Cumberland, where he captained the rugby fifteen, and St Catharine's College, Cambridge (1931–4), he took a second in the natural science tripos and played rugby for Cambridge (but was not a blue). Having been commissioned into the Royal Air Force in September 1934, he completed his pilot training and joined 99 squadron, flying Heyford bombers. Selected for specialist armament training, he served at armament establishments and then at the Air Ministry joint directorate of research and development. Meanwhile he played rugby for Blackheath, Yorkshire, Eastern Counties, and the Barbarians, and was capped twice for England in 1939. He captained the RAF rugby fifteen from 1936 to 1939.

Walker was promoted squadron leader in April 1939 and wing commander in November. He commanded 50 squadron flying Hampden bombers from Lindholme in Yorkshire, and made many raids on industrial targets in Germany, as well as, on 6 July 1941, the capital ships *Scharnhorst* and *Gneisenau* in Brest harbour. His courage and leadership impressed Lord Moran, who took him as one of his models for his book *The Anatomy of Courage* (1945). In July 1941 he moved 50 squadron to RAF Swinderby, Lincolnshire, and was appointed to the DSO for his leadership, particularly on low-level bombing raids, and for the inspiring example he provided to his crews. In October 1941 he was awarded the DFC for his accurate identification and incendiary attack on the Buna synthetic rubber plant at Krefeld. After a year of successful bombing, mining, and other operations, including helping develop the Lindholme air sea rescue apparatus, he was promoted group captain and, in October 1941, was made station commander of RAF North Luffenham, where he flew both Hampden and Manchester bombers.

In April 1942 Walker took command of the Lancaster base at RAF Syerston, Nottinghamshire, and on 5 September 1942 he married (Dorothy) Brenda Willcox (b. c.1919), a WAAF plotter. She was the widow of a brother officer killed on bomber operations in September 1941, and the daughter of Hewitt Brewis of Westcliff-on-sea, Essex. They had one son and one daughter.

In December 1942, with Wing Commander Guy Gibson, Walker was observing his 'bombed-up' Lancaster squadrons taxiing for takeoff from Syerston when he noticed burning incendiaries falling from one aircraft. Walker set off across the airfield to warn the crew and arrived with the fire tender but, as he ran towards the aircraft, a 4000 lb bomb exploded, severely injuring him and the fire crew. His right arm was amputated, just above the elbow joint, that evening. But he was back at his desk within two months and was flying again in May 1943, attaching his false arm to the aircraft control column and with his left hand working twice as hard. In March 1943, now an air commodore, he was made base commander at Pocklington, commanding three local Halifax bomber bases. By May 1944 he commanded some 100 heavy bombers, including two squadrons manned by French personnel. After two years as base commander, he was appointed CBE (1945) and made senior air staff officer at 4 group, responsible for thirteen Halifax squadrons on some fourteen airfields in eastern Yorkshire. In November 1945 he flew to Bordeaux to receive the Croix de Guerre and Légion d'honneur presented by the French government in recognition of his outstanding war record and the support he had given his French squadrons.

In May 1946, reverting to the rank of group captain, Walker went to the Air Ministry as deputy director of operational training until February 1948, when he moved to Bulawayo as senior air staff officer of the air training wing in Rhodesia. On his return to England in August 1950 he spent a period at the Joint Services Staff College before commanding RAF Coningsby, with its four RAF squadrons equipped with Washington (American B-29) bombers. In 1953 he attended the Imperial Defence College, then in February 1954 became commandant of the RAF Flying College at Manby in Lincolnshire. Here, again leading from the front, he flew the Hastings transport aircraft on polar navigation flights and, having converted to jet aircraft, the Canberra bomber.

Walker was awarded the AFC (1956) for his polar flights and, promoted air vice-marshal, was made air officer commanding no. 1 group of Bomber Command in October 1956. During his three years in this post he flew nearly 600 hours in eight different aircraft types, including 281 hours in the new Vulcan bomber. In April 1959 he led a three Vulcan detachment to the air display in Las Vegas. Two months later he was appointed CB and moved back to the Air Ministry as chief information officer, heading the public relations department of the RAF. In September 1961, as air officer commanding-in-chief of Flying Training Command, with the rank of air marshal, he oversaw, for three years, the training of all RAF aircrew. In January 1962 he was knighted (KCB) and was made inspector-general of the RAF, undertaking special tasks for the air board visiting units across the world. In March 1967, now air chief marshal, Sir Gus became deputy commander-in-chief of allied forces central Europe. He was appointed GCB in 1969 and retired from the RAF in 1970.

In retirement Walker served as chairman, then president, of the Royal Air Force Association, where his memory for recalling names of colleagues met years before was legendary. He was always greatly respected by those he led and never asked his men to do anything which he would not himself attempt, despite the loss of his arm. On the golf course he played a single-handed game with great success. He became a first-class rugby referee, officiating at a county match in his year as president of the Rugby Football Union (1965–6), impressively handling his whistle, watch, notebook, and pencil in his one hand. He served for many years on numerous volunteer, ex-service, and youth organizations. He died, of a heart attack, on 11 December 1986 in Queen Elizabeth Hospital, King's Lynn, Norfolk, and was buried at Burnham Deepdale church, Norfolk.

ROBIN WOOLVEN

Sources D. Sawden, ed., *Our tribute to Air Chief Marshal Sir Augustus Walker (1912–86)* (1998) · Lord Moran, *The anatomy of courage* (1945), 110–12 · J. Mace, *The history of Royal Air Force rugby, 1919–1999* (2000) · *Centenary history of the Rugby Football Union* (1970) · *The Times* (12 Dec 1986) · RAF Syerston operational record (form 540), Dec 1942, PRO · I. Broom, *Air Mail* (spring 1987) · *Royal Air Force Lists* (1935–70) · WW (1951–86) · Burke, *Peerage* (1967) · b. cert. · m. cert. · private information (2004) [Librarian, Museum of Rugby, Twickenham; M. Tomkins, RAF Association; M. Knight; D. Parry-Evans; R. McConnell; J. Mace]
Archives priv. coll., medals · Yorkshire Air Museum, Royal Air Force flying log books, uniforms, flying helmet, and (single) flying glove | King's Lond., Liddell Hart C., letters to Basil Liddell Hart | FILM Thames Television, *Whirlwind - Bombing Germany, September 1939 – April 1944*, in series *World at War* (1973), Walker shown escorting ACM Sir Arthur ('Bomber') Harris when the CinC Bomber Command visited Walker's station
Likenesses photographs, priv. coll. · photographs, RAF · photographs, Rugby Football Union photographic archives
Wealth at death £192,219: probate, 1987, CGPLA Eng. & Wales

Walker, Sir Baldwin Wake, first baronet (1802–1876), naval officer, was born on 6 January 1802. He was the only surviving son of John Walker of Whitehaven (d. 1822) and Frances (d. 1812), daughter of Captain Drury Wake of the 17th dragoons (second son of Sir William Wake, seventh baronet; 1742–1846). He entered the navy in July 1812, was made a lieutenant on 6 April 1820, and served for two years on the Jamaica station, then for three years on the coast of South America and the west coast of Africa. In 1827 he went to the Mediterranean in the *Rattlesnake*, and in 1828 was first lieutenant of the bomb-vessel *Etna* at the capture of Kastro Morea. For this service he received the cross of the Légion d'honneur and that of the Redeemer of Greece. He continued in the Mediterranean, serving in the

Asia, *Britannia*, and *Barham*, and was made commander on 15 July 1834. He served in the *Vanguard*, in the Mediterranean, from September 1836 until his promotion to post rank on 24 November 1838. With Admiralty permission he then accepted a command in the Turkish navy, in which he was known at first as Walker Bey, and afterwards as Yavir Pasha.

In July 1839, on hearing of the death of Sultan Mahmud II, and anticipating Russian dominance at Constantinople, instead of sailing to attack the Egyptian fleet the Capitan Pasha took his ships to Alexandria and delivered them to Mehmet Ali, who then refused to let them go. Walker was taken with them. He summoned the Turkish captains to a council of war and proposed to them to land in the night, surround the palace, carry off Mehmet Ali, and send him to Constantinople. But the plan was not attempted and Walker went back to Constantinople alone on a steamer sent by Sir Robert Stopford, the British naval commander-in-chief. In the capital Walker in effect acted as commander-in-chief of the Turkish navy. In the summer of 1840 he prepared and took command of a combined expedition to Syria, slipping at night past a reputedly hostile French squadron watching off the Dardanelles. In September and November he co-operated with Turkey's allies in the reduction of Beirut, Sidon, and Acre, showing great gallantry, both in organizing naval operations and in landing and leading detachments of Turkish troops to seize the towns in the name of the sultan. In January 1841 he had the pleasure of arriving at Alexandria to reconduct the Turkish fleet to Constantinople. He was nominated a KCB on 12 January 1841; he received from the allied sovereigns the second class of the Iron Crown of Austria, of St Anne of Russia, of the Red Eagle of Prussia, and was made a hereditary pasha of the Turkish empire.

Walker was responsible for important reforms in the Turkish navy, but intrigue ensured his dismissal in January 1844. He returned to England, and in 1845 he commanded the *Queen*, designed by the surveyor Sir William Symonds, which, in sailing trials, beat all rivals. In 1846–7 he commanded the frigate *Constance* in the Pacific, being recalled to succeed Symonds. His first duty as surveyor was to bring calm to an office disturbed by controversy, but soon he became engaged with planning the change to a steam line of battle. With the Crimean War, Walker became the main naval adviser to the first lord, and on occasions the only one. His advice was important in prompting the expedition to Sevastopol. He was created a baronet on 19 July 1856, and on 5 January 1858 he became a rear-admiral. By 1858 the question of the introduction of the seagoing ironclad was coming to the fore, and Walker was responsible for proposing the *Warrior*, whose size and speed owed much to his advice. In 1860 Walker was given greater powers of control and independent judgement over the dockyards, his title changing to controller.

Walker did not avoid controversy during his time in office. In 1851–2 he defeated an attempt to introduce political criteria into dockyard officer appointments. Late in the decade there were accusations of gross waste in warship construction and conversion; these were very trying to Walker, involving disputes within the Admiralty as well as without, and heavy demands from parliament for returns and for Walker himself to give evidence before investigating committees. By the end of 1860, after years of long office hours and strain, Walker was exhausted, scarcely able to write a letter. The board accepted his resignation in January 1861, appointing him to the Cape command (1861–4) in the hope that the climate would re-establish his health. He left just in time to avoid another parliamentary inquiry, his flagship outpacing the steamer sent to recall him; this led to some comment, including satirical verses in *Punch* (on 23 March 1861).

Walker's quick recovery at the Cape was especially fortunate since he had to prepare for hostilities with the USA after the *Trent* incident, and did so with enthusiasm, primarily through a wish to teach 'Brother Jonathan' a lesson but also hoping for prize money and to improve his fortune, over which he had several times been disappointed. The dispute was settled, but Walker still had to deal with complications with the Americans, largely because of the visit of the Confederate commerce raider *Alabama* to the Cape. Other responsibilities included slave trade patrols, David Livingstone's expedition, the extension of the dockyard at Simonstown, a quiet conflict over precedence with the Cape chief justice, and the protection of his three unmarried daughters from importunate naval officers.

Walker became a vice-admiral on 10 February 1865. His next employment was his last, as commander-in-chief at Sheerness (1866–9). He became a full admiral on 27 February 1870, shortly afterwards going on to the retired list. He had married, on 9 September 1834, Mary Catherine Sinclair (*d.* 1889), only daughter of Captain John Worth RN of Oakley House, Suffolk; they had five sons and four daughters. He lost both a son, Charles, and a son-in-law, Captain Hugh Talbot Burgoyne, when the *Captain* went down on 7 September 1870. Walker died at his home, The Depperhaugh, Hoxne, Suffolk, on 12 February 1876. He was succeeded in the baronetcy by his eldest son, Sir Baldwin Wake Walker (1846–1905), a naval officer and at one time assistant director of torpedoes. A grandson, Sir William Frederic Wake-*Walker, was controller of the navy from 1942 to 1945.

Walker was highly regarded as a seaman. He was also hard-working and generally popular with colleagues and subordinates. In matters of personal honour he was punctilious, this circumscribing a sense of humour that was perhaps never highly developed. One of his great strengths was what Sir William Symonds described as his 'own quiet mild and discreet persuasive manner' (W. Symonds to Walker, 7 Jan 1848). His tenure as surveyor–controller was historically significant, marking the change from that officer being a naval architect to a policy maker, and an important stage on his development into becoming the acknowledged head of naval *matériel* and a lord of the Admiralty. Walker was a good and careful administrator, but did not possess much imagination or prescience, above all concerning the supersession of the screw liner by the ironclad battleship, where, despite the *Warrior*, his influence was often retrograde. Surviving photographs principally suggest the administrator, but a painting of Walker in Turkish service, in the possession of the family, is in a heroic tradition suitable to the subject's undeniable gallantry.   C. I. HAMILTON

Sources B. W. Walker, 'Memorandum on his Turkish services', University of Cape Town, Cape Town, South Africa, Jagger Library, Walker MSS, Bc 356/1575/7/h · W. Symonds, letter to Walker, 7 Jan 1848, University of Cape Town, Cape Town, South Africa, Jagger Library, Walker MSS, Symonds's letters, Bc 356/1646 · *The Times* (15 Feb 1876) · O'Byrne, *Naval biog. dict.* · *The early correspondence of Richard Wood, 1831–1841*, ed. A. B. Cunningham, CS, 4th ser., 3 (1966) · H. Reeve, *Memoirs*, ed. J. K. Laughton (1898) · 'Walker's warbler', *Punch*, 40 (1861), 119 · H. W. V. Temperley, *England and the Near East: the Crimea* (1936) · C. I. Hamilton, *Anglo-French naval rivalry, 1840–1870* (1993) · A. D. Lambert, *The last sailing battlefleet: maintaining naval mastery, 1815–1850* (1991) · *Dod's Peerage* (1958) · Burke, *Peerage* (1967) · *DNB*
Archives NMM, corresp. and papers · University of Cape Town, corresp. and papers [some photocopies in NMM] | Cumbria AS, Carlisle, Graham MSS · NL Scot., corresp. with David Livingstone · U. Durham L., letters to Viscount Ponsonby
Likenesses D. Wilkie, oils, 1840–44, priv. coll. · photograph, 1860–69, Dockyard Naval Museum, Simonstown · J. Nash, lithograph (after D. Wilkie), BM; repro. in D. Wilkie, *Sir David Wilkie's sketches in Turkey, Syria and Egypt, 1840 and 1841* (1843)
Wealth at death £12,000: probate, 1 April 1876, *CGPLA Eng. & Wales*

Walker, Sir Byron Edmund (1848–1924), banker in Canada, the eldest son of Alfred Edmund Walker and his wife, Fanny, the daughter of William Murton, of East Stour, Kent, was born on a farm in Seneca township, Haldimand county, Canada West, on 14 October 1848. Both his parents were of English origin. He went to the central school in Hamilton, Ontario, at the age of four, but left when he was only twelve on account of ill health. In 1861 he was taken into the exchange office of an uncle, J. W. Murton, in Hamilton, where he became an expert in currencies and the detection of counterfeit money. In July 1868 he entered the Canadian Bank of Commerce in Hamilton as a discount clerk, and remained for the rest of his life in the bank. In 1872 he became chief accountant in Toronto; in 1873 accountant in the New York agency; in 1875 manager in Windsor, Ontario; in 1878 manager in London, Ontario; in 1879 inspector at the head office; in 1880 manager in Hamilton; in 1881 joint agent in New York; in 1886 general manager; in 1906 director; and in 1907 president. Not only was the growth of the Bank of Commerce due in great part to Walker's skill and personality, but the Canadian banking system as a whole owes its present form largely to his efforts. He was a lifelong advocate of the branch-banking system, and always strenuously opposed attempts to change the Canadian branch system to the system of local banks which prevails in the United States. As the branch-banking system demanded co-operation among the Canadian banks, he and others founded in 1891 the Canadian Bankers' Association, of which he was successively vice-president and president.

Walker became recognized as an authority on Canadian finance. In 1899 he chaired a royal commission which investigated the finances of Ontario; in 1909 he was elected vice-president of the American Bankers' Association; and in the last years of his life he was consulted by the English authorities about the public finance of England. As director of many companies, he had a wide influence on Canadian business and finance. The greatest tribute to his financial ability was the stability of Canadian finance during the First World War, which was due in large part to a plan of his making.

Walker was much interested in the University of Toronto, as a trustee (1892), which office he held until the reorganization of the university following the report of the royal commission of 1905, of which he was a member. Thereafter he served as a governor, as chairman (1910–23), and then as chancellor. He was honorary president of the Mendelssohn Choir of Toronto from 1900, and chairman of the governors of the Toronto Conservatory of Music. He took an active interest in the acquisitions as well as the management of the Royal Ontario Museum, which opened in 1914, particularly in its palaeontological collection. In 1907 he was made one of three members of a government arts council (later the board of trustees of the National Gallery). He was a keen and knowledgeable collector, particularly of Japanese prints. He was involved in politics only in the general election of 1911, when he and other Liberals of Toronto opposed the Laurier government's policy of reciprocity with the United States, in which he and they saw serious political and economic harm to Canada.

Walker's writings include 'Canadian banking' in Palgrave's *Dictionary of Political Economy* (1894–1908) and *A History of Banking in Canada* (1896). His private papers shed important light on Canadian and international finance.

Walker married in 1874 Mary (*d.* 1923), the daughter of Alexander Alexander, of Hamilton, and had four sons and three daughters. He was knighted in 1910, and received honorary degrees from Trinity University, Toronto, and the University of Toronto (1906). He died in Toronto on 27 March 1924.

W. P. M. KENNEDY, *rev.* ELIZABETH BAIGENT

Sources V. Ross, *A history of the Canadian Bank of Commerce*, 3 vols. (1920) [vol. 3 by A. St L. Trigge] · personal knowledge (1937) · private information (1937) · K. A. Jordan, *Sir Edmund Walker, print collector* (1974)
Likenesses J. Lavery, oils, National Gallery of Canada, Ottawa
Wealth at death £1812 10s.: administration with will, 19 Dec 1924, *CGPLA Eng. & Wales*

Walker, Sir Charles Pyndar Beauchamp (1817–1894), army officer, was born on 7 October 1817, the eldest son of Charles Ludlow Walker of Redland, JP and deputy lieutenant of Gloucestershire, and Mary Anne, daughter of Revd Reginald Pyndar of Hadsor, Worcestershire, and Kempley, Gloucestershire, cousin of the first Earl Beauchamp. He was a commoner at Winchester College from 1831 to 1833. He was commissioned ensign in the 33rd foot on 27 February 1836, and became lieutenant on 21 June 1839 and captain on 22 December 1846. He served with the regiment at Gibraltar, in the West Indies, and in North America. On 16 November 1849 he exchanged into the 7th dragoon guards. He married in 1845 Georgiana, daughter of Captain Richard Armstrong of the 100th foot. She survived him.

On 25 March 1854 Walker was appointed aide-de-camp to Lord Lucan, who commanded the cavalry division in the Crimea. He was present at Alma, Balaklava, and Inkerman, and was mentioned in dispatches. He was also present at the naval attack on Sevastopol on 17 October, where he acted as aide-de-camp to Lord George Paulet on board the *Bellerophon*, and was awarded the Mejidiye (fifth class).

On 8 December 1854 Walker was promoted major in his regiment, and in anticipation of this he left the Crimea at the beginning of that month. He was appointed assistant quartermaster-general in Ireland on 9 July 1855, and on 9 November he was given an unattached lieutenant-colonelcy. On 7 December 1858 he became lieutenant-colonel of the 2nd dragoon guards (the Queen's Bays). He joined them in India, and took part in the later operations against the rebels. He commanded a field force in Oudh, with which he defeated the rebels at Bungdon on 27 April 1859, and a month afterwards served in the action of the Jirwah Pass under Sir Hope Grant. He was mentioned in dispatches.

From India Walker went on to China, being appointed on 14 May 1860 assistant quartermaster-general of cavalry in Sir Hope Grant's expedition. He was present at the actions of Sinho, Changkiawan (Zhangjiawan), and Palichiao (Baliqiao). In the advance on Peking (Beijing) he went ahead to select the camping-grounds, and on 16 September, when Sir Harry Smith Parkes and others were treacherously seized during the truce, he narrowly escaped. His sword was found when Changkiawan was stormed and sacked later in the day, 18 September 1860. He was mentioned in dispatches, and was made CB on 28 February 1861. He had become colonel in the army on 14 December 1860.

Back in England, Walker went on half pay on 11 June 1861, and on 1 July was appointed assistant quartermaster-general at Shorncliffe. He remained there until 31 March 1865. On 26 April he was made military attaché at Berlin, and he held that post for nearly twelve years. In the Austro-Prussian War of 1866 he was attached to the headquarters of the crown prince's army as British military commissioner, and was present at the battles of Nachod and Königgrätz. He was again attached to the crown prince's army in the Franco-Prussian War, and was present at Weissenburg, Wörth, Sedan, and throughout the siege of Paris. He was given the medal and the Iron Cross. The irritation of the Germans against England and the number of roving Englishmen made his task difficult, but he was tactful and genial and his action had the approval of the government.

Walker was promoted major-general on 29 December 1873 (afterwards antedated to 6 March 1868). He resigned his post at Berlin on 31 March 1877, and became lieutenant-general on 1 October. He was inspector-general of military education from January 1878 until 7 October 1884, when he was retired with the honorary rank of general. He had been made KCB on 24 May 1881, and colonel of the 2nd dragoon guards on 22 December 1881. He died at his London residence, 97 Onslow Square, South Kensington, on 19 January 1894, and was buried in Brompton cemetery. Extracts from his letters and journals during active service were published after his death as *Days of a Soldier's Life* (1894).   E. M. LLOYD, *rev.* JAMES LUNT

Sources C. P. B. Walker, *Days of a soldier's life* (1894) · *The Standard* (22 Jan 1894) · *Hart's Army List* · M. Mann, *History of 1st the queen's dragoon guards* (1993) · M. Mann, *China, 1860* (1989) · A. W. Kinglake, *The invasion of the Crimea*, 8 vols. (1863–87) · R. Swinhoe, *Narrative of the north China campaign* (1861) · R. Cannon, ed., *The second, or queen's regiment of dragoon guards* (1837)
Archives PRO, letters to Odo Russell, FO 918
Wealth at death £58,179 9s. 1d.: probate, 13 Feb 1894, *CGPLA Eng. & Wales*

Walker, Charles Vincent (1812–1882), technical editor and electrical engineer, was born on 20 March 1812 in Marylebone, Middlesex, the son of Vincent Walker and his wife Ann, *née* Blake. Details of his education are unknown, although he was said to have been trained as an engineer. By 1838 he was drawn to the study of electricity, and was a founder and active member of the London Electrical Society, serving as its secretary and treasurer and editing its *Proceedings* from 1841–3. On its winding-up, he started the *Electrical Magazine*, of which only two volumes appeared, in 1841–3. He acquired a wider reputation in 1841 by completing the second volume and editing the entire manuscript of Dionysius Lardner's *Manual of Electricity, Magnetism and Meteorology*, which formed part of Lardner's *Cabinet Cyclopedia*. Walker's own book on *Electrotype Manipulation* was published in 1841, and ran through many editions, and, like his telegraph manual, *Electric Telegraph Manipulation* (1850), was translated into French and German. He also edited and translated into English sundry other scientific works.

In 1845 Walker was appointed electrician to the South-Eastern Railway Company. During his lifelong tenure of this post, he was responsible for many improvements: when telegraph wires had to be laid underground, he was the first to make use of gutta-percha as an insulant; he devised an instrument to protect telegraph apparatus from damage by atmospheric electric discharge; and he improved graphite batteries. In 1866 he patented apparatus to enable train passengers to communicate with the guard, and in 1876 he patented a 'train describer' for indicating trains on a distant dial.

Walker also interested himself in submarine telegraphy and on 13 October 1848 he sent the first submarine message, through a 2 mile loop of cable laid from Folkestone to a ship anchored offshore and back, the shore end being connected with the railway company's telegraph to London Bridge Station. In 1849 he collaborated with George Biddell Airy, astronomer royal, in the introduction of time signals, which were telegraphed from Greenwich observatory to stations on the South-Eastern Railway.

Walker was elected to the Meteorological Society in 1850, where he held various offices and served as president in 1869–70. He encouraged the society to publish its

Proceedings, of which he was editor from 1861 to 1864. On 7 June 1855 he was elected to the Royal Society; on 8 January 1858 to the Royal Astronomical Society; and in 1876 he was president of the Society of Telegraph Engineers and Electricians. Walker died of heart failure at his residence, 26 Upper Grosvenor Road, Tunbridge Wells, Kent, on 24 December 1882. The probate record described him as a widower, but nothing is known of his wife.

ANITA MCCONNELL

Sources K. R. Haigh, Cableships and submarine cables, [new edn] (1978), 26–7 · D. Howse, Greenwich time (1980), 89–92 · Nature, 14 (1876), 50–52, 110–13 · Nature, 27 (1882–3), 228 · Monthly Notices of the Royal Astronomical Society, 43 (1882–3), 183–4 · Quarterly Journal of the Meteorological Society, 9 (1883), 99–100 · Journal of the Society of Telegraph Engineers, 12 (1883), 1–3 · Telegraphic Journal and Electrical Review, 12 (1883), 16 · Proceedings of London Electrical Society (1841–3) · d. cert. · CGPLA Eng. & Wales (1883)
Archives RAS, letters to Royal Astronomical Society
Likenesses M. Thomas, oils, 1876, Inst. EE
Wealth at death £2467 6s. 10d.: administration with will, 29 March 1883, CGPLA Eng. & Wales

Walker, Clement [pseud. Theodorus Verax] (d. 1651), political pamphleteer, was born at Cliffe, in the parish of Tincleton, Dorset. His father was Thomas Walker of Westminster. Clement may have attended Christ Church, Oxford, though there is no record of his matriculation. In 1611 he was admitted to Middle Temple. Soon afterwards he inherited the office of usher of receipt in the exchequer, but he always employed a deputy to do the work. In the 1630s he was also marshal of common pleas.

Some time before 1626 Walker married Frances (d. 1631), daughter of Sir William Pitt, a teller of the exchequer. They had three children, born between 1626 and 1631, but it was not a happy marriage. There were rumours that Frances had been unfaithful, and in June 1629 Walker stabbed and seriously wounded her; the whalebones of her stomacher saved her life. Her father wanted to hush it up, but his son told him that this was impossible, because 'the whole Sheir of Dorsett doth ring with the Infamous fame therof' (BL, Add MS 29974, fol. 118). Frances eventually recovered, and the couple were at least partly reconciled before her death in 1631, although her husband still remained on bad terms with her family. In 1634 Walker was married a second time, to Mary, daughter of Sir William Button. She claimed to have brought him a large marriage portion; in return he settled his office on her as jointure. A son, John, was born to this marriage. The attempt on Frances's life blotted Walker's reputation: Anthony Wood later said that his hands were 'stained with his own wife's blood' (Wood, Ath. Oxon., 3.293).

By 1640 Walker had acquired an estate at Charterhouse-on-Mendip, Somerset. He supported parliament in the civil war and early in 1643 was appointed to the Somerset assessment and sequestration committees. Soon afterwards he served as advocate in the trial of Robert Yeomans and George Bourchier for attempting to betray Bristol to Prince Rupert. Walker remained in Bristol, and was there when the city fell to Rupert at the end of July 1643. The governor, Colonel Nathaniel Fiennes, defended himself from charges that he had not put up a resolute defence,

provoking Walker to accuse him of cowardice. On 25 September 1643 Walker was sent for by the House of Lords, charged with having scandalized Fiennes's father, Lord Saye and Sele. When taken into custody Walker said that Saye was 'a base beggarly Lord, and that his Sons were Cowards' (JHL, 6.240–41). The Lords fined him £100, awarded Saye £500 damages, and required Walker to make submission at the bar of the house. He refused to submit, claiming that the Lords' judgment 'was against the Liberty of the Subject', and that they had no right to try 'a Commoner of England' (JHL, 6.247). He was sent to the Tower, but released on bail on 17 October so that he and William Prynne could prosecute the charges against Fiennes. The colonel was court-martialled and sentenced to death, though subsequently pardoned by his commander, the earl of Essex.

After his release Walker may have spent several years in London; there is no sign that he ever attended meetings of the Somerset committee. He claimed to have lost his whole estate during the war (£10,000 according to his later estimate), to have spent another £3000 in the parliament's service, and to be liable for £5000 borrowed for the defence of Bristol. These sums are almost certainly exaggerations. In 1646 he was elected to the House of Commons for Wells; according to Wood, he curried favour with the local puritans in order to win the seat. He took the covenant on 24 June. In the same year he was named an elder of the Somerset presbyterian classis, though he was critical of clergy who wished to impose an oppressive discipline on the Scottish model. He was one of those accused of instigating the 'presbyterian' London riots of 26 July 1647. He stayed at Westminster when the speakers fled to the army at the end of that month, and on 1 August he was named as chairman of a committee charged with drawing up a protest against the army's actions; his notes for this declaration were soon confiscated.

By this time Walker was writing the first of his numerous pamphlets against the parliamentary radicals. The Mystery of the Two Juntoes was written in 1647 under the pseudonym Theodorus Verax; in 1648 it was incorporated, along with the first volume of Walker's History of Independency, in his Relations and Observations, Historical and Politick, upon the Parliament Begun anno Dom. 1640. Walker argued that the increasing polarization of parliament between 'Presbyterians' and 'Independents' was a sham to enable the leaders of the factions to divide offices and patronage between them. He claimed to express the views of the non-partisan back-benchers, 'the honest middle men of the House' (C. Walker, Mystery, 1647, 6). Their desire for a moderate settlement, he said, had been betrayed by their leaders: 'the controversie between the 2 Juntoes being no more than whose slaves we shall be' (ibid., 17). Despite his later reputation as a presbyterian, Walker was even-handed in his criticisms of the two factions, blaming the presbyterians for needlessly antagonizing Fairfax's army, and for trying to constitute a countervailing force against the New Model out of disbanded supernumerary forces.

However, by May 1648 Walker was convinced that it was the radical Independents who were responsible for the illegalities being perpetrated by parliament. In part one of *The History of Independency* he argued that the army and its allies in the Commons were obstructing a settlement with the king, aiming at achieving power for themselves. His case against the Independents was further developed in *Anarchie Anglicana, or, The History of Independency, the Second Part* (1649), which focused largely on the events of the previous year. A third part of the series, entitled *The High Court of Justice, or, Cromwells New Slaughter House in England*, appeared in 1651.

There are few signs of Walker's parliamentary activities in 1648. On 17 June he joined the presbyterians in demanding an investigation of an alleged plot to poison Charles I, and he was sometimes involved in Somerset affairs, joining with other MPs in October to ask for the disbandment of military forces in the county. On 2 December he was named to the presbyterian militia commission for Somerset. In the great all-night debate in the Commons on 4–5 December, Walker spoke in favour of accepting the king's recent answers in the treaty of Newport. He also supported the subsequent motion that the king's answers were a satisfactory basis for continuing negotiations. He was imprisoned in Pride's Purge on 6 December, and remained in custody until some time in January 1649. During that month he joined William Prynne in publishing *A Declaration and Protestation* against the army's recent actions.

Walker was again arrested soon after the publication of the second part of *The History of Independency*. On 24 October 1649 his papers were seized by order of the House of Commons; soon afterwards he was committed to the Tower on a charge of treason, though he was never brought to trial. During his imprisonment the committee of revenue took away his exchequer office and conferred it upon another MP, Humphrey Edwards, whom Walker publicly denounced in a broadside entitled *The Case between Clement Walker Esq. and Humphrey Edwards, Truely Stated* (1650); his wife wrote a similar attack. Walker died in the Tower in October 1651, and was buried at the nearby church of All Hallows Barking. No known portrait has survived, but a 1647 deposition described Walker as being of short stature, and in 1650 George Wither spoke sneeringly of his red nose and wrinkled face.

Anthony Wood said that Walker was 'notably vers'd in the liberties and privileges of parliament, and in the statute law of the kingdom' (Wood, *Ath. Oxon.*, 3.293), but he is chiefly important as a political pamphleteer. *The History of Independency* was a highly effective piece of propaganda against the radicals in parliament, the army, and the counties, especially Somerset. It was still in demand after the Restoration, and was reprinted in 1661. Walker may have begun a continuation, but the one that appeared in 1661 was written by a certain 'T. M'.   DAVID UNDERDOWN

Sources Thomason tracts [BL] · *DNB* · Wood, *Ath. Oxon.*, new edn, 3.292 · D. Underdown, *Pride's Purge: politics in the puritan revolution* (1971) · *JHC*, 5 (1646–8) · *JHC*, 6 (1648–51) · *JHL*, 6 (1643–4) · BL, Pitt MSS, Add. MS 29974 · G. E. Aylmer, *The king's servants: the civil service of Charles I, 1625–1642* (1961) · G. E. Aylmer, *The state's servants: the civil service of the English republic, 1649–1660* (1973) · C. H. Firth and R. S. Rait, eds., *Acts and ordinances of the interregnum, 1642–1660*, 3 vols. (1911) · D. Underdown, *Somerset in the civil war and interregnum* (1973) · J. Hutchins, *The history and antiquities of the county of Dorset*, 2 vols. (1774)

Walker, Cyril Frederick [Bob] **Danvers-** (1906–1990), newsreel commentator and radio and television broadcaster, was born on 11 October 1906 at Wylma, Burdon Lane, Cheam, Surrey, the son of an Australian insurance clerk, William Charles Walker, and his wife, Lilian Danvers. He grew up in Tasmania, where his father was helping to set up the first woollen mills, and he was educated there at Launceston church grammar school. After leaving school he worked as a motor mechanic, raced in the first Australian Grand Prix, and spent time on a sheep station, before moving to Melbourne, where in 1925 he became a junior announcer at the Herald broadcasting station 3DB. In 1926 he moved to the Australian Broadcasting Company's stations 3LO and 3AR, and from there in 1932 to 2FC in Sydney, where he was the first to broadcast from an aircraft in flight when he joined the search for the wreckage of an airliner lost in the mountains. He moved back to England with his family later in 1932, and on 14 October 1933 he married Vera Nita White (*b.* 1910/11), daughter of Albert Edmund White, of the Royal Navy; they had one son and one daughter.

Walker (he began to use the name Danvers-Walker only in the 1950s) joined the newly formed International Broadcasting Company in London in 1932, and went to Fécamp, on the French coast, to be chief announcer for Radio Normandy, installed in a farmyard stable. Radio Normandy beamed radio programmes into southern England, broadcasting records of popular dance music after the BBC closed down for the night. Walker helped to set up Radio Toulouse, Radio Lyons, Poste Parisien, Union Radio Madrid, and stations in Barcelona and Valencia, all part of the IBC network of commercial radio stations. He also recorded programmes for Radio Luxemburg, a separate company. With the outbreak of war in 1939, Radio Normandy closed down for two months, but when it returned to the airwaves in November as Radio International, Walker was one of the announcers, presenting music recorded in America and news bulletins for the British expeditionary force in France, and making broadcasts for the French government to counter German propaganda, which led to his inclusion on a Nazi blacklist. After Radio International closed down in January 1940 Walker returned to England, where he was employed by the Entertainments National Service Association (ENSA) as manager for the Will Hay Empire Variety Company, taking the show to France to provide entertainment for the troops, until the invasion of France in May 1940. He brought the company out on the last convoy to leave Cherbourg, three weeks after Dunkirk.

Walker joined Pathé Gazette in July 1940 as a newsreel commentator, reading narratives written by the Pathé scriptwriters, and for the next thirty years, until the newsreels came to an end in February 1970, his fruity voice became known to millions in cinemas and news theatres. He was also wartime editor of the newsreel from 1944 to 1945. Pathé Gazette became Pathé News in 1946, and he continued to cover all the major national and international events. He also spoke the commentary for many of the promotional and educational films, and documentaries, made by Pathé, and for the Pathé Pictorial films.

From 1943 Walker also worked as an announcer and scriptreader for the BBC European and overseas services, once the BBC had removed its ban on employing pre-war radio 'pirates', on programmes including *London Calling Europe*, *Round and About*, and *Radio Newsreel*. He was never on the permanent staff of the BBC, though he would have liked to have been, but he continued to work for the BBC after the war, and was a regular presenter of *Housewives' Choice* from 1947 to 1960. He contributed to the *Countryside* series from 1965 until 1982, and went to destinations including Sicily, Tangier, and the Costa Brava to collect material for the Light Programme series *Holiday Hour* from 1959 to 1963, and later for *Holidays Abroad* on Radio 4 from 1967 to 1969. His full-length programmes included *The Gracie Fields Story* (1958) and *A World of Sound* (1969). He also made programmes for the BBC Pacific service, including *This is Britain* from 1950 to 1951.

When commercial television began in 1955, Danvers-Walker launched ABC Television's weekend service during the radio show at Earl's Court by taking part in a high wire act crossing the Earl's Court Road. This led to regular appearances as a stuntman on the BBC television show *Saturday Night Out*, including taking part in a seaborne commando landing, and *Now*, in which he filmed Jacques Cousteau underwater in Marseilles harbour. For eighteen years he announced the prizes on the ITV quiz show *Take your Pick*. Bob Danvers-Walker died of cancer on 17 May 1990 in Sobell House, at the Churchill Hospital, Oxford. His wife survived him.   ANNE PIMLOTT BAKER

Sources C. F. Danvers-Walker, interview, 1981, IWM SA, 5200/3 · R. Nichols, *Radio Luxembourg* (1983) · 'Bob Danvers-Walker', *ABC Film Review*, 13 (Dec 1954) · *The Times* (19 May 1990) · *Daily Telegraph* (18 May 1990) · *The Independent* (26 May 1990) · BBC WAC · b. cert. · m. cert. · d. cert.
Archives FILM British Pathé archive of newsreels, New Pathé House, 57 Jamestown Road, London NW1 7XX | SOUND IWM SA, interview 1981, 5200/3
Likenesses two photographs, *c*.1938, BBC WAC · photograph, repro. in *The Times*
Wealth at death £246,807: probate, 5 March 1991, *CGPLA Eng. & Wales*

Walker, Deane Franklin (1778–1865). *See under* Walker, Adam (1730/31–1821).

Walker, Sir Edward (1612–1677), herald, was born on 24 January 1612 at Roobers, Nether Stowey, Somerset, the second son of Edward Walker (*d.* 1635/6) of Roobers and Barbara, daughter of Edward Salkeld of Corby Castle, Cumberland.

Early years and civil war In 1633 Walker entered the service of Thomas Howard, earl of Arundel, earl marshal, who was attending Charles I's unpopular coronation as king of Scotland on 18 June 1633 in Edinburgh. On 24 May 1635 he was appointed Blanch Lyon pursuivant-extraordinary, thanks to his patron, by whose warrant of 27 August to the

Sir Edward Walker (1612–1677), by William Dobson

master of the wardrobe he acquired 'a coat of arms [tabard] embroidered with satin upon damask enriched with gold thread' (*CSP dom.*, 1635, 355). In 1636 Walker attended Arundel on his lengthy but abortive mission to the ailing holy Roman emperor, Ferdinand II, in Regensburg. In 1637 he was appointed Rouge Dragon pursuivant and in 1638 Chester herald. In 1639 he was secretary at war in Arundel's bloodless expedition against the Scots leading to the treaty of Berwick, for which he wrote the minutes. He also wrote a short life of his patron, which became the fourth book of Walker's *Historical Discourses*. On 23 April 1640 he was made paymaster to the garrison at Carlisle and the following year he was paid to disband it.

On 24 April 1642, shortly before the start of the civil war, Charles I sent Walker and another herald to demand the surrender of Kingston upon Hull and to proclaim Sir John Hotham a traitor in case of refusal. By autumn that year the king had constituted Walker his secretary at war. Following the battle of Edgehill in 1642 Walker remained with the king at Oxford (where he was created MA in 1642) until its siege and surrender in 1646. He was made secretary extraordinary of the privy council on 13 April 1644 and Norroy king of arms in the same year. He was sent to offer a pardon to Waller's army after the battle of Cropredy Bridge of 29 June 1644 and played a similar role on 12 August 1644 prior to the defeat of Essex at Lostwithiel. His account of the 1644 campaigns was an important source for the relevant section of Edward Hyde, earl of Clarendon's *History of the Rebellion*.

Walker became Garter king of arms in 1645, having been knighted on 2 February of that year in Oxford. One of his first tasks as Garter was to call on Prince Rupert in Oxford, with the chancellor and register of the order, with messages from the king about the prince's future installation as a knight of the Garter. Following the royalist defeat at Naseby (1645), the capture of the king by the Scots at Newark (1646), and the surrender of Oxford on 24 June 1646, Walker went briefly to France, where he saw at Le Mans the famous enamel memorial plate of Geoffrey Plantagenet, count of Anjou, said to be the earliest surviving example of a true coat of arms. Charles I having escaped in 1647 from Hampton Court to the Isle of Wight, Walker was permitted by parliament to act as his chief secretary at the abortive treaty of Newport. The documentary records of this treaty were published as a supplement to Walker's *Historical Discourses* but a fuller account by his secretary, Nicholas Oudart, is printed in Peck's *Desiderata curiosa*.

Royal service in exile The execution of Charles I on 30 January 1649 did not end Walker's career in the royal service. That same year he was in The Hague with Charles II who appointed him clerk of the council in ordinary and receiver of the king's moneys. On 6 June the king sent him a list of debts to be settled immediately and Walker complied. Anxious to preserve his rights in troubled times he petitioned the king to confirm his right as Garter to carry the warrants and insignia to foreign princes and others who were elected to the Order of the Garter. The king, having referred the matter to three companions of the order, confirmed Garter's rights in his declaration at Breda on 28 May 1650. In the following month Walker accompanied Charles to Scotland and his name was included in a list (10 July 1650) of those ordered by the Scots parliament to be banished from the court and/or the country. He was still in Scotland during the battle of Dunbar on 3 September 1650 but on 4 October he was ordered to leave the court within twenty-four hours and he finally embarked for the Netherlands via Aberdeen in late October. From 30 October to 9 November 1650 he reported to Cottington from The Hague on the king's movements following Dunbar.

Walker had already invested Edward count palatine of the Rhine, first cousin of the king, as a knight of the Garter on 19 September 1649 at St Germain-en-Laye. He later invested three more companions at The Hague in 1653: Henry, duke of Gloucester, brother of Charles II; the prince of Taranto; and William Henry, prince of Orange (later William III). In 1654 he undertook a mission to Berlin to invest (on 3 April) Frederick William, elector of Brandenburg. Nevertheless, Walker was seldom satisfied and his endless complaints irritated his superiors. Secretary Nicholas in 1653 called him importunate, ambitious, and foolish, and in the same year Hyde described him as a correspondent not to be endured, and continued

> he has written impertinent letters either of expostulation or request, every week; he was troubled about Lane's appointment to be Clerk of the Council; next he asked for a letter to the Prince Elector, asking for Lord Stafford's liberty; and now he expostulates severely upon Sir W Ballentyne's being charged with the Garter for the Swedish Prince. (Ogle and others, 2.175)

In the following year Hyde wrote to Nicholas 'Why should [you] wonder that a herald who is naturally made up of embroidery, should adorn his own services?' (ibid., 2.346). However both men sometimes found him useful, as on 5 May 1656 when Hyde recorded that he had heard from Walker in Amsterdam who suggested a scheme for getting money from Dutch Catholics by means of some priests. On 23 March 1657 Hyde wrote to Ormond that Walker, like Hyde himself, desired plenty and to live according to his quality as herald, but that it was no more in Hyde's power to help him than to restore him to his lodging in Windsor Castle. This refers to Garter's Tower in the lower ward which successive garters petitioned unsuccessfully to have repaired.

Walker was on good terms with Elias Ashmole but apparently disliked Sir William Dugdale, though after borrowing the latter's splendid *Monasticon Anglicanum* for three days in Amsterdam he wrote to him enthusiastically on 6 August 1655 saying 'I have almost made myself blind perusing it' and offered to supply a plate by W. Hollar (Hamper, 293). He was also a friend of the astrologer William Lilly and took an interest in horoscopes himself. The Ashmolean manuscripts contain much of this material including Walker's nativity 'Calculated and interpreted by Capt. G Wharton at Oxford 1645' (Bodl. Oxf., MS Ashmole 179, 2.1–9). However, he took exception to a book about Charles I published by Lilly in July 1651, *Monarchy and No Monarchy*, and admonished him in a letter from The Hague dated 24 May 1652 which became the fifth book of his *Historical Discourses*. In November 1655 Walker joined Charles II at Cologne and became once more secretary of the council and the following year secretary at war.

Restoration At the Restoration, Walker returned to his post as Garter displacing the intruded Edward Bysshe who, with parliamentary sanction, had been Garter from 1646 to 1660 and Clarenceux from 1650 to 1658. Sir William Le Neve, who had been appointed Clarenceux in 1635, was found insane in March 1661, and although Walker tried to get the post for himself Bysshe was appointed on 10 March 1661. He was frequently attacked by Walker, notably for having allegedly forged his own pedigree, but Walker's motives were partly selfish, namely to hinder the grant to Bysshe of a commission to carry out a heraldic visitation, or else to get himself included in it. In fact on 7 July 1663 Clarenceux (Bysshe) and Norroy (John Dugdale) received commissions in their own right to visit their respective provinces, thus resuming a practice which had been halted by the civil war. Walker's self interest had already led him, while still in exile in 1657, to draft a proposal for uniting the offices of Clarenceux and Norroy with that of Garter. He further angered his colleagues by making grants of arms without reference to the provincial kings (Clarenceux and Norroy) or to the earl marshal. On 6 May 1645 he had received a warrant from Charles I at Oxford authorizing him to grant augmentations (special marks of honour) to the arms of the king's faithful adherents, or to grant them new arms as he saw fit. On 3 September 1660 he obtained a further warrant confirming and amplifying that of 1645.

Meanwhile, away from the College of Arms, on 27 May 1660 Walker had invested with the Garter, on board ship, Sir Edward Montagu, who had just escorted Charles II back to England and in July of that year Walker, John Nicholas, and Sir George Lane were made clerks of the privy council in ordinary. Walker and Nicholas received a substantial pay rise on 18 April 1665. Walker also played an important part in the coronation of Charles II, which took place in Westminster Abbey during a thunderstorm on 23 April 1661. He wrote a detailed account of the event in fifty-two manuscript folios dated 25 May 1661, subsequently published in 1820 as *A Circumstantial Account of the Preparations for the Coronation*. Ashmole also wrote a brief narrative of the coronation and banquet as part of a book by John Ogilby but withdrew his name from the second and subsequent editions, possibly for fear of upsetting Walker.

Disputes within the College of Arms In 1668 the College of Arms submitted to the commissioners draft orders for the regulation of the college based on those of 1568 but dealing in more detail with the control of unauthorized herald painters, certain duties of the kings of arms such as the recording of their grants of arms at the college, and the conduct of visitations and funerals. These were largely accepted by the commissioners but Walker and Bysshe both seemed to ignore the requirement to register their grants. Meanwhile in 1672 Charles II revived the office of hereditary earl marshal, which had been in commission since 1662, conferring it on Henry (Howard) earl of Norwich, later duke of Norfolk. The latter decided that the kings of arms needed stricter control and on 21 May 1673 he made an order requiring every grant to be made by all three kings jointly, following a warrant from the earl marshal, and recorded before it went to the grantee. He also laid down minimum fees, both Bysshe and Walker having been accused of making cheap grants surreptitiously. Next day the earl marshal directed a warrant to all three kings to make a grant to one Nevinson Fox. Walker considered the earl marshal had exceeded his powers and, perhaps unwisely, petitioned the privy council. The king referred the petition to the lord privy seal, whose lengthy opinion strongly supported the earl marshal, whereupon the king, on 16 June 1673, issued a declaration of the earl marshal's authority over the officers of arms. The loyal Ashmole tried to assist Walker by drafting a statement claiming that while Garter was subject to the earl marshal's authority as a member of the college he was not so as an officer of the Order of the Garter. The exercise was in vain, for on 22 January 1675 an order in council confirmed the validity of the king's declaration of 1673.

Fuller details of Walker's grievances against his colleagues and the earl marshal during the period 1673–6 may be found in Ashmole manuscript 1133. He singled out for particular blame Andrew Hay, the earl marshal's secretary, and Thomas Lee, Chester herald. Lee was one of a triumvirate (with Francis Sandford and Henry St George) who disagreed with Walker over details of the plans to rebuild the College of Arms on the site of Derby House, destroyed in the great fire of 1666. Many similar disputes

were chronicled in letters sent to Sir Joseph Williamson in Cologne by his clerk Henry Ball. Letters of June 1673 indicate that Bysshe was in disgrace over the inadequacy of his grant and visitation records and that Walker proposed to sell his place and retire. He did not in fact do so and he even obeyed the earl marshal's warrant for the grant of arms to Nevinson Fox. However, further disagreements followed and it is regrettable that these disputes clouded the final years of his distinguished career, to the prejudice of the office of Garter and of the College of Arms itself.

On 18 May 1675 Walker bought for £1060 from the surviving trustee of Elizabeth, Lady Barnard, William Shakespeare's grandchild and heir, a house called New Place in Stratford upon Avon, which had been the poet's last home. However, he does not seem to have lived there but at Clopton in Warwickshire. He married at an unknown date Agnes (*d.* in or before 1676), daughter of John Reeve of Bookham, Surrey, and had an only child, Barbara, who married, in 1662, Sir John Clopton of Clopton; their eldest son, Edward, was baptized at the College of Arms in 1663. Walker died at Whitehall on 20 February 1677 and was buried in the Lady (or Clopton) Chapel in Stratford upon Avon church. His epitaph was composed by his successor William Dugdale. In his will he left the college the library of Sir William Le Neve, which he had purchased in 1663, having already presented it with a collection of original grants of arms in 1673. He also bequeathed to his successors as Garter two volumes of the arms of the nobility and two relating to the Order of the Garter. He was probably the first Garter to keep a continuous record of the order, and Dugdale was to continue the second of Walker's volumes. HUBERT CHESSHYRE

Sources W. H. Godfrey, A. Wagner, and H. Stanford London, *The College of Arms, Queen Victoria Street* (1963) · A. Wagner, *Heralds of England: a history of the office and College of Arms* (1967) · DNB · *Elias Ashmole (1617–1692): his autobiographical and historical notes*, ed. C. H. Josten, 5 vols. (1966 [i.e. 1967]) · *The manuscripts of J. Eliot Hodgkin … of Richmond, Surrey*, HMC, 39 (1897) · *Calendar of the Clarendon state papers preserved in the Bodleian Library*, ed. O. Ogle and others, 5 vols. (1869–1970) · E. Walker, *Historical discourses upon several occasions* (1705) · *The life, diary, and correspondence of Sir William Dugdale*, ed. W. Hamper (1827) · CSP dom. · E. Ashmole, *The institution, laws and ceremonies of the most noble order of the Garter* (1672) · Bodl. Oxf., MSS Ashmole · P. G. Begent and H. Chesshyre, *The most noble Order of the Garter: 650 years* (1999) · W. D. Christie, ed., *Letters addressed from London to Sir Joseph Williamson*, 2 vols., CS, new ser., 8–9 (1874) · *The statutes of the most noble Order of the Garter* (privately printed, 1972) · A. R. Wagner, *The records and collections of the College of Arms* (1952) · *The Nicholas papers*, ed. G. F. Warner, 4 vols., CS, new ser., 40, 50, 57, 3rd ser., 31 (1886–1920) · heraldic visitation of Somerset, 1623, Coll. Arms, 2C22, fol. 292b · Coll. Arms, MS ped 4D14 (1734), fols. 186–9 · funeral certificate, 1635, Coll. Arms, I24, fol. 47 · Foster, *Alum. Oxon.* · grant of arms, 1660, Coll. Arms, R22, fols. 44b, 50b · VCH *Warwickshire* · J. O. Halliwell, *An historical account of the New Place, Stratford upon Avon* (1864) · 'Shakespeare, William', DNB · Wood, *Ath. Oxon.: Fasti*, new edn

Archives BL, corresp. and papers · Bodl. Oxf., account of progress and successes of Charles I · Coll. Arms, collections; College of Arms grants of arms, arms of the nobility, paper on Order of the Garter; papers · HLRO, draft letters and warrants · Hunt. L., historical discourses · S. Antiquaries, Lond., heraldic papers · U. Edin. L., journal of activities of Charles II in Scotland | Arundel Castle, West Sussex, corresp. with sixth duke of Norfolk · BL, Add. MS ·

BL, Harley MSS · Bodl. Oxf., MSS Ashmole · NL Wales, annotated transcript of Rice Merrick's *Morganiae Archaiographia*
Likenesses P. Lely, black chalk on paper, 1660?–1669, Courtauld Inst., Witt Library · W. Dobson, oils, Shakespeare Birthplace Trust RO, Stratford upon Avon [*see illus.*] · attrib. W. Dobson, oils, Coll. Arms · double portrait, oils (with Charles I), NPG · engraving (after unknown artist), repro. in Walker, *Historical discourses*; formerly at Melton Constable Park, Norfolk
Wealth at death property in Warwickshire and certain valuable items: will

Walker [*née* Sadler], **Elizabeth** (1623–1690), autobiographer, was born on 12 July 1623 in Bucklersbury, London, and baptized in the City on 20 July in the parish of St Stephen Walbrook, the eldest of the three children of John Sadler (*b.* 1587, *d.* in or after 1650), citizen of London, and his wife, Elizabeth (*b. c.*1600, *d.* in or after 1650), daughter of the Revd Dackum, minister of Portsmouth. In their native Stratford upon Avon in Warwickshire the Sadlers had close ties to William Shakespeare: Elizabeth's grandfather John Sadler (1561–1625) was probably a schoolfellow of Shakespeare, and her father's brother-in-law and business partner was Richard Quiney, elder brother of Thomas Quiney who married Shakespeare's daughter Judith in 1618. Most information about Elizabeth comes from a volume of autobiographical reminiscences and other writings entitled 'Some memorials of God's providences to my husband, self, and children', no longer extant. Selections were printed posthumously by Anthony Walker in his biographical memoir, *The Holy Life of Mrs. Elizabeth Walker* (1690). Walker's assurance that all quoted passages were taken verbatim from Elizabeth's autograph MS is consistent with independent evidence such as contemporary parish registers.

Elizabeth was a sickly infant, her parents' first child after five years of marriage, and they took 'exceedingly tender' care of her. Yet she almost starved from neglect at Lewisham, Kent, where she was put to nurse: the meat the Sadlers had sent to supplement the nurse's wages was found to be 'ready to stink for want of dressing' (Walker, 12). As the eldest child she helped in the London grocers shop of her father, a prosperous druggist and tobacconist, being trusted with management of the petty cash of £100 or more. Later she recalled with Augustinian scrupulosity various 'temptations' associated with her youthful responsibilities. Sent by her mother to the locked cupboard where apples were stored, she took one for herself, but thinking she had stolen it, reluctantly put the apple back. When civil war broke out, Elizabeth was sent to Ipswich for her safety; she was courted there by a wealthy merchant but her father overruled the match. Next she visited her father's Stratford relatives. There, she recalled, 'a gentleman of a very considerable Estate was importunate with me for my liking; but though his Estate was a great Temptation to me, I could not fancy his Person' (Walker, 15–16).

In youth Elizabeth's most agonizing 'temptation', suffered intermittently throughout her life, was the doubt of God's existence: she recalled wishing she could apprehend a God 'all Vengeance and Terrour, rather than no God at all' (Walker, 19). As an adolescent she feared her

atheistic doubts were unique, and expected to hear 'books and ballads' cried about her in the streets (Walker, 19–20). Attempting to combat these thoughts with the argument from Creation, she studied the intricate forms of the potted plants her father (a great lover of flowers) kept all year round in the parlour window of his shop:

> With others there was then in flower a Calcedon Iris, full of the impresses of God's curious workmanship, which the Lord was pleased to make use of to raise my poor heart and thoughts to the admiring and adoring of him.   (Walker, 19)

She confided her doubts to Mr Watson, minister of the local Warwickshire parish, as well as her beloved aunt Eleanor Quiney, who assured Elizabeth that she herself had experienced the same sceptical thoughts during her own youth. Later her father called a physician, Dr Bathurst, who diagnosed Elizabeth's complaint as mostly 'Dejectedness and Melancholy' (Walker, 20). Finally, she asked to stay with a private family in the country where she was not known. The minister's wife, Mrs Watson, arranged for Elizabeth to join the household of Mrs Watson's father, Dr John Beadle, minister of Banston, Essex, where she was kindly treated. Nevertheless, she led an ascetic life, allowing herself almost no food or sleep for six months, fearful that if she gratified her sensual appetites she would be vulnerable to the devil's temptations.

Living with the Beadles, Elizabeth found her depression gradually wear off. It was there that she first met her future husband, Anthony *Walker (*bap.* 1622, *d.* 1692), the earl of Warwick's household chaplain, who had come to exchange a Sunday service with John Beadle. The couple fell in love and were married by Mr Watson at Hammersmith on 22 July 1650, with Elizabeth's parents and friends accompanying her. She described how the cloudy weather at first troubled her as a well-known portent of an unhappy marriage, but soon 'the Sun expelled the Clouds to my comfort … [leaving] as clear and bright a day as ever my Eyes beheld. Thus God was pleased to condescend to my [superstitious] weakness' (Walker, 27–8). Her husband also had a weakness for portents. Waiting in Elizabeth's father's London parlour to propose marriage, he had casually opened the Bible on the desk there to the verse 'a prudent Wife is from the Lord' (Proverbs 19: 14). When he went to buy a wedding ring, the first offered to him had the posy 'Joined in one by Christ alone'; it fitted Elizabeth's finger exactly (Walker, 28). In the event, the portents were fulfilled, for the marriage during its forty-year span was an ideally loving and companionate one. For their first year the couple lived in Elizabeth's father's London house. Walker spent the rest of her married life in Fyfield, Essex, where her husband was rector, aside from the couple's annual visits to Tunbridge Wells from 1661 to 1689 to restore their health.

From 1651 until she ceased childbearing fifteen years later, Elizabeth Walker bore eleven children, including three stillbirths, as well as suffering several miscarriages. She noted each delivery in her book of memoirs, reporting many difficult and dangerous births. In 1659 her seventh child, a son, was born after a 'long hard labour' of 'three days and three nights in extremity … all about me despairing of life' (Walker, 62). The following year her eighth child, also a son, was stillborn after a 'hard labour'. At this time Walker experienced post-partum depression in which she was again attacked by atheistic doubts: 'In this Lying-in I fell into Melancholy, which much disturbed me with Vapours, and was very ill. It pleased God to suffer my old Enemy [the devil] very impetuously to assault me' (Walker, 63). Of eight live births, only two daughters survived to adolescence, one dying at age sixteen of smallpox, and the other while bearing her first child, Elizabeth's only grandchild, to whom she was intensely devoted. She educated all her children at home, teaching them to read as soon as they could pronounce their letters, then giving them a simple catechism and passages from scripture to memorize. Fearing what she regarded as the pernicious effects of popular culture, Walker would 'strictly charge the Servants not to tell them foolish Stories, or teach them idle songs' (Walker, 89). She taught her two surviving daughters the skills of housewifery, including the preparation and use of medicines. Although brought up in London, Walker herself became remarkably proficient in country arts, including wine and cider making. When Anthony Walker was complimented on 'his' cider, his wife jokingly retorted 'His sider! 'tis my Sider; I have all the Pains and Care, and he hath all the Praise who never meddles with it' (Walker, 89).

Celebrated for hospitality to friends (the Walkers turned their wedding anniversary into an annual feast for the entire Essex neighbourhood), Elizabeth was even more renowned for her charity to the poor, on whom she bestowed more than half of her own disposable income of £23 per annum. Active in medical charity among her neighbours, she would go at any hour of the day or night to assist women in childbirth. After a short sickness complicated by 'Rheumatism, Erysipelas, and Peripneumonia' she died on 23 February 1690 at Fyfield and was buried there in the parish church on 27 February (Walker, 210). Her husband's parish register entry expresses his grief:

February 27th. My Dear wife mrs Elizabeth Walker who fell asleep in Jesus the Lords day before 23, was Decently and Honorably buryed after liveing with mee 39 years and 7 months in a scarce to be exampled state of constant uninterrupted most endeared and endearing affections. The Best of wives and women. Shee was buryed in Linnen as she had desired and the law satisfyed … the 50s penalty to the poor exceeded neer ten times. (Crisp, 102)

SARA H. MENDELSON

Sources A. Walker, The holy life of Mrs. Elizabeth Walker (1690) • A. Pritchard, 'Elizabeth Walker and Shakespeare's Stratford', N&Q, 223 (1978), 156–8 • F. A. Crisp, ed., The parish registers of Fyfield, Essex, 1538–1700 (1896) • H. Smith, 'Anthony Walker', Essex Review, 44 (1935), 156–72 • IGI • J. A. Scott, 'Shepherdess of the flock: an Anglican minister's wife in seventeenth-century England', MA diss., University of Rochester, 1994

Walker, Elizabeth (1800–1876). See under Walker, William (1791–1867).

Walker, Sir Emery (1851–1933), process engraver and typographer, was born at 10 Pickering Terrace, Paddington, Middlesex, on 2 April 1851, the eldest of the five children of Emery Walker (d. 1891), a coach-builder, originally from Norfolk, and his wife, Mary Anne, née Barber. After receiving a little schooling at St Mark's College, Chelsea, he was obliged by the onset of his father's blindness in 1864 to earn his living. After a succession of more or less laborious occupations, the trend of his life was fixed by an encounter with Alfred Dawson, who had perfected 'glyptography', a form of etching devised in the 1840s by a certain Palmer. In 1872 Dawson founded the Typographic Etching Company, and in the following year Walker joined him. On 7 June 1877 Walker married Mary Grace (1849/50–1920), daughter of William Jones, an Inland Revenue supervisor. They had one daughter. Walker remained with Dawson's company until 1883, when he joined his brother-in-law, Robert Dunthorne, in business as a printseller and occasional publisher. Finding this change uncongenial, he returned in 1886 to his old pursuit and, in partnership with Walter Boutall, founded the firm of 'process and general engravers, draughtsmen, map-constructors, and photographers of works of art' known first as Walker and Boutall, later as Walker and Cockerell, and finally as Emery Walker, Ltd. Its office was at 16 Clifford's Inn, next door to the chambers of Samuel Butler, who became a close friend. The works were at a Georgian house not far from Walker's home in Hammersmith Terrace, London.

By good fortune there was another riverside dweller at Hammersmith who shared Walker's tastes to the full. This was William Morris. Their acquaintance, begun in 1883, quickly ripened into an affectionate comradeship which grew only the stronger as long as Morris lived. Although Morris was the more forceful character, each could tell the other much that he did not know, and they saw eye to eye on all important topics. In 1888 they joined Walter Crane and others in founding the Arts and Crafts Exhibition Society, the parent stock from which many kindred societies sprang. At about the same period Walker was elected to the committee of the Society for the Protection of Ancient Buildings, founded in 1877 by Morris and Philip Webb. They were prominent in a group supporting the then young and unpopular socialist movement. As secretary to the Hammersmith Socialist Society, Walker's duty was to organize Sunday evening lectures, some of them by men afterwards famous.

Among the subjects in which they were both deeply interested was the art of typography, then at a low ebb. Out of the lecture on printing and illustration which Walker delivered at the Arts and Crafts Exhibition in 1888 and the seminal essay on typography which he wrote (and Morris expanded) for the exhibition catalogue, arose the Kelmscott Press, the first of the great private presses, which they established early in 1891 in modest premises close to Morris's Kelmscott House. Its output during the seven years of its existence was astonishing. It comprised fifty-two works in sixty-six volumes, all printed by hand, with type and ornaments designed by Morris and many illustrations drawn by Edward Burne-Jones and engraved on wood by W. H. Hooper. Walker declined to be a partner in this costly enterprise, having (he said) 'some sense of proportion' and no capital to risk. Nevertheless, he was all the while a virtual partner, and no important step was taken without his advice and approval. This was not the only field in which he co-operated with Morris.

Morris's death in 1896 was a crushing blow, but Walker continued his artistic labours more persistently than ever. In 1900, in conjunction with T. J. Cobden-Sanderson, he founded the Doves Press in a house in Hammersmith Terrace. For this renowned press a type of great beauty and legibility, based on the fifteenth-century Venetian type used by the Frenchman Nicolas Jenson, was cut from drawings made under Walker's eye. Unfortunately, after nearly twenty volumes had appeared, including the five volumes of an English Bible (1903–5), a profound disagreement caused the severance of the partnership, and from 1909 to the close of the Doves Press in 1916 Cobden-Sanderson carried it on alone.

The Kelmscott, Doves, and Ashendene presses will go down in typographical history as the stately precursors of the numerous private presses that followed them. Walker's name is inseparably connected with all three: together with Sydney Cockerell he was instrumental in guiding St John Hornby's choice of Subiaco type for his Ashendene Press. But his great reputation among students of typography rests on a far wider basis, for he was keenly preoccupied with the appearance of the everyday book, and not only with its rich relations. It is scarcely too much to say that his influence, direct or indirect, can be discerned in nearly every well-designed traditional typographical page that now appears, and that to him more than to any other man the twentieth century's great improvement in book production in Britain was due. Walker's exacting taste demanded close, even typesetting, perfect harmony between text and illustration, and excellent materials; above all he admired the finest incunabula. He also enjoyed considerable influence on German book design through his friendship with Count Harry Kessler, owner of the Cranach Press, and he designed a series of classics for Insel-Verlag. He later collaborated with the great American typographer Bruce Rogers in the production of two fine limited editions, published in 1917 and 1928. Walker was proud to be elected master of the Art Workers' Guild in 1904. He was knighted in 1930, and in May 1933 was elected an honorary fellow of Jesus College, Cambridge. He delivered the Sandars lectures in bibliography at Cambridge University for 1924–5 entitled 'Modern Printing'. Although his schooling ended at the age of thirteen, his erudition was extraordinary. So was his endless generosity in helping and advising others, combined with great modesty and a most lovable nature. He died at his home, 7 Hammersmith Terrace, on 22 July 1933. After cremation at Golders Green, Middlesex, the ashes were interred at Sapperton, Gloucestershire.

SYDNEY COCKERELL, rev. JOHN TREVITT

Sources R. C. H. Briggs, 'Sir Emery Walker: a memoir', 1959, priv. coll. · D. Harrop, *Emery Walker* (1986) · J. Dreyfus, *Italic quartet* (privately printed, Cambridge, 1966) · private information (2004) · C. Franklin, *Emery Walker* (privately printed, Cambridge, 1973) · N. Rooke, 'Sir Emery Walker, 1851–1933', *Penrose Annual* (1954) · C. V. Nordlunde, *Sir Emery Walker and the revival of printing* (privately printed, Copenhagen, 1959) · V. Meynell, ed., *Friends of a lifetime: letters to Sydney Carlyle Cockerell* (1940) · C. Franklin, *The private presses* (1969) · m. cert.

Archives Cheltenham Art Gallery and Museum, MSS · priv. coll., MSS | BL, corresp. with Sir Sydney Cockerell, Add. MS 52758 · BL, minutes of Hammersmith Socialist Society · Bodl. Oxf., corresp. with Lord and Lady Lovelace · U. Texas, MSS · William Morris Gallery, London, corresp. with May Morris

Likenesses photograph, c.1904, repro. in Dreyfus, *Italic quartet* · W. Strang, etching, 1906, NPG · G. Clausen, oils, exh. RA 1926, Art Workers' Guild, Queen Square, London · photograph, 1930, repro. in Nordlunde, *Sir Emery Walker* · H. Coster, photographs, NPG · Elliott & Fry, photograph, NPG · W. Strang, line drawing, BM; repro. in Rooke, 'Sir Emery Walker' · E. Walker?, photographs, NPG · photo, repro. in W. S. Peterson, *The Kelmscott press* (1991) · two portraits, Art Workers Guild, Queen Square, London

Wealth at death £33,223 16s. 2d.: probate, 19 Sept 1933, CGPLA Eng. & Wales

Walker, Ernest (1870–1949), musicologist, was born in Bombay, India, on 15 July 1870, the son of Edward Walker, partner in a firm of East India merchants, and his wife, Caroline Cooper. His parents brought him to England in 1871 where he was taught first by his grandmother and aunt, before entering the Bowdon and Penalvern School at Anerley, Surrey. He frequented the concerts at the Crystal Palace, then under the direction of August Manns. He studied privately with E. Pauer and A. Richter before being admitted to Balliol College, Oxford. Benjamin Jowett, the master of the college, took a special interest in him. He was placed in the second class of the honours list in classical moderations (1889) and *literae humaniores* (1891). Philosophy was his chief interest in his work for the schools and he was deeply influenced by R. L. Nettleship and W. R. Hardie. He became a close friend of the college organist, John Farmer, and he helped Farmer in the Balliol Sunday evening concerts. He proceeded to take the degrees of BMus (1893) and DMus (1898), and he was assistant organist at Balliol from 1891 until, on Farmer's death in 1901, he succeeded as organist and director of music. In this capacity he greatly raised the standard of the concerts by bringing artists such as Plunket Greene, Steuart Wilson, Fanny Davies, and Adolf Busch to Oxford. In 1913 he resigned the organistship, thinking participation in chapel services inconsistent with his views on religion (a fact made plain by his article 'Free thought and the musician' for *Music and Letters* in July 1921), but he held the directorship until 1925, when he retired in order to devote himself to composition. He was elected an honorary fellow of the college in 1926.

Walker took a large part in all the musical activities of the university—indeed his name became synonymous with all aspects of Oxford music. He was most active as a teacher and examiner; added to which he did much to improve and reform the standard of the BMus and DMus degrees with Sir Hugh Allen.

Subsequently Walker was best known for his contribution to British musicology. Early in his career he edited the quarterly journal the *Musical Gazette* (1899–1902), contributed to the *Oxford Magazine*, presented a paper on Brahms for the Musical Association (1898), and wrote articles for Fuller Maitland's second edition of *Grove's Dictionary of*

Music and Musicians (1902). He also wrote articles for *The Times* and the *Manchester Guardian*. Walker was less interested in musical biography; rather he was keen to illuminate musical issues through analysis, historical context, and philosophical argument (much influenced by Parry's amalgam of Ruskin, utilitarian rationalism, and social Darwinism). This is apparent in his first book, *Beethoven* (1905), written for the Music of the Masters series edited by John Lane, a work that also emphasizes his devotion to the nineteenth-century German masters. As a critic and reviewer he was incisive and open-minded, which gained the admiration of Donald Tovey (who knew him at Balliol), Philip Heseltine, William Walton, Adrian Boult, and Thomas Armstrong. In 1946 a compilation of his most influential articles and reviews was published as *Free Thought and the Musician*, which contained important discussions on Mendelssohn, Schumann, Brahms, and Joachim as well as a review of C. L. Graves's two-volume biography of Sir Hubert Parry. Walker's most enduring achievement, however, was *A History of Music in England* (1907) which, in an era of national reappraisal, attempted to rationalize the English musical renaissance at the end of the nineteenth century by means of the nation's earlier heritage, notably in the music of Dunstaple, Tallis, Byrd, and Purcell. A second, revised edition appeared in 1924, and a third edition, enlarged and extensively amended by Jack Westrup, was published in 1952. Though much changed from its original form, Westrup's revision stands as a major tribute to Walker's initial effort.

An accomplished pianist and performer, Walker gave much time to his beloved German masters (being credited with the English premières of Brahms's op. 117 piano pieces and the rhapsody from op. 119), but he was also well known for his interest in Hugo Wolf and in the early works of Debussy. As a productive composer—and this appears to have been the greatest compulsion among his talents—he tended to cleave to the German Romantic tradition assimilated during the 1890s. This is clearly demonstrated in the *Six Songs* (1893); the *Two Anthems*, op. 16 (of which the solemn 'Lord, thou hast been our refuge' is still occasionally sung); the *Duets for Tenor and Contralto* (1904); and the wide array of chamber works that increasingly dominated his output. Earlier in his life he also showed a propensity for vocal music—the inventive *Five Songs from 'England's Helicon'*, op. 10, for vocal quartet and piano; the choral *Hymn to Dionysus*, op. 13 (1906); and *Ode to a Nightingale*, op. 14 (1908), are notable examples—but this gave way later to a more astringent, chromatic style in his chamber works, of which, arguably, the cello sonata, op. 41 (1914), is the best and most passionate example.

Naturally a retiring, even shy, man, Walker was gentle and quiet in his ways, but always strong in his protest against anything false or shoddy. He was unmarried, but made many friends, especially among his pupils and fellow musicians. Early in life he tended to high-church Anglicanism, but that gave way to agnosticism and ultimately to atheistic rationalism, yet there was always something of the mystic in him, which found expression both in his music and in his lasting love of nature. He continued to live in Oxford after his retirement and he died there, at his home, 19 Norham Gardens, on 21 February 1949.   CYRIL BAILEY, *rev.* JEREMY DIBBLE

Sources M. Deneke, *Ernest Walker* (1951) · T. Armstrong, 'Ernest Walker, 1870–1949', *MT*, 90 (1949), 73–5 · F. Flindell, 'Walker, Ernest', *Die Musik in Geschichte und Gegenwart*, ed. F. Blume (Kassel and Basel, 1949–86) · R. Hull, 'Ernest Walker', *Music Review*, 10 (1949), 205–6 · d. cert. · personal knowledge (1959) · *DNB*
Archives Balliol Oxf., diary and MSS · Bodl. Oxf., MSS
Likenesses F. Dodd, drawing, 1934, Balliol Oxf. · M. Bone, drawing, 1946, probably Balliol Oxf.
Wealth at death £35,951 7s. 5d.: probate, 2 July 1949, *CGPLA Eng. & Wales*

Walker, Dame Ethel (1861–1951), painter and sculptor, was born in Melville Street, Edinburgh, on 9 June 1861, the younger child of Arthur Abney Walker and his second wife, Isabella Robertson. In the early 1870s Arthur Walker moved his family from Clifton House, Rotherham, Yorkshire, where he was an iron-founder, to Beech Lodge, Wimbledon, Surrey. Here Walker attended a private day school where her artistic talent was quickly recognized. However, lessons consisting of slavish copying caused her to reject any suggestion of further study. It was only after a visit to a private collection of oriental art, when she was in her early twenties, that Walker decided to train as a painter. Chinese painting and Taoist philosophy were to exercise a lifelong influence upon her work.

Walker went first to the Ridley School of Art, London, and then to Putney School of Art. Later she attended Westminster School of Art, run by Frederick Brown, who perceived great promise in Walker. Indeed she used to say that she owed everything to Brown and Walter Sickert, whose evening painting classes she also attended. Thus, when in 1892 Brown was appointed Slade professor at University College, London, she followed her teacher and remained at the Slade School of Fine Art for a further two years. She returned to the Slade again in 1912 and 1916 to learn fresco and tempera painting and once more in 1921 to study sculpture with James Harvard Thomas. Few pieces of her sculpture survive. Her masterly portrait of fellow sculptor Mary Buchanan (1922; Tate collection) demonstrates that painting was her preferred and most successful medium.

Walker's early paintings are heavily influenced by the Slade's teaching and its links with the New English Art Club (NEAC). They mainly depict figures in interiors which are well drawn and carefully executed in dark rich tones; for example *The Honourable Mrs. Adams* (1901; Tate collection), *The Forgotten Melody* (1902; Laing Art Gallery, Newcastle upon Tyne), and her first major success, *Angela* (priv. coll., reproduced in Rothenstein). *Angela*, whose subject stands in a full-skirted white dress in front of a mantlepiece, is clearly derived from a similarly composed painting by Whistler. Yet it is a *tour de force*, which prompted Walker's immediate election to the NEAC. This was another major achievement: only seven women were elected to the NEAC's forty-strong membership between 1886 and 1918 despite an ever-increasing number of female exhibitors (40 per cent by 1918).

Dame Ethel Walker (1861–1951), self-portrait, c.1925

his followers. Most notable are *The Zone of Hate* (1914–15) and *The Zone of Love* (1930–32; both Tate collection). *The Zone of Hate* is a strong anti-war statement in which a centrally placed earth mother mourns the loss of life in front of the gods of war, greed, and revenge, surrounded by a chorus of aggressive youths and grieving mothers. Its companion piece sets out an idyllic world in which women commune together with nature and music.

These visionary and allegorical compositions represent Walker's own search for an idyllic state of equality with her male peers. Many accounts exist of Walker's supreme confidence in her own abilities, of her fanatical independence, and of her superhuman energy. If sometimes Walker appeared vain or self-absorbed it is important to remember that she took her painting extremely seriously and ensured that nothing in her lifestyle obstructed a total commitment. Her dedication eventually brought her recognition. In the inter-war years Ethel Walker was widely celebrated as one of Britain's leading women painters. Her work was widely seen in group and regular one-person shows. Critics praised the 'strange exotic beauty' of her decorative panels (F. Rutter, *Sunday Times*, Oct 1936) and 'the charm of her feminine portraiture' (*Daily Telegraph*, Nov 1947). In 1938 Walker was made a CBE. Two years later she was elected an associate of the Royal Academy and in 1943 was created a DBE.

Since Walker's death at 20 Glazbury Road, Fulham, London, on 2 March 1951 her reputation has declined. This is probably more a consequence of the changing fashion of artistic taste rather than any reflection upon her intrinsic skills as a painter. Undoubtedly Walker produced some of the most individual works of the twentieth century.

ALISON THOMAS

Sources B. L. Pearce, *Dame Ethel Walker: an essay in reassessment* (1997) · K. Deepwell, *Dictionary of women artists*, 2 (1997), 1419–21 · J. Kenyon, 'Ethel Walker (1861–1951): in pursuit of heaven', *Women's Art Magazine*, 47 (July–Aug 1992), 17–19 · J. Rothenstein, *Modern English painters*, 1: *Sickert to Smith* (1952) · G. English, 'Ethel Walker', [n.d.], Tate collection · A. Thomas, *NEAC annual open exhibition* (1998) [feature on Ethel Walker] · *Ethel Walker, Frances Hodgkins, Gwen John* (1952) [exhibition catalogue, Tate Gallery, 7 May – 15 June 1952] · M. Chamot, *Apollo*, 13 (1931), 307–8 · M. Chamot, 'Paintings by Ethel Walker', *Country Life*, 77 (1935), 98–9 · M. Chamot, *Painting in England* (1937) · M. Sorrell, *Apollo*, 45 (1947), 119–21 · CGPLA Eng. & Wales (1951)
Archives Tate collection, letters to Grace English · Tate collection, letters to J. B. de Graaf
Likenesses E. Walker, self-portrait, oils, c.1925, NPG [see illus.] · E. Walker, self-portrait, oils, c.1930, Tate collection
Wealth at death £1542 0s. 3d.: probate, 21 Aug 1951, CGPLA Eng. & Wales

Walker exhibited at the NEAC for many years, yet she soon broke away from the New English tonal tradition. Informed by the deep impact that the work of Velázquez and the impressionists had made upon her during visits to Madrid and Paris in the 1890s, she evolved a looser and more expressive style in which to paint her many flower pieces, seascapes, and portraits. When painting flowers Walker often employed a vaguely pointillist approach; for example, *Flower Piece No. 4* (1930; Courtauld Inst.) or *Bouquet of Flowers* (1938–9; Manchester City Galleries). These floral pictures were generally painted in her large studio overlooking the River Thames at 127 Cheyne Walk, Chelsea; while her sea pieces were the products of trips to her Yorkshire cottage perched precariously on the cliffs above Robin Hood's Bay. Here she would paint rapidly at one sitting an atmospheric vista, full of movement and life; for example, *October Morning* (c.1938; Royal Collection) or *Landscape at Robin Hood's Bay* (1945; York City Art Gallery).

Although she was highly regarded as a painter of flowers and seascapes, Walker's favourite subject was the female portrait, sensitively painted in one dominant key of radiant colour; for example, *Jean Werner Laurie* (1927–8; Tate collection), *Vanessa Bell* (1937; Tate collection), and her own self-portraits (c.1925; NPG; and c.1930; Tate collection). Walker also regularly employed women to model for her series of reclining nudes. These were beautifully modelled in strong, clean contours, hinting at Modigliani, yet distinctively her own, as are her extraordinary large-scale imaginative compositions of various classical, allegorical, and biblical themes. These gatherings of tall, slender women represent a synthesis of fine draughtsmanship and the romantic symbolism of Puvis de Chavannes and

Walker, Frederick (1840–1875), painter and illustrator, was born at 90 Great Titchfield Street, London, on 26 May 1840, the son of William Henry Walker (d. c.1847), a jeweller, and his wife, Ann Powell (d. 1874). W. H. Walker died while Frederick was still a child, from which time he and his seven siblings were supported by their mother, who was a skilled embroiderer. Frederick's paternal grandfather, William Walker, had been a painter of portraits

Frederick Walker (1840–1875), self-portrait, c.1865

and nature subjects who exhibited at the Royal Academy between 1782 and 1808.

Education and illustration work Walker attended the North London Collegiate School in Camden Town until the age of fifteen, when he was placed as an apprentice and draughtsman in the office of Messrs Baker and Harris, architects in Gower Street. In 1857 he enrolled at Leigh's academy, and in March the following year he entered the Royal Academy Schools. During this time he regularly drew from antique sculpture in the British Museum. Walker was notoriously inattentive as a student, both at Leigh's and at the Royal Academy. Towards the end of 1858 he was employed by Josiah Wood Whymper in Lambeth as an apprentice designer of woodblock illustrations, where he was to work three days a week for two years. There he met Charles Green and John William North, both fellow apprentices; the latter became Walker's closest friend. In 1859 he enrolled at the Langham Artists' Society, a club where young painters worked together on specified subjects and then compared the resulting sketches.

By 1860 Walker's reputation as a designer of black and white illustrations was sufficiently well established for him to embark on a freelance career. His output as an illustrator during the first half of the 1860s was considerable, contributing as he did to periodicals such as *Good Words*, *Once a Week*, and the *Cornhill Magazine*. His series of illustrations for Thackeray's novel *The Adventures of Philip*, which was serialized in the *Cornhill Magazine* in 1861–2, were admired by a wide public and by the author himself.

Walker had been asked in the first instance to adapt Thackeray's own sketches, but after the first two and following his plea that he should be allowed to contribute designs of his own invention he was given virtually a free hand. The illustration entitled *Thanksgiving*, later worked up as the watercolour drawing known as *Philip in Church* (Tate collection), ended the series and was published in August 1862. In addition, Walker made drawings for the Dalziel brothers, for publications including both *Hard Times* and *Reprinted Pieces* by Charles Dickens. Dalziel commissioned a series of thirty illustrations of countryside subjects from Walker, but found that increasing pressure of work meant that only about a third of the project was fulfilled. Other artists, among them George John Pinwell and J. W. North, were brought in, and the resulting volume was entitled *A Round of Days* (1866). This was followed by *Wayside Posies* (1867), also produced by Dalziel and published by Routledge. The engraver Joseph Swain, who cut many of the woodblocks that Walker designed, wrote of Walker's method: 'In working out the minutest detail Walker was painfully conscientious. This was even shown in the backgrounds of his illustrations, most of which were drawn on the blocks from nature' (Goldman, *Victorian Illustration*, 125).

Watercolour paintings In the early 1860s Walker was turning increasingly to painting, treating domestic and genre subjects, some of which were derived from his work as an illustrator, and working both in oil and watercolour. His first exhibited work at the Royal Academy—*The Lost Path* (priv. coll.), shown in 1863—was badly hung, but none the less attracted admiring attention. In February the following year he was elected as an associate member of the Old Watercolour Society and exhibited the watercolour version of *Philip in Church*, previously treated as an illustration, as a trial piece. At the society's summer exhibition of 1864 he showed the elaborate watercolour *Spring*, while the following year he sent its pendant, *Autumn* (both V&A). He was also regularly represented in the society's winter exhibitions of drawings and sketches.

Walker's use of bodycolour was elaborate and very personal, and as a technique identified him as one of the younger generation who believed that the method of blending pigment with commercially manufactured Chinese white paint to give opaque areas of colour was a legitimate way of gaining depth of tone and richness of compositional effect. This was a technique still regarded with disfavour by the older members of the Watercolour Society, and about 1865 Walker caricatured himself squeezing paint out of an enormous tube, with the caption 'What *would* "The Society" say if it could only see me?' In 1876, on the occasion of the memorial exhibition of Walker's paintings and drawings, John Ruskin commented unkindly on the artist's 'semi-miniature, quarter fresco, quarter wash manner of his own—exquisitely clever, and reaching, under such clever management, delightfullest results here and there, but which betrays his genius into perpetual experiment instead of achievement' (*Works of John Ruskin*, 14.340).

In his watercolour compositions of the 1860s and early

1870s Walker devised his most characteristic subject type, in which figures go about their daily routines in either rustic or urban settings. A subject such as *My Front Garden* (Harris Museum and Art Gallery, Preston), exhibited at the Watercolour Society in the winter of 1864–5, shows the immediate precinct of the house in St Petersburgh Place, Bayswater, which he shared with his mother and siblings from 1863, and a postman handing letters to a housekeeper. Of his careful attention to the forms of nature, but avoidance of mechanical realism, J. W. North wrote of his friend's method:

> Walker painted direct from nature, not from sketches. His ideal appeared to be to have suggestiveness in his work; not by leaving out, but by painting in, detail, and then partly erasing it. [His work] frequently passed through a stage of extreme elaboration of drawing, to be afterwards carefully worn away, so that a suggestiveness and softness resulted—not emptiness, but veiled detail. His knowledge of nature was sufficient to disgust him with the ordinary conventions which do duty for grass, leaves, and boughs; and there is scarcely an inch of his work that has not been at one time a careful, loving study of fact. (Marks, 168)

Oil paintings Walker had ambitions to be known for large-scale oils as well as for watercolours. In 1867 he returned as an exhibitor at the Royal Academy, with the remarkable canvas *The Bathers* (Lady Lever Art Gallery, Port Sunlight), showing boys swimming and playing together beside the River Thames. From the early 1860s Walker had been connected with the group of St John's Wood artists who called themselves The Clique, and among which his fellows were P. H. Calderon, G. D. Leslie, J. E. Hodgson, W. F. Yeames, G. A. Storey, and H. Stacy Marks. It was perhaps contact with artists in this circle that caused Walker to introduce symbolical elements and a more generalized evocation of the landscape in his academy exhibits. Walker was much praised for his oil *The Old Gate* (Tate collection) when it was exhibited at the Royal Academy in 1869, and in fact received a personal commendation from Frederic Leighton, who served on the hanging committee that year. The following year he showed another Somerset subject, *The Plough* (Tate collection), a work that secured his election as an associate of the Royal Academy in January 1871.

Travel and final years Although Walker was based in London, most of his work was done in different parts of the countryside—his most favoured haunts being the Thames valley around the village of Cookham, where his mother had a cottage; the Quantock Hills in north Somerset, where he stayed with J. W. North at Halsway Manor, and later at Woolstone Moor; and the Scottish highlands, to which he went on fishing expeditions to Corrichoillie with Richard Ansdell and often stayed with his friend and patron William Graham MP, at Stobhall on the River Tay. Occasionally he ventured overseas—to Paris in 1863 and 1866; and to Venice in 1868 and 1870. A breakdown in his health in 1873—presumably the first symptom of the consumption that was to cause his death two years later—led to his visiting Algiers, in company with North, in the winter of 1873–4. Whenever he was abroad he found himself desperately homesick; in Algiers he cried piteously: 'I shall never see a hansom cab again' (Marks, 291).

Walker remained busy through the year 1874, taking up various unfinished canvases, such as *Mushroom Gatherers*, and completing *The Right of Way* (National Gallery of Victoria, Melbourne). In May 1875 he travelled to Scotland, and this was despite worries about his deteriorating state of health. At St Fillans on Loch Earn in Perthshire he collapsed; his twin sister Mary Marks was sent for, and she was with him when he died on 4 June, at the Drummond Arms Hotel. His body was taken south, and was buried on 8 June 1875 in Cookham churchyard, beside that of his mother, Ann, who had died in the previous November. He was unmarried. Henry Armstead's sculpted profile portrait of Walker remains in Cookham church, and conveys the same distinctive appearance that the artist himself had often shown in his delightful self-portrait caricatures, a number of which are reproduced in J. G. Marks's biography of his late brother-in-law, *The Life and Letters of Frederick Walker* (1896).

A memorial exhibition of Walker's works was held at Deschamps Gallery in New Bond Street in the spring of 1876. A notice of the exhibition in the *Art Journal* made the observation that, 'like Millet, and Mason, and Pinwell, [Walker's] sympathies went forth to what was lowly and familiar, and his genius sublimed common things into the region of poetry and Art' (*Art Journal*, 38, 1876, 85).

CHRISTOPHER NEWALL

Sources The remaining works of Frederick Walker (1875) [sale catalogue, London, 17 July 1875] · T. Taylor, introduction, *Catalogue of the exhibition of Walker's works* (1876) [exhibition catalogue, Deschamps Gallery, London, 1876] · 'Exhibition of works by Frederick Walker, ARA', *Art Journal*, 38 (1876), 85 · J. C. Carr, 'Frederick Walker', *Essays on art* (1897), 198–222 · J. Swain, 'Frederick Walker', *Good Words* (July 1888), 471–7 · G. D. Leslie, *Our river: personal reminiscences of an artist's life on the River Thames* (1888) · J. E. Hodgson, 'An artist's holidays', *Magazine of Art*, 12 (1888–9), 385–91 · C. Phillips, *Frederick Walker and his works* (1894) · J. G. Marks, *The life and letters of Frederick Walker* (1896) · [G. Dalziel and E. Dalziel], *The brothers Dalziel: a record of fifty years' work … 1840–1890* (1901), 193–205 · *The works of John Ruskin*, ed. E. T. Cook and A. Wedderburn, library edn, 39 vols. (1903–12), vol. 14, pp. 339–48 · J. Treuherz, *Hard times: social realism in Victorian art* (1987), 49–52 [exhibition catalogue, Man. City Gall., 14 Nov 1987 – 10 Jan 1988] · P. Goldman, *Victorian illustrated books, 1850–1870: the heyday of wood-engraving, the Robin de Beaumont collection* (1994) · P. Goldman, *Victorian illustration: the Pre-Raphaelites, the idyllic school and the high Victorians* (1996), 123–6

Likenesses D. W. Wynfield, photograph, c.1860–1869, NPG · F. Walker, self-portrait, watercolour drawing, c.1865, NPG [*see illus.*] · R. Ansdell, woodcut, BM · H. H. Armstead, marble medallion, Cookham church; repro. in Marks, *Life and letters*, 313 · F. Barnard, woodcut, BM; repro. in *The cream of 'Fun'* (1873) · London Stereoscopic Co., two cartes-de-visite, NPG · H. Schell, woodcut (after J. E. Hodgson), BM · F. Walker, self-portraits, caricature, repro. in Marks, *Life and letters*, 4, 51, 56, 58, 69, 73, 76, 83, 101, 111, 148, 156, 220, 249, 254, 268, 277 · J. Watkins, carte-de-visite, NPG · prints, BM · woodcuts, BM

Wealth at death under £4000: administration, 1 July 1875, *CGPLA Eng. & Wales*

Walker, Frederick John (1896–1944), naval officer, was born at Plymouth on 3 June 1896, the second son of Lieutenant (later Captain) Frederic Murray Walker RN and his

Frederick John Walker (1896–1944), by White, 1944

wife, Lucy Selina, the daughter of Major Horace William Scriven. He was a grandson of Colonel Sir George Walker KCB of Crawfordton, Dumfries. Inevitably known as Johnnie after Johnnie Walker's whisky, he entered the Royal Naval College at Osborne in 1909 and Dartmouth in 1911, and quickly showed conspicuous officer-like qualities, for which he was awarded the king's medal for his term. He went to sea as a cadet in the training cruiser *Cornwall* in 1913 and joined the battleship *Ajax* as a midshipman in 1914. Promoted sub-lieutenant in 1916 and lieutenant in 1918, he served in the destroyers *Mermaid* and *Sarpedon*.

In 1919 Walker married Jessica Eileen Ryder, the daughter of William Ryder Stobart, a businessman of Etherley Lodge, Bishop Auckland, co. Durham. They had three sons and one daughter, of whom the eldest surviving son, Lieutenant John Timothy Ryder Walker RNVR, was lost in HM submarine *Parthian* in August 1943; the daughter joined the Women's Royal Naval Service. His wife survived him.

After the First World War Walker served for two years as a watchkeeper in the battleship *Valiant* before starting technical courses. In 1921 he became one of the navy's first anti-submarine specialists, and after training in *Osprey*, the anti-submarine school at Portland, he was anti-submarine officer of the Atlantic Fleet from 1926 to 1928 and then of the Mediterranean Fleet until promoted commander in 1931. Between 1931 and 1935 he commanded successively but briefly the destroyer *Shikari*, which controlled by radio the target battleship *Centurion*, and then the sloop *Falmouth* on the China station, where she was the commander-in-chief's yacht. This was an unfortunate appointment for so dedicated an officer, but worse was to

follow: after two years as executive officer back in the *Valiant*, whose singularly ambitious captain reported that he 'lacked powers of leadership', Walker was passed over for promotion to captain, seemingly because of his personality. From 1937 to 1940 he was again in *Osprey*, as experimental commander responsible for development in anti-submarine material and methods. He joined the staff of Admiral Bertram Ramsay at Dover in January 1940 and was mentioned in dispatches for his services at Dunkirk. And in October 1941 he joined the sloop *Stork* as senior officer of the 36th escort group. Seldom has there been so felicitous an appointment.

Walker rapidly became the doyen of U-boat killers. In December 1941 his group, escorting its first convoy, destroyed four of their seven opponents within five days. In April 1942 it sank another. In June Walker was promoted captain and in 1943, after temporarily commanding the escort base in Liverpool, returned to sea in the sloop *Starling* as captain (D) and senior officer of the famous second support group. Success followed success, based on Walker's combination of leadership and professionalism. His commander-in-chief, Admiral Sir Max Horton, noted his 'outstanding leadership and determination'. He had undoubtedly the total loyalty and confidence of every ship's company he commanded, and he came into his own in the last four years of his life. Between June 1943 and his untimely death, on 9 July 1944 in the Royal Naval Hospital, Seaforth, Liverpool, from a stroke, officially attributed to his sea time by the lords of the Admiralty in a general message to the fleet, his frigates and sloops destroyed another sixteen submarines. On account of what Admiral Horton described as his relentless, unceasing, and conspicuously successful war against the U-boats, Walker was appointed CB and DSO with three bars. What gave him especial pleasure was the extremely unusual reward of two years' additional seniority as captain, which restored him to his peers and accelerated his progress to the flag list. His career ended with a service funeral on 11 July 1944 in Liverpool Cathedral, where his commander-in-chief pronounced that 'not dust, or the light weight of a stone, but all the sea of the Western Approaches shall be his tomb', and whence his body was buried at sea in Liverpool Bay from the destroyer *Hesperus*. His group went on to destroy seven more enemy submarines in the way he had taught them. Perhaps he died at the right time: he might have fretted on the flag list.   A. B. SAINSBURY

Sources *DNB* · *Navy List* (1939) · PRO, ADM 1/16682 · S. W. Roskill, *The war at sea, 1939–1945*, 3 vols. in 4 (1954–61) · T. Robertson, *Walker, RN* (1956) · A. Burn, *The fighting captain* (1993) · S. Howarth and D. Law, eds., *The battle of the Atlantic: the 50th anniversary International Naval Conference* [Liverpool 1993] [1994] · PRO, ADM 199/1998, 5.16–37 · PRO, ADM 1/11895 · PRO, ADM 199/932 · *CGPLA Eng. & Wales* (1944)

Archives PRO, Admiralty MSS, ADM | FILM BFI NFTVA, news footage · IWM FVA, actuality footage · IWM FVA, news footage | SOUND IWM SA, oral history interview

Likenesses White, photograph, 1944, Sci. Mus., Science and Society Picture Library [*see illus.*] · photograph, 1944, repro. in Burn, *Fighting captain*, jacket · T. Murphy, statue, 1998, Liverpool Pier Head · T. Murphy, maquette, repro. in *Navy News* (April 1998), 3 ·

A. R. Sims, oils, HMS *Vernon*, Portsmouth, Creasy Building · photographs, repro. in Robertson, *Walker, RN*

Wealth at death £709 7s.: probate, 4 Oct 1944, *CGPLA Eng. & Wales*

Walker, Frederick William (1830–1910), headmaster, was born in Bermondsey, London, on 7 July 1830, the only son of Thomas Walker, hatter, of Northern Irish descent, and his wife, Elizabeth Elkington. He was educated from 1841 at St Saviour's Grammar School, Southwark, and suffered as a day boy at Rugby (1844–9). He was open scholar of Corpus Christi College, Oxford, where he won first class honours in Greats and second in mathematics, prizes in law and Sanskrit, the respect of Mark Pattison, and the lifelong friendship of Benjamin Jowett. He graduated BA in 1853, MA in 1856, was philosophy tutor of Corpus from 1856 to 1859, and held a fellowship there from 1859 to 1867.

Although his former headmaster, A. C. Tait, now bishop of London, wanted him as his examining chaplain, Walker (who became an admirer of Comte and J. S. Mill) had probably already lost any conventional religious faith. He was called to the bar at Lincoln's Inn in 1858, but the following year reluctantly accepted the high mastership of Manchester grammar school, to which the president of Corpus had the right of appointment. Since the 1830s the school had been a political battleground, catchment and curriculum being equally at issue. Its buildings were obsolete, its income was inadequate, its staff were demoralized and eccentric. Walker set to work with the 'determined will' which he himself called 'the chief requisite for success'. He willed a secure and enlarged school with an enviable reputation for academic achievement. Although a Rugbeian, his educational philosophy owed more to Germany, where he had recently studied (at Dresden) for six months, than to Thomas Arnold. His own scholarly field was comparative philology. 'I believe in Latin grammar and the cane,' he remarked (in characteristic self-parody), 'they are cheap and efficient.' But, though he normally allowed the classical sixth form, which he taught himself, to study nothing but Latin, Greek, and Palgrave's *Golden Treasury*, he introduced for the rest of the school physics, chemistry, German, and an art master (whom he paid partly out of his own pocket). He also acquired a cricket pitch. He did not believe in games as character building, but in exercise as essential for health. Later, at St Paul's School, he was to announce publicly 'I know nothing about cricket', and used not to attend the annual sports day; but games became compulsory there in 1897.

Walker's rapid and dictatorial changes at Manchester made him enemies. He abolished the semi-separate 'English', or commercial, school; he introduced entrance examinations and fees; he dismissed masters who refused to carry out supervision during the dinner hour. One local newspaper called him a tyrant. But a powerful and enthusiastic group of nonconformists had recently been admitted as feoffees (or governors) of the school. These provided Walker with loyal supporters, and in 1867 he married Maria, the daughter of one of them, Richard Johnson, a

Frederick William Walker (1830–1910), by Sir William Rothenstein, 1906

wealthy cable manufacturer and art collector. Her death, only two years after their marriage, left him with a son and the financial independence that no doubt set the seal on his fearless and truculent individualism, and began the long widowerhood that perhaps contributed to his rather unkempt appearance, occasional devastating rudeness, and idiosyncratic reserve.

Walker's early unpopularity at Manchester was shown by a sharp fall in the number of boys; this was soon reversed, and numbers grew from 250 in 1865 to 750 in 1876. He took every opportunity of obtaining, and broadcasting, measurable success, entering boys for as many reputable external examinations as he could find, and parading their results at annual speech days, which he revived. Above all he treasured entrance awards at Oxford and Cambridge and in 1867 the Taunton commission attributed the school's outstanding success in gaining these to his 'ability and exertion' and his admissions policy. Growing local confidence in Walker was reflected in his success in persuading Manchester magnates to contribute financially. They founded prizes, and closed awards for Mancunians at Oxford and Cambridge, and provided the land and much of the money for new buildings, which were occupied in 1872.

Although Walker turned down two opportunities (including the Corpus professorship of Latin in 1869) to return to Oxford with a chair, he also made two unsuccessful bids for London headmasterships (Charterhouse 1863, King's College School 1866), before his appointment to St Paul's School in 1876. His achievements at Manchester made him an obvious choice for St Paul's, which had similar problems; but his friendship with Jowett, an Old Pauline and governor, probably secured him the post. The two men shared a passionate commitment to classical education both as ladder and as end in itself. One of Walker's *obiter dicta* was that 'a boy will not take kindly to commerce when he has once tasted Greek iambics'; but he also advised an able, poor, boy that, if he stuck to his classics, he would pay for his education in scholarships, and soon be earning £400 a year. Jowett may also have sympathized with Walker's lack of religious dogmatism. Until the latter's arrival at St Paul's, entrants had had to produce a certificate of baptism and it was in his day that the school began to admit Jewish boys, soon in fairly large numbers. He was the first high master for over a century not to be in holy orders. Nor can Jowett have been displeased by Walker's veneration for Balliol scholarships.

The year before Walker's appointment to St Paul's, the decision had been taken to move it from its cramped premises beside the cathedral to broader ones on the Hammersmith Road. Walker was involved in planning the new site and buildings (whose architect was Waterhouse), but numbers were already growing and he allowed the high master's house to be used as classrooms during his eight years in the City, and lived (as he said) 'in squalor', in an attic. At Hammersmith, however, a house was built for him, connected to the school by a cloister, where he liked to walk and think. Numbers, already growing, rose rapidly (211 in 1884, 650 in 1905).

As at Manchester, Walker sought, and achieved, principally academic success and reputation. The classics were at the heart of this; but, though their supremacy was unchallenged, Walker continued the development of a broader curriculum already begun by his predecessor, Herbert Kynaston, whose reputation has suffered from the near idolatry accorded to Walker's memory at St Paul's. But it was Walker who introduced science there, earning the praise of his first science master for his encouragement and enthusiasm; and in 1893 he allowed the foundation of a senior history class (though he castigated Compton Mackenzie for joining it). In his first ten years Paulines won 173 entrance awards at Oxford and Cambridge, twenty-six more than any other school. Walker had made St Paul's the leading academic school in England, or, as his detractors put it, the most notorious forcing house.

Between 1890 and 1899 Walker found the school's governors (a majority of whom were representatives of the Mercers' Company) deeply engaged in a struggle with the charity commissioners who, together with local pressure groups, wanted to divert its funds to broader educational purposes, including a separate 'modern' department with places for boys from elementary schools. Walker, who enjoyed the governors' full confidence, circumvented or ignored the commission's rulings with the help of influential Old Paulines, legal finesse, and sheer bravado. The separate school would have meant another, independent, headmaster; but 'I will have no democracy where I rule.' Walker hated snobbery: he remembered, and often referred to, his own early poverty. At Manchester he had taught evening classes for nothing at Owens College, and at St Paul's he secretly paid the fees of poor boys out of his own pocket. He would teach Latin and Greek to peasants, he proclaimed, if he had the means and the staff; but they must be initiated into his world—it was not to be diluted to their needs. From Manchester he brought with him his secretary, Samuel Bewsher, who started a preparatory school across the Hammersmith Road.

Walker made a powerful, often terrifying, impression on his pupils. Two of them vividly portray him in novels: Compton Mackenzie in *Sinister Street* and (as Dr Hodder) Ernest Raymond in *Mr Olim*. He was a short man with a large, sometimes soup-stained beard. He smelt of cigar smoke. He would 'bellow in a paralysing bass', seize boys by the ear, sit down on the bench beside them, pushing them aside, and (according to Raymond) roar: 'Can't you recognise a Past Unfulfilled Protasis when you see one? If you can't, go to some school where they put up with work like this.' But his rages were simulated or short lived.

After Walker retired in 1905 he never revisited St Paul's. He was made an honorary fellow of Corpus Christi College, Oxford, in 1894 and was awarded the honorary degree of LittD at Manchester in 1899. He died at his home, 7 Holland Villas Road, Kensington, London, on 13 December 1910 and was buried in the Kensington Hanwell cemetery, Ealing, after a service in St Paul's Cathedral. His only child was Richard Johnson Walker (1868–1934), who won a scholarship at Balliol College, Oxford, from St Paul's. He was private assistant to his father, and then a master at St Paul's until 1905, when his application to succeed his father was unsuccessful. He took Anglican orders in 1902 and became a Roman Catholic in 1912, devoting himself to literary work and a collection of *objets d'art*.

ARTHUR HUGH MEAD

Sources R. B. Gardiner and J. Lupton, eds., *Res Paulinae* (1911) · M. F. J. McDonnell, *A history of St Paul's School* (1909) · A. H. Mead, *A miraculous draught of fishes, a history of St Paul's School, 1509–1990* (1990) · J. Bentley, *Dare to be wise: a history of the Manchester grammar school* (1990) · *The Pauline* [magazine of St Paul's School, London], 29 (1911) · C. Mackenzie, *My life and times*, 10 vols. (1963–71), vol. 2 · *CGPLA Eng. & Wales* (1911) · *DNB*
Likenesses H. R. Hope Pinker, marble bust, *c.*1889, St Paul's School, London · T. M. Rooke, pencil drawing, 1893, St Paul's School, London · W. Rothenstein, oils, 1906, St Paul's School, London [*see illus.*] · Spy [L. Ward], chromolithograph caricature, NPG; repro. in *VF* (27 June 1901) · Spy [L. Ward], tinted drawing, cartoon, St Paul's School, London · photographs, Manchester grammar school · photographs, St Paul's School, London · sketch, repro. in E. H. Shepherd, *Drawn from life* (1961), 70
Wealth at death £29,965 13s. 5d.: resworn administration, 18 Feb 1911, *CGPLA Eng. & Wales*

Walker, Sir Frederick William Edward Forestier Forestier- (1844–1910), army officer, born at the Manor House, Bushey, Hertfordshire, on 17 April 1844, was eldest of the four sons of General Sir Edward Walter Forestier-Walker (1812–1881) of Bushey and his first wife, Lady Jane, only daughter of Francis Grant, sixth earl of Seafield. His grand-uncle was Sir George Townshend Walker, first baronet. Educated at Sandhurst, he entered the Scots guards as lieutenant on 5 September 1862, and was promoted captain on 11 July 1865. In 1866–7 he served as aide-de-camp to the major-general at Mauritius, and from 1869 to 1873 was adjutant of his regiment. On 1 February 1873 he became lieutenant-colonel.

From 1873 to 1879 Forestier-Walker was on the staff at the Cape as assistant military secretary to the general officer. In that capacity, or on special service, he experienced much warfare in South Africa. In 1875 he served in the expedition to Griqualand West. During 1877–8 he was with Lieutenant-General Sir Arthur Cunynghame through the Cape Frontier War. He was mentioned in dispatches, and was made colonel on 15 October 1878 and CB on 11 November. In the course of 1878 he became military secretary to Sir Bartle Frere, the high commissioner. Throughout the Anglo-Zulu War, Forestier-Walker was employed on special service. In the early campaign he was principal staff officer to no. 1 column, being present at the action of Inyezane and during the occupation of Eshowe. Subsequently he was on the line of communications and in command of Fort Pearson and the Lower Tugela district. He was mentioned in dispatches.

Returning to England, Forestier-Walker was from 1 August to 14 November 1882 assistant adjutant and quartermaster-general of the home district, but from 12 November 1884 until December 1885 he was again in South Africa, serving with the Bechuanaland expedition under Sir Charles Warren as assistant adjutant and quartermaster-general. He was nominated CMG on 27 January 1886 and major-general on 31 December 1887. In 1887 he married Mabel Louisa, daughter of Lieutenant-Colonel A. E. Ross, late Northumberland Fusiliers, and they had one son.

From 1 April 1889 to December 1890 Forestier-Walker served as brigadier-general at Aldershot, and from 19 December 1890 to 30 September 1895 he was major-general commanding the British troops in Egypt. On 26 May 1894 he was created KCB. Subsequently he was lieutenant-general commanding the western district of England from 1 November 1895 to 18 August 1899. Shortly before the outbreak of the Second South African War, Sir William Butler was recalled from the command of the forces at the Cape, and the appointment was accepted at short notice by Forestier-Walker, who arrived at Cape Town on 6 September 1899. Placed in command of the lines of communication, he performed his important duties with thoroughness, and was active in support of Sir Redvers Buller's advance. In 1900 he was made GCMG.

On 18 April 1901 Forestier-Walker handed over his post to Major-General Wynne, and embarked for England. On 7 July 1902 he attained the rank of general, and on 1 September 1905 became governor and commander-in-chief of Gibraltar. On 31 July of the same year he was nominated colonel of the King's Own Scottish Borderers. Thomas Pakenham's later description of him as 'a charming nonentity' (Pakenham, 96) was unduly dismissive. Forestier-Walker died from heart failure at Tenby on 30 August 1910, and was buried at Bushey.

H. M. VIBART, rev. JAMES FALKNER

Sources Army List · Hart's Army List · The Times (1 Sept 1910) · J. F. Maurice and M. H. Grant, eds., History of the war in South Africa, 1899–1902, 4 vols. (1906–10) · LondG (5 March 1879) · LondG (18 May 1879) · T. Pakenham, The Boer War (1979) · J. Martineau, The life and correspondence of Sir Bartle Frere, 2 (1895) · Burke, Peerage
Likenesses Spy [L. Ward], caricature, watercolour study, NPG; repro. in VF (25 Dec 1902) · photograph, repro. in Navy and Army Illustrated (18 Feb 1898)
Wealth at death £38,964 18s. 10d.: probate, 15 Dec 1910, CGPLA Eng. & Wales

Walker, George (bap. 1582?, d. 1651), Church of England clergyman, was born at Hawkshead in Furness, Lancashire, and was probably the son of Edward Walker baptized in Hawkshead on 7 October 1582. Educated first at Hawkshead grammar school, founded by his kinsman Archbishop Edwin Sandys, he then went to St John's College, Cambridge, where he graduated BA early in 1609 and proceeded MA in 1611, and where his teachers included Christopher Foster and Alexander Richardson. Ordained deacon in London on 22 September 1611, 'aged twenty-eight', he may have been curate of Ware, Hertfordshire, before being ordained priest on 7 June 1612.

In 1611 Walker attracted attention by attacking the celebrated London puritan divine Anthony Wotton for perversion of the orthodox doctrine of justification. Their dispute, which was initially conducted in private conference and from various city pulpits, centred on whether or not Christ's righteousness was imputed to the believer, Wotton having claimed in defiance of Calvinist orthodoxy that this was not the case. Walker believed he detected in Wotton's position a thinly veiled Socinianism, and he noisily accused the older preacher of heresy and blasphemy. The dispute ultimately led in 1614 to an informal (but semi-sanctioned) conclave of some of London's most distinguished godly divines—including Lewis Bayly, Richard Westfield, William Gouge, Richard Stock, and Thomas Gataker—which gathered to adjudicate the quarrel. The result was a qualified victory for Wotton. This neither hindered Walker's career nor ended his campaign, however. On the presentation of the dean and chapter of Canterbury Cathedral he was inducted on 29 April 1614 to the living of St John the Evangelist, Watling Street, London, resigned in his favour by his former tutor Foster. Later in the decade he wrote a long manuscript polemical attack on the renowned nonconformist divine William Bradshaw, whose A Treatise of Justification (1615) had attempted to clarify the dispute. Walker's appointment on 2 March 1619 as chaplain to the widely respected bishop of Ely, Nicholas Felton, suggests that despite his godly connections and tendencies he also had friends in the ecclesiastical establishment and was regarded as a conformist. That year he proceeded BD, being incorporated of Oxford in 1621.

While in the early 1620s Walker apparently accused the London minister William Chibald of errors similar to Wotton's, he also took aim at a very different polemical target, Roman Catholicism. In May 1623 Walker agreed to an informal conference with a priest named Sylvester Norris; a month later, accompanied by his fellow London minister Henry Burton, Walker engaged in a disputation with the notorious Jesuit John Fisher (real name Percy). Walker's accounts of these encounters were published respectively as *The Sum of a Disputation* (1624) and *Fishers Folly Unfolded* (1624).

Only with the accession of William Laud to the bishopric of London in 1628 did Walker begin to experience difficulties with the ecclesiastical authorities. In November 1631 he found himself summoned before the high commission. Although no articles or accusations survive, the fact that the court ordered him at one point to 'give in a Coppy of the sermon' suggests that he was in trouble for some matter uttered by him from the pulpit (CUL, MS Dd. ii. 21, fol. 85r). His case dragged on for two years, although in the end Walker appears to have escaped serious censure. Yet this was only the beginning of his troubles with Laud. As the latter, now archbishop, observed to King Charles in his annual report for 1635, Walker

> had all his time been but a disorderly and peevish man, and now of late hath very forwardly preached against the Lord Bishop of Ely [Francis White] his book concerning the Lord's Day, set out by authority; but upon a canonical admonition given him to desist he hath recollected himself, and I hope will be advised. (*Works*, 5.332)

Perhaps unsurprisingly given his temperament, this warning served only to provoke Walker, who in 1638 brazenly published a work of sabbatarian extremism, *The Doctrine of the Sabbath*, printed illicitly at Amsterdam. In 1638–9 he came under official scrutiny again for his theological disputes with John Goodwin, an affray that drew the intervention of Bishop William Juxon of London.

Walker's final confrontation with the Caroline authorities came on 14 November 1638, when he was called before the king and privy council and 'Charged to have uttered and delivered in a Sermon … the fourth of October Last, divers thinges tending to publique faction, and disobedience to Authority' (Bodl. Oxf., MS Bankes 23, fol. 27r). On Walker's account, Laud (perhaps not without some warrant) 'accused to the king' that Walker had been 'a seditious fellow ever since he the said Archbishop knew London, and a preacher of factious and mutinous doctrine and the greatest troubler of London who had raysed upp more troubles and stirres then any other in the City' (PRO, SP 16/500/6, fols. 35–8). Among other things, it was alleged that Walker had preached that 'wee must not too much fear great men kings and potentates', that '[h]e teaches inferiors to examine and dispute the commands of their superiors', that '[h]e blames officers and ministers who execute the warrants of judges and magistrates by taking away mens goods and Haling them to prison calling them executions of unjust decrees', a claim that the councillors saw as a reference to ship money (Bodl. Oxf., MS Bankes 44, fol. 13r). For his pains Walker found himself suspended and committed to the Gatehouse, where he languished for ten weeks until he grew perilously ill and was transferred to his brother's house in the country. Walker remained under house arrest for the next year and a half.

On 20 May 1641 Walker was freed by order of parliament, and his imprisonment declared illegal. Restored to his parsonage, he published that year a number of theological works which acknowledged his debt to Londoners and others who had supported him in his afflictions, including *The Key of Saving Knowledge* (dedicated to his parishioners), *The History of the Creation* (dedicated to the earl of Bedford), and *God Made Visible in his Works* (dedicated to Sir Thomas Barrington, Sir Gilbert Gerard, Sir William Masson, and Sir Martin Lumley). Twenty-five years after the Wotton affair, he also continued to spar in print over its exact details. His *Socinianism in the Fundamental Point of Justification* (1641) and *A True Relation* (1642) were countered by Thomas Gataker's *Mr Anthony Wotton's Defence* (1641). He went on to become an active member of the Westminster assembly of divines in 1643, to preach a fast sermon before parliament on 29 January 1645, and (as a zealous presbyterian) to become a leader of the first London classis upon its foundation in 1645, serving alongside William Gouge as a trier. His anonymous advocacy of the new discipline appeared as *A Modell of the Government of the Church under the Gospell* (1646).

During this period Walker likewise devoted considerable effort to raising funds for the establishment of lectureships in parts of England that, in the words of his will, had hitherto been 'most barren and destitute of meanes to maintayne the preaching of the Gospell', especially his native Lancashire. Indeed, when he died late in 1651 he bequeathed land in his birthplace of Hawkshead for the establishment of a perpetual lectureship there. Walker was survived by his wife, Katherine, who proved his will on 22 January 1652, a married daughter, and his apparently estranged son, George (who against Walker's wishes had abandoned study for the ministry and secretly married a poor, undowried woman). DAVID R. COMO

Sources P. Lake and D. Como, '"Orthodoxy" and its discontents: dispute settlement and the production of "consensus" in the London (puritan) "underground"', *Journal of British Studies*, 39 (2000), 34–70 • Venn, *Alum. Cant.* • *Chetham miscellanies*, new ser., 1, Chetham Society, new ser., 47 (1902) • *The works of the most reverend father in God, William Laud*, ed. J. Bliss and W. Scott, 7 vols. (1847–60) • *Calendar of the correspondence of Richard Baxter*, ed. N. H. Keeble and G. F. Nuttall, 1 (1991), 58 • will, PRO, PROB 11/220, sig. 16, fols. 127v–128r • STC, 1475–1640 • Wing, STC

Walker, George (1645/6–1690), Church of Ireland clergyman, was the son of the Revd George Walker (c.1600–1677) and Ursula (d. 1654), the daughter of Sir John Stanhope of Melwood, Yorkshire. His parents settled in Ireland but fled following the 1641 rising. Although Walker is generally supposed to have been born and brought up in Yorkshire, he claimed to have an 'affection to the Scottish nation where he had his education' (Walker, *Vindication*, preface, 3). The family returned to Ireland after the Restoration and Walker matriculated at Dublin University in 1662 and took holy orders. He married, about 1668, Isabella Barclay (b. c.1650), with whom he had five sons and three daughters. In 1674 he was appointed rector of Donoghmore, co. Tyrone, which had been devastated during the civil war. He built a rectory there in 1683 and a mill in the village in 1684.

The siege of Londonderry In early 1689, when Ireland was again on the brink of war, Walker rallied the protestants in the area and raised men to garrison Dungannon. Orders to abandon the town were received on 14 March from Colonel Robert Lundy, who planned to consolidate the forces under his command. When King James's army marched on Londonderry, Walker commanded five companies in St Johnstown. On 13 April he rode to Lundy to alert him to the danger, and was present that night at Clady when the Irish advance was temporarily checked. On the following morning he was posted with his troops to Long Causey, north of Lifford, but once the Irish army crossed the Finn he was forced to abandon his position and fall back on Londonderry. Walker arrived at night to find the gates shut, and he and his men were obliged to sleep outside the walls. He gained entry the next day only after the sentry had been threatened.

Lundy's decision to treat with the enemy once King James arrived outside the city provoked a mutiny. Lundy refused to continue as governor and on 19 April, after a hurried election, Henry Baker succeeded him and nominated Walker as a joint governor, a choice that was ratified by the electorate. Both Walker and Baker begged Lundy to remain, but without success, and Walker arranged Lundy's escape from the city the following evening. The division of responsibilities between the new governors was such that Walker took charge of the civil administration of the city and all the provisioning, while Baker looked after military affairs. Walker was also elected colonel of one of the regiments in the city and took an active part in its defence throughout the ensuing three months. He proved to be an inspirational leader. John Michelburne, never quick to praise others, wrote of Walker that: 'Truly much Praise was due to him for having been so great an Animator of the Protestant Cause in those worst of Times' (Michelburne, *An Account*, x). When Baker died on 30 June, Michelburne succeeded him to become joint governor with Walker.

After the Irish failed to storm the defences on 4 June, the siege developed into a blockade. Provisions in the city ran low and the garrison was reduced to eating horseflesh, cats, mice, seaweed, and dogs 'fattened by eating the bodies of the slain Irish' (Walker, *True Account*, 39). The desperate circumstances of the city prompted occasional outbreaks of rioting fuelled by wild rumours that Walker was either embezzling the stores or treating with the enemy. A later cause of discontent in some quarters was the suggestion that Walker's intransigence was preventing an honourable capitulation. In early June, he was forced to take refuge in Baker's house while a violent mob searched for him outside, and later that month a group of officers signed a petition to have him removed. Nevertheless, the complaints against Walker were rejected by the overwhelming majority of the garrison as, after the city was finally relieved on 28th July, he and Michelburne welcomed General Percy Kirke into the city on behalf of the inhabitants and led the celebrations.

Celebrity After handing over the command of his regiment, Walker was entrusted with a loyal address to King William signed by 145 officers, clergymen, 'and other gentlemen' of Londonderry. On 9 August he set sail for Scotland and began a triumphant progress to London. He was made a burgess and guild-brother of the city of Glasgow on 13 August. He received the same honours in Edinburgh on the next day, and on his journey south he was mobbed and dined in Chester on 22 August.

Walker's reputation in London had been made not only by the newsletters but by the publication of a speech and two sermons supposedly given by him during the siege. He was met at Barnet by a coach belonging to Sir Robert Cotton, the MP for Chester, and was brought discreetly into the city. Nevertheless, 'The prime citizens treated him with all the demonstrations of joy and gratitude; and the vulgar even stifled him with gazing, crowding and acclamations' (Macrory, 325). A week after his arrival, he was taken to Hampton Court to be presented to the king. William drank to his health, gave him £5000, commissioned Kneller to paint his portrait, and promised him the bishopric of Derry when it fell vacant. Walker was banqueted by the Irish Society, the sheriffs of London, and the lord mayor, and was made a doctor of divinity by the universities of Oxford and Cambridge.

In November 1689 Walker presented a petition to the House of Commons on behalf of the 2000 widows and orphans in Londonderry, and was invited to the bar of the house to be told by the speaker that £10,000 had been voted for the relief of the sufferers and that note had been taken of the 'extraordinary service you have done to their Majesties and to England and Ireland'.

Walker's self-effacing manner was much admired. He told the House of Commons: 'As for the service I have done, it is very little, and does not deserve this favour you have done me' (Hempton, 403). The *London Gazette* noted that 'The applauses of the People as he passes are very troublesome to him, for his modesty is as great, and as deservedly admired, as his courage and Conduct' (*London Gazette*, no. 2484). Narcissus Luttrell described Walker as 'a very modest person' (Luttrell, 555), and John Tillotson, yet to become archbishop of Canterbury, wrote approvingly of 'Walker, whose modesty is equal to his merit' (Milligan, 360).

Bishop Burnet saw Walker as being 'but a man of ordinary parts, but they were well suited to this work, for he did wonders in this siege' (BL, Add. MS 63057B, fol. 278). The caricature of Walker in King James's *Memoirs* (p. 334) as a 'fierce Minister of the gospel, being of the true Cromwelian or Cameronian stamp' is quite false, especially as Walker described himself as 'a true son of the Church of England' (Walker, *Vindication*, 13).

Pamphlet wars Walker took lodgings in Fetter Lane, London, where he hurriedly wrote his *True Account of the Siege of London-Derry*. Although this proved a popular and vivid description of the siege, it drew immediate criticism, especially from Presbyterians, and sparked off a pamphlet war. In an attempt to placate his critics, Walker published later in the year *A Vindication of the Account of the Siege of Derry*. Sensitive to the suggestion that as a clergyman he should not have taken up arms, he pleaded that his Case has all the authority that the greatest necessity in the World can give to any Action—the lives of thousands, besides his own, were at stake; his Religion, that is dearer than all, and the *English* and *Scotch* equally dear to him, next door to an utter Extirpation out of Ireland.   (Walker, *Vindication*, 23)

Walker's *True Account* was in early 1690 attacked in print by the Irish Presbyterian minister John Mackenzie, who had been his regimental chaplain during the siege. 'Walker', wrote Mackenzie, 'was a man of peace all the time and was guilty of shedding no other blood to stain his coat but the blood of the grape' (Mackenzie, *Invisible Champion*, 8). The *True Account* was criticized for falsely playing up Walker's own part in the siege at the expense of others: 'Gov. Baker has been thus injuriously pilfered of several of his deserved plumes, and Dr Walker adorned with them' (Mackenzie, *Narrative*, preface, iii).

Mackenzie took particular exception to Walker's describing himself throughout the *True Account* as 'The Governor', thereby giving the impression that he stood above Baker and Michelburne. Whenever Baker or Michelburne signed a document first, Mackenzie asserted, Walker 'seldom failed to crowd in his name before them' (Mackenzie, *Narrative*, 62). Whatever the truth of that, Mackenzie's claim that Walker was not a governor at all, but merely the commissary of stores, is certainly false. This is clear from Michelburne's barbed remark of 1692 that he 'was in joynt Command with the Doctor, whose conduct appear'd more conspicuous in the Eating part than the Fighting, and reason good, the Charge of the Stores, and Provision being committed to him alone' (Michelburne, *An Account*, x).

In recounting a surprise attack by the defenders in the early hours of 6 May, Walker described himself as leading 'at the head of them with all imaginable silence' (Walker, *True Account*, 26). Mackenzie retorted: 'if he did so, it was not only with all imaginable silence, but with so wonderful secrecy too, as to be neither seen nor heard by any of those that are said to follow him' (Mackenzie, *Invisible Champion*, 8).

Walker was also criticized for belittling the part in the defence played by the Presbyterians in the city. In the *True Account*, he listed the names of seventeen other clergymen who were in the city during the siege. There were also seven nonconforming ministers, he wrote, 'whose names I could not learn' (Hempton, 146), but noted that they 'were equally careful of their people and kept them obedient and quiet' (ibid., 113). This statement, with its suggestion that the Presbyterians were naturally disobedient and noisy, still caused anger two centuries after his death. 'Perhaps no other passage could be produced from the whole range of English literature in which an equal amount of deliberate and stinging malice is conveyed under the garb of innocence and praise' (Witherow, 300).

To the Presbyterians, Walker's crime was aggravated by his printing a misspelt list of those nonconforming ministers at the end of his *Vindication*. William Gilchrist of Kilrea was spelt as 'Mr W. KilChrist'. 'The mischievious intent cannot be mistaken', wrote Doctor Killen (Killen,

xvi). It was 'a puerile attempt to annoy the Presbyterians' (ibid.).

The Boyne Walker travelled back to Ireland in February 1690 and was in Carrickfergus to greet King William on his arrival on 14 June. The see of Derry became vacant on the death of Ezekiel Hopkins on 19 June, but Walker was never consecrated bishop, as he accompanied the army on its march south. While encouraging the troops forward, he was shot dead at the battle of the Boyne on 1 July 1690. The account published by Sir John Dalrymple in 1771 that, on being told of Walker's death by the river, King William enquired sarcastically 'Fool that he was, what had he to do there?' (Dalrymple, 1.40) is apocryphal. Walker's corpse was stripped by camp followers and was buried on the field of battle on the same day.

Thirteen years later Walker's widow paid for his remains to be disinterred and reburied in the church at Castlecaufield, co. Tyrone. The Latin inscription on his monument there reads: 'His fame shall be more durable than rock.' When the bones were inspected in 1838 it was found that they belonged to more than one man. 'A cast was taken of the skull, which was perfectly sound, and in which the organs of intelligence and firmness were remarkably developed' (*Newry Telegraph*, 30 Oct 1838). In 1826 a statue of Walker on an 81 foot stone column was erected on the walls of Londonderry. It was destroyed by a bomb in 1973.   PIERS WAUCHOPE

Sources G. Walker, *A true account of the siege of London-Derry* (1689) • G. Walker, *A vindication of the true account of the siege of Derry* (1689) • J. MacKenzie, *A narrative of the siege of London-Derry* (1690) • J. Mackenzie, *Dr Walker's invisible champion foyl'd* (1690) • J. Michelburne, *Ireland preserv'd, or, The siege of London-Derry*, 2 pts (privately printed, London, 1708) • J. Michelburne, *An account of the transactions in the north of Ireland anno domini 1691* (1692) • J. Dalrymple, *Memoirs of Great Britain and Ireland*, 2 vols. (1771–3), vol. 1 • A. Dawson, 'Biographical notice of George Walker', *Ulster Journal of Archaeology*, 2 (1854), 129–35, 261–77 • J. Hempton, ed., *The siege and history of Londonderry* (1861) • W. D. Killen, ed., *John Mackenzie's narrative* (1861) • T. Witherow, *Derry and Enniskillen in the year 1689* (1879) • P. Dwyer, *The siege of Londonderry in 1689* (1893) • T. U. Sadleir, 'The descendants of George Walker', *Genealogists Magazine*, 2 (1926), 90 • W. S. Kerr, *Walker of Derry* (1938) • C. D. Milligan, *History of the siege of Londonderry* (1951) • P. Macrory, *The siege of Derry* (1980) • N. Luttrell, *A brief historical relation of state affairs from September 1678 to April 1714*, 6 vols. (1857) • R. Lundy, 'Ane acounte of Coll: Robt Lundies proceedings in Ireland', 1689, NA Scot., GD 26/7/37/2

Likenesses P. Vanderbank, line engraving, pubd 1689 (after oil portrait by G. Kneller, *c*.1690), NG Ire. • Irish school, stipple, 18th cent. (after portrait, Irish school, 18th cent.), NG Ire. • J. Brooks, group portrait, mezzotint, pubd 1747 (*The battle of the Boyne, 1st July 1690*; after J. Wyck), NG Ire. • R. De Hoghe, group portrait, etching (*The battle of the Boyne, below the flight of King James II from Ireland on the 12th July, 1690*), NG Ire. • A. Haelwegh, line engraving (after oil portrait by G. Kneller, *c*.1685), NG Ire. • D. Loggan, engraving, BM • E. Nunzer, line engraving (after portrait, English school, 17th cent.), NG Ire. • E. H. Nunzer, engraving, BM • P. Schenck, engraving, Royal unmounted Dutch and Flemish series, Schenck H. 933 • L. Smids, mezzotint (after I. Gole), NPG • P. Vanderbank, line engraving (after G. Kneller, 1689), BM, NPG • R. White, engraving, BM; repro. in Milligan, *History of the siege of Londonderry* • oils, NPG

Walker, George (*d.* 1777), privateer, is of unknown origins. As a boy and a young man he served in the Dutch navy and was employed in the Levant, apparently for the protection of trade against Turkish or Greek pirates. Later he became the owner of a merchant ship and commanded her for some years. In 1739 he was principal owner and commander of the *William* (20 guns and only 32 men), trading from London to South Carolina. The Carolina coast was heavily populated by Spanish privateers, and in the absence of a British man-of-war Walker put the *William* at the service of the colonial government. His offer was accepted, whereupon he increased the crew to 130 and presently succeeded in driving the Spaniards off the coast. In late 1742 he sailed for England with three merchantmen in convoy, but his ship foundered in a December gale. On his eventual arrival in London he learned that his agents had allowed the insurance to lapse and that he was a ruined man.

The following year Walker was master of the *Russia Merchant*, trading to the Baltic. With the outbreak of war with France in 1744 he was offered the command of the *Mars*, a private ship of war of 26 guns, to cruise in company with another, the *Boscawen*, somewhat larger and belonging to the same owner. They sailed from Dartmouth in November, and in early January 1745 encountered two homeward-bound French ships of the line, which captured the *Mars* after the *Boscawen* had hurriedly deserted her. Walker was sent as prisoner in the *Fleuron*. On 6 January the two ships and their prize were sighted by a British squadron of four ships of the line, including the *Sunderland* (Captain John Brett), the *Captain* (Thomas Griffin), and the *Hampton Court* (Savage Mostyn). The four British ships now divided, with two giving chase but failing to engage the Frenchmen, who escaped to safety at Brest. The crews of the *Fleuron* and *Neptune*, though sickly and depleted, were jubilant and boastful at their escape from the controversial British action. At Brest, Walker was landed as a prisoner at large and was exchanged within a month. On his return to England he was put in command of the *Boscawen* and sent out in company with the *Mars*, which had been recaptured and bought by her former owners. In this cruise Walker met another privateer, the *Sheerness*, and agreed to sail in company. Next day, north-west of Cape Finisterre, they sighted eight homeward-bound West Indiamen under the French flag. Walker boldly attacked them, sank one, and with the aid of the *Sheerness* captured five, which were safely brought to Bristol. On a second cruise, coming into the channel in December the weakly built *Boscawen* almost fell to pieces, and was preserved to be run ashore near St Ives, on the Cornish coast, only through Walker's exertions. His conduct was widely reported in London, with the result that he was almost immediately offered a much more important command.

Walker now left the employ of his Dartmouth owners, following an offer from a London syndicate who had formed a squadron to attack the powerful ships increasingly employed by France and Spain to bring their cargoes across the Atlantic. This force, known collectively as the Royal Family, had already achieved one notable success; Walker was to have the command of what proved to be the culminating effort of British privateering. The squadron, comprising four ships—the *King George*, *Prince Frederick*, *Duke*, and *Princess Amelia*—carried an aggregate of 121 guns and 970 men. Its prestige was very high, for in the summer of 1745, off Louisbourg, it had made an enormously rich prize that, after the owners' share of £700,000 had been deducted, yielded £850 to each seaman, and to the officers in proportion. After cruising for nearly a year and having made prizes well in excess of £200,000 the Royal Family put into Lisbon; they sailed again in July 1747, and had watered in Lagos Bay, when on 6 October the Spanish ship *Glorioso* (70 guns) was sighted standing in towards Cape St Vincent. Walker rightly assumed that she had treasure and boldly attacked her in the *King George*, a 32-gun frigate. In an action of several hours' duration, in smooth water and fine weather, the *King George* was nearly beaten; but on the *Prince Frederick*'s coming up, the *Glorioso* fled to the westward, where she was met and engaged by the *Dartmouth*, a king's ship of 50 guns that accidentally blew up, with the loss of all but one of her crew. Some hours later the 80-gun *Russell* brought the *Glorioso* to action and succeeded in taking her. Only half-manned, the *Russell* was largely dependent on the privateers to take the prize into the Tagus. The Royal Family then continued cruising, but with moderate success owing to the absence of enemy shipping, until the end of the war; none the less the total prizes taken by the four ships under Walker's command were valued at about £400,000.

Walker is generally regarded as the most successful British privateer. He was evidently a good and resourceful seaman, who rose to the occasion and won his crews' regard by taking care of them, although he maintained strict discipline, and exercised his men both physically and in evolutions and in gunnery. Further, he always carried a number of musicians on board. It is unfortunate that so little is known of him. After the peace of Aix-la-Chapelle he involved himself in the venture of the Society of the Free British Fishery and carried out surveys of the Orkneys and of the Hebrides in its interest. But the syndicate that owned the Royal Family proved none too scrupulous and refused to admit his expenses and delayed settling his claims, and indeed those of his crews. Eventually he was imprisoned for debt and then declared bankrupt, and was released only after four years. Little is known of his subsequent life; he died on 20 September 1777 at Seething Lane, in the City of London, and was buried at All Hallows Barking, Great Tower Street, London.

J. K. LAUGHTON, rev. A. W. H. PEARSALL

Sources D. J. Starkey, *British privateering enterprise in the eighteenth century* (1990) · H. S Vaughan, ed., *The voyages and cruises of Commodore Walker* (1928) · J. K. Laughton, *Studies in naval history: biographies* (1887)

Walker, George (1734?–1807), Presbyterian minister and mathematician, was born at Newcastle upon Tyne. At the age of ten he was placed in the care of his uncle at Durham, Thomas Walker (*d.* 1763), who was successively minister at Cockermouth (1732), Durham (1736), and Leeds (1748). He attended the Durham grammar school under Richard Dongworth. In autumn 1749 he was admitted to

George Walker (1734?–1807), by George Clint, pubd 1805 (after Richard Bonington)

the dissenting academy at Kendal under Caleb Rotherham; here, among the lay students, he met his lifelong friend John Manning (1730–1806). On Rotherham's retirement in 1751 he was for a short time a pupil of Hugh Moises at Newcastle upon Tyne. In November 1751 he entered at Edinburgh University with Manning, where he studied mathematics under Matthew Stewart, who interested him in that subject. He moved to Glasgow University in 1752 to attend divinity lectures of William Leechman; he continued his mathematical studies under Robert Simson and heard the lectures of Adam Smith, but learned more from all three in their private conversation than their public performances. Among his contemporaries at Glasgow were Newcome Cappe, Nicholas Clayton, and John Millar (1735–1801), members with him of a college debating society. After leaving Glasgow in 1754 without graduating, he did occasional preaching at Newcastle and Leeds, and injured his health by excessive study; at Glasgow he had allowed himself only three hours' sleep. He apparently recovered through a course of sea bathing. In 1756, while seeking to become what he himself termed the 'spiritual consul' to 'any presbyterian tribe' (Walker, xxxi), he declined an invitation to succeed Robert Andrews as minister of Platt Lane Chapel, Manchester, partly on financial grounds: the salary was only £40 p.a. But later in that year he accepted a call (in succession to Joseph Wilkinson) to serve his uncle's former congregation, at Durham, and was ordained there in 1757.

At Durham, Walker finished, but did not immediately publish, his *Doctrine of the Sphere*, begun in Edinburgh. With the signature P. M. D. (presbyterian minister, Durham) he contributed to the *Ladies' Diary* a collection of mathematical papers, published in serial form and edited by Thomas Simpson (1710–1761). He left Durham at the beginning of 1762 to become minister at Filby, Norfolk, and assistant to John Whiteside (d. 1784) at Great Yarmouth. Here he resumed his friendship with Manning, who was by then practising as a physician at Norwich. He began a treatise on conic sections, inspired by Isaac Newton's *Arithmetica universalis* of 1707. He took pupils in mathematics and navigation. Through Richard Price he was elected fellow of the Royal Society, and in 1772 was recommended to William Petty, second earl of Shelburne (afterwards first marquess of Lansdowne), for the post of his librarian, subsequently filled by Joseph Priestley. He declined it owing to his approaching marriage in that year, when he also became mathematical tutor at Warrington Academy in succession to John Holt (d. 1772). Here Walker prepared his treatise on the sphere for publication, himself cutting out all the illustrative figures, of which there were 20,000, for an edition of 500 copies. It appeared in quarto in 1775, and was reissued in 1777. Joseph Johnson gave him for the copyright £40, remitted by Walker on finding the publisher had lost money.

The emoluments at Warrington did not answer Walker's expectations, and he resigned in two years, becoming colleague to John Simpson (1746–1812) at High Pavement Chapel, Nottingham, in autumn 1774. Here he remained for twenty-four years and devoted himself to congregational and political work. He made his mark as a pulpit orator, reconciled a division in his congregation, founded a charity school in 1788, and published a hymnbook. In conjunction with Gilbert Wakefield, the controversialist and classical scholar, he formed a literary club, meeting weekly at the members' houses. Wakefield described him as possessing 'the greatest variety of knowledge, with the most masculine understanding' of any man he ever knew (*Memoirs of the Life of Gilbert Wakefield*, ed. J. T. Rutt and A. Wainewright, 2 vols., 1804, 1.227). Nottingham was a focus of political opinion, which Walker led both by special sermons and by drafting petitions and addresses sent forward by the town in 1775 in favour of the independence of the United States and the advocacy of parliamentary reform (1782) and religious liberalization (1789–90). His ability and his whiggish constitutional opinions won the high commendation of Edmund Burke. His reform speech at the county meeting at Mansfield on 28 October 1782 led William Henry Cavendish Cavendish-Bentinck, third duke of Portland, to compare him with Cicero, to the disadvantage of the latter. From 1787 Walker was chairman of the associated dissenters of Nottinghamshire, Derbyshire, and part of Yorkshire, an organization aiming to achieve the repeal of the Test Acts and secure religious liberty for Unitarians. His *Dissenters' Plea* (n.d. [1790]) was praised by Charles James Fox as the best publication on the subject. He was an early advocate of the abolition of the slave trade. The variety of his interests is shown by his publication in 1794 of his treatise on conic sections, while he was agitating against government measures for the suppression of public opinion which culminated in the 'Gagging Act' of 1795.

Towards the end of 1797 Walker was invited to succeed Thomas Barnes as professor of theology in Manchester College. Feeling it a duty to comply, he resigned his Nottingham charge on 5 May 1798. There was one other tutor, but the funds were low, and Walker's appeal in April 1799 for increased subscriptions met with little response. From 1800 the entire burden of teaching, including classics and mathematics, fell on him, with no increase of salary. In addition he served the congregation at Dob Lane Chapel, Failsworth, from 1801 to 1803. Samuel Pipe-Wolferstan, whose son Stanley studied under Walker at Manchester, recorded in his diary that Walker was overworked and embroiled in financial disputes with the college trustees. He resigned in 1803, and the college was moved to York.

Walker remained for two years in the neighbourhood of Manchester, and continued to take an active part in its Literary and Philosophical Society, of which he was elected president on the death of Thomas Percival (1740–1804). In 1805 he moved to Wavertree, near Liverpool, still keeping up a connection with Manchester. In the spring of 1807 he went to London on a publishing errand. His health declined suddenly, and he died at Draper Hall, London, on 21 April 1807. He was buried in Bunhill Fields. His only son, George Walker, his biographer and author of *Letters to a Friend* (1843) on his reasons for nonconformity, became a resident in France. His only daughter, Sarah (*d.* 1854), married on 9 July 1795 Sir George Cayley, bt, of Brompton, near Scarborough.

Walker's theology, which he described as a 'tempered Arianism', plays a considerable part in his own compositions, and also shows itself in omissions and alterations in his *Collection of Psalms and Hymns* (1788). James Tayler, in a funeral sermon, described him as 'averse to … contradiction' and prone in controversy to 'an unbecoming warmth of expression'. As J. E. Bradley has shown, Walker was an important figure in late eighteenth-century English radicalism and his controversial writing endured for longer than that of most of his contemporaries.

ALEXANDER GORDON, rev. G. M. DITCHFIELD

Sources G. Walker, 'Memoir', in G. Walker, *Essays on various subjects*, 2 vols. (1809), vol. 1 · J. Tayler, *A sermon containing a sketch of the character of the late Revd George Walker* (1807) · V. D. Davis, *A history of Manchester College* (1932) · B. Smith, ed., *Truth, liberty, religion: essays celebrating two hundred years of Manchester College* (1986) · G. M. Ditchfield, 'The early history of Manchester College', *Transactions of the Historic Society of Lancashire and Cheshire*, 123 (1971), 81–104 · J. E. Bradley, *Religion, revolution and English radicalism: nonconformity in eighteenth century politics and society* (1990) · *Monthly Repository*, 2 (1807), 217 · *Monthly Repository*, 5 (1810), 264, 351–2, 475–7, 500–03, 504–11 · 'On Dr Priestley's connection with the marquis of Lansdown', *Monthly Repository*, 6 (1811), 17–19 · B. Carpenter, *Some account of the original introduction of Presbyterianism in Nottingham and the neighbourhood*, ed. [J. J. Tayler] (1862?) · R. Halley, *Lancashire: its puritanism and nonconformity*, 2 vols. (1869) · H. McLachlan, *English education under the Test Acts: being the history of the nonconformist academies, 1662–1820* (1931) · H. McLachlan, *Warrington Academy: its history and influence*, Chetham Society, 107, new ser. (1943) · B. Nightingale, *Lancashire nonconformity*, 6 vols. [1890–93], vol. 5, p. 4
Archives BL, Add. MS 41423 · Harris Man. Oxf., lecture notes | William Salt Library, Stafford, Samuel Pipe-Wolferstan

Likenesses G. Clint, mezzotint, pubd 1805 (after R. Bonington), BM, NPG [*see illus.*] · R. Earlom, portrait, Manchester Literary and Philosophical Society; repro. in Smith, ed., *Truth, liberty, religion*

Walker, George (1772–1847), writer and publisher, was born in Falcon Square, Cripplegate, London, on 24 December 1772. At fifteen he was apprenticed to a bookseller named Cuthell in Middle Row, Holborn, and two years later opened his own business with a capital of a few shillings. He married the daughter of a local tradesman with some property and prospered. He transferred to Great Portland Street, adding a musical publishing department, and finally, as a music publisher solely, moved to Soho Square, and took his son George *Walker (1803–1879) into partnership.

Walker wrote numerous Gothic novels in the manner of Ann Radcliffe, including *The Romance of the Cavern* (1792), *Cinthelia* (1797), and *The Three Spaniards* (1800). The latter two works were translated into French for sale in Paris. He also published a volume of poetry in 1801, and *The Battle of Waterloo: a Poem* in 1815. His *Adventures of Timothy Thoughtless* (1813) is a children's book. More notable was a satirical novel, *The Vagabond* (1799). A. D. Harvey regards this 'picaresque masterpiece', with Godwin as its target, as the best of the anti-reform novels, exhibiting 'the anxious repudiation of the new ideals about woman's role' (Harvey, 292). George Walker died on 8 February 1847 and was buried in Highgate cemetery.

J. R. MACDONALD, rev. JOHN D. HAIGH

Sources *London Directory* (1899) · 'Walker, George', *Biographie universelle, ancienne et moderne*, ed. L. G. Michaud and E. E. Desplaces, new edn, 45 vols. (Paris, 1843–65), vol. 44 · A. D. Harvey, 'George Walker and the anti-revolutionary novel', *Review of English Studies*, new ser., 28 (1977), 290–300 · [J. Watkins and F. Shoberl], *A biographical dictionary of the living authors of Great Britain and Ireland* (1816) · will, PRO, PROB 11/2058, fols. 313–14
Wealth at death see will, PRO, PROB11/2058, fols. 313–14

Walker, George (1803–1879), writer on chess, was born in Great Portland Street, London, on 20 March 1803 and baptized at St Marylebone on 17 April. He was the son of the novelist and publisher George *Walker (1772–1847). Working in his father's music publishing business at 17 Soho Square, he was a partner by 1836. After his father's death, George Walker went on to the stock exchange, where he practised until 1873 in partnership with William Bull. He died on 23 April 1879 at his home, 40 Albion Road, Stoke Newington, leaving a widow, Matilda, and was buried at Kensal Green cemetery.

As a chess player Walker was bright without being extremely brilliant. His recorded games with masters show that he was an adept in developing his pieces and making exchanges, but he admits that players of the strength of Morphy or Macdonnell could always give him the odds of the pawn and move. His particular hero was Labourdonnais, whom he tended in his last illness, and buried at his own expense in Kensal Garden cemetery (December 1840). Walker wrote a memoir of the 'roi d'échecs' for *Bell's Life*, which was translated for the Parisian *Palamède* (15 December 1841) as 'Derniers moments de

Labourdonnais'. From 1840 to 1847, when he ceased play-ing first-rate chess, Walker was inferior only to Buckle and Staunton among English players.

More significant, however, were Walker's administrat-ive and literary activities. As a young man, he founded the Percy chess club in Rathbone Place in 1823; impressed by defeats at the hands of William Lewis, he defected to the latter's chess school. He was a prime mover in the West-minster chess club (1831–43; secretary to 1838)—host to the Macdonnell–Labourdonnais match at Bedford Street, Covent Garden, and later based in the Strand—and helped resurrect it in the form of the St George's club, before the enmity of Howard Staunton caused him to migrate to the London chess club. As early as 1823 he attempted a chess column (in *The Lancet*); in 1838 he sought to start a special-ist magazine (*The Philidorian*). Longer-lived was his chess column for *Bell's Life* (1835–73).

As a writer on the game, George Walker's reputation was European, although the *Oxford Companion to Chess* now considers his work 'more enthusiastic than accurate' (Hooper and Whyld, 444–5). His production of cheap books had a significant publicizing role. 'No writer has produced so many books upon the subject of chess as Mr. Walker' (*ILN*, 427). His first publication, a pamphlet of twenty-four pages, on *New Variations in the Muzio Gambit* (1831), was followed in less than a year by his *New Treatise* (reprinted thrice to 1846), which gradually supplanted the chess *Studies* of Peter Pratt (1803) and the far from thor-ough *Treatise* by J. H. Sarratt (1808), as amended by Lewis in 1821; of the *New Treatise*, a German translation went through several editions. Walker's *Chess Studies, Comprising one Thousand Games actually Played during the Last Half-Century* (1844), also an improvement on Lewis's previous work, was re-edited by E. Freeborough in 1893; it finally established the principle that games of major masters (even quite casual ones) should be recorded. The year 1847 largely saw the end of Walker's writing. He is to be distin-guished from William Greenwood Walker, who published *A Selection of Games at Chess* in 1836.

THOMAS SECCOMBE, rev. JULIAN LOCK

Sources D. Hooper and K. Whyld, *The Oxford companion to chess*, 2nd edn (1992), 444–5 · P. W. Sergeant, *A century of British chess* (1934) · Boase, *Mod. Eng. biog.* · *ILN* (3 May 1879), 427 · *Chess Player's Chronicle* (1 June 1879) · *Westminster Papers*, 9 (1876), 140–42 · R. N. Coles, 'One hundred years ago', *British Chess Magazine*, 99 (1979), 177–8 · G. Walker, *Chess studies: comprising one thousand games*, ed. E. Freeborough (1893) · H. Staunton, *The chess-player's handbook* (1847); facs. edn (1985) · private information (1899) · *CGPLA Eng. & Wales* (1879) · IGI

Likenesses engraving, repro. in F. M. Edge, *Exploits and triumphs of Paul Morphy* (1973), facing p. 196 · portrait, repro. in *Illustrated News of the World*, 8 (1861)

Wealth at death under £1500: probate, 19 May 1879, *CGPLA Eng. & Wales*

Walker, George Alfred (1807–1884), sanitary reformer, was born on 27 February 1807 at Nottingham, the second son of William Walker, a plumber, and his wife, Elizabeth Williamson, of Barton under Needwood, Staffordshire; he also had at least one sister. His earliest teacher was Henry

Wild, a Quaker of 'Notten'. Later Walker moved to London and studied at Aldersgate Street School. In 1829 he became a licentiate of the Society of Apothecaries, and, in 1831, a member of the Royal College of Surgeons. In 1835 he stud-ied at St Bartholomew's Hospital, and the following year at the Hôtel Dieu in Paris. While there, he visited the great cemeteries which had been recently established outside the city boundaries, his interest in interment having first been awakened when, as a boy in Nottingham, he had wit-nessed shocking mutilations and upturning of human remains in the overcrowded graveyards of the town.

In 1837 Walker returned to London and set up in medical practice at 101 Drury Lane. Within a short distance of his surgery were seven of the most overcrowded and pestilen-tial graveyards in London. These included the Green Ground in Portugal Street and the notorious Enon Chapel in St Clement's Lane, where between 10,000 and 12,000 people were buried under the floorboards in a cellar meas-uring only 59 by 29 feet. A believer in the miasmic theory of disease, Walker was convinced that the smell emanat-ing from these overcrowded graveyards was poisonous and could ruin the health of those who lived nearby.

In *Gatherings from Graveyards* (1839) he exposed the appalling state of urban graveyards and, drawing on his extensive knowledge of health, sanitation, and mortality, sought to prove the connection between disease and burial. His solution was to propose the prohibition of intramural interment and the establishment of new cem-eteries outside the towns. This was the first of a series of publications on the subject which was instrumental in securing the appointment in 1842 of the parliamentary select committee on intramural interments. It was chaired by W. A. Mackinnon (Conservative MP for Lyming-ton, the most active campaigner in the Commons on the issue) and included Anthony Ashley Cooper, earl of Shaftesbury, who, in the following years, continued to support burial reform. Its report (1842) recommended the ending of burials in large towns, enabling parishes to establish suburban cemeteries, and the establishment of a central authority. Following this report, Sir James Gra-ham (home secretary, 1841–6), apparently as a delaying ploy, asked Edwin Chadwick (secretary of the poor-law commission, 1834–46) to report on intramural inter-ments. His report (1843) further publicized insanitary and disgusting burial areas (also exploitation, fraud, and infanticide) and recommended ending most intramural burial, and establishing a comprehensive nationalized system of interment. However, Graham's refusal to act, and the complacency of many of the medical and ecclesi-astical authorities, who profited much from burial fees, prevented much immediate progress towards closing the metropolitan graveyards. Walker continued his cam-paign, establishing the National Society for the Abolition of Burials in Towns in 1845. He also continued to lecture and write on the subject, publishing *Interment and Disinter-ment* (1843), *Burial Ground Incendiarism* (1846), and *A Series of Lectures on the Actual Conditions of Metropolitan Graveyards*

(1847). Some time in 1846–7, Walker purchased or leased Enon Chapel, with the intention of removing the remains. At his own expense, he arranged for these to be reburied at Norwood cemetery, and 6000 people witnessed their removal in four van loads.

Walker's campaign was given a significant boost by the cholera epidemic of 1848, which convinced most people of a connection between disease and the state of public hygiene and sanitation. The Society for the Abolition of Burials in Towns campaigned vigorously in 1849. Among the legislation that followed were measures forbidding any further burials in London's inner-city graveyards and prohibiting interment anywhere in the metropolis if such action were necessary for the protection of public health; the bodies were subsequently removed from most of these graveyards to the large new out-of-town cemeteries, as Walker had proposed. Also, burial inspectors were appointed.

Walker's other principal interest was the use of warm vapour baths to treat diseases such as rheumatism, gout, and indigestion. He established the first warm vapour baths in London at 11 St James's Place in 1844, and published *The Warm Vapour Cure* (1847) to publicize his methods of treatment. However, the baths were destroyed by fire in 1854.

Walker retired to Ynysfaig House, Arthog, Dolgellau, Merioneth, in 1855. He spent his last years writing his memoirs, called 'Grave reminiscences: some experiences of a sanitary reformer', but these were never completed. Following a sudden paralytic seizure about a week before, he died, unmarried, at his home on 6 July 1884 and was buried at the Quaker burial-ground near Tywyn, Merioneth.   JOHN PINFOLD

Sources P. C. Jupp and G. Howarth, eds., *The changing face of death* (1997) • C. Brooks, *Mortal remains* (1989) • *Men of the time* (1884) • *The Athenaeum* (12 July 1884) • *Medical Times and Gazette* (12 July 1884), 68 • R. Mellors, *Men of Nottingham and Nottinghamshire* (1924) • R. Richardson, *Death, dissection and the destitute*, pbk edn (1988) • Boase, *Mod. Eng. biog.* • S. E. Finer, *The life and times of Sir Edwin Chadwick* (1952) • A. Brundage, *England's 'Prussian minister': Edwin Chadwick and the politics of government growth, 1832–1854* (1988) • D. Roberts, *Victorian origins of the British welfare state* (1960) • personal knowledge (2004) • *CGPLA Eng. & Wales* (1884)
Wealth at death £9163 17s. 9d.: probate, 1 Dec 1884, *CGPLA Eng. & Wales*

Walker, Sir George Townshend, first baronet (1764–1842)

Walker, Sir George Townshend, first baronet (1764–1842), army officer, was born on 25 May 1764, the eldest son of Major Nathaniel Walker (1740–1780), who served in the Royal American rangers during the Anglo-American War, and Henrietta (d. 1829), only daughter and heir of Captain John Bagster RN, of West Cowes, Isle of Wight. His great-great-grandfather Sir Walter Walker, of Bushey Hall, Hertfordshire, was advocate to Catherine of Braganza, the wife of King Charles II.

By Queen Charlotte's wish Walker was commissioned ensign in the 95th foot on 4 March 1782; he became lieutenant on 13 March 1783, and on 22 June was transferred to

Sir George Townshend Walker, first baronet (1764–1842), by Thomas Heaphy, 1813–14

the 71st, the 95th being disbanded. The 71st was also disbanded soon afterwards, and on 15 March 1784 he was transferred to the 36th. He joined it in India, and served with General (afterwards Sir Henry) Cosby's force against the Poligars in the neighbourhood of Tinnevelly in February 1786, in charge of the quartermaster-general's department. He was invalided home in 1787, and exchanged on 25 July to the 35th foot. In 1788 he was employed on the staff in Ireland as aide-de-camp to General Bruce. On 13 March 1789 he was made captain-lieutenant in the 14th foot, but, instead of making plans to join it in Jamaica, he obtained leave to go to Germany to study tactics and the German language.

On 4 May 1791 Walker obtained a company in the 60th, all the battalions of which were in America; but he seems to have remained at the depot. In 1793 he went to Flanders with a body of recruits who had volunteered for active service. He was present at the action of 10 May 1794 near Tournai, and was employed on various missions while serving in the quartermaster-general's department during the retreat of the duke of York's army. When the army embarked for England he was made an inspector of foreign corps, and was sent to the Black Forest and Switzerland to superintend the raising of Baron de Roll's regiment. After making arrangements for its passage through Italy and embarkation at Civitavecchia, he returned to England in August 1796.

Walker was promoted major in the 60th on 27 August. In March 1797 he went to Portugal and was aide-de-camp first to General Simon Fraser (d. 1777), and afterwards to the prince of Waldeck, who commanded the Anglo-Portuguese army; but ill health obliged him to go home in June. He was inspecting field officer of recruiting at Manchester from February 1798 until March 1799. He then joined the 50th in Portugal, having become lieutenant-colonel in that regiment on 6 September 1798; but in October he was summoned to the Netherlands to act as British commissioner with the Russian troops under the duke of York. He afterwards accompanied them to the Channel Islands, and so missed the campaign in Egypt, in which his regiment served. He took over the command of the 50th at Malta in October 1801, returned with it to Ireland in 1802, and served with it in the expedition to Copenhagen in 1807, being in Spencer's brigade of Baird's division.

In January 1808 he went with the 50th to the Peninsula, as part of Spencer's force. It was one of the regiments particularly mentioned by Sir Arthur Wellesley (later Viscount Wellington) in his report of the battle of Vimeiro. It formed part of Fane's brigade, which, with Anstruther's brigade and Robe's guns, occupied a hill in front of Vimeiro, and was attacked by a strong column under Laborde. The French had nearly reached the guns when Walker wheeled his right wing round to the left by companies, poured a volley into the flank of the column, charged it both in front and flank, and drove it in confusion down the hillside.

In the autumn Walker went to England. He returned with dispatches for Moore, but reached Corunna two days after the battle. He was made colonel in the army on 25 September 1808. In 1809 he served in the Walcheren expedition, at first in command of his regiment, and afterwards as brigadier.

In August 1810 Walker went back to the Peninsula with the rank of brigadier-general. He was employed for a year in the north of Spain, aiding and stimulating the authorities of Galicia and the Asturias to raise troops and take a more active part in the war. He had persuaded Lord Liverpool to let him take 3000 British troops to Santona, but the men were sent to Wellington after the latter had intervened. Finding that he could do no good with the Spaniards, and having become major-general on 4 June 1811, Walker applied to join the army in Portugal, and in October he was given command of a brigade in the 5th (Leith's) division.

At the storming of Badajoz, on the night of 6 April 1812, Walker's brigade was ordered to make a false attack on the San Vincente bastion, to be turned into a real attack if circumstances were favourable. After a confused action Walker forced his way along the ramparts, and captured three bastions. Then a sudden scare (fear of a mine, according to Napier) made the men turn, and they were chased back to the San Vincente bastion, where they rallied on a battalion in reserve. Walker was shot while trying to overcome this panic. The ball, fired by a man not two yards distant, struck the edge of a watch which he was wearing in his breast, turned downwards and passed out between his ribs, splintering one of them. He also

received four bayonet wounds. He was taken care of for a time by a French soldier, whom he was afterwards able to repay. He was so weakened by loss of blood that his life was for some time in danger, and he had to remain three months at Badajoz before he could be sent home. His brigade had lost about half its effective strength, but its success had decided the fall of Badajoz. Wellington in his dispatch wrote of his conspicuous gallantry. On 24 October he was given the colonelcy of De Meuron's regiment, one of the 'foreign' corps raised for garrison duties.

Walker was still suffering from his wounds when he returned to the Peninsula in June 1813. The army was in the Pyrenees, covering the blockade of Pamplona, when he joined it on 4 August at Ariscun, and was placed in command of the 1st brigade (50th, 71st, and 92nd regiments) of the 2nd (Stewart's) division. Stewart had been wounded in the action of Maya ten days before, and in his absence the division was commanded by Walker for a month. He was present at the battle of the Nivelle on 10 November, but his brigade, which had suffered very severely at Maya, was not actively engaged. Shortly afterwards he was given temporary command of the 7th (Lord Dalhousie's) division, which formed part of Beresford's corps. At the passage of the Nive and the actions near Bayonne (10–13 December) this division was in second line. It helped to drive the French out of their works at Hastingues and Oeyergave on 23 February 1814. At Orthez, four days later, it was at first behind the 4th division, but it had a prominent share in the latter part of the battle, and in the pursuit. Walker was wounded while leading one of his brigades. He was mentioned in Wellington's dispatch, and was included in the thanks of parliament.

In March he reverted to his former brigade, but in the middle of that month his own wound and the recent death of his wife caused him to leave the army and return to England. He received the gold medal with two clasps for his services in the Peninsula, was made KCB in January 1815, and knight commander of the Portuguese order of the Tower and Sword in May.

Walker was governor of Grenada from 7 April 1815 to 17 February 1816. On 21 April 1817 he received the GCB. He was made a member of the consolidated board of general officers, and groom of the chamber to the duke of Sussex. On 19 July 1821 he was promoted lieutenant-general, and on 11 May 1825 he was appointed commander-in-chief at Madras. He took over that command on 3 March 1826, and held it until May 1831. On 28 March 1835 he was made a baronet, and received a grant of arms commemorating Vimeiro, Badajoz, and Orthez.

On 24 May 1837 Walker was appointed lieutenant-governor of Chelsea Hospital, and on 28 June 1838 he was promoted general. He had been made a colonel-commandant of the rifle brigade on 21 May 1816, De Meuron's regiment being disbanded in that year. He was transferred to the 84th regiment on 13 May 1820, to the 52nd on 19 September 1822, and, finally, to the 50th on 23 December 1839. He had married in July 1789, Anna (d. 15

Feb 1814), only daughter of Richard Allen of Bury, Lancashire; they had two daughters. On 15 August 1820 he married Helen (d. 23 Aug 1859), youngest daughter of Alexander Caldcleugh of Croydon, Surrey; they had four sons and two daughters. A handsome soldierly man, Walker died at Chelsea Hospital on 14 November 1842.

E. M. LLOYD, rev. JAMES LUNT

Sources United Service Magazine, 3 (1842), 583 · GM, 2nd ser., 19 (1843), 88 · Colonel Fyler [A. E. Fyler], The history of the 50th or (the queen's own) regiment, from the earliest date to the year 1881 (1895) · Selections from the dispatches and general orders of Field Marshall the duke of Wellington, ed. J. Gurwood, new edn (1851) · W. F. P. Napier, History of the war in the Peninsula and in the south of France, 3 vols. (1882) · J. T. Jones, Journals of sieges carried on by the army under the duke of Wellington in Spain, ed. H. D. Jones, 3rd edn, 3 vols. (1846) · J. Philippart, ed., The royal military calendar, 3 (1816) · C. W. C. Oman, Wellington's army, 1809–1814 (1912); repr. (1968) · R. Holloway, The queen's own royal west Kent regiment (1973) · Burke, Peerage (1959) · private information (1899)

Likenesses T. Heaphy, watercolour drawing, 1813–14, NPG [see illus.] · W. Theed junior, plaster bust, 1860, Royal Military Academy, Sandhurst

Walker, George Washington (1800–1859), missionary, was born in London on 19 March 1800, the twenty-first child of John Walker (1726–1821) and his second wife, Elizabeth, née Ridley. His mother died early and his father moved to Paris, and he was brought up by a grandmother at Newcastle upon Tyne as a Unitarian. He was confirmed by a bishop, and sent to a Wesleyan school at Barnard Castle. Apprenticed to a Quaker linen draper in Newcastle in 1814, he attended meetings of the Society of Friends; in 1827, influenced in part by James Backhouse, the York Quaker, he joined the society. An attachment to his master's daughter, who soon after became blind and died on 3 November 1828, much influenced his character at this time.

In 1831, in obedience to a 'call', Walker accompanied Backhouse on what turned out to be a twenty-seven-year mission to the southern hemisphere. They landed at Hobart Town on 8 February 1832, after a five months' voyage. Encouraged by the governor of Van Diemen's Land, Sir George Arthur, they visited convicts, and reported on the living conditions of convicts and Aborigines (there and on Flinders Island). In Launceston they gathered a body of Quakers, who held their first yearly meeting in 1834. By that meeting Walker was acknowledged a minister. After three years in Van Diemen's Land, Walker and Backhouse went to Sydney and made the acquaintance of Samuel Marsden, the senior chaplain there. When they returned to Hobart, at the request of the new governor, Sir John Franklin, they assisted Alexander Maconochie in the writing of his controversial report on penal conditions. In 1838 they travelled to Cape Town, visiting Mauritius on the way. They toured all the mission stations in South Africa, regardless of denomination, in a journey of 6000 miles.

When they parted on leaving South Africa in September 1840, Walker returned to Hobart Town and on 15 December 1840 married Sarah Benson Mather, a member of a Wesleyan family which had joined the Friends; they had ten children and were prominent members of the Quaker community, with both parents becoming noted philanthropists. Walker set up as a linen draper but devoted himself chiefly to moral causes, attaching a savings bank and a Bible distribution centre to his business. Regardless of considerable opposition—on one occasion threatened with being tarred and feathered—he preached the virtues of temperance and was active in convict and Aborigine welfare programmes. He and his wife (also a Quaker minister) became active in finding employment for destitute women. Walker possessed 'the gentle methodological persuasion of a Quaker resolved to effect a change in a vicious brutal world' (AusDB). He died in Hobart Town on 2 February 1859 and was buried on 4 February in the Friends' burial-ground, Providence Valley, West Hobart, Tasmania. His house, Narryna, later became the Van Diemen's Land Folk Museum.

CHARLOTTE FELL-SMITH, rev. H. C. G. MATTHEW

Sources J. Backhouse and C. Tylor, Life and labours of George Washington Walker (1862) · J. Backhouse, Visit to Australian colonies, 8 vols. (1838–41) · J. Backhouse, Visit to Mauritius (1844) · J. Backhouse, Extracts from letters, 3rd edn (1838) · AusDB

Archives RS Friends, Lond. · University of Tasmania

Walker, Sir Gilbert Thomas (1868–1958), applied mathematician and meteorologist, was born in Rochdale, Lancashire, on 14 June 1868, the fourth child in a family of eight of Thomas H. Walker, civil engineer, and his wife, Charlotte (or Elizabeth) Haslehurst. His father moved to Croydon and became borough engineer. Walker was educated first at Whitgift Grammar School (1876–1881) and then at St Paul's School (to 1886), from which he gained a mathematical scholarship to Trinity College, Cambridge. He was senior wrangler in part one of the mathematical tripos in 1889 and again in part two in 1890, and was elected a fellow of Trinity in 1891. In 1890 his health broke down and he had to spend the following three winters in Switzerland, where he became interested in skating. On his recovery he became lecturer in mathematics at Trinity in 1895.

From 1892 onwards Walker published a series of papers on electromagnetism for one of which, 'Aberration and some other problems connected with the electromagnetic field', he was awarded an Adams prize in 1899. This interest appears to have come to a close with the publication of his lectures on the Theory of Electromagnetism in 1910. An equally early but more sustained interest was in the physics of projectiles, ball games, and flight. Here his work was both practical and theoretical, for he became expert in the design and use of primitive projectiles, such as the boomerang and stone-age celt—he was known to his early Cambridge friends as Boomerang Walker—and he contributed a fine article entitled 'Spiel und Sport' to the great Enzyklopädie der mathematischen Wissenschaften in 1900. His interest in flight was later stimulated, in India, by the magnificent soaring and gliding of Himalayan birds whose actions in relation to their environment he did much to clarify. An article by him on natural flight in the *Encyclopaedia Britannica* placed much of this work on permanent record. Later still this interest was extended to human gliding and soaring and he greatly encouraged the sport in England in its early days.

Walker left Cambridge for India in 1904 to become director-general of observatories, which post he retained until retiring age in 1924. In 1908 he married May Constance (*d.* 1955), daughter of Charles Stephen Carter, gentleman farmer. They had one son and one daughter. Walker's administration of the Indian state meteorological service was most enlightened and in particular he gave their heads to the notable young scientists, like George Simpson and Charles Normand, whom he collected round him. From the beginning of his appointment he became much concerned with the vital problem for India of the variability of monsoon rainfall—the great Indian famine of 1899–1900 was much in people's minds—and he set out to find sound methods of forecasting the incidence of the Indian monsoon. This was a highly intractable problem for there was practically no quantitative theory of the monsoon nor therefore of its changes from year to year. Walker was thus led to seek empirical relations between antecedent events in and outside India and the Indian monsoon itself. Such relations are not difficult to find from the meteorological records over any given span of years but their persistence into the future, when lacking any theoretical basis, is uncertain. (Any two series of random numbers may show quite high but chance correlations over some part of their course.) Walker was well aware of the pitfalls pertaining to the method and he adopted the most stringent statistical tests of his analysis. Useful results were achieved but in spite of his tremendous effort to break it the monsoon problem really remained unsolved at the end of his term of office.

On retirement from India, Walker became professor of meteorology at the Imperial College of Science and Technology in London and he continued to explore the relations between weather in different parts of the world in a series of memoirs entitled 'World Weather' to the Royal Meteorological Society. He also engaged with students on a series of laboratory researches on the forms of motion in shallow fluids when heated gently from below (Bénard cells), and on the changes induced in these motions when a horizontal motion, varying with height, was imposed on the fluid. These experiments enabled Walker to identify the conditions of formation of many beautiful thin layer clouds (altocumulus) which commonly occur in the middle troposphere.

Walker retired from his chair to Cambridge in 1934 but remained active scientifically and in music (he was responsible for improvements in the design of the flute) until well over eighty years of age. He was president of the Royal Meteorological Society (1926–8), was its Symons gold medallist (1934), and editor of its *Quarterly Journal* (1935–41). He was elected FRS in 1904, appointed CSI in 1911, and knighted in 1924. These and other honours he wore lightly and ever remained modest, kindly, liberal minded, wide of interest, and a very perfect gentleman.

He left Cambridge in 1950, living mainly in Sussex and Surrey thereafter. He died at Coulsdon, Surrey, on 4 November 1958.

P. A. SHEPPARD, *rev.* ISOBEL FALCONER

Sources *Indian Journal of Meteorology and Geophysics* (Jan 1959) · G. I. Taylor, *Memoirs FRS*, 8 (1962), 167–74 · private information (1971) · personal knowledge (1971) · *CGPLA Eng. & Wales* (1959)
Archives Sci. Mus., corresp.
Likenesses Maull & Fox, photograph, RS · J. Russell & Sons, photograph, RS · photograph, RS; repro. in *Memoirs FRS*, facing p. 167
Wealth at death £8370 4s. 6d.: probate, 27 Feb 1959, *CGPLA Eng. & Wales*

Walker, Sir Harold Thomas Coulthard (1891–1975), naval officer, was born on 18 March 1891 at Plymstock, Devon, the younger son of Lieutenant-General Sir Harold Bridgwood Walker (1862–1934), and his wife, Harriet Edith Coulthard. Harold entered the Royal Naval College, Osborne, in 1903 among the earliest entries under the Selborne scheme, passing on to Dartmouth in 1905. He went to sea as a midshipman in 1908, and was promoted sub-lieutenant in 1911. That year, while serving in the destroyer *Bulldog*, the ship was involved in a collision with the French sailing vessel *Yvonne* and Walker was officially censured. He was, however, receiving excellent reports on his zeal, capability, and reliability and he was promoted lieutenant in 1913. He spent most of the First World War in the battleship *Bellerophon* in the Grand Fleet but also took part in the raids on Zeebrugge and Ostend in April 1918 where he showed great gallantry, being mentioned in dispatches and placed in the ballot for the Victoria crosses awarded. He was also seriously wounded and lost an arm, which earned him the nickname Hookey.

Promoted lieutenant-commander in 1921, Walker's qualities of leadership prevented his being subject to the Geddes 'axe' and he was promoted commander in 1926. He earned a commendation in the battleship *Warspite* in 1927 for his action in securing the safety of the ship after she struck a submerged obstruction. He then moved on to HMS *Ganges*, the boys' training establishment, where he was promoted captain at the end of 1931. In that year, on 3 October, he married Olive Marjorie, youngest daughter of Major J. A. Knowles of Woolverstone Park, Ipswich. They had a son and a daughter.

After a short time in command of the reserve cruiser *Canterbury* on trooping duty, Walker went ashore in 1933 for senior officer's courses, before being lent to the Royal Australian Navy in 1934–6 to command the cruiser *Canberra*. Service then followed in the Admiralty as deputy director, training and staff duties, before Walker went back to sea in HMS *Hood* as flag captain and chief staff officer to the vice-admiral battle-cruiser squadron.

In 1939 Walker moved to the 1st battle squadron as flag captain in the battleship *Barham*. Ill luck struck again when she hit the mole at Gibraltar and Walker was cautioned by the Admiralty. This may have accounted for his being sent ashore for his next appointment in 1940, when he was placed in command of the royal naval barracks, Portsmouth, in the rank of commodore. On promotion to rear-admiral he remained ashore as director of personnel services from 1941 to 1943, being appointed to head the Mediterranean and Levant manpower committee.

The war against Japan allowed Hookey Walker a welcome opportunity to return to sea and he was appointed first to the 5th cruiser squadron and then to the 3rd battle squadron in the East Indies fleet. In December 1944 he was promoted vice-admiral. Operating from Trincomalee and flying his flag in the battleships *Queen Elizabeth* and *Nelson* and the escort carrier *Empress*, Walker led the fleet in offensive operations against Japanese forces. In May 1945 special intelligence revealed that a Japanese heavy cruiser was about to operate in the eastern Indian Ocean and Walker put to sea with every available ship. This led to the sinking of the *Haguro*. After facing suicide bombers (kamikazes) in July 1945 and being appointed additionally second in command of the fleet in August, Walker was mentioned in dispatches in September for gallantry, skill, and devotion to duty in the *Haguro* action. He had been made CB in January 1944 and was gazetted KCB at the beginning of 1946.

In March 1946 Walker became commander of British naval forces in Germany, overseeing with enthusiasm the rigorous disarmament of the Kriegsmarine. He retired in September 1947 and was promoted admiral on the retired list. Walker died on 25 December 1975 at Rowley Bristow Hospital, Pyrford, Woking.   ERIC J. GROVE

Sources PRO, ADM 196/53, fol. 11 · *WWW, 1929–40* · *WWW, 1971–80* · J. Winton, *Sink the Haguro* (1979) · *CGPLA Eng. & Wales* (1976) · b. cert. · d. cert.

Wealth at death £40,377: probate, 14 April 1976, *CGPLA Eng. & Wales*

Walker, Henry (*fl.* 1638–1660), journalist and preacher, was born in Derbyshire of unknown parentage. On 28 October 1638 he was admitted a pensioner at Queens' College, Cambridge; though he appears not to have proceeded BA, he claimed to have been ordained a deacon by a representative of the bishop of Lincoln. He apparently worked as an ironmonger (apprenticed to a Mr Holland in Newgate market), served out his apprenticeship, but was unsuccessful at the trade. This would suggest that his Cambridge career followed his apprenticeship, though the account of his mechanic years may be exaggerated, if not fabricated. He subsequently became involved in the book trade as a bookseller (vending anti-episcopal books) and author. At the same time he operated as a preacher, a 'tub' or 'mechanic' preacher (meaning a preacher without a benefice, usually of Independent or nonconformist tendencies). In his *Modest Vindication* (1642), Walker professes, 'I was never yet a member of any separated congregation' (p. 6).

During 1641 Walker was repeatedly in trouble for writings and publications. In March he was briefly committed to the Fleet prison for two libellous pamphlets provocatively conflating episcopacy with popery, *The Prelates Pride* and *Verses on the Wren and Finch*. In December 1641 the Commons sent for him as a delinquent. Sudden notoriety came on 5 January 1642 when he threw into the king's carriage a pamphlet (now lost) entitled *To Your Tents, O Israel*. He was

arrested, escaped, and was recaptured before coming to trial. He denied authorship but was convicted on the testimony of the printer. After begging the king's pardon he was sentenced to the pillory.

During 1642 Walker engaged in a pamphlet exchange with John Taylor, who repeatedly stigmatized him as an ignoramus ironmonger and a scandalous preacher. Except when engaged in polemical mud-slinging Walker's tone was conciliatory, godly, informed, and submissive to the king. During the 1640s he published about thirty pamphlets (his anonymity makes certain attribution difficult), including an eight-page history of the church, proposals for further reformation of the English church, proposals to reform parliament, and a short exposition of Genesis based on lectures delivered at the academy of Balthasar Gerbier. Walker's learning was not extensive, and he did not wear it lightly, but like others he acquired during the 1640s rudimentary knowledge of Hebrew.

Walker's career took a new turn in January 1644 when he began to edit a newsbook, initially entitled *Occurrences of Certain Speciall and Remarkable Passages* and subsequently *Perfect Occurrences*. For this and other items he used the anagrammatic pseudonym Luke Harruney. The newsbook spoke to his religious nonconformity, journalistic ambition, and political opinions, including close support for Cromwell. It also pioneered an innovative element in newsbooks, perhaps a precursor of the crossword puzzle: from 1648 each issue began with a Hebrew transliteration of the name of a figure prominent in the news, which was then translated back into English to obtain a hidden meaning. Walker's relationship with parliament was chequered. He was questioned in March and April 1647 for expressions in *Perfect Occurrences*, and asked to verify a report therein; in the same year he was given a privilege for printing army papers. In 1648 and 1649 he successfully struggled to retain possession of his title. Walker petitioned for the right to be his own licenser in January 1649; this was granted but suspended by the Lords, and events soon overtook Walker's ambition. *Perfect Occurrences* disappeared in October 1649, killed off by the Commonwealth's act against unlicensed and scandalous books and pamphlets. One of the weekly newsbooks authorized following the act was *Severall Proceedings in Parliament*, apparently edited by Henry Scobell, clerk to the parliament; Walker later took control of this title and edited it until a second newsbook purge in 1655.

It is likely that Walker was involved in other short-lived periodicals, less colourful than *Perfect Occurrences*, most probably *A Perfect Summary of Chiefe Passages in Parliament* (1646); *Packets of Letters* (1648); *A Declaration, Collected out of the Journalls of Both Houses of Parliament* (1648); and *Tuesdaies Journall of Perfect Passages in Parliament* (1649). His newsbooks profited from advertising, and in August 1649 he advertised an 'Office of Entries' at the Fountain in King's Street, Westminster. In 1647 an anonymous pamphleteer remonstrated of Walker: 'I do think that his, and many other scurrilous Pamphlets, have done more mischief in this Kingdome then ever all my Lord of *Essex's* or Sir *Thomas Fairfaxes* whole train of Artillery ever did' (*A Fresh*

Whip, London, 1647, 6). Walker's contemporary notoriety was chiefly as a newsbook editor, perhaps second only to Marchamont Nedham in prominence, in which trade he was competent and engaging if not eloquent.

Wood credits Walker with responsibility for editing selections from *A Conference about the Next Succession* (1595) by the Jesuits William Allen and Robert Persons, which was published as *Severall speeches at a conference concerning the power of parliament, to proceed against their king for misgovernment* (1648[1649]), and reports that Walker was rewarded with £30 for his pains. Walker preached in the king's chapel at Whitehall on 15 July 1649, which sermon was printed. Perhaps it was not only because of his red hair and beard, but on account of his former expressions of allegiance to the king, that royalist pamphleteers nicknamed Walker Judas; they also labelled him a Jew, presumably because of his interest in Hebrew, and described his sexual predilections and the promiscuous conduct of his wife. The only two known contemporary likenesses of Walker are unlikely to be accurate: both appear in woodcuts on title-pages of John Taylor's pamphlets *A Reply as True as Steele* (1641), showing Walker being discharged from the anus of the devil, and *A Seasonable Lecture* (1642), showing Walker preaching from a tub.

Royalist journalists also report in August 1649 that Walker was given a benefice at Uxbridge, Middlesex, with a stipend of £100. A printed sermon delivered by him before Cromwell at Somerset House on 27 June 1650 describes him as 'minister of Gods word, at Knightsbridge in Middlesex' (*A Sermon Preached in the Chappell at Somerset-House*, 1650). He was appointed to the living of St Martin Vintry, College Hill, London, in 1655. He may have been the author of a pamphlet describing Cromwell's last hours published in 1659, which described its author as a groom of the protector's bedchamber and an eyewitness to his death. His last extant publication is *Serious Observations Lately Made, Touching his Majesty Charles the Second* (1660), a royalist work that began with one of his Hebrew word plays. He may have been appointed to the chapel at Hounslow, Middlesex, in 1664; otherwise nothing further is heard of him.   JOAD RAYMOND

Sources J. B. Williams, 'Henry Walker, journalist of the Commonwealth', *Nineteenth Century and After*, 63 (1908), 454–64 · H. Walker, *A modest vindication* (1642) · J. Taylor, *The whole life and progress of Henry Walker* (1642) · *Seventh report*, HMC, 6 (1879) · A. N. B. Cotton, 'London newsbooks in the civil war: their political attitudes and sources of information', DPhil diss., U. Oxf., 1972 · J. Raymond, *The invention of the newspaper: English newsbooks, 1641–1649* (1996) · *JHL*, 4–10 (1628–48) · *JHC*, 2–6 (1640–51) · *CSP dom.*, 1638–49 · *Mercurius Aulicus (for King Charles II)* (14–21 Aug 1649) · *Man in the Moon*, 20 (30 Aug–5 Sept 1649) · Venn, *Alum. Cant.*
Likenesses J. Taylor, caricature, repro. in Taylor, *A reply as true as steele* (1641) · J. Taylor, caricature, repro. in Taylor, *A seasonable lecture* (1642)

Walker, Sir Herbert Ashcombe (1868–1949), railway manager, was born on 16 May 1868 at 75 Talbot Road, Paddington, London, the only child of Dr George Stephen Walker MRCS, and his wife, Ellen Frances Ley. He was educated at the North London Collegiate School, and studied medicine for one year at St Francis Xavier College, Bruges.

It was intended that he should enter the medical profession but for financial reasons this became impossible, and when only seventeen he joined the office of the district superintendent of the line of the London and North Western Railway (LNWR) at Euston. He loved the work and soon grasped the essentials of railway operation. By 1910 he was outdoor goods manager for the large southern division of the LNWR and a year later became assistant to the general manager, Sir Frank Ree.

In 1911 Walker was chosen to become general manager of the London and South Western Railway (LSWR) and remained there until 1923. At Waterloo, the LSWR headquarters, there was much to do; many platforms had to be replanned and the rebuilding of the terminus speeded up, but Walker saw at once that he must entice more commuters, and his electrification of the London suburban lines, which was to be pursued long after he was running the future Southern Railway, was of lasting significance. At the outbreak of the First World War, though not the most senior of chief railway officers, he was made chairman of the railway executive committee, which controlled all aspects of railway operation. With characteristic confidence and zeal Walker did both this exacting job and his work at Waterloo. He was knighted in 1915, and in 1917 was appointed KCB.

The Railways Act of 1921 called for the establishment of four groups in Britain. The southern group, which became the Southern Railway, included the LSWR. Walker emerged as its sole general manager, from 1923 to 1937. Walker knew what he wanted to do at Waterloo and he had the backing of the Southern board. Under his aegis the tentacles of the electrified lines stretched south and west. The port of Southampton was enlarged so that ocean-going liners were attracted to its facilities and in 1933 what was then the largest dry dock in the world was opened by King George V. The programme gave the Southern Railway the biggest electrified suburban system in the world.

Though a firm manager, Walker was no dictator. He appointed able men, such as Alfred and Gilbert Szlumper, Alfred Raworth, E. C. Cox, and John Elliot. Walker fostered cross-channel traffic; in 1929 the Golden Arrow service was inaugurated which, in its prime, ran with almost French *élan*. In 1931 the autocarrier with room for forty cars appeared, the vehicles being hoisted aboard from the quayside. Yet Walker also knew that railways were no longer omnipotent; he became associated with the Great Western Railway in running a coach service to the west and acquired for his company a financial interest in Imperial Airways. He also kept a watchful eye on channel tunnel plans as they came and went. Walker retired in 1937 and joined the Southern board, on which he sat until railway nationalization in 1947.

Walker was physically well made, having stamina and a commanding presence. He looked what he was, a man who knew his job and meant to do it. He wore pince-nez spectacles, a round-ended stiff collar, and a moustache. On board days he would wear a tailcoat. He lacked social graces and had no small talk but this, to some extent, was compensated for by his unfailing memory. He was reputed to be able to stand by the footplate of a steam locomotive knowing at once the names of driver and fireman who, for their part, knew that he had a very good idea of what each did and how he did it. He had a taste for the theatre and when on the continent enjoyed a little gambling at a casino. He became a grand officer of the Légion d'honneur and a lieutenant of the City of London. A plaque in Walker's memory was erected at Waterloo Station after his death.

In 1894 Walker married Ethel Louisa (1867–1909), daughter of John Robert Griffith, a solicitor, of Llanrwst, north Wales. After her death he married, in 1910, Lorina Elizabeth (b. 1874/5), widow of A. Shield, a member of the stock exchange. She was the daughter of Alfred Webb, mechanical engineer. There were no children of either marriage. Walker died on 29 September 1949 at 9 Maresfield Gardens, Hampstead, London.   COLIN WATSON, rev.

Sources C. F. Klapper, *Sir Herbert Walker's Southern Railway* (1973) · *The Times* (30 Sept 1949) · J. Simmons, *The railways of Britain* (1961) · b. cert. · b. cert. [Ethel Louisa Griffith] · m. certs. · d. cert. · *CGPLA Eng. & Wales* (1950)
Wealth at death £38,058 17s.: probate, 18 Jan 1950, *CGPLA Eng. & Wales*

Walker, Horace (1910–1994), Church of Scotland minister and administrator, was born on 16 August 1910 in Aberdeen, the youngest of five children of William Telfer Walker (c.1865–c.1937), a sales representative, and his wife, Sarah Jackson (c.1867–1949). From Aberdeen grammar school he went, in 1928, to Aberdeen University, and graduated with honours in English (MA, 1932) before studying divinity (BD, 1935). He worked for three years as Scottish travelling organizer of the Student Christian Movement (SCM), which then encompassed both liberal and evangelical theology. The appointment was a joint arrangement between the SCM and the home board of the Church of Scotland, whose Aberdeen presbytery ordained Walker in December 1935.

In 1938–9 Walker was assistant minister at St Mary's, Dundee, and when the Second World War broke out was in the process of induction (completed 27 September 1939) into his first parish charge at West Port, Hawick. He remained there for most of the war, apart from secondment to Orkney with the Church of Scotland huts and canteens serving the forces. Hawick introduced him to a Scottish regional culture as distinctive as Aberdeen's and to his future wife, Annie Wyles Duncan (b. 1918), a nurse whom he married on 28 April 1945, shortly after he had moved back to Aberdeen. They had two daughters. From 1944 to 1948 he was minister of the church extension parish of High Hilton, an Aberdeen area developed between the wars.

Walker left the parish ministry to become secretary-depute of the Church of Scotland's home board in 1948 and from 1 November 1957 to August 1977 was its secretary, a managing co-ordinator, and executive director as far as Presbyterian structures allowed. He was bureaucrat and diplomat, even entrepreneur, involved in creating nearly fifty new parishes and in 150 building projects at a

time when urban redevelopment, new town projects, Glasgow overspill, and suburban expansion changed the face of Scotland.

Walker's ministry extended beyond planning and administering these changes. He sought to extend as well as organize concepts of ministry and to integrate parish based church life with initiatives of a different kind. These tried to respond to social and intellectual trends as well as population changes. His commitment to traditional church extension which had sustained and often revived the Church of Scotland in inter-war and post-war years went with enthusiasm for industrial and hospital chaplaincy and church involvement with science, technology, and the arts, as well as conference and lay training centres. There were initiatives for groups from immigrants to weekend skiers, as well as a sustained 'Tell Scotland' movement.

These endeavours flourished in an age when church membership in Scotland was still around its peak (a decline set in from the early 1960s) and residual attachment and respect remained strong among those with no formal connection. This approach recognized that many congregational activities had become less relevant to life patterns among a more mobile population, though it depended for long-term viability on the ability of traditional parishes to pay their own way and sustain central funds.

Most of the initiatives remained vigorous when Walker retired, though further expansion and experiment were limited by straitened circumstances in the church and a less universally friendly perception of it. Hospital chaplaincy thrived but industrial chaplaincy, originally linked to Scottish heavy industry, found that it was not only parish life that had to cope with social and economic change. One fresh success was a chaplaincy to the North Sea oil industry. Some other initiatives wilted or were scaled down, but Walker's concepts continued to influence the Church of Scotland's perception of its history, theology, and mission, most spectacularly demonstrated in its ownership of a theatre and arts centre through the wall from the building accepted by tradition as John Knox's house.

In demeanour Horace Walker could show a reserve which only briefly concealed a warm heart. Literally and metaphorically he walked upright, visible from afar by a shining head of white hair unthinned with age. He was a receptive listener, generally shrewd in judgement, and strong willed but fair-minded. Some of those working with him called him prophetic. He was not most notable as visionary of the distant scene, but as team leader, planner, and negotiator with a liberal evangelical faith. He could share visions and work out practical steps to give them substance. He also achieved considerable success in harmonizing parish efforts of different trends in the church, notably the Iona Community emphasis on social gospel and the growth of a self-conscious conservative evangelicalism.

After retirement in 1977 Walker was chairman of the ecumenical Scottish Churches Council for four years before ill health weakened him. He died in Edinburgh after years of increasing infirmity on 5 December 1994 and was cremated on 8 December at Warriston crematorium. He was survived by his wife. Aberdeen University conferred a DD on him in 1967. He was made OBE in 1978.

R. D. KERNOHAN

Sources *Fasti Scot.*, new edn, vols. 9–11 · *Reports to general assembly of Church of Scotland (home board)* (1948–78) · *The Scotsman* (7 Dec 1994) · *The Scotsman* (14 Dec 1994), 14 · *Life and Work* (June 1977), 24 · *Church of Scotland Yearbooks* (1936–95) · private information (2004) [family]

Archives Church of Scotland, Edinburgh, department of national mission, Church of Scotland general assembly, verbatim reports · Church of Scotland, Edinburgh, department of national mission, Home Board annual reports and meeting minutes

Likenesses photographs, Church of Scotland Press Office, Edinburgh · photographs, *The Scotsman* Photo Library

Wealth at death £8248.34: confirmation, Scotland, 1995

Walker, Sir Hovenden (1666?–1725), naval officer, was the second son of Colonel William Walker of Tankardstown, Queen's county, Ireland, and Elizabeth, daughter of the physician Peter *Chamberlen (1601–1683). There is some doubt over his date of birth, some sources giving 1656 and others 1666: the latter is more likely, as in June 1678 he was admitted to Trinity College, Dublin, though he never completed his degree. In April 1686 he was at Nevis, where he volunteered to join the *Dartmouth* for the pursuit of a Spanish pirate. His account of the voyage found its way into Samuel Pepys's papers, and he subsequently visited Boston in the *Dartmouth*, where he entertained the crew with an anti-Spanish poem of his own composition. He was appointed second lieutenant of the *Saint David* on 30 October 1688, and obtained post rank as captain of the fireship *Vulture* on 17 February 1692.

In the *Vulture* Walker was present at the battle of Barfleur, but had no actual share in it, nor in the destruction of the French ships at La Hogue. He was shortly afterwards appointed to the *Sapphire* on the Irish station, and in 1694 to the armed ship *Friends' Adventure*. In 1695 he commanded the *Foresight* (50 guns), in which, when off the Lizard, in charge of a convoy, and with the *Sheerness* in company, he fought a gallant action with two French ships of 60 and 70 guns, on 29 April 1696, and beat them off. In January 1697 he was appointed to the *Kent*, in June to the *Content Prize*, in September to the *Royal Oak*, and in February 1698 to the *Boyne* as flag-captain to Vice-Admiral Matthew Aylmer, going to the Mediterranean as commander-in-chief. On the return of the *Boyne* to England in November 1699 the ship was ordered to pay off, and Walker asked for leave of absence to go to Ireland, where, he explained, he had a case pending in the court of chancery, in which his interests were involved to the extent of £1000. As the Admiralty refused him leave until the ship was safe in Hamoaze and her powder discharged, he begged to 'lay down' the command.

In December 1701 Walker was appointed to the *Burford*, one of the fleet off Cadiz under Sir George Rooke in 1702; and afterwards of a squadron detached to the West Indies with Walker as commodore. After calling at the Cape Verde Islands and at Barbados he arrived at Antigua in the middle of February, and was desired by Colonel Christopher Codrington to co-operate in an attack on Guadeloupe. The first part of the co-operation was to provide the land forces with ammunition, which was done by making up cartridges with large-grained cannon powder and bullets taken from the case-shot. There were no flints, mortars, bombs, pickaxes, spades, and such like, necessary for a siege. The ships took the men over to Guadeloupe, put them safely on shore, cleared the enemy out of such batteries as were within reach of the sea, and kept open the communications. When the French, driven out of the towns and forts, were permitted to retire to the mountains, the English were incapable of pursuing them, and finally withdrew after destroying the town, forts, and plantations. At the end of May the squadron returned to Nevis, where, a few weeks later, it was joined by Vice-Admiral John Graydon, with whom it went to Jamaica, and later on to Newfoundland and England.

From 1705 to 1707 Walker commanded the *Cumberland*, in which, in the summer of 1706, he took out a reinforcement to Sir John Leake in the Mediterranean, and took part in the relief of Barcelona. In December 1707 he was appointed to the *Royal Oak*, in January 1708 to the *Ramillies*, and in June, under a recent order in council (18 January), to be captain resident at Plymouth, to superintend and hasten the work of the port, and to be commander-in-chief in the absence of a flag-officer. On 15 March 1711 he was promoted rear-admiral of the white. About the same time he was knighted, and on 3 April he was appointed commander-in-chief 'of a secret expedition', with an order to wear the union flag at the main when clear of the channel. The 'expedition' intended against Quebec—consisting of ten ships of the line, with several smaller vessels and some thirty transports, carrying upwards of 5000 soldiers, commanded by Brigadier-General John Hill—sailed from Plymouth in the beginning of May, and arrived in New England on 24 June. The supplies and reinforcements which were expected to be waiting for it were not ready, and the fleet did not sail for the St Lawrence until 30 July. As they entered the river it began to blow hard, and on 21 August a dense fog and an easterly gale compelled them, on the advice of the pilots, to lie to for the night. By the next morning they had drifted on to the north shore, among rocks and islands, where eight transports were cast away with the loss of nearly 900 men, and the rest of the fleet was saved with the greatest difficulty.

The storms continued, and the locally recruited pilots were unanimous in stating the fleet could not reach Quebec. In any case the ships were short of provisions, a consequence of the earl of Oxford's policy of keeping the expedition's purpose as secret as possible even from the Admiralty—and, indeed, from Walker himself. A council of war was of the opinion that, with only ten weeks' provisions on short allowance, nothing could be done but to return to England as soon as possible. They arrived at St Helen's on 9 October, and not long afterwards, Walker's flagship, the *Edgar* (70 guns), blew up while at anchor at Spithead. When the *Edgar* blew up Walker was on shore; but—among other things—all his papers were still on the ship and were lost, a circumstance which afterwards caused him much trouble. On 14 March 1712 he was appointed commander-in-chief at Jamaica, where he quarrelled with the governor, and sailed finally from Plymouth on 30 April with the small squadron and a convoy of 100 merchant ships. The command was uneventful, and is important mainly in showing that nothing in the conduct of the expedition to the St Lawrence was considered by the Admiralty prejudicial to Walker's character as an officer. On the peace he was ordered to England, and arrived off Dover on 26 May 1713.

Walker retired to Somersham, his country estate near St Ives in Huntingdonshire, where he was a JP. In March 1715 he was ordered to send a justification of his conduct at Quebec to the Admiralty, but the loss of his papers in the *Edgar* delayed him. He had not responded when he learned in April that his half pay had been stopped and he had been removed from the flag-officers' list, almost certainly more because of his closeness to the tories, and especially to Viscount Bolingbroke, than because of genuine misconduct in Canada. Thereafter Walker left England for a plantation in South Carolina: in 1719 he attempted to justify his departure to the Admiralty, arguing that 'being struck out of half pay … I looked upon myself at liberty, in order to provide for myself … [being] a drowning man, catching in haste at any twig to save himself'. In the same letter he referred to himself living in Carolina on 'Indian corn, and potatoes (because I could not afford to buy plumb cake in London)', and to his part of Carolina as 'the most poor and beggarly settlement in that new discovered world' (PRO, ADM 1/577, Walker to Admiralty, 11 Sept 1719). Shortly afterwards he published *A Journal, or Full Account of the Late Expedition to Canada* (1720), an attempt at self-justification which actually betrayed the writer's *naïveté* and mediocrity as a commander. Walker was back in England by 1722, soliciting for his half pay and even for the post of controller of the navy, and two months before his death he even applied audaciously for back pay from his 1702 command.

By the mid-1720s Walker had moved to Germany where he was well acquainted with Thomas Lediard in Hamburg and Hanover. 'I found him', wrote Lediard, 'a gentleman of letters, good understanding, ready wit, and agreeable conversation; and withal the most abstemious man living; for I never saw or heard that he drank anything but water, or eat anything but vegetables' (Lediard, 855). He was twice married: first to Jane Pudsey and second to Margaret Jefferson, who survived him and with whom he had one daughter, Margaret (*d. c.*1777). Walker died in Dublin, of apoplexy, on 24 December 1725.

J. K. LAUGHTON, *rev.* J. D. DAVIES

Sources G. S. Graham, ed., *The Walker expedition to Quebec, 1711*, Navy Records Society (1953) · PRO, ADM 1/230, ADM 1/577, ADM 6/424, ADM 8 · G. S. Graham, 'Walker, Sir Hovenden', *DCB*, vol. 2 · Bodl. Oxf., MS Rawl. A. 189, fol. 337ff. · NMM, Sergison MSS, SER/136 · Burtchaell & Sadleir, *Alum. Dubl.*, 2nd edn, 847 · BL, Add. MS 31137, fols. 338, 340 · letters to Lord Strafford, 1712–13, BL, Add. MS 31138, fol. 72 · J. H. Owen, *War at sea under Queen Anne, 1702–1708* (1938) · *GM*, 1st ser., 94/2 (1824), 38–9 · T. Lediard, *The naval history of England*, 2 vols. (1735)

Archives National Library of Jamaica, Jamaica journal | PRO, Admiralty MSS

Walker, Humphrey (*d.* in or before **1516**), gun-founder, about whose early life nothing is known, first appears in documentary sources with his payment of quarterage in 1497/8 as a freeman of the Founders' Company of London. By 1499 Walker was acting as a deputy gunner in the Tower of London for Thomas Greves; and in 1509 he was appointed gunner in his own right, an office he held until his death. In 1507 Walker estimated that it would take 6400 lb of bronze to make the images of Henry VII and his wife, Queen Elizabeth, and the other castings for their tomb at Westminster Abbey, designed by the Italian sculptor Torrigiani. It is probable that Walker cast the effigies; he certainly attended the funeral of Henry VII in his capacity as groom of the office of ordnance.

From the accession of Henry VIII in 1509 Walker played a key role in facilitating his sovereign's military ambitions. In the early years of his reign Henry VIII was anxious to build up his navy and arsenals so that he could compete on the European stage. Walker was the only English gun-founder able to compete with the continental founders, who also cast guns for the crown. From Henry's accession until Walker's death about 1516, he regularly cast cannon for the king, in all sizes from the enormous 'King's Basiliscus' down through culverins and demi-culverins to the smaller falcons. He also cast other bronze items for the office of ordnance, such as shears and moulds, as well as supplying other ordnance requirements such as bill hafts and gunstocks.

The location of Walker's workshops in London is not known. However, during the early years of Henry VIII's reign new foundries were set up in the Tower of London and Houndsditch and Walker seems to have been involved in both. Certainly the basiliscus was cast in the Tower. Walker was also involved in other branches of the ordnance supply, including the new techniques of casting iron. In 1512 he took over the lease of the pioneering blast furnace at Newbridge, Sussex, where he cast iron shot for the crown.

Walker was an active member of the Founders' Company of London throughout his career. He was a freeman by 1497 and in 1502/3 he paid the fee to admit an apprentice. In 1509 he was paid for the sizing of brass. By 1510 he had become a liveryman and the second, or master warden in 1511–12. An inventory of the company's possessions taken about 1512 includes a standing cup presented by Walker. He died at some date before 20 May 1516, when John Mayer was appointed gunner in his place. There were no English-born founders to replace him until the 1530s, when the Owen brothers began supplying the crown with great bronze pieces. In the years immediately after Walker's death, Henry had to invite foreign founders to continue the workshops established by him.

RUTH RHYNAS BROWN

Sources *LP Henry VIII*, vol. 1 · G. Parsloe, *Wardens' accounts of the Worshipful Company of Founders of the City of London, 1497–1681* (1964) · H. Cleare and D. Crossley, *The iron industry of the Weald* (1985)

Walker, Jack (1929–2000), businessman, was born on 19 May 1929 at 96 Randal Street in the Little Harwood area of Blackburn, Lancashire, the youngest son in the family of three sons and one daughter of Charlie Walker (d. 1951), a sheet-metal worker, and his wife, Annie Louisa, née Farrar. On leaving Bangor Street School at the age of fourteen, he was apprenticed as a sheet-metal worker in the factory where his father worked. After the latter was invalided out of his job and set up his own sheet-metal works and car repair business in a garage in St Peter Street, Blackburn, in 1943, Walker joined him in 1945. He did his national service in the Royal Electrical and Mechanical Engineers (REME), then returned to the family business, and when his father died in 1951 he and his brother Fred took over the firm. On 25 October 1952 he married Eleanor Joan Moore, the daughter of Francis Moore, a driver.

The Walkers moved into steel stockholding, buying steel when the price was low, storing it, and selling it when the price went up. As the business grew, they moved to larger premises on several sites, and in 1968 they bought a 54 acre site at Guide, near Blackburn, and built a warehouse measuring 1 million square feet, which when it opened in 1970 was the largest steel stockholding site in the world. Walker moved to Jersey in 1974, and in 1983 Walkersteel took over the small Jersey European Airways, which was combined within the Walker Aviation Group with the charter airline Spacegrand, already owned by the company, in 1985: the airline was estimated to be worth £100 million at his death. By 1990, when Walkersteel was sold to British Steel for £330 million, at that time the largest amount ever paid for a private company, the firm had a workforce of 3400 in sixty locations in the United Kingdom and Ireland, and was one of the largest steel stockists in the world, with an annual profit of £48 million.

A lifelong supporter of Blackburn Rovers Football Club, Walker bought a 62 per cent share in the club in 1991, which he increased to 99 per cent by 1993, and went on to pour millions of pounds into the club. Blackburn Rovers had been in the second division of the Football League since 1980, and had not been in the first division since 1966, with periods in the third division in the 1970s. After Walker persuaded Kenny Dalglish, a former Scottish international and manager of Liverpool Football Club, to become manager in October 1991, the fortunes of the club began to change. Walker made money available to Dalglish in order to strengthen the playing squad; he signed eleven new players during the 1991–2 season, while selling fifteen, and on 25 May 1992, after beating Leicester City 1–0 in the second division play-off final at Wembley, Blackburn Rovers won the last place in the new premier league. With promotion, Dalglish continued to build up the squad, signing Alan Shearer from Southampton in July 1992 for a then record fee of £3.3 million and Graeme le Saux from Chelsea in March 1993.

Blackburn Rovers finished fourth in the premier league in the 1992–3 season and second in 1993–4, and in 1995 it won the premier league, its first championship since 1914, at the end of a season in which six members of the team played for England, and Dalglish won the Football Association Carling premiership manager of the year award. Attendance went up by 300 per cent between 1991 and 1995, and the new 25,000-seat stadium at Ewood Park, paid for by Walker, opened at the beginning of the 1995–6 season. But after 1995, despite Walker's continuing to pour in money, Blackburn Rovers lost its position at the top of the premier league. Dalglish, who became director of football after his three-year contract ended, left the club in August 1996, while several of the leading players moved elsewhere, including Alan Shearer, sold to Newcastle United in July 1996 for £15 million. Other premier league clubs began to spend on the same scale, and after a succession of less successful managers Blackburn Rovers was relegated to the first division in 1999. It was thought that Walker had spent over £100 million on the club.

A shy and reclusive man, who refused to be chairman of the club but flew over from Jersey for every match, Walker was very popular with the club's supporters, who always referred to him as Uncle Jack. He was a generous benefactor to other Blackburn causes, usually anonymously, and his Walker Park estate helped to create hundreds of jobs in the area. In Jersey he subsidized the local amateur football club, First Tower United, and paid for a training ground. He died on 17 August 2000 in Jersey, leaving a fortune estimated at between £500 and £700 million. He was survived by his second wife, Carol, his two sons and two daughters, and his brother Fred. A memorial fund was set up, and in 2001 the Jack Walker memorial garden was unveiled in Blackburn. ANNE PIMLOTT BAKER

Sources M. Jackman, *Blackburn Rovers: an illustrated history* (1995) · S. F. Kelly, *Dalglish* (1992) · K. Dalglish, *My autobiography* (1996) · *Lancashire Evening Telegraph* (18 Aug 2000) · *The Independent* (19 Aug 2000) · *The Guardian* (19 Aug 2000) · b. cert. · m. cert.

Likenesses photograph, 1994, repro. in *The Independent* · photograph, 1995, repro. in *The Guardian* (19 Aug 2000) · statue, Ewood Park, Blackburn

Wealth at death est. £500 million–700 million: *Lancashire Evening Telegraph*

Walker, James (1758×60–1822×5?), engraver in mezzotint and stipple, son (according to Redgrave) of a captain in the merchant service, was apprenticed to the London engraver Valentine Green on 28 January 1773. He left Green in 1780, the year of his earliest published plate, dated 2 July, which depicted Sir Hyde Parker, after Romney; this was followed by other portraits, notably after Romney, as well as the subject pieces for which Green's studio was renowned. He engraved a portrait of Empress Catherine II from a painting belonging to the Russian ambassador, Ivan Simolin, and it was probably Simolin who recruited him to go to Russia in 1784, where he was appointed engraver to Catherine. Walker was accompanied by his wife, Mary, and possibly a daughter. Two more children were born while they were in Russia: Catherine (born and died in 1791) and a son, Charles James (1786–1788). Walker was also accompanied by John Augustus *Atkinson (1774×6–1830), probably his stepson, who later trained under Walker and developed into a competent painter in Russia.

Walker's principal task was to engrave important pictures by old and contemporary masters in the imperial collection, but he also produced some forty-three portraits of the imperial family and the Russian aristocracy. On 30 December 1786 he was made an associate of the Academy of Arts at St Petersburg, and in September 1794 a full academician. His appointment as imperial engraver was renewed by Emperor Alexander I. Walker returned to England from time to time to arrange publication of his engravings. During one such visit, in 1792, when he also took out the freedom of the Russia Company, he published two parts of *A collection of prints, from the most celebrated pictures in the gallery of her imperial majesty Catherine II, empress and autocratix of all the Russias*. These were retailed for him by the landscape painter William Hodges and the bookseller R. Blamire. Back in Russia, Walker's other duties included showing distinguished British and other foreign visitors round the Hermitage, and the training of pupils. He returned to England with a pension in 1802, but twenty-four of his plates were lost in a shipwreck off Yarmouth.

In London, Walker continued to publish mezzotints and also to collaborate with Atkinson. He engraved several of Atkinson's pictures but he also wrote the text for *A Picturesque Representation of the Manners, Customs and Amusements of the Russians* (1803–4), in three volumes, illustrated with 100 aquatints by Atkinson, and dedicated to Alexander I. In 1807 they launched a similar collaboration on *A picturesque representation of the naval, military and miscellaneous costumes of Great Britain*, although only the first volume appeared. Walker wrote a light-hearted account of his experiences in *Paramythia, or, Mental pastimes: being original anecdotes, historical, descriptive, humourous, and witty, collected chiefly during a long residence at the court of Russia, by the author*; probably written by 1816, it was published anonymously in 1821. A sale of his surviving prints took place on 29 November 1822; Walker may have died shortly before that date, although the existence in the British Museum of a plate by him published in 1825 suggests, if it was not a reprint, that he died a few years later.

TIMOTHY CLAYTON and ANITA MCCONNELL

Sources Redgrave, *Artists* · J. C. Smith, *British mezzotinto portraits*, 4 vols. in 5 (1878–84) · A. Cross, ed., *Engraved in the memory: James Walker, engraver to the empress Catherine the Great, and his Russian anecdotes* (1993) · D. Alexander, 'James Walker: a British engraver in Russia', *Print Quarterly*, 12 (1995), 412–14 · I. Maxted, *The British book trades, 1710–1777* (1983)

Walker, James (1764–1831), naval officer, was son of James Walker of Innerdovat in Fife and his wife, Mary, daughter of Alexander Melville, fifth earl of Leven and fourth earl of Melville. He entered the navy in 1776 on the frigate *Southampton*, in which he served for five years, in the West Indies, then in the channel. He was appointed to the *Princess Royal*, the flagship of Sir Peter Parker (1721–1811), who, on 18 June 1781, promoted him lieutenant of the *Torbay*, one of the squadron that accompanied Sir Samuel Hood to North America. The *Torbay* took part in the action off Chesapeake on 5 September, in the operations at St Kitts in January 1782, and in the battle of Dominica on 12 April.

Walker, whose father was an intimate friend of George Brydges Rodney, was on the point of being promoted when Rodney was superseded by Admiral Pigot, and the chance was gone; he was still in the *Torbay* when, on 17 October 1782, in company with the *London*, she destroyed the French *Scipion* in Samana Bay, Haiti.

After the peace, Walker spent some years in France, Italy, and Germany. While in Vienna in 1787 he heard of the Dutch armament and immediately started for England. Near Aschaffenburg, the diligence in which he was travelling, and which was carrying a considerable sum of money, was attacked by robbers. Walker put up resistance but was knocked on the head, stripped, and thrown into the ditch. He was carried into Aschaffenburg, where his wounds were dressed. Although the Frankfurt lodge of freemasons offered financial assistance, the delay prevented his reaching England until the crisis with the Dutch was over, so he returned to Germany. In 1788 he was offered command of a Russian ship, but the Admiralty refused him permission to accept it. In 1789 he was appointed to the *Champion* on the coast of Scotland. After postings to the *Winchelsea* and, in 1793, the *Boyne*, he was moved as first lieutenant into the frigate *Niger*, which was attached to the Channel Fleet under Lord Howe and was one of the repeating ships in the battle of 1 June 1794 in the north Atlantic.

On 6 July Walker was rewarded with the rank of commander. Short commissions as acting captain of the *Gibraltar* and commander of the bomb-vessel *Terror* led to his appointment in June 1795 as acting captain of the *Trusty*, in which, having escorted five East Indiamen to a latitude of safety, he learned that some forty English merchant ships were at Cadiz waiting for convoy. Disregarding orders to return to Spithead, he went to Cadiz and brought the ships home, with property, as represented by the merchants in London, of the value of upwards of £1 million, 'which but for his active exertions would have been left in great danger at a most critical time, when the Spaniards were negotiating a peace with France' (Ralfe, 159). It was probably this very circumstance that made the government attentive to the Spanish complaint that money had been smuggled on board the *Trusty* on account of the merchants. Walker was accordingly tried by court martial for disobeying orders and dismissed the service. In March 1797, after war had broken out with Spain, he was reinstated, and soon appointed to a gunboat intended to act against the Nore mutineers; afterwards, as acting captain of the *Garland*, he convoyed the Baltic trade as far as Elsinore. On his return he was appointed, still as acting captain, to the *Monmouth*, which he commanded in the battle of Camperdown on 11 October. As they were bearing down on the enemy, Walker addressed the hands:

> My lads, you see your enemy; I shall lay you close aboard and give you an opportunity of washing the stain off your characters [alluding to the recent mutiny] in the blood of your foes. Now, go to your quarters and do your duty.
> (Ralfe, 160)

In the battle two of the Dutch ships surrendered to the *Monmouth*. On 17 October Walker's promotion as captain was confirmed. Temporary command of various ships in the North Sea followed, and in 1801 he commanded the *Isis* (50 guns) in the fleet sent to the Baltic, and was in Nelson's squadron at the battle of Copenhagen. In addition to a 14 gun battery, Walker engaged both his own intended target and that of Nelson, whose flagship, the *Elephant*, had run aground. When the *Elephant* was refloated and sailed past, Nelson took off his hat, waved it, and cried, 'Well done, brave Walker! Go on as you have begun; nothing can be better' (Marshall, *Royal Naval Biography*, 1/2, 1823, 161). After four and a half hours' fighting the two Danish block-ships were reduced to silence, but at the heavy cost of 33 killed and 88 wounded out of the *Isis*'s complement of 350.

Walker shortly afterwards took a convoy to the West Indies in the frigate *Tartar*. There he was appointed to the *Vanguard*, and on the renewal of the war took an active part in the blockade of San Domingo, in the capture of the French *Duquesne* on 25 July 1803, and in the capture of St Marc, taking off its garrison of 1100 men, who were on the verge of starvation, to save them from the vengeance of the local people. Walker returned to England in the *Duquesne* and was then appointed to the frigate *Thalia*, in which, after taking convoys to the East Indies and to Quebec, he commanded a squadron of three frigates on the Guernsey station.

In October 1807 he was appointed to the *Bedford*, one of the ships that went to Lisbon and to Rio de Janeiro with Sir William Sidney Smith. When the fleet dispersed in a gale, Walker's ship alone escorted the two Portuguese men-of-war carrying the Portuguese royal family for the thirteen-week voyage to Rio. For the next two years Walker remained at Rio, where he was admitted to the friendship of the prince regent of Portugal, who on 30 April 1816 conferred on him the order of the Tower and Sword, and, when Walker was recalled to England, presented him with his portrait set with diamonds and a valuable diamond ring. The *Bedford* was afterwards employed in the North Sea and in the channel, and in September 1814 went out to the Gulf of Mexico, where, during the absence of the flag officers at New Orleans, Walker was left as senior officer in command of the large ships. He was reportedly an officer of pleasing and cheerful disposition who won the respect of his crew by lenity and goodness, and was complimented by his admiral, Sir William Young, for once going five months and three weeks on the *Bedford* without a flogging while the ship remained in the highest state of discipline.

In the summer of 1814 Walker was selected to accompany the duke of Clarence to Boulogne to bring over the emperor of Russia and king of Prussia. On 4 June 1815 he was nominated a CB. After the peace he commanded the *Albion*, *Queen*, and *Northumberland*, which last was paid off on 10 September 1818, ending his long service afloat. He was promoted rear-admiral on 19 July 1821.

He was twice married: his first wife was a daughter of General Sir John Irvine; his second was the third daughter of Arnoldus Jones Skelton MP (first cousin of the Marquess

Cornwallis); they had three sons. Walker died after a few days' illness, on 13 July 1831, at Blatchington, near Seaford; he was survived by his second wife.

J. K. LAUGHTON, rev. MICHAEL DUFFY

Sources J. Marshall, *Royal naval biography*, 1/2 (1823), 848–53, 882–3 · J. Ralfe, *The naval biography of Great Britain*, 4 (1828), 155–72 · *GM*, 1st ser., 101/2 (1831), 270 · D. Syrett and R. L. DiNardo, *The commissioned sea officers of the Royal Navy, 1660–1815*, rev. edn, Occasional Publications of the Navy RS, 1 (1994)
Likenesses G. Noble and J. Parker, group portrait, line engraving, pubd 1803 (*Commemoration of 11th Oct 1797*; after *Naval victories* by J. Smart), BM, NPG

Walker, James (*bap.* 1770, *d.* 1841), Scottish Episcopal bishop of Edinburgh, the son of Alexander Walker, was baptized in Fraserburgh, Aberdeenshire, on 24 January 1770. He was tutored by Alexander Jolly (1756–1838), bishop of Moray, and later attended Marischal College, Aberdeen, and afterwards St John's College, Cambridge, graduating BA in 1793, MA in 1796, and DD in 1826. He returned to Scotland in 1793, where he was ordained deacon in the Scottish Episcopal church. Later he became a sub-editor of the third edition of the *Encyclopaedia Britannica*, edited by George Gleig (1753–1840), bishop of Brechin. About 1800 he became tutor to Sir John Hope bt, of Craighall, and for two or three years he travelled with him in Europe. While in Germany he sought the acquaintance of the foremost philosophers and men of letters, devoting particular attention to metaphysics. The article on Kant's system in the supplement to the *Encyclopaedia* was the result of his researches at Weimar.

In 1805 Walker was ordained priest by the bishop of Kildare, possibly to overcome the legal disqualification preventing those in Scottish orders holding a living in the Church of England. But in the same year he received the charge of St Peter's Chapel, Edinburgh, although he was always a scholar rather than a pastor; in 1808 he became dean of Edinburgh. On 30 November 1819, during a visit to Rome, he conducted the first regular Anglican service held in the city, for British residents. Eschewing proselytism, the service, using the English rather than the Scottish liturgy, was unofficially tolerated by Pope Pius VII.

In 1829 Walker resigned his charge of St Peter's to his colleague Charles Hughes Terrot (1790–1872): chronic rheumatism made his health uncertain and he wished to conserve his energies for his recent appointment as the first Pantonian professor at the Episcopal Theological College, an office which he retained until his death. In 1829 Walker published *Sermons on Various Occasions*; he was also the author of several single sermons, and translated Jean Joseph Mounier's treatise under the title *On the influence attributed to philosophers, freemasons, and to the illuminati on the revolution of France* (1810).

Walker was the most distinguished scholar of his day in the Episcopal church, and his wide theological knowledge gave him great influence across the Episcopal church and with the bishops. As a result he was elected bishop of Edinburgh by the clergy of Edinburgh, Glasgow, and Fife, and consecrated bishop at Stirling on 7 March 1830. As a native

of the north of Scotland, with Scottish and English education, the appointment further consolidated the unity
between northern and southern Episcopalians assisted by
the appointment of his predecessor, Daniel Sandford, an
Englishman. At the Episcopal synod in Aberdeen on 24
May 1837, on the resignation of George Gleig, Walker was
elected primus of the Scottish Episcopal church, though
his health made some of the burdens of office difficult. He
died at his home at 22 Stafford Street, Edinburgh, on 5
March 1841, and was buried in the cemetery of St John's
Episcopal Church, Princes Street, Edinburgh. He was married, and was survived by two daughters.

                        E. I. CARLYLE, *rev.* ROWAN STRONG

Sources G. Grub, *An ecclesiastical history of Scotland*, 4 vols. (1861) ·
J. P. Lawson, *History of the Scottish Episcopal church* (1843) · T. Stephen,
The history of the Church of Scotland, 4 vols. (1843–5) · W. Walker, *Life of
the Rt Rev Alexander Jolly* (1878) · Venn, *Alum. Cant.* · *Edinburgh Evening
Courant* (12 March 1841) · parish register (baptism), Fraserburgh,
Aberdeenshire, 24 Jan 1770
Archives NA Scot., corresp. and papers | NA Scot., Scottish Epis-
copal Church records · NRA Scotland, letters to Lady Hope
Likenesses T. Dick, mezzotint (after K. MacLeay), NPG · engraving, repro. in Stephen, *History of the Church of Scotland* (1845), vol. 4,
p. 518

Walker, James (1781–1862), civil engineer, was born on 28
October 1781 in his father's house at the corner of the Law
Wynd in Falkirk, the first of five children of James Walker,
farmer, merchant, and banker, and his wife, Margaret,
daughter of Robert Smith, a merchant linen draper of Falkirk. At the age of four he was sent to the parish English
school. In October 1794 he began a five-year course of studies at Glasgow University, the first two years devoted to
classics, the third to logic, and the final years to combined
natural philosophy and mathematics, in which he distinguished himself. In the summer of 1800, on a chance visit
to London, he stayed in Blackwall with his uncle Ralph
Walker, an engineer with a large practice in London, who
was then involved with the preliminary works of the West
India docks on the Isle of Dogs. Ralph discussed drawings
and specifications with Walker and was most impressed
with his nephew's abilities.

Thus began one of the most distinguished engineering
careers in nineteenth-century Britain. Walker was soon
articled to his uncle and his first appointment, in 1803,
was as engineer to the Commercial Road Trustees in east
London. In 1807 the Commercial Dock Company was
formed with Ralph Walker as engineer and James superintending the new lock and keeping the accounts. On his
uncle's death James became engineer to the Commercial
Dock Company and also succeeded him as engineer to the
East India Dock Company. During the 1820s and 1830s
Walker developed his career as a consulting engineer and
was elected a member of the Institution of Civil Engineers
in 1823. His connection with railways was brief but significant. In 1829 he was, with J. U. Rastrick, an adjudicator at
the Rainhill locomotive trials on the Liverpool and Manchester Railway. In the same year he reported on a railway
route from Leeds to Selby, and in 1834 was engaged to
extend the railway from Selby to Hull. Both lines were

constructed under his supervision. The Hull and Selby directors described Walker as 'at once prompt and decided,
and at the same time, prudent and cautious'. By then he
had begun his characteristic work on harbour design,
making reports on Great Yarmouth (1826) and Sunderland
(1832) among others. While living in the East India Dock
Road he married his childhood friend from Falkirk, Janet
Cook. They had three daughters followed by a son who
was stillborn.

On the death of Thomas Telford in 1834 Walker became
the second president of the Institution of Civil Engineers
and inherited much of the work that Telford had in progress at the time. Walker's practice developed and by 1830
he had taken Alfred Burges into partnership and soon
established an office at 23 Great George Street, Westminster. In 1853 he promoted one of his assistants, James
Cooper, to a partnership, the firm being then known as
Walker, Burges, and Cooper. Many of the next generation
of eminent civil engineers were trained in Walker's Westminster office. His consulting work comprised inland and
marine navigation works (canals, river improvements,
harbours, and lighthouses) and the design and maintenance of bridges. He was first consulted by Trinity House
about 1824 and he was associated with them until his
death. He was appointed initially as inspector-general of
the lights, with a retaining fee, and afterwards as consulting engineer. He designed and built all the important
lighthouses in the first half of the nineteenth century,
including Belle Toute, Start Point, St Catherine's, the
Needles, the Smalls, and Menai Strait, but his greatest
work was Bishop Rock lighthouse at the Isles of Scilly.
Walker's firm designed some twenty-nine towers for Trinity House.

Walker was consulted, and retained, as engineer to various harbour schemes by both the Admiralty and civil harbour commissioners. His improvement schemes included
those of Belfast, Whitehaven, Dover, Harwich, Leith,
Granton, the Tyne piers, Alderney, and the completion of
Plymouth breakwater. His canal schemes included design
work on the Tame valley Canal and the Netherton Tunnel
and major repair works to the Caledonian and Crinan
canals. Walker undertook extensive work in London—
tide surveys on the Thames and embankment schemes
including the coffer-dam and river wall of the houses of
parliament. He designed Vauxhall Bridge, the first iron
bridge over the Thames, opened in June 1816, and was
extensively involved in the maintenance of Westminster
and Blackfriars bridges. In addition, he was frequently
consulted about the drainage of the Middle Level on the
fens.

Walker said in his diary: 'I have never courted business
abroad partly from a dislike of sea voyages, & partly from
this obliging me to neglect business at home of which I
have always had as much as I could manage.' During his
eleven-year tenure of the presidency of the Institution of
Civil Engineers he was described as 'most active, persever-
ing, punctual and constant in his attendance, liberal in his
gifts, courteous in the chair … though somewhat wanting
in dignity' ('Institution of Civil Engineers: notes', 15).

However, his period as president ended in acrimony and led to the limiting of the presidential terms to three years. Walker's portrait, by P. J. Knight, hangs in the institution's building in Great George Street.

Walker was elected a fellow of the Royal Society, received the degree of doctor of laws from Glasgow University, and was elected a member of the senate of the University of London in 1858. He endowed prizes at both Glasgow University and the Institution of Civil Engineers. In 1861 he suffered a slight paralysis and in May 1862 he wrote to Trinity House saying that, owing to ill health, he wished to retire. He died on 8 October 1862 at 23 Great George Street, Westminster, but by his own wish was buried in the family vault in St John's episcopal burial-ground in Edinburgh.   DENIS SMITH

Sources PICE, 22 (1862–3), 630–33 · J. Walker, diary, Inst. CE · 'Institution of Civil Engineers: notes of the session, Tuesday 12 January 1841', Surveyor, Engineer, and Architect (1 Feb 1841), 15 · d. cert.
Archives Inst. CE, autobiography, diary, and notebook | BL, corresp. with Sir Robert Peel · Trinity House, London · U. Southampton L., letters to first duke of Wellington
Likenesses P. J. Knight, oils, Inst. CE
Wealth at death under £300,000: probate, 15 Nov 1862, CGPLA Eng. & Wales

Walker, Sir James (1809–1885), colonial governor, the son of Andrew Walker of Edinburgh, was born at Edinburgh on 9 April 1809, and educated at the high school and the university there. After entering the Colonial Office as a junior clerk in 1826 he served under several secretaries of state, and on 11 February 1837 he became registrar of British Honduras, from where he was transferred on 18 February 1839 to be treasurer of Trinidad; here he acted as colonial secretary from June 1839 to September 1840. On 15 October 1839 Walker married Anne, the daughter of George Bland of Trinidad. They had a son and three daughters.

In January 1841 Walker became secretary to Sir Henry Macleod, special commissioner to British Guiana, for the purpose of settling the difficulties with the legislature over the civil list. In 1842 he was appointed colonial secretary of Barbados. This colony was at that time the seat of the government for the Windward Islands, and during his service there Walker was sent in September 1856 to act as lieutenant-governor of Grenada and in 1857 to fill a similar position at St Vincent. He acted as governor of Barbados and the Windward Islands from 13 March to 25 December 1859, and as lieutenant-governor of Trinidad from 20 April 1860 to 25 March 1862, when he was appointed governor-in-chief of Barbados and the Windward Islands. A careful official rather than an able administrator, he became a CB in 1860 and KCMG in 1869. On 4 January 1869 he was transferred to the Bahamas, which were then going through a time of severe financial depression. He retired on a pension of £400 on 3 May 1871, and lived a quiet country life, first at Uplands, near Taunton, and later at Southerton, Ottery St Mary, Devon, where he died on 28 August 1885. Walker's son, Sir Edward Noel-Walker, was lieutenant-governor and colonial secretary of Ceylon.

C. A. HARRIS, rev. LYNN MILNE

Sources Colonial Office List · The Times (31 Aug 1885) · Boase, Mod. Eng. biog. · D. P. Henige, Colonial governors from the fifteenth century to the present (1970) · CGPLA Eng. & Wales (1885)
Wealth at death £10,244 4s. 1d.: probate, 29 Sept 1885, CGPLA Eng. & Wales

Walker, Sir James (1863–1935), chemist, was born on 6 April 1863 at Dundee, the only son of James Walker, a flax merchant in the town, and his wife, Susan Hutchison, daughter of Arthur Cairns, also of Dundee. Walker showed an interest in science at Dundee high school, but although he passed the entrance examination for St Andrews University at the age of sixteen, he became an apprentice to a flax and jute spinner for three years. He finally entered Edinburgh University in 1882, where his teachers included Alexander Crum Brown (1838–1922), who diverted Walker's interests towards chemistry. Graduating BSc in 1885, he carried out experimental work with Thomas Carnelley in University College, Dundee, during his vacations and graduated DSc (Edinburgh) in 1886. He then spent three years in Germany studying with Ludwig Claisen and Adolf Baeyer in Munich and with the influential Wilhelm Ostwald (1853–1932) at Leipzig. Having obtained his PhD at Leipzig in 1889 he carried his new-found enthusiasm for physical chemistry back to Edinburgh where he had been appointed research assistant to Crum Brown. He held this post for three years, his chief work being on electrolytic synthesis. In 1892 he joined the laboratory of William Ramsay in University College, London, at that time the leading centre for physical chemistry in the United Kingdom. In 1893 he became Ramsay's second assistant.

In 1894 Walker was elected professor of chemistry at University College, Dundee. He succeeded Crum Brown as professor of chemistry in Edinburgh in 1908. The First World War interfered with academic work, and Walker devoted himself instead to the manufacture of trinitrotoluene (TNT), then in great demand as a high explosive. In 1918 he returned to the manifold problems of the postwar period. He planned and saw built at Edinburgh one of the finest university chemical laboratories in the country, and established a research school there in order to provide the higher training for chemistry being demanded by the greatly expanded British chemical industry. He retired in 1928.

As Ostwald's first British pupil and disciple, Walker had the unenviable responsibility of being the chief English-speaking protagonist of the new physical chemistry of Ostwald, J. H. van't Hoff, and S. A. Arrhenius, which was largely based on the last's controversial ionic theory. He proved an able propagandist, chiefly through his translation in 1890 of Ostwald's textbook, *Grundriss der allgemeinen Chemie* (*Outlines of General Chemistry*), and most notably through his own readable textbook, *Introduction to Physical Chemistry* (1899), which went through ten editions and was a set book in many British university chemistry courses. His most important work in this field was the elaboration of methods of electrolysis in the synthesis of dicarboxylic acids, and in finding support for the ionic theory. He published researches on hydrolysis, the affinity

Sir James Walker (1863–1935), by Walter Stoneman, 1918

constants of weak acids and bases, investigated amphoteric electrolytes and reaction velocities, and determined molecular weights by freezing-point depressions.

Although Walker made no important discoveries, his experimental work and his influence as a teacher did much to win support for physical chemistry in Great Britain. His advice was widely sought on a great variety of matters and given with equal readiness. He was a fine musician and possessed a flair for languages; Ramsay once mistook him for a German, while as a young man he was in great demand as a Russian translator. He was a founder member of the Alembic Club of Edinburgh which became well known for sponsoring reprints of historical chemical papers. He received many honours, both for his academic and industrial activities, including a knighthood in 1921 for his war work. The honorary degree of LLD was conferred upon him by the universities of St Andrews (1909) and Edinburgh (1929). In 1900 he was elected a fellow of the Royal Society, by which he was awarded the Davy medal in 1926.

On 1 September 1897 Walker married Annie Purcell Sedgwick [**Annie Purcell Walker**, Lady Walker (1871–1950)], chemist, elder daughter of Lieutenant-Colonel William Sedgwick of Godalming. She was born in Cork on 4 December 1871 and educated at Girton College, Cambridge, where she gained second-class honours in the science tripos in 1893. She then joined Norman Collie as a research student at University College, London, where she met her husband. She published three papers on organic chemistry, but abandoned research after 1905. There was

one son, Frederick, who became a geologist. Walker died at 5 Wester Coates Road, Edinburgh, on 6 May 1935; his wife died in the same city on 7 September 1950.

H. W. MELVILLE, *rev.* W. H. BROCK

Sources J. Kendall, *Obits. FRS*, 1 (1932–5), 537–49 · J. Kendall, *JCS* (1935), 1347–54 [incl. Walker's autobiographical note] · J. Kendall, *Nature*, 135 (1935), 863–4 · *The Times* (8 May 1935), 16c · *The Times* (14 May 1935), 21a · *The Times* (18 May 1935), 9a · *The Times* (19 Nov 1935), 12e · *WWW* · J. Kendall, 'The Alembic Club', *Endeavour*, 13 (1954), 94–6 · E. L. Hirst, 'Schools of chemistry: the University of Edinburgh', *Journal of the Royal Institute of Chemistry*, 77 (1953), 505–11 · *CGPLA Eng. & Wales* (1935) · K. T. Butler and H. I. McMorran, eds., *Girton College register, 1869–1946* (1948)

Likenesses W. Stoneman, photograph, 1918, NPG [*see illus.*] · black and white photograph, RS, portrait collection · photograph, RS, portrait collection · photograph

Wealth at death £34,000: *The Times* (27 June 1935), 12e

Walker, James (1883–1945), trade unionist and politician, was born at 817 Great Eastern Road, Parkhead, Glasgow, on 12 May 1883, the son of John Walker, a steel smelter, and his wife, Jane (Jeanie), *née* Harwood. He was educated at Parkhead public school, worked on a farm, and then became a steel smelter's apprentice. Having served his time he joined the British Steel Smelters' Association in November 1904. Two years later he won a union scholarship to Ruskin College, Oxford; having in 1907 successfully completed his course he became a steel smelters' organizer and was based largely in Glasgow. On 5 January 1910 he married Ada (*b.* 1886/7), daughter of John Chivers of Oxford; she was a sewing machinist. They had a daughter (who predeceased him) and a son (who became a solicitor specializing in trade union issues).

In 1917, when the British Steel Smelters' Association federated with other unions to form the Iron and Steel Trades Confederation (ISTC), Walker became the confederation's Scottish divisional officer. This rapid rise within his union was accompanied by political activities. As a teenager he was attracted to secularist and socialist movements, and in 1902 he enrolled in the Glasgow Social Democratic Federation's class on Marxist economics. In 1904 he became a member of the Independent Labour Party, and from 1912 to 1929 he sat on the Glasgow city council. With the restructuring of steel trade unionism in 1917, the affiliate to the Labour Party became the British Iron, Steel, and Kindred Trades Association. Sponsored by his union, he unsuccessfully contested Rotherham in the general elections of 1918 and 1922; he was successful at Newport, Monmouthshire, in 1929.

Walker was very prominent in the Scottish Trades Union Congress (STUC) throughout the 1920s. He sat on its parliamentary committee, subsequently reformed as the general council, and was its president in 1921. His post-war industrial concerns highlighted the problems and practices of his own union. A collapse in steel prices, which precipitated a decline in employment and pressures on wage standards, caused him to question a strict adherence to free-trade principles. The centralized structures of steel trade unionism reflected leaders' distaste for rank and file initiatives. Walker, like his colleagues, was a vigorous opponent of the Communist Party, and indeed of any critic who seemed to threaten the solidarity of the labour movement. The ISTC was notable for promoting consensual industrial relations policies; politically Walker's union stood firmly on the right of the labour movement.

Loss of his parliamentary seat in 1931 did not indicate any decline in Walker's political significance. He was elected to the trade union section of the Labour Party's national executive committee (NEC) in 1932 and played a significant part in the formulation of the party's proposals for the public ownership of the iron and steel industry. These were incorporated into the policy document *For Socialism and Peace* (1934). He returned to parliament in November 1935, appropriately as member for the Scottish steel making centre of Motherwell. In the Parliamentary Labour Party (PLP) and on the NEC, he took a firm line in favour of rearmament. He worked closely with Hugh Dalton and made a typically vigorous contribution to the PLP discussions in July 1937 that resulted in the abandonment of opposition to the defence estimates. His value to the party leadership was indicated and strengthened by his membership of the NEC's international sub-committee from 1937. He remained a strict disciplinarian, opposed to overtures from communists and hostile to calls for a popular front.

Walker's eyesight deteriorated badly in the late thirties and he intended to retire from parliament at the next election. The outbreak of war meant that this was delayed and he continued to make trenchant contributions on the NEC and within the PLP. His poor eyesight meant that as party chairman he could not preside over the 1941 Labour Party conference, but he nevertheless gave the opening address. This rejected any distinction between Nazis and other Germans. All were responsible for government policies and only a thorough reform of German values could make Europe safe for political and social democracy (*Labour Party Conference Report*, 1941, 110–11). Despite opposition from many, such views—close to those of Lord Vansittart—became more influential within the Labour Party. They were promoted by Dalton, by some trade union leaders, and by the party's international secretary, William Gillies. One consequence was an estrangement between the Labour Party and many exiled German Social Democrats. Walker was very active in mobilizing support for this line. Apart from his interventions within the party, he set up the Fight for Freedom Editorial and Publishing Service, which produced a stream of books and pamphlets arguing that the Third Reich was the predictable outcome of German history.

Walker's wartime denunciations of Germans were combined with the dismissal of those who disagreed with him. 'Credulous fool' and 'overweening vanity' were two of his typical characterizations (*War Diary of Hugh Dalton*, 732, citing Walker's letter to Dalton, 17 April 1944). For his political allies Walker's robust interventions combined common sense and remorseless logic pitted against loose thinking and sentimentality. Dalton referred approvingly to his 'intellectual mallet' (ibid., 73, 14 Aug 1940). Walker died on 5 January 1945 at Royal Sussex County Hospital, Brighton, of injuries sustained after being knocked down by a lorry, which he was too blind to see, when crossing Marine Drive, Saltdean, near his home. He was cremated on 10 January at Golders Green.   DAVID HOWELL

Sources A. Pugh, *Men of steel* (1951) · W. Knox, ed., *Scottish labour leaders, 1918–39: a biographical dictionary* (1984) · A. Glees, *Exile politics during the Second World War: the German social democrats in Britain* (1982) · I. Tombs, 'The victory of socialist "Vansittartism": labour and the German question, 1941–1945', *Twentieth Century British History*, 7/3 (1996), 287–309 · H. Dalton, *The fateful years: memoirs, 1931–1945* (1957) · *The Second World War diary of Hugh Dalton, 1940–1945*, ed. B. Pimlott (1986) · b. cert. · m. cert. · d. cert. · WWW · *Biographical dictionary of British members of parliament*

Archives BLPES, Dalton MSS · Labour History Archive and Study Centre, Manchester, labour party national executive committee minutes · NL Scot., Scottish trades union congress material · University of Warwick, Iron and Steel Trades Confederation archive

Wealth at death £6084 2s. 1d.: administration, 21 June 1945, CGPLA Eng. & Wales

Walker, James Robertson- (1783–1858), naval officer, was born on 22 June 1783, the eldest son of James Robertson, deputy lieutenant of Ross-shire, and for many years collector of the customs at the port of Stornoway. His mother was Annabella, daughter of John Mackenzie of Ross. He probably served a few years in merchant ships; he entered the navy in April 1801 as able seaman on board the sloop *Inspector* at Leith, but was moved into the frigate *Princess Charlotte*, in which, as midshipman and master's mate, he served for two years on the Irish station. In May 1803 he joined the *Canopus*, flagship of Rear-Admiral George Campbell off Toulon in 1804. From her in March 1805 he was moved to the *Victory*, in which he was present at Trafalgar. When she was paid off in January 1806, Robertson was sent, at the request of Captain Hardy, to the frigate *Thames*, in which he went to the West Indies; there in April 1807 he was moved to the *Northumberland*, flagship of Sir Alexander Forrester Inglis Cochrane, with whom in December he went to the *Belle Isle*. In April 1808 he was appointed acting lieutenant of the *Fawn*, in which, and afterwards in the sloop *Hazard*, he was repeatedly engaged in boat actions with the batteries round the coast of Guadeloupe. On 21 July 1809 his rank of lieutenant was confirmed. He continued in the *Hazard* until October 1812, and was repeatedly engaged with the enemy's batteries, either in the boats or in the ship herself. Several times he won the approval of the admiral, but it did not take the form of promotion; and in October 1812 he was appointed to the *Antelope*, flagship of Sir John Thomas Duckworth. In her in 1813 he was in the Baltic, and in November was moved to the *Vigo*, the flagship of Rear-Admiral Graham Moore. A few weeks later the *Vigo* was ordered to be paid off, and in February 1814 Robertson was sent out to North America for service on the lakes.

In September Robertson joined the *Confiance* (37 guns), a ship newly launched on Lake Champlain, and being fitted out by Captain George Downie. The British army of 11,000 men, under the command of Sir George Prevost (1767–1816), had advanced against Plattsburg on the Saranac, then held by an American force estimated at 2000 men, but supported by a strong and heavily armed flotilla. Prevost sent repeated messages urging Downie to co-operate with him in the capture of this place, and in language which, coming from an officer of Prevost's rank, admitted of no delay. The *Confiance* was not ready for service, her guns not fitted, her men made up of drafts of bad characters from the fleet, and only just got together when she weighed anchor on 11 September and, in company with three smaller vessels and ten gunboats, crossed over to Plattsburg Bay. The American squadron was of nearly double the force; but Downie, relying on the promised co-operation of Prevost, closed with the enemy and engaged. But Prevost did not move; the gunboats shamefully ran away; one of the small vessels struck on a reef; Downie was killed; and Robertson, left in command, was obliged to surrender after the *Confiance* had lost 41 killed and 83 wounded, out of 270, and was sinking. Sir James Lucas Yeo, the naval commander-in-chief, preferred charges of gross misconduct against Prevost, who, however, died before he could be brought to trial. At the peace Robertson returned to England, was tried for the loss of the *Confiance*, and honourably acquitted. The next day, 29 August 1815, he was promoted commander. He had no further service; on 28 July 1851 he was promoted captain on the retired list.

On 24 June 1824 he married Ann, only daughter and heir of William Walker of Gilgarran, near Whitehaven, Cumberland, and thereupon assumed the additional surname of Walker. He married, secondly, Catherine (*d.* 1892), daughter of John Mackenzie of Ross. He died at Gilgarran on 26 October 1858, leaving a widow but no children.

J. K. LAUGHTON, rev. ANDREW LAMBERT

Sources T. Roosevelt, *The naval war of 1812* (1882) · J. M. Hitsman, *The incredible war of 1812* (1965) · O'Byrne, *Naval biog. dict.* · *CGPLA Eng. & Wales* (1859)
Wealth at death under £4000: probate, 29 April 1859, *CGPLA Eng. & Wales*

Walker, James Thomas (1826–1896), army officer and surveyor, eldest son of John Walker of the Madras civil service, sometime judge at Cannanore, and his wife, Margaret Allan (*d.* 1830) of Edinburgh, was born at Cannanore, India, on 1 December 1826. He was educated by a private tutor in Wales, and at Addiscombe in 1843–4, before being commissioned second lieutenant in the Bombay Engineers on 9 December 1844. After training at Chatham, he went to India, arriving at Bombay on 10 May 1846. The following year he went to Sind as executive engineer at Sukkur.

From 1848 to 1853 Walker served in a succession of frontier campaigns. He was several times mentioned in dispatches, but his active service was incidental to his surveying, which he vigorously prosecuted. It was dangerous work, and in the country between the Khyber and Kohat passes he was fired at on several occasions. He reconnoitred the approaches to the Ambela Pass, which ten years later was the scene of protracted fighting between British and local forces. On the completion of the military survey of the Peshawar frontier, he received the thanks of the government of India. He was promoted lieutenant on

2 July 1853, and, in recognition of his survey services on the frontier, was appointed on 1 December second assistant on the great trigonometrical survey of India under Sir Andrew Scott Waugh. He was promoted first assistant on 24 March 1854, and on 27 April married (in India) Alicia Mary (*d.* in or after 1896), daughter of General Sir John Scott KCB, and Alicia, granddaughter of Dr William Markham, archbishop of York. He worked first on the measurement of the Chach base, near Attock, and then had charge of the northern section of the Indus series of triangulation connecting the Chach and the Karachi bases. From 1852 to 1856 he taught at the newly opened Thomason Engineering College at Roorkee.

On the outbreak of the Indian mutiny in 1857, Walker was once more involved in fighting. Acting with conspicuous courage at Delhi, he was severely wounded by a bullet in the left thigh, and shortly afterwards narrowly escaped death from cholera. He was promoted captain on 4 December 1857, and for his services in the mutiny received the medal, with clasp for Delhi, and the brevet rank of major on 19 January 1858. He returned to his survey duties and resumed work on the Indus series, which was completed in 1860; and he was afterwards employed in the Jogi Tila meridional series. In 1860 he served under Sir Neville Chamberlain in the expedition against the Mahsud Wazirs, for which he received the medal and clasp. Here again he made every effort to extend the survey, and sent a map which he had made of the country to the surveyor-general.

In September 1860 Walker was appointed astronomical assistant, and on 12 March 1861 superintendent, of the great trigonometrical survey of India. In the next two years the three last meridional series in the north of India were completed, and Walker's first independent work was the measurement of the Vizagapatam baseline, which was completed in 1862. The accuracy achieved was such that the difference between the measured length and the length computed from triangles, starting 480 miles away at the Calcutta baseline and passing through dense jungles, was only half an inch. By 1863 the main triangulation of India was brought back to its starting point at Madras, and Walker thus oversaw the completion of the work of Lambton, Everest, and Waugh. He next undertook a revision of Lambton's triangulation in the south of India, with remeasurements of the baselines.

On 27 February 1864 Walker was promoted lieutenant-colonel, and went home on furlough by way of Russia, establishing friendly relations with the geodesists of the Russian survey, which led to the exchange of geodetic and geographical information with St Petersburg. In 1864 he proposed a series of gravity pendulum observations, which were intended to contribute to the survey's aim of furnishing data for determining the figure of the earth. From 1865 to 1871 observations were made, but the method was subsequently proved unreliable.

On 27 February 1869 Walker was promoted brevet colonel, and about this time it was decided to publish an *Account of the Operations of the Great Trigonometrical Survey of*

India, in twenty volumes. The first nine were published under Walker's supervision, beginning in 1871. The volumes describe the course and technical character of the survey and remain the standard authority on one of the most remarkable and extensive surveys ever undertaken. In 1871–2, when in England on leave from India, Walker (with Sir Oliver Beauchamp Coventry St John) fixed the difference of longitude between Tehran and London. He remained in England to investigate the condition of the plates of the Indian atlas, and to write a memorandum on the projection and scale of the atlas. In 1873 he turned his attention to the dispersion of unavoidable minute errors in the triangulation, to ensure high standards of accuracy in the trigonometrical survey.

Walker's work as superintendent of the great trigonometrical survey was as much that of a geographer as of a geodesist. At his office at Dehra Dun explorers were trained, survey parties for military expeditions organized, and Indian surveyors dispatched to make discoveries, while their observations were reduced and combined. Many valuable maps were published, and Walker's map of Turkestan, compiled using information from his Russian colleagues, went through many editions. He also initiated a scheme of tidal observations at different ports on the Indian coast and devised the method of analysing the observations. Beginning in 1858 he arranged an extensive scheme of spirit-levelling, connecting the tidal observation stations by lines of levels (sometimes extending across the continent), in order to fix the exact heights above sea level of the survey baselines. The network proved of great value to canal and railway engineers who used it to provide datum points for their surveys.

On 2 June 1877 Walker was made a companion of the Bath, military division. He was appointed surveyor-general of India on 1 January 1878, retaining the office of superintendent of the trigonometrical survey. On 31 December of the same year he was promoted major-general, and on 10 May 1881 lieutenant general. He retired on 12 February 1883, and received the honorary rank of general on 12 January 1884, but his services in India received no official recognition.

Walker, like his cousin Clements Markham (with whom he had corresponded professionally while the latter was geographer at the India Office), was keenly interested in geography. He was elected fellow of the Royal Geographical Society in 1859, and from 1885 to 1896 served on its council. In 1885 he was president of the geographical section of the British Association at Aberdeen. He was elected fellow of the Royal Society in 1865, was made a member of the Russian geographical society in 1868, and of the French in 1887. In June 1883 he was made an honorary LLD of Cambridge University. In 1895 he took charge of the geodetic work of the international geographical congress at the Imperial Institute in London. He contributed to the ninth edition of the *Encyclopaedia Britannica*, and to the *Journal of the Asiatic Society of Bengal*, the *Transactions of the Royal Society*, and the Royal Geographical Society's *Journal*. Walker died at his home, 13 Cromwell Road, London, on 16

February 1896, and was buried on 20 February in Brompton cemetery. His wife, a son, Herbert John (lieutenant in the Royal Engineers), and three daughters survived him.

R. H. Vetch, *rev.* Elizabeth Baigent

Sources *The Times* (18 Feb 1896) · *The Times* (21 Feb 1896) · C. R. M., *PRS*, 59 (1895–6), xliii–xlvi · *GJ*, 7 (1896), 320–23 · E. W. C. Sandes, *The military engineer in India*, 2 vols. (1933–5) · H. M. Vibart, *Addiscombe: its heroes and men of note* (1894) · private information (1899) · *Nature*, 53 (1895–6), 469–70 · *Scottish Geographical Magazine*, 13 (1897), 23–4 · C. E. D. Black, *A memoir on the Indian surveys, 1875–1890* (1891) · C. R. Markham, *A memoir on the Indian surveys*, 2nd edn (1878) · *CGPLA Eng. & Wales* (1896)
Archives RGS, corresp. and papers relating to India and Afghanistan | CUL, letters to Sir George Stokes
Likenesses portrait, repro. in Sandes, *Military engineer in India*, vol. 2, pl. facing p. 206
Wealth at death £9046 3s. 11d.: probate, 26 May 1896, *CGPLA Eng. & Wales*

Walker, Jane Harriett (1859–1938), physician and specialist in the open-air treatment of tuberculosis, was born on 24 October 1859 at Canal Cottage, Dewsbury, Yorkshire. She was the eldest daughter, one of eight children, three boys and five girls, of John Walker (1834–1900), then a wool merchant, later a prosperous local blanket manufacturer, and his wife, Dorothy Ann, *née* Clay (1834–1884) also of Dewsbury. Little is known about Walker's early years, except that she was educated at a school in Southport and at the Yorkshire College of Science (established 1874). Defying the conventions of the day, but with the encouragement of her father, she decided upon a career as a doctor and in 1879 enrolled as a student at the London School of Medicine for Women (established in 1877). As only London matriculates could take the English qualification, she qualified LRCP (Ire.) in 1884, LRCS (Edin.) in 1888, and MD (Brussels) in 1890.

Early on in her medical career Walker, who never married, established a private practice at her home in Harley Street, London, and she also held a number of posts which reflected her deep interest in the treatment of women and children. The course of her career changed dramatically in 1892 when a young friend fell victim to tuberculosis. The tubercle bacillus, causal agent of the disease, had been discovered in 1882 by the German bacteriologist Robert Koch, though there was as yet no effective treatment for this highly infectious disease. While many doctors in Britain advocated that sufferers be kept in a warm stuffy atmosphere, there were those elsewhere who believed that fresh air was an important factor in effecting a cure. Seeking further knowledge Jane Walker visited the sanatorium opened by Otto Walther in 1888 at Nordrach, Germany, to study his use of the open-air method of treating tubercular patients. So convinced was she by its merits that she returned to England determined to introduce a similar programme into the country.

Walker's pioneering work, for which she was to gain wide acclaim, began modestly in a farmhouse in Downham Market, Norfolk, with beds for six patients. Encouraged by the success of this experiment, and with the financial backing of family and friends, she was able to expand, and in 1901 the East Anglian Sanatorium opened at Nayland, Suffolk. Here she adopted the best of the latest ideas on the treatment of tuberculosis, including putting patients to sleep in the open air. This practice led a mischievous nephew to joke that if tuberculosis did not kill Jane's patients, then pneumonia probably would. In everything at Nayland, Dr Walker's word was law, and a member of her staff there recalled that she professed to being 'a socialist in politics, but her own methods were those of a benevolent dictator' (private information).

Initially the sanatorium took only paying patients, but in 1904 a department for poorer patients, the Maltings Farm Sanatorium, opened, and eventually all those treated were referred by county and municipal authorities. Further developments included the East Anglian Children's Sanatorium, which in the course of twenty-five years treated some 2700 children. Of great significance was the ethos of the sanatorium, which encouraged a community rather than a hospital spirit, largely due to Dr Walker's pioneering use of occupational therapy. Patients were employed in gardening, clerical work, baking, toy making, and jewellery repair and manufacture, while others received training in industrial and agricultural work to enable them to lead useful lives. Many ex-patients worked as members of the staff. Not surprisingly, Walker's centre became a model for similar institutions both at home and abroad.

It is a testimony to her vitality and strength of character that Walker managed to involve herself in innumerable activities outside of Nayland and her Harley Street practice. She was a founder member (1917) and first president of the Medical Women's Federation, established to represent the views of medical women, and was one of the first women on the Royal Society of Medicine Council. A co-founder of Godstowe, the first preparatory school for girls, she maintained a long-term involvement with this establishment, and also sat as a magistrate in Suffolk. Her extensive literary contributions and her innumerable committee appointments reflected the variety of her major interests outside of tuberculosis: these included infant mortality, agricultural wages, maternal education, inebriety, the illnesses of women and children, Dr Barnado's, the work of borstal institutions, nutrition, housing problems, and the improvement of social and economic conditions. Beyond this she was a gifted and persuasive speaker. Her outstanding achievements were honoured in 1931 when she was made a Companion of Honour, and was awarded an honorary doctorate from Leeds University.

Some of her family regarded Jane Walker as a bossy, eccentric woman, but others found her to be friendly, kind, and helpful. She certainly cut a somewhat unconventional figure, being short, of stocky build, with a round face, ruddy complexion, and heavy eyebrows. Her outspoken nature often brought her into conflict with others—she had a quick temper, but was broad-minded, shrewd, determined, and a firm supporter of women's rights. Renowned for her hospitality, guests at her dinner parties were wined and dined in style, and entertained by her knowledgeable discussions on religion, to which she

was deeply committed, as well as music, art, and politics. Walker died of a coronary thrombosis at her London home, 122 Harley Street, on 17 November 1938, and was buried two days later in the churchyard at Wiston, Suffolk.   SUSAN L. COHEN

Sources L. Bryder, *Below the magic mountain: a social history of tuberculosis in twentieth century Britain* (1988) · C. Stewart, 'History of the federation: the origin of the Medical Women's Federation', *Journal of the Medical Women's Federation*, 49 (April 1967), 71–2 · *Medical Women's Federation Quarterly* (Jan 1939), 17–253 · *The Lancet* (26 Nov 1938), 1259–60 · R. Dubos and J. Dubos, *The white plague: tuberculosis, man and society* (1953) · *WWW*, 1929–40, 1402 · corresp. and MSS, East Anglian Sanatorium Co. Ltd, Suffolk RO, Bury St Edmunds · M. Vogeler, 'People Gissing knew: Dr Jane Walker', *Gissing Journal*, 39/2 (April 1993), 1–10 · *Dewsbury District News* (30 June 1900) · Medical Women's Federation archive, Wellcome L. · private information (2004) [colleague; bursar, Godstowe preparatory school, High Wycombe, Buckinghamshire; librarian, U. Leeds archive] · b. cert. · d. cert. · register of students, Royal Free Hospital Archives · *The Times* (21 Nov 1938), 15

Archives Suffolk RO, Bury St Edmunds, corresp. and MSS, East Anglian Sanatorium Co. Ltd · Wellcome L., Medical Women's Federation archive, press cuttings, and issues of the magazine of the School of Medicine for Women, Royal Free Hospital, London · Wellcome L., Medical Women's Federation archive

Likenesses W. de Glehn, oils, 1921, Royal Society of Medicine, London · photographs, Wellcome L., Medical Women's Federation Collection archive

Wealth at death £12,386 16s. 1d.: resworn probate, 1938, *CGPLA Eng. & Wales*

Walker, John (*d.* 1588), Church of England clergyman, is of obscure origins. Having graduated BA at Peterhouse, Cambridge, early in 1548 and proceeded MA in 1551, he was a fellow of Peterhouse from 1550 to 1555. His activities during the Marian years are unknown. Following Elizabeth's accession he became a preacher in Ipswich, his sermons winning a reputation for him throughout Suffolk. He was appointed one of the twelve university preachers in 1562, served as proctor for the Suffolk clergy in the convocation of 1563, and in 1564 was made a parish chaplain of St Peter's, Norwich. He was granted the degree of BTh in 1562 and became DTh in 1568. He voted with the reformers in convocation in February 1563 in favour of altering or abolishing some of the rites and ceremonies of the church, notably making the sign of the cross in baptism and kneeling at communion.

Walker's abilities and reputation brought him preferment. He became rector of Little Wilbraham, Cambridgeshire, in 1567 but was deprived, probably for non-residency, on 15 August 1570. He was also rector of Alderton, Suffolk, from 1568 to 1571; but appears to have been most active in Norwich where his sermons continued to be much admired. Presented by the lord keeper, Sir Nicholas Bacon, to the third prebend in Norwich Cathedral on 25 January 1570, his appointment, together with that of Edmund Chapman, Robert Johnson, and Jeffrey Johnson, helped to bring the reformers within the cathedral chapter into a majority. This position of strength, combined with a distaste for the unreformed nature of the cathedral services, appears to have goaded Walker and others into action. Precisely what happened is unclear, but a hostile report sent to the queen complained of innovations attempted and specifically that four of the prebendaries (Walker, George Gardiner, Thomas Fowle, and Chapman) with others had broken up the organs and committed 'other outrages'. Elizabeth sent a stinging letter on 25 September 1570 to the bishop of Norwich, John Parkhurst, insisting that the offenders be discovered and sent to Archbishop Parker for punishment. It seems doubtful that any disciplinary action was actually taken, for on 10 October 1570 the queen conveyed her continuing anger, through a letter from Leicester to Parker, that the matter had been 'so far excused' by him. It was grudgingly accepted that the prebendaries were seeking to rid the cathedral of 'popish ceremonies', but their claim that they acted with the dean's consent was disputed (*Pepys MSS*, 174–6).

The Norwich affair brought no loss for Walker: he was collated to the archdeaconry of Essex on 10 July 1571 by Edwin Sandys, bishop of London. He did not hasten to take up his new appointment as he was still in Norwich in August, giving advice on the dispute between the city's governors and the ministers of the Dutch church, and in 1572 his name was included in a proposed ecclesiastical commission for the diocese which never seems to have materialized. He seldom adjudicated on cases in court, remaining active instead as an itinerant preacher. His preface to Robert Norton's translation of Rodolph Gualter's sermons entitled *Certaine godlie homelies or sermons upon the prophets Abdias and Jonas: conteyning a most fruitefull exposition of the same* (1573) was dedicated to William Blennerhasset of Norfolk and sheds light on the godly circles with which Walker associated in Norfolk and Suffolk. Further preferment followed his appointment as archdeacon. He became rector of the parish of Laindon, Essex, on 12 November 1573, and of St Botolph, Billingsgate, in 1574. He resigned his prebend in Norwich when collated prebendary of Mora in St Paul's Cathedral on 14 August 1575, and the archdeaconry about August 1585; but he held his other livings until his death in 1588.

Although Walker's life is ill-documented, his career mirrors that of other protestants of his generation—those early evangelicals who urged further reform in Elizabeth's early years but were prepared as time passed to live with the anomalies of the Elizabethan settlement. Once ensconced within the London diocesan hierarchy Walker made himself useful both to Sandys and to his successor John Aylmer. In October 1573 it was reported (possibly wrongly) that Edward Dering's lecture in St Paul's Cathedral 'is bestowed upon Mr Dr Walker' (Smith, 1.90). In 1578 with the plague spreading, he was named with others to appoint from the London clergy sixty visitors of the sick. He was actively involved in the disciplinary proceedings against Robert, third Lord Rich, and his puritan chaplains in 1581, and on 27 September that year assisted William Charke in a fourth day of conference with Edmund Campion in the Tower. Aylmer employed him on a team to collect material to answer Campion's *Decem rationes* and he was appointed in 1582 to confer with captured Catholic priests. He appears to have been most active in the chapter of St Paul's, whether estimating the costs of Sir Nicholas Bacon's funeral or preaching at Aylmer's visitation of the cathedral in 1583, and he worked closely with Dean Alexander Nowell and fellow prebendaries like John Mullins, archdeacon of London. On 8 May 1583 he witnessed Archbishop Grindal's will.

Walker drew up his own will on 14 September 1588, as 'residentiary' of St Paul's. He requested burial among other Christians 'in simple manner without any pompe or vanitie' (PRO, PROB 11/72, fol. 429v). His 'faithfull and lovinge' wife, Anne (probably *née* Thackham), pregnant at the time, was made his sole executor. She became his widow within the week as the will was granted probate on 21 September 1588.

JOHN CRAIG

Sources J. P. Anglin, 'The court of the archdeacon of Essex, 1571–1609: an institutional and social study', PhD diss., U. Cal., Los Angeles, 1965 • BL, Lansdowne MS 443, fol. 180v • BL, Add. MS 5843, fol. 131 • Cooper, *Ath. Cantab.*, vol. 2 • J. H. Crosby, ed., 'Ely episcopal registers, 1337–1587', *Ely Diocesan Remembrancer* (1889–1914) • *Report on the Pepys manuscripts*, HMC, 70 (1911), 174–6 • *The letter book of John Parkhurst, bishop of Norwich*, ed. R. A. Houlbrooke, Norfolk RS, 43 (1974–5) • R. Gualter, *Certaine godlie homelies or sermons upon the prophets Abdias and Jonas*, trans. R. Norton (1573) • R. Houlbrooke, 'Refoundation and Reformation, 1538–1628', *Norwich Cathedral: church, city and diocese, 1096–1996*, ed. I. Atherton and others (1996), 507–39 • A. Nowell and W. Day, *A true report of the disputation or rather private conference had in the Tower of London with Ed. Campion Jesuite, the last of August 1581 set downe by the reverend learned men themselves that dealt therein* (1583) • state papers domestic, Elizabeth I, PRO, SP 12/73, fol. 171 • *The papers of Nathaniel Bacon of Stiffkey*, ed. A. H. Smith, G. M. Baker, and R. W. Kenny, 1–2, Norfolk RS, 46, 49 (1979–83) • J. Strype, *Annals of the Reformation and establishment of religion … during Queen Elizabeth's happy reign*, new edn, 4 vols. (1824) • J. Strype, *The history of the life and acts of the most reverend father in God Edmund Grindal*, new edn (1821) • J. Strype, *The life and acts of Matthew Parker*, new edn, 3 vols. (1821) • Venn, *Alum. Cant.*, 1/4.317 • will, PRO, PROB 11/72, sig. 55

Walker, John (*c.*1550–1626), cartographer, was born probably in West Hanningfield, Essex, one of three sons of John Walker (*c.*1516–1589), and his wife, Eleanor (*c.*1525–1589). The family had occupied the copyhold farm of Kents in West Hanningfield from about 1503 or soon after, his father being a yeoman and carpenter, an occupation in Essex that signified a builder of timber-framed houses. His younger brother Cyprian (*d.* 1631) continued in his father's trade and John Walker himself seems to have derived his early livelihood from building houses, and as late as 1584 to 1597 he was styling himself 'architector'. His marriage has not been traced, but he and his wife, Lucy (*c.*1555–1627), had three children, all baptized at West Hanningfield: Joan in 1574, John in 1577, and Jane in 1579. Walker's early familiarity with the skills of measuring led him to the new practice of surveying landed estates and into an emerging profession otherwise dominated by minor or professional gentry. His earliest extant work was on the manor of West Tilbury for Andrew Jenour in 1584. It is the third oldest surviving scaled map of an Essex estate, remarkable for its thoughtful layout, attention to detail, and careful drawings of buildings, all of which were to be hallmarks of the maps of Walker and, later, his son. It was clearly not the work of a novice but the source of his training as a surveyor and draughtsman is unknown. Although Ralph Agas might have been his tutor, it is more likely to have been Israel Amyce of Wakes Colne (Edwards and Newton, 24). Walker's first surveys of West Tilbury in 1584 and Boxted in 1586 are reminiscent of Amyce's style and much of his early work was for clients or in places plausibly connected with Amyce. In 1589, when he was residing at Ballingdon-cum-Brundon on the Suffolk–Essex boundary, he surveyed Earls Colne, where Amyce lived, and their names occur together as contributors to the Armada loan collected at the spring assizes in Chelmsford; Walker contributed the surprisingly large sum of £25.

Walker's introduction to the county gentry led to commissions to survey the mid-Essex estates of Sir Thomas Mildmay in 1591, Edward Neville, Baron Bergavenny in 1592, Sir John Tyrell in 1597, and Sir John Petre in 1598. In the maps produced for them he established his reputation for accuracy in fieldwork and a distinctive style of draughtsmanship with fresh colouring and clear handwriting, notably in maps of Chelmsford and Horndon. Further work followed for these and other clients, from 1599 mostly in a partnership with his son in which he directed the fieldwork and his son drew the maps. Although clearly based in mid-Essex throughout this period he occurs irregularly at West Hanningfield until after 1609, when he was elected bailiff of the manor in 1612, 1615, and 1616. He apparently trained Samuel Walker, son of his brother Cyprian Walker, who continued map making in a debased style until 1645, but he himself gave up all surveying after his son's death in 1618. He was buried at West Hanningfield on 8 June 1626.

John Walker (*bap.* 1577, *d.* 1618), cartographer, was baptized at West Hanningfield on 24 June 1577. He and his father produced twelve maps together between 1599 and 1616. Careful analysis of their similar calligraphy has shown that John Walker junior, who had the better hand, was the draughtsman of all their joint maps after 1601. His ability may partly explain a widening demand for their surveys. These included Mascalls Bury in White Roding for Sir John Poyntz in 1609, which was John Walker junior's first commission by himself. In 1614 he undertook the family's only survey outside Essex, albeit for an Essex landowner, Sir Edward Barrett. This was a fine map of the manor of Foxcote in Hampshire. For a new client perhaps unused to interpreting a large-scale map he adopted his father's earlier practice of explaining its purpose 'to be as it were a Lanthorne and light for the Lord or Owner of the landes … for the readier and easier finding out of any thing in the sayde Survey that they doe desier' (Edwards and Newton, 64).

In 1611 John Walker married Penelope Warner of South Hanningfield and they lived in West Hanningfield for their short and childless marriage. Two crudely drawn maps in 1616 betray a sudden decline; he was buried at West Hanningfield on 9 April 1618. The two John Walkers were accomplished map makers in a formative period of English cartography. Twenty-nine of their maps and surveys have survived, the great majority in Essex Record Office.   BRIAN S. SMITH

Sources A. C. Edwards and K. C. Newton, *The Walkers of Hanningfield: surveyors and mapmakers extraordinary* (1984) • B. S. Smith, 'Notes on the Walkers of West Hanningfield', 1960, Essex RO, Chelmsford, T/Z 382 • A. S. Mason, 'An upstart art: early mapping in Essex', 1996, Essex RO, Chelmsford, T/Z 438/2/1 [also in BL] • F. G. Emmison, ed., *Catalogue of maps in the Essex Record Office, 1566–1855* (1947) • F. G. Emmison, ed., *Catalogue of maps in the Essex Record Office: supplements 1–3*, 3 vols. in 1 (1952–68) • I. E. Gray, 'Notes on the Walkers', 1947, Essex RO, Chelmsford, T/G 9 • F. W. Steer and others, *Dictionary of land surveyors and local map-makers of Great Britain and Ireland, 1530–1850*, ed. P. Eden, 2nd edn, ed. S. Bendall, 2 vols. (1997) • S. Tyacke, ed., *English map-making, 1500–1650: historical essays* (1983) • P. D. A. Harvey, *The history of topographical maps: symbols, pictures and surveys* (1980) • 'Agas, Radulph or Ralph', *DNB* • I. Gray, 'Maps of 350 years ago', *Country Life*, 101 (1947), 914–15 • D. MacCulloch, 'Radulph Agas: virtue unrewarded', *Proceedings of the Suffolk Institute of Archaeology*, 33 (1973–5), 275–84 • J. Schofield, ed., *The London surveys of Ralph Treswell* (1987) • A. C. Edwards, *John Petre* (1975) • West Hanningfield parish registers

Archives Essex RO, Chelmsford, estate maps and surveys by John Walker senior, John Walker junior, and Samuel Walker

Walker, John (*bap.* 1577, *d.* 1618). *See under* Walker, John (*c.*1550–1626).

Walker, John (*bap.* 1674, *d.* 1747), Church of England clergyman and historian, son of Endymion Walker, was baptized at St Kerrian's, Exeter, on 21 January 1674. His father was mayor of Exeter from 1682 to 1683. On 19 November 1691 he matriculated at Exeter College, Oxford, was admitted fellow on 3 July 1695, and became full fellow on 4 July 1696 (vacated 1700). On 16 January 1698 he was ordained deacon by Sir Jonathan Trelawny, then bishop of Exeter; he graduated BA on 4 July 1698 and was instituted to the rectory of St Mary Major, Exeter, on 22 August after the death of the previous incumbent, Richard Carpenter. On 13 October 1699 he graduated MA (apparently incorporated at Cambridge, 1702).

The publication of Edmund Calamy's *Account* (1702–13) of nonconformist ministers silenced and ejected after the Restoration in 1660 suggested simultaneously to Charles Goodall and to Walker the idea of rendering a similar service to the memory of the conforming clergy who were deprived and sequestered by the puritans in the period before the Restoration. Goodall advertised for information in the *London Gazette*; finding that Walker was engaged on a similar task, he gave him the materials he had collected. Walker collected particulars by help of query sheets, circulated in various dioceses. (Those for Exeter—very minute—and Canterbury are printed by Calamy in his *Church and Dissenters Compar'd as to Persecution*, 1719.) Walker's helpers in this task included Mary Astell. His diligence in amassing materials may be estimated from the detailed account given in the preface to his *Attempt towards recovering an account of the numbers and sufferings of the clergy of the Church of England, heads of colleges, fellows, scholars, &c., who were sequester'd, harrass'd, &c. in the late times of the grand rebellion* (1714). A remarkable subscription list contains over thirteen hundred names. The work consists of two parts: first, a history of ecclesiastical affairs from 1640 to 1660, the object being to show that the ejection of the puritans by the Act of Uniformity (1662) was a just reprisal for their actions when in power; second, a catalogue, well arranged and fairly well indexed, of the deprived clergy with particulars of their sufferings.

The plan falls short of Calamy's, as it does not give biographies. A third part, announced in the title-page as an examination of Calamy's work, was deferred and never appeared, though Calamy is plentifully attacked in the preface.

The work was hailed by Thomas Bisse in a sermon before the sons of the clergy (6 December 1716) as a 'book of martyrology' and 'a record which ought to be kept in every sanctuary'. However, John Lewis, whom Calamy calls a 'chumm' of Walker's, and who had formed high expectations of the book, disparages it, in *Remarks* on Bisse, as 'a farrago of false and senseless legends'. It was criticized, from the nonconformist side, by John Withers of Exeter, in an appendix to his *Reply* (1714) to two pamphlets by John Agate, an Exeter clergyman; and by Calamy in *The Church and the Dissenters Compar'd*. Walker's work, though strongly polemical and full of anti-puritan sentiments, shows evidence of careful historical consideration of his materials, and he does not try to ignore the charges made against some of his 'sufferers' which led to their ejection.

Walker married Martha Brooking (1679/80–1747), in Exeter Cathedral on 17 November 1704. On 7 December 1714 he was made DD by diploma at Oxford in recognition of his literary work on the sufferings of the clergy. On 20 December of the same year he became a prebendary of Exeter Cathedral. On 17 October 1720 he was instituted to the rectory of Upton Pyne in Devon, after the death of the previous rector, James Gray. He was presented to the living by Hugh Stafford of Pyne. He seems to have spent the rest of his life there.

Walker died in 1747, probably at Upton Pyne. He was buried on the north side of the chancel at Upton Pyne church on 20 June 1747. Before his death Walker had expressed an intention to deposit the material he had collected for his work in a library. In 1754 his son William, a druggist in Exeter, presented these papers to the Bodleian Library, where they remain. They were bound up in the nineteenth century, making twelve folio and eleven quarto volumes. Walker also left a large collection of pamphlets, and several letters, which have proved awkward to decipher because of his eccentric handwriting. He was survived by his wife who, according to her tombstone, was buried on 12 September 1747, aged sixty-seven.

ALEXANDER DU TOIT

Sources C. W. Boase, *Registrum Collegii Exoniensis*, 2 vols. (1879–94) · Foster, *Alum. Oxon.* · *N&Q*, 2nd ser., 12 (1861), 435 · *N&Q*, 4th ser., 3 (1869), 483, 566 · W. D. Macray, *Annals of the Bodleian Library, Oxford* (1868), 167 · *A catalogue of all graduates … in the University of Oxford, between … 1659 and … 1850* (1851), 689 · *Mayors of Exeter from the thirteenth century to the present day* (1964), 15
Archives Bodl. Oxf., working papers for *Sufferings of the clergy* | BL, Harley, Sloane, Thoresby MSS · Bodl. Oxf., Brett, Clarendon Press, Viner, Whiston MSS

Walker, John (1692/3–1741), classical and biblical scholar, was, according to the admission registers of Trinity College, Cambridge, the son of Thomas Walker of Huddersfield. The entry for his admission to Trinity College as a pensioner on 24 May 1710 also records that he had been educated at Wakefield School under Mr Clark (Edward Clarke) and that he was aged seventeen. A search in the parish registers in the West Riding of Yorkshire provides only one baptismal entry that could be his. A John, son of a Thomas Walker, was baptized in Hartshead parish church on 14 October 1694. If this is the same person who was admitted to Trinity aged seventeen, he was born in 1692 or 1693. In 1731 Slaithwaite Free School received an endowment by the terms of the will of a Thomas Walker of Huddersfield, salter, dated 9 May 1719. The surname is a common one in the area, and that this is the subject's father can hardly be expressed as more than a possibility.

Walker's Cambridge career was a successful one. He graduated BA in 1713, and was elected a minor fellow of his college in 1716. He took his MA in 1717. He should not be confused with his two contemporaries at Trinity, Richard Walker, the vice-master, and Samuel Walker. Walker's preference was for collaborative research, to which he brought considerable learning as well as a pleasant personality. The only evidence of an independent publication is his projected edition of the Christian apologist Arnobius. Both the first and the last of his works to be published were contributions to the work of others. The first was a set of emendations to Cicero's *De natura deorum*, printed at the end of the edition by Dr John Davies of 1718. The last consisted of some notes which he had prepared on Cicero's *De officiis* which were incorporated by Zachary Pearce into his edition of 1745. The emendations, which show a wide range of reading, are mostly bold or ingenious conjectures after the manner of Richard Bentley. Bentley also had been a pupil at Wakefield, and their education and scholarly interests were to continue to coincide. Walker was to provide Bentley with variant readings in manuscripts both of Suetonius and of Cicero's *Tusculan Disputations*. But the greatest part of his assistance to Bentley was in New Testament work. In fact, assistance is rather too weak a word, as the end of Bentley's *Proposals for Printing* (a new edition of the Greek and Vulgate New testaments published in 1720), makes clear:

> The Overseer and Corrector of the Press will be the Learned Mr. John Walker of Trinity-College in *Cambridge*; who with great accurateness has collated many MSS. at *Paris* for the present Edition. And the Issue of it, whether Gain or Loss, is equally to fall on Him and the Author.

In the summer or autumn of 1719 Walker went to Paris on Bentley's behalf, in order to collate Latin and Greek manuscripts of the New Testament. Walker was received kindly at Paris, especially by the Benedictines. He seems to have remained in Paris for almost a year. Collations of fourteen Latin manuscripts at Paris are extant, the whole New Testament in five, and part of it in nine others. He also noted the readings of four Tours manuscripts collated by Léon Chevallier, which were given him by Sabatier. These collections are contained in Trinity College, Cambridge Library, B.17.5.

The following year (1721) Walker returned to Paris, to concentrate on Greek manuscripts. The readings of manuscripts from various collections now to be found in the Bibliothèque Nationale that are contained in the Trinity College volume B.17.42, 43 probably belong to this period. Plague in Paris in the winter of 1721–2 drove Walker to Brussels. A letter describing this removal suggests that he may have been travelling with Lord Preston, either as his chaplain or in his entourage. During this stay he collated further manuscripts, including a Greek New Testament then in the library of a convent at Corsendonck near Turnhout, now at Vienna (Österreichische Nationalbibliothek, MS suppl. Gr. 52; Gregory-Aland 3), and succeeded in identifying many of the manuscripts used by Lucas Brugensis. When the epidemic had abated, Walker returned to Paris, and seems to have remained there until 1723.

Walker's work on Arnobius must have taken shape in these years. Of this, as he wrote in the letter already quoted, there is 'only one MS. in the world, which is lodged in the library of the King of France [now Bibl. Nat. Lat. 1661], and which I have often seen and examin'd there'. During his visit to Brussels, he discovered and collated a second manuscript (now Brussels, Bibl. Royale 10846–7), which is now generally regarded as a copy of the Paris manuscript. Two quarto volumes containing these collations, as well as notes and conjectures, along with other notes, were left in his will to Dr Richard Meade. One of these volumes subsequently came into the hands of J. E. B. Mayor.

At about this time Walker became friends with William Wake, archbishop of Canterbury, and after his return to England, he received a series of ecclesiastical preferments. He became dean and rector of Bocking, Essex, in the archbishop's patronage, on 15 November 1725. At Lady day 1726 he received his last dividend as fellow of Trinity. He became chancellor of St David's on 17 July 1727. He was made DD under royal commission (together with Richard Walker the vice-master) on 25 April 1728. A year later Wake appointed him archdeacon of Hereford (on 3 February 1729). In 1730 he was instituted rector of the adjacent parishes in the city of London of St Mary Aldermary and St Thomas the Apostle, both in the archbishop's patronage. He was also chaplain to George II.

Walker married Charlotte Sheffield (d. in or after 1762) on 26 January 1728, and they had six sons and four daughters. Charlotte was a natural daughter of John *Sheffield, duke of Normanby and Buckinghamshire (1647–1721), and Frances Stewart (d. 1751), who afterwards married the Hon. Oliver Lambart. Her father's will provided Mrs Walker with a fortune of £6000. One of their sons went into the East India trade, another (Henry) became a fellow of King's College, Cambridge, whence he graduated BA (1757), and a third an officer in Germany, who married and had children. A fourth studied in the Temple, and then took orders.

Walker continued to collate manuscripts, including those acquired by Wake, now in the library of Christ Church, Oxford. Some of these collations are in Trinity College, Cambridge (B.17.42, 43 and others in B.17.34) and those of eight of the manuscripts are in a Greek Testament in Christ Church Library (MS Wake Gr. 35). A note by

Walker at the end of the volume states that this work was carried out in 1732. He certainly went on collating Greek manuscripts until after 1735, as he entered some collations in a Greek Testament printed in that year (Trinity College, B.17.44, 45). Altogether, ninety-six of Walker's collations of Greek manuscripts are known, containing the whole or parts of the New Testament. It was John Wordsworth's informed opinion that his 'collations of Latin manuscripts are decidedly better than Bentley's, although they are not as perfect as his reputation for scholarship and his neat writing would lead one to hope' (DNB). In the volume Wake Gr. 35, Walker wrote accurate descriptions and datings of the manuscripts, which were used by Kitchin in his catalogue of Christ Church manuscripts.

Walker's health was increasingly delicate, and he signed his will on 29 May 1741. He died on 9 November 1741. Mrs Walker caused to be erected a monument to him in the chancel of Bocking church where he was buried. Its laudatory character is confirmed by all the evidence. It asserts that his 'uncommon learning and sweetness of temper, joined to all other Christian perfections, and accompanied with a pleasing form of body, justly rendered him the delight and ornament of mankind'. Mrs Walker afterwards married a Welshman named Griffiths, from whom she soon separated, resuming the name of Walker, and lived first in Bedford and then in Yarmouth. She was still living in 1762.

Wordsworth believed that the collapse of the projected Greek Testament was due to Walker's death much more than to Bentley's, since Walker continued collating at least until 1737, while Bentley seems to have turned his attention to other tasks long before. If this was indeed the case, then his early death may have deprived Walker of a place beside Mill, Tregelles, and Hort, as well as of the opportunity of anticipating Lachmann with the first acceptable replacement to the received text. As it is, Walker's place in history is as the successor of Mill in the collation of manuscripts, and as a pioneer among British scholars in studying manuscripts abroad. The degree to which he contributed to the text selected in Bentley's notes and drafts is a matter for speculation.

D. C. PARKER

Sources W. Coles, MS collections, vol. 32, BL, Add. MS 5833, Plut. CLXXXI F., fols. 115B and 116 • A. A. Ellis, *Bentleii critica sacra* (1862) • A. Fox, *John Mill and Richard Bentley: a study of the textual criticism of the New Testament, 1675–1729* (1954), 119–26 • I. Hutter, *Corpus der Byzantinischen Miniaturenhandschriften: Band 4.1, Oxford Christ Church, Textband* (Stuttgart, 1993), xxviii–xxix • H. J. Moorhouse and C. A. Hulbert, *Extracts from the diary of the Rev. Robert Meeke, minister of the ancient chapelry of Slaithwaite, near Huddersfield … to which are added notes, illustrations, and a brief sketch of his life and character, by Henry James Moorhouse, also a continuation of the history of Slaithwaite free school by Charles Augustus Hulbert* (1874) • W. W. Rouse Ball and J. A. Venn, eds., *Admissions to Trinity College, Cambridge*, 3 (1911), vii, xii, 32 • D. F. E. Sykes, *The history of Huddersfield and its vicinity* (1898) • Venn, *Alum. Cant.* • *The correspondence of Richard Bentley*, ed. C. Wordsworth, 2 vols. (1842), letters 211, 213, 215–17, 219, 230 • J. Wordsworth, ed., *The gospel according to St Matthew, from the St Germain MS. (g¹)* (1883), xxiii–xxvi, 54–67 • *GM*, 1st ser., 11 (1741), 609 •

DNB · will, PRO, PROB 11/713, fols. 393*v*–397*r* · memorial inscription, 1741, Bocking church, Essex
Archives Christ Church Oxf., MS Wake Gr. 35 · Trinity Cam., B.17.5, 34, 42, 43 | Trinity Cam., Richard Bentley MSS
Likenesses monument, Bocking church, Essex
Wealth at death see will, PRO, PROB 11/713, fols. 393*v*–397*r*

Walker, John (1731–1803), natural historian and Church of Scotland minister, was born in the Canongate, Edinburgh, son to John Walker, rector of Canongate School, and Eupham Morison, lady-in-waiting to Lady Dirleton. From his father's grammar school he went to the University of Edinburgh (1746–9) in preparation for the ministry. He records that he was an avid collector of natural specimens from at least 1746, and from 1750 his interest in natural history was further heightened by the remains of the museum left by Sir Robert Sibbald and Sir Andrew Balfour. He was licensed to preach on 3 April 1754, and on 13 September 1758 was ordained minister of Glencorse, 7 miles south of Edinburgh, where in 1750 he had made the acquaintance of Henry Home, Lord Kames, a member of the board of annexed estates.

On 8 June 1762 Walker was transferred to Moffat, from which parish he undertook extensive fieldwork. In 1764 he was appointed, through Kames's patronage, to survey the Hebrides, and to make a report to the Society in Scotland for the Propagation of Christian Knowledge. Walker travelled 3000 miles in seven months. His report, together with his 1771 tour and four other trips between 1766 and 1786, formed the basis of his manuscripts on the natural history of the Hebrides, partly published posthumously as *An Economical History of the Hebrides* (2 vols., 1808; reissued in 1812), and printed by Charles Stewart, the university printer, Walker's friend, executor, and former student. His other main work was also published posthumously: *Essays on Natural History and Rural Economy* (1812).

Walker was appointed regius professor of natural history and keeper of the university's museum at Edinburgh on 3 November 1779, while retaining his clerical post at Moffat. His lectures were considered clear but dry and formal. His teaching emphasized a utilitarian natural history. His students came mainly from Scotland but some were from Europe and from North and South America. They included James Edward Smith, Tobias Smollett, and Robert Jameson, his successor as natural history professor. Many former students provided him with natural specimens for his museum. Works printed by Walker during his lifetime comprised mainly syllabuses for his students: *Schediasma fossilium* (1781); *Delineatio fossilium* (1782); *Classes fossilium* (1787); and *Institutes of Natural History* (1792). His guide to collecting, *Preservatio naturalium*, came out in 1796 followed in 1800 by a work on the discovery of coal for Colonel Dirom, quartermaster-general of Scotland. Walker produced a large body of important but unpublished work including geological observations, a flora of Edinburgh, anticipations of Linnaean classification within the genus *Alga*, and an account of species of the genus *Salix*. He corresponded with Linnaeus and Thomas Pennant among others, was a close friend to William Cullen and Joseph Black, and greatly developed the natural history museum

at Edinburgh. His breadth of expertise was remarkable but his posthumous reputation suffered from his not having published much during his lifetime.

On 24 November 1789 Walker married Jane Wallace (Jean) Wauchope of Niddrie, who died on 4 May 1827. On 7 June 1764 he was elected a freeman and burgess of Campbeltown in Argyll. On 28 February 1765 he received the honorary degree of MD from Glasgow University, and on 22 March 1765 that of DD from Edinburgh University.

On 7 January 1783 Walker was transferred from his parish at Moffat to Colinton, near Edinburgh. On 2 March 1782, he was the leading figure in plans for 'a Society for the Advancement of Learning and Usefull Knowledge', a body established in 1783 as the Royal Society of Edinburgh. Walker was secretary to the physical class, 1784–1803. He contributed seven papers to that society's *Transactions* on subjects ranging from the motion of sap in trees to whales, and five to the *Transactions* of the Highland Society of Scotland on peat and the salmon among other subjects. He was elected an honorary member of the Highland Society in 1789, and a member of the Edinburgh Natural History Society, founded by James Edward Smith, on 5 April 1782. Walker's lectures on agriculture prompted Sir William Pulteney to found the chair of agriculture in Edinburgh in 1790. On 20 May 1790 Walker was elected moderator of the general assembly of the Scottish church. He was made a fellow of the Royal Society in 1794. He wrote parochial accounts of Glencorse (1795) and Colinton (1797) for Sir John Sinclair's *Statistical Account of Scotland* (20 vols., 1791–9). During his last years he was blind. He died at Somerville Wynd, Canongate, on 31 December 1803 and was buried in Canongate churchyard.

CHARLES W. J. WITHERS

Sources U. Edin. L., special collections division, university archives · *The Rev. Dr. Walker's report on the Hebrides of 1764 and 1771*, ed. M. McKay (1980) · H. W. Scott, ed., *Lectures on geology including hydrography, mineralogy, and meteorology* (1966) · G. Taylor, 'John Walker, DD, FRSE, 1731–1803: a notable Scottish naturalist', *Transactions of the Botanical Society* [Edinburgh], 38 (1959), 180–203 · U. Glas., Archives and Business Records Centre · U. Aberdeen, archives · Edinburgh City Archives · Royal College of Physicians of Edinburgh, Archives · C. W. J. Withers, 'The Rev. Dr. John Walker and the practice of natural history in late eighteenth-century Scotland', *Archives of Natural History*, 18 (1991), 201–20 · F. J. Grant, ed., *Parish of Holyroodhouse or Canongate register of marriages, 1564–1800*, Scottish RS, 46 (1911–15)
Archives Edinburgh City Archives · Royal College of Physicians of Edinburgh, lecture notes · U. Aberdeen · U. Edin. L., notes, memoranda, lectures, and papers · U. Glas. L., papers | BL, King's MS, 105 · NA Scot., letters to Lord Kames and Lady Kames
Likenesses J. Kay, caricature, etching, 1789, BM; repro. in J. Kay, *Original portraits*, 2 vols. (1842), vol. 2, after p. 178 · engraving, repro. in W. Jardine, *Birds of Great Britain and Ireland* (1842), pt 3 [vol. 12 of *Naturalist's Library*]
Wealth at death after death, natural history specimens removed by executors from University of Edinburgh's museum and sold; house and property to be sold after wife's death and proceeds halved between University of Edinburgh's museum and library

Walker, John (1732–1807), elocutionist, orthoepist, and lexicographer, was born on 18 March 1732 at Colney Heath, a hamlet in the parish of Friern Barnet, Middlesex,

John Walker (1732–1807), by Henry Ashby, 1802

on the eastern side of Finchley Common. Nothing is known about his father, except that he died when John was a child. His mother came from Nottingham and was the sister of the Revd James Morley, a dissenting minister in Painswick, Gloucestershire. Walker attended grammar school, but left early to learn a trade, of which he tried several, but none suited him. On his mother's death, when he was about seventeen, he decided to pursue a career on the stage and joined a succession of provincial theatre companies, the last of which was in Gloucester. In 1757 he joined Garrick's company at Drury Lane, where he at first played minor characters, such as Angus in *Macbeth*, but was soon promoted to play the second parts in tragedy, and those of a grave and sententious nature in comedy.

In May 1758 Walker married Miss Sybilla Minors (Myners; 1723–1802), a well-known comic actress at Drury Lane. Shortly after their marriage they were both engaged by Spranger Barry and Henry Woodward to join the Crow Street Theatre in Dublin, where Walker took on many of Henry Mossop's characters after Mossop joined the Smock Alley Theatre. While he was engaged in Dublin he also played summer seasons in Bristol. In June 1762 he returned to London, where he and his wife joined Beard's company at Covent Garden. His first appearance on this stage was on 25 October 1762 as Downright in *Every Man in his Humour*, which was considered to be his best performance, though his Cato and Brutus were also commended. Walker left Covent Garden in 1767 and, after a year's stay in Dublin and a final summer season in Bristol, quit the stage in 1768. Although he achieved a certain level of fame as an actor, it was acknowledged that 'though a judicious

and correct, he was far from a perfect actor. His gesture was ungraceful and … his enunciation monotonous' (*The Athenaeum*, 78).

In January 1769 Walker started a school at Kensington gravel pits with the Revd James Usher. Under Usher's influence he had converted to Roman Catholicism shortly after his marriage, and he continued to adhere to this faith for the rest of his life. Although the school was a success, Walker left after two years, following a disagreement with Usher, to become a teacher of elocution. He was very successful in this, attracting more pupils than he could accommodate, mainly young men aiming to qualify for the senate or the bar. By 1775 Walker's reputation was such that he was invited to give a series of lectures in Edinburgh. These were so popular that he was invited back, and he also gave the lectures in Dublin and in Oxford, where he was subsequently invited by the heads of several colleges to give private lectures in the university. Walker's pupils included the emperor of Russia's prime minister, the sons of Lord Erskine, and several members of parliament. As well as Garrick, his friends and patrons included Samuel Johnson, John Milner, the Roman Catholic bishop of Castabala, and Edmund Burke, who introduced him to an acquaintance as 'Mr Walker, whom not to know, by name at least, would argue want of knowledge of the harmonies, cadences, and proprieties of our language' (Emerson, 115).

Walker was the leader of the 'mechanical' school of elocution, in which detailed rules concerning voice production, posture, and gesture were laid down, as opposed to the 'natural' school led by Thomas Sheridan. Although Walker's first publication was *A General Idea of a Pronouncing Dictionary* (1774), and he also published *Exercises for Improvement in Elocution* (1777) and *Hints for Improvement in the Art of Reading* (1783), it was his *Elements of Elocution* (1781), *Rhetorical Grammar* (1785), and *The Melody of Speaking* (1787) which sealed his reputation as an elocutionist. His major contribution was his theory of inflections, whereby the pitch of the voice moves up or down, or both up and down, within a single syllable. These ideas were not original, having been put forward by Joshua Steele in *Prosodia rationalis* (1775), but Steele's work, with its elaborate musical notation, was much more difficult for the public to understand. It is unlikely that Walker actually plagiarized Steele because, by his own admission, he had a 'total want of knowledge in music' and found himself incapable of understanding Steele's notation (*Elements of Elocution*, 1781, xi–xii).

Walker's ideas on elocution continued to be influential throughout the nineteenth century, but it is as an orthoepist and lexicographer that he is best known. His most important and frequently reprinted works are his *Rhyming Dictionary*, first published in 1775 but still in press throughout the twentieth century, and, above all, his *Critical Pronouncing Dictionary* (1791). This was the most successful and authoritative pronouncing dictionary of the late eighteenth and the nineteenth century. It was reprinted over 100 times up to 1904 and was the basis of over 20 other dictionaries published in the nineteenth century, including

B. H. Smart's *Walker Remodelled* (1836). The *Critical Pronouncing Dictionary* was successful and influential in the United States as well as Britain, the first American edition appearing in 1803. The success of this work was due to its detailed and authoritative pronouncements on correct pronunciation, set out in 545 'rules' prefaced to the dictionary proper as well as in notes to any word whose pronunciation was controversial. Walker used the same system of notation as Sheridan, marking the different pronunciations of vowels with superscripted numbers, but criticized him for 'numerous instances ... of impropriety, inconsistency, and want of acquaintance with the analogies of the Language' (*Critical Pronouncing Dictionary*, 1791, 1). Walker was acknowledged to have 'settled all doubts on the subject' of English pronunciation, and his *Critical Pronouncing Dictionary* came to be regarded as the 'statute book of English orthoepy' (*The Athenaeum*, 81). By the end of the nineteenth century Walker had become a byword for linguistic correctness, so that those who used an affected pronunciation were accused of trying to 'out-Walker Walker' (Mugglestone, *Talking Proper*, 41). In the twentieth century his authority came to be superseded by that of Daniel Jones, and he has come to be regarded as an arch-prescriptivist. This criticism was first levelled at him by Alexander Ellis, who, while acknowledging his 'good and hard work', accused Walker of being one of 'these word-peddlars, those letter-drivers, those stiff-necked pedantic philosophical, miserably informed, and therefore supremely certain, self-confident and self-conceited orthographers' (*On Early English Pronunciation*, 1869, 2.629, 1.155).

After the *Critical Pronouncing Dictionary* Walker published *A Key to the Classical Pronunciation of Greek and Latin Proper Names* (1798), which, as 'Walker's key', was appended to several dictionaries in the nineteenth century, including an edition of Webster's American dictionary in 1829, Joseph Worcester's *Universal and Critical Dictionary of the English Language* (1846), and several later editions of the *Critical Pronouncing Dictionary*. His last works were *The Academic Speaker* (1801), *The Teacher's Assistant in English Composition* (1801), and *Outlines of English Grammar* (1805).

Walker died at Tottenham Court Road, London, on 1 August 1807, his wife having died in April 1802. He was buried at St Pancras on 7 August, and left about £7000, most of which was bequeathed to distant relatives and the rest to friends. Although, as his authoritative pronouncements suggest, he was dogmatic and opinionated, and at times irritable and impatient, he was scrupulously honest, generous, and charitable, and a loyal friend even to those who disagreed with him.   JOAN C. BEAL

Sources *Athenaeum: a Magazine of Literary and Miscellaneous Information*, 3 (1808), 77–84 • *GM*, 1st ser., 77 (1807), 112–13, 786 • R. K. O'Neill, *English language dictionaries, 1604–1900* (1988) • R. Alston, *A bibliography of the English language from the invention of printing to the year 1800* [1965–73], vols. 5–6 • W. Benzie, *The Dublin orator* (1972) • G. W. Stone, ed., *The London stage, 1660–1800*, pt 4: *1747–1776* (1962) • L. Mugglestone, *Talking proper* (1995) • L. Mugglestone, 'John Walker and Alexander Ellis: antedating R. P.', *N&Q*, 242 (1997), 103–

7 • J. H. Lamb, 'John Walker and Joshua Steele', *Speech Monographs*, 32 (1965), 411–19 • E. K. Sheldon, 'Walker's influence on the pronunciation of English', *Proceedings of the Modern Language Association of America*, 62 (1947), 130–46 • R. H. Emerson, 'The distribution of eighteenth-century prerhotic *o*-phonemes in Walker's *Critical pronouncing dictionary*', *American Speech*, 68/2 (1993), 115–38 • D. Lysons, *Supplement to the first edition of 'The environs of London'* (1811), 270

Likenesses H. Ashby, oils, 1802, NPG [*see illus.*] • R. Hicks, stipple, pubd 1825 (after J. Barry), BM, NPG • J. Barry, miniature, V&A • Heath, engraving (after J. Barry), repro. in J. Walker, *A key to the classical pronunciation of Greek and Latin proper names*, 2nd edn (1804) • watercolour drawing, NPG

Wealth at death approx. £7000: *Athenaeum*

Walker, John (1759–1830), vaccinator and writer, was born on 31 July 1759 at Cockermouth, Cumberland, one of the several children of a blacksmith and ironmonger. He was educated at the free grammar school in the town and was intended for an artistic career. However, plans for an apprenticeship were abandoned and he spent five years in his father's business, engraving ornamental metalwork. During this time he received some training in drawing. In 1779 Walker travelled to Dublin with the romantic ambition of joining a privateer. The ship had already been taken by the French, so he resumed his artistic studies and within a year was publishing engravings in magazines. In 1784 he took up teaching, gradually building up a large and successful school on Usher's Island, Dublin. However, he continued to produce engravings and began to write to supplement his income, publishing an *Elements of Geography and of Natural and Civil History* in 1788 and a *Universal Gazetteer* in 1795.

By this time Walker had settled in London and had again changed his career, this time for medicine. He undertook a conventional course of study, spending three years at Guy's Hospital, with a brief visit to Paris in 1797. He reportedly spent time in Edinburgh in 1799–1800, although he did not matriculate at the university. Walker graduated MD from Leiden University in 1799, and later published his thesis on the function of the heart and blood vessels. He became a licentiate of the Royal College of Physicians, London, in 1812, and was for a long time member of the Physical Society of Guy's Hospital. According to his first biographer, Walker was able to pursue these studies through the generosity of Anne Bowman, a native of Cockermouth, whom he married in a civil ceremony in Glasgow on 23 October 1799. The couple had no children.

If Walker's medical education was conventional, his career was not. He never set up in practice, but always worked in vaccine institutions, then a new arena of practice. This unusual career path was dictated largely by Walker's confrontational character, his scepticism of the merits of orthodox medical treatment, and his unconventional views in religion and politics. Walker was brought up a Baptist but in the 1780s he attempted to join the Society of Friends. He was never formally accepted in the Quaker faith, because of his doubts about the divinity of Christ and his critical views of contemporary Quaker principles. However, he rigidly adhered to the outward conventions of Quaker life, attending meetings and adopting their distinctive style of address and garb. The latter caused difficulty on numerous occasions, when Walker refused to remove his hat at table as etiquette demanded. In Paris this behaviour provoked a minor scandal at the Conseil des Anciens. Walker's politics were radical. In Paris he was acquainted with Thomas Paine, Thomas Muir, and James Napper Tandy, and translated the manifesto of the Theophilanthropists, an atheistic society. He embraced a number of radical causes that included opposition to slavery, to the employment of children as chimney sweeps, and to cruelty to animals.

Walker first became involved in vaccination against smallpox in 1800, when he was asked by Dr Marshall to join an expedition to the Mediterranean. The two practitioners carried out successful vaccinations in Gibraltar, Minorca, Malta, and Naples, and Walker went on to join Sir Ralph Abercromby's expedition to Egypt, vaccinating the troops and working as a surgeon. He also undertook various journeys in Egypt, which provided the material for his travel book *Fragments of Letters and Other Papers* (1802). In Egypt he caused much confusion by persistently sporting a large beard, by which he was mistaken for a Jew and assaulted.

On his return in 1802 Walker immediately began to practise vaccination in London, and in 1803 he was appointed resident vaccinator to the Royal Jennerian Society, a charity which provided free vaccination to the poor. The post offered a small salary and a house at the main vaccine station in Salisbury Court, Fleet Street. Walker's singular temperament did not, however, allow a quiet life. In 1806 he became embroiled in a dispute with Jenner, ostensibly over vaccination technique, although the true causes are now obscure. The society split into factions: Jenner and the society's medical board demanded Walker's dismissal, while the lay board of directors, which included a number of Quakers, consistently supported him. Walker was forced to resign, but did not go gracefully. He published a scurrilous 'Jenneric opera' in the anti-vaccination *Medical Observer*, which drew a similarly bad-tempered response from Jenner's camp. The society alleged that Walker refused to hand over vaccination registers and had taken a shop at the entrance to Salisbury Court from which he waylaid patients before they could reach the vaccination station. Walker and his supporters set up a rival charity, the London Vaccine Institution, which flourished as the Jennerian Society declined. In 1813 Walker added insult to injury by reviving the moribund Royal Jennerian Society, which was eventually amalgamated with the London Vaccine Institution. Despite its controversial beginnings, and Walker's rough and ready style of dealing with patients, the London Vaccine Institution proved the most successful vaccine charity of its day, providing free vaccination to thousands of Londoners. It also sought to encourage free vaccination in the provinces by recruiting local practitioners as associate vaccinators. Walker himself worked hard in the cause until a few days of his death. He continued to publish on a wide range of topics, such as vaccination and popular science; he even made Latin translations. He died in London on 23 June 1830 from a lung disease, probably tuberculosis.

DEBORAH BRUNTON

Sources J. Epps, *The Life of John Walker M.D.* (1832) · R. B. Fisher, *Edward Jenner* (1991) · Munk, *Roll* · H. Lonsdale, *The worthies of Cumberland*, 6 (1875) · *DNB*
Likenesses G. Cruikshank, coloured etching, 1812, Wellcome L.

Walker, John (*fl.* **1784–1802**). *See under* Walker, Anthony (1726–1765).

Walker, John (**1769–1833**), founder of the Church of God and classical scholar, was born in co. Roscommon, the son of Matthew Walker, a Church of Ireland clergyman. He entered Trinity College, Dublin, on 18 January 1786, was chosen a scholar in 1788, graduated BA in 1790, was elected a fellow in 1791, and proceeded MA in 1796, and BD in 1800.

Walker was ordained a Church of Ireland priest and served as a chaplain in Bethesda Chapel, Dublin, from 1793; he composed a moderately well-known hymn, 'Thou God of power and God of love', in honour of the chapel's move to Dorset Street, Dublin, on 22 June 1794. From about 1803 he began to study the principles of Christian fellowship prevailing among the earliest Christians. Convinced that later departures were erroneous, he joined with a small band of followers who attempted to live what they believed to be the practice of the apostles, rejecting all church authority and discipline and calling themselves members of the Church of God. His views from this period can be found in his *Expostulatory Address to Members of the Methodist Society in Ireland* (1804) and his *Letters to Alexander Knox* (1803).

On 8 October 1804 Walker became convinced that he could no longer honestly hold the position of a clergyman of the Church of Ireland. Informing the provost of Trinity College of his theological position, he offered to resign his fellowship, but was formally expelled on the following day. He joined a congregation of fellow believers at their meeting-place for worship in Stafford Street, Dublin, and supported himself by lecturing on subjects of university study, completing his edition of Livy's *Historiarum libri qui supersunt* (1797–1813) and publishing *The First, Second and Sixth Books of Euclid's Elements* (1808) and *Selections from Lucian* (1816). After paying several visits to Scotland, he moved to London in 1819, where he wrote *A Full and Plain Account of the Horatian Metres* (1822). It was probably while in London that he married and that his daughter Mary was born.

In 1833, after Trinity College, Dublin, had granted Walker a pension of £600 in amends for their earlier treatment of him, he returned to Dublin where he died on 25 October. His theological work, *The Sabbath: a Type of the Lord Jesus Christ* (1866), was published posthumously, and his *Essays and Correspondence* (1838), edited by W. Burton, went to press five years after his death. His followers were known by the pejorative terms Separatists or Walkerites.

E. I. CARLYLE, *rev.* DAVID HUDDLESTON

Sources A. J. Webb, *A compendium of Irish biography* (1878), 544 · *GM*, 1st ser., 103/2 (1833), 540–42 · J. Julian, ed., *A dictionary of hymnology*, rev. edn (1907), 1231 · *Essays and correspondence, chiefly on scriptural subjects, by the late John Walker*, ed. W. Burton, 3 vols. (1838) · J. B. Leslie, biographical succession list of clergy for the diocese of Dublin, PRO NIre., T 1075/1 · Allibone, *Dict.* · Burtchaell & Sadleir, *Alum. Dubl.* · [J. H. Todd], ed., *A catalogue of graduates who have proceeded to degrees in the University of Dublin, from the earliest recorded commencements to … December 16, 1868* (1869), 586 · *Millennial Harbinger* (1835), 344 · S. Madden, *Memoir of the Late Rev. Peter Roe* (1842), 116
Likenesses etching, repro. in Burton, ed., *Essays and correspondence*, vol. 1

Walker, John (*bap.* 1770, *d.* 1831), antiquary, son of John and Mary Walker of London, was baptized at the church of St Katharine Cree, London, on 18 February 1770, and was elected scholar at Winchester College in 1783. He matriculated from Brasenose College, Oxford, in 1788, and graduated BCL in 1797. In the same year he was elected fellow of New College; he retained his fellowship until 1820. He also filled the posts of bursar, librarian, and dean of canon law. In 1809 he published *A Selection of Curious Articles from the 'Gentleman's Magazine'* in four volumes. This undertaking had been suggested by Edward Gibbon to the magazine's editor, John Nichols, in 1792, but, as he recorded in *Literary Anecdotes of the Eighteenth Century* (8.557), Nichols never found time to pursue the idea. Inspired by Gibbon's suggestion, Walker began work on a selection and in April 1805 wrote to Nichols asking if he would publish it (Bodl. Oxf., MS Eng. lett. c. 367, fol. 206). The popularity of the work, published by Longman, led to a second edition in 1811 and a third in 1814.

Walker's other literary and antiquarian pursuits were centred on Oxford. In 1809 he brought out *Oxoniana*, four volumes of selections from books and manuscripts in the Bodleian Library relating to university matters, 'to exhibit a view of the customs and manners which have prevailed at different periods' (*Oxoniana*, 1809, advertisement, vol. 1, p. i). This was followed in 1813 by a similar work, *Letters Written by Eminent Persons … from the Originals in the Bodleian Library and Ashmolean Museum* (2 vols.). Both proved valuable sources of quotation for succeeding writers. Walker was also the author of *Curia Oxoniensis, or, Observations on the Statutes which Relate to the University Court* (2nd edn, 1822). He was one of the original proprietors of the *Oxford University and City Herald and Midland County Chronicle*, first published on 31 May 1806, and for several years assisted in the editorial work. He was also, from 1810, the first editor of the *Oxford University Calendar*.

In 1819 Walker was presented by the warden and fellows of New College to the vicarage of Hornchurch in Essex, and resided there, apparently unmarried, during the rest of his life. He died of a violent cold and inflammation of the chest, at the vicarage on 5 April 1831. His library was sold by Sothebys in 739 lots on 2 June the same year.

E. I. CARLYLE, *rev.* MARY CLAPINSON

Sources *GM*, 1st ser., 101/1 (1831), 474 · *DNB* · *Oxford University Calendar* (1810–21) · Foster, *Alum. Oxon.*

Walker, John (1781–1859), chemist and inventor of a friction match, was born at 104 High Street, Stockton-on-Tees, on 29 May 1781, the third son of John Walker (1748–1812), a grocer, and wine and spirits merchant, and his wife, Mary Peacock (1752–1840). He was educated in the town and afterwards apprenticed to Watson Alcock, Stockton's principal surgeon. He then moved to London—probably to complete his medical training—before returning to Stockton as assistant surgeon to Alcock. However, he came to dislike this work, and, as he was interested in botany and chemistry, he moved first to Durham and then to York, where he was employed by wholesale druggists. He then returned to Stockton and in June 1819 opened a chemist and druggist's shop at 59 High Street, where he made up prescriptions and supplied medicines for animals.

Walker also enjoyed experimenting with chemicals. One day, at home, he prepared a mixture in which a dipped splint, probably used as a stirrer, became coated and dried. When the splint was scraped on the hearth, either accidentally or in an effort to remove the coating, it suddenly sparked and caught fire. Realizing that he had found a simple method of making an instant sustainable flame or light, he decided to prepare further splints that he could sell or give away. His only surviving daybook contains the earliest recorded sale of these friction matches (first entered as 'Sulphurata Hyperoxygenata Frict.') to a local solicitor on 7 April 1827. As it appears that this was the thirtieth batch to have been produced, it seems likely that he made his important discovery some time in 1826.

In September 1827 Walker started calling the new matches 'friction lights', which became his usual name for them. The cost of 100 of these was 1s., with a round tin case for 2d., though the matches were often sold loose. A piece of folded glasspaper was supplied with each box, and the matches, at first made of pasteboard (later wood), were flat and about 3 inches long. A match was lit by pinching the head between the folds of glasspaper and then quickly withdrawing it—the friction igniting the chemical tip. The composition of this tip was antimony sulphide and potassium chlorate mixed with gum arabic, starch, and water.

Walker did not think his invention was worth patenting, considering it trivial and preferring to leave its full commercial potential to others. As a result, Samuel Jones of London introduced an imitation of the friction light in 1829, which he called the Lucifer, a name that Walker disliked. Lucifers quickly became established and Walker ceased making his own matches, probably about 1830 or 1831, though he continued with his original trade until he retired. However, his invention should not be underestimated, as it was the first really practical match and an improvement on earlier methods of making fire, which could sometimes be dangerous. Friction matches gradually replaced the cumbersome tinderbox, and although expensive at the time, they eventually developed into the modern, mass-produced safety match, which could be bought very cheaply.

Walker was small and thin in appearance, and had a courteous but cheerful nature. Clever and knowledgeable, he was always willing to give advice. His dress was neat, usually consisting of a brown coat with tails, drab knee-breeches, and grey stockings. He never married. In retirement he lived at 1b The Square in Stockton, where, suffering from heart disease and dropsy, he died on 1 May 1859. He was buried in St Mary's churchyard, Norton, Stockton-on-Tees, on 5 May 1859.

CHRISTOPHER F. LINDSEY

Sources D. Thomas, *Strike a light: John Walker, 1781–1859, who invented the friction match in 1826*, 2nd edn (1990) · D. Thomas, *The day-book of John Walker, inventor of friction matches* (1981) · M. Christy, *The Bryant & May museum of fire-making appliances: catalogue of the exhibits* (1926), 14, 106–9; suppl. (1928), 269 · 'Instantaneous Light Apparatus', *The Royal Institution Quarterly Journal* (July–Sept 1829), 180 · M. Heavisides, ed., *The true history of the invention of the Lucifer match* (1909) · W. A. Bone, 'The centenary of the friction match', *Nature*, 119 (1927), 495–6 · *DNB* · R. W. Foss, 'The tinder-box, and its practical successor', *Archaeologia Aeliana*, new ser., 7 (1876), 217–26 · parish register (baptism), 6 July 1781, Stockton-on-Tees · d. cert. · parish register (burial), 5 May 1859, Stockton-on-Tees, St Mary

Archives Green Dragon Museum, Theatre Yard, Stockton-on-Tees · North of England Open Air Museum, Beamish, co. Durham, fittings of pharmacy · Sci. Mus., day-book and items reputedly used by him · Stockton Reference Library, Church Road, Stockton-on-Tees

Wealth at death under £3000: probate, 12 July 1859, *CGPLA Eng. & Wales*

Walker, John (1900–1964), numismatist, was born on 4 September 1900 at Glasgow, the youngest of the seven children of John Walker, a master carpenter, and his wife, Isabella Watson. His education was at Glasgow, at the John Street and Whitehill schools, until after a brief period of service in the army he entered Glasgow University in 1918. He studied a wide variety of subjects, including classics, although his principal subject was Semitic languages, and he took first classes in Hebrew and Arabic in 1922. He was a Lanfine bursar and John Clark scholar. To his master's degree he proceeded to add the diploma of the Jordanhill Training College and in 1924 went to teach, as first assistant, at St Andrew's Boys School in Alexandria in Egypt until 1927. He was next assistant lecturer in Arabic at Glasgow for a year, but went back to Egypt to work for the Ministry of Education from 1928 to 1930. By this time he had already published numerous articles in, for instance, the *Encyclopaedia of Islam* (to which he continued to contribute throughout his life), and had prepared works on *Bible Characters in the Koran* (1931) and *Folk Medicine in Modern Egypt* (1934), based on his close knowledge of Egypt and the Islamic world.

In 1931 Walker was appointed assistant keeper in the department of coins and medals at the British Museum. Thenceforth his scholarship and experience were to be applied mainly to the field of Islamic numismatics, which had been somewhat neglected since the compilation of the museum's *Catalogue of Oriental Coins* by Stanley Lane-Poole. The two volumes which Walker produced at the museum were the monument of his life's work. The first of these, dealing with the Arab–Sassanian coins, was finished in 1939 but published only in 1941; it was at once recognized by the award of the degree of DLitt of Glasgow University. At precisely this moment Walker was taken from the museum to serve until 1945 in the air staff intelligence, on account of his special knowledge of Arabic and

of the Near East. On his return to the museum he set to work on the next volume of his catalogue, despite the circumstances of post-war disorganization and the assumption of ever more extensive responsibilities. In 1948 he was elected secretary of the Royal Numismatic Society and in 1949 he became deputy keeper of his department at the museum; in 1952 he succeeded as keeper and became at the same time an editor of the *Numismatic Chronicle*. He had also from 1937 to 1947 been an additional lecturer at the School of Oriental and African Studies in London University. His own work was maintained, however, and in 1956 there appeared the second volume of his catalogue, devoted to the Arab–Byzantine coins. Only three years later he was responsible, as keeper, for the removal of the department of coins and medals from its temporary housing into rebuilt quarters. His work as secretary of, and from 1956 as chief editor for, the Royal Numismatic Society was assiduous and exemplary, and it was largely his achievement that, by the time of his death, the society's total membership had trebled to about 600 members in all parts of the world.

Walker's scholarly and numismatic publications, over and above the catalogues, include many remarkable and original works. He broke new ground with his fundamental studies of Islamic coinage in Africa with his monograph on the sultans of Kilwa, and of that in central Asia with his treatise on the second Saffarid dynasty in Sistan; and above all with his discovery of a series of coins issued by Arab governors in Crete in the ninth century, whose existence had previously been unsuspected. One of his keenest interests was in pre-Islamic Arabia, on which he wrote a number of articles, and another masterly stroke was his identification of a coinage of mixed Arab–Roman type as being of the city of Hatra in Mesopotamia. The scope of his activity at the museum was further attested by articles on such disparate topics as Italian medals, a Roman coin hoard, and a find of Anglo-Saxon pennies from Tetney in Lincolnshire. His mastery and acumen in all branches of the Semitic languages, ancient and modern, were always of the greatest value in dealing with otherwise intractable problems, and the history of Cyprus in the fourth century BC was changed, at a blow, by Walker's reading, correct and unhesitating, of a new Phoenician inscription on a coin of the island.

The two-volume *Catalogue of Muhammadan Coins in the British Museum* (1941 and 1956) constituted Walker's chief glory. It dealt with the initial and transitional stages of the Arab coinage, those crucial and almost intolerably intractable sections of the subject which, as Walker sometimes remarked drily, but with a twinkle, 'Lane-Poole had found too difficult' (private information). This was nothing less than the truth, and it was well that these topics had been left over, for a far greater degree of organized knowledge, and especially a mastery of modern numismatic techniques, only developed after Poole's day, were needful to cope effectively with such complexities. In the first volume, the Arab–Sassanian coins comprise all those issues of Sassanian-derived type made for Arab governors in Iran until the general currency reform of ʿAbd-al-Malik; and the wide range of interlocking problems, linguistic, epigraphic, and historical, was successfully treated by Walker on the basis of an ordered collection of material from every source, going far beyond the contents of the British Museum's own collection. In particular the interpretation of mint marks and chronology was such as to throw much new light also on the Sassanians, a topic to which Walker had ever hoped to devote himself one day. The second volume covered the equally complex first period of the coinage of the Arab caliphate, in which extensive use was made of prototypes from the Byzantine empire, together with the Latin-inscribed Arab coins of north Africa and Spain, as well as the Ummayad coins of the post-reform period. The depth and thoroughness with which Walker investigated every ramification of this vast material, and its masterly presentation, form as fundamental a contribution as the first volume to the historical understanding of the vital formative period of the Islamic civilization, in its relationships to Byzantium and to Iran.

Recognition of Walker's achievement in numismatic scholarship was attested by the award of the Huntington medal of the American Numismatic Society in 1955 and of the medal of the Royal Numismatic Society in 1956. He was elected a corresponding member of the Swedish Royal Academy and a member of the Institut d'Egypte, and in 1958 a fellow of the British Academy; a year before his death he was appointed CBE. A portrait medal of Walker by Paul Vincze was struck for the occasion of his retirement, due in 1965.

Walker's work was his life. He remained a bachelor, but he shared his life with J. Harrison Ball. Many remember him as a most human personality and the kindest of colleagues, ever generous and helpful with his advice to any who sought it. His very Scottish and sometimes unexpected sense of humour would not only rejoice his friends but on occasion serve to turn a tricky situation. He genuinely delighted in the good things of life, in music and opera, in the civilized enjoyment of food and drink, wherein he was a considerable connoisseur, and in the peace of the home where he lived latterly in the Essex countryside. He remained ever a devoted member of the Roman Catholic church, into which he was received as a young man, and endured his last illness with stoic courage. He died at St John's Hospital, Chelmsford, on 12 November 1964.   G. K. JENKINS, *rev.*

Sources E. S. G. Robinson, 'John Walker, 1900–1964', *PBA*, 52 (1966), 287–91 · *Numismatic Chronicle*, 7th ser., 5 (1965), 255 · *The Times* (14 Nov 1964) · *WWW* · *CGPLA Eng. & Wales* (1965) · private information (1981)
Likenesses P. Vincze, medal, c.1964–1965
Wealth at death £11,352: probate, 23 Feb 1965, *CGPLA Eng. & Wales*

Walker, Jonathan (1710–1778). *See under* Walker family (*per.* 1741–1833).

Walker, Joseph (1673–1729). *See under* Walker family (*per.* 1741–1833).

Walker, Joseph Cooper (1761–1810), antiquary, was probably born in Dublin, the son of Cooper Walker (1725–1799) of Dublin, and his wife and second cousin, Mary, daughter of William Gordon. He was educated in Dublin by the Revd Thomas Ball. He began work as a clerk in the Irish treasury, but suffered all his life from acute asthma, and travelled abroad frequently in the hope of improving his health. For many years he lived in Italy, where he became acquainted with Sir William and Lady Hamilton. He studied Italian literature and Irish antiquities, and published several works on both subjects, including *A Historical Memoir on Italian Tragedy* (1799) and *A Historical Essay on the Dress of the Ancient and Modern Irish* (1788). But his most significant work was his earliest, the *Historical Memoirs of the Irish Bards* (1786), which—like Charlotte Brooke's *Reliques of Irish Poetry* (1789)—was remarkable as a pioneering study of contemporary literature and vernacular poetry, intended to illustrate the Irish past.

After his return to Ireland Walker settled in his house, St Valeri, Bray, co. Wicklow, where he kept his various art treasures and his large library. He was one of the original members of the Royal Irish Academy, elected in 1785, and contributed various papers to its *Transactions*. Walker died on 12 April 1810 at St Valeri, and was buried on 14 April in St Mary's churchyard, Dublin. He left several works in manuscript, including a journal of his travels; his *Memoirs of Alessandro Tassoni* were published posthumously in 1815. Francis Hardy, the biographer of the earl of Charlemont, completed an inadequate memoir of Walker in 1812, which his family decided to withhold. After Hardy's death the materials were handed to Edward Berwick, who failed to complete it.

D. J. O'DONOGHUE, *rev.* MARIE-LOUISE LEGG

Sources R. A. Breatnach, 'Two eighteenth-century Irish scholars: Joseph Cooper Walker and Charlotte Brooke', *Studia Hibernica*, 5 (1965), 88–97 · S. Walker, 'Preface', in J. C. Walker, *Memoirs of Alessandro Tassoni* (1815), i–lxxix · *GM*, 1st ser., 57 (1787), 34–5 · *GM*, 1st ser., 80 (1810), 487–9 · Burke, *Gen. Ire.*
Archives Mitchell L., Glas., letters · NRA, priv. coll., papers · TCD, corresp. | BL, letters to Bishop Thomas Percy, Egerton MS 201 · Castle Howard, Yorkshire, letters to fifth earl of Carlisle · Dublin City Library, Gilbert collection · FM Cam, letters to Thomas Percy · Hunt. L., letters to Charles O'Conor · NA Scot., corresp. with countess of Moira · Royal Irish Acad.

Walker, Kenneth MacFarlane (1882–1966), urologist and author, was born on 6 June 1882 in Hampstead, London, the third child of William James Walker (1844–1905), a Ceylon merchant, and his wife, Isabella MacFarlane (1881–1921), *née* Currie. Both his parents were Scottish but were permanently settled in the south and Walker spent much of his childhood on a small estate in Essex where he acquired a taste for, and some skill in, country sports. He attended Leys School in Cambridge and, having chosen medicine rather than the family business, entered Gonville and Caius College, Cambridge, to work for the natural sciences tripos. He gained first-class honours in 1904. He went on to St Bartholomew's Hospital medical school in London where, having overcome his initial repugnance for the unsavoury aspects of advanced disease, he developed a lifelong commitment to his profession. His autobiographical writings reveal the conflicting ambitions of these early years, the craving for adventure, for exploration, for a missionary role in bringing relief to the sick and suffering, and more prosaically for attaining fame and fortune as a Harley Street consultant. He took opportunities during his training to explore Iceland, to climb in Switzerland, to tour India, and to trek in east Africa. His successful student career and house surgeoncy gave him hopes of professional advancement.

Walker qualified in 1906, gained the fellowship of the Royal College of Surgeons at the minimum age, and set about research into disorders of the bladder. However, the prospect of many unrewarding years in a junior capacity seemed altogether too unadventurous and in 1910 he took a resident post in Argentina at the British Hospital in Buenos Aires. There he soon built up a private surgical practice, and also kept in touch with the London surgical scene, and at the outbreak of war he returned to serve in the Royal Army Medical Corps. In 1918 he was appointed OBE but refused to accept it, believing that honour to be little better than a music-hall joke and that he deserved something better.

Walker next contemplated going into research but nothing was on offer and Harley Street beckoned. He was appointed officer in charge of the venereal diseases department at St Bartholomew's, where his work resulted in a particular concern with the social and psychological consequences of sexual disorders. In the previous century such expertise could well have led to a place on the full surgical staff, but in the 1920s it was considered appropriate only for genito-urinary surgeons and the teaching hospital could not yet contemplate such specialization. Walker thus became a urologist with appointments at smaller London voluntary hospitals and at St Paul's Hospital for Urinary Diseases in Covent Garden. One of the first in Britain to attempt the endoscopic operation for the relief of prostatic obstruction, he was quick to take up new ideas and to publish his experience, but he was not himself responsible for any major advance. With an established consulting practice dealing with psycho-sexual as well as surgical problems he was particularly conscious of the mental as well as the physical aspects of disease, a concern which was to lead him on to philosophical speculations.

A handsome, athletic, and good-humoured man, Walker was popular with his professional colleagues and on the hunting field, but being curiously careless in his clothing he never quite adopted the style of the complete Harley Street consultant. On 24 April 1926 he married Eileen Marjorie (1903–1983), only daughter of Frederick H. Wilson, with whom he had a son and a daughter. This marriage ended in divorce in 1944. His second wife, whom he married on 23 September 1944, was Mary Gabrielle Piggot (née Ginnett; b. 1908), the divorced wife of an artist. In addition to his Harley Street house he had a country home, Woodcutters, at Little London, South Ambersham in Sussex, where he enjoyed the garden and walking beneath the arching trees of what he called the Cathedral Wood. He remained active and in good health until the last years of his life, when he gradually withdrew from medical practice and gave more and more time to authorship.

Writing came easily to Walker and no fewer than fifty-three books by him are held in the British Library, though there is considerable repetition of the major themes. His prose is straightforward, readily comprehensible, and displays in a multiplicity of quotations a wide acquaintance with the literature of history and philosophy. His first non-medical publication was a children's book, *The Log of the Ark*. His professional works included *Enlarged Prostate* (1926) and *Manual of Male Disorders of Sex* (1939), but he endeavoured to interpret modern medicine to the laity in *The Circle of Life* (1942) and *A Doctor Digresses* (1950). At a time when there was little factual information available to the general public on the subject, his *Physiology of Sex and its Social Implications*, published in the Pelican series in 1940, was well received. In *The Intruder: an Unfinished Self-Portrait* (1936) and *I Talk of Dreams* (1946), he interweaves the story of his life with an exploration of the nature of the human mind.

It was Walker's search for a true philosophy of medicine and for an understanding of the relationship between body and mind which became the pre-occupation of his later years. In 1923 Walker had been introduced to a discussion group led by P. D. Ouspensky, a Russian journalist then expounding the esoteric philosophy of G. I. Gurdjieff, and Walker found in his teachings much to resolve his earlier difficulties. He met the philosopher himself in 1948 and subsequently wrote a series of books, starting with *Venture with Ideas* (1951), in which he endeavours to explain in simple language the amalgam of analysis and mysticism in Gurdjieff's philosophy. Walker's prose is lucid but for most readers the matter remains obscure. The Buddhist element in his beliefs came increasingly to the fore; happily for his family he never attempted to proselytize. Walker died at Pendean, West Lavington, Sussex, on 22 January 1966; his body was cremated and his ashes scattered in the woods near his Sussex home.

DAVID INNES WILLIAMS

Sources *The Lancet* (5 Feb 1966) · *BMJ* (29 Jan 1966), 300 [with portrait] · J. P. Ross and W. R. Le Fanu, *Lives of the fellows of the Royal College of Surgeons of England, 1965–1973* (1981), 377 · K. M. Walker, *The intruder* (1936) · K. M. Walker, *I talk of dreams* (1949) · K. M. Walker, *Venture with ideas* (1951) · private information (2004) · d. cert. · m. certs.

Archives University of Bristol, corresp. and statements relating to trial of *Lady Chatterley's lover*

Likenesses portrait, repro. in *BMJ*, 300

Wealth at death £10,404: probate, 30 June 1966, *CGPLA Eng. & Wales*

Walker, Lucy (1836–1916), mountaineer, was the eldest child of Frank Walker (1808–1872), a lead merchant in Liverpool, and his wife, Jane McNeile, who married in 1835. Her father and younger brother Horace (1838–1908) were both early members of the Alpine Club, and Lucy began her climbing career in 1858 after walking had been prescribed by her doctor as a cure for rheumatism. At that date many women had made expeditions below the snowline, on foot or muleback; some had walked round Monte Rosa and Mont Blanc and crossed high passes; a very few

Lucy Walker (1836–1916), by unknown photographer [sitting, with Frank Walker, and (standing, left to right) unknown, Melchior Anderegg, and A. W. Moore]

had reached the top of Mont Blanc. Lucy Walker was the first woman to climb regularly in the Alps, season after season, with her father, brother, and the Oberland guide Melchior Anderegg. She started modestly with a crossing of the Monte Moro and Théodul passes; by 1862 she had climbed the Finsteraarhorn, Monte Rosa, and Mont Blanc. In the following years she added major peaks of the Valais and Oberland, including the Weisshorn, and made the fourth ascent of the Eiger. There were few mountain huts, and, with the party starting from the valley at midnight or soon after, expeditions were long; Lucy Walker showed that in pace, endurance, and determination, she was the equal of any climber. She was a large, spectacled young woman, who climbed on a diet of sponge cake and champagne.

Only friends and fellow alpinists noticed that, with her father, brother, and Anderegg, she had made the first ascent of the Balmhorn (1864), and had been the first woman up the Wetterhorn (1866), Lyskamm (1868), and Piz Bernina (1869). However, when, on 22 August 1871, climbing with her father and Anderegg, and wearing her usual white print dress, she was the first woman up the Matterhorn, she became famous. It was only six years since Whymper had been the first to climb it, and the accident on the way down, when four of his party were killed, had given the peak a lurid fame. Lucy Walker's feat brought some criticism from those who thought ladies should stick to the valleys, but it was robustly celebrated in *Punch*, in verses beginning 'A lady has clomb to the Matterhorn's summit':

No glacier can baffle, no precipice balk her,
No peak rise above her, however sublime,

Give three times three cheers for intrepid Miss Walker,
I say, my boys, doesn't she know how to climb!
(*Punch*, 61, 26 Aug 1871, 86)

In 1872 Lucy Walker's father died; but by 1873 she was back in the Alps with her brother and Anderegg, whom she described as 'one of the finest and most well-bred gentlemen I have ever known' (*Ladies' Alpine Club Year Book*, 1915, 4); they climbed the Jungfrau, Täschhorn, and Weisshorn, and she continued to add new peaks to her record until 1879, when her doctor advised her to give up long expeditions. (This occasioned a rather mawkish poem by Fanny Kemble in *Temple Bar* (1889), on past glories now denied.) Lucy Walker continued to walk in the Alps with Anderegg and other friends. 'Her energies were immense', wrote Charles Pilkington (Gardiner and Pilkington, 101), who found that travelling in her company was always lightened by her vivacity and pithy remarks. She seldom talked of her own climbs, and though she did make a list of her ninety-eight expeditions, she published no account of them. Acclaimed as the pioneer of women climbers, in 1909 she joined the newly formed Ladies' Alpine Club, and was its second president, in 1913–15.

Away from the mountains, Lucy Walker led the life of a cultured Victorian lady at her home in Liverpool. She was a charming hostess, an expert needlewoman, and was fluent in several languages. She died at her home, South Lodge, Prince's Park, Toxteth Park, Liverpool, after a long illness on 10 September 1916.   JANET ADAM SMITH

Sources F. Gardiner and C. Pilkington, 'In memoriam: Miss Lucy Walker', *Alpine Journal*, 31 (1917), 97–102 • 'S', *Ladies' Alpine Club Year Book* (1917), 23–7 • A. L. Mumm, *The Alpine Club register*, 1 (1923) • M. Morin, *Encordées* (1936) • C.-E. Engel, *They came to the hills* (1952) • C. Williams, *Women on the rope* (1973) • 'A climbing girl', *Punch*, 61 (1871), 86 • F. Kemble, 'Lines addressed to Miss L. W.', *Temple Bar*, 85 (1889), 350 • d. cert.
Likenesses E. Whymper, engraving, 1864 (*The club room of Zermatt*), repro. in E. Whymper, *Scrambles amongst the Alps in the years 1860–1869* (1871), 262 • photograph, 1870 • photographs, 1871, repro. in Gardiner and Pilkington, 'In memoriam: Miss Lucy Walker', facing pp. 98–9 • group portrait, photograph, Alpine Club, London [see illus.]
Wealth at death £12,034 10s.: probate, 2 Jan 1917, *CGPLA Eng. & Wales*

Walker, Sir Mark (1827–1902), army officer, was born at Gore Port on 24 November 1827, the eldest of three sons of Captain Alexander Walker of Gore Port, Finea, co. Westmeath, and Elizabeth, daughter of William Elliott, of Ratherogue, co. Carlow. His father, of the 97th (West Kent) regiment, served at the battles of Vimeiro, Salamanca, Talavera, Busaco, and Albuera, and at Talavera saved the colours of his regiment, which he carried, by tearing them off the pole and tying them round his waist. Sir Samuel *Walker and Alexander Walker, captain 38th South Staffordshire regiment, who died unmarried at Aden of cholera in 1867, were younger brothers. Educated at Arlington House, Portarlington, under the Revd John Ambrose Wall, Mark Walker entered the army on 25 September 1846, in the 30th foot, without purchase, on account of his father's services. In 1851 the regiment embarked for Cephalonia, and was detached in the Ionian Islands.

Walker was appointed adjutant to the company depot at Walmer, then at Dover, and in 1853 at Fermoy. In October 1853 he went with a draft to Cork, and embarked for Gibraltar, where the regiment was then stationed. On 4 February 1854 he was promoted lieutenant and appointed adjutant. On 1 May 1854 the regiment embarked for Turkey; it camped at Scutari, and formed part of the 1st brigade under Brigadier-General Pennefather, and of the 2nd division under Sir De Lacy Evans. He served with his regiment in the Crimea, was wounded at the Alma, and won the Victoria Cross at Inkerman. He was with the regiment during the winter of 1854, serving continually in the trenches. On the night of 21 April, when on trench duty, he volunteered and led a party which took and destroyed a Russian rifle pit, for which he was mentioned in dispatches and promoted into the 'Buffs' (later the East Kent regiment). On the night of 9 June in the trenches he was severely wounded by a piece of howitzer shell and had his right arm amputated that night. He received a brevet majority (6 June 1856) and the Mejidiye (fifth class).

Walker served with the Buffs in England, Ireland, the Ionian Islands, and India, from where, in November 1859, he went with a wing of the regiment to Canton (Guangzhou). Serving through the China campaign, he was on 30 March 1860 appointed brigade major of the 4th brigade, which was in the 2nd division, commanded by Sir Robert Napier. He was at the capture of Chushan, the battle of Sinho, the assault of the Taku (Dagu) forts, the surrender of Peking (Beijing), and the signing of the treaty of peace by Lord Elgin. He was promoted brevet lieutenant-colonel on 15 February 1861. He returned with the regiment to England, arriving on 15 April 1862.

In July 1867, when the Buffs went to India, Walker remained in command of the company depot at home, and after two years exchanged into the 2nd battalion at Aldershot. He was promoted brevet colonel on 15 February 1869, and on 3 August 1870 was advanced to a regimental majority in the 1st battalion, then quartered at Sitapur in Oudh. He served with them in India from 1871 to 1873 at Benares, Lucknow, and Calcutta. On 10 December 1873 he was appointed to command the 45th regiment (Sherwood Foresters), with which he served in Burma and India. In May 1875 he was made CB, and in August was appointed a brigadier-general to command the Nagpur force, with headquarters at Kamptee. He vacated this command on 4 November 1879, owing to promotion to major-general (11 November 1878).

On 22 November 1879 Walker proceeded to England. He married on 6 June 1881 Catharine, daughter of Robert Bruce Chichester, barrister, of Arlington, Devon, brother of Sir John Palmer Bruce Chichester, first baronet, of Arlington; she survived him. On 1 April 1883 he was appointed to the command the 1st brigade at Aldershot. From 1 April 1884 to 1 April 1888 he commanded the infantry at Gibraltar. On 16 December 1888 he became lieutenant-general, and general on 15 February 1893. He retired on 1 April 1893, and on 3 June following was appointed KCB. On 27 September 1900 he was appointed

colonel of the Sherwood Foresters. He died at Arlington rectory, near Barnstaple, on 18 July 1902, and was buried at Folkestone.   H. M. VIBART, rev. JAMES LUNT

Sources A. W. Kinglake, *The invasion of the Crimea*, [new edn], 8 (1888) · M. Mann, *China, 1860* (1989) · G. Blaxland, *The buffs* (1972) · Burke, *Gen. GB* · *Army List* · *Hart's Army List* · *Dod's Peerage* · *The XXX: Journal of the 1st battalion east Lancashire regiment*
Likenesses Giore, oils, 1891; bequeathed to the Buffs · memorial tablet, Canterbury Cathedral · oils, Institute of Directors, Pall Mall · print (in uniform; after photograph?); formerly in possession of United Services and Royal Aero Club, London
Wealth at death £15,240 16s. 3d.: probate, 17 Oct 1902, *CGPLA Eng. & Wales*

Walker [*née* Leslie; *known as* Hamilton], **Lady Mary** (1736–1822), novelist, was born on 8 May 1736 at Melville House, by Cupar, Fife, the youngest child of Alexander Leslie, fifth earl of Leven and fourth earl of Melville (*c.*1699–1754), and his second wife, Elizabeth (1699–1783), daughter of David Monypenny of Pitmilly. On 3 January 1762 Lady Mary married Dr James Walker of Inverdovat, a physician in Edinburgh. The Walkers had three sons and one daughter, but it was probably an unhappy marriage. In a late letter (of 1818), Lady Mary says that 'with a family of young children … abandoned by their father' she was forced to publish to 'cloath, feed, and educate them' (Fraser, 2.329). Lady Mary's first two novels—*Letters from the Duchess de Crui and Others* (1775) and *Memoirs of the Marchioness de Louvoi* (1777)—are epistolary and didactic. *Munster Village* followed in 1778, and *The Life of Mrs Justman* in 1782 (the latter was referred to in a notice to the later *La famille du duc de Popoli*, although no copy seems to have survived). The novels have little to offer modern readers, although *Munster Village* was seriously reviewed in the *Gentleman's Magazine* (48, 1778, 424–5). Its concern with female education and intellectual equality in marriage shows Lady Mary sufficiently advanced for her time, and the novel was one of the earlier works of the period to feature an ideal community, yet the writing is marred by sententiousness and relentless intellectual name-dropping. All the fictions attempt to combine romance and morality but lack perception of nuances of character. Jane Austen may have read the novels: her use of the names Bingley and Bennet from *Munster Village* and Dashwood from *Louvoi* seems more than coincidence.

It is unclear how long Lady Mary and her husband lived together or when Walker died, but by 1784 Lady Mary had formed a relationship with George Robinson Hamilton, who owned the estate Success in Jamaica; the couple moved to France, initially to Lille. Hamilton is usually referred to as her second husband; she certainly entered into a financial agreement with him and they had two daughters, but there may never have been a marriage—she does not refer to him in her will as having been her husband. Lady Mary's daughter Henrietta-Isabella Walker married the soldier and playwright Étienne de Jouy in 1793; another daughter, presumably with Hamilton, later married General Thiébault. After Hamilton's death Lady Mary made the acquaintance of the eccentric English scholar Sir Herbert *Croft, and the pair moved to Amiens, setting up house there entirely on the basis of friendship.

Croft engaged the struggling young writer Charles Nodier as his secretary, and Nodier's tasks included translating *Munster Village* and assisting Lady Mary to write a novel in French, *La famille du duc de Popoli*. Nodier's letters reveal an indulgent, if sometimes exasperated, stance towards his employers. He recognizes Lady Mary's goodness, while describing her French as 'macaronique' and her writing as perhaps 'trop fécond' (*Charles Nodier: Correspondence*, 1.352–3). Nodier saw his versions of *Popoli* (1810), and *Munster Village* (1811), through the press, even producing in 1812 a sequel to *Popoli*, called *Auguste et Jules de Popoli*. Lady Mary had been aware for some time that she was being cheated of her proper rents from the Jamaican estate, and she went in 1815 to Jamaica to settle her affairs. After this successful journey until her death in Brompton, Middlesex, she lived in and around London with her widowed daughter Sophia Saint John Hamilton Alderson. Her will proved in July 1822 divided her estate between her daughter Sophia and her son Lieutenant-Colonel Leslie Walker.

DOROTHY MCMILLAN

Sources W. Fraser, ed., *The Melvilles, earls of Melville, and the Leslies, earls of Leven*, 3 vols. (1890) · *Charles Nodier: Correspondence de jeunesse*, ed. J.-R. Dahan, 2 vols. (Geneva, 1995) · P.-L. Jacob, 'Charles Nodier chez Lady Hamilton', *Le Bibliophile Français*, 4 (1869), 204–12, 276–87 · S. F. B. de Genlis, *Mémoires inédits de madame la comtesse de Genlis* (1825), 4.126–7, 133 · review, *GM*, 1st ser., 48 (1778), 425–5 · A. R. Oliver, *Charles Nodier: pilot of Romanticism* (1964) · J. Balteau and others, eds., *Dictionnaire de biographie française* (Paris, 1979–), vol. 18
Wealth at death £10,000 and personal effects: will, proved 5 July 1822

Walker, Mary Russell (1846–1938), headmistress and promoter of women's education, was born in Edinburgh, the first of two daughters of William Walker, accountant of the National Bank of Scotland, and his wife, Margaret Gray. She had what she described as 'a somewhat desultory' private education in Glasgow. Then her father's work took the family to Sweden and California. Back in Edinburgh after her father's retirement in 1873, she was frustrated by the genteel pastimes of polite, professional New Town society. She joined a group of bright and articulate young women who had already begun to campaign for admission to Edinburgh University, establishing herself as both the chief intellect and administrator of the group.

The campaign had started in 1867 with the founding of the Edinburgh Ladies' Educational Association, later the Edinburgh Association for the University Education of Women. It offered classes for women only, taught by male lecturers, at the end of which the university could award a certificate in arts, intended to be of similar standard and standing to an MA degree. Mary Walker was awarded the first class in all seven subjects.

The Scottish educational tradition had allowed a ladder of opportunity for the 'lad o' pairts', the bright boy from humble circumstances who could work his way through school and university, but girls had rarely reached even the lowest rungs. Mary Walker and her group believed that the universities would not take women seriously until large numbers had acquired more than the most basic elementary education. In 1876 they advertised in *The Scotsman*, offering classes for women who wished to reach university entrance standards. Premises were secured in St George's Hall in the centre of Edinburgh and a tutor, Mr M'Glashan, was appointed to 'the singular task of teaching the rudiments of grammar and arithmetic to grown-up women with all the zest and freshness of one who makes an experiment' (Shepley, 7). The response was so great that in 1877 Mary Walker took charge as full-time superintendent, secretary, and treasurer of the St George's Hall oral and correspondence classes.

From all over Scotland, from women of all ages, Mary Walker received letters seeking help. She devised a system of learning by correspondence which included preparation for examinations from the most basic to the LLA (lady literate in arts) of St Andrews University, the nearest a Scotswoman could then come to a degree. She provided the smooth administration which allowed St George's Hall classes to become a kind of open university for nineteenth-century Scotswomen. She was not always successful, as she later recalled: 'From time to time students withdrew—from ill-health usually, but occasionally the work appeared to interfere with other duties, in one case with attendance at balls—and the balls carried the day' (Welsh, 16). By 1893 there were 193 students attending classes in Edinburgh and 657 learning by correspondence.

In 1882 Mary Walker moved to the Bishopgate (later Maria Grey) Training College in London to work for the Cambridge University teachers' certificate. Here she formed a strong personal link between the English pioneers and the Edinburgh group. She headed the list of candidates in her year and was appointed lecturer in the college, specializing in psychology. In 1885 she was persuaded to return to manage the classes in Edinburgh. Supported by Edinburgh's first professor of education, Simon Laurie, she convinced her friends on the committee that Scotland must have its own training college for women secondary teachers. St George's Training College for Women Teachers opened in 1886, with Mary Walker as principal, funds of £501 8*s*. 6*d*., and seven students. She was involved in the kindergarten movement, the development of arts and crafts teaching (using her knowledge of Swedish to translate teachers' handbooks on *slöjd* methods), and in educational psychology.

In 1888 St George's High School for Girls opened with Mary Walker taking on the additional duties of headmistress. It was the first academic day school of its kind for girls in Scotland, four years before the Scottish universities finally admitted women. The school provided teaching practice for the college students and the college provided well-qualified teachers for the school. Here she could introduce many of the ideas and methods, including the Ling system of physical training, which had so excited her in England. By 1900 a steady stream of her pupils had passed through Scottish and English universities. She was always careful in her dress, writing of 'the injury that can be done by untidiness in the teacher's person or general arrangements' (Welsh, 88).

Mary Walker retired in 1910 after fighting her last battle

with the educational establishment, resisting the demands of the inspectors of the Scottish education department to increase the teaching of sewing and domestic science. In retirement she set up house with her sister, Elizabeth Walker, and continued to take an interest in college and school. Mary Walker died on 20 November 1938 at her home, 2 Rochester Terrace, Edinburgh. Her funeral was held at the Edinburgh crematorium.

NIGEL SHEPLEY

Sources St George's High School for Girls, Edinburgh, archive · B. W. Welsh, *After the dawn: a record of the pioneer work in Edinburgh for the higher education of women* (1939) · N. Shepley, *Women of independent mind: St George's School, Edinburgh, and the campaign for women's education, 1888–1988* (1988) · d. cert.
Archives St George's High School for Girls, Edinburgh
Likenesses oils, c.1938, St George's High School for Girls archive, Edinburgh · photograph, repro. in Welsh, *After the dawn*, frontispiece · photographs, St George's High School for Girls archive, Edinburgh

Walker, Sir Norman Purvis (1862–1942), dermatologist, was born at the Free Church manse, Dysart, Fife, on 2 August 1862, the only son of the Revd Dr Norman Macdonald Lockhart Walker, for many years editor of the journal of the Free Church of Scotland, and his wife, Christian Alexander Normand. He was educated at the Edinburgh Academy and graduated MB CM of Edinburgh University (1884) and MD (1888), having also spent some time in Europe. His first post (1883) was as resident physician to Claude Muirhead at the Edinburgh Royal Infirmary. For the next five years he was in general practice in Dalston, Cumberland. He became honorary secretary and president of the Carlisle Medical Society. He married Annie (b. 1864/5), only daughter of Edward Trimble, a Dalston brewer, on 24 August 1887. It was a long and happy marriage; they had three sons and one daughter.

Walker then studied with the great names in dermatology. He went to its world centre in Vienna, where Ferdinand Ritter von Hebra's son, Hans von Hebra, and son-in-law, Moriz Kohn Kaposi, continued the elder Hebra's tradition. In Prague, Walker studied with Professor Filipp Josef Pick and learned the new scientific basis of dermatology in histopathology and bacteriology, which influenced his own book on skin diseases. Finally Walker became a favourite student of Paul Gerson Unna in Hamburg.

After returning to Edinburgh, Walker was appointed assistant physician to the skin department of the Royal Infirmary (1892–1906), under Allan Jamieson. When Jamieson retired, Walker became full physician, in charge of the skin wards (1906–24), and consultant physician (1925–42). He was also lecturer in dermatology in the university and royal colleges and had a private practice. Walker ran a special clinic on Wednesday afternoons to treat lupus vulgaris, a rare form of skin tuberculosis which causes severe disfigurement. Here patients were not embarrassed as they met only those who were similarly afflicted. Walker used injection of tuberculin, X-rays and ultraviolet light, and continued this clinic after he retired. He also translated G. H. A. Hansen and C. Looft's German text as *Leprosy in its Clinical and Pathological Aspects*

(1895). He then translated one of the seminal texts in dermatology, by his friend Paul Gerson Unna, as *The Histopathology of Diseases of the Skin* (1896). Walker's *Introduction to Dermatology*, based on his lectures to undergraduates, was published in 1899. The tenth edition appeared in 1939 with Walker and G. H. Percival as authors. For some time Walker was editor of the *Scottish Medical and Surgical Journal*, and joint editor of the *Edinburgh Medical Journal* after the two journals merged.

Walker had a natural aptitude for university administration and became deeply involved in academic affairs. He became a member of the Edinburgh University court and curator of patronage, and was inspector of anatomy for Scotland. He was elected fellow of the Royal College of Physicians of Edinburgh in 1892, and was treasurer in 1908–29, and president from 1929 to 1931. Walker's business acumen served the college well. He took a conspicuous part in the organization of medical services in Scotland as convenor of the Scottish medical service committee during the First World War. He was especially involved after the war in the work of the Highlands and Islands Medical Service Board, which had been established in 1913.

Walker was the directly elected representative of Scottish practitioners on the General Medical Council (GMC) from 1906 to 1941. After being chairman of business, he was elected president in 1931, succeeding the outstanding president, Sir Donald MacAlister, and held office until 1939. Few men could rival MacAlister's brilliance. However, Walker was an able, businesslike president, with profound knowledge of the council's history and procedure, which he combined with a rare attention to detail. In 1922 and 1927 he visited India at the instance of the secretary of state, Edwin Samuel Montague, after the GMC became aware of laxity in the conduct of examinations there. Walker's tact and judgement were invaluable, and his report on the recognition of Indian qualifications contributed greatly to improving medical education in India. He was knighted (India Office list) in 1923.

In 1906 Walker was president of the Fife Medical Association. He was an honorary member of the American, and a corresponding member of the New York, American, French, and Danish dermatological associations; he was also an honorary fellow of the American Medical Association and an honorary member of the Association of Military Surgeons of the United States. His other distinctions included honorary degrees of LLD at St Andrews (1920), Edinburgh (1926), and Bristol (1933), and MD Dublin (1935).

Walker had a rather aloof and unapproachable manner, but possessed the judicial approach needed in the work of the GMC. He was among the first people in Scotland to receive insulin: he developed diabetes shortly after the First World War and Low (*Edinburgh Medical Journal*) considered that he was only saved by insulin sent to him by its discoverers from Toronto before it was available on the market. Walker died at home in Greensyke, Balerno, Midlothian, on 7 November 1942. He was survived by his wife and children. His second son, Edward Robert Charles Walker (*c*.1899–1986), became Scottish secretary of the British Medical Association and served on the GMC.

GEOFFREY L. ASHERSON

Sources *The Times* (10 Nov 1942) · *BMJ* (21 Nov 1942), 622 · J. T. Crissey and L. C. Parish, *The dermatology and syphilology of the nineteenth century* (1981) · R. Low, 'Scotland: Norman Walker', *The Lancet* (5 Dec 1942), 683 · R. Low, *The Lancet* (21 Nov 1942), 630–31 · R. C. Low, *Edinburgh Medical Journal*, 3rd ser., 49 (1942), 776–8 · R. Low, *British Journal of Dermatology and Syphilis*, 55 (1943), 102–5 · J. Macleod, 'Milestones on a dermatological journey', *British Journal of Dermatology and Syphilis*, 61 (1949), 1–16 · b. cert. · m. cert. · d. cert. · *DNB*

Archives Royal College of Physicians of Edinburgh, notes

Likenesses J. Bowie, oils, *c*.1931–1939, General Medical Council, London · portrait, 1932, repro. in R. C. Low, *Edinburgh Medical Journal*, 776–8 · W. & E. Drummond Young, photograph, repro. in *BMJ* · W. & E. Drummond Young, photograph, Wellcome L. · photograph, Royal College of Physicians of Edinburgh

Wealth at death £13,491 3*s*. 6*d*.: confirmation, 2 March 1943, *CCI*

Walker, Obadiah (1616–1699), college head and author, was born at Darfield, near Barnsley, the son of William Walker of Worsbrough Dale in the West Riding of Yorkshire. He was baptized at his father's parish on 17 September 1616. Nothing is known of his schooling. He matriculated at Oxford on 5 April 1633, having previously entered University College. The learned Abraham Woodhead, a Yorkshire compatriot, was assigned his tutor. The appointment marked the beginning of a lifelong intimacy between them. A ready scholar with an aptitude for languages Walker displayed an appetite for learning well beyond the bounds of the arts curriculum. He was elected Freiston exhibitioner on 1 October 1633 and a perpetual fellow on 10 August 1635. He graduated BA on 4 July 1635, and MA on 23 April 1638. Shortly afterwards he received ordination in the Church of England. A born teacher he inspired intellectual endeavour and personal affection in his tutorial pupils.

In the great rebellion Walker took the king's side. On 1 September 1642 he and Woodhead were nominated delegates for the defence of the university, a tribute to his standing in Oxford. Membership of the delegacy brought him into contact with the leaders of Anglican royalism, especially Gilbert Sheldon. Unlike Woodhead, Walker remained at his post throughout the war, and discharged the office of college bursar. He preached before Charles I: a privilege which earned him his grace for the degree of BD in June 1646. Modestly, he waived the degree.

With the surrender of Oxford, Walker was exposed to the wrath of the victorious rebel parliament. Arraigned before the parliamentary visitors he deferred submission on 19 May 1648, 'as beinge yet unsatisfied' of the lawfulness of the visitation. Three days later he was ordered to be expelled, and was finally ejected from his fellowship on 7 July for 'high contempt of the authoritie of Parliament' (Burrows, 103, 143).

Interregnum and Restoration Walker made a virtue of necessity by electing to travel. Intent on improving himself 'in all kinds of polite literature' (*DNB*), he visited Paris and Rome. His time abroad stimulated his interest in different societies. Already a classicist he developed a passion for numismatics and antiquities that stayed with him for life. For the first time he encountered the splendours and challenges of Counter-Reformation Catholicism. He undertook, about 1650, on the recommendation of John Evelyn, to act as tutor to Henry and Charles, the sons of Henry Hildyard, of Horsley, Surrey. In October 1655 he and his pupils were at Basel. The conversion to Rome of his elder pupil, Henry Hildyard, suggested that Walker was, to say no more, complacent in his attitude to Catholicism.

After wandering 'a long time up and down' (*DNB*) Walker returned to England. In 1659 he published at London his first book, *Some Instruction Concerning the Art of Oratory*, the fruit of his years of study and teaching. At his return it is likely that he renewed his acquaintance with Sheldon through his friend Abraham Woodhead, whose poverty Sheldon is known to have relieved. Following the Restoration both Walker and Woodhead, as well as Sheldon, were reinstated in their Oxford preferment. On 15 August 1660 Charles II's commissioners for visiting the university ordered the removal of the intruded fellows and the restoration of Walker and Woodhead, the 'lawfull and undoubted Fellowes of the said Colledg[e]' (Beddard, *Restoration Oxford*, 1.164).

Walker found it difficult to settle down. He soon set off on his travels. Again, he made for Rome as a private tutor. The college gave him repeated leave of absence, granting him four terms away in August 1661, on 31 January 1663, and 23 March 1664, and a further two terms on 14 January 1665, after the expiry of which he kept residence. On the death of the royalist master, Dr Thomas Walker, he voted for his successor, Richard Clayton, on 6 December 1665. Abroad he observed the 'divers communities' through which he passed and conversed with 'their most eminent directors and professors', experiences which distinguished him from most stay-at-home Oxford dons. At his homecoming he was, according to the Benedictine monk Richard Reeve, in every way 'best qualified for the advancement and direction of collegiate and academicall studies' (Beddard, 'James II', 922–3).

Walker was soon drawn back into the intellectual and administrative life of the university. He found a powerful patron in Dean John Fell of Christ Church. As a royalist cleric who reverenced the early fathers and a seasoned tutor who loved history and the classics, he fitted easily into Restoration Oxford. Fell did more than befriend him, he employed him in some of his enterprises. In 1667 Walker became a delegate of the newly founded university press. It was his influence that brought Anthony Wood the offer to publish his pioneering *History and Antiquities of Oxford*. A connoisseur of Roman antiquity he joined Evelyn to secure the Arundel marbles for the university in 1667.

Walker's knowledge of European scholarship and continental contacts enabled him to swell the foreign holdings of the public library. In the early 1670s he obtained Ciacconius's *Columna Trajani*, Peruta's *Book of Medals*, and 'other bookes from Rome'. An informed bibliophile he helped to price duplicates in Bodley's library, the sale of which added to the book purchasing fund. In 1673 he published two works: *Of Education. Especially of Young Gentlemen*, a distillation of his teaching experience, which in 1699 reached its sixth edition; and *Artis rationis ad mentem nominalium libri tres*, an introduction to logic that made use of the medieval nominalists. He was behind the Oxford publication of Ockham's *Summa totius logicae* of 1675.

Master of University College At the death of Richard Clayton on 14 June 1676 Walker, already the senior fellow, was an obvious choice for the mastership. He was unanimously elected on 22 June. He proved an active and popular head of house. An epistolary campaign, addressed to grandees and old members, raised money to complete the main quadrangle by erecting the eastern range. Following Fell's example he aspired to give an intellectual lead to his college. Calling on the assistance of his fellows he undertook an edition in Latin of Sir John Spelman's unpublished 'Life of Alfred', the reputed founder of University College. The work was chiefly intended to let the world know that its benefactions were, as he put it, 'not bestowed on mere drones' (Beddard, 'Tory Oxford', 864).

Paradoxically, the publication in 1678 of the *Vita Aelfredi* turned out to be a mixed blessing. While the elegantly printed folio, augmented by Walker's Old English erudition and illustrated by engravings of contemporary coinage, achieved its primary aim of justifying continuing financial support for his college, it also attracted condemnation in 1679 in—of all places—parliament. In the Commons that veteran sniffer out of popery, Sir Harbottle Grimston, detected a whiff of Romanism about the book. Walker's dedication to Charles II, who was fulsomely compared to the Catholic King Alfred, and seeming reconciliation of the royal supremacy with papal obedience, offended protestant prejudices. Grimston's anti-Catholicism, stirred up by Gilbert Burnet, had been directed against the master by two parliamentarian quondams of the college: Israel Tonge (Tongue) and William Shippen, who spied a chance to supplant him.

Matters were compounded by Walker's known friendship with the Catholic convert Abraham Woodhead. At his demise in May 1678 Woodhead had left Walker a property at Hoxton that was believed to be a popish school, and, though a Catholic and non-resident, Woodhead had been permitted to draw his fellowship stipend from the college since 1660. Notwithstanding the master's negative return when called on by the vice-chancellor to identify suspected Catholics in his society in February 1679, suspicions lingered on the score of his religion. This was not helped by the preaching in June 1680 of a 'popishly affected' university sermon by one of his erstwhile pupils, Francis Nicholson, and by his publication of Woodhead's *Of the Benefits of Our Saviour Jesus Christ to Mankind*, also in 1680 (Beddard, 'James II', 918). Against the background of whig exertions to exclude a Catholic successor from the throne, the suggestion that any tory don sympathized with popery provoked widespread public concern.

Less controversially Walker published *Propositions Concerning Optic Glasses* (1679), proof of his interest in the experimental sciences, and 'A description of Greenland', which he contributed to volume one of *The English Atlas* (1680). In 1682 he submitted proposals to Elias Ashmole regarding his donation of the Tradescant 'Rarities' to the university and the foundation of his museum.

The Catholic challenge Whatever the inner state of his convictions Walker did not avow himself a Catholic until 1686, the second year of James II's reign. In 1685 he published an anonymous life of Christ, which was instantly ascribed to him, albeit it was probably of Woodhead's composing. The honour which the volume accorded to Our Lady and the Petrine claims of Rome caused the vice-chancellor, Timothy Halton, to ban the sale of the master's books in Oxford, following a failed attempt to remove the unacceptable passages before it was printed. Fell, hitherto a friend, deleted Walker from his will as a lessee of the university's privilege of printing.

Unintimidated Walker stood his ground. He was joined by further converts: Nathaniel Boyse and Thomas Deane, fellows of University College, and John Barnard, fellow of Brasenose. Known as the master's 'three disciples' they were in October 1686 joined by John Massey of Merton, Walker's former servitor. All four academics had long ago fallen under the spell of his cosmopolitan learning and attractive personality. In January 1686 the master was summoned to court. There he consulted John Leyburn, bishop of Adrumetum, the recently arrived vicar apostolic sent from Rome, and was persuaded to declare his conversion. Together they laid plans for protecting him and his companions. On returning to college he abstained from chapel prayers.

On 3 May James issued his dispensation, allowing the converts to retain their posts, and permitted free access to the royal court, which was to be their lifeline against Oxonian opposition. The accompanying licence authorized Walker to print, reprint, publish, and sell some thirty-six Catholic works, with an annual limit prescribed of 20,000 copies for any one title. James's optimism expected Walker, with his knowledge of the press, to make a massive contribution to the missionizing effort which, under royal auspices, began to forge ahead. Aided by Francis Nicholson, Walker began to publish apologetical pieces taken from Woodhead's manuscript writings.

Eager to gain converts Walker boldly erected a Catholic altar in the spring of 1686, using a garret in his lodgings. Growing attendances quickly overwhelmed the capacity of this and its downstairs successor. Armed with James's mandate in August, he annexed two ground floor rooms and made them into an oratory. Mass began to be celebrated publicly on the feast of the assumption. Walker invited the Jesuit priests Edward Humberston and Joseph Wakeman to act as chaplains. In January 1687 James commanded the appropriation of the sequestrated revenue of a fellowship to be applied to their upkeep. The king attended vespers in Walker's oratory during his state visit to Oxford in September 1687. Meanwhile, assured of

James's countenance, Walker embarked on a policy of Catholic imperialism. He succeeded in advancing Massey to the deanery of Christ Church, and Barnard to the moral philosophy lectureship. He even admitted Catholic undergraduates to his college.

Denied access to the university press by his protestant adversaries Walker established his own in University College in 1687, from which he issued his first overtly Catholic work, Woodhead's *Two Discourses Concerning the Adoration of our Blessed Saviour in the Holy Eucharist*: a tract which elicited protestant replies, and, in turn, begot Walker's *Animadversions* (1688) on Henry Aldrich's strictures. His maintenance of the crown's traditional powers to make and unmake corporations, academical, ecclesiastical, and municipal, added political resentment to mounting confessional hatred. Unable to touch him the wits of Christ Church were reduced to bribing 'a poor natural' to sing rhymed doggerel at his door:

> Oh, old Obadiah,
> Sing *Ave Maria*,
> But so will not I-a,
> For why-a?
> I had rather be a fool than a knave-a.
> (*Le Fleming MSS*, 25, 200)

His gratitude to the king was shown by his erection of James's statue over the inner gatehouse of the college in 1688. University College was one of the few societies in Oxford to celebrate the birth of the Catholic prince of Wales in June.

Revolution, imprisonment, and destitution The protestant reckoning, when it came, was swift. On 9 November 1688, four days after William of Orange's invasion, Walker packed up his books, barred his door, and left his lodgings for London to be near a monarch who could no longer protect him. Seeing flight as his only option he made for the coast. On 11 December he was arrested at Sittingbourne in the company of Bishop Giffard of Madura, former president of Magdalen, and Father Poulton, schoolmaster of the Savoy. Committed to Maidstone gaol they were subsequently removed to the Tower. Meantime, acting on a complaint from the fellows, the vice-chancellor, Ironside, and the visitors of University College proceeded on 4 February 1689 to declare the mastership vacant and to confirm the election of a new master.

On 23 October, the first day of term, a writ of habeas corpus was moved for Walker, whereupon the House of Commons ordered him to be brought to the bar. He was charged with being reconciled to the Church of Rome and other 'high crimes and misdemeanours', and remanded back to the Tower as a traitor. He remained a prisoner until 30 January 1690 when, after an appearance in king's bench, he was reluctantly freed 'on great security' (*Life and Times of Anthony Wood*, 3.324). His bail was discharged on 2 June. He was excepted from the Act of Indemnity. Thereafter he lived privately in London, regained his customary equipoise, and reapplied his mind to scholarship, publishing *Some Instruction in the Art of Grammar* (1691) for would-be Latinists, and a *Greek and Roman History Illustrated by Coins and Medals* (1692). He never married.

Walker's former scholar, the eminent physician Dr John Radcliffe, whom he had tried unsuccessfully to convert to Rome, 'sent him once a year a new suit of clothes, with ten broad pieces and twelve bottles of richest canary to support his drooping spirits' (*DNB*). Increasingly infirm with age he was offered a home by Radcliffe. He died in London on 21 January 1699, and was interred in St Pancras's churchyard, where Radcliffe erected a tombstone with the memorial inscription: 'O. W. per bonam famam et infamiam' ('Obadiah Walker through good fame and ill'). The extent of his infamy was that, like James II, to whom he remained loyal to the end, he had preferred the Catholic religion to the Church of England. Stripped of confessional obloquy his reputation as one of the most productive scholars of Restoration Oxford still stands. His ghost is reputed to haunt staircase 8 of University College.

R. A. P. J. BEDDARD

Sources R. A. Beddard, 'Tory Oxford', *Hist. U. Oxf.* 4: *17th-cent. Oxf.*, 863–906 • R. A. Beddard, 'James II and the Catholic challenge', *Hist. U. Oxf.* 4: *17th-cent. Oxf.*, 907–54 • R. Beddard, ed., *A kingdom without a king: the journal of the provisional government in the revolution of 1688* (1988) • Wood, *Ath. Oxon.*, new edn • *The life and times of Anthony Wood*, ed. A. Clark, 5 vols., OHS, 19, 21, 26, 30, 40 (1891–1900) • R. A. Beddard, *Restoration Oxford, 1660–1667*, 1– (2002–) • M. Burrows, ed., *The register of the visitors of the University of Oxford, from AD 1647 to AD 1658*, CS, new ser., 29 (1881) • Evelyn, *Diary* • *A dialogue between Father Gifford, the late popish president of Maudlin, and Obadiah Walker, master of University, upon their new colledge preferment in Newgate* (1689) • A. E. Firth, 'Obadiah Walker', *University College Record*, 4 (1962), 95–106, 261–73 • R. Darwall-Smith, 'Obadiah Walker in his own words', *University College Record*, 12/2 (1998), 56–68 • L. Mitchell, 'Obadiah Walker: addendum', *University College Record*, 12/2 (1998), 69–73 • *DNB* • *The manuscripts of S. H. Le Fleming*, HMC, 25 (1890)

Archives University College, Oxford, corresp. and papers | Bodl. Oxf., MSS Ballard, MSS Wood F, MS J. Walker c. 8, MSS Tanner, MSS Rawlinson C. • PRO, SP 31, SP 44 • University College, Oxford, Registrum I

Walker, Patrick Chrestien Gordon, Baron Gordon-Walker (1907–1980), politician and author, was born on 7 April 1907 at Worthing, Sussex, the eldest son and child of Alan Lachlan Gordon Walker (d. 1932), an Indian civil servant, and his wife, Dora Marguerite Chrestien. Brought up in the Punjab, where his father was a land settlement officer from 1913, and later a judge in Lahore, he was educated at Wellington College, Berkshire, from 1921 to 1925. In his final year, when he was a prefect and head of house, he won a scholarship to Christ Church, Oxford. Failure to win a first in history in 1928 was mitigated when he became Gladstone memorial exhibitioner in 1929 and received a BLitt in 1931 for a thesis on the national debt. He was then, remarkably, elected a history tutor of Christ Church, as a result of his reputation for 'sound scholarship' and 'reliable games-playing' (Pakenham, 251). In 1934 he married Audrey Muriel Rudolf, who had come to study in Oxford from Jamaica, where her father owned a coconut plantation. They subsequently had twin sons and three daughters. In 1935 he published *The Sixteenth and Seventeenth Centuries*, and two years later an article in the *Economic History Review*. Yet increasingly Gordon Walker

Patrick Chrestien Gordon Walker, Baron Gordon-Walker (1907–1980), by Kenneth Green, 1966

began to forsake the life of a cultured Oxford don for political involvement.

Gordon Walker spent much of 1930 at German universities, particularly Heidelberg. Here he perfected his knowledge of German and, with articles for the *Daily Telegraph*, began a prolific career as a journalist. He twice saw Goebbels speak, and once Hitler. These experiences deepened his political interests, which might have originated with his father's reputed early Fabianism and with the influence of the left-wing Oxford academic G. D. H. Cole. During his trips to Germany after 1933 he was used by the Labour Party—at least once at considerable personal risk—to maintain clandestine links with the underground social democratic movement, and he became an active figure in Labour politics—secretary of the university Labour Party and official candidate for Oxford City in the 1935 general election. But Oxford was safe tory territory, and he later described his first campaign as 'a flag-waving exercise against hopeless odds' (*Political Diaries*, 6).

An admittedly slim chance to enter parliament seemed to come after the Oxford MP died in August 1938: Gordon Walker, Labour's official candidate, intended to stand against the Conservative Quintin Hogg. Now, he believed, the electorate could repudiate Chamberlain's policy of appeasement. Yet the voters were influenced by other than solely foreign policy considerations, and influential local Labour supporters, including Frank Pakenham and Richard Crossman, favoured a popular front candidate, the master of Balliol, A. D. Lindsay. When the national party refused to bring the local men to heel, Gordon

Walker insisted that he was not voluntarily standing down but that the local party was withdrawing its candidate. Hogg subsequently beat Lindsay by about 2500 votes. The episode was a painful one, harming Gordon Walker's relations with both the local party and Transport House, and he was replaced as the city's prospective candidate for the next election. Perhaps because of this he devoted more time to the National Council of Labour Colleges, which provided correspondence courses for trade unionists, and for which body in 1939 he wrote *An Outline of Man's History*.

The advent of war saw Gordon Walker organizing the city's 2000 evacuees from the East End, housing several mothers and their families himself. Along with Anthony Crosland and Roy Jenkins, he was also one of the founders of the Oxford University Democratic Socialist Club, formed when the existing Labour Club became dominated by the far left. But his major occupation was with the European service of the BBC. Occasional talks led to an offer of permanent employment, and he joined the team assembled by Hugh Carleton Greene on the fourth floor of Bush House. By 1942 he was arranging the daily schedule of broadcasts to Germany. Change came in the late summer of 1944, when American forces reached Luxembourg and took over its radio station. The BBC then seconded some of its most senior staff to help run it. It was from his post at Radio Luxemburg that Gordon Walker travelled with the troops into Germany. His broadcasts describing the tragic scenes at Belsen are among the most powerful and disturbing pieces of reportage of the twentieth century. His findings were published in part as *The Lid Lifts* (1945) and in full in his diaries (1991).

The death of the MP for Smethwick in a car crash enabled Gordon Walker to win the first by-election of the new parliament, in October 1945. Later in life Gordon Walker had the image of an unambitious, totally disinterested man, but at this point his sights were set on 10 Downing Street (8 Aug 1945; *Political Diaries*, 165). His progress was indeed rapid. In October 1946 he became parliamentary private secretary to Herbert Morrison, the number two in the government. A year later, in October 1947, he became under-secretary of state at the Commonwealth Relations Office. One achievement was to make this new office, formed from the old dominions and India offices, into a more harmonious and effective body under a single permanent under-secretary, Sir Percivale Liesching. Another was to help devise the 1949 London declaration, one of the key statements in the history of the Commonwealth, which asserted that henceforth the monarch was 'the symbol of the free association' of the member states and, as such, 'head of the Commonwealth'. This allowed the republic of India to remain a member, and indeed it was Gordon Walker himself who visited Pakistan, Ceylon, and India to secure acceptance of the new formula. The prime minister, Clement Attlee, believed he had shown 'exceptional ability' (*Political Diaries*, 18), and on 28 February 1950, after the general election, he made him secretary of state. After fewer than five years in parliament, and at the age of forty-three, Gordon Walker was a cabinet minister and a privy councillor.

Joe Garner, who became head of the Commonwealth Relations Office in the 1960s, judged that Gordon Walker was 'one of the most effective Commonwealth Secretaries and also one of the most popular with the staff generally' (Garner, 282), and Liesching called him 'a grand leader and a great personal friend' (*Political Diaries*, 23). Certainly he made a major contribution to the growth of the multiracial Commonwealth. Yet it was as secretary of state that he became associated with the unpopular exile of Seretse Khama, the chief of the Ngwato tribe in Bechuanaland (later Botswana), who had married a white woman, Ruth Williams. A storm of unjustified criticism was levelled at Gordon Walker. The decision to exile Seretse had, in fact, been made in cabinet before he became secretary of state; and in addition there seemed strong geo-political reasons for bowing to pressure from the Union of South Africa not to endorse a mixed-race marriage. Any other course would, it seemed, lead the union to strangle the three high commission territories economically. Gordon Walker was convinced that he was right to elevate the liberties of nearly two million Africans over the rights of two individuals. He may well have been insensitive towards Seretse and Ruth, but it is hard to find him guilty of the racial prejudice his critics charged him with.

Gordon Walker expected Labour to win the general election of 1951. It narrowly lost, and his own majority at Smethwick fell marginally to 9727. But he remained optimistic. He pinned his hopes partly on the Commonwealth, which he believed might take its place as 'a giant in the world' (*Political Diaries*, 31). He became the party's pre-eminent Commonwealth expert, publishing an authoritative 400-page work, *The Commonwealth*, in 1962. Yet he had undoubtedly overestimated popular enthusiasm for the institution. Furthermore his support for the Central African Federation, which the Conservatives inaugurated in 1953 with far fewer safeguards for African interests than Labour had originally envisaged, ran counter to official Labour policy. He spoke the rhetoric of Central African 'partnership' long after it ceased to have any reality, in the process showing no real understanding of black Africa.

In home affairs Gordon Walker was an instinctive modernizer. In the 1951 cabinet squalls he had sided with Gaitskell against Bevan; and in 1955 he voted for Gaitskell, and not his old mentor Morrison, in the leadership contest that followed Attlee's resignation. His was an important voice in the policy reappraisals prompted by electoral defeats in 1955 and 1959, when his own majority fell to 6495 and then 3544, broadly in line with west midland trends. He called for a loosening of the links with the trade unions and the jettisoning of the commitment to nationalization. He was also one of the leading figures in the Campaign for Democratic Socialism, which emerged in 1960 partly as a result of the party conference's vote in favour of unilateral nuclear disarmament. The following year, when the vote was reversed, Gaitskell wrote to thank Gordon Walker for the 'absolutely vital part' he had played in this (*Political Diaries*, 38).

Gaitskell's death in January 1963 led to some speculation that Gordon Walker might stand for the leadership. The *Sunday Times* judged him to be 'the leader of the Labour Party the Conservatives would regard as hardest to beat' (*Political Diaries*, 39). The tall, balding, pipe-smoking Gordon Walker was compared with Stanley Baldwin as a solid, reassuring figure. Instead, he acted as campaign manager for George Brown, who lost to Harold Wilson. Wilson then divided his enemies and strengthened his front bench by making Gordon Walker shadow foreign secretary.

Labour won the 1964 general election and Gordon Walker duly became foreign secretary, on 16 October, but in fact he had lost the contest at Smethwick by 1174 votes after a racist campaign by his opponents. A national swing to Labour of 3.5 per cent was transformed, in Smethwick, into a 7.2 swing to the Conservatives. The tory candidate, Peter Griffiths, refused to condemn the slogan 'If you want a nigger neighbour, vote Labour' and called for a complete ban on coloured immigration. This was the first major eruption of racism in modern British politics, and many considered the election result to be a major national scandal. The fact that Gordon Walker had opposed the limitations on immigration imposed by the 1962 Commonwealth Immigrants Act was used against him. The Seretse issue had finally been forgotten—with a vengeance. A seemingly safe seat was hastily found for the foreign secretary at Leyton, whose incumbent MP was sent reluctantly to the Lords. But on 21 January 1965 Gordon Walker again lost, by 205 votes. Immigration was not a key issue in Leyton, though the National Front campaigned violently against him and the press gloried in portraying—unrealistically but effectively—a lugubrious patrician statesman too disdainful to beg the votes of the plebs. He resigned as foreign secretary the following day.

Gordon Walker's career never recovered. Yet he did win Leyton at the 1966 general election and again in 1970; he was minister without portfolio from 7 January to 21 August 1967, conducting a review of the social services and negotiating defence arrangements with Malta, and minister of education from 29 August 1967 to 6 April 1968, when the need for post-devaluation cuts meant he had to suspend the raising of the school leaving age. In June 1968 he became a Companion of Honour. Out of office, he devoted more time to writing, and in 1970 published his most readable and influential book *The Cabinet*, whose essential—and some said optimistic—message was that real cabinet government still existed. His last three books, a novel and two biographies, remained unpublished. He entered the House of Lords as Lord Gordon-Walker in 1974 and was a member of the European parliament in 1975–6. He was found dead, of natural causes, in the back of a taxi at the Palace of Westminster on 2 December 1980. The *Times* obituary judged that 'No politician was less susceptible to the allurements of intrigue. He was far too honest to practise the meretricious arts of the demagogue'. This was not a bad reputation for a politician in the Wilson years. It is hard to believe that, in different circumstances, he might have become prime minister. Yet it is very easy to imagine that, with a little less bad luck, he might have been a distinguished foreign secretary.

ROBERT PEARCE

Sources *Patrick Gordon Walker: political diaries, 1932–1971*, ed. R. Pearce (1991) · F. Pakenham, *Five lives* (1964) · J. Garner, *The commonwealth office, 1925–1968* (1978) · *The Times* (3 Dec 1980) · CAC Cam., Gordon Walker MSS · A. Thompson, *The day before yesterday* (1971)
Archives Bodl. RH, corresp. on colonial issues · CAC Cam., diaries, corresp., papers · PRO, corresp. and papers, CAB 127/296–325 · PRO, CRO MSS | Bodl. Oxf., Attlee MSS, corresp. with Attlee · Bodl. RH, Perham MSS, corresp. with Margery Perham and related papers
Likenesses photographs, 1965–8, Hult. Arch. · K. Green, oils, 1966, NPG [*see illus.*]
Wealth at death £87,247: probate, 3 April 1981, *CGPLA Eng. & Wales*

Walker, Richard (1679–1764), horticulturist and college administrator, was the son of Robert Walker, of Tanfield, near Ripon, Yorkshire. After school in Tanfield, he was admitted as sizar in Trinity College, Cambridge, in 1703, matriculated in 1704, and graduated BA in 1707. He obtained a fellowship in 1709, proceeded MA in 1710, and was vice-master in 1734–64. From 1744 to 1764 he was Knightbridge professor of moral philosophy. Walker, a friend and protégé of the master of Trinity, Richard Bentley, played an important part in the long-running battle between Bentley and the fellows of Trinity, in particular, by refusing as vice-master to act on the sentence passed by the college visitor, the bishop of Ely, to deprive Bentley of his post.

Walker was an enthusiastic gardener, and especially interested in growing exotics in his small garden in Trinity, where his hothouse displayed banana, coffee, pineapple, and many other fashionable foreign plants. He clearly felt that the university lacked a garden and associated regular botanical instruction, and on 16 July 1760 purchased a 5 acre plot of land, including the 'Mansion House' to provide lecture rooms, on a central site on which an Augustinian friary had once stood; he conveyed this land to the university on 25 August 1762 in trust 'for the purpose of a public Botanic Garden'. In a pamphlet by him published anonymously in 1763 and entitled *A Short Account of a Late Donation of a Botanic Garden to the University of Cambridge*, Walker made clear his design, referring to the fact that 'we have generally had titular Professors of Botany, but nothing worth mentioning left behind them', and the first 'Statute or order' of his new garden states that 'by making use of the plants grown there, trials and experiments shall be regularly made and repeated, in order to discover their virtues, for the benefit of mankind'. In contrast, he states: 'Flowers and Fruits must be looked upon as amusements only; though, as these do not want their excellences and uses, they need not be totally neglected'.

Unfortunately, Walker's death in 1764 cut short his enthusiastic promotion of the new garden, but his bequest provided for two salaried posts, a reader on plants

Richard Walker (1679–1764), by Peter Spendelowe Lamborn, pubd 1771 (after D. Heins)

and a curator; to the first of these posts he appointed Thomas Martyn, who had just succeeded his father John Martyn as professor of botany; the curator's post was filled by Charles Miller, brother of Philip Miller, curator of the Chelsea Physic Garden. Walker died on 15 December 1764, unmarried, in Cambridge. The 'Walkerian garden', inside which the university built its first scientific laboratory in 1787, laid the foundation for the great development of science on the 'New Museums site' between Bene't Street and Downing Street. His name is perpetuated in the Walkerian Society run by the horticultural students in the botanic garden on its present site.

E. I. CARLYLE, *rev.* S. MAX WALTERS

Sources S. M. Walters, *The shaping of Cambridge botany* (1981), 40–43 · Venn, *Alum. Cant.* · B. Henrey, *British botanical and horticultural literature before 1800*, 2 (1975), 236–8
Likenesses D. Heins, oils, 1751, Trinity Cam. · P. S. Lamborn, line engraving, pubd 1771 (after D. Heins), BM, NPG [*see illus.*]

Walker, Richard Stuart (1918–1985), angler and engineer, was born on 29 May 1918 at 16 Fishpond Road, Hitchin, Hertfordshire, the only child of Richard Harry Walker (1892–1956), government clerk, and his wife, Elsie May (1892–1990), daughter of Frederick A. Cooper of Stanbridge, Bedfordshire. Both his maternal grandfather, Frederick, and his paternal grandfather, Richard, were important influences upon him and enthused their grandson with their respective passions for the natural world and angling. It was from this background that Britain's most perceptive, informed, and celebrated angler of the twentieth century emerged to become possibly 'the single most important writer in angling history … not even Walton was in the same class' (C. Dyson in Paisley, 33).

Raised largely by his mother and grandparents, Richard Walker first went to school in Hitchin before attending the notable Quaker Friends' school, at Saffron Walden, Essex. From the age of sixteen he attended the Quaker St Christopher School, Letchworth, Hertfordshire. His scholastic activities included a spell as centre forward in the first eleven, occasional success as a lower order batsman, and keen support of the camera club.

In 1936 Walker went to Gonville and Caius College, Cambridge, where he read engineering. Regrettably the Second World War put an end to his formal academic career and although he took to studying genetics in his spare time he never graduated. During the conflict he served as a military technician based at St Athans, Glamorgan, and then Farnborough, Hampshire. In that capacity not only did he contribute to the ground breaking work on aircraft radar and other installation works, he acquired a bullet scar on his shin, a lifelong dislike of the sea, and two nominal ranks. On the advent of peace Walker joined his family's lawnmower manufactory, Lloyd's of Letchworth, initially as chief designer and ultimately for some thirty years as technical director and general manager. On 21 March 1940 Walker married Ruth Maud (1914–1971), daughter of Henry Burdett-Holcroft, watchmaker and jeweller, and they had three sons.

It was, however, as an innovative and inspirational angler that Walker was to illuminate post-war Britain. He was only four years old when he caught his first fish; a superb 4 lb trout from the River Lea at Hertford. He placed his first order for twelve trout wet flies from the Hardy catalogue in 1926; it is characteristic of the man that his evident youthful enthusiasm merited a personal reply from the great Laurence R. Hardy himself. This began a fruitful association that lasted for the rest of his life, resulting, among other things, in the production of the world's first carbon fibre rod some forty years later. It is also typical that although this first note of his angling interest refers to the pursuit of game fish, his passion was never restricted to one particular branch of fresh water fishing. Indeed it was in the realm of coarse fishing that the name of Walker exploded upon the angling world.

In 1950, despite the evidence of Walker's own catches and the writings of Denys Watkins-Pitchford (B.B.), it was still generally considered that catching all but the smallest of carp was next to impossible. Having applied his mind to dispel many of the stale angling conventions of the day by first-hand experience and thorough experimentation with new tackle innovations such as electronic bite alarms and the personally designed and wonderfully effective Mark IV carp rods, Richard Walker and a small group of other famous anglers (Watkins-Pitchford, Pete Thomas, and Maurice Ingham) shared their knowledge and enthusiasm in an informal association called the Carp Catchers' Club. On a very dark September night in 1952 from a small lake in Herefordshire, after an epic struggle now familiar to generations of anglers, Richard Walker landed a huge female common carp of 44 lb, over 25 per cent more than the existing record. This momentous,

headline-grabbing, record-breaking triumph and the planned manner of the conquest was soon followed in 1953 by Walker's first major book, *Still Water Angling*—a seminal work that succinctly outlined five essentials for catching good fish, defined his approach to angling, and inspired readers with lucid accounts of his captures. Simultaneously, the new weekly magazine *Angling Times* signed up Richard Walker for a contribution to be known as 'Walker's pitch'. From the rather conservative and sedate pre-war pastime when father's tackle and techniques would be passed on wholesale to the son, coarse angling became the most rapidly evolving area of angling with specimen groups, new tackle, new baits, and new methods adding to the knowledge and success of its many participants. Walker was the inspiration and catalyst for much of this change.

Always mindful of the advice proffered to him by R. L. Marston, editor of the *Fishing Gazette* on submission of his second angling article in 1936 (he also wrote under the name Water Rail), Walker always wrote from his own experience. His articles became a *tour de force* of angling journalism. Considered, provocative, clearly written, and entertaining, his wide reading, phenomenal memory, acute powers of observation, and sheer enthusiasm sustained a weekly journal that only Alistair Cooke's *Letter from America* has emulated for quality and surpassed for duration. His deserved reputation for original thinking, strong views, relish for an argument, and unconcealed contempt for ill-founded opinion were, mercifully, allied to a generosity and understanding that impressed all who knew him. In his later years, after notable work on other coarse species such as perch and pike, and again developing tackle and techniques and exploring new locations to enhance their capture, his attentions were increasingly drawn to the attractions of trout angling in the burgeoning still waters of England. Dick Walker was thus the most significant advocate of the shooting head, inventor of a truly effective floating and sinking agent, developer of some of the first new generation lures, and captor of an unclaimed 'record' rainbow trout. He was also a strident supporter of the Anglers' Co-operative Association and fiercely critical of both government agencies and the small conservation lobby for their evident disregard for the current fate or future prospects for British fish species and watercourses.

An active and well-informed man, Walker's enthusiasms included photography, music, poetry, and latterly palaeoanthropology. He was featured on *Desert Island Discs* on BBC Radio 4 in July 1974, where he revealed his fondness for classic operas and his love and affinity for the rural England captured in Rudyard Kipling's *Puck of Pook's Hill*. The programme records the 'polite, dignified and gentlemanly' Walker very well (F. Taylor in Paisley, 40). What it fails to reveal is the wicked sense of humour that many close friends had cause to remember in their dealings with him. From his talent for imitating accents to his relish for practical jokes this side to his character was aptly summarized by Ken Sutton: 'Dick, despite his age and fame, had never left the sixth form' (F. Buller in Paisley, 43). Following the death of his first wife Walker married on 6 May 1971 Patricia (b. 1932), of *Fishing Gazette* fame, daughter of Robert Leslie Marston, publisher. They had another son.

Although in the early 1980s Walker was diagnosed with the cancer that was ultimately to claim his life, he continued to fish, write, and contribute to the angling world with undiminished zeal and inventiveness. He died on 2 August 1985 at his home, 37 Ivel Gardens, Biggleswade, Bedfordshire, and was cremated in Cambridge. He was the author of sixteen books and countless articles, and is widely regarded as the most celebrated British angler to have emerged in the twentieth century, its leading participant, and most accomplished advocate.

RICHARD IAN HUNTER

Sources T. Paisley, ed., *Dick Walker … a memoir* (1988) · private information (2004) [P. M. Walker; R. Hunter; S. Walker] · T. Scott, 'The angling books of Richard Walker', *Book and Magazine Collector*, 148 (July 1996), 57–64 · BBC Radio 4 programme, *Desert island discs*, 6 July 1974 · *CGPLA Eng. & Wales* (1985) · b. cert. · m. certs. · d. cert. · Church of England baptismal records, County Hall, Hertford · b. cert. [R. H. Walker]
Archives priv. colls., letters | SOUND BBC WAC, *Desert island discs*, BBC Radio 4, 6 July 1974
Wealth at death £69,156: probate, 1985

Walker, Robert (1595×1610–1658), portrait painter, was by 1637 an independent master, and in 1650 he became a member of the Painter–Stainers' Company. 'He lived in Oliver Cromwell's days, and drew the portraits of that Usurper, and all his Officers' (Vertue, *Note books*, 2.142). There is no firm evidence that he either trained in Italy, as has been suggested, or that he worked as an assistant in the studio of Van Dyck, but his portraiture is much influenced by that master. Walker's poses are often stiff and his colour schemes limited compared to Van Dyck's. A prolific artist, his style is much more obviously derivative than that of his royalist counterpart William Dobson. This is evident in, for example, his portrait of Cromwell in the Cromwell Museum, Huntingdon, in which the pose is closely based on that used by Van Dyck in his portrait of Sir Kenelm Digby in armour (NPG). Though his work lacks any of the painterly qualities of Dobson, Walker occasionally demonstrated wit and originality, and his portraits possess a distinctive soft quality that is his own. His portraits were much popularized by the engravings of William Faithorne, and many images (including those of the parliamentarians John Lambert and Thomas Fairfax) are known only through engravings after lost originals. Walker also had a reputation for copying works by Italian masters. Signed and dated portraits by Walker are few. His best-known paintings are his striking *Self-Portrait* in the Ashmolean Museum, Oxford, which is signed and datable to c.1640–45; *John Evelyn*, a portrait of the diarist contemplating a skull, a *memento mori* (1648; on loan to the NPG); *Oliver Cromwell with his Page* (versions at Althorp, Northamptonshire; NPG; Justitsministieriet, Copenhagen, in 1935; and, best known, signed version at Leeds City Art Gallery); and *Colonel John Hutchinson and his Son* (priv. coll.).

Walker's *Self-Portrait* in the Ashmolean Museum is closely related to Van Dyck's famous *Self-Portrait with a Sunflower* (priv. coll.). The pose is similar but Walker alters the format to give a more vertical emphasis to the composition and points not to a sunflower, which symbolizes loyalty to the crown, but to a statue of Mercury, god of eloquence and feats of skill and patron of vagabonds. While Van Dyck shows himself as confident, at the height of his powers (and wealth), a sophisticated figure drawing attention to his gold chain, Walker reveals his own youth and naïvety, his serious expression hiding the sardonic wit of his tribute to Van Dyck. A later, more conventional self-portrait is in the National Portrait Gallery, London. *John Evelyn* is one of his most accomplished and Italianate portraits. Evelyn is shown in a half-length view wearing a white shirt and blue gown, at a table and leaning on a skull.

Having recently become engaged to be married, Evelyn had sat to Walker on 1 July 1648, an event he recorded in his diary, and the painting was intended to accompany a treatise he had written for his young wife as a guide to married life: *Instruction œconomique*. Originally the portrait showed Evelyn holding a miniature or medal of his wife; the skull was added later. It is the image of *Oliver Cromwell with his Page* with which Walker is most associated. The finest version of this work, dated 1649, at Leeds, shows the protector in a three-quarter length view, standing, wearing armour and holding a baton, with a page. The pose is related to Van Dyck's *The First Earl of Strafford* (studio versions at NPG and Petworth House, Sussex). The several versions of this portrait which Walker continued to produce until 1656 are based on a number of sittings by Cromwell in 1649. Other accomplished portraits such as his *A Portrait of a Tutor and his Pupil* (London art market, 1994) (formerly incorrectly called *Lord Fairfax and his Daughter*), with its Greek inscription on the bookshelf which translates as 'Ever growing older and learning less', again reveal Walker's wit. His portrait of a man of the Shirley family, signed and dated 1656, shows signs of a fading talent.

Walker, who chiefly painted the portraits of the great parliamentarians of the period, died between July and December 1658, two years before the restoration of the monarchy in 1660. His estate passed to his daughter, Jane Walker; his sister, Katherine, and a servant, Mary Nicholson, also received bequests.

ANN SUMNER

Sources Vertue, *Note books*, 2.142 · C. H. C. Baker, *Lely and the Stuart portrait painters: a study of English portraiture before and after van Dyck*, 1 (1912), 106–10 · E. K. Waterhouse, *The dictionary of British 16th and 17th century painters* (1988), 289 · E. Waterhouse, *Painting in Britain, 1530–1790*, 5th edn (1994), 86–8 · O. Millar, *The age of Charles I: painting in England, 1620–1649* (1972) [exhibition catalogue, Tate Gallery, London, 15 Nov 1972 – 14 Jan 1973] · will, PRO, PROB 11/285, sig. 716 · NPG, Heinz Archive and Library
Likenesses P. Lombart, line engraving, c.1633, BM, NPG · R. Walker, self-portrait, c.1640–1645, NPG; version, AM Oxf.
Wealth at death £5 bequeathed to servant, Mary; residue to daughter: will, PRO, PROB 11/285, sig. 716

Walker, Robert (c.1709–1761), printer and distributor of patent medicines, details of whose parentage and upbringing remain the subject of speculation, was a prolific entrepreneur in print based in London, who was probably apprenticed through the Stationers' Company. Two entries under this name appear in the registers. The first, a Scot, was apprenticed to a writing master in 1699 and freed in 1706. The second, and more likely candidate, was the son of Thomas Walker, gentleman, deceased, of St Bride's parish in London. This Robert Walker was apprenticed in 1724, presumably at an age close to fourteen, to the City printer James Read, but did not formally complete his term of seven years. Read's interests centred on the publication of his pro-Walpole weekly journal and the sale of patent medicines, while his son Thomas was active in the publication of part-works and cheap newspapers. All these elements figured prominently in the career of Robert Walker. The first imprints to carry his name were published during 1728 and they included a virulent anti-Walpole pamphlet, *The Dunghill and the Oak*, printed for Walker and 'W. R.'. The initials were undoubtedly those of William Rayner, whose career interlocked with Walker's and who may have had some direct commercial links with him. Between them, Walker and Rayner dominated the trade in the cheaper forms of print into the early 1740s. Walker's appearance on this contentious publication fits with the image of a young man, free of parental control, whose rash and active nature, combined perhaps with financial necessity, were likely to push him into confrontations with authority. His willingness to engage with this material led to his arrest in December 1729, at which time he was described as a pamphlet seller and printer. With his wife he was running a shop at the sign of the White Hart in the Strand adjacent to Devereux Court. The proprietor and distributor of the famous Anodyne Necklace lived on the first floor, while E. Lynn, a whip maker with some interest in publishing, and an unidentified pamphleteer were also on the premises. Walker was taken into custody but made fulsome offers of discovery and was not proceeded against. His unnamed wife figured prominently but, although the details of Walker's family circumstances are obscure, the timing of what is known, checked against the content of his will (1761), may suggest a second marriage in the 1730s. Circumstantial evidence seems to point to a first wife, Elizabeth Hoseley (d. 1731), and a second, Judith (second name unknown), who survived him. Their daughter Judith was baptized at St Sepulchre Church (1738) as were four other children—Anne (1740), Robert (1743), Mary (1745), and Franklin (1749). Samuel Walker was baptized at St Botolph without Bishopsgate in 1750.

Meanwhile Walker's erratic and dynamic career was moving in several directions. He continued to publish potentially libellous pamphlets, and an equivocal disclaimer of responsibility for one of them which he inserted in the *Daily Journal* in 1731 was supported by an affidavit signed by William Rayner. Party-political material hostile to the administration continued to form an identifiable element within his mixed output as printer and publisher. In 1732 he was again arrested, this time in a sweep of the trade centred on a cluster of anti-Walpole

material for which Rayner was arrested and finally imprisoned (1733). It may have been because of the force of this process that Walker moved into another, more directly commercial, area of attack. In 1734 he became embroiled in a flat-out battle over material claimed by Jacob Tonson and associates, high-status members of the respectable London trade, under the shaky notion of perpetual copyright. Walker had apparently moved his main centre of operations to Turnagain Lane, one of the streets embedded in the dense networks of courts and alleys abutting the Fleet market and prison and adjacent to the complex formed by Newgate prison, the Sessions House, and the College of Physicians in the Old Bailey. He remained in this neighbourhood for the rest of his life. From his printing office he began to issue cut-price editions of the plays of Shakespeare and others which were being simultaneously published by the booksellers whom in his advertisements he described as 'the monopolists'. Legal proceedings followed but Walker remained in business and may have reached a financial accommodation with his competitors. He continued to confront the claims of the respectable trade and in 1739 and 1752 faced injunctions over his serial publication of *Paradise Lost*. He remained undaunted. During the skirmishes with Tonson in 1734 Walker worked out of a number of shops under his truculent sign of Shakespeare's Head and his premises at the Royal Exchange and in Fleet Street, among other central locations, figured on his fluctuating imprints. In the mid-1730s he moved his printing office to Fleet Lane, where he consolidated his business and began to develop what were to become his main lines of publication— cheap newspapers and part works. The bibliography of Walker's increasingly voluminous output is bewildering. Non-survival, disguised imprints, multiple and overlapping series in a variety of forms help to obscure the networks of material that flowed through Walker's office and across the nation.

Initially, Walker's publications are hard to distinguish from those of William Rayner and others. However, by 1737 he had begun to publish sequences of cheap newspapers specifically directed at the local market. With their geographical target identified in their titles by county, these publications represented the first attempt to provide cheap serial print specifically for readers outside London. The newspapers formed one part of Walker's marketing strategy. It was combined with the issue of works in parts, some of which used material already in print and often claimed under copyright; others were composed of original material written by authors for whom Walker acted as sole publisher. These serials were sometimes supplementary to the newspapers with which they were issued, sometimes the newspaper simply formed the wrapper for each part. The third element of Walker's output was provided by medical specifics.

From 1739 Walker consolidated his newspaper interest in the *London and Country Journal*. Until 1741 this was published in conjunction with the *History of the Bible* in parts which was incorporated into the title of the paper. The *Journal* appeared in different series published from Fleet

Lane on different days of the week and directed at readers in counties extending through the midlands and into the north-west. Walker's interventions in places outside London brought him into a series of conflicts with established local printers such as Thomas Aris in Birmingham. To ensure a foothold in the local market he began from the late 1730s to work directly with printers who moved into several of the main urban centres as his representative. John Berry in Manchester (1738) and Joseph Collett in Bristol (1739) centred their activities on the distribution of Walker's print and medicines, while Walker himself played an occasional part in the conduct of the local business.

By the mid-1740s Walker's business may have needed a new impetus. He had resolved the problems arising out of his attempt to evade the taxes on newspapers, pamphlets, and advertisements and in most local centres agreement seems to have been reached with his main competitors. In 1744 Walker left London with the printers Rene Le Butte and Thomas James to set up a new printing office in Cambridge, from which the first newspaper to appear locally was to be produced. The *Cambridge Journal and Weekly Flying Post* proved successful and two years later Walker moved on. In another joint venture, this time with the printer William Jackson, Walker targeted Oxford. In 1746 they opened a printing office and began to publish the *Oxford Flying Weekly Journal*. In spite of entrenched university interests, the corporation of the city of Oxford granted Walker the right to hang out his sign at the office and Jackson to do the same at their medical warehouse (1746/7). In 1749 the newspaper ceased publication and Walker, who had also published a number of part works in association with Jackson, probably returned to London. Four years later Jackson set up a new journal under his own name and in 1761 was named as an executor in Walker's will.

Walker continued to run his London printing and publishing business, probably with the help of his wife, who must have taken over during his absences, and to distribute those medicines in which he had a special interest. The Fleet Lane printing office itself or adjacent premises appeared in advertisements as Walker's Daffy's Elixir Warehouse (1738) or the British Oil Warehouse (1748). Walker, like his competitors, made extensive promotional use of royal grants under letters patent. These sometimes applied to original printed material particularly vulnerable to low-level piracy and increasingly to such medicines as the British Oil, which was granted to Walker during the 1740s. His business, like that of most printer–publishers in London and elsewhere, was essentially miscellaneous. His *Journal* carried advertisements for prints, songs, shrub (a lemon mixer), as well as his usual cheap print and medicine. Print was always part of a broad spectrum of commercial interests and at the end of the 1740s, although he was still living at his house in the Little Old Bailey, near Fleet Street, his move away from publication may already have begun. In 1752 he issued the serial edition of *Paradise Lost*, to which Tonson took exception, and announced the trials of Mary Blandy and others. In a notice published in the papers he expressed outrage

at those who were already pirating these trials 'in the most scandalous and mangled Manner'.

Such remarks suggest a build-up in pressure. Shortly after this Walker fled abroad to avoid his creditors, although by 1755 he had returned and surrendered himself to the keeper of the Fleet prison. In July he claimed benefit of the latest Act for Insolvent Debtors, describing himself as 'formerly of Fleet Lane, late of the Little Old Bailey … and last of Dunkirk in French Flanders' (*London Gazette*, 9492, Saturday 12 July 1755). His release was followed in 1756 by a brief flourish of material issued from the Fleet Lane office under the imprint of Judith Walker. He must have found the return to an increasingly active market in print discouraging and from 1755 Walker himself reappears in the exclusive guise of a specialist supplier of a patent medicine called the Jesuit Drops or Elixir of Health and Long Life.

This was one of many specifics for venereal disease and was available under a plain wrapper from Walker's warehouse at the Bible and Crown in Fleet Lane. Walker described himself as the inventor and patentee of the drops and in his advertisements rehearsed his accumulation of grants for its exclusive production and sale—for England and for the Plantations (1755), for Scotland (1756), and for Ireland (1759). He may have kept up the printing office to produce books of direction, handbills, labels, and other necessary items, but his interest in other forms of print was over. His medical business was managed by Joseph Wessells, who was praised in Walker's will for his 'capacity in the practice of Physick and Surgery' as well as for his knowledge of Walker's medicines. In 1761 Wessells was earning a salary of 2 guineas a week and was probably responsible for a number of 'Common and Necessary Servants' employed in 'Bottling, Corking, Tying, Papering &c.'. Walker's established distribution networks extending overseas must have been fully employed. At his death he owned a £150 share in the brig *Happy Success*, presumably for use in the export trade.

Suddenly, in 1759, his advertisements without comment began to refer to Dr Robert Walker (MD), a title which he insisted on using in all areas of his personal life. Working almost opposite the College of Physicians, his self-identification as doctor of physick may have been a last contemptuous gesture towards the claims of authority. In 1761 Walker was running a 'chariot' (hired for health reasons, he claimed) drawn by his own horses and the assumption of the title may also have reflected a rise in his financial status. Much of his long will was taken up with an attempt to ensure the continuation of the medical business, with Joseph Wessells holding the major share. His property and personal effects were to be shared between his wife, Judith, and his three daughters, Judith Burling, Elizabeth Croft, and Anne Walker. He died shortly after making his will, which was proved on 15 September 1761. No notice of his death was placed in the newspapers and advertisements for the Jesuit Drops continued to carry the name and address of 'the well-known Robert Walker' long after his demise.

MICHAEL HARRIS

Sources R. M. Wiles, *Freshest advice: early provincial newspapers in England* (1965) · M. Harris, *London newspapers in the age of Walpole* (1987) · R. M. Wiles, *Serial publication in England before 1750* (1957) · M. Harris, 'Paper pirates: the alternative book trade in mid-eighteenth century London', *Fakes and frauds*, ed. R. Myers and M. Harris (1989), 47–69 · H. L. Foord, *Shakespeare, 1700–1740* (1935) · D. F. McKenzie, ed., *Stationers' Company apprentices*, [3]: 1701–1800 (1978) · newspapers in the Burney collection, BL · Nichols, *Lit. anecdotes* · *Cambridge Journal and Weekly Flying Post* (1746–57) · *Jackson's Oxford Journal* (1753–62) · H. R. Plomer and others, *A dictionary of the printers and booksellers who were at work in England, Scotland, and Ireland from 1726 to 1775* (1932) · *Boyd's miscellaneous marriage index*, ed. Society of Genealogists, 2nd ser. · *Boyd's London burials* · IGI
Archives GL, land tax assessments · PRO, examination papers, SP 36/15, 16, 17

Walker, Robert [*called* Wonderful Walker] (1710–1802), Church of England clergyman, was born on 21 February 1710 at Undercrag in Seathwaite near Broughton in Furness in the Duddon valley, Lancashire, the last of twelve children of Nicholas Walker (*d.* 1728), yeoman, and his wife, Elizabeth. As they thought him too delicate to earn his living by fell farming or slate quarrying, his parents resolved to 'breed him a scholar'. To complete his education and qualify for ordination, Walker left Seathwaite for Eskdale and then the Vale of Lorton, enduring for the best part of a decade the itinerant and impoverished life of schoolmaster, deacon, and curate, and acquiring in the process habits of application and frugality that he never subsequently forsook. During this period his efforts were supported by James Stephenson, curate of Seathwaite, Thomas Parker, curate of Eskdale, and Christopher Denton, rector of Gosforth. Finally in 1736 he was nominated to the curacy of his native Seathwaite. On 5 January 1736 he married Ann Tyson (1707/8–1800), a domestic servant from Brackenthwaite whom he had met in Buttermere, and they set up house in the cottage adjoining the chapel where he was to officiate for over sixty-six years. Ann had a portion of £40, Robert a stipend of £5 per annum to begin with. They were to have ten children, eight of whom survived to adulthood.

Yet in spite of his straitened circumstances Walker became a prosperous man by local standards, and left about £1500 at his death. Remarkably, he had become wealthy without seriously jeopardizing the dignity of his office or forfeiting the affections of his parishioners. His successor wrote in the parish register that he was a man 'Singular for his Temperance, Industry and Integrity'. In *The Excursion* Wordsworth reported that the local shepherds called him 'Wonderful', and the poet later celebrated him in Sonnet 17 of *The River Duddon* as

A Pastor such as Chaucer's verse portrays;
Such as the heaven-taught skill of Herbert drew.
(Wordsworth)

On weekdays Walker taught the local children in the chapel, plying his spinning wheel as he listened to them recite their lessons. He then carried the wool in 16 or 32 lb bales over the high cross 7 miles to Broughton market. He farmed his small glebe and hired himself out to local farmers. When he called on him in 1755, the Broughton curate found Walker at 'one of the most servile of the country's employments, which out of regard to persons of

our profession, I shall forbear to mention' (*GM*, 30, 1760, 318). He was equally industrious with the pen, writing deeds and wills and keeping accounts. About 1754 he became steward of the manor of Dunnerdale with Seathwaite, and subsequently served his patron in that capacity for forty years, presiding over the annual court baron and recording its proceedings in his beautiful hand. The position not only brought him the customary fees but enabled him to purchase parcels of land around the manor, and he eventually became owner of a nearby farm at Longhouse. Later he invested in industry both locally and further afield as his eldest son (1736–1808) and then grandson (1768–1822), both named Zaccheus, rose to partnership status in Boulton and Watt. Walker died at the Chapelhouse, Seathwaite, on 25 June 1802, and was buried in the churchyard there three days later.

Robert Walker had supplemented his stipend by selling ale. Though not uncommon among poverty-ridden curates, the practice was frowned upon and the fact was suppressed by some early eulogists. It explains why his successor put 'Temperance' at the head of his virtues. Indeed, all reports agree on the austere simplicity of the Walkers' way of life; their diet was devoid of luxuries such as tea and coffee. But their hospitality to parishioners and passing travellers was famed. Their eldest daughter, Elizabeth (1738–1820), carried on the tradition as proprietor of the Black Bull in Coniston and her daughter, as Mrs Casson, kept the Newfield inn in Seathwaite just 200 yards down the valley from her grandfather's church. To that inn in 1804 came William and Dorothy Wordsworth, enquiring about the late curate. The result of those enquiries appeared in the passage in *The Excursion* (Book 7, lines 351ff.), published in 1814. Then in October 1819 a descendant, Robert Walker Bamford (1796–1838), published a prose tribute to his great-grandfather in the *Christian Remembrancer*, probably too late to influence the treatment of Walker by Wordsworth in the eighteenth sonnet of *The River Duddon*, published in the spring of the following year, but in time to be quoted in the prose memoir of him that Wordsworth included in the notes to that volume.

Walker's posthumous reputation owes much to Wordsworth's praise. Indubitably, Wordsworth, Bamford, and later Canon Richard Parkinson (1797–1858)—in his novel *The Old Church Clock* (1843)—idealized the mountain curate. For example, Wordsworth not only suppressed the matter of ale-selling but also misrepresented Walker's failed attempt to add the neighbouring curacy of Ulpha to that of Seathwaite as a modest refusal of an unsolicited offer made by the bishop. However, Walker's local reputation and the testimony inscribed in the register preceded their public tributes; and not only his descendants, but his parishioners and their descendants assisted in the preservation of the memory of 'a varra good man'. Visitors to the Seathwaite chapel graveyard afford ample evidence that his modest fame has outlasted the mere century predicted for it in *The Excursion*:

A simple stone
May cover him; and by its help, perchance,

A century shall hear his name pronounced,
With images attendant on the sound;
Then shall the slowly gathering twilight close
In utter night; and of his course remain
No cognizable vestiges, no more
Than of this breath, which shapes itself in words
To speak of him, and instantly dissolves.
(W. Wordsworth, *Poetical Works*, ed. E. de Selincourt and
H. Darbishire, 1946, 5.242)

FELICITY A. HUGHES

Sources W. Wordsworth, 'Memoir of the Rev. Robert Walker', *The poetical works of William Wordsworth*, ed. E. de Selincourt and H. Darbishire, 3 (1946), 508–22 [notes to *The River Duddon*, sonnet 18] · *GM*, 1st ser., 30 (1760), 317–19 · *GM*, 1st ser., 73 (1803), 17–19, 103 · Philacribos [R. W. Bamford], 'An account of the Rev. Mr. Walker, formerly curate of Seathwaite, in the north of Lancashire', *Christian Remembrancer*, 2 (1819), 604–9 · J. Thorne, 'Rambles by rivers', *Knights Weekly Volume for All Readers*, 16 (1843) · R. Parkinson, *The old church clock*, ed. J. Evans, 5th edn (1880) · E. Waugh, 'Seaside lakes and mountains', *Rambles in the lake country and other travel sketches*, ed. G. Milner (1893?) · F. A. Malleson, 'Wordsworth and the Duddon', *The North Lonsdale Magazine and Furness Miscellany* (June 1896), 4–20 · J. D. Marshall and M. Davies-Shiel, *The industrial archaeology of the lake counties*, 2nd edn (1977) · J. Dawson, *Torver: the story of a lakeland community* (1985) · parish register, Seathwaite, Cumbria AS · parish register, Broughton, Cumbria AS · Seathwaite parish bundle, Lancs. RO, Diocese of Chester papers
Archives NRA, priv. coll., court baron book of the manor of Dunnerdale with Seathwaite · Wordsworth Trust, Dove Cottage, Grasmere, corresp. and MSS, A/Walker R/1–5
Wealth at death £1483 5*s*.—purse and apparel £8 5*s*.; money upon speciality £1459; ditto £16: will

Walker, Robert (1716–1783), Church of Scotland minister, was born in the Canongate, Edinburgh, the son of John Walker (1680–1741), Church of Scotland minister of the Canongate, and Mary, daughter of Adam Leslie of Dumfries, merchant. He was educated at the University of Edinburgh and then lived for a time with a clergyman in Galloway, where in 1737 he was licensed to preach by the presbytery of Kirkcudbright. In 1738, following a unanimous call by the parishioners, he was ordained by the presbytery of Ayr to the ministry of the Ayrshire parish of Straiton. He would later recall his years in rural Straiton as among the happiest in his life. He married Magdalen Dickson on 27 May 1743, a marriage that would last for forty years, until his death. In 1746 he accepted a call to the second charge of the parish of South Leith, in the presbytery of Edinburgh. Eight years later, in 1754, he was translated to the first charge of St Giles, the high church of Edinburgh—one of the most influential positions in the Church of Scotland.

Walker's reputation within the church and nation rested largely on his eloquence as an evangelical preacher. A devout Calvinist, his sermons emphasized the sinful nature of humankind, the vanity of worldly wealth and status, the absolute dependence of each individual on divine grace and the vital importance of such practical expressions of the faith as humility, gratitude, godliness, and benevolence. These values were forcefully expressed in his popular *Sermons on Practical Subjects* (1765), which is probably the clearest exposition of the social ethics of the popular party in the eighteenth-century Scottish Church.

Walker also associated with the popular party in ecclesiastical politics, and resisted efforts by the moderate clergy to move the church towards greater accommodation with the polite society of enlightened Edinburgh. Unlike his moderate opponents, he did not aspire to literary fame, and was simple and unassuming in his tastes and manners. He was bold in denouncing deviations from a strict Christian morality among the rich as well as the poor. He opposed, for example, theatrical performances as encouraging human vanity and deceit, and made a memorable impression on 31 January 1757 when he condemned from the St Giles pulpit the Edinburgh performance of the play, *Douglas*, written by the moderate clergyman, John Home. A leading proponent of missions and charitable societies, he published in 1748 *A Short Account of the Rise, Progress and Present State of the SSPCK*, and was also known for his personal generosity to the poor.

Despite their differences in piety and ecclesiastical politics, Walker maintained a close friendship with his ministerial colleague at St Giles, the celebrated moderate preacher Hugh Blair, who wrote the preface to his *Sermons on Practical Subjects*. While Blair's congregations were drawn from the wealthier social orders, Walker's appeal was to the less opulent; in financial terms it was said 'that it took *twenty-four* of Mr Walker's hearers to equal *one* of Dr Blair's' (Kay, 1.348). In 1771 Walker was elected to the one-year office of moderator of the general assembly. He experienced a seizure after preaching on Sunday 4 April 1783, and died two hours later at his home on Castle Hill, Edinburgh. He was buried in Edinburgh on 13 April. He was survived by his wife.　　STEWART J. BROWN

Sources J. Kay, *A series of original portraits and caricature etchings … with biographical sketches and illustrative anecdotes*, ed. [H. Paton and others], 1 (1837), 347–9 · R. Walker, *Sermons on practical subjects, to which is prefixed a character of the author by Hugh Blair*, 4th edn, 3 vols. (1804) · *Fasti Scot.*, new edn, vol. 1 · R. Walker, *We have nothing which we did not receive … a sermon* (1776) · J. R. McIntosh, *Church and theology in Enlightenment Scotland: the popular party, 1740–1800* (1998)
Likenesses D. Lizars, engraving, 1779, Scot. NPG · J. Kay, portrait, repro. in Kay, *Series of original portraits and caricature etchings*, vol. 1, facing p. 347

Walker, Robert [called the Skating Minister] (1755–1808), Church of Scotland minister and subject of a painting by Henry Raeburn, was born on 30 April 1755 at Monkton, Ayrshire, the second son of the Revd William Walker (1719–1774), minister of that parish, and Susanna, *née* Sturment, widow of Thomas Latimer, a Virginian merchant. In 1760 William Walker was translated to the Scottish church at Rotterdam, where no doubt the young Robert learned to skate. Following his mother's death, Robert's father married Elizabeth Lawson, widow of William Robertson, merchant of Rotterdam.

Robert Walker returned to Scotland and on 24 April 1770 was licensed to preach, at the unusually early age of fifteen, by the presbytery of Edinburgh. It was not until 27 November 1776 that he was ordained to the charge of Cramond, near Edinburgh, to which he was presented by Willielma, Lady Glenorchy. On 19 August 1784 he was called to the first charge of the Canongate Kirk, Edinburgh. He remained there for his entire career with what

Robert Walker (1755–1808), by Sir Henry Raeburn, c.1792–4 [The Skating Minister]

was then a good stipend. Clearly a popular and sociable man, in 1779 he was elected a member of the Royal Company of Archers and was appointed their chaplain in 1798. In January of the following year he joined Edinburgh's Skating Society and in 1784 his name first appears in the minute book of the Wagering Club.

On 8 May 1778 Walker married Jean (d. 1831), daughter of John Fraser of Borlum, writer to the signet, and his wife, Jean, née Brown. The couple had two daughters and three sons. During his career Walker published a modest number of works, including a collection of Sermons (1791), along with a further three sermons which appeared individually, his Observations on the national character of the Dutch and the family character of the house of Orange and The Psalms of David Methodized (both 1794). He also contributed a description on the Dutch table game of kolf to John Sinclair's Statistical Account (vol. 16).

Walker's celebrity rests today on his being the subject of Henry Raeburn's The Skating Minister, though it is not known how the two men met. Considerable debate has surrounded the dating and attribution of the work, and the identity of the skater. Formerly identified as one of Raeburn's earlier works (claimed by the sitter's family to have been completed in 1784), it is now regarded as a product of the experimentation and intense activity that followed the artist's return from Rome in 1786, which would date the portrait to the early 1790s. The Skating Minister was privately owned until 1949, when it was purchased by the National Gallery of Scotland. Walker's portrait continues to attract considerable interest among scholars and the public, and is now one of Raeburn's most popular and best-known works. Walker died in Edinburgh on 13 June

1808. By his will, of which Raeburn was a trustee, he left all his movable goods to his eldest son, John; no mention of skates appears in the bequest.   DAVID MACKIE

Sources D. Mackie, 'Raeburn: life and art', PhD diss., U. Edin., 1994 · D. Thomson, 'Raeburn': the art of Sir Henry Raeburn, 1756–1823 (1997) [exhibition catalogue, Royal Scot. Acad., 1 Aug 1997 – 5 Oct 1997, and NPG, 24 Oct 1997 – 1 Feb 1998] · Fasti Scot., new edn, vol. 3 · C. Thompson and H. Brigstocke, Shorter catalogue: National Gallery of Scotland, 2nd edn (1978) · Raeburn bi-centenary exhibition, Arts Council, Scottish Committee (1956) [exhibition catalogue, NG Scot., 16 July – 16 Sept 1956] · A. G. Pearson, 'Gilbert Stuart's The skater (Portrait of William Grant) and Henry Raeburn's The Reverend Robert Walker DD, skating on Duddingston Loch: a study of sources', Rutgers Art Review, 8 (1987), 55–70 · [F. J. Grant], A history of the Society of Writers to Her Majesty's Signet (1890) · will, NA Scot., register of deeds, RD 3/327, fols. 773–86 · private information (2004) [S. Lloyd, Scot. NPG]

Archives NL Scot., Edinburgh Skating Society collection
Likenesses H. Raeburn, oils, c.1792–1794, NG Scot. [see illus.]

Walker, Robert (1801–1865), university teacher, was born in Dover, the third of at least five sons of Robert Walker, gentleman, and his wife, Elizabeth Mozier, both of Dover. On 20 January 1819 he entered Wadham College, Oxford, where he was an exhibitioner. He obtained a second class in literae humaniores and a first in mathematics in 1822. He took holy orders as a deacon in 1826, and was ordained priest in 1827. Walker was appointed junior chaplain of Wadham College in 1826, but had to relinquish the post when he married, in 1831, Elizabeth Holdsworth of Alverstoke, Hampshire; they had at least two sons and two daughters, of whom the elder son, Robert Holdsworth Walker (b. 1834), followed his father to Wadham and into the teaching profession.

As early as 1826 Walker served as a university examiner in mathematics, the first of many occasions. From 1828 until 1853 he was mathematics tutor of Wadham College, though he was never a fellow. He was elected FRS in 1831. In 1839 he succeeded Stephen Rigaud as reader in experimental philosophy (physics) at Oxford, becoming responsible not only for a well-established course but also for an extensive collection of apparatus with an endowment for its development. One of the first pieces that he added was the Oxford dry pile, an extremely durable battery. Walker's appointment as reader (upgraded to professor in 1860) was significant, for he was the first to hold the post in its own right, rather than annexed to a professorship in another subject.

Inspired by the meeting of the British Association for the Advancement of Science in Oxford in 1847, at which he was one of the local secretaries and president of the physics section, Walker, along with Henry Acland, Charles Daubeny, and Philip Duncan, launched a vigorous campaign for the reform of scientific education in Oxford. The eventual results were the creation of a new degree in natural science in 1850 and the building of a new scientific teaching centre, which became known as the university museum. Walker was one of the most active members of the steering committee appointed in 1853 to establish the museum; and as secretary of the British Association in 1859–61 he helped organize the Oxford meeting of 1860, which inaugurated the museum but became famous for its discussion of Darwinism.

Walker was not an original physicist, but kept pace with the work of his great contemporaries in order to demonstrate their experiments to his students, and also to senior members of the university in the Ashmolean Society. He made his lecture demonstrations as lively as possible in order to capture the interest of the undergraduates. A brief account of them occurs in the memoirs of William Tuckwell.

Walker's vocation as a clergyman was not eclipsed by his scientific career. He was one of the university's select preachers in 1840–42 and 1847–9, and became vicar of Culham, Oxfordshire, in 1848, moving with his family to Culham vicarage. He resigned this living in 1862. Little is known about Walker's personality, though Tuckwell describes him as cheery. He died at Rose Hill, Iffley, near Oxford, on 28 September 1865.   A. V. SIMCOCK, rev.

Sources Boase, *Mod. Eng. biog.*, vol. 3 • R. B. Gardiner, ed., *The registers of Wadham College, Oxford*, 2 (1895) • W. Tuckwell, *Reminiscences of Oxford* (1900) • H. M. Vernon and K. D. Vernon, *A history of the Oxford Museum* (1909) • IGI • d. cert. • CGPLA Eng. & Wales (1865)

Wealth at death under £7000: resworn probate, July 1866, CGPLA Eng. & Wales (1865)

Walker, Robert Francis (1789–1854), Church of England clergyman and translator, was born in Oxford on 15 January 1789, the son of Robert Walker. At the age of eleven he was sent to Magdalen College School, where as a chapel chorister his voice was said to have so impressed Lord Nelson that he gave the boy half a guinea. He matriculated at New College, Oxford, in 1806, and graduated BA in 1811, proceeding to an MA in 1813. In 1812 he was appointed chaplain of New College, and from 1813 to 1815 he was curate at St Ebbe's, the evangelical centre in Oxford, becoming curate at Taplow, Buckinghamshire, in 1815, and at the end of 1816 or the beginning of 1817 moving to Henley-on-Thames. In 1819 he went to Purleigh, Essex, where he was curate-in-charge to an absentee rector, the provost of Oriel College, Oxford.

Walker was twice married: first, in 1814, to Frances, *née* Langton (d. 1824), at Cookham, Berkshire, with whom he had four sons and one daughter; second, on 30 September 1830, to Elizabeth, *née* Palmer (d. 1876), at Olney, with whom he had five sons.

Walker was a talented poet and an accomplished musician, but he particularly excelled as a linguist. His interest in missions and his contact with German missionary students ultimately led him to translate a substantial number of works by German evangelical theologians, notably the writings of F. W. Krummacher and C. G. Barth.

In 1848, stricken with paralysis, Walker was compelled to resign his living and retired to Great Baddow in Essex, where he died on 31 January 1854. He was buried at Purleigh.   J. R. MACDONALD, rev. STEPHEN GREGORY

Sources T. Pyne, *A memoir of the Rev. Robert Francis Walker* (1855) • J. S. Reynolds, *The evangelicals at Oxford, 1735–1871: a record of an unchronicled movement* (1953) • Boase, *Mod. Eng. biog.* • D. M. Lewis, ed., *The Blackwell dictionary of evangelical biography, 1730–1860*, 2 vols. (1995) • Foster, *Alum. Oxon.* • GM, 2nd ser., 41 (1854), 438 • private information (1899)

Likenesses lithograph, repro. in Pyne, *Memoir of the Rev. Robert Francis Walker*

Walker, Samuel (*bap.* 1713, *d.* 1761), Church of England clergyman, was baptized on 30 December 1713 at St Paul's, Exeter. He was the fourth son, and the seventh and youngest child, of Robert Walker (1665?–1749?) of Withycombe Raleigh, Devon, and his wife, Margaret (b. 1669?), daughter of Richard Hall, rector of St Edmund's and All Hallows, Exeter; Sir Thomas Walker, merchant and MP for Exeter, was his grandfather. Members of his family, including a cousin, Dr John *Walker (*bap.* 1674, *d.* 1747), had been prominent as clergymen in Exeter. His three brothers also became clergymen.

Walker attended Exeter grammar school (founded by an ancestor) from 1722 to 1731, during the headmastership of the Revd Dr John Reynolds, who was from another local family and great-uncle of Sir Joshua Reynolds. On 4 November 1732 he matriculated from Exeter College, Oxford, becoming BA on 25 June 1736. Disappointed in his hope of a fellowship, he was made deacon by Dr Stephen Weston, bishop of Exeter, on 25 September 1737, to serve as curate at Doddiscombsleigh, near Exeter, and was ordained priest on 28 May 1738 on the same title. In August of the same year he resigned this curacy to accompany, as tutor and companion, young Mr Rolle—whose relatives were prominent at Withycombe Raleigh and elsewhere in Devon—on a visit to France. Returning early in 1740 Walker became curate to his friend Nicholas Kendall at Lanlivery in Cornwall. Kendall was archdeacon of Totnes, and on his death Walker succeeded as vicar of Lanlivery (3 March 1740), holding the benefice under bond and resigning it in favour of a nephew of Walter Kendall, the patron, in 1746.

In the same year Walker accepted the curacy of Truro parish church (St Mary's, later incorporated in Truro Cathedral), where the Revd St John Elliot (also of Exeter College, but after Walker's time) was instituted as rector on 3 June 1746. By 5 May 1749 Elliot had become non-resident at Truro, having been instituted also to the rectory of Ladock, 10 miles north-east of Truro, where he chose to live. In recognition of the inadequate stipendiary arrangements at Truro, Bishop Clagett instituted Walker as vicar of Talland, a village some 25 miles north-east of Truro, on 13 July 1747, but Walker came to believe that this arrangement was morally wrong and resigned Talland in 1752.

Until this time Walker, tall and handsome with a notable presence, had been a cleric of nominal religious conviction, who particularly enjoyed dancing. Contact with the able headmaster of Truro grammar school, George Conon, a Scottish layman and graduate of the University of Aberdeen, attracted him towards a more biblical faith, and evangelical conversion followed. Walker soon preached in a different strain; large numbers of parishioners came under spiritual instruction and conviction. Soon half the population of Truro, some 800, attended Sunday services, and were organized during the week into religious societies; their children were catechized publicly. Opposition arose and the non-resident rector tried to dismiss Walker, finding however that he was unable to bring himself to do it.

In spite of hostility to evangelicals shown by contemporary bishops of Exeter (Clagett and Lavington, 1742–62), Walker remained a fully convinced churchman (accepting now the moderate Calvinism of article 17) and in 1750 formed a club for like-minded clergymen, of whom a sprinkling had appeared in Cornwall. Unlike Berridge and others, Walker believed that evangelical clergy should minister strictly within their parish boundaries. Nevertheless, the Wesley brothers were in touch with him, and in 1756 Walker was instrumental in preventing, for the time being, the Methodists' leaving the Church of England. Walker was also in contact with evangelical clergy elsewhere in England, notably Thomas Adam, vicar of Wintringham in Lincolnshire. In spite of a favourable opportunity to wed a lady of similar Christian outlook, he refrained from marriage.

Three young men from Truro, in Walker's time, became well-known as evangelical leaders: Thomas Haweis, Thomas Wills, and George Burnett, subsequently vicar of Elland in Yorkshire, and founder of the Elland Society for educating young men for the ministry, which still operates. John Martyn, father of Henry Martyn, pioneer missionary in India, was an active member of Walker's congregation. Haweis, Wills, and Burnett went up to Oxford, where Haweis was subsequently ordained as curate to the Revd Joseph Jane, senior student of Christ Church, at St Mary Magdalen, Jane's father having been Elliot's predecessor as rector of Truro. Walker's occasional visits to Oxford made him better known to the small band of evangelicals in the university, of which the leader was the Revd James Stillingfleet, fellow of Merton College (1752–68), who subsequently published, as a preface to Walker's *Sermons* (1763), what was for many years the only account of Walker's life.

The strain of his parochial and other activities, amid frequent opposition, proved too much for Walker's health. He recovered from serious illness in 1744 but ten years later his physical health had seriously deteriorated. In 1758 his rector insisted on receiving a larger proportion of the meagre financial returns (collected annually, and in person from parishioners) of the benefice. Walker was obliged to move back into lodgings and was no longer able to provide a home for the elderly sister who had kept house for him. (Nevertheless he survived Elliot, who died in June 1761.) On 27 April 1760 Walker preached for the last time at Truro. He travelled to Bath and elsewhere, seeking to restore his health; Truro friends helped to meet his financial and other needs. But he was dying, apparently from consumption, and the second earl of Dartmouth, a leading benefactor of evangelicals, who had helped Walker financially on at least one occasion, took him into his house at Blackheath. For his last few weeks Walker was transferred to lodgings, where Haweis and Burnett attended him. He died at Lewisham, Kent, on 19 July 1761, aged forty-seven, and was buried on 23 July in Lewisham churchyard, where a memorial remained in 1889. In his lifetime, though his writing was cogent and succinct,

Walker published little apart from eleven sermons, printed as *The Christian* (1755), which reached a twelfth edition in 1879. His sermons were considered by Charles Simeon of Cambridge, a leading figure in the later evangelical revival, to be 'the best in the English language' (Brown, 320).   J. S. REYNOLDS

Sources C. S. Gilbert, *An historical survey of the county of Cornwall*, 2 (1820), 324–7 • G. C. Boase, *Collectanea Cornubiensia: a collection of biographical and topographical notes relating to the county of Cornwall* (1890), 1689 • J. S. [J. Stillingfleet], preface, in S. Walker, *Fifty-two sermons on the baptismal covenant, the creed, the ten commandments*, 1 (1763), 3–96 • E. Middleton, ed., *Biographia evangelica*, 4 (privately printed, London, 1786), 350–74 • C. Simeon, introduction, in S. Walker, *The Christian: being a course of practical sermons* (1825), 5–18 • E. Sidney, *Life, ministry & select further remains of Rev. S. Walker* (1835), 1–283 • Boase & Courtney, *Bibl. Corn.*, 2.846–8, 3.1358 • A. W. Brown, *Recollections of the conversation parties of the Rev Charles Simeon* (1863), 320 • H. C. Kirby and L. L. Duncan, eds., *Memorial inscriptions in the church and churchyard of S. Mary, Lewisham* (1889), 53, no. 527 • J. C. Ryle, *The Christian leaders of the last century* (1869), 306–27 • G. C. B. Davies, *The early Cornish evangelicals, 1735–60* (1951) • A. S. Wood, *Thomas Haweis, 1734–1820* (1957) • J. S. Reynolds, *The evangelicals at Oxford, 1735–1871: a record of an unchronicled movement*, [2nd edn] (1975) • *Memoirs of … the Rev. Thomas Wills* (1804) • F. W. B. Bullock, *History of the parish church of St. Mary, Truro* (1948) • D. M. Lewis, ed., *The Blackwell dictionary of evangelical biography, 1730–1860*, 2 vols. (1995) • parish register, Exeter, St Paul, 30 Dec 1713 [baptism] • IGI • Foster, *Alum. Oxon.*

Walker, Samuel (1715–1782). *See under* Walker family (*per.* 1741–1833).

Walker, Sir Samuel, first baronet (1832–1911), judge, was born at Gore Port, Finea, co. Westmeath, on 19 June 1832, the second son of Captain Alexander Walker of Gore Port, and his wife, Elizabeth, daughter of William Elliott of Rathrogie, co. Carlow; Mark *Walker was his elder brother. He was educated at Arlington House, Portarlington, King's county, under the Revd John Ambrose Wall. On 23 June 1849 he matriculated at Trinity College, Dublin, where he won a scholarship in 1851, a year before the usual time, and graduated BA in 1855 as first senior moderator in classics and winner of the large gold medal. He was called to the Irish bar in Trinity term 1855. In the same year, on 9 October, he married Cecilia Charlotte, née Green. They had two sons and four daughters before her death on 18 June 1880.

Walker quickly attained a large practice both in equity and in common law on the home circuit. Never a particularly fluent or attractive speaker, he had a solid knowledge of the law and shrewd common sense, which made him a valued advocate. He took silk on 6 July 1872, and soon became a prominent member of the inner bar. He is perhaps most famous for his conduct of the defence of Charles Parnell and the other traversers during the state trial in 1881. Francis MacDonagh QC, who had been leading the defence, fell ill and so Walker took over. The trial ended with a jury disagreement and a triumph of sorts for the traversers.

On 17 August 1881, a year and two months after his first wife's death, Walker married Eleanor MacLaughlin; they had one son and one daughter, making the total number of children in the family eight. In Trinity term 1881 he had been appointed a bencher of the King's Inns. He was made solicitor-general for Ireland on 19 December 1883, when Andrew Porter, the attorney-general, was made master of the rolls. A Liberal in politics, in January 1884 he entered the House of Commons unopposed as one of the members for the county of Londonderry, filling the seat vacated by Porter. He had been an enthusiastic upholder of the tenants' side in the land controversy, which had reached an acute stage. In the House of Commons, he spoke only when compelled to do so, and then briefly and to the point—the dry humour of his contributions in keeping with parliamentary style. When Sir George Trevelyan, who was chief secretary to the lord lieutenant, left owing to poor health in 1884, Walker as solicitor-general—the attorney-general John Naish not being a member of the House of Commons—was the acting Irish secretary until the appointment of Sir Henry Campbell-Bannerman to the chief secretaryship later in the same year. Walker became attorney-general for Ireland and was sworn of the Irish privy council in May 1885, but within a few weeks the Gladstone administration resigned on a defeat in the House of Commons (8 June 1885) and he lost the post.

At the general election of 1885, Walker stood as a Liberal for Londonderry North but was defeated by Henry Lyle Mulholland (second Lord Dunleath) on 1 December 1885. A month earlier, at a banquet in the Ulster Hall, Belfast, he had said: 'The liberals of Ireland will not permit the union to be tampered with, and any attempt in that direction, no matter by what party, will not be tolerated'. Yet when Gladstone's adoption of home rule split the Liberal Party, Walker cast in his lot with the Gladstonian Liberals. On the appointment of Gladstone as prime minister on 6 February 1886, Walker, though without a seat in the House of Commons, again filled the office of attorney-general for Ireland, and he held the post until the fall of Gladstone's third administration on 3 August 1886.

While the Liberal Party was in opposition (1886–92) Walker pursued his practice at the Irish bar and took a prominent part in the meetings of the Liberal Party held in Dublin. He was defeated in his candidature for Londonderry South in July 1892; but on the formation of Gladstone's fourth administration in August 1892, Walker was appointed lord chancellor of Ireland.

On the bench Walker sustained his reputation as an able lawyer. Perhaps his best judgment is that in *Clancarty* v. *Clancarty*. which dealt with precatory trusts. As lord chancellor he presided over the court of appeal in Ireland, and he continued in his duty even after his retirement from the chancellorship on 8 July 1895, when the Liberal administration fell. Although no longer president of the court of appeal nor receiving a salary, he was unremitting in his judicial duties. In 1897 he was appointed by Earl Cadogan, the Unionist lord lieutenant, to preside over the commission on Irish fisheries. Walker was reappointed lord chancellor by Sir Henry Campbell-Bannerman on 14 December 1905; he was created a baronet on 12 July 1906. Walker held the great seal until his death in Dublin on 13

August 1911. He was buried in Mount Jerome cemetery, Dublin, and survived by his second wife.

Walker resided at Pembroke House, Upper Mount Street, Dublin. During his life he enjoyed fishing and shooting; his long vacations were generally spent fishing in the Connemara lakes, and entertaining his many friends. J. G. S. MACNEILL, rev. SINÉAD AGNEW

Sources J. S. Crone, *A concise dictionary of Irish biography*, rev. edn (1937), 258 • F. E. Ball, *The judges in Ireland, 1221–1921*, 2 (1926), 318, 322, 327, 379 • Burtchaell & Sadleir, *Alum. Dubl.*, 2nd edn • *The Times* (14 Aug 1911), 9 • J. Foster, *The register of admissions to Gray's Inn, 1521–1889, together with the register of marriages in Gray's Inn chapel, 1695–1754* (privately printed, London, 1889), 475 • *Men and women of the time* (1899), 1126 • A. T. C. Pratt, ed., *People of the period: being a collection of the biographies of upwards of six thousand living celebrities*, 2 (1897), 469 • *Irish Times* (14 Aug 1911) • *Freeman's Journal* [Dublin] (14 Aug 1911)

Wealth at death £19,190 14s. 8d.: probate, 29 Aug 1911, CGPLA Ire.

Walker, Sayer (1748–1826), physician, whose family came from Bocking, Essex, was born in London. About 1763 he attended the Mile End dissenting academy and in 1770 became assistant minister in Bocking under the Revd T. Davidson. While at Bocking he became friendly with his future father-in-law, Joseph Savill, a wealthy cloth maker who arranged for the collection of rents for property in Essex that belonged to Guy's Hospital. Walker then became acquainted with William Saunders of Guy's Hospital. On 5 November 1772 Walker married Mary (d. 1822), daughter of Joseph Savill; they had at least one child. From this year until 1777 Walker was assistant minister in charge at Castle Green church, Bristol. After his wife inherited money from an aunt and received a cash gift from her father, Walker was able to spend two years studying medicine. In 1779 he attended lectures on materia medica given by William Saunders at Guy's before studying possibly at Montpellier, and certainly at Edinburgh. Later that year he became Presbyterian minister at the Baker Street mission in Enfield, where he treated his poor parishioners. He held this post until 1792. On new year's day 1790 Walker preached a sermon in London in which he praised scientific education, spoke of the progress being made in the treatment of the insane, and supported the French revolutionaries' attack on tyranny and stagnation.

Walker received his MD from Aberdeen on 31 December 1791 and on 25 June 1792 became a licentiate of the Royal College of Physicians. He resigned from the ministry in this year, possibly as a result of his asthma. He was elected physician to the London Lying-in Hospital in June 1794, where J. C. Lettsom was a colleague. Walker later became treasurer and orator of the Medical Society of London. He published *The Importance of Religious Instruction* (1790), *A Treatise on Nervous Diseases* (1796), and *Observations on the Constitution of Women* (1803). In 1826 Walker's asthma forced him to move to Clifton, Bristol, where he died on 9 November 1826.

About a year later Walker's body was exhumed and buried in Bunhill Fields, London, in the tomb of the Revd John

Owen (1616–1683), dean of Christ Church, vice-chancellor of Oxford University, and friend of John Sayer (1633–1686), after whom Walker had been named.

MICHAEL BEVAN

Sources Munk, *Roll* · *GM*, 1st ser., 96/2 (1826), 470 · A. S. Paterson, 'Sayer Walker MD (1748–1826)', *Proceedings of the Royal Society of Medicine*, 65 (1972), 553–6
Likenesses N. Branwhite, group portrait, stipple, pubd 1801 (*Institutors of the Medical Society of London*; after S. Medley), BM · portrait, repro. in Paterson, 'Sayer Walker MD (1748–1826)'

Walker, (Richard) Sebastian Maynard (1942–1991), publisher, was born on 11 December 1942 at the Imperial Nursing Home, Cheltenham, Gloucestershire, the only son and elder child of Richard Fife Walker, mechanical engineer, and his first wife, Christine Mary Wilkes (d. 1968). The family owned Walker Crosweller, makers of thermostats and shower valves. Sebastian attended the junior school of Cheltenham College and boarded at Rugby School (1956–61) before going to New College, Oxford, where he took a second in French in 1965 and developed his passions for gourmet cuisine and social climbing.

Abandoning a doctoral thesis on French historian Jules Michelet, Walker spent a couple of years (1968–70) in management training at two light engineering firms in greater London, B. Elliott of Acton and Max Fordham of Camden Town. His mother, who suffered from mental illness, committed suicide in December 1968. Walker had intended to enter the family business, but he suddenly decided otherwise in October 1970 and went into publishing. Engaged by the Chatto and Windus/Bodley Head/Jonathan Cape consortium as a sales representative, he soon became its European sales manager, travelling in France, West Germany, and Italy. In 1973 he set up home in Alwyne Place, Canonbury, London, with his homosexual lover, Donald Richards (1950/51–1990), an Australian student, later a writer and stockbroker. They underwent a form of wedding ceremony. The part-work publishers Marshall Cavendish employed Walker from 1975 to 1977. Though still primarily a salesman, he also started their children's imprint. Chatto and Windus then called him back as director of children's books (1977–9).

Perceiving a gap in the market, Walker borrowed £20,000 in 1978 and formed Sebastian Walker Associates, an independent publishing house, operating from his spare bedroom. Picture books for infants were his speciality. Other publishers devoted relatively little attention to them, but they possessed two commercial advantages: a long shelf-life and international appeal. With editor Wendy Boase and designer Amelia Edwards, Walker brought to these publications the production values normally associated with books for adults. Rechristened Walker Books, his company issued its first seventeen titles in 1980. The following year it went into profit with a popular series of board books for babies by Helen Oxenbury.

Walker declared that he would stop at nothing to get the best children's authors and illustrators. Walker Books offered top-quality paper and colour printing and paid appreciably larger advances than competitors, who, after bitter complaints about 'poaching', had to follow suit.

Aggressive marketing culminated in an unprecedented deal with Sainsbury's in 1985, whereby cut-price titles went on sale alongside groceries in supermarkets. Traditional booksellers were outraged; Walker Books boomed, moving via Tottenham Court Road to spacious offices in Vauxhall Walk. Its list included works by Hugh Scott, Quentin Blake, Nicola Bayley, and Jill Murphy. Critics grumbled about the low ratio of words to pictures, but Walker maintained that his products coaxed infants over the threshold of literacy.

Sebby Walker, a trim figure usually in an open-necked shirt, appeared to take children's books very seriously and himself not at all. Effervescent, boastful, gossipy, and apt to fantasize, he made a habit of archness, and his curly dark hair, bright eyes, and toothy grin combined with his favourite exclamations—'Crumbs!' 'Golly!' 'Horrid!'—to create a boyish air that neither large rimless spectacles nor latterly a beard much diminished. Money matters were 'a bore' but being 'mega-rich' was rather fun. He had separated from Richards (who was having an affair with Bruce Chatwin) and moved in 1982 to a fashionably minimalist studio apartment in Holland Park Road, dominated by his collection of modern British art and a concert grand piano on which he earnestly practised every day. He was a sponsor of Glyndebourne Opera and a director of the Rambert Dance Company. Best of all he liked to give parties, especially for musicians, artists, and aristocrats. While his charm and intelligence won him scores of carefully tended friendships, he still seemed an essentially solitary man without much instinctive understanding of people's feelings. He suffered a nervous breakdown in 1986.

Employees found Walker inspirational and autocratic. There were fresh flowers on every desk and free hot lunches, but he wanted total loyalty. His obsessive perfectionism sometimes spilt over into petulance, so departures from Walker Books frequently grew acrimonious. By 1990 it was producing 300 titles per year and had an annual turnover of £18 million. When he gave 51 per cent of the company to a discretionary trust for the benefit of staff, authors, and illustrators in May 1990, business rivals were puzzled, unaware that he had been diagnosed as HIV positive in autumn 1989. Sebastian Walker died at his home in Holland Park Road, London, on 16 June 1991 of an AIDS-related brain disease. He was credited with the revitalization of publishing for the very young.

JASON TOMES

Sources M. Cecil, *Sebastian Walker 1942–91: a kind of Prospero* (1995) · *The Independent* (18 June 1991) · *The Times* (19 June 1991) · *Daily Telegraph* (18 June 1991) · *The Guardian* (20 June 1991) · V. Grove, 'Publishing wizard casts a sweet spell of success', *Sunday Times* (6 May 1990) · C. Fitzsimons, 'On a personal quest for perfection', *The Guardian* (27 March 1990) · N. Jones, 'From circus clown to publisher', *The Times* (9 Aug 2000) · 'Walker on the wild side', *Independent on Sunday* (6 May 1990) · N. Shakespeare, *Bruce Chatwin* (1999)
Likenesses B. Schroeder, watercolour, 1976 · C. Riddell, caricature, 1987 · S. Soames, photograph, c.1990, repro. in Grove, 'Publishing wizard casts a sweet spell' · photograph, c.1990, repro. in D. Heaton and J. Higgins, eds., *Lives remembered: the Times obituaries*

of 1991 (1991) • portraits, repro. in Cecil, *Sebastian Walker*, frontispiece and 94
Wealth at death £4,045,651: probate, 25 Feb 1992, *CGPLA Eng. & Wales*

Walker, (William) Sidney (1795–1846), literary scholar, was born at Pembroke, south Wales, on 4 December 1795, the eldest of the six children of John Walker, a naval officer who died at Twickenham in 1811 from the effects of war wounds, and his wife (*née* Fullman or Falconer). Sidney Walker was named after his godfather, Admiral Sir Sidney Smith, under whom his father had served. Sidney Walker, who was always called by his second forename, was a precocious child of weak physique. After spending some years first at a school at Doncaster, run by his mother's brother, and then with a private tutor at Forest Hill in Kent, he entered Eton College in 1811. He had already shown a remarkable literary ability which, however, was never fully realized. At ten he translated many of Anacreon's odes. At eleven he planned an epic in heroic verse on the career of Gustavus Vasa, and in 1813 he published by subscription the first four books of this epic in a volume entitled *Gustavus Vasa, and other Poems*, an immature work, showing little promise of 'any high and distinctive poetic power' (Moultrie, xv). At Eton he learned the whole of Homer's *Iliad* and *Odyssey* by heart, and wrote Greek verse with unusual correctness and ease. There, too, he began lifelong friendships with Winthrop Mackworth Praed and John Moultrie. Walker was of diminutive stature and uncouth appearance and manner, and abnormally absent-minded, and suffered much bullying at school, although he retaliated with 'relentless sarcasm' (Moultrie, xi). After winning many distinctions at Eton, he was entered as a sizar at Trinity College, Cambridge, on 16 February 1814, and began his university career in October 1814. There he maintained the promise of his schooldays. In the next few years he published verse and translations, which included *The Heroes of Waterloo: an Ode* and a translation, *Poems from the Danish, Selected by Andreas Andersen Feldborg*, both in 1815. Walker won the Craven scholarship in 1817 and the Porson prize for Greek verse in 1818, and was admitted scholar of Trinity on 3 April of that year. Although his ignorance of mathematics made it extremely difficult for him to pass the examination for his BA in 1819, he was elected on the strength of his classical attainments to a fellowship at his college in 1820. His awkward manners and slovenly bearing did not improve, but he retained his close friendship with Praed and Moultrie, and formed a new and lasting friendship with Derwent Coleridge, who later attended him in the last days of his life. In 1824 Walker applied unsuccessfully for the Greek professorship at the university and thereafter made no further effort to obtain any similar work. While a fellow of Trinity he lived in seclusion, although his wish 'for the married life … was intense and soul-consuming' (Moultrie, lxxiv). He contributed philological essays to the *Classical Journal*, and both verse and prose to Charles Knight's *Quarterly Magazine*. In 1824 he prepared for publication a two-volume edition of Milton's newly discovered treatise *De doctrina Christiana*. Charles Richard Sumner, then librarian at Windsor, was ostensibly the editor and translator, but Walker took it on himself to revise 'not only the printer's, but the translator's labour' (Moultrie, lxxviii). In 1828 he edited for Knight a useful *Corpus poetarum Latinorum*, which was reprinted in 1848 and 1854.

As an undergraduate Walker had been troubled by religious doubts, and had asked William Wilberforce for guidance. During 1817–18 Wilberforce wrote him letters attempting to strengthen his beliefs. Charles Simeon, an important influence at Cambridge during these years, allayed his concerns for a time, but Walker felt that his sceptical views regarding eternal punishment disqualified him from taking holy orders. Therefore, because of the university regulations of the time, he was forced to resign his fellowship in 1829. The loss of his fellowship meant the loss of his income and, owing to his unbusinesslike habits and trusting nature, he found himself with debts totalling £300. In 1830 his old friend Praed paid his debts and settled on him an income of £52 a year for life, to which Trinity College added £20 p.a., and on this income Walker supported himself for the rest of his life. In 1831 he moved to London and was lodging at 26 Melton Crescent, Euston Square, in 1836, and in the neighbourhood of St James's Street from 1838 until his death. His reason became disturbed, so that he thought himself possessed by a demon, and social intercourse with him became impossible. However, he remained capable of occasional literary work, which bore few signs of his mental state, and at times he was able to describe the symptoms of his illness calmly and rationally. After a life which was 'almost as uneventful as it was unhappy' (Moultrie, i), Walker died of 'the stone' (Moultrie, cxxxiv), probably kidney failure, at his lodgings, a single room on the top floor of 41 St James's Place, on 15 October 1846. He was buried in Kensal Green cemetery. On the tomb were engraved some lines from Moultrie's poem called 'The Dream of Life', in which the writer mourned the 'shapeless wreck' to which Walker's fine mind had been reduced. Moultrie published in 1852 a collection of Walker's letters and poems, the former being entertaining to read, under the title, *The poetical remains of William Sidney Walker, formerly fellow of Trinity College, Cambridge, with a memoir of the author.*

Walker left a voluminous collection of manuscripts, including critical essays and numerous notes on the text and versification of Shakespeare. William Nanson Lettsom, one of Walker's school and college friends, tried without much success to bring some order into Walker's Shakespearian papers, and in 1854 published *Shakespeare's versification, and its apparent irregularities explained by examples from early and late English writers*. Lettsom also edited *A critical examination of the text of Shakespeare, with remarks on his language and that of his contemporaries, together with notes on his plays and poems*, which appeared in three volumes in 1860. The cost of printing both works was borne by George Crawshay, a wealthy Cambridge undergraduate. These two works, which mainly deal with minute points of Shakespearian prosody and syntax, embody the results of Walker's vast and close reading and have

proved of some value to succeeding students of Elizabethan and Shakespearian literature. Their defects are the
want of logical arrangement of the material and the lack
of an index, although the British Library copy of the *Critical examination* has a partial handwritten index (1869),
bound in at the end of volume 2.

SIDNEY LEE, *rev.* PENELOPE HICKS

Sources J. Moultrie, 'A memoir of the author', in *The poetical
remains of William Sidney Walker, formerly fellow of Trinity College, Cambridge*, ed. J. Moultrie (1852) · W. N. Lettsom, 'Preface', in W. S.
Walker, *Shakespeare's versification, and its apparent irregularities
explained by examples from early and late English writers*, ed. W. N. Lettsom (1854) · W. N. Lettsom, preface, in W. S. Walker, *A critical examination of the text of Shakespeare*, ed. W. N. Lettsom, 3 vols. (1860) ·
private information (1899)

Archives CUL, letters, poems, and papers

Wealth at death £72 p.a.: Moultrie, 'Memoir'

Walker, Thomas (*bap.* 1698, *d.* 1744), actor and playwright,
was baptized on 5 June 1698 at St Anne's, Soho, London,
the son of Francis Walker and his wife, Elizabeth. He was
educated locally at Mr Midon's school. In 1714 he joined
Shepherd's company to play Paris in the droll *The Siege of
Troy*. Barton Booth then recruited him for the Drury Lane
company, where he first appeared on 2 June 1715 as the
third whore in Elkanah Settle's *The City Ramble*. During his
first season he was given more sizeable roles, as Young
Fashion in Sir John Vanbrugh's *The Relapse*, Captain Jolly in
Johnson's *The Cobbler of Preston*, and King in Dryden and
Nathaniel Lee's *The Duke of Guise*, as well as a solo benefit.
Walker stayed with the company, playing Granius in
Thomas Otway's *Caius Marius*, Hilliard in Richard Brome's
A Jovial Crew, Pisander in Philip Massinger's *The Bondman*,
Cornwall and Edmund in *King Lear*, and Sir Charles in
Thomas Shadwell's *The Fair Quaker of Deal*, and originating
Cardono in Susannah Centlivre's *The Cruel Gift* and Charles
in Colley Cibber's *The Non-Juror*. His engagement appears
to have been uninterrupted by his indictment, according
to the *Evening Post* of 4–7 May 1717, for the murder of an
abbot and a bailiff near the playhouse. Davies reports he
was acquitted, and nothing further seems to have transpired.

Like many Drury Lane comedians, Walker did not abandon the summer fairs. He excelled in drolls, those short,
comic sketches that were often cobbled-together excerpts
from popular plays. In September 1720 he collaborated
with a booth owner called Lee on *The Siege of Bethulia*, a
Southwark fair droll, and the following year he worked
Lee's booth at both Bartholomew fair and Southwark fair,
appearing in the droll *The Noble Englishman*. By 1722 Walker
was running his own great booth in Bird Cage Alley at
Southwark fair, where he produced two drolls, *The Royal
Revenge* and *Valentine and Orson*, with actors from Drury
Lane. This popular entertainment required a performer
with a strong voice, able to establish an easy rapport with
an audience. Walker offered these qualities in abundance;
indeed, Hill, in *The Actor*, thought that on occasion 'the
vehemence of his feeling took away his utterance' (Hill,
82).

In 1721 Walker was poached by John Rich for the company at Lincoln's Inn Fields where, during the 1720s, he

earned £1 6s. 8d. daily, with modest annual benefits, which
may have netted him £20. Davies thought Walker an
inheritor of Barton Booth's roles and his easy, natural
manner, and particularly praised his Faulconbridge in
King John for his 'manly deportment, vigorous action, and
a humour which descended to an easy familiarity in conveying a jest or sarcasm with uncommon poignancy'
(Davies, 1.15). Walker's expanded range of roles with Rich
included noble, if compromised, heroes, such as the
eponymous roles in Dryden's *Don Sebastian* and Thomas
Southerne's *Oroonoko*, Alexander in Lee's *The Rival Queens*
and Massinissa in his *Sophonisba*, Ulysses in *Troilus and Cressida*, and Juba in Joseph Addison's *Cato*. He had the comic
timing for such roles as Young Valere in Centlivre's *The
Gamester*, Harcourt in William Wycherley's *The Country
Wife*, Lovemore in Thomas Betterton's *The Amorous Widow*,
and Dick in Vanbrugh's *The Confederacy*, as well as the stage
presence to carry such sexually threatening parts as Lorenzo in Dryden's *The Spanish Fryar* and Polydore in Otway's
The Orphan. Although not originally designed for him, but
rather for James Quin, who refused the role, Macheath in
John Gay's *The Beggar's Opera* was the kind of role Walker
excelled in, and it was the part that made him, despite his
limited singing experience. The play had an extended run,
and Walker is captured in the role of Macheath in
Hogarth's painting of the prison scene.

Walker's extracurricular activities during this period
stretched to playwriting. On 31 July 1724 his compression
of Thomas D'Urfey's *Massaniello* was printed, and he took
the title role at Lincoln's Inn Fields that season. In the September after his success in *The Beggar's Opera* he produced
an imitation called *The Quaker's Opera* at Southwark fair,
which made it indoors to the Haymarket in October 1728.
Two years later he tried out *The Fate of Villainy* at Goodman's Fields Theatre, but it quickly disappeared; however, when rewritten as *Love and Loyalty*, it was well
received at its one and only performance in Dublin in
1744. Walker also returned to his source of summer
income when in September 1732 he and Rayner produced
Centlivre's afterpiece *A Wife Well Managed* and *The Humours
of Harlequin* at a Tottenham Court booth. This seems to
have been his last sortie into the London fairs. He stayed
with Rich's company when it moved to the new Covent
Garden Theatre in 1732, accepting a reduced daily rate of
16s. 8d. During the next few years he added more demanding roles to his repertory, such as Bajazet in Nicholas
Rowe's *Tamerlane*, Angelo in *Measure for Measure*,
Sempronius in *Cato*, Kite in George Farquhar's *The Recruiting Officer*, Faulconbridge in *King John*, and Fainall in William Congreve's *The Way of the World*.

Walker's life appears to have been beset by debt, and by
the late 1730s his problems were compounded by the
death of his wife, Mary, on 20 March 1737. She was buried
at St Paul's, Covent Garden, three days later. By 1739 Walker's employment was patchy, and he made only two benefit appearances at Drury Lane that year. The following
season, 1741–2, he moved to the company at Goodman's
Fields Theatre, which had staged his *Fate of Villainy*, and he
was made much use of by Henry Giffard, but managed

only one benefit performance in 1742. During the summer of 1742 he went to the Smock Alley Theatre, Dublin, and had occasional roles at Aungier Street, where he managed to persuade the management to mount his redrafted play *Love and Loyalty*. However, despite receiving critical applause, Walker could not cover the house charges for a second night, and the play closed. Chetwood thought 'this Disappointment hasten'd his Death' (Chetwood, 248), for Walker died a few days later, on 5 June 1744.

J. MILLING

Sources Highfill, Burnim & Langhans, *BDA* · T. Davies, *Dramatic miscellanies: consisting of critical observations on several plays of Shakespeare*, 3 vols. (1783–4) · W. R. Chetwood, *A general history of the stage, from its origin in Greece to the present time* (1749) · [J. Hill], *The actor, or, A treatise on the art of playing* (1755) · IGI
Likenesses J. Faber junior, mezzotint, 1728 (after J. Ellys), BM, NPG · W. Hogarth, group portrait, oils, 1728 (*A scene from 'The beggar's opera'*), Tate collection; version, Yale U. CBA · attrib. Hogarth, oils, NPG

Walker, Thomas (1749–1817), cotton merchant and political reformer, was born on 3 April 1749 in Manchester, the eldest son of a local merchant who originally lived in Bristol. Although very little is known of Walker's childhood, it was during these formative years that he became acquainted with the writings of Rousseau, Hume, Locke, and Voltaire. It was, however, James Burgh, the radical schoolmaster, and in particular his treatise *Political Disquisitions*, that was to have the most important influence on Walker's mind during these early years. Indeed, Walker recalled in 1794 that Burgh was 'an able writer, endeared to me, as the instructor of my youth' (Walker, 5). In 1775 Walker married Hannah Shore, with whom he had three daughters and three sons, including Thomas *Walker (1784–1836), police magistrate and author.

Through his marriage, Walker came to know the Unitarian gentleman of Derbyshire Samuel Shore, his wife's brother, who, as an associate of Christopher Wyvill and a member of the Society of the Friends of the People, perhaps first aroused Walker's interest in reform politics. Walker quickly became a prominent figure in Manchester's community and politics, serving as an adviser on numerous local boards during the 1770s and 1780s, including that of the Manchester Infirmary, where the dissenter Dr Thomas Percival was a physician. As an outspoken protectionist, Walker earned national fame in 1785 when he successfully led a local campaign to oppose the government's introduction a year earlier of a fustian tax. That same year he founded the General Chamber of Manufactures, incorporated to fight William Pitt's Irish trade arrangements, and in 1786 he was a vocal opponent of the Eden–Vergennes treaty. By the end of 1787 Walker had become chairman of a Manchester anti-slavery committee, holding the post for several years. These efforts endeared him to many leading Foxite whigs, especially the earl of Derby, who became godfather to one of Walker's sons and who sponsored Walker's election to the Whig Club in 1788. Walker was also associated with the Manchester Revolution Society and on 1 February 1788 he

became a member of the Society for Constitutional Information.

Following the outbreak of the French Revolution Walker was elected a steward of the London Revolution Society, and on 22 January 1790 he joined the Manchester Literary and Philosophical Society, founded by Thomas Percival, but resigned at the end of 1791 after the society refused to offer their sympathies to Priestley following the riots of July. In October 1790 Walker became borough reeve of Manchester, a position he found beneficial in the early days of the Manchester Constitutional Society, which he helped organize on 5 October 1790. With Walker as president of the society moderate parliamentary reform was its primary objective, and, despite the Anglican persuasion of its founder, the society advocated equality for dissenters in the light of ongoing and increasing repression and intimidation.

Walker's political activities attracted conservative attention and loyalist reprisal. In November 1790 at a dinner meeting of the Manchester Revolution Society, Walker clashed with William Roberts, a tory lawyer and American émigré, who subsequently published a handbill that led to charges of libel being laid, albeit unsuccessfully, against Walker. Within a year he had helped establish the *Manchester Herald* and his house became a rendezvous for reformers after they were excluded from local taverns and public houses. On 11 December 1792, however, Walker's house on South Parade and the offices of the *Manchester Herald* were besieged by a 'church and king' mob. By June 1793 the Manchester Constitutional Society was dissolved when legal action commenced against him. Manchester authorities and loyalists had bribed an Irish weaver and local radical named Thomas Dunn to give false evidence against Walker and, despite failing to indict him of high treason, he and nine other Manchester reformers were charged with conspiring to overthrow the king, constitution, and government. Walker, who employed the defence of Thomas Erskine and Felix Vaughan, was tried at Lancaster assizes on 2 April 1794, but he was acquitted largely on account of Dunn's perjury. He was similarly exonerated on the same day on a separate charge of damning the king.

Despite writing and publishing *A review of some of the political events which have occurred in Manchester during the last five years* (1794) soon after his trials, Walker remained aloof from active reform politics, emerging only briefly in 1795 to oppose the 'Gagging Acts'. By 1799 his business enterprise had collapsed and in 1806 he was twice unsuccessful in obtaining positions in the public service. By this time he was living on a small farm at Longford, Lancashire, surviving on a legacy bequeathed by Felix Vaughan. Walker died on 2 February 1817 at Longford and his body was interred at Chorlton-cum-Hardy, Lancashire.

MICHAEL T. DAVIS

Sources T. Walker, *A review of some of the political events which have occurred in Manchester during the last five years* (1794) · W. Hone, *Memoir of Thomas Walker* (1819) · F. Knight, *The strange case of Thomas Walker* (1957)

Likenesses W. Sharp, line engraving, pubd 1794 (after G. Romney), BM, NPG · J. Tassie, paste medallion, 1798, Scot. NPG
Wealth at death lived final years by benefit of a bequeathal: Knight, *Strange case*

Walker, Thomas (1784–1836), police magistrate and author, the son of Thomas *Walker (1749–1817) and Hannah Shore, was born at Barlow Hall, Chorlton-cum-Hardy, near Manchester, on 10 October 1784. His father, a Manchester cotton merchant, was the head of the town's whig or reform party and in 1785 led the successful opposition to Pitt's fustian tax.

The younger Thomas Walker attended a school at Manchester before going up to Trinity College, Cambridge, where he graduated BA in 1808 and MA in 1811. He was called to the bar at the Inner Temple on 8 May 1812, and, after the death of his father, lived for some years at Longford Hall, Stretford, engaging in township affairs and dealing successfully with the problem of pauperism, which became his special study. A Malthusian, in 1826 he published *Observations on the Nature, Extent, and Effects of Pauperism, and on the Means of Reducing it* (2nd edn, 1831), and in 1834 *Suggestions for a Constitutional and Efficient Reform in Parochial Government*. In 1829 he was appointed a police magistrate at the Lambeth Street court.

On 20 May 1835 Walker began the publication of a weekly periodical entitled *The Original*, which he continued until the following December. It was a collection of his thoughts on many subjects, intended to raise 'the national tone in whatever concerns us socially or individually'; his papers on health and gastronomy, however, were the chief attraction of the work. Many editions of *The Original* were published: one, with memoirs of the two Walkers by William Blanchard Jerrold, came out in 1874; another, edited by William Augustus Guy, in 1875; and one, with an introduction by Henry Morley, in 1887. A selection, entitled *The Art of Dining and of Attaining High Health*, was printed at Philadelphia in 1837, and another selection, by Felix Summerley (Sir Henry Cole), was published in 1881 under the title *Aristology, or, The Art of Dining*.

Walker died unmarried at Brussels on 20 January 1836, and was buried in the cemetery there. A tablet to his memory was placed in London at St Mary's, Whitechapel.

C. W. SUTTON, *rev.* MARK CLEMENT

Sources F. Espinasse, *Lancashire worthies*, 2 (1877) · W. B. Jerrold, ed., *The Original*, 1 (1874) · *GM*, 2nd ser., 5 (1836), 324–6 · Venn, *Alum. Cant.*

Walker, Thomas (1822–1898), journalist, was born on 5 February 1822, at Marefair, Northampton. His parents sent him to a local school at the age of six where he remained until he was ten. His father had died when he was young, and his mother accepted the offer of relatives at Oxford to take charge of him. He was apprenticed to a carpenter and, when his apprenticeship was completed, began in business. However, he found carpentry uncongenial and abandoned his trade at twenty-four, determined instead to become a journalist. Walker had already begun his lifelong pursuit of learning by an exhaustive programme of reading. He followed his self-imposed task with much earnestness, teaching himself German so that he could read Kant in the original. To be better equipped for a career in journalism he also taught himself shorthand.

Walker moved to London and in September 1846 advertised for a position in *The Times*, but without success. He was in danger of starving to death in the street when he chanced upon the surgery of Frederick Knight Hunt, who offered Walker casual employment. Hunt was impressed by the younger man's willingness to undertake with enthusiasm the humblest task. By a combination of good fortune and diligence, Walker eventually realized his ambition and established himself as a journalist. T. P. Healey, proprietor of the *Medical Times*, engaged him as a reporter; he also contributed to *Eliza Cook's Journal*. But the most important factor was Hunt's becoming assistant editor of the *Daily News*. At first Walker made occasional contributions to the paper and then he obtained a junior post on the editorial staff. He served as the foreign sub-editor's general factotum, providing him with translations and précis of articles in European and South American journals. In 1851 Walker was promoted to foreign and general sub-editor. The *Daily News* now entered into a period of increasing success, first under the editorship of Walker's mentor, Hunt, and, after his death in 1854, under William Weir. When Weir died in 1858, Walker was appointed the *Daily News*'s political editor, with John Robinson as managing editor. This proved to be a most successful partnership.

This rapid change in Walker's fortunes did not change his demeanour. He remained austere and was never known to make a joke. In domestic affairs, he declared his intention that the *Daily News* would pursue a 'perfectly independent course'. Lord John Russell's new administration was afforded 'a fair trial', and its performance judged with generosity. In foreign politics he was a steadfast friend to the cause of Italian liberty, while in the American Civil War, much influenced by Harriet Martineau, he sturdily supported the northern states. However, what above all else set the tone of Walker's editorship was his unflagging devotion to Gladstone. When, in 1869, failing health obliged Walker to resign the editorship of the *Daily News*, Gladstone rewarded his loyalty by giving him charge of the *London Gazette*. This much less onerous position Walker held for twenty years until July 1889. Despite his uncertain health and other duties, Walker's respect and admiration for Gladstone determined that he should return temporarily to the *Daily News* at the time of the Turkish Bulgarian outrages, to guide the news reporting and editorial comment.

An enthusiastic churchman, Walker served as president of the London branch of the Congregational church. He devoted his retirement years to philanthropic works for his church. He married twice and was survived by one daughter. He died on 16 February 1898 at his house, 53 Addison Road, Kensington, and was buried in Brompton cemetery. Political candour distinguished Walker as an editor. T. P. O'Connor described him as 'very brilliant' but discerned a marked cynicism (Koss, 1.96). T. H. S. Escott thought him 'blameless and rather colourless' (p. 214). All were agreed on Walker's devotion to Gladstone. Frederick

Greenwood generously acknowledged in his *Pall Mall Gazette* that Walker 'always held aloof from partisan excess [and was] at all times anxious to do justice to opponents— not common merits'. All men were equally in awe of Walker's vast store of knowledge to which, over the years, he added judgement that grew ever more formidable and statesmanlike.   W. F. RAE, *rev.* A. J. A. MORRIS

Sources *Fifty years of Fleet Street: being the life and recollections of Sir John R. Robinson*, ed. F. M. Thomas (1904), 40–41 · S. E. Koss, *The rise and fall of the political press in Britain*, 1 (1981) · *The Times* (20 Feb 1898) · *The Athenaeum* (26 Feb 1898), 279 · *Daily Chronicle* [London] (19 Feb 1898) · T. H. S. Escott, *Masters of English journalism* (1911)
Wealth at death £14,796 17s. 1d.: probate, 25 March 1898, *CGPLA Eng. & Wales*

Walker, Thomas Andrew (1828–1889), civil engineering contractor, was born on 15 October 1828 at Kerrymore, Brewood, Staffordshire, the first of three children of Robert Walker, land agent of Brewood, and Ann Hay. In 1845, after a brief course in applied science at King's College, London, he began his professional career by undertaking work on parliamentary surveys. Walker became one of the most important civil engineering contractors of the nineteenth century, demonstrating exceptional management abilities in undertaking some of the largest contracts of his day. In 1847 he was employed by Thomas Brassey on the North Staffordshire Railway and remained with him until 1854 working on the Royston and Hitchin, and Newcastle and Ashbourne, railways, and for the last two years on the Grand Trunk Railway of Canada. On 6 January 1852 Walker married Fanny Beetlestone; they had four surviving daughters. In 1854 he began his own contracting career in Canada, building railways for the government of the Lower Provinces for a further seven years.

Walker returned to England in 1861. Then, as assistant to P. Pritchard Baly, in 1863 he made a survey for the Oryol and Vitebsk Railway in Russia. During 1864–5 he made extensive railway surveys for Charles Manby in Egypt and the Sudan. He returned to England in 1865 and managed the contracts for the Metropolitan Railway extension and the construction of the Metropolitan District line. He undertook these works, from Edgware Road to the Mansion House, jointly with Peto and Betts, Kelk, and Waring Brothers, completing the work by 1 July 1871. From this date to his death he was engaged, at first in partnership with his brother Charles and then alone, in a series of contracts for some of the largest engineering projects of the late nineteenth century. He undertook the extension of the East London Railway from the north end of the Thames Tunnel to its junction with the Great Eastern line at Shoreditch. This work involved tunnelling under the London docks and was completed in 1876. The engineer for the East London line, Sir John Hawkshaw, was so impressed with Walker's work that he entrusted him with the construction of the Severn railway tunnel, designed to shorten the Great Western route from Bristol to south Wales. Work had begun on the tunnel in 1873, but, after slow progress, was handed over to Sir John Hawkshaw as chief engineer and Thomas Walker as contractor on 18 December 1879. Characteristically, Walker employed a great deal of steam-powered machinery on this job. The work was one of great difficulty owing to the irruption of water, but was completed in 1889, when the tunnel was opened to goods traffic. Walker spoke of the 'ever-varying and strangely contorted strata, and the dangers from flood above and flood below' and said 'one sub-aqueous tunnel is quite enough for a lifetime' (Walker, preface). During the tunnel works he was also engaged on the Deal and Dover Railway (1880); the Elham Valley Railway (Canterbury–Folkestone, 1889); completion of the Prince of Wales Dock, Swansea (1881); extension of Penarth Dock (1884); Barry Dock (1889), and part of the Barry railway; and completion of the Lisvane Reservoir for Cardiff corporation (1886).

Walker's last undertaking was his greatest work. In June 1887 he obtained the contract for the whole works of the Manchester Ship Canal, at £5.75 million. As soon as he had possession of the land the chief engineer said that Walker 'showed great energy in commencing to erect huts, hospitals, and chapels for the workmen' (Williams, 419). Walker was renowned for the care and provisions made for his army of navvies. He established the administrative structure and amassed the largest group of steam-powered contractor's plant assembled for one contract up to that time. This included locomotives, waggons, cranes, and excavating machinery, and the first 'steam navvy' was at work in December 1887. Unfortunately within two years of starting work Walker died, and the ship canal company took over the work and the construction plant, valued at over £860,000. Walker died, of Bright's disease, at his home, Mount Balan, in Caer-went, Monmouthshire, on 25 November 1889. He was buried at St Stephen's Church, Caer-went. Walker's success as a contracting engineer is indicated by the fact that his estate was valued at nearly £1 million.   DENIS SMITH

Sources *PICE*, 100 (1889–90), 416–19 · T. A. Walker, *The Severn Tunnel: its construction and difficulties, 1872–1887* (1888) · Inst. CE, Frank Smith deposit, file FSB 075 · b. cert. · d. cert. · *CGPLA Eng. & Wales* (1890) · E. Leader Williams, 'On the mechanical appliances employed in the construction of the Manchester ship canal', *Institution of Mechanical Engineers: Proceedings* (1891), 418–27
Archives Inst. CE
Wealth at death £982,243 7s.: probate, 1 May 1890, *CGPLA Eng. & Wales*

Walker, Thomas Larkins (*bap.* 1811, *d.* 1860), architect, was baptized on 20 May 1811 in Dysart, Fife, the son of Adam Walker and Elizabeth Larkins. He studied architectural draughtsmanship with Augustus Charles Pugin in London from about 1827 until Pugin's death in 1832. He was later a co-executor of Pugin's will and completed Pugin's last work, *Examples of Gothic Architecture* (3 vols., 1836–8), to which he added his own studies of *The History and Antiquities of the Manor House and Church at Great Chalfield, Wilts* (1837) and *The History and Antiquities of the Manor House of South Wraxhall, and the Church of St. Peter at Biddlestone, Wiltshire* (1838). Walker's unpublished 'Essay on the study of architecture' of 1833 (MS in RIBA BAL) shows how his theory and practice were influenced by Pugin and his son A. W. N. Pugin.

Walker was in practice with Benjamin Ferrey, another alumnus of the Pugin school, from 1833 to 1838, in which year he became a fellow of the Royal Institute of British Architects. Walker designed All Saints' Church, Spicer Street, Mile End (1838–9); Camphill House, Warwickshire, for J. Craddock (1839); a church at Attleborough, Nuneaton, Warwickshire, for Lord Harrowby (1839–40); and St Philip's Church, Mount Street, Bethnal Green (1840–42). In 1840 he designed the Chamberlaine almshouses at Bedworth, Warwickshire. They are in a red brick Tudor style and looked, to Nikolaus Pevsner, precocious for their date. They are described by Walker as a hospital in *Architectural Precedents* (ed. C. Davy, 1841). Walker lived for a time in Nuneaton and was later in partnership with Robert Johnson Goodacure in Leicester from 1851 to 1856. After this he went to Hong Kong, possibly to recover from a failed business venture, and died there, apparently unmarried, on 10 October 1860.   ROSEMARY HILL

Sources *Dir. Brit. archs.* · [W. Papworth], ed., *The dictionary of architecture*, 11 vols. (1853–92) · *GM*, 3rd ser., 10 (1861), 337 · A. Wedgwood, *Catalogue of the drawings collection of the Royal Institute of British Architects: the Pugin family* (1977) · *Warwickshire*, Pevsner (1966) · *IGI* · drawings and papers, RIBA BAL
Archives RIBA, nomination papers · RIBA BAL, biog. file · RIBA BAL, drawings and MSS · V&A, drawings

Walker, Vyell Edward (1837–1906), cricketer, was the fifth of seven sons of Isaac Walker of Southgate and his wife, Sarah Sophia Taylor, of Palmer's Green, Middlesex. He was born at Southgate House, Southgate, Middlesex, on 20 April 1837. His father was a brewer and the family had bought Arnos Grove, a seventeenth-century mansion in Southgate, in the 1790s. Four of his brothers—John, the eldest (1826–1885), Alfred (1827–1870), Frederick (1829–1889), and Arthur Henry (1833–1878)—made occasional appearances for Middlesex. The others, Isaac Donnithorne (1844–1898) and Russell Donnithorne (1842–1922), played a substantial number of matches for the county. From 1868 to 1874 the latter two, with Vyell, were a formidable trio in the Middlesex team.

Walker was educated at a preparatory school in Stanmore, where he learned his cricket under Mr A. Woodmass, and at Bayford, Hertfordshire, before going to Harrow School (1850–54). He played in the matches against both Eton and Winchester in 1853 and 1854. On leaving school he devoted himself mainly to cricket until some twenty years later he joined the family brewing firm, Taylor, Walker & Co. In 1856, at the age of nineteen, he appeared at Lord's for the Gentlemen against the Players and scored 16 runs. With three of his brothers—John, Frederick, and Arthur—he played for the Gentlemen in the following year, when the match against the Players took place at Kennington Oval for the first time. He regularly played for the side until 1869, captaining it on ten occasions. In July 1859 he scored 108 for England v. Surrey at the Oval, and took all ten Surrey wickets in the first innings for 74 runs. His feat was equalled by both E. M. *Grace in 1862 for the MCC v. Kent and by W. G. Grace in

1886 for the MCC v. Oxford University. Twice more Walker took ten wickets in an innings, for Middlesex against Sussex and Lancashire in 1864 and 1865 respectively. For a brief spell in the early 1860s, before the emergence of W. G. Grace, he was considered the best all-round cricketer in the country.

In 1858 Walker's eldest brother, John, founded the Southgate cricket club, on his own land. The club became a chief centre of local cricket in which all his brothers were closely involved until July 1877, when it ceased to be their private property. It was there, in 1859, that John Walker invited the Kent eleven to play a Middlesex eleven that included five members of his family.

John Walker and his brothers were also mainly responsible for the formal creation of the Middlesex County Cricket Club in 1864, and began renting a ground in Islington. After many wanderings the club found a permanent home at Lord's in 1877. Vyell was secretary of Middlesex (1864–70), joint captain with John (1864–5), and sole captain (1866–72). He was succeeded in the captaincy (1873–84) by his youngest brother, Isaac Donnithorne. Later Vyell was vice-president (1887–97), treasurer (from 1895), and president and a trustee (from 1898). In 1891 he served his term as president of the MCC.

As a batsman Walker played in an orthodox style; he was a powerful hitter, but had a safe defence. As a slow 'lob' bowler he was second only to William Clarke. He tossed the ball higher than was customary, with deceptive flight and varied pace. In the field he was exceptionally quick, especially in backing up his own bowling. As a captain he was 'the very best of his time' (*Wisden*, 1907), a view endorsed by Lord Harris. He helped Middlesex to become one of the leading cricketing counties.

Walker took over 300 wickets in his first-class career and in 1887, some years after retiring, he captained an eighteen-man Veterans' team against the MCC, led by W. G. Grace, in the MCC's centenary celebrations. Six years later, he was instrumental in persuading the club to publish the fourteenth and final volume of Arthur Haygarth's mammoth *Scores and Biographies*.

On his brother Frederick's death in 1889 Walker succeeded to the family mansion and estate of Arnos Grove, Southgate, and in 1890 he presented to the new Southgate local board 15 acres of land (then valued at £5000) for use as a public recreation ground; in 1894 he gave a further sum of £1000 to complete its laying out. He became in 1891 a JP and in 1899 deputy lieutenant for Middlesex, and he was an active magistrate. He died at his home, Arnos Grove, Southgate, unmarried, on 3 January 1906. By his will he left the house to his only surviving brother, Russell Donnithorne, and made bequests (amounting to £24,500) to London hospitals, societies, and churches, and to the Cricketers' Fund Friendly Society. He was buried in Southgate church, where a chapel built at his expense was completed, a month after his death, in February 1906. Not long before he died Walker's name was in the national press for rescuing a policeman who was overpowered while making an arrest.   W. B. OWEN, *rev.* GERALD M. D. HOWAT

Sources W. A. Bettesworth, *The Walkers of Southgate* (1900) · *The Times* (5 Jan 1906) · *Cricket* (25 Jan 1906) · *Wisden* (1907) · A. Haygarth, *Arthur Haygarth's cricket scores and biographies*, 15 vols. (1862–1925), vol. 4 · R. Daft, *Kings of cricket* (1893) · W. J. Ford, *Middlesex CCC* (1900) · P. Bailey, P. Thorn, and P. Wynne-Thomas, *Who's who of cricketers* (1984)
Likenesses photograph, *c*.1867, repro. in Daft, *Kings of cricket* · Cote, photograph, *c*.1890, repro. in Ford, *Middlesex CCC* · Dickinson, photograph, *c*.1890, Lord's, London · T. W. Wilson, pencil sketch, *c*.1890, Lord's, London · Parker, portrait, 1891, Lord's, London · Alwood, photograph, *c*.1900, repro. in *Cricket* · photograph, *c*.1900, repro. in Bettesworth, *Walkers of Southgate*
Wealth at death £1,598,177 2*s*. 6*d*.: probate, 20 March 1906, *CGPLA Eng. & Wales*

Walker, William (1623–1684), schoolmaster and author, was born in Lincoln to unknown parents. Educated at Lincoln School under John Clarke, in 1640 he matriculated from Trinity College, Cambridge, graduating BA early in 1644. He was an usher at Louth grammar school, Lincolnshire, from about 1646 and headmaster of that school from 1651 to 1657. By 1661 he had married, but his wife's name is unknown. In 1666 he was awarded the degree of BD *per literas regias* and from some time after 1662 until 1681 was rector of Colsterworth (and an acquaintance of Sir Isaac Newton). From 1671 to his death he was master of Grantham grammar school.

Noted as an author of textbooks dealing with grammar, his best-known work, *A Treatise of English Particles* (1655), was the first systematic treatment of English particles for students of Latin. *Some Improvements to the Art of Teaching* (1669) and his revision of Lily's 'authorized' grammar, *The Royal Grammar* (1670), also stress the use of English in teaching Latin grammar. Walker was a diffident man and a poor public speaker. His defence of the Church of England, made in *A Modest Plea for Infants Baptism* (1677) and *The Doctrine of Baptisms* (1678), aimed to pacify rather than provoke.

In 1677 Walker's wife died and by that time he was himself suffering from gout, stone, and other illnesses. When he made his will on 31 July 1684 he had two sons, William (*b.* 1661/2) and Thomas, two married daughters, and another daughter, Margaret. He died, probably at Colsterworth, on 1 August 1684 aged sixty-one, and was buried in the parish church. His will was proved on 15 September by his executor, son-in-law, and successor as rector of Colsterworth, George Parish. W. R. MEYER

Sources W. Walker, *A treatise of English particles* (1655), dedication · W. Walker, *Some improvements to the art of teaching* (1669) · W. Walker, *The royal grammar* (1670) · Venn, *Alum. Cant.* · Wood, *Ath. Oxon.*, new edn, 3.407 · PRO, PROB 11/377, fols. 178r–178v · E. Turner, *Collections for the history of the town and soke of Grantham* (1806), 154–5 · W. W. Rouse Ball and J. A. Venn, eds., *Admissions to Trinity College, Cambridge*, 2 (1913), 370 · Nichols, *Illustrations*, 4.28 · *VCH Lincolnshire*, vol. 2

Walker, William (*bap.* 1729, *d.* 1793). *See under* Walker, Anthony (1726–1765).

Walker, William (*bap.* 1766, *d.* 1816). *See under* Walker, Adam (1730/31–1821).

Walker, William (1791–1867), engraver, was born on 1 August 1791 at Markton, Musselburgh, Midlothian, the son of Alexander Walker and his wife, Margaret Somerville, of Lauder. His father manufactured salt from sea water until this business became unprofitable; the family then moved to Edinburgh, where Walker was apprenticed to the engraver E. Mitchell. In 1815 Walker moved to London and studied line engraving with James Stewart, stipple engraving with Thomas Woolnoth, and mezzotinting with Thomas Lupton. In 1819 he returned to Scotland and was employed to make the engraving of Sir Henry Raeburn's equestrian portrait of the fourth earl of Hopetoun (1821), which established his reputation; he also engraved a number of portraits after Raeburn, notably those of Sir Walter Scott and Raeburn himself (both 1826), which are often cited as among the finest examples of stipple work ever produced. In 1828 he published an engraving of Lord Brougham, after a painting by Sir Thomas Lawrence, which he himself had commissioned.

In 1829 Walker married Elizabeth Reynolds [*see below*], the daughter of the engraver Samuel William *Reynolds, and settled in London at 64 Margaret Street, where he lived for the rest of his life. They had six children: William, Samuel Alexander, Elizabeth, Marion, Kate, and Jane. Walker's total *œuvre* included 107 plates (twenty-three stipple, eighty-one mezzotint, and three in mixed method), of which 100 are portraits of contemporary figures which he published himself. He also produced historical group pictures. He collaborated with other engravers, among them his brother-in-law, Samuel William Reynolds the younger, and a pupil of his father-in-law, the mezzotinter Samuel Cousins. It was Cousins who did the mezzotinting on Walker's portrait *Robert Burns*, after Alexander Nasmyth (1830), which Nasmyth is said to have considered a better likeness than his own picture. Walker's most important historical pictures are *The Reform Bill Receiving the Royal Assent in 1832*, after S. W. Reynolds, engraved with Reynolds (1836); *The Reformers Presenting their Protest at the Diet of Spires*, after G. Cattermole (1844, larger version 1845); *The Aberdeen Cabinet Deciding upon the Expedition to the Crimea*, after John Gilbert (1857); and *The Distinguished Men of Science*, engraved with assistance from G. Zobel, after a drawing by John Gilbert, J. L. Skill, and Walker himself (1862). This last work includes fifty-one portraits and occupied Walker for six years. Late in life Walker set up a commercial portrait photography business. He died at his house in Margaret Street on 7 September 1867 and was buried in Brompton cemetery. Examples of his prints are in the British Museum, the Victoria and Albert Museum, and the National Portrait Gallery, London.

Elizabeth Walker (1800–1876), miniature painter, wife of William Walker, was the second daughter of the engraver Samuel William Reynolds (1773–1835) and his wife, Jane Cowen. Her father taught her to paint and to engrave in mezzotint at an early age; she later studied engraving with Thomas Lupton and miniature painting with George Clint and William Northcote, and herself became a popular miniaturist. She was a frequent exhibitor at the Royal Academy and the Society of British Artists between 1818 and 1850, and in 1830 she was appointed miniature painter to William IV. Among her many eminent sitters were five prime ministers. She also painted in oils, and after her marriage she assisted her husband with his engravings. She died on 9 November 1876 and was buried with her husband. Her miniature of her father is in the National Portrait Gallery, London, and her full-size portrait of the earl of Devon is at Christ Church, Oxford.

F. M. O'DONOGHUE, rev. LOIS OLIVER

Sources Thieme & Becker, *Allgemeines Lexikon* · B. Hunnisett, *Engraved on steel: the history of picture production using steel plates* (1998) · R. Walker, *National Portrait Gallery: Regency portraits*, 2 vols. (1985) · Graves, *RA exhibitors* · D. Foskett, *Miniatures: dictionary and guide* (1987) · R. K. Engen, *Dictionary of Victorian engravers, print publishers and their works* (1979) · B. S. Long, *British miniaturists* (1929) · Bryan, *Painters* (1886–9) · Graves, *Artists* · CGPLA Eng. & Wales (1868) · NPC (wills), 1868, 12/105 · d. cert. [Elizabeth Walker]
Likenesses E. Reynolds, mezzotint (Elizabeth Walker; after portrait by J. Opie), BM · T. Woolnoth, stipple (Elizabeth Walker; after miniature by E. Reynolds), BM, NPG; repro. in *Ladies' Monthly Museum* (1825)
Wealth at death under £600: probate, 14 Feb 1868, CGPLA Eng. & Wales

Walker, William (1840–1931), folklorist and film-maker, was born in Aberdeen, the son of James Walker from Old Deer, Aberdeenshire, who was a Chartist and one of the last hand-loom weavers, and his wife, Mary, *née* Dingwall, who was originally from Strath Kildonan in Sutherland. His education appears to have finished when he left Blackfriars Street dame-school, Aberdeen, at the age of eight, although later he studied at the mechanics' institute. He started work for the Equitable Loan Company, rising from lowly message boy to successful managing director; his profession at his death was given as retired pawnbroker. Writing and books were his main outside interests, culminating in the local classic *The Bards of Bon-Accord* (1887), a thorough study of north-east poets from Barbour to the mid-nineteenth century.

Walker's extensive interest in balladry, folk-song, and related literature led to his becoming one of Professor Francis James Child's principal informants for *English and Scottish Popular Ballads* (1882–98). In addition he aided Gavin Greig and James Duncan in amassing their monumental north-east folk-song collection in the decade before the First World War. After their premature deaths, he oversaw the final editing by Alexander Keith of the classical balladry in the collection, which was published as *Last Leaves of Traditional Ballads and Ballad Airs* (1925). In 1915 Walker had published *Peter Buchan and other Papers*, a celebration of an earlier local ballad collector whose working methods were regarded as suspect by many authorities. He persuaded Keith not only to give *Last Leaves* its unjustifiably elegiac title (the local folk-song tradition was, and still is, thriving) but also to write an introduction which was largely a justification of Peter Buchan. Walker had examined the Greig–Duncan collection in 1919 and had been horrified by its catholicity (later regarded as an indicator of both comprehensiveness and authenticity). In his eyes it contained far too much that was not 'genuine' folk-song, such as chap-book and music-hall versions, for Greig and Duncan had been uniquely thorough and

non-selective in collecting all that their informants could give, altering virtually nothing in the process. Walker therefore determined that only the classical story songs (as categorized by Child) should see the light of day, in order that Aberdeenshire's reputation for fine balladry (for which he was partly responsible) should not be sullied by the publication of what he regarded as inconsequential rubbish. His great influence and standing ensured that only the *Last Leaves* ballad selection (including a statement—against all the evidence—that the great songs it contained had almost disappeared) ever saw the light of day and that any thought of publishing the collection in full was dismissed for almost half a century.

Walker amassed one of the most comprehensive and valuable libraries in private hands, covering both general song and balladry (especially works concerning Burns), general English and north-east literature, and works on theology, philosophy, and economics, in all of which he was well versed. From this foundation he wrote and published extensively—newspaper articles, pamphlets, and books. The last of these contained the delightful *Letters on Scottish Ballads from Professor Francis J. Child to W. W. Aberdeen* (1930), which gave many insights into Child's mind, character, and working methods. Walker's Peter Buchan manuscripts, including the notorious *Songs of Silence*, were accepted by Harvard University after being refused by a shocked Aberdeen Public Library.

As well as being an expert on fiddle music (and a good performer) and an authoritative collector of coins and medals, Walker was a skilled film-maker, recording many aspects of local life, including Queen Victoria at Balmoral. He presented the north-east's first film show in Aberdeen in 1896. His extensive knowledge, generous, sociable, and friendly nature, together with his fund of anecdotes, songs, and fiddle tunes made him a popular local citizen respected for making a successful way in life as a typical Scottish 'lad o' pairts'; his extensive and wide-ranging self-taught knowledge also made him an influential international authority, especially in the field of balladry. He was married for fifty-two years to Elsie, *née* Noble; they had no children. He died at his home, 65 Argyll Place, Aberdeen, on 26 December 1931 and was buried, on 29 December, at Allenvale cemetery, Aberdeen.

IAN A. OLSON

Sources *Aberdeen Press and Journal* (28 Dec 1931) · *Scottish Notes and Queries*, 3rd ser., 10 (1932), 1–2 · R. M. Lawrance, *Bibliography of the writings of the late William Walker, Aberdeen* (1932) · F. Ross, 'William Walker, 1840–1931', *Aberdeen University Review*, 39 (1961–2), 317–22 · A. Keith, 'William Walker', *Eminent Aberdonians* (1984), 97–101 · I. A. Olson, 'Scottish traditional song and the Greig–Duncan collection: last leaves or last rites?', *The history of Scottish literature*, 4: *Twentieth century*, ed. C. Craig (1987), 37–48 · I. A. Olson, 'The Greig-Duncan folk song collection: last leaves of local culture?', *Review of Scottish Culture*, 5 (1989), 79–85 · M. E. Brown, *The bedesman and the hodbearer* (2001) · d. cert.
Archives Aberdeen Central Library · U. Aberdeen, corresp. and papers on *Scottish ballads*; notebooks and other papers · University of Florida, Gainsville | Harvard U., Houghton L., Child MSS | FILM Scottish Film Archives
Likenesses photographs, repro. in Lawrance, *Bibliography* · photographs, repro. in Ross, 'William Walker'

Wealth at death £8498 16*s.* 10*d.*: confirmation, 6 April 1932, *CCI* · £16 1*s.* 9*d.*—additional estate: 15 June 1932, *CCI*

Walker, William (1871–1918), trade union official and socialist, was born on 9 January 1871 at 35 McCluny Street, Belfast, the son of Francis Walker, a boilermaker, and his wife, Sarah McLaughlin. He was educated at St George's National School, Belfast, and entered Harland and Wolff's shipyard as an apprentice joiner in 1885. By the early 1890s he was playing a prominent role in the city's trade union movement and in the first attempts to develop a socialist politics with strong links to developments in the rest of the United Kingdom. He was elected delegate to the Belfast Trades Council for the Amalgamated Society of Carpenters and Joiners (ASC&J) in 1892 and rapidly emerged as the champion of 'new unionism' in the local labour movement, playing a central role in establishing unions for unorganized female linen workers and unskilled labourers in the shipyards and engineering factories. In 1892 he was a member of the Belfast branch of what became the Independent Labour Party. Speaking regularly at the Custom House steps (Belfast's version of Speakers' Corner), he had often to brave verbal and physical abuse from ultra-protestant and loyalist groups who identified socialism with irreligion and support for home rule.

Walker was elected to the Belfast corporation for the Duncairn ward in north Belfast in 1904. By this time he was a full-time union official, having been elected district delegate of the ASC&J in 1901. He was Belfast's leading Labour figure and was well known in the Irish and British movements. A regular delegate to the Irish Trade Union Congress he was elected president at its 1904 congress, and his active role in the development of British Labour politics was recognized when he was elected to the executive of the Labour Party in 1907.

Walker's union adopted him as a parliamentary candidate in 1905. He had been at the centre of efforts to establish a local branch of the Labour Representation Committee (LRC) in 1902 and became the LRC's candidate for the North Belfast parliamentary constituency. In a by-election in September 1905 Walker came within 500 votes of winning North Belfast. The Conservatives had alleged that the LRC in Britain was in favour of home rule and that many of the British Labour politicians who campaigned for Walker, including Ramsay MacDonald, who was his election agent, were sympathizers with Irish nationalism. Walker's response was to develop a strongly pro-union and anti-home rule form of Labour politics. Home rule would mean an Irish parliament dominated by the political representatives of a conservative peasantry and a reactionary Catholic church; it would produce an inward-looking society and would cut off Belfast's industries from their British and imperial markets. Continuation of the constitutional status quo would guarantee all Irish workers the benefits of Britain's developing welfare state. Walker went even further in attempting to establish his Unionist credentials by answering an anti-Catholic questionnaire produced by the Belfast Protestant Association. This probably lost him the seat by alienating the 1000 Catholic voters in the constituency.

Walker contested North Belfast in the 1906 general election and narrowed the Conservative majority to 291 but by the time he next contested it, in a by-election in April 1907, the Liberal government's Irish Council Bill had heightened sectarian tensions in the city and the Conservatives' majority rose to 1800. Walker would never contest another Irish election, although he did stand unsuccessfully as a Labour candidate in the Scottish seat of Leith burghs at the January 1910 general election. His final contribution to the cause of Labour unionism was his famous debate with the socialist and Irish nationalist James Connolly in the pages of the Scottish socialist journal *Forward* in 1911. Against Connolly's support for the creation of a separate Irish Labour Party Walker argued that, just as many Irish workers were members of British-based unions, they should go forward politically as part of the developing British Labour Party. For all their differences on the Irish national question both men were united in the mistaken belief that sectarian divisions were a thing of the past.

Walker gave up trade union and political involvement in 1912, when he took up a position under the new National Insurance Act. When he died, at the Royal Victoria Hospital, Belfast, after a long illness, on 23 November 1918 he was an inspector under the act and also a justice of the peace. He was buried on 26 November at Newtown Breda burying-ground, Belfast, and was survived by his wife, Margaret, *née* Adams.   HENRY PATTERSON

Sources A. Morgan, *Labour and partition: the Belfast working class, 1905–1923* (1991) · H. Patterson, *Class conflict and sectarianism* (1980) · J. W. Boyle, *The Irish labour movement in the nineteenth century* (1988) · *The Connolly/Walker controversy*, Cork Workers' Club (1974) · *Irish News and Belfast Morning News* (25 Nov 1918) · *Northern Whig* (25 Nov 1918) · *Belfast Telegraph* (27 Nov 1918) · b. cert. · d. cert.

Walker, Sir William Frederic Wake- (1888–1945), naval officer, was born at Watford, Hertfordshire, on 24 March 1888, the younger of the two sons in the six children of Frederic George Arthur Wake-Walker (1857–1931), solicitor, and his wife, Mary Eleanor (*d.* 1928), daughter of William Forster, barrister, of London. He was the grandson of Admiral Sir Baldwin Wake *Walker, first baronet. He was educated for a short time at Haileybury College, but left to become a naval cadet at the Royal Naval College, Dartmouth, in January 1903. He went to sea as a midshipman in May 1904 and for three years served in the *Good Hope*, flagship of Sir Wilmot Fawkes, commander of the 1st cruiser squadron. He spent some months as sublieutenant in the battleship *Illustrious* and after passing first class in all his examinations at Greenwich and winning a prize, he received rapid promotion to the rank of lieutenant. After short spells in the *Eclipse* and the *Warrior*, he joined the *Invincible*, one of the three original battle cruisers, as a watchkeeper in March 1909. He transferred to the *Vernon*, torpedo school, in August 1910 and by 1912 had qualified as a torpedo specialist.

In January 1913 Wake-Walker joined the *Cochrane*, 2nd cruiser squadron, as torpedo lieutenant and was still serving in her at the outbreak of war in August 1914. At the end of September 1915 he rejoined the *Vernon* and in July 1916,

Sir William Frederic Wake-Walker (1888–1945), by Walter Stoneman, 1942

the month of his promotion to lieutenant-commander, he was transferred to the new battleship *Ramillies*, which was so severely damaged during her launching on the Clyde in September 1916 that she was unable to join the Grand Fleet until November 1917. He was appointed OBE for his war services in 1919. On 19 January 1916 he married Muriel (*d*. 1963), daughter of Sir Collingwood Hughes, tenth baronet. They had two sons, both of whom entered the Royal Navy, and two daughters.

In April 1919 Wake-Walker was appointed to the *Coventry* and though promoted commander in June 1920 remained in her until August 1921. From September 1921 to December 1925 he was employed ashore, first at the Royal Naval College, Greenwich, then on the naval staff of the Admiralty, and finally at the tactical school, Portsmouth. He returned to sea at the end of 1925 as executive officer of the *Royal Oak*, and was promoted captain at the end of 1927 at the early age of thirty-nine. After taking the senior officers' technical and war courses he commanded the *Castor*, 3rd cruiser squadron, on the Mediterranean and China stations until July 1930, when he became deputy director of the training and staff duties division of the naval staff at the Admiralty. From September 1932 until July 1935 he was again at sea, in command of the *Dragon* on the America and West Indies station, but in October 1935 returned to the Admiralty as director of torpedoes and mining. In January 1938 he took over the command of the *Revenge* in the Home Fleet and remained in command until he reached flag rank on 10 January 1939.

After a senior officers' war course Wake-Walker became in September 1939 rear-admiral commanding the 12th cruiser squadron, in the northern patrol. He returned to the Admiralty at the end of October as rear-admiral in charge of mine-laying, but at the end of November he became responsible for co-ordinating all technical measures for dealing with the German magnetic mine, a task he discharged with great success. Wake-Walker played a crucial role in the evacuation from Dunkirk in May 1940. Sent hurriedly to Dover, he spent six days and nights under almost constant attack off the beaches and was chiefly responsible for the control of the 'little ships' which helped to bring the allied armies safely back to the United Kingdom. For this service he was appointed CB.

Wake-Walker then commanded successively: the newly formed 1st mine-laying squadron, from June 1940, flying his flag in the *Southern Prince*; force K, from December 1940, with his flag in the aircraft-carrier *Formidable*; and, from January 1941, the 1st cruiser squadron, with his flag in the *Norfolk*. It was he who on 23 May 1941 first reported the German battleship *Bismarck* and the cruiser *Prinz Eugen* in the Denmark Strait. He played a leading role in the subsequent operations and took part in the final attack which led to the destruction of the enemy battleship on 27 May. For this he was appointed CBE. *The Times* noted that while it was for this operation that Wake-Walker was best known to the public, quite generally his '1939–45 war service was brilliant' (*The Times*, 26 Sept 1945, 7).

In February 1942 Wake-Walker hauled down his flag and in April was promoted vice-admiral. In May he became third sea lord and controller of the navy, and was appointed KCB in 1943. As controller he played a significant part in the great development of landing craft which made possible the victorious allied invasions of northern and southern Europe. He reached admiral's rank on VE-day, 8 May 1945, but died suddenly on 24 September 1945 at 2 Wellington Square, Chelsea, London, only a few hours after formally accepting the appointment of commander-in-chief, Mediterranean. He was buried at St Mary's, East Bergholt, Suffolk, on 27 September.

J. H. LLOYD-OWEN, *rev.* MARC BRODIE

Sources *The Times* (26 Sept 1945) · Burke, *Peerage* · *Annual Register* (1945), 425–6 · S. Roskill, *The navy at war, 1939–45* (1960) · *WWW* · personal knowledge (1959) · private information (1959) · *CGPLA Eng. & Wales* (1945)
Archives IWM, papers | FILM IWM FVA, actuality footage | SOUND IWM SA, 'Sinking of the *Bismarck*, 26/5/1941', BBC, 28 May 1941, 2384
Likenesses W. Stoneman, photograph, 1940, NPG · W. Stoneman, photograph, 1942, NPG [*see illus.*] · M. Codner, oils, *c*.1945–1946, Haileybury and Imperial Service College, Hertfordshire · photograph, repro. in *The Times*, 7
Wealth at death £3780 4*s.* 3*d.*: probate, 27 Nov 1945, *CGPLA Eng. & Wales*

Walker [*formerly* Bellenie, Bellenie-Walker], **William Robert** (1869–1918), diver, was born William Robert Bellenie on 21 October 1869 at 124 Hill Street, Walworth, Surrey, one of four sons and one daughter in the family of William John Bellenie, a carpenter of Italian ancestry, and his

William Robert Walker (1869–1918), by Charles Edward
Shuttleworth Beloe, 1907 [left, with his assistant, William West]

wife, Frances Jane Rose. As an adult William Robert
changed his surname by deed poll to Bellenie-Walker, and
later shortened it to Walker at the request of his second
wife.

Walker joined the Royal Navy as a boy entrant aged sixteen, and in 1887 he started training as a deep-sea diver at
HMS *Vernon*, graduating as a first-class diver. During this
period he gave the future George V, then a cadet, his first
lesson in diving. In 1892 Walker left the navy to become an
employee of the diving firm Siebe Gorman & Co. of Westminster Bridge Road, London. He worked for four years in
Gibraltar on the new dockyard, and, as his skill was recognized, was in constant demand to deal with flooded coal
and lead mines, and to undertake wreck work. He participated in experiments for his firm, whose doctors were collaborating with Admiralty physicians on the subject of
underwater pressure, and he made a near record dive to
189 feet. Walker was working on a new jetty at the Victoria
docks, London, when he was sent to Winchester Cathedral for the five-year project for which he was to achieve
national fame.

The repair works at Winchester had begun in November
1905 under the direction of Thomas Jackson, then diocesan architect, and the consultant engineer Francis Fox.
A decision had been made to underpin the cathedral by
digging a random series of trenches (drifts) at right angles

to the cathedral walls and replacing the inadequate medieval footings by cement concrete, down to the solid gravel
24 feet below ground level. The high water table in Winchester (only 10 feet below the surface) meant that a
powerful pump was initially used in an attempt to empty
the drifts; this was felt to be hazardous as there was a risk
of removing solid material from beneath the cathedral
walls. Progress was slow, and the problems were resolved
only at the end of March 1906, when Francis Fox suggested
that the initial stages of the underpinning work might be
done under water, using a diver and obviating the need for
pumping. Walker and another diver began work in Winchester within a week. It was intended that they should
work alternate shifts, using one set of equipment, but
Walker's output and skill proved far superior to that of his
colleague who eventually was taken off the project.

Walker quickly achieved popular renown as the key figure in the preservation operation at Winchester, in which
up to 150 other workmen were involved. He worked for
two four-hour shifts a day, which allowed time for two
three-hour periods under water. There, in almost total
darkness caused by the turbidity of the water, Walker
worked at a depth of some 15–20 feet, completing the
excavation of the drifts, and laying two to three layers of
bags of cement concrete, which sealed the ingress of
water from below. It was then possible to pump out the
drift so that masons could complete the underpinning.
Eventually the foundations of all the outer walls of the
cathedral were renewed in this way.

Walker's work at Winchester was completed by August
1911. On 15 July 1912, St Swithun's day, the preservation
works were commemorated by a service of national
thanksgiving, attended by the king and queen. Walker
was present at the service and received an honourable
mention in the sermon given by the archbishop of Canterbury, Randall Davidson, who presented Walker to George
V after the service. His former pupil congratulated him
'upon [his] feat in saving the Cathedral' (Henderson and
Crook, 118). At the end of 1912 Walker was made a member
of the Royal Victorian Order, an honour in the gift of the
sovereign.

Walker was a robust man. His job required considerable
stamina, and he scarcely lost a day's work through ill
health, attributing this to the pipe which he regularly
smoked in silence between shifts, claiming that it preserved him from the harmful effects of working in ground
then considered to be infected by 900-year-old graves. He
returned each weekend to his family home at South Norwood, on one occasion making the journey by bicycle. A
modest man, he spoke little about his exploits, despite
constant media attention.

Walker was a Freemason: a member of the Royal Jubilee
Lodge, and grand master of Malta. He married Hannah,
daughter of Thomas John Cashman, a scaffolder, of Cork.
The marriage produced five children, the last, Edward,
being born in Gibraltar in 1900 while Walker was working
in the dockyard there. Hannah died within a year of
Edward's birth, and Walker sent the young family home
to the care of Hannah's younger sister, Alice, then aged

nineteen. On the children's arrival Alice discovered that two of them had contracted typhoid fever during the voyage home. She nursed them back to health and married their father on 30 December 1907. Seven children resulted from this second marriage.

On 27 October 1918 Walker fell victim to the Spanish influenza epidemic, and died on 30 October of acute lobar pneumonia at his home, 112 Portland Road, South Norwood. He was buried in Elmers End cemetery, Beckenham. He was survived by his second wife. In 1964 a statuette of a diver by Sir Charles Wheeler was unveiled in Winchester Cathedral in honour of the man who had 'saved the cathedral with his own two hands' (Henderson and Crook, 126); owing to a confusion the effigy was in fact modelled on a photograph of Francis Fox in diver's dress. In 1989 Walker's neglected grave was restored by public subscription. In June 2001 the error over the diver's memorial was finally corrected when a bronze portrait bust of Walker by Glyn Williams was unveiled. Walker is remembered annually at Winchester Cathedral's patronal festival. JOHN CROOK

Sources I. T. Henderson and J. Crook, *The Winchester diver: the saving of a great cathedral* (1984) · 8 vols. of miscellaneous items, 2 vols. of contemporary photographs, 6 vols. of press cuttings, Winchester Cathedral, Walker Collection · T. G. Jackson, 'Winchester Cathedral: an account of the building and of the repairs now in progress', *Transactions of the St Paul's Ecclesiological Society*, 6 (1910), 218–36 · F. Fox, 'The restoration of Winchester Cathedral', *Sixty-three years of engineering: scientific and social work* (1924), 124–45 · J. Patton, 'William Robert Walker, the family man', *Winchester Cathedral Record*, 57 (1988), 11–12 · b. cert. · m. cert. [Alice Ellen Cashman] · d. cert. · *CGPLA Eng. & Wales* (1919) · *Hampshire Observer* (2 Sept 1911) · *Norwood Echo* (8 Nov 1918) · private information (2004) [family]
Likenesses photograph, *c*.1885, Winchester Cathedral archives · C. E. S. Beloe, photograph, 1907, priv. coll. [*see illus.*] · Ishibashi, pastel, *c*.1913, Winchester Cathedral · G. Williams, bronze bust, 2001, Winchester Cathedral · photographs, Winchester Cathedral archives
Wealth at death £1397 12*s*. 9*d*.: probate, 2 Jan 1919, *CGPLA Eng. & Wales*

Walkingame, Francis (*bap.* 1723, *d.* 1783), schoolmaster and writer on arithmetic, was baptized on 25 July 1723 at St Giles-in-the-Fields, London, the only surviving son of John Walkingame (*d.* 1752), agent to the Marchant Water Works, and Elizabeth (*d.* in or before 1752), probably daughter of Hugh Marchant, founder of the works. His education is unknown. On 18 May 1746 he married Mary Hider (*d.* 1763/4) of Kensington; their first child was baptized there in 1747, and another in 1750.

In the following year, 1751, appeared the first edition of Walkingame's outstandingly successful school arithmetic book, *The Tutor's Assistant: being a Compendium of Arithmetic; and a Complete Question Book*. The title-page describes the author as 'writing-master and accomptant and master of the boarding-school in Kensington', while the preface says that it was compiled 'for the use of my own school'. Walkingame returned his thanks to all 'whose kind approbation and encouragement have now established the use of this book in almost every school of eminence throughout the kingdom'. He was referring to the schoolmasters and accountants among his 238 subscribers, who included

also carpenters and plumbers. The fourth edition came out in 1760, and the twentieth in 1784, shortly after the author's death. Afterwards there were in many years two or three editions, variously edited, the main series from London and others in the provinces, notably from Gainsborough, York, and Derby. Further editions later appeared in Canada. An incomplete listing comprises 276 editions, the last in 1885; often an edition numbered 5000 or 10,000 copies. There were also close imitations, not always acknowledging the original. The York editions, starting in 1797, were corrected by Thomas Crosby of that city. To provide teachers and autodidacts with the working to the questions, in the same year Crosby published a *Key*, more substantial than the original work. It achieved at least sixty editions, with diverse authors and editors.

From 1751 to 1800 *The Tutor's Assistant* was one of the two most popular arithmetics (the other being by Thomas Dilworth), and thereafter reigned supreme for another half-century, its perpetuation assisted by the advent of stereotyping. Walkingame disclaimed originality. He aimed to equip his pupils to solve problems by using formulae, without necessarily understanding their validity. His success was based on inclusion of contemporary commercial topics, worked examples, and many practice questions with answers.

The second edition of the *Assistant* in 1752 no longer referred to 'the boarding-school in Kensington'. It seems likely that about then Walkingame moved his family into his parental home at the Water Office in St Martin's Lane. By 1764 his wife must have died, possibly as a result of giving birth to a son the previous year, and on 22 December 1764 he married Elizabeth Maria Steere. Their youngest child, Jane, was born in 1781. From 1771 for about ten years he lived in Great Russell Street, before returning to Kensington, where he died in February or early March 1783, probably predeceased by his wife.

Walkingame's fame rests on his single publication. Augustus De Morgan commented: 'this book is by far the most used of all school-books, and deserves to stand high among them' (*Arithmetical Books*, 1847, 80). It must have suited the educational requirements of the century during which it flourished. RUTH WALLIS

Sources P. J. Wallis, 'An early best seller', *Mathematical Gazette*, 47 (1963), 199–208 · P. J. Wallis, 'Francis Walking(h)am(e) and "The tutor's assistant"', *N&Q*, 201 (1956), 258–61 · R. V. Wallis and P. J. Wallis, eds., *Biobibliography of British mathematics and its applications*, 2 (1986), 380–92 · *DNB* · will, PRO, PROB 11/1102, sig. 153 · PRO, C 11/1328/44 and 2737/57
Wealth at death left estates in Enfield: will, PRO, PROB 11/1102, sig. 153

Walkington, Nicholas of (*supp. fl.* before 1200), supposed historical writer and Augustinian canon, may have been a native of Walkington, Yorkshire, who became canon of Holy Trinity Priory at Kirkham. All information concerning him derives ultimately from John Bale. In his *Index Britanniae scriptorum* Bale ascribes two works to Nicholas, whom he describes as a 'canonicus de Kirkeham', later emending to 'Cisterciensis monachus de Kirkeham': a *De virtutibus et vitiis* with the incipit 'Dominus dicit'; and a

Historiola de Gualtero Espec, fundatore cenobii Kirkhamensis. He gives Leland's collections as his source. In fact, Leland's surviving papers provide no reference to a Nicholas of Walkington, although Leland did see a *Historiola de virtute Gualteri Espec, autore Alredo, abbate Riaevallensi* at Kirkham (*Collectanea*, 4.36). In his *Scriptorum illustrium maioris Brytanniae … catalogus* Bale states that Nicholas flourished at the end of the twelfth century. He also gives a fuller incipit, 'Dominus dicit, Sancti estote' for the *De virtutibus et vitiis*: no surviving treatise on the virtues and vices begins with this phrase. BL, Cotton MS Titus A.xix, whose medieval provenance was Kirkstead Abbey, contains on folio 144*r* a fifteenth-century copy of an account of the battle of Brémule taken with some slight amplification from Henry of Huntingdon's *Historia Anglorum*, book 7. This is followed (on folios 144*v*–149*v*) by a somewhat corrupt copy in the same hand of Ailred of Rievaulx's *De bello standardii*, with some additions from Henry of Huntingdon. At some point in the very late sixteenth century a reader, presumably familiar with Bale, added 'Nicholaus de Walkinton de Kirkeham' in the upper margin of folio 144*r*. Having seen Titus A.xix, Thomas Tanner attributed both a *Narratio de bello inter Henrico I, et Ludovicum Grossum regem* and a *Narratio de bello de Standardo* to Nicholas, and it was his account that formed the basis for the entry in Hardy's *Descriptive Catalogue*.   JAMES P. CARLEY

Sources Bale, *Index*, 310 · Bale, *Cat.*, 1.232 · Tanner, *Bibl. Brit.-Hib.*, 749 · T. D. Hardy, *Descriptive catalogue of materials relating to the history of Great Britain and Ireland*, 2, Rolls Series, 26 (1865), 204–5 · BL, Cotton MS Titus A.xix · *Joannis Lelandi antiquarii de rebus Britannicis collectanea*, ed. T. Hearne, [3rd edn], 6 vols. (1774)
Archives BL, Cotton MS Titus A.xix

Walkington, Thomas (*c*.1575–1621), Church of England clergyman and author, was born in Lincoln, possibly the son of Thomas Walkington (*c*.1548–1620?), a Lincolnshire clergyman. He matriculated as a pensioner from St John's College, Cambridge, graduating BA in 1597 and MA in 1600. On 26 March 1602 he was elected fellow of the college, and in 1607 he published the work for which he is primarily remembered, *The Optick Glasse of Humors, or, The Touchstone of a Golden Temperature*. Dedicated to Sir Justinian Lewin from Walkington's college study on 10 March, this engaging account of Galen's four temperamental types went beyond the usual expository tradition of such treatises, and has been regarded as something of a curiosity. Lively, witty, and concerned at least as much to entertain as instruct, it foreshadowed the literary culmination of the tradition in Burton's *Anatomy of Melancholy*.

Although Walkington henceforth turned his attention to a clerical career, his few surviving sermons show a continuing fascination with the effects of language and style. In 1608 he completed his BD and published a sermon on Ecclesiastes 12: 10, preached at Thetford 'before his Majestie, by Thomas Walkington Batchelour in Divinitie, and fellow of S. Johns Colledge in Cambridge'. *Salomon's Sweete Harpe; Consisting of Five Words, Like so many Golden Strings* is a paean to the 'heavenly art' of speaking (p. 9), and was dedicated to a fellow Johnsman, Thomas Howard,

earl of Suffolk and lord chamberlain, on 28 June. In it Walkington also advocated strong measures against Brownism and other divisive movements within the church, and it is perhaps not coincidental that he was presented the same year to the vicarage of Raunds, Northamptonshire, an area closely associated with Brownist activity. In 1610 Walkington became rector of Waddingham St Mary, Lincolnshire; he was incorporated BD at Oxford on 14 July 1612, proceeded DD at Cambridge in 1613, and finally on 25 May 1615 was appointed vicar of Fulham, Middlesex.

In 1620 Walkington published his last known work, *Rabboni*, an elegiac sermon on John 20: 16 'preached at S. Paulls Crosse … By Thomas Walkington, Doctor in Divinity and Minister of the Word at Fulham'. For its dedication, 'To Rabboni' or Christ, Walkington now turned inwards to a spiritual rather than worldly patron; and in another virtuoso display of passion and rhetoric, he invoked the glory of the life to come—'the day of our life is far spent' (sig. A7). Walkington died at Fulham the following year; the administration of his goods was granted on 29 October 1621.

After his death *The Optick Glasse* went into several further editions. An undated edition, which cannot be dated earlier than 1627, was printed by William Turner at Oxford. This issue retains the 1607 dedication but substitutes a title-page elaborately engraved on steel, showing an optic glass held aloft by two graduates in cap and gown, who represent respectively the universities of Oxford and Cambridge. The universities are further depicted in a facing engraving, above a diagram of the humours abstracted from page 39 of the 1607 text. An identical London edition appeared in 1639; and in 1664 an edition appeared with both a printed title-page (dated 1664) and the later engraved version (dated 1663). W. C. Hazlitt describes an Oxford edition containing an extra leaf of dedication to the author's 'worshippefull, good friend M. Carye' (Hazlitt, *Bibliographical Collections*, 624), but, although the engravings may suggest Walkington's personal involvement with an edition published some time after 1612, there are no copies extant of such an edition.

JILLIAN KEARNEY

Sources Wood, *Ath. Oxon.: Fasti* (1815) · Foster, *Alum. Oxon.*, 1500–1714, vol. 4 · Venn, *Alum. Cant.*, 1/4 · G. Hennessy, *Novum repertorium ecclesiasticum parochiale Londinense, or, London diocesan clergy succession from the earliest time to the year 1898* (1898) · W. C. Hazlitt, *Collections and notes, 1867–1876* (1876) · W. C. Hazlitt, *Second series of bibliographical collections and notes on early English literature, 1474–1700* (1882) · F. Madan, *The early Oxford press: a bibliography of printing and publishing in Oxford, 1468–1640*, OHS, 29 (1895), vol. 1 of *Oxford books: a bibliography of printed works* (1895–1931) · *VCH Northamptonshire*, vol. 2 · *VCH Northamptonshire*, vol. 4 · W. P. W. Phillimore and A. K. Maples, eds., *Lincolnshire parish registers*, 1–11 (1905–21) · R. Farmer, *An essay on the learning of Shakespeare: addressed to Joseph Craddock*, 2nd edn (1767) · *DNB*

Walkinshaw, Clementine, styled countess of Albestroff (*c*.1720–1802), mistress of Prince Charles Edward Stuart, was the youngest of ten children, all daughters, of John

Clementine Walkinshaw, styled countess of Albestroff
(*c*.1720–1802), by unknown artist

Walkinshaw (1671–1731) of Barrowfield and his wife, Katharine (1683–1780), daughter of Sir Hugh Paterson of Bannockburn. Clementine was a staunch Roman Catholic and supporter of the exiled Stuarts.

Detail of her early life hangs on tradition and conjecture: she was almost certainly named after Clementina Sobieska, wife of James Francis Edward Stuart, the Old Pretender, but no firm evidence supports claims that she was born in Rome and Clementina was her godmother, or that as a child she was the 'little playmate' of *Charles Edward Louis Philip Stuart (1720–1788), Stuart claimant to the throne. It is not certain that she was with Charles while he was in Glasgow in December 1745, but they met a month later at Bannockburn House, home of Clementine's uncle, when the prince fell ill, and according to Lord Elcho she became his mistress. Tradition in the Lake District of England claims they had a daughter, Clementina Johannes Sobieski Douglas (a surname used by Charles), known as the Finsthwaite princess. She lived near Newby Bridge, but died young, and her grave can be seen in Finsthwaite churchyard.

Following the prince's return to France, Clementine Walkinshaw's relations with her family turned cold, and for no apparent reason she was ostracized for thirty-two years. The suggestion that she met the prince again in London when he came to England in 1750, a story that features in Sir Walter Scott's *Redgauntlet*, has been dismissed by Leo Berry.

According to a memoir laid before the French king, Louis XV, in 1774, the prince made Clementine promise at Bannockburn to join him if he sent for her. He did so in

1752 as she was about to enter a religious order in the Low Countries. Since her sister was a member of the household of the princess dowager of Wales, English Jacobites suspected Clementine of being a British spy, and violently opposed her joining Charles: he insisted, however, and they were reunited in Paris in June or July 1752. When the Elibank plot to capture the Hanoverian royal family was betrayed later that year, Clementine was blamed, although the real 'mole' was Alexander Macdonnell of Glengarry, also known as Pickle the Spy, who was not exposed until 150 years later by Andrew Lang in his book *Pickle the Spy*. Many bitter and disillusioned supporters now abandoned the Jacobite cause.

Charles and Clementine settled in 'a preti house' in the rue des Vernopeles in Ghent, and later in Liège as Count and Countess de Johnson. At first they were happy together, and even Alexander Macdonnell admitted that 'the Pretender keeps her well and seems very fond of her' (Lang, 213). A daughter, Charlotte, born in October 1753, was baptized in the church of Ste Marie-des-Fonts in Liège on the 29th of that month. Sir Compton Mackenzie asserts that the couple's first serious quarrel was over Charlotte's baptism into the Catholic faith because Charles had converted to protestantism in London.

Jacobites continued to blame Clementine for every folly the prince committed and for every secret leaked to London; at the same time spies hunted the pair down relentlessly, until they were forced to abandon Liège for secret hiding places, and eventually the relative safety of Basel in Switzerland. There they lived, modestly but comfortably, as an English doctor named Thomson and his wife, but when their presence in Basel became widely known they returned to Liège in 1756. Later they moved to the Château de Carlsbourg, near Sedan, which belonged to the prince's uncle, the duke of Bouillon. James Francis Edward Stuart, the Old Pretender, tried to persuade his son to abandon Clementine and marry, but to his credit Charles refused, bringing about the final rift between father and son.

Charles subjected Clementine to outbursts of temper and beatings, and eventually, on the night of 22 July 1760, while he was absent, she took her child and fled. The prince was beside himself with anger, not because his mistress had left him but at the loss of his child, his beloved Pouponne, as he called her. With the connivance of Louis XV and the prince's father Clementine had taken refuge in the convent of the Visitation de Ste Marie, in the rue du Bac in Paris, and had no intention of returning. Anger, humiliation, and grief at losing his child led to physical and mental collapse, and for almost five years Charles scarcely left Carlsbourg. He paid Clementine nothing and, taking the style countess of Albestroff, she lived for twenty-four years with her daughter in near penury at convents around Paris. The Pretender in Rome gave her a pension of 10,000 livres, and after his death in 1766 she received half that amount from Charles's brother Henry, Cardinal York. But the price was high: Henry forced her to sign an affidavit on 9 March 1767 swearing she was never married to Charles, a declaration which she withdrew almost immediately. In 1772 the prince married Louisa, countess of Albany. Charlotte worked ceaselessly to have the world accept that her parents were husband and wife under the law of Scotland. Only ill health put an end to her pursuit of the claim. In 1784 the prince sent for his daughter, declared her legitimate, and gave her the title duchess of Albany. Within a month of joining him in Florence Charlotte persuaded her father to provide for Clementine.

Charlotte kept in close touch with her mother, writing as many as 100 letters to her in a single year, and after Charles's death in 1788 did all she could to help her. At the French Revolution in 1789 the French cut off Charlotte's financial help, and Clementine had to flee to Switzerland for safety. Then in November that same year Charlotte died, leaving Clementine to live out a lonely life of genteel poverty at Fribourg, in Switzerland. She died there in November 1802, and was buried at the town's St Nicholas's Cathedral.   HUGH DOUGLAS

Sources DNB · C. L. Berry, *The Young Pretender's mistress* (1977) · H. Tayler, *Prince Charlie's daughter* (1951) · C. Stuart, duchess of Albany, letters to her mother, Bodl. Oxf., MSS North · Charlotte Stuart's memoranda to King Louis XV, Archives Etrangères, Paris · H. Tayler, *A Jacobite miscellany* (1948) · W. Duke, *The ship of fools* (1956) · H. Douglas, *The private passions of Bonnie Prince Charlie* (1998) · E. H. Coleridge, *The life of Thomas Coutts, banker*, 2 vols. (1920) · T. Cross, *A Lakeland princess* (1945) · A. Lang, *Pickle the Spy* (1897) · C. Mackenzie, *Prince Charlie* (1932)
Likenesses miniature in oils, Blair Castle, Perthshire · oils, Derby Museums and Art Gallery · oils, Scot. NPG [*see illus.*]
Wealth at death negligible: Berry, *Young Pretender's mistress*, 196–7

Walkley, Arthur Bingham (1855–1926), theatre and literary critic, was born at Bedminster, Bristol, on 17 December 1855, the only child of Arthur Hickman Walkley, a bookseller, and his wife, Caroline Charlotte, the daughter of Joseph Bingham, also a bookseller of Bristol. From Warminster School he gained an exhibition at Balliol College, Oxford, and matriculated there in October 1873. In January 1874 he was admitted a scholar of Corpus Christi College, Oxford. He obtained a first class in both the mathematical moderations (1875) and the final school of mathematics (1877).

In June 1877 Walkley was appointed a third-class clerk in the secretary's office of the General Post Office. On 29 March 1881 he married Frances Eldridge, the daughter of Charles Eldridge, a bookmaker's manager. They had a daughter, Beatrix. In November 1882 Walkley was promoted second-class clerk, in January 1892 first-class clerk, in November 1899 principal clerk, and in August 1911 assistant secretary (in charge of the telegraph branch). In 1897 he was secretary to the British delegation to the Washington Postal Congress, in 1898 secretary to the Imperial Penny Postage Conference, and in 1906 a delegate to the Rome Postal Congress. He retired in June 1919.

Side by side with his career as a civil servant ran Walkley's more brilliant career as a writer. He began by reviewing books in the periodical press. Interested by the reviews written by his friend the theatre critic William Archer, and especially by his book *English Dramatists of To-Day* (1882), Walkley turned his attention to the theatre.

When *The Star* evening newspaper was founded in January 1888 he was appointed its theatre critic, a post he held until 1900. As Spectator, besides his notices of plays, he wrote an occasional piece on theatrical affairs and the drama in general; this prepared his way as an essayist. In *The Star* he also wrote, under his own name, a series of miscellaneous papers entitled 'Fly leaves', some of which concerned a certain Pettifer, who was intended for a 'fantasticated, burlesqued, and belittled projection' of the writer. In November 1890 he became theatre critic of *The Speaker*, a weekly paper, and held the post until the paper changed hands at the end of September 1899.

In 1892 Walkley published *Playhouse Impressions*, a collection of reviews which he had written for *The Speaker*, the *National Observer*, and other periodicals. A selection from his miscellaneous papers in *The Speaker*, *The Star*, and other journals was published as *Frames of Mind* in 1899. In that year he began to contribute reviews of plays to *The Times*, his first notice being a review in the issue of 21 September 1899 of Herbert Beerbohm Tree's production of *King John*. On 1 March 1900 he was formally engaged as the paper's theatre critic. He contributed in 1900 and 1901 to *Literature*, a weekly paper published by *The Times*, and to the *Times Literary Supplement* after its foundation in January 1902. Some of these articles composed his volume *Drama and Life* (1907). In February 1903 he delivered three lectures at the Royal Institution, which he published as *Dramatic Criticism* (1903). After his retirement from the Post Office he began the series of miscellaneous articles published in *The Times* on Wednesdays on dramatic, social, and literary subjects, including articles on Dr Johnson, Dickens, Jane Austen, Hazlitt, Lamb, and Proust, some of which he collected into his three volumes *Pastiche and Prejudice* (1921), *More Prejudice* (1923), and *Still More Prejudice* (1925).

Walkley's view of criticism may best be understood from his book *Dramatic Criticism*. He professed himself an 'impressionist', one whose task was to estimate and analyse his own sensations in the presence of a work of art, not to judge it by rule. In practice he was not entirely consistent, being inclined, as Archer told him, to let aesthetic and philosophical theory intrude between him and the work of art; but his idea of criticism enabled him to come unprejudiced and fresh to each new book or play. This, especially in his earlier years, was of great help to English drama, which was then beginning a new period and breaking free from certain conventions of dramatic form and content. In particular Walkley's welcome of Ibsen, not as a moralist or reformer, but as a great artist in playmaking, did much to counteract the abuse and the misunderstanding with which Ibsen's plays were at first received in London. Later in life Walkley's fastidious love of form, clarity, and finish gave him a distaste for the developments, in plays by Bernard Shaw and others, of the very 'drama of ideas' which his admiration for the French drama of the period had led him to desire. He lost his love of Ibsen and came to prefer light comedy of the more conventional type. The theatrical profession found him too much of the essayist and too little of the reporter for its taste; and his fearless gaiety in attack led to his being turned away in March 1903 from the doors of the Garrick Theatre, to which, as critic of *The Times*, he had been invited to see *Whitewashing Julia*, a new play by Henry Arthur Jones produced by Arthur Bourchier. The insult did nothing to prevent Jones and Walkley from later becoming firm friends.

Whatever his opinions, Walkley's criticisms were always in themselves works of art. He was widely read in French drama, fiction, and criticism (he liked to be as French as possible in appearance and in bearing), fairly well read in the classics and in English prose, and had some knowledge of Spanish and Italian. Next to criticism, Walkley was most interested in fruit-growing and rock gardening, which he practised at his country home at Pound Hill, near Crawley in Sussex. In 1919 he left this for a house at Brightlingsea in Essex, Little Orchard, 25 Upper Park Road, where he died on 7 October 1926.

H. H. CHILD, *rev.* NILANJANA BANERJI

Sources *The Times* (9 Oct 1926) · WWW · B. Hunt and J. Parker, eds., *The green room book, or, Who's who on the stage* (1906–9) · H. Child, 'Arthur Bingham Walkley', *The post Victorians*, ed. [W. R. Inge] (1933), 619–32 · P. Hartnoll, ed., *The Oxford companion to the theatre* (1951); 2nd edn (1957); 3rd edn (1967) · P. Hartnoll, ed., *The concise Oxford companion to the theatre* (1972) · m. cert. · d. cert.
Archives News Int. RO, papers | BL, corresp. with William Archer, Add. MS 45297
Likenesses M. Beerbohm, caricature drawing, 1907 (*Dramatic critics arboricultural and otherwise*), U. Cal., Los Angeles, William Andrews Clark Memorial Library · M. Beerbohm, caricature drawings, U. Cal., Los Angeles, William Andrews Clark Memorial Library · M. Beerbohm, caricature sketch, U. Texas · M. Beerbohm, miniature, repro. in *Academy* (1898) · photograph, repro. in *The Theatre* (1892)
Wealth at death £6896 14s.: probate, 5 Nov 1926, *CGPLA Eng. & Wales*

Wall [*née* Baring], **Harriet** (1768–1838), religious controversialist, was born in the parish of St Gabriel Fenchurch, London, on 13 September 1768, the eldest daughter of Sir Francis *Baring (1740–1810) MP, founder of Baring's Bank, and chairman of the East India Company, who was heralded by Lord Erskine as 'the first merchant of Europe', and his wife, Harriet (d. 1804), daughter and coheir of William Herring of Croydon (cousin and coheir of Thomas *Herring, archbishop of Canterbury). Harriet was born into considerable wealth; so formidable was the reputation of Baring's by the early nineteenth century that the duc de Richelieu, Louis XVIII's prime minister, was reputed to have exclaimed, 'there are six great powers in Europe: England, France, Prussia, Austria, Russia and Baring Brothers'. Educated privately, Harriet Baring married, on 1 September 1790, at Beddington, Surrey, Charles Wall (d. 1815), a partner in Baring's Bank, with whom she had one son, Charles Baring Wall (1795–1853), Liberal MP, and Hampshire landowner and magistrate. The Walls lived in the parish of St Peter-le-Poer, London; at Albury, Surrey; and at Norman Court, West Tytherley, Hampshire.

Throughout much of her life Harriet Wall was attracted to the excesses of 'serious religion', as evangelicalism has been described. After her conversion, which occurred sometime prior to 1815, her country house at Albury

became the focus of much local devotional activity. Here, Wall organized (and sometimes officiated at) twice-daily scriptural readings and prayers, attracting large congregations.

During 1815, after the sudden death of her husband, Harriet Wall moved to Everton, near Lymington, Hampshire, to be nearer her brother, Sir Thomas Baring, of Stratton Park, Micheldever, and her son, Charles, of Norman Court. Bursting with evangelistic zeal, she quickly set about converting her rural circle; in this she enjoyed no little success, drawing into her coterie several members of her extended family as well as a number of neighbouring clergymen. Meeting regularly for discussion, the group soon began to develop—and promote—its own unique interpretation of Christian doctrine, which included a mixture of antinomian, Sabellian, and separatist teachings. Opposed to the inclusive ecclesiology inherent in a national religious establishment, in 1815 the Western Schism (as the group was quickly labelled by its critics) seceded *en masse*, the first collective secession from the Church of England since the non-jurors.

Harriet Wall, in partnership with her brothers, Sir Thomas and George *Baring, occupied a prominent position as one of the Schism's principal patrons and organizers. Its rapid progress produced much national excitement—and opposition—for the party was composed of wealthy, prominent, and highly impressionable young adherents including, as well as members of the Baring family, Thomas Snow, the MP Thomas Mead Kemp, the Revd George Bevan, and the Revd James Harington Evans. In their proselytizing zeal, they seemed to threaten the foundations of Anglican evangelicalism, if not those of the established church itself.

By 1819, as the leading members of the Schism began to moderate their views and disperse geographically, it appears that Harriet Wall continued to adhere to some of the movement's more extreme teachings, though she remained willing to promote the less controversial aspects of 'personal religion' among the English aristocracy. Eventually her interest in the 'novelties of doctrine' led her, together with Henry Drummond, another prominent member of the Schism, to fall under the spell of the Scottish evangelical Edward Irving and to adhere to the new movement which coalesced around him. Perhaps because her resources—financial as well as psychological—had been somewhat depleted by the excesses of the Western Schism, it appears that Wall played no significant role in the early formation and progress of the Irvingites. She may have been content to pass on the baton of leadership and patronage to the wealthier, and more doctrinally eccentric, Drummond, who had recently purchased her substantial country house at Albury (which would later serve as the venue for the Albury conferences and as the spiritual headquarters of the Irvingites, or Catholic Apostolic church).

Harriet Wall died on 5 March 1838. Described by contemporaries as possessing a 'dexterous intelligence' and a 'cool temperament' (both of which she inherited from her celebrated father), she held an obvious superiority over the 'heated brains and crude notions' of her mostly male disciples (Baring-Gould, 96). GRAYSON CARTER

Sources G. Carter, 'Evangelical seceders from the Church of England, c.1800–1850', DPhil diss., U. Oxf., 1990 • S. Nicholson, *Select remains of the Revd John Mason, late pastor of the Church of Christ in Bartholemew-Terrace, Exeter, with a memoir of his life* (1836) • S. Baring-Gould, *The church revival* (1914) • P. Ziegler, *The sixth great power: Barings, 1762–1929* (1988) • *GM*, 2nd ser., 9 (1838), 442 • Surrey RO, Drummond MSS, MS 1322 • M. Levey, *Sir Thomas Lawrence, 1769–1830* (1979), 100 [exhibition catalogue, NPG, 9 Nov 1979 – 16 March 1980]
Archives ING Barings, London, Northbrook MSS
Likenesses T. Lawrence, portrait, c.1805–1810, Baring Brothers & Co., London • E. Scriver, print, 1816 (after H. Edridge), Baring Brothers & Co., London

Wall, John (1588–1666), Church of England clergyman, was born into a gentry family in Holborn, Middlesex, and educated at Westminster School. Having matriculated at Oxford from Christ Church in 1604, he graduated BA in 1608 and proceeded MA in 1611. Appointed rector of St Aldates, Oxford, in 1617, he gained his BD and licence to preach in 1618 and his DD in 1623.

Wall gained wide recognition as a preacher. In the 1620s he published several sermons dedicated to members of the Berkeley and Stanhope families and to Bishop Williams of Lincoln, the 'lord and patron of my studies and fortunes' (Wall, *Apollos*), who in turn described Wall as 'the best read in the fathers of any he ever knew' (Wood, *Ath. Oxon.*, 3.734). Exhibiting a combination of learning, sycophancy, and high-flown language, Wall's sermons are characterized by Christocentricity and by a scorn of separatists and of Roman Catholics, the 'bloudie instruments of voluntarie penance' (J. Wall, *Alae seraphicae: the Seraphins Wings to Raise Us to Heaven*, 1627). About this time he was chaplain to Philip Stanhope, first earl of Chesterfield, at whose Shelford seat he preached *Christ in Progresse* (1627) and *The Lion in the Lambe, or, Strength in Weaknes* (1628).

Preferment followed as Wall was made a canon of Christ Church, Oxford, in 1632, vicar of Chalgrove, Oxfordshire, in 1637, and a canon of Salisbury in 1644. Deprived of his canonry at Christ Church by the parliamentary visitors in March 1648, in September he was the sole member of the chapter to be restored following a submission apparently given with 'reluctance' (Wood, *History*, 4.811–12). Remaining at Christ Church through the 1640s and 1650s, he became subdean and moderator, and in *Ramus olivae*, preached in the university church in 1653, hailed Oliver Cromwell, the dedicatee, as 'most invincible leader of the troops of … Britain and Ireland … most honorable chancellor of the academy of Oxford … [and] most extraordinary propagator of arts and sciences'; just as Alexander the Great had civilized the barbarians, so the campaigning Cromwell had brought the people to the true faith and recognition of Jesus. However, by 1658 Wall had experienced some disillusionment: *Christian Reconcilement*, while celebrating the peace Christ had obtained, regretted that 'we should live to make debate among our selves, striving and struggling, like Jacob and Esau in the wombe, and bowels

of Church and Country, not as true Israelites, but as vaine Ishmaelites' (*Christian Reconcilement*, 1658, 18).

Wall publicly welcomed the Restoration with a sermon in the university church on 1 May, *Solomon in solio* (1660), and asserted in dedicating *A Divine Theater, or, A Stage for Christians* (1662) to Bishop George Morley, lately dean of Christ Church, that he had 'wept for joy' when he read Morley's coronation sermon, 'perform'd, to the … Gracious settlement of Church and State in their Ancient and Fundamentall Government and Splendour, the continuance whereof I do heartily pray for'. According to Anthony Wood's account, however, he was unpopular with his newly installed colleagues and with students because of insufficient loyalty to Christ Church and excessive generosity towards the town of Oxford. Although he subscribed to the college's rebuilding in 1660, it was to Pembroke College that he willed his 'Great Bible … in severall languages' (PRO, PROB 11/322, fol. 257), and the £100 left to the poor of Holborn on his death was apparently on top of much larger donations during the last years of his life to the poor of Oxford. Friends and executors Dr Sebastian Smith of Christ Church and Richard Croke of Marston, city recorder, did not, as Wood claimed, receive 'an incredible mass of money that he had hid' (*Life and Times of Anthony Wood*, 2.91)—they in fact received £100 each—but Croke, a leading local parliamentarian during the civil war, was deeply distrusted by many in the university, and the association would not have helped Wall. After he died, unmarried, at Christ Church on 20 October 1666, none of his colleagues, Wood asserted, joined the funeral procession to the cathedral, where he was buried.

J. R. MACDONALD, rev. VIVIENNE LARMINIE

Sources Wood, *Ath. Oxon.*, new edn, 3.734–5 • Wood, *Ath. Oxon.*: *Fasti* (1815), 325, 342, 382, 412 • A. Wood, *The history and antiquities of the University of Oxford*, ed. J. Gutch, 2 (1796), 3.447, 512 • *The life and times of Anthony Wood*, ed. A. Clark, 2, OHS, 21 (1892), 90–91 • *Hist. U. Oxf. 4: 17th-cent. Oxf.*, 811–12 • F. Madan, *The early Oxford press: a bibliography of printing and publishing in Oxford, 1468–1640*, OHS, 29 (1895), vol. 1 of *Oxford books: a bibliography of printed works* (1895–1931), 106, 128, 131, 136, 142 • J. Wall, *The watering of Apollos* (1625) • J. Wall, *A divine theater, or, A stage for Christians* (1662) • will, PRO, PROB 11/322, fol. 257 • Foster, *Alum. Oxon.*
Likenesses J. Taylor, oils, Oxford Town Hall
Wealth at death left considerable amounts to poor: will, PRO, PROB 11/322, fol. 257

Wall, John (*bap.* 1708, *d.* 1776), physician and a founder of the Worcester Porcelain Company, was baptized on 12 October 1708 at St Peter and St Lawrence Church, Powick, Worcestershire, the second child of John Wall (1662–1734), a Worcester grocer, and his second wife, Catherine, *née* Cleve (1678–1722). Following his father's bankruptcy, he was educated at King's School, Worcester, until June 1726, when he gained a Cookes scholarship to Worcester College, Oxford; he obtained a BA in 1730. He moved to Merton College, where he was elected a fellow in 1734 and became MA and BM in 1736; he took his MD in 1759. By July 1736, however, he had left Oxford and begun practice in Worcester. In 1740 he married Catherine (*bap.* 1709, *d.* 1797?), the daughter of Martin Sandys, town clerk of Worcester and cousin of Samuel Sandys, first Baron Sandys of

John Wall (*bap.* 1708, *d.* 1776), by William Daniell (after George Dance)

Ombersley. They lived in Foregate Street, Worcester, where Wall had built a house, with their five children, one of whom died young; their two sons, John Wall and Martin *Wall, both became physicians.

Wall's medical practice was said to consist of three-quarters of the city and much of the surrounding countryside; his patients included Lord Dudley at Halesowen Grange, the Lytteltons at Hagley Hall, and Lady Luxborough at Barrells, Warwickshire. Wall actively supported the efforts of the bishop, Isaac Maddox, to establish an infirmary at Worcester in 1745; he served as its first treasurer and was one of the four honorary physicians there until his death; he was also on the building committee for the new hospital in 1766. A regular subscriber, he left the hospital a legacy of £20 in 1776; his widow bequeathed £100 in 1797. His influence beyond the city was felt through his work as a steward of the Three Choirs festival and in 1757 through his promotion of a scheme to build accommodation at Malvern Wells for visiting patients. Politically, he was a whig.

Wall published quite widely, often on controversial topics. His first essay was on the local typhus epidemic of 1740–42. He wrote on the uses of musk as a medication in 1744; on the efficacy of bark in smallpox, in 1747, claiming that Richard Mead had not given him credit for his therapy; on the 'putrid' sore throat in 1751; and on the rinderpest epidemic then raging among cattle. He described treatment for worms in children, in 1758, and wrote about inoculation (1764), lead-poisoning from cider (1768), and angina pectoris (1775). His son Martin published a collection of these writings under the title *Medical Tracts*, in 1780. Wall's interest in hydrotherapy, which began in 1743,

centred on the waters at nearby Malvern Wells. His monograph, *Experiments and Observations on the Malvern Waters* (1756, with enlarged editions in 1757 and 1763), helped to make the spa fashionable.

Apart from his medical interests, John Wall was a co-founder, with William Baylies and Edward Cave, of the Worcester Porcelain Company, in 1751. He was also one of the original fifteen shareholders. Wall was credited with inventing a new process for the manufacture of Worcester porcelain and the years 1751–76 are known as the Wall period. An amateur artist, his earliest published etching was in 1736, though most of his work cannot now be traced. He produced frontispieces to three contemporary volumes, as well as some twelve classical and religious scenes, five of which were later hung in the museum of Worcester Porcelain and one in the Worcester city museum. In 1773 and 1774 he exhibited at the Royal Academy. Wall was also interested in glass painting, and about 1750 he designed the windows for the rebuilt Hartlebury Castle chapel; these were largely removed in 1898. In 1767 he designed an east window for Oriel College chapel, Oxford, which was executed by William Peckitt of York.

John Wall reputedly suffered from gout and in 1774 he left Worcester for Bath; he died there on 27 June 1776 and was buried in the abbey. His white marble monument, with its coat of arms and fulsome verse, illustrates the two aspects of his life, the palette of an artist and the caduceus of a practitioner. In his will, prepared a month before his death, his wife and children were the chief beneficiaries; and bequests were made to four Bath practitioners. His paintings were divided among his children.

JOAN LANE

Sources W. H. McMenemey, *A history of the Worcester Royal Infirmary* (1947) · J. Lane, 'Worcester Infirmary in the eighteenth century', *Worcestershire Historical Society Occasional Paper*, 6 (1992) · V. Green, *The history and antiquities of the city and suburbs of Worcester*, 2 (1796) · J. Chambers, *Biographical illustrations of Worcestershire* (1820) · *Worcestershire*, Pevsner (1968) · M. Craze, *King's School, Worcester* (1972) · *Berrow's Worcester Journal* (1753) · Worcs. RO, infirmary archives, 010:6 BA 5161 · parish registers, Worcs. RO · John Wall's will, PRO, PROB 11/1025 · Merton Oxf. · King's School, Worcester · Foster, *Alum. Oxon.*
Likenesses oils, *c.*1765, Dyson Perrins Museum, Worcester · oils, *c.*1765, Worcester Royal Infirmary · R. E. Pine, portrait, 1774 · E. F. Burney, portrait? (after R. E. Pine, 1774) · W. Daniell, lithograph (after G. Dance), NPG [*see illus.*] · J. Ross, engraving (after R. E. Pine, 1774), S. Antiquaries, Lond.

Wall, Joseph (1737–1802), army officer and murderer, was born in Dublin, the eldest son of Gereld or Garrett Wall, a well-to-do tenant farmer on the estate of Sir John Denny Vesey, second baronet, near Abbeyleix in Queen's county. Details of his early life are sparse. His family were Roman Catholic but he and his brothers converted to protestantism. Most accounts state that at the age of fifteen he attended Trinity College, Dublin, where he studied and mastered classical languages, but he is not recorded in college lists, nor did he take a degree.

It is said that about 1760 Wall volunteered for military service as a cadet, with his younger brother Augustine (*d.* 1780), later a barrister and the first Irish law reporter to

Governor Wall at the condemned Sermon
given to my Friend Smith Tho.s Rowlandson

Joseph Wall (1737–1802), by Thomas Rowlandson, 1802

include names of speakers in his accounts. He served with distinction at the siege of Havana in 1762, returning home with the rank of captain. Lieutenant Charles Forbes of the 1st Royal Scots regiment referred to Wall's brave conduct at the siege when testifying at his trial forty years later. However, the army lists record no regimental commission, leaving the possibility of a brevet field promotion. Upon his return Wall obtained an appointment with the East India Company at Bombay, but he left this service after a few years following a duel. Although a tall man of 'genteel appearance' (*Life*, 40), he 'lacked proper balance and suffered from a very short temper' (Gray, 248). He returned to Ireland to look for a rich heiress, but he courted a Miss Gregory, whom he met at an inn near his father's tenancy, 'in a style so coercive' that she prosecuted him for assault and defamation and 'succeeded in his conviction and penal chastisement' (*Life*, 4).

Wall moved to England and spent his time in gaming and amorous intrigues in London and the spa towns. To relieve his debts, in 1773 he procured a captaincy in what was to become the African corps, consisting of three independent companies of foot stationed at St Louis on the River Senegal for the defence of the recently created province of Senegambia. The governor, Charles O'Hara, placed great confidence in Wall, and he was left as senior military officer when O'Hara left Senegambia in 1776.

Ensign Matthias Macnamara, lieutenant-governor of the Gambia, 'a man without education, extremely brutal,

vulgar and avaricious' (Gray, 244), then returned to St Louis as acting governor and quickly removed his principal rival by appointing Wall lieutenant-governor of the Gambia in his stead. This was more a punishment than a promotion. The post at James Island was regarded as little more than a penal colony and its troops were of the poorest quality. Wall treated his position as an independent command, ignoring Macnamara's orders, and relations between the two quickly deteriorated. When rumours reached St Louis that Wall was acting in an arbitrary manner towards his subordinates, an investigation by the governor and council of Senegal was convened. Despite much conflicting evidence and signs of perjury and bias among the witnesses, the investigation showed the charges had substance.

Wall, by now a sick man, continued to ignore Macnamara's orders. Matters were brought to a head when on 8 August 1776 he returned to St Louis and confronted Macnamara. He was placed under arrest for quitting his post without orders, and sent back to James Island, where he was kept in close confinement for ten months. No effort was made to bring him to trial, and Wall's health deteriorated further. In the meantime news of Macnamara's maladministration and cruel treatment of local people had reached Britain, and Captain John Clarke was appointed permanent governor; he arrived at St Louis on 8 April 1777. Wall's case was brought before the council in June, when the sickly Wall conducted his own defence. Macnamara's charges of disobedience, mistreatment of subordinates, and private trading were proved to be grossly embellished and were dismissed. Released from prison, Wall commenced several actions against Macnamara for damages over the removal of goods and false imprisonment. The council in Senegal awarded him £1527 for the former. On 28 May 1778 Wall replaced Macnamara as lieutenant-governor of Senegambia. The following year he brought a further civil action against Macnamara in London at the court of common pleas, which decided that, while his arrest might have been at first legal on the grounds that he left his post without orders, his subsequent imprisonment was malicious, and it awarded him £1000.

Governor Clarke had died on 18 August 1778, and in Wall's absence the British administration in Senegambia surrendered to the attacking French fleet on 11 February 1779. Wall returned with a contingent of the African corps in a naval squadron under Sir Edward Hughes to occupy the island of Goree, which could be used to control the mouth of the River Gambia but which the French had left undefended. Leaving a small force to rebuild and garrison the dismantled forts, Wall, as acting governor of Goree, proceeded with four men-of-war to the Gambia. He reached James Island on 31 May, but the fort was found to be in a dilapidated state, beyond repair. Wall then sailed with the squadron to Barbados, returning to Goree in 1780. His younger brother Ensign Patrick Wall accompanied him to Goree, but died shortly after their arrival, allegedly from the shock of watching a man named Paterson flogged to death on board ship by order of his brother. Under Wall's protection, British merchants began trading on the Gambia River again, and a series of settlements were built along the river bank. However, after he had been governor and superintendent of trade for two years Wall's health gave way, and he prepared to leave the colony.

On 10 July 1782 a deputation of the African corps, who had been on short allowance, waited on him to ask for a settlement. Wall caused their leader, Sergeant Benjamin Armstrong, and two others to be arrested on a charge of mutiny. Without holding a court martial he ordered Armstrong and the others to be flogged with a knotted rope by black slaves, which was contrary to military practice. Armstrong and the others received 800 lashes. Wall left Goree the next day. Armstrong and the other men died of their wounds several days later. In England, Wall made no mention of a mutiny in his official report, but rumours began to circulate of the tyrannical and arbitrary nature of his governorship. Charges were laid against him by Captain Roberts, one of his officers. Wall was brought before a court martial, but the charges were allowed to drop as the ship in which the witnesses were returning was believed to be lost. Wall then retired to Bath. In October 1784, following the arrival of the witnesses, he was arrested and charged with murder by two king's messengers. They began to escort him to London, but Wall escaped at Reading, walking '60 miles across country before he took a carriage, when he proceeded to Scotland, and there remained until a favourable occasion offered for his passage to the continent' (*The Times*, 1 Feb 1802). There he met Frances, the sixth daughter of Kenneth Mackenzie, styled Lord Fortrose (d. 1761), whom he married.

For many years the couple lived in France and Italy, where they were admitted into society. Wall made several secret visits to Britain, and in 1797 both he and his wife returned to London, living under the assumed name of Thompson, at a house in Upper Thornhaugh Street, Bedford Square. Wall had returned to surrender himself for trial but lacked resolve, and it was not until 25 October 1801 that he wrote to Thomas Pelham, home secretary, about this intention. He was arrested soon after.

Wall's motive was primarily financial. A large property belonging to his wife was in the hands of trustees, which he had frequently applied for, 'but they, knowing the circumstances in which he was placed, and that he could not legally sue them for it, without exposing himself to the dangers of a criminal prosecution, consistently resisted his applications for money' (*The Times*, 1 Feb 1802). To free himself of this difficulty Wall had to clear his name. The death of Captain Roberts in Ireland some ten years before and the 'supposed dissolution or dispersion of the other principal witnesses taught him to rely with perfect security in his surrendering himself for trial' (*Life*, 6). He was tried for the murder of Armstrong on 20 January 1802 at the Old Bailey by a special commission, presided over by Sir Archibald Macdonald, chief baron of the exchequer. The chief evidence for the prosecution was given by the surgeon, Mr Ferrit, and the orderly sergeant who were on duty during Armstrong's punishment. The evidence was not shaken on any point and the charge of mutiny was not

sustained. The absence of a court martial, and of any record of a mutiny in the garrison records or in Wall's official report upon his return, proved telling. The trial lasted from 9 a.m. until 11 o'clock at night and resulted in a verdict of guilty. Efforts were made by a relative of his wife's, Charles Howard, eleventh duke of Norfolk, to obtain a pardon for Wall. The privy council held several deliberations on the case, but it had become a subject of great public interest and popular indignation, and a pardon was politically inexpedient. It would have been unwise to spare the life of an officer condemned for brutality to his soldiers when at the same time sailors were being executed at Spithead for mutiny against their officers.

After two respites, on 28 January 1802, at 8 o'clock, Wall emerged from his cell at Newgate, to the hostile cheers of an immense crowd. 'He did not remain above two minutes on the scaffold before the platform dropped, but owing to the rope slipping a little … he was a considerable time in dying, during which time he appeared to be much convulsed' (*The Times*, 29 Jan 1802). Following the execution the body was only formally dissected and not exposed to public view. Upon payment of 50 guineas to the Philanthropic Society by his family his remains were handed over and buried in St Pancras churchyard.

The execution was at the time considered a triumph of justice—the administration of the criminal law making no distinction between the classes—but the poet Robert Southey pointed out:

> Nobody seems to recollect that he has been hanged, not for having flogged three men to death, but for the informality in the mode of doing it … The martial laws of England are the most barbarous which at this day exist in Europe. (Southey, 3.109)

Wall was survived by his wife and a son aged about nine at the time of his death. She was at Harrogate in September 1821 at the same time as the poet James Montgomery, who, observing her solitary walks, 'recollected how faithfully she clung to her husband through the period of his desertion, disgrace and suffering' (Holland and Everett, 3.253). Her example suggested the theme of a poem he then commenced on 'Woman', later published as 'Tale without a Name'.   JONATHAN SPAIN

Sources *The life, trial and execution of Joseph Wall Esq., late governor of Goree, for the wilful murder of Benjamin Armstrong* (1802) · *The authentic trial of Joseph Wall, late governor of Goree* (1802) · *The trial of Governor Wall* (1867) · *N&Q*, 3rd ser., 8 (1865), 438, 550 · *N&Q*, 6th ser., 8 (1883), 208 · *N&Q*, 9th ser., 1 (1898), 503; 2 (1898), 129–30 · G. L. Browne, *Narrative of state trials in the nineteenth century, first period, 1801–11*, 1 (1882) · review, *EdinR*, 157 (1883), 81–108, esp. 83–5 · *Annual Review* (1802), 560–68 · *Morning Chronicle* (21 Jan 1802) · *Morning Chronicle* (29 Jan 1802) · *The Times* (11 Jan 1802) · *The Times* (29 Jan 1802) · *The Times* (1 Feb 1802) · *GM*, 1st ser., 72 (1802), 81 · *European Magazine and London Review*, 41 (1802), 74, 154–6 · J. M. Gray, *A history of the Gambia* (1940) [new edn, 1966] · P. H. Nicolas, *Historical record of the royal marine forces*, 1 (1845), 70 · F. R. Hart, *The siege of Havanna* (1931) · H. Bleackley, *Some distinguished victims of the scaffold* (1905) · Army List (1759–65) · *Memoirs of the life and writings of James Montgomery*, ed. J. Holland and J. Everett, 7 vols. (1854–6), 3.253 · *The poetical works of James Montgomery, collected by himself*, 3 (1841), 287 · R. Southey [M. Alvarez Espriella], *Letters from England*, 2nd edn, 3 vols. (1808), vol. 3, pp. 97–108, 109 · *Scots peerage*
Archives NAM, papers, MS 9310

Likenesses T. Rowlandson, drawing, 1802, NG Ire. [*see illus.*] · Chapman, stipple, pubd 1804, NPG · etching, NPG; repro. in *Life, trial and execution*, frontispiece

Wall, Martin (*bap.* **1747**, *d.* **1824**), physician, youngest son of John *Wall (*bap.* 1708, *d.* 1776), physician, and his wife, Catherine Sandys (*bap.* 1709, *d.* 1797?), daughter of Martin Sandys, town clerk of Worcester, was baptized at Worcester on 24 June 1747. He went to Winchester College, then to New College, Oxford, in 1763. He graduated BA in 1767, MA in 1771, BM in 1773, and DM in 1777, and was a fellow of New College until 1778. He studied medicine at St Bartholomew's Hospital, and in Edinburgh.

Wall began practice at Oxford in 1774; on 2 November 1775 he was elected physician to the Radcliffe Infirmary and in his *Letter* of 1785 he replied to John Howard's criticisms of the infirmary. He became reader in chemistry in 1781. Having previously edited his father's essays (1780), in 1783 he published his 1781 inaugural dissertation together with two more essays, one of them on the diseases prevalent in the south sea islands. He drank tea with Dr Johnson at Oxford in June 1784 and his essay on the south sea islands was presumably the origin of their conversation on the advantage of physicians travelling among barbarous nations.

Wall was Lichfield professor of clinical medicine from 1785 until his death. His work on the use of opium in low fevers and on the typhus epidemic at Oxford appeared in 1786. He was elected a fellow of the College of Physicians in 1787, and Harveian orator and FRS in 1788.

Wall died in Oxford on 21 June 1824; an obituary records his capacity for exhilarating conversation and his hilarity of temper, lively anecdotes, and urbanity, as well as his free treatment of poor patients. His wife, Mary, survived him, dying in Oxford in 1841, aged ninety. They had at least two daughters and a son, Martin Sandys Wall (1786/7–1871), who was chaplain-in-ordinary to the prince regent and to the British embassy at Vienna.

NORMAN MOORE, *rev.* JEAN LOUDON

Sources *GM*, 1st ser., 94/2 (1824), 183–4 · Foster, *Alum. Oxon.* · *The Lancet* (3 July 1824), 30–31 · Munk, *Roll* · *GM*, 1st ser., 98/2 (1828), 283 · *GM*, 2nd ser., 2 (1834), 220 · *GM*, 2nd ser., 16 (1841), 108 · M. Wall, *A letter to John Howard esq. FRS on the state of the Radcliffe Infirmary* (1785) · J. Boswell, *The life of Samuel Johnson*, 2 vols. (1791) · *Monthly Gazette of Health*, 9 (1824), 1021
Likenesses oils, New College, Oxford

Wall, Max [*real name* Maxwell George Lorimer] (**1908–1990**), comedian and actor, was born on 12 March 1908 at 37 Glenshaw Mansions, Brixton Road, Brixton, London, the second of the three children, all sons, of John Gillespie Lorimer (*d.* 1922), music-hall artiste, formerly of Forres, Scotland, and his wife, Maud Clara, dancer and singer, daughter of William and Maud Mitchison of Newcastle upon Tyne, both music-hall entertainers. He had sporadic schooling of a disjointed kind, being brought up in the music-hall theatre by his parents, who were known as Jack Lorimer and Stella Stahl. He was first taken on stage, in a kilt, at the age of two. Later he changed his name to Max Wall by deed poll.

After the break up of his parents' marriage and the

Max Wall (1908–1990), by Maggi Hambling, 1981

death of his father, Max Wall began his long show-business career. At the age of fourteen he made his stage début in *Mother Goose* (1922), and, much encouraged by his stepfather, Harry Wallace—from whom he took his stage surname—he soon became a fully-fledged professional entertainer, concentrating on eccentric dance routines and funny walks. He made his first London appearance in 1925 at the London Lyceum in *The London Revue*. Thereafter he appeared in several musical comedies and revues, including C. B. Cochran's *One Dam Thing After Another* (1927), and he appeared in the 1930 and 1950 royal variety performances. He now established himself as a prominent music-hall artiste, variously billed as 'the boy with the obedient feet' or 'Max Wall and his independent legs'. He served in the Royal Air Force from 1941 to 1943, when he was invalided out on account of 'anxiety neurosis', and returned to the music hall stage.

With his inventive patter, Wall also enjoyed radio success, notably in *Hoopla!* (1944), *Our Shed* (in which he popularized the character of Humphrey, 1946), and *Petticoat Lane* (1949). He next had a major success as Hines in the musical *The Pajama Game* (1955), and soon starred in his first television series, *The Max Wall Show* (1956). He had also perfected his role as Professor Wallofski, a weird spidery figure of a musical clown, clad in black tights, straggling wig, a short dishevelled jacket, and monstrously huge boots. His idols were the clown Grock and Groucho Marx.

By now the old variety theatre was in decline, and, with domestic problems also taking some toll, Wall had a lean period, during which he mainly played dates in northern clubland. In 1966 his mordant style found fresh opportunities on the legitimate stage, first as Père Ubu in Ian Cuthbertson's adaptation of *Ubu Roi* (1966), and then, *inter alia*, in Arnold Wesker's *The Old Ones* (1972), as Archie Rice in John Osborne's *The Entertainer* (1974), and in Samuel Beckett's *Krapp's Last Tape* (1975) and *Waiting for Godot* (1980). He also appeared, in 1973, in *Cockie!*, a musical version of C. B. Cochran's life, and the *International Herald Tribune* said he was 'quite simply, the funniest comedian in the world'. He acted in several films, for instance as Flintwich in *Little Dorrit* (1987).

In 1974 Wall first produced what was to become a famous one-man show with songs, *Aspects of Max Wall*. In his later years he became something of a cult entertainer and in 1975 published his autobiography, *The Fool on the Hill*. He was a fluent mime, hilarious and eccentric dancer, competent musician, and an acidic stand-up comedian. His stage persona had an air of melancholy, even of cynicism, and his countenance was clown-like, with glaring eyes, a prominent nose, and leering mouth.

Following an unstable upbringing, Wall married, in 1942, Marion Ethel (Pola) Pollachek, dancer, the divorced wife of Thomas Patrick Charles and daughter of Alexander Pollachek, mechanical engineer, who ran a sponge rubber business in Islington. They had four sons and one daughter. The marriage was dissolved, with colourful attendant publicity, in 1956, and Wall became estranged from his family. In the same year he married a beauty queen, Jennifer Chimes, of north Staffordshire, daughter of John William Schumacher, master plumber. That marriage was dissolved in 1969, and he had a third marriage, to Christine Clements, in 1970, which was dissolved in 1972.

Max Wall rarely sought the camaraderie of show business in his later years, and, despite considerable wealth, lived almost as a recluse in a bedsitting room in south London. He died in the Westminster Hospital, London, on 22 May 1990, having fractured his skull in a fall outside a London restaurant. A celebration of his life was held at St Paul's, Covent Garden, London, on 9 August 1990.

ERIC MIDWINTER, rev.

Sources M. Wall, *The fool on the hill* (1975) [autobiography] · *The Times* (23 May 1990) · *The Guardian* (23 May 1990) · *The Independent* (23 May 1990) · Archives of Theatre Museum, London · private information (1996) · *CGPLA Eng. & Wales* (1990) · J. Walker, ed., *Halliwell's filmgoer's companion*, 12th edn (1997)

Likenesses M. Hambling, oils, 1981, NPG [*see illus.*] · photograph, repro. in *The Times* · photograph, repro. in *The Independent* · photographs, Hult. Arch.

Wealth at death £193,004: probate, 19 Dec 1990, *CGPLA Eng. & Wales*

Wall, Richard (1694–1778), politician and diplomatist for Spain, was born in 1694, probably at Coolnamuck, co. Waterford, Ireland, where a branch of that family was settled. He is first heard of in 1718, when he served as a volunteer in the Spanish fleet which was defeated off Sicily by George Byng, Viscount Torrington. In 1727, as a captain of dragoons, he went to St Petersburg as secretary with the duke of Liria, the eldest son of the duke of Berwick and grandson of James II, who had been appointed Spanish ambassador to that city. They had an interview on their way with the Old Pretender at Bologna, and halted also at Vienna, Dresden, and Berlin. Despite the trust placed in him by Liria, Wall returned to Spain prematurely, apparently suffering from depression.

After rejoining the Spanish army, Wall served under Don Philip in Lombardy and under Montemar in Naples, and was next dispatched to the West Indies, where he conceived a plan for recovering Jamaica. In 1747 he was sent to Aix-la-Chapelle and London to negotiate peace, returned to Spain by way of France in February 1748 to report progress, and on the conclusion of the peace of Aix-la-Chapelle in October 1748 he was formally appointed to the London embassy. Wall's priorities in Britain were to obtain diplomatic concessions for Spanish commerce while simultaneously using espionage to further Spain's economic recovery. Attempts were made, with limited success, to smuggle skilled men and equipment from Britain to Spain's dockyards and woollen industry. Wall, in conjunction with the Spanish secretary of state Carvajal in Madrid, successfully ended the asiento, obtained by Britain for forty years in 1713 and interrupted by war, by which she had won the right to import Africans as slave labour into Spanish America. Unfortunately they had to cede Britain other trade concessions in return.

In 1752 Wall was appointed lieutenant-general and in October of the same year was briefly recalled on account of his services being required at Madrid in settling commercial arrangements with the English ambassador, Sir Benjamin Keene. Although he had occasional differences with Keene and his successor, Lord Bristol, Wall was regarded as the head of the English party, and the French intrigued against him. He was finally recalled in April 1754, following Carvajal's death, when he succeeded the latter as foreign minister. He was reluctant to leave England, where he was very popular and had made the acquaintance of the elder Pitt and many others. That autumn, supplanting Ensenada, Wall became secretary of state. His administration was compromised by internal conflicts revolving around centralizing policies, such as the campaign against the Jesuits, and the aristocratic conservatism of his courtier colleagues.

Wall had reached an understanding with the queen dowager, Elizabeth Farnese, and enjoyed enduring good relations with her son the king of Naples. Nevertheless, when on the death of Ferdinand VI in 1759 the king of Naples acceded to the Spanish throne as Charles III, Wall began to be eclipsed in Madrid. The king preferred a more belligerent foreign policy, leading to an alliance with France and the other Bourbon states in December 1761 and entry into the war with Britain. Wall's handling of the conflict was half-hearted and of mixed success, and after many attempts he was allowed to resign in August 1763. Some of his protégés remained in office, and Charles III continued to consult him on some matters. Among his labours in office had been the restoration of the Alhambra, which he incongruously roofed with red tiles.

On his retirement, Wall received a pension of 100,000

crowns, the full pay of a lieutenant-general, and the possession for life of the Soto di Roma, a royal hunting seat near Granada, later presented to the duke of Wellington. This he decorated with English furniture. He also drained its 4000 acres of fields and woods, made new drives, and improved the economic condition of his tenants. He resided there from October to May, attended the court at Aranjuez for a month, and spent the summer at Mirador, a villa near Granada. Henry Swinburne (1743–1803) visited him at Soto di Roma in 1776, and was delighted with his sprightly conversation, for which he had always been noted. He died in 1778.

J. G. ALGER, rev. MATTHEW KILBURN

Sources A. H. Hull, *Charles III and the revival of Spain* (1980) · J. Lynch, *Bourbon Spain, 1700–1788* (1989) · J. O. McLachlan, *Trade and peace with old Spain, 1667–1750* (1940) · W. N. Hargreaves-Mawdsley, *Eighteenth-century Spain, 1700–1788* (1979) · Walpole, *Corr.*, 20.170–71, 426 · E. Armstrong, *Elisabeth Farnese: the termagant of Spain* (1892) · C. Dalton, ed., *English army lists and commission registers, 1661–1714*, 6 vols. (1892–1904) · [R. L. de Voyer de Paulmy and Marquis d'Argenson], *Journal et mémoires du marquis d'Argenson*, ed. E. J. B. Rathery, 9 vols. (Paris, 1859–67) **Wealth at death** 100,000 crowns; pension in last fifteen years of life: *DNB*

Wall, Richard (1777/8–1838). *See under* Wall, Thomas (1846–1930).

Wall, Thomas (1817–1884). *See under* Wall, Thomas (1846–1930).

Wall, Thomas (1846–1930), sausage entrepreneur and philanthropist, was born at 113 Jermyn Street, London, on 30 August 1846 into a family of pork butchers and sausage manufacturers. His grandfather **Richard Wall** (1777/8–1838), pork butcher, had in 1790 been apprenticed to Edmund Cotterill, a pork butcher in St James's Market, subsequently becoming a partner and in 1807 the shop's sole owner. The shop supplied meat to nearby Carlton House, the London residence of George, prince of Wales, and in 1812 George (by then prince regent) granted Wall a royal warrant as 'purveyor of pork'. That was renewed when the prince succeeded as George IV in 1820, and also by William IV on his accession ten years later.

By 1834 Richard Wall was prosperous enough to lease from the crown 113 Jermyn Street, where he built up his trade in sausages. The meat was prepared in the basement, hard by a donkey which ploddingly worked the rotary machinery for 'chopping' or mixing the sausage contents. He died there on 19 June 1838 and his widow, Ann, temporarily took over the running of the business.

Richard Wall's son (he also had a younger daughter), Thomas Wall's father, also named **Thomas Wall** (1817–1884), sausage maker, was born in St James's, Westminster, in 1817, and was barely of age when his father died. On 21 June 1842 he married Mary (1821–1900), daughter of George Charlton, gentleman. They had two sons and three daughters. He had already received a royal warrant from Queen Victoria, the head chef at Buckingham Palace regularly sending over for inclusion in the sausages his own seasoning, enriched with new-laid eggs. The queen

duly appointed Thomas, in a strange reversal of anthropomorphism, as 'pork-in-ordinary' to herself. He died at 113 Jermyn Street on 25 April 1884.

Thomas Wall, elder son of the foregoing Thomas Wall and his wife, Mary Charlton, was apprenticed as a teenager to his father and was made a partner in 1870. He was joined in 1878 by his brother, Frederick (1855–1924), when the firm became Thomas Wall & Sons.

The two brothers' subsequent efforts transformed the firm into Britain's best-known sausage enterprise. Their burgeoning royal and commercial connections generated plentiful business, with no need to advertise, in high-quality meat and its products for hotels, clubs, restaurants, department stores, and houses of the élite throughout London's West End. After his father's death Thomas became general manager, while Frederick in the butcher's department purchased requirements of meat in Smithfield market at 4 a.m. each weekday. Other departments made pork and other pies, and sausage rolls, brawns, patés, bottled soups, and cured hams.

By 1900 the firm was beginning to go wholesale countrywide. Wall's sausages were then made by factory production, in a new works opened at Battersea. It became T. Wall & Sons Ltd in 1905, when it acquired a sausage making rival in Acton, west London. However, through a refusal to raise sausage prices despite the cost of premium meat, turnover in 1905–14 totalled £1,250,000 but yielded less than £19,260 as profit; losses were made in three of those years. Other high costs sprang from having to operate in the three scattered localities of Jermyn Street, Battersea, and Acton. Efforts to find a suitable central production site, eventually at Acton, were fruitless until 1920. The highly seasonal pattern of sausage sales, which plummeted in summer, involved wasteful lay-offs of workers each year.

Despite the support of a dedicated brother and able senior managers recruited through acquisitions, Thomas Wall as chairman did not provide the drive to unravel these corporate tangles. Burly and bearded, a confirmed bachelor who lived frugally, he devoted most of his energies and resources to assisting almost every known charity that offered recreational, sporting, and educational facilities to boys and young men, including the Boy Scouts; females were helped by the provision of nursery schools and a Working Women's College. His most spectacular benefaction was the Thomas Wall Trust, endowed with £200,000 to support students at university and college, no fewer than 200 receiving bursaries at his death. He built workmen's dwellings, and liberally contributed towards purchasing open spaces for parks and playing fields in areas of south London. Among his other favourite charities were the YMCA, the Adult School Movement, and the Workers' Educational Association.

Meanwhile Wall's company was a prime target for a take-over by some mogul willing to enforce a clear business strategy. It was the super-mogul of the age, William Hesketh Lever, first Viscount Leverhulme, who purchased Wall's in 1920. His object was to bolster the fishing interests he had assembled for his personally owned

MacFisheries venture, since he viewed sausages as ideal extra foodstuffs for sale in fish shops. Two years later he sold Wall's and MacFisheries to Lever Brothers Ltd, which in 1929 became part of Unilever Ltd.

Doubtless at Leverhulme's behest, Wall's solved its seasonal problem by diversifying into ice-cream production, using American know-how. As most ordinary shops lacked refrigerators to house ice cream, the company created a sales force to roam the streets in box tricycles (with bells) under the much anthologized slogan 'Stop me and buy one'. The sabbatarian Thomas would permit their deployment on Sundays, the most promising day for impulse buying at the roadside, only after attendance at a religious service, under his supervision. His childlike simplicity of mind, easiness to please, and enthusiasm in all branches of his life were widely noted. He died at his home, Blythewood, Worcester Road, Sutton, Surrey, on 2 January 1930.   T. A. B. CORLEY

Sources L. Cooper, 'The Wall's meat company', unpublished, 1980, Unilever historical archives · Wall's way, T. Wall & Sons Ltd (1960) · C. Wilson, The history of Unilever: a study in economic growth and social change, 2 vols. (1954) · T. Heald, By appointment: 150 years of the royal warrant and its holders (1989) · T. Heald, A peerage for trade: a history of the royal warrant (2001) · J. Trager, The food chronology (1995) · J. P. Johnston, A hundred years eating (1977) · The Times (3 Jan 1930) · Sutton and Cheam Advertiser (9 Jan 1930) · K. Mercer, Thomas Wall [n.d.] · b. cert. · d. cert. · m. cert. [Thomas Wall (1817–1884)] · d. cert. [Richard Wall] · d. cert. [Thomas Wall (1817–1884)] · census returns, 1881 · Society of Genealogists, London, one name index
Archives Unilever, London, archives
Likenesses photograph, c.1920, repro. in Sutton and Cheam Advertiser
Wealth at death £285,087 7s. 5d.: resworn probate, 1930, CGPLA Eng. & Wales · £42,587 13s. 3d.—Thomas Wall (1817–1884): resworn probate, July 1885, CGPLA Eng. & Wales (1884)

Wall, William (1647–1728), Church of England clergyman, was born at Maranto Court Farm in the parish of Chevening, Kent, on 6 January 1647, the son of William Wall, and his wife, probably Mary Rich (a couple of those names had married in Chevening on 14 January 1646). He had at least one brother, Geoffrey, and a sister, Elizabeth, who were alive when he made his will in 1725. Wall graduated BA from Queen's College, Oxford, in 1667 and proceeded MA in 1670, being incorporated in the latter degree at Cambridge in 1676. After taking holy orders he became vicar of Shoreham, Kent, in December 1674, where he continued until his death.

Wall married Catharine (1657/8–1706), daughter of Edward Davenant, at St Martin-in-the-Fields, Westminster, London, on 1 May 1677 (parish register). Their children were as follows: Catharine, baptized on 9 April 1678, who married Richard Waring and had eight sons and eight daughters; William, baptized on 9 November 1679, who became a citizen of London and was buried on 20 June 1725 at Shoreham; Richard, baptized on 2 January 1681; Elizabeth, baptized on 18 December 1681, and buried on 12 February 1683; Edward, baptized on 17 December 1682; Rebekka, baptized on 17 December 1683, and buried on 2 March 1685; and Thomas, baptized on 20 March 1685, also a citizen of London, and buried at Shoreham on 3 February 1710.

Wall once had the offer of a living of £300 a year at Chelsfield, 3 miles from Shoreham, which he declined because his 'conscience would not let him take [it]' (GM, 54/1, 1784, 435). Later, about 1708, he took the living at Milton, near Gravesend, at about one-fifth of the value, and 12 miles from Shoreham. At Milton he had the assistance of a curate, Mr Thomas.

Wall's major publication was A History of Infant Baptism (1705), followed by expanded second (1707) and third editions (1720). In it he defended the validity of infant baptism by using much material from ancient church fathers, and he explored a variety of topics related to baptism. The last chapter made a plea for not dividing the Church of England over the age of baptism: a plea made to Antipaedobaptists (Baptists) who remained separate from the established church. Because of that book he was awarded the degree of DD by the University of Oxford in 1720. John Wesley (1703–1791) published some twenty pages of extracts from it under the title Thoughts upon Infant-Baptism (1751; reprinted 1780 and 1791). Wall's book was reprinted several times in the nineteenth century. The circumstances of Wall's history were that David Russen had written a book against Baptists, Fundamentals without Foundation (1703), to which, for Baptists, Joseph Stennett (1663–1713) published An Answer to Mr. David Russen's Book (1704). Wall's book then followed; he consulted with Stennett and respected him. Wall was in turn opposed by a Baptist, John Gale, in Reflections on Mr. Wall's History (London, 1711); the two men held a conference in 1719. In connection with the topic of infant baptism Wall also published A Conference between Two Men … about Infant-Baptism (1706) and A Defence of the History of Infant Baptism (1720). Several small works complete his publications.

Catharine Wall died on 10 May 1706, aged forty-eight; William Wall died on 13 January 1728, probably at Shoreham, and was buried in the parish church there six days later.   OSCAR C. BURDICK

Sources will, PRO, PROB 11/621, sig. 131 · parish register, Chevening, Kent [baptism] · parish register, Shoreham, Kent [burial, burial of spouse] · parish register, St Martin-in-the-Fields, London [marriage] · The miscellaneous works of Bishop Atterbury, ed. J. Nichols, 5 vols. (1789–98), vol. 5, pp. 301–2 · Foster, Alum. Oxon. · J. Thorpe, ed., Registrum Roffense, or, A collection of antient records, charters and instruments … illustrating the ecclesiastical history and antiquities of the diocese and cathedral church of Rochester (1769), 1014 · The works of … Joseph Stennett, 4 vols. (1731–2), vol. 1, first numbering, p. 23 · GM, 1st ser., 54 (1784), 435 · Venn, Alum. Cant.
Wealth at death £600 in cash bequests; plus land in Wiltshire and house and land in Kent; also share of two other properties; also household goods: will, PRO, PROB 11/621, sig. 131

Wallace family (per. 1841–1925), merchants, came to prominence with the sons of Lewis Alexander Wallace (1789–1861), builder and merchant of Edinburgh, and his wife, Isabella Clerk. The couple had six sons and five daughters. In the late eighteenth century Lewis Wallace's father, William Wallace, had established William Wallace & Co., leading builders and architects, which participated notably in the building of Edinburgh's New Town. A director of the National Bank of Scotland, Lewis Wallace lived in comfortable circumstances in Regent Terrace in the New Town, in a house he had designed and built himself. However, like numerous Scottish businessmen he recognized greater opportunities in employing his capital in international trade, especially that centred on India and the East. Thus in 1841 he provided J. G. Frith, a merchant recently returned from India, with capital for the development of a merchant business in London linked to Frith's well-established business in Bombay. Lewis's eldest son, **William Wallace** (1818–1888), born in Edinburgh on 24 March 1818, joined Frith & Co. of Bombay in 1841. In due course all the sons were to follow in William's footsteps and forsake the family's Edinburgh connections.

In 1844 William, who apparently disliked India, returned to establish, with Frith, the London firm of Frith, Wallace & Co., East India merchants. Acting in tandem with the Bombay house this became a major London agency firm and survived as Wallace Brothers until the 1980s. Almost all the brothers made significant and diverse contributions to its success, but William and his siblings Lewis and Alexander played the most important roles in a family firm where relationships were especially close-knit. After William's return the third son, **Lewis Alexander Wallace** (1821–1906), went out aged twenty-seven to join the Bombay partnership, which in 1848 was reformed as Wallace & Co.; it specialized not just in merchanting but in the provision of shipping agency services, and it acted as financial agents for the Ceylon government and, of increasing importance, imported Lancashire textiles. Born on 20 September 1821, Lewis emerged as a major figure in Bombay's business community, beginning an important family connection through his directorship and later chairmanship of the Commercial Bank of India. In 1850 he was joined as a partner by the fourth son, George. Subsequently both returned to become partners in London and were replaced in Bombay by their three other brothers, Alexander, Robert, and Richard.

William, having participated in the establishment of a viable business in London, returned to India in 1853 and set about establishing connections with Burma. In either 1856 or 1857 he went there as the Bombay firm's representative to purchase teak for India's fast-expanding railways. Using the Bombay firm's capital he established William Wallace & Co., timber merchants and shipbuilders, at Rangoon and Moulmein, and purchased land. In 1862 he travelled to Mandalay to negotiate with King Mindon for the lease of teak forests in northern Burma and his firm became a major shipper of Burma teak around the world. The business rapidly diversified as other opportunities were recognized, but the extent of the investment drained the Bombay firm's resources—a major point of friction between William, who had a reputation for determination and impatience, and his brothers.

At the end of 1862 the two brothers then resident in London, Lewis and George, broke with their non-family partners and established Wallace Brothers & Co. with £100,000 capital. At the same time Alexander reorganized the Bombay business and thus family control was consolidated in their two interlocking partnerships. These were already of considerable size as the first balance sheet of

the London firm totalled more than £450,000. This manoeuvre was followed by the equally significant transfer in 1863 of the family's Burma assets to a newly formed, publicly owned company registered in India, the Bombay Burmah Trading Corporation Ltd, in exchange for a large and lucrative shareholding. By the 1880s it was the largest business in Burma and acted as a major force for the country's modernization and for the extension of British economic imperialism. It was dominated by the Wallaces, who acted as its 'perpetual' secretaries, treasurers, and managers through to the 1950s.

The youngest of the brothers, **Alexander Falconer Wallace** (1836–1925), was the guiding hand in Bombay behind this innovative and immensely successful transaction which removed many of the risks faced by the London and Bombay firms while ensuring for them a lucrative commission income. Born on 30 June 1836, he first went out to Bombay in 1856. He became the corporation's first chairman and emerged as a major business figure at Bombay and a worthy successor there to William and Lewis. William was to play no part in the new company's affairs, but retired from business, aged forty-six, on his return to London in 1864; for most of the rest of his life he lived at the Union Club. Little is known about him in retirement. He never married but in Burma had an illegitimate child whom he supported through remittances to Rangoon. He died on 28 January 1888 at 29 Hyde Park Place, London, leaving his estate to Lewis and Alexander.

Alexander himself left for England in 1867, and from then on the day-to-day management was in the hands of local partners; none of the brothers were to return to India. Shortly after his return, on 25 February 1868 Alexander married Katharine Louisa, daughter of William Harter of Hope Hall, Eccles; they had a son and a daughter. Alexander then moved to Manchester to supervise, along with his brother Robert, the family's interests there, as an important part of its business was the export of Lancashire textiles to India. After a decade running Wallace & Co. (formed in 1864), Alexander moved back to London, to assist in the management of the London house.

Under the direction of Lewis and Alexander (as joint senior partners), the London business went from strength to strength. Lewis, in his sixties, was concerned with financial and investment matters and Alexander, fifteen years younger, with expansion into new ventures; they enjoyed 'a complete and perfect confidence' in one another (Pointon, *Wallace Brothers*, 50). From the 1880s Alexander—energetic, alert, shrewd, and the most entrepreneurial of all the brothers—led the family and Bombay Burmah businesses in new directions, ranging from the importation of kerosene into India to the extension of the teak business to Siam, and from oil prospecting in Sumatra to the ownership of rubber plantations. Very often these new interests were carried on through the establishment of new companies controlled by the Wallaces. However, the core of the family firm's business continued to be in timber, and the trade of textiles and other exports and imports.

Alexander's growing reputation in the City was confirmed in 1887 through his appointment to the Bank of England's court; he served as a director for thirty-one years and was governor between 1905 and 1907. By the end of the 1880s the size of their business meant that both brothers had withdrawn from managing day-to-day transactions and were focusing instead upon policy and strategy. A sign of this withdrawal was their acquisition in the 1890s of estates at Strathdon, Aberdeenshire, Lewis through the lease of Castle Newe and Alexander through the purchase of Candacraig, though both had possessed country houses in England prior to this.

Lewis died on 9 September 1906, aged eighty-five, at Castle Newe. Throughout his life he had devoted himself single-mindedly to Wallace's affairs and had purposefully avoided charitable and committee work. He never married. Although still a partner at his death, a few years earlier he had handed his duties as senior to his brother. It was Alexander who in 1911 oversaw the London firm's conversion to a limited company and who was its first chairman and major shareholder. Alexander died on 24 January 1925 at 20 Hyde Park Gardens, London. By this time the family's influence had waned, if only because of a shortage of male heirs produced by the six founding brothers. The firm was finally acquired by Standard Chartered Bank.

JOHN ORBELL

Sources A. C. Pointon, *Wallace Brothers* (1974) · A. C. Pointon, *The Bombay Burmah Trading Corp. Ltd, 1863–1963* (1964) · R. H. Macaulay, *History of the Bombay Burmah Trading Corp. Ltd* (1934) · *CGPLA Eng. & Wales* (1925) · *CGPLA Eng. & Wales* (1906) · *CGPLA Eng. & Wales* (1888) · d. certs. [Alexander Falconer Wallace, Lewis Alexander Wallace] · m. cert. [Alexander Falconer Wallace] · *WWW*
Archives GL, Wallace Brothers archives | GL, Bombay Burmah Trading Corp. Ltd, archives
Likenesses K. MacLeay, group portrait, watercolour, 1842 (family of Lewis Wallace senior, showing William Wallace, Lewis Alexander Wallace, Alexander Falconer Wallace, and others) · C. Smith, oils, *c*.1850–1859 (Lewis Wallace) · portraits (of each of Lewis Wallace's sons), repro. in Pointon, *Wallace Brothers* · portraits (of each of Lewis Wallace's sons), repro. in Pointon, *Bombay Burmah Trading Corp. Ltd*
Wealth at death £315,289 1s. 1d.—Alexander Falconer Wallace: probate, 11 June 1925, *CGPLA Eng. & Wales* · £489,696 8s. 2d.—Lewis Alexander Wallace: probate, 13 Nov 1906, *CGPLA Eng. & Wales* · £10,959 7s. 8d.—William Wallace: probate, 5 June 1888, *CGPLA Eng. & Wales*

Wallace, Alexander Falconer (1836–1925). *See under* Wallace family (*per.* 1841–1925).

Wallace, Alfred Russel (1823–1913), naturalist, evolutionary theorist, and social critic, was born on 8 January 1823, at Kensington Cottage, Usk, Monmouthshire, the third of four sons and eighth of the nine children of Thomas Vere Wallace and Mary Anne Greenell. Early biographical treatments give the year of his birth as 1822 through an oversight on Wallace's own part. The spelling 'Russel' was perpetuated from a mistake made when the birth was recorded.

Early life, 1823–1848 Wallace's childhood was happy but not without hardship. His mother came from a respectable middle-class English family; his father, of Scottish descent, was to have taken up the law. Despite being

Alfred Russel Wallace (1823–1913), by Reginald Haines, *c.*1909

sworn in as an attorney in 1792, however, he apparently never practised, the income from inherited property allowing him to live a life of leisure for the next fifteen years. In 1807 he married and shortly thereafter entered into the first of a long series of largely unprofitable ventures, most notably the publication of a literary magazine. He was swindled out of his remaining property about 1835 and the family, already foundering financially, fell on hard times. Wallace was forced to withdraw from the grammar school at Hertford at the end of 1836 and was sent to London to board with his elder brother John. The ensuing stay of several months produced the first critical influence on his overall intellectual development: contact with supporters of the socialist Robert Owen. Indeed, at some point during this period Wallace actually heard Owen lecture in person; the effect was such that from that time onward he would characterize himself as a disciple.

By mid-1837 Wallace had joined the eldest brother, William, in Bedfordshire to learn the surveying trade. In January 1839 he was temporarily apprenticed to a watchmaker, but less than a year later was back with William, by then working in Hereford. In these and the following years he gained a good practical education in a number of technical trades (surveying, drafting and map-making, mechanics, building design and construction, agricultural chemistry, and so on), and began to develop an amateur's interest in natural history subjects, especially geology, astronomy, and botany. In 1841 he became associated with the newly formed Kington Mechanics' Institution and in that same year or the next, on moving to the Welsh town of Neath, began attending lectures sponsored by the Neath area's scientific societies. Soon he was frequenting the local libraries and giving his own lectures on various popular science subjects at the Neath Mechanics' Institute. In the early 1840s he also began to write: one of his first efforts, on the disposition of mechanics' institutes, was composed about 1841 and reached print in a history of Kington published in 1845.

During a work slowdown in late 1843 William Wallace was forced to let his brother go, whereupon Alfred secured the position of master at the collegiate school in Leicester. Here he again had access to a good library, and encountered several works that would profoundly influence his future endeavours. Here, too, he was fortunate enough to make the acquaintance of Henry Walter Bates, a young entomologist whose enthusiasm for neighbourhood collecting excursions soon attracted Wallace's involvement. It was also during this period that he attended some lectures on mesmerism, and proceeded to become a skilled practitioner of the then little credited art. His early experiments in this realm were a revelation to him; as he later recalled, he had learned his

> first great lesson in the inquiry into these obscure fields of knowledge, never to accept the disbelief of great men, or their accusations of imposture or of imbecility, as of any weight when opposed to the repeated observation of facts by other men admittedly sane and honest.   ('Notes on the growth of opinion', *Religio-Philosophical Journal*, new ser., 4, 1893, 229)

The sudden death of William in February of 1845 drew Wallace back to surveying, where there was again plenty of work thanks to the railroad boom. He still enjoyed the outdoor labour, but the trials of managing the business, even with the assistance of his brother John, began to test his patience. He had meanwhile been keeping up his natural history collecting and lecturing activities on the side, and was even made a curator of the Neath Philosophical and Literary Institute's museum. Eventually, natural history won out: inspired by William H. Edwards's new book, *A Voyage up the River Amazon*, Wallace commenced plans for an extended collecting expedition. Bates was quickly enlisted, and on 25 April 1848 the two young naturalists left Liverpool for Pará (now Belém), at the mouth of the Amazon.

Collecting in the Amazon, 1848–1852, and the Malay archipelago, 1854–1862 Apart from meeting their immediate goal of earning a living through natural history collecting, Wallace and Bates had a broader purpose for travelling to the Amazon: solving the mystery of the causes of organic evolution. Though Wallace had unreservedly embraced the notion of social progress from his early teens and apparently leaned toward a uniformitarianism-based but progressive view of change in physical nature even before turning twenty, he had not been a convert to biological evolution until he read Robert Chambers's controversial, anonymously published *Vestiges of the Natural History of Creation* about 1845, the year it was published. That one might demonstrate the fact of evolution through a detailed tracing out of individual phylogenies over time and space was

apparent to him early on, and the Amazon was to afford a natural laboratory to this end. He would eventually stay in the area four years, gaining invaluable field experience and sending home a sizeable quantity of biological specimens, largely of birds and insects.

The two men split up in March 1850 (or possibly earlier), Wallace choosing to concentrate on the central Amazon and Rio Negro regions. There he first came into contact with native peoples unaffected by European influence, an experience that left an indelible positive impression on him. A map he prepared of the Rio Negro proved reliable and became a standard reference for many years. Most of his time was spent studying the area's ornithology, entomology, physical geography, primatology, botany, and ichthyology, and he soon became fascinated by two problems in particular: first, how geography influenced species distribution boundaries, and second, the way the adaptive suites of many populations seemed more attuned to ecological station than to closeness of affinity with other forms.

By early 1852 the stresses of tropical exploration had undermined Wallace's health to the extent that he decided to leave the region. On returning to Pará he was told that his younger brother Herbert, who had joined the expedition in 1849, had succumbed to yellow fever some months earlier. Earlier he had discovered that through an unfortunate misunderstanding his collections from the year before had not been forwarded on to England. Passage for both himself and his treasures (including a number of living specimens) was arranged, but after several days at sea the brig on which he was sailing caught fire. Although everyone on board was safely evacuated to a pair of lifeboats all of Wallace's possessions, save a few drawings, notes, and odds and ends, perished. The party was finally rescued—after ten anxious days of paddling and bailing—by a passing cargo vessel making a return run to England. Their new carrier too, was old and decrepit, and barely managed to survive a series of storms encountered over the remainder of the voyage.

The Amazon experience left Wallace, now twenty-nine, with a solid reputation as a naturalist. But the sea disaster had robbed him of materials for further study, and—most significantly—the mechanism of organic change had eluded him. He was initially undecided as to what course to pursue next. While making up his mind he made good use of what was to be an eighteen-month stay in London; in addition to vacationing briefly in Paris and Switzerland and reading several papers at professional society meetings, he put together two reasonably well-received books: *Palm Trees of the Amazon* (1853), a short systematic ethnobotanical survey, and *A Narrative of Travels on the Amazon and Rio Negro* (1853). When finally he decided to soldier on with his collecting activities, this time in the Malay archipelago (the Indonesia region), passage to Singapore was secured through a grant from the Royal Geographical Society.

By the time he left the Malay archipelago, just less than eight years after his arrival in Malaya on 20 April 1854, Wallace had visited every important island in the group, many on multiple occasions. His efforts, drawing on perhaps 70 separate expeditions (requiring some 14,000 miles of island-to-island sailing in native crafts), reaped the astonishing harvest of 126,500 natural history specimens, including more than 200 new species of birds and well over 1000 new insects. His many experiences are imperishably detailed in his splendidly successful book *The Malay archipelago* (1869), a work that remained in print in multiple editions more than a century later, and which continues to make for fascinating reading. In it are recorded, among other exploits, his efforts to capture specimens of the bird of paradise, his pursuit of the orang-utan, his activities in New Guinea (where he was one of the first Europeans to set up a residence), his various dealings with the region's many native peoples, and numerous vignettes conveying the joys and vicissitudes of the field naturalist's work.

It was during the period from 1854 to 1862 that Wallace fully came into his own as a zoogeographer. The Malay archipelago provided the ideal geographical setting for species distribution studies, not only as an end in themselves, but as evidence critical to elucidation of the evolutionary process. His 1859 paper 'On the zoological geography of the Malay archipelago' (*Journal and Proceedings of the Linnean Society, Zoology*, 4, 1860, 172–84), a classic in that field, included his delineation of the abrupt zoogeographical discontinuity between the oriental and Australian faunal realms that now bears his name: Wallace's Line.

The discovery of natural selection While collecting in Sarawak in February 1855 Wallace wrote out his first important contribution to theoretical biology, 'On the law which has regulated the introduction of new species' (*Annals and Magazine of Natural History*, 16, 1855, 184–96). When it appeared in print it caught the attention of the celebrated geologist Sir Charles Lyell, who specially brought it to the notice of Charles Darwin, then labouring over his work, planned in several volumes, on 'the species problem'. As most of its ideas were not new to Darwin he was not particularly impressed, and indeed the essay, though a model of clarity, did no more than rather generally outline connections between the geological and geographical distribution of organisms that even Wallace himself had taken for granted for a good ten years at that point. But it was an indication of things to come, as were the several further studies based in the same evolutionary train of thought that he penned over the next three years.

While staying in the Moluccas in February 1858, during a bout of malaria, Wallace arrived at the notion of natural selection. His discovery was an independent one: Darwin's commitment to the same idea, privately reached twenty years earlier, was still only known to a handful of confidants. The ideas of Thomas Malthus figured prominently in this revolutionary concept: given the limited resources of earth, the ability of populations to reproduce in numbers testing those limits, and the inherent variability of expression of traits in such populations, it was logical to suppose that only the better-adapted individuals would tend to win out in the continuing competition for survival and pass their particular characteristics on to

their progeny. On recovering from his illness Wallace jotted down his ideas in essay form and sent the work—'On the tendency of varieties to depart indefinitely from the original type'—off to Darwin, with whom he had recently begun a correspondence, for 'possible forwarding' to Lyell. Darwin recognized in its message the very essence of his last twenty years of labour, and was quite understandably taken aback. The exact chain of events that followed is still not known, but it appears that Darwin decided to place the matter—an issue of priority—in the hands of two of his most trusted scientific friends, Lyell and the botanist Joseph Hooker. It was their altogether reasonable solution to present Wallace's paper, along with two extracts from Darwin's unpublished writings on natural selection, at the next meeting of the Linnean Society on 1 July 1858. This compromise has been viewed by most observers as having satisfied all involved, both then and later, yet it must be pointed out that as the initiating work Wallace's paper rightfully should have been read first, but instead was presented third; and that his permission to have it read and then published was not obtained prior to the act. The second matter, especially, is of great historical interest: it had not been Wallace's intention to have his communication published immediately, and it is now difficult to judge just how far—and in what directions—his thoughts had actually progressed at that point.

While the essential similarity between the Darwin and Wallace versions of natural selection as of 1858 is apparent enough, a number of observers have noted that Wallace tended to address competition in population level terms, whereas Darwin dwelled on the relative superiorities of individual organisms. This may be one result of Wallace's early exposure to socialist views. However, it is still not clear what Wallace's views on evolution in general were at that time. Among the remarkable features of 'On the tendency …' is the absence of any reference to the concepts earlier set out in 'On the law …'; further, 'On the tendency …' contains no discussions of the possible relation of natural selection to the emergence of mankind. Yet there is conclusive evidence that the question of man's origins had been on Wallace's mind for ten years or more by 1858. Wallace, like Darwin, believed that the struggle for existence was a conservative force incapable of shaping unnecessary adaptational refinements, but this position, added to his Owenist views on societal perfectibility and his acquaintance with the moral and intellectual capabilities of native tropical peoples, may well have led him to a pre-1858 evolutionary perspective differing considerably from Darwin's.

Later life, 1862–1913 Although Wallace later referred to his Malay adventure as 'the central and controlling incident of my life' (*My Life*, 1.336), his work had really just begun when he returned to England in the spring of 1862. Over fifty-one years of fruitful attention to a formidable array of subjects lay ahead, with the ultimate result that by the end of his life he had become one of the best-known scientists in the world—'the Grand Old Man of Science', as he was often referred to. He appears to have retained his travelling habit even after 'settling' in England, residing at at least ten separate addresses between 1862 and 1903. In the spring of 1866 he married Annie (1845/6–1914), the twenty-year-old daughter of his friend the botanist William Mitten. Their marriage was a long and happy one; Annie Wallace shared her husband's consuming love of nature (and, especially, gardening), and assisted him from time to time with his literary work. Two children, Violet and William, survived to adulthood (a third died in infancy).

For a couple of years Wallace busied himself primarily with study of his vast personal collection of specimens, but it was not long before he realized that he did not want to spend the rest of his life immersed in species-level systematics. At first living in London, he was able to take part in the meetings of several scientific institutions, notably the Entomological (of which he was president in 1870–71), Ethnological, Linnean, Zoological, and Anthropological societies. To the last of these bodies in March 1864 he delivered the important paper, 'The origin of human races and the antiquity of man deduced from the theory of "natural selection"', in which he theorized that physical evolution in our species had probably largely ceased once the action of natural selection had begun to focus itself on the human mind.

Wallace quickly developed a warm personal and professional relationship with Darwin. In 1863 he wrote his first reply to a criticism of Darwinian tenets; dozens more followed. However, in 1869 he showed the first definite sign of parting with Darwin's logic when he opined that the higher intellectual and moral faculties of humankind could be explained only on supposition of the influence of preternatural causal agencies. At about the same time he began seriously to question Darwin's model of sexual selection—the notion that female choice of mates could account for the gaudy coloration and other secondary sexual characteristics of the males of many species of birds and other animals.

Meanwhile, scores of articles, reviews, and letters to the editor on various other matters ranging from geodesy and animal instinct to museum organization and the power of the vote had been appearing in various newspapers and reviews under his name. Over a period of nine years (1862–70) Wallace presented ten papers at the annual meetings of the British Association for the Advancement of Science. He met nearly every British naturalist of note and counted many as intimates, including Darwin, Lyell, Hooker, Thomas Huxley, St George Mivart, Philip Sclater, Edward Poulton, Herbert Spencer, William Crookes, Francis Galton, John Lubbock, William Barrett, and Edward Tylor.

After *The Malay archipelago* appeared in 1869 and the essay collection *Contributions to the Theory of Natural Selection* a year later, Wallace turned his attention to an in-depth study of the geographical distribution of animals. In 1876 he produced the two-volume classic *The Geographical Distribution of Animals*; this was followed by *Tropical Nature and other Essays* in 1878, and in 1880 by another definitive work, *Island Life*. By now he had tired of city living and embarked on a series of removals to more rural

settings. The first relocation out of London was to Grays, Essex, in 1872; this was followed by moves to Dorking (1876), Croydon (1878), Godalming (1881), Parkstone (1889), and, finally, Broadstone, near Wimborne, Dorset (1902).

Though Wallace and his family managed to live reasonably comfortably right through to the end, they were never able to achieve financial security. Bad and carelessly speculative investments led to his losing most of the considerable profits accrued from the sale of his Malay archipelago collections; meanwhile, none of his applications for permanent income-yielding positions proved successful. As a result he was forced to take on a variety of short-term employments (notably, editing other naturalists' writings, working part-time as an assistant examiner in physical geography, and engaging in various lecturing and creative literary activities). In 1870 he attempted to take an easy profit by answering a £500 challenge posed by a flat-earther; this proved to be a mistake, for although Wallace won the wager he was unable to collect and the man harassed him and his family for years. By 1881 his financial situation had so deteriorated that a mutual friend intervened and, largely through Darwin's influence, was able to secure him a civil-list pension.

Wallace's professional attention in the post-Malay period was by no means exhausted, or perhaps even dominated, by natural science subjects. In 1866, to the wonder of many of his colleagues, he publicly embraced spiritualism. Earlier he had been a self-proclaimed agnostic; his conversion was precipitated by several factors, including long-held opinions on the nature of belief as related to the evidence of the senses, an attraction to spiritualism's moral teachings, an interest in its apparent connection to natural processes, an extensive personal investigation of séance phenomena, and perhaps (though this has never been conclusively demonstrated, and he denied it himself) a general dissatisfaction with the materialist limitations of Darwinian natural selection. As soon as he was convinced of the reality of the phenomena, he began writing on spiritualism as well. His first three major treatments of the subject were later brought out as the collection *On Miracles and Modern Spiritualism* in 1875. He quickly gained recognition as one of the movement's leading voices. Three of his essays on spiritualism, 'A defence of modern spiritualism' (1874), 'Modern spiritualism—are its phenomena in harmony with science?' (1885), and 'If a man die, shall he live again?' (1887), were in his own time his most reprinted works.

It will be recalled that Wallace had committed himself to Owenist ideals as far back as 1837; further important early influences on the development of his social conscience included his involvement as a surveyor with the enclosure movement c.1840–1841, his reading in 1853 of Herbert Spencer's *Social Statics* and adoption of its 'social justice' message, and his admiration for the innate qualities of 'uncivilized' peoples. When by 1880 he had completed the major part of his studies on geographical distribution, Wallace began devoting much of his time to social issues. That same year his essay 'How to nationalize the land' (*Contemporary Review*, 38, 1880, 716–36) attracted such attention that a new organization called the Land Nationalisation Society, dedicated to retrieving control of the land from large holders, was created and he was made its first president. He held the office to his death in 1913, working persistently for the organization's success until about 1896, at which point he effectively retired to the role of figurehead. Another of what he ironically termed his 'heresies' was an active involvement in the anti-vaccination movement, especially from 1883 to 1898. His conclusions on this matter appeared in a series of three pamphlets and the final report of a royal commission that took up the matter. The most visible of these efforts was *Vaccination a Delusion* in 1898; it was issued simultaneously as a pamphlet and as part of the book *The Wonderful Century*.

Meanwhile, Wallace's natural science studies had been given a boost by an invitation to deliver a series of lectures on evolutionary theory at the Lowell Institute in Boston in late 1886. On completing this obligation he took the series (plus talks on at least three non-science subjects) across the United States over a period of ten months, along the way meeting countless dignitaries of science, politics, and letters, up to and including President Cleveland. While in California in the summer of 1887 he was reunited with his expatriate brother John, whom he had not seen in nearly forty years. In San Francisco he gave the spectacularly successful public lecture 'If a man die, shall he live again?' The California visit was also marked by strong impressions produced by visits to redwood groves (in the company of John Muir), the Yosemite valley, and the future site of Stanford University (with Leland Stanford, whom he had befriended in Washington, DC, earlier that year).

On returning to England, Wallace used his American lectures as the point of departure for a new book, *Darwinism* (1889), which achieved considerable popularity and ranks among his best-known works. Encouraged by this success, he spent most of the 1890s writing on a mixture of social and natural science topics. In 1889, after reading Edward Bellamy's best-selling novel *Looking Backward*, he finally declared himself a socialist (until that point he had remained unconvinced that the change-over to a socialistic state was feasible). In 1898, expanding on some lectures on scientific progress he had delivered two years earlier in Switzerland, he fashioned an idiosyncratic rendering of the nineteenth century's successes and failures under the title *The Wonderful Century*. In 1900 he brought out the two-volume collection of his essays *Studies Scientific and Social*, and three years later the study *Man's Place in the Universe*, in which he created a stir by arguing for the soleness of advanced life on earth and its centrality of location in the universe (then thought to extend no further than our own galaxy). Some of the arguments used in the latter work were applied in 1907 to the more special case of Mars in an attempt (*Is Mars Habitable?*) to debunk Percival Lowell's theory that the red planet was inhabited. In these two works Wallace fully anticipated the anthropic principle and all but founded another study for which he has been given but little credit: exobiology.

In 1905 Wallace's well-received two-volume autobiography *My Life* came out. In 1908 his name appeared—this time as editor—at the head of yet another two-volume work: the botanical papers and diaries of his friend and co-Amazonian explorer Richard Spruce, who had died in 1894. His last public appearance took place in 1909, when he gave a lecture to the Royal Institution that evolved into the teleological popular science study *The World of Life* (1910). Two short works of social criticism, *Social Environment and Moral Progress* and *The Revolt of Democracy* (both published in 1913) were his final monographic productions, at the age of ninety. The full list of Wallace's books is rounded out by the inclusion of *Australasia* (1879), a commissioned volume for a travel series, *Land Nationalisation* (1882), *Bad Times* (1886), an essay on the depression of trade, and *Natural Selection and Tropical Nature* (1891), another collection of previously published works.

Appearance, character, and historical significance Physically, Wallace was tall (6 feet 1 inch in his youth) and lean but robust with sparkling, bespectacled blue eyes. He was bearded from the time of his Malay travels; his hair turned prematurely snow white in his fifties, and in old age he came to walk with a considerable stoop. Apart from a moderate number of passing but occasionally troubling ills, his health was generally good throughout his life.

Wallace was especially celebrated for his forthright honesty. Decent to a fault (he refused to blame others for their blemishes of character and on occasion was duped accordingly), he was held in the highest respect even by most of his adversaries. Though shy and self-effacing by nature, he was good company when at ease and was much in demand as a lecturer. Further, he was sought out as a reviewer and popular expositor for his easy, lucid writing style. Among colleagues of equal standing his professional reputation was excellent, and those who knew best considered him to be among the greatest scientific reasoners of the era.

Numerous important honours came Wallace's way during his long and productive life—there might have been even more, but after receiving honorary doctorates from Dublin in 1882 and Oxford in 1889 he politely let it be known he desired no further academic honoraria. He received medals from the Royal Society in 1868, 1890, and 1908, the Société de Géographie in 1870, and the Linnean Society in 1892 and 1908, as well as the Order of Merit in 1908. A mark of his dissenting status within the scientific élite was that he was only elected FRS as late as 1893. His main professional affiliations were with the Royal Geographical Society, Linnean Society, Royal Entomological Society, and Zoological Society. He also belonged to the Ethnological Society, British Association for the Advancement of Science, Batavian Society of Arts and Sciences, British National Association of Spiritualists, Anti-Vaccination League, and a few lesser institutions.

In an assessment of Wallace's long-term significance, his contributions to natural science occupy the primary position. The vast range of his attention to natural science, however, precludes more than a brief summary of his main contributions. Above all, of course, he is recognized as the independent realizer of the theory (actually, and revealingly, he usually referred to it as the 'law') of natural selection; and his action was also the main spur for Darwin's decision to publish. But his work in this sphere went far beyond the setting of the general principle. He also established the role of protective coloration and other aspects of coloration in the evolutionary process, originated the concepts of polymorphism and recognition marks, explored the influences of geography on the processes of evolution, contributed significantly to the development of Batesian and Müllerian mimicry theory, and produced important arguments on the forces at work in human evolution, instinct, adaptation, the evolution of island biotas, and the relation of hybrid sterility to species divergence, among other subjects.

The Geographical Distribution of Animals (1876) has long been viewed as a cornerstone work in the history of the science of zoogeography, the study of the causes of the distribution of animal species and faunas. As its effective 'father' Wallace argued for the field's recognition as a subject worthy of enquiry, established principles of faunal regionalization, and introduced methods of analysis. Further, he linked the characteristics of distribution to other sciences such as geology, climatology, and anthropology. Among his outstanding contributions to zoogeography were his defence of ornithologist Philip L. Sclater's faunal regionalization scheme, the corridor model of dispersal along mountain chains into tropical regions, the theory of air- and water-borne dispersal of colonizing propagules to oceanic islands, his conservative stance regarding posed connective land bridges between now separated land masses, his recognition of the scope of worldwide latitudinal diversity gradients, his model of the causes of discontinuous (disjunct) distribution patterns, and his attention to the problems of tropical nature in general.

Wallace the physical geographer and geologist is perhaps most celebrated for his theory of continental glaciation, in which he was the first to propose a modern synthetic model drawing on both geographical–climatological and astronomical lines of reasoning. He also developed a coherent theory of ice movement, marshalling an array of evidence demonstrating the validity of the glacial excavation model of alpine lake basin evolution. He is also remembered for his support of the theory of the permanence of ocean basins and continental masses; further contributions were made to the study of land surface erosion rates, the classification of islands, the age of the earth, and the record of pre-Cenozoic and southern hemisphere glaciation episodes. His work on astronomical subjects was entirely derivative, yet it too was significant in that he was one of the first investigators to apply logically climatological and physical geography principles to the study of planetary environments.

In physical anthropology Wallace is most frequently cited for his early applications of natural selection to human evolution and racial differentiation, his field observations on the orang-utan and on primates in general, and his conclusions regarding the racial affinities of the native inhabitants of Australia, New Guinea, and Polynesia. He is also known for his early championing of

what he termed the 'mouth-gesture' theory of the origin of language.

Wallace's contributions as a social critic should also not be ignored. Many of his schemes for social progress were quite ingeniously argued, and some have actually come to pass, if sometimes in variant form or under a different name. Indeed, his individuality as a social critic has often been overlooked altogether (he is usually viewed as a 'follower' of the social theories of the American social critic Henry George, for example, but most of Wallace's ideas on related subjects had actually already been worked out by the time he came into contact with George's writings). The foundation of his land nationalization plan was a novel thinking out of the concept of rent which took into account both the locational value of a parcel of land and value added to it over time. In *Land Nationalisation* (1882) Wallace proposed planning strategies such as green belts and the legislated protection of rural lands and historic monuments; in this work he also developed elaborate plans for the divestiture of large land holdings (including a compensation programme for landlords) and the subsequent monitoring of state-owned properties. His concern with the ownership and distribution of land, and with social geography, drew in part on his experiences in early life, when he worked as a surveyor.

An interesting side-contribution of Wallace's involvement in the anti-vaccination campaign was his groundbreaking use of comparative statistics-based argumentation in epidemiology. There was much resistance to the non-anecdotal approach at first, especially by members of the medical profession, but most of Wallace's figures were apparently never seriously challenged. Among Wallace's other interventions were suggestions for reforming the House of Lords and the Church of England, a plea that strikers redirect their efforts toward concentrating on employee-based buy-outs, analyses of the depopulation of the Scottish highlands and the Irish land problem, and protests against colonial imperialism and 'might makes right' arguments. His explorations into currency stabilization theory presaged the 'Chicago school' of thought of the 1930s and were insightful enough to impress the American economist Irving Fisher, who dedicated his book *Stabilizing the Dollar* to him in 1920.

Wallace was greatly admired by leaders of the women's movement, both for his vocal support of suffrage and for his position that women's release from economic indenture was the prerequisite for a form of mate selection that would tend to raise the moral standards of humanity. Here, as elsewhere in his social criticism writings, the underlying theory was one linking the morality of spiritualist philosophy to Benjamin Kidd's notion of social 'equality of opportunity'. This idiosyncratic blend of concepts allowed him to envision a social direction governed by both societal and personal concerns, thereby avoiding the ethical crudities of much of the contemporary Darwinist and eugenicist formulations.

Wallace also made a significant, albeit indirect, mark as an educator. He devoted several studies to the proper design of museums and display of collections, inventing the concept of the 'faunal diorama' (since extended to the 'biome exhibit' of zoological parks). His collections and travel and tropical nature works, moreover, proved an inspiration to the next generation of travelling naturalist–explorers and novelists alike (*Malay archipelago*, for example, was a major influence on the writings of Joseph Conrad).

The general assessment of Wallace's role in the history of evolutionary theory has not been without controversy. Historians have sometimes implied that, by virtue of his deferral of priority to Darwin, he got something of a raw deal. This assessment, however, neglects his rather special character and talents. The logician Charles Peirce once described Wallace as 'a man conscious of superior powers of sound and solid reasoning, … [but] with … a moral sense … which will not allow him to approve anything illogical or wrong, though it be upon his own side of a question' (Peirce, 36). Thus, he played a significant role in drawing attention to the moral and ethical problems involved in applying natural selection to man; his example served to counter the influence of the more rigorist evolutionary philosophers, such as Herbert Spencer. While continuing, unlike other critics of Darwin, to insist on the centrality of natural selection, and indeed to extend and refine the concept in many ways, he sought nevertheless to accomplish this within a broader concept of evolution, one that admitted of a place for more than just the amorality of gross competition. It should be noted, for example, that it is Wallace's then little accepted view of the intellectual and moral comparability of primitive peoples with their 'civilized' counterparts that has been the one adopted by the best twentieth-century anthropologists.

Although, in the later twentieth century, Wallace's name became less well known to the general public than that of Huxley or Darwin, his position in the history of science remains secure: the essay on natural selection (of February 1858) alone identifies him with the front rank of scientific discoverers. On the several major subjects on which he disagreed with Darwin—the origin of humankind's higher moral and intellectual faculties, the manner of operation of sexual selection, the possibility of inheritance of acquired characters, the importance of the production of sterile hybrids to the evolutionary process, and the mode of dispersal of organic propagules along glacial corridors and across oceanic expanses—his positions have on the whole not fared badly. However, progress in understanding and contextualizing his world-view has been slow. About the exact relation between his spiritualism and social criticism, and his zoology, for example, little can be stated confidently at this time. Perhaps the most significant result of recent Wallace studies has been a growing appreciation that his involvement in social issues was part and parcel of his overall cosmology and not, as many earlier thought, the faddist hobbies of a crank.

Nevertheless, the trajectory of Wallace's career remains a remarkable one. From a young radical of impoverished background working as a surveyor, to a successful traveller, collector, and ethnographer; a leading evolutionary theorist and pioneering scientific geographer; a partial dissenter within the ranks of the Darwinists; and a prominent social critic he was, much more than Darwin, the founder of a true 'social Darwinism'. His life highlights some of the lesser-known aspects of nineteenth-century English society. Though some have drawn attention to a deep-seated idiosyncrasy in his opinions, it remains a proof of the quality of his vision that many of the issues to which he drew attention continue to be viable concerns a century later.

After a general weakening of his health in his last few weeks, Wallace died peacefully in his sleep at Broadstone on 7 November 1913. He had apparently not been ready to call it quits until the very end as only a short time earlier he had been contracted to write yet another two books. His remains were buried three days later in Broadstone, where there is a small memorial stone made from fossilized wood. On 1 November 1915 a medallion bearing his name was placed in Westminster Abbey.

CHARLES H. SMITH

Sources A. R. Wallace, *My life: a record of events and opinions*, 2 vols. (1905) · J. L. Brooks, *Just before the origin: Alfred Russel Wallace's theory of evolution* (1984) · *Alfred Russel Wallace: an anthology of his shorter writings*, ed. C. H. Smith (1991) · H. L. McKinney, *Wallace and natural selection* (1972) · J. Marchant, ed., *Alfred Russel Wallace: letters and reminiscences*, repr. of 1916 edn (1975) · W. George, *Biologist philosopher: a study of the life and writings of Alfred Russel Wallace* (1964) · M. J. Kottler, 'Alfred Russel Wallace, the origin of man, and spiritualism', *Isis*, 65 (1974), 144–92 · M. J. Kottler, 'Charles Darwin and Alfred Russel Wallace: two decades of debate over natural selection', *The Darwinian heritage*, ed. D. Kohn (1985), 367–432 · B. G. Beddall, 'Wallace, Darwin, and the theory of natural selection: a study in the development of ideas and attitudes', *Journal of the History of Biology*, 1 (1968), 261–323 · B. G. Beddall, 'Darwin and divergence: the Wallace connection', *Journal of the History of Biology*, 21 (1988), 1–68 · R. Smith, 'Alfred Russel Wallace: philosophy of nature and man', *British Journal for the History of Science*, 6 (1972–3), 177–99 · A. Brackman, *A delicate arrangement: the strange case of Charles Darwin and Alfred Russel Wallace* (1980) · H. Clements, *Alfred Russel Wallace: biologist and social reformer* (1983) · M. J. Kottler, 'Darwin, Wallace, and the origin of sexual dimorphism', *Proceedings of the American Philosophical Society*, 124 (1980), 203–26 · R. E. Hughes, 'Alfred Russel Wallace: some notes on the Welsh connection', *British Journal for the History of Science*, 22 (1989), 401–18 · H. L. McKinney, 'Alfred Russel Wallace and the discovery of natural selection', *Journal of the History of Medicine and Allied Sciences*, 21 (1966), 333–57 · G. Scarpelli, '"Nothing in nature that is not useful"; the anti-vaccination crusade and the idea of *harmonia naturae* in Alfred Russel Wallace', *Nuncius*, 7 (1992), 109–30 · M. Fichman, 'Wallace: zoogeography and the problem of land bridges', *Journal of the History of Biology*, 10 (1977), 45–63 · J. S. Schwartz, 'Darwin, Wallace, and the descent of man', *Journal of the History of Biology*, 17 (1984), 271–89 · C. S. Peirce, review, *The Nation*, 72 (1901), 36–7 [*Studies scientific and social*] · election certificate, RS · M. Shermer, *In Darwin's shadow: the life and science of Alfred Russel Wallace* (2002) · P. Raby, *Alfred Russel Wallace: a life* (2001) · G. Jones, 'Alfred Russel Wallace, Robert Owen and the theory of natural selection', *British Journal for the History of Science*, 35 (2002), 73–96 · D. Quammen, *The song of the dodo: island biogeography in an age of extinctions* (1996) · M. Fichman, 'Science in theistic contexts: a case study of Alfred Russel Wallace on human evolution', *Osiris*, 2nd ser., 16 (2001), 227–50

Archives BL, corresp. and papers, Add. MSS 3794, 46414–46442 · Linn. Soc., corresp. and papers · NHM, drawings and notebooks · Oxf. U. Mus. NH, Hope Library, corresp. and papers relating to spiritualism · Zoological Society of London, MSS of published communications | BL, corresp. with Macmillans, Add. MS 55221 ·

John Innes Centre, Norwich, letters to Sir W. H. Flower • Man. CL, Manchester Archives and Local Studies, letters to Matthew Slater • NHM, letters to Samuel Stevens [copies] • NHM, letters to Lord Walden and to G. A. Boulenger and C. O. Waterhouse • Oxf. U. Mus. NH, letters to Robert McLachlan; letters to Raphael Meldola; letters to F. D. Morice; corresp. with Sir E. B. Poulton; letters to J. O. Westwood • RGS, corresp. with Royal Geographical Society • UCL, letters to Sir Francis Galton | FILM BFI NFTVA, 'Wild islands', 4 Aug 1997

Likenesses W. Strang, drawing, 1908, Royal College • R. Haines, photograph, c.1909, NPG [*see illus.*] • A. B. Joy, sculpture, Linn. Soc. • W. Rothenstein, lithograph, NPG • photographic plate (age 66), repro. in A. R. Wallace, *Darwinism*, frontispiece • photographic plates (at ages of 25, 30, 46, 55 and 79), repro. in A. R. Wallace, *My life: a record of events and opinions*, 2 vols. (1905) • portrait (painted over a photograph by T. Sims, 1869), NPG

Wealth at death £5823 0s. 6d.: probate, 24 Dec 1913, *CGPLA Eng. & Wales*

Wallace, Sir Cuthbert Sidney, baronet (1867–1944), surgeon, was born at Kingston upon Thames, Surrey, on 20 June 1867, the third son of the Revd John Wallace, of Haslemere, and his wife, Marion K. J. Agnes, daughter of Francis Howard *Greenway of Sydney, New South Wales. He was educated at Haileybury College and at St Thomas's Hospital, London, from which he qualified in medicine in 1891. He became FRCS in 1893 and graduated MB BS (London) in 1894, obtaining the gold medal in obstetric medicine and qualifying for the gold medal in surgery.

Wallace's appointment as resident assistant surgeon at St Thomas's Hospital in 1897 coincided with the need to remodel the theatres and wards along aseptic lines rather than antiseptic Listerian principles. It was largely through Wallace's vision and enthusiasm that this took place. His belief in asepsis had a major impact on his practice both at the Portland Hospital during the Second South African War and later as a consulting surgeon to the First Army in France in 1914. Despite the conditions of a field hospital he was able to maintain the principles of aseptic surgery. His belief in the early evacuation of abdominal injuries to casualty clearing stations saved many lives.

Wallace's surgical work in the front line was perhaps his most important contribution, and the experience he gained is recorded in a number of works. He collaborated with Anthony Bowlby and other colleagues on writing an account of their experiences in South Africa, entitled *A Civilian War Hospital* (1901). His books *War Surgery of the Abdomen* (1918) and (in collaboration with John Fraser) *Surgery at a Casualty Clearing Station* (1918) remain important source books of surgery at the battle front. He was one of the editors of and contributors to the *Official History of the Great War, Medical Services, Surgery of War* (2 vols., 1922). In addition to his work on military abdominal surgery he was remembered by his dictum, 'The surgeon who does not trust the peritoneum is not fit to do abdominals'.

At St Thomas's Hospital, Wallace was assistant surgeon (1900–13), dean of the medical school (1907–9 and 1918–28), and full surgeon (1913–30). He was also surgeon to the East London Hospital for Children and dean of the medical faculty of London University. He was closely associated with the work of the Royal College of Surgeons, being a member of the board of examiners and of council,

Bradshaw lecturer (1927), Hunterian orator (1934), and president (1935–8).

For a long period Wallace was a member of the radium commission and of the Medical Research Council, and in June 1940 he was made chairman of the committee on war wounds. For his military services he was appointed CMG (1916) and CBE (1918), and promoted KCMG (1919). He was also awarded the American DSM, and became an officer of the Légion d'honneur in 1937, the year in which he was also created a baronet. He received honorary doctorates from three universities: DSc, Oxford (1936), DCL, Durham (1937), and LLD, Birmingham (1938).

On 6 July 1912 Wallace married Florence Mildred, youngest daughter of Herbert Jackson, of Sussex Place, Regent's Park, London; they had no children. They lived at 5 Cambridge Terrace, Regent's Park, and he died in Mount Vernon Hospital, London, on 25 May 1944, survived by his wife. He was of middle height and upright carriage and in later years had a bright complexion and white hair. He wore a blue and white spotted bow-tie, and despite a somewhat brusque manner he was never known to say a vindictive word.   W. J. BISHOP, rev. HARVEY WHITE

Sources *BMJ* (10 June 1944), 797–8 • *BMJ* (1 July 1944), 28–9 • *The Lancet* (10 June 1944) • *The Times* (31 May 1944) • *St Thomas's Hospital Gazette*, 42 (1944), 134–5 • D'A. Power and W. R. Le Fanu, *Lives of the fellows of the Royal College of Surgeons of England, 1930–1951* (1953), 810–13 • *CGPLA Eng. & Wales* (1944) • WWW

Likenesses W. Stoneman, photograph, 1918, NPG • G. Harcourt, oils, c.1931, St Thomas's Hospital Medical School • M. Ayoub, group portrait, oils (*Council of the Royal College of Surgeons, 1926–27*), RCS Eng.

Wealth at death £68,387 19s. 2d.: probate, 24 Oct 1944, *CGPLA Eng. & Wales*

Wallace, Sir Donald Mackenzie (1841–1919), journalist and author, the son of Robert Wallace, of Boghead, Dunbartonshire, and his wife, Sarah, daughter of Donald Mackenzie, was born on 11 November 1841. He lost both parents before he was ten years old, and at about the age of fifteen, having adequate private means, he conceived, in his own words, 'a passionate love of study, and determined to devote my life to it'. Accordingly, he spent all the years of his early manhood, until he was twenty-eight, in continuous study at various universities: about half the time at Glasgow and Edinburgh, where he was occupied mainly with metaphysics and ethics; the remainder at the École de Droit, Paris, and at the universities of Berlin and Heidelberg, where he applied himself particularly to Roman law and modern jurisprudence, taking the degree of doctor of laws at Heidelberg in 1867. During the vacations he travelled extensively over the continent of Europe, acquiring fluency in its principal languages.

While he was engaged in qualifying himself in Germany for a professorship of comparative law, Wallace accepted a private invitation to visit Russia, as he had a strong desire to study the Ossetes, a peculiar Aryan tribe in the Caucasus. He remained in Russia from early in 1870 until late in 1875, studying not the Ossetes but the Russians, whom he found more worthy of attention. He familiarized himself thoroughly with the life of the people, not

Sir Donald Mackenzie Wallace (1841–1919), by unknown photographer

merely visiting the great towns and the showplaces, but settling for a considerable period in a remote country village. In 1876 he went back to England with the material that he utilized in his famous work *Russia*, published in two volumes in the beginning of 1877, just before the outbreak of the Russo-Turkish War. The book had a great and instant success, went through several editions, and was translated into many languages, the French translation being 'crowned' by the Académie Française. It was twice revised by its author, in 1905 and in 1912, and remains a very important source for the history of late-tsarist Russia.

Wallace now entered active life as a foreign correspondent of *The Times*, which he represented at St Petersburg in 1877–8; at the Berlin Congress in June and July 1878, where he assisted Henri de Blowitz, the famous Paris correspondent of *The Times*, and carried the text of the treaty from Berlin to Brussels sewn into the lining of his greatcoat; and afterwards for six years at Constantinople (1878–84). From that point of vantage he was able to investigate the Balkan peoples and their problems; and thence he went on behalf of *The Times* on a special mission to Egypt, the outcome being his book, *Egypt and the Egyptian Question* (1883). In 1884 Lord Dufferin, who, as British ambassador at Constantinople, had learned to appreciate Wallace's unusual attainments, tact, and discretion, took him to India as his private secretary during his viceroyalty, and

testified at its close in 1888 to the 'incomparable' nature of his assistance, which was rewarded by the KCIE in 1887.

After a further period of travel in the Near and Middle East, Wallace was selected to accompany, as political officer, the tsarevich, afterwards the ill-fated Tsar Nicholas II of Russia, in his Indian tour during the winter of 1890–91. Then he returned to the service of *The Times*, as foreign assistant editor, a new and important post, for Wallace effectively deposed De Blowitz as the paper's leading foreign affairs authority. Wallace believed the Turkish empire was no longer sustainable, and encouraged Salisbury in his reorientation of tory policy on this point. He was cautious about German expansionism, but carefully controlled Valentine Chirol's anti-German hostility. He was (for a tory) an early proponent of Anglo-Russian amity. In 1899, when *The Times* took over the *Encyclopaedia Britannica*, Wallace was persuaded, with Hugh Chisholm as colleague, to edit the extra volumes of the tenth edition needed to bring the work up to date. In 1901 he accompanied, as assistant private secretary, the duke and duchess of Cornwall and York (afterwards George V and Queen Mary) in their tour of the British dominions—a tour which he commemorated in a book, *The Web of Empire* (1902). In 1905 he acted once more as a correspondent of *The Times*, attending the conference at Portsmouth, New Hampshire, USA, which produced peace between Russia and Japan; he was also correspondent for the Algeciras conference in 1906.

In his last years Wallace reverted to his youthful ideal, and devoted himself to persistent study, varied by occasional travel; but he published nothing further. In spite of being essentially a student he had a genius for friendship, with contacts in all European and several non-European countries, and in many walks of life—savants, artists, journalists, travellers, diplomatists, statesmen, social magnates, great ladies, courtiers, and, to a remarkable degree, royal personages. He never married, and died at Lymington, Hampshire, on 10 January 1919.

G. E. BUCKLE, rev. H. C. G. MATTHEW

Sources *The Times* (11 Jan 1919) · [S. Morison and others], *The history of The Times*, 3 (1947) · A. J. A. Morris, *The scaremongers: the advocacy of war and rearmament, 1896–1914* (1984)

Archives CUL, *History of foreign policy* and notes on Russian revolution of 1905 · London Library, notes · News Int. RO, papers · Balliol Oxf., letters to Sir Robert Morier · BL, corresp. with Sir Alfred Lyall, MS Eur. F 132 · BL, letters to viceroy of India, MS Eur. F 102 · BL OIOC, corresp. with Sir Henry Durand, MSS Eur. D 727 · Bodl. Oxf., corresp. with Lord Kimberley · Bodl. Oxf., letters to John Wodehouse · CAC Cam., corresp. with Lord Randolph Churchill · NL Scot., letters to Lord Rosebery and notes

Likenesses W. Stoneman, photograph, before 1917, NPG · J. Russell & Sons, photograph, NPG · photograph, NPG [*see illus.*] · portrait, repro. in *ILN* (1902)

Wallace, (Richard Horatio) Edgar (1875–1932), writer, was born on 1 April 1875 at 7 Ashburnham Grove, Greenwich, London, and was legally registered as the son of Walter Wallace, comedian, and Mary Jane (Polly) Wallace, previously Richards, *née* Blair (1843–1903). He was in fact, however, the illegitimate son of Polly and Richard Horatio

(**Richard Horatio**) **Edgar Wallace** (1875–1932), by Howard Coster, 1930

Edgar, both of whom were minor players in a touring theatre company based in London. His mother arranged for him to be fostered by the family of George Freeman, Billingsgate fish-porter, who adopted Wallace when she was no longer able to pay for his keep. The Freeman household was largely semi-literate with a rough-edged respectability in which hard work, hard drinking, and piety were closely interwoven. Wallace left school at twelve, though he had already begun to play truant in order to sell newspapers in Ludgate Circus, where a bronze commemorative plaque was erected after his death to mark the beginning of his long association with the press. A variety of jobs followed: as a printer's boy, a shoe shop assistant, a worker in a mackintosh cloth factory, a milk roundsman, a builder's labourer and road maker, and, most unhappily of all, a very brief spell on a Grimsby trawler. In 1894 he enlisted as a private in the Royal West Kent regiment, quickly transferring to the medical staff corps when picket duty and infantry training proved too unpalatable.

It is difficult to date Wallace's decision to become a writer with any precision; but at the beginning of his time in the army he was bold enough to send a song that he had written to the music-hall comedian Arthur Roberts, who performed it on the London stage. In 1896 Wallace was posted to South Africa and there he set about writing in earnest, supplementing his army pay by contributing occasional columns on local events and politics to the Cape Colony press. He also began to publish poetry, much of it inspired by Kipling, whom he was to meet on a visit to

Cape Town in 1898. Wallace's first book, a collection of his ballads with the Kiplingesque title *The Mission that Failed!*, appeared later that same year. His growing ambition, combined with his senior officers' disapproval of his unofficial career, led him to buy himself out of the army in 1899. During the Second South African War he worked briefly for Reuters before becoming the *Daily Mail*'s war correspondent in 1900. His assiduous intelligence-gathering and flagrant evasion of the military censors enabled the *Mail* to scoop the signing of the peace treaty twenty-four hours ahead of the official announcement, a violation which prompted an outraged Lord Kitchener to rescind Wallace's war correspondent's pass. He was appointed the first editor of the *Rand Daily Mail* in 1902, but the following year, after a quarrel with its proprietor, he returned to England where he resumed working for the *Daily Mail* as a general reporter. Badly in debt and eager for a quick windfall, he also began work on what was to be the first of his many thrillers.

The Four Just Men (1905) proved to be both a financial disaster and one of Wallace's most enduring novels. It was conceived as a locked-room mystery with a difference: readers were invited to send in their own solutions as to how Britain's foreign secretary had been murdered by a band of mysterious anarchists in his study in Downing Street, and those with the correct answer would receive cash prizes. Unable to find a publisher, Wallace set up his own company and brought out the book himself, but his lavish spending on promotion and advertising left hardly any money with which to pay the lucky winners, despite brisk sales. He was bailed out by the owner of the *Daily Mail*, Alfred Harmsworth, who was worried that any adverse publicity would damage the paper's reputation. Never a very judicious reporter, Wallace's relations with Harmsworth went from bad to worse when inaccuracies in one of his stories were used against the *Mail* in an embarrassing and costly libel action. A second libel suit led to his dismissal in 1907. At this point in his career Wallace's standing in Fleet Street was so low that no editor would employ him.

By this time Wallace had a family to support. In April 1901, while in South Africa, he had married Ivy Maude Caldecott (1880?–1926), the daughter of a Wesleyan minister in Simonstown. The Wallaces' first child, Eleanor, died from meningitis in March 1903, but a son, Bryan, was born in April 1904 and early in 1908 Ivy gave birth to a second daughter, named Patricia. In a perpetual state of near-bankruptcy, Wallace continued to write, but it was not until the end of 1909 that he hit upon a successful popular formula. As his last assignment for the *Mail*, Wallace had been sent to the Congo to investigate the horrific reports of atrocities committed against the indigenous population by the Belgian rubber companies, and a chance meeting with the editor of a penny magazine called the *Weekly Tale-Teller* suggested that he might turn his African experiences into a series of short stories. These adventures of empire, with their resolute district commissioner, gullible missionaries, child-like natives, and wily Arabs, quickly found an enthusiastic audience, and *Sanders of the*

River (1911), the first of eleven books of stories, became a best-seller.

Wallace's change of fortune helped to rehabilitate his name as a journalist and he began to develop a new sideline as a tipster and horse-racing correspondent on the *Week-End* and the *Evening News*. A keen though decidedly maladroit gambler, he became shareholding editor of the *Week-End Racing Supplement* and started two racing papers of his own, *Bibury's* and *R. E. Walton's Weekly*. In September 1916 Ivy gave birth to another son, Michael, but the couple were divorced in 1919. To cope with his growing volume of work, Wallace relied upon a Dictaphone and hired a succession of typists and personal assistants. On 17 May 1921 he married one of his secretaries, Ethel Violet King (1896/7–1933), daughter of Frederick King, financier. Their daughter Penelope was born on 30 May 1923.

The last decade of Wallace's life was undoubtedly his most prolific. Represented by the literary agent A. S. Watt, he stopped selling his books outright for relatively small fixed sums and in 1921 signed a contract with the publishers Hodder and Stoughton, which for the first time provided him with generous advances and a sliding scale of royalties. Hodder and Stoughton concentrated on promoting a handful of celebrity authors, selling large print runs through aggressive marketing campaigns. Wallace was crowned the 'King of Thrillers' and dust jackets and posters carried the slogan 'It is impossible not to be thrilled by Edgar Wallace'. Each book was adorned with a distinctive trademark: a crimson circle (based on Wallace's first Hodder and Stoughton title) embossed with the author's signature. His output was extraordinary. He could work on three different stories at once, switching from one to the other, and could polish off a 70,000-word novel in three days. It has been estimated that by 1928 one in four of all the books printed and sold in England, apart from the Bible, was written by him.

Wallace perfected the modern thriller. Exploiting the crisp demotic style pioneered by the *Daily Mail*, he wrote sensational, fast-paced suspense stories in which anything could happen, no matter how improbable: a shop girl might awaken from a drugged sleep to learn that she is really a millionaire's daughter (*Green Rust*, 1919), or a criminal genius might use an army of tramps to hold the country to ransom (*The Fellowship of the Frog*, 1925). But Wallace was the master of many genres. His books ranged from low-life comedies, to science fiction, to imperial romance, and his non-fiction included a ten-volume history of the First World War. In May 1926 he had his first West End theatrical success with *The Ringer*, starring Gerald Du Maurier, and over the next six years a further seventeen of his plays were staged. His stories were also eagerly sought by the film industry, and in 1927 he was invited to serve as chairman of the new British Lion Film Corporation, for whom he directed several of his own productions.

During these years Wallace was an ostentatiously public figure who enjoyed living in the grand style: he was a box holder at Ascot, owned a stable of lacklustre racehorses, ran a flamboyant yellow Rolls Royce, and lost vast sums on the turf. In 1923 he was elected chairman of the Press Club, where he inaugurated a fund for impoverished journalists in 1928. Yet his popularity had its limits: an ill-judged foray into politics ended in humiliating defeat when he stood as the Liberal candidate for Blackpool in the 1931 general election, losing by over 33,000 votes. The following November Wallace accepted a job in the United States as a scriptwriter with RKO Studios in Hollywood, where he died suddenly from diabetes and double pneumonia at North Maple Drive, Beverly Hills, California, on 10 February 1932 while working on the film subsequently released as *King Kong* (1933). He was buried close to his country home, Chalklands, Bourne End, Buckinghamshire. Although he left behind massive debts, the enormous demand for his work produced enough royalties to permit settlement of his estate in full just two years later.

Wallace's daughter Penelope (1923–1997) married George Halcrow in 1955, and ran what became the Edgar Wallace industry from their north Oxford home. She managed her father's literary estate from 1960, founded the internationally subscribed Edgar Wallace Society, edited the *Edgar Wallace Mystery Magazine*, and lectured on her father's life.

DAVID GLOVER

Sources M. Lane, *Edgar Wallace: the biography of a phenomenon*, rev. 2nd edn (1964) · J. R. Cox, 'Edgar Wallace', *British mystery writers, 1860–1919*, ed. B. Benstock and T. F. Staley, DLitB, 70 (1988) · J. Attenborough, *A living memory: Hodder & Stoughton publishers, 1868–1975* (1975) · E. Wallace, *People: a short autobiography* (1926) · E. Wallace, *My Hollywood diary* (1932) · E. V. Wallace, *Edgar Wallace by his wife* (1932) · R. Curtis, *Edgar Wallace: each way* (1932) · W. O. G. Lofts and D. Adley, *The British bibliography of Edgar Wallace* (1969) · J. E. Nolan, 'Edgar Wallace', *Films in Review*, 18 (1967), 71–85 · b. cert. · m. cert.
Archives BL, letters · Bodl. Oxf., letters · Mitchell L., Glas., letters · New York University, letters · NRA, corresp. and literary papers · U. Leeds, letters · U. Reading, letters · U. Sussex, letters · Wellcome L., letters | BL, corresp. with Society of Authors, Add. MS 56840 | FILM BFI NFTVA, news footage | SOUND BL NSA, performance recording
Likenesses H. Coster, photographs, 1930, NPG [*see illus.*] · E. Kapp, four drawings, 1931–40, U. Birm. · T. Cole, oils, Press Club, London · J. Davidson, bust · R. S. Sherrifs, ink caricature, NPG · cigarette card, NPG · relief portrait on bronze plaque, Ludgate Circus, London
Wealth at death £18,335 5s. 0d.: probate, 5 May 1932, CGPLA Eng. & Wales

Wallace [*née* Maxwell], **Eglantine**, styled Lady Wallace (*d.* 1803), writer, was the youngest daughter of Sir William Maxwell, third baronet (*d.* 1771), of Monreith, Wigtownshire, and his wife, Magdalene Blair. Her sister was Jane *Gordon, duchess of Gordon (1748/9–1812). A boisterous hoyden in her youth, and a woman of violent temper in her maturer years, Eglantine Maxwell was married on 4 September 1770 to Thomas Dunlop, son of John Dunlop of Dunlop, and Frances Anna, daughter and heir of Sir Thomas Wallace, fourth and last baronet (1702–1770), of Craigie. On his grandfather's death Dunlop inherited Craigie, took the name of Wallace, and assumed the style of fifth baronet; but the property was deeply indebted, and in 1783 he was obliged to sell all that remained of Craigie. His wife obtained a legal separation in 1778, on the ground, it is said, of her husband's cruelty, but the quarrel may have been due to pecuniary embarrassment.

Lady Wallace was herself a little later summoned for assaulting a woman—apparently a humble companion—and was directed by the magistrate to compound the matter. She left Edinburgh, and seems to have settled in London, but when her play *The Whim: a Comedy* (1795) was banned from the stage by the licenser, she left England in disgust. In October 1789 she was arrested at Paris as a British agent, and narrowly escaped with her life. In 1792 she was in Brussels. There she contracted a friendship with General Charles François Dumouriez, whom in 1793 she entertained in London, where she seems to have been well received in society.

Lady Wallace was author of *Letter to a Friend, with a Poem called The Ghost of Werter* (1787), *Diamond Cut Diamond: a Comedy* (from the French, 1787), and *The Ton: a Comedy* (1788), which was produced at Covent Garden on 8 April 1788 with a good cast, but was a failure. Other works include *The Conduct of the King of Prussia and General Dumouriez* (1793) and *An Address to the People on Peace and Reform* (1798).

Lady Wallace died at Munich on 28 March 1803, leaving two sons, the elder of whom was General Sir John Alexander Dunlop Agnew *Wallace (1774/5–1857).

J. K. LAUGHTON, rev. REBECCA MILLS

Sources Blain, Clements & Grundy, *Feminist comp.* · J. Todd, ed., *A dictionary of British and American women writers, 1660–1800* (1985), 314–15 · D. E. Baker, *Biographia dramatica, or, A companion to the playhouse*, rev. I. Reed, new edn, rev. S. Jones, 1/2 (1812), 733 · C. Rogers, *The Book of Wallace*, Grampian Club, 1 (1889), 87–8 · *GM*, 1st ser., 73 (1803), 386 · Watt, *Bibl. Brit.*, vol. 2 · IGI · GEC, *Baronetage*, 4.278
Archives NA Scot., letters to H. Dundas

Wallace, George (1730–1805). *See under* Wallace, Robert (1697–1771).

Wallace [*née* Stein], **Grace Jane**, Lady Wallace (1804–1878), translator, was born on 20 February 1804, the eldest daughter of John Stein of Carron Mills, Edinburgh (1769–1814), distiller and MP, and Grace Bushby, daughter of John Bushby of Tinwald Downs, Dumfries. Her father was the sixth in descent from John Stein Craig, of Alloa. He was returned to parliament on 31 May 1796 for Bletchingley as a paying guest of Sir Robert Clayton, but he did not seek re-election in 1802. There is no information about Grace Jane's early education, which might have been carried out at home.

On 18 July 1824 Grace Jane Stein married Sir Alexander Don, sixth baronet (c.1779–1826), of Newton Don, Berwickshire, widower of Lucretia Montgomerie (d. 1817), and MP for Roxburghshire (from 25 July 1814 to 11 March 1826). Don had been detained in Verdun after the resumption of war with France and was freed only after seventeen years. He was a good friend of Sir Walter Scott who remarked that 'he possessed strong natural parts, and in particular few men could speak better in public when he chose' (*Journal*, 125). In fact Don was not a regular attender in parliament: on 5 March 1816 he gave a speech supporting his contributors' petition against the property tax and on 10 June 1819 he voted for the Foreign Enlistment Bill. Grace had two children with him: Sir William Henry *Don

(1825–1862), the celebrated actor, and Alexina Harriet Elizabeth (c.1826–1919), who married in 1844 Sir Frederick Acclom Milbank esquire. Sir Walter Scott wrote about Grace Jane in a letter to his son in 1825 'Mamma and Anne are quite well. They are with me on a visit to Sir Alexr. Don and his new Lady, who is a very pleasant woman and plays on the harp delightfully' (*Letters*, 9.228). Sir Alexander died in 1826.

On 2 April 1836 Grace Jane Don married Sir James Maxwell Wallace (1783–1867), fifth son of John Wallace of Kelly. Sir James entered the army in 1805, was promoted captain in 1807, served in the campaign of 1815, and took part in the battle of Waterloo. In September 1823 he was appointed lieutenant-colonel and in 1831 he received the honour of the knighthood. He was then promoted colonel (1838), major-general (1851), general (1863), and colonel of the 17th lancers (1864). Sir James and Lady Wallace had no children.

Grace Jane Wallace started her career as a translator in the latter years of her second marriage. She worked on German children's books and works of folkloric and historical interest. She translated some of Friedrich Wilhelm rittern von Hackländer's widely popular works, publishing *Katherine and the Moment of Fortune* (1857), *The Old Monastery* (1857), and *Clara, or, Slave-Life in Europe* (1855), and also took an interest in the works of contemporary women writers, such as Marie Petersen (1816–1859), Wilhelmine von Hillern (1836–1916), Cecilia Böhl de Faber, known as Fernán Caballero (1796–1877), and Elise Polko (1823–1899). She caught the attention of the publishers Longman with her preface to the translation of Schiller's *Life and Works* (1860) by Emil Palleske (1823–1880), one of the few critical statements left by her, and one which reveals her reading of Carlyle's 'fine tribute to Schiller' (*The Life of Schiller*, xi). For Longmans she translated the lives and letters of contemporary musicians, publishing the *Letters of Felix Mendelssohn Bartholdy from 1833 to 1847*, edited by Paul Mendelssohn Bartholdy and Dr Carl Mendelssohn Bartholdy (1863); Mendelssohn's *Letters from Italy and Switzerland* (1862); *Beethoven's Letters* (1790–1826) *from the Collection of Dr Ludwig Nohl* (1866); and *The Letters of Wolfgang Amadeus Mozart* (1769–1791), edited by Nohl (1865). These works were widely reviewed and remained the standard English translations until Emily Anderson's new editions for Macmillan. The *Edinburgh Review*, however, criticized Lady Wallace's translation of Mozart's letters for 'the perpetual repetition of the foolish expression "our maestro"' and for 'the musical blunders' (*EdinR*, 150, Oct 1879, 358) in translating German musical terminology. Her translation of Mendelssohn's letters was largely commended for its prose. Her last work was the translation of the *Memoirs of the Empress Alexandra Feodorowna Empress of Russia* by August Theodor von Grimm (1870). Evidence to corroborate Charles Rogers's statement that Grace Jane Wallace was also a composer has not been found. Grace Jane Wallace died on 12 March 1878 at Isaberdour, Fife, Scotland.

ANTONELLA BRAIDA

Sources *Members of parliament: return to two orders of the honorable the House of Commons*, House of Commons, 2 (1878), 207 · R. G.

Thorne, 'Don, Alexander', HoP, *Commons, 1790–1820* • B. Murphy and R. G. Thorne, 'Stein, John', HoP, *Commons, 1790–1820* • C. Rogers, *The Book of Wallace*, Grampian Club, 2 (1889), 110–12 • E. Lodge, *The peerage and baronetage of the British empire*, 29th edn (1860) • NL Scot., MSS 4144, fol. 66; 4254, fols. 69–71; 15953, fol. 126 • NA Scot., ref. 401; 465/7; 685 1/63 • *The journal of Sir Walter Scott*, ed. W. E. K. Anderson (1972) • *The letters of Sir Walter Scott*, ed. H. J. C. Grierson and others, centenary edn, 12 vols. (1932–79) • Allibone, *Dict.* • Grove, *Dict. mus.* (1927) • *EdinR*, 138 (1873), 366–94 • *EdinR*, 150 (1879), 339–66 • bap. reg. Scot. • *IGI* • d. cert.

Archives U. Reading L., letters to George Bell & Sons

Wallace, James (*d.* 1678), army officer, was the only son of Matthew Wallace (*d. c.*1641), laird of Dundonald in Ayrshire, and his wife, Agnes Somervell. In 1629 James Wallace married Jean Hay, daughter of the late John Hay of Renfield, minister at Renfrew; she died before 5 March 1638. In that year James Wallace's father sold the estate of Dundonald to Sir William Cochrane; even after the sale James was still sometimes called Wallace of Auchans after an important part of the Dundonald estate.

In 1642 Wallace went to Ireland as a captain in Major-General Robert Munro's regiment. In April 1644 he was one of the petitioners of the Ulster army to the Scottish estates for arrears of pay and supplies. In 1645 he was recalled with 200 men of the regiment as part of Home's commanded foot to oppose the progress of Montrose. He joined the covenanters under General Baillie and was taken prisoner at the battle of Kilsyth.

Wallace returned to Ireland before 1647. In November 1648 the Scottish committee of estates sent Wallace, now a major, to Ulster to recruit anti-engager troops for the Scottish army. On 30 March 1649 he was noted as being an officer in one of Monck's Ulster regiments along with the crypto-royalist Lord Montgomery of Ards. About the same time he was appointed governor of Belfast, but he was deprived of this position in June. Soon afterwards he removed to Kedhall, Ballycarry, near Carrickfergus, where he married in 1649 or 1650 a daughter of Mr Edmonstone of Ballycarry. On 10 August 1649 the estates gave him the lieutenant-colonelcy of the Irish foot, which was recruited from the anti-royalist refugees of the Ulster civil war of March–July. In May 1650 Wallace acted as warden of Montrose during the latter's imprisonment before his execution in Edinburgh. Following Charles II's return to Scotland, Wallace's regiment (commanded by Archibald, Lord Lorne), owing to its fierce loyalty to the kirk party regime, was named His Majesty's life guard of foot. Wallace served with it during Lieutenant-General David Leslie's successful defence of Edinburgh. At the battle of Dunbar, Wallace was again made prisoner. On his colonel's petition, as a reward for his services, he was referred to the committee of estates for him to be assigned part of the 'excise or maintenance' due from Ayrshire.

After the Restoration Wallace seems initially to have lived in retirement. However, he may have been connected with the plans for a general rising in Ireland, the Dublin Plot of 1663. In September 1665 he was named as one of those leading dissidents ordered to be rounded up by the Scottish authorities, but he escaped to Ireland and took refuge with his wife's kin near Carrickfergus. By the

autumn of 1666 he was back in Edinburgh, part of a committee almost certainly planning a general rising which was in contact with the dissidents of Galloway. When the Pentland rising flared up independently of such schemes Wallace was one of those resolute that it 'was our duty to own our brethren in Galloway, yea, and to go with them, and take share with them in what should be their lot' (Wallace, 389). On 18 November, a few days after the rising had sparked off, he set off to join them, and on 21 November he took command at the bridge of Doon, and led them in their march on Edinburgh. One of his earliest prisoners was Sir James Turner, who had been his companion in arms twenty-three years before. During his captivity Turner was constantly with Wallace, of whose character and rebellion he gives a detailed account in his *Memoir* (1829). On 28 November Wallace's forces and the king's, under the command of his former comrade in Munro's foot, General Tam Dalzell of the Binns, met at Rullion Green, 7 miles from Edinburgh. Wallace and his heavily outnumbered force of 600–700 foot and 800 horse were defeated at the ensuing, hard-fought battle. With his followers, he fled. He escaped to the Netherlands where he took the name of Forbes and wrote 'A narrative of the rising at Pentland'. He was condemned and forfaulted on 15 August 1667 by the justice court at Edinburgh, and this sentence was ratified by parliament on 15 December 1669. At the time of the assassination of Archbishop Sharp in July 1668 he was thought to have been in hiding in Edinburgh and then escaped to Ireland.

In exile Wallace was obliged to move from place to place for several years to avoid his enemies, who were on the look-out for him. He afterwards lived at Rotterdam, where he became an elder of the Scottish church; but on the complaint of Henry Wilkie, whom the king had placed at the head of the Scottish factory at Kamperveen, Wallace was ordered to return from Zealand. Wallace, however, went back to the Netherlands some time afterwards, and died at Rotterdam at the end of 1678. He left one son, who succeeded to his father's property because the sentence of death and fugitation passed against him after the Pentland rising was rescinded at the revolution of 1688.

George Stronach, *rev.* Edward M. Furgol

Sources D. Stevenson, *Scottish covenanters and Irish confederates* (1981) • J. Turner, *Memoirs of his own life and times, 1632–1670*, ed. T. Thomson, Bannatyne Club, 28 (1829) • J. Spalding, *Memorialls of the trubles in Scotland and in England, AD 1624 – AD 1645*, ed. J. Stuart, 2 vols., Spalding Club, [21, 23] (1850–51) • P. Adair, *A true narrative of the rise and progress of the Presbyterian church in Ireland (1623–1670)*, ed. W. D. Killen (1866) • M. Napier, ed., *Memorials of Montrose and his times*, 2 vols., Maitland Club, 66 (1848–50) • *Report on the manuscripts of the late Reginald Rawdon Hastings*, 4 vols., HMC, 78 (1928–47) • *The diary of Mr John Lamont of Newton, 1649–1671*, ed. G. R. Kinloch, Maitland Club, 7 (1830) • R. Wodrow, *The history of the sufferings of the Church of Scotland from the Restoration to the revolution*, ed. R. Burns, 4 vols. (1828–30) • Chambers, *Scots.* (1855) • W. Steven, *The history of the Scottish church, Rotterdam* (1832, 1833) • Lord Strathallan [W. Drummond], *History of the house of Drummond* (1889) • J. Wallace, 'Narrative of the rising at Pentland', *Memoirs of Mr. William Veitch, and George Brysson*, ed. T. M'Crie (1825), 388–432 • E. M. Furgol, *A regimental history of the covenanting armies, 1639–1651* (1990) • G. Wishart, *The memoirs of James, marquis of Montrose, 1639–1650*, ed. and trans. A. D. Murdoch and H. F. M. Simpson (1893) · R. L. Greaves, *Enemies under his feet: radicals and nonconformists in Britain, 1664–1677* (1990) · J. Buckroyd, *Church and state in Scotland, 1660–1681* (1980) · private information (2004) · J. M. Thomson and others, eds., *Registrum magni sigilli regum Scotorum / The register of the great seal of Scotland*, 11 vols. (1882–1914), vol. 8, pp. 652–3; vol. 9, pp. 289–90

Wallace, James (1642–1688), Church of Scotland minister and writer on Orkney, was born in Banffshire of unknown parentage. He entered King's College, Aberdeen, in 1655 and graduated MA in 1659, thereafter becoming schoolmaster at Fortrose. He was appointed minister of Ladykirk in 1668, then responded to an appeal for ministers to go to Orkney, where he was admitted minister at Kirkwall in November 1672. In October 1678 he was collated to the prebend of St John in the cathedral church of St Magnus-the-Martyr at Kirkwall. His marriage to Elizabeth Cuthbert (*d.* 1685), probably of the Inverness family of that name, brought them three sons, Andrew (*b.* 1675), Alexander (who died young), and James *Wallace (*b.* 1684), and a daughter, Jean, who also died young. Wallace was known as 'a man of great industry and scholarship' (*Fasti Scot.*, 222), with a thorough grounding in philosophy, theology, history, and mathematics. He owned a house in Albert Street, Kirkwall, distinguished with the words 'Welcome, welcome' and a double heart above the entrance.

When Sir Robert Sibbald (1641–1722), the king's geographer for Scotland, advertised in 1682 for contributions to his projected description of the kingdom Wallace was one of those who sent him materials; he became a prolific correspondent and also provided Sibbald with information on Shetland. Wallace left in manuscript various sermons and other religious pieces, a complete history of the Orkney islands, and the work for which he is known, *A Description of the Isles of Orkney*, which his son James issued in 1693, dedicating it to Sibbald and including Sibbald's 'An Essay Concerning the Thule of the Ancients'. A second edition of 1700, purporting to be the work of the younger Wallace and dedicated to the earl of Dorset, cut some of the earlier text but added a section on the plants and shells of Orkney. The original version, edited by John Small, was reprinted in 1883.

In the closing months of his life, and in consequence of the revolution of 1688–9, Wallace was deprived by the council of his preferments. He died of a fever on 18 September 1688, 'in the flower of his age, to the regrate of all that knew him' (Craven, preface). He gave a large number of books to the town, together with 100 merks, with which two communion cups were bought and inscribed with his name. ANITA McCONNELL

Sources J. Small, preface, in J. Wallace, *A description of the Isles of Orkney* (1883) · J. B. Craven, *A history of the episcopalian church in Orkney* (1883), 18–19 · *Fasti Scot.*, new edn, 7.222–3 · *N&Q*, 2nd ser., 5 (1858), 89–90; 6 (1858), 533–4
Archives NL Scot., account of the ancient and present state of Orkney

Wallace, James (*b.* 1684), botanist and writer, was the eldest son of the four children of James *Wallace (*d.* 1688),

minister of Kirkwall, Orkney, and his wife, Elizabeth Cuthbert (*d.* 1685). He gained the degree of MD—probably from Edinburgh University as his father held a great admiration for Sir Robert Sibbald, who taught medicine there. His father died in September 1688 leaving his book *A Description of the Isles of Orkney* unpublished, and Wallace brought it out in Edinburgh in 1693, later adding to it a chapter on the shells and plants of the islands. This edition was dedicated to Sir Robert Sibbald, who is thought to have contributed an essay entitled 'The Thule of the ancients'. In 1700 Wallace brought out a new edition of the book dedicated to the ninth earl of Dorset—a man of some learning—but without making it clear that he was not himself the author.

Wallace took part in the first voyage of the Darien scheme, the attempt by 'the Company of Scotland trading to Africa and the Indies', the Scottish rival to the East India Company, to found a colony in the isthmus of Panama. He sailed in the *Endeavour*, which left Leith on 19 July 1698. The diary that he kept on the journey, now in the possession of the Royal Society of London, is the only source of information for the first six weeks of the expedition, to Madeira. In Darien he was impressed by the range of animal and vegetable life, particularly by what he described as 'the legion of monstrous plants' (Wallace, 'Journal'), from which he collected some samples. He also noted species similar to those of Europe. The limited amount of shipping space meant that he could not bring back to Britain any large species, but he collected some leaves and ferns. Following the *Endeavour*'s sinking he returned to Scotland in December 1699 with the other survivors of the expedition in the company's remaining ship, the *Caledonia*. Wallace gave some botanic specimens to James Petiver, the demonstrator at Chelsea Physic Garden, and three of these found their way into the Sloane herbarium, the great reference collection in London. Wallace was made a fellow of the Royal Society. He had connections in London, and is said to have been in the employment of the East India Company.

In 1724 Wallace published in Dublin *The History of the Kingdom of Scotland from Fergus the First King to the Union*, taking kingship back to 330 BC. The work is mostly derivative, following a line of descent from the imaginary early kings listed by Hector Boece and accepted by George Buchanan. Wallace diverged from Buchanan's hostility to Mary, queen of Scots, because of a strong belief in monarchy: 'kings derive their power from God alone', he asserted (Wallace, *The History of the Kingdom of Scotland*, introduction). His mastery of history, even when he was not misled by Boece, was not great; there appears to be some confusion between the covenant and the solemn league and covenant. He went beyond the nominal limiting date of his work by including an 'impartial' account of the Jacobite rising of 1715, which he presented as a letter from some Scottish gentleman to a friend in New England. He was scornful of the military performance of both sides at Sheriffmuir, claiming that the encounter should not be referred to as a battle. His concern in the rising as a whole is with the various members of the aristocracy who participated in it. Nothing is known of Wallace after the publication of the *History*.   ROSALIND MITCHISON

Sources J. Wallace, *A description of the Isles of Orkney* (1693); rev. edn (1700) · J. Wallace, *The history of the kingdom of Scotland*, new edn (1724) · J. Wallace, 'Part of a journal kept from Scotland to New Caledonia in Darien', *PTRS*, 22 (1700–01), 536–43 · G. P. Insh, *The Company of Scotland trading to Africa and the Indies* (1932) · G. P. Insh, *Papers relating to the ships and voyages of the Company of Scotland* (1924) · *Fasti Scot.*, new edn, 7.227 · M. Spence, *Flora Orcadiensis* (1914) · Desmond, *Botanists* · W. Nicolson, *Scottish historical library* (1702) · J. Britten and J. E. Dandy, eds., *The Sloane herbarium* (1958) · J. Britten and G. S. Boulger, eds., *A biographical index of deceased British and Irish botanists*, 2nd edn, ed. A. B. Rendle (1931) · *N&Q*, 2nd ser., 6 (1858), 533–4
Archives RS, journal

Wallace, James (*bap.* 1729, *d.* 1783), lawyer and politician, was born at Brampton, Cumberland, and baptized on 12 March 1729. He was the eldest son of Thomas Wallace (1697–1728) of Asholme, Northumberland, attorney, and his wife, Dulcebella Sowerbye (*b.* 1705). According to William Hutchinson in his *History of the County of Cumberland*, the family claimed a distinguished Scottish descent and included among its ancestry the celebrated patriot William Wallace. Hutchinson also relates that James Wallace had a 'common school education' at Thornton, Yorkshire. His family was not wealthy, and Wallace had to rely on ability and diligence to pursue his chosen career in the law. He was admitted to Lincoln's Inn on 22 November 1754 and to the Middle Temple on 2 January 1755. He was called to the bar at Middle Temple on 8 June 1761, becoming a bencher in 1769 and reader in 1778. He became a KC in 1769. On 8 January 1767 he married Elizabeth Simpson (*d.* 1811), daughter of Thomas Simpson of Carleton Hall, Cumberland; they had a son and a daughter.

Crucial to Wallace's entry into politics was his close friendship with Alexander Wedderburn. In April 1770 he was returned on the interest of Henry Ingram, Viscount Irwin, as member of parliament for Horsham, a burgage borough of some eighty voters, which he represented for the remainder of his life, and where he never had to face a contested election. In the same year he declined an offer of appointment as a judge of the court of king's bench. In the House of Commons he generally supported the administration of Lord North, although his Cumberland connections led him to assist a leading opposition peer, the duke of Portland, in a protracted land dispute with Sir James Lowther. North recognized his ability and loyalty in 1778, when Wallace became solicitor-general. It is clear that he was a more effective lawyer than parliamentarian, and on several occasions found himself in difficulties when defending the ministry's American policy. North described him and the attorney-general, James Mansfield, as 'sensible men, & good lawyers', but doubted whether 'we shall draw from them all the assistance we shall want' (Fortescue, 3.116–17). He was none the less promoted to be attorney-general in 1780, and early in March 1782 it fell to him to move for leave to introduce a bill 'to enable his Majesty to conclude a truce or peace with the revolted American colonies' (Wheatley, 2.210).

Wallace left office on the fall of North in March 1782, but remained loyal to his leader in opposition, opposing the second earl of Shelburne's peace preliminaries in February 1783. On the formation of the Fox–North coalition the following April he became attorney-general for the second time. By then, however, his health was failing and he was obliged to delegate some of his duties to the solicitor-general, John Lee. He wrote to Lee on 12 April from the Hotwells, Bristol, in the expectation of a complete recovery after 'a very strict diet & exercise & … the operations of bleeding & blistering' (John Lee MSS). In the autumn of 1783, however, a troublesome cough obliged him to seek relief, first at Margate and then in Devon, where he intended to remain until January 1784. But he died on 16 November 1783, and was buried in Exeter Cathedral.

Wraxall considered Wallace to be one of the most outstanding lawyers of his generation (Wheatley, 3.129). He moved in the circles of, and clearly charmed, Hester Thrale Piozzi (Balderston, 1.356, 467, 500). The respect in which he was held by the king is reflected in George III's description of him, immediately after his death, as 'the late worthy Attorney-General' (Fortescue, 4.468). In the professional, if not in the political, sense, he died at the very threshold of the highest rewards. He was not quite the self-made, rough-hewn, northern attorney in the mould of John Lee and John Scott, but his life none the less is an example of the career open to talents.

G. M. DITCHFIELD

Sources Burke, *Gen. GB* (1855) · *HoP, Commons, 1754–90* · W. Hutchinson, *The history of the county of Cumberland*, 1 (1794), 129 · A. Valentine, *The British establishment, 1760–1784: an eighteenth-century biographical dictionary*, 2 (1970), 898 · *The correspondence of King George the Third from 1760 to December 1783*, ed. J. Fortescue, 6 vols. (1927–8) · *The historical and the posthumous memoirs of Sir Nathaniel William Wraxall, 1772–1784*, ed. H. B. Wheatley, 5 vols. (1884) · *Thraliana: the diary of Mrs. Hester Lynch Thrale (later Mrs. Piozzi), 1776–1809*, ed. K. C. Balderston, 2nd edn, 2 vols. (1951) · *The correspondence of Edmund Burke*, ed. T. W. Copeland and others, 10 vols. (1958–78) · J. B. Williamson, ed., *The Middle Temple bench book*, 2nd edn, 1 (1937) · H. A. C. Sturgess, ed., *Register of admissions to the Honourable Society of the Middle Temple, from the fifteenth century to the year 1944*, 3 vols. (1949) · W. P. Baildon, ed., *The records of the Honorable Society of Lincoln's Inn: admissions*, 1 (1896) · *GM*, 1st ser., 53 (1783), 982 · *IGI* · J. Wallace, letter to J. Lee, 12 April 1783, U. Mich., Clements L., John Lee MSS
Archives BL, corresp. and opinions · BL, opinions on legal cases, Add. MSS 6709, 8935 | BL, Liverpool MSS, Add. MSS 38307, fols. 109, 145, 155; 38308, fol. 82; 38309, fol. 41 · U. Mich., Clements L., John Lee MSS
Likenesses G. Romney, portrait; in possession of executors for J. Hope-Wallace, at Featherstone Castle, Northumberland, 1804 · photograph (after G. Romney), NPG

Wallace, Sir James (1731–1803), naval officer, details of whose parents and upbringing are unknown, entered the navy as a scholar in the Royal Naval Academy at Portsmouth in 1746. He afterwards served in the *Syren*, *Vigilant*, and *Intrepid* and passed his lieutenant's examination on 3 January 1753, being described on his certificate as 'appearing to be 21' (PRO, ADM 107/4). On 11 March 1755 he was promoted lieutenant in the *Greenwich* under Captain Robert Roddam and was in her when she was captured off Cape François in the West Indies on 16 March 1757. In April 1758 he was appointed to the *Ripon* (60 guns, Captain

Edward Jekyl), one of the squadron under Sir John Moore at the reduction of Guadeloupe in April 1759. In January 1760 he was appointed to the *Neptune* (90 guns) when she went to the Mediterranean as flagship of Sir Charles Saunders. On 1 November 1762 he was promoted commander and in the following April he was appointed to the sloop *Trial* (14 guns) for the North American station. He later commanded the *Dolphin* (24 guns) in the East Indies and the *Bonetta* in the English Channel. On 10 January 1771 Wallace was promoted captain of the *Unicorn*, and in November 1771 he was appointed to the frigate *Rose* (20 guns) which he took to the North American station in 1774. In the course of 1775 and the first part of 1776 the *Rose* was actively engaged in operations designed to maintain a sense of insecurity among the rebels in the small towns and harbours along the coast. His activity attracted the attention of Rear-Admiral Shuldham who wrote to Philip Stephens at the Admiralty: 'Captain Wallace's services deserve every reward that can be conferred on him. I humbly recommend it to their Lordships' consideration sending him out a larger and better ship' (ibid., 1/484, fol. 378). Perhaps as a consequence he was given the *Experiment* (50 guns) in July 1776. In her, he was sent to England with dispatches in January 1777, a service for which he was knighted on 13 February.

In July Wallace returned to the North American station and to his earlier cruising activities. In July 1778 the *Experiment* became one of the small squadron which Vice-Admiral Richard Howe assembled for the defence of the channel past Sandy Hook against the fleet under d'Estaing. The *Experiment* continued with the squadron when Howe followed the French to Rhode Island, and took part in the manoeuvres on 10–11 August at the end of which, just as battle was to be joined, both fleets were scattered by a storm. The *Experiment* remained in the area and on 20 August was off Newport when the French were standing in towards it. On 23 August the *Experiment* was chased into Long Island Sound by three French line ships, thus becoming 'the first two decker that ever attempted that dangerous passage' (that is, Hell Gate, the East River connecting Long Island Sound and New York harbour) (Beatson, 4.354), and rejoined Howe at Sandy Hook on 25 August. In the following December, while cruising on the coast of Virginia, the *Experiment* was blown off the land in a violent westerly gale. Wallace, conscious that his ship would find it hard to get to New York in her distressed condition, and knowing that the dockyard could not supply the spars and rigging he needed, bore away to the east to be refitted in an English dockyard. When ready, Wallace joined the squadron which sailed from St Helens under Admiral Marriot Arbuthnot on 1 May 1779 and with him turned aside for the relief of Jersey, then threatened by a French force of five ships of the line under the prince of Nassau. Hearing that Nassau had been repulsed and that some frigates had been sent from Portsmouth, Arbuthnot pursued his voyage, leaving the *Experiment* to strengthen the force at Jersey. When Wallace was joined by Captain Gidoin, commanding the expected frigates, the two captains concerted an attack on the French squadron which

had gone towards the mainland and was endeavouring to reach St Malo. Wallace, now benefiting from the tide, drove them into Cancale Bay, following them in, despite the refusal of the pilot to navigate the channels. He then succeeded in silencing a six-gun battery under which they had sheltered, and burnt two of the frigates and a small cutter that were fast on shore. The third frigate, the *Danae* (34 guns), and two smaller vessels were brought off and sent to England.

Wallace then rejoined Arbuthnot, who had been forced by foul winds to wait in Torbay, and sailed with him for New York. In September 1779 he was sent to the southward with a considerable sum of money for the payment of the troops in Georgia. On 24 September he fell in with a detachment of d'Estaing's fleet, and was captured after a spirited resistance. In the action Wallace lost his secret signal books to the enemy, making it necessary for Arbuthnot to issue a new set to the fleet. Wallace was exonerated at the court martial he faced on the loss of his ship and was given command of the *Nonsuch* (64 guns) in March 1780, a position he fulfilled '*dress'd or rather undress'd* in a white Jacket, Night cap and Flannel Trowsers' (NMM, JOD/23). In July, cruising off the coast of France, Wallace captured the corvette *Hussard*, followed soon afterwards by the famous frigate *Belle Poule*, commanded by Raymond-Marie Kergariou de Coatlès, the former captain of the *Danae*, who was killed in the engagement. In April 1781 the *Nonsuch* was with Admiral Darby's fleet at the relief of Gibraltar. Darby praised all the captains who 'had greatly exerted themselves in their attacks on the gunboats' which had threatened the relief (ADM 1/95). On the homeward voyage the *Nonsuch* was lookout vessel of the van squadron and chased and brought to action a French line-of-battle ship. According to Wallace the fight started at half past ten at night when he brought the *Nonsuch* alongside the Frenchman, exchanging broadsides and for a time being caught in her rigging. Wallace considered he had the best of the action when, about midnight, his opponent seized the chance to sail away. The *Nonsuch* continued to chase and the action was resumed at 5 a.m. and in the early light of dawn Wallace said she appeared to be an 80-gun ship and some 'who pretended to know say she is the *Languedoc*' (ADM 1/95, fol. 210). By half past six, with much damage and many casualties, Wallace thought it prudent to disengage and rejoined the fleet, the *Languedoc* pursuing her course to Brest. Darby ordered Wallace to make his own way back to Plymouth to send his sixty wounded men to hospital and to dock the *Nonsuch*.

In October Wallace was appointed to the *Warrior* (74 guns), which sailed for the West Indies in January 1782 with Sir George Rodney and took part in the battle of the Saints on 12 April 1782, sailing in Hood's rear division. He returned to England in 1783 and for the next seven years was on half pay. In the Spanish armament of 1790 he commanded the *Swiftsure* for a few months and, in 1793, the *Monarch*, in which he went to the West Indies, returning at the end of the year. On 12 April 1794 he was promoted rear-admiral of the white and appointed commander-in-chief at Newfoundland with his flag in the *Romney* (50 guns). He was further promoted rear-admiral of the red on 4 July 1794. The remainder of his squadron was composed of frigates and smaller vessels intended for the protection of trade from the enemy's privateers. Wallace was therefore unable to offer any serious resistance to a French squadron of seven ships of the line and three frigates commanded by Rear-Admiral Richery which came out to North America, having been freed from Cadiz (August 1796) by the Spanish declaration of war. The French were free to inflict considerable damage on the fishermen, plundering their huts, stages, and boats. Wallace was bitterly mortified; but the colonists and traders, realizing that he had done all that was possible under the circumstances, passed a vote of thanks to him. He returned to England early the next year and had no further service. He had been made a vice-admiral of the white on 1 June 1795, vice-admiral of the red on 14 February 1799, and finally admiral of the blue on 1 January 1801.

At the time of his death on 6 January 1803 Wallace was living at Hanworth in Middlesex (will, PRO, PROB 11/1389), but he died, according to James Ralfe, in Gloucester Place, Portman Square, London. He left to his wife, Anne, the estates which had come to her from her father, Sir James *Wright, a former governor of Georgia. After some other bequests Wallace left the remainder of his property and various moneys including prize money and arrears of pay equally to his wife and their daughter, Mary. The amount of his fortune is not clear from his will but it is evident that he died a wealthy man with estates in Middlesex and Huntingdon and cash bequests in excess of £20,000.

KENNETH BREEN

Sources DNB · lieutenant's passing certs., PRO, ADM 107/4 · dispatches of Shuldham, PRO, ADM 1/484 · dispatches of Arbuthnot, PRO, ADM 1/486 · dispatches of Howe, PRO, ADM 1/487-8 · dispatches of Darby, PRO, ADM 1/95 · dispatches of Rodney, PRO, ADM 1/314 · captain's log, *Experiment*, PRO, ADM 51/331 · will, PRO, PROB 11/1389 · D. Syrett and R. L. DiNardo, *The commissioned sea officers of the Royal Navy, 1660–1815*, rev. edn, Occasional Publications of the Navy RS, 1 (1994) · R. Beatson, *Naval and military memoirs of Great Britain*, 2nd edn, 6 vols. (1804) · GM, 1st ser., 73 (1803), 270 · W. James, *The naval history of Great Britain, from the declaration of war by France, in February 1793, to the accession of George IV in January 1820*, 5 vols. (1822–4) · J. Ralfe, *The naval biography of Great Britain*, 4 vols. (1828)

Wealth at death over £20,000—in bequests, and estates in Middlesex and Huntingdon: will, PRO, PROB 11/1389

Wallace, John Alexander Dunlop Agnew [styled Sir John Wallace, sixth baronet] (**1774/5–1857**), army officer, was the only son of Thomas Dunlop Wallace (d. 1835), of Craigie, Ayrshire, who assumed the style of fifth baronet, and his first wife, Eglantine (d. 1803), known as Lady *Wallace, youngest daughter of Sir William Maxwell, third baronet (d. 1771), of Montreith, Wigtownshire.

Wallace was given a commission as ensign in the 75th (Highland) regiment on 28 December 1787, his family having helped to raise it. He joined it in India in 1789, became lieutenant on 6 April 1790, and served in Cornwallis's operations against Tipu in 1791–2, including the siege of Seringapatam. He acted as aide-de-camp to Colonel Maxwell, who commanded the left wing of the army. He obtained a company in the 58th regiment on 8 June 1796, and returned to England to join it. He went with it to the Mediterranean in 1798, and was present at the capture of Minorca, and in the 1801 campaign in Egypt. It formed part of the reserve under Moore, and was hotly engaged in the battle of Alexandria. It came home in 1802. He was promoted major on 9 July 1803, and became a lieutenant-colonel in the 11th foot on 28 August 1804. At the end of 1805 he was transferred to the 88th (Connaught Rangers) to command a newly raised 2nd battalion.

Wallace went to the Peninsula with this battalion in 1809. With 300 men from it he joined the 1st battalion at Campo Mayor, while the rest went on to Cadiz. The 1st battalion had suffered in the Talavera campaign; he set himself vigorously to restore it, and made it one of the finest in the army. It greatly distinguished itself at Busaco. It was on the left of the 3rd division, and when the French had gained the ridge, and seemed to have cut the army in two, a charge made by the 88th, with one wing of the 45th, drove them down headlong. Wellington, riding up, said, 'Wallace, I never saw a more gallant charge than that just made by your regiment.' Picton gave Wallace the credit for 'that brilliant exploit'.

Wallace commanded the 88th at Fuentes de Oñoro, and was again particularly mentioned in Wellington's dispatch. He was also mentioned in the dispatch after Salamanca, where he was in command of the right brigade of the 3rd division (Pakenham's). During the retreat of the army from Burgos, he had a very severe attack of fever at Madrid. Conveyance in a cart to Santarem in very bad weather aggravated its effects, and he was dangerously ill for nearly eight months. He had no further service in the Peninsula; but he commanded a brigade in the army of occupation in France in the latter part of 1815. He received the gold medal with two clasps, and was made CB in 1815.

Wallace became colonel in the army on 4 June 1813, and on 12 August 1819 major-general. He was made colonel of the 88th on 20 October 1831, and a KCB on 16 September 1833. On the death of his father in 1835, he called himself sixth baronet. He became lieutenant-general on 10 August 1837, and general on 11 November 1851.

On 23 June 1829 Wallace married Janette (d. 1862), daughter of William Rodger, and they had five sons and one daughter. He died at Lochryan House, Stranraer, Wigtownshire, on 10 February 1857, aged eighty-two.

E. M. LLOYD, rev. ROGER T. STEARN

Sources GM, 3rd ser., 2 (1857), 497 · R. Cannon, ed., *Historical record of the eighty-eighth regiment of foot, or Connaught rangers* (1838) · *The dispatches of … the duke of Wellington … from 1799 to 1818*, ed. J. Gurwood, 13 vols. in 12 (1834–9) · H. B. Robinson, *Memoirs of Lieutenant-General Sir Thomas Picton*, 1 (1836) · W. F. P. Napier, *History of the war in the Peninsula and in the south of France*, rev. edn, 4 (1851) · Boase, *Mod. Eng. biog.* · GEC, *Baronetage*, 4.278

Wallace, Lewis Alexander (1821–1906). *See under* Wallace family (*per.* 1841–1925).

Wallace, Nellie [*real name* Eleanor Jane Wallace; *married name* Eleanor Jane Liddy] (**1870–1948**), music-hall entertainer, was born in Glasgow on 18 March 1870 to parents

Nellie Wallace (1870–1948), by Sir Cecil Beaton

who both worked in the music-hall: her father gave 'lectures', and her mother played the piano. By the age of twelve she had made her own début as a clog dancer at the Steam Clock Music-Hall, Birmingham, and she subsequently worked solo as La Petite Nellie, and as one of the Three Sisters Wallace in pantomime and in music-hall. About 1892 she married actor and manager William J. Liddy and attempted to establish a career in the legitimate theatre for herself; she found, however, that as the doomed Little Willie in Alfred Kempe's version of *East Lynne* she tended to elicit laughter rather than tears, and she liked to claim that she abandoned her acting career after being sneezed off her horse while playing Joan of Arc. In 1894 Nellie Wallace returned to pantomime as second girl and understudy to the star, Ada Reeve, in *Jack and Jill* at the Comedy Theatre, Manchester, where the cast included the young George Robey. On 9 March 1895 Reeve left the show to have a child, and Wallace took over as principal girl. Her music-hall career blossomed, and her appearance at the London Palladium in 1910 confirmed the success of the image she had established, as the 'essence of eccentricity'. While there were other performers who adopted the old-maid persona expressed in songs such as 'Blasted Oak' and 'I've been jilted by the baker, Mister White', Wallace gave it a new dimension. Along with 'the wife's mother', the old maid was a staple topic for jokes that represented woman as a threat while continuing to endorse a conservative ideology of the family. Wallace, however, completely eschewed the predatory aspect of the persona: when she narrated her search for a man ('Crossed in love?', asked her stooge. 'No', she replied,

'I've been run over'), the effect was of a vitality so powerful that she would wear out an ordinary man in a couple of hours. At the same time she exempted members of the audience from her search. Rather than potential mates they became members of her own family, listening to the confidences of a much-loved spinster aunt, at a time when aunts were a vital part of the family unit, contributing both earnings and caring skills in households struggling to cope with recession and often deprived by war of their main breadwinners.

Wallace's stage spinsterhood liberated her into anarchy, what *The Times* called her 'saving touch of the devil' (25 Nov 1948). The true focus of her act was her enjoyment of her power as a performer. One of her songs had a chorus that ran 'It's excitement, all excitement—if you're after anything tasty, what price me?' As Wilson Disher commented, 'Just to be let loose on the stage gives her so much joy that she performs an *entrechat* in each corner' (Green, 287). She had a weird beauty, a face of aquiline elegance, marred only by buck teeth, which she transformed into a clownish mask with elaborately arched black brows. Her clothes were a parody of middle-class respectability, with elastic-sided boots, a sensible tartan skirt (that occasionally revealed enormous red flannel bloomers), and a moth-eaten fur tippet ('my little bit of vermin'). She sometimes varied it with an evening dress of impossible extravagance, its skirt so tight that her efforts to pick up a dropped fan involved outrageous contortions. Her songs were charged with energy, erupting into high-spirited yodelling and arguments with the orchestra; her sketches tipped the balance from the merely eccentric to the surreal: in one, which captivated the young Alec Guinness, she deconstructed one of the archetypal images of spinsterhood, the nurse assisting the noble (male) doctor:

> Nellie stood by looking very prim, but every now and then she would dive under the sheet and extract with glee and a shout of triumph quite impossible articles—a hot water bottle, a live chicken … Finally she inserted, with many wicked looks, a long rubber tube which she blew down. The body inflated rapidly to huge proportions and then, covered in its sheet, took slowly to the air.   (Guinness, 10)

With the decline of variety Wallace took to revue, notably in Albert de Courulles' *Whirl of the World*, which ran for 627 performances at the London Palladium in 1924, and in George Black's 'crazy' shows between 1931 and 1934. She was also associated with the comedian with whom she shared her pantomime début, George Robey: one of the few female pantomime dames, she replaced him as Dame Trot at the London Hippodrome in 1922, and in March 1925 she opened with him in the London Palladium revue *Sky High*, which ran for 309 performances.

During the Second World War Wallace toured with the Entertainments National Service Association, her surreal humour in tune with the popular radio comedies of the day. In February 1948 she began touring with Don Ross's company in *Thanks for the Memory*. The cast were invited to appear at that year's royal variety performance at the London Palladium on 1 November. Wallace sang 'A Boy's Best

Friend is his Mother', and then collapsed. She rallied to finish the show, but was admitted to hospital and died three weeks later at the Bethanie Nursing Home, 12 Hornsey Lane, Upper Holloway, London, on 24 November 1948. She had been a widow for many years, and her only daughter had died in March 1948. FRANCES GRAY

Sources R. Busby, *British music hall: an illustrated who's who from 1850 to the present day* (1976) · B. Green, ed., *The last empires: a music hall companion* (1986) · A. Guinness, *Blessings in disguise* (1985) · M. W. Disher, *Winkles and champagne: comedies and tragedies of the music hall* (1938) · M. Banks and A. Swift, *The joke's on us* (1987) · F. Gray, *Women and laughter* (1994) · *The Times* (25 Nov 1948) · d. cert. · J. Parker, ed., *Who's who in the theatre*, 6th edn (1930) · *CGPLA Eng. & Wales* (1949)
Likenesses C. Beaton, photograph, NPG [*see illus.*] · photograph, repro. in Banks and Swift, *The joke's on us*
Wealth at death £8439 8s. 11d.: probate, 18 Feb 1949, *CGPLA Eng. & Wales*

Wallace, Philip Adrian Hope- (1911–1979), music and theatre critic, was born in London on 6 November 1911, the only son (there were two elder sisters) of Charles Nugent Hope-Wallace MBE, charity commissioner, and his wife, Mabel, daughter of Colonel Allan Chaplin, Madras army, of Dorking. He grew up a tall boy but with a weak constitution, and after attending Charterhouse School he was sent to a sanatorium in Germany and then to lodge with a protestant pastor in Normandy. By the time he went up to Balliol College, Oxford, to read modern languages in 1930 he had already acquired a thorough grasp of French and German and a lifelong passion for Racine and Goethe. He graduated with third-class honours (1933) at the worst point of the depression and for a while found it impossible to obtain congenial employment, or indeed any at all. He worked briefly and disastrously (1933–4) for the International Broadcasting Company in France, at Fécamp radio station, and then (1935–6) as press officer for the Gas Light and Coke Company. In later life he claimed he had hawked appliances as a door-to-door salesman.

In 1935 Hope-Wallace got his first chance as a critic, covering song recitals for *The Times*. By the time war came he had established himself as a sensitive and exceptionally knowledgeable judge of theatre and music (especially opera), being sent to Zürich in 1938 for the world première of Paul Hindemith's *Mathis der Maler* and to Frankfurt for the drama festival. Ill health prevented active war service, and he spent six years in the Air Ministry press office. With peace he became, and remained to his death, one of the most prolific and influential arts critics in the West, first with the *Daily Telegraph* (1945–6) and with *Time and Tide* (1945–9), and then for a quarter-century (1946–71) on the arts staff of *The Guardian*. He was for many years the paper's chief drama critic, though for the last decade of his life he concentrated almost exclusively on opera. He was also a mainstay of *The Gramophone*, a member of the editorial board of *Opera*, and a frequent contributor to *The Listener*, the *New Statesman*, and other journals. For thirty-five years he broadcast with great success, especially on such key programmes as *The Critics* and *Music Magazine*. In 1958 he was president of the Critics' Circle, and in 1975 he was appointed CBE for services to the arts.

Hope-Wallace was the least assertive of men, but he had

Philip Adrian Hope-Wallace (1911–1979), by Howard Coster, 1955

an imperturbable confidence in his own artistic judgement and so remained serenely impervious to fashion. As a young critic he championed Handel and Verdi, then little regarded, and he always admired uncerebral but theatrical masters like Gounod, Massenet, and Bizet. In the theatre he appreciated a good Shavian argument but anything which smacked of dogma, ideology, or 'message' filled him with dismay; from the mid-1960s he quite lost sympathy with most contemporary playwrights. He was concerned, above all, with what actually happened on stage, and was perhaps the last great British critic to regard assessment of the performance as his chief function. He did not see the critic as a privileged high priest but as spokesman for the theatregoers. 'The best critic', he wrote, 'will be the epitome of the best part of any given audience, its head, heart and soul'. Hence, though mandarin in mind, he was democratic at heart, and in spirit always close to the ordinary London theatre and opera patron. Loving skilled performance, he enjoyed Chinese acrobats, Kabuki players, or the royal tournament almost as much as great actors and singers. He admitted he was easily moved to tears: by Emlyn Williams reading the death of Paul Dombey, for instance, or by Irina's line 'They are gone away' from *The Three Sisters*.

Hope-Wallace's sense of theatrical occasion, his intuitive sympathy with performers, and his vast experience and wonderful memory made him the outstanding judge, in his generation, of dramatic celebrities, especially women. He wrote with superb precision of such fine actresses as Edith Evans, Edwige Feuillère, Peggy Ashcroft, and Sybil Thorndike. But his greatest enthusiasm was for the diva: 'I love a soprano', he wrote, 'a loud soprano, even a lame one'. He treasured the personalities, follies, triumphs, and misadventures of the prima donna, and much of his best writing revolved around stars like Elisabeth Schwarzkopf, Birgit Nillson, Kirsten Flagstad, Maria Callas, and Joan Sutherland.

Hope-Wallace was close to Bloomsbury in its silver age, but he was essentially a journalist rather than a literary man. His only books were *A Key to Opera* (written in collaboration with Frank Howes), published in 1939, and *A Picture History of Opera* (1959), though a selection of his notices and essays, *Words and Music*, was published posthumously in 1981. He gently rejected the entreaties of his friends to write an autobiography.

For Hope-Wallace immediacy of impression was everything: many of his best notices were dictated straight to the copy-takers from a call box. He worshipped words but drew no hard distinction between their written and spoken forms. Indeed his real genius lay in conversation. For many years some of the best talk in London could be heard at his favourite table at El Vino's in Fleet Street. His noble head, his mellifluous voice, his thesaurus of anecdotes, and the shafts of wit, sharp but never cruel, which he played on the personalities of the day, attracted a gifted circle of writers, editors, lawyers, and public men, over which he presided with grace, generosity, and a quiet but unmistakable moral authority. To his younger admirers, who were legion, he epitomized the best characteristics of the pre-war generation: breadth of culture, fine breeding, flawless manners, and delightful urbanity. At the age of sixty-seven a visit to a health farm led to a fall and a broken hip, providing him with his last, ironic joke; he never left Guildford Hospital and died there on 3 September 1979. With his death, his circle broke up, and it contained, alas, no Boswell. He was unmarried.   PAUL JOHNSON, *rev.*

Sources personal knowledge (1986) · private information (1986) · *CGPLA Eng. & Wales* (1980) · *Daily Telegraph* (4 Sept 1979) · I. Elliott, ed., *The Balliol College register, 1900–1950*, 3rd edn (privately printed, Oxford, 1953)
Archives JRL, letters to *Manchester Guardian*
Likenesses H. Coster, photograph, 1955, NPG [*see illus.*]
Wealth at death £41,136: probate, 19 March 1980, *CGPLA Eng. & Wales*

Wallace [*formerly* Jackson], **Sir Richard**, baronet (1818–1890), philanthropist and art collector, was the illegitimate son of Richard Seymour-Conway, Viscount Beauchamp, later fourth marquess of Hertford (1800–1870). His mother, Mrs Agnes Jackson, *née* Wallace, was very probably Eliza Agnes Wallace (1789–1864), daughter of Sir Thomas Wallace of Craigie, who had married Samuel Bickley in 1808. Richard was born in London on 21 June 1818, when his father was just eighteen years old, and was given the surname Jackson. He spent his first six years in London with his mother who then took him to Paris, where she left him with his father and grandmother Maria Seymour-*Conway, marchioness of Hertford (1770/71–1856) [*see under* Conway, Francis Ingram-Seymour], and Lady Hertford's second, illegitimate, son, Lord Henry Seymour (1805–1859). Thereafter Richard led a privileged life in Paris. Since his father spent much time travelling before settling permanently in Paris, at 2 rue Laffitte, in 1835, Richard was brought up by his grandmother in the rue Taitbout with the eccentric Lord Henry as a companion. In April 1842, a month after his father's succession as fourth marquess of Hertford, Richard had himself baptized in the Anglican church, taking the surname Wallace (his mother's maiden name). He was

Sir Richard Wallace, baronet (1818–1890), by J. J. Thomson, 1888

already the father of a son, Edmond (1840–1887), with Amélie-Julie Charlotte Castelnau (1819–1897), the daughter of a French officer, Bernard Castelnau.

Lord Hertford now embarked on making his extraordinary collection of works of art. Wallace was employed as his secretary, with an annual allowance, and from at least 1843 as his saleroom agent. In 1854 and 1856 Lord Hertford settled Wallace's debts, sustained through speculation, but in 1857 he made Wallace settle further debts by selling a small collection of works of art he had made in his own name. Following the death of the dowager marchioness in 1856, Lord Hertford, who had always been misanthropic, further withdrew from society, and Wallace, as the well-mannered agent of one of the richest, but most reclusive, collectors in Europe, became a figure of interest. In October 1859 Sir Charles Eastlake, director of the National Gallery, met 'Lord Hertford's son "Monsieur Richard"' at a sale in Hanover and immediately recognized a rival 'against whom there is little chance of contending' (*Journals … of Lady Eastlake*, 2.134–5). This acknowledgement of Wallace's parentage, recorded in Lady Eastlake's *Journal*, is of interest, since Lord Hertford never publicly declared his paternity.

When Lord Hertford died at Bagatelle in August 1870, on the eve of the Prussian defeat of France at Sedan, Wallace unexpectedly succeeded to his father's collections and to his unentailed properties in Paris (2 rue Laffitte and the château of Bagatelle in the Bois-de-Boulogne), London (houses in Piccadilly, Berkeley Square, and Manchester

Square), and Ireland (the Lisburn estates). Having lived in his father's shadow all his life, he was now able to express his good nature through his inherited fortune. Among the many donations he made during the Prussian siege of Paris (from September 1870 to January 1871), he gave £12,000 towards the cost of a field ambulance (attached to the army corps in which his son was serving), he chaired a British charitable fund, and he subscribed £4000 to start a subscription for victims of the shelling. The armistice was signed on 28 January 1871, and on 15 February Wallace married Amélie-Julie at the *mairie* in the rue Drouot, both parties giving their address as 3 rue Taitbout. From March to May of the same year there ensued the uprising of the Paris commune. Throughout these months of violence Wallace kept his Paris collections boarded up in the rue Laffitte. When peace returned he was quickly rewarded for his extraordinary philanthropy: he was made a member of the Légion d'honneur and, in August 1871, received a baronetcy from Queen Victoria. One of Wallace's last public acts in Paris was to present the city with fifty cast-iron drinking fountains, known to this day as *wallaces*.

Wallace now resolved to remove as much of his collection as he could to Manchester House in London, although much was to remain in the rue Laffitte and at Bagatelle. While Manchester House, now renamed Hertford House, was being prepared, he exhibited his London collection from 1872 to 1875, at his own expense, in the new outstation of the South Kensington Museum at Bethnal Green. Meanwhile, in 1871–2, he had purchased collections of medieval and Renaissance armour and *objets d'art*, extending the historical scope of his father's collection which, principally, contained outstanding seventeenth-century old master paintings with a spectacular collection of French fine and applied art of the *ancien régime*. Although never an extravagant collector like his father, Wallace continued to make occasional purchases.

Wallace's subsequent years were spent principally either in Hertford House or at Bagatelle, but he also bought a country residence, Sudbourne Hall in Suffolk, from the fifth marquess of Hertford and, after some litigation, established his right to the Hertford Irish estates in Lisburn. He was a conscientious Conservative MP for that constituency from 1873 to 1885; he gave the town a public park, known as Wallace Park, and built Castle House as his Lisburn residence. He remained generous with both his fortune and his time: he was a commissioner for the Paris Exhibition of 1878, and was made KCB the same year; he was a trustee of both the National Portrait Gallery (1879–90) and the National Gallery (1884–90), and a generous lender to special exhibitions.

Wallace was a small, dapper figure, and his later portraits always give him a serious expression. He wore a French imperial moustache and his English remained tainted with a French accent. Although Wallace was highly respected as a public figure, his final years were not without their disappointments. Lady Wallace was unable to adapt satisfactorily to the life of an English aristocrat, and Wallace failed in his attempt to have his baronetcy made transferable to his illegitimate son, who then died

suddenly in 1887 (leaving four illegitimate children, whose descendants survive today). Wallace afterwards spent an increasing amount of time alone at Bagatelle, where he died on 20 July 1890, in the same room and bed in which his father had died. He was buried on 23 July in the Hertford family vault in the cemetery of Père Lachaise, beneath the body of his great friend Lord Henry Seymour.

Although Wallace had considered leaving his London collection to the nation, he had been deterred by the government's indifference towards the question of a suitable home. Instead he left all his estate to Lady Wallace, who continued to live in Hertford House. On her death in 1897 she bequeathed the contents to the nation as the Wallace Collection and, in the event, Hertford House itself became the museum. The works of art remaining in Paris were eventually dispersed by the Paris dealer Seligmann.

JOHN INGAMELLS

Sources P. Hughes, *The founders of the Wallace Collection* (1992) · B. Falk, *'Old Q's' daughter: the history of a strange family* (1951) · *Journals and correspondence of Lady Eastlake*, ed. C. E. Smith, 2 (1895), 134–5 · Hertford House, London, Wallace Collection catalogues, 1962–95 · Hertford House, Wallace Collection, letters, invoices, sales catalogues, inventories, 1843–90 · CGPLA Eng. & Wales (1890)
Archives Wallace Collection, London · Warks. CRO, letters and papers relating to bequest and lawsuits
Likenesses C. Blaize, watercolour drawing, 1826, V&A · H. J. Brooks, oils, 1833 (*Private view of the Old Masters Exhibition, Royal Academy, 1888*), NPG · Chant & Cie, photograph, 1857, Wallace Collection, London · Adolphe, group portrait, photograph, 1871 (with members of the British Charitable Fund), NPG · Elliott & Fry, photographs, 1872, Wallace Collection, London · C. Baudry, etching, after 1873, Wallace Collection, London · W. R. Symonds, oils, 1885, Wallace Collection, London · J. J. Thomson, photograph, 1888, NPG [*see illus.*] · J. J. Thomson, photographs, 1888, Wallace Collection, London · E. Hannaux, marble bust, 1899 (with Bath Star), Wallace Collection, London · A. C. F. Decaen, oils (*A shooting party at the Great Wood, Sudbourn Hall, 1876*), Orford town hall, Suffolk · J. Jacquemart, etching (after P. Baudry), BM, NPG; repro. in *Gazette des Beaux Arts*, vol. 7 · Spy [L. Ward], chromolithograph cartoon, NPG; repro. in *VF* (29 Nov 1873)
Wealth at death £1,226,353 7s. 4d.: resworn probate, April 1892, CGPLA Eng. & Wales (1890)

Wallace, Robert (1697–1771), Church of Scotland minister and writer on population, was born on 7 January 1697 in Kincardine, Perthshire, the only son of Matthew Wallace (*d.* 1727), Church of Scotland minister for the parish, and his wife, Margaret Stewart. Robert was educated at Stirling grammar school and matriculated at Edinburgh University in 1711. He studied divinity, excelled in mathematics under Professor James Gregory at Edinburgh, and taught the professor's classes in 1720. In 1722 he was licensed to preach by the presbytery of Dunblane, Perthshire, and assigned to the parish of Moffat the following year. On 14 October 1726 he married Helen Turnbull (1706–1776), daughter of George Turnbull, minister of Tyninghame. They had three children: one daughter and two sons, including George Wallace (1730–1805) [*see below*].

In 1729 Robert Wallace was elected moderator of the provincial synod of Dumfries. His synod sermon, *The Regard due to Divine Revelation*, published in 1731 together with a prefatory response to Matthew Tindal's *Christianity as Old as the Creation*, was well received by Queen Caroline, who arranged his translation to the Edinburgh pulpit of New Greyfriars in 1733. He moved to New North Church, Edinburgh, in 1738.

Though predisposed toward a life of reflection Wallace emerged as a leader in ecclesiastical politics. In the 1730s he became identified with the squadrone opposition interest. Aligning himself with Robert Dundas, Lord Arniston, he opposed the efforts of Archibald Campbell, third earl of Ilay, Sir Robert Walpole's Scottish manager, to implement a system of church patronage designed to pacify the kirk. His identification with opposition politics solidified during the Porteous affair of 1736. The Porteous Act, against harbouring 'rioters' who participated in the murder of Captain Porteous, required ministers to read the act monthly from their pulpits. Wallace, in council with Arniston, led a group of Edinburgh ministers who successfully resisted complying. In August 1739 Wallace was appointed chaplain in Scotland for Frederick, prince of Wales, then a magnate for the opposition. The following year he preached against the government from the New North pulpit when he suggested that Walpole was managing the war in accord with his own private interests rather than those of Britain.

With the change of ministry in 1742 Wallace was chosen to manage the crown's patronage of kirk benefices by the new minister for Scottish affairs, John, fourth marquess of Tweeddale. Conciliatory in discharging these duties, Wallace attempted to balance the interests of heritors and local elders. He was elected moderator of the general assembly in the following year and was appointed a royal chaplain for Scotland and dean of the Chapel Royal in 1744. His formal leadership in the kirk ceased in 1746 with the demise of Tweeddale's ministry.

Thereafter Wallace turned increasingly to his scholarly interests, though he was still occasionally visible in political controversies. As an Edinburgh minister he was also a trustee of George Heriot's Hospital, a responsibility he took seriously. In 1759 and 1760 he and several other ministers publicly opposed efforts by the town provost, George Drummond, to appropriate hospital land for the construction of Edinburgh's New Town. Two years later he opposed the town council's attempt to circumvent the kirk's general sessions in filling an Edinburgh pulpit with John Drysdale, an issue which focused popular sentiment against the city's managerial élite. Late in life Wallace's political sympathies were with the new spirit of radicalism associated with John Wilkes.

While leading the kirk in the 1740s Wallace was instrumental in the establishment of the widow's fund, a project uniting his mathematical interests, political skills, and reformist inclinations. The fund was an insurance scheme to provide for the widows and orphans of kirk ministers. With assistance from Colin MacLaurin, Wallace performed the calculations on the data collected by Alexander Webster and derived a suitable formula for the plan. As moderator in 1743 he used his connections with Arniston and Tweeddale to gain support for the proposals in parliament. When the political climate appeared favourable Wallace and George Wishart were commissioned for London to request passage of the plan, which, once implemented in 1744, became one of the first truly successful insurance programmes in Britain.

Wallace contributed to the intellectual fermentation then under way in Edinburgh. A founding member of the Rankenian Club during his university days, he was also active in the Philosophical and Select societies. He was in the vanguard of the new moderate church leadership that helped create the milieu in which Edinburgh's literati thrived after mid-century. Ecclesiastically latitudinarian, he favoured an incorporating national church without creedal ordination tests, a church capable of mitigating the effects from dangerous factional extremes like popular enthusiasm and radical freethinking. For instance, he quietly opposed the revivalism that spread through Scotland in the 1740s in the conviction that such preaching presented unscrupulous, politically ambitious men with dangerous influence over the passions of the lower orders.

Wallace's intellectual curiosity, spirit of liberality, and commitment to the free exchange of ideas made him a role model for members of the ecclesiastical moderate party of younger men who gained control of church politics in the 1750s under William Robertson's leadership. Wallace shared with the moderates a fundamental opposition to the evangelical and Calvinistic forces in the church. Even so, his political and social outlook contained a radical, egalitarian edge that kept him from close alignment with Robertson's coterie. He could not abide their unequivocal support for the law of patronage, the tool by which they gained control of church politics, and one of the issues at stake in the Drysdale 'Bustle' of 1762, in which Wallace and the moderates took opposing sides. Nor did Wallace share in their enthusiasm for James Macpherson's controversial 'recovery' of the Ossianic poetry, which Hugh Blair promoted as a Homeric production of an ancient, virtuous, and noble race of Scots. Less sanguine about such an ancient, noble race, Wallace attributed the success of Ossian to moderate party factionalism that threatened to distort good judgement and taste. Nor was he in sympathy with the moderates' attempt to revive the Edinburgh theatre by staging John Home's *Douglas* in 1756 over and against the popular cry that the stage was a breeding ground for sin and vice. Wallace opposed this Calvinistic attack on *Douglas*, but argued on classical republican grounds that an active theatre would tempt Edinburgh's social élite with another indulgent diversion of economic resources from useful projects of public service. Ideologically out of step as he was with both emerging church parties, Wallace's tendency from the 1750s was to dissociate himself from church politics, finding consolation in quiet walks, stoic philosophy, and scholarly pursuits.

Wallace's publications typically sought to counter the influence of various freethinkers whose ideas threatened to erode commitment either to virtue or to liberty. Among these Bernard Mandeville, author of *Fable of the Bees*, was a favourite target. Wallace developed an innovative response to Mandeville's provocative political economy of passions and interests, private vices producing public benefits. In his *Dissertation on the Numbers of Mankind* (1753) Wallace argued that the traditional agrarian virtues of 'frugality, temperance, simplicity, contentment with a little, and patience of labour' were more rational and more efficient at producing happiness than the commercial vices of Mandeville's imagined bees; to argue the case, he presented an elaborate history of population based on the extensive research in ancient history that he had originally presented to the Philosophical Society some time before 1745.

Wallace opened the *Dissertation* with a hypothetical model for the geometrical rate of world population growth, beginning from an assumed original pair. The model demonstrated that present world population was far below its potential—a fact which, coupled with his historical argument for greater populations in the past, begged an explanation for humankind's failure to populate the earth. For this he attended to the impact of economic forces and cultural tastes on marriage patterns. Traditional agrarian societies produce an inexpensive subsistence, encouraging men and women toward early, fruitful marriages. Appetites and tastes are correspondingly simple. Economies of large, modern commercial states, by contrast, are driven by exchanges of nonessential luxuries. With a smaller percentage of the workforce in agriculture essential goods are correspondingly expensive. Tastes and appetites become attuned to luxuries, or 'overrefinement', delaying marriage and setting off a decline in both population and civic virtue.

As Wallace was completing work on the *Dissertation* in 1751 he showed it to fellow Philosophical Society member David Hume, who reciprocated with the essay he published in the *Political Discourses* of 1752: 'Of the populousness of ancient nations'. Hume questioned the accuracy of population estimates in ancient sources, and argued for the superiority of modern assessments of population. Nevertheless, his essay included a graciously worded acknowledgement of debt to Wallace, that 'eminent clergyman in Edinburgh', whose work, if published, would shed additional light on this 'the most curious and important of all questions of erudition' (Heinemann, 10). Wallace published the *Dissertation* the following year with a long appendix addressing Hume's essay. This polite exchange was widely celebrated as a model for the pursuit of truth in an enlightened age. Montesquieu supervised the translation of both works into French. In the *Confessions* Rousseau acknowledged the spirit of the debate, praising Hume in particular for having helped edit Wallace's text.

Underneath this population debate were fundamental assumptions about the nature of a rationally organized society, issues to which Wallace devoted considerable attention. He composed, for instance, an unorthodox essay on sexual and marital practices, 'Of venery' (published by Norah Smith in *Texas Studies in Literature and Language*, 15, 1973, 429–44), in which he lamented an onerous injustice suffered by women in the present age of over-

refined tastes and indulgent appetites. Men, instead of acting on natural sexual urges and being relatively indiscriminate in the selection of partners, now sought marriage guided by artificially high standards of feminine beauty, consigning many women to remaining single and lonely. He wanted marriage redefined as a freely negotiable and dissolvable contract. Hence sexual relationships would become less exclusive, more democratic, less prone to jealousy, more widely disseminated, and more conducive to happiness and population growth. In this and other proposals his thoughts were inspired by the image of Thomas More's ideal society.

Wallace also took an interest in agrarian reform. He decried the lack of attention to agriculture among leading families who directed their sons toward the liberal professions or the military rather than toward agricultural improvement. His unpublished essay 'Of the prices and dearth of provisions in different numbers referring to one another' (Edinburgh University Library, Laing II 620:11) proposed planned villages with more equitably divided farm land, safeguards against enclosure, and integration of agriculture with small scale manufactures, a model he felt would be morally and culturally superior to both British town and hamlet. These concerns are likewise reflected in his 'Treatise on taste' (Edinburgh University Library, DC 1 55), an unpublished response to Lord Kames's *Elements of Criticism*, in which Wallace argued that aristocratic houses should be designed without courtyards to better direct a great family's view toward its chief proper concern, the fields.

Among Wallace's other published works, *The Characteristics of the Present Political State of Great Britain* (1758) defended the British constitution and culture against John Brown's assault in *An Estimate of the Manners and Principles of the Times*. While Wallace was not unsympathetic to elements of Brown's critique, the latter's accusations of national effeminacy, coming as they did in the midst of critical failures in the British war against despotic France, did not serve the cause of constitutional government. The *Various Prospects of Mankind, Nature and Providence* (1761), a metaphysical defence of a morally ordered universe, is best remembered today as a principal source of Thomas Malthus's population calculus in the *Essay on the Principle of Population*. The *Various Prospects* revisited two of Wallace's favourite themes, a perfected human order modelled after More's *Utopia*, and his population calculus from the *Dissertation*. He reasoned that a perfected constitution, once established, would be victimized by its own success in the unforgiving calculus of geometric population growth. Wallace again appealed to More's ideal republic in a sermon preached for the Scottish Society for Propagating Christian Knowledge, *Ignorance and Superstition a Source of Violence and Cruelty* (1746), in which he preferred its design to Mandeville's social theory. A prolific author, a large collection of his unpublished works is held in the Laing collection, Edinburgh University Library. Wallace died in Edinburgh on 29 July 1771.

His youngest son, **George Wallace** (1730–1805), lawyer and writer, was admitted to the Faculty of Advocates in

Edinburgh in 1754. He was a member with his father of the Rankenian Club, and a member of the Royal Society of Edinburgh. He wrote a memoir of his father that appeared in the *Scots Magazine* for July 1771. He also published *A System of the Principles of the Law of Scotland* (1760), which deserves recognition as the source for the article on *Thoughts on the Origin of Feudal Tenures and the Descent of Ancient Peerages in Scotland* (1783), with a second edition; *Nature and Descent of Ancient Peerages Connected with the State of Scotland*, (8 vols., 1785); and *Prospects from Hills in Fife* (1796), a poem modelled after James Thomson's 'Seasons'. He died in 1805.   B. BARNETT COCHRAN

Sources *DNB* · N. Smith, 'The literary career and achievement of Robert Wallace', PhD diss., U. Edin., 1973 · B. Barnett Cochran, 'Grace, virtue, and law: political discourse and the search for national identity in the early Scottish Enlightenment', PhD diss., Emory University, 1997 · R. B. Sher, *Church and university in the Scottish Enlightenment: the moderate literati of Edinburgh* (1985) · G. Wallace, 'Memoirs of Dr Wallace of Edinburgh', *Scots Magazine*, 33 (1771), 340–44 · H. R. Sefton, 'Rev. Robert Wallace: an early moderate', *Records of the Scottish Church History Society*, 16 (1966–8), 1–22 · H. R. Sefton, 'The early development of moderatism in the Church of Scotland', PhD diss., U. Glas., 1962 · D. J. Peterson, 'Political economy in transition: from classical humanism to commercial society—Robert Wallace of Edinburgh', PhD diss., University of Illinois at Urbana-Champaign, 1994 · M. Winsor, 'Robert Wallace: predecessor of Malthus and pioneering actuary', *Acta Historica Scientiarum Naturalium et Medicinalium*, 39 (1985), 215–24 · E. C. Mossner, *The forgotten Hume: le bon David* (1943) · F. H. Heinemann, *David Hume, the man and the science of man: containing some unpublished letters of Hume* (Paris, 1940) · J. M. Hartwick, 'Robert Wallace and Malthus and the ratios', *History of Political Economy*, 20 (1988), 357–80 · R. B. Luehrs, 'Population and Utopia in the thought of Robert Wallace', *Eighteenth-Century Studies*, 20 (1986–7), 313–35 · J. B. Dow, 'Early actuarial work in eighteenth-century Scotland', *Transactions of the Faculty of Actuaries*, 33/240 (1975), 193–229 · D. B. Davis, 'New sidelights on early anti-slavery radicalism', *William and Mary Quarterly*, 28 (1971), 585–94 · N. M. [N. Morren], *Annals of the general assembly of the Church of Scotland*, 2 vols. (1838–40)
Archives LUL, notes on paper credit and banking · U. Edin. L., corresp. and papers | NA Scot., Ministers' Widows' Fund records, Ch 9/9/5, Ch 9/17/6, Ch 9/17/10, Ch 9/17/23 · NA Scot., letters to Sir Andrew Mitchell
Likenesses Millar, portrait, 1764, Offices of the Trustees of the Widows' Fund, George Street, Edinburgh

Wallace, Robert (1773–1855), politician and postal reformer, was the second son of John Wallace (1712–1805) of Cessnock and Kelly in Ayrshire, and his third wife, Janet, third daughter of Robert Colquhoun of the island of St Kitts. His father was a merchant in Glasgow, who amassed a large fortune trading in the West Indies and became proprietor of several important estates. Wallace's older brother was Sir James Maxwell Wallace [see Wallace, Grace]. By his father's will Robert Wallace received the estate of Kelly and part of the West Indian property, and was known by the designation of Wallace of Kelly. He married Margaret, daughter of Sir William Forbes of Craigievar; they had no children.

Wallace was a devoted whig, and, as a vigorous orator, his services were in demand during the reform agitation before 1832. After the passing of the Reform Bill he was the first member of parliament for Greenock under the act, and held that seat continuously until 1846. In parliament his chief efforts were directed towards law reform, especially cheaper and simpler methods for the transfer of heritable property; though he did not carry through any measure specially for this purpose, he gave an impetus to reforms, and suggested plans that were subsequently adopted. In 1833 Wallace attacked the Post Office as expensive and inefficient: the pressure he exerted on the government led in 1835 to the appointment of a royal commission to which he gave evidence. After inaction from the tories in 1834–5, the whigs in 1837 made Wallace chairman of a select committee to examine Rowland Hill's plan for a penny post; Wallace's committee offered unqualified support when it reported in 1838, the penny post being enacted in 1839.

In 1846 Wallace became embarrassed financially by the depreciation in value of some of his West Indian estates, and deemed it prudent to resign his seat in parliament. The estate of Kelly was sold, and Wallace lived in retirement at Seafield Cottage, Greenock. After his resignation a liberal public subscription was made for him, which provided an annuity of £500 p.a. Wallace died at Seafield on 1 April 1855. His sister, Anne Wallace, died unmarried in 1873 in her 102nd year.

A. H. MILLAR, *rev.* H. C. G. MATTHEW

Sources Boase, *Mod. Eng. biog.* · *Glasgow Herald* (2 April 1855) · M. J. Daunton, *Royal Mail: the Post Office since 1840* (1985) · A. H. Millar, *The castles and mansions of Ayrshire, illustrated in seventy views* (1885) · Irving, *Scots*.
Archives Watt Library, letters | BL, letters to Rowland Hill, Add. MS 31978 · BL, corresp. with Sir Robert Peel, Add. MSS 40503–40611 · NL Scot., corresp. mainly with Lord Rosebery
Likenesses bust, Greenock town hall, Strathclyde

Wallace, Robert (1791–1850), Unitarian minister and biographer, second son and child (of six) born to Robert Wallace (1749/50–1830) and his wife, Phoebe (1756/7–1837), was born at Dudley, Worcestershire, on 26 February 1791. He was baptized on 19 March by the name of Robert, to which in early life he sometimes added William. His father was a pawnbroker, his grandfather a Dumfriesshire farmer. Two younger brothers also became Unitarian ministers: James Cowdan Wallace (1793?–1841), a prolific writer of hymns, served at Totnes (1824–6), York Street, London (1827–8), Brighton (1828–9), and Wareham (1831–41); and Charles Wallace (1796–1859), who studied at the University of Glasgow (MA, 1817) and Manchester College, York (1817–19), and was minister at Altrincham and Hale, Cheshire, in 1829–56.

Wallace's father had been raised in the Church of Scotland but in Dudley attended the Presbyterian chapel in Wolverhampton Street. Until 1807 the younger Wallace was educated by John Todd (1775?–1838), curate of Frankley and St Kenelm, Worcestershire. In 1808 he came under the influence of James Hews Bransby, who had come to Wolverhampton Street in 1805. Bransby made Wallace a Unitarian and prepared him to enter Manchester College, York, in September 1810. He left York in 1815 and became in September minister at Elder Yard, Chesterfield, where he also conducted a school for sixteen years. In 1825 he married Sophia (*d.* 1835), daughter of Michael Lakin of Birmingham; they had a daughter, who survived her father.

Wallace distinguished himself as a theological writer and was a regular contributor to the *Monthly Repository* and the *Christian Reformer* on biblical and patristic topics. In 1834, in the latter journal, he reviewed J. H. Newman's *Arians of the Fourth Century*, a work, Robert Aspland said in commissioning the review, that contained 'some ingenuity and some learning, but quite enough paradox and high-church presumption, and even *papism*, to keep a reviewer alive' (Aspland to Wallace, 24 Jan 1834). His essay of 1835, again in the *Reformer*, 'On the parenthetical and digressive style of John's gospel', is a very able piece of criticism.

In 1840 Manchester College returned to Manchester from York, and Wallace was appointed to succeed Charles Wellbeloved as professor of critical and exegetical theology; in 1842 he was made principal of the theological department. His theological position was conservative, but he was the first in his own denomination to bring to his classroom the processes and results of German critical research. He was held in great respect and affection by his students.

The change to Manchester did not suit Wallace's health; after six years he resigned and in June 1846 became minister of Trim Street Chapel, Bath. He was made visitor of his college, became a fellow of the Geological Society, and worked hard at the completion of his *Antitrinitarian Biography*, which was published in March 1850. He preached for the last time on 10 March and died at 20 Camden Place, Walcot, Bath, on 13 May 1850. He was buried in the Trim Street Chapel graveyard at Lyncombe, near Bath.

His three-volume *Antitrinitarian Biography* was the result of nearly twenty-four years of labour. A few of the earlier biographies were published anonymously in the *Monthly Repository* in 1831 and part of the introduction in the *Christian Reformer* in 1845–6. In breadth of treatment and in depth of original research Wallace's work is inferior to that of Thomas Rees (1777–1864), but he covers more ground than any previous writer, dealing with continental and English figures from the Reformation to the opening of the eighteenth century. His introduction deals mainly with the development of opinion in England during that period. His careful array of authorities is especially useful. An extended list of his separate and periodical publications appears at the conclusion of the obituary by his brother Charles in the *Christian Reformer* in 1850.

R. K. Webb

Sources [C. Wallace], *Christian Reformer, or, Unitarian Magazine and Review*, new ser., 6 (1850), 549–60 · *DNB* · registers, Wolverhampton Street Chapel, Dudley, Worcestershire · *Christian Reformer, or, Unitarian Magazine and Review*, 2 (1835), 510 · R. Aspland, *Christian Reformer, or, Unitarian Magazine and Review*, new ser., 6 (1850), 23 [letter to R. Wallace, 24 Jan 1834] · *GM*, 2nd ser., 10 (1838), 104
Likenesses oils, Harris Man. Oxf.
Wealth at death under £7000: PRO, death duty registers, PC2/309

Wallace, Robert (1831–1899), Church of Scotland minister and politician, second son of Jasper Wallace, master gardener, was born at Kincaple near Cupar, Fife, on 24 June 1831. His mother claimed to be the illegitimate daughter of a peer, according to Wallace's autobiography. In his home he was taught a strict Calvinism. He was educated at the Geddes Institution, Culross; the high school, Edinburgh; and at the University of St Andrews, where he won special distinction and graduated MA in 1853. After teaching for some time in private families, and attending the 1853–4 session at the Divinity Hall, Edinburgh, he was appointed on 22 April 1854 classical master at the Madras Academy in Cupar. In October 1855 he resumed his theological studies at Edinburgh University. He was licensed to preach in 1857, and shortly afterwards appointed to the charge of Newton-on-Ayr. In 1858 he married Margaret, daughter of James Robertson of Cupar; they had four sons and a daughter. In 1860 he moved to Trinity College Church, Edinburgh. In 1866 he was appointed examiner in philosophy in the University of St Andrews, and two years later the Edinburgh corporation presented him with the charge of Old Greyfriars. In 1869 the University of Glasgow conferred upon him the degree of DD.

As a churchman Wallace was noted for the support he gave both in the Edinburgh presbytery and in the general assembly of the Church of Scotland to broad views on theology and to the reform of worship, of which Dr Robert Lee, his predecessor at Greyfriars, was the chief champion. To the latter controversy he contributed *Reform of the Church of Scotland in Worship, Government, and Doctrine*, and to the former an essay entitled 'Church tendencies in Scotland', published in *Recess Studies* (1870), which led to much controversy and ultimately to his impeachment for heresy. In 1872 he was appointed by the crown to the chair of church history in Edinburgh University, and his ecclesiastical and political opponents protested. His inaugural lecture, published as *The Study of Ecclesiastic History* (1873), declared not the truth of theology but 'the truth of its history' and led to his prosecution. Wallace won his case mainly owing to his own remarkable powers as a debater, but in 1876 he determined to leave the church—resigning his chair, charge, and orders—and became editor of *The Scotsman* newspaper. For some years previously he had been contributing to that newspaper, but his editorship was not a success, and he resigned in 1880.

In 1881 Wallace entered the Middle Temple, and in 1883 was called to the bar. In 1886 he was elected to parliament as a radical to represent East Edinburgh, which he held until his death. In parliament he maintained an unusual independence, and though he took only an occasional part in the debates, he kept up the reputation he had won in the ecclesiastical courts. While about to address the House of Commons on 5 June 1899 he fell down in a fit, and died in Westminster Hospital on the following day. He was buried in Kensal Green cemetery. His wife predeceased him. At the time of his death he was engaged on a biography of George Buchanan, completed by J. C. Smith and published in 1899, and on his autobiography, published in 1903 in a memorial volume prepared by J. C.

Robert Wallace (1831–1899), by Sir Benjamin Stone, 1898

Smith and W. Wallace. Wallace was in later life irascible and unsettled: his loss of vocation increased rather than diminished his intellectual difficulties. The element of bitterness was reflected by his always placing the word 'minister' in inverted commas (Drummond and Bulloch, 260).   J. R. MacDonald, *rev.* H. C. G. Matthew

Sources *Fasti Scot.* · *The Scotsman* (7 June 1899) · R. Lawson, *Reminiscences of the late Robert Wallace* (1899) · J. C. Smith and W. Wallace, eds., *Robert Wallace: life and last leaves* (1903) [incl. section entitled 'Reminiscences' by Robert Wallace, pp. 3–73] · A. L. Drummond and J. Bulloch, *The church in Victorian Scotland, 1843–1874* (1975)
Archives NL Scot., corresp. with Lord Rosebery
Likenesses B. Stone, photograph, 1898, NPG [*see illus.*]
Wealth at death £997 11s. 1d.: probate, 14 July 1899, *CGPLA Eng. & Wales*

Wallace, Thomas, Baron Wallace (1768–1844), politician, only son of James Wallace, barrister (afterwards solicitor- and attorney-general under Lord North to George III), and his wife, Elizabeth, daughter and heir of Thomas Simpson, Carleton Hall, Cumberland, was born at Brampton, Cumberland. He was educated at Eton College (1777–84) and Christ Church, Oxford, where he was the contemporary and associate of the earl of Liverpool and of George Canning. He graduated MA on 18 March 1790 and DCL on 5 July 1793. At the general election in 1790 Wallace was elected MP for Grampound, which he held until 1796. His subsequent constituencies were: Penrhyn (1796–1802), Hindon (1802–6), Shaftesbury (1807–12), Weymouth (1812–13), Cockermouth (1813–18), and Weymouth again (1818–28). He was from the first a Pittite, except for his strong opposition to Catholic emancipation. In July 1797 he was

appointed to a seat at the Admiralty, from which he was removed in May 1800 to become one of the commissioners for the affairs of India. When Pitt retired in 1801, Wallace continued to hold office under his successor, Addington, and was made a privy councillor on 21 May 1801. When Pitt resumed office in 1804, Wallace was included in the new government, and he went with the Pittites who opposed the Grenville ministry in 1806. He resumed his commissionership in 1807, holding it until 1816 but without the promotion to the peerage for which he yearned and which his family had failed to gain owing to his father's early death. Having resigned in 1816 after not becoming president of the Board of Control, Wallace accepted in 1818 the vice-presidency of the Board of Trade. Chairing the various committees on foreign trade between 1820 and 1824 gained him a reputation, and his work for the committees and their subsequent legislative proposals marked the formal start of the movement towards 'free trade' (Hilton, 173).

In April 1823 Wallace was succeeded by William Huskisson at the Board of Trade, but was soon appointed chairman of the committee inquiring into irregularities and abuses in the Irish revenue. The recommendations of the committee were adopted. In October 1823 he was appointed master of the mint in Ireland, a post that he held until the change of administration in May 1827, and in May 1825 he successfully proposed the assimilation of the currencies of England and Ireland. Canning pressed him to join his government, but he refused. On the death of Canning he finally gained a peerage (on 2 February 1828), as Baron Wallace of Knaresdale.

Wallace married, on 16 February 1814, Jane, sixth daughter of John Hope, second earl of Hopetoun, and second wife of Henry Dundas, first Viscount Melville. The marriage was childless; Jane died on 9 June 1829. Wallace lived at his seat, Featherstone Castle, Northumberland, and died there on 23 February 1844, the peerage becoming extinct and the estates going to the Hope family.

George Stronach, *rev.* H. C. G. Matthew

Sources *GM*, 2nd ser., 21 (1844), 425–30 · HoP, *Commons* · *The letter-journal of George Canning, 1793–1795*, ed. P. Jupp, CS, 4th ser., 41 (1991) · B. Hilton, *Corn, cash, commerce: the economic policies of the tory governments, 1815–1830* (1977) · GEC, *Peerage*
Archives Northumbd RO, corresp., letter-book, MS memoirs · Northumbd RO, corresp. and papers | BL, corresp. with John Charles Herries, Add. MS 57401 · BL, corresp. with second earl of Liverpool, Add. MSS 38243–38300, 38410, 38425, 38572 · BL, corresp. with Sir Robert Peel, Add. MSS 40354–40388 · St Deiniol's Library, corresp. with Sir John Gladstone
Likenesses C. Bestland, stipple, pubd 1795 (after W. Beechey), NPG · C. Turner, mezzotint, pubd 1801 (after T. Clarke), BM, NPG · W. Holl, stipple, pubd 1823 (after A. Wivell), BM, NPG · J. Brown, stipple, BM, NPG; repro. in *Eminent conservative statesmen* (1823) · G. Romney, oils, Eton

Wallace, Thomas (1891–1965), agricultural chemist, was born on 5 September 1891 at Newton on the Moor, near Alnwick, the eighth child of the family of three sons and six daughters of Thomas Wallace, blacksmith and agricultural engineer, and his wife, (Isabella) Mary Thompson. He won a county scholarship to Rutherford College in Newcastle upon Tyne in 1905 and five years later entered Armstrong College of the University of Durham, where he took his BSc degree in 1913, with distinction in chemistry.

Wallace was then staff sergeant in the university's Officers' Training Corps, and on the outbreak of war in 1914 he was commissioned and posted to the 3rd Border regiment. Almost immediately he was sent to France and attached to the Royal West Kent regiment during early fighting in France and Flanders, receiving the 1914 Mons star. In 1915 he returned to the Border regiment, serving with the 29th division in Gallipoli, where he was awarded the Military Cross. The following year he was sent back to France and appointed adjutant to the 11th Sussex regiment. At Richebourg in July 1917 he received a severe wound which left him with a permanently stiff left knee. He was subsequently seconded to the Royal Engineers for service in the anti-gas department, which continued until his demobilization in 1919.

At the suggestion of C. T. Gimingham, who served with him in the anti-gas department, Wallace joined the staff of the Long Ashton Agricultural and Horticultural Research Station of the University of Bristol in 1919, serving as the former's assistant. When Gimingham left in 1920 Wallace was appointed agricultural research chemist at Long Ashton and advisory officer in agricultural chemistry for the Bristol province, an area which covered the west of England and the west midlands. This was a daunting assignment for one not familiar with crops, but Wallace quickly demonstrated to the fruit growers of Hereford and the Vale of Evesham that the crippling malady of leaf scorch in plums and apples was a deficiency disease curable by the application of potash. This practical help secured the lasting confidence of the growers and opened up a new field of research.

Wallace and his rapidly growing team established the effects of four major plant nutrients and eleven micronutrients on forty-eight crops. These results were published in *The Diagnosis of Mineral Deficiencies in Plants by Visual Symptoms* (1943 and later editions), which for some time remained the standard authority on the subject. During the Second World War, when he also organized the Long Ashton Local Defence Volunteers, Wallace's work was of immense value in correcting soil deficiencies and so bringing into full production thousands of acres previously considered infertile.

In 1924 Wallace was appointed deputy director at Long Ashton. It soon became apparent that the director, Professor B. T. P. Barker, was very willing to transfer to his deputy much of the burden of station administration. Consequently, although Wallace held the title of director and professor of horticultural chemistry only during the period 1943 to 1957, he exerted a decisive influence on the development of the station for three decades, during which he organized a sevenfold increase in scientific staff with a corresponding growth in buildings and equipment. Outside Long Ashton, Wallace played a major part in the post-war reorganization of the agricultural research and advisory services: he served on numerous committees of the Ministry of Agriculture, the Agricultural Research Council, and the National Agricultural Advisory Service, and on the governing bodies of many of the agricultural and horticultural stations, colleges, and institutes. He was a governor of the Royal Agricultural College, Cirencester, in 1944.

As editor from 1943 to 1958 of the *Journal of Horticultural Science* Wallace established its reputation among scientific journals. An Agricultural Research Council unit was set up within his institute in 1952. Wallace was honorary director of this unit of plant nutrition (micronutrients), and his standing was further recognized by requests for advice which took him to Australia, New Zealand, the United States, France, Spain, and the Caribbean.

Wallace was regarded as a man of complete integrity, forthright in his approach both to people and to his scientific work. In his research and in his administrative sphere he would accept nothing improvised or uncertain. He figures in Edmund Blunden's *Undertones of War* (1928) as 'the austere Wallace' and indeed he scorned any form of self-aggrandizement. His director's room was an uncarpeted laboratory with a battered desk and a few wooden chairs. He maintained his soldierly carriage and, to those who did not know him well, he seemed inflexible, but his friends remembered him as a brave, kindly man and an inspiring leader, whose great ability was clothed with modesty.

His honours and awards included the DSc of the University of Durham (1931), the Victoria medal of honour of the Royal Horticultural Society (1952), and CBE (1947). He became FRIC (1946) and FRS (1953).

Wallace married in 1917 Gladys Mary, daughter of Robert Johnson Smith, a merchant navy captain, and had a daughter, Jean, and a son, Alan, both of whom qualified in medicine. After the death of his wife in 1936, his second marriage, in 1938, was to Elsie Stella, daughter of Colonel John Smyth of the Indian Medical Service. They had one son. Alan and his wife were tragically killed in a plane accident in 1963, leaving two young children to become the responsibility of their grandparents. In 1958 Wallace had a severe illness, but made an excellent recovery. At about that time he went to live at Redwings, Old Church Road, Nailsea. On 1 February 1965 he visited his office at Long Ashton, where he had remained actively involved after the end of his term as director, looking fit and well: on the next day he collapsed and died in the General Hospital, Bristol, survived by his wife.   R. W. MARSH, *rev.*

Sources W. K. Slater and H. G. H. Keaths, *Memoirs FRS*, 12 (1966), 503–19 · personal knowledge (1981) · *CGPLA Eng. & Wales* (1965)
Likenesses W. Stoneman, photograph, c.1953, RS · J. Whitlock, oils, 1957, University of Bristol
Wealth at death £11,652: probate, 3 May 1965, *CGPLA Eng. & Wales*

Wallace, Sir William (d. 1305), patriot and guardian of Scotland, is a man whose origins, once thought secure, have now become uncertain.

Early life: fiction and facts The name Wallace originally meant a Welshman, and William's descent has been confidently traced from a Ricardus Wallensis, or Richard Wallace, who went to Scotland from the lordship of Oswestry in the mid-twelfth century in the train of Walter fitz Alan, soon to become first hereditary steward of the Scottish king. Richard's great-grandson Malcolm, who held Auchenbothie near Kilmacolm as well as the five-pound land of Elderslie near Paisley, both in Renfrewshire, and who married Margaret, daughter of Sir Reginald or Rainald Crawford of Corsbie, sheriff of Ayr, has been equally confidently identified as William's father. However, the rediscovery of a deed sealed by Wallace in 1297 casts considerable doubt on this, for in the inscription on his seal Wallace identifies himself as 'son of Alan Walais'. Much of what has in the past been accepted concerning Wallace, and especially his early life, derives from the late fifteenth-century poet Blind *Hary, who here, as so often, now appears to have been a source of confusion. For in the light of the seal inscription it seems highly likely that William's father was in fact the Alan Wallace recorded as a crown tenant in Ayrshire in the late thirteenth century, and that his son's presumed links with the stewards were consequently less important than was previously supposed. In this context it may be significant that evidence for Hary's story that Sir Malcolm Wallace, his hero's father, was killed in 1291 by an English knight called Fenwick, is entirely lacking. There is no doubt, however, that Wallace had brothers named Malcolm and John.

The year of Wallace's birth is unknown. According to Hary, Wallace was eighteen when he killed the son of Selby, the constable of Dundee (book 1), an event which has been placed in 1291 or 1292, but for which there is no recorded evidence and which probably never happened, but forty-five when he was betrayed to the English in 1305 (book 11). Certainty on this subject, as in so much concerning Wallace, is impossible; it is enough, perhaps, to see Wallace as a young man, as does the English chronicler Rishanger, when he emerged from obscurity in 1297. What Hary has to say about Wallace's education, by two uncles who were priests, and about his meeting John Blair, said to have been later his chaplain and the author of a biography to which Hary acknowledges his indebtedness, must also be regarded as fiction, arising from Hary's desire to confer respectability upon both his subject and himself. One intriguing piece of evidence does survive, however, from the period before 1297. A document of 8 August 1296 records the conviction of one Matthew of York, a cleric, of robbery at Perth on 14 June 'in the company of a thief, one William le Waleys' (*CDS*, 2.191). There is no means of establishing the connection between the patriot and Matthew's confederate, but English references to Wallace as a thief and brigand, although clearly part of a propaganda campaign against him, may refer to a less than creditable period in his career.

The rebellion of 1297 By the time of the Perth incident, Scotland was occupied territory. Following the defeat of the Scots and Edward I's conquest of their country in the spring and early summer of 1296, the English king had imposed English administration upon it, with John de Warenne, earl of Surrey (d. 1304), as keeper or lieutenant, and Hugh of Cressingham as treasurer. Believing Scotland conquered, Edward left for England, to prepare for war against France. His confidence was misplaced. Within months unrest was widespread; disturbances occurred as far apart as the west highlands, Aberdeenshire, and Galloway in the south-west. In the north Andrew Murray of Petty led the resistance to English rule. The response by Warenne and Cressingham was ineffectual and disaffection spread. It was not, however, until May 1297, when Wallace slew William Heselrig, the English sheriff of Lanark, that unrest became full-blown rebellion.

Hary presents the death of Heselrig as Wallace's revenge for the murder of his mistress, Marion Braidfute, who had spurned Heselrig's son. The truth is almost certainly less romantic. Heselrig represented a repressive and alien regime and at the time of his death was in Lanark to hold an assize, a symbol of English authority. An attempt on an English official on such an occasion was therefore an act of great and symbolic importance. An eyewitness account in the *Scalacronica* reveals that the attack on Heselrig was carefully planned and ruthlessly executed. The impact of Lanark was immediate. Wallace's original band of some thirty men now grew. The Scottish chronicler Fordun saw his followers as 'those who were bitter in heart, and heavily oppressed by the intolerable servitude of English domination' (Fordun, 2.321). The English verdict, in Guisborough, is that they were 'vagrants, fugitives, and outlaws' (*Chronicle of Walter of Guisborough*, 294). Recruitment was aided by a rumour that Edward meant to impress the 'middle folk of Scotland' into his army against France. For such as these, rebellion against Edward was preferable to service abroad in a war against Scotland's ally, Philippe IV.

The killing of Heselrig was the only specific charge in the indictment against Wallace in 1305. He was now no longer unknown but notorious in English eyes if an inspiration to the Scots. Soon after Lanark he struck again. His target was a figure senior to Heselrig, William Ormsby, Edward's justiciar, then at Scone. In this endeavour Wallace was joined by Sir William Douglas 'le Hardi', a man of fearsome reputation, captured at Berwick in 1296 but released. This, Wallace's first recorded association with a nobleman, failed, but narrowly. Ormsby somehow learned of the approach of the Scots and fled, leaving much booty behind. The raid, as daring as the attack on Heselrig, gave further encouragement to the patriotic cause and added to Wallace's reputation. He and Douglas separated after Scone. Wallace overran the Lennox, while Douglas was active in Nithsdale. The English maintained that behind Wallace was to be discovered the influence of Robert Wishart, bishop of Glasgow, and James Stewart. The chronicle of Lanercost is emphatic on this point: 'They [Wishart and Stewart] caused a certain bloody man, William Wallace, who had formerly been a chief of brigands in Scotland, to revolt against the King, and assemble the people in his support' (*Chronicle of Lanercost*, 163). The belief that Wallace the rebel was the creation of the two men has persisted. His devotion to the church and his maintenance, when in power, of the established order suggest an innate conservatism. In this characteristic, however, he was not unique and the events of 1297 were to show that he was very much his own man.

The capitulation of Irvine In June the English at last moved against the Scots. Henry Percy and Robert Clifford had been given the task by Edward of suppressing the rebellion. From Cumberland they crossed into Annandale, where they burnt Lochmaben before proceeding to Irvine, arriving there by the end of the month. A Scottish army had assembled to meet the threat. In command were Wishart, Stewart, Douglas, and a recent convert to the patriotic cause, Robert Bruce, lord of Annandale, the future King *Robert I. At the sight of the English cavalry the Scots sought terms. The negotiations leading to their submission were lengthy; Guisborough avers that the Scots were gaining time for Wallace to collect an army, an opinion which has found favour with historians. This denies Wallace the credit to which he is entitled by once more making him dependent on others. His presence at Irvine is not attested and the compromise which the negotiations represented was foreign to his nature. In a letter of 23 July to Edward, Cressingham described Wallace, then in the Forest of Selkirk, as 'like one who holds himself against your peace' (Stevenson, *Documents*, 2, no. 453). Cressingham, for once more perceptive than his colleagues, raised an army and would have acted but for Percy and Clifford who, with Irvine in mind, claimed to have subdued Scotland south of the Forth. Their confidence, like that of their king in the previous year, was misplaced, if understandable. Irvine had been deceptively easy. Wishart and Douglas were imprisoned. Stewart escaped this fate, as did Bruce, but their authority had been damaged. Wallace, however, was untainted by Irvine and, aided by a lack of response from the English, was free to assume the role in which Guisborough portrayed him: 'the common folk of the land followed him as their leader and ruler; the retainers of the great lords adhered to him; and even though the lords themselves were present with the English king in body, at heart they were on the opposite side' (*Chronicle of Walter of Guisborough*, 299).

The battle of Stirling Bridge From the Forest of Selkirk, Wallace went north. According to Hary he reached Aberdeen, where he burnt 100 English ships. If this incident occurred, it was more probably the work of Andrew *Murray, soon to be Wallace's colleague. Wallace himself was busy enough, clearing Fife and Perthshire of the English. In early August he began the siege of Dundee. Warenne, loath to continue as Edward's lieutenant in Scotland but disappointed in his hopes of relief, finally acted. He left Berwick at the head of what Lanercost calls 'a great army'. How many men exactly he had at his disposal is unknown. Guisborough's figures of 1000 horse and 50,000 foot in the English army, and 180 horse and 40,000 foot for the Scots, must be regarded as fanciful. Cressingham, who accompanied Warenne, informed Edward that he himself had mustered at Roxburgh 300 horse and 10,000 foot, a respectable contribution. Whatever the total number at Warenne's command, Cressingham thought it adequate for its purpose, refusing an offer of reinforcements from Percy and Clifford on the grounds of cost.

To Warenne the strategic importance of Stirling was clear, and he had reached there by the first week of September. The Scottish army which faced him was under the joint leadership of Wallace and Murray. The two had linked up towards the end of August, possibly at Dundee. Fordun tells us that before leaving Dundee Wallace entrusted the siege of the castle to the people of the town on 'pain of loss of life and limb' (Fordun, 2.322). The Scottish army at Stirling was certainly smaller than the English and almost entirely infantry. Unlike Warenne, neither Wallace nor Murray could claim extensive military experience, least of all in command of large forces; their victories over the English had been on a limited scale. Yet at Stirling they inflicted on the English a wholly unexpected defeat, the first in a pitched battle in the war. The battle of Stirling Bridge was fought on 11 September, after abortive attempts at arbitration by Stewart and Malcolm, earl of Lennox (*d.* 1333). Warenne was obviously reluctant to fight, despite his superiority in numbers and the contempt for the Scots which he shared with Cressingham after Dunbar and Irvine. Even after Stewart and Lennox had failed in their negotiations, Warenne was not done with talking. He sent two Dominican friars to the Scots to seek their surrender. To them Wallace made a justly celebrated response:

> Go back and tell your people that we have not come here for peace: we are ready, rather, to fight to avenge ourselves and to free our country. Let them come up to us as soon as they like, and they will find us prepared to prove the same in their beards. (*Chronicle of Walter of Guisborough*, 300)

This was the response of one committed to a cause and sure of the outcome. Wallace and Murray had drawn up their army on the south-facing slope of the Abbey Crag, where the Wallace monument stands today, looking towards Stirling Castle and the narrow wooden bridge across the Forth which stood below it. The English army was stationed on the south side of the Forth, between it and the castle. To come to grips with the Scots, who made no attempt to advance, the English had to cross the bridge. On the morning of 11 September this manoeuvre began. Some 5000 men had crossed, only to be recalled because Warenne had overslept and now insisted on creating several new knights. Dissension broke out in the English camp. An intelligent suggestion from Sir Richard Lundie to outflank the Scots at a nearby ford was overruled by Warenne on the intervention of Cressingham and the crossing resumed. The bridge was so narrow that only two horsemen could cross abreast. Wallace and Murray watched the English from the Abbey Crag until they were sure that enough of the enemy had reached the far side for their purposes. They then released their infantry down from the slope along the narrow causeway to the bridge. The terrain was, if suitable for infantry, too soft to permit the effective deployment of the English cavalry. In the words of Guisborough 'there was, indeed, no better place in all the land to deliver the English into the hands of the Scots, and so many into the power of the few' (*Chronicle of Walter of Guisborough*, 301). The Scots seized the northern end of the bridge so that the English vanguard was isolated and no reinforcements could reach it. The vanguard suffered appalling casualties, while the remainder of the army watched, unable to assist. Some 5000 infantry and 100 knights are said to have perished, killed by the Scots or drowned in the Forth. Sir Marmaduke Tweng, a Yorkshire knight, made a heroic escape, and some of the Welsh infantry swam to safety, but Cressingham died on the Scottish spears. Warenne had not crossed the bridge and fled to Berwick after ordering the destruction of the bridge to hinder a pursuit by the victorious Scots. With the battle won, Stewart and Lennox reappeared and with their men fell on the retreating English, killing some and capturing the baggage-train.

The Scots flayed the body of Cressingham and cut the skin into strips to be used as trophies. Lanercost states that Wallace had a sword-belt made from one of the strips. The English showed no sympathy for the treasurer, in whose incompetence as a general and refusal to countenance the expense of additional troops they found an explanation for their defeat. Warenne, no less incompetent, continued to enjoy his king's confidence.

The guardianship The failure of the English leadership at Stirling Bridge should not be allowed to detract from the achievement of Wallace and Murray. They had deployed their army, inferior in numbers to the English but more disciplined, with intelligence, and on terrain suited to their purpose. Stirling did not end the war but its significance was not lost on contemporaries. In its aftermath Dundee Castle surrendered, as did Stirling itself. Edinburgh and Berwick also fell to the Scots, although their castles remained in English hands. Haddington and Roxburgh were burnt. The English hold on Scotland had been severely weakened. The collaboration of Wallace and Murray was not destined to last; wounded at Stirling, Murray died early in November. On Wallace alone thus fell the burden of leading the Scots in the continuing war. He soon gave evidence of his qualities. As he had in the military field, he demonstrated an unexpected talent in the diplomatic. On 11 October he and Murray wrote from Haddington to the mayors and communes of Hamburg and Lübeck. The style of the document, and that of others issued by them, indicates that they saw themselves as leaders of the army of Scotland in the name of King John (John Balliol). The letter of 11 October was doubtless one of a series intended to restore trading relations with Germany. Nor was Wallace unaware of the importance of the church in the struggle with England. On 3 November he secured the election of William Lamberton as bishop of St Andrews in succession to William Fraser. The wisdom of Wallace's action became apparent in time, with Lamberton until his death in 1328 a strong opponent of the English.

By the time of Lamberton's election Wallace had invaded England. His army had grown in size and become a drain on the limited resources of a Scotland stricken by famine. The Scots, moreover, were intent on retribution and Wallace saw no reason to restrain them. About 18 October he marched into Northumberland, catching the inhabitants by surprise. The Scots plundered and slaughtered at will. From Northumberland the Scots crossed into the north-west, reaching as far as Cockermouth. Without siege equipment they were unable to take any town of consequence, but such was their ferocity that, Guisborough relates, 'the services of God totally ceased in all the monasteries and churches between Newcastle and Carlisle, for all the canons, monks and priests fled before the face of the Scots, as did nearly all the people' (*Chronicle of Walter of Guisborough*, 304). The barbarous acts committed by the Scots under Wallace, like those ordered by Edward I at Berwick, had the purpose of breaking resistance, and were of a kind often repeated by both sides. But Wallace was on occasion capable of mercy. At Hexham, whose priory had suffered from the depredations of his soldiers, he invited the canons to celebrate mass and issued a letter of protection to them. His treatment of the canons was not enough, however, to alleviate the reputation for cruelty which the raid guaranteed him in English eyes; henceforth he was the object of an unremitting campaign of vilification. The raid into England ended in late November, with the Scots foiled in their attempt to ravage the bishopric of Durham by increasingly severe weather and, it was believed, by the intervention of St Cuthbert himself.

Back in Scotland, Wallace began to prepare for the inevitable clash with Edward. To what extent he could rely on the support of the magnates in this is debatable; many had agreed to serve Edward I in Flanders in 1296, and Scottish tradition suggests that some at least were not reconciled to Wallace's rise to power. If Fordun is to be believed, Wallace did not hesitate to employ harsh measures against these recalcitrants, imprisoning them until they submitted to his will. To others he was no less brutal. One source relates that he hanged some citizens of Aberdeen as an example to those who refused to obey him, while the case of Michael Miggel further illustrates Wallace's methods. Summoned to Perth after Wallace's death to explain his association with him, Michael told how he had twice escaped from Wallace's army only to be recaptured and warned that a third escape would mean death. He had remained with Wallace 'through fear of death and not of his own will' (*CDS*, 2, no. 1689). His story was credible enough to save him from punishment and can scarcely have been unusual. Such was Wallace's military genius that he created from a mixture of volunteers and pressed men an army capable of standing against Edward.

The campaign of 1298 The shock of Stirling had reunited the English behind their king who, in the wake of a truce with France, returned from Flanders on 14 March 1298. The nobles and clergy of England, both sources of disaffection, were won over by the need to defeat Wallace. In pursuit of this aim the king was his usual careful self, obsessed with detail and the need for legal justification for his actions. To facilitate the administration of the war the seat of government was moved north to York, and there Edward held a council in April to discuss the forthcoming campaign. The disregard by the Scottish magnates of the summons to attend the council allowed Edward to announce the forfeiture of the lands of his Scottish enemies. His army was instructed to muster at Roxburgh on 25 June. Edward, having made a pilgrimage to the shrine of St John of Beverley, was at Roxburgh in early July. Estimates of the force at his disposal vary but by the standards of the time it was formidable, composed of some 2000–3000 horse and about 14,000 infantry, of whom the greater proportion were Welsh. Edward advanced into Scotland through Lauderdale, over country devastated by Wallace and empty of inhabitants so that, as Guisborough has it, the English 'could not discover a single soul to tell them the whereabouts of the Scottish army' (*Chronicle of Walter of Guisborough*, 324).

Wallace's movements between his return from England and the start of the Falkirk campaign are uncertain. The winter of 1297–8 saw limited incursions by the English, under Clifford in Annandale and Warenne in the east, but what part Wallace played in these events is unknown. No major English activity was possible until Edward's return from Flanders, and it must be assumed that Wallace used the time to assemble and train his army and to devise the strategy which brought him so close to victory against Edward. His presence at Torphichen in Linlithgowshire on 29 March 1298 is attested by a grant of that date to Alexander Scrymgeour, the hereditary standard-bearer of the Balliols, and himself subsequently executed for treason by Edward. In the grant to Scrymgeour, Wallace styles himself both knight and guardian of the kingdom and, as before, leader of the army in the name of King John. When he was knighted and by whom is not recorded, although an English source suggests that one of the premier earls of Scotland was involved in the ceremony. His election to the guardianship as the first sole occupant of the office arose naturally from his military achievements; whether or not the magnates approved, he was the obvious choice. The English were unimpressed by his new status. One of their political songs comments that 'from a robber he becomes a knight, just as a swan is made out of a raven; an unworthy man takes the seat, when a worthy man is not by' (*Wright's Political Songs*, 174). As guardian Wallace now imposed on the Scots a strategy hitherto alien, eschewing confrontation on the line of advance, and instead withdrawing to the north behind country systematically wasted.

The wisdom of Wallace's strategy was soon apparent. Edward, frustrated by his inability to bring Wallace to battle, moved deeper into Scotland. As he did so, his problems increased. Food was short, Wallace's situation was undiscovered, it was impossible to live off the land, and Edward for once had failed to ensure the supply of provisions by sea. A detachment under Antony Bek, bishop of Durham, sent by Edward to attack the castles of Dirleton and Tantallon, had no food other than beans and peas from the fields and the rest of the army was in no better condition. By 19 July Edward was at Temple Liston, on the right bank of the Almond. The few supplies which reached him contained 200 tuns of wine. This Edward unwisely distributed. The Welsh, their morale and loyalty equally suspect, became drunk and rioted, killing a number of priests. The cavalry thereupon charged the Welsh. Eighty were killed and the rest spent the night apart from the main army, threatening to change sides. Edward stated that if necessary he would, with God's help, defeat the Welsh and Scots together. He recognized the true nature of his predicament, however, in his decision to fall back on Edinburgh, as a possible preliminary to the abandonment of the campaign. A withdrawal from Scotland by Edward at this time would not have ended the war but the blow to his prestige and the likely resumption of his struggle with his barons would have given Wallace the opportunity further to strengthen his position and thus have affected the course of the war.

The battle of Falkirk The most renowned of Plantagenet kings, outgeneralled by a man for whom he and his people had nothing but contempt, was saved from disaster by news from a scout brought to him on 21 July by two earls, Patrick of Dunbar and Gilbert Umfraville of Angus. From the scout Edward learned that the Scots were no more than 18 miles away, at Falkirk. According to Guisborough, who gives the fullest account of these events, the scout also revealed Wallace's plans. He had discovered Edward's intention to retire on Edinburgh and thought to attack the retreating English by night, when they were most vulnerable. A set-piece battle was not part of Wallace's strategy. Edward's response was both spirited and immediate; praising God who had delivered the enemy to him, he declared that he would not wait upon an attack by the Scots but would instead seek them out. He led his army in the direction of Falkirk and by this action seized the initiative from Wallace. That night, 21 July, the English camped to the east of Linlithgow. Despite his apparent confidence Edward was still conscious of the possibility of attack by the Scots; his men were to rest with their horses beside them. During the night he was injured by his horse but he quelled the panic in his camp when he proved his fitness by mounting his horse. At dawn on the next day, the feast of St Mary Magdalene, Tuesday 22 July, he led his army through Linlithgow towards Falkirk.

Shortly afterwards the English had their first sight of the enemy. On the top of a hill a large body of Scottish spearmen was sighted. The English took this to be the main body of Wallace's army but the spearmen disappeared. What their function was is unclear. If, however, the information from Edward's scout was correct, the spearmen may have constituted the leading element in the proposed attack on the English. Events had overtaken Wallace and he was faced with a battle he had not sought. His dispositions, however, indicate that he had clearly understood that, ultimately, he would have to meet Edward in battle. The English saw a Scottish army divided into four schiltroms, composed of infantry armed with spears with 12 inch iron tips. Each schiltrom, in the words of Guisborough, 'was made up wholly of spearmen, standing shoulder to shoulder in deep ranks and facing towards the circumference of the circle, with their spears slanting outwards at an oblique angle' (*Chronicle of Walter of Guisborough*, 327). A fence of stakes protected each schiltrom. The Scots could not match the English in heavy cavalry, the latter's principal weapon; if the schiltrom thwarted the expected cavalry assault, the fence could be moved aside to allow the spearmen an offensive role. The numbers in each schiltrom are unrecorded. Wallace had stationed his archers, a small force from the Forest of Selkirk under Sir John Stewart of Jedburgh, brother of James Stewart, between the schiltroms. The cavalry, probably controlled by John Comyn the younger of Badenoch, 'the Red', was to the rear. Behind the Scots lay Callander Wood, in front the Westquarter Burn and a small loch hidden from the English. Wallace had chosen neither the moment nor the location for his meeting with Edward; in the circumstances his dispositions were sound. Retreat was not an option; it would have damaged his credibility and given the English cavalry its opportunity. A remark attributed to him at Falkirk suggests that he recognized the parlous situation of his army. To his spearmen he said: 'I have brought you to the ring; now see if you can dance' (Rishanger, *Chronicle*, 187).

Wallace's dispositions were such as to give Edward pause. He was opposed to an immediate engagement and wished to allow his army rest and refreshment. His subordinates would not listen and the earls of Norfolk, Hereford, and Lincoln led the vanguard forward. Their momentum was slowed by the loch between them and the Scots and they were forced to swing westward. Antony Bek, in charge of the English right wing, was apparently, like Edward, in favour of caution but was overruled by his commanders. The two wings then clashed with the schiltroms. At this juncture the Scottish cavalry fled, whether from treachery, as was later asserted in Scottish accounts, or from fear as at Irvine, cannot be known. The loss of the cavalry was to prove a great blow to Wallace. The schiltroms, however, trained and controlled by him, proved their worth against the repeated cavalry charges; more than 100 English horses were killed. Edward's strategy during the campaign had been flawed; his tactics now restored his reputation. He withdrew his cavalry and advanced his Welsh longbowmen and Genoese crossbowmen. At Bannockburn, sixteen years later, Robert Bruce kept in reserve a small cavalry force against such an eventuality, a lesson learned from Falkirk. Wallace was deprived of the use of the cavalry by its flight and the schiltroms, with Stewart and his archers slain in the early English charges, were unprotected. They stood, an increasingly easy target, their discipline a credit to Wallace. The slaughter of the infantry was immense, both under the hail of missiles and the subsequent renewed cavalry assaults. One English chronicler relates that the Scots fell like blossoms in an orchard when the fruit had ripened. The majority of those who perished at Falkirk were of the common people who had discerned in Wallace their best hope of salvation. Not all of their betters left them to their fate. Sir John Stewart died with his men as, according to Fordun, did Macduff, son of Earl Malcolm

of Fife. Guisborough reports that while most of the knights fled, a handful remained to direct the schiltroms.

Attempts at diplomacy Wallace himself left the field before the end. The inevitable English charge of cowardice can safely be discounted. There is reason to believe that Wallace supervised the escape of Scottish survivors, while the ambush of Brian le Jay, master of the English Templars, was an action of the kind in which Wallace excelled. The English, exhausted by the battle and still without adequate supplies, could not follow up their victory and Wallace had time to reach Stirling, where he burnt the town and castle. Edward restored both, then began a phased withdrawal from Scotland by way of Ayr and Lochmaben, reaching Carlisle on 9 September. Of Wallace's movements at this time we have, as so often, little evidence. At some date between Falkirk and the following December he resigned the guardianship, to be succeeded by Robert Bruce, earl of Carrick, and John Comyn the younger of Badenoch, an uneasy coalition reflecting Scottish conservatism. Historians have seen Wallace's resignation as inevitable after Falkirk. Scottish tradition is, however, less positive. Fordun, for example, places the resignation 'at the water of Forth' soon after Falkirk, and blames it on Scottish treachery, but indicates that Wallace chose to resign 'of his own accord' (Fordun, 2.324). Despite Falkirk no credible alternative to him as commander existed; had he determined to remain as guardian, he could scarcely have been forced from the position without damage to Scottish unity, a fragile thing at any time. He rejected this option, as he did, according to an allegation at his trial in 1305, an offer of clemency from Edward. A year after Falkirk he was in the field against the English. He then went abroad to argue the Scottish case.

We know something of Wallace's intentions from a letter of 20 August 1299 from Robert Hastings, the English constable of Roxburgh, to his king. Hastings passed to Edward an account by an informant of a council of Scots magnates at Peebles:

> at the council, Sir David Graham demanded the lands and goods of Sir William Wallace because he was leaving the kingdom without the leave or approval of the Guardians. And Sir Malcolm, Sir William's brother, answered that neither his lands nor his goods should be given away, for they were protected by the peace in which Wallace had left the kingdom, since he was leaving for the good of the kingdom. (Barrow, *Robert Bruce*, 107)

A description follows of a violent altercation between Graham and Malcolm Wallace, in which Bruce and Comyn, still ostensibly colleagues in the guardianship, joined on opposing sides. It required intervention by Stewart and others to prevent bloodshed.

The letter does not reveal what decision was taken on Wallace's lands. He had in any case reached France, where he remained for at least a year, by early November 1299. Wallace went to the court of Philippe IV to try to persuade him once more to support the Scots against Edward. Philippe, whose sister Margaret had married Edward in September, was at first hostile to Wallace. He had him arrested and offered to surrender him to Edward. In thanking Philippe, Edward asked merely that Wallace be kept in France. With time Philippe's attitude to Wallace changed. In a letter of 7 November 1300, a year after Wallace's arrival in France, Philippe wrote to 'his lieges destined for the Roman court' with the request that they obtain 'the Pope's favour for his beloved William le Walois, knight, in the matter which he wishes to forward with His Holiness' (Stevenson, *Documents Illustrative of Sir William Wallace*, 163). French records name a number of Scots associated with Wallace in France, all of them devoted to the restoration of Balliol, and Wallace's presence in France and possibly in Rome was part of a larger initiative. In May–June 1301 a powerful Scottish delegation, in which Master Baldred Bisset played a leading role, was in Rome to present a rebuttal of Edward's claim to Scotland and it was natural that Wallace should wish to support this endeavour in person. A safe-conduct from Hakon V, found on Wallace at his capture, hints at a visit to Norway but no proof exists that it occurred.

Resistance renewed The date of Wallace's return to Scotland is unknown. That he was once more in the field against Edward in 1303 is certain, although the assertion in an English chronicle that in that year the Scots 'began to rebel, making William Wallace their commander and captain' (Rishanger, *Chronicle*, 213) does not accurately reflect his role. In his absence, the Scots had met with varying fortune. Campaigns in Scotland by Edward in 1300 and 1301 had been inconclusive and hopes of a Balliol restoration were high in 1301. The next year, however, was not a happy one for the Scots. In January Robert Bruce submitted to Edward. At Courtrai in July the French met with a defeat so serious at the hands of the Flemings that Philippe IV, in order to retrieve the position, sought an accommodation with Edward. In August Pope Boniface VIII (r. 1294–1303), hitherto sympathetic to Scotland, wrote to the Scottish bishops to seek peace with Edward. A year which had begun well for the Scots with a truce of nine months with Edward had by the autumn so deteriorated that the very real danger of an Anglo-French peace which excluded Scotland was recognized. To avert the danger a Scottish delegation was sent to Paris. Among those involved were John Soules, sole guardian since early 1301, and Bishop Lamberton. John Comyn remained in Scotland to direct the war and it was he rather than Wallace therefore who was at this time the principal figure in the resistance to Edward. On 24 February 1303 Comyn inflicted a defeat on the English under Sir John Segrave at Roslin. The delegation to Paris, however, failed in its purpose and on 20 May the feared Anglo-French treaty was agreed. In the summer of 1303 Edward carried out an extensive campaign, and by September he had reached Kinloss Abbey before wintering at Dunfermline.

Wallace is not known to have been at Roslin. Yet he was not inactive. In June 1303, with Comyn and Simon Fraser, he left the Forest of Selkirk to raid through Annandale and Liddesdale and into Cumberland. This raid and other individual acts of defiance could not turn the tide against Edward, with whom Comyn, acting for the Scots, was forced to negotiate. On 9 February 1304, at Strathord,

Comyn submitted. From the relatively lenient terms imposed on the Scots Wallace was specifically excluded: 'as for Sir William Wallace, it is agreed that he may render himself up to the will and mercy of our sovereign lord the king, if it shall seem good to him' (*RotP*, 1.213). An English chronicle relates that early in 1304 Wallace had sought through friends to submit to Edward. It adds that Wallace's request for an inducement to submit so angered Edward that he offered 300 marks to any man who killed Wallace. Edward continued to use every means to bring Wallace to account. A parliament at St Andrews in March outlawed Wallace, Simon Fraser, and the garrison of Stirling, which still held out against Edward. In July Fraser submitted and Stirling fell to Edward, but Wallace remained at large, the search for him growing increasingly intense.

The pursuit of Wallace had apparently begun soon after his return to Scotland. On 15 March 1303 certain Scots had been rewarded with money by Edward for an attempted ambush of Wallace and Fraser. On 10 September reimbursement was made for the loss of two horses in a similar venture. From his winter quarters Edward in March 1304 sent against Wallace and Fraser a large force under Segrave, Sir Robert Clifford, and Sir William Latimer. With them went Robert Bruce. The raid failed in its primary purpose of capturing Wallace and Fraser, but defeated them at Happrew near Peebles. Edward rewarded Nicholas Oysel, who had brought news of Happrew, and John of Musselburgh, who had guided the English force, but was displeased at the escape of the two Scots. Wallace was not easily to be taken; nor had he lost his skill as a soldier. In September 1304, in a skirmish 'below Earnside', in Stirlingshire, he inflicted casualties on a superior force under Aymer de Valence and made his escape. Edward put considerable pressure on the Scots to ensure Wallace's capture. James Stewart, Sir John Soules, and Sir Ingram Umfraville were not to be given letters of safe-conduct until Wallace was taken. Comyn, Sir Alexander Lindsay, Sir David Graham, and Fraser would have their sentences of exile or otherwise remitted if they captured Wallace before the twentieth day after Christmas. Lest there should still be doubt in the minds of the Scots, Edward informed Alexander Abernethy that 'it is not at all our pleasure that you hold out any word of peace to him, or to any other of his company, unless they place themselves absolutely and in all things at our will without any reservation whatsoever' (Stevenson, *Documents Illustrative of Sir William Wallace*, 2, no. 471).

Capture and death In such circumstances it was only a matter of time before Wallace was captured. He survived, by means unknown, until 3 August 1305, when he was seized, in or near Glasgow, by servants of Sir John Menteith, Edward's keeper of Dumbarton. For his part in the capture Menteith was rewarded with land and other marks of Edward's favour. Sixty marks were distributed to those who had assisted in the capture, and forty marks given to 'the servant who had spied out William Wallace' (Stevenson, *Documents Illustrative of Sir William Wallace*, 169). English accounts emphasize that Wallace was betrayed by his own countrymen, but it has been argued that Menteith, at least, was merely carrying out his sworn duty. After Edward had refused to see him, Wallace was brought to London by Sir John Segrave on 22 August, amid great popular excitement, and lodged overnight in the property of William Leyre, an alderman, in Fenchurch. Early the next morning, again to great excitement, he was taken to Westminster Hall on horseback in a procession which included Segrave, his brother Geoffrey, and justices, sheriffs and aldermen. Inside the hall he was made to stand on a scaffold at the south end. A laurel crown had been placed on his head, to mock, it was said, his boast that one day he would wear a crown there. The principal figure in the commission of gaol delivery appointed to try Wallace was the justice Peter Mallore, and it was he who presented the indictment. Wallace denied the charge of treason, since he had never sworn allegiance to Edward, but admitted the other charges. There was no trial in the modern sense. The proceedings were a formality, as was the judgment, given on the same day by Segrave. Wallace, disregarding his fealty and allegiance, had risen in arms against the English king; he had exercised authority 'as if a superior' in Scotland, making an alliance with France in the process; he had waged destructive war in both Scotland and northern England; and he had continued in his resistance to Edward I even after his defeat at Falkirk. Since his legal standing was by 1305 that of an outlawed thief, the law allowed him no defence. Consequently he was to be drawn on a hurdle to the gallows at Smithfield, hanged, his heart and bowels taken out and burnt, his body quartered. His head was to be cut off and placed on London Bridge, his quarters displayed at Newcastle, Berwick, Stirling, and Perth. The sentence, the standard one for treason, was carried out immediately. To Sir John Segrave fell the task of distributing the severed limbs to their various destinations in Scotland; 'for the carriage of the body of William le Waleys' he received the sum of fifteen shillings (*CDS*, 2, no. 485).

Patriot and hero No contemporary equalled Wallace in courage and constancy in the cause of Scottish independence. Others (some of them unjustly overlooked since) met the same end but, unlike such as Simon Fraser and John, earl of Atholl (*d.* 1306), Wallace could not be guilty of treason since he had never taken an oath to Edward. When he might have saved his life by submission, he judged the price, the abandonment of the cause to which he had devoted himself, too great. That he could have saved his life before 1303 seems certain; Edward's offer of clemency after Falkirk and his response to Philippe IV's news of the apprehension of Wallace suggest that Edward was then less intransigent than he became in the matter of Wallace. The latter's continued defiance of Edward after his return to Scotland accelerated the search for Wallace. It is sometimes argued today that in 1303 Wallace was already something of a spent force. Yet the view of Rishanger, albeit unsubstantiated, that Wallace then again assumed the leadership of the Scots reflects the persistent English perception of Wallace as the source of Scottish resistance. His defeat at Falkirk had cost him an army but

not, for the English, that pre-eminent position. At Stirling and in the Falkirk campaign Wallace demonstrated military qualities which Edward, a vastly experienced soldier, could not fail to appreciate. Where Wallace acquired those qualities, and that political and diplomatic skill of which there are few but significant indications, it is impossible to say. But the combination made him unique in a society unprepared for his emergence and, ultimately, unable to tolerate him. Of his time in his devotion to religion and his cruelty to enemies, he was in advance of it in his challenge to current doctrines in war and politics. In rebelling against Edward he threatened revolution. His isolation, pursued by the English and alienated from the ruling classes in Scotland, was inevitable. He was the victim of his own success.

Wallace remained, chiefly through the poem by Blind Hary, a popular figure in Scottish folklore in the seventeenth and eighteenth centuries. The Latin poetry of Thomas Ruddiman (1674–1757) presented Wallace as a popular, radical bastion against imperial power. Robert Burns's verses 'Scots wha hae wi' Wallace bled' were for two centuries in effect the Scottish national anthem. Early in the nineteenth century consideration was given to a national memorial of 'the Scottish hero', as Victorians often referred to Wallace. *Traditions, &c. Respecting Sir William Wallace* (1856) records much Wallace folklore. The nationalism characteristic of the 1850s reached its culmination when, on 24 June 1861, the duke of Atholl laid the foundation stone of the national Wallace monument, designed by J. T. Roach of Glasgow. The monument, 220 feet high and placed on the Abbey Crag, north of Stirling overlooking the battlefield, is rivalled as a monument to a Scot only by that to Sir Walter Scott in Edinburgh. At its foot is a 'hall of [Scottish] heroes', such as Bruce, Buchanan, Knox, Burns, Livingstone, and Gladstone. The hall also contains what is thought to be Wallace's sword. Derivative monuments to Wallace reflected reviving Scottish patriotism in many parts of the empire; that at Ballarat, Victoria, unveiled in 1889, was the best known, a focus of Scottish national sentiment in Australia. Wallace's pre-eminence in the Scottish historical tradition is also marked by the positioning of his statue, together with that of Robert Bruce, at the entrance to Edinburgh Castle. Wallace's reputation received a different but equally fervent memorial in the film *Braveheart*, which Mel Gibson directed in 1995, also playing the starring role of Wallace and achieving a great international success. This modern retelling of Wallace's story reflected the approach to the subject adopted by Hary. There is the same distortion of fact and manipulation of chronology, the same ability to arouse a range of emotions, and the same anti-English sentiment. Present, too, is the view of Wallace as the inspiration behind Bruce's conversion to the cause of Scottish independence. Despite the potency of this mixture, the Wallace who emerges in the film is as two-dimensional as Hary's creation; to that extent, epic and film alike do him a disservice. Our knowledge of Wallace is limited, but such reliable evidence as we have points to a quite exceptional figure whose reputation is secure without the need for invention. The status of Hary's work as an authority on Wallace has in any case declined with the acknowledgement of its true function. Hary was intent on countering the pro-English policies of James III, and the adventures of Wallace, inveterate foe of the English and patriotic martyr, were admirably suited to his purpose. Even so, Hary's poem established a national stereotype of such remarkable force that Wallace remains not merely the first but the most durable and heroic of Scottish patriots.					ANDREW FISHER

Sources CDS • Rymer, *Foedera* • John of Fordun, *Scotichronicon*, ed. W. F. Skene, 2 vols. (1871–2) • *The chronicle of Walter of Guisborough*, ed. H. Rothwell, CS, 3rd ser., 89 (1957) • H. Maxwell, ed., *Chronicle of Lanercost* (1913) • F. Palgrave, ed., *Documents and records illustrating the history of Scotland* (1837) • *Hary's Wallace*, ed. M. P. McDiarmid, 2 vols., STS, 4th ser., 4–5 (1968–9) • J. Stevenson, ed., *Documents illustrative of Sir William Wallace* (1841) • J. Stevenson, ed., *Documents illustrative of the history of Scotland*, 2 vols. (1870) • [W. Rishanger], *The chronicle of William de Rishanger, of the barons' wars*, ed. J. O. Halliwell, CS, 15 (1840) • W. Stubbs, ed., *Chronicles of the reigns of Edward I and Edward II*, 2 vols., Rolls Series, 76 (1882–3) • P. Coss, ed., *Thomas Wright's political songs of England* (1996) • A. Fisher, *William Wallace* (1986); new edn (2001) • G. W. S. Barrow, *Robert Bruce*, 3rd edn (1988) • J. G. Bellamy, *The law of treason in England in the later middle ages* (1970) • M. G. H. Pittock, *The invention of Scotland* (1991) • *Proceedings at the laying of the foundation stone of the national Wallace monument* (1861) • *Guide to the national Wallace monument* (1904)

Likenesses A. Carrick, statue, Edinburgh Castle • R. Forrest, statue, Lanark • portrait, National Wallace Monument, Stirling

Wallace, William (*d.* 1631), architect, was appointed principal master mason to all his majesty's works in Scotland on 18 April 1617. Nothing is known of his family background or earlier career, except that he was of Scottish nationality and had worked at Edinburgh Castle as a carver in 1616; he had also provided moulds for the plasterers there. Although he appears to have lived at Musselburgh, 5 miles east of Edinburgh (he was paid for travelling from there in 1618), he became a master of the Edinburgh masons' lodge by 1624 and its deacon by 1628.

Wallace worked closely with James Murray of Kilbaberton, principal master of works from 1607 to 1634. At a period of transition in the relative roles of the principal officers of the royal works, when the king was rarely in Scotland, it remains debatable who took the lead in designing the buildings on which they jointly worked. Nevertheless, analysis of the details of those with which Wallace was involved, both in an official and in an unofficial capacity, reveals shared traits, which suggest an identifiably personal approach to design. These traits include: strong articulation of the elevations by salient stair turrets, which are sometimes set on the principal axes; extensive use above windows and doorways of strapwork gablets or of pediments with carved tympana; prominent dormer windows flanked by pilasters; carved quoins; and prominent chimney stacks with volutes at their bases. None of these features is unique to Wallace, although the confident permutations on these themes in his work suggest that he was a central figure in the evolution of a Scottish synthesis of architectural ideas, in which inspiration from English, Netherlandish, and possibly Danish prototypes and pattern books was particularly important.

With such lavish embellishment, his buildings clearly required patrons with deep pockets.

Some buildings can be definitely associated with Wallace. From 1615 he took part in remodelling the palace within Edinburgh Castle in anticipation of the 'homecoming' of James I (James VI of Scotland) in 1617. This brief royal visit to Scotland in turn led to the rebuilding of the collapsed north range of Linlithgow Palace, between 1618 and 1624, in which Wallace was closely involved. In 1625, in anticipation of the homecoming of Charles I in 1633, Wallace carved the royal beasts for the roof ridges of the great hall and palace at Stirling Castle; in the following year he was working at the palace of Holyroodhouse. From 1628 he was active on what was probably his most important single building, Heriot's Hospital in Edinburgh, although this school and charitable foundation was not to be finished until *c.*1700. Its quadrangular plan with towered angle pavilions shows an awareness of the designs of Sebastiano Serlio, the north Italian architect whose treatise of architecture exercised such a powerful classicizing influence on early modern British architecture; the elevations, however, are in the Anglo-Netherlandish idiom seen elsewhere in Wallace's work. His contribution to the design process is in little doubt here, since his widow agreed to hand over his moulds and drawings in return for financial help from the school's governors.

It is clear, from money recorded as owing to him after his death, that Wallace had also worked on Winton House, Haddingtonshire, for the third earl of Wintoun, and on Moray House in Edinburgh, for the dowager countess of Home. In addition to domestic architecture, he designed monuments, including that of John Byres of Coates (*d.* 1629), in the Edinburgh Greyfriars churchyard. Wallace's name has attracted many other attributions, including Argyll's Lodging in Stirling, nearing completion for Sir William Alexander (the future first earl of Stirling) in the early 1630s. Sir William was the father of Sir Anthony Alexander, a joint master of works to the crown from 1629 and thus a colleague of Wallace's. The family connections, together with the stylistic similarities of the lodging with Wallace's work elsewhere, make this attribution particularly attractive.

Wallace married Agnes, daughter of Andrew Blackhall, minister of Inveresk (near Musselburgh); at his death, in late October 1631, after what was possibly a protracted illness, she and their young children were left in needy circumstances.					RICHARD FAWCETT

Sources J. Imrie and J. G. Dunbar, eds., *Accounts of the masters of works for building and repairing royal palaces and castles*, 2 (1982) • R. S. Mylne, *The master masons to the crown of Scotland and their works* (1893) • W. Wallace, testament, NA Scot., CC 8/8/56, fols. 39v–40v • D. Howard, *Scottish architecture: Reformation to Restoration, 1560–1660* (1995), vol. 2 of *The architectural history of Scotland* • C. B. Gunn, ed., *George Heriot's Hospital* (1906) • A. Rowan, 'George Heriot's Hospital, Edinburgh [pt 1]', *Country Life*, 157 (1975), 554–7 • A. Rowan, 'George Heriot's Hospital, Edinburgh [pt 2]', *Country Life*, 157 (1975), 634–7 • Colvin, *Archs.* • J. G. Dunbar, *The historic architecture of Scotland* (1966); 2nd edn (1978)

Wealth at death apparently poor; widow had to seek financial help

Wallace, William (1768–1843), mathematician, was born on 23 September 1768 at Dysart, Fife, the eldest son of Alexander Wallace, a leather manufacturer, and his wife, Janet Simson. He received an inadequate school education, but was instructed in arithmetic by his father. In 1784 his family moved to Edinburgh where he was apprenticed to a bookbinder. Here, by his own industry, he mastered geometry, fluxions, and astronomy. In 1788 he attended John Robison's lectures on natural philosophy. Robison introduced him to John Playfair, who assisted him and who remained his patron thereafter. Subsequently he exchanged his occupation for that of a warehouseman in a printing office, and also took on work as a private tutor, learning Latin and French so that he could study continental mathematics.

In 1794, after briefly working as a bookseller's shopman, Wallace was appointed mathematical teacher in Perth Academy on Playfair's recommendation. In the same year he married. In 1796 he submitted his first paper (on geometrical porisms) to the *Transactions of the Royal Society of Edinburgh*, and wrote the article 'Porism' for the third edition of the *Encyclopaedia Britannica* (1801). His next paper, submitted to the Royal Society of Edinburgh in 1802, concerned the application of an ingenious method for the rectification of the ellipse to a problem of physical astronomy. This paper established Wallace's reputation as a mathematician, although it later emerged that his method had been anticipated by A. M. Legendre (1752–1833), in a memoir of 1794. This induced Wallace to publish a translation of Legendre's memoir in Leybourn's *Mathematical Repository* (1809 and 1814).

In 1803, following his patron's advice, Wallace applied for the office of mathematical master in the Royal Military College at Marlow (later at Sandhurst), a post obtained after hard competition. After he moved there his family increased rapidly, and he had three daughters and a son. In 1804 he was elected a fellow of the Royal Society of Edinburgh. A regular contributor of encyclopaedia articles, he submitted papers of a geometrical nature, incorporating applications to geodesy and astronomy; he also contributed several translations of French memoirs and some geometrical problems to the *Mathematical Repository*. In 1804, writing as 'Scoticus', he proposed for proof a problem, now known as Wallace's theorem, which states 'if four lines intersect each other to form four triangles by omitting one line in turn, the circumcircles of these triangles have a point in common' (*Mathematical Repository*, n.s. 1, 1804, 22). Wallace was one of those individuals who realized very early the need for a mathematical renaissance in Britain. A decade before the Cambridge reform in 1816, he and his colleague at Marlow, James Ivory, abandoned the fluxional calculus in their contributions to the *Repository*. However, Wallace considered his most significant step towards fostering mathematics to be his article 'Fluxions' published in the *Edinburgh Encyclopaedia* in 1815—the first systematic presentation of the continental calculus in Britain.

In 1819 Wallace succeeded John Leslie as professor of mathematics in Edinburgh University. This position was the crowning object of his ambition and he cherished being held in high esteem by his students, such as D. F. Gregory and T. Galloway. Delight in practical applications induced him to invent, and give his name to, the eidograph, with which drawings could be copied to a larger or smaller scale, and the chorograph, a simple calculating device for cartographers to find the position of a station given the angles made to it from three points in the same plane. He superintended the erection of two observatories, one at Sandhurst and another on Calton Hill, Edinburgh, with the nearby monument to Napier, the inventor of logarithms. In 1838 he retired due to ill health, and was accorded a civil pension of £300 a year. He received the degree of LLD from the university on 17 November 1838. He published two books, *Conic Sections* (1837) and *Geometrical Theorems and Analytical Formulae* (1839). He died at Edinburgh on 28 April 1843.

GEORGE STRONACH, rev. MARIA PANTEKI

Sources *Monthly Notices of the Astronomical Society of London*, 6 (1843–5), 31–41 · M. Panteki, 'William Wallace and the introduction of continental calculus to Britain: a letter to George Peacock', *Historia Mathematica*, 14 (1987), 119–32 · Chambers, *Scots.* (1872) · d. cert. · A. D. D. Craik, 'Calculus and analysis in early 19th-century Britain: the work of William Wallace', *Historia Mathematica*, 26 (1999), 239–67 · A. D. D. Craik, 'Geometry versus analysis in early 19th-century Scotland: John Leslie, William Wallace, and Thomas Carlyle', *Historia Mathematica*, 27 (2000), 133–63
Archives Institute of Actuaries, London, MSS · U. Edin. L., notebook | BL, Macvey Napier corresp. · LUL, letter to G. Peacock, A.L.483 1833 · RS, Herschel collection, HS 18: 21–27 · U. Edin., New Coll. L., letters to Thomas Chalmers
Likenesses J. Thomson, oils, c.1825, U. Edin. · A. Geddes, pencil and chalk drawing, Scot. NPG · A. Geddes, portrait, Scot. NPG
Wealth at death £1725 12s. 0d.: confirmation, 1843, Scotland

Wallace, William (1818–1888). *See under* Wallace family (*per.* 1841–1925).

Wallace, William (1844–1897), philosopher, was born at Cupar, Fife, on 11 May 1844, the son of James Cooper Wallace, builder, and his wife, Jean, *née* Kelloch, both persons of considerable originality and force of character. After attending Madras Academy in Cupar and spending four years at the University of St Andrews, and electing not to pursue theological studies as his parents had hoped, Wallace gained an exhibition at Balliol College, Oxford, in 1864, and in 1867 became fellow of Merton College. He graduated BA in 1868 and proceeded MA in 1871. In 1868 he was appointed a tutor of Merton, and in 1871 he became its librarian. In 1872 he married Janet Barclay, whom he had known from his childhood; a daughter and two sons were born to them. His brother Edwin Wallace, author of *Outlines of the Philosophy of Aristotle* (1883), was vice-provost of Worcester College from 1881 to his death in 1884. In 1882 Wallace succeeded T. H. Greene as Whyte professor of moral philosophy, and he held that office, along with the Merton tutorship, until his death fifteen years later.

As a professor, Wallace had a great influence upon many generations of students of philosophy at Oxford. In his lectures he aimed not so much at the detailed exposition of philosophical systems as at encouraging students to think critically. He lectured without notes, and seemed to develop his subject as he spoke. His humorous, elegant, and yet earnest lectures produced a unique impression of insight and sincerity.

Wallace's writings are almost all devoted to the exposition of German philosophy, particularly the philosophy of Hegel. In 1873 he published *The Logic of Hegel*, translated from the work known as the *Encyclopaedia of the Philosophical Sciences*. The first full English translation entitled this work Wallace's *Logic* and was a free and creative rendition, accompanied by notes explicating difficult parts of the text. Wallace drew parallels between classical philosophy and contemporary German and British thinkers, connecting, for example, Hegel's Idea and the Idea of Plato and Aristotle; he also highlighted the links between Hegelianism and Christianity. Reissued a little more than one hundred years after its first publication, it was still deemed 'the most masterly and influential of all English translations of Hegel' (Findlay, v). Such idiosyncratic, often amusing, notes as 'the Absolute Idea may be compared to the old man who utters the same creed as a child, but for whom it is pregnant with the significance of a lifetime' (ibid., v) contributed to the distinctiveness of Wallace's translation. Well read in both classical and modern literature, Wallace was particularly successful in freeing philosophical conceptions from technical terms and reclothing them in language of much literary force and beauty. In 1892 he produced a second edition of *The Logic of Hegel*, which was reissued the following year with the addition of a long analytical introduction. His work on Hegel culminated in his translation entitled *The Philosophy of Mind* (1894), which was also republished almost a century after its first publication. Regarding Hegel as fundamentally a German philosopher whose thought was alien to a British audience, Wallace's introduction and notes accentuated those elements of the texts which resonated with British readers, especially with fellow idealists. Accordingly, he treated the dialectic fleetingly but fully discussed themes of unity and community in Hegel.

In addition to his monumental translations of Hegel, Wallace's brief biographical account of Kant (1882), which depicted Kant as engaged in a dialogue with Locke and Hume, added to the growing Kantian scholarship by J. H. Stirling, Edward Caird, John Watson, and others. In his spirited and forceful biography of Schopenhauer, published in 1890, Wallace traced the alternating depth and shallowness of the philosopher's repudiation of empiricism and materialism, complaining of his 'unconquerable vanity' (*The Life of Arthur Schopenhauer*, 112) but praising his insight into the power of art and his belief that the best life is one predicated on the underlying unity of all experience. He read widely and travelled to various parts of Germany to acquaint himself with the geographical and cultural environment. Wallace's Gifford lectures on the history of natural theology, delivered at the University of Glasgow in 1892, were posthumously published in a collection of essays and lectures edited by Edward Caird.

Wallace was a keen botanist, cyclist, and mountaineer

whose rather abrupt manner concealed a generous and affectionate nature. His knowledge of Kant, Fichte, Herder, and Hegel was exceptional and his contribution towards the reception of German thought in Britain singular. Wallace died at the Rock of Gibraltar inn, Bletchington, near Oxford, on 19 February 1897, the day after a bicycling accident from which he never fully recovered consciousness. He was buried at Holywell cemetery, Oxford, on 22 February.

S. M. DEN OTTER

Sources J. N. Findlay, 'Introduction', in W. Wallace, *The logic of Hegel*, 3rd edn (1975) · W. Wallace, *Lectures and essays on natural theology and ethics*, ed. E. Caird (1898) [incl. memoir] · G. R. G. Mure, *A study of Hegel's logic* (1950) · *Mind*, new ser., 6 (1897), 287–8 · *Oxford Magazine* (24 March 1897), 217–18 · *Oxford Times* (27 Feb 1897) · *CGPLA Eng. & Wales* (1897) · *DNB*

Likenesses photograph, repro. in Wallace, *Lectures and essays on natural theology and ethics*, ed. Caird

Wealth at death £7434 0s. 1d.: administration, 30 March 1897, *CGPLA Eng. & Wales*

Wallace, (Charles) William [Bill] **(1855–1916)**, oil industrialist, was born in Calcutta on 21 November 1855, the elder son of Alexander Wallace, an East India merchant, and his wife, Helen, *née* Davidson. He was educated at Framlingham College, Suffolk (*c*.1866–1874), and in 1874 joined a Calcutta mercantile firm (not his father's). He rose rapidly in that business, helping to sort out its chaotic accounts, and in 1886 he refounded it as Shaw, Wallace & Co. In 1881 he married Ellen Charlotte, daughter of Captain George Fulton of the Royal Engineers, a veteran of the siege of Lucknow in 1857; they had two sons and three daughters.

One of the agencies held by Shaw Wallace was for marketing kerosene in India for the Burmah Oil Company. When in 1892 Wallace returned to London, he found himself helping out in the nearby London office of Burmah Oil, of which he became a director in 1902. There he assisted the chairman, John Cargill, who was based in Glasgow, over negotiating with the Admiralty an agreement, signed in 1905, to supply fuel oil from Rangoon.

Cargill and Wallace, aided by the company's consultant, Sir Boverton Redwood, jointly agreed to buy for Burmah Oil some Persian oil concessions from William Knox D'Arcy; Wallace thereafter maintained contacts with government departments in London. Despite bouts of severe liver disorder, Wallace agreed to become vice-chairman and managing director of a new firm, the Anglo-Persian Oil Company, set up in 1909 after oil had been discovered in Persia. His chairman was the aged imperialist Donald Alexander Smith, first Baron Strathcona. Wallace's executive assistant, and successor as managing director in 1910, was Charles Greenway, a former employee in Shaw Wallace.

From 1912 onwards, Greenway attempted to persuade the British government to purchase a majority stake in Anglo-Persian, and this was finally agreed in 1914. These negotiations, which involved a number of government departments, were protracted and arduous. Wallace monitored every move taken by Greenway, but remained largely in the background, emerging only when Greenway needed powerful support.

Wallace possessed the intellectual capacity and the

(Charles) **William Wallace** (1855–1916), by unknown
photographer

vision to have become one of the country's outstanding
oil entrepreneurs of his day. As an old India hand, he
grasped the immense economic and strategic advantages
to Britain of a presence in Persia, to forestall Russian
expansionist designs on Britain's route to the east. However, he exercised his talents mainly behind the scenes,
partly because of illness; yet he would not have been
happy as a high-profile tycoon. His influence sprang from
a thorough knowledge of commercial conditions in the
East and from his patent integrity and reliable judgement.
The latter was not infallible, however, as he thought that
the allies were going to lose the First World War; and he
could be crusty, sceptical, and outspoken to a fault. His
marriage ended in separation, but he got on well with his
children and was devastated by the death of his younger
son in action. A human touch was his legacy to a daughter's friend, Gwen Ffrangcon-Davies, to help her in what
later became an acting career of distinction.

Equally human were Wallace's idiosyncrasies, such as
his rule in Shaw Wallace that no one could be appointed
who was related to those already in the firm. Again, believing that wealth acquired from the people should be appropriately returned, he bequeathed the residue of his
£125,966 estate to the treasuries of Britain and India. In
1977 the British exchequer received from this source £1
million, and the governments of India, Pakistan, Bangla-
desh, and Burma shared in a further £1 million. Wallace
had no particular interests outside his work, apart from
recreational travel in company with one or more of his
daughters. Had he been a more contented man, his
achievements might have been less considerable.

On Strathcona's death in 1914, Wallace's reputation in
Whitehall was so high that he was officially recommended to be chairman of the Anglo-Persian Oil Company. He declined because of poor health; a year later he
had to give up all business commitments. By the time of
his death he had lost his sight; he died of kidney failure on
2 August 1916 at his London home, 76 Avenue Road, St
John's Wood.   T. A. B. CORLEY

Sources H. Townend, *A history of Shaw Wallace & Co. and Shaw Wallace & Co. Ltd* (1965) · T. A. B. Corley, *A history of the Burmah Oil Company*, 1: *1886–1924* (1983) · R. W. Ferrier, *The history of the British Petroleum Company*, 1: *The developing years, 1901–1932* (1982) · *Daily Telegraph*
(25 May 1977) · BL OIOC · m. cert.
Archives Burmah Castrol plc, Swindon, archives · U. Warwick
Mod. RC, archives of British Petroleum Co. plc
Likenesses W. Orpen, oils, priv. coll. · photograph, priv. coll. [*see
illus.*] · photographs, Swindon, archives of Burmah Castrol plc ·
photographs, U. Warwick Mod. RC, archives of British Petroleum
Co. plc
Wealth at death £125,966 0s. 6d.: probate, 2 Dec 1916, *CGPLA Eng.
& Wales*

Wallace, Sir William (1881–1963), marine engineer, was
born on 25 August 1881 in Paisley, Renfrewshire, the son of
Mathew Wallace, master dyer, and his wife, Agnes Reid.
His early education was at Paisley grammar school, after
which he was taken into apprenticeship in the Paisley
shipyard of Bow, McLachlan & Co.; during this time he
also attended technical classes at the West of Scotland
Technical College in Glasgow. His next step was to gain
engineering experience and, as was common at that time,
that meant a position as an engineering officer in a prominent shipping line. Wallace joined the British and Burm-
ese Steam Navigation Company, with whom he gained the
Board of Trade first class certificate and rose to the rank of
chief engineer.

Wallace spent nearly ten years at sea before he came
ashore in 1910 and joined the prominent Edinburgh firm
of Brown Brothers, hydraulic and general engineers and
iron-founders, whose premises were at the Rosebank ironworks. A talent for invention was quickly demonstrated,
and Brown Brothers took out patents for his developments with steering gear and hydraulic equipment. In
1916 Wallace was appointed managing director and celebrated his advancement by marrying, on 24 March, Christina, daughter of John Stewart, a coachman. They had a
son and a daughter. Brown Brothers was then deeply
involved in naval work, especially in supplying gear for
submarines; and in 1917 Wallace was on the submarine
K13 on a test in the Gareloch when it sank with seventy-
seven men on board. He is reported to have stopped water
flooding the boat by blocking off the hydraulic system,
and was one of the forty-six survivors rescued after being
submerged for fifty-seven hours.

Wallace's most long-lasting engineering innovations
came in the 1930s, when he was again undertaking work
for the Admiralty. He was among the first to develop cata-
pults for the early aircraft-carriers and regularly risked his
life by being his own test pilot, insisting that he be the first
to be catapulted by each of his improved devices. His most
important development came in 1936, when he took out a

patent to improve the stability of ships; the device was the first activated fin-ship stabilizer. The idea was ingenious but required considerable development, which was undertaken in co-operation with Maurice Denny (1886–1955) of the famous Dumbarton firm of shipbuilders. Their collaboration finally produced the Denny–Brown stabilizer, the first commercial version being installed in 1937 in the *Isle of Park*. The innovation was widely used by the Royal Navy during the Second World War to help stabilize gun-platforms, and in the post-war period it came into widespread use in merchant ships.

Brown Brothers prospered under Wallace's engineering inventiveness and shrewd management, and war work greatly extended its facilities until it employed over a thousand men, twice the size it had been when he had joined it before the First World War. Wallace's leadership and contributions to engineering earned him the CBE in 1944 and the KB in 1951. He was an active member of numerous professional associations, notably as vice-president of the Institution of Engineers and Shipbuilders in Scotland, and also of the Institute of Marine Engineers. His inventive talent and distinction won for his firm in 1951 a royal commission award of £27,510 for his work on stabilizers (shared with Denny of Dumbarton), and in 1954 the Society of Engineers awarded him the Churchill gold medal. The following year he received the gold medal of the Institution of Engineers and Shipbuilders in Scotland, and in 1956 he was elected a fellow of the Royal Society of Edinburgh and had an honorary LLD conferred on him by the University of Edinburgh.

At Brown Brothers, Wallace enjoyed a long and successful career as an inventor and engineer. He was managing director of the firm from 1916 to 1957, and then became chairman for a further two years before retiring. He was well known and respected in the business community and held positions on the boards of the British Linen Bank, Alex Cowan & Son, and the North British Rubber Company. He was also a director of the First, Second, and Third Edinburgh investment trusts, of William Beardmore & Co., and of the Leith shipbuilders Henry Robb & Co. His active business life was backed by his passion for golf. He was a member of the Honourable Company of Edinburgh Golfers (Muirfield) and captain of his local Bruntsfield Links Golfing Society. He was a family man whose son, William, succeeded him on the board of Brown Brothers. When he died on 27 May 1963 in a nursing home at 12 Drumsheugh Gardens, Edinburgh, his entire gross estate was worth over £45,000. His wife survived him. The company with which he was associated almost all his life did not outlast him for very long, as it was taken over by Vickers Ltd in 1970.   ANTHONY SLAVEN

Sources A. Slaven, 'Wallace, Sir William', *DSBB* · *WWW, 1961–70* · *The Scotsman* (29 May 1963) · *Glasgow Herald* (29 May 1963) · *The Times* (29 May 1963) · m. cert. · d. cert. · NA Scot., SC 70/1/1536, SC 70/4/1305
Likenesses J. Burgh, portrait, Brown Bros., Edinburgh
Wealth at death £45,458 17s. 0d.: confirmation, 30 July 1963, NA Scot., SC 70/1/1536/205–10

Wallace, William Arthur James (1842–1902), army officer and railway engineer, was born at Kingstown, co. Dublin, on 4 January 1842, the son of William James Wallace JP of co. Wexford. Educated at private schools and the Royal Military Academy, Woolwich, he was commissioned lieutenant in the Royal Engineers on 19 December 1860. After two years' training at Chatham and two years' service at home stations, Wallace in 1864 joined the railway branch of the public works department in India. He became executive engineer in 1871, then deputy consulting engineer for guaranteed railways administered from Calcutta. Promoted captain on 25 August 1873, and appointed officiating consulting engineer to the government of India at Lucknow in 1877, he went to Europe in 1878 in connection with the railway exhibits to the Paris Exhibition, and on his return to India in the autumn was appointed secretary to the railway conference at Calcutta. He worked out the details of a policy, advocated at the conference, of vigorous railway construction in India, a result of experience gained in the recent famine.

At the end of 1878 Wallace received the thanks of the commander-in-chief, Sir Frederick Haines, for conducting the transport of General Sir Donald Stewart's division over 300 miles of new railway on the Indus valley line between Multan and Sukkur, on its march to Kandahar. Serving under Sir Frederick Roberts as field engineer to the Kurram valley column in the Afghan campaign of 1879, Wallace was mentioned in dispatches, and commended for his work on road making and for his energy and skill in the management of the Ahmad Khel Jagis. When he returned from active service to railway work in August, Wallace was appointed engineer-in-chief and manager of the Northern Bengal Railway at Saidpur, was promoted major on 1 July, and arrived home on furlough in June 1882. On the recommendation of Major-General Sir Andrew Clarke, inspector-general of fortifications, Wallace was made director of a new railway corps, formed of the 8th company of Royal Engineers, to work the Egyptian railways in the coming Egyptian campaign. The railway corps contributed largely to the success of the operations in Egypt. Wallace's improvised corps proved how essential in war such an organization was, and led to its establishment in the service in an expanded form and on a more permanent basis. Wallace was present at the battle of Tell al-Kebir, was mentioned in dispatches, and received a brevet lieutenant-colonelcy on 18 November 1882 and the Osmanieh (4th class). When he returned to India in October 1884 Wallace was appointed acting chief engineer to the government of India for guaranteed railways at Lahore. In the spring of the following year, when the Panjdeh incident caused preparations for war with Russia, Wallace was appointed controller at Lahore of military troops and stores traffic for the frontier. The Afghanistan boundary question was settled in September 1885, but Wallace remained at Lahore as chief engineer for guaranteed railways until his transfer to Agra in April 1886. A brevet colonelcy was given to him on 18 November, and in the following year he returned to Lahore as chief engineer of the north-western railway.

In 1888 Wallace reported for the government of India on the Abt system of railways in Switzerland. On 1 January 1890 he was made CIE. He retired from the service on 19 December 1892. He died unmarried at 62 Elm Park Gardens, London, on 6 February 1902.

R. H. VETCH, *rev.* M. G. M. JONES

Sources *The Times* (11 Feb 1902) · Army List · War Office records · Royal Engineers records · W. Porter, *History of the corps of royal engineers*, 2 vols. (1889) · R. H. Vetch, *Life of Lieutenant-General Sir Andrew Clarke* (1905) · Susan, countess of Malmesbury [S. Ardagh], *The life of Major-General Sir John Ardagh* (1909) · *CGPLA Eng. & Wales* (1902)

Wealth at death £15,360 10s. 2d.: probate, 14 March 1902, *CGPLA Eng. & Wales*

Wallace, William Francis Stuart (1860–1940), composer and writer on music, was born at 62 Regent Street, Greenock, on 3 July 1860, the first son of James Wallace (1826–1904), a prominent Scottish physician and surgeon, and his wife, Mary Cecilia Williamson. Educated at Fettes College in Edinburgh, he won a trustees' exhibition to Edinburgh University. This he later resigned, and he entered Glasgow University where he graduated MB and MCh in 1886. In Vienna, Paris, and Moorfields he studied ophthalmology before returning to Glasgow to take his MD in 1888. He practised medicine briefly in London, but his attraction to music led him to terminate his medical career in 1889 when he studied for two terms under A. C. Mackenzie and F. W. Davenport at the Royal Academy of Music. The decision to study music served to aggravate a volatile relationship with his father, who was ambitious for his son. His time at the Royal Academy of Music constituted his only period of formal training; after that he worked independently.

In the early 1890s Wallace began to produce a series of orchestral and vocal works including the scena *Lord of Darkness* (1890), the suite *A Scots Fantasy* (1891), *An American Rhapsody* (1891), and also *The Lady from the Sea* (1892), based on Henrik Ibsen's play. However, it was his first symphonic poem, *The Passing of Beatrice* (arguably the first modern British work in the genre), based on canto xxxi from Dante's 'Paradiso' in *The Divine Comedy*, that made the greatest impression at its first performance at the Crystal Palace on 26 November 1892 under August Manns. With Howard Orsmond Anderton, Wallace assisted Granville Bantock, a fellow Royal Academy of Music student, with the production of the *New Quarterly Musical Review* from May 1893 until February 1897. Bantock also did much to promote Wallace's music, first at a concert in London on 15 December 1896, and later at The Tower, New Brighton, where Bantock was musical director. At The Tower not only did Wallace have the opportunity to conduct entire concerts of his own work (particularly in 1898 and 1899) but, as Bantock's rehearsal conductor, he gained much experience from directing the music of other composers.

During a holiday in Hilders, Switzerland, in 1895, he met Ottilie Helen McLaren (1875–1947), daughter of John, Lord McLaren (1831–1910), judge of the court of sessions, MP, and lord advocate. In spite of Ottilie's being fifteen years younger, they fell in love and became engaged. Lord McLaren insisted that Wallace's income as a musician should be

no less than £600 a year before he and Ottilie could marry, a condition which prolonged their engagement for nine years. They were finally married on 11 April 1905 in St Giles' Cathedral, Edinburgh. Ottilie studied sculpting in Edinburgh under James Pittendrigh MacGillivray, before working in Paris under Auguste Rodin between 1897 and 1901. Her separation from Wallace provoked a sizeable correspondence between them—Wallace wrote almost daily—which Wallace preserved in a series of small books, covered with white vellum and fastened with coloured ribbon, now preserved in the National Library of Scotland.

For much of his creative life as a composer Wallace remained independent of musical institutions and societies. Later, however, he was a committee member of the Associated Board of the Royal Schools of Music and served as honorary secretary of the Royal Philharmonic Society and the Society of British Musicians in the years before the outbreak of war. During the war he returned to the medical profession, first as an eye specialist at the military hospital in Colchester before moving to the ophthalmic department in London's Second General Hospital. For five months Wallace was an inspector of ophthalmic centres in the eastern command and in 1919 he retired as a captain in the Royal Army Medical Corps. In 1924, at the invitation of John Blackwood McEwen, he joined the staff of the Royal Academy as a professor of harmony and composition, a post he retained until the year before his death. Though based in London, he and Ottilie bought a retirement home, Westport House, in Malmesbury, where he died on 16 December 1940 from bronchitis and the effects of Parkinson's disease.

External stimuli, be they Scottish, British, or more broadly European, were essential to Wallace's musical sensibility as he freely declared in his paper 'The scope of programme music' for the Musical Association on 9 May 1899. This is evident in his output of six symphonic poems, *The Passing of Beatrice* (1892), *Amboss oder Hammer* (1896), *Sister Helen* (1897), *Greeting to the New Century* (1901), *Sir William Wallace AD, 1305–1905* (1905), and *Villon* (1909), and his largest work, the *Creation Symphony*, begun in 1896 but not performed until 1899 at New Brighton. Several other symphonic poems including *Asperges*, *The Covenanters*, and *The Forty-Five* (all 1898) were unfinished, as was a three-movement choral symphony based on texts from Ecclesiastes. Wallace's musical language was heavily informed by Liszt, Wagner, and the progressivist spirit of late nineteenth-century Europe, and this preoccupation gave rise to his books *Richard Wagner as he Lived* (1925) and *Liszt, Wagner, and the Princess* (1927). It was also fuelled by his friendship with Granville Bantock, and set him apart from what he perceived as the more conservative, Brahms-orientated disposition of the Royal College of Music and the ancient universities. Unintimidated by his contemporaries he openly criticized the college in a letter to *The Times* in 1904 over the administration of the patron's fund. He nevertheless found a common cause with Charles Villiers Stanford in the Copyright Act of 1906.

Wallace's interest in the theatre (and Christian conviction) resulted in a mystery play, *The Divine Surrender* (1893), with incidental music (only the vocal scene *The Rhapsody of Mary Magdalene* survives), a prelude to Aeschylus's *The Eumenides*, and an unperformed lyric tragedy in one act, *Brassolis* (1896), as well as music for Shakespeare's *Romeo and Juliet* (1896) and Maurice Maeterlinck's *Pélléas et Mélisande* (1897). Dubbed 'A Protean Spirit' in *Musical Opinion* in 1920, Wallace evinced a broad interest in literature, drama, the visual arts, and science. He habitually mixed with painters such as Norman Hirst, Edwin James, Augustus John, Sholto Johnstone, James Douglas, and Detmar Blow—together they briefly formed a circle called the Anonymous Academicians—and later he was well acquainted with the 'Glasgow Boys'—the Irish painter John Lavery, and the sculptors John Tweed and Alfred Gilbert. He was active as a writer for the *National Review*, *The Musician*, and the *Royal Academy of Music Club Magazine*, wrote a set of short stories, *The Lighter Life* (1896), and authored two books, *The Threshold of Music* (1908) and *The Musical Faculty* (1914), in which he examined the physiological and psychological properties of music. He also contributed to the third edition of *Grove's Dictionary of Music and Musicians* (1927–8) and as a translator his work included Richard Strauss's *Feuersnot* and Frederick Delius's *A Mass of Life*.

JEREMY DIBBLE

Sources H. O. Anderton, 'Cameo portraits no. 9: "A Protean spirit"', *Musical Opinion* (May 1920), 627–9 · V. Carson, '"A Protean spirit": William Wallace, artist, composer and catalyst', MA diss., U. Durham, 1999 · L. Foreman, *From Parry to Britten: British music in letters, 1900–45* (1945), 26–8 · J. Purser, *Scotland's music* (1992) · M. Bantock, *Granville Bantock: a personal portrait* (1972) · CGPLA Eng. & Wales (1941) · b. cert.

Archives NL Scot., 'books' of letters · NL Scot., notes and score of *Mass* | NL Scot., corresp. mainly with Ottilie Wallace

Likenesses T. Roussel, portrait, 1897

Wealth at death £441 11s. 8d.: administration, 10 March 1941, CGPLA Eng. & Wales

Wallace, William Vincent (1812–1865), composer, was born at Waterford, Ireland, on 11 March 1812, the first of the three children of Sergeant William Wallace, a Scot, who was bandmaster of the 29th or Worcestershire regiment. As a child, instructed in music by his father, he learned to play many instruments, including piano, violin, clarinet, and guitar. In 1825 his father was discharged from the army and the family moved to Dublin, where the elder Wallace apparently played bassoon in the orchestra of the Theatre Royal. His two sons, William and Wellington, played violin and flute respectively in the same orchestra, and William sometimes deputized for the leader, James Barton. During these years William studied piano with W. S. Conran and organ with Haydn Corri. He was appointed organist of the Roman Catholic cathedral of Thurles in 1830 and professor of music at Thurles Ursuline convent. He sought the hand of Isabella Kelly (d. 1900), one of his pupils at the convent and, to gain her father's consent, converted to Roman Catholicism in 1830, taking the additional name of Vincent, which he thereafter used as his principal Christian name. The marriage took place the following year, and in August 1831 the

couple returned together to Dublin, where Wallace rejoined the theatre orchestra. Paganini's visit to Dublin stimulated him greatly. In May 1834 he made his début as a composer and violinist, playing his own concerto at a concert of the Anacreontic Society.

On 9 July 1835 Wallace left Liverpool on a ship bound for Van Diemen's Land with his wife, his son, William, and his sister-in-law Anna Kelly. On 31 October they arrived in Hobart, where Wallace gave a number of concerts, and in January 1836 they moved to Sydney, where he began to establish himself as a performer of note. At a concert given under the patronage of the governor of New South Wales, Sir Richard Bourke, at the Royal Hotel on 12 February he played a piano concerto by Herz and a violin concerto by Mayseder. His performances, particularly on the violin, excited the awe of the Australian press. In the wake of several successful concerts, together with his wife and his sister, Eliza (1814–1879), who was an accomplished singer, on 4 April 1836 he founded an academy of music for the instruction of young ladies in Bridge Street. He may also have been involved in sheep farming but this remains uncertain. Within two years he had run up debts of nearly £2000 and, abandoning his family, set sail from Sydney on 11 February 1838. His wife and child probably returned to Ireland shortly afterwards. An improbable tale of adventures, involving Maori cannibals and tiger hunting during a three- or four-month journey to Chile via New Zealand and India, is colourfully related by Berlioz in his *Les soirées de l'orchestre* (1853), apparently on the basis of information supplied by Wallace. He was certainly in Valparaiso, Chile, by 3 June 1838, when he gave a concert on violin and piano. During the next five years he slowly made his way northwards, visiting Buenos Aires, Lima, Jamaica, Cuba, and Mexico. In Mexico City he conducted the opera season of 1841 and composed a mass for the cathedral. He then proceeded to New Orleans (1841), Philadelphia (1842), Boston (1843), and New York, where his début at the Apollo Saloon on 6 June established him as a leading figure in New York's musical society; he astonished his listeners by playing his own brilliant *Introduction and Variations on La Cracovienne* on either violin or piano. In 1844, having reputedly lost a fortune by poor investments, he left for Europe. After a period in Germany and the Low Countries he arrived in London, where he performed as a pianist at the Hanover Square Rooms on 8 May 1845.

It was only at this point that Wallace's public career as a composer began in earnest, after the veteran librettist Edward Fitzball, to whom he had been introduced by an old Dublin friend, Heyward St Leger, invited him to set his latest text. The result of their collaboration was the opera *Maritana*, written in a very short time (probably incorporating much musical material from Wallace's earlier unpublished compositions) and produced under Alfred Bunn's direction at Drury Lane on 15 November 1845. It gained immediate and decisive success with a public and press that was already intrigued by tales of Wallace's exotic adventures, and came to rival Balfe's *The Bohemian Girl* (1843) in popularity. A major reason for its success was its eclectic yet at the same time vigorous and inventive musical idiom, so different from that of the conventional English operas of the time; Wallace's musical styles ranged from the robust sumptuousness of Meyerbeerian grand opera, through the gentle melancholy of Chopin, to the intriguing unfamiliarity of Spanish-American popular music; this occasioned the critic of *The Athenaeum*, H. F. Chorley, to observe that Wallace was 'in search of a style, since there are half-a-dozen different manners tried in as many portions of the opera', but such sophisticated quibbles hardly troubled the average listener, who enjoyed a succession of stirring and memorable pieces. *Maritana* also shared with *The Bohemian Girl* the distinction of being one of the very few English operas to obtain recognition abroad; it was produced in Vienna, Hamburg, and Prague as well as in far-flung places in the English-speaking world such as Sydney and Cape Town. Though it did not gain such a decisive place in the repertory as Balfe's opera, it continued to be performed in England well into the twentieth century. It has been suggested by Nicholas Temperley in the *New Grove Dictionary of Music and Musicians* that Wallace's unorthodox harmonies were directly derived from genuine Spanish-American folk music and that, in this aspect of the opera, may have had a direct influence on Bizet's *Carmen*.

Bunn hoped to follow up the success of *Maritana* with Wallace's next opera, *Matilda of Hungary*, to Bunn's own libretto, which the composer had set to music in a more ambitious grand opera style. However, when produced at Drury Lane on 22 February 1847, it was coolly received, largely on account of the banal libretto. Wallace almost immediately began work on a new opera, *Lurline*, to a libretto by Fitzball, based on the Loreley legend. It was announced for performance at the Paris Opéra and at Covent Garden in 1848, but did not reach the stage; it seems probable that, on account of serious eye trouble, Wallace failed to complete the score in time. Abandoning composition for a while he sailed for Brazil in 1849 and, after an eight-month stay there, made his way to New York. In 1850, having apparently obtained advice that his marriage to Isabella Kelly was invalid because he had been under age at the time and 'bred up a Protestant', he married an American pianist, Hélène Stoepel (d. 1885), who had made her New York début on 16 June 1850; she appeared in concert programmes from January 1851 as Mrs Wallace.

For much of the 1850s Wallace's activities are largely uncertain. He may have returned to England in 1853, and it has been suggested that *Lurline* was staged in Germany as *Loreley* in 1854, though no firm evidence has so far come to light. In the same year he experienced the first symptoms of the heart disease that was eventually to cause his death. He is known to have been in Germany between September 1858 and January 1859, whence he probably travelled to London, and here, on 18 March 1859, he assigned the copyright of *Lurline* to the Pyne–Harrison Opera Company, which produced it at Covent Garden on 23 February 1860. Later in 1860 he revisited New York, where extracts from his latest opera were performed at a reception held in his honour. The success of *Lurline*, though not as great as that of *Maritana*, was considerable, especially with those

critics who approved of Wallace's greater reliance on their favourite German models, such as Weber and Mendelssohn. The opera was extended to the end of the season and eventually earned some £50,000 for the company, though Wallace, who had sold the copyright for 10*s*., did not benefit financially. Nevertheless, encouraged by the critical reception of *Lurline*, he immediately set to work on a new opera, *The Amber Witch*, to a libretto by Chorley, which was brought out in a rather inadequate production at Her Majesty's Theatre on 28 February 1861. The critics again were favourable, and a late twentieth-century commentator has described it as the work in which 'Wallace's style reached its full maturity' (Burton, 'Wallace'). Wallace himself regarded *The Amber Witch* as his finest work, but the public was lukewarm. He continued his attempt to interest the London public in English grand opera with *Love's Triumph*, to a libretto by Planché, produced at Covent Garden on 3 November 1862; however, the production had only a short run. His last completed opera, *The Desert Flower*, received its première at Covent Garden on 12 October 1863, but, like the previous two operas, achieved no more than a *succès d'estime*. Wallace was working on a new opera, *Estrella*, in 1864 when he again became seriously ill with heart trouble, in consequence of which he retired to Passy near Paris, where he was visited by Rossini and other notable musicians. His condition deteriorated, and in September 1865 he travelled to the Château de Haget, at Vieuzos in the Pyrenees, with his wife, Hélène, who nursed him through his final illness. He died on 12 October 1865 and his body was transported back to London, where it was buried at Kensal Green cemetery on 23 October.

CLIVE BROWN

Sources W. Guernsey, *Musical World* (21 Oct 1865), 656–8 · 'Wallace', *Cyclopedia of music and musicians*, ed. J. D. Champlin, 3 vols. (1888–90) · A. Pougin, *William Vincent Wallace: étude biographique et critique* (1866) · H. Berlioz, *Les soirées de l'orchestre* (1853) · [H. F. Chorley], *The Athenaeum* (22 Nov 1845) · 'American notions of modern violinists', *Musical World* (6 June 1844), 188 · 'Mr Wallace's new opera', *Musical World* (20 Nov 1845), 553 · notice of *Lurline*, *Musical World* (29 July 1848), 482 · *Musical World* (4 Aug 1860), 499 · *Musical World* (11 Aug 1860), 512 · N. Burton, 'Wallace, Vincent', *The new Grove dictionary of opera*, ed. S. Sadie, 4 (1992) · N. Burton, 'Maritana', *The new Grove dictionary of opera*, ed. S. Sadie, 3 (1992) · N. Burton, 'Lurline', *The new Grove dictionary of opera*, ed. S. Sadie, 3 (1992) · N. Temperley, 'Wallace, Vincent', *New Grove* · CGPLA Eng. & Wales (1865)

Archives NL Scot., corresp. and papers

Likenesses J. Hanshew, NG Ire.; repro. in Temperley, 'Wallace, Vincent' · lithograph (after photograph), BM; repro. in supplement to *The Orchestra* (1865) · wood-engraving, NPG; repro. in *ILN* (18 Nov 1865)

Wealth at death under £800: administration, 6 Dec 1865, CGPLA Eng. & Wales

Wallack, Henry John (1790–1870). *See under* Wallack, James William (1795–1864).

Wallack, James William (1795–1864), actor, born on 20 August 1795 at Hercules Buildings in Lambeth, London, was the second son of William Wallack (d. 1805) and his wife, Elizabeth Granger, née Field, an actress who had been a member of David Garrick's company for a time,

James William Wallack (1795–1864), by Samuel John Stump

and who died on 6 March 1850 at Clarendon Square, London, at the age of ninety. Both William and Elizabeth Wallack were well-known performers at Astley's Amphitheatre. Following in their footsteps, James William made his first appearance on stage at the age of four in the pantomime *Blue Beard* at the Royal Circus, afterwards known as the Surrey Theatre. His father originally intended him to have a naval career, but later allowed him to follow his own desires and take to the stage. At the age of twelve Wallack appeared with a troupe of the Academic Theatre in London and impressed Sheridan into obtaining him an engagement at Drury Lane. When the house burnt down in 1809 he went to the Royal Hibernian Theatre, Dublin, at the age of seventeen, to play Laertes to the Hamlet of R. W. Elliston. This was followed by roles such as Rob Roy, Rolla in *Pizarro*, Benedick in *Much Ado about Nothing*, Petruchio in *The Taming of the Shrew*, Mercutio in *Romeo and Juliet*, and Iago in *Othello*, all of which were highly successful.

In 1817 Wallack eloped with and married Susan Johnstone (d. 1851), the daughter of the celebrated popular singer and Irish comic actor John Henry *Johnstone, and then departed for the USA. He made his American début on 7 September 1818 as Macbeth, at the Park Theatre, New York, and went on to play in Boston and other American cities, mainly in a variety of Shakespearian roles. After a short season at Drury Lane in England in 1820, he continued with his theatrical career in New York. He received a compound fracture of the leg when a stagecoach in which he was travelling to Philadelphia was involved in an accident near Brunswick, and was slightly lame for the rest of his life. However, he adapted his career to his disability and appeared in New York in *The Birthday* in the role of an old sailor on crutches. On his return to England he became stage-manager in the autumn of 1823 under Elliston at Drury Lane Theatre, where he played Doricourt, Lovemore, Faulkland in *The Rivals*, Harry Dornton in Thomas Holcroft's *The Road to Ruin*, the original Earl of Leicester in *Kenilworth*, and other leading

roles in comedy. He continued to portray Shakespearian characters too, and in 1827 was Iago to the Othello of Edmund Kean, whom he also supported in the roles of Edgar, Malcolm, and Macduff. He supported both Macready and Kean in such parts as Charalois in Philip Massinger's *The Fatal Dowry*, Valentine in Congreve's *Love for Love*, and Charles Surface in Sheridan's *The School for Scandal*.

Between 1827 and 1837 Wallack alternated between performances in England and America, his greatest hits being, in romantic drama, Allessandro Massani in J. R. Planché's adaptation of Scribe's *The Brigand* (1829) and, in domestic drama, Martin in Douglas Jerrold's *The Rent Day* (1832). In September 1837 he assumed management of the National Theatre, New York, the first of the four Wallack theatres, with his brother Henry [see below] as stage-manager. When the house burnt down in September 1839 he took over Niblo's Garden for a time. After appearing at London and Dublin in 1840 and touring America, he was seen for the first time at the Princess's Theatre, London, in October 1844, as the leading actor in a popular version of the famous French play *Don Caesar de Bazan*, by Gilbert à Beckett and Mark Lemon. He stayed on there as stage-manager until 1846. He spent the next five years in America, touring Philadelphia, Boston, and New Orleans. In 1851 he was once again in London, this time at the Haymarket. His wife's death that year grieved him greatly and brought on an illness, on his recovery from which he made his last appearance in England as St Pierre in Sheridan Knowles's *The Wife*.

Back in New York in 1852, Wallack took over Brougham's Lyceum at Broadway and Broome Street. With his sons (John Johnstone) Lester [see below] and Charles, as stage-manager and treasurer, he opened it in September 1852 as Wallack's Theatre with Thomas Morton's *The Way to Get Married*. For nine years this second of the Wallack theatres flourished. Wallack played many roles himself, such as Sir Edward Mortimer in Colman's *The Iron Chest* and Shylock in *The Merchant of Venice*. In 1861 he and his son Lester opened the new Wallack's Theatre at Broadway and 13th Street, and, most importantly, continued to provide opportunities for many new and young actors from England to make their début on the American stage. By this time Wallack had given up acting and was spending most of his leisure at The Hut, his country seat at Long Beach. At the close of the season in 1862 he spoke a farewell address, which was his last public appearance. His health declined rapidly, and he died in New York on 25 December 1864.

Wallack belonged to the school of Charles Kemble and appeared at his best in light comedy, his dark, handsome figure lending itself easily to romance. His performance in tragedy never achieved quite as much success but he was greatly admired in melodrama. His brother Henry John and his sisters Mary and Elizabeth also had a certain amount of success on the stage. Mary played at the Coburg Theatre, London, as Mrs Stanley, and made her American début at the Chatham Theatre, New York, in June 1827. However, she retired into private life after a couple of seasons, and died in New Orleans in 1834. Elizabeth, the only member of the family who never visited the United States, married an actor named Pincott and became the mother of Leonora, who in turn married the actor Alfred Wigan.

Henry John Wallack (1790–1870), the eldest son of William Wallack and Elizabeth Granger, and the elder brother of James William Wallack, born in London, was also a well-known actor. He made his first appearance on stage at the Surrey Theatre. He was more successful in America than in England, and made his American début in Baltimore in 1819. His first appearance in New York was in May 1821 at the Anthony Street Theatre, where he continued to play in tragedy and in heroic drama. His most popular roles were those of Rob Roy, Coriolanus, Brutus in *Julius Caesar*, Captain Bertram in *Eternal Discord*, and Gambia in the opera *The Slave*. On this trip he was accompanied by his wife, the former Fanny Jones, a beautiful dancer. After the birth of their youngest daughter, Fanny, in 1822, his wife also became a dramatic actress, and was attached to the Park Theatre, New York, for about ten years. Following an extended tour of the country, Henry John Wallack became the leading man at the Chatham Garden Theatre in 1824. He returned to England in 1828 and remained at Covent Garden until 1832. He also appeared as Julius Caesar at Drury Lane in October 1829. His wife divorced him in 1833 and about a year later he married again. His second wife was a Liverpool-born singer named Maria Turpin, who had just joined the Covent Garden company, having appeared in London for the first time at the Haymarket in 1830 as Polly in *The Beggar's Opera*.

After spending the years 1834 to 1836 at Covent Garden as stage-manager and leading actor, Wallack went to New York once more in September 1837, as stage-manager of the National Theatre which his brother James William had opened there. In 1839 he gave several important performances against Edwin Forrest, notably as Iago to the latter's Othello. In the same year he and his wife began a long engagement at the New Chatham Theatre, where his two daughters Fanny and Julia also made their stage début, with their father in Sheridan Knowles's *The Hunchback* (23 December 1839). The following summer Wallack returned to England, where he rented Covent Garden for a short, unsuccessful season in 1843. His next appearance was in New York, as Sir Peter Teazle in *The School for Scandal* (September 1847), when the Wallacks opened the Broadway Theatre. Throughout that season his daughter Fanny was the leading lady. He himself played a varied repertory, his parts ranging from the chief Shakespearian heroes to Fagin in *Oliver Twist*, Rolla in *Pizarro*, and Sir Anthony Absolute in *The Rivals*. Thereafter he spent most of his time in the United States. He died in New York at the age of eighty, on 30 August 1870. Both his wives predeceased him: his first wife, Fanny, died in New Orleans in 1845, and his second wife, Maria, died of cancer in London on 18 July 1860.

James William Wallack (1818–1873), the son of Henry John Wallack and Fanny Wallack, *née* Jones, affectionately referred to as Young Jim Wallack, became an extremely successful actor. He was born in London on 24 February 1818 and taken to the USA by his parents the following year. His first appearance on stage was at the age of four at the Chesnut Street Theatre, Philadelphia, playing the part of Cora's child with his uncle James William Wallack (1795–1864) in *Pizarro*. He was educated at private schools in New York and England, and at the age of fourteen he became a call boy at the Bowery Theatre, New York, where he also played small parts. In 1835, after three years of touring England with various provincial companies, he joined his father, then stage-manager at Covent Garden. In 1837 he was engaged for the National Theatre, New York, by his uncle James William, who opened there in *The Rivals*, young James playing the role of Fag. By 1844 he had married at New Orleans a Mrs Ann Sefton (1815–1879), formerly Ann Duff Waring, a tragic actress, who subsequently appeared with him in many plays. They had two children, who both died young. Among the more successful roles played by the younger James William in the next few years were Othello at the Haymarket, London, in 1851 and Macbeth at the Arch Street Theatre, Philadelphia, in 1852. In 1853 and 1855 he made attempts at management in London and Paris without much success. Afterwards he remained in the United States, where he built a highly successful and lucrative career. In 1865 he joined the stock company of his cousin Lester Wallack at the latter's theatre in New York, and in December 1867 he appeared for the first time in the role of Fagin in *Oliver Twist*. At Booth's Theatre, in the winter of 1872–3, he made a good impression on the public as Mercutio in *Romeo and Juliet*, Jaques in *As You Like It*, and other classic Shakespearian characters. Soon, however, he was forced by tuberculosis to retire from the stage. He died a few months later, on 24 May 1873, on a train near Aiken in South Carolina, where he had gone for the benefit of his health.

(John Johnstone) Lester Wallack (1820–1888), actor and playwright, the son of James William Wallack (1795–1864) and Susan Wallack, *née* Johnstone, was ultimately perhaps the best known of the family, though mainly in the United States. He was born in New York on 1 January 1820 and made his début as a professional actor in England as Angelo in *Tortesa the Usurer* around 1841. Initially in the provinces he took the stage name of Allan Field and then played as John Lester. In 1844 he became stage-manager at the Theatre Royal, Southampton, but left the following year for the Queen's Theatre, Manchester, to play Benedick in *Much Ado about Nothing* and Mercutio in *Romeo and Juliet*. He did not get the chance to make an appearance in London until November 1846, when he played at the Haymarket Theatre. His American début was on 27 September 1847, as Sir Charles Coldstream in the farce *Used up* at the Broadway Theatre, New York, when he used the name John Wallack Lester. From then he built his career exclusively in the United States. Within a couple of years he had been successful in such varied roles as Captain Absolute in *The Rivals*, Sir Frederick Blount in Bulwer-Lytton's *Money*, and Edmond Dantes in *The Count of Monte Cristo*, and had appeared at the Chatham and Bowery theatres as Don Caesar de Bazan and Dick Dashall and in other highly successful roles. His own dramatizations of Alexander Dumas—*The Three Guardsmen* and *The Four Musketeers, or, Ten Years after*—were produced at the Bowery

Theatre in November. He played D'Artagnan and his cousin James William Wallack (1818–1873) played Athos. In 1848 he had married Emily Millais; they had four children.

Wallack played with Burton's company at the Chambers Street Theatre for a while in such roles as Charles Surface in *The School for Scandal*, Harry Dornton in *The Road to Ruin*, and Sir Andrew Aguecheek in *Twelfth Night*. He came into his own in September 1852 on Broadway at his father's reopening of Brougham's Lyceum as Wallack's Theatre. Here he had the opportunity to stage many of his own works, notably *Two to One, or, The King's Visit* (1854), *First Impressions* (1856), *The Veteran* (1859), and *Central Park* (1861), as well as to take the lead in many plays, such as Orlando in *As You Like It*, Bassanio in *The Merchant of Venice*, and Tom Dexter in Tom Taylor's *The Overland Route*. Wallack became more closely involved in management when this theatre was closed down and a new Wallack's Theatre was opened by his father, at the corner of Broadway and 13th Street, with Taylor's new comedy *The New President*, in which Wallack, playing La Rampe, appeared as Lester Wallack for the first time. He was active manager of this establishment from the beginning and became sole proprietor on his father's death in 1864. For more than fifteen years he ran the theatre with great fame and success, continuing his father's policy of encouraging both known and unknown British actors to make their first appearance on the American stage at his house. Towards the end, however, he was unable to compete with Booth's and Daly's theatres, and he closed down in 1881. He made one more effort at management in January 1882, when he opened the last of the Wallack theatres on Broadway and 30th Street; he was forced to transfer the lease in 1887, though the house retained the name of Wallack until 1896. Lester Wallack died at his country home near Stamford, Connecticut, on 6 September 1888, and was buried in Woodlawn cemetery on 9 September 1888. His *Memories of Fifty Years* was published posthumously in 1889. As actor and manager he was, for about forty years, one of the most prominent figures of the American stage, and much renowned also in England. With his death, the name of Wallack passed from the world of theatre.

NILANJANA BANERJI

Sources *The Era* (15 Jan 1865) · *Era Almanack and Annual* (1871) · *Era Almanack and Annual* (1889) · *Who was who in America: historical volume, 1607–1896* (1963) · T. A. Brown, *History of the American stage* (1870) · Hall, *Dramatic ports.* · DAB · L. Wallack, *Memories of fifty years* (1889) · P. Hartnoll, ed., *The Oxford companion to the theatre* (1951); 2nd edn (1957); 3rd edn (1967) · *The biography of the British stage, being correct narratives of the lives of all the principal actors and actresses* (1824) · J. D. Hart, ed., *Oxford companion to American literature* (1965) · *The life and reminiscences of E. L. Blanchard, with notes from the diary of Wm. Blanchard*, ed. C. W. Scott and C. Howard, 2 vols. (1891) · J. C. Dibdin, *The annals of the Edinburgh stage* (1888)
Likenesses T. Woolnoth, stipple, pubd 1818 (after T. C. Wagemann), BM, NPG · G. Clint, oils, Garr. Club · S. J. Stump, miniature, Metropolitan Museum of Art, New York [*see illus.*] · S. J. Stump, oils (as Hotspur?), Garr. Club · forty-three prints (John Johnstone Lester Wallack), Harvard TC · line engraving, NPG · prints, BM, NPG · six prints (Henry John Wallack), Harvard TC

Wallack, James William (1818–1873). *See under* Wallack, James William (1795–1864).

Wallack, (John Johnstone) Lester (1820–1888). *See under* Wallack, James William (1795–1864).

Wallas, Graham (1858–1932), political psychologist and educationist, was born at Monkwearmouth, Sunderland, on 31 May 1858, the fifth child and elder son of Gilbert Innes Wallas and his wife, Frances Talbot Peacock. Katharine Talbot *Wallas was his sister. Another sister, Mary Talbot Wallas, married the philosopher J. H. Muirhead. His father, an evangelical in religion and a Liberal in politics, was curate at Bishopwearmouth at the time of Graham's birth but became in 1861 vicar of Barnstaple and later rector of Shobrooke, Devon.

Wallas was educated at Shrewsbury School and went as a scholar to Corpus Christi College, Oxford, where he matriculated on 23 October 1877 and obtained a second class in classical moderations (1879) and in *literae humaniores* (1881). While at Oxford he lost his religious faith, pronouncing himself a rationalist, but also confirmed a lifelong devotion to Greek civic ideals. On leaving Oxford he became a classical schoolmaster.

Wallas left schoolmastering in 1885, resigning his post at the Highgate School in London rather than take communion with his pupils. For the next five years he lived on money which his father had left him. Through his college friend Sydney Olivier, who had entered the Colonial Office, Wallas had met Sidney Webb, another Colonial Office clerk, and Bernard Shaw, and in early 1886 he followed them into the fledgeling Fabian Society. These four dominated the society through its early years. Wallas lectured around the country for the society. In 1888 he began lecturing on Chartism. He contributed the essay 'Property under socialism' to the *Fabian Essays in Socialism* (1889). Within the Fabian Society, Wallas was perhaps the firmest 'opportunist', urging fellow socialists to take part in the existing system of politics. He became chairman of the Fabian Parliamentary League in 1887, and of its successor the political committee of the Fabian Society. Through this position he worked to establish liaison between socialists and advanced Liberals. He remained one of the leaders of the Fabian Society until 1895, coming near or at the top of the poll in the annual elections for the executive committee. However, as the society (increasingly dominated by Webb and Shaw) distanced itself from Liberalism, he came to feel isolated. He strongly objected to the society's support of the Conservative Education Act of 1902, opposed its growing sympathy for imperialism, and finally resigned in 1904 in disapproval of its endorsement of Joseph Chamberlain's tariff policy. A difference in interests between Wallas and the Webbs also became increasingly apparent: as he later remarked, the Webbs were interested in town councils, while he was interested in town councillors. The break was carried out with characteristic goodwill, and he kept his friendships with his former Fabian colleagues. Thereafter, he was a prominent 'new Liberal' intellectual, writing frequently for *The Nation* and supporting a number of Liberal causes. Wallas

Graham Wallas (1858–1932), by Sir William Rothenstein, 1923

married on 18 December 1897 Ada Radford (*b.* 1859/60), daughter of George David Radford, a draper from a Plymouth family well known in the public life of that area. Herself an author, she shared in her husband's work and interests. Her book on early literary women in England, *Before the Bluestockings* (1929), like his book on Francis Place, helped to rescue a significant part of the past from obscurity. They had one child, a daughter, May, who graduated at Newnham College, Cambridge, in 1920, took a London PhD, and taught at Morley College, the London School of Economics, and Cambridge.

By the time he left the Fabian Society, Wallas was deeply involved in two new careers—as an educationist, and as an academic historian and political scientist. In 1894 he had been elected to the London school board on the Progressive slate, and from then until electoral defeat in 1907 he was engrossed in educational administration and London politics, becoming chairman of the board's school management committee in 1897. His chief goal while on the board, apart from the general improvement of state education through day-to-day administrative supervision, was to increase the 'academic' education of the mass of working-class pupils, most importantly by expanding the role and the quality of the higher elementary schools. His ideal was always the Athenian *polis*, and his educational efforts were meant to make his political ideal possible under modern conditions. It was this *polis* ideal that caused him to oppose the 1902 Education Act, drafted in

part by Sidney Webb, with its destruction of the higher elementary schools in favour of a more separate system of elementary schools for the masses and grammar schools for the few (including, of course, working-class scholarship boys). It would be ahistoric to claim Wallas as a forerunner of the comprehensive school movement, but he did argue against the trend toward a two-track state school system.

Wallas's academic career began in 1890, when he was appointed a university extension lecturer. In 1895 he became a lecturer at the London School of Economics and Political Science, newly founded through a bequest from a wealthy follower of the Fabian Society. In 1898, having discovered in the British Museum a large archive of material deposited by the early nineteenth-century utilitarian radical Francis Place, he published a pioneering and very influential biography of that almost forgotten figure. Both these new careers led to his most important work, *Human Nature in Politics* (1908), one of the founding books of the modern study of political psychology. School board campaigning immersed him in the disillusioning realities of democratic politics, while writing Place's life made him aware of the yawning gap between these realities and the high expectations of the pioneers of democracy. Asked years later by Beatrice Webb why he had launched into psychology when the Webbs had stuck to the study of institutions, he replied that by the later 1890s he had found himself pondering whether he believed in the psychological basis of democracy as set out by the utilitarians. He had found that he did not, and his books were the result.

These books, particularly *Human Nature in Politics* and its successors *The Great Society* (1914) and *Our Social Heritage* (1921), presciently explored the fragile psychological underpinnings of both democracy and modern urban–industrial society more generally, and have had much influence on social and political thinking, particularly in America. Wallas lectured in the United States on five visits between 1897 and 1928, teaching for a semester at Harvard in 1910. The American political commentator Walter Lippmann was a Harvard student of his, and did much thereafter to spread his ideas. Indeed, for two decades Wallas played the role of intellectual godfather to the circle of American liberal intellectuals gathered around the important periodical the *New Republic*. By the later 1920s, however, the underlying theme of his writings—the tensions between a relatively fixed human nature (seen through Darwinian eyes) and a drastically transformed social environment—was passing out of favour in the reaction against all forms of 'social Darwinism'. The revival of socio-biological modes of thought means that this sort of evolutionary psychology looks a great deal less antiquated at the turn of the twenty-first century than it did in the decades following his death.

Wallas was also influential in Britain, through decades of inspiring teaching, and particularly among the younger members of the civil service. He served on the 1912–14 royal commission on the civil service, suggesting many reforms that had to wait for implementation until the later twentieth century. Among these was the recommendation that specialist expertise be brought into the civil service by a system of short-term appointments. He was created the first fellow of the Institute of Public Administration in 1922. In 1914 he was appointed to the newly created chair of political science in the University of London, which he held until 1923. He received honorary degrees from the universities of Manchester (1922) and Oxford (1931).

Wallas's last books, *The Art of Thought* (1926) and the unfinished *Social Judgment* (1934), turned more completely to psychology, as he came to feel that the key to social change lay not in institutions and movements, but in the cultivation and management of ideas and feelings. To most of his friends and students, they seemed a diversion: his friend and successor at the London School of Economics Harold Laski characterized the former book as 'elegant trifling'. None the less, after his death Laski hailed him as 'the supreme teacher of social philosophy in the last forty years'. Wallas died at Portloe, Cornwall, on 9 August 1932. His wife survived him. MARTIN J. WIENER

Sources M. J. Wiener, *Between two worlds: the political thought of Graham Wallas* (1971) • P. Clarke, *Liberals and social democrats* (1978) • W. Wolfe, *From radicalism to socialism* (1975) • *DNB* • Foster, *Alum. Oxon.* • *CGPLA Eng. & Wales* (1932)

Archives BLPES, annotated proofs of *The Queen v. Frost* • BLPES, corresp., diaries, and papers • BLPES, draft paper for tract *A ministry of justice* | BL, corresp. with George Bernard Shaw, Add. MS 50553 • BLPES, letters to the Fabian Society • BLPES, letters to the Webbs • Bodl. Oxf., letters to Sir Alfred Zimmern • HLRO, letters to Herbert Samuel • Internationaal Instituut voor Sociale Geschiedenis, Amsterdam, letters to Harold Laski • Keele University Library, LePlay Collection, corresp. and minute book entries as member of Sociological Society committees • University of Illinois, Urbana-Champaign, H. G. Wells collection • Yale U., W. Lippmann MSS

Likenesses W. Rothenstein, sanguine drawing, 1923, London School of Economics [*see illus.*] • R. Austin, drawing, London School of Economics

Wealth at death £3971 3s. 4d.: probate, 4 Oct 1932, *CGPLA Eng. & Wales*

Wallas, Katharine Talbot (1864–1944), educationist and local government official, was born at the vicarage in Barnstaple, north Devon, on 11 April 1864, the eldest daughter of the Revd Gilbert Innes Wallas (1820–1890) and his wife, Frances Talbot Peacock. She had one brother, Graham *Wallas, the political scientist, and two sisters, Mary and Marion (the latter married the Revd P. J. Wodehouse, rector of Bratton Fleming, Barnstaple). She was educated at Maida Vale high school and Bedford College, London, before spending four years at Girton College, Cambridge (1883–7). She soon made her presence felt in college life, serving as president of the college amateur dramatic society; she played the part of Aegisthus 'in a masterly way' (Lady Nathan). She took the mathematics tripos in 1887 and was placed among the senior optimes. Twenty years later she crossed the Irish Sea as one of the so-called Steamboat Ladies to make use of the privilege extended by Trinity College when, for a period of three years from 1904 to 1907, women who had passed final examinations but were disqualified by their sex from

Katharine Talbot Wallas (1864–1944), by Mary Sargant, 1883

graduating at Oxford or Cambridge universities could apply for Dublin degrees: she thus obtained her Dublin MA in 1907. In that year she edited with Robert Pickett Scott an anthology of English verse, *The Call of the Homeland*. A devoted member of Girton's old students' association, in 1908 she was elected a member of the college and of the executive committee and resigned in 1913 only because of the pressure of other work.

On leaving college Katharine Wallas began her teaching career as mathematics mistress at Notting Hill and Ealing high school (one of the group belonging to the Girls' Public Day School Company, founded in 1872) in 1888. Her sister Mary was already on the teaching staff but left in 1892 to marry the philosopher J. H. Muirhead, while her nieces Helen and Christine Wodehouse were sent to Notting Hill in 1893 and 1896 as boarders (Helen Wodehouse later became mistress of Girton College).

Leaving Notting Hill in 1898 Katharine Wallas devoted the rest of her life to the new education committee of the London county council, set up in 1904 when the council took over responsibility for education from the London school board. Initially she took the place of her brother

Graham while he was away in America in 1909, but was co-opted onto the education committee in 1910 and was chosen as an alderman of the council in 1913, a position she retained until 1934, after which she served for a further three years as a co-opted member of the education committee. During the years 1918 to 1919 she became the first female deputy chair of the London county council, a significant achievement at a time when there were only eleven women members (including Henrietta Adler, Susan Lawrence, and Jessie Wilton Phipps) out of a total of 124 elected members and twenty aldermen. She also served on the finance and public control committees. During 1899–1900 Katharine Wallas was president of the Association of Assistant Mistresses, devoting her 1900 presidential address to the issue of women's work in local government, mindful of their recent exclusion from the London borough councils and the impending threat to the school board system with its inclusion of women as elected representatives. She herself accepted an invitation to serve on a special committee of the National Union of Women Workers to secure the presence of women on local authorities responsible for secondary education. She also became vice-president of the Teachers' Registration Council and later honorary treasurer of the Association of University Women Teachers. Her outstanding service on the London county council was in connection with the work of the teaching staff sub-committee, 'where her unique knowledge of the members of the teaching staff, and their work and achievements, and her shrewd judgement of personality, made her exceptionally valuable when new appointments were to be made' (Lady Nathan). For a considerable period up to 1934 she was one of the council's representatives on the Burnham committee to determine teachers' pay, and in 1933 she was appointed CBE in recognition of her work from 1920 to 1932 on the unemployment grants committee. Her 'sound judgment, her high sense of duty, her keen sense of humour and undemonstrative affection for her friends' (ibid.) made her a greatly respected 'elder statesman' at County Hall, whose opinion was greatly valued and constantly sought. Yet she could rarely be persuaded to speak at council meetings and regarded herself as an educational administrator rather than a party politician. Katharine Wallas, who was unmarried, died at her home, 34 Princes House, Kensington Park Road, London, on 14 April 1944.

JANE MARTIN

Sources Lady Nathan, *Girton Review*, Easter term (1944) · J. E. Sayers, *The fountain unsealed: a history of the Notting Hill and Ealing high school* (privately printed, Broadwater Press, 1973) · *WW* · S. M. Parkes, 'The Steamboat Ladies', *Girton College Newsletter* (1994) · *CGPLA Eng. & Wales* (1944)
Archives Girton Cam., college register · LMA, London county council MSS · University of Warwick, Association of Assistant Mistresses
Likenesses M. Sargant, portrait, 1883, Girton Cam. [*see illus.*] · photograph, 1890–92, repro. in Sayers, *Fountain unsealed*, pl. 18
Wealth at death £11,467 7s. 5d.: probate, 3 Aug 1944, *CGPLA Eng. & Wales*

Wallensis, John. *See* Galensis, John (*fl.* 1210).

Wallensis, Thomas. *See* Waleys, Thomas (*fl.* 1318–1349).

Waller [*née* Paget], **Anne**, **Lady Waller** [*other married name* Anne Harcourt, Lady Harcourt] (*d.* **1661**), diarist and patron of clergy, was the youngest daughter of William *Paget, fourth Baron Paget (1572–1629), and his wife, Lettice Knollys (*d.* 1655); William *Paget, fifth Baron Paget (1609–1678), was the eldest of her three brothers. Extracts from her diary, which was begun after her second marriage in 1652 but contained some retrospective material, were published in *The Harcourt Papers*. Anne recalled in her diary that her education was 'strickt' and deeply religious; an important influence on her was Sir Gilbert Gerard, a family friend and member of the godly Barrington circle, who acted as a sort of godfather. About 1630 she married Sir Simon *Harcourt (*bap.* 1601?, *d.* 1642), who had inherited the ancient Stanton Harcourt estate near Oxford. They had two sons, Philip and Frederick, one of whom was born in 1638. Correspondence in *The Harcourt Papers* suggests that the marriage was very affectionate, though the pair were often separated while Sir Simon was on military expeditions abroad. He was governor of the city of Dublin when he died, on 27 March 1642, of wounds sustained in an engagement with rebels the previous day.

Lady Harcourt was left responsible for the Stanton Harcourt estate, which was in grave disrepair and did not bring her a sufficient income. None the less, according to Edmund Calamy, she hired a preacher for the parish at her own cost because the incumbent was old and unable to carry out his duties. In 1648, in recognition of her husband's services in Ireland, she received a parliamentary grant of lands in co. Dublin, but it is not clear how much difference this made to her financial circumstances.

On 13 April 1652 Anne married, as his third wife, Sir William *Waller (*bap.* 1598?, *d.* 1668), the former parliamentarian army officer, whom she describes as a good husband and 'the anser of my prayer'. Their three children died young. In her diary, written primarily for the purpose of spiritual reflection, she meditates on the signs of God's providence in her life, and the mercies which she discerns in otherwise trying circumstances. Her life with Waller could not always have been easy since, after spells of imprisonment for opposition to the government prior to their marriage, he remained under a cloud and was in clandestine touch with royalists. In his *Recollections* Waller recorded that when he was a prisoner in Denbigh Castle in Wales in 1658, Anne 'came to me disguised in mean apparell … thinking itt the duty of a wife to riske all thing for the satisfaction of her husband'. Arriving after a difficult journey, she seemed 'like the Angell who appeared unto Peter in like circumstances' (*The Poetry of Anna Matilda*, 1788). In spite of chronic financial problems, he managed to buy Osterley Park, Middlesex, in 1654. Lady Waller's diary reveals how, in presiding over a country house, she was required to be omnicompetent, practising medicine, accountancy, and estate management, as well as performing many of the functions of a teacher or clergyman within the household. As at Stanton Harcourt, she provided for the spiritual needs of the parish, this time by setting up a lectureship.

Evidently some saw Lady Waller as a wicked, or at least unwelcome, stepmother since on her deathbed she was anxious for her husband to exonerate her from charges that she had ever caused or aggravated the enmity between him and his eldest son. He did so. She died in October 1661, after a long and painful illness. At her funeral at Westminster on 31 October, Edmund Calamy's eulogy emphasized the piety and godliness of the 'Elect Lady', and her role in instilling piety in others. She was survived by her husband, who died in 1668, and by her son Philip Harcourt, who in the year of her death married Anne, Waller's daughter from his second marriage.

JULIA GASPER

Sources E. Calamy, *The happiness of those who sleep in Jesus … a sermon preached at the funeral of Lady Anne Waller* (1662) • E. W. Harcourt, ed., *The Harcourt papers*, 14 vols. (privately printed, London, [1880–1905]) • GEC, *Peerage* • *DNB*
Likenesses portrait; in possession of Harcourt family, Nuneham Courtenay, Oxfordshire, in the nineteenth century; copy, attrib. Mrs Beale

Waller, Augustus Désiré (1856–1922), physiologist, was born in Paris on 12 July 1856, the only son and younger child of Augustus Volney *Waller FRS (1816–1870), physiologist, and his wife, Matilda Margaret Walls, daughter of John Walls, a solicitor. The family lived in turn in Paris, England, and Switzerland until the death of his father in 1870 when, with his mother and his sister, Matilda Amelia (*b.* 1845), he moved to Aberdeen. He was educated at the Collège de Genève and entered the University of Aberdeen in 1874, where he graduated MB in 1878 and MD in 1881. He joined the department of physiology at University College, London, in 1879 as a research scholar of the British Medical Association. In 1883 he became lecturer in physiology at the Royal Free Hospital and in 1884 lecturer in physiology at St Mary's Hospital. He remained there until 1903, when he was appointed the first, and only, director of the newly founded University of London Physiological Laboratory, established in the former Imperial Institute in South Kensington mainly as a result of Waller's initiative. In 1885 he married Alice Mary (1859–1922), daughter of George *Palmer, MP for Reading and founder of the biscuit manufacturers Huntley and Palmer. They had three sons and two daughters; there were no grandchildren.

Waller's research interests started in the emerging field of electro-physiology, in which he made useful contributions to the study of fatigue in muscle and the nature of cardiac potentials. He made the first recording of the human electrocardiogram in 1887, an important advance which, in other hands, had widespread applications in medicine. He studied the physiological actions of volatile anaesthetics, stressing the importance of quantitative measurement. Other subjects included human energy metabolism, bio-electro phenomena in tissues, and psycho-physiology. He was dedicated to experimental work and wrote many scientific papers; he also wrote a manual of experimental physiology for medical students, and a major *Introduction to Human Physiology* (1891).

Physiology dominated Waller's adult life. He was ambitious to be recognized as a physiologist as successful as his father. But physiology was also a family activity; he had a laboratory at his spacious home in London. His wife and children took part in experiments, entertained visiting scientists, and travelled with him to conferences at home and abroad. He was a keen motorist, enjoyed skiing, skating, golf, and billiards, and kept a large family of bulldogs. One of these, Jimmie, was used by him for a harmless demonstration of the electrocardiogram at the Royal Society and became the subject of a famous parliamentary reply to a question from the anti-vivisection lobby (*Hansard 5C*, 8 July 1909). Waller was argumentative, opinionated, and sometimes outspoken, but he had a sense of humour ('I am the Wallerian degeneration' in reference to his father's eponymous discovery) and he retained an unworldly delight in science throughout his life.

Waller was elected FRS in 1892 and gave the Croonian lecture in 1896. Other honours included the Monthyon medal of the French Académie des Sciences (1888), the Prix Aldini from Bologna (1892), and honorary degrees from the universities of Edinburgh (1905), Western Australia (1914), and Tomsk (1914). He was Fullerian professor of physiology at the Royal Institution in 1897 and became a professor in the University of London in 1912. Waller died in London on 11 March 1922 and was buried in a family grave in Finchley cemetery.   A. H. SYKES, *rev.*

Sources W. D. H., *PRS*, 93B (1922), xxvii–xxx • E. Besterman and R. Creese, 'Waller—pioneer of electrocardiography', *British Heart Journal*, 42/1 (1929), 61–4 • A. H. Sykes, 'A. D. Waller and the electrocardiogram', *BMJ* (30 May 1987) • U. Lond. • private information (1993) • A. H. Sykes, 'A. D. Waller: a biographical note', *St Mary's Gazette*, 91/3 (1985), 19–20
Archives ICL, scientific equipment • LUL, medical notebook • RS • Sci. Mus., scientific equipment | BL, letters to W. J. Ashley, Add. MS 42244 • Wellcome L., corresp. with Sir Edward Sharpey-Schafer
Likenesses A. Zeitlin, bronze bust, 1901, ICL • photograph, repro. in Sykes, 'A. D. Waller and the electrocardiogram' • photographs, ICL, Wellcome L.
Wealth at death £1141 13s. 8d.: administration with will, 25 May 1922, *CGPLA Eng. & Wales*

Waller, Augustus Volney (1816–1870), physiologist, was one of the seven children of William Waller (*d.* 1829) and his wife, Jessie (*née* Eagle), of Elverton Farm, near Faversham, Kent. An entry in the parish records of Preston church, near Faversham, gives the date of Waller's baptism as 11 December 1833, with a note appended stating, on the authority of the surgeon in attendance, that he was born on 9 November 1816. This date also appears on his University of Paris diploma and may be taken as correct. His baptism at the age of seventeen is consistent with the belief that soon after his birth the family emigrated to Nice, where his father died in 1829. Waller returned to England with his mother, who later remarried, and he is believed to have been brought up by a friend of his father, William *Lambe, a medical practitioner in London, and later with his son Lacon Lambe (1797–1871), a medical practitioner in Herefordshire. The elder Lambe was a vegetarian who wrote on the subject, and Waller followed the same diet until he left his adopted home to study in Paris. He matriculated *bachelier ès lettres* in 1834 and went on to study medicine. In 1840 he obtained his MD with a thesis on indirect percussion, returned to England to qualify as a licentiate of the Society of Apothecaries, and established himself in practice at St Mary Abbott's Terrace, Kensington, London. Waller married on 6 January 1844 Matilda Margaret Walls (1815–1888), daughter of John Walls, solicitor, of Fulham. They had one daughter, Matilda Amelia (1845–1908), and one son, Augustus Désiré *Waller (1856–1922), later professor of physiology in the University of London.

Between 1840 and 1850 Waller combined medicine with private scientific research, in which he had a deep interest. His first published work was on microscopical observations of hailstones, but he soon turned to what became his main interest, the physiology of nerves, which secured him an enduring reputation. In 1851 he was elected a fellow of the Royal Society at the early age of thirty-five, having published two papers in the *Philosophical Transactions*. The first, in 1849, was on the histology of the frog's tongue. The second, in 1850, was on the changes undergone by nerve fibres following bisection: this was his seminal contribution to physiology.

Waller relinquished his medical practice in 1851 to move to the University of Bonn, where he worked with the ophthalmologist J. L. Budge. His papers, mainly in French, on the pathways of the cervical autonomic nerves, were well received and he and Budge were jointly awarded the Monthyon prize of the French Académie des Sciences in 1852. He left Bonn for Paris in 1856 to work in M. J. P. Flourens's laboratory at the Jardin des Plantes. In 1856 he was awarded a second Monthyon prize, this time in his sole name, but he left for England soon after, owing to ill health. Waller applied, unsuccessfully, for a teaching post at University College, London, under William Sharpey, but in 1858, with improving health, he was appointed professor of physiology at Queen's College medical school, Birmingham.

This offered Waller a permanent academic post with time for research, which was his métier; but he also kept in touch with clinical work by taking the additional post of physician to Queen's College Hospital, and obtaining his membership of the Royal College of Physicians. Birmingham did not suit him; the two medical schools in the city were active rivals (until their merger in 1868), and after failing to obtain the newly created Linacre chair of anatomy and physiology at Oxford in 1859, he resigned to live at St Leonards, Sussex. He kept in touch with science and in 1860 he was awarded a gold medal by the Royal Society, in recognition of the importance of his physiological researches. In 1862 he went to live abroad again, first in Bruges and then in the canton of Vaud, Switzerland. He was in medical practice, but still drawn to scientific investigations, and he received some support from the Royal

Society. In 1868 he moved to Geneva, where he undertook clinical investigations and also physiological experiments at the university. In May 1870 he went to London to deliver the Croonian lecture to the Royal Society, but soon after his return he fell ill again and died of 'angina pectoris' (coronary heart disease) at his home, 4 rue du Mont-Blanc, Geneva, on 18 September 1870. He was buried at the Cimetière de Plainpalais, Geneva, on 21 September, but his grave can no longer be traced.

Waller's principal technique was microscopy, which he learned as a medical student under Alfred Donné, the pioneer French histologist. He made no technical advances in the subject, beyond introducing the frog tongue for the examination of the capillary circulation, but he devised simple, yet crucial, experiments based on the bisection of nerves supplying the eye, tongue, and blood vessels and observing changes in the function and appearance of these organs. The pathways between brain and body organ were traced by following the degenerative changes which took place below the point of bisection distal to the nerve-cell body. Thus the nerve was effectively stained by its own chemistry in a manner analogous to the tracing of blood vessels by injected dyes. These histological changes became known as 'Wallerian degeneration'. Their importance in physiology lies in their use in mapping the course of nerve fibres within nerve trunks and in the central nervous system: this has been called the Wallerian method. By its use Waller and Budge were able to demonstrate that the sympathetic nerve to the eye has its motor roots in the cervical spinal cord, the cilio-spinal centre. From his work on degenerating nerve Waller came to understand the essential nutritive function of the cell body, at a time when the connection between nerve cell and nerve fibre was not clearly established. Cut off from the cell, the fibre withers and dies.

The discovery of vasomotor nerves was made by the combined but independent work of Claude Bernard, C. E. Brown-Sequard, and Waller in 1852–3. Waller's contribution was an elegant experiment on the action of the sympathetic nerve on blood flow in the ear, and he appreciated, more than the others, the importance of vascular control throughout the body.

Another discovery for which Waller can claim priority is that of diapedesis, the process by which white blood cells can move across the capillary wall into the interstitial space without the leakage of other blood components. This observation was made in 1846 in London, but he never explored it further and the subject is now usually associated with Julius Cohnheim, whose work did not appear until 1867.

Waller was always aware of the problems of clinical medicine, and throughout his career he undertook investigations which might have had some practical application. Thus he examined cooling as a form of local anaesthesia and the use of what he termed vagal compression in the treatment of migraine and seasickness. He was always prepared to carry out these procedures on himself, but they were never widely adopted.

A. H. SYKES

Sources *DNB* · LUL, University of London collection · *Medical Directory* · bishops' transcripts of parish records, Canterbury Cathedral · private information (2004) · UCL · d. cert.
Likenesses portrait, repro. in W. Stirling, *Some apostles of physiology* (1902) · portrait, repro. in 'Notice obituaire', *Mémoires de la Société de Physique et d'Histoire Naturelle de Genève*, 21 (1871)
Wealth at death £366: probate, 1883, *CGPLA Eng. & Wales*

Waller, Benjamin (1716–1786), lawyer and politician in America, was born on 1 October 1716 at Endfield, King William county, Virginia, the fifth child of John Waller (1673–1754), planter and public official, and Dorothy King (c.1675–c.1759). When he was about ten years old, John Carter, member of the council of state and secretary of the colony, noticed his intelligence and became his mentor. Carter took him to Williamsburg and entered him in the College of William and Mary.

When his studies were completed, about 1734, Carter put Waller to work in the secretary's office. He also encouraged him to study law, and obtained permission for him to use the law library of the late Sir John Randolph. Waller was granted a licence to practise law in 1738. Carter was clearly grooming him for important positions. He was successively, between 1737 and 1740, deputy clerk and clerk of the James City county court, as well as the king's attorney there. He also served briefly as king's attorney for Gloucester county, and was assistant clerk of the committee of propositions and grievances in the house of burgesses. In 1740 he became clerk assistant of that body. Four years later he was appointed clerk of the general court, a powerful and lucrative position. Earlier, Waller had caught the eye of Lieutenant-Governor William Gooch, who in 1742 appointed him advocate of the court of Admiralty. All of this took place in a remarkably short period, which was capped by his election to the house of burgesses from James City county in 1744. Two years later Waller married Martha Hall (1728–1780), a native of North Carolina. The union produced ten children, all of whom lived to maturity.

For the next fifteen years Benjamin Waller played a key leadership role in the house of burgesses. He was a member of the important committee for the revisal of the laws in 1746, served on the most important standing committees through the 1750s, and in 1759 was made a member of a committee of correspondence which directed the activities of an agent who represented the general assembly in Britain. He was initially a close associate of Speaker John Robinson, but he quickly established his independence and reportedly played an important role in exposing Robinson's 'enormous fraud' ('Sketches of his own family') of illegally lending over £100,000 of public money to needy friends and relations.

Waller was not returned to the house of burgesses in 1761. He continued to serve as clerk of the general court and, until 1772, advocate for the court of Admiralty. His law practice prospered with a wide clientele, including George Washington, and he represented British mercantile firms in collecting debts owed them by Virginians. He did not play an important role in the movement for independence, but under the new state government he served

on the council of state in 1778 and 1779, and was then elected judge of the Admiralty court. In that capacity he also sat on the state's court of appeals. The capital was moved to Richmond in 1781 and Waller, in ill health, found it difficult to carry out his duties. He resigned these offices in 1785, and died on 1 May 1786 in Williamsburg.

EMORY G. EVANS

Sources 'Sketches of his own family written by Littleton Waller Tazewell for the use of his children', 1823, Library of Virginia · A. L. Riffe and C. Torrence, 'The Wallers of Endfield, King William county Virginia', *Virginia Magazine of History and Biography*, 59 (1951), 337–52, 458–70 · M. H. Harris, *Old New Kent county: some account of the planters, plantations and places in New Kent county*, 2 vols. (1977) · L. G. Tyler, *Encyclopedia of Virginia biography*, 5 vols. (New York, 1915) · H. R. McIlwaine and J. P. Kennedy, eds., *Journals of the house of burgesses of Virginia, 1619–1776*, 13 vols. (1905–15), vols. 7–9 · *Executive journals of the council of colonial Virginia*, 4, ed. H. R. McIlwaine (1930); 5, ed. W. L. Hall (1945); 6, ed. B. J. Hillman (1956) · H. R. McIlwaine and others, eds., *Journals of the council of state of Virginia*, 2 and 5 (1932–82) · *The papers of George Washington*, ed. W. W. Abbot and others, [10 vols.] (1983–), 7–8 · *The diary of Colonel Landon Carter of Sabine Hall, 1752–1778*, ed. J. P. Greene, 2 vols. (1965) · J. P. Greene, 'Foundations of political power in the Virginia house of burgesses, 1720–1776', *William and Mary Quarterly*, 16 (1959), 485–506 · *The papers of James Madison*, ed. R. A. Rutland and others, 8 (1973) · F. N. Mason, ed., *John Norton and Sons: merchants of London and Virginia* (1937) · *The official letters of Francis Fauquier: lieutenant governor of Virginia, 1758–1768*, ed. G. Reese, 3 vols. (1980) · G. Reese, ed., *Proceedings of the vice admiralty court of Virginia, 1658–1775* (1983) · B. Waller, letter to Col. Jones, 2 June 1750, L. Cong., Jones family MSS
Likenesses portrait, priv. coll.; repro. in Riffe and Torrence, 'The Wallers of Endfield'

Waller, Charles Henry (1840–1910), Church of England clergyman and college head, was born at Ettingshall, Staffordshire, on 23 November 1840. He was the eldest son of the Revd Stephen Richard Waller and his wife, Lucy, eldest daughter of the Revd Charles Richard Cameron and his wife, Lucy Lyttelton *Cameron (1781–1858), children's author. Waller was educated at Bromsgrove School and at University College, Oxford, where he graduated BA in 1863 and MA in 1867; in 1891 he became BD and DD. He was ordained deacon in 1864 and priest in 1865.

Waller settled in London. He was briefly curate to the Revd W. Pennefather (1816–1873), vicar of St Jude's, Mildmay Park, Islington, but resigned owing to ill health. Although the Revd A. M. W. Christopher (1820–1913) considered him to be a shy person, he recommended him as a tutor to the Revd T. P. Boultbee (1818–1884), principal of the London College of Divinity (LCD). Waller was appointed in 1865 when the college was situated at Kilburn, and he remained on the staff after it moved in the following year to Highbury. From 1882 to 1899 he was the first McNeile professor of biblical exegesis at the college, a post founded by Dean Francis Close (1797–1882) in memory of Dean Hugh McNeile (1795–1879) 'for the duty of preaching and expounding to the people the true meaning and application of Holy Scripture' (McNeile professorship, 24 Jan 1882, University of Birmingham, Special Collections, St John's archive). Waller succeeded Boultbee as principal in 1884 and remained in office until 1899. During his time as tutor and principal more than 700 men were trained at LCD. In 1957 a window was erected in his memory in the chapel of LCD at Northwood, Middlesex (later the library of the London Bible College).

Alongside his college commitments Waller was the Sunday curate of Christ Church, Mayfair, from 1865 to 1869, reader at Curzon Chapel, Mayfair, in 1869, minister of St John's Chapel, Downshire Hill, Hampstead, from 1870 to 1872, and examining chaplain to Bishop J. C. Ryle (1816–1900). On 22 July 1865 he married Arabella Maria Stubbs (1832–1914) and they had a family of four sons (three were ordained and two were briefly tutors of LCD) and three daughters (one of whom became a missionary with the Church Missionary Society).

Waller was an evangelical whose faith had been enriched while he was an undergraduate at Oxford. He had heard the Revd J. W. Burgon (1813–1888) preach a series of seven sermons on the inspiration and interpretation of scripture, which profoundly influenced his attitude to the Bible. The first sermon was particularly significant: 'I can never forget what I heard that afternoon. … To his teaching, under God, I owe all I know of divinity' (*The Record*, 17 Aug 1888). Waller's publications included a number of biblical commentaries and sermons, and in 1887 he published *The authoritative inspiration of Holy Scripture as distinct from the inspiration of its human authors*. It was his conviction that biblical criticism was responsible for unsettling Christian faith, and that 'the one shortcoming of the church at the present day was its neglect of the study of dogmatic Christianity' (*Church Association Monthly Intelligencer*, 171).

In his last year as principal Waller was in poor health and took a six months' sea cruise to Australia. He retired on a pension of £400 a year to Little Coxwell, Faringdon, Berkshire, where he died on 9 May 1910, survived by his wife. He was buried in Little Coxwell churchyard later in the month. A. F. MUNDEN

Sources *The Times* (11 May 1910) · *The Record* (17 Aug 1888) · *DNB* · *Church Association Monthly Intelligencer* (1 Aug 1870) · L. L. Cameron, *The life of Mrs. Cameron*, ed. [C. Cameron], rev. G. T. Cameron, 2nd edn [1873], 222–3

Archives Durham Cath. CL, sermons

Likenesses photograph, U. Birm. L.

Wealth at death £4645 14s. 9d.: probate, 16 June 1910, CGPLA Eng. & Wales

Waller, Edmund (1606–1687), poet and politician, was born on 3 March 1606 at Stocks Place, Coleshill, Hertfordshire, and baptized on 9 March 1606 at Amersham, Buckinghamshire, the eldest son of Robert Waller (1560–1616) and his wife, Anne (1581–1653), daughter of Griffith Hampden. His father, originally a barrister, retired to the care of his extensive estates in Buckinghamshire, Oxfordshire, and Bedfordshire, taking up residence in Beaconsfield, Buckinghamshire, early in the poet's life. After attending Eton, he was admitted to King's College, Cambridge, in 1621, not taking a degree, and in 1622 he was admitted to Lincoln's Inn. In 1624 the Waller family purchased Hall Barn, Beaconsfield, which remained the poet's principal residence for the rest of his life.

Family and fortune At the death of his father in 1616, Waller was heir to an estate estimated at £2100–£2500 a year,

Edmund Waller (1606–1687), by David Loggan, 1685

and in 1631 he married a wealthy heiress, Anne Banks (c.1609–1634), daughter of a London mercer, John Banks (1571–1630), who brought him an additional £8000. His first wife died in childbirth in October 1634, and he married for a second time, in 1644, during his imprisonment for 'Waller's plot'. An interesting letter to his cousin Walter Waller suggests that this marriage took place while he was a prisoner in the Tower, and was for a time kept secret. His second wife, Mary Bressy (d. 1677), bore him thirteen children, of whom four sons and seven daughters survived him. His son Robert (b. 1633), from his first marriage, who at one point was tutored by Hobbes and, like his father, was a student at Lincoln's Inn, died young, probably during the 1650s.

At the time of his death Waller had an estate of £40,000. Besides Hall Barn in Beaconsfield, he owned a house in St James's Street, London, and extensive properties elsewhere. Even after paying a fine of £10,000 at the time of his exile, he remained a wealthy man; leaving his mother to manage his estates, he lived comfortably in Rouen and Paris, selling some of his wife's jewels to meet expenses: according to the 'Life' in *Poems*, 1711 (p. xxviii), 'there was no *English* Table but Mr. *Waller's*' in Paris during this period. Before his period of exile, Waller was one of the richest men in Buckinghamshire: Thorn-Drury says that with the exception of the banker Samuel Rogers 'the history of English literature can show no richer poet' (*Poems*, ed. Thorn-Drury, 1.xxi). Clarendon, who had reason to dislike and distrust Waller, described him as 'born to a very fair estate' and 'resolved to improve it with his utmost care', commenting tartly on Waller's well-attested social skills: 'He was a very pleasant discourser, in earnest and in jest, and therefore very grateful to all kind of company, where he was not the less esteemed for being very rich' (*Life of … Clarendon*, 1.45).

Waller the courtier The two main intellectual influences upon the early Waller were his friends George Morley (later bishop of Winchester) and Lucius Cary, Lord Falkland. Waller had paid Morley's debts and in return Morley had, over a period of years beginning in the late 1620s, 'assisted and instructed him in the reading many good books … especially the poets' (*Life of … Clarendon*, 44). Nearly all of Waller's poetry was written after he met Morley, and most of it after Morley had introduced him to the Falkland circle in the 1630s. Falkland's ideas of moderation and tolerance, of humane learning and urbane conversation, exercised a lasting influence over Waller long after Falkland's death during the early stages of the civil war. Other close friends, from a later stage in his life, were Thomas Hobbes and John Evelyn. Many of Waller's poems, and in particular the 'Panegyrick' to Cromwell, are strongly influenced by Hobbes, whose *De cive* Waller proposed to translate at one point. Characteristically, when asked by Aubrey to 'write some Verses in praise' of Hobbes, he declined on the grounds of being 'afrayd of the Churchmen', though he admitted to Aubrey that he greatly admired the way Hobbes in *Leviathan* had 'dispelled the mists of Ignorance, and layd-open their Priestcraft' (*Brief Lives*, 156).

Although Waller held no court office under Charles I and, as a substantial country gentleman, cultivated a degree of independence, he was, as Aubrey says, 'very much admired at Court' during the 1630s, and his poems are very much products of a court culture. Thomas Corns has described Waller as a central figure among those poets associated with the court of Charles I whose writings 'refracted a brilliant image of Charles and his queen in poems of compliment, in song and in masque' (T. Corns, *The Royal Image: Representations of Charles I*, 1999, 17). After the Restoration, Waller remained closely associated with the court: 'no man's conversation', Aubrey writes, 'is more esteemed at Court now then his' (*Brief Lives*, 309). Waller was pre-eminently an occasional poet, and a poet of compliment: Rochester, in *An Allusion to Horace* (1675), expresses a view of him widely held at the time:

> Waller, by Nature for the Bayes design'd,
> With force, and fire, and fancy unconfin'd,
> In Panigericks does Excell Mankind:
> He best can turne, enforce, and soften things,
> To praise great Conqu'rours, or to flatter Kings.

Waller's skills as panegyrist, addressing poems in praise, successively, of Charles I, Cromwell, Charles II, and James II, have frequently led later writers to see him as a Vicar of Bray. Samuel Johnson, for example, writes disapprovingly:

> Neither Cromwell nor Charles could value his testimony as the effect of conviction, or receive his praises as effusions of reverence; they could consider them but as the labour of invention and the tribute of dependence … He that has flattery ready for all whom the vicissitudes of the world happen to exalt must be scorned as a prostituted mind that may retain the glitter of wit, but has lost the dignity of virtue.　(Johnson, *Poets*, 1.271)

Yet the view of Waller's poems, in the 1630s and later, as merely offering servile support to the king in verse, underestimates the complexity of the political stance in a number of the poems, tuned precisely to a particular audience, context, and persuasive purpose.

In 1645, shortly after Waller went into exile, the publisher Humphrey Moseley, a committed royalist, issued a collection of Waller's *Poems*, identifying the author as 'lately a Member of the Honourable House of Commons'. A series of poems placed at the beginning of the volume are all political statements, with overt persuasive intent. For example, 'Upon his Majesties Repairing of Pauls' (1635) seeks to counter puritan attacks on Laudian innovation (the poem tactfully omits all mention of Archbishop Laud) by presenting Charles I as moderate reformer with a

> grand design
> To frame no new Church but the old refine.

'To the King on his Navy' (1636) again turns its elegant praise to a concrete political end, arguing for a maintenance of a strong navy used for pacific aims rather than being involved in the wars of continental Europe. In responding to the pressure of opposing views of royal power and its uses, these poems rely much more on 'comely grace' than on the cut and thrust of polemic, presenting 'a bloodlesse conquest' as the best of all.

In changing circumstances, Waller's allegiances may have changed over the years, but, it can be argued, his fundamental beliefs remained consistent. The role he habitually assumed both in his poems on state affairs and in parliament was that of a peacemaker, a broker between opposing factions, and his career as a whole can be seen as illustrative of the strengths and weaknesses of the ideology of moderation and compromise.

Waller in parliament Waller was first elected to parliament in 1624 at the unusually young age of eighteen—Clarendon describes him as having been 'nursed in parliaments' (*Life of … Clarendon*, 1.45). Between 1624 and 1629 he represented Ilchester, Chipping Wycombe, and Amersham in the House of Commons. He was elected to the Short Parliament in 1640, again representing Amersham, and sat for St Ives, Cornwall, in the Long Parliament until his expulsion in 1643. Although after the discovery of 'Waller's plot' he was banished and excluded from ever sitting again as a member of parliament, in 1651 he was pardoned and his sentence of banishment was revoked. He was elected to parliament in 1661, representing Hastings. He continued to serve until two years before his death, and Burnet describes how in his later parliamentary career 'he was the delight of the House, and though old, said the liveliest things of any among them' (*Bishop Burnet's History*, 2.83).

When parliament was summoned in 1640 after eleven years of the personal rule of Charles I, Waller played an active role in both the Short and Long parliaments, arguing a position similar to that of Falkland and other moderates: conservative, distrustful of innovation and extreme measures, critical of those advisers to the king 'who thought to disswade his Majesty from this way of Parliaments' and of the doctrine that 'a Monarch can be absolute, and that the King may doe all things *ad libidinem*', while avoiding any direct criticism of the king himself. The right to property, the desire of 'a true hearted *Englishman* ... to leave his ... Inheritance as intire to posterity, as he received it from his Ancestors', is to Waller the keystone of all rights: 'The propriety of our goods is the mother of courage and nurse of Industry, which makes us valiant in warre and good husbands in peace' (*A Worthy Speech*, 1, 2, 4). Waller's speeches, packed with Latin tags and classical allusions, were circulated widely during the 1640s, suggesting that they are as much addressed to a general public audience as to his fellow MPs. Abuses, the result of a 'misunderstanding betwixt the King and the people', can and will be corrected, and temporary disunities resolved by an appeal to reason and the public interest:

> for let the Commonwealth flourish and then, he that hath the Soveraignty can never want or doe amisse so as he governes not according to the interest of others, but goe the shortest and safest wayes to his owne and the Common good. (ibid., 3, 4)

In the Short Parliament and the early stages of the Long Parliament, Waller was sufficiently trusted by his colleagues to manage the impeachment of the ship-money judge Sir Francis Crawley, and the evil counsellors he inveighs against in speeches in 1640 and 1641 include clerical and lay exponents of absolutism.

But where in 1640 he could attack 'the Prelates Innovations' in urging absolutist counsels, Waller's speech of July 1641, urging reform rather than abolition of episcopal church government, sees the danger of 'great Innovation' and disrespect for law and tradition as coming from below, rather than above: 'the *Roman* Story tels us, that when the people began to flock about the Senate, and were more curious to direct and know what was done, then to obey, that Common-wealth soon came to ruine'. In this speech, unsuccessfully urging caution on his colleagues, Waller appeals to class solidarity in depicting law and property as under siege by mob pressure, in the form of petitions:

> I look upon Episcopacy, as a Counter-scar[p], or outwork, which if it be taken by this assault of the people, and withall this Mysterie once revealed, that we must deny them nothing when they aske it thus in troopes, we may in the next place, have as hard a taske to defend our propriety, as we have lately had to recover it from the prerogative. (*Speech Concerning Episcopacie*, 4–5)

In the months that followed, Waller and his allies among the constitutional moderates were more and more forced to choose sides, as partisan bitterness increased in the House of Commons, and by October 1641 Waller was listed in a letter by Sir Edward Nicholas to the king as prominent among the 'Champions in maynten'nce of your Prerogative' (*Poems*, ed. Thorn-Drury, 1.xxxvi). As late as July 1642, according to D'Ewes, Waller was urging 'an accommodation to be had with his majesty and that a civil war might be avoided', though the 'fiery spirits' in the house would

not hear of it (V. Snow and A. Steele Young, eds., *Private Journals of the Long Parliament*, 1992, 264).

Waller's plot The most discreditable episode in Waller's life, and one which has blackened his later reputation, is the fiasco of 'Waller's plot'. Here the ideology of moderation and compromise shows itself in the worst possible light. After the outbreak of the civil war Waller remained in parliament with the king's approval, speaking 'with great sharpness and freedom ... as the boldest champion the Crown had in both Houses' (Clarendon, *Hist. rebellion*, 3.38–9). He was thus in a position to capitalize on the strong sentiment for peace that had grown up in the City of London and in those parliamentary moderates who still hoped for a reconciliation with the king. In its original form, 'Waller's plot' seems to have entailed some form of passive resistance by citizens of London, backed by members of both houses, to urge a negotiated settlement upon parliament. One of the plotters, Richard Chaloner, a wealthy linen draper, described its inception as follows:

> It came from Mr. *Waller* under this notion, that if we could make a moderate party here in *London*, to stand betwixt the gappe, and in the gappe, to unite the King and the Parliament, it would be a very acceptable work, for now the three Kingdomes lay a bleeding, and unless that were done there was no hopes to unite them.   (Challenor, 4)

But the peace plan quickly turned to war: in its final form, the plot apparently called for an armed rising and seizure of the key points of the City in order to let the king's army in. When Pym, in a highly dramatic speech, revealed the alleged plot to the House of Commons, he placed particular emphasis on the contrast between the 'pretences' of peace and the actuality of 'blood and violence'—'such a combustion, as to have your swords imbrued in one anothers bloud' (*Discovery*, sigs. A2, A3). Even if Waller cannot be held fully responsible for the plot's final form—in his speech before the House of Commons pleading for his life, he claimed to have 'utterly rejected ... the Propositions of letting in part of the Kings Army' (*Mr Waller's Speech*, 3)—the readiness with which the plot and one of its chief actors were diverted from their course is an index to their fundamental weakness.

Pym and his allies in parliament used the plot as a pretext to annihilate the moderates, destroying any possibility of peace. Members of the House of Commons who had spoken up for a negotiated settlement in the previous months were hard pressed to clear themselves of charges of complicity in the plot. The peace party, which comprised a majority in the House of Lords and a large minority in the House of Commons, was in a moment reduced to impotence. Moreover, a covenant was imposed upon the parliament, the City, and the army, by which all signatories declared their innocence of the plot and vowed support of 'the Forces raised by the Two Houses of Parliament ... for the defence of the true Protestant Religion and Libertie of the Subject, against the Forces raised by the King' (*Sacred Vow and Covenant*, 1643, 2).

When Waller was questioned in prison after his arrest on 31 May 1643, he confessed his own guilt and implicated others freely. He was, as Clarendon put it, 'so confounded with fear and apprehension that he confessed whatsoever he had said, heard, thought, or seen, all that he knew of himself, and all that he suspected of others, without concealing any person, of what degree or quality soever' (Clarendon, *Hist. rebellion*, 3.44). In accusing such figures as the earls of Portland and Northumberland of complicity in the plot, Waller hoped to save his own life by shifting the blame on others whom the House of Commons and the army would be unable, because of their rank, to punish. Apparently Waller agreed to co-operate fully with his captors; in a petition to the house the following year, he speaks of 'the free and ingenuous confession and discoveries made upon promised favour' (*Sixth Report*, HMC, 28). But his behaviour after his arrest caused his reputation to plummet: Clarendon accuses him of 'abjectness and want of courage' in seeking to preserve his life 'in an occasion when in which he ought to have been ambitious to have lost it' (*Life of … Clarendon*, 1.45).

Waller managed to have his trial put off until the furore had died down, and then was allowed to appear before the house. Aubrey claims that during his imprisonment the poet 'bribed the whole House, which was the first time a house of Commons was ever bribed' (*Brief Lives*, 309), while Clarendon and the author of the 'Life' in *Poems* (1711), more modestly, make the bribes selective, directed to 'some leading Members' of the house and influential puritan clergymen. When he appeared before the house in July 1643, his air of 'despairing dejectedness', 'all clothed in mourning', impressed his viewers: 'divers of the House seeing his sad and dejected condition at the barre whom they had formerly heard speake in publique with so much applause could not forbeare shedding of teares' (D'Ewes, MS diary). Clarendon, whose account of the incident is generally hostile to Waller, pays tribute to his oratorical skills as 'a man … very powerful in language, and who, by what he spoke and in the manner of speaking it, exceedingly captivated the good-will and benevolence of his hearers; which is the highest part of an orator': 'so that, in truth, he does as much owe the keeping his head to that oration as Catiline did the loss of his to those of Tully' (Clarendon, *Hist. rebellion*, 3.52). After remaining a year and a half in prison without trial, Waller was fined £10,000 and permitted to go into exile in November 1644. Although he had saved his life, he had managed by his conduct to alienate all parties.

Protectorate and Restoration As early as 1645, near the beginning of his period of exile, Waller was described by his friend Hobbes as 'meditating how you may to your Contentment and wthout blame passe the seas' and return to England, making peace with the new regime, and on 27 November 1651 the House of Commons revoked his sentence of banishment (Wikelund, 'Hobbes', 266). In January 1652 he returned to England, and before long was on terms of familiarity with his kinsman Cromwell (Waller was Cromwell's second cousin by marriage, John Hampden's first cousin, and brother-in-law to Adrian Scrope, the regicide, who may have been instrumental in securing his pardon). Cromwell appointed Waller a commissioner

of trade in 1655. Waller's 'Panegyrick to my Lord Protector' (1655) is an argument for the legitimacy of Cromwell's protectorate, seeking to demonstrate to former royalists 'the present Greatness and joynt Interest of His Highness, and this Nation'. Using arguments closely akin to those of Hobbes's *Leviathan* (1651), 'to set before men's eyes the mutual relation between protection and obedience' (*Leviathan*, review and conclusion), the 'Panegyrick' presents Cromwell as *de facto* monarch, a restorer of order rather than a feared agent of destruction:

> Your drooping Countrey torn with Civill Hate,
> Restor'd by you, is made a Glorious State.

In elegant quatrains, the poem deploys a series of classical and biblical analogies to present England as 'the seat of Empire' and Cromwell as a new Augustus:

> As the vext world to finde repose at last
> It self into *Augustus* Arms did cast;
> So *England* now, doth with like toyle opprest
> Her weary head upon your bosome rest.

The 'Panegyrick' thus concerns itself with the most important political issue of the 1650s, the settlement of the state, the transformation of the rule of the sword into the rule of law.

The publication of the 'Panegyrick' prompted a number of satiric poems, anti-panegyrics, by royalists and republicans who sought to refute Waller's arguments for accepting the legitimacy of the Cromwellian regime (see Norbrook, 311–16). In 'Upon the Present War with *Spain*, and the First Victory Obtained at Sea' (1658–9), a much-elaborated heroic poem about a naval victory in 1656, Waller concludes by explicitly urging Cromwell to accept the title of king, arguing that the state can be 'fixt' by 'making him a Crown' and 'a Royal Scepter, made of Spanish Gold'. It has been suggested that the publication of a broadside version of Waller's poem in 1658 was part of a 'concerted propaganda campaign' to counter republican and royalist objections to a proposal to offer a crown to Cromwell (Stocker and Raylor, 134–7). These schemes came to nothing, and though Waller continues to praise Cromwell in a poem the following year as one who 'gave us peace and empire', bringing the nation glory in 'conquering abroad', the occasion of that poem was the lord protector's sudden death, and Waller makes no predictions about the future.

In addressing lines 'To the King, upon his Majesties Happy Return' (1660), Waller faced a particularly delicate task, as one of the many Englishmen who had gone over to the support of Cromwell's regime. He solves his problem by praising the returning Charles II for possessing those virtues which serve his own purpose best, by implication urging upon the king a policy of toleration and general amnesty, forgiveness for the 'Frailty' of others. In the years after the Restoration, Waller at frequent intervals commemorated particular occasions with a panegyric addressed to one or another member of the royal family: 'On St James's Park as Lately Improved by his Majesty', 'Upon her Majesties New Buildings at Somerset-House', 'Of the Lady Mary, Princess of Orange', 'A Presage of the Ruine of the Turkish Empire, Presented to his Majestie on his Birth-Day'. In such poems, the tendency toward idealization, already marked in his poems of the 1630s, is even more pronounced. Waller provides an implicit defence of his practice in a poem of 1680 which defines 'the use of poetry' in traditional ethical terms:

Well sounding verses are the Charm we use,
Heroick thoughts, and vertue to infuse.

Yet the 'great Acts' singled out for praise, here as in Waller's poems addressed to Cromwell, are open to conflicting interpretations. The longest and most ambitious of his heroic panegyrics, *Instructions to a painter, for the drawing of the posture and progress of his majesties forces at sea, under the command of his highness-royal; together with the battel and victory obtained over the Dutch* (1666), turns the inconclusive battle of Lowestoft into a second Actium and the duke of York into a peerless hero of romance. As earlier with the 'Panegyrick to my Lord Protector', Waller's poem gave rise to a whole series of parodies and refutations, portraying similar events in unflattering terms, as exemplifying cowardice and greed. Marvell's *Last Instructions to a Painter*, written a year later, is representative of these anti-court satires in the way it makes the events it describes indicative not of England's glory but of England's shame.

Throughout the reign of Charles II, Waller played an active role in parliament, and the stance he habitually assumed there was more independent of the court than in such poems as *Instructions to a painter* or 'On St James's Park'. Over 180 speeches by him are recorded in Grey's *Debates*, and he was appointed to 209 parliamentary committees between 1661 and 1681 (HoP, *Commons, 1660–90*, 3.654). Although allied to the court by his position on the council of trade and plantations, as well as by personal ties, he was found a good part of the time in the parliamentary opposition. Party organization lists drawn up in the 1670s show him now a seeming ally of one side, now of the other. His allegiance, as under Cromwell's protectorate, was not to a particular ruler or administration, but to his idea of the nation, as expressed, for example, in a speech of 1675 critical of Charles II and his ministers: 'We believed, when the King was called back, that the Law was come again … No Government can be more advantageous to him than this. 'Tis a monarchy. The King governs by Law' (Grey, 3.302). In the bitterness between the parliament and the king over such issues as the king's declarations of indulgence in 1662 and 1672, the Third Anglo-Dutch War, and the crown's management of finances, he endeavoured to reconcile the opposing parties. While he jealously guarded parliament's privileges, the poet repeatedly cautioned the House of Commons against the dangers of meddling where they had no right and of attempting to eat into the king's prerogative.

Waller was a steadfast proponent of religious toleration in a house bent on persecution of papists and dissenters, arguing that severe laws would have an effect opposite to that intended: 'the people of *England* are a generous people, and pity sufferers … He would not have the Church of *England*, like the elder brother of the *Ottoman* family, strangle all the younger brothers' (Grey, 1.128). Throughout his parliamentary career, he was concerned with the growth of trade, arguing that 'the riches and strength of all nations is proportionable to their trade' (*Memoirs of Sir John Reresby*, 2nd edn, 1991, 99). Again and again on the floor of parliament he urged the example of other nations and of history to argue against the narrow, tight-fisted provincialism of many of his colleagues: 'At *Paris* there are many bridges—at *Venice* hundreds—We are still obstructing public things' (Grey, 1.415). Whether defending or attacking the government, Waller emphasized the primacy of the national interest, the importance of law, and common sense.

During the agitation over the Popish Plot, Waller characteristically sought to act as broker between opposing factions, yet found his attempts in the House of Commons to 'persuade them to Union among themselves, agreement with the Lords & a better understanding with his Maj[ty]' did not meet with success: 'I thinke both the Weather & the House at this tyme too hot for mee' (BL, Egerton MS 922). Initially sympathetic to the whigs, he later opposed their attempts to exclude the duke of York from the succession. Waller did not serve in the three Exclusion parliaments of 1679–81, and it may be that at the height of the crisis he prudently chose to withdraw from active politics. When James II ascended the throne, he greeted him with two poems, both of which are thinly disguised pleas to the new king to pursue a policy of reconciliation and national unity. According to the 'Life' in *Poems* (1711), his private opinion was that 'the King would be left like a Whale upon the Strand' (p. xxxvi).

Death and reputation Waller suffered from ill health in his last years, and his *Divine Poems* (1685) are explicitly the product of old age and physical decline. His poem 'Of the Last Verses in the Book' includes the memorable lines,

The Soul's dark Cottage, batter'd and decay'd
Lets in new Light thro' chinks that time has made.

He died at his house in St James's Street, London, on 21 October 1687, and was buried five days later in Beaconsfield.

Waller's oldest surviving son, also Edmund Waller (1652–1699), was an active whig, closely associated with republicans during the later years of the reign of Charles II, served as MP for Amersham after 1689, and became a Quaker towards the end of his life. The poet's favourite daughter, Margaret (1648–1690), who remained unmarried, served as her father's amanuensis, and many manuscripts survive in her hand (and possibly also in the hand of her sister Elizabeth) among the Waller family papers (Beal, 548–51). The younger Edmund Waller is not mentioned in his father's will, which names his brother Stephen (1654–1706) as executor, and leaves £1000 apiece to Stephen and to his sisters Margaret, Mary, Elizabeth, Anne, Cicely, and Octavia, with the residue of the estate to be divided equally among them, and leaves smaller sums to Benjamin (of unsound mind, and left in the care of his sister Margaret) and Dorothy, a dwarf; a codicil leaves an equal £1000 share in the estate to another son, William. Evidently there was ill feeling between the brothers Edmund and Stephen after their father's death, since in 1688 Edmund sued Stephen and his sisters to recover money allegedly owed him by his father and to gain access to the London house left to Stephen in their father's will (private information).

In the editions of his poems published in 1645 at the time of his exile, Waller is presented as primarily a lyric poet: the title-page of *Poems* (1645), incidentally signalling Waller's association with the court of Charles I, includes the statement that 'All the Lyrick Poems in this Booke were set by Mr. Henry Lawes, Gent. of the Kings Chappell, and one of his Majesties Private Musick.' Settings of sixteen Waller poems can be found in a manuscript by Lawes dating from the 1630s (BL, Add. MS 53723), and six of them appear in Lawes's *Ayres and Dialogues* (1653). Waller's poems appear to have circulated widely in scribal manuscript collections, several of which are still extant ('this parcell of exquisit Poems, have pass'd up and downe through many hands amongst persons of the best quallity', according to the 'advertisement to the Reader' in *Poems*, 1645). In a dedicatory epistle he casually dismisses these poems as 'the diversions of … youth', and their characteristic titles maintain the fiction of being by-products of a courtier's life, attuned to particular occasions: 'Of the Lady who can Sleep when she Pleases', 'Of her Passing through a Crowd of People', 'On the Friendship betwixt Sacharissa and Amoret', 'To a Lady from whom he Receiv'd a Silver Pen', 'In Answer of Sir John Suckling's Verses'. Waller is a highly traditional poet, who consistently chose to work in themes and forms that other writers had cultivated before him, and adhered to the classical ideal of the poet as craftsman:

> Our lines reform'd, and not compos'd in haste,
> Polisht like Marble, would like Marble last.
> (Prologue to *The Maid's Tragedy Altered*, 1690)

Waller's love poems tend to be relatively formal, decorous, and impersonal, as compared to the colloquial tone and jaunty cynicism of his fellow Caroline poet Suckling. His advice in one poem ('To Flavia') is to 'dissemble well': unobtrusive wit, poise, and attention to nuance characterize such lyrics as 'Go Lovely Rose', 'To a Lady in Retirement', and 'On a Girdle'. His poetical courtship of Lady Dorothy Sidney, daughter of the earl of Leicester, as 'Sacharissa' is tactful rather than passionate, and the same graceful and elegant praise can be found in a congratulatory letter on her marriage in 1639 (*Poems*, ed. Thorn-Drury, 1.xxviii–xxx) as in the poems for which she provided the occasion. As 'The Story of Phoebus and Daphne Apply'd' wittily suggests, even if the poet loves 'in vain', he is more than amply compensated by the applause of his coterie audience: 'He catcht at love, and fill'd his arm with bayes'.

Although the edition of 1664 describes Waller's poems as 'Written only to please himself, and such particular persons to whom they were directed' (sig. A3), his poems were widely read during the late seventeenth and early eighteenth centuries. At least four separate editions were published in 1645, and during his lifetime there were further collected editions, each containing new poems, in 1664, 1668, 1682, and 1686. Two posthumous volumes of previously uncollected writings, *The Maid's Tragedy Altered* and *The Second Part of Mr Waller's Poems*, were published in 1690. Waller's reputation as a poet was at its highest during this period, when Gerard Langbaine described his writings as 'fit to serve as a Standard, for all succeeding poems' (*An Account of the English Dramatick Poets*, 1691, 507) and his editor Francis Atterbury could speak of him as 'the Parent of English Verse, and the first that shew'd us our Tongue had Beauty and Numbers in it' (*Second Part*, sig. A3).

As a poet Waller is to an unusual degree poised precisely between two ages: F. W. Bateson describes him as 'a minor Renaissance poet and a major Augustan poet' (*English Poetry: a Critical Introduction*, 1966, 117). During Waller's lifetime and afterwards, the terms regularly used to describe his poems were 'sweet', 'soft', and 'smooth': these characteristics helped make his poems particularly suited for musical setting, and helped ensure his continuing popularity in Restoration salons. Etherege's Dorimant and Congreve's Mirabell both quote Waller at every available opportunity. What Augustan poets and critics singled out for praise in Waller was his technical skill in 'numbers' or versification and in the control of diction. Dryden, who greatly admired Waller and consistently treated him as mentor and precursor, claimed that 'the well-placing of words, for the sweetness of pronunciation, was not known till Mr. Waller introduced it' (*Of Dramatic Poesy and other Essays*, 2 vols., 1962, 1.175). In paying tribute to Waller, Dryden, like Atterbury, particularly emphasizes his role in showing later writers 'the excellence and dignity' of rhyme: 'he first made writing easily an art; first showed us to conclude the sense most commonly in distichs' (ibid., 1.7). When neo-classical canons of correctness fell out of fashion in the nineteenth century, Waller's poetic reputation plummeted, and it has never fully recovered. Where the inscription on his monument in Beaconsfield reads 'inter poetas sui temporis facile princeps' ('easily the prince of poets in his time'), Douglas Bush in 1945 could confidently proclaim that 'there is little attraction in Waller … a fluent trifler' and that 'no poetical reputation of the seventeenth century has been so completely and irreparably eclipsed' (*English Literature in the Earlier Seventeenth Century*, 1945, 166–7). A renewed interest in court culture and in the intersection of literature and history toward the end of the twentieth century has led to a modest Waller revival, notably in studies by Chernaik, Norbrook, Hammond, and Corns.

There is no twentieth-century edition of Waller (other than George Thorn-Drury's edition of 1905, long out of print), and no modern biography. In 2000 a biography by John Safford and a critical edition by Michael Parker and Timothy Raylor were in preparation. Useful biographical materials can be found in the 'Life' prefixed to the 1711 *Poems*, in the 'Observations on some of Mr Waller's poems' in the fine edition prepared by Elijah Fenton in 1729 (*The Works of Edmund Waller, Esq., in Verse and Prose*), and in Thorn-Drury's introduction. An indispensable guide to the extensive Waller archives (some in the possession of Waller's descendants) can be found in Peter Beal, *Index of English Literary Manuscripts*, volume 2, *1625–1700*, part 2 (1993).   WARREN CHERNAIK

Sources *The poems of Edmund Waller*, ed. G. Thorn-Drury, 2 vols. (1905) · P. Beal and others, *Index of English literary manuscripts*, ed. P. J. Croft and others, [4 vols. in 11 pts] (1980–), vol. 2, pt 2 · 'Life', E. Waller, *Poems &c. written upon several occasions and to several persons*, 8th edn (1711) · *The life of Edward, earl of Clarendon … written by himself*, 2 vols. (1857) · Clarendon, *Hist. rebellion* · *Aubrey's Brief lives*, ed. O. L. Dick (1949); repr. (1962) · S. Johnson, *Lives of the English poets*, ed. G. B. Hill, [new edn], 3 vols. (1905) · *Bishop Burnet's History* · A. Grey, ed., *Debates of the House of Commons, from the year 1667 to the year 1694*, 10 vols. (1763) · W. Chernaik, *The poetry of limitation: a study of Edmund Waller* (1968) · D. Norbrook, *Writing the English republic: poetry, rhetoric and politics, 1627–1660* (1999) · private information (2004) [John Safford] · E. Waller, *Poems* (1645) · *The second part of Mr Waller's poems* (1690) · *Fifth report*, HMC, 4 (1876) · *Sixth report*, HMC, 5 (1877–8) · HoP, *Commons, 1660–90* · P. Hardacre, 'A letter from Edmund Waller to Thomas Hobbes', *Huntington Library Quarterly*, 11 (1947–8), 431–3 · P. Wikelund, 'Edmund Waller's fitt of versifying', *Philological Quarterly*, 49 (1970), 68–91 · P. R. Wikelund, '"Thus I passe my time in this place"; an unpublished letter of Thomas Hobbes', *English Language Notes*, 6 (1968–9), 263–8 · M. Stocker and T. Raylor, 'A new Marvell manuscript: Cromwellian patronage and politics', *English Literary Renaissance*, 20 (1990), 106–62 · *The works of Edmund Waller, esq., in verse and prose: published by Mr Fenton* (1729) · Mr Waller [E. Waller], *A worthy speech* (1641) [Thomason tract E 198(11)] · *A speech made by Master Waller … concerning episcopacie* (1641) [Thomason tract E 198(30)] · *Mr Wallers speech … being brought to the barre* (1643) [Thomason tract E 60(11)] · *Mr Challenor: his confession and speech made upon the ladder before his execution* (1643) [Thomason tract E 59(7)] · *A discovery of the great plot for the utter ruine of the city of London … as it was at large made known by John Pym esq. on Thursday, being the eighth of June, 1643* (1643) [Thomason tract E 105(21)] · S. D'Ewes, parliamentary diary, BL, Harley MS 165 · Henry Lawes, settings of poems by Waller, BL, Add. MS 53723 · letters from Waller to Jane Middleton, BL, Egerton MS 922 · T. Corns, 'The poetry of the Caroline court', British Academy Warton Lecture on English Poetry, 1997 · G. Hammond, *Fleeting things: English poets and poems, 1616–1660* (1990) · Venn, *Alum. Cant.* · T. Raylor, 'Moseley, Walkley, and the 1645 editions of Waller', *The Library*, 7th ser., 2 (2001), 236–65

Archives Morgan L., Latin notebook · priv. coll., family papers | BL, corresp. with John Evelyn, JEA 16 · BL, Sir Simonds D'Ewes, parliamentary diary, Harley MS 165 · BL, Henry Lawes MS, Add. MS 53723 · BL, letters to Jane Middleton, Egerton MS 922

Likenesses C. Johnson, oils, 1629 (aged twenty-three), priv. coll. · P. Oliver, miniature, c.1635, Welbeck Abbey, Nottinghamshire · A. Van Dyck, oils, c.1638 (possibly of Waller); photograph, NPG · attrib. I. Fuller, oils, c.1640–1650, Rousham House, Oxfordshire · P. Lely, oils, c.1665, priv. coll.; on loan to Plymouth Art Gallery, Clarendon collection · J. Riley, oils, 1682, priv. coll.; copies at NPG, Hall Barn, Buckinghamshire · P. Vanderbank, engraving, c.1682 (aged seventy-six; after J. Riley, 1682), BM, NPG; repro. in E. Waller, *Poems* (1682) · P. Vanderbank, line engraving, c.1682 (aged twenty-three; after portrait by C. Johnson, 1629), BM, NPG · G. Kneller, oils, priv. coll. · D. Loggan, graphite on vellum drawing, 1685, NPG [*see illus.*] · G. White, graphite on vellum drawing, c.1710, BM · G. Vertue, line engraving, 1727 (after G. Kneller), BM, NPG · M. Rysbrack, marble bust, 1728, Hall Barn, Buckinghamshire · W. Bromley, line engraving (aged twenty-three; after C. Johnson), BM, NPG; repro. in B. W. Procter, *Effiges poeticae* (1824) · oils (after J. Riley, c.1685), NPG

Wealth at death £40,000: estimate by John Safford, based on will and various financial transactions involving Waller

Waller, Sir Hardress

Waller, Sir Hardress (c.1604–1666), parliamentarian army officer and regicide, was the son of George Waller of Groombridge, Kent, and Mary, daughter of Richard Hardress; both parents were dead by 1622. He was descended from the fifteenth-century soldier and administrator Richard Waller and was the first cousin of the parliamentarian general Sir William Waller. Hardress was knighted in 1629, and in the same year married Elizabeth Dowdall, the daughter of Sir John Dowdall, an Old English (but protestant) landowner from co. Limerick, and acquired a large estate centred on Castletown, on the River Shannon. In the 1630s Waller was involved in Munster society, and became a close ally of the lord president of the province, Sir William St Leger, whom he would later describe as 'so dear a friend, and may I say, a father' (Bodl. Oxf., MS Carte 3, fol. 498). He was elected for the borough of Askeaton in co. Limerick in the Irish parliaments of 1634 and 1640. In the latter he became a prominent opponent of Thomas Wentworth, first earl of Strafford, and worked with both Old English and New English opponents of the Dublin administration, travelling to London to present the Commons' petition to the king. He was the only New Englishman to join an Old English petition offering composition payments to avert further plantation in the west of Ireland.

Waller's sympathies with the Old English were crushed by the Irish rising of 1641. When Munster rebelled in late November St Leger appointed Waller governor of Askeaton, and in 1642 he became lieutenant-colonel of St Leger's regiment of foot. On the death of St Leger in June 1642 Waller took control of his regiment, and became an ally of Lord Inchiquin (Morrough O'Brien) in his factional rivalry with the Boyle family, led by Richard Boyle, first earl of Cork. In September 1642 Waller travelled to England to advance Inchiquin's claim to the presidency of Munster, and to lobby for Irish interests in general. His early reports were bleak. In December 1642 he told the earl of Ormond 'that they are there so involved in their own danger that a word of Ireland will not be heard' (Bodl. Oxf., MS Carte 4, fol. 83). For the next year Waller remained in England, trying to persuade the king and parliament to settle their differences and turn their attention towards Ireland. Waller's outspoken criticism of Charles I's plan to sign a cessation of arms with the Irish rebels was badly received at court, and he left Oxford in disgrace. In January 1644, when Inchiquin went to Oxford to prevent a peace treaty with the Irish, Waller was left in charge of Munster, and his open hostility towards the cessation riled the confederates, who accused him of being 'devoted and affected to the Parliament' (Bodl. Oxf., MS Carte 10, fol. 536). On his return from court Inchiquin sent Waller back to Oxford to lobby the king once more, but he was unable to make any headway before July 1644, when Inchiquin and the other Munster protestants declared for parliament. By the end of August Waller had fled to London.

Waller was appointed colonel of a regiment of foot in the New Model Army in April 1645, and fought at Naseby in June of that year. In October he was wounded leading his men in the assault against Basing House. During this period Waller caught the spiritual enthusiasm of the New Model officers, becoming a religious Independent. He also developed a lasting admiration for Oliver Cromwell. By December 1645 he proclaimed that ''Tis certain that our greatest hopes for Ireland is from this army, about which I have had many free and serious discourse with Lieutenant-General Cromwell, whose spirit leads much that way' (*Egmont MSS*, 1.264–5). His support for Cromwell as commander-in-chief was a snub to Inchiquin, and indicates how far Waller had changed his political allegiances since the summer of 1644. Even the choice of the Independent peer Viscount Lisle as lord lieutenant of Ireland proved insufficiently radical for Waller, who complained that 'I do not hear the work is like to be carried on by such as carry a two-edged sword in their hearts as well as their hands' (ibid., 1.280). Despite his initial misgivings Waller supported Lisle, and in December 1646 joined Sir William Parsons, Sir John Temple, Arthur Annesley, and others in calling for the new lord lieutenant's immediate dispatch for Munster. Waller accompanied Lisle in his expedition in February 1647, and tried to take over Inchiquin's army when the lord lieutenant's commission expired in April. The failure of the coup left Waller vulnerable, and for a few days he tried to placate his old commander, in the hope of saving his Munster commissions. When Inchiquin rejected his advances—saying 'I would not willingly be joined here with any Independent'—Waller had little option but to return to England (ibid., 1.395).

From June 1647 Waller was heavily involved in the politics of the New Model Army. His regiment had been prominent in the Saffron Walden debates in May, and he represented the army in its meetings with MPs and the City of London, and presented the army's remonstrance to parliament on 23 June. In August he joined Fairfax's committee of officers, and in October he was chosen to consider the *Case of the army*. During the Putney debates which followed Waller was keen to prevent religion becoming a cause of division, and urged that such issues should not be discussed. This did not signal a softening of his radical political stance: when it came to negotiating with parliament or the king, Waller was forthright, telling the army 'to let them know that these are our rights, and if we have them not, we must get them the best way we can' (Firth, 1.344). Waller's readiness to use force may have quietened dissent in his own regiment, at least: through the disturbances of late 1647 his men were unanimous in their loyalty to Fairfax. Waller's radicalism continued in the winter of 1648–9. After playing an important part in suppressing the royalist rising in Devon and Cornwall during the second civil war, he returned to London in December 1648, where he seconded Pride's Purge, Thomas Pride's purge of the presbyterian members of the House of Commons, and personally prevented William Prynne from taking his seat. In January 1649 he was appointed a commissioner to the high court of justice which tried Charles I, and he was to miss only one of its meetings. On 29 January he signed the king's death warrant [*see also* Regicides].

Cromwell's appointment as lord lieutenant of Ireland in March 1649 was welcomed by Waller, but his regiment was not chosen for the invasion, and he returned to his policing duties in the west country. By the end of November, however, he had been given command of a new regiment for Ireland, and by June 1650 he had been promoted

major-general. Waller's Irish service confirmed his reputation as a soldier. He led the siege of Carlow, fought at Limerick, and pursued the defeated Irish into the mountains of counties Kerry and Clare. Having been appointed governor of Limerick in 1651 he used his military position to extend his influence over the whole county, and throughout the 1650s continued to control the local administration and to ensure that his own men were elected MPs for the protectorate parliaments. At first Waller was closely allied to the army interest in Ireland. In 1652–3 he was one of the army's agents in England, where (in February 1653) he presented the 'humble representation of the officers of Ireland' against John Weaver, and argued that the army should be treated generously in the Irish land settlement. It was hardly surprising that one commentator saw Waller as having 'a great interest in the soldiery' at this time (*Fifth Report*, HMC, 193). The formation of the protectorate undermined Waller's position within the army. Many of the Irish officers were suspicious of Oliver Cromwell's ambition, and began to work against his regime. This grated with Waller's personal loyalty to the new protector, which had been reinforced by the marriage of his daughter to Cromwell's relative Henry Ingoldsby in August 1653. It is significant that when the protector was proclaimed in Dublin on 30 January 1654, Waller was one of only two senior officers present. In later years he worked closely with Henry Cromwell, who governed Ireland from 1655, and this alliance brought him back into contact with the Munster protestants, and especially Cromwell's closest adviser, Lord Broghill (Roger Boyle), some of whose relatives in the Clayton and Fenton families were married to Waller's children. Although Waller did not take his seat as MP for counties Kerry, Limerick, and Clare in the protectorate parliaments, his friends and clients would support the attempts by Broghill and others to establish a civilian 'settlement' in the Commonwealth, and (in 1657) they were involved in the attempt to persuade Cromwell to accept the crown.

Waller's loyalty to the regime was based on his personal fealty to Oliver Cromwell. In the late 1650s Waller showed signs of restlessness, and Henry Cromwell warned his father that 'your old servant Sir Hardress Waller thinks himself forgotten' (Thurloe, *State papers*, 7.734). Grants of baronetcies to his sons-in-law Maurice Fenton and Henry Ingoldsby were designed to placate Waller, but with the death of Oliver Cromwell in September 1658 there was little to restrain him, and Henry Cromwell included him among the untrustworthy officers who should be recalled to England. From then on, Waller behaved erratically. With the collapse of the protectorate in May 1659, he immediately threw in his lot with the Rump Parliament, and proved his new allegiance by seizing Henry Cromwell at Phoenix Park. His new friends did not trust him, however, and the Irish commander-in-chief, Edmund Ludlow, refused to put him in charge of the army in his absence. In October and November 1659 Waller continued to support the republicans, and signed the Irish officers' letter in support of John Lambert and the English army. In December, however, he joined the Irish protestants' coup in Dublin and refused Ludlow permission to land at Ringsend. In the early months of 1660, as secluded MPs were returned to Westminster and the restoration of the monarchy was expected, Waller panicked, and again seized Dublin Castle. This second coup was short-lived, and he was imprisoned, on Sir Charles Coote's orders, at Athlone, only being released on the intervention of his cousin Sir William Waller.

On the Restoration Waller fled to France, but he returned in the hope of benefiting from the leniency offered to repentant regicides. During his trial in October 1660 he claimed to have signed the death warrant unwillingly, 'finding that no dissent of his could have prevented it', and denied supporting the offer of the crown to Cromwell (BL, Egerton MS 2549, fol. 93). Such lies seem to justify Edmund Ludlow's attack on Waller as 'one who would say anything to save his life' (Ludlow, 209). Waller was one of only two regicides to plead guilty to the charges against him. He was attainted, but the death sentence was commuted, and he was imprisoned in Mont Orgueil Castle, Jersey, where he died in 1666. After his final arrest most of Waller's friends and family deserted him; but the marriages he had secured for his children ensured that the Wallers regained the estate at Castletown, and remained important figures in Munster into the twentieth century.

PATRICK LITTLE

Sources HoP, *Commons* [draft] · Bodl. Oxf., MSS Carte · *Report on the manuscripts of the earl of Egmont*, 2 vols. in 3, HMC, 63 (1905–9), vol. 1, pt 1 · *CSP Ire.*, 1633–47 · *The Clarke papers*, ed. C. H. Firth, [new edn], 2 vols. in 1 (1992) · *Fifth report*, HMC, 4 (1876) · Thurloe, *State papers* · BL, Egerton MS 2549 · E. Ludlow, *A voyce from the watch tower*, ed. A. B. Worden, CS, 4th ser., 21 (1978) · *JHC*, 2–7 (1640–59) · J. Rushworth, *Historical collections*, new edn, 8 vols. (1721–2) · BL, Add. MS 5711, fols. 74*v*–75*r* [Sussex pedigrees] · W. A. Shaw, *The knights of England*, 2 vols. (1906)
Archives BL, corresp. with Sir P. Perceval, Add. MSS 46922–46923, 46929, 46931 · Bodl. Oxf., MSS Carte
Wealth at death attainted in 1660

Waller, Henry Hirst [Harry] (1861–1949), rugby administrator, was born on 11 August 1861 at Waring Green, Brighouse, Yorkshire, the elder of two sons of Abraham Waller, one of Brighouse's leading textile manufacturers, and his wife, Martha Ann Crossley. His grandfather had introduced cotton spinning to the town. Educated at Silcoates grammar school, near Wakefield, he helped to found the local rugby club, Brighouse Rangers, in 1878 and played until he received four broken ribs in a game in 1894. He then became a leading campaigner for a relaxation of rugby's amateur rules and for paying working-class players compensation for 'broken time', or time lost from work.

On 29 August 1895 Waller chaired the historic meeting at the George Hotel in Huddersfield at which twenty-two leading northern rugby clubs voted to leave the Rugby Football Union and found the Northern Rugby Football Union (NU), which in 1922 became the Rugby Football League. The first decision of the new body was to legalize payments of no more than 6s. per day for broken time. At this meeting Waller was elected president, a position he was to hold for the next two years, during which the NU grew from its original 22 clubs to over 150. As president of

the NU, he oversaw a number of rule changes, such as the abolition of the line-out, which were to lay the basis for the modern game of rugby league football. After stepping down from the presidency in 1897, he continued to play a leading role on the sport's general committee until 1902, most notably in helping to steer the game towards professionalism.

An articulate public speaker, Waller played the central role in developing the NU's self-image as a democratic sport. A lifelong Liberal, he became the Liberal chairman of Greetland urban district council in 1905, was the founding senior vice-chairman of the Urban District Councils' Association, and in 1906 was appointed a JP. His political principles guided his philosophy for rugby, and he believed that 'the game brought men together and united them in brotherhood which could hardly be found elsewhere' (*Yorkshire Post*, 30 April 1894). In 1890 he had taken over the running of the family business, and this experience informed his belief in the importance of the social role of the NU. He saw rugby as a means of assisting working-class players to better themselves, and was instrumental in introducing the NU's 1898 'work clauses', whereby only those in regular employment were allowed to play, arguing that 'the Northern Union was anxious to make football the means of improving the positions of players' (*Yorkshire Post*, 23 May 1898).

After Brighouse Rangers disbanded in 1906 owing to financial problems, Waller became a regular spectator at Halifax rugby league club's matches. In November 1945, as the only surviving founder of the NU, he was guest of honour of the Rugby Football League at the game's jubilee banquet. He died on 19 May 1949 at Lyndhurst, Greetland, Halifax, Yorkshire, leaving a widow and two sons, and a daughter from his first marriage; he was buried three days later in Brighouse cemetery.

TONY COLLINS

Sources 'H. H. Waller', *Athletic News Football Annual* (1897), 7 · 'Northern Union AGM', *Yorkshire Post* (28 Aug 1896) · 'Football notes', *Yorkshire Post* (22 April 1897) · 'Football', *Yorkshire Post* (23 May 1898) · *Brighouse Echo* (20 May 1949) · T. Delaney, *The roots of rugby league* (1984) · G. Moorhouse, *A people's game* (1995) · b. cert. · d. cert.

Waller, Horace (1833–1896), missionary and slavery abolitionist, was born in Tavistock Square, London, on 16 February 1833, the first son of six children of John Waller (*c*.1791–1865), stockbroker, and his wife, Mary Ann. He had three brothers and two sisters. From 1840 to May 1846 he attended Eagle House School, Brook Green, in Hammersmith, run by Dr Wickham, and spent his early years in Walthamstow, Essex, learning a love for country sports which continued throughout his life. He apprenticed as a stockbroker, growing up lanky and 6 feet tall with a long beard. At Whitsuntide 1859 a new sense of religious dedication led Waller, an evangelical Anglican, to join the first Universities' Mission to Central Africa (UMCA). By October 1860 he was a lay missionary bound for Nyasaland. He spent three years there supervising supplies, helping fight Yao slave raiders, and becoming friends with David Livingstone and John Kirk. He left the mission in protest when its second leader, Bishop William George Tozer, decided to keep only the boys of the mission, who had been rescued along with women and girls in 1861 by Bishop Charles Frederick Mackenzie (d. 31 Jan 1862). Convinced that the women and girls would be re-enslaved if left in Nyasaland, he took them to Cape Town. In 1864 he was elected FRGS.

In 1865, a year after Waller's return home, his father died, leaving Waller to support the family. He divided his time, applying for business ventures and government posts and aiding Livingstone, who was writing a book on his Zambezi travels. By 1867 he found his vocation in the church. False rumours of Livingstone's death in Africa that year made Waller's African experiences and his letters from Kirk, then vice-consul in Zanzibar, valuable to geographical and humanitarian circles. In August 1867 he spoke at an international anti-slavery convention in Paris; and in December, through Bishop Samuel Wilberforce, president of the UMCA (Waller's missionary experience being accepted in lieu of educational requirements), he was ordained deacon, and in 1868 priest. He was curate of St John's, Chatham (1867–70), vicar of St John's, Leytonstone, Essex (1870–74), and rector of Twywell, near Thrapston, Northamptonshire (1874–95). This career enabled him to earn a living, to focus on religion and Africa, and on 13 April 1869 to marry Alice, daughter of Thomas Brown of Kent; they had three daughters and a son, and she survived her husband.

Correspondence with Livingstone and Kirk, augmented over time by other missionaries, officials, and businessmen going to Africa, enabled Waller to command a continuing supply of African news, making him a key person for humanitarians and businessmen who were convinced of Britain's duty to end the slave trade and develop Africa's natural resources—in the name of 'Christianity, commerce, and civilization'. His position was recognized by his election in 1870 to the committee of the British and Foreign Anti-Slavery Society and in 1882 to the home committee of the UMCA.

When Livingstone's body and diaries were brought to England in 1874, Waller was asked to edit his *Last Journals*. He set out to ensure that Livingstone's name would continue as synonymous with the anti-slavery cause. He omitted all Livingstone's complaints about other travellers and his African attendants, depicting him as a gentle, saintly martyr. The death scene embodied this Livingstone legend. Livingstone's attendants Susi and Chuma had found him in death on his knees on his cot, his head on his pillow. Waller transmuted it into a powerful, moving image of the missionary doctor offering up a final prayer for the end to the 'great open sore' of Africa.

Waller received letters with African news which he regularly sent on to the *Anti-Slavery Reporter* and, in over eighty letters to the editor, to *The Times*. His correspondents included Colonel George Gordon and Captain Frederick Lugard, men Waller hoped would become Livingstone's successors. Waller also consulted with the Scots sent to Nyasaland—where he owned a large estate—to create a Livingstone memorial mission, and kept in touch with Scottish businessmen attempting to extend legitimate trade in Africa. One, Sir William Mackinnon, eventually formed the Imperial British East Africa Company.

Convinced that British expansion would benefit Great Britain and Africa alike, Waller wrote for journals and published pamphlets, including *The Title-Deeds to Nyassa-Land* (1887), *Nyassaland: Great Britain's Case Against Portugal* (1890), and *Heligoland for Zanzibar, or, One Island Full of Free Men for Two Full of Slaves* (1893). In 1895 Waller retired from Twywell to Hampshire and died unexpectedly of pneumonia at Overcombe, Hill Brow, East Liss, on 22 February 1896; he was buried at Milland church, near Liphook, Hampshire, on 26 February.

Polemicist and advocate of British empire in Africa, Waller was a Conservative in politics and an evangelical in religion. He dedicated his life to opening up Africa to British influence. For him the British flag was the hope of Africa, and, indeed, it did bring an end to the slave trade, though the immediate benefits for Africans proved more illusory.   DOROTHY O. HELLY

Sources Bodl. RH, Waller MSS · H. Waller, diaries, 1875–6, Yale U., divinity school · Bodl. RH, British and Foreign Anti-Slavery MSS · Universities' Mission to Central Africa, Bodl. RH, United Society for the Propagation of the Gospel MSS · Bodl. RH, Lugard MSS · John Murray, London, archives, copybook (outgoing letters), incoming letters, outgoing correspondence, ledger journals · NL Scot., Blackwood MSS · NL Scot., Cameron MSS · Livingstonia and Blantyre Mission Papers, NL Scot., Church of Scotland Foreign Mission MSS · NL Scot., Gordon MSS · NL Scot., Livingstone MSS · NL Scot., Mackinnon MSS · NL Scot., Stanley MSS · RGS, Cameron MSS · correspondence files, council minute books, newspaper clippings, RGS · National Archives of Zimbabwe, Livingstone and Stewart MSS · *Anti-Slavery Reporter* (1865–96) · SOAS, Mackinnon MSS · English letters, 1857–1900, RBG Kew · *Church Missionary Intelligencer*, 16–47 (1865–96) · BL, Gordon MSS · general minute books, 1874–9, RSA, African section · letters to the editor, *The Times* (1874–96) · 'Editorial diary', *The Times* (1886–96) · D. O. Helly, *Livingstone's legacy: Horace Waller and Victorian mythmaking* (1987) · *The Times* (26 Feb 1896) · *The Guardian* (26 Feb 1896) · *The Guardian* (4 March 1896) · *Black and White* (7 March 1896) · *GJ*, 7 (1896), 558–9 · *Anti-Slavery Reporter* (Jan–Feb 1896) · A. E. M. Anderson-Morshead, *The history of the Universities' Mission to Central Africa, 1859–1909*, 5th edn (1909) · Boase, *Mod. Eng. biog.* · d. cert. · m. cert.

Archives Bodl. RH, corresp. and MSS | BL, Gordon MSS · Bodl. RH, British and Foreign Anti-Slavery MSS · Bodl. RH, corresp. with Lord Lugard · Bodl. RH, Universities' Mission to Central Africa MSS · National Archives of Zimbabwe, Livingstone and Stewart MSS · NL Scot., Blackwood MSS · NL Scot., Gordon MSS · NL Scot., corresp., mainly with David Livingstone · NL Scot., letters to Sir William Mackinnon · NL Scot., Stanley MSS · NL Scot., Stewart MSS · NRA, priv. coll., letters to David Livingstone · RBG Kew, English letters · RGS, Cameron MSS · RSA, African section, general minute books · SOAS, letters to Sir William Mackinnon · Wellcome L., letters to Henry Lee

Likenesses portrait, c.1860, Bodl. RH; repro. in Helly, *Livingstone's legacy* · group photograph, 1874, RGS; repro. in Helly, *Livingstone's legacy* · portrait, c.1890, Bodl. RH, MS. Brit. Emp.s99[n]; repro. in Helly, *Livingstone's legacy* · portrait, repro. in *Black and White*

Wealth at death £1320 13s. 10d.: probate, 17 April 1896, CGPLA Eng. & Wales

Waller, John Francis [*pseud.* Jonathan Freke Slingsby] (c.1809–1894), writer, was born in Limerick, the third son of Thomas Maunsell Waller of Finnoe House, co. Tipperary, and his wife, Margaret, daughter of John Vereker. He entered Trinity College, Dublin, in 1827, and graduated BA in 1831. He was called to the Irish bar in 1833, and while studying in the chambers of Joseph Chitty he began to contribute to periodicals.

Waller served in the court of chancery for some years, and in 1835 married Anna, the daughter of William Hopkins, with whom he had six daughters and two sons. He was one of the founders of the *Dublin University Magazine*, contributing prose and verse for more than forty years, and in 1845 succeeding Charles James Lever as its editor. He became well known under the pseudonym of Jonathan Freke Slingsby, and *The Slingsby Papers*, a collection of his comic and sentimental contributions, appeared in book form in 1852, and ran to several editions.

The success of *The Slingsby Papers* marked the start of a prolific literary career. In 1852 Trinity College, Dublin, conferred the honorary degree of LLD on him in recognition of his literary and legal work, and later that year Waller published two volumes of poems, one, *Ravenscroft Hall*, under his own name, and the second, *St Patrick's Day in my Own Parlour*, under the Slingsby pseudonym. Further volumes appeared as *Poems* (1854) and *The Dead Bridal* (1856). From 1856 until 1861 he was honorary secretary of the Royal Dublin Society.

From 1857 until 1866 Waller edited and wrote many of the articles for the *Imperial Dictionary of Universal Biography*. He was elected vice-president of the Royal Irish Academy in 1864. His biographical work led him to edit, with short biographies, *The Works of Oliver Goldsmith* (1864), *Gulliver's Travels* (1864), and *The Illustrated Family Moore* (1866). He was appointed registrar of the rolls in 1867, and in 1870 he bought the ailing *Dublin University Magazine* from Sheridan Le Fanu for £1700, selling it on to Kennington Cooke in its final year.

On his retirement in 1870, Waller moved to London, where he contributed to *Cassell's Biographical Dictionary*, and continued to write. *Festival Tales* appeared in 1873, and *The Adventures of a Protestant in Search of a Religion* later that year, a work which was particularly popular in America, going through three editions in New York in a decade. In 1881 he published *Boswell and Johnson: their Companions and Contemporaries*. Waller died at his home, Windhill, near Bishop's Stortford, Hertfordshire, on 19 January 1894.

Waller was best known for his verse, in particular 'Kitty Neil', which was anthologized in many collections of Irish poetry well into the twentieth century. *The Athenaeum* commented that 'his thought was so clear and his verse so graceful that his lyrics lent themselves readily to music' (p. 149), and many of his poems were turned into popular songs. In 1874 a long article on Waller and his works appeared in the *Dublin University Magazine*, and was later reprinted as a pamphlet.   KATHERINE MULLIN

Sources *The Athenaeum* (3 Feb 1894), 149 · R. Welch, ed., *The Oxford companion to Irish literature* (1996) · A. M. Brady and B. Cleeve, eds., *A biographical dictionary of Irish writers*, rev. edn (1985) · Allibone, *Dict.* · W. D. Adams, *Dictionary of English literature*, rev. edn [1879–80] · Boase, *Mod. Eng. biog.* · D. J. O'Donoghue, *The poets of Ireland: a biographical and bibliographical dictionary* (1912) · *Dublin University Magazine*, 1 (1833), 83 · Burke, *Gen. GB* · DNB

Archives BL, letters to Royal Literary Fund · NL Scot., letters to Blackwoods

Wealth at death £19,922 3s. 10d.: resworn probate, May 1894, CGPLA Eng. & Wales

Waller, Lewis [*real name* William Waller Lewis] (1860–1915), actor and theatre manager, was born in Bilbao, Spain, on 3 November 1860, the eldest son of William James Lewis, civil engineer, and his wife, Carlotta, daughter of Thomas Vyse. He changed his name when he began his professional stage career in 1883.

Educated at King's College School, London, Waller worked in his uncle's commercial firm as a clerk from 1879 until 1883. He began his professional career playing Claude Lorrimer in H. J. Byron's *Uncle Dick's Darling* (Toole's Theatre, 16 March 1883). During his first season he married the actress Florence West (1862–1912), the daughter of Horatio Brandon, solicitor. For the next ten years he consolidated his theatrical skills, working both on extensive provincial tours and at most of the West End London theatres as a supporting actor. His first London success came in the role of Roy Carlton in George Sims's and Clement Scott's *Jack in the Box* (Strand Theatre, 7 February 1887). This brought him to the attention of established actor-managers such as John Hare and Wilson Barrett. Waller was in Hare's company, which opened the Garrick Theatre (24 April 1889), playing Hugh Murray in A. W. Pinero's *The Profligate*. His most celebrated performance during this early period was as Fyodor Ivanovich in Robert Buchanan's version of Dostoevsky's *Crime and Punishment*, entitled *The Sixth Commandment* (Shaftesbury Theatre, 8 October 1890).

In 1893 Waller's engagement by Herbert Beerbohm Tree to play Orestes in Stuart Ogilvie's *Hypatia* (Haymarket Theatre, 2 January 1893) and his matinée performances in Ibsen brought him to the serious attention of William Archer, Jacob Grein, and Bernard Shaw. Waller played Oswald in *Ghosts* (Athenaeum Theatre, 26 January 1893, and at the Opera Comique), Lovborg in *Hedda Gabler* (29 May 1893), Rosmer in *Rosmersholm* (31 May 1893), and Solness in *The Master Builder* (2 June 1893). Archer was delighted that an established West End actor had contributed to the Ibsen revival but was aware that Waller could overcome neither the plays' inadequate rehearsal period nor his background of florid West End performances.

Waller's career as an actor-manager began in October 1893 when, with his own company, he toured Wilde's *A Woman of No Importance* playing Lord Illingworth. He then leased the Haymarket Theatre and opened his management with the première of Wilde's *An Ideal Husband*, playing Sir Robert Chiltern to his wife's Mrs Cheveley (3 January 1895). Waller's Shakespearian potential, however, emerged only when he played Hotspur in a matinée performance of *1 Henry IV* (Haymarket Theatre, 8 May 1896). The performance persuaded Beerbohm Tree to employ Waller as a member of his permanent company when Her Majesty's Theatre opened on 28 April 1897. Meanwhile he

Lewis Waller (1860–1915), by Dover Street Studios

had also managed the Shaftesbury Theatre (October 1895–January 1897), where his most notable role was Philip Christian in Wilson Barrett's adaptation of Hall Caine's *The Manxman* (18 November 1895). Archer did not care for the version but was enthusiastic about Waller as Hotspur: he ideally matched the character's 'fire, energy, turbulence, impatient pride and indomitable daring' (Archer, 148). Shaw, however, was unimpressed and felt that 'our miserable theatre has left Mr. Waller a novice' (*Our Theatres*, 130).

From 1897 to 1900 Waller remained in Tree's regular company, although he continued to tour as well. At Her Majesty's Theatre his Shakespearian roles included Brutus in *Julius Caesar* (22 January 1898) and Faulconbridge in *King John* (20 September 1899). Although Shaw was again unimpressed by Waller's Brutus, it was hugely popular. His performance as D'Artagnan in Henry Hamilton's adaptation of *The Three Musketeers* transformed him from a flamboyant West End actor into a stage idol, an image Waller's fans forced him to enshrine for the remainder of his career. The play opened at the Metropole Theatre, Camberwell (12 September 1898), with Florence West as Miladi, and transferred to the Globe Theatre (22 October 1898). According to Jacob Grein, Waller's 'delightful impetuosity fired the audience to frantic applause' (*Dramatic Criticism*, 108), even though the play itself was a hotchpotch of 'plot, passion and pyrotechnics'.

From 1900 Waller was largely his own manager, principally at the Imperial Theatre from 1903 to 1906 and the Lyric Theatre from 1906 to 1910. He consolidated his position as the foremost Edwardian heroic actor as Henry V (Lyceum Theatre, 22 December 1900) and pre-eminently in the title role of Evelyn Sutherland's adaptation of Booth Tarkington's story, *Monsieur Beaucaire*. The play opened in Liverpool (Shakespeare Theatre, 6 October 1902) and then transferred to the Comedy Theatre, London (25 October 1902), for a long run of 430 performances. Edward VII saw it and invited Waller to perform the role at Windsor in one of the actor's four royal command performances up to 1908. Though Waller continued to add new roles to his repertory, the range became increasingly narrow as he came to rely on both past successes and new roles that replicated performance qualities his fans wished to see. Max Beerbohm described him as Alexander Mackenzie in Somerset Maugham's *The Explorer* (Lyric Theatre, 13 June 1908): 'see him standing in the centre of the drawing room, his heels joined … his eyes flashing luminous shafts as he turns his profile … with the abruptness of a ventriloquist's dummy' (*Last Theatres*, 378).

After once again touring the English provinces and appearing at the Palladium as Mark Antony in the forum scene from *Julius Caesar* (23 January 1911), Waller began a two-year tour of the USA, Canada, and Australia. He opened in New York in an adaptation of Robert Hichens's novel *The Garden of Allah* (Century Theatre, 21 October 1911), an oriental pastiche that attracted a lukewarm reception. Waller's performance as Boris Androvsky, however, was much praised (*New York Times*, 22 Oct 1911). Yet perhaps somewhat ominously, notices began to point out that Waller's vehicles were hardly new. The *New York Times* (12 March 1912) referred to the fact that *Monsieur Beaucaire* had been already seen with Richard Mansfield some years before. When he performed the role of de Candale in Sydney Grundy's *A Marriage of Convenience*, in Australia, the *Sydney Morning Herald* (30 August 1913) mentioned that Waller's role had been more than adequately filled by Charles Thursby fifteen years before.

Florence West died in 1912, while Waller was away on tour. After his return to England in 1914 he appeared in a patriotic compilation at the Empire music hall, reciting Kipling ballads and the St Crispin's day speech from *Henry V* (17 August 1914), and began a further series of provincial tours. His last play was May Martindale's *Gamblers All*, which opened at Wyndham's Theatre (9 June 1915), and it was while touring this in Nottingham that he developed pneumonia. He died at the Rufford Hotel, Goldsmith Street, Nottingham, on 1 November 1915 and was buried in Kensal Green cemetery on 4 November 1915.

Waller was probably the first English stage actor to develop a cult following based on his physical attractiveness and aggressive masculinity. Nevertheless, his dependence upon bravura roles in costumed melodrama disappointed the supporters of 'the new drama'. Ultimately, 'the puerile nature of the plays … and the adolescent behaviour of his female admirers, prevented many people from appreciating his superb gift as a declaimer of Shakespeare's rhetoric, and frequently exposed him to ridicule' (Donaldson, 42).   VICTOR EMELJANOW

Sources C. Scott, *The drama of yesterday and today*, 2 vols. (1899) · F. Donaldson, *The last actor-managers* (1970) · *Who was who in the theatre, 1912–1976*, 4 vols. (1978) · [L. Waller], *Parts I have played* [1909] [with a biography by R. de Cordova] · W. Macqueen-Pope, *Carriages at eleven* (1947) · J. T. Grein, *Dramatic criticism* (1899) · W. Archer, *The theatrical 'World'* (1894–6); repr. (1969–71) · G. B. Shaw, *Our theatres in the nineties*, rev. edn, 3 vols. (1932) · M. Beerbohm, *Last theatres, 1904–1910* (1970) · *The Times* (2 Nov 1915) · *The Era* (3 Nov 1915) · *New York Times* (2 Nov 1915) · *DNB* · d. cert. · *CGPLA Eng. & Wales* (1915)
Archives FILM BFI NFTVA, performance footage | SOUND BL NSA, documentary recording · BL NSA, performance recordings
Likenesses McNab, Glasgow, photograph, 1885, repro. in Waller, *Parts I have played* · G. W. W. Legg, 1909, University of Newcastle, New South Wales, Australia, Michael R. Booth Theatre Collection · Dover Street Studios, photograph, NPG [*see illus.*] · photographs, repro. in Donaldson, *Last actor-managers* · portraits, repro. in Waller, *Parts I have played*
Wealth at death £5845 18s. 11d.: probate, 17 Dec 1915, *CGPLA Eng. & Wales*

Waller, Richard (*c*.1395–*c*.1462), soldier and administrator, was the son of John Waller of Groombridge, Kent, and Margaret Landsdale of Landsdale, Sussex. Groombridge had been purchased from William Clinton by Waller's grandfather Thomas, who came originally from Lamberhurst in Sussex. Richard Waller served in the French wars under Henry V, and was present at Agincourt in 1415, being said to have captured Charles, duke of Orléans. Waller was rewarded for his role in the battle with the custody of the duke, and from its profits was able to rebuild his Groombridge house. The custody also left its mark on the family's crest, through the addition of the duke's shield of arms hanging from a walnut tree. On 17 August 1424 Waller served under John, duke of Bedford, at the battle of Verneuil, but retired from military life in 1431, after holding numerous positions of command, and turned his attention to legal and political concerns. In 1433–4 he was sheriff of the joint county of Surrey and Sussex, and in 1437–8 sheriff of Kent. In 1437 Orléans's brother, the count of Angoulême, was also entrusted to Waller's keeping, after being held by the Beauforts since 1412.

Waller became a retainer of Cardinal Beaufort; by 1434 he was receiving from Beaufort an annuity worth £20 from Farnham, Surrey, and was appointed steward of Downtown by the cardinal in 1435. By 1439 Waller had become master of Beaufort's household, and he accompanied the cardinal on his embassy to France in that year. Not long before his death Beaufort made Waller (who had also served Louis de Luxembourg as steward) steward for life of the bishopric's lands and temporalities, and in his will, dated 20 January 1446, appointed Waller one of his executors. Waller then became increasingly attached to the court. In March 1443 he served with Sir John Fastolf as treasurer of the expedition to Guyenne led by John Beaufort, duke of Somerset, and on 3 April he presented to the council a schedule of necessary purveyances for the army. He acted as receiver and treasurer of a subsidy in 1450, and was probably also joint chamberlain of the exchequer

with Sir Thomas Tyrell. On 12 July of that year he was commissioned to arrest John Mortimer, alias Jack Cade, while in September he was sent on an errand to Richard of York, the purpose of which may have been to secure the duke's arrest. On 8 June 1456 he was summoned to attend an assize of oyer and terminer at Maidstone to punish rioters, and he was one of the commissioners appointed on 31 July 1458 to inquire into Warwick's attack on a fleet of Lübeck merchantmen. He must have made his peace with the Yorkists after Edward IV's accession, since on 26 February 1461 he was made receiver of the king's castles, manors, and lands in Kent, Surrey, Sussex, and Hampshire.

Waller's eldest son, Richard (*d*. 21 Aug 1474), who had represented Hindon in the parliament of 1453, was made a commissioner of array for Kent on 10 May 1461. Waller presumably died soon afterwards, as his name appears in no further records. With his wife, Silvia Gulby, he had two sons, Richard and John, and a daughter, Alice, who married Sir John Guildford. The second son, John (*d*. 1517), was the ancestor both of Edmund *Waller the poet, and of Sir William *Waller, the parliamentary general.

A. F. POLLARD, *rev.* E. L. O'BRIEN

Sources G. L. Harriss, *Cardinal Beaufort: a study of Lancastrian ascendancy and decline* (1988) · *CPR, 1461–7* · J. C. Wedgwood and A. D. Holt, *History of parliament*, 1: *Biographies of the members of the Commons house, 1439–1509* (1936) · *Letters of Queen Margaret of Anjou and Bishop Beckington and others written in the reigns of Henry V and Henry VI*, ed. C. Monro, CS, 86 (1863) · R. A. Griffiths, *King and country: England and Wales in the fifteenth century* (1991)

Waller, Richard (*c*.1660–1715), natural philosopher and translator, is of unknown origin except that his mother, Mary, who later married a Mr More, was educated in the classics and was an artist of note in her day. About 1683 Waller married Anna (surname unknown), with whom he had several children and lived sometime near St Helen's, Bishopsgate, London. He had a business in Broad Street and owned estates in Hertfordshire, Middlesex, and Gloucestershire. His education and the sources of his estates are unknown.

A cultivated man, Waller was described by Evelyn in 1694 as 'an extraordinary young Gent. & of great accomplishments; skild in Mathematics, Anatomie, Musick, … Painting … an excellent Botanist, [he] Ingraves rarely in Brasse, writes in Latine and is a Poet' (Evelyn, *Diary*, 4.325). He was elected to the Royal Society in 1681, was its secretary (1687–1709, 1710–14), served on its council, and edited its transactions (1691–5). His connection with the society was due primarily to Robert Hooke, who filled the society with many friends. Waller featured almost daily in Hooke's diary in 1688, and belonged to a group of London fellows—including James Petiver, Abraham Hill, and Alexander Pitfield, Waller's brother-in-law—with business and professional backgrounds; he was on equally good terms with Edmond Halley and Sir Hans Sloane.

While latterly a rather reluctant secretary, Waller became a man of considerable standing and contributed to the society in a number of ways. He was inspired by

Hooke to spend his life seeking accurate knowledge across the whole range of objects and phenomena, and his papers on frog spoor, glow-worms, and the East Indies were published in the *Philosophical Transactions*. Among the fellows he became known for his artistic skills: he submitted a drawing of Dr Jonathan Goddard, experimented with turpentine, drew up tables of colours, and oversaw the engravings for Francis Willoughby's and John Ray's *History of Fishes*. However, his greatest contribution to the society and to the international aspect of the new attitude to science was his correspondence with natural philosophers in the counties and abroad. He was an active reformer on the society's council and often acted as auditor of accounts.

Waller's publications display his talents as a virtuoso and man of letters. Between 1674 and 1676 he produced and illustrated a manuscript translation of part of the *Aeneid*. In 1684 he brought out *Essayes of Natural Experiments Made in the Academia del Cimento*, a translation intended to provide access to the experimental work of the Florentine academy published in 1667. He devised an emblematic engraving for the frontispiece of the book, which was dedicated to Sir John Hoskins, then president of the Royal Society. He gave a copy of *An Account of the Meanes of the Measure of the Great Circle of the Earth*, which he translated from the French in 1688, to Hooke. Apart from these major works he also translated shorter pieces from Latin, French, and Italian. As a designer and engraver of frontispieces and illustrator of botanical, geological, and mechanical items for the works of others, he displayed his Baconian epistemological purpose: 'to give an Idea of the Difference of Plants by *Pictures* … rather than by *Words*' (*Philosophical Letters*, 210).

As Hooke's friend and protégé, Waller inherited his papers: he produced *The Posthumous Works of Robert Hooke* (1705) and edited versions of some of Hooke's lectures and writings. Although he saw his role as editor 'not to Methodize them anew … much less adding … any Epitome distorting … the Author's true sense', he nevertheless editorialized throughout and added summaries as well as illustrations. Where he thought Hooke dangerously mechanical (as in his account of the soul), he used his editor's voice both to excuse the author's views and to distance himself from them. The volume was dedicated to Newton as president of the Royal Society, and in his prefatory life of Hooke, Waller made no mention of Hooke's quarrels with Sir Isaac. Here the politics of contemporary natural philosophy made the task of dispassionately representing his old patron difficult. Despite his professed aim to give a plain account of Hooke's scientific contributions, he chose to refer to his old friend's 'Errors and Blemishes' and ended with the dictum 'humanum est errare', encapsulating the contemporary predilection to condemn the use of rhetoric while employing its tropes. Waller was active with his Royal Society friends until shortly before his death, which took place at his estate in Northaw, Hertfordshire, in January 1715.

LOTTE MULLIGAN

Sources BL, Sloane MSS, MS 4065, fol. 61; MS 4036, fols. 194, 249, 266 · Trinity Cam. · *The posthumous works of Robert Hooke*, ed. R. Waller (1705) · T. Birch, *The history of the Royal Society of London*, 4 vols. (1756–7); repr. with introduction by A. R. Hall (1968) · [L. Magalotti], *Essayes of natural experiments made in the Academia del Cimento*, trans. R. Waller (1684); repr. with new introduction by A. R. Hall (1964) · R. T. Gunther, *Early science in Oxford*, 6: *The life and work of Robert Hooke* (1930) · M. J. M. Ezell, 'Richard Waller, SRS: in the pursuit of nature', *Notes and Records of the Royal Society*, 38 (1983–4), 215–34 · H. J. Lyons, 'Richard Waller', *Notes and Records of the Royal Society*, 3 (1940–41), 92–4 · L. Mulligan and D. G. Mulligan, 'Reconstructing restoration science: styles of leadership and social composition of the early Royal Society', *Social Studies of Science*, 11 (1981), 327–64 · H. Lyons, *The Royal Society, 1660–1940: a history of its administration under its charters* (1944) · *Philosophical letters: between the late learned Mr Ray and several of his ingenious correspondents*, ed. W. Derham (1718), 210 · PRO, PROB 11/546, sig. 104

Archives RS, corresp. and papers · Trinity Cam. | BL, Sloane MSS, letters mainly to Sir Hans Sloane

Likenesses T. Murray, print, RS · R. Waller, pencil sketch, BL, Add. MS 27347

Waller, Samuel Edmund (1850–1903), genre and animal painter, was born at Wotton, Kingsholm, Gloucester, on 16 June 1850, the son of Frederick Sandham Waller, an architect and farmer, and his wife, Anne Elizabeth Hitch. Waller was educated at Cheltenham College with a view to joining the army, but he showed artistic inclinations and was sent to the Gloucester School of Art instead. This period was important for his development as an artist. He made many drawings of animals while working on his father's farm, and a course of architectural studies in his father's office equipped him to paint the Elizabethan houses that featured so often in the backgrounds of his pictures. At eighteen he entered the Royal Academy Schools and three years later, in 1871, he exhibited his first pictures at Burlington House, sending two small paintings, *A Winter's Tale* and *The Illustrious Stranger*. In 1872 he went to Ireland and later published an illustrated account of his travels, entitled *Six Weeks in the Saddle* (1874). In 1873 he joined the staff of *The Graphic* as an illustrator. The next year he appeared at the Royal Academy with a work called *Soldiers of Fortune*, and he was afterwards a steady exhibitor there until 1902. On 8 April 1874 he married Mary Lemon (1851–1931), daughter of the Revd Hugh Fowler of Burnwood, Gloucestershire. A portrait painter, Mary had also attended Gloucester School of Art and the Royal Academy Schools. She exhibited at the Royal Academy from 1877 to 1904 and was elected to the Royal Society of Portrait Painters in its foundation year of 1891. They had one son.

Old English country life strongly attracted Waller's imagination, and furnished him with the romantic incidents that formed the subjects of his most notable pictures, which include *Jealous* (1875), *The Way of the World* (1876), *Home* (1877), and *Sweethearts and Wives* (1882), which is in the Tate collection. Many of his pictures became well known throughout the English-speaking world by reproductions and engravings, most notably *The Empty Saddle* (1879), which has an architectural setting taken from Burford Priory, Oxfordshire; *Success* (1881; Tate collection); and *The Day of Reckoning* (1883). The originals are in many cases in private ownership in America and Australia, as well as in England, and Waller is represented at the Sydney and Melbourne national galleries.

Waller's great knowledge of horses and his skill in representing them gave his work much vogue among sportsmen. He took great pains in studying animals, and related some of his experiences in articles contributed to the *Art Journal* (1893; 1896). These were written in a humorous and engaging style; in one he recalled an exchange with a distinguished lady who registered surprise at the fact that he painted using models: '"I thought only students and, excuse me, second-rate artists needed them." I hastened to assure her I *was* second-rate' (*Art Journal*, 1896, 289–92). His pictures usually tell a story effectively and dramatically, but he was more of an illustrator than a genuine artist.

Waller died at his studio, 6 Wynchcombe Studios, England's Lane, Haverstock Hill, London, on 9 June 1903, after a long illness, and was buried at Golders Green.

F. W. GIBSON, *rev.* MARK POTTLE

Sources *The Times* (15 June 1903) · Wood, *Vic. painters*, 3rd edn · J. Johnson and A. Greutzner, *The dictionary of British artists, 1880–1940* (1976), vol. 5 of *Dictionary of British art* · B. Stewart and M. Cutten, *The dictionary of portrait painters in Britain up to 1920* (1997) · S. H. Pavière, *A dictionary of British sporting painters* (1965) · *Art Journal*, new ser., 13 (1893) · *Art Journal*, new ser., 16 (1896) · *WWW* · private information (1912) · b. cert. · m. cert. · d. cert.
Likenesses J. Pettie, oils; priv. coll. in 1912

Waller, Sir William (*bap.* **1598**?, *d.* **1668**), parliamentarian army officer, was born at Knole House, Kent, the son of Sir Thomas Waller (*d.* 1613) and his wife, Margaret Lennard. The parish register of Sevenoaks records his baptism as having taken place on 3 December 1598. Given sixteenth-century practice, Waller would almost certainly have been baptized no more than a few weeks after birth, but a little doubt is cast on the accuracy of the register by Waller's recorded age at matriculation at Oxford, which suggests that he was born in 1597 or even 1596, rather than 1598.

The Wallers, long established in Kent and of Norman descent, had been seated at Groombridge, near Tunbridge Wells, since the early fifteenth century. Sir Thomas, a younger son, had an active official career in the county and in 1604, through the patronage of the earl of Northampton, became lieutenant of Dover Castle. His wife, Margaret, was the daughter of Sampson Lennard of Chevening, Kent, and the lessee of Knole, whose wife, Margaret Fiennes, became Baroness Dacre in her own right in 1604. William Waller was thus part of a well-connected upper gentry family with aristocratic links which the Wallers were—to judge from the name of Waller's sister, Fenes—anxious to preserve. His cousins, close or more distant, included the parliamentarians Sir Hardress *Waller and Lord Dacre, and the royalist and poet Edmund *Waller.

Early years and education The 'stormy sea' ('Recollections', 103) of Waller's life was filled with escapes from danger that he saw as evidence of God's protecting providence and as signs that he had been preserved to be an active instrument of God's purpose. As a child he had narrow

Sir William Waller (*bap.* 1598?, *d.* 1668), by Cornelius Johnson, 1643

escapes from a casually discharged bullet, from drowning, and in a fall from his horse. Later, as he was about to leave for Oxford, he fell dangerously ill with pleurisy and 'hardly escaped the danger of itt' ('Experiences', Wadham College, Oxford, 9). He nevertheless matriculated safely at Magdalen Hall, Oxford, on 2 December 1612, when his age was recorded as fifteen, but shortly afterwards migrated to Hart Hall. He left without taking a degree, and on his return home was again providentially preserved when, after he contracted smallpox, an eminent doctor intervened to prevent the administration of potentially lethal medicine.

Waller's education continued in Paris, where he learned fencing and the management of 'the great horse' (Wood, *Ath. Oxon.*, 3.814). Later he went to Italy, where his practical military formation began. He served with the English volunteers who arrived in late 1617 to aid the Venetians in their siege of Gradisca, near Trieste, in their war against piratical Christian refugees from the Turks. His fellows in the enterprise included representatives of old English military families, notably Sir John Vere, with whom he shared another providential delivery when a 'neere shotte' fell between them as they 'sate close together by the battery' ('Recollections', 108). Waller's Italian travels took him beyond battlefields to Venice, Florence, Padua, and Bologna, and it has been suggested that his later 'vanity in furniture' (ibid., 131; Adair, 7) was formed on this Italian expedition, while in 1645 the connection was recalled by an abortive proposal that he return to Venetian service. Waller's Italian venture had thus grounded his military education and introduced him to English professional soldiers, and had also widened his cultural horizons.

In 1620 Waller left England again, one of the small band of Englishmen who actively rallied to the support of James I's daughter Elizabeth, the 'winter queen' of Bohemia. For Waller she was to remain 'that queen of women … whom I had the honour to serve at Prague in the first breaking out of the German warr' (*Vindication*, 213–14). He and Ralph Hopton, the future royalist commander, were members of the troop of horse sent to Prague to act as her life guard. After the defeat of the Bohemian army at the battle of the White Mountain (8 November 1620) they escorted the pregnant queen through the snow in her flight to Frankfurt. On this expedition too Waller had providential escapes, from Cossacks of the imperial army and from shipwreck on his way home to England. The episode had furthered his military education and demonstrated his commitment to an active protestantism.

A domestic interval When Waller came of age he inherited a substantial income from the prisage and butlerage on wine entering the kingdom, a grant previously held by his grandmother and his father which brought him between £1000 and £3000 a year. He was thus already comfortably established economically, and his standing was reinforced when on 20 June 1622 he was knighted by James I. He was then described as of Brenchley, Kent, where his mother held the manor of Barnes, some 10 miles from Groombridge.

On 12 August 1622 Waller married Jane Reynell (d. 1633), the only daughter and heir of Sir Richard Reynell of the Middle Temple and Forde House, Wolborough, Devon, and his godly wife, Lucy Brandon (d. 1652). The Reynells were an old Devon family, and Sir Richard devoted much of the proceeds of his profitable career at the exchequer to extending his estates in the county. The young couple lived at Forde House, and in 1622 Reynell granted Waller an annuity of £133 6s. 8d., and settled land on them after his and his wife's deaths. Jane gave birth to a son, Richard, in 1631, and a daughter, Margaret, in 1633 before dying in Bath in May 1633. Waller commissioned a splendid monument to her in Bath Abbey in which he himself was represented in armour beside her. She was, he said, 'a vertuous discreet loving and beloved wife' ('Experiences', Wadham College, Oxford, 55). Sir Richard Reynell died the next year, and was followed in 1636 by the child Richard.

In his wife and son Waller had lost 'very deare blessings' ('Recollections', 127), but he resolved to marry again and moved to London to seek 'a religious woman, or none', a wife who would be 'an help to me in the way of [God's] service' (ibid.). God in his providence directed him to Anne Finch, a daughter of Thomas Finch, first earl of Winchilsea, an intrepid and aggressively puritan young woman. At her suggestion they 'sett a day apart to seeke God' to assure themselves of His blessing, and indeed after a somewhat troubled start arising from 'some little differences in … natures, and judgments', the marriage proved happy. She was 'a deare and sweet Comforter', said Waller: 'I may say wee were but as one soul, in two bodyes' (ibid., 128, 131). Four children were born to them, two sons who lived to unsatisfactory adulthood and two daughters.

At first Sir William and Lady Waller lived in London, but on 23 May 1638 he acquired Winchester Castle and forest lands in Hampshire, and they thereupon set about repairing the castle; more providential deliverances ensued, in the shape of escapes from falling masonry. Waller also demonstrated a keen eye for his own property rights. In later life he admitted to 'a covetuous desire to gaine a good bargaine' ('Recollections', 130), and saw God's chastising hand in the troubles that arose from such covetously inspired ventures as his attempt to supplant, by legal but sharp practice, the previous possessor of the market of Newton Abbot, Devon, which led to 'all that trouble … in Kings Bench' (ibid.). He was soon embroiled in similar trouble in Hampshire. In 1639 he instigated twenty-eight suits against local people who had cut wood from his forest at West Bere, as they had customarily done, to fulfil their obligation to repair a nearby beacon. They petitioned the privy council for relief, and met with a sympathetic reception (*CSP dom.*, 1639, 215).

Before the civil war Waller's life seems to have been confined to personal and domestic matters, although on 21 November 1632 he had been admitted to Gray's Inn. He was not a member of parliament nor, apparently, active with the county militia; he was an inactive justice of the peace; and he played no part in the Scottish wars. When in later life he looked back on his 'retired way' in these years he observed with some complacency,

> I … desired no greater preferment than to be mine own man. GOD hath blessed me with a competent fortune, and given me a minde (it is his gift) fitted to enjoy that blessing. In that retired way, I enjoyed myself freely. (*Vindication*, 107)

That this was no false boast is suggested by the depth of feeling with which he later wrote of the pleasures of country life: the goods that earth and wealth brought were to be enjoyed so long, he said, as we do not 'bottom … our selves' on them or abandon responsibilities (*Divine Meditations*, 88–9). Only in November 1640 did he seek—and at first fail to achieve—election to parliament, and not until 3 May 1642, after a successful challenge to his opponent's election, was he finally approved as member for Andover (*JHC*, 2.554).

Civil war Once on the public stage Waller showed no uncertainty about the side he would choose in the imminent conflict. Royalists attributed his choice of parliament to his wife's influence or to resentment at a fine of £1500 imposed on him in Star Chamber following a quarrel and exchange of blows with a kinsman of his first wife who, unfortunately for Waller, was a royal servant. In fact his grounds were religious and constitutional, although his intentions were unrevolutionary.

The religious background of the Waller family remains obscure, but Jane Reynell's mother, Lucy, was notably pious, while Anne Finch's puritan sympathies went beyond private prayer over their marriage to public support in 1640 of the reformer John Dury (whom Waller also supported). She was later to become notorious as a 'Wonderfull Lady' who accompanied Waller on his campaigns (she was 'his pretty portable Armie') and preached to sometimes ungrateful troops who accused her of usurping 'the general's baton' (*Mercurius Aulicus*, 6 Sept 1644, 1147; *CSP Venice, 1643–7*, 135). Waller's providential account of his own life, in which God preserved him to 'arise, and be doing' in his cause (*Divine Meditations*, 16–17), was no retrospective construct but represented the guiding principle of his conduct once open conflict broke out. Yet his puritanism also appears to have been less aggressive and unshaded than his wife's. He was suspicious of outward displays of religiosity for public effect, scenting hypocrisy; he was not always an enthusiastic sermon-goer; and he later regretted that he had allowed professional criteria to outweigh godliness in appointing officers.

Politically, once in parliament Waller was 'an active person against the prerogative' (Wood, *Ath. Oxon.*, 3.814). Even in later disillusion he reaffirmed 'the constancy of [his] affection to the service of the Parliament' (*Vindication*, 317). He 'abhorred' the war, but

> acted in it, as upon the defensive (which I thought justifiable), … ever with a wish … that the difference might end, rather in a peace than a conquest; … with saving of honour to King and Parliament, whereby both might have best. (ibid., 7–8)

He wanted to preserve the monarchy 'according to our laws and fundamental constitutions' (ibid., 316), and he hoped that 'GOD might have … his fear; the King his honour; the Houses of Parliament their priviledges; the people of the kingdome their liberties and proprieties' (ibid., 304). To defend this conservative equilibrium, however, it was necessary to resort to arms in 1642.

Waller quickly emerged as an active member of the House of Commons. Within days of taking his seat he was appointed to the committee to raise money for the war against the Irish rebels, a cause which he supported generously, and in June he contributed to an appeal to raise a parliamentary army. In July he volunteered to raise his own regiment of horse, and in August he was listed as colonel of one of parliament's six cavalry regiments. Yet this willingness is not enough to explain his speedy rise to military eminence. His own limited soldiering was twenty years in the past, nor did he come from a family with a strong military tradition. Wood attributed the authority so quickly granted to him to 'his great knowledge in martial affairs' (Wood, *Ath. Oxon.*, 3.814). This, taken in conjunction with Waller's insistence that his serious reading was such as would 'fit [him] for *action, which is the true end of all learning*, and for *the service of God, which is the true end of all action*' (*Divine Meditations*, 31), suggests that he profited from the ample supply of books on modern military practice available in England in the decades before the war. His 'Military discourse of the ordering of soldiers' (a manuscript now lost) indicates an interest in military theory. That he chose to be represented in armour on his first wife's tomb in 1633, ten years after his palatine expedition, also suggests that he wished to retain his military persona. There is thus circumstantial evidence to explain his readiness for action in 1642. Thereafter his early successes undoubtedly contributed to his rapid rise.

In August 1642 Waller led his fledgeling forces to besiege the important arsenal and port of Portsmouth, then in royalist hands, and on 7 September the town surrendered. It was the first of his 'prosperous successes' ('Recollections', 120), and one in which his talents for speed, night actions, and choice of ground were already manifest. Less happily, he was present at Edgehill on 23 October, where he fled with the rest of the cavalry when it broke under royalist attack. It has been suggested that this experience convinced him of the need to train a body of horse equal to that of the cavaliers, and also of the inadequacy of a passive defence against a cavalry charge, and hence to his practice of trotting forward to meet such an attack (Adair, 39).

A string of successes now followed. On 1 December Waller took Farnham Castle, Surrey, strategically situated between Winchester and London. Then, with a substantial force of six mounted regiments, he advanced towards Winchester which he entered on 12 December after breaching the town walls; the next day the castle itself surrendered. Some 600 prisoners were taken and Waller yielded to the demands of his soldiers to sack the town. Technically he was justified, on the ground that its resistance had forced a storm, but he came to regret his decision and to see the destruction of his own house there as God's punishment for allowing the plunder of a city which, as one of its freemen, he should have protected. Winchester was soon recovered by the royalists but other successes followed. By the end of December Waller had also captured the town and castle of Arundel on his way to Chichester, which surrendered on 27 December. His reputation as 'William the Conqueror' was established (Clarendon, 2.215).

At the beginning of 1643 royalist successes in the west threatened the Severn valley and Bristol. On 11 February 1643 the earl of Essex appointed Waller major-general of the west. He reached Bristol after rapid night marches but with only 2000 men: this lack of men was to be a continuing source of friction between him and Essex. In late March, after another night march, he had a 'great victory' when he took Malmesbury in Wiltshire, where the enemy quickly surrendered, in part persuaded by Waller's noisy pretended preparations for an assault under cover of darkness (*A Letter from Sir William Waller … to … Essex … of a Great Victory … at Malmesbury, 23 Martii*, 1643). He had suffered, however, from the half-heartedness of some of his men and a shortage of ammunition, and it was a costly victory. Nevertheless his successes continued and on 24 March, after ferrying his men across the Severn, he and Lieutenant-Colonel Edward Massey demolished Lord Herbert's newly raised Welsh army at Highnam. Frustrated in his intention of moving on to Devon and Cornwall by a pacification treaty between both parties that he thought ill judged, Waller advanced into Monmouthshire, taking Monmouth and Chepstow. He then returned to Gloucester and from there supervised the taking of Tewkesbury by Massey on 12 April 1643.

These 'Victorious … Proceedings' (W. Waller, *The Victorious and Fortunate Proceedings of Sir William Waller*, 1643) were immediately followed by a sharp setback at Ripple Field at the hands of Prince Maurice, but Waller, though outmanned and outgunned, made a skilful retreat to Gloucester. He next advanced on Hereford and the city quickly fell on 25 April. Then, contrary to Essex's instructions to prevent the junction of the two royalist western armies, he besieged Worcester in order to consolidate control of the region, but he was forced to retire again to Gloucester at the end of May. Hereford too quickly returned to royalist hands, and Waller devoted himself to building up forces to confront the now combined royalist armies. He was hampered by shortages of men and lack of pay for those he had, by mutinous troops, and by a terrain unsuitable for action by his able cavalry. On 22 June 1643 he wrote from Bath to the speaker of the House of Commons,

> [I]t grieves our souls we dare not attempt what we desire. We must not hazard your trust like fools. Neither can we stay here and starve. We have long and often supplicated you for money find us but a way to live without it or else we humbly beg a present supply if not this horse will certainly disband which thought makes our hearts to bleed.   (Bodl. Oxf., MS Tanner 62/1A, fol. 128)

Exasperation at the failure to provide money to enable his army to perform the services required of it was joined to worsening relations with the lord-general; henceforth the 'jealousies and peeks' between Waller and Essex were public knowledge and a constant irritant from which, Waller observed, 'the country did suffer' (B. Whitelocke, *Memorials of the English Affairs*, 1732, 90; 'Recollections', 120–21). '[T]he General thought himself undervalued', observed Whitelocke, 'and *Waller* was high enough. Nor did there want Pick-thanks to blow those Coals of jealousy; and this proved unhappy to the Parliament Affairs' (B. Whitelocke, *Memorials of the English Affairs*, 1732, 90).

Waller's uncomplicated record of successes was now over. The war's operations and demands grew more complex, and in the south and west the royalists had a very capable general in his friend Hopton. On 5 July 1643 they faced each other in an inconclusive battle at Lansdown, near Bath, which left the royalists in possession of the field but badly mauled, while Waller conducted another a skilful retreat. He pursued the royalists to Devizes, Wiltshire, but his army was in a deplorable condition, prone to panic, flight, and confusion. On 13 July Waller was unequivocally beaten at nearby Roundway Down and a 'miserable rout' ensued. Losses of men, arms, and baggage were severe. It was, Waller said, 'the most heavy stroke of any that did ever befall me' (Adair, 96; 'Recollections', 131). His army was effectively destroyed. He had been sure of success, and attributed his 'dismal defeat' to Essex's 'heartburnings and jealoucies' and failure to support him. It had 'pleas'd the Lord to turn my victory into mourning, and my glory into shame' (ibid., 123, 124).

Despite this disaster Waller made a triumphal entry into London on 25 July. His achievements were magnified, the Venetian envoy wrote sceptically, to raise civilian morale (*CSP Venice*, 1643–7, 2). He had the support of the citizens and was allied with the Independents and others in the House of Commons anxious for active prosecution of the war and suspicious that Essex sought a soft peace with the king. On 27 July he was thanked by the house and recommended to Essex for command of a new army in the west, but the earl successfully dragged his feet for a month before granting the extensive authority requested by parliament on 26 August.

Waller meanwhile had taken the solemn league and covenant on 1 August, had been appointed to the new council of war designed to exercise unified oversight over operations, and had been ordered to send a force to relieve Gloucester. On 9 August his horse—'Waller's dogs' (Adair, 114)—had brutally suppressed a demonstration for peace by London women. After a summer of acerbic political manoeuvring by the two generals and their supporters Essex's reputation revived, and on 7 October he threatened to resign and leave the country, claiming that Waller's commission was inconsistent with his authority. Parliament thereupon cancelled Waller's independent command, but on 4 November 1643, threatened by a new royalist army under Hopton in the west, they named him major-general of the troops raised by the newly associated counties of Hampshire, Sussex, Surrey, and Kent.

Waller was already prepared for action, and on 7 November he marched from Farnham to the royalist stronghold of Basing House. After several expensive assaults he was forced to abandon the siege by bad weather, the approach of royalist forces, and soldiers who, blaming him for heavy casualties, mutinied or deserted, leaving him 'enfeebled and abandoned' (*CSP Venice*, 1643–7, 46). On 13 December, however, he attacked royalist forces at Alton, and in a brutal fight centred around the church the royalist commander Colonel Bolles and at least forty of his men were killed and over 700 prisoners taken. On 6 January 1644 he took Arundel Castle, and then retired to winter quarters.

In late March 1644, now with some 8000 men, Waller advanced towards Winchester by way of Alresford. Confused though it was, the battle of Cheriton that followed on 29 March counted as a major parliamentarian victory, and although the royalists made an orderly retreat their casualties were severe. The battle demonstrated that parliament's cavalry was now the equal of the enemy's, and left parliamentarian forces in control of Hampshire and Wiltshire. Several months of marches and countermarches by the armies of both sides followed until Essex and Waller parted angrily and Essex marched towards the west. On 29 June Waller, attempting to prevent the king from advancing into the eastern counties, faced him at Cropredy Bridge, near Banbury, and was decisively beaten. His London troops, with 'their old song of home, home' (*CSP dom.*, 1644, 301), were mutinous. This hindered his pursuit of the victorious royalists, but Waller followed them on their circuitous march as best he could. 'I am of opinion', he wrote to the committee of both kingdoms, 'before this business be done, we shall be the longest winded army in England' (ibid., 303). Meanwhile he continued to beg parliament for men, money, and supplies.

After the humiliating surrender of Essex's army at Lost-withiel, Cornwall, on 2 September he was too weak to prevent the king's return to Oxford. On 27 October, however, his men performed with distinction at the second battle of Newbury. After the ensuing winter lull he campaigned again in the west where he and Cromwell, who served under him, had some success, notably at Devizes in March 1645, but he was still beset by mutinous and disorderly troops and a shortage of money.

It was Waller's last campaign. The ordinance of 17 February 1645 creating the New Model Army under the command of Sir Thomas *Fairfax largely abolished the old structure of divided armies under competing and quarrelling commanders, and the self-denying ordinance of 3 April required members of parliament to resign their military offices. Waller left the army disillusioned. He felt 'slighted and disesteemed' by his mutinous troops and frustrated by the 'discouragements' of parliament (Gardiner, 2.192; *Egmont MSS*, 1.237).

Disillusion, disgrace, and revival Waller, now increasingly identified with the presbyterians, continued to be an active member of the committee of both kingdoms, of which he was a founding member, and of the council of state. He had not abandoned all hopes of a revived military career. Although he refused to consider command in Ireland when it was mooted in December 1645, citing his previous 'discouragements', he was at the same time, from October 1645 to March 1646, engaged in detailed negotiations with the Venetians to raise and command a substantial force for amphibious operations in the eastern Mediterranean. Nothing came of these plans, and for a time prosperity returned at home. Waller was again able to enjoy his 'estate, and the comforts of [his] family'. Winchester Castle was restored to him; in December 1645 the House of Commons voted him an annuity of £2500 and a barony was suggested; and in July 1646 parliament voted payment of £7307 due in wages. He was, he confessed, 'puffed upp' and felt unduly secure ('Recollections', 132; B. Whitelocke, *Memorials of the English Affairs*, 1732, 182; *Calendar of the … Committee for Compounding*, 1.794). As a member of parliament's committee for Irish affairs he sought to persuade disbanding soldiers to re-enlist for Irish service, and in March and April 1647 he was one of the commissioners dispatched by parliament to Saffron Walden to persuade the restive soldiers to do so. As tension between army and parliament escalated Waller was one of the eleven members of the House of Commons accused on 16 June of attacking the rights of subjects and soldiers and fomenting a new war. When the Independent members of both houses left London to take refuge with the army in July, Waller remained behind with the presbyterian majority and was appointed to its committee of safety. After the triumphant return of the Independents he fled to France. His ship was intercepted by a parliamentarian frigate but he nevertheless reached Calais safely on 17 August 1647, whence he sailed to Flushing with £46 in his pocket. He had already prudently sent household goods to Rotterdam. Later he received some of his English rents, and when his wife and family joined him they brought £500. They settled first at Leiden and then at The Hague, where he was able to wait once again on Elizabeth of Bohemia.

'Banishment' was only the first of the 'chastisements' that God visited on Waller's 'puffed upp … presumption' of good fortune: 'imprisonment, sickness, the death of [his] wife, poverty' followed ('Recollections', 132). A vote of 27 January 1648 disabled him from sitting in parliament, but it was annulled on 3 June and he returned prematurely to England. Excluded and confined after Pride's Purge on 6 December, he was arrested on 12 December on charges of inviting the Scots into England and conspiring with Queen Henrietta Maria.

For Waller, politics had become a 'labyrinth' (*Vindication*, 224). He passed the next ten years '[i]n prisons frequent' and in trying to negotiate his way past suspicion and entrapment in 'so insnaring a time' ('Recollections', 104, 120). He spent eighteen months as a prisoner at St James's Palace before being moved to Windsor Castle and finally to Denbigh Castle in north Wales. He was not ill-treated, and he successfully evaded attempts by 'false brethren' (ibid., 116) to trap him into criminal indiscretion. Thanks to God's special mercy, he said, 'I came off with an intire innocency, not only uncondemned, but unaccused' (ibid., 105). He asserted the integrity and freedom of the captive whose soul, abandoning worldly ambition, walked with God, yet he felt the disgrace of imprisonment and the affront to status keenly: the language of ignominy, of being in 'an obscure base condition', of being the prey of malice and jealousy, is pervasive (*Divine Meditations*, 66). One of the few consolations of his imprisonment was the resource and courage of Lady Anne, who found her way over the Welsh mountains to Denbigh 'disguised in mean apparell' and whose 'sweet converse and behaviour' lightened his sufferings ('Recollections', 104–5). He employed his time in writing his *Vindication … of Sir William Waller* (1793), in which he defended himself against charges of deserting his 'first principles' and aligning himself with 'malignants', of attempting to 'break the Army' and ignite a new war, of transporting 'great summs of mony' to the Netherlands and accepting a commission from the prince of Wales, and of implication in the second civil war (*Vindication*, 5–6). The catalogue reveals the distrust in which he was now held by non-presbyterians. Even after his release in early 1652 he remained at risk.

Lady Anne died in Wales and Waller sought a third wife. He found a 'rich … blessing' in Anne, Lady Harcourt (*d.* 1661) [see Waller, Anne, Lady Waller], widow of Sir Simon Harcourt, who was killed in Ireland in 1643. They married on 13 April 1652 and were, Waller said, 'not only one flesh, but one spirit; one in our affections, judgments, wayes, ends, (as if wee had been cut out of one and the same peece)' ('Experiences', Wadham College, Oxford, 59). His material fortunes also improved, although in the 1650s he was embroiled for years in proceedings against the customs commissioners over his grant of prisage. Nevertheless he now had access both to that income and to his rents. In 1656 he sold the slighted ruins of Winchester Castle to the town corporation. In 1654 he had bought

Osterley House, Middlesex, with some 758 acres. He raised £5000 by mortgages on the property, but in 1663 he sold half his acreage for £5250 with which he paid off much of the debt. He had thus not abandoned his entrepreneurial ways, although he had also made a vow in thanksgiving on his third marriage to devote a tenth of the income from his estate to 'pious uses' ('Recollections', 133). His failure to observe this vow led God, who would 'never suffer [him] to sin prosperously', justly to punish him by taking Lady Anne from him ('Experiences', Wadham College, Oxford, 62). She died in 1661; in the nine years of their marriage she bore Waller three children, cared solicitously for the children of his second marriage, and was an intelligent and godly partner to her husband, to whom she brought 'blessing and happiness' ('Recollections', 133).

In the uncertain 1650s Waller evaded implication in Penruddock's rising in 1655, but on 22 March 1658 his house was searched and he was taken to Whitehall to be questioned by Cromwell. Nothing could be proved against him and he was promptly released, but Waller recorded that Cromwell, although courteous, examined him 'as a stranger, not as one whome he had aforetime … obeyed' ('Recollections', 116). He was suspected, probably correctly, of implication in Booth's abortive rising of 1659 and spent ten weeks as a prisoner in the Tower of London, where he and his wife found kindness and reasonable comfort until their release on 31 October 1659. On 27 December he courageously joined other old parliamentarians at the door of the House of Commons seeking admission to the reconstituted Rump, and in January and February he was active in the negotiations for the return of Charles II. On 21 February 1660 he re-entered the House of Commons, but farce mingled with triumph. In the procession of formerly secluded members William Prynne's long basket-hilt sword 'got between Sir W. Waller's short legs and threw him down, which caused laughter' (*Memoirs of Edmund Ludlow … 1625–1672*, ed. C. H. Firth, 2 vols., 1894, 2.235). Two days later he was appointed a member of the new council of state. He was elected to the Convention Parliament as member for Westminster in 1660 but did not sit in the next parliament. Henceforth he retired from public life. Unlike some of his fellow presbyterians he neither sought nor received reward.

By 1660 Waller had already fallen out with his eldest son, William *Waller, and his hopes of the second, Thomas, were not high. His two older daughters married in 1648 and 1649, and Anne, the daughter of Anne Finch, married Sir Philip Harcourt, son of Waller's third wife, in 1661 and died in 1664. His three youngest children had predeceased their mother, Anne. In his retirement he wrote his *Divine Meditations* (published posthumously in 1680). He apparently maintained old religious associations, for at his death he left £10 each to two ejected London ministers, Thomas Case and Gabriel Sangar, as well as £200 to be disbursed at their discretion for charitable uses. A close friend was Dr Thomas Coxe, who had previously served in the parliamentarian army, a fellow of the Royal College of Physicians, an original member of the Royal Society, and

Waller's 'faythfull and dearlie respected friend', who was one of the executors of his will and to whom, in thanks for his 'inviolable friendship both to mee and mine', Waller left £250 (PRO, PROB 11/330, sig. 78). Meanwhile relations with his heir deteriorated further, and in 1666 the younger William brought an unsuccessful suit in chancery against his in-laws and his father over his wife's portion. In his will Waller directed that Osterley House and park be sold and the proceeds used to buy lands to enable his executors to discharge William's debts and pay him an annuity. In the event of the failure of William's male line the annuity would go to Thomas and his heirs. The will is notable both for the control exerted over his sons' wayward financial propensities and for the absence of any affective language applied to them, in contrast to the warmth of his reference to Coxe.

Waller died at Osterley House on 19 September 1668 and was buried with pomp on 9 October in the New Chapel in Tothill Street, Westminster. On 17 October, however, the heralds removed the heraldic displays, either because they were 'false and beyond his quality' or because his son, to save money, had employed counterfeit heralds (Adair, 274; Wood, *Ath. Oxon.*, 3.817).

Conclusion Waller's public reputation derives from his part as parliament's 'famous and fortunate Commander' of the first phases of the civil war (J. Vicars, *Jehovah-Jireh*, 1644, 375). Anthony Wood dismissed many of his victories as 'little, or inconsiderable' (Wood, *Ath. Oxon.*, 3.815) but cumulatively, transitory as the fruits of victory sometimes were, his campaigns were crucial to parliament's ultimate control of south-central England and the approaches to the Welsh border. His military talents are difficult to assess beyond his well-known tactical skills for 'nimble and successful marches', exploitation of darkness, and choice of ground (Clarendon, 2.179). His comments are always sensible, if defensively self-serving, but there is no evidence of a wider strategic grasp. In this, however, he did not differ from other commanders in a fluid, reactive, and fragmented war. His efforts were undoubtedly undercut by chronic shortages of men and money and by what an observer called Essex's 'inertia or malice' (*CSP Venice*, 1643–7, 2). Although Waller marched in Essex's magnificent funeral procession in October 1646 his retrospective writings still breathed resentment. He was a victim of the splintered command structure and imperfect system of taxation and disbursement of the early war years. As he said, 'Possibly I might have made more brick, if I had had more straw' (*Vindication*, 317). Yet although soldiers on both sides were notoriously volatile, the frequency of references to Waller's troops as mutinous, disorderly, and unwilling to follow him suggests that he lacked the touch that generals like Fairfax and Cromwell and other lesser commanders had in dealing with their soldiers.

Waller was notably short—'little in person' but a 'brave little spark' (Wood, *Ath. Oxon.*, 3.814; Adair, x). Portraits show a thoughtful and determined face with a long nose and direct gaze. He was a sociable friend, an uxorious husband, a disappointed father, and a vivid and pithy writer. His writings provide invaluable evidence of gentry life in peace and war. His was, in part from the circumstances of enforced retirement, an examined life, and through his reflections it is possible to discern the views of many of the substantial conservative revolutionaries of 1642 without whom there could have been no civil war. His sociability, humour, and intense pleasure in the comfortable material world of books, gardens, and pictures (the 'long gallery' at Osterley held twenty-four at his death), notably revealed in his *Divine Meditations* (1680), tell us much not only about Waller's mind and milieu but also about the texture of other gentry lives. The importance of a sense of personal worth and social status is illuminated by his response to the demeaning conditions of imprisonment, while the fragility of seventeenth-century health and the need for stoicism in bearing afflictions are evident in his references to attacks of the stone and other illnesses and in the vivid intensity of his account of his gout, that 'terrible disease' of seventeenth-century men (Wood, *Ath. Oxon.*, 4.270). 'I am *an infirmity of the world*', he wrote, 'a *living Hospital … the Ghost of my departed self … My pain is my life*' (*Divine Meditations*, 49–50). Through it all ran his conviction that all life was a manifestation of God's purpose and that the most trivial events as well as the greatest were evidence of God's oversight and intentions: God expected action from his instruments and he corrected and encouraged them on the way to his ends. Waller saw everything—even defeat, his wives' deaths, his gout—as sent from God for his ultimate good. The real terror, he believed, would come if it seemed that God did not care and that one was outside '*the pale of his providence*'. He prayed, 'Lord, do *any thing* to me, rather *then nothing*: Let thy pruning knife be never *so sharp*, and *cutting*, it can do me no *hurt*, so long as it *tends to make me good*' (ibid., 119).

In his disappointed later years Waller was to 'humbly acquiesce in the good Providence of GOD', but it was a sad acquiescence for 'GOD had determined a judgment upon the land' (*Vindication*, 197, 125 [*recte* 325]). He remained a moderate parliamentarian and constitutionalist and a moderate presbyterian. He had wished to tame the king but not to destroy him:'I was borne under a monarchy; and I desire to dy under it' (ibid., 317). He had preserved the 'integrity of [his] heart according to the principles upon which [he] first engaged' (ibid., 225): his allegiance to parliament remained constant, and he rebuffed approaches from the king during the war. Parliaments, like kings, however, could decline from the ideal, and as parliament bowed before the 'incendiaries of the state' Waller became alienated and disillusioned (ibid., 11). In religion too he faced threats to the moderate reform he had hoped for. His puritanism was neither austere nor intolerant. He denied that 'Religion is a dull flat melancholy thing'; instead the 'Communion of Saints' brought 'merry hearts' together (*Divine Meditations*, 32, 34). Adherence to the solemn league and covenant allowed moderate toleration given agreement on the essentials of faith, for though there could be no compromise on these there could be flexibility on its indifferent aspects. Nevertheless God required '*decency and order*'; 'the *Garden of his Church*' must not be 'overgrown with *errours* or *prophaneness*'.

When that threatened, 'weeding', 'lopping, and cutting' were required (ibid., 118). As he confronted the 'labyrinth' of the interregnum Waller clung to the belief that it was the world and his former allies, not he, who had changed. 'This change is not in me, but in others', he said (*Vindication*, 9–10).

Yet Waller still believed that there were 'many saints' among his 'former brethren', and he found it 'a misery to think … that there should be saints on two sides' (*Vindication*, 10). To his former enemies too he had tried to extend all the 'civilities' he could, and had endeavoured to fight the war in such a way 'that so our differences might be kept in a reconcileable condition; and we might still look upon one another … as enemies that might live to be friends' (ibid., 8). He combined principled parliamentarianism, godliness, and active and committed conduct of hostilities with hope for restoration of a socially and politically conservative, religiously reformed, but unrevolutionary society. In this Waller was typical of many who started a revolution without hesitation in 1642, were alarmed and disillusioned by its progress, and looked for the return of the monarchy in 1660 as the solution to the dangers, personal and public, that it had unleashed.

BARBARA DONAGAN

Sources W. Waller, *Divine meditations upon several occasions* (1680) • W. Waller, 'Recollections', in *The poetry of Anna Matilda* (1788), 103–39 • 'Sir Wm Waller's remarks—experiences', Wadham College, Oxford [variant of 'Recollections'] • [W. Waller], *Vindication of the character and conduct of Sir William Waller* (1793) • E. W. Harcourt, ed., *The Harcourt papers*, 14 vols. (privately printed, London, [1880–1905]) • Wood, *Ath. Oxon.*, new edn, 3.814–18 • J. Adair, *Roundhead general: the campaigns of Sir William Waller*, new edn (1997) • E. Hyde, earl of Clarendon, *The history of the rebellion and civil wars in England*, 3 vols. (1702–4) • DNB • S. R. Gardiner, *History of the great civil war, 1642–1649*, 4 vols. (1893); repr. (1987) • CSP dom., 1638–60, passim • CSP Venice, 1643–7 • *The manuscripts of his grace the duke of Portland*, 10 vols., HMC, 29 (1891–1931), vol. 3, pp. 240–41 • *Seventh report*, HMC, 6 (1879) • JHC, 3–8 (1642–67) • B. Donagan, 'Understanding providence: the difficulties of Sir William and Lady Waller', *Journal of Ecclesiastical History*, 39 (1988), 433–44 • J. T. Cliffe, *The world of the country house in seventeenth-century England* (1999) • Foster, *Alum. Oxon.* • W. Berry, *County genealogies … of Kent* (1830) • E. Hasted, *The history and topographical survey of the county of Kent*, 2nd edn, 3 (1797) • will, PRO, PROB 11/330, sig. 78 • J. Foster, *The register of admissions to Gray's Inn, 1521–1889, together with the register of marriages in Gray's Inn chapel, 1695–1754* (privately printed, London, 1889) • W. A. Shaw, *The knights of England*, 2 (1906), 179 • M. A. E. Green, ed., *Calendar of the proceedings of the committee for advance of money, 1642–1656*, 3 vols., PRO (1888) • M. A. E. Green, ed., *Calendar of the proceedings of the committee for compounding … 1643–1660*, 1, PRO (1889)
Likenesses C. Johnson, oils, 1643, NPG [*see illus.*] • Rodttemmondt, etching, 1643 (after C. Johnson), BM, NPG • engraving, 1643, AM Oxf. • P. Lely, oils, c.1645, Goodwood House, West Sussex • attrib. E. Bower, oils, NPG • N. Yeates, line engraving (after P. Lely, c.1645), BM, NPG; repro. in Waller, *Divine meditations* • oils, NPG • silver badge, BM
Wealth at death Osterley House to be sold to establish annuity for heir; separate indenture disposed of remaining forty years' prisage income; trusts established for portions: will, PRO, PROB 11/330, sig. 78 • est £1000–£3000 from prisage: Adair, *Roundhead general*, 7

Waller, Sir William (*c*.1639–1699), politician, was the second, but first surviving, son of Sir William *Waller (*bap.*

1598?, *d.* 1668), parliamentarian army officer, and his second wife, Lady Anne Finch (*d.* 1651/2), daughter of Thomas Finch, first earl of Winchilsea. He was educated at the University of Leiden in 1647 and travelled abroad with a tutor in France in 1656, where he acquired a reputation as a vicious profligate. His father had closely supervised his strict presbyterian education, but William later went his own 'rebellious way' (*Portland MSS*, 3.240–41), leaving the elder Waller fearful of William's influence upon his younger stepbrother. Under the father's will both sons were left in the hands of trustees, but William soon began to sell off his father's property. A number of customs posts that came his way, however, proved less profitable. In 1667 he married Catherine, daughter of Bussy Mansel of Briton Ferry, Glamorgan. He was at Utrecht during the Third Anglo-Dutch War and on his return to England he was targeted as a frequenter of conventicles. As a result a recommendation that Waller should be given the post of minister at Hamburg was ignored. Nevertheless, he was knighted in 1675.

It was during the period of the Popish Plot in 1678–81 that Waller became prominent as a London JP. He was particularly noted for his anti-Catholic fervour as well as his actions to seize both Catholic priests and their goods. As one contemporary noted:

> God's Providence and Waller's studious care,
> Hath laid the Bottom of their secrets bare.
> (*England's Remembrancer*)

Waller swiftly established himself in the popular mind as a zealous justice, being often in the vanguard in searches for hidden priests by raiding their homes, as well as the Savoy and other regular Catholic haunts. He also made many conspicuous appearances in the satirical literature of the day, being described as one whose 'Argus Eyes, the Secret'st Corners spy' (*Sir William Waller's Kindness*). In early February 1679 he seized some 1500 popish books and other material in Holborn. Three cartloads of popish goods were subsequently burnt on 11 February under his supervision in a public ceremony lasting from eleven in the morning until one in the afternoon. His anti-Catholicism also brought him into close contact with the great informers of the day and made him a number of enemies. In 1679 he was closely involved in uncovering Thomas Dangerfield's Meal-Tub Plot. Thomas Blood, with whom Waller came into conflict in 1680, claimed to have 'broke the neck' (*CSP dom.*, 1679–80, 556) of Waller when the latter was removed from the bench in April for his overzealous pursuit of Blood and Edward Christian's plot to implicate the duke of Buckingham in the crime of sodomy. Nevertheless Waller continued to be involved in various underhand activities such as suborning witnesses and was a prominent member of the Green Ribbon Club.

Waller represented Westminster in the parliaments of 1679 and 1681. In March of the latter year he was prominent in the entrapment of the conspirator Edward Fitzharris, acting as a witness at Fitzharris's trial for high treason. In May 1681 Waller was arrested for debt and placed in the Fleet prison, but was soon released. With the reaction against plots, informers, and the whigs he fled abroad and

was at Amsterdam to greet the earl of Shaftesbury on his arrival there in December 1682. He eventually settled at Bremen in Germany where he became a colonel of the city militia, although he was removed from this post in May 1684. Despite this other miscreants, including Sir Thomas Armstrong and Robert Ferguson, soon gathered around him and were given a warm welcome. English agents noted that Waller played the 'devill … and many more of that stamp … style [him] a second Cromwell' (*Seventh Report*, HMC, 386). In 1685 he was made governor of Lüneburg, given a regimental command, and established an English factory there. In the wake of the Williamite revolution of 1688 he returned to England, initially leading a regiment (that was soon disbanded), and continued his actions to seize Catholics, for which he had a warrant from William III in March 1689. Thereafter the new king 'did not seem inclin'd to do anything for' him, and 'would not hear of [him as governor] for the Leeward Islands' (Foxcroft, 2.215, 224). His final years are obscure and he died in poverty on 18 July 1699.

Waller's genuinely held, although slightly unbalanced, anti-Catholicism permeated all of his actions. At the height of the Popish Plot he was never very scrupulous about his methods and was undoubtedly guilty of bullying, suborning, and intimidating many witnesses, as well as seizing their goods for his own benefit. As he plied his trade one contemporary noted that:

> You let them Plot, then shew their Priests a trick,
> You catch the plotters in the very Nick.
> Many by your Industry have been taken,
> For fear of you, some have the land forsaken.
> (*Sir William Waller's Kindness*)

Scorned by his enemies for his short stature Waller seems to have delighted in his duties and, for a time, successfully strove to make himself as conspicuous as possible in the affair of the Popish Plot.　　　　　　ALAN MARSHALL

Sources *The manuscripts of his grace the duke of Portland*, 10 vols., HMC, 29 (1891–1931), vol. 3 · *England's remembrancer for the late discovery of the horrid plot found in a meal tub* (1679) · *Sir William Waller's kindness to the cities of London and Westminster particularly exprest* (1675) · *Seventh report*, HMC, 6 (1879) · *The life and letters of Sir George Savile … first marquis of Halifax*, ed. H. C. Foxcroft, 2 (1898) · N. Luttrell, *A brief historical relation of state affairs from September 1678 to April 1714*, 6 vols. (1857) · J. Adair, *Roundhead general: a military biography of Sir William Waller* (1969) · *An impartial and exact accompt of divers popish books, beads, crucifixes and images taken at the Savoy by Sir William Waller one of his majesties justices of the peace and burnt by his order in the New Palace-yard Westminster the 11th of February* (1679) · W. Waller, *Notorious fraud of the Romish priests and Jesuits* (1692) · *Dagon's fall, or, The knight turned out of commission* (1680) · *An elergy on the much lamented Sir William Waller who valiantly hang'd himself at Rotterdam 21 August 1683* (1683) · *CSP dom.*, 1660–85 · E. Cruickshanks and B. D. Henning, 'Waller, Sir William', HoP, *Commons, 1660–90*, 3.658–60

Archives Bodl. Oxf., autograph copy of his Apology, MS Don U. 57

Likenesses group portrait, engraving (W. Waller?), repro. in *A tale of the Tubbs, or, Rome's master peice defeated*

Wallich, George Charles (1815–1899), military surgeon and oceanographer, was born on 16 November 1815 in Calcutta, India, the eldest of seven children of Nathaniel

*Wallich (1785–1854), a Danish-born surgeon and botanist, and his second wife, Sophia Colling. He was educated at King's College, Aberdeen, and at the University of Edinburgh, where he studied medicine and graduated MD in 1836; he became a licentiate of the College of Surgeons (Edinburgh) the following year.

Wallich returned to India in 1838 as assistant surgeon in the Indian army and saw considerable active service during the next nineteen years, taking part in the Sutlej and Punjab campaigns of 1842 and 1847 and acting as field surgeon during the Santal rebellion of 1855–6. In 1851, during his single furlough spent in England, he married Caroline Elizabeth, daughter of Edmund Norton, a solicitor in Lowestoft. They had four sons and four daughters. Wallich returned to England on sick leave in 1857 and retired from the Indian army in 1859 with the rank of surgeon-major.

During the homeward voyage Wallich collected a variety of marine organisms, thus beginning the study of oceanography which was to dominate the remainder of his life. His reports on the collections brought him to the notice of the British scientific establishment and led to his appointment as naturalist in HMS *Bulldog* during a voyage under the command of Sir Leopold McClintock in 1860 to investigate a possible northern route for the proposed north-Atlantic telegraph cable.

Wallich reported the results of the *Bulldog* cruise in his most important publication, *The North-Atlantic Sea-Bed* (1862), which included his general views on deep-sea biology and in particular a refutation of the 'azoic theory', put forward by Edward Forbes in 1843, according to which the depths of the ocean beyond a few hundred metres were devoid of life. Wallich based his refutation mainly on a *Bulldog* sounding, at a depth of some 2300 metres, which brought up a number of brittle-stars entangled in the line. However, this evidence was generally regarded as inconclusive by the scientific world, and the credit for disproving the azoic theory went to Charles Wyville Thomson and W. B. Carpenter for their dredging results during the cruises of the *Lightning* and the *Porcupine* in 1868 and 1869.

Wallich published several significant scientific papers during the 1870s and 1880s, mainly on the classification of foraminiferans and on the role of the lower organisms in the formation of geological deposits. He also became an accomplished photographer, publishing privately a volume of excellent portraits of contemporary scientists. But his main preoccupation during the latter part of his life was about obtaining the public recognition which he felt he had been denied. This led him into a series of acrimonious exchanges, both private and public, with several notable scientists of the day, but mainly with Carpenter and Thomson, whom he also accused of plagiarizing his results, particularly those dealing with the biology of the foraminiferans. The controversy culminated in 1877 with Wallich's unsuccessful demand that the Royal Society should censure his two opponents; he believed that the society had tacitly condoned their misdemeanours by publishing their results in its prestigious journal, from which Wallich was debarred since he was not a fellow.

Although Wallich was never elected to the fellowship of the Royal Society, his work was recognized in 1898 by the award of the gold medal of the Linnean Society. Wallich undoubtedly felt that this recognition was too little and too late, and he remained bitter and resentful to his death, on 31 March 1899, at his home, 11 Nottingham Place, Baker Street, London. He was survived by his wife.

A. L. RICE, *rev.*

Sources A. L. Rice, H. L. Burstyn, and A. G. E. Jones, 'G. C. Wallich, MD—megalomaniac or mis-used oceanographic genius?', *Journal of the Society of the Bibliography of Natural History*, 7 (1974–6), 423–50 · NHM, Wallich MSS · *CGPLA Eng. & Wales* (1899)
Archives NHM, corresp., diaries, and papers; corresp., drawings, and private journal · University of British Columbia Library, Vancouver, notebooks and annotated publications · Wellcome L., notebooks and papers
Wealth at death £3053 2s. 1d.: administration, 14 April 1899, *CGPLA Eng. & Wales*

Wallich, Nathaniel [*formerly* Nathanael Wulff Wallich] **(1785–1854)**, botanist, was born at Copenhagen on 28 January 1785, the son of Købmand Wulff Lazarus Wallich (1756–1843), merchant, and his wife, Hanne, *née* Jacobson (1757–1839). Having graduated MD in 1806 in his native city, where he studied botany under Martin Vahl, he was appointed surgeon to the Danish factory at Serampore, near Calcutta, where he arrived in 1807. When this place was captured by the East India Company in 1808, Wallich, with other officers, was allowed to enter the company's service, and in March 1809 was appointed to assist William Roxburgh at the Royal Botanic Garden, Calcutta. On 30 May 1812 Wallich married Juliane Marie Hals (b. 1797), who was subsequently known as Mary Ann Wallich, but she died just two months later. In 1813 he married Sophia Colling. Together they had at least seven children, two of whom died in infancy. Their son, George Charles *Wallich, was a distinguished oceanographer. On 10 May 1814 Wallich was appointed assistant surgeon, and on 1 August 1817 superintendent of the garden. He at once distinguished himself by his great activity in collecting and describing new plants, causing them to be drawn, and distributing specimens to the chief European and North American gardens and herbaria.

In 1820 Wallich, in conjunction with William Carey (1761–1834), began to publish William Roxburgh's *Flora Indica*, to which Wallich added much original matter. In the same year he was officially directed to explore Nepal; besides sending many plants home to Banks, Smith, Lambert, Rudge, and Roscoe, he subsequently issued two fascicles of his *Tentamen florae Napalensis illustratae, consisting of botanical descriptions and lithographic figures of select Nipal plants* (1824 and 1826), printed at the newly established Asiatic Lithographic Press in Serampore. In 1825 he inspected the forests of western Hindustan, and in 1826 and 1827 those of Ava and Lower Burma. He was invalided to England in 1828, and took with him some eight thousand specimens of plants, duplicates of which were widely distributed to both public and private collections. *A numerical list of dried specimens of plants in the East India Company's museum, collected under the superintendence of Dr. Wallich* (1828–49) contains in all 9148 species. The best set of these was presented by the company to the Linnean Society. From 1829 to 1832 he published his most important work, *Plantae Asiaticae rariores, or, Descriptions and figures of a select number of unpublished East Indian plants* (3 vols.). He then returned to India, where, among other official duties, he made an extensive exploration of Assam with reference to the discovery of the wild tea shrub. His health, which had been weak for some years, deteriorated further despite a visit to the Cape of Good Hope in 1842–3, and he was finally forced to resign on 9 April 1846. Returning to London in that year Wallich remained active as a botanist. As vice-president of the Linnean Society, of which he was fellow from 1818, he frequently presided over its meetings. He received the degree of MD from Marischal College, Aberdeen, in 1819, was a fellow of the Royal Society of Edinburgh and of the Danish Royal Society of Copenhagen, and was elected fellow of the Royal Society in 1829; he was also a fellow of the Royal Asiatic Society and of the Geological Society of London. In addition to the more important works already mentioned, he is credited with thirty-five papers, mostly botanical, contributed between 1816 and 1854 to various journals including the *Asiatick Researches*, *Edinburgh Philosophical Journal*, *Transactions of the Linnean Society*, *Journal of Botany, British and Foreign*, and the journals of the Asiatic Society of Bengal and the Horticultural Society.

Wallich died at his home, 5 Upper Gower Street, London, on 28 April 1854 and was buried in Kensal Green cemetery on 3 May 1854. An obelisk was erected to his memory by the East India Company in the botanical garden at Calcutta. The genus *Wallichia*, of the Palmae, and many species commemorate his name.

G. S. BOULGER, rev. ANDREW GROUT

Sources [S. Raffles], *Letters of Sir Stamford Raffles to Nathaniel Wallich, 1819–1824*, ed. J. Bastin, Malaysian Branch of the Royal Asiatic Society, reprint, 8 (1981) · R. de Candolle and A. Radcliffe-Smith, 'Nathaniel Wallich (1786–1854) and the herbarium of the Honourable East India Company, and their relation to the de Candolles of Geneva and the *Great Prodromus*', *Botanical Journal of the Linnean Society*, 83 (1981), 325–48 · R. Desmond, *The European discovery of the Indian flora* (1992) · C. Christensen, *Den Danske botaniks historie med tilhørende bibliography*, 2 (1924–6), 157–60 · F. A. Stafleu and R. S. Cowan, *Taxonomic literature: a selective guide*, 2nd edn, 7, Regnum Vegetabile, 116 (1988), 37–40 · C. G. G. J. Van Steenis, ed., *Flora Malesiana*, 1st ser., 1 (1950), 557–8 · C. G. G. J. Van Steenis, ed., *Flora Malesiana*, 1st ser., 8 (1974), 104 · *The Bengal obituary, or, A record to perpetuate the memory of departed worth*, Holmes & Co. (1851) · *Gardeners' Chronicle* (6 May 1854), 284 · *Memoir and correspondence of the late Sir James Edward Smith*, ed. Lady Smith, 2 (1832), 246, 262

Archives BL OIOC, catalogue and drawings, MSS Eur. G 32, 36 · Calcutta Botanic Garden, Calcutta, India · Linn. Soc., papers relating to Burma · RBG Kew, corresp. and papers · RBG Kew, herbarium · U. Edin. L., corresp. | BL, letters to Sir Joseph Banks, Add. MS 33982 · BL, letters to Thomas Hardwicke, Add. MSS 9869–9870 · Linn. Soc., letters to Sir James Smith · RBG Kew, letters to Sir William Hooker · RS, Herschel MSS (and other MSS)

Likenesses J. Lucas, oils, *c.*1833, Linn. Soc. · M. Gauci, engraving (after A. Robertson), RS · M. Gauci, lithograph (after A. Robertson), BM, Linn. Soc. · D. Macnee, crayon, RBG Kew · T. H. Maguire, lithograph, BM; repro. in T. H. Maguire, *Portraits of the honorary members of the Ipswich Museum* (1852) · engraving, RS

PICTURE CREDITS

Ussher, James (1581–1656)—private collection

Uttley, Alice Jane (1884–1976)—© Jane Bown

Uvarov, Sir Boris Petrovich (1889–1970)—© Diana Willson

Vachell, Horace Annesley (1861–1955)—© National Portrait Gallery, London

Vale, Samuel (1797–1848)—© National Portrait Gallery, London

Valence, William de, earl of Pembroke (d. 1296)—© Dean and Chapter of Westminster

Valentine, James (1815–1879)—courtesy of St Andrews University Library

Valera, Eamon De (1882–1975)—by courtesy of Felix Rosenstiel's Widow & Son Ltd., London, on behalf of the Estate of Sir John Lavery; courtesy the Hugh Lane Municipal Gallery of Modern Art, Dublin

Valpy, Abraham John (1787–1854)—© National Portrait Gallery, London

Valpy, Richard (1754–1836)—© Copyright The British Museum

Vanbrugh, Dame Irene (1872–1949)—© National Portrait Gallery, London

Vanbrugh, Sir John (1664–1726)—© National Portrait Gallery, London

Vandeleur, Sir John Ormsby (1763–1849)—© National Portrait Gallery, London

Vane, Anne (d. 1736)—© National Portrait Gallery, London

Vane [Stewart], Charles William, third marquess of Londonderry (1778–1854)—© National Portrait Gallery, London

Vane, Frances Anne, Viscountess Vane (bap. 1715, d. 1788)—Lord Inglewood - Hutton-in-the-Forest

Vane, Frances Anne, marchioness of Londonderry (1800–1865)—private collection. Photograph: Photographic Survey, Courtauld Institute of Art, London

Vane, Sir Henry (1589–1655)—photograph by courtesy Sotheby's Picture Library, London

Vane, Sir Henry, the younger (1613–1662)—reproduced with the permission of Lord Barnard, Raby Castle, Staindrop, Darlington, co. Durham. Photograph: Photographic Survey, Courtauld Institute of Art, London

Vansittart, Henry (1732–1770?)—© Fitzwilliam Museum, University of Cambridge

Vansittart, Nicholas, first Baron Bexley (1766–1851)—© National Portrait Gallery, London

Vansittart, Robert Gilbert, Baron Vansittart (1881–1957)—© National Portrait Gallery, London

Vardon, Henry William [Harry] (1870–1937)—reproduced by kind permission of the Royal and Ancient Golf Club of St Andrews

Varley, John (1778–1842)—photograph by courtesy Sotheby's Picture Library, London

Vassall, (William) John Christopher (1924–1996)—© News International Newspapers Ltd

Vaughan, Charles John (1816–1897)—Collection: the Keepers & Governors of Harrow School

Vaughan, David James (1825–1905)—Vaughan College, Univeristy of Leicester

Vaughan, Dame Helen Charlotte Isabella Gwynne- (1879–1967)—© National Portrait Gallery, London

Vaughan, Henry Halford (1811–1885)—© National Portrait Gallery, London

Vaughan, Herbert Alfred Henry Joseph Thomas (1832–1903)—© National Portrait Gallery, London

Vaughan, Dame Janet Maria (1899–1993)—© National Portrait Gallery, London

Vaughan, Kate (1852?–1903)—V&A Images, The Victoria and Albert Museum

Vaughan, Richard (c.1553–1607)—© Bodleian Library, University of Oxford

Vaughan, Richard, second earl of Carbery (1600?–1686)—Collection and photograph Carmarthenshire County Museum; purchased with aid from Resource / V&A Purchase Grant Fund

Vaughan, Robert (1795–1868)—© National Portrait Gallery, London

Vaux, Thomas, second Baron Vaux (1509–1556)—The Royal Collection © 2004 HM Queen Elizabeth II

Vavasour, Anne (fl. 1580–1621)—The Worshipful Company of Armourers and Brasiers in the City of London

Veitch, William (1794–1885)—Scottish National Portrait Gallery

Venables, Sir Percy Frederick Ronald (1904–1979)—© National Portrait Gallery, London

Venn, Henry (1725–1797)—© National Portrait Gallery, London

Venn, Henry (1796–1873)—© The President and Fellows of Queens' College, Cambridge

Vere, Aubrey de, twentieth earl of Oxford (1627–1703)—© National Portrait Gallery, London

Vere, Aubrey Thomas de (1814–1902)—© National Portrait Gallery, London

Vere, Sir Charles Broke (1779–1843)—© National Portrait Gallery, London

Vere, Edward de, seventeenth earl of Oxford (1550–1604)—private collection; on loan to the National Portrait Gallery, London

Vere, Sir Francis (1560/61–1609)—private collection; on loan to the National Portrait Gallery, London

Vere, Horace, Baron Vere of Tilbury (1565–1635)—Ashdown House, The Craven Collection (The National Trust). Photograph: Photographic Survey, Courtauld Institute of Art, London

Vereker, John Standish Surtees Prendergast, sixth Viscount Gort in the peerage of Ireland and first Viscount Gort in the peerage of the United Kingdom (1886–1946)—The Imperial War Museum, London

Vermigli, Pietro Martire [Peter Martyr] (1499–1562)—© National Portrait Gallery, London

Verney, Sir Edmund (1590–1642)—The Verney Family. Photographic Survey, Courtauld Institute of Art, London

Verney, Sir Harry, second baronet (1801–1894)—unknown collection / Christie's; photograph National Portrait Gallery, London

Verney, Margaret Maria, Lady Verney (1844–1930)—The Verney Family. Photograph: Photographic Survey, Courtauld Institute of Art, London

Vernon, Edward (1684–1757)—© National Portrait Gallery, London

Vertue, George (1684–1756)—© National Portrait Gallery, London

Vesey, Elizabeth (c.1715–1791)—© National Portrait Gallery, London

Vestey, William, first Baron Vestey (1859–1940)—© National Portrait Gallery, London

Vestris, Lucia Elizabeth (1797–1856)—© National Portrait Gallery, London

Vezin, Hermann (1829–1910)—© National Portrait Gallery, London

Vezin, Jane Elizabeth (1827–1902)—© National Portrait Gallery, London

Vicious, Sid (1957–1979)—photograph Ebet Roberts / Redferns

Vickers, Sir (Charles) Geoffrey (1894–1982)—© National Portrait Gallery, London

Vickers, Joan Helen, Baroness Vickers (1907–1994)—© Yevonde Portrait Archive; collection National Portrait Gallery, London

Vickers, Thomas Edward (1833–1915)—photograph by courtesy Sotheby's Picture Library, London

Victoria, Princess, duchess of Kent (1786–1861)—The Royal Collection © 2004 HM Queen Elizabeth II

Victoria (1819–1901)—The Royal Collection © 2004 HM Queen Elizabeth II

Victoria, princess royal (1840–1901)—© National Portrait Gallery, London

Victoria, Vesta (1873–1951)—private collection

Villiers, Charles Amherst (1900–1991)—© News International Newspapers Ltd

Villiers, Charles Pelham (1802–1898)—© National Portrait Gallery, London

Villiers [Hamilton], Elizabeth, countess of Orkney (c.1657–1733)—unknown collection; photograph Sotheby's Picture Library, London / National Portrait Gallery, London

Villiers, Frances, countess of Jersey (1753–1821)—private collection; photograph National Portrait Gallery, London

Villiers, George, first duke of Buckingham (1592–1628)—Palazzo Pitti, Florence / Bridgeman Art Library

Villiers, George, second duke of Buckingham (1628–1687)—private collection. Photograph: Photographic Survey, Courtauld Institute of Art, London

Villiers, George William Frederick, fourth earl of Clarendon (1800–1870)—private collection

Villiers, Henry Montagu (1813–1861)—© National Portrait Gallery, London

Villiers, John Henry de, first Baron de Villiers (1842–1914)—© National Portrait Gallery, London

Villiers, Margaret Elizabeth Child-, countess of Jersey (1849–1945)—private collection; photograph © National Portrait Gallery, London

Villiers, Mary, duchess of Lennox and Richmond (1622–1685)—The Royal Collection © 2004 HM Queen Elizabeth II

Villiers, Sarah Sophia Child-, countess of Jersey (1785–1867)—private collection; © reserved in the photograph

Vinaver, Eugène (1899–1979)—© reserved; photograph National Portrait Gallery, London

Vincent, Edgar, Viscount D'Abernon (1857–1941)—Christie's Images Ltd. (2004)

Vincent, Henry (1813–1878)—© National Portrait Gallery, London

Vincent, Sir (Charles Edward) Howard (1849–1908)—© National Portrait Gallery, London

Vincent, William (1739–1815)—© National Portrait Gallery, London

Vinogradoff, Sir Paul Gavrilovitch (1854–1925)—© National Portrait Gallery, London

Vivekananda (1863–1902)—© National Portrait Gallery, London

Vivian, Richard Hussey, first Baron Vivian (1775–1842)—© National Portrait Gallery, London

Vivian, Valentine Patrick Terrell (1886–1969)—© reserved; collection The British Library; photograph, National Portrait Gallery, London

Vizetelly, Henry Richard (1820–1894)—© National Portrait Gallery, London

Vorticists (act. 1914–1919)—© Estate of the Artist / Tate, London, 2004

Voysey, Charles (1828–1912)—© National Portrait Gallery, London

Voysey, Charles Francis Annesley (1857–1941)—© National Portrait Gallery, London

Vyner, Sir Thomas, first baronet (1588–1665)—© National Portrait Gallery, London

Waagen, Gustav Friedrich (1794–1868)—© Copyright The British Museum

Wace, Henry (1836–1924)—© National Portrait Gallery, London

Waddilove, Robert Darley (1736–1828)—© National Portrait Gallery, London

Wadding, Luke (1588–1657)—unknown collection; photograph Sotheby's

Picture Library, London / National Portrait Gallery, London

Wade, Sir Claude Martine (1794–1861)—Ashmolean Museum, Oxford

Wade, George (1673–1748)—courtesy of the Royal Aero Club of the United Kingdom

Wade, Sir Thomas Francis (1818–1895)—© National Portrait Gallery, London

Wadham, Dorothy (1534/5–1618)—The Lord Egremont. Photograph: Photographic Survey, Courtauld Institute of Art, London

Wadham, Nicholas (1531/2–1609)—The Lord Egremont. Photograph: Photographic Survey, Courtauld Institute of Art, London

Wager, Lawrence Rickard (1904–1965)—Godfrey Argent Studios / Royal Society

Waghorn, Thomas (1800–1850)—© National Portrait Gallery, London

Wagner, Sir Anthony Richard (1908–1995)—© National Portrait Gallery, London

Wain, John Barrington (1925–1994)—© Mark Gerson; collection National Portrait Gallery, London

Wainwright, Alfred (1907–1991)—© reserved; collection National Portrait Gallery, London

Waite, Arthur Edward (1857–1942)—© National Portrait Gallery, London

Wake, William (1657–1737)—© National Portrait Gallery, London

Wakefield, Edward Gibbon (1796–1862)—© National Portrait Gallery, London

Wakefield, Gilbert (1756–1801)—© National Portrait Gallery, London

Wakefield, Gordon Stevens (1921–2000)—© News International Newspapers Ltd

Wakefield, Priscilla (1750–1832)—© National Portrait Gallery, London

Wakefield, (William) Wavell, Baron Wakefield of Kendal (1898–1983)—Getty Images - Hulton Archive

Wakley, Thomas (1795–1862)—by kind permission of The Lancet

Walcot, William (1874–1943)—© National Portrait Gallery, London

Waldegrave, James, first Earl Waldegrave (1684–1741)—© National Portrait Gallery, London

Waley, Arthur David (1889–1966)—© Estate of Rex Whistler 2004. All rights reserved, DACS; collection National Portrait Gallery, London

Walford, Edward (1823–1897)—© National Portrait Gallery, London

Walker, Sir Alexander (1869–1950)—© National Portrait Gallery, London

Walker, Sir Edward (1612–1677)—The Shakespeare Birthplace Trust, Stratford-upon-Avon

Walker, Dame Ethel (1861–1951)—© National Portrait Gallery, London

Walker, Frederick (1840–1875)—© National Portrait Gallery, London

Walker, Frederick John (1896–1944)—© Science & Society Picture Library;

photograph National Portrait Gallery, London

Walker, Frederick William (1830–1910)—by courtesy of the Estate of Sir William Rothenstein; collection St Paul's School, London

Walker, George (1734?–1807)—© National Portrait Gallery, London

Walker, Sir George Townshend, first baronet (1764–1842)—© National Portrait Gallery, London

Walker, Sir James (1863–1935)—© National Portrait Gallery, London

Walker, John (1732–1807)—© National Portrait Gallery, London

Walker, Lucy (1836–1916)—Alpine Club Photo Library, London

Walker, Patrick Chrestien Gordon, Baron Gordon-Walker (1907–1980)—© National Portrait Gallery, London

Walker, Richard (1679–1764)—© National Portrait Gallery, London

Walker, Robert (1755–1808)—National Gallery of Scotland

Walker, Sir William Frederic Wake- (1888–1945)—© National Portrait Gallery, London

Walker, William Robert (1869–1918)—private collection

Walkinshaw, Clementine, styled countess of Albestroff (c.1720–1802)—Scottish National Portrait Gallery

Wall, John (bap. 1708, d. 1776)—© National Portrait Gallery, London

Wall, Joseph (1737–1802)—by courtesy of the National Gallery of Ireland

Wall, Max (1908–1990)—© National Portrait Gallery, London

Wallace, Alfred Russel (1823–1913)—© National Portrait Gallery, London

Wallace, Sir Donald Mackenzie (1841–1919)—© National Portrait Gallery, London

Wallace, (Richard Horatio) Edgar (1875–1932)—© National Portrait Gallery, London

Wallace, Nellie (1870–1948)—© Cecil Beaton Archive, Sotheby's; collection National Portrait Gallery, London

Wallace, Philip Adrian Hope- (1911–1979)—© National Portrait Gallery, London

Wallace, Sir Richard, baronet (1818–1890)—© National Portrait Gallery, London

Wallace, Robert (1831–1899)—© National Portrait Gallery, London

Wallace, (Charles) William (1855–1916)—from the collection of T. A. B. Corley

Wallack, James William (1795–1864)—private collection

Wallas, Graham (1858–1932)—by courtesy of the Estate of Sir William Rothenstein; collection London School of Economics and Political Science

Wallas, Katharine Talbot (1864–1944)—The Mistress and Fellows, Girton College, Cambridge

Waller, Edmund (1606–1687)—© National Portrait Gallery, London

Waller, Lewis (1860–1915)—© National Portrait Gallery, London

Waller, Sir William (bap. 1598?, d. 1668)—© National Portrait Gallery, London

Ref DA 28 .O95 2004 v.56

Oxford dictionary of
national biography